WHO'S WHO
OF
CRICKETERS

WHO'S WHO OF CRICKETERS

a complete who's who of all cricketers who have played first-class cricket in the British Isles, with full career records

PHILIP BAILEY PHILIP THORN
PETER WYNNE-THOMAS

HAMLYN

Published by Hamlyn in association with
THE ASSOCIATION OF CRICKET STATISTICIANS

The Association of Cricket Statisticians and Historians
Enquiries about the publications, or membership, of the Association of Cricket Statisticians and Historians should be addressed to the Secretary at
3 Radcliffe Road, West Bridgford, Nottingham NG2 5FF

First published in 1984
This revised and updated edition published in 1993
by Hamlyn an imprint of Reed Consumer Books Limited
Michelin House, 81 Fulham Road, London SW3 6RB
and Auckland, Melbourne, Singapore and Toronto

ISBN 0 600 57729 5

A CIP catalogue record for this book is available at the British Library

Typeset by Limlow Books Ltd in Ventura Times Roman 9 on 10 pt.
Printed in Great Britain

Introduction to First Edition

The concept of a volume containing the biographies of every notable English cricketer is not a new one. Arthur Haygarth, whilst at Harrow School in the 1840s, began a search for famous players of the past, a search which was to last a lifetime. Haygarth died in 1903 and his work was continued by F. S. Ashley-Cooper, who edited the fifteenth and final volume of Haygarth's monumental *Scores and Biographies*. The task of researching and collating biographical material on English cricketers, other than contemporary players, more or less died with Ashley-Cooper, except for certain specialist areas, such as specific clubs or families.

When the Association of Cricket Statisticians was formed in 1973, it was found that a number of members had an interest in reviving the type of biographical research formerly undertaken by Haygarth and Ashley-Cooper, and had in fact been quietly ferreting out details of the cricketers who had eluded their predecessors. The Association was anxious to continue this research and to try to direct the footsteps of the researchers in order to avoid duplication of effort. It was decided to publish brief biographical details of English first-class cricketers on a County by County basis. Before much progress could be made, however, it was necessary to solve a problem that had confounded cricket historians and statisticians for fifty years, the compilation of a precise list of English first-class matches, for without such a list, it was impossible to compose a list of English first-class cricketers.

Although the modern concept of first-class cricket evolved during the 1860s, it was not until 1947 that a 'first-class' match was officially defined. For about eighty years therefore, the decision as to which matches to include in the season's 'First-class Averages' was largely in the hands of the sporting press, though since 1890 the MCC had decided which Counties could boast first-class status.

The Association of Cricket Statisticians gathered in the views of all known interested parties, held meetings, published preliminary lists, conducted fresh research into contemporary newspapers and periodicals, held further meetings, and the result of three years intensive study was *A Guide to First Class Cricket Matches Played in the British Isles*, published in 1976. This work found general acceptance among statisticians, because it gave historical reasons for the inclusion, or exclusion, of the matches on the borderline of first-class status. The guide commences with the 1864 season when the modern concept of 'first-class' cricket was being evolved. Further research led to the publication of *A Guide to Important Cricket Matches Played in the British Isles 1709-1863*, published in 1981.

This publication gives a list of important matches from 1801-1863 and a list of 18th century matches which includes most matches that are known to have been played. The career records in this book start from 1801.

Now, at last, the biographical researchers could produce a list of 'first-class' cricketers and the task of detection, with its blind alleys, false trails, and, in most cases, eventual success, could begin in earnest. The story of the tracing of these hundreds of 'lost' cricketers is a saga on its own. We can only thank all those members of the Association who have helped in our 'County' booklets, and indeed the many first-class cricketers, their friends or relatives, who have provided the clues without which many of the facts contained in this volume could not have been discovered. There are still a few 'lost' cricketers; we will of course continue to search for them, but we would be most grateful for any clues that might help that research and any addenda or errata will be published and acknowledged in the next edition of this book.

May we close this introduction by dedicating this work to all the cricketers contained herein, for the pleasure they have given to cricket followers throughout the British Isles.

Philip J. Bailey
Philip R. Thorn
April 1984 Peter Wynne-Thomas

Introduction to Second Edition

Following the publication of the First Edition of this work in 1984, research into the biographical details of first-class cricketers did not cease. A number of players had not been identified and many more were partially detailed in the First Edition. Work on filling the biographical gaps has continued and the information discovered will be found in this edition. Over 600 new players (those whose first-class careers in the British Isles began between 1984 and 1992 inclusive) have been added and the several hundred players in the First Edition whose careers continued after 1983 have had their details suitably amended. In order to ascertain the accurate dates and places of birth and death of many players, certificates have been purchased and this has cleared up a number of identification problems. Research by S.T.Harper-Scott revealed that two cricketers surnamed Marshall, not one, played for Cambridgeshire in the 1860s. Therefore two separate entries are now given. Many of the people who assisted with the first volume continued to help; in particular we would like to thank Lionel King, Peter Griffiths and Peter Arnold. A list of additional helpers is given elsewhere.

Philip J. Bailey
Philip R. Thorn
Peter Wynne-Thomas

West Bridgford, Nottingham
January 1993

As this book went to press the ICC ruled that some matches played on tours to South Africa should no longer be regarded as first-class. As it is not yet clear which, and as delegates might change the decision when the implications become clear (a large number of career records are involved), the figures in this book follow the generally accepted rulings made by the South African authorities.

About the Authors

Philip Bailey, Philip Thorn and Peter Wynne-Thomas are all prominent members of the Association of Cricket Statisticians and Historians.

Peter Wynne-Thomas, the Association's Honorary Secretary, is a frequent contributor to cricketing periodicals, and has published a number of cricket books, including *Nottinghamshire Cricketers 1821-1914* which won the Cricket Society's Award as the best book of 1971. He is a Committee Member of Nottinghamshire County Cricket Club and the Club's archivist. He runs the specialist sports bookshop Sport in Print, opposite the Trent Bridge ground.

He was born in Manchester in 1934 and educated at Lancing College. He is married with a daughter and two stepsons and lives a cricket ball's throw from the ground in Nottingham.

Philip Thorn has been involved with the publications of the Association of Cricket Statisticians and Historians since 1973, being primarily concerned with biographical researches. He was born in 1936 and educated at Sutton High School, Surrey. He is an insurance consultant. Married, with three daughters, he lives at Colsterworth, Lincolnshire.

Philip Bailey is a Committee Member of the Association of Cricket Statisticians and Historians, and is the editor of the Association's journal, *The Cricket Statistician*. He is the Association's authority on cricketers' career records. He was educated at Eltham College and Churchill College, Cambridge, where he gained a degree in mathematics. He is a computer programmer for the London Borough of Lewisham and is a regular bridge player having represented Cambridge University against Oxford.

ACKNOWLEDGEMENTS

The authors acknowledge their debt to the many previously published works that have given biographical details of cricketers. Apart from the work of Arthur Haygarth and F. S. Ashley-Cooper, noted in the Introduction, a major source has been all the cricket annuals, ranging from the *Wisden Cricketers' Almanack* and *Playfair Annual* of the present day to the many Annuals, both national and local, which have appeared only briefly, and all the County Yearbooks, as well as the biographies of players. The number of books consulted runs into four figures; the principal ones are listed on another page.

As stated in the Introduction the present research began with the Association of Cricket Statisticians' 'County' booklets in 1973, and the names of those who researched for these booklets are included below. We particularly wish however to acknowledge our thanks to Maurice Alexander for his very extensive researches during the last two years, to Peter Arnold for his guidance throughout the project and to Leigh Scaife for her assistance.

The help of the following was also much appreciated:

C. D. Adams
R. L. Arrowsmith
N. S. Asgarali
D. St. E. Atkinson
Sir John Aubrey-Fletcher
G. L. B. August
S/Ldr A. Bacon
J. A. Baiss
I. H. S. Balfour
P. Banham
C. J. Bartlett
A. Beecroft
K. E. Bridger
R. W. Brooke
D. Brookes
R. B. Bruce-Lockhart
J. Burrell
G. N. J. Byrne
J. H. Cameron
D. S. Carmichael
E. Cawston
P. B. Clift
R. H. Cobbold
J. R. Cole
F. Collins
H. R. Cox
B. A. C. Croudy
R. L. B. Cunliffe
J. H. Doggart
A. Dossa
M. Down
W. M. Eadon
R. M. Edwards
J. S. Emsley
J. A. Evetts
J. Featherstone
M. Featherstone
L. C. Fielding
T. E. J. Fitton
C. B. Fordham
R. A. C. Forrester
T. W. Fraser
R. E. G. Fulljames
P. F. Garthwaite
P. W. Gooden
J. Goulstone
E. W. Greenhalgh
J. N. Grover
R. J. L. Hammond
L. W. Hancock
M. N. Harbottle
S. T. Harper-Scott
R. Harragan
T. M. Hart
S. B. Hassan
L. Hatton
D. Heesom
I. C. Henry
G. E. Hewan
Gen Sir R.Hewetson
A. K. Hignell
B. J. W. Hill
M. F. Hill
J. W. Holder
R. A. A. Holt
R. H. Horsley
R. E. H. Hudson
B. Hunt
V. H Isaacs
R. Isherwood
D. H. James
N. Jenkinson
H. H. H. Johnson
W. R. H. Joynson
W. G. Kalaugher
M. A. C. P. Kaye
D. King
F. King
L. King
N. S. Knight
C. H. Knott
H. J. H. Lamb
D. A. Lambert
P. D. Lashley
J. H. Lee
J. E. Liddle
W. S. P. Lithgow
R. A. Lord
C. W. S. Lubbock
R. E. Luyt
S. Lynch
A. E. Mallalieu
D. A. Marriott
R. W. S. Miller
J. M. Mills
H. Milton
M. J. H. Morton
A. H. Musson
C. J. Myburgh
P. G. E. Nash
L. T. Newell
L. F. Newnham
Capt D. Oakley
P. C. Oldfield
H. A. Osborne
D. G. Oswald

R. K. Page
Roger Page
F. G. Peach
S. S. Perera
S. Pether
R. H. Priestley
S. Proffitt
T. B. Raikes
O. L. Roberts
H. B. O. Robinson
B. W. Rought-Rought
J. V. D. Rowley
G. W. Russ
R. Sargent
G. G. A. Saulez
H. E. Scott
P. Sichel
R. G. Simons
F. W. Simpson
R. W. Skene
D. Smith
E. E. Snow
R. G. Stainton
J. W. Stockwell
D. W. Stokes
P. M. Studd
G. C. Tovey
K. S. C. Trushell
K. C. Turner
A. W. Tyler
A. H. Wagg
P. Wakefield
R. Warburton
K. Warsop
A. Wharton
R. C. C. Whittaker
A. Wiggett
K. Williams
D. Wilshin
D. C. Wilson
M. Wong
A. Woodhouse
A. J. Wreford-Brown
J. E. L. Wright
D. E. Young

Additional information for the Second Edition was provided by many of those who helped with the First Edition and also the following:

W. B. Ambrose
D.J.Baggett
R. Baker
L. Birkett
P.Bolton
C. J. Clynes
R.Coggins
C. N. Collyns
D.G.Crampton
J. B. Crofts
P. Crush
S. Draper
W. H. Frindall
D. E. J. Frith
P. D. Frost
Patricia Gaywood
K. Gerrish
M. Gilbert
J. A. Goulder
J. F. Griffiths
T. Harrison
W. Harte
D. Q. Harvey
J. M. Harvie
A. M. Hastilow
J. W. Hearne
N. A. Johns
M. I. H. Kamardeen
D. Kendix
H. C. Kidson
W. Lane
Anne Leitch
N. Leitch
M. G. Lorimer
A. J. M. Mansell
D. W. Mathias
A. Miller
K. Montgomery
G. Mortimer
E. A. Morton
P. Norman
P. Oxley
J. Parkinson
M. Pope
N. Rogers
J. A. Sangster
R. Sethi
M. C. Spurrier
D. Steele
Lt Col J. R. Stephenson
Rev T. Treanor
R. Webster
Prof T. West
I. Whyte
G. S. Wilde

First Class Teams 1864 to 1992

The following is the list of teams considered to have played first-class cricket matches in the British Isles since 1864.

All England Eleven (1864–78)
L. E. G. Ames' XI (1957)
Army (1912–39)
Australians (1878 to date)
Australian Imperial Forces (AIF) (1919)
Australian Services (1945)
J. Bamford's XI (1907–09)
Barbados (1969)
R. G. Barlow's XI (1883)
Sir Julien Cahn's XI (1932–38)
F. S. G. Calthorpe's XI (1926)
Cambridgeshire (1864–71)
Cambridgeshire and Yorkshire (1864)
Cambridge University (1864 to date)
Cambridge University Past and Present (1882–90)
Canada (1954)
Capped (1923)
Civil Service (1927)
D. B. Close's XI (1982-86)
S. H. Cochrane's XI (1909)
Combined Services (1920-64)
Commonwealth (1950-61)
Lord Cowdray's XI (1923-24)
R. Daft's XI (1870-80)
Demobilised Officers (1919)
Derbyshire (1871 to date)
Dominions (1945)
Dublin University (1895-1926)
Durham (1992)
East (1892-1948)
East Africa (1975)
T. Emmett's XI (1881-83)
England / England XI (1864 to date)
Essex (1894 to date)
Essex and Middlesex (1947)
H. K. Foster's XI (1912-19)
Free Foresters (1912-68)
C. B. Fry's XI (1912)
Gentlemen (1864-1962)
Gentlemen of Kent (1864-80)
Gentlemen of Middlesex (1865)
Gentlemen of the North (1867-80)
Gentlemen of the South (1864-1920)
A. E. R. Gilligan's XI (1925-66)
Glamorgan (1921 to date)
Gloucestershire (1870 to date)
Gloucestershire and Yorkshire (1877)
W. G. Grace's XI (1871-1907)
L. Hall's XI (1885-91)
Hambledon XII (1908)
Hampshire (1864 to date)
Harlequins (1924-28)
Lord Hawke's XI (1885-1930)
H. T. Hewett's XI (1892)
Home Counties (1899)
Hurst Park Club (1890)
Indians (1911 to date)
International Cavaliers (1969)
International XI (1975)
Ireland (1902 to date)
I Zingari (1866-1904)
Jamaica (1970)
D. R. Jardine's XI (1955-58)
G. L. Jessop's XI (1911)
V. W. C. Jupp's XI (1926)
Kent (1864 to date)
Kent and Gloucestershire (1874-76)
Kent and Nottinghamshire (1864)
Kent and Surrey (1947)
Kent and Sussex (1902)
Kent and Yorkshire (1913)
Lancashire (1865 to date)
Lancashire and Yorkshire (1883-1909)
W. H. Laverton's XI (1890)
Left-handed (1870)
Leicestershire (1894 to date)
H. D. G. Leveson-Gower's XI (1902-50)
M. Leyland's XI (1947)
Liverpool and District (1882-94)
Lord Londesborough's XI (1886-1913)
London County (1900-04)
London United (1879)
Lyric Club (1890)
Lord March's XI (1886)
Married (1871-92)
MCC (1864-1991)
MCC Australian XI (1904-63)
MCC President's XI (1964-68)
MCC South African XI (1910-48)
MCC Tour XI (1973)
MCC West Indian XI (1935)
J. R. Mason's XI (1913)
Middlesex (1864 to date)
Midland Counties (1896-99)
Minor Counties (1912 to date)
Navy (1912-29)
Navy and Army (1910-19)
New Zealanders (1927 to date)
New Zealand Services (1945)
Non-Smokers (1884)
North (1864-1961)
Northamptonshire (1905 to date)
Nottinghamshire (1864 to date)
Nottinghamshire and Lancashire (1883)
Nottinghamshire and Yorkshire (1872-83)
Old Oxford University (1881)
Orleans Club (1878-83)
Oxford University (1864 to date)
Oxford and Cambridge Universities (1910-92)
Oxford University Past and Present (1888-99)
Oxford and Cambridge Universities, Past and Present (1874-92)
Over 30 (1879-1949)

Over 32 (1950)
Over 33 (1945)
Pakistanis (1954 to date)
Pakistan Eaglets (1963)
Sir L. Parkinson's XI (1933-35)
T. N. Pearce's XI (1951-78)
Philadelphians (1897-1908)
H. Philipson's XI (1891)
R. Pilling's XI (1889)
Players (1864-1962)
Players of the North (1873-87)
Players of the South (1864-1920)
Rest of England (1901-76)
Rest of the World / World XI / M.Parkinson's World XI (1965-92)
A. W. Ridley's XI (1879)
Right-handed (1870)
D.H. Robins' XI (1969-78)
L. Robinson's XI (1912-21)
RAF (1927-46)
RAF (Ex-Service) (1922)
Scotland (1905 to date)
Second Class Counties (1893)
J. Sharp's XI (1923)
A. Shaw's XI (1881-85)
Lord Sheffield's XI (1881-96)
M. Sherwin's XI (1889-91)
A. Shrewsbury's XI (1888-93)
Single (1871-92)
Smokers (1884)
Somerset (1882 to date)
South (1864-1961)
South Africans (1901-65)
South African Fezelas (1961)
South African Universities (1967)
South Americans (1932)
Southgate (1864-68)
South Wales (1912)
Sri Lankans (1975 to date)
L. C. Stevens' XI (1960-61)
A. E. Stoddart's XI (1895-98)
Surrey (1864 to date)
A Surrey XI (1949)
Surrey and Middlesex (1868-1912)
Surrey and Sussex (1867-1900)
Surrey Club (1865-73)
Sussex (1864 to date)
Hon. L. H. Tennyson's XI (1923-26)
TCCB XI (1981-86)
TCCB Under 25 XI (1990)
C. I. Thornton's XI (1882-1929)
C. E. de Trafford's XI (1896)
Uncapped (1923)
Under 25 (1968-90)
Under 30 (1879-1949)
Under 32 (1950)
Under 33 (1945)
United Eleven (1882)
United All England Eleven (1864-69)
United North of England Eleven (1870-76)
United South of England Eleven (1870-80)
Victoria (1991)
Wales (1923-30)
R. D. Walker's XI (1866)
P. F. Warner's XI (1903-47)
Earl de la Warr's XI (1896)
Warwickshire (1894 to date)
G. J. V. Weigall's XI (1904-14)
A. J. Webbe's XI (1885-1901)
Wembley Park (1896)
West (1892-1948)
West Indians (1906 to date)
Woodbrook Club and Ground (1912)
Worcestershire (1899 to date)
G. N. Wyatt's XI (1886)
Sir F. M. M. Worrell's West Indian XI (1964)
Yorkshire (1864 to date)
Young England (1963-78)
Zimbabweans (1982 to date)

Bibliography

Of the many books and journals consulted, the authors found the following particularly useful, and thank the authors and publishers.

Abrahams, H. M. and Bruce-Kerr, J. C. *Oxford versus Cambridge* (Faber, 1931)

Adamson, J. A. *Denstone Cricket 1874-1952* (Wilde, Shrewsbury, 1952)

Aitchison, Rev James *Kilmarnock C. C. Hundred Not Out* (Kilmarnock, 1952)

All England Cricket and Football Journal 1877-79 (Hurst, Sheffield, 1877-79)

American Cricket Annual 1890-1901 (various publishers, New York)

Anthony, Edwyn *Herefordshire Cricket* (the author, Hereford, 1903)

Ashley-Cooper, F. S. *New Zealand Cricket Guide* 1927, 1931 (Richards, Nottingham)

Ashley-Cooper, F. S. *West Indies Cricket Guide* 1928 (Richards, Nottingham)

Ashley-Cooper, F. S. manuscript biographical notes

ACS County Series, including all first-class counties to 1991 together with *Scotland, Ireland, Barbados* and *Cambridge Univ.* (ACS, 1973-1992)

ACS Guides to First-Class Matches British Isles, Australia, South Africa, New Zealand, West Indies, Pakistan, America, Sri Lanka, India (ACS, various years)

Athletic News Cricket Annual 1888-1939 (London and Manchester)

Ayres' Cricket Companion 1902-1932 (Ayres, London)

Betham, J. D. *Oxford and Cambridge, Scores and Biographies* (Simpkin, Marshall, London, 1905)

Bettesworth, W. A. *Chats on the Cricket Field* (Merritt and Hatcher, London, 1910)

British Sports and Sportsmen (London, 1917)

Brooke, R. W. *The Collins Who's Who of English First Class Cricket 1946-84* (Collins, 1985)

Brooke, R. W. and Goodyear, D. *A Who's Who of Lancashire CCC* (Breedon, 1991)

Brooke, R. W. and Goodyear, D. *A Who's Who of Warwickshire CCC* (Hale, 1989)

Brooke, R. W. and Goodyear, D. *A Who's Who of Worcestershire CCC* (Hale, 1990)

Burke's Peerage (London, various years)

Burke's Landed Gentry (London, various years)

Canynge Caple, S. *The Cricketers' Who's Who* (Williams, London, 1934)

Cambridge University Calendar

Canynge Caple, S. *The Cricketer's Who Who A – E* (C. B. S., Hunstanton, 1947)

Clarke, James *History of Cricket in Kendal* (Thompson, Kendal, 1906)

Coldham, J. D. *Northamptonshire Cricket* (Heinemann, London, 1959)

Cochrane, A. *Records of the Harlequin Cricket Club* (Eyre and Spottiswoode, London, 1930)

Cricket: A Weekly Record of the Game 1882 to 1914 (London, various years)

Cricket Field 1892-95 (London, various years)

Cricket Quarterly 1963-70 (Bowen, Eastbourne and Mullion, various years)

Cricket Society Journal 1961 to date (Cricket Society)

Cricket Spotlight 1957 to 1970 (Barker, Northampton, various years)

The Cricketer 1921 to date (London)

The Cricketer Quarterly 1973 to date (Tunbridge Wells)

Crockford's Clerical Directory

Daily News Cricket Annual 1913 to 1930 (*Daily News*, London)

De Lugo, A. B. *Surrey at the Wicket* (the author, Madrid, 1888)

Derbyshire County Year Book 1957 to date (Derby, various years)

Dorey, H. V. *Cricket Who's Who 1909 to 1913* (London)

Duffus, Louis *South African Cricket, Vol 3* (Johannesburg, 1948)

Essex County Cricket Club Year Book (London and Chelmsford, various years)

Flagstaff Cricket Annual 1953 to 1969 (Flagstaff, London, various years)

Frith, D. *By His Own Hand* (Stanley Paul, London, 1991)

Glamorgan County Cricket Club Year Books 1933 to date (Cardiff)
Gloucestershire County Cricket Club Year Books 1923 to date (Bristol)
Gordon, Home *Cricket Form at a Glance* (Constable, London, 1902)
Goulstone, John *Sports Quarterly* (the author, Bexleyheath, various years)
Hampshire County Cricket. Club Guides 1892 to 1939 (Southampton)
Harris, Lord *The History of Kent Cricket* (Eyre and Spottiswoode, London, 1907)
Haygarth, A. *Lillywhite's Scores & Biographies, Vols 1-4* (London, 1862)
Haygarth, A. *MCC Scores & Biographies, Vols 5-15* (Longmans, London, various years)
Hignell, A. K. *A Who's Who of Glamorgan CCC* (Breedon, 1991)
Indian Cricket Almanacks 1946 to date (Kasturi and Sons, Madras, various years)
Indian Cricket Field Annual 1957 to 1964 (Rutnagur, Bombay, various years)
Kent County Cricket Club Year Book (Blue Book) 1877-1945
James Lillywhite's Cricketer's Annual 1872-1900 (London, various years)
John Lillywhite's Cricketers' Companion 1865-85 (London, various years)
Luckin, M. W. *South African Cricket, Vols 1* (Hortor, Johannesburg, 1915) *and 2* (Johannesburg, 1928)
Lyon, W. R. *The Elevens of Three Great Schools* (Spottiswoode, Eton, 1930)
Martin-Jenkins, C. D. A. *Who's Who of Test Cricketers* (Orbis, London, 1983)
Miller, A. *Allan's Australian Cricket Annual* 1987/8 to date (Busselton, various years)
Morning Leader Cricket Annual 1907-12
News Chronicle Cricket Annual 1932-62 (London, various years)
New Zealand Cricket Almanack 1948 to date
Norman, Philip *Scores and Annals of the West Kent C. C.* (Eyre and Spottiswoode, London, 1897)
Pentelow, J. N. *Guide to Cricketers* (Simpkin, Marshall, Kent, 1911)
Playfair Cricket Annual 1948 to date (London, various years)
Playfair Cricket Monthly 1960 to 1973 (London, various years)
Pullin, A. W. *Talks with Old English Cricketers* (Blackwood, Edinburgh, 1900)
Pullin, A. W. *Talks with Old Yorkshire Cricketers* (*Yorkshire Post*, Leeds, 1898)
Reese, T. W. *New Zealand Cricket, Vols 1* (Simpson & Williams, Christchurch, 1927) *and 2* (Whitcombe & Toombs, Auckland, 1936)
Richards, C. H. *Notts Cricket Scores & Biographies* (Richards, Nottingham, 1901)
Roebuck, P. M. *From Sammy to Jimmy* (Partridge, 1991)
Rysden, O. *The Book of Blues* (Robinson, 1900)
Snow, E. E. *A History of Leicestershire Cricket, Vols 1* (Backus, Leicester, 1949) *and 2* (Stanley Paul, London, 1977)
South African Cricket Annual 1951 to date (Durban, various years)
Sproat, I. *The Cricketers' Who's Who* 1981 to date
Standing, P. C. *The Cricketers' Birthday Book* (Dent, London, 1898)
Surrey County Cricket Club Yearbooks 1884 to date (London, various years)
Thomas, P. *Yorkshire Cricketers 1839-1939* (Hodgson, Cheshire 1973)
Trinidad Cricket Council Yearbook (Port of Spain, various years)
Washbrook, C. *Cricket Annual 1949* (Sportsguide, London, 1949)
Webster, R. *First Class Cricket in Australia 1850 to 1942* (The Author, 1991)
West Indies Cricket Annual 1970 to date
Who's Who/Who was Who (A. and C. Black, London, various years)
Wisden Cricketers' Almanack 1864 to date
Wisden Cricket Monthly 1979 to date (London)
Woodhouse, A. *A Who's Who of Yorkshire CCC* (Breedon, 1991)
Wynne-Thomas, P. *Notts Cricketers, Vols 1 and 2* (Nottingham, 1971, 1981)
Wynne-Thomas, P. *England on Tour* (Hamlyn, London, 1982)
Yorkshire County Cricket Club Yearbooks 1893 to date

Explanation of the Entries

Scope
This book contains every cricketer who played in a first-class match in the British Isles from 1864 to 1992. Some of the most prominent players before this date are also included. A list of first-class teams appears on a separate page in this book.

The Order
Players are listed in alphabetical order; those of the same surname are listed in order of their forenames (*note:* this is a change from the first edition, in which players of the same name were listed in order of their initials). Those who in the course of their lives changed their names, are shown under the names they used when playing cricket, except for the handful who played under aliases. Cricketers who changed their name during the course of their cricket career are cross-referenced.

Names
For players born in the British Isles the forenames given are those on their birth certificates. If a player adopted an additional name, for example Robert George (Dylan) Willis, the adopted name is given in brackets. Nicknames are not shown. Relatives are shown only where the exact relationship is known.

Decorations are not given unless they were awarded for services to cricket. Services ranks, because of the complexity of the subject, especially in the 19th century, are not shown except for ranks of General and above and the Navy and RAF equivalents.

Status
The players are described as professional or amateur if their career began before 1963. Those whose career began after 1962 are shown as 'cricketer', since the distinction, in first-class cricket, was abolished in 1963. The convention of describing overseas tourists as 'amateur' is followed in most cases.

Dates and places of birth and death
For players born or dying in England, Wales or Scotland, dates and places have been checked, where possible, against the records of the General Register Office, London, or Register House, Edinburgh, and thus many details given will differ from previously published information. Counties are shown as they were prior to modern reorganisation as the names of the county teams have remained unchanged.

The cause of death is stated if it is unusual, or, when known, for a player who died young. There are players who may be presumed dead because of their birth date but for whom no definite information about date of death exists.

Type of Player

A player's style may vary at different stages of his career, for example a fast bowler may become medium pace, or in the 19th century, an under-arm bowler change to round-arm, or a lower order batsman in County cricket may be an opening batsman in local club cricket. The description given here is of the player during his first-class career only, unless stated to the contrary. The description is in the order of batting, bowling and fielding characteristics, whatever the player's principal activity.

School

A player's school is given only if the school is one of those whose records are usually found in cricketing periodicals.

Teams

The first-class County(ies) for which the player appeared are given with dates indicating the extent of his career and number of first-class matches. Dates are also given for appearances for London County, Cambridge Town Club, Scotland, Wales, Ireland, Oxford U, Cambridge U and Dublin U. If a player did not represent a first-class County then the principal first-class team is given with appropriate dates. The overseas equivalents of English first-class Counties are given as appropriate with dates, but the number of matches are only included for the Australian States. In the case of players of Oxford and Cambridge Universities, the year(s) in which blues were obtained are stated.

If a player made his first-class debut, or his final first-class appearance, for a side not mentioned under 'teams', the details are given separately.

Tours

All tours involving first-class matches or limited overs internationals are shown as appropriate, plus those tours which the authors feel are of significance to the biography.

Test Matches

The countries for which the player appeared in an official Test match are given with seasons of first and last appearance and number of matches.

Career Records

The first-class career record for each player is given, except for 18th century players. Details of the matches included can be found in the various 'Guides' published by the Association of Cricket Statisticians. The Career records are complete to the end of the 1992 English season. The line of batting figures is composed as follows:

matches–innings–not outs–runs–highest score–average–100s–catches –stumpings

The line of bowling figures is:

runs conceded–wickets–average–five wickets in an innings –ten wickets in a match–best bowling in an innings

In cases where a bowler took wickets but no bowling analyses are extant then these wickets are shown thus (+ 21) between the wickets figure and the average.

A bowler who did not take a wicket is given an abbreviated record, for example: 27–0.

Where no bowling figures are given, it is to be assumed that the player did not bowl in first-class cricket. Test career records are set out in similar fashion.

Abbreviations

The abbreviations used in the entries are:

b: born *c:* christened *d:* died *Sch* School *ct* caught *st* stumped * not out

Seasons

Seasons overseas, where the cricket season takes place in the English winter, are indicated in the style: 1981/2. Career spans are shown thus: 1975–79, except where an overseas season is concerned, when the style is: 1975 to 1978/9.

WHO'S WHO *OF* CRICKETERS

A

Aamer Hameed
Cricketer. *b:* 18.10.1954, Lahore, Pakistan. Lower order right-hand batsman, right-arm medium fast bowler. *Teams* Universities (1972/3 to 1973/4); Lahore (1974/5 to 1976/7); Punjab (1974/5 to 1977/8); Servis Industries (1975/6 to 1977/8); National Bank (1976/7); United Bank (1977/8); Oxford U (1979, blue). *Tour* Pakistan to England 1978.
Career batting
54–70–10–895–103–14.91–2–*ct* 15
Bowling 4138–110–37.61–5–1–7/36

Although awarded his blue in 1979, Aamer Hameed's bowling record for the University was a very modest 7 wickets (av 74.57). He appeared for Pakistan in one-day internationals.

Aamer Sohail
Cricketer. *b:* 14.9.1966, Lahore, Pakistan. Opening left-hand batsman, slow left-arm bowler. *Teams* Lahore (1983/4 to 1986/7); Habib Bank (1987/8 to 1991/2); Sargodha (1990/1). *Tours* Pakistan B to Zimbabwe 1986/7; Pakistan A to Sri Lanka 1990/1; Pakistan to Sharjah (not first-class) 1990/1, 1991/2, to Australia 1991/2, to Australia and New Zealand (World Cup) 1991/2, to England 1992. *Tests* Pakistan (1992, 5 matches).
Career batting
106–177–14–6527–205–40.04–14–*ct* 79
Bowling 3256–90–36.17–1–1–7/53
Test batting
5–9–1–413–205–51.62–1–*ct* 3
Bowling 14–0

On the 1992 tour to England he hit 1,110 runs, av 42.69. Playing in all five Tests, he scored 205 in the Third Test at Old Trafford.

Aaqib Javed
Cricketer. *b:* 5.8.1972, Sheikhupura, Pakistan. Lower order right-hand batsman, right-arm fast medium bowler. *Teams* Lahore Division (1984/5 to 1986/7); PACO (1989/90); Hampshire (1991, 18 matches). *Tours* Pakistan to Australia and New Zealand 1988/9, 1991/2 (World Cup), to Australia 1989/90, 1991/2, to India 1989/90 (not first-class), to Sharjah (not first-class) 1988/9, 1989/90, 1990/1, to England 1992. *Tests* Pakistan (1988/9 to 1992, 13 matches).
Career batting
53–41–18–154–32*–6.69–0–0–*ct* 5
Bowling 4125–125–33.00–4–0–6/91
Test batting
13–10–3–26–10–3.71–0–*ct* 1
Bowling 1013–25–40.52–0–0–4/100

For Hampshire in 1991 he took 53 wickets, av 31.24. Touring England with Pakistan in 1992 he played in all five Tests, but was very much overshadowed by Wasim and Waqar. If his published birth date is correct, he made his first-class debut at the age of 12.

Abberley, Robert Neal
Cricketer. *b:* 22.4.1944, Stechford, Birmingham. Opening or middle order right-hand batsman, occasional right-arm medium pace bowler. *Team* Warwickshire (1964–79, 258 matches). *Tour* MCC Under 25 to Pakistan 1966/7.
Career batting
261–439–27–10082–117*–24.47–3–*ct* 171
Bowling 294–5–58.80–0–0–2/19

He had his best season in 1966 with 1,315 runs (av 28.58) and exceeded 1,000 runs on two other occasions, but never lived up to his early promise. He was Warwickshire chief coach from 1981, later taking charge of the 2nd XI.

Abbey, David Robert
Cricketer. *b:* 11.12.1941, Edmonton, Middlesex. Lower order right-hand batsman, slow left-arm bowler. *Team* Middlesex (1967, 2 matches).
Career batting
2–2–0–14–12–7.00–0–*ct* 0
Bowling 23–0

Abbott, Alan Wesley
Professional. *b:* 15.11.1926, Sutton-in-the-Elms, Leicestershire. Lower order right-hand batsman, off break bowler. *Team* Leicestershire (1946, 1 match).
Career batting
1–2–0–5–5–2.50–0–*ct* 0
Bowling 8–0

Abbott, Frederick Julius
Amateur. *b:* 25.11.1901, Wellington, New Zealand. *d:* 4.5.1952, Banstead, Surrey. Middle order right-hand batsman. *Sch* Malvern. *Team* Worcestershire (1919–20, 3 matches).
Career batting
3–5–0–63–42–12.60–0–*ct* 0

Abbott, Herbert Edward Stacy
Amateur. *b:* 6.4.1855, Alipore, India. *d:* 13.6.1939, Richmond, Surrey. Middle order batsman. *Sch* Elizabeth College, Guernsey. *Team* MCC (1902).
Career batting
1–2–0–19–18–9.50–0–*ct* 0

Abbott, William
Amateur. *b:* 28.10.1856, Rydens, Walton-on-Thames, Surrey. *d:* 22.12.1935, Maybury, Woking, Surrey. Son of C. J. (Surrey 1844). Middle order batsman, wicket-keeper. *Sch* Winchester. *Team* Surrey (1877, 3 matches).
Career batting
3–5–0–9–5–1.80–0–*ct* 7–*st* 2

Abdul Hafeez (*see under* Kardar, A. H.)

Abdul Qadir Khan
Cricketer. *b:* 15.9.1955, Lahore, Pakistan. Brother of Ali Bahadur (WAPDA). Lower order right-hand batsman, leg break and googly bowler. *Teams* Punjab (1975/6); Lahore (1975/6 to 1984/5); Habib Bank (1975/6 to 1990/1). *Tours* Pakistan to England 1978, 1982, 1983 (World Cup), 1987, to India 1979/80, 1986/7, 1989/90 (not first-class), to Australia 1983/4, 1988/9, 1989/90, to Sharjah (not first-class) 1983/4, 1985/6, 1986/7, 1988/9, 1989/90, to New Zealand 1984/5, 1988/9, to Sri Lanka 1985/6, to West Indies 1987/8, to Bangladesh (not first-class) 1988/9; Rest of World to England 1987. *Tests* Pakistan (1977/8 to 1990/1, 67 matches).
Career batting
198–234–40–3636–112–18.74–2–*ct* 76
Bowling 21017–897–23.43–70–19–9/49
Test batting
67–77–11–1029–61–15.59–0–*ct* 15
Bowling 7742–236–32.80–15–5–9/56

His Test debut against England came in 1977/8 when he baffled the English cricketers and topped the Test bowling averages. Coming to England in 1978 however he achieved little and was not required for the Tests. Returning in 1982 he was Pakistan's leading wicket-taker with 57 victims, av 20.82. In 1982/3 he became the first bowler to capture 100 wickets in a single Pakistan season. He caused all sorts of problems with his spin bowling in the 1983/4 series in Pakistan, taking 19 wickets, av 23.73, and being the outstanding bowler on either side. He missed the first seven weeks of the 1987 tour to England and showed his best form only in the final Test at the Oval. He was the second Pakistan bowler to capture more than 200 Test wickets, reaching this landmark in 1987/8 when he took 9 for 56 in the Lahore Test. His best bowling was 9/49 for Habib Bank v Rawalpindi at Rawalpindi in 1982/3.

Abdy, Brig-Gen Anthony John
Amateur. *b:* 26.4.1856, Cambridge. *d:* 4.7.1924, La Tour-de-Peilz, Switzerland. Brother-in-law of L. G. Bonham-Carter (Hampshire), uncle of S. S. Bonham-Carter (Royal Navy). Useful opening batsman. *Sch* Charterhouse. *Team* Hampshire (1881, 1 match).
Career batting
1–2–0–30–23–15.00–0–*ct* 0

Notable Army cricketer with Royal Artillery, Southern Division, etc. He also played for Essex (pre first-class) in 1876.

Abdy, Robert Burlton
Amateur. *b:* 1.8.1857, Carlton, Worksop, Nottinghamshire. *d:* 21.5.1899, Great Yarmouth, Norfolk. Middle order batsman. *Team* MCC (1888).
Career batting
2–4–0–8–6–2.00–0–*ct* 1

a'Beckett, Edward Lambert
Amateur. *b:* 11.8.1907, East St Kilda, Melbourne, Victoria, Australia. *d:* 2.6.1989, Terang, Melbourne, Victoria, Australia. Father of E. C. (Victoria). Attractive middle order right-hand batsman, right-arm fast medium bowler, good field anywhere. *Team* Victoria (1927/8 to 1931/2, 25 matches). *Tour* Australia to England 1930. *Tests* Australia (1928/9 to 1931/2, 4 matches).
Career batting
47–64–8–1636–152–29.21–2–*ct* 35
Bowling 3062–105–29.16–3–0–6/119
Test batting
4–7–0–143–41–20.42–0–*ct* 4
Bowling 317–3–105.66–0–0–1/41

Illness on his tour to England in 1930 deprived him of the opportunity of acclimatising himself and he therefore had a moderate tour. His only real moment was the brilliant catch he took in the third Test to dismiss Hobbs. He left first-class cricket while still young, to concentrate on his career as a barrister, also having received a head injury playing Australian football.

Abel, Robert
Professional. *b:* 30.11.1857, Rotherhithe, Surrey. *d:* 10.12.1936, Stockwell, London. Father of T. E. (Surrey and Glamorgan) and W. J. (Surrey), great-uncle of R. W. Wilkinson (Kent). Very sound opening right-hand batsman, who could hit if required, off break bowler. *Team* Surrey (1881–1904, 514 matches). *Tours* Vernon to Australia 1887/8; Warton to S. Africa 1888/9; Sheffield to Australia 1891/2. *Tests* England (1888–96, 13 matches).
Career batting
627–1007–73–33124–357*–35.46–74–*ct* 587
Bowling 6314–263–24.00–3–0–6/15
Test batting
13–22–2–744–132*–37.20–2–*ct* 13

'The Guv'nor', as he was affectionately termed, did not make his first-class debut until he was 23 and then made little impact on the cricketing world for the next six years. It was an innings of 144 in 1886 against the Australians which really made his name and in the same summer he reached 1,000 runs for the first of 14 times. An eye infection seemed likely to close prematurely his career in 1893, but happily he recovered and the next decade saw his run tally vastly increase. For eight successive seasons (1895–02) he exceeded 2,000 runs, and in one glorious summer acquired no less than 3,309 to create a new first-class record. That was in 1901, but two years earlier he had hit 357 not out for Surrey v Somerset at the Oval, an innings that was then the second highest ever in Championship cricket.

After 1902 he again suffered from eye trouble and, although wearing glasses helped a little, his first-class days were brought to a rather abrupt end in 1904. He was Surrey coach in 1907. As an opening batsman he shared in many large partnerships, usually for the first wicket with W. Brockwell, but his record-breaking effort was for the fourth wicket with T. W. Hayward, the pair adding 448 for Surrey against Yorkshire at the Oval in 1899 – a world record for nearly fifty years and the English record until 1982.

Abel was on the short side for a batsman and somewhat ungainly, but his perseverance during his early years at the Oval, when the authorities retained him as much for his fielding as batting, paid dividends in the long term, both for himself and for Surrey.

Abel, Thomas Ernest
Professional. *b:* 10.9.1890, Kennington, London. *d:* 23.1.1937, Lambeth, London. Son of Robert (Surrey), brother of W. J. (Surrey). Hard hitting opening right-hand batsman, slow right-arm bowler. *Teams* Surrey (1919–20, 12 matches); Glamorgan (1922–25, 32 matches).
Career batting
44–68–2–1045–107–15.83–1–*ct* 19
Bowling 976–31–31.48–0–0–3/30

Abel, William John
Professional. *b:* 29.8.1887, South Bermondsey, Surrey. *d:* 23.3.1934, Stockwell, London. Son of Robert (Surrey), brother of T. E. (Surrey and Glamorgan). Hard hitting right-hand batsman, right-arm fast medium, later leg break and googly bowler, good slip field. *Team* Surrey (1909–26, 170 matches).
Career batting
171–246–29–4988–117–22.98–1–*ct* 146
Bowling 5753–187–30.76–3–0–5/28

His health was seriously affected while serving in the First World War, and this led to his death at the early age of 46.

Abell, Sir George Edmond Brackenbury
Amateur. *b:* 22.6.1904, Worcester. *d:* 11.1.1989, Whittonditch, Ramsbury, Wiltshire. Father of J. N. (Oxford) and T. G. (Free Foresters), nephew of E. L. Sale (Europeans), brother-in-law of C. T. Ashton (Essex). Hard-hitting middle order right-hand batsman, wicket-keeper. *Sch* Marlborough. *Teams* Worcestershire (1923–39, 34 matches); Oxford U (1924–27, blue 1924, 1926 and 1927); Europeans (1928/9 to 1929/30); Northern India (1934/5 to 1941/2).
Career batting
75–124–16–2674–210–24.75–4–*ct* 97–*st* 33
Bowling 4–0

His most famous innings was on his debut in the Ranji Trophy when he hit 210 for Northern India v Army at Lahore 1934/5. From 1946 to 1967 he was the First Civil Service Commissioner. He also won blues for rugby and hockey.

Abell, John Norman
Amateur. *b:* 18.9.1931, Chelsfield House, Kent. Son of G. E. B. (Worcestershire), brother of T. G. (Free Foresters), great-nephew of E. L. Sale (Europeans). Forcing middle order right-hand batsman, wicket-keeper. *Sch* Marlborough. *Team* Oxford U (1952–53).
Career batting
3–5–0–56–25–11.20–0–*ct* 2–*st* 5

Abell, Roy Beverley
Cricketer. *b:* 21.1.1931, Small Heath, Birmingham. Tail end right-hand batsman, leg break bowler. *Team* Warwickshire (1967, 1 match).
Career batting
1 match, did not bat–*ct* 1
Bowling 112–4–28.00–0–0–3/64

Abell, Timothy George
Amateur. *b:* 29.4.1930, Lahore, India. Son of G. E. B. (Worcestershire), brother of J. N. (Oxford U), great-nephew of E. L. Sale (Europeans). Lower order right-hand batsman, off break bowler. *Sch* Marlborough. *Team* Free Foresters (1954).
Career batting
1–2–1–4–4*–4.00–0–*ct* 0
Bowling 1–0

Abercrombie, Cecil Halliday
Amateur. *b:* 12.4.1886, Mozufferpore, India. *d:* 31.5.1916. Killed in the naval action off Jutland (HMS *Defence*). Dashing middle order right-hand batsman. *Sch* Berkhamsted. *Team* Hampshire (1913, 13 matches).
Career batting
16–31–3–1126–165–40.21–4–*ct* 11
Bowling 329–8–41.12–0–0–3/27

His first-class debut was for Navy and Army in 1910. He scored a century for Navy v Army at Lord's in 1912 and was drafted into the Hampshire side in 1913, hitting 126 on his debut v Oxford U at Southampton. Owing to Service commitments he could not appear for Hampshire in 1914. He represented Scotland at rugby.

Aberdare, Lord
(*see under* Bruce, Hon C. N.)

Abid Ali, Syed
Cricketer. *b:* 9.9.1941, Hyderabad, India. Middle order right-hand batsman, right-arm medium fast bowler. *Team* Hyderabad (1959/60 to 1978/9). *Tours* India to England 1971, 1974, 1975 (World Cup), to Australia and New Zealand 1967/8, to West Indies 1970/1; State Bank of India to Ceylon 1968/9; Rest of World to Pakistan 1970/1. *Tests* India (1967/8 to 1974/5, 29 matches).
Career batting
212–333–35–8732–173*–29.30–13–*ct* 190–*st* 5
Bowling 11336–397–28.55–14–0–6/23
Test batting
29–53–3–1018–81–20.36–0–*ct* 32
Bowling 1980–47–42.12–1–0–6/55

He was for several years the best seam bowler in India, but his returns in Test cricket were very modest, and though he could show the lowest average in first-class matches during the 1974 tour to England, his 32 wickets cost 30.15 runs apiece.

Abington, Michael Barringer
Cricketer. *b:* 8.3.1965, Lusaka, Zambia. Lower order right-hand batsman, slow left-arm bowler. *Sch* Bedford. *Team* Cambridge U (1992, blue).
Career batting
7–7–0–20–6–2.85–0–*ct* 4
Bowling 530–10–53.00–0–0–3/33

Ablack, Robert Kenneth
Amateur. *b:* 5.1.1919, Port of Spain, Trinidad. Lower order batsman, slow left-arm bowler. *Team* Northamptonshire (1946–49, 3 matches).
Career batting
3–4–2–24–16–12.00–0–*ct* 0
Bowling 220–6–36.66–0–0–3/32

He became well-known as a cricket commentator on radio.

Aboyne, Earl of, Charles Gordon
(also known as Lord Strathavon 1794–1836 and 10th Marquis of Huntly 1853–1863)
Amateur. *b:* 4.1.1792, Orton Longueville, Huntingdonshire. *d:* 18.9.1863, Orton Longueville, Huntingdonshire. Brother of F. A. Gordon (Cambridge U). Lower order right-hand batsman. *Teams* Hampshire (1819–21); Kent (1827–36); Surrey(1831).
Career batting
33–61–13–193–19–4.02–0–*ct* 9

As he backed the Players (v Gentlemen) in 1819, he was allowed to appear in the professional ranks; in 1827 he appeared for the Gentlemen. His first first-class match was for W. Ward's XI in 1818 and his last for MCC in 1843. He was President of MCC in 1821.

Abraham, Thomas Smyth
Amateur. *b:* 19.6.1838, Exeter, Devon. *d:* 14.12.1873, Algiers, Algeria. Lower order batsman. *Team* Gentlemen of England (1870).
Career batting
1–2–0–9–9–4.50–0–*ct* 0
Bowling 45–0

He also played for Cornwall (1859), Devon (1862–71), Wiltshire (1867) and Somerset (1871).

Abrahams, John
Cricketer. *b:* 21.7.1952, Salt River, Cape Town, South Africa. Middle order left-hand batsman, off break bowler, cover field. *Team* Lancashire (1973–88, 251 matches).
Career batting
252–390–52–10059–201*–29.76–14–*ct* 162
Bowling 2811–56–50.19–0–0–3/27

He hit 1,000 runs in a season four times (best 1,261, av 39.40, in 1983). In 1984 and 1985 he captained Lancashire. He also played for Shropshire (1989–91). His highest score was 201* for Lancashire v Warwickshire at Nuneaton in 1984.

Absolom, Charles Alfred
Amateur. *b:* 7.6.1846, Blackheath, Kent. *d:* 30.7.1889, Port-of-Spain, Trinidad. He was employed as purser on SS *Muriel* which was loading sugar cane when a crane collapsed, crushing him. He lingered on in great agony for three days before dying. Opening or middle order right hand batsman, being a lively but eccentric hitter, useful right-arm medium pace bowler, good field. Privately educated. *Teams* Cambridge U (1866–69, blue each year); Kent (1868–79, 57 matches). *Tour* Harris to Australia 1878/9. *Test* England (1878/9, 1 match).
Career batting
99–178–11–2515–94–15.05–0–*ct* 127
Bowling 5472–281 + 1–19.47–19–3–7/45
Test batting
1–2–0–58–52–29.00–0–*ct* 0

He was an all round athlete, representing Cambridge at putting the shot and the long jump, and a noted footballer. The last ten years of his life were spent roving America, spending much time with the Spokane Red Indians. As a cricketer he always played for his side and never for himself, a philosophy which he carried into other walks of life. He also played for Essex (pre first-class) in 1865–72.

Aburrow, Edward
Professional. *b:* 1747, Hambledon, Hampshire *d:* 6.10.1835, Hambledon, Hampshire. Safe and steady right-hand batsman, right-hand under-arm bowler, good long-field. *Team* Hampshire.

He played before 1801, so career records are inapplicable.

Acfield, David Laurence
Cricketer. *b:* 24.7.1947, Chelmsford, Essex. Lower order right-hand batsman, off break bowler. *Sch* Brentwood. *Teams* Essex (1966–86, 378 matches); Cambridge U (1966–68, blue 1967 and 1968). *Tour* MCC to East Africa 1973/4.

Career batting
420–417–212–1677–42–8.18–0–*ct* 137
Bowling 26800–950–28.21–34–4–8/55

His best season was 1981 with 76 wickets, av 22.61. A noted fencer, he represented Cambridge and Great Britain in the Olympic Games and was British sabre champion.

Acheson, Lord Archibald Brabazon-Sparrow (4th Earl of Gosford)
Amateur. *b:* 19.8.1841, Worlingham Hall, Beccles, Suffolk. *d:* 11.4.1922, Paddington, London. Brother of E. A. B. (MCC), uncle of G. S. Foljambe (Nottinghamshire) and G. A. T. Foljambe (MCC), great-uncle of E. W. S. Foljambe (Oxford U). Lower order right-hand batsman, right medium pace round-arm bowler. *Sch* Harrow. *Team* MCC (1864).
Career batting
1–2–1–6–4*–6.00–0–*ct* 1
Bowling 7–1–7.00–0–0–1/7

He succeeded to the Earldom in 1864. He was Vice-Chamberlain to Queen Alexandra. He appeared for Ireland (not first-class) in 1867.

Acheson, Major General Hon Edward Archibald Brabazon
Amateur. *b:* 22.5.1844, Worlingham Hall, Beccles, Suffolk. *d:* 3.7.1921, Westminster, London. Brother of A. B. S. (MCC), uncle of G. S. Foljambe (Nottinghamshire) and G. A. T. Foljambe (MCC), great-uncle of E. W. S. Foljambe (Oxford U). Lower order right-hand batsman, round-arm bowler, excellent field. *Sch* Harrow. *Team* MCC (1866).
Career batting
1–1–0–0–0–0.00–0–*ct* 1

Achong, Ellis Edgar
Amateur. *b:* 16.2.1904, Belmont, Port of Spain, Trinidad. *d:* 30.8.1986, St Augustine, Port of Spain, Trinidad. Lower order left-hand batsman, slow left-arm bowler. *Team* Trinidad (1929/30 to 1934/5). *Tour* West Indies to England 1933. *Tests* West Indies (1929/30 to 1934/5, 6 matches).
Career batting
38–55–20–503–45*–14.37–0–*ct* 20
Bowling 3326–110–30.23–3–1–7/73
Test batting
6–11–1–81–22–8.10–0–*ct* 6
Bowling 378–8–47.25–0–0–2/64

Of Chinese descent – the first such to play in a Test match – Achong was the leading slow bowler of the 1933 touring side, but achieved little due to the unresponsive wickets that year. It is sometimes said that the term 'Chinaman', for a left-hander's wrist spinner, was inspired by him, but this appears to have no basis in fact.

Ackerman, Hylton Michael
Cricketer. *b:* 28.4.1947, Springs, Transvaal, South Africa. Sound opening or middle order left-hand batsman, right-arm medium pace bowler. *Teams* Border (1963/4 to 1965/6); North East Transvaal (1966/7 to 1967/8); Northamptonshire (1967–71, 98 matches); Natal (1968/9 to 1969/70); Western Province (1970/1 to 1981/2). *Tours* Rest of World to Australia 1971/2, South Africa to Australia 1971/2 (tour cancelled).
Career batting
234–409–33–12219–208–32.49–20–*ct* 199
Bowling 1400–32–43.75–0–0–4/61

He hit 1,000 runs in a season three times (best 1,565, av 33.29, in 1970). His only double century in England was 208 for Northamptonshire v Leicestershire at Leicester in 1970.

Ackroyd, Alfred
Amateur. *b:* 29.8.1858, Oakroyd Hall, Birkenshaw, Leeds, Yorkshire. *d:* 3.10.1927, Eccles, Lancashire. Lower order right-hand batsman, right-arm fast bowler. *Sch* Uppingham. *Team* Yorkshire (1879, 1 match).
Career batting
2–3–2–15–13*–15.00–0–*ct* 0
Bowling 32–3–10.66–0–0–3/25

His first-class debut was for an England XI in 1878.

Ackroyd, Archibald
Professional. *b:* 18.5.1897, Heanor, Derbyshire. *d:* 25.6.1968, Dixon's Green, Dudley, Worcestershire. Lower order right-hand batsman, right-arm medium fast bowler. *Teams* Derbyshire (1924–25, 11 matches); Scotland (1937).
Career batting
12–20–1–79–15–4.15–0–*ct* 5
Bowling 707–20–35.35–0–0–4/63

A'Court, Dennis George
(also known as Kenneth)
Professional. *b:* 27.7.1937, Markham, Bedwellty, Monmouth. Tail end right-hand batsman, right-arm fast medium bowler. *Team* Gloucestershire (1960–63, 49 matches).
Career batting
49–68–31–420–47*–11.35–0–*ct* 10
Bowling 3890–145–26.82–5–0–6/25

He was on the Gloucestershire staff for ten years, but rarely commanded a regular place in the Eleven.

Acton, James
Amateur. Lower order batsman. *Team* Hampshire (1880–82, 2 matches).
Career batting
2–3–0–41–31–13.66–0–*ct* 0
Bowling 12–0

Adair, John Frederick
Amateur. *b:* 1851, St Stephen's Green, Dublin, Ireland. *d:* 1.4.1913, Ballsbridge, Co Dublin, Ireland. Middle order batsman, wicket-keeper. *Team* Cambridge U (1875).

Adair, Robert Emile

Career batting
2–2–1–31–17–31.00–0–*ct* 2

Adair, Robert Emile
Amateur. *b:* 1876, Ireland. *d:* 18.3.1951, Prittlewell, Westcliff-on-Sea, Essex. Middle order right-hand batsman, right-arm fast medium bowler. *Team* Ireland (1902).
Career batting
4–7–1–86–32–14.33–0–*ct* 3
Bowling 37–1–37.00–0–0–1/29

Adams, Alfred
Professional. *b:* 14.11.1814, Saffron Walden, Essex. *d:* 1.10.1868, Saffron Walden, Essex. Brother of James (Essex). Fine hitter.
His chief claim to fame is an innings of 279 which he hit in a minor match in 1837 – at the time the highest recorded score. He never appeared in first-class matches.

Adams, Christopher John
Cricketer. *b:* 6.5.1970, Whitwell, Derbyshire. Middle order right-hand batsman, off break bowler. *Sch* Repton. *Team* Derbyshire (1988–92, 69 matches).
Career batting
69–103–13–3014–140*–33.48–8–*ct* 71
Bowling 375–10–37.50–0–0–4/29
He scored 1,109 runs, av 41.07, in 1992.

Adams, Cyril Douglas
Amateur. *b:* 18.9.1897, Penn Hall, Parkstone, Dorset. *d:* 19.8.1988, Milford-on-Sea, Hampshire. Useful middle order right-hand batsman, right-arm fast bowler. *Team* RAF (1928–32).
Career batting
5–10–1–173–46*–19.22–0–*ct* 4
Bowling 373–11–33.90–0–0–3/62
His County cricket was for Dorset (1923–27).

Adams, Donald
Professional. *b:* 8.6.1880, Ockley, Surrey. *d:* 8.1.1976, Walton-on-Thames, Surrey. Lower order batsman, opening bowler. *Team* Surrey (1902, 1 match).
Career batting
1–2–0–26–14–13.00–0–*ct* 2
Bowling 83–1–83.00–0–0–1/28
His only first-class wicket was that of W. G. Grace, the match being Surrey v London County at Crystal Palace, 1902.

Adams, Douglas Howe
Amateur. Middle order batsman. *Sch* Haverford College. *Team* Philadelphia (1898–1908). *Tour* Philadelphia to England 1908.
Career batting
4–7–0–101–74–14.42–0–*ct* 2
Bowling 46–0
His first-class debut was for Players of USA in 1894.

Adams, Edmund Joe
Amateur. *b:* 1.2.1915, Shepton Mallet, Somerset. Middle order batsman. *Team* Somerset (1935, 1 match).
Career batting
1–1–0–5–5–5.00–0–*ct* 0

Adams, Geoffrey Coker Arding
Amateur. *b:* 24.5.1909, Hampstead, London. Hard-hitting middle order right-hand batsman, excellent cover-point, fair change bowler. *Sch* Radley. *Team* Hampshire (1928–30, 18 matches).
Career batting
18–33–2–421–42–13.58–0–*ct* 3
Bowling 162–4–40.50–0–0–1/0
He played in various trial matches at Cambridge with little success, and for Hampshire in the vacation.

Adams, Henry James
Professional. *b:* 25.4.1852, Croydon, Surrey. *d:* 21.2.1922, Edmonton, Middlesex. Tail end right-hand batsman, wicket-keeper, right-arm medium pace bowler. *Team* Surrey (1887–89, 4 matches).
Career batting
5–9–4–25–9–5.00–0–*ct* 4–*st* 2

Adams, Keith
Amateur. *b:* 6.6.1932, Aberford, Leeds, Yorkshire. Stylish opening right-hand batsman. *Sch* St Peter's, York. *Team* Cambridge U (1954).
Career batting
1–2–0–34–34–17.00–0–*ct* 1

Adams, Lestock Handley
Amateur. *b:* 10.9.1887, Ormskirk, Lancashire. *d:* 22.4.1918. He was killed in action at Placaut Wood, France. Tail end batsman, useful bowler. *Sch* St Lawrence College, Ramsgate. *Team* Cambridge U (1908–10).
Career batting
6–10–5–61–21*–12.20–0–*ct* 1
Bowling 531–17–31.23–1–0–6/86

Adams, Percy William
Amateur. *b:* 5.9.1900, Northampton. *d:* 28.9.1962, Pimlico, Westminster, London. Lower order right-hand batsman, wicket-keeper. *Sch* Cheltenham. *Team* Sussex (1922, 1 match).
Career batting
1–2–1–2–1*–2.00–0–*ct* 0–*st* 1

Adams, Sidney Clarke
Amateur. *b:* 17.8.1904, Northampton. *d:* 24.3.1945, Berlin, Germany. Middle order right-hand batsman, useful leg break bowler. *Team* Northamptonshire (1926–32, 10 matches).
Career batting
11–16–1–158–87–10.53–0–*ct* 5
Bowling 250–13–19.23–1–0–6/32
On his first-class debut for Northamptonshire v Dublin Univ at Northampton, Adams hit 87 and took

two wickets with the first two balls he delivered, ending with 6/32.

Adams, Thomas Miles
Professional. *b:* 2.5.1813, Gravesend, Kent. *d:* 20.1.1894, Milton, Gravesend, Kent. Fine, punishing middle order right-hand batsman, medium pace round-arm bowler. *Teams* Kent (1836–58, 99 matches); Hampshire (1848, 1 match); Lancashire (1851, 1 match).
Career batting
157–290–11–3435–78–12.31–0–*ct* 144
Bowling 449–33 + 117–13.60–5–1–7/?

He played County cricket for about 20 years, and unusually for round-arm bowlers bowled over the wicket. On 18 July 1849 in the match between I Zingari and Royal Artillery, he had a hand in dismissing all ten of his opponents in both innings.

Adams, William
Amateur. *b:* 17.4.1885, Staple Claydon, Buckinghamshire. *d:* 6.4.1957, Ashton, Northamptonshire. Defensive opening left-hand batsman. *Team* Northamptonshire (1920–29, 37 matches).
Career batting
38–67–5–1125–154*–18.14–2–*ct* 5
Bowling 67–0

Adamson, Charles Lodge
Amateur. *b:* 18.5.1906, Neville's Cross, Durham. *d:* 18.11.1979, Durham. Son of C. Y. (Queensland). Middle order right-hand batsman. *Sch* Durham. *Team* Minor Counties (1934).
Career batting
1–2–0–15–15–7.50–0–*ct* 0

His County cricket was for Durham (pre first-class, 1926–39).

Adcock, Neil Amwin Treharne
Amateur. *b:* 8.3.1931, Sea Point, Cape Town, South Africa. Tail end right-hand batsman, hostile right-arm fast bowler. *Teams* Transvaal (1952/3 to 1959/60); Natal (1960/1 to 1962/3). *Tours* South Africa to England 1955, 1960; Commonwealth to New Zealand 1961/2. *Tests* South Africa (1953/4 to 1961/2, 26 matches).
Career batting
99–117–35–451–41–5.50–0–*ct* 23
Bowling 6989–405–17.25–19–4–8/39
Test batting
26–39–12–146–24–5.40–0–*ct* 4
Bowling 2195–104–21.10–5–0–6/43

Adcock appeared in Test cricket after only 9 first-class matches, but initially his career was plagued by injuries and it was not until the 1960 tour to England that he was physically capable of playing continuous first-class cricket. In this tour he was South Africa's principal bowler, equalling the record for the most wickets by a South African in a Test Series in England (26) and taking more wickets in an English season (108 at 14.02) than any previous South African fast bowler.

Adcock, Robert Alfred
Professional. *b:* 3.11.1916, Ibstock, Leicestershire. Middle order right-hand batsman, right-arm medium pace bowler. *Team* Leicestershire (1938, 5 matches).
Career batting
5–9–0–89–27–9.88–0–*ct* 2
Bowling 29–1–29.00–0–0–1/29

He also played for Lincolnshire (1939).

Adderley, Charles Henry
Amateur. *b:* 16.9.1912, Kings Heath, Birmingham. *d:* 28.2.1985, Moseley, Birmingham. Lower order right-hand batsman, right-arm medium pace bowler. *Team* Warwickshire (1946, 5 matches).
Career batting
5–8–2–27–12–4.50–0–*ct* 1
Bowling 255–4–63.75–0–0–1/19

Addis, Charles Frederick
Amateur. *b:* 2.2.1902, Finedon, Northamptonshire. *d:* 15.8.1983, Northampton. Lower order left-hand batsman, left-arm medium pace bowler. *Team* Northamptonshire (1924–26, 2 matches).
Career batting
2–1–0–38–38–38.00–0–*ct* 1
Bowling 155–5–31.00–0–0–3/78

Addison, Jonathan Paul
Cricketer. *b:* 14.11.1965, Leek, Staffordshire. Middle order right-hand batsman, slow left-arm bowler. *Team* Leicestershire (1983, 1 match).
Career batting
1–2–0–67–51–33.50–0–*ct* 0

He also played for Staffordshire (1986–92).

Adhikari, Hemchandra Ramachandra
Amateur. *b:* 31.7.1919, Poona, Maharashtra, India. Middle order right-hand batsman, occasional leg break bowler, brilliant cover point. *Teams* Gujarat (1936/7); Baroda (1937/8 to 1949/50); Hindus (1941/2 to 1944/5); Services (1950/1 to 1959/60). *Tours* India to Australia 1947/8, to England 1952. *Tests* India (1947/8 to 1958/9, 21 matches).
Career batting
152–236–28–8683–230*–41.74–17–*ct* 97
Bowling 1859–49–37.93–0–0–3/2
Test batting
21–36–8–872–114*–31.14–1–*ct* 8
Bowling 82–3–27.33–0–0–3/68

Although he began his first-class career as an attractive stroke playing batsman, the weakness of the Indian batting in the 1950s changed him into a dour defensive player. In the field he was regarded as second only to R. N. Harvey at cover. His highest score was 230* for Services v Rajasthan at Ajmer in 1951/2. He captained India in one Test.

Adshead, Frank Hand
Amateur. *b:* 9.2.1894, Tividale, Dudley, Worcestershire. *d:* 22.11.1977, Twyford Abbey, Ealing, Middlesex. Brother of W. E. (Worcestershire). Middle order right-hand batsman. *Team* Worcestershire (1927, 2 matches).
Career batting
2–3–0–26–14–8.66–0–*ct* 2

Adshead, Dr William Ewart
(later known as Barnie-Adshead)
Amateur. *b:* 10.4.1901, Tividale, Dudley, Worcestershire. *d:* 26.1.1951, Edgbaston, Birmingham. Brother of F. H. (Worcestershire). Middle order right-hand batsman. *Team* Worcestershire (1922–28, 12 matches).
Career batting
12–22–1–244–51–11.61–0–*ct* 15
A noted soccer player, he appeared for Aston Villa, and England in amateur internationals.

Aers, David Roland
Cricketer. *b:* 3.10.1946, Lahore, India. Middle order right-hand batsman, slow left-arm bowler. *Sch* Tonbridge. *Team* Cambridge U (1966–68, blue 1967).
Career batting
15–26–2–288–48–12.00–0–*ct* 3
Bowling 882–18–49.00–1–0–5/116

Afaq Hussain
Cricketer. *b:* 31.12.1939, Lucknow, India. Lower order right-hand batsman, off break bowler, good field. *Teams* Karachi (1957/8 to 1963/4); Karachi University (1959/60 to 1960/61); Universities (1959/60); PIA (1964/5 to 1973/4); PWD (1967/8). *Tours* Pakistan to England 1962, to Australia 1964/5; Pakistan Eaglets to England 1963; PIA to Ireland 1969 (not first-class). *Tests* Pakistan (1961/2 to 1964/5, 2 matches).
Career batting
67–83–24–1448–122*–24.54–1–*ct* 52
Bowling 4156–214–19.42–14–5–8/108
Test batting
2–4–4–66–35*–no av–0–*ct* 2
Bowling 106–1–106.00–0–0–1/40

Afford, John Andrew
Cricketer. *b:* 12.5.1964, Crowland, Lincolnshire. Lower order right-hand batsman, slow left-arm bowler. *Team* Nottinghamshire (1984–92, 113 matches). *Tour* England A to Zimbabwe 1989/90.
Career batting
115–99–41–208–22*–3.58–0–*ct* 36
Bowling 9900–296–33.44–9–2–6/68
He also played for Lincolnshire (1991).

Aftab Baloch
Cricketer. *b:* 1.4.1953, Karachi, Pakistan. Son of M. S. Baloch (Gujarat and Karachi). Sound middle order right-hand batsman, off break bowler. *Teams* PWD (1969/70); PIA (1970/1 to 1984/5); Karachi (1971/2 to 1984/5); Sind (1972/3 to 1975/6); National Bank (1973/4 to 1976/7). *Tours* Pakistan Under 25 to Sri Lanka 1973/4; Pakistan to England 1974; PIA to Zimbabwe 1981/2. *Tests* Pakistan (1969/70 to 1974/5, 2 matches).
Career batting
172–265–46–9166–428–41.85–20–*ct* 134–*st* 3
Bowling 7017–223–31.46–11–2–8/171
Test batting
2–3–1–97–60*–48.50–0–*ct* 0
Bowling 17–0
On his 1974 tour to England he hit 101 runs, av 25.25, and did not appear in the Tests. He hit 428 for Sind v Baluchistan at Karachi in 1973/4. He scored 1,000 runs in a season in Pakistan twice (best 1,457, av 52.03, in 1973/4).

Aftab Gul
Cricketer. *b:* 31.3.1946, Gujar Khan, India. Opening right-hand batsman, leg break bowler. *Teams* Punjab University (1964/5 to 1969/70); Lahore (1964/5 to 1975/6); Punjab (1972/3 to 1977/8); Servis Industries (1976/7). *Tours* Pakistan to England 1971, 1974. *Tests* Pakistan (1968/9 to 1971, 6 matches).
Career batting
101–173–7–6129–140–36.92–11–*ct* 46
Bowling 475–14–33.28–0–0–2/20
Test batting
6–8–0–182–33–22.75–0–*ct* 3
Bowling 4–0
He was most successful on his 1971 visit to England, hitting 1,154 runs (av 46.16) and appearing in all 3 Tests, but on his return in 1974 failed to strike form and did not play against England. He played in a Test for Pakistan whilst on bail. He scored 1,008 runs (av 40.32) in Pakistan in 1973/4.

Agar, Charles
Professional. *b:* 20.5.1877, Rothley, Leicestershire. *d:* 10.11.1921, Southfields, Leicester. Lower order right-hand batsman, useful right-arm medium pace bowler. *Team* Leicestershire (1898–1900, 23 matches).
Career batting
23–40–6–381–48–11.20–0–*ct* 14
Bowling 1711–38–45.02–0–0–4/80

Agnew, Jonathan Philip
Cricketer. *b:* 4.4.1960, Macclesfield, Cheshire. Lower order right-hand batsman, right-arm fast bowler. *Sch* Uppingham. *Team* Leicestershire (1978–90, 205 matches). *Tour* Leicestershire to Zimbabwe 1980/1; England to India 1984/5, to Australia 1984/5 (not first-class); England B to Sri Lanka 1985/6. *Tests* England (1984–85, 3 matches).
Career batting
218–232–49–2118–90–11.57–0–*ct* 39
Bowling 19485–666–29.25–37–6–9/70

Test batting
3–4–3–10–5–10.00–0–*ct* 0
Bowling 373–4–93.25–0–0–2/51

He took 101 wickets, av 24.26, in 1987. His early career was dogged by injury, but he overcame these difficulties and produced his best bowling in 1987, only to be ignored by the selectors. He retired still at his peak in 1990 to take up a career in journalism and broadcasting. He reappeared for Leicestershire in emergency in one limited overs match in 1992. His best bowling was 9/70 for Leicestershire v Kent at Leicester in 1985.

Agnew, Vice-Adm Sir William Gladstone
Amateur. *b:* 2.12.1898, Paddington, London. *d:* 12.7.1960, Alverstoke, Hampshire. Nephew of W. B. Anderson (Middlesex). Opening batsman. *Team* Royal Navy (1920).
Career batting
1–2–0–68–48–34.00–0–*ct* 0

Ahangama, Franklyn Saliya
Cricketer. *b:* 14.9.1959, Colombo, Ceylon. Lower order left-hand batsman, right-arm medium pace bowler. *Team* Sinhalese SC (1989/90 to 1991/2). *Tours* Sri Lanka to Pakistan 1985/6, to England 1988, 1990, 1991. *Tests* Sri Lanka (1985/6, 3 matches).
Career batting
35–26–9–211–51–12.41–0–*ct* 10
Bowling 2203–115–19.15–6–2–7/30
Test batting
3–3–1–11–11–5.50–0–*ct* 1
Bowling 348–18–19.33–1–0–5/52

He did not appear in the Tests played during his tours to England, and easily his best tour was his first in 1988 when he topped the tourists' first-class bowling averages.

Ahl, Frank Douglas
Professional. *b:* 24.11.1908, Potchefstroom, Transvaal, South Africa. *d:* 3.5.1967, Stanwell, Middlesex. Punishing middle order right-hand batsman, right-arm bowler, wicket-keeper. *Team* Worcestershire (1931–33, 35 matches).
Career batting
35–53–3–592–43–11.84–0–*ct* 24–*st* 2
Bowling 384–13–29.53–0–0–4/44

Ahluwalia, Manraj Singh
Cricketer. *b:* 27.12.1965, Isleworth, Middlesex. Opening right-hand batsman, off break bowler. *Sch* Latymer. *Team* Cambridge U (1985–87, blue 1986).
Career batting
14–25–1–306–36–12.75–0–0–*ct* 4

Ahsan ul Haq
Amateur. *b:* 16.7.1878, Jullundur City, Punjab, India. *d:* 29.12.1957, Karachi, Pakistan. Father of Inam ul Haq (Muslims). Good right-hand batsman with excellent drive, useful right-arm medium pace change bowler. *Teams* Middlesex (1902, 3 matches); Muslims (1923/4 to 1924/5).
Career batting
7–9–1–172–100*–21.50–1–*ct* 4
Bowling 90–0

He made his first-class debut for MCC in 1901. Coming to England to study the law, he scored many runs for Hampstead in club cricket, but when he had just gained his place in the Middlesex side, he was called to the bar and returned to India. He hit 100* in about 40 minutes batting at number eleven in his first first-class match in India, batting last due to his late arrival at the ground.

Aikman, Andrew Miller
Amateur. *b:* 9.4.1885, Galashiels, Selkirkshire, Scotland. *d:* 14.4.1959, Galashiels, Selkirkshire, Scotland. Lower order right-hand batsman, wicket-keeper. *Team* Scotland (1921).
Career batting
1–1–0–1–1–1.00–0–*ct* 0

Ainley, Joe
Professional. *b:* 28.10.1878, Huddersfield, Yorkshire. *d:* 18.11.1907, Sparkbrook, Birmingham. Tail end right-hand batsman, good wicket-keeper. *Team* Worcestershire (1905–06, 19 matches).
Career batting
19–25–16–64–13–7.11–0–*ct* 25–*st* 5

Ainley died of consumption when only 29 – his obituary in Wisden is mistakenly given under Hinley.

Ainscough, Thomas
Amateur. *b:* 23.2.1865, Lancaster House, Parbold, Lancashire. *d:* 20.11.1927, Lancaster House, Parbold, Lancashire. Middle order left-hand batsman. *Sch* Ampleforth. *Team* Lancashire (1894–1906, 2 matches).
Career batting
5–9–1–194–61*–24.25–0–*ct* 3

He played first-class cricket for Liverpool and District, for whom he made his first-class debut in 1891, and was a prolific batsman in club cricket in the Liverpool area.

Ainsworth, Cyrus Gerald
Amateur. *b:* 4.8.1888, Bury, Lancashire. *d:* 20.2.1940, Elton, Lancashire. Hard hitting lower order batsman. *Team* Royal Navy (1919).
Career batting
1–2–0–77–71–38.50–0–*ct* 0

Ainsworth, George William Bromilow
Amateur. *b:* 21.3.1876, Freshfield, Formby, Lancashire. *d:* 3.3.1941, Bushey, Hertfordshire. Brother of J. L. (Lancashire). Middle order batsman. *Sch* Marlborough. *Team* Leveson-Gower's XI (1902).
Career batting
1–1–1–10–10*–no av–0–*ct* 0

Ainsworth, Jerry Lionel
Amateur. *b:* 11.9.1877, Freshfield, Formby, Lancashire. *d:* 30.12.1923, Falmouth, Cornwall. Brother of G. W. B. (Leveson-Gower's XI). Lower order batsman, good left-arm slow bowler. *Sch* Marlborough. *Teams* Lancashire (1899, 4 matches); Europeans (1904/5). *Tour* Warner to North America 1898.
Career batting
11–16–5–44–11–4.00–0–*ct* 7
Bowling 791–50–15.82–5–2–7/61

He had great success in America taking 75 wickets (av 6.33) including 11 for 67 against the Philadelphians. This success led to his four matches with Lancashire, when he took 18 wickets. He would probably have obtained a regular place in the County side if he had cared to play cricket. He was a well-known racehorse owner.

Ainsworth, Michael Lionel Yeoward
Amateur. *b:* 13.5.1922, Hooton, Cheshire. *d:* 28.8.1978, Hillingdon, Middlesex. He died whilst playing cricket. Excellent middle order right-hand batsman with good off-drive. *Sch* Shrewsbury. *Team* Worcestershire (1948–50, 17 matches).
Career batting
49–86–2–2034–137–24.21–3–*ct* 26
Bowling 126–2–63.00–0–0–1/4

His first-class debut was for Combined Services in 1946. Service duties prevented him from appearing regularly in County cricket, but he captained the Combined Services in 1950 and did not make his final first-class appearance until 1964, playing for the Free Foresters.

Aird, Ronald
Amateur. *b:* 4.5.1902, Paddington, London. *d:* 16.8.1986, West Down House, Yapton, Sussex. Middle order stylish right-hand batsman, right-arm medium pace bowler, brilliant cover-point. *Sch* Eton. *Teams* Hampshire (1920–38, 108 matches); Cambridge U (1923, blue).
Career batting
136–223–19–4482–159–21.97–4–*ct* 52
Bowling 413–7–59.00–0–0–2/35

His best year was 1924 when he hit 1,072 runs (av 24.36). He is best remembered for his work for MCC being Assistant Secretary (1926–52), Secretary (1952–62) and President 1968/9. He was Hampshire President 1971–83. He also won a blue for rackets.

Airey, Robert Berkeley
Amateur. *b:* 21.9.1874, Southminster, Essex. *d:* 23.6.1933, Westminster Pier, London. Middle order right-hand batsman. *Sch* Tonbridge. *Team* Hampshire (1911, 3 matches).
Career batting
3–5–0–52–30–10.40–0–*ct* 2

Aislabie, Benjamin
Amateur. *b:* 14.1.1774, City of London. *d:* 2.6.1842, Regent's Park, London. Tail-end right-hand batsman. *Sch* Eton. *Teams* Surrey (1808–17); Hampshire (1819); Kent (1823); Sussex (1827).
Career batting
56–100–29–224–15*–3.15–0–*ct* 7

Though he played his last match of importance in 1841 – MCC v Cambridge U – at the age of 67 and had therefore appeared for the MCC in all grades of cricket for about 40 seasons, he was never more than a moderate cricketer. His fame rests with the fact that he was Secretary of MCC (1822–42) and as such organised many matches: 'He doats on the game, has played many a year, Weighs at least seventeen stones, on his pins rather queer, But he still takes the bat, and there's no better fun, Than to see him when batting attempting a run.' He was President of MCC in 1823.

Aitchison, Rev James
Amateur. *b:* 26.5.1920, Kilmarnock, Ayrshire, Scotland. Opening right-hand batsman, right-arm medium pace bowler. *Team* Scotland (1946–63).
Career batting
50–87–2–2786–190*–32.77–5–*ct* 22
Bowling 3–0

Aitchison, John Edward
Professional *b:* 27.12.1928, Gillingham, Kent. Lower order right-hand batsman, left arm bowler. *Team* Kent (1949–50, 3 matches).
Career batting
3–3–0–6–4–2.00–0–*ct* 0
Bowling 88–3–29.33–0–0–3/33

Aizazuddin, Fakir Syed
Amateur. *b:* 17.8.1935, Lahore, India. Middle order right-hand batsman, leg break bowler. *Teams* Cambridge U (1957); Khairpur (1959/60 to 1968/9); Karachi (1965/6 to 1971/2). *Tours* Pakistan Eaglets to England 1963; Pakistan to Ceylon 1964/5, to England 1967.
Career batting
43–79–4–1872–187–24.96–3–*ct* 13
Bowling 761–19–40.05–0–0–4/36

He was known as S. A. U. Fakir whilst at Cambridge U.

Akers-Douglas, Ian Stanley
Amateur. *b:* 16.11.1909, Kensington, London. *d:* 16.12.1952, Frant, Sussex, as the result of a shot-gun accident. Grandson of S. Christopherson (Kent), nephew of P. Christopherson (Kent). Stylish middle order right-hand batsman with excellent cover-drive. *Sch* Eton. *Teams* Oxford U (1929–30); Kent (1929–38, 48 matches). *Tour* Martineau to Egypt 1929 (not first-class).
Career batting
60–86–3–1965–123–23.67–2–*ct* 12
Bowling 100–4–25.00–0–0–2/20

He hit 158 for Eton v Harrow in 1928 and scored centuries in both the Freshmen's match of 1929 and the Senior's match of 1930. In 1933 he won the Open Rackets Championship of the British Isles.

Akroyd, Bayly Nash
Amateur. *b:* 27.4.1850, Streatham, Surrey. *d:* 24.11.1926, Marylebone, London. Brother of S. H. (Surrey). Steady middle order right-hand batsman, occasional slow round-arm bowler, good field at point. *Sch* Radley. *Team* Surrey (1872–73, 6 matches).
Career batting
8–15–0–129–30–8.60–0–*ct* 9
Bowling 14–0
His final first-class match was for MCC in 1879.

Akroyd, Swainson Howden
Amateur. *b:* 13.11.1848, Streatham, Surrey. *d:* 5.12.1925, Marylebone, London. Brother of B. N. (Surrey). Useful opening right-hand batsman, good field. *Sch* Radley. *Team* Surrey (1869–78, 23 matches).
Career batting
33–55–1–930–87–17.22–0–*ct* 7
He was captain of Surrey in 1869 and 1870.

Alabaster, John Chaloner
Amateur. *b:* 11.7.1930, Invercargill, Otago, New Zealand. Brother of G. D. (Otago, Canterbury and Northern Districts). Lower order right-hand batsman, leg break and googly bowler. *Team* Otago (1956/7 to 1971/2). *Tours* New Zealand to India and Pakistan 1955/6, to England 1958, to South Africa 1961/2, to Australia 1967/8, to West Indies 1971/2. *Tests* New Zealand (1955/6 to 1971/2, 21 matches).
Career batting
143–212–30–2427–82–13.33–0–*ct* 94
Bowling 12687–500–25.37–25–4–7/41
Test batting
21–34–6–272–34–9.71–0–*ct* 7
Bowling 1863–49–38.02–0–0–4/46
The unusual aspect of Alabaster's career was that he had not appeared at all in first-class cricket when he visited India and Pakistan as part of the 1955/6 New Zealand side. His only visit to England was not very successful, though he appeared in two of the Tests.

Alban, Mark Timothy
Cricketer. *b:* 19.4.1966, Kendal, Westmorland. Middle order right-hand batsman, leg break bowler. *Sch* Sedbergh. *Team* Cambridge U (1989, blue).
Career batting
3–4–0–134–86–33.50–0–*ct* 0
Bowling 21–0

Alderman, Albert Edward
Professional. *b:* 30.10.1907, Allenton, Derby. *d:* 6.6.1990, Frimley Park, Surrey. Grandfather of T. A. J. Dawson (Oxford U). Sound right-hand opening batsman, off break bowler, smart field, occasional wicket-keeper. *Team* Derbyshire (1928–48, 318 matches).
Career batting
318–529–52–12376–175–25.94–12–*ct* 202–*st* 2
Bowling 171–4–42.75–0–0–3/37
He completed 1,000 runs each season from 1934 to 1939 (best 1,509, av 32.53, in 1937). He was a first-class umpire (1966–68). He also played for Berkshire (1950). He played soccer for Burnley and Derby County.

Alderman, Terence Michael
Cricketer. *b:* 12.6.1956, Subiaco, Perth, Western Australia. Brother of Denise Emerson (Australia Women). Lower order right-hand batsman, right-arm fast medium bowler. *Team* Western Australia (1974/5 to 1991/2, 103 matches); Kent (1984–86, 40 matches); Gloucestershire (1988, 20 matches). *Tours* Australia to England 1981, 1989, to New Zealand 1981/2, 1989/90, to Pakistan 1982/3, to West Indies 1983/4, 1990/1, to Sharjah (not first-class) 1984/5, 1989/90, to India 1989/90 (not first-class); Australian XI to South Africa 1985/6, 1986/7. *Tests* Australia (1981 to 1990/1, 41 matches).
Career batting
238–257–104–1276–52*–8.34–0–*ct* 189
Bowling 21974–936–23.47–53–8–8/46
Test batting
41–53–22–203–26*–6.54–0–*ct* 27
Bowling 4616–170–27.15–14–1–6/17
He was signed for Kent at the last moment in 1984 when Baptiste was required by West Indies and Dilley was unavailable due to injury. Alderman proved a very useful acquisition, taking 76 wickets, av 22.69. Selected to tour England in 1985, he was deleted from the party when he agreed to visit South Africa in 1985/6 with an Australian side. He returned to Kent for 1986 and was outstandingly successful with 98 wickets, av 19.20. His two Test tours to England were in 1981 and 1989. On both tours he topped the Test and the first-class bowling tables. The accuracy and control of his bowling, especially in 1989, was altogether too much for the English batsmen. In the First Test of 1982/3 at Perth v England, he badly dislocated a shoulder whilst trying to arrest a spectator who had attacked him. This injury affected his cricket for more than a year.

Alderson, Ralph
Professional. *b:* 7.6.1919, Newton-le-Willows, Lancashire. *d:* 2.4.1988, Glazebury, Leigh, Lancashire. Sound middle order right-hand batsman. *Team* Lancashire (1948–49, 2 matches).
Career batting
2–2–0–55–55–27.50–0–*ct* 0
He scored 55 in his only Championship match, adding 120 for the 4th wicket with G. A. Edrich.

Alderwick, Ernest Ewart Gladstone
Amateur. *b:* 4.4.1886, Montpelier, Bristol, Gloucestershire. *d:* 26.8.1917, Peronne, France. He was killed in action. Middle order right-hand batsman. *Team* Gloucestershire (1908, 2 matches).
Career batting
2–3–0–7–5–2.33–0–*ct* 0
He also played for Suffolk (1914).

Aldridge, Keith John
Professional. *b:* 13.3.1935, Evesham, Worcestershire. Tail end right-hand batsman, right-arm fast medium bowler. *Teams* Worcestershire (1956–60, 73 matches); Tasmania (1961/2 to 1963/4, 6 matches).
Career batting
79–112–35–511–24*–6.63–0–*ct* 33
Bowling 6033–256–23.56–7–0–6/26
In July 1959 he was no-balled for throwing by J. S. Buller; and no-balled again in 1960 for the same reason.

Alexander, Charles Dallas
Amateur. *b:* 25.12.1839, Calcutta, India. *d:* 22.1.1917, Kingsdown Park, Tankerton, Kent. Middle order batsman. *Sch* Cheltenham and Harrow. *Team* Kent (1864, 1 match).
Career batting
1–2–0–11–8–5.50–0–*ct* 0

Alexander, Charles Robert
Amateur. *b:* 8.11.1847, Westminster, London. *d:* 17.2.1902, Westminster, London. Steady opening right-hand batsman, good field at longstop. *Sch* Eton. *Teams* Kent (1867–69, 4 matches); Cambridge U (1870–71).
Career batting
6–9–0–88–41–9.77–0–*ct* 2
In 1867 he is reported to have scored 1,016 runs for Eton, being the captain that year. He was also a noted sprinter.

Alexander, Franz Copeland Murray
Amateur. *b:* 2.11.1928, Kingston, Jamaica. Aggressive middle order right-hand batsman, skilful wicket-keeper. *Sch* Wolmer's (Jamaica). *Teams* Cambridge U (1952–53, blue both years); Jamaica (1956/7 to 1959/60). *Tours* West Indies to England 1957, to India and Pakistan 1958/9, to Australia 1960/1; played for Governor-General's XI v MCC in New Zealand 1960/61. *Tests* West Indies (1957 to 1960/1, 25 matches).
Career batting
92–141–30–3238–108–29.17–1–*ct* 217–*st* 39
Bowling 7–0
Test batting
25–38–6–961–108–30.03–1–*ct* 85–*st* 5
Known as 'Gerry', Alexander's last Test series was undoubtedly the highlight of his career, for he not only hit his single Test hundred (at Sydney in the 3rd match), but also ended the series at the top of the West Indies batting averages (484 runs, av 60.50). Usually coming in at no. 7 or 8, he hit at least one fifty in each of the five Tests. He also played for Cambridgeshire (1954–1955). He won a blue for soccer, and also appeared in amateur internationals for England.

Alexander, Frederick Russell
Professional. *b:* 4.6.1924, Acton Green, Middlesex. *d:* 17.5.1984, Harrow, Middlesex. Forcing middle order right-hand batsman, right-arm medium, or off break, bowler. *Team* Middlesex (1951, 2 matches).
Career batting
2–3–0–15–8–5.00–0–*ct* 0
He 'appeared' for England in the fill-up game played when the Lord's Test of 1951 finished early.

Alexander, George
Amateur. *b:* 22.4.1851, Fitzroy, Melbourne, Victoria, Australia. *d:* 6.11.1930, Richmond, Melbourne, Victoria, Australia. Dashing opening or middle order right-hand batsman, fast right round-arm bowler, excellent field. *Team* Victoria (1875/6 to 1879/80, 6 matches). *Tours* Australia to England 1880, 1884. *Tests* Australia (1880 to 1884/5, 2 matches).
Career batting
24–35–5–466–75–15.53–0–*ct* 16
Bowling 607–33–18.39–1–0–5/57
Test batting
2–4–0–52–33–13.00–0–*ct* 2
Bowling 93–2–46.50–0–0–2/69
Alexander acted as manager to both the 1880 and 1884 Australian teams in England.

Alexander, George Caledon
Amateur. *b:* 4.10.1842, Epsom, Surrey. *d:* 8.4.1913, Westminster, London. Opening batsman. *Team* Surrey (1869, 1 match).
Career batting
3–4–0–14–10–3.50–0–*ct* 0
Apart from his match with Surrey his only other first-class appearances were for Gentlemen of South in 1866 and Gentlemen of England in 1876.

Alexander, Gilbert William Arbuthnot
Amateur. *b:* 7.9.1895. *d:* 10.4.1957, Finchley, Middlesex. Brother of L. A. (Europeans). Middle order right-hand batsman, right-arm medium pace bowler. *Sch* Glenalmond. *Team* Scotland (1922–32).
Career batting
13–22–0–617–136–28.04–1–*ct* 12
Bowling 113–3–37.66–0–0–2/30

Alexander, Robert
Amateur. *b:* 24.9.1910, Belfast, Ireland. *d:* 19.7.1943, near Catania, Sicily. Tail-end right-hand batsman, right-arm fast medium bowler. *Sch* Royal Belfast Academical Institution. *Team* Ireland (1932).

Career batting
1–2–0–29–22–14.50–0–*ct* 0
Bowling 55–0
He was also an Irish rugby international, and toured South Africa with the British Lions in 1938.

Ali, Inshan
Cricketer. *b:* 25.9.1949, Preysal Village, Trinidad. Lower order left-hand batsman, slow left-arm bowler. *Team* Trinidad (1965/6 to 1979/80). *Tours* West Indies to England 1973, to Australia 1975/6. *Tests* West Indies (1970/1 to 1976/7, 12 matches).
Career batting
90–118–21–1341–63–13.82–0–*ct* 44
Bowling 9491–328–28.93–17–4–8/58
Test batting
12–18–2–172–25–10.75–0–*ct* 7
Bowling 1621–34–47.67–1–0–5/59
On his visit to England in 1973, Inshan Ali bowled well, taking 38 wickets (av 26.84) and was unfortunate not to play in more than one Test.

Alikhan, Rehan Iqbal
Cricketer. *b:* 28.12.1962, Westminster, London. Opening right-hand batsman, off break bowler. *Sch* KCS, Wimbledon. *Teams* Sussex (1986–88, 47 matches); PIA (1986/7); Surrey (1989–92, 41 matches).
Career batting
101–173–14–4547–138–28.59–2–*ct* 56
Bowling 274–7–39.14–0–0–2/19
He hit 1,055 runs, av 32.96, in 1991.

Alim-ud-Din
Amateur. *b:* 15.12.1930, Ajmer, India. Brother of Azim-ud-Din (Rajputana) and Salim-ud-Din (Karachi). Opening or middle order right-hand batsman, occasional leg break bowler. *Teams* Rajputana (1942/3); Gujarat (1944/5 to 1947/8); Muslims (1945/6); Sind (1948/9); Bahawalpur (1953/4); Karachi (1954/5 to 1965/6); PWD (1967/8). *Tours* Pakistan to Ceylon 1948/9, to England 1954, 1962, to West Indies 1957/8, to India 1960/1. *Tests* Pakistan (1954–62, 25 matches).
Career batting
140–238–16–7276–142–32.77–14–*ct* 65
Bowling 959–40–23.97–0–0–4/33
Test batting
25–45–2–1091–109–25.37–2–*ct* 8
Bowling 75–1–75.00–0–0–1/17
He was the youngest cricketer in first-class matches when he appeared for Rajputana v Baroda at Rajkot in 1942/3, aged 12 years and 73 days. He hit 1,083 runs, av. 30.94, in 1954. He also hit 1,020 runs, av 51.00, in 1961/2 in Pakistan.

Alison, Charles Hugh
Amateur. *b:* 5.3.1883, Preston, Lancashire. *d:* 20.10.1952, Woodstock, Cape Town, South Africa. Lower order batsman. *Sch* Malvern. *Team* Somerset (1902–05, 4 matches).
Career batting
4–5–2–36–20–12.00–0–*ct* 3
Bowling 23–0
He played in the Oxford Freshmen's match of 1902. He also played for Buckinghamshire (1911–12). He was a well known golf course designer.

Allan, David Walter
Cricketer. *b:* 5.11.1937, Hastings, Christ Church, Barbados. Lower order right-hand batsman, wicket-keeper. *Team* Barbados (1955/6 to 1965/6). *Tours* West Indies to England 1963, 1966. *Tests* West Indies (1961/2 to 1966, 5 matches).
Career batting
54–64–12–764–56–14.69–0–*ct* 117–*st* 24
Test batting
5–7–1–75–40*–12.50–*ct* 15–*st* 3
Allan came to England as the wicket-keeper on the 1963 tour, and was regarded as the principal keeper on the 1966 visit, but lost his Test place following a poor performance in the Second Test.

Allan, Francis Erskine
Amateur. *b:* 2.12.1849, Allansford, Victoria, Australia. *d:* 9.2.1917, Flinders Lane, Latrobe, Melbourne, Australia. Tail-end right-hand batsman, excellent fast medium left round-arm bowler, slip field. *Team* Victoria (1867/8 to 1882/3, 14 matches). *Tour* Australia to England and USA 1878. *Test* Australia (1878/9, 1 match).
Career batting
31–50–16–371–35*–10.91–0–*ct* 14
Bowling 1638–123–13.31–11–2–8/20
Test batting
1–1–0–5–5–5.00–0–*ct* 0
Bowling 80–4–20.00–0–0–2/30
He was one of the first Australian bowlers to develop the art of swerving the ball in the air and deceived many batsmen, especially on his visit to England in 1878. He was picked for the first ever Test in 1877, but decided instead to go to an agricultural show.

Allan, James Moffat
Amateur. *b:* 2.4.1932, Leeds, Yorkshire. Brother of W. R. (Scotland). Determined right-hand batsman, who went in at no. 11 for Oxford in 1953 but by 1955 opened for Kent, accurate slow left-arm bowler. *Sch* Edinburgh Academy. *Teams* Oxford U (1953–56, blue all four years); Kent (1954–57, 40 matches); Warwickshire (1966–68, 48 matches); Scotland (1954–72).
Career batting
179–268–45–4988–153–22.36–5–*ct* 124
Bowling 11179–435–25.69–18–2–7/54
He had an amazing start to his first-class career, bowling ten successive maidens and taking three wickets before conceding a run. In 1955 he was just 5

wickets short of achieving the 'double'. He hit 1,000 runs in a season twice (best 1,369, av 27.93, in 1955).

Allan, John
Amateur. *b:* 20.1.1911, Hamilton, Lanarkshire, Scotland. Tail-end right-hand batsman, right-arm medium pace bowler. *Team* Scotland (1951).
Career batting
1–2–0–2–2–1.00–0–*ct* 1
Bowling 78–3–26.00–0–0–3/78

Allan, Dr Walter Ramsay
Amateur. *b:* 26.10.1927, Riccarton, Ayrshire, Scotland. Brother of J. M. (Kent, Warwickshire and Scotland). Middle order right-hand batsman. *Sch* Edinburgh Academy. *Team* Scotland (1950).
Career batting
3–6–0–73–30–12.16–0–*ct* 3

Allbrook, Mark Edward
Cricketer. *b:* 15.11.1954, Frimley, Surrey. Tail end right-hand batsman, off break bowler. *Sch* Tonbridge. *Teams* Cambridge U (1975–78, blue all four years); Nottinghamshire (1976–80, 12 matches).
Career batting
47–56–19–320–39–8.64–0–*ct* 15
Bowling 3504–76–46.10–2–0–7/79

Allchurch, Thomas
Amateur. *b:* 24.4.1883, Old Swinford, Worcestershire. *d:* 23.10.1934, Halesowen, Worcestershire. Middle order right-hand batsman, off break bowler. *Team* Worcestershire (1919–20, 3 matches).
Career batting
3–6–0–74–51–12.33–0–*ct* 2
Bowling 280–10–28.00–1–0–5/70

Allcock, Charles Howard
Amateur. *b:* 16.4.1855, Ravenhurst, Harborne, Staffordshire. *d:* 30.9.1947, Aberdovey, Merioneth. Brother of Rev. A. E. (Warwickshire, non-first-class). Lower order right-hand batsman, slow round-arm bowler, slip field. *Sch* King Edward's School, Birmingham. *Team* Cambridge U (1878).
Career batting
5–8–0–29–14–3.62–0–*ct* 4
Bowling 250–14–17.85–0–0–4/51
His County cricket was for Staffordshire (1876–91) and later Buckinghamshire (1895–98), being a master at Eton College. His final first-class match was for Cambridge U (Past and Present) in 1884.

Allcott, Cyril Francis Walter
Amateur. *b:* 7.10.1896, Lower Moutere, New Zealand. *d:* 19.11.1973, Auckland, New Zealand. Attacking middle order left-hand batsman, slow left-arm bowler. *Teams* Hawke's Bay (1920/1); Auckland (1921/2 to 1931/2); Otago (1945/6). *Tours* New Zealand to Australia 1925/6, 1927/8, to England 1927, 1931. *Tests* New Zealand (1929/30 to 1931/32, 6 matches).
Career batting
82–116–26–2514–131–27.93–5–*ct* 61
Bowling 5892–220–26.78–13–2–7/75
Test batting
6–7–2–113–33–22.60–0–*ct* 3
Bowling 541–6–90.16–0–0–2/102
Originally Allcott made his mark as a bowler, but by 1927 had developed into an all-rounder. On the 1931 tour to England he acted as assistant manager and treasurer.

Alldis, James Stephen
Cricketer. *b:* 27.12.1949, Paddington, London. Lower order left-hand batsman, slow left-arm bowler. *Team* Middlesex (1970, 2 matches).
Career batting
2–4–1–7–4*–2.33–0–*ct* 0
Bowling 37–1–37.00–0–0–1/33

Allen, Antony William
Amateur. *b:* 22.12.1912, Evenley Hall, Brackley, Northamptonshire. Brilliant right-hand opening batsman. *Sch* Eton. *Teams* Cambridge U (1932–34, blue 1933–34); Northamptonshire (1932–36, 8 matches).
Career batting
35–64–1–1928–144–30.60–4–*ct* 13
Allen hit a century (112) before lunch for Eton v Harrow at Lord's in 1931, helping in a record opening stand of 208. It was Northamptonshire's misfortune that he gave up serious cricket after leaving Cambridge. His final first-class match was for Free Foresters in 1947. He won a blue for real tennis.

Allen, Basil Oliver
Amateur. *b:* 13.10.1911, Clifton, Bristol. *d:* 1.5.1981, Wells, Somerset. Solid middle order left-hand batsman, who could hit if required, fine close leg-side field. *Sch* Clifton. *Teams* Cambridge U (1932–33, blue 1933); Gloucestershire (1932–51, 285 matches).
Career batting
308–512–20–14195–220–28.85–14–*ct* 310
Bowling 429–3–143.00–0–0–2/80
He captained Gloucestershire 1937–38 and 1947–50. His highest score was 220 v Hampshire at Bournemouth in 1947. He scored 1,000 runs in a season seven times (best 1,785, av 34.32, in 1938). He was President of Gloucestershire 1978–79.

Allen, Charles
Amateur. *b:* 1878. *d:* 22.5.1958, Cirencester, Gloucestershire. Hard hitting middle order batsman. *Sch* Cranleigh. *Team* Gloucestershire (1909, 2 matches).
Career batting
2–3–0–51–35–17.00–0–*ct* 2

Allen, David Arthur
Professional. *b:* 29.10.1935, Horfield, Bristol. Dependable lower order right-hand batsman, consistent off spin bowler with subtle variations of flight,

fine outfield with accurate throw. *Team* Gloucestershire (1953–72, 349 matches). *Tours* MCC to West Indies 1959/60, New Zealand 1960/1, Ceylon, India and Pakistan 1961/2, Australia 1962/3, South Africa 1964/5, Australia and New Zealand 1965/6; Commonwealth to Pakistan 1967/8. *Tests* England (1959/60 to 1966, 39 matches).
Career batting
456–641–147–9291–121*–18.80–1–*ct* 252
Bowling 28586–1209–23.64–56–8–8/34
Test batting
39–51–15–918–88–25.50–0–*ct* 10
Bowling 3779–122–30.97–4–0–5/30

Though making his debut in 1953, Allen did not come to the fore until 1959, when he gained a regular place in the Gloucestershire side and was chosen for the winter tour to West Indies. As a useful all-rounder he then remained on the Test scene for six years. His best season was 1961, when he performed the double. He hit 1,000 runs twice (best 1,165, av 24.78, in 1964) and took 100 wickets once (124, av 19.43, in 1961).

Allen, Ernest George
Amateur. *b:* 24.6.1880, Holme, Worksop, Nottinghamshire. *d:* 28.5.1943, Harrogate, Yorkshire. Middle order right-hand batsman. *Sch* Lancing. *Team* Nottinghamshire (1903, 2 matches).
Career batting
2–3–0–48–19–16.00–0–*ct* 0

Allen, Sir George Oswald Browning, CBE
Amateur. *b:* 31.7.1902, Bellevue Hill, Sydney, New South Wales, Australia. *d:* 29.11.1989, St John's Wood, London. Nephew of R. C. (New South Wales and Australia). Forceful middle order right-hand batsman, fast right-arm bowler. *Sch* Eton. *Teams* Middlesex (1921–50, 146 matches); Cambridge U (1922–23, blue both years). *Tours* MCC to South America 1926/7, to Australia and New Zealand 1932/3, 1936/7, to West Indies 1947/8. *Tests* England (1930 to 1947/8, 25 matches).
Career batting
265–376–54–9232–180–28.67–11–*ct* 131
Bowling 17518–788–22.23–48–9–10/40
Test batting
25–33–2–750–122–24.19–1–*ct* 20
Bowling 2379–81–29.37–5–1–7/80

Although he was never really a regular County player, due to business commitments, Allen nevertheless remained for most of the period between the First and Second World Wars one of the leading fast bowlers in the game. He first appeared for Middlesex in the year that he was regarded as the best Public School bowler, and his performances for the County won immediate praise. His success continued during two years at Cambridge, but not a great deal was seen of him in the following seasons, and his selection for the MCC team to Australia in 1932/33 was the subject of some controversy, which was subsequently silenced by his all-round performances on that 'Bodyline' tour – it was notable that he himself did not use leg-theory bowling. His best bowling was 10/40 for Middlesex v Lancashire at Lord's in 1929.

He led England on the next visit to Australia and had the mortification to find his side winning the first two Tests but still losing the series.

After the Second World War he was persuaded to lead England on the ill-fated tour of West Indies, when not a single match was won. In all he captained England in 11 Tests. He played his last first-class match for Free Foresters in 1954.

After his first-class career Allen became one of the most influential figures behind the scenes at Lord's. He was chairman of the Test selectors from 1955 to 1961; treasurer of MCC from 1964 to 1976 and held the office of President in 1963/4. He was President of Middlesex 1977–79.

Allen, Ian Basil Alston
Cricketer. *b:* 6.10.1965, Coull's Hill, St Vincent. Lower order right-hand batsman, right-arm fast medium bowler. *Team* Windward Islands (1988/9 to 1991/2). *Tours* Young West Indies to Zimbabwe 1989/90; West Indies to England 1991. *Tests* West Indies (1991, 2 matches).
Career batting
33–39–16–290–36–12.60–0–*ct* 15
Bowling 2832–78–36.30–2–0–7/48
Test batting
2–2–2–5–4*–no av–*ct* 1
Bowling 180–5–36.00–0–0–2/69

Although he played in two Tests on the 1991 tour of England, his bowling return in Tests and first-class matches was very modest.

Allen, James Stephen
Professional. *b:* 4.11.1881, Croydon, Surrey. *d:* 4.4.1958, Creaton, Northamptonshire. Tail end left-hand batsman, slow left-arm bowler. *Team* Northamptonshire (1905, 2 matches).
Career batting
2–3–1–0–0*–0.00–0–*ct* 0
Bowling 154–1–154.00–0–0–1/58

Allen, John Wallace
Amateur. *b:* 17.2.1921, Waterside, Londonderry, Ireland. *d:* 10.9.1987, Derry, Ireland. Middle order right-hand batsman. *Team* Ireland (1948).
Career batting
1–1–0–0–0–0.00–0–*ct* 0

Allen, Michael Henry John
Professional. *b:* 7.1.1933, Bedford. Tail end right-hand batsman, accurate slow left-arm bowler, good close field. *Sch* Bedford School. *Teams* Northamptonshire (1956–63, 155 matches); Derbyshire (1964–66, 31 matches).

Allen, Spencer

Career batting
193–231–56–1723–59–9.84–0–*ct* 171
Bowling 11219–500–22.43–25–3–8/48

He took 8/88 in the first first-class innings in which he bowled (it was his second first-class match). He also played for Bedfordshire (1950).

Allen, Spencer
Amateur. *b:* 20.12.1893, Halifax, Yorkshire. *d:* 9.10.1978, Bradford, Yorkshire. Lower order left-hand batsman, slow left-arm bowler. *Team* Yorkshire (1924, 1 match).
Career batting
1–2–0–8–6–4.00–0–*ct* 0
Bowling 116–2–58.00–0–0–2/116

Allen played for Yorkshire when four of the first eleven were appearing in a 'Test Trial'.

Allen, Wentworth
Amateur. *b:* 30.1.1894, Dublin, Ireland. *d:* 22.2.1943, Shankhill, Co Dublin, Ireland. Lower order right-hand batsman, right-arm medium pace bowler. *Teams* Ireland (1920–25); Dublin University (1926).
Career batting
7–10–5–23–10*–4.60–0–*ct* 3
Bowling 435–15–29.00–0–0–2/20

Allen, William Reginald
Professional. *b:* 14.4.1893, Sharlston, near Wakefield, Yorkshire. *d:* 14.10.1950, Normanton, Yorkshire. Lower order right-hand batsman, wicket-keeper. *Team* Yorkshire (1921–25, 30 matches).
Career batting
30–32–10–475–95–21.59–0–*ct* 45–*st* 21

In his later years, when playing for Castleford in the Yorkshire Council, he weighed about 20 stones.

Allenby, Marmaduke Cecil
Amateur. *b:* 30.8.1873, Elvington Hall, Brinkworth, York. *d:* 16.4.1932, Mannamead, Plymouth, Devon. Lower order batsman. *Team* Hampshire (1900, 1 match).
Career batting
1–1–0–0–0–0.00–0–*ct* 0

He also appeared for Devon (1902).

Allerton, Jeremy William Orde
Cricketer. *b:* 2.2.1944, Windsor, Berkshire. Middle order left-hand batsman, right-arm medium pace bowler. *Sch* Stowe. *Team* Oxford U (1967–69, blue 1969).
Career batting
15–26–1–605–67–24.20–0–*ct* 2
Bowling 7–0

Alletson, Edwin Boaler
Professional. *b:* 6.3.1884, Welbeck Woodhouse, Nottinghamshire. *d:* 5.7.1963, Worksop, Nottinghamshire. Hard hitting middle order right-hand batsman, occasional right-arm medium leg break bowler. *Team* Nottinghamshire (1906–14, 118 matches).
Career batting
119–179–6–3217–189–18.59–1–*ct* 74
Bowling 628–33–19.03–1–0–6/74

Alletson created a sensation in the match between Nottinghamshire and Sussex at Hove in 1911, when he hit 189 in 90 minutes, the last 142 coming in 40 minutes, including 34 off one over from Killick. He was never able to reproduce this form, though earlier in his career he hit several fast fifties.

Alley, William Edward
Professional. *b:* 3.2.1919, Hornsby, Sydney, New South Wales, Australia. Uncle of P. J. S. (South Australia and New South Wales). Aggressive middle order left-hand batsman, right-arm fast-medium or medium pace bowler. *Teams* New South Wales (1945/6 to 1947/8, 12 matches); Somerset (1957–68, 350 matches). *Tours* Commonwealth to India, Pakistan and Ceylon 1949/50, to Rhodesia 1962/3, to Pakistan 1963/4; Cavaliers to South Africa 1962/3.
Career batting
400–682–67–19612–221*–31.88–31–*ct* 293
Bowling 17421–768–22.68–30–1–8/65

After a moderate cricket career in Australia and nine years in League cricket in Lancashire, Alley joined Somerset at the age of 38 and began a most successful all-round career in County cricket. The highlight of this was his aggregate of 3,019 runs (av 56.96) in 1961, and in all he reached 1,000 runs on 10 occasions. His highest innings was 221* v Warwickshire at Nuneaton in 1961. He performed the 'double' in 1962, taking 112 wickets, av 20.74. He became a first-class umpire from 1969–84, umpiring in 10 Test matches between 1974–81. His first first-class match in England was for Commonwealth XI in 1953.

Alley is a colourful character and a great inspiration to lesser players – nothing daunts him. In his early years he was a noted boxer, winning all his 28 professional fights at welterweight.

Alleyne, Hartley Leroy
Cricketer. *b:* 28.2.1957, Derricks, St James, Barbados. Lower order right-hand batsman, right-arm fast bowler. *Teams* Barbados (1978/9 to 1982/3); Worcestershire (1980–82, 38 matches); Natal (1984/5 to 1989/90); Kent (1988–89, 9 matches). *Tours* Young West Indies to Zimbabwe 1981/2; West Indian XI to South Africa 1983/4.
Career batting
85–96–25–709–72–9.98–0–*ct* 17
Bowling 7028–254–27.66–9–2–8/43

He also played for Lincolnshire (1979) and Buckinghamshire (1984–85). In his first season with Kent an injury to his heel meant he missed nearly the whole season; in his second year Pienaar was preferred in most matches.

Alleyne, Mark Wayne
Cricketer. *b:* 23.5.1968, Tottenham, Middlesex. Aggressive middle order right-hand batsman, right-arm medium pace bowler, occasional wicket-keeper. *Team* Gloucestershire (1986–92, 124 matches). *Tour* Gloucestershire to Sri Lanka 1986/7.
Career batting
124–194–25–5082–256–30.07–5–*ct* 103–*st* 2
Bowling 2505–62–40.40–0–0–4/48
He scored 1,000 runs in a season twice (best 1,121, av 32.02, in 1991). His highest score was 256 for Gloucestershire v Northamptonshire at Northampton in 1990.

Allin, Anthony William
Cricketer. *b:* 20.4.1954, Raleigh Park, Barnstaple, Devon. Lower order right-hand batsman, excellent slow left-arm bowler. *Sch* Belmont College, Barnstaple. *Team* Glamorgan (1976, 13 matches).
Career batting
13–16–8–108–32–13.50–0–*ct* 3
Bowling 1011–44–22.97–4–1–8/63
He headed the Glamorgan bowling averages in 1976 with 44 wickets (av 22.97), his best bowling being 8/63 v Sussex at Cardiff. He declined an offer of a two-year contract with Glamorgan, preferring to return to farming and Minor County cricket with Devon, for whom he played 1975–92.

Allison, David Farquhar
Cricketer. *b:* 26.6.1948, Marylebone, London. Lower order right-hand batsman, wicket-keeper. *Sch* Greenmore College. *Team* Oxford U (1970, blue).
Career batting
6–9–2–48–21–6.85–0–*ct* 4

Alliston, Cyril George Prat
Amateur. *b:* 1.11.1891, West Kensington, London. *d:* 21.7.1973, Southport, Lancashire. Lower order right-hand batsman, right-arm medium pace bowler. *Sch* Repton. *Team* Kent (1922, 1 match).
Career batting
1–1–0–0–0–0.00–0–*ct* 0

Allom, Anthony Thomas Carrick
Amateur. *b:* 21.10.1938, Bletchingley, Surrey. Son of M. J. C. (Surrey). Hard-hitting lower order right-hand batsman, accurate right-arm medium fast bowler, fine slip field. *Sch* Charterhouse. *Team* Surrey (1960, 1 match).
Career batting
5–8–3–94–34*–18.80–0–*ct* 1
Bowling 439–15–29.26–1–0–5/79
His debut was for the Free Foresters in 1959 and final match for the same team in 1961. He was one of the tallest ever first-class cricketers, at 6 feet 9 inches.

Allom, Maurice James Carrick
Amateur. *b:* 23.3.1906, Northwood, Middlesex. Father of A. T. C. (Surrey), son-in-law of O. T. Norris (Oxford U). Useful lower order right-hand batsman, effective right-arm medium fast bowler. *Sch* Wellington. *Teams* Cambridge U (1926–28, blue 1927–28); Surrey (1927–37, 100 matches). *Tours* MCC to Australia and New Zealand 1929/30, to South Africa 1930/1; Tennyson to Jamaica 1927/8. *Tests* England (1929/30 to 1930/1, 5 matches).
Career batting
179–203–51–1953–64–12.84–0–*ct* 83
Bowling 14291–605–23.62–30–3–9/55
Test batting
5–3–2–14–8*–14.00–0–*ct* 0
Bowling 265–14–18.92–1–0–5/38
Allom's most noteworthy feat was the dismissal of four men in five balls (including the hat-trick) on his Test debut for England v New Zealand at Christchurch in 1929/30. His best English season was 1930 when he took 108 wickets (av 23.33). His best bowling was for 9/55 for Cambridge U v Army at Cambridge in 1927. His final first-class match was for Free Foresters in 1938. He was President of MCC 1969/70 and of Surrey 1970.

Allott, Paul John Walter
Cricketer. *b:* 14.9.1956, Altrincham, Cheshire. Lower order right-hand batsman, right-arm fast medium bowler, good deep field. *Teams* Lancashire (1978–91, 205 matches); Wellington (1985/6 to 1986/7). *Tours* England to India and Sri Lanka 1981/2, to India 1984/5; International XI to Jamaica 1982/3; Lancashire to Jamaica 1986/7, to Zimbabwe 1988/9. *Tests* England (1981–85, 13 matches).
Career batting
245–262–64–3360–88–16.96–0–*ct* 136
Bowling 16665–652–25.55–30–0–8/48
Test batting
13–18–3–213–52*–14.20–0–*ct* 4
Bowling 1084–26–41.69–1–0–6/61
He took 85 wickets, av 23.09, in 1981. He also played for Cheshire (1976).

Allsop, Richard
Professional. *b:* 10.6.1849, Wirksworth, Derbyshire. *d:* 20.3.1908, Burton-on-Trent, Staffordshire. Lower order right-hand batsman, slip field. *Team* Derbyshire (1872–74, 3 matches).
Career batting
3–5–0–42–33–8.40–0–*ct* 3

Allsopp, Hon Frederic Ernest
Amateur. *b:* 21.9.1857, Hindlip Hall, Worcestershire. *d:* 20.12.1928, Hadzor, Droitwich, Worcestershire. Brother of H. T. (Cambridge U). Sound middle order right-hand batsman, slow round-arm bowler. *Sch* Cheltenham. *Team* MCC (1884).

Allsopp, Hon Herbert Tongue

Career batting
2–3–0–46–34–15.33–0–*ct* 1
Bowling 23–2–11.50–0–0–1/8
His County cricket was for Worcestershire (pre first-class, 1874–77).

Allsopp, Hon Herbert Tongue
Amateur. *b:* 5.12.1855, Foremark Hall, Derbyshire. *d:* 31.1.1920, Barnwood, Gloucestershire. Brother of F. E. (MCC), brother-in-law of G. M. Buckston (Derbyshire). Lower order right-hand batsman, fast round-arm bowler, good field at third man. *Sch* Cheltenham. *Team* Cambridge U (1876, blue).
Career batting
5–8–1–80–22–11.42–0–*ct* 4
Bowling 58–6–9.66–0–0–3/15
His County cricket was for Worcestershire (pre first-class, 1874–80).

Allsopp, Thomas Charlesworth
Professional. *b:* 18.12.1880, Leicester. *d:* 7.3.1919, Norwich, Norfolk. He died from influenza. Lower order left-hand batsman, good slow left-arm bowler. *Team* Leicestershire (1903–05, 36 matches).
Career batting
37–55–17–347–32–9.13–0–*ct* 10
Bowling 2490–88–28.29–4–1–6/85
He made quite an impression as a bowler in 1904, but was dropped from the Leicestershire side the following year and later played with success for Norfolk (1907–12). A well-known soccer player, he played for Leicester Fosse.

Almaer, Simon Ashley
Cricketer. *b:* 12.7.1969, Wanstead, Essex. Opening right-hand batsman, right-arm medium pace bowler. *Team* Oxford U (1988–90, blue 1988–89).
Career batting
15–24–1–441–67–19.17–0–*ct* 6

Alpass, Herbert John Hampden
Amateur. *b:* 7.8.1906, Berkeley, Gloucestershire. Lower order right-hand batsman, slow left-arm bowler, who could spin or swing the ball. *Sch* Clifton. *Team* Gloucestershire (1926–28, 7 matches).
Career batting
7–9–2–36–18*–5.14–0–*ct* 3
Bowling 114–4–28.50–0–0–2/42
He was a brilliant schoolboy bowler, who might well have developed into a good County cricketer.

Alston, Hallam Newton Egerton
Amateur. *b:* 10.6.1908, Cheltenham, Gloucestershire. *d:* 20.10.1985, Gloucester. Middle order right-hand batsman, right-arm medium pace bowler. *Sch* Cheltenham. *Team* Somerset (1933, 1 match).
Career batting
1–2–0–6–4–3.00–0–*ct* 0
Bowling 6–1–6.00–0–0–1/6

Altham, Harry Surtees, CBE
Amateur. *b:* 30.11.1888, Camberley, Surrey. *d:* 11.3.1965, Fulwood, Sheffield, Yorkshire. Father of R. J. L. (Oxford U), father-in-law of A. H. Brodhurst (Gloucestershire). Middle order right-hand batsman, occasional right-arm medium pace bowler. *Sch* Repton. *Teams* Oxford U (1909–12, blue 1911–12); Surrey (1908–12, 10 matches); Hampshire (1919–23, 24 matches).
Career batting
55–87–9–1537–141–19.70–1–*ct* 26
Bowling 47–0
He was better known 'behind the scenes' rather than on the field; cricket coach at Winchester for 30 years; member of MCC Committee for 25 years being Treasurer 1950–63 and President 1959/60; Test Selector in 1954; author with E. W. Swanton of 'A History of Cricket', which was the standard work on the game. His final first-class match was for Gentlemen of England v New Zealand in 1931. He was President of Hampshire from 1946 until his death.

Altham, Richard James Livingstone
Amateur. *b:* 19.1.1924, Winchester, Hampshire. Son of H. S. (Surrey and Hampshire), brother-in-law of A. H. Brodhurst (Gloucestershire). Middle order right-hand batsman, right-arm medium pace bowler. *Sch* Marlborough. *Team* Oxford U (1947).
Career batting
2–3–0–14–14–4.66–0–*ct* 2
His County cricket was for Hertfordshire (1952). His final first-class match was for Free Foresters in 1948. He won a blue for hockey.

Alwyn, Nicholas
Amateur. *b:* 13.6.1938, Finchley, Middlesex. Opening right-hand batsman. *Team* Cambridge U (1961).
Career batting
5–10–0–141–41–14.10–0–*ct* 0

Amar Singh, Ladhabhai Nakum
Amateur. *b:* 4.12.1910, Rajkot, India. *d:* 21.5.1940, Jamnagar, India. He died of pneumonia. Brother of L. Ramji (India), uncle of Vajehsingh Nakum (Nawanagar and Saurashtra). Punishing middle order right-hand batsman, right-arm fast medium bowler. *Teams* Patiala (1931/2 to 1932/3); Western India (1933/4 to 1935/6); Hindus (1934/5 to 1939/40); Nawanagar (1936/7 to 1939/40). *Tours* India to England 1932, 1936; also appeared in England in 1935 and 1938, and in Ceylon in 1933/4. *Tests* India (1932–36, 7 matches).
Career batting
92–150–12–3344–140*–24.23–5–*ct* 77
Bowling 9286–506–18.35–42–14–8/23
Test batting
7–14–1–292–51–22.46–0–*ct* 3
Bowling 858–28–30.64–2–0–7/86

The best Indian fast bowler of his generation, he died at the early age of 29. He was the first man to take 100 wickets in Ranji Trophy matches and he was a brilliant hitter – in a minor match at Rajkot he hit a century in 22 minutes. He took 111 wickets, av. 20.78, in 1932. His first class debut was for Rest of India in 1930/1.

Amarnath, Mohinder
Cricketer. *b:* 24.9.1950, Patiala, India. Son of Nanik (India), brother of Surinder (India) and Rajinder (Punjab and Delhi). Middle order right-hand batsman, right-arm medium pace bowler. *Teams* Punjab (1966/7 to 1973/4); Delhi (1974/5 to 1988/9); Baroda (1984/5). *Tours* Indian Universities to Sri Lanka 1970/1; India to England 1975 (World Cup), 1979, 1983 (World Cup), 1986, to West Indies 1975/6, 1982/3, to New Zealand 1975/6, to Australia 1977/8, 1984/5 (not first-class), 1985/6, to Pakistan 1978/9, 1982/3, 1984/5, to Sharjah (not first-class) 1984/5, 1985/6, 1987/8, 1988/9, 1989/90, to Sri Lanka 1985/6, to Bangladesh (not first-class) 1988/9. *Tests* India (1969/70 to 1987/8, 69 matches).
Career batting
248–379–61–13747–207–43.22–30–*ct* 152
Bowling 9107–277–32.87–8–1–7/27
Test batting
69–113–10–4378–138–42.50–11–*ct* 47
Bowling 1782–32–55.68–0–0–4/63

His two Test tours to England were in 1979 and 1986. On both visits he appeared in two out of three Tests and returned good batting figures. He was omitted from the 1982 tour, as well as several other India Test series about the same period, because of his suspected weakness against fast bowling. His overall Test record shows that he proved his critics wrong. He hit over 2,000 runs in the 1982/3 season, whilst playing in India, Pakistan and West Indies. His highest score was 207 for North Zone v East Zone at Bombay 1982/3. He also played for Durham (pre first-class, 1976–78) and Wiltshire (1984).

Amarnath, Nanik
(known as Lala Amarnath)
Amateur. *b:* 11.9.1911, Lahore, India. Father of Mohinder (India), Surinder (India) and Rajinder (Delhi and Punjab). Middle order right-hand batsman, excellent right-arm medium pace bowler, originally wicket-keeper. *Teams* Hindus (1929/30 to 1939/40); Southern Punjab (1933/4 to 1951/2); Gujarat (1952/3); Patiala (1953/4 to 1957/8); Uttar Pradesh (1956/7); Railways (1958/9 to 1960/61). *Tours* India to England 1936, 1946, to Ceylon 1944/5, to Australia 1947/8, to Pakistan 1954/5; Indian Starlets to Pakistan 1959/60; also appeared in Ceylon 1933/4. *Tests* India (1933/4 to 1952/3, 24 matches).
Career batting
186–286–34–10426–262–41.38–31–*ct* 96–*st* 2
Bowling 10644–463–22.98–19–3–7/27
Test batting
24–40–4–878–118–24.38–1–*ct* 13
Bowling 1481–45–32.91–2–0–5/96

At Aligarh University, Amarnath was principally a wicket-keeper, but by the time of the 1933/4 MCC tour to India, he had developed into an attacking batsman and hit a century on his Test debut. It was whilst in the nets prior to this Test that Amarnath's bowling potential was discovered, and within a short while he became one of the best all-rounders in India. He was expected to play a leading part in the 1936 tour to England, but was sent home for disciplinary reasons on the eve of the first Test. On the 1946 Tour he headed the Test bowling averages – the peculiarity of his bowling was that he bowled off the wrong foot, using a three pace run-up. His highest score was 262 for Indians in England v Rest at Calcutta in 1946/7. His final first class match was for Maharashtra Governor's XI in 1963/4. He scored 1,071 runs, av 59.94, in India in 1935/6, and 1,162 runs, av 58.10, in Australia in 1947/8.

Ambler, Joe
Professional. *b:* 12.2.1860, Lascelles Hall, Yorkshire. *d:* 10.2.1899, Lascelles Hall, Yorkshire. Middle order right-hand batsman, right-arm fast medium bowler. *Teams* Somerset (1883, 4 matches); Yorkshire (1886, 4 matches).
Career batting
8–14–0–197–76–14.07–0–*ct* 5–*st* 2
Bowling 222–7–31.71–0–0–4/54

According to MCC 'Scores and Biographies', vol XIV, p lxxxvi, the cricketer who appeared for Yorkshire was John Ambler of Lascelles Hall, b 1845, but this is incorrect.

Ambrose, Curtly Elconn Lynwall
Cricketer. *b:* 21.9.1963, Swetes Village, Antigua. Cousin of R. M. Otto (Leeward Islands). Lower order left-hand batsman, right-arm fast bowler. *Teams* Leeward Islands (1985/6 to 1991/2); Northamptonshire (1989–92, 42 matches). *Tours* West Indies to England 1988, 1991, to Australia 1988/9, to India 1989/90 (not first-class), to Sharjah (not first-class) 1988/9, 1989/90, to Pakistan 1990/1, 1991/2 (not first-class), to Australia and New Zealand 1991/2 (World Cup). *Tests* West Indies (1987/8 to 1991/2, 34 matches).
Career batting
110–140–37–1603–59–15.56–0–*ct* 26
Bowling 9293–420–22.12–19–3–8/45
Test batting
34–51–9–513–53–12.21–0–*ct* 7
Bowling 3322–148–22.44–6–1–8/45

A very tall cricketer (6ft 7in), he took over the role of Joel Garner in the West Indies Test side and was very successful during his first English tour in 1988. His Test record that year was 22 wickets, av 20.22. Heading both Test and first-class bowling averages on his second England tour in 1991, he demonstrated that he had become the equal of any of the current world Test bowlers.

Ames, Leslie Ethelbert George, CBE
Professional. *b:* 3.12.1905, Elham, Kent. *d:* 27.2.1990, Canterbury, Kent. Forcing middle order right-hand batsman, brilliant wicket-keeper, occasional leg break bowler. *Team* Kent (1926–51, 430 matches). *Tours* MCC to Australia 1928/9, 1932/3, 1936/7, to South Africa 1938/39, to West Indies 1929/30, 1934/5, to New Zealand 1932/3; Commonwealth to Ceylon and India 1950/1. *Tests* England (1929 to 1938/9, 47 matches).
Career batting
593–951–95–37248–295–43.51–102–*ct* 704–*st* 417
Bowling 801–24–33.37–0–0–3/23
Test batting
47–72–12–2434–149–40.56–8–*ct* 74–*st* 23

The outstanding wicket-keeper-batsman of the 1930s, Ames joined the Kent staff in 1923 as a batsman, but soon took up wicket-keeping. He obtained a regular place in the County side for the first time in 1927, scoring over 1,000 runs in the season, a feat he was to accomplish 17 times, his highest being in 1933 when 3,058 runs, av. 58.80, flowed from his bat. In 1927 he also hit the first of 102 centuries – completing his century of centuries in 1950. His highest innings was 295 for Kent v Gloucestershire at Folkestone in 1933 and he hit eight other double centuries.

In 1928 he created a new seasonal first-class record by picking up 122 dismissals behind the stumps, but the following year he again broke the record with a total of 128, which remains the English record. In 1932 he achieved 100 dismissals for the third time (104), but this time included 64 stumpings in his bag, another record which still stands. In his career he achieved 417 stumpings, another first-class record. Most of his triumphs behind the wicket were accomplished in harness with A. P. Freeman, the prolific leg spinner.

Ames played regularly for England as a wicket-keeper-batsman through the 1930s, but when first-class cricket resumed after the Second World War, he forsook his position behind the wicket (giving way to T. G. Evans) and remained in the County side purely as a batsman. In 1950 he was the first professional to be appointed as a Test Selector and served for eight seasons, then from 1957 to 1974 he took the post as Manager to Kent, being also Secretary from 1961 to 1973. He was President of Kent in 1975. On three occasions, including the riot-torn Pakistan tour of 1968/9, he managed MCC teams abroad.

In one capacity or another his career in first-class cricket spanned over 50 years. He also played soccer for Clapton Orient and Gillingham. His niece married J. G. Spanswick (Kent).

Ames, Neville Lawrenson
Amateur. *b:* 31.7.1891, Fulham, London. *d:* 21.3.1956, Marylebone, London. Lower order right-hand batsman, right-arm fast medium bowler, good field. *Sch* Radley. *Team* Leveson-Gower's XI (1912).
Career batting
1–2–0–0–0–0.00–0–*ct* 0
Bowling 11–0

Amherst, Hon Josceline George Herbert
Amateur. *b:* 7.6.1846, Westminster, London. *d:* 1.2.1900, Darlington, Western Australia. Brother of P. A. (MCC). Steady middle order right-hand batsman, slow round-arm bowler. *Sch* Harrow. *Teams* Gentlemen of Kent (1864); MCC (1866).
Career batting
2–4–0–15–7–3.75–0–*ct* 0
Bowling 36–3–12.00–0–0–2/26

It is very difficult to separate the performances of this player and his brother (Hon Jeffrey Charles Amherst, 1845–1877), but it is believed that the two appearances in first-class matches were by J. G. H. Amherst. He held various high political offices.

Amherst, Rev Hon Percy Arthur
Amateur. *b:* 30.11.1839, Montreal Park, Sevenoaks, Kent. *d:* 30.1.1910, Ossington, Nottinghamshire. Brother of J. G. H. (MCC). Lower order batsman. *Sch* Eton. *Team* MCC (1871).
Career batting
1–2–0–2–2–1.00–0–*ct* 0

His County cricket was for Northamptonshire (pre first-class, 1864).

Amir Elahi
Amateur. *b:* 1.9.1908, Lahore, India. *d:* 28.12.1980, Multan, Pakistan. Lower order right-hand batsman, right-arm medium pace, later leg-break and googly bowler. *Teams* Northern India (1934/5 to 1943/4); Muslims (1935/6 to 1944/5); Southern Punjab (1937/8 to 1949/50); Baroda (1944/5 to 1949/50); Bahawalpur (1953/4). *Tours* India to England 1936, to Australia 1947/8; Pakistan to India 1952/3. *Tests* India (1947/8, 1 match); Pakistan (1952/3, 5 matches).
Career batting
125–172–20–2562–96–16.35–0–*ct* 67
Bowling 13221–513–25.77–30–6–8/94
Test batting
6–9–1–82–47–10.25–0–*ct* 0
Bowling 248–7–35.42–0–0–4/134

Neither on the tour to England in 1936, nor the visit to Australia in 1947/8 did he attain much distinction, but he was comparatively successful in his later years for Pakistan when he not only became one of the few cricketers to represent two countries, but also one of the oldest (44) of Test players. He took 5 wickets in 5 balls in the Surat Tournament, 1944/5, a match which might be first-class if the full details could be discovered.

Amiss, Dennis Leslie, MBE
Professional. *b:* 7.4.1943, Harborne, Birmingham. Sound opening right-hand batsman, slow left-arm bowler, good close field. *Team* Warwickshire (1960–87, 547 matches). *Tours* MCC Under 25 to Pakistan 1966/7, to India, Pakistan and Sri Lanka 1972/3, to West Indies 1973/4, to Australia and New Zealand 1974/5, to India, Sri Lanka and Australia 1976/7; International XI to India, Ceylon and Pakistan 1967/8; Rest of World to Pakistan 1970/1; SAB England XI to South Africa 1981/2. *Tests* England (1966–77, 50 matches).
Career batting
658–1139–126–43423–262*–42.86–102–*ct* 418
Bowling 718–18–39.88–0–0–3/21
Test batting
50–88–10–3612–262*–46.30–11–*ct* 24
He hit 1,000 runs in a season in England 23 times, going on to 2,000 three times (best 2,239, av 55.97, in 1984). Of his three double centuries two were for England and one for Warwickshire, the highest being 262* for England v West Indies at Kingston in 1973/4. His career in Test cricket ended when he signed for Packer's World Series Cricket. In 1992 he was Chairman of the Cricket Committee of Warwickshire CCC.

Amor, Stanley Long
Amateur. *b:* 22.7.1887, Bath, Somerset. *d:* 7.8.1965, Bloomfield, Bath, Somerset. Lower order right-hand batsman, wicket-keeper. *Sch* Bath College. *Team* Somerset (1908–30, 26 matches).
Career batting
29–51–20–220–21–7.09–0–*ct* 29–*st* 22
He also represented Somerset at hockey.

Amory, J. H. (*see under* Heathcoat-Amory, J.)

Amory, L. H. (*see under* Heathcoat-Amory, L.)

Anderson, Albert Edwin
Amateur. *b:* 13.4.1889, Comber, Co Down, Ireland. *d:* 21.9.1944, Comber, Co Down, Ireland. Middle order right-hand batsman. *Team* Ireland (1926).
Career batting
1–2–0–18–18–9.00–0–*ct* 1

Anderson, Charles Stewart
Amateur. *b: circa* 1881. *d:* 1.3.1943, Portrush, Co Antrim, Ireland. Middle order right-hand batsman, right-arm medium pace off break bowler. *Team* Ireland (1926).
Career batting
1–1–0–0–0–0.00–0–*ct* 0
Bowling 25–0

Anderson, Desmond John
Cricketer. *b:* 17.10.1968, Johannesburg, South Africa. Lower order right-hand batsman, right-arm medium pace bowler. *Sch* Repton. *Team* Oxford U (1992, blue).
Career batting
8–8–4–18–9–4.50–0–*ct* 3
Bowling 511–9–56.77–0–0–2/68

Anderson, Ewan William
Amateur. *b:* 28.3.1938, Bromley, Kent. Lower order right-hand batsman, right-arm fast medium bowler. *Sch* Dulwich. *Team* Oxford U (1961–62).
Career batting
12–15–5–38–13*–3.80–0–*ct* 1
Bowling 727–18–40.38–0–0–3/69
He won a blue for rugby.

Anderson, George
Professional. *b:* 20.1.1826, Bedale, Yorkshire. *d:* 27.11.1902, Aiskew, Bedale, Yorkshire. Hard-hitting middle order right-hand batsman, excellent mid-wicket or long-leg field. *Team* Yorkshire (1850–69, 33 matches). *Tour* Parr to Australia 1863/4.
Career batting
99–171–16–2535–99*–16.35–0–*ct* 74
One of the most prominent professionals of his day, Anderson appeared for the All England Eleven for about 20 years. Late in his career he was offered the captaincy of Yorkshire but refused because it would mean playing against Surrey, there being a dispute between the leading Northern professionals and the authorities at the Oval. Anderson's refusal resulted in him missing a number of County matches – the argument continuing for several years (1862–66). He also played for Northumberland (1851).

Anderson, Iain Mair
Amateur. *b:* 11.5.1931, Ballygunge, Calcutta, India. Opening right-hand batsman, right-arm fast medium bowler. *Sch* Dollar. *Team* Scotland (1951–53).
Career batting
5–8–0–114–40–14.25–0–*ct* 2

Anderson, Iain Stuart
Cricketer. *b:* 24.4.1960, Derby. Opening or middle order right-hand batsman, off break bowler. *Teams* Derbyshire (1978–87, 134 matches); Boland (1983/4).
Career batting
140–225–27–4726–112–23.86–2–*ct* 106
Bowling 1356–22–61.63–0–0–4/35
He hit 1,233 runs, av 37.36, in 1983.

Anderson, Ivan John
Cricketer. *b:* 13.8.1944, Armagh, Ireland. Middle order right-hand batsman, off break bowler. *Team* Ireland (1966–82).
Career batting
19–33–8–947–147–37.88–3–*ct* 9
Bowling 249–17–14.64–1–0–5/21

Anderson, James Duncan
Amateur. *b:* 17.12.1931, Melbourne, Victoria, Australia. Lower order right-hand batsman, right-arm medium pace off break bowler. *Sch* Melbourne GS.

Anderson, John Theodore

Team Oxford U (1955).
Career batting
2–3–2–4–4*–4.00–0–*ct* 3
Bowling 118–4–29.50–0–0–4/68

He won a half-blue for athletics and represented Australia at Australian Rules Football.

Anderson, John Theodore
Amateur. *b:* 10.8.1878, Warrnambool, Victoria, Australia. *d:* 20.8.1926, Geelong, Victoria, Australia. Lower order right-hand batsman. *Teams* Scotland (1905–06); Western Australia (1908/9 to 1909/10, 4 matches).
Career batting
6–11–2–68–17*–7.55–0–*ct* 4
Bowling 351–16–21.93–0–0–4/51

Anderson, Joseph
Amateur. *b:* 31.1.1878, Perth, Scotland. *d:* 10.6.1961, Perth, Scotland. Opening right-hand batsman. *Team* Scotland (1906–12).
Career batting
5–9–0–139–31–15.44–0–*ct* 3

Anderson, Michael Herbert
Amateur. *b:* 11.12.1916, Devonport, Devon. *d:* 10.5.1940, Spijkenisse, Holland. He was killed in action (with 600 Squadron, based at Manston, Kent). Opening right-hand batsman, wicket-keeper. *Sch* Clifton. *Team* Cambridge U (1937–38).
Career batting
4–7–2–92–60–18.40–0–*ct* 3–*st* 3

His County cricket was for Hertfordshire (1936).

Anderson, Paul Napier
Cricketer. *b:* 28.4.1966, Driffield, Yorkshire. Lower order right-hand batsman, right-arm medium pace bowler. *Team* Yorkshire (1988, 1 match).
Career batting
1–1–0–0–0–0.00–0–*ct* 1
Bowling 47–1–47.00–0–0–1/47

Anderson, Reginald Mervyn Bulford
Amateur. *b:* 25.4.1914, Brynhyfryd, Swansea, Glamorgan. *d:* 12.8.1972, Uplands, Swansea, Glamorgan. Tail end right-hand batsman, right-arm fast medium bowler. *Team* Glamorgan (1946, 1 match).
Career batting
1–1–0–0–0–0.00–0–*ct* 0
Bowling 60–0

Anderson, Robert Wickham
Cricketer. *b:* 2.10.1948, Christchurch, New Zealand. Son of W. McD. (New Zealand). Attacking opening right-hand batsman, leg break bowler, good deep field. *Teams* Canterbury (1967/8); Northern Districts (1969/70); Otago (1971/2 to 1976/7); Central Districts (1977/8 to 1981/2). *Tours* New Zealand to England 1973, 1978, to Pakistan 1976/7. *Tests* New Zealand (1976 to 1978/9, 9 matches).
Career batting
111–197–14–5609–155–30.65–8–*ct* 79
Bowling 154–5–30.80–0–0–4/49
Test batting
9–18–0–423–92–23.50–0–0–*ct* 1

He played in all three Tests on the 1978 tour, scoring 739 runs, av 35.19, in first-class matches.

Anderson, William Alexander
Amateur. *b:* 28.7.1909, Sandwich, Kent. *d:* 21.4.1975, Much Hadham, Hertfordshire. Brother-in-law of J. H. Pawle (Essex). Middle order left-hand batsman. *Sch* Charterhouse. *Team* Free Foresters (1946).
Career batting
1–1–0–14–14–14.00–0–*ct* 0

Anderson, William Burn
Amateur. *b:* 12.11.1871, Westminster, London. *d:* 31.1.1948, Langham Hall, Bury St Edmunds, Suffolk. Uncle of W. G. Agnew (Royal Navy). Lower order right-hand batsman, right-arm medium fast bowler, good field. *Sch* Harrow. *Team* Middlesex (1891, 1 match).
Career batting
1–2–0–2–2–1.00–0–*ct* 1

Anderson, William Williamson
Amateur. *b:* 27.11.1894, Dunfermline, Fife, Scotland. *d:* 16.6.1973, Dunfermline, Fife, Scotland. Lower order right-hand batsman, right-arm fast bowler. *Team* Scotland (1922–36).
Career batting
16–26–3–241–27–10.47–0–*ct* 14
Bowling 1147–54–21.24–3–0–6/51

Anderton, Rev Frederic Michael
Amateur. *b:* 8.12.1931, Agra, India. Middle order right-hand batsman, off break bowler. *Sch* Sherborne. *Team* Cambridge U (1953).
Career batting
3–5–1–64–38–16.00–0–*ct* 2
Bowling 11–0

Andreae, Charles Montagu
Amateur. *b:* 16.12.1906, Marylebone, London. *d:* 22.6.1970, Broomhall, Sunningdale, Berkshire. He married the granddaughter of W. B. Harrison (MCC). Attacking middle order right-hand batsman, slow right-arm bowler. *Sch* Harrow. *Team* Cambridge U (1929).
Career batting
2–3–0–44–18–14.66–0–*ct* 1
Bowling 118–2–59.00–0–0–2/60

Andrew, Christopher Robert
Cricketer. *b:* 18.2.1963, Richmond, Yorkshire. Middle order left-hand batsman, off break bowler. *Sch* Barnard Castle. *Team* Cambridge U (1984–85, blue both years).

Career batting
17–33–2–658–101*–21.22–1–*ct* 6
Bowling 847–12–70.58–0–0–3/77

He captained Cambridge in 1985. An outstanding fly-half, he gained a blue at Cambridge and has since played regularly for England and toured Australia with the British Lions in 1989.

Andrew, Frederick James
Professional. *b:* 29.5.1937, Southmead, Bristol. Tail end right-hand batsman, right-arm fast medium opening bowler. *Team* Gloucestershire (1959–63, 21 matches).
Career batting
21–26–7–53–6–2.78–0–*ct* 13
Bowling 1366–57–23.96–2–1–5/8

His only performance of note was for Gloucestershire v Kent at Dartford in 1962, when he took 5/8 and 5/83 in the two innings.

Andrew, Keith Vincent
Professional. *b:* 15.12.1929, Greenacres, Oldham, Lancashire. Lower order right-hand batsman, occasional leg break bowler, brilliant wicket-keeper. *Team* Northamptonshire (1953–66, 351 matches). *Tours* MCC to Australia and New Zealand 1954/5, to West Indies 1959/60; Commonwealth to Pakistan 1963/4, to India 1964/5. *Tests* England (1954/5 to 1963, 2 matches).
Career batting
390–476–160–4230–76–13.38–0–*ct* 723–*st* 181
Bowling 31–2–15.50–0–0–2/9
Test batting
2–4–1–29–15–9.66–0–*ct* 1

By some he was regarded as the most talented wicket-keeper of his generation, but his lack of batting ability meant few Test calls. He captained Northamptonshire from 1962 to 1966. His debut was for Combined Services in 1952. He became the NCA Director of Coaching and in 1992 was the Chief Executive of that body.

Andrew, Stephen Jon Walter
Cricketer. *b:* 27.1.1966, Marylebone, London. Lower order right-hand batsman, right-arm medium fast bowler. *Teams* Hampshire (1984–89, 57 matches); Essex (1990–92, 43 matches).
Career batting
100–69–31–292–35–7.68–0–*ct* 21
Bowling 8349–260–32.11–5–0–7/92

Andrew, Walter
(known as William Andrew)
Amateur. *b:* 22.3.1869, Bournemouth, Hampshire. *d:* 30.3.1911, Sligo, Ireland. Middle order right-hand batsman, right-arm medium pace bowler. *Team* Hampshire (1897–98, 12 matches).
Career batting
12–22–1–312–106–14.85–1–*ct* 3
Bowling 626–23–27.21–1–0–5/157

His fame rests with an innings of 106 for Hampshire v Warwickshire at Southampton in 1897, when he shared a partnership of 222 with A. J. L. Hill and saved the match. He was tried in several matches the following season, but could not repeat his success. He also played for Dorset (1902–06).

Andrews, Arthur John
Amateur. *b:* 26.8.1856, Southampton, Hampshire. *d:* 26.2.1943, Aldershot, Hampshire. Defensive middle order right-hand batsman, wicket-keeper. *Team* Hampshire (1880–85, 7 matches).
Career batting
7–12–1–236–62*–21.45–0–*ct* 6–*st* 2
Bowling 2–0

He also played for Wiltshire (1895). His last match for Hampshire was in 1887 (not first-class).

Andrews, Clifford Jack
Amateur. *b:* 6.8.1912, Swindon, Wiltshire. *d:* 11.12.1973, Eastleigh, Hampshire. Brother of W. H. R. (Somerset). Lower order right-hand batsman, wicket-keeper. *Team* Hampshire (1938–48, 7 matches).
Career batting
7–10–1–127–29–14.11–0–*ct* 6–*st* 1

Andrews, Henry Wyche
Amateur. *b:* 4.10.1821, Eling, Hampshire. *d:* 13.12.1865, Dulwich Common, Surrey. Father of W. H. (Sussex). Middle order right-hand batsman, wicket-keeper. *Team* Kent (1852–63, 16 matches).
Career batting
41–75–7–915–58–13.45–0–*ct* 31–*st* 8
Bowling 9–0

He was one of the few cricketers of his day to wear spectacles whilst playing. His first-class debut was for Gentlemen of Kent in 1849.

Andrews, Norman Palmer
Amateur. *b:* 1.5.1899, Sydenham, Kent. *d:* 5.11.1971, Westminster School, London. Opening or middle order right-hand batsman. *Sch* Westminster. *Team* Northamptonshire (1922–23, 6 matches).
Career batting
6–12–1–122–45*–11.09–0–*ct* 1

Andrews, Oscar
Amateur. *b:* 24.7.1876, West Derby, Liverpool, Lancashire. *d:* 30.10.1956, Belfast, Ireland. Lower order right-hand batsman, right-arm medium pace bowler. *Sch* Rossall. *Team* Ireland (1902). *Tour* Ireland to North America 1909.
Career batting
6–11–2–94–29*–10.44–0–*ct* 6
Bowling 94–4–23.50–0–0–2/8

He also played hockey for Ireland.

Andrews, Thomas James Edwin
Amateur. *b:* 26.8.1890, Newtown, New South Wales, Australia. *d:* 28.1.1970, Croydon, Sydney, New

South Wales, Australia. Attractive middle order right-hand batsman, leg break and googly bowler. *Teams* New South Wales (1912/3 to 1928/9, 74 matches). *Tours* Australia to England 1921, 1926, to South Africa 1914/15 (tour cancelled), 1921/2; New South Wales to New Zealand 1923/4. *Tests* Australia (1921–26, 16 matches).
Career batting
151–222–17–8095–247*–39.48–14–*ct* 85
Bowling 3050–95–32.10–3–0–6/109
Test batting
16–23–1–592–94–26.90–0–*ct* 12
Bowling 116–1–116.00–0–0–1/23

Andrews toured England twice and on both occasions appeared in the Tests. He never made his mark in International cricket, though he was a successful member of the New South Wales side for many years. His play was characterised by the straightness of his bat. He hit 1,000 runs in a season twice (best 1,234, av. 38.56, in 1926). His highest score was 247* for New South Wales v Victoria at Sydney in 1919/20.

Andrews, Walter Herman
Amateur. *b:* 17.4.1865, Dulwich Common, Surrey. *d:* 26.11.1908, Stanger, Natal, South Africa. Son of H. W. (Kent). Hard-hitting middle order left-hand batsman, left-arm fast bowler, good field. *Sch* Radley. *Team* Sussex (1888–92, 37 matches).
Career batting
37–69–4–864–67–13.29–0–*ct* 27
Bowling 1–0

Andrews, William Harry Russell
Professional. *b:* 14.4.1908, Swindon, Wiltshire. *d:* 9.1.1989, Worlebury, Somerset. Brother of C. J. (Hampshire). Aggressive lower order right-hand batsman, right-arm fast medium bowler. *Team* Somerset (1930–47, 226 matches).
Career batting
231–371–54–5000–80–15.77–0–*ct* 96
Bowling 18033–768–23.48–40–6–8/12

Andrews was unfortunate to be released by Somerset at the end of the 1932 season due to economy measures, but returning to the staff in 1935 he looked a much improved player and in 1937 and 1938 achieved the 'double'. He hit 1,000 runs in a season twice (best, 1,141, av 20.74, in 1937) and took 100 wickets four times (best 143, av 20.53, in 1937). His bowling, with a deceptive swing and accurate length, was little short of the highest standard. He was released by the County a second time in 1947, but returned later as coach (1955–57 and 1968). He also played for Devon (1950).

Angell, Frederick Leslie
Amateur turned professional in 1949. *b:* 29.6.1922, Norton St Philip, Somerset. Steady opening right-hand batsman, good slip field. *Team* Somerset (1947–56, 132 matches).
Career batting
132–251–11–4596–114–19.15–1–*ct* 54
Bowling 31–0

He scored 1,125, av 22.95, in 1954.

Angus, Alexander William
Amateur. *b:* 11.11.1889, Sydney, New South Wales, Australia. *d:* 23.3.1947, Edinburgh, Scotland. Opening right-hand batsman. *Sch* George Watson's College. *Team* Scotland (1921–22).
Career batting
4–7–0–108–29–15.42–0–*ct* 2

He played rugby for Scotland.

Angus, Thomas
Professional. *b:* 23.11.1934, Gateshead, Co Durham. *d:* 14.5.1988, Englefield Green, Surrey. He died whilst playing in a club match. Tail end left-hand batsman, useful right-arm fast medium bowler. *Team* Middlesex (1956–57, 7 matches).
Career batting
7–11–5–49–18*–8.16–0–*ct* 4
Bowling 353–23–15.34–0–0–4/81

In 1958 it was announced that he would be having a trial with Somerset, but in fact he did not appear in that side.

Anscombe, John Parker
Professional. *b:* 4.1.1838, Brighton, Sussex. *d:* 2.3.1881, Hurstpierpoint, Sussex. Tail end right-hand batsman, wicket-keeper. *Sch* Hurstpierpoint. *Team* Sussex (1862–66, 3 matches).
Career batting
3–5–1–7–2–1.75–0–*ct* 1–*st* 3

Anson, Claude Esmond
Amateur. *b:* 14.10.1889, Bradford, Yorkshire. *d:* 26.3.1969, Selby, Yorkshire. Opening right-hand batsman. *Sch* Pocklington. *Team* Yorkshire (1924, 1 match).
Career batting
1–2–0–27–14–13.50–0–*ct* 1

Anson, Geoffrey Frank
Amateur. *b:* 8.10.1922, Sevenoaks, Kent. *d:* 4.12.1977, Hastings, Sussex. Attacking middle order right-hand batsman. *Sch* Harrow. *Teams* Cambridge U (1947); Kent (1947, 7 matches).
Career batting
10–18–0–460–106–25.55–1–*ct* 6

Anson was originally at Cambridge in 1942, but returned in 1947 and looked certain to get his blue when he abruptly took up an appointment in the Colonial Service and left the University.

Anson, Hon Rupert
Amateur. *b:* 7.11.1889, Marylebone, London. *d:* 20.12.1966, Blandford St Mary, Dorset. Grandson of Earl of Leicester (MCC 1851). Middle order right-hand batsman, slow right-arm bowler. *Sch* Harrow. *Team* Middlesex (1910–14, 30 matches).

Career batting
33–49–4–1030–97–22.88–0–*ct* 16
Bowling 233–10–23.30–1–0–5/39

His final first-class match was for Leveson-Gower's XI in 1919.

Anson, Rev Thomas Anchitel
Amateur. *b:* 14.10.1818. *d:* 3.10.1899, Longford, Derbyshire. Middle order right-hand batsman, but with ugly style, wicket-keeper. *Sch* Eton. *Teams* Cambridge U (1839–42, blue all four years); Cambridge Town Club (1840–41).
Career batting
45–80–7–901–72*–12.34–0–*ct* 29–*st* 21

He played little first-class cricket after leaving Cambridge and his final match for Gentlemen of South in 1862 came 17 years after his previous appearance. He captained Cambridge in his last three years. His County cricket was for Norfolk (1843–48).

Anstead, Walter Henry
Professional, but Amateur in 1872. *b:* 26.2.1845, Twickenham, Middlesex. *d:* 14.5.1933, Winton, Bournemouth, Hampshire. Father of R. D. (Europeans). Middle order right-hand batsman, excellent right-arm fast bowler. *Team* Surrey (1870–72, 7 matches).
Career batting
7–12–2–61–17–6.10–0–*ct* 2
Bowling 542–48–11.29–5–1–6/27

He performed brilliantly for Surrey in the school holidays of 1870 – his occupation being that of a schoolmaster in Weybridge – but in 1871 he was appointed Assistant-Inspector of Schools and this virtually ended his important cricket. He also played for Bedfordshire (1871). His bowling action was the subject of unfavourable comment.

Anstruther, Alexander William
(he changed his name to Anstruther-Duncan in 1897) Amateur. *b:* 3.10.1846, Rajahmundry, Madras, India. *d:* 18.10.1902, Naughton, Wormit, Fife, Scotland. Uncle of R. A. (Europeans). Opening right-hand batsman, excellent field at long-stop or short-leg. *Team* Sussex (1875–78, 7 matches).
Career batting
14–27–3–281–43–11.70–0–*ct* 4
Bowling 12–0

His most notable innings was 120 for Gentlemen of England v Gentlemen of Kent in 1877 – the match was XIII-a-side and not first-class. His first-class debut was for MCC in 1873, and his final match for the same team in 1887.

Anthony, Alfred Feargus O'Connor
Professional. *b:* 22.5.1841, Arnold, Nottinghamshire. *d:* 10.6.1900, Park Hill, Sheffield, Yorkshire. Uncle of George (Nottinghamshire) and Henry (Nottinghamshire). Lower order right-hand batsman, wicket-keeper, occasional under-arm or round-arm bowler. *Team* Nottinghamshire (1875–76, 3 matches).
Career batting
3–6–0–14–11–2.33–0–*ct* 2–*st* 2

Anthony, George
Professional. *b:* 25.6.1875, Arnold, Nottinghamshire. *d:* 13.5.1907, Arnold, Nottinghamshire. Brother of Henry (Nottinghamshire), nephew of A. F. O'C. (Nottinghamshire). Middle order right-hand batsman, right-arm fast medium bowler. *Team* Nottinghamshire (1900–05, 85 matches).
Career batting
85–126–13–1721–89–15.23–0–*ct* 33
Bowling 2619–82–31.93–3–0–6/72

He died of consumption aged 31, which cut short a promising career.

Anthony, Hamish Arbeb Gervais
Cricketer. *b:* 16.1.1971, Urlings Village, Antigua. Cousin of G. J. F. Ferris (Leicestershire). Lower order right-hand batsman, right-arm fast medium bowler. *Teams* Leewards Islands (1989/90 to 1991/2); Glamorgan (1990, 6 matches). *Tours* West Indies to England 1991, to Australia 1991/2.
Career batting
33–40–5–592–82–16.91–0–*ct* 15
Bowling 2798–99–28.26–2–0–5/23

He showed promise as a potential Test all-rounder on the 1991 tour of England, but was not called upon for any internationals.

Anthony, Henry
Professional. *b:* 20.9.1876, Arnold, Nottinghamshire. *d:* 13.7.1928, Mansfield, Nottinghamshire. Brother of George (Nottinghamshire), nephew of A. F. O'C. (Nottinghamshire). Middle order right-hand batsman, right-arm medium pace bowler. *Team* Nottinghamshire (1898–1902, 4 matches).
Career batting
4–7–1–52–13*–8.66–0–*ct* 3
Bowling 81–2–40.50–0–0–1/15

He also played for Cheshire (1920).

Antliff, William Norris
Amateur. *b:* 23.8.1848, Bottesford, Leicestershire. *d:* 29.4.1909, Draycott, Derbyshire. Opening right-hand batsman. *Sch* Shireland Hall, Birmingham. *Team* Derbyshire (1880, 2 matches).
Career batting
2–4–0–17–5–4.25–0–*ct* 0

Anton, John Hamish Hugh
Amateur. *b:* 19.9.1926, Aggborough, Kidderminster, Worcestershire. Attractive hard-hitting middle order right-hand batsman, right-arm medium pace bowler. *Sch* Rugby. *Teams* Cambridge U (1949–50); Worcestershire (1950, 4 matches).
Career batting
14–24–1–361–45–15.69–0–*ct* 2

Antrobus, Edward Philip
Cricketer. *b:* 28.9.1938, Long Acre, Cradock, Cape Province, South Africa. Nephew of G. J. (Cambridge U). Middle order right-hand batsman, leg break bowler. *Team* Cambridge U (1963).
Career batting
2–4–0–53–31–13.25–0–*ct* 1
Bowling 20–0

Antrobus, Geoffrey John
Amateur. *b:* 26.5.1904, Cradock, Cape Province, South Africa. Uncle of E. P. (Cambridge U). Tail end right-hand batsman, leg break bowler. *Team* Cambridge U (1925).
Career batting
2–4–0–2–1–0.50–0–*ct* 1
Bowling 194–3–64.66–0–0–3/121

Antrobus, Robert Crawford
Amateur. *b:* 21.3.1830. *d:* 12.2.1911, Westminster, London. Lower order batsman. *Sch* Eton. *Teams* Gentlemen of England (1850); I Zingari (1866).
Career batting
2–4–1–17–12*–5.66–0–*ct* 0
Bowling 10–1 + 1–10.00–0–0–1/10

Anurasiri, Sangarange Don
Cricketer. *b:* 25.2.1966, Panadura, Ceylon. Lower order right-hand batsman, slow left-arm bowler. *Team* Panadura (1988/9 to 1991/2). *Tours* Sri Lanka to England 1984, 1988, 1991, to Sharjah (not first-class) 1985/6, 1986/7, 1987/8, to India 1986/7, 1989/90 (not first-class), 1990/1 (not first-class), to Bangladesh (not first-class) 1988/9, to India and Pakistan (World Cup) 1987/8, to Pakistan 1991/2, to Australia and New Zealand (World Cup) 1991/2. *Tests* Sri Lanka (1985/6 to 1991/2, 8 matches).
Career batting
57–62–15–637–74–13.55–0–*ct* 24
Bowling 3727–164–22.72–12–4–8/53
Test batting
8–10–3–33–16–4.71–0–*ct* 1
Bowling 493–13–37.92–0–0–4/71

After very modest results on his first two tours to England, he improved in 1991 and played in the Test match with fair success.

Appleby, Arthur
Amateur. *b:* 22.7.1843, Enfield, near Clayton le Moors, Lancashire. *d:* 24.10.1902, Mill House, Enfield, near Clayton le Moors, Lancashire. Free-hitting middle order left-hand batsman, left-hand fast medium bowler with a round-arm action. *Sch* Grange School, Yorkshire. *Team* Lancashire (1866–87, 58 matches). *Tour* FitzGerald to North America 1872 (not first-class).
Career batting
81–131–22–1249–99–11.45–0–*ct* 55
Bowling 5267–336–15.67–24–3–9/25

His best bowling was 9/25 for Lancashire v Sussex at Hove in 1877. He was twice invited to tour Australia (1873/4 and 1878/9) but had to decline for business reasons. During the 1870s he was perhaps the best amateur fast bowler in England.

Appleton, Charles
Amateur. *b:* 15.5.1844, Kirk Ella, Hull, Yorkshire. *d:* 26.2.1925, Bradley Hall, Standish, Wigan, Lancashire. Lower order right-hand batsman, wicket-keeper. *Sch* Rossall. *Team* Yorkshire (1865, 3 matches).
Career batting
3–6–1–56–18–11.20–0–*ct* 0

An all-round athlete he excelled at running, pole-jumping and putting 'the stone'. He left Yorkshire shortly after playing for the County and appeared regularly in London Club cricket.

Appleyard, Francis
Amateur. *b:* 26.9.1905, Clifton, Yorkshire. *d:* 12.10.1971, Stevenage, Hertfordshire. Lower order right-hand batsman, steady right-arm fast medium bowler. *Team* Essex (1946–47, 14 matches).
Career batting
18–25–14–74–15*–6.72–0–*ct* 10
Bowling 1210–30–40.33–2–0–5/14

A leading bowler with Hertfordshire (1931–1939, 1950) and with the British Empire XI during the 1939–45 war. His first-class debut was for Minor Counties in 1939 and his final match for MCC in 1950.

Appleyard, Robert
Professional. *b:* 27.6.1924, Wibsey, Bradford, Yorkshire. Tail end right-hand batsman, versatile right-arm bowler – medium pace or off-breaks. *Team* Yorkshire (1950–58, 133 matches). *Tour* MCC to Australia and New Zealand 1954/5. *Tests* England (1954–56, 9 matches).
Career batting
152–145–54–776–63–8.52–*ct* 80
Bowling 10965–708–15.48–57–17–8/76
Test batting
9–9–6–51–19*–17.00–0–*ct* 4
Bowling 554–31–17.87–1–0–5/51

Appleyard took the cricket world by storm, when in 1951, virtually as an unknown, he took 200 wickets (av 14.14) and headed the first-class averages. The secret of his success lay in the way he concealed his variation of pace. A prolonged illness prevented him from playing except on one occasion in 1952 and he was not seen at all in 1953, but quite astonishingly he came back in 1954 to come second in the averages with 154 wickets (av 14.42) and win his Test cap, also a place in the MCC side to Australia the following winter. Appleyard was dropped from the Yorkshire side during 1958 and then left County cricket.

Apte, Arvindrao Laxmanrao
Amateur. *b:* 24.10.1934, Bombay, India. Brother of M. L. (India). Opening right-hand batsman, right-arm medium pace bowler. *Teams* Bombay (1957/8 to 1964/5); Rajasthan (1968/9 to 1970/1). *Tour* India to England 1959. *Test* India (1959, 1 match).
Career batting
58–91–8–2782–165–33.51–6–*ct* 14–*st* 1
Bowling 76–2–38.00–0–0–1/21
Test batting
1–2–0–15–8–7.50–0–*ct* 0
His debut was for Indian Universities in 1955/6.

Arber, Ralph Herbert
Professional. *b:* 10.5.1846, Cambridge. Tail end batsman, useful bowler. *Team* Cambridgeshire (1871, 1 match).
Career batting
1–2–0–6–6–3.00–0–*ct* 0
Bowling 51–2–25.50–0–0–2/29

Arbuthnot, Reginald James Hugh
Amateur. *b:* 2.6.1853, Brighton, Sussex. *d:* 19.9.1917, Brighton, Sussex. Uncle of W. H. Spottiswoode (Kent). Lower order right-hand batsman, good field. *Sch* Rugby. *Team* Kent (1881–90, 2 matches).
Career batting
2–4–0–8–5–2.00–0–*ct* 0
The reason for the nine years gap between his appearances for Kent was that he lived in India in the interim.

Archdale, Arthur Somerville
Amateur. *b:* 8.9.1882, Baldock, Hertfordshire. *d:* 30.3.1948, Camberley, Surrey. Lower order batsman. *Sch* Repton. *Teams* Army (1920–21); Services (1920–21).
Career batting
5–8–3–91–38*–18.20–0–*ct* 5
Bowling 447–19–23.52–0–0–4/102

Archdale, J.
Amateur. Tail end batsman. *Team* MCC (1876).
Career batting
1–2–0–7–7–3.50–0–*ct* 0

Archer, Alfred German
Amateur. *b:* 6.12.1871, Richmond, Surrey. *d:* 15.7.1935, Seaford, Sussex. Lower order right-hand batsman, good wicket-keeper. *Sch* Haileybury. *Team* Worcestershire (1900–01, 4 matches). *Tour* Hawke to South Africa 1898/9. *Test* England (1898/9, 1 match).
Career batting
12–24–3–231–43–11.00–0–*ct* 10–*st* 2
Test batting
1–2–1–31–24*–31.00–0–*ct* 0
The unusual aspect of Archer's career was that not only did he appear in a Test for England before playing in first-class County cricket, but he was not even in the XI at Haileybury. He did not keep wicket in his only Test, but played in emergency, owing to the absence through injury of Bromley-Davenport. He also played for Shropshire (1904) and his final first-class match was for MCC in 1903.

Archer, Graeme Francis
Cricketer. *b:* 26.9.1970, Carlisle, Cumberland. Middle order right-hand batsman, right-arm medium pace bowler. *Team* Nottinghamshire (1992, 7 matches).
Career batting
7–13–3–475–117–47.50–1–*ct* 6
He also played for Staffordshire (1990–91).

Archer, Kenneth Alan
Amateur. *b:* 17.1.1928, Yeerongpilly, Queensland, Australia. Brother of R. G. (Australia). Middle order right-hand batsman, off break bowler. *Team* Queensland (1946/7 to 1956/7, 58 matches). *Tour* Australia to South Africa 1949/50. *Tests* Australia (1950/1 to 1951/2, 5 matches).
Career batting
82–139–13–3774–134–29.95–3–*ct* 56–*st* 1
Bowling 698–13–53.69–0–0–2/16
Test batting
5–9–0–234–48–26.00–0–*ct* 0
His one appearance in England for Commonwealth XI at Hastings was made when he was professional for Accrington in the Lancashire League in 1954, when he hit a record 1,116 runs, av 93.00, for the club.

Archer, Ronald Graham
Amateur. *b:* 25.10.1933, Highgate Hill, Brisbane, Queensland, Australia. Brother of K. A. (Australia). Hard-hitting middle order right-hand batsman, excellent right-arm fast bowler. *Team* Queensland (1951/2 to 1958/9, 35 matches). *Tours* Australia to England 1953, 1956, to West Indies 1954/5, to Pakistan 1956/7. *Tests* Australia (1952/3 to 1956/7, 19 matches).
Career batting
98–137–19–3768–148–31.93–4–*ct* 106
Bowling 5958–255–23.36–9–1–7/56
Test batting
19–30–1–713–128–24.58–1–*ct* 20
Bowling 1318–48–27.45–1–0–5/53
The peak of his brief career was the 1956 Test series in England, when his bowling was most effective and he was hailed as Lindwall's successor. He was forced to retire at the age of 25 due to injury.

Ardagh, Osmond Charles
Amateur. *b:* 1.11.1900, Courts Hill, Haslemere, Surrey. *d:* 1.2.1954. He drowned in River Thames, near Wallingford, Berkshire. Useful middle order left-hand batsman. *Sch* Epsom. *Team* Oxford U (1922).
Career batting
1–1–0–2–2–2.00–0–*ct* 0

Arden-Davis, Rev Richard
Amateur. *b:* 31.1.1855, Malins Lee, Shropshire. *d:* 29.6.1917, Branksome Park, Dorset. Middle order batsman. *Team* Middlesex (1881, 1 match).
Career batting
1–2–0–14–14–7.00–0–*ct* 1
He also played for Suffolk (1877–82).

Ardington, Anthony John
Cricketer. *b:* 26.3.1940, Howick, Natal, South Africa. Middle order right-hand batsman. *Team* Oxford U (1965).
Career batting
3–5–0–29–11–5.80–0–*ct* 1.

Arenhold, John Adolf
Amateur. *b:* 9.5.1931, Plumstead, Cape Town, South Africa. Forcing right-hand batsman, right-arm fast medium bowler, slip-field. *Sch* Diocesan College, South Africa. *Teams* Oxford U (1953–55, blue 1954); Ceylon (1956/7); Orange Free State (1959/60).
Career batting
33–47–7–403–45–10.07–0–*ct* 14
Bowling 2226–82–27.14–4–1–7/97
He also represented Ceylon at rugby.

Argent, E.
Professional. *b:* 6.2.1902. Lower order right-hand batsman, off break bowler. *Team* Worcestershire (1928, 2 matches).
Career batting
2–4–1–22–19–7.33–0–*ct* 0
Bowling 63–0

Arif Butt
Cricketer. *b:* 17.5.1944, Lahore, India. Brother of Saeed Butt (Railways). Opening or middle order right-hand batsman, right-arm fast medium bowler. *Teams* Lahore (1960/1 to 1961/2); Railways (1962/3 to 1977/8). *Tours* Pakistan to Australia and New Zealand 1964/5, to England 1967. *Tests* Pakistan (1964/5, 3 matches).
Career batting
97–154–16–4017–180–29.10–4–*ct* 44
Bowling 5386–201–26.79–10–2–8/45
Test batting
3–5–0–59–20–11.80–0–*ct* 0
Bowling 288–14–20.57–1–0–6/89

Arkell, Henry John Denham
Amateur. *b:* 26.6.1898, Edmonton, Middlesex. *d:* 12.3.1982, Oxford. Father of R. H. M. (Cambridge U). Middle order right-hand batsman. *Team* Northamptonshire (1921, 2 matches).
Career batting
2–2–0–11–6–5.50–0–*ct* 0

Arkell, Richard Henry Myles
Amateur. *b:* 16.6.1932, Abington, Northampton. Son of H. J. D. (Northamptonshire). Lower order right-hand batsman, slow left-arm bowler. *Sch* Aldenham. *Team* Cambridge U (1953–55).
Career batting
3–5–1–18–10–4.50–0–*ct* 1
Bowling 125–6–20.83–0–0–3/39
He played hockey for Northamptonshire.

Arkwright, Francis Godfrey Bertram
Amateur. *b:* 30.1.1905, Bromley, Kent. *d:* 1.7.1942, Knightsbridge, near Acroma, Libya. Nephew of H. F. (New Zealand Minor Associations). Hard hitting lower order right-hand batsman, rather weak in defence. *Sch* Eton. *Team* Hampshire (1923, 3 matches).
Career batting
4–7–0–67–23–9.57–0–*ct* 2
His best innings was 175 for Eton v Winchester in 1923, on the strength of which he appeared later in the year for Hampshire. He also represented the Army, for whom he played his last first-class match in 1925.

Arkwright, Harold Arthur
Amateur. *b:* 10.11.1872, Oswestry, Shropshire. *d:* 10.12.1942, Virginia Water, Surrey. Nephew of Henry (Cambridge U). Lower order right-hand batsman, useful right-arm medium pace bowler. *Sch* Eton. *Teams* Oxford U (1893–95, blue 1895); Essex (1894–95, 3 matches). *Tour* Mitchell to North America 1895.
Career batting
24–42–4–453–38–11.92–0–*ct* 16
Bowling 1696–72–23.55–5–1–8/40
His final first-class match was for MCC in 1903. He also played for Cambridgeshire (1898). He first played for Essex (pre first-class) in 1893.

Arkwright, Henry
Amateur. *b:* 16.12.1837, Hampton Court, Leominster, Herefordshire. *d:* 13.10.1866. He was killed by avalanche whilst ascending Mont Blanc, France. Uncle of H. A. (Essex). Free hitting lower order right-hand batsman, fast underhand bowler, but changed to slow round-arm in 1853. *Sch* Harrow. *Team* Cambridge U (1858, blue).
Career batting
17–32–3–144–26–4.96–0–*ct* 16
Bowling 976–86 + 11–11.34–10–2–9/43
For Gentlemen of MCC v Gentlemen of Kent at Canterbury in 1861 he took 18 of the 22 wickets to fall (12-a-side match), including 9/43, being his best innings bowling analysis. He was Aide-de-camp to Lord Lieutenant of Ireland at his death. He also played for Herefordshire (1855–61) and his final first-class match was for Gentlemen of MCC in 1866. His body was recovered perfectly preserved 30 years after his death.

Arlington, George Harewood Ashley
Amateur. *b:* 28.5.1871, Dover, Kent. *d:* *circa* 1940, Queensland, Australia. Free hard-hitting middle order

right-hand batsman, good wicket-keeper. *Sch* Brighton GS. *Team* Sussex (1894–98, 29 matches).
Career batting
29–50–0–614–73–12.28–0–*ct* 27–*st* 3
Bowling 36–1–36.00–0–0–1/13

In club cricket in Sussex it is believed that he scored over 100 centuries, his highest being 309 for Sheffield Park v Nutley in 1897.

Armitage, Alan Kenneth
Amateur. *b:* 25.1.1930, Nottingham. Middle order right-hand batsman, wicket-keeper. *Sch* Nottingham HS. *Teams* Nottinghamshire (1950–51, 5 matches); Oxford U (1951).
Career batting
7–12–2–348–115–34.80–1–*ct* 3

Armitage, Charles Ingram
Amateur. *b:* 28.4.1849, Birkby Grange, Huddersfield, Yorkshire. *d:* 24.4.1917, High Royd House, Honley, Yorkshire. Middle order right-hand batsman, good left-arm fast bowler. *Team* Yorkshire (1873–78, 3 matches).
Career batting
3–5–0–26–12–5.20–0–*ct* 0
Bowling 29–0

Armitage, Edward Leathley
Amateur. *b:* 26.4.1891, Omagh, Co Tyrone, Ireland. *d:* 24.11.1957, St Leonards, Sussex. Middle order right-hand batsman. *Sch* Cheltenham. *Teams* Hampshire (1919–25, 8 matches); Europeans (1929/30). *Tour* Martineau to Egypt 1935 (not first-class).
Career batting
20–35–2–576–105–17.45–1–*ct* 11
Bowling 476–26–18.30–1–0–5/67

His final first-class match was in India for Viceroy's XI in 1932/3.

Armitage, Thomas
Professional. *b:* 25.4.1848, Walkley, Sheffield, Yorkshire. *d:* 21.9.1922, Pullman, Chicago, USA. Excellent opening or middle order right-hand batsman, both in attack and defence, right-arm medium pace bowler or underhand lobs, all-round fieldsman. *Team* Yorkshire (1872–79, 51 matches). *Tour* Lillywhite to Australia 1876/7. *Tests* England (1876/7, 2 matches).
Career batting
56–92–8–1122–95–13.35–0–*ct* 23
Bowling 1699–119–14.27–12–3–7/26
Test batting
2–3–0–33–21–11.00–0–*ct* 0
Bowling 15–0

Although principally a batsman, Armitage had some startling successes as a lob bowler and in 1876 returned figures of 13 for 46 for Yorkshire v Surrey at Bramall Lane.

Armitage, Vernon Kirk
Amateur. *b:* 20.10.1842, Hope Hall, Eccles, Lancashire. *d:* 8.5.1911, Birkdale, Lancashire. Lower order right-hand batsman, good cover point. *Sch* Harrow. *Teams* Cambridge U (1864).
Career batting
1–1–0–6–6–6.00–0–*ct* 0

Armitstead, Rev Sydney Henry
Amateur. *b:* 13.6.1837, Holmes Chapel, Cheshire. *d:* 29.1.1912, Glyn Garth, Llandegean, Anglesey. Brother of W. G. (Oxford U). Useful middle order batsman, medium pace round-arm bowler, wicket-keeper. *Sch* Charterhouse. *Teams* Gentlemen of North (1862); MCC (1864).
Career batting
2–2–0–0–0–0.00–0–*ct* 1

He was one of the founder-members of the Free Foresters. He also played for Cheshire (1855–63), Herefordshire (1861) and Shropshire (1863).

Armitstead, Rev William George
Amateur. *b:* 22.3.1833, Holmes Chapel, Cheshire. *d:* 12.3.1907, Goostrey, Cheshire. Brother of S. H. (MCC). Hard hitting opening right-hand batsman, excellent long-stop. *Sch* Westminster. *Team* Oxford U (1853–57, blue 1853, 1854, 1856 and 1857).
Career batting
14–25–1–293–38–12.20–0–*ct* 6
Bowling 2 wickets (no analyses)–0–0–2/?

His first-class debut was for Manchester in 1852 and his last match for MCC in 1864. He also played for Oxfordshire (1853), Cheshire (1855–78) and Shropshire (1863).

Armstrong, Gregory de Lisle
Cricketer. *b:* 11.5.1950, Bank Hall, St Michael, Barbados. Tail end right-hand batsman, right-arm fast bowler. *Teams* Barbados (1973/4 to 1977/8); Glamorgan (1974–76, 30 matches).
Career batting
40–54–12–642–93–15.28–0–*ct* 13
Bowling 3199–91–35.15–2–0–6/91

He signed on a three-year contract after glowing reports on his prospects, but never realised his promise in County cricket.

Armstrong, H. H.
Amateur. Tail end right-hand batsman, useful right-arm medium pace bowler. *Team* Hampshire (1882–85, 23 matches).
Career batting
23–42–7–502–68–14.34–0–*ct* 10
Bowling 1376–68–20.23–2–0–7/33

His last match for Hampshire (not first-class) was in 1888.

Armstrong, Norman Foster
Amateur, but turned professional in 1926. *b:* 22.12.1892, Loughborough, Leicestershire. *d:*

Armstrong, Philip Alexander Nikolas

19.1.1990, Bournemouth, Hampshire. Sound defensive middle order right-hand batsman, right-arm medium pace change bowler. *Team* Leicestershire (1919–39, 386 matches).
Career batting
386–637–61–19002–186–32.98–36–*ct* 223
Bowling 4459–110–40.53–0–0–4/21

Though he did not take up regular County cricket until well into his thirties, Armstrong developed into the mainstay of the batting – so often did he rescue the side from collapse that he was known as the 'Valiant Armstrong'. In 1933 he became the first man to hit 2,000 runs in a season for the County, totalling 2,113, av 43.12, for the summer. He reached 1,000 runs in a season 13 times: every season between 1927 and 1939.

Armstrong, Philip Alexander Nikolas
Cricketer. *b:* 23.1.1962, Lambeth, London. Middle order right-hand batsman, right-arm medium pace bowler. *Sch* Eastbourne. *Team* Oxford U (1982).
Career batting
1–2–0–34–34–17.00–0–*ct* 0

Armstrong, Robert Lloyd George
Amateur. *b:* 22.5.1914, Donaghcloney, Co Armagh, Ireland. *d:* 9.4.1959, Downpatrick, Co Down, Ireland. Opening right-hand batsman, right-arm medium pace bowler. *Team* Ireland (1948–53).
Career batting
5–10–1–121–29*–13.44–0–*ct* 1
Bowling 129–6–21.50–0–0–4/16

Armstrong, Thomas
Professional. *b:* 16.3.1872, Keyworth, Nottinghamshire. *d:* 5.7.1938, Keyworth, Nottinghamshire. Lower order right-hand middle order batsman, right-arm medium pace bowler, useful outfield. *Teams* Nottinghamshire (1892–96, 6 matches).
Career batting
6–11–2–67–20*–7.44–0–*ct* 1

Armstrong, Thomas Hugh
Amateur. *b:* 21.4.1849, Wingate Grange, Co Durham. *d:* 27.1.1929, Leigh House, East Grinstead, Sussex. Lower order batsman. *Sch* Rossall. *Team* Oxford U (1869).
Career batting
1–2–0–6–6–3.00–0–*ct* 0
Bowling 43–1–43.00–0–0–1/43

His County cricket was for Shropshire (1868).

Armstrong, Thomas Riley
Professional. *b:* 13.10.1909, Clay Cross, Derbyshire. Tail end left-hand batsman, useful slow left-arm bowler. *Team* Derbyshire (1929–50, 58 matches).
Career batting
58–83–33–314–28*–6.28–0–*ct* 18
Bowling 3239–133–24.35–7–0–7/36

His career was, for a professional, most unusual, spanning 22 years, but he never commanded a regular place in the County side. He played for the most part in place of regular bowlers, injured or otherwise absent.

Armstrong, Warwick Windridge
Amateur. *b:* 22.5.1879, Kyneton, Victoria, Australia. *d:* 13.7.1947, Darling Point, Sydney, New South Wales, Australia. Brother of T. G. (Victoria). Excellent middle order right-hand batsman, originally fast medium right-arm, but by 1905 leg-break, bowler. *Team* Victoria (1898/9 to 1921/2, 83 matches). *Tours* Australians to England 1902, 1905, 1909, 1921, to South Africa 1902/3, 1914/15 (tour cancelled), to New Zealand 1904/5, 1909/10, 1913/14. *Tests* Australia (1901/2 to 1921, 50 matches).
Career batting
269–406–61–16158–303*–46.83–45–*ct* 273
Bowling 16405–832–19.71–50–5–8/47
Test batting
50–84–10–2863–159*–38.68–6–*ct* 44
Bowling 2923–87–33.59–3–0–6/35

Of all the cricketers to visit England, Armstrong has the most remarkable all-round record – on three of his four tours, 1905, 1909 and 1921 he achieved the 'double', and indeed in 1905 narrowly missed 2,000 runs. His best season in England was 1905 with 1,902 runs, av 50.05, and 122 wickets, av 18.20.

Considering also that he captained Australia to eight successive Test victories over England, the stature of Armstrong is apparent – his physical stature in fact matched his performances, for he was over 1.83m (6 feet) in height and on his last tour to England weighed over 127kg (20 stone). He was known as 'The Big Ship'. In all he captained Australia in 10 Tests.

In his later career, he was accused, as many successful men have been, of arrogance, and no-one can deny that he was a man who liked his own way, but he had certainly earned that right! It was however, unfortunate that in his retirement he should put his name to press articles which were almost designed to cause bitterness and ill-feeling.

Armstrong was a splendid stroke-player, but his real worth was to be found on difficult wickets. He survived long after his so-called equals were back in the pavilion. As a bowler he used accuracy of length and variation of flight rather than an ability to turn the ball, and he could bottle up one end with no difficulty. His highest score was 303* v Somerset at Bath on the 1905 tour, but a better innings was his 248* against the Gentlemen at Lord's on the same visit.

Arnall, Harry Thompson
(he assumed the name of Arnall-Thompson in 1885)
Amateur. *b:* 7.4.1864, Belgrave, Leicestershire. *d:* 28.12.1916, Anstey Frith, Leicester. Brother of W. E. (Leicestershire, pre first-class). Lower order right-

hand batsman, capital slow left-arm bowler (fast until 1878), slip field. *Sch* Rugby. *Team* Oxford U (1886, blue).
Career batting
6–9–3–56–25–9.33–0–*ct* 5
Bowling 352–16–22.00–1–0–7/82

His County cricket was for Leicestershire (pre first-class) 1882–90, being captain 1886–89. Batting for Leicestershire v MCC in 1889, the ball flew off his bat on to his eyebrow from whence it rebounded to the bowler. After being stunned and stemming the flow of blood Arnall-Thompson prepared to continue batting only to be informed he was out 'caught'.

His first-class debut was for Gentlemen of England in 1885 and his final match for MCC in 1887.

Arnold, Alban Charles Phidias
Amateur. *b:* 19.11.1892, Tattenhall, Chester, Cheshire. *d:* 7.7.1916. He was killed in action at Ovilliers La Boiselle, France. Good middle order right-hand batsman, wicket-keeper. *Sch* Malvern. *Teams* Cambridge U (1912–14, blue 1914); Hampshire (1912–14, 16 matches).
Career batting
22–35–2–836–89–25.33–0–*ct* 13–*st* 2
Bowling 0–0

Arnold, Arnold Peter
Professional. *b:* 16.10.1926, Wellington, New Zealand. Attacking right-hand opening batsman, occasional right-arm medium pace bowler. *Teams* Northamptonshire (1951–60, 167 matches); Canterbury (1953/4).
Career batting
174–306–15–8013–122–27.53–7–*ct* 79
Bowling 85–3–28.33–0–0–1/5

He played as a middle order batsman for the first three years with Northamptonshire, but had only limited success. Being promoted to open in 1954 made all the difference. Hit 1,000 runs in a season three times (best 1,699, av 30.89, in 1955). In 1992 he was Chairman of the Cricket Committee of Northamptonshire.

Arnold, Charles
Professional. *b:* 10.2.1822, Cambridge. *d:* 1.2.1873, Cambridge. Brother of Mark (Cambridge Town Club). Lower order batsman, a 'tremendous-paced round-armed bowler delivering many shooting balls, which have proved very fatal and destructive' (Scores and Biographies, vol IV p514). *Teams* Cambridge Town Club (1843–56); Cambridgeshire (1857, 1 match).
Career batting
22–35–5–203–29–6.76–0–*ct* 23
Bowling 258–27 + 106–9.55–13–5–8/?

For a few years about 1850, Arnold was one of the most notable bowlers in England, and in 1853 was engaged by the All England Eleven. He also played for Suffolk (1847), Herefordshire, Essex (pre first-class), Warwickshire (pre first-class, 1863), Huntingdonshire and Worcestershire (pre first-class, 1851).

Arnold, Edward George
Professional. *b:* 7.11.1876, Exmouth, Devon. *d:* 25.10.1942, Worcester. Uncle of John Price (Worcestershire) and W. H. Price (Worcestershire). Middle order right-hand batsman, medium to fast medium right-arm bowler, safe close field. *Teams* Worcestershire (1899–1913, 301 matches); London County (1900). *Tour* MCC to Australia 1903/4. *Tests* England (1903/4 to 1907, 10 matches).
Career batting
343–592–62–15853–215–29.91–24–*ct* 187
Bowling 24763–1069–23.16–63–13–9/64
Test batting
10–15–3–160–40–13.33–0–*ct* 8
Bowling 788–31–25.41–1–0–5/37

Arnold was the best all-round cricketer in the Worcestershire side of 1897, but ill-health more or less stopped his cricket in 1898. When Worcestershire were promoted to the Championship in 1899, he did nothing spectacular, but in 1902 he achieved the 'double' for the first of four times. The following year he won a place in the MCC team to Australia and performed well in both Tests and other matches. He had the knack of making the ball lift off a good length, even on docile wickets, and bowled with a beautiful action. Ill-health (he was never very strong physically) brought his career to a close in 1913. He hit 1,000 runs in a season ten times (best 1,767, av 50.48, in 1906) and took 100 wickets four times (best 143, av 17.44, in 1903). His highest score was 215 for Worcestershire v Oxford U at Oxford in 1910, and his best bowling 9/64 v Oxford U at Oxford in 1905. He also played for Devon (1893). He first appeared for Worcestershire (pre first-class) in 1895.

Arnold, Frederick George
Amateur. *b:* 18.11.1899, Dover, Kent. *d:* 16.12.1980, Broughton, Hampshire. Tail end right-hand batsman, right-arm fast medium bowler. *Teams* Army (1926–30); Europeans (1935/6).
Career batting
6–6–4–33–15–16.50–0–*ct* 2
Bowling 493–18–27.38–1–0–6/41

Arnold, Geoffrey Graham
Cricketer. *b:* 3.9.1944, Earlsfield, Surrey. Lower order right-hand batsman, right-arm fast medium bowler. *Teams* Surrey (1963–77, 218 matches); Sussex (1978–82, 77 matches); Orange Free State (1976/7). *Tours* MCC Under 25 to Pakistan 1966/7; MCC to Ceylon 1969/70, to India, Pakistan and Sri Lanka 1972/3, to West Indies 1973/4, to Australia and New Zealand 1974/5; International XI to India and Pakistan 1967/8. *Tests* England (1967–75, 34 matches).

Arnold, James Frederick

Career batting
365–379–90–3952–73–13.67–0–*ct* 122
Bowling 24761–1130–21.91–46–3–8/41
Test batting
34–46–11–421–59–12.02–0–*ct* 9
Bowling 3254–115–28.29–6–0–6/45

He took 109 wickets, av 18.22, in 1967. About 1970 he was one of the most effective bowlers in England and his Test place would have been more secure if he had been as deadly overseas as he was on damp English wickets. He also suffered more than his fair share of injuries. He appeared in one Sunday League game for Surrey in emergency in 1989, having been Surrey coach since 1984.

Arnold, James Frederick
Amateur. *b:* 2.3.1869, Withington, Manchester, Lancashire. *d:* 26.3.1944, Worthing, Sussex. Good middle order right-hand batsman. *Team* Lancashire (1896, 3 matches).
Career batting
3–5–0–94–37–18.80–0–*ct* 2

Arnold, John
Professional. *b:* 30.11.1907, Cowley, Oxford. *d:* 4.4.1984, Southampton, Hampshire. Attractive opening right-hand batsman, particularly effective against spin bowling, right-arm slow bowler, excellent deep field with strong throw. *Team* Hampshire (1929–50, 396 matches). *Test* England (1931, 1 match).
Career batting
402–710–45–21831–227–32.82–37–*ct* 184
Bowling 1182–17–69.52–0–0–3/34
Test batting
1–2–0–34–34–17.00–0–*ct* 0

He scored 1,000 runs in season 14 times (best 2,261, av 48.10, in 1934); his highest score being 227 for Hampshire v Glamorgan at Cardiff in 1932. He also played for Oxfordshire (1923). He became a first-class umpire (1961–72). He played soccer as outside left for Southampton and Fulham and played for England v Scotland 1932–33.

Arnold, Keith Andrew
Cricketer. *b:* 27.5.1960, Solihull, Warwickshire. Lower order left-hand batsman, right-arm fast medium bowler. *Team* Minor Counties (1985–90).
Career batting
2 matches, did not bat–*ct* 3
Bowling 221–6–36.83–1–0–5/57

His county cricket was for Oxfordshire (1980–92).

Arnott, Kevin John
Cricketer. *b:* 8.3.1961, Salisbury, Rhodesia. Opening right-hand batsman. *Team* Zimbabwe (1979/80 to 1991/2). *Tours* Zimbabwe to England 1990, to India (World Cup) 1987/8, to Australia and New Zealand (World Cup) 1991/2.
Career batting
22–40–5–973–121–27.80–1–*ct* 13

Arnott, Trevor
Amateur. *b:* 16.2.1902, Radyr, Glamorgan. *d:* 2.2.1975, Wilton, Ross-on-Wye, Herefordshire. Hard-hitting middle order right-hand batsman, right-arm fast medium pace swing bowler. *Sch* Wycliffe and Monmouth. *Teams* Glamorgan (1921–30, 188 matches); Wales (1924–30). *Tours* MCC to West Indies 1934/5; Tennyson to Jamaica 1927/8; Cahn to South America 1929/30.
Career batting
216–370–30–5791–153–17.03–3–*ct* 104
Bowling 13511–408–33.11–10–0–7/40

He captained Glamorgan in 1928 and also played for Monmouthshire (1931–34). His final first-class match was MCC in 1931.

Arrowsmith, Robert
Cricketer. *b:* 21.5.1952, Denton, Lancashire. Lower order right-hand batsman, slow left-arm bowler. *Team* Lancashire (1976–79, 43 matches).
Career batting
43–40–12–286–39–10.21–0–*ct* 13
Bowling 2796–99–28.24–4–0–6/29

He also played for Northumberland (1983–85).

Arscott, Jonathan Paul
Cricketer. *b:* 4.7.1970, Tooting, London. Middle order right-hand batsman, right-arm medium pace bowler, wicket-keeper. *Sch* Tonbridge. *Team* Cambridge U (1990–92, blue 1991–92).
Career batting
21–30–5–573–79–22.92–0–*ct* 18–*st* 8
Bowling 252–7–36.00–0–0–1/17

Arshad Pervez
Cricketer. *b:* 1.10.1953, Sargodha, Pakistan. Opening right-hand batsman, right-arm medium pace bowler. *Teams* Sargodha (1969/70 to 1991/2); Lahore (1971/2); Universities (1972/3 to 1974/5); Punjab University (1973/4); Servis Industries (1975/6); Habib Bank (1975/6 to 1991/2), Punjab (1976/7). *Tour* Pakistan to England 1978.
Career batting
242–408–41–14776–251*–40.26–39–*ct* 206
Bowling 754–22–34.27–0–0–3/37

He played in only three first-class matches on the 1978 tour. He hit four double hundreds, the highest being 251* for Habib Bank v Karachi Whites at Karachi in 1976/7. He has appeared for Pakistan in one-day internationals. He has scored 1,000 runs in a season in Pakistan 5 times (best 1,364, av 85.25, in 1977/8).

Arthurton, Keith Lloyd Thomas
Cricketer. *b:* 21.2.1965, Charlestown, Nevis. Middle order left-hand bastman, slow left-arm bowler, brilliant field. *Team* Leeward Islands (1985/6 to 1991/2). *Tours* West Indies to England 1988, to Australia 1988/9, 1991/2, to Sharjah (not first-class) 1988/9, 1989/90, 1991/2, to India 1989/90 (not first-class), to

Pakistan 1991/2 (not first-class), to Australia and New Zealand (World Cup) 1991/2. *Tests* West Indies (1988 to 1991/2, 6 matches).
Career batting
53–88–13–3235–154–43.13–9–*ct* 29
Bowling 379–13–29.15–0–0–3/14
Test batting
6–10–2–186–59–23.25–0–*ct* 2
Bowling 46–0
He was included on the 1988 tour to England as a promising youngster and played in one Test.

Asgarali, Nyron Sultan
Amateur. *b:* 28.12.1920, St James, near Port of Spain, Trinidad. Father of Gregory (Trinidad). Opening right-hand batsman, right-arm medium pace bowler. *Team* Trinidad (1940/1 to 1961/2). *Tour* West Indies to England 1957. *Tests* West Indies (1957, 2 matches).
Career batting
50–89–5–2761–141*–32.86–7–*ct* 29
Bowling 966–23–42.00–0–0–4/72
Test batting
2–4–0–62–29–15.50–0–*ct* 0
His first first-class match in England was for Commonwealth XI in 1956. He hit 1,011 runs, av 29.73, in 1957.

Ash, David Leslie
Cricketer. *b:* 18.2.1944, Bingley, Yorkshire. Lower order right-hand batsman, slow left-arm bowler. *Team* Yorkshire (1965, 3 matches).
Career batting
3–3–0–22–12–7.33–0–*ct* 0
Bowling 22–0
He also played for Cumberland (1968–84).

Ash, Edward Philip
Amateur. *b:* 25.12.1842, Brisley, Norfolk. *d:* 25.5.1909, Petersfield, Hampshire. Middle order right-hand batsman. *Sch* Rugby. *Team* Cambridge U (1865, blue).
Career batting
5–10–0–126–47–12.60–0–*ct* 3
His County cricket was for Warwickshire (pre first-class, 1864), Norfolk (1865–77), hitting 130 for that County v I Zingari in 1866, Suffolk (1866–67) and Hertfordshire (1870–76).

Ashby, David Alexander
Professional. *b:* 11.6.1852, Beddington, Surrey. *d:* 2.6.1934, Christchurch, New Zealand. Lower order right-hand batsman, right-arm medium to fast bowler. *Teams* Surrey (1874, 1 match); Canterbury (1875/6 to 1889/90).
Career batting
17–31–4–468–59–17.33–0–*ct* 12
Bowling 586–53–11.05–4–1–6/27
His first-class debut was for Surrey Club in 1873.

Ashby, William
Professional. *b:* 12.1.1786, Linton, Maidstone, Kent. *d:* 10.4.1847, London. Tail end batsman, excellent slow round-arm bowler. *Teams* Kent (1815–29); Sussex (1823); Hampshire (1825–26); Surrey (1830).
Career batting
45–78–24–242–18–4.48–0–*ct* 26
Bowling 164 wickets (no analyses)–8–1–8/?
After John Willes he was, perhaps, the first bowler of note to bowl 'round-arm'. His first first-class match was for England in 1808.

Ashcroft, Dr Edward Maynard
Amateur. *b:* 27.9.1875, Chorlton, Manchester, Lancashire. *d:* 26.2.1955, Upton-by-Chester, Cheshire. Free scoring middle order right-hand batsman, occasional off break bowler. *Sch* Owens College. *Team* Derbyshire (1897–1906, 100 matches).
Career batting
101–170–13–4581–162–29.17–8–*ct* 33
Bowling 1186–24–49.41–1–0–5/18
He was joint captain of Derbyshire 1904–05. He also played for Herefordshire (1893).

Ashdown, William Henry
Professional. *b:* 27.12.1898, Bromley, Kent. *d:* 15.9.1979, Rugby, Warwickshire. Opening right-hand batsman, noted for the square drive and cut, right-arm medium fast bowler, good field. *Team* Kent (1920–37, 482 matches).
Career batting
487–812–77–22589–332–30.73–39–*ct* 400–*st* 1
Bowling 19551–602–32.47–13–0–6/23
Ashdown actually made his first-class debut aged 15 for G. J. V. Weigall's Team v Oxford in 1914 and his final first-class match was for M. Leyland's XI at Harrogate in 1947. Thus he is the only cricketer to appear in first-class matches in England both before the First World War and after the Second.
He is among the very few batsmen to hit two triple centuries in County cricket: 332 v Essex at Brentwood in 1934 and 305* v Derbyshire at Dover in 1935. He reached 1,000 runs in a season 11 times, his best being 2,247 (av 43.21) in 1928. He was a first-class umpire (1948–50), standing in 4 Test matches (1949–50). He was Leicestershire coach 1951–61 and scorer 1966–69.

Ashenden, Martin
Professional. *b:* 4.8.1937, Bexhill-on-Sea, Sussex. Lower order right-hand batsman, right-arm fast medium bowler. *Teams* Northamptonshire (1959–61, 19 matches); Gloucestershire (1962–65, 15 matches).
Career batting
34–41–12–70–15–2.41–0–*ct* 9
Bowling 2095–64–32.73–0–0–4/50
He created a sensation by taking all 10 wickets (for 15) for Bedfordshire v Shropshire in 1958 and then signed as a professional first for Northamptonshire

and later Gloucestershire, but he never gained a regular place in first-class cricket. He also played for Bedfordshire (1957–58, 1966).

Asher, Sir Augustus Gordon Grant
(also known as Grant-Asher)
Amateur. *b:* 18.12.1861, Poona, Maharashtra, India. *d:* 15.7.1930, Kingussie, Inverness, Scotland. Middle order right-hand batsman, right-arm fast-medium bowler, good deep field. *Sch* Loretto. *Team* Oxford U (1883–84, blue 1883).
Career batting
10–17–0–346–182–20.35–1–*ct* 2
Bowling 88–3–29.33–0–0–3/62

He was a noted rugby footballer, playing at half-back against Cambridge University in 1881 and the next three years. He also represented Scotland seven times. He won a third blue for athletics, being the Oxford champion long-jumper and later champion pole-vaulter for Scotland.

Ashley, Derek John
Cricketer. *b:* 22.1.1956, Whitchurch, Shropshire. Lower order right-hand batsman, wicket-keeper. *Team* Minor Counties (1986).
Career batting
1–2–0–4–4–2.00–0–*ct* 0–*st* 1

His county cricket was for Shropshire (1981–90).

Ashley, Richard
Amateur. *b:* 27.10.1902, Axbridge, Somerset. *d:* 7.8.1974, Selsey, Sussex. Lower order right-hand batsman, good opening bowler. *Teams* Somerset (1932, 2 matches); Mysore (1937/8); Europeans (1939/40).
Career batting
4–6–0–61–17–10.16–0–*ct* 1
Bowling 180–8–22.50–0–0–3/26

Ashman, John Robert
Professional. *b:* 20.5.1926, Rotherham, Yorkshire. Tail end left-hand batsman, useful slow left-arm bowler. *Teams* Yorkshire (1951, 1 match); Worcestershire (1953–54, 33 matches).
Career batting
34–41–15–149–24–5.73–0–*ct* 26
Bowling 2546–61–41.73–3–0–7/111

Ashman had an extended trial in the Worcestershire side of 1953 due to Jenkins' injury, but did not realise his promise.

Ashmore, William Scott
Professional. *b:* 29.10.1929, St John's Wood, London. Lower order left-hand batsman, useful left-arm medium fast bowler. *Team* Middlesex (1946–47, 2 matches).
Career batting
3–5–3–24–15*–12.00–0–*ct* 1
Bowling 129–3–43.00–0–0–2/37

Both his matches for Middlesex were against Cambridge U at Fenner's – in 1948 he made a single appearance for Combined Services.

Ashton, Claude Thesiger
Amateur. *b:* 19.2.1901, Calcutta, India. *d:* 31.10.1942, Caernarvon. He was killed on active service with the RAF. Brother of Gilbert (Worcestershire), Hubert (Essex) and Percy (Essex), nephew of A. M. Inglis (Kent) and J. F. Inglis (Kent), brother-in-law of G. E. B. Abell (Worcestershire). Attacking middle order right-hand batsman, right-arm medium pace bowler. *Sch* Winchester. *Teams* Cambridge U (1921–23, blue all three years); Essex (1921–38, 89 matches).
Career batting
127–204–15–4723–118–24.98–4–*ct* 113
Bowling 4299–139–30.92–5–1–7/51

An all-round sportsman, he played soccer for England and obtained his blue for soccer and hockey as well as cricket. Three of the brothers captained Cambridge at cricket in successive seasons, C. T. in 1923. Whilst flying his plane he collided with the plane of R. de W. K. Winlaw, both men being killed.

Ashton, Gilbert
Amateur. *b:* 27.9.1896, Bromley, Kent. *d:* 6.2.1981, Abberley, Worcestershire. Brother of C. T. (Essex), Hubert (Essex) and Percy (Essex), nephew of A. M. Inglis (Kent) and J. F. Inglis (Kent), brother-in-law of R. C. Huband (Cambridge U). Fine middle order right-hand batsman, excellent cover-point, occasional leg break bowler. *Sch* Winchester. *Teams* Cambridge U (1919–21, blue all three years); Worcestershire (1922–36, 27 matches).
Career batting
62–100–3–2329–125–24.01–2–*ct* 24
Bowling 521–14–37.21–0–0–3/49

He captained Cambridge U in 1921 and played in the match v Australians at Eastbourne that year. He lost a thumb in action in the First World War, but this did not seem to impede his cricket. The headmaster of a private school in Worcestershire after leaving University, his appearances for the County were confined to the school holidays. He also won a blue for soccer. He was President of Worcestershire 1967–69.

Ashton, Sir Hubert
Amateur. *b:* 13.2.1898, Calcutta, India. *d:* 17.6.1979, South Weald, Essex. Brother of C. T. (Essex); Gilbert (Worcestershire) and Percy (Essex), nephew of A. M. Inglis (Kent) and J. F. Inglis (Kent), brother-in-law of Rt. Hon. Hugh Gaitskell, leader of the Labour Party. Attractive and sound middle order right-hand batsman, fine outfield. *Sch* Winchester. *Teams* Cambridge U (1920–22, blue all three years); Essex (1921–39, 21 matches); Europeans (1926/7); Burma (1926/7).

Career batting
71–115–11–4025–236*–38.70–8–*ct* 72
Bowling 14–0

His highest score was 236* for Cambridge U v Free Foresters at Fenner's in 1920, but his most famous innings was 75 for an England XI v Australians at Eastbourne in 1921, when with G. A. Faulkner he added 154 runs for the 5th wicket, a partnership which enabled his side to defeat the tourists. He hit 1,000 runs in a season twice (best 1,294, av 39.21, in 1921). He captained Cambridge in 1922.

He played soccer for Clapton Orient and Bristol Rovers. He was MP for Chelmsford 1950–64 and President of MCC 1960. He was Essex Chairman 1946–51 and President 1949–70. He also won blues for soccer and hockey.

Ashton, Nicholas Charles Ellis
Amateur. *b:* 8.10.1904, Scaftworth, Nottinghamshire. *d:* 17.7.1986, Merrow, Surrey. Lower order right-hand batsman, wicket-keeper. *Sch* Repton. *Team* Oxford U (1924).
Career batting
1–1–0–0–0–0.00–0–*ct* 1–*st* 2

He won a blue for soccer.

Ashton, Percy
Amateur. *b:* 27.2.1895, Calcutta, India. *d:* 18.9.1934, Bigbury-on-Sea, Devon. Brother of C. T. (Essex), Gilbert (Worcestershire) and Hubert (Essex), nephew of A. M. Inglis (Kent) and J. F. Inglis (Kent). Lower order batsman, right-arm fast medium bowler. *Sch* Winchester. *Team* Essex (1924, 1 match).
Career batting
1–2–0–52–31–26.00–0–*ct* 0
Bowling 55–1–55.00–0–0–1/55

He also played for Cornwall. He lost an eye in the 1914–18 War.

Ashwell, Arthur Harry
Professional. *b:* 2.8.1908, Charing, Kent. *d:* 19.8.1985, Birkenhead, Cheshire. Lower order right-hand batsman, right-arm medium pace bowler. *Team* Kent (1933–34, 4 matches).
Career batting
4–5–2–42–21*–14.00–0–*ct* 1
Bowling 139–0

Ashwell, Arthur Thomas
Amateur. *b:* 8.2.1853, Nottingham. *d:* 30.9.1925, Canterbury, Kent. Brother of C. T. (Gentlemen of North). Middle order right-hand batsman. *Sch* Rugby. *Team* Nottinghamshire (1876, 2 matches).
Career batting
2–2–0–0–0–0.00–0–*ct* 0

He represented Notts County at the inaugural meeting of the Football League in 1888.

Ashwell, Charles Tebbutt
Amateur. *b:* 31.1.1851, Nottingham. *d:* 18.4.1928, The Park, Nottingham. Brother of A. T. (Nottinghamshire). Tail end batsman. *Team* Gentlemen of North (1870).
Career batting
1–2–1–21–19–21.00–0–*ct* 0

Ashwell, Thomas Geoffrey Lyon
Amateur. *b:* 18.7.1897, Nottingham. *d:* 21.12.1969, Chelsea, London. Lower order right-hand batsman, leg break bowler. *Sch* Rugby. *Team* Oxford U (1919).
Career batting
1–2–1–3–2–3.00–0–*ct* 2
Bowling 19–0

Ashworth, David Anthony
Cricketer. *b:* 18.7.1944, Rani, India. Middle order right-hand batsman, off break bowler. *Sch* Uppingham. *Team* Oxford U (1966–67).
Career batting
7–13–0–173–67–13.30–0–*ct* 3

Ashworth, John Thomas
Amateur. *b:* 27.2.1850, New Hall, Haslingden, Lancashire. *d:* 20.10.1901, Werneth, Oldham, Lancashire. Middle order batsman. *Team* Lancashire (1871–73, 2 matches).
Career batting
2–3–0–28–19–9.33–0–*ct* 0

Asif Ahmed
Cricketer. *b:* 1.4.1942, Karachi, India. Middle order right-hand batsman, wicket-keeper. *Teams* Oxford U (1963–64); Karachi University (1959/60 to 1960/1); Universities (1959/60); Karachi (1961/2 to 1970/1); PWD (1971/2). *Tour* Pakistan to England 1962.
Career batting
61–96–14–2186–148–26.65–4–*ct* 28
Bowling 97–0

He scored 148 for Universities v East Pakistan at Karachi in 1959/60 on his first-class debut.

Asif Din, Mohamed
Cricketer. *b:* 21.9.1960, Kampala, Uganda. Middle order right-hand batsman, leg break bowler. *Team* Warwickshire (1981–92, 199 matches). *Tour* Warwickshire to South Africa 1991/2.
Career batting
199–326–44–8423–158*–29.86–8–*ct* 108
Bowling 4256–73–58.30–1–0–5/100

He hit 1,000 runs in a season twice, best 1,425, av 38.41, in 1988.

Asif Iqbal Razvi
Professional. *b:* 6.6.1943, Hyderabad, India. Nephew of Ghulam Ahmed (India). Attacking middle order right-hand batsman, right-arm medium pace bowler, good cover field. *Teams* Hyderabad (1959/60 to 1960/1); Karachi (1961/2 to 1968/9); PIA (1964/5 to 1979/80); National Bank (1976/7); Kent (1968–82,

243 matches). *Tours* Pakistan to Australia and New Zealand 1964/5, 1972/3, 1978/9, to England 1967, 1971, 1974, 1975 (World Cup), 1979 (World Cup), to Australia and West Indies 1976/7, to India 1979/80, to Ceylon 1964/5, 1972/3; Pakistan Eaglets to England 1963; PIA to East Africa 1964/5. *Tests* Pakistan (1964/5 to 1979/80, 58 matches).
Career batting
440–701–75–23329–196–37.26–45–*ct* 303
Bowling 8776–291–30.15–5–0–6/45
Test batting
58–99–7–3575–175–38.85–11–*ct* 36
Bowling 1502–53–28.33–2–0–5/48

After playing in India, he emigrated to Pakistan in 1961. He appeared in all three Tests on the 1967 tour to England, his most successful match being the third Test when he hit 146. In 1971 he again appeared in all three Tests and hit a century in the first. On his final English tour in 1974, he made little impression in the Tests, though he played in all three. He was vice-captain on both the 1971 and 1974 tours and he led Pakistan in six Tests, all against India. He also captained Kent in 1977 and in 1981–82. He hit 1,000 runs in England seven times (best 1,379, av 39.40, in 1970).

Asif Masood
Cricketer. *b:* 23.1.1946, Lahore, India. Tail end right-hand batsman, right-arm fast medium bowler. *Teams* Lahore (1963/4 to 1968/9); Punjab U (1965/6 to 1968/9); PIA (1969/70 to 1976/7). *Tours* Pakistan to England 1971, 1974, 1975 (World Cup), to Sri Lanka, New Zealand and Australia 1972/3, to West Indies and Australia 1976/7, to Sri Lanka 1975/6; Rest of World to Australia 1971/2; PIA to Ireland (not first-class) 1969. *Tests* Pakistan (1968/9 to 1976/7, 16 matches).
Career batting
121–119–46–635–34–8.69–0–*ct* 38
Bowling 8854–305–29.02–9–0–8/97
Test batting
16–19–10–93–30*–10.33–0–*ct* 5
Bowling 1568–38–41.26–1–0–5/111

In 1971 on his first Test tour to England he took 13 wickets (av 26.46) in the three Tests, but in 1974 was not so successful. He also played for Northumberland (1975–76).

Asif Mujtaba
Cricketer. *b:* 4.11.1967, Karachi, Pakistan. Middle order left-hand batsman, slow left-arm bowler. *Teams* Karachi (1984/5 to 1991/2); PIA (1987/8 to 1991/2). *Tours* Pakistan to England 1987, 1992, to Australia 1986/7 (not first-class), to India 1986/7, to Sharjah (not first-class) 1986/7; Pakistan B to Zimbabwe 1986/7, 1990/1. *Tests* Pakistan (1987/8 to 1992, 8 matches).
Career batting
128–201–40–7765–193*–48.22–20–*ct* 114
Bowling 3960–178–22.24–10–2–6/19
Test batting
8–13–0–292–59–22.46–0–*ct* 7
Bowling 32–1–32.00–0–0–1/0

In 1987 he achieved little with the bat, but won great praise as a fielder. On the 1992 tour to England he hit 1,074 runs, av 56.52, and played in all five Tests. In Pakistan in 1989/90 he scored 1,587 runs (av 52.90).

Askew, John Garbutt
Amateur. *b:* 2.9.1908, Gateshead, Co Durham. *d:* 31.8.1942, North Shotton, Northumberland. Middle order right-hand batsman. *Sch* Durham. *Team* Cambridge U (1931).
Career batting
2–4–0–30–11–7.50–0–*ct* 1

His County cricket was for Durham (1928–31). A noted rugby footballer, he appeared both for Cambridge U and England.

Askham, Sydney Thomas
Amateur. *b:* 9.9.1896, Wellingborough, Northamptonshire. *d:* 21.8.1916. He was killed in action at Maillet Wood, Sheepal, France. Lower order right-hand batsman, right-arm fast medium bowler. *Sch* Wellingborough. *Team* Northamptonshire (1914, 5 matches).
Career batting
5–9–3–83–28*–13.83–0–*ct* 0
Bowling 86–2–43.00–0–0–2/68

He appeared for Northamptonshire with still a full year left at school and in 1915 was regarded as one of the best Public School players in England – it was tragic that he should die at the age of 19.

Aslett, Derek George
Cricketer. *b:* 12.2.1958, Dover, Kent. Middle order right-hand batsman, leg break bowler. *Team* Kent (1981–87, 119 matches).
Career batting
119–199–20–6128–221*–34.23–12–*ct* 82
Bowling 1253–17–73.70–0–0–4/119

He hit 1,000 runs in a season twice, best 1,491, av 35.50, in 1984. His only double century was 221* for Kent v Sri Lankans at Canterbury in 1984. On his first-class debut in 1981 he made 146* for Kent v Hampshire at Bournemouth.

Aspinall, Frederick
Amateur. *b:* 2.9.1859, West Kirby, Cheshire. Middle order batsman. *Team* Liverpool and District (1892).
Career batting
1–2–1–27–16–27.00–0–*ct* 0

His County cricket was for Cheshire (1881–92).

Aspinall, Ronald
Professional. *b:* 26.10.1918, Almondbury, Huddersfield, Yorkshire. Hard hitting right-hand batsman, right-arm fast medium bowler, good field. *Team*

Yorkshire (1946–50, 36 matches).
Career batting
36–48–8–763–75*–19.07–0–*ct* 18
Bowling 2670–131–20.38–8–2–8/47

His bowling in 1947 and 1948 was such that he was regarded as an England prospect, but a strained Achilles tendon ended his first-class career in 1950. He then played for Durham (pre first-class, 1951–57), and became a first-class umpire (1960–81).

Aspinall, Walter
Professional. *b:* 24.3.1858, Elland, Yorkshire. Moderate right-hand batsman, wicket-keeper, occasional fast bowler. *Team* Yorkshire (1880, 2 matches).
Career batting
3–4–0–19–14–4.75–0–*ct* 5

His final first-class match was for Under 30s in 1882.

Asquith, Frederick Thomas
Professional. *b:* 5.2.1870, Kirkstall, Leeds, Yorkshire. *d:* 11.1.1916, Hull, Yorkshire. Middle order batsman, wicket-keeper. *Team* Yorkshire (1903, 1 match).
Career batting
1–1–0–0–0–0.00–0–*ct* 2

Asquith, John Patrick Kenyon
Amateur. *b:* 1.2.1932, Carshalton, Surrey. Brother-in-law of D. R. W. Silk (Somerset). Lower order right-hand batsman, wicket-keeper. *Sch* Purley GS. *Team* Cambridge U (1953–54).
Career batting
5–8–1–46–12–6.57–0–*ct* 4–*st* 1

He won a rugby blue 1953–54.

Astill, William Ewart
Professional. *b:* 1.3.1888, Ratby, Leicestershire. *d:* 10.2.1948, Stoneygate, Leicester, after a long illness. Nephew of T. Jayes (Leicestershire). Originally a tail end right-hand batsman, he developed into a good middle order player, right-arm slow to medium bowler, turning the ball either way, excellent slip field. *Team* Leicestershire (1906–39, 628 matches). *Tours* MCC to West Indies 1925/6, 1929/30, to India and Ceylon 1926/7, to South Africa 1927/8; Cahn to Jamaica 1928/9; Joel to South Africa 1924/5; Tennyson to West Indies 1930/1. *Tests* England (1927/8 to 1929/30, 9 matches).
Career batting
733–1153–145–22731–164*–22.55–1.5–*ct* 464
Bowling 57783–2431–23.76–140–22–9/41
Test batting
9–15–0–190–40–12.66–0–*ct* 7
Bowling 856–25–34.24–0–0–4/58

After making his first-class debut with a single appearance for Leicestershire during 1906, Astill then appeared in every match for the County during the next four seasons. He headed the County's bowling averages in both 1907 and 1908 and an international career was confidently forecast for him. Curiously, however, he seemed to lose his bowling and by 1911 was dropped from the Leicestershire team for several matches.

He appeared to be re-born after demobilisation and in 1921 completed his first of nine 'doubles'. For year after year he was near the top of both Leicestershire's batting and bowling and in his 40th year – in 1927/28 – finally made his England debut. If he had represented a more fashionable County, no doubt his tally of 9 Tests would have been much higher. He captained Leicestershire in 1935.

His best season with the bat was 1925 with 1,601 runs (av 32.03), having 1,000 runs in a season 11 times, and with the ball, 1921 with 153 wickets (av 20.99), having 100 wickets in a season 9 times and the 'double' 9 times. His best bowling was 9/41 v Warwickshire at Birmingham in 1923. He was an accomplished billiards player, winning several titles, whilst he was also a noted vocalist, singing to his own piano accompaniment. In his final years he did much coaching, showing himself to be an expert in this field.

Aston, John Gordon
Amateur. *b:* 20.11.1882, Dublin, Ireland. *d:* 9.1.1951, Selly Oak, Birmingham. Middle order right-hand batsman, right-arm medium pace bowler. *Team* Ireland (1925). *Tour* Ireland to North America 1909.
Career batting
4–8–1–73–53*–10.42–0–*ct* 1
Bowling 101–9–11.22–1–0–5/58

Atapattu, Marvan Samson
Cricketer. *b:* 22.11.1972, Kalutara, Sri Lanka. Middle order right-hand batsman. *Team* Sinhalese SC (1990/1 to 1991/2). *Tours* Sri Lanka to England 1990, 1991, to India 1990/1, to Pakistan 1991/2. *Test* Sri Lanka (1990/1, 1 match).
Career batting
38–48–15–1525–110*–46.21–3–*ct* 25
Bowling 226–10–22.60–0–0–3/19
Test batting
1–2–0–0–0–0.00–0–*ct* 0

He is a promising young batsman, who learnt a great deal from his two tours to England. His first-class debut was for Youth XI in 1988/9.

Ata-ur-Rehman
Cricketer. *b:* 28.3.1975, Lahore, Pakistan. Lower order right-hand batsman, right-arm fast medium bowler. *Teams* Lahore (1991/2); PACO (1991/2). *Tours* Pakistan A to Sri Lanka 1990/1; Pakistan to England 1992. *Test* Pakistan (1992, 1 match).
Career batting
19–11–3–57–17–7.12–0–*ct* 4
Bowling 1335–40–33.37–1–0–8/87
Test batting
1 match, did not bat–*ct* 0

Bowling 69–3–23.00–0–0–3/69

He had little success on the 1992 tour to England, but played in the first Test, having arrived as a replacement.

Atfield, Alfred John
Professional. *b:* 3.3.1868, Ightham, Kent. *d:* 1.1.1949, Caterham, Surrey. Lower order right-hand batsman, right-arm medium pace bowler, good field. *Teams* Gloucestershire (1893, 3 matches); Natal (1897/8); London County (1900); Transvaal (1906/7).
Career batting
8–13–2–137–45–12.45–0–*ct* 5
Bowling 102–3–34.00–0–0–3/102

He was principally known as a coach in South Africa and a first-class umpire, both in South Africa and England. He also played for Wiltshire (1897–99). He was on the umpires list 1905–24, and stood in 8 Test matches in South Africa (1909/10 to 1913/14).

Atherton, Michael Andrew
Cricketer. *b:* 23.3.1968, Manchester, Lancashire. Attractive opening right-hand batsman, leg break bowler. *Sch* Manchester GS. *Teams* Cambridge U (1987–89, blue all three years); Lancashire (1987–92, 66 matches). *Tours* England A to Zimbabwe 1989/90; England to Australia 1990/1, to New Zealand 1990/1 (not first-class). *Tests* England (1989–92, 21 matches).
Career batting
123–211–26–8424–199–45.53–26–*ct* 108
Bowling 4666–106–44.01–3–0–6/78
Test batting
21–39–1–1311–151–34.50–3–*ct* 20
Bowling 282–1–282.00–0–0–1/60

He hit 1,193 runs (av 38.48) in his debut season of 1987, reaching 1,000 runs in four seasons in all (best 1,924, av 71.25, in 1990). He captained Cambridge in 1988 and 1989.

Athey, Charles William Jeffrey
Cricketer. *b:* 27.9.1957, Middlesbrough, Yorkshire. Brother-in-law of C. R. Cook (Middlesex). Middle order right-hand batsman, off break bowler, slip field. *Teams* Yorkshire (1976–83, 151 matches); Gloucestershire (1984–92, 183 matches). *Tours* Robins to New Zealand 1979/80; England to West Indies 1980/1, to Australia 1986/7, 1987/8, to New Zealand 1987/8, to India and Pakistan (World Cup) 1987/8, to Pakistan 1987/8; England B to Sri Lanka 1985/6; England XI to South Africa 1989/90. *Tests* England (1980–88, 23 matches).
Career batting
387–639–62–20129–184–34.88–42–*ct* 369–*st* 2
Bowling 2339–45–51.97–0–0–3/3
Test batting
23–41–1–919–123–22.97–1–*ct* 13

He hit 1,000 runs in a season ten times (best 1,812 av 37.75, in 1984). In 1989 he captained Gloucestershire. Although he batted well for Gloucestershire, he was never consistently successful for England, his best Test series being in Australia in 1986/7, when he opened the batting with Broad.

Atkins, Frederick Mark
Amateur. *b:* 28.3.1864, Boxley, Kent. *d:* 13.1.1941, Rochester, Kent. Lower order left-hand batsman, useful wicket-keeper. *Team* Kent (1882–97, 25 matches).
Career batting
25–46–2–425–52–9.65–0–*ct* 21–*st* 1

He scored very heavily in club cricket in Kent, including 364 for Mote Park v Shorncliffe Camp in 1887.

Atkins, Gerald
Amateur. *b:* 14.5.1938, Great Missenden, Buckinghamshire. Middle order left-hand batsman, leg break bowler. *Sch* Challenors, Amersham. *Team* Cambridge U (1960–61, blue 1960).
Career batting
20–36–3–394–49–11.93–0–*ct* 8
Bowling 96–2–48.00–0–0–2/25

His County cricket was for Buckinghamshire (1957–72). His first-class debut was for Combined Services in 1958.

Atkins, Paul David
Cricketer. *b:* 11.6.1966, Aylesbury, Buckinghamshire. Opening right-hand batsman, off break bowler. *Team* Surrey (1988–92, 17 matches).
Career batting
17–32–3–853–114*–29.41–1–*ct* 5

He also played for Buckinghamshire (1985–91). In 1988 he hit 114* on his first-class debut for Surrey v Cambridge U at the Oval.

Atkinson, Bernard Gerard Wensley
Amateur. *b:* 11.9.1900, Puddington, Devon. *d:* 4.9.1966, Hampstead, London. Brother of N. S. M. (Middlesex). Hard-hitting middle order right-hand batsman, useful right-arm fast medium bowler. *Sch* St Paul's. *Teams* Northamptonshire (1922–25, 13 matches); Middlesex (1933–34, 9 matches).
Career batting
22–37–2–554–94–15.82–0–*ct* 17
Bowling 867–25–34.68–0–0–4/97

He went to Cambridge University where he captained his college at cricket and had trials for the University at both cricket and rugby, but failed to obtain a blue at either. A master at Edinburgh Academy, he appeared in four non-first-class matches for Scotland (1935–48).

Atkinson, Colin Ronald Michael
Cricketer. *b:* 23.7.1931, Thornaby, Yorkshire. *d:* 25.6.1991, Glastonbury, Somerset. Father of J. C. M. (Somerset). Middle order right-hand batsman, leg break bowler, but altered to right-arm medium in 1965 due to arthritis in the hand. *Team* Somerset

(1960–67, 163 matches).
Career batting
164–240–41–3796–97–19.07–0–*ct* 77
Bowling 5982–192–31.15–7–0–7/54

He also played for Northumberland (1951–58) and Durham (pre first-class, 1959) and his first-class debut was for Minor Counties in 1959. He retired in 1963 from County cricket, but was released by Millfield School, where he was a master, to captain Somerset 1965–67. He hit 1,120 runs, av 26.04, in 1966. He was Somerset Chairman 1972–74 and President from 1976 until his death.

Atkinson, Denis St Eval
Amateur. *b:* 9.8.1926, Rockley, Christ Church, Barbados. Brother of E. St. E. (West Indies). Good middle order right-hand batsman, right-arm medium pace off-break bowler. *Teams* Barbados (1946/7 to 1960/1); Trinidad (1947/8 to 1949/50). *Tours* West Indies to India, Pakistan and Ceylon 1948/9, to Australia 1951/2, to New Zealand 1951/2, 1955/6, to England 1957. *Tests* West Indies (1948/9 to 1957/8, 22 matches).
Career batting
78–115–16–2812–219–28.40–5–*ct* 39
Bowling 5291–200–26.45–6–2–8/58
Test batting
22–35–6–922–219–31.79–1–*ct* 11
Bowling 1647–47–35.04–3–0–7/53

Atkinson captained West Indies in 7 Tests, including the fourth Test v Australia at Bridgetown, when he hit his only first-class double-century (219) and in the process created a new 7th wicket Test partnership record of 348 with C. C. Depeiaza. He was by far the best West Indian bowler in this series, heading the averages and taking most wickets. On his only visit to England he suffered from injury and was rarely seen on the top of his form.

Atkinson, Geoffrey Bean
Amateur. *b:* 29.1.1896, Lambeth, London. *d:* 1.9.1951, Bognor Regis, Sussex. Middle order right-hand batsman, right-arm fast-medium bowler. *Sch* Forest. *Team* Middlesex (1930, 2 matches).
Career batting
3–6–2–25–14–6.25–0–*ct* 2
Bowling 57–2–28.50–0–0–2/27

His final first-class match was for Leveson-Gower's XI in 1933.

Atkinson, George Robert
Professional. *b:* 21.9.1830, Ripon, Yorkshire. *d:* 3.5.1906, West Bowling, Bradford, Yorkshire. Stylish lower order right-hand batsman, right medium fast round-arm bowler, good slip field. *Team* Yorkshire (1861–70, 31 matches).
Career batting
62–95–21–935–66–12.63–0–*ct* 32
Bowling 2782–161 + 3–17.27–8–2–6/18

Atkinson was 29 before he took part in the major matches of the day, but through the 1860s was one of the leading Yorkshire all-rounders. The great facet of his bowling was its accuracy at a time when the faster round-arm bowlers tended to be wayward in direction. His first-class debut was for Yorkshire and Durham in 1858. His final first-class match was for United North in 1871. He also played for Wiltshire (1874). He was a first-class umpire 1893–94.

Atkinson, Graham
Professional. *b:* 29.3.1938, Lofthouse, Wakefield, Yorkshire. Sound opening right-hand batsman, occasional off break bowler, good outfield. *Teams* Somerset (1954–66, 271 matches); Lancashire (1967–69, 62 matches).
Career batting
347–608–41–17654–190–31.13–27–*ct* 188
Bowling 260–5–52.00–0–0–4/63

He made his first-class debut for Somerset at the age of 16; reached 1,000 runs in a season 9 times: best 2,078 (av 37.10) in 1961.

Atkinson, Harry
Professional. *b:* 1.2.1881, Sculcoates, Hull, Yorkshire. *d:* 22.12.1959. Lower order batsman. *Team* Yorkshire (1907, 1 match).
Career batting
1–2–0–0–0–0.00–0–*ct* 0
Bowling 17–0

He was drafted into the Yorkshire side when three of the regulars were appearing for England, but had no success.

Atkinson, John
Professional. *b:* 7.6.1878, Nether Green, Nottinghamshire. *d:* 20.11.1951, Bentley with Arksey, Doncaster, Yorkshire. Lower order left-hand batsman, useful slow left-arm bowler. *Team* Nottinghamshire (1899–1901, 7 matches).
Career batting
7–12–4–40–19–5.00–0–*ct* 1
Bowling 236–10–23.60–0–0–4/22

He was dismissed in five consecutive innings for 0 (1899–1900).

Atkinson, Jonathan Colin Mark
Cricketer. *b:* 10.7.1968, Butleigh, Somerset. Son of C. R. M. (Somerset). Middle order right-hand batsman, right-arm medium fast bowler. *Sch* Millfield. *Teams* Somerset (1985–89, 14 matches); Cambridge U (1988–90, blue all three years).
Career batting
41–64–5–1316–79–22.30–0–*ct* 19
Bowling 639–6–106.50–0–0–2/80

He captained Cambridge in 1990.

Atkinson, Nigel Samuel Mitford
Amateur. *b:* 26.7.1899, Hong Kong. *d:* 24.10.1966, St John's Wood, London. Brother of B. G. W. (Middle-

sex and Northamptonshire). Lower order right-hand batsman, useful slow/medium left-arm bowler. *Sch* St Paul's. *Team* Middlesex (1923, 2 matches).
Career batting
2–2–0–41–39–20.50–0–*ct* 2
Bowling 147–12–12.25–1–0–5/16

He was a leading figure with Hampstead CC for many years. He played in the trial matches at Cambridge U, but not in first-class games.

Atkinson, Stephen Robert
Cricketer. *b:* 8.12.1952, Birtley, Durham. Opening right-hand batsman. *Team* Minor Counties (1985).
Career batting
1–1–0–63–63–63.00–0–*ct* 1

His County cricket was for Durham (pre first-class, 1972–91). He played for Holland in ICC Trophy in 1986.

Atkinson, Thomas
Professional. *b:* 27.9.1930, Millom, Cumberland. *d:* 2.9.1990, Glasgow, Scotland. Useful middle order right-hand batsman, right-arm fast medium bowler. *Team* Nottinghamshire (1957–60, 64 matches).
Career batting
64–104–19–1127–48–13.25–0–*ct* 30
Bowling 5157–116–44.45–2–1–6/61

He also played for Cumberland (1955, 1961–67).

Atkinson-Clark, John Cecil
Amateur. *b:* 9.7.1912, Kensington, London. *d:* 2.10.1969, Alderwasley Lodge, Derbyshire. Nephew of C. T. Weatherby (MCC), J. T. Weatherby (Europeans) and F. Weatherby (Oxford U), brother-in-law of W. E. Harbord (Yorkshire). Middle order right-hand batsman. *Sch* Eton. *Team* Middlesex (1930–32, 8 matches).
Career batting
8–12–0–116–66–9.66–0–*ct* 2
Bowling 13–1–13.00–0–0–1/13

He hit 135 for Eton v Harrow at Lord's in 1930 and made his first-class debut for Middlesex with still a full school year ahead of him.

Attenborough, Thomas
Professional. *b:* July 1833, Ilkeston, Derbyshire. *d:* 21.1.1907, Gallows Inn, Ilkeston, Derbyshire. He died by his own hand. Middle order right-hand batsman, good slow left-arm bowler. *Team* Derbyshire (1871–74, 6 matches).
Career batting
6–9–0–72–27–8.00–0–*ct* 2
Bowling 29–2–14.50–0–0–1/9

A good all-rounder, his best days were prior to Derbyshire being first-class. He also played for Lincolnshire (1875).

Attewell, Thomas
Professional. *b:* 7.11.1869, Keyworth, Nottinghamshire. *d:* 6.7.1937, Standard Hill, Nottingham. Brother of William (Nottinghamshire), cousin of Walter (Nottinghamshire). Lower order right-hand batsman, right-arm medium pace bowler. *Team* Nottinghamshire (1891–94, 7 matches).
Career batting
7–10–3–53–23*–7.57–0–*ct* 2
Bowling 12–0

He was on the MCC staff at Lord's 1893 to 1925.

Attewell, Walter
Professional. *b:* 29.1.1865, Keyworth, Nottinghamshire. *d:* 3.2.1919, Keyworth, Nottinghamshire. Cousin of Thomas (Nottinghamshire) and William (Nottinghamshire). Opening right-hand batsman, excellent field. *Teams* Nottinghamshire (1891, 1 match); Players of USA (1894).
Career batting
5–6–1–44–19–8.80–0–*ct* 2
Bowling 262–9–29.11–1–0–5/81

He was the cricket coach at Shrewsbury School from 1906 to 1912 and is immortalised in the writing of Neville Cardus.

Attewell, William
Professional. *b:* 12.6.1861, Keyworth, Nottinghamshire. *d:* 11.6.1927, Long Eaton, Derbyshire. Brother of Thomas (Nottinghamshire), cousin of Walter (Nottinghamshire). Useful lower order right-hand batsman, accurate right-arm medium pace bowler, excellent mid-field. *Team* Nottinghamshire (1881–99, 283 matches). *Tours* Lillywhite, Shaw and Shrewsbury to Australia 1884/5; Vernon to Australia 1887/8; Sheffield to Australia 1891/2. *Tests* England (1884/5 to 1891/2, 10 matches).
Career batting
429–644–68–8083–102–14.03–1–*ct* 364
Bowling 29896–1951–15.32–134–27–9/23
Test batting
10–15–6–150–43*–16.66–0–*ct* 9
Bowling 626–28–22.35–0–0–4/42

Accuracy of length and direction was the prime facet of Attewell's bowling, and throughout the 1880s and 1890s he returned a continuous string of very economical bowling analyses. Three examples for Nottinghamshire are: 10–9–2–3 v MCC (Lord's) 1881; 52.2–42–19–4 v Kent (Trent Bridge) 1887; 14–12–6–4 v Sussex (Trent Bridge) 1891.

He first took 100 wickets in a season in 1884 and in all performed the feat on ten occasions (best 153 wickets, av 13.93, in 1891). His best bowling was 9/23 for Nottinghamshire v Sussex at Trent Bridge in 1886.

All but one of his ten Test appearances were in Australia and on the last two of his three tours there he was the most successful bowler. His first-class batting is remarkable for the fact that his first and only century came in 1897 – sixteen seasons after his debut. His last first-class match was for MCC in 1900. He was a first-class umpire 1902–07.

He was a man who never got on anyone's nerves and whose good nature was proverbial.

Aubrey-Fletcher, Sir John Henry Lancelot
Amateur. *b:* 22.8.1912, Kensington, London. *d:* 19.6.1992, Oxford. Middle order right-hand batsman, right-arm medium pace bowler. *Sch* Eton. *Team* Oxford U (1933).
Career batting
2–3–3–66–48*–no av–0–*ct* 2
Bowling 133–5–26.60–0–0–2/46
His County cricket was for Buckinghamshire (1931–48), and his first-class debut for Minor Counties in 1933. He was High Sheriff of Buckinghamshire in 1961.

Audland, Rev John Heslop
Amateur. *b:* 5.10.1852, Tintern, Monmouth. *d:* 4.10.1931, Ackenthwaite, Westmorland. Lower order batsman, wicket-keeper. *Team* Oxford U (1875).
Career batting
1–1–0–2–2–2.00–0–*ct* 1–*st* 1
His County cricket was for Wiltshire (1894).

August, George Lawrence Bagley
Amateur. *b:* 16.9.1917, Mymensingh, Bangalore, India. *d:* 13.10.1991, Bedford. Middle order right-hand batsman. *Sch* Bedford. *Team* Minor Counties (1950–53).
Career batting
2–4–0–41–27–10.25–0–*ct* 0
His County cricket was for Bedfordshire (1935–60), and he was later Secretary of the County Club (1969–84).

Austen-Leigh, S. (*See under* Leigh, S. A.)

Austin, Edward James
Amateur. *b:* 25.9.1847, Buckland Ripers, Weymouth, Dorset. *d:* 13.4.1891, Pimlico, London. Tail end right-hand batsman, medium pace round-arm bowler. *Sch* Sherborne. *Team* Oxford U (1869).
Career batting
1–2–1–10–10–10.00–0–*ct* 1
Bowling 58–2–29.00–0–0–2/58
His County cricket was for Dorset (1869).

Austin, Geoffrey Lewis
Amateur. *b:* 11.9.1837, Canterbury, Kent. *d:* 29.5.1902, Chelsea, London. Middle order batsman. *Team* Kent (1861–68, 2 matches).
Career batting
3–6–0–64–23–10.66–0–*ct* 1

Austin, Sir Harold Bruce Gardiner
Amateur. *b:* 15.7.1877, Enmore, St Michael, Barbados. *d:* 27.7.1943, Collymore Rock, St Michael, Barbados. Brother of A. P. G. (British Guiana), M. B. G. (British Guiana), J. G. (Barbados) and F. E. W. G. (Barbados), father-in-law of G. W. White (Army). Middle order right-hand batsman. *Sch* Harrison College, Barbados. *Teams* Barbados (1894/5 to 1927/8); MCC (1909–26). *Tours* West Indies to England 1906, 1923.
Career batting
65–100–7–2643–129–28.41–1–*ct* 45–*st* 3
Bowling 302–15–20.13–0–0–3/7
Austin was the captain of both the first and second first-class West Indies tours to England. Knighted in 1935, he was Speaker of the House of Assembly, Barbados.

Austin, Harold McPherson
Amateur. *b:* 8.3.1903, Skipton, Victoria, Australia. *d:* 31.7.1981, Timboon, Victoria, Australia. Middle order right-hand batsman, leg break bowler. *Sch* Melbourne GS. *Teams* Cambridge U (1924, blue); Victoria (1924/5, 6 matches – all on tour of New Zealand). *Tour* Victoria to New Zealand 1924/5.
Career batting
17–25–2–599–87–26.04–0–*ct* 11
Bowling 1047–41–25.53–3–0–6/79
He also won a blue for athletics.

Austin, Harry
Professional. *b:* 17.4.1892, Moseley, Birmingham. *d:* 29.8.1968, Canterbury, Kent. Lower order left-hand batsman, slow left-arm bowler. *Teams* Warwickshire (1919, 4 matches); Worcestershire (1928, 2 matches).
Career batting
6–10–2–67–13–8.37–0–*ct* 3
Bowling 290–3–96.66–0–0–1/41
He also played for Cornwall (1932–34).

Austin, Ian David
Cricketer. *b:* 30.5.1966, Haslingden, Lancashire. Lower order left-hand batsman, right-arm medium pace bowler. *Team* Lancashire (1987–92, 51 matches). *Tour* Lancashire to Zimbabwe 1988/9.
Career batting
51–66–17–1249–115*–25.48–2–*ct* 7
Bowling 2919–78–37.42–1–0–5/79

Austin, Mervyn Neville
Amateur. *b:* 1.8.1913, Melbourne, Victoria, Australia. Tail end right-hand batsman, leg break and googly bowler. *Sch* Melbourne GS. *Team* Oxford U (1938).
Career batting
4–5–4–14–6–14.00–0–*ct* 2
Bowling 234–7–33.42–0–0–4/36

Austin, Robert Gordon Lefroy
Amateur. *b:* 28.12.1871, Cheltenham, Gloucestershire. *d:* 26.5.1958, Stellenbosch, Cape Province, South Africa. Hard-hitting lower order right-hand batsman, but liable to throw away his wicket, good field. *Sch* Cheltenham. *Team* Oxford U (1894).
Career batting
1–2–0–7–7–3.50–0–*ct* 0
Bowling 4–0

Avery, Alfred Victor
Professional. *b:* 19.12.1914, New Beckton, Essex. Sound opening right-hand batsman, slow left-arm bowler, close field. *Team* Essex (1935–54, 268 matches).
Career batting
269–455–35–14137–224–33.65–25–*ct* 119
Bowling 627–9–69.66–0–0–1/11

His highest score was 224 for Essex v Northamptonshire at Northampton in 1952. He scored 1,000 runs in a season seven times (best 1,890, av 46.09, in 1948). He was Gloucestershire coach 1957–58.

Avory, Henry Kemp
Amateur. *b:* 4.10.1848, Clapham, Surrey. *d:* 16.4.1918, Weybridge, Surrey. Hard-hitting opening right-hand batsman, useful outfield. *Team* Surrey (1876, 2 matches).
Career batting
2–4–0–82–42–20.50–0–*ct* 0

A solicitor, he was for many years Clerk to the Central Criminal Court.

Awdry, Charles Edwin
Amateur. *b:* 29.4.1906, Paddington, London. *d:* 16.11.1965, Bowden Hill, Lacock, Wiltshire. Nephew of R. W. (Oxford U), son-in-law of E. C. Mordaunt (Middlesex and Kent). Middle order batsman, right-arm fast-medium bowler, good extra cover. *Sch* Winchester. *Teams* West of England (1927); Minor Counties (1937).
Career batting
2–3–0–16–8–5.33–0–*ct* 1
Bowling 80–3–26.66–0–0–2/56

He was the leading all-rounder in the Wiltshire side for many years, playing for the county from 1924 to 1939.

Awdry, Robert William
Amateur. *b:* 20.5.1881, Kensington, London. *d:* 3.2.1949, Devizes, Wiltshire. Uncle of C. E. (Minor Counties), nephew of J. C. Moberly (Hampshire). Good opening right-hand batsman. *Sch* Winchester. *Team* Oxford U (1902–04, blue 1904).
Career batting
9–16–0–383–72–23.93–0–*ct* 5

He was a mainstay of Wiltshire cricket for many years, first as player (1900–34) then as Hon Secretary and Treasurer. He was a Chairman of Wiltshire County Council.

Aworth, Christopher John
Cricketer. *b:* 19.2.1953, Wimbledon, Surrey. Good middle order left-hand batsman, occasional slow left-arm bowler. *Sch* Tiffin. *Teams* Cambridge U (1973–75, blue all three years); Surrey (1974–76, 26 matches).
Career batting
56–104–6–2552–135–26.04–3–*ct* 22
Bowling 476–7–68.00–0–0–2/23

His best season was 1975 when he hit 1,057 runs (av 31.08). He captained Cambridge in 1975.

Axford, William Ian
Amateur. *b:* 2.1.1933, Dannevirke, Hawke's Bay, New Zealand. Middle order right-hand batsman, right-arm medium pace bowler. *Team* Cambridge U (1960).
Career batting
2–2–0–13–7–6.50–0–*ct* 1

Ayling, Cyril Edgar
Amateur. *b:* 26.10.1910, Buenos Aires, Argentina. Brother of D. E. (Argentine), Cecil (Argentine) and Eric (Argentine, not first-class). Lower order right-hand batsman, right-arm fast medium bowler. *Team* Argentine (1937/8). *Tour* South America to England 1932.
Career batting
9–15–2–200–50–15.38–0–*ct* 8
Bowling 674–24–28.08–1–0–5/48

Ayling, Dennet Ernest
Amateur. *b:* 8.6.1906, Buenos Aires, Argentina. *d:* 18.12.1987, Los Cocos, Cordoba, Argentina. Brother of Cecil (Argentine), Cyril (Argentine) and Eric (Argentine, not first-class). Middle order right-hand batsman, off spin bowler. *Team* Argentine (1926/7 to 1937/8). *Tour* South America to England 1932.
Career batting
16–29–2–653–88–24.18–0–*ct* 6
Bowling 1297–79–16.41–7–2–6/10

Ayling, Jonathan Richard
Cricketer. *b:* 13.6.1967, Portsmouth, Hampshire. Middle order right-hand batsman, right-arm medium pace bowler. *Team* Hampshire (1988–92, 56 matches).
Career batting
56–84–11–1993–121–27.30–1–*ct* 14
Bowling 3254–131–24.83–1–0–5/12

Ayling, William
Professional. *c:* 30.9.1766, Cocking, Chichester, Sussex. *d:* 1826, Bromley, Kent. Brother of R. Ayling (Kent 1796). Hard-hitting batsman, fine outfield. *Teams* Kent (1806); England (1801–10).
Career batting
21–38–5–271–45–8.21–0–*ct* 7

In his early days he was a bit of a poacher and on this account moved from Sussex. When batting he stood square to the bowler and held the bat in his right hand only, grasping it with his left immediately before receiving the ball.

Aylmer, Edward Arthur
Amateur. *b:* 20.3.1892, Tredouvra, Falmouth, Cornwall. *d:* 30.10.1974, Askerswell House, Dorset. Lower order batsman. *Team* Royal Navy (1920).

Career batting
1–2–1–20–10*–20.00–0–*ct* 1
Bowling 38–1–38.00–0–0–1/19

Aylward, James
Professional. *b:* 1741, Warnford, Droxford, Hampshire. *d:* 27.12.1827, Marylebone, Middlesex. Brother of John and Thomas (both noted players in their day). Excellent left-hand batsman. *Team* Hampshire.

He played almost entirely before 1801, so career records are inapplicable. He hit 167 for Hampshire v England at Sevenoaks in 1777 – at the time the highest score ever made in an important match. He continued to play cricket until 1802, when his age was 61, his career thus being one of the longest on record, but many of his early scores are lost. In his later years he became well-known as a captain.

Aymes, Adrian Nigel
Cricketer. *b:* 4.6.1964, Southampton, Hampshire. Lower order right-hand batsman, wicket-keeper. *Team* Hampshire (1987–92, 50 matches).
Career batting
50–63–17–1402–75*–30.47–0–*ct* 121–*st* 9
Bowling 75–1–75.00–0–0–1/75

Ayres, George White
Professional. *b:* 5.7.1871, Thames Ditton, Surrey. *d:* 28.8.1934, Riverside Park, Felpham, Sussex. Steady middle order right-hand batsman, brilliant fieldsman and change bowler. *Teams* Surrey (1892–96, 25 matches); Essex (1899, 12 matches). *Tour* Read to South Africa 1891/2 (he did not play in a first-class match).
Career batting
38–52–2–672–83–13.44–0–*ct* 22
Bowling 166–5–33.20–0–0–1/2

Azad, Kirtivardhan Bhagwat Jha
Cricketer. *b:* 2.1.1959, Purnea, India. Middle order right-hand batsman, off break bowler, good outfield. *Team* Delhi (1977/8 to 1991/2). *Tours* India to Australia and New Zealand 1980/1, to England 1983 (World Cup), to Sharjah (not first-class) 1983/4, 1985/6. *Tests* India (1980/1 to 1981/2, 4 matches).
Career batting
134–170–13–6435–215–40.98–20–*ct* 87
Bowling 6755–218–30.98–4–0–7/63
Test batting
4–6–0–107–24–17.83–0–*ct* 2
Bowling 158–1–158.00–0–0–1/35

His first-class debut was for India Under 22s in 1976/7. His only first-class match in England was for D. B. Close's XI in 1983.

Azeem Hafeez
Cricketer. *b:* 29.7.1963, Jhelum, Pakistan. Lower order left-hand batsman, left-arm medium pace bowler. *Teams* Allied Bank (1982/3); Karachi (1985/6); PNSC (1986/7 to 1988/9); PIA (1989/90). *Tours* Pakistan to India 1983/4, to Australia 1983/4, 1984/5 (not first-class), to Sharjah (not first-class) 1983/4, to New Zealand 1984/5, to England 1987; Pakistan Under 23 to Sri Lanka 1984/5. *Tests* Pakistan (1983/4 to 1984/5, 18 matches).
Career batting
73–92–21–828–69–11.66–0–*ct* 15
Bowling 6760–200–33.80–6–0–7/68
Test batting
18–21–5–134–24–8.37–0–*ct* 1
Bowling 2204–63–34.98–4–0–6/46

He was drafted into the 1987 touring team to England for one match, being on holiday at the time.

Azharuddin, Mohammad
Cricketer. *b:* 8.2.1963, Hyderabad, India. Stylish middle order right-hand batsman, right-arm medium pace bowler. *Teams* Hyderabad (1981/2 to 1990/1); Derbyshire (1991, 22 matches). *Tours* India to Australia 1984/5 (not first-class), 1985/6, 1991/2, to Sharjah (not first-class) 1984/5, 1985/6, 1986/7, 1987/8, 1988/9, 1989/90, 1991/2, to Sri Lanka 1985/6, to England 1986, 1990, to West Indies 1988/9, to Bangladesh (not first-class) 1988/9, to New Zealand 1989/90, to Pakistan 1989/90, to Australia and New Zealand (World Cup) 1991/2; Young Indians to Zimbabwe 1983/4. *Tests* (1984/5 to 1991/2, 46 matches).
Career batting
128–197–24–9378–226–54.20–31–*ct* 110
Bowling 533–7–76.14–0–0–2/33
Test batting
46–70–3–3168–199–47.28–11–*ct* 35
Bowling 8–0

He scored hundreds in each of his first three Test matches, the only player to do this. Coming to England in 1986, Azharuddin scored most first-class runs for the Indian tourists and played in all three Tests. When he returned in 1990, he captained the side. Topping both Test and first-class averages, he hit hundreds in the Tests at both Lord's and Old Trafford. Joining Derbyshire in 1991, he reached 2,016 runs (av 59.29). He has captained India in 12 Tests. His highest score was 226 for South Zone v Central Zone at Jamadoba in 1983/4. He scored 1,058 runs, av 70.53, in India in 1986/7.

Azmat Rana
Cricketer. *b:* 3.11.1951, Lahore, Pakistan. Twin brother of Sultan Rana (Habib Bank), brother of Shafqat Rana (PIA) and Shakoor Rana (Lahore), uncle of Mansoor Rana (Lahore) and Maqsood Rana (Lahore). Opening or middle order left-hand batsman, off break bowler. *Teams* Bahawalpur (1969/70); PIA (1969/70 to 1974/5); Punjab (1976/7 to 1977/8); Muslim Commercial Bank (1976/7 to 1983/4). *Tours* Pakistan to England 1971, to New Zealand 1972/3. *Test* Pakistan (1979/80, 1 match).

Babington, Andrew Mark

Career batting
94–142–18–5984–206*–48.25–16–*ct* 74
Bowling 85–0
Test batting
1–1–0–49–49–49.00–0–*ct* 0

He hit 192 runs, av 21.33, on the 1971 tour to England and did not appear in the Tests.

B

Babington, Andrew Mark
Cricketer. *b:* 22.7.1963, Marylebone, London. Lower order left-hand batsman, right-arm fast medium bowler. *Teams* Sussex (1986–90, 60 matches); Gloucestershire (1991–92, 27 matches).
Career batting
87–92–37–475–58–8.63–0–*ct* 31
Bowling 6911–194–35.62–3–0–8/107

He performed the hat-trick in taking his first three wickets in first-class cricket.

Bacchus, Sheik Faoud Ahamul Fasiel
Cricketer. *b:* 31.1.1954, Campbellville, Georgetown, British Guiana. Opening or middle order right-hand batsman, right-arm medium pace bowler, good outfield. *Teams* Guyana (1972/3 to 1982/3); Western Province (1984/5); Border (1985/6). *Tours* West Indies to India and Sri Lanka 1978/9, to England 1980, 1983 (World Cup), to Pakistan 1980/1, to Australia 1981/2; Young West Indies to Zimbabwe 1981/2; West Indian XI to South Africa 1983/4. *Tests* West Indies (1977/8 to 1981/2, 19 matches).
Career batting
111–182–13–5944–250–35.17–8–*ct* 88
Bowling 197–8–24.62–0–0–2/18
Test batting
19–30–0–782–250–26.06–1–*ct* 17
Bowling 3–0

His first-class debut was for Demerara in 1971/2. In first-class matches on the 1980 tour he hit 710 runs, av 33.80, and played in all five Tests, but with little success.

Bache, Harold Godfrey
Amateur. *b:* 20.8.1889, Churchill, Worcestershire. *d:* 15.2.1916, Comines Canal Bank, Ypres, Belgium. He was killed in action. Lower order left-hand batsman, slow left-arm bowler. *Sch* KES, Birmingham. *Teams* Worcestershire (1907–10, 17 matches); Cambridge U (1909–10).
Career batting
20–31–1–270–36–9.00–0–*ct* 5
Bowling 39–3–13.00–0–0–2/4

He was better known as a soccer player, playing for Cambridge U, West Bromwich and the Corinthians. He also represented Cambridge U at lawn tennis.

Bacher, Dr Aron
(known as Ali Bacher)
Amateur. *b:* 24.5.1942, Roodeport, Johannesburg, South Africa. Uncle of Michael (Transvaal) and W. Kirsh (Northern Transvaal), nephew of A. Nickel (Transvaal). Middle order right-hand batsman, leg break bowler, brilliant field. *Team* Transvaal (1959/60 to 1973/4). *Tour* South Africa to England 1965. *Tests* South Africa (1965 to 1969/70, 12 matches).
Career batting
120–212–10–7894–235–39.07–18–*ct* 110–*st* 1
Bowling 87–2–43.50–0–0–1/8
Test batting
12–22–1–679–73–32.33–0 *ct* 10

On his only visit to England Bacher hit 1,008 runs (av 40.32) and was one of the successes of the tour. In 1969/70 he captained South Africa to a great victory over the Australians, winning all four of the Tests. His highest score was 235 for Transvaal v Australians at Johannesburg in 1966/7.

He was one of the prominent figures in organising rebel tours to South Africa, and then in seeing the return of South Africa to Test cricket as the United Board of Cricket in South Africa was formed.

Backhouse, Edgar Norman
Professional. *b:* 13.5.1901, Sheriff Hutton, Yorkshire. *d:* 1.11.1936. He was killed in a motor accident at High Wycombe, Buckinghamshire. Lower order right-hand batsman, left-arm medium pace bowler. *Team* Yorkshire (1931, 1 match).
Career batting
2–3–0–3–2–1.00–0–*ct* 0
Bowling 134–3–44.66–0–0–3/130

Oldroyd was taken ill when Yorkshire arrived in London to play as Champion County v The Rest and as they brought only 11 men, Backhouse, on the staff at Lord's, was brought into the County side at the last moment. It proved to be one of two appearances in first-class cricket, the other being for MCC in 1932. He also played for Staffordshire (1932–36).

Bacmeister, Lucas Henry
Amateur. *b:* 22.11.1869, Islington, London. *d:* 23.5.1962, Woolage Green, Barham, Kent. Lower order right-hand batsman, useful right-arm fast-medium bowler. *Team* Middlesex (1889–90, 9 matches).
Career batting
11–17–4–59–15–4.53–0–*ct* 9
Bowling 688–31–22.19–1–0–5/22

He made his first-class debut for Gentlemen of England v Oxford U in May 1889 and took 5/22 in the second innings. He was immediately drafted into the Middlesex side, but discarded after a handful of games, though his record was most promising. After an interval of 14 years he reappeared in first-class cricket in one match in 1904 for Weigall's XI.

Bacon, Francis Hugh
Originally professional, but turned amateur in 1903. *b:* 24.6.1869, Colombo, Ceylon. *d:* 31.10.1915. He was drowned off the coast of Belgium, the ship, *Yacht Aries*, in which he was serving being sunk by a mine. Middle order right-hand batsman, slow right-arm bowler. *Sch* St Augustine's, Canterbury. *Team* Hampshire (1895–1911, 75 matches).
Career batting
75–132–11–1909–110–15.77–1–*ct* 34
Bowling 190–6–31.66–0–0–2/23

Bacon hit 114 in 130 minutes on his debut for Hampshire v Warwickshire in 1894 (this match is not ranked as first-class). He was appointed Secretary of Hampshire in 1903 and remained in that post until his death.

Bacon, John
Professional. *b:* 30.5.1871, Enderby, Leicestershire. *d:* 16.10.1942, Broughton Astley, Leicestershire. Lower order right-hand batsman, useful right-arm medium pace bowler. *Team* Leicestershire (1895, 4 matches).
Career batting
4–8–1–42–14–6.00–0–*ct* 0
Bowling 21–1–21.00–0–0–1/18

He also played for Cambridgeshire (1900–04).

Badat, Yunus
Cricketer. *b:* 1943, Northern Rhodesia. Middle order right-hand batsman. *Team* East Africa (1975). *Tour* East Africa to England 1975.
Career batting
1–2–0–3–3–1.50–0–*ct* 0

Badcock, Clayvel Lindsay
Amateur. *b:* 10.4.1914, Exton, Tasmania, Australia. *d:* 13.12.1982, Exton, Tasmania, Australia. Punishing opening or middle order right-hand batsman. *Teams* Tasmania (1929/30 to 1933/4, 19 matches); South Australia (1934/5 to 1940/1, 40 matches). *Tour* Australia to England 1938. *Tests* Australia (1936/7 to 1938, 7 matches).
Career batting
97–159–16–7371–325–51.54–26–*ct* 41
Bowling 44–0
Test batting
7–12–1–160–118–14.54–1–*ct* 3

His only success in Test matches came at Melbourne in 1936/7 when, in the fifth Test, he hit 118 in 205 minutes. On his visit to England in 1938, he batted well in the ordinary matches, returning an aggregate of 1,604 runs (av 45.82) but totally failed in the Tests – in 8 innings his best score was 9. His highest score was 325 for South Australia v Victoria at Adelaide in 1935/6. He suffered from lumbago and had to retire at the age of 27.

Badcock, Frederick Theodore
Professional. *b:* 9.8.1897, Abbottabad, India. *d:* 19.9.1982, South Perth, Western Australia. Attacking opening or middle order right-hand batsman, right-arm fast-medium bowler. *Sch* Wellington (UK). *Teams* Wellington (1924/5 to 1929/30); Otago (1930/1 to 1936/7). *Tour* New Zealand Services to England 1945. *Tests* New Zealand (1929/30 to 1932/3, 7 matches).
Career batting
53–96–3–2383–155–25.62–4–*ct* 38
Bowling 5211–221–23.57–14–5–7/50
Test batting
7–9–2–137–64–19.57–0–*ct* 1
Bowling 610–16–38.12–0–0–4/80

Badcock went out to New Zealand as coach to Wellington in 1924/5 and after six years moved on to Otago. He played for New Zealand only in home Tests and his two appearances in English first-class cricket occurred in 1945 playing for the New Zealand Forces team, and for L. Parkinson's XI in 1935.

Badcock, John
Professional. *b:* 4.10.1883, Christchurch, Hampshire. *d:* 24.8.1940, Marylebone, London. Useful tail end right-hand batsman, right-arm fast bowler. *Team* Hampshire (1906–08, 63 matches).
Career batting
63–102–19–1199–74–14.44–0–*ct* 30
Bowling 5414–212–25.53–12–3–8/44

Badcock had a most successful debut season with 96 wickets (av 24.81), but his first-class career lasted only three years.

Bader, Sir Douglas Robert Steuart
Amateur. *b:* 21.2.1910, Marylebone, London. *d:* 4.9.1982, Chiswick, London. Hard hitting middle order right-hand batsman, fast bowler. *Sch* St Edward's, Oxford. *Team* RAF (1931).
Career batting
1–2–0–66–65–33.00–0–*ct* 0

Also a noted rugby footballer for the RAF and Combined Services, Bader lost both legs in a flying accident in 1931. The way in which he overcame this disability and returned to the RAF to become a hero of the Second World War was the subject of books and a film. He was a Battle of Britain pilot. He was shot down in 1941 and was a prisoner of war in Colditz until 1945. He set out to encourage other disabled people to conquer their difficulties and lead an ordinary life.

Badger, Henry Dixon
Amateur. *b:* 7.3.1900, Clifton, York. *d:* 10.8.1975, Barnard Castle, Co Durham. Lower order right-hand batsman, right-arm fast bowler. *Sch* Shrewsbury. *Teams* Yorkshire (1921–22, 2 matches); Oxford U (1921).

Badham, Peter Henry Christopher

Career batting
5–7–4–33–17*–11.00–0–*ct* 2
Bowling 325–15–21.66–0–0–4/53

Badham, Peter Henry Christopher
Amateur. *b:* 11.2.1911, Bagworth, Leicestershire. *d:* 10.4.1983, Upton, Dorset. Lower order right-hand batsman, right-arm medium pace bowler. *Sch* Winchester. *Teams* Leicestershire (1933, 1 match); Oxford U (1934).
Career batting
4–6–0–67–38–11.16–0–*ct* 4
Bowling 311–10–31.10–0–0–4/70

He played for Leicestershire v Oxford University only, appearing in 1933–34 for Buckinghamshire in the Minor Counties Championship. He also played for Dorset (1937–47).

Baggallay, Mervyn Eric Claude
Amateur. *b:* 7.12.1887, Kensington, London. *d:* 19.3.1961, West Brompton, Kensington, London. Brother of R. R. C. (Derbyshire), cousin of T. W. (Surrey). Hard hitting lower order right-hand batsman, wicket-keeper. *Sch* Eton. *Team* Cambridge U (1911, blue).
Career batting
8–14–3–119–22–10.81–0–*ct* 6–*st* 4

Though at Cambridge in 1908, he did not play in a first-class match for the University until 1911.

Baggallay, Richard Romer Claude
Amateur. *b:* 4.5.1884, Kensington, London. *d:* 12.12.1975, Kensington, London. Brother of M. E. C. (Cambridge U), cousin of T. W. (Surrey). Middle order right-hand batsman, wicket-keeper. *Sch* Marlborough. *Team* Derbyshire (1912–19, 31 matches).
Career batting
31–59–1–688–88–11.86–0–*ct* 25

He captained Derbyshire 1913–1919 (jointly with J. Chapman in 1919).

Baggallay, Thomas Weeding
(he changed his name to T. W. Weeding in 1868)
Amateur. *b:* 11.6.1847, St Pancras, London. *d:* 19.12.1929, Addlestone, Surrey. Cousin of R. R. C. (Derbyshire) and M. E. C. (Cambridge U). Opening or middle order right-hand batsman, slow round-arm bowler, wicket-keeper. *Sch* Marlborough. *Team* Surrey (1865–74, 8 matches).
Career batting
9–15–0–181–82–12.06–0–*ct* 4

A keen yachtsman, he took up sailing to the detriment of his cricket.

Bagguley, Robert
Professional. *b:* 10.7.1873, Ruddington, Nottinghamshire. *d:* 8.10.1946, Brackcliffe Farm, Bradmore, Nottinghamshire. Brother of William (Derbyshire). Middle order right-hand batsman, useful left-arm medium pace bowler. *Team* Nottinghamshire (1891–96, 45 matches).
Career batting
48–76–12–766–110–11.96–1–*ct* 25
Bowling 930–38–24.47–3–0–6/74

On the staff at Lord's from 1893 to 1902, Bagguley made his final appearance in first-class cricket for MCC in 1900.

Bagguley, William
Professional. *b:* 9.9.1866, Ruddington, Nottinghamshire. *d:* 18.4.1936, Standard Hill, Nottingham. Brother of Robert (Nottinghamshire). Useful middle order batsman. *Team* Derbyshire (1905, 1 match).
Career batting
1–1–0–5–5–5.00–0–*ct* 0

Bagnall, Hamer Fraser
Amateur. *b:* 18.2.1904, Farnham, Surrey. *d:* 2.9.1974, Marylebone, London. Middle order right-hand batsman with splendid off-drive, leg break bowler. *Sch* Harrow. *Teams* Northamptonshire (1921–28, 64 matches); Cambridge U (1923–25, blue 1923). *Tour* Tennyson to Jamaica 1931/2 (but played no first-class matches).
Career batting
85–158–3–2956–128*–19.07–3–*ct* 40
Bowling 59–0

He made his debut for Northamptonshire with still a full year to go at school. He scored well on fast wickets and against fast bowlers, but failed too often against the slower bowlers. His final first-class match was for MCC in 1929.

Bagshaw, Henry
Professional. *b:* 1.9.1859, Foolow, Tideswell, Derbyshire. *d:* 31.1.1927, Woodhead, Cheshire. Free hitting opening left-hand batsman, useful right-arm medium pace bowler. *Team* Derbyshire (1887–1902, 123 matches).
Career batting
125–218–9–5456–127*–26.10–7–*ct* 36
Bowling 2119–73–29.02–2–0–5/18

He was buried in his umpire's coat and with a cricket ball in his hand. He hit 1,055 runs, av 29.30, in 1900. He was a first-class umpire 1907–23.

Baig, Abbas Ali
Amateur. *b:* 19.3.1939, Hyderabad, India. Brother of Murtuza Ali (Oxford U) and Mazhar Ali (Hyderabad). Attractive middle order right-hand batsman, leg break bowler. *Teams* Hyderabad (1954/5 to 1975/6); Oxford U (1959–62, blue all four years); Somerset (1960–62, 23 matches). *Tours* India to England 1959, 1971; Hyderabad Blues to Ceylon 1966/7; Swanton to West Indies 1960/1. *Tests* India (1959 to 1966/7, 10 matches).
Career batting
235–391–29–12367–224*–34.16–21–*ct* 154
Bowling 432–9–48.00–0–0–2/26

Test batting
10–18–0–428–112–23.77–1–*ct* 6
Bowling 15–0

Baig's only Test hundred was made on his debut for India v England at Old Trafford in 1959 – he made 112 – when he was co-opted into the touring side after being at Oxford. His first first-class century was scored in his second first-class match: 105 for Hyderabad v Mysore in 1954/5.

He hit over 1,000 runs in each of his 3 full seasons in England (best 1821, av 39.58, in 1959). His highest score was 224* for South Zone v North Zone at Delhi in 1966/7.

Baig, Murtuza Ali
Amateur. *b:* 8.11.1941, Hyderabad, India. Brother of A. A. (Somerset and India) and Mazhar Ali (Hyderabad). Middle order right-hand batsman, off break bowler. *Teams* Hyderabad (1958/9 to 1970/1); Oxford U (1961–64, blue 1962–64).
Career batting
47–81–12–1898–103–27.50–1–*ct* 13
Bowling 299–6–49.83–0–0–4/44

In 1962 both M. A. Baig and his brother appeared for Oxford at Lord's – the first time two brothers had done this since 1928.

Bail, Paul Andrew Clayden
Cricketer. *b:* 23.6.1965, Burnham-on-Sea, Somerset. Middle order right-hand batsman, off break bowler. *Sch* Millfield. *Teams* Somerset (1985–86, 7 matches); Cambridge U (1986–88, blue all three years).
Career batting
29–49–2–1016–174–21.61–1–*ct* 7
Bowling 103–1–103.00–0–0–1/36

He also played for Wiltshire (1989–91).

Bailey, Albert E.
Professional. *b:* 14.3.1872, Norwood, Surrey. Lower order right-hand batsman, good slow left-arm bowler. *Teams* Somerset (1900–11, 40 matches); Scotland (1908–09).
Career batting
43–70–27–322–25*–7.48–0–*ct* 15
Bowling 3541–133–26.62–7–2–8/46

He also played for Surrey in non-first-class matches in 1892.

Bailey, David
Cricketer. *b:* 9.9.1944, West Hartlepool, Co Durham. Brother of H. J. (Minor Counties). Middle order right-hand batsman, off break bowler, excellent cover point. *Sch* Malvern. *Team* Lancashire (1968–69, 27 matches). *Tour* Minor Counties to Kenya 1977/8 (not first-class).
Career batting
32–46–2–1265–136–28.75–1–*ct* 13
Bowling 139–3–46.33–0–0–3/67

His cricket has been mainly in the Minor Counties Championship, with Durham 1961–67 and Cheshire 1973–83. He has appeared regularly in representative Minor Counties sides. His final first-class match was for Minor Counties in 1981.

Bailey, Sir Derrick Thomas Louis
Amateur. *b:* 15.8.1918, Marylebone, London. Son of Sir Abe Bailey (Transvaal), son-in-law of R. S. Darling (Oxford U). Middle order right-hand batsman, right-arm medium pace change bowler. *Sch* Winchester. *Team* Gloucestershire (1949–52, 60 matches).
Career batting
60–95–12–2029–111–24.44–2–*ct* 36
Bowling 398–12–33.16–0–0–2/19

He captained Gloucestershire, 1951–52. He hit 1,003, av 30.39, in 1951. He also played for Oxfordshire (1937) and Herefordshire. He played in trial matches at Oxford U but not in first-class games.

Bailey, Frederick Raymond
Amateur. *b:* 2.11.1919, Newcastle-under-Lyme, Staffordshire. *d:* 8.5.1985, Wolstanton, Staffordshire. Opening left-hand batsman. *Team* Minor Counties (1950–60).
Career batting
3–5–1–118–79–29.50–0–*ct* 0

His County cricket was for Staffordshire (1939–63).

Bailey, George Herbert
Amateur. *b:* 29.10.1853, Colombo, Ceylon. *d:* 10.10.1926, Hobart, Tasmania, Australia. Father of G. K. B. (Tasmania), son-in-law of G. Gibson (Tasmania). Hard hitting lower order right-hand batsman, right-hand fast round-arm bowler, deep field. *Sch* Elizabeth College, Guernsey, C.I. *Team* Tasmania (1872/3 to 1892/3, 2 matches). *Tour* Australia to England and North America 1878.
Career batting
15–27–5–367–57*–16.68–0–*ct* 9
Bowling 102–4–25.50–0–0–1/5

He was also invited to tour England with the 1880 Australians, but had to decline for business reasons.

Bailey, Harry John
Cricketer. *b:* 23.4.1940, West Hartlepool, Co Durham. Brother of David (Lancashire). Middle order right-hand batsman, left-arm medium pace bowler. *Sch* Malvern. *Team* Minor Counties (1967–69).
Career batting
3–4–0–50–25–12.50–0–*ct* 1
Bowling 68–3–22.66–0–0–2/20

His County cricket was for Durham (pre first-class, 1961–71).

Bailey, Jack Arthur
Amateur. *b:* 22.6.1930, Brixton, London. Lower order right-hand batsman, right-arm fast medium bowler. *Sch* Christ's Hospital. *Teams* Essex (1953–58, 71 matches); Oxford U (1956–58, blue all three years).

Bailey, James

Career batting
112–148–38–641–29*–5.82–0–*ct* 67
Bowling 7504–347–21.62–20–2–8/24

He was Assistant Secretary of MCC 1967–74 and Secretary from June 1974 until January 1987, when he retired in controversial circumstances. He has since become well-known as a cricket journalist. During the 1960s he appeared frequently in MCC matches. He took 7/32 in the second innings of his first-class debut match for Essex v Nottinghamshire at Southend in 1953. His final first-class match was for Free Foresters in 1968. He captained Oxford in 1958.

Bailey, James
Professional. *b:* 6.4.1908, Otterbourne, Hampshire. *d:* 10.2.1988, Southampton, Hampshire. Solid left-hand opening batsman, good slow left-arm bowler, gully fielder. *Team* Hampshire (1927–52, 242 matches).
Career batting
248–418–37–9500–133–24.93–5–*ct* 64
Bowling 12886–473–27.24–25–5–7/7

Hitting 1,000 runs in a season four times (best 1,410, av 30.00, in 1946), he did not play regularly for the County through the 1930s, being engaged in League cricket. His outstanding year was 1948 when he performed the 'double' with 1,399 runs (av 31.79) and 121 wickets (av 18.13).

Bailey, Keith Richard
Cricketer. *b:* 21.2.1964, Dublin, Ireland. Lower order right-hand batsman, wicket-keeper. *Team* Ireland (1991).
Career batting
1 match, did not bat–*ct* 1–*st* 1

Bailey, Michael John
Cricketer. *b:* 1.8.1954, Cheltenham, Gloucestershire. Lower order left-hand batsman, off break bowler. *Team* Hampshire (1979–82, 20 matches).
Career batting
20–29–9–228–24–11.40–0–*ct* 8
Bowling 996–18–55.33–1–0–5/89

He also played for Wiltshire (1983–84) and Herefordshire (1992).

Bailey, Raymond Reginald
Cricketer. *b:* 16.5.1944, Bedford. Lower order right-hand batsman, right-arm fast medium bowler. *Team* Northamptonshire (1964–73, 48 matches).
Career batting
49–48–21–253–25–9.37–0–*ct* 27
Bowling 2906–108–26.90–5–0–5/25

He also played for Bedfordshire (1963) and Buckinghamshire (1975–80). He played soccer for Bedford Town, Gillingham and Northampton Town as centre half.

Bailey, Robert John
Cricketer. *b:* 28.10.1963, Biddulph, Staffordshire. Middle order right-hand batsman, off break bowler. *Team* Northamptonshire (1982–92, 222 matches). *Tours* England to Sharjah (not first-class) 1984/5, to India 1988/9 (tour cancelled), to West Indies 1989/90; Northamptonshire to South Africa 1991/2. *Tests* England (1988 to 1989/90, 4 matches).
Career batting
233–390–60–13725–224*–41.59–29–*ct* 166
Bowling 2361–55–42.92–0–0–3/27
Test batting
4–8–0–119–43–14.87–0–*ct* 0

He hit 1,000 runs in a season nine times (best 1,987, av 64.09, in 1990). His highest score was 224* for Northamptonshire v Glamorgan at Swansea in 1986. He also played for Staffordshire (1980).

Bailey, Ronald Anthony
Amateur. *b:* 30.7.1923, Camberwell, London. *d:* 28.9.1990, Sissinghurst, Kent. Tail end right-hand batsman, right-arm medium pace bowler. *Team* Kent (1948, 3 matches).
Career batting
3–5–1–0–0*–0.00–0–*ct* 0
Bowling 250–2–125.00–0–0–1/76

Bailey, Trevor Edward
Amateur. *b:* 3.12.1923, Westcliff-on-Sea, Essex. Tenacious middle order right-hand bat, right-arm fast-medium bowler, brilliant close field. *Sch* Dulwich. *Teams* Essex (1946–67, 482 matches); Prime Minister's XI in India (1963/64); Cambridge U (1947–48, blue both years). *Tours* MCC to Australia and New Zealand 1950/1, 1954/5, to West Indies 1953/4, to South Africa 1956/7, to Australia 1958/9; Cavaliers to West Indies 1963/4, 1964/5. *Tests* England (1949 to 1958/9, 61 matches).
Career batting
682–1072–215–28641–205–33.42–28–*ct* 427
Bowling 48170–2082–23.13–110–13–10/90
Test batting
61–91–14–2290–134*–29.74–1–*ct* 32
Bowling 3856–132–29.21–5–1–7/34

The best English all-round cricketer of the 1950s, Bailey became famous for his defensive batting against the Australians, particularly in the 1953 and 1954/5 series when he time and again saved England from collapse. His great innings at Lord's v Australia in 1953 went a long way towards bringing back the Ashes to England for the first time since the war. In the record books his two most dogged innings were: 68 in 458 minutes v Australia at Brisbane in 1958/9 and 8 in 120 minutes v South Africa at Headingley in 1955. He opened the England bowling for several series with A. V. Bedser and on the latter's retirement from Tests, Bailey continued as the main back-up bowler to Statham and Tyson. He hit 1,000 runs 17 times, going on to 2,000 once (2,011, av 46.76, in

1959) and took 100 wickets 9 times (best 133, av 21.01, in 1961). In County cricket he was Essex's leading bowler and his batting was much more attractive than in the Test arena. Achieving the 'double' on eight occasions, he performed the feat of 2,000 runs and 100 wkts in 1959, the only post-war cricketer to attain this milestone. His highest innings was 205 for Essex v Sussex at Eastbourne in 1947 and his best bowling 10/90 for Essex v Lancashire at Clacton in 1949. From 1961 to 1966 he captained the County and from 1955 to 1967 was the County Secretary. His first-class debut was for Under-33s in 1945.

A talented soccer player, Bailey won his blue at Cambridge and went on to obtain an FA Amateur Cup medal with Walthamstow in 1951/2. He is the author of several books and other publications on cricket and is well-known as a sports commentator.

Bailey, W. P.
Amateur. Opening batsman. *Team* Hampshire (1864, 1 match).
Career batting
1–2–0–14–10–7.00–0–*ct* 0

Bailey, William Henry
Professional. *b:* 2.10.1870, Melton Mowbray, Leicestershire. *d:* 19.10.1930, Melton Mowbray, Leicestershire. Hard hitting right-hand batsman. *Team* Leicestershire (1896, 2 matches).
Career batting
2–4–0–49–15–12.25–0–*ct* 1
He first played for Leicestershire (pre first-class) in 1891.

Baillie, William Hunter
Amateur. *b:* 12.11.1838, Duntisbourne House, Cheltenham, Gloucestershire. *d:* 17.3.1895, Paddington, London. Middle order batsman. *Sch* Eton. *Team* Gloucestershire (1870, 1 match).
Career batting
1–1–0–7–7–7.00–0–*ct* 1

Baily, Cyril Alexander Highett
Amateur. *b:* 17.7.1880, Beckery House, Glastonbury, Somerset. *d:* 21.9.1924, Burnham-on-Sea, Somerset. Lower order right-hand batsman. *Team* Somerset (1902, 1 match).
Career batting
1–2–1–8–4*–8.00–0–*ct* 2

Baily, Edward Peter
Amateur. *b:* 18.1.1852, St John's Wood, London. *d:* 21.1.1941, Tupsley, Hereford. Father of R. E. H. (Surrey). Middle order right-hand batsman, wicket-keeper. *Sch* Harrow. *Teams* Cambridge U (1872–74, blue 1872 and 1874); Middlesex (1872, 1 match).
Career batting
10–17–3–172–26–12.28–0–*ct* 15–*st* 2
He also played for Somerset (pre first-class) in 1880.

Baily, Henry Paul
Amateur. *b:* 3.9.1868, Philadelphia, USA. Lower order right-hand batsman, off break bowler. *Sch* Haverford College. *Team* Philadelphia (1890–1903). *Tour* Philadelphia to England 1897.
Career batting
28–45–7–392–40–10.31–0–*ct* 24
Bowling 2019–99–20.39–4–1–7/65
He also visited England with the non-first-class side in 1889 and was most successful on that visit. He appeared 3 times for United States v Canada 1890, 1892 and 1894.
He was always cheerful and nothing could change his tranquil manner.

Baily, Robert Edward Hartwell
Amateur. *b:* 6.6.1885, Limpsfield, Surrey. *d:* 19.9.1973, Hereford. Son of E. P. (Middlesex). Opening or middle order right-hand batsman, wicket-keeper. *Sch* Harrow. *Teams* Surrey (1904–06, 5 matches); Cambridge U (1905–08, blue 1908).
Career batting
28–51–2–825–61–16.83–0–*ct* 37–*st* 12
His cricket career was short as he was in the Sudan political service 1909–32.

Bainbridge, Alfred Brian
Cricketer. *b:* 15.10.1932, Middlesbrough, Yorkshire. Lower order right-hand batsman, useful off break bowler. *Team* Yorkshire (1961–63, 5 matches).
Career batting
5–10–0–93–24–9.30–0–*ct* 3
Bowling 358–20–17.90–2–1–6/53
In his second match for Yorkshire (v Essex at Harrogate, 1961) he took 12 for 111.

Bainbridge, Herbert William
Amateur. *b:* 29.10.1862, Ghowhatti, Assam, India. *d:* 3.3.1940, Leamington Spa, Warwickshire. Opening right-hand batsman, slow round-arm, later changed to fast, good field. *Sch* Eton. *Teams* Surrey (1883–85, 11 matches); Cambridge U (1884–86, blue all three years); Warwickshire (1894–1902, 118 matches). *Tour* Sanders to North America 1886.
Career batting
177–288–21–6878–162–25.76–7–*ct* 101
Bowling 988–31–31.87–0–0–3/21
He first appeared for Warwickshire (pre first-class) in 1886, but was unqualified and an objection by Leicestershire was upheld by MCC. From 1888 to 1902 he captained Warwickshire and in 1903 he was appointed Hon Secretary of the County Club, remaining in the position until his death and he was also Chairman 1931–39. He was a Test selector in 1899 and 1902. He scored 1,000 runs in a season twice (best 1,162, av 34.17, in 1895).

Bainbridge, Rear-Admiral John Hugh
Amateur. *b:* 31.5.1845, Frankfield, Douglas, Co Cork, Ireland. *d:* 10.8.1901, on board yacht *Vanadis*

off Bergen, Norway. Middle order batsman. *Team* MCC (1882).
Career batting
1–2–0–0–0–0.00–0 *ct* 0

Bainbridge, Philip
Cricketer. *b:* 16.4.1958, Sneyd Green, Stoke-on-Trent, Staffordshire. Cousin of S. G. Wilkinson (Somerset). Middle order right-hand batsman, right-arm medium pace bowler, good field. *Teams* Gloucestershire (1977–90, 255 matches); Durham (1992, 17 matches). *Tours* English Counties to Zimbabwe 1984/5; Gloucestershire to Sri Lanka 1986/7.
Career batting
274–454–69–13276–169–34.48–22–*ct* 118
Bowling 10554–287–36.77–8–0–8/53

He hit 1,000 runs in a season eight times (best 1,644, av 56.68, in 1985). He first played for Durham (pre first-class) in 1991.

Baines, Francis Edmund
Amateur. *b:* 18.6.1864, Ecclesall, Sheffield, Yorkshire. *d:* 17.11.1948, Worksop, Nottinghamshire. Lower order batsman, right-arm medium fast bowler. *Team* Yorkshire (1888, 1 match).
Career batting
1–1–0–0–0–0.00–0–*ct* 0

Baines, Matthew Talbot
Amateur *b:* 19.9.1863, East Molesey, Surrey. *d:* 6.5.1925, Beckley, Sussex. Uncle of M. F. T. (Army) and T. W. T. (Cambridge U). Middle order right-hand batsman, fast bowler, brilliant field at point. *Sch* Harrow. *Team* Cambridge U (1883).
Career batting
8–14–1–109–29–8.38–0–*ct* 1

Baines played two of the best innings ever seen in a Freshmen's match – 104 and 48* – in 1883, both innings made without a chance, but he did little in other matches for Cambridge. His final first-class match was for MCC in 1890.

Baines, Michael Fitzroy Talbot
Amateur. *b:* 3.9.1898, Kasauli, India. *d:* 9.3.1990, South Newton, Salisbury, Wiltshire. Cousin of T. W. T. (Cambridge U), nephew of M. T. (Cambridge U). Tail end batsman, right-arm medium fast bowler. *Sch* Cheltenham. *Team* Army (1926).
Career batting
1–2–1–0–0*–0.00–0–*ct* 0
Bowling 39–0

Baines, Threlfall Werge Talbot
Amateur. *b:* 20.6.1908, Johannesburg, South Africa. Cousin of M. F. T. (Army), nephew of M. T. (Cambridge U). Opening right-hand batsman, leg break bowler. *Teams* Cambridge U (1930); Eastern Province (1925/6 to 1926/7); Transvaal (1931/2 to 1936/7).
Career batting
20–33–1–1045–96–32.65–0–*ct* 18
Bowling 453–2–226.50–0–0–1/8

Bairamian, Robert
Amateur. *b:* 18.3.1935, Nicosia, Cyprus. Middle order right-hand batsman, off break bowler. *Sch* Dover College. *Team* Cambridge U (1957).
Career batting
2–3–1–45–24–22.50–0–*ct* 1
Bowling 6–1–6.00–0–0–1/6

Baird, Henry Hume Chisholm
Amateur. *b:* 13.4.1878, Haverfordwest, Pembrokeshire. *d:* 22.2.1950, Sandwich, Kent. Hard hitting middle order right-hand batsman. *Sch* Cheltenham. *Teams* MCC (1910); Army (1912–13). *Tour* MCC to South America 1911/12.
Career batting
9–16–0–308–81–19.25–0–*ct* 10
Bowling 451–31–14.54–2–0–5/43

He hit 111* in 130 minutes for the Army v Navy at Lord's in 1910 (non-first-class).

Bairstow, Arthur
Professional. *b:* 14.8.1868, Great Horton, Bradford, Yorkshire. *d:* 7.12.1945, Bucklow Hill, Cheshire. Tail end right-hand batsman, wicket-keeper. *Team* Yorkshire (1896–1900, 24 matches).
Career batting
26–26–12–79–12–5.64–0–*ct* 41–*st* 18

His final first-class match was for an England XI v Australians in 1902.

Bairstow, David Leslie
Cricketer. *b:* 1.9.1951, Horton, Bradford, Yorkshire. Hard hitting middle or lower order right-hand batsman, wicket-keeper, right-arm medium pace bowler. *Teams* Yorkshire (1970–90, 429 matches); Griqualand West (1976/7 to 1977/8). *Tours* England to Australia 1978/9 (not first-class), 1979/80, to West Indies 1980/1; Yorkshire to Windward Islands 1986/7. *Tests* England (1979 to 1980/1, 4 matches).
Career batting
459–647–119–13961–145–26.44–10–*ct* 961–*st* 138
Bowling 308–9–34.22–0–0–3/25
Test batting
4–7–1–125–59–20.83–0–*ct* 12–*st* 1

In the match between Yorkshire and Derbyshire at Scarborough in 1981 he caught out 11 batsmen, equalling the world first-class record. He hit 1,000 runs in a season three times (best 1,181, av 47.24, in 1985). From 1984 to 1986 he captained Yorkshire. His last first-class match was for Rest of World in the 1990 Scarborough Festival. He played soccer for Bradford City.

Baiss, James Archibald
Amateur. *b:* 27.5.1909, Kensington, London. *d:* 17.11.1984, Tresithick, St Erme, Cornwall. Son of

R. S. H. (Kent). Sound opening right-hand batsman, leg break bowler. *Sch* Tonbridge. *Team* Oxford U (1929).
Career batting
3–5–0–59–19–11.80–0–*ct* 4
His final first-class match was for Free Foresters in 1937.

Baiss, Reginald Sydney Habershon
Amateur. *b:* 6.3.1873, Belvedere, Kent. *d:* 2.5.1955, Mount Ephraim, Tunbridge Wells, Kent. Father of J. A. (Oxford U). Middle order right-hand batsman with strong defence, wicket-keeper. *Sch* Tonbridge. *Teams* Oxford U (1895); Kent (1895–1901, 7 matches).
Career batting
10–19–4–379–52*–25.26–0–*ct* 7
He also played rugby for Oxford U.

Baitup, Frederick Henry
Professional. *b:* 9.1.1896, Tunbridge Wells, Kent. *d:* 3.2.1991, Whipps Cross, Leytonstone, Essex. Tail end batsman, change bowler. *Team* Somerset (1924, 1 match).
Career batting
1–1–0–11–11–11.00–0–*ct* 1
Bowling 8–0
At the time of his death he was the oldest living County cricketer.

Bajana, Manek Pallon
Amateur. *b:* 14.9.1886, India. *d:* 28.4.1927, Bethnal Green, London. Opening right-hand batsman, change bowler. *Team* Somerset (1912–20, 51 matches). *Tour* India to England 1911.
Career batting
55–96–1–1975–115–20.78–3–*ct* 36
Bowling 132–4–33.00–0–0–2/14
He never appeared in first-class cricket in India.

Baker, Albert
Professional. *b:* 28.11.1872, Hale, Farnham, Surrey. *d:* 17.4.1948, Hale Common, Upper Hale, Farnham, Surrey. Sound defensive middle order right-hand batsman. *Teams* Surrey (1900–07, 104 matches); Ireland (1912).
Career batting
108–168–18–3863–155*–25.75–5–*ct* 40
Bowling 116–2–58.00–0–0–1/3
Easily his best season was 1905 when he hit 1,257 runs (av 31.42). After his County career, Baker was engaged in Ireland by S. H. Cochrane at Bray.

Baker, Air Marshal Sir Brian Edmund
Amateur. *b:* 31.8.1896, Hertford. *d:* 8.10.1979, Nocton Hall, Lincolnshire. Middle order right-hand batsman. *Sch* Haileybury. *Team* RAF (1927–32).
Career batting
8–13–1–303–66–25.25–0–*ct* 5
His County cricket was for Hertfordshire (1914).

Baker, Charles Shaw
Professional. *b:* 5.1.1883, Moss Side, Manchester, Lancashire. *d:* 16.12.1976, Lelant, Cornwall. Sound middle order left-hand batsman, leg break and googly bowler. *Sch* Hulme GS. *Team* Warwickshire (1905–20, 214 matches).
Career batting
214–355–42–9244–155*–29.53–10–*ct* 98
Bowling 1017–22–46.22–0–0–4/59
He hit 1,000 runs in a season on three occasions (best 1,242, av 33.56, in 1913). After leaving Warwickshire he appeared for Cornwall (1925–30) as an amateur with considerable success. He also became a well-known cartoonist and worked for some time on the *Daily Express*. He played soccer for Aston Villa.

Baker, Clare Valentine
Amateur. *b:* 23.11.1885, Marylebone, London. *d:* 7.12.1947, Broome, Buckland, Betchworth, Surrey. Middle order right-hand batsman. *Sch* Harrow. *Team* Middlesex (1906–12, 31 matches).
Career batting
38–58–5–726–53–13.69–0–*ct* 19

Baker, Cyril
Amateur. *b:* 22.11.1885, Northampton. *d:* 8.10.1949, Northampton. Lower order right-hand batsman, right-arm medium pace bowler. *Team* Northamptonshire (1906–22, 4 matches).
Career batting
4–8–1–17–7–2.42–0–*ct* 2
Bowling 198–11–18.00–0–0–3/38
Baker's career in first-class County cricket was unusual in that he played in three matches at the beginning of the 1906 season for Northamptonshire and headed the season's bowling averages, then reappeared once only – in 1922.

Baker, David William
Cricketer. *b:* 26.7.1935, Hull, Yorkshire. Lower order right-hand batsman, leg break and googly bowler. *Teams* Kent (1961–63, 27 matches); Nottinghamshire (1964–65, 7 matches).
Career batting
34–37–13–101–15–4.20–0–*ct* 11
Bowling 2856–78–36.61–3–0–5/47

Baker, Edward
Professional. *b:* 9.2.1846, Plaxtol, Kent. *d:* 30.6.1913, Maidenhead, Berkshire. Tail end batsman, right-arm medium pace bowler. *Team* Kent (1875, 1 match).
Career batting
1–2–0–0–0–0.00–0–*ct* 0
Bowling 19–1–19.00–0–0–1/19

Baker, Edward Conrad
Amateur. *b:* 7.1.1892, Carmarthen. *d:* 8.4.1969, Maidenhead, Berkshire. Lower order right-hand batsman, right-arm fast medium bowler. *Sch* Brighton. *Teams* Cambridge U (1912–14, blue 1912 and 1914);

Baker, Edward Stanley

Sussex (1912–19, 8 matches); Somerset (1921, 1 match).
Career batting
25–43–14–334–63*–11.51–0–*ct* 5
Bowling 1815–69–26.30–2–0–5/18

Baker, Edward Stanley
Amateur. *b:* 9.11.1910, Moseley, Birmingham. *d:* 15.3.1992, Great Dunmow, Essex. Tail end right-hand batsman, wicket-keeper. *Sch* KES, Birmingham. *Team* Worcestershire (1933–34, 32 matches).
Career batting
32–44–19–160–21*–6.40–0–*ct* 35–*st* 5

Baker, Francis
Amateur. *b:* 5.12.1847, Cirencester, Gloucestershire. *d:* 15.4.1901. Fine free left-hand batsman, occasional right-arm medium pace bowler (or left-arm slow bowler in another report). *Sch* Cheltenham. *Team* Gloucestershire (1875, 1 match).
Career batting
8–15–2–199–53–15.30–0–*ct* 4

He made his first-class debut for Gentlemen of the South in 1866 when he still had a further year at Cheltenham.

Baker, Frank Adam Conyers
Amateur. *b:* 6.12.1889, Lismacue, Bansha, Co Tipperary, Ireland. *d:* 17.3.1961, Witley, Surrey. Middle order batsman. *Team* Royal Navy (1920).
Career batting
1–2–0–34–28–17.00–0–*ct* 0

Baker, George Dashwood
Amateur. *b:* 4.3.1849, Compton-Martin, Somerset. *d:* 21.12.1879, Ayot St Lawrence, Hertfordshire. Middle order right-hand batsman, occasional right-arm fast bowler. *Sch* Rugby. *Team* Middlesex (1872, 1 match).
Career batting
1–2–0–5–5–2.50–0–*ct* 2

He also played for Hertfordshire (1870–72).

Baker, George Robert
Professional. *b:* 18.4.1862, Malton, Yorkshire. *d:* 6.2.1938, Wing, Buckinghamshire. Sound right-hand batsman, useful right-arm medium pace bowler, good field. *Teams* Yorkshire (1884, 7 matches); Lancashire (1887–99, 228 matches).
Career batting
249–382–30–7563–186–21.48–4–*ct* 153
Bowling 3616–145–24.93–6–0–6/18

His best season was 1897 when he hit 1,444 runs (av 32.81). In all he hit 1,000 runs in three seasons, but his form was very variable and he went through long periods when he was unable to build a good innings. He was coach at Harrow for 12 years after leaving County cricket.

Baker, Harold Frank
Amateur. *b:* 4.5.1884, Walsall, Staffordshire. *d:* 5.5.1954, West Hagley, Worcestershire. Lower order right-hand batsman, slow left-arm bowler. *Team* Worcestershire (1911, 2 matches).
Career batting
2–4–1–21–8*–7.00–0–*ct* 1
Bowling 66–0

Baker, Herbert Zouch
Amateur. *b:* 7.2.1880, Beckenham, Kent. *d:* 26.8.1958, Orpington, Kent. Brother of P. C. (Kent). Middle order right-hand batsman. *Sch* Wellington. *Team* Kent (1903 (USA)–04, 11 matches). *Tour* Kent to North America 1903.
Career batting
12–18–0–211–82–11.72–0–*ct* 5
Bowling 108–5–21.60–0–0–2/68

His final first-class match was for J. R. Mason's XI in 1913.

Baker, Hugh Thomas
Amateur. *b:* 19.7.1906, Midleton, Co Cork, Ireland. *d:* 1989, Harare, Zimbabwe. Lower order right-hand batsman. *Team* Dublin University (1926).
Career batting
1–2–1–2–2–2.00–0–*ct* 0

Baker, John
Amateur. *b:* 18.5.1933, Weston-super-Mare, Somerset. Middle order right-hand batsman, right-arm medium pace bowler. *Sch* Taunton. *Teams* Somerset (1952–54, 9 matches); Oxford U (1955).
Career batting
15–24–6–338–91*–18.77–0–*ct* 4
Bowling 424–9–47.11–0–0–2/26

His last appearance in first-class cricket was for Combined Services in 1956. He also played for Dorset (1960–71).

Baker, Dr Leslie George
Amateur. *b:* 19.5.1904, High Wycombe, Buckinghamshire. *d:* 9.8.1976, High Wycombe, Buckinghamshire. Opening right-hand batsman. *Sch* Bedford. *Team* Minor Counties (1939).
Career batting
1–1–0–6–6–6.00–0–*ct* 1

His County cricket was for Buckinghamshire (1924–47).

Baker, Nigel Ernest Westby
Amateur. *b:* 9.1.1914, Westminster, London. *d:* 10.3.1968, Balcombe, Sussex. Tail end right-hand batsman, fast bowler. *Sch* Eton. *Team* Cambridge U (1934–35).
Career batting
3–3–2–19–10*–19.00–0–*ct* 3
Bowling 190–11–17.27–0–0–4/22

His County cricket was for Berkshire (1934).

Baker, Percy Charles
Amateur. *b:* 2.5.1874, Bromley, Kent. *d:* 30.12.1939, Northwood, Middlesex. Brother of H. Z. (Kent). Fast scoring middle order right-hand batsman. *Sch* Uppingham. *Team* Kent (1900–02, 41 matches).
Career batting
41–67–2–1600–130–24.61–2–*ct* 14
Though Baker failed to get into the Eleven at either Uppingham or Oxford, he batted so well for Beckenham that he obtained a place in the Kent side of 1900. His highest innings was 130 v Nottinghamshire at Trent Bridge in 1900, but in the same year he also hit an excellent 89 v Yorkshire at Headingley.

Baker, Raymond Paul
Cricketer. *b:* 9.4.1954, Carshalton, Surrey. Lower order right-hand batsman, right-arm medium pace bowler. *Team* Surrey (1973–78, 54 matches).
Career batting
54–56–30–563–91–21.65–0–*ct* 24
Bowling 2942–104–28.28–1–0–6/29
In 1977 he headed the season's batting averages – but with only three completed innings.

Baker, Richard Kenneth
Cricketer. *b:* 28.4.1952, Gidea Park, Essex. Middle order right-hand batsman, wicket-keeper. *Sch* Brentwood. *Teams* Essex (1972, 1 match); Cambridge U (1973–74, blue both years).
Career batting
20–34–3–505–59*–16.29–0–*ct* 24–*st* 1
He also won a soccer blue.

Baker, Robert
Amateur. *b:* 3.7.1849, Hunmanby, Yorkshire. *d:* 21.6.1896, Scarborough, Yorkshire. Lower order right-hand batsman, right-arm fast medium bowler, slip field. *Team* Yorkshire (1874–75, 3 matches).
Career batting
3–5–1–45–22–11.25–0–*ct* 3
Bowling 43–0
He was for about 25 years the leading light in Scarborough cricket and organised the annual Festival. In a minor match, but involving good class batsmen, he once took 5 wickets with 5 balls for Scarborough.

Baker, W.
Amateur. Lower order batsman, change bowler. *Team* Worcestershire (1920, 2 matches).
Career batting
2–4–0–24–7–6.00–0–*ct* 1
Bowling 38–1–38.00–0–0–1/38

Baker, William Beresford
Amateur. *b:* 31.10.1849. *d:* 20.2.1933, Buckland, Dover, Kent. Middle order right-hand batsman. *Team* MCC (1895).
Career batting
1–2–0–33–30–16.50–0–*ct* 0
His County cricket was for Hertfordshire (1881–84).

Baker, William De Chair
Amateur. *b:* 21.4.1823, Canterbury, Kent. *d:* 20.2.1888, St Stephen's, Canterbury, Kent. Brother-in-law of J. F. Fagge (Kent). Stylish middle order right-hand batsman. *Teams* Kent (1841–53, 14 matches); Cambridge U (1843).
Career batting
22–41–6–312–29*–8.91–0–*ct* 9
The Beverley Ground at Canterbury was on the Baker family estate and he was for many years the Secretary of the Canterbury Cricket Week. He was also Hon Secretary to Kent CCC from 1870 to 1875. In 1887 he was presented with a Testimonial to the value of about £200 for his services to Kent cricket.

Bakewell, Alfred Harry
Professional. *b:* 2.11.1908, Walsall, Staffordshire. *d:* 23.1.1983, Westbourne, Dorset. Opening right-hand batsman, useful change bowler, brilliant short-leg. *Team* Northamptonshire (1928–36, 227 matches). *Tour* MCC to India and Ceylon 1933/4. *Tests* England (1931–35, 6 matches).
Career batting
250–453–24–14570–257–33.96–31–*ct* 225
Bowling 1271–22–57.77–0–0–2/17
Test batting
6–9–0–409–107–45.44–1–*ct* 3
Bowling 8–0
Coming into the Northamptonshire team midway through the 1928 season, Bakewell was an immediate success, and from 1929 to 1936 exceeded 1,000 runs each season: 2,149 (av 46.71) in 1933 being his best. He also scored two double centuries in 1933, including 257 v Glamorgan at Swansea, the highest innings till then ever made for Northamptonshire. His career was brought to a sudden end due to a motor accident at the end of the 1936 season – his right arm being badly injured.

Bakker, Paul-Jan
Cricketer. *b:* 19.8.1957, Vlaardingen, Netherlands. Lower order right-hand batsman, right-arm medium fast bowler. *Team* Hampshire (1986–92, 69 matches).
Career batting
69–54–19–333–22–9.51–0–*ct* 9
Bowling 5406–193–28.01–7–0–7/31
He played for Netherlands in the 1986 and 1990 ICC Trophy competitions.

Balaskas, Xenophon Constantine
Amateur. *b:* 15.10.1910, Kimberley, South Africa. Useful middle order right-hand batsman, leg break and googly bowler. *Teams* Griqualand West (1926/7 to 1932/3); Border (1933/4); Western Province (1934/5 to 1935/6); Transvaal (1936/7 to 1946/7); North East Transvaal (1938/9). *Tours* South Africa to Australia and New Zealand 1931/2, to England 1935.

Tests South Africa (1930/1 to 1938/9, 9 matches).
Career batting
75–107–13–2696–206–28.68–6–*ct* 47
Bowling 6656–276–24.11–20–9–8/60
Test batting
9–13–1–174–122*–14.50–1–*ct* 5
Bowling 806–22–36.63–1–0–5/49

Owing to an elbow injury, he missed many matches on his single visit to England, but when fit he was most effective. His highest score was 206 for Griqualand West v Rhodesia at Kimberley in 1929/30.

Balderstone, John Christopher
Professional. *b:* 16.11.1940, Longwood, Huddersfield, Yorkshire. Opening or middle order right-hand batsman, slow left-arm bowler, gully field. *Teams* Yorkshire (1961–69, 68 matches); Leicestershire (1971–86, 319 matches). *Tour* Leicestershire to Zimbabwe 1980/1. *Tests* England (1976, 2 matches).
Career batting
390–619–61–19034–181*–34.11–32–*ct* 210
Bowling 8160–310–26.32–5–0–6/25
Test batting
2–4–0–39–35–9.75–0–*ct* 1
Bowling 80–1–80.00–0–0–1/80

He hit 1,000 runs in a season eleven times (best 1,482, av 39.00, in 1982). A good soccer player, he appeared for Huddersfield Town, Carlisle United, Doncaster Rovers and Queen of the South. He became a first-class umpire in 1988. On September 15 1975 he played Championship cricket for Leicestershire until 6.30 and then appeared in League soccer for Doncaster Rovers at 7.30 the same evening.

Baldock, William Frederick
Amateur. *b:* 1.8.1900, Wellington, Somerset. *d:* 30.12.1941, Jabor Valley, Trengganu, Malaya. He was taken prisoner and then shot by the Japanese. Son of W. S. (Hampshire), grandson of William (Gentlemen of Kent), son-in-law of J. Daniell (Somerset). Middle order right-hand batsman. *Sch* Winchester. *Team* Somerset (1920–36, 10 matches).
Career batting
10–16–2–238–63*–17.00–0–*ct* 2

Baldock, William Stanford
Amateur. *b:* 20.1.1847, Chilworth Common, Hampshire. *d:* 30.8.1923, Wellington, Somerset. Son of William (Gentlemen of Kent), father of W. F. (Somerset). Middle order batsman, change bowler. *Sch* Winchester. *Team* Hampshire (1877–82, 7 matches).
Career batting
7–13–1–155–40–12.91–0–*ct* 4
Bowling 48–2–24.00–0–0–1/10

He played in 1878 as W. Stanford.

Baldry, Dennis Oliver
Professional. *b:* 26.12.1931, Acton, Middlesex. Middle order right-hand batsman, useful off-break bowler. *Teams* Middlesex (1953–58, 49 matches); Hampshire (1959–62, 85 matches).
Career batting
139–242–19–4661–151–20.90–3–*ct* 63
Bowling 3076–83–37.06–1–0–7/76

After six seasons with Middlesex without achieving a great deal, Baldry hit 151 for Hampshire on his debut (v Glamorgan at Portsmouth in 1959) and later in the same season took 7/76 v Lancashire at Old Trafford. This initial success with his adopted county however did not develop into an extended first-class career and he dropped out of first-class county cricket in 1962. His best season was in 1959 with 1,715 runs, av 29.06.

Baldwin, Charles
Professional. *b:* 29.12.1864, Bury St Edmunds, Suffolk. *d:* 2.5.1947, Tylers Green, Penn, Buckinghamshire. Son of Thomas (pro for Suffolk in 1860s). Sound middle order right-hand batsman, occasional medium pace bowler, good field at point. *Team* Surrey (1892–98, 80 matches).
Career batting
80–126–12–2757–234–24.18–3–*ct* 55
Bowling 87–0

His best year was 1897 when he scored 1,211 runs (av 30.27) including an innings of 234 for Surrey v Kent at the Oval – easily the highest score of his career. After leaving Surrey he appeared in the ranks of his native county in 1904.

Baldwin, George Frederick
Professional. *b:* 3.4.1878, Northampton. *d:* 15.5.1970, Burton-on-Trent, Staffordshire. Lower order batsman, useful bowler. *Team* Northamptonshire (1906, 1 match).
Career batting
1–1–0–6–6–6.00–0–*ct* 0
Bowling 18–0

Baldwin, Harry
Professional. *b:* 27.11.1860, Wokingham, Berkshire. *d:* 12.1.1935, Aldershot, Hampshire. Father of H. G. (Surrey). Hard-hitting lower order right-hand batsman, off break bowler. *Team* Hampshire (1877–1905, 150 matches).
Career batting
151–241–66–1873–55*–10.70–0–*ct* 54
Bowling 14383–580–24.79–41–6–8/74

Unfortunately the best ten years of his career occurred whilst Hampshire were not ranked as first-class. His best first-class season was 1895 when he took 114 wickets (av 15.80). He was the first Hampshire professional to be granted a benefit. He was a first-class umpire (1907–09).

Baldwin, Herbert George
Professional. *b:* 16.3.1893, Hartley Wintney, Hampshire *d:* 7.3.1969, Hartley Wintney, Hampshire. Son of Harry (Hampshire). Middle order right-hand batsman, leg break bowler, brilliant field at cover-point.

Team Surrey (1922–30, 32 matches).
Career batting
32–46–8–509–63*–13.39–0–*ct* 10
Bowling 321–3–107.00–0–0–2/83

After his playing career, Baldwin became a noted umpire (1932–60), standing in nine Tests (1946–53). He caused a sensation in 1938, when, in the opening match of the Australian tour, he no-balled McCormick 19 times in three overs.

Bale, Ernest William
Professional. *b:* 18.9.1878, Mitcham, Surrey. *d:* 6.7.1952, Carshalton, Surrey. Lower order right-hand batsman, wicket-keeper. *Teams* Surrey (1904, 1 match); Worcestershire (1908–20, 138 matches); London County (1904).
Career batting
148–233–86–1222–43–8.31–*ct* 252–*st* 90
Bowling 230–9–25.55–0–0–3/46

Bale, Frank
Professional. *b:* 7.1.1891, Leicester. *d:* 16.1.1969, Leicester. Lower order left-hand batsman, slow medium left-arm bowler, slip field. *Team* Leicestershire (1920–28, 134 matches).
Career batting
134–202–53–1426–52–9.57–0–*ct* 62
Bowling 6431–231–27.83–3–0–5/62

A most promising all-rounder, Bale never really realised his full potential.

Balfour, Edward
Amateur. *b:* 2.1.1833, Marylebone, London. *d:* 11.8.1856, Genoa, Italy. Brother of Archibald (MCC 1862) and R. D. (Cambridge U). Stylish middle order right-hand batsman, slow round-arm bowler. *Sch* Westminster. *Team* Oxford U (1852–54, blue all three years).
Career batting
28–50–4–586–62–12.73–0–*ct* 13–*st* 2
Bowling 20–2 + 42–10.00–3–1–5/?

Balfour, Leslie Melville
(changed name to Balfour-Melville in 1893)
Amateur. *b:* 9.3.1854, Bonnington, Edinburgh, Scotland. *d:* 16.7.1937, Westgate, North Berwick, Scotland. Father of J. E. (Scotland). Excellent opening right-hand batsman, wicket-keeper. *Sch* Edinburgh Academy. *Teams* I Zingari (1888); MCC (1892); Scotland (1909–10).
Career batting
4–7–0–121–91–17.28–0–*ct* 6–*st* 1

Known as 'The W. G. Grace of Scotland', no Scottish representative eleven was complete without him for about 40 years (1874–1914). He captained Scotland in their first 'official' match with Ireland in 1909. Aside from cricket he excelled at golf, winning the Amateur Championship in 1895; he won the Scottish Lawn Tennis Championship, also the billiards title, and represented Scotland at rugby.

Balfour, Robert Drummond
Amateur. *b:* 1.3.1844, Putney, Surrey. *d:* 7.5.1915, Sherrards, Welwyn, Hertfordshire. Brother of Archibald (MCC 1862) and Edward (Oxford U). Steady middle order right-hand batsman, wicket-keeper. *Sch* Westminster and Bradfield. *Team* Cambridge U (1863–66, blue all four years).
Career batting
32–59–4–685–82–12.45–0–*ct* 22–*st* 11

He played for I Zingari and MCC, playing his final first-class match for MCC in 1873.

He won a blue for royal tennis.

Balfour-Melville, James Elliot
(changed name from Balfour in 1893)
Amateur. *b:* 9.7.1882, Edinburgh, Scotland. *d:* 25.9.1915, Loos, France. Son of L. M. (Scotland). Lower order right-hand batsman, wicket-keeper. *Sch* Malvern. *Team* Scotland (1913).
Career batting
2–4–0–46–32–11.50–0–*ct* 1

He was at Oxford, but did not play in any first-class matches whilst there. He won a soccer blue.

Ball, Edgar Cedric
Amateur. *b:* 11.1.1892, Richmond, Surrey. *d:* 15.5.1969, Vancouver, British Columbia, Canada. Son of E. W. (Gloucestershire). Middle order left-hand batsman, occasional left-arm bowler. *Sch* Clifton. *Team* Somerset (1914, 3 matches).
Career batting
3–6–0–35–20–5.83–0–*ct* 0

He also played for Devon (1909–12).

Ball, Edward William
Amateur. *b:* 10.2.1859, Clifton, Bristol. *d:* 31.7.1917, Tonbridge, Kent. Father of E. C. (Somerset). Lower order batsman. *Sch* Clifton. *Team* Gloucestershire (1880–81, 3 matches).
Career batting
3–3–0–0–0–0.00–0–*ct* 3

Ball, George Armstrong
Amateur. *b:* 27.2.1914, Barwell, Leicestershire. Middle order right-hand batsman. *Team* Leicestershire (1933–36, 11 matches).
Career batting
11–17–2–206–44*–13.73–0–*ct* 7

Ball, Kenneth John
Professional. *b:* 16.5.1889, Northampton. *d:* 16.1.1958, Eastfield, Northampton. Middle order right-hand batsman, change bowler. *Team* Northamptonshire (1921, 12 matches).
Career batting
12–22–1–178–49–8.47–0–*ct* 7
Bowling 384–13–29.53–0–0–4/52

Ball, Martyn Charles John
Cricketer. *b:* 26.4.1970, Bristol. Lower order right-hand batsman, off break bowler. *Team* Gloucester-

shire (1988–92, 32 matches).
Career batting
32–44–9–379–54–10.82–0–*ct* 23
Bowling 2449–70–34.98–2–0–5/101

Ball, Wilfred Joseph
Professional. *b:* 24.4.1895, Thrapston, Northamptonshire. *d:* 23.7.1965, Hollowell, Northamptonshire. Tail end right-hand batsman, wicket-keeper. *Team* Northamptonshire (1924–31, 4 matches).
Career batting
4–6–2–10–8–2.50–0–*ct* 2

Ballance, Tristan George Lance
Amateur. *b:* 21.4.1916, Norwich, Norfolk. *d:* 4.12.1943. He was killed in action near Naples, Italy. Lower order right-hand batsman, slow left-arm bowler. *Sch* Uppingham. *Team* Oxford U (1935–37, blue 1935 and 1937).
Career batting
23–32–12–190–63–9.50–0–*ct* 18
Bowling 1875–51–36.76–2–0–5/30

He appeared for Norfolk from 1932 to 1939 with great success.

Ballantyne, David
Amateur. *b:* 31.10.1914, Peebles, Scotland. Opening right-hand batsman. *Sch* Merchiston. *Team* Scotland (1937).
Career batting
1–2–0–11–10–5.50–0–*ct* 0

Baloo, Babaji Palwankar
Amateur. *b:* 19.3.1876, Bombay, India. *d:* 4.7.1955, Bombay, India. Father of Y. B. Palwankar (Bombay), brother of P. Shivram (Hindus), P. Ganpat (Hindus) and P. Vithal (Hindus). Useful lower order batsman, slow left-arm bowler. *Team* Hindus (1905/6 to 1920/1). *Tour* India to England 1911.
Career batting
33–58–3–753–75–13.69–0–*ct* 12
Bowling 2724–179–15.21–17–4–8/103

He was easily the best bowler of the 1911 Indians in England and in all matches on the tour took 114 wickets, av 18.86. In India he performed well for the Hindus for over ten years.

Bamber, Martin John
Cricketer. *b:* 7.1.1961, Cheam, Surrey. Middle order right-hand batsman, right-arm medium pace bowler. *Sch* Millfield. *Team* Northamptonshire (1982–84, 13 matches).
Career batting
13–26–2–638–77–26.58–0–*ct* 6
Bowling 3–0

Bancroft, Claude Keith
Amateur. *b:* 30.10.1885, Fontabelle, St Michael, Barbados. *d:* 12.1.1919, Toronto, Canada. Fair middle order right-hand batsman, wicket-keeper. *Team* Barbados (1904/5). *Tour* West Indies to England 1906.
Career batting
14–27–7–293–53–14.65–0–*ct*–14–*st* 6

He appeared in some trials for Cambridge but not in any first-class matches for the University.

Bancroft, John
Professional. *b:* 9.10.1879, Swansea, Glamorgan. *d:* 7.1.1942, Swansea, Glamorgan. Brother of W. J. (South Wales). Tail end right-hand batsman, wicket-keeper. *Team* Glamorgan (1922, 9 matches).
Career batting
9–18–3–36–5*–2.40–0–*ct* 4–*st* 3

He first played for Glamorgan (pre first-class) in 1908. He played rugby for Wales.

Bancroft, William James
Professional. *b:* 2.3.1871, Swansea, Glamorgan. *d:* 3.3.1959, Swansea, Glamorgan. Brother of John (Glamorgan). Opening right-hand batsman. *Teams* West of England (1910); South Wales (1912).
Career batting
2–4–0–38–16–9.50–0–*ct* 3

He played for Glamorgan from 1889 to 1914 and was perhaps the county's leading batsman of the non-first-class days. He was more famous on the rugby field, representing Wales on 33 successive occasions as full back – his local club was Swansea.

Banerjee, Sarobindu Nath
Amateur. *b:* 3.10.1911, Calcutta, India. *d:* 14.10.1980, Calcutta, India. Lower order right-hand batsman, right-arm fast-medium bowler. *Teams* Hindus (1935/6 to 1945/6); Bengal (1935/6 to 1936/7); Nawanagar (1937/8 to 1941/2); Bihar (1942/3 to 1957/8); Madhya Pradesh (1959/60). *Tours* India to England 1936, 1946, to Ceylon 1944/5; Indian Univ Occasionals to Ceylon 1935/6. Also Combined XI v Commonwealth in Ceylon 1950/1. *Test* India (1948/9, 1 match).
Career batting
138–209–29–3715–138–20.63–5–*ct* 74
Bowling 10274–385–26.68–15–2–8/25
Test batting
1–2–0–13–8–6.50–0–*ct* 0
Bowling 127–5–25.40–0–0–4/54

His first-class debut was for Patiala's XII in 1931/2. Although he performed well in Indian domestic cricket, he was not very successful on his two tours to England and is remembered chiefly for his 10th wicket partnership with Sarwate v Surrey at the Oval in 1946 when 249 runs were added: Banerjee hit 121.

Banes-Walker, Frederick Cecil
Amateur. *b:* 19.6.1888, North Petherton, Somerset. *d:* 9.5.1915. He was killed in action near Ypres, Belgium. Aggressive middle order right-hand batsman. *Sch* Tonbridge. *Team* Somerset (1914, 5 matches).
Career batting
5–10–1–172–40–19.11–0–*ct* 3

He played hockey for Gloucestershire.

Banfield, Arthur Ernest
Amateur. *b:* 28.1.1897, Hackney, London. *d:* 3.1.1972, Raynes Park, Surrey. Lower order batsman, useful bowler. *Team* Essex (1921, 1 match).
Career batting
1–2–1–0–0*–0.00–0–*ct* 0
Bowling 62–2–31.00–0–0–2/62

Banham, Stanley Tattersall
Professional. *b:* 21.9.1913, Bacup, Lancashire. *d:* 29.12.1984, Peterborough, Northamptonshire. Tail end right-hand batsman, wicket-keeper. *Team* Lancashire (1939, 1 match).
Career batting
1 match, did not bat–*ct* 1

Banister, Stephen Michael Alvin
Amateur. *b:* 7.10.1918, Llandegai, Caernarvon. Tail end right-hand batsman, off break bowler. *Sch* Eton. *Team* Cambridge U (1938–39).
Career batting
6–5–2–8–4*–2.66–0–*ct* 2
Bowling 350–5–70.0–0–0–2/73

Banks, David Andrew
Cricketer. *b:* 11.1.1961, Pensnett, Staffordshire. Middle order right-hand batsman, right-arm medium pace bowler. *Teams* Worcestershire (1983–85, 19 matches); Warwickshire (1988–89, 11 matches).
Career batting
30–45–7–1034–100–27.21–1–*ct* 15
Bowling 30–0

He hit 100 and 53 on his first-class debut for Worcestershire v Oxford U at Oxford in 1983. He also played for Staffordshire (1986–92).

Banks, Percy d'Aguilar
Amateur. *b:* 9.5.1885, Bath, Somerset. *d:* 26.4.1915. He was killed in action near La Bricque, Ypres, Belgium. Attractive middle order right-hand batsman. *Sch* Cheltenham. *Team* Somerset (1903–08, 7 matches).
Career batting
7–14–1–161–30–12.38–0–*ct* 1

He hit 103 for Cheltenham v Haileybury at Lord's in 1902 – an innings regarded as the best ever made by a schoolboy at Lord's. He also played with success in India and was well-known as a polo player.

Banner, George
Professional. *b:* 21.1.1864, Sutton-in-Ashfield, Nottinghamshire. *d:* 20.3.1890, Sutton-in-Ashfield, Nottinghamshire. Lower order right-hand batsman, right-arm fast bowler. *Team* Nottinghamshire (1885, 1 match).
Career batting
1–1–0–5–5–5.00–0–*ct* 0
Bowling 33–2–16.50–0–0–2/33

Bannerman, Alexander Chalmers
Began as amateur, but professional for most of his first-class career. *b:* 21.3.1854, Paddington, Sydney, New South Wales, Australia. *d:* 19.9.1924, Paddington, Sydney, New South Wales, Australia. Brother of Charles (Australia). Defensive opening right-hand batsman, right-hand medium pace round-arm bowler, excellent field. *Team* New South Wales (1876/7 to 1893/4, 46 matches). *Tours* Australia to England 1878, 1880, 1882, 1884, 1888, 1893, to North America 1878, 1893. *Tests* Australia (1878/9 to 1893, 28 matches).
Career batting
219–381–28–7816–134–22.14–5–*ct* 154
Bowling 656–22–29.81–0–0–3/12
Test batting
28–50–2–1108–94–23.08–0–*ct* 21
Bowling 163–4–40.75–0–0–3/111

He was described as the most famous of all Australian stonewall batsmen, his patience being inexhaustible. His most notable innings was 91 for Australia v England at Sydney in 1891/2 when he batted for seven and a half hours to win the match for his side. He took his cricket very seriously indeed. He hit 1,000 runs twice (best 1,144, av 22.88, in 1882).

Bannerman, Charles
Professional. *b:* 3.7.1851, Woolwich, Kent. *d:* 20.8.1930, Surry Hills, Sydney, New South Wales, Australia. Brother of A. C. (Australia). Excellent opening right-hand batsman, fine outfield, occasional bowler. *Team* New South Wales (1870/1 to 1887/8, 23 matches). *Tour* Australia to England and North America 1878. *Tests* Australia (1876/7 to 1878/9, 3 matches).
Career batting
44–84–6–1687–165*–21.62–1–*ct* 20
Bowling 44–0
Test batting
3–6–2–239–165*–59.75–1–*ct* 0

His most noteworthy innings and his only first-class century was the first ever Test hundred; he hit 165 retired hurt v England at Melbourne in 1876/7. On his only visit to England he headed the tourists' batting averages. He umpired 12 Tests (1886/7 to 1901/2).

Bannister, Arthur Frederick
Professional. *b:* 18.6.1875, Somers Town, London. *d:* 17.11.1958, Islington, London. Tail-end batsman, slow right-arm bowler with plenty of spin, or slow left-arm bowler in another account. *Team* Worcestershire (1900–02, 38 matches).
Career batting
38–62–16–354–44–7.69–*ct* 18
Bowling 2175–92–23.64–5–1–7/29

In his debut season of 1900, Bannister had the encouraging return of 65 wickets at a cost of 20.47, but he fell away badly in 1901 and lost his place in the County side. He was a first-class umpire in 1911.

Bannister, Charles Stuart
Cricketer. *b:* 22.5.1956, Redhill, Surrey. Middle order right-hand batsman, right-arm medium pace bowler. *Sch* Caterham. *Team* Cambridge U (1975–77, blue 1976).
Career batting
17–30–2–383–50–13.67–0–*ct* 2
Bowling 813–19–42.78–1–0–5/50
His County cricket was for Hertfordshire (1982–85).

Bannister, Herbert Milburn
Amateur. *b:* 3.6.1889, Lutterworth, Leicestershire. *d:* 18.6.1959, Hammersmith, London. Lower order right-hand batsman, right-arm medium pace bowler. *Sch* Tonbridge. *Team* Leicestershire (1912–21, 11 matches).
Career batting
11–20–3–227–64–13.35–0–*ct* 4
Bowling 793–26–30.50–1–0–5/90
Business prevented him from appearing regularly in first-class cricket, but he was a stalwart of the Bank of England team for many years.

Bannister, John David
Professional. *b:* 23.8.1930, Wolverhampton, Staffordshire. Lower order right-hand batsman, right-arm fast medium bowler. *Sch* KES, Birmingham. *Team* Warwickshire (1950–68, 368 matches).
Career batting
374–456–123–3140–71–9.42–0–*ct* 168
Bowling 26258–1198–21.91–53–6–10/41
He took 100 wickets in a season on four occasions (best 137, av 20.83, in 1961). His best bowling performance was 10 for 41 for Warwickshire v Combined Services in 1959 and in 1955 he took 9 for 35 v Yorkshire at Bramall Lane. He is well-known as a television commentator.

Bannon, Bernard Douglas
Amateur. *b:* 7.12.1874, Goudhurst, Kent. *d:* 18.12.1938, Virginia Water, Surrey. Stylish right-hand opening batsman. *Sch* Tonbridge. *Teams* Kent (1895–1900, 25 matches); Oxford U (1897–98, blue 1898).
Career batting
36–60–4–1078–78–19.25–0–*ct* 10
He played for Oxford in the University Hockey match of 1897 and threw the hammer in the University Sports of 1898. Owing to his profession, the Law, he was unable to devote much time to County cricket.

Baptiste, Eldine Ashworth Elderfield
Cricketer. *b:* 12.3.1960, Liberta, Antigua. Middle order right-hand batsman, right-arm fast medium bowler, deep field. *Teams* Kent (1981–87, 87 matches); Leeward Islands (1981/2 to 1990/1); Northamptonshire (1991, 18 matches); Eastern Province (1991/2). *Tours* West Indies to India 1983/4, 1987/8, to Australia 1983/4 (not first-class), 1984/5, to England 1984, to Pakistan (World Cup) 1987/8; Young West Indies to Zimbabwe 1986/7. *Tests* West Indies (1983/4 to 1989/90, 10 matches).
Career batting
180–251–32–6180–136*–28.21–3–*ct* 88
Bowling 13268–522–25.41–22–3–8/76
Test batting
10–11–1–233–87*–23.30–0–*ct* 2
Bowling 563–16–35.18–0–0–3/31
His only Test tour to England was in 1984, when he played in all five Tests and his accurate bowling provided an excellent back-up to Marshall, Garner and Holding. His best season with Kent was 1985 when he took 58 wickets, av 28.63, and hit 972 runs, av 31.35. West Indies won every Test match in which he played.

Baqa Khan Jilani, Mohammad
Amateur. *b:* 20.7.1911, Jullundur, India. *d:* 2.7.1941, Jullundur, India. He died following an accidental fall from a balcony. Uncle of Sherandaz Khan (Sargodha), Imran Khan (Pakistan), Javed Burki (Pakistan), Majid Khan (Pakistan), A. J. Khan (Oxford U), Javed Zaman (Lahore) and Humayun Zaman (Lahore), brother-in-law of M. Jahangir Khan (India). Lower order right-hand batsman, right-arm medium-fast bowler. *Teams* Northern India (1934/5 to 1938/9); Muslims (1934/5). *Tour* India to England 1936. *Test* India (1936, 1 match).
Career batting
30–54–4–928–113–18.56–1–*ct* 12
Bowling 1655–83–19.93–3–1–7/37
Test batting
1–2–1–16–12–16.00–0–*ct* 0
Bowling 55–0

Barber, Alan Theodore
Amateur. *b:* 17.6.1905, Ecclesall, Sheffield, Yorkshire. *d:* 10.3.1985, Ludgrove, Wokingham, Berkshire. Fine middle order or opening right-hand batsman. *Sch* Shrewsbury. *Teams* Oxford U (1927–29, blue all three years); Yorkshire (1929–30, 42 matches.)
Career batting
70–100–3–2261–119–23.30–2–*ct* 52
Bowling 0–0
Brought in to captain Yorkshire in 1930, with virtually no County Cricket experience, he proved to be the best leader Yorkshire had had for some years. Unfortunately owing to his profession, a schoolteacher, he had to retire from first-class cricket at the end of 1930. He captained Oxford in 1929. An all-round sportsman, he also won blues for soccer and golf.

Barber, Arthur Norman
Professional. *b:* 23.11.1898, West Ham, Essex. Lower order batsman, opening bowler. *Team* Essex (1925, 2 matches).

Career batting
2–4–0–46–31–11.50–0–*ct* 2
Bowling 76–1–76.00–0–0–1/42

Barber, Eric George
Professional. *b:* 22.7.1915, Bishopsgate Green, Coventry, Warwickshire. Middle order right-hand batsman. *Team* Warwickshire (1936, 2 matches).
Career batting
2–3–0–31–13–10.33–0–*ct* 2

Barber, Frederick Arthur
Professional. *b:* 13.5.1887, Ilkeston, Derbyshire. *d:* 4.6.1943, The Pastures, Mickleover, Derbyshire. Tail-end batsman, useful change bowler. *Team* Derbyshire (1907–20, 5 matches).
Career batting
5–10–1–30–10–3.33–0–*ct* 3
Bowling 267–9–29.66–0–0–2/19
He also played for Cumberland (1910).

Barber, Henry William
Amateur. *b:* 5.11.1841, Bloomsbury, London. *d:* 10.7.1924, Draycott, Cheddar, Somerset. Hard hitting lower order right-hand batsman, right-hand fast round-arm bowler. *Sch* King's School, Canterbury. *Team* Kent (1861–64, 9 matches).
Career batting
13–26–5–218–45–10.38–0–*ct* 4
Bowling 18–0
He did not appear in first-class matches whilst at Oxford U.

Barber, Horatio William
Amateur. *b:* 27.2.1843, Broughton, Salford, Lancashire. *d:* 27.4.1869, St Leonards-on-Sea, Sussex. Middle order left-hand batsman, right-arm bowler. *Sch* Rossall. *Team* Lancashire (1866–67, 3 matches).
Career batting
5–10–0–69–20–6.90–0–*ct* 6

Barber, John Benjamin
Amateur. *b:* 6.2.1849, Trafford Park, Manchester, Lancashire. *d:* 21.2.1908, Southwark, London. Middle order batsman. *Team* Lancashire (1874–76, 3 matches).
Career batting
3–6–3–39–12*–13.00–0–*ct* 2

Barber, Robert William
Amateur. *b:* 26.9.1935, Withington, Manchester, Lancashire. Attractive left-hand opening batsman, leg break and googly bowler. *Sch* Ruthin. *Teams* Lancashire (1954–62, 155 matches); Cambridge U (1955–57, blue 1956–57); Warwickshire (1963–69, 124 matches). *Tours* MCC to New Zealand 1960/1, to Ceylon, India and Pakistan 1961/2, to South Africa 1964/5, to Australia 1965/6; Swanton to West Indies 1960/1; Rest of World to Barbados 1966/7. *Tests* England (1960–68, 28 matches).
Career batting
386–651–52–17631–185–29.43–17–*ct* 210
Bowling 16176–549–29.46–12–0–7/35
Test batting
28–45–3–1495–185–35.59–1–*ct* 21
Bowling 1806–42–43.00–0–0–4/132
An outstanding schoolboy cricketer – he achieved the 'double' at Ruthin in 1953 – his initial County career with Lancashire was one surrounded in controversy and it was not until he moved to Warwickshire that his full potential was realised. The highest and best innings of his career was 185 for England v Australia at Sydney in 1965/6. He hit 1,000 runs in a season seven times, his best being 1,573 (av 31.46) in 1964. He also played for Cheshire (1952). He captained Lancashire 1960–61.

Barber, Thomas David
Amateur. *b:* 18.11.1937, Carlton-in-Lindrick, Nottinghamshire. Great-nephew of W. D. (Nottinghamshire). Middle order right-hand batsman, off break bowler. *Sch* Eton. *Team* Nottinghamshire (1960, 1 match).
Career batting
2–3–1–5–3–2.50–0–*ct* 2
He did not play in a first-class match for the University, whilst at Cambridge.

Barber, Wilfred
Professional. *b:* 18.4.1901, Cleckheaton, Yorkshire. *d:* 10.9.1968, Bradford, Yorkshire. Defensive middle order or opening right-hand batsman, right-arm fast medium bowler, brilliant outfield. *Team* Yorkshire (1926–47, 354 matches). *Tour* MCC to New Zealand and Australia 1935/6. *Tests* England (1935, 2 matches).
Career batting
373–526–49–16402–255–34.38–29–*ct* 182
Bowling 419–16–26.18–0–0–2/1
Test batting
2–4–0–83–44–20.75–0–*ct* 1
Bowling 0–1–0.00–0–0–1/0
He did not obtain a regular place in the Yorkshire team until 1932, after which he was a model of consistency. He hit 1,000 runs in a season on eight occasions (best 2,147, av 42.09, in 1935) – his highest innings of 255 for Yorkshire v Surrey at Bramall Lane came in the same year.

Barber, William Douglas
Amateur. *b:* 17.10.1881, Lambclose House, Eastwood, Nottinghamshire. *d:* 26.4.1971, Ranby Hall, Nottinghamshire. Great-uncle of T. D. (Nottinghamshire). Lower order right-hand batsman, wicket-keeper. *Sch* Eton. *Team* Nottinghamshire (1904, 1 match).
Career batting
2–3–0–13–7–4.33–0–*ct* 2–*st* 1

For many years he appeared in Army matches and in 1924 made his second and final appearance in first-class cricket for the Army v Oxford U at Oxford.

Barber, William Henry
Professional. *b:* 23.7.1906, Nuneaton, Warwickshire. *d:* 14.1.1981, Coventry, Warwickshire. Lower order right-hand batsman, right-arm fast-medium bowler. *Team* Warwickshire (1927–33, 5 matches).
Career batting
5–6–1–71–23–14.20–0–*ct* 0
Bowling 253–7–36.14–0–0–3/81
He also played for Cheshire (1934–39).

Barber, William Langan Frederick
Amateur. *b:* 25.10.1919, Hackney, London. *d:* 26.11.1989, Middleton-on-Sea, Sussex. Lower order right-hand batsman, wicket-keeper. *Team* Combined Services (1946).
Career batting
1–2–1–4–4–4.00–0–*ct* 3
He also appeared for the Army at Lord's in 1946.

Barbery, Alfred Edward
Professional. *b:* 13.10.1884, Marylebone, London. *d:* 23.5.1973, Solihull, Warwickshire. Tail end right-hand batsman, right-arm fast-medium bowler. *Team* Warwickshire (1906–07, 2 matches).
Career batting
2–3–0–13–6–4.33–0–*ct* 0
Bowling 245–3–81.66–0–0–2/64

Barbour, Robert Roy Pitty
Amateur. *b:* 29.3.1899, Ashfield, Sydney, New South Wales, Australia. Brother of E. P. (New South Wales). Opening right-hand batsman. *Teams* Queensland (1919/20, 2 matches); Oxford U (1922–23).
Career batting
6–11–0–172–41–15.63–0–*ct* 2
He won blues for lacrosse and lawn tennis.

Barchard, Harry George
Amateur. *b:* 25.6.1860, Crumpsall, Manchester, Lancashire. *d:* 28.7.1935, Seaton, Devon. Middle order batsman. *Sch* Uppingham. *Team* Lancashire (1888, 1 match).
Career batting
1–2–0–45–40–22.50–0–*ct* 1

Barclay, John Robert Troutbeck
Cricketer. *b:* 22.1.1954, Bonn, West Germany. Great-nephew of F. G. J. Ford (Middlesex). Opening or middle order right-hand batsman, off break bowler, good slip field. *Sch* Eton. *Teams* Sussex (1970–86, 265 matches); Orange Free State (1978/9). *Tours* MCC to West Africa 1975/6, to Bangladesh 1976/7 (neither first-class).
Career batting
274–434–44–9677–119–24.81–9–*ct* 214
Bowling 9936–324–30.66–9–1–6/61

He hit 1,000 in a season four times (best 1,093, av 32.14, in 1979). From 1981 to 1986 he captained Sussex.

Barcroft, Peter
Professional. *b:* 14.8.1929, Sharneyford, Bacup, Lancashire. *d:* 26.8.1977, Bacup, Lancashire. Middle order right-hand batsman, leg break bowler. *Team* Lancashire (1956, 3 matches).
Career batting
3–3–0–40–29–13.33–0–*ct* 1

Bardsley, Robert Vickers
Amateur. *b:* 28.6.1890, Prestwich, Lancashire. *d:* 26.7.1952, Coldwaltham, Pulborough, Sussex. Useful middle order right-hand batsman, leg break bowler. *Sch* Shrewsbury. *Teams* Oxford U (1910–13, blue 1911–13); Lancashire (1910–20, 7 matches).
Career batting
31–52–0–964–72–18.53–0–*ct* 19
Bowling 344–12–28.66–0–0–3/15
He represented Oxford at billiards and golf. He was Governor of the Blue Nile Province, Sudan, 1928–32. His final first-class match was for Free Foresters in 1922.

Bardsley, Warren
Amateur. *b:* 6.12.1882, Nevertire, Warren, New South Wales, Australia. *d:* 20.1.1954, Collaroy Plateau, Bondi, Sydney, New South Wales, Australia. Brother of Raymond (New South Wales). Stylish opening left-hand batsman. *Team* New South Wales (1903/4 to 1925/6, 83 matches). *Tours* Australia to England 1909, 1912, 1921, 1926, to South Africa 1914/15 (tour cancelled), 1921/2, to New Zealand 1909/10, to North America 1913; New South Wales to New Zealand 1923/4. *Tests* Australia (1909 to 1926, 41 matches).
Career batting
250–376–35–17025–264–49.92–53–*ct* 113
Bowling 41–0
Test batting
41–66–5–2469–193*–40.47–6–*ct* 12
Regarded as one of the most correct of batsmen, he was exceedingly successful on all his visits to England, hitting over 2,000 runs on three of the four trips (best 2,365, av 51.41, in 1912). His highest score was 264 for Australian XI v Rest at Melbourne in 1908/9. He hit six other double centuries. He was the first batsman to score a hundred in each innings of a Test, a feat he accomplished at the Oval in 1909. In 1926 he hit 193 in the Lord's Test – the highest score made up to that date in a Lord's Test. His final first-class match was for Australian XI in 1926/7. He captained Australia in 2 Tests.

Bardswell, Gerald Roscoe
Amateur. *b:* 7.12.1873, Woolton, Liverpool, Lancashire. *d:* 29.12.1906, New Orleans, USA. He died following an operation. Useful middle order right-hand

batsman, right-arm medium pace bowler, brilliant slip field. *Sch* Uppingham. *Teams* Oxford U (1894–97, blue 1894, 1896, 1897); Lancashire (1894–1902, 21 matches). *Tours* Lord Hawke to North America 1894, to West Indies 1896/7.
Career batting
59–92–13–1585–97–20.06–0–*ct* 104
Bowling 1618–63–25.68–4–0–6/36
He was on both the Lancashire and MCC Committees. Owing to business, Bardswell was unable to play regularly in County cricket. He captained Oxford in 1897 and Lancashire (jointly) in 1899.

Barford, Michael Thomas
Cricketer. *b:* 7.6.1950, Eastbourne, Sussex. Opening right-hand batsman, right-arm medium pace bowler. *Sch* Eastbourne. *Team* Cambridge U (1970–71, blue both years).
Career batting
15–27–4–606–95–26.34–0–*ct* 7

Baring, Amyas Evelyn Giles
Amateur. *b:* 21.1.1910, Roehampton, London. *d:* 29.8.1986, Newcastle upon Tyne, Northumberland. Tail end right-hand batsman, right-arm fast bowler. *Sch* Gresham's Holt. *Teams* Cambridge U (1930–31); Hampshire (1930–39, 62 matches).
Career batting
70–103–27–664–46–8.73–0–*ct* 29
Bowling 5607–197–28.46–10–2–9/26
Making a promising debut, Baring was unfortunate to dislocate both knees in a motor accident in 1931, which prevented him appearing at all in 1932, though he was able to play occasionally in later seasons. He was easily the fastest Hampshire bowler of his time. His final first-class match was for MCC in 1946. His best bowling was 9/26 for Hampshire v Essex at Colchester in 1931.

Barkass-Wiliamson, J. G
(*see under* Williamson, J. G. B.)

Barker, Andrew Hunter
Cricketer. *b:* 7.8.1945, Salisbury, Wiltshire. Middle order left-hand batsman, slow left-arm bowler. *Sch* Charterhouse. *Team* Oxford U (1964–67, blue 1964, 1965 and 1967).
Career batting
44–67–8–864–94–14.64–0–*ct* 24
Bowling 2906–70–41.51–2–0–5/42
His County cricket was for Wiltshire (1963–82).

Barker, Antony Royston Paul
Cricketer. *b:* 30.5.1947, May Bank, Newcastle-under-Lyme, Staffordshire. Middle order right-hand batsman, off break bowler, good close field. *Team* Worcestershire (1967–69, 27 matches).
Career batting
27–43–3–544–67–13.60–0–*ct* 12
He also played for Staffordshire (1970).

Barker, Gordon
Professional. *b:* 6.7.1931, Bramley, Leeds, Yorkshire. Opening right-hand batsman, occasional right-arm medium pace bowler, fine field. *Team* Essex (1954–71, 444 matches).
Career batting
451–809–46–22288–181*–29.21–30–*ct* 236
Bowling 200–5–40.00–0–0–2/34
He scored a century on his first-class debut (Essex v Canadians 1954) and hit 1,000 runs in 15 seasons (best 1,741, av 36.27, in 1960). He played soccer for Southend United.

Barker, J.
Professional. Lower order batsman. *Team* North (1880).
Career batting
1–2–1–19–16–19.00–0–*ct* 0

Barker, Kenneth Edgar Mylne
Amateur. *b:* 27.10.1877, Godstone, Surrey. *d:* 6.8.1938, Blakeney, Norfolk. Sound middle order right-hand batsman, right-arm fast medium bowler. *Sch* Uppingham. *Teams* Cambridge U (1899); Surrey (1899–03, 6 matches).
Career batting
10–14–0–203–52–14.50–0–*ct* 2
Bowling 31–0
He made his first-class debut for MCC in 1898.

Barker, Maurice Percy
Amateur. *b:* 4.2.1917, Leamington Spa, Warwickshire. Lower order right-hand batsman, right-arm fast medium bowler. *Team* Warwickshire (1946, 5 matches).
Career batting
5–9–2–55–17–7.85–0–*ct* 1
Bowling 378–16–23.62–1–0–7/68
His one day of triumph in County cricket was at the expense of Yorkshire, when at Edgbaston in 1946 he took 7 for 68.

Barker, Montague Merton
Amateur. *b:* 20.7.1867, Paddington, London. *d:* 12.1.1954, Epsom Downs, Surrey. Attacking middle order right-hand batsman, occasional bowler, excellent cover field. *Sch* Radley. *Team* MCC (1895–96). *Tour* Lucas to West Indies 1894/5.
Career batting
10–15–1–106–30–7.57–0–*ct* 11
Bowling 7–0
A brilliant hockey player, he captained England in 1898.

Barker, Philip David
Cricketer. *b:* 22.9.1951, Edmonton, Middlesex. Opening right-hand batsman, left-arm medium or slow bowler. *Sch* Latymer GS. *Team* Oxford U (1974).

Barker, Thomas

Career batting
1–2–0–15–14–7.50–0–*ct* 0
His County cricket was for Suffolk (1972–88). He won a blue for hockey and also played for Suffolk.

Barker, Thomas
Professional. *b:* 15.11.1798, Carlton, Nottinghamshire. *d:* 2.3.1877, Nottingham. Good right-hand batsman, fast under-arm, then fast round-arm bowler. *Teams* Nottinghamshire (1826–45); Yorkshire (1836).
Career batting
72–132–12–1269–58–10.57–0–*ct* 34
Bowling 266–18 + 192–14.77–15–4–7/?
In 1843, whilst travelling with the Nottinghamshire team to Southampton to play Hampshire, he was involved in an accident, being thrown out of a horse-drawn cab in London and breaking a leg. This virtually ended his career.

Barker, W.
Amateur. Tail end right-hand batsman, left-arm fast bowler. *Team* Surrey (1882, 1 match).
Career batting
1–2–0–1–1–1.00–0–*ct* 0
Bowling 40–0

Barkham, Frederick
Amateur. *b:* 26.10.1905, Scarborough, Yorkshire. Middle order right-hand batsman, right-arm medium pace bowler. *Team* Scotland (1948–49).
Career batting
2–4–1–7–3*–2.33–0–*ct* 0

Barley, Jack Charles
Amateur. *b:* 4.12.1887, Eton, Buckinghamshire. *d: circa* 1960, Surfers' Paradise, Queensland, Australia. Lower order right-hand batsman, wicket-keeper. *Sch* Tonbridge. *Teams* Sussex (1908, 1 match); Oxford U (1909); Worcestershire (1909, 1 match).
Career batting
4–7–2–12–8–2.40–0–*ct* 4–*st* 1

Barling, Henry Thomas
(known as Thomas Henry Barling)
Professional. *b:* 1.9.1906, Kensington, London. *d:* 2.1.1993, Hastings, Sussex. Forcing middle order right-hand batsman. *Team* Surrey (1927–48, 389 matches).
Career batting
391–609–54–19209–269–34.61–34–*ct* 171
Bowling 550–7–78.57–0–0–3/46
His best season was 1946 when he hit 2,014 runs (av 43.78). In all he exceeded 1,000 runs in a season nine times. His two double centuries were both for Surrey: 269 v Hampshire at Southampton in 1933 and 233* v Nottinghamshire at the Oval in 1946. A good soccer player, he represented Surrey.

Barlow, Alfred
Professional. *b:* 31.8.1915, Little Lever, Lancashire. *d:* 9.5.1983, Middleton, Lancashire. Lower order right-hand batsman, wicket-keeper. *Team* Lancashire (1947–51, 74 matches). *Tour* Commonwealth to Ceylon and India 1950/1.
Career batting
85–100–25–863–44–11.50–0–*ct* 116–*st* 52
Bowling 0–0

Barlow, Charles Sydney
Amateur. *b:* 10.5.1905, Durban, South Africa. *d:* 1.6.1979, Sotto Grande, Spain. Forcing lower order right-hand batsman, steady right-arm medium fast bowler, brilliant field. *Sch* Clifton. *Team* Somerset (1925–26, 2 matches).
Career batting
2–4–0–24–23–6.00–0–*ct* 1
Bowling 120–2–60.00–0–0–2/98
He played no first-class cricket at Cambridge U but won a blue for rugby. He also played rugby for Natal.

Barlow, Edgar John
Professional. *b:* 12.8.1940, Pretoria, South Africa. Sound opening right-hand batsman, right-arm medium pace bowler, excellent slip field. *Teams* Transvaal (1959/60 to 1967/8); Eastern Province (1964/5 to 1965/6); Western Province (1968/9 to 1980/1); Derbyshire (1976–78, 60 matches); Boland (1981/2 to 1982/3). *Tours* South Africa to Australia and New Zealand 1963/4, to England 1965, 1970 (tour cancelled); South Africa Fezela to England 1961; International Wanderers to South Africa 1974/5; Rest of the World to England 1965, 1967, 1968, 1970. *Tests* South Africa (1961/2 to 1969/70, 30 matches).
Career batting
283–493–28–18212–217–39.16–43–*ct* 335
Bowling 13785–571–24.14–16–2–7/24
Test batting
30–57–2–2516–201–45.74–6–*ct* 35
Bowling 1362–40–34.05–1–0–5/85
On the 1965 tour to England he hit 971 runs, av 38.84, and played in all three Tests. In England he hit 1,000 runs in a season twice (best 1,162, av 29.05, in 1976). His highest score in England was 217 for Derbyshire v Surrey at Ilkeston on 1976. He captained Derbyshire from midway through 1976 to the close of the 1978 season. For the Rest of the World v England at Headingley in 1970 he took 4 wickets in 5 balls. He was Senior coach to Gloucestershire in 1990–91.

Barlow, Edwin Alan
Amateur. *b:* 24.2.1912, Ashton-under-Lyne, Lancashire. *d:* 27.6.1980, Gretton, Gloucestershire. Useful lower order right-hand batsman, slow-medium off break bowler. *Sch* Shrewsbury. *Teams* Oxford U (1932–34, blue all three years); Lancashire (1932, 7 matches).

Career batting
36–53–11–582–46–13.85–0–*ct* 21
Bowling 2793–102–27.38–4–0–6/44

He also played for Denbighshire (1930–35).

Barlow, Graham Derek
Cricketer. *b:* 26.3.1950, Folkestone, Kent. Determined opening or middle order left-hand batsman, right-arm medium pace bowler, excellent cover field. *Team* Middlesex (1969–86, 239 matches). *Tour* MCC to India, Sri Lanka and Australia 1976/7. *Tests* England (1976/7 to 1977, 3 matches).
Career batting
251–404–59–12387–177–35.90–26–*ct* 136
Bowling 68–3–22.66–0–0–1/6
Test batting
3–5–1–17–7*–4.25–0–*ct* 0

He hit 1,000 runs in a season seven times (best 1,545, av 48.28, in 1983). He retired due to injury.

Barlow, Keith
Amateur. *b:* 27.8.1890, Kensington, London. *d:* 5.4.1930, Kensington, London. Middle order right-hand batsman. *Team* Kent (1910, 2 matches).
Career batting
2–3–0–11–6–3.66–0–*ct* 1

Barlow, Micah Yates
Amateur. *b:* 6.2.1873, Bury, Lancashire. *d:* 13.1.1936, Grange-over-Sands, Lancashire. Middle order batsman, good field at cover. *Sch* Harrow. *Team* Oxford U (1894).
Career batting
1–2–0–9–6–4.50–0–*ct* 0

Barlow, Richard Gorton
Professional. *b:* 28.5.1851, Barrow Bridge, Bolton, Lancashire. *d:* 31.7.1919, Stanley Park, Blackpool, Lancashire. Defensive opening right-hand batsman, left-arm medium pace bowler, excellent field. *Team* Lancashire (1871–91, 249 matches). *Tours* Shaw and Shrewsbury to Australia 1881/2, 1886/7; Bligh to Australia 1882/3. *Tests* England (1881/2 to 1886/7, 17 matches).
Career batting
351–608–64–11217–117–20.61–4–*ct* 268
Bowling 13799–950–14.52–66–14–9/39
Test batting
17–30–4–591–62–22.73–0–*ct* 14
Bowling 767–34–22.55–3–0–7/40

Runs were always at a premium when Barlow was playing – the epitome of the 'stonewaller', the accurate bowler and brilliant field, he served Lancashire well for over 20 years.

As a batsman he concentrated on defending his wicket; it was reckoned that his opening partner, Hornby, made a 100 runs for every 10 that Barlow scored. On two occasions, Lancashire v Sussex at Old Trafford in 1876, and v Nottinghamshire at Trent Bridge in 1882, he batted two and a half hours for 5 runs and in the latter innings spent 80 minutes without scoring. In first-class matches he carried his bat through a completed innings 11 times and in all on 51 occasions. Although he never scored a Test century, his batting materially assisted in the winning of two Tests – at Lord's in 1884 and at Old Trafford in 1886. He hit 1,000 runs in a season once (1,138, av 27.09, in 1882) and took 100 wickets three times (best 130, av 13.18, in 1884). His best bowling was 9/39 for Lancashire v Sussex at Old Trafford in 1886.

The best performance of his career was for the North against the Australians in 1884 at Trent Bridge: he hit a century on a wicket on which Spofforth claimed the entire side would not make 60, and Barlow also took ten wickets for 48 in the match.

His bowling was rarely off a length and in the Lancashire v Sussex match at Old Trafford in 1885 he bowled for an hour conceding just a single.

Physically he kept himself very fit and played football for 12 years, keeping goal for Lancashire. In addition he won numerous awards as a sprint runner.

In contrast to his dour cricket, Barlow was the most amiable of men. He claimed that no one could possibly have enjoyed a career in first-class cricket as much as he had done. He is the Barlow remembered in Francis Thompson's famous poem 'At Lord's'.

He was a first-class umpire (1894–1914), standing in one Test match in 1899.

Barmby, Francis James
Amateur. *b:* 21.12.1863, Pittington, Durham. *d:* 30.9.1936, Summertown, Oxford. Stylish middle order right-hand batsman, useful right-arm medium pace bowler, good slip field. *Sch* Charterhouse. *Team* Oxford U (1885).
Career batting
1–2–0–6–6–3.00–0–*ct* 1

He was awarded his soccer blue in 1886. His County cricket was for Berkshire (1900).

Barnard, Francis Herbert
Amateur. *b:* 6.5.1902, Castries, St Lucia. Hard hitting middle order right-hand batsman, right-arm medium pace bowler. *Sch* Charterhouse. *Team* Oxford U (1922–24, blue 1922 and 1924).
Career batting
23–37–1–571–61–15.86–0–*ct* 19
Bowling 766–28–27.35–0–0–3/17

He also won a blue for soccer.

Barnard, Henry Michael
Professional. *b:* 18.7.1933, Portsea, Portsmouth, Hampshire. Middle order right-hand batsman, occasional right-arm medium pace bowler. *Sch* Portsmouth GS. *Team* Hampshire (1952–66, 276 matches).
Career batting
276–463–41–9314–128*–22.07–6–*ct* 313
Bowling 563–16–35.18–0–0–3/35

His best year was 1962 when he reached 1,000 runs for the only time in his career (1,114, av 27.17). He played soccer for Portsmouth.

Barnardo, Freeman Frederick Thomas
Amateur. *b:* 16.5.1918, Bombay, India. *d:* 25.10.1942, ten miles west of El Alamein, Egypt. Middle order right-hand batsman. *Sch* Eton. *Teams* Middlesex (1939, 1 match); Cambridge U (1939).
Career batting
2–3–0–75–75–25.00–0–*ct* 0

Barnato, Joel Woolf
Amateur. *b:* 27.9.1895, Westminster, London. *d:* 27.7.1948, Marylebone, London. Tail end right-hand batsman, wicket-keeper. *Sch* Charterhouse. *Team* Surrey (1928–30, 6 matches).
Career batting
6–8–1–23–7–3.28–0–*ct* 19–*st* 1
He was best known as a long distance motor racing driver and was the son of the diamond merchant, Barney Barnato.

Barnby, Arthur Charles
Amateur. *b:* 10.9.1881, Westminster, London. *d:* 30.10.1937, Rochester Airport, Bridgewood, Kent. Lower order right-hand batsman, wicket-keeper. *Sch* Westminster. *Team* Royal Navy (1913).
Career batting
1–2–1–1–1*–1.00–0–*ct* 0

Barne, Rev George Dunsford
Amateur. *b:* 6.5.1879, Jamaica. *d:* 18.6.1954, Ravenscourt Park, Hammersmith, London. Brother-in-law of A. M. Streatfeild (Kent) and E. C. Streatfeild (Surrey). Lower order batsman. *Sch* Clifton. *Team* Somerset (1904, 1 match).
Career batting
1–2–1–10–9*–10.00–0–*ct* 0
He was Bishop of Lahore. He played no first-class matches at Oxford U but won a blue for golf.

Barnes, Alan Sedgwick
Amateur. *b:* 9.10.1850, Anfield, Liverpool, Lancashire. *d:* 17.5.1915, Twyford Abbey, Willesden, Middlesex. Uncle of R. G. (Oxford U). Middle order right-hand batsman. *Team* Derbyshire (1878, 3 matches).
Career batting
13–20–2–107–16–5.94–0–*ct* 4
He was at Cambridge, but not in the Eleven. His first-class debut was for MCC in 1877 and his final first-class match was for MCC in 1879.

Barnes, Frederic Barrie
Amateur. *b:* 4.5.1923, King William's Town, South Africa. Lower order left-hand batsman, wicket-keeper. *Team* Cambridge U (1948).
Career batting
2–2–0–61–39–30.50–0–*ct* 3

Barnes, George Corbett
Amateur. *b:* 9.3.1847, Umballa, India. Lower order batsman. *Sch* Brighton. *Team* Gentlemen of Kent (1866).
Career batting
1–1–0–3–3.00–0–*ct* 1

Barnes, Henry Marshall
Amateur. *b:* 27.6.1869, Newbridge, Co Kildare, Ireland. *d:* 8.6.1946, Ipswich, Suffolk. Son of C. H. (MCC 1860). Middle order batsman. *Sch* Marlborough. *Team* MCC (1907).
Career batting
1–1–1–3–3*–no av–0–*ct* 0

Barnes, James William
Professional. *b:* 14.8.1886, Sutton-in-Ashfield, Nottinghamshire. *d:* 9.9.1963, Mansfield, Nottinghamshire. Son of William (Nottinghamshire), nephew of Thomas (Nottinghamshire). Lower order batsman, right-arm medium pace bowler. *Team* Nottinghamshire (1908–10, 3 matches).
Career batting
3–5–0–19–12–3.80–0–*ct* 0
Bowling 105–2–52.50–0–0–1/30

Barnes, John Hamilton
Amateur. *b:* 14.11.1916, Armagh, Ireland. *d:* 22.4.1943, Kneesall, Nottinghamshire. Brother of R. J. (Ireland). Tail end right-hand batsman, right-arm fast bowler. *Team* Ireland (1937).
Career batting
1–2–0–0–0–0.00–0–*ct* 0
Bowling 7–0

Barnes, John Reginald
Amateur. *b:* 18.5.1897, Aughton, Ormskirk, Lancashire. *d:* 22.7.1945, Grange-over-Sands, Lancashire. Stylish middle order right-hand batsman, occasional leg break bowler, good field. *Sch* Marlborough. *Team* Lancashire (1919–30, 89 matches).
Career batting
94–145–23–3643–133–29.86–4–*ct* 40
Bowling 53–0
Barnes scored heavily in Lancashire club cricket, but business (he was a Liverpool cotton merchant) limited his first-class appearances. His final first-class match was for MCC in 1931.

Barnes, Rev Robert James
Amateur. *b:* 25.3.1911, Armagh, Ireland. *d:* 12.3.1987, Musgrave Park, Belfast, Ireland. Brother of J. H. (Ireland). Middle order left-hand batsman, slow left-arm bowler. *Team* Ireland (1930–47).
Career batting
8–15–1–199–48–14.21–0–*ct* 7
Bowling 99–9–11.00–0–0–4/18
He was an Irish rugby international.

Barnes, Hon Ronald Gorell
(succeeded as 3rd Baron Gorell in 1917)
Amateur. *b:* 16.4.1884, Kensington, London. *d:* 2.5.1963, Burpham, Sussex. Nephew of A. S. (Derbyshire). Lower order right-hand batsman, left-arm medium pace bowler. *Sch* Winchester and Harrow. *Team* Oxford U (1906–07, blue both years).
Career batting
19–33–2–431–77–13.90–0–*ct* 17
Bowling 1127–43–26.20–1–0–5/48

His final first-class match was for MCC in 1920, and his County cricket for Suffolk (1905–09). He was a well-known author and poet.

Barnes, Sidney George
Amateur. *b:* 5.6.1916, Charters Towers, Queensland, Australia. *d:* 16.12.1973, Collaroy, Sydney, New South Wales, Australia. Excellent opening right-hand batsman, leg break bowler. *Team* New South Wales (1936/7 to 1952/3, 56 matches). *Tours* Australia to England 1938, 1948, to New Zealand 1945/6. *Tests* Australia (1938–48, 13 matches).
Career batting
110–164–10–8333–234–54.11–26–*ct* 80–*st* 4
Bowling 1836–57–32.21–0–0–3/0
Test batting
13–19–2–1072–234–63.05–3–*ct* 14
Bowling 218–4–54.50–0–0–2/25

He was unfortunate to fracture a wrist on his 1938 visit to England and thereby miss the first half of the tour; in 1948 on his second visit, however, he was a great success, averaging 82.25 in the Tests and hitting a century in the Lord's Test. In the 1946/7 series in Australia he made 234 at Sydney, creating a record 405 fifth wicket stand with Bradman. He hit 1,354 runs, av 56.81, in 1948. After 1948 he was increasingly at loggerheads with the Australian authorities and wrote many caustic criticisms in the press, which ended his first-class career.

Barnes, Stuart Neil
Cricketer. *b:* 27.6.1970, Bath, Somerset. Lower order right-hand batsman, right-arm medium pace bowler. *Team* Gloucestershire (1990–91, 11 matches).
Career batting
11–10–3–23–12*–3.28–0–*ct* 3
Bowling 625–16–39.06–0–0–4/51

Barnes, Sydney Francis
Professional. *b:* 19.4.1873, Smethwick, Staffordshire. *d:* 26.12.1967, Chadsmoor, Staffordshire. Lower order right-hand batsman, right-arm fast-medium to slow-medium bowler. *Teams* Warwickshire (1894–96, 4 matches); Lancashire (1899–1903, 46 matches); Wales (1927–30). *Tours* MacLaren to Australia 1901/2; MCC to Australia 1907/8, 1911/12, to South Africa 1913/14. *Tests* England (1901/2 to 1913/14, 27 matches).
Career batting
133–173–50–1573–93–12.78–0–*ct* 72
Bowling 12289–719–17.09–68–18–9/103
Test batting
27–39–9–242–38*–8.06–0–*ct* 12
Bowling 3106–189–16.43–24–7–9/103

Regarded by his contemporary players as the greatest of bowlers, Barnes was not only a master of length and of deception in flight, but also had the knack of making the ball turn either to the off or the leg. He could alter his bowling to suit all types of wicket and few if any batsmen were happy against him.

A rather gaunt, cold character, he remained aloof from the humdrum world of first-class county cricket. Twice he tried it – with Warwickshire, then Lancashire – but soon rejected it as too irksome. Those in authority at Lord's were very wary of him and though his career spanned over 40 years and for most of that time he was taking wickets at minimal cost – he captured all ten wickets in an innings seven times – his name is to be found in only ten Test Matches played in England.

MacLaren really introduced him to the public at large when the Lancashire amateur picked him for the 1901/2 tour to Australia. His visit was only a partial success due to injury, and it was not until the tours of 1911/12 to Australia and 1913/14 to South Africa that he demonstrated his art to its full. On the latter tour, with only four Tests, he took 49 wickets, whilst on the former he took 34. He took 100 wickets in a season once: 131, av 17.85, in 1903 and his best bowling was 9/103 for England v South Africa at Johannesburg in 1913/14.

After the First World War Barnes confined himself mainly to League cricket and Minor Counties Championship matches with Staffordshire (1904–35) – at the age of 55 he took 76 wickets (av 8.21) for his native County. According to his biography he took 6,229 wickets (av 8.33) in competitive matches during his career.

Barnes, Terry Peter
Professional. *b:* 13.11.1933, Radford, Coventry, Warwickshire. Lower order right-hand batsman, wicket-keeper. *Sch* King Henry VIII, Coventry. *Team* Warwickshire (1956, 1 match).
Career batting
1–1–0–7–7–7.00–0–*ct* 1

Barnes, Thomas
Professional. *b:* 11.5.1849, Sutton-in-Ashfield, Nottinghamshire. *d:* 22.9.1873, Sutton-in-Ashfield, Nottinghamshire. He died of typhoid. Brother of William (Nottinghamshire), uncle of J. W. (Nottinghamshire). Lower order right-hand batsman, right-arm medium pace bowler. *Team* Nottinghamshire (1872, 5 matches).

Career batting
6–8–0–70–33–8.75–0–*ct* 2
Bowling 23–2–11.50–0–0–2/23

His first-class debut was in 1870 for R. Daft's XI v United North of England Eleven.

Barnes, William
Professional. *b:* 27.5.1852, Sutton-in-Ashfield, Nottinghamshire. *d:* 24.3.1899, Mansfield Woodhouse, Nottinghamshire. Brother of Thomas (Nottinghamshire), father of J. W. (Nottinghamshire). Middle order right-hand batsman, right-arm fast medium bowler. *Team* Nottinghamshire (1875–94, 257 matches). *Tours* Daft to North America 1879 (not first-class); Bligh to Australia 1882/3; Shaw and Shrewsbury to Australia 1884/5, 1886/7. *Tests* England (1880–90, 21 matches).
Career batting
459–725–60–15425–160–23.19–21–*ct* 342–*st* 3
Bowling 15448–902–17.11–45–10–8/64
Test batting
21–33–2–725–134–23.38–1–*ct* 19
Bowling 793–51–15.54–3–0–6/28

A regular member of the England team during the 1880s, Barnes was the leading professional all-rounder of his day. His greatest triumphs occurred on the second of his three visits to Australia, when he finished the tour at the head of both batting and bowling tables – his batting on that tour included a brilliant 134 in the first Test on a tricky wicket at Adelaide. In the second Test he took 6 for 31 in Australia's second innings to enable England to win by ten wickets. The third Test was the scene of his refusal to bowl when asked to do so by the England captain and in fact his rather rumbustious character caused him more trouble on his third visit to Australia for he got involved in a fracas with one of the Australian players and so injured his hand that he missed many of the matches.

In England he exceeded 1,000 runs in a season five times, his best being 1,308, av 27.82, in 1883, but the nearest he got to 100 wickets was 97 in both 1885 and 1888. He was at loggerheads with the Nottinghamshire Committee on several occasions and due to this was omitted from the County side two or three years earlier than might otherwise have been the case.

Barnett, Alexander Anthony
Cricketer. *b:* 11.9.1970, Malaga, Spain. Great-nephew of C. J. (Gloucestershire). Lower order right-hand batsman, slow left-arm bowler. *Teams* Middlesex (1988–91, 3 matches); Lancashire (1992, 22 matches).
Career batting
25–20–12–92–17–11.50–0–*ct* 7
Bowling 2559–56–45.69–2–0–5/78

Barnett, Benjamin Arthur, AM
Amateur. *b:* 23.3.1908, Auburn, Melbourne, Victoria, Australia. *d:* 29.6.1979, Newcastle, New South Wales, Australia. Middle order left-hand batsman, occasional slow bowler, wicket-keeper. *Team* Victoria (1929/30 to 1946/7, 73 matches). *Tours* Australia to England 1934, 1938, to South Africa 1935/6; Commonwealth to India 1953/4. *Tests* Australia (1938, 4 matches).
Career batting
173–243–42–5531–131–27.51–4–*ct* 215–*st* 142
Bowling 20–1–20.00–0–0–1/3
Test batting
4–8–1–195–57–27.85–0–*ct* 3–*st* 2

After a relatively successful career in first-class and Test cricket, Barnett moved to London in 1949 and appeared for Buckinghamshire from 1951 to 1964. During this time he took part in a number of first-class matches, usually end of season festival games, and his last first-class game was in 1961 for Commonwealth XI in England. He was an excellent Australian Rules footballer and represented Victoria.

Barnett, Charles John
Amateur on debut but turned professional in 1929. *b:* 3.7.1910, Fairview, Cheltenham, Gloucestershire. Son of C. S. (Gloucestershire), nephew of E. P. (Gloucestershire) and P. P. (Gloucestershire), great-uncle of A. A. (Middlesex and Lancashire). Excellent opening or middle order right-hand batsman, good right-arm medium pace bowler, fine outfield. *Sch* Wycliffe. *Teams* Gloucestershire (1927–48, 424 matches). *Tours* MCC to Ceylon and India 1933/4, to Australia 1936/7; Commonwealth to India 1953/4. *Tests* England (1933–48, 20 matches).
Career batting
498–821–45–25389–259–32.71–48–*ct* 319
Bowling 12207–394–30.98–12–2–6/17
Test batting
20–35–4–1098–129–35.41–2–*ct* 14
Bowling 93–0

For the first few years of his career Barnett was a hard-hitting middle order batsman, but in 1932 he began opening the innings for Gloucestershire and became much more consistent. He reached 1,000 runs in a season twelve times, including over 2,000 on four occasions, his best being 2,489 (av 40.14) in 1937. He also hit four double centuries, the highest 259 for MCC v Queensland at Brisbane in 1936/7. His benefit realised £4,164 in 1947, a Gloucestershire record at that time. His last first-class match in England was for the Commonwealth XI in 1952.

Barnett, Charles Sherborne
Amateur. *b:* 24.2.1884, Cheltenham, Gloucestershire. *d:* 20.11.1962, Coney Hill, Gloucester. Brother of E. P. (Gloucestershire) and P. P. (Gloucestershire), father of C. J. (Gloucestershire). Opening right-hand batsman. *Sch* Wycliffe. *Team* Gloucestershire (1904–

26, 107 matches).
Career batting
107–191–18–3690–157–21.32–2–*ct* 51
Bowling 66–0

His best season was 1921 when he hit two centuries, but he was unable to play regularly for the County.

Barnett, E. E.
Amateur. Middle order batsman. *Team* MCC (1908).
Career batting
1–2–0–71–70–35.50–0–*ct* 1

His County cricket was for Shropshire (1899) and Buckinghamshire (1913).

Barnett, Edgar Playle
Amateur. *b:* 22.3.1885, Cheltenham, Gloucestershire. *d:* 20.1.1922, Cheltenham, Gloucestershire. He died of meningitis. Brother of C. S. (Gloucestershire) and P. P. (Gloucestershire), uncle of C. J. (Gloucestershire). Good right-hand batsman. *Sch* Wycliffe. *Team* Gloucestershire (1903–21, 64 matches).
Career batting
64–119–8–1925–95–17.34–0–*ct* 57

Barnett, Kim John
Cricketer. *b:* 17.7.1960, Stoke-on-Trent, Staffordshire. Opening right-hand batsman, leg break bowler, cover field. *Teams* Derbyshire (1979–92, 300 matches); Boland (1982/3 to 1987/8). *Tour* Robins to New Zealand 1979/80; England B to Sri Lanka 1985/6; England to India 1988/9 (tour cancelled); England XI to South Africa 1989/90. *Tests* (1988–89, 4 matches).
Career batting
333–533–47–18495–239*–38.05–38–*ct* 216
Bowling 5324–137–38.86–2–0–6/28
Test batting
4–7–0–207–80–29.57–0–*ct* 1
Bowling 32–0

He hit 1,000 runs in a season ten times (best 1,734, av 45.63, in 1984). He captained Derbyshire from 1983 to 1992. His highest score was 239* for Derbyshire v Leicestershire at Leicester in 1988. He also played for Staffordshire (1976).

Barnett, Percival Playle
Amateur. *b:* 8.10.1889, Cheltenham, Gloucestershire. *d:* 17.1.1966, Kendal, Westmorland. Brother of C. S. (Gloucestershire) and E. P. (Gloucestershire), uncle of C. J. (Gloucestershire). Middle order batsman. *Sch* Wycliffe. *Team* Gloucestershire (1908–09, 4 matches).
Career batting
4–7–0–36–16–5.14–0–*ct* 2

Barnfather, James David
Professional. *b:* 22.7.1896, Leicester. *d:* 21.8.1957, Grays, Thurrock, Essex. Lower order right-hand batsman, right-arm fast medium bowler. *Team* Essex (1924, 5 matches).
Career batting
5–5–3–50–28*–25.00–0–*ct* 1
Bowling 355–13–27.30–1–0–6/32

Barnie-Adshead, W. E.
(see under Adshead, W. E.)

Barnsdale, John Davison
Amateur. *b:* 24.5.1878, Mapperley Park, Nottingham. *d:* 5.8.1960, Lower Bourne, Farnham, Surrey. Lower order right-hand batsman, wicket-keeper. *Sch* Nottingham HS and Sedbergh. *Team* Nottinghamshire (1905, 1 match).
Career batting
1–2–0–10–10–5.00–0–*ct* 0–*st* 1

He played soccer for Nottingham Forest.

Barnwell, Charles John Patrick
Amateur. *b:* 23.6.1914, Stoke-on-Trent, Staffordshire. Uncle of L. M. L. (Somerset). Middle order right-hand batsman, right-arm medium pace bowler. *Sch* Repton. *Team* Somerset (1935–48, 69 matches).
Career batting
69–111–6–1592–83–15.16–0–*ct* 18
Bowling 40–0

Barnwell, Lionel Michael Lowry
Cricketer. *b:* 12.8.1943, Crewkerne, Somerset. Nephew of C. J. P. (Somerset). Opening right-hand batsman, right-arm medium pace bowler. *Sch* Repton. *Teams* Cambridge U (1965–66); Somerset (1967–68, 6 matches); Eastern Province (1969/70 to 1970/1).
Career batting
19–33–2–612–74–19.74–0–*ct* 10
Bowling 194–3–64.66–0–0–1/11

He was awarded a blue for soccer at Cambridge.

Baroda, The Gaekwad of, HH Maharajkumar Shiyajirao
Amateur. *b:* 31.8.1890, Baroda, India. *d:* 24.11.1919, India. Father of U. S. Gaekwar (Cambridge U), uncle of F. P. Gaekwad (Baroda), R. P. Gaekwad (Baroda) and S. P. Gaekwad (Baroda). Stylish opening or middle order right-hand batsman. *Teams* Oxford U (1911–12); Hindus (1909/10). *Tour* India to England 1911.
Career batting
14–27–1–406–62–15.61–0–*ct* 4–*st* 1

An accident in 1912 which resulted in concussion of the brain cut short his cricket at Oxford when he would probably have gained a blue. His last first-class match in England was for Gentlemen in 1913 and his final first-class match for Hindus and Muslims in 1917/8.

Barr, Douglas
Amateur. *b:* 1.2.1935, Dalry, Edinburgh, Scotland. Middle order right-hand batsman, right-arm fast medium bowler. *Team* Scotland (1954–70).

Barraclough, Eric Scott

Career batting
41–70–9–1199–86–19.65–0–*ct* 34
Bowling 2747–88–31.21–2–0–6/89

Barraclough, Eric Scott
Professional. *b:* 30.3.1923, Great Horton, Bradford, Yorkshire. Lower order right-hand batsman, right-arm fast medium bowler. *Team* Yorkshire (1949–50, 2 matches).
Career batting
2–4–2–43–24*–21.50–0–*ct* 2
Bowling 136–4–34.00–0–0–2/39

Barratt, Edward (D'Oyley)
Professional. *b:* 21.4.1844, Stockton-on-Tees, Durham. *d:* 27.2.1891, Kennington, Surrey. Hard-hitting lower order left-hand batsman, excellent slow left-arm bowler, good field. *Team* Surrey (1876–85, 130 matches).
Career batting
153–245–57–1595–67–8.48–0–*ct* 75
Bowling 13861–790–17.54–69–18–10/43

He created a sensation in 1872, when, as an unknown, he took 8/60 on his first-class debut in the second innings of North v South at Prince's. He then joined the Oval staff and qualified by residence for Surrey. He took 100 wickets in a season three times, his best being 148, av 17.25, in 1883. The best performance of his career was for Players v Australians at the Oval in 1878 when he took all ten wickets in an innings (for 43). He also played for Durham (pre first-class, 1874–75). His final first-class match was for C. I. Thornton's XI in 1886. He was a first-class umpire (1889–90).

Barratt, Fred
Professional. *b:* 12.4.1894, Annesley, Nottinghamshire. *d:* 29.1.1947, Standard Hill, Nottingham. Powerful lower order right-hand batsman, right-arm fast bowler. *Team* Nottinghamshire (1914–31, 353 matches). *Tour* MCC to New Zealand and Australia 1929/30. *Tests* England (1929 to 1929/30, 5 matches).
Career batting
371–467–52–6445–139*–15.53–2–*ct* 174
Bowling 27811–1224–22.72–69–11–8/26
Test batting
5–4–1–28–17–9.33–0–*ct* 2
Bowling 235–5–47.00–0–0–1/8

Barratt took 100 wickets in his debut season of 1914 and in all obtained 100 wickets in five seasons (best 129, av 21.24, in 1929). His great year was 1928 when he also hit 1,000 runs and achieved the 'double' for the only time, scoring 1,167 runs, av 29.17, that year. He was noted for hitting sixes and twice hit three in succession. His highest score of 139 v Warwickshire at Coventry in 1928 took 84 minutes. He played soccer for Aston Villa and Sheffield Wednesday.

Barratt, Roy James
Professional. *b:* 3.5.1942, Aylestone, Leicester. Lower order left-hand batsman, slow left-arm bowler. *Team* Leicestershire (1961–70, 70 matches).
Career batting
70–88–16–604–39–8.38–0–*ct* 50
Bowling 4007–141–28.41–7–1–7/35

Barratt left the Leicestershire staff after 1962 and did not play at all in 1963, 1966 or 1967.

Barrell, Ben
Professional. *b:* 14.5.1885, Orford, Suffolk. *d:* 14.7.1969, Bootle, Lancashire. Middle order batsman, useful change bowler. *Team* Lancashire (1911–23, 3 matches).
Career batting
3–3–1–45–25–22.50–0–*ct* 1
Bowling 135–9–15.00–0–0–3/10

He also played for Cheshire (1913) and represented Anglesey.

Barrett, Alexander Gould
Amateur. *b:* 17.11.1866, Moredon, North Curry, Taunton, Somerset. *d:* 12.3.1954, Galmington, Taunton, Somerset. Middle order batsman. *Sch* Eton. *Team* Somerset (1896, 1 match).
Career batting
1–2–0–6–6–3.00–0–*ct* 0

He was President of Somerset 1931–32.

Barrett, Arthur George
Cricketer. *b:* 4.4.1944, Kingston, Jamaica. Lower order right-hand batsman, leg break and googly bowler. *Team* Jamaica (1966/7 to 1980/1). *Tours* Jamaica to England 1970; West Indies to India and Pakistan 1974/5. *Tests* West Indies (1970/1 to 1974/5, 6 matches).
Career batting
57–75–13–1086–102*–17.51–1–*ct* 54
Bowling 5276–169–31.21–9–2–7/90
Test batting
6–7–1–40–19–6.66–0–*ct* 0
Bowling 603–13–46.38–0–0–3/43

His appearances in English first-class cricket were limited to four, on the Jamaican tour of 1970.

Barrett, Brian Joseph
Cricketer. *b:* 16.11.1966, Auckland, New Zealand. Lower order right-hand batsman, right-arm fast medium bowler. *Teams* Worcestershire (1985, 1 match); Auckland (1985/6); Northern Districts (1986/7 to 1989/90). *Tour* New Zealand to England 1986.
Career batting
31–28–14–124–25*–8.85–0–*ct* 4
Bowling 2355–73–32.26–0–0–4/32

He achieved little success on the 1986 tour to England; the previous summer he had played for Worcestershire by virtue of a qualification for Ireland!

Barrett, Edward
Amateur. *b:* 11.6.1846. *d:* 23.12.1923, London. Father of E. I. M. (Hampshire). Lower order batsman, useful bowler. *Sch* Cheltenham. *Team* Hampshire (1885, 2 matches).
Career batting
2–4–2–22–13*–11.00–0–*ct* 1
Bowling 48–0

Barrett, Edward Ivo Medhurst
Amateur. *b:* 22.6.1879, Churt, Frensham, Surrey. *d:* 10.7.1950, Boscombe, Hampshire, following an accident. Son of Edward (Hampshire). Fine hard-hitting middle order right-hand batsman. *Sch* Cheltenham. *Team* Hampshire (1896–1925, 80 matches).
Career batting
86–133–15–3804–215–32.23–6–*ct* 36
Bowling 40–0

Service abroad prevented him from appearing regularly for the County, but in 1912 he hit 1,381 runs (av 40.61) and also exceeded 1,000 runs in 1920. His highest score was 215 for Hampshire v Gloucestershire at Southampton in 1920. When Commissioner for Police in Shanghai, he appeared often in the matches between Shanghai and Hong Kong and in 1921 hit a record 165 in this match series. An excellent rugby footballer, he represented England in 1903.

Barrett, Dr John Edward
Amateur. *b:* 15.10.1866, South Melbourne, Victoria, Australia. *d:* 6.2.1916, Peak Hill, Western Australia. Brother of E. A. (Victoria). Defensive opening or middle order left-hand batsman, right-arm medium pace bowler. *Team* Victoria (1884/5 to 1892/3, 15 matches). *Tour* Australia to England 1890. *Tests* Australia (1890, 2 matches).
Career batting
50–91–12–2039–97–25.81–0–*ct* 16
Bowling 336–21–16.00–3–1–6/49
Test batting
2–4–1–80–67*–26.66–0–*ct* 1

His batting was regarded as the success of the 1890 Australian tour to England and his great innings came at Lord's in the Test when he carried out his bat, having gone in first, for 67*. His profession considerably reduced his opportunities in first-class cricket. He hit 1,226 runs, av 20.03, in 1890.

Barrett, Peter
Cricketer. *b:* 3.6.1955, Winchester, Hampshire. *d:* 28.10.1983, Everton, Hampshire. He was killed in a moped accident. Opening left-hand batsman. *Team* Hampshire (1975–76, 6 matches).
Career batting
6–11–0–138–26–12.54–0–*ct* 0
Bowling 4–0

Barrick, Desmond William
Professional. *b:* 28.4.1926, Fitzwilliam, Yorkshire. Attractive middle order right-hand batsman, useful leg-break and googly bowler, good outfield. *Team* Northamptonshire (1949–60, 267 matches). *Tours* Commonwealth to India 1953/4; Norfolk to Jamaica 1956/7.
Career batting
301–490–62–13970–211–32.64–20–*ct* 116
Bowling 3575–79–45.25–2–0–5/71

He scored 1,000 runs in a season seven times (best 1,570, av 37.38, in 1952). His highest score was 211 for Northamptonshire v Essex at Northampton in 1952.

Barrington, George Bainbridge
(registered at birth as G. Bainbridge)
Amateur. *b:* 20.4.1857, Pimlico, London. *d:* 29.3.1942, Kirk Langley, Derbyshire. Middle order right-hand batsman, slow round-arm bowler. *Sch* Repton. *Team* Derbyshire (1880–87, 24 matches).
Career batting
25–48–1–455–50–9.68–0–*ct* 7
Bowling 27–1–27.00–0–0–1/27

Barrington, Kenneth Frank
Professional. *b:* 24.11.1930, Reading, Berkshire. *d:* 14.3.1981, Needham's Point, Bridgetown, Barbados. Very sound middle order right-hand batsman, leg break bowler, fine field. *Team* Surrey (1953–68, 362 matches). *Tours* MCC to Pakistan 1955/6, to West Indies 1959/60, to Ceylon, India and Pakistan 1961/2, to Australia and New Zealand 1962/3, to India 1963/4, to South Africa 1964/5, to Australia 1965/6, to West Indies 1967/8; Surrey to Rhodesia 1959/60; Cavaliers to South Africa 1960/1. *Tests* England (1955–68, 82 matches).
Career batting
533–831–136–31714–256–45.63–76–*ct* 515
Bowling 8907–273–32.62–8–0–7/40
Test batting
82–131–15–6806–256–58.67–20–*ct* 58
Bowling 1300–29–44.82–0–0–3/4

The key to Barrington's success in County and Test cricket was determination. He was no infant prodigy, for although he joined the Oval staff in 1948, it was not until 1953 that he made his first-class debut for the County and it took another six years to establish himself in the Test side. The England selectors gave him a chance in 1955, but he failed and this made him practise until he had eliminated every risky stroke from his repertoire. By 1959, when he became an integral part of the England Eleven, he was technically the soundest bat in the team.

The highlight of his career was the 1962/3 MCC tour to Australia – his Test average that winter was 72.75 and his average in all first-class matches 80.13. No-one else approached either figure and without him the series would undoubtedly have been lost. He was at times criticised for slow play and sometimes justifiably – against the weak New Zealanders of 1965 he took seven and a quarter hours to make 137. The selectors disciplined him by omitting him from the side for the next match. It is true that he was a match saver rather than a winner and perhaps Surrey suffered because of this. He hit 2,000 runs in a season three times (best 2,499, av 54.32, in 1959) and reached 1,000 runs on nine other occasions in England. His highest score was 256 in the 1964 Test at Old Trafford v Australia. He also compiled one 200 for Surrey and one for MCC in Australia.

A heart attack in 1968 brought his first-class career to a premature end, but he continued to play an active role as manager/coach until he suffered a second fatal heart attack in the West Indies, whilst assistant manager to the English touring party. He was a Test selector from 1975 until his death.

Barrington, William Edward James
Cricketer. *b:* 4.1.1960, Carshalton, Surrey. Middle order right-hand batsman. *Sch* Lancing. *Team* Cambridge U (1982, blue).
Career batting
4–6–1–174–59–34.80–0–*ct* 1

Barrington-Chance, G. H.
(*see under* Chance, G. H. B.)

Barron, William
Professional. *b:* 26.10.1917, Herrington, Co Durham. Forcing middle order left-hand batsman, leg break bowler, slip field, occasional wicket-keeper. *Teams* Lancashire (1945, 1 match); Northamptonshire (1946–51, 118 matches).
Career batting
120–200–13–4772–161*–25.51–6–*ct* 98–*st* 2
Bowling 200–5–40.00–0–0–1/1

He hit 1,000 runs in a season twice (best 1,123, av 26.11, in 1946). He also played for Durham (pre first-class, 1937–39). He played soccer at full-back for Northampton Town, Charlton and Wolverhampton Wanderers.

Barrow, Arthur William
Professional. *b:* 19.7.1897, Cheltenham, Gloucestershire. *d:* 19.7.1943, Stoke Bishop, Bristol. Fair lower order batsman, useful change bowler. *Team* Gloucestershire (1919, 6 matches).
Career batting
6–11–1–162–37–16.20–0–*ct* 2
Bowling 196–3–65.33–0–0–2/51

Barrow, Charles Deans
Amateur. *b:* 4.4.1875, Paddington, London. *d:* 20.9.1944, Farmington, Gloucestershire. Middle order right-hand batsman. *Sch* Eton. *Team* MCC (1903).
Career batting
2–2–0–25–25–12.50–0–*ct* 0

Barrow, Ivan
Amateur. *b:* 6.1.1911, Kingston, Jamaica. *d:* 2.4.1979, Kingston, Jamaica. Opening right-hand batsman, wicket-keeper. *Team* Jamaica (1928/9 to 1945/6). *Tours* West Indies to England 1933, 1939, to Australia 1930/1. *Tests* West Indies (1929/30 to 1939, 11 matches).
Career batting
68–113–6–2551–169–23.84–3–*ct* 73–*st* 27
Bowling 34–0
Test batting
11–19–2–276–105–16.23–1–*ct* 17–*st* 5

His most illustrious innings was at Old Trafford in the second Test v England in 1933. He hit 105, becoming the first West Indian to make a Test hundred in England. In the course of his innings he added 200 for the second wicket with G. A. Headley. He hit 1,046 runs, av 23.77, in 1933.

Barrow, Patrick Lindsay
Amateur. *b:* 22.1.1893, Plaistow, Bromley, Kent. *d:* 7.5.1974, Adstock, Buckinghamshire. Useful middle order left-hand batsman. *Sch* Wellington. *Team* Essex (1922, 1 match).
Career batting
1–1–0–0–0–0.00–0–*ct* 0
Bowling 43–1–43.00–0–0–1/21

He also played for Dorset (1914–20). He played ice hockey for England. He was a composer of some repute.

Barrs, Frank Arthur
Amateur. *b:* 24.4.1871, Repton, Derbyshire. *d:* 16.12.1963, Vancouver, British Columbia, Canada. Middle order left-hand batsman, left-arm fast bowler. *Team* Derbyshire (1900–01, 3 matches).
Career batting
3–5–0–68–58–13.60–0–*ct* 0
Bowling 29–1–29.00–0–0–1/17

Barry, Edward Albert
Amateur. *b:* 8.6.1898, Hong Kong. *d:* 24.11.1965, Liphook, Hampshire. Lower order left-hand batsman, left-arm medium pace bowler. *Team* Ireland (1926).
Career batting
2–3–1–20–15–10.00–0–*ct* 1
Bowling 70–1–70.00–0–0–1/44

Barry, Gerald
Amateur. *b:* 18.12.1896, Westminster, London. *d:* 21.2.1977, Lake House, Great Witchingham, Norfolk. Brother-in-law of G. N. Capel-Cure (Essex). Tail end batsman, opening bowler. *Sch* Eton. *Team* Combined Services (1922).
Career batting
1–2–0–2–2–1.00–0–*ct* 1
Bowling 68–0

Bartels, Clarence Wilfred
Professional. *b:* 24.6.1922, Colombo, Ceylon. Middle order right-hand batsman, right-arm medium pace bowler. *Team* Ceylon (1952/3 to 1953/4). *Tour* Ceylon to India 1952/3.
Career batting
5–8–1–215–88–30.71–0–*ct* 8
Bowling 317–14–22.64–0–0–3/24
He was engaged by Ashton in the Central Lancashire League when he appeared for the Commonwealth XI in 1957 and 1958.

Bartholomew, Amos
Professional. *b:* 26.5.1825, Sevenoaks, Kent. *d:* 4.11.1907, Sevenoaks, Kent. Lower order right-hand batsman. *Team* Kent (1858–64, 2 matches).
Career batting
4–7–0–17–6–2.42–0–*ct* 2
Bowling 11–2–5.50–0–0–2/11
His first first-class match was for Combined Kent and Sussex in 1853.

Bartholomew, Arthur Churchill
Amateur. *b:* 21.2.1846, Lympstone, Devon. *d:* 29.3.1940, Reading, Berkshire. Brother of Robert (MCC). Steady middle order right-hand batsman, good field in the covers. *Sch* Marlborough. *Team* Oxford U (1866–68, blue 1868).
Career batting
8–13–3–158–54–15.80–0–*ct* 5
His County cricket was for Devon (1865–71).

Bartholomew, Robert
Amateur. *b:* 27.1.1841, Lympstone, Devon. *d:* 25.3.1918, Marylebone, London. Brother of A. C. (Oxford U). Middle order batsman. *Sch* Uppingham. *Team* MCC (1872).
Career batting
1–1–0–0–0–0.00–0–*ct* 1
His County cricket was for Devon (1871).

Bartlett, Edward Lawson
Amateur. *b:* 10.3.1906, Flint Hall, St Michael, Barbados. *d:* 21.12.1976, Bayville, St Michael, Barbados. Quick scoring middle order right-hand batsman. *Team* Barbados (1923/4 to 1938/9). *Tours* West Indies to England 1928, to Australia 1930/1. *Tests* West Indies (1928 to 1930/1, 5 matches).
Career batting
42–72–4–1581–109–23.25–1–*ct* 8
Test batting
5–8–1–131–84–18.71–0–*ct* 2
A broken finger on the West Indies tour to England in 1928 forced him to miss some matches in mid-tour and later he could not recover his confidence.

Bartlett, Ezra William
Amateur. *b:* 26.9.1861, Doncaster, Yorkshire. *d:* 16.3.1942, Taunton, Somerset. Lower order batsman, wicket-keeper. *Team* Somerset (1894–95, 6 matches).
Career batting
6–12–1–126–40–11.45–0–*ct* 2
Bowling 16–0
He first played for Somerset (not first-class) in 1889.

Bartlett, Hugh Tryon
Amateur. *b:* 7.10.1914, Balaghat, India. *d:* 26.6.1988, Hove, Sussex. Middle order hard-hitting left-hand batsman. *Sch* Dulwich. *Teams* Surrey (1933–35, 3 matches); Cambridge U (1934–36, blue all three years); Sussex (1937–49, 152 matches). *Tours* MCC to South Africa 1938/9, to India 1939/40 (tour cancelled).
Career batting
216–350–34–10098–183–31.95–16–*ct* 70
Bowling 269–10–26.90–0–0–1/0
His greatest season was his first full year with Sussex, 1938. He hit 175 for the Gentlemen v Players at Lord's and also the fastest hundred of the year – for Sussex v Australians at Hove in 57 minutes. His record for 1938 was 1,548 runs, av 57.33 – he also hit 1,000 runs in 1939, 1947 and 1948. He was captain of Cambridge in 1936 and Sussex from 1947 to 1949, but then resigned after a disagreement with the County Committee. His final first-class appearance was Free Foresters in 1951. He was President of Sussex 1977–79.

Bartlett, John Norton
Amateur. *b:* 26.6.1928, Mickleover, Derbyshire. Lower order right-hand batsman, slow left-arm bowler. *Teams* Oxford U (1946–51, blue 1946 and 1951); Sussex (1946–50, 7 matches). *Tour* MCC to Canada 1951.
Career batting
49–70–32–351–28–9.23–0–*ct* 34
Bowling 3443–107–32.17–2–0–5/77
An unusual feature of Bartlett's career is that he was awarded his blue in 1946 and then not again until 1951 – he was on National Service in 1947 and 1948. His final first-class match was for Free Foresters in 1953.

Bartlett, Richard James
Cricketer. *b:* 8.10.1966, Ash Priors, Somerset. Middle order right-hand batsman, off break bowler. *Sch* Taunton. *Team* Somerset (1986–92, 50 matches).
Career batting
51–82–6–1856–117*–24.42–2–*ct* 35
Bowling 145–4–36.25–0–0–1/9
He scored 117* on his first-class debut for Somerset v Oxford U at Oxford in 1986.

Bartley, Edward Leslie Dayrell
Amateur. *b:* 2.3.1896, Stockport, Cheshire. *d:* 7.10.1969, Stonehouse, Plymouth, Devon. Middle order left-hand batsman, wicket-keeper. *Team* Hampshire (1931, 3 matches). *Tour* Joel to South Africa 1924/5.

Barton, Arthur

Career batting
27–44–12–649–84–20.28–0–*ct* 43–*st* 19

He was for many years a leading figure in Naval cricket and made his first-class debut for the Royal Navy in 1914.

Barton, Arthur
Professional. *b:* 30.9.1874, Shipley, Ilkeston, Derbyshire. *d:* 19.1.1949, Ealing, Middlesex. Middle order right-hand batsman, change bowler. *Team* Derbyshire (1901, 3 matches).
Career batting
3–6–0–24–7–4.00–0–*ct* 0
Bowling 61–0

Barton, Charles Gerard
Amateur. *b:* 26.4.1860, Sherfield English, Romsey, Hampshire. *d:* 3.11.1919, Hatfield-Peverel, Essex. Lower order right-hand batsman, good slow left-arm bowler. *Sch* Sherborne and Tonbridge. *Teams* Hampshire (1895–96, 4 matches); Europeans (1893/4).
Career batting
6–8–2–29–22–4.83–0–*ct* 0
Bowling 206–9–22.88–1–0–6/27

His best County cricket was played whilst Hampshire were not considered first-class, making his debut in 1881, and in 1891 he took 42 wickets (av 9.79) for the County.

Barton, George
Amateur. *b:* 8.6.1808, Dartford, Kent. *d:* 20.6.1864, Uckfield, Sussex. Hard hitting middle order right-hand batsman. *Team* Sussex (1835–56, 34 matches).
Career batting
37–65–8–388–34–6.80–0–*ct* 20

Barton, Harold George Mitford
Amateur. *b:* 10.10.1882, Mudeford, Christchurch, Hampshire. *d:* 3.7.1970, Bassett, Southampton, Hampshire. Middle order right-hand batsman. *Sch* Sherborne. *Team* Hampshire (1910–12, 8 matches).
Career batting
8–15–2–146–31–11.23–0–*ct* 2

He also played for Buckinghamshire (1907).

Barton, Joseph
Professional. *b:* 10.1.1860, Smethwick, Staffordshire. *d:* 31.1.1945, Selly Oak, Birmingham. Tail end right-hand batsman, right-arm fast bowler. *Team* Warwickshire (1895–96, 3 matches).
Career batting
3–4–0–38–16–9.50–0–*ct* 0
Bowling 165–7–23.57–1–0–5/73

He took 5 for 73 in the first County Championship match ever played by Warwickshire (v Essex at Edgbaston in 1895). He also played for Staffordshire (1902).

Barton, Michael Richard
Amateur. *b:* 14.10.1914, Dereham, Norfolk. Sound middle order right-hand batsman, good slip field. *Sch* Winchester. *Teams* Oxford U (1935–37, blue 1936–37); Surrey (1948–54, 110 matches).
Career batting
147–247–16–5965–192–25.82–7–*ct* 117

Barton played for Norfolk from 1933 to 1947, but joined Surrey in 1948 and captained that County from 1949 to 1951. His final first-class appearance was for Free Foresters in 1955. He hit 1,000 runs in a season three times (best 1,187, av 22.82, in 1948). He was President of Surrey in 1983.

Barton, Victor Alexander
Professional. *b:* 6.10.1867, Hound, Netley, Hampshire. *d:* 23.3.1906, Belle Vue, Southampton, Hampshire. Attractive hard-hitting middle order right-hand batsman, useful right-arm medium pace bowler. *Teams* Kent (1889–90, 11 matches); Hampshire (1895–1902, 143 matches). *Tour* Read to South Africa 1891/2. *Test* England (1891/2, 1 match).
Career batting
157–282–15–6411–205–24.01–6–*ct* 101
Bowling 4036–141–28.62–3–0–6/28
Test batting
1–1–0–23–23–23.00–0–*ct* 0

Barton first came to notice when playing for the Royal Artillery v MCC at Lord's in 1889 – he hit 91 and 102 and took 6 for 53. He then appeared for Kent as 'Bombardier Barton', but in 1891 purchased his discharge from the Army and began his career with Hampshire. His highest score was 205 for Hampshire v Sussex at Hove in 1900. His on-drives were noted for their power and fieldsmen at mid-on had a 'wholesome dread of him'. He hit 1,000 runs in a season twice (best 1,060, av 27.17, in 1900).

Barwell, Terence Ian
Cricketer. *b:* 29.4.1937, Bloemhof, Transvaal, South Africa. Middle order right-hand batsman, wicket-keeper. *Team* Somerset (1959–68, 43 matches).
Career batting
44–77–8–1344–84*–19.47–0–*ct* 39–*st* 1

His final first-class match was in 1973 for Minor Counties – he played for Wiltshire from 1971 to 1976.

Barwick, Stephen Royston
Cricketer. *b:* 6.9.1960, Neath, Glamorgan. Low order right-hand batsman, right-arm medium pace bowler. *Team* Glamorgan (1981–92, 173 matches).
Career batting
173–162–62–724–30–7.24–0–*ct* 37
Bowling 12931–378–34.20–9–1–8/42

A serious road accident in August 1988 ended his cricket for that summer.

Base, Simon John
Cricketer. *b:* 2.1.1960, Maidstone, Kent. Lower order right-hand batsman, right-arm medium fast bowler. *Teams* Western Province (1981/2 to 1982/3); Glamorgan (1986–87, 20 matches); Boland (1987/8 to

1988/9); Derbyshire (1988–92, 55 matches); Border (1989/90 to 1991/2).
Career batting
103–130–33–1135–58–11.70–0–*ct* 45
Bowling 8915–323–27.60–12–1–7/60

Bashford, Rev Alfred Myddleton
Amateur. *b:* 23.7.1881, Wickhampton, Norfolk. *d:* 31.7.1949, Colham Green, Hillingdon, Middlesex. Middle order right-hand batsman. *Sch* Merchant Taylors'. *Team* Middlesex (1906, 2 matches).
Career batting
2–4–0–27–14–6.75–0–*ct* 1
Bowling 29–1–29.00–0–0–1/12
He played in the Seniors' Match at Cambridge in 1903, but never in a first-class game for the University.

Baskervyle-Glegg, John
Amateur. *b:* 10.11.1940, Windsor, Berkshire. Opening right-hand batsman, wicket-keeper. *Sch* Eton. *Team* Combined Services (1962).
Career batting
1–2–0–43–35–21.50–0–*ct* 0

Bass, Hamar Alfred
Amateur. *b:* 30.7.1842, Yoxall, Burton-on-Trent, Staffordshire. *d:* 8.4.1898, Byrkly Lodge, Callingwood, Staffordshire. Middle order batsman. *Sch* Cheltenham and Harrow. *Team* MCC (1865).
Career batting
1–2–0–6–3–3.00–0–*ct* 0
His County cricket was for Derbyshire (pre first-class, 1866) and Staffordshire (1875–77). From 1878 to 1885 he was MP for Tamworth, then for West Staffordshire until his death.

Bass, Henry John
Professional. *b:* 14.10.1852, Canterbury, Kent. *d:* 24.1.1904, Canterbury, Kent. *Team* Kent (1871–75, 3 matches).
Career batting
3–5–0–11–8–2.20–0–*ct* 1
He was employed as groundsman at Canterbury from 1879 until his death.

Bass, John George
Amateur. *b:* 9.8.1903, Abington, Northampton. Lower order right-hand batsman, right-arm medium pace change bowler. *Team* Northamptonshire (1935, 2 matches).
Career batting
2–4–0–43–16–10.75–0–*ct* 0
Bowling 31–0

Bassett, Hubert
Amateur. *b:* 5.10.1867, Stanton St John, Oxford. *d:* 13.6.1943, Oxford. Middle order left-hand batsman, left-arm medium pace bowler. *Team* Oxford U (1888–91, blue last three years).
Career batting
21–39–6–292–54*–8.84–0–*ct* 15
Bowling 1722–78–22.07–4–0–6/50
He also played for Oxfordshire (1895–1906) and Suffolk (1908–14).

Bastard, Edward William
Amateur. *b:* 28.2.1862, Wilton, Somerset. *d:* 2.4.1901, Taunton, Somerset. Tail end left-hand batsman, excellent slow left-arm bowler, slip field. *Sch* Sherborne. *Teams* Oxford U (1882–85, blue 1883–85); Somerset (1883–85, 15 matches).
Career batting
37–60–19–278–47–6.78–0–*ct* 15
Bowling 2887–137–21.07–8–2–8/54
He continued to appear for Somerset in non-first-class matches until 1889. He also played for Dorset (1881).

Bastien, Steven
Cricketer. *b:* 13.3.1963, Stepney, London. Lower order right-hand batsman, right-arm medium fast bowler. *Team* Glamorgan (1988–92, 44 matches). *Tour* Glamorgan to Zimbabwe 1990/1.
Career batting
44–33–13–152–36*–7.60–0–*ct* 5
Bowling 3715–96–38.69–5–0–6/75

Bastow, John
Professional. *b:* 30.10.1850, Bromley-by-Bow, London. *d:* 1.6.1927, Haverstock Hill, London. Grandfather of F. C. Hawker (Essex). Lower order right-hand batsman, wicket-keeper. *Team* Middlesex (1874–77, 5 matches).
Career batting
5–10–2–118–35–14.75–0–*ct* 3–*st* 5
He also played for Essex (pre first-class, 1886–89).

Batchelor, Rev William Jesse
Amateur. *b:* 14.11.1846, Hayes, Kent. *d:* 19.11.1917, Epsom, Surrey. Good middle order right-hand batsman, fine field. *Sch* Perse. *Team* Cambridgeshire (1868, 2 matches).
Career batting
2–4–0–14–7–3.50–0–*ct* 1
Bowling 42–0
He was educated at Cambridge and was asked to play for the University but declined, as he was the senior mathematical scholar of his college. He appeared for Warwickshire (pre first-class) from 1872–77. His scores in minor matches were quite extraordinary.

Bate, Richard
Cricketer. *b:* 27.12.1966, Finchley, Middlesex. Middle order right-hand batsman. *Sch* Haberdashers' Aske's, Elstree. *Team* Cambridge U (1987–89, blue 1988).
Career batting
11–17–2–225–45–15.00–0–*ct* 2

Bateman, Dr Arthur Cyril
Amateur. *b:* 31.10.1890, Bailieborough, Co Cavan, Ireland. *d:* 28.3.1918, near Arras, France. Middle order right-hand batsman. *Sch* Portora Royal School. *Team* Ireland (1913–14).
Career batting
2–4–0–149–52–37.25–0–*ct* 2

Bateman, Edward Louis
Amateur. *b:* 15.9.1834, Mickleover, Derbyshire. *d:* 25.1.1909, Rowditch Lodge, Derbyshire. Brother of Augustus (Nottinghamshire). Middle order right-hand batsman, excellent field. *Sch* Marlborough and Repton. *Teams* Oxford U (1854–55, blue both years); Nottinghamshire (1855, 1 match).
Career batting
8–15–1–269–68*–19.21–0–*ct* 4

His last first-class match was for the Gentlemen of England v Gentlemen of Middlesex at Islington in 1865. He was on the MCC Committee for many years and was Auditor to the Club from 1904 to his death. He also played for Leicestershire (pre first-class, 1855).

Bateman, Richard
Amateur. *b:* 29.4.1849, Farnham, Surrey. *d:* 5.11.1913, Ash Vale, Surrey. Middle order batsman. *Team* Hampshire (1883, 1 match).
Career batting
1–2–1–18–14*–18.00–0–*ct* 0

Bateman-Champain, Claude Edward
Amateur. *b:* 30.3.1875, Richmond, Surrey. *d:* 13.10.1956, Budleigh Salterton, Devon. Brother of F. H. (Gloucestershire), H. F. (Gloucestershire) and J. N. (Gloucestershire), nephew of F. Currie (Gentlemen of Kent), F. L. Currie (Cambridge U), R. G. Currie (Gentlemen of Surrey and Sussex), W. C. Currie (Gentlemen of Surrey and Sussex), brother-in-law of F. A. Currie (MCC). Middle order right-hand batsman, slow right-arm bowler. *Sch* Cheltenham. *Team* Gloucestershire (1898–1907, 16 matches).
Career batting
18–28–4–226–29–9.41–0–*ct* 8
Bowling 14–0

Bateman-Champain, Francis Henry
Amateur. *b:* 17.6.1877, Richmond, Surrey. *d:* 29.12.1942, Tiverton, Devon. Brother of C. E. (Gloucestershire), H. F. (Gloucestershire) and J. N. (Gloucestershire), nephew of F. Currie (Gentlemen of Kent), F. L. Currie (Cambridge U), R. G. Currie (Gentlemen of Surrey and Sussex), W. C. Currie (Gentlemen of Surrey and Sussex), brother-in-law of F. A. Currie (MCC). Stylish opening/middle order right-hand batsman, slow right-arm bowler, good field. *Sch* Cheltenham. *Teams* Gloucestershire (1895–1914, 83 matches); Oxford U (1897–1900, blue all four years).
Career batting
114–198–8–4677–149–24.61–5–*ct* 101
Bowling 418–17–24.58–1–0–6/62

He captained Oxford in 1899. He also won a blue for rugby.

Bateman-Champain, Brig-Gen Hugh Frederick
(name changed from Champain in October 1870)
Amateur. *b:* 6.4.1869, Ashford, Middlesex. *d:* 7.10.1933, Swinley Park, Ascot, Berkshire. Brother of C. E. (Gloucestershire), F. H. (Gloucestershire) and J. N. (Gloucestershire), nephew of F. Currie (Gentlemen of Kent), F. L. Currie (Cambridge U), R. G. Currie (Gentlemen of Surrey and Sussex), W. C. Currie (Gentlemen of Surrey and Sussex), brother-in-law of F. A. Currie (MCC). Middle order right-hand batsman. *Sch* Cheltenham. *Team* Gloucestershire (1888–1902, 11 matches).
Career batting
12–18–1–142–35–8.35–0–*ct* 8

Owing to his military duties he was unable to play much County cricket, but he appeared in Army and other matches in India.

Bateman-Champain, Rt Rev John Norman
Amateur. *b:* 14.3.1880, Richmond, Surrey. *d:* 22.10.1950, Westbury-on-Trym, Gloucestershire. Brother of C. E. (Gloucestershire), F. H. (Gloucestershire) and H. F. (Gloucestershire), nephew of F. Currie (Gentlemen of Kent), F. L. Currie (Cambridge U), R. G. Currie (Gentlemen of Surrey and Sussex), W. C. Currie (Gentlemen of Surrey and Sussex), brother-in-law of F. A. Currie (MCC). Middle order right-hand batsman. *Sch* Cheltenham. *Team* Gloucestershire (1899, 2 matches).
Career batting
5–9–2–36–17–5.14–0–*ct* 2
Bowling 7–0

His final first-class match was for Free Foresters in 1920. Whilst at Cambridge he played in both the Freshmen's and Seniors' Trials, but never in a first-class match. He also played for Shropshire. He was Bishop of Knaresborough 1938–1948.

Bates, Arthur John
Professional. *b:* 18.6.1852, New Radford, Nottinghamshire. *d:* 13.2.1925, Old Lenton, Nottinghamshire. Lower order right-hand batsman, slow right-arm bowler. *Team* Nottinghamshire (1878, 2 matches).
Career batting
2–4–0–5–5–1.25–0–*ct* 0

He played soccer at right wing for Nottingham Forest in 1879.

Bates, Donald Lawson
Professional. *b:* 10.5.1933, Hove, Sussex. Lower order right-hand batsman, right-arm fast medium bowler, good field. *Team* Sussex (1950–71, 315 matches).

Career batting
315–358–157–1525–37*–7.58–0–*ct* 118
Bowling 22776–880–25.88–34–2–8/51

Bates took 100 wickets in a season three times (best 113, av 22.65, in 1961). His benefit in 1968 realised £8,000. A talented soccer player, he appeared at right-half for Lewes and Brighton and Hove Albion.

Bates, F. H.
Amateur. *b:* 1875, Philadelphia, USA. Middle order right-hand batsman, right-arm medium pace bowler. *Team* Philadelphia (1897–1903). *Tours* Philadelphia to England 1897, 1903.
Career batting
16–30–1–224–24–7.72–*ct* 8
Bowling 355–7–50.71–0–0–2/17

He scored prolifically in club cricket in the United States, but failed completely on both his visits to England. He appeared for United States v Canada in 1898 and 1899.

Bates, Frederick Stanley
Amateur. *b:* 25.2.1899, Lambourn, Berkshire. *d:* 13.8.1969, Hammersmith, London. Middle order batsman. *Sch* Marlborough. *Team* Hampshire (1920, 2 matches).
Career batting
2–3–0–18–9–6.00–0–*ct* 0

Bates, Henry Albert
Amateur. *b:* 3.12.1880, Hoxton New Town, Shoreditch, London. *d:* 9.9.1942, Reading, Berkshire. Middle order right-hand batsman, right-arm medium pace bowler. *Team* Middlesex (1909, 2 matches).
Career batting
2–3–0–18–10–6.00–0–*ct* 0

Bates, James
Professional. *b:* 10.1.1856, Paddington, London. *d:* 7.12.1915, City of London. Middle order right-hand batsman, right-arm medium pace bowler. *Team* Middlesex (1880, 1 match).
Career batting
1–2–0–9–8–4.50–0–*ct* 2

Bates, Leonard Thomas Ashton
Professional. *b:* 20.3.1895, in the groundsman's house at Edgbaston, Birmingham. *d:* 11.3.1971, Coldwaltham, Sussex. Brother of S. H. (Warwickshire), father-in-law of D. J. Weekes (Sussex). Sound middle order right-hand batsman, right-arm medium pace bowler. *Team* Warwickshire (1913–35, 441 matches).
Career batting
444–749–53–19380–211–27.84–21–*ct* 160
Bowling 471–9–52.33–0–0–2/16

He exceeded 1,000 runs in a season twelve times (best 1,518, av 33.73, in 1926). His highest score was 211 for Warwickshire v Gloucestershire at Gloucester in 1932.

Bates, Samuel Harold
Professional. *b:* 16.6.1890, Edgbaston Cricket Ground, Birmingham. *d:* 28.8.1916. He was killed in action near Hardecourt, France. Brother of L. T. A. (Warwickshire). Lower order right-hand batsman, slow left-arm bowler. *Team* Warwickshire (1910–12, 5 matches).
Career batting
5–9–1–24–13–3.00–0–*ct* 0
Bowling 182–6–30.33–0–0–3/56

Bates, William Ederick
Professional. *b:* 5.3.1884, Kirkheaton, Yorkshire. *d:* 17.1.1957, Belfast, Ireland. Son of Willie (Yorkshire). Opening or middle order right-hand batsman, slow left-arm bowler, brilliant field. *Teams* Yorkshire (1907–13, 113 matches); Glamorgan (1921–31, 283 matches); Wales (1923–30).
Career batting
406–684–30–15964–200*–24.40–13–*ct* 250
Bowling 8671–230–37.70–4–0–8/93

After being unable to obtain a regular place in the Yorkshire side, Bates became one of the mainstays of Glamorgan. He reached 1,000 runs in seven seasons (best 1,692, av 43.48, in 1927). His highest score was 200* for Glamorgan v Worcestershire at Kidderminster in 1927. He also played for Cheshire (1933–36). He played soccer for Leeds City and Bolton Wanderers. He first played for Glamorgan (pre first-class) in 1914.

Bates, Willie
Professional. *b:* 19.11.1855, Lascelles Hall, Huddersfield, Yorkshire. *d:* 8.1.1900, Lepton, Yorkshire. Father of W. E. (Yorkshire and Glamorgan). Very hard-hitting middle order right-hand batsman, off break bowler. *Team* Yorkshire (1877–87, 202 matches). *Tours* Daft to North America 1879 (not first-class); Shaw and Shrewsbury to Australia 1881/2, 1884/5, 1886/7; Bligh to Australia 1882/3; Vernon to Australia 1887/8. *Tests* England (1881/2 to 1886/7, 15 matches).
Career batting
299–495–20–10249–144*–21.57–10–*ct* 238
Bowling 14979–874–17.13–52–10–8/21
Test batting
15–26–2–656–64–27.33–0–*ct* 9
Bowling 821–50–16.42–4–1–7/28

An excellent all-rounder, though his fielding tended to let him down, Bates took 121 wickets av 16.28, in 1881 and scored 1,000 runs five times (best 1,161, av 25.23, in 1885). His most famous feat was the hat-trick he performed against Australia in 1882/3 when his victims were McDonnell, Giffen and Bonnor. During net practice on the 1887/8 tour to Australia, Bates was hit in the eye and nearly lost his sight – the accident ended his first-class career.

Bather, Rev William Henry
Amateur. *b:* 12.12.1861, Meole Brace, Shropshire. *d:* 3.1.1939, Boscombe, Hampshire. Hard hitting middle order right-hand batsman. *Sch* Rossall. *Team* Cambridge U (1882–83).
Career batting
6–10–1–119–33–13.22–0–*ct* 6
He also played for Shropshire (1884).

Bathurst, F. H. H
(*see under* Hervey-Bathurst, F. H)

Bathurst, F. T. A. H
(*see under* Hervey-Bathurst, F. T. A)

Bathurst, L. H.
(*see under* Hervey-Bathurst, L.)

Bathurst, Lawrence Charles Villebois
Amateur. *b:* 4.6.1871, Gressenhall, Dereham, Norfolk. *d:* 22.2.1939, Bonchurch, Isle of Wight. Steady middle order right-hand batsman, useful left-arm medium pace bowler, good field. *Sch* Radley. *Teams* Oxford U (1893–94, blue both years); Middlesex (1894–95, 8 matches). *Tour* Lord Hawke to North America 1894.
Career batting
33–56–11–671–45*–14.91–0–*ct* 19
Bowling 1908–96–19.87–6–2–8/44
His final first-class match was for MCC in 1899. He also played for Norfolk (1896–1904).

Batson, Dr Richard Erstine
Amateur. *b:* 11.6.1891, Belleville, St Michael, Barbados. *d:* 25.1.1971, Islington, London. Middle order right-hand batsman. *Teams* Barbados (1909/10 to 1911/12); Scotland (1920–23).
Career batting
6–10–0–260–111–26.00–1–*ct* 2

Batson, W.
Amateur. Middle order right-hand batsman. *Team* Northamptonshire (1920-21, 2 matches).
Career batting
2–4–0–45–34–11.25–0–*ct* 0

Battcock, Oliver Gordon
Amateur. *b:* 16.9.1903, Slough, Buckinghamshire. *d:* 26.9.1970, Southwark, London. Lower order left-hand batsman, right-arm medium pace bowler. *Sch* Harrow. *Team* MCC (1938–39).
Career batting
2–2–1–30–27–30.00–0–*ct* 0
Bowling 102–2–51.00–0–0–1/10
His County cricket was for Buckinghamshire (1923–52) and he was reputed to have captured about 6,000 wickets in local cricket. He appeared on the stage as 'Oliver Gordon'.

Battersby, Terence Esmond Maxwell
Amateur. *b:* 29.10.1893, Meerut, Bengal, India. *d:* 10.1.1972, Goring Heath, Berkshire. Opening left-hand batsman, change bowler. *Sch* Marlborough. *Teams* Army (1926); Europeans (1923/4).
Career batting
3–6–0–110–41–18.33–0–*ct* 1
Bowling 126–2–63.00–0–0–2/60
His County cricket was for Suffolk (1913) and Devon (1930–32).

Battersea, Howard Lawrence Paley
Amateur. *b:* 3.8.1881, Martley, Worcestershire. *d:* 4.12.1922, Ide Hill, Sevenoaks, Kent. Tail end batsman, bowler. *Team* H. K. Foster's XI (1919).
Career batting
1–1–0–1–1–1.00–0–*ct* 0
Bowling 163–0

Batty, Jeremy David
Cricketer. *b:* 15.5.1971, Bradford, Yorkshire. Lower order right-hand batsman, off break bowler. *Team* Yorkshire (1989–92, 45 matches). *Tour* Yorkshire to South Africa 1991/2.
Career batting
45–41–13–403–51–14.39–0–*ct* 15
Bowling 3864–99–39.03–2–0–6/48

Baucher, Frederick William
Amateur. *b:* 6.11.1878, Wigan, Lancashire. *d:* 7.6.1947, Blundellsands, Lancashire. Lower order right-hand batsman, wicket-keeper. *Team* Lancashire (1903, 1 match).
Career batting
1–2–0–12–8–6.00–0–*ct* 0

Bawtree, John Francis
Amateur. *b:* 26.11.1873, Witham, Essex. *d:* 25.3.1938, Great Totham, Essex. Useful batsman, slow left-arm bowler. *Sch* Haileybury. *Team* Essex (1895–96, 5 matches).
Career batting
5–9–1–96–47–12.00–0–*ct* 5
Bowling 66–2–33.00–0–0–1/16

Baxter, Arthur Douglas
Amateur. *b:* 20.1.1910, West End, Edinburgh, Scotland. *d:* 28.1.1986, Edenbridge, Kent. Tail end right-hand batsman, right-arm fast medium bowler. *Sch* Loretto. *Teams* Scotland (1929–37); Lancashire (1933–34, 3 matches); Middlesex (1938, 2 matches). *Tour* MCC to Australia and New Zealand 1935/6.
Career batting
42–56–18–273–26*–7.18–0–*ct* 10
Bowling 4109–189–21.74–16–4–7/33
His final first-class match was for Free Foresters in 1939. He also played for Devon (1930).

Baxter, Austin Godfrey
Amateur. *b:* 21.9.1931, West Bridgford, Nottingham. *d:* 17.1.1993, Lenton, Nottinghamshire. Nephew of

H. W. Radford (Derbyshire). Stylish middle order right-hand batsman, occasional right-arm medium pace bowler. *Sch* Ratcliffe College. *Team* Nottinghamshire (1952–53, 13 matches).
Career batting
13–22–1–314–98–14.95–0–*ct* 4
Bowling 8–0
He was a most promising batsman, but unable to play regularly in County cricket owing to business commitments.

Baxter, Herbert Wood
Amateur. *b:* 2.4.1883, Stockport, Cheshire. *d:* 25.4.1962, Shaw Heath, Stockport, Cheshire. Hard-hitting middle order batsman. *Team* Glamorgan (1921, 1 match).
Career batting
1–2–0–11–10–5.50–0–*ct* 0
He first played for Glamorgan (pre first-class) in 1920.

Bayes, George William
Professional. *b:* 27.2.1884, Flamborough, Yorkshire. *d:* 6.12.1960, Flamborough, Yorkshire. Tail end right-hand batsman, right-arm fast bowler. *Team* Yorkshire (1910–21, 18 matches).
Career batting
18–24–11–165–36–12.69–0–*ct* 7
Bowling 1534–48–31.95–1–0–5/83

Bayford, Robert Augustus
Amateur. *b:* 13.3.1838, Albury, Surrey. *d:* 24.8.1922, Netley Hill, Hampshire. Hard-hitting middle order right-hand batsman, slow round-arm bowler. *Teams* Cambridge U (1857–60, blue 1857–59); Cambridgeshire (1858, 1 match); Surrey (1860–61, 4 matches); Middlesex (1861–64, 5 matches).
Career batting
30–51–1–822–92–16.44–0–*ct* 7–*st* 4
Bowling 128–7 + 5–18.28–0–0–4/42
His final first-class appearance was for Southgate in 1867. He captained Cambridge in 1859.

Bayley, Henry Peter
Amateur. *b:* 9.4.1916, Georgetown, British Guiana. Sound middle order right-hand batsman, good field. *Team* British Guiana (1935/6 to 1950/1). *Tour* West Indies to England 1939.
Career batting
28–50–4–1577–268–34.28–3–*ct* 11
Bowling 10–0
Coming to England with a reputation built on his record breaking innings of 268 for British Guiana v Barbados at Bridgetown in 1937/8, Bayley failed to find any sort of form and was not selected for the Tests.

Bayley, John
Professional. *b:* 17.5.1794, Mitcham, Surrey. *d:* 7.11.1874, Mitcham, Surrey. Uncle of Morton (Surrey). Fair hard-hitting right-hand batsman, good slow round-arm bowler. *Teams* Middlesex (1830); Surrey (1839–47, 5 matches); Hampshire (1843).
Career batting
83–144–17–936–54–7.37–0–*ct* 52–*st* 5
Bowling 259–12 + 338–21.58–31–9–7/?
His first first-class match was for the Bs v England in 1822 and from 1823 to 1854 he was on the staff at Lord's. His bowling was at its best in the late 1830s when he was well over 40 years of age. His final first-class match was for MCC in 1850.

Bayley, Rev Sir John Robert Laurie Emilius
(changed his name to Laurie in 1887)
Amateur. *b:* 16.5.1823, Bloomsbury, London. *d:* 4.12.1917, Maxwelltown, Dumfries, Scotland. Son of J. E. G. (Hampshire), brother of L. H. (Kent). Fine free hitting middle order right-hand batsman. *Sch* Eton. *Team* Kent (1842–44, 9 matches).
Career batting
29–53–12–515–50–12.56–0–*ct* 8
His most famous innings was his 152 in the Eton v Harrow match of 1841, a record which stood for over 60 years. He was not in the Eleven at Cambridge. His last first-class match was for Gentlemen of Kent in 1845.

Bayley, Martin George
Cricketer. *b:* 10.7.1952, Leamington Spa, Warwickshire. Lower order right-hand batsman, slow left-arm bowler. *Team* Warwickshire (1969, 2 matches).
Career batting
2–2–1–2–1*–2.00–0–*ct* 2
Bowling 125–3–41.66–0–0–2/54

Bayley, Morton
Professional. *b:* 7.5.1843, Mitcham, Surrey. *d:* 6.3.1926, Mitcham, Surrey. Nephew of John (Surrey). Lower order right-hand batsman, right-arm medium pace bowler. *Team* Surrey (1866, 1 match).
Career batting
1–1–1–8–8*–no av–0–*ct* 1
Bowling 19–0

Baylis, Keith Rodney
Cricketer. *b:* 5.11.1947, Redditch, Worcestershire. Lower order right-hand batsman, leg break bowler, good close field. *Sch* Ellesmere. *Team* Worcestershire (1966–67, 6 matches).
Career batting
6–7–1–89–26–14.83–0–*ct* 2
Bowling 495–14–35.35–0–0–4/112

Bayliss, Edward George
Amateur. *b:* 5.1.1918, Worcester. *d:* 21.11.1989, Aston Fields, Bromsgrove, Worcestershire. Lower order right-hand batsman. *Team* Worcestershire (1939, 1 match).
Career batting
1–2–0–0–0–0.00–ct 0

Baynton, Robert Geoffrey
Amateur. *b:* 5.3.1900, Moseley, Birmingham. *d:* 26.9.1924, Highbury Park, Moor Green, Birmingham after a motor accident. Lower order right-hand batsman, left-arm medium pace bowler. *Team* Warwickshire (1921–23, 13 matches).
Career batting
13–19–1–212–36–11.77–0–*ct* 3
Bowling 479–14–34.21–0–0–4/56

Beadle, Sydney Wilford
Amateur. *b:* 9.11.1885, Wadhwan, India. *d:* 24.7.1937, Reading Street, Tenterden, Kent. Middle order right-hand batsman, slow right-arm bowler. *Sch* Rossall. *Team* Hampshire (1911, 1 match).
Career batting
3–6–0–88–28–14.66–0–*ct* 2
Bowling 53–0
He also represented the Navy v Army at Lord's in 1911 and 1912.

Beadsmoore, Walter Arthur
Amateur. *b:* 15.10.1891, Basford, Nottinghamshire. *d:* 13.4.1964, Watford, Hertfordshire. Lower order left-hand batsman, slow left-arm bowler. *Team* Minor Counties (1924).
Career batting
1–2–1–10–7–10.00–0–*ct* 0
Bowling 55–5–11.00–0–0–4/53
His county cricket was for Norfolk (1921–31).

Beagley, Thomas
Professional. *b:* 5.10.1789, Farringdon, Alton, Hampshire. *d:* 21.2.1858, Paddington, London. Brother of Henry (Hampshire) and John (Hampshire). Fine batsman, splendid long-stop. *Team* Hampshire (1816–28).
Career batting
70–127–15–1916–113*–17.10–1–*ct* 32
Bowling 7 wickets (no analyses)–0–0–3/?
His most celebrated innings was 113* – the first century ever scored in the Gentlemen v Players series of matches – hit at Lord's in 1821. His last first-class match was for England in 1839.

Beal, Charles William
Amateur. *b:* 24.6.1855, Sydney, New South Wales, Australia. *d:* 5.2.1921, Randwick, New South Wales, Australia. Nephew of J. C. (New South Wales). *Tours* Manager of the 1882 and 1888 Australians to England.
Career batting
1–1–0–5–5–5.00–0–*ct* 0
He appeared in first-class cricket in England in 1882, playing in emergency for the Australian tourists. He was Secretary to the New South Wales Cricket Association.

Beal, David
Cricketer. *b:* 17.7.1966, Butleigh, Somerset. Lower order right-hand batsman, right-arm medium pace bowler. *Team* Somerset (1991, 3 matches).
Career batting
3–2–0–1–1–0.50–0–*ct* 1
Bowling 320–3–106.66–0–0–1/37

Bean, George
Professional. *b:* 7.3.1864, Sutton-in-Ashfield, Nottinghamshire. *d:* 16.3.1923, Mansfield, Nottinghamshire. Brother of Joseph (Sussex). Hard-hitting middle order or opening right-hand batsman, right-arm medium pace bowler, good cover-point. *Teams* Nottinghamshire (1885, 5 matches); Sussex (1886–98, 202 matches). *Tour* Sheffield to Australia 1891/2. *Tests* England (1891/2, 3 matches).
Career batting
247–438–21–8634–186–20.70–9–*ct* 154
Bowling 7086–260–27.25–9–2–8/29
Test batting
3–5–0–92–50–18.40–0–*ct* 4
He reached 1,000 runs in a season twice (best 1,277, av 28.38, in 1893). He was a first-class umpire (1902–03).

Bean, John Reginald
Amateur. *b:* 16.1.1913, Bangalore, India. Middle order right-hand batsman, leg break bowler. *Sch* Ampleforth. *Team* Army (1936).
Career batting
1–2–0–20–19–10.00–0–*ct* 0

Bean, Joseph
Professional. *b:* 16.2.1876, Sutton-in-Ashfield, Nottinghamshire. *d:* 12.1.1922, Sutton-in-Ashfield, Nottinghamshire. Brother of George (Nottinghamshire and Sussex). Middle order batsman, change bowler. *Team* Sussex (1895–1903, 40 matches).
Career batting
40–57–4–453–46–8.54–0–*ct* 27
Bowling 841–35–24.02–1–0–5/34

Bean, Leslie Hugh
Amateur. *b:* 2.2.1906, Burnham-on-Sea, Somerset. *d:* 13.1.1988, Accra, Ghana. Middle order right-hand batsman, leg break and googly bowler. *Sch* Sherborne. *Team* Somerset (1929, 3 matches).
Career batting
3–6–0–35–17–5.83–0–*ct* 1
Bowling 24–1–24.00–0–0–1/14
He also played for Dorset (1928–39) with some success. He captained Sierra Leone for six years and also appeared for the Gold Coast.

Bear, Michael John
Professional. *b:* 23.2.1934, Brentwood, Essex. Opening left-hand batsman, occasional leg break bowler, excellent outfield. *Team* Essex (1954–68, 322 matches). *Tour* MCC to New Zealand 1960/1 (played in emergency in non-first-class match).

Career batting
322–562–44–12564–137–24.25–9–*ct* 113
Bowling 53–0

He hit 1,000 runs in a season four times (best 1,833, av 32.15, in 1966). He played soccer for Romford.

Beard, Bertram Ferryman
Amateur. *b:* 1.11.1874, Brighton, Sussex. *d:* 2.12.1959, Westminster, London. Middle order right-hand batsman, right-arm medium pace bowler. *Sch* Wellington. *Team* Sussex (1899, 2 matches).
Career batting
2–2–0–4–4–2.00–0–*ct* 1
Bowling 9–0

Beard, Graeme Robert
Cricketer. *b:* 19.8.1950, Auburn, Sydney, New South Wales, Australia. Lower order right-hand batsman, right-arm medium pace off break bowler. *Team* New South Wales (1975/6 to 1981/2, 39 matches). *Tours* Australia to Pakistan 1979/80, to Sri Lanka 1980/81, to England 1981. *Tests* Australia (1979/80, 3 matches).
Career batting
54–71–10–1441–75–23.62–0–*ct* 22
Bowling 3524–125–28.19–7–1–5/33
Test batting
3–5–0–114–49–22.80–0–*ct* 0
Bowling 109–1–109.00–0–0–1/26

He was given few opportunities on the 1981 tour to England and did not appear in the Tests.

Beardmore, William Joseph Montague
Amateur. *b:* 18.7.1894, Renfrew, Scotland. *d:* 29.12.1978, Haywards Heath, Sussex. Middle order right-hand batsman. *Sch* Loretto. *Team* Scotland (1924).
Career batting
1–2–0–5–3–2.50–0–*ct* 0

Beardshall, Mark
Cricketer. *b:* 10.1.1962, Barnsley, Yorkshire. Lower order right-hand batsman, right-arm medium pace bowler. *Team* Derbyshire (1987, 8 matches).
Career batting
8–8–3–47–25–9.40–0–*ct* 2
Bowling 572–12–47.66–0–0–4/68

Beart, Frederick Robert
Amateur. *b:* 6.7.1850, Godmanchester, Huntingdonshire. *d:* 4.3.1895, Godmanchester, Huntingdonshire. Father of C. W. (Europeans). Hard hitting middle order batsman, moderate field. *Sch* Marlborough. *Team* Oxford U (1871).
Career batting
1–1–0–0–0–0.00–0–*ct* 1

His County cricket was for Huntingdonshire (1869–79).

Beasley, Joseph Noble
Amateur. *b:* 5.12.1881, Chapel Brayton, Northampton. *d:* 23.1.1960, Stony Stratford, Buckinghamshire. Brother of R. N. (Northamptonshire). Hard-hitting tail end right-end batsman, right-arm fast medium bowler. *Team* Northamptonshire (1911–19, 16 matches).
Career batting
16–22–6–100–21–6.25–0–*ct* 9
Bowling 261–5–52.20–0–0–1/6

From 1911 to 1914 he lived in Australia. He was a good rugby footballer, appearing for Northampton.

Beasley, Rev Robert Noble
Amateur. *b:* 17.12.1882, Chapel Brayton, Northampton. *d:* 21.1.1966, Lakeview, Northampton. Brother of J. N. (Northamptonshire). Lower order batsman. *Team* Northamptonshire (1907–11, 10 matches).
Career batting
10–15–0–109–28–7.26–0–*ct* 4

He was an excellent rugby footballer, appearing for Northampton.

Beattie, Fred Demetrius
Amateur. *b:* 18.8.1909, Ashton-on-Mersey, Cheshire. *d:* 20.3.1989, Llanystumdwy, Caernarvon. Middle order right-hand batsman, right-arm medium pace bowler. *Sch* Rossall. *Team* Lancashire (1932, 5 matches).
Career batting
7–12–2–172–36–17.20–0–*ct* 0

He also played for the Minor Counties in first-class matches in 1930 and 1933. He was President of Lancashire in 1975–76.

Beauclerk, Rev Lord Frederick
Amateur. *b:* 8.5.1773. *d:* 22.4.1850, Westminster, London. Father of A. F. J. (MCC 1837) and C. W. (Oxford U 1836). Brilliant right-hand batsman, slow under-arm bowler, slip field. *Teams* Hampshire (1805–07); Kent (1806).
Career batting
99–181–15–4555–129*–27.43–4–*ct* 81–*st* 1
Bowling 252 wickets (no analyses)–3–0–7/?

He followed William Beldham as the best batsman in England and for some years was regarded as the finest amateur single-wicket cricketer in the country. Like Beldham's, his career was a very long one, extending over 35 years, and in his retirement he was a frequenter of Lord's, being regarded as the autocrat of the game. His uncontrollable temper made him a man with whom few cared to cross swords. His final first-class match was for the Bs in 1825. He was President of MCC in 1826.

Beaumont, David John
Cricketer. *b:* 17.9.1944, West Bridgford, Nottingham. Middle order right-hand batsman, off break bowler. *Team* Cambridge U (1977–78, blue 1978).

Beaumont, Harold

Career batting
11–16–1–258–44–17.20–0–*ct* 4

Beaumont, Harold
Professional. *b:* 14.10.1916, Thongs Bridge, Yorkshire. Hard hitting middle order right-hand batsman, right-arm medium pace bowler. *Team* Yorkshire (1946–47, 28 matches).
Career batting
28–46–6–716–60–17.90–0–*ct* 11
Bowling 236–9–26.22–0–0–4/31

Beaumont, John
Professional. *b:* 16.9.1854, Armitage Bridge, Yorkshire. *d:* 1.5.1920, Lambeth, London. Lower order right-hand batsman, right-arm fast bowler. *Teams* Yorkshire (1877–78, 4 matches); Surrey (1885–90, 91 matches). *Tour* Vernon to Australia 1887/8.
Career batting
112–158–52–881–60–8.31–0–*ct* 37
Bowling 7808–467–16.71–31–7–8/40

Easily his best season was his first with Surrey, when he captured 129 wickets, av 16.57, the only time in his career he passed 100.

Beaumont, Rolland
Amateur. *b:* 4.2.1884, Newcastle, Natal, South Africa. *d:* 25.5.1958, Berea, Durban, South Africa. Hard hitting middle order right-hand batsman, fine field. *Team* Transvaal (1911/12 to 1913/14). *Tour* South Africa to England 1912. *Tests* South Africa (1912 to 1913/14, 5 matches).
Career batting
31–47–4–1086–121–25.25–1–*ct* 11
Bowling 2–0
Test batting
5–9–0–70–31–7.77–0–*ct* 2
Bowling 0–0

His first-class debut was for Wanderers CC in South Africa in 1908/9.

Becher, Adrian William Bay
Amateur. *b:* 12.5.1897, Bourton-on-the-Water, Gloucestershire. *d:* 29.3.1957, Swindon Hall, Cheltenham, Gloucestershire. Middle order right-hand batsman. *Sch* Repton. *Teams* Gloucestershire (1925–29, 9 matches); Europeans (1924/5 to 1925/6).
Career batting
12–21–0–327–64–15.57–0–*ct* 18
Bowling 209–0

Becher, Arthur William Reddie
Amateur. *b:* 6.12.1842, Allahabad, India. *d:* 25.3.1926, Maida Vale, London. Middle order batsman. *Team* MCC (1872).
Career batting
1–2–0–13–8–6.50–0–*ct* 1

Becher, Sir William Fane Wrixon
Amateur. *b:* 7.9.1915, Roxborough, Co Limerick, Ireland. Middle order right-hand batsman. *Sch* Harrow. *Team* Sussex (1939, 3 matches).
Career batting
3–5–0–48–20–9.60–0–*ct* 0

He also played for Wiltshire (1949–53).

Beck, Rev Geoffrey Edward
Amateur. *b:* 16.6.1918, Wisbech, Cambridgeshire. Opening or middle order right-hand batsman, off break bowler. *Sch* Whitgift. *Team* Oxford U (1946).
Career batting
3–6–0–72–50–12.00–0–*ct* 0

He played for Oxford U v Cambridge U in 1945 (not first-class). His County cricket was for Oxfordshire (1951). He won a blue for hockey.

Beckett, Samuel Barclay
Amateur. *b:* 13.4.1906, Foxrock, Dublin, Ireland. *d:* 22.12.1989, Paris, France. Opening left-hand batsman, left-arm medium pace bowler. *Sch* Portora Royal School. *Team* Dublin University (1925–26).
Career batting
2–4–0–35–18–8.75–0–*ct* 2
Bowling 64–0

A well-known author whose works include 'Waiting for Godot', 'Murphy' and 'Molloy', he was awarded the Nobel Prize for Literature in 1969.

Beddow, Alan Michael
Cricketer. *b:* 12.10.1941, St Helens, Lancashire. Attacking middle-order right-hand batsman, right-arm medium pace bowler. *Team* Lancashire (1962–66, 33 matches).
Career batting
33–54–3–775–112*–15.19–1–*ct* 14
Bowling 473–15–31.53–0–0–3/10

He was a well-known Rugby League footballer with St Helens.

Bedford, Edward Henry Riland
Amateur. *b:* 7.6.1903, Aston, Birmingham. *d:* 9.10.1976, Chelmsford, Essex. Grandson of Rev W. K. R. Bedford (co-founder of Free Foresters). Middle order right-hand batsman. *Sch* Winchester. *Team* Derbyshire (1924, 1 match).
Career batting
1–2–0–3–3–1.50–0–*ct* 0

Bedford, H.
Amateur. Lower order batsman, useful leg break bowler. *Team* Hampshire (1882, 1 match).
Career batting
1–1–0–3–3–3.00–0–*ct* 0
Bowling 5–1–5.00–0–0–1/5

He also played for Essex (pre first-class) in 1881.

Bedford, Harry
Professional. *b:* 17.7.1907, Morley, Leeds, Yorkshire. *d:* 5.7.1968, Croydon, Surrey. Lower order right-hand batsman, leg break and googly bowler. *Team* Yorkshire (1928, 5 matches).

Career batting
5–5–1–57–24–14.25–0–*ct* 0
Bowling 179–8–22.37–1–0–6/91

Bedford, Philip Ian
Amateur. *b:* 11.2.1930, Friern Barnet, Middlesex. *d:* 18.9.1966, on way to Wanstead Hospital, Essex. Lower order right-hand batsman, leg break bowler. *Team* Middlesex (1947–62, 65 matches). *Tours* MCC to South America 1958/9, 1963/4, to North America 1959 (all not first-class).
Career batting
77–84–24–979–75*–16.31–0–*ct* 45
Bowling 4208–128–32.87–5–0–6/52

As a 17-year-old he created a most favourable impression in 1947, when he came second in the Middlesex bowling averages with 25 wickets, av 19.36, but he failed to maintain this form and soon left County cricket. He was recalled by Middlesex in 1961 as captain, and led the side for two seasons. He collapsed whilst batting in a club match at Buckhurst Hill in 1966 and died on the way to hospital; he had played his last first-class match – for MCC – only a fortnight before his death.

Bedford, Walter
Professional. *b:* 24.2.1879, Barnsley, Yorkshire. *d:* 28.7.1939, Balby, Doncaster, Yorkshire. Hard hitting lower order right-hand batsman, right-arm fast-medium bowler. *Team* Yorkshire (1903, 2 matches).
Career batting
2–2–1–38–30*–38.00–0–*ct* 1
Bowling 117–2–58.50–0–0–2/38

Bedi, Bishan Singh
Cricketer. *b:* 25.9.1946, Amritsar, India. Hard-hitting tail end right-hand batsman, slow left-arm bowler. *Teams* Northern Punjab (1961/2 to 1966/7); Delhi (1968/9 to 1980/1); Northamptonshire (1972–77, 110 matches). *Tours* India to England 1967, 1971, 1974, 1975 (World Cup), 1979, to Australia and New Zealand 1967/8, to Australia 1977/8, to East Africa 1967/8, to West Indies 1970/1, 1975/6, to New Zealand 1975/6, to Pakistan 1978/9; State Bank of India to Ceylon 1968/9; Rest of the World to Australia 1971/2; International XI to Pakistan 1981/2. *Tests* India (1966/7 to 1979, 67 matches).
Career batting
370–426–111–3584–61–11.37–0–*ct* 172
Bowling 33843–1560–21.69–106–20–7/5
Test batting
67–101–28–656–50*–8.98–0–*ct* 26
Bowling 7637–266–28.71–14–1–7/98

He played in all but one of the Tests during his four tours to England, but was not very successful, his best Test series being 1971 with 11 wickets, av 29.54. In 1971 and 1974 he took 58 wickets and 53 wickets respectively. He proved, however, most effective for Northamptonshire and twice reached 100 wickets in a season (best 112, av 24.64, in 1974). He captained India in 22 Tests, but none in England.

Bedser, Alec Victor, OBE
Professional. *b:* 4.7.1918, Reading, Berkshire. Twin brother of E. A. (Surrey). Lower order right-hand batsman, outstanding right-arm medium fast bowler. *Team* Surrey (1939–60, 371 matches). *Tours* MCC to Australia and New Zealand 1946/7, 1950/1, to Australia 1954/5, to South Africa 1948/9; Howard to India 1956/7; Surrey to Rhodesia 1959/60. *Tests* England (1946–55, 51 matches).
Career batting
485–576–181–5735–126–14.51–1–*ct* 289
Bowling 39279–1924–20.41–96–16–8/18
Test batting
51–71–15–714–79–12.75–0–*ct* 26
Bowling 5876–236–24.89–15–5–7/44

Although he played for Surrey in 1939, Bedser's first-class career really began in 1946, when he was quickly recognised as the principal seam bowler in England. His Test debut – the first post-war Test – provided him with figures of 11 for 145, and in the second Test he captured another 11 wickets (for 93). From that moment until 1954 he was the major force in the England attack. His total of 236 Test wickets created a new world record and if he had not declined invitations to go on several winter tours he would probably have topped the 300 mark.

Bedser's name is inseparably linked with the first four post-war series against Australia – in the 1950/1 matches he took 30 wickets (av 16.06) and in the 1953 matches 39 wickets (av 17.48). The latter included 14 for 99 at Trent Bridge – the outstanding performance of his career. His most effective delivery was the one which went from leg to off, but unlike many bowlers of his pace, he employed a number of subtle variations which were undoubtedly the essence of his success. The way in which he uncovered a flaw in Bradman's technique and dismissed the master batsman on several occasions was a credit to Bedser's endeavour.

He took 100 wickets in a season on eleven occasions with 162 (av 16.67) in 1953 his best, and he constituted a major force in Surrey's famous run of seven consecutive Championships.

From 1962 until 1985 he was appointed as an England selector and from 1969 to 1981 was Chairman of the Selection Committee. He managed the tours to Australia of 1974/5 and 1979/80, after being assistant manager on the 1962/3 visit. He was awarded an OBE for his services to cricket. He captained Surrey in 1960 in the absence due to illnes of May. He was President of Surrey in 1987.

Bedser, Eric Arthur
Professional. *b:* 4.7.1918, Reading, Berkshire. Twin brother of A. V. (Surrey). Middle order or opening right-hand batsman, off break bowler. *Team* Surrey

(1939–61, 443 matches). *Tours* MCC to Australia 1950/1 (one match in emergency); Surrey to Rhodesia 1959/60.
Career batting
457–692–79–14716–163–24.00–10–*ct* 236
Bowling 20784–833–24.95–24–4–7/33

He hit 1,000 runs in a season six times (best 1,740, av 34.11, in 1949). His final first-class match was for MCC in 1962. He was President of Surrey in 1990.

Bee, Andrew
Cricketer. 24.1.1965, Bridgnorth, Shropshire. Lower order right-hand batsman, right-arm medium fast bowler. *Team* Scotland (1988–92).
Career batting
3–3–3–41–21*–no av–0–*ct* 1
Bowling 219–3–73.00–0–0–2/20

Beech, Andrew Robert
Cricketer. *b:* 17.4.1962, Perth, Western Australia. Opening right-hand batsman, off break bowler. *Team* Oxford U (1987, blue).
Career batting
4–7–0–49–33–7.00–0–*ct* 1

Beeching, Thomas Hugh Pitt
Amateur. *b:* 10.3.1900, Maidstone, Kent. *d:* 31.12.1971, Aldershot, Hampshire. Hard hitting middle order right-hand batsman. *Sch* Charterhouse. *Team* Kent (1920–21, 10 matches).
Career batting
10–13–0–217–38–16.69–0–*ct* 1

Beers, Hector George
Amateur. *b:* 29.4.1876, Wakefield Lawn, Potterspury, Northamptonshire. *d:* 11.2.1954, Northampton. Middle order right-hand batsman, slow right-arm bowler. *Sch* Wellingborough. *Team* Northamptonshire (1914–21, 17 matches).
Career batting
17–30–1–175–31–6.03–0–*ct* 9
Bowling 232–4–58.00–0–0–1/8

Beet, George
Professional. *b:* 24.4.1886, Somercotes, Derbyshire. *d:* 13.12.1946, Somercotes, Derbyshire. Father of G. H. C. (Derbyshire), grandfather of G. A. (Derbyshire). Middle order right-hand batsman, wicket-keeper. *Team* Derbyshire (1910–25, 47 matches).
Career batting
48–88–10–1277–92*–16.37–0–*ct* 59–*st* 11
Bowling 27–0

He was a noted umpire (1929–46) after retiring from County cricket, standing in one Test match in 1946.

Beet, George Hector Cook
Professional. *b:* 30.5.1904, Somercotes, Derbyshire. *d:* 22.8.1949, Somercotes, Derbyshire. Uncle of G. A. (Derbyshire), son of George (Derbyshire). Middle order right-hand batsman, wicket-keeper. *Team* Derbyshire (1928–32, 5 matches).
Career batting
11–19–2–277–61–16.29–0–*ct* 14–*st* 2

His last match in first-class cricket was for MCC in 1938.

Beet, Gordon Albert
Professional. *b:* 5.5.1939, Heanor, Derbyshire. Nephew of G. H. C. (Derbyshire), grandson of George (Derbyshire). Lower order right-hand batsman, slow left-arm bowler. *Team* Derbyshire (1956–61, 6 matches).
Career batting
6–7–2–36–17–7.20–0–*ct* 3
Bowling 100–2–50.00–0–0–1/42

Beevor, John Grosvenor
Amateur. *b:* 1.1.1845, Barnby Moor, Nottinghamshire. *d:* 5.5.1903, Barnby Moor, Nottinghamshire. Hard-hitting middle order right-hand batsman, slow right-hand round-arm bowler. *Sch* Uppingham. *Team* Nottinghamshire (1868–70, 5 matches).
Career batting
7–13–1–322–88–26.83–0–*ct* 2

His final first-class match was for Gentlemen of North in 1871.

Begbie, Denis Warburton
Amateur. *b:* 12.12.1914, Middelburg, Transvaal, South Africa. Middle order right-hand batsman, leg break and googly bowler. *Team* Transvaal (1933/4 to 1949/50). *Tour* South Africa to England 1947. *Tests* South Africa (1948/9 to 1949/50, 5 matches).
Career batting
58–85–9–2727–207*–35.88–6–*ct* 27
Bowling 2085–88–23.69–5–2–7/96
Test batting
5–7–0–138–48–19.71–0–*ct* 2
Bowling 130–1–130.00–0–0–1/38

He had only limited success on his tour to England and did not appear in any of the Tests. His best innings against English bowling was for Transvaal v MCC in 1948/9, when he hit 154. His highest score was 207* for Transvaal v Orange Free State at Johannesburg in 1937/8.

Beisiegel, Walter Karl
Amateur. *b:* 13.7.1907, Uppingham, Rutland. *d:* 8.1.1973, Halton, Buckinghamshire. Middle order right-hand batsman, excellent cover field. *Sch* Uppingham. *Team* Leicestershire (1934, 10 matches).
Career batting
15–25–3–357–54–16.22–0–*ct* 9

His debut in first-class matches was for RAF in 1928.

Belcher, Charles Frank
Amateur. *b:* 15.12.1872, Berkeley, Gloucestershire. *d:* 1.4.1938, Caernarvon. Sound right-hand middle order batsman, right-arm medium pace bowler. *Team*

Gloucestershire (1890–92, 7 matches).
Career batting
7–12–2–157–60*–15.70–0–*ct* 2
Bowling 55–1–55.00–0–0–1/13

Belcher, Gordon
Amateur. *b:* 26.9.1885, Kemp Town, Brighton, Sussex. *d:* 16.5.1915. He was killed in action near Richebourg L'Avoue, Belgium. Son of T. H. (Oxford U). Middle order right-hand batsman, right-arm medium pace bowler. *Sch* Brighton. *Team* Hampshire (1905, 1 match).
Career batting
1–2–0–0–0–0.00–0 *ct* 0
Bowling 3–0
He appeared in the Freshmen's match of 1905 at Cambridge, but did not play in any first-class games for the University. He also played for Berkshire (1910–13).

Belcher, Rev Thomas Hayes
Amateur. *b:* 12.9.1847, Faringdon, Berkshire. *d:* 26.11.1919, Bramley, Hampshire. Father of Gordon (Hampshire). Lower order right-hand batsman, right-arm fast round-arm bowler. *Sch* Magdalen College School. *Team* Oxford U (1869–70, blue 1870).
Career batting
7–13–8–58–23–11.60–*ct* 4
Bowling 391–19 + 1–20.57–0–0–4/22
His County cricket was for Herefordshire (1873) and Worcestershire (pre first-class, 1877).

Beldam, Cyril Asplan
Amateur. *b:* 15.10.1869, Northfleet, Kent. *d:* 7.9.1940, Marylebone, London. Brother of G. W. (Middlesex), cousin of E. A. (Middlesex). Lower order right-hand batsman. *Sch* King's College School, London. *Team* Middlesex (1896, 2 matches). *Tour* Priestley to West Indies 1896/7.
Career batting
11–18–4–172–24*–12.28–0–*ct* 5
Bowling 272–7–38.85–1–0–5/97

Beldam, Ernest Asplan
Amateur. *b:* 30.6.1879, Brentford, Middlesex. *d:* 28.11.1958, Horsell, Surrey. Cousin of C. A. (Middlesex) and G. W. (Middlesex). Middle order right-hand batsman. *Team* Middlesex (1903–07, 37 matches).
Career batting
39–63–5–1225–105–21.12–1–*ct* 19
His only first-class hundred was made for Middlesex v Somerset at Lord's in 1904, when he and his cousin, G. W., both reached three figures and featured in a partnership of 201 for the fifth wicket.

Beldam, George William
Amateur. *b:* 1.5.1868, New Cross, Kent. *d:* 23.11.1937, Lower Bourne, Farnham, Surrey. Brother of C. A. (Middlesex), cousin of E. A. (Middlesex). Sound middle order right-hand batsman, right-arm medium slow bowler. *Teams* Middlesex (1900–07, 102 matches); London County (1900–03).
Career batting
142–235–16–6575–155*–30.02–9–*ct* 83
Bowling 3278–107–30.63–4–0–5/28
He hit 1,000 runs in a season three times (best 1,158, av 38.60, in 1901). A pioneer in action photography, he produced the plates for 'Great Batsmen, Their Methods at a Glance' published in 1907 and a remarkable book for its time. Beldam also wrote books on golf and tennis. His first-class debut was for A. J. Webbe's XI in 1899.

Beldham, William
Professional. *b:* 5.2.1766, Wrecclesham, Farnham, Surrey. *d:* 26.2.1862, Tilford, Surrey. Uncle of George (Surrey), brother-in-law of J. Wells (Surrey). Excellent right-hand batsman, medium pace under-arm bowler. *Teams* Surrey (1801–17); Hampshire (1805–07); Kent (1806).
Career batting
72–131–8–2374–82–19.30–0–*ct* 111–*st* 42
Bowling 48 wickets (no analyses)–0–0–4/?
He was regarded as the best batsman of his time, his career in great matches lasting 35 seasons. He was the last survivor of the famous cricketers of the Hambledon era and details of many of his early performances are unfortunately lost. His final first-class match was for Godalming in 1821. He was generally known as 'Silver Billy' Beldham.

Bell, Alexander John
Amateur. *b:* 15.4.1906, East London, South Africa. *d:* 1.8.1985, Mowbray, Cape Town, South Africa. Tail end right-hand batsman, right-arm fast-medium bowler. *Teams* Western Province (1925/6 to 1930/31); Rhodesia (1938/9). *Tours* South Africa to England 1929, 1935, to Australia and New Zealand 1931/2. *Tests* South Africa (1929–35, 16 matches).
Career batting
63–79–45–311–32*–9.14–0–*ct* 27
Bowling 5312–228–23.29–10–1–8/34
Test batting
16–23–12–69–26*–6.27–0–*ct* 6
Bowling 1567–48–32.64–4–0–6/99
On his first visit to England, Bell's best performance was his 6/99 in the Lord's Test. His second visit was unfortunately marred by injury.

Bell, Alexander Patrick
Amateur. *b:* 23.2.1915, Rosario, Argentina. *d:* 12.4.1956, Oxford. Middle order right-hand batsman. *Sch* Warwick. *Team* Northamptonshire (1934, 3 matches).
Career batting
3–6–0–37–24–6.16–0–*ct* 2
He also played for Hertfordshire (1946–49).

Bell, David Lauder
Cricketer. *b:* 28.4.1949, Warriston, Edinburgh, Scotland. Middle order right-hand batsman. *Teams* Oxford U (1971); Scotland (1979–81).
Career batting
7–13–3–234–60–23.40–0–*ct* 3
He played rugby for Scotland.

Bell, Frederick William
Professional. *b:* 2.1.1830, St Neots, Huntingdonshire. *d:* 18.9.1871, Cambridge. Lower order right-hand batsman, round-arm medium pace bowler, brilliant outfield. *Teams* Cambridge Town Club (1846–56); Cambridgeshire (1857–64, 17 matches).
Career batting
58–100–18–921–50*–11.23–0–*ct* 23
Bowling 1118–70 + 9–15.91–4–1–6/25
He also played for Worcestershire (pre first-class, 1849), Dorset (1850–54) and Herefordshire (1852).

Bell, Geoffrey Foxall
Amateur. *b:* 16.4.1896, Stapenhill, Staffordshire. *d:* 17.1.1984, Haslemere, Surrey. Cousin of E. Evershed (Derbyshire), S. H. Evershed (Derbyshire) and W. Evershed (Derbyshire). Middle order right-hand batsman. *Sch* Repton. *Teams* Derbyshire (1914–20, 5 matches); Oxford U (1919, blue).
Career batting
12–21–0–336–64–16.00–0–*ct* 6

Bell, John Thomson
Professional. *b:* 16.6.1895, Batley, Yorkshire. *d:* 8.8.1974, Guiseley, Leeds, Yorkshire. Stylish opening right-hand batsman. *Teams* Yorkshire (1921–23, 7 matches); Glamorgan (1924–31, 166 matches); Wales (1924–30).
Career batting
184–307–20–8391–225–29.23–12–*ct* 63
Bowling 205–2–102.50–0–0–1/2
He hit 1,000 runs in a season four times (best 1,701, av 31.50, in 1929). He hit two double centuries, the higher being 225 for Glamorgan v Worcestershire at Dudley in 1926. He was a first-class umpire (1948–51).

Bell, Michael Anthony Vincent
Cricketer. *b:* 19.12.1966, Birmingham. Lower order right-hand batsman, left-arm fast medium bowler. *Team* Warwickshire (1992, 3 matches).
Career batting
3–5–2–10–5–3.33–0–*ct* 0
Bowling 247–8–30.87–0–0–3/78

Bell, Percy Harrison
Amateur. *b:* 26.7.1892, Headington, Oxfordshire. *d:* 4.2.1956, Morningside, Durban, South Africa. Middle order batsman. *Teams* Gloucestershire (1911–12, 8 matches); Orange Free State (1912/3, 2 matches).
Career batting
10–18–1–293–64–17.23–0–*ct* 9
This cricketer has two obituary notices in Wisden, one for 1956 and the other for 1971. It is believed, but is by no means certain, that 1956 is correct.

Bell, Richard Moor
Amateur. *b:* 1.1.1874, Wigton, Cumberland. *d:* 10.6.1953, Elm Grove, Brighton, Sussex. Lower order right-hand batsman, off break bowler. *Sch* The Leys. *Team* London County (1902–04). *Tour* Brackley to Egypt 1909 (not first-class).
Career batting
15–26–6–225–31*–11.25–0–*ct* 10
Bowling 889–31–28.67–2–0–6/88
He was a noted cricketer in London Club cricket, appearing for Sutton CC (Surrey) for about 40 years.

Bell, Robert Malcolm Hamilton
Cricketer. *b:* 26.2.1969, Hugh Town, St Mary's, Isles of Scilly. Lower order right-hand batsman, right-arm medium pace bowler. *Sch* Truro. *Team* Gloucestershire (1990–91, 3 matches).
Career batting
3–2–1–0–0*–0.00–0–*ct* 0
Bowling 123–3–41.00–0–0–2/38
He also played for Cornwall (1990–92).

Bell, Roland
Amateur. *b:* 16.5.1857, Bishops Stortford, Hertfordshire. *d:* 29.1.1935, Leamington Spa, Warwickshire. Middle order right-hand batsman, slow round arm bowler. *Team* Surrey (1876, 1 match).
Career batting
1–2–0–4–3–2.00–0–*ct* 0

Bell, Ronald Victor
Professional. *b:* 7.1.1931, Chelsea, London. *d:* 26.10.1989, Farnham, Surrey. Tail end left-hand batsman, slow left-arm bowler. *Teams* Middlesex (1952–54, 5 matches); Sussex (1957–64, 183 matches).
Career batting
189–233–54–1558–53*–8.70–0–*ct* 150
Bowling 11111–392–28.34–19–1–8/54
He also played for Norfolk (1967–69). He played soccer for Chelsea.

Bellamy, Benjamin Walter
Professional. *b:* 22.4.1891, Wollaston, Northamptonshire. *d:* 22.12.1985, Wellingborough, Northamptonshire. Middle order right-hand batsman, wicket-keeper. *Team* Northamptonshire (1920–37, 353 matches).
Career batting
354–625–66–9247–168–16.54–4–*ct* 529–*st* 125
Bowling 57–0
His best season with the bat was 1928 when he hit 1,116 runs, av 22.77 – this was the only time he reached 1,000 runs for the season. He played soccer for Northampton Town.

Belle, Brian Henry
Amateur. *b:* 7.4.1914, Woodford Green, Essex. Middle order right-hand batsman, right-arm medium pace bowler. *Sch* Forest. *Teams* Essex (1935–37, 26 matches); Oxford U (1935–36, blue 1936). *Tour* Oxford and Cambridge to Jamaica 1938/9.
Career batting
43–72–5–1235–70–18.43–0–*ct* 29
Bowling 33–1–33.00–0–0–1/10
He also played for Suffolk (1939–57) and appeared in first-class matches for the Minor Counties in 1949 and 1950. His first-class debut was for MCC in 1934.

Beloe, Gerald Harry
Amateur. *b:* 21.11.1877, Clifton, Bristol. *d:* 1.10.1944, Brandon Hill, Clifton, Bristol. Middle order left-hand batsman, slow left-arm bowler. *Sch* Marlborough. *Team* Gloucestershire (1898–99, 6 matches).
Career batting
6–11–2–153–52*–17.00–0–*ct* 4

Bembridge, Henry
Professional. *b:* 27.6.1852, Bulwell, Nottinghamshire. Lower order right-hand batsman, right-arm fast bowler. *Team* Nottinghamshire (1878, 1 match).
Career batting
1–2–1–17–15*–17.00–0–*ct* 0
Bowling 34–0

Benaud, Richard, OBE
Amateur. *b:* 6.10.1930, Penrith, New South Wales, Australia. Brother of John (Australia). Forcing middle-order right-hand batsman, excellent leg break and googly bowler. *Team* New South Wales (1948/9 to 1963/4, 86 matches). *Tours* Australia to England 1953, 1956, 1961, to West Indies 1954/5, to New Zealand 1956/7, to Pakistan and India 1956/7, 1959/60, to South Africa 1957/8; Cavaliers to South Africa 1960/1, to India, Pakistan and New Zealand 1961/2, to India and South Africa 1962/3; Swanton to India 1963/4; Commonwealth to Pakistan 1967/8. *Tests* Australia (1951/2 to 1963/4, 63 matches).
Career batting
259–365–44–11719–187–36.50–23–*ct* 254
Bowling 23371–945–24.73–56–9–7/18
Test batting
63–97–7–2201–122–24.45–3–*ct* 65
Bowling 6704–248–27.03–16–1–7/72
Although originally selected for New South Wales as a batsman, Benaud developed into the best Australian all-rounder of his generation, and indeed his bowling latterly became even more effective than his batting. It was the tour to South Africa in 1957/8, when he took 106 wickets in addition to making 817 runs, that really established him. The following year he was chosen to lead Australia against England and his shrewd captaincy plus brilliant bowling won the Ashes by four Tests to nil. He captained Australia in England in 1961 and again won the series, though injury curtailed his bowling ability. In all he captained Australia in 28 Tests. He is a noted journalist and broadcaster.

Benbow, Herbert Clifton
Amateur. *b:* 4.10.1861, Hillingdon, Middlesex. *d:* 2.2.1941, Brampton, Cumberland. Useful middle order right-hand batsman, wicket-keeper. *Sch* Westminster. *Team* Cambridge U (1881).
Career batting
2–4–1–28–12–9.33–0–*ct* 2–*st* 3

Bencraft, Dr Sir Henry William Russell
(also known as Russell-Bencraft)
Amateur. *b:* 4.3.1858, Southampton, Hampshire. *d:* 25.12.1943, Compton, Winchester, Hampshire. Middle order right-hand batsman, fast right-arm bowler. *Sch* St Edward's, Oxford. *Team* Hampshire (1876–96, 44 matches).
Career batting
46–78–18–932–62*–15.53–0–*ct* 31
Bowling 197–5–39.40–0–0–2/15
For many years he was Hampshire cricket, being Treasurer to the County Club from 1880 to 1893, Secretary from 1882 to 1904, captain from 1880 to 1882 and 1893 to 1895 and on the Committee of the Club for many years, being Chairman 1919–34 and President 1911–12 and 1935. He was also a noted rugby player.

Bendall, Frederick George
Professional. *b:* 18.12.1865, Cheltenham, Gloucestershire. *d:* 27.4.1941, Tivoli, Cheltenham, Gloucestershire. Lower order right-hand batsman, right-arm medium pace bowler. *Team* Gloucestershire (1887, 1 match).
Career batting
1–2–0–3–3–1.50–0–*ct* 0
Bowling 42–1–42.00–0–0–1/42

Bengough, Clement Stuart
Amateur. *b:* 14.1.1861, Latteridge, Frampton-Cotterell, Bristol. *d:* 19.11.1934, Laramie, Wyoming, USA. Lower order hard-hitting right-hand batsman, wicket-keeper. *Sch* Marlborough. *Team* Gloucestershire (1880, 2 matches).
Career batting
2–3–0–8–8–2.66–0–*ct* 3

Benham, Charles Edward
Professional. *b:* 24.6.1880, East Ham, Essex. *d:* 13.12.1961, Bangour Hospital, Broxburn, West Lothian, Scotland. Father of F. C. (Scotland). Lower order right-hand batsman, right-arm fast bowler. *Teams* Essex (1904–09, 57 matches); Scotland (1912).
Career batting
59–84–11–1047–65*–14.34–0–*ct* 33
Bowling 2338–70–33.40–4–0–7/60

Benham, Frederick Charles
Professional. *b:* 18.12.1903, Bexley, Kent. *d:* 29.11.1985, Bangour Hospital, Broxburn, West Lothian, Scotland. Son of C. E. (Essex). Middle order right-hand batsman. *Team* Scotland (1949).
Career batting
1–2–1–9–9–9.00–0–*ct* 0

Benjamin, Harold Lewis
Amateur. *b:* 13.4.1892, St Thomas Parish, Birmingham. *d:* 7.8.1942, Tettenhall, Staffordshire. Lower order right-hand batsman, right-arm fast medium bowler. *Teams* Warwickshire (1919, 2 matches); Northamptonshire (1928, 1 match).
Career batting
3–4–0–37–23–9.25–0–*ct* 1
Bowling 182–6–30.33–0–0–3/38

Benjamin, Joseph Emmanuel
Cricketer. *b:* 2.2.1961, Christ Church, St Kitts. Lower order right-hand batsman, right-arm medium fast bowler. *Teams* Warwickshire (1988–91, 25 matches); Surrey (1992, 18 matches).
Career batting
43–40–16–341–42–14.20–0–*ct* 12
Bowling 3800–109–34.86–6–0–6/30
He also played for Staffordshire (1986–89).

Benjamin, Kenneth Charlie Griffith
Cricketer. *b:* 8.4.1967, Liberta, Antigua. Lower order right-hand batsman, right-arm fast bowler. *Team* Leeward Islands (1988/9 to 1991/2). *Tour* Rest of World to England 1992. *Test* West Indies (1991/2, 1 match).
Career batting
25–33–10–321–52*–13.95–0–*ct* 2
Bowling 1943–81–23.98–2–0–7/51
Test batting
1–2–0–8–7–4.00–0–*ct* 0
Bowling 108–2–54.00–0–0–2/87

Benjamin, Winston Keithroy Matthew
Cricketer. 31.12.1964, All Saints, Antigua. Lower order right-hand batsman, right-arm fast bowler. *Teams* Leeward Islands (1985/6 to 1991/2); Leicestershire (1986–92, 75 matches). *Tours* West Indies to Australia 1986/7, 1988/9, to Pakistan 1986/7, to Sharjah (not first-class) 1986/7, 1988/9, 1989/90, 1991/2, to India 1987/8, 1989/90 (not first-class), to England 1988, to India and Pakistan (World Cup) 1987/8, to Australia and New Zealand (World Cup) 1991/2; Rest of World to England 1985. *Tests* West Indies (1987/8 to 1988/9, 8 matches).
Career batting
124–148–34–2630–101*–23.07–1–*ct* 60
Bowling 8946–343–26.08–17–2–7/54
Test batting
8–10–1–124–40*–13.77–0–*ct* 3
Bowling 564–26–21.69–0–0–4/52
His first-class debut was for Rest of the World v D. B. Close's XI at Scarborough in 1985. He also played for Cheshire (1985). He played in three Tests on the 1988 tour of England and in first-class matches took 33 wickets (av 14.15). His best season to date in England was 1989 when he took 69 wickets (av 17.94).

Benka, Herbert Frank
Amateur. *b:* 27.10.1909, Regent's Park, London. *d:* 22.4.1970, Westminster, London. Middle order right-hand batsman, slow left-arm bowler. *Team* Middlesex (1933–36, 11 matches).
Career batting
13–23–1–359–59–16.31–0–*ct* 12
Bowling 331–12–27.58–0–0–4/78
His last first-class match was for MCC in 1939.

Benke, Andrew Frederick
Amateur. *b:* 3.9.1938, Southampton, Hampshire. Lower order right-hand batsman, off break bowler. *Sch* Cheltenham. *Team* Cambridge U (1962, blue).
Career batting
19–29–4–240–26–9.60–0–*ct* 4
Bowling 1964–50–39.28–2–0–5/75
He did not make his first-class debut for the University until his third year and then proceeded to win his blue and capture 50 wickets in the University season.

Benn, Anthony
Amateur. *b:* 7.10.1912, Kensington, London. Middle order right-hand batsman, right-arm medium pace bowler. *Sch* Harrow. *Team* Oxford U (1934–35, blue 1935).
Career batting
12–20–0–378–90–18.90–0–*ct* 6
Bowling 135–0

Bennet, Ferdinando Wallis
Amateur. *b:* 13.12.1850, East Newlyn, Cornwall. *d:* 17.10.1929, Northam, Devon. Middle order right-hand batsman, right-arm slow bowler, good field. *Sch* Sherborne. *Team* Kent (1874, 1 match).
Career batting
4–6–1–119–47–23.80–0–*ct* 2
Bowling 40–1–40.00–0–0–1/22
He was a prolific batsman in military cricket. His final first-class match was for MCC in 1878.

Bennett, Albert
Professional. *b:* 21.5.1910, St Helens, Lancashire. Lower order right-hand batsman, leg break and googly bowler. *Teams* New South Wales (1930/1, 1 match); Lancashire (1932–33, 16 matches).
Career batting
17–16–1–254–51–16.93–0–*ct* 12
Bowling 906–24–37.75–0–0–4/49

Bennett, Alfred Charles Leopold
Amateur. *b:* 31.12.1914, West Norwood, London. *d:* 24.9.1971, Thames Ditton, Surrey. Middle order right-hand batsman. *Sch* Dulwich. *Team* Northamp-

tonshire (1947–49, 16 matches).
Career batting
16–29–0–586–68–20.20–0–*ct* 8

A noted batsman in London Club cricket and one time captain of the Club Cricket Conference, his work with the BBC prevented him from playing regular County cricket.

Bennett, Arthur Robert
Amateur. *b:* 16.11.1868, Mapperley, Nottinghamshire. *d:* 7.5.1899, Marylebone, London. Tail end right-hand batsman, right-arm fast medium bowler. *Team* Nottinghamshire (1893–96, 7 matches).
Career batting
7–11–1–40–17–4.00–0–*ct* 2
Bowling 498–17–29.29–1–0–5/81

Bennett, Barry William Prosser
Cricketer. *b:* 6.2.1955, RAF Abyad, Ismailia, Egypt. Middle order left-hand batsman. *Team* Cambridge U (1979, blue).
Career batting
2–2–0–4–4–2.00–0–*ct* 0

Bennett, Cecil Tristram
Amateur. *b:* 10.8.1902, Tulse Hill, London. *d:* 3.2.1978, Islington, London. Opening or middle order right-hand batsman, good slip field. *Sch* Harrow. *Teams* Surrey (1922, 4 matches); Cambridge U (1923–25, blue 1923 and 1925); Middlesex (1926–27, 3 matches). *Tour* MCC to West Indies 1925/6.
Career batting
50–85–9–1335–88–17.56–0–*ct* 43
Bowling 4–0

He was regarded as one of the most promising cricketers at Harrow, but never made his mark in County cricket. His last first-class match was for MCC in 1928. He captained Cambridge in 1925.

Bennett, Charles Oatley
Amateur. *b:* 15.8.1872, Ticehurst, Sussex. *d:* 23.5.1921, Walcot, Bath, Somerset. Middle order right-hand batsman, leg break bowler. *Sch* Haileybury. *Team* Somerset (1902, 2 matches).
Career batting
2–4–2–10–6–5.00–0–*ct* 1

Bennett, Donald
Professional. *b:* 18.12.1933, Wakefield, Yorkshire. Middle order right-hand batsman, right-arm fast medium bowler. *Team* Middlesex (1950–68, 392 matches).
Career batting
404–612–125–10656–117*–21.88–4–*ct* 159
Bowling 20598–784–26.27–24–1–7/47

He scored 1,000 runs in a season twice (1,144, av 22.00, best). He has been Middlesex coach since 1969. A noted soccer player, he appeared for Arsenal and Coventry City.

Bennett, Edwin Howard
Amateur. *b:* 21.12.1893, Shifnal, Shropshire. *d:* 9.7.1929, East Worthing, Sussex. Hard hitting middle order batsman. *Sch* Wolverhampton GS. *Team* Worcestershire (1925, 3 matches).
Career batting
4–8–0–157–73–19.62–0–*ct* 1

In 1927 he played for the Civil Service against the New Zealanders and scored 73 and 60 – easily the best batting for his side. This match is regarded as first-class. He also played for Staffordshire (1921–24).

Bennett, Geoffrey Michael
Amateur. *b:* 17.12.1909, Bruton, Somerset. *d:* 26.7.1982, Toronto, Ontario, Canada. Middle order right-hand batsman, right-arm medium pace bowler. *Sch* King's Bruton. *Team* Somerset (1928–39, 109 matches).
Career batting
109–173–21–2330–73–15.32–0–*ct* 52
Bowling 448–14–32.00–0–0–4/39

Bennett, George
Professional. *b:* 12.2.1829, Shorne Ridgeway, Gravesend, Kent. *d:* 16.8.1886, Shorne Ridgeway, Gravesend, Kent. Very defensive middle order right-hand batsman, slow right-hand round arm bowler, good outfield. *Team* Kent (1853–73, 126 matches). *Tour* Stephenson to Australia 1861/2.
Career batting
169–307–22–4199–100–14.73–1–*ct* 122
Bowling 10250–607 + 5–16.85–41–12–9/113

He was one of the best all-rounders of his day. His most notable innings was 100 for South v North in 1865. His bowling was very slow, flighted high in the air and most deceptive. His best bowling was 9/113 for Kent v Sussex at Hove in 1871.

Bennett, George Guy Marsland
Amateur. *b:* 22.4.1883, Chorlton, Lancashire. *d:* 6.2.1966, Sunningdale, Berkshire. Middle order right-hand batsman. *Sch* Harrow. *Team* Oxford U (1903–05).
Career batting
8–16–0–380–131–23.75–1–*ct* 6
Bowling 49–2–24.50–0–0–1/20

His County cricket was for Berkshire (1902–26).

Bennett, Henry Simpson
Professional. *b:* 3.9.1869, Pilsley, Derbyshire. *d:* 18.2.1965, Flowery Field, Hyde, Cheshire. Tail end batsman, wicket-keeper. *Team* Lancashire (1894, 1 match).
Career batting
1–2–0–16–11–8.00–0–*ct* 4

Bennett, Howard Alfred
Amateur. *b:* 20.8.1892, Alcester, Warwickshire. *d:* 13.1.1973, Southbourne, Hampshire. Lower order

right-hand batsman, leg break bowler. *Sch* Wellingborough. *Team* Northamptonshire (1920, 1 match).
Career batting
1–2–0–1–1–0.50–0–*ct* 1
Bowling 51–0

'He was surprised to be invited to play for Northamptonshire in 1920 as he had played no cricket of any sort since 1914 having been wounded in the Great War and in poor health since.'

Bennett, Rev Hugh Frederic
Amateur. *b:* 10.11.1862, Pirton, Pershore, Worcestershire. *d:* 26.7.1943, Malvern, Worcestershire. Middle order right-hand batsman, slow right-hand bowler. *Sch* Bradfield. *Team* Worcestershire (1901, 2 matches).
Career batting
2–3–1–63–31*–31.50–0–*ct* 0

He also played for Shropshire (1891). He first played for Worcestershire (pre first-class) in 1895.

Bennett, John
Professional. *b:* 1777, Kingsley, Hampshire. *d:* July 1857, Kingsley, Hampshire. Cousin of James (Hampshire 1803). Free hitting left-hand batsman, fast bowler, wicket-keeper. *Team* Hampshire (1797–1818).
Career batting
51–93–7–1200–72–13.95–0–*ct* 37–*st* 1
Bowling 49 wickets (no analyses)–1–0–5/?

His career in great matches lasted about 20 years, during which he was one of the leading Hampshire cricketers.

Bennett, John William
(registered at death as William Bennett)
Professional. *b:* 22.2.1864, Lower Whitfield, Glossop, Derbyshire. *d:* 10.11.1928, Stepping Hill, Stockport, Cheshire. Lower order right-hand batsman, left-arm medium or slow bowler. *Team* Derbyshire (1895–96, 16 matches).
Career batting
16–25–2–257–43–11.17–0–*ct* 7
Bowling 701–35–20.02–3–0–5/8

He played for Cheshire (1888–94) before representing his native County.

Bennett, Montague Valentine
Amateur. *b:* 19.2.1912, Glentham, Lincolnshire. *d:* 17.12.1940, at sea, serving in HMS *Acheron*, sunk by a mine off the Isle of Wight. Lower order batsman, opening bowler. *Team* Minor Counties (1935).
Career batting
1–2–1–22–16*–22.00–0–*ct* 2
Bowling 54–2–27.00–0–0–2/27

His County cricket was for Lincolnshire (1932–39).

Bennett, Murray John
Cricketer. *b:* 6.10.1956, Brisbane, Queensland, Australia. Lower order right-hand batsman, slow left-arm bowler. *Team* New South Wales (1982/3 to 1987/8, 52 matches). *Tours* Young Australia to Zimbabwe 1982/3; Australia to India 1984/5 (not first-class), to Sharjah (not first-class) 1984/5, to England 1985. *Tests* Australia (1984/5 to 1985, 3 matches).
Career batting
67–85–25–1437–59*–23.95–0–*ct* 49
Bowling 4856–157–30.92–5–0–6/32
Test batting
3–5–2–71–23–23.66–0–*ct* 5
Bowling 325–6–54.16–0–0–3/79

Bennett, Nigel Harvie
Amateur. *b:* 23.9.1912, Walton-on-Thames, Surrey. Lower order right-hand batsman. *Sch* Stowe. *Team* Surrey (1946, 31 matches).
Career batting
31–45–2–688–79–16.00–0–*ct* 6
Bowling 25–1–25.00–0–0–1/1

He was captain of Surrey in 1946.

Bennett, Dr Norman Osborn
Amateur. *b:* 21.9.1922, Putney, London. Middle order batsman. *Sch* Epsom. *Team* Worcestershire (1946, 1 match).
Career batting
1–2–0–10–8–5.00–0–*ct* 1

He played rugby for England.

Bennett, Richard Alexander
Amateur. *b:* 12.12.1872, Holdenhurst, Bournemouth, Hampshire. *d:* 16.7.1953, Thornbury Park, Gloucestershire. Brother-in-law of A. S. Crawley (MCC) and C. J. B. Webb (Middlesex). Steady middle order right-hand batsman, wicket-keeper. *Sch* Eton. *Team* Hampshire (1896–99, 23 matches). *Tours* Warner to North America 1897; Bennett to West Indies 1901/2.
Career batting
37–60–6–683–47–12.64–0–*ct* 44–*st* 29

His final first-class match was for Gentlemen in 1903.

Bennett, Robert
Professional. *b:* 1831, Tunbridge Wells, Kent. *d:* 5.10.1875, Chichester, Sussex. Lower order batsman, wicket-keeper. *Teams* Sussex (1860, 1 match); Kent (1863–64, 6 matches).
Career batting
7–14–0–35–12–2.50–0–*ct* 9–*st* 2

Bennett, Robert
Cricketer. *b:* 16.6.1940, Bacup, Lancashire. Opening right-hand batsman, off break bowler. *Sch* Rossall. *Team* Lancashire (1962–66, 49 matches).
Career batting
49–82–3–1814–112–22.96–2–*ct* 13
Bowling 0–0

He has been Chairman of Lancashire CCC since 1988.

Bennett, Sydney John
Professional. *b:* 7.2.1905, Hackleton, Northamptonshire. *d:* 15.8.1969, Margate, Kent. Lower order right-hand batsman, slow right-arm bowler. *Team* Northamptonshire (1933–34, 3 matches).
Career batting
3–6–1–37–19*–7.40–0–*ct* 0
Bowling 107–2–53.50–0–0–1/40

Benskin, William Ewart
Professional. *b:* 8.4.1880, Leicester. *d:* 1.6.1956, Leicester. Lower order right-hand batsman, right-arm fast bowler. *Teams* Leicestershire (1906–24, 100 matches); Scotland (1912–13).
Career batting
105–162–48–954–79*–8.36–0–*ct* 30
Bowling 8408–325–25.87–17–5–8/86
After appearing briefly for Leicestershire, Benskin took an engagement in Scotland, playing in five first-class matches for that country, and did not return to County cricket until 1919. Injury ended his first-class cricket in 1924. A noted soccer player he was a half-back with Leicester Fosse.

Benson, Edward Turk
Amateur. *b:* 20.11.1907, Tredegarville, Cardiff. *d:* 11.9.1967, Newlands, Cape Town, South Africa. Tail end right-hand batsman, wicket-keeper. *Sch* Blundell's. *Teams* Oxford U (1928–29, blue both years); Gloucestershire (1929–31, 5 matches). *Tour* MCC to Australia and New Zealand 1929/30.
Career batting
38–55–14–520–42–12.68–0–*ct* 49–*st* 12
Bowling 0–0
Whilst he was in New Zealand in 1929/30, he was adjudged out 'handled ball', though there was some doubt as to whether he actually touched it. He also won a blue for rugby. He was the brother of the actor George Benson.

Benson, Gwynfor Leonard
Professional. *b:* 7.1.1941, Handsworth, Birmingham. Middle order right-hand batsman, off break bowler. *Sch* KES, Birmingham. *Team* Warwickshire (1959–61, 3 matches).
Career batting
3–5–2–102–46–34.00–0–*ct* 1
Bowling 32–2–16.00–0–0–2/25
He played hockey for Warwickshire and Wales.

Benson, Justin David Ramsay
Cricketer. *b:* 1.3.1967, Dublin, Ireland. Middle order right-hand batsman, right-arm medium pace bowler, slip field. *Sch* The Leys. *Team* Leicestershire (1988–92, 50 matches).
Career batting
50–76–8–1854–133*–27.26–3–*ct* 52
Bowling 488–8–61.00–0–0–2/24
He also played for Cambridgeshire (1984–89).

Benson, Mark Richard
Cricketer. *b:* 6.7.1958, Shoreham-by-Sea, Sussex. Opening left-hand batsman, off break bowler. *Sch* Sutton Valence. *Team* Kent (1980–92, 246 matches). *Test* England (1986, 1 match).
Career batting
248–419–31–16035–257–41.32–42–*ct* 120
Bowling 493–5–98.60–0–0–2/55
Test batting
1–2–0–51–30–25.50–0–*ct* 0
He hit 1,000 runs in a season eleven times (best 1,725, av 44.23, in 1987). He captained Kent in 1991 and 1992. His highest score was 257 for Kent v Hampshire at Southampton in 1991.

Benstead, Charles Richard
Amateur. *b:* 21.4.1896, Cambridge. *d:* 3.7.1980, Solihull, Warwickshire. Lower order right-hand batsman, right-arm medium pace bowler. *Teams* Cambridge U (1920–21); Royal Navy (1923).
Career batting
3–4–1–28–16–9.33–0–*ct* 2
Bowling 259–11–23.54–1–0–5/32
His County cricket was for Cambridgeshire (1921–23).

Bent, Paul
Cricketer. *b:* 1.5.1965, Worcester. Opening right-hand batsman, off break bowler. *Sch* Worcester RGS. *Team* Worcestershire (1985–91, 32 matches).
Career batting
32–54–2–1289–144–24.78–2–*ct* 4
Bowling 5–0
He also played for Herefordshire (1992).

Benthall, William Henry
Amateur. *b:* 3.7.1837, Westminster, London. *d:* 4.1.1909, St Leonard's-on-Sea, Sussex. Middle order right-hand batsman, good field at point, occasional slow bowler. *Sch* Marlborough and Westminster. *Teams* Cambridge U (1858–60, blue all three years); Middlesex (1862–68, 6 matches).
Career batting
37–70–8–1030–103–16.61–1–*ct* 33
Bowling 74–4 + 1–18.50–0–0–3/24
He also represented Cambridge at rackets and played cricket for Buckinghamshire (1859–68) and Devon (1865). Owing to his duties at the India Office, his appearances in first-class cricket were very limited, though he appeared seven times for the Gentlemen v Players.

Bentinck, Bernhard Walter
Amateur. *b:* 16.7.1877, South Warnborough, Hampshire. *d:* 27.6.1931, Winchester, Hampshire. Brother-in-law of C. R. Seymour (Hampshire), his niece married Dom Mintoff, Prime Minister of Malta. Hard-hitting right-hand batsman. *Sch* Winchester. *Team* Hampshire (1900–02, 2 matches).

Bentley, Henry

Career batting
2–4–0–26–15–6.50–0–*ct* 1

Bentley, Henry
Professional. *b:* 19.2.1782, Westminster, London. *d:* 18.9.1857, Hereford. Brother of John (Middlesex, Hampshire and Surrey) and Charles (Middlesex). Middle order batsman. *Teams* Middlesex (1807–16); Kent (1816); Hampshire (1819).
Career batting
66–124–14–1176–56–10.69–0–*ct* 17–*st* 1
Bowling 26 wickets (no analyses)–0–0–4/?

His first-class debut was for Turner's XI in 1801 and his last match for Players in 1822. After finishing playing he became the most notable umpire of his day. In 1823 he published a book of cricket scores 1786 to 1822. He also played for Hertfordshire (1816), Norfolk (1823) and Herefordshire (1839).

Bentley, Michael
Professional. *b:* 14.2.1934, Rotherham, Yorkshire. Opening left-hand batsman. *Team* Derbyshire (1957, 1 match).
Career batting
1–2–0–12–10–6.00–0–*ct* 0

Benton, Charles Henry
Amateur. *b:* 8.1.1868, Glossop, Derbyshire. *d:* 19.5.1918, Knutsford, Cheshire. He died by his own hand. Middle order right-hand batsman, occasional left-arm medium pace bowler. *Sch* Harrow. *Team* Lancashire (1892–1901, 29 matches).
Career batting
29–50–6–663–68–15.06–0–*ct* 15

He also played for Cheshire and was on the MCC Committee.

Benton, Rev William Manstead
Amateur. *b:* 11.7.1873, Chelsea, London. *d:* 17.8.1916. He was killed in action on the Somme, Belgium. Middle order batsman. *Sch* Framlingham. *Team* Middlesex (1913, 2 matches).
Career batting
2–3–1–25–19*–12.50–0–*ct* 0

Beresford, Richard Augustus Agincourt
Amateur. *b:* 12.8.1869, Castor, near Peterborough, Northamptonshire. *d:* 12.7.1941, Derby. Hard-hitting middle order right-hand batsman, useful change bowler. *Sch* Oundle. *Team* Cambridge U (1889–91).
Career batting
7–14–1–177–40–13.61–0–*ct* 2
Bowling 6–0

He put the weight for Cambridge in 1891 and 1892. His County cricket was for Northamptonshire (pre first-class, 1887–91) and Norfolk (1901–1910).

Beresford, Hon Seton Robert de la Poer Horsley
Amateur. *b:* 25.7.1868, Leixlip, Co Kildare, Ireland. *d:* 28.5.1928, Cap d'Ail, France. Nephew of M. H. Milner (Cambridge U), his widow married the father of R. H. Cobbold (Cambridge U) in 1929. Middle order batsman. *Sch* Eton. *Team* Middlesex (1909, 2 matches).
Career batting
8–13–0–161–45–12.38–0–*ct* 9

His final first-class match was for MCC in 1910.

Bergin, Bernard Francis
Amateur. *b:* 20.9.1913, Dublin, Ireland. *d:* 17.6.1985, Dublin, Ireland. Brother of S. F. (Ireland). Opening right-hand batsman. *Team* Ireland (1937).
Career batting
1–2–0–16–12–8.00–0–*ct* 0

Bergin, Stanley Francis
Amateur. *b:* 18.12.1926, Dublin, Ireland. *d:* 4.8.1969, Dublin, Ireland. Brother of B. F. (Ireland). Opening left-hand batsman. *Team* Ireland (1949–65).
Career batting
27–52–5–1610–137–34.25–2–*ct* 6

Berkeley, George Fitz-Hardinge
Amateur. *b:* 29.1.1870, Dublin, Ireland. *d:* 14.11.1955, Hanwell Castle, Banbury, Oxfordshire. Lower order right-hand batsman, good left-arm medium pace bowler. *Sch* Wellington. *Team* Oxford U (1890–93, blue all four years).
Career batting
32–60–28–324–38–10.12–0–*ct* 17
Bowling 2719–131–20.75–9–1–8/70

His County cricket was for Oxfordshire (1904–06). His final first-class match was for Leveson-Gower's XI in 1906. He played for Ireland (non first-class) in 1890–91.

Berkeley, Robert George Wilmot
Amateur. *b:* 23.4.1898, Warley Place, Romford, Essex. *d:* 28.8.1969, Bristol. Middle order right-hand batsman. *Sch* Downside and Oratory. *Team* Worcestershire (1919–22, 4 matches).
Career batting
4–7–0–37–16–5.28–0–*ct* 0

In 1933 he was High Sheriff of Worcestershire.

Berkley, Rev Maurice
Amateur. *b:* 6.9.1872, Navestock, Essex. *d:* 9.8.1947, Bangor, Caernarvonshire. Lower order right-hand batsman, slow right-arm bowler. *Sch* Fettes. *Team* Essex (1894, 2 matches).
Career batting
2–3–1–6–5–3.00–0–*ct* 2
Bowling 103–7–14.71–1–0–6/50

He appeared in a number of trials whilst at Oxford (1892–94), but never in first-class games for the University.

Bernard, Charles Albert
Amateur. *b:* 16.2.1876, Bristol. *d:* 26.9.1953, Clifton, Bristol. Opening right-hand batsman, moderate field. *Team* Somerset (1896–1901, 33 matches).

Career batting
33–62–6–1705–122–30.44–2–*ct* 21
Bowling 30–0

Bernard, Dr John Richard
Amateur. *b:* 7.12.1938, Clifton Hill, Bristol. Middle order right-hand batsman, right-arm medium pace bowler. *Sch* Clifton. *Teams* Gloucestershire (1956–61, 11 matches); Cambridge U (1958–60, blue all three years).
Career batting
56–100–17–1891–119*–22.78–1–*ct* 28
Bowling 1705–35–48.71–0–0–4/44
His final first-class match was for MCC in 1964.

Bernau, Ernest Henry Lovell
Amateur. *b:* 6.4.1896, Napier, Hawke's Bay, New Zealand. *d:* 7.1.1966, Wanganui, Wellington, New Zealand. Hard hitting lower order left-hand batsman, left-arm medium pace bowler, moderate field. *Teams* Hawke's Bay (1914/5); Wellington (1922/3 to 1927/8). *Tour* New Zealand to England 1927.
Career batting
28–39–2–651–117–17.59–1–*ct* 10
Bowling 1672–58–28.82–1–0–6/35

Berners, John Anstruther
Amateur. *b:* 23.9.1869, Westminster, London. *d:* 2.3.1934, Woolverstone Park, Suffolk. Middle order batsman. *Sch* Eton. *Team* Middlesex (1904, 1 match).
Career batting
2–4–0–59–50–14.75–0–*ct* 0
He also played for Suffolk (1904–09).

Bernstein, Rodney Elliott
Amateur. *b:* 15.12.1937, Dublin, Ireland. Lower order right-hand batsman, right-arm fast medium bowler. *Team* Ireland (1960–62).
Career batting
6–10–0–89–18–8.90–0–*ct* 1
Bowling 406–16–25.37–0–0–4/23

Berridge, Edward Henry Stuart
Amateur. *b:* 19.4.1873, Islington, London. *d:* 30.1.1927, Charing Cross, Westminster, London. Middle order batsman. *Team* London County (1900).
Career batting
1–1–0–0–0–0.00–0–*ct* 0

Berridge, William
Professional. *b:* 7.9.1892, Leicester. *d:* 1.4.1968, Leicester. Middle order right-hand batsman, right-arm medium pace bowler. *Team* Leicestershire (1923–24, 13 matches).
Career batting
13–21–0–146–33–6.95–0–*ct* 5
Bowling 27–0

Berridge, Dr William Claude Morpott
Amateur. *b:* 2.12.1894, Enderby, Leicestershire. *d:* 25.2.1973, Oxshott, Surrey. Useful right-hand batsman, right-arm slow-medium bowler. *Sch* Malvern. *Team* Leicestershire (1914–22, 22 matches).
Career batting
23–40–5–411–61–11.74–0–*ct* 6
Bowling 839–30–27.96–1–0–5/58

Berrington, Edwin Henry
Professional. *b:* 20.4.1850, Waterloo, London. *d:* 11.5.1880, Uxbridge, Middlesex. Lower order batsman, right-arm medium pace bowler. *Team* Surrey (1872, 1 match).
Career batting
1–2–0–16–8–8.00–0–*ct* 0
Bowling 4–0

Berry, Darren Shane
Cricketer. *b:* 10.12.1969, Melbourne, Victoria, Australia. Lower order right-hand batsman, wicket-keeper. *Teams* South Australia (1989/90, 12 matches); Victoria (1990/1 to 1991/2, 24 matches). *Tour* Victoria to England 1991.
Career batting
36–46–5–671–98–16.36–0–*ct* 124–*st* 10

Berry, Fred
Professional. *b:* 13.2.1910, Kirkheaton, Yorkshire. *d:* 2.1.1989, Bracknell, Berkshire. Useful lower order right-hand batsman, right-arm medium fast bowler. *Team* Surrey (1934–39, 46 matches).
Career batting
47–66–11–1053–104*–19.14–1–*ct* 28
Bowling 2376–83–28.62–2–0–6/81
He also played for Berkshire (1947–50).

Berry, George Leslie
(known as Leslie George)
Professional. *b:* 28.4.1906, Dorking, Surrey. *d:* 5.2.1985, Great Glen, Leicester. Attractive opening right-hand batsman, good field. *Team* Leicestershire (1924–51, 605 matches).
Career batting
609–1056–57–30225–232–30.25–45–*ct* 181
Bowling 606–10–60.60–0–0–1/1
For many years the mainstay of Leicestershire's batting, Berry hit 1,000 runs in a season 18 times between 1925 and 1950. His best year, and the only time he exceeded 2,000 runs, was 1937 with 2,446, av 52.04. His highest score was 232 for Leicestershire v Sussex at Leicester in 1930. He hit one other double century for the County. He captained Leicestershire from 1946 to 1948. A good soccer player, he appeared for Sheffield Wednesday, Bristol Rovers and Swindon Town.

Berry, John
Professional. *b:* 10.1.1823, Dalton, Yorkshire. *d:* 26.2.1895, Haslingden, Lancashire. Nephew of George (Yorkshire 1845–53). Sound middle order right-hand batsman, round-arm medium pace bowler. *Team* Yorkshire (1849–67, 37 matches).

Berry, Joseph

Career batting
47–83–7–1069–78–14.06–0–*ct* 34
Bowling 247–17 + 23–14.52–3–0–6/31
He also played for Warwickshire (pre first-class, 1851), Cheshire (1855) and Northumberland (1855).

Berry, Joseph
Professional. *b:* 29.11.1829, Dalton, Yorkshire. *d:* 20.4.1894, Hillhouse, Fartown, Huddersfield, Yorkshire. Opening right-hand batsman, right-arm medium pace bowler. *Team* Yorkshire (1861–74, 5 matches).
Career batting
5–8–0–82–30–10.25–0–*ct* 2

Berry, Philip John
Cricketer. *b:* 28.12.1966, Saltburn, Yorkshire. Lower order right-hand batsman, off break bowler. *Teams* Yorkshire (1986–90, 7 matches); Durham (1992, 9 matches).
Career batting
16–22–9–281–76–21.61–0–*ct* 6
Bowling 1050–24–43.75–1–1–7/113

Berry, Robert
Professional. *b:* 29.1.1926, West Gorton, Manchester, Lancashire. Tail end left-hand batsman, slow left-arm bowler, good outfield. *Teams* Lancashire (1948–54, 93 matches); Worcestershire (1955–58, 94 matches); Derbyshire (1959–62, 54 matches). *Tours* MCC to Australia 1950/51; Commonwealth to India 1953/4. *Tests* England (1950, 2 matches).
Career batting
273–305–112–1463–40–7.58–0–*ct* 138
Bowling 17389–703–24.73–34–5–10/102
Test batting
2–4–2–6–4*–3.00–0–*ct* 2
Bowling 228–9–25.33–1–0–5/63
A most promising spin bowler, he failed miserably on his only tour to Australia in 1950/1 and despite gaining County Caps with both Worcestershire and Derbyshire (in addition to his Lancashire one) he never really fulfilled early promise. His best year was 1953 (98 wickets, av 18.97) and in the same year he took all 10 wickets (for 102) for Lancashire v Worcestershire at Blackpool.

Berry, Wilfred Ernest
Amateur. *b:* 12.10.1897, Hertford. *d:* 1951. Lower order batsman, useful bowler. *Team* Somerset (1926, 1 match).
Career batting
1–1–1–1–1*–no av–0–*ct* 0
Bowling 34–0

Berwick, John Albert
Professional. *b:* 30.7.1867, Northampton. *d:* 31.7.1946, Glossop, Derbyshire. Lower order left-hand batsman, left-arm fast medium bowler. *Team* Derbyshire (1895–1901, 16 matches).
Career batting
16–29–6–138–27–6.00–0–*ct* 7
Bowling 892–24–37.16–2–0–5/61
He also played for Northamptonshire (pre first-class, 1898).

Beslee, George Prior
Professional. *b:* 27.3.1904, Cliffe, Kent. *d:* 3.11.1975, Tonbridge, Kent. Lower order right-hand batsman, right-arm fast medium bowler. *Team* Kent (1925–30, 63 matches).
Career batting
63–86–25–439–24–7.19–0–*ct* 30
Bowling 4199–133–31.57–0–0–4/27

Bessant, John George William Thomas
Professional. *b:* 11.11.1892, Bedminster, Somerset. *d:* 17.1.1982, Frenchay, Bristol. Lower order right-hand batsman, right-arm medium pace bowler. *Team* Gloucestershire (1921–28, 113 matches).
Career batting
113–170–53–1200–50–10.25–0–*ct* 81
Bowling 4615–130–35.50–5–0–5/29

Best, Carlisle Alonza
Cricketer. *b:* 14.5.1959, Richmond Gap, St Michael, Barbados. Middle order right-hand batsman, right-arm medium pace or off break bowler. *Team* Barbados (1979/80 to 1991/2). *Tours* Young West Indies to Zimbabwe 1986/7; West Indies to India 1987/8 (World Cup), 1989/90 (not first-class), to Sharjah (not first-class) 1989/90, to Pakistan 1990/1, to Australia 1991/2; Rest of World to England 1989. *Tests* West Indies (1985/6 to 1990/1, 8 matches).
Career batting
81–138–14–5021–179–40.49–13–*ct* 102
Bowling 605–21–28.80–0–0–3/29
Test batting
8–13–1–342–164–28.50–1–*ct* 8
Bowling 21–0
He scored 100 in his first, and only, first-class match in England for Rest of World at Scarborough in 1989.

Best, William Finlay
Amateur. *b:* 30.5.1865, Smarden, Staplehurst, Kent. *d:* 3.8.1942, Ruthin Castle, Denbighshire. Opening right-hand batsman, slow right-arm bowler. *Team* Kent (1890–92, 5 matches).
Career batting
5–8–0–103–26–12.87–0–*ct* 2
Bowling 69–5–13.80–0–0–3/29
For Kent v Somerset at Taunton in 1891, Best performed the hat-trick. His first-class cricket however was very limited and his most noted performances were for Preston in Lancashire.

Bestwick, Robert Saxton
Professional. *b:* 29.9.1899, Heanor, Derbyshire. *d:* 3.7.1980, St Ouen's, Jersey. Son of William (Derby-

shire). Tail end right-hand batsman, right-arm fast medium bowler. *Team* Derbyshire (1920–22, 5 matches).
Career batting
5–9–1–29–10–3.62–0–*ct* 2
Bowling 151–2–75.50–0–0–2/47

Bestwick, William
Professional. *b:* 24.2.1875, Heanor, Derbyshire. *d:* 2.5.1938, Standard Hill, Nottingham. Father of R. S. (Derbyshire). Tail end right-hand batsman, excellent right-arm fast medium bowler. *Team* Derbyshire (1898–1925, 321 matches).
Career batting
323–524–183–1607–39–4.71–0–*ct* 89
Bowling 30998–1457–21.27–104–27–10/40

Employing a short run up, he was able to bowl for long spells without tiring. He took 100 wickets in a season four times (best 147, av 16.72 in 1921). In 1921 he also took 10 wickets in an innings (for 40) v Glamorgan at Cardiff. Owing to his intemperance, the Derbyshire Committee dispensed with his services in 1909 and he moved to South Wales where he qualified by residence for Glamorgan and played for that County (pre first-class) in 1914. He resumed his first-class career with Derbyshire in 1919. He was a first-class umpire (1927–37), standing in three Test matches (1929–30).

Betham, Sir Geoffrey Lawrence
Amateur. *b:* 8.4.1889, Belgaum, India. *d:* 6.11.1963, Chelsea, London. Opening right-hand batsman, change bowler. *Sch* Dulwich. *Teams* Free Foresters (1922); Europeans (1917/8 to 1926/7); Rajputana (1937/8).
Career batting
7–13–3–129–30–12.90–0–*ct* 3
Bowling 139–4–34.75–0–0–2/27

Bethell, John Arthur Lionel
Cricketer. *b:* 18.12.1940, Bowmanston, St John, Barbados. Sound middle order left-hand batsman, left-arm medium pace bowler. *Team* Barbados (1963/4 to 1969/70). *Tour* Barbados to England 1969.
Career batting
16–25–6–496–84*–26.10–0–*ct* 7
Bowling 391–10–39.10–0–0–2/16

Bethune, Henry Beauclerk
Amateur. *b:* 16.11.1844, Worth, Horsham, Sussex. *d:* 16.4.1912, Denne Park, Horsham, Sussex. Middle order right-hand batsman, slow bowler, latterly under-arm. *Team* Hampshire (1885–97, 2 matches).
Career batting
2–4–1–26–9–8.66–0–*ct* 1
Bowling 27–1–27.00–0–0–1/27

He made many large scores in club cricket, notably in the army and for Gentlemen of Hampshire.

Beton, Sydney Lionel
Professional. *b:* 22.11.1895, Paddington, London. *d:* 30.11.1972, St John's Wood, London. Middle order right-hand batsman. *Team* Middlesex (1923–28, 32 matches).
Career batting
32–46–10–688–49–19.11–0–*ct* 7

Bettesworth, Walter Ambrose
Amateur. *b:* 24.11.1856, Horndean, Hampshire. *d:* 23.2.1929, Hampstead, London. Middle order right-hand batsman, slow round-arm bowler, good cover field. *Sch* Ardingly. *Team* Sussex (1878–83, 21 matches).
Career batting
22–43–3–716–77–17.90–0–*ct* 12
Bowling 986–38–25.94–2–0–5/66

A noted author and journalist, he was cricket editor of 'The Field' from 1906 to 1928 and wrote several books on the game.

Bettington, Brindley Cecil John
Amateur. *b:* 2.9.1898, Oatlands, Parramatta, New South Wales, Australia. *d:* 26.8.1931, Brindley Park, Merriwa, New South Wales, Australia. Brother of R. H. B. (Middlesex and New South Wales). Middle order right-hand batsman, leg break and googly bowler. *Teams* Oxford U (1920–22); New South Wales (1927/8, 1 match).
Career batting
4–7–2–153–69–30.60–*ct* 1
Bowling 229–8–28.62–0–0–3/35

Bettington, Dr Reginald Henshall Brindley
Amateur. *b:* 24.2.1900, Oatlands, Parramatta, New South Wales, Australia. *d:* 24.6.1969, Gisborne, New Zealand. He was killed in a motor accident. Brother of B. C. J. (Oxford U and New South Wales). Hard hitting middle order right-hand batsman, leg-break and googly bowler. *Teams* Oxford U (1920–23, blue all four years); Middlesex (1928, 15 matches); New South Wales (1928/9 to 1931/2, 5 matches).
Career batting
86–142–21–3314–127–27.38–4–*ct* 60
Bowling 8496–357–23.79–21–5–8/66

A fine all-round sportsman, he also obtained his blue for rugby and golf. He qualified for Middlesex whilst studying medicine at St Bartholomew's. His final first-class match was for Free Foresters in 1938. He captained Oxford in 1923. He was Australian Amateur Golf Champion in 1932.

Betts, George
Professional. *b:* 19.9.1841, Sheffield, Yorkshire. *d:* 26.9.1902, Brightside, Sheffield, Yorkshire. Hard-hitting middle order right-hand batsman. *Team* Yorkshire (1873–74, 2 matches).
Career batting
2–4–1–56–44*–18.66–0–*ct* 0

Betts, Gilbert Frederick
Amateur. *b:* 21.12.1916, Fulbrook, Oxfordshire. *d:* 5.1.1982, Abingdon, Oxfordshire. Lower order right-hand batsman, right-arm fast medium bowler. *Team* Minor Counties (1951).
Career batting
1–2–0–1–1–0.50–0–*ct* 1
Bowling 95–5–19.00–1–0–5/95
His County cricket was for Oxfordshire (1950–56).

Betts, Morton Peto
Amateur. *b:* 30.8.1847, Bloomsbury, London. *d:* 19.4.1914, Mentone, France. Middle order batsman. *Sch* Harrow. *Teams* Middlesex (1872, 1 match); Kent (1872–81, 2 matches).
Career batting
3–5–2–83–39*–27.66–0–*ct* 0
He also played for Essex (pre first-class, 1884). From 1887 to 1890 he was Secretary to Essex CCC. He was well-known on the soccer field, playing for Wanderers in the first FA Cup final of 1872, when he played under a pseudonym, A. H. Chequer (he had played for Harrow Chequers in an earlier round), and scored the only goal. He also played for England in 1877.

Betts, William Hammond
Amateur. *b:* 25.8.1846, Islington, London. *d:* 14.6.1884, Diss, Norfolk. Middle order batsman. *Sch* Harrow. *Team* MCC (1866).
Career batting
1–2–0–1–1–0.50–0–*ct* 0

Bevan, David George
Cricketer. *b:* 11.6.1943, Gloucester. Middle order right-hand batsman, right-arm medium pace bowler. *Teams* Gloucestershire (1964–70, 33 matches); Eastern Province (1973/4).
Career batting
36–57–4–706–80–13.32–0–*ct* 13
Bowling 30–3–10.00–0–0–3/30
He left the Gloucestershire staff after the 1967 season to become a lecturer at Cape Town University, but returned to Gloucestershire for 1970. He also played for Suffolk (1977).

Bevan, Thomas
Amateur. *b:* 14.2.1900, Crayford, Kent. *d:* 12.6.1942, Tobruk, Libya. Middle order right-hand batsman. *Sch* Eton. *Team* Army (1928).
Career batting
1–2–0–7–6–3.50–0–*ct* 0
His County cricket was for Suffolk (1933).

Beveridge, Robert
Professional. *b:* 16.9.1909, Paddington, London. Lower order right-hand batsman, slow left-arm bowler. *Team* Middlesex (1930–34, 41 matches).
Career batting
41–57–19–352–49–9.26–0–*ct* 21
Bowling 1350–41–32.92–2–0–6/66
He emigrated to New Zealand.

Beves, Gordon
Amateur. *b:* 15.3.1862, Brighton, Sussex. *d:* 22.3.1927, Auckland Park, Johannesburg, South Africa. Lower order right-hand batsman, change bowler. *Sch* The Leys. *Teams* Nottinghamshire (1888–91, 9 matches); Transvaal (1894/5 to 1898/9).
Career batting
18–31–1–370–60–12.33–0–*ct* 11
Bowling 201–8–25.12–0–0–2/13
A noted rugby footballer he represented Sussex. He was Chairman of the South African Cricket Association. He umpired in one Test match in South Africa in 1895/6.

Bevington, John Currey
Amateur. *b:* 6.4.1872, Sydenham, Kent. *d:* 4.4.1933, Woodham-Ferrers, Chelmsford, Essex. Brother of T. A. D. (Middlesex). Middle order right-hand batsman. *Sch* Harrow. *Team* Middlesex (1900, 1 match).
Career batting
1–2–0–8–6–4.00–0–*ct* 1
He did not appear in a first-class match whilst at Cambridge. He also played for Essex (pre first-class, 1891).

Bevington, Timothy Arthur Dent
Amateur. *b:* 22.8.1881, Amwell, Hertfordshire. *d:* 4.5.1966, Vancouver, British Columbia, Canada. Brother of J. C. (Middlesex). Middle order left-hand batsman. *Sch* Harrow. *Team* Middlesex (1900–04, 6 matches).
Career batting
14–22–2–359–91–17.95–0–*ct* 4
Bowling 77–3–25.66–0–0–3/21
He emigrated to Winnipeg, Canada, and played a large part in cricket in Canada in the years immediately prior to the First World War. He represented Canada v United States in 1911. His last first-class match was for USA and Canada v Australia in 1913.

Bevins, Stuart Roy
Cricketer. *b:* 8.3.1967, Solihull, Warwickshire. Lower order right-hand batsman, wicket-keeper. *Sch* Solihull. *Team* Worcestershire (1989–91, 6 matches).
Career batting
6–6–2–34–10–8.50–0–*ct* 18

Bewick, Alfred William George
Professional. *b:* 25.1.1876, Hempstead, Gloucestershire. *d:* 15.10.1949, Cheltenham, Gloucestershire. Tail end left-hand batsman, left-arm fast bowler. *Team* Gloucestershire (1903, 1 match).
Career batting
1–2–0–5–5–2.50–0–*ct* 0
Bowling 51–1–51.00–0–0–1/31

Bezer, Arthur Herbert
Professional. *b:* 20.10.1875, Bath, Somerset. *d:* 11.7.1944, Bath, Somerset. Lower order batsman, left-arm bowler. *Team* Somerset (1914, 1 match).
Career batting
1–2–0–1–1–0.50–0–*ct* 1
Bowling 12–0

Bhatia, Anand Narain
Cricketer. *b:* 23.1.1947, Lucknow, India. Lower order right-hand batsman, off break bowler. *Teams* Delhi (1966/7); Cambridge U (1969, blue).
Career batting
13–21–2–277–43–14.57–0–*ct* 7
Bowling 866–30–28.86–0–0–4/36

Bick, Donald Albert
Professional. *b:* 22.2.1936, Hampstead, London. *d:* 24.1.1992, Ware, Hertfordshire. Lower order right-hand batsman, off break bowler. *Team* Middlesex (1954–67, 145 matches).
Career batting
147–190–31–2221–85–13.96–0–*ct* 35
Bowling 6482–234–27.70–5–0–5/22
He also played for Hertfordshire (1968–74).

Bickley, John
Professional. *b:* 16.1.1819, Keyworth, Nottinghamshire. *d:* 15.11.1866, Nottingham. Lower order right-hand batsman, right-hand fast round-arm bowler, good slip. *Teams* Nottinghamshire (1847–60, 15 matches); Surrey (1852, 1 match as given man); Kent (1854, 1 match as given man).
Career batting
38–60–8–228–27–4.38–0–*ct* 37
Bowling 1639–140 + 1–11.70–9–4–8/7
For England against Kent and Sussex at Lord's in 1856 he took 8 wickets for 7 runs. He also played for Worcestershire (pre first-class, 1848–51).

Bickmore, Arthur Frederic
Amateur. *b:* 19.5.1899, Tonbridge, Kent. *d:* 18.3.1979, Tonbridge, Kent. Good right-hand opening batsman, brilliant outfield. *Sch* Clifton. *Teams* Kent (1919–29, 48 matches); Oxford U (1920–21, blue both years).
Career batting
64–104–7–2254–120–23.23–2–*ct* 41
Bowling 120–0
In both his University matches he hit the highest score for his side and in 1921 also made the highest score for Kent in the match v Australians. Owing to his scholastic duties his first-class appearances were very limited.

Bicknell, Darren John
Cricketer. *b:* 24.6.1967, Guildford, Surrey. Brother of M. P. (Surrey). Opening left-hand batsman, left-arm medium pace bowler. *Team* Surrey (1987–92, 107 matches). *Tours* England A to Zimbabwe 1989/90, to Pakistan and Sri Lanka 1990/1, to West Indies 1991/2.
Career batting
122–213–22–7364–186–38.55–17–*ct* 45
Bowling 265–3–88.33–0–0–2/62
He shared a record 3rd wicket stand for Surrey with D. M. Ward of 413 v Kent at Canterbury in 1990. He reached 1,000 runs in a season four times (best 1,888, av 47.20, in 1991).

Bicknell, Martin Paul
Cricketer. *b:* 14.1.1969, Guildford, Surrey. Brother of D. J. (Surrey). Lower order right-hand batsman, right-arm fast medium bowler. *Team* Surrey (1986–92, 112 matches). *Tours* England A to Zimbabwe 1989/90; England to Australia 1990/1, to New Zealand 1990/1 (not first-class).
Career batting
119–133–40–1563–88–16.80–0–*ct* 38
Bowling 10298–383–26.88–13–0–9/45
On the England tour of 1990/1, he appeared in 5 one-day internationals, but no Tests. He took 71 wickets, av 25.66, in 1992. His best bowling was 9/45 for Surrey v Cambridge U at the Oval in 1988.

Biddle, Lynford Arthur
Amateur. *b:* 1876, Chestnut Hill, Philadelphia, USA. *d:* 24.1.1941, Philadelphia, USA. Sound opening left-hand batsman. *Team* Philadelphia (1893–97). *Tour* Philadelphia to England 1897.
Career batting
13–21–4–216–45*–12.70–0–*ct* 11
Bowling 23–2–11.50–0–0–2/16
He represented the United States v Canada in 1893, 1894, 1896 and 1903.

Biddolph, George Henry
Amateur. *b:* 28.3.1858, Manchester, Lancashire. *d:* 21.4.1937, Melbourne, Victoria, Australia. Middle order right-hand batsman, right-arm medium pace bowler. *Team* Lancashire (1885, 1 match).
Career batting
1–2–0–19–18–9.50–0–*ct* 1
Bowling 13–0

Biddulph, Kenneth David
Professional. *b:* 29.5.1932, Chingford, Essex. Tail end right-hand batsman, right-arm fast medium bowler. *Team* Somerset (1955–61, 91 matches).
Career batting
91–119–50–468–41–6.78–0–*ct* 37
Bowling 7457–270–27.61–10–0–6/30
He also played for Durham (1962–72).

Biddulph, Samuel
Professional. *b:* 23.12.1840, Hyson Green, Nottinghamshire. *d:* 7.3.1876, Nottingham. Tail end right-hand batsman, wicket-keeper, occasional right-hand round-arm medium pace bowler. *Team* Nottinghamshire (1862–75, 76 matches).

Bielby, Stephen Richard

Career batting
176–291–51–2287–60–9.52–0–*ct* 164–*st* 123
Bowling 117–5 + 2–23.40–0–0–3/31
From 1863 to his death he was on the staff at Lord's and played in many MCC matches.

Bielby, Stephen Richard
Cricketer. *b:* 9.3.1947, Windsor, Berkshire. Middle order right-hand batsman, off break bowler. *Sch* Radley. *Team* Nottinghamshire (1967–71, 43 matches).
Career batting
43–58–12–837–62–18.19–0–*ct* 16
Bowling 161–3–53.66–0–0–1/14
He also played for Buckinghamshire (1965).

Bigg, George Ashburner
Amateur. *b:* 24.7.1861, Barrow-in-Furness, Lancashire. *d:* 27.10.1931, Barrow-in-Furness, Lancashire. *Team* Lancashire (1887, 1 match).
Career batting
1–1–0–16–16–16.00–0–*ct* 0
Bowling 13–1–13.00–0–0–1/13

Bigge, George Orde
Amateur. *b:* 13.1.1869, Ferezepore, India. *d:* 26.3.1935, Stone-in-Oxney, Kent. Brother-in-law of H. M. Braybrooke (Kent). Middle order right-hand batsman, right-arm medium pace bowler. *Sch* Mill Hill. *Team* MCC (1898).
Career batting
1–2–0–12–11–6.00–0–*ct* 0
His County cricket was for Hertfordshire (1896–1903).

Biggs, Anthony Llewellyn
Amateur. *b:* 26.4.1946, Graaff-Reinet, Cape Province, South Africa. Opening right-hand batsman, off break bowler. *Team* Eastern Province (1964/5 to 1980/1). *Tours* SA Universities to England 1967; South Africa to Australia 1971/2 (tour cancelled).
Career batting
62–112–8–3409–156–32.77–8–*ct* 35
Bowling 2811–82–34.28–4–1–7/62

Bignall, Thomas
Professional. *b:* 8.1.1842, Chilwell, Nottinghamshire. *d:* 19.9.1898, Hyson Green, Nottinghamshire. Powerful opening right-hand batsman, occasional fast round-arm bowler. *Team* Nottinghamshire (1863–78, 60 matches).
Career batting
90–155–10–2656–116*–18.31–1–*ct* 19
Bowling 104–1 + 1–104.00–0–0–1/12
He also played for Devon (1864).

Bignell, Guy Newcombe
Amateur. *b:* 3.12.1886, Mozufferpore, India. *d:* 10.6.1965, Lausanne, Switzerland. Brother of H. G. (Hampshire). Middle order right-hand batsman, right-arm medium pace bowler. *Sch* Haileybury. *Teams* Hampshire (1904–25, 55 matches); Europeans (1923/4).
Career batting
58–86–5–1670–109–20.61–1–*ct* 27
Bowling 759–17–44.64–0–0–3/67
In 1908 for Hambledon XII he appeared under the assumed name of G. N. Deer and in 1919 for Hampshire under the assumed name G. Newcombe.

Bignell, Hugh Glennie
Amateur. *b:* 4.10.1882, Mozufferpore, India. *d:* 6.5.1907, of enteric fever, Rawalpindi, India. Brother of G. N. (Hampshire). Middle order right-hand batsman, right-arm fast bowler. *Sch* Haileybury. *Teams* Hampshire (1901–02, 5 matches); Europeans (1901/2).
Career batting
6–11–2–140–49*–15.55–0–*ct* 2
Bowling 29–0

Bigwood, Alfred
Professional. *b:* 3.8.1857, Mortlake, Surrey. *d:* 12.9.1940, East Putney, London. Lower order right-hand batsman, slow round-arm bowler. *Team* Surrey (1878, 1 match).
Career batting
1–2–1–5–4–5.00–0–*ct* 2

Bilbie, Anthony Robin
Professional. *b:* 29.4.1942, Sherwood, Nottingham. Middle order right-hand batsman. *Team* Nottinghamshire (1960–63, 14 matches).
Career batting
14–27–1–291–39–11.19–0–*ct* 12

Billham, Frank Denis
Amateur. *b:* 27.9.1896, Georgetown, British Guiana. *d:* 16.11.1980, Sudbury, Suffolk. Lower order right-hand batsman, slow left-arm bowler. *Sch* Framlingham. *Team* Essex (1924, 2 matches).
Career batting
2–3–1–12–12*–6.00–0–*ct* 0
Bowling 72–0
For many years he was on the Council of the Club Cricket Conference.

Billingsley, Charles William
Amateur. *b:* 1.1.1910, Belfast, Ireland. *d:* 4.11.1951, Belfast, Ireland. Tail end right-hand batsman, right-arm fast medium bowler. *Team* Ireland (1936–38).
Career batting
5–10–5–19–6*–3.80–0–*ct* 1
Bowling 265–18–14.72–0–0–4/19

Billington, David James
Cricketer. *b:* 6.12.1965, Leyland, Lancashire. Middle order right-hand batsman. *Team* Leicestershire (1985, 1 match).
Career batting
1–1–0–19–19–19.00–0–*ct* 1

Billyeald, James
Amateur. *b:* 20.1.1835, Hyson Green, Nottingham. *d:* 8.7.1890, Hyson Green, Nottingham. Middle order right-hand batsman, round-arm medium pace bowler. *Team* Derbyshire (1871, 1 match).
Career batting
1–2–1–15–11*–15.00–0–*ct* 0

Bilton, Edmund John
Professional. *b:* 23.5.1839, Cambridge. *d:* 24.8.1916, Cambridge. Middle order batsman. *Teams* Cambridge Town Club (1859–60); Cambridgeshire (1866, 1 match).
Career batting
3–5–0–25–10–5.00–0–*ct* 3

Bingham, Dr Frank Miller
Amateur. *b:* 17.9.1874, Alfreton, Derbyshire. *d:* 22.5.1915. He was killed in action, Sanctuary Wood, Ypres, Belgium. Lower order batsman, right-arm medium pace bowler. *Sch* St Peter's, York. *Team* Derbyshire (1896, 1 match).
Career batting
1–2–0–17–11–8.50–0–*ct* 0
He played rugby for Blackheath.

Binks, James Graham
Professional. *b:* 5.10.1935, Hull, Yorkshire. Lower order right-hand batsman, occasional leg break bowler, wicket-keeper. *Team* Yorkshire (1955–69, 491 matches). *Tours* MCC to Ceylon, India and Pakistan 1961/2, to India 1963/4. *Tests* England (1963/4, 2 matches).
Career batting
502–598–129–6910–95–14.73–*ct* 895–*st* 176
Bowling 82–0
Test batting
2–4–0–91–55–22.75–0–*ct* 8
Binks appeared in 412 consecutive County Championship matches for Yorkshire between 1955 and 1969. In 1960 he dismissed 107 batsmen (96 ct, 11 st). He also played for Lincolnshire (1972–73). His last first-class match was for International XI in 1975.

Binns, John
Professional. *b:* 31.3.1870, Woodhouse Carr, Leeds, Yorkshire. *d:* 8.12.1934, Leeds, Yorkshire. Lower order batsman, wicket-keeper. *Team* Yorkshire (1898, 1 match).
Career batting
1–1–0–4–4–4.00–0–*ct* 0–*st* 3

Binny, Roger Michael Humphrey
Cricketer. *b:*19.7.1955, Bangalore, India. Middle order right-hand batsman, right-arm medium pace bowler. *Teams* Karnataka (1975/6 to 1989/90); Goa (1991/2). *Tours* India to Australia 1980/1, 1984/5 (not first-class), 1985/6, to New Zealand 1980/1, to England 1983 (World Cup), 1986, to Sharjah (not first-class) 1983/4, 1984/5, 1985/6, 1986/7, to Pakistan 1984/5, to Sri Lanka 1985/6. *Tests* India (1979/80 to 1986/7, 27 matches).
Career batting
136–215–22–6579–211*–34.08–14–*ct* 91
Bowling 7386–205–36.02–5–0–8/22
Test batting
27–41–5–830–83*–23.05–0–*ct* 11
Bowling 1534–47–32.63–2–0–6/56
He proved a useful all-rounder on the 1986 tour to England and played in all three Tests. He scored 211* for Karnataka v Kerala at Chickmagalur in 1977/8 and in the process added 451 unbroken for the first wicket with S. Desai.

Birch, Albert Edgar
Professional. *b:* 11.8.1868, Bethnal Green, London. *d:* 6.11.1936. Lower order batsman, right-arm fast medium bowler. *Team* Kent (1894, 1 match).
Career batting
1–2–0–3–3–1.50–0–*ct* 0

Birch, John Dennis
Cricketer. *b:* 18.6.1955, Aspley, Nottingham. Hard hitting middle order right-hand batsman, right-arm medium pace bowler, gully field. *Team* Nottinghamshire (1973–88, 250 matches).
Career batting
250–374–59–8673–125–27.53–6–*ct* 182
Bowling 2446–50–48.92–1–0–6/64
He hit 1,000 runs in a season twice (best 1,086, av 30.16, in 1983). He was Nottinghamshire Cricket Manager from October 1990 to May 1992.

Birch, William
Professional. *b:* 10.2.1863, Isleworth, Middlesex. *d:* 11.12.1940, Isleworth, Middlesex. Lower order batsman, useful bowler. *Team* Middlesex (1887, 2 matches).
Career batting
2–4–1–6–4–2.00–0–*ct* 0
Bowling 95–2–47.50–0–0–2/28

Bird, Albert
Professional. *b:* 17.8.1867, Moseley, Warwickshire. *d:* 16.6.1927, Worcester. Lower order right-hand batsman, off break bowler, good field. *Team* Worcestershire (1899–1909, 143 matches).
Career batting
143–225–63–1951–64*–12.04–0–*ct* 55
Bowling 7403–292–25.35–20–3–7/41
He also played for Warwickshire (pre first-class, 1887–90) and began his career with Worcestershire (pre first-class) in 1892.

Bird, Austin Carlos
Amateur. *b:* 26.1.1884, Sefton Park, Liverpool, Lancashire. *d:* 4.1.1938, Buxted, Sussex. Son of George (Middlesex and Lancashire), brother of M. C. (Lancashire and Surrey), father of A. C. (Army in India),

nephew of Walter (MCC). Middle order batsman. *Sch* Malvern. *Team* MCC (1914).
Career batting
1–2–0–3–3–1.50–0–*ct* 0

Bird, Rev Frederick Nash
Amateur. *b:* 13.12.1875, Framlingham, Suffolk. *d:* 3.3.1965, Chichester, Sussex. Middle order right-hand batsman, right-arm medium pace bowler. *Teams* Gloucestershire (1899–1900, 6 matches); Northamptonshire (1908–09, 10 matches).
Career batting
16–28–4–398–61*–16.58–0–*ct* 11

He also played for Buckinghamshire (1896–1907), Suffolk (1910–14) and Devon (1920–24).

Bird, George
Amateur. *b:* 30.7.1849, Crouch Hall, Hackney, London. *d:* 28.10.1930, Esher, Surrey. Father of M. C. (Lancashire and Surrey) and A. C. (MCC), brother of Walter (MCC), grandfather of A C. (Army in India). Elegant middle order right-hand batsman. *Sch* Highgate. *Teams* Middlesex (1872–77, 13 matches); Lancashire (1880, 1 match).
Career batting
21–36–3–477–75–14.45–0–*ct* 6–*st* 5
Bowling 0–0

He was a member of the MCC for 60 years. His best innings was 112 for Fifteen of the MCC v Anglo-American Team of 1872 at Lord's in 1873 (non-first-class).

Bird, Harold Dennis, MBE
Professional. *b:* 19.4.1933, Barnsley, Yorkshire. Opening right-hand batsman, off break bowler. *Teams* Yorkshire (1956–59, 14 matches); Leicestershire (1960–64, 79 matches).
Career batting
93–170–10–3314–181*–20.71–2–*ct* 28
Bowling 22–0

He hit 1,028 runs, av 21.41, in 1960.

Appointed as a first-class umpire in 1970, he stood in a Test match for the first time in 1973, since when he has been regularly on the panel of Test match umpires, standing in 47 Tests as at the end of the 1992 season.

Bird, Morice Carlos
Amateur. *b:* 25.3.1888, St Michael's Hamlet, Liverpool, Lancashire. *d:* 9.12.1933, Broadstone, Dorset. Son of George (Middlesex and Lancashire), brother of A. C. (MCC), nephew of Walter (MCC), uncle of A. C. (Army in India). Fine forcing middle order right-hand batsman, right-arm medium pace bowler. *Sch* Harrow. *Teams* Lancashire (1907, 5 matches); Surrey (1909–21, 127 matches); Cooch-Behar's XI (1917/18); Bird's XI (1918/19). *Tours* MCC to South Africa 1909/10, 1913/14, to Argentine 1911/12; Leveson-Gower to Rhodesia 1909/10. *Tests* England (1909/10 to 1913/14, 10 matches).
Career batting
192–306–14–6938–200–23.76–7–*ct* 111
Bowling 3827–149–25.68–2–1–5/48
Test batting
10–16–1–280–61–18.66–0–*ct* 5
Bowling 120–8–15.00–0–0–3/11

The outstanding schoolboy cricketer of 1907, Bird hit a century in each innings (100 and 131) for Harrow v Eton at Lord's, the only boy ever to perform such a feat in that fixture. In County cricket he hit 1,000 runs in a season three times (best 1,404, av 30.52, in 1919). He captained Surrey from 1910 to 1913 and was coach in 1924 and 1925. His highest score, 200, was made for MCC v Orange Free State at Bloemfontein in 1913/14, but his record on his two tours to South Africa was a modest one.

Bird, Percy John
Amateur. *b:* 27.5.1877, West Cowes, Isle of Wight. *d:* 11.11.1942, Freshwater Bay, Isle of Wight. Middle order left-hand batsman, slow left-arm bowler. *Sch* Cheltenham. *Team* Hampshire (1900, 1 match).
Career batting
1–2–0–37–28–18.50–0–*ct* 0

Bird, Ronald Ernest
Amateur. *b:* 4.4.1915, Quarry Bank, Staffordshire. *d:* 20.2.1985, Feckenham, Worcestershire. Forcing middle order right-hand batsman, occasional right-arm fast medium bowler. *Team* Worcestershire (1946–54, 190 matches).
Career batting
195–327–32–7700–158*–26.10–7–*ct* 157
Bowling 1121–23–48.73–0–0–3/26

He hit 1,000 runs in a season three times (best 1,591, av 37.00, in 1952). He captained Worcestershire 1952–54. His last first-class match was for MCC in 1958.

Bird, Walter
Amateur. *b:* 22.7.1845, Crouch Hall, Hackney, London. *d:* 27.7.1921, Upperton, Eastbourne, Sussex. Brother of George (Middlesex and Lancashire), uncle of M. C. (Surrey and Lancashire) and A. C. (MCC). Middle order batsman. *Sch* Highgate. *Team* MCC (1880).
Career batting
1–2–0–13–13–6.50–0–*ct* 2

Bird, Wilfred Stanley
Amateur. *b:* 28.9.1883, Yiewsley, Middlesex. *d:* 9.5.1915, Richebourg St Vaast, France. Lower order right-hand batsman, wicket-keeper. *Sch* Malvern. *Teams* Oxford U (1904–06, blue all three years); Middlesex (1905–08, 11 matches).
Career batting
55–92–16–969–57–12.75–0–*ct* 93–*st* 17

His final first-class appearance was for MCC in 1913. He captained Oxford in 1906.

Birkenshaw, Jack
Professional. *b:* 13.11.1940, Rothwell, Yorkshire. Middle or lower order left-hand batsman, off break bowler, good slip field. *Teams* Yorkshire (1958–60, 30 matches); Leicestershire (1961–80, 420 matches); Worcestershire (1981, 10 matches). *Tours* MCC to Pakistan, India and Sri Lanka 1972/3, to West Indies 1973/4; International XI to India and Pakistan 1967/8; Norfolk to West Indies 1969/70. *Tests* England (1972/3 to 1973/4, 5 matches).
Career batting
490–665–123–12780–131–23.57–4–*ct* 318
Bowling 29276–1073–27.28–44–4–8/94
Test batting
5–7–0–148–64–21.14–0–*ct* 3
Bowling 469–13–36.07–1–0–5/57

He took 100 wickets in a season twice (best 111, av 21.41, in 1967). He was a first-class umpire (1982–88, standing in 2 Test matches 1986–88). He was appointed Cricket Manager of Leicestershire in 1992, having previously served in the same post for Somerset 1989–91.

Birkett, William
(also known as William Burkitt)
Professional. *b:* 27.2.1874, Coal Aston, Derbyshire. *d:* 2.5.1934, Norton, Sheffield, Yorkshire. Lower order batsman. *Team* Derbyshire (1898–1901, 4 matches).
Career batting
4–7–0–20–10–2.85–0–*ct* 0
Bowling 115–3–38.33–0–0–2/28

Birks, Douglas Thomas Montague
Amateur. *b:* 4.7.1919, Roche, Cornwall. Middle order right-hand batsman, right-arm fast medium bowler. *Sch* Radley. *Team* Free Foresters (1949).
Career batting
1–1–0–3–3–3.00–0–*ct* 0

His County cricket was for Suffolk (1938–48).

Birley, Francis Hornby
Amateur. *b:* 14.3.1850, Chorlton, Manchester, Lancashire. *d:* 1.8.1910, Dormans Land, Surrey. Brother-in-law of J. Kenrick (Surrey). Lower order right-hand batsman, useful slow right-arm bowler, excellent field. *Sch* Winchester. *Teams* Lancashire (1870–72, 4 matches); Surrey (1879, 1 match).
Career batting
5–8–1–65–18–9.28–0–*ct* 1
Bowling 120–4–30.00–0–0–3/76

He also played for Cheshire (1868). He played in the Freshmen's match of 1869 but not in any first-class matches for Oxford U. A well-known soccer player, he was a member of the Oxford side which won the FA Cup in 1874 and of the Wanderers who won it in 1876 and 1877. He appeared in two internationals for England. He won a blue for athletics.

Biron, Rev Henry Brydges
Amateur. *b:* 13.6.1835, Lympne, Hythe, Kent. *d:* 7.4.1915, Derringstone, Canterbury, Kent. Middle order right-hand batsman. *Sch* King's School, Canterbury. *Team* Kent (1857–64, 15 matches).
Career batting
20–33–3–314–53–10.46–0–*ct* 9
Bowling 64–2–32.00–0–0–1/29

He scored many runs in club cricket, including an innings of 214 for the Quidnuncs at Brighton in 1864.

Birrell, Henry Benson
Amateur. *b:* 1.12.1927, Pietermaritzburg, South Africa. Father of A. V. (Eastern Province), uncle of W. V. Rippon (Eastern Province). Middle order right-hand batsman, right-arm medium or slow bowler, brilliant cover field. *Sch* St Andrews, South Africa. *Teams* Eastern Province (1947/8 to 1956/7); Rhodesia (1957/8 to 1959/60); Oxford U (1953–54, blue both years).
Career batting
54–95–3–2446–134–26.58–3–*ct* 18
Bowling 1939–55–35.25–2–0–5/20

He was also awarded his rugby blue 1953/4.

Birtle, Thomas William
Professional. *b:* 28.3.1926, Stockton-on-Tees, Durham. Lower order right-hand batsman, right-arm fast medium bowler. *Team* Nottinghamshire (1952, 7 matches).
Career batting
7–7–2–12–4*–2.40–0–*ct* 4
Bowling 593–8–74.12–0–0–2/68

He also played for Durham (pre first-class, 1946 and 1955).

Birtles, Thomas James Denton
Professional. *b:* 26.10.1886, Higham, Barnsley, Yorkshire. *d:* 13.1.1971, Attenborough, Nottinghamshire. Middle order right-hand batsman. *Team* Yorkshire (1913–24, 37 matches).
Career batting
37–57–11–876–104–19.04–1–*ct* 19
Bowling 20–0

He played soccer for Barnsley, Swansea Town and Portsmouth.

Birtwell, Alexander Joseph
Amateur. *b:* 17.12.1908, Burnley, Lancashire. *d:* 20.11.1974, Nelson, Lancashire. Tail end right-hand batsman, leg break bowler. *Team* Lancashire (1937–39, 14 matches).
Career batting
14–16–6–103–31–10.30–0–*ct* 12
Bowling 999–25–39.96–0–0–4/78

Prior to playing for Lancashire he had appeared for Buckinghamshire (1934–36), but his best cricket was for Nelson in the Lancashire League.

Bisgood, Bertram Lewis
Amateur. *b:* 11.3.1881, Glastonbury, Somerset. *d:* 19.7.1968, Canford Cliffs, Hampshire. Brother of E. D. P. (Somerset). Middle order right-hand batsman, wicket-keeper. *Sch* Prior Park College. *Team* Somerset (1907–21, 67 matches).
Career batting
67–126–12–2143–116*–18.79–2–*ct* 23–*st* 1
Bisgood made a remarkable first-class debut; playing for Somerset v Worcestershire at Worcester in 1907 he hit 82 and 116*.

Bisgood, Eustace Denis Piers
Amateur. *b:* 6.2.1878, Glastonbury, Somerset. *d:* 4.3.1958, Sidmouth, Devon. Brother of B. L. (Somerset). Lower order batsman. *Team* Somerset (1909, 1 match).
Career batting
1–2–0–6–6–3.00–0–*ct* 1

Bishop, Arthur Theodore
Amateur. *b:* 2.9.1863, West Ham, Essex. *d:* 8.9.1931, St John's Wood, London. Brother of F. A. (Essex). Lower order right-hand batsman, useful bowler. *Team* Middlesex (1883, 1 match).
Career batting
1–2–2–0–0*–no av–0–*ct* 0
Bowling 76–2–38.00–0–0–2/72
He also played for Essex (pre first-class, 1885–88).

Bishop, Charles Frederick
Amateur. *b:* 19.8.1879, Down End, Horsley, Gloucestershire. *d:* 27.10.1943, Stonehouse, Plymouth, Devon. Middle order batsman. *Team* Somerset (1920–21, 2 matches).
Career batting
2–4–1–9–3*–3.00–0–*ct* 0

Bishop, Francis Augustus
Amateur. *b:* 11.6.1862, Wanstead, Essex. *d:* 11.4.1942, Finchley, Middlesex. Brother of A. T. (Middlesex). Tail end right-hand batsman, useful right-arm fast bowler. *Team* Gentlemen (1889).
Career batting
1–2–0–1–1–0.50–0–*ct* 1
Bowling 108–1–108.00–0–0–1/74
His County cricket was for Essex (pre first-class, 1885–91). He was one of the principal bowlers of the Essex team in 1889 when he was chosen to represent the Gentlemen – the selection was criticised on account of his doubtful bowling action.

Bishop, Ian Raphael
Cricketer. *b:* 24.10.1967, Port of Spain, Trinidad. Nephew of R. J. (Trinidad). Lower order right-hand batsman, right-arm fast bowler. *Teams* Trinidad (1986/7 to 1990/1); Derbyshire (1989–92, 45 matches). *Tours* West Indies to England 1988, 1991, to Australia 1988/9, to India 1989/90 (not first-class), to Sharjah (not first-class) 1988/9, 1989/90, 1991/2, to Pakistan 1990/1, 1991/2 (not first-class). *Tests* West Indies (1988/9 to 1990/1, 11 matches).
Career batting
88–115–32–1342–103*–16.16–1–*ct* 19
Bowling 6660–325–20.49–18–1–7/34
Test batting
11–17–7–156–30*–15.60–0–*ct* 1
Bowling 1091–53–20.58–3–0–6/87
Although regarded as one of the up and coming fast bowlers on the 1988 tour to England he was not selected for any of the Tests. Signed by Derbyshire for 1989, he shared the overseas spot with Holding. In 1990 however he was the County's leading bowler. Injury prevented him from playing, except in one festival match, on the 1991 tour.

Bishop, Jamie
Cricketer. *b:* 14.1.1971, Swansea, Glamorgan. Middle order left-hand batsman, wicket-keeper. *Team* Glamorgan (1992, 1 match).
Career batting
1–1–1–51–51*–no av–0–*ct* 4
He played for Wales (1989–92) in the Minor Counties Championship.

Bishop, John Fillingham
Amateur. *b:* 21.11.1891, Radcliffe-on-Trent, Nottinghamshire. *d:* 14.12.1963, Hove, Sussex. Opening right-hand batsman, slip field. *Sch* Uppingham. *Team* Nottinghamshire (1923–25, 3 matches).
Career batting
3–4–2–21–15*–10.50–0–*ct* 4

Bishop, Michael Mark
Cricketer. *b:* 20.10.1952, Marlborough, Wiltshire. Tail end right-hand batsman, right-arm medium pace bowler. *Team* Cambridge U (1976–78).
Career batting
3–4–1–4–3–1.33–0–*ct* 1
Bowling 165–2–82.50–0–0–1/13

Bishop, S.
Amateur. Lower order batsman, change bowler. *Team* H. K. Foster's XI (1919).
Career batting
1–2–0–30–20–15.00–0–*ct* 0
Bowling 54–1–54.00–0–0–1/54

Bisseker, Rev Robert Godlonton
Amateur. *b:* 19.11.1878, Port Elizabeth, South Africa. *d:* 9.3.1965, Hindhead, Surrey. Lower order batsman, change bowler. *Sch* KES, Birmingham. *Team* Cambridge U (1904).
Career batting
1–1–1–9–9*–no av–0–*ct* 1
Bowling 44–2–22.00–0–0–1/16
He won a blue for soccer.

Bisset, Arthur Vintcent Crossley
Amateur. *b:* 15.1.1879, Kenilworth, Cape Town, South Africa. *d:* 8.3.1955, Wynberg, Cape Town,

South Africa. Brother of Murray (Western Province). Middle order right-hand batsman. *Team* Western Province (1902/3 to 1921/2). *Tour* South Africa to England 1901.
Career batting
25–47–2–697–94–15.48–0–*ct* 13
Bowling 265–7–37.85–0–0–2/33

Bisset, Sir Murray
Amateur. *b:* 14.4.1876, Port Elizabeth, South Africa. *d:* 24.10.1931, Salisbury, Rhodesia. Brother of A. V. C. (Western Province), brother-in-law of A. N. Difford (Western Province). Good middle order right-hand batsman, occasional left-arm bowler, wicket-keeper. *Team* Western Province (1894/5 to 1909/10). *Tour* South Africa to England 1901. *Tests* South Africa (1898/9 to 1909/10, 3 matches).
Career batting
40–70–9–1436–184–23.54–2–*ct* 51–*st* 13
Bowling 122–5–24.40–0–0–2/20
Test batting
3–6–2–103–35–25.75–0–*ct* 2–*st* 1
He captained the tourists on the 1901 visit to England and also led South Africa in two Tests in 1898/9. At the time of his death he was the acting Governor of Rhodesia.

Bissett, George Finlay
Amateur. *b:* 5.11.1905, Kimberley, Griqualand West, South Africa. *d:* 14.11.1965, Botha's Hill, near Durban, South Africa. Tail end right-hand batsman, right-arm fast bowler. *Teams* Griqualand West (1922/3 to 1923/4); Western Province (1927/8); Transvaal (1929/30). *Tour* South Africa to England 1924. *Tests* South Africa (1927/8, 4 matches).
Career batting
21–31–12–294–33–15.47–0–*ct* 8
Bowling 1816–67–27.10–5–0–7/29
Test batting
4–4–2–38–23–19.00–0–*ct* 0
Bowling 469–25–18.76–2–0–7/29
Injury considerably reduced his cricket in England in 1924, but he was very effective in the 1927/8 series in South Africa, and the press deplored the fact that he did not come to England with the 1929 tourists.

Bissex, Michael
Cricketer. *b:* 28.9.1944, Newbridge, Bath, Somerset. Middle order right-hand batsman, slow left-arm bowler. *Team* Gloucestershire (1961–72, 204 matches). *Tour* MCC Under 25 to Pakistan 1966/7.
Career batting
212–354–35–6492–104*–20.35–2–*ct* 133
Bowling 6783–237–28.62–11–2–7/50
He hit 1,316 runs, av 37.60, in 1970. He also played for Cheshire (1977–78) and Cornwall (1984).

Blaber, Archibald
Professional. *b:* 15.12.1867, Ludwell Farm, Horsted Keynes, Sussex. *d:* 15.5.1905, Cuckfield, Sussex. Lower order batsman, change bowler. *Team* Sussex (1890–94, 2 matches).
Career batting
2–3–1–29–28*–14.50–0–*ct* 0
Bowling 68–1–68.00–0–0–1/32

Black, Christopher James Robert
Cricketer. *b:* 15.12.1947, Johannesburg, South Africa. Lower order right-hand batsman, right-arm medium pace bowler. *Sch* Stowe. *Team* Middlesex (1970–73, 17 matches).
Career batting
17–26–1–400–71–16.00–0–*ct* 8
Bowling 649–13–49.92–0–0–3/51
He was also a noted hockey player.

Black, George Gordon
Amateur. *b:* 19.1.1885, Darling Point, Sydney, New South Wales, Australia. *d:* 6.12.1954, Orange, New South Wales, Australia. Middle order right-hand batsman, right-arm medium pace bowler. *Teams* London County (1903); New South Wales (1903/4, 1 match).
Career batting
2–3–0–104–72–34.66–0–*ct* 1
Bowling 143–2–71.50–0–0–2/41

Black, Lennox Graham
Amateur. *b:* 1880, Toronto, Ontario, Canada. *d: circa* 1950, Quebec, Canada. Lower order right-hand batsman, right-arm fast bowler. *Team* Hampshire (1903–19, 4 matches).
Career batting
4–5–0–36–21–7.20–0–*ct* 3
Bowling 229–1–229.00–0–0–1/27
His first-class career for Hampshire was confined to 1903 and 1919. He appeared for Canada v USA in 1907.

Black, Thomas MacMillan
Cricketer. *b:* 7.2.1956, Greenock, Renfrew, Scotland. Middle order right-hand batsman, right-arm medium pace bowler. *Team* Scotland (1979).
Career batting
1–2–0–88–57–44.00–0–*ct* 2

Blackburn, Benjamin Fielding
Amateur. *b:* 10.9.1855, Meadows, Nottingham. *d:* 6.5.1907, West Cliff, Bournemouth, Hampshire. Middle order right-hand batsman. *Team* Nottinghamshire (1879, 2 matches).
Career batting
2–3–1–6–4*–3.00–0–*ct* 2

Blackburn, John Derek Hepburn
Amateur. *b:* 27.10.1924, Headingley, Leeds, Yorkshire. *d:* 19.2.1987, Steeton, Keighley, Yorkshire. Middle order right-hand batsman. *Team* Yorkshire (1956, 1 match).
Career batting
1–2–0–18–15–9.00–0–*ct* 0

Blackburn, Joseph Scott
Professional *b:* 24.9.1852, Holbeck, Yorkshire. *d:* 8.7.1922, New Wortley, Leeds, Yorkshire. Useful lower-order right-hand batsman, right-arm fast bowler. *Team* Yorkshire (1876–77, 6 matches).
Career batting
7–13–1–122–28–10.16–0–*ct* 4
Bowling 218–8–27.25–0–0–2/19

Blackburn, Paul Hamer
Amateur. *b:* 29.3.1934, Heaton Moor, Stockport, Cheshire. Tail end right-hand batsman, right-arm medium pace bowler. *Sch* Cheltenham. *Team* Cambridge U (1954).
Career batting
1–2–0–7–5–3.50–0–*ct* 0
Bowling 30–0

Blackburn, William Edward
(registered as W. E. Blackburne at death)
Amateur. *b:* 24.11.1888, Clitheroe, Lancashire. *d:* 3.6.1941, Heaton, Bolton, Lancashire. Tail end right-hand batsman, right-arm fast medium bowler. *Team* Yorkshire (1919–20, 10 matches).
Career batting
10–13–6–26–6*–3.71–0–*ct* 9
Bowling 1113–45–24.73–4–0–5/17

Blacker, William
Amateur. *b:* 29.9.1853, Dublin, Ireland. *d:* 21.11.1907, Weston Straffan, Co Kildare, Ireland, as the result of a hunting accident. Opening/middle order right-hand batsman. *Sch* Harrow. *Team* Cambridge U (1873–76, blue all four years).
Career batting
32–55–2–856–86–16.15–0–*ct* 10
Bowling 34–1–34.00–0–0–1/24

He played for Ireland (not first-class) 1879 to 1888.

Blackett, Mark
Cricketer. *b:* 3.2.1964, Edmonton, Middlesex. Middle order right-hand batsman. *Team* Leicestershire (1985, 2 matches).
Career batting
2–4–2–41–28*–20.50–0–*ct* 0

Blackham, John McCarthy
Amateur. *b:* 11.5.1854, North Fitzroy, Melbourne, Victoria, Australia. *d:* 28.12.1932, Flinders Lane, Latrobe, Melbourne, Victoria, Australia. Brother-in-law of G. E. Palmer (Victoria). Stubborn defensive lower order right-hand batsman, brilliant wicket-keeper. *Team* Victoria (1874/5 to 1894/5, 45 matches). *Tours* Australia to England 1878, 1880, 1882, 1884, 1886, 1888, 1890, 1893, to North America 1878, 1893. *Tests* Australia (1876/7 to 1894/5, 35 matches).
Career batting
275–442–61–6395–109–16.78–1–*ct* 274–*st* 180
Bowling 138–2–69.00–0–0–1/8
Test batting
35–62–11–800–74–15.68–0–*ct* 37–*st* 24

He went on every one of the first eight tours made by the Australians to England. Though at the start of his career he had a rival in W. L. Murdoch, he was soon regarded as the 'Prince' of Australian wicket-keepers. Generally standing up very close to the stumps he was able to gather the ball and whip off the bails in a single movement. Unlike some keepers of his day he never played to the gallery. He captained Australia in 8 Tests.

Blackledge, Joseph Frederick
Amateur. *b:* 15.4.1928, Chorley, Lancashire. Lower order right-hand batsman. *Sch* Repton. *Team* Lancashire (1962, 26 matches).
Career batting
26–41–4–569–68–15.37–0–*ct* 9
Bowling 10–0

A useful club cricketer, Blackledge was appointed captain of Lancashire for 1962 without ever having appeared in first-class cricket. This experiment was not successful. He is the uncle of Bill Beaumont, the TV personality and former England rugby captain.

Blacklidge, Henry George
Professional. *b:* 14.7.1884, Stoughton, Surrey. *d:* 23.5.1917, Amara, Mesopotamia. Lower order left-hand batsman, left-arm fast medium bowler or slow left-arm in another account. *Team* Surrey (1908–13, 7 matches).
Career batting
7–9–2–100–45–14.28–0–*ct* 8
Bowling 334–10–33.40–0–0–4/26

He moved to Derbyshire in 1914 as coach in order to qualify for that County.

Blackman, Arthur
Amateur. *b:* 13.10.1853, Dartford, Kent. *d:* 6.4.1908, Preston, Sussex. Half-brother of F. Martin (Kent). Lower order right-hand batsman, right-hand medium pace round-arm bowler, good deep field. *Teams* Surrey (1878, 1 match); Kent (1879–80, 3 matches); Sussex (1881–87, 15 matches).
Career batting
20–35–1–399–73–11.73–0–*ct* 9
Bowling 263–7–37.57–0–0–2/20

Blackman, William
Amateur. *b:* 27.11.1862, Arundel, Sussex. *d:* 2.6.1885, Fitzroy, Melbourne, Victoria, Australia. Hard hitting middle-order right-hand batsman, right-arm fast bowler, good outfield. *Sch* Ardingly. *Team* Sussex (1881–84, 34 matches).
Career batting
34–65–7–1070–89–18.44–0–*ct* 21
Bowling 1882–87–21.63–3–0–7/86

His bowling was objected to in 1882 as unfair. He went to Australia for the benefit of his health, but died within a few months of consumption.

Blackmore, David
Amateur. *b:* 19.12.1909, Swansea, Glamorgan. *d:* 15.6.1988, Swansea, Glamorgan. Middle order batsman. *Team* Glamorgan (1934, 1 match).
Career batting
1–1–0–34–34–34.00–0–*ct* 1

Blackmore, Ernest George
Amateur. *b:* 21.5.1895, Bedminster, Somerset. *d:* October 1955, Pretoria, South Africa. Tail end right-hand batsman, right-arm fast medium bowler. *Team* Gloucestershire (1925, 3 matches).
Career batting
3–5–0–11–5–2.20–0–*ct* 0
Bowling 140–2–70.00–0–0–1/38

Blackmore, George Patrick Maxwell
Amateur. *b:* 8.10.1908, Gillingham, Kent. *d:* 29.1.1984, Isleworth, Middlesex. Tail end right-hand batsman, right-arm fast medium bowler. *Sch* Blundell's. *Teams* Europeans (1944/5); Kent (1948, 2 matches).
Career batting
3–3–0–12–8–4.00–0–*ct* 1
Bowling 127–2–63.50–0–0–1/14

Blackstock, Richard
Amateur. *b:* 13.7.1838, Oxton, Cheshire. *d:* 3.2.1893, Oxton, Cheshire. Middle order right-hand batsman. *Team* Lancashire (1865, 1 match).
Career batting
4–8–1–154–47–22.00–0–*ct* 3–*st* 1
Bowling 11–1–11.00–0–0–1/11
His first-class debut was for Gentlemen of North in 1858.

Blackwell, Henry
Amateur. *b:* 16.12.1876, Wirksworth, Derbyshire. *d:* 24.1.1900, Wirksworth, Derbyshire. Middle order right-hand batsman, right-arm medium pace bowler. *Team* Derbyshire (1895–98, 4 matches).
Career batting
4–6–2–41–15–10.25–0–*ct* 1
Bowling 105–4–26.25–0–0–2/23

Blades, Colin Francis
Cricketer. *b:* 13.8.1944, Clarkes Hill, St Philip, Barbados. Middle order right-hand batsman, right-arm medium pace bowler. *Team* Barbados (1963/4 to 1969/70). *Tour* Barbados to England 1969.
Career batting
12–22–0–406–75–18.45–0–*ct* 11
Bowling 21–0
He represented Bermuda in the ICC Trophy in 1979 and 1982.

Blagg, Edward Arthur
Professional. *b:* 9.2.1918, Shireoaks, Nottinghamshire. *d:* 28.10.1976, Shireoaks, Nottinghamshire. Lower order right-hand batsman, right-arm fast medium bowler. *Team* Nottinghamshire (1948, 1 match).
Career batting
1 match, did not bat–*ct* 0
Bowling 20–0
He was a noted League footballer with Nottingham Forest and Southport.

Blagg, Peter Henry
Amateur. *b:* 11.9.1918, Basford, Nottinghamshire. *d:* 18.3.1943, near Donbaik, Burma. He was presumed killed in action. Tail end right-hand batsman, wicket-keeper. *Sch* Shrewsbury. *Team* Oxford U (1939).
Career batting
10–13–5–67–28*–8.37–0–*ct* 17–*st* 12

Blagrave, Herbert Henry Gratwicke
Amateur. *b:* 3.3.1899, Cheltenham, Gloucestershire. *d:* 4.7.1981, Beckhampton Grange, Wiltshire. Lower order batsman, slow bowler. *Sch* Cheltenham. *Team* Gloucestershire (1922, 1 match).
Career batting
1–2–0–12–12–6.00–0–*ct* 0
He was a well-known racehorse trainer.

Blaikie, Kenneth Guy
Amateur. *b:* 8.5.1897, Johannesburg, South Africa. *d:* 8.6.1968, Lennoxville, Quebec, Canada. Hard-hitting middle order left-hand batsman, left-arm medium or slow bowler. *Teams* Oxford U (1921–24, blue 1924); Somerset (1921–23, 9 matches).
Career batting
27–48–1–1080–120–22.97–2–*ct* 20
Bowling 1196–46–26.00–0–0–4 /14
Blaikie produced perhaps the best all-round performance seen in an Oxford Freshmen's match, scoring a century and taking 13/58, but could not obtain a regular place in the Oxford team until 1924, when he hit two brilliant hundreds and topped the Oxford batting averages. He also won a blue for hockey.

Blain, Tony Elston
Cricketer. *b:* 17.2.1962, Nelson, New Zealand. Middle order right-hand batsman, wicket-keeper. *Team* Central Districts (1982/3 to 1991/2). *Tours* New Zealand to Sharjah (not first-class) 1985/6, 1987/8, to Sri Lanka 1985/6 (not first-class), to England 1986, to Australia 1987/8 (not first-class), to India 1988/9; Young New Zealand to Zimbabwe 1988/9. *Tests* New Zealand (1986 to 1988/9, 3 matches).
Career batting
90–148–21–4550–161–35.82–7–*ct* 158–*st* 20
Bowling 119–2–59.50–0–0–1/12
Test batting
3–5–0–73–37–14.60–0–*ct* 1
He proved a useful wicket-keeper batsman on the 1986 tour to England and appeared in one Test.

Blair, Major-Gen Everard McLeod
Amateur. *b:* 26.7.1866, Bangalore, India. *d:* 16.5.1939, Northampton. Hard hitting middle order

right-hand batsman, leg break bowler. *Sch* Cheltenham. *Team* Kent (1893–1900, 7 matches).
Career batting
7–10–0–190–61–19.00–0–*ct* 2
He was also a noted rackets player.

Blair, Philbert Duncan
Cricketer. *b:* 30.10.1943, Georgetown, British Guiana. Tail end right-hand batsman, right-arm fast bowler. *Team* Guyana (1967/8 to 1973/4). *Tour* West Indies to England 1969.
Career batting
31–34–10–142–30–5.91–0–*ct* 5
Bowling 2630–77–34.15–3–0–5/60
He made little impact on his only visit to England and did not appear in any of the Tests.

Blair, Robert William
Amateur. *b:* 23.6.1932, Petone, Wellington, New Zealand. Aggressive tail-end right-hand batsman, right-arm fast medium bowler. *Teams* Wellington (1951/2 to 1964/5); Central Districts (1955/6). *Tours* New Zealand to South Africa and Australia 1953/4, to England 1958. *Tests* New Zealand (1952/3 to 1963/4, 19 matches).
Career batting
119–172–36–1672–79–12.29–0–*ct* 46
Bowling 9961–537–18.54–41–12–9/72
Test batting
19–34–6–189–64*–6.75–0–ct 5
Bowling 1515–43–35.23–0–0–4/85
On his single visit to England he did very little in the Tests, and in first-class matches took 51 wickets (av 23.58). He was the leading wicket-taker in New Zealand first-class cricket, until overtaken by H. J. Howarth. His best bowling was 9/72 for Wellington v Auckland at Wellington in 1956/7.

Blair-White, Arthur
Amateur. *b:* 3.7.1891, Ashton Park, Monkstown, Co Dublin, Ireland. *d:* 29.4.1975, Murlough, Ballindrait, Lifford, Co Donegal, Ireland. Opening right-hand batsman, wicket-keeper. *Sch* Rugby. *Team* Ireland (1913).
Career batting
1–2–0–30–25–15.00–0–*ct* 0

Blake, David Eustace
Amateur. *b:* 27.4.1925, Havant, Hampshire. Brother of J. P. (Hampshire). Attractive middle order left-hand batsman, wicket-keeper. *Sch* Aldenham. *Team* Hampshire (1949–58, 50 matches). *Tours* Swanton to West Indies 1955/6; Norfolk to Jamaica 1956/7.
Career batting
73–129–9–2909–100–24.24–2–*ct* 91–*st* 30
His County cricket was restricted due to his profession, a dentist. His final first-class match was for Free Foresters in 1961.

Blake, John Philip
Amateur. *b:* 17.11.1917, Portsmouth, Hampshire. *d:* 3.6.1944, near Neresisce, Brac Island, Yugoslavia. Brother of D. E. (Hampshire). Free scoring opening/middle order right-hand batsman. *Sch* Aldenham. *Teams* Hampshire (1937–39, 14 matches); Cambridge U (1938–39, blue 1939).
Career batting
29–51–3–1095–88–22.81–0–*ct* 18

Blake, Rev Peter Douglas Stuart
Amateur. *b:* 23.5.1927, Calcutta, India. Stylish middle order right-hand batsman, right-arm medium pace bowler, fine field. *Sch* Eton. *Teams* Sussex (1946–51, 23 matches); Oxford U (1950–52, blue all three years).
Career batting
58–99–6–2067–130–22.22–3–*ct* 26
Bowling 52–0
His final first-class match was for Free Foresters in 1953. He captained Oxford in 1952.

Blake, Wilfred
Professional. *b:* 29.11.1854, Embsay, Skipton, Yorkshire. Middle order right-hand batsman, right-hand medium pace round-arm bowler, good deep field. *Teams* Lancashire (1877, 1 match); Yorkshire (1880, 2 matches).
Career batting
3–4–0–70–26–17.50–0–*ct* 0
Bowling 17–1–17.00–0–0–1/17

Blake-Kelly, G. N.
(*see under* Kelly, G. N. B.)

Blake-Kelly, G. W. F.
(*see under* Kelly, G. W. F. B.)

Blaker, Richard Norman Rowsell
Amateur. *b:* 24.10.1879, Bayswater, London. *d:* 11.9.1950, Eltham, Kent. His twin daughters, Barbara and Joan, both played cricket for England. Grandson of R. N. (Cambridge U 1842–43). Hard-hitting middle order right-hand batsman, right-arm fast bowler, brilliant field. *Sch* Westminster. *Teams* Kent (1898–1908, 119 matches); Cambridge U (1899–1902, blue 1900–02). *Tour* Bennett to West Indies 1901/2.
Career batting
162–262–25–5359–122–22.61–2–*ct* 143
Bowling 226–9–25.11–0–0–2/1
He also played for Oxfordshire (1902). He was President of Kent in 1950. He also obtained a soccer blue, playing as centre-forward.

Blakey, George Matthew
Professional. *b:* 20.1.1907, St Anne's-on-Sea, Lancashire. *d:* 12.1.1968, Meir, Stoke-on-Trent, Staffordshire. Middle order right-hand batsman, right-arm bowler. *Team* Worcestershire (1939, 3 matches).

Career batting
3–4–1–46–42–15.33–0–*ct* 1
Bowling 87–0

He also played for Shropshire (1954).

Blakey, Richard John
Cricketer. *b:* 15.1.1967, Huddersfield, Yorkshire. Middle order right-hand batsman, wicket-keeper. *Team* Yorkshire (1985–92, 151 matches). *Tours* Yorkshire to Windward Islands 1986/7, to South Africa 1991/2; England A to Zimbabwe 1989/90, to Pakistan and Sri Lanka 1990/1.
Career batting
157–254–35–7242–221–33.06–9–*ct* 252–*st* 25
Bowling 68–1–68.00–0–0–1/68

He reached 1,000 runs four times (best 1,361, av 41.24, in 1987). His highest score was 221 for England A v Zimbabwe at Bulawayo in 1989/90. He has played in one one-day international for England.

Blamires, Emmanuel
(registered at birth as Nimrod)
Professional. *b:* 31.7.1850, Bradford, Yorkshire. *d:* 22.3.1886, Bradford, Yorkshire. Lower order left-hand batsman, left-hand fast round-arm bowler. *Teams* Yorkshire (1877, 1 match); Surrey (1878–81, 32 matches).
Career batting
36–61–15–440–31–9.56–0–*ct* 28
Bowling 2743–137–20.02–9–2–8/77

He was a noted player of the game called knur and spell.

Blanckenberg, James Manuel
Amateur. *b:* 31.12.1892, Claremont, Cape Town, South Africa. *d: circa* 1955, West Berlin, West Germany. Brother of Nicholas (Western Province), uncle of C. B. Van Ryneveld (South Africa) and A. J. Van Ryneveld (Oxford U). Middle order right-hand batsman, right-arm medium pace bowler. *Teams* Western Province (1912/13 to 1922/3); Natal (1923/4). *Tour* South Africa to England 1924. *Tests* South Africa (1913/14 to 1924, 18 matches).
Career batting
74–116–16–2232–171–22.32–1–*ct* 53
Bowling 6230–293–21.26–21–3–9/78
Test batting
18–30–7–455–59–19.78–0–*ct* 9
Bowling 1817–60–30.28–4–0–6/76

Although he took 119 wickets (av 22.40) on his single tour to England, Blanckenberg was ineffective against the major English batsmen and admitted that he could not bowl well on turf wickets. His most successful series was the 1913/14 Tests in South Africa. His style of bowling was similar to T. G. Wass, in that he delivered a fast leg break. His best bowling was 9/78 for Western Province v Transvaal at Johannesburg in 1920/1.

Bland, Cyril Herbert George
Professional. *b:* 23.5.1872, Old Leake, Boston, Lincolnshire. *d:* 1.7.1950, Greenlands Drain, Maud Foster Canal, Cowbridge, Lincolnshire. He died by his own hand. Tail end right-hand batsman, right-arm fast bowler. *Team* Sussex (1897–1904, 145 matches).
Career batting
147–190–35–998–59–6.43–0–*ct* 80
Bowling 13524–557–24.28–44–11–10/48

Bland's career was short but brilliant. He took 129 wickets (av 21.69) in his debut season of 1897, 82 wickets in 1898, 108 in 1899 and 112 in 1900 and then faded completely away. This sudden failure was perhaps due to his being warned that his bowling action was suspect. In 1899 he took all ten wickets in the innings (for 48) for Sussex v Kent at Tonbridge. He also played for Lincolnshire (1891–95).

Bland, Kenneth Colin
Amateur. *b:* 5.4.1938, Bulawayo, Rhodesia. Middle order right-hand batsman, right-arm medium pace bowler, brilliant outfield. *Teams* Rhodesia (1956/7 to 1968/9); Eastern Province (1969/70 to 1970/1); Orange Free State (1972/3 to 1973/4). *Tours* South Africa to Australia and New Zealand 1963/4, to England 1965; SA Fezela to England 1961; International XI to Pakistan 1961/2; Rest of World to England 1966, 1967. *Tests* South Africa (1961/2 to 1966/7, 21 matches).
Career batting
131–219–28–7249–197–37.95–13–*ct* 51
Bowling 1512–43–35.16–0–0–4/40
Test batting
21–39–5–1669–144*–49.08–3–*ct* 10
Bowling 125–2–62.50–0–0–2/16

On his only Test playing visit to England, Bland was most successful, batting well in two of the three internationals, hitting 906 runs (av 39.39) in first-class matches and bringing delight to the crowds with his outstanding fielding, his pick-ups and returns to the wicket being rarely equalled for speed. He hit 1,048 runs, av 69.86, in South Africa in 1964/5.

Bland, Robert Dennis Fraser
Amateur. *b:* 16.5.1911, West Bridgford, Nottingham. Lower order right-hand batsman, left-arm medium pace bowler. *Sch* Shrewsbury. *Team* Nottinghamshire (1929–34, 33 matches).
Career batting
33–39–14–240–20*–9.60–0–*ct* 13
Bowling 2697–73–36.94–1–0–5/61

His daughter, Jane, played bridge for England.

Blaney, Frederick Andrews
Amateur. *b:* 17.3.1918, Lisburn, Co Antrim, Ireland. *d:* 2.2.1988, Ireland. Middle order right-hand batsman. *Sch* Royal Belfast Academical Institution. *Team* Ireland (1939).

Blatcher, Richard Brian

Career batting
1–2–0–14–13–7.00–0–*ct* 0

Blatcher, Richard Brian
Amateur. *b:* 2.4.1934, Miri, Sarawak. Lower order right-hand batsman, right-arm medium fast bowler. *Sch* Kingston Grammar School. *Team* Cambridge U (1955).
Career batting
2–3–1–16–15–8.00–0–*ct* 1
Bowling 120–4–30.00–0–0–2/42
He won a blue for hockey.

Blaxland, Rev Lionel Bruce
Amateur. *b:* 25.3.1898, Lilleshall, Shropshire. *d:* 29.4.1976, Temple Ewell, Kent. Great-uncle of J. M. H. Graham-Brown (Kent and Derbyshire). Middle order right-hand batsman, right-arm fast medium bowler, good field. *Sch* Shrewsbury. *Team* Derbyshire (1925–47, 19 matches).
Career batting
19–31–1–483–64–16.10–0–*ct* 7
Bowling 18–0
Whilst at Oxford he was awarded his blue for soccer and played in some cricket trials, but not in first-class matches for the University. He played soccer for Corinthians.

Bleackley, Edward Overall
Amateur. *b:* 10.3.1898, Salford, Lancashire. *d:* 17.2.1976, Twyford Abbey, Ealing, Middlesex. Middle order batsman. *Sch* Harrow. *Team* Lancashire (1919, 2 matches).
Career batting
3–5–0–31–21–6.20–0–*ct* 0

Blenkiron, William
Professional. *b:* 21.7.1942, Newfield, Co Durham. Lower order right-hand batsman, right-arm fast medium bowler. *Team* Warwickshire (1964–74, 117 matches). *Tour* MCC to Ceylon 1969/70 (not first-class).
Career batting
118–139–30–1467–62–13.45–0–*ct* 55
Bowling 8149–287–28.39–7–0–5/37
He also played for Durham (1975–76).

Blewitt, Charles Percy
Amateur. *b:* 15.10.1877, Kates Hill, Worcestershire. *d:* 15.12.1937, Danesford, Shropshire. Lower order right-hand batsman. *Team* Worcestershire (1912, 1 match).
Career batting
1–2–0–7–4–3.50–0–*ct* 0

Bligh, Algernon Stuart
Amateur. *b:* 6.10.1888, Marylebone, London. *d:* 27.12.1952, Minehead, Somerset. Son of L. E. (Kent), grandson of E. V. (Kent and Middlesex). Middle order right-hand batsman, wicket-keeper. *Sch* Eton. *Team* Somerset (1922–26, 14 matches).
Career batting
14–27–1–455–73*–17.50–0–*ct* 13
Bowling 14–0

Bligh, General The Hon Edward
Amateur. *b:* 19.9.1769. *d:* 2.11.1840, Thames Ditton, Surrey. Brother of the 4th Earl of Darnley (Kent 1790), uncle of J. D. (MCC 1822). One of the best amateur batsmen of his day. *Sch* Eton. *Teams* Kent (1806); Hampshire (1806).
Career batting
25–46–10–382–42*–10.61–0–*ct* 14
His final first-class match was for his own XI in 1813.

Bligh, Hon and Rev Edward Vesey
Amateur. *b:* 28.2.1829, Belgravia, London. *d:* 22.4.1908, Farthingwell Hall, West Malling, Kent. Brother of 6th Earl of Darnley (Gentlemen of Kent 1848) and Henry (Kent 1853), father of L. E. (Kent), grandfather of A. S. (Kent), uncle of I. F. W. (Kent) and Lord Clifton (Kent), nephew of J. D. (MCC 1822), grandson of 4th Earl of Darnley (Kent 1790). Hard-hitting lower order right-hand batsman, slow round-arm bowler. *Sch* Eton. *Teams* Kent (1849–64, 23 matches); Oxford U (1850, blue); Middlesex (1862, 1 match).
Career batting
40–73–10–786–53–12.47–0–*ct* 21–*st* 2
Bowling 178–9 + 14–19.77–1–0–6/?
From 1850 to 1855 his cricket was limited as he was successively Attache at Hanover, Florence and Berlin. He later left the Diplomatic Service and entered the Church. His first first-class match was for Gentlemen of Kent in 1848. He also played for Oxfordshire (1850).

Bligh, Hon Ivo Francis Walter
(became 8th Earl of Darnley in 1900)
Amateur. *b:* 13.3.1859, Westminster, London. *d:* 10.4.1927, Puckle Hill House, Shorne, Kent. Son of 6th Earl of Darnley (Gentlemen of Kent 1848), brother of Lord Clifton (Kent), nephew of E. V. (Kent and Middlesex) and Henry (Kent 1853), great-grandson of 6th Earl of Darnley (Kent 1790), nephew of F. G. Pelham (Sussex). Opening right-hand batsman, good deep field. *Sch* Eton. *Teams* Kent (1877–83, 47 matches); Cambridge U (1878–81, blue all four years). *Tour* Bligh to Australia 1882/3. *Tests* England (1882/3, 4 matches).
Career batting
84–143–11–2733–113*–20.70–2–*ct* 81
Test batting
4–7–1–62–19–10.33–0–*ct* 7
He hit 1,013 runs, av 30.69, in 1880.
Owing to ill-health his career in first-class cricket was relatively brief and he is remembered for his team which went to Australia in the winter of 1882/3 and recaptured 'The Ashes' for England. He cap-

tained Cambridge in 1881 and was President of Kent in 1892 and of MCC in 1900. Apart from cricket he represented Cambridge at royal tennis, both singles and doubles, and rackets.

Bligh, Lodovick Edward
Amateur. *b:* 24.11.1854, Dover, Kent. *d:* 16.5.1924, Minehead, Somerset. Son of E. V. (Kent), father of A. S. (Somerset), nephew of Henry (Kent 1853) and 6th Earl of Darnley (Gentlemen of Kent 1848), great-grandson of 4th Earl of Darnley (Kent 1790). Sound middle order right-hand batsman, right-arm fast bowler. *Sch* Eton. *Team* Kent (1878–84, 10 matches).
Career batting
10–18–4–107–20–7.64–0–*ct* 6
Bowling 157–5–31.40–0–0–2/36
He was not in the Eleven whilst at Eton or Cambridge.

Blitz, Rayner John
Cricketer. *b:* 25.3.1968, Watford, Hertfordshire. Lower order right-hand batsman, wicket-keeper. *Team* Somerset (1986, 5 matches).
Career batting
5–5–0–33–18–6.60–0–*ct* 8
He also played for Dorset (1988).

Block, Spencer Allen
Amateur. *b:* 15.7.1908, Esher, Surrey. *d:* 7.10.1979, Meadle, Buckinghamshire. Attacking opening or middle order right-hand batsman, brilliant deep field. *Sch* Marlborough. *Teams* Cambridge U (1928–29, blue 1929); Surrey (1928–33, 30 matches). *Tour* Martineau to Egypt 1929 (not first-class).
Career batting
58–93–4–2488–117–27.95–2–*ct* 33
Bowling 40–2–20.00–0–0–1/0
His final first-class match was for Free Foresters in 1948. He won a blue for hockey and also represented England. He also excelled at rugby football.

Blofeld, Henry Calthorpe
Amateur. *b:* 23.9.1939, Hoveton Home Farm, Norfolk. Nephew of F. S. G. Calthorpe (Sussex and Warwickshire). Opening right-hand batsman, wicket-keeper. *Sch* Eton. *Team* Cambridge U (1958–59, blue 1959).
Career batting
17–32–1–758–138–24.45–1–*ct* 11
Bowling 15–0
His County cricket was for Norfolk (1956–65). He is a well-known cricket journalist and broadcaster. His final first-class match was for Free Foresters in 1960.

Blomley, Benjamin
Professional. *b:* 10.6.1879, Chadderton, Lancashire. *d:* 12.3.1949, Chadderton, Lancashire. Tail end right-hand batsman, wicket-keeper. *Team* Lancashire (1903–22, 70 matches).
Career batting
70–87–32–316–41–5.74–0–*ct* 109–*st* 33

Bloodworth, Bernard Sydney
Professional. *b:* 13.12.1893, Cheltenham, Gloucestershire. *d:* 19.2.1967, Bristol. Impetuous middle order left-hand batsman, slow left-arm bowler, wicket-keeper. *Team* Gloucestershire (1919–32, 142 matches).
Career batting
142–237–9–3714–115–16.28–1–*ct* 74–*st* 27
Bowling 47–0
He was also a good rugby footballer, playing for Cheltenham. After he finished as a first-class cricketer he remained with the County Club as scorer and groundsman at Bristol until 1965.

Bloom, George Raymond
Cricketer. *b:* 13.9.1941, Aston, Sheffield, Yorkshire. Middle order left-hand batsman. *Team* Yorkshire (1964, 1 match).
Career batting
1–1–0–2–2–2.00–0–*ct* 2

Bloomfield, Horace Orlando
Amateur. *b:* 15.7.1891, Brixton, Surrey. *d:* 31.5.1973, Hillhead, near Fareham, Hampshire. Son-in-law of F. C. Holland (Surrey). Middle order right-hand batsman. *Team* Surrey (1921–22, 4 matches).
Career batting
4–7–2–180–107*–36.00–1–*ct* 2
He scored 107* on his first-class debut v Northamptonshire at Northampton in 1921. He was a noted figure in London club cricket and appeared in representative matches for the Club Cricket Conference.

Bloor, James Henry
Amateur. *b:* 29.9.1857, Clifton, Bristol. *d:* 9.3.1935, Brynmawr, Breconshire. Middle order batsman, change bowler. *Team* Gloucestershire (1887, 3 matches).
Career batting
3–5–0–44–22–8.80–0–*ct* 2
Bowling 14–0

Blore, Rev Edward William
Amateur. *b:* 24.1.1828, Marylebone, London. *d:* 24.6.1885, Trinity College, Cambridge. Lower order right-hand batsman, slow round-arm bowler. *Sch* Eton. *Team* Cambridge U (1848–54, blue 1848–51).
Career batting
18–34–6–230–22–8.21–0–*ct* 5
Bowling 41–0 + 104–no av–7–2–8/?
He was the greatest schoolboy bowler of his day, taking no fewer than 68 wickets for Eton against Harrow and Winchester in three seasons. He was also successful at Cambridge and captained the University in his fourth year. He also played for Buckinghamshire (1846). His final first-class match was for MCC in 1855.

Blount, Albert
Professional. *b:* 8.8.1889, Morton, Derbyshire. *d:* 10.11.1961, New Rossington, Yorkshire. Tail end right-hand batsman, slow left-arm bowler. *Team* Derbyshire (1912–26, 7 matches).
Career batting
7–11–2–52–17–5.77–0–*ct* 3
Bowling 215–7–30.71–0–0–4/53

Blount, Air Vice Marshal Charles Hubert Boulby
Amateur. *b:* 26.10.1893, Kampti, India. *d:* 23.10.1940, Hendon Aerodrome, Colindale, Middlesex. He was killed in an air crash. Hard hitting middle order right-hand batsman, slow right-arm bowler. *Sch* Harrow. *Teams* Services (1920–24); RAF (1927–30).
Career batting
10–17–0–575–110–33.82–1–*ct* 9
Bowling 303–12–25.25–0–0–3/16
His County cricket was for Suffolk (1910–12).

Bloy, Nigel Clement Francis
Amateur. *b:* 2.1.1923, Mannamead, Plymouth, Devon. *d:* 7.1.1989, Sherborne, Dorset. Middle order left-hand batsman, leg break bowler. *Sch* Dover. *Team* Oxford U (1946–48, blue 1946–47).
Career batting
31–53–9–964–77–21.90–0–*ct* 15
Bowling 613–8–76.62–0–0–3/80
His final first-class match was for MCC in 1958. His County cricket was for Devon (1951–57) and Dorset (1958–61).

Bluett, John Douglas Jeremy
Amateur. *b:* 29.5.1930, Kensington, London. Stylish middle-order right-hand batsman, off break bowler. *Sch* Cranbrook. *Team* Kent (1950, 2 matches).
Career batting
2–2–0–16–10–8.00–0–*ct* 1

Blundell, Dermot Howard Blundell Hollinshead
Amateur. *b:* 27.2.1874, Westminster, London. *d:* 26.10.1910, Kensington, London. Brother-in-law of G. E. F. Ward (MCC), his widow married M. D. F. Wood (Hampshire). Middle order right-hand batsman. *Sch* Wellington. *Team* MCC (1902).
Career batting
1–1–0–45–45–45.00–0–*ct* 0
His County cricket was for Berkshire (1897–1904).

Blundell, Sir Edward Denis
Amateur. *b:* 29.5.1907, Wellington, New Zealand. *d:* 24.9.1984, Townsville, Queensland, Australia. Tail end left-hand batsman, right-arm fast medium bowler. *Teams* Cambridge U (1928–29, blue both years); Wellington (1930/1 to 1937/8). *Tour* New Zealand to England 1927 (one match).
Career batting
48–68–22–400–27*–8.69–*ct* 16
Bowling 4924–195–25.25–12–1–6/25
He was Governor-General of New Zealand from 1972 to 1977.

Blundell, Frederick John
Amateur. *b:* 19.11.1850, South Stoneham, Hampshire. *d:* 26.4.1929, Botley, Southampton, Hampshire. Lower order right-hand batsman, slow right-arm bowler. *Team* Hampshire (1880, 1 match).
Career batting
1–1–0–2–2–2.00–0–*ct* 1
Bowling 22–2–11.00–0–0–2/22

Blundell, Joseph Wagstaff
Amateur. *b:* 15.2.1845, Droitwich, Worcestershire. *d:* 11.1.1933, Hove, Sussex. Middle order batsman. *Team* MCC (1882).
Career batting
1–2–0–3–2–1.50–0–*ct* 0

Blunden, Arthur
Professional. *b:* 5.9.1906, East Malling, Kent. *d:* 27.7.1984, Skinburness, Carlisle, Cumberland. Tail end right-hand batsman, right-arm fast medium bowler. *Team* Kent (1931–33, 11 matches).
Career batting
11–12–4–33–9*–4.12–0–*ct* 3
Bowling 586–18–32.55–0–0–4/31
He also played for Durham (pre first-class, 1939).

Blunt, Leonard
Professional. *b:* 29.3.1921, Worcester. Tail end right-hand batsman, right-arm fast medium bowler. *Teams* Worcestershire (1946–48, 14 matches); Europeans (1942/3).
Career batting
15–20–5–109–18–7.26–0–*ct* 4
Bowling 966–37–26.10–1–0–5/60
He also played for Cheshire (1950–53).

Blunt, Roger Charles, MBE
Amateur. *b:* 3.11.1900, Durham. *d:* 22.6.1966, Westminster, London. Middle order right-hand batsman, leg break bowler. *Teams* Canterbury (1917/18 to 1924/5); Otago (1926/7 to 1931/2); MCC (1934). *Tours* New Zealand to Australia 1925/6, 1927/8, to England 1927, 1931. *Tests* New Zealand (1929/30 to 1931/2, 9 matches).
Career batting
123–209–15–7953–338*–40.99–15–*ct* 88
Bowling 6638–214–31.01–5–1–8/99
Test batting
9–13–1–330–96–27.50–0–*ct* 5
Bowling 472–12–39.33–0–0–3/17
His highest innings was 338* for Otago v Canterbury at Christchurch in 1931/2. He was originally purely a leg break bowler, but developed into a fine bat. His two visits to England were most successful. In 1927 he hit 1,540 runs (av 44.00) and in 1931, 1,592 (av 43.02). His highest innings in England was

225 v Gentlemen at Eastbourne in 1931. His final first-class match was for Sir J. Cahn's XI in 1935.

Blythe, Colin
Professional. *b:* 30.5.1879, Deptford, Kent. *d:* 8.11.1917. He was killed in action on the Forest Hall to Pimmern military railway line near Passchendaele, Belgium. Tail end right-hand batsman, slow left-arm bowler. *Team* Kent (1899–1914, 381 matches). *Tours* MacLaren to Australia 1901/2; MCC to Australia 1907/8, to South Africa 1905/6, 1909/10; Kent to North America 1903. *Tests* England (1901/2 to 1909/10, 19 matches).
Career batting
439–587–137–4443–82*–9.87–0–*ct* 206
Bowling 42099–2503–16.81–218–71–10/30
Test batting
19–31–12–183–27–9.63–0–*ct* 6
Bowling 1863–100–18.63–9–4–8/59

Blythe and Rhodes were the two principal left-arm spin bowlers of the Edwardian era. Contemporaries were in two minds as to which was the greater. Ranjitsinhji chose Blythe, but others equally qualified picked the Yorkshireman. Blythe's great quality was his deceptive flight, but he was also a master of the sticky or crumbling wicket, and the fact that he could deliver a faster ball coming through with his arm without any noticeable change of action proved the downfall of many batsmen.

He appeared in first-class cricket for 15 full seasons (1900–14) and in 14 of them captured over 100 wickets – in 1901 ill-health hampered him, but he still had 93 victims to his name. His best year was 1909 when his total reached 215 (av 14.54). His best bowling was 10/30 for Kent v Northamptonshire at Northampton in 1907.

Blythe first played for England during MacLaren's 1901/2 tour to Australia and on both that visit and his return in 1907/8 he came second in the bowling table to the redoubtable Barnes. Both his visits to South Africa were also most successful.

His best Test performances in England occurred in the 1909 series against Australia, when in the Edgbaston Test he took 11 for 102, which brought England victory by 10 wickets. His international career was marred to some extent by the fact that he suffered from epilepsy and for this reason he was omitted from the England team on several occasions.

Blythe's death in the First World War was a major loss to cricket since, in normal circumstances, his career would have lasted about another ten seasons and in 1914 he was still at the top of his profession.

Boak, John
Professional. *b:* 27.6.1837, Edinburgh, Scotland. *d:* 29.10.1876, Bermondsey, London. He was killed by a train whilst crossing the line. Tail end right-hand batsman, right-arm fast bowler. *Sch* Royal High School, Edinburgh. *Team* Middlesex (1873, 1 match).
Career batting
1–2–0–19–11–9.50–0–*ct* 2
Bowling 37–1–37.00–0–0–1/20

He emigrated to Australia in 1858 and was employed as a professional cricketer there, but returned to England about 1868. He played for New South Wales and Queensland, but not in first-class matches.

Board, John Henry
Professional. *b:* 23.2.1867, Clifton, Bristol. *d:* 15.4.1924, on board ss *Kenilworth Castle* en route from South Africa from heart failure. Sound middle order right-hand batsman, wicket-keeper. *Teams* Gloucestershire (1891–1914, 430 matches); London County (1900–04); Hawke's Bay (1910/11 to 1914/15). *Tours* Stoddart to Australia 1897/8; Hawke to South Africa 1898/9; MCC to South Africa 1905/6. *Tests* England (1898/9 to 1905/6, 6 matches).
Career batting
525–906–97–15674–214–19.37–9–*ct* 851–*st* 355
Bowling 46–0
Test batting
6–12–2–108–29–10.80–0–*ct* 8–*st* 3

He hit 1,000 runs in a season six times (best 1,132, av 24.08, in 1900). He went abroad most winters coaching, either in South Africa or New Zealand. His highest score was 214 for Gloucestershire v Somerset at Bristol in 1900. He was a first-class umpire from 1921 until his death.

Boardman, Alfred Joseph
Professional. *b:* 11.5.1859, Islington, London. *d:* 11.11.1928, Carshalton, Surrey. Middle order right-hand batsman, right-arm medium pace bowler. *Team* Surrey (1878–80, 9 matches).
Career batting
10–19–2–162–33–9.52–0–*ct* 1
Bowling 37–0

Bocking, Henry
Professional. *b:* 10.12.1835, Sheffield, Yorkshire. *d:* 22.1.1907, Sharrow, Sheffield, Yorkshire. Lower order batsman. *Team* Yorkshire (1865, 2 matches).
Career batting
2–2–0–14–11–7.00–0–*ct* 0

He appeared for Yorkshire in two matches in 1865, when the leading five County players were in dispute with the Committee.

Boddam-Whetham, John Whetham
(changed his name from Boddam in April 1870)
Amateur. *b:* 25.5.1843, Kirklington Hall, Southwell, Nottinghamshire. *d:* 23.3.1918, Folkestone, Kent. Middle order batsman. *Team* Gentlemen of North (1870).
Career batting
1–2–0–12–7–6.00–0–*ct* 0
Bowling 13–0

Boddington, Myles Alan
Amateur. *b:* 30.11.1924, Hale, Cheshire. Son of R. A. (Lancashire). Tail end left-hand batsman, right-arm fast medium bowler. *Sch* Rugby. *Team* RAF (1946).
Career batting
1–2–0–23–23–11.50–0–*ct* 1
Bowling 13–0

Boddington, Robert Alan
Amateur. *b:* 30.6.1892, Kersal, Manchester, Lancashire. *d:* 5.8.1977, Fifield Manor, Oxford. Father of M. A. (RAF). Middle order right-hand batsman, wicket-keeper. *Sch* Rugby. *Teams* Lancashire (1913–24, 52 matches); Oxford U (1914).
Career batting
56–83–19–801–69–12.51–0–*ct* 76–*st* 21
He won a blue for rackets. He was Treasurer of Lancashire 1949–58 and President 1959–60.

Bodell, Ernest Herbert
Amateur. *b:* 17.8.1928, Dublin, Ireland. Tail end right-hand batsman, right-arm fast medium pace bowler. *Team* Ireland (1954–59).
Career batting
5–8–4–25–11*–6.25–0–*ct* 1
Bowling 464–11–42.18–0–0–4/27

Boden, Rev Cecil Arthur
Amateur. *b:* 18.12.1890, Countesthorpe, Leicestershire. *d:* 31.5.1981, Hampstead Marshall, Newbury, Berkshire. Opening right-hand batsman, occasional right-arm medium pace bowler. *Sch* Christ's Hospital. *Team* Leicestershire (1911–13, 11 matches).
Career batting
11–19–0–196–40–10.31–0–*ct* 5

Boden, David Jonathan Peter
Cricketer. *b:* 26.11.1970, Eccleshall, Staffordshire. Lower order right-hand batsman, right-arm medium fast bowler. *Teams* Middlesex (1989, 1 match); Essex (1992, 1 match).
Career batting
2–1–0–5–5–5.00–0–*ct* 2
Bowling 68–4–17.00–0–0–4/11
He joined the Essex staff in 1990.

Boden, John George
Amateur. *b:* 27.12.1848, Birstall, Leeds, Yorkshire. *d:* 3.1.1928, Ilkley, Yorkshire. Lower order right-hand batsman, wicket-keeper. *Team* Yorkshire (1878, 1 match).
Career batting
1–1–0–6–6–6.00–0–*ct* 1

Boden, Reginald George
Professional. *b:* 13.9.1884, Ashby-de-la-Zouch, Leicestershire. *d:* 11.2.1966, Bowness-on-Windermere, Cumberland. Middle order batsman. *Team* Lancashire (1907, 1 match).
Career batting
1–2–0–8–5–4.00–0–*ct* 0

Boden, Timothy Walter
Amateur. *b:* 19.5.1901, Sherborne, Dorset. *d:* 5.9.1969, Churchill, Axminster, Devon. Grandson of Henry (Gentlemen of North 1861), great nephew of Walter (Derbyshire). Middle order batsman. *Sch* Eton. *Team* Derbyshire (1920, 1 match).
Career batting
1–2–0–14–9–7.00–0–*ct* 0

Boden, Walter
Amateur. *b:* 6.8.1837, Derby. *d:* 16.9.1905, The Pastures, Mickleover, Derbyshire. Brother of Henry (Gentlemen of North 1861), great uncle of T. W. (Derbyshire), brother-in-law of H. O. Peacock (MCC). Lower order right-hand batsman. *Sch* Rugby. *Team* Derbyshire (1874, 1 match).
Career batting
2–4–2–18–11–9.00–0–*ct* 0
His only other first-class match was for Gentlemen of the North at the Oval in 1859. Boden was one of the prime movers in the creation of Derbyshire CCC in 1870. He was hon secretary to the County Club from 1870 to 1881 and President 1895 to 1898.

Bodington, Cecil Herbert
Amateur. *b:* 20.1.1880, Suffield, Norfolk. *d:* 11.4.1917. He was killed in action near Arras, France. Middle order right-hand batsman, change bowler. *Sch* Charterhouse and King's, Canterbury. *Team* Hampshire (1901–02, 10 matches).
Career batting
10–18–4–154–36–11.00–0–*ct* 4
Bowling 287–9–31.88–0–0–3/19
He appeared in the Seniors' match at Cambridge in 1901 and 1902, but not in any first-class matches at the University.

Bodkin, Dr Peter Ernest
Amateur. *b:* 15.9.1924, Barnet, Hertfordshire. Middle order right-hand batsman, left-arm medium pace bowler. *Sch* Bradfield. *Team* Cambridge U (1946, blue).
Career batting
9–17–0–328–52–19.29–0–*ct* 9
Bowling 330–8–41.25–0–0–2/27
He captained Cambridge in 1946, having appeared in the non-first-class war time matches v Oxford, and led Cambridge in the 1945 game. His County cricket was for Hertfordshire (1946–47). He also won a blue for soccer.

Boger, Alnod John
Amateur. *b:* 31.8.1871, Stonehouse, Plymouth, Devon. *d:* 3.6.1940, Oxford. Middle order right-hand batsman, right-arm slow bowler, slip field. *Sch* Winchester. *Team* Oxford U (1891–92, blue 1891).
Career batting
6–12–1–143–41*–13.00–0–*ct* 1
Bowling 225–9–25.00–1–0–6/63

His County cricket was for Hertfordshire (1889–97). In 1925 he was appointed Sheriff of Cornwall. He won a blue for golf.

Bohlen, Francis Hermann
Amateur. *b:* 31.7.1868, Philadelphia, USA. *d:* 9.12.1942, USA. Forcing middle order right-hand batsman, occasional right-arm fast medium bowler. *Teams* Philadelphians (1890–1908); MCC (1894–1904); London County (1904). *Tours* Philadelphia to England 1897, 1903, 1908.
Career batting
65–115–5–2568–162–23.34–3–*ct* 20
Bowling 6–0
In Philadelphia he played for the Germantown Club. He appeared regularly in the USA v Canada match, but his most famous innings was 118 for the Gentlemen of Philadelphia v Australians in 1893. He was a brilliant batsman on hard fast wickets, but never really flourished on English pitches. He scored 162 on his first-class debut for Philadelphia v English Residents at Manheim in 1890.

Boiling, James
Cricketer. *b:* 8.4.1968, New Delhi, India. Lower order right-hand batsman, off break bowler. *Sch* Rutlish. *Team* Surrey (1988–92, 28 matches).
Career batting
28–34–15–250–29–13.15–0–*ct* 27
Bowling 2286–62–36.87–1–1–6/84

Boissier, Arthur Paul
Amateur. *b:* 25.1.1881, Bloxham, Oxfordshire. *d:* 2.10.1953, Stockethill, Aberdeen, Scotland. Middle order batsman, change bowler. *Sch* St John's, Leatherhead. *Team* Derbyshire (1901–06, 2 matches).
Career batting
2–4–0–13–6–3.25–0–*ct* 0
Bowling 32–2–16.00–0–0–2/32
He batted well in the Oxford Freshmen's match of 1901, but did not appear in first-class cricket for the University. He was awarded his blue for soccer in 1904. He also played for Oxfordshire (1903).

Bokhari, Iftikhar Ali
Amateur. *b:* 6.7.1935, Lahore, India. Opening right-hand batsman, right-arm medium pace bowler. *Teams* Cambridge U (1957); Punjab (1957/8); Lahore (1958/9 to 1965/6); Sargodha (1964/5).
Career batting
18–30–6–938–203*–39.08–3–*ct* 4
Bowling 25–0
His highest score was 203* for Lahore v Punjab U at Lahore in 1960/1. He also played for Cambridgeshire in 1956, leading the Minor County batting averages.

Bolitho, William Edward Thomas
Amateur. *b:* 2.7.1862, Polwithien, Penzance, Cornwall. *d:* 21.2.1919, Bath, Somerset. Brother-in-law of R. J. McNeill (MCC). Middle order right-hand batsman, excellent cover field. *Sch* Harrow. *Team* Oxford U (1883 and 1885, blue both years; injury prevented him playing in 1884). *Tour* Sanders to North America 1885.
Career batting
10–19–1–338–45*–18.77–0–*ct* 1
He played for and captained Cornwall, being one of the mainstays of cricket in the West Country for many years.

Bollon, Sidney
Amateur. *b:* 3.12.1899, Edmonton, Middlesex. *d:* 28.10.1986, Tavistock, Devon. Lower order batsman, opening bowler. *Team* Demobilised Officers (1919).
Career batting
1–1–0–9–9–9.00–0–*ct* 2
Bowling 81–6–13.50–1–0–5/59

Bolton, Alan
Professional. *b:* 1.7.1939, Darwen, Lancashire. Opening or middle order right-hand batsman, off break bowler. *Team* Lancashire (1957–61, 40 matches).
Career batting
40–71–6–1223–96–18.81–0–*ct* 15
Bowling 80–2–40.00–0–0–1/17

Bolton, Benjamin Charles
Amateur. *b:* 23.9.1861, Cottingham, Yorkshire. *d:* 18.11.1910, Hull, Yorkshire. He died from injuries sustained falling from an express train. Tail end right-hand batsman, right-arm fast medium bowler. *Team* Yorkshire (1890–91, 4 matches).
Career batting
4–6–0–25–11–4.16–0–*ct* 2
Bowling 252–13–19.38–1–0–5/40
He took 8 for 26 on his Yorkshire debut v Warwickshire in 1890 – not first-class.

Bolton, Robert Henry Dundas
Amateur. *b:* 13.1.1893, Koppa Kadur, Mysore, India. *d:* 30.10.1964, St Pancras, London. He married a niece of E. H. Rivett-Carnac (MCC). Middle order right-hand batsman. *Sch* Rossall. *Team* Hampshire (1913–22, 7 matches).
Career batting
7–12–0–121–24–10.08–0–*ct* 2
He played for Dorset whilst still at school (1910–12) and later, when Chief Constable of Northamptonshire, he was on the Committee of that County Club.

Bolus, Frank
Professional. *b:* 2.11.1864, Wolverhampton, Staffordshire. *d:* 15.9.1939, Coventry, Warwickshire. Middle order right-hand batsman. *Team* Somerset (1893–94, 10 matches).
Career batting
10–18–3–111–23–7.40–0–*ct* 5
Bowling 7–0

Bolus, John Brian
Cricketer. *b:* 31.1.1934, Whitkirk, Leeds, Yorkshire. Opening right-hand batsman, occasional left-arm medium pace bowler. *Teams* Yorkshire (1956–62, 107 matches); Nottinghamshire (1963–72, 269 matches); Derbyshire (1973–75, 64 matches). *Tour* MCC to India 1963/4. *Tests* England (1963 to 1963/4, 7 matches).
Career batting
469–833–81–25598–202*–34.03–39–*ct* 201
Bowling 886–24–36.91–0–0–4/40
Test batting
7–12–0–496–88–41.33–0–*ct* 2
Bowling 16–0

He hit 1,000 runs in a season on 14 occasions, including two seasons over 2,000 (best 2,190, av 41.32, in 1963). His only double century was 202* for Nottinghamshire v Glamorgan at Nottingham in 1963. He captained Nottinghamshire in 1972 and Derbyshire in 1973–75. He was awarded his County Cap for all three of his first-class Counties.

Bomford, Sir Hugh
Amateur. *b:* 12.8.1882, Fort William, Calcutta, India. *d:* 19.1.1939, Meerut, India. Lower order right-hand batsman, wicket-keeper. *Sch* Marlborough. *Team* Oxford U (1901–03).
Career batting
9–11–4–52–16*–7.42–0–*ct* 19–*st* 9

He won a blue for hockey.

Bompas, Hugh Steele
Amateur. *b:* 9.12.1881, Hampstead, London. *d:* 19.7.1944, Chelsea, London. Opening right-hand batsman, wicket-keeper. *Sch* Westminster. *Teams* Cambridge U (1901–03); London County (1901).
Career batting
7–11–2–35–15–3.88–0–*ct* 5–*st* 4

He was most successful with the bat in his final year (1900) at school and then hit 109 and 59 in the Cambridge Freshmen's match of 1901, but totally failed to make runs in first-class cricket.

Bond, John David
Cricketer. *b:* 6.5.1932, Kearsley, Lancashire. Middle order right-hand batsman, occasional leg break bowler. *Teams* Lancashire (1955–72, 344 matches); Nottinghamshire (1974, 17 matches).
Career batting
362–548–80–12125–157–25.90–14–*ct* 222
Bowling 69–0

He hit over 1,000 runs in a season twice (best 2,125, av 36.01, in 1962). He was appointed captain of Lancashire in 1968 when the County was at a low ebb and took the team to the top with three Gillette Cup Championships and two John Player League successes. After retiring in 1972, having led Lancashire for five seasons, he was appointed joint Lancashire coach in 1973 and then captain and manager of Nottinghamshire in 1974, but had little success. From 1980–86 he held the post of manager of Lancashire. He became a first-class umpire in 1988. He was a Test selector in 1974.

Bond, Raymond Ernest
Cricketer. *b:* 7.9.1944, Burnham, Buckinghamshire. Tail end left-hand batsman, right-arm medium fast bowler. *Team* Minor Counties (1973).
Career batting
1 match, did not bat–*ct* 0
Bowling 107–2–53.50–0–0–1/33

His County cricket was for Buckinghamshire (1965–79).

Bonham-Carter, Lothian George
Amateur. *b:* 29.9.1858, Adhurst St Mary, Petersfield, Hampshire. *d:* 13.1.1927, Buriton, Hampshire. Father of S. S. (Royal Navy), brother-in-law of A. J. Abdy (Hampshire). Free hitting opening right-hand batsman, useful slow round-arm bowler. *Sch* Clifton. *Team* Hampshire (1880–85, 8 matches).
Career batting
8–15–0–260–67–17.33–0–*ct* 5
Bowling 63–2–31.50–0–0–2/22

He last played for Hampshire (not first-class) in 1888.

Bonham-Carter, Sir Maurice
Amateur. *b:* 11.10.1880, Paddington, London. *d:* 7.6.1960, Bayswater, London. Uncle of P. H. (Royal Navy), grandson of G. W. Norman (Kent), nephew of C. L. Norman (Kent), F. H. Norman (Kent) and P. Norman (Gentlemen of Kent). Middle order right-hand batsman, slow bowler, wicket-keeper. *Sch* Winchester. *Teams* Oxford U (1901–02, blue 1902); Kent (1902, 1 match).
Career batting
14–23–3–391–86–19.55–0–*ct* 8–*st* 1
Bowling 430–9–47.77–0–0–2/2

From 1910 to 1916 he was Private Secretary to the Prime Minister, Herbert Asquith, whose daughter, Violet, he married.

Bonham-Carter, Philip Herman
Amateur. *b:* 12.11.1891, Karachi, India. *d:* 7.1.1934, South End, Hampstead, London. Nephew of Maurice (Kent), great-grandson of G. W. Norman (Kent), grandson of W. H. Wathen (Kent). Middle order batsman. *Team* Royal Navy (1919–29).
Career batting
3–6–0–35–16–5.83–0–*ct* 0

Bonham-Carter, Admiral Sir Stuart Sumner
Amateur. *b:* 9.7.1889, Portsmouth, Hampshire. *d:* 5.9.1972, Petersfield, Hampshire. Son of L. G. (Hampshire), nephew of A. J. Abdy (Hampshire). Middle order batsman. *Sch* Clifton. *Team* Royal Navy (1925–26).

Career batting
2–4–0–47–18–11.75–0–*ct* 0

Boning, John
Professional. *b:* 21.9.1805, Cambridge. *d:* 12.4.1879, Cambridge. Middle order batsman. *Team* Cambridge Town Club (1825–47).
Career batting
35–60–5–704–65–12.80–0–*ct* 39
Bowling 54 wickets (no analyses)–6–1–5/?

Bonner, John Wardell
Amateur. *b:* 3.4.1869, Mile End, London. *d:* 26.11.1936, East Cliff, Bournemouth, Hampshire. Middle order right-hand batsman. *Sch* Forest. *Team* Essex (1896–98, 16 matches).
Career batting
16–27–1–339–59–13.03–0–*ct* 5

Bonnor, George John
Amateur. *b:* 25.2.1855, Bathurst, New South Wales, Australia. *d:* 27.6.1912, East Orange, New South Wales, Australia. Very hard-hitting middle order right-hand batsman, right-arm medium pace bowler. *Teams* Victoria (1881/2 to 1884/5, 10 matches); New South Wales (1884/5 to 1890/1, 5 matches). *Tours* Australia to England 1880, 1882, 1884, 1886, 1888. *Tests* Australia (1880–88, 17 matches).
Career batting
148–244–17–4820–128–21.23–5–*ct* 128–*st* 1
Bowling 470–12–39.16–0–0–3/34
Test batting
17–30–0–512–128–17.06–1–*ct* 16
Bowling 84–2–42.00–0–0–1/5
Known as 'The Colonial Hercules', Bonnor was the most powerful hitter of his day – he stood about 6ft 6in and weighed 16st. His best innings in England, though not his highest, was 119 for Australians v Gentlemen at Lord's in 1888, whilst his outstanding innings in Test cricket came at Sydney in 1884/5, when he hit the fastest Test hundred (in 100 mins) up to that date. From 1886 to 1889 he lived in England. He hit 1,000 runs in a season twice (best 1,155, av 20.26, in 1886).

Boobbyer, Brian
Amateur. *b:* 25.2.1928, Ealing, Middlesex. Opening right-hand batsman, right-arm medium pace bowler, brilliant field. *Sch* Uppingham. *Team* Oxford U (1949–52, blue all four years).
Career batting
40–75–2–1970–126–26.98–2–*ct* 35
Bowling 19–0
In addition to his cricket he was a brilliant rugby footballer, obtaining his blue at Oxford and also being capped for England at centre.

Boock, Stephen Lewis
Cricketer. *b:* 20.9.1951, Dunedin, Otago, New Zealand. Lower order right-hand batsman, slow left-arm bowler. *Teams* Otago (1973/4 to 1989/90); Canterbury (1975/6 to 1977/8). *Tours* New Zealand to England 1978, to Australia 1980/1, 1985/6, to Sri Lanka 1983/4, 1984/5 (not first-class), to Pakistan 1984/5, to West Indies 1984/5, to India (World Cup) 1987/8. *Tests* New Zealand (1977/8 to 1988/9, 30 matches).
Career batting
164–195–67–1092–37–8.53–0–*ct* 83
Bowling 14314–640–22.36–40–5–8/57
Test batting
30–41–8–207–37–6.27–0–*ct* 14
Bowling 2564–74–34.64–4–0–7/87
He came second in the first-class bowling averages for the 1978 tour to England with 39 wickets, av 22.17, and played in all three Tests.

Booden, Christopher Derek
Cricketer. *b:* 22.6.1961, Newport Pagnell, Buckinghamshire. Lower order right-hand batsman, right-arm medium pace bowler. *Team* Northamptonshire (1980–81, 4 matches).
Career batting
4–3–2–10–6*–10.00–0–*ct* 2
Bowling 258–3–86.00–0–0–2/30
He also played for Buckinghamshire (1983–92).

Bookman, Louis
(orignally L. Buckhalter)
Amateur. *b:* 1890, Zagaren, Lithuania. *d:* 10.6.1943, Dublin, Ireland. Opening or middle order left-hand batsman, slow left-arm bowler. *Team* Ireland (1920–29).
Career batting
9–17–0–342–53–20.11–0–*ct* 5
Bowling 189–3–63.00–0–0–2/32
He also played for Bedfordshire (1921). He played soccer for Bradford City, West Bromwich Albion and Luton Town, and was an international for Northern Ireland, 1914–22.

Boon, David Clarence, MBE
Cricketer. *b:* 29.12.1960, Launceston, Tasmania, Australia. Opening or middle order right-hand batsman, right-arm medium pace bowler. *Team* Tasmania (1978/9 to 1991/2, 90 matches). *Tours* Australia to England 1985, 1989, to New Zealand 1985/6, 1989/90, 1991/2 (World Cup), to Sharjah (not first-class) 1985/6, 1986/7, 1989/90, to India 1986/7, 1989/90 (not first-class), to India and Pakistan (World Cup) 1987/8, to Pakistan 1988/9, to West Indies 1990/1. *Tests* Australia (1984/5 to 1991/2, 63 matches).
Career batting
190–321–30–13508–227–46.41–41–*ct* 163
Bowling 302–5–60.40–0–0–1/12
Test batting
63–115–12–4538–200–44.05–13–*ct* 62
Bowling 5–0

On the 1985 tour to England he played in the first four Tests, but with little success and was then omitted from the Test side. In 1989 he appeared in all six Tests, hit 442 runs, av 55.25, and in first-class games scored 1,306 runs, av 56.78. He scored 1,287 runs, av 67.73, in Australia in 1987/8. His highest score was 227 for Tasmania v Victoria at Melbourne in 1983/4.

Boon, Ronald Winston
Amateur. *b:* 11.6.1909, Barry, Glamorgan. Middle order right-hand batsman, right-arm medium pace bowler. *Team* Glamorgan (1931–32, 11 matches).
Career batting
11–19–2–229–33–13.47–0–*ct* 4
Bowling 40–0

Boon was much better known on the rugby field, being a Welsh cap.

Boon, Timothy James
Cricketer. *b:* 1.11.1961, Balby, Doncaster, Yorkshire. Opening right-hand batsman, right-arm medium pace bowler. *Team* Leicestershire (1980–92, 208 matches). *Tour* Leicestershire to Zimbabwe 1980/1.
Career batting
208–350–39–10117–144–32.53–12–*ct* 106
Bowling 525–11–47.72–0–0–3/40

He hit 1,000 runs in a season seven times (best 1,539, av 37.53, in 1990). He missed all of the 1985 season due to injury. He played limited overs cricket for Natal in 1991/2.

Boot, Jesse
Professional. *b:* 18.3.1860, South Normanton, Derbyshire. *d:* 1.3.1940, Chesterfield, Derbyshire. Lower order right-hand batsman, wicket-keeper. *Team* Derbyshire (1895, 1 match).
Career batting
1–2–0–4–4–2.00–0–*ct* 2

Booth, Arthur
Professional. *b:* 3.11.1902, Featherstone, Yorkshire. *d:* 17.8.1974, Rochdale, Lancashire. Tail end right-hand batsman, slow left-arm bowler. *Team* Yorkshire (1931–47, 36 matches).
Career batting
38–40–16–137–29–5.70–0–*ct* 12
Bowling 1931–131–14.74–7–1–6/21

His career was altogether a remarkable one. Given a brief trial in County cricket in 1931, Booth was not again seen in Yorkshire matches until 1945 when he played twice. In 1946 however he carried all before him and ended the season at the head of the first-class bowling averages with 111 wickets (av 11.61). The following year he appeared in just four matches and then retired back into League cricket. He also played for Northumberland (1935–39).

Booth, Arthur
Professional. *b:* 8.1.1926, Droylsden, Lancashire. Middle order right-hand batsman. *Team* Lancashire (1950–51, 4 matches).
Career batting
4–5–0–81–49–16.20–0–*ct* 1

His most notable performance was an innings of 253 for Lancashire 2nd XI v Lincolnshire in 1950.

Booth, Brian Charles
Amateur. *b:* 19.10.1933, Perthville, Bathurst, New South Wales, Australia. Elegant middle order right-hand batsman, right-arm medium pace or off-break bowler, good field. *Team* New South Wales (1954/5 to 1968/9, 93 matches). *Tours* Australia to England 1961, 1964, to West Indies 1964/5, to India and Pakistan 1964/5, to New Zealand 1959/60, 1966/7. *Tests* Australia (1961 to 1965/6, 29 matches.)
Career batting
183–283–35–11265–214*–45.42–26–*ct* 119
Bowling 956–16–59.75–0–0–2/29
Test batting
29–48–6–1773–169–42.21–5–*ct* 17
Bowling 146–3–48.66–0–0–2/33

On his first tour to England he forced his way into the Australian Test side and proved a most useful acquisition. In first-class matches he hit 1,279 runs (av 44.10). Returning in 1964 as Australia's vice-captain he hit 1,551 runs (av 55.39) but had only one good Test innings. His only first-class double century (214*) was made v Central Districts at Palmerston North on his 1966/7 tour to New Zealand. He captained Australia in two Tests. He played hockey for Australia in the 1956 Olympic Games.

Booth, Brian Joseph
Professional. *b:* 3.12.1935, Billinge End, Blackburn, Lancashire. Opening right-hand batsman, leg break and googly bowler. *Teams* Lancashire (1956–63, 117 matches); Leicestershire (1964–73, 232 matches).
Career batting
350–600–52–15298–183*–27.91–18–*ct* 135
Bowling 4677–146–32.03–1–0–7/143

He hit over 1,000 runs in a season eight times (best 1,752, av 31.85, in 1961).

Booth, Rev Cecil
Amateur. *b:* 21.2.1896, Aylesbury, Buckinghamshire. *d:* 13.6.1988, Peterborough, Northamptonshire. Middle/lower order right-hand batsman, leg break bowler. *Sch* Alleyn's. *Team* Cambridge U (1923).
Career batting
7–10–1–94–24*–10.44–0–*ct* 1
Bowling 382–7–54.57–0–0–2/16

Booth, Clement
Amateur. *b:* 11.5.1842, Friskney, Boston, Lincolnshire. *d:* 14.7.1926, Hundleby, Spilsby, Lincolnshire. Brother-in-law of H. G. Alington (Oxford U 1859). Opening or middle order right-hand batsman, excellent deep field. *Sch* Rugby. *Teams* Cambridge U (1862–65, blue all four years); Hampshire (1875–80, 20 matches).

Career batting
75–131–6–1922–78–15.37–0–*ct* 34
Bowling 186–5–37.20–0–0–1/4

He also represented Cambridge at athletics. He also played for Lincolnshire (1863–89) and Huntingdonshire (1876). He was hon secretary of Lincolnshire 1867–71. In 1874 he was appointed hon secretary to Hampshire, resigning in 1879. He captained Cambridge in 1864 and Hampshire in 1875–78. His final first-class match was for MCC in 1886.

Booth, Frank Stanley
Professional. *b:* 12.2.1907, Cheetham Hill, Lancashire. *d:* 21.1.1980, Shoreham-by-Sea, Sussex. Tail end right-hand batsman, right-arm fast-medium bowler. *Team* Lancashire (1927–37, 140 matches).
Career batting
140–157–25–1330–54–10.07–0–*ct* 56
Bowling 11180–457–24.46–24–3–7/59

He joined the Lancashire staff in 1924, but after a few years with limited opportunity in County cricket left to play in the Leagues. Returning in 1932 to Old Trafford he quickly gained a regular place in the County Eleven and remained for six seasons before retiring due to injury. His best year was 1934 when he took 101 wickets (av 23.46). He also played for Durham (pre first-class, 1939).

Booth, Lionel Edward Blakeney
Amateur. *b:* 21.12.1850, Marylebone, London. *d:* 9.7.1912, Billingham Manor, Newport, Isle of Wight. Middle order batsman. *Sch* Wellington. *Team* MCC (1885).
Career batting
1–1–0–8–8–8.00–0–*ct* 1

Booth, Major William
Professional. *b:* 10.12.1886, Lowtown, Pudsey, Yorkshire. *d:* 1.7.1916. He was killed in action near La Cigny, France. Middle/lower order right-hand batsman, right-arm medium fast bowler. *Team* Yorkshire (1908–14, 144 matches). *Tour* MCC to South Africa 1913/14. *Tests* England (1913/14, 2 matches).
Career batting
162–243–39–4753–210–23.29–2–*ct* 120
Bowling 11953–603–19.82–43–9–8/47
Test batting
2–2–0–46–32–23.00–0–*ct* 0
Bowling 130–7–18.57–0–0–4/49

Major was his Christian name, not rank. His career was tragically cut short, for he did not obtain a regular place in the Yorkshire team until 1910 and was at the top of his profession when the war broke out. He scored 1,000 runs in a season twice (best 1,239, av 25.81, in 1911) and took 100 wickets in a season three times (best 181, av 18.46, in 1913) – in 1913 he performed the 'double'. His only double century was 210 for Yorkshire v Worcestershire at Worcester in 1911.

Booth, Paul Antony
Cricketer. *b:* 5.9.1965, Crossland Moor, Huddersfield, Yorkshire. Lower order left-hand batsman, slow left-arm bowler. *Teams* Yorkshire (1982–89, 23 matches); Warwickshire (1990–92, 29 matches). *Tour* Warwickshire to South Africa 1991/2.
Career batting
52–69–15–686–62–12.70–0–*ct* 15
Bowling 3804–91–41.80–1–0–5/98

Booth, Peter
Cricketer. *b:* 2.11.1952, Shipley, Yorkshire. Lower order right-hand batsman, right-arm fast medium bowler. *Team* Leicestershire (1972–81, 90 matches). *Tour* Leicestershire to Zimbabwe 1980/1.
Career batting
90–80–21–767–58*–13.00–0–*ct* 27
Bowling 4549–162–28.08–1–0–6/93

Booth, Roy
Professional. *b:* 1.10.1926, Marsden, Yorkshire. Lower order right-hand batsman, occasional right-arm medium pace bowler, wicket-keeper. *Teams* Yorkshire (1951–55, 65 matches); Worcestershire (1956–70, 402 matches). *Tours* Worcestershire on World Tour (Rhodesia first-class) 1964/5, to Jamaica 1965/6.
Career batting
468–671–135–10138–113*–18.91–2–*ct* 948–*st* 177
Bowling 3–0

In 1959 he exceeded 1,000 runs in a season for the only time (1,042, av 27.42). In 1960 he had 101 victims behind the wicket and in 1964 100.

Booth, Stephen Charles
Cricketer. *b:* 30.10.1963, Cross Gates, Leeds, Yorkshire. Lower order right-hand batsman, slow left-arm bowler. *Team* Somerset (1983–85, 33 matches).
Career batting
33–34–15–202–42–10.63–0–*ct* 33
Bowling 3159–87–36.31–0–0–4/26

Booth-Jones, Timothy Douglas
Cricketer. *b:* 6.8.1952, Dover, Kent. Middle order right-hand batsman. *Team* Sussex (1980–81, 26 matches).
Career batting
26–44–1–1034–95–24.04–0–*ct* 8

Booton, Walter Thomas
Amateur. *b:* 13.1.1941, Kidderminster, Worcestershire. Lower order right-hand batsman, right-arm fast medium bowler. *Team* Ireland (1970).
Career batting
1–1–0–12–12–12.00–0–*ct* 0
Bowling 72–2–36.00–0–0–2/72

Borde, Chandrakant Gulabrao
Amateur. *b:* 21.7.1934, Poona, Maharashtra, India. Brother of R. G. (Maharashta). Middle order right-hand batsman, leg break bowler. *Teams* Baroda

(1952/3 to 1953/4); Maharashtra (1953/4 to 1972/3). *Tours* India to England 1959, 1967, to West Indies 1961/2, to Australia and New Zealand 1967/8, to Pakistan 1954/5; Commonwealth to Rhodesia 1962/3. *Tests* India (1958/9 to 1969/70, 55 matches).
Career batting
251–370–57–12805–207*–40.91–30–*ct* 159
Bowling 9044–331–27.32–14–3–8/52
Test batting
55–97–11–3061–177*–35.59–5–*ct* 37
Bowling 2417–52–46.48–1–0–5/88

He was the great success of the 1959 Indian tour to England, hitting 1,060 runs and taking 72 wickets, but returning in 1967 he had given up bowling and did very little in the Tests. His highest score was 207* for Maharashtra v Bengal at Poona in 1972/3. Borde's greatest achievement was early in his career when he scored 109 and 96 for India v West Indies at Delhi against the formidable attack of Hall and Gilchrist. He also played for Northumberland (1955), but not in the Minor Counties Championship. His last first-class match was for Birhan Maharashtra Sugar Syndicate XI (1973/4). He captained India in one Test.

Border, Allan Robert
Cricketer. *b:* 27.7.1955, Cremorne, Sydney, New South Wales, Australia. Middle order left-hand batsman, slow left-arm bowler, slip field. *Teams* New South Wales (1976/7 to 1979/80, 25 matches); Gloucestershire (1977, 1 match); Queensland (1980/1 to 1991/2, 68 matches); Essex (1986–88, 40 matches). *Tours* Australia to England 1979 (World Cup), 1980, 1981, 1983 (World Cup), 1985, 1989, to India 1979/80, 1984/5 (not first-class), 1986/7, 1989/90 (not first-class), to Pakistan 1979/80, 1982/3, 1988/9, to Sri Lanka 1980/1, 1982/3, to New Zealand 1981/2, 1985/6, 1989/90, 1991/2 (World Cup), to West Indies 1983/4, 1990/1, to Sharjah (not first-class) 1984/5, 1986/7, 1989/90, to India and Pakistan (World Cup) 1987/8; Rest of World to England 1987. *Tests* Australia (1978/9 to 1991/2, 130 matches).
Career batting
316–519–85–22818–205–52.57–62–*ct* 309
Bowling 3410–89–38.31–2–1–7/46
Test batting
130–224–42–9532–205–52.37–23–*ct* 135
Bowling 1339–37–36.18–2–1–7/46

The outstanding Australian cricketer of the past ten years, Border has achieved remarkable success both for himself and for his country. He has made more appearances in Test and one-day international matches than any other cricketer. On his three major tours to England he has rarely known failure. In 1981 he topped both Test and first-class batting averages; in 1985 he repeated these distinctions, when in Tests he hit 597 runs, av 66.33, and first-class matches 1,355, av 71.31. In that season he captained Australia and lost the Ashes, but returned in 1989, again as captain when he beat England four wins to nil. In Australia in 1990/1 he led his side to a second unbeaten series against England, and has now captained Australia in 67 Tests.

He scored 1,000 runs in both his seasons for Essex, best 1,393, av 58.64, in 1988. He has also scored 1,000 runs in a season in Australia five times, best 1,247, av 73.35, in 1985/6. His highest score was 205 for Australia v New Zealand at Adelaide in 1987/8. Possibly under-employed as a bowler, he took 11 wickets in a Test v West Indies at Sydney in 1987/8.

Bore, Michael Kenneth
Cricketer. *b:* 2.6.1947, East Hull, Yorkshire. Lower order right-hand batsman, left-arm medium pace bowler, deep field. *Teams* Yorkshire (1969–78, 74 matches); Nottinghamshire (1979–88, 85 matches).
Career batting
159–158–52–874–37*–8.24–0–*ct* 51
Bowling 11243–372–30.22–9–0–8/89

He has been the Director of Coaching at the Yorkshire Cricket Academy since 1990. He also played for Lincolnshire (1989).

Borgnis, Richard Peter
(later Hammond-Chambers-Borgnis)
Amateur. *b:* 25.8.1910, Newbury, Berkshire. Middle order right-hand batsman, right-arm medium pace bowler. *Team* Combined Services (1937).
Career batting
1–2–0–124–101–62.00–1–*ct* 1
Bowling 57–3–19.00–0–0–3/38

He hit 101 for Combined Services v New Zealanders at Portsmouth in 1937 in his only first-class match. His County cricket was for Berkshire (1931).

Boroughs, William Frederick
Professional. *b:* 30.12.1864, Cheltenham, Gloucestershire. *d:* 16.1.1943, Birmingham. Tail end batsman, wicket-keeper. *Team* Gloucestershire (1899–1901, 5 matches).
Career batting
5–7–3–45–25–11.25–0–*ct* 3–*st* 4

Borradaile, Oswell Robert
Amateur. *b:* 9.5.1859, Westminster, London. *d:* 11.5.1935, Bexhill, Sussex. Opening or middle order right-hand batsman, right-arm medium pace bowler, good field at point. *Sch* Westminster. *Team* Essex (1894, 1 match).
Career batting
1–2–0–7–5–3.50–0–*ct* 1

He was Secretary to Essex CCC from 1891 to 1921 and had much to do with the promotion of Essex to first-class status, first playing for the county in 1891. He captained Stoics CC for 10 years and was a major force in London Club cricket.

Borrett, Norman Francis
Amateur. *b:* 1.10.1917, Wanstead, Essex. Middle order right-hand batsman, slow left-arm bowler. *Sch* Framlingham. *Team* Essex (1937–46, 3 matches).
Career batting
3–4–2–33–15*–16.50–0–*ct* 2
Bowling 43–0

At Cambridge he performed the hat-trick in the Seniors' Match of 1939, but did not appear in a first-class match whilst there. He also played for Devon (1949–59).

Borrill, Peter David
Cricketer. *b:* 4.7.1951, Burmantofts, Leeds, Yorkshire. Tail end right-hand batsman, right-arm fast medium bowler. *Team* Yorkshire (1971, 2 matches).
Career batting
2 matches, did not bat–*ct* 0
Bowling 61–5–12.20–0–0–2/6

Borrington, Anthony John
Cricketer. *b:* 8.12.1948, Spondon, Derbyshire. Middle order right-hand batsman, leg break bowler, occasional wicket-keeper. *Team* Derbyshire (1971–80, 122 matches).
Career batting
122–203–24–4230–137–23.63–3–*ct* 57
Bowling 19–0

Borrowes, Sir Kildare Dixon, 10th Bart
Amateur. *b:* 21.9.1852, Exeter, Devon. *d:* 19.10.1924, Wateringbury, Kent. Free hitting middle order right-hand batsman, wicket-keeper. *Sch* Cheltenham. *Team* Middlesex (1882, 5 matches).
Career batting
6–9–0–40–20–4.44–0–*ct* 8–*st* 7

He appeared in the Essex side in 1878, when his regiment was stationed at Colchester, and was prominent in military cricket in Natal when stationed in South Africa in the 1890s.

Borwick, Peter Malise
Amateur. *b:* 21.11.1913, Aldby Park, York. *d:* 23.12.1983, Haselbeach, Northamptonshire. Grandson of W. G. Middleton (MCC). Lower order right-hand batsman, slow left-arm bowler. *Sch* Harrow. *Team* Northamptonshire (1932, 3 matches).
Career batting
3–6–0–25–11–4.16–0–*ct* 0
Bowling 98–3–32.66–0–0–1/25

Bosanquet, Bernard James Tindal
Amateur. *b:* 13.10.1877, Bulls Cross, Enfield, Middlesex. *d:* 12.10.1936, Wykehurst, Ewhurst, Surrey. Hard-hitting middle order right-hand batsman, right-arm fast bowler until 1900, later leg-break and googly. *Sch* Eton. *Teams* Oxford U (1898–1900, blue all three years); Middlesex (1898–1919, 123 matches). *Tours* Warner to North America 1898; Ranjitsinhji to North America 1899; Bosanquet to North America 1901; Bennett to West Indies 1901/2; Hawke to New Zealand and Australia 1902/3; MCC to Australia 1903/4. *Tests* England (1903/4 to 1905, 7 matches).
Career batting
235–382–32–11696–214–33.41–21–*ct* 191
Bowling 14972–629–23.80–45–11–9/31
Test batting
7–14–3–147–27–13.36–0–*ct* 9
Bowling 604–25–24.16–2–0–8/107

One of the most remarkable of all English cricketers, Bosanquet holds a place in the history of the game by virtue of perfecting the googly – an off-break bowled with a leg-break action. Despite the fact that his length when delivering this ball tended to be wayward, for several seasons he baffled the best batsmen even on good wickets.

His outstanding summer with the ball was 1904 when he took 132 wickets (av 21.62). In the previous winter he had taken 6 for 51 for England in the fourth Test v Australia to bring victory to his side. In 1905 he performed the feat of taking 11 wickets and hitting a century in each innings of the same match – Middlesex v Sussex at Lord's.

His bowling declined after 1905, but as a batsman he grew in stature until his astonishing success in 1908, when he headed the first-class averages with 1,081 runs (av 54.05) and hit his most famous innings of 214 in 195 minutes for the Rest of England v Champion County at the Oval. In all he topped 1,000 runs in a season six times (best 1,405, av 36.02, in 1904) – in 1904 he achieved the 'double' for the only time in his career. His best bowling was 9/31 for Oxford U v Sussex at Oxford in 1900.

After 1908 Bosanquet played very infrequently in first-class matches but it was not until 1919 that he made his final appearance for Middlesex.

Apart from cricket he achieved a considerable reputation at other sports, representing Oxford at throwing the hammer and at billiards, whilst also being an accomplished ice-hockey player. He was the father of television news-reader and personality Reginald Bosanquet.

Bose, Gopal
Cricketer. *b:* 20.5.1947, Calcutta, India. Opening right-hand batsman, off break bowler. *Team* Bengal (1968/9 to 1977/8). *Tours* India to England 1974, to Sri Lanka 1973/4.
Career batting
77–126–5–3741–170–30.91–8–*ct* 39
Bowling 1905–71–26.83–1–0–5/67

He failed to make any impression on his single tour of England, hitting 328 runs, av 18.22, and was not selected for the Tests. His last first-class match was for East Zone 1978/9.

Boshier, Brian Stanley
Professional. *b:* 6.3.1932, Leicester. Tail end right-hand batsman, right-arm medium pace bowler. *Team* Leicestershire (1953–64, 169 matches).
Career batting
170–226–92–579–30–4.32–0–*ct* 56
Bowling 11742–510–23.02–23–2–8/45

He took 100 wickets in a season twice – each time 108 (in 1958, av 18.77; in 1961, av 17.87). In 1955 he began the season with nine successive scoreless innings.

Bosomworth, William Edward
Professional. *b:* 8.3.1847, Carlton-Husthwaite, Thirsk, Yorkshire. *d:* 7.6.1891, Norton, Malton, Yorkshire. Lower order right-hand batsman, right-arm fast round-arm bowler. *Team* Yorkshire (1872–80, 4 matches).
Career batting
4–7–1–20–7–3.33–0–*ct* 2
Bowling 140–9–15.55–0–0–2/5

In 1874 Bosomworth joined the short-lived Yorkshire United team, and thus his opportunities to appear in bona fide Yorkshire matches were limited.

Bostock, Herbert
Professional. *b:* 4.5.1869, Ilkeston, Derbyshire. *d:* 20.2.1954, Ilkeston, Derbyshire. Middle order right-hand batsman. *Team* Derbyshire (1897, 4 matches).
Career batting
4–6–2–75–36–18.75–0–*ct* 1

Bostock, Lionel Carrington
Amateur. *b:* 13.2.1888, Castries, St Lucia. *d:* 30.1.1962, The Mount, Ifield, Sussex. Lower order right-hand batsman, right-arm medium pace bowler. *Sch* Marlborough. *Team* Army (1925).
Career batting
1–2–1–5–3–5.00–0–*ct* 1
Bowling 58–2–29.00–0–0–2/58

Bostock-Hill, A. J. (*see under* Hill, A. J. B.)

Boston, Granger Farwell
Amateur. *b:* 24.5.1921, Mossley Hill, Liverpool, Lancashire. *d:* 4.2.1958, Marylebone, London. Middle order right-hand batsman. *Sch* Wellington. *Team* Cambridge U (1946).
Career batting
3–6–0–38–19–6.33–0–*ct* 0

Boswell, Cecil Stanley Reginald
Professional. *b:* 19.1.1910, Edmonton, Middlesex. *d:* 15.8.1985, Brundall, Norfolk. Tail end right-hand batsman, leg break and googly bowler. *Team* Essex (1932–36, 30 matches).
Career batting
30–46–8–406–69–10.68–0–*ct* 12
Bowling 1345–36–37.36–0–0–4/22

After leaving Essex he appeared with some success for Norfolk (1939–55).

Boswell, William Gerald Knox
Amateur. *b:* 24.6.1892, Chelsea, London. *d:* 28.7.1916. He died of wounds, Thiepval, France. Middle order right-hand batsman, change bowler. *Sch* Eton. *Team* Oxford U (1912–14, blue 1913–14).
Career batting
14–26–1–756–101*–30.24–1–*ct* 2
Bowling 343–14–24.50–0–0–4/22

Bosworth-Smith, B. N.
(*see under* Smith, B. N. B.)

Botham, Ian Terence, OBE
Cricketer. *b:* 24.11.1955, Oldfield, Heswall, Cheshire. Attacking middle order right-hand batsman, right-arm fast medium bowler, good close field. *Teams* Somerset (1974–86, 172 matches); Worcestershire (1987–91, 54 matches); Queensland (1987/8, 11 matches); Durham (1992, 15 matches). *Tours* England to Pakistan 1977/8, 1983/4, to New Zealand 1977/8, 1982/3 (not first-class), 1983/4, 1991/2, to Australia 1978/9, 1979/80, 1982/3, 1986/7, to India 1979/80, 1981/2, to West Indies 1980/1, 1985/6, to Sri Lanka 1981/2, to Australia and New Zealand (World Cup) 1991/2; Worcestershire to Zimbabwe 1990/1. *Tests* England (1977–92, 102 matches).
Career batting
392–600–45–18983–228–34.20–37–*ct* 346
Bowling 31386–1159–27.08–59–8–8/34
Test batting
102–161–6–5200–208–33.54–14–*ct* 120
Bowling 10878–383–28.40–27–4–8/34

Since his Test debut he has been the outstanding English Test cricketer, his reputation both on and off the cricket field being the subject of press headlines throughout his international career. Of his many outstanding performances, the greatest was perhaps achieved in Bombay in 1979/80 for England v India, when he hit 114 in his single innings and took 13 for 106 (6/58 and 7/48). This was the first time that the all-round feat of scoring a century and taking ten wickets had been accomplished in a Test match. He reached the Test career double of 1,000 runs and 100 wickets in 21 matches. His tally of 100 wickets was reached after 2 years and 9 days. Both these feats created new records. He was also the youngest cricketer to take 200 wickets in a Test career. More records came his way when he reached the second double of 2,000 runs and 200 wickets after 42 Tests. He was the first player to hit 5,000 runs and take 300 wickets in Tests. A serious back injury in 1988 threatened to end his career, but he came back to Test cricket in 1989 and despite further injuries his international career has continued until 1992. His highest Test innings and best bowling were 208 v India at the Oval 1982 and 8 for 34 v Pakistan at Lord's in 1978.

The fact that he has appeared in more than 100 Tests and over 100 one-day internationals has meant that his appearances in County matches have been restricted. He has hit 1,000 runs in a season four times (best 1,530, av 69.54, in 1985). In the same summer he hit no fewer than 80 sixes, which is believed to be a record. He took 100 wickets, av 16.40, in 1978. His highest first-class innings was 228 for Somerset v Gloucestershire at Taunton in 1980. He first played for Somerset in Sunday League matches in 1973. He captained England in 12 Tests including the 1980/1 tour to West Indies. In 1984 and 1985 he captained Somerset.

He was a useful soccer player and appeared for Scunthorpe United. His charity walks in aid of Leukaemia Research have attracted much publicity for that cause and in 1992 he was awarded the OBE for services to cricket and his work for charity. In recent years he has also appeared in the theatre, both giving talks on cricket and acting in pantomime.

Botten, James Thomas
Amateur. *b:* 21.6.1938, Pretoria, South Africa. Lower order right-hand batsman, right-arm fast medium bowler. *Team* North East Transvaal (1957/8 to 1971/2). *Tours* South Africa to England 1965; SA Fezela to England 1961. *Tests* South Africa (1965, 3 matches).
Career batting
98–143–31–1775–90–15.84–0–*ct* 52
Bowling 8125–399–20.36–24–5–9/23
Test batting
3–6–0–65–33–10.83–0–*ct* 1
Bowling 337–8–42.12–0–0–2/56

He had a very rapid rise to fame, when in 1958/9 he took 55 wickets in the Currie Cup, creating a new record in what was his first full season in the competition. With the Fezelas in England in 1961, he was the most successful bowler with over 70 wickets in all matches. In 1965, on his only Test tour to England, he bowled well without being outstanding. His best bowling was 9/23 for North East Transvaal v Griqualand West at Pretoria in 1958/9.

Botting, Stephen Hovey
Professional. *b:* 5.11.1845, Higham, Kent. *d:* 23.1.1927, Shorne, Gravesend, Kent. Middle order right-hand batsman, right-arm medium pace bowler. *Team* Kent (1867–75, 2 matches).
Career batting
2–4–0–27–20–6.75–0–6–*ct* 0

Bottom, Daniel
Professional originally, but amateur in 1901. *b:* 2.10.1864, Whitwell, Derbyshire. *d:* 16.2.1937, Sherwood, Nottingham. Lower order right-hand batsman, right-arm medium pace bowler. *Teams* Derbyshire (1894–1901, 3 matches); Nottinghamshire (1899, 3 matches).
Career batting
6–10–0–42–9–4.20–0–*ct* 2
Bowling 250–9–27.77–1–0–5/34

Bottom had a rather unusual if brief first-class career, playing three times for Derbyshire – once each in 1894, 1898 and 1901 – and three times for Nottinghamshire in 1899, for whom he was qualified by residence. He first-played for Derbyshire (not first-class) in 1891.

Bottomley, Isaac Henry
Amateur. *b:* 9.4.1855, Shelf, Halifax, Yorkshire. *d:* 23.4.1922, Heysham, Lancashire. Middle order right-hand batsman, right-arm fast round-arm bowler. *Team* Yorkshire (1878–80, 9 matches).
Career batting
9–12–0–166–32–13.83–0–*ct* 1
Bowling 75–1–75.00–0–0–1/17

Bottomley, Thomas
Professional. *b:* 26.12.1910, Rawmarsh, Yorkshire. *d:* 19.2.1977, Rotherham, Yorkshire. Middle order right-hand batsman, right-arm medium pace bowler. *Team* Yorkshire (1934–35, 6 matches).
Career batting
6–7–0–142–51–20.28–0–*ct* 5
Bowling 188–1–188.00–0–0–1/46

Botton, Norman Denis
Cricketer. *b:* 21.1.1954. Hammersmith, London. Lower order left-hand batsman, left-arm medium pace bowler. *Team* Oxford U (1974–75, blue 1974).
Career batting
15–30–6–286–38*–11.91–0–*ct* 10
Bowling 714–11–64.90–0–0–2/53

Bouch, Herbert Edward
Amateur. *b:* 15.4.1868, Bickley, Kent. *d:* 28.7.1929, Keston, Kent. Lower order right-hand batsman, right-arm bowler. *Sch* Eastbourne. *Team* Kent (1892, 1 match).
Career batting
1–2–0–7–7–3.50–0–*ct* 1
Bowling 52–1–52.00–0–0–1/52

Boucher, James Chrysostom
Amateur. *b:* 22.12.1910, Phoenix Park, Dublin, Ireland. Lower order right-hand batsman, off break bowler. *Team* Ireland (1930–54).
Career batting
28–51–5–625–85–13.58–0–*ct* 23
Bowling 2359–168–14.04–18–5–7/13

He was for many years the outstanding Irish cricketer, and after retiring from first-class cricket was Hon Secretary to the Irish Cricket Union 1954–73.

Boucher, Sidney
Amateur. *b:* 17.9.1899, Rochester, Kent. *d:* 4.8.1963, Wadhurst, Sussex. Lower order left-hand batsman, left-arm seam bowler. *Teams* Kent (1922, 1 match); Royal Navy (1923–29).
Career batting
9–15–0–147–43–9.80–0–*ct* 4
Bowling 613–14–43.78–0–0–2/15

Boughton, Hubert James
Amateur. *b:* 11.10.1858, Westbury-on-Severn, Gloucestershire. *d:* 26.3.1902, Gloucester. Brother of W. A. (Gloucestershire). Middle order right-hand batsman. *Team* Gloucestershire (1884–88, 7 matches).
Career batting
7–12–2–114–41–11.40–0–*ct* 3

Boughton, William Albert
Amateur. *b:* 23.12.1854, Westbury-on-Severn, Gloucestershire. *d:* 26.11.1936, Pontcanna, Canton, Cardiff. Brother of H. J. (Gloucestershire). Middle order right-hand batsman, right-arm medium pace bowler. *Team* Gloucestershire (1879–83, 3 matches).
Career batting
3–3–0–3–3–1.00–0–*ct* 1

Boult, Farrington Holker
Amateur. *b:* 12.6.1852, Bath, Somerset. *d:* 21.5.1882, Marylebone, London, of consumption. Steady middle order right-hand batsman, fast round-arm bowler, good point field. *Sch* Epsom. *Team* Surrey (1872–73, 22 matches). *Tour* Grace to Australia 1873/4 (not first-class).
Career batting
25–46–0–570–65–12.39–0–*ct* 15
Bowling 1161–55–21.10–1–0–5/32

Boultbee, St John
Amateur. *b:* 30.4.1843, Bedford. *d:* 4.9.1898, Minster, Kent. Lower order right-hand batsman, slow round-arm bowler. *Team* Surrey (1867, 2 matches).
Career batting
3–6–2–57–35–14.25–0–*ct* 5
Bowling 94–3–31.33–0–0–2/54
He also played for Bedfordshire.

Boumphrey, Colin
Amateur. *b:* 7.1.1897, Birkenhead, Cheshire. *d:* 1.2.1945, Liverpool, Lancashire. Brother of Donald (Wales). Middle order right-hand batsman. *Sch* Shrewsbury. *Team* RAF (1932).
Career batting
1–2–0–31–31–15.50–0–*ct* 0
His County cricket was for Cheshire (1920–26).

Boumphrey, Donald
Amateur. *b:* 4.10.1892, Birkenhead, Cheshire. *d:* 12.9.1971, Holt Green, Aughton, Lancashire. Brother of Colin (RAF). Opening batsman. *Sch* Shrewsbury. *Team* Wales (1928).
Career batting
1–2–0–10–6–5.00–0–*ct* 0
His County cricket was for Cheshire (1913–33) and Denbighshire (1925–27).

Boundy, Gerald Oscar
Amateur. *b:* 17.7.1895, Great Torrington, Devon. *d:* 8.2.1964, Hammersmith, London. Middle order right-hand batsman. *Team* Somerset (1926–30, 2 matches).
Career batting
2–4–1–22–10*–7.33–0–*ct* 1

Bourchier, Rev Canon Wilfred La Rive
Amateur. *b:* 22.3.1884, Cahir, Co Tipperary, Ireland. *d:* 7.9.1973, Cork, Ireland. Opening right-hand batsman. *Team* Ireland (1908–09).
Career batting
3–6–0–47–19–7.83–0–*ct* 0

Bourdillon, Thomas Edmund
Amateur. *b:* 31.5.1890, Bloemfontein, South Africa. *d:* 28.5.1961, Salisbury, Rhodesia. Brother of V. E. (Sussex). Middle order batsman. *Sch* Tonbridge. *Teams* Sussex (1919, 1 match); Rhodesia (1909/10 to 1924/5).
Career batting
7–13–0–176–60–13.53–0–*ct* 4
Bowling 173–3–57.66–0–0–2/51

Bourdillon, Victor Edmund
Amateur. *b:* 18.6.1897, Bloemfontein, South Africa. *d:* 16.9.1985, Borrowdale, Harare, Zimbabwe. Brother of T. E. (Sussex). Middle order right-hand batsman. *Sch* Brighton. *Team* Sussex (1919, 3 matches).
Career batting
3–6–0–15–7–2.50–0–*ct* 0

Bourne, Alfred Allinson
Amateur. *b:* 16.4.1848, Atherstone, Warwickshire. *d:* 17.7.1931, Cheltenham, Gloucestershire. Lower order right-hand batsman, slow left-arm bowler, good close field. *Sch* Rugby. *Team* Cambridge U (1870, blue).
Career batting
4–6–2–6–3*–1.50–0–*ct* 1
Bowling 494–28–17.64–3–1–7/65
His County cricket was for Warwickshire (pre first-class) in 1876.

Bourne, Edmund Horace
Amateur. *b:* 14.2.1885, Stoke-on-Trent, Staffordshire. *d:* 7.8.1962, Earlswood, Redhill, Surrey. Middle order right-hand batsman, right-arm slow bowler. *Team* Minor Counties (1912).
Career batting
1–1–0–16–16–16.00–0–*ct* 0
His County cricket was for Staffordshire (1904–22).

Bourne, John James
Professional. *b:* 2.11.1872, Church Gresley, Derbyshire. *d:* 23.12.1952, Burton-on-Trent, Staffordshire. Tail end batsman, left-arm medium pace bowler. *Team* Derbyshire (1898, 1 match).
Career batting
1–1–0–6–6–6.00–0–*ct* 0
Bowling 103–3–34.33–0–0–2/63

Bourne, William Anderson
Cricketer. *b:* 15.11.1952, Clapham, St Michael, Barbados. Lower order right-hand batsman, right-arm fast medium bowler. *Teams* Barbados (1970/1); Warwickshire (1973–77, 59 matches).
Career batting
60–78–15–1325–107–21.03–1–*ct* 39
Bowling 4164–128–32.53–2–0–6/47
He played for East Africa in the ICC Trophy in 1982.

Bousfield, Donald Greenhill
Amateur. *b:* 9.4.1914, Broxbourne, Hertfordshire. Middle order right-hand batsman, leg break bowler. *Sch* Winchester. *Team* Cambridge U (1935).
Career batting
2–4–0–38–37–9.50–0–*ct* 0
He also played for Hertfordshire (1932–36) and Buckinghamshire (1947–49).

Bousfield, Edwin James
Amateur. *b:* 21.5.1838, Chorlton, Manchester, Lancashire. *d:* 8.1.1895, Torquay, Devon. Middle order right-hand batsman, splendid deep field, wicket-keeper. *Team* Lancashire (1865–78, 12 matches).
Career batting
16–27–2–321–32–12.84–0–*ct* 23–*st* 5
His first-class debut was for Gentlemen of North in 1860.

Bovill, Walter Denman
Amateur. *b:* 12.8.1857, Worplesdon, Surrey. *d:* 5.1.1940, St James, Westminster, London. Middle order right-hand batsman, medium pace round-arm bowler. *Sch* Clifton. *Team* MCC (1874).
Career batting
1–2–1–30–19–30.00–0–*ct* 1
In a minor match in 1886 he took all ten wickets in an innings and hit 28* and 115, going in first and being last man out. He was only 16 years old at the time of his only first-class match – as he seems to have been successful in minor matches, it is not known why he was not seen again in first-class cricket.

Bowden, Ernest
Amateur. *b:* 13.6.1892, Lancaster. *d:* 14.10.1972, Slyne with Hest, Lancashire. Tail end batsman, right-arm fast medium bowler. *Team* Lancashire (1914, 4 matches).
Career batting
4–6–0–27–10–4.50–0–*ct* 5
Bowling 453–12–37.75–1–0–6/78

Bowden, Jack
Amateur. *b:* 17.10.1916, Lisburn, Co Antrim, Ireland. *d:* 22.12.1988, Lisburn, Co Antrim, Ireland. Lower order right-hand batsman, leg break bowler. *Team* Ireland (1946–55).
Career batting
6–9–0–52–34–5.77–0–*ct* 6
Bowling 369–19–19.42–2–0–6/23
He played hockey for Ireland.

Bowden, Joseph
Professional. *b:* 8.10.1884, Glossop, Derbyshire. *d:* 1.3.1958, Glossop, Derbyshire. Sound opening right-hand batsman, right-arm medium pace bowler. *Team* Derbyshire (1909–30, 231 matches).
Career batting
231–395–25–7613–120–20.57–4–*ct* 75
Bowling 54–1–54.00–0–0–1/0
He hit 1,000 runs in a season twice (best 1,221, av 30.52, in 1926).

Bowden, Montague Parker
Amateur. *b:* 1.11.1865, Stockwell, Surrey. *d:* 19.2.1892, near Laurencedale (now Umtali), Mashonaland, Rhodesia. He died after a fall from a cart. Middle order right-hand batsman, wicket-keeper. *Sch* Dulwich. *Teams* Surrey (1883–88, 72 matches); Transvaal (1889/90). *Tours* Vernon to Australia 1887/8; Warton to South Africa 1888/9. *Tests* England (1888/9, 2 matches).
Career batting
86–132–17–2316–189*–20.13–3–*ct* 73–*st* 14
Bowling 35–2–17.50–0–0–2/7
Test batting
2–2–0–25–25–12.50–0–*ct* 1
He captained the England team in the second Test of 1888/9 v South Africa, owing to the absence of C. A. Smith. After the 1888/9 tour, Bowden remained in Southern Africa.

Bowell, Horace Alexander William
Professional. *b:* 27.4.1880, Oxford. *d:* 28.8.1957, Oxford. Father of N. H. (Hampshire and Northamptonshire). Sound right-hand opening batsman, latterly middle order, right-arm medium fast bowler, brilliant cover-point. *Team* Hampshire (1902–27, 473 matches).
Career batting
475–810–43–18509–204–24.13–25–*ct* 255–*st* 2
Bowling 1766–34–51.94–0–0–4/20
He hit 1,000 runs in a season 8 times (best 1,627, av 31.28, in 1913). His only double century was 204 for Hampshire v Lancashire at Bournemouth in 1914.

Bowell, Norman Henry
Professional. *b:* 2.2.1904, Oxford. *d:* 5.3.1943, at sea off the coast of Singapore. Son of H. A. W. (Hampshire). Middle order right-hand batsman, slow right-arm bowler. *Teams* Hampshire (1924, 2 matches); Northamptonshire (1925, 1 match).
Career batting
3–3–0–56–48–18.66–0–*ct* 0
Bowling 72–0
His only appearance for Northamptonshire was v Dublin University, when the County fielded a very weak side. He also played for Oxfordshire (1930–31).

Bowen, Edward Ernest
Amateur. *b:* 30.3.1836, Glenmore, Co Wicklow, Ireland. *d:* 8.4.1901, Moux, Cote D'or, France, whilst on a cycling tour. Brother of C. S. C. (Hampshire). Middle order right-hand batsman, occasional wicket-keeper. *Sch* Kings College, London. *Team* Hampshire (1864, 1 match).
Career batting
1–2–0–0–0–0.00–0–*ct 0*
He was educated at Cambridge, but was not in the Eleven. He played soccer for England in the first unofficial match with Scotland in 1870, and also appeared for Wanderers on the winning side in the first two FA Cup finals, 1872 and 1873.

Bowen, Elvyn
Professional. *b:* 10.7.1907, Llannon, Llanelly, Carmarthen. *d:* 24.8.1965, Brynlliw Colliery, Gorseinon, Glamorgan. Middle order left-hand batsman, slow left-arm bowler. *Team* Glamorgan (1928–33, 3 matches).
Career batting
3–5–1–40–22–10.00–0–*ct* 0
Bowling 14–0

Bowen, Mark Nicholas
Cricketer. *b:* 6.12.1967, Redcar, Yorkshire. Tail-end right-hand batsman, right-arm fast medium bowler. *Team* Northamptonshire (1991/2 to 1992, 3 matches). *Tour* Northamptonshire to South Africa 1991/2.
Career batting
3–3–2–26–13*–26.00–0–*ct* 0
Bowling 247–2–123.50–0–0–1/23
He played hockey for Durham.

Bower, Joseph
Professional. Tail end batsman, opening bowler. *Team* Hampshire (1897–98, 3 matches).
Career batting
3–4–1–14–8–4.66–0–*ct* 0
Bowling 166–8–20.75–0–0–4/43

Bower, Philip Salkeld Syndercombe
Amateur. *b:* 24.9.1898, Holtby, York. *d:* 12.10.1978, Magaliesberg, Transvaal, South Africa. Grandfather of C. E. B. Rice (Transvaal and Nottinghamshire), great-nephew of C. Nevill (Cambridge U 1821). Middle order right-hand batsman. *Sch* Repton. *Team* Oxford U (1919).
Career batting
5–7–0–105–78–15.00–0–*ct* 7
Bowling 467–11–42.45–0–0–3/103

Bower, Wallace
Professional. *b:* 2.1.1895, Eastwood, Nottinghamshire. *d:* 10.2.1971, Welbeck Colliery Village, Nottinghamshire. Lower order right-hand batsman, right-arm fast medium bowler. *Team* Nottinghamshire (1914, 1 match).
Career batting
1–1–0–0–0–0.00–*ct* 0
Bowling 51–1–51.00–0–0–1/31

Bower, William Henry
Professional. *b:* 17.10.1857, Bradford, Yorkshire. *d:* 31.1.1943, Nelson, Lancashire. Middle order right-hand batsman, good field. *Teams* Yorkshire (1883, 1 match); Lancashire (1885–86, 4 matches).
Career batting
5–8–0–55–23–6.87–0–*ct* 1

Bowerman, Alfred James
Amateur. *b:* 22.11.1873, Haygrove, Bridgwater, Somerset. *d:* 1959, Brisbane, Queensland, Australia. Middle order batsman. *Team* Somerset (1900–05, 2 matches).
Career batting
2–4–0–8–3–2.00–0–*ct* 1
He played in the 1900 Olympic cricket match.

Bowers, Robert Bruce
Amateur. *b:* 1.3.1897, Lambeg, Co Antrim, Ireland. *d:* 25.11.1956, Belfast, Ireland. Lower order right-hand batsman, right-arm medium pace bowler. *Team* Ireland (1926).
Career batting
1–2–0–10–5–5.00–0–*ct* 2
Bowling 52–0

Bowes, John Barton
Professional. *b:* 2.1.1918, Stretford, Manchester, Lancashire. *d:* 22.5.1969, Manchester, Lancashire. Lower order batsman, right-arm medium pace bowler. *Team* Lancashire (1938–48, 10 matches).
Career batting
10–13–1–106–39–8.83–0–*ct* 6
Bowling 602–21–28.66–0–0–4/103
He was a first-class umpire (1958–59).

Bowes, William Eric
Professional. *b:* 25.7.1908, Elland, Yorkshire. *d:* 4.9.1987, Otley, Yorkshire. Tail end right-hand batsman, fast medium/medium right-arm bowler. *Team* Yorkshire (1929–47, 301 matches). *Tours* MCC to Australia and New Zealand 1932/3; Yorkshire to Jamaica 1935/6. *Tests* England (1932–46, 15 matches).
Career batting
372–326–148–1528–43*–8.58–0–*ct* 138
Bowling 27470–1639–16.76–116–27–9/121
Test batting
15–11–5–28–10*–4.66–0–*ct* 2
Bowling 1519–68–22.33–6–0–6/33
It would not be an injustice to other County cricketers to state that Bowes was the most intelligent bowler of his era, and because of that he was one of the very few performers who never had an 'off' season, right from his first games with MCC to his retirement at the close of the 1947 season.

Perhaps due to his poor batting and rather moderate showing as a fieldsman, he appeared in only 15 Tests for England, but his true worth can be demonstrated by the standing of Yorkshire in the County Championship between 1929 and 1939, when the County attack was built around Bowes and Verity.

Bowes studied the weaknesses of each batsman and exploited them through his controlled use of both the out and in-swinger. He could also make the ball come very sharply off the wicket, though he was never one to over-use the bouncer or to employ leg theory. He took 100 wickets in a season nine times (best 193, av 15.44, in 1935). His best bowling was 9/121 for Yorkshire v Essex at Scarborough in 1932.

During the Second World War he was taken prisoner and physically never really recovered from the time spent in enemy hands, but in 1946 he still proved an effective bowler, even if his pace was slowed to a brisk medium. After retiring from first-class cricket he built himself a considerable reputation as a cricket writer. His first-class debut was for MCC in 1928.

Bowes-Lyon, Hon John Herbert
Amateur. *b:* 1.4.1886, Glamis, Scotland. *d:* 7.2.1930, Glamis, Scotland. Brother of Queen Elizabeth, the Queen Mother, grandson of Claude (MCC 1843). Lower order batsman, opening bowler. *Sch* Eton. *Team* Oxford U (1906–07).
Career batting
3–5–2–50–28–16.66–0–*ct* 2
Bowling 165–2–82.50–0–0–2/17

Bowie, Thomas Alexander
Amateur. *b:* 21.2.1877, Alloa, Clackmannan, Scotland. *d:* 23.1.1974, Stirling, Scotland. Middle order right-hand batsman, right-arm medium pace bowler. *Team* Scotland (1906–13).
Career batting
8–15–1–252–66–18.00–0–*ct* 4
Bowling 156–4–39.00–0–0–3/35

Bowler, Peter Duncan
Cricketer. *b:* 30.7.1963, Plymouth, Devon. Opening right-hand batsman, off break bowler, occasional wicket-keeper. *Teams* Leicestershire (1986, 8 matches); Tasmania (1986/7, 2 matches); Derbyshire (1988-92, 118 matches).
Career batting
128–223–22–8256–241*–41.07–18–*ct* 82–*st* 1
Bowling 1449–20–72.45–0–0–3/41

He performed the unique double feat of a century on first-class debut for Leicestershire, 100* v Hampshire at Leicester in 1986, and for Derbyshire, 155* v Cambridge U at Cambridge in 1988. He completed 1,000 runs in a season five times, going on to 2,000 once, namely 2,044, av 65.93, in 1992. His highest score was 241* for Derbyshire v Hampshire at Portsmouth in 1992.

Bowles, John Jesse
Professional. *b:* 3.4.1890, Lower Slaughter, Gloucestershire. *d:* 27.11.1971, Salisbury, Wiltshire. Lower order right-hand batsman, left-arm medium or slow bowler. *Teams* Gloucestershire (1911–20, 18 matches); Worcestershire (1926–28, 62 matches).
Career batting
80–136–15–1392–73–11.50–0–*ct* 46–*st* 1
Bowling 3457–83–41.65–1–0–5/56

He was a first-class umpire (1931).

Bowles, Roger Andrew
Amateur. *b:* 1.2.1936, Carshalton, Surrey. Opening right-hand batsman, leg break bowler. *Team* Oxford U (1957).
Career batting
3–6–0–92–43–15.33–0–*ct* 0

Bowley, Edward Henry
Professional. *b:* 6.6.1890, Leatherhead, Surrey. *d:* 9.7.1974, Winchester, Hampshire. Sound right-hand opening batsman, leg break bowler. *Teams* Sussex (1912–34, 458 matches); Auckland (1926/7 to 1928/9). *Tours* Joel to South Africa 1924/5; MCC to New Zealand and Australia 1929/30; Tennyson to Jamaica 1931/2. *Tests* England (1929 to 1929/30, 5 matches).
Career batting
510–859–47–28378–283–34.94–52–*ct* 373
Bowling 19257–741–25.98–28–2–9/114
Test batting
5–7–0–252–109–36.00–1–*ct* 2
Bowling 116–0

He reached 1,000 runs in a season fifteen times and on four of those exceeded 2,000 (best 2,360, av 43.70, in 1929). He hit four double centuries, all for Sussex, his highest of 283 being against Middlesex at Hove in 1933. During this innings he was involved in a record Sussex 1st wicket stand of 490 with J. G. Langridge. His best bowling was 9/114 for Sussex v Derbyshire at Hove in 1919.

Bowley, Frederick James
Professional. *b:* 20.2.1909, Ratby, Leicestershire. Brother of H. B. (Leicestershire). Tail end right-hand batsman, slow left-arm bowler. *Team* Leicestershire (1930–31, 13 matches).
Career batting
13–17–7–33–6–3.30–0–*ct* 4
Bowling 770–23–33.47–0–0–4/46

Bowley, Frederick Lloyd
Professional. *b:* 9.11.1873, Brecon. *d:* 31.5.1943, Worcester. Sound opening right-hand batsman, excellent deep field. *Team* Worcestershire (1899–1923, 396 matches).
Career batting
405–738–25–21122–276–29.62–38–*ct* 148
Bowling 101–4–25.25–0–0–1/6

He exceeded 1,000 runs in a season 14 times (best 1,629, av 39.73, in 1906). He scored three double centuries, all for Worcestershire, the highest being 276 v Hampshire at Dudley in 1914. He first played for Worcestershire (pre first-class) in 1895.

Bowley, Herrick Browett
Professional. *b:* 10.1.1911, Kirby-Muxloe, Leicestershire. *d:* December 1991. Brother of F. J. (Leicestershire). Middle order right-hand batsman, leg break bowler. *Team* Leicestershire (1933–37, 13 matches).
Career batting
13–18–1–113–25–6.64–0–*ct* 3
Bowling 919–17–54.05–0–0–4/17

Bowley, Thomas
Professional. *b:* 28.2.1857, Old Basford, Nottinghamshire. *d:* 8.11.1939, Sherborne, Dorset. Lower order right-hand batsman, right-arm fast bowler. *Team* Surrey (1885–91, 76 matches).
Career batting
83–111–26–730–46–8.58–0–*ct* 42
Bowling 4441–264–16.82–9–1–7/64
He played for Northamptonshire (pre first-class, 1880–84) before joining the Oval staff, and for Dorset (1896–1903).

Bowling, Kenneth
Professional. *b:* 10.11.1931, Fulwood, Preston, Lancashire. Nephew of J. Iddon (Lancashire). Stylish middle order right-hand batsman, good deep field. *Team* Lancashire (1954, 1 match).
Career batting
1–2–1–7–4*–7.00–0–*ct* 0

Bowman, Richard
Amateur. *b:* 26.1.1934, Cleveleys, Lancashire. Lower order right-hand batsman, right-arm fast bowler. *Sch* Fettes. *Teams* Oxford U (1955–57, blue 1957); Lancashire (1957–59, 9 matches).
Career batting
26–37–9–454–75–16.21–0–*ct* 15
Bowling 1902–51–37.29–2–0–7/60
His final first-class match was for MCC in 1964. He also played for Cumberland (1955–59).

Bowmer, Herbert Edgar
Amateur. *b:* 4.7.1891, Wirksworth, Derbyshire. *d:* 1.6.1966, Derby. Middle order right-hand batsman, right-arm fast-medium bowler. *Sch* Wellingborough. *Team* Derbyshire (1909–11, 3 matches).
Career batting
3–6–0–6–3–1.00–0–*ct* 1

Bowring, Charles James
Professional. *b:* 27.8.1887, Portland, Weymouth, Dorset. *d:* 16.1.1959, Preston, Yeovil, Somerset. Middle order batsman. *Team* Somerset (1913, 4 matches).
Career batting
4–7–0–42–15–6.00–0–*ct* 0
Bowling 26–3–8.66–0–0–3/24

Bowring, Trevor
Amateur. *b:* 8.11.1887, Upper Long Ditton, Surrey. *d:* 7.8.1908, Ditton Hill, Surrey. Cousin of W. B. Stoddart (Lancashire). Opening right-hand batsman, slow bowler. *Sch* Rugby. *Team* Oxford U (1907–08, blue both years).
Career batting
17–32–2–722–228–24.06–1–*ct* 5
Bowling 535–20–26.75–0–0–3/10
In 1908 he hit 228 in 210 minutes, adding 338 for the 1st wicket with H. Teesdale for Oxford U v Gentlemen, but within two months of this great innings he died from blood poisoning aged only 20.

Bowstead, John
Amateur. *b:* 14.5.1872, Edenhall, Penrith, Cumberland. *d:* 17.1.1939, Ealing, Middlesex. Middle order right-hand batsman, slow round-arm bowler. *Sch* Repton. *Team* Middlesex (1909, 1 match).
Career batting
1–2–0–21–16–10.50–0–*ct* 0

Box, Joseph William
Professional. *b:* 14.6.1842, Queens Road, Peckham, London. *d:* 2.10.1873, Bow Common, London. Lower order batsman, wicket-keeper. *Team* Middlesex (1866–68, 4 matches).
Career batting
4–7–1–33–17–5.50–0–*ct* 3–*st* 1

Box, Thomas
Professional. *b:* 7.2.1808, Ardingly, Sussex. *d:* 12.7.1876, Prince's Cricket Ground, London. Middle order right-hand batsman, wicket-keeper. *Teams* Sussex (1826–56, 108 matches); Surrey (1849, 2 matches as given man); Hampshire (1844–45); Cambridge Town Club (1846).
Career batting
247–456–43–4936–79–11.95–0–*ct* 236–*st* 162
Bowling 66–5+3–13.20–1–0–5/45
He was regarded in his day as the best wicket-keeper in England. After retiring he kept the Brunswick Cricket Ground in Brighton and latterly was ground-keeper at Prince's, where he fell down dead during the Middlesex v Nottinghamshire match of 1876 – the match was abandoned as soon as his death was known. He also played for Essex (pre first-class, 1846).

Boxall, Thomas
Professional. Excellent bowler. *Teams* Kent (pre 1801); England (1801–03).
Career batting
5–9–2–42–17*–6.00–0–*ct* 3
Bowling 10 wickets (no analyses)–0–0–2/?

For about fifteen seasons commencing 1790 he was regarded as one of the best bowlers in England, but nowhere is his type of bowling recorded. It is believed that he was born in Ripley in Surrey and played for Kent by reason of residing at Barming. He published a cricket guide, the first of its kind.

Boxill, Darnley Da Costa
Cricketer. *b:* 2.10.1944, Christchurch, Christ Church, Barbados. Lower order right-hand batsman, wicket-keeper. *Team* Barbados (1964/5 to 1971/2). *Tour* Barbados to England 1969.
Career batting
15–19–1–149–38–8.27–0–*ct* 28–*st* 14

Boyce, Keith David
Cricketer. *b:* 11.10.1943, Castle, St Peter, Barbados. Hard hitting middle order right-hand batsman, right-arm fast medium bowler, excellent field. *Teams* Barbados (1964/5 to 1974/5); Essex (1966–77, 211 matches). *Tours* West Indies to England 1973, 1975 (World Cup), to India, Sri Lanka and Pakistan 1974/5, to Australia 1975/6; Commonwealth to Pakistan 1967/8; Rest of World to Pakistan 1973/4. *Tests* West Indies (1970/1 to 1975/6, 21 matches).
Career batting
285–420–27–8800–147*–22.39–4–*ct* 215
Bowling 21324–852–25.02–35–7–9/61
Test batting
21–30–3–657–95*–24.33–0–*ct* 5
Bowling 1801–60–30.01–2–1–6/77

The high point of his career was the 1973 Test series between West Indies and England, when he took 19 wickets (av 15.47) in the three matches and averaged 25.80 with the bat, being the major factor in winning the rubber for his country. He was outstandingly successful in limited overs matches for Essex and was the first player ever to reach 1,000 runs and 100 wickets in the John Player League. In first-class matches he hit 1,000 runs in 1972 (1,023, av 30.08). His best bowling was 9/61 for Essex v Cambridge U at Brentwood in 1966, on his County debut. A serious knee injury prematurely ended his career in 1977.

Boycott, Geoffrey, OBE
Professional. *b:* 21.10.1940, Fitzwilliam, Yorkshire. Very sound and determined opening right-hand batsman, right-arm medium pace bowler. *Teams* Yorkshire (1962–86, 414 matches); Northern Transvaal (1971/2). *Tours* MCC to South Africa 1964/5, to Australia and New Zealand 1965/6, to Australia 1970/1, to West Indies 1967/8, 1973/4, to Ceylon 1969/70; England to Pakistan and New Zealand 1977/8, to Australia 1978/9, to Australia and India 1979/80, to West Indies 1980/1, to India and Sri Lanka 1981/2; SAB England XI to South Africa 1981/2. *Tests* England (1964 to 1981/2, 108 matches).
Career batting
609–1014–162–48426–261*–56.83–151–*ct* 264
Bowling 1459–45–32.42–0–0–4/14
Test batting
108–193–23–8114–246*–47.72–22–*ct* 33
Bowling 382–7–54.57–0–0–3/47

The most prolific and controversial batsman of recent years, he is the only cricketer to average more than 100 in an English first-class season twice. His two great years were 1979 with 1,538 runs, av 102.53, and 1971 with 2,503, av 100.12. 1971 was his own record aggregate season, but he exceeded 1,000 runs in England 23 times and went on to 2,000 three times. Of his ten double centuries, seven were for Yorkshire, two for MCC (including his highest which was 261* v President's XI in Bridgetown in 1973/4) and one for England – 246* v India at Headingley in 1967. He performed the feat of scoring his 100th 100 in first-class cricket on the same ground in the 1977 Test v Australia.

His aggregate of 8,114 runs set a world record (now beaten) for Test cricket (he passed Sobers' total in 1981) and would be larger had it not been for two factors: first that he indicated that he was not available for selection for England in 1975 and 1976 and for several overseas tours, and secondly that he was banned from Test cricket for three years following his 1981/2 tour to South Africa.

He captained England in four Tests in 1977/8 and led Yorkshire from 1971 to 1978. At the close of the 1983 season his contract with Yorkshire was not renewed and this action caused a resumption of the discontent within the Yorkshire Club which had flared up when he was dropped as County captain.

In 1984 he was elected to the Yorkshire Committee, thereby being a contracted player and a member of the ruling club committee for the last three seasons of his career. This was clearly a difficult duality. He continued to top the Yorkshire first-class averages until he retired, but criticism of his slow scoring became more strident. He has become well-known as a television summariser.

Boyd, James Lawrence
Amateur. *b:* 18.8.1891, Amoy, China. *d:* 15.6.1930, Arosa, Switzerland. Lower order batsman, bowler. *Team* Royal Navy (1913–19).
Career batting
2–4–1–25–10*–8.33–0–*ct* 1
Bowling 56–1–56.00–0–0–1/30

He played rugby for Scotland.

Boyd-Moss, Robin James
Cricketer. *b:* 16.12.1959, Hatton, Ceylon. Middle order right-hand batsman, slow left-arm bowler. *Sch* Bedford. *Teams* Cambridge U (1980–83, blue all four years); Northamptonshire (1980–87, 115 matches).
Career batting
153–257–20–7171–155–30.25–13–*ct* 61
Bowling 2198–51–43.09–1–0–5/27

He hit 1,000 runs in a season three times (best 1,602, av 44.50, in 1982). He scored 139 and 124 for Cambridge v Oxford in the 1983 match at Lord's, the first time two hundreds had been hit by one batsman in this fixture. A good rugby footballer, he appeared in the University matches of 1980/1 and 1981/2. He also played for Bedfordshire (1977–79).

Boyers, Michael John Herbert
Cricketer. *b:* 16.4.1948, Plaistow, Essex. Lower order right-hand batsman, right-hand fast medium bowler. *Team* Essex (1969, 1 match).
Career batting
1–2–0–2–2–1.00–0–*ct* 0

Boyes, George Stuart
Amateur in 1921 but turned professional in 1922. *b:* 31.3.1899, Southampton, Hampshire. *d:* 11.2.1973, Southampton, Hampshire. Lower order right-hand batsman, slow left-arm bowler, splendid field at short-leg. *Team* Hampshire (1921–39, 474 matches). *Tour* MCC to India, Burma and Ceylon 1926/7.
Career batting
504–709–169–8078–104–14.95–2–*ct* 498
Bowling 34610–1472–23.51–74–11–9/57

He took 100 wickets in a season three times (best 111, av 26.75, in 1933). His best bowling was 9/57 for Hampshire v Somerset at Yeovil in 1938.

Boyle, Cecil William
Amateur. *b:* 16.3.1853, Westminster, London. *d:* 5.4.1900, killed in action near Boshof, Orange Free State, South Africa. Cousin of C. E. (Oxford U), uncle of L. H. Tennyson (Hampshire). Lower order right-hand batsman, right-arm fast bowler, slip field. *Team* Oxford U (1873–74, blue 1873).
Career batting
6–8–3–52–16–10.40–0–*ct* 3
Bowling 309–30–10.30–2–1–7/33

He excelled on the rugby field and represented England. By some he was regarded as one of the three fastest bowlers of his day.

Boyle, Sir Courtenay Edmund
Amateur. *b:* 21.10.1845, Newcastle, Jamaica. *d:* 18.5.1901, Marylebone, London. Cousin of C. W. (Oxford U), brother-in-law of C. G. Lane (Surrey). Steady middle order right-hand batsman, change bowler, wicket-keeper. *Sch* Charterhouse. *Team* Oxford U (1865–67, blue all three years).
Career batting
24–41–0–575–55–14.02–0–*ct* 21–*st* 6

In 1866 and 1867 he was champion tennis player at Oxford and in both years defeated the Cambridge champion. At the time of his death he was Permanent Secretary to the Board of Trade. His final first-class match was for MCC in 1872, and his County cricket was for Northamptonshire (pre first-class, 1863–65) and Buckinghamshire (1866–68).

Boyle, Henry Frederick
Amateur. *b:* 10.12.1847, Sydney, New South Wales, Australia. *d:* 21.11.1907, East Bendigo, Victoria, Australia. Lower order right-hand batsman, right-hand medium pace round-arm bowler, good field. *Team* Victoria (1871/2 to 1887/8, 28 matches). *Tours* Australia to England 1878, 1880, 1882, 1884, 1888 and as player/manager in 1890, to North America 1878. *Tests* Australia (1878/9 to 1884/5, 12 matches).
Career batting
140–215–48–1711–108–10.24–1–*ct* 126
Bowling 5692–370–15.38–26–6–7/32
Test batting
12–16–4–153–36*–12.75–0–*ct* 10
Bowling 641–32–20.03–1–0–6/42

Boyle was an invaluable bowler for keeping down the runs; he kept an immaculate length and proved an excellent foil to Spofforth, especially in the 1882 Tests in England. He took 125 wickets, av 12.18, in 1882.

Boyns, Cedric Nigel
Cricketer. *b:* 14.8.1954, Starbeck, Harrogate, Yorkshire. Middle order right-hand batsman, right-arm medium pace bowler. *Teams* Cambridge U (1976); Worcestershire (1976–79, 33 matches).
Career batting
37–54–7–871–95–18.53–0–*ct* 37
Bowling 1668–36–46.33–0–0–3/24

He also played for Shropshire (1973 and 1980–85).

Boys, Frank Cecil
Amateur. *b:* 21.6.1918, Kensington, London. Middle order right-hand batsman, right-arm medium pace bowler. *Team* Combined Services (1947–51).
Career batting
7–13–0–273–84–21.00–0–*ct* 4

Boys, John James
Professional. *b:* 17.8.1856, Titchfield, Hampshire. *d:* 1.8.1883, Woolwich, Kent. Opening right-hand batsman, right-arm fast round-arm bowler, wicket-keeper. *Team* Kent (1875–81, 3 matches).
Career batting
3–5–0–34–21–6.80–0–*ct* 4–*st* 2

A musician in the band of the Royal Artillery stationed at Woolwich, he could only occasionally obtain leave to play County cricket. His end was a melancholy one, for he died, aged 26, on the day on which he was to be married, having been busy preparing on the previous day.

Boys, Richard
Professional. *b:* 17.6.1849, Burnley, Lancashire. *d:* 4.1.1896, Burnley, Lancashire. Lower order right-hand batsman, wicket-keeper. *Team* Lancashire (1877, 1 match).
Career batting
1–2–1–13–10–13.00–0–*ct* 2

He did not keep wicket in his only first-class match. He was killed when an industrial chimney collapsed on him.

Bracewell, Brendon Paul
Cricketer. *b:* 14.9.1959, Auckland, New Zealand. Brother of J. G. (New Zealand), D. W. (Canterbury) and M. A. (Otago). Lower order right-hand batsman, right-arm medium pace bowler. *Teams* Central Districts (1977/8 to 1979/80); Otago (1981/2 to 1982/3); Northern Districts (1983/4 to 1989/90). *Tours* New Zealand to England 1978, to Australia 1980/1, 1989/90. *Tests* New Zealand (1978 to 1984/5, 6 matches).
Career batting
77–106–24–965–57*–11.76–0–*ct* 32
Bowling 5642–194–29.08–2–0–6/49
Test batting
6–12–2–24–8–2.40–0–*ct* 1
Bowling 585–14–41.78–0–0–3/110

He took 24 wickets, av 28.91, on the 1978 tour to England and played in all three Tests.

Bracewell, John Garry
Cricketer. *b:* 15.4.1958, Auckland, New Zealand. Brother of B. P. (New Zealand), D. W. (Canterbury) and M. A. (Otago). Lower order right-hand batsman, off break bowler. *Teams* Otago (1978/9 to 1981/2); Auckland (1982/3 to 1989/90). *Tours* New Zealand to Australia 1980/1, 1984/5 (not first-class), 1985/6, 1987/8, 1989/90, to England 1983, 1986, 1990, to Sri Lanka 1983/4, 1985/6 (not first-class), 1986/7, to Pakistan 1984/5, to West Indies 1984/5, to Sharjah (not first-class) 1985/6, 1989/90, to India 1987/8 (World Cup), 1988/9; Young New Zealand to Zimbabwe 1984/5; Rest of World to England 1987. *Tests* New Zealand (1980/1 to 1990, 41 matches).
Career batting
149–208–40–4354–110–25.91–4–*ct* 125
Bowling 13919–522–26.66–33–9–8/81
Test batting
41–60–11–1001–110–20.42–1–*ct* 32
Bowling 3653–102–35.81–4–1–6/32

He bowled well on his three tours to England and during the 1990 visit he completed the career Test double of 1,000 runs and 100 wickets. An attacking, rather than containing, off spinner his strike rate in Tests was rather better than his contemporaries. His batting was more than useful and he topped the batting averages on the 1986 tour to England, mainly due to an innings of 110 in the Second Test at Trent Bridge.

Bracey, Frederick Cecil
(also known as Frederick Robert Bracey)
Professional. *b:* 20.7.1887, Glossop, Derbyshire. *d:* 28.3.1960, Derby. Lower order left-hand batsman, slow left-arm bowler. *Team* Derbyshire (1906–14, 77 matches).
Career batting
77–132–54–562–28–7.20–0–*ct* 20
Bowling 3122–132–23.65–5–1–6/36

A noted soccer player, he appeared for Leicester Fosse and Bradford Park Avenue.

Bracher, Frederick Charles
Amateur. *b:* 25.10.1868, Bedminster, Somerset. *d:* 23.12.1947, Portishead, Somerset. Middle order batsman. *Team* Gloucestershire (1895–97, 13 matches).
Career batting
13–23–1–163–21–7.40–0–*ct* 9

Brackin, Thomas
Professional. *b:* 5.1.1859, Thornes, Wakefield, Yorkshire. *d:* 7.10.1924, Darton, Yorkshire. Opening right-hand batsman, right-arm slow bowler, good field. *Team* Yorkshire (1882, 3 matches).
Career batting
3–6–0–12–9–2.00–0–*ct* 0

Brackley, Lord John Francis Granville Scrope Egerton
(succeeded as 4th Earl of Ellesmere in 1914)
Amateur. *b:* 14.11.1872, Bridgewater House, Westminster, London. *d:* 24.8.1944, Mertoun, Berwickshire, Scotland. Brother-in-law of G. Kemp (Lancashire). Middle order right-hand batsman. *Sch* Eton. *Team* MCC (1898–1905). *Tours* Brackley to West Indies 1904/5; MCC to Egypt 1909 (not first-class).
Career batting
12–18–3–210–34–14.00–0–*ct* 6–*st* 1

Brackpool, Alfred
Professional. *b:* 11.10.1857, Crawley Down, Sussex. *d:* 24.10.1927, Crawley Down, Sussex. Middle order right-hand batsman, right-arm medium pace bowler. *Team* Sussex (1880, 1 match).
Career batting
1–2–0–2–2–1.00–0–*ct* 0
Bowling 62–1–62.00–0–0–1/62

Bradbury, Leslie
Cricketer. *b:* 19.4.1938, Matlock, Derbyshire. Lower order right-hand batsman, right-arm fast medium bowler. *Team* Derbyshire (1971, 1 match).
Career batting
1 match, did not bat –*ct* 1
Bowling 53–1–53.00–0–0–1/53

Bradbury, Thomas Farrell
Amateur. *b:* 1856. *d:* 26.4.1934, Cadishead, Lancashire. *Team* Lancashire (1881, 1 match).
Career batting
1–2–1–6–6*–6.00–0–*ct* 1

Bradby, Edward Hugh Falkwin
Amateur. *b:* 8.11.1866, Harrow, Middlesex. *d:* 7.11.1947, Kensington, London. Brother of H. C. (Oxford U), brother-in-law of A. J. Chitty (Oxford

U). Middle order right-hand batsman, change bowler. *Sch* Rugby. *Team* Oxford U (1886).
Career batting
1–2–0–4–4–2.00–0–*ct* 0
He represented Oxford at athletics and in the inter-university sports.

Bradby, Henry Christopher
Amateur. *b:* 28.12.1868, Haileybury, Hertfordshire. *d:* 28.6.1947, Ringshall, Hertfordshire. Brother of E. H. F. (Oxford U), brother-in-law of A. J. Chitty (Oxford U). Middle order right-hand batsman. *Sch* Rugby. *Team* Oxford U (1890, blue).
Career batting
6–11–2–178–40*–19.77–0–*ct* 5
His County cricket was for Hertfordshire (1889).

Braddell, Robert Lyttleton Lee
Amateur. *b:* 14.12.1888, Malacca, Malaya. *d:* 17.3.1965, Thiago, Sintra, Portugal. Middle order right-hand batsman, right-arm medium pace bowler. *Sch* Charterhouse. *Team* Oxford U (1908–11, blue 1910–11).
Career batting
20–37–2–648–96–18.51–0–*ct* 11
Bowling 247–11–22.45–0–0–2/1
His County cricket was for Suffolk (1908–09). His final first-class match was for Leveson-Gower's XI in 1926. He also won a blue for soccer.

Braddock, J.
Professional. Opening batsman. *Team* Lancashire (1873, 1 match).
Career batting
1–2–0–13–11–6.50–0–*ct* 0

Bradfield, Arthur
Professional. *b:* 5.1.1892, Box, Wiltshire. *d:* 25.12.1978, Mochdre, Colwyn Bay, Denbighshire. Tail end right-hand batsman, wicket-keeper. *Team* Essex (1922, 5 matches).
Career batting
5–7–3–7–4*–1.75–0–*ct* 2–*st* 3

Bradfield, Geoffrey Winston
Cricketer. *b:* 28.2.1948, Grahamstown, South Africa. Middle order right-hand batsman. *Team* Northamptonshire (1970, 1 match).
Career batting
1–1–0–50–50–50.00–0–*ct* 0

Bradford, Sir Evelyn Ridley, 2nd Bart
Amateur. *b:* 16.4.1869, Goonah, India. *d:* 14.9.1914. He was killed in action near Bucy-le-Long, Soissons, France. Grandson of E. Knight (Hampshire and Kent). Opening right-hand batsman, right-arm fast bowler. *Sch* Eton. *Team* Hampshire (1895–1905, 8 matches).
Career batting
8–14–2–311–102–25.91–1–*ct* 5
Bowling 328–20–16.40–2–1–6/28

In 1899 his name was on the list of bowlers with 'doubtful' deliveries.

Bradley, George
Professional. *b:* 29.4.1850, Derby. *d:* 24.4.1887, Derby. Lower order right-hand batsman, change bowler. *Team* Derbyshire (1875, 1 match).
Career batting
1–2–0–1–1–0.50–0–*ct* 0
Bowling 17–0

Bradley, James
Professional. *b:* 3.10.1913, Pleasley Hill, Nottinghamshire. Tail end batsman, slow left-arm bowler. *Team* Nottinghamshire (1937–39, 9 matches).
Career batting
9–8–3–30–13–6.00–0–*ct* 4
Bowling 781–19–41.10–0–0–4/116

Bradley, Michael Ewart
Amateur. *b:* 29.3.1934, Halesowen, Worcestershire. Tail end right-hand batsman, slow left-arm bowler. *Team* Worcestershire (1951–52, 9 matches).
Career batting
9–9–7–9–6*–4.50–0–*ct* 0
Bowling 867–23–37.69–1–0–6/162

Bradley, Peter
Cricketer. *b:* 3.3.1937, Gee Cross, Hyde, Cheshire. Lower order left-hand batsman, right-arm medium pace bowler. *Team* Minor Counties (1973–74).
Career batting
2–3–2–11–9*–11.00–0–*ct* 3
Bowling 249–9–27.66–0–0–4/57
His County cricket was for Shropshire (1957–76).

Bradley, Walter Morris
Amateur. *b:* 2.1.1875, Sydenham, London. *d:* 19.6.1944, Wandsworth Common, London. Very moderate tail end right-hand batsman, right-arm fast bowler. *Sch* Alleyn's. *Teams* Kent (1895–1903, 123 matches); London County (1903). *Tour* Kent to North America 1903. *Tests* England (1899, 2 matches).
Career batting
144–216–57–956–67*–6.01–0–*ct* 80
Bowling 14341–633–22.65–44–10–9/87
Test batting
2–2–1–23–23*–23.00–0–*ct* 0
Bowling 233–6–38.83–1–0–5/67
His two great seasons were 1899 (156 wickets, av 19.10) and 1901 (128, av 23.39) – these were the only years in which he took 100 wickets. His best bowling was 9/87 for Kent v Hampshire at Tonbridge in 1901. He regarded himself as one of the poorest batsmen of all time, but once or twice rose above this modest description. His final first-class match was for G. J. V. Weigall's XI in 1904.

Bradman, Sir Donald George
Amateur. *b:* 27.8.1908, Cootamundra, New South Wales, Australia. Outstanding middle order right-

hand batsman, occasional leg break bowler. *Teams* New South Wales (1927/8 to 1933/4, 41 matches); South Australia (1935/6 to 1948/9, 44 matches). *Tours* Australia to England 1930, 1934, 1938, 1948. *Tests* Australia (1928/9 to 1948, 52 matches).
Career batting
234–338–43–28067–452*–95.14–117–*ct* 131–*st* 1
Bowling 1367–36–37.97–0–0–3/35
Test batting
52–80–10–6996–334–99.94–29–*ct* 32
Bowling 72–2–36.00–0–0–1/8

The most effective batsman the game has yet produced, Bradman was as successful in England as he was in his native Australia. By the time of his first English tour in 1930 he had established himself as Australia's leading batsman and he followed one triumph after another as the season progressed. His return in 1934 was no less triumphant and though his first tour as captain, in 1938, resulted only in a drawn series of Tests, his final visit in 1948 was totally successful, both from the team's results and his own, save perhaps for his failure in the fifth Test at the Oval on his farewell appearance against England. His record during his four English tours is so remarkable that it deserves being chronicled in full:

	M	I	NO	R	HS	Avge	100s
1930	27	36	6	2960	334	98.66	10
1934	22	27	3	2020	304	84.16	7
1938	20	26	5	2429	278	115.66	13
1948	23	31	4	2428	187	89.92	11

Both the triple hundreds noted above were hit in the Leeds Test matches – in 1930 he actually hit 309* by the close of the first day's play. His 334 was a new Test record. The previous winter in Australia he scored 452* for New South Wales v Queensland at Sydney which was the world record for first-class cricket; a record which stood for almost thirty years, and remains unbeaten in Australia. He scored 118 on his first-class debut for New South Wales v South Australia at Adelaide in 1927/8. He captained Australia in 24 Tests.

No other cricketer has remotely challenged his career average either in Tests or in all first-class matches. Bradman's achievements remain without parallel.

Bradshaw, James Cecil
Amateur, but changed to professional in 1926. *b:* 25.1.1902, Romford, Essex. *d:* 8.11.1984, Minehead, Somerset. Brother of W. H. (Leicestershire), cousin of J. W. M. (Leicestershire). Stylish middle order right-hand batsman, brilliant field. *Sch* Stamford. *Team* Leicestershire (1923–33, 181 matches).
Career batting
181–286–20–5051–140–18.98–3–*ct* 68
Bowling 80–0

He hit 1,000 runs in a season once – 1,119, av 25.43, in 1929. An excellent hockey player, he represented Leicestershire for six seasons.

Bradshaw, James William Montgomery
Amateur. *b:* 23.11.1906, Oakham, Rutland. *d:* 5.12.1938, Oakham, Rutland. Cousin of J. C. (Leicestershire) and W. H. (Leicestershire). Middle order left-hand batsman, right-arm bowler. *Sch* Oakham. *Team* Leicestershire (1935–38, 3 matches).
Career batting
3–3–0–95–82–31.66–0–*ct* 3
Bowling 103–1–103.00–0–0–1/25

Bradshaw, Stanley William
Amateur. *b:* 16.1.1898, Leicester, *d:* 9.1.1980, Oadby, Leicestershire. Middle order right-hand batsman. *Team* Leicestershire (1923, 3 matches).
Career batting
3–6–0–9–5–1.50–0–*ct* 2

Bradshaw, Walter Harry
Professional. *b:* 2.8.1906, Teddington, Middlesex. *d:* 30.10.1989, Leicester. Brother of J. C. (Leicestershire), cousin of J. W. M. (Leicestershire). Middle order right-hand batsman. *Sch* Stamford. *Team* Leicestershire (1929, 3 matches).
Career batting
3–5–0–38–20–7.60–0–*ct* 0

Bradshaw, Walter Hulatt
Amateur. *b:* 22.1.1909, Adelaide, South Australia. *d:* 13.7.1986, Adderbury, Banbury, Oxfordshire. Lower order right-hand batsman, right-arm fast medium bowler. *Sch* Malvern. *Team* Oxford U (1929–31, blue 1930–31); Rajputana (1935/6 to 1938/9); Europeans (1936/7 to 1937/8).
Career batting
25–37–7–330–81–11.00–0–*ct* 12
Bowling 2001–76–26.32–3–1–8/68

His County cricket was for Buckinghamshire (1948). He also won a blue for soccer.

Brailsford, Frank Colliss
Professional. *b:* 26.8.1933, Hepthorne Lane, Derbyshire. Opening right-hand batsman, right-arm medium pace in-swing bowler. *Team* Derbyshire (1958, 3 matches).
Career batting
3–5–0–41–14–8.20–0–*ct* 1
Bowling 2–1–2.00–0–0–1/2

He dismissed Ted Dexter with his first ball in first-class cricket.

Brain, Brian Maurice
Professional. *b:* 13.9.1940, Worcester. Lower order right-hand batsman, right-arm fast medium bowler. *Sch* Kings, Worcester. *Teams* Worcestershire (1959–75, 149 matches); Gloucestershire (1976–81, 110 matches). *Tours* Worcestershire World Tour (Rhodesia first-class) 1964/5, to Jamaica 1965/6.
Career batting
259–271–68–1704–57–8.39–0–*ct* 50
Bowling 20194–824–24.50–33–6–8/55

Whilst at Worcestershire he left the staff twice (in 1960 and 1971), but rejoined after a break of a season or two. He also played for Shropshire (1982).

Brain, John Henry Patrick
Amateur. *b:* 17.3.1896, Caerau, Cardiff, Glamorgan. *d:* 11.12.1945, Dinas Powis, Glamorgan. Son of W. H. (Gloucestershire), brother of M. B. (Glamorgan), nephew of J. H. (Gloucestershire). Lower order right-hand batsman, wicket-keeper. *Sch* Winchester. *Team* Glamorgan (1921–28, 6 matches).
Career batting
7–13–3–86–19*–8.60–0–*ct* 4–*st* 1
He first played for Glamorgan (pre first-class) in 1920.

Brain, Joseph Hugh
Amateur. *b:* 11.9.1863, Kingswood, Bristol, Gloucestershire. *d:* 26.6.1914, Bonvilston, Cardiff, Glamorgan. Brother of W. H. (Gloucestershire), uncle of J. H. P. (Glamorgan) and M. B. (Glamorgan). Opening or middle order right-hand batsman, right-arm medium pace bowler, occasional wicket-keeper. *Sch* Clifton. *Teams* Gloucestershire (1883–89, 68 matches); Oxford U (1884–87, blue all four years).
Career batting
101–180–6–3393–143–19.50–3–*ct* 84–*st* 4
Bowling 306–8–38.25–0–0–4/54
The most promising schoolboy batsman of his year, although he did reasonably well in County cricket, he never realised his promise. In 1891 he began playing for Glamorgan and was one of the mainstays of the Welsh County until 1908 in its pre first-class days, also being Secretary 1893–1908. His final first-class match was for MCC in 1901. He captained Oxford in 1887.

Brain, Michael Benjamin
Amateur. *b:* 13.4.1910, Cardiff, Glamorgan. *d:* 24.8.1971, Trelleck, Monmouth. Son of W. H. (Gloucestershire), brother of J. H. P. (Glamorgan), nephew of J. H. (Gloucestershire). Middle order right-hand batsman, wicket-keeper. *Sch* Repton. *Team* Glamorgan (1930, 1 match).
Career batting
1–2–0–9–9–4.50–0–*ct* 0
He played no first-class matches, but did appear in trials, whilst at Cambridge.

Brain, William Henry
Amateur. *b:* 21.7.1870, Clifton, Bristol, Gloucestershire. *d:* 20.11.1934, Dinas Powis, Glamorgan. Brother of J. H. (Gloucestershire), father of J. H. P. (Glamorgan) and M. B. (Glamorgan). Lower order right-hand batsman, wicket-keeper. *Sch* Clifton. *Teams* Oxford U (1891–93, blue all three years); Gloucestershire (1893, 7 matches).
Career batting
30–55–15–458–65*–11.45–0–*ct* 39–*st* 22
In 1891 he began to play for Glamorgan under residential qualification, playing until 1908. Whilst at Oxford he was awarded his soccer blue, being a goalkeeper. His great feat as wicket-keeper came for Gloucestershire v Somerset at Cheltenham in 1893 when he achieved a hat-trick of stumpings, the bowler being C. L. Townsend.

Bramhall, Stephen
Cricketer. *b:* 26.11.1967, Warrington, Lancashire. Lower order right-hand batsman, wicket-keeper. *Teams* Lancashire (1990, 2 matches); Nottinghamshire (1992, 8 matches).
Career batting
10–13–5–115–37*–14.37–0–*ct* 18–*st* 6
He also played for Cheshire (1988–91).

Brampton, Charles
Professional. *b:* 5.2.1828, Hyson Green, Nottingham. *d:* 12.6.1895, Marlborough, Wiltshire. Opening right-hand batsman, right-arm medium pace round-arm bowler. *Team* Nottinghamshire (1854–67, 36 matches).
Career batting
73–133–12–1973–89–16.30–0–*ct* 38
Bowling 760–40 + 16–19.00–2–1–6/18
He also played for Herefordshire (1856), Wiltshire (1859–63), Monmouthshire (1859), Lincolnshire (1861) and Devon (1862).

Bramwell, Thomas Young
Amateur. *b:* 15.10.1850, North Shields, Northumberland. *d:* 23.4.1924, Green Bank, Carleton, Wetherall, Cumberland. Middle order batsman. *Sch* Cheltenham. *Team* MCC (1875).
Career batting
1–2–0–44–44–22.00–0–*ct* 0
His County cricket was for Northumberland (1868–73).

Brancker, Rawle Cecil
Cricketer. *b:* 19.11.1937, Emmerton, St Michael, Barbados. Middle order left-hand batsman, slow left-arm bowler. *Team* Barbados (1955/6 to 1969/70). *Tours* West Indies to England 1966; Barbados to England 1969.
Career batting
47–68–7–1666–135*–27.31–5–*ct* 21
Bowling 2895–106–27.31–4–0–7/77
He had only very modest success during his 1966 tour of England.

Brand, Hon David Francis
(succeeded to the title 5th Viscount Hampden in 1965)
Amateur. *b:* 14.6.1902, Westminster, London. *d:* 4.9.1975, Trevor House, Glynde, Sussex. Grandson of H. R. (Sussex), nephew of G. W. M. Scott (Middlesex), H. F. M. Scott (Philipson's XI) and Earl of Dalkeith (MCC), brother-in-law of B. S. Hill-Wood

(Derbyshire). Attractive middle order right-hand batsman, right-arm medium pace bowler. *Sch* Eton. *Team* Cambridge U (1922). *Tour* MCC to New Zealand and Australia 1922/3.
Career batting
14–18–2–246–60–15.37–0–*ct* 5
Bowling 757–27–28.03–0–0–4/31

He was regarded as a most promising all-rounder, but gave up first-class cricket after his tour to Australia and New Zealand. His County cricket was for Hertfordshire.

Brand, Rt Hon Henry Robert
(succeeded to the title 2nd Viscount Hampden in 1892)
Amateur. *b:* 2.5.1841, Devonport, Devon. *d:* 22.11.1906, Pimlico, Westminster, London. Grandfather of D. F. (Cambridge U), brother-in-law of F. F. Thomas (Sussex). Middle order right-hand batsman, good field. *Sch* Rugby. *Team* Sussex (1860–67, 2 matches).
Career batting
2–4–0–16–9–4.00–0–*ct* 2

He also played for Hertfordshire (1873). He was MP for Hertfordshire 1868–73 and for Stroud 1880–86, and Governor of New South Wales 1895–99.

Brand, James Samson
Amateur. *b:* 5.3.1913, Arbroath, Angus, Scotland. *d:* 8.1.1988, Stracathro, Brechin, Scotland. Lower order right-hand batsman, wicket-keeper. *Team* Scotland (1939).
Career batting
1–2–0–12–12–6.00–0–*ct* 1–*st* 1

Brander, Edward Richard Spieker
Amateur. *b:* 21.7.1845, Dartford, Kent. *d:* 2.5.1883, Southbourne-on-Sea, Hampshire. *Sch* Cheltenham. *Team* Orleans Club (1878).
Career batting
1–1–0–2–2–2.00–0–*ct* 0

Brandes, Eddo André
Cricketer. *b:* 5.3.1963, Port Shepstone, Natal, South Africa. Lower order right-hand batsman, right-arm fast medium bowler. *Team* Zimbabwe (1985 to 1991/2). *Tours* Zimbabwe to England 1985, 1990, to India (World Cup) 1987/8, to Australia and New Zealand (World Cup) 1991/2.
Career batting
30–43–6–471–94–12.72–0–*ct* 16
Bowling 2652–82–32.34–5–0–6/59

Brandt, Druce Robert
Amateur. *b:* 20.10.1887, Streatham, London. *d:* 6.7.1915, Boesinghe, Belgium. Middle order right-hand batsman, wicket-keeper. *Sch* Harrow. *Team* Oxford U (1907–08, blue 1907).
Career batting
8–15–3–105–23–8.75–0–*ct* 6–*st* 3

At Harrow he was a noted lightweight boxer, winning the Public School Championship.

Brann, George
Amateur. *b:* 23.4.1865, near Eastbourne, Sussex. *d:* 14.6.1954, Surbiton Hill, Surrey. Originally a hard-hitting but latterly, stubborn defensive, middle order right-hand batsman, right-arm fast bowler, good deep field. *Sch* Ardingly. *Team* Sussex (1883–1905, 271 matches). *Tours* Shrewsbury to Australia 1887/8; Read to South Africa 1891/2 (no first-class matches); Ranjitsinhji to North America 1899.
Career batting
291–479–43–11205–161–25.69–25–*ct* 146–*st* 2
Bowling 3058–69–44.31–1–0–5/73

He reached 1,000 runs in a season twice (best 1,626, av 36.42, in 1897). An excellent soccer player, he was capped for England in 1886 and 1891.

Branston, George Trevor
Amateur. *b:* 3.9.1884, The Friary, Newark, Nottinghamshire. *d:* 12.8.1969, Regent's Park, London. Attacking middle order right-hand batsman, right-arm medium pace bowler. *Sch* Charterhouse. *Teams* Nottinghamshire (1903–13, 44 matches); Oxford U (1904–06, blue all three years). *Tours* MCC to New Zealand 1906/7, to North America 1907, to Egypt 1909 (not first-class).
Career batting
89–144–16–3301–194*–25.78–3–*ct* 96
Bowling 4303–153–28.12–6–0–6/66

He also won a blue for rackets.

Branston, John Richard Martin
Amateur. *b:* 20.4.1932, Nuneaton, Warwickshire. Lower order right-hand batsman, right-arm medium pace bowler. *Team* Oxford U (1956).
Career batting
5–6–2–32–19–8.00–0–*ct* 2
Bowling 235–9–26.11–0–0–3/50

His first-class debut was for Free Foresters in 1955.

Brassington, Andrew James
Cricketer. *b:* 9.8.1954, Bagnall, Staffordshire. Lower order right-hand batsman, wicket-keeper. *Team* Gloucestershire (1974–88, 128 matches).
Career batting
128–156–46–882–35–8.01–0–*ct* 216–*st* 49
Bowling 10–0

He has been Marketing Manager with Gloucestershire since 1988.

Braund, Leonard Charles
Professional. *b:* 18.10.1875, Clewer, Berkshire. *d:* 23.12.1955, Putney Common, London. Middle order right-hand batsman, leg break bowler, excellent slip field. *Teams* Surrey (1896–98, 21 matches); Somerset (1899–1920, 281 matches); London County (1900–04). *Tours* MacLaren to Australia 1901/2; MCC to Australia 1903/4, 1907/8. *Tests* England (1901/2 to

1907/8, 23 matches).
Career batting
432–752–57–17801–257*–25.61–25–*ct* 545–*st* 1
Bowling 30388–1114–27.27–80–16–9/41
Test batting
23–41–3–987–104–25.97–3–*ct* 39
Bowling 1810–47–38.51–3–0–8/81

As a young man Braund played County cricket for Surrey but with little success. In 1899 he switched his allegiance to Somerset, only to discover that he was not qualified, and he thus spent a year appearing in non-Championship cricket for London County. Re-appearing for Somerset in 1901 he took the critics by surprise, completing the 'double' and being rewarded by selection for the England team to Australia in 1901/2. His success continued through 1902; he again completed the 'double' and represented England in all five Tests. A third and last 'double' was completed in 1903, and though he went with MCC on two further visits to Australia and appeared for Somerset until 1920, his career showed a gradual decline from those three great summers of 1901, 1902 and 1903. His highest score was 257* for Somerset v Worcestershire at Worcester in 1913 and best bowling 9/41 for Somerset v Yorkshire at Sheffield in 1902.

In all he hit 1,000 runs in a season 6 times (best 1,587, av 36.06, in 1901) and took 100 wickets 4 times (best 172, av 19.80, in 1902). His great asset which does not show in the averages was his slip fielding and several catches he took during his Test career were quite exceptional. He was a player who could rise to the big occasion and he never appeared to suffer from nerves. After leaving County cricket he was a first-class umpire from (1923–38), standing in three Test matches (1926–29).

Bray, Charlie
Amateur. *b:* 6.4.1898, Portslade, Brighton, Sussex. Defensive middle order right-hand batsman, right-arm medium pace bowler. *Team* Essex (1927–37, 95 matches).
Career batting
95–154–14–3474–129–24.81–5–*ct* 54
Bowling 104–2–52.00–0–0–1/1

He was a noted sporting journalist with the *Daily Herald*.

Bray, Sir Edward
Amateur. *b:* 19.8.1849, The Manor House, Shere, Surrey. *d:* 19.6.1926, Kensington, London. Father of E. H. (Middlesex). Lower order right-hand batsman, right-arm slow bowler. *Sch* Westminster. *Teams* Surrey (1870–78, 14 matches); Cambridge U (1871–72, blue both years).
Career batting
30–52–10–389–38–9.26–0–*ct* 18
Bowling 1757–108–16.26–8–2–7/32

His final first-class match was for MCC in 1879. At the time of his death he was County Court Judge for Bloomsbury and Brentford.

Bray, Sir Edward Hugh
(registered as H. E. Bray at birth)
Amateur. *b:* 15.4.1874, Kensington, London. *d:* 27.11.1950, Playden, Rye, Sussex. Son of Edward (Surrey). Middle/lower order right-hand batsman, wicket-keeper. *Sch* Charterhouse. *Teams* Middlesex (1895–1906, 21 matches); Cambridge U (1896–97, blue both years). *Tour* Warner to North America 1898.
Career batting
42–60–9–684–49–13.41–0–*ct* 71–*st* 12

He also won a blue for soccer. He was in business in Bengal for many years.

Bray, James
Professional. *b:* 18.1.1853, Limehouse, London. *d:* 30.8.1898, St Pancras, London. Tail end right-hand batsman, right-arm medium pace bowler. *Team* Kent (1879–82, 22 matches).
Career batting
22–37–10–74–9–2.74–0–*ct* 16
Bowling 1464–87–16.82–6–1–8/103

He also played for Essex (pre first-class, 1887).

Bray, Leslie Lingwood
Amateur. *b:* 14.1.1895, West Ham, Essex. *d:* 29.11.1957, Ampthill, Bedfordshire. Lower order batsman. *Team* RAF (1927).
Career batting
1–1–1–10–10*–no av–0–*ct* 1

Braybrooke, Henry Mellor
Amateur. *b:* 11.2.1869, Kandy, Ceylon. *d:* 28.10.1935, Hawkhurst, Kent. Brother-in-law of G. O. Bigge (MCC). Opening/middle order right-hand batsman, right-arm medium pace bowler. *Sch* Wellington. *Teams* Kent (1891–99, 21 matches); Cambridge U (1891).
Career batting
28–51–3–690–53–14.37–0–*ct* 15
Bowling 21–0

He represented Cambridge against Oxford at golf in 1890 and 1891 and was also a noted runner and tobogganer.

Brayshay, Peter Beldon
Amateur. *b:* 14.10.1916, Headingley, Leeds, Yorkshire. Tail end right-hand batsman, right-arm fast bowler. *Teams* Yorkshire (1952, 2 matches); Europeans (1945/6).
Career batting
3–5–1–23–13–5.75–0–*ct* 0
Bowling 223–4–55.75–0–0–2/48

He played badminton for England.

Brazier, Alan Frederick
Professional. *b:* 7.12.1924, Paddington, London. Middle order right-hand batsman, right-arm medium pace bowler. *Teams* Surrey (1948–54, 36 matches); Kent (1955–56, 20 matches).
Career batting
58–94–14–1366–92–17.07–0–*ct* 20
Bowling 158–4–39.50–0–0–2/45

In 1949 he created a new aggregate run record for Minor County cricket, hitting 1,212 runs (av 80.80) for Surrey 2nd XI.

Breakwell, Dennis
Cricketer. *b:* 2.7.1948, Brierley Hill, Staffordshire. Middle order left-hand batsman, slow left-arm bowler. *Teams* Northamptonshire (1969–72, 64 matches); Somerset (1973–83, 165 matches).
Career batting
231–306–64–4792–100*–19.80–1–*ct* 80
Bowling 13008–422–30.82–12–1–8/39

Brearley, Horace
Amateur. *b:* 26.6.1913, Heckmondwike, Yorkshire. Father of J. M. (Middlesex). Middle order right-hand batsman. *Teams* Yorkshire (1937, 1 match); Middlesex (1949, 2 matches).
Career batting
5–10–0–134–37–13.40–0–*ct* 3

Brearley, John Michael, OBE
Amateur. *b:* 28.4.1942, Harrow, Middlesex. Son of Horace (Yorkshire and Middlesex). Sound opening right-hand batsman, right-arm medium pace bowler, occasional wicket-keeper. *Sch* City of London. *Teams* Cambridge U (1961–68, blue 1961–64); Middlesex (1961–83, 291 matches). *Tours* MCC to South Africa 1964/5, to East Africa 1973/4, to India and Australia 1976/7; MCC Under 25 to Pakistan 1966/7; England to Pakistan 1977/8, to Australia 1978/9, to Australia and India 1979/80; Kent to West Indies 1972/3 (not first-class); International XI to Pakistan 1973/4; Middlesex to Zimbabwe 1980/1; Overseas XI to India 1980/1. *Tests* England (1976–81, 39 matches).
Career batting
455–768–102–25185–312*–37.81–45–*ct* 418–*st* 12
Bowling 192–3–64.00–0–0–1/6
Test batting
39–66–3–1442–91–22.88–0–*ct* 52

He hit 1,000 runs in a season eleven times, going on to 2,000 once: 2,178, av 44.44, in 1964. His highest innings was 312* for MCC v North Zone at Peshawar in 1966/7, and both his double centuries were also for MCC overseas. He captained Cambridge (1963–64), Middlesex with great success from 1971 to 1982 and England in 31 Tests, including the overseas tours of 1966/7, 1977/8, 1978/9 and 1979/80. He is generally regarded as England's best captain in recent years and in fact commanded a place in the Test team rather for his flair as leader than for his batting. He also played for Cambridgeshire (1966).

Brearley, Walter
Amateur. *b:* 11.3.1876, Bolton, Lancashire. *d:* 13.1.1937, Marylebone, London. Tail end right-hand batsman, right-arm fast bowler. *Teams* Lancashire (1902–11, 106 matches); London County (1904). *Tests* England (1905–12, 4 matches).
Career batting
134–185–31–907–38–5.88–0–*ct* 52
Bowling 16305–844–19.31–93–27–9/47
Test batting
4–5–2–21–11*–7.00–0–*ct* 0
Bowling 359–17–21.11–1–0–5/110

His first-class career was marred by continual quarrels with the Lancashire Committee. He refused to play for the County for most of 1906 and all of 1907 and the final break came at the end of the 1911 season, so that in 1912 he played Test cricket for England whilst appearing for Cheshire. He was the epitome of the explosive fast bowler. In three seasons he took over 100 wickets (best 181, av 19.25, in 1905). His final first-class match was for an England XI v Australians in 1921. His best bowling was 9/47 for Lancashire v Somerset at Old Trafford in 1905.

Breddy, Martin Nicholas
Cricketer. *b:* 23.9.1961, Torquay, Devon. Middle order right-hand batsman. *Team* Cambridge U (1984, blue).
Career batting
10–20–1–339–61–17.84–0–*ct* 2

Bredin, Andrew Michael
Cricketer. *b:* 12.1.1962, Wimbledon, Surrey. Lower order right-hand batsman, slow left-arm bowler. *Sch* KCS, Wimbledon. *Team* Sussex (1986, 7 matches).
Career batting
7–6–2–26–8*–6.50–0–*ct* 1
Bowling 385–7–55.00–0–0–2/50

Breeden, Carl Louis
Amateur. *b:* 10.2.1891, Moseley, Warwickshire. *d:* 2.11.1951, Claverdon, Warwickshire. Middle order right-hand batsman, right-arm medium pace bowler. *Sch* KES, Birmingham. *Team* Warwickshire (1910, 5 matches).
Career batting
5–8–1–80–27–11.42–0–*ct* 4
Bowling 29–0

Brelsford, James
(also known as James Bralsford)
Professional. *b:* 19.12.1855, Brimington, Derbyshire. *d:* 24.12.1924, Hale, Cheshire. Lower order right-hand batsman, right-arm medium pace bowler. *Team* Derbyshire (1883–86, 8 matches).
Career batting
8–14–1–56–16–4.30–0–*ct* 4

Bowling 482–24–20.08–1–0–5/31

He also played for Cheshire (1889–91) under residential qualification.

Bremner, Colin David
Amateur. *b:* 29.1.1920, Hawthorn, Melbourne, Victoria, Australia. Lower order right-hand batsman, wicket-keeper. *Teams* Dominions (1945); Australian Services (1945/6). *Tour* Australian Services to India 1945/6.
Career batting
7–9–6–8–4*–2.66–0–*ct* 4–*st* 6

He was a member of the RAAF team stationed in England in 1945.

Brennan, Donald Vincent
Amateur. *b:* 10.2.1920, Eccleshill, Yorkshire. *d:* 9.1.1985, Ilkley, Yorkshire. Lower order right-hand batsman, wicket-keeper. *Sch* Downside. *Team* Yorkshire (1947–53, 204 matches). *Tour* MCC to India, Pakistan and Ceylon 1951/2. *Tests* England (1951, 2 matches).
Career batting
232–258–74–1937–67*–10.52–0–*ct* 318–*st* 122
Test batting
2–2–0–16–16–8.00–0–*ct* 0–*st* 1

His last first-class match was for MCC in 1964.

Brent, Jonathan Peveritt
Cricketer. *b:* 29.1.1956, Salisbury, Rhodesia. Middle order left-hand batsman, right-arm medium pace bowler. *Team* Zimbabwe (1988/9 to 1990). *Tour* Zimbabwe to England 1990.
Career batting
3–5–2–101–34*–33.66–0–*ct* 0
Bowling 99–2–33.00–0–0–2/28

Bretherton, James
Amateur. *b:* 5.1.1862, Whiston, Lancashire. *d:* 9.6.1926, Raby, Cheshire. Tail end right-hand batsman, right-arm fast medium bowler, slip field. *Team* Liverpool and District (1890–94).
Career batting
6–11–1–165–50–16.50–0–*ct* 2
Bowling 396–24–16.50–1–0–5/30

His County cricket was for Cheshire (1885–95).

Brett, Patrick John
Amateur. *b:* 18.4.1910, Johannesburg, South Africa. *d:* 9.12.1982, Hook Heath, Surrey. Brother-in-law of J. L. T. Guise (Free Foresters). Middle order right-hand batsman, right-arm medium fast bowler. *Sch* Winchester. *Team* Oxford U (1929, blue).
Career batting
8–13–1–490–106–40.83–1–*ct* 2
Bowling 242–4–60.50–0–0–2/32

Brett, Thomas
Professional. *b:* 1747, Catherington, Hampshire. *d:* 31.12.1809, Kingston Cross, Portsmouth, Hampshire. Hard hitting lower order batsman, very fast under-arm bowler. *Team* Hampshire.

First-class career figures are inappropriate as he played before 1801. In the 1770s he was regarded as the fastest and straightest of the Hambledon Club bowlers, but about 1778 he left the Club and seems to have retired from the game.

Brettell, David Norman
Cricketer. *b:* 10.3.1956, Woking, Surrey. Brother of J. G. (Oxford U). Lower order left-hand batsman, slow left-arm bowler. *Sch* Cheltenham. *Team* Oxford U (1975–78, blue 1977).
Career batting
13–19–4–175–39–11.66–0–*ct* 4
Bowling 549–18–30.50–0–0–3/22

Brettell, James Gordon
Cricketer. *b:* 19.12.1962, Woking, Surrey. Brother of D. N. (Oxford U). Lower order right-hand batsman, slow left-arm bowler. *Sch* Cheltenham. *Team* Oxford U (1984–85).
Career batting
5–4–2–0–0*–0.00–0–*ct* 2
Bowling 340–5–68.00–0–0–2/87

Brewer, Thomas Tanner
Amateur. *b:* 23.8.1868, Huntspill, Bridgwater, Somerset. Middle order batsman. *Team* London County (1903).
Career batting
5–8–1–88–59–12.57–0–*ct* 5

His final first-class match was for Gentlemen of England in 1905. His County cricket was for Cheshire (1909).

Brewster, Vincent Crescedo
Cricketer. *b:* 2.1.1940, Bridgetown, Barbados. Lower order left-hand batsman, slow left-arm bowler. *Team* Warwickshire (1965, 2 matches).
Career batting
2–4–1–58–35*–19.33–0–*ct* 1
Bowling 175–10–17.50–1–0–7/58

Briant, Gavin Aubrey
Cricketer. *b:* 11.4.1969, Salisbury, Rhodesia. Middle order right-hand batsman, right-arm medium pace bowler, occasional wicket-keeper. *Team* Zimbabwe (1990 to 1990/1). *Tour* Zimbabwe to England 1990.
Career batting
4–6–0–151–69–25.16–0–*ct* 4

Brice, Edward Archibald
(changed his name to Bruce in 1875)
Amateur *b:* 1.9.1849, Secunderabad, India. *d:* 14.11.1918, Hove, Sussex. Middle/lower order right-hand batsman, right-arm fast bowler. *Sch* Cheltenham. *Team* Gloucestershire (1872–73, 4 matches).
Career batting
6–9–0–22–13–2.44–0–*ct* 3
Bowling 264–20–13.20–2–1–6/34

In 1874 he was stationed in India and therefore lost to County cricket. After retiring from the Army he was Hon Sec (1909–12) and Chairman of Sussex CCC. He played for Somerset in non-first-class matches (1879).

Brice, Gordon Harry Joseph
Professional. *b:* 4.5.1924, Goldington, Bedford. Lower order right-hand batsman, right-arm fast medium bowler. *Sch* Bedford Modern. *Team* Northamptonshire (1949–52, 25 matches).
Career batting
25–35–5–412–82*–13.73–0–*ct* 14
Bowling 2426–72–33.69–4–1–8/124

He also played for Bedfordshire (1953–55). He was an excellent soccer player, appearing at centre half for Reading, Luton, Fulham, Wolves and Ayr United.

Bridge, Derek James Wilson
Amateur. *b:* 30.11.1921, Crumpsall, Manchester, Lancashire. Uncle of R. C. G. Fortin (Oxford U). Lower order right-hand batsman, off break bowler. *Teams* Northamptonshire (1947, 3 matches); Oxford U (1947).
Career batting
4–7–1–55–25*–9.16–0–*ct* 1
Bowling 261–5–52.20–0–0–2/14

An excellent rugby player he was awarded his blue at Oxford. He also played for Dorset (1949–69).

Bridge, Walter Basil
Professional. *b:* 29.5.1938, Selly Oak, Birmingham. Lower order right-hand batsman, off break bowler. *Team* Warwickshire (1955–68, 98 matches).
Career batting
99–133–33–1058–56*–10.58–0–*ct* 59
Bowling 7438–283–26.28–13–2–8/56

He took 123 wickets, av 22.99, in 1961.

Bridgeman, Charles George Orlando
Amateur. *b:* 13.7.1852, Wells, Somerset. *d:* 19.12.1933, St John's Wood, London. Stylish lower order right-hand batsman, right-hand slow round-arm bowler, excellent deep field. *Sch* Harrow. *Team* Cambridge U (1872).
Career batting
3–6–1–87–27–17.40–0–*ct* 1
Bowling 20–0

His County cricket was for Cheshire (1872) and Staffordshire (1874–75). His last first-class match was for an England XI in 1874.

Bridgeman, William Clive
(created 1st Viscount Bridgeman in 1929)
Amateur. *b:* 31.12.1864, Marylebone, London. *d:* 14.8.1935, Leigh Manor, Shropshire. Middle order right-hand batsman, good field at point. *Sch* Eton. *Team* Cambridge U (1887–88, blue 1887).
Career batting
13–20–3–361–162*–21.23–1–*ct* 5

His County cricket was for Shropshire (1884–85) and Staffordshire (1890). His final first-class match was for MCC in 1894. He was President of MCC in 1931. A well-known MP, he was Home Secretary in 1922 and First Lord of the Admiralty in 1924. He represented Oswestry from 1906 to 1929.

Bridger, Rev John Richard
Amateur. *b:* 8.4.1920, Dulwich, Surrey. *d:* 14.7.1986, Burley, Hampshire, in a motor accident. Stylish opening right-hand batsman, leg break bowler. *Sch* Rugby. *Team* Hampshire (1946–54, 38 matches).
Career batting
40–69–4–1883–142–28.96–2–*ct* 30
Bowling 56–0

He appeared for Cambridge U against Oxford in 1941 and 1943. His first-class debut was for Under 33s in 1945. Being in the scholastic profession his County cricket was limited mainly to August.

Bridges, James John
Professional to 1914, amateur from 1919. *b:* 28.6.1887, Timsbury, Somerset. *d:* 26.9.1966, Hackney, London. Tail end right-hand batsman, right-arm fast medium bowler. *Team* Somerset (1911–29, 214 matches).
Career batting
216–348–108–2418–99*–10.07–0–*ct* 128
Bowling 17613–685–25.71–44–4–7/41

Bridges, John Henry
Amateur. *b:* 26.3.1852, Horsham, Sussex. *d:* 12.2.1925, Eastbourne, Sussex. Father-in-law of G. Marks (Middlesex), brother-in-law of E. W. Tritton (Middlesex). Free scoring middle order right-hand batsman, good deep field. *Sch* Winchester. *Team* Surrey (1876, 2 matches).
Career batting
2–2–0–9–8–4.50–0–*ct* 0

He did not appear in any first-class matches whilst at Oxford, but won his blue for soccer. He was Champion Archer of Scotland in 1905 and from 1919 to 1920 High Sheriff of Surrey.

Bridges, Leslie Walter
Amateur. *b:* 14.2.1890, Christchurch, New Zealand. *d:* 6.8.1959, Antwerp, Belgium. Middle order batsman, change bowler. *Team* Cambridge U (1911).
Career batting
1–2–0–34–25–17.00–0–*ct* 0
Bowling 39–0

He performed well in the Seniors' match at Cambridge in 1911, taking 13 wickets and hitting 74, but did little in his other trials at the University.

Brierley, Thomas Leslie
Professional. *b:* 15.6.1910, Southampton, Hampshire. *d:* 7.1.1989, Vancouver, British Columbia, Canada. Middle order right-hand batsman, wicket-keeper. *Teams* Glamorgan (1931–39, 181 matches); Lanca-

shire (1946–48, 46 matches); Canada (1951–54). *Tour* Canada to England 1954.
Career batting
232–362–33–6244–116*–18.97–4–*ct* 215–*st* 91
Bowling 45–0
He hit 1,183 runs, av 23.66, in 1938. He emigrated to Canada after leaving Lancashire and appeared for Canada against the MCC touring team in 1951.

Briers, Mark Paul
Cricketer. *b:* 21.4.1968, Kegworth, Leicestershire. Middle order right-hand batsman, leg break bowler. *Team* Durham (1992, 16 matches).
Career batting
16–28–4–460–62*–19.16–0–*ct* 7
Bowling 621–12–51.75–0–0–3/109
He also played for Bedfordshire (1990). He first played for Durham (pre first-class) in 1991.

Briers, Nigel Edwin
Cricketer. *b:* 15.1.1955, Southfields, Leicester. Cousin of Norman (Leicestershire). Opening right-hand batsman, right-arm medium pace bowler, cover field. *Team* Leicestershire (1971–92, 335 matches). *Tour* Leicestershire to Zimbabwe 1980/1.
Career batting
335–547–55–15977–201*–32.47–26–*ct* 144
Bowling 988–32–30.87–0–0–4/29
He hit 1,000 runs in a season nine times (best 1,996, av 49.90, in 1990). His highest innings was 201* for Leicestershire v Warwickshire at Edgbaston in 1983. He captained Leicestershire 1990 to 1992.

Briers, Norman
Cricketer. *b:* 10.2.1947, Highfields, Leicester. Cousin of N. E. (Leicestershire). Lower order right-hand batsman, right-arm fast medium bowler. *Team* Leicestershire (1967, 1 match).
Career batting
1–1–0–1–1–1.00–0–*ct* 0
Bowling 31–0

Briggs, Rev Charles Edward
Amateur. *b:* 17.9.1873, Ashbourne, Derbyshire. *d:* 16.12.1949, Sherborne, Dorset. Middle order batsman. *Sch* Winchester. *Team* Hampshire (1900, 6 matches).
Career batting
6–10–0–158–58–15.80–0–*ct* 4
He also played for Buckinghamshire (1909).

Briggs, Jack
Professional. *b:* 8.4.1916, Haslingden, Lancashire. *d:* 1.6.1984, Rawtenstall, Lancashire. Tail end right-hand batsman, slow left-arm bowler. *Team* Lancashire (1939, 4 matches).
Career batting
4–2–2–0–0*–no av–0–*ct* 2
Bowling 391–10–39.10–0–0–4/48
He also played for Cheshire (1948).

Briggs, John
Professional. *b:* 3.10.1862, Sutton-in-Ashfield, Nottinghamshire. *d:* 11.1.1902, Heald Green, Cheadle, Cheshire. Brother of J. B. (Nottinghamshire). Hard-hitting middle/lower order right-hand batsman, slow left-arm bowler, brilliant cover field. *Team* Lancashire (1879–1900, 391 matches). *Tours* Lillywhite, Shaw and Shrewsbury to Australia 1884/5, 1886/7, 1887/8; Warton to South Africa 1888/9; Sheffield to Australia 1891/2; Stoddart to Australia 1894/5, 1897/8. *Tests* England (1884/5 to 1899, 33 matches).
Career batting
535–826–55–14092–186–18.27–10–*ct* 258
Bowling 35430–2221–15.95–200–52–10/55
Test batting
33–50–5–815–121–18.11–1–*ct* 12
Bowling 2095–118–17.75–9–4–8/11
'Boy' Briggs – he was only 5ft 5in tall and made his first-class debut at the age of 16 – was one of the most popular professionals of his generation. He is remembered now chiefly for his slow bowling, but in 1879 he won his place in the Lancashire team as a fieldsman and retained it for six years as a batsman. It was not until 1885 that his skill with the ball was of paramount importance – in 1884 he had only 9 first-class wickets to his credit. The first of his many good performances for England came in the Lord's Test of 1886, when he took 11 for 74 to win the match for England. He exceeded 100 wickets in a season 12 times, but it is difficult to pinpoint his best year, so consistent was his success. In 1893 he took most wickets in his career with 166 (av 15.89), but he had effectively headed the bowling table in 1890 with 158 wickets (av 12.34) and in 1888 his 160 wickets were obtained at the low cost of 10.49 runs each. His best bowling was 10/55 for Lancashire v Worcestershire at Old Trafford in 1900. He visited Australia with no fewer than six English Test-playing sides and was a success on all but the last trip.
From about 1889 he suffered from a form of epilepsy which became increasingly serious. He had a particularly bad seizure during the Leeds Test of 1899 and it seemed as if his career were at an end, but he recovered and bowled with all his old skill in 1900. That, however, was the farewell season, for he had another more serious attack and was confined to Cheadle Asylum where he died in the winter of 1901/2 at the early age of 39.

Briggs, Joseph Banner
Professional. *b:* 4.6.1860, Sutton-in-Ashfield, Nottinghamshire. *d:* 1.12.1902, Bramley, Leeds, Yorkshire. Brother of John (Lancashire). Lower order right-hand batsman, slow left-arm bowler. *Team* Nottinghamshire (1888, 6 matches).
Career batting
7–11–0–26–9–2.36–0–*ct* 2
Bowling 168–14–12.00–1–0–5/34

His first-class debut was in 1885 for L. Hall's XI v A. Shaw's XI.

Briggs, Kenneth Robert
Amateur. *b:* 17.7.1933, Woking, Surrey. Middle order right-hand batsman, off break bowler. *Sch* KCS, Wimbledon. *Team* Combined Services (1961).
Career batting
1–2–1–29–17*–29.00–0–*ct* 2
Bowling 44–1–44.00–0–0–1/32
His County cricket was for Lincolnshire (1956).

Briggs, Patrick David
Cricketer. *b:* 24.8.1940, Timperley, Cheshire. Middle order right-hand batsman, right-arm medium pace bowler. *Sch* Pocklington. *Team* Cambridge U (1963–64).
Career batting
21–35–2–533–91–16.15–0–*ct* 17
Bowling 7–0
His County cricket was for Cheshire (1960–68) and Bedfordshire (1969–75).

Briggs, Canon Rawdon
Amateur. *b:* 30.12.1853, Warkworth, Northumberland. *d:* 21.8.1936, Bedford. Middle order right-hand batsman, right-hand fast round-arm bowler. *Sch* Winchester. *Team* Oxford U (1875–76, blue both years).
Career batting
10–17–1–342–71–21.37–0–*ct* 8
Residing in Yorkshire in the 1870s, he was a notable player with the Gentlemen of that County and also appeared for the breakaway Yorkshire United side.

Bright, Raymond James
Cricketer. *b:* 13.7.1954, Footscray, Melbourne, Victoria, Australia. Lower order right-hand batsman, slow left-arm bowler. *Team* Victoria (1972/3 to 1987/8, 114 matches). *Tours* Australia to New Zealand 1973/4, 1976/7, 1981/2, 1985/6, to England 1977, 1980, 1981, to Pakistan 1979/80, 1982/3, to Sri Lanka 1980/1, to Sharjah (not first-class) 1985/6, to India 1986/7. *Tests* Australia (1977 to 1986/7, 25 matches).
Career batting
184–247–51–4130–108–21.07–2–*ct* 107
Bowling 15114–471–32.08–24–2–7/87
Test batting
25–39–8–445–33–14.35–0–*ct* 13
Bowling 2180–53–41.13–4–1–7/87
He headed the first-class bowling averages on the 1977 tour to England with 39 wickets, av 20.35, and played in three Tests. He appeared in the Centenary Test of 1980 and in five Tests on the 1981 tour, but made little impression.

Brindle, Reginald Gordon
Professional. *b:* 3.10.1925, Warrington, Lancashire. Middle order right-hand batsman. *Team* Warwickshire (1949, 1 match).
Career batting
1–2–0–74–42–37.00–0–*ct* 0

Brindley, Thomas
Amateur. *b:* 3.6.1841, Chester. *d:* 1.3.1911, West Cliff, Bournemouth, Hampshire. Hard hitting lower order right-hand batsman, slow under-arm bowler. *Team* MCC (1867).
Career batting
2–4–1–31–13*–10.33–0–*ct* 0
His County cricket was for Warwickshire (pre first-class, 1858), Gloucestershire (pre first-class, 1868), Dorset (1869) and Staffordshire (1876–77),

Brindley, William Thomas
Amateur. *b:* 4.12.1896, High Wycombe, Buckinghamshire. *d:* 13.8.1958, Virginia Water, Surrey. Opening right-hand batsman, change bowler. *Teams* Ceylon (1925/6 to 1933/4); Minor Counties (1930–35).
Career batting
9–15–2–221–59*–17.00–0–*ct* 4
Bowling 389–14–27.78–1–0–5/40
His County cricket was for Buckinghamshire (1925–35), but he joined the Ceylon Police Force and his English cricket was thereby very restricted.

Brinton, Rev Percival Robert
Amateur. *b:* 5.2.1873, Moor Hall, Lower Mitton, Worcestershire. *d:* 14.5.1958, Oxford. Brother of R. S. (Worcestershire). Middle order batsman. *Sch* Winchester. *Team* Worcestershire (1904, 1 match).
Career batting
1–1–0–1–1–1.00–0–*ct* 0

Brinton, Reginald Seymour
Amateur. *b:* 15.12.1869, Moor Hall, Lower Mitton, Worcestershire. *d:* 23.2.1942, Kidderminster, Worcestershire. Brother of P. R. (Worcestershire). Steady middle order right-hand batsman, right-arm fast medium bowler. *Sch* Winchester. *Team* Worcestershire (1903–09, 13 matches).
Career batting
13–24–7–332–72*–19.52–0–*ct* 3
Bowling 13–0
He first played for Worcestershire (pre first-class) in 1892.

Brinton, Ronald Lewis
Amateur. *b:* 26.2.1903, Kidderminster, Worcestershire. *d:* 19.4.1980, Malvern, Worcestershire. Lower order right-hand batsman, change bowler. *Sch* Shrewsbury. *Team* Worcestershire (1924, 2 matches).
Career batting
2–4–0–22–10–5.50–0–*ct* 0
Bowling 22–0

Briscoe, Henry
Professional. *b:* 20.5.1861, Bonehill, Staffordshire. *d:* 7.3.1911, Fenton, Staffordshire. Lower order right-

hand batsman, right-arm fast medium bowler. *Team* An England XI (1888).
Career batting
1–2–1–4–4*–4.00–0–*ct* 0
Bowling 28–0
His County cricket was for Staffordshire (1885–95).

Bristow, John
Professional. *b:* 13.4.1840, Esher, Surrey. *d:* 25.1.1912, Knaphill, Brookwood, Surrey. Lower order right-hand batsman, left-arm medium pace bowler, occasional wicket-keeper. *Team* Surrey (1867–73, 32 matches).
Career batting
32–58–8–514–79–10.28–0–*ct* 17–*st* 1
Bowling 1503–73–20.58–5–0–7/45

Bristowe, Orme Cheshyre
Amateur. *b:* 12.4.1895, Watford, Hertfordshire. *d:* 27.12.1938, of heart failure whilst out shooting at Freiston Shore, Lincolnshire. Hard hitting lower order right-hand batsman, leg break and googly bowler, good field. *Sch* Eton. *Teams* Essex (1913–14, 11 matches); Oxford U (1914, blue).
Career batting
21–33–2–567–81–18.29–0–*ct* 6
Bowling 1751–74–23.66–4–0–6/81
He also played for Cheshire. He also won a blue for golf.

Bristowe, William Robert
Cricketer. *b:* 17.11.1963, Woking, Surrey. Middle order right-hand batsman, off break bowler. *Sch* Charterhouse. *Team* Oxford U (1984–85, blue both years).
Career batting
10–16–4–260–42*–21.66–0–*ct* 5
Bowling 5–0

Britton, George
Professional. *b:* 7.2.1843, Hunslet, Leeds, Yorkshire. *d:* 3.1.1910, Leeds, Yorkshire. Opening right-hand batsman. *Team* Yorkshire (1867, 1 match).
Career batting
1–2–0–3–3–1.50–0–*ct* 0
In 1870 he performed the unusual feat of carrying his bat through the completed innings of a team of Twenty-Two of Hull v All England.

Broad, Brian Christopher
Cricketer. *b:* 29.9.1957, Knowle, Bristol. Opening left-hand batsman, right-arm medium pace bowler. *Sch* Colston's. *Team* Gloucestershire (1979–83, 89 matches); Nottinghamshire (1984–92, 173 matches); Orange Free State (1985/6). *Tours* England to Australia 1986/7, 1987/8, to India and Pakistan (World Cup) 1987/8, to New Zealand 1987/8, to Pakistan 1987/8; English Counties to Zimbabwe 1984/5; England XI to South Africa 1989/90. *Tests* England (1984–89, 25 matches).
Career batting
311–557–38–20147–227*–38.81–47–*ct* 174
Bowling 1036–16–64.75–0–0–2/14
Test batting
25–44–2–1661–162–39.54–6–*ct* 10
Bowling 4–0
He hit 1,000 runs in a season ten times, going on to 2,000 once (2,226, av 54.29, in 1990). His highest score was 227* for Nottinghamshire v Kent at Tunbridge Wells in 1990. Regarded as one of the best opening batsmen in England, his career has been a controversial one, his outspokenness not being appreciated in some quarters. He scored hundreds in three consecutive Tests in Australia in 1986/7.

Broadbent, Arthur
Professional. *b:* 7.6.1879, Armley, Yorkshire. *d:* 19.7.1958, Aberdeen, Scotland. Middle order right-hand batsman, right-arm fast medium bowler. *Teams* Scotland (1907–12); Yorkshire (1909–10, 3 matches).
Career batting
6–11–1–141–32–14.10–0–*ct* 1
Bowling 545–16–34.06–0–0–4/61
He was a most successful player for Yorkshire 2nd XI, taking 100 wickets in 1910 (av 13.20), but did little in first-class matches.

Broadbent, Robert Gillespie
Amateur for first season, professional afterwards. *b:* 21.6.1924, Beckenham, Kent. Aggressive middle order right-hand batsman, occasional right-arm fast medium bowler, good field. *Sch* Caterham. *Team* Worcestershire (1950–63, 307 matches).
Career batting
307–520–56–12800–155–27.58–13–*ct* 297
Bowling 382–4–95.50–0–0–1/16
He hit 1,000 runs in a season 7 times (best 1,556, av 33.10, in 1952). He also played for Hertfordshire (1964).

Broadbridge, James
Professional. *c:* 25.6.1795, Duncton, Sussex. *d:* 12.2.1843, Duncton, Sussex. Brother of Robert (Sussex) and William (Sussex). Hard hitting opening left-hand or right-hand batsman, right-arm medium pace round-arm bowler. *Teams* Sussex (1815–40, 53 matches); Godalming (1822–24); Kent (1828); Surrey (1829).
Career batting
102–184–23–2671–135–16.59–1–*ct* 51
Bowling 243–13 + 310–18.69–8–1–6/?
He was considered for some seasons the best all round cricketer in England and was partly responsible for the introduction of round-arm bowling in 1827. When batting he stood at the wicket 'with his bat over his shoulder'. In 1825 in first-class matches he hit 552 runs, av 46.00. His first first-class match was for G. Osbaldeston's XI in 1814.

Broadbridge, William
Professional. *b:* 1.10.1790, Duncton, Sussex. *d:* 19.4.1860, Duncton, Sussex. Brother of James (Sussex) and Robert (Sussex). Hard-hitting right-hand batsman, wicket-keeper. *Team* Sussex (1817–30, 21 matches).
Career batting
25–45–2–609–61–14.16–0–*ct* 14–*st* 22
Bowling 3 wickets (no analyses)–0–0–1/?
He was one of the mainstays of the old Sussex team for many years, commencing 1817, but details of his early performances have been lost.

Broadhead, Wilfred Bedford
Professional. *b:* 31.5.1903, East Ardsley, Yorkshire. *d:* 2.4.1986, Wath-on-Dearne, Yorkshire. Opening right-hand batsman, leg break bowler. *Team* Yorkshire (1929, 1 match).
Career batting
1–2–0–5–3–2.50–0–*ct* 1

Broadhurst, Mark
Cricketer. *b:* 20.6.1974, Worsborough Common, Barnsley, Yorkshire. Lower order right-hand batsman, right-arm fast medium bowler. *Team* Yorkshire (1991, 2 matches).
Career batting
2–1–0–1–1–1.00–0–*ct* 0
Bowling 130–6–21.66–0–0–3/61
He was the third youngest player ever to play for Yorkshire in a first-class match, aged 16 years and 359 days.

Broadley, Vaughan John Pascal
Cricketer. *b:* 4.4.1972, Sutton-in-Ashfield, Nottinghamshire. Lower order right-hand batsman, right-arm medium fast bowler. *Team* Nottinghamshire (1991, 1 match).
Career batting
1–1–0–6–6–6.00–0–*ct* 0
Bowling 111–1–111.00–0–0–1/92

Broberg, Ralph Francis
Amateur. *b:* 21.7.1899, Balsall Heath, Birmingham, *d:* 3.9.1938, Hall Green, Birmingham. Lower order batsman, slow left-arm bowler. *Sch* KES, Birmingham. *Team* Warwickshire (1920, 1 match).
Career batting
1–1–0–4–4–4.00–0–*ct* 0
Bowling 16–0

Brockbank, John
Amateur. *b:* 22.8.1848, Whitehaven, Cumberland. *d:* 4.2.1896, Fulham, London. Grandfather of W. M. E. White (Cambridge U). Middle order right-hand batsman. *Sch* Shrewsbury. *Team* MCC (1874).
Career batting
1–2–0–5–4–2.50–0–*ct* 0
His County cricket was for Shropshire (1870), Cumberland (1874–78), Cambridgeshire, Brecon (1876), Herefordshire (1877) and Staffordshire (1877). He was not however in the Eleven whilst at Cambridge U, being better known as a soccer player. He was awarded his soccer blue and went on to play for England in 1873. By profession he was an actor.

Brocklebank, Sir John Montague, Bart
Amateur. *b:* 3.9.1915, Hoylake, Cheshire. *d:* 13.9.1974, Palazz Zeitun, Malta. Brother of T. A. L. (Cambridge U), nephew of F. S. Jackson (Yorkshire). Tail end right-hand batsman, medium pace leg break bowler. *Sch* Eton. *Teams* Cambridge U (1936, blue); Lancashire (1939, 4 matches); Bengal (1947/8). *Tours* MCC to Canada 1937 (not first-class); MCC to India 1939/40 (tour cancelled).
Career batting
21–26–14–112–23–9.33–0–*ct* 7
Bowling 1998–68–29.38–4–2–6/92
His final first-class match was for Free Foresters in 1949. He also played for Cheshire. Chairman of the Cunard shipping line, he placed the order for the QE2.

Brocklebank, Sir Thomas Aubrey Lawies
Amateur. *b:* 23.10.1899, Chelsea, London. *d:* 15.9.1953, Bathafarn Hall, Ruthin, Denbighshire. Brother of J. M. (Lancashire), nephew of F. S. Jackson (Yorkshire). Middle order batsman. *Sch* Eton. *Team* Cambridge U (1919).
Career batting
2–4–2–42–37*–21.00–0–*ct* 2
His County cricket was for Cheshire (1921).

Brocklehurst, Benjamin Gilbert
Amateur. *b:* 18.2.1922, Knapton, Norfolk. Father-in-law of R. A. Hutton (Yorkshire). Hard-hitting middle order right-hand batsman. *Sch* Bradfield. *Team* Somerset (1952–54, 64 matches).
Career batting
64–116–9–1671–89–15.61–0–*ct* 26
Bowling 36–1–36.00–0–0–1/9
He was Captain of Somerset 1953–54. He also played for Berkshire (1955). He is Managing Director and Proprietor of *The Cricketer* Magazine.

Brockwell, George
Professional. *b:* 14.8.1809, Kingston-upon-Thames, Surrey. *d:* 12.12.1876, Hackney, London. Uncle of William (Surrey). Very hard-hitting lower order left-hand batsman, left-hand slow round-arm bowler. *Team* Surrey (1844–57, 34 matches).
Career batting
44–77–7–790–57–11.28–0–*ct* 17
Bowling 208–9 + 77–23.11–2–1–7/?
When bowling he had a very curious delivery, striking himself on the chest just before the ball left his hand. In wet weather this left a large round mark in the centre of his shirt. He was employed at the Oval from the opening of the ground in 1845 to 1862, when he was retired on half-pay.

Brockwell, William
Professional. *b:* 21.1.1865, Kingston-upon-Thames, Surrey. *d:* 30.6.1935, Richmond, Surrey. Nephew of George (Surrey). Stylish opening right-hand batsman, right-arm fast medium bowler, good slip field. *Teams* Surrey (1886–1903, 314 matches); Kimberley (1889/90); London County (1901–03). *Tours* Read to South Africa 1891/2 (no first-class matches); Stoddart to Australia 1894/5. *Tests* England (1893–99, 7 matches).
Career batting
357–539–47–13285–225–27.00–21–*ct* 250–*st* 1
Bowling 13680–553–24.73–24–1–8/22
Test batting
7–12–0–202–49–16.83–0–*ct* 6
Bowling 309–5–61.80–0–0–3/33

He exceeded 1,000 runs in a season 6 times, his highest aggregate being 1,686, av 38.31, in 1898, but his best being 1,491, av 38.23, in 1894, when he headed the first-class averages, that season being a very difficult one for batsmen. His highest score was 225 for Surrey v Hampshire at the Oval in 1897. His single visit to Australia was not very successful. In 1899 he took 105 wickets, av 25.26, his best season with the ball, and he completed the double that year. He fell on hard times after leaving first-class cricket and died in abject poverty.

Broderick, Vincent
Professional. *b:* 17.8.1920, Bacup, Lancashire. Opening/middle order left-hand batsman, slow left-arm bowler. *Team* Northamptonshire (1939–57, 245 matches).
Career batting
253–384–44–7530–190–22.14–6–*ct* 65
Bowling 15007–548–27.38–23–4–9/35

He performed the 'double' in 1948 (1,066 runs, av 26.65, and 100 wickets, av 22.77); he also exceeded 1,000 runs in one other season. His best bowling was 9/35 for Northamptonshire v Sussex at Horsham in 1948.

Brodhurst, Arthur Hugh
Amateur. *b:* 21.7.1916, Buenos Aires, Argentina. Son-in-law of H. S. Altham (Surrey and Hampshire), brother-in-law of R. J. L. Altham (Oxford U). Middle order right-hand batsman, off break bowler, excellent field. *Sch* Malvern. *Teams* Cambridge U (1937–39, blue 1939); Gloucestershire (1939–46, 6 matches). *Tours* Oxford and Cambridge Universities to Jamaica 1938/9; MCC to Canada 1951.
Career batting
20–33–2–658–111–21.22–2–*ct* 8
Bowling 321–6–53.50–0–0–4/83

Brodhurst, Bernard Maynard Lucas
Amateur. *b:* 6.8.1873, Benares, India. *d:* 27.4.1915. He was killed in action near Canadian Farm, St Juliens, Ypres, Belgium. Lower order right-hand batsman, right-arm fast medium bowler. *Sch* Clifton. *Team* Hampshire (1897, 1 match).
Career batting
1–1–0–9–9–9.00–0–*ct* 1
Bowling 23–0

Brodie, James Bruce
Amateur. *b:* 19.3.1937, Graaff-Reinet, Cape Province, South Africa. Lower order right-hand batsman, right-arm fast medium bowler. *Teams* Cambridge U (1959–60, blue 1960); Eastern Province (1961/2 to 1963/4).
Career batting
22–36–11–305–37–12.20–0–*ct* 7
Bowling 1743–48–36.31–2–0–5/47

He appeared for Berkshire with considerable success in 1960.

Brodie, James Lothian
Amateur. *b:* 17.10.1893, Glasgow, Scotland. *d:* 2.7.1939, Newlands, Glasgow, Scotland. Middle order right-hand batsman. *Team* Scotland (1924–25).
Career batting
3–5–0–57–20–11.40–0–*ct* 0

Brodrick, Peter Dawson
Amateur. *b:* 11.5.1937, North Shields, Northumberland. Lower order right-hand batsman, slow left-arm bowler. *Sch* Newcastle GS. *Team* Cambridge U (1959–61, blue 1961).
Career batting
22–34–11–321–49–13.95–0–*ct* 7
Bowling 1927–44–43.79–0–0–4/74

His County cricket was for Northumberland (1956–68).

Bromfield, Harry Dudley
Amateur. *b:* 26.6.1932, Mossel Bay, Cape Province, South Africa. Lower order right-hand batsman, off break bowler. *Team* Western Province (1956/7 to 1968/9). *Tour* South Africa to England 1965. *Tests* South Africa (1961/2 to 1965, 9 matches).
Career batting
62–91–32–374–44–6.33–0–*ct* 68
Bowling 5256–205–25.63–13–1–7/60
Test batting
9–12–7–59–21–11.80–0–*ct* 13
Bowling 599–17–35.23–1–0–5/88

On his single visit to England he failed to do himself justice and appeared in only one Test, with little success.

Bromley, Ernest Harvey
Amateur. *b:* 2.9.1912, Fremantle, Perth, Western Australia. *d:* 1.2.1967, Clayton, Melbourne, Victoria, Australia. Nephew of O. H. Kelly (Western Australia) and W. H. Kelly (Western Australia). Middle order left-hand batsman, slow left-arm bowler, brilliant field. *Teams* Western Australia (1929/30 to 1931/2, 6 matches); Victoria (1932/3 to 1938/9, 22 matches);

Europeans (1936/7). *Tour* Australia to England 1934. *Tests* Australia (1932/3 to 1934, 2 matches).
Career batting
52–78–6–2055–161–28.54–3–*ct* 43
Bowling 1651–39–42.33–0–0–4/50
Test batting
2–4–0–38–26–9.50–0–*ct* 2
Bowling 19–0

Although he appeared in one of the Tests on his single tour to England, he had few days of success during the visit, save that his fielding was always a great asset to the team.

Bromley, Philip Harry
Professional. *b:* 30.7.1930, Stratford-on-Avon, Warwickshire. Middle order right-hand batsman, off break bowler. *Sch* Warwick. *Team* Warwickshire (1947–56, 49 matches).
Career batting
49–66–11–1183–121*–21.50–1–*ct* 37
Bowling 1264–35–36.11–1–0–5/61

Bromley, Richard Charles
Cricketer. *b:* 23.6.1946, Oxted, Surrey. Middle order left-hand batsman, wicket-keeper. *Team* Cambridge U (1970, blue).
Career batting
5–9–0–78–18–8.66–0–*ct* 6

Bromley-Davenport, Hugh Richard
Amateur. *b:* 18.8.1870, Capesthorne Hall, Chelford, Cheshire. *d:* 23.5.1954, South Kensington, London. Brother-in-law of J. R. Head (Middlesex). Lower order right-hand batsman, left-arm fast bowler, slip field. *Sch* Eton. *Teams* Cambridge U (1892–93, blue both years); Middlesex (1896–98, 28 matches). *Tours* Lucas to West Indies 1894/5; Hawke to West Indies 1896/7; Hawke to South Africa 1895/6, 1898/9. *Tests* England (1895/6 to 1898/9, 4 matches).
Career batting
76–119–21–1801–91–18.37–0–*ct* 48
Bowling 3352–187–17.92–12–1–7/17
Test batting
4–6–0–128–84–21.33–0–*ct* 1
Bowling 98–4–24.50–0–0–2/46

He was one of the few players of his era to play cricket wearing glasses. His most successful cricket was on his two visits to the West Indies, when he headed the bowling averages each time. From 1886 to 1895 he appeared for Cheshire. His final first-class match was for A. J. Webbe's XI in 1899. His brother William played soccer for England.

Bromley-Martin, Eliot George
Amateur. *b:* 2.10.1866, St Cloud, Callow End, Worcester. *d:* 23.1.1946, Downton, Walton, Radnorshire. Brother of G. E. (Worcestershire), uncle of D. D. E. Holland-Martin (Royal Navy). Lower order right-hand batsman, right-arm slow bowler. *Sch* Eton. *Team* Worcestershire (1899–1900, 10 matches).
Career batting
12–17–1–257–42–16.06–0–*ct* 2
Bowling 274–10–27.40–0–0–4/33

Whilst at Oxford he appeared in various trials, but no first-class matches. He did, however, win his soccer blue in 1888. Most of his County cricket for Worcestershire was played before that side was in the County Championship. He acted as Hon Sec to the County Club in the 1890s.

Bromley-Martin, Granville Edward
Amateur. *b:* 18.10.1875, St Cloud, Callow End, Worcester. *d:* 31.5.1941, Streat Place, Streat, Sussex. Brother of E. G. (Worcestershire), uncle of D. D. E. Holland-Martin (Royal Navy). Middle order right-hand batsman, slow right-arm bowler. *Sch* Eton. *Teams* Oxford U (1897–98, blue both years); Worcestershire (1899–1904, 32 matches).
Career batting
48–83–1–1779–137–21.69–2–*ct* 21
Bowling 93–1–93.00–0–0–1/11

He was also an excellent fives player. He first appeared for Worcestershire (pre first-class) in 1891.

Brook, Arthur John
Amateur. *b:* 18.9.1844, Bexhill, Sussex. *d:* 19.12.1917, Sidley, Bexhill, Sussex. Middle order batsman. *Team* Sussex (1873, 1 match).
Career batting
1–1–0–10–10–10.00–0–*ct* 0

Brook, George Wilfred
Professional. *b:* 30.8.1888, Mirfield, Yorkshire. *d:* 24.7.1966, Bournemouth, Hampshire. Lower order right-hand batsman, slow left-arm bowler. *Team* Worcestershire (1930–35, 150 matches).
Career batting
150–218–17–1877–56–9.33–0–*ct* 77
Bowling 12841–461–27.85–23–4–7/50

He enjoyed great success in his initial County Championship season of 1930 taking 132 wickets (av 21.88) at the age of 41.

Brook, James William
Professional. *b:* 1.2.1897, Ossett, Yorkshire. *d:* 3.3.1989, Selby, Yorkshire. Middle order right-hand batsman, right-arm medium pace bowler. *Team* Yorkshire (1923, 1 match).
Career batting
1–1–0–0–0–0.00–0–*ct* 0

His obituary incorrectly appeared in Wisden 1988.

Brooke, Vice Admiral Basil Charles Barrington
Amateur. *b:* 6.4.1895, Boddington, Northamptonshire. *d:* 20.1.1983, Saffron Walden, Essex. Grandson of John Brooke, the Rajah of Sarawak, son-in-law of C. Toppin (Cambridge U), brother-in-law of C. G. Toppin (Worcestershire) and J. F. T. Toppin (Worcestershire). Middle order batsman, bowler. *Sch* Malvern. *Team* Royal Navy (1919–26)

Brooke, Bernard

Career batting
2–4–0–61–28–15.25–0–*ct* 3
Bowling 59–3–19.66–0–0–2/48

Brooke, Bernard
Professional. *b:* 3.3.1930, Newsome, Huddersfield, Yorkshire. Tail end right-hand batsman, right-arm medium fast bowler. *Team* Yorkshire (1950, 2 matches).
Career batting
2–4–0–16–14–4.00–0–*ct* 0
Bowling 191–2–95.50–0–0–1/64

Brooke, Francis Ralph Russell
Amateur. *b:* 2.10.1884, Bowdon, Cheshire. *d:* 20.6.1960, Greywell Manor, Basingstoke, Hampshire. Brother-in-law of George Mallory, the well-known mountaineer lost on Mount Everest in 1924. Middle/lower order hard-hitting right-hand batsman, wicket-keeper. *Sch* Harrow. *Teams* Lancashire (1912–13, 29 matches); Europeans (1910/11 to 1926/7); Ceylon (1925/6 to 1926/7).
Career batting
62–92–6–2197–115–25.54–2–*ct* 85–*st* 21
Bowling 9–1–9.00–0–0–1/9

Owing to his military career he played little County cricket, but was one of the mainstays of the Army team, his final first-class match being for the Army in 1929.

Brooke, Rev Richard Hubert John
Amateur. *b:* 6.6.1909, Eton, Buckinghamshire. *d:* 3.5.1973, Great Canfield, Essex. Opening right-hand batsman, right-arm medium pace bowler. *Sch* St Edward's, Oxford. *Teams* Oxford U (1931–32, blue 1931); Gloucestershire (1931, 1 match). *Tour* Martineau to Egypt 1933 (not first-class).
Career batting
18–29–3–1043–140–40.11–5–*ct* 14
Bowling 331–14–23.64–0–0–3/7

He played with success for Buckinghamshire (1929–35) and his final first-class match was for Minor Counties in 1935.

Brooker, Mervyn Edward William
Cricketer. *b:* 24.3.1954, Burton-on-Trent, Staffordshire. Lower order right-hand batsman, right-arm medium pace bowler. *Sch* Lancaster RGS. *Team* Cambridge U (1974–76, blue 1976).
Career batting
15–28–15–43–9–3.30–0–*ct* 3
Bowling 1149–25–45.96–0–0–4/58

His County cricket was for Cambridgeshire (1976–80) and Staffordshire (1982–86).

Brookes, Dennis
Professional. *b:* 29.10.1915, Kippax, Leeds, Yorkshire. Sound stylish opening right-hand batsman, right-arm medium pace bowler. *Team* Northamptonshire (1934–59, 492 matches). *Tour* MCC to West Indies 1947/8. *Test* England (1947/8, 1 match).
Career batting
525–925–70–30874–257–36.10–71–*ct* 205
Bowling 127–3–42.33–0–0–1/7
Test batting
1–2–0–17–10–8.50–0–*ct* 1

He hit 1,000 runs in a season 17 times, exceeding 2,000 on six occasions (best 2,229, av 47.42, in 1952). His highest score was 257 for Northamptonshire v Gloucestershire at Bristol in 1949 and he made five other double centuries, all for Northamptonshire. On his only MCC tour overseas he was unlucky to be injured and return home early. He was captain of Northamptonshire 1954–57, coach 1961–73 and President 1982–85.

Brooke-Short, Cecil
Amateur. *b:* 1894. *d:* 28.6.1937, Wei-Hai-Wei, China. Lower order batsman. *Team* Royal Navy (1925).
Career batting
1–2–1–4–3*–4.00–0–*ct* 0

Brooke-Taylor, David Charles
Amateur. *b:* 15.6.1920, Bakewell, Derbyshire. Nephew of G. P. (Derbyshire). Middle order right-hand batsman. *Sch* Cheltenham. *Team* Derbyshire (1947–49, 15 matches).
Career batting
15–26–1–375–61*–15.00–0–*ct* 6

Brooke-Taylor, Geoffrey Parker
Amateur. *b:* 25.10.1895, Bakewell, Derbyshire. *d:* 13.1.1968, Hurlingham, Buenos Aires, Argentina. Uncle of D. C. (Derbyshire). Middle order left-hand batsman, wicket-keeper. *Sch* Cheltenham. *Teams* Cambridge U (1919–20, blue both years); Derbyshire (1920, 1 match); Argentine (1926/7 to 1929/30).
Career batting
25–40–1–778–84–19.94–0–*ct* 13–*st* 3

He played in the North v South match in Argentina.

Brooks, Abraham Worthington
Professional. *b:* 1853. *d:* 7.5.1925, Breighmet Fold, Bolton, Lancashire. Tail end batsman, wicket-keeper. *Team* Lancashire (1877, 1 match).
Career batting
1–1–0–6–6–6.00–0–*ct* 2

Brooks, Alfred James
Professional. *b:* 24.3.1846, Sutton-in-Ashfield, Nottinghamshire. *d:* 20.11.1911, Sutton-in-Ashfield, Nottinghamshire. Lower order right-hand batsman, right-arm fast medium bowler, cover field. *Team* Nottinghamshire (1877, 2 matches).
Career batting
2–4–1–10–6–3.33–0–*ct* 0
Bowling 85–5–17.00–0–0–2/10

He also played for Dorset (1873–74) and Somerset (pre first-class, 1880).

Brooks, Edward William John
Professional. *b:* 6.7.1898, Camberwell, London. *d:* 10.2.1960, Rustington, Sussex. Lower order right-hand batsman, occasional right-arm medium pace bowler, wicket-keeper. *Team* Surrey (1925–39, 354 matches).
Career batting
359–442–98–4497–70–13.07–0–*ct* 725–*st* 96
Bowling 6–0

Brooks, J.
Professional. Tail end batsman, medium pace bowler. *Team* Gloucestershire (1892, 1 match).
Career batting
1–2–0–0–0–0.00–0–*ct* 1
Bowling 31–1–31.00–0–0–1/31

Brooks, Joseph
Professional. *b:* 10.9.1870, South Normanton, Derbyshire. *d:* 15.5.1937, Shuttlewood, Derbyshire. Tail end batsman, left-arm fast-medium bowler. *Team* Derbyshire (1895–96, 5 matches).
Career batting
5–7–4–8–6–2.66–0–*ct* 1
Bowling 190–2–95.00–0–0–1/22

Brooks, Kevin Graham
Cricketer. *b:* 15.10.1959, Caversham, Reading, Berkshire. Lower order right-hand batsman, right-arm medium pace bowler. *Team* Derbyshire (1980, 1 match).
Career batting
1–2–0–11–8–5.50–0–*ct* 2
He also played for Lincolnshire (1983) and Suffolk (1986–87). He is the nephew of Johnny Brooks, the Tottenham Hotspur and England footballer.

Brooks, Paul Wilson
Professional. *b:* 28.5.1921, Marylebone, London., *d:* 26.1.1946, Paddington, London, as a result of wounds received whilst on active service in Italy. Middle order left-hand batsman, left-arm fast medium bowler. *Team* Middlesex (1939, 1 match).
Career batting
1–1–1–44–44*–no av–0–*ct* 0

Brooks, Gen Sir Reginald Alexander Dallas
(also known as R. A. Dallas-Brooks)
Amateur. *b:* 2.8.1896, Cambridge. *d:* 22.3.1966, Frankston, Victoria, Australia. Middle order right-hand batsman, right-arm medium pace bowler. *Sch* Dover. *Team* Hampshire (1919–21, 9 matches).
Career batting
29–53–1–1070–143–20.57–2–*ct* 15
Bowling 1092–38–28.73–1–0–8/90
His final first-class match was for Combined Services in 1931. A prominent sportsman, he captained the Royal Navy at golf and at hockey, also representing England in the latter. From 1949 to 1963 he was Governor of Victoria.

Brooks, Richard
(generally known as R. B. Brooks, but he had only one Christian name)
Amateur. *b:* 29.7.1863, Sutton-on-Sea, Lincolnshire. *d:* 9.4.1927, Kensington, London. Lower order right-hand batsman, wicket-keeper. *Sch* Cranleigh. *Teams* Surrey (1889, 1 match); London County (1900–03).
Career batting
7–8–1–56–18*–8.00–0–*ct* 8–*st* 12
He was regarded as one of the best wicket-keepers of his day, but owing to his profession of solicitor could not afford the time for County cricket. He appeared mainly in London Club matches for the Wanderers CC.

Brooks, Richard Alan
Cricketer. *b:* 14.6.1943, Edgware, Middlesex. Lower order right-hand batsman, wicket-keeper. *Teams* Oxford U (1967, blue); Somerset (1968, 26 matches).
Career batting
35–45–16–317–44–10.93–0–*ct* 53–*st* 7
After one full season with Somerset, Brooks took up a teaching post at Bradfield College, which ended his first-class career. He also played for Berkshire (1977).

Brooks, Ronald Clifton
Amateur. *b:* 3.3.1899, East Molesey, Surrey. *d:* 14.8.1980, Chelsea, London. Son-in-law of M. W. Payne (Middlesex). Lower order right-hand batsman, wicket-keeper. *Sch* Haileybury. *Team* Cambridge U (1919).
Career batting
5–6–2–99–27–24.75–0–*ct* 1–*st* 2
His final first-class match was for Free Foresters in 1929.

Brooks, Victor Charles George
Cricketer. *b:* 29.6.1948, East Ham, Essex. Middle order left–hand batsman. *Team* Essex (1970–71, 3 matches).
Career batting
3–5–0–53–22–10.60–0–*ct* 1

Brooks, Walter Tyrrell
Amateur. *b:* 23.2.1884, Kensington, London. *d:* 3.6.1965, Tunbridge Wells, Kent. Son-in-law of J. N. Tonge (Kent). Lower order batsman, bowler. *Sch* Marlborough. *Team* Leveson-Gower's XI (1906).
Career batting
1–2–1–14–13*–14.00–0–*ct* 0
Bowling 47–2–23.50–0–0–1/9
His County cricket was for Oxfordshire (1902–24).

Broome, Ian
Cricketer. *b:* 6.5.1960, Bradenstoke-cum-Clack, Wiltshire. Tail end right-hand batsman, right-arm fast medium bowler. *Team* Derbyshire (1984, 2 matches).
Career batting
2–4–3–35–26*–35.00–0–*ct* 1

Bowling 82–2–41.00–0–0–1/17

He appeared for Gloucestershire in a Sunday League match in 1980.

Brophy, James Noel

Amateur. *b:* 8.1.1912, Cork, Ireland. Lower order right-hand batsman, wicket-keeper. *Team* Ireland (1938).

Career batting

1–2–0–13–9–6.50–0–*ct* 0

Brotherhood, Rowland

Amateur. *b:* 18.11.1841, Brinkworth, Wiltshire. *d:* 4.3.1883, Redland, Bristol, Gloucestershire. Lower order left-hand batsman, left-hand fast under-arm bowler, good deep field. *Sch* King's College, Wimbledon. *Team* Gloucestershire (1875, 3 matches).

Career batting

3–6–2–3–2–0.75–0–*ct* 1

Bowling 67–2–33.50–0–0–2/49

From 1869 to 1874 he was residing in South America. He belonged to a family of eleven brothers and on several occasions the eleven played as a team.

Brougham, Henry

Amateur. *b:* 8.7.1888, Wellington College, Berkshire. *d:* 18.2.1923, La Croix, Var, France. Brother-in-law of J. H. Bruce-Lockhart (Cambridge U), uncle of R. B. Bruce-Lockhart (Cambridge U), his widow married T. C. Fitzherbert (Trinidad). Opening/middle order right-hand batsman, brilliant field. *Sch* Wellington. *Team* Oxford U (1911, blue).

Career batting

5–9–0–214–84–23.77–0–*ct* 1

His County cricket was for Berkshire (1905–14). A noted rugby footballer, he appeared for Harlequins and England. He represented Oxford at rackets in 1908 and 1909. Invalided out of the Army in 1917, he died in 1923 after five years illness. His final first-class match was for Minor Counties in 1912.

Broughton, Ernest Alfred

Amateur. *b:* 22.4.1905, Wigston, Leicestershire. *d:* 19.2.1982, Wigston, Leicestershire. Middle order right-hand batsman, off break bowler. *Sch* Wyggeston GS. *Team* Leicestershire (1928–33, 25 matches).

Career batting

25–38–1–482–61–13.02–0–*ct* 12

Bowling 18–0

He was Treasurer of Leicestershire 1974–80.

Broughton, John Jarvis

Professional. *b:* 8.9.1873, Grantham, Lincolnshire. *d:* 3.4.1952, Orrell, Billinge, Lancashire. Middle order right-hand batsman. *Team* Lancashire (1901–02, 6 matches).

Career batting

6–7–0–153–99–21.85–0–*ct* 3

Bowling 69–2–34.50–0–0–2/28

He had the unusual distinction of scoring 99 on his Championship debut – Lancashire v Essex 1901. He also played for Lincolnshire (1907–14).

Broughton, Peter Norman

Professional. *b:* 22.10.1935, Castleford, Yorkshire. Tail end right-hand batsman, right-arm fast medium bowler. *Teams* Yorkshire (1956, 6 matches); Leicestershire (1960–62, 24 matches).

Career batting

30–33–17–162–17*–10.12–0–*ct* 12

Bowling 2430–85–28.58–5–0–6/38

He also played for Cumberland (1963–69).

Broughton, Robert John Porcher

Amateur. *b:* 11.7.1816, Farnham, Surrey. *d:* 15.6.1911, Callipers Hall, Chipperfield, Hertfordshire. Grandfather of J. N. Cowley (Free Foresters). Hard-hitting middle order batsman, round-arm slow bowler, excellent cover field. *Sch* Harrow. *Teams* Cambridge U (1836–39, blue 1836, 1838 and 1839.). Cambridge Town Club (1838).

Career batting

26–49–6–523–40–12.15–0–*ct* 5

Bowling 2 wickets (no analyses)–0–0–1/?

His final first-class match was for MCC in 1864.

Brown, Adrian Desmond

Cricketer. *b:* 18.5.1962, Clacton-on-Sea, Essex. Lower order right-hand batsman, wicket-keeper. *Team* Cambridge U (1986, blue); Essex (1988–92, 5 matches).

Career batting

14–16–4–99–30–8.25–0–*ct* 28–*st* 5

He also played for Suffolk (1984–91). He reappeared in emergency for Essex in 1992, having left the staff in 1988.

Brown, Alan

Professional. *b:* 17.10.1935, Rainworth, Nottinghamshire. Lower order right-hand batsman, right-arm fast medium bowler. *Team* Kent (1957–70, 237 matches). *Tour* MCC to India, Pakistan and Ceylon 1961/2. *Tests* England (1961/2, 2 matches).

Career batting

251–312–87–2189–81–9.72–0–*ct* 104

Bowling 18326–743–24.66–26–4–8/47

Test batting

2–1–1–3–3*–no av–0–*ct* 1

Bowling 150–3–50.00–0–0–3/27

He took 100 wickets in a season once – 116, av 19.04, in 1965. Also a useful soccer player, he appeared for Gravesend at centre forward.

Brown, Alan

Cricketer. *b:* 23.12.1957, Darwen, Lancashire. Lower order right-hand batsman, wicket-keeper. *Team* Worcestershire (1979, 1 match).

Career batting

1 match, did not bat–*ct* 2

Brown, Albert
Amateur. *b:* 10.7.1911, Aston, Birmingham. Lower order right-hand batsman, right-arm fast medium bowler. *Team* Warwickshire (1932, 1 match).
Career batting
1–1–1–1–1*–no av–0–*ct* 1
Bowling 96–2–48.00–0–0–2/96

He was a well-known snooker and billiards player.

Brown, Alexander
Cricketer. *b:* 7.10.1950, Coatbridge, Lanark, Scotland. Opening or middle order right-hand batsman, wicket-keeper. *Team* Scotland (1977–87).
Career batting
9–13–0–256–74–19.69–0–*ct* 13–*st* 3

Brown, Alfred
Professional. *b:* 10.6.1854, Old Malton, Yorkshire. *d:* 2.11.1900, Malton, Yorkshire. Opening right-hand batsman, right-hand fast round-arm bowler, good field. *Team* Yorkshire (1872, 2 matches).
Career batting
2–3–0–9–5–3.00–0–*ct* 4
Bowling 47–3–15.66–0–0–2/17

Brown, Alistair Duncan
Cricketer. *b:* 11.2.1970, Beckenham, Kent. Middle order right-hand batsman, leg break bowler, occasional wicket-keeper. *Sch* Caterham. *Team* Surrey (1992, 11 matches).
Career batting
11–16–1–740–175–49.33–3–*ct* 6
Bowling 78–0

Brown, Andrew John Trevor
Amateur. *b:* 27.6.1935, Haymarket, Edinburgh, Scotland. Middle order left-hand batsman, off break bowler. *Sch* Sherborne. *Team* Combined Services (1960).
Career batting
2–4–1–41–40*–13.66–0–*ct* 1

Brown, Andrew Mark
Cricketer. *b:* 6.11.1964, Heanor, Derbyshire. Opening left-hand batsman, off break bowler. *Team* Derbyshire (1985–92, 22 matches).
Career batting
22–31–3–815–139*–29.10–1–*ct* 19
Bowling 9–0

Brown, Anthony Stephen
Professional. *b:* 24.6.1936, Clifton, Bristol, Gloucestershire. Middle/lower order right-hand batsman, right-arm medium fast bowler, excellent close field. *Team* Gloucestershire (1953–76, 489 matches). *Tours* Robins to South Africa 1972/3; International XI to South Africa 1974/5.
Career batting
496–808–99–12851–116–18.12–3–*ct* 494
Bowling 31546–1230–25.64–54–8–8/80

He exceeded 1,000 runs in a season once (1,149, av 20.15, in 1964) and 100 wickets twice (best 110, av 23.08, in 1959).

For Gloucestershire v Nottinghamshire at Trent Bridge in 1966, he held 7 catches in one innings, equalling the world first-class record. He was captain of Gloucestershire 1969–76 and on retirement was appointed secretary-manager of Gloucestershire 1977–82, moving to Somerset in a similar position 1983–88. Since 1988 he has been Administration Secretary of TCCB.

Brown, Air Vice Marshal Cecil Leonard Morley
Amateur. *b:* 16.7.1895, Melton Mowbray, Leicestershire. *d:* 6.12.1955, Crowthorne, Berkshire. Middle order right-hand batsman, right-arm medium pace bowler. *Sch* Worksop. *Team* Leicestershire (1920–21, 7 matches).
Career batting
7–11–0–74–33–6.72–0–*ct* 1

Brown, Charles
Professional. *b:* 22.1.1815, Nottingham. *d:* 28.9.1875, Nottingham. Middle order right-hand batsman, occasional round-arm bowler, wicket-keeper. *Team* Nottinghamshire (1842–61, 25 matches).
Career batting
33–59–10–435–43*–8.87–0–*ct* 32–*st* 26
Bowling 92–6 + 3–15.33–0–0–4/27

He was regarded as one of the leading wicket-keepers of his day and played for the England team v Kent in 1844, 1848 and 1849. He could bowl 'behind his back' i.e. putting his right-arm behind his back and delivering from his left side and in minor matches was quite successful with this strange delivery. He also played for Oxfordshire (1849).

Brown, Charles Atherton
Amateur. *b:* 8.6.1854, Sydney, New South Wales, Australia. *d:* 8.7.1917, Grendon Hill, Warwickshire. Tail end right-hand batsman, left-hand fast round-arm bowler. *Sch* Highgate. *Team* Sussex (1876–78, 11 matches).
Career batting
11–20–5–137–26–9.13–0–*ct* 10
Bowling 575–25–23.00–2–0–7/58

Brown, Colin Edwin
Amateur. *b:* 12.10.1878, North Curry, Taunton, Somerset. *d:* 25.6.1936, Whitby, Yorkshire. Middle order batsman, change bowler. *Team* Somerset (1902–05, 8 matches).
Career batting
8–15–3–151–53–12.58–0–*ct* 6
Bowling 15–0

Brown, David
Amateur. *b:* 29.7.1900, Dunfermline, Fife, Scotland. *d:* 30.1.1951, Dunfermline, Fife, Scotland. Middle order right-hand batsman, right-arm medium pace

bowler. *Team* Scotland (1927–30).
Career batting
2–3–0–21–13–7.00–0–*ct* 1
Bowling 43–1–43.00–0–0–1/10

Brown, David Basil Stuart
Cricketer. *b:* 14.6.1941, Insch, Aberdeenshire, Scotland. Opening left-hand batsman. *Team* Scotland (1973–76).
Career batting
3–6–0–115–58–19.16–0–*ct* 2

Brown, David John
Professional, *b:* 30.1.1942, Walsall, Staffordshire. Lower order right-hand batsman, right-arm fast medium bowler. *Team* Warwickshire (1961–82, 326 matches). *Tours* MCC to South Africa 1964/5, to Australia and New Zealand 1965/6, to West Indies 1967/8, to Ceylon and Pakistan 1968/9; MCC Under 25 to Pakistan 1966/7; Rest of World to Pakistan 1970/1; Robins to South Africa 1972/3. *Tests* England (1965–69, 26 matches).
Career batting
390–446–111–4110–79–12.26–0–*ct* 157
Bowling 28961–1165–24.85–46–5–8/60
Test batting
26–34–5–342–44*–11.79–0–*ct* 7
Bowling 2237–79–28.31–2–0–5/42

He captained Warwickshire from 1975–77 and was manager of the County 1980–87. He appeared in one match in 1982 in emergency.

Brown, David Wyndham James
Cricketer. *b:* 26.2.1942, Sandfields, Cheltenham, Gloucestershire. Middle order right-hand batsman, off break bowler. *Team* Gloucestershire (1964–67, 88 matches).
Career batting
89–153–11–2863–142–20.16–1–*ct* 37
Bowling 84–3–28.00–0–0–3/84

Brown, Douglas Robert
Cricketer. *b:* 29.10.1969, Stirling, Scotland. Lower order right-hand batsman, right-arm fast medium bowler. *Teams* Scotland (1989); Warwickshire (1991/2 to 1992, 2 matches). *Tour* Warwickshire to South Africa 1991/2.
Career batting
3–3–2–54–44*–54.00–0–*ct* 2
Bowling 204–8–25.50–0–0–3/27

Brown, Edward
Professional. *b:* 27.11.1911, Newcastle upon Tyne, Northumberland. *d:* 14.4.1978, Birmingham. Lower order right-hand batsman, right-arm medium fast bowler. *Team* Warwickshire (1932–34, 28 matches).
Career batting
28–29–9–134–19*–6.70–0–*ct* 10
Bowling 1877–56–33.51–3–0–8/35

He also played for Durham (pre first-class, 1929) and Northumberland (1936).

Brown, Frederick Richard, MBE
Amateur. *b:* 16.12.1910, Lima, Peru. *d:* 24.7.1991, Ramsbury, Wiltshire. Brother of Aline (England Women). Hard hitting middle order right-hand batsman, right-arm medium or leg break and googly bowler. *Sch* The Leys. *Teams* Cambridge U (1930–31, blue both years); Surrey (1931–48, 106 matches); Northamptonshire (1949–53, 102 matches). *Tours* MCC to Australia and New Zealand 1932/3, 1950/1; Martineau to Egypt 1934, 1936, 1939 (not first-class); MCC to South Africa 1956/7 (manager, but appeared in one match); MCC to East Africa 1957/8 (not first-class); Brown to East Africa 1961/2 (not first-class). *Tests* England (1931–53, 22 matches).
Career batting
335–536–49–13325–212–27.36–22–*ct* 212
Bowling 32007–1221–26.21–62–11–8/34
Test batting
22–30–1–734–79–25.31–0–*ct* 22
Bowling 1398–45–31.06–1–0–5/49

After a short but brilliant career at Cambridge, where he headed the batting averages as a Freshman, then in his only other season headed the bowling table, Brown made a tremendous impact in his first full season of County cricket by performing the 'double' and being selected to tour Australia with Jardine's 1932/33 team. His talents were scarcely required on this venture and afterwards his County cricket career seemed to be destined to follow the pattern of so many other amateurs – just appearing in a handful of first-class games each season. During the Second World War he was a POW for three years and afterwards very little was seen of him – in three seasons he made one solitary appearance in a Championship match for Surrey.

In 1949 however came his appointment as captain of Northamptonshire and overnight he was transformed back into the brilliant all-rounder of the early 1930s – he performed the 'double' for the second time in his career and was soon recalled to the England team, this time as captain. His leadership revitalised England on the 1950/51 tour to Australia, just as it had revitalised Northamptonshire. This second career lasted until 1953, when he retired from the Northamptonshire captaincy, but he went on appearing in occasional first-class matches until 1961 – his farewell match being for Free Foresters. He captained England in 15 Tests. He hit 1,000 runs in a season 4 times (best 1,135, av 32.42, in 1932), and took 100 wickets three times (best 120, av 20.46 in 1932), achieving the 'double' twice. His only double century was 212 for Surrey v Middlesex at the Oval in 1932.

He was a Test Selector from 1951 to 1953, being Chairman in the last year, President of MCC in 1971/2 and Chairman of the Cricket Council 1974–79. He was awarded the MBE for services to cricket.

Brown, Gary Kevin
Cricketer. *b:* 16.6.1965, Welling, Kent. Brother of K. R. (Middlesex). Middle order right-hand batsman, off break bowler. *Teams* Middlesex (1986, 1 match); Durham (1992, 4 matches).
Career batting
6–10–1–345–103–38.33–1–*ct* 5
Bowling 103–1–103.00–0–0–1/39

He first played for Durham (pre first-class) in 1988, and played for Minor Counties in 1990.

Brown, George
Professional. *b:* 27.4.1783, Stoughton, Sussex. *d:* 25.6.1857, Sompting, Sussex. Father of G. G. (Sussex) and John (Hampshire). Hard hitting right-hand batsman, very fast under-arm bowler. *Teams* Hampshire (1819–23); Sussex (1825–38, 32 matches).
Career batting
51–96–4–1053–70–11.44–0–*ct* 51
Bowling 68–6 + 83–11.33–5–1–6/?

He was rated as the fastest of bowlers, placing nearly all his fieldsmen behind the wicket and his wicket-keeper, Dench, had a sack stuffed with straw fastened to his chest for protection. He was the father of no fewer than 17 children.

Brown, George
Professional. *b:* 6.10.1887, Cowley, Oxfordshire. *d:* 3.12.1964, Winchester, Hampshire. Opening or middle order left-hand batsman, right-arm medium pace bowler, wicket-keeper/brilliant close field. *Team* Hampshire (1908–33, 539 matches). *Tours* MCC to West Indies 1910/11, to South Africa 1922/3, to India, Burma and Ceylon 1926/7; Tennyson to Jamaica 1931/2. *Tests* England (1921 to 1922/3, 7 matches).
Career batting
612–1012–52–25649–232*–26.71–37–*ct* 568–*st* 78
Bowling 18666–626–29.81–23–2–8/55
Test batting
7–12–2–299–84–29.90–0–*ct* 9–*st* 3

In his day one of the most brilliant all-round cricketers ever seen, Brown's batting tended to be inconsistent as well as moving unpredictably from attack to dour defence. He could be given the wicket-keeper's job at a moment's notice and perform to Test match standard. He made 1,000 runs in a season 11 times, exceeding 2,000 once – 2,040 runs, av 40.00, in 1926. The highest of his three double-centuries was 232* for Hampshire v Yorkshire at Leeds in 1920. He was a first-class umpire (1935–36).

Brown, George Grainger
Professional. *b:* 16.6.1821, Brighton, Sussex. *d:* 21.3.1875, Battersea, London. Son of George (Sussex), brother of John (Hampshire). Steady middle order right-hand batsman, slow under-arm bowler, long-stop. *Team* Sussex (1851–58, 37 matches).
Career batting
46–78–10–898–86–13.20–0–*ct* 18
Bowling 508–35–14.51–3–0–5/25

Brown, George Rainy Reynolds
Amateur. *b:* 8.12.1905, Maldon, Essex. Lower order right-hand batsman, slow left-arm bowler. *Sch* Felsted. *Teams* Essex (1924–32, 23 matches); Cambridge U (1925); Europeans (1936/7 to 1945/6).
Career batting
29–46–12–396–38*–11.64–0–*ct* 15
Bowling 1358–46–29.52–1–0–5/55

Brown, Graham Elliott
Cricketer. *b:* 11.10.1966, Balham, London. Lower order right-hand batsman, wicket-keeper. *Team* Surrey (1986–88, 10 matches).
Career batting
10–11–8–59–13*–19.66–0–*ct* 19–*st* 2

Brown, H. W.
Amateur. Middle order batsman, useful bowler. *Team* Gloucestershire (1890–94, 16 matches).
Career batting
16–31–5–210–41–8.07–0–*ct* 4
Bowling 1023–36–28.41–1–0–6/155

Brown, James
Amateur. *b:* 7.2.1864, Gainford, Co Durham. *d:* December 1916, Copenhagen, Denmark. Middle order left-hand batsman, left-arm medium fast bowler, slip field. *Team* Sussex (1890, 2 matches).
Career batting
3–4–0–31–19–7.75–0–*ct* 0
Bowling 26–0

He also played for Durham (pre first-class, 1891–99). His final first-class match was for the South in 1896.

Brown, James, MBE
Amateur. *b:* 24.9.1931, Perth, Scotland. Middle order right-hand batsman, wicket-keeper. *Team* Scotland (1953–73).
Career batting
59–85–18–1306–90–19.49–0–*ct* 83–*st* 23

Brown, John
Professional. *b:* 1862, Bingham, Nottinghamshire. Brother of Thomas (Nottinghamshire). Middle order left-hand batsman, left-arm medium pace bowler. *Team* Nottinghamshire (1888, 3 matches).
Career batting
3–6–2–33–24–8.25–0–*ct* 1
Bowling 15–0

He also played for Staffordshire (1895).

Brown, John Dowell
Professional. *b:* 25.8.1890, Coventry, Warwickshire. *d:* 18.3.1968, Leamington, Warwickshire. Lower order left-hand batsman, slow left-arm bowler. *Team* Warwickshire (1913–14, 9 matches)

Brown, John Thomas

Career batting
9–12–5–12–7–1.71–0–*ct* 4
Bowling 264–9–29.33–0–0–4/18

Brown, John Thomas
Professional. *b:* 20.8.1869, Great Driffield, Yorkshire. *d:* 4.11.1904, Pimlico, Westminster, London. Opening right-hand batsman, leg break bowler, excellent field. *Team* Yorkshire (1889–1904, 346 matches). *Tour* Stoddart to Australia 1894/5. *Tests* England (1894/5 to 1899, 8 matches).
Career batting
383–634–47–17920–311–30.52–29–*ct* 230
Bowling 5627–190–29.61–4–0–6/52
Test batting
8–16–3–470–140–36.15–1–*ct* 7
Bowling 22–0

One of the greatest of Yorkshire's batsmen, Brown was the only one to hit two triple centuries for the County – 311 v Sussex at Bramall Lane in 1897 and 300 v Derbyshire at Chesterfield in 1898. During the latter innings he and Tunnicliffe created a new first-class record first wicket partnership of 554. His only other score over 200 was 203 v Middlesex at Lord's in 1896, in which match he and Tunnicliffe added 139 in the first innings and 147 without being parted in the second.

He scored over 1,000 runs in a season in 10 successive years (1894 to 1903) with 1,873, av 35.33, in 1896 best. He went to Australia in 1894/5 and hit his only Test hundred whilst there. His career was marred by ill-health. Though he made his first-class debut in 1889, it was not until 1893 that he did anything exceptional and then after a decade of run getting he was obliged to drop out of first-class cricket in May 1904 due to heart trouble, which initially was not regarded as serious, but he in fact never recovered, and died in November of the same year, aged only 35. His love of tobacco unfortunately did little to help his health, for apart from his heart condition he suffered with asthma.

Brown, John Thomas
Professional. *b:* 24.11.1874, Darfield, Yorkshire. *d:* 12.4.1950, Duckmanton, Derbyshire. Brother of William (Yorkshire). Tail end right-hand batsman, right-arm fast bowler. *Team* Yorkshire (1897–1903, 30 matches).
Career batting
30–32–3–333–37*–11.48–0–*ct* 18
Bowling 2071–97–21.35–8–2–8/40

Regarded as one of the fastest bowlers of his time, his career ended suddenly when he dislocated his shoulder.

Brown, Joseph Henry
Professional. *b:* 26.1.1872, Earl Shilton, Leicestershire. *d:* 27.4.1915, Earl Shilton, Leicestershire. Brother of Lewis (Leicestershire). Middle order right-hand batsman, off break bowler. *Team* Leicestershire (1898–1905, 15 matches).
Career batting
15–28–3–305–53*–12.20–0–*ct* 16
Bowling 325–7–46.42–0–0–2/6

Brown, Keith Robert
Cricketer. *b:* 18.3.1963, Edmonton, Middlesex. Brother of G. K. (Middlesex and Durham). Middle order right-hand batsman, right-arm slow medium bowler, wicket-keeper. *Team* Middlesex (1984–92, 136 matches).
Career batting
136–212–36–6059–200*–34.42–10–*ct* 180–*st* 11
Bowling 162–5–32.40–0–0–2/7

He scored 1,000 runs in a season twice (best 1,505, av 53,75, in 1990). His highest score was 200* for Middlesex v Nottinghamshire at Lord's in 1990.

Brown, Lewis
Professional. *b:* 12.3.1874, Earl Shilton, Leicestershire. *d:* 14.10.1951, Earl Shilton, Leicestershire. Brother of J. H. (Leicestershire). Opening right-hand batsman, right-arm medium pace bowler. *Team* Leicestershire (1896–1903, 62 matches).
Career batting
62–110–7–1660–110–16.11–1–*ct* 23
Bowling 385–7–55.00–0–0–3/39

Brown, Rev Lionel George
Amateur. *b:* 23.4.1872, Ancaster, Lincolnshire. *d:* 16.12.1938, Chapel, Chorlton, Staffordshire. Middle/lower order right-hand batsman, wicket-keeper. *Sch* Bedford Modern. *Team* Oxford U (1892).
Career batting
1–2–0–22–14–11.00–0–*ct* 1

His County cricket was for Bedfordshire (1891–1903) and Berkshire (1901). He won a blue for billiards.

Brown, Malcolm Edward Osborne
Cricketer. *b:* 19.8.1961, Durban, South Africa. Middle order right-hand batsman, right-arm medium pace bowler. *Team* Oxford U (1988, blue).
Career batting
3–5–2–71–47–23.66–0–*ct* 0

Brown, Reynolds Driver
Amateur. *b:* 6.5.1869, Newcastle, Delaware, USA. *d:* 6.4.1956, Charleston, South Carolina, USA. Son of H. W. (Philadelphia), brother of H. I. (Philadelphia). Defensive middle order right-hand batsman, right-arm fast bowler. *Sch* Harvard. *Team* Philadelphia (1886–1903). *Tours* Philadelphians to England 1889 (not first-class), 1903.
Career batting
20–37–2–536–103–15.31–1–*ct* 7
Bowling 47–1–47.00–0–0–1/12

He achieved very little on his 1903 visit to England, but hit two hundreds in minor matches on the 1889 trip. His best innings was probably 103 for Philadelphia v Bosanquet's Team of 1901. He appeared in three matches for USA v Canada.

Brown, Robin David
Cricketer. *b:* 11.3.1951, Gatooma, Rhodesia. Middle order right-hand batsman, wicket-keeper. *Team* Rhodesia/Zimbabwe (1976/7 to 1989/90). *Tour* Zimbabwe to England 1982, 1983 (World Cup), to Sri Lanka 1983/4, to India (World Cup) 1987/8.
Career batting
63–117–7–2597–200*–23.60–4–*ct* 66–*st* 12
Bowling 4–0

On his first-class appearances in England he played almost invariably as a specialist batsman. His highest score was 200* for Rhodesia B v Eastern Province B at Salisbury in 1978/9.

Brown, Samuel
Professional. *b:* 26.2.1857, Kimberley, Nottinghamshire. *d:* 5.9.1938, Edgley, Cheshire. Lower order right-hand batsman, right-arm fast medium bowler. *Team* Nottinghamshire (1896–97, 14 matches).
Career batting
17–23–3–288–43–14.40–0–*ct* 7
Bowling 1159–49–23.65–3–0–6/55

His first-class debut was for North v South at Lord's in 1884. Nottinghamshire first asked him to play for the County in 1883, but his club, Stockport, refused to release him and later in the same year he made his debut for Cheshire, but his appearance was objected to as he was not qualified. He played for Cheshire until 1895. He was a first-class umpire in 1907.

Brown, Sidney J.
Professional. Middle order batsman. *Team* MCC (1930–33).
Career batting
2–3–0–26–21–8.66–0–*ct* 1

His County cricket was for Hertfordshire (1926–34).

Brown, Simon John Emmerson
Cricketer. *b:* 29.6.1969, Cleadon, Co Durham. Tail end right-hand batsman, left-arm fast medium bowler. *Teams* Northamptonshire (1987–90, 15 matches); Durham (1992, 20 matches).
Career batting
35–38–19–267–47*–14.05–0–*ct* 9
Bowling 2787–83–33.57–3–0–7/105

He first played for Durham (pre first-class) in 1991.

Brown, Stevens William
Professional. *b:* 15.4.1875, Cliffe, Kent. *d:* 21.10.1957, Watford, Hertfordshire. Lower order batsman, bowler. *Team* Kent (1899, 3 matches).
Career batting
3–6–1–3–1*–0.60–0–*ct* 1
Bowling 217–5–43.40–0–0–2/36

Brown, Sydney Maurice
Professional. *b:* 8.12.1917, Eltham, Kent. *d:* 28.12.1987, Rickmansworth, Hertfordshire. Forcing right-hand opening batsman, good deep field, occasional wicket-keeper. *Team* Middlesex (1937–55, 313 matches).
Career batting
329–580–40–15756–232*–29.17–22–*ct* 152–*st* 2
Bowling 80–3–26.66–0–0–2/19

He hit 1,000 runs in a season nine times, exceeding 2,000 once – 2,078, av 37.78, in 1947. He scored two double centuries, both for Middlesex, his higher being 232* v Somerset (Lord's) 1951.

Brown, Thomas
Professional. *b:* 9.8.1845, Rusper, Sussex. Lower order right-hand batsman, right-hand medium pace round-arm bowler. *Team* Surrey (1868–74, 9 matches).
Career batting
9–15–2–58–10–4.46–0–*ct* 6
Bowling 123–7–17.57–0–0–4/16

Brown, Thomas
Professional. *b:* 14.6.1848, Bingham, Nottinghamshire. *d:* 2.7.1919, Netherfield, Nottinghamshire. Brother of John (Nottinghamshire). Middle order right-hand batsman, right-arm medium pace bowler. *Team* Nottinghamshire (1881, 4 matches).
Career batting
4–7–0–118–74–16.85–0–*ct* 0
Bowling 42–0

Brown, Thomas Austin
Professional. *b:* 11.4.1863, Wollaston, Northamptonshire. *d:* 12.3.1930, Dunstable, Bedfordshire. Lower order right-hand batsman, right-arm fast bowler. *Team* MCC (1894–1901).
Career batting
12–22–3–333–64*–17.52–0–*ct* 9
Bowling 342–12–28.50–1–0–6/82

His County cricket was for Northamptonshire (pre first-class, 1895–99), Bedfordshire (1901–06) and Hertfordshire (1909–10), but he was mainly involved in cricket at Lord's, being on the MCC staff, until forced to retire through ill-health. He was a first-class umpire (1905–22).

Brown, Thomas Charles
Professional. *b:* 25.3.1854, Ampthill, Bedfordshire. *d:* 26.4.1936, Isleworth, Middlesex. Lower order right-hand batsman, right-hand fast medium round-arm bowler. *Team* Sussex (1890, 6 matches).
Career batting
6–12–1–142–38–12.90–0–*ct* 3
Bowling 161–1–161.00–0–0–1/38

In 1877 and 1878 he resided in Surrey to qualify for the County, but never in fact was included in the County side. He also played for Bedfordshire (1876–83) and Northamptonshire (pre first-class, 1890–91).

Brown, Walter Medlicott Rodney
Amateur. *b:* 31.7.1868, Benares, India. *d:* 13.8.1954, Lansdown, Cheltenham, Gloucestershire. Middle order right-hand batsman. *Sch* Cheltenham. *Team* Gloucestershire (1895, 1 match).
Career batting
1–2–0–19–11–9.50–0–*ct* 0

Brown, William
Professional. *b:* 13.6.1866, Brierley Hill, Staffordshire. Middle order right-hand batsman, left-arm medium pace bowler. *Team* Lancashire (1894, 2 matches).
Career batting
2–3–0–17–7–5.66–0–*ct* 1
Bowling 12–0
He also played for Staffordshire (1890–99).

Brown, William
Professional. *b:* 19.11.1876, Darfield, Yorkshire. *d:* 27.7.1945, Barnsley, Yorkshire. Brother of J. T. (Darfield) (Yorkshire). Tail end right-hand batsman, right-arm fast bowler. *Team* Yorkshire (1902–08, 2 matches).
Career batting
2–2–1–2–2–2.00–0–*ct* 0
Bowling 84–4–21.00–0–0–3/61

Brown, William
Professional. *b:* 11.4.1888, Old Woodhouse, Leicestershire. *d:* 3.9.1964, Heywood, Lancashire. Lower order left-hand batsman, left-arm slow medium bowler. *Team* Leicestershire (1910–19, 46 matches).
Career batting
46–72–23–347–35–7.08–0–*ct* 22
Bowling 3161–114–27.72–4–1–7/51

Brown, William
Professional. *b:* 17.1.1889, Accrington, Lancashire. Lower order batsman, opening bowler. *Team* Lancashire (1919–22, 10 matches).
Career batting
10–17–2–239–39–15.93–0–*ct* 10
Bowling 474–22–21.54–0–0–4/22

Brown, William Alfred
Amateur. *b:* 31.7.1912, Toowoomba, Queensland, Australia. Excellent opening right-hand batsman, off break bowler, brilliant field. *Team* New South Wales (1932/3 to 1934/5, 22 matches); Queensland (1936/7 to 1949/50, 50 matches). *Tours* Australia to England 1934, 1938, 1948, to South Africa 1935/6, to New Zealand 1945/6, 1949/50. *Tests* Australia (1934–48, 22 matches).
Career batting
189–284–15–13838–265*–51.44–39–*ct* 110–*st* 1
Bowling 110–6–18.33–0–0–4/16
Test batting
22–35–1–1592–206*–46.82–4–*ct* 14

On each of his three visits to England he hit over 1,000 runs, having an almost identical average on the last two tours – 1,854 (av 57.93) in 1938 and 1,448 runs (av 57.92) in 1948. His two great innings in England were both at Lord's. In 1934 he hit 105, the only score of substance for Australia in that match, and 1938 he made 206*. Despite his high scoring in 1948, he was not required in three of the Tests. At times Brown could be a most stubborn batsman, but usually he was an elegant quick-scoring player. His highest score was 265* for Australians v Derbyshire at Chesterfield in 1938. He captained Australia in one Test.

Brown, William Cecil
Amateur. *b:* 13.11.1900, Wellingborough, Northamptonshire. *d:* 20.1.1986, Hove, Sussex. Middle order right-hand batsman. *Sch* Charterhouse and Wellingborough. *Team* Northamptonshire (1925–37, 127 matches).
Career batting
127–214–29–2601–103*–14.05–1–*ct* 57
Bowling 1–0
He captained Northamptonshire 1932–35 and was later Honorary Secretary 1938–39.

Brown, William Stanley Alston
Amateur. *b:* 23.5.1877, Clifton, Bristol, Gloucestershire. *d:* 12.9.1952, Kingsdown, Bristol, Gloucestershire. Attractive middle order right-hand batsman, left-arm medium slow bowler, excellent field. *Sch* Leys School. *Team* Gloucestershire (1896–1919, 161 matches); London County (1900).
Career batting
164–277–23–4820–155–18.97–2–*ct* 139
Bowling 6510–195–33.38–3–0–6/56
One of the leading all-round sportsmen of his County, Brown represented Gloucestershire at soccer, hockey, lacrosse, golf and bowls, as well as playing rugby for Bristol.

Browne, Cyril Ross
Amateur. *b:* 7.2.1893, King's Norton, Warwickshire. *d:* 30.4.1948, Eastbourne, Sussex. Brother of F. B. R. (Sussex). Middle order right-hand batsman, right-arm medium pace bowler. *Teams* Cambridge U (1913–19); Sussex (1913–19, 3 matches).
Career batting
10–18–0–146–23–8.11–0–*ct* 2
Bowling 329–11–29.90–0–0–4/8

Browne, Cyril Rutherford
Amateur. *b:* 8.10.1890, Robert's Tenantry, St Michael, Barbados. *d:* 12.1.1964, Georgetown, British Guiana. Brother of C. A. (Barbados). Hard-hitting middle/lower order right-hand batsman, right-arm googly bowler. *Teams* Barbados (1908/9 to 1910/11); British Guiana (1921/2 to 1938/9). *Tours* West Indies to England 1923, 1928. *Tests* West Indies (1928 to 1929/30, 4 matches).

Career batting
74–115–11–2077–103–19.97–3–*ct* 59
Bowling 6228–278–22.40–17–6–8/58
Test batting
4–8–1–176–70*–25.14–0–*ct* 1
Bowling 288–6–48.00–0–0–2/72

On both tours to England he produced some useful all-round performances, without doing anything outstanding. Before the First World War he was seen in London Club cricket, being in England to study law.

Browne, David William
Cricketer. *b:* 4.4.1964, Stamford, Lincolnshire. Middle order right-hand batsman. *Sch* Stamford. *Team* Cambridge U (1985–86, blue 1986).
Career batting
8–14–4–238–61*–23.80–0–*ct* 5
Bowling 76–1–76.00–0–0–1/13

Browne, Rev Elliott Kenworthy
Amateur. *b:* 10.10.1847. Goldington Hall, Bedfordshire. *d:* 10.3.1915, Bournemouth, Hampshire. Brother of G. E. K. (Gloucestershire). Middle order right-hand batsman, right-arm fast bowler, useful deep field. *Sch* Rugby. *Team* Gloucestershire (1872, 4 matches).
Career batting
4–6–1–136–52–27.20–0–*ct* 1
Bowling 19–1–19.00–0–0–1/7

He was not in the Eleven whilst at Oxford. In 1868 he appeared for the Gentlemen of Hampshire, but never for that County in first-class matches.

Browne, Canon Francis Bernard Ross
Amateur. *b:* 28.7.1899, Eastbourne, Sussex. *d:* 11.3.1970, Pewsey, Wiltshire. Brother of C. R. (Sussex). Lower order right-hand batsman, right-arm fast medium bowler. *Sch* Eastbourne. *Teams* Sussex (1919–32, 49 matches); Cambridge U (1921–22, blue 1922).
Career batting
75–89–31–333–26*–5.74–0–*ct* 34
Bowling 5223–252–20.72–15–1–8/39

He had a very strange delivery, bowling off the wrong foot, which earned him the soubriquet 'Tishy', after a cross-legged racehorse of the time.

Browne, Franklin Doughty
Amateur. *b:* 4.3.1873, Tufnell Park, London. *d:* 12.8.1946, Cobham, Kent. Middle order right-hand batsman. *Sch* Dulwich. *Team* Kent (1899–1903, 10 matches).
Career batting
10–17–3–262–53*–18.71–0–*ct* 8

Whilst at Oxford he captained Trinity College, but did not appear in any first-class matches.

Browne, George Fairbrother
Amateur. *b:* 1835. *d:* 28.5.1919, Lowestoft, Suffolk. Middle order batsman. *Teams* Sussex (1864, 1 match); Middlesex (1864, 1 match).
Career batting
2–3–0–19–11–6.33–0–*ct* 0

Since he played for Sussex against Middlesex, it is probable that he was a native of the former County, but resided in the latter in 1864 – both his first-class appearances took place on the Middlesex home ground at Islington.

Browne, Gerald Elliott Kenworthy
(later Kenworthy-Browne)
Amateur. *b:* 14.5.1850, Goldington Hall, Bedfordshire. *d:* 6.7.1910, Glencormac, Co Wicklow, Ireland. Brother of E. K. (Gloucestershire). Middle order right-hand batsman. *Sch* Rugby. *Team* Gloucestershire (1874, 2 matches).
Career batting
2–3–0–20–12–6.66–0–*ct* 0

He also played non-first-class cricket for Somerset (1877).

Browne, Horace James
Amateur. *b:* 1.12.1842, Cambridge. *d:* 19.3.1896, Byfleet, Surrey. Middle order batsman. *Sch* Bury St Edmunds. *Team* Cambridgeshire (1865–69, 7 matches).
Career batting
7–13–2–111–28–10.09–0–*ct* 0

Brownell, Eric Lindsay Douglas
Amateur. *b:* 7.11.1876, Hobart, Tasmania, Australia. *d:* 22.10.1945, Windsor, New South Wales, Australia. Middle order right-hand batsman. *Team* Worcestershire (1908, 1 match).
Career batting
1–2–0–28–21–14.00–0–*ct* 1

He also played in Ceylon but not in first-class matches.

Brownfield, Douglas Harold
Amateur. *b:* 30.3.1856, Hanley, Staffordshire. *d:* 5.8.1917, Llandudno, Caernarvonshire. Middle order right-hand batsman. *Sch* Rugby. *Team* An England XI (1888).
Career batting
1–2–0–4–4–2.00–0–*ct* 0

His County cricket was for Staffordshire (1885–1900).

Brownhill, Thomas
Professional. *b:* 10.10.1838, Ecclesfield, Sheffield, Yorkshire. *d:* 6.1.1915, Wortley, Yorkshire. Middle order right-hand batsman, excellent deep field. *Team* Yorkshire (1862–71, 12 matches).
Career batting
14–26–4–202–25–9.18–0–*ct* 12

He was a first-class umpire (1883–85).

Browning, Francis Henry
Amateur. *b:* 23.6.1868, Kingstown, Dublin, Ireland. *d:* 26.4.1916, Dublin, Ireland. Middle order right-

hand batsman, wicket-keeper. *Sch* Marlborough. *Team* Ireland (1902–09). *Tour* Ireland to North America 1909.
Career batting
11–22–2–363–56–18.15–0–*ct* 9–*st* 4
He was 'killed by the Irish rebels'.

Browning, Frederick Henry
Amateur. *b:* 1.8.1870, Barton Mere, Bury St Edmunds, Suffolk. *d:* 13.10.1929, Flaxley, Gloucestershire. Father-in-law of Daphne du Maurier, the author. Sound middle order right-hand batsman, wicket-keeper. *Sch* Wellington. *Team* MCC (1907). *Tour* MCC to North America 1907.
Career batting
3–5–1–38–27–9.50–0–*ct* 0
He did not appear in any first-class matches whilst at Oxford, but represented his University at rackets in 1893 and 1895.

Brownlee, Leigh Dunlop
Amateur. *b:* 17.12.1882, Redland, Bristol, Gloucestershire. *d:* 22.9.1955, Clifton, Bristol, Gloucestershire. Brother of W. M. (Gloucestershire). Middle order right-hand batsman, slow right-arm bowler, good deep field. *Sch* Clifton. *Teams* Gloucestershire (1901–09, 65 matches); Oxford U (1902–04, blue 1904); Somerset (1902, 1 match).
Career batting
82–138–5–1946–103–14.63–1–*ct* 62
Bowling 407–15–27.13–0–0–3/40
He also won a blue for golf.

Brownlee, Wilfred Methven
Amateur. *b:* 18.4.1890, Cotham, Bristol, Gloucestershire. *d:* 12.10.1914, Wyke Regis, Dorset. He died of meningitis. Brother of L. D. (Gloucestershire and Somerset). Free scoring middle order right-hand batsman, right-arm fast medium bowler, brilliant field. *Sch* Clifton. *Team* Gloucestershire (1909–14, 32 matches).
Career batting
33–53–4–773–68–15.77–0–*ct* 26
Bowling 1251–46–27.19–3–0–6/61

Brownrigg, George Neville
Professional. *b:* 16.7.1896, Queen's County, Ireland. *d:* 20.1.1981, Westminster, London. Lower order batsman, left-arm bowler. *Sch* Rossall. *Team* Sussex (1921–22, 3 matches).
Career batting
3–5–2–26–11–8.66–0–*ct* 2
Bowling 103–4–25.75–0–0–4/31

Bruce, Hon Clarence Napier
(succeeded to the title 3rd Baron Aberdare in 1929)
Amateur. *b:* 2.8.1885, Pimlico, Westminster, London. *d:* 4.10.1957, Moring, near Kotor, Yugoslavia. He was drowned when the car in which he was travelling went over a precipice into a river. Brother-in-law of Lord Dalmeny (Surrey) and K. A. Muir-Mackenzie (MCC). Hard-hitting middle order right-hand batsman. *Sch* Winchester. *Teams* Oxford U (1905–08, blue 1907–08); Middlesex (1908–29, 62 matches); Wales (1925–29).
Career batting
96–159–10–4326–149–29.03–6–*ct* 34
Bowling 13–0
A brilliant rackets player he was the Amateur Champion in 1922 and 1931 and ten times Doubles Champion. He was Amateur Champion at real tennis in 1932 and 1938. He represented Oxford at rackets, real tennis and golf and for 20 years was on the International Olympic Executive.

Bruce, William
Amateur. *b:* 22.5.1864, South Yarra, Melbourne, Victoria, Australia. *d:* 3.8.1925, Elwood, St Kilda, Melbourne, Victoria, Australia. He was found drowned. He took his own life. Aggressive middle order left-hand batsman, left-arm medium pace bowler. *Team* Victoria (1882/3 to 1903/4, 61 matches). *Tours* Australia to England 1886, 1893, to North America 1893. *Tests* Australia (1884/5 to 1894/5, 14 matches).
Career batting
145–250–11–5731–191–23.97–4–*ct* 102
Bowling 4244–143–29.67–5–0–7/72
Test batting
14–26–2–702–80–29.25–0–*ct* 12
Bowling 440–12–36.66–0–0–3/88
He was an excellent hitter, but had little defence. His first visit to England in 1886 was not successful, but in 1893 he scored 1,227 runs (av 25.01) and his best innings was 191 v Combined Universities, made in 220 minutes. His best year in Test cricket was 1891/2 in Australia.

Bruce-Lockhart, John Harold
Amateur. *b:* 4.3.1889, Beith, Ayrshire, Scotland. *d:* 4.6.1956, Marylebone, London. Father of R. B. (Cambridge U), brother-in-law of H. Brougham (Oxford U). Lower order right-hand batsman, leg break and googly bowler. *Sch* Sedbergh. *Teams* Cambridge U (1909–11, blue 1909–10); Scotland (1910–11, 2 matches).
Career batting
24–38–3–306–42–8.74–0–*ct* 12
Bowling 2418–121–19.98–10–3–8/45
Cambridge were greatly criticised for omitting him from the 1911 University match. His County cricket was for Berkshire (1911–12). An excellent rugby footballer, he represented Cambridge and Scotland at fly half.

Bruce-Lockhart, Rab Brougham
Amateur. *b:* 1.12.1916, Rugby, Warwickshire. *d:* 1.5.1990, Burneside, Cumberland. Son of J. H. (Cambridge U and Scotland), nephew of H. Brougham (Oxford U), son-in-law of S. T. Crump (Europeans).

Middle/lower order right-hand batsman, leg break bowler. *Sch* Edinburgh Academy. *Team* Cambridge U (1937–38).
Career batting
3–5–1–32–17–8.00–0–*ct* 3
Bowling 146–1–146.00–0–0–1/76
He represented Scotland at rugby.

Brumfitt, Jack
Amateur. *b:* 18.2.1917, Guiseley, Yorkshire. *d:* 16.3.1987, Ilkley, Yorkshire. Middle order right-hand batsman. *Team* Yorkshire (1938, 1 match).
Career batting
1–1–0–9–9–9.00–0–*ct* 0

Brune, Charles Julius
Amateur. *b:* 16.4.1843, Cuba. *d:* 13.1.1877, Boulogne, France. Stubborn defensive lower order right-hand batsman, right-hand medium fast pace round-arm bowler, good deep field. *Team* Cambridge U (1866–70, blue 1867–69); Middlesex (1866–75, 19 matches).
Career batting
56–91–20–738–41–10.39–0–*ct* 21
Bowling 1872–107–17.49–6–1–8/31
He was the first Treasurer of the Incogniti (commencing 1861). He also played for Hertfordshire (1871–72) and Staffordshire (1876). He was Middlesex joint Hon Secretary 1873–75.

Brunskill, Dr John Handfield
Amateur. *b:* 17.4.1875, Rathmines, Dublin, Ireland. *d:* 21.7.1940, Lincoln. Middle order left-hand batsman, right-arm medium pace bowler. *Team* Dublin University (1895).
Career batting
4–8–0–134–58–16.75–0–*ct* 0
Bowling 50–0
He played for Ireland (not first-class) in 1895.

Brunton, Rev John du Vallon
Amateur. *b:* 23.7.1869, Benares, India. *d:* 12.11.1962, Knutsford, Cheshire. Middle order right-hand batsman. *Sch* Lancaster GS. *Team* Cambridge U (1894, blue).
Career batting
6–11–0–258–66–23.45–0–*ct* 4
He was also a rugby blue, playing three times against Oxford, and a hockey blue.

Brunwin, Herbert Jack
Amateur. *b:* 28.4.1912, Layer-de-la-Haye, Essex. *d:* 17.1.1990, Colchester, Essex. Tail end right-hand batsman, right-arm medium fast bowler. *Team* Essex (1937, 1 match).
Career batting
1–1–1–2–2*–no av–0–*ct* 0
Bowling 5–1–5.00–0–0–1/5

Bruton, Charles Lamb
Amateur. *b:* 6.4.1890, Wotton, Gloucester. *d:* 26.3.1969, Henley-on-Thames, Oxfordshire. Middle order right-hand batsman. *Sch* Radley. *Team* Gloucestershire (1922, 3 matches).
Career batting
3–6–1–60–24–12.00–0–*ct* 0
He was Resident Commissioner in Swaziland 1937–42 and Commissioner of the East African Refugee Association 1942–47.

Brutton, Charles Phipps
Amateur. *b:* 20.1.1899, Southsea, Hampshire. *d:* 11.5.1964, Ticehurst House, Sussex. Son of Septimus (Hampshire), nephew of E. B. (Liverpool). Middle order right-hand batsman. *Sch* Winchester. *Team* Hampshire (1921–30, 81 matches).
Career batting
82–129–12–2055–119*–17.56–1–*ct* 36
Bowling 125–0
He also played for Cheshire (1934), Denbighshire (1935) and Dorset (1937–38).

Brutton, Rev Ernest Bartholomew
Amateur. *b:* 29.7.1864, Tynemouth, Newcastle upon Tyne, Northumberland. *d:* 19.4.1922, Aylesbeare, Devon. Brother of Septimus (Hampshire), uncle of C. P. (Hampshire). Hard-hitting middle order right-hand batsman, right-arm fast bowler. *Sch* Durham. *Teams* C. I. Thornton's XI (1885); Liverpool and District (1892).
Career batting
2–4–1–33–18*–11.00–0–*ct* 1
Bowling 37–0
His County cricket was for Northumberland (1881–91) and Devon (1901–14). An excellent rugby footballer, he gained a blue at Cambridge and went on to represent England. He also represented Cambridge at athletics.

Brutton, Septimus
Amateur. *b:* 26.7.1869, Tynemouth, Newcastle upon Tyne, Northumberland. *d:* 29.9.1933, Marylebone, London. Brother of E. B. (Liverpool), father of C. P. (Hampshire). Middle order batsman. *Sch* Leatherhead. *Team* Hampshire (1904, 1 match).
Career batting
1–2–0–22–15–11.00–0–*ct* 1
Before playing for Hampshire he played for Northumberland (1887–1901).

Bruyns, André
Cricketer. *b:* 19.9.1946, Pietermaritzburg, South Africa. Excellent middle order right-hand batsman, wicket-keeper. *Teams* Western Province (1965/6 to 1976/7); Natal (1972/3). *Tours* South African Universities to England 1967; Isaacs to England 1969 (not first-class).

Career batting
90–160–9–5050–197–33.44–11–*ct* 106
Bowling 25–1–25.00–0–0–1/1
He was also a notable rugby footballer.

Bryan
Professional. *b:* West Indies. Middle order batsman, change bowler. *Team* MCC (1902).
Career batting
1–2–0–10–5–5.00–0–*ct* 0
Bowling 15–0

Bryan, Frank
Amateur. *b:* 12.9.1853, Amersham, Buckinghamshire. *d:* 11.6.1923, Quainton, Buckinghamshire. Lower order batsman, wicket-keeper. *Team* Middlesex (1891, 1 match).
Career batting
1–2–0–0–0–0.00–0–*ct* 0

Bryan, Godfrey James
Amateur. *b:* 29.12.1902, Beckenham, Kent. *d:* 24.3.1991, Canterbury, Kent. Brother of J. L. (Kent) and R. T. (Kent). Excellent opening or middle order left-hand batsman, right-arm medium pace bowler. *Sch* Wellington. *Team* Kent (1920–33, 51 matches).
Career batting
70–114–8–3192–229–30.11–6–*ct* 46
Bowling 1753–35–50.08–1–0–5/148
Bryan was an exceptional schoolboy batsman, hitting 699 runs (av 116.50) in his last year at Wellington. On his first-class debut in August of the same year (Kent v Nottinghamshire, Trent Bridge, 1920) he hit 124, the youngest player to score a Championship hundred. Joining the Army and being stationed abroad meant that his County cricket was very limited. His final first-class match was for the Army in 1935. His highest score was 229 for Combined Services v South Africans at Portsmouth in 1924.

Bryan, John
Amateur. *b:* 17.10.1841, Lower Slaughter, Gloucestershire. *d:* 24.6.1909, Minchinhampton, Gloucestershire. Middle order right-hand batsman, excellent long-stop. *Sch* Gloucester College. *Team* Gloucestershire (1873, 2 matches).
Career batting
2–3–1–34–24–17.00–0–*ct* 4

Bryan, John Lindsay
Amateur. *b:* 26.5.1896, Beckenham, Kent. *d:* 23.4.1985, Eastbourne, Sussex. Brother of G. J. (Kent) and R. T. (Kent). Opening/middle order left-hand batsman, excellent cover field. *Sch* Rugby. *Teams* Kent (1919–32, 119 matches); Cambridge U (1921, blue). *Tour* MCC to Australia 1924/5.
Career batting
165–260–20–8702–236–36.25–17–*ct* 89
Bowling 675–15–45.00–0–0–2/18
Bryan had a most unusual career at Cambridge; in 1919 and 1920 he was not even afforded a trial, but in 1921 hit a century in the Seniors' match and ended the season top of the batting table, being so successful that he was chosen as a Wisden 'Cricketer of the Year'. In 1921 he hit 1,858 runs, av 50.21. Thereafter he could only play County cricket in August owing to his scholastic duties, but in most seasons produced a few brilliant innings. He hit two double centuries, the higher being 236 for Kent v Hampshire at Canterbury in 1923. His final first-class match was for Leveson-Gower's XI in 1933.

Bryan, Ronald Thurston
Amateur. *b:* 30.7.1898, Beckenham, Kent. *d:* 27.7.1970, Pevensey Bay, Sussex. Brother of G. J. (Kent) and J. L. (Kent). Middle order left-hand batsman, leg break and googly bowler. *Sch* Rugby. *Team* Kent (1920–37, 40 matches).
Career batting
40–60–9–1154–89*–22.62–0–*ct* 30
Bowling 22–1–22.00–0–0–1/9
Like his brothers his profession of banker prevented his regular participation in County cricket, though in 1937 he obtained three months' leave of absence to captain Kent.

Bryan, William
Professional. *b:* 22.9.1856, Kimberley, Nottinghamshire. *d:* 22.5.1933, Brooklands, Cambridge. Lower order right-hand batsman, right-arm medium pace bowler. *Team* South (1886).
Career batting
1–2–0–11–7–5.50–0–*ct* 0
Bowling 14–0
His County cricket was for Essex (pre first-class, 1887–88) and Cambridgeshire (1891–1903).

Bryans, F. A.
Amateur. *b:* 3.7.1901. *d:* 15.12.1963, Buenos Aires, Argentina. Lower order batsman. *Teams* Leveson-Gower's XI (1933); Argentina (1926/7 to 1929/30).
Career batting
9–17–2–240–65–16.00–0–*ct* 3
Bowling 420–18–23.33–1–0–5/67

Bryant, David John
Cricketer. *b:* 29.10.1950, Wandsworth, London. Tail end right-hand batsman, right-arm fast medium bowler. *Team* Oxford U (1970–71).
Career batting
6–10–7–19–6*–6.33–0–*ct* 1
Bowling 423–8–52.87–0–0–3/40

Bryant, Edwin Harvey
Amateur. *b:* 12.9.1886, Bromsgrove, Worcestershire. *d:* 24.10.1948, Barnt Green, Worcestershire. Middle order batsman. *Sch* Bromsgrove. *Team* Worcestershire (1923–25, 16 matches).

Career batting
16–30–0–329–63–10.96–0–*ct* 5

Bryant, Herbert William
Amateur. *b:* 30.6.1867, Uxbridge, Middlesex. *d:* 23.2.1910, St Mary, Azores. Punishing lower order right-hand batsman, excellent wicket-keeper. *Team* Middlesex (1888–89, 8 matches).
Career batting
8–12–3–71–38–7.88–0–*ct* 13–*st* 12
The demands of business took him abroad in 1890 and he was therefore lost to County cricket.

Bryant, James Mark
Professional. *c:* 24.10.1826, Caterham, Surrey. *d:* 10.12.1881, Sale, Victoria, Australia. Lower order right-hand batsman, right-arm medium pace bowler. *Teams* Surrey (1852, 2 matches); Victoria (1856/7 to 1861/2, 8 matches).
Career batting
11–19–2–182–32–10.70–0–*ct* 9
Bowling 238–22–10.81–0–0–3/11
He emigrated to Australia shortly after appearing for Surrey and was for some years the curator of the Melbourne Cricket Ground.

Bryant, Leonard Eric
Professional. *b:* 2.6.1936, Weston-super-Mare, Somerset. Tail end left-hand batsman, slow left-arm bowler. *Team* Somerset (1958–60, 22 matches).
Career batting
22–29–14–133–17–8.86–0–*ct* 10
Bowling 943–34–27.73–1–0–5/64

Bryant, Michael
Cricketer. *b:* 5.4.1959, Beacon, Camborne, Cornwall. Middle order right-hand batsman, right-arm fast medium bowler. *Team* Somerset (1982, 2 matches).
Career batting
2–2–0–6–6–3.00–0–*ct* 1
Bowling 158–2–79.00–0–0–1/29
He also played for Cornwall (1978–84).

Bryson, Rudi Edwin
Cricketer. *b:* 25.7.1968, Springs, Transvaal, South Africa. Lower order right-hand batsman, right-arm fast medium bowler. *Teams* Northern Transvaal (1987/8 to 1988/9); Eastern Province (1988/9 to 1991/2); Surrey (1992, 11 matches).
Career batting
39–43–11–750–100–23.43–1–*ct* 9
Bowling 3735–136–27.46–10–2–7/68

Buchanan, David
Amateur. *b:* 16.1.1830, Edinburgh, Scotland. *d:* 30.5.1900, Northfield, Rugby, Warwickshire. Lower order left-hand batsman, originally fast left round-arm bowler, but changed to slow medium spin bowling about 1864. *Sch* Rugby. *Team* Cambridge U (1850–51, blue 1850).
Career batting
62–106–39–257–27–3.83–0–*ct* 17
Bowling 5718–366 + 42–15.62–40–11–9/82
His County cricket was for Warwickshire (pre first-class, 1862–85). He was about 40 years old before he made much of a mark in first-class cricket and declined an invitation to tour Australia with the 1878/9 team. Regarded by many as the best amateur slow bowler in the 1870s, he wrote a much valued essay on the subject, which was published in 1894. He also played for Lincolnshire (1872–73). His final first-class match was for Gentlemen in 1881. His best bowling was 9/82 for Gentlemen v Players at the Oval in 1868. He was Warwickshire Chairman 1882–85 and Treasurer 1885–91.

Buchanan, John Nevile
Amateur. *b:* 30.5.1887, Grahamstown, South Africa. *d:* 31.10.1969, St John's Wood, London. Uncle of E. B. Leigh (Bihar). Opening/middle order right-hand batsman, right-arm medium fast bowler, brilliant field. *Sch* Charterhouse. *Team* Cambridge U (1906–09, blue all four years).
Career batting
34–60–2–1536–118–26.48–4–*ct* 45
Bowling 1094–26–42.07–0–0–4/56
His County cricket was for Buckinghamshire (1925). His final first-class match was for Free Foresters in 1922.

Buck, William Dalton
Cricketer. *b:* 30.9.1946, Portswood, Southampton, Hampshire. Lower order right-hand batsman, right-arm medium pace bowler. *Teams* Somerset (1969, 1 match); Hampshire (1969, 1 match).
Career batting
2–2–0–11–6–5.50–0–*ct* 0
Bowling 135–2–67.50–0–0–2/54
Buck's career in first-class cricket is a curiosity – he played for Somerset and for Hampshire in the same season, but neither game was in the County Championship, the Somerset match being against New Zealanders and the Hampshire one against West Indians.

Buckenham, Claude Percival
Professional. *b:* 16.1.1876, Herne Hill, Surrey. *d:* 23.2.1937, Dundee, Angus, Scotland. Middle or lower order right-hand batsman, right-arm fast bowler. *Sch* Alleyn's. *Team* Essex (1899–1914, 258 matches). *Tour* MCC to South Africa 1909/10. *Tests* England (1909/10, 4 matches).
Career batting
307–468–79–5641–124–14.50–2–*ct* 172
Bowling 29110–1150–25.31–85–17–8/33
Test batting
4–7–0–43–17–6.14–0–*ct* 2
Bowling 593–21–28.23–1–0–5/115

He took 100 wickets in a season 6 times (best 135, av 24.13, in 1906). Regarded as one of the deadliest fast bowlers of his time, he would have had a much better record had it not been for catches missed in the slips.

Buckingham, Amyand David
Amateur. *b:* 28.1.1930, Pymble, Sydney, New South Wales, Australia. Opening/middle order right-hand batsman, off break bowler. *Team* Cambridge U (1955).
Career batting
10–20–1–349–61–18.36–0–*ct* 3
Bowling 43–0
His final first-class match was for Free Foresters in 1960.

Buckingham, John
Professional. *b:* 21.1.1903, Grimethorpe, Yorkshire. *d:* 25.1.1987, Moseley, Birmingham. Forcing middle/lower order right-hand batsman, wicket-keeper. *Team* Warwickshire (1933–39, 93 matches).
Career batting
93–142–23–2840–137*–23.86–3–*ct* 132–*st* 92
He hit 1,054 runs, av 31.00, in 1938.

Buckland, Edward Hastings
Amateur. *b:* 20.6.1864, Laleham-on-Thames, Middlesex. *d:* 10.2.1906, Southgate, Winchester, Hampshire. Brother of F. M. (Oxford U and Middlesex), his widow married G. W. Ricketts (Surrey). Middle order right-hand batsman, originally fast under-arm, afterwards slow off break bowler. *Sch* Marlborough. *Teams* Oxford U (1884–87, blue all four years); Middlesex (1885–88, 9 matches); Hampshire (1895, 4 matches). *Tour* Sanders to North America 1886.
Career batting
48–82–4–1414–148–18.12–1–*ct* 54
Bowling 2159–110–19.62–8–1–7/17
He also represented Oxford U at rackets and played both soccer and golf to a high standard. He also played for Wiltshire (1883).

Buckland, Francis Matthew
Amateur. *b:* 27.8.1854, Laleham-on-Thames, Middlesex. *d:* 7.3.1913, Bexhill-on-Sea, Sussex. Brother of E. H. (Middlesex and Hampshire). Middle order right-hand batsman, right-hand medium pace round-arm bowler, close field. *Sch* Eton. *Teams* Oxford U (1874–77, blue 1875–77); Middlesex (1877–78, 5 matches).
Career batting
24–40–5–829–117*–23.68–2–*ct* 21
Bowling 1199–71–16.88–4–2–6/48
Whilst at Eton he bowled leg-breaks, but in first-class cricket relied entirely on accuracy of length and direction. His final first-class match was for MCC in 1891.

Buckland, Joseph Edwin
Professional. *b:* 24.9.1916, Lingfield, Surrey. Lower order left-hand batsman, left-arm fast medium bowler. *Team* Somerset (1948, 1 match).
Career batting
1–2–2–17–17*–no av–0–*ct* 2
Bowling 55–3–18.33–0–0–2/35

Buckland, Tom George
(birth registered as T. G. Beastall)
Professional. *b:* 20.11.1860, Sutton-in-Ashfield, Nottinghamshire. *d:* 18.7.1915, Sutton-in-Ashfield, Nottinghamshire. Lower order right-hand batsman, right-arm fast medium bowler. *Team* Nottinghamshire (1888, 2 matches).
Career batting
2–3–1–23–12–11.50–0–*ct* 0
Bowling 68–4–17.00–0–0–2/13

Buckle, Frederick
Professional. *b:* 25.9.1849, Thames Ditton, Surrey. *d:* 7.11.1884, Long Ditton, Surrey. Lower order right-hand batsman, wicket-keeper, change bowler. *Team* Surrey (1867–72, 15 matches).
Career batting
15–25–4–156–31–7.42–0–*ct* 4
Bowling 165–6–27.50–0–0–2/40

Buckley, Cyril Francis Stewart
Amateur. *b:* 21.2.1905, Chelsea, London. *d:* 11.6.1974, Chelsea, London. Great-nephew of A. (MCC) and D. F. (MCC). Middle order batsman. *Sch* Eton. *Team* Leveson-Gower's XI (1934–36).
Career batting
3–5–0–53–50–10.60–0–*ct* 5
His County cricket was for Berkshire (1927–35).

Buckley, George Arthur
Amateur. *b:* 3.2.1889, Skegby, Nottinghamshire. *d:* 1.12.1935, Norton Lees, Yorkshire. Middle order right-hand batsman, right-arm fast medium bowler. *Team* Derbyshire (1921, 1 match).
Career batting
1–2–0–10–8–5.00–0–*ct* 1
Bowling 48–0
Buckley was selected to play for Nottinghamshire in 1913 v Leicestershire, but forced to withdraw due to injury. He also played for Cheshire (1909).

Bucknell, John
Professional. *b:* 7.6.1872, Bedminster, Somerset. *d:* 5.3.1925, Darlington, Co Durham. Lower order batsman, right-arm medium pace bowler. *Team* Somerset (1895–1905, 10 matches).
Career batting
10–19–7–144–33–12.00–0–*ct* 3
Bowling 617–10–61.70–0–0–3/93
He also played for Durham (pre first-class, 1909).

Buckston, George Moreton
Amateur. *b:* 12.3.1881, Hope, Derbyshire. *d:* 24.11.1942, Sutton Hall, Sutton-on-the-Hill, Derbyshire. Father of R. H. R. (Derbyshire), brother-in-law of H. T. Allsopp (Cambridge U). Lower order right-hand batsman, wicket-keeper. *Sch* Eton. *Teams* Cambridge U (1903); Derbyshire (1905–21, 33 matches).
Career batting
39–75–3–852–96–11.83–0–*ct* 8–*st* 1

Most of his first-class cricket was confined to 1921, when he was appointed captain of Derbyshire and served the County well at a time of great difficulty. He was Derbyshire joint Hon Secretary 1927–29.

Buckston, Robin Henry Rowland
Amateur. *b:* 10.10.1908, Kensington, London. *d:* 16.5.1967, Burton-on-Trent, Staffordshire. Son of G. M. (Derbyshire). Lower order right-hand batsman, wicket-keeper. *Sch* Eton. *Team* Derbyshire (1928–39, 72 matches).
Career batting
74–104–24–944–60*–11.80–0–*ct* 18–*st* 2
Bowling 10–0

He captained Derbyshire from 1937 to 1939 and was Hon Secretary from 1950 to 1959.

Budd, Edward Hayward
Amateur. *b:* 23.2.1785, Great Missenden, Buckinghamshire. *d:* 29.3.1875, Wroughton, Wiltshire. Hard-hitting middle order right-hand batsman, medium pace under-arm bowler, but with his hand extended from his side, wicket-keeper. *Teams* Middlesex (1808); Norfolk (1820); Hampshire (1823).
Career batting
73–125–9–2728–105–23.51–1–*ct* 51–*st* 27
Bowling 173 wickets (no analyses)–4–0–5/?

He first played at Lord's in 1802 and for about 30 years was one of the best all-rounder cricketers in England, his complete career extending over 50 years. His first first-class match was for H. C. Woolridge's XI in 1803 and his last for England in 1831.

Budd, William Lloyd
Professional. *b:* 25.10.1913, Hawkley, Hampshire. *d:* 23.8.1986, Southampton, Hampshire. Lower order right-hand batsman, right-arm fast medium bowler. *Team* Hampshire (1934–46, 60 matches).
Career batting
60–98–16–941–77*–11.47–0–*ct* 24
Bowling 2506–64–39.15–0–0–4/22

He became a first-class umpire (1969–82), standing in four Test matches (1976–78).

Budden, Charles
Professional. *b:* 18.7.1879, Fareham, Hampshire. *d:* 26.11.1969, Winchester, Hampshire. Lower order batsman, bowler. *Team* Hampshire (1900, 2 matches).
Career batting
2–3–1–35–32*–17.50–0–*ct* 0
Bowling 102–2–51.00–0–0–1/30

Budden, James Thomas William Frederick
Amateur. *b:* 25.7.1882, Bevois Town, Southampton, Hampshire. *d:* 5.9.1965, St Denys, Southampton, Hampshire. Lower order batsman. *Team* Hampshire (1912, 1 match).
Career batting
1 match, did not bat –*ct* 0
Bowling 46–0

He also played for Devon (1906).

Budgen, Harry
Amateur. *b:* 1.4.1879, Reigate, Surrey. *d:* 13.3.1944, Earlswood, Redhill, Surrey. Lower order right-hand batsman, slow left-arm bowler. *Team* Surrey (1904–09, 3 matches).
Career batting
3–4–0–58–30–14.50–0–*ct* 1
Bowling 213–3–71.00–0–0–3/112

Budgen, Henry Richard
Professional. *b:* 4.7.1865, Brighton, Sussex. *d:* 13.3.1929, Ilford, Essex. Lower order right-hand batsman. *Team* Sussex (1886–92, 10 matches).
Career batting
10–20–4–120–32–7.50–0–*ct* 6
Bowling 19–0

Buggé, David Anthony Bowdell
Cricketer. *b:* 12.12.1956, Tarshine, Steamer Point, Aden. Tail end right-hand batsman, right-arm medium fast bowler. *Sch* Cranleigh. *Team* Oxford U (1977).
Career batting
1 match, did not bat –*ct* 0
Bowling 22–0

Bulcock, Leslie
Professional. *b:* 5.1.1913, Colne, Lancashire. Opening right-hand batsman, off break bowler. *Team* Lancashire (1946, 1 match).
Career batting
1–1–0–1–1–1.00–0–*ct* 0
Bowling 90–2–45.00–0–0–2/41

Bull
Professional. Lower order batsman, change bowler. *Team* Kent (1871, 1 match).
Career batting
1–2–1–10–8*–10.00–0–*ct* 0
Bowling 22–0

Bull, Arthur Herbert
Amateur. *b:* 23.1.1892, Wellingborough, Northamptonshire. *d:* 18.12.1965, Ingoldisthorpe, Norfolk. Lower order right-hand batsman. *Sch* Wellingborough and Mill Hill. *Team* Northamptonshire (1913–24, 36 matches).
Career batting
36–57–4–538–44–10.15–0–*ct* 12

He captained Northamptonshire in 1923 and 1924. Much better known as a bowls player, he represented

England 45 times and captained the national side in 1939.

Bull, Charles Harry
Professional. *b:* 29.3.1909, Lewisham, London. *d:* 28.5.1939. He was killed in a road accident at Margaretting, Chelmsford, Essex. Opening or middle order right-hand batsman. *Teams* Kent (1929–30, 4 matches); Worcestershire (1931–39, 171 matches).
Career batting
175–308–20–6801–161–23.61–5–*ct* 63
Bowling 120–0
He hit 1,000 runs in a season 4 times with 1,619, av 28.40, in 1937 his best.

Bull, Eric Alister
Amateur. *b:* 28.9.1886, Bourke, New South Wales, Australia. *d:* 14.5.1954, Mount Ku-ring-gai, Sydney, New South Wales, Australia. Middle order right-hand batsman, right-arm medium pace or leg break bowler. *Team* New South Wales (1913/14 to 1914/15, 3 matches). *Tours* AIF to England 1919, to South Africa 1919/20.
Career batting
23–33–2–595–42–19.19–0–*ct* 8
Bowling 100–4–25.00–0–0–2/8
He had a very modest record in English first-class cricket in 1919.

Bull, Frederick George
Amateur, but changed to professional in 1905. *b:* 2.4.1875, Hackney, London. *d:* 16.9.1910. He was found drowned at St Annes-on-Sea, Lancashire. He took his own life. Tail end right-hand batsman, off break bowler. *Teams* Essex (1895–1900, 88 matches); Scotland (1905). *Tour* Warner to United States 1897.
Career batting
95–138–35–1274–51–12.36–0–*ct* 46
Bowling 9042–416–21.73–34–7–9/93
He took 100 wickets in a season twice (best 120, av 21.95, in 1897). His best bowling was 9/93 for Essex v Surrey at the Oval in 1897.

Bull, G.
Professional. Lower order batsman, bowler. *Team* Hampshire (1900, 2 matches).
Career batting
2–3–1–12–10–6.00–0–*ct* 0
Bowling 25–0

Bull, Henry Edward
Amateur. *b:* 8.3.1843, Lathbury Rectory, Newport Pagnell, Buckinghamshire. *d:* 31.5.1905, Maids Moreton, near Buckingham. Opening right-hand batsman, excellent deep field. *Sch* Westminster. *Team* Oxford U (1863, blue).
Career batting
21–36–1–494–46–14.11–0–*ct* 9
Bowling 20–0
His County cricket was for Bedfordshire (1860), Oxfordshire (1863–64), Northamptonshire (pre first-class, 1863), Hertfordshire (1863) and Buckinghamshire (1864–71). He was the first Hon Sec of the Buckinghamshire County Club. His final first-class match was for MCC in 1876.

Bullen, Christopher Keith
Cricketer. *b:* 5.11.1962, Clapham, London. Middle order right-hand batsman, off break bowler. *Team* Surrey (1982–91, 30 matches).
Career batting
30–35–7–663–65–23.67–0–*ct* 30
Bowling 1078–38–28.36–1–0–6/119
He was regarded as a specialist one-day player.

Buller, Charles Edward
Professional. *b:* 23.8.1892, Wellingborough, Northamptonshire. *d:* 16.12.1969, Northampton. Tail end right-hand batsman, bowler. *Team* Northamptonshire (1931, 1 match).
Career batting
1–2–1–2–1*–2.00–0–*ct* 0
Bowling 35–0

Buller, Charles Francis
Amateur. *b:* 26.5.1846, Colombo, Ceylon. *d:* 22.11.1906, Cobb, Lyme Regis, Dorset. Son of Arthur (Gentlemen 1836). He married the former wife of H. B. Kingscote (Kent and Gloucestershire). Very stylish middle order right-hand batsman, right-hand slow round-arm bowler, excellent deep field. *Sch* Harrow. *Team* Middlesex (1865–77, 24 matches).
Career batting
90–158–14–3140–106–21.80–2–*ct* 46
Bowling 220–7 + 5–31.42–1–0–5/?
His debut in first-class matches was for England v XIII of Kent in 1864. He also played for Devon (1862). An excellent athlete, he was a noted long jumper.

Buller, Eric Tremayne
(later Buller-Leybourne-Popham)
Amateur. *b:* 3.1.1894, Highworth, Wiltshire. *d:* 8.8.1973, Bath, Somerset. Grandson of F. L. Popham (Oxford U). Lower order batsman, useful bowler. *Sch* Harrow. *Team* Army (1919).
Career batting
1–2–1–58–46–58.00–0–*ct* 0
Bowling 71–0
His County cricket was for Devon (1924–31).

Buller, John Sydney, MBE
Professional. *b:* 23.8.1909, Wortley, Leeds, Yorkshire. *d:* 7.8.1970, Edgbaston, Birmingham. Lower order right-hand batsman, wicket-keeper. *Teams* Yorkshire (1930, 1 match); Worcestershire (1935–46, 110 matches).
Career batting
112–171–44–1746–64–13.74–0–*ct* 178–*st* 71

He was better known as an umpire than a player and was the leading figure in the elimination of 'throwing' in the early 1960s, notably in the case of the South African bowler, Griffin. Buller became a first-class umpire in 1951 and died at Edgbaston whilst officiating in the match between Warwickshire and Nottinghamshire. He stood regularly as an umpire in 32 Test matches (1956–69) and was awarded the MBE for his services to cricket.

Bullock, Burnett Wedlake
Professional. *b:* 5.10.1896, Redhill, Surrey. *d:* 22.12.1954, Balham, London. Middle order right-hand batsman. *Team* Surrey (1922–24, 5 matches).
Career batting
6–8–1–121–40–17.28–0–*ct* 0

Bullock, Mark
Professional. *b:* 24.10.1872, Dudley, Worcestershire. *d:* 22.4.1925, Leicester. Middle order batsman. *Team* Worcestershire (1900, 4 matches).
Career batting
4–6–0–59–27–9.83–0–*ct* 1

Bullock, Percy George
Professional. *b:* 28.8.1893, Balsall Heath, Worcestershire. *d:* 1.12.1986, Wythall, Worcestershire. Middle or lower order right-hand batsman, slow left-arm bowler. *Team* Worcestershire (1921, 3 matches).
Career batting
3–5–0–11–9–2.20–0–*ct* 3

Bullough, John
Professional. *b:* 1893, Bolton, Lancashire. *d:* 3.6.1967, Westhoughton, Lancashire. Tail end right-hand batsman, slow right-arm bowler. *Team* Lancashire (1914–19, 8 matches).
Career batting
8–8–3–24–17–4.80–0–*ct* 3
Bowling 573–13–44.07–1–0–5/123

Bulmer, John Robert Leopold
Professional. *b:* 28.12.1867, Guisborough, Yorkshire. *d:* 20.1.1917, Werneth, Oldham, Lancashire. Tail end batsman, right-arm fast medium bowler. *Team* Yorkshire (1891, 1 match).
Career batting
1–2–0–0–0–0.00–0–*ct* 0
Bowling 79–1–79.00–0–0–1/51

Bulpett, Charles William Lloyd
Amateur. *b:* 18.8.1852, Sandgates, Chertsey, Surrey. *d:* 11.7.1939, Chiromo, Nairobi, Kenya. Lower order right-hand batsman, right-arm fast bowler. *Sch* Rugby. *Team* Middlesex (1880, 1 match).
Career batting
5–9–2–76–23*–10.85–0–*ct* 2
Bowling 163–5–32.60–0–0–4/21

His first appearance in first-class cricket was for MCC in 1877. He was at Oxford, but not in the Eleven. His final first-class match was for Gentlemen in 1882. He appeared in some matches under the name 'C. W. Lloyd'. In 1887 he backed himself for £200 to walk a mile, run a mile and ride a mile in 18 minutes and won the bet. In 1888 for a bet of £1,000 to £400 he set himself 16 minutes 30 seconds to achieve the same feat and again won. He won a blue for athletics.

Bulsara, Maneksha Dadabhai
Amateur. *b:* 2.9.1877, Daman, Portugese India. Lower order right-hand batsman, right-arm medium fast bowler. *Team* Parsis (1899/1900 to 1921/2). *Tour* India to England 1911.
Career batting
30–47–14–228–24*–6.90–0–*ct* 14
Bowling 1885–119–15.84–7–2–8/31

Bunce, William Newman
Amateur. *b:* 17.4.1911, Pill, Bristol. *d:* 29.5.1981, Pill, Bristol. Lower order left-hand batsman, right-arm medium fast bowler. *Team* Somerset (1936–37, 14 matches).
Career batting
14–21–3–227–46–12.61–0–*ct* 5
Bowling 186–4–46.50–0–0–3/81

He played soccer for Bristol Rovers and Bristol City.

Bunting, Dr Edward Lancelot
Amateur. *b:* 10.12.1883, Tillington, Staffordshire. *d:* 26.2.1962, Barnwood, Gloucestershire. Middle order right-hand batsman, leg break and googly bowler. *Sch* Blundell's. *Team* Worcestershire (1922, 1 match).
Career batting
1–2–0–1–1–0.50–0–*ct* 1
Bowling 38–0

Bunting, Rodney Alan
Cricketer. *b:* 25.4.1965, East Winch, Norfolk. Lower order right-hand batsman, right-arm fast medium bowler. *Team* Sussex (1988–91, 38 matches).
Career batting
38–40–14–366–73–14.07–0–*ct* 5
Bowling 3047–80–38.08–3–0–5/44

He also played for Norfolk (1985–87 and 1992).

Bunting, Walter Henry
Professional. *b:* 18.6.1854, Cambridge. *d:* 28.10.1922, Burnham, Somerset. Lower order right-hand batsman, right-arm fast bowler. *Team* Middlesex (1877, 3 matches).
Career batting
3–6–1–6–2*–1.20–0–*ct* 3
Bowling 107–0

He played under the assumed name of Walter Gray.

Bunyard, Graham Stuart
Amateur. *b:* 17.10.1939, Port Elizabeth, South Africa. Lower order right-hand batsman, right-arm fast bowler. *Teams* Transvaal (1959/60 to 1960/1); Rhodesia (1962/3). *Tour* SA Fezela to England 1961.

Burbidge, Arthur

Career batting
14–17–3–192–35–13.71–0–*ct* 7
Bowling 1082–48–22.54–1–0–5/35

Burbidge, Arthur
Amateur. *b:* 1836, Camberwell, Surrey. *d:* 18.12.1890, Swanage, Dorset. Brother of Frederick (Surrey). Middle order batsman. *Team* Surrey (1857, 2 matches).
Career batting
4–8–1–54–13–7.71–0–*ct* 0
His last first-class match was for Gentlemen of South in 1862.

Burbidge, Frederick
Amateur. *b:* 23.11.1832, Champion Hill, London. *d:* 12.12.1892, Micklefield, Rickmansworth, Hertfordshire. Brother of Arthur (Surrey). Sound middle order right-hand batsman, good field. *Team* Surrey (1854–66, 41 matches).
Career batting
64–110–11–1475–101–14.89–1–*ct* 58
His last first-class match was for Gentlemen of South in 1868. Owing to his profession of a wholesale druggist he was unable to appear regularly for Surrey, but he was the appointed captain 1858–65. He also played for Bedfordshire (1856).

Burch, Geoffrey Worth
Professional. *b:* 12.4.1937, Braunstone, Leicester. Useful lower order right-hand batsman, wicket-keeper, occasional right-arm medium pace bowler. *Team* Leicestershire (1958–64, 46 matches).
Career batting
46–79–10–1067–64*–15.46–0–*ct* 55
Bowling 3–0

Burchell, Thomas James
Professional in 1905, but amateur in 1919. *b:* 26.4.1875, Steyning, Sussex. *d:* 16.2.1951, Hollingbury, Brighton, Sussex. Tail end batsman, wicket-keeper. *Team* Sussex (1905–19, 2 matches).
Career batting
2–4–2–13–6*–6.50–0–*ct* 8–*st* 1

Burchnall, Richard Langley
Cricketer. *b:* 8.8.1948, Oxford. Opening right-hand batsman. *Sch* Winchester. *Team* Oxford U (1968–71, blue 1970–71).
Career batting
32–57–2–874–85–15.89–0–*ct* 14

Burden, Mervyn Derek
Professional. *b:* 4.10.1930, Southampton, Hampshire. *d:* 9.11.1987, Whitchurch, Hampshire. Lower order right-hand batsman, off break bowler. *Sch* KES, Southampton. *Team* Hampshire (1953–63, 174 matches).
Career batting
174–191–59–901–51–6.82–0–*ct* 76
Bowling 12559–481–26.11–23–4–8/38

Burdett, John Willder
Amateur. *b:* 16.8.1888, Blaby, Leicestershire. *d:* 16.4.1974, Melton Mowbray, Leicestershire. Son of Thomas (Hon Sec, Leicestershire CCC 1883–1907). Middle order right-hand batsman. *Sch* Oundle. *Team* Leicestershire (1919, 1 match).
Career batting
1–2–0–1–1–0.50–0–*ct* 0

Burge, Gerard Rodon
Amateur. *b:* 9.8.1857, Dinapore, India. *d:* 15.2.1933, Edmonton, Middlesex. Lower order right-hand batsman, right-arm fast bowler. *Sch* Marlborough. *Team* Middlesex (1885, 1 match).
Career batting
2–4–1–1–1–0.33–0–*ct* 1
Bowling 103–5–20.60–1–0–5/46
His last first-class appearance was for Gentlemen at Scarborough in 1886. He also played for Bedfordshire and Hertfordshire.

Burge, Peter John Parnell
Amateur. *b:* 17.5.1932, Kangaroo Point, Brisbane, Queensland, Australia. Sound middle order right-hand batsman, right-arm medium pace bowler. *Team* Queensland (1952/3 to 1967/8, 91 matches). *Tours* Australia to England 1956, 1961, 1964, to West Indies 1954/5, to New Zealand 1956/7, 1966/7, to South Africa 1957/8, to India 1956/7, 1959/60, 1964/5, to Pakistan 1959/60, 1964/5. *Tests* Australia (1954/5 to 1965/6, 42 matches).
Career batting
233–354–46–14640–283–47.53–38–*ct* 166–*st* 4
Bowling 129–1–129.00–0–0–1/0
Test batting
42–68–8–2290–181–38.16–4–*ct* 23
He hit 1,000 runs in a season twice on his tours to England (best 1,376, av 55.04, in 1961). His two great innings in England were 181 in the Oval Test of 1961 and 160 in the Leeds Test of 1964. His highest score was 283 for Queensland v New South Wales at Brisbane in 1963/4.

Burger, Christopher George de Villiers
Amateur. *b:* 12.7.1935, Randfontein, Transvaal, South Africa. Middle order right-hand batsman, right-arm medium pace bowler, fine field. *Teams* Free Foresters (1955); Natal (1955/6 to 1965/6). *Tour* SA Fezela to England 1961. *Tests* South Africa (1957/8, 2 matches).
Career batting
48–74–5–2073–131–30.04–2–*ct* 47
Bowling 17–1–17.00–0–0–1/8
Test batting
2–4–1–62–37*–20.66–0–*ct* 1

Burgess, Alan Thomas
Amateur. *b:* 1.5.1920, Christchurch, New Zealand. Lower order right-hand batsman, left-arm bowler. *Team* Canterbury (1940/1 to 1951/2). *Tour* New Zea-

land Services to England 1945.
Career batting
14–23–2–466–61*–22.19–0–*ct* 12
Bowling 491–16–30.68–1–0–6/52

Burgess, Alec Andrews
Amateur. *b:* 2.1.1906, Peterborough, Northamptonshire. *d:* 20.11.1990, Waveney, Norfolk. Lower order right-hand batsman, leg break bowler. *Sch* Wellingborough. *Team* Northamptonshire (1929, 1 match).
Career batting
1–2–0–14–13–7.00–0–*ct* 1
Bowling 13–0
He also played for Suffolk (1934–35).

Burgess, Charles Thomas
Amateur. *b:* 30.6.1886, Hastings, Sussex. *d:* 14.1.1978, Crediton, Devon. Middle order right-hand batsman, slow right-arm bowler. *Team* Sussex (1919, 1 match).
Career batting
1–2–0–2–1–1.00–0–*ct* 1
Bowling 39–3–13.00–0–0–3/39

Burgess, Graham Iefvion
Cricketer. *b:* 5.5.1943, Glastonbury, Somerset. Middle/lower order right-hand batsman, right-arm medium pace bowler. *Sch* Millfield. *Team* Somerset (1966–79, 252 matches).
Career batting
252–414–37–7129–129–18.90–2–*ct* 120
Bowling 13543–474–28.57–18–2–7/43
He also played for Wiltshire (1981–82) and Cambridgeshire (1983–84). He became a first-class umpire in 1991.

Burgess, Henry
Amateur. *b:* 5.5.1879, Carlton-Curlieu, Leicestershire. *d:* 16.4.1964, Middleton, Northamptonshire. Brother of John (Leicestershire), uncle of C. B. R. Fetherstonhaugh (MCC). Lower order right-hand batsman, right-arm fast bowler. *Sch* Wellingborough and Oakham. *Teams* Leicestershire (1900–02, 8 matches); Northamptonshire (1905, 1 match).
Career batting
9–13–1–63–20–5.25–0–*ct* 4
Bowling 556–11–50.54–0–0–3/106

Burgess, John
Amateur. *b:* 22.11.1880, Carlton-Curlieu, Leicestershire. *d:* 2.11.1953, East Carlton, Northamptonshire. Brother of Henry (Leicestershire and Northamptonshire), uncle of C. B. R. Fetherstonhaugh (MCC). Hard-hitting middle order right-hand batsman, wicket-keeper. *Sch* Oakham. *Team* Leicestershire (1902–13, 12 matches).
Career batting
12–18–0–230–39–12.77–0–*ct* 7–*st* 2

Burgess, Mark Gordon
Cricketer. *b:* 17.7.1944, Auckland, New Zealand. Son of G. C. (Auckland). Middle order right-hand batsman, off break bowler. *Team* Auckland (1966/7 to 1979/80). *Tours* New Zealand to England 1969, 1973, 1978, 1979 (World Cup), to Australia 1967/8, 1969/70, 1970/1, 1980/1, to West Indies 1971/2, to India and Pakistan 1969/70, 1976/7. *Tests* New Zealand (1967/8 to 1980/1, 50 matches).
Career batting
192–322–35–10281–146–35.82–20–*ct* 152
Bowling 1148–30–38.26–0–0–3/23
Test batting
50–92–6–2684–119*–31.20–5–*ct* 34
Bowling 212–6–35.33–0–0–3/23
His first-class debut was for New Zealand Under 23 in 1963/4. The most successful of his three tours to England was in 1973 when he hit 836 runs, av 49.17, including a Test hundred. He captained the 1978 touring side and in all captained New Zealand in 10 Tests.

Burgess, Thomas
Professional. *b:* 1861, Harrogate, Yorkshire. *d:* 22.2.1922, Harrogate, Yorkshire. Useful middle order right-hand batsman, right-arm fast medium bowler. *Team* Yorkshire (1895, 1 match).
Career batting
1–2–1–0–0*–0.00–*ct* 2
The professional with the Harrogate Club, he played in emergency for Yorkshire in one match at Harrogate, when one of the County team failed to arrive.

Burgess, William Arthur
Amateur. *b:* 31.1.1888, Williton, Somerset. *d:* 20.6.1970, Minehead, Somerset. Middle order right-hand batsman, left-arm bowler. *Team* Somerset (1921–22, 7 matches).
Career batting
7–12–0–211–79–17.58–0–*ct* 7
Bowling 246–6–41.00–0–0–2/39

Burghes, Arthur
Professional. *b:* 8.9.1848, Southwark, London. *d:* 18.8.1916, Bow, London. Middle or lower order right-hand batsman, right-hand medium pace round-arm bowler. *Team* Middlesex (1876–77, 7 matches).
Career batting
7–11–1–245–104–24.50–1–*ct* 4
Bowling 82–0
He also played for Essex (pre first-class, 1876).

Burgin, Eric
Professional. *b:* 4.1.1924, Pitsmoor, Sheffield, Yorkshire. Lower order right-hand batsman, right-arm medium pace bowler. *Team* Yorkshire (1952–53, 12 matches).
Career batting
12–10–3–92–32–13.14–0–*ct* 0

Bowling 795–31–25.64–2–0–6/43

A noted soccer player, he appeared for York City and Sheffield United.

Burke, Cecil
Amateur. *b:* 27.3.1914, Ellerslie, Auckland, New Zealand. Defensive lower order right-hand batsman, leg break and googly bowler, good close field. *Team* Auckland (1937/8 to 1953/4). *Tour* New Zealand to England 1949. *Test* New Zealand (1945/6, 1 match).
Career batting
60–73–18–959–51–17.43–0–*ct* 31
Bowling 5199–200–25.99–7–1–6/23
Test batting
1–2–0–4–3–2.00–0–*ct* 0
Bowling 30–2–15.00–0–0–2/30

On his single tour to England he was not selected for any of the Tests, but in all first-class matches took 54 wickets, av 29.83.

Burke, Charles Carrington
Amateur. *b:* 8.7.1853, Bayswater, London. *d:* 22.5.1904, Mitchen, Godalming, Surrey. Lower order batsman. *Sch* Harrow. *Team* MCC (1882).
Career batting
1–2–0–7–7–3.50–0–*ct* 0

Burke, George Humphrey
Professional. *b:* 18.8.1847, Greenwich, Kent. *d:* 21.7.1920, Peckham, London. Lower order right-hand batsman, right-arm fast bowler. *Team* Kent (1877, 1 match).
Career batting
1–1–0–9–9–9.00–0–*ct* 2
Bowling 51–4–12.75–0–0–3/16

Burke, James Wallace
Amateur. *b:* 12.6.1930, Mosman, Sydney, New South Wales, Australia. *d:* 2.2.1979, Manly, Sydney, New South Wales, Australia. He died by his own hand. Defensive opening right-hand batsman, off break bowler. *Team* New South Wales (1948/9 to 1958/9, 67 matches). *Tours* Australia to New Zealand 1949/50, to England 1956, to Pakistan and India 1956/7, to South Africa 1957/8. *Tests* Australia (1950/1 to 1958/9, 24 matches).
Career batting
130–204–36–7563–220–45.01–21–*ct* 58
Bowling 2941–101–29.11–3–0–6/40
Test batting
24–44–7–1280–189–34.59–3–*ct* 18
Bowling 230–8–28.75–0–0–4/37

He was one of the few successful players of the 1956 Australian tour of England, heading the Test batting averages and in all first-class matches hitting 1,339 runs, av 47.82. His highest score was 220 for New South Wales v South Australia at Adelaide in 1956/7. An injury on his 1957/8 tour to South Africa put an end to his career, undermining his confidence. As a bowler he was more than useful, but a suspect action curtailed his career in this direction. After retiring he was a well-known sports commentator.

Burke, Joseph Patrick
Amateur. *b:* 31.1.1923, Dublin, Ireland. Lower order right-hand batsman, right-arm fast medium bowler. *Team* Ireland (1953–58).
Career batting
3–4–1–36–19*–12.00–0–*ct* 2
Bowling 105–3–35.00–0–0–2/32

Burki, Javed
Amateur. *b:* 8.5.1938, Meerut, India. Middle order right-hand batsman, right-arm medium pace bowler. Nephew of M. Baqa Jilana (India) and M. Jahangir Khan (India), cousin of Imran Khan (Pakistan), Majid Jahangir Khan (Pakistan), A. J. Khan (Oxford U), Humayun Zaman (Lahore) and Javed Zaman (Lahore). *Teams* Oxford U (1958–60, blue all three years); Punjab (1955/6 to 1956/7); Lahore (1961/2 to 1970/1); Karachi (1963/4 to 1967/8); Rawalpindi (1967/8 to 1972/3); NWFP (1974/5). *Tours* Pakistan to England 1962, 1967, to India 1960/1, to Australia and New Zealand 1964/5, to Ceylon 1964/5. *Tests* Pakistan (1960/1 to 1969/70, 25 matches).
Career batting
177–290–31–9421–227–36.37–22–*ct* 101
Bowling 1553–35–44.37–0–0–4/13
Test batting
25–48–4–1341–140–30.47–3–*ct* 7
Bowling 23–0

Although he had an excellent cricket career at Oxford, neither of his visits to England with the Pakistani team was very successful. He captained the 1962 side and hit 1,257 runs, av 33.07, including a century in the Lord's Test, but his leadership came in for considerable criticism and these were his only five Tests as captain. In 1967, he was promoted to opening batsman, an experiment which failed. His highest score was 227 for Karachi Whites v Khairpur at Karachi in 1963/4.

Burkitt, W.
(*see under* Birkett, W.)

Burls, Charles William
Amateur. *b:* 8.3.1847, Peckham Rye Common, Surrey. *d:* 17.12.1923, Datchet, Buckinghamshire. Middle order right-hand batsman, change bowler. *Team* Surrey (1873–80, 10 matches).
Career batting
17–29–0–304–37–10.48–0–*ct* 8
Bowling 23–0

His final first-class match was for Gentlemen in 1887.

Burlton, Arthur Temple
Amateur. *b:* 10.3.1900, Coimbatore, India. *d:* 10.2.1980, Ballochneck, Thornhill, Stirling, Scotland. Middle order right-hand batsman, off break bowler.

Sch Repton. *Team* Worcestershire (1922, 5 matches).
Career batting
5–10–1–114–35*–12.66–0–*ct* 3
Bowling 38–1–38.00–0–0–1/22

He also played for Devon (1934). He wrote a book on 'cricketing manners.'

Burman, John
Professional. *b:* 5.10.1838, Bramham, Yorkshire. *d:* 14.5.1900, Halton, Leeds, Yorkshire. Tail end batsman. *Team* Yorkshire (1867, 1 match).
Career batting
1–2–1–1–1*–1.00–0–*ct* 0

Burn, Edmund Holcroft Miller
Amateur. *b:* 6.10.1922, Brigg, Lincolnshire. *d:* 22.10.1969. He was killed in a road accident at Grimsby Beach, Ontario, Canada. Middle order right-hand batsman, right-arm medium pace bowler. *Team* Canada (1954). *Tour* Canada to England 1954.
Career batting
2–4–0–31–12–7.75–0–*ct* 1

He appeared for Canada v MCC (non-first-class) in 1951 and was one of the mainstays of cricket in Ontario. He produced, edited and published '*The Canadian Cricketer*' from 1952 to 1965.

Burn, Edwin James Kenneth
Amateur. *b:* 17.9.1862, Richmond, Tasmania, Australia. *d:* 20.7.1956, Hobart, Tasmania, Australia. Opening/middle order right-hand batsman. *Team* Tasmania (1883/4 to 1909/10, 25 matches). *Tours* Australia to England 1890; Tasmania to New Zealand 1883/4. *Tests* Australia (1890, 2 matches).
Career batting
48–90–9–1750–119–21.60–2–*ct* 31
Bowling 320–14–22.85–0–0–3/15
Test batting
2–4–0–41–19–10.25–0–*ct* 0

Burn was chosen as reserve wicket-keeper on the 1890 tour to England owing to a dispute among the selectors, but on the voyage to England it was then discovered that he had never kept wicket! He was a prolific batsman in Tasmania, but never came to terms with conditions in England.

Burn, Paul
Cricketer. *b:* 31.10.1963, Sacriston, Durham. Middle order right-hand batsman, right-arm medium pace bowler. *Team* Minor Counties (1990).
Career batting
1–2–1–47–47*–47.00–0–*ct* 0

His County cricket was for Durham (pre first-class, 1985–91) and Northumberland (1992).

Burn, Sir Roland Clive Wallace
Amateur. *b:* 29.10.1882, Streatham, London. *d:* 8.5.1955, Westminster, London. Lower order batsman, slow left-arm bowler. *Sch* Winchester and Merchant Taylors. *Team* Oxford U (1902–05, blue all four years). *Tours* Brackley to West Indies 1904/5; MCC to North America 1905.
Career batting
45–71–23–420–59–8.75–0–*ct* 30
Bowling 3284–123–26.69–4–0–6/66

His final first-class match was for Leveson-Gower's XI in 1919.

Burnand, Lewis Whitmore
Amateur. *b:* 5.5.1839, Bloomsbury, London. *d:* 31.1.1923, Worthing, Sussex. Lower order batsman, bowler. *Sch* Harrow. *Team* MCC (1863–64).
Career batting
2–3–0–4–4–1.33–0–*ct* 1
Bowling 11–0

His County cricket was for Hertfordshire (1863).

Burnell, Henry Blomfield
Amateur. *b:* 14.11.1853, Upper Clapton, London. *d:* 19.10.1910, St John's Wood, London. Lower order batsman. *Sch* Harrow. *Team* MCC (1879).
Career batting
1–1–0–1–1–1.00–0–*ct* 0

Burnell, Philip John
Cricketer. *b:* 12.6.1945, Woodford Green, Essex. Lower order right-hand batsman, wicket-keeper. *Sch* Chigwell. *Team* Oxford U (1967).
Career batting
6–10–3–71–28–10.14–0–*ct* 3–*st* 1

Burnet, John Ronald
Amateur. *b:* 11.10.1918, Saltaire, Shipley, Yorkshire. Middle order right-hand batsman. *Team* Yorkshire (1958–59, 54 matches).
Career batting
55–77–6–897–54–12.63–0–*ct* 7
Bowling 26–1–26.00–0–0–1/8

Appointed captain of Yorkshire in 1958, without previously having appeared in first-class cricket, he led the County for two seasons.

Burnett, Anthony Compton
(later known as Compton-Burnett)
Amateur. *b:* 26.10.1923, Chipstead, Surrey. Father of R. J. Compton-Burnett (Cambridge U). Middle order right-hand batsman, good close field, occasional wicket-keeper. *Sch* Lancing. *Teams* Cambridge U (1949–50, blue 1949); Glamorgan (1958, 8 matches).
Career batting
27–40–6–790–79*–23.23–0–*ct* 20
Bowling 16–0

Burnett, Ernest Wildman
Amateur. *b:* 22.9.1844, Brighton, Sussex. *d:* 22.12.1931, Oxford. Cousin of J. D. (Surrey). Hard-hitting lower order right-hand batsman, slow round-arm bowler. *Sch* Harrow. *Teams* Gentlemen of South (1867); Southgate (1868).
Career batting
5–7–0–45–26–6.42–0–*ct* 1

Bowling 60–2–30.00–0–0–2/39

He also played for Staffordshire (1868–78). His first-class debut was for the South in 1862.

Burnett, John David
Amateur. *b:* 25.2.1840, Vauxhall, London. *d:* 18.6.1878, Pietermaritzburg, Natal, South Africa. Cousin of E. W. (Gentlemen of South). Middle order right-hand batsman, brilliant cover field. *Sch* Harrow. *Team* Surrey (1862, 1 match).
Career batting
5–7–0–68–39–9.71–0–*ct* 4

He appeared in several trials whilst at Oxford, but not against Cambridge. His first-class debut was for Gentlemen of South in 1861 and his final first-class match for the same side in 1863.

Burnett, Neil William
Cricketer. *b:* 16.12.1961, Wolstanton, Newcastle-under-Lyme, Staffordshire. Middle order right-hand batsman, right-arm medium pace bowler. *Team* Scotland (1986).
Career batting
1–1–0–4–4–4.00–0–*ct* 0
Bowling 30–0

Burnham, George Joseph
Professional. *b:* 5.11.1878, Nottingham. *d:* 7.3.1971, Nottingham. Middle order right-hand batsman. *Team* Derbyshire (1912, 5 matches).
Career batting
5–6–1–30–15–6.00–0–*ct* 3

Burnham, Gordon Le Roy
Amateur. *b:* 18.12.1886. *d:* 1.9.1964, Gessenay, Berne, Switzerland. Middle order batsman, useful change bowler. *Teams* Europeans (1910/11); Sussex (1914, 1 match).
Career batting
3–4–0–42–18–10.50–0–*ct* 2
Bowling 60–3–20.00–0–0–2/48

Burnham, John William
Professional. *b:* 6.6.1839, Nottingham. *d:* 20.4.1914, Derby. Opening/middle order right-hand batsman. *Team* Derbyshire (1871–76, 6 matches).
Career batting
6–11–0–55–31–5.00–0–*ct* 2

He also played for Suffolk (1866).

Burnley, Ian David
Cricketer. *b:* 11.3.1963, Darlington, Co Durham. Opening right-hand batsman. *Team* Cambridge U (1984, blue).
Career batting
3–6–0–232–86–38.66–0–*ct* 1

Burns, James
Professional. *b:* 20.6.1866, Liverpool, Lancashire. *d:* 11.9.1957, Hampstead, London. Opening right-hand batsman, slow left-arm bowler. *Team* Essex (1894–96, 26 matches).
Career batting
41–70–4–1134–114–17.18–1–*ct* 15
Bowling 460–15–30.66–1–0–6/41

He appeared in non-first-class matches for Lancashire from 1884 to 1886 and commenced his connection with Essex in 1887. His first-class debut was for MCC in 1890 and his final first-class match for the same club in 1901. An excellent soccer player, he appeared for West Bromwich Albion and Notts County.

Burns, Michael
Cricketer. *b:* 2.6.1969, Barrow-in-Furness, Lancashire. Lower order right-hand batsman, wicket-keeper. *Team* Warwickshire (1992, 2 matches).
Career batting
2–3–0–85–78–28.33–0–*ct* 7–*st* 1

He also played for Cumberland (1988–92).

Burns, Neil David
Cricketer. *b:* 19.9.1965, Chelmsford, Essex. Middle order left-hand batsman, occasional slow left-arm bowler, wicket-keeper. *Teams* Western Province (1985/6); Essex (1986, 2 matches); Somerset (1987–92, 137 matches).
Career batting
143–211–50–4870–166–30.24–4–*ct* 279–*st* 28
Bowling 8–0

Burns, William Beaumont
Amateur. *b:* 29.8.1883, Rugeley, Staffordshire. *d:* 7.7.1916, Contalmaison, France. Hard-hitting middle order right-hand batsman, right-arm fast bowler, brilliant field. *Sch* King's School, Ely. *Team* Worcestershire (1903–13, 196 matches). *Tour* MCC to New Zealand 1906/7.
Career batting
217–374–23–9479–196–27.00–12–*ct* 147
Bowling 6334–214–29.59–8–1–7/58

He hit 1,000 runs in a season 5 times (best 1,438, av 31.95, in 1911). His bowling was very fast, but the fairness of his delivery was often in question. He also played for Staffordshire (1901–02). At the close of the 1913 season he emigrated to Canada.

Burnup, Cuthbert James
Amateur. *b:* 21.11.1875, Blackheath, Kent. *d:* 5.4.1960, North End, Golders Green, Middlesex. Sound right-hand opening batsman, slow right-arm bowler, splendid outfield. *Sch* Malvern. *Teams* Cambridge U (1895–98, blue 1896–98); Kent (1896–1907, 157 matches); London County (1901). *Tours* Warner to North America 1898; Hawke to New Zealand and Australia 1902/03; Kent to North America 1903.
Career batting
228–395–25–13614–200–36.79–26–*ct* 107
Bowling 3178–98–32.42–4–0–6/36

He hit 1,000 runs in a season 8 times (best 2,048, av 39.38, in 1902). His only double century was 200 for Kent v Lancashire at Old Trafford in 1900. He captained Kent in 1903. An excellent soccer player he was awarded his blue at Cambridge and went on to gain an England cap in 1896.

Burr, Frederick Bonham
Amateur. *b:* 2.8.1887, Blacklands, Hastings, Sussex. *d:* 12.3.1915, Kemmel, Belgium. Middle order batsman. *Sch* Denstone. *Team* Worcestershire (1911, 1 match).
Career batting
1–2–1–46–39–46.00–0–*ct* 1
He played in trial matches at Oxford U, but not in first-class games.

Burrell, Rev Herbert John Edwin
Amateur. *b:* 15.11.1866, Kirtling, Cambridgeshire. *d:* 22.5.1949, Trumpington, Cambridge. Brother of R. J. (Essex). Middle order right-hand batsman, right-arm medium pace bowler. *Sch* Charterhouse. *Teams* Essex (1895, 2 matches); Oxford U (1889).
Career batting
3–5–0–15–10–3.00–0–*ct* 0
Bowling 78–2–39.00–0–0–1/37
He first played for Essex (pre first-class) in 1888. He also played for Hertfordshire (1901–04).

Burrell, Reginald John
Amateur. *b:* 26.8.1870, Kirtling, Cambridgeshire. *d:* 16.3.1948, Risby Place, Suffolk. Brother of H. J. E. (Essex). Middle order batsman. *Sch* Charterhouse. *Team* Essex (1894–95, 6 matches).
Career batting
10–17–1–200–40–12.50–0–*ct* 2
His final first-class match was for MCC in 1897. He also played for Suffolk (1904).

Burridge, Alan James
Cricketer. *b:* 8.10.1936, Sunderland, Co Durham. Middle order left-hand batsman, right-arm slow bowler. *Team* Minor Counties (1973).
Career batting
1–2–0–42–37–21.00–0–*ct* 0
His County cricket was for Durham (pre first-class, 1961–72), Lincolnshire (1973–74) and Hertfordshire (1975–78). He was Secretary of Middlesex in 1980.

Burrington, George
Amateur. *b:* 5.7.1864, Tiverton, Devon. *d:* 22.1.1942, Newhaven, Sussex. Middle order batsman. *Team* Somerset (1901–02, 3 matches).
Career batting
3–5–0–40–15–8.00–0–*ct* 1

Burrington, Humphrey Sandford
Amateur. *b:* 5.4.1882, Bridgwater, Somerset. *d:* 15.4.1957, Barnstaple, Devon. Middle order batsman. *Sch* Haileybury. *Team* Somerset (1903–05, 5 matches).
Career batting
5–7–1–65–20–10.83–0–*ct* 3
Bowling 10–0

Burrough, George Baker
Amateur. *b:* 8.2.1907, Glastonbury, Somerset. *d:* 9.5.1965, Butleigh, Somerset. Lower order batsman, useful spin bowler. *Team* Somerset (1936, 1 match).
Career batting
1–1–0–27–27–27.00–0–*ct* 2
Bowling 38–1–38.00–0–0–1/23

Burrough, Herbert Dickinson
Amateur. *b:* 6.2.1909, Wedmore, Somerset. Son of W. G. (Somerset), cousin of J. W. (Gloucestershire), nephew of John (Cambridge U). Sound middle order right-hand batsman. *Sch* King's, Bruton. *Team* Somerset (1927–47, 171 matches).
Career batting
171–272–18–5316–135–20.92–4–*ct* 83
Bowling 14–0
He appeared in the Seniors' match whilst at Cambridge, but not in first-class matches. His best season was 1933 when he reached 1,007 runs, av 25.17 – the only year he exceeded 1,000 runs. He played hockey for England.

Burrough, Rev John
Amateur. *b:* 5.9.1873, Clun, Shropshire. *d:* 26.12.1922, St Leonards-on-Sea, Sussex. Brother of W. G. (Somerset), uncle of H. D. (Somerset) and J. W. (Gloucestershire). Middle order right-hand batsman, right-arm medium pace bowler. *Sch* King's, Bruton and Shrewsbury. *Team* Cambridge U (1893–95, blue 1895).
Career batting
24–39–5–780–127–22.94–1–*ct* 15
Bowling 1929–65–29.67–4–2–6/29
His County cricket was for Herefordshire (1890). His final first-class match was for Free Foresters in 1914. An excellent athlete, he put the shot.

Burrough, Rev John Wilson
Amateur. *b:* 17.6.1904, Summertown, Oxford. *d:* 11.9.1969. He was killed in a road accident at Seale, Surrey. Nephew of John (Cambridge U) and W. G. (Somerset), cousin of H. D. (Somerset). Middle order right-hand batsman, right-arm fast medium bowler. *Sch* Lancing. *Teams* Oxford U (1924–26); Gloucestershire (1924–37, 7 matches).
Career batting
10–16–4–146–46–12.16–0–*ct* 6
Bowling 349–6–58.16–0–0–2/26

Burrough, William George
Amateur. *b:* 22.7.1875, Clun, Shropshire. *d:* 30.12.1939, Wedmore, Somerset. Brother of John (Cambridge U), father of H. D. (Somerset), uncle of J. W. (Gloucestershire). Lower order batsman, opening bowler. *Sch* King's, Bruton. *Team* Somerset

(1906, 4 matches).
Career batting
4–7–0–40–11–5.71–0–*ct* 2
Bowling 344–7–49.14–0–0–2/102

Burrowes, Dr James Taylor
Amateur. *b:* 28.2.1914, Rae Town, Kingston, Jamaica. Opening right-hand batsman, right-arm bowler. *Team* Oxford U (1934).
Career batting
1–1–0–3–3–3.00–0–*ct* 0
Bowling 37–0
He won a blue for soccer.

Burrows, Arthur Dixon
Professional. *b:* 2.7.1865, Awsworth, Nottinghamshire. *d:* 6.2.1890, Eastwood, Nottinghamshire. Middle order right-hand batsman, right-arm fast medium bowler. *Team* Nottinghamshire (1887, 1 match).
Career batting
1–2–0–2–1–1.00–0–*ct* 1
Bowling 19–0

Burrows, Dean Andrew
Cricketer. *b:* 20.6.1966, Peterlee, Co Durham. Lower order right-hand batsman, right-arm medium fast bowler. *Team* Gloucestershire (1984–87, 2 matches).
Career batting
2–1–0–0–0–0.00–0–*ct* 0
Bowling 103–0
He also played for Durham (pre first-class, 1984–87).

Burrows, Matthew
Professional. *b:* 18.8.1855, Chesterfield, Derbyshire. *d:* 29.5.1893, Beeston, Leeds, Yorkshire. Middle order right-hand batsman, occasional right-hand fast round-arm bowler. *Teams* Yorkshire (1880, 6 matches); Derbyshire (1884, 1 match).
Career batting
7–12–0–95–23–7.91–0–*ct* 2
Bowling 10–0

Burrows, Lieut-General Montagu Brocas
Amateur. *b:* 31.10.1894, Kinnersley Manor, Reigate, Surrey. *d:* 17.1.1967, Marylebone, London. Nephew of R. V. Le Bas (MCC). Middle order right-hand batsman, right-arm fast medium bowler. *Sch* Eton. *Teams* Oxford U (1914–21); Surrey (1921, 1 match). *Tour* Incogniti to North America 1920 (not first-class).
Career batting
28–45–5–1283–112–32.07–1–*ct* 29
Bowling 1998–85–23.50–2–0–6/27
He appeared in many Army matches and his last first-class game was for the Army in 1932. He also played for Oxfordshire (1923–24).

Burrows, Robert Dixon
Professional. *b:* 6.6.1871, Eastwood, Nottinghamshire. *d:* 12.2.1943, Hill Top, near Eastwood, Nottinghamshire. Hard-hitting lower order right-hand batsman, right-arm fast bowler. *Team* Worcestershire (1899–1919, 277 matches).
Career batting
277–436–65–5223–112–14.07–2–*ct* 138
Bowling 23604–894–26.40–57–9–8/48
He twice took exactly 100 wickets in a season 1910 (av 23.46) and 1913 (av 21.41). After retiring from first-class cricket he became a noted umpire (1924–37), standing in one Test match (1926). He first played for Worcestershire (pre first-class) in 1895.

Burrows, William
Professional. *b:* 31.12.1844, Preston, Lancashire. Lower order batsman, right-hand medium pace round-arm bowler, good long-stop. *Team* Lancashire (1867–73, 14 matches).
Career batting
14–26–1–255–39–10.20–0–*ct* 2
Bowling 6–0

Burt, George Peter
Amateur. *b:* 11.11.1886, Dennistoun, Glasgow, Scotland. *d:* 20.1.1935, Murtle, Aberdeenshire, Scotland. Lower order right-hand batsman. *Team* Scotland (1924–25).
Career batting
2–3–0–35–26–11.66–0–*ct* 1

Burton, Clifford
Amateur. *b:* 15.6.1931, Moston, Manchester. *d:* 20.5.1978, Oldham, Lancashire. Tail end right-hand batsman, right-arm fast medium bowler. *Team* Lancashire (1956, 2 matches).
Career batting
2–1–0–0–0–0.00–0–*ct* 2
Bowling 80–0

Burton, David Cecil Fowler
(registered at birth as C. D. F. Burton)
Amateur. *b:* 13.9.1887, Bridlington Quay, Yorkshire. *d:* 24.9.1971, Chertsey, Surrey. Brother of R. C. (Yorkshire), cousin of D. S. G. (MCC in West Indies), nephew of A. B. Trollope (Hampshire). Middle order right-hand batsman, excellent field at cover. *Sch* Rugby. *Teams* Cambridge U (1907–08); Yorkshire (1907–21, 104 matches). *Tours* MCC to West Indies 1910/11, 1912/13.
Career batting
130–171–20–3057–142*–20.24–2–*ct* 54
He captained Yorkshire 1919–21. His final first-class match was for MCC in 1922. At Cambridge he was awarded his blue for rugby football and was also a noted sprinter.

Burton, Frederick Alfred
Professional. *b:* 28.12.1885, Islington, London. *d:* 7.1.1978, Weston-super-Mare, Somerset. Son of George (Middlesex). Lower order right-hand batsman, right-arm medium fast bowler. *Teams* MCC

(1921–25); Minor Counties (1924).
Career batting
7–13–5–99–35*–12.37–0–*ct* 0
Bowling 564–11–51.27–0–0–4/101

During the 1920s he was the principal Hertfordshire bowler, playing for the County 1907–32. His final first-class match was for East of England in 1927.

Burton, Geoffrey Cecil
Amateur. *b:* 14.12.1909, Stamford Hill, Middlesex. *d:* 4.4.1986, Eastbourne, Sussex. Middle order right-hand batsman. *Sch* Cheltenham. *Team* Middlesex (1930, 1 match).
Career batting
1–2–0–1–1–0.50–0–*ct* 0

Burton, George
Professional. *b:* 1.5.1851, Hampstead, London. *d:* 7.5.1930, Covent Garden, Westminster, London. Father of F. A. (MCC). Lower order right-hand batsman, right-hand slow round-arm bowler. *Team* Middlesex (1881–93, 111 matches).
Career batting
128–205–62–1150–34–8.04–0–*ct* 98
Bowling 10446–608–17.18–47–12–10/59

For Middlesex v Surrey at the Oval in 1888 he took all ten wickets (for 59) in the first innings. He was a first-class umpire (1898–99).

Burton, Henry Herbert
Amateur. *b:* 27.3.1874, Lambeth, London. *d:* 4.2.1964, Streatham, London. Middle order right-hand batsman. *Teams* Surrey (1904, 3 matches); London County (1904).
Career batting
6–12–1–261–59–23.72–0–*ct* 0

His final first-class match was for Gentlemen in 1905.

Burton, John Chambers
Professional. *b:* 7.5.1837, Oare, Faversham, Kent. *d:* 19.2.1887, East Sittingbourne, Kent. Stylish middle order right-hand batsman, good field. *Team* Kent (1862–64, 12 matches).
Career batting
12–24–2–162–40–7.36–0–*ct* 3

Burton, Joseph Parkin
Professional. *b:* 10.12.1873, Somercotes, Derbyshire. *d:* 25.1.1940, Somercotes, Derbyshire. Middle order right-hand batsman. *Team* Derbyshire (1901, 7 matches).
Career batting
7–12–1–200–51*–18.18–0–*ct* 4

Burton, Michael St John Whitehead
Cricketer. *b:* 14.2.1944, Bulawayo, Rhodesia. Middle order right-hand batsman, off break bowler. *Teams* Eastern Province (1964/5 to 1967/8); Oxford U (1969–71, blue all three years).
Career batting
37–59–5–821–84–15.20–0–*ct* 15
Bowling 3317–77–43.07–2–0–5/96

He captained Oxford in 1970.

Burton, Oswald
Professional. *b:* 21.8.1874, Gorton, Lancashire. *d:* 4.7.1944, Kingsdown, Bristol. Lower order right-hand batsman, right-arm medium fast bowler. *Team* Derbyshire (1901–05, 3 matches).
Career batting
3–4–4–21–9*–no av–0–*ct* 2
Bowling 156–5–31.20–0–0–2/44

Burton, Reginald Henry Markham
Amateur. *b:* 23.3.1900, Leamington, Warwickshire. *d:* 19.10.1980, Rugby, Warwickshire. Middle order right-hand batsman. *Team* Warwickshire (1919, 1 match).
Career batting
1–1–0–47–47–47.00–0–*ct* 0

Burton, Robert Claude
Amateur. *b:* 11.4.1891, Bridlington Quay, Yorkshire. *d:* 30.4.1971, Stone Cross, Pevensey, Sussex. Brother of D. C. F. (Yorkshire), cousin of D. S. G. (MCC in West Indies), nephew of A. B. Trollope (Hampshire). Hard-hitting lower order right-hand batsman, right-arm medium fast bowler. *Sch* Malvern. *Teams* Oxford U (1911–13); Yorkshire (1914, 2 matches).
Career batting
12–16–2–312–71–22.28–0–*ct* 8
Bowling 886–33–26.84–0–0–4/95

He played much cricket with the Harlequins and Free Foresters. His final first-class match was for Harlequins in 1928.

Burton, W. J.
Professional. *b:* 31.1.1878, Barbados. Hard-hitting lower order batsman, medium pace bowler. *Team* British Guiana (1901/2 to 1904/5). *Tours* West Indians to England 1900 (non-first-class), 1906.
Career batting
10–18–4–161–38*–11.50–0–*ct* 14
Bowling 857–57–15.03–5–3–7/54

Burton was regarded as the best bowler in the West Indies at the turn of the century and performed well on the 1900 tour with 78 wickets (av 21.55) and the remarkable figures of 10.4–7–9–8 v Norfolk, but in 1906 he played in few games and had no success.

Burtt, Leonard Lionel
Amateur. *b:* 4.2.1886, Hammersmith, London. *d:* 8.11.1942, Hampstead, London. Middle order right-hand batsman, change bowler. *Team* Middlesex (1921, 2 matches).
Career batting
2–4–1–78–50–26.00–0–*ct* 1
Bowling 9–1–9.00–0–0–1/8

Burtt, Thomas Browning
Amateur. *b:* 22.1.1915, Christchurch, New Zealand. *d:* 24.5.1988, Christchurch, New Zealand. Brother of N. V. (Canterbury), uncle of J. W. (Canterbury and Central Districts). Lower order right-hand batsman, slow left-arm bowler. *Team* Canterbury (1943/4 to 1954/5). *Tour* New Zealand to England 1949. *Tests* New Zealand (1946/7 to 1952/3, 10 matches).
Career batting
84–124–29–1644–68*–17.30–0–*ct* 53
Bowling 9054–408–22.19–29–5–8/35
Test batting
10–15–3–252–42–21.00–0–*ct* 2
Bowling 1170–33–35.45–3–0–6/162
On his single tour to England, Burtt was easily the most successful New Zealand bowler, both in terms of wickets taken and average: 128 wickets, av 22.88. He played hockey for New Zealand.

Bury, Lindsay
Amateur. *b:* 9.7.1857, Withington, Manchester, Lancashire. *d:* 30.10.1935, Stanford-Dingley, Bradfield, Berkshire. Lower order right-hand batsman, right-hand fast round-arm bowler. *Sch* Eton. *Teams* Cambridge U (1877–78, blue 1877); Hampshire (1877, 1 match).
Career batting
9–15–3–115–21–9.58–0–*ct* 6
Bowling 249–18–13.83–0–0–4/26
A well-known soccer player, he was awarded his blue at Cambridge and went on to be capped by England at full-back. He also threw the hammer for Cambridge in the University sports and was a noted sprinter.

Bury, Thomas Edmund Oswell
Cricketer. *b:* 14.5.1958, Chelmsford, Essex. Lower order right-hand batsman, wicket-keeper. *Sch* Charterhouse. *Team* Oxford U (1979–80, blue 1980).
Career batting
4–4–1–32–22–10.66–0–*ct* 2

Bury, Rev William
Amateur. *b:* 14.10.1839, Radcliffe-on-Trent, Nottinghamshire. *d:* 21.5.1927, West Bank, Wrotham, Borough Green, Kent. Brother of T. W. (Cambridge U 1855), brother-in-law of G. S. Foljambe (Nottinghamshire). Hard-hitting right-hand batsman, brilliant deep field. *Teams* Cambridge U (1860–62, blue 1861–62); Nottinghamshire (1861–62, 3 matches).
Career batting
9–13–0–245–121–18.84–1–*ct* 9
Bowling 4–0
He also played for Northamptonshire (pre first-class, 1867–70). In 1920 he had the odd experience of reading his own obituary notice twice within a few months.

Buse, Herbert Francis Thomas
Professional. *b:* 5.8.1910, Ashley Down, Bristol. *d:* 23.2.1992, Combe Park, Bath, Somerset. Steady middle or lower order right-hand batsman, right-arm medium pace bowler. *Team* Somerset (1929–53, 304 matches).
Career batting
304–523–55–10623–132–22.69–7–*ct* 151
Bowling 18908–657–28.77–20–0–8/41
He hit 1,000 runs in a season 5 times (best 1,279, av 26.10, in 1948).

Bush, Damien Jonathon
Cricketer. *b:* 19.5.1968, Solihull, Warwickshire. Lower order left-hand batsman, left-arm medium pace bowler. *Sch* KES, Birmingham. *Team* Cambridge U (1989–91, blue 1989).
Career batting
16–15–5–115–28–11.50–0–*ct* 6
Bowling 1111–15–74.06–0–0–3/64

Bush, Frederick William
Amateur. *b:* 27.2.1852, East Dulwich, Surrey. *d:* 8.1.1937, West Cliff, Bournemouth, Hampshire. Brother of H. S. (Surrey). Lower order right-hand batsman, slow round-arm bowler. *Sch* Dulwich. *Team* Surrey (1879–85, 7 matches). *Tours* Lucas to West Indies 1894/5; Priestley to West Indies 1896/7.
Career batting
22–35–1–481–101–14.14–1–*ct* 10
Bowling 1071–65–16.47–5–2–7/25
His last appearance in first-class cricket was in the West Indies in 1896/7. He also played for Shropshire (1902) and Suffolk (1906).

Bush, Harry Stebbing
Amateur. *b:* 7.10.1871, Dulwich, Surrey. *d:* 18.3.1942, South Farnborough, Hampshire. Brother of F. W. (Surrey). Stylish middle order right-hand batsman, right-arm medium pace bowler. *Sch* Dover. *Team* Surrey (1901–12, 70 matches).
Career batting
72–113–7–2607–135–24.59–4–*ct* 40
Bowling 204–2–102.00–0–0–1/12
His final first-class match was for the Army in 1914 – he was most successful in County cricket, but his military duties prevented him from appearing at all frequently.

Bush, James Arthur
Amateur. *b:* 28.7.1850, Cawnpore, India. *d:* 21.9.1924, Clevedon, Somerset. Brother of R. E. (Gloucestershire). Lower order left-hand batsman, wicket-keeper. *Sch* Clifton. *Team* Gloucestershire (1870–90, 136 matches). *Tour* Grace to Australia 1873/4 (not first-class).
Career batting
148–224–67–1263–57–8.04–0–*ct* 206–*st* 93
Bowling 65–0

He also excelled as a rugby footballer and gained five international caps.

Bush, John Edgar
Amateur. *b:* 20.8.1928, Oxford. Opening right-hand batsman. *Sch* Magdalen School, Oxford. *Team* Oxford U (1950–52, blue 1952).
Career batting
8–15–1–417–67–29.78–0–*ct* 6
His County cricket was for Oxfordshire (1949–73), and in 1949 he assisted in an opening partnership of 264 v Buckinghamshire.

Bush, Robert Edwin
Amateur. *b:* 11.10.1855, Redland, Bristol, Gloucestershire. *d:* 29.12.1939, Bishops Knoll, Stoke Bishop, Bristol. Brother of J. A. (Gloucestershire). Middle order right-hand batsman, wicket-keeper. *Sch* Clifton. *Team* Gloucestershire (1874–77, 16 matches).
Career batting
17–24–1–221–42–9.60–0–*ct* 6
He emigrated to Australia in the 1880s, remaining there as a sheep-farmer for about 30 years. He was President of Gloucestershire 1919–20 and 1923–24.

Bush, Robert Thompson
Professional. *b:* 14.1.1839, Kennington, London. *d:* 24.12.1874, Kennington Park, London. Steady middle order right-hand batsman, fine field. *Team* Surrey (1864–68, 2 matches).
Career batting
2–4–1–21–8*–7.00–0–*ct* 0

Bushby, Edward
Professional. *b:* 3.4.1817, Sompting, Sussex. *d:* 29.2.1856, Henfield, Sussex. Fine free hitting right-hand batsman. *Team* Sussex (1843–54, 50 matches).
Career batting
64–114–12–1485–86–14.55–0–*ct* 27
Bowling 25–0
He was regarded as one of the best bats of his day, but latterly suffered from ill-health and died aged only 38.

Bushby, Michael Howard
Amateur. *b:* 29.7.1931, Macclesfield, Cheshire. Sound opening right-hand batsman, leg break bowler. *Sch* Dulwich. *Team* Cambridge U (1952–54, blue all three years).
Career batting
46–78–1–1919–113–24.92–3–*ct* 12
Bowling 11–1–11.00–0–0–1/7
His final first class match was for MCC in 1966. He captained Cambridge in 1956. An excellent rugby footballer he toured Japan with Cambridge U in 1953.

Bushe, Edwin Alexander
Cricketer. *b:* 11.4.1951, Lurgan, Co Armagh, Ireland. Brother-in-law of D. W. Harrison (Ireland), R. Harrison (Ireland), J. Harrison (Ireland) and G. D. Harrison (Ireland). Tail end right-hand batsman, wicket-keeper. *Team* Ireland (1979–80).
Career batting
2–2–1–14–14–14.00–0–*ct* 7 *st* 1

Busher, Harold Aston
Amateur. *b:* 2.8.1876, Sparkhill, Birmingham. *d:* 3.10.1954, McMahon's Point, Sydney, New South Wales, Australia. Brother of S. E. (Surrey and Worcestershire). Middle order right-hand batsman. *Team* Warwickshire (1908, 1 match).
Career batting
1–2–1–15–15–15.00–0–*ct* 0
He also played for Suffolk (1913–14).

Busher, Sydney Edmund
Amateur. *b:* 19.12.1882, Solihull, Warwickshire. *d:* 28.5.1953, Turramurra, Sydney, New South Wales, Australia. Brother of H. A. (Warwickshire). Lower order right-hand batsman, right-arm fast-medium bowler. *Teams* Surrey (1908, 1 match); Worcestershire (1908–10, 4 matches).
Career batting
5–8–1–84–52–12.00–0–*ct* 2
Bowling 380–26–14.61–3–0–6/63
He lived in Australia for many years.

Busk, Richard Dawson
Amateur. *b:* 21.6.1895, Marylebone, London. *d:* 24.12.1961, Uphall, Rampisham, Dorset. Middle or lower order right-hand batsman, right-arm fast bowler. *Sch* Marlborough. *Team* Hampshire (1919, 2 matches).
Career batting
5–6–2–50–43–12.50–0–*ct* 1
Bowling 365–11–33.18–0–0–4/60
His last first-class appearance was for West of England in 1927. He played regularly for Dorset (1912–39).

Buss, Antony
Professional. *b:* 1.9.1939, Brightling, Sussex. Brother of M. A. (Sussex). Lower order right-hand batsman, right-arm fast medium bowler. *Team* Sussex (1958–74, 304 matches).
Career batting
310–412–76–4415–83–13.13–0–*ct* 131
Bowling 23989–958–25.04–44–3–8/23
He took 100 wickets in a season three times (best 120, av 20.30, in 1965 and 120, av 22.55, in 1966). He was Sussex coach 1977–78.

Buss, Clarence Harold Henry
Amateur. *b:* 19.2.1913, Weybridge, Surrey. *d:* 6.12.1974, Addlestone, Surrey. Lower order left-hand batsman, slow left-arm bowler. *Team* Surrey (1934, 1 match).
Career batting
1–2–0–47–42–23.50–0–*ct* 0
Bowling 143–2–71.50–0–0–2/90

Buss, Michael Alan
Professional. *b:* 24.1.1944, Brightling, Sussex. Brother of Antony (Sussex). Middle order, then from 1966 opening left-hand batsman, slow left-arm, later medium pace bowler. *Teams* Sussex (1961–78, 297 matches); Orange Free State (1972/3 to 1977/8). *Tour* MCC Under 25 to Pakistan 1966/7.
Career batting
316–547–47–11996–159–23.99–11–*ct* 230
Bowling 15349–547–28.06–18–0–7/58
He hit 1,000 runs in a season 4 times (best 1,379, av 37.27, in 1970).

Buswell, John Edgar
Professional. *b:* 3.7.1909, Barnwell, Northamptonshire. Tail end right-hand batsman, right-arm medium pace bowler. *Team* Northamptonshire (1936–39, 61 matches).
Career batting
61–99–29–525–30–7.50–0–*ct* 19
Bowling 5653–172–32.86–5–1–7/61

Buswell, Walter Alfred
Professional. *b:* 12.1.1875, Welford, Northamptonshire. *d:* 24.4.1950, Swinford, Leicestershire. Son of Alfred (Leicestershire 1879–83). Lower order hard-hitting right-hand batsman, wicket-keeper. *Team* Northamptonshire (1906–21, 205 matches).
Career batting
205–327–76–2670–101*–10.63–1–*ct* 288–*st* 115
He was a first-class umpire (1923–37). He played for Leicestershire in 1903 in a non-first-class match.

Butchart, Iain Peter
Cricketer. *b:* 9.5.1960, Bulawayo, Rhodesia. Sound middle order right-hand batsman, right-arm medium pace bowler. *Team* Zimbabwe (1980/1 to 1990). *Tours* Zimbabwe to England 1982, 1983 (World Cup), 1985, 1990, to Sri Lanka 1983/4, to India (World Cup) 1987/8, to Australia and New Zealand (World Cup) 1991/2.
Career batting
43–68–10–1083–82–18.67–0–*ct* 36
Bowling 2052–62–33.09–1–0–5/65
He achieved only moderate success on his three tours to England.

Butcher, Alan Raymond
Cricketer. *b:* 7.1.1954, Croydon, Surrey. Brother of I. P. (Leicestershire and Gloucestershire) and M. S. (Surrey), father of M. A. (Surrey). Attractive opening left-hand batsman, left-arm medium or slow bowler, good close field. *Teams* Surrey (1972–86, 283 matches); Glamorgan (1987–92, 111 matches). *Tours* Overseas XI to India 1980/1; International XI to Jamaica 1982/3; Glamorgan to Zimbabwe 1990/1. *Test* England (1979, 1 match).
Career batting
401–682–60–22633–216*–36.38–46–*ct* 185
Bowling 5433–141–38.53–1–0–6/48
Test batting
1–2–0–34–20–17.00–0–*ct* 0
Bowling 9–0
He hit 1,000 runs in a season twelve times, going on to 2,000 once (2,116, av 58.77, in 1990). His highest score was 216* for Surrey v Cambridge U at Fenner's in 1980. He was appointed Glamorgan captain during the 1989 season. He missed much of the 1992 season due to injury and then resigned the captaincy. He played against his son in a Sunday League game in 1991.

Butcher, Arthur
Amateur. *b:* 8.11.1863, Tring, Hertfordshire. *d:* 17.9.1955, Kensington, London. Middle order right-hand batsman, right-arm slow bowler. *Sch* Mill Hill. *Team* MCC (1902–05).
Career batting
2–4–1–35–24*–11.66–0–*ct* 0
His County cricket was for Hertfordshire (1898–1909).

Butcher, Basil Fitzherbert
Professional. *b:* 3.9.1933, Sugar Estate near Port Mourant, Berbice. Excellent middle order right-hand batsman, leg break bowler, fine field. *Team* British Guiana (1954/5 to 1970/1). *Tours* West Indies to England 1963, 1966, 1969, to Australia and New Zealand 1968/9, to India and Pakistan 1958/9, to India and Ceylon 1966/7; Rest of World to England 1968; Commonwealth to Pakistan 1963/4. *Tests* West Indies (1958/9 to 1969, 44 matches).
Career batting
169–262–29–11628–209*–49.90–31–*ct* 67
Bowling 1217–40–30.42–1–0–5/34
Test batting
44–78–6–3104–209*–43.11–7–*ct* 15
Bowling 90–5–18.00–1–0–5/34
He was very successful on all of his three tours to England, hitting 1,294 runs (av 44.62) in 1963, 1,105 (av 48.04) in 1966 and 984 (av 61.50) in 1969. His best innings in England was his 133 in the Lord's Test of 1963, but he also hit a splendid 209* in the Trent Bridge Test of 1966, saving his side. His final first-class match was for Berbice in 1971/2.

Butcher, Cecil Frank
Professional. *b:* 31.10.1872, Brighton, Sussex. *d:* 22.3.1929, Portslade, Sussex. Tail end right-hand batsman, right-arm fast medium bowler. *Team* Sussex (1894–96, 6 matches).
Career batting
6–12–0–36–13–3.00–*ct* 1
Bowling 355–9–39.44–0–0–3/107

Butcher, Douglas Harry
Amateur. *b:* 15.5.1876, Mitcham, Surrey. *d:* 4.7.1945, Wallington, Surrey. Middle order right-hand batsman. *Team* Surrey (1900–13, 7 matches).

Career batting
7–11–1–187–71–18.70–0–*ct* 1

Butcher, Ian Paul
Cricketer. *b:* 1.7.1962, Farnborough, Kent. Brother of A. R. (Surrey and Glamorgan) and M. S. (Surrey), uncle of M. A. (Surrey). Middle order right-hand batsman. *Teams* Leicestershire (1980–87, 94 matches); Gloucestershire (1988–90, 30 matches).
Career batting
124–201–16–5480–139–29.62–11–*ct* 87
Bowling 43–1–43.00–0–0–1/2

He hit 1,000 runs in a season twice (best 1,349, av 32.90, in 1984).

Butcher, Mark Alan
Cricketer. *b:* 23.8.1972, Croydon, Surrey. Son of A. R. (Surrey and Glamorgan), nephew of I. P. (Leicestershire and Gloucestershire) and M. S. (Surrey). Middle order left-hand batsman, right-arm medium pace bowler. *Team* Surrey (1992, 2 matches).
Career batting
2–2–1–52–47–52.00–0–*ct* 0
Bowling 115–1–115.00–0–0–1/95

Butcher, Martin Simon
Cricketer. *b:* 17.5.1958, Thornton Heath, Surrey. Brother of A. R. (Surrey and Glamorgan) and I. P. (Leicestershire and Gloucestershire), uncle of M. A. (Surrey). Middle order right-hand batsman. *Team* Surrey (1982, 1 match).
Career batting
1 match, did not bat– *ct* 1
Bowling 2–0

Butcher, Roland Orlando
Cricketer. *b:* 14.10.1953, East Point, St Philip, Barbados. Hard-hitting middle order right-hand batsman, right-arm medium pace bowler, good close field. *Teams* Middlesex (1974–90, 251 matches); Barbados (1974/5); Tasmania (1982/3, 12 matches). *Tours* Middlesex to Zimbabwe 1980/1; England to West Indies 1980/1; International XI to Pakistan 1981/2, to Jamaica 1982/3. *Tests* England (1980/1, 3 matches).
Career batting
277–428–43–12021–197–31.22–17–*ct* 290–*st* 1
Bowling 182–4–45.50–0–0–2/37
Test batting
3–5–0–71–32–14.20–0–*ct* 3

He hit 1,000 runs in a season four times (best 1,326, av 40.18, in 1984). He qualified for England by residence and became the first black West Indian born cricketer to represent England in a Test, when he toured West Indies in 1980/1. His selection for the touring team was somewhat of a surprise and based as much on his batting in limited overs cricket as in first-class matches. He achieved only modest success on the tour. He also played for Suffolk (1991).

Butler, Hon Brian Danvers
Amateur. *b:* 18.4.1876, Lanesborough Lodge, Belturbet, Co Cavan, Ireland. *d:* 18.8.1916, Longueval, France. Middle order batsman. *Sch* Eton. *Team* MCC (1913–14).
Career batting
2–4–0–42–29–10.50–*ct* 0

Butler, Edward Henry
Amateur. *b:* 15.3.1851, Hobart, Tasmania, Australia. *d:* 5.1.1928, Lower Sandy Bay, Hobart, Tasmania, Australia. Brother of C. W. (Tasmania), father of E. L. A. (Tasmania). Middle order right-hand batsman, right-arm fast bowler. *Teams* Tasmania (1870/1 to 1883/4, 5 matches); Victoria (1872/3, 1 match); MCC (1877). *Tour* Tasmania to New Zealand 1883/4.
Career batting
10–17–3–98–26–7.00–0–*ct* 7
Bowling 148–7–21.14–1–0–6/62

Butler, Edward Montagu
Amateur. *b:* 3.12.1866, Harrow-on-the-Hill, Middlesex. *d:* 11.2.1948, Rogate, Sussex. Middle order right-hand batsman. *Sch* Harrow. *Teams* Middlesex (1885, 2 matches); Cambridge U (1888–89, blue both years).
Career batting
13–22–2–362–47–18.10–0–*ct* 4
Bowling 11–0

He was an all-round athlete, representing Cambridge at both royal tennis and rackets and winning the 100 yards at the University sports in 1885. He also played for Cambridgeshire (1894–95).

Butler, F. L.
Amateur. Tail end batsman. *Team* South (1877).
Career batting
1–2–2–3–3*–no av–0–*ct* 0

Butler, Frederick
Professional. *b:* 29.12.1857, Radcliffe-on-Trent, Nottinghamshire. *d:* 26.2.1923, Sailors' Snug Harbor, Staten Island, New York, USA. Brother of Robert (Nottinghamshire), nephew of G. Parr (Nottinghamshire). Opening or middle order right-hand batsman. *Teams* Nottinghamshire (1881–90, 45 matches); Players of USA (1885–86).
Career batting
50–78–7–1084–171–15.26–1–*ct* 30
Bowling 65–5–13.00–1–0–5/54

He did not play for Nottinghamshire in 1885–86, being in America, where he went to live permanently about 1900. He also played for Durham (pre first-class, 1891–94) and Northumberland (1896).

Butler, George
Professional. *b:* 20.2.1810, Mansfield, Nottinghamshire. *d:* 23.4.1887, Nottingham. Hard hitting middle order right-hand batsman, slow right-hand round-arm bowler. *Team* Nottinghamshire (1841–52, 15

matches).
Career batting
36–65–5–650–40–10.83–0–*ct* 20
Bowling 96–8 + 1–12.00–0–0–3/19

After retiring he umpired county matches and was the groundsman at Trent Bridge until 1877.

Butler, George Stephen
Amateur. *b:* 16.12.1900, Kennett, Marlborough, Wiltshire. *d:* 21.9.1969, Kingswear, Devon. Attractive opening right-hand batsman. *Sch* Marlborough. *Team* Somerset (1920, 1 match).
Career batting
8–14–0–411–121–29.35–1–*ct* 7
Bowling 22–0

He played regularly for Wiltshire from 1920 to 1939 and made several appearances in first-class cricket for the Minor Counties, the final one being in 1939. He also played for Devon (1946).

Butler, Harold James
Professional. *b:* 12.3.1913, Clifton, Nottingham. *d:* 17.7.1991, Lenton, Nottingham. Hard-hitting lower order right-hand batsman, right-arm fast medium bowler. *Teams* Nottinghamshire (1933–54, 306 matches); Services in India (1943/4 to 1944/5). *Tour* MCC to West Indies 1947/8. *Tests* England (1947 to 1947/8, 2 matches).
Career batting
319–381–100–2962–62–10.54–0–*ct* 112
Bowling 23276–952–24.44–46–6–8/15
Test batting
2–2–1–15–15*–15.00–0–*ct* 1
Bowling 215–12–17.91–0–0–4/34

He took 100 wickets in a season twice (best 106, av 22.55, in 1947).

Butler, John
Professional. *b:* 29.8.1863, Clifton, Nottingham. *d:* 21.5.1945, Belper, Derbyshire. Nephew of G. Wootton (Nottinghamshire), brother-in-law of J. Moss (Nottinghamshire). Middle order right-hand batsman. *Team* Nottinghamshire (1889, 6 matches).
Career batting
6–8–1–111–56–15.85–0–*ct* 1

He also played for Durham (pre first-class, 1898–1905).

Butler, Keith Andrew
Cricketer. *b:* 20.1.1971, Camden Town, London. Middle order right-hand batsman, right-arm medium pace bowler. *Team* Essex (1989, 1 match).
Career batting
1–1–1–10–10*–no av–0–*ct* 0

Butler, Robert
Generally amateur but played as professional in a few matches. *b:* 8.3.1852, Radcliffe-on-Trent, Nottinghamshire. *d:* 18.12.1916, Sutton-cum-Granby, Nottinghamshire. Brother of Frederick (Nottinghamshire), nephew of G. Parr (Nottinghamshire). Middle order right-hand batsman. *Team* Nottinghamshire (1870–77, 7 matches).
Career batting
10–16–0–163–60–10.18–0–*ct* 8–*st* 1

Butler, Samuel Evan
Amateur. *b:* 15.4.1850, Colombo, Ceylon. *d:* 30.4.1903, Bath, Somerset. Lower order right-hand batsman, right-hand fast round-arm bowler, good field. *Sch* Eton. *Team* Oxford U (1870–73, blue all four years).
Career batting
21–34–6–256–31–9.14–0–*ct* 17
Bowling 1419–99 + 17–14.33–10–3–10/38

His fame rests with the feat of taking all ten wickets (for 38) in the first innings of Cambridge during the University match at Lord's in 1871. He also played for Devon (1871) and Somerset (pre first-class, 1878).

Butt, Henry Rigden
Professional. *b:* 27.12.1865, Sands End, Fulham, Middlesex. *d:* 21.12.1928, West Hill, Hastings, Sussex. Hard-hitting tail end right-hand batsman, wicket-keeper. *Team* Sussex (1890–1912, 517 matches). *Tour* Hawke to South Africa 1895/6. *Tests* England (1895/6, 3 matches).
Career batting
550–801–225–7391–96–12.83–0–*ct* 953–*st* 275
Bowling 33–0
Test batting
3–4–1–22–13–7.33–0–*ct* 1–*st* 1

He was a first-class umpire (1913–28), standing in six Test matches (1921–26).

Butt, John Alec Steuart
Amateur. *b:* 7.5.1892, Sutton, Surrey. *d:* 30.10.1966, Kensington, London. Middle order left-hand batsman. *Sch* Marlborough. *Team* Sussex (1923, 1 match).
Career batting
1–2–0–10–8–5.00–0–*ct* 0

Butterfield, Edward Banks
Amateur. *b:* 22.10.1848, Keighley, Yorkshire. *d:* 6.5.1899, Keighley, Yorkshire. Opening right-hand batsman. *Team* Yorkshire (1870, 1 match).
Career batting
1–2–0–18–10–9.00–0–*ct* 0

Butterfield, Walter
Professional. *b:* 6.8.1870, Dewsbury, Yorkshire. *d:* 19.7.1954, West Bridgford, Nottingham. Lower order right-hand batsman, right-arm medium pace bowler. *Team* Derbyshire (1896, 2 matches).
Career batting
2–4–0–11–7–2.75–0–*ct* 0
Bowling 20–1–20.00–0–0–1/10

Butterworth, Henry Rhodes Whittle
Amateur. *b:* 4.2.1909, Rochdale, Lancashire. *d:* 9.10.1958, Hollingworth Lake, near Littleborough, Lancashire. Middle or lower order right-hand batsman, leg break bowler. *Sch* Rydal. *Teams* Cambridge U (1929–30, blue 1929); Lancashire (1931–36, 25 matches).
Career batting
47–68–11–1014–107–17.78–1–*ct* 23
Bowling 2909–80–36.36–3–1–6/50
His final first-class match was for Minor Counties in 1937. He also played for Denbighshire (1927).

Butterworth, Hugh Montagu
Amateur. *b:* 1.11.1885, Saffron Walden, Essex. *d:* 25.9.1915. He was killed in action, Hooge, Belgium. Opening batsman. *Sch* Marlborough. *Team* Oxford U (1906).
Career batting
3–6–0–78–31–13.00–0–*ct* 2
His County cricket was for Wiltshire (1904–06). He represented Oxford at rackets in 1905 and 1906. After leaving the University he emigrated to Wanganui, New Zealand, and his name can be found in matches there – in the 1914/15 season he hit consecutive innings of 296 and 311.

Butterworth, John Compton
Amateur. *b:* 17.8.1905, Samarang, Java. *d:* 18.3.1941, Shooter's Hill, London. Brother of R. E. C. (Middlesex). Middle order right-hand batsman. *Sch* Harrow. *Teams* Middlesex (1925, 1 match); Oxford U (1926).
Career batting
3–6–1–49–16*–9.80–0–*ct* 1

Butterworth, Reginald Edmund Compton
Amateur. *b:* 16.8.1906, Samarang, Java. *d:* 21.5.1940, St Martin-au-Laert, France. He was killed in action. Brother of J. C. (Middlesex). Opening right-hand batsman, right-arm fast medium bowler. *Sch* Harrow. *Teams* Oxford U (1926–27, blue 1927); Middlesex (1935–37, 14 matches). *Tour* Cahn to Ceylon 1936/7.
Career batting
38–63–2–1189–110–19.49–2–*ct* 15
Bowling 2078–50–41.56–0–0–3/11
His final first-class match was for MCC in 1939. He also won a blue for golf.

Butterworth, Wilfred Selkirk
Amateur. *b:* 11.10.1855, Rochdale, Lancashire. *d:* 9.4.1908, Rochdale, Lancashire. Middle order right-hand batsman, wicket-keeper. *Sch* Lancing. *Team* Lancashire (1876–82, 9 matches).
Career batting
9–14–1–73–22–5.61–0–*ct* 4

Buttery, John
Professional. *b:* 21.12.1814, Nottingham. *d:* 5.12.1873, Nottingham. Lower order batsman, excellent bowler. *Teams* Nottinghamshire (1843–45, 4 matches); Lancashire (1849, 1 match); Manchester (1852).
Career batting
9–16–1–148–36–9.86–0–*ct* 6
Bowling 47–3 + 19–15.66–1–0–8/?
He also played for Monmouthshire (1855).

Buttle, Cecil Frederick Douglas
Professional. *b:* 11.1.1906, Norton Fitzwarren, Somerset. *d:* 15.12.1988, Taunton, Somerset. Lower order right-hand batsman, right-arm fast medium bowler. *Team* Somerset (1926–28, 2 matches).
Career batting
2–4–1–8–4*–2.66–0–*ct* 0
Bowling 54–0
He was head groundsman at Taunton, retiring in 1971 after 50 years service with the County.

Buttress, William
Professional. *b:* 25.11.1827, Cambridge. *d:* 25.8.1866, Cambridge. Lower order batsman, right-arm medium pace spin bowler. *Team* Cambridge Town Club (1849–61); Cambridgeshire (1857–61, 3 matches).
Career batting
17–27–10–65–9*–3.82–0–*ct* 11
Bowling 558–37 + 46–15.08–9–2–7/35
He was regarded as one of the best bowlers of his day, but was rarely selected for important matches because he drank – once when required to bat at Lord's he was found sitting up a tree singing. He also played for Suffolk (1848), Norfolk (1850), Huntingdonshire (1851), Leicestershire (pre first-class, 1851–55), Devon (1853), Dorset (1854), Cheshire (1854–55), Durham (pre first-class, 1856) and Bedfordshire (1860).

Buxton, Cyril Digby
Amateur. *b:* 25.6.1865, Knighton, Woodford Wells, Essex. *d:* 10.5.1892, Woodford Wells, Essex, by his own hand. Nephew of K. E. Digby (Oxford U) and R. Digby (Oxford U). Opening right-hand batsman, right-arm medium pace bowler, brilliant field. *Sch* Harrow. *Team* Cambridge U (1885–88, blue all four years).
Career batting
40–68–4–1213–108*–18.95–1–*ct* 30
Bowling 1522–60–25.36–2–1–5/16
His County cricket was for Essex (pre first-class, 1883–91), being captain 1889–91. He captained Cambridge in 1888. His final first-class match was for MCC in 1891. He also excelled at tennis and rackets, winning blues at both sports.

Buxton, Ian Ray
Professional. *b:* 17.4.1938, Cromford, Derbyshire. Middle order right-hand batsman, right-arm medium pace bowler. *Team* Derbyshire (1959–73, 350 matches).
Career batting
350–579–86–11803–118*–23.94–5–*ct* 199
Bowling 12742–483–26.38–12–2–7/33
He hit 1,000 runs in a season 5 times (best 1,219, av 28.34, in 1964). He was captain of Derbyshire 1970–72. He was also a good soccer player, appearing for Derby County, Luton Town, Notts County and Port Vale.

Buxton, Joseph Herbert
Professional. *b:* 20.12.1912, Kirkby-in-Ashfield, Nottinghamshire. Nephew of Noah (Derbyshire). Lower order right-hand batsman, right-arm fast medium bowler. *Team* Nottinghamshire (1937, 1 match).
Career batting
1–1–0–6–6–6.00–0–*ct* 2
Bowling 90–1–90.00–0–0–1/54

Buxton, Noah
Professional. *b:* 6.11.1876, Codnor, Derbyshire. *d:* 26.5.1967, Pontefract, Yorkshire. Uncle of J. H. (Nottinghamshire). Lower order right-hand batsman, right-arm fast medium bowler. *Team* Derbyshire (1902–11, 7 matches).
Career batting
7–14–2–40–7–3.33–0–*ct* 1
Bowling 171–5–34.20–0–0–2/14
He also played for Staffordshire (1905) and Cheshire (1909–12).

Buxton, Robert Vere
Amateur. *b:* 29.4.1883, Westminster, London. *d:* 1.10.1953, Abbey House, Itchen-Abbas, Hampshire. Opening or middle order right-hand batsman. *Sch* Eton. *Teams* Oxford U (1906, blue); Middlesex (1906–09, 10 matches).
Career batting
17–31–1–664–76–22.13–*ct* 10
Bowling 15–0
He also played for Hertfordshire (1902).

Buzza, Alan Jan
Cricketer. *b:* 3.3.1966, Beverley, Yorkshire. Lower order right-hand batsman, slow left-arm bowler. *Team* Cambridge U (1989–90, blue both years).
Career batting
17–17–5–86–25*–7.16–0–*ct* 6
Bowling 1842–43–42.83–1–0–6/102
His County cricket was for Cornwall (1984–90). He gained his rugby blue and captained the University in 1989/90.

Byas, David
Cricketer. *b:* 26.8.1963, Kilham, Yorkshire. Middle order left-hand batsman, right-arm medium pace bowler. *Team* Yorkshire (1986–92, 99 matches). *Tour* Yorkshire to South Africa 1991/2.
Career batting
99–161–17–4488–153–31.16–8–*ct* 99
Bowling 612–10–61.20–0–0–3/55
He scored 1,557 runs (av 44.48) in 1991.

Byass, John Edmund
Amateur. *b:* 8.5.1854, Upper Clapton, London. *d:* 6.6.1936, Shepparton, Victoria, Australia. Middle order right-hand batsman, right-arm fast bowler, slip field. *Sch* Christ College, Finchley. *Team* Kent (1874–76, 3 matches).
Career batting
4–8–0–34–17–4.25–0–*ct* 2
He emigrated to Australia as a young man and was therefore lost to County cricket.

Byng, Arthur Maitland
Amateur. *b:* 26.10.1872, Southsea, Hampshire. *d:* 14.9.1914. He was killed in action at Vailly, France. Brother of J. A. (Transvaal), grandson of W. F. Maitland (Oxford U), nephew of F. Stephens (MCC), cousin of F. G. R. B. Stephens (Weigall's XI) and B. J. B. Stephens (Europeans). Sound middle order right-hand batsman. *Teams* Hampshire (1905, 3 matches); Jamaica (1896/7).
Career batting
8–15–0–252–70–16.80–0–*ct* 8
Bowling 168–7–24.00–0–0–3/53
He was one of the best batsmen in Army cricket during the ten years prior to the First World War.

Bynoe, Michael Robin
Cricketer. *b:* 23.2.1941, Alleynedale, Black Rock, St Michael, Barbados. Grandson of H. F. Austin (Barbados). Opening right-hand batsman, slow left-arm bowler. *Team* Barbados (1957/8 to 1971/2). *Tours* West Indies to India and Pakistan 1958/9, to India and Ceylon 1966/7; Barbados to England 1969. *Tests* West Indies (1958/9 to 1966/7, 4 matches).
Career batting
56–97–10–3572–190–41.05–6–*ct* 45
Bowling 246–9–27.33–0–0–2/7
Test batting
4–6–0–111–48–18.50–0–*ct* 4
Bowling 5–1–5.00–0–0–1/5

Byrne, George Robert
Amateur. *b:* 28.5.1892, Northfield, Birmingham. *d:* 23.6.1973, Torteval, Guernsey. Nephew of J. F. (Warwickshire). Middle order right-hand batsman, right-arm medium pace bowler. *Sch* Downside. *Team* Warwickshire (1912, 8 matches); Worcestershire (1914–21, 4 matches).
Career batting
12–20–0–64–18–3.20–0–*ct* 1
Bowling 239–7–34.14–0–0–3/9
He took 3 wickets in 4 balls during his first-class debut match for Warwickshire in 1912.

Byrne, James Frederick
Amateur. *b:* 19.6.1871, Penns, Warwickshire. *d:* 10.5.1954, Edgbaston, Birmingham. Uncle of G. R. (Warwickshire and Worcestershire), great-grandfather of J. N. Perry (Cambridge U). Middle order right-hand batsman, right-arm fast medium bowler. *Sch* Downside. *Team* Warwickshire (1897–1912, 138 matches).
Career batting
140–219–10–4766–222–22.80–4–*ct* 81
Bowling 2248–74–30.37–1–0–5/37
His highest score was 222 for Warwickshire v Lancashire at Edgbaston in 1905. He captained Warwickshire 1903–06. A brilliant rugby footballer, he played for Moseley and England at fullback, leading England in the 1897/8 season. He first played for Warwickshire (pre first-class) in 1892.

Byrom, John Lewis
Amateur. *b:* 20.7.1851, Saddleworth, Yorkshire. *d:* 24.8.1931, Delph, Oldham, Lancashire. Middle order right-hand batsman, right-arm medium pace bowler, good field. *Team* Yorkshire (1874, 2 matches).
Career batting
3–5–0–20–11–4.00–0–*ct* 1
His final first-class match was for Gentlemen of North in 1877.

Bythell, William John
Amateur. *b:* 9.9.1862, Poona, India. *d:* 30.6.1920, Elm Grove, Southsea, Hampshire. Lower order batsman. *Team* MCC (1903).
Career batting
1–2–0–8–6–4.00–0–*ct* 0

C

Caddick, Andrew Richard
Cricketer. *b:* 21.11.1968, Christchurch, New Zealand. Lower order right-hand batsman, right-arm medium bowler. *Team* Somerset (1991–92, 22 matches).
Career batting
22–20–6–261–54*–18.64–0–*ct* 7
Bowling 2169–76–28.53–3–1–6/52
He took 71 wickets, av 27.01, in 1992. He took a record 96 wickets in the 2nd XI competition in 1991 whilst qualifying by residence.

Cadell, Alexander Richard
Amateur. *b:* 19.8.1900, Ferozepore, India. *d:* 14.5.1928, Petersfield Cottage Hospital, Hampshire, as the result of a motor accident. Middle/lower order right-hand batsman, right-arm medium fast bowler. *Team* Hampshire (1923–27, 2 matches).
Career batting
12–19–2–226–48–13.29–0–*ct* 6
Bowling 854–21–40.66–0–0–3/37
His first-class debut was for Royal Navy in 1922.

Cadman, Samuel William Anthony
Professional. *b:* 29.1.1877, Gibraltar, Haughton Green, Cheshire. *d:* 6.5.1952, Glossop, Derbyshire. Steady opening or middle order right-hand batsman, right-arm medium pace bowler. *Team* Derbyshire (1900–26, 375 matches).
Career batting
377–690–34–14077–126–21.45–8–*ct* 277
Bowling 20370–807–25.24–30–2–8/70
He hit 1,000 runs in a season twice (best 1,036, av 29.60, in 1911). After leaving first-class cricket he played for Glossop and continued with that club until the age of 70.

Cadogan, Edward Henry
Amateur. *b:* 11.9.1908, Kasauli, India. Lower order right-hand batsman, right-arm fast bowler. *Sch* Winchester. *Teams* Europeans (1929/30); Hampshire (1933–35, 5 matches).
Career batting
9–15–5–148–36*–14.80–0–*ct* 4
Bowling 652–29–22.48–1–0–5/52
His last first-class match was for the Army in 1936.

Caesar, Julius
Professional. *b:* 25.3.1830, Godalming, Surrey. *d:* 6.3.1878, Godalming, Surrey. Son of Benjamin (Surrey), brother of F. B. (Surrey). Opening or middle order right-hand batsman, occasional right-hand fast round-arm bowler, excellent field. *Teams* Surrey (1849–67, 121 matches); Lancashire (1851, 2 matches as given man). *Tours* Parr to North America 1859 (not first-class), to Australia 1863/4.
Career batting
194–333–24–4879–132*–15.78–3–*ct* 181
Bowling 134–6 + 8–22.33–0–0–3/?
He was one of the best batsmen of his day and excelled at the on-drive. Unfortunately he was also very temperamental, getting most dejected when he made a small score. Out with a shooting party, his gun went off accidentally and killed one of the gamekeepers; Caesar never really recovered from the shock.

Caesar, William Cecil
Amateur. *b:* 25.11.1899, Clapham, London. *d:* 5.4.1988, Richmond, Surrey. Lower order right-hand batsman, right-arm medium fast bowler. *Teams* Surrey (1922, 1 match); Somerset (1946, 3 matches).
Career batting
4–4–1–14–7–4.66–0–*ct* 3
Bowling 252–10–25.20–0–0–4/59
A noted soccer player, he represented England in amateur internationals and appeared for Dulwich Hamlet, Darlington, Fulham, Walsall and Brentford.

Caffarey, James
(birth registered as J. Caffray)
Professional. *b:* 16.5.1859, Mitcham, Surrey. *d:* 25.12.1913, Tooting Grove, London. Middle order

batsman, change bowler. *Team* Surrey (1881–82, 3 matches).
Career batting
3–5–0–18–6–3.60–0–*ct* 2
Bowling 44–0

Caffyn, William
Professional. *b:* 2.2.1828, Reigate, Surrey. *d:* 28.8.1919, Reigate, Surrey. Nephew of W. W. (Surrey 1844). Stylish middle order right-hand batsman, right-hand medium pace round-arm bowler. *Teams* Surrey (1849–73, 89 matches); Lancashire (1851, 1 match as given man); Kent (1858, 2 matches as given man); New South Wales (1865/6 to 1870/1, 5 matches). *Tours* Parr to North America 1859 (not first-class), to Australia 1863/4; Stephenson to Australia 1861/2.
Career batting
200–350–23–5885–103–17.99–2–*ct* 149
Bowling 7770–577 + 24–13.46–49–11–9/29

Regarded as one of the leading batsmen of his time, Caffyn stayed behind in Australia after the 1863/4 tour and his coaching had much to do with raising the standard of cricket in Australia. He returned to England in 1871. His best bowling was 9/29 for Surrey and Sussex v England at the Oval in 1857. He also played for Suffolk (1849) and Bedfordshire (1860).

Cahn, Sir Julien
Amateur. *b:* 21.10.1882, Cardiff, Glamorgan. *d:* 26.9.1944, Stanford Hall, Nottinghamshire. Tail end right-hand batsman, right-arm slow bowler. *Team* Cahn's XI (1928/9 to 1935). *Tours* Cahn to Jamaica 1928/9, to Argentine 1929/30, to North America 1933 (not first-class), to Ceylon 1936/7 (no first-class matches), to New Zealand 1938/9 (no first-class matches).
Career batting
6–9–2–70–17–10.00–0–*ct* 0
Bowling 149–2–74.50–0–0–1/1

The major patron of English cricket between the two World Wars, Cahn ran his own cricket team with its home ground at Loughborough Road, West Bridgford, Nottingham. He was Nottinghamshire President 1931, 1935 and 1938, and Leicestershire President 1940–41.

Cairns, Bernard Lance
Cricketer. *b:* 10.10.1949, Picton, Marlborough, New Zealand. Father of C. L. (Nottinghamshire and New Zealand). Hard hitting lower order right-hand batsman, right-arm medium pace bowler. *Teams* Central Districts (1972/3 to 1975/6); Otago (1976/7 to 1979/80); Northern Districts (1981/2 to 1984/5). *Tours* New Zealand to Australia 1973/4, 1974/5 (not first-class), 1980/1, 1982/3 (not first-class), 1984/5 (not first-class), 1985/6, to England 1975 (World Cup), 1978, 1979 (World Cup), 1983, to Pakistan 1976/7, 1984/5, to India 1976/7, to Sri Lanka 1983/4, 1984/5 (not first-class), to West Indies 1984/5; Rest of World to England 1988. *Tests* New Zealand (1973/4 to 1985/6, 43 matches).
Career batting
148–226–25–4165–110–20.72–1–*ct* 89
Bowling 12544–473–26.52–24–5–8/46
Test batting
43–65–8–928–64–16.28–0–*ct* 30
Bowling 4279–130–32.91–6–1–7/74

He took 35 wickets, av 25.20, on the 1978 tour to England and played in two Tests, but with little success. In 1983 he played in all four Tests and after Hadlee was the leading bowler with 16 wickets, av 28.81. His first-class debut was for New Zealand Under 23 in 1971/2. He played for Durham (pre first-class, 1979–81 and 1988).

Cairns, Christopher Lance
Cricketer. *b:* 13.6.1970, Picton, Marlborough, New Zealand. Son of B. L. (New Zealand). Middle order right-hand batsman, right-arm fast medium bowler. *Teams* Nottinghamshire (1988–92, 31 matches); Northern Districts (1988/9); Canterbury (1990/1 to 1991/2). *Tour* New Zealand to Australia 1989/90. *Tests* New Zealand (1989/90 to 1991/2, 5 matches).
Career batting
59–77–14–1945–110–30.87–3–*ct* 24
Bowling 5619–187–30.04–6–2–7/34
Test batting
5–8–0–165–61–20.62–0–*ct* 4
Bowling 700–20–35.00–2–0–6/52

In his first full season of English cricket, 1992, he scored 984 runs, av 41.00, and took 56 wickets, av 35.25.

Cairns, Dr John David
Amateur. *b:* 10.2.1925, Gibraltar. Opening right-hand batsman. *Sch* Highgate. *Team* Oxford U (1946).
Career batting
7–14–0–179–36–12.78–0–*ct* 2

His final first-class match was for Free Foresters in 1949.

Caldecourt, William Henry
Professional. *b:* 28.9.1802, Blisworth, Northamptonshire. *d:* 21.6.1857, St John's Wood, London. Powerful attacking middle order batsman, medium pace under-arm bowler. *Teams* Hampshire (1821); Kent(1828); Cambridge Town Club (1832–38).
Career batting
42–68–8–650–59*–10.83–0–*ct* 18
Bowling 0–0 + 48–no av–5–1–5/?

Most of his cricket was for MCC as he was first engaged at Lord's at the age of nine as a ground boy and then as a practice bowler at the age of fifteen. He retained this post until his death. In a minor match in Hertfordshire he hit six sixes off a single six-ball over. He was the principal umpire at Lord's for many years.

Calder, Henry
Amateur. *b:* 14.4.1858, South Stoneham, Hampshire. *d:* 19.5.1938, Southampton, Hampshire. Middle order batsman, useful change bowler. *Teams* Hampshire (1882–85, 5 matches); Western Province (1892/3 to 1894/5); Eastern Province (1896/7).
Career batting
10–19–2–288–44–16.94–0–*ct* 5
Bowling 222–10–22.20–0–0–3/24
He last played for Hampshire (not first-class) in 1888.

Caldwell, Rev William Somerville
Amateur. *b:* 26.2.1878, Altrincham, Cheshire. *d:* 14.1.1964, Littlemore, Oxfordshire. Patient middle order right-hand batsman. *Team* Worcestershire (1901–04, 20 matches).
Career batting
20–33–1–673–133–21.03–2–*ct* 6
Bowling 40–2–20.00–0–0–2/23
He also played for Cheshire (1910) and Oxfordshire (1928–29).

Callaghan, David John
Cricketer. *b:* 1.2.1965, Queenstown, Cape Province, South Africa. Middle order right-hand batsman, right-arm medium pace bowler. *Teams* Eastern Province (1983/4 to 1991/2); Griqualand West (1985/6); Nottinghamshire (1988, 1 match).
Career batting
63–100–11–2845–171–31.96–3–*ct* 48
Bowling 1376–40–34.40–0–0–4/50

Callington, A. (*see under* Lord, A.)

Calnan, Clement Noel
Amateur. *b:* 25.12.1888, Mile End, London, *d:* 30.1.1974, Southend, Essex. Middle order batsman, change bowler. *Team.* Essex (1919–29, 4 matches).
Career batting
4–8–0–49–24–6.12–0–*ct* 1
Bowling 25–0

Calthorpe, Hon Frederick Somerset Gough
Amateur. *b:* 27.5.1892, Kensington, London. *d:* 19.11.1935, Worplesdon, Surrey. Uncle of H. C. Blofeld (Cambridge U), his widow married G. A. I. Dury (Army). Middle order right-hand batsman, right-arm medium pace bowler. *Sch* Repton. *Teams* Sussex (1911–12, 2 matches); Cambridge U (1912–14, 1919, blue all four years); Warwickshire (1919–30, 231 matches). *Tours* MCC to Australia and New Zealand 1922/3, to West Indies 1925/6, 1929/30. *Tests* England (1929/30, 4 matches).
Career batting
369–576–52–12596–209–24.03–13–*ct* 216
Bowling 23390–782–29.91–18–0–6/17
Test batting
4–7–0–129–49–18.42–0–*ct* 3
Bowling 91–1–91.00–0–0–1/38

He captained England in the four Tests in which he appeared and also captained Warwickshire from 1920 to 1929. He hit 1,000 runs in a season five times (best 1,546 av 30.92, in 1925). His only double century was 209 for Warwickshire v Hampshire at Edgbaston in 1921. He took 100 wickets, av 24.26, in 1920, performing the 'double' in the same season. His final first-class match was for MCC in 1935.

Calvert, Charles
Amateur. *b:* 21.3.1833, Kneller Hall, Middlesex. *d:* 7.4.1905, Ecclefechan, Dumfriesshire, Scotland. Uncle of J. C. Hibbert (MCC). Middle order right-hand batsman, right-hand fast round-arm bowler. *Sch* Rugby. *Teams* Middlesex (1865–66, 9 matches); Surrey (1868, 13 matches).
Career batting
27–43–4–541–67*–13.87–0–*ct* 14
Bowling 102–2–51.00–0–0–1/9
He was captain of Surrey in 1868.

Camacho, George Stephen
Cricketer. *b:* 15.10.1945, Georgetown, British Guiana. Son of G. A. (British Guiana), grandson of G. C. Learmond (Barbados and Trinidad). Opening right-hand batsman, leg break and googly bowler. *Team* British Guiana/Guyana (1964/5 to 1978/9). *Tours* West Indies to England 1969, 1973, to Australia and New Zealand 1968/9. *Tests* West Indies (1967/8 to 1970/1, 11 matches).
Career batting
76–125–8–4079–166–34.86–7–*ct* 47
Bowling 216–8–27.00–0–0–3/10
Test batting
11–22–0–640–87–29.09–0–*ct* 4
Bowling 12–0
He was most successful on his 1969 tour of England, heading the Test batting averages, but in 1973 he had the misfortune to suffer a severe injury and played in only two first-class matches. He was appointed Secretary of the West Indies Board of Control in 1983.

Came, Kenneth Charles
Amateur. *b:* 29.10.1925, Caversham, Reading, Berkshire. *d:* 29.1.1986, Up Nately, Basingstoke, Hampshire. Son-in-law of R. W. V. Robins (Middlesex), brother-in-law of R. V. C. Robins (Middlesex). Lower order left-hand batsman, right-arm medium pace bowler. *Team* Free Foresters (1957).
Career batting
1–2–0–12–6–6.00–0–*ct* 1
Bowling 46–0
His County cricket was for Berkshire (1956–57).

Cameron, Francis James
Amateur. *b:* 22.6.1923, Kingston, Jamaica. Son of J. J. (Jamaica), brother of J. H. (Somerset and West Indies), nephew of E. G. Hull (Jamaica). Middle order right-hand batsman, off-break bowler. *Teams*

Jamaica (1945/6 to 1958/9); Canada (1954). *Tours* West Indies to India, Pakistan and Ceylon 1948/9; Canada to England 1954. *Tests* West Indies (1948/9, 5 matches).
Career batting
21–27–5–551–75*–25.04–0–*ct* 9
Bowling 1411–29–48.65–0–0–4/52
Test batting
5–7–1–151–75*–25.16–0–*ct* 0
Bowling 278–3–92.66–0–0–2/74

Cameron, Francis James, MBE
Amateur. *b:* 1.6.1932, Dunedin, New Zealand. Tail end right-hand batsman, right-hand medium-fast bowler. *Team* Otago (1952/3 to 1966/7). *Tours* New Zealand to South Africa and Australia 1961/2, to India and Pakistan 1964/5, to England 1965. *Tests* New Zealand (1961/2 to 1965, 19 matches).
Career batting
119–176–92–993–43–11.82–0–*ct* 26
Bowling 9658–447–21.60–21–0–7/27
Test batting
19–30–20–116–27*–11.60–0–*ct* 2
Bowling 1849–62–29.82–3–0–5/34

Although he ended the 1965 tour to England with 47 wickets av 24.42, he was ineffective in the two Tests in which he played. By dint of having 12 not out innings he headed the first-class batting averages for the tour.

Cameron, Horace Brakenridge
Amateur. *b:* 5.7.1905, Port Elizabeth, South Africa. *d:* 2.11.1935, Joubert Park, Johannesburg, South Africa, of enteric fever. Excellent middle order right-hand batsman, wicket-keeper. *Teams* Transvaal (1924/5 to 1934/5); Eastern Province (1929/30); Western Province (1930/1). *Tours* South Africa to England 1929, 1935, to Australia and New Zealand 1931/2. *Tests* South Africa (1927/8 to 1935, 26 matches).
Career batting
107–161–17–5396–182–37.47–11–*ct* 155–*st* 69
Bowling 13–0
Test batting
26–45–4–1239–90–30.21–0–*ct* 39–*st* 12

In 1935 he was regarded as a wicket-keeper the equal of the Australian, Oldfield, and his batting was of great value to South Africa – in first-class matches he hit 1,458 runs, av 41.65. He captained the South Africans in Australia in 1931/2, and was vice-captain in 1935. He captained South Africa in 9 Tests. He died after only three weeks illness, having just returned to South Africa from England.

Cameron, John Hemsley
Amateur. *b:* 8.4.1914, Kingston, Jamaica. Son of J. J. (Jamaica), brother of F. J. (Jamaica and Canada), nephew of E. G. Hull (Jamaica). Middle order right-hand batsman, off break, leg break and googly bowler. *Sch* Taunton. *Teams* Somerset (1932–47, 48 matches); Cambridge U (1934–37, blue 1935–37); Jamaica (1945/6). *Tours* West Indies to England 1939; Oxford and Cambridge U to Jamaica 1938/9. *Tests* West Indies (1939, 2 matches).
Career batting
105–164–12–2772–113–18.23–4–*ct* 63
Bowling 5662–184–30.77–7–0–7/73
Test batting
2–3–0–6–5–2.00–0–*ct* 0
Bowling 88–3–29.33–0–0–3/66

His greatest triumph was in The Rest v Public Schools match at Lord's in 1931, when in one innings his return read: 19.1–3–49–10.

Cameron, Dr John Joseph
Amateur. *b:* 18.5.1882, Kingston, Jamaica. *d:* 12.12.1954, Kingston, Jamaica. Father of J. H. (Somerset and West Indies) and F. J. (Jamaica and Canada), brother-in-law of E. G. Hull (Jamaica). Lower order right-hand batsman, right-arm slow bowler. *Teams* Jamaica (1908/9 to 1927/8); Gentlemen of England (1908). *Tour* West Indies to England 1906.
Career batting
13–21–2–272–52–14.31–0–*ct* 7
Bowling 213–10–21.30–1–0–5/83

Cammish, James William
Professional. *b:* 21.5.1921, Scarborough, Yorkshire. *d: circa* 1975, New Zealand. Lower order right-hand batsman, leg break and googly bowler. *Teams* Auckland (1950/1); Yorkshire (1954, 2 matches).
Career batting
7–10–3–31–7*–4.42–0–*ct* 8
Bowling 781–25–31.24–2–0–6/93

Campbell, Alastair Keyon
Amateur. *b:* 29.5.1890, South Stoneham, Hampshire. *d:* 16.6.1943, Cosham, Hampshire. Middle order right-hand batsman. *Sch* KES, Southampton. *Team* Hampshire (1908–09, 7 matches).
Career batting
7–10–0–91–21–9.10–0–*ct* 1

He played soccer for Southampton.

Campbell, Andrew Neville
Cricketer. *b:* 17.6.1949, Chesham Bois, Buckinghamshire. Middle order left-hand batsman. *Sch* Berkhamsted. *Team* Oxford U (1968–70, blue 1970).
Career batting
15–27–1–530–73–20.38–0–*ct* 5

His County cricket was for Buckinghamshire (1970–72).

Campbell, Donald
Amateur. *b:* 18.9.1851, Loddon Plains, Victoria, Australia. *d:* 14.9.1887, South Yarra, Melbourne, Victoria, Australia. He died from paralysis. Opening right-hand batsman. *Teams* Oxford U (1873–76, blue 1874–76); Victoria (1868/9 to 1880/1, 8 matches).

Career batting
25–44–3–643–55–15.68–0–*ct* 13
Bowling 61–2–30.50–0–0–1/0

His County cricket was for Cheshire (1872).

Campbell, Euly Anthony
Cricketer. *b:* 25.9.1950, Kingston, Jamaica. Opening/middle order right-hand batsman, wicket-keeper. *Team* Jamaica (1969/70 to 1979/80). *Tour* Jamaica to England 1970.
Career batting
22–35–3–509–48*–15.90–0–*ct* 49–*st* 9

Campbell, Frederick
Amateur. *b:* 15.6.1843, Edinburgh, Scotland. *d:* 13.9.1926, Sydenham Hill, London. Father of J. M. (Middlesex). Middle order batsman, bowler. *Team* MCC (1867–69).
Career batting
4–6–0–52–34–8.66–0–*ct* 4
Bowling 116–13–8.92–1–0–6/37

He was a well-known club cricketer for many years, appearing for I Zingari, Gentlemen of Hampshire and in military matches.

Campbell, G.
Amateur. Middle order batsman, change bowler. *Team* W. G. Grace's XI (1871).
Career batting
1–1–0–0–0–0.00–0–*ct* 1
Bowling 73–1–73.00–0–0–1/73

Campbell, George Augustus
Amateur. *b:* 7.7.1847, Tunbridge Wells, Kent. *d:* 12.9.1930, Brackley, Northamptonshire. Father-in-law of H. F. J. Eaton (Cambridge U). Lower order batsman. *Sch* Wellington. *Team* Lancashire (1866, 1 match).
Career batting
1–2–0–18–10–9.00–0–*ct* 0

Campbell, George Gordon
Amateur. *b:* 12.9.1893, Durban, South Africa. *d:* 5.5.1977, Durban, South Africa. Middle order batsman. *Team* Scotland (1921).
Career batting
1–2–0–9–6–4.50–0–*ct* 0

Campbell, Gerald Victor
Amateur. *b:* 29.4.1884, Kensington, London. *d:* 26.3.1950, Lymington, Hampshire. Brother of H. G. (Royal Navy). Lower order right-hand batsman, right-arm medium pace bowler. *Sch* Eton. *Teams* Surrey (1912, 1 match); Europeans (1905/6).
Career batting
2–3–0–16–14–5.33–0–*ct* 0
Bowling 86–0

He was for many years a stalwart of the Sussex Martlets, taking over 1,000 wickets for the Club. He also played for Norfolk (1906).

Campbell, Gregory Dale
Cricketer. *b:* 10.3.1964, Launceston, Tasmania, Australia. Lower order right-hand batsman, right-arm fast medium bowler. *Team* Tasmania (1986/7 to 1991/2, 29 matches). *Tours* Australia to England 1989, to New Zealand 1989/90, to Sharjah (not first-class) 1989/90. *Tests* Australia (1989 to 1989/90, 4 matches).
Career batting
44–50–9–347–41–8.46–0–*ct* 10
Bowling 4016–120–33.46–5–0–6/80
Test batting
4–4–0–10–6–2.50–0–*ct* 1
Bowling 503–13–38.69–0–0–3/79

A surprise selection for the 1989 tour to England, he played only in the First Test and then was dropped. In all first-class matches he took 30 wickets, av 27.46.

Campbell, Sir Harold George
Amateur. *b:* 6.4.1888, Westminster, London. *d:* 9.6.1969, Strood House, Rolvenden, Kent. Brother of G. V. (Surrey). Lower order right-hand batsman, right-arm medium pace bowler. *Team* Royal Navy (1912–14).
Career batting
2–4–1–76–38–25.33–0–*ct* 2
Bowling 65–2–32.50–0–0–2/45

Campbell, Iain Parry
Amateur. *b:* 5.2.1928, Purley, Surrey. Hard-hitting middle or lower order right-hand batsman, wicket-keeper. *Sch* Canford. *Teams* Kent (1946, 1 match); Oxford U (1949–51, blue 1949–50). *Tour* MCC to Canada 1951.
Career batting
22–36–4–482–60*–15.06–0–*ct* 24–*st* 17

His fame as a cricketer rests with his quite remarkable achievement at Canford School. In 1945 he hit 1,027 runs (av 79.00) and in 1946 1,277 runs (av 116.00) including three double centuries. In first-class cricket his performances were quite modest, but he was also a noted rugby footballer for Kent and London Counties and was awarded a blue for hockey at Oxford. His final first-class match was for MCC in 1954.

Campbell, Ion Percy Fitzgerald
Amateur. *b:* 25.11.1890, Palampur, Kangra Valley, Punjab, India. *d:* 25.12.1963, Waukmill, Redgorton, Perthshire, Scotland. Nephew of I. D. F. (India). Middle order right-hand batsman, change bowler. *Sch* Repton. *Teams* Surrey (1910–27, 25 matches); Oxford U (1911–13, blue all three years); Europeans (1925/6 to 1926/7).
Career batting
59–102–3–2413–120–24.37–3–*ct* 28
Bowling 205–5–41.00–0–0–3/12

He also was awarded his blue for soccer and was an excellent fives player. His final first-class match was for Indian XI v MCC in 1933/4. He captained Oxford in 1913.

Campbell, John Maxwell
(known as Ian Maxwell Campbell)
Amateur. *b:* 3.10.1870, Kensington, London. *d:* 6.3.1954, Amersham, Buckinghamshire. Son of Frederick (MCC). Middle order right-hand batsman, right-arm medium pace bowler. *Sch* Dulwich. *Teams* Middlesex (1900, 1 match); London County (1900–02).
Career batting
4–6–0–65–37–10.83–0–*ct* 2
Bowling 57–1–57.00–0–0–1/57

Campbell, Percivale
(registered at death as Percival Campbell)
Amateur. *b:* 26.12.1887, West Ham, Essex. *d:* 18.3.1960, South Woodford, Essex. Middle order batsman, change bowler. *Sch* Eastbourne. *Team* Essex (1911–19, 13 matches).
Career batting
13–21–2–270–35–14.21–0–*ct* 6
Bowling 26–0

Campbell, Thomas
Amateur. *b:* 9.2.1882, Edinburgh, Scotland. *d:* 5.10.1924, Milndale Railway Siding, Natal, South Africa, in a railway accident. Middle/lower order right-hand batsman, wicket-keeper. *Team* Transvaal (1906/7 to 1909/10). *Tours* South Africa to Australia 1910/11, to England 1912. *Tests* South Africa (1909/10 to 1912, 5 matches).
Career batting
29–42–12–365–48–12.16–0–*ct* 40–*st* 12
Test batting
5–9–3–90–48–15.00–0–*ct* 7–*st* 1
On his single visit to England he was deputy wicket-keeper to Sherwell and had little to do. In view of the nature of his death it should be recorded that he fell out of a train in 1916 and suffered severe head injuries, from which it was thought he would not recover. His last first-class match in South Africa was for South Africa XI in 1910/11. He played rugby for Scotland.

Candler, Rev David Cecil
Amateur. *b:* 18.10.1924, Bulawayo, Rhodesia. Middle order right-hand batsman, leg break bowler. *Team* Oxford U (1950–51).
Career batting
5–7–0–115–54–16.42–0–*ct* 2
Bowling 4–0

Candler, Dr John Pycock
Amateur. *b:* 7.10.1873, Tendring, Essex. *d:* 4.12.1942, Finsbury, London. Tail end batsman, bowler. *Sch* Merchant Taylors. *Team* Cambridge U (1894–95).
Career batting
7–10–5–8–8*–1.60–0–*ct* 5
Bowling 662–18–36.77–0–0–3/91
He failed to score in his first nine first-class innings.

Candlett, William
Professional. *b: circa* 1847. *d:* 20.6.1904, Salford, Lancashire. Tail end right-hand batsman, right-arm medium pace bowler. *Team* Kent (1880, 1 match).
Career batting
1–2–1–3–3–3.00–0–*ct* 0
Bowling 29–0

Cangley, Barron George Merriman
Amateur. *b:* 12.9.1922, Blakesley, Towcester, Northamptonshire. Middle order right-hand batsman. *Sch* Weymouth College and Felsted. *Team* Cambridge U (1947).
Career batting
8–14–1–295–76–22.69–0–*ct* 3
His County cricket was for Cambridgeshire (1946). He won a blue for hockey and also played for Natal.

Cann, Michael James
Cricketer. *b:* 4.7.1965, Cardiff, Glamorgan. Middle order left-hand batsman, off break bowler. *Teams* Glamorgan (1986–91, 36 matches); Orange Free State (1989/90); Griqualand West (1990/1 to 1991/2).
Career batting
52–84–6–2250–141–28.84–4–*ct* 23
Bowling 1780–38–46.84–0–0–4/54

Canning, Ernest George
Professional. *b:* 11.8.1902, Marylebone, London. Middle order right-hand batsman. *Team* Middlesex (1929–31, 36 matches).
Career batting
37–62–7–829–85–15.07–0–*ct* 11
Bowling 12–0
He also played for Hertfordshire (1935–38).

Cannings, Victor Henry Douglas
Professional. *b:* 3.4.1919, Bighton, Hampshire. Lower order right-hand batsman, right-arm medium pace bowler. *Teams* Warwickshire (1947–49, 53 matches); Hampshire (1950–59, 230 matches).
Career batting
285–373–128–2660–61–10.85–0–*ct* 103
Bowling 21077–927–22.73–42–4–7/52
He took 100 wickets in a season 4 times (best 112, av 21.56, in 1952). He also played for Buckinghamshire (1960–62).

Cantelupe, Viscount
(*see under* De La Warr, Earl)

Cantlay, Charles Peter Thrale
Cricketer. *b:* 4.2.1954, Victoria, London. Lower order right-hand batsman, right-arm medium fast

bowler. *Sch* Radley. *Team* Oxford U (1975).
Career batting
6–9–5–19–9–4.75–0–*ct* 0
Bowling 419–11–38.09–0–0–4/85

Cantrell, Arthur Stanley
Amateur. *b:* 8.5.1883. *d:* 22.5.1954, Black-Notley, Essex. Lower order right-hand batsman, right-arm medium fast bowler. *Sch* Bedford. *Team* Royal Navy (1913–29).
Career batting
15–27–14–308–32*–23.69–0–*ct* 6
Bowling 1256–49–25.63–3–0–6/58

Cantwell, Noel Euchuria Cornelious
Amateur. *b:* 28.12.1932, Cork, Ireland. Middle order left-hand batsman, right-arm medium pace bowler. *Team* Ireland (1956).
Career batting
1–2–1–48–31–48.00–0–*ct* 0
Bowling 13–0
He played soccer for West Ham and Manchester United, and was an international for the Republic of Ireland.

Capel, David John
Cricketer. *b:* 6.2.1963, Northampton. Middle order right-hand batsman, right-arm medium pace bowler. *Teams* Northamptonshire (1981–92, 223 matches); Eastern Province (1985/6 to 1986/7). *Tours* England to Sharjah (not first-class) 1986/7, to New Zealand 1987/8, to Pakistan 1987/8, to Australia 1987/8, to West Indies 1989/90. *Tests* England (1987 to 1989/90, 15 matches).
Career batting
261–394–58–10068–134–29.96–12–*ct* 126
Bowling 14350–439–32.68–12–0–7/46
Test batting
15–25–1–374–98–15.58–0–*ct* 6
Bowling 1064–21–50.66–0–0–3/88
He hit 1,000 runs in a season three times (best 1,311, av 36.41, in 1989). His best season with the ball was 1986 when he took 63 wickets, av 32.44. Selected for the twin tours of 1987/8, he failed to make the most of his England opportunities, his bowling not coming up to Test standard and being unable to command a Test place as a specialist batsman. The same comment applies to his 1989/90 visit to West Indies, though his enthusiasm and dedication were an example to his colleagues.

Capel-Cure, George Nigel
Amateur. *b:* 28.9.1908, Kensington, London. Nephew of Arthur and Francis (both Essex, pre first-class), brother-in-law of G. Barry (Combined Services). Opening left-hand batsman, leg break bowler. *Sch* Eton. *Team* Essex (1929, 1 match).
Career batting
1–2–0–6–6–3.00–0–*ct* 0
Bowling 58–2–29.00–0–0–2/58

He played in Cambridge Freshmen's match of 1928 and the Seniors' of 1930, but in no first-class matches at the University. He won a blue for squash.

Capes, Charles John
Amateur. *b:* 5.1.1898, Forest Hill, London. *d:* 16.2.1933, Ospedaletti, Italy. Hard-hitting lower order right-hand batsman, left-arm medium pace bowler. *Sch* Malvern. *Team* Kent (1923–28, 33 matches).
Career batting
33–41–8–534–65*–16.18–0–*ct* 16
Bowling 1381–55–25.10–2–0–7/20
He was better known as an English International hockey player.

Caplan, Jeremy John Notley
Amateur. *b:* 9.10.1941, Kolar Gold Mine, Champion Reef, Mysore, India. Lower order right-hand batsman, off break bowler. *Sch* Cheltenham. *Team* Cambridge U (1962).
Career batting
2–3–0–38–26–12.66–0–*ct* 0
Bowling 97–3–32.33–0–0–1/25

Caple, Robert Graham
Professional. *b:* 8.12.1939, Chiswick, Middlesex. Middle order left-hand batsman, off break bowler. *Teams* Middlesex (1959, 2 matches); Hampshire (1961–67, 65 matches).
Career batting
68–103–17–1581–64*–18.38–0–*ct* 32
Bowling 1235–34–36.32–1–0–5/54
His first-class debut was for MCC in 1958.

Caplen, Tom
Amateur. *b:* 23.11.1879, Rusthall, Tunbridge Wells, Kent. *d:* 17.4.1945, Hove, Sussex. Lower order right-hand batsman, right-arm fast bowler. *Team* Kent (1897, 1 match).
Career batting
1–2–1–6–5*–6.00–0–*ct* 0
Bowling 74–2–37.00–0–0–2/74
He appeared for Cornwall in 1898, but later moved to India, and his name can be found in a number of important matches there.

Capon, Stephen
Amateur. *b:* 25.4.1927, Snodland, Kent. Lower order right-hand batsman, right-arm fast medium bowler. *Team* Kent (1950, 1 match).
Career batting
1–1–0–4–4–4.00–0–*ct* 0
Bowling 98–0

Caprani, Joseph Desmond
Amateur. *b:* 27.5.1920, Clontarf, Co Dublin, Ireland. Middle order right-hand batsman. *Team* Ireland (1948–60).
Career batting
5–10–0–95–44–9.50–0–*ct* 5

Capron, Frederick William
Amateur. *b:* 1.10.1860, Westminster, London. *d:* 18.1.1942, Kensington, London. Middle order right-hand batsman. *Sch* Tonbridge and Rugby. *Team* MCC (1881–82).
Career batting
2–3–0–13–11–4.33–0–*ct* 0
He played in trial matches at Cambridge U, but in no first-class games.

Carbutt, Noel John Obelin
Amateur. *b:* 25.12.1895, Gingindhlovu, Zululand. *d:* 31.10.1964, Durban, South Africa. Lower order right-hand batsman, leg break and googly bowler. *Teams* Essex (1923, 2 matches); Madras (1926/7).
Career batting
15–19–5–135–45–9.64–0–*ct* 7
Bowling 1386–36–38.50–2–0–5/20
He was a noted figure in Army cricket for many years. His first-class debut was for Combined Services in 1920 and last match for the Army in 1928.

Card, Anthony John
Professional. *b:* 13.9.1929, Doncaster, Yorkshire. Lower order batsman, slow left-arm bowler. *Team* MCC (1955–58).
Career batting
2–4–2–51–19*–25.50–0–*ct* 2
Bowling 87–7–12.42–0–0–4/26

Carew, Michael Conrad
Amateur. *b:* 15.9.1937, Woodbrook, Port of Spain, Trinidad. Father of M. P. (Trinidad). Opening left-hand batsman, right-arm medium pace or off break bowler. *Team* Trinidad (1955/6 to 1972/3). *Tours* West Indies to England 1963, 1966, 1969, to Australia and New Zealand 1968/9. *Tests* West Indies (1963 to 1971/2, 19 matches).
Career batting
129–221–18–7810–182–38.47–13–*ct* 83
Bowling 3215–108–29.76–5–0–5/28
Test batting
19–36–3–1127–109–34.15–1–*ct* 13
Bowling 437–8–54.62–0–0–1/11
Of his three tours to England his best was in 1969, when he hit 677 runs, av 45.13; in 1963 he made 1,060 runs, av 30.28. His final first-class match was for North Trinidad 1973/4.

Carey, P. A. D.
(*see under* Dobree-Carey, P. A. H.)

Carey, Thomas Falkland
Amateur. *b:* 12.2.1903, California, USA. *d:* 4.12.1966, Thorpe St Andrew, Norfolk. Lower order right-hand batsman, right-arm medium pace bowler. *Team* Dublin University (1924).
Career batting
1–2–0–21–15–10.50–0–*ct* 0
Bowling 41–2–20.50–0–0–2/41

Carkeek, William (Barlow)
Amateur. *b:* 17.10.1878, Walhalla, Victoria, Australia. *d:* 20.2.1937, Prahran, Melbourne, Victoria, Australia. Lower order left-hand batsman, wicket-keeper. *Team* Victoria (1903/4 to 1914/15, 53 matches). *Tours* Australia to England 1909, 1912, to North America 1912, to South Africa 1914/15 (tour cancelled). *Tests* Australia (1912, 6 matches).
Career batting
95–146–32–1388–68–12.17–0–*ct* 114–*st* 46
Test batting
6–5–2–16–6*–5.33–0–*ct* 6
Although he was the principal wicket-keeper on the 1912 tour, he did not approach the standard of his contemporary, H. Carter.

Carless, Ernest Francis
Professional in 1934, amateur in 1946. *b:* 9.9.1912, Barry, Glamorgan. *d:* 26.9.1987, Barry, Glamorgan. Lower order right-hand batsman, occasional off break bowler, wicket-keeper. *Team* Glamorgan (1934–46, 3 matches).
Career batting
3–3–0–35–25–11.66–0–*ct* 1
He also played for Devon (1947–49). A noted soccer player he appeared for Cardiff City and Plymouth Argyle.

Carlin, John
Professional. *b:* 3.11.1861, New Eastwood, Nottinghamshire. *d:* 28.11.1944, Mansfield, Nottinghamshire. Originally a left-hand batsman, he changed to right-hand when being tried for Nottinghamshire, wicket-keeper. *Team* Nottinghamshire (1887–1901, 58 matches).
Career batting
76–113–20–1578–85–16.96–0–*ct* 101–*st* 39
Bowling 121–5–24.20–0–0–3/25
From 1888 to 1912 he was on the staff at Lord's. He was a first-class umpire (1902–21), standing in 4 Test matches (1905–09).

Carlin, Robert McKenzie
Professional. *b:* 24.1.1871, Eastwood, Nottinghamshire. *d:* 10.3.1950, Conisbrough, Yorkshire. Middle order right-hand batsman, right-arm medium pace bowler. *Team* Derbyshire (1905–08, 15 matches).
Career batting
15–28–1–306–37–11.33–0–*ct* 5
Bowling 208–5–41.60–0–0–2/53

Carling, Philip George
Cricketer. *b:* 25.11.1946, Carshalton, Surrey. Sound opening left-hand batsman, wicket-keeper. *Sch* Kingston GS. *Team* Cambridge U (1967–70, blue 1968 and 1970).
Career batting
30–55–3–1160–104–22.30–1–*ct* 13
Bowling 25–0

He was Chief Executive of Nottinghamshire CCC 1979–82 and Glamorgan CCC 1983–90. His County cricket was for Cambridgeshire (1972).

Carlisle, Frederick
Amateur. *b:* 4.11.1849, Chorley Hall, Liverpool, Lancashire. *d:* 22.10.1920, Pevensey, Eastbourne, Sussex. Uncle of K. M. (Oxford U) and M. M. (MCC), great-uncle of K. R. M. (Sussex). Middle order batsman. *Sch* Harrow. *Team* Lancashire (1869, 2 matches).
Career batting
2–4–0–37–18–9.25–0–*ct* 0
He also played for Cheshire.

Carlisle, Kenneth Methven
Amateur. *b:* 7.8.1882, Foxley Hall, Lymm, Cheshire. *d:* 15.5.1967, Wyker Hall, Bardwell, Suffolk. Father of K. R. M. (Sussex), brother of M. M. (MCC), nephew of Frederick (Lancashire). Middle order right-hand batsman, slow right-arm bowler. *Sch* Harrow. *Team* Oxford U (1903–05, blue all three years).
Career batting
30–55–4–1211–114*–23.74–2–*ct* 19
Bowling 279–6–46.50–0–0–2/39
He was captain of Oxford in 1905. In 1908 he represented South v North Argentine.

Carlisle, Kenneth Ralph Malcolm
Amateur. *b:* 28.3.1908, Buenos Aires, Argentina. *d:* 23.7.1983, Kensington, London. Son of K. M. (Oxford U), nephew of M. M. (MCC), great-nephew of Frederick (Lancashire). Middle or lower order right-hand batsman, right-arm medium pace bowler. *Sch* Harrow. *Teams* Sussex (1927–28, 3 matches); Oxford U (1929).
Career batting
5–7–0–101–34–14.42–0–*ct* 2

Carlisle, Malcolm Methven
Amateur. *b:* 5.7.1884, Foxley Hall, Lymm, Cheshire. *d:* 24.5.1906, Lucknow, India. Brother of K. M. (Oxford U), uncle of K. R. M. (Sussex), nephew of Frederick (Lancashire). Middle order right-hand batsman. *Sch* Harrow. *Team* MCC (1904).
Career batting
1–2–0–12–12–6.00–0–*ct* 0
Bowling 26–0

Carlstein, Peter Rudolph
Amateur. *b:* 28.10.1938, Klerksdorp, Transvaal, South Africa. Middle order right-hand batsman, leg break bowler, fine field, occasional wicket-keeper. *Teams* Orange Free State (1954/5 to 1957/8); Transvaal (1958/9 to 1971/2); Natal (1964/5 to 1966/7); Rhodesia (1967/8 to 1979/80). *Tours* South Africa to England 1960, to Australia 1963/4. *Tests* South Africa (1957/8 to 1963/4, 8 matches).
Career batting
148–255–16–7554–229–31.60–9–*ct* 82
Bowling 480–9–53.33–0–0–3/37
Test batting
8–14–1–190–42–14.61–0–*ct* 3
He appeared in all five Tests on his 1960 tour to England, but averaged only 13.22; in all first-class matches he just missed reaching 1,000 runs. His highest score was 229 for Transvaal v Cavaliers at Johannesburg in 1962/3.

Carmichael, Duncan Smart
Amateur. *b:* 8.11.1915, Matelli, Jailpaiguri, India. *d:* 28.11.1984, Holybourne, Alton, Hampshire. Lower order right-hand batsman, right-arm medium pace bowler. *Sch* Fettes. *Team* Cambridge U (1936–37).
Career batting
9–11–4–13–5–1.85–0–*ct* 1
Bowling 658–20–32.90–1–0–6/103

Carmichael (of Carmichael), Evelyn George Massey
Amateur. *b:* 3.4.1871, Upper Wick, Worcester. *d:* 14.7.1959, Berrington Hall, Shrewsbury, Shropshire. Middle order right-hand batsman, right-arm medium pace bowler. *Sch* Harrow. *Team* Worcestershire (1903, 1 match).
Career batting
1–2–0–6–5–3.00–0–*ct* 1
He did not appear in first-class cricket whilst at Oxford U. He first played for Worcestershire (pre first-class) in 1891.

Carmichael, Ian Robert
Cricketer. *b:* 17.12.1960, Hull, Yorkshire. Lower order right-hand batsman, left-arm fast medium bowler. *Teams* South Australia (1983/4 to 1987/8, 26 matches); Leicestershire (1984, 7 matches).
Career batting
33–35–17–142–24–7.88–0–*ct* 9
Bowling 3741–86–43.50–4–0–6/112

Carmichael, John
Amateur. *b:* 4.7.1858, Bubwith, Howden, Yorkshire. *d:* 24.8.1914, USA, as the result of a motor accident. Middle order right-hand batsman, wicket-keeper. *Sch* Cranleigh. *Team* Surrey (1876–81, 14 matches).
Career batting
14–24–1–243–47–10.56–0–*ct* 11–*st* 3
Bowling 9–0

Carmody, Douglas Keith
Amateur. *b:* 16.2.1919, Mosman, Sydney, New South Wales, Australia. *d:* 21.10.1977, Concord, Sydney, New South Wales, Australia. Opening or middle order right-hand batsman, right-arm medium pace bowler. *Teams* New South Wales (1939/40 to 1946/7, 13 matches); Western Australia (1947/8 to 1955/6, 35 matches). *Tours* Australian Services to England 1945, to India 1945/6.
Career batting
65–123–2–3496–198–28.89–2–*ct* 39–*st* 3

Bowling 187–3–62.33–0–0–1/0

He was captain of the RAAF team in England in 1945, after being a prisoner-of-war. In 1947/8 he captained West Australia to its Sheffield Shield Championship and his close-to-the-wicket field placings earned the name 'Carmody Umbrella'.

Carnegie-Brown, Dr George
Amateur. *b:* 28.1.1906, Jerusalem. *d:* 26.3.1964, Lincoln. Attractive middle order left-hand batsman, good field. *Sch* Leys. *Team* Cambridge U (1926).
Career batting
4–7–0–78–32–11.14–0–*ct* 2

His County cricket was played for Cambridgeshire (1921–31), Dorset (1935–46) and Lincolnshire (1947). His final first-class match was for the Minor Counties in 1937.

Carnie, William
Amateur. *b:* 27.1.1907, Caputh, Perthshire, Scotland. *d:* 1980, Montreal, Quebec, Canada. Lower order right-hand batsman, right-arm fast medium bowler. *Team* Scotland (1925).
Career batting
1–2–1–6–6*–6.00–0–*ct* 1
Bowling 21–0

Carnill, Denys John
Amateur. *b:* 11.3.1926, Hampstead, London. Lower order left-hand batsman, leg break bowler. *Sch* Hitchin GS. *Team* Oxford U (1950).
Career batting
1–1–0–8–8–8.00–0–*ct* 0
Bowling 33–1–33.00–0–0–1/33

His County cricket was for Hertfordshire (1949–56). An excellent hockey player, he represented Oxford and England.

Carpenter, Charles Wilson
Amateur. *b:* 1837, Brighton, Sussex. *d:* 5.3.1876, Nagpore, India as the result of a fall from his horse whilst steeplechasing. Middle order right-hand batsman. *Sch* Brighton College. *Team* Sussex (1868, 2 matches).
Career batting
3–6–0–47–15–7.83–0–*ct* 2
Bowling 45–3–15.00–0–0–3/32

His debut in first-class matches was for Gentlemen of Kent and Sussex in 1857.

Carpenter, David
Professional. *b:* 12.9.1935, Rodborough, Stroud, Gloucestershire. Opening right-hand batsman, off break bowler. *Team* Gloucestershire (1954–63, 117 matches).
Career batting
117–210–6–3741–95–18.33–0–*ct* 72
Bowling 36–0

He reached 1,000 runs in a season once: 1,353, av 23.32, in 1961.

Carpenter, Herbert Arthur
Professional. *b;* 12.7.1869, Cambridge. *d:* 12.12.1933, Whipps Cross, Essex. Son of R. P. (Cambridgeshire), nephew of George (Cambridge Town Club) and William (Cambridge Town Club), uncle of J. O'Connor (Essex). Opening right-hand batsman, off break bowler. *Team* Essex (1894–1920, 262 matches).
Career batting
310–551–26–14939–199–28.45–25–*ct* 257
Bowling 2246–50–44.92–0–0–4/57

He scored 1,000 runs in a season 7 times (best 1,852, av 37.04, in 1901). His career with Essex commenced in 1888. Latterly he was handicapped by ill-health and left first-class cricket to appear for Cambridgeshire (1913), but made a final appearance for Essex in 1920. His debut in first-class matches was for MCC in 1893.

Carpenter, Robert Pearson
Professional. *b:* 18.11.1830, Mill Road, Cambridge. *d:* 14.7.1901, Cambridge. Father of H. A. (Essex), brother of George (Cambridge Town Club) and William (Cambridge Town Club). Fine middle order right-hand batsman, brilliant point field. *Teams* Cambridgeshire (1861–71, 32 matches), Cambridge Town Club (1855–61). *Tours* Parr to North America 1859 (not first-class), to Australia 1863/4.
Career batting
141–233–19–5220–134–24.39–4–*ct* 190–*st* 1
Bowling 290–18+1–16.11–0–0–4/29

About 1860 he was regarded as the finest batsman in England but for various reasons he did not play in important matches at Lord's as often as he deserved. He was associated mainly with the United All England Eleven. His final first-class match was for the North in 1876. He also played for Bedfordshire (1860). He umpired in 2 Test matches (1886–88).

Carr, Arthur William
Amateur. *b:* 21.5.1893, Mickleham, Surrey. *d:* 7.2.1963, West Witton, Yorkshire. Hard-hitting middle order right-hand batsman, right-arm medium pace bowler. *Sch* Sherborne and Eton. *Team* Nottinghamshire (1910–34, 416 matches). *Tour* MCC to South Africa 1922/3. *Tests* England (1922/3 to 1929, 11 matches).
Career batting
468–709–42–21051–206–31.56–45–*ct* 393–*st* 1
Bowling 1150–31–37.09–0–0–3/14
Test batting
11–13–1–237–63–19.75–0–*ct* 3

An inspiring but controversial captain, Carr led Nottinghamshire from 1919 to 1934 and England in the first four Tests v Australia in 1926 and in two Tests v South Africa in 1929. He was dismissed from the England captaincy in 1926 and the Nottinghamshire captaincy in 1934, in each case in circumstances that resulted in much ill-feeling.

An attacking batsman, he hit 1,000 runs in a season 11 times, exceeding 2,000 runs once (2,338, av 51.95, in 1925). He hit two double centuries, his highest being 206 for Nottinghamshire v Leicestershire at Leicester in 1925. Also in 1925 he hit no fewer than 48 sixes, which is believed to have created a new record. The close of his first-class career was brought about by the arguments concerning 'bodyline' bowling. He was dismissed by the Nottinghamshire Committee in December 1934, but forced an Extraordinary General Meeting of the County Club which demanded the sacking of the Committee and reinstatement of Carr. Subtle manoeuvring however managed to reverse the decision of the Extraordinary Meeting at the club's AGM and Carr was not seen again in County cricket, though he appeared in a final first-class match for Sir Lindsay Parkinson's XI in 1935. He was a Test selector 1927–28.

Carr, Austin Michael
Amateur. *b:* 29.9.1898, Lower Hall, Broxton, Chester, Cheshire. *d:* 20.12.1946, Great Witley, Worcestershire. Middle order right-hand batsman, *Sch* Eton. *Team* Worcestershire (1921–25, 6 matches).
Career batting
6–10–0–150–82–15.00–0–*ct* 2
Bowling 10–0

Carr, Donald Bryce, OBE
Amateur. *b:* 28.12.1926, Wiesbaden, Germany. Son of J. L. (Army), father of J. D. (Middlesex). Attractive middle order right-hand batsman, slow left-arm bowler, excellent close field. *Sch* Repton. *Teams* Derbyshire (1946–63, 336 matches); Oxford U (1948–51, blue 1949–51). *Tours* MCC to India, Pakistan and Ceylon 1951/2, to Pakistan 1955/6, to South America 1958/9 (not first-class). *Tests* England (1951/2, 2 matches).
Career batting
446–745–72–19257–170–28.61–24–*ct* 500
Bowling 11396–328–34.74–5–0–7/53
Test batting
2–4–0–135–76–33.75–0–*ct* 0
Bowling 140–2–70.00–0–0–2/84

His first-class debut was for England v Australian Services in the Victory 'Test' of 1945 at Lord's. He reached 1,000 runs 11 times (best 2,292, av 44.07, in 1959). On his 1951/2 MCC tour, he captained England in the Madras Test v India. He captained Oxford in 1950 and Derbyshire 1955 to 1962. He was Secretary of the County from 1960 to 1962, Assistant Secretary of MCC 1962–73, Secretary of TCCB 1973–86 and Secretary of the Cricket Council 1974–86. He managed three MCC Test tours: to South Africa 1964/5, to India and Pakistan 1972/3, to West Indies 1973/4. His final first-class match was for Free Foresters in 1968. He also gained a soccer blue and appeared in the Amateur FA Cup Final for Pegasus in 1950/1 and 1952/3.

Carr, Douglas Ward
Amateur. *b:* 17.3.1872, Cranbrook, Kent. *d:* 23.3.1950, Salcombe Hill, Sidmouth, Devon. Lower order right-hand batsman, right-arm medium pace bowler, changed to googly bowler about 1906. *Sch* Sutton Valence. *Team* Kent (1909–14, 49 matches). *Test* England (1909, 1 match).
Career batting
58–68–18–447–48–8.94–0–*ct* 19
Bowling 5585–334–16.72–31–8–8/36
Test batting
1–1–0–0–0–0.00–0–*ct* 0
Bowling 282–7–40.28–1–0–5/146

At Oxford he played in the Freshmen's match of 1891, but a football injury prevented him appearing in any major matches. After years in good class club cricket, he suddenly developed an aptitude for bowling 'googlies' and achieved almost instant fame in 1909, when soon after being introduced into the Kent team he was selected for the Gentlemen and then for England.

Carr, Harry Lascelles
Amateur. *b:* 8.10.1907, Lambeth, London. *d:* 18.8.1943, Marylebone, London. He died following an operation. Lower order right-hand batsman, wicket-keeper. *Sch* Clifton. *Team* Glamorgan (1934, 1 match).
Career batting
3–5–0–54–33–10.80–0–*ct* 4–*st* 2

His debut in first-class matches was for Leveson-Gower's XI in 1931. He played no first-class cricket whilst at Cambridge U, but did win blues for golf and billiards.

Carr, John Donald
Cricketer. *b:* 15.6.1963, St John's Wood, London. Son of D. B. (Derbyshire), grandson of J. L. (Army). Opening right-hand batsman, off break bowler. *Sch* Repton. *Teams* Oxford U (1983–85, blue all three years); Middlesex (1983–92, 117 matches).
Career batting
138–223–28–6623–156–33.96–12–*ct* 123
Bowling 2866–64–44.78–3–0–6/61

He also played for Hertfordshire (1982–84 and 1990–91). At the close of 1989, after a patchy season, he decided to retire from first-class County cricket, but returned to Middlesex in 1992. He hit 1,000 runs in a season three times (best 1,541, av 41.64, in 1987).

Carr, John Lillingston
Amateur. *b:* 16.5.1892, Palamcottah, India. *d:* 3.2.1963, Derby. Father of D. B. (Derbyshire), grandfather of J. D. (Middlesex). Middle order right-hand batsman. *Sch* Repton and St Lawrence, Ramsgate. *Teams* MCC (1913); Army (1926).
Career batting
4–7–0–114–46–16.28–0–*ct* 3

His County cricket was for Berkshire (1926–31). He played in trial matches at Oxford U, but not in first-class games.

Carr, Michael Lewis
(originally Kerner-Cohen)
Amateur. *b:* 24.6.1933, Alexandria, Egypt. Lower order right-hand batsman, wicket-keeper. *Sch* Malvern. *Team* Cambridge U (1953).
Career batting
1–2–1–1–1*–1.00–0–*ct* 2

Carr, Ronald Bernard
Professional. *b:* 12.1.1938, Johannesburg, South Africa. Lower order right-hand batsman, leg break and googly bowler. *Teams* Essex (1960, 1 match); Transvaal (1964/5).
Career batting
2–3–2–35–28*–35.00–0–*ct* 2
Bowling 107–0

Carrick, James Stewart
Amateur. *b:* 4.9.1855, Blythswood, Glasgow, Scotland. *d:* 2.1.1923, Seattle, Washington, USA. Hard-hitting middle order left-hand batsman, slow bowler, good field. *Sch* Glasgow Academy. *Team* MCC (1882).
Career batting
1–2–0–13–10–6.50–0–*ct* 0
In 1885 he hit 419* for West of Scotland v Priory Park at Chichester, batting 11¼ hours. For many years the best bat in Scotland he regularly appeared for his Country. Also an excellent rugby player, he represented Scotland v England. In addition he was a noted golfer.

Carrick, Phillip
Cricketer. *b:* 16.7.1952, Armley, Leeds, Yorkshire. Middle or lower order right-hand batsman, slow left-arm bowler. *Teams* Yorkshire (1970–92, 422 matches); Eastern Province (1976/7); Northern Transvaal (1982/3). *Tours* Robins to South Africa 1975/6, to Sri Lanka 1977/8; Yorkshire to Windward Islands 1986/7, to South Africa 1991/2.
Career batting
441–568–102–10255–131*–22.00–3–*ct* 197
Bowling 32115–1078–29.79–47–5–8/33
He was captain of Yorkshire 1987–89.

Carrington, Elijah
Professional. *b:* 25.3.1914, Blackwell, Derbyshire. Middle order right-hand batsman. *Team* Derbyshire (1934–37, 50 matches).
Career batting
50–77–4–1470–80–20.13–0–*ct* 18
Bowling 32–0

Carris, Bertram Dudley
Amateur. *b:* 23.10.1917, Flixton, Lancashire. Brother of H. E. (Middlesex). Opening right-hand batsman. slow left-arm bowler. *Sch* Harrow. *Teams* Middlesex (1937–39, 12 matches); Cambridge U (1938–39, blue both years).
Career batting
32–55–2–1214–87–22.90–0–*ct* 14
Bowling 955–26–36.73–0–0–4/59

Carris, Harold Edward
Amateur. *b:* 7.7.1909, Flixton, Lancashire. *d:* 29.7.1959, Cheadle Hulme, Cheshire. Brother of B. D. (Middlesex). Middle order left-hand batsman, right-arm bowler. *Sch* Mill Hill. *Teams* Middlesex (1928–33, 36 matches); Cambridge U (1930, blue).
Career batting
44–71–3–1418–98–20.85–0–*ct* 11
Bowling 65–2–32.50–0–0–1/5
He was awarded his rugby blue in 1929.

Carroll, James Thomas
Professional. *b:* 18.3.1843, Gravesend, Kent. *d:* 1.4.1926, Windmill Hill, Gravesend, Kent. Opening or middle order right-hand batsman, right-arm fast medium bowler, good outfield. *Team* Kent (1865–69, 33 matches).
Career batting
33–56–6–610–48–12.20–0–*ct* 12
Bowling 257–8–32.12–0–0–2/21

Carroll, John Paul
Cricketer. *b:* 14.7.1972, Bebington, Cheshire. Middle order right-hand batsman, right-arm medium pace bowler. *Sch* Rendcomb. *Team* Cambridge U (1992, blue).
Career batting
5–9–0–175–92–19.44–0–*ct* 1

Carroll, Dr Peter Robert
Cricketer. *b:* 7.11.1941, Mosman, Sydney, New South Wales, Australia. Middle order right-hand batsman, right-arm medium pace bowler. *Team* Oxford U (1969–71, blue 1971).
Career batting
14–27–2–403–60*–16.12–0–*ct* 11
Bowling 64–0
He also won a blue for rugby.

Carse, James Alexander
Cricketer. *b:* 13.12.1958, Salisbury, Rhodesia. Lower order right-hand batsman, right-arm fast medium bowler. *Teams* Rhodesia (1977/8 to 1979/80); Western Province (1980/1); Eastern Province (1981/2 to 1986/7); Northamptonshire (1983, 11 matches); Border (1985/6 to 1987/8).
Career batting
57–70–29–444–44–10.82–0–*ct* 16
Bowling 4237–133–31.85–3–0–6/50
A good all-round sportsman, he represented Rhodesia at rugby football and athletics.

Carson, William Nicol
Amateur. *b:* 16.7.1916, Gisborne, East Coast, New Zealand. *d:* 8.10.1944, He died on board ship

between Bari, Italy and Egypt of wounds received in Italy. Uncle of J. R. (Auckland and Northern Districts), nephew of William (Otago). Middle order left-hand batsman, left-arm fast medium bowler. *Team* Auckland (1936/7 to 1939/40). *Tours* New Zealand to England 1937, to Australia 1937/8.
Career batting
31–51–7–1535–290–34.88–4–*ct* 27
Bowling 752–35–21.48–0–0–4/20

Coming to England with a big reputation, Carson had a very modest tour and was not selected for the Tests. He shared the world record 3rd wicket stand (since broken) of 445 with P. E. Whitelaw for Auckland v Otago at Dunedin in 1936/7, making his highest score of 290. He was perhaps better known as a rugby player, and played for New Zealand.

Carter, Rev Arthur
Amateur. *b:* 1847, Slingsby, Yorkshire. *d:* 9.4.1923, Thrussington, Leicestershire. Lower order right-hand batsman, right-hand fast round-arm bowler. *Team* MCC (1885).
Career batting
1–1–0–8–8–8.00–0–*ct* 1

He was at Cambridge but not in the Eleven. His County cricket was for Hertfordshire (1878–83).

Carter, Arthur Gervase
(known as Jarvis Carter)
Professional. *b:* 22.12.1867, Wilford, Nottinghamshire. *d:* 19.7.1933, Standard Hill, Nottingham. Middle order right-hand batsman, right-arm medium pace bowler. *Team* Nottinghamshire (1895, 2 matches).
Career batting
2–3–1–16–13–8.00–0–*ct* 1

Carter, Charles Edward Peers
Cricketer. *b:* 7.8.1947, Richmond, Surrey. Tail end right-hand batsman, wicket-keeper. *Sch* Radley. *Team* Somerset (1968–69, 26 matches).
Career batting
26–35–10–73–16–2.92–0–*ct* 47–*st* 6

Carter, Claude Padgett
Amateur, but professional for Cornwall. *b:* 23.4.1881, Durban, South Africa. *d:* 8.11.1952, Addington, Durban, South Africa. Lower order right-hand batsman, slow left-arm bowler. *Teams* Natal (1897/8 to 1923/4); Transvaal (1910/11). *Tours* South Africa to England 1912, 1924. *Tests* South Africa (1912–24, 10 matches).
Career batting
107–142–28–1333–80*–11.69–0–*ct* 64
Bowling 6796–366–18.56–23–2–7/37
Test batting
10–15–5–181–45–18.10–0–*ct* 2
Bowling 694–28–24.78–2–0–6/50

During the 1924 tour to England, he headed the tourists' bowling averages with 51 wickets, av 21.64. His real skill however was on the South African batting pitches. He came back to England after the 1924 visit to play for Cornwall (1930–35), returning to South Africa in 1939.

Carter, Rev Edmund Sardinson
Amateur. *b:* 3.2.1845, Malton, Yorkshire. *d:* 23.5.1923, Scarborough, Yorkshire. Middle order right-hand batsman, right-hand fast round-arm and lob bowler, good slip field. *Sch* Durham. *Teams* Oxford U (1865–68, blue 1866 and 1867); Victoria (1868/9, 1 match); Yorkshire (1876–81, 14 matches).
Career batting
29–44–7–503–63–13.59–0–*ct* 16
Bowling 601–36 + 3–16.69–0–0–4/58

He played for Victoria whilst on holiday recovering from pleurisy. He is one of the few cricket blues who also won a rowing blue at Oxford. His last first-class match was for I Zingari in 1882.

Carter, Frederic Asgill
Amateur. *b:* 13.6.1853, Newnham, Gloucestershire. *d:* 1.8.1924, Hurlingham, London. Lower order right-hand batsman, right-hand fast round-arm bowler. *Sch* Cheltenham. *Team* Gloucestershire (1871–73, 10 matches).
Career batting
10–13–3–75–13*–7.50–0–*ct* 6
Bowling 88–2–44.00–0–0–1/15

Carter, George
Amateur. *b:* 4.8.1846, Warblington, Hampshire. Opening right-hand batsman, right-hand fast round-arm bowler, good field. *Team* Hampshire (1869–78, 12 matches).
Career batting
12–23–0–274–34–11.91–0–*ct* 4
Bowling 12–1–12.00–0–0–1/11

He also played for Herefordshire (1885).

Carter, George
Amateur. *b:* 10.5.1901, Stoke Newington, London. Middle order right-hand batsman, right-arm medium pace bowler. *Team* Essex (1921–23, 7 matches).
Career batting
7–11–1–163–44*–16.30–0–*ct* 3
Bowling 18–0

He later played in Canada, and now lives in Florida, USA.

Carter, Hanson
Amateur. *b:* 15.3.1878, Northowram, Halifax, Yorkshire. *d:* 8.6.1948, Bellevue Hill, Sydney, New South Wales, Australia. Lower order right-hand batsman, wicket-keeper. *Team* New South Wales (1897/8 to 1924/5, 44 matches). *Tours* Australia to England 1902, 1909, 1921, to South Africa 1902/3, 1921/2. *Tests* Australia (1907/8 to 1921/2, 28 matches).
Career batting
128–175–31–2897–149–20.11–2–*ct* 181–*st* 89

Carter, Horatio Stratton

Test batting
28–47–9–873–72–22.97–0–*ct* 44–*st* 21

After being reserve on the 1902 tour, he was principal wicket-keeper in 1909 and 1921 and was regarded as the best Australia had had since Blackham. He was in addition a more than useful lower order batsman.

Carter, Horatio Stratton
Professional. *b:* 21.12.1913, Hendon, Sunderland, Co Durham. Lower order right-hand batsman, right-arm medium pace bowler. *Team* Derbyshire (1946, 3 matches).
Career batting
3–4–0–8–7–2.00–0–*ct* 1
Bowling 46–2–23.00–0–0–2/39

He also played for Durham (pre first-clss, 1933–34). One of the great soccer players, he appeared as inside-forward for Sunderland, Derby County and Hull City winning FA Cup winners' medals with Sunderland in 1937 and Derby County in 1946, a League Championship medal in 1935/6, and an Irish Cup Winners' medal in 1953 with Cork Athletic. He was capped 13 times by England 1934–47.

Carter, John William
Professional. *b:* 23.6.1935, Oxford. Middle order right-hand batsman. *Sch* Magdalen College School. *Team* Leicestershire (1959, 7 matches).
Career batting
7–14–0–209–41–14.92–0–*ct* 0

He also played for Oxfordshire (1953–57 and 1961).

Carter, Raymond George
Professional. *b:* 14.4.1933, Billesley, Birmingham. Lower order right-hand batsman, right-arm fast medium or off break bowler. *Team* Warwickshire (1951–61, 88 matches).
Career batting
89–109–20–635–37–7.13–0–*ct* 43
Bowling 6759–243–27.81–7–1–8/82

Carter, Reginald
Professional. *b:* 7.11.1933, Whitwell, Derbyshire. Lower order right-hand batsman. slow left-arm bowler. *Team* Derbyshire (1953–55, 17 matches).
Career batting
17–22–4–130–25–7.22–0–*ct* 6
Bowling 752–30–25.06–1–0–7/46

A useful soccer player, he was left half for Worksop.

Carter, Richard Dring
Amateur. *b:* 19.7.1891, Boston, Lincolnshire. *d:* 24.8.1969, Crabb's Abbey, Wiggenhall, St Mary Magdalen, Norfolk. Middle order right-hand batsman. *Team* East of England (1927).
Career batting
1–2–0–1–1–0.50–0–*ct* 0

His County cricket was for Norfolk (1920–25).

Carter, Robert George Mallaby
Professional. *b:* 11.7.1937, Horden, Co Durham. Lower order left-hand batsman, right-arm fast medium bowler. *Team* Worcestershire (1961–72, 177 matches).
Career batting
178–165–95–324–23–4.62–0–*ct* 55
Bowling 13714–523–26.22–17–2–7/61

His final first-class match was for MCC in 1973.

Carter, Robert Michael
Cricketer. *b:* 25.5.1960, Kings Lynn, Norfolk. Lower order right-hand batsman, right-arm medium pace bowler. *Teams* Northamptonshire (1978–82, 51 matches); Canterbury (1982/3 to 1984/5).
Career batting
60–85–16–1112–79–16.11–0–*ct* 35
Bowling 1566–39–40.15–0–0–4/27

He has been Northamptonshire coach since 1987. He played soccer for Norwich City.

Carter, Wilfred
Professional. *b:* 19.6.1896, Annesley, Nottinghamshire. *d:* 1.11.1975, Watford, Hertfordshire. Middle order right-hand batsman, slow right-arm donkey-drop bowler. *Teams* Derbyshire (1920–26, 65 matches).
Career batting
65–112–10–1812–145–17.76–2–*ct* 26
Bowling 707–16–44.18–0–0–3/12

He played soccer at left-half for Watford.

Carter, William John
Professional. *b:* 21.1.1841, Kennington, London. *d:* 18.11.1888, Kingston-upon-Thames, Surrey. Lower order right-hand batsman, right-arm fast bowler. *Team* Surrey (1871–74, 7 matches).
Career batting
8–14–3–91–21*–8.27–0–*ct* 2
Bowling 41–4–10.25–0–0–2/15

At the time of his death he was in the service of the Jockey Club as a kind of private detective.

Carter-Shaw, Robert
Amateur. *b:* 21.11.1941, Berkhamsted, Hertfordshire. Tail end right-hand batsman, slow left-arm bowler. *Sch* Radley. *Team* Cambridge U (1962).
Career batting
1–1–0–2–2–2.00–0–*ct* 0
Bowling 78–1–78.00–0–0–1/33

Cartledge, J. (or W.)
Professional. *b: circa* 1857. *Team* Derbyshire (1878, 1 match).
Career batting
1–2–0–1–1–0.50–0–*ct* 0

It is not clear from the match report whether the player involved is John Cartledge of Burton Joyce, Nottinghamshire, who died at Stoke Bardolph, Nottinghamshire on 8 July 1907 aged 50, or W. Cartledge of Woodsetts, Derbyshire.

Cartman, William Henry
Professional. *b:* 20.6.1861, Skipton, Yorkshire. *d:* 16.1.1935, Skipton, Yorkshire. Middle order right-hand batsman. *Team* Yorkshire (1891, 4 matches).
Career batting
5–9–0–129–49–14.33–0–*ct* 1

Cartridge, Donald Colin
Professional. *b:* 31.12.1933, Sholing, Southampton, Hampshire. Middle order right-hand batsman, off break bowler. *Team* Hampshire (1953, 3 matches).
Career batting
3–6–0–6–4–1.00–0–*ct* 2

Cartwright, George Hamilton Grahame Montagu
Amateur. *b:* 23.4.1889, Westminster, London. *d:* 4.8.1976, Westminster, London. Middle order right-hand batsman, right-arm fast medium bowler. *Sch* Eton. *Team* Oxford U (1909–10).
Career batting
17–28–5–523–65*–22.73–0–*ct* 2
Bowling 1143–32–35.71–0–0–4/79
He was Secretary of the Eton Ramblers 1919–55 and then President until his death. His final first-class match was for MCC in 1928.

Cartwright, Harold
Cricketer. *b:* 12.5.1951, Half Way Houses, Derbyshire. Middle order right-hand batsman. *Team* Derbyshire (1973–79, 82 matches).
Career batting
82–128–16–2384–141*–21.28–1–*ct* 31
Bowling 11–0

Cartwright, Philip
Amateur. *b:* 26.9.1880, Gibraltar. *d:* 21.11.1955, Virginia Water, Surrey. Defensive middle order left-hand batsman, left-arm medium pace bowler. *Team* Sussex (1905–22, 84 matches).
Career batting
84–134–7–2463–101–19.39–1–*ct* 36
Bowling 547–16–34.18–0–0–3/29

Cartwright, Thomas William
Professional. *b:* 22.7.1935, Alderman's Green, Coventry, Warwickshire. Middle order right-hand batsman, right-arm medium pace bowler. *Teams* Warwickshire (1952–69, 353 matches); Somerset (1970–76, 101 matches); Glamorgan (1977, 7 matches). *Tours* MCC to South Africa 1964/5, to East Africa 1963/4, 1973/4; Warwickshire to East Africa 1967/8 (not first-class). *Tests* England (1964–65, 5 matches).
Career batting
479–737–94–13710–210–21.32–7–*ct* 332
Bowling 29357–1536–19.11–94–18–8/39
Test batting
5–7–2–26–9–5.20–0–*ct* 2
Bowling 544–15–36.26–1–0–6/94
He hit 1,000 runs in a season three times (best 1,668, av 30.88, in 1961) and took 100 wickets in a season 8 times (best 147, av 15.52 in 1967). He accomplished the 'double' in 1962. His highest innings and only double century was 210 for Warwickshire v Middlesex at Nuneaton in 1962. It was his withdrawal from the England touring party to South Africa in 1968/9 and his replacement by d'Oliveira that led to the cancellation of the tour, the 'd'Oliveira Affair' and the cessation of Test matches with South Africa. He was Somerset coach 1974–76, Glamorgan coach 1977–83 and since 1979 has been Director of Coaching to the Welsh CA.

Cartwright, Vincent Henry
Amateur. *b:* 10.9.1882, The Park, Nottingham. *d:* 25.11.1965, Loughborough, Leicestershire. Opening right-hand batsman, good slip field. *Sch* Rugby. *Team* Nottinghamshire (1901–04, 7 matches).
Career batting
7–8–0–60–22–7.50–0–*ct* 4
Whilst at Oxford he appeared in various Trials, but no first-class matches. He was a famous rugby footballer, gaining his blue at Oxford and going on to play for England, being captain in 1905 and 1906. He was later an England selector and President of the Rugby Union.

Carty, Richard Arthur
Professional. *b:* 28.7.1922, Chapel, Southampton, Hampshire. *d:* 31.3.1984, Bishops Waltham, Hampshire. Lower order right-hand batsman, right-arm fast medium bowler. *Team* Hampshire (1949–54, 55 matches).
Career batting
55–79–25–798–53–14.77–0–*ct* 24
Bowling 4164–138–30.17–8–1–7/29

Carver, George James
Professional. *b:* 4.5.1879, Long Ditton, Surrey. *d:* 1.10.1912, Bootle, Lancashire. He was killed in an accident at the docks. Brother-in-law of F. J. Mathews (Surrey). Lower order batsman, opening bowler. *Team* Surrey (1907, 1 match).
Career batting
1–2–0–36–36–18.00–0–*ct* 0
Bowling 42–1–42.00–0–0–1/42

Caryer, Reginald George
Professional. *b:* 28.9.1895, Hougham, Dover, Kent. *d:* 7.6.1957, Reading, Berkshire. Tail end right-hand batsman, right-arm medium fast bowler. *Team* Sussex (1922, 1 match).
Career batting
1–2–0–12–7–6.00–0–*ct* 0
Bowling 13–0
He also played for Berkshire (1928–35).

Case, Cecil Charles Coles
Amateur. *b:* 7.9.1895, Frome, Somerset. *d:* 11.11.1969, Keyford, Somerset. Defensive middle order right-hand batsman. *Sch* King's, Bruton. *Team* Somerset (1925–35, 255 matches).
Career batting
257–424–36–8574–155–22.09–9–*ct* 47
Bowling 128–0

He reached 1,000 runs in a season four times (best 1,146, av 26.65, in 1933). He also played for Dorset (1923).

Case, Dr George Henry
Amateur. *b:* 4.4.1839, Fareham, Hampshire. *d:* 21.4.1911, Fareham, Hampshire. Middle order right-hand batsman. *Sch* University College, London. *Team* Hampshire (1864, 2 matches).
Career batting
2–3–0–85–48–28.33–0–*ct* 0
Bowling 21–0

Case, Thomas
Amateur. *b:* 14.7.1844, Liverpool, Lancashire. *d:* 31.10.1925, Swanpool, Falmouth, Cornwall. Father of T. B. (Oxford U) and W. S. (MCC). Middle order right-hand batsman, good long-stop. *Sch* Rugby. *Teams* Oxford U (1864–67, blue 1864, 1865 and 1867); Middlesex (1864–68, 12 matches).
Career batting
35–56–4–982–116–18.88–1–*ct* 12

His final first-class match was for MCC in 1869.

Case, Thomas Bennett
Amateur. *b:* 19.2.1871, Upton, Berkshire. *d:* 10.11.1941, Donnybrook, Co Dublin, Ireland. Son of Thomas (Middlesex), brother of W. S. (MCC). Opening right-hand batsman. *Sch* Winchester. *Team* Oxford U (1891–92, blue both years).
Career batting
15–28–2–330–55–12.69–0–*ct* 5

His County cricket was for Oxfordshire (1891–94). In 1891 he gained his blue only because Thesiger was injured whilst fielding on the first day and Case took his place with the consent of the opposing captain. His debut in first-class cricket was for Gentlemen of England in 1890.

Case, William Sterndale
Amateur. *b:* 24.8.1873, Northam, Oxford. *d:* 18.3.1922, St Giles, Oxford. Son of Thomas (Middlesex), brother of T. B. (Oxford U). Defensive opening left-hand batsman, slow left-arm bowler. *Sch* Winchester. *Teams* Gentlemen of England (1895); MCC (1896).
Career batting
2–4–0–26–11–6.50–0–*ct* 0

He did not appear in any first-class matches whilst at Oxford U. His County cricket was for Oxfordshire (1891–1906).

Cass, George Rodney
Cricketer. *b:* 23.4.1940, Overton, Yorkshire. Opening or middle order left-hand batsman, wicket-keeper. *Teams* Essex (1964–67, 45 matches); Worcestershire (1969–75, 104 matches); Tasmania (1970/1 to 1972/3, 6 matches).
Career batting
155–231–34–4304–172*–21.84–2–*ct* 213–*st* 28

He also played for Shropshire (1976–81).

Cassels, Field Marshal Sir Archibald James Halkett
Amateur. *b:* 28.2.1907, Quetta, India. Son of R. A. (Europeans). Middle or lower order right-hand batsman, right-arm medium fast, or off break, bowler. *Sch* Rugby. *Teams* Europeans (1927/8); Army (1932–35).
Career batting
5–6–1–197–72–39.40–0–*ct* 5
Bowling 415–20–20.75–2–0–6/51

Cassidy, John Joseph
Cricketer. *b:* 31.1.1963, Leeds, Yorkshire. Lower order right-hand batsman, right-arm medium pace bowler. *Team* Oxford U (1982).
Career batting
1–1–0–0–0–0.00–0–*ct* 0
Bowling 12–0

Casswell, Arthur Henry Seymour
Amateur. *b: circa* 1894. *d:* 29.10.1940, High House Farm, Tardebigg, Bromsgrove, Worcestershire. Lower order batsman, opening bowler. *Team* Royal Navy (1927).
Career batting
1–2–1–7–7*–7.00–0–*ct* 1
Bowling 44–0

Castell, Alan Terry
Professional, *b:* 6.8.1943, Oxford. Lower order right-hand batsman, leg break and googly bowler, changing in 1966 to right-arm medium. *Team* Hampshire (1961–71, 110 matches). *Tour* Cavaliers to Jamaica 1963/4.
Career batting
112–141–39–1622–76–15.90–0–*ct* 89
Bowling 7094–229–30.97–8–1–6/22

He also played for Berkshire (1971–73).

Castle, Frederick
Amateur. *b:* 8.4.1909, Elham, Kent. Fast-scoring middle order right-hand batsman, leg break bowler, good field. *Team* Somerset (1946–49, 23 matches).
Career batting
23–36–3–686–60*–20.78–0–*ct* 6
Bowling 43–1–43.00–0–0–1/16

Being in the scholastic profession he was only able to appear during the school holidays.

Castle, Sidney
Amateur. *b:* 21.1.1864, Westminster, London. *d:* 5.12.1937, Furzehatt, Plymstock, Devon. Stylish middle order right-hand batsman. *Sch* Rugby. *Team* Kent (1890–93, 5 matches).
Career batting
5–6–0–25–6–4.16–0–*ct* 6

Castledine, Stafford William Thomas
Professional. *b:* 10.4.1912, Bingham, Nottinghamshire. *d:* 17.4.1986, Nottingham. Middle order right-hand batsman, slow left-arm bowler. *Team* Nottinghamshire (1933–34, 5 matches).
Career batting
5–7–0–22–15–3.14–0–*ct* 6
Bowling 25–0

Castor, Brian Kenneth
Amateur. *b:* 21.10.1889, Mahaica, British Guiana. *d:* 2.10.1979, Maida Hill, London. Middle order right-hand batsman. *Team* Essex (1932, 1 match).
Career batting
1–1–0–13–13–13.00–0–*ct* 0
He was Secretary of Essex CCC 1930–46 and of Surrey CCC 1947–57.

Cater, Charles Alexander
Amateur. *b:* 24.1.1844, Liverpool, Lancashire. *d:* 3.2.1892, Roxeth, Harrow, Middlesex. Opening or middle order right-hand batsman. *Sch* Harrow. *Team* Middlesex (1866–67, 3 matches).
Career batting
3–4–0–22–20–5.50–0–*ct* 2

Catling, William
Professional. *b:* 9.9.1836, Highgate, Middlesex. *d:* 10.6.1899, Camden Town, London. Lower order right-hand batsman, right-hand medium pace round-arm bowler. *Team* Middlesex (1864–65, 8 matches).
Career batting
8–12–7–53–24*–10.60–0–*ct* 5
Bowling 150–18–8.33–1–0–5/29

Catlow, Charles Stanley
Amateur. *b:* 21.2.1908, Darwen, Lancashire. *d:* 7.3.1986, Northampton. Middle order right-hand batsman. *Sch* Haileybury. *Team* Northamptonshire (1929, 2 matches).
Career batting
2–3–1–18–10*–9.00–0–*ct* 0

Catt, Anthony Waldron
Professional. *b:* 2.10.1933, Edenbridge, Kent. Lower order right-hand batsman, wicket-keeper. *Teams* Kent (1954–64, 126 matches); Western Province (1965/6 to 1967/8).
Career batting
138–218–37–3123–162–17.25–1–*ct* 284–*st* 37
Bowling 2–0
After the 1964 English season, he emigrated to South Africa. Playing for Kent v Leicestershire at Maidstone in 1962 he was put in to bat as night-watchman and proceeded to hit 162, including making 121 before lunch on the second morning.

Catterall, Robert Hector
Amateur. *b:* 10.7.1900, Port Elizabeth, South Africa. *d:* 3.1.1961, Kempton Park, Johannesburg, South Africa. Middle order, later opening, right-hand batsman, right-arm medium pace bowler, excellent deep field. *Teams* Transvaal (1920/1 to 1933/4); Rhodesia (1924/5); Natal (1925/6 to 1927/8); Orange Free State (1928/9). *Tours* South Africa to England 1924, 1929. *Tests* South Africa (1922/3 to 1930/1, 24 matches).
Career batting
124–203–8–5849–147–29.99–9–*ct* 52
Bowling 1629–53–30.73–0–0–4/22
Test batting
24–43–2–1555–120–37.92–3–*ct* 12
Bowling 162–7–23.14–0–0–3/15
He did very well on his two visits to England – on the first, as a free scoring middle order batsman, he hit 1,329 runs, av 28.27, and on the second 1,411, av 28.79, as a defensive opener.

Cattley, Arthur Cyril
Amateur. *b:* 27.11.1861, Croydon, Surrey. *d:* 21.9.1895, Dorking, Surrey. Brother of S. W. (Surrey). Middle order right-hand batsman, right-arm fast or medium bowler. *Sch* Eton. *Team* Surrey (1882, 1 match).
Career batting
1–2–0–45–45–22.50–0–*ct* 1

Cattley, Stephen Wildman
Amateur. *b:* 28.10.1860, Croydon, Surrey. *d:* 11.4.1925, Dean, Sparsholt, Winchester, Hampshire. Brother of A. C. (Surrey). Middle or lower order right-hand batsman, occasional wicket-keeper. *Sch* Eton. *Team* Surrey (1879–83, 23 matches).
Career batting
23–41–1–562–89–14.05–0–*ct* 9
Bowling 13–0

Causton, Edward Postle Gwyn
Amateur. *b:* 27.11.1876, Hammersmith, London. *d:* 18.4.1957, Torquay, Devon. Middle order batsman. *Team* Hampshire (1919, 1 match).
Career batting
1–1–0–21–21–21.00–0–*ct* 0
Bowling 4–0

Cave, Sir Basil Shillito
Amateur. *b:* 14.11.1865, Mill Hill, Middlesex. *d:* 9.10.1931, Bishops Down, Tunbridge Wells, Kent. Lower order right-hand batsman, wicket-keeper. *Sch* Merchant Taylors. *Team* MCC (1902).
Career batting
1–1–0–13–13–13.00–0–*ct* 1
He was Consul-General at Algiers.

Cave, Henry Butler
Amateur. *b:* 10.10.1922, Wanganui, Wellington, New Zealand. *d:* 15.9.1989, Wanganui, Wellington, New Zealand. Lower order right-hand batsman, right-arm medium pace bowler. *Teams* Wellington (1945/6 to 1949/50); Central Districts (1950/1 to 1958/9). *Tours* New Zealand to England 1949, 1958, to India and Pakistan 1955/6. *Tests* New Zealand (1949–58, 19 matches).
Career batting
117–175–39–2187–118–16.08–2–*ct* 69
Bowling 8664–362–23.93–13–1–7/31
Test batting
19–31–5–229–22*–8.80–0–*ct* 8
Bowling 1467–34–43.14–0–0–4/21

His bowling on the two tours he made to England was steady and reliable, but he did very little in the Tests. He captained the 1955/6 New Zealand team to India and Pakistan, in all captaining New Zealand in 9 Tests.

Cave, Walter Frederick
Amateur. *b:* 17.9.1863, Stoneleigh House, Clifton, Bristol, Gloucestershire. *d:* 7.1.1939, Westminster, London. Sound middle order right-hand batsman. *Sch* Eton. *Team* Gloucestershire (1883, 3 matches).
Career batting
4–8–0–74–42–9.25–0–*ct* 0

He was a well-known architect.

Cave-Rogers, R. A.
(*see under* Rogers, R. A. C.)

Cawston, Edward
Amateur. *b:* 16.1.1911, Wantage, Berkshire. Opening or middle order right-hand batsman, right-arm medium fast bowler. *Sch* Lancing. *Teams* Sussex (1928–31, 6 matches); Cambridge U (1932–33, blue 1932). *Tours* Martineau to Egypt 1934, 1936 (not first-class).
Career batting
25–43–3–668–93–16.70–0–*ct* 16
Bowling 1305–39–33.46–2–0–7/53

An outstanding schoolboy cricketer, he appeared for Sussex with still another year to complete at Lancing. He also played for Berkshire (1937–46) and Suffolk (1947–50). He also won blues for athletics and relay racing.

Cawthray, George
Professional. *b:* 28.9.1913, Brayton, Selby, Yorkshire. Middle/lower order left-hand batsman, right-arm medium pace bowler. *Team* Yorkshire (1939–52, 4 matches).
Career batting
4–6–0–114–30–19.00–0–*ct* 1
Bowling 304–4–76.00–0–0–2/64

He was groundsman at Headingley 1964–78.

Cazalet, Peter Victor Ferdinand
Amateur. *b:* 15.1.1907, Westminster, London. *d:* 29.5.1973, Fairlawn, Plaxtol, Kent. Great-nephew of J. H. Maxwell-Heron (Gentlemen of England), he married the daughter of P. G. Wodehouse, the author. Opening right-hand batsman. *Sch* Eton. *Teams* Oxford U (1927–28, blue 1927); Kent (1927–32, 4 matches).
Career batting
22–36–2–744–150–21.88–1–*ct* 6

He also represented Oxford at rackets, royal tennis, lawn tennis and squash. Later he was a steeplechase jockey until a bad fall ended his career in 1938. For 25 years he was in charge of the horses of Queen Elizabeth the Queen Mother. In 1960 he was High Sheriff of Kent.

Cecil, Aubrey Bruce Cooper
Amateur. *b:* 10.3.1847, Toddington, Bedfordshire. *d:* 26.8.1918, South Brisbane, Queensland, Australia. Brother of E. D. C. (Hampshire). Lower order batsman. *Sch* Chatham House, Ramsgate. *Team* Hampshire (1876, 1 match).
Career batting
1–2–0–6–4–3.00–0–*ct* 0

He also played for Bedfordshire (1876–78).

Cecil, Egerton Dodge Cooper
(birth registered as E. D. C. Cecill)
Amateur. *b:* 4.7.1853, Worthing, Sussex. *d:* 25.9.1928, Mortlake, Surrey. Brother of A. B. C. (Hampshire). Lower order batsman. *Team* Hampshire (1875, 1 match).
Career batting
1–1–0–4–4–4.00–0–*ct* 0
Bowling 8–0

Chadd, John Etheridge
Professional. *b:* 27.10.1933, Whitestone, Hereford. Lower order right-hand batsman, off break bowler. *Sch* Hereford Cathedral School. *Team* Worcestershire (1955–56, 2 matches).
Career batting
2–1–0–4–4–4.00–0–*ct* 1
Bowling 98–2–49.00–0–0–2/84

Chadwick, Edmund Leach
Amateur. *b:* 31.8.1847, Rochdale, Lancashire. *d:* 6.8.1918, Parkstone, Dorset. Middle order right-hand batsman, good long-stop. *Sch* Marlborough. *Team* Lancashire (1875–81, 13 matches).
Career batting
13–24–3–254–42–12.09–0–*ct* 2

Chadwick, John Peter Granville
Professional. *b:* 8.11.1934, Pateley Bridge, Yorkshire. Middle order right-hand batsman, right-arm medium pace bowler, slip field. *Team* Yorkshire (1960–65, 6 matches).

Career batting
6–9–3–106–59–17.66–0–*ct* 7
Bowling 67–2–33.50–0–0–2/58

Chadwick, Mark Robert
Cricketer. *b:* 9.2.1963, Milnrow, Rochdale, Lancashire. Opening right-hand batsman, right-arm medium pace bowler. *Team* Lancashire (1983–87, 33 matches). *Tour* Lancashire to Jamaica 1986/7.
Career batting
33–56–1–1197–132–21.76–1–*ct* 15
Bowling 71–0

Chakorsab, Prince (*see under* Rajkot, T. S.)

Chalk, Frederick Gerald Hudson
(registered at birth as G. F. H. Chalk)
Amateur. *b:* 7.9.1910, Sydenham, London. *d:* 17.2.1943, Louches, near Calais, France. Nephew of H. E. W. Prest (Kent), son-in-law of G. N. Foster (Worcestershire and Kent). Forcing middle order right-hand batsman, occasional bowler. *Sch* Uppingham. *Teams* Oxford U (1931–34, blue all four years); Kent (1933–39, 101 matches).
Career batting
156–259–20–6732–198–28.16–11–*ct* 62
Bowling 409–7–58.42–0–0–2/22

He hit 1,000 runs in a season 4 times (best 1,306, av 29.02, in 1939). For several seasons his cricket was limited due to his profession of a teacher, but in 1938 and 1939 he captained Kent. He captained Oxford in 1934 where he also obtained a hockey blue and was a noted rugby footballer and fives player. His body was identified by his RAF disc when the wreckage of his plane was discovered in 1989.

Challen, John Bonamy
Amateur. *b:* 26.3.1863, Ruthin, Denbighshire. *d:* 5.6.1937, Eastbourne, Sussex. Hard-hitting middle order right-hand batsman, right-arm fast medium bowler, excellent cover-point. *Sch* Marlborough. *Team* Somerset (1884–99, 52 matches).
Career batting
52–90–6–1656–108–19.71–1–*ct* 32
Bowling 572–16–35.75–0–0–4/43

Being in the scholastic profession, his appearances in County cricket were limited. He first played for Somerset (pre first-class) in 1880. An excellent soccer player, he was chosen to represent Wales in five matches.

Challenor, Brig-Gen Edward Lacy
Amateur. *b:* 10.3.1873, Speightstown, St Peter, Barbados. *d:* 15.9.1935, Hampstead Garden Suburb, London. Brother of George (West Indies), V. C. (Barbados) and Robert (Barbados), nephew of G. D. Whitehall (Barbados), great-uncle of M. L. Sealy (Barbados). Middle order right-hand batsman. *Teams* Barbados (1894/5 to 1895/6); Western Province (1895/6 to 1896/7); Natal (1897/8); Leicestershire (1906–14, 10 matches).
Career batting
29–52–1–1106–111–21.68–1–*ct* 23
Bowling 15–0

His final first-class match was for MCC in 1914. He also played in important matches in India.

Challenor, George
Amateur. *b:* 28.6.1888, Waterloo, St Michael, Barbados. *d:* 30.7.1947, Collymore Rock, St Michael, Barbados. Brother of E. L. (Leicestershire), V. C. (Barbados) and Robert (Barbados), grandfather of M. L. Sealy (Barbados), nephew of G. D. Whitehall (Barbados). Fine opening right-hand batsman, right-arm medium pace bowler. *Team* Barbados (1905/6 to 1929/30). *Tours* West Indies to England 1906, 1923, 1928. *Tests* West Indies (1928, 3 matches).
Career batting
95–160–9–5822–237*–38.55–15–*ct* 25
Bowling 1290–54–23.88–0–0–4/16
Test batting
3–6–0–101–46–16.83–0–*ct* 0

He reached 1,000 runs in 1923 and 1928, the former year being his great season with 1,556 runs (av 51.86). His highest score was 237* for Barbados v Jamaica at Bridgetown in 1924/5.

Chalmers, George Keay
Amateur. *b:* 13.6.1881, Dundee, Angus, Scotland. *d:* 5.1.1946, Carnoustie, Angus, Scotland. Lower order right-hand batsman, wicket-keeper. *Team* Scotland (1908–20).
Career batting
7–11–4–118–40*–16.85–0–*ct* 7–*st* 7

Chamberlain, William Richard Frank
Amateur. *b:* 13.4.1925, Elton, Huntingdonshire. Middle order right-hand batsman, leg break bowler. *Sch* Uppingham. *Team* Northamptonshire (1946, 6 matches).
Career batting
6–9–0–67–14–7.44–0–*ct* 3

He was Northamptonshire Chairman 1985–90 and President 1990–92. He was appointed Chairman of the Cricket Council in TCCB in 1990.

Chambers, Charles Graham
Amateur. *b:* 12.7.1870, West Ilsley, Berkshire. *d:* 30.1.1921, Reading, Berkshire. Hard-hitting middle order right-hand batsman, good cover point. *Sch* Marlborough. *Team* Liverpool and District (1894).
Career batting
1–2–0–21–16–10.50–0–*ct* 0
Bowling 13–0

His County cricket was for Cheshire (1894) and Dorset (1896).

Chambers, George Henry
Professional. *b:* 6.10.1875, The Meadows, Nottingham. Lower order batsman, left-arm fast bowler.

Chambers, George Henry

Team Nottinghamshire (1896–99, 3 matches).
Career batting
3–4–2–25–16–12.50–0–*ct* 2
Bowling 235–6–39.16–0–0–3/44

Chambers, George Henry
Professional. *b:* 24.3.1884, Kimberley, Nottinghamshire. *d:* 13.9.1947, Bentley, Doncaster, Yorkshire. Lower order right-hand batsman, slow left-arm bowler. *Team* Nottinghamshire (1903–05, 4 matches).
Career batting
4–6–1–58–30–11.60–0–*ct* 1
Bowling 54–0

Chambers, Meshach
Professional. *b:* 23.12.1867, Awsworth, Nottinghamshire. *d:* 23.6.1920, Leazes Park, Newcastle upon Tyne, Northumberland. Lower order batsman, medium pace bowler. *Team* Nottinghamshire (1894, 1 match).
Career batting
1–2–0–6–4–3.00–0–*ct* 0
Bowling 22–1–22.00–0–0–1/22
He also played for Northumberland (1899–1911).

Chambers, Robert Edwin Jeffery
Cricketer. *b:* 19.11.1943, Bexhill-on-Sea, Sussex. Opening right-hand batsman, off break bowler. *Sch* Forest. *Team* Cambridge U (1966, blue).
Career batting
12–22–0–386–58–17.54–0–*ct* 9
Bowling 4–0
His County cricket was for Staffordshire (1969) and Hertfordshire (1972–74).

Champain, C. E. B.
(*see under* Bateman-Champain, C. E.)

Champain, F. H. B.
(*see under* Bateman-Champain, F. H.)

Champain, H. F. B.
(*see under* Bateman-Champain, H. F.)

Champain, J. N. B.
(*see under* Bateman-Champain, J. N.)

Champion, Albert
Professional. *b:* 27.12.1851, Hollins End, Handsworth, Yorkshire. *d:* 30.6.1909, Wortley, Sheffield, Yorkshire. Middle order left-hand batsman, right-arm medium pace bowler. *Teams* Yorkshire (1876–79, 14 matches); Lancashire (1886, 1 match).
Career batting
18–31–4–218–29–8.07–0–*ct* 9
Bowling 17–1–17.00–0–0–1/10
His final first-class match was for Liverpool and District in 1890.

Champion, George Ernest
Amateur. *b:* 15.7.1867, Stockbury, Kent. *d:* 30.9.1933, Linton, Kent. Middle order right-hand batsman, right-arm medium pace bowler. *Team* Kent (1892, 1 match).
Career batting
1–2–0–0–0–0.00–0–*ct* 0

Chance, Geoffrey Henry Barrington
(also known as Barrington-Chance)
Amateur. *b:* 16.12.1893, Burghfield, Berkshire. *d:* 11.7.1987, Minety, Wiltshire. Hard-hitting lower order left-hand batsman, right-arm medium pace bowler. *Sch* Eton. *Team* Hampshire (1913, 1 match).
Career batting
2–2–1–0–0*–0.00–0–*ct* 0
Bowling 47–0
His final first-class match was for MCC in 1922. He also played for Berkshire (1912–13).

Chandler, Allen
Amateur. *b:* 5.12.1849, Kensington, London. *d:* 25.12.1926, Haslemere, Surrey. Middle order right-hand batsman, good field. *Sch* Cheltenham. *Team* Surrey (1873–77, 27 matches).
Career batting
29–50–1–716–74–14.61–0–*ct* 17
He captained Surrey in 1876.

Chandler, G.
Professional. Lower order batsman, wicket-keeper. *Team* Hampshire (1865, 1 match).
Career batting
1–2–0–16–16–8.00–0–*ct* 1–*st* 2

Chandler, Gordon Mountford
Amateur. *b:* 23.10.1909, Purley, Surrey. Lower order right-hand batsman, right-arm medium pace bowler. *Sch* Uppingham. *Team* Cambridge U (1929).
Career batting
2–1–0–11–11–11.00–0–*ct* 3
Bowling 173–2–86.50–0–0–1/39

Chandless, John
Amateur. *b:* 21.8.1884, Cardiff, Glamorgan. *d:* 1.6.1968, Whitchurch, Cardiff, Glamorgan. Lower order right-hand batsman, right-arm medium pace bowler. *Teams* Wales (1926); Glamorgan (1927, 1 match).
Career batting
2–1–0–2–2–2.00–0–*ct* 0
Bowling 95–6–15.83–0–0–3/13
He first played for Glamorgan (pre first-class) in 1911.

Chandrasekhar, Bhagwat Subramanya
Cricketer. *b:* 17.5.1945, Mysore, India. Tail end right-hand batsman, right-arm medium pace leg break bowler. *Teams* Mysore/Karnataka (1963/4 to 1979/80). *Tours* India to England 1967, 1971, 1974, 1979, to Australia 1967/8, 1977/8, to West Indies 1975/6, to New Zealand 1975/6, to Pakistan 1978/9, to East Africa 1967/8. *Tests* India (1963/4 to 1979, 58 matches).

Career batting
246–244–114–600–25–4.61–0–*ct* 107
Bowling 25547–1063–24.03–75–19–9/72
Test batting
58–80–39–167–22–4.07–0–*ct* 25
Bowling 7199–242–29.74–16–2–8/79

He was successful on his first two visits to England, taking 57 wickets, av 22.21, in 1967 and 50, av 24.86, in 1971, but his 1974 and 1979 tours were not so fruitful. His best bowling was 9/72 for Mysore v Kerala at Bijapur in 1969/70.

Chanmugam, Dennis Ravindran
Cricketer. *b:* 13.8.1948, Colombo, Ceylon. Brother of Neil (Ceylon). Lower order right-hand batsman, right-arm fast medium bowler. *Team* Sri Lanka (1973/4 to 1975/6). *Tours* Sri Lanka to Pakistan 1973/4, to India 1974/5, 1975/6, to England 1975.
Career batting
14–18–2–180–35–11.25–0–*ct* 8
Bowling 780–19–41.05–0–0–4/60

His first-class debut was for R. Senanayake's XI in Sri Lanka in 1972/3.

Chapel, David
Amateur. *b:* 23.6.1882, St Vigeans, Angus, Scotland. *d:* 4.5.1912, Arbroath, Angus, Scotland. Lower order right-hand batsman, left-arm fast medium bowler. *Team* Scotland (1909–11).
Career batting
4–6–1–68–36–13.60–0–*ct* 2
Bowling 325–18–18.05–2–0–5/34

Chaplin, Herbert Percy
Amateur. *b:* 1.3.1883, Westminster, London. *d:* 6.3.1970, Deal, Kent. Middle order right-hand batsman, right-arm medium pace bowler. *Sch* Harrow. *Teams* Sussex (1905–14, 169 matches); Europeans (1904/5 to 1906/7).
Career batting
176–292–26–6497–213*–24.42–7–*ct* 59
Bowling 370–8–46.25–0–0–3/47

His single double century was 213* for Sussex v Nottinghamshire at Hove in 1914 and in the same season he hit 1,158 runs, av 33.08, his best year – in all he reached 1,000 runs in 4 seasons. He captained Sussex 1910–14 and was coach 1946–47.

Chapman, Allinson George
Amateur. *b:* 7.3.1892, Langton, Kent. *d:* 21.10.1982, Tunbridge Wells, Kent. Lower order right-hand batsman, right-arm fast bowler. *Team* Civil Service (1927).
Career batting
1–2–0–22–22–11.00–0–*ct* 0
Bowling 73–3–24.33–0–0–3/73

Chapman, Arthur Percy Frank
Amateur. *b:* 3.9.1900, The Mount. Reading, Berkshire. *d:* 16.9.1961, Alton, Hampshire. Great-nephew of C. E. (Cambridge U), brother-in-law of T. C. Lowry (Somerset and New Zealand). Attacking middle order left-hand batsman, brilliant close field, slow left-arm, later medium pace, bowler. *Sch* Oakham and Uppingham. *Teams* Cambridge U (1920–22, blue all three years); Kent (1924–38, 194 matches). *Tours* MCC to Australia and New Zealand 1922/3, to Australia 1924/5, 1928/9, to South Africa 1930/1; Tennyson to Jamaica 1931/2; Martineau to Egypt 1938 (not first-class). *Tests* England (1924 to 1930/1, 26 matches).
Career batting
394–554–44–16309–260–31.97–27–*ct* 356
Bowling 921–22–41.86–1–0–5/40
Test batting
26–36–4–925–121–28.90–1–*ct* 32
Bowling 20–0

In the 1920s and early 1930s, Chapman was regarded as the epitome of the English amateur cricketer. A brilliant career at school – in 1917 he hit 668 runs at an average of 111.33 – was crowned by a century on his first-class debut for Cambridge U v Essex in 1920 and later a century in the University match of 1922. His carefree batting won him an England cap in 1924 in spite of the fact that his County cricket had been only for Berkshire (1920–24). In that season however began his connection with Kent. He was in splendid form in 1926, when he was selected to captain England at the Oval and won back the Ashes – winning this Test, after the first four of the series had all been drawn. He captained England on the 1928/9 tour to Australia and returned home victorious by 4 matches to 1. His leadership of England was ended temporarily for the final Test of 1930, when on the grounds that his batting was too unpredictable, Wyatt was selected, but Chapman led England to South Africa the following winter. This, however, proved to be the close of his Test career – at the early age of 30. He captained England in 17 Tests. He captained Kent from 1931 to 1936, though not regularly. His final first-class match was for MCC in 1939.

Considering his ability it is surprising that he reached 1,000 runs in only three seasons (best 1,387, av 66.04, in 1927) and hit only one double century – 260 for Kent v Lancashire at Maidstone in 1927, but his qualities as a leader and fieldsman must be added to his batting to give a complete picture of Chapman as a cricketer.

Chapman, Rev Charles Edward
Amateur. *b:* 26.8.1860, Swinstead, Lincolnshire. *d:* 23.8.1901, Scrivelsby, Lincolnshire. He died by his own hand. Great-uncle of A. P. F. (Kent). Lower order right-hand batsman, right-arm fast bowler. *Sch* Trent. *Team* Cambridge U (1882–83).
Career batting
5–8–2–59–33*–9.83–0–*ct* 1
Bowling 190–7–27.14–0–0–3/19

His County cricket was for Lincolnshire (1880–83) and Berkshire (1896–1900). A noted rugby footballer, he represented Cambridge and England.

Chapman, Colin Anthony
Cricketer. *b:* 8.6.1971, Bradford, Yorkshire. Middle order right-hand batsman, wicket-keeper. *Team* Yorkshire (1990–92, 3 matches).
Career batting
3–5–1–55–20–13.75–0–*ct* 3

Chapman, Rev David Macklin Braby
Amateur. *b:* 12.9.1855, St Paul's, Ruperts Land, Red River, Canada. *d:* 24.3.1934, Hailsham, Sussex. Lower order batsman, bowler. *Sch* Trent. *Team* Cambridge U (1876–77).
Career batting
2–4–0–7–5–1.75–0–*ct* 0
Bowling 128–4–32.00–0–0–3/56

Chapman, Ivan
Amateur. *b:* 12.10.1906, Pudsey, Yorkshire. *d:* February 1976, Hamilton, New Zealand. Middle order right-hand batsman, right-arm fast medium bowler. *Team* Essex (1929, 1 match).
Career batting
1–1–0–9–9–9.00–0–*ct* 0
Bowling 18–0

Chapman, John
Professional and amateur at various times. *b:* 28.11.1814, Nottingham. *d:* 14.4.1896, Gainsborough, Lincolnshire. Stepson of William Clarke (Nottinghamshire 1826–55). Middle order right-hand batsman, right-arm fast bowler. *Team* Nottinghamshire (1842–48, 8 matches).
Career batting
13–22–4–179–41–9.94–0–*ct* 3
Bowling 167–8 + 2–20.87–0–0–2/6

He succeeded William Clarke as manager of Trent Bridge Cricket Ground and ran the ground for about four seasons. He also played for Durham (pre first-class, 1849).

Chapman, John
Amateur. *b:* 11.3.1877, Frocester, Gloucestershire. *d:* 12.8.1956, Carlecoates, Dunford Bridge, Yorkshire. Attractive middle order right-hand batsman, excellent cover field. *Sch* Uppingham. *Team* Derbyshire (1909–20, 113 matches).
Career batting
113–210–15–3624–198–18.58–2–*ct* 35
Bowling 241–1–241.00–0–0–1/42

He was Derbyshire captain, 1910 to 1912, and joint-captain, 1919 and 1920. With A. Warren he created a world record 9th wicket partnership of 283 for Derbyshire v Warwickshire at Blackwell in 1910.

Chapman, Mat
Professional. *b:* 13.4.1865, Arnesby, Leicestershire. *d:* 28.11.1909, Narborough, Leicestershire. Middle order right-hand batsman, right-arm medium pace bowler, wicket-keeper. *Team* Leicestershire (1894–95, 27 matches).
Career batting
28–54–6–633–56–13.18–0–*ct* 21–*st* 2
Bowling 30–0

His first-class debut was for Liverpool and District in 1893. He first played for Leicestershire (pre first-class) in 1890.

Chapman, Robert James
Cricketer. *b:* 28.7.1972, Nottingham. Lower order right-hand batsman, right-arm fast medium bowler. *Team* Nottinghamshire (1992, 1 match).
Career batting
1 match, did not bat–*ct* 0
Bowling 77–2–38.50–0–0–1/38

Chapman, Thomas Alan
Professional. *b:* 14.5.1918, Barwell, Leicestershire. *d:* 19.2.1979, Marandellas, Rhodesia. Middle order right-hand batsman, fine field. *Teams* Leicestershire (1946–50, 53 matches); Rhodesia (1952/3).
Career batting
58–95–5–1413–124*–15.70–1–*ct* 20–*st* 1
Bowling 23–0

He emigrated to Rhodesia at the end of the 1950 season.

Chappell, Gregory Stephen, MBE
Cricketer. *b:* 7.8.1948, Unley, Adelaide, South Australia. Brother of I. M. (Australia) and T. M. (Australia), grandson of V. Y. Richardson (Australia). Stylish middle order right-hand batsman, right-arm medium pace bowler, brilliant slip field. *Teams* South Australia (1966/7 to 1972/3, 57 matches); Somerset (1968–69, 52 matches); Queensland (1973/4 to 1983/4, 61 matches). *Tours* Australia to New Zealand 1969/70, 1973/4, 1976/7, 1981/2, to England 1972, 1975, 1977, 1980, to West Indies 1972/3, to Pakistan 1979/80, to Sri Lanka 1982/3; International Wanderers to South Africa 1975/6. *Tests* Australia (1970/1 to 1983/4, 87 matches).
Career batting
321–542–72–24535–247*–52.20–74–*ct* 376
Bowling 8717–291–29.95–5–0–7/40
Test batting
87–151–19–7110–247*–53.86–24–*ct* 122
Bowling 1913–47–40.70–1–0–5/61

He hit 1,260 runs, av 70.00, in first-class matches on his first tour to England in 1972 and 437 runs, av 48.55, in the Tests. In 1975 he was not very successful, but in 1977, when he captained the tourists, he hit 1,182 runs, av 59.10, in first-class matches and 371, av 41.22, in the Tests, being the leading batsman of the tour. He hit 1,000 runs during both his seasons with Somerset. His highest score was 247* for Australia v New Zealand at Wellington in 1973/4, when he also hit 133 in the second innings. He was one of the leading players to join Packer's World Series Cricket and announced his retirement from Test cricket at that time, but resumed as Australia's captain in 1979; however he declined to come to England on the 1981 tour. He captained Australia in 48 Tests.

Chappell, Ian Michael
Cricketer. *b:* 26.9.1943, Unley, Adelaide, South Australia. Brother of G. S. (Australia) and T. M. (Australia), grandson of V. Y. Richardson (Australia). Brilliant middle order right-hand batsman, leg break and googly bowler, excellent slip field. *Teams* South Australia (1961/2 to 1979/80, 109 matches); Lancashire (1963, 1 match). *Tours* Australia to England 1968, 1972, 1975, to South Africa 1966/7, 1969/70, to West Indies 1972/3, to India and Sri Lanka 1969/70; International Wanderers to South Africa 1974/5, 1975/6. *Tests* Australia (1964/5 to 1979/80, 75 matches).
Career batting
262–448–41–19680–209–48.35–59–*ct* 312–*st* 1
Bowling 6614–176–37.57–2–0–5/29
Test batting
75–136–10–5345–196–42.42–14–*ct* 105
Bowling 1316–20–65.80–0–0–2/21

He reached 1,000 runs on all 3 tours to England (best 1,261, av 48.50, in 1968) and also hit 1,000 runs six times in Australia. He was the captain of both the 1972 and 1975 tours, in all captaining Australia in 30 Tests. Of his three double centuries, the highest is 209 for Australians v Barbados at Bridgetown in 1972/3. He came out of retirement to play for Packer's World Series Cricket, and resumed his first class career for one season. He is a well-known television commentator in Australia.

Chappell, Trevor Martin
Cricketer. *b:* 21.10.1952, Glenelg, Adelaide, South Australia. Brother of I. M. (Australia) and G. S. (Australia), grandson of V. Y. Richardson (Australia). Middle order right-hand batsman, right-arm medium pace bowler. *Teams* South Australia (1972/3 to 1975/6, 17 matches); Western Australia (1976/7, 4 matches); New South Wales (1979/80 to 1984/5, 51 matches). *Tours* Australia to England 1981, 1983 (World Cup); Robins to South Africa 1975/6. *Tests* Australia (1981, 3 matches).
Career batting
88–151–14–4049–150–29.55–5–*ct* 47
Bowling 1462–59–24.77–0–0–4/12
Test batting
3–6–1–79–27–15.80–0–*ct* 2

Although he played in three Tests on the 1981 tour of England he achieved very little.

Chapple, Glen
Cricketer. *b:* 23.1.1974, Skipton, Yorkshire. Lower order right-hand batsman, right-arm medium pace bowler. *Team* Lancashire (1992, 2 matches).
Career batting
2–2–1–19–18–19.00–0–*ct* 0
Bowling 128–5–25.60–0–0–3/40

Chard, Herbert William
Amateur. *b:* 17.10.1869, Westbury, Clifton, Bristol. *d:* 9.1.1932, Cotham, Gloucestershire. Middle or lower order right-hand batsman, right-arm medium pace bowler. *Team* Gloucestershire (1889, 2 matches).
Career batting
2–4–0–35–32–8.75–0–*ct* 3
Bowling 136–3–45.33–0–0–2/27

Charles, Stephen Flockton
Amateur. *b:* 17.8.1858, Romford, Essex. *d:* 24.6.1950, Wroxham House, Norfolk. Lower order right-hand batsman, wicket-keeper. *Sch* Harrow. *Teams* MCC (1895–1905); Gentlemen (1897–98)
Career batting
8–12–5–143–30–20.42–0–*ct* 4–*st* 5

His County cricket was for Norfolk (1905–07).

Charlesworth, Albert Percy
Professional. *b:* 19.2.1865, Potternewton, Leeds, Yorkshire. *d:* 11.5.1926, Hull, Yorkshire. Free-hitting middle order right-hand batsman. *Team* Yorkshire (1894–95, 7 matches).
Career batting
7–12–1–241–63–21.90–0–*ct* 2

Charlesworth, Alfred
Amateur. *b:* 9.5.1865, Simmondley, Glossop, Derbyshire. *d:* 4.12.1928, St Annes-on-Sea, Lancashire. Lower order batsman, change bowler. *Team* Derbyshire (1898, 7 matches).
Career batting
7–10–1–92–23–10.22–0–*ct* 2
Bowling 47–0

He first played for Derbyshire (not first-class) in 1888.

Charlesworth, Crowther
Professional. *b:* 12.2.1875, Swinton, Lancashire. *d:* 15.6.1953, Halifax, Yorkshire. Middle order right-hand batsman, right-arm fast medium bowler. *Team* Warwickshire (1898–1921, 372 matches).
Career batting
372–632–27–14289–216–23.61–15–*ct* 194
Bowling 8878–295–30.09–7–1–6/45

He reached 1,000 runs in a season 5 times (best 1,376, av 38.22, in 1911). He hit two double centuries, the highest being 216 for Warwickshire v Derbyshire at Blackwell in 1910. He was a first-class umpire (1925–26).

Charlton, Dr Percie Chater
Amateur. *b:* 9.4.1867, Surry Hills, Sydney, New South Wales, Australia. *d:* 30.9.1954, Pymble, Sydney, New South Wales, Australia. Uncle of C. J. Tozer (New South Wales). Tail end right-hand bats-

man, right-arm fast medium bowler. *Team* New South Wales (1888/9 to 1897/8, 14 matches). *Tour* Australia to England 1890. *Tests* Australia (1890, 2 matches).
Career batting
40–65–13–648–50–12.46–0–*ct* 39
Bowling 1937–97–19.96–6–1–7/44
Test batting
2–4–0–29–11–7.25–0–*ct* 0
Bowling 24–3–8.00–0–0–3/18

He had only modest success during his tour to England, not being able to adapt his bowling to English conditions.

Charlwood, Alexander Evelyn
Professional. *b:* 25.11.1888, Eastbourne, Sussex. *d:* 23.6.1974, Hove, Sussex. Middle/lower order right-hand batsman. *Team* Sussex (1911–14, 12 matches).
Career batting
12–17–2–165–34–11.00–0–*ct* 1

Charlwood, Charles Robert
Professional. *b:* 22.11.1842, Horsham, Sussex. *d:* 16.5.1880, Horsham, Sussex. Brother of H. R. J. (Sussex). Opening right-hand batsman, right-arm medium pace bowler. *Team* Sussex (1866–69, 3 matches).
Career batting
3–5–0–40–15–8.00–0–*ct* 6

Charlwood, Henry Rupert James
Professional. *b:* 19.12.1846, Horsham, Sussex. *d:* 6.6.1888, Scarborough, Yorkshire. Brother of C. R. (Sussex). Fine middle order right-hand batsman, lob bowler, excellent cover point. *Team* Sussex (1865–82, 127 matches). *Tours* Willsher to North America 1868 (not first-class); Lillywhite to Australia 1876/7. *Tests* England (1876/7, 2 matches).
Career batting
197–350–19–7017–155–21.19–5–*ct* 89
Bowling 89–4–22.25–0–0–2/12
Test batting
2–4–0–63–36–15.75–0–*ct* 0

He was regarded as one of the best batsmen in England and was referred to as the 'Hope of Sussex'. About 1872 he moved to Chesterfield and then to Scarborough and for this reason ceased to play for Sussex earlier than would otherwise have been the case.

Charlwood, John Armstrong
Professional. *b:* 8.3.1871, East Grinstead, Sussex. *d:* 18.9.1923, Westminster, London. Middle order batsman, fine field. *Team* Sussex (1890, 3 matches).
Career batting
3–6–1–44–23*–8.80–0–*ct* 3

Charman, William
Amateur. *b:* 23.9.1850, Epsom, Surrey. *d:* 8.12.1924, Hove, Sussex. Opening right-hand batsman, occasional right-arm fast medium bowler. *Team* Surrey (1875, 1 match).
Career batting
1–2–0–11–7–5.50–0–*ct* 0
Bowling 24–0

Charteris, Hon Hugo Francis Wemyss
(Lord Elcho)
Amateur. *b:* 28.12.1884, Wilbury House, Salisbury, Wiltshire. *d:* 23.4.1916. He was killed in action, Katia, Egypt. Nephew of Richard (MCC 1847), brother-in-law of A. Windsor-Clive (Cambridge U). Lower order right-hand batsman, change bowler. *Sch* Eton. *Team* Gloucestershire (1910, 1 match).
Career batting
1–1–0–1–1–1.00–0–*ct* 0

He was at Oxford, but did not appear in first-class cricket whilst there. His niece married Ian Fleming, the author.

Charters, Frank Henry
Professional. *b:* 17.1.1884, Plymouth, Devon. *d:* 25.1.1953, Boscombe, Bournemouth, Hampshire. Middle order right-hand batsman. *Team* Hampshire (1913, 1 match).
Career batting
1–2–0–14–9–7.00–0–*ct* 0

Chater, Leathley
Amateur. *b:* 23.12.1858, Camberwell, London. *d:* 5.5.1931, Littlehampton, Sussex. Middle order right-hand batsman, good field at long stop. *Sch* Harrow. *Team* MCC (1881).
Career batting
1–1–1–6–6*–no av–0–*ct* 0

Chatfield, Ewen John, MBE
Cricketer. *b:* 3.7.1950, Dannevirke, Hawkes Bay, New Zealand. Tail end right-hand batsman, right-arm medium fast bowler. *Team* Wellington (1973/4 to 1989/90). *Tours* New Zealand to Australia 1974/5 (not first-class), 1980/1, 1982/3, 1984/5 (not first-class), 1985/6, 1987/8, to England 1979 (World Cup), 1983, 1986, to Sri Lanka 1983/4, 1984/5 (not first-class), 1985/6 (not first-class), 1986/7, to West Indies 1984/5, to Pakistan 1984/5, to Sharjah (not first-class) 1985/6, 1987/8, to India 1987/8 (World Cup), 1988/9. *Tests* New Zealand (1974/5 to 1988/9, 43 matches).
Career batting
157–135–71–582–24*–9.09–0–*ct* 51
Bowling 13429–587–22.87–27–8–8/24
Test batting
43–54–33–180–21*–8.57–0–*ct* 7
Bowling 3958–123–32.17–3–1–6/73

On the 1983 tour to England he took 28 wickets, av 29.21, and played in three Tests. He was knocked unconscious whilst batting for New Zealand v England at Auckland in 1974/5, when a ball from P. Lever hit him on the temple. He did not regain consciousness until he had been taken to hospital, but happily fully recovered from his injury. He disappointed on his second visit to England in 1986, playing in only one Test. In contrast on the following visit of England to New Zealand in 1987/8, he proved to be New Zealand's best bowler and topped the averages.

Chatham, Charles Henry
Amateur. *b:* 18.6.1910, Tewkesbury, Gloucestershire. Middle order right-hand batsman, right-arm medium pace bowler. *Sch* Wycliffe. *Team* Worcestershire (1934, 1 match).
Career batting
1–2–0–12–8–6.00–0–*ct* 0
Bowling 65–1–65.00–0–0–1/49

Chatterton, George
Professional. *b:* 23.9.1821, Sheffield, Yorkshire. *d:* 1.10.1881, Park, Sheffield, Yorkshire. Fine middle order right-hand batsman, slow right-hand under-arm lob bowler, wicket-keeper. *Team* Yorkshire (1849–55, 11 matches).
Career batting
79–132–14–1611–109–13.65–1–*ct* 66–*st* 56
Bowling 269–20 + 5–13.45–2–0–7/21

His first-class debut was for Sheffield in 1846. He was on the ground staff at Lord's for 14 seasons, and his last first-class match was for MCC in 1861. He was later well-known as an umpire.

Chatterton, James
Professional. *b:* 1.4.1836, Newark, Nottinghamshire. *d:* 13.2.1891, Newark, Nottinghamshire. Hard-hitting opening right-hand batsman, right-hand slow round-arm bowler. *Team* Nottinghamshire (1856–65, 6 matches).
Career batting
21–39–4–414–47*–11.82–0–*ct* 6
Bowling 44–5 + 1–8.80–0–0–2/14

His final first-class match was for MCC in 1867. He was a first-class umpire (1886–89).

Chatterton, Joseph Deeley
Professional. *b:* 14.2.1867, Thornsett, Derbyshire. *d:* 7.11.1886, Derby, of typhoid fever aged 19. Brother of William (Derbyshire). Middle order right-hand batsman, slow right-arm bowler. *Team* Derbyshire (1884–86, 11 matches).
Career batting
11–22–2–108–21–5.40–0–*ct* 3
Bowling 119–5–23.80–0–0–1/9

Chatterton, William
Professional. *b:* 27.12.1861, Thornsett, Derbyshire. *d:* 19.3.1913, Flowery Field, Hyde, Cheshire. He died from consumption. Brother of J. D. (Derbyshire). Middle order right-hand batsman, slow right-arm bowler, excellent field. *Team* Derbyshire (1882–1902, 196 matches). *Tour* Read to South Africa 1891/2. *Test* England (1891/2, 1 match).
Career batting
289–510–39–10914–169–23.17–8–*ct* 239–*st* 4
Bowling 4465–208–21.46–4–1–6/42
Test batting
1–1–0–48–48–48.00–0–*ct* 0

He reached 1,000 runs in a season three times (best 1,193, av 38.49, in 1896). He captained Derbyshire jointly in 1887 and solely in 1888 and 1889. In the period when Derbyshire were not first class (1888–93), he appeared regularly in first-class matches for MCC, being on the Lord's staff. He played soccer for Derby County.

Chauhan, Chetandra Pratap Singh
Cricketer. *b:* 21.7.1947, Bareilly, India. Sound opening right-hand batsman, off break bowler. *Teams* Maharashtra (1967/8 to 1974/5); Delhi (1975/6 to 1984/5). *Tours* India to Australia 1977/8, to Pakistan 1978/9, to England 1979, to Australia and New Zealand 1980/1. *Tests* India (1969/70 to 1980/1, 40 matches).
Career batting
179–299–22–11143–207–40.22–21–*ct* 190
Bowling 1741–51–34.13–1–0–6/26
Test batting
40–68–2–2084–97–31.57–0–*ct* 38
Bowling 106–2–53.00–0–0–1/4

He hit 561 runs, av 28.05, on the 1979 tour to England and appeared in all four Tests. His highest score was 207 for Maharashtra v Vibarbha at Poona in 1972/3.

Chauhan, Sanjay
Cricketer. *b:* 12.12.1966, Delhi, India. Lower order right-hand batsman, off break bowler. *Team* Oxford U (1989–90).
Career batting
6–6–0–51–25–8.50–0–*ct* 2
Bowling 59–1–59.00–0–0–1/58

Chaytor, Joshua David Gerald
Amateur. *b:* 13.5.1903, Knockmaroon, Co Dublin, Ireland. *d:* 4.3.1937, Meerut, India as the result of a polo accident. Hard-hitting middle or lower order right-hand batsman, right-arm fast medium bowler. *Sch* Wellington. *Team* Free Foresters (1924).
Career batting
1–1–1–9–9*–no av–0–*ct* 0

He played in the Freshmen's match and Seniors' match at Cambridge but not in first-class matches.

Cheatle, Robert Giles Lenthall
Cricketer. *b:* 31.7.1953, Paddington, London. Lower order left-hand batsman, slow left-arm bowler, good field. *Sch* Stowe. *Teams* Sussex (1974–79, 42 matches); Surrey (1980–83, 18 matches).
Career batting
60–44–18–338–49–13.00–0–*ct* 54
Bowling 3303–104–31.75–6–0–6/32

Checksfield, Martin Frederic James
Amateur. *b:* 29.4.1939, Marylebone, London. Middle order right-hand batsman. *Sch* Bryanston. *Team* Oxford U (1961).
Career batting
2–4–0–59–42–14.75–0–*ct* 0
His first-class debut was for Free Foresters in 1960.

Cheetham, Albert George
Amateur. *b:* 7.12.1915, Ryde, Sydney, New South Wales, Australia. Nephew of H. S. B. Love (Australia). Middle order right-hand batsman, right-arm fast medium bowler. *Team* New South Wales (1936/7 to 1939/40, 20 matches). *Tour* Australian Services to England 1945.
Career batting
24–46–3–899–85–20.90–0–*ct* 7
Bowling 1517–42–36.11–0–0–4/75
His final first-class match was for Australian Services in Australia 1945/6.

Cheetham, John Erskine
Amateur. *b:* 26.5.1920, Mowbray, Cape Province, South Africa. *d:* 21.8.1980, Park Town, Johannesburg, South Africa. Brother of R. W. S. (North East Transvaal), father of J. R. (Western Province and Transvaal) and R. S. (Transvaal). Defensive middle order right-hand batsman, leg break bowler, excellent field. *Team* Western Province (1939/40 to 1954/5). *Tours* South Africa to England 1951, 1955, to Australia and New Zealand 1952/3. *Tests* South Africa (1948/9 to 1955, 24 matches).
Career batting
108–170–35–5697–271*–42.20–8–*ct* 67
Bowling 376–8–47.00–0–0–2/38
Test batting
24–43–6–883–89–23.86–0–*ct* 13
Bowling 2–0
On his 1951 visit to England he hit 1,196 runs, av 42.71, and appeared in all five Tests, but in 1955, when he captained the team, he missed two Tests through injury and did not complete 1,000 runs. Good though his batting was, his reputation rests mainly on his splendid captaincy, especially during the 1952/3 tour to Australia, when his unsung side drew the rubber two-all and confounded all the critics. He captained South Africa in 15 Tests. His highest score was 271* for Western Province v Orange Free State at Bloemfontein in 1950/1.

Cheetham, John Leslie
Amateur. *b:* 17.3.1918, Hull, Yorkshire. Lower order right-hand batsman, wicket-keeper. *Team* Gentlemen (1947).
Career batting
1–2–0–9–6–4.50–0–*ct* 1

Chenery, Charles John
Amateur. *b:* 1.1.1850, Lambourn Woodlands, Berkshire. Middle order right-hand batsman, right-arm fast bowler, excellent field. *Team* Surrey (1872–73, 12 matches).
Career batting
13–24–2–309–40*–14.04–0–*ct* 4
Bowling 48–1–48.00–0–0–1/11
He also played non-first-class cricket for Northamptonshire (1877). One of the best soccer players of his day, he appeared for England in three matches in 1873 and 1874.

Cherrington, Peter Ralph
Professional. *b:* 24.11.1917, Newark, Nottinghamshire. *d:* 20.1.1945, Monywa, Burma. Middle/lower order right-hand batsman, leg break and googly bowler. *Sch* Wellingborough. *Team* Leicestershire (1938, 10 matches).
Career batting
10–14–0–85–33–6.07–0–*ct* 3
Bowling 127–0

Chessher, John Robert
Cricketer. *b:* 21.8.1962, Banstead, Surrey. Middle order right-hand batsman, right-arm medium pace bowler. *Sch* Ipswich. *Team* Oxford U (1982–83).
Career batting
4–6–1–78–47–15.60–0–*ct* 0

Chester, Arthur
Professional. *b:* 18.12.1851, Kingston-upon-Thames, Surrey. *d:* 13.5.1915, Lambeth, London. Son of James (Surrey). Middle order right-hand batsman, change bowler. *Team* Surrey (1872–83, 17 matches).
Career batting
17–27–2–272–54*–10.88–0–*ct* 5
He was a mainstay of Kingston-upon-Thames CC for many years and captained the Club for nine seasons. He was a first-class umpire (1895–99), standing in one Test in 1896.

Chester, Charles
Professional. *b:* 7.2.1869, Eastwood, Nottinghamshire. *d:* 9.2.1940, Forest Town, Mansfield, Nottinghamshire. Lower order right-hand batsman, right-arm medium pace bowler. *Team* Derbyshire (1899, 1 match).
Career batting
1–2–0–0–0–0.00–0–*ct* 1
Bowling 9–1–9.00–0–0–1/9

Chester, Frank
Professional. *b:* 20.1.1895, Bushey, Hertfordshire. *d:* 8.4.1957, Bushey, Hertfordshire. Middle order left-hand batsman, slow left-arm bowler. *Team* Worcestershire (1912–14, 54 matches).
Career batting
55–92–18–1773–178*–23.95–4–*ct* 25
Bowling 2561–81–31.61–2–0–6/43
Having lost an arm below the elbow in the First World War, he became a first-class umpire in 1922 and stood in 48 Tests, retiring in 1955, by which time

he had become the most respected member of his profession.

Chester, James
Professional. *b:* 30.5.1823, Kingston-upon-Thames, Surrey. *d:* 23.6.1888, Wimbledon, Surrey. Father of Arthur (Surrey). Hard-hitting middle order right-hand batsman, right-hand medium pace round-arm bowler. *Team* Surrey (1846–58, 26 matches).
Career batting
45–79–5–853–64–11.52–0–*ct* 15
Bowling 7–0 + 46–no av–3–1–9/?

He was regarded as one of the best all-round cricketers of his day, but he did not play regularly in important matches. His final first-class match was for MCC in 1859. His best bowling was for MCC v Cambridge U at Cambridge in 1850.

Chester-Master, Algernon William
(registered as A. W. C. Master at death)
Amateur. *b:* 27.9.1851, Almondsbury, Gloucestershire. *d:* 1.9.1897, Rushmere, Northampton. Father of Edgar (Gloucestershire). *Sch* Marlborough. *Team* Gloucestershire (1870, 2 matches).
Career batting
2–2–1–5–5–5.00–0–*ct* 4

Chester-Master, Edgar
(registered as E. C. Master at birth)
Amateur. *b:* 6.5.1888, Westminster, London. *d:* 17.9.1979, Durban, South Africa. Son of A. W. (Gloucestershire). *Sch* Repton. *Team* Gloucestershire (1911, 1 match).
Career batting
1–2–1–4–4–4.00–0–*ct* 0
Bowling 25–1–25.00–0–0–1/9

He also played for Dorset (1908–21).

Chesterton, George Herbert
Amateur. *b:* 15.7.1922, Chirbury, Shropshire. Lower order right-hand batsman, right-arm medium pace bowler. *Sch* Malvern. *Teams* Oxford U (1949, blue); Worcestershire (1950–57, 47 matches). *Tour* MCC to Canada 1951 (no first-class matches).
Career batting
72–102–34–598–43–8.79–0–*ct* 37
Bowling 5993–263–22.78–18–1–7/14

His first-class debut was for Free Foresters in 1948 and his final first-class appearance for MCC in 1966. He also played for Cornwall (1948–49). He was elected President of Worcestershire in 1990.

Chichester-Constable, Raleigh Charles Joseph
(changed name from Chichester in 1895)
Amateur. *b:* 21.12.1890, Great Marlow, Buckinghamshire. *d:* 26.5.1963, Burton-Constable, Yorkshire. Lower order right-hand batsman, right-arm fast bowler. *Sch* Stonyhurst. *Team* Yorkshire (1919, 1 match). *Tour* MCC to India, Burma and Ceylon 1926/7.
Career batting
24–19–2–152–47*–8.94–0–*ct* 7
Bowling 243–4–60.75–0–0–2/42

He captained Yorkshire 2nd XI 1926–38. His final first-class match was for Minor Counties in 1935.

Chidgey, Graham James
Amateur. *b:* 5.1.1937, Lambeth, London. Middle order right-hand batsman, off break bowler. *Sch* City of London. *Team* Free Foresters (1962–64).
Career batting
3–6–0–164–113–27.33–1–*ct* 6

He score 113 on his first-class debut for Free Foresters v Cambridge U at Cambridge in 1962.

Chidgey, Harry
Amateur for first match, professional thereafter. *b:* 25.7.1879, Flax Bourton, Somerset. *d:* 16.11.1941, Flax Bourton, Somerset. Tail end right-hand batsman, wicket-keeper. *Team* Somerset (1900–21, 98 matches).
Career batting
99–169–64–717–45–6.82–0–*ct* 135–*st* 55

He was a first-class umpire (1925–27), standing in one Test match (1926).

Chignell, Thomas Alexander
Amateur. *b:* 31.10.1880, Havant, Hampshire. *d:* 25.8.1965, Milton, Portsmouth, Hampshire. Lower order left-hand batsman, right-arm medium slow bowler. *Team* Hampshire (1901–04, 18 matches).
Career batting
18–28–10–181–29*–10.05–0–*ct* 11
Bowling 1108–33–33.57–1–0–5/68

Childs, John Henry
Cricketer. *b:* 15.8.1951, Lipson, Plymouth, Devon. Tail end left-hand batsman, slow left-arm bowler, deep field. *Teams* Gloucestershire (1975–84, 165 matches); Essex (1985–92, 157 matches). *Tour* England to India 1988/9 (tour cancelled). *Tests* England (1988, 2 matches).
Career batting
326–290–136–1391–43–9.03–0–*ct* 103
Bowling 25095–840–29.87–45–8–9/56
Test batting
2–4–4–2–2*–no av–0–*ct* 1
Bowling 183–3–61.00–0–0–1/13

His best season with the ball was 1986 when he took 89 wickets, av 16.28, and was the outstanding England-qualified bowler by a large margin. He was aged 36 years and 320 days on his Test debut in 1988. His best bowling was 9/56 for Gloucestershire v Somerset at Bristol in 1981. He also played for Devon (1973–74).

Childs-Clarke, Arthur William
Amateur. *b:* 13.5.1905, Exeter, Devon. *d:* 19.2.1980, Mevagissey, Cornwall. Middle/lower order right-hand batsman, change bowler. *Sch* Christ's Hospital.

Chinnery, Esmé Fairfax

Teams Middlesex (1923–34, 10 matches); Northamptonshire (1947–48, 53 matches). *Tours* Martineau to Egypt 1936, 1937, 1938, 1939 (not first class).
Career batting
66–107–9–1674–68–17.08–0–*ct* 31
Bowling 1098–25–43.92–0–0–3/72

He captained Northamptonshire in 1947 and 1948.

Chinnery, Esmé Fairfax
Amateur. *b:* 28.3.1886, Hatchford Park, Cobham, Surrey. *d:* 18.1.1915. He was killed in a plane crash at Issy, Paris, France. Half-brother of H. B. (Middlesex and Surrey). Middle order right-hand batsman. *Sch* Eton. *Team* Surrey (1906, 1 match).
Career batting
1–1–0–47–47–47.00–0–*ct* 0

He played no first-class cricket whilst at Oxford U but did win a blue for athletics.

Chinnery, Harry Brodrick
Amateur. *b:* 6.2.1876, Teddington, Middlesex. *d:* 28.5.1916. He was killed in action at Monchy-le-Preux, France. Half-brother of E. F. (Surrey). Stylish opening right-hand batsman, slow left-arm bowler. *Sch* Eton. *Teams* Surrey (1897–1904, 30 matches); Middlesex (1899–1902, 9 matches). *Tours* Warner to North America 1897; Oxford U Authentics to India 1902/3.
Career batting
66–108–6–2536–165–24.86–4–*ct* 25
Bowling 554–12–46.16–0–0–4/51

Although he retired from first-class County cricket relatively young, he was a noted player for MCC, Eton Ramblers and I Zingari until 1914. His final first-class match was for Gentlemen of England in 1910.

Chipperfield, Arthur Gordon
Amateur. *b:* 17.11.1905, Ashfield, Sydney, New South Wales, Australia. *d:* 29.7.1987, Ryde, Sydney, New South Wales, Australia. Middle order right-hand batsman, leg break bowler, excellent slip field. *Team* New South Wales (1933/4 to 1939/40, 30 matches). *Tours* Australia to England 1934, 1938, to South Africa 1935/6. *Tests* Australia (1934–38, 14 matches).
Career batting
96–129–17–4295–175–38.34–9–*ct* 91
Bowling 2582–65–39.72–1–1–8/66
Test batting
14–20–3–552–109–32.47–1–*ct* 15
Bowling 437–5–87.40–0–0–3/91

Although failing to reach 1,000 runs on either of his visits to England, he appeared in all 5 Tests on the 1934 tour, hitting 99 on his Test debut at Trent Bridge. On his visit in 1938 he was struck down with appendicitis and appeared in only one Test.

Chisholm, Jack Richardson
Professional. *b:* 9.10.1924, Enfield, Middlesex. *d:* 24.8.1977, Leytonstone, Essex. Lower order right-hand batsman, right-arm fast bowler. *Team* Middlesex (1947, 1 match).
Career batting
1–2–0–14–12–7.00–0–*ct* 0
Bowling 33–1–33.00–0–0–1/15

He also played for Bedfordshire (1949–51) and Devon (1956). He was better known as a soccer player with Brentford, Tottenham Hotspur, Sheffield United and Plymouth Argyle.

Chisholm, Ronald Harry Eddie
Amateur. *b:* 22.5.1927, Aberdeen, Scotland. Opening right-hand batsman, leg break and googly bowler. *Team* Scotland (1948–71).
Career batting
61–106–6–2354–105–23.54–1–*ct* 18
Bowling 839–26–32.26–0–0–4/9

Chitty, Arthur John
Amateur. *b:* 27.5.1859, Marylebone, London. *d:* 6.1.1908, South Kensington, London. Son of J. W. (Oxford U 1848–49), brother-in-law of E. H. F. Bradby (Oxford U) and H. C. Bradby (Oxford U). Lower order right-hand batsman, wicket-keeper. *Sch* Eton. *Team* Oxford U (1879).
Career batting
2–3–1–23–10*–11.50–0–*ct* 2

Chivers, Ian James
Cricketer. *b:* 5.11.1964, Southampton, Hampshire. Lower order right-hand batsman, off break bowler. *Team* Hampshire (1985–87, 2 matches).
Career batting
2–1–1–20–20*–no av–0–*ct* 0
Bowling 76–2–38.00–0–0–1/4

Chowdhury, Nirode Ranjan
Amateur. *b:* 23.5.1923, Jamshedpur, India. *d:* 14.12.1979, Durgapur, Pakistan. Tail end right-hand batsman, right-arm medium pace off break bowler. *Teams* Bengal (1944/5 to 1954/5); Bihar (1941/2 to 1957/8). *Tour* India to England 1952. *Tests* India (1948/9 to 1951/2, 2 matches).
Career batting
58–85–27–419–30*–7.22–0–*ct* 22
Bowling 5029–200–25.14–10–2–7/79
Test batting
2–2–1–3–3*–3.00–0–*ct* 0
Bowling 205–1–205.00–0–0–1/130

He was given very few opportunities on his 1952 tour to England and did not appear in a Test. His final first-class match was for Bihar Governor's XI in 1958/9.

Christen, Brian
Amateur. *b:* 27.11.1926, Bradford, Yorkshire. Lower order batsman, left-arm fast medium bowler. *Team*

Canada (1951–54). *Tour* Canada to England 1954.
Career batting
5–7–3–29–9*–7.25–0–*ct* 2
Bowling 384–17–22.58–1–0–7/80

He was the leading opening bowler in Canada for several seasons.

Christian of Schleswig-Holstein, HRH Prince Victor Albert Ludwig Ernest Anton
Amateur. *b:* 14.4.1867, Windsor Castle, Berkshire. *d:* 29.10.1900, Pretoria, South Africa, of enteric fever whilst serving in the Boer War. Grandson of Queen Victoria. Middle order right-hand batsman, wicket-keeper. *Sch* Wellington. *Team* I Zingari (1887).
Career batting
1–2–0–35–35–17.50–0–*ct* 1

Most of his cricket was played in India in the 1890s. He was at Oxford but did not appear in any first-class matches there.

Christiani, Cyril Marcel
Amateur. *b:* 28.10.1913, Georgetown, British Guiana. *d:* 4.4.1938, Georgetown, British Guiana. He died of malaria. Brother of E. S. (British Guiana), Harry (British Guiana) and R. J. (British Guiana). Lower order right-hand batsman, wicket-keeper. *Team* British Guiana (1931/2 to 1937/8). *Tour* West Indies to England 1933. *Tests* West Indies (1934/5, 4 matches).
Career batting
28–44–4–658–79–16.45–0–*ct* 44–*st* 20
Bowling 6–0
Test batting
4–7–2–98–32*–19.60–0–*ct* 6–*st* 1

As reserve wicket-keeper on his only tour of England, his opportunites were very limited. He was a good batsman in club cricket and with his brother E. S. Christiani added 296 for the 1st wicket in a match in British Guiana.

Christiani, Robert Julian
Amateur. *b:* 19.7.1920, Georgetown, British Guiana. Brother of C. M. (British Guiana), Harry (British Guiana) and E. S. (British Guiana). Middle order right-hand batsman, off break bowler, wicket-keeper. *Team* British Guiana (1938/9 to 1953/4). *Tours* West Indies to India, Ceylon and Pakistan 1948/9, to England 1950, to Australia and New Zealand 1951/2. *Tests* West Indies (1947/8 to 1953/4, 22 matches).
Career batting
88–142–16–5103–181–40.50–12–*ct* 96–*st* 12
Bowling 1088–18–60.44–0–0–3/11
Test batting
22–37–3–896–107–26.35–1–*ct* 19–*st* 2
Bowling 108–3–36.00–0–0–3/52

On his tour to England he hit 1,094 runs, av 45.58, and played in all four Tests.

Christie, John Cubie
Amateur. *b:* 12.7.1903, Edinburgh, Scotland. *d:* 27.5.1978, Wroxham, Norfolk. Lower order right-hand batsman. *Team* Scotland (1923).
Career batting
2–3–2–13–11*–13.00–0–*ct* 3
Bowling 132–6–22.00–0–0–3/31

Christie, Paul
Cricketer. *b:* 9.2.1971, Sunderland, Co Durham. Lower order right-hand batsman, left-arm medium fast bowler. *Team* MCC (1989).
Career batting
1–1–0–0–0–0.00–0–*ct* 0
Bowling 120–3–40.00–0–0–3/57

His County cricket was for Durham (pre first-class, 1991).

Christie, Robert Douglas
Cricketer. *b:* 7.3.1942, New Delhi, India. Lower order right-hand batsman, right-arm medium pace bowler. *Sch* Eton. *Team* Oxford U (1964).
Career batting
4–6–2–47–21–11.75–0–*ct* 0
Bowling 315–8–39.37–0–0–4/44

Christopherson, John Clifford
Amateur. *b:* 1.6.1909, Blackheath, Kent. Middle order right-hand batsman, right-arm medium pace bowler. *Sch* Uppingham. *Teams* Cambridge U (1931, blue); Kent (1931–35, 3 matches).
Career batting
16–29–2–486–75–18.00–0–*ct* 5
Bowling 32–1–32.00–0–0–1/8

His final first-class match was for Leveson Gower's XI in 1936.

Christopherson, Percy
Amateur. *b:* 31.3.1866, Kidbrooke, Blackheath, Kent. *d:* 4.5.1921, Folkestone, Kent. Brother of Stanley (Kent), great-uncle of I. S. Akers-Douglas (Kent). Middle order right-hand batsman, right-arm medium pace bowler, good field. *Sch* Bedford Grammar and Marlborough. *Teams* Kent (1887, 1 match); Oxford U (1889).
Career batting
2–3–0–27–27–9.00–0–*ct* 0

He also played for Berkshire (1897). An excellent rugby footballer, he represented Oxford and England.

Christopherson, Stanley
Amateur. *b:* 11.11.1861, Kidbrooke, Blackheath, Kent. *d:* 6.4.1949, St John's Wood, London. Brother of Percy (Kent), grandfather of I. S. Akers-Douglas (Kent). Lower order right-hand batsman, very fast right-arm bowler, fine field. *Sch* Uppingham. *Team* Kent (1883–90, 50 matches). *Tests* England (1884, 1 match).
Career batting
66–109–12–923–47–9.51–0–*ct* 41
Bowling 5332–241–22.12–13–3–8/41
Test batting
1–1–0–17–17–17.00–0–*ct* 0

Bowling 69–1–69.00–0–0–1/52

He played little serious cricket after 1886, when an injury to his arm affected his bowling. He was President of Kent in 1924 and from 1939 to 1946 President of MCC. He was one of ten brothers, and the family, with his father, fielded a fairly strong Eleven in a few matches in the 1880s. He played hockey for England.

Christy, James Alexander Joseph
Amateur. *b:* 12.12.1904, Pretoria, South Africa. *d:* 1.2.1971, Brighton Beach, Durban, South Africa. Stylish opening/middle order right-hand batsman, right-arm medium pace bowler. *Teams* Transvaal (1925/6 to 1929/30); Queensland (1934/5 to 1935/6, 13 matches). *Tours* South Africa to England 1929, to Australia and New Zealand 1931/2. *Tests* South Africa (1929 to 1931/2, 10 matches).
Career batting
65–108–9–3670–175–37.07–11–*ct* 33
Bowling 894–32–27.93–0–0–4/19
Test batting
10–18–0–618–103–34.33–1–*ct* 3
Bowling 92–2–46.00–0–0–1/15

Owing to a finger injury, his opportunities were limited during his single visit to England.

Chubb, Geoffrey Walter Ashton
Amateur. *b:* 12.4.1911, East London, South Africa. *d:* 28.8.1982, East London, South Africa. Brother of A. P. A. (Border). Originally opening, later lower order right-hand batsman, right-arm medium fast bowler. *Teams* Border (1931/2); Transvaal (1936/7 to 1950/1). *Tour* South Africa to England 1951. *Tests* South Africa (1951, 5 matches).
Career batting
49–61–15–835–71*–18.15–0–*ct* 12
Bowling 3826–160–23.91–7–0–7/54
Test batting
5–9–3–63–15*–10.50–0–*ct* 0
Bowling 577–21–27.47–2–0–6/51

Chosen for his first tour to England at the age of 40, Chubb completely justified his selection and appeared in all five Tests. He bowled most overs on the tour and took most wickets: 76, av 26.38.

Church, Lewis Girling
Amateur. *b:* 17.10.1928, Peterborough, Northamptonshire. Middle order right-hand batsman, leg break bowler. *Team* D. R. Jardine's XI (1957).
Career batting
1–2–0–1–1–0.50–0–*ct* 0
Bowling 16–0

Churchill, Rev Smith Wild
Amateur. *b:* 17.5.1838, Shepshed, Leicestershire. *d:* 13.2.1902, Mapperley, Nottinghamshire. *Sch* Christ's Hospital. *Team* MCC (1865).
Career batting
1–2–2–1–1*–no av–0–*ct* 0

Churchill, William
Amateur. *b:* 6.10.1840, Winterborne-Stickland, Dorset. *d:* 20.10.1907, Woking, Surrey. Opening/middle order batsman. *Sch* Brighton. *Team* MCC (1870–72).
Career batting
2–3–0–16–12–5.33–0–*ct* 0

His County cricket was for Dorset (1863).

Churchill, Rev William Henry
Amateur. *b:* 9.4.1855, Satara, India. *d:* 8.9.1936, South Kensington, London. Middle order right-hand batsman, change bowler. *Sch* Marlborough. *Team* An England XI (1877).
Career batting
1–2–0–13–13–6.50–0–*ct* 2

A noted athlete, he represented Cambridge at soccer and also in the quarter mile in 1877 and 1878, but did not appear in any first-class matches whilst at University.

Clapp, Albert Edward
Amateur until 1890, then professional. *b:* 3.5.1867, Chelsea, London. *d:* 3.6.1936, Bristol. Middle order right-hand batsman, right-arm medium pace bowler. *Team* Somerset (1885–95, 10 matches).
Career batting
10–17–3–152–60*–10.85–0–*ct* 1
Bowling 12–0

He also played for Shropshire commencing 1886 – appearing for both that County and Somerset in the same year. He was a first-class umpire in 1906.

Clapp, Robert John
Cricketer. *b:* 12.12.1948, Weston-super-Mare, Somerset. Lower order right-hand batsman, right-arm medium pace bowler. *Sch* Queen's College, Taunton. *Team* Somerset (1972–77, 15 matches).
Career batting
15–16–5–49–32–4.45–0–*ct* 1
Bowling 734–25–29.36–0–0–3/15

A schoolmaster, his first-class cricket was very limited, but in Limited Overs County matches in 1974 he took 51 wickets (av 15.90).

Clapperton, Dr Thomas James Milner
Amateur. *b:* 3.9.1875, Bourn, Cambridge. *d:* 26.5.1939, Corby, Northamptonshire. Lower order batsman, change bowler. *Sch* Epsom. *Team* Northamptonshire (1909, 1 match).
Career batting
1–1–0–0–0–0.00–0–*ct* 0
Bowling 29–0

Clare, Thomas
Amateur. *b:* 20.8.1883, Brierley Hill, Staffordshire. *d:* 6.5.1940, Hagley, Worcestershire. Middle order right-hand batsman. *Team* Worcestershire (1920–25, 2 matches).
Career batting
2–4–0–63–34–15.75–0–*ct* 3

Clark, Antony Roy
Cricketer. *b:* 7.11.1956, Grahamstown, South Africa. Middle order right-hand batsman. *Team* Cambridge U (1981).
Career batting
1–2–0–13–12–6.50–0–*ct* 0

Clark, Arthur Henry Seymour
Professional. *b:* 26.3.1902, Weston-super-Mare, Somerset. Tail end right-hand batsman, wicket-keeper. *Team* Somerset (1930, 5 matches).
Career batting
5–9–2–0–0*–0.00–0–*ct* 8
He had a most unfortunate batting record in first-class matches, failing to score a run in any of 9 innings.

Clark, Augustus Gilbert Finnis
Professional. *b:* 31.7.1862, Dover, Kent. *d:* 7.5.1928, Hastings, Sussex. Lower order left-hand batsman, left-arm medium pace bowler. *Team* Sussex (1886, 1 match).
Career batting
1–2–0–1–1–0.50–0–*ct* 0
Bowling 19–0
He was for many years associated with cricket in Hastings.

Clark, Charles Manning Hope
Amateur. *b:* 3.3.1915, Burwood, New South Wales, Australia. *d:* May 1991, Canberra, Australia. Middle order right-hand batsman, wicket-keeper. *Sch* Melbourne GS, Australia. *Team* Oxford U (1939).
Career batting
3–6–0–87–22–14.50–0–*ct* 1–*st* 1
He was Australia's 'foremost historian'.

Clark, David Graham
Amateur. *b:* 27.1.1919, Hall Place, Barming, Kent. Stubborn opening/middle order right-hand batsman, right-arm slow bowler, good close field. *Sch* Rugby. *Team* Kent (1946–51, 75 matches).
Career batting
75–133–9–1959–78–15.79–0–*ct* 46
Bowling 44–1–44.00–0–0–1/19
He was captain of Kent 1949–51, Chairman 1970–74 and President 1990; President of MCC 1977/8, he was appointed Treasurer in 1981 but resigned as treasurer and Trustee, as well as a Committee Member of MCC in December 1986 over the relationship of the club with the TCCB. He was Chairman of a sub-committee set up in 1966 to examine the future of County cricket.

Clark, Edward Austen
Professional. *b:* 15.4.1937, Balham, London. Middle order right-hand batsman, left-arm medium pace bowler. *Team* Middlesex (1959–76, 196 matches). *Tours* MCC to East Africa 1973/4; he also captained MCC on three minor tours: West Africa 1975/6, Bangladesh 1976/7 and 1978/9.
Career batting
200–339–39–8733–149–29.11–6–*ct* 106
Bowling 1883–58–32.46–2–0–5/61
He reached 1,000 runs in a season 5 times (best 1,454, av 32.31 in 1964). He ceased to appear regularly in County cricket after 1966. He scored 100* on his first-class debut for Middlesex v Cambridge U at Cambridge in 1959.

Clark, Edward Winchester
Professional. *b:* 9.8.1902, Elton, Huntingdonshire. *d:* 28.4.1982, West Winch, King's Lynn, Norfolk. Tail end left-hand batsman, left-arm fast bowler. *Team* Northamptonshire (1922–47, 307 matches). *Tours* Tennyson to Jamaica 1927/8; MCC to India and Ceylon 1933/4. *Tests* England (1929–34, 8 matches).
Career batting
338–510–195–1971–30–6.25–0–*ct* 104
Bowling 25967–1208–21.49–63–15–8/59
Test batting
8–9–5–36–10–9.00–0–*ct* 0
Bowling 899–32–28.09–1–0–5/98
He took 100 wickets in a season twice (best 149, av 19.10, in 1929). Although his County career extended from 1922 to 1947, it contained two breaks – in 1927 and in 1938 – when he left Northamptonshire to play in League cricket. He also played for Cambridgeshire (1948) and Huntingdonshire (1950).

Clark, Herbert Lincoln
Amateur. *b:* 8.1.1866, Germantown, Philadelphia, USA. *d:* 8.2.1940, Bryn Mawr, Philadelphia, USA. Brother of P. H. (Philadelphia) and E. W. (Philadelphia). Middle order right-hand batsman, good field. *Team* Philadelphia (1894–97). *Tour* Philadelphia to England 1897.
Career batting
7–11–0–92–22–8.36–0–*ct* 2
He was completely unable to find his form on his visit to England.

Clark, Horace George
Amateur. *b:* 23.1.1889, West Ham, Essex. *d:* 28.2.1967, Epping Plain, Essex. Middle order batsman. *Team* Essex (1923, 2 matches).
Career batting
2–3–0–13–11–4.33–0–*ct* 0
He was Secretary of Essex 1951–54.

Clark, John
Cricketer. *b:* 9.12.1943, Greenock, Renfrew, Scotland. Lower order right-hand batsman, right-arm fast medium bowler. *Team* Scotland (1969–82).
Career batting
13–16–3–104–29–8.00–0–*ct* 13
Bowling 800–43–18.60–0–0–4/10

Clark, Leonard Stanley
Amateur. *b:* 6.3.1914, Manor Park, Essex. Opening right-hand batsman, right-arm medium pace bowler. *Team* Essex (1946–47, 24 matches).
Career batting
24–44–3–745–64–18.17–0–*ct* 11
Bowling 15–0

Clark, Percy Hamilton
Amateur. *b:* 7.8.1873, Germantown, Philadelphia, USA. *d:* 12.8.1965, Villanova, Pennsylvania, USA. Brother of E. W. (Philadelphia) and H. L. (Philadelphia). Lower order right-hand batsman, right-arm fast medium bowler. *Team* Philadelphia (1896–1913). *Tours* Philadelphia to England 1897, 1903.
Career batting
52–87–17–897–67–12.81–0–*ct* 31
Bowling 4374–199–21.97–11–4–8/91

On his second visit to England in 1903 he was most successful, taking 85 wickets (av 20.50) in all matches. He appeared regularly for USA v Canada and was regarded as one of the best bowlers in North American cricket.

Clark, Robert Selbie
Amateur. *b:* 11.9.1882, Aberdeen, Scotland. *d:* 29.9.1950, Aberdeen, Scotland. Middle order right-hand batsman. *Team* Scotland (1912–24).
Career batting
2–4–0–19–10–4.75–0–*ct* 2

Clark, Ronald Disston
Amateur. *b:* 22.2.1895, Romford, Essex. *d:* 20.2.1983, East Wittering, Sussex. Lower order right-hand batsman, wicket-keeper. *Sch* Christ's Hospital. *Team* Essex (1912–19, 7 matches).
Career batting
7–11–1–61–14–6.10–0–*ct* 10–*st* 1

Clark, Thomas Henry
Professional. *b:* 5.10.1924, Luton, Bedfordshire. *d:* 14.6.1981, Luton, Bedfordshire. Sound opening or middle order right-hand batsman, off break bowler. *Team* Surrey (1947 to 1959/60, 260 matches). *Tour* Surrey to Rhodesia 1959/60.
Career batting
263–426–35–11490–191–29.38–12–*ct* 104
Bowling 2314–75–30.85–1–0–5/23

He reached 1,000 runs in a season 6 times (best 1,570, av 32.70, in 1957). He also played for Bedfordshire (1946). He was forced to retire due to arthritis. He played soccer for Walsall and Aston Villa.

Clark, William
Amateur. *b:* 8.9.1905, Crieff, Perthshire, Scotland. Middle order right-hand batsman, wicket-keeper. *Team* Scotland (1946).
Career batting
1–2–0–13–9–6.50–0–*ct* 1–*st* 1

Clarke, A.
Professional. Lower order batsman, right-arm fast bowler. *Team* Leicestershire (1902, 1 match).
Career batting
1 match, did not bat–*ct* 0
Bowling 70–2–35.00–0–0–2/70

Clarke, Alfred
Professional. *b:* 16.2.1831, Nottingham. *d:* 23.10.1878, Ruddington, Nottinghamshire. Son of William Clarke (Nottinghamshire 1826–55). Middle order right-hand batsman, good deep field. *Team* Nottinghamshire (1851–63, 25 matches). *Tour* Parr to Australia and New Zealand 1863/4.
Career batting
55–95–10–936–57–11.01–0–*ct* 30

Clarke, Alfred Ferrier
Amateur. *b:* 12.8.1865, Farnworth, Lancashire. *d:* 12.6.1935, Hastings, Sussex. Lower order right-hand batsman, wicket-keeper. *Sch* University College School, London. *Team* Surrey (1890–92, 8 matches).
Career batting
8–8–2–61–30–10.16–0–*ct* 8–*st* 6

Clarke, Andrew Russell
Cricketer. *b:* 23.12.1961, Patcham, Sussex. Lower order right-hand batsman, leg break bowler. *Team* Sussex (1988–89, 26 matches).
Career batting
26–37–9–406–68–14.50–0–*ct* 7
Bowling 1872–53–35.32–2–0–5/60

His leg breaks created quite a stir in 1988, particularly in Sunday League cricket.

Clarke, Basil Frederick
Amateur. *b:* 26.9.1885, Madras, India. *d:* 4.5.1940, Hove, Sussex. Middle order right-hand batsman. *Sch* Marlborough. *Teams* Gloucestershire (1914–20, 12 matches); Leicestershire (1922, 5 matches).
Career batting
20–32–3–349–108*–12.03–1–*ct* 10
Bowling 24–0

Clarke, Dr Carlos Bertram
Amateur. *b:* 7.4.1918, Lakes Folly, Cats Castle, St Michael, Barbados. Lower order right-hand batsman, leg break and googly bowler. *Teams* Barbados (1937/8 to 1938/9); Northamptonshire (1946–49, 49 matches); Essex (1959–60, 18 matches). *Tour* West Indies to England 1939. *Tests* West Indies (1939, 3 matches).
Career batting
97–145–40–1292–86–12.30–0–*ct* 42
Bowling 8782–333–26.37–20–1–7/75
Test batting
3–4–1–3–2–1.00–0–*ct* 0
Bowling 261–6–43.50–0–0–3/59

He captained the British Empire XI in England during the Second World War and in post-war years played club cricket in the Home Counties. His final first-class match was for MCC in 1961.

Clarke, Charles
Professional. *b:* 11.4.1878, Partick, Lanarkshire, Scotland. Son of W. B. (Nottinghamshire and Middlesex). Lower order batsman, left-arm medium pace bowler. *Team* Sussex (1902, 3 matches).
Career batting
3–4–2–17–10–8.50–0–*ct* 2
Bowling 122–1–122.00–0–0–1/56

Clarke, Charles Cyril
Amateur. *b:* 22.12.1910, Burton-on-Trent, Staffordshire. Middle order right-hand batsman. *Sch* Repton. *Teams* Derbyshire (1929–33, 25 matches); Sussex (1947, 3 matches).
Career batting
28–43–3–472–35*–11.80–0–*ct* 8
He also played for Staffordshire (1935–39).

Clarke, Charles Frederick Carlos
Amateur. *b:* 26.4.1853, Welton, Northamptonshire. *d:* 29.1.1931, Virginia Water, Surrey. Brother of M. C. (Surrey), father-in-law of N. C. Tufnell (Surrey). Middle order right-hand batsman, right-arm slow bowler. *Team* Surrey (1873–82, 10 matches).
Career batting
24–40–3–437–65–11.81–0–*ct* 19–*st* 1
Bowling 154–4–38.50–0–0–2/50
His final first-class match was for I Zingari in 1890.

Clarke, Donald Hugh
Amateur. *b:* 15.5.1926, Bromborough, Cheshire. Opening right-hand batsman. *Sch* Oundle. *Team* Cambridge U (1946).
Career batting
2–4–0–32–24–8.00–0–*ct* 0

Clarke, Frank
Professional. *b:* 8.10.1936, Heath, Cardiff. Lower order right-hand batsman, right-arm fast medium bowler. *Team* Glamorgan (1956–60, 31 matches).
Career batting
31–41–15–98–31–3.76–0–*ct* 10
Bowling 1868–50–37.36–1–0–5/66

Clarke, George William
Amateur. *b:* 10.4.1869, Northampton. *d:* 26.8.1955, Northampton. Lower order batsman, bowler. *Team* Northamptonshire (1908, 1 match).
Career batting
1–2–0–0–0–0.00–0–*ct* 1
Bowling 58–2–29.00–0–0–2/58

Clarke, J.
Professional. Lower order batsman, bowler. *Team* Lancashire (1905, 1 match).
Career batting
1–1–0–0–0–0.00–0–*ct* 0
Bowling 35–0

Clarke, John Michael
Cricketer. *b:* 25.12.1948, Barcombe, Sussex. Middle order left-hand batsman, right-arm medium fast bowler. *Team* Sussex (1969, 1 match).
Career batting
1–2–0–0–0–0.00–0–*ct* 1

Clarke, Morice Carlos
Amateur. *b:* 1852, Welton, Northamptonshire. *d:* 14.7.1887, Virginia Water, Surrey. Brother of C. F. C. (Surrey). Middle order right-hand batsman. *Team* Surrey (1875–80, 9 matches).
Career batting
9–17–1–115–26–7.18–0–*ct* 6
He also played for Northamptonshire (pre first-class, 1884–85).

Clarke, Peter
Professional. *b:* 19.5.1881, Paddington, London. *d:* December, 1915, Dublin, Ireland. Tail end right-hand batsman, leg break and googly bowler. *Teams* Ireland (1912); Middlesex (1913–14, 11 matches).
Career batting
19–28–12–125–28–7.81–0–*ct* 7
Bowling 1376–47–29.27–2–0–5/62
He bowled with great success for Woodbrook Club and Ground in Ireland and as a result was given a place in the Test Trial of 1912, without ever having appeared in English County cricket.

Clarke, Robert Wakefield
Professional. *b:* 22.4.1924, Finedon, Northamptonshire. *d:* 3.8.1981, Sherborne, Dorset. Hard-hitting tail end left-hand batsman, left-arm fast bowler, fine close field. *Team* Northamptonshire (1947–57, 208 matches).
Career batting
212–263–84–2745–56–15.33–0–*ct* 150
Bowling 16749–484–34.60–16–1–8/26
He also played for Devon (1960).

Clarke, Simon John Scott
Amateur. *b:* 2.4.1938, Westcliff-on-Sea, Essex. Middle order right-hand batsman. *Sch* Wellington. *Team* Cambridge U (1961–62).
Career batting
8–14–0–99–19–7.07–0–*ct* 5
His first-class debut was for Combined Services in 1958. An excellent rugby footballer, he represented Cambridge U and England.

Clarke, Sylvester Theophilus
Cricketer. *b:* 11.12.1954, Lead Vale, Christ Church, Barbados. Half-brother of R. O. Estwick (Barbados). Attacking lower order right-hand batsman, right-arm fast bowler, gully field. *Teams* Barbados (1977/8 to 1981/2); Surrey (1979–88, 152 matches); Transvaal (1983/4 to 1985/6); Orange Free State (1987/8); Northern Transvaal (1988/9 to 1989/90). *Tours* West Indies to India and Sri Lanka 1978/9, to Pakistan

1980/1, to Australia 1981/2; West Indian XI to South Africa 1982/3, 1983/4. *Tests* West Indies (1977/8 to 1981/2, 11 matches).
Career batting
238–265–44–3269–100*–14.79–1–*ct* 146
Bowling 18397–942–19.52–59–10–8/62
Test batting
11–16–5–172–35*–15.63–0–*ct* 2
Bowling 1170–42–27.85–1–0–5/126

A devastating fast bowler, his Test cricket ended when he opted to tour South Africa. He was the spearhead of the Surrey attack. He took 85 wickets, av 19.95, in 1982 and was even more impressive in 1988 when he effectively topped the first-class averages with 63 wickets, av 14.49. His County career was abruptly terminated after a single Benson & Hedges match in 1989 for 'persistent breaches of the terms and conditions of his contract'. He was also a very hard hitting batsman and in 1981 hit the fastest 100 of the season, in 62 minutes. He missed all of the 1985 season due to injury.

Clarke (or Clark), William
Professional. *b:* 24.12.1798, Nottingham. *d:* 25.8.1856, Wandsworth, Surrey. Father of Alfred (Nottinghamshire), step-father of John Chapman (Nottinghamshire). Lower order right-hand batsman, slow right-hand under-arm bowler. *Teams* Nottinghamshire (1826–55); Surrey (1852, 1 match as given man); Sussex (1854, 1 match as given man); Kent (1854, 1 match as given man).
Career batting
143–243–37–2133–75–10.35–0–*ct* 55
Bowling 4144–409 + 386–10.13–82–25–9/29

He did not become prominent as a player, outside his native County, until he was about 45 years old, and then for some ten seasons his bowling was most successful – he practised the art of under-arm deliveries, an art which had more or less died with the coming of round-arm bowling.

In 1838 he laid out Trent Bridge cricket ground and in 1846 created the All England Eleven – the first professional wandering cricket team, which proved to be immensely popular. His best bowling was 9/29 for Nottinghamshire v Kent at Trent Bridge in 1845. He also played for Suffolk (1847).

Clarke, William
Professional. *b:* 17.3.1849, Kirkby-in-Ashfield, Nottinghamshire. *d:* 29.5.1935, Woodthorpe Park, Mapperley, Nottinghamshire. Lower order left-hand batsman, right-arm fast bowler. *Team* Nottinghamshire (1876–77, 6 matches).
Career batting
6–10–0–82–17–8.20–0–*ct* 1
Bowling 126–4–31.50–0–0–2/60

Clarke, William Benjamin
Professional. *b:* 5.11.1846, Old Basford, Nottingham. *d:* 18.8.1902, Hyson Green, Nottingham. Father of Charles (Sussex). Lower order right-hand batsman, right-hand medium pace round-arm bowler. *Teams* Nottinghamshire (1874–76, 13 matches); Middlesex (1880–84, 21 matches).
Career batting
39–64–13–409–40–8.01–0–*ct* 38
Bowling 1741–101–17.23–10–0–7/51

He was a first-class umpire (1883-99).

Clarkson, Anthony
Cricketer. *b:* 5.9.1939, Killinghall, Harrogate, Yorkshire. Opening right-hand batsman, off break bowler. *Teams* Yorkshire (1963, 6 matches); Somerset (1966–71, 104 matches).
Career batting
110–189–12–4458–131–25.18–2–*ct* 52
Bowling 367–13–28.23–0–0–3/51

He reached 1,000 runs in a season twice (best 1,346, av 27.68, in 1970). He also played for Devon.

Clarkson, William
Professional. *b:* Lancashire. Lower order left-hand batsman, left-arm medium pace bowler. *Team* Warwickshire (1922–23, 2 matches).
Career batting
2–4–0–59–41–14.75–0–*ct* 0
Bowling 52–2–26.00–0–0–2/24

Claughton, Hugh Marsden
Professional 1914, amateur 1919. *b:* 24.12.1891, Guiseley, Leeds, Yorkshire. *d:* 17.10.1980, Middleton-in-Wharfedale, Yorkshire. Great-uncle of J. A. (Warwickshire). Middle/lower order right-hand batsman, right-arm medium fast bowler. *Team* Yorkshire (1914–19, 4 matches).
Career batting
4–6–0–39–15–6.50–0–*ct* 1
Bowling 176–3–58.66–0–0–1/27

Claughton, John Alan
Cricketer. *b:* 17.9.1956, Guiseley, Leeds, Yorkshire. Great-nephew of H. M. (Yorkshire). Opening right-hand batsman, slow left-arm bowler, brilliant field. *Sch* KES, Birmingham. *Teams* Oxford U (1976–79, blue all four years); Warwickshire (1979–80, 18 matches).
Career batting
55–96–7–1910–130–21.46–4–*ct* 21
Bowling 4–0

He scored 51 and 112 for Oxford U v Gloucestershire at Oxford in 1976 on his first-class debut. He captained Oxford in 1978. He also played for Berkshire (1982–86) and Dorset (1988–92).

Clay, John Charles
Amateur. *b:* 18.3.1898, Bonvilston, Glamorgan. *d:* 11.8.1973, St Hilary, near Cowbridge, Glamorgan.

Great nephew of H. Boden (Gentlemen of North). Lower order right-hand batsman, originally right-arm fast medium bowler, off break bowler from about 1924. *Sch* Winchester. *Teams* Glamorgan (1921–49, 358 matches); Wales (1923–26). *Test* England (1935, 1 match).

Career batting
373–555–90–7186–115*–15.45–2–*ct* 177
Bowling 26028–1317–19.76–105–28–9/54
Test batting
1 match, did not bat –*ct* 1
Bowling 75–0

He took 100 wickets in a season three times (best 176, av 17.34, in 1937). He was captain of Glamorgan 1924–27, jointly in 1929 and 1946, Treasurer 1933–38, Secretary 1946 and President from 1960 until his death. He was a Test Selector 1947–48. His best bowling was 9/54 for Glamorgan v Northamptonshire at Llanelly in 1935.

Clay, John Desmond
Professional. *b:* 25.10.1924, West Bridgford, Nottingham. Opening right-hand batsman, good slip field. *Team* Nottinghamshire (1948–61, 236 matches).
Career batting
236–400–17–9991–192–26.08–11–*ct* 164
Bowling 133–0

He hit 1,000 runs 6 times (best 1,497, av 25.81, in 1961). In 1961 he captained Nottinghamshire.

Clayton, Frederick George Hugh
Amateur. *b:* 5.5.1873, Wylam Hall, Northumberland. *d:* 20.3.1946, Warkworth, Northumberland. Middle order right-hand batsman, right-arm medium pace bowler. *Sch* Harrow. *Team* Oxford U (1893–96). *Tour* Oxford U Authentics to India 1902/3.
Career batting
9–16–0–332–68–20.75–0–*ct* 5
Bowling 525–18–29.16–1–0–7/70

Appearing in the Oxford Freshmen's match of 1893 he hit 230 and 70* – a remarkable feat – but failed to obtain his blue. His County cricket was for Northumberland (1893–1906). He won a blue for rackets.

Clayton, Geoffrey
Professional. *b:* 3.2.1938, Mossley, Lancashire. Lower order right-hand batsman, wicket-keeper. *Teams* Lancashire (1959–64, 183 matches); Somerset (1965–67, 89 matches).
Career batting
274–415–66–6154–106–17.63–1–*ct* 605–*st* 65

His first-class debut was for Combined Services in 1957.

Clayton, John Morton
Amateur. *b:* 17.11.1857, Chesterfield, Derbyshire. *d:* 1.4.1938, West Southbourne, Hampshire. Lower order right-hand batsman, right-arm fast medium bowler. *Team* Derbyshire (1881–83, 2 matches).
Career batting
2–3–0–3–2–1.00–0–*ct* 1
Bowling 11–0

Clayton, Robert Owen
Professional. *b:* 1.1.1844, Penygroes, Caernarvonshire. *d:* 26.11.1901, Gainsborough, Lincolnshire. Hard-hitting lower order right-hand batsman, right-arm fast bowler. *Team* Yorkshire (1870–79, 70 matches).
Career batting
121–201–34–1709–62–10.23–0–*ct* 48
Bowling 4255–254–16.75–18–2–8/66

He joined the MCC ground staff in 1872 and remained there until his death. He also played for Northumberland (1870) and Lincolnshire (1881). His final first-class match was for MCC in 1881. He was a first-class umpire (1895–99).

Clayton, William Clayton
(changed name from W. C. Walters in 1849)
Amateur. *b:* 23.4.1839, Stella Hall, Newcastle upon Tyne, Northumberland. *d:* 25.12.1876, Delhi, India, as the result of a polo accident. Lower order right-hand batsman, wicket-keeper. *Sch* Harrow. *Teams* Gentlemen of England (1858–59); MCC (1861–67).
Career batting
6–8–0–90–26–11.25–0–*ct* 0–*st* 4

In a minor match in Sheffield, he was responsible as wicket-keeper for the dismissal of 4 batsmen in 4 balls, stumping one, catching two and running out the last. At the time of his death he was aide-de-camp to the Viceroy of India.

Cleal, Matthew William
Cricketer. *b:* 23.7.1969, Yeovil, Somerset. Lower order right-hand batsman, right-arm fast medium bowler. *Team* Somerset (1988–89, 15 matches).
Career batting
15–19–1–165–30–9.16–0–*ct* 4
Bowling 909–26–34.96–0–0–4/41

Cleaton, Howard
Cricketer. *b:* 15.11.1949, Merthyr Tydfil, Glamorgan. Lower order right-hand batsman, off break bowler. *Sch* Bristol GS. *Team* Gloucestershire (1971, 1 match).
Career batting
1–1–0–1–1–1.00–0–*ct* 1
Bowling 23–0

Clegg, Henry
Professional. *b:* 8.12.1850, Dewsbury, Yorkshire. *d:* 30.12.1920, Dewsbury, Yorkshire. Middle order right-hand batsman, fine field. *Team* Yorkshire (1881, 6 matches).
Career batting
8–11–2–96–27–10.66–0–*ct* 2

His final first-class match was for T. Emmett's XI in 1883.

Clegg, William Gavin
Amateur. *b:* 29.6.1869, Altrincham, Cheshire. *d:* 18.5.1949, Delamere, Cheshire. Hard-hitting lower order right-hand batsman, right-arm medium pace bowler. *Sch* Winchester. *Team* Oxford U (1891).
Career batting
2–4–0–35–35–8.75–0–*ct* 1
Bowling 62–5–12.40–0–0–3/35

Clements, Simon Mark
Cricketer. *b:* 29.4.1956, Felixstowe, Suffolk. Middle order left-hand batsman, right-arm medium pace bowler. *Sch* Ipswich. *Team* Oxford U (1976–79, blue 1976 and 1979).
Career batting
29–47–5–860–91–20.47–0–*ct* 18
Bowling 205–3–68.33–0–0–1/29
His County cricket was for Suffolk (1974–92). He captained Oxford in 1979.

Cleveley, Alan Barnard
Professional. *b:* 5.1.1932, Chaddesden, Derbyshire. Lower order right-hand batsman, right-arm fast medium bowler. *Team* Nottinghamshire (1955, 1 match).
Career batting
1–2–1–4–4*–4.00–0–*ct* 0
Bowling 107–3–35.66–0–0–3/63

Cliff, Alfred Talbot
Amateur. *b:* 27.10.1878, Scawby Grove, Brigg, Lincolnshire. *d:* 25.1.1966, Oxford. Middle order right-hand batsman, slow left-arm bowler. *Team* Worcestershire (1912–20, 39 matches).
Career batting
39–74–2–986–81*–13.69–0–*ct* 12
Bowling 410–8–51.25–0–0–1/4

Clifford, Christopher Craven
Cricketer. *b:* 5.7.1942, Hovingham, Yorkshire. Lower order right-hand batsman, off break bowler. *Teams* Yorkshire (1972, 11 matches); Warwickshire (1978–80, 36 matches).
Career batting
47–45–16–210–26–7.24–0–*ct* 16
Bowling 4740–126–37.61–6–0–6/89
He appeared for Yorkshire 2nd XI in 1963, but lived in South Africa 1969–72.

Clifford, Francis Seath
Professional. *b:* 17.12.1822, Bearsted, Kent. *d:* 17.11.1869, Gravesend, Kent. Brother of William (Kent), grandson of Robert (Kent 1779). Middle order right-hand batsman with a forward style of play, wicket-keeper. *Team* Kent (1849–60, 43 matches).
Career batting
53–95–7–907–60*–10.30–0–*ct* 28–*st* 8

Clifford, Frank Leonard
Professional. *b:* 29.8.1891, Westminster, London. *d:* 13.6.1982, Enfield, Middlesex. Lower order batsman. *Team* Middlesex (1921, 1 match).
Career batting
1–2–2–0–0*–no av–0–*ct* 0
Bowling 7–0

Clifford, George
Professional. *b:* 19.4.1852, Barnes, Surrey. *d:* 4.2.1941, Thames Ditton, Surrey. Middle or lower order right-hand batsman, change bowler. *Team* Surrey (1871–78, 15 matches).
Career batting
16–30–1–282–45–9.72–0–*ct* 7
Bowling 355–13–27.30–0–0–3/15
His final first-class match was for the South in 1879.

Clifford, William
Professional. *c:* 14.12.1811, Bearsted, Kent. *d:* 5.9.1841, Gravesend, Kent. Brother of F. S. (Kent), grandson of Robert (Kent 1779). Middle order right-hand batsman, wicket-keeper. *Team* Kent (1834–41, 17 matches).
Career batting
29–51–10–521–49–12.70–0–*ct* 20–*st* 3

Clift, Patrick Bernard
Cricketer. *b:* 14.7.1953, Salisbury, Rhodesia. Middle order right-hand batsman, right-arm medium pace bowler, slip field. *Teams* Rhodesia (1971/2 to 1979/80); Leicestershire (1975–87, 219 matches); Natal (1980/1 to 1987/8).
Career batting
319–446–91–8383–106–23.61–2–*ct* 161
Bowling 21610–876–24.66–26–2–8/17
Although he did not complete 1,000 runs in any single season, or take 100 wickets, he was a very dependable all-rounder for his County.

Clift, Phil Brittain
Professional. *b:* 3.9.1918, Usk, Monmouth. Opening right-hand batsman, off break bowler, brilliant field at short leg. *Team* Glamorgan (1937–55, 183 matches).
Career batting
183–306–21–6055–125*–21.24–7–*ct* 169
Bowling 675–11–61.36–0–0–3/6
He hit 1,000 runs in a season three times (best 1,226, av 26.08, in 1949). He was Secretary of Glamorgan, 1978–82, having been coach 1958–76.

Clifton, Cecil Cooper
Professional. *b:* 8.12.1885, Eastwood, Nottinghamshire. *d:* 12.3.1930, Anfield, Liverpool, Lancashire. Lower order right-hand batsman, right-arm fast medium bowler. *Team* Nottinghamshire (1908–10, 24 matches).
Career batting
24–36–10–154–22–5.92–0–*ct* 10
Bowling 1334–50–26.68–0–0–4/25
He also played for Cheshire (1920–23).

Clifton, Charles
Professional. *b:* 13.1.1846, Ruddington, Nottinghamshire. Son-in-law of James Grundy (Nottinghamshire), brother-in-law of John Grundy (England XI). Middle order right-hand batsman, right-hand fast round-arm bowler, good field. *Team* Nottinghamshire (1873–76, 9 matches).
Career batting
10–18–2–168–45–10.50–0–*ct* 9

Clifton, Lord Edward Henry Stuart
(succeeded as 7th Earl of Darnley in 1896)
Amateur. *b:* 21.8.1851, Cobham Hall, Gravesend, Kent. *d:* 31.10.1900, Cobham Hall, Kent. Son of 6th Earl Darnley (Gentlemen of Kent 1848), brother of I. F. W. Bligh (Kent), great-grandson of 4th Earl of Darnley (Kent 1790), nephew of Henry Bligh (Kent), E. V. Bligh (Kent and Middlesex) and F. G. Pelham (Sussex). Hard-hitting middle order right-hand batsman, right-hand fast round-arm bowler. *Sch* Eton. *Team* Kent (1871–79, 6 matches).
Career batting
11–21–2–200–52–10.52–0–*ct* 2
Bowling 22–0
His final first-class match was for MCC in 1880.

Clifton, Ernest George
Cricketer. *b:* 15.6.1939, Lambeth, London. Lower order right-hand batsman, wicket-keeper. *Team* Middlesex (1962–66, 25 matches).
Career batting
25–29–16–128–25–9.84–0–*ct* 43–*st* 7

Clinton, Grahame Selvey
Cricketer. *b:* 5.5.1953, Sidcup, Kent. Opening left-hand batsman, right-arm medium pace bowler. *Teams* Kent (1974–78, 32 matches), Surrey (1979–90, 234 matches); Zimbabwe-Rhodesia (1979/80).
Career batting
270–450–53–13118–192–33.04–20–*ct* 96
Bowling 201–4–50.25–0–0–2/8
He scored 1,000 runs in a season seven times (best 1,292, av 46.14, in 1990).

Clitheroe, Roger Ian
Cricketer. *b:* 18.11.1966, Radcliffe, Lancashire. Opening right-hand batsman, wicket-keeper. *Team* Cambridge U (1987–91, blue 1991).
Career batting
13–21–2–291–36–15.31–0–*ct* 8–*st* 2
He did not play any first-class cricket from 1988 to 1990.

Clode, Harry Pile
Professional. *b:* 7.9.1877, Kensington, London. *d:* 19.10.1964, Sunderland, Co Durham. Lower order right-hand batsman, slow right-arm bowler. *Team* Surrey (1899–1903, 40 matches).
Career batting
40–56–6–596–50*–11.92–0–*ct* 20
Bowling 2884–111–25.98–6–1–6/31
He also played for Durham (pre first-class, 1912–21).

Close, Dennis Brian, CBE
Professional. *b:* 24.2.1931, Rawdon, Leeds, Yorkshire. Versatile left-hand batsman, right-arm medium pace or off break bowler. *Teams* Yorkshire (1949–70, 536 matches); Somerset (1971–77, 142 matches). *Tours* MCC to Australia 1950/1, to Pakistan 1955/6; Commonwealth to South Africa 1959/60, to India 1964/5; Yorkshire to North America 1964 (not first-class); International Wanderers to Rhodesia 1972/3, to South Africa 1974/5; Robins to South Africa 1973/4, 1974/5. *Tests* England (1949–76, 22 matches).
Career batting
786–1225–173–34994–198–33.26–52–*ct* 813–*st* 1
Bowling 30947–1171–26.42–43–3–8/41
Test batting
22–37–2–887–70–25.34–0–*ct* 24
Bowling 532–18–29.55–0–0–4/35
Close achieved so much in his first year in first-class cricket that any subsequent success was almost bound to be an anti-climax – at the age of 18 in 1949 he became the youngest player to attain the 'double', the youngest to gain a Yorkshire cap and the youngest to represent England in Test cricket. Looking back on his County career, which spanned 29 seasons to 1977, it is apparent, however, that he might well have remained as successful as he was in 1949 had not he become a magnet for controversy. Several times he won himself the praise of all connected with the game, only then to be entangled in discord. In 1963 he was made captain of Yorkshire and took to the responsibility with such success that he was recalled to the England side and held the country's batting together. In 1966 he was given the English captaincy and looked to be set for a long reign when suddenly he was at loggerheads with the authorities and his international career abruptly ended.
He captained Yorkshire from 1963 to 1970, Somerset from 1972 to 1977 and England in seven Tests. In all he reached 1,000 runs in a season 20 times (best 1,985, av 35.44, in 1961) and took 100 wickets in a season twice (best 114, av 24.08, in 1952). In 1949 and 1952 he achieved the 'double'. His final first-class match was for D. B. Close's XI in 1986. He was a Test selector 1979–81. He was elected to the Yorkshire CCC Committee in 1984 and has been Chairman of the Cricket Sub-Committee since that date.
Apart from his cricketing ability, he was a good soccer player, and was on the books of Leeds United, Arsenal and Bradford City before a knee injury forced him to retire.

Close, Peter Alwen
Cricketer. *b:* 1.6.1943, Murree, India. Middle order right-hand batsman, off break bowler. *Sch* Hailey-

bury. *Team* Cambridge U (1964–65, blue 1965).
Career batting
15–27–2–344–54–13.76–0–*ct* 15
Bowling 44–1–44.00–0–0–1/6
His County cricket was for Dorset (1963–66).

Clowes, Henry
Amateur. *b:* 1.7.1863, Cheadle, Cheshire. *d:* 6.4.1899, Bloomsbury, London. Middle order right-hand batsman, occasional wicket-keeper. *Sch* Cheltenham. *Team* Gloucestershire (1884, 4 matches).
Career batting
4–8–0–82–22–10.25–0–*ct* 1

Clube, Stace Victor Murray
Amateur. *b:* 22.10.1934, Tooting, London. Lower order right-hand batsman, off break bowler. *Sch* St John's, Leatherhead. *Team* Oxford U (1956–57, blue 1956).
Career batting
17–25–3–132–25–6.00–0–*ct* 11
Bowling 1514–47–32.21–1–0–5/49
His final first-class match was for Free Foresters in 1959.

Clugston, David Lindsay
Amateur. *b:* 5.2.1908, Belfast, Ireland. Lower order left-hand batsman, slow left-arm bowler. *Team* Warwickshire (1928–46, 6 matches).
Career batting
6–9–0–64–17–7.11–0–*ct* 3
Bowling 475–4–118.75–0–0–2/75

Coates, Arthur Edward
Amateur. *b:* 2.8.1848, Pemberton, Wigan, Lancashire. *d:* 19.8.1897, Los Angeles, California, USA. Middle order right-hand batsman, useful change bowler. *Sch* Shrewsbury. *Team* Gloucestershire (1873, 1 match).
Career batting
1–1–0–2–2–2.00–0–*ct* 0
He was Vice-President of California CA.

Coates, Crawford
Amateur. *b:* 24.5.1866, Cape Town, South Africa. *d:* 9.10.1944, Manhattan Beach, California, USA. Middle order right-hand batsman, good outfield. *Team* Philadelphia (1886–97). *Tour* Philadelphia to England 1897.
Career batting
21–33–0–602–84–18.24–0–*ct* 18
Bowling 59–0
Although he did well for Belmont in Philadelphian Club cricket, he achieved little either on his 1897 visit to England or his five appearances for USA v Canada.

Coates, Joseph
Amateur. *b:* 13.11.1844, Huddersfield, Yorkshire. *d:* 9.9.1896, Sydney, New South Wales, Australia. Lower order left-hand batsman, left-arm medium pace bowler. *Teams* New South Wales (1867/8 to 1879/80, 13 matches); North (1877).
Career batting
15–26–6–158–36*–7.90–0–*ct* 3
Bowling 887–76–11.67–5–1–7/39
In 'Scores and Biographies' it is incorrectly stated that he played for Surrey.

Cobb, Arthur Rhodes
Amateur. *b:* 12.3.1864, Cotefield House, Adderbury, Banbury, Oxfordshire. *d:* 6.11.1886, Cotefield House, Adderbury, Banbury, Oxfordshire, of typhoid fever. Brother of C. E. (Webbe's XI). Middle order right-hand batsman, wicket-keeper. *Sch* Winchester. *Team* Oxford U (1884–86, blue 1886). *Tours* Sanders to America 1885, 1886.
Career batting
17–30–2–323–51–11.53–0–*ct* 15–*st* 4
His County cricket was for Warwickshire (pre first-class, 1885–86). He had only just returned from America at the time of his death.

Cobb, Charles Edward
Amateur. *b:* 24.5.1863, Cotefield House, Adderbury, Banbury, Oxfordshire. *d:* 6.7.1922, Marylebone, London. Brother of A. R. (Oxford U). Lower order right-hand batsman, wicket-keeper. *Sch* Rugby. *Team* A. J. Webbe's XI (1900).
Career batting
1–2–0–36–19–18.00–0–*ct* 1
His County cricket was for Buckinghamshire (1891–1903).

Cobb, Humphry Henry
Amateur. *b:* 12.7.1873, Kensington, London. *d:* 13.12.1949, Links End, Camber, Sussex. Middle order right-hand batsman. *Sch* Sedbergh. *Team* Middlesex (1898–1901, 10 matches).
Career batting
11–16–4–160–55*–13.33–0–*ct* 10
His first-class debut was for MCC in 1896. He captained Rosslyn Park FC for three seasons and was at one time President of the Bear Skating Club. He also played for Hertfordshire (1894–97).

Cobb, Russell Alan
Cricketer. *b:* 18.5.1961, Leicester. Opening right-hand batsman, left-arm medium pace bowler. *Sch* Trent College. *Teams* Leicestershire (1980–89, 118 matches); Northern Transvaal (1988/9). *Tours* Robins to New Zealand 1979/80 (no first-class matches); Leicestershire to Zimbabwe 1980/1.
Career batting
122–195–15–4388–91–24.37–0–*ct* 73
Bowling 49–0
He scored 1,092 runs, av 28.73, in 1986.

Cobbett, James
Professional. *b:* 12.1.1804, Frimley, Surrey. *d:* 31.3.1842, Marylebone, London. Middle order right-hand batsman, right-hand slow round-arm bowler. *Teams* Middlesex (1826); Yorkshire (1835); Surrey (1839, 1 match).
Career batting
100–172–17–1573–60–10.14–0–*ct* 71–*st* 5
Bowling 111–9 + 525–12.33–41–14–8/?

He was on the staff at Lord's for 16 seasons and was regarded as one of the best all-round cricketers of his day. His final first-class match was for MCC in 1841.

Cobbold, Philip Wyndham
Amateur. *b:* 5.1.1875, Holywells, Ipswich, Suffolk. *d:* 28.12.1945, Tattingstone, Ipswich, Suffolk. Uncle of R. H. (Cambridge U). Lower order right-hand batsman, leg break bowler, fine slip field. *Sch* Eton. *Team* Cambridge U (1896, blue).
Career batting
18–31–5–249–49*–9.57–0–*ct* 13
Bowling 1601–67–23.89–3–0–6/56

His County cricket was for Suffolk (1902–11), captaining the County for several seasons. His final first-class match was for Free Foresters in 1922. He represented Cambridge at both tennis and rackets. He was Mayor of Ipswich 1910/11 and 1933/4.

Cobbold, Ralph Hamilton
Amateur. *b:* 22.5.1906, Calne, Wiltshire. *d:* 1.9.1987, Ipswich, Suffolk. Nephew of P. W. (Cambridge U), brother-in-law of C. S. Crawley (Hampshire and Middlesex), his father married the widow of S. R. D. Beresford (Middlesex) in 1929. Middle order right-hand batsman, off break bowler. *Sch* Eton. *Team* Cambridge U (1926–27, blue 1927).
Career batting
14–18–1–456–100*–26.82–1–*ct* 6
Bowling 558–9–62.00–0–0–4/81

His final first-class match was for Free Foresters in 1928.

Cobden, Frank Carroll
Amateur. *b:* 14.10.1849, Marylebone, London. *d:* 7.12.1932, Capel Curig, Caernarvonshire. Brother of H. S. (Gloucestershire). Hard-hitting lower order right-hand batsman, right-arm fast bowler. *Sch* Highgate, Brighton and Harrow. *Team* Cambridge U (1870–72, blue all three years).
Career batting
22–37–4–471–73*–14.27–0–*ct* 9
Bowling 1118–65–17.20–4–1–6/35

His most famous feat on the cricket field occurred in the 1870 University Match. Oxford required only 4 to win with three wickets in hand when Cobden bowled the last over. A single was hit off the first delivery, then Cobden performed the 'hat-trick' to win the game for Cambridge by 2 runs. For many years he ran Radnor CCC. His County cricket was for Shropshire (1868–78) and Herefordshire (1883).

Cobden, Halsted Sayer
Amateur. *b:* 20.11.1845, Marylebone, London. *d:* 5.1.1909, Wincanton, Somerset. Brother of F. C. (Cambridge U). Lower order right-hand batsman, right-hand fast round-arm bowler. *Sch* Repton and Brighton. *Team* Gloucestershire (1872, 4 matches).
Career batting
4–5–2–11–5*–3.66–0–*ct* 0
Bowling 21–1–21.00–0–0–1/21

Cobham, Michael David
Amateur. *b:* 11.5.1930, Boynton, Yorkshire. Middle order right-hand batsman, right-arm medium fast bowler. *Sch* Stowe. *Team* Free Foresters (1953).
Career batting
1–2–0–0–0–0.00–0–*ct* 0
Bowling 54–2–27.00–0–0–2/21

His County cricket was for Berkshire (1948).

Cobham, 8th Viscount
(*see under* Lyttelton, Hon C. G.)

Cobham, 9th Viscount
(formerly Lyttelton, Hon John Cavendish, succeeded to title in 1922)
Amateur. *b:* 23.10.1881, Westminster, London. *d:* 31.7.1949, Bromsgrove, Worcestershire. Son of C. G. (Cambridge U), brother of C. F. (Worcestershire), father of C. J. (Worcestershire), grandson of 4th Lord Lyttelton (Cambridge U), nephew of Alfred (Middlesex), Edward (Middlesex), A. T. (MCC), R. H. (MCC), G. W. S. (Cambridge U). Lower order right-hand batsman, change bowler. *Sch* Eton. *Team* Worcestershire (1924–25, 3 matches).
Career batting
3–6–1–63–30–12.60–0–*ct* 0

He was Conservative MP for Droitwich, 1910–16 and Parliamentary Secretary of State for War, 1939–40. He was President of MCC 1935, and at the time of his death he was Treasurer of MCC (since 1938) and President of Worcestershire (since 1936).

Cobham, 10th Viscount
(*see under* Lyttelton, Hon C. J.)

Cobley, Arthur
Professional. *b:* 5.10.1874, Barwell, Leicestershire. *d:* 21.4.1960, Evington, Leicester. Lower order right-hand batsman, right-arm medium pace bowler. *Team* Leicestershire (1897–1904, 9 matches).
Career batting
9–18–0–139–22–7.72–0–*ct* 4
Bowling 142–1–142.00–0–0–1/9

Cochrane, Alfred Henry John
Amateur. *b:* 26.1.1865, Moka, Mauritius. *d:* 14.12.1948, Elmhurst, Batheaston, Somerset. Lower order right-hand batsman, left-arm medium pace off-

break bowler. *Sch* Repton. *Teams* Derbyshire (1884–86, 4 matches); Oxford U (1885–88, blue 1885, 1886 and 1888)
Career batting
28–48–15–347–61*–10.51–0–*ct* 16
Bowling 1956–103–18.99–4–0–7/66

Injury prevented him from appearing in the University match of 1887. He also played for Northumberland (1891–97). He was a noted writer and apart from books on cricket, contributed many articles to cricket magazines. His brother married the daughter of E. Mathews (Oxford U).

Cochrane, Roy Dundonald
Amateur. *b:* 13.2.1892, Kensington, London. *d:* 5.12.1968, Kensington, London. Middle order batsman. *Sch* Marlborough. *Team* Sussex (1913, 1 match).
Career batting
1–1–0–6–6–6.00–0–*ct* 0
Bowling 37–2–18.50–0–0–2/37

Whilst at Cambridge he appeared in the Seniors' match, but no first-class games.

Cochrane, Sir Stanley Herbert
Amateur. *b:* 19.9.1877, Dublin, Ireland. *d:* 23.10.1949, Bray, Co Dublin, Ireland. Lower order batsman, wicket-keeper. *Team* Woodbrook C and G (1912).
Career batting
1–1–0–5–5–5.00–0–*ct* 1

He was the originator of Woodbrook CC which played on his private ground at Bray.

Cock, David Frederick
Amateur. *b:* 22.10.1914, Great Dunmow, Essex. *d:* 26.9.1992. Middle order right-hand batsman. *Sch* Bishops Stortford. *Team* Essex (1939–46, 14 matches).
Career batting
14–20–2–355–98–19.72–0–*ct* 5

He also played for Hertfordshire (1936) and Cambridgeshire (1951).

Cockbain, Ian
Cricketer. *b:* 19.4.1958, Bootle, Lancashire. Opening or middle order right-hand batsman, slow left-arm bowler. *Team* Lancashire (1979–83, 46 matches).
Career batting
46–78–9–1456–98–21.10–0–*ct* 22
Bowling 14–0

He also played for Cheshire (1984–92).

Cockburn, Sir William Robert Marshall
Amateur. *b:* 26.4.1891, Paisley, Renfrew, Scotland. *d:* 1.9.1957, Winchester, Hampshire. Middle order batsman. *Team* Scotland (1921).
Career batting
1–2–0–11–11–5.50–0–*ct* 0
Bowling 20–1–20.00–0–0–1/20

Cockburn-Hood, Rev J. S. E.
(*see under* Hood, J. S. E.)

Cockerell, Rev Louis Arthur
Amateur. *b:* 20.11.1836, North Weald, Essex. *d:* 4.3.1929, Oxford. Brother-in-law of R. A. Benson (MCC 1845). Lower order batsman, useful bowler. *Sch* Rugby and Radley. *Team* Gentlemen of Kent (1865).
Career batting
1–1–0–8–8–8.00–0–*ct* 0
Bowling 10–0

He appeared for Essex and at the time of his death was the oldest member of the Harlequins.

Cockett, John Ashley
Amateur. *b:* 23.12.1927, Reading Street, Broadstairs, Kent. Middle order right-hand batsman. *Sch* Aldenham. *Team* Cambridge U (1951, blue).
Career batting
8–15–2–311–121–23.92–1–*ct* 3
Bowling 6–0

His County cricket was for Buckinghamshire (1949–62). His final first-class match was for Minor Counties in 1953. He played hockey for England and took part in the 1952 and 1956 Olympic Games.

Cocks, Arthur Denis Bradford
Amateur. *b:* 29.7.1904, Dharmsala, India. *d:* 6.6.1944, La Breche, Ouistreham, Normandy, France. Lower order right-hand batsman, useful bowler. *Sch* Bedford. *Team* Army (1927).
Career batting
2–3–1–30–26*–15.00–0–*ct* 3
Bowling 113–0

He played in trials but no first-class matches at Cambridge U. His County cricket was for Bedfordshire (1924).

Coe, Geoffrey
Cricketer. *b:* 29.3.1943, Earl Shilton, Leicestershire. Lower order right-hand batsman, left-arm medium pace bowler. *Team* Leicestershire (1963, 1 match).
Career batting
1 match, did not bat –*ct* 0
Bowling 77–2–38.50–0–0–1/26

Coe, Samuel
Professional. *b:* 3.6.1873, Earl Shilton, Leicestershire. *d:* 4.11.1955, Earl Shilton, Leicestershire. Middle order left-hand batsman, left-arm slow medium bowler. *Teams* Leicestershire (1896–1923, 448 matches); London County (1900–04).
Career batting
452–775–69–17438–252*–24.69–19–*ct* 176
Bowling 10789–335–32.20–3–0–6/38

He reached 1,000 runs in a season 7 times (best 1,258, av 37.00, in 1914). His only double century was 252* for Leicestershire v Northamptonshire at Leicester in 1914, which was the highest score for the

County. From 1931 until 1949 he was the Leicestershire scorer.

Cogger, Gerald Lyndley
Professional. *b:* 7.9.1933, Uckfield, Sussex. Uncle of K. B. Smith (Sussex). Tail end right-hand batsman, right-arm medium fast bowler. *Team* Sussex (1954–57, 8 matches).
Career batting
8–8–1–12–5–1.71–0–*ct* 5
Bowling 286–7–40.85–0–0–3/20

Coghlan, Timothy Boyle Lake
Amateur. *b:* 29.3.1939, Chelsea, London. Lower order right-hand batsman, right-arm fast bowler. *Sch* Rugby. *Team* Cambridge U (1958–60, blue 1960).
Career batting
20–33–8–257–24–10.28–0–*ct* 12
Bowling 1622–30–54.06–0–0–3/70
His final first-class match was for L. C. Stevens' XI in 1961.

Cohen, Mark Francis
Cricketer. *b:* 27.3.1961, Cork, Ireland. Middle order right-hand batsman. *Team* Ireland (1980–91).
Career batting
9–16–0–282–60–17.62–0–*ct* 4
He was on the Middlesex staff in 1981.

Cohen, Neville
Amateur. *b:* 11.9.1913, Calcutta, India. *d:* 4.10.1987, Oxford. Middle order right-hand batsman, leg break bowler. *Sch* Cheltenham. *Team* Oxford U (1934).
Career batting
3–3–2–27–15*–27.00–0–*ct* 2
Bowling 269–4–67.25–0–0–2/79

Cohen, Rudolph Alexander
Cricketer. *b:* 4.8.1942, Kingston, Jamaica. Lower order right-hand batsman, right-arm fast medium bowler. *Team* Jamaica (1963/4 to 1966/7). *Tour* West Indies to England 1966.
Career batting
37–42–20–160–32*–7.27–0–*ct* 15
Bowling 2576–81 + 1–31.80–1–0–6/71
Visiting England in 1966 in the place of the injured Lester King, Cohen, though not obtaining a place in the Tests, proved fairly effective with 40 wickets, av 24.22.

Cokayne-Frith, Colin
Amateur. *b:* 27.3.1900, St Stephen's, Canterbury, Kent. *d:* 18.5.1940, Assche, Belgium. He was killed in action. Middle order batsman. *Sch* Eton. *Team* Army (1939).
Career batting
1–1–0–54–54–54.00–0–*ct* 1

Colah, Sorabji Hormasji Munchersha
Amateur. *b:* 22.9.1902, Bombay, India. *d:* 11.9.1950, Ahmedabad, India. Brother of N. H. (Parsis). Middle order right-hand batsman, right-arm medium pace bowler, fine close field. *Sch* St Xavier's College, Bombay. *Teams* Parsis (1922/3 to 1939/40); Bombay (1926/7 to 1933/4); Western India (1934/5 to 1935/6); Nawanagar (1936/7 to 1941/2). *Tour* India to England 1932. *Tests* India (1932 to 1933/4, 2 matches).
Career batting
75–132–9–3578–185*–29.08–6–*ct* 51
Bowling 279–6–46.50–0–0–2/14
Test batting
2–4–0–69–31–17.25–0–*ct* 2
He had a moderate tour to England in 1932 – his fielding being perhaps his major asset.

Colbeck, Leonard George
Amateur. *b:* 1.1.1884, Harrow, Middlesex. *d:* 3.1.1918. He died off the Cape of Good Hope in HMS *Ormonde*. Middle order right-hand batsman. *Sch* Marlborough. *Teams* Cambridge U (1905–06, blue both years); Middlesex (1906–08, 10 matches); Europeans (1913/14).
Career batting
32–60–5–1368–175*–24.87–3–*ct* 16
His great innings was for Cambridge in the University match of 1905 when he hit 107 and added 143 for the 7th wicket after 6 batsmen had gone for 77. His last first-class match in England was for MCC in 1911. He also won a blue for hockey.

Colchin, Robert
Professional. *c:* 12.11.1713, Chailey, Sussex. *d:* believed to be April 1750, Bromley, Kent.
Known as 'Long Robin' he was one of the best known cricketers of the 1740s; his name certainly occurs more frequently than any other in the brief cricket notices of the period. He was of rather humble origins, but apparently became relatively wealthy and it is suggested that this wealth may have come from smuggling – cricket matches in Bromley in the 1740s were played as cover for smugglers.

Coldham, John Maurice
Amateur. *b:* 17.1.1901, Cheadle, Cheshire. *d:* 25.7.1986, Woking, Surrey. Middle order right-hand batsman. *Sch* Repton. *Team* Oxford U (1925).
Career batting
2–4–0–73–40–18.25–0–*ct* 0
His first-class debut was for the Minor Counties in 1924 and his County cricket was for Norfolk (1924–32).

Coldwell, Leonard John
Professional. *b:* 10.1.1933, Newton Abbot, Devon. Tail end right-hand batsman, right-arm fast medium bowler. *Team* Worcestershire (1955–69, 296 matches). *Tours* MCC to Australia and New Zealand 1962/3; Worcestershire World Tour (Rhodesia first-class) 1964/5, to Jamaica 1965/6. *Tests* England (1962–64, 7 matches).

Coldwell, William Rodney

Career batting
310–347–100–1474–37–5.96–0–*ct* 90
Bowling 22791–1076–21.18–60–7–8/38
Test batting
7–7–5–9–6*–4.50–0–*ct* 1
Bowling 610–22–27.72–1–0–6/85

He took 100 wickets in a season twice (best 152, av 17.90, in 1962). He also played for Devon (1953–54).

Coldwell, William Rodney
Professional. *b:* 4.6.1932, Petersfield, Hampshire. Middle order right-hand batsman, off break bowler. *Team* MCC (1954–55).
Career batting
2–4–0–15–8–3.75–0–*ct* 0

Cole, A.
Professional. Middle/lower order batsman, bowler. *Team* Middlesex (1879, 2 matches).
Career batting
3–6–0–45–21–7.50–0–*ct* 0
Bowling 51–3–17.00–0–0–3/29

He also played for Essex (pre first-class, 1880).

Cole, Colin Gibson
Professional. *b:* 7.7.1916, Sittingbourne, Kent. Lower order right-hand batsman, right-arm fast medium bowler. *Team* Kent (1935–38, 27 matches).
Career batting
27–43–14–228–23*–7.86–0–*ct* 15
Bowling 2110–61–34.59–2–0–6/62

Cole, Derek Henry
Amateur. *b:* 9.3.1925, Dawlish, Devon. Opening right-hand batsman, right-arm fast medium and off-break bowler. *Team* Minor Counties (1959–67).
Career batting
3–4–0–86–36–21.50–0–*ct* 1
Bowling 82–2–41.00–0–0–1/11

His County cricket was for Devon (1947–70). He made his first-class debut for South v North in 1956.

Cole, Major-General Eric Stuart
Amateur. *b:* 10.2.1906, Imtarfa, Malta. *d:* 19.12.1992. Middle or lower order right-hand batsman, right-arm medium pace bowler. *Sch* Dover College. *Team* Kent (1938, 3 matches).
Career batting
10–15–0–147–36–9.80–0–*ct* 13
Bowling 912–25–36.48–0–0–4/78

His first-class debut was for Free Foresters in 1931 and he also played regularly for the Army.

Cole, Frederick Livsey
Amateur. *b:* 4.10.1852, Patricroft, Lancashire. *d:* 1.7.1941, Sheffield, Yorkshire. Middle order right-hand batsman, right-arm medium pace bowler. *Team* Gloucestershire (1879–90, 15 matches).
Career batting
15–25–2–188–36–8.17–0–*ct* 8–*st* 1
Bowling 41–0

He also played for Somerset (pre first-class, 1886–88).

Cole, Canon George Lamont
Amateur. *b:* 5.9.1885, St Leonard's-on-Sea, Sussex. *d:* 14.10.1964, Boughton Street, Faversham, Kent. Middle order right-hand batsman. *Sch* Sherborne. *Teams* Cambridge U (1908); Hampshire (1909–11, 6 matches).
Career batting
7–12–1–122–33–11.09–0–*ct* 4

Cole, George Thomas
(known as Thomas George Cole)
Amateur. *b:* 16.2.1846, Poplar, London. *d:* 6.12.1900, Islington, London. Middle order right-hand batsman, right-hand fast round-arm bowler. *Team* Surrey Club (1873).
Career batting
2–4–0–55–21–13.75–0–*ct* 0

Cole, John Richard
Amateur. *b:* 15.2.1907, Clapham, London. Opening right-hand batsman. *Sch* Emanuel. *Team* Army (1930–32).
Career batting
4–8–0–112–63–14.00–0–*ct* 5

Cole, Terence George Owen
Amateur. *b:* 14.11.1877, Llanrhaiadr, Denbighshire. *d:* 15.12.1944, Stoke Court, near Taunton, Somerset. Opening or middle order right-hand batsman, slow left-arm bowler. *Sch* Harrow. *Teams* Cambridge U (1898); Lancashire (1904, 1 match); Derbyshire (1913, 6 matches); Somerset (1922, 1 match). *Tour* Brackley to West Indies 1904/5.
Career batting
20–35–3–499–68–15.59–0–*ct* 9
Bowling 17–0

He also played for Denbighshire (1905).

Colebrooke, Rev Edward Lotherington
Amateur. *b:* 29.10.1858, Southborough, Kent. *d:* 10.8.1939, Canterbury, Kent. Uncle of F. V. Hutchings (Kent), K. L. Hutchings (Kent) and W. E. C. Hutchings (Kent and Worcestershire). Opening or middle order right-hand batsman. *Sch* Charterhouse. *Teams* Oxford U (1880, blue); Gentlemen of Kent (1880).
Career batting
7–14–2–161–34*–13.41–0–*ct* 6

He made his first-class debut for Gentlemen of England in 1879.

Colegrave, Henry Manby
Amateur. *b:* 3.6.1872, Paddington, London. *d:* 21.4.1955, Brighton, Sussex. Uncle of W. F. Q. Shuldham (Somerset). Middle order right-hand batsman, right-arm fast bowler. *Sch* Oscott College. *Team* London County (1901).

Career batting
2–2–1–36–36*–36.00–0–*ct* 2

Coleman, Charles Alfred Richard
Professional. *b:* 7.7.1906, Gumley, Leicestershire. *d:* 14.6.1978, Market Harborough, Leicestershire. Hard-hitting lower order batsman, right-arm fast medium bowler. *Team* Leicestershire (1926–35, 114 matches).
Career batting
114–170–10–2403–114–15.01–1–*ct* 60
Bowling 3576–100–35.76–1–0–5/30
He was a first-class umpire (1946–57), standing in two Test matches (1947).

Coleman, Edward Charles
Amateur. *b:* 5.9.1891, Southend, Essex. *d:* 2.4.1917, Salonica, Greece. He was killed in action. Lower order left-hand batsman, wicket-keeper. *Sch* Dulwich. *Team* Essex (1912, 2 matches).
Career batting
3–5–1–14–6–3.50–0–*ct* 2–*st* 1
He did not appear in a first-class match whilst at Cambridge. His first-class debut was for Combined Oxford and Cambridge Universities in 1911.

Coleman, William Ezra
Professional. *b:* 5.12.1878, Hitchin, Hertfordshire. *d:* 27.1.1960, Napsbury, St Albans, Hertfordshire. Middle/lower order right-hand batsman, right-arm fast medium bowler. *Team* MCC (1902–09).
Career batting
10–18–2–180–37–11.25–0–*ct* 4
Bowling 483–23–21.00–1–0–6/30
His County cricket was for Hertfordshire (1896–1914).

Coles, George Edward
Amateur. *b:* 11.2.1851, Ratnagiri, India. *d:* 21.6.1903, Naini Tal, India. Middle order right-hand batsman, right-hand fast round-arm bowler. *Team* Kent (1873, 2 matches).
Career batting
2–4–0–39–19–9.75–0–*ct* 0
Bowling 98–11–8.90–1–1–6/23

Coles, Percival
Amateur. *b:* 2.5.1865, Eastbourne, Sussex. *d:* 24.2.1920, Bohemia, St Leonard's-on-Sea, Sussex. Opening right-hand batsman, occasional right-arm fast medium bowler, good field. *Sch* Rugby. *Teams* Sussex (1885, 4 matches); Oxford U (1885–86).
Career batting
10–20–2–174–45–9.66–0–*ct* 3
He played in the Oxford Rugby XV for three years, being captain in 1886.

Coles, Walter Neill
Amateur. *b:* 11.2.1928, Northwood, Middlesex. Middle order right-hand batsman. *Sch* Eton. *Team* Cambridge U (1949).
Career batting
2–3–0–26–14–8.66–0–*ct*

Colhoun, Osmund David
Amateur. *b:* 6.6.1938, Sion Mills, Co Tyrone, Ireland. Cousin of A. J. Finlay (Ireland). Tail end right-hand batsman, wicket-keeper. *Team* Ireland (1959–79).
Career batting
28–35–19–74–9*–4.62–0–*ct* 44–*st* 2

Colledge, Fred
Amateur. *b:* 7.5.1915, Moorpark, Renfrew, Scotland. *d:* 6.10.1985, Paisley, Renfrewshire, Scotland. Tail end right-hand batsman, right-arm fast medium bowler. *Team* Scotland (1949–52).
Career batting
4–4–2–21–12*–10.50–0–*ct* 2
Bowling 267–6–44.50–0–0–2/50

Collett, Gilbert Faraday
Amateur. *b:* 18.7.1879, Wynstone Place, near Gloucester. *d:* 25.2.1945, Huddlecote, Barnwood, near Gloucester. Middle order right-hand batsman, change bowler, good slip field. *Sch* Cheltenham. *Team* Gloucestershire (1900–14, 9 matches).
Career batting
9–16–0–155–41–9.68–0–*ct* 8
Bowling 144–4–36.00–0–0–2/37
He played no first-class matches whilst at Cambridge U, but did win a blue for rugby, and toured South Africa with the British team in 1903.

Collett, William Eustace
Professional. *b:* 23.9.1839, Lambeth, London. *d:* 1.5.1904, Lambeth, London. Middle order right-hand batsman, right-hand fast round-arm bowler. *Team* Surrey (1869–74, 4 matches).
Career batting
4–8–0–44–19–5.50–0–*ct* 1

Colley, David John
Cricketer. *b:* 15.3.1947, Mosman, Sydney, New South Wales, Australia. Lower order right-hand batsman, right-arm fast medium bowler. *Team* New South Wales (1969/70 to 1977/8, 71 matches). *Tour* Australia to England 1972. *Tests* Australia (1972, 3 matches).
Career batting
87–123–23–2374–101–23.74–1–*ct* 44
Bowling 7459–236–31.60–8–0–6/30
Test batting
3–4–0–84–54–21.00–0–*ct* 1
Bowling 312–6–52.00–0–0–3/83
Although he had a place in three of the five Tests on the 1972 tour to England, his performance on the visit was a modest one, his 33 first-class wickets costing 28.66 runs each.

Collier, Christopher George Arthur
Professional. *b:* 23.8.1886, Banff, Scotland. *d:* 25.8.1916, near Mametz, France. He was killed in

action. Middle order right-hand batsman, slow right-arm bowler. *Team* Worcestershire (1910–14, 52 matches).
Career batting
53–87–8–1021–72–12.92–0–*ct* 13
Bowling 369–10–36.90–0–0–3/28

Collier, Robert
(succeeded as 2nd Baron Monkswell in 1886)
Amateur. *b:* 26.3.1845, Chelsea, London. *d:* 22.12.1909, Chelsea, London. Middle order batsman. *Sch* Eton. *Team* Cambridgeshire (1866–67, 3 matches).
Career batting
3–6–0–33–14–5.50–0–*ct* 0
Bowling 15–0
He was Under Secretary for War in 1895.

Collin, Spencer Compton
Amateur. *b:* 1.8.1852, Saffron Walden, Essex. *d:* 25.11.1923, Brighton, Sussex. Middle order batsman, excellent cover field. *Sch* Winchester. *Team* An All England Eleven (1873).
Career batting
1–2–0–4–4–2.00–0–*ct* 0
Whilst at Cambridge he did not appear in any first-class matches. His County cricket was for Essex (pre first-class, 1881).

Collin, Thomas
Professional, amateur after 1937. *b:* 7.4.1911, South Moor, Co Durham. Middle order left-hand batsman, slow left-arm bowler. *Team* Warwickshire (1933–36, 52 matches).
Career batting
52–75–7–1399–105*–20.57–1–*ct* 35
Bowling 1302–26–50.07–0–0–3/45
He also played for Durham (pre first-class, 1938–46).

Collinge, John Gregory
Cricketer. *b:* 10.5.1939, Mahara, Hastings, Hawke's Bay, New Zealand. Middle order right-hand batsman, off break bowler. *Team* Oxford U (1964).
Career batting
2–3–0–18–9–6.00–0–*ct* 1

Collinge, Rex Alan
Amateur. *b:* 23.4.1935, Nottingham. Lower order right-hand batsman, right-arm fast medium bowler. *Sch* Bedford. *Team* Combined Services (1962).
Career batting
2–4–0–101–41–25.25–0–*ct* 2
Bowling 186–11–16.90–1–0–6/52
His County cricket was for Suffolk (1955–62).

Collinge, Richard Owen
Cricketer. *b:* 2.4.1946, Wellington, New Zealand. Lower order right-hand batsman, left-arm medium fast bowler. *Teams* Central Districts (1963/4 to 1969/70); Wellington (1967/8 to 1974/5); Northern Districts (1975/6 to 1977/8). *Tours* New Zealand to England 1965, 1969, 1973, 1975 (World Cup), 1978, to Australia 1967/8, 1969/70, 1970/1, 1974/5 (not first-class), to India and Pakistan 1964/5, 1976/7. *Tests* New Zealand (1964/5 to 1978, 35 matches).
Career batting
163–178–50–1848–68*–14.43–0–*ct* 57
Bowling 12793–524–24.41–22–4–8/64
Test batting
35–50–13–533–68*–14.40–0–*ct* 10
Bowling 3393–116–29.25–3–0–6/63
Of his four tours to England, his 1973 visit was easily the most successful, in that he headed both first-class and Test bowling averages with 51 wickets, av 21.92, and 12 wickets, av 24.08, respectively.

Collings, Algernon William
Amateur. *b:* 4.9.1853, Guernsey. *d:* 14.5.1945, Burghfield Common, Berkshire. Middle order batsman, good field. *Sch* Winchester. *Team* Gloucestershire (1874, 1 match).
Career batting
1–1–0–1–1–1.00–0–*ct* 0

Collings, Edward Peter
Amateur. *b:* 30.1.1892, Lichfield, Staffordshire. *d:* 14.9.1968, Combe Down, Somerset. Lower order right-hand batsman, right-arm bowler. *Sch* King's, Canterbury. *Team* Somerset (1921–25, 4 matches).
Career batting
4–8–1–42–16–6.00–0–*ct* 2
Bowling 156–2–78.00–0–0–2/125

Collingwood, Boris Esmond
Amateur. *b:* 8.1.1920, Hither Green, London. *d:* 18.11.1968, Storrington, Sussex. Middle order right-hand batsman, good outfield. *Sch* Dulwich. *Teams* Cambridge U (1948); Somerset (1953, 1 match).
Career batting
2–3–0–21–15–7.00–0–*ct* 2

Collins, Arthur
Amateur. *b:* 7.9.1871, East Grinstead, Sussex. *d:* 22.7.1945, Hadlow Down, Sussex. Middle or lower order right-hand batsman, slow left-arm bowler. *Team* Sussex (1895–1902, 53 matches).
Career batting
53–89–18–1812–102–25.52–1–*ct* 29
Bowling 1656–36–46.00–1–0–5/61

Collins, Bernard Abdy
Amateur. *b:* 17.2.1880, Saxmundham, Suffolk. *d:* 22.10.1951, Bedford. Lower order right-hand batsman, wicket-keeper. *Sch* Malvern. *Team* Oxford U (1901).
Career batting
1–2–1–83–83*–83.00–0–*ct* 1
His County cricket was for Suffolk (1904). He was Director-General of Commerce and Industry in

Hyderabad State. His score of 83* is the highest ever made by a number 11 batsman on his debut.

Collins, Brian George
Cricketer. *b:* 11.8.1941, Enfield, Middlesex. Lower order right-hand batsman, right-arm fast medium bowler. *Team* Minor Counties (1979). *Tour* Minor Counties to Kenya 1977/8 (not first-class).
Career batting
1 match, did not bat–*ct* 0
Bowling 110–3–36.66–0–0–3/83
His County cricket was for Hertfordshire (1965–87).

Collins, Christopher
Professional. *b:* 14.10.1859, Cobham, Kent. *d:* 11.8.1919, Gravesend, Kent. Son of Benjamin (Kent 1856), brother of George (Kent), father of G. C. (Kent). Lower order right-hand batsman, right-arm fast medium bowler. *Team* Kent (1881–85, 8 matches).
Career batting
8–13–2–97–41–8.81–0–*ct* 5
Bowling 305–16–19.06–0–0–4/9
Owing to his bowling action being suspect, his County career was of short duration.

Collins, Dr David Charles
Amateur. *b:* 1.10.1887, Wellington, New Zealand. *d:* 2.1.1967, Tauranga, New Zealand. Son of W. E. (Wellington), nephew of J. U. (Canterbury). Opening right-hand batsman, right-arm medium pace bowler. *Sch* Wellington College, New Zealand. *Teams* Cambridge U (1908–11, blue 1910–11); Wellington (1905/6 to 1926/7).
Career batting
53–96–8–2604–172–29.59–6–*ct* 33–*st* 1
Bowling 870–32–27.18–0–0–4/10
He returned to New Zealand after coming down from Cambridge. His final first-class match in England was for Free Foresters in 1912. He rowed in the 1912 Boat Race which was re-rowed when both crews sank in the first race.

Collins, Frank
Professional. *b:* 3.2.1903, Eastbourne, Sussex. *d:* 24.7.1988, Eastbourne, Sussex. Tail end right-hand batsman, right-arm medium pace bowler. *Team* Sussex (1923, 1 match).
Career batting
1–2–0–27–27–13.50–0–*ct* 0
Bowling 33–0

Collins, Geoffrey Albert Kirwan
Amateur. *b:* 16.5.1909, Hove, Sussex. *d:* 7.8.1968, Hove, Sussex. Opening right-hand batsman. *Sch* Lancing. *Team* Sussex (1928–34, 49 matches).
Career batting
50–72–12–1140–90–19.00–0–*ct* 17
He was a useful soccer player, appearing for The Casuals. Demands of business restricted his County cricket.

Collins, Geoffrey Allan
Professional. *b:* 10.6.1918, Brighton, Sussex. Opening right-hand batsman. *Team* Sussex (1939, 1 match).
Career batting
1–2–0–19–17–9.50–0–*ct* 1
He also played for Wiltshire.

Collins, George
Professional. *b:* 29.10.1851, Cobham, Kent. *d:* 11.3.1905, Tunbridge Wells, Kent. Son of Benjamin (Kent 1856), brother of Christopher (Kent), uncle of G. C. (Kent). Lower order right-hand batsman, right-hand fast round-arm bowler. *Team* Kent (1874–82, 13 matches).
Career batting
14–22–4–183–36–10.16–0–*ct* 5
Bowling 68–3–22.66–0–0–2/15
His first-class debut was for W. G. Grace's XI in 1873.

Collins, George Christopher
Professional. *b:* 21.9.1889, Gravesend, Kent. *d:* 23.1.1949, Rochester, Kent. Son of Christopher (Kent), nephew of George (Kent), grandson of Benjamin (Kent 1856). Middle or lower order left-hand batsman, right-arm fast-medium bowler. *Team* Kent (1911–28, 212 matches). *Tour* MCC to West Indies 1925/6.
Career batting
218–321–37–6280–110–22.11–4–*ct* 81–*st* 1
Bowling 9065–379–23.91–24–3–10/65
In 1923 he hit 1,036 runs, av 22.04. His best bowling was 10/65 for Kent v Nottinghamshire at Dover in 1922.

Collins, Gordon Thomas
Professional. *b:* 26.12.1914, Sunbury-on-Thames, Middlesex. *d:* 3.3.1986, Manchester, Lancashire. Opening right-hand batsman, wicket-keeper. *Team* Northamptonshire (1938, 3 matches).
Career batting
3–5–0–44–17–8.80–0–*ct* 0
He also played for Cambridgeshire (1947–49).

Collins, Herbert Leslie
Amateur. *b:* 21.1.1889, Darlinghurst, Sydney, New South Wales, Australia. *d:* 28.5.1959, Little Bay, Sydney, New South Wales, Australia. Brother of R. S. (Civil Service). Sound opening right-hand batsman, slow left-arm bowler. *Team* New South Wales (1909/10 to 1925/6, 52 matches). *Tours* Australia to England 1921, 1926, to South Africa 1921/2, to New Zealand 1913/4, to North America 1913; AIF to England 1919, to South Africa 1919/20. *Tests* Australia (1920/1 to 1926, 19 matches).

Collins, Ian Glen

Career batting
168–258–10–9924–282–40.01–32–*ct* 115
Bowling 3871–181–21.38–8–2–8/31
Test batting
19–31–1–1352–203–45.06–4–*ct* 13
Bowling 252–4–63.00–0–0–2/47

Captaining the AIF in England in 1919, he was most successful, performing the 'double' with 1,615 runs, av 38.45, and 106 wickets, av 16.55. On his two official tours, however, he was beset by injury and neither time reached 1,000 runs in first-class matches, whilst his bowling was of little account. He captained Australia on the 1926 tour, and in all captained Australia in 11 Tests. Of his three double centuries, two were made in South Africa, including 203 in the Johannesburg Test of 1921/2, and the other, his highest score, was 282 for New South Wales v Tasmania at Hobart in 1912/3.

Collins, Ian Glen
Amateur. *b:* 23.4.1903, Glasgow, Scotland. *d:* 20.3.1975, Bearsden, Dunbartonshire, Scotland. Opening or middle order right-hand batsman, change bowler. *Sch* Harrow. *Teams* Oxford U (1925); Scotland (1927).
Career batting
2–4–0–69–34–17.25–0–*ct* 1

A broken leg prevented him from playing cricket in his first year at Oxford. He gained half-blues for golf and lawn tennis and represented Great Britain in the Davis Cup.

Collins, Lionel Peter
Amateur. *b:* 27.11.1878, Reading, Berkshire. *d:* 28.9.1957, Fleet, Hampshire. Father-in-law of L. E. Hunt (Cambridge U), brother-in-law of S. R. Olivier (Hampshire). Middle order right-hand batsman. *Sch* Marlborough. *Team* Oxford U (1899, blue). *Tour* MCC to North America 1907.
Career batting
19–35–3–858–102*–26.81–1–*ct* 5

His County cricket was for Berkshire (1898–1913). For several years commencing 1901 he was stationed in India. His final first-class match was for Free Foresters in 1913. He also won a blue for hockey.

Collins, R. S.
Amateur. *b:* 1890, Darlinghurst, Sydney, New South Wales, Australia. Brother of H. L. (Australia). Lower order batsman, bowler. *Team* Civil Service (1927).
Career batting
1–2–0–11–11–5.50–0–*ct* 1
Bowling 47–2–23.50–0–0–2/47

Collins, Ross Phillip
Cricketer. *b:* 9.12.1945, Paddington, Sydney, New South Wales, Australia. Middle order right-hand batsman, right-arm medium pace bowler. *Teams* New South Wales (1967/8 to 1975/6, 22 matches); International Cavaliers (1969).
Career batting
23–43–3–1061–88*–26.52–0–*ct* 20
Bowling 910–31–29.35–1–0–5/54

Collins, Roy
Professional. *b:* 10.3.1934, Clayton, Manchester, Lancashire. Brother-in-law of J. Cumbes (Lancashire). Middle/lower order right-hand batsman, off break bowler, good slip field. *Team* Lancashire (1954–62, 119 matches).
Career batting
120–183–18–3436–107*–20.82–2–*ct* 80
Bowling 4831–159–30.38–4–0–6/63

He also played for Cheshire (1963–73).

Collins, Thomas Hugh
Professional. *b:* 4.3.1895, Nottingham. *d:* 19.5.1964, Edwalton, Nottinghamshire. Lower order left-hand batsman, left-arm slow medium bowler. *Teams* Nottinghamshire (1921, 2 matches); Hampshire (1935, 2 matches).
Career batting
4–6–0–32–13–5.33–0–*ct* 2
Bowling 80–4–20.00–0–0–1/17

Collins, William Edmund Wood
Amateur. *b:* 16.6.1848, Cheriton, Glamorgan. *d:* 7.1.1932, Summerhill, Heacham, Norfolk. Hard-hitting lower order right-hand batsman, left-arm fast bowler. *Sch* Radley. *Team* Gentlemen (1884).
Career batting
7–10–2–157–56*–19.62–0–*ct* 3
Bowling 448–19–23.57–3–0–6/35

Although considered one of the best amateur cricketers of his day, he rarely appeared in first-class matches, confining himself mainly to Free Foresters and Country House games, though he played occasionally for Shropshire, Northamptonshire (1867) and Hertfordshire (1875). His final first-class match was for H. Philipson's XI in 1891. He was a noted author, his subjects including cricket.

Collins, William Ronald
Amateur. *b:* 29.1.1868, Hackney, London. *d:* 10.12.1942, Clapton, Thrapston, Northamptonshire. Middle order right-hand batsman, right-arm fast bowler. *Sch* Wellington, *Team* Middlesex (1892, 1 match).
Career batting
1–2–0–0–0–0.00–0–*ct* 0

Collinson, John
Amateur. *b:* 2.10.1911, Sotterley, Suffolk. *d:* 29.8.1979, Hove, Sussex. Middle order right-hand batsman, off break bowler. *Sch* St John's, Leatherhead. *Teams* Middlesex (1939, 2 matches); Worcestershire (1946, 1 match).
Career batting
3–6–0–109–34–18.16–0–*ct* 1

Collinson, Robert Whiteley
Amateur. *b:* 6.11.1875, Halifax, Yorkshire. *d:* 26.12.1963, Thorpe St Andrew, Norwich, Norfolk. Middle order right-hand batsman. *Team* Yorkshire (1897, 2 matches).
Career batting
2–3–0–58–34–19.33–0–*ct* 0
He also played for Norfolk (1910–12).

Collishaw, William Frederick
Professional. *b:* 2.10.1860, Hickling, Nottinghamshire. *d:* 31.1.1936, Saltley, Birmingham. Middle order right-hand batsman, right-arm medium pace bowler. *Team* An England XI (1886).
Career batting
1–1–0–0–0–0.00–0–*ct* 0
His County cricket was for Warwickshire (pre first-class, 1884–92). He was a first-class umpire (1894–97).

Collyer, Francis Edward
Cricketer. *b:* 4.2.1947, Brentford, Middlesex. Lower order right-hand batsman, wicket-keeper. *Team* Cambridge U (1967–69).
Career batting
5–8–1–96–46–13.71–0–*ct* 11–*st* 1
His County cricket was for Hertfordshire (1965–87), playing first-class matches for Minor Counties between 1973 and 1979.

Collyer, William James
Amateur. *b:* 1.6.1841, Halebourne, Chobham, Surrey. *d:* 1.9.1908, Bruges, Belgium. Opening or middle order right-hand batsman, good long-stop. *Sch* Windlesham House School. *Team* Surrey (1866–69, 18 matches).
Career batting
18–34–3–386–69–12.45–0–*ct* 6
He did not appear in any first-class matches whilst at Oxford U. He captained Surrey in 1867.

Collyer, William Robert
Amateur. *b:* 11.1.1842, Camberwell, London. *d:* 27.10.1928, Hackford-by-Reepham, Norfolk. Middle order right-hand batsman. *Sch* Rugby. *Team* Cambridge U (1864).
Career batting
1–2–0–2–2–1.00–0–*ct* 2
His County cricket was for Norfolk (1868). From 1903 until 1906 he was Attorney-General of the Straits Settlements.

Colman, Geoffrey Russell Rees
Amateur. *b:* 14.3.1892, Bracondale, Norwich, Norfolk. *d:* 18.3.1935, Framingham, Norwich, Norfolk. Cousin of Stanley (Surrey), brother-in-law of C. F. Lyttleton (Worcestershire) and D. G. Wigan (Oxford U). Attractive opening right-hand batsman, occasional slow bowler, brilliant cover point. *Sch* Eton. *Team* Oxford U (1912–14, blue 1913–14). *Tour* Incogniti to North America 1913 (not first-class).
Career batting
23–41–2–958–127–24.56–1–*ct* 17
Bowling 14–1–14.00–0–0–1/14
His County cricket was for Norfolk (1911–30). He was obliged to retire due to ill-health. His final first-class match was for Minor Counties in 1924.

Colman, Stanley
Amateur. *b:* 6.1.1862, Clapham Common, London. *d:* 27.2.1942, Walton-on-the-Hill, Surrey. Cousin of G. R. R. (Oxford U). Opening or middle order right-hand batsman. *Team* Surrey (1882, 6 matches).
Career batting
6–10–0–81–63–8.10–0–*ct* 2
Captain of the South London club, Wanderers CC, for over 50 years, he was regarded as the 'W. G. Grace' of club cricket.

Colquhoun, James Clifton
Amateur. *b:* 1.12.1893, Scotland. *d:* 9.2.1977, City of London. Opening right-hand batsman, wicket-keeper. *Sch* Glenalmond. *Team* G. J. V. Weigall's XI (1914).
Career batting
1–2–0–30–15–15.00–0–*ct* 0
His County cricket was for Cornwall (1930). He played in trial matches at Cambridge U, but not in first-class games.

Comber, George
Professional. *b:* 12.10.1856, Redhill, Surrey. *d:* 18.10.1929, Redhill, Surrey. Middle/lower order right-hand batsman, wicket-keeper. *Team* Surrey (1880–85, 6 matches).
Career batting
6–11–2–44–19–4.88–0–*ct* 2–*st* 1

Comber, John Howard
Professional. *b:* 8.1.1861, Brighton, Sussex. Middle/lower order batsman, change bowler. *Team* Sussex (1885, 3 matches).
Career batting
3–6–1–28–8–5.60–0–*ct* 0
Bowling 20–0
He emigrated to Philadelphia in 1886.

Comber, Joseph Thomas Henry
Amateur. *b:* 26.2.1911. *d:* 3.5.1976, Chelsea, London. Lower order right-hand batsman, wicket-keeper. *Sch* Marlborough. *Team* Cambridge U (1931–33, blue all three years).
Career batting
57–78–18–833–62–13.88–*ct* 84–*st* 42
His County cricket was for Cambridgeshire (1931). His final first-class match was for MCC in 1948. He was the adopted son of H. G. Comber who was at various times the Treasurer of the Cambridge University rugby, hockey and cricket clubs.

Commaille, John McIllwaine Moore
Amateur. *b:* 21.2.1883, Cape Town, South Africa. *d:* 28.7.1956, Sea Point, Cape Town, South Africa. Opening right-hand batsman. *Teams* Western Province (1905/6 to 1923/4); Orange Free State (1924/5 to 1928/9); Griqualand West (1929/30 to 1930/1). *Tours* South Africa to Australia 1910/11, to England 1924. *Tests* South Africa (1909/10 to 1927/8, 12 matches).
Career batting
96–169–13–5026–186–32.21–9–*ct* 32
Bowling 33–1–33.00–0–0–1/15
Test batting
12–22–1–355–47–16.90–0–*ct* 1

Over 40 when he came to England as vice-captain of the 1924 team, he hit 1,170 runs, av 26.00, and whilst doing nothing extraordinary achieved as much as was expected of him. He also played soccer for South Africa, and was a well-known singer.

Compton, Denis Charles Scott, CBE
Professional, changed to amateur after 1957 season. *b:* 23.5.1918, Hendon, Middlesex. Brother of L. H. (Middlesex). Brilliant middle order right-hand batsman, slow left-arm bowler. *Teams* Middlesex (1936–58, 296 matches); Holkar (1944/5); Europeans (1944/5 to 1945/6). *Tours* MCC to Australia and New Zealand 1946/7, 1950/1, 1954/5, to South Africa 1948/9, 1956/7, to West Indies 1953/4; Commonwealth to South Africa 1959/60; Cavaliers to Jamaica 1963/4. *Tests* England (1937 to 1956/7, 78 matches).
Career batting
515–839–88–38942–300–51.85–123–*ct* 416
Bowling 20074–622–32.27–19–3–7/36
Test batting
78–131–15–5807–278–50.06–17–*ct* 49
Bowling 1410–25–56.40–1–0–5/70

Of his many achievements on the cricket field all are dwarfed by Compton's incredible success in 1947. Scoring 3,816 runs at an average of 90.85 with 18 centuries, he created new records both for the most runs in first-class cricket in a season and most centuries. The South African tourists, who visited England that summer, suffered greatly from his appetite, conceding 6 centuries to him and in the Tests 753 runs at an average of 94.12. His success continued, though slightly reduced, through 1948 and the tour to South Africa in 1948/9, when he hit his highest innings of 300 for MCC v North-East Transvaal – this innings, which took 181 minutes, was the fastest triple hundred ever made in a first-class match. In both 1948 and 1949, Compton reached 2,000 runs in a season, as he had done in 1939 and 1946, but his run glut was halted by an old soccer injury, which meant that despite several operations he was never as fluent after 1949 as he had been previously. In all he exceeded 1,000 runs in a season 14 times in England and three more times overseas.

He scored nine double hundreds, his highest in England being 278 for England v Pakistan at Trent Bridge in 1954. Owing to his football commitments he did not tour overseas with MCC until 1946/7, but he made many runs whilst serving in India during the Second World War. He played outside left for Arsenal, gaining an FA Cup winner's medal in 1950, and, in wartime internationals, for England.

He captained Middlesex jointly with W. J. Edrich in 1951 and 1952 and was vice-captain of MCC on the 1950/1 tour to Australia. His final first-class match was for MCC in 1964. He was President of Middlesex 1991–92.

Compton, Edward Denison
Amateur. *b:* 11.4.1872, Frome, Somerset. *d:* 11.10.1940, Rye, Sussex. Lower order right-hand batsman, wicket-keeper. *Sch* Lancing. *Teams* Somerset (1894–1907, 4 matches); Oxford U (1896).
Career batting
6–11–4–51–22*–7.28–0–*ct* 4–*st* 1

He also played for Oxfordshire (1897–1902). He won a blue for soccer.

Compton, Leslie Harry
Professional. *b:* 12.9.1912, Woodford, Essex. *d:* 27.12.1984, Hendon, Middlesex. Brother of D. C. S. (Middlesex). Lower order right-hand batsman, wicket-keeper, right-arm medium pace bowler. *Team* Middlesex (1938–56, 272 matches).
Career batting
274–393–46–5814–107–16.75–1–*ct* 468–*st* 131
Bowling 569–12–47.41–0–0–2/21

A noted soccer player, he was centre-half for Arsenal, winning an FA Cup winners medal in 1950, and in 1950/1 gained two caps for England, being at 38 the oldest player to make his debut for England.

Compton-Burnett, A.
(*see under* Burnett, A. C.)

Compton-Burnett, Richard James
Cricketer. *b:* 1.7.1961, Windsor, Berkshire. Son of A. C. Burnett (Glamorgan). Middle order right-hand batsman. *Sch* Eton. *Team* Cambridge U (1981).
Career batting
1–2–0–23–18–11.50–0–*ct* 0

Comyn, Andrew Daniel
Amateur. *b:* 23.9.1872, Ballinderry, Kilconnell, Co Galway, Ireland. *d:* 23.5.1949, Dublin, Ireland. Uncle of A. W. B. Kelly (Ireland) and G. N. B. Kelly (Ireland), brother-in-law of G. W. F. B. Kelly (Ireland). Opening right-hand batsman, leg break bowler. *Teams* Dublin University (1895); Ireland (1902).
Career batting
8–16–0–290–54–18.12–0–*ct* 1
Bowling 102–0

Conan Doyle, Dr Sir Arthur Ignatius
Amateur. *b:* 22.5.1859, Edinburgh, Scotland. *d:* 7.7.1930, Crowborough, Sussex. Lower order right-hand batsman, slow bowler. *Sch* Stonyhurst. *Team*

MCC (1900–07).
Career batting
10–18–6–231–43–19.25–0–*ct* 1
Bowling 50–1–50.00–0–0–1/4

He was a well-known author, the creator of Sherlock Holmes. His only victim in first-class cricket was W. G. Grace and he wrote a poem about it.

Conde-Williams, Maurice Marcel Frederic
Amateur. *b:* 16.1.1885. *d:* 16.11.1967, Chelsea, London. Opening batsman. *Sch* Brighton. *Team* Royal Navy (1913–23).
Career batting
2–4–0–54–30–13.50–0–*ct* 2
Bowling 10–0

His County cricket was for Devon (1912–13).

Coney, Jeremy Vernon, MBE
Cricketer. *b:* 21.6.1952, Wellington, New Zealand. Brother of C. J. (Wellington). Sound middle order right-hand batsman, right-arm medium pace bowler. *Team* Wellington (1971/2 to 1986/7). *Tours* New Zealand to Australia 1973/4, 1980/1, 1982/3, 1984/5 (not first-class), 1985/6, to England 1979 (World Cup), 1983, 1986, to Sri Lanka 1983/4, 1984/5 (not first-class), to Pakistan 1984/5, to West Indies 1984/5. *Tests* New Zealand (1973/4 to 1986/7, 52 matches).
Career batting
165–272–48–7872–174*–35.14–8–*ct* 192
Bowling 3460–111–31.17–1–0–6/17
Test batting
52–85–14–2668–174*–37.57–3–*ct* 64
Bowling 966–27–35.77–0–0–3/28

He proved a useful all-rounder on the 1983 tour to England and played in all four Tests. In 1985/6 Coney captained New Zealand in two series of Tests against Australia and proved victorious in both. He then came to England in 1986 as leader of the touring party and won a third successive Test rubber. In these series he proved a very useful all-rounder without producing any outstanding personal performances. In the following New Zealand season, he led his country in a drawn series v West Indies and then retired from international cricket. He captained New Zealand in 15 Tests. His first-class debut was for New Zealand Under 23s in 1970/1.

Congdon, Bevan Ernest, OBE
Amateur. *b:* 11.2.1938, Motueka, Nelson, New Zealand. Opening or middle order right-hand batsman, right-arm medium pace bowler. *Teams* Central Districts (1960/1 to 1970/1); Wellington (1971/2); Otago (1972/3 to 1973/4); Canterbury (1974/5 to 1977/8). *Tours* New Zealand to England 1965, 1969, 1973, 1978, to Australia 1967/8, 1969/70, 1970/1, 1972/3, 1973/4, 1974/5 (not first-class), to West Indies 1971/2, to India and Pakistan 1964/5, 1969/70. *Tests* New Zealand (1964/5 to 1978, 61 matches).
Career batting
241–416–40–13101–202*–34.84–23–*ct* 201
Bowling 6125–204–30.02–4–0–6/42
Test batting
61–114–7–3448–176–32.22–7–*ct* 44
Bowling 2154–59–36.50–1–0–5/65

Although touring England four times and playing in all three Tests on each visit, he was only really successful in 1973, when he hit 1,081 runs, av 60.05, and averaged 72.40 in the Tests. He captained New Zealand on the 1973 tour, and in all in 17 Tests. His highest score was 202* for Central Districts v Otago at Nelson in 1968/9.

Congdon, Charles Hector
Amateur. *b:* 29.8.1891. *d:* 11.1.1958, Fairbrook, Boughton Street, Kent. Opening right-hand batsman. *Team* Royal Navy (1921–29).
Career batting
9–17–0–652–128–38.35–2–*ct* 4
Bowling 75–3–25.00–0–0–2/11

Conibere, William John
Amateur. *b:* 11.8.1923, Wiveliscombe, Somerset. *d:* 19.8.1982, Lawes Bridge, Torquay, Devon. Lower order right-hand batsman, left-arm medium fast bowler. *Team* Somerset (1950, 4 matches).
Career batting
4–5–0–16–8–3.20–0–*ct* 4
Bowling 220–7–31.42–0–0–4/66

A rugby footballer, he appeared for Somerset.

Coningham, Arthur
Amateur. *b:* 14.7.1863, Emerald Hill, South Melbourne, Victoria, Australia. *d:* 13.6.1939, Gladesville, Sydney, New South Wales, Australia. Middle or lower order left-hand batsman, left-arm fast medium bowler, brilliant field. *Teams* New South Wales (1892/3 to 1898/9, 13 matches); Queensland (1893/4 to 1895/6, 4 matches). *Tour* Australia to England and North America 1893. *Test* Australia (1894/5, 1 match).
Career batting
35–59–2–896–151–15.71–1–*ct* 27
Bowling 2603–112–23.24–7–0–6/38
Test batting
1–2–0–13–10–6.50–0–*ct* 0
Bowling 76–2–38.00–0–0–2/17

For some unexplained reason he was given very few opportunities to bowl on his only visit to England, but did well when called upon. He was a noted athlete, holding records for the quarter-mile hurdles, half-mile flat, one-mile flat and five mile flat races.

Connaughton, Joseph Maurice Francis
Amateur. *b:* 15.8.1918, Paddington, London. *d:* 12.2.1944, drowned when HMT *Khedive Ismail* torpedoed in One and a Half Degree Channel, Maldive Islands, and officially declared dead one year later. Lower order right-hand batsman, leg break bowler.

Connell, Francis Gerard

Sch Oratory. *Teams* Oxford U (1939); Middlesex (1939, 1 match).
Career batting
2–3–1–22–16*–11.00–0–*ct* 1
Bowling 85–3–28.33–0–0–3/19

Connell, Francis Gerard
Amateur. *b:* 13.1.1902, Dublin, Ireland. *d:* 16.3.1983, Dublin, Ireland. Opening right-hand batsman. *Team* Ireland (1934–38).
Career batting
5–10–0–262–87–26.20–0–*ct* 2

Connolly, Alan Norman
Amateur. *b:* 29.6.1939, Skipton, Victoria, Australia. Lower order right-hand batsman, right-arm fast medium bowler. *Team* Victoria (1959/60 to 1970/1, 83 matches); Middlesex (1969–70, 44 matches). *Tours* Australia to England 1964, 1968, to South Africa 1969/70, to India 1964/5, 1969/70, to New Zealand 1966/7. *Tests* Australia (1964/5 to 1970/1, 29 matches).
Career batting
201–215–93–1073–40–8.79–0–*ct* 77
Bowling 17974–676–26.58–25–4–9/67
Test batting
29–45–20–260–37–10.40–0–*ct* 17
Bowling 2981–102–29.22–4–0–6/47
Minor injuries affected his 1964 tour to England and he did not appear in any Tests, but in 1968 he headed both Test and first-class bowling averages. He continued in 1969 to bowl well for Middlesex taking 74 wickets, av 23.24, but retired from first-class cricket in 1970/1 due to back trouble. His best bowling was 9/67 for Victoria v Queensland at Brisbane in 1964/5.

Connor, Cardigan Adolphus
Cricketer. *b:* 24.3.1961, The Valley, Anguilla. Lower order right-hand batsman, right-arm fast medium bowler. *Team* Hampshire (1984–92, 160 matches).
Career batting
160–129–38–889–51–9.76–0–*ct* 47
Bowling 13326–405–32.90–10–1–7/31
He also played for Buckinghamshire (1979–84).

Connor, Edward James
Professional. *b:* 9.11.1872, Folkestone, Kent. *d:* 11.1.1947, Enfield, Middlesex. Lower order batsman, right-arm medium pace bowler. *Team* Essex (1905, 2 matches).
Career batting
2–4–0–43–26–10.75–0–*ct* 0
Bowling 131–2–65.50–0–0–2/21

Conradi, Eric Ralph
Amateur. *b:* 25.7.1920, Kensington, London. *d:* 22.8.1972, Droitwich, Worcestershire. Middle order left-hand batsman, excellent field. *Sch* Oundle. *Team* Cambridge U (1946, blue).
Career batting
7–13–3–164–50*–16.40–0–*ct* 8
He was very successful for Cambridge U in the wartime matches of 1940.

Considine, Stanley George Ulick
Amateur. *b:* 11.8.1901, Bilaspur, India. *d:* 31.8.1950, Bath, Somerset. Middle order right-hand batsman. *Sch* Blundell's. *Team* Somerset (1919–35, 89 matches).
Career batting
89–155–16–2965–130*–21.33–1–*ct* 43
Bowling 0–0
An excellent rugby footballer, he represented Bath, Somerset and England.

Constable, Bernard
Professional. *b:* 19.2.1921, East Molesey, Surrey. Brother of Dennis (Northamptonshire). Middle order right-hand batsman, leg-break bowler, excellent cover-point. *Team* Surrey (1939–64, 434 matches). *Tour* Surrey to Rhodesia 1959/60.
Career batting
446–701–82–18849–205*–30.45–27–*ct* 180
Bowling 3017–64–47.14–1–0–5/131
He reached 1,000 runs in a season 12 times (best 1,799, av 39.97, in 1961). His only double century was 205* for Surrey v Somerset at the Oval in 1952.

Constable, Dennis
Professional. *b:* 14.8.1925, East Molesey, Surrey. Brother of Bernard (Surrey). Lower order right-hand batsman, wicket-keeper. *Team* Northamptonshire (1949, 2 matches).
Career batting
2–2–0–20–12–10.00–0–*ct* 5–*st* 1

Constable, William Thomas
Professional. *b:* 21.3.1851, Poplar, London. *d:* 31.1.1894, Rochester, Kent. Middle order right-hand batsman, right-hand fast round-arm bowler. *Team* Kent (1876, 1 match).
Career batting
1–2–0–1–1–0.50–0–*ct* 0

Constant, David John
Professional. *b:* 9.11.1941, Bradford-on-Avon, Wiltshire. Son-in-law of G. E. E. Lambert (Gloucestershire and Somerset). Middle order left-hand batsman, slow left-arm bowler. *Teams* Kent (1961–63, 8 matches); Leicestershire (1965–68, 53 matches).
Career batting
61–93–14–1517–80–19.20–0–*ct* 33
Bowling 36–1–36.00–0–0–1/28
He was appointed a first-class umpire in 1969 and stood in 36 Test matches (1971–88).

Constantine, Baron Learie Nicholas, MBE
Amateur. *b:* 21.9.1901, Petit Valley, Diego Martin, Trinidad. *d:* 1.7.1971, Brondesbury, Hampstead, London. Son of L. S. (Trinidad), brother of Elias (Trini-

dad), nephew of V. S. Pascall (West Indies). Hard-hitting middle order right-hand batsman, right-arm fast bowler, later also medium, brilliant fielder. *Teams* Trinidad (1921/2 to 1934/5); Freelooters (India) (1934/5); Barbados (1938/9). *Tours* West Indies to England 1923, 1928, 1933, 1939, to Australia 1930/1. *Tests* West Indies (1928–39, 18 matches).

Career batting
119–197–11–4475–133–24.05–5–*ct* 133
Bowling 8991–439–20.48–25–4–8/38
Test batting
18–33–0–635–90–19.24–0–*ct* 28
Bowling 1746–58–30.10–2–0–5/75

The best West Indian all-rounder of his generation, he first toured England in 1923, when fielding was his most notable asset; in 1928 he performed the 'double' and was the outstanding figure of the visit, but in 1933 he was playing for Rochdale and assisted the tourists in only five matches. In 1939 he was easily the best bowler, again taking 100 wickets. His best season's batting was in 1928 with 1381 runs, av 34.52; he took 107 wickets that season, but at 22.95 each compared with 103, at 17.77, in 1939. His final first-class match was for Dominions in 1945. He was knighted in 1962. He was High Commissioner for Trinidad and Tobago from 1962 to 1964 and was created a Life Peer in 1969.

Constantine, Lebrun Samuel
Amateur. *b:* 25.5.1874, Maraval, Trinidad. *d:* 5.1.1942, Tunapuna, Trinidad. Father of L. N. (Trinidad) and Elias (Trinidad), brother-in-law of V. S. Pascall (West Indies). Opening/middle order right-hand batsman, wicket-keeper. *Team* Trinidad (1893/4 to 1922/3). *Tours* West Indies to England 1900 (not first-class), 1906.

Career batting
56–100–4–2433–116–25.34–1–*ct* 95–*st* 18
Bowling 632–46–13.73–1–0–6/17

He was one of the best West Indian batsmen on both of his visits to England, but the tourists were of modest strength on each occasion.

Contractor, Nariman Jamshedji
Amateur. *b:* 7.3.1934, Godhra, Gujarat, India. Father of H. N. (Bombay). Opening left-hand batsman, right-arm medium pace bowler. *Teams* Gujarat (1952/3 to 1970/1); Railways (1958/9 to 1959/60). *Tours* India to England 1959, to West Indies 1961/2, to Ceylon 1956/7. *Tests* India (1955/6 to 1961/2, 31 matches).

Career batting
138–234–18–8611–176–39.86–22–*ct* 72
Bowling 1040–26–40.00–0–0–4/85
Test batting
31–52–1–1611–108–31.58–1–*ct* 18
Bowling 80–1–80.00–0–0–1/9

He scored a century in each innings on his first-class debut: 152 and 102 for Gujarat v Baroda at Baroda in 1952/3. When visiting England in 1959 he hit 1,183 runs, av 31.13. He captained India in 12 Tests, including 1961/2 series v England, which India won 2–0. His skull was fractured by a ball from C. C. Griffith in the match between Indians and Barbados in 1961/2 and this ended his Test career.

Conway, Arthur Joseph
Professional. *b:* 1.4.1885, Stirchley, Worcestershire. *d:* 29.10.1954, Blackpool, Lancashire. Lower order right-hand batsman, right-arm fast bowler. *Team* Worcestershire (1910–19, 29 matches).

Career batting
31–52–14–165–20*–4.34–0–*ct* 6
Bowling 2039–57–35.77–2–1–9/38

He played soccer for Wolverhampton Wanderers. His best bowling was 9/38 for Worcestershire v Gloucestershire at Moreton-in-Marsh in 1914.

Coode, Arthur Trevenen
Amateur. *b:* 5.2.1876, St Helier, Jersey. *d:* 28.12.1940, Hazlemere, Buckinghamshire. Opening right-hand batsman. *Sch* Beccles. *Teams* Cambridge U (1898, blue); Middlesex (1898, 1 match).

Career batting
11–19–2–280–38–16.47–0–*ct* 3
Bowling 3–0

His last first-class match was for MCC in 1901. A noted soccer player, he obtained his blue for Cambridge and also appeared for Middlesex.

Cook, Cecil
Professional. *b:* 23.8.1921, Tetbury, Gloucestershire. Tail end right-hand batsman, slow left-arm bowler. *Team* Gloucestershire (1946–64, 498 matches). *Test* England (1947, 1 match).

Career batting
506–612–249–1965–35*–5.41–0–*ct* 153
Bowling 36578–1782–20.52–99–15–9/42
Test batting
1–2–0–4–4–2.00–0–*ct* 0
Bowling 127–0

He took 100 wickets in a season 9 times (best 149, av 14.16, in 1956). His best bowling was 9/42 for Gloucestershire v Yorkshire at Bristol in 1947. He was a first-class umpire (1971–86).

Cook, Charles John
Cricketer. *b:* 5.6.1946, Retford, Nottinghamshire. Lower order right-hand batsman, off break bowler. *Team* Nottinghamshire (1974–75, 2 matches).

Career batting
2–2–1–1–1–1.00–0–*ct* 1
Bowling 105–1–105.00–0–0–1/50

Cook, Colin Roy
Cricketer. *b:* 11.1.1960, Edgware, Middlesex. Brother-in-law of C. W. J. Athey (Yorkshire and Gloucestershire). Middle order right-hand batsman. *Sch* Merchant Taylors. *Team* Middlesex (1981–84, 11

matches).
Career batting
11–18–2–393–79–24.56–0–*ct* 8

Cook, David Roland
Cricketer. *b:* 2.9.1936, Edgbaston, Birmingham. Brother of M. S. (Warwickshire). Lower order right-hand batsman, left-arm fast medium bowler. *Sch* Warwick School. *Team* Warwickshire (1962–68, 9 matches).
Career batting
9–13–5–108–28*–13.50–0–*ct* 7
Bowling 534–23–23.21–0–0–4/66

He played once for Warwickshire in 1962, but did not re-appear until 1967. A noted rugby footballer, he represented Coventry and Warwickshire.

Cook, Enoch
Professional. *b:* 23.4.1845, Sandiacre, Derbyshire. *d:* 14.4.1927, Long Eaton, Derbyshire. Middle order right-hand batsman. *Teams* Derbyshire (1878–79, 8 matches).
Career batting
8–15–2–92–23*–7.07–0–*ct* 3

Cook, Geoffrey
Cricketer. *b:* 9.10.1951, Middlesbrough, Yorkshire. Sound opening right-hand batsman, slow left-arm bowler, good close field. *Teams* Northamptonshire (1971–90, 415 matches); Eastern Province (1978/9 to 1980/1). *Tours* England to India and Sri Lanka 1981/2, to Australia 1982/3, to New Zealand 1982/3 (not first-class). *Tests* England (1981/2 to 1982/3, 7 matches).
Career batting
460–793–65–23277–203–31.97–37–*ct* 419–*st* 3
Bowling 806–15–53.73–0–0–3/47
Test batting
7–13–0–203–66–15.61–0–*ct* 9
Bowling 27–0

He hit 1,000 runs in a season twelve times (best 1,759, av 43.97, in 1981). His highest score was 203 for Northamptonshire v Yorkshire at Scarborough in 1988. He was Northamptonshire captain 1981–88. In 1991 he was appointed Director of Cricket to Durham CCC, playing for the County in Minor Counties Championship, and in 1992 he appeared in limited overs matches.

Cook, Dr Geoffrey William
Amateur. *b:* 9.2.1936, Beckenham, Kent. Middle order right-hand batsman, off break bowler. *Sch* Dulwich. *Teams* Cambridge U (1956–58, blue 1957–58); Kent (1957, 4 matches). *Tour* MCC to East Africa 1957/8 (not first-class).
Career batting
47–77–11–1858–140–28.15–3–*ct* 26
Bowling 2309–64–36.07–0–0–4/45

He also played for Berkshire (1967–70). His final first-class match was for Free Foresters in 1961.

Cook, Jeremy
Cricketer. *b:* 20.7.1941, Leicester. Lower order right-hand batsman, right-arm fast medium bowler. *Team* MCC (1961–63).
Career batting
2–4–0–52–35–13.00–0–*ct* 3
Bowling 103–7–14.71–1–0–5/48

Cook, John Gilbert
Amateur. *b:* 16.5.1911, Houghton Regis, Bedfordshire. *d:* 10.9.1979, Overstrand, Norfolk. Opening right-hand batsman. *Sch* Bedford. *Team* Ireland (1936).
Career batting
1–2–0–27–21–13.50–0–*ct* 0
Bowling 31–1–31.00–0–0–1/15

His County cricket was for Bedfordshire (1928–32). He was a rugby international for England.

Cook, Lawrence Whalley
Professional. *b:* 28.3.1885, Preston, Lancashire. *d:* 2.12.1933, Mesnes, Wigan, Lancashire. Brother of William (Lancashire). Lower order right-hand batsman, right-arm medium pace bowler. *Team* Lancashire (1907–23, 203 matches).
Career batting
206–263–93–2126–54*–12.50–0–*ct* 137
Bowling 17791–839–21.20–46–8–8/39

He took 100 wickets in a season three times (best 156, av 14.88, in 1920).

Cook, Michael Stephen
Amateur. *b:* 19.2.1939, Edgbaston, Birmingham. Brother of D. R. (Warwickshire). Opening left-hand batsman, wicket-keeper. *Sch* Warwick School. *Team* Warwickshire (1961–62, 2 matches).
Career batting
2–4–0–110–52–27.50–0–*ct* 0

Cook, Nicholas Grant Billson
Cricketer. *b:* 17.6.1956, Leicester. Lower order right-hand batsman, slow left-arm bowler. *Teams* Leicestershire (1978–85, 153 matches); Northamptonshire (1986–92, 148 matches). *Tours* Robins to New Zealand 1979/80; Leicestershire to Zimbabwe 1980/1; England to New Zealand 1983/4, to Pakistan 1983/4, 1987/8, to India 1989/90 (not first-class); English Counties to Zimbabwe 1984/5; England B to Sri Lanka 1985/6. *Tests* England (1983–89, 15 matches).
Career batting
337–344–94–2989–75–11.95–0–*ct* 191
Bowling 24380–854–28.54–31–4–7/34
Test batting
15–25–4–179–31–8.52–0–*ct* 5
Bowling 1689–52–32.48–4–1–6/65

His best season with the ball was 1982 when he took 90 wickets, av 23.25. In 1983 he obtained a Test place when Edmonds was injured and in two matches took 17 wickets, av 16.17; on the twin tours the following winter he was the leading wicket-taker for

England. Although he has been successful in County cricket since then, his opportunities at Test level have been very restricted.

Cook, Stephen James
Cricketer. *b:* 31.7.1953, Johannesburg, South Africa. Opening right-hand batsman, off break bowler. *Teams* Transvaal (1972/3 to 1991/2); Somerset (1989–91, 71 matches). *Tour* South Africa to India 1991/2 (not first-class).
Career batting
243–428–49–18946–313*–49.98–55–*ct* 137
Bowling 107–3–35.66–0–0–2/25

At the age of 35, Cook joined Somerset and, considering he had no previous experience of English cricket, had a remarkable success scoring 2,241 runs, av 60.56, in 1989, 2,608, av 76.70, in 1990 and 2,755, av 81.02, in 1991. He was respectively first, sixth and second in the first-class batting averages for those seasons. His highest innings was 313* for Somerset v Glamorgan at Cardiff in 1990. He also hit two separate hundreds in a match twice and carried his bat through a completed innings twice for the county in the same match. He played in every unofficial Test for South Africa during the 1980s, and captained his country in 1989/90. He scored 1,000 runs in a season in South Africa twice.

Cook, Thomas Edwin Reed
Professional. *b:* 5.2.1901, Cuckfield, Sussex. *d:* 15.1.1950, Brighton, Sussex. He died by his own hand. Middle order right-hand batsman, right-arm medium pace bowler. *Team* Sussex (1922–37, 459 matches).
Career batting
460–730–65–20198–278–30.37–32–*ct* 169–*st* 1
Bowling 2880–80–36.00–1–0–5/24

He reached 1,000 runs in a season ten times including once over 2,000: 2,132, av 54.66, in 1934. He hit three double centuries, all for Sussex, the highest being 278 v Hampshire at Hove in 1930. In 1937 he left County cricket for a coaching position in South Africa. A noted soccer player with Brighton and Hove Albion and Bristol Rovers, he appeared as centre-forward for England in 1925.

Cook, William
Professional. *b:* 16.1.1882, Preston, Lancashire. *d:* 18.12.1947, Burnley, Lancashire. Brother of L. W. (Lancashire). Lower order batsman, right-arm fast medium bowler. *Team* Lancashire (1905–07, 11 matches).
Career batting
11–17–3–307–46–21.92–0–*ct* 4
Bowling 946–51–18.54–3–1–7/64

He played soccer for Preston and Oldham Athletic.

Cook, William Thomas
Amateur. *b:* 6.12.1891, Westbury, Wiltshire. *d:* 22.9.1969. Shirley, Surrey. Middle order left-hand batsman, right-arm medium pace bowler. *Team* Surrey (1921–33, 32 matches).
Career batting
39–66–4–1441–92–23.24–0–*ct* 12
Bowling 111–2–55.50–0–0–1/1

He was for many years captain of Surrey 2nd XI and appeared for the Minor Counties in several matches.

Cooke, Air Marshal Sir Cyril Bertram
Amateur. *b:* 28.6.1895, Dorking, Surrey. *d:* 27.9.1972, Rustington, Sussex. Lower order batsman, right-arm fast bowler. *Team* RAF (1927–30).
Career batting
6–8–2–51–20–8.50–0–*ct* 4
Bowling 490–23–21.30–2–0–7/76

Cooke, Geoffrey Charles Sidney Bancroft
Amateur. *b:* 8.9.1897, Westminster, London. *d:* 4.12.1980, Broomhall, Sunningdale, Berkshire. Lower order right-hand batsman, bowler. *Sch* Charterhouse. *Team* Army (1925–26).
Career batting
2–3–1–25–13–12.50–0–*ct* 3
Bowling 120–6–20.00–0–0–4/39

Cooke, John
Professional. *b:* 7.3.1851, Wirksworth, Derbyshire. *d:* 22.11.1908, Wirksworth, Derbyshire. Lower order right-hand batsman, wicket-keeper. *Team* Derbyshire (1874, 1 match).
Career batting
1–2–0–6–6–3.00–0–*ct* 0

Cooke, Noel Henry
Professional. *b:* 5.1.1935, West Derby, Liverpool, Lancashire. Middle order right-hand batsman, off break bowler. *Sch* Liverpool College. *Team* Lancashire (1958–59, 12 matches).
Career batting
12–16–0–242–33–15.12–0–*ct* 2
Bowling 93–3–31.00–0–0–2/10

He also played for Cheshire (1962–63).

Cooke, Robert
Professional. *b:* 25.5.1900, Selly Oak, Birmingham. *d:* 14.1.1957, Bournbrook, Birmingham. Tail end right-hand batsman, right-arm fast medium bowler. *Team* Warwickshire (1925–26, 15 matches).
Career batting
15–21–4–66–14–3.88–0–*ct* 6
Bowling 507–16–31.68–1–0–5/22

Cooke, Robert Michael Oliver
Cricketer. *b:* 3.9.1943, Adlington, Cheshire. Middle order left-hand batsman, leg break and googly bowler. *Sch* Rossall. *Team* Essex (1973–75, 40 matches).
Career batting
42–70–5–1450–139–22.30–2–*ct* 25
Bowling 184–4–46.00–0–0–2/55

He played for Cheshire (1969–72) and returned to that County (1976–84) after leaving Essex. His first-class debut was for Minor Counties in 1972 and his final match for the same side in 1976.

Cooke, W.
Amateur. Lower order batsman. *Team* Hurst Park Club (1890).
Career batting
1–2–0–1–1–0.50–0–*ct* 0

Cookson, William Whicher
Amateur. *b:* 29.8.1862, Mufsoorie, India. *d:* 23.12.1922, Winscombe, Somerset. Lower order batsman. *Sch* Clifton. *Team* Somerset (1882, 1 match).
Career batting
1–1–0–8–8–8.00–0–*ct* 0

Cooley, Bertram Clifford
Amateur. *b:* 1874, Durban, South Africa. *d:* 17.8.1935, Durban, South Africa. Middle order right-hand batsman, bowler. *Team* Natal (1893/4 to 1906/7). *Tour* South Africa to England 1901.
Career batting
19–32–4–564–126*–20.14–2–*ct* 11
Bowling 361–15–24.06–0–0–4/34
He returned very modest results on his only visit to England.

Coomaraswamy, Indrajit
Cricketer. *b:* 3.4.1950, Colombo, Ceylon. Middle order right-hand batsman, slow left-arm bowler. *Sch* Harrow. *Team* Cambridge U (1971–72).
Career batting
2–4–0–7–4–1.75–0–*ct* 0

Coomb, Arthur Grenfell
Amateur. *b:* 3.3.1929, Kempston, Bedford. Lower order right-hand batsman, right-arm medium fast bowler. *Sch* Bedford Modern. *Team* Combined Services (1948–49).
Career batting
5–10–4–55–16–9.16–0–*ct* 1
Bowling 321–8–40.12–0–0–3/61
His County cricket was for Bedfordshire (1947–55) and Norfolk (1956–63) and his last first-class match for Minor Counties in 1953.

Coombs, Robert Vincent Jerome
Cricketer. *b:* 20.7.1959, Barnet, Hertfordshire. Lower order right-hand batsman, slow left-arm bowler. *Sch* King's, Taunton. *Team* Somerset (1985–86, 13 matches).
Career batting
13–9–3–32–18–5.33–0–*ct* 3
Bowling 1112–32–34.75–1–0–5/58
He also played for Dorset (1979–90).

Coope, Miles
Professional. *b:* 28.11.1916, Gildersome, Yorkshire. *d:* 5.7.1974, Gildersome, Yorkshire. Hard-hitting middle order right-hand batsman, leg break bowler. *Team* Somerset (1947–49, 70 matches).
Career batting
71–136–4–2789–113–21.12–2–*ct* 20
Bowling 479–8–59.87–0–0–3/29
He hit 1,172 runs, av 22.11, in 1948.

Cooper, Albert Vincent
Amateur. *b:* 3.12.1893, Stoke Newington, London. *d:* 3.5.1977, Stoke Newington, London. Middle order right-hand batsman, right-arm slow bowler. *Sch* Bancroft's. *Team* Essex (1923, 1 match).
Career batting
1–2–0–14–12–7.00–0–*ct* 0

Cooper, Dr Alfred William Madison
Amateur. *b:* 12.6.1932, Dublin, Ireland. Middle order right-hand batsman, right-arm fast medium bowler. *Team* Ireland (1954).
Career batting
1–2–0–50–31–25.00–0–*ct* 0
Bowling 38–2–19.00–0–0–2/35

Cooper, Archibold Henry Hedges
Professional. *b:* 14.8.1878, Cowley, Oxfordshire. *d:* 13.1.1922, Chesterfield, Derbyshire. Lower order batsman, bowler. *Team* Derbyshire (1902, 1 match).
Career batting
1–1–0–0–0–0.00–0–*ct* 1
Bowling 12–0

Cooper, Bransby Beauchamp
Amateur. *b:* 15.3.1844, Dacca, India. *d:* 7.8.1914, Geelong, Victoria, Australia. Middle order right-hand batsman, wicket-keeper. *Sch* Rugby. *Teams* Middlesex (1863–67, 8 matches); Kent (1868–69, 9 matches); Victoria (1870/1 to 1877/8, 11 matches). *Test* Australia (1876/7, 1 match).
Career batting
50–83–5–1600–101–20.51–1–*ct* 41–*st* 20
Test batting
1–2–0–18–15–9.00–0–*ct* 2
In 1870 he moved to the USA and his name is found in some matches there, then he settled permanently in Australia.

Cooper, Charles Osborn
Amateur. *b:* 5.8.1868, Plaistow, Essex. *d:* 23.11.1943, Southborough, Kent. Brother-in-law of E. H. Simpson (Kent). Steady right-hand batsman, right-arm medium pace bowler, good slip. *Sch* Dulwich. *Team* Kent (1894–96, 10 matches).
Career batting
10–19–1–237–44–13.16–0–*ct* 7

Cooper, Edgar
Amateur. *b:* 12.11.1891, Briton Ferry, Glamorgan. *d:* 15.3.1959, Kettering, Northamptonshire. Lower order right-hand batsman, right-arm fast medium bowler. *Team* Glamorgan (1921, 4 matches).

Career batting
4–8–0–46–14–5.75–0–*ct* 3
Bowling 406–10–40.60–0–0–4/61

He first played for Glamorgan (pre first-class) in 1912.

Cooper, Edwin
Professional. *b:* 30.11.1915, Bacup, Lancashire. *d:* 29.10.1968, Birmingham. Brother of Fred (Lancashire and Worcestershire). Sound opening right-hand batsman, fine deep field. *Team* Worcestershire (1936–51, 249 matches).
Career batting
250–444–28–13304–216*–31.98–18–*ct* 99
Bowling 44–0

He reached 1,000 runs nine times (best 1,916, av 43.54, in 1949). His only double century was 216* for Worcestershire v Warwickshire at Dudley in 1938. He also played for Devon (1953–54).

Cooper, Fred
Professional. *b:* 18.4.1921, Bacup, Lancashire. *d:* 22.12.1986, Stourbridge, Worcestershire. Brother of Edwin (Worcestershire). Opening right-hand batsman, leg break bowler. *Teams* Lancashire (1946, 4 matches); Worcestershire (1947–50, 39 matches).
Career batting
44–84–13–1369–113*–19.28–1–*ct* 17
Bowling 30–0

Cooper, Frederick Joseph
Amateur. *b:* 16.3.1888, Wetherby, Yorkshire. *d:* 27.6.1958, York. Lower order batsman, right-arm medium pace bowler. *Team* Essex (1921–23, 10 matches).
Career batting
10–18–1–170–52–10.00–0–*ct* 3
Bowling 385–8–48.12–1–0–5/71

He also appeared for Shropshire. A useful soccer player he represented Bradford Park Avenue. In 1921 it is believed that he played in two matches under the assumed name of A. Brown, but this is by no means certain and A. Brown may perhaps be another cricketer altogether.

Cooper, Graham Charles
Professional. *b:* 2.9.1936, East Grinstead, Sussex. Middle/lower order right-hand batsman, off break bowler. *Team* Sussex (1955–69, 252 matches).
Career batting
252–407–56–8134–142–23.17–2–*ct* 150
Bowling 3677–100–36.77–5–0–5/13

He reached 1,000 runs in three seasons (best 1095, av 28.81, in 1961). He played soccer for Hastings United.

Cooper, Herbert
Professional. *b:* 25.12.1883, Dukinfield, Cheshire. *d:* 6.12.1963, Moorhey, Oldham, Lancashire. Middle order right-hand batsman. *Team* Derbyshire (1905–10, 15 matches).
Career batting
15–28–4–216–23–9.00–0–*ct* 7

Cooper, Howard Pennett
Cricketer. *b:* 17.4.1949, Great Horton, Bradford, Yorkshire. Lower order left-hand batsman, right-arm medium pace bowler. *Teams* Yorkshire (1971–80, 98 matches); Northern Transvaal (1973/4).
Career batting
101–113–30–1191–56–14.34–0–*ct* 61
Bowling 6529–233–28.02–4–1–8/62

Cooper, John Frederick
Amateur. *b:* 14.2.1855, Henley-on-Thames, Oxfordshire. *d:* 30.1.1928, Henley-on-Thames, Oxfordshire. Middle order right-hand batsman. *Sch* Marlborough. *Team* MCC (1881).
Career batting
1–1–0–0–0–0.00–0–*ct* 0

His County cricket was for Shropshire (1874–75) and Wiltshire (1878).

Cooper, Kevin Edwin
Cricketer. *b:* 27.12.1957, Sutton-in-Ashfield, Nottinghamshire. Lower order left-hand batsman, right-arm fast medium bowler, deep field. *Team* Nottinghamshire (1976–92, 272 matches). *Tour* Robins to New Zealand 1979/80 (no first-class matches).
Career batting
273–281–67–2141–46–10.00–0–*ct* 85
Bowling 19332–711–27.18–25–1–8/44

He took 101 wickets, av 21.57, in 1988. In 1991 and 1992 his appearances were very restricted due to a back injury.

Cooper, Nicholas Henry Charles
Cricketer. *b:* 14.10.1953, Bristol, Gloucestershire. Opening left-hand batsman, off break bowler. *Teams* Gloucestershire (1975–78, 17 matches); Cambridge U (1979, blue).
Career batting
24–39–2–825–106–22.29–1–*ct* 10
Bowling 277–7–39.57–0–0–2/11

After being on the Gloucestershire staff, he went on a one-year post-graduate course at Cambridge. He also played for Hertfordshire (1981).

Cooper, Norman Charles
Amateur. *b:* 12.7.1870, Norbiton, Surrey. *d:* 30.7.1920, Hampden Park, Eastbourne, Sussex. Opening/middle order right-hand batsman, right-arm medium pace bowler. *Sch* Brighton. *Team* Cambridge U (1891–92).
Career batting
13–24–1–275–45–11.95–0–*ct* 10
Bowling 15–0

His first-class debut was for Oxford and Cambridge, Past and Present v Australians 1890. His final first-class match was for C. I. Thornton's XI in 1893.

He also played for Surrey (1891), but not in a first-class match. An excellent soccer player, he represented both Cambridge U and England at wing half.

Cooper, Philip Edward
(later Whiteoak-Cooper)
Amateur. *b:* 19.2.1885, Rotherham, Yorkshire. *d:* 21.5.1950, Hoveton, Norfolk, on board motor launch *Sea Maiden*. Middle order right-hand batsman. *Sch* Queen's College, Taunton. *Team* Yorkshire (1910, 1 match).
Career batting
1–2–0–0–0–0.00–0–*ct* 0

Cooper, Richard Claude
Cricketer. *b:* 9.12.1945, Malmesbury, Wiltshire. *d:* 14.3.1990, Crudwell, Wiltshire. He died from a heart attack. Middle order right-hand batsman, right-arm medium pace bowler. *Team* Somerset (1972, 1 match).
Career batting
1–2–0–4–4–2.00–0–*ct* 0
Originally he played for Wiltshire, commencing 1967, and returned to that County (1975–89), being on the Somerset staff 1972–74.

Cooper, Rustom Sorabji
Amateur. *b:* 15.12.1922, Bombay, India. Attractive middle order right-hand batsman. *Teams* Parsis (1941/2 to 1944/5); Bombay (1943/4 to 1944/5); Middlesex (1949–51, 8 matches).
Career batting
22–29–6–1205–127*–52.39–3–*ct* 7
Bowling 61–0

Cooper, Sydney Hyde
Amateur. *b:* 5.2.1913, Carshalton, Surrey. *d:* 20.1.1982, Wallington, Surrey. Lower order right-hand batsman, wicket-keeper. *Team* Surrey (1936, 2 matches).
Career batting
2–2–1–11–11*–11.00–0–*ct* 2–*st* 3

Cooper, Walter
Professional. Middle order left-hand batsman, slow left-arm bowler. *Team* Essex (1905–10, 3 matches).
Career batting
3–6–0–32–18–5.33–0–*ct* 1
Bowling 69–0
He was a first-class umpire in 1928.

Cooper, William Henry
Amateur. *b:* 11.9.1849, Maidstone, Kent. *d:* 5.4.1939, Malvern, Melbourne, Victoria, Australia. Great grandfather of A. P. Sheahan (Australia). Lower order right-hand batsman, leg break and googly bowler. *Team* Victoria (1878/9 to 1882/3, 15 matches). *Tour* Australia to England 1884. *Tests* Australia (1881/2 to 1884/5, 2 matches).
Career batting
26–39–15–247–46–10.29–0–*ct* 16
Bowling 1739–71–24.49–5–0–7/37
Test batting
2–3–1–13–7–6.50–0–*ct* 1
Bowling 226–9–25.11–1–0–6/120
His only visit to England was a complete failure: in all matches he took just 7 wickets, av 46.43, and he did not appear in any of the Tests. His final first-class match was for Non-Smokers in 1886/7.

Cooper-Key, Charles Aston Whinfield
Amateur. *b:* 13.11.1856, Stretton Sugwas, Hereford. *d:* 13.7.1936, Paddington, London. Middle order right-hand batsman, right-arm fast bowler. *Sch* Rugby. *Team* Oxford U (1877).
Career batting
1–2–1–2–1*–2.00–0–*ct* 1
Bowling 11–3–3.66–0–0–3/8
His County cricket was for Herefordshire (1881–82).

Coote, Charles Purdon
Amateur. *b:* 8.8.1847, Weymouth, Dorset. *d:* 20.9.1893, Ballyclough, Co Cork, Ireland. Nephew of Algernon (Oxford U 1837). Middle order right-hand batsman, change bowler. *Sch* Harrow. *Team* MCC (1869–74).
Career batting
13–21–0–192–35–9.14–0–*ct* 5
His County cricket was for Warwickshire (pre first-class, 1872–73).

Coote, Cyril Ernest
Amateur. *b:* 13.4.1909, Cambridge. *d:* 24.1.1990, Cottenham, Cambridgeshire. Opening left-hand batsman, left-arm medium pace bowler. *Team* Minor Counties (1935).
Career batting
4–6–0–120–49–20.00–*ct* 1
His County cricket was for Cambridgeshire (1932–49). He was for many years the Head Groundsman at Fenner's.

Coote, David Edward
Cricketer. *b:* 8.4.1955, Winkburn, Nottinghamshire. Middle order left-hand batsman. *Team* Nottinghamshire (1977, 1 match).
Career batting
1–1–0–20–20–20.00–0–*ct* 0

Cope, Geoffrey Alan
Cricketer. *b:* 23.2.1947, Burmantofts, Leeds, Yorkshire. Lower order right-hand batsman, off break bowler. *Team* Yorkshire (1966–80, 230 matches). *Tours* Robins to South Africa 1975/6; MCC to India and Sri Lanka 1976/7; England to Pakistan and New Zealand 1977/8. *Tests* England (1977/8, 3 matches).
Career batting
246–261–93–2383–78–14.18–*ct* 71
Bowling 16948–686–24.70–35–6–8/73

Test batting
3–3–0–40–22–13.33–0–*ct* 1
Bowling 277–8–34.62–0–0–3/102

His first-class career was marred by doubts concerning his bowling action and he was twice suspended by the TCCB (1972 and 1978). He also played for Lincolnshire (1981–84).

Cope, James Edward Bailye
Cricketer. *b:* 5.5.1966, Leigh-on-Sea, Essex. Lower order right-hand batsman, wicket-keeper. *Sch* St John's, Leatherhead. *Team* Oxford U (1986–88, blue 1986–87).
Career batting
12–12–5–28–8*–4.00–0–*ct* 13–*st* 1

Cope, John James
Amateur. *b:* 1.8.1908, Ellesmere Port, Cheshire. Middle order right-hand batsman. *Team* Glamorgan (1935, 3 matches).
Career batting
3–5–1–27–14*–6.75–0–*ct* 1

He also played for Monmouthshire (1930–34).

Cope, Sidney Alfred
Professional. *b:* 12.8.1904, Hastings, Sussex. *d:* 14.4.1986, Dartford, Kent. Lower order left-hand batsman, left-arm fast bowler. *Team* Kent (1924, 1 match).
Career batting
1–1–0–0–0–0.00–0–*ct* 1
Bowling 27–1–27.00–0–0–1/27

Copeland, William
Professional. *b:* 10.6.1856, Trimdon, Co Durham. *d:* 28.1.1917, South Shields, Co Durham. Lower order batsman, left-arm medium pace bowler. *Team* Lancashire (1885, 1 match).
Career batting
1–2–1–21–21*–21.00–0–*ct* 0
Bowling 23–1–23.00–0–0–1/23

He appeared for Durham (pre first-class) between 1882 and 1894, being for about 30 years professional with South Shields.

Copland-Crawford, Robert Erskine Wade
(added Copland to his name in 1872)
Amateur. *b:* 5.9.1852. *d:* 23.5.1894, Hendon, Middlesex. Stylish middle order right-hand batsman, lob bowler. *Sch* Harrow. *Team* MCC (1872–73).
Career batting
3–6–0–20–9–3.33–0–*ct* 0

Copley, Sydney Herbert
Professional. *b:* 1.11.1905, Hucknall Torkard, Nottinghamshire. *d:* 1.4.1986, Isle of Man. Middle order right-hand batsman, slow left-arm bowler, brilliant field. *Team* Nottinghamshire (1930, 1 match).
Career batting
1–2–0–7–4–3.50–0–*ct* 0
Bowling 28–0

Whilst fielding as substitute in the England v Australia Test at Trent Bridge in 1930, he took a magnificent catch which changed the course of the game. A useful soccer player, he played for Rotherham United.

Coppinger, Charles
Amateur. *b:* 10.4.1851, Bexleyheath, Kent. *d:* 1.8.1877, New Cross, Kent. Brother of E. T. (Kent) and William (Kent), nephew of Septimus (Sussex). Lower order batsman. *Team* Kent (1870, 1 match).
Career batting
1–2–1–13–11*–13.00–0–*ct* 0

Coppinger, Edward Thomas
Professional. *b:* 25.11.1846, Bexley, Kent. *d:* 26.2.1927, Surbiton, Surrey. Brother of Charles (Kent) and William (Kent), nephew of Septimus (Sussex). Middle order right-hand batsman, wicket-keeper. *Team* Kent (1873, 2 matches).
Career batting
2–4–0–17–10–4.25–0–*ct* 1
Bowling 29–5–5.80–1–0–5/29

In 1890/1 he was Mayor of Kingston-upon-Thames.

Coppinger, Septimus
Professional. *b:* 15.9.1828, Northiam, Sussex. *d:* 8.4.1870, Epsom, Surrey. Uncle of Charles (Kent), E. T. (Kent) and William (Kent). Middle order right-hand batsman. *Team* Sussex (1857–61, 8 matches).
Career batting
9–16–1–126–43–8.40–0–*ct* 2

One of eight brothers – the family occasionally put an eleven into the field – his youngest brother, Octavius, was a noted local cricketer, but never appeared in first-class matches. His final first-class match was for the New All England Eleven in 1862.

Coppinger, William
Professional. *b:* 3.6.1849, Bexley, Kent. Brother of Charles (Kent), E. T. (Kent), nephew of Septimus (Sussex). Middle order right-hand batsman, slow under-hand bowler, good field. *Team* Kent (1868–73, 7 matches).
Career batting
7–14–3–52–16–4.72–0–*ct* 1
Bowling 98–2–49.00–0–0–2/49

Copson, William Henry
Professional. *b:* 27.4.1908, Stonebroom, Derbyshire. *d:* 13.9.1971, Clay Cross, Derbyshire. Lower order right-hand batsman, right-arm fast medium bowler with short run. *Team* Derbyshire (1932–50, 261 matches). *Tour* MCC to Australia and New Zealand 1936/7. *Tests* England (1939–47, 3 matches).
Career batting
279–359–108–1711–43–6.81–0–*ct* 103
Bowling 20752–1094–18.96–66–6–8/11
Test batting
3–1–0–6–6–6.00–0–*ct* 1

Bowling 297–15–19.80–1–0–5/85

He took 100 wickets in a season three times (best 160, av 13.34, in 1936). For Derbyshire v Warwickshire at Derby in 1937 he obtained four wickets in four balls. He became a first-class umpire (1958–67).

Corbett, Alexander Melvin
Amateur. *b:* 25.11.1855, Aston, Rotherham, Yorkshire. *d:* 7.10.1934, Kimberworth, Rotherham, Yorkshire. Middle order batsman. *Team* Yorkshire (1881, 1 match).
Career batting
1–2–0–0–0–0.00–0–*ct* 1

Corbett, Bertie Oswald
Amateur. *b:* 15.5.1875, Thame, Oxfordshire. *d:* 30.11.1967, Waddon, Portesham, Dorset. Brother of C. J. (Derbyshire). Middle order right-hand batsman. *Team* Derbyshire (1910, 1 match).
Career batting
1–2–0–1–1–0.50–0–*ct* 0

He also appeared for Buckinghamshire. A noted soccer player, he represented England as an outside-left and played for Oxford U and the Corinthians.

Corbett, Cornelius John
(known as John Cornelius Corbett)
Amateur. *b:* 8.3.1883, Thame, Oxfordshire. *d:* 10.4.1944, Chandlers Ford, Hampshire. Brother of B. O. (Derbyshire). Middle order right-hand batsman, change bowler. *Sch* Eastbourne. *Team* Derbyshire (1911–24, 27 matches).
Career batting
27–48–4–633–61–14.38–0–*ct* 7
Bowling 54–0

Corbett, Leonard James
Amateur. *b:* 12.5.1897, Bristol, Gloucestershire. *d:* 26.1.1983, Taunton, Somerset. Middle order right-hand batsman. *Team* Gloucestershire (1920–25, 9 matches).
Career batting
9–18–0–373–55–20.72–0–*ct* 9
Bowling 19–0

He played rugby as a three-quarter for England.

Corbett, Percival Thomas
Professional. *b:* 20.2.1900, Fernhill Heath, Worcestershire. *d:* 26.6.1944, West Malvern, Worcestershire. Middle/lower order right-hand batsman, change bowler. *Team* Worcestershire (1922–23, 7 matches).
Career batting
7–13–3–57–20–5.70–0–*ct* 2
Bowling 77–0

Cordaroy, Terence Michael
Cricketer. *b:* 26.5.1944, Hampstead, London. Middle order right-hand batsman. *Team* Middlesex (1968, 2 matches). *Tour* MCC to West Africa 1975/6 (not first-class).
Career batting
2–3–0–104–81–34.66–0–*ct* 1

He also played for Buckinghamshire (1977–79).

Corden, Charles Frederic
Professional. *b:* 30.12.1874, Croydon, Surrey. *d:* 26.2.1924, Croydon, Surrey. Middle order right-hand batsman. *Team* Worcestershire (1900–03, 17 matches).
Career batting
17–33–4–479–64–16.51–0–*ct* 6

He played for Surrey 2nd XI in the 1890s.

Cording, George Ernest
Amateur. *b:* 1.1.1878, Tredegar, Monmouthshire. *d:* 2.2.1946, Llanrumney, St Mellons, Monmouthshire. Middle order right-hand batsman, occasional wicket-keeper, fine slip field. *Team* Glamorgan (1921–23, 19 matches).
Career batting
19–34–4–498–101–16.60–1–*ct* 16–*st* 2

He first played for Glamorgan (pre first-class) in 1900.

Cordingley, Albert
Professional. *b:* 13.5.1871, Eccleshill, Bradford, Yorkshire. *d:* 30.4.1945, Horsham, Sussex. Lower order batsman, slow left-arm bowler. *Team* Sussex (1901–05, 15 matches).
Career batting
15–14–5–47–24*–5.22–0–*ct* 9
Bowling 546–16–34.12–1–0–5/22

He appeared once for Yorkshire, in 1898 v Worcestershire (a non-first-class match).

Cordle, Elton Anthony
(known as Anthony Elton Cordle)
Cricketer. *b:* 21.9.1940, Carrington Village, Bridgetown, Barbados. Half-brother of F. M. King (West Indies). Lower order right-hand batsman, right-arm fast medium bowler, deep field. *Team* Glamorgan (1963–80, 312 matches). *Tour* Glamorgan to West Indies 1969/70.
Career batting
312–433–76–5239–81–14.67–0–*ct* 141
Bowling 19281–701–27.50–19–2–9/49

His best bowling was 9/49 for Glamorgan v Leicestershire at Colwyn Bay in 1969.

Cordner, Arthur Douglas
Amateur. *b:* 30.8.1887. *d:* 3.7.1946, Dublin, Ireland. Tail end right-hand batsman, wicket-keeper. *Team* Ireland (1926).
Career batting
1–2–1–3–3*–3.00–0–*ct* 0

He played for Canada v USA in 1909.

Cordner, John Pruen
Amateur. *b:* 20.3.1929, Diamond Creek, Victoria, Australia. Second cousin of L. O. (Victoria). Lower order right-hand batsman, left-arm fast medium

bowler. *Teams* Victoria (1951/2, 3 matches); Warwickshire (1952, 1 match).
Career batting
4–4–2–13–8*–6.50–0–*ct* 3
Bowling 236–3–78.66–0–0–2/37

Cork, Dominic Gerald
Cricketer. *b:* 7.8.1971, Newcastle-under-Lyme, Staffordshire. Lower order right-hand batsman, right-arm fast medium bowler. *Team* Derbyshire (1990–92, 38 matches). *Tour* England A to West Indies 1991/2.
Career batting
42–56–12–1022–72*–23.22–0–*ct* 23
Bowling 3155–115–27.26–3–1–8/53
He also played for Staffordshire (1989–90). He played in a one-day international for England in 1992.

Corke, Martin Dewe
Amateur. *b:* 8.6.1923, Murree, India. Opening or middle order right-hand batsman. *Sch* Radley. *Team* Free Foresters (1953–58).
Career batting
5–10–0–116–53–11.60–0–*ct* 0
His County cricket was for Suffolk (1946–64).

Corlett, Samuel
Professional. *b:* 8.5.1852, Withington, Lancashire. *d:* 2.1.1921, Rusholme, Manchester, Lancashire. Lower order right-hand batsman, right-arm medium fast bowler. *Team* Lancashire (1871–75, 2 matches).
Career batting
2–3–0–6–4–2.00–0–*ct* 0

Corlett, Simon Charles
Cricketer. *b:* 18.1.1950, Blantyre, Nyasaland. Lower order right-hand batsman, right-arm fast medium bowler. *Sch* Worksop. *Teams* Oxford U (1970–72, blue 1971–72); Ireland (1974–87).
Career batting
33–47–9–697–60–18.34–0–*ct* 26
Bowling 2331–79–29.50–4–0–7/82

Corley, Harry Hagarty
Amateur. *b: circa* 1879, Dublin, Ireland. *d:* February 1936, Dublin, Ireland. Middle order right-hand batsman. *Team* Ireland (1907–09).
Career batting
4–8–1–50–27–7.14–0–*ct* 4
He was a rugby international for Ireland.

Corling, Grahame Edward
Cricketer. *b:* 13.7.1941, Waratah, Newcastle, New South Wales, Australia. Lower order right-hand batsman, right-arm fast medium bowler. *Team* New South Wales (1963/4 to 1968/9, 46 matches). *Tour* Australia to England 1964. *Tests* Australia (1964, 5 matches).
Career batting
65–78–32–484–42*–10.52–0–*ct* 11
Bowling 5546–173–32.05–6–0–5/44
Test batting
5–4–1–5–3–1.66–0–*ct* 0
Bowling 447–12–37.25–0–0–4/60
The youngest member of the 1964 tourists to England, he appeared in all five Tests and in first-class matches took 44 wickets, av 31.38.

Cornelius, Bernard William
Amateur. *b:* 16.3.1919, Kingsley Park, Northampton. *d:* 26.8.1987, Towcester, Northamptonshire. Middle order right-hand batsman, leg break bowler. *Team* Northamptonshire (1947, 1 match).
Career batting
1–2–1–9–9*–9.00–0–*ct* 1

Cornelius, Norman Stanley
Amateur. *b:* 5.6.1886, Blundellsands, Lancashire. *d:* 21.10.1963, West Felton, Shropshire. Middle order right-hand batsman, brilliant outfield. *Sch* Malvern. *Team* Gloucestershire (1910–11, 6 matches).
Career batting
6–9–1–99–40–12.37–0–*ct* 0
He appeared in the Freshmen's and Seniors' matches at Cambridge, but not in first-class cricket. He won a blue for soccer.

Cornell, William
(also known as William Cornwell)
Professional. *c:* 27.8.1838, Lode, Cambridgeshire. *d:* 21.4.1915, Bottisham, Lode, Cambridgeshire. Lower order batsman. *Team* Cambridgeshire (1864–68, 5 matches).
Career batting
5–8–3–22–12–4.40–0–*ct* 3–*st* 1

Cornford, James Henry
Professional. *b:* 9.12.1911, Crowborough, Sussex. *d:* 17.6.1985, Harare, Zimbabwe. Tail end right-hand batsman, right-arm fast medium bowler. *Team* Sussex (1931–52, 330 matches).
Career batting
332–399–145–1357–34–5.34–0–*ct* 135
Bowling 26999–1019–26.49–39–6–9/53
He several times took 90 wickets in a season, but never reached 100 (best 97, av 25.52, in 1949). His best bowling was 9/53 for Sussex v Northamptonshire at Rushden in 1949.

Cornford, Walter Latter
Professional. *b:* 25.12.1900, Hurst Green, Sussex. *d:* 6.2.1964, Elm Grove, Brighton, Sussex. Lower order right-hand batsman, wicket-keeper. *Team* Sussex (1921–47, 484 matches). *Tour* MCC to Australia and New Zealand 1929/30. *Tests* England (1929/30, 4 matches).
Career batting
496–649–211–6554–82–14.96–0–*ct* 675–*st* 342
Bowling 65–0
Test batting
4–4–0–36–18–9.00–0–*ct* 5–*st* 3

He retired from first-class cricket in 1939, but appeared once in 1947 in emergency. He was only just over 5 feet tall.

Cornish, Harry Hemming
Amateur. *b:* 19.2.1871, Westminster, London. *d:* 1918, Philadelphia, USA. Lower order batsman, bowler. *Team* Middlesex (1893, 1 match).
Career batting
1–2–0–7–6–3.50–0–*ct* 0
Bowling 27–0
He emigrated to the USA and was Editor of the *American Cricketer* commencing 1906. He appeared in Philadelphian Club cricket for Belmont and in 1909, in emergency, made a single appearance for USA v Canada. He died in the influenza epidemic that swept the USA in 1918.

Cornock, Walter Berkeley
Professional. *b:* 1.1.1921, Waverley, New South Wales, Australia. Middle order right-hand batsman, left-arm medium pace bowler. *Team* Leicestershire (1948, 26 matches).
Career batting
26–43–2–801–60–19.53–0–*ct* 24
Bowling 1007–15–67.13–0–0–3/46
He played soccer for Rochdale.

Cornu, Geoffrey
Amateur. *b:* 29.6.1913, Sheffield, Yorkshire. Lower order right-hand batsman, leg break and googly bowler. *Sch* Malvern. *Team* Free Foresters (1934–37).
Career batting
5–5–3–60–21*–30.00–0–*ct* 4
Bowling 513–13–39.46–0–0–3/92

Cornwall, Alan Edward Cripps
Amateur. *b:* 12.8.1898, Monmouth. *d:* 26.2.1984, Wreyland Down, Lustleigh, Devon. Middle order right-hand batsman. *Sch* Marlborough. *Team* Gloucestershire (1920, 1 match).
Career batting
1–2–0–5–3–2.50–0–*ct* 2

Cornwallis, Hon Oswald Wykeham
Amateur. *b:* 16.3.1894, Linton Park, Kent. *d:* 28.1.1974, Froxfield, Hampshire. Brother of W. S. (Kent). Opening right-hand batsman. *Team* Hampshire (1921, 1 match).
Career batting
4–6–0–91–31–15.16–0–*ct* 0
He also played first-class matches for the Royal Navy (1920–26).

Cornwallis (2nd Baron), Wykeham Stanley
Amateur. *b:* 14.3.1892, Linton Park, Kent. *d:* 4.1.1982, Ashurst Park, Fordcombe, Kent. Brother of O. W. (Hampshire). Lower order right-hand batsman, right-arm fast medium bowler. *Team* Kent (1919–26, 105 matches).
Career batting
106–129–47–964–91–11.75–0–*ct* 35
Bowling 3830–118–32.45–5–0–6/37
He was captain of Kent from 1924 to 1926.

Cornwell, Anthony Ewart Frank
Amateur. *b:* 19.8.1929, Parkstone, Devon. Lower order right-hand batsman, right-arm fast medium bowler. *Sch* Radley. *Team* Free Foresters (1949).
Career batting
1–2–0–0–0–0.00–0–*ct* 4
Bowling 60–3–20.00–0–0–3/60
His County cricket was for Dorset (1947–50).

Cornwell, Henry
(also known as Henry Cornell)
Professional. *b:* 19.12.1822, Cambridge. *d:* October 1869, Cambridge. Brother of Edward (Cambridge Town Club). Hard-hitting right-hand batsman, good long-stop. *Team* Cambridge Town Club (1844–49).
Career batting
11–18–1–266–61–15.64–0–*ct* 5
The leading batsman of the Cambridge Town Club in the 1840s, he appeared for England v Kent in 1846.

Corrall, Percy
Professional. *b:* 16.7.1906, Aylestone Park, Leicester. Lower order right-hand batsman, wicket-keeper. *Teams* Leicestershire (1930–51, 285 matches); Europeans (1944/5); Services (1944/5).
Career batting
288–422–126–2846–64–9.61–0–*ct* 381–*st* 187
In 1933 he received a serious injury, being struck on the head by an opponent's bat whilst keeping wicket – it was feared that the accident would end his career, but happily he fully recovered. He was a first-class umpire (1952–58).

Corran, Andrew John
Amateur. *b:* 25.11.1936, Eaton, Norwich, Norfolk. Lower order right-hand batsman, right-arm medium pace bowler. *Sch* Gresham's. *Teams* Oxford U (1958–60, blue all three years); Nottinghamshire (1961–65, 101 matches).
Career batting
132–207–55–2476–75–16.28–0–*ct* 77
Bowling 10556–410–25.74–21–1–7/45
He captained Nottinghamshire in 1962. He also played for Norfolk (1955–60). An excellent hockey player he was awarded his blue at Oxford. He took 111 wickets, av 20.31, in 1965.

Corry, Charles Victor
Amateur. *b:* 26.11.1940, Ormeau, Belfast, Ireland. Middle order right-hand batsman. *Team* Ireland (1959–66).
Career batting
4–7–1–40–17–6.66–0–*ct* 2

Cosh, Nicholas John
Cricketer. *b:* 6.8.1946, Denmark Hill, London. Middle order right-hand batsman, off break bowler. *Sch* Dulwich. *Teams* Cambridge U (1966–68, blue all three years); Surrey (1969, 6 matches).
Career batting
36–64–6–1731–138–29.84–2–*ct* 25
Bowling 34–1–34.00–0–0–1/8
A noted rugby footballer, he was awarded his blue and played for Blackheath.

Cosh, Stephen Hunter
Amateur. *b:* 31.1.1920, Ayr, Scotland. Middle order right-hand batsman, wicket-keeper. *Sch* Edinburgh Academy. *Team* Scotland (1950–59).
Career batting
36–57–3–873–99–16.16–0–*ct* 36–*st* 7
Bowling 7–0

Cosier, Gary John
Cricketer. *b:* 25.4.1953, Richmond, Victoria, Australia. Middle order right-hand batsman, right-arm medium pace bowler. *Teams* Victoria (1971/2 to 1980/1, 4 matches); South Australia (1974/5 to 1976/7, 24 matches); Queensland (1977/8 to 1979/80, 26 matches). *Tours* Australia to England 1977, 1979 (World Cup), to New Zealand 1976/7, to West Indies 1977/8. *Tests* Australia (1975/6 to 1978/9, 18 matches).
Career batting
91–161–9–5005–168–32.92–7–*ct* 75
Bowling 2301–75–30.68–0–0–3/20
Test batting
18–32–1–897–168–28.93–2–*ct* 14
Bowling 341–5–68.20–0–0–2/26
He achieved only modest results on his 1977 tour of England and was not selected for the Tests.

Coskerry, Joseph Whiteside
Amateur. *b:* 22.7.1895, Ballynahinch, Co Down, Ireland. *d:* 24.9.1965, Bangor, Co Down, Ireland. Middle order left-hand batsman. *Team* Ireland (1924).
Career batting
1–2–1–7–4*–7.00–0–*ct* 0

Cottam, Andrew Colin
Cricketer. *b:* 14.7.1973, Northampton. Son of R. M. H. (Hampshire and Northamptonshire). Lower order right-hand batsman, slow left-arm bowler. *Team* Somerset (1992, 6 matches).
Career batting
6–8–1–43–31–6.14–0–*ct* 1
Bowling 280–6–46.66–0–0–1/1
He also played for Devon (1990).

Cottam, Francis William
Amateur. *b:* 6.6.1900, Redhill, Surrey. *d:* 19.5.1987, Redhill, Surrey. Lower order right-hand batsman, slow left-arm bowler. *Team* Essex (1922, 1 match).
Career batting
1 match, did not bat–*ct* 0
Bowling 25–0

Cottam, Robert Michael Henry
Cricketer. *b:* 16.10.1944, Cleethorpes, Lincolnshire. Father of A. C. (Somerset). Lower order right-hand batsman, right-arm fast medium bowler. *Team* Hampshire (1963–71, 188 matches); Northamptonshire (1972–76, 76 matches). *Tours* MCC to Ceylon and Pakistan 1968/9, to India, Pakistan and Sri Lanka 1972/3; Robins to West Indies 1974/5 (not first-class); Commonwealth to Pakistan 1970/1. *Tests* England (1968/9 to 1972/3, 4 matches).
Career batting
289–280–97–1278–62*–6.98–0–*ct* 153
Bowling 21125–1010–20.91–58–6–9/25
Test batting
4–5–1–27–13–6.75–0–*ct* 2
Bowling 327–14–23.35–0–0–4/50
He took 100 wickets in a season three times (best 130, av 17.56, in 1968). His best bowling was 9/25 for Hampshire v Lancashire at Old Trafford in 1965. He also played for Devon (1977–78). He was coach to Warwickshire (1988–90) and Somerset (1992).

Cotter, Albert
Amateur. *b:* 3.12.1884, Philip Street, Macquarie, Sydney, New South Wales, Australia. *d:* 31.10.1917. He was a stretcher bearer and was buried 2 miles south of Beersheba, Palestine. Lower order right-hand batsman, right-arm fast bowler. *Team* New South Wales (1901/2 to 1913/14, 38 matches). *Tours* Australia to England 1905, 1909, to New Zealand 1904/5. *Tests* Australia (1903/4 to 1911/12, 21 matches).
Career batting
113–157–10–2484–82–16.89–0–*ct* 62
Bowling 10730–442–24.27–31–4–7/15
Test batting
21–37–2–457–45–13.05–0–*ct* 8
Bowling 2549–89–28.64–7–0–7/148
He was the fastest bowler on both his visits to England and though prone to inaccuracy, his sheer pace proved too much for many batsmen. He took 119 wickets, av 20.41 in 1905, but did not exceed 100 in 1909.

Cotterell, Thomas Archbold
Cricketer. *b:* 12.5.1963, Marylebone, London. Lower order right-hand batsman, slow left-arm bowler. *Sch* Downside. *Team* Cambridge U (1983–85, blue all three years).
Career batting
29–40–8–617–69*–19.28–0–*ct* 6
Bowling 2574–41–62.78–1–0–5/89
He also represented Cambridge at royal tennis.

Cotterill, Rev George Edward
Amateur. *b:* 28.7.1839, Madras, India. *d:* 2.6.1913, Cambridge. Brother of J. M. (Sussex), father of G. H. (Sussex). Hard-hitting middle order right-hand batsman, right-arm medium fast, or slow underhand, bowler, good deep field. *Sch* Brighton. *Teams* Cambridge U (1858–60, blue all three years); Cambridgeshire (1858, 1 match); Sussex (1869–74, 8 matches).
Career batting
18–32–1–447–55–14.41–0–*ct* 5–*st* 2
Bowling 182–14–13.00–1–0–5/23
He also played for Norfolk in 1866 and 1867.

Cotterill, George Huth
Amateur. *b:* 4.4.1868, Brighton, Sussex. *d:* 1.10.1950, Llandaff, Glamorgan. Son of G. E. (Sussex), nephew of J. M. (Sussex). Middle order right-hand batsman, slow right-arm bowler. *Sch* Brighton. *Teams* Sussex (1886–90, 8 matches); Cambridge U (1888–90).
Career batting
17–31–1–305–27–10.16–0–*ct* 9
Bowling 115–3–38.33–0–0–2/59
An excellent soccer player, he was awarded his blue at Cambridge and appeared for the Corinthians and for England as centre-forward in four matches 1891–94. He also played rugby for Richmond and Surrey, was an excellent long-jumper and rowed with Weybridge RC.

Cotterill, Dr Sir Joseph Montagu
Amateur. *b:* 23.11.1851, Kemp Town, Brighton, Sussex. *d:* 30.12.1933, Edinburgh, Scotland. Brother of G. E. (Sussex), uncle of G. H. (Sussex). Sound middle order right-hand batsman, right-arm medium pace bowler, good deep field. *Sch* Brighton. *Team* Sussex (1870–88, 27 matches).
Career batting
37–65–2–1708–191–27.11–1–*ct* 16
Bowling 214–6–35.66–0–0–2/44
He moved to Edinburgh in 1871 and this greatly restricted his appearances in first-class cricket. He was famous for throwing the cricket ball – his own authenticated record being 121 yards in 1875. He captained Sussex 1874–75. He was one of the best-known surgeons of his day.

Cottey, Phillip Anthony
Cricketer. *b:* 2.6.1966, Swansea, Glamorgan. Middle order right-hand batsman, off break bowler. *Team* Glamorgan (1986–92, 83 matches); Eastern Transvaal (1991/2). *Tour* Glamorgan to Zimbabwe 1990/1.
Career batting
88–136–22–3582–156–31.42–5–*ct* 45
Bowling 303–6–50.50–0–0–2/42
He reached 1,000 in a season twice (best 1,076, av 46.79, in 1992). He played soccer for Swansea City.

Cotton, Daniel Charles
Cricketer. *b:* 3.9.1968, Bletchley, Buckinghamshire. Lower order right-hand batsman, right-arm medium fast bowler. *Sch* Merchant Taylors. *Team* Cambridge U (1989-91).
Career batting
4–6–2–4–4–1.00–0–*ct* 0
Bowling 273–4–68.25–0–0–1/43

Cotton, John
Professional. *b:* 7.11.1940, Newstead, Nottinghamshire. Hard-hitting lower order right-hand batsman, right-arm fast medium bowler. *Teams* Nottinghamshire (1958–64, 138 matches); Leicestershire (1965–69, 94 matches).
Career batting
239–298–107–1631–58–8.53–0–*ct* 74
Bowling 16674–652–25.57–21–1–9/29
His best bowling was 9/29 for Leicestershire v Indians at Leicester in 1967.

Cotton, Robert Henry
Amateur. *b:* 5.11.1909, Birmingham. *d:* 17.1.1979, Warley, Staffordshire. Lower order right-hand batsman, right-arm fast bowler. *Team* Warwickshire (1947, 2 matches).
Career batting
2–3–1–0–0*–0.00–0–*ct* 0
Bowling 128–2–64.00–0–0–2/42

Cottrell, Clement Edward
Amateur. *b:* 28.5.1854, Westminster, London. *d:* 21.1.1897, Brighton, Sussex. Middle/lower order right-hand batsman, right-arm fast medium bowler. *Sch* Harrow. *Team* Middlesex (1876–85, 14 matches). *Tour* Sanders to North America 1886.
Career batting
26–43–6–464–46–12.54–0–*ct* 14
Bowling 1407–59–23.84–4–0–5/55
He was a noted club cricketer in the London area, appearing mainly for Esher.

Cottrell, Graham Allan
Cricketer. *b:* 23.3.1945, Datchet, Slough, Buckinghamshire. Middle order right-hand batsman, right-arm medium pace bowler. *Sch* Kingston GS. *Team* Cambridge U (1966–68, blue all three years).
Career batting
39–70–4–1108–81–16.78–0–*ct* 17
Bowling 2121–60–35.35–0–0–4/31
His County cricket was for Cambridgeshire (1976). He captained Cambridge in 1968, and also won a hockey blue.

Cottrell, Dr Peter Richard
Cricketer *b:* 22.5.1957, Welling, Kent. Lower order right-hand batsman, wicket-keeper. *Team* Cambridge U (1979, blue).
Career batting
10–9–1–119–34–14.87–0–*ct* 17–*st* 4

Coulson, Sydney Samuel
Professional. *b:* 17.10.1898, South Wigston, Leicestershire. *d:* 3.10.1981, Gainsborough, Lincolnshire. Steady opening right-hand batsman. *Team* Leicestershire (1923–27, 53 matches).
Career batting
53–94–6–1094–80–12.43–0–*ct* 11
He also played for Lincolnshire (1933).

Coulthurst, Josiah
Amateur. *b:* 24.12.1893, Blackburn, Lancashire. *d:* 6.1.1970, Lytham, Lancashire. Lower order batsman, left-arm fast medium bowler. *Team* Lancashire (1919, 1 match).
Career batting
1 match, did not bat–*ct* 0
He was one of the best amateur bowlers ever to appear in the Lancashire League, and in 1919 created a record for the East Lancashire Club by taking 101 wickets, av 9.78.

Coup, Edwin
(known as Coupe)
Professional. *b:* 9.6.1861, Ripley, Derbyshire. *d:* 2.7.1892, Mickleover, Derbyshire. Middle order left-hand batsman, excellent field at point. *Team* Derbyshire (1885–87, 13 matches).
Career batting
13–26–3–195–33–8.47–0–*ct* 2

Court, Richard Charles Lucy
(later Lucy-Court)
Professional. *b:* 23.10.1916, Ambala, India. *d:* 10.4.1974, Southampton, Hampshire. Lower order right-hand batsman, right-arm fast bowler. *Team* Hampshire (1937–39, 18 matches).
Career batting
18–27–5–224–35–10.18–0–*ct* 8
Bowling 1228–33–37.21–0–0–4/53
He was joint Secretary of Hampshire 1948–50.

Court, William Thomas
Amateur. *b:* 1842, Sydney, New South Wales, Australia. *d:* 31.5.1910, Red Hill, Wateringbury, Kent. Middle order right-hand batsman, wicket-keeper. *Team* Kent (1867, 1 match).
Career batting
1–2–0–11–11–5.50–0–*ct* 0

Courtenay, Geofry William List
Amateur. *b:* 16.12.1921, Castle Cary, Somerset. *d:* 17.10.1980, Comely Bank, Edinburgh, Scotland. Brother of P. J. S. (Somerset). Middle order right-hand batsman. *Sch* Sherborne. *Teams* Somerset (1947, 4 matches); Scotland (1955–57).
Career batting
8–14–0–168–69–12.00–0–*ct* 1
He also played for Dorset (1952–57).

Courtenay, Peter Jeofry Searle
Amateur. *b:* 11.3.1914, Weymouth, Dorset. *d:* 7.4.1959, Broadstone, Dorset. Brother of G. W. L. (Somerset). Attractive middle order right-hand batsman. *Sch* Marlborough. *Team* Somerset (1934, 2 matches).
Career batting
2–4–0–15–9–3.75–0–*ct* 2
He went up to Cambridge in 1933, but did not appear in any first-class matches whilst there. He won a blue for hockey.

Cousens, Peter
Professional. *b:* 15.5.1932, Durban, South Africa. Lower order right-hand batsman, slow left-arm bowler. *Team* Essex (1950–55, 39 matches).
Career batting
39–50–26–72–13–3.00–0–*ct* 3
Bowling 1707–44–38.79–0–0–4/63

Coutts, Ian Douglas Freeman
Amateur. *b:* 27.4.1928, Herne Hill, London. Lower order right-hand batsman, right-arm medium fast bowler. *Sch* Dulwich. *Team* Oxford U (1951–52, blue 1952).
Career batting
15–25–5–108–16*–5.40–0–*ct* 4
Bowling 1180–33–35.75–1–0–5/64
A noted rugby footballer, he was awarded his blue at Oxford and won a cap for Scotland.

Coventry, Hon Henry Thomas
Amateur. *b:* 3.5.1868, Regent's Park, London. *d:* 2.8.1934, Westminster, London. Brother of C. J. (England in South Africa), uncle of J. B. (Worcestershire). Middle order right-hand batsman, slow right-arm bowler, good field. *Sch* Eton. *Team* MCC (1888).
Career batting
2–4–0–28–15–7.00–0–*ct* 0
Bowling 12–1–12.00–0–0–1/12
His County cricket was for Worcestershire (pre first-class, 1888). He did not appear in first-class matches at Oxford U.

Coventry, Hon John Bonynge
Amateur. *b:* 9.1.1903, Westminster, London. *d:* 4.7.1969, Pirton Court, Worcestershire. Nephew of C. J. (England in South Africa) and H. T. (MCC). Lower order right-hand batsman, slow left-arm bowler. *Sch* Eton. *Team* Worcestershire (1919–35, 75 matches).
Career batting
75–133–13–1774–86–14.78–0–*ct* 28
Bowling 733–16–45.81–0–0–2/18
He did not appear in any first-class matches whilst at Oxford U. He captained Worcestershire 1929–30.

Coverdale, Stephen Peter
Cricketer. *b:* 20.11.1954, York. Opening right-hand batsman, wicket-keeper. *Sch* St Peter's, York. *Teams*

Yorkshire (1973–80, 6 matches); Cambridge U (1974–77, blue all four years); Northamptonshire (1987, 1 match).
Career batting
46–75–6–1245–85–18.04–0–*ct* 41–*st* 10
Bowling 0–1–0.00–0–0–1/0

He was appointed Secretary-Manager of Northamptonshire at the start of 1985 and in 1992 was Chief Executive. After a gap of seven years he reappeared in first-class cricket in one match (v Cambridge U at Fenner's) in 1987.

Coverdale, Walter William
Professional. *b:* 30.5.1912. *d:* 6.10.1972, Gateshead, Co Durham. Middle order right-hand batsman, right-arm medium pace bowler. *Team* Northamptonshire (1931–32, 31 matches).
Career batting
31–53–4–512–35*–10.44–0–*ct* 4
Bowling 62–1–62.00–0–0–1/25

He also played for Hertfordshire (1934–38) and Durham (1946–51).

Coverdale, William
Amateur. *b:* 8.7.1862, Pickering, Yorkshire. *d:* 23.9.1934, Bridlington, Yorkshire. Middle order batsman, wicket-keeper. *Team* Yorkshire (1888, 2 matches).
Career batting
2–2–0–2–1–1.00–0–*ct* 2

Covill, Reginald John
Professional. *b:* 10.8.1905, Cambridge. Middle order right-hand batsman, right-arm fast bowler. *Team* MCC (1930–35).
Career batting
12–19–3–322–48–20.12–0–*ct* 4
Bowling 589–23–25.60–1–0–5/31

His County cricket was for Norfolk (1926–27) and Cambridgeshire (1928–39). His first-class debut was for East of England in 1927.

Covington, Frederick Ernest
Amateur. *b:* 29.10.1912, Kingston-upon-Thames, Surrey. Steady middle order left-hand batsman, slow left-arm bowler. *Sch* Harrow. *Teams* Cambridge U (1935); Middlesex (1936, 6 matches). *Tour* Brinckman to South America 1937/8.
Career batting
12–21–4–301–83–17.70–0–*ct* 4
Bowling 25–0

Cowan, Charles Frederic Roy
Amateur. *b:* 18.9.1883, Glangrwyney, Crickhowell, Breconshire. *d:* 22.3.1958, Leamington Spa, Warwickshire. Middle order right-hand batsman. *Sch* Uppingham. *Team* Warwickshire (1909–21, 27 matches).
Career batting
29–53–3–846–78–16.92–0–*ct* 10
Bowling 9–0

He captained Warwickshire 2nd XI in the 1930s and was later Treasurer to the County Club (1943–57).

Cowan, David
Cricketer. *b:* 30.3.1964, St Andrews, Fife, Scotland. Lower order right-hand batsman, right-arm fast medium bowler. *Team* Scotland (1991).
Career batting
1–1–1–2–2*–no av–0–*ct* 1
Bowling 133–5–26.60–0–0–3/41

Cowan, James Ferguson
Amateur. *b:* 17.5.1929, Penicuik, Midlothian, Scotland. Lower order left-hand batsman. *Team* Scotland (1960–62).
Career batting
3–5–0–52–18–10.40–0–*ct* 1

Cowan, Michael Joseph
Professional. *b:* 10.6.1933, Leeds, Yorkshire. Lower order right-hand batsman, left-arm fast medium bowler. *Team* Yorkshire (1953–62, 91 matches). *Tour* MCC to Pakistan 1955/6.
Career batting
99–94–52–233–22–5.54–0–*ct* 40
Bowling 6784–276–24.57–13–2–9/43

His first-class career was marred by injury. On the tour to Pakistan in 1955/6 he went home early due to back strain and missed most of the 1956 English season in consequence. He also missed the 1959 and most of 1961 seasons due to injury and illness. His best bowling was 9/43 for Yorkshire v Warwickshire at Edgbaston in 1960. He also played for Northumberland (1964).

Cowan, Ralph Stewart
Cricketer. *b:* 30.3.1960, Hamlin, West Germany. Middle order right-hand batsman, right-arm medium pace bowler. *Teams* Oxford U (1980–82, blue all three years); Sussex (1982–83, 6 matches).
Career batting
28–52–5–1406–143*–29.91–3–*ct* 17–*st* 1
Bowling 798–9–88.66–0–0–2/75

He also won a blue for soccer.

Cowans, Norman George
Cricketer. *b:* 17.4.1961, Enfield, St Mary, Jamaica. Lower order right-hand batsman, right-arm fast bowler, deep field. *Team* Middlesex (1980–92, 182 matches). *Tours* Middlesex to Zimbabwe 1980/1; England to Australia 1982/3, 1984/5 (not first-class), to New Zealand 1982/3 (not first-class), 1983/4, to Pakistan 1983/4, to Sri Lanka 1984/5, to India 1984/5; England B to Sri Lanka 1985/6. *Tests* England (1982/3 to 1985, 19 matches).
Career batting
221–228–61–1531–66–9.16–0–*ct* 59
Bowling 15241–620–24.58–23–1–6/31

Test batting
19–29–7–175–36–7.95–0–*ct* 9
Bowling 2003–51–39.27–2–0–6/77

In 1984 and again in 1985 he took 73 wickets, av 21.82 and 22.95, these being his most successful seasons. He also excels at squash and real tennis.

Coward, Cornelius
Professional. *b:* 27.1.1838, Preston, Lancashire. *d:* 15.7.1903, Preston, Lancashire. Brother of Frederick (Lancashire). Middle order right-hand batsman, right-arm medium pace bowler, fine deep field. *Team* Lancashire (1865–76, 36 matches).
Career batting
49–86–5–1210–85–14.93–0–*ct* 15
Bowling 44–0

He also played for Denbighshire (1865) and Northamptonshire (pre first-class, 1869). He was a first-class umpire (1883–90).

Coward, Frederick
Professional. *b:* 11.2.1842, Preston, Lancashire. *d:* 15.12.1905, Broadgate, Preston, Lancashire. Brother of Cornelius (Lancashire). Middle order right-hand batsman, good field. *Team* Lancashire (1867–68, 7 matches).
Career batting
8–14–1–38–9–2.92–0–*ct* 5

He was a first-class umpire (1889–94).

Cowderoy, John
Professional. *b:* 19.4.1851, Battersea, London. *d:* 15.1.1934, Fulham, London. Lower order right-hand batsman, left-hand fast round-arm bowler. *Team* Surrey (1876, 1 match).
Career batting
1–2–0–4–2–2.00–0–*ct* 0
Bowling 11–0

Cowdrey, Christopher Stuart
Cricketer. *b:* 20.10.1957, Farnborough, Kent. Son of M. C. (Kent), grandson of E. A. (Europeans), brother of G. R. (Kent). Middle order right-hand batsman, right-arm medium pace bowler, good field. *Sch* Tonbridge. *Teams* Kent (1977–91, 280 matches); Glamorgan (1992, 2 matches). *Tours* Robins to Sri Lanka 1977/8, to New Zealand 1979/80; England to India 1984/5, to Australia 1984/5 (not first-class); England XI to South Africa 1989/90. *Tests* England (1984/5 to 1988, 6 matches).
Career batting
299–452–68–12252–159–31.90–21–*ct* 295
Bowling 7962–200–39.81–2–0–5/46
Test batting
6–8–1–101–38–14.42–0–*ct* 5
Bowling 309–4–77.25–0–0–2/65

He hit 1,000 runs in a season four times (best 1,364, av 56.83, in 1983). From 1985 to 1990 he captained Kent; in 1988 he was appointed captain of England for the final two Tests v West Indies. An injury meant that he was unavailable for the fifth Test, and Gooch replaced him.

Cowdrey, Graham Robert
Cricketer. *b:* 27.6.1964, Farnborough, Kent. Brother of C. S. (Kent and Glamorgan), son of M. C. (Kent), grandson of E. A. (Europeans). Middle order right-hand batsman, right-arm medium pace bowler. *Sch* Tonbridge. *Team* Kent (1984–92, 124 matches).
Career batting
124–193–37–6009–147–38.51–11–*ct* 66
Bowling 749–11–68.09–0–0–1/5

He reached 1,000 runs three times (best 1,576, av 47.75, in 1990).

Cowdrey, Sir Michael Colin
Amateur. *b:* 24.12.1932, Bangalore, India. Father of C. S. (Kent) and G. R. (Kent), son of E. A. (Europeans). Brilliant middle order right-hand batsman, leg break bowler, slip field. *Sch* Tonbridge. *Teams* Kent (1950–76, 402 matches); Oxford U (1952–54, blue all three years). *Tours* MCC to Australia and New Zealand 1954/5, 1958/9, 1962/3, 1965/6, 1970/1, to Australia 1974/5, to South Africa 1956/7, to West Indies 1959/60, 1967/8, to India 1963/4, to Ceylon and Pakistan 1968/9; Swanton to West Indies 1955/6; International XI to India and Pakistan 1961/2; Commonwealth to India 1964/5; Norfolk to West Indies 1969/70; Kent to West Indies 1972/3 (not first-class); MCC to West Africa 1975/6 (not first-class). *Tests* England (1954/5 to 1974/5, 114 matches).
Career batting
692–1130–134–42719–307–42.89–107–*ct* 638
Bowling 3329–65–51.21–0–0–4/22
Test batting
114–188–15–7624–182–44.06–22–*ct* 120
Bowling 104–0

Beginning his public career as the youngest cricketer to appear in an important match at Lord's – aged 13 for Tonbridge School – Cowdrey developed into the most accomplished batsman in England. He broke many batting records, but lacking the ruthlessness of some he made comparatively few high scores – only three innings over 200 in a total of 107 centuries. Most cricketers with 100 hundreds had at least 10 double centuries.

In the opinion of many his best innings came on the first of his six tours to Australia – a brilliant 102, when England were all out for 191 in the third Test at Melbourne, 1954/5. The highest innings of his first-class career was 307 for MCC v South Australia at Adelaide in 1962/3. He exceeded 1,000 runs in a season 21 times, but only in 1959 and 1965 did he reach 2,000: 2,093, av 63.42, in the latter season being his best. He also exceeded 1,000 runs in an overseas season on six occasions.

He created a new record of 114 for appearances in Test cricket and his partnership of 411 for the 4th wicket with P. B. H. May for England v West Indies at Edgbaston in 1957 was also a new record stand for England. He captained Oxford in 1954, from 1957 to 1971 he captained Kent, and between 1959 and 1968/9 he led England in 27 Tests. On four of his Australian tours he was the vice-captain, but he was never chosen as captain for this major overseas trip, the selectors apparently under the impression that he was not quite rigorous enough for the task.

He was President of MCC in 1986/7, and has been Chairman of the ICC since 1989 – previously the Chairman of ICC had been the MCC President. He was knighted in the 1992 New Year Honours list.

Cowell, Edward
Professional. *b:* 22.3.1848, Cambridge. *d:* 17.11.1885, Cambridge. Lower order right-hand batsman, right-arm fast bowler. *Team* Cambridgeshire (1867, 3 matches).
Career batting
3–5–0–37–13–7.40–0–*ct* 1
Bowling 61–4–15.25–0–0–3/11

Cowie, Alexander Gordon
Amateur. *b:* 27.2.1889, Yeatton House, Hordle, Lymington, Hampshire. *d:* 7.4.1916, Amara, Mesopotamia. He died of wounds. Lower order right-hand batsman, right-arm fast bowler. *Sch* Charterhouse. *Teams* Cambridge U (1910–11, blue 1910); Hampshire (1910, 2 matches).
Career batting
14–20–6–98–28–7.00–0–*ct* 6
Bowling 1395–58–24.05–5–0–6/87

He created a sensation in the University match of 1910, bowling 2 wides and taking 2 wickets in his opening over – he was a very fast bowler, but erratic. His last first-class match was for the Army in 1913.

Cowie, John
Amateur. *b:* 30.3.1912, Auckland, New Zealand. Lower order right-hand batsman, right-arm fast medium bowler. *Team* Auckland (1932/3 to 1949/50). *Tours* New Zealand to England 1937, 1949, to Australia 1937/8. *Tests* New Zealand (1937–49, 9 matches).
Career batting
86–104–29–762–54–10.16–0–*ct* 35
Bowling 8001–359–22.28–20–1–6/3
Test batting
9–13–4–90–45–10.00–0–*ct* 3
Bowling 969–45–21.53–4–1–6/40

The outstanding player of the 1937 tourists, he took 114 wickets, av 19.95, in first-class matches and 19 wickets, av 20.78, in the Tests, heading both bowling tables. In 1949 he was at the veteran stage as a fast bowler and, suffering from various strains, was not as effective, but he played in all four Tests and came second in the Test bowling figures with 14 wickets, av 32.21. He umpired 3 Test matches in New Zealand (1955/6 to 1958/9).

Cowley, John Norman
Amateur. *b:* 7.2.1885, Marylebone, London. *d:* 5.8.1957, Bovingdon, Hertfordshire. Grandson of R. J. P. Broughton (Cambridge U). Lower order batsman. *Sch* Harrow. *Team* Free Foresters (1914).
Career batting
1–2–0–0–0–0.00–*ct* 0

His County cricket was for Hertfordshire (1908–11).

Cowley, Nigel Geoffrey
Cricketer. *b:* 1.3.1953, Shaftesbury, Dorset. Middle order right-hand batsman, off break bowler. *Teams* Hampshire (1974–89, 257 matches); Glamorgan (1990, 14 matches).
Career batting
271–375–62–7309–109*–23.35–2–*ct* 105
Bowling 14879–437–34.04–5–0–6/48

He reached 1,000 runs once, 1,042, av 30.64, in 1984. He also played for Dorset (1972).

Cownley, John Michael
Amateur. *b:* 24.2.1929, Wales, near Sheffield, Yorkshire. Middle order left-hand batsman, right-arm medium fast, later leg break bowler. *Team* Yorkshire (1952, 2 matches); Lancashire (1962, 2 matches).
Career batting
4–6–1–64–25–12.80–0–*ct* 1
Bowling 155–3–51.66–0–0–2/36

He also played for Cheshire (1961). A noted amateur boxer at light-heavyweight, he represented Sheffield University.

Cowper, Robert Maskew
Amateur. *b:* 5.10.1940, Kew, Melbourne, Victoria, Australia. Brother of D. R. (Victoria). Middle order left-hand batsman, off break bowler. *Teams* Victoria (1959/60 to 1969/70, 66 matches); MCC (1966); Western Australia (1968/9, 3 matches). *Tours* Australia to England 1964, 1968, to West Indies 1964/5, to India and Pakistan 1964/5, to South Africa 1966/7. *Tests* Australia (1964–68, 27 matches).
Career batting
147–228–31–10595–307–53.78–26–*ct* 152
Bowling 5709–183–31.19–1–0–7/42
Test batting
27–46–2–2061–307–46.84–5–*ct* 21
Bowling 1139–36–31.63–0–0–4/48

Despite hitting 1,286 runs, av 51.44, he appeared in only one Test on his first visit to England in 1964. On his return in 1968, he played in four Tests, being omitted from the last only due to injury, but was nothing like as successful – 744 runs, av 37.20. His most famous innings was 307 for Australia v England at Melbourne in 1965/6, but it was a feat of endurance rather than entertainment.

Cox, Alexander Robb
Amateur. *b:* 6.8.1865, West Derby, Liverpool, Lancashire. *d:* 21.11.1950, Warren, Newmarket, Suffolk.

Brother of G. R. (Liverpool). Lower order batsman, wicket-keeper. *Sch* Harrow. *Team* Cambridge U (1887).
Career batting
2–3–0–6–4–2.00–0–*ct* 4
He was a well-known racehorse owner.

Cox, Arthur Leonard
Professional. *b:* 22.7.1907, Abington, Northampton. *d:* 13.11.1986, Northampton. Son of Mark (Northamptonshire), brother of M. H. D. (Northamptonshire). Middle order right-hand batsman, medium slow leg break bowler. *Team* Northamptonshire (1926–47, 229 matches).
Career batting
230–410–31–6631–104–17.49–1–*ct* 121
Bowling 7926–199–39.82–4–0–7/91

Cox, David William
Cricketer. *b:* 19.5.1946, Oakhill, Somerset. Lower order right-hand batsman, right-arm fast medium bowler. *Team* Somerset (1969, 1 match).
Career batting
1–2–0–8–8–4.00–0–*ct* 2
Bowling 77–1–77.00–0–0–1/50

Cox, Dennis Frank
Professional. *b:* 21.12.1925, Bermondsey, London. Lower order right-hand batsman, right-arm fast medium bowler. *Team* Surrey (1949–57, 42 matches).
Career batting
42–52–17–660–57–18.85–0–*ct* 39
Bowling 2316–68–34.05–2–1–7/22
He also played for Cheshire (1961–67).

Cox, E.
Amateur. Lower order batsman. *Team* London County (1900).
Career batting
1–2–0–9–7–4.50–0–*ct* 1

Cox, George
Professional. *b:* 23.8.1911, Warnham, Sussex. *d:* 30.3.1985, Burgess Hill, Sussex. Son of G. R. (Sussex). Aggressive middle order right-hand batsman, right-arm medium pace bowler, excellent cover field. *Team* Sussex (1931–60, 448 matches).
Career batting
455–754–57–22949–234*–32.92–50–*ct* 139
Bowling 5935–192–30.91–3–0–6/125
He reached 1,000 runs in a season 13 times, twice going on to 2,000 (best 2,369, av 49.35, in 1950). All four of his double centuries were for Sussex, the highest being 234* v Indians at Hove in 1946. His final first-class match was for L. C. Stevens' XI in 1961. A noted soccer player he appeared as centre-forward for Arsenal, Fulham and Luton.

Cox, George Robert
Amateur. *b:* 9.11.1859, Twickenham, Middlesex. *d:* 24.2.1936, Hoylake, Cheshire. Brother of A. R. (Cambridge U). Middle order right-hand batsman. *Sch* Uppingham. *Team* Liverpool and District (1884).
Career batting
1–2–0–0–0–0.00–0–*ct* 0

Cox, George Rubens
Professional. *b:* 29.11.1873, Warnham, Sussex. *d:* 23.3.1949, Dorking, Surrey. Father of George (Sussex). Sound middle order right-hand batsman, left-arm medium pace bowler, later slow, good field. *Team* Sussex (1895–1928, 618 matches).
Career batting
634–978–198–14643–167*–18.77–2–*ct* 549
Bowling 42136–1843–22.86–111–13–9/50
He reached 1,000 runs once – 1,158, av 25.73, in 1906 and 100 wickets five times (best 170, av 21.87, in 1905). During four winters he went out coaching in South Africa and once to India at Cooch Behar. His best bowling was 9/50 for Sussex v Warwickshire at Horsham in 1926. He played soccer for Fulham.

Cox, Gilbert Clifford
Amateur. *b:* 5.7.1908, Stroud, Gloucestershire. *d:* 31.3.1974, Alcester, Warwickshire. Middle order right-hand batsman. *Sch* Worcester RGS. *Team* Worcestershire (1935, 2 matches).
Career batting
2–4–0–28–19–7.00–0–*ct* 0

Cox, Henry Ramsay
Amateur. *b:* 19.5.1911, Radcliffe-on-Trent, Nottinghamshire. Middle/lower order right-hand batsman, right-arm medium pace bowler. *Sch* Uppingham. *Teams* Nottinghamshire (1930–54, 23 matches); Cambridge U (1934).
Career batting
30–42–9–419–64–12.69–0–*ct* 12
Bowling 1556–47–33.10–2–0–6/30
He was also a useful soccer player.

Cox, Joseph Lovell
Amateur. *b:* 28.6.1886, Pietermaritzburg, South Africa. *d:* 4.7.1971, Bulawayo, Rhodesia. Uncle of L. Tuckett (South Africa), brother-in-law of L. R. Tuckett (South Africa). Lower order right-hand batsman, right-arm medium fast bowler, good slip field. *Sch* St Charles's College, Pietermaritzburg. *Team* Natal (1910/11 to 1921/2). *Tour* South Africa to England 1912. *Tests* South Africa (1913/14, 3 matches).
Career batting
42–55–12–357–51–8.30–0–*ct* 14
Bowling 2704–120–22.53–4–1–8/20
Test batting
3–6–1–17–12*–3.40–0–*ct* 1
Bowling 245–4–61.25–0–0–2/74
He was not given enough bowling to do on his only visit to England, and his results were therefore moderate.

Cox, Mark
Professional. *b:* 10.5.1879, Northampton. *d:* 18.12.1968, Northampton. Father of A. L. (Northamptonshire) and M. H. D. (Northamptonshire). Originally tail end left-hand batsman, developing into a defensive opener, right-arm medium pace bowler. *Team* Northamptonshire (1905–19, 75 matches).
Career batting
75–134–10–1808–78–14.58–0–*ct* 22
Bowling 984–25–39.36–0–0–3/22
His career with Northamptonshire commenced in the pre-first-class days in 1897. He retired in 1909, but returned briefly in 1919.

Cox, Mark Henry David
Professional. *b:* 5.12.1905, Abington, Northampton. *d:* 27.3.1979, Pontypridd, Glamorgan. Son of Mark (Northamptonshire), brother of A. L. (Northamptonshire). Middle order right-hand batsman, slow right-arm bowler. *Team* Northamptonshire (1932, 3 matches).
Career batting
3–4–0–8–5–2.00–0–*ct* 1
Bowling 62–2–31.00–0–0–2/11

Cox, Roger
Cricketer. *b:* 27.4.1947, Luton, Bedfordshire. Middle order right-hand batsman, right-arm medium pace bowler. *Team* Minor Counties (1971).
Career batting
1–2–1–24–24–24.00–0–*ct* 0
His County cricket was for Bedfordshire (1967–75).

Cox, Rupert Michael Fiennes
Cricketer. *b:* 20.8.1967, Guildford, Surrey. Middle order left-hand batsman, off break bowler. *Sch* Bradfield. *Team* Hampshire (1990–92, 9 matches).
Career batting
9–12–2–287–104*–28.70–1–*ct* 5
Bowling 1-0

Cox, Sydney
Professional. *b:* 23.5.1905, Northampton. *d:* 5.3.1969, Northampton. Middle order right-hand batsman, right-arm medium pace bowler. *Team* Northamptonshire (1932, 6 matches).
Career batting
6–11–1–89–25–8.90–0–*ct* 2
Bowling 45–1–45.00–0–0–1/10

Coxhead, Maurice Edward
Amateur. *b:* 24.5.1889, Kensington, London. *d:* 3.5.1917. He was killed in action near Monchy, France. Middle/lower order right-hand batsman, right-arm fast bowler. *Sch* Eastbourne. *Teams* Oxford U (1909–10); Middlesex (1911, 1 match).
Career batting
6–8–0–29–9–3.62–0–*ct* 4
Bowling 300–13–23.07–1–0–5/53

Coxon, Alan John
Amateur. *b:* 18.3.1930, Clapton, London. Aggressive lower order left-hand batsman, left-arm fast medium bowler. *Team* Oxford U (1951–54, blue 1952).
Career batting
18–26–14–144–43*–12.00–0–*ct* 4
Bowling 1350–28–48.21–0–0–3/55
His final first-class match was for MCC in 1958. His County cricket was for Buckinghamshire (1978).

Coxon, Alexander
Professional. *b:* 18.1.1916, Huddersfield, Yorkshire. Lower order right-hand batsman, right-arm medium fast bowler. *Team* Yorkshire (1945–50, 142 matches). *Test* England (1948, 1 match).
Career batting
146–188–33–2817–83–18.17–0–*ct* 127
Bowling 9893–473–20.91–24–2–8/31
Test batting
1–2–0–19–19–9.50–0–*ct* 0
Bowling 172–3–57.33–0–0–2/90
He took 100 wickets in a season twice (best 131, av 18.60, in 1950). He left County cricket after the 1950 season to go into the Leagues. He also played for Durham (pre first-class, 1951–54).

Coxon, Ernest James De Veuille
Amateur. *b:* 10.12.1857, Taunton, Somerset. *d:* 8.4.1924, Neuilly-sur-Seine, Paris, France. Lower order left-hand batsman, left-arm medium pace bowler. *Team* Gentlemen of England (1890).
Career batting
1–2–0–31–21–15.50–0–*ct* 2
Bowling 5–0
He was no-balled for throwing in his only first-class match and was therefore taken off after three overs.

Coyle, Frederick Thomas
Professional. *b:* 1869, Taunton, Somerset. *d:* 12.9.1925, Halifax, Yorkshire. Middle/lower order right-hand batsman, right-arm fast medium bowler. *Team* Somerset (1903–05, 2 matches).
Career batting
2–3–2–14–10–14.00–0–*ct* 4
Bowling 54–0
He also played for Northumberland (1898).

Crabtree, Frederick
Professional. *b:* 10.3.1867, Baildon, Shipley, Yorkshire. *d:* 28.11.1893, Nelson, Lancashire, of ulceration of the stomach caused by a cricket ball. Lower order batsman, wicket-keeper. *Team* Lancashire (1890, 1 match).
Career batting
1–1–0–1–1–1.00–0–*ct* 1
He appeared for Yorkshire in a few matches in 1893, but only in non-first-class matches.

Crabtree, Frederick Lane
Amateur. *b:* 13.9.1872, Darlington, Co Durham. *d:* 19.8.1951, Canterbury, Kent. Middle order right-hand batsman, left-arm medium pace bowler. *Sch* Eton. *Team* Cambridge U (1894).
Career batting
3–6–1–66–27*–13.20–0–*ct* 2
His County cricket was for Hertfordshire (1898).

Crabtree, Harry Pollard
Amateur. *b:* 30.4.1906, Barnoldswick, Yorkshire. *d:* 28.5.1982, Great Baddow, Essex. Opening right-hand batsman, right-arm medium pace bowler. *Sch* St Peters, York. *Team* Essex (1931–47, 24 matches).
Career batting
24–41–1–1281–146–32.02–4–*ct* 12
Bowling 63–0
Owing to his scholastic duties he was unable to appear regularly for Essex.

Crabtree, Herbert
Professional. *b:* 25.5.1880, Colne, Lancashire. *d:* 2.3.1951, Colne, Lancashire. Middle order right-hand batsman, medium pace bowler, brilliant slip field. *Team* Lancashire (1902–08, 5 matches).
Career batting
5–8–0–116–49–14.50–0–*ct* 1
Bowling 34–0

Craddy, Wilfred Hartland
Amateur. *b:* 1.9.1905, Rose Green, Bristol, Gloucestershire. *d:* 4.1.1979, Westbury-on-Trym, Bristol. Middle order left-hand batsman. *Team* Gloucestershire (1928, 3 matches).
Career batting
3–5–0–47–29–9.40–0–*ct* 0

Cragg, James Richard Allen
Cricketer. *b:* 28.10.1946, Edgeley, Stockport, Cheshire. Grandson of J. S. (Lancashire). Middle order right-hand batsman. *Sch* King's, Macclesfield. *Team* Cambridge U (1970).
Career batting
7–13–0–149–55–11.46–0–*ct* 2
His County cricket was for Cheshire (1966–79).

Cragg, James Stanley
Amateur. *b:* 18.10.1886, Stockport, Cheshire. *d:* 27.7.1979, Manchester, Lancashire. Grandfather of J. R. A. (Cambridge U). Middle order batsman. *Team* Lancashire (1908, 1 match).
Career batting
1–2–0–10–9–5.00–0–*ct* 0
He also played for Cheshire (1912–23). He was President of Lancashire CCC 1965–66 and 1968.

Craib, James Derek Graham
Amateur. *b:* 27.11.1917, Kandy, Ceylon. Lower order right-hand batsman, right-arm fast medium bowler. *Sch* Eastbourne. *Team* Cambridge U (1937).
Career batting
2–3–0–100–62–33.33–0–*ct* 0
Bowling 109–4–27.25–0–0–2/34

Craig, Edward John
Amateur. *b:* 26.3.1942, Formby, Lancashire. Opening right-hand batsman, off break bowler. *Sch* Charterhouse. *Teams* Cambridge U (1961–63, blue all three years); Lancashire (1961–62, 6 matches).
Career batting
50–93–7–3103–208*–36.08–7–*ct* 43
Bowling 16–0
He reached 1,000 runs in a season twice (best 1,528, av 42.44 in 1961). He was one of the few Cambridge cricket blues to be placed in the First Class in three Triposes. His highest score was 208* for Cambridge U v L. C. Stevens' XI at Eastbourne in 1961.

Craig, Hartley Samuel
Amateur. *b:* 19.9.1917, Prospect, Adelaide, South Australia. Brother of R. J. (South Australia). Opening left-hand batsman. *Team* Dominions (1945).
Career batting
1–2–0–88–56–44.00–0–*ct* 0

Craig, Ian David
Amateur. *b:* 12.6.1935, Yass, New South Wales, Australia. Middle order right-hand batsman, slow right-arm bowler, excellent deep field. *Teams* New South Wales (1951/2 to 1961/2, 55 matches); Free Foresters (1957). *Tours* Australia to England 1953, 1956, to South Africa 1957/8, to India and Pakistan 1956/7, to New Zealand 1956/7, 1959/60; Commonwealth to South Africa 1959/60, to New Zealand and India 1961/2. *Tests* Australia (1952/3 to 1957/8, 11 matches).
Career batting
144–208–15–7328–213*–37.96–15–*ct* 70
Bowling 127–1–127.00–0–0–1/3
Test batting
11–18–0–358–53–19.88–0–*ct* 2
Only 17 years of age when he toured England in 1953, he had a very modest tour and did not appear in the Tests; his second visit was an improvement, but he failed to reach 1,000 runs and did little in either of the Tests for which he was chosen. He captained Australia in five Tests. His highest score was 213* for New South Wales v South Africans at Sydney in 1952/3.

Craig, Ian Thornton
Amateur. *b:* 26.1.1931, Maidstone, Kent. Lower order right-hand batsman, right-arm medium fast bowler. *Sch* Leys. *Team* Minor Counties (1959).
Career batting
1–1–0–1–1–1.00–0–*ct* 0
Bowling 85–2–42.50–0–0–2/46
His County cricket was for Cambridgeshire (1955–59).

Craig, Dr Leslie
Amateur. *b:* 14.10.1904, Edinburgh, Scotland. *d:* 3.10.1971, Willington Quay, Northumberland. Opening batsman, wicket-keeper. *Team* Scotland (1928–29).
Career batting
2–3–0–30–17–10.00–0–*ct* 4–*st* 1

Craig, Victor Alexander
Amateur. *b:* 27.7.1917, Strabane, Co Tyrone, Ireland. Lower order left-hand batsman, wicket-keeper. *Team* Ireland (1948).
Career batting
1–1–0–12–12–12.00–0–*ct* 2

Craig, Walter Reid
Amateur. *b:* 29.12.1846, Radcliffe Bridge, Pilkington, Lancashire. *d:* 6.7.1923, Hangleton, Sussex. Opening batsman. *Sch* Shrewsbury. *Team* Lancashire (1874, 1 match).
Career batting
1–2–0–8–7–4.00–0–*ct* 0

Craigie, Edmund Warren
Amateur. *b:* 8.5.1842, Goruckpore, India. *d:* 8.6.1907, Putney, London. Lower order batsman. *Sch* Harrow. *Team* MCC (1870).
Career batting
1–2–0–0–0–0.00–0–*ct* 0

Crake, Eric Hamilton
Amateur. *b:* 25.1.1886, Madras, India. *d:* 3.2.1948, Nakuru, Kenya. Brother of R. H. (MCC). Middle order batsman. *Sch* Harrow. *Team* MCC (1912).
Career batting
1–1–0–1–1–1.00–0–*ct* 0
He emigrated to Kenya about 1912.

Crake, Ralph Hamilton
Amateur. *b:* 13.4.1882, Madras, India. *d:* 26.1.1952, Dean, Edinburgh, Scotland. Brother of E. H. (MCC). Lower order batsman, wicket-keeper. *Sch* Harrow. *Teams* MCC (1901); Europeans (1920/1).
Career batting
2–4–0–47–37–11.75–0–*ct* 1

Cranfield, Beaumont
Professional. *b:* 28.8.1872, Bath, Somerset. *d:* 20.1.1909, Montpelier, Bristol, of pneumonia contracted whilst watching a soccer match. Tail end batsman, slow left-arm bowler. *Teams* Somerset (1897–1908, 125 matches); London County (1902–03).
Career batting
137–228–95–1307–42–9.82–0–*ct* 64
Bowling 14896–621–23.98–47–12–8/39
He took 100 wickets in a season three times (best 141, av 18.56, in 1902).

Cranfield, Lionel Lord
Professional. *b:* 11.10.1883, Brixton, London. *d:* 17.5.1968, Sale, Cheshire. Father of L. M. (Gloucestershire). Lower order right-hand batsman, slow left-arm bowler. *Teams* Gloucestershire (1903–22, 25 matches); Somerset (1906, 4 matches).
Career batting
29–51–5–612–51*–13.30–0–*ct* 15
Bowling 1760–59–29.83–2–0–6/67

Cranfield, Lionel Montague
Professional. *b:* 29.8.1909, Bristol. Son of L. L. (Gloucestershire and Somerset). Lower order right-hand batsman, off break bowler. *Team* Gloucestershire (1934–51, 162 matches).
Career batting
162–228–55–2466–90–14.25–0–*ct* 38
Bowling 7670–233–32.91–8–2–8/45
He was on the Old Trafford staff in 1933. He was Gloucestershire scorer 1950–52.

Crankshaw, Sir Eric Norman Spencer
Amateur. *b:* 1.7.1885, Over Peover, Cheshire. *d:* 24.6.1966, Reading, Berkshire. Brother-in-law of J. F. Ireland (Cambridge U). Opening/middle order right-hand batsman. *Sch* Eton. *Team* Gloucestershire (1909, 1 match).
Career batting
1–2–0–2–1–1.00–0–*ct* 0

Cranmer, Peter
Amateur. *b:* 10.9.1914, Acocks Green, Birmingham. Middle order right-hand batsman, right-arm medium fast bowler, good field. *Sch* St Edward's School, Oxford. *Teams* Warwickshire (1934–54, 166 matches); Europeans (1944/5); Services (1944/5).
Career batting
175–284–13–5853–113–21.59–4–*ct* 126
Bowling 1208–29–41.65–1–0–7/52
He played in the Freshmen's match at Oxford, but no first-class matches. He reached 1,000 runs in a season three times (best 1,192, av 22.49, in 1947). He captained Warwickshire 1938–47. His final first-class match was for MCC in 1959. A noted rugby footballer, he played at centre three-quarter for Oxford and England. He later became a well-known sporting journalist and commentator.

Cranston, James
Amateur. *b:* 9.1.1859, Bordesley, Birmingham. *d:* 10.12.1904, Bristol. Middle order left-hand batsman, left-arm bowler, fine outfield. *Sch* Taunton College. *Team* Gloucestershire (1876–99, 103 matches). *Test* England (1890, 1 match).
Career batting
118–195–20–3450–152–19.71–5–*ct* 49
Bowling 19–0
Test batting
1–2–0–31–16–15.50–0–*ct* 1

He also played for Worcestershire (pre first-class, 1885) and Warwickshire (pre first-class, 1886–87) but returned to Gloucestershire in 1889. During a match for the latter County in 1891 he was seized with a fit and this ended his first-class career, apart from a brief reappearance in 1899.

Cranston, Kenneth
Amateur. *b:* 20.10.1917, Aigburth, Liverpool, Lancashire. Middle order right-hand batsman, right-arm medium pace bowler. *Team* Lancashire (1947–48, 50 matches). *Tour* MCC to West Indies 1947/8. *Tests* England (1947–48, 8 matches).
Career batting
78–104–15–3099–156*–34.82–3–*ct* 47
Bowling 4985–178–28.00–10–1–7/43
Test batting
8–14–0–209–45–14.92–0–*ct* 3
Bowling 461–18–25.61–0–0–4/12

He captained Lancashire in 1947–48 and England in one match v West Indies 1947/8. He hit 1,000 runs in a season twice (best 1,228, av 33.18, in 1947). A dentist by profession, he retired from regular first-class cricket after the 1948 season. His final first-class match was for Leveson-Gower's XI in 1950.

Cranston, Robert S.
Amateur. Lower order right-hand batsman, wicket-keeper. *Team* Scotland (1922–23).
Career batting
3–5–3–35–31–17.50–0–*ct* 4–*st* 2

Crapp, John Frederick
Professional. *b:* 14.10.1912, St Columb Major, Cornwall. *d:* 13.2.1981, Knowle, Somerset. Sound middle order left-hand batsman, excellent slip field. *Team* Gloucestershire (1936–56, 422 matches). *Tours* MCC to South Africa 1948/9; Commonwealth to India 1953/4. *Tests* England (1948 to 1948/9, 7 matches).
Career batting
452–754–80–23615–175–35.03–38–*ct* 385
Bowling 306–6–51.00–0–0–3/24
Test batting
7–13–2–319–56–29.00–0–*ct* 7

He reached 1,000 runs in a season 14 times, but 2,000 runs only once – 2,014, av 45.77, in 1949. He captained Gloucestershire in 1953 and 1954. After retiring from first-class cricket, he became a noted umpire (1957–78), officiating in 4 Tests (1964–65).

Crawford, Alexander Basil
Amateur. *b:* 24.5.1891, Coleshill, Warwickshire. *d:* 10.5.1916, Laventie, Richebourg, France. He was killed in action. Hard-hitting middle order right-hand batsman, right-arm fast medium bowler. *Sch* Oundle. *Teams* Warwickshire (1911, 7 matches); Nottinghamshire (1912, 11 matches).
Career batting
18–27–4–381–51–16.56–0–*ct* 5
Bowling 607–21–28.90–1–0–6/36

Crawford, Frank Fairbairn
Amateur. *b:* 17.6.1850, Hastings, Sussex. *d:* 16.1.1900, at the military base hospital, Pietermaritzburg, South Africa. Brother of J. C. (Kent), uncle of V. F. S. (Surrey and Leicestershire), J. N. (Surrey and South Australia) and R. T. (Leicestershire). Middle order right-hand batsman, splendid outfield. *Sch* Maidstone. *Teams* Kent (1870–79, 15 matches); Natal (1889/90).
Career batting
25–48–6–579–38–13.78–0–*ct* 13
Bowling 17–0

He went to India with his Regiment in 1874/5 and then to South Africa, his appearances in County cricket being therefore very limited. His last first-class match in England was for MCC in 1884.

Crawford, George Henry
Professional. *b:* 15.12.1890, Hull, Yorkshire. *d:* 28.6.1975, Cottingham, Hull, Yorkshire. Lower order right-hand batsman, right-arm fast bowler. *Team* Yorkshire (1914–26, 9 matches).
Career batting
9–8–0–46–21–5.75–0–*ct* 3
Bowling 541–21–25.76–1–0–5/59

After playing for Yorkshire in 1914, he was not seen again in the County side until 1925.

Crawford, Ian Cunningham
Cricketer. *b:* 13.9.1954, Bristol. Middle order right-hand batsman, off break bowler. *Sch* Colstons. *Team* Gloucestershire (1975–78, 5 matches).
Career batting
5–7–0–104–73–14.85–0–*ct* 5
Bowling 174–3–58.00–0–0–1/18

He did not play in first-class cricket in either 1976 or 1977.

Crawford, Rev John Charles
Amateur. *b:* 29.5.1849, Hastings, Sussex. *d:* 21.2.1935, Wimbledon Chase, Surrey. Brother of F. F. (Kent), father of R. T. (Leicestershire), J. N. (Surrey and South Australia) and V. F. S. (Surrey and Leicestershire). Middle order batsman, being right-hand usually, but left-hand when hitting out; also right-hand fast bowler and left-hand slow bowler, brilliant deep field. *Sch* Maidstone. *Team* Kent (1872–77, 10 matches).
Career batting
11–22–1–202–35–9.61–0–*ct* 0
Bowling 174–6–29.00–0–0–3/5

He did not play in any first-class matches whilst at Oxford. In 1878 he was a curate in Leicester and appeared for that County. At one time he was reputed to be the fastest bowler in England. He also played for Herefordshire (1874). His debut in first-class matches was for W. G. Grace's XI 1871.

Crawford, John Neville
Amateur. *b:* 1.12.1886, Cane Hill, Surrey. *d:* 2.5.1963, Epsom, Surrey. Son of J. C. (Kent), brother of R. T. (Leicestershire) and V. F. S. (Surrey and Leicestershire), nephew of F. F. (Kent). Middle order right-hand batsman, right-arm medium pace off break bowler. *Sch* Repton. *Teams* Surrey (1904–21, 120 matches); South Australia (1909/10 to 1913/14, 22 matches); Otago (1914/15); Wellington (1917/18). *Tours* MCC to South Africa 1905/6, to Australia 1907/8; Australia to New Zealand 1913/14, to North America 1913/14. *Tests* England (1905/6 to 1907/8, 12 matches).
Career batting
210–325–34–9488–232–32.60–15–*ct* 162
Bowling 16842–815–20.66–57–12–8/24
Test batting
12–23–2–469–74–22.33–0–*ct* 13
Bowling 1150–39–29.48–3–0–5/48

As a schoolboy with still a year ahead of him at Repton, Crawford made his first-class debut for Surrey in August 1904. By the season's close he had taken 44 wickets at a cost of 16.93 each, only two occasional bowlers standing ahead of him in the first-class averages. Shortly after leaving school in 1905 he was on his way to South Africa with the MCC team and made his Test debut in the first match of the 1905/6 series. Back in England for the 1906 season he accomplished the 'double', repeated the feat in 1907 and missed it by two wickets in 1908. A quarrel in the middle of the 1909 summer abruptly ended his career with Surrey. He quit England and began a new life in Australia, playing for South Australia. Only the outbreak of war in 1914 brought him back to England and after it was over, his quarrel forgotten, he reappeared for Surrey and demonstrated how much his County had missed by coming third in the first-class batting table with an average of 61.00. That was more or less the swansong of one of England's most remarkable players, though his final first-class match was not until 1921.

In all he reached 1,000 runs in three seasons (best 1,371, av 37.05, in 1908) and 100 wickets twice (best 124, av 16.95, in 1907). His single 200 was 232 for Surrey v Somerset at the Oval in 1908, but mention should be made of his 354 in 330 minutes for an Australian XI v XV of South Canterbury in 1914, he and Trumper adding 298 in 69 minutes!

Crawford, Michael Grove
Amateur. *b:* 30.7.1920, Moortown, Leeds, Yorkshire. Father of N. C. (Cambridge U). Middle order right-hand batsman, good cover point. *Sch* Shrewsbury. *Team* Yorkshire (1951, 1 match).
Career batting
1–2–0–22–13–11.00–0–*ct* 1

He played no first-class cricket at Cambridge U, but did win a blue for soccer. He was Chairman of Yorkshire CCC (1980–84).

Crawford, Neil Cameron
Cricketer. *b:* 26.11.1958, Chapel Allerton, Leeds, Yorkshire. Son of M. G. (Yorkshire). Lower order right-hand batsman, right-arm medium pace bowler. *Sch* Shrewsbury. *Team* Cambridge U (1978–80, blue 1979–80).
Career batting
22–22–2–262–46–13.10–0–*ct* 5
Bowling 1030–32–32.18–1–0–6/80

Crawford, R. E. W.
(see *under* Copland-Crawford, R. E. W.)

Crawford, Reginald Trevor
Amateur. *b:* 11.6.1882, Leicester. *d:* 15.11.1945, Swiss Cottage, London, after a long illness. Son of J. C. (Kent), brother of J. N. (Surrey and South Australia) and V. F. S. (Surrey and Leicestershire), nephew of F. F. (Kent). Middle order right-hand batsman, right-arm fast medium bowler. *Team* Leicestershire (1901–11, 96 matches).
Career batting
112–187–13–3190–99*–18.33–0–*ct* 100
Bowling 5686–221–25.72–15–5–7/71

A well known singer, his concert engagements limited his appearances in first-class cricket.

Crawford, Robert Ogilvy
(registered at death as Robert Ogilvie Crawford)
Amateur. *b:* 1.10.1869, Bedford. *d:* 27.2.1917, Weston-super-Mare, Somerset. Middle order right-hand batsman. *Sch* Monkton Combe and Highgate. *Team* Cambridge U (1891).
Career batting
1–2–0–8–4–4.00–0–*ct* 0

Crawford, Thomas Alan
Amateur. *b:* 18.2.1910, Hoo, Kent. *d:* 6.12.1979, Westminster, London. Attacking middle order right-hand batsman, occasional off break bowler, good close field. *Sch* Tonbridge. *Team* Kent (1930–51, 13 matches).
Career batting
13–16–1–150–32–10.00–0–*ct* 2
Bowling 13–0

He appeared in the Cambridge Freshmen's match of 1931, but not in first-class matches whilst at University. Most of his cricket was for Kent Second XI. He was Kent President 1968 and Chairman 1969.

Crawford, Vivian Frank Shergold
Amateur. *b:* 11.4.1879, Leicester. *d:* 21.8.1922, Merton, Surrey. He died from pneumonia. Son of J. C. (Kent), brother of J. N. (Surrey and South Australia) and R. T. (Leicestershire), nephew of F. F. (Kent). Hard-hitting middle order right-hand batsman, right-arm fast bowler. *Sch* Whitgift. *Teams* Surrey (1896–1902, 110 matches); Leicestershire (1903–10, 165 matches). *Tour* Bosanquet to North America 1901.

Career batting
293–479–32–11909–172*–26.64–16–*ct* 262
Bowling 875–17–51.47–0–0–3/14

He reached 1,000 runs in a season five times (best 1,511, av 32.14, in 1901). In 1903 he was appointed Secretary to Leicestershire CCC and therefore, being qualified by birth, removed from Surrey to his native County. He was one of the greatest of schoolboy batsmen, hitting 1,340 runs for his school in 1897. After leaving Leicestershire he emigrated to Ceylon, becoming a tea-planter, but returned to serve in the First World War.

Crawford, Sir Walter Ferguson
Amateur. *b:* 11.4.1894, Malvern, Melbourne, Victoria, Australia. *d:* 28.3.1978, Churt, Surrey. Middle or lower order batsman, bowler. *Team* Oxford U (1919).
Career batting
3–5–0–23–11–4.60–0–*ct* 3
Bowling 136–3–45.33–0–0–2/43

Crawford, William Patrick Anthony
Amateur. *b:* 3.8.1933, Dubbo, New South Wales, Australia. Lower order right-hand batsman, right-arm fast bowler. *Team* New South Wales (1954/5 to 1957/8, 14 matches). *Tours* Australia to England 1956, to India 1956/7. *Tests* Australia (1956 to 1956/7, 4 matches).
Career batting
37–42–20–424–86–19.27–0–*ct* 18
Bowling 2313–110–21.02–5–1–6/55
Test batting
4–5–2–53–34–17.66–0–*ct* 1
Bowling 107–7–15.28–0–0–3/28

On his only tour of England in 1956, he achieved a modest return and appeared in a single Test, in which his bowling was scarcely required.

Crawfurd, John William Frederick Arthur
Amateur. *b:* 15.11.1878, Dulwich, London. *d:* 22.6.1939, Dublin, Ireland. Lower order left-hand batsman, left-arm fast medium bowler. *Sch* Merchant Taylors. *Teams* Oxford U (1900–01, blue both years); Ireland (1907–23).
Career batting
19–31–3–644–72–23.00–0–*ct* 15
Bowling 403–13–31.00–0–0–3/30

He played for Surrey in 1900 in a non-first-class match. His last first-class match was for Harlequins in 1927. A noted rugby player he gained his blue in 1900.

Crawley, Aidan Merivale
Amateur. *b:* 10.4.1908, Benenden, Kent. Son of A. S. (MCC), brother of C. S. (Hampshire and Middlesex), nephew of Eustace (Cambridge U) and H. E. (Cambridge U), cousin of C. L. (Essex) and L. G. (Essex and Worcestershire). Attacking opening right-hand batsman, right-arm medium pace off break bowler. *Sch* Harrow. *Teams* Oxford U (1927–30, blue all four years); Kent (1927–47, 33 matches).
Career batting
87–141–6–5061–204–37.48–11–*ct* 44
Bowling 565–15–37.66–0–0–2/40

He also played for Buckinghamshire (1948). He hit 1,316 runs, av 48.74, in 1928 and his highest score was 204 for Oxford U v Northamptonshire at Wellingborough in 1929. His final first-class match was for Free Foresters in 1949. He was President of MCC 1971/2. He was Labour MP for Buckingham 1945–51 and Conservative MP for West Derbyshire 1962–67. A noted journalist and author, he was at one time Editor-in-Chief of Independent Television News. From 1967 to 1971 he was Chairman of London Weekend Television.

Crawley, Canon Arthur Stafford
Amateur. *b:* 18.9.1876, Tressady, Rogart, Sutherland, Scotland. *d:* 8.10.1948, Clewer, Berkshire. Brother of Eustace (Cambridge U) and H. E. (Cambridge U), father of A. M. (Kent) and C. S. (Hampshire and Middlesex), uncle of C. L. (Essex) and L. G. (Essex and Worcestershire), brother-in-law of R. A. Bennett (Hampshire). Middle order right-hand batsman, good cover point. *Sch* Harrow. *Team* MCC (1897–98).
Career batting
3–4–0–19–12–4.75–0–*ct* 4

He appeared in the Freshmen's and Seniors' matches at Oxford, but no first-class games. He played a little for Hertfordshire (1895–96). He won blues for royal tennis and rackets.

Crawley, Charles Lambart
Amateur. *b:* 1.5.1908, Brandon, Park, Suffolk. *d:* 24.7.1935, Sunderland, Co Durham. Brother of L. G. (Essex and Worcestershire), nephew of Eustace (Cambridge U), A. S. (MCC) and H. E. (Cambridge U), cousin of C. S. (Hampshire and Middlesex) and A. M. (Kent). His widow married M. V. Milbank (Army). Middle order batsman. *Sch* Harrow. *Team* Essex (1929, 1 match).
Career batting
1–2–0–3–3–1.50–0–*ct* 1

Crawley, Cosmo Stafford
Amateur. *b:* 27.5.1904, Chelsea, London. *d:* 10.2.1989, Westminster, London. Son of A. S. (MCC), brother of A. M. (Kent), nephew of Eustace (Cambridge U) and H. E. (Cambridge U), cousin of C. L. (Essex) and L. G. (Essex and Worcestershire), brother-in-law of R. H. Cobbold (Cambridge U). Middle order right-hand batsman, right-arm medium pace bowler. *Sch* Harrow. *Teams* Hampshire (1923, 1 match); Oxford U (1924–25); Middlesex (1929, 1 match).
Career batting
6–11–0–243–81–22.09–0–*ct* 1

He won blues for royal tennis and rackets.

Crawley, Eustace
Amateur. *b:* 19.4.1868, Highgate, Middlesex. *d:* 2.11.1914, Wytschaete, Hollebeke, Belgium. He was killed in action. Brother of H. E. (Cambridge U) and A. S. (MCC), uncle of A. M. (Kent), C. L. (Essex), C. S. (Hampshire and Middlesex) and L. G. (Essex and Worcestershire). Opening right-hand batsman, good field. *Sch* Harrow. *Team* Cambridge U (1887–89, blue all three years).
Career batting
17–28–2–424–103*–16.30–1–*ct* 8
He played occasional County cricket for Hertfordshire (1886–88) and Worcestershire (1892). An excellent royal tennis player he represented Cambridge.

Crawley, Henry Ernest
Amateur. *b:* 19.8.1865, Highgate, Middlesex. *d:* 18.6.1931, Walton-on-the-Hill, Surrey. Brother of Eustace (Cambridge U) and A. S. (MCC), uncle of A. M. (Kent), C. L. (Essex), C. S. (Hampshire and Middlesex) and L. G. (Essex and Worcestershire). Middle order right-hand batsman, good field. *Sch* Harrow. *Team* Cambridge U (1886).
Career batting
4–8–0–132–54–16.50–0–*ct* 3
His debut in first-class matches was for C. I. Thornton's XI 1885 and his final match for MCC in 1887. His County cricket was for Hertfordshire (1886). He was amateur royal tennis champion in 1892 to 1894 and represented Cambridge and also won a blue for rackets. He was also a noted chess champion.

Crawley, John Paul
Cricketer. *b:* 21.9.1971, Maldon, Essex. Brother of M. A. (Lancashire and Nottinghamshire) and P. M. (Cambridge U). Middle order right-hand batsman, right-arm medium pace bowler. *Sch* Manchester GS. *Teams* Lancashire (1990–92, 12 matches); Cambridge U (1991–92, blue both years).
Career batting
32–52–6–2127–172–46.23–3–*ct* 25
Bowling 104–1–104.00–0–0–1/90
He was captain of Cambridge in 1992. He scored 1,175 runs, av 45.19, in 1992.

Crawley, Leonard George
Amateur. *b:* 26.7.1903, Nacton, Suffolk. *d:* 9.7.1981, Worlington, Suffolk. Brother of C. L. (Essex), nephew of Eustace (Cambridge U), H. E. (Cambridge U) and A. S. (MCC), cousin of C. S. (Hampshire and Middlesex) and A. M. (Kent). Opening or middle order right-hand batsman, right-arm fast medium bowler. *Sch* Harrow. *Teams* Worcestershire (1922–23, 6 matches); Cambridge U (1923–25, blue all three years); Essex (1926–36, 56 matches). *Tour* MCC to West Indies 1925/6.
Career batting
109–177–9–5227–222–31.11–8–*ct* 42
Bowling 57–0
Regarded as one of the most talented cricketers of his generation, he unfortunately was unable to play regularly in County cricket. He was disqualified from County cricket 1924–25 on the grounds that he was not properly qualified for Worcestershire. His single 200 was 222 for Essex v Glamorgan at Swansea in 1928. His final first-class match was for MCC in 1939. He was a talented golfer, being English Amateur Champion in 1931 and appearing four times in the Walker Cup and for Cambridge, and also a good rackets player, representing Cambridge.

Crawley, Mark Andrew
Cricketer. *b:* 16.12.1967, Newton-le-Willows, Lancashire. Brother of J. P. (Lancashire) and P. M. (Cambridge U). Middle order right-hand batsman, right-arm medium pace bowler. *Sch* Manchester GS. *Teams* Oxford U (1987–90, blue all four years); Lancashire (1990, 1 match); Nottinghamshire (1991–92, 36 matches).
Career batting
62–94–19–2900–160*–38.66–8–*ct* 52
Bowling 2682–57–47.05–1–0–6/92
He scored 1,297 runs, av 37.05, in 1992. He was captain of Oxford in 1989, and also won a blue for soccer.

Crawley, Peter Matthew
Cricketer. *b:* 4.1.1969, Newton-le-Willows, Lancashire. Brother of M. A. (Lancashire and Nottinghamshire) and J. P. (Lancashire). Middle order right-hand batsman, right-arm medium pace bowler. *Sch* Manchester GS. *Team* Cambridge U (1992).
Career batting
4–6–2–118–45–29.50–0–*ct* 0
Bowling 236–3–78.66–0–0–2/36

Crawley, Rev William Parry
Amateur. *b:* 24.8.1842, Bryngwyn, Monmouthshire. *d:* 9.5.1907, Walberton, Sussex. Uncle of C. G. E. Farmer (MCC). Middle order batsman. *Sch* Marlborough. *Team* MCC (1867).
Career batting
1–1–0–0–0–0.00–0–*ct* 0
Had several Trials whilst at Cambridge, but did not appear for the University. His County cricket was for Somerset (pre first-class, 1870).

Cray, Stanley James
Professional. *b:* 29.5.1921, Stratford, Essex. Opening right-hand batsman. *Teams* Essex (1938–50, 99 matches); Europeans (1943/4 to 1944/5).
Career batting
102–177–6–4218–163–24.66–7–*ct* 24
Bowling 40–1–40.00–0–0–1/0
He hit 1,000 runs twice (best 1,339, av 26.78, in 1947). He also played for Devon (1954–57).

Creber, Arthur Brynley
Professional. *b:* 11.10.1909, Sketty, Glamorgan. *d:* 10.8.1966, Colwyn Bay, Denbighshire. Son of Harry (Glamorgan). Middle order right-hand batsman, right-arm medium pace bowler. *Teams* Glamorgan (1929, 1 match); Scotland (1937).
Career batting
2–4–0–45–23–11.25–0–*ct* 1
Bowling 80–1–80.00–0–0–1/80

Creber, Harry
Professional. *b:* 30.4.1872, Birkenhead, Cheshire. *d:* 27.3.1939, Uplands, Swansea, Glamorgan. Father of A. B. (Glamorgan). Lower order right-hand batsman, left-arm medium pace bowler. *Team* Glamorgan (1921–22, 33 matches).
Career batting
34–60–29–157–13*–5.06–0–*ct* 6
Bowling 2671–98–27.25–5–1–7/47

He was a leading figure in South Wales cricket prior to the First World War and for 40 years professional and groundsman at St Helens, Swansea. His first-class debut was for South Wales in 1912. He first played for Glamorgan (pre first-class) in 1898.

Creese, William Charles Leonard
Professional. *b:* 27.12.1907, Park Town North, Transvaal, South Africa. *d:* 9.3.1974, Buckland, Dover, Kent. Son of W. H. (Transvaal). Hard-hitting middle order left-hand batsman, left-arm medium pace bowler. *Team* Hampshire (1928–39, 278 matches).
Career batting
281–455–42–9938–241–24.06–6–*ct* 192
Bowling 11246–410–27.42–15–1–8/37

He reached 1,000 runs in a season five times (best 1,421, av 28.42, in 1938) and missed the 'double' by only five wickets in 1936. His highest score was 241 for Hampshire v Northamptonshire at Northampton in 1939. His last first-class match was for Combined Services in 1946. He also played for Dorset (1949–51). He was head groundsman at Hove.

Cregar, Edward Mathews
Amateur. *b:* 28.12.1868, Philadelphia, USA. *d:* 6.5.1916, Philadelphia, USA. Hard-hitting middle or lower order right-hand batsman, right-arm fast medium, later slow, bowler. *Team* Philadelphia (1894–1908). *Tours* Philadelphia to England 1897, 1903, 1908.
Career batting
39–69–6–755–57–11.98–0–*ct* 14
Bowling 1840–74–21.90–3–0–8/35

He achieved a fairly good bowling record on his first two visits to England, but was clearly too old for the 1908 tour. Appearing in ten matches for USA v Canada, he took 25 wickets, av 14.12, and also performed usefully with the bat.

Creighton, Ernest
Professional. *b:* 9.7.1859, Hemsworth, Yorkshire. *d:* 17.2.1931, Leeds, Yorkshire. Lower order batsman, slow left-arm bowler. *Team* Yorkshire (1888, 4 matches)
Career batting
4–8–2–33–10–5.50–0–*ct* 0
Bowling 181–10–18.10–0–0–4/22

Crerar, George Graham
Amateur. *b:* 1.10.1914, Glasgow, Scotland. *d:* 6.12.1986, Worthing, Sussex. Middle order right-hand batsman, slow left-arm bowler. *Sch* Glasgow Academy. *Team* Scotland (1947–48).
Career batting
2–4–0–76–36–19.00–0–*ct* 1

Cresswell, George Fenwick
Amateur. *b:* 22.3.1915, Wanganui, Wellington, New Zealand. *d:* 10.1.1966, Blenheim, Marlborough, New Zealand. He was found dead with a shot gun by his side. Brother of A. E. (Wellington). Tail end left-hand batsman, right-arm slow medium bowler. *Teams* Wellington (1949/50); Central Districts (1950/1 to 1954/5). *Tour* New Zealand to England 1949. *Tests* New Zealand (1949 to 1950/51, 3 matches).
Career batting
33–36–19–89–12*–5.23–0–*ct* 11
Bowling 2794–124–22.53–8–0–8/100
Test batting
3–5–3–14–12*–7.00–0–*ct* 0
Bowling 292–13–22.46–1–0–6/168

He had only appeared in one first-class match when he was selected to tour England in 1949, but proved successful with 62 wickets, av 26.09. He played only in the final Test however, when he took 6 for 168 in the single innings. His first-class debut was for Rest of New Zealand in 1948/9.

Cresswell, James Arthur
Professional. *b:* 16.3.1903, Marehay, Derbyshire. Nephew of Joseph (Warwickshire). Lower order right-hand batsman, left-arm fast medium bowler. *Team* Derbyshire (1923–27, 21 matches).
Career batting
21–34–13–160–28–7.61–0–*ct* 17
Bowling 1022–25–40.88–0–0–4/65

Cresswell, Joseph
Professional. *b:* 22.12.1865, Denby, Derbyshire. *d:* 19.7.1932, Birmingham. Uncle of J. A. (Derbyshire). Lower order right-hand batsman, right-arm medium fast bowler, good close field. *Team* Warwickshire (1895–99, 15 matches).
Career batting
15–22–9–137–16–10.53–0–*ct* 12
Bowling 1144–42–27.23–1–0–6/69

He first appeared for Warwickshire in 1889 and his best years occurred before the County was raised to first-class status.

Cressy-Hall, John Walter
Amateur. *b:* 4.8.1843, Brighton, Sussex. *d:* 7.4.1894, Kimberley, South Africa. Brother of Edward Marshall Hall, the barrister. Middle order batsman, change bowler. *Sch* Merchant Taylors and Brighton. *Team* MCC (1873–80).
Career batting
3–5–0–27–12–5.40–0–*ct* 4
Bowling 48–2–24.00–0–0–2/48

Crichton, Henry Thompson
Amateur. *b:* 18.5.1884, Edgbaston, Birmingham. *d:* 1.7.1968, Branksome Park, Poole, Dorset. Middle or lower order right-hand batsman, right-arm medium pace bowler. *Sch* KES, Birmingham. *Team* Warwickshire (1908, 2 matches).
Career batting
2–3–0–26–26–8.66–0–*ct* 0
Bowling 30–2–15.00–0–0–2/21
He also played for Berkshire (1913).

Crichton, Ian Gordon
Cricketer. *b:* 7.1.1943, St Annes-on-Sea, Lancashire. Tail end left-hand batsman, left-arm medium fast bowler. *Sch* St Paul's. *Team* Oxford U (1963).
Career batting
1–1–0–4–4–4.00–0–*ct* 0
Bowling 61–0
He retired from serious cricket following a motor scooter accident in 1964.

Crick, Harry
Professional. *b:* 29.1.1910, Ecclesall, Sheffield, Yorkshire. *d:* 10.2.1960, Lower Wyke, Bradford, Yorkshire, in a road accident. Lower order right-hand batsman, wicket-keeper. *Team* Yorkshire (1937–47, 8 matches).
Career batting
11–15–2–124–22–9.53–0–*ct* 20–*st* 8
His last first-class match was for Combined Services in 1949.

Crisp, James George
Amateur. *b:* 15.11.1927, Newtown, Montgomeryshire. Lower order right-hand batsman, right-arm fast medium bowler. *Sch* Alleyns. *Team* Oxford U (1951).
Career batting
1–2–1–12–12–12.00–0–*ct* 0
Bowling 26–0
His County cricket was for Suffolk (1957–58).

Crisp, Robert James
Amateur. *b:* 28.5.1911, Calcutta, India. Lower order right-hand batsman, right-arm fast bowler. *Teams* Rhodesia (1929/30 to 1930/1); Western Province (1931/2 to 1935/6); Worcestershire (1938, 8 matches). *Tours* South Africa to England 1935; Cahn to Ceylon 1936/7. *Tests* South Africa (1935 to 1935/6, 9 matches).
Career batting
62–82–14–888–45–13.05–0–*ct* 27
Bowling 5487–276–19.88–21–4–9/64
Test batting
9–13–1–123–35–10.25–0–*ct* 3
Bowling 747–20–37.35–1–0–5/99
His single tour to England proved most successful: 107 wickets, av 19.58. He moved to England in 1936 and during that summer and the following one played for Sir Julien Cahn's XI, taking 105 wickets in 1936 and 165 in 1937. In 1938 he appeared for Worcestershire, but an injury limited his County matches. His best bowling was 9/64 for Western Province v Natal at Durban in 1933/4. He twice took four wickets in four balls for Western Province.

Cristofani, Desmond Robert
Amateur. *b:* 14.11.1920, Waverley, New South Wales, Australia. Middle/lower order right-hand batsman, right-arm medium leg break bowler. *Team* New South Wales (1941/2 to 1946/7, 3 matches). *Tours* Australian Services to England 1945, to India and Ceylon 1945/6.
Career batting
18–30–2–749–110*–26.75–1–*ct* 13
Bowling 1581–48–32.93–2–0–5/49

Critchley-Salmonson, Humphrey Seymour Ramsay
Amateur. *b:* 19.1.1894, Chalbury Lodge, Preston, Dorset. *d:* 24.4.1956, Ottery St Mary, Devon. Brother-in-law of G. R. Pedder (Gloucestershire). Lower order right-hand batsman, right-arm fast medium bowler. *Sch* Winchester. *Team* Somerset (1910–28, 14 matches). *Tour* Cahn to Argentine 1929/30.
Career batting
16–23–0–205–66–8.91–0–*ct* 16
Bowling 773–25–30.92–1–0–5/23
He was regarded as the best Public School bowler of his day, bowling at the speed of S. F. Barnes and having the knack of making the ball swerve in late.

Crocker, Christopher Simon Codrington
Cricketer. *b:* 25.1.1963, Edgbaston, Birmingham. Lower order right-hand batsman, right-arm medium pace bowler. *Team* Oxford U (1989).
Career batting
1–2–0–9–7–4.50–0–*ct* 0
Bowling 50-0

Crocker, Jonathan Alfred
Amateur. *b:* 8.10.1874, Kensington, London. *d:* 21.7.1944, Westminster, London. Middle order batsman, change bowler. *Sch* Eton. *Team* Cambridge U (1894).
Career batting
4–7–1–65–29–10.83–0–*ct* 2
Bowling 132–5–26.40–0–0–2/27
His County cricket was for Hertfordshire (1891–95).

Crockford, Eric Bertram
Amateur. *b:* 13.10.1888, Wylde Green, Warwickshire. *d:* 17.1.1958, Four Oaks, Sutton Coldfield, Warwickshire. Middle order right-hand batsman. *Sch* Eastbourne. *Team* Warwickshire (1911–22, 21 matches).
Career batting
21–35–0–394–55–11.25–0–*ct* 6
Bowling 199–2–99.50–0–0–1/7
He played hockey for England.

Croft, Colin Everton Hunte
Cricketer. *b:* 15.3.1953, Lancaster Village, Demerara, British Guiana. Lower order right-hand batsman, right-arm fast bowler, deep field. *Teams* Guyana (1971/2 to 1981/2); Lancashire (1977–82, 49 matches). *Tours* West Indies to Australia and New Zealand 1979/80, to England 1979 (World Cup), 1980, to Pakistan 1980/1, to Australia 1981/2; West Indian XI to South Africa 1982/3 (no first-class matches), 1983/4. *Tests* West Indies (1976/7 to 1981/2, 27 matches).
Career batting
121–136–54–865–46*–10.54–0–*ct* 25
Bowling 10527–428–24.59–17–1–8/29
Test batting
27–37–22–158–33–10.53–0–*ct* 8
Bowling 2913–125–23.30–3–0–8/29
He played in three Tests on the 1980 tour to England, but took only 9 wickets, av 34.00, and was scarcely more successful in the other first-class matches. After he retired he became an airline pilot in the USA.

Croft, Peter Downton
Amateur. *b:* 7.7.1933, Croydon, Surrey. Middle order right-hand batsman, off break bowler. *Sch* Gresham's Holt. *Team* Cambridge U (1955–57, blue 1955).
Career batting
18–29–2–402–47*–14.88–0–*ct* 8
Bowling 29–0
He played hockey for England and also appeared in the Olympics.

Croft, Robert Damien Bale
Cricketer. *b:* 25.5.1970, Morriston, Glamorgan. Middle order right-hand batsman, off break bowler. *Team* Glamorgan (1989–92, 71 matches). *Tours* Glamorgan to Zimbabwe 1990/1; England A to West Indies 1991/2.
Career batting
73–100–27–1902–91*–26.05–0–*ct* 28
Bowling 6076–143–42.48–6–1–8/66

Croft, Sydney James
Amateur. *b:* 14.1.1883, Gravesend, Kent. *d:* 16.7.1965, Dartford Marshes, Kent. Middle order right-hand batsman. *Team* Kent (1902, 2 matches).
Career batting
2–4–0–18–13–4.50–0–*ct* 0

Crofton, Edward Hugh
Amateur. *b:* 7.9.1854, Plymouth, Devon. *d:* 15.5.1882, Kilmainham, Dublin, Ireland. Middle order batsman, bowler. *Team* Hampshire (1881, 3 matches).
Career batting
3–5–0–32–23–6.40–0–*ct* 0
Bowling 42–1–42.00–0–0–1/21

Crofts, Edmund Sclater
Amateur. *b:* 23.1.1859, Winchester, Hampshire. *d:* 23.12.1938, Carlton, Bedford. Middle order batsman. *Sch* Winchester. *Team* Hampshire (1885, 1 match).
Career batting
1–2–0–5–3–2.50–0–*ct* 0

Crole, Gerard Bruce
Amateur. *b:* 7.6.1894, Calton, Edinburgh, Scotland. *d:* 31.3.1965, Aberdeen, Scotland. Middle order batsman. *Sch* Edinburgh Academy. *Teams* Oxford U (1920); Scotland (1920).
Career batting
2–3–0–90–47–30.00–0–*ct* 1
Bowling 16–3–5.33–0–0–3/16
He won blues for rugby and golf, and also represented Scotland at rugby.

Cromack, Bernard
Professional. *b:* 5.6.1937, Rothwell, Leeds, Yorkshire. Lower order right-hand batsman, slow left-arm bowler. *Team* Leicestershire (1959–68, 34 matches).
Career batting
34–55–2–626–55–11.81–0–*ct* 13
Bowling 1006–38–26.47–1–0–6/48
He left the Leicestershire staff at the end of the 1961 season, but re-appeared for the County in one match in 1968.

Cromb, Ian Burns
Amateur. *b:* 25.6.1905, Christchurch, New Zealand. *d:* 6.3.1984, Christchurch, New Zealand in a car accident. Hard-hitting lower/middle order right-hand batsman, right-arm fast medium bowler. *Team* Canterbury (1929/30 to 1946/7). *Tour* New Zealand to England 1931. *Tests* New Zealand (1931 to 1931/2, 5 matches).
Career batting
88–148–12–3950–171–29.04–3–*ct* 103
Bowling 6152–222–27.71–10–2–8/70
Test batting
5–8–2–123–51*–20.50–0–*ct* 1
Bowling 442–8–55.25–0–0–3/113
He bowled usefully on his 1931 visit to England and was expected to develop into a very effective bowler, but his later career was confined mainly to Provincial cricket in which he was a leading all-rounder.

Crommelin-Brown, John Louis
Amateur. *b:* 20.10.1888, Delhi, India. *d:* 11.9.1953, Old Town, Minehead, Somerset. Father-in-law of J. D. Eggar (Derbyshire). Opening or middle order right-hand batsman. *Sch* Winchester. *Team* Derbyshire (1922–26, 16 matches).
Career batting
16–28–2–659–74–25.34–0–*ct* 9
Bowling 70–1–70.00–0–0–1/29

At Cambridge he appeared in the Freshmen's match, but no first-class matches. He was Hon Secretary of Derbyshire 1945–49. He won a blue for soccer and played for the Corinthians and was a fine billiard player.

Crooke, Frederick James
Amateur. *b:* 21.4.1844, Liverpool, Lancashire. *d:* 6.8.1923, Southsea, Hampshire. Middle order right-hand batsman, right-hand fast round-arm bowler. *Sch* Winchester. *Teams* Lancashire (1865, 1 match); Gloucestershire (1874–75, 8 matches).
Career batting
21–35–1–573–56*–16.85–0–*ct* 10
Bowling 12–0

From 1866 to 1886 he lived in India and was for many years captain of Calcutta CC. His appearances for Gloucestershire were made whilst home on leave.

Crookes, Dennis Victor
Amateur. *b:* 18.6.1931, Berea, Durban, South Africa. Cousin of N. S. (Natal). Middle/lower order right-hand batsman, leg break bowler. *Sch* Michaelhouse. *Team* Cambridge U (1953–54, blue 1953).
Career batting
11–16–3–227–33–17.46–0–*ct* 4
Bowling 125–3–41.66–0–0–1/0

Crookes, John Edward
Amateur. *b:* 7.3.1890, Horncastle, Lincolnshire. *d:* 8.9.1948, Cuddington, Surrey. Middle order batsman. *Team* Hampshire (1920, 3 matches).
Career batting
3–5–1–50–36*–12.50–0–*ct* 3
Bowling 6–0

He also played for Lincolnshire (1909–10). He was a sergeant-major in the army.

Crookes, Norman Samuel
Cricketer. *b:* 15.11.1935, Renishaw, Natal, South Africa. Father of D. N. (Natal), cousin of D. V. (Cambridge U). Lower order right-hand batsman, off break bowler. *Team* Natal (1962/3 to 1969/70). *Tour* South Africa to England 1965.
Career batting
50–64–5–1123–68–19.03–0–*ct* 51
Bowling 4489–153–29.33–6–1–8/47

Although he was not selected for any of the Tests on his visit to England, he returned the satisfactory figures of 47 wickets, av 19.44.

Crookes, Ralph
Professional. *b:* 9.10.1846, Sheffield, Yorkshire. *d:* 15.2.1897, Ecclesall, Sheffield, Yorkshire. Lower order batsman, bowler. *Team* Yorkshire (1879, 1 match).
Career batting
1–2–1–2–2*–2.00–0–*ct* 0
Bowling 14–0

Croom, Alfred John William
Professional. *b:* 23.5.1896, Reading, Berkshire. *d:* 16.8.1947, Whiteheath Gates, Oldbury, Worcestershire. Father of L. C. B. (Warwickshire). Opening/middle order right-hand batsman, off break bowler. *Team* Warwickshire (1922–39, 394 matches).
Career batting
398–628–65–17692–211–31.42–24–*ct* 296
Bowling 6072–138–44.00–2–0–6/65

He reached 1,000 runs in a season 12 times (best 1,584, av. 38.63, in 1931). His only double century was 211 for Warwickshire v Worcestershire at Edgbaston in 1934. He appeared for Berkshire (1914–22) as an amateur before joining Warwickshire.

Croom, Leslie Charles Brian
Professional. *b:* 20.4.1920, Wybunbury, Cheshire. *d:* 20.12.1989, Dudley, Worcestershire. Son of A. J. W. (Warwickshire). Opening right-hand batsman, off break bowler. *Team* Warwickshire (1949, 4 matches).
Career batting
4–8–0–73–26–9.12–0–*ct* 0

Croome, Arthur Capel Molyneux
Amateur. *b:* 21.2.1866, Stroud, Gloucestershire. *d:* 11.9.1930, Taplow, Berkshire. Father of Victor (RAF). Middle order right-hand batsman, slow right-arm bowler. *Sch* Wellington. *Teams* Gloucestershire (1885–92, 30 matches); Oxford U (1887–89, blue 1888–89).
Career batting
51–86–13–978–81–13.39–0–*ct* 38
Bowling 1539–53–29.03–1–1–6/73

He suffered a terrible accident whilst playing for Gloucestershire at Old Trafford in 1887 – in attempting to stop a ball travelling over the boundary he impaled himself in the spike of the railings, the spike entering his neck, and it was at first thought that the injury would prove fatal. Happily he recovered completely. His final first-class appearance was for Gentlemen of England in 1908. He also played for Berkshire (1896–1905). A noted athlete, he took part in the University Sports of 1886 to 1889, winning the hurdles in 1886.

Croome, Victor
Amateur. *b:* 30.11.1899, Westminster, London. *d:* 1.9.1973, Thaxted, Essex. Son of A. C. M. (Gloucestershire). Lower order right-hand batsman, wicket-keeper. *Sch* Westminster. *Team* RAF (1928–30).

Career batting
5–8–1–124–36–17.71–0–*ct* 6–*st* 4

Cropper, William
Professional. *b:* 27.12.1862, Brimington, Derbyshire. *d:* 13.1.1889, Grimsby, Lincolnshire, as the result of an accident on the football field. Middle order right-hand batsman, left-arm medium pace bowler. *Team* Derbyshire (1882–87, 56 matches).
Career batting
60–113–4–1636–93–15.00–0–*ct* 26
Bowling 2930–171–17.13–8–0–7/25
His final first-class match was for an England XI in 1888. He last played for Derbyshire (not first-class) in 1888.

Crosdale, Gordon
(name changed from G. Fatt in 1883)
Amateur. *b:* 14.7.1880, Islington, London. *d:* 12.9.1954, Cold Ash, Newbury, Berkshire. Lower order right-hand batsman, wicket-keeper. *Sch* Charterhouse. *Team* Middlesex (1905, 3 matches).
Career batting
3–4–2–30–17*–15.00–0–*ct* 1

Crosfield, Sydney Morland
Amateur. *b:* 12.11.1861, Warrington, Lancashire. *d:* 30.1.1908, Las Palmas, Canary Islands. Hard hitting middle order right-hand batsman, right-arm fast, but after 1882, slow bowler, good cover field. *Sch* Wimbledon School. *Team* Lancashire (1883–99, 90 matches).
Career batting
96–150–14–2027–82*–14.90–0–*ct* 49
Bowling 151–3–50.33–0–0–1/1
He also played for Cheshire (1885–87). He was joint captain of Lancashire 1892–93. A fine shot, he won the Grand Prix de Casino at Monte Carlo in two successive years.

Cross, Anthony John
Cricketer. *b:* 5.8.1945, Fulmer Chase, Buckinghamshire. Middle order right-hand batsman, off break bowler. *Teams* Cambridge U (1966–67); Warwickshire (1969, 1 match).
Career batting
6–10–1–151–39*–16.77–0–*ct* 2
Bowling 19–0

Cross, Eric Percival
Amateur. *b:* 25.6.1896, Handsworth, Birmingham. *d:* 27.2.1985, Birmingham. Lower order right-hand batsman, wicket-keeper. *Sch* Denstone. *Team* Warwickshire (1921–23, 7 matches).
Career batting
7–12–4–61–12*–7.62–0–*ct* 9–*st* 1
He also played for Staffordshire (1928–34).

Cross, Graham Frederick
Professional. *b:* 15.11.1943, Leicester. Middle or lower order right-hand batsman, right-arm medium pace bowler. *Team* Leicestershire (1961–76, 83 matches).
Career batting
83–128–15–2079–78–18.39–0–*ct* 61
Bowling 2756–92–29.95–0–0–4/28
He was a noted soccer player, appearing for Leicester City, Brighton and Hove Albion, Chesterfield, Preston North End and Lincoln City, and in England Under-23 Internationals.

Cross, James
Professional. *b:* 6.2.1862, Leyland, Lancashire. *d:* 22.3.1927, Great Harwood, Lancashire. Lower order batsman, bowler. *Team* Derbyshire (1897, 9 matches).
Career batting
9–15–4–82–29*–7.45–0–*ct* 4
Bowling 634–22–28.81–0–0–4/68

Cross, Joseph John
Amateur. *b:* 23.2.1849, Merriott, Somerset. *d:* 2.11.1918, Lambridge, Bath, Somerset. Middle order right-hand batsman. *Sch* Uppingham. *Team* Gloucestershire (1870, 2 matches).
Career batting
2–2–0–5–5–2.50–0–*ct* 0
He also played for Devon.

Crosse, Charles William
Amateur. *b:* 13.6.1854, Bushey, Hertfordshire. *d:* 28.5.1905, Paris, France. Middle order right-hand batsman, good field. *Sch* Rugby. *Team* Oxford U (1875).
Career batting
1–2–0–13–8–6.50–0–*ct* 1
He also played for Devon (1886). He was an excellent rugby footballer, winning a blue and representing England.

Crosse, Edmund Mitchell
Amateur. *b:* 11.12.1882, Camberwell, London. *d:* 28.6.1963, Putney, London. Opening or middle order right-hand batsman. *Sch* Cheltenham. *Team* Northamptonshire (1905–10, 48 matches).
Career batting
48–90–4–1168–65–13.58–0–*ct* 16
He captained Northamptonshire in 1907. He first played for Northamptonshire (pre first-class) in 1903.

Crosskey, Thomas Roland
Professional. *b:* 4.7.1905, Hastings, Sussex. *d:* 25.3.1971, Totnes, Devon. Opening right-hand batsman, right-arm fast medium bowler. *Team* Scotland (1949–50).
Career batting
4–8–0–236–81–29.50–0–*ct* 2
Bowling 26–0
He played for Northumberland in 1957 but not in a Minor County Championship game. He played soccer for Crystal Palace, Hearts and Albion Rovers.

Crossland, Andrew
Professional. *b:* 30.11.1816, Dalton, Huddersfield, Yorkshire. *d:* 17.11.1902, Hull, Yorkshire. Brother of Joseph (Yorkshire 1850), father of S. M. (Yorkshire). Middle order right-hand batsman, right-hand medium pace round-arm bowler. *Team* Yorkshire (1844–55, 5 matches).
Career batting
8–16–1–138–28–9.20–0–*ct* 3–*st* 2
Bowling 146–11+1–13.27–0–0–4/11
He was regarded as the best Yorkshire bowler of his day. He also played for Northumberland (1852). His final first-class match was for AEE in 1857.

Crossland, John
Professional. *b:* 2.4.1852, Sutton-in-Ashfield, Nottinghamshire. *d:* 26.9.1903, Blackburn, Lancashire. Hard-hitting lower order batsman, very fast right-arm bowler, excellent deep field. *Team* Lancashire (1878–85, 71 matches).
Career batting
84–132–25–1172–51–10.95–0–*ct* 32
Bowling 4019–322–12.48–25–6–8/57
His bowling was regarded a 'pure throw' by many experts and several counties refused to play Lancashire so long as Crossland and Nash were in the County Eleven. He was finally forced out of County cricket on the grounds that he was not qualified for Lancashire – his *bona fide* residence being in the County of his birth. His final first-class match was for C. I. Thornton's XI in 1887. He took 112 wickets, av 10.06, in 1882.

Crossland, Samuel Moorhouse
Professional. *b:* 16.8.1851, Leeds, Yorkshire. *d:* 11.4.1906, Wakefield, Yorkshire. Son of Andrew (Yorkshire), nephew of Joseph (Yorkshire 1850). Middle or lower order right-hand batsman, wicket-keeper. *Team* Yorkshire (1883–86, 4 matches).
Career batting
4–6–2–32–20–8.00–0–*ct* 3–*st* 5

Crossman, George Lytton
Amateur. *b:* 18.2.1877, Hambrook, Bristol. *d:* 17.1.1947, Colchester, Essex. Middle order right-hand batsman, leg break bowler. *Sch* Radley. *Team* Gloucestershire (1896, 2 matches).
Career batting
2–4–0–11–5–2.75–0–*ct* 0

Crothers, George Marcus
Amateur. *b:* 30.1.1909, Belfast, Ireland. *d:* 5.2.1982, Lisburn, Co Antrim, Ireland. Tail end right-hand batsman, wicket-keeper. *Sch* Royal Belfast Academical Institution. *Team* Ireland (1931–47).
Career batting
10–19–1–174–41–9.66–0–*ct* 6–*st* 3

Crothers, Dr Joseph Graham
Cricketer. *b:* 8.4.1949, Belfast, Ireland. Middle order right-hand batsman. *Sch* Royal Belfast Academical Institution. *Team* Ireland (1972).
Career batting
1–2–0–10–10–5.00–0–*ct* 1
He won a blue at Cambridge U for rugby.

Crouch, Henry Russell
Amateur. *b:* 10.2.1914, Calcutta, India. *d:* 17.4.1991, Claygate, Surrey. Nephew of E. R. (Queensland) and G. S. (Queensland). Middle order right-hand batsman, right-arm medium pace bowler. *Sch* Tonbridge. *Team* Surrey (1946, 1 match). *Tour* Martineau to Egypt 1939 (not first-class).
Career batting
3–3–0–11–7–3.66–0–*ct* 1
Bowling 101–2–50.50–0–0–1/34
His debut in first-class matches was for Minor Counties in 1935 – he was a mainstay of Surrey 2nd XI for many years.

Crouch, Maurice Alfred
Amateur. *b:* 9.8.1917, Wisbech, Cambridgeshire. Opening right-hand batsman. *Sch* Oundle. *Teams* MCC (1950); Minor Counties (1952).
Career batting
4–7–0–205–81–29.28–0–*ct* 7
His County cricket was for Cambridgeshire (1936–63).

Crowder, Alfred Joseph
Amateur. *b:* 3.4.1878, Clipston, Northamptonshire. *d:* 12.10.1961, Isleworth, Middlesex. Opening or middle order batsman. *Team* Somerset (1908, 3 matches).
Career batting
3–6–0–44–24–7.33–0–*ct* 1

Crowder, Frederick
Amateur. *b:* 8.10.1845. *d:* 27.3.1938, Oxford. Opening batsman. *Sch* Rugby. *Team* MCC (1874).
Career batting
3–6–1–25–14–5.00–0–*ct* 1
His first-class debut was for Gentlemen of England in 1873 and his County cricket for Berkshire (1869). He was a rowing blue at Oxford U in 1866 and 1867.

Crowdy, Rev James Gordon
Amateur. *b:* 2.7.1847, Westrop House, Highworth, Wiltshire. *d:* 16.12.1918, Sarum, Winchester, Hampshire. Middle order right-hand batsman. *Sch* Rugby. *Team* Hampshire (1875–84, 6 matches).
Career batting
7–12–0–112–21–9.33–0–*ct* 0
Bowling 31–1–31.00–0–0–1/31
He did not appear in any first-class matches whilst at Oxford. His first-class debut was for MCC in 1872, playing against Oxford U. He also played for Berkshire (1869–70), Worcestershire (pre first-class, 1871–72) and Devon (1874).

Crowe, George Lawson
Amateur. *b:* 8.1.1885, Worcester. *d:* 23.6.1976, Bromley, Kent. Middle order right-hand batsman. *Sch* Westminster and Tonbridge. *Team* Worcestershire (1906–13, 23 matches).
Career batting
23–38–2–584–78–16.22–0–*ct* 5
Bowling 35–2–17.50–0–0–1/6

Crowe, Jeffrey John
Cricketer. *b:* 14.9.1958, Cornwall Park, Auckland, New Zealand. Son of D. W. (Wellington), brother of M. D. (New Zealand). Middle order right-hand batsman. *Teams* South Australia (1977/8 to 1981/2, 34 matches); Auckland (1982/3 to 1991/2). *Tours* New Zealand to Australia 1982/3 (not first-class), 1984/5 (not first-class), 1985/6, 1987/8, 1989/90, to England 1983, 1986, 1990, to Sri Lanka 1983/4, 1984/5 (not first-class), 1985/6 (not first-class), 1986/7, to Pakistan 1984/5, to West Indies 1984/5, to Sharjah (not first-class) 1985/6, to India 1987/8 (World Cup); Young New Zealand to Zimbabwe 1984/5. *Tests* New Zealand (1982/3 to 1989/90, 39 matches).
Career batting
180–304–34–10233–159–37.90–22–*ct* 199
Bowling 55–1–55.00–0–0–1/10
Test batting
39–65–4–1601–128–26.24–3–*ct* 41
Bowling 9–0
Although he played in two Tests on the 1983 tour of England, and all three Tests in 1986, he achieved only modest results. On the 1990 visit he failed to obtain a place in the Test side. He captained New Zealand in 6 Test matches. He scored 1,063 runs, av 62.52, in New Zealand in 1991/2.

Crowe, Martin David, MBE
Cricketer. *b:* 22.9.1962, Henderson, Auckland, New Zealand. Son of D. W. (Wellington), brother of J. J. (New Zealand). Middle order right-hand batsman, right-arm medium pace bowler. *Teams* Auckland (1979/80 to 1982/3); Central Districts (1983/4 to 1989/90); Somerset (1984–88, 48 matches); Wellington (1990/1 to 1991/2). *Tours* New Zealand to Australia 1982/3, 1984/5 (not first-class), 1985/6, 1987/8, 1989/90, 1990/1 (not first-class), to England 1983, 1986, 1990, to Sri Lanka 1983/4, 1984/5 (not first-class), 1985/6 (not first-class), 1986/7, to Pakistan 1984/5, 1990/1, to West Indies 1984/5, to Sharjah (not first-class) 1985/6, 1989/90, to India 1987/8 (World Cup); Rest of World to England 1985, 1989. *Tests* New Zealand (1981/2 to 1991/2, 59 matches).
Career batting
210–345–54–16602–299–57.05–58–*ct* 197
Bowling 3817–117–32.62–4–0–5/18
Test batting
59–98–10–4205–299–47.78–13–*ct* 58
Bowling 651–14–46.50–0–0–2/25

A very sound batsman who plays his strokes in accordance with the coaching manual, he has topped the tourists' batting averages on each of his three tours to England and appeared in all the Tests on each visit. His Test batting in England however has never quite reached the heights expected, but on his first season in County cricket, for Somerset in 1984, he hit 1,870 runs, av 53.42. He completed 1,000 runs in England in one other season. His highest Test innings is also his highest first-class score, 299 for New Zealand v Sri Lanka at Wellington in 1990/1. During that innings he added a record 467 for the 3rd wicket with A. H. Jones. In 1990/1 he also took over as New Zealand's regular Test captain, in 8 matches to date. His first-class debut in England was for D. B. Close's XI in 1982. He scored 1,676 runs, av 93.11, in New Zealand in 1986/7, including 8 hundreds, both national records.

Crowe, Dr Philip John
Cricketer. *b:* 27.10.1955, Westminster, London. Lower order left-hand batsman, left-arm medium pace bowler. *Team* Oxford U (1982).
Career batting
1–2–0–11–11–5.50–0–*ct* 0
Bowling 121–1–121.00–0–0–1/105
A good rugby footballer, he gained his blue at Oxford and was capped six times for Australia.

Crowhurst, William
Amateur. *b:* 24.10.1849, Chislehurst, Kent. *d:* 4.7.1915, St Mary Cray, Kent. Tail end batsman, right-arm fast bowler. *Team* Kent (1877, 1 match).
Career batting
1–2–0–1–1–0.50–0–*ct* 0
Bowling 46–1–46.00–0–0–1/26

Crowther, Arthur
Professional. *b:* 1.8.1878, Leeds, Yorkshire. *d:* 4.6.1946, East Bierley, Bradford, Yorkshire. Lower order batsman. *Team* Yorkshire (1905, 1 match).
Career batting
1–2–0–0–0–0.00–0–*ct* 1

Crowther, Fred
Amateur. *b:* 22.1.1857, Birstall, Leeds, Yorkshire. *d:* 16.10.1899, Wyke, North Bierley, Yorkshire. Opening right-hand batsman. *Team* L. Hall's XI (1891).
Career batting
1–2–1–60–43*–60.00–0–*ct* 0
He appeared for Yorkshire in 1890 in a non-first-class match.

Crowther, Peter Gwynne
Cricketer. *b:* 26.4.1952, Neath, Glamorgan. Middle order right-hand batsman, off break bowler. *Team* Glamorgan (1977–78, 9 matches).
Career batting
9–14–0–185–99–13.21–0–*ct* 3
Bowling 22–1–22.00–0–0–1/22

He hit 99 for Glamorgan v Cambridge U at Fenner's on his first-class debut.

Croxford, Henry
Professional. *b:* 14.6.1845, Hadlow, Kent. *d:* 15.12.1892, Faversham, Kent. Hard-hitting lower order right-hand batsman, right-hand fast round-arm bowler. *Team* Kent (1869–77, 27 matches).
Career batting
27–51–11–472–53–11.80–0–*ct* 9
Bowling 683–31–22.03–2–0–6/45

Crozier, William Magee
Amateur. *b:* 5.12.1873, Roebuck Hall, Dundrum, Dublin, Ireland. *d:* 1.7.1916, Thiepval, France. Lower order right-hand batsman. *Sch* Repton. *Team* Dublin University (1895).
Career batting
1–2–0–7–4–3.50–0–*ct* 0
Bowling 42–0

Crump, Brian Stanley
Professional. *b:* 25.4.1938, Chell, Stoke-on-Trent, Staffordshire. Cousin of D. S. Steele (Northamptonshire and Derbyshire) and J. F. Steele (Leicestershire and Glamorgan). Middle order right-hand batsman, right-arm medium pace off break bowler. *Team* Northamptonshire (1960–72, 317 matches).
Career batting
321–479–111–8789–133*–23.88–5–*ct* 144
Bowling 20163–814–24.77–30–5–7/29

He reached 1,000 runs in a season twice (best 1,396, av 29.08, in 1961) and 100 wickets in a season also twice (best 112, av 18.88, in 1965). He also played for Staffordshire (1955–58).

Crump, Rev Thomas
Amateur. *b:* 5.7.1845, Bristol. *d:* 8.1.1907, East Pennard, Somerset. Middle order right-hand batsman, lob bowler. *Team* Somerset (1885, 1 match).
Career batting
1–1–0–8–8–8.00–0–*ct* 0

He also played for Herefordshire (1877).

Crush, Edmund
Amateur. *b:* 25.4.1917, Crabble, Dover, Kent. Lower order right-hand batsman, right-arm medium pace off break bowler. *Team* Kent (1946–49, 45 matches).
Career batting
45–72–5–1078–78–16.08–0–*ct* 23
Bowling 3163–83–38.10–2–0–6/50

Crutchley, Edward
Amateur. *b:* 2.4.1922, Paddington, London. *d:* 18.10.1982, Guildford, Surrey. Son of G. E. V. (Middlesex), great-nephew of P. E. (MCC). Middle order right-hand batsman. *Sch* Harrow. *Team* Middlesex (1947, 2 matches).
Career batting
2–4–0–28–14–7.00–0–*ct* 1

Crutchley, Gerald Edward Victor
Amateur. *b:* 19.11.1890, Chelsea, London. *d:* 17.8.1969, St John's Wood, London. Father of Edward (Middlesex), nephew of P. E. (MCC), son-in-law of W. H. Spottiswoode (Kent). Opening or middle order batsman, right-arm medium pace leg break bowler. *Sch* Harrow. *Teams* Oxford U (1910–12, blue 1912); Middlesex (1910–30, 54 matches).
Career batting
123–200–17–4112–181–22.46–5–*ct* 53
Bowling 2191–67–32.70–0–0–4/52

In the 1912 University match he made 99 not out on the first day, then was found to be ill with measles overnight and compelled to retire from the match. His last first-class match was for Leveson-Gower's XI in 1932. He was President of Middlesex 1958–62. During the First World War he was a prisoner in Germany for almost four years.

Crutchley, Percy Edward
Amateur. *b:* 24.7.1855, Parson's Town, King's County, Ireland. *d:* 16.10.1940, Sunninghill, Berkshire. Uncle of G. E. V. (Middlesex), great-uncle of Edward (Middlesex). Hard-hitting middle order right-hand batsman, right-hand slow round-arm bowler, excellent long-stop. *Sch* Harrow. *Team* MCC (1876).
Career batting
3–5–1–128–84–32.00–0–*ct* 0
Bowling 68–2–34.00–0–0–2/68

Whilst at Cambridge he did not appear in any first-class matches. His final first-class match was for Gentlemen in 1878.

Cruwys, Rev Robert Geoffrey
Amateur. *b:* 10.3.1884, Cruwys-Morchard, Devon. *d:* 25.8.1951, Cruwys-Morchard, Devon. Middle order batsman, useful bowler. *Sch* Blundell's. *Team* Oxford U (1907).
Career batting
1–2–0–29–19–14.50–0–*ct* 0

His County cricket was for Devon (1903–13).

Crwys-Williams, Gareth
Amateur. *b:* 27.12.1907, Crickhowell, Breconshire. *d:* 8.3.1970, Llangollen, Denbighshire. Lower order batsman, left-arm medium fast bowler. *Sch* Bancrofts and Mill Hill. *Team* MCC (1934).
Career batting
1–1–1–0–0*–no av–0–*ct* 0
Bowling 18–0

His County cricket was for Monmouthshire (1930–33) and Lincolnshire (1949–51). He played in the trial matches at Cambridge U, but not in first-class games.

Cudworth, Henry
Amateur. *b:* 6.12.1873, Burnley, Lancashire. *d:* 5.4.1914, Burnley, Lancashire. Middle order batsman. *Team* Lancashire (1900, 1 match).

Career batting
1–1–0–4–4–4.00–0–*ct* 0

He hit a fine century for Lancashire v West Indies in 1900 – the West Indies tour that year however was not first class.

Cuffe, Charles Richard
Amateur. *b:* 5.8.1914, Dublin, Ireland. *d:* 10.11.1972, Dublin, Ireland. Lower order left-hand batsman, wicket-keeper. *Sch* Stonyhurst. *Team* Ireland (1936–39).
Career batting
3–6–2–61–18–15.25–0–*ct* 2–*st* 4

Cuffe, John Alexander
Professional. *b:* 26.6.1880, Sydney, New South Wales, Australia. *d:* 16.5.1931. He was found drowned at Burton-on-Trent, Staffordshire. He took his own life. Middle order right-hand batsman, slow left-arm bowler. *Teams* New South Wales (1902/3, 1 match); Worcestershire (1903–14, 215 matches).
Career batting
221–368–32–7476–145–22.25–4–*ct* 126
Bowling 18803–738–25.47–33–7–9/38

He reached 1,000 runs in a season three times (best 1,112, av 31.77, in 1906) and 100 wickets twice (best 110, av 23.56, in 1911). In 1911 he performed the 'double'. His best bowling was 9/38 for Worcestershire v Yorkshire at Bradford in 1907. He played soccer for Glossop. At the time of his death he had just taken up an appointment as coach at Repton School. He was a first-class umpire (1925–27).

Cull, George
Professional. *b:* 3.3.1856, Lymington, Hampshire. *d:* 9.5.1898, Sandown, Isle of Wight. Lower order batsman, wicket-keeper. *Team* Hampshire (1877, 2 matches).
Career batting
2–4–0–14–7–3.50–0–*ct* 1

Cullen, Alexander Coney
Amateur. *b:* 17.1.1889, Uddingston, Lanarkshire, Scotland. *d:* 25.2.1922, Glasgow, Scotland. Lower order left-hand batsman, leg break bowler. *Team* Scotland (1912–21).
Career batting
4–7–2–34–11–6.80–0–*ct* 2
Bowling 42–0

Cullen, Leonard
Professional. *b:* 23.11.1914, Johannesburg, South Africa. *d:* 15.9.1984, South Africa. Lower order right-hand batsman, right-arm medium pace bowler. *Sch* St Andrew's College, Bloemfontein, South Africa. *Team* Northamptonshire (1934–35, 18 matches).
Career batting
18–31–1–253–40–8.43–0–*ct* 4
Bowling 650–11–59.09–0–0–3/73

Whilst playing for Northamptonshire v Glamorgan at Llanelly in 1935, he had the frightening experience of falling out of his bedroom window whilst sleepwalking and was badly bruised.

Cullimore, Martin Henry
Amateur. *b:* 4.12.1908, Stroud, Gloucestershire. Middle order right-hand batsman. *Sch* Wycliffe. *Team* Gloucestershire (1929, 3 matches).
Career batting
3–3–0–19–15–6.33–0–*ct* 0

Cullinan, Mark Ronald
Cricketer. *b:* 3.4.1957, Johannesburg, South Africa. Lower order right-hand batsman, wicket-keeper. *Team:* Oxford U (1983–84, blue both years).
Career batting
16–21–2–215–59–11.31–0–*ct* 18–*st* 1
Bowling 4–1–4.00–0–0–1/4

His first-class debut was for South African Universities in 1979/80.

Cumberbatch, C. P.
Professional. *b:* 22.11.1882, Barbados. *d:* 15.2.1922, Port of Spain, Trinidad. Lower order batsman, right-arm medium pace bowler. *Team* Trinidad (1904/5 to 1921/2). *Tour* West Indies to England 1906.
Career batting
30–50–10–804–127*–20.10–1–*ct* 31
Bowling 1636–92–17.78–6–2–8/27

He performed moderately on his single tour to England.

Cumberlege, Barry Stephenson
Amateur. *b:* 5.6.1891, Newcastle upon Tyne, Northumberland. *d:* 22.9.1970, Sandgate, Folkestone, Kent. Son of C. F. (Surrey). Opening right-hand batsman. *Sch* Durham. *Teams* Cambridge U (1913, blue); Kent (1923–24, 6 matches).
Career batting
14–23–3–763–172–38.15–1–*ct* 5
Bowling 13–0

He also played for Durham (pre first-class, 1909) and Northumberland (1911–12). A noted rugby footballer, he played for Cambridge against Oxford four times as scrum-half and for Blackheath and England in the 1920s.

Cumberlege, Charles Farrington
Amateur. *b:* 29.7.1851, Kurreebee, India. *d:* 12.2.1929, Ealing Common, Middlesex. Father of B. S. (Kent). Middle order right-hand batsman. *Sch* Rossall. *Team* Surrey (1872, 2 matches).
Career batting
2–4–0–30–26–7.50–0–*ct* 1

He also played for Wiltshire (1867) and Northumberland (1875–92).

Cumbes, James
Cricketer. *b:* 4.5.1944, East Didsbury, Manchester, Lancashire. Brother-in-law of R. Collins (Lanca-

shire). Lower order right-hand batsman, right-arm fast medium bowler. *Teams* Lancashire (1963–71, 9 matches); Surrey (1968–69, 29 matches); Worcestershire (1972–81, 109 matches); Warwickshire (1982, 14 matches).
Career batting
161–133–67–498–43–7.54–0–*ct* 38
Bowling 11447–379–30.20–13–0–6/24

He was Commercial Manager of Warwickshire CCC 1982–87 and has held a similar position with Lancashire since 1988. A good soccer player, he kept goal for Tranmere Rovers, West Bromwich Albion, Aston Villa, Southport and Worcester City.

Cuming, Thomas
Amateur. *b:* 21.4.1893, Woolwich, Kent. *d:* 18.8.1960, Cooden Beach, Bexhill, Sussex. Stylish middle order batsman, change bowler. *Sch* Malvern. *Teams* Middlesex (1913, 1 match); Ceylon (1925/6 to 1930/1).
Career batting
5–8–0–112–36–14.00–0–*ct* 1
Bowling 22–1–22.00–0–0–1/12

Cumming, Bruce Leonard
Amateur. *b:* 11.7.1916, Germiston, Transvaal, South Africa. *d:* 5.5.1968, Johannesburg, South Africa. Cousin of A. Melville (South Africa) and C. M. Melville (Oxford U). Hard-hitting middle order right-hand batsman, right-arm medium pace bowler. *Teams* Oxford U (1936–37); Sussex (1936–38, 17 matches).
Career batting
24–36–1–684–60–19.54–0–*ct* 10
Bowling 52–2–26.00–0–0–2/19

Cunis, Robert Smith
Cricketer. *b:* 5.1.1941, Whangarei, Auckland, New Zealand. Middle or lower order right-hand batsman, right-arm fast medium bowler. *Teams* Auckland (1960/1 to 1973/4); Northern Districts (1975/6 to 1976/7). *Tours* New Zealand to England 1969, to India and Pakistan 1969/70, to Australia 1969/70, 1970/1, to West Indies 1971/2; Rest of World to Australia 1971/2. *Tests* New Zealand (1965/6 to 1971/2, 20 matches).
Career batting
132–157–45–1849–111–16.50–1–*ct* 30
Bowling 10287–386–26.65–18–2–7/29
Test batting
20–31–8–295–51–12.82–0–*ct* 1
Bowling 1887–51–37.00–1–0–6/76

On his 1969 visit to England he was unable to find his form until late in the tour. His 38 first-class wickets cost 27.76.

Cunliffe, Charles Morley
Amateur. *b:* 2.9.1858, Leyton, Essex. *d:* 15.10.1884, Davos-Platz, Switzerland, of consumption. Middle order right-hand batsman, right-hand medium pace round-arm bowler. *Sch* Rugby. *Team* Kent (1877–80, 23 matches).
Career batting
25–44–4–378–47–9.45–0–*ct* 18
Bowling 1395–93–15.00–11–3–7/25

Cunliffe, Sir Foster Hugh Egerton
Amateur. *b:* 17.8.1875, Westminster, London. *d:* 10.7.1916, of wounds at Ovilliers La Boiselle, France. Lower order left-hand batsman, left-arm medium pace bowler. *Sch* Eton. *Teams* Oxford U (1895–98, blue all four years); Middlesex (1897–1903, 18 matches).
Career batting
56–85–16–1053–70–15.26–0–*ct* 25
Bowling 5120–235–21.78–15–5–8/26

He also played for Shropshire (1895). His final first-class match was for I Zingari in 1904. He captained Oxford in 1898. He was a distinguished military historian.

Cunliffe, Robert Lionel Brooke
Amateur. *b:* 15.3.1895, Woolwich, London. *d:* 29.11.1990, Pakenham, Bury St Edmunds, Suffolk. Lower order right-hand batsman, leg break and googly bowler. *Team* Royal Navy (1914–29).
Career batting
10–18–2–335–87–20.93–0–*ct* 2
Bowling 582–16–36.37–1–0–5/78

Cunningham, Alec George Gordon
Amateur. *b:* 15.7.1905, Knowle, Somerset. *d:* 21.7.1981, Keynsham, Somerset. Tail end right-hand batsman, wicket-keeper. *Team* Somerset(1930, 2 matches).
Career batting
2–3–2–10–6*–10.00–0–*ct* 3–*st* 1

Cunningham, Edward James
Cricketer. *b:* 16.5.1962, Oxford. Nephew of F. G. Mann (Middlesex) and J. P. Mann (Middlesex), great-nephew of F. T. Mann (Middlesex). Middle order left-hand batsman, off break bowler. *Sch* Marlborough. *Team* Gloucestershire (1982–84, 14 matches).
Career batting
14–23–6–271–61*–15.94–0–*ct* 4
Bowling 264–4–66.00–0–0–2/55

Cunningham, William Henry Ranger
Amateur. *b:* 23.1.1900, Christchurch, New Zealand. *d:* 29.11.1984, Christchurch, New Zealand. Uncle of G. F. Anderson (Canterbury). Lower order right-hand batsman, right-arm medium fast bowler. *Team* Canterbury (1922/3 to 1930/1). *Tours* New Zealand to Australia 1925/6, to England 1927.
Career batting
32–50–16–396–33*–11.64–0–*ct* 8
Bowling 3122–91–34.30–4–0–6/33

Although he proved the best bowler on his tour to Australia, his form in England in 1927 was a complete disappointment.

Cupitt, Joseph
(registered at birth as J. Cupit)
Professional. *b:* 25.9.1867, Barrow Hill, Derbyshire. *d:* 6.5.1932, South Kirkby, Yorkshire. Lower order batsman, left-arm medium pace off break bowler. *Team* Derbyshire (1905, 2 matches).
Career batting
2–4–2–19–13–9.50–0–*ct* 0
Bowling 145–3–48.33–0–0–2/24
He first played for Derbyshire (not first-class) in 1892.

Curgenven, Gilbert
Amateur. *b:* 1.12.1882, Derby. *d:* 26.5.1934, Birmingham. Brother of H. G. (Derbyshire), son of W. G. (Derbyshire). Middle order right-hand batsman, slow bowler. *Sch* Repton. *Team* Derbyshire (1901–22, 95 matches).
Career batting
95–169–5–3440–124–20.97–3–*ct* 40
Bowling 1163–25–46.52–0–0–3/32

Curgenven, Henry Grafton
Amateur. *b:* 22.12.1875, Derby. *d:* 14.2.1959, Bryncethin, Bridgend, Glamorgan. Brother of Gilbert (Derbyshire), son of W. G. (Derbyshire). Middle order right-hand batsman, right-arm fast medium bowler. *Sch* Repton. *Teams* Derbyshire (1896–97, 9 matches); Cambridge U (1897).
Career batting
11–14–1–125–26–9.61–0–*ct* 6
Bowling 223–7–31.85–0–0–2/9
He was later engaged as a club professional.

Curgenven, Dr William Grafton
Amateur. *b:* 30.11.1841, Plymouth, Devon. *d:* 18.3.1910, Fareham, Hampshire. Father of Gilbert (Derbyshire) and H. G. (Derbyshire). Middle order right-hand batsman. *Sch* Wellingborough and Aldenham. *Team* Derbyshire (1872–78, 17 matches).
Career batting
17–30–0–376–71–12.53–0–*ct* 5
He also played for Devon (1862–66).

Curle, Arthur Charles
Amateur. *b:* 27.7.1895, Milverton, Leamington Spa, Warwickshire. *d:* 2.2.1966, Aylesbury, Buckinghamshire. Brother of Gerald (Warwickshire). Middle order left-hand batsman, left-arm bowler. *Teams* Warwickshire (1920, 3 matches); Rhodesia (1922/3).
Career batting
4–6–1–102–40–20.40–0–*ct* 0
Bowling 14–0

Curle, Gerald
Amateur. *b:* 7.6.1893, Milverton, Leamington Spa, Warwickshire. *d:* 4.3.1977, Budleigh Salterton, Devon. Brother of A. C. (Warwickshire). Middle order right-hand batsman, off break bowler. *Sch* King Edward's, Birmingham. *Team* Warwickshire (1913, 5 matches).
Career batting
5–9–0–54–34–6.00–0–*ct* 2
Bowling 3–1–3.00–0–0–1/3

Curley, Simon Andrew
Amateur. *b:* 21.7.1917, Pembroke, Dublin, Ireland. *d:* 11.3.1989, Dublin, Ireland. Middle order left-hand batsman. *Team* Ireland (1948–51).
Career batting
5–10–1–175–43–19.44–0–*ct* 6

Curran, Kevin Malcolm
Cricketer. *b:* 7.9.1959, Rusape, Rhodesia. Son of K. P. (Rhodesia). Middle order right-hand batsman, right-arm fast medium bowler. *Teams* Zimbabwe (1980/1 to 1987/8); Gloucestershire (1985–90, 139 matches); Natal (1988/9); Northamptonshire (1991–92, 42 matches). *Tours* Zimbabwe to England 1982, 1983 (World Cup), to Sri Lanka 1983/4, to India (World Cup) 1987/8.
Career batting
210–320–53–9441–144*–35.35–18–*ct* 118
Bowling 10589–409–25.88–12–4–7/47
He hit 1,000 runs in a season five times (best 1,353, av 43.64, in 1986). At the close of 1990 his contract with Gloucestershire was not renewed; this caused some controversial newspaper comment.

Currie, Cecil Edmund
Amateur. *b:* 4.4.1861, Bright Waltham, Berkshire. *d:* 2.1.1937, Staines, Middlesex. Son of F. L. (Cambridge U 1845), nephew of Fendall (Gentlemen of Kent), R. G. (Gentlemen of Surrey and Sussex) and W. C. (Gentlemen of Surrey and Sussex), cousin of F. A. (MCC). Lower order right-hand batsman, right-arm slow bowler, splendid field. *Sch* Marlborough. *Teams* Hampshire (1881–85, 16 matches); Cambridge U (1883).
Career batting
20–35–10–300–32–12.00–0–*ct* 9
Bowling 1426–64–22.28–2–1–8/57
His last first-class appearance was for Oxford and Cambridge, Past and Present in 1890. He last played for Hampshire (not first-class) in 1893.

Currie, Frederick Alexander
Amateur. *b:* 23.9.1851, India. *d:* 13.6.1902, Aldeburgh, Suffolk. Nephew of R. G. (Gentlemen of Surrey and Sussex), F. L. (Cambridge U), Fendall (Gentlemen of Kent) and W. C. (Gentlemen of Surrey and Sussex), cousin of C. E. (Hampshire), brother-in-law of E. F. Dyke (Cambridge U), C. E. Bateman-Champain (Gloucestershire), F. H. Bateman-Champain (Gloucestershire), H. F. Bateman-Champain (Gloucestershire) and J. N. Bateman-Champain (Gloucestershire). Middle order right-hand batsman.

Currie, John David

Sch Harrow. *Team* MCC (1894).
Career batting
1–2–0–10–7–5.00–0–*ct* 1
His County cricket was for Norfolk (1881–87).

Currie, John David
Amateur. *b:* 3.5.1932, Clifton, Bristol. *d:* 8.12.1990, Leicester. Attacking middle order right-hand batsman. *Sch* Bristol GS. *Teams* Somerset (1953, 1 match); Oxford U (1956–57).
Career batting
10–20–1–283–38–14.89–0–*ct* 4
An excellent rugby footballer he played for Gloucester, Oxford U and England.

Cursham, Arthur William
Amateur. *b:* 14.3.1853, Nottingham. *d:* 24.12.1884, Florida, USA, of yellow fever. Brother of H. A. (Nottinghamshire). Middle order right-hand batsman, slow round-arm bowler, brilliant cover field. *Sch* Oakham School. *Teams* Nottinghamshire (1876–78, 12 matches); Derbyshire (1879–80, 9 matches).
Career batting
21–35–0–314–67–8.97–0–*ct* 10
Bowling 49–1–49.00–0–0–1/39
A noted soccer player with Notts County and Nottingham Forest, he represented England six times at outside right 1876–83, on two occasions with his brother H. A. in the side. He emigrated to Florida, but died within a year of reaching there.

Cursham, Henry Alfred
Amateur. *b:* 27.11.1859, Wilford, Nottinghamshire. *d:* 6.8.1941, Holme Pierrepont, Nottinghamshire. Brother of A. W. (Nottinghamshire and Derbyshire). Lower order right-hand batsman, wicket-keeper. *Sch* Repton. *Team* Nottinghamshire (1880–1904, 2 matches).
Career batting
2–3–1–41–25*–20.50–0–*ct* 1
Bowling 43–0
His two appearances in first-class cricket were separated by 24 years. A noted soccer player for Notts County and Corinthians, he appeared in eight internationals for England, 1880–84, on two occasions with his brother A. W. in the side.

Curteis, Edward Witherden
Amateur. *b:* 17.4.1853, Corsley Hall, Wiltshire. *d:* 25.2.1902, Mottram, Macclesfield, Cheshire. Middle order right-hand batsman. *Sch* Tonbridge. *Team* Kent (1877, 1 match).
Career batting
2–3–0–17–8–5.66–0–*ct* 0
His final first-class match was for MCC in 1887.

Curteis, Brig Gen Francis Algernon
Amateur. *b:* 26.6.1856, Bideford, Devon. *d:* 1.5.1928, Tenby, Pembrokeshire. Lower order batsman, fast bowler. *Sch* Malvern. *Team* Gloucestershire (1884, 6 matches).
Career batting
6–10–1–72–27*–8.00–0–*ct* 3
Bowling 127–0
He also played for Devon (1883).

Curteis, Herbert
Amateur. *b:* 14.4.1849, Windmill Hill, Hailsham, Sussex. *d:* 28.10.1919, Windmill Hill Place, Hailsham, Sussex. Son of H. M. (Sussex), brother of R. M. (Sussex). Lower order right-hand batsman, right-hand medium round-arm bowler. *Sch* Westminster. *Team* Sussex (1873, 1 match).
Career batting
4–6–1–48–25–9.60–0–*ct* 0
His last first-class match was for MCC in 1880. He did not appear in any first-class matches whilst at Oxford U.

Curteis, Herbert Mascall
Amateur. *b:* 8.1.1823, Florence, Italy. *d:* 16.6.1895, Windmill Hill Place, Hailsham, Sussex. Father of Herbert (Sussex) and R. M. (Sussex). Middle order right-hand batsman, slow round-arm bowler, good deep field. *Sch* Westminster. *Teams* Oxford U (1841–42, blue both years); Sussex (1846–60, 43 matches).
Career batting
57–102–20–560–29–6.82–0–*ct* 11
Bowling 27–1+10–27.00–0–0–3/?
He was for many years a liberal supporter of Sussex cricket and was President of the County Club 1869–78. He was MP for Rye 1847–52.

Curteis, Robert Mascall
Amateur. *b:* 12.10.1851, Windmill Hill, Hailsham, Sussex. *d:* 21.1.1927, Uckfield, Sussex. Son of H. M. (Sussex), brother of Herbert (Sussex). Middle order right-hand batsman, good field. *Sch* Westminster. *Team* Sussex (1873–78, 9 matches).
Career batting
11–18–1–117–41–6.88–0–*ct* 6
He did not appear in any first-class matches whilst at Oxford U. His last first-class match was for MCC in 1881.

Curteis, Rev Thomas Spencer
Amateur. *b:* 10.3.1843, Shelton, Norfolk. *d:* 5.6.1914, Brampton, Suffolk. Lower order batsman, left-hand fast round-arm bowler. *Sch* Bury St Edmunds School and Felsted. *Team* Cambridge U (1864–65, blue both years).
Career batting
7–13–4–65–16–7.22–0–*ct* 6
Bowling 447–23+1–19.43–0–0–4/23
His County cricket was for Norfolk (1864–72), Cheshire (1866–67) and Suffolk (1870–83).

Curtis, Andrew David
Cricketer. *b:* 12.1.1943, Bedford. Opening right-hand batsman. *Sch* Bedford Modern. *Team* Oxford U

(1966).
Career batting
1–1–0–15–15–15.00–0–*ct* 0

His County cricket was for Bedfordshire (1964–81).

Curtis, David Michael
Cricketer. *b:* 10.4.1965, Salisbury, Rhodesia. Middle order right-hand batsman, leg break bowler. *Team* Oxford U (1990, blue).
Career batting
4–4–0–89–43–22.25–0–*ct* 0
Bowling 8-0

He also won a rugby blue and played for Ireland.

Curtis, Ian James
Cricketer. *b:* 13.5.1959, Purley, Surrey. Lower order left-hand batsman, slow left-arm bowler. *Sch* Whitgift. *Teams* Oxford U (1980–82, blue 1980 and 1982); Surrey (1983–84, 14 matches).
Career batting
31–30–14–77–20*–4.81–0–*ct* 7
Bowling 2109–51–41.35–2–0–6/28

He also played for Oxfordshire (1985–92). He represented Oxford at rugby fives.

Curtis, John Stafford
Professional. *b:* 21.12.1887, Barrow-upon-Soar, Leicestershire. *d:* 8.3.1972, Leicester. Lower order right-hand batsman, off break bowler. *Team* Leicestershire (1906–21, 36 matches).
Career batting
36–57–4–868–66–16.37–0–*ct* 14
Bowling 2334–71–32.87–4–0–7/75

Curtis, Timothy Herbert William
(registered at birth as Roderick Herbert William Curtis)
Amateur. *b:* 3.8.1882, Folkestone, Kent. *d:* 11.6.1966, Little Waltham, Essex. Middle order batsman. *Sch* Harrow. *Team* Sussex (1912, 1 match).
Career batting
1–2–0–3–2–1.50–0–*ct* 0

Curtis, Timothy Stephen
Cricketer. *b:* 15.1.1960, Chislehurst, Kent. Opening right-hand batsman, leg break bowler. *Sch* Worcester RGS. *Teams* Worcestershire (1979–92, 233 matches); Cambridge U (1983, blue). *Tour* Worcestershire to Zimbabwe 1990/1. *Tests* England (1988–89, 5 matches).
Career batting
249–423–54–15311–248–41.49–27–*ct* 139
Bowling 657–11–59.72–0–0–2/17
Test batting
5–9–0–140–41–15.55–0–*ct* 3
Bowling 7–0

He hit 1,000 runs in a season nine times (best 1,829, av 50.80, in 1992). His highest score was 248 for Worcestershire v Somerset at Worcester in 1991. In 1992 he was appointed captain of Worcestershire.

Curtis, William Frederick
Amateur. *b:* 29.5.1881, Leicester. *d:* 23.12.1962, Southfields, Leicester. Middle order right-hand batsman. *Team* Leicestershire (1911–20, 5 matches).
Career batting
5–8–0–69–38–8.62–0–*ct* 0

Being in the legal profession he was unable to appear regularly in County cricket, but was a stalwart of the Leicester Ivanhoe Club.

Curwen, Wilfred John Hutton
Amateur. *b:* 14.4.1883, Beckenham, Kent. *d:* 9.5.1915, near Poperinghe, Belgium. He was killed in action. Brother-in-law of C. Wreford-Brown (Gloucestershire). Middle or lower order right-hand batsman, right-arm fast medium bowler. *Sch* Charterhouse. *Teams* Oxford U (1906, blue); Surrey (1909, 4 matches). *Tours* MCC to New Zealand 1906/7, to Australia 1911/12 (minor matches only).
Career batting
25–44–5–511–76–13.10–0–*ct* 12
Bowling 851–26–32.73–1–0–5/81

His final first-class match was for MCC in 1910, after which he went to Australia, and thus played in emergency for MCC in 1911/12. An excellent soccer player he was awarded his blue at Oxford.

Curzon, Christopher Colin
Cricketer. *b:* 22.12.1958, Lenton, Nottinghamshire. Brother of J. T. (Nottinghamshire). Lower order right-hand batsman, wicket-keeper. *Teams* Nottinghamshire (1978–80, 17 matches); Hampshire (1981, 1 match).
Career batting
18–23–5–307–45–17.05–0–*ct* 32–*st* 3

Curzon, John Timothy
Cricketer. *b:* 4.6.1954, Lenton, Nottinghamshire. Brother of C. C. (Nottinghamshire and Hampshire). Lower order right-hand batsman, right-arm medium pace bowler. *Team* Nottinghamshire (1978, 1 match).
Career batting
1–1–0–1–1–1.00–0–*ct* 1
Bowling 22–0

Cushing, Vincent Gordon Burke
Cricketer. *b:* 17.1.1950, Chichester, Sussex. Middle order right-hand batsman. *Sch* KCS, Wimbledon. *Team* Oxford U (1971–73, blue 1973).
Career batting
14–25–5–565–77*–28.25–0–*ct* 7

Cuthbertson, Arthur
Professional. *b:* 25.8.1901, Belford, Northumberland. *d:* 13.2.1979, Reading, Berkshire. Lower order right-hand batsman, right-arm medium pace bowler. *Team* MCC (1924).

Cuthbertson, Edward Hedley

Career batting
1–2–0–7–6–3.50–0–*ct* 0
Bowling 33–1–33.00–0–0–1/23

His County cricket was for Hertfordshire (1926–29).

Cuthbertson, Edward Hedley
Amateur. *b:* 15.12.1887, Hackney, London. *d:* 24.7.1917, Amara, Mesopotamia. He was killed in action. Brother of G. B. (Sussex, Middlesex and Northamptonshire). Sound defensive left-hand batsman, wicket-keeper. *Sch* Malvern and Charterhouse. *Team* Cambridge U (1908–10).
Career batting
3–6–1–32–18–6.40–0–*ct* 4–*st* 3

His County cricket was for Hertfordshire (1906–13). His final first-class match was for MCC in 1914. He obtained his blue for soccer.

Cuthbertson, Geoffrey Bourke
Amateur. *b:* 23.3.1901, Hampstead, London. Brother of E. H. (Cambridge U). Hard-hitting opening right-hand batsman. *Sch* Malvern. *Teams* Cambridge U (1920–22); Sussex (1920, 1 match); Middlesex (1921–27, 17 matches); Northamptonshire (1935–38, 43 matches).
Career batting
79–140–9–1991–96–15.19–0–*ct* 32

He captained Northamptonshire in 1936 and 1937. He also played for Hertfordshire (1920–25).

Cuthbertson, John Layton
Amateur. *b:* 24.2.1942, Bombay, India. Middle order right-hand batsman, right-arm medium pace bowler. *Sch* Rugby. *Teams* Oxford U (1962–63, blue both years); Surrey (1963, 7 matches).
Career batting
28–51–7–1294–94–29.40–0–*ct* 21
Bowling 1646–34–48.41–1–0–5/32

He was awarded his hockey blue whilst at Oxford.

Cutler, Roy William
Cricketer. *b:* 28.3.1945, West Hartlepool, Co Durham. Lower order right-hand batsman, right-arm medium fast bowler. *Team* Cambridge U (1965–66).
Career batting
6–12–1–79–18–7.18–0–*ct* 1
Bowling 341–9–37.88–1–0–5/39

He won a blue for soccer.

Cutmore, James Albert
Professional. *b:* 28.12.1898, Walthamstow, Essex. *d:* 30.11.1985, Brentwood, Essex. Opening right-hand batsman, right-arm medium pace bowler. *Team* Essex (1924–36, 342 matches).
Career batting
342–593–36–15937–238*–28.61–15–*ct* 121
Bowling 687–11–62.45–0–0–2/31

He reached 1,000 runs in 11 seasons (best 1,876, av 40.78, in 1934). His single double century was 238* for Essex v Gloucestershire at Bristol in 1927.

Cuttell, William
Professional. *b:* 28.1.1835, Sheffield, Yorkshire. *d:* 10.6.1896, Sheffield, Yorkshire. Father of W. R. (Lancashire). Middle order right-hand batsman, 'excellent' bowler. *Team* Yorkshire (1862–71, 15 matches).
Career batting
15–29–7–272–56–12.36–0–*ct* 4
Bowling 596–36+2–16.55–2–0–6/48

Cuttell, Willis Robert
Professional. *b:* 13.9.1864, Sheffield, Yorkshire. *d:* 9.12.1929, Nelson, Lancashire. Son of William (Yorkshire). Middle or lower order right-hand batsman, right-arm slow medium leg break bowler. *Team* Lancashire (1896–1906, 213 matches). *Tour* Hawke to South Africa 1898/9. *Tests* England (1898/9, 2 matches).
Career batting
227–315–31–5938–137–20.90–5–*ct* 140
Bowling 15519–792–19.59–50–8–8/105
Test batting
2–4–0–65–21–16.25–0–*ct* 2
Bowling 73–6–12.16–0–0–3/17

He appeared in two non-first-class matches for Yorkshire in 1890. He scored 1,000 runs in a season twice (best 1,054, av 26.35, in 1899) and took 100 wickets in a season four times (best 120, av 16.45, in 1897). In 1898 he performed the 'double'. He was a first-class umpire (1927–28).

Cuyler, Sir Charles
Amateur. *b:* 15.8.1867, Oakleaze, Gloucestershire. *d:* 1.10.1919, Shotover House, Oxfordshire. Middle order left-hand batsman. *Sch* Clifton. *Team* MCC (1895).
Career batting
1–2–0–0–0–0.00–0–*ct* 0

D

Da Costa, Oscar Constantine
Amateur. *b:* 11.9.1907, Kingston, Jamaica, *d:* 1.10.1936, Kingston, Jamaica. Middle order right-hand batsman, right-arm medium pace bowler. *Team* Jamaica (1928/9 to 1934/5). *Tour* West Indies to England 1933. *Tests* West Indies (1929/30 to 1934/5, 5 matches).
Career batting
39–64–11–1563–105*–29.49–1–*ct* 30
Bowling 1766–44–40.13–0–0–4/31
Test batting
5–9–1–153–39–19.12–0–*ct* 5

Bowling 175–3–58.33–0–0–1/14

In 1933 in England he hit 1,046 runs, av 26.82.

Dacre, Charles Christian Ralph
Amateur, but changed to professional in 1930. *b:* 15.5.1899, Devonport, New Zealand. *d:* 2.11.1975, Devonport, New Zealand. Brother of L. M. (Auckland), uncle of D. D. Coleman (Auckland). Middle order right-hand batsman, slow left-arm bowler, good field. *Teams* Auckland (1914/15 to 1932/3); Gloucestershire (1928–36, 191 matches). *Tours* New Zealand to England 1927, to Australia 1925/6, 1927/8; Tennyson to Jamaica 1931/2.
Career batting
268–439–20–12223–223–29.17–24–*ct* 166–*st* 6
Bowling 1219–39–31.25–1–0–5/35

An outstanding schoolboy cricketer, he hit 1,817 runs and took 149 wickets in all cricket 1912/13, and made his first-class debut in 1914/15. He hit 1,000 runs in a season seven times (best 1,413, av 33.64, in 1930). His only double century was 223 for Gloucestershire v Worcestershire at Worcester in 1930.

Daer, Arthur George
Amateur. *b:* 22.11.1905, Bishopsgate, London. *d:* 16.7.1980, Torquay, Devon. Brother of H. B. (Essex). Lower order right-hand batsman, right-arm fast medium bowler. *Teams* Essex (1925–35, 100 matches).
Career batting
100–141–42–1469–59–14.83–0–*ct* 48
Bowling 6183–195–31.70–3–0–6/38

Daer, Harry Bruce
Professional. *b:* 10.12.1918, Hammersmith, London. *d:* 19.12.1980, Plymouth, Devon. Brother of A. G. (Essex). Tail end right-hand batsman, right-arm medium pace bowler. *Team* Essex (1938–39, 9 matches).
Career batting
9–12–3–60–17–6.66–0–*ct* 4
Bowling 387–11–35.18–0–0–3/21

D'Aeth, Edward Knatchbull Hughes
Amateur. *b:* 11.9.1866, Knowlton Court, Wingham, Kent. *d:* 19.9.1923, New York, USA. Brother of L. N. H. (MCC), grandson of H. Knight (Sussex). Hard-hitting middle order right-hand batsman, right-arm fast medium bowler. *Sch* Haileybury. *Team* Oxford U (1885).
Career batting
3–5–0–44–22–8.80–*ct* 1

D'Aeth, Lewis Narbrough Hughes
Amateur. *b:* 13.3.1858, Knowlton Court, Wingham, Kent. *d:* 21.10.1920, Mark Cross, Sussex. Brother of E. K. H. (Oxford U), grandson of H. Knight (Sussex). Useful middle order batsman. *Sch* Harrow. *Team* MCC (1894).
Career batting
1–2–0–0–0–0.00–0–*ct* 0

Daffen, Arthur
Amateur. *b:* 30.12.1861, East Retford, Nottinghamshire. *d:* 9.7.1938, Victoria Park, Perth, Western Australia. Sound middle order right hand batsman, right-arm fast bowler, good deep field. *Team* Kent (1890–91, 16 matches).
Career batting
16–27–3–399–72*–16.62–0–*ct* 8
Bowling 144–7–20.57–0–0–4/5

He also played for Berkshire (1896–97).

Daft, Charles Frederick
Professional. *b:* 8.6.1830, Nottingham. *d:* 9.3.1915, Nottingham. Brother of Richard (Nottinghamshire), uncle of H. B. (Nottinghamshire) and R. P. (Nottinghamshire). Middle order right-hand batsman, right-hand medium pace round arm bowler. *Team* Nottinghamshire (1862–64, 14 matches).
Career batting
17–29–1–392–46–14.00–0–*ct* 6

Daft, Harry Butler
Amateur until 1890, professional from 1891. *b:* 5.4.1866, Radcliffe-on-Trent, Nottinghamshire. *d:* 12.1.1945, High Cross, Hertfordshire. Son of Richard (Nottinghamshire), brother of R. P. (Nottinghamshire), nephew of C. F. (Nottinghamshire). Defensive middle order right-hand batsman, occasional slow bowler. *Sch* Trent College. *Team* Nottinghamshire (1885–99, 190 matches).
Career batting
200–309–34–4370–92*–15.89–0–*ct* 81
Bowling 2239–86–26.03–1–0–5/79

An excellent soccer player he was outside left for Notts County, Nottingham Forest, and England; he also played in the lacrosse England trials.

Daft, Richard
Amateur to 1858, professional 1859 to 1880, amateur 1881 to retirement. *b:* 2.11.1835, Nottingham. *d:* 18.7.1900, Radcliffe-on-Trent, Nottinghamshire. Brother of C. F. (Nottinghamshire), father of H. B. (Nottinghamshire) and R. P. (Nottinghamshire). Brilliant middle order right-hand batsman, occasional slow bowler, good field. *Team* Nottinghamshire (1858–91, 157 matches). *Tour* Daft to North America 1879 (not first-class).
Career batting
254–431–46–9788–161–25.42–7–*ct* 155
Bowling 1070–51–20.98–2–0–6/59

About 1870 he was regarded as the best professional batsman in England. He captained Nottinghamshire 1871–80. He headed the first-class batting averages in 1867 (377 runs, av 53.85) and was second to W. G. Grace in 1869, 1870, 1871 and 1873. He was a first-class umpire (1898–99).

Daft, Richard Parr
Amateur. *b:* 25.10.1863, Radcliffe-on-Trent, Nottinghamshire. *d:* 27.3.1934, South Croydon, Surrey. Son

of Richard (Nottinghamshire), brother of H. B. (Nottinghamshire), nephew of C. F. (Nottinghamshire). Middle order right-hand batsman, right-arm medium pace bowler. *Sch* Trent College. *Team* Nottinghamshire (1886, 1 match).
Career batting
1–1–0–5–5–5.00–0–*ct* 0
He also played for Berkshire (1896).

Daily, Charles Edwin
Professional. *b:* 28.4.1900, Ockley, Surrey. *d:* 30.6.1974, Ockley, Surrey. Middle order right-hand batsman. *Team* Surrey (1923–29, 45 matches).
Career batting
45–60–4–998–91–17.82–0–*ct* 15
Bowling 11–1–11.00–0–0–1/11

Dainty, Harold William
Amateur. *b:* 2.6.1892, Rushton, Northamptonshire. *d:* 17.4.1961, Kettering, Northamptonshire. Lower order right-hand batsman, right-arm fast bowler. *Team* Northamptonshire (1922, 3 matches).
Career batting
3–5–2–20–8–6.66–0–*ct* 0
Bowling 47–0
He played soccer for New Brighton and Leicester City.

Dakin, Samuel
Professional. *b:* 12.4.1808, Sileby, Leicestershire. *d:* 27.12.1876, Cambridge. Middle order right-hand batsman, medium pace round arm bowler. *Teams* Nottinghamshire (1845, 1 match); Cambridge Town Club (1853).
Career batting
45–80–10–834–64–11.91–0–*ct* 21
Bowling 9–8 + 27–1.12–0–0–4/3
His first-class debut was for the North in 1840, and his last match for MCC in 1855. He also played for Somerset (pre first-class, 1845–46), Leicestershire (pre first-class, 1847) and Derbyshire (pre first-class, 1848–49).

Dale, Adrian
Cricketer. *b:* 24.10.1968, Germiston, Transvaal, South Africa. Middle order right-hand batsman, right-arm medium pace bowler. *Team* Glamorgan (1989–92, 53 matches). *Tours* Glamorgan to Zimbabwe 1990/1.
Career batting
53–83–12–2509–150*–35.33–4–*ct* 23
Bowling 1547–38–40.71–0–0–3/21
He moved to England at the age of six months. In 1992 he scored 1,159 runs, av 41.39.

Dale, Christopher Stephen
Cricketer. *b:* 15.12.1961, Canterbury, Kent. Lower order right-hand batsman, off break bowler. *Teams* Gloucestershire (1984, 8 matches); Kent (1986, 3 matches).
Career batting
11–11–3–118–49–14.75–0–*ct* 1
Bowling 609–7–87.00–0–0–3/10

Dale, Jack Hillen
Amateur. *b:* 29.10.1901, Northampton. *d:* 28.4.1965, Battle, Sussex. Son of P. W. (Northamptonshire Secretary). Middle order right-hand batsman, slow right-arm bowler. *Team* Northamptonshire (1922, 7 matches).
Career batting
9–17–1–323–76–20.18–0–*ct* 2
Bowling 119–2–59.50–0–0–1/19
His last first-class match was for the Royal Navy in 1928; his career in the Royal Navy curtailed his appearances in County cricket.

Dale, John Ronald
Professional. *b:* 24.10.1930, Cleethorpes, Lincolnshire. Lower order right hand batsman, slow left-arm bowler. *Team* Kent (1958, 1 match).
Career batting
1–1–0–0–0–0.00–0–*ct* 0
Bowling 31–1–31.00–0–0–1/31
He also played for Lincolnshire (1949–52, 1973–79).

Dale, John William
Amateur. *b:* 21.6.1848, Lincoln. *d:* 26.6.1895, Westminster. London. Opening or middle order right-hand batsman, right-hand fast round arm bowler. *Sch* Tonbridge. *Teams* Cambridge U (1868–70, blue all three years); Middlesex (1874–78, 7 matches).
Career batting
56–98–2–1625–132–16.92–1–*ct* 39
Bowling 174–6–29.00–0–0–2/16
His final first-class match was for MCC in 1882. He also played for Lincolnshire (1867–72). He also won a blue for rugby.

Dales, Hartley Horace
Amateur. *b:* 12.5.1909, Zoutpansburg, Transvaal, South Africa. Middle/lower order right-hand batsman, wicket keeper. *Team* Cambridge U (1929–31).
Career batting
4–6–2–6–3–1.50–0–*ct* 9–*st* 1

Dales, Hugh Lloyd
Amateur. *b:* 18.5.1888, Medomsley, Co Durham. *d:* 4.5.1964, Whitley Bay, Northumberland. Opening left-hand batsman, slow left-arm bowler. *Team* Middlesex (1920–30, 108 matches). *Tour* MCC to West Indies 1925/6.
Career batting
118–190–15–4643–143–26.53–8–*ct* 32
Bowling 206–4–51.50–0–0–2/28
He also played for Durham (1911–14). He hit 1,000 runs in a season twice (best 1,138, av 29.17, in 1923).

Daley, James Arthur
Cricketer. *b:* 24.9.1973, Sunderland, Co Durham. Middle order right-hand batsman, right-arm medium pace bowler. *Team* Durham (1992, 2 matches).
Career batting
2–4–1–190–88–63.33–0–*ct* 2

Daley, John Valiant
Professional. *b:* 1.2.1906, Beccles, Suffolk. *d:* 14.6.1986, East Margate, Kent. Tail end right-hand batsman, slow left-arm bowler. *Team* Surrey (1936–38, 28 matches).
Career batting
28–34–24–75–26*–7.50–0–*ct* 13
Bowling 1942–67–28.98–3–1–6/47

He was nine years in the Army before starting his County cricket career. He also played for Norfolk (1930–31) and Suffolk (1939). A well-known soccer player, he appeared for Kingstonian in the FA Amateur Cup Final.

Dalkeith, Earl of
(Walter Henry Montagu-Douglas-Scott, known as Lord Eskdaill until 1884)
Amateur. *b:* 17.1.1861, Westminster, London. *d:* 18.9.1886, Farrochmore Hill, Achnacarry Forest, Loch Arkaig, Fort William, Inverness, Scotland. Brother of G. W. M. Scott (Middlesex) and H. F. M. Scott (Philipson's XI), grandson of Viscount Drumlanrig (MCC), uncle of D. F. Brand (Cambridge U). Opening or middle order batsman. *Sch* Eton. *Team* MCC (1881–85).
Career batting
3–4–0–9–7–2.25–0–*ct* 0

He accidentally shot himself whilst deer-stalking.

Dallas-Brooks, R. A.
(*see under* Brooks, R. A. D.)

Dalmeny, Lord Albert Edward Harry Mayer Archibald Primrose
(succeeded as 6th Earl of Rosebery in 1929)
Amateur. *b:* 8.1.1882, Mayfair, Westminster, London. *d:* 30.5.1974, Mentmore House, Buckinghamshire. Father of Lord Dalmeny (Middlesex), brother-in-law of C. N. Bruce (Middlesex). Middle order right-hand batsman, right-arm fast bowler. *Sch* Eton. *Teams* Middlesex (1902, 2 matches); Surrey (1903–08, 94 matches); Scotland (1905).
Career batting
102–164–6–3551–138–22.47–2–*ct* 50
Bowling 100–3–33.33–0–0–2/16

He captained Surrey 1905–07. He also played for Buckinghamshire (1899–1901). His final first-class match was for MCC in 1920. He hit 1,000 runs in a season twice (best 1,150, av 25.55, in 1907). He was MP for Midlothian 1906–1910. He left £9,650,986 net.

Dalmeny, Lord Archibald Ronald Primrose
Amateur. *b:* 1.8.1910, Westminster, London. *d:* 11.11.1931, Oxford, of blood poisoning. Son of Lord Dalmeny (Middlesex and Surrey). Middle order right-hand batsman, right-arm fast medium bowler. *Sch* Eton. *Teams* Middlesex (1929–31, 2 matches); Oxford U (1930).
Career batting
3–3–0–29–29–9.66–0–*ct* 6
Bowling 62–2–31.00–0–0–1/15

Dalrymple, John James Hamilton
Cricketer. *b:* 14.10.1957, St John's Wood, London. Tail end right-hand batsman, right-arm fast medium bowler. *Sch* Ampleforth. *Team* Oxford U (1978).
Career batting
3–4–2–27–15–13.50–0–*ct* 1
Bowling 260–7–37.14–0–0–3/34

Dalton, Andrew John
Cricketer. *b:* 14.3.1947, Horsforth, Yorkshire. Middle order right-hand batsman. *Sch* Leeds GS. *Team* Yorkshire (1969–72, 21 matches).
Career batting
21–31–2–710–128–24.48–3–*ct* 6

Dalton, Eric Londesbrough
Amateur. *b:* 2.12.1906, Durban, South Africa. *d:* 3.6.1981, Entabeni Hospital, Durban, South Africa. Son of G. L. (Natal), nephew of L. D. (Natal). Middle order right-hand batsman, leg break bowler. *Team* Natal (1924/5 to 1946/7). *Tours* South Africa to England 1929, 1935, to Australia and New Zealand 1931/2. *Tests* South Africa (1929 to 1938/9, 15 matches).
Career batting
121–180–19–5333–157–33.12–13–*ct* 72
Bowling 3588–139–25.81–5–0–6/42
Test batting
15–24–2–698–117–31.72–2–*ct* 5
Bowling 490–12–40.83–0–0–4/59

He hit 1,446 runs, av 37.07, in 1935. After retiring from first-class cricket he became a noted golfer and won the South African Amateur Championship.

Daly, Arthur Raine
Amateur. *c:* 1.5.1833, Marylebone, London. *d:* 1.2.1898, Marylebone, London. Lower order left-hand batsman, left-hand medium pace round arm bowler. *Team* Middlesex (1866, 1 match).
Career batting
1–1–0–0–0–0.00–*ct* 1
Bowling 26–1–26.00–0–0–1/26

Daly, Guy Nolan
(known as G. N. O'Daly)
Amateur. *b:* 4.9.1908, Bramley, Hampshire. *d:* 29.9.1991, Basingstoke, Hampshire. Lower order right-hand batsman, right-arm medium pace bowler. *Team* Glamorgan (1938, 1 match)

Daniel, Adrian Richard Huw

Career batting
1–1–0–9–9–9.00–0–*ct* 0
Bowling 17–0

Daniel, Adrian Richard Huw
Cricketer. *b:* 17.1.1955, Ealing, Middlesex. Middle order right-hand batsman, right-arm medium pace bowler. *Team* Cambridge U (1976–77).
Career batting
4–5–0–96–75–19.20–0–*ct* 0

Daniel, Arthur William Trollope
Amateur. *b:* 3.1.1841, St Pancras, London. *d:* 26.1.1873, Clapham, London, of consumption. Middle order right-hand batsman, brilliant field. *Sch* Harrow. *Teams* Cambridge U (1861–64, blue all four years); Middlesex (1861–69, 16 matches).
Career batting
37–64–2–1102–87–17.77–0–*ct* 23–*st* 6
Bowling 74–4–18.50–0–0–2/8
In 1861 he was rackets champion at Cambridge and in 1864 won the 120 yards hurdles in the inter-University athletics meeting. He also played for Leicestershire (pre first-class, 1860).

Daniel, Wayne Wendell
Cricketer. *b:* 16.1.1956, Brereton Village, St Philip, Barbados. Tail end right-hand batsman, right-arm fast bowler, deep field. *Teams* Barbados (1975/6 to 1984/5); Middlesex (1977–88, 214 matches); Western Australia (1981/2, 2 matches). *Tours* West Indies to England 1976, 1983 (World Cup), to India 1983/4, to Australia 1983/4 (not first-class); Young West Indies to Zimbabwe 1981/2. *Tests* West Indies (1975/6 to 1983/4, 10 matches).
Career batting
266–241–106–1551–53*–11.48–0–*ct* 63
Bowling 19490–867–22.47–31–7–9/61
Test batting
10–11–4–46–11–6.57–0–*ct* 4
Bowling 910–36–25.27–1–0–5/39
On the 1976 tour to England he appeared in four of the five Tests and took 13 wickets, av 24.38, his record in first-class matches being 52, av 21.26. His two best seasons for Middlesex were 1978, with 76 wickets, av 14.65, and 1985 with 79, av 26.72. His best bowling was 9/61 for Middlesex v Glamorgan at Swansea in 1982. Although his Test record was a modest one, he was one of the most feared bowlers in County cricket and his commitment to his county was total.

Daniell, John
Amateur. *b:* 12.12.1878, Bath, Somerset. *d:* 24.1.1963, Holway, Somerset. Father-in-law of W. F. Baldock (Somerset). Hard hitting middle order right-hand batsman, right-arm fast bowler, brilliant close field. *Sch* Clifton. *Teams* Somerset (1898–1927, 287 matches); Cambridge U (1899–1901, blue all three years).
Career batting
304–531–54–10468–174*–21.94–9–*ct* 231
Bowling 171–7–24.42–0–0–1/0
Despite scoring over 10,000 runs in his first-class career, he never hit 1,000 in a season. He captained Somerset 1908–12 and 1919–26. He was Hon Secretary of Somerset 1932–36 and President 1947–49, and was a Test selector 1921–24. An excellent rugby footballer, he was awarded his blue and went on to captain England. He was later President of the Rugby Football Union.

Daniels, David Michael
Cricketer. *b:* 29.3.1942, Bexleyheath, Kent. Opening right-hand batsman. *Team* Cambridge U (1964–65, blue both years).
Career batting
18–32–0–562–82–17.56–0–*ct* 7
Bowling 7–0
His County cricket was for Dorset (1966–75) and Bedfordshire (1976–83).

Daniels, John Giles Upton
Cricketer. *b:* 25.1.1942, Edgbaston, Birmingham. Brother of R. C. (Oxford U). Middle order right-hand batsman. *Sch* Winchester. *Team* Gloucestershire (1964, 1 match).
Career batting
2–4–0–51–22–12.75–0–*ct* 1
Apart from his appearance for Gloucestershire, his only other first-class match was for Combined Services, also in 1964.

Daniels, Rupert Chandos
Cricketer. *b:* 28.6.1945, Edgbaston, Birmingham. Brother of J. G. U. (Gloucestershire). Middle order right-hand batsman, off break bowler. *Sch* Eton. *Team* Oxford U (1965–66).
Career batting
7–14–1–97–26–7.46–0–*ct* 1
Bowling 148–1–148.00–0–0–1/29

Daniels, Simon Antony Brewis
Cricketer. *b:* 23.8.1958, Darlington, Co Durham. Lower order right-hand batsman, right-arm fast medium bowler. *Sch* Sedbergh. *Team* Glamorgan (1981–82, 16 matches).
Career batting
16–23–10–227–73–17.46–0–*ct* 7
Bowling 1162–28–41.50–0–0–3/33
He also played for Durham (pre first-class, 1979–80 and 1983).

Darby, James Herbert
Amateur. *b:* 26.10.1865, Fareham, Hampshire. *d:* 7.11.1943, Fareham, Hampshire. Middle order batsman. *Team* Hampshire (1884–97, 4 matches).
Career batting
4–7–1–78–35–13.00–0–*ct* 1
Bowling 24–0

Darbyshire, Rev Benjamin Stewart
Amateur. *c:* 13.6.1845, West Derby, Liverpool, Lancashire. *d:* 18.1.1907, Birkdale, Lancashire. Father-in-law of C. E. Moon (London County). Middle/lower order batsman, bowler. *Team* Oxford U (1864–66).
Career batting
2–2–0–4–4–2.00–0–*ct* 0
Bowling 9–3 + 5–3.00–1–0–5/?
He won a blue for athletics.

D'Arcy, John William
Amateur. *b:* 23.4.1936, Christchurch, New Zealand. Opening right-hand batsman. *Teams* Canterbury (1955/6 to 1958/9); Wellington (1959/60); Otago (1960/1 to 1961/2). *Tour* New Zealand to England 1958. *Tests* New Zealand (1958, 5 matches).
Career batting
53–90–3–2009–89–23.09–0–*ct* 26
Bowling 12–1–12.00–0–0–1/0
Test batting
5–10–0–136–33–13.60–0–*ct* 0
Despite hitting only 522 runs, av 16.31, on the 1958 tour to England, he appeared in all five Tests as as an opening bat.

Dare, Reginald Arthur
Professional. *b:* 26.11.1921, Blandford, Dorset. Middle order right-hand batsman, slow left-arm bowler. *Team* Hampshire (1949–54, 109 matches).
Career batting
109–169–32–1679–109*–12.25–1–*ct* 70
Bowling 6479–185–35.02–5–0–6/28
He also played for Buckinghamshire (1958–63). He played soccer for Southampton and Exeter.

Dargan, Michael James
Amateur. *b:* 9.10.1929, Dublin, Ireland. Opening right-hand batsman. *Team* Ireland (1954).
Career batting
1–2–0–10–7–5.00–0–*ct* 3
He was an Irish rugby international.

Darke, Robert Henry
Amateur. *b:* 25.1.1876, Dunsden Green, Oxfordshire. *d:* 19.7.1961, Balham, London. Lower order batsman. *Sch* Dulwich. *Team* Gentlemen of England (1905).
Career batting
1 match, did not bat–*ct* 0

Darks, Geoffrey Chalton
Professional. *b:* 28.6.1926, Bewdley, Worcestershire. Lower order right-hand batsman, right-arm medium pace bowler. *Team* Worcestershire (1946–50, 7 matches).
Career batting
7–8–3–89–39–17.80–0–*ct* 6
Bowling 452–13–34.76–1–0–5/49

Darling, Joseph
Amateur. *b:* 21.11.1870, Glen Osmond, Adelaide, South Australia. *d:* 2.1.1946, Hobart, Tasmania, Australia. Great-uncle of W. M. (Australia). Opening or middle order left-hand batsman, slow bowler, good field. *Team* South Australia (1893/4 to 1907/8, 42 matches). *Tours* Australia to England 1896, 1899, 1902, 1905, to South Africa 1902/3, to North America 1896. *Tests* Australia (1894/5 to 1905, 34 matches).
Career batting
202–333–25–10635–210–34.52–19–*ct* 148
Bowling 55–1–55.00–0–0–1/5
Test batting
34–60–2–1657–178–28.56–3–*ct* 27
He captained the Australian teams to England in 1899, 1902 and 1905, also to South Africa 1902/3. In all, he captained Australia in 21 Tests. He hit 1,000 runs on all four of his tours to England (best 1,941, av 41.29, in 1899). His only double century was 210 for South Australia v Queensland at Brisbane in 1898/9. He was a member of the Tasmanian Parliament from 1921 until his death.

Darling, Leonard Stuart
Amateur. *b:* 14.8.1909, South Yarra, Melbourne, Victoria, Australia. *d:* 24.6.1992, Daw Park, Adelaide, South Australia. Middle order left-hand batsman, right-arm medium pace bowler. *Team* Victoria (1926/7 to 1936/7, 47 matches). *Tours* Australia to England 1934, to South Africa 1935/6. *Tests* Australia (1932/3 to 1936/7, 12 matches).
Career batting
100–143–7–5780–188–42.50–16–*ct* 59
Bowling 1502–32–46.93–0–0–3/57
Test batting
12–18–1–474–85–27.88–0–*ct* 8
Bowling 65–0
On his 1934 tour to England he hit 1,022 runs, av 34.06. He appeared in four out of five Tests on that tour, but had little success. He played baseball for Victoria and South Australia.

Darling, Robert Stormonth
Amateur. *b:* 6.6.1880, Kerfield, Kelso, Roxburghshire, Scotland. *d:* 20.5.1956, Rosebank, Kelso, Roxburghshire, Scotland. Father-in-law of D. T. L. Bailey (Gloucestershire). Middle order right-hand batsman, right-arm medium bowler. *Sch* Winchester. *Team* Oxford U (1902–03).
Career batting
10–16–0–188–54–11.75–0–*ct* 3
Bowling 84–3–28.00–0–0–2/35
He won a blue for soccer.

Darnton, Thomas
Professional. *b:* 12.2.1836, Stockton-on-Tees, Durham. *d:* 25.10.1874, Stockton-on-Tees, Durham, of consumption. Opening right-hand batsman, right-

hand medium pace round arm bowler. *Team* Yorkshire (1864–68, 13 matches).
Career batting
20–35–2–402–81*–12.18–0–*ct* 4
Bowling 492–18–27.33–0–0–3/57
He also played for Durham (pre first-class, 1856). His first-class debut was for Yorkshire and Durham in 1858.

Darvell, Bruce Stanley
Professional. *b:* 29.4.1931, Chipperfield, Hertfordshire. Lower order right-hand batsman, off break bowler. *Team* Kent (1952, 1 match).
Career batting
1–1–0–5–5–5.00–0–*ct* 1
Bowling 2–0
He also played for Hertfordshire (1956–58).

Darwall-Smith, John Anderton
Amateur. *b:* 12.4.1912, Marylebone, London. *d:* 22.6.1976, Lockers Park, Hemel Hempstead, Hertfordshire. Brother of R. F. H. (Sussex). Lower order right-hand batsman, right-arm fast medium bowler. *Sch* Winchester. *Team* Oxford U (1933–34).
Career batting
5–9–1–98–36–12.25–0–*ct* 2
Bowling 393–13–30.23–0–0–4/106
His final first-class match was for Free Foresters in 1937. He was awarded his soccer blue and also played for Corinthians.

Darwall-Smith, Randle Frederick Hicks
Amateur. *b:* 11.7.1914, Westminster, London. Brother of J. A. (Oxford U). Lower order right-hand batsman, right-arm fast medium bowler. *Sch* Charterhouse. *Teams* Oxford U (1935–38, blue all four years); Sussex (1946, 5 matches).
Career batting
46–69–16–649–54–12.24–0–*ct* 16
Bowling 4153–151–27.50–6–1–7/44

Das, Shonu Sanjeev Kumar
Cricketer. *b:* 15.11.1967, Newcastle upon Tyne, Northumberland. Opening right-hand batsman, right-arm medium pace bowler. *Sch* Queen Elizabeth GS, Wakefield. *Team* Cambridge U (1992).
Career batting
3–5–1–38–24*–9.50–0–*ct* 1

Dashwood, Thomas Henry Knyvett
Amateur. *b:* 3.1.1876, Hitchin, Hertfordshire. *d:* 24.1.1929, Fulham, London. Middle order right-hand batsman, good field. *Sch* Wellington. *Teams* Oxford U (1899); Hampshire (1904, 2 matches). *Tour* Bennett to West Indies 1901/2.
Career batting
18–29–1–334–70–11.92–0–*ct* 14
He also played for Hertfordshire (1898–1907) and Cornwall (1903).

Datta, Punya Brata
Amateur. *b:* 21.6.1924, Sylhet, India. Middle order left-hand batsman, slow left-arm bowler. *Teams* Cambridge U (1947, blue); Bengal (1944/5 to 1955/6).
Career batting
34–52–3–1459–143–29.77–4–*ct* 12
Bowling 1520–41–37.07–1–0–5/52
His County cricket was for Cambridgeshire (1947).

Dauglish, Maurice John
Amateur. *b:* 2.10.1867, St Pancras, London. *d:* 30.4.1922, Hunton Bridge, Hertfordshire. Middle order right-hand batsman, lob bowler, wicket-keeper. *Sch* Harrow. *Teams* Middlesex (1886–90, 9 matches); Oxford U (1889–90, blue both years).
Career batting
14–24–3–165–46*–7.85–0–*ct* 11–*st* 5
Bowling 13–0
He also played for Berkshire (1896–99).

Dauncey, John Gilbert
Professional. *b:* 9.4.1936, Ystalyfera, Glamorgan. Middle order right-hand batsman. *Team* Glamorgan (1957, 2 matches).
Career batting
2–4–0–54–34–13.50–0–*ct* 1

Davenport, Rev Edward
Amateur. *b:* 26.3.1844, Oxford. *d:* 5.3.1915, Stoke Talmage, Oxfordshire. Steady middle order right-hand batsman, excellent long stop. *Sch* Rugby. *Team* Oxford University (1864–66, blue 1866).
Career batting
7–10–0–318–107–31.80–1–*ct* 2–*st* 1
His County cricket was for Oxfordshire (1863–64), Northamptonshire (pre first-class, 1866) and Buckinghamshire (1866).

Davenport, George
Professional. *b:* 5.5.1860, Nantwich, Cheshire. *d:* 4.10.1902, Nantwich, Cheshire. Middle order right-hand batsman, wicket-keeper, right-arm medium pace bowler. *Team* MCC (1884–96).
Career batting
27–46–8–625–101*–16.44–1–*ct* 22–*st* 12
He appeared with great success for Cheshire, (1883–95).

Davenport, H. R. B.
(*see under* Bromley-Davenport, H. R.)

Davenport, Horace John
Amateur. *b:* 11.1.1875, Camberwell, London. *d:* 20.8.1946. Opening right-hand batsman. *Sch* Repton. *Team* MCC (1898).
Career batting
1–2–0–2–2–1.00–0–*ct* 1
He played no first-class cricket whilst at Cambridge U but won blues for hockey and athletics.

Davey, Clive Frederick
Amateur. *b:* 2.6.1932, North Petherton, Somerset. Middle order right-hand batsman, leg break bowler. *Team* Somerset (1953–55, 13 matches).
Career batting
13–25–4–261–46–12.42–0–*ct* 4

Davey, Jack
Cricketer. *b:* 4.9.1944, Tavistock, Devon. Tail end left-hand batsman, left-arm fast medium bowler. *Team* Gloucestershire (1966–78, 175 matches).
Career batting
175–208–90–918–53*–7.77–0–*ct* 32
Bowling 11720–411–28.51–9–0–6/95
He also played for Devon (1964–65, 1981 and 1985).

Davey, John George
Professional. *b:* 21.6.1847, Brighton, Sussex. *d:* 4.5.1878, Brighton, Sussex. Lower order right-hand batsman, right-hand medium pace round arm bowler, wicket-keeper. *Team* Sussex (1869–73, 4 matches).
Career batting
7–13–3–80–32–8.00–0–*ct* 8
His final first-class match was for MCC in 1876.

Davey, Philip John
Amateur. *b:* 10.8.1913, Bishop's Hull, Taunton, Somerset. Tail end right-hand batsman, right-arm medium bowler. *Sch* Taunton. *Team* Somerset (1934–37, 16 matches).
Career batting
16–26–3–235–30–10.21–0–*ct* 10
Bowling 621–22–28.22–1–0–6/9
He played in trial matches at Cambridge U but not in first-class games.

David, Rodney Felix Armine
Amateur. *b:* 19.6.1907, Cardiff, Glamorgan. *d:* 2.7.1969, Hellingly, Hailsham, Sussex. Middle order right-hand batsman. *Sch* Wellington. *Team* Glamorgan (1925–29, 3 matches).
Career batting
3–5–0–20–17–4.00–0–*ct* 0

Davidge, Guy Mortimer Coleridge
Amateur. *b:* 2.3.1878, Woolwich, Kent. *d:* 17.2.1956, Hove, Sussex. Middle order right-hand batsman. *Sch* Newton College. *Team* Worcestershire (1911, 1 match).
Career batting
1–1–0–0–0–0.00–0–*ct* 1

Davidson, Alan Keith, OBE
Amateur. *b:* 14.6.1929, Lisarow, Gosford, New South Wales, Australia. Middle order left-hand batsman, left-arm fast medium bowler. *Team* New South Wales (1949/50 to 1962/3, 72 matches). *Tours* Australia to New Zealand 1949/50, to England 1953, 1956, 1961, to West Indies 1954/5, to India and Pakistan 1956/7, 1959/60, to South Africa 1957/8. *Tests* Australia (1953 to 1962/3, 44 matches).
Career batting
193–246–39–6804–129–32.86–9–*ct* 168
Bowling 14048–672–20.90–33–2–7/31
Test batting
44–61–7–1328–80–24.59–0–*ct* 42
Bowling 3819–186–20.53–14–2–7/93
Although he did not reach 1,000 runs or take 100 wickets in a season on any of his three visits to England (in 1956 he missed many matches due to injury), he was one of the best all-rounders of his day and his bowling was especially effective in England in 1961, when he topped the Test averages with 23 wickets, av 24.86.

Davidson, Frank
Professional. *b:* 1.10.1872, Brimington, Derbyshire. *d:* 7.6.1951, Chesterfield, Derbyshire. Son of Joseph (Derbyshire), brother of G. A. (Derbyshire). Lower order right-hand batsman, right-arm medium pace bowler. *Team* Derbyshire (1897–99, 14 matches).
Career batting
14–23–4–129–43–6.78–0–*ct* 11
Bowling 1094–43–25.44–2–0–6/36

Davidson, George Arthur
Professional. *b:* 29.6.1866, Brimington, Derbyshire. *d:* 8.2.1899, Tividale, Staffordshire, of pneumonia. Son of Joseph (Derbyshire), brother of Frank (Derbyshire). Stylish middle order right-hand batsman, right-arm fast-medium bowler, good field. *Team* Derbyshire (1886–98, 95 matches).
Career batting
158–260–27–5546–274–23.80–3–*ct* 135
Bowling 11341–621–18.26–43–10–9/39
The best all-rounder in the Derbyshire side, his appearances in first-class matches were restricted, first because of the demotion of Derbyshire and then because of his sudden death at the early age of 32. He hit 1,000 runs in a season three times (best 1,296, av 28.18, in 1895); in the same year he took over 100 wickets, for the only time – 138, av. 16.79 – thus completing the 'double'. His only double century, 274 for Derbyshire v Lancashire at Old Trafford in 1896, remains the highest individual innings for the County. His best bowling was 9/39 for Derbyshire v Warwickshire at Derby in 1895.

Davidson, Ian Charles
Cricketer. *b:* 21.12.1964, Roe Green, Worsley, Lancashire. Lower order right-hand batsman, off break bowler. *Team* Lancashire (1985 to 1986/7, 2 matches). *Tour* Lancashire to Jamaica 1986/7.
Career batting
2–4–0–14–13–3.50–0–*ct* 2
Bowling 85–4–21.25–0–0–2/24

Davidson, James Norman Grieve
Amateur. *b:* 28.1.1931, Hawick, Roxburgh, Scotland. Middle order right-hand batsman. *Team* Scotland

(1951).
Career batting
4–7–1–86–40–14.33–0–*ct* 1
He was a Scottish rugby international.

Davidson, John Edward
Cricketer. *b:* 23.10.1964, Aberystwyth, Cardiganshire. Lower order right-hand batsman, right-arm fast medium bowler. *Team* Cambridge U (1985–87, blue 1985–86).
Career batting
15–18–5–144–41*–11.07–0–*ct* 5
Bowling 1526–40–38.15–2–0–5/35

Davidson, John Ewen
Amateur. *b:* 2.3.1841, Westminster, London. *d:* 2.9.1923, Oxford. Middle order batsman. *Sch* Harrow. *Team* MCC (1864, 1 match).
Career batting
1–2–0–13–13–6.50–0–*ct* 0
His County cricket was for Hertfordshire (1863).

Davidson, Joseph
Professional. *b:* 9.8.1846, Brimington, Derbyshire. *d:* 3.12.1901, Brimington Common, Derbyshire. Father of Frank (Derbyshire) and G. A. (Derbyshire). Tail end right-hand batsman, right-arm medium pace off break bowler. *Team* Derbyshire (1871–74, 4 matches).
Career batting
4–6–3–14–8–4.66–0–*ct* 2
Bowling 96–6–16.00–0–0–3/33

Davidson, Kenneth Richard
Amateur in 1933, then professional from 1934. *b:* 24.12.1905, Calverley, Yorkshire. *d:* 25.12.1954, Prestwick Aerodrome, Ayr, Scotland, in a plane crash. Middle order right-hand batsman. *Teams* Yorkshire (1933–35, 30 matches); Scotland (1938).
Career batting
31–48–5–1355–128–31.51–2–*ct* 18
Bowling 4–0
He hit 1,241 runs, av 34.47, in 1934. He emigrated to USA in 1935 and became a noted badminton player. It was during a badminton world tour with a United States team that he was killed.

Davidson, William Leslie
Amateur. *b:* 31.1.1850. Inchmarlo, Kincardineshire, Scotland. *d:* 3.8.1915, Rouen, France. Middle order batsman. *Team* MCC (1877, 1 match).
Career batting
1–1–0–0–0–0.00–0–*ct* 0
His County cricket was for Northamptonshire (pre first-class, 1873). He was killed in action at the age of 65 and is thought to be the oldest first-class cricketer to be killed in the First World War.

Davidson, Rev William Watkins
Amateur. *b:* 20.3.1920, Poplar, London. Lower order right-hand batsman, wicket-keeper. *Sch* Brighton. *Teams* Oxford U (1947–48, blue both years); Sussex (1948–51, 5 matches).
Career batting
22–23–6–118–31–6.94–0–*ct* 34–*st* 6
His final first-class match was for MCC in 1956.

Davies, Alec George
Cricketer. *b:* 14.8.1962, Rawalpindi, Pakistan. Middle order right-hand batsman, wicket-keeper. *Sch* Monmouth. *Team* Surrey (1985, 1 match).
Career batting
1–1–1–26–26*–no av–0–*ct* 3

Davies, Andrew George
Cricketer. *b:* 15.5.1962, Altrincham, Cheshire. Nephew of H. G (Glamorgan) and D. R. (Glamorgan). Tail end right-hand batsman, wicket-keeper. *Sch* Birkenhead. *Team* Cambridge U (1982–89, blue 1984–85).
Career batting
22–33–7–494–69–19.00–0–*ct* 28–*st* 4
He was not in residence in 1989 when recalled to the University side in emergency for one match, having gone down in 1985. His County cricket was for Buckinghamshire (1989).

Davies, Conrad Stephen
Amateur. *b:* 27.6.1907, Edgbaston, Birmingham. Lower order right-hand batsman, slow left-arm bowler. *Sch* Chatham House, Ramsgate. *Team* Warwickshire (1930–36, 8 matches).
Career batting
8–11–0–112–63–10.18–0–*ct* 3
Bowling 672–14–48.00–0–0–3/26

Davies, David
(known as Dai Davies)
Professional. *b:* 26.8.1896, Llanelly, Carmarthen. *d:* 16.7.1976, Llanelly, Carmarthen. Middle order right-hand batsman, right-arm medium pace off break bowler. *Teams* Glamorgan (1923–39, 411 matches); Wales (1923–30).
Career batting
421–696–62–15390–216–24.27–16–*ct* 197
Bowling 9633–275–35.02–4–0–6/50
He hit 1,000 runs in a season seven times (best 1,539, av 34.97, in 1930). His only double century was 216 for Glamorgan v Somerset at Newport in 1939. He was a noted first-class umpire (1946–61), standing in 22 Test matches (1947–58).

Davies, David Aubrey
Professional. *b:* 11.7.1915, Swansea, Glamorgan. Lower order right-hand batsman, leg break and googly bowler. *Team* Glamorgan (1934–38, 46 matches).
Career batting
46–64–16–600–55–12.50–0–*ct* 28
Bowling 760–14–54.28–0–0–3/63
He also played for Devon (1946–50).

Davies, David Emrys
Professional. *b:* 27.6.1904, Sandy, Llanelly, Carmarthen. *d:* 10.11.1975, Llanelly, Carmarthen. Brother of Gwynfor (Glamorgan). Opening left-hand batsman, slow left-arm bowler, sound deep field. *Teams* Glamorgan (1924–54, 612 matches); Wales (1926–29). *Tour* MCC to India 1939/40 (tour cancelled).
Career batting
621–1032–80–26564–287*–27.90–32–*ct* 215
Bowling 26458–903–29.30–32–2–6/24

He hit 1,000 runs in a season 16 times, exceeding 2,000 once – 2,012, av 40.24, in 1937. He took 100 wickets in a season twice (best 103, av 23.03, in 1937). In 1935 and 1937 he performed the 'double', in the latter year achieving the feat of 2,000 runs and 100 wickets in the same year. He hit two double centuries, the higher being 287* for Glamorgan v Gloucestershire at Newport in 1939. He was a first-class umpire (1955–60) and stood in 9 Test matches (1956–59).

Davies, David Roy
Professional. *b:* 12.8.1928, Llanelly, Carmarthen. Brother of H. G. (Glamorgan), uncle of A. G. (Cambridge U). Middle order right-hand batsman. *Team* Glamorgan (1950, 1 match),
Career batting
1–1–0–7–7–7.00–0–*ct* 0

He played squash for Wales.

Davies, Geoffrey Boisselier
Amateur. *b:* 26.10.1892, Poplar, London. *d:* 26.9.1915, Hulluch, France. He was killed in action. Opening/middle order right-hand batsman, right-arm slow medium bowler. *Sch* Rossall. *Teams* Essex (1912–14, 32 matches); Cambridge U (1913–14, blue both years).
Career batting
54–90–9–1487–118–18.35–2–*ct* 43
Bowling 2935–141–20.81–4–1–8/67

Davies, Gwyn Llewelyn
Professional. *b:* 10.6.1919, Cathays, Cardiff, Glamorgan. Middle order right-hand batsman, right-arm medium pace bowler. *Team* Glamorgan (1947–48, 2 matches).
Career batting
2–2–0–9–7–4.50–0–*ct* 1

He played rugby for Cardiff.

Davies, Gwynfor
Professional. *b:* 12.8.1908, Sandy, Llanelly, Carmarthen. *d:* 10.3.1972, Llanelly, Carmarthen. Brother of D. E. (Glamorgan). Middle/lower order right-hand batsman, right-arm medium bowler. *Team* Glamorgan (1932, 7 matches).
Career batting
7–9–1–77–44–9.62–0–*ct* 2
Bowling 134–3–44.66–0–0–2/18

Davies, Harry Donald
Amateur. *b:* 13.3.1892, Pendleton, Manchester, Lancashire. *d:* 6.2.1958, Riem Airport, near Munich, Germany. He was killed in air crash involving the Manchester United football team. Middle order right-hand batsman. *Team* Lancashire (1924–25, 11 matches).
Career batting
11–15–0–260–46–17.33–0–*ct* 4

He played soccer for Bolton Wanderers and obtained an Amateur International cap with England. Latterly he was a well-known journalist, reporting soccer for *The Guardian* under the title 'An Old International'.

Davies, Haydn George
Professional. *b:* 23.4 1912, Llanelly, Carmarthen. Brother of D. R. (Glamorgan), uncle of A. G. (Cambridge U). Lower order right-hand batsman, wicket-keeper. *Team* Glamorgan (1935–58, 423 matches).
Career batting
427–602–96–6615–80–13.07–0–*ct* 585–*st* 204
Bowling 20–1–20.00–0–0–1/20

He was also a noted squash player.

Davies, Henry Gwyn Saunders
(later Davies-Scourfield. He was also known as Saunders-Davies)
Amateur. *b:* 2.2.1865, Pentre, Pembroke. *d:* 4.12.1934, Patching, Sussex. Middle order right-hand batsman. *Sch* Winchester. *Team* Hampshire (1883, 1 match).
Career batting
1–2–0–45–42–22.50–0–*ct* 0

A noted rider, he headed the Gentlemen Riders Steeplechasing for four years 1891–94.

Davies, Henry Richard
Cricketer. *b:* 2.9.1970, Camberwell, London. Lower order left-hand batsman, off break bowler. *Sch* St Dunstan's. *Team* Oxford U (1990–92, blue 1992).
Career batting
17–20–6–178–39–12.71–0–*ct* 0
Bowling 1377–13–105.92–0–0–3/93

Davies, Hugh Daniel
Professional. *b:* 23.7.1932, Pembrey, Llanelly, Carmarthen. Tail end right-hand batsman, right-arm medium fast bowler. *Team* Glamorgan (1955–60, 52 matches).
Career batting
52–70–26–247–28–5.61–0–*ct* 16
Bowling 3659–115–31.81–4–0–6/85

Davies, Jack Gale Wilmot, OBE
Amateur. *b:* 10.9.1911, Broad Clyst, Devon. *d:* 5.11.1992, Cambridge. Stylish middle order right-hand batsman, off break bowler. *Sch* Tonbridge. *Teams* Cambridge U (1931–34, blue 1933–34); Kent (1934–51, 99 matches).

Davies, John Anthony

Career batting
153–262–12–5982–168–23.92–4–*ct* 87
Bowling 7847–258–30.41–6–1–7/20

He scored 1246 runs, av 32.78, in 1946. His final first-class match was for MCC in 1961. He was Treasurer of MCC 1976–80 and President in 1985/6. A noted rugby footballer, he appeared for Blackheath and Kent.

Davies, John Anthony
Amateur. *b:* 3.2.1926, Pontypridd, Glamorgan. Hard hitting middle order right-hand batsman, leg break and googly bowler. *Team* Glamorgan (1952, 1 match).
Career batting
1–2–0–11–11–5.50–0–*ct* 0

Davies, John Trevor
Amateur. *b:* 26.12.1932, Shrewsbury, Shropshire. Middle order right-hand batsman. *Team* Cambridge U (1956–58).
Career batting
8–15–0–94–29–6.26–0–*ct* 4

His County cricket was for Shropshire (1957–58) and Dorset (1959–64).

Davies, Llewellyn John
Amateur. *b:* 17.5.1894, Northampton. *d:* 28.10.1965, Bournbrook, Selly Oak, Birmingham. Lower order right-hand batsman, bowler. *Team* Northamptonshire (1919–21, 6 matches).
Career batting
6–9–1–43–20–5.37–0–*ct* 2
Bowling 96–2–48.00–0–0–1/9

He played no first-class cricket whilst at Cambridge U, but did win a blue for soccer. He also played soccer for Northampton Town.

Davies, Mark
Cricketer. *b:* 18.4.1969, Neath, Glamorgan. Lower order right-hand batsman, slow left-arm bowler. *Teams* Glamorgan (1990, 1 match); Gloucestershire (1992, 19 matches).
Career batting
20–24–11–153–32*–11.76–0–*ct* 11
Bowling 1677–56–29.94–0–0–4/73

He also played for Wales in the Minor Counties Championship (1991).

Davies, Mark Nicholas
Cricketer. *b:* 28.12.1959, Maesteg, Glamorgan. Middle order left-hand batsman, off break bowler. *Team* Glamorgan (1982, 2 matches).
Career batting
2–1–0–0–0–0.00–0–*ct* 1

Davies, Morean Kimsley
Cricketer. *b:* 13.10.1954, Clydach, Glamorgan. Lower order left-hand batsman, wicket-keeper. *Team* Glamorgan (1975–76, 2 matches).
Career batting
2–2–1–14–12–14.00–0–*ct* 2–*st* 2

He played rugby for Aberavon.

Davies, Philip Havelock
Amateur. *b:* 30.8.1893, Brighton, Sussex. *d:* 30.1.1930, Catterick Camp, Yorkshire. Lower order right-hand batsman, right-arm slow bowler. *Sch* Brighton. *Teams* Oxford U (1913–14, blue both years); Sussex (1914, 1 match).
Career batting
27–41–8–286–55–8.66–0–*ct* 23
Bowling 2370–98–24.18–3–0–6/59

His final first-class match was for the Army in 1927.

Davies, Richard John
Cricketer. *b:* 11.2.1954, Selly Oak, Birmingham. Opening right-hand batsman, right-arm medium pace bowler. *Team* Warwickshire (1976, 1 match).
Career batting
1–2–0–18–18–9.00–0–*ct* 1

He also played for Berkshire (1979).

Davies, Terry
Cricketer. *b:* 25.10.1960, St Albans, Hertfordshire. Lower order right-hand batsman, wicket-keeper. *Team* Glamorgan (1979–86, 100 matches).
Career batting
100–121–36–1775–75–20.88–0–*ct* 165–*st* 27

Having acted as the regular Glamorgan wicket-keeper from 1984 to 1986, he decided to emigrate to Australia and this abruptly ended his County career.

Davies, Thomas Clive
Cricketer. *b:* 7.11.1951, Pontrhydyfen, Glamorgan. Lower order right-hand batsman, slow left-arm bowler. *Team* Glamorgan (1971–72, 7 matches).
Career batting
7–6–4–9–5–4.50–0–*ct* 0
Bowling 625–18–34.72–0–0–3/22

Davies, Trefor Elliott
Professional. *b:* 14.3.1938, Stourbridge, Worcestershire. Middle order right-hand batsman, leg break bowler. *Team* Worcestershire (1955–61, 20 matches).
Career batting
20–30–5–481–76–19.24–0–*ct* 8
Bowling 169–6–28.16–0–0–2/22

Davies, William David Edward
Professional. *b:* 26.8.1906, Briton Ferry, Glamorgan. *d:* 1.10.1971, Briton Ferry, Glamorgan. Middle order right-hand batsman, leg break and googly bowler. *Team* Glamorgan (1932–35, 7 matches).
Career batting
7–12–1–122–32–11.09–0–*ct* 2
Bowling 60–0

Davies, William George
Professional. *b:* 3.7.1936, Barry, Glamorgan. Opening right-hand batsman, right-arm medium fast bowler. *Team* Glamorgan (1954–60, 32 matches).
Career batting
32–58–0–674–64–11.62–0–*ct* 14
Bowling 646–16–40.37–0–0–2/23

Davies, William Henry
Amateur. *b:* 7.8.1901, Briton Ferry, Glamorgan. Lower order right-hand batsman, right-arm medium pace bowler. *Team* Glamorgan (1922–27, 5 matches).
Career batting
5–10–2–33–8*–4.12–0–*ct* 0
Bowling 130–3–43.33–0–0–2/35

Davis, Anthony Tilton
Cricketer. *b:* 14.8.1931, Reading, Berkshire. *d:* 20.11.1978, Reading, Berkshire. He died by his own hand. Middle order right-hand batsman, slow left-arm bowler. *Sch* Reading. *Teams* Minor Counties (1967); MCC (1967).
Career batting
2–3–0–57–47–19.00–0–*ct* 0
He was a mainstay of Berkshire, playing for the County 1950–71 and captaining the side 1960–70.

Davis, Arthur Edward
Amateur. *b:* 4.8.1882, Victoria Park, Leicester. *d:* 4.11.1916, near Albert, France. He was killed in action. Middle order right-hand batsman, wicket-keeper. *Sch* Mill Hill. *Team* Leicestershire (1901–08, 21 matches).
Career batting
21–31–4–334–55–12.37–0–*ct* 37–*st* 10

Davis, Bryan Allan
Cricketer. *b:* 2.5.1940, Belmont, Port of Spain, Trinidad. Brother of C. A. (Trinidad), father of G. A. (Trinidad). Opening or middle order right-hand batsman, off break bowler. *Teams* Trinidad (1959/60 to 1970/1); Glamorgan (1968–70, 60 matches). *Tours* West Indies to India and Ceylon 1966/7; Glamorgan to West Indies 1969/70. *Tests* West Indies (1964/5, 4 matches).
Career batting
112–193–14–6231–188*–34.81–5–*ct* 127
Bowling 434–9–48.22–0–0–4/79
Test batting
4–8–0–245–68–30.62–0–*ct* 1
He hit 1,000 runs in a season twice (best 1,532, av 31.26, in 1970).

Davis, Charles Allan
Cricketer. *b:* 1.1.1944, Belmont, Port of Spain, Trinidad. Brother of B. A. (Trinidad and Glamorgan), uncle of G. A. (Trinidad). Middle order right-hand batsman, right-arm medium pace bowler. *Team* Trinidad (1960/1 to 1974/5). *Tours* West Indies to Australia and New Zealand 1968/9, to England 1969. *Tests* West Indies (1968/9 to 1972/3, 15 matches).
Career batting
90–152–18–5538–41.32–14–*ct* 44
Bowling 2480–63–39.36–3–0–7/106
Test batting
15–29–5–1301–183–54.20–4–*ct* 4
Bowling 330–2–165.00–0–0–1/27
He was successful on his tour of England, scoring 848 runs, av 42.40, and was the only tourist to hit a century in the Tests. His final first-class match was for North Trinidad in 1975/6.

Davis, Charles Percy
(known as Percy Charles Davis)
Professional. *b:* 24.5.1915, Brackley, Northamptonshire. Brother of Edward (Northamptonshire). Sound opening right-hand batsman, right-arm medium pace bowler, wicket-keeper. *Team* Northamptonshire (1935–52, 169 matches).
Career batting
169–303–22–6363–237–22.64–10–*ct* 72–*st* 10
Bowling 492–6–82.00–0–0–2/13
He hit 1,000 runs in a season three times (best 1,435, av 32.61, in 1946). His only double century was 237 for Northamptonshire v Somerset at Northampton in 1947.

Davis, Edward
Professional. *b:* 8.3.1922, Brackley, Northamptonshire. Brother of C. P. (Northamptonshire). Middle order right-hand batsman. *Team* Northamptonshire (1947–56, 104 matches).
Career batting
104–159–14–4126–171–28.45–3–*ct* 27
Bowling 8–1–8.00–0–0–1/0
He also played for Cambridgeshire (1958–63).

Davis, Francis John
Amateur. *b:* 26.3.1939, Whitchurch, Cardiff, Glamorgan. Brother of R. C. (Glamorgan). Lower order right-hand batsman, slow left-arm bowler. *Sch* Blundell's. *Teams* Glamorgan (1959–67, 14 matches); Oxford U (1963, blue).
Career batting
28–47–13–552–63–16.23–0–*ct* 17
Bowling 1694–52–32.57–2–0–5/67
He was at Oxford on a one-year course only. He also played for Hertfordshire (1977–78).

Davis, Ian Charles
Cricketer. *b:* 25.6.1953, North Sydney, New South Wales, Australia. Stylish opening or middle order right-hand batsman. *Teams* New South Wales (1973/4 to 1982/3, 46 matches); Queensland (1975/6, 9 matches). *Tours* Australia to New Zealand 1973/4, 1976/7, to England 1977. *Tests* Australia (1973/4 to 1977, 15 matches).
Career batting
88–147–9–4609–156–33.39–7–*ct* 48
Bowling 7–0

Davis, John Percy

Test batting
15–27–1–692–105–26.61–1–*ct* 9
On the 1977 tour to England he hit 608 runs, av 30.40,but in three Tests had little success.

Davis, John Percy
Amateur. *b:* 26.1.1884, Lye, Worcestershire. *d:* 16.2.1951, Heath, Stourbridge, Worcestershire. Brother of Major (Worcestershire). Middle order right-hand batsman. *Team* Worcestershire (1922, 4 matches).
Career batting
4–8–1–48–38*–6.85–0–*ct* 0
Bowling 45–0

Davis, John William
Professional. *b:* 10.4.1882, Ironville, Derbyshire. *d:* 29.10.1963, Ripley, Derbyshire. Middle order right-hand batsman. *Team* Derbyshire (1920, 1 match).
Career batting
1–2–0–9–8–4.50–0–*ct* 2
He played soccer for Grimsby Town and Derby County.

Davis, Major
Amateur. *b:* 27.3.1882, Lye, Worcestershire. *d:* 27.4.1959, Blakebrook, Kidderminster, Worcestershire. Brother of J. P. (Worcestershire). Middle order right-hand batsman, wicket-keeper. *Team* Worcestershire (1911, 1 match).
Career batting
1–2–0–35–29–17.50–0–*ct* 1
Major was his Christian name not rank.

Davis, Mark Richard
Cricketer. *b:* 26.2.1962, Kilve, Somerset. Tail end left-hand batsman, left-arm fast medium bowler. *Team* Somerset (1982–87, 77 matches). *Tour* English Counties to Zimbabwe 1984/5 (not first-class).
Career batting
77–79–24–803–60*–14.60–0–*ct* 29
Bowling 5308–149–35.62–4–1–7/55
He also played for Wiltshire (1989).

Davis, Michael John
Professional. *b:* 18.8.1943, Bolton, Lancashire. Lower order right-hand batsman, right-arm fast medium bowler. *Sch* King's School, Macclesfield. *Team* Northamptonshire (1963, 1 match).
Career batting
1 match, did not bat–*ct* 1
Bowling 58–2–29.00–0–0–1/21
He also played for Cheshire (1961 and 1965–69).

Davis, Percy Vere
Professional. *b:* 4.4.1922, Forest Hill, London. Middle order right-hand batsman. *Team* Kent (1946, 6 matches).
Career batting
10–17–0–276–136–16.23–1–*ct* 4

Davis, Richard Peter
Cricketer. *b:* 18.3.1966, Westbrook, Margate, Kent. Brother-in-law of R. Sharma (Derbyshire). Lower order right-hand batsman, slow left-arm bowler. *Team* Kent (1986–92, 110 matches).
Career batting
110–136–37–1620–67–16.36–0–*ct* 94
Bowling 10010–280–35.75–11–1–7/64
His best season was 1992 when he took 74 wickets, av 21.74.

Davis, Roger Clive
Cricketer. *b:* 1.1.1946, Whitchurch, Cardiff, Glamorgan. Brother of F. J. (Glamorgan). Opening right-hand batsman, off break bowler. *Sch* Blundell's. *Team* Glamorgan (1964–76, 213 matches). *Tour* Glamorgan to West Indies 1969/70.
Career batting
214–371–30–7367–134–21.60–5–*ct* 208
Bowling 7793–241–32.33–6–0–6/82
He hit 1,000 runs in a season once; 1,243, av 31.07, in 1975. He suffered a very bad injury in 1971 when hit fielding close to the wicket but happily made a complete recovery.

Davis, Thomas
Professional. *b:* 27.11.1827, Nottingham. *d:* 29.5.1898, Nottingham. Middle order right-hand batsman, right-arm medium pace bowler. *Team* Nottinghamshire (1854–65, 12 matches).
Career batting
18–31–2–326–72–11.24–0–*ct* 16

Davis, W.
Professional. Middle or lower order batsman, change bowler. *Team* Essex (1920, 4 matches).
Career batting
4–6–0–26–13–4.33–0–*ct* 2
Bowling 69–1–69.00–0–0–1/67

Davis, William Ernest
Professional. *b:* 26.11.1880, Wimbledon, Surrey. *d:* 27.1.1959, Balham, London. Middle order right-hand batsman, leg break bowler. *Teams* Surrey (1903–11, 111 matches); London County (1904).
Career batting
113–178–12–3504–112–21.10–3–*ct* 76
Bowling 919–17–54.05–0–0–4/51

Davis, Winston Walter
Cricketer. *b:* 18.9.1958, Sion Hill, Kingstown, St Vincent. Lower order right-hand batsman, right-arm fast medium bowler. *Teams* Windward Islands (1979/80 to 1991/2); Glamorgan (1982–84, 45 matches); Tasmania (1985/6, 8 matches); Northamptonshire (1987–90, 57 matches), Wellington (1990/1). *Tour* Young West Indies to Zimbabwe 1981/2; West Indies to England 1983 (World Cup), 1984, to India 1983/4, 1987/8, to Australia 1983/4 (not first-class), 1984/5; Wellington to Australia 1990/1; Rest of

World to England 1991. *Tests* West Indies (1982/3 to 1987/8, 15 matches).
Career batting
181–227–61–2346–77–14.13–0–*ct* 57
Bowling 17316–608–28.48–28–7–7/52
Test batting
15–17–4–202–77–15.53–0–*ct* 10
Bowling 1472–45–32.71–0–0–4/19

His best season in England was 1988 when he took 73 wickets, av 22.10. He never came to England as a member of a West Indies Test side, but was co-opted into the 1984 team and was largely responsible for victory in his single Test of that series. His outstanding feat in international cricket came in the 1983 World Cup when he took a record 7 for 51 v Australia at Headingley. He also played for Durham (pre first-class, 1980).

Davison, Brian Fettes
Cricketer. *b:* 21.12.1946, Bulawayo, Rhodesia. Attacking middle order right-hand batsman, right-arm medium pace bowler, good field. *Teams* Rhodesia (1967/8 to 1978/9); Leicestershire (1970–83, 303 matches); Tasmania (1979/80 to 1987/8, 49 matches); Gloucestershire (1985, 24 matches).
Career batting
467–766–79–27453–189–39.96–53–*ct* 338
Bowling 2688–82–32.78–1–0–5/52

He hit 1,000 runs in a season 13 times (best 1,818, av 56.81, in 1976). His career in County cricket came to an abrupt halt just before the start of the 1986 season. The Home Office turned down his application for British Citizenship, without which he could not play as an English qualified player. An appeal to the Home Secretary failed to reverse the decision. He captained Leicestershire in 1980. A good hockey player, he represented Rhodesia.

Davison, Ian Joseph
Professional. *b:* 4.10.1937, Hemel Hempstead, Hertfordshire. Lower order right-hand batsman, right-arm medium fast bowler. *Sch* Berkhamsted. *Team* Nottinghamshire (1959–66, 177 matches).
Career batting
178–246–65–1641–60*–9.06–0–*ct* 91
Bowling 15588–541–28.81–22–2–7/28

He took 111 wickets, av 21.92, in 1963. He also played for Bedfordshire (1955–58 and 1967–69).

Davy, Charles Vinicombe Butler
Amateur. *b:* 24.10.1869, Mercara, India. *d:* 10.9.1931, Vancouver, British Columbia, Canada. Middle or lower order left-hand batsman, slow left-arm bowler. *Sch* Cheltenham. *Team* Kent (1892).
Career batting
1–2–0–35–32–17.50–0–*ct* 1
Bowling 41–1–41.00–0–0–1/6

Dawes, Albert George
Professional. *b:* 23.4.1907, Frimley Green, Surrey. *d:* 23.6.1973, Goring-by-Sea, Sussex. Middle order batsman. *Team* Northamptonshire (1933, 1 match).
Career batting
1–2–0–16–16–8.00–0–*ct* 1

He was a noted soccer player with Northampton, Crystal Palace and Luton Town.

Dawes, Joseph
Professional. *b:* 14.2.1836, Hallam, Sheffield, Yorkshire. Lower order right-hand batsman, right-hand fast round arm bowler. *Team* Yorkshire (1865, 5 matches).
Career batting
6–11–2–104–28*–11.55–0–*ct* 3
Bowling 236–6–39.33–0–0–2/24

His last first-class match was for the North in 1866.

Dawkes, George Owen
Professional. *b:* 19.7.1920, Aylestone Park, Leicester. Lower order right-hand batsman, wicket-keeper. *Teams* Leicestershire (1937–39, 63 matches); Derbyshire (1947–61, 392 matches). *Tour* Commonwealth to India and Pakistan 1949/50.
Career batting
482–736–105–11411–143–18.08–1–*ct* 895–*st* 148
Bowling 20–0

A good soccer player, he appeared as goalkeeper for Leicester City.

Dawson, Edward William
Amateur. *b:* 13.2.1904, Paddington, London. *d:* 4.6.1979, Idmiston, Wiltshire. His brother married the daughter of M. N. Kenyon (Lancashire). Opening right-hand batsman. *Sch* Eton. *Teams* Leicestershire (1922–34, 174 matches); Cambridge U (1924–27, blue all four years). *Tours* MCC to South Africa 1927/8, to Australia and New Zealand 1929/30; Cahn to Jamaica 1928/9; Martineau to Egypt 1932, 1933 (not first-class). *Tests* England (1927/8 to 1929/30, 5 matches).
Career batting
282–482–17–12598–146–27.09–14–*ct* 110
Bowling 68–0
Test batting
5–9–0–175–55–19.44–0–*ct* 0

He hit 1,000 runs in a season six times (best 1,909, av 31.29, in 1929). He captained Cambridge in 1927 and Leicestershire in 1928, 1929, 1931 and 1933.

Dawson, Edwin
Professional. *b:* 1.5.1835, Dalton, Huddersfield, Yorkshire. *d:* 1.12.1888, Bradford, Yorkshire, whilst watching a football match. Middle order right-hand batsman, right-hand medium pace round arm bowler. *Team* Yorkshire (1862–74, 16 matches).
Career batting
16–27–1–256–30–9.84–0–*ct* 5

Dawson, G. A.
Amateur. Lower order batsman, wicket-keeper. *Team* MCC (1871).
Career batting
2–4–0–24–18–6.00–0–*ct* 3
He played County cricket for Brecon. His first-class debut was for Gentlemen of South in 1860.

Dawson, Gilbert Wilkinson
Professional. *b:* 9.12.1916, Bradford, Yorkshire. *d:* 24.5.1969, Paisley, Glasgow, Scotland. He was found dead in his crashed car. Opening right-hand batsman. *Team* Hampshire (1947–49, 60 matches).
Career batting
60–107–7–2643–158*–26.43–4–*ct* 36
Bowling 7–0
He hit 1,000 runs in a season twice (best 1,229, av 23.63, in 1948).

Dawson, Harold
Professional. *b:* 10.8.1914, Todmorden, Yorkshire. Middle order right-hand batsman, right-arm medium pace bowler. *Team* Hampshire (1947–48, 10 matches).
Career batting
10–19–1–236–37–13.11–0–*ct* 6
Bowling 8–0
He also played for Devon (1949).

Dawson, Oswald Charles
Amateur. *b:* 1.9.1919, Rossburgh, Durban, South Africa. Father of K. D. (Natal), cousin of J. C. Watkins (Natal). Middle order right-hand batsman, right-arm medium pace bowler, good slip field. *Teams* Natal (1938/9 to 1949/50); Border (1951/2 to 1961/2). *Tour* South Africa to England 1947. *Tests* South Africa (1947 to 1948/9, 9 matches).
Career batting
75–119–9–3804–182–34.58–6–*ct* 76
Bowling 3427–123–27.86–3–0–5/42
Test batting
9–15–1–293–55–20.92–0–*ct* 10
Bowling 578–10–57.80–0–0–2/57
In England in 1947 he hit 1,002 runs, av 32.32.

Dawson, Robert Ian
Cricketer. *b:* 29.3.1970, Exmouth, Devon. Middle order right-hand batsman, right-arm medium pace bowler. *Sch* Millfield. *Team* Gloucestershire (1992, 6 matches).
Career batting
6–8–0–88–29–11.00–0–*ct* 2
He also played for Devon (1988–91).

Dawson, Timothy Andrew John
Cricketer. *b:* 29.1.1963, Münster, West Germany. Grandson of A. E. Alderman (Derbyshire). Lower order right-hand batsman, off break bowler. *Sch* Mill Hill. *Team* Oxford U (1986, blue).
Career batting
7–9–5–32–10*–8.00–0–*ct* 2
Bowling 649–13–49.92–0–0–3/65

Dawson, William Arthur
Amateur. *b:* 3.12.1850, Bradford, Yorkshire. *d:* 6.3.1916, Ilkley, Yorkshire. Lower order right-hand batsman, right-arm medium pace bowler. *Sch* Marlborough. *Team* Yorkshire (1870, 1 match).
Career batting
1–2–0–0–0–0.00–0–*ct* 1
He did not appear in first-class matches whilst at Cambridge, but represented the University in the 100 yards, being Champion of England at that distance. He also represented Yorkshire at rugby.

Day, Alan Richard
Cricketer. *b:* 12.11.1938, Muswell Hill, Middlesex. Middle order right-hand batsman. *Sch* Aldenham. *Team* MCC (1968).
Career batting
1–1–0–5–5–5.00–0–*ct* 0
His County cricket was for Hertfordshire (1962–75) and Berkshire (1977–80).

Day, Albert George
Amateur. *b:* 20.9.1865, Dewsbury, Yorkshire. *d:* 16.10.1908, Dewsbury, Yorkshire. Middle order right-hand batsman. *Sch* Mill Hill. *Team* Yorkshire (1885–88, 6 matches).
Career batting
6–10–0–78–25–7.80–0–*ct* 3

Day, Anthony Samuel
Amateur. *b:* 20.6.1930, Ascot, Berkshire. Son of S. H. (Kent), nephew of A. P. (Kent) and S. E. (Kent), cousin of D. A. S. (Europeans). Middle order right-hand batsman. *Sch* Harrow. *Team* Cambridge U (1953).
Career batting
1–2–0–3–2–1.50–0–*ct* 1

Day, Arthur Percival
Amateur. *b:* 10.4.1885, Kidbrooke, Blackheath, Kent. *d:* 22.1.1969, Budleigh Salterton, Devon. Father of D. A. S. (Europeans), brother of S. E. (Kent) and S. H. (Kent), uncle of A. S. (Cambridge U), C. G. Toppin (Worcestershire) and J. F. T. Toppin (Worcestershire). Middle order right-hand batsman, right-arm fast and leg break bowler. *Sch* Malvern. *Team* Kent (1905–25, 143 matches).
Career batting
157–243–25–7174–184*–32.90–13–*ct* 92
Bowling 3480–132–26.36–4–0–8/49
He scored 1,000 runs in a season twice (best 1,149, av 32.82, in 1905). For Kent v Hampshire at Southampton in 1911 he hit 100* in 55 minutes.

Day, Daniel
Professional. *b:* 14.6.1807, Streatham, London. *d:* 22.11.1887, Southampton, Hampshire. Lower order

right-hand batsman, right-hand fast medium round arm bowler, good close field. *Teams* Hampshire (1843–50, 13 matches); Surrey (1846–52, 23 matches).
Career batting
50–86–15–395–70–5.56–0–*ct* 36
Bowling 1077–91 + 161–11.83–22–8–8/?

He also played for Dorset (1849–51) and Norfolk (1849). His first-class debut was for England in 1842.

Day, Frederick Gordon Kenneth
Amateur. *b:* 25.6.1919, Yatton, Somerset. *d:* 9.12.1991, Whitchurch, Bristol, Gloucestershire. Lower order right-hand batsman, wicket-keeper. *Team* Somerset (1950–56, 7 matches).
Career batting
7–13–2–201–56*–18.27–0–*ct* 7–*st* 8

Day, Harold Lindsay Vernon
Amateur. *b:* 12.8.1898, Darjeeling, India. *d:* 15.6.1972, Hadley Wood, Hertfordshire. Middle order right-hand batsman. *Sch* Bedford Modern. *Team* Hampshire (1922–31, 78 matches).
Career batting
80–129–5–3142–142–25.33–4–*ct* 26
Bowling 46–0

He played for Bedfordshire (1920–22) before joining Hampshire. A well-known rugby player, he represented Leicestershire and England as wing three quarter.

Day, James John
Amateur. *b:* 8.2.1850, Holborn, London. *d:* 19.2.1895, Battersea, London. Middle order batsman. *Teams* Gentlemen of South (1870); W. G. Grace's XI (1871–73).
Career batting
3–3–0–1–1–0.33–0–*ct* 2

Day, John William
Professional. *b:* 15.4.1881, Sutton-on-Trent, Nottinghamshire. *d:* 9.11.1949, Saxilby, Lincolnshire. Middle order right-hand batsman, medium pace bowler. *Team* Nottinghamshire (1903–07, 61 matches).
Career batting
61–96–8–1233–88–14.01–0–*ct* 36
Bowling 950–27–35.18–1–0–5/50

He also played for Lincolnshire (1909–27). He played soccer for Gainsborough Trinity. He was a first-class umpire (1926–36).

Day, Kenneth Brian
Professional. *b:* 19.5.1935, Hendon, Middlesex. *d:* 19.1.1971, Fulham, London. Lower order right-hand batsman, wicket-keeper. *Team* Middlesex (1959, 2 matches).
Career batting
3 matches, did not bat–*ct* 4–*st* 4

He made his first-class debut in 1958 for MCC.

Day, Leonard Morrison
Amateur. *b:* 24.12.1859, York. *d:* 25.4.1943, Crouch End, Hornsey, Middlesex. Middle/lower order right-hand batsman, lob bowler, wicket-keeper. *Team* Gloucestershire (1880–82, 15 matches).
Career batting
16–23–8–164–34*–10.93–0–*ct* 7–*st* 3

Day, Samuel Hulme
Amateur. *b:* 29.12.1878, Peckham Rye, London. *d:* 21.2.1950, Chobham, Surrey. Brother of A. P. (Kent) and S. E. (Kent), father of A. S. (Cambridge U), uncle of D. A. S. (Europeans), C. G. Toppin (Worcestershire) and J. F. T. Toppin (Worcestershire). Middle order right-hand batsman, right-arm fast bowler. *Sch* Malvern. *Teams* Kent (1897–1919, 128 matches); Cambridge U (1899–1902, blue all four years).
Career batting
171–285–25–7722–152*–29.70–7–*ct* 58
Bowling 317–8–39.62–0–0–3/46

He twice hit 1,000 runs in a season (best 1,167, av 34.32, in 1901). He captained Cambridge in 1901. He scored 101* on debut for Kent v Gloucestershire at Cheltenham in 1897. A noted soccer player, he appeared for Corinthians and England.

Day, Sydney Ernest
Amateur. *b:* 9.2.1884, Kidbrooke, Blackheath, Kent. *d:* 7.7.1970, West Malling, Kent. Brother of A. P. (Kent) and S. H. (Kent), uncle of A. S. (Cambridge U), D. A. S. (Europeans), C. G. Toppin (Worcestershire) and J. F. T. Toppin (Worcestershire). Middle order right-hand batsman. *Sch* Malvern. *Team* Kent (1922–25, 11 matches).
Career batting
11–17–4–245–45*–18.84–0–*ct* 4

He was President of Kent 1954. An excellent soccer player, he appeared for Corinthians.

Days, John Edward
Professional. *b:* 10.7.1872, Peopleton, Worcestershire. *d:* 19.8.1947, Walsall, Staffordshire. Lower order batsman, bowler. *Team* Worcestershire (1900–07, 2 matches).
Career batting
2–3–0–8–5–2.66–0–*ct* 0
Bowling 42–2–21.00–0–0–2/42

Deakin, Michael John
Cricketer. *b:* 6.5.1957, Bury, Lancashire. Lower order right-hand batsman, wicket-keeper. *Team* Derbyshire (1981, 4 matches).
Career batting
4–6–0–45–15–7.50–0–*ct* 9

De Alwis, Ronald Guy
Cricketer. *b:* 15.2.1959, Colombo, Ceylon. Lower order right-hand batsman, wicket-keeper. *Team* Sinhalese SC (1988/9). *Tours* Sri Lanka to New Zealand 1982/3, to Australia 1982/3, 1987/8, to Zimbabwe

1982/3, to England 1983 (World Cup), 1984, to Sharjah (not first-class) 1985/6, 1986/7, 1987/8, to India 1986/7. *Tests* Sri Lanka (1982/3 to 1987/8, 11 matches).
Career batting
36–48–4–673–74–15.29–0–*ct* 68–*st* 6
Test batting
11–19–0–152–28–8.00–0–*ct* 21–*st* 2

He came to England as Sri Lanka's principal wicket-keeper in 1984, but a broken finger meant he appeared in only two first-class matches. His last first-class match was for Western Province (Sri Lanka) in 1989/90.

Dean, David
Professional. *b:* 27.7.1847, Duncton, Sussex. *d:* 19.6.1919, Graffham, Sussex. Brother of James jun (Sussex), nephew of James sen (Sussex). Middle order batsman. *Team* Sussex (1871, 2 matches).
Career batting
2–3–0–8–6–2.66–0–*ct* 1

Dean, Harry
Professional. *b:* 13.8.1884, Burnley, Lancashire. *d:* 12.3.1957, Garstang, Lancashire. Lower order left-hand batsman, left-arm fast medium bowler. *Team* Lancashire (1906–21, 256 matches). *Tests* England (1912, 3 matches).
Career batting
267–370–122–2559–49*–10.31–0–*ct* 121
Bowling 23606–1301–18.14–97–24–9/31
Test batting
3–4–2–10–8–5.00–0–*ct* 2
Bowling 153–11–13.90–0–0–4/19

He took 100 wickets in a season eight times (best 183, av 17.43, in 1911). His best bowling was 9/31 for Lancashire v Somerset at Old Trafford in 1909. He also played for Cheshire (1922–23).

Dean, James (sen)
Professional. *b:* 4.1.1816, Duncton, Sussex. *d:* 25.12.1881, Duncton, Sussex. Uncle of David (Sussex) and James jun (Sussex). Lower order right-hand batsman, right-hand fast round arm bowler, wicket-keeper. *Team* Sussex (1835–60, 112 matches).
Career batting
305–548–63–5115–99–10.54–0–*ct* 207
Bowling 6805–491 + 649–13.85–85–18–9/34

He often bowled from one end and then remained there to keep wicket for the following over. His best bowling was 9/34 for MCC v Nottinghamshire at Trent Bridge in 1843. He took 100 wickets in 1845. His final first-class match was for MCC in 1861. He also played for Dorset (1845) and Northamptonshire (pre first-class, 1852).

Dean, James (jun)
Professional. *b:* 7.4.1842, Petworth, Sussex. *d:* 6.3.1869, Duncton, Sussex. Brother of David (Sussex), nephew of James sen (Sussex). Hard hitting middle order right-hand batsman. *Team* Sussex (1862–66, 12 matches).
Career batting
12–22–4–220–39*–12.22–0–*ct* 5
Bowling 23–1–23.00–0–0–1/13

Dean, Philip James
Cricketer. *b:* 4.6.1955, Skipton, Yorkshire. Middle order left-hand batsman. *Sch* Mill Hill. *Team* Oxford U (1978).
Career batting
2–4–0–75–39–18.75–0–*ct* 1

Dean, T.
Professional. Middle order batsman. *Team* Gloucestershire (1908, 1 match).
Career batting
1–2–0–15–11–7.50–0–*ct* 0

Dean, Thomas Arthur
Professional. *b:* 21.11.1920, Gosport, Hampshire. Lower order right-hand batsman, leg break bowler. *Teams* Hampshire (1939–49, 28 matches); Eastern Province (1956/7).
Career batting
29–46–13–285–26–8.63–0–*ct* 31
Bowling 1706–54–31.59–4–1–7/51

He was brought up in South Africa and returned there as a cricket coach after leaving Hampshire. He also played for Devon (1954).

Dean, William
Professional. *b: circa* 1882, Australia. Lower order batsman. *Team* Hampshire (1907, 1 match).
Career batting
1–1–1–3–3*–no av–0–*ct* 2
Bowling 52–2–26.00–0–0–2/52

Dean, William Henry
Professional. *b:* 25.11.1928, Leeds, Yorkshire. Lower order right-hand batsman, right-arm fast medium bowler. *Team* Somerset (1952, 1 match).
Career batting
1–2–1–21–21–21.00–0–*ct* 0
Bowling 17–0

Deane, Charles Gerrard
Amateur. *b:* 8.3.1885, Oakhill, Somerset. *d:* 14.12.1914, Multan, India, of fever. Middle order right-hand batsman, right-arm medium pace bowler. *Sch* Taunton. *Team* Somerset (1907–13, 36 matches).
Career batting
36–69–6–753–78–11.95–0–*ct* 25
Bowling 206–8–25.75–0–0–2/36

Deane, Hubert Gouvaine
Amateur. *b:* 21.7.1895, Eshowe, Zululand. *d:* 21.10.1939, Lower Houghton, Johannesburg, South Africa. He died from a heart attack. Son of H. P. (Natal). Middle order right-hand batsman, brilliant close field. *Teams* Natal (1919/20 to 1922/3); Trans-

vaal (1923/4 to 1929/30). *Tours* South Africa to England 1924, 1929. *Tests* South Africa (1924 to 1930/1, 17 matches).
Career batting
100–138–12–3795–165–30.11–6–*ct* 63
Bowling 99–3–33.00–0–0–3/23
Test batting
17–27–2–628–93–25.12–0–*ct* 8
He hit 1,239, av 34.41, runs on his 1929 tour of England. He captained the South Africans in England in 1929 and in all led his country in 12 Tests. His final first-class match was in South Africa in 1930/1.

Deane, Marmaduke William
Professional. *b:* 25.3.1857, Petersham, Surrey. *d:* 7.11.1936, Dorking, Surrey. Lower order right-hand batsman, wicket-keeper. *Teams* Surrey (1880, 1 match); Hampshire (1895, 4 matches).
Career batting
5–9–2–16–8–2.28–0–*ct* 6–*st* 4

Dearden, John
Amateur. *b:* 26.12 1891, St Helens, Lancashire. *d:* 4.5.1972, Belfast, Ireland. Lower order right-hand batsman, wicket-keeper. *Team* Ireland (1922–26).
Career batting
2–3–0–84–84–28.00–0–*ct* 1–*st* 1

Dearlove, Alfred John
Amateur. *b:* 3.8.1869, Kingsdown, Bristol. *d:* 17.3.1955, Southmead, Bristol. Middle order right-hand batsman, change bowler. *Team* Gloucestershire (1895–1900, 6 matches).
Career batting
6–10–1–129–34*–14.33–0–*ct* 1
Bowling 141–5–28.20–0–0–3/56

Dearlove, John Alban
Amateur. *b:* 30.4.1931, Woking, Surrey. Lower order right-hand batsman, right-arm medium pace bowler. *Sch* Downside. *Team* Cambridge U (1954).
Career batting
1–1–0–6–6–6.00–0–*ct* 1
Bowling 74–0

Dearnaley, Irvine
Professional in 1900, but amateur 1905–07. *b:* 18.2.1877, Glossop, Derbyshire. *d:* 14.3.1965, Ashton-under-Lyne, Lancashire, following a road accident. Middle order right-hand batsman. *Team* Derbyshire (1905–07, 4 matches).
Career batting
4–8–0–51–34–6.37–0–*ct* 3
He played for Derbyshire v West Indies (pre first-class) in 1900.

Deas, Kenneth Robin
Amateur. *b:* 10.7.1927, Papatoetoe, New Zealand. Middle order right-hand batsman, slow left-arm bowler. *Teams* Scotland (1955–56); Auckland (1947/8 to 1960/1).
Career batting
18–34–4–522–73–17.40–0–*ct* 7
Bowling 313–9–34.77–0–0–4/81

Debnam, Alexander Frederick Henry
Amateur in 1948, professional from 1949. *b:* 12.10.1921, Belvedere, Kent. Middle or lower order right-hand batsman, leg break bowler. *Teams* Kent (1948–49, 11 matches); Hampshire (1950–51, 10 matches).
Career batting
21–33–6–327–64–12.11–0–*ct* 12
Bowling 862–20–43.10–1–0–5/87

De Burgh, Hubert Henry
Amateur. *b:* 16.2.1879, Oldtown, Naas, Co Kildare, Ireland. *d:* 6.10.1960, Oldtown, Naas, Co Kildare, Ireland. Middle order right-hand batsman. *Teams* Ireland (1926); Europeans (1905/6).
Career batting
2–3–0–39–28–13.00–0–*ct* 0

De Courcy, James Harry
Amateur. *b:* 18.4.1927, Newcastle, New South Wales, Australia. Middle order right-hand batsman, leg break bowler. *Team* New South Wales (1947/8 to 1957/8, 50 matches). *Tour* Australia to England 1953. *Tests* Australia (1953, 3 matches).
Career batting
79–113–11–3778–204–37.03–6–*ct* 51
Bowling 67–0
Test batting
3–6–1–81–41–16.20–0–*ct* 3
In 1953 in England he hit 1,214 runs, av 41.86. His only double century was made during that tour v Combined Services at Kingston.

Deed, John Arthur
Amateur. *b:* 12.9.1901, Bessels Green, Sevenoaks, Kent. *d:* 19.10.1980, Ide Hill, Kent. Opening or middle order right-hand batsman. *Sch* Malvern. *Team* Kent (1924–30, 62 matches).
Career batting
62–99–17–1863–133–22.71–2–*ct* 16
He appeared in the Seniors' match whilst at Cambridge, but no first-class games. He was President of Kent in 1965.

DeFreitas, Phillip Anthony Jason
Cricketer. *b:* 18.2.1966, Scotts Head, Dominica. Middle order right-hand batsman, right-arm fast medium bowler. *Teams* Leicestershire (1985–88, 65 matches); Lancashire (1988/9 to 1992, 56 matches). *Tours* England to Australia 1986/7, 1987/8 (not first-class), 1990/1, to New Zealand 1987/8, 1990/1 (not first-class), 1991/2, to Pakistan 1987/8, to India 1989/90 (not first-class), to West Indies 1989/90, to Sharjah (not first-class) 1986/7, to India and Pakistan (World Cup) 1987/8, to Australia and New Zealand (World Cup) 1991/2; Lancashire to Zimbabwe 1988/9. *Tests*

De Grandhomme, Laurence Leonard

England (1986/7 to 1992, 31 matches).
Career batting
167–224–24–4295–113–21.47–4–*ct* 43
Bowling 14847–542–27.39–27–2–7/21
Test batting
31–46–4–527–55*–12.54–0–*ct* 6
Bowling 3017–93–32.44–3–0–7/70

He took 94 wickets (av 23.09) in 1986. His career in Test cricket has been uneven, but he went to Australia in 1990/1 as a replacement for Small and proved very effective; in 1991 he topped the England bowling averages against West Indies, but in 1992 was not so successful.

De Grandhomme, Laurence Leonard
Cricketer. *b:* 22.11.1956, Ndola, Northern Rhodesia. Son of H. L. (Rhodesia). Middle order right-hand batsman, off break bowler. *Team* Zimbabwe (1979/80 to 1987/8). *Tours* Zimbabwe to England 1985.
Career batting
16–25–7–428–60–23.78–0–*ct* 12
Bowling 937–26–36.04–0–0–3/56

De Grey, Rev Hon Arnald
Amateur. *b:* 11.9.1856, Westminster, London. *d:* 15.11.1889, Hyères, France. Half-brother of Thomas (Cambridge U), son-in-law of S. C. B. Ponsonby (Surrey and Middlesex). Middle order right-hand batsman. *Sch* Eton. *Team* I Zingari (1880).
Career batting
1–1–0–1–1–1.00–0–*ct* 1
Bowling 32–0

De Grey, Hon Thomas
(succeeded as 6th Baron Walsingham in 1870)
Amateur. *b:* 29.7.1843, Mayfair, London. *d:* 3.12.1919, Hampstead, London. Half-brother of Arnald (I Zingari). Opening or middle order right-hand batsman, excellent cover point. *Sch* Eton. *Team* Cambridge U (1862–65, blue 1862–63).
Career batting
15–27–1–380–62–14.61–0–*ct* 9

His final first-class match was for MCC in 1866. He would have played in the University match of 1864 but for rheumatism. He also played for Norfolk (1868). He was at one time the best shot in England and had a record of 1,070 grouse in one day. He was MP for West Norfolk, 1865–70.

Deighton, John Harold Greenway
Amateur. *b:* 5.4.1920, Prestwich, Lancashire. Hard hitting middle/lower order right-hand batsman, right-arm fast medium bowler. *Sch* Denstone. *Team* Lancashire (1948–50, 7 matches).
Career batting
35–63–13–994–79–19.88–0–*ct* 17
Bowling 3081–127–24.25–6–1–6/50

Most of his first-class cricket was for the Combined Services. He made his first-class debut in 1947 and played his last match in for he same team in 1962. He also played for Northumberland (1947).

Delacombe, William Barclay
Amateur. *b:* 20.7.1860, Georgetown, Ascension Island. *d:* 14.10.1911, Nottingham. Lower order batsman, change bowler, good field. *Sch* King's, Bruton. *Team* Derbyshire (1894–1900, 10 matches).
Career batting
10–13–3–95–23*–9.50–0–*ct* 2
Bowling 44–0

He was Secretary to Derbyshire CCC from 1889 to 1907 and, as a good club cricketer, appeared for the County if required. He first played for Derbyshire (not first-class) in 1891.

De La Pêna, Jason Michael
Cricketer. *b:* 16.9.1972, Hammersmith, London. Lower order right-hand batsman, right-arm fast medium bowler. *Sch* Stowe. *Team* Gloucestershire (1991, 2 matches).
Career batting
2–2–1–1–1*–1.00–0–*ct* 0
Bowling 138–3–46.00–0–0–2/69

De La Warr, Earl, Gilbert George Reginald Sackville-West
(Viscount Cantelupe, becoming 8th Earl in 1896)
Amateur. *b:* 22.3.1869, Westminster, London. *d:* 16.12 1915, Messina, Sicily. Brother-in-law of F. F. Thomas (Sussex). Lower order batsman. *Sch* Charterhouse. *Teams* Lord Sheffield's XI (1891); Earl De La Warr's XI (1896)
Career batting
2–2–0–2–1–1.00–0–*ct* 2

His son married the sister of Rex Harrison, the actor.

Delisle, Gustave Peter Sapenne
Amateur. *b:* 25.12.1934, Basseterre, St Kitts. Middle order right-hand batsman, off break bowler. *Sch* Stonyhurst. *Teams* Oxford U (1954–56, blue 1955–56); Middlesex (1954–57, 55 matches). *Tour* Surridge to Bermuda 1961 (not first-class).
Career batting
91–163–16–3283–130–22.33–3–*ct* 40

His last first-class class was for Combined Services in 1958. He hit 1,185 runs, av 22.78, in 1955.

De Lisle, John Adrian Frederick March Phillipps
Amateur. *b:* 27.9.1891, Kensington, London. *d:* 4.11.1961, Stockerston, Leicestershire. Middle or lower order right-hand batsman. *Sch* Downside and Beaumont. *Team* Leicestershire (1921–30, 33 matches).
Career batting
33–50–4–530–88–11.52–0–*ct* 13

He captained Leicestershire in 1930, his only season playing regularly in County cricket.

De Little, Ernest Robert
Amateur. *b:* 19.6.1868, Melbourne, Victoria, Australia. *d:* 1.10.1926, Caramut, Victoria, Australia. Lower order right-hand batsman, right-arm fast bowler, good field. *Team* Cambridge U (1888–89, blue 1889). *Tour* Vernon to India 1889/90 (not first-class).
Career batting
9–16–7–104–22–11.55–0–*ct* 4
Bowling 548–27–20.29–2–1–7/27

Deller, Reginald Patrick
Professional. *b:* 27.3.1933, Paddington, London. Lower order right-hand batsman, right-arm fast medium bowler. *Team* Middlesex (1951–53, 3 matches).
Career batting
3–3–3–4–3*–no av–0–*ct* 0
Bowling 127–2–63.50–0–0–1/35

Delmé-Radcliffe, Arthur Henry
Amateur. *b:* 23.11.1870, South Tidworth, Hampshire. *d:* 30.6.1950, Branksome Park, Dorset. Middle order right-hand batsman, slow bowler. *Sch* Sherborne. *Team* Hampshire (1896–1900, 7 matches).
Career batting
7–13–0–190–43–14.61–0–*ct* 3
Whilst at Oxford he played in the Freshmen's match, but no first-class games. His County cricket began with Hampshire in 1889, during a period when Hampshire were not considered first-class, and he also played for Berkshire (1897).

De Mel, Ashantha Lakdasa Francis
Cricketer. *b:* 9.5.1959, Colombo, Ceylon. Lower order right-hand batsman, right-arm fast medium bowler. *Team* Sri Lanka (1980/1 to 1986/7). *Tours* Sri Lanka to India 1980/1, 1982/3, 1986/7, to England 1981, 1983 (World Cup), 1984, to Pakistan 1981/2, 1985/6, to Australia 1982/3, 1984/5, to New Zealand 1982/3, to Zimbabwe 1982/3, to Sharjah (not first-class) 1985/6, 1986/7, to India and Pakistan (World Cup) 1987/8. *Tests* Sri Lanka (1981/2 to 1986/7, 17 matches).
Career batting
42–57–9–918–100*–19.12–1–*ct* 22
Bowling 4132–109–37.90–3–0–6/109
Test batting
17–28–5–326–34–14.17–0–*ct* 9
Bowling 2180–59–36.94–3–0–6/109
After achieving modest results on the 1981 tour to England, he came a second time in 1984 and showed much improved form. He was not however fully fit when he appeared in the 1984 Lord's Test.

De Montezuma, Leonidas De Toledo Marcondes
Amateur. *b:* 16.4.1869, Crowborough, Sussex. *d:* 18.3.1937, Stone, Dartford, Kent. Middle order right-hand batsman, useful change bowler. *Teams* Sussex (1898, 7 matches); London County (1904).
Career batting
9–15–4–285–80*–25.90–0–*ct* 2
Bowling 83–4–20.75–0–0–4/71
His family originated from Ecuador.

De Montmorency, Reymond Hervey
Amateur. *b:* 6.10.1871, Gondah, India. *d:* 19.12.1938, Sunningdale, Berkshire. Father-in-law of E. W. Swanton (Middlesex). Middle order right-hand batsman, right-arm slow medium bowler. *Sch* Cheltenham and St Paul's. *Team* Oxford U (1899, blue).
Career batting
4–7–0–230–62–32.85–0–*ct* 1
Bowling 123–5–24.60–0–0–3/16
His first-class debut was for Oxford U, Past and Present in 1897. His County cricket was for Hertfordshire (1899) and Buckinghamshire (1907–09). A useful all round sportsman, he represented Oxford at golf and rackets.

Dempsey, General Sir Miles Christopher
Amateur. *b:* 15.12.1896, Wallasey, Cheshire. *d:* 5.6.1969, Newbury, Berkshire. Middle order right-hand batsman, slow left-arm bowler. *Sch* Shrewsbury. *Team* Sussex (1919, 2 matches).
Career batting
2–3–0–5–4–1.66–0–*ct* 1
He also played for Berkshire (1926–29). He commanded the Second Army in the 1944 invasion of Normandy.

Dempster, Charles Stewart
Amateur. *b:* 15.11.1903, Wellington, New Zealand. *d:* 14.2.1974, Wellington, New Zealand. Opening or middle order right-hand batsman, right-arm slow bowler. *Teams* Wellington (1921/2 to 1947/8); Scotland (1934); Leicestershire (1935–39, 69 matches); Warwickshire (1946, 3 matches). *Tours* New Zealand to England 1927, 1931, to Australia 1927/8; Cahn to Ceylon 1936/7, to New Zealand 1938/9. *Tests* New Zealand (1929/30 to 1932/3, 10 matches).
Career batting
184–306–36–12145–212–44.98–35–*ct* 94–*st* 2
Bowling 300–8–37.50–0–0–2/4
Test batting
10–15–4–723–136–65.72–2–*ct* 2
Bowling 10–0
One of the greatest of all New Zealand batsmen, he began in County cricket after two successful tours to England with the New Zealand team. He hit 1,000 runs in a season five times (best 1,778, av 59.26, in 1931). The highest of his two double centuries was 212 for New Zealanders v Essex at Leyton in 1931. He captained Leicestershire 1936–38.

Dench, Charles Edward
Professional. *b:* 6.9.1873, East Stoke, Nottinghamshire. *d:* 28.6.1958, Sherwood, Nottingham. Middle or lower order right-hand batsman, right-arm medium pace bowler. *Team* Nottinghamshire (1897–1902, 91 matches).

Denham, Harold Alfred

Career batting
91–136–17–2660–88–22.35–0–*ct* 61
Bowling 2191–78–28.08–4–0–7/28

He took 7 for 28 on his first-class debut, for Nottinghamshire v MCC at Lord's in 1897. He was a first-class umpire (1906–12), standing in one Test (1909).

Denham, Harold Alfred
Amateur. *b:* 13.10.1872, Howrah, India. *d:* 25.2.1946, Wilmington, Eastbourne, Sussex. Middle order batsman. *Team* Hampshire (1896, 1 match).
Career batting
1–2–0–8–7–4.00–0–*ct* 0

He played for Ireland (not first-class) in 1901.

Denman, Henry Wynne
Amateur. *b:* 5.7.1929, Tue Brook, Liverpool, Lancashire. Lower order right-hand batsman, wicket-keeper. *Sch* Oundle. *Team* Cambridge U (1950–52).
Career batting
7–5–4–4–3–4.00–0–*ct* 5–*st* 2

Denman, John
Cricketer. *b:* 13.6.1947, Horley, Surrey. Lower order right-hand batsman, right-arm medium pace bowler. *Team* Sussex 1970–73, 49 matches).
Career batting
49–65–20–713–50*–15.84–0–*ct* 26
Bowling 3065–70–43.78–1–0–5/45

Denness, Michael Henry
Cricketer. *b:* 1.12.1940, Bellshill, Lanarkshire, Scotland. Opening or middle order right-hand batsman, right-arm medium pace off break bowler. *Sch* Ayr Academy. *Teams* Scotland (1959–67); Kent (1962–76, 333 matches); Essex (1977–80, 83 matches). *Tours* International XI to India, Pakistan and Ceylon 1967/8; Norfolk to West Indies 1969/70; MCC to India, Pakistan and Sri Lanka 1972/3, to West Indies 1973/4, to Australia and New Zealand 1974/5; International Wanderers to South Africa 1975/6; Robins to Sri Lanka 1977/8. *Tests* England (1969–75, 28 matches).
Career batting
501–838–65–25886–195–33.48–33–*ct* 411
Bowling 62–2–31.00–0–0–1/7
Test batting
28–45–3–1667–188–39.69–4–*ct* 28

He reached 1,000 runs in a season 14 times (best 1,606, av 31.49, in 1966). He captained Kent from 1972 to 1976 and England in 19 Tests between 1973/4 and 1975, including the Test tours of 1973/4 and 1974/5. He dropped himself from the fourth Test in Australia in 1974/5, but resumed his place later.

Dennett, Edward George
Professional. *b:* 27.4.1879, Upway, Dorset. *d:* 15.9.1937, Leckhampton, Cheltenham, Gloucestershire. Lower order left-hand batsman, slow left-arm bowler. *Teams* Gloucestershire (1903–26, 387 matches); Bengal Governor's XI (1917/18).
Career batting
401–651–254–4102–71–10.33–0–*ct* 297
Bowling 42640–2151–19.82–211–57–10/40

He took 100 wickets in a season 12 times, exceeding 200 once – 201, av 16.05, in 1907. He performed the feat of taking all ten wickets in an innings (for 40 runs) for Gloucestershire v Essex at Bristol in 1906. An all-round sportsman, he also excelled at soccer, fives, billiards and shooting.

Denning, Peter William
Cricketer. *b:* 16.12.1949, Chewton Mendip, Somerset. Middle order left-hand batsman, off break bowler, deep field. *Sch* Millfield. *Team* Somerset (1969–84, 269 matches).
Career batting
269–447–44–11559–184–28.68–8–*ct* 132
Bowling 96–1–96.00–0–0–1/4

He hit 1,000 runs in a season six times (best 1,222, av 42.13, in 1979). His achievements for Somerset were as much in limited overs cricket as in first-class, and he hit centuries in all three one-day competitions.

Dennis, Frank
Professional. *b:* 11.6.1907, Holbeck, Leeds, Yorkshire. Uncle of S. J. (Yorkshire), R. A. Hutton (Yorkshire) and J. L. Hutton (MCC in East Africa), brother-in-law of L. Hutton (Yorkshire). Lower order left-hand batsman, right-arm fast bowler. *Team* Yorkshire (1928–33, 89 matches).
Career batting
92–105–29–1500–95–19.73–0–*ct* 59
Bowling 4770–163–29.26–5–0–6/42

He also played for Cheshire (1935–39) and his final first-class match was for Minor Counties in 1939. After the Second World War he lived in New Zealand and was an official of the Canterbury Club.

Dennis, John Newman
Amateur. *b:* 4.1.1913, Leytonstone, Essex. Middle order right-hand batsman. *Sch* Forest. *Team* Essex (1934–39, 22 matches).
Career batting
22–33–3–530–53–17.66–0–*ct* 13

Dennis, Joseph
Professional. *c:* 6.1.1779, Nottingham. *d:* 16.11.1831, Nottingham. Lower order batsman, wicket-keeper. *Team* Nottingham (1803–29).
Career batting
7–13–0–48–14–3.69–0–*ct* 4–*st* 4

He was regarded as one of the greatest wicket-keepers of his era.

Dennis, Simon John
Cricketer. *b:* 18.10.1960, Scarborough, Yorkshire. Nephew of L. Hutton (Yorkshire) and F. Dennis (Yorkshire), cousin of R. A. Hutton (Yorkshire) and

J. L. Hutton (MCC in East Africa). Lower order right-hand batsman, left-arm fast medium bowler. *Teams* Yorkshire (1980–88, 67 matches); Orange Free State (1982/3); Glamorgan (1989–91, 32 matches). *Tour* Yorkshire to Windward Islands 1986/7.
Career batting
104–100–29–669–53*–9.42–0–*ct* 26
Bowling 8426–254–33.17–7–0–5/35

Dennison, David George
Cricketer. *b:* 22.12.1961, Banbridge, Co Down, Ireland. Opening right-hand batsman. *Team* Ireland (1983–87).
Career batting
2–4–0–32–16–8.00–0–*ct* 1

Denny, Christopher Mark
Cricketer. *b:* 22.4.1964, Farnborough, Kent. Lower order right-hand batsman, slow left-arm bowler. *Sch* St Dunstan's. *Team* Oxford U (1985).
Career batting
4–6–1–28–19–5.60–0–*ct* 3

Denny, Ernest Wriothesley
Amateur. *b:* 5.2.1872, Kensington, London. *d:* 20.10.1949, Garboldisham Manor, Norfolk. Lower order right-hand batsman, right-arm fast medium bowler. *Sch* Wellington. *Team* Oxford U (1891).
Career batting
1–2–2–1–1*–no av–0–*ct* 0
Bowling 14–0

Dent, Henry James
Amateur. *b:* 23.6.1875, Dilwyn, Herefordshire. *d:* 27.8.1929, Perton, Stoke Edith, Herefordshire. Lower order batsman, useful bowler. *Team* H. K. Foster's XI (1919).
Career batting
1–1–0–1–1–1.00–0–*ct* 0
Bowling 38–0
His County cricket was for Herefordshire (1898–99).

Denton, Arthur Donald
Amateur. *b:* 21.10.1896, Rushden, Northamptonshire. *d:* 23.1.1961, Higham Ferrers, Northamptonshire. Brother of J. S. (Northamptonshire) and W. H. (Northamptonshire). Middle order right-hand batsman, lob bowler. *Sch* Wellingborough. *Team* Northamptonshire (1914–20, 7 matches).
Career batting
7–13–2–276–51*–25.09–0–*ct* 3
Bowling 5–0
He lost part of a leg in the First World War, but continued to play cricket with the aid of a runner.

Denton, David
Professional. *b:* 4.7.1874, Thornes, Wakefield, Yorkshire. *d:* 16.2.1950, Thornes, Wakefield, Yorkshire. Brother of Joe (Yorkshire). Middle order right-hand batsman, right-arm medium fast bowler, brilliant outfield. *Team* Yorkshire (1894–1920, 676 matches). *Tours* MCC to South Africa 1905/6, 1909/10. *Tests* England (1905 to 1909/10, 11 matches).
Career batting
741–1161–70–36440–221–33.40–69–*ct* 396–*st* 1
Bowling 983–34–28.91–1–0–5/42
Test batting
11–22–1–424–104–20.19–1–*ct* 8
He hit 1,000 runs in a season 21 times, exceeding 2,000 on five occasions (best 2,405, av 42.19, in 1905). His three double centuries were all for Yorkshire, the highest being 221 v Kent at Tunbridge Wells in 1912. He was a first-class umpire (1925–36).

Denton, Joe
Professional. *b:* 3.2.1865, Thornes, Wakefield, Yorkshire. *d:* 17.7.1946, Purston-Jaglin, Yorkshire. Brother of David (Yorkshire). Middle order right-hand batsman. *Team* Yorkshire (1887–88, 15 matches).
Career batting
15–24–1–222–57–9.65–0–*ct* 6

Denton, John Sidney
Amateur. *b:* 2.11.1890, Rushden, Northamptonshire. *d:* 9.4.1971, Rushden, Northamptonshire. Twin brother of W. H. (Northamptonshire) and brother of A. D. (Northamptonshire). Opening right-hand batsman, leg break and googly bowler. *Sch* Wellingborough. *Team* Northamptonshire (1909–19, 104 matches).
Career batting
104–178–26–3298–124–21.69–2–*ct* 53
Bowling 1883–67–28.10–2–0–5/39
He hit 1,007 runs, av 17.97, in 1913.

Denton, William Herbert
Amateur. *b:* 2.11.1890, Rushden, Northamptonshire. *d:* 23.4.1979, Bedford. Twin brother of J. S. (Northamptonshire) and brother of A. D. (Northamptonshire). Opening right-hand batsman, good field. *Sch* Wellingborough. *Team* Northamptonshire (1909–24, 119 matches).
Career batting
119–205–19–4449–230*–23.91–4–*ct* 54
Bowling 42–0
In 1913 he hit 1,055 runs, av 34.03. He also scored his only double century in the same year: 230* for Northamptonshire v Essex at Leyton.

De Paravicini, Harry Farquhar
Amateur. *b:* 20.10.1859, Kensington, London. *d:* 28.10.1942, Hove, Sussex. Brother of P. J. (Middlesex). Middle order right-hand batsman. *Sch* Harrow. *Team* MCC (1882–85).
Career batting
6–9–3–64–28*–10.66–0–*ct* 1

He was not in the eleven at Cambridge, but excelled at rackets. His final first-class match was for I Zingari in 1888. He was President of Sussex in 1924.

De Paravicini, Percy John
Amateur. *b:* 15.7.1862, Kensington, London. *d:* 11.10.1921, Pangbourne, Berkshire. Brother of H. F. (MCC). Middle order right-hand batsman, right-hand slow round arm bowler, excellent deep field. *Sch* Eton. *Teams* Middlesex (1881–92, 62 matches); Cambridge U (1882–85, blue all four years).
Career batting
121–200–26–2699–77–15.51–0–*ct* 70
Bowling 1048–32–32.75–0–0–4/26

In a minor match he went to the wicket with time nearly up and fifteen runs required – he hit the first ball for eight and the second for seven! He also played for Buckinghamshire (1899–1911). He played soccer for Cambridge University and England, and played in two FA Cup finals for Old Etonians, being on the winning side against Blackburn Rovers in 1882.

Dermont, Roger Wayne Archie
Cricketer. *b:* 1.4.1945, Whitwell, Hertfordshire. Lower order right-hand batsman, right-arm medium fast bowler. *Team* MCC (1967).
Career batting
1–1–0–0–0–0.00–0–*ct* 0
Bowling 31–2–15.50–0–0–2/23

His County cricket was for Hertfordshire (1967–74).

Derrick, John
Cricketer. *b:* 15.1.1963, Cwmaman, Glamorgan. Middle order right-hand batsman, right-arm medium pace bowler. *Team* Glamorgan (1983–91, 95 matches). *Tour* Glamorgan to Zimbabwe 1990/1.
Career batting
95–125–38–1995–78*–22.93–0–*ct* 40
Bowling 5213–137–38.05–2–0–6/54

He also played for Wales in the Minor Counties Championship (1992). He appeared in one-day matches for Northern Districts in 1986/7.

Desai, Avinash Harkant
Professional. *b:* 7.8.1932, Surat, India. Son of Harkant (Baroda and Gujarat). Lower order right-hand batsman, leg break and googly bowler. *Teams* Rajputana (1947/8); Bombay (1952/3 to 1957/8); Railways (1958/9 to 1963/4).
Career batting
41–51–12–1700–147*–43.58–5–*ct* 18
Bowling 1378–54–25.51–4–1–6/108

His only first-class match in England was for Commonwealth XI in 1957.

Desai, Ramakant Bhikaji
Amateur. *b:* 20.6.1939, Bombay, India. Lower order right-hand batsman, right-arm fast medium bowler. *Team* Bombay (1958/9 to 1968/9). *Tours* India to England 1959, to West Indies 1961/2, to Australia and New Zealand 1967/8; Wadekar to Sri Lanka 1975/6. *Tests* India (1958/9 to 1967/8, 28 matches).
Career batting
150–179–48–2384–107–18.19–1–*ct* 50
Bowling 11282–468–24.10–22–2–7/46
Test batting
28–44–13–418–85–13.48–0–*ct* 9
Bowling 2761–74–37.31–2–0–6/56

He took 45 wickets, av 41.42, on the 1959 tour to England and played in all five Tests. His final first-class match in India was for ACC in 1971/2.

De Saram, Frederick Cecil
Amateur. *b:* 5.9.1912, Colombo, Ceylon. *d:* 11.4.1983, Colombo, Sri Lanka. Brother of F. J. (Ceylon), nephew of D. L. (Ceylon) and F. R. (Ceylon). Middle order right-hand batsman. *Teams* Oxford U (1934–35, blue both years); Ceylon (1930/1 to 1953/4). *Tour* Ceylon to India 1940/1.
Career batting
40–74–4–2789–208–39.84–6–*ct* 17
Bowling 81–0

In 1934 he hit 1,119 runs, av 50.86, and scored his only double century, 208 for Oxford U v Leveson-Gower's XI at Reigate. His County cricket was for Hertfordshire (1933–36). He was jailed in Ceylon in 1962 for being a political activist.

Deshon, David Peter Tower
Amateur. *b:* 19.6.1923, Marylebone, London. *d:* 18.1.1992, Heathrow Airport, Middlesex. Middle order right-hand batsman. *Sch* Sherborne. *Team* Somerset (1947–53, 4 matches).
Career batting
4–8–1–82–21–11.71–0–*ct* 1

De Silva, Dandeniyage Somachandra
Cricketer. *b:* 11.6.1942, Galle, Ceylon. Brother of D. H. (Ceylon) and D. P. (Ceylon). Middle order right-hand batsman, leg break and googly bowler. *Team* Sri Lanka (1966/7 to 1984). *Tours* Sri Lanka to India 1972/3, 1975/6, 1982/3, to Pakistan 1973/4, 1981/2, to England 1975, 1979, 1981, 1983 (World Cup), 1984, to Australia and New Zealand 1982/3, to Zimbabwe 1982/3, to Sharjah (not first-class) 1983/4, to Australia 1984/5 (not first-class). *Tests* Sri Lanka (1981/2 to 1984, 12 matches).
Career batting
64–95–16–1735–97–21.96–0–*ct* 34
Bowling 6714–238–28.21–15–5–8/46
Test batting
12–22–3–406–61–21.36–0–*ct* 5
Bowling 1347–37–36.40–1–0–5/59

Although he achieved no outstanding performances in England, he was a major figure in Sri Lankan cricket during the 1970s, when that country was striving for Test match status. His only Test match in England was on the 1984 visit. He also played for Lincolnshire (1976–78) and Shropshire (1980–83). He captained Sri Lanka in 2 Test matches in 1982/3.

De Silva, Deva Lokesh Stanley
Cricketer. *b:* 17.11.1956, Ambalangoda, Ceylon. *d:* 12.4.1980, Balapitiya, Sri Lanka, in a motor cycle accident. Tail end right-hand batsman, right-arm fast medium bowler. *Team* Sri Lanka (1979). *Tour* Sri Lanka to England 1979.
Career batting
4–3–1–11–7–5.50–0–*ct* 2
Bowling 199–6–33.16–0–0–2/28
He was the principal seam bowler on the 1979 tour to England. He appeared in one-day Internationals for Sri Lanka.

De Silva, Ginigalgodage Ramba Ajit
Cricketer. *b:* 12.12.1952, Ambalangoda, Ceylon. Lower order left-hand batsman, slow left-arm bowler. *Team* Sri Lanka (1973/4 to 1982/3). *Tours* Sri Lanka to Pakistan 1973/4, 1981/2, to India 1974/5, 1975/6, 1976/7, 1982/3, to England 1975, 1979, 1981; Arosa Sri Lankan XI to South Africa 1982/3. *Tests* Sri Lanka (1981/2 to 1982/3, 4 matches).
Career batting
53–68–27–317–75–7.73–0–*ct* 21
Bowling 4418–161–27.44–4–0–6/30
Test batting
4–7–2–41–14–8.20–0–*ct* 0
Bowling 385–7–55.00–0–0–2/38

De Silva, John Albert
Amateur. *b:* 19.1.1901, Novella, Colombo, Ceylon. *d:* 30.11.1981, Colombo, Sri Lanka. Brother of C. E. (Ceylon 1919). Middle order left-hand batsman, right-arm medium pace bowler. *Teams* Oxford U (1924–27); Ceylon (1929/30 to 1930/1).
Career batting
8–14–3–214–65–19.45–0–*ct* 4
Bowling 187–4–46.75–0–0–1/5

De Silva, Pinnaduwage Aravinda
Cricketer. *b:* 17.10.1965, Colombo, Ceylon. Middle order right-hand batsman, off break bowler. *Team* Nondescripts CC (1988/9 to 1991/2). *Tours* Sri Lanka to England 1984, 1988, 1990, 1991, to Australia 1984/5, 1987/8, 1989/90, to Pakistan 1985/6, 1991/2, to India 1986/7, 1989/90 (not first-class), 1990/1, to Sharjah (not first-class) 1983/4, 1985/6, 1986/7, 1987/8, 1988/9, 1989/90, 1990/1, to India and Pakistan (World Cup) 1987/8, to Bangladesh (not first-class) 1988/9, to New Zealand 1990/1, to Australia and New Zealand (World Cup) 1991/2. *Tests* Sri Lanka (1984 to 1991/2, 25 matches).
Career batting
85–125–15–4967–267–45.15–12–*ct* 54
Bowling 805–12–67.08–0–0–2/16
Test batting
25–44–2–1639–267–39.02–5–*ct* 16
Bowling 220–3–73.33–0–0–2/65
He captained Sri Lanka on the 1990 and 1991 tours to England and has captained 4 Tests. In 1990 he hit 221* v Hampshire at Southampton. He created a national Test record, scoring 267 v New Zealand at Wellington in 1990/1. His first-class debut was for Sri Lanka in 1983/4.

De Soysa, Gahmini Ryle Johannes
Amateur. *b:* 21.6.1917, Colombo, Ceylon. Middle order left-hand batsman, leg break and googly bowler. *Sch* Newton College. *Teams* Oxford U (1938); Ceylon (1944/5). *Tour* Oxford and Cambridge U to Jamaica 1938/9.
Career batting
8–16–1–314–67–20.93–0–*ct* 0
Bowling 15–2–7.50–0–0–2/15

Dessaur, Wayne Anthony
Cricketer. *b:* 4.2.1971, Nottingham. Middle order right-hand batsman, right-arm medium pace bowler. *Team* Nottinghamshire (1992, 2 matches).
Career batting
2–3–0–164–148–54.66–1–*ct* 1

De Trafford, Charles Edmund
Amateur. *b:* 21.5.1864, Trafford Park, Manchester, Lancashire. *d:* 11.11.1951, Rothley Temple, Leicestershire. Brother-in-law of T. C. O'Brien (Middlesex). Hard hitting middle order right-hand batsman. *Sch* Beaumont. *Teams* Lancashire (1884, 1 match); Leicestershire (1894–1920, 231 matches); London County (1904). *Tours* Hawke to North America 1894; MCC to New Zealand 1906/7, to South America 1911/12.
Career batting
292–526–13–9581–137–18.67–6–*ct* 98
Bowling 95–2–47.50–0–0–2/47
He played for Leicestershire from 1888 and led the County from 1890 to 1906. He was President of Leicestershire 1909–10. He also played for Northamptonshire (pre first-class).

De Uphaugh, Richard George Duppa
Amateur. *b:* 12.3.1895, Camberwell, London. *d:* 25.10.1972, Morning Dawn, Hollingbourne, Kent. Middle order batsman. *Sch* Harrow. *Team* Oxford U (1919).
Career batting
1–2–1–47–43*–47.00–0–*ct* 0

Devapriya, Hettiwatte Hemantha
Cricketer. *b:* 12.4.1958, Galle, Ceylon. Middle order right-hand batsman, wicket-keeper. *Team* Colts (1988/9 to 1991/2). *Tours* Sri Lanka to India 1980/1,

to England 1981; Arosa Sri Lankan XI to South Africa 1982/3.
Career batting
39–59–4–1240–95–22.54–0–*ct* 63–*st* 10

Deverell, Sir Colville Montgomery
Amateur. *b:* 21.2.1906. Clonskea, Dublin, Ireland. Opening right-hand batsman. *Sch* Portora Royal School, Enniskillen. *Team* Dublin University (1926).
Career batting
1–2–0–3–2–1.50–0–*ct* 0
He played for Ireland (not first-class) in 1930.

Devereux, Louis Norman
Professional. *b:* 20.10.1931, Heavitree, Exeter, Devon. Middle order right-hand batsman, off break bowler, fine field. *Teams* Middlesex (1949, 2 matches); Worcestershire (1950–55, 79 matches); Glamorgan (1956–60, 106 matches).
Career batting
192–327–47–5560–108*–19.85–1–*ct* 107
Bowling 6286–178–35.31–2–0–6/29
He hit 1,039 runs, av 22.58, in 1957. He represented England at table tennis in 1949.

Devereux, Richard Jaynes
Cricketer. *b:* 26.12.1938, Castle Bromwich, Warwickshire. Hard hitting lower order right-hand batsman, left-arm medium pace bowler. *Sch* Malvern. *Team* Worcestershire (1963, 11 matches).
Career batting
11–16–3–216–55*–16.61–0–*ct* 13
Bowling 581–13–44.69–0–0–3/44

Devey, John Henry George
Professional. *b:* 26.12.1866, Birmingham. *d:* 11.10.1940, Moseley, Birmingham. Opening or middle order right-hand batsman, right-arm medium pace bowler. *Team* Warwickshire (1894–1907, 153 matches).
Career batting
154–253–20–6550–246–28.11–8–*ct* 68
Bowling 655–16–40.93–0–0–3/65
His best season was 1906 when he hit 1,237 runs, av 41.23. His only double century was 246 for Warwickshire v Derbyshire at Birmingham in 1900. He first played for Warwickshire (pre first-class) in 1888.
A noted soccer player he represented West Bromwich Albion, Aston Villa and England as a forward, and won three FA Cup winners medals, one with West Brom and two with Villa.

De Ville, Roger Thomas
Cricketer. *b:* 21.1.1935, Uttoxeter, Staffordshire. Middle/lower order right-hand batsman, leg break bowler. *Sch* Denstone. *Team* Derbyshire (1963–64, 3 matches)
Career batting
3–5–2–26–17–8.66–0–*ct* 0
Bowling 146–2–73.00–0–0–2/47
He also played for Staffordshire (1959–73).

De Villiers, Petrus Stephanus
Cricketer. *b:* 13.10.1964, Vereeniging, Transvaal, South Africa. Lower order right-hand batsman, right-arm fast medium bowler. *Teams* Northern Transvaal (1985/6 to 1991/2); Kent (1990, 12 matches).
Career batting
55–76–25–953–50–18.68–0–*ct* 28
Bowling 4643–195–23.81–9–0–6/47
He played for South Africa against rebel touring teams.

De Villiers, John Olivier
Amateur. *b:* 28.2.1930, Cape Town, South Africa. *d:* 3.7.1969, Tarkastad, Cape Province, South Africa. He died following an accident. Middle order right-hand batsman. *Teams* Oxford U (1951–52); Orange Free State (1953/4).
Career batting
11–20–4–347–81–21.68–0–*ct* 3
Bowling 38–0

Dew, David Gerveys du Breul
Amateur. *b:* 16.9.1935, Marylebone, London. Lower order right-hand batsman, wicket-keeper. *Sch* Stowe. *Team* Cambridge U (1959).
Career batting
2–2–0–4–4–2.00–0–*ct* 1

Dew, Dr John Alexander
Amateur. *b:* 12.5.1920, Horsham, Sussex. Middle order right-hand batsman, wicket-keeper. *Sch* Tonbridge. *Team* Sussex (1947, 2 matches).
Career batting
3–5–0–60–29–12.00–0–*ct* 5
His final first-class match was for L. C. Stevens' XI in 1961. He played in trial matches at Cambridge U during the Second War.

Dewar, Arthur
Amateur. *b:* 15.3.1934, Perth, Scotland. Tail end right-hand batsman, right-arm fast medium bowler. *Team* Scotland (1960–62).
Career batting
5–7–4–15–4*–5.00–0–*ct* 1
Bowling 366–11–33.27–1–0–7/71

Dewdney, David Thomas
Amateur. *b:* 23.10.1933, Kingston, Jamaica. Lower order right-hand batsman, right-arm fast bowler. *Team* Jamaica (1954/5 to 1957/8). *Tours* West Indies to New Zealand 1955/6, to England 1957, to Australia 1960/1. *Tests* West Indies (1954/5 to 1957/8, 9 matches).
Career batting
40–49–19–171–37*–5.70–0–*ct* 6
Bowling 2828–92–30.73–4–0–7/55
Test batting
9–12–5–17–5*–2.42–0–*ct* 0

Bowling 807–21–38.42–1–0–5/21

He performed only modestly on his tour of England. His last first-class match was for Commonwealth XI in 1961.

Dewé, Charles Douglas Eyre
Amateur. *b:* 2.5.1879, Kingsdown, Kent. *d:* 24.5.1955, Fleet, Hampshire. Lower order batsman, fast medium bowler. *Sch* Marlborough. *Team* Cambridge U (1901).
Career batting
2–4–1–33–16–11.00–0–*ct* 0
Bowling 130–2–65.00–0–0–2/66

Dewes, Anthony Roy
Cricketer. *b:* 2.6.1957, Rugby, Warwickshire. Son of J. G. (Middlesex). Middle order right-hand batsman, leg break bowler. *Sch* Dulwich. *Team* Cambridge U (1978–79, blue 1978).
Career batting
14–21–1–368–84–18.40–0–*ct* 3
Bowling 146–1–146.00–0–0–1/52

Dewes, John Gordon
Amateur. *b:* 11.10.1926, North Latchford, Cheshire. Father of A. R. (Cambridge U). Opening left-hand batsman, right-arm medium pace bowler, excellent outfield. *Sch* Aldenham. *Teams* Cambridge U (1948–50, blue all 3 years); Middlesex (1948–56, 62 matches). *Tour* MCC to Australia and New Zealand 1950/1. *Tests* England (1948 to 1950/1, 5 matches).
Career batting
137–229–24–8564–212–41.77–18–*ct* 48
Bowling 71–2–35.50–0–0–1/0
Test batting
5–10–0–121–67–12.10–0–*ct* 0

He made his first-class debut for England v Australia at Lord's in 1945 and his final first-class appearance for L. E. G. Ames' XI in 1957. His batting at Cambridge was quite exceptional, but his appearances in County cricket after 1950 were very restricted due to his profession of teaching. He hit 1,000 runs in a season three times (best 2,432, av 59.31, in 1950). The highest of his two double centuries (both for Cambridge) was 212 v Sussex at Hove in 1950. A good hockey player he gained his blue in 1949 and 1950.

Dewfall, Ernest George
Amateur. *b:* 12.8.1911, Long Ashton, Somerset. *d:* 11.11.1982, Cleeve, Somerset. Lower order right-hand batsman, right-arm fast bowler. *Team* Gloucestershire (1938, 2 matches).
Career batting
2–2–0–0–0–0.00–0–*ct* 1
Bowling 148–4–37.00–0–0–3/82

Dewhurst, George Alric R.
Amateur. *b:* 31.10.1894, Trinidad. *d:* 4.1.1954, Trinidad. Lower order right-hand batsman, wicket-keeper. *Team* Trinidad (1919/20 to 1929/30). *Tour* West Indies to England 1923.
Career batting
31–51–10–665–58–16.21–0–*ct* 47–*st* 13

Dewhurst, Robert
Amateur. *b:* 11.5.1851, Clitheroe, Lancashire. *d:* 13.10.1924, Blackpool, Lancashire. Middle order right-hand batsman, right-arm medium round or under arm bowler, good field. *Team* Lancashire (1872–75, 13 matches).
Career batting
13–22–1–266–59–12.66–0–*ct* 8

He also played for Cheshire (1871).

Dewing, Edward May
Amateur. *b:* 21.5.1823, Carbrooke Hall, Norfolk. *d:* 29.10.1899, Nowton, Suffolk. Attractive middle order batsman. *Sch* Harrow. *Team* Cambridge U (1842–45, blue all four years).
Career batting
39–69–4–536–43–8.24–0–*ct* 6
Bowling 3 wickets (no analyses)–0–0–2/?

He played almost no important cricket after leaving Cambridge, his last match being for MCC in 1848. His County cricket was for Norfolk (1848).

De Winton, George Seaton
Amateur. *b:* 5.9.1869, Clifton, Bristol. *d:* 28.6.1930, Froxfield, Wiltshire. Middle order left-hand batsman. *Team* Gloucestershire (1890–1901, 28 matches).
Career batting
28–51–9–669–80–15.92–0–*ct* 13
Bowling 3–0

Dews, George
Professional. *b:* 5.6.1921, Ossett, Yorkshire. Forcing middle order right-hand batsman, brilliant outfield. *Team* Worcestershire (1946–61, 374 matches).
Career batting
376–642–53–16803–145–28.52–20–*ct* 355
Bowling 202–2–101.00–0–0–1/31

He hit 1,000 runs in a season 11 times (best 1,752, av 41.71, in 1959). A well-known soccer player he appeared at inside left for Plymouth Argyle, Walsall and Middlesbrough.

Dewse, Harry
Professional. *b:* 23.2.1836, York. *d:* 8.7.1910, York. Lower order batsman, lob bowler, wicket-keeper. *Team* Yorkshire (1873, 1 match).
Career batting
1–2–0–14–12–7.00–0–*ct* 1
Bowling 15–0

He also played for Northumberland (1860).

Dexter, Edward Ralph
Amateur. *b:* 15.5.1935, Milan, Italy. Son-in-law of T. C. Longfield (Kent). Brilliant middle order right-hand batsman, right-arm medium pace bowler. *Sch* Radley. *Teams* Cambridge U (1956–58, blue all three

years); Sussex (1957–68, 137 matches). *Tours* MCC to Australia and New Zealand 1958/9, 1962/3, to West Indies 1959/60, to India, Pakistan and Ceylon 1961/2, to South Africa 1964/5; Cavaliers to Jamaica 1963/4, 1969/70, to South Africa 1962/3. *Tests* England (1958–68, 62 matches).
Career batting
327–567–48–21150–205–40.75–51–*ct* 233
Bowling 12539–419–29.92–9–2–7/24
Test batting
62–102–8–4502–205–47.89–9–*ct* 29
Bowling 2306–66–34.93–0–0–4/10

Regarded, when he was in his first year at Cambridge, as one of the greatest of modern batsmen, Dexter's career was unfortunately barely ten years in length, first because he chose to retire from regular first-class cricket after 1965, and secondly because he suffered a number of injuries which reduced his opportunites, even in this period. He was captain of Sussex from 1960 to 1965 and captain of England in 30 Tests from 1961/2 in India to the series in 1964 against Australia. After this he decided to stand, unsuccessfully as it happened, for Parliament and lost the leadership in the meanwhile. His best summer was 1962 when he hit 2,148 runs and took 76 wickets. In all he hit over 1,000 runs in a season eight times, going on to 2,000 on three occasions, with 2,217 (av 43.47) in 1960 his highest.

Of his two double centuries, the higher was 205 for England v Pakistan at Karachi in 1961/2 and the other 203 for Sussex v Kent at Hastings in 1968, when he made a brief reappearance in first-class cricket.

He was at his best attacking the bowling, but often found himself forced to play a defensive game. As a bowler he was under-rated and he might easily have achieved the 'double' had his ambitions been in that direction. After retiring from cricket he became a noted golfer. He was appointed the Chairman of the England Cricket Committee in 1989.

Dexter, Hermon Walter
Professional. *b:* 2.5.1877, Nottingham. *d:* 31.1.1961, Nottingham. Middle/lower order batsman, right-arm fast medium bowler. *Team* Nottinghamshire (1902–03, 10 matches).
Career batting
10–17–6–223–38*–20.27–0–*ct* 3
Bowling 33–0

Dexter, Roy Evatt
Cricketer. *b:* 13.4.1955, Nottingham. Middle order right-hand batsman. *Sch* Nottingham HS. *Team* Nottinghamshire (1975–81, 22 matches).
Career batting
22–36–6–464–57–15.46–0–*ct* 23

Deyes, George
Professional. *b:* 11.2.1878, Sculcoates, Hull, Yorkshire. *d:* 11.1.1963, Tipperlin, Edinburgh, Scotland. Lower order right-hand batsman, right-arm fast bowler. *Team* Yorkshire (1905–07, 17 matches).
Career batting
17–24–4–44–12–2.20–0–*ct* 6
Bowling 944–41–23.02–3–0–6/62

In 1907 he had 14 successive innings and scored just three singles. He also played for Staffordshire (1910–14).

De Zoete, Herman Walter
Amateur. *b:* 13.2.1877, Bromley Common, Kent. *d:* 26.3.1957, Ipswich, Suffolk. Brother-in-law of C. J. Round (Essex). Lower order right-hand batsman, left-arm medium pace/spin bowler. *Sch* Eton. *Teams* Cambridge U (1897–98, blue both years); Essex (1897, 2 matches).
Career batting
18–26–4–151–29–6.86–0–*ct* 7
Bowling 1033–55–18.78–3–0–6/53

An excellent golfer, he represented Cambridge in 1896, 1897 and 1898.

Dias, Roy Luke
Cricketer. *b:* 18.10.1952, Colombo, Ceylon. Middle order right-hand batsman, excellent cover field. *Team* Colombo CC (1988/9 to 1991/2). *Tours* Sri Lanka to India 1974/5, 1975/6, 1976/7, 1982/3, 1986/7, to England 1979, 1981, 1983 (World Cup), 1984, to Pakistan 1981/2, 1985/6, to Zimbabwe 1982/3, to Australia 1982/3, 1983/4 (not first-class), 1984/5, to New Zealand 1982/3, to Sharjah (not first-class) 1985/6, to India and Pakistan (World Cup) 1987/8; Sri Lanka B to Zimbabwe 1987/8. *Tests* Sri Lanka (1981/2 to 1986/7, 20 matches).
Career batting
93–147–13–4296–144–32.05–5–*ct* 36
Bowling 118–1–118.00–0–0–1/9
Test batting
20–36–1–1285–109–36.71–3–*ct* 6
Bowling 17–0

On the 1981 tour to England he hit 607 runs, av 40.46, and scored the only first-class century of the tour. Although he played in the Test match on the 1984 tour, his batting form, compared with 1981, was very poor.

Dible, William Guy
(known as William Charles Dible)
Professional. *b:* 5.11.1861, Sholing Common, Southampton, Hampshire. *d:* 15.8.1894, Fareham, Hampshire. Middle or lower order right-hand batsman, right-arm fast bowler. *Teams* Surrey (1882, 1 match); Hampshire (1883–85, 25 matches).
Career batting
26–47–8–503–68–12.89–0–*ct* 18
Bowling 1996–90–22.17–5–1–7/60

His last match for Hampshire was in 1890 (not first-class).

Dick, Arthur Edward
Cricketer. *b:* 10.10.1936, Middlemarch, Otago, New Zealand. Middle order right-hand batsman, wicket-keeper. *Teams* Otago (1956/7 to 1960/1); Wellington (1962/3 to 1968/9). *Tours* New Zealand to Australia and South Africa 1961/2, to Pakistan 1964/5, to England 1965. *Tests* New Zealand (1961/2 to 1965, 17 matches).
Career batting
78–126–12–2315–127–20.30–1–*ct* 148–*st* 21
Bowling 20–0
Test batting
17–30–4–370–50*–14.23–0–*ct* 47–*st* 4
On his tour of England in 1965, he appeared in two of the three Tests.

Dick, Robert Douglas
Amateur. *b:* 16.4.1889, Middlesbrough, Yorkshire. *d:* 14.12.1983, Guisborough, Yorkshire. Tail end right-hand batsman, right-arm fast bowler. *Team* Yorkshire (1911, 1 match).
Career batting
1–1–0–2–2–2.00–0–*ct* 1
Bowling 37–2–18.50–0–0–1/3

Dickens, Alfred
Amateur. *b:* 9.12.1883, Brixworth, Northamptonshire. *d:* 30.1.1938, Bedford. Lower order batsman, bowler. *Team* Northamptonshire (1907, 1 match).
Career batting
1–2–0–3–3–1.50–0–*ct* 0
Bowling 4–1–4.00–0–0–1/4

Dickens, Frederick
Professional. *b:* 23.4.1873, Stratford-on-Avon, Warwickshire. *d:* 20.2.1935, Warwick. Lower order batsman, left-arm medium pace bowler. *Team* Warwickshire (1898–1903, 29 matches).
Career batting
29–32–6–172–35–6.61–0–*ct* 7
Bowling 1782–75–23.76–3–1–6/23

Dickins, George Caldwell
Amateur. *b:* 17.11.1821, North Elmham, Norfolk. *d:* 5.12.1903, Coldstream, Berwickshire, Scotland. Middle order left-hand batsman, right-arm lob bowler. *Sch* Harrow. *Team* Kent (1849–64, 2 matches).
Career batting
7–13–2–158–44–14.36–0–*ct* 1
His debut in first-class matches was for Gentlemen of Kent in 1848. He also played for Northumberland (1851–70).

Dickinson, David Christopher
Amateur. *b:* 11.12.1929, Blackheath, Kent. Lower order right-hand batsman, right-arm medium pace bowler. *Sch* Clifton. *Team* Cambridge U (1953, blue).
Career batting
13–18–7–111–36*–10.09–0–*ct* 4
Bowling 653–24–27.20–0–0–4/22
His final first-class match was for Free Foresters in 1957.

Dickinson, Harold John
Professional. *b:* 26.11.1911, Barry, Glamorgan. Lower order batsman, right-arm fast medium bowler. *Team* Glamorgan (1934–35, 7 matches).
Career batting
7–13–6–37–14*–5.28–0–*ct* 3
Bowling 335–6–55.83–0–0–3/91

Dickinson, John Edward
Amateur. *b:* 20.5.1914, Ashby-de-la-Zouch, Leicestershire. Forcing middle order left-hand batsman, slow left-arm bowler. *Team* Leicestershire (1933–35, 2 matches).
Career batting
2–4–0–27–16–6.75–0–*ct* 1
Bowling 63–0
He also played for Devon (1947–53).

Dickinson, Patrick John
Amateur. *b:* 28.8.1919, Upper Barian, India. *d:* 28.5.1984, St Pancras, London. Middle/lower order right-hand batsman, right-arm medium slow bowler. *Sch* KCS Wimbledon. *Teams* Cambridge U (1939, blue); Surrey (1939, 10 matches); Bombay (1947/8 to 1948/9); Madras (1950/1 to 1952/3).
Career batting
27–39–1–782–122–20.57–2–*ct* 16
Bowling 1052–28–37.57–1–0–5/95

Dickinson, Stanley Patrick
Amateur. *b:* 7.3.1890, Norton, Derbyshire. *d:* 25.6.1972, Wern, Caernarvonshire. Middle or lower order right-hand batsman, right-arm fast medium bowler. *Sch* Haileybury. *Team* Derbyshire (1909, 2 matches).
Career batting
2–3–1–13–10*–6.50–0–*ct* 0
Bowling 45–1–45.00–0–0–1/38

Dickinson, Thomas Eastwood
Amateur. *b:* 11.1.1931, Parramatta, New South Wales, Australia. Lower order left-hand batsman, right-arm fast medium bowler. *Team* Lancashire (1950–51, 4 matches); Somerset (1957, 5 matches).
Career batting
9–12–6–21–9–3.50–0–*ct* 5
Bowling 419–20–20.95–1–0–5/36

Dickinson, William Vicris Digby
Amateur. *b:* 2.11.1889, Swansea, Glamorgan. *d:* 24.11.1948, Nairobi, Kenya. Middle order right-hand batsman, left-arm fast medium bowler. *Sch* Cheltenham. *Team* Army (1919–23).
Career batting
14–23–4–614–150–32.31–1–*ct* 8
Bowling 1286–59–21.79–5–1–7/111
He opened the batting whilst at Cheltenham, but in post-war Services matches usually went in at 7 or 8.

Dickson, A. W.
(*see under* Dixon, A. W.)

Dickson, Maurice Rhynd
Amateur. *b:* 2.1.1882, Panbride, Angus, Scotland. *d:* 10.1.1940, Woodville House, Arbroath, Angus, Scotland. Middle order right-hand batsman, right-arm medium pace bowler. *Sch* Marlborough. *Team* Scotland (1905–14).
Career batting
13–26–1–723–98–28.92–0–*ct* 6
Bowling 16–1–16.00–0–0–1/9
He played no first-class cricket whilst at Oxford U but won a blue for rugby. He was a Scottish rugby international.

Digby, Reginald
Amateur. *b:* 30.4.1847, Tittleshall, Norfolk. *d:* 29.9.1927, Colehill, Wimborne, Dorset. Brother of K. E. (Oxford U 1856–59), uncle of A. K. Watson (Middlesex), H. D. Watson (Oxford U) and C. D. Buxton (Cambridge U). Middle order right-hand batsman, good cover point. *Sch* Harrow. *Team* Oxford U (1867–69, blue all three years).
Career batting
14–25–2–429–88–18.65–0–*ct* 3
His County cricket was for Norfolk (1866–70).

Dilawar Hussain, Dr
Amateur. *b:* 19.3.1907, Lahore, India. *d:* 26.8.1967, Lahore, Pakistan. Father of Waqar Ahmed (Lahore) and Nadeem Ahmed (Lahore), brother of Jamaluddin (Muslims). Very steady opening right-hand batsman, wicket-keeper. *Teams* Muslims (1924/5 to 1939/40); Northern India (1926/7 to 1934/5); Central India (1934/5 to 1938/9); Uttar Pradesh (1940/1). *Tours* India to England 1936; Vizianagram's XI to India and Ceylon 1930/1. *Tests* India (1933/4 to 1936, 3 matches).
Career batting
57–94–9–2394–122–28.16–4–*ct* 70–*st* 32
Bowling 40–0
Test batting
3–6–0–254–59–42.33–0–*ct* 6–*st* 1
In residence at Cambridge, he was co-opted into the 1936 touring team and was most successful, coming second in the batting table (620 runs, av 44.28) and appearing in one Test. He did not appear in any first-class matches for Cambridge, missing the 1935 summer through illness. He scored 112 on debut for Muslims v Europeans at Lahore in 1924/5. A notable figure in Pakistan cricket he was a member of the Board of Control and a Test selector.

Dilley, Graham Roy
Cricketer. *b:* 18.5.1959, Dartford, Kent. Brother-in-law of G. W. Johnson (Kent). Lower order left-hand batsman, right-arm fast bowler, deep field. *Teams* Kent (1977–86, 109 matches); Natal (1985/6); Worcestershire (1987–92, 52 matches). *Tours* England to Australia 1979/80, 1986/7, 1987/8, to West Indies 1980/1, to India 1981/2, 1988/9 (tour cancelled), to Sri Lanka 1981/2, to New Zealand 1983/4, 1987/8, to Pakistan 1983/4, 1987/8; England XI to South Africa 1989/90. *Tests* England (1979/80 to 1989, 41 matches).
Career batting
234–252–93–2339–81–14.71–0–*ct* 75
Bowling 17395–648–26.84–34–3–7/63
Test batting
41–58–19–521–56–13.35–0–*ct* 10
Bowling 4107–138–29.76–6–0–6/38
Such was the immediate promise of his fast bowling that he played Test cricket before gaining his County Cap. From 1979/80 to 1981/2 he appeared regularly for England, then injury and lack of confidence undermined his performances. His next regular spell with England began in 1986, in which season he took more Test wickets than any home bowler. The height of his career was the 1986/7 tour to Australia when he took 16 wickets, av 31.93, in the series, though he also bowled well against the West Indies in 1988. The following summer he was ineffective in two Tests against Australia and then chose to join the touring side to South Africa. He missed all of the 1984 season due to injury, and later in his career suffered more injuries which forced his retirement.

Dilley, Michael Reginald
Professional. *b:* 28.3.1939, Rushden, Northamptonshire. Lower order right-hand batsman, right-arm fast medium bowler. *Sch* Wellingborough. *Team* Northamptonshire (1957–63, 33 matches).
Career batting
33–38–16–232–31*–10.54–0–*ct* 13
Bowling 2471–80–30.88–2–0–6/74

Dillon, Edward Wentworth
Amateur. *b:* 15.2.1881, Penge, Kent. *d:* 20.4.1941, Totteridge, Hertfordshire. Hard hitting left-hand opening batsman, leg break bowler. *Sch* Rugby. *Teams* Kent (1900–23, 223 matches); Oxford U (1901–02, blue both years); London County (1900). *Tours* Bennett to West Indies 1901/2; Kent to North America 1903.
Career batting
260–414–25–11006–143–28.29–15–*ct* 213
Bowling 2426–74–32.78–0–0–4/11
He scored 108 on debut for London County v Worcestershire (Crystal Palace) 1900. He captained Kent 1909–13. A noted rugby footballer, he played three-quarter for Blackheath and England.

Diment, Robert Anthony
Amateur. *b:* 9.2.1927, Tortworth, Gloucestershire. Middle order right-hand batsman, right-arm medium pace bowler. *Teams* Gloucestershire (1952, 1 match); Leicestershire (1955–58, 59 matches).

Career batting
60–102–5–1595–71–16.44–0–*ct* 35
Bowling 4–0
He was Secretary of Leicestershire, 1958–59.

Dindar, Andrew
Cricketer. *b:* 26.6.1942, Johannesburg, South Africa. Lower order right-hand batsman, right-arm medium pace bowler. *Team* Gloucestershire (1962–63, 7 matches).
Career batting
7–10–2–100–55–12.50–0–*ct* 2
Bowling 70–3–23.33–0–0–3/32
He also played for Hertfordshire (1976–80) and Berkshire (1981–84).

Dineen, Patrick Joseph
Amateur. *b:* 13.5.1938, Cork, Ireland. Middle order left-hand batsman. *Team* Ireland (1962–71).
Career batting
7–12–2–179–84–17.90–0–*ct* 3

Dines, William James
Professional. *b:* 14.9.1916, Colchester, Essex. *d:* 16.6.1992, Gidea Park, Essex. Lower order right-hand batsman, right-arm medium pace off break bowler. *Team* Essex (1947–49, 20 matches).
Career batting
20–30–7–431–69*–18.73–0–*ct* 7
Bowling 980–15–65.33–0–0–3/35

Dinsdale, Stephen Charles
Cricketer. *b:* 30.12.1948, Buckhurst Hill, Essex. Opening or middle order left-hand batsman, left-arm medium pace bowler. *Teams* Rhodesia (1969/70); Essex (1970, 5 matches); Transvaal (1974/5 to 1975/6).
Career batting
15–26–2–581–88–24.20–0–*ct* 8
Bowling 160–8–20.00–0–0–4/24

Dinwiddy, Hugh Pochin
Amateur. *b:* 16.10.1912, Kensington, London. Opening/middle order right-hand batsman, leg break and googly bowler, excellent cover field. *Sch* Radley. *Teams* Kent (1933–34, 10 matches); Cambridge U (1934–35).
Career batting
15–24–3–258–45–12.28–0–*ct* 9
Bowling 35–0

Dipper, Alfred Ernest
Professional. *b:* 9.11.1885, Apperley, Gloucestershrie. *d:* 7.11.1945, Lambeth, London. Solid opening right-hand batsman, right-arm medium pace bowler, moderate field. *Team* Gloucestershire (1908–32, 478 matches). *Test* England (1921, 1 match).
Career batting
481–865–69–28075–252*–35.27–53–*ct* 210
Bowling 4903–161–30.45–5–1–7/46
Test batting
1–2–0–51–40–25.50–0–*ct* 0
He hit 1,000 runs in a season 15 times, going on to complete 2,000 five times (best 2,365, av 55.00, in 1928). He scored three double centuries, all for Gloucestershire, the highest being 252* v Glamorgan at Cheltenham in 1923. He was a first-class umpire (1933–36). He was also a noted bowls player.

Dippie, William Russell Hennessy
Amateur. *b:* 9.6.1907, Edinburgh, Scotland. Tail end right-hand batsman, right-arm fast medium bowler. *Team* Scotland (1939).
Career batting
1–2–1–7–7*–7.00–0–*ct* 1
Bowling 71–3–23.66–0–0–3/41

Disbury, Brian Elvin
Professional. *b:* 30.9.1929, Bedford. Opening right-hand batsman, right-arm medium pace bowler. *Sch* Bedford School. *Team* Kent (1954–57, 14 matches).
Career batting
14–21–3–288–74*–16.00–0–*ct* 11
Bowling 204–5–40.80–0–0–2/76
He also played for Bedfordshire (1946–53).

Disney, Charles Ronald
Amateur. *b:* 21.11.1894, Stourbridge, Worcestershire. *d:* 11.4.1963, Linthorpe, Yorkshire. Middle order right-hand batsman, right-arm fast medium bowler. *Sch* Clifton and Rossall. *Team* Gloucestershire (1923, 1 match).
Career batting
1–2–0–2–2–1.00–0–*ct* 0

Disney, James Joseph
Professional. *b:* 20.11.1859, Butterley, Derbyshire. *d:* 24.6.1934, Ripley, Derbyshire. Lower order right-hand batsman, wicket-keeper. *Team* Derbyshire (1881–87, 53 matches).
Career batting
57–101–30–377–27*–5.30–0–*ct* 97–*st* 12
His final first-class match was for Liverpool and District in 1894. His last match for Derbyshire (not first-class) was in 1890. He also played for Cheshire (1893–94).

Disney-Roebuck, Claude Delaval
Amateur. *b:* 1.3.1876, Morice Town, Plymouth, Devon. *d:* 10.5.1947, Hindhead, Surrey. Middle order batsman. *Sch* Weymouth. *Team* MCC (1906–07).
Career batting
2–4–1–20–8*–6.66–0–*ct* 1
His County cricket was for Dorset (1903–06).

Disney-Roebuck, Francis Henry Algernon
Amateur. *b:* 7.10.1846, Trinidad. *d:* 9.1.1919, Kensington, London. Middle order batsman. *Sch* Wimbledon. *Team* MCC (1878–82).

Divecha, Ramesh Vithaldas

Career batting
4–6–0–33–10–5.50–0–*ct* 1
His County cricket was for Devon.

Divecha, Ramesh Vithaldas
Amateur. *b:* 18.10.1927, Kakadwadi, Bombay, India. Brother of A. V. (Maharashtra). Middle order right-hand batsman, right-arm fast medium or slow off break bowler. *Teams* Oxford U (1948–51, blue 1950–51): Northamptonshire (1948, 1 match); Bombay (1951/2); Madhya Pradesh (1954/5); Saurashtra (1962/3). *Tour* India to England 1952. *Tests* India (1951/2 to 1952/3, 5 matches).
Career batting
61–88–18–1423–92–20.32–0–*ct* 35
Bowling 5401–217–24.88–9–0–8/74
Test batting
5–5–0–60–26–12.00–0–*ct* 5
Bowling 361–11–32.81–0–0–3/102
He also played for Oxfordshire (1949).

Diver, Alfred John Day
Professional. *b:* 6.7.1824, Cambridge. *d:* 25.3.1876, Rugby, Warwickshire. Uncle of E. J. (Surrey and Warwickshire). Middle order right-hand batsman, right-hand fast medium round arm and lobs. *Teams* Cambridge Town Club (1843–55); Middlesex (1850, 1 match); Cambridgeshire (1857–66, 15 matches); Nottinghamshire (1858, 1 match). *Tour* Parr to North America 1859 (not first-class).
Career batting
84–152–13–1701–65–12.23–0–*ct* 43–*st* 3
Bowling 282–15 + 72–18.80–6–1–7/?
He also played for Norfolk (1848), Suffolk (1848–49), Huntingdonshire (1851) and Cheshire (1854).

Diver, Edwin James
Amateur to 1885, then professional. *b:* 20.3.1861, Cambridge. *d:* 27.12.1924, Pontardawe, Glamorgan. Nephew of A. J. D. (Middlesex and Nottinghamshire). Opening or middle order right-hand batsman, right-arm medium pace bowler, wicket-keeper. *Sch* Perse School. *Teams* Surrey (1883–86, 75 matches); Warwickshire (1894–1901, 118 matches).
Career batting
205–329–14–7245–184–23.00–5–*ct* 117–*st* 4
Bowling 311–6–51.83–1–0–6/58
He hit 1,096 runs, av 29.62, in 1899. He first played for Warwickshire (pre first-class) in 1893. He also played for Cambridgeshire (1889–92), being appointed joint Secretary and Treasurer of the County Club in 1889, and later he played for Monmouthshire (1903–14). He played soccer for Aston Villa.

Dixie-Smith, J. W. (*see under* Smith, J. W. D.)

Dixon, Alan Leonard
Professional. *b:* 27.11.1933, Dartford, Kent. Middle order right-hand batsman, right-arm medium pace off break bowler, excellent cover field. *Team* Kent (1950–70, 378 matches). *Tour* MCC to East Africa (1973/4).
Career batting
381–580–71–9589–125*–18.83–3–*ct* 155
Bowling 24060–935–25.73–46–10–8/61
He hit 1,000 runs in a season three times (best 1,170, av 24.37, in 1961). He created a Gillette Cup record (since broken) in taking 7/15 for Kent v Surrey at the Oval in 1967. He took 100 wickets three times (best 122, av 23.89, in 1964).

Dixon, Alexander Willoughby
(birth registered as A. W. Dickson)
Professional. *b:* 4.8.1876, Toxteth Park, Liverpool, Lancashire. *d:* 1.3.1953, Houghton-on-the-Hill, Leicestershire. Lower order left-hand batsman, slow left-arm bowler. *Team* Leicestershire (1900, 5 matches).
Career batting
5–9–1–36–18–4.50–0–*ct* 2
Bowling 266–5–53.20–0–0–2/79

Dixon, Anthony Sumner
Cricketer. *b:* 17.11.1948, Clifton, Bristol. Middle order right-hand batsman. *Sch* Clifton. *Team* Cambridge U (1971).
Career batting
1–2–0–12–12–6.00–0–*ct* 0

Dixon, Cecil Donovan
Amateur. *b:* 12.2.1891, Potchefstroom, Transvaal, South Africa. *d:* 9.9.1969, Illovo, Johannesburg, South Africa. Lower order right-hand batsman, right-arm medium pace bowler. *Team* Transvaal (1912/13 to 1924/5) *Tour* South Africa to England 1924. *Test* South Africa (1913/14, 1 match).
Career batting
33–39–8–184–27–5.93–0–*ct* 21
Bowling 2556–106–24.11–6–1–7/16
Test batting
1–2–0–0–0–0.00–0–*ct* 1
Bowling 118–3–39.33–0–0–2/62
He only returned very modest figures on his visit to England and did not appear in the Tests.

Dixon, Cecil Egerton
Amateur. *b:* 21.7.1903, Ayton, Berwickshire, Scotland. *d:* 3.3.1973, Battle, Sussex. Middle order batsman, change bowler. *Sch* Wellington. *Team* Hampshire (1929, 2 matches).
Career batting
2–4–0–10–5–2.50–0–*ct* 0

Dixon, Eric John Hopkins
Amateur. *b:* 22.9.1915, Horbury, Yorkshire. *d:* 20.4.1941, killed on active service flying from HMS *Formidable* off the coast of Tripoli, Libya. Solid right-hand opening batsman. *Sch* St Edward's School, Oxford. *Teams* Oxford U (1937–39, blue all three years); Northamptonshire (1939, 8 matches). *Tour*

Oxford and Cambridge U to Jamaica 1938/9.
Career batting
49–86–4–2356–123–28.73–2–*ct* 19
Bowling 29–0
He captained Oxford in 1939.

Dixon, Dr Francis
Amateur. *b:* 31.7.1855, Derby. *d:* 20.8.1943, Eastwood, Nottinghamshire. Middle order right-hand batsman, off break bowler. *Team* Derbyshire (1885, 1 match).
Career batting
2–4–0–23–15–5.75–0–*ct* 1
Bowling 7–0
His last first-class match was for M. Sherwin's XI in 1891.

Dixon, J.
Amateur. Tail end batsman. *Team* Lancashire (1878, 1 match).
Career batting
1–2–0–2–2–1.00–0–*ct* 0

Dixon, J. T.
Amateur. Lower order batsman, right-arm slow medium bowler. *Team* Middlesex (1908, 1 match).
Career batting
1–2–0–7–7–3.50–0–*ct* 2
Bowling 22–0

Dixon, John Auger
Amateur. *b:* 27.5.1861, Grantham, Lincolnshire. *d:* 8.6.1931, The Park, Nottingham. Opening or middle order right-hand batsman, right-arm medium pace bowler. *Sch* Nottingham HS. *Team* Nottinghamshire (1882–1905, 235 matches).
Career batting
253–419–25–9527–268*–24.18–13–*ct* 180
Bowling 5080–184–27.60–2–0–5/28
He hit 1,100 runs, av 44.00, in 1897. His only double century was 268* for Nottinghamshire v Sussex in 1897. He captained Nottinghamshire 1889–99, and was a Test selector in 1905. A noted soccer player, he appeared for Notts County and England as a forward.

Dixon, John Henry
Cricketer. *b:* 3.3.1954, Westbourne, Bournemouth, Hampshire. Tail end right-hand batsman, right-arm medium fast bowler. *Sch* Monkton Combe. *Team* Gloucestershire (1973–81, 16 matches).
Career batting
16–20–8–77–13*–6.41–0–*ct* 6
Bowling 1136–21–54.09–2–0–5/44
Whilst at Oxford, he appeared for the University in the Benson and Hedges Cup, but not in first-class matches. He also played for Wiltshire (1978 and 1988).

Dixon, Joseph Gilbert
Amateur. *b:* 3.9.1895, Chelmsford, Essex. *d:* 19.11.1954, Great Baddow, Essex. Middle order right-hand batsman, right-arm fast medium bowler. *Sch* Felsted. *Team* Essex (1914–22, 93 matches).
Career batting
93–148–12–2214–173–16.27–3–*ct* 48
Bowling 6484–206–31.47–9–2–7/61

Dixon, Patrick O'Madigan
Amateur. *b:* 9.10.1907, Rohtak, India. *d:* 14.9.1987, Nakuru, Kenya. Brother of T. H. (Ireland). Middle order right-hand batsman, right-arm medium pace or leg break and googly bowler. *Teams* Dublin University (1926); Ireland (1932).
Career batting
3–6–0–69–47–11.50–*ct* 1
Bowling 30–0

Dixon, Thomas Hartigan
Amateur. *b:* 22.1.1906, Dhaipai, India. *d:* 12.4.1985, Nakuru, Kenya. Brother of P. O'M. (Ireland). Middle order right-hand batsman, right-arm fast medium bowler. *Teams* Dublin University (1926); Ireland (1927–32); Delhi (1934/5 to 1936/7).
Career batting
14–27–5–312–45*–14.18–0–*ct* 4
Bowling 1043–50–20.86–3–1–7/51

Dobell, Percy
Amateur. *b:* 29.4.1864, Huyton, Liverpool, Lancashire. *d:* 5.1.1903, Freshfield, Liverpool, Lancashire. Middle order right-hand batsman. *Sch* Birkenhead. *Team* Lancashire (1886–87, 7 matches).
Career batting
10–17–2–142–28–9.46–0–*ct* 4
His final first-class match was for Liverpool and District in 1888.

Dobree-Carey, Paul Alexander Huntly
(also known as P. A. D. Carey)
Professional. *b:* 21.5.1920, Horsham, Sussex. Lower order left-hand batsman, right-arm fast bowler. *Teams* Baroda (1942/3); Services (1943/4); Bengal (1944/5); Europeans (1944/5 to 1945/6); Sussex (1946–48, 42 matches).
Career batting
52–81–16–869–96–13.36–0–*ct* 23
Bowling 4448–136–32.70–7–0–6/80
He also played for Dorset (1938) and Durham (pre first-class, 1950–52).

Dobson, Alban Tabor Austin
Amateur. *b:* 29.6.1885, Ealing, Middlesex. *d:* 19.5.1962, Hardwick, Bury St Edmunds, Suffolk. Middle order batsman. *Sch* Clifton. *Team* Gentlemen (1905).
Career batting
1–2–0–1–1–0.50–0–*ct* 0
He played in trial matches at Cambridge U, but not in first-class games.

Dobson, Arthur
Professional. *b:* 22.2.1854, Ilkley, Yorkshire. *d:* 17.9.1932, Horsforth, Yorkshire. Lower order right-hand batsman, right-arm medium pace bowler, fine cover point. *Team* Yorkshire (1879, 2 matches).
Career batting
2–3–0–1–1–0.33–0–*ct* 1

Dobson, Frederick
Amateur. *b:* 12.10.1898, Olton, Solihull, Warwickshire. *d:* 15.10.1980, Burley, Hampshire. Lower order right-hand batsman, slow left-arm bowler. *Team* Warwickshire (1928, 3 matches).
Career batting
3–3–0–9–7–3.00–0–*ct* 0
Bowling 138–7–19.71–0–0–3/51

Dobson, Kenneth William Cecil
Amateur. *b:* 28.8.1900, Barrow-on-Trent, Derbyshire. *d:* 6.3.1960, Torquay, Devon. Nephew of J. T. C. Eadie (Derbyshire) and W. S. Eadie (Derbyshire). Lower order right-hand batsman, right-arm medium pace bowler. *Sch* Repton. *Teams* Derbyshire (1920, 3 matches); Warwickshire (1925, 2 matches).
Career batting
5–10–3–33–12*–4.71–0–*ct* 0
Bowling 123–1–123.00–0–0–1/25
He also played for Staffordshire (1923).

Dobson, Mark Christopher
Cricketer. *b:* 24.10.1967, Canterbury, Kent. Middle order right-hand batsman, slow left-arm bowler. *Teams* Kent (1989–91, 9 matches); Glamorgan (1992, 1 match).
Career batting
10–15–3–211–52–17.58–0–*ct* 2
Bowling 486–9–54.00–0–0–2/20

Dobson, Thomas Kell
Amateur. *b:* 27.1.1901, South Shields, Durham. *d:* 3.10.1940, Whitburn, Sunderland, Durham. Middle order left-hand batsman, bowler. *Team* Minor Counties (1929–34).
Career batting
8–12–2–305–126–30.50–1–*ct* 6
Bowling 377–6–62.83–0–0–4/70
His County cricket was for Durham (pre first-class, 1922–36).

Docker, Cyril Talbot
Amateur. *b:* 3.3.1884, Ryde, Sydney, New South Wales, Australia. *d:* 26.3.1975, Double Bay, Sydney, New South Wales, Australia. Brother of K. B. (New South Wales) and P. W. (New South Wales), nephew of E. B. (New South Wales) and A. R. (New South Wales), cousin of G. A. M. (MCC). Lower order right-hand batsman, right-arm fast medium bowler. *Team* New South Wales (1909/10, 1 match). *Tours* AIF to England 1919, to South Africa 1919/20.
Career batting
24–32–10–371–52*–16.86–0–*ct* 17
Bowling 1091–58–18.81–5–0–5/20

Docker, Frank Dudley
Amateur. *b:* 26.8.1862, Smethwick, Staffordshire. *d:* 8.7.1944, Coleshill, Amersham, Buckinghamshire. Brother of L. C. (Derbyshire and Warwickshire) and Ralph (Derbyshire). Middle order batsman. *Sch* KES, Birmingham. *Team* Derbyshire (1881–82, 2 matches).
Career batting
2–3–0–33–25–11.00–0–*ct* 3
He also played for Warwickshire (pre first-class, 1884–89).

Docker, George Arthur Murray
Amateur. *b:* 18.11.1876, Sydney, New South Wales, Australia. *d:* 17.11.1914, near Le Touquet, Belgium. Son of A. R. (New South Wales), nephew of E. B. (New South Wales), cousin of C. T. (New South Wales), K. B. (New South Wales) and P. W. (New South Wales). Hard hitting middle order right-hand batsman, right-arm fast bowler. *Sch* Highgate. *Team* MCC (1911–14). *Tour* MCC to West Indies 1912/13.
Career batting
11–18–2–185–34*–11.56–0–*ct* 3
Bowling 169–5–33.80–0–0–2/66

Docker, Ludford Charles
Amateur. *b:* 26.11.1860, Smethwick, Staffordshire. *d:* 1.8.1940, Alveston Leys, Warwickshire. Brother of F. D. (Derbyshire) and Ralph (Derbyshire). Opening or middle order right-hand batsman, right-arm fast, later medium fast bowler. *Sch* KES, Birmingham. *Teams* Derbyshire (1881–86, 48 matches); Warwickshire (1894–95, 11 matches). *Tour* Shrewsbury to Australia 1887/8.
Career batting
77–136–8–2665–107–20.82–1–*ct* 41
Bowling 280–9–31.11–0–0–3/38
He captained Derbyshire in 1884, but in 1887 moved to Warwickshire. He also occasionally played for Worcestershire. He was President of Warwickshire 1915–30.

Docker, Ralph
Amateur. *b:* 31.8.1855, Harborne, Staffordshire. *d:* 7.7.1910, Tunbridge Wells, Kent. Brother of F. D. (Derbyshire) and L. C. (Derbyshire and Warwickshire). Middle order batsman. *Team* Derbyshire (1879, 2 matches).
Career batting
2–4–0–9–6–2.25–0–*ct* 2
He also played non-first-class cricket for Worcestershire (1878), Staffordshire (1880) and Warwickshire (1883–85).

Docwra, Edward David
Cricketer. *b:* 24.4.1953, Paddington, London. Opening right-hand batsman, leg break bowler. *Sch*

Canford. *Team* Oxford U (1974).
Career batting
1–2–0–26–20–13.00–0–*ct* 0

Dodd, William Thomas Francis
Professional. *b:* 8.3.1908, Steep, Hampshire. Lower order left-hand batsman, slow left-arm bowler. *Team* Hampshire (1931–35, 10 matches).
Career batting
10–16–2–95–31–6.78–0–*ct* 3
Bowling 321–10–32.10–1–0–5/63

Dodds, Thomas Carter
Amateur in 1946, professional from 1947. *b:* 29.5.1919, Bedford. Opening right-hand batsman, right-arm medium pace or leg break bowler. *Sch* Wellingborough and Warwick. *Teams* Essex (1946–59, 380 matches); Services (in India) (1943/4).
Career batting
396–693–18–19407–157–28.75–17–*ct* 186
Bowling 1126–36–31.27–0–0–4/34

He hit 1,000 runs in a season 13 times, exceeding 2,000 once – 2,147, av 38.33, in 1947. His final first-class match was for MCC in 1961.

Dodemaide, Anthony Ian Christopher
Cricketer. *b:* 5.10.1963, Williamstown, Melbourne, Victoria, Australia. Middle order right-hand batsman, right-arm fast medium bowler. *Teams* Victoria (1983/4 to 1991/2, 74 matches); Sussex (1989–91, 63 matches). *Tours* Young Australia to Zimbabwe 1985/6; Australia to Pakistan 1988/9; Victoria to England 1991. *Tests* Australia (1987/8 to 1988/9, 8 matches).
Career batting
148–224–56–5029–117*–29.93–4–*ct* 77
Bowling 13836–436–31.73–13–0–6/58
Test batting
8–12–3–171–50–19.00–0–*ct* 6
Bowling 803–28–28.67–1–0–6/58

He was an all-round success during his three seasons with Sussex; his best season with the bat being 1990 with 1,001 runs, av 33.36, and with the ball 1989 with 65 wickets, av 30.32.

Dods, Harold William
Amateur. *b:* 25.3.1909, Gosberton, Lincolnshire. *d:* 18.6.1944, Westminster, London. Middle order left-hand batsman. *Sch* Tonbridge. *Team* Minor Counties (1936–38). *Tour* Brinckman to South America 1937/8.
Career batting
3–5–0–172–104–34.40–1–*ct* 0

His County cricket was for Lincolnshire (1927–39), and he was that side's leading batsman for many years.

Dodsworth, George Edward
Amateur. *b:* 2.12.1841, York. *d:* 14.6.1876, Morar, Gwalior, India. Middle order left-hand batsman. *Sch* Repton. *Team* MCC (1868).
Career batting
1–2–1–5–3–5.00–0–*ct* 0

Doggart, Alexander Graham
Amateur. *b:* 2.6.1897, Bishop Auckland, Co Durham. *d:* 7.6.1963, Bayswater, London, whilst chairing the AGM of the Football Association. Father of A. P. (Sussex) and G. H. G. (Sussex), brother of J. H. (Cambridge U), grandfather of S. J. G. (Cambridge U). Middle order right-hand batsman, right-arm medium pace bowler. *Sch* Bishop's Stortford. *Teams* Cambridge U (1919–22, blue 1921–22); Middlesex (1925, 4 matches).
Career batting
46–69–9–1716–116–28.60–2–*ct* 53
Bowling 2582–85–30.37–2–0–5/58

He also played for Durham (pre first-class, 1920–24). His final first-class match was for Free Foresters in 1930. A noted soccer player he appeared for Cambridge U, Darlington, Corinthians and England (amateur) as inside left.

Doggart, Arthur Peter
Amateur. *b:* 3.12.1927, Earl's Court, London. *d:* 17.3.1965, Woodcote, Epsom, Surrey. He died by his own hand. Son of A. G. (Middlesex), brother of G. H. G. (Sussex), uncle of S. J. G. (Cambridge U), nephew of J. H. (Cambridge U). Middle order right-hand batsman, right-arm medium pace bowler. *Sch* Winchester. *Team* Sussex (1947–51, 9 matches).
Career batting
9–16–3–228–43–17.53–0–*ct* 3
Bowling 41–2–20.50–0–0–2/8

He was on the staff of *The Cricketer* magazine until his death.

Doggart, George Hubert Graham
Amateur. *b:* 18.7.1925, Earl's Court, London. Son of A. G. (Middlesex), brother of A. P. (Sussex), father of S. J. G. (Cambridge U), nephew of J. H. (Cambridge U). Middle order right-hand batsman, off break bowler, brilliant close field. *Sch* Winchester. *Teams* Cambridge U (1948–50, blue all 3 years); Sussex (1948–61, 155 matches). *Tours* Swanton to West Indies 1955/6; MCC to East Africa 1957/8, to South America 1958/9 (neither first-class). *Tests* England (1950, 2 matches).
Career batting
210–347–28–10054–219*–31.51–20–*ct* 199
Bowling 2057–60–34.28–0–0–4/50
Test batting
2–4–0–76–29–19.00–0–*ct* 3

He hit 1,000 runs in a season four times (best 2,063, av. 45.84, in 1949). Both his double centuries were for Cambridge U, the higher being 219* v Essex at Cambridge in 1949, when he and J. G. Dewes put on 429* for the 2nd wicket, constituting a new record in English first-class cricket, and he scored 215* v Lancashire at Cambridge on debut in 1948. He captained Cambridge in 1950 and Sussex in 1954. He was President of MCC 1981/2 and Treasurer in 1987. A brilliant all round sportsman, he was awarded his blue for soccer and also represented Cambridge at squash, rackets and rugby fives.

Doggart, Dr James Hamilton
Amateur. *b:* 22.1.1900, Bishop Auckland, Co Durham. *d:* 15.10.1989, Guildford, Surrey. Brother of A. G. (Middlesex), uncle of A. P. (Sussex) and G. H. G. (Sussex). Middle order right-hand batsman, right-arm fast bowler. *Sch* Bishops Stortford. *Team* Cambridge U (1919).
Career batting
1–1–0–0–0–0.00–0–*ct* 1
Bowling 69–1–69.00–0–0–1/50
He also played for Durham (pre first-class, 1919–22).

Doggart, Simon Jonathon Graham
Cricketer. *b:* 8.2.1961, Winchester, Hampshire. Son of G. H. G. (Sussex), grandson of A. G. (Cambridge U), nephew of A. P. (Sussex). Middle order left-hand batsman, off break bowler. *Sch* Winchester. *Team* Cambridge U (1980–83, blue all four years).
Career batting
35–50–11–878–70–22.51–0–*ct* 14
Bowling 2223–34–65.38–0–0–3/3

Doidge, Matthew James
Cricketer. *b:* 2.7.1970, Horsforth, Yorkshire. Middle order left-hand batsman, slow left-arm bowler. *Team* Yorkshire (1990, 1 match).
Career batting
1 match, did not bat–*ct* 0
Bowling 106–0

Dolbey, Hugh Owen
Amateur. *b:* 27.11.1879, Sutton, Surrey. *d:* 14.7.1936, Stanstead, Glemsford, Suffolk. Lower order right-hand batsman, right-arm fast bowler. *Sch* Dulwich and Cranleigh. *Team* Surrey (1899–1902, 3 matches).
Career batting
3–6–2–21–18*–5.25–0–*ct* 1
Bowling 235–7–33.57–0–0–4/96
His career in County cricket was very brief since he worked in East Africa, where he was a District Judge. He also played for Shropshire (1898).

Dolding, Desmond Leonard
Professional. *b:* 13.12.1922, Oordegem, Belgium. *d:* 23.11.1954, Wembley, Middlesex, as the result of a motor accident. Lower order right-hand batsman, leg break bowler, brilliant field. *Team* Middlesex (1951, 1 match).
Career batting
3–3–1–11–8–5.50–0–*ct* 0
Bowling 103–3–34.33–0–0–3/43
He made his first-class debut in 1950 for MCC. A noted soccer player he appeared for QPR, Chelsea and Norwich City as wing forward.

D'Oliveira, Basil Lewis, OBE
Cricketer. *b:* 4.10.1931, Signal Hill, Cape Town, South Africa. Brother of Ivan (Leicestershire), father of D. B. (Worcestershire). Middle order right-hand batsman, right-arm medium pace or off break bowler. *Team* Worcestershire (1964–80, 278 matches). *Tours* International XI to Rhodesia 1961/2; Commonwealth to Rhodesia 1962/3, to Pakistan 1963/4; Worcestershire World Tour (Rhodesia first-class) 1964/5, to Jamaica 1965/6; Rest of World to West Indies 1966/7; MCC to West Indies 1967/8, to Ceylon and Pakistan 1968/9, to Australia and New Zealand 1970/1; International Wanderers to Rhodesia 1972/3. *Tests* England (1966–72, 44 matches).
Career batting
362–566–88–18918–227–39.57–43–*ct* 211
Bowling 15021–548–27.41–17–2–6/29
Test batting
44–70–8–2484–158–40.06–5–*ct* 29
Bowling 1859–47–39.55–0–0–3/46
After attaining great success in local club cricket in South Africa, d'Oliveira, a Cape Coloured, was forced to emigrate to England in order to achieve an opportunity of playing cricket at the highest standard. He began in 1960 with Middleton in the Central Lancashire League and then in 1965 qualified to play for Worcestershire. The following summer he won a place in the England team. When he was chosen as a member of the MCC team to tour South Africa, his acceptance caused the cancellation of the tour and brought the problems of apartheid more forcibly before the British public.
His first-class debut had been made in Rhodesia in 1961/2 and he appeared in a handful of first-class matches before his regular County cricket commenced in 1965. He hit over 1,000 runs in a season nine times with 1,691, av 43.35, in 1965 as his best. His only double century was 227 for Worcestershire v Yorkshire at Hull in 1974. He was made an OBE in the 1969 Birthday Honours list. Receipts from his benefit in 1975 amounted to £27,000.
On retiring from first-class cricket he was coach to Worcestershire 1980–91.

D'Oliveira, Damian Basil
Cricketer. *b:* 19.10.1960, Signal Hill, Cape Town, South Africa. Son of B. L. (Worcestershire), nephew of Ivan (Leicestershire). Middle order right-hand batsman, right-arm medium pace or off break bowler. *Team* Worcestershire (1982–92, 210 matches). *Tours* English Counties to Zimbabwe 1984/5; Worcestershire to Zimbabwe 1990/1.
Career batting
212–331–22–8667–237–28.04–10–*ct* 187
Bowling 1712–37–46.27–0–0–2/17

He hit 1,000 runs in a season four times (best 1,263, av 38.27, in 1990). His highest score was 237 for Worcestershire v Oxford U at Oxford in 1991.

D'Oliveira, Ivan
Cricketer. *b:* 19.3.1941, Cape Town, South Africa. Brother of B. L. (Worcestershire), uncle of D. B. (Worcestershire). Middle order right-hand batsman, right-arm medium pace bowler. *Team* Leicestershire (1967, 1 match).
Career batting
1–1–0–0–0–0.00–0–*ct* 0

Doll, Christian Charles Tyler
Amateur. *b:* 22.3.1880, Kensington, London. *d:* 5.4.1955, Meldreth, Cambridgeshire. Brother of M. H. C. (Middlesex). Middle order right-hand batsman, excellent field. *Sch* Charterhouse. *Teams* MCC (1900–04); Cambridge U (1901).
Career batting
27–45–9–774–224*–21.50–2–*ct* 17
Bowling 15–0
His County cricket was for Hertfordshire (1901–09). His highest score was 224* for MCC v London County at Crystal Palace in 1901.

Doll, Mordaunt Henry Caspers
Amateur. *b:* 5.4.1888, Camberwell, London, *d:* 30.6.1966, Devizes, Wiltshire. Brother of C. C. T. (Cambridge U). Hard hitting middle order right-hand batsman. *Sch* Charterhouse. *Teams* Cambridge U (1908); Middlesex (1912–19, 24 matches). *Tour* MCC to West Indies 1912/13.
Career batting
43–63–4–1097–102*–18.59–1–*ct* 32
Bowling 655–15–43.66–1–0–5/52
He also played for Hertfordshire (1907–09).

Dollery, Horace Edgar
Amateur to 1933, professional from 1934. *b:* 14.10.1914, Reading, Berkshire. *d:* 20.1.1987, Edgbaston, Birmingham. Excellent middle order right-hand batsman, fine slip field. occasional wicket-keeper. *Sch* Reading. *Teams* Warwickshire (1934–55, 413 matches); Wellington (1950/1). *Tour* MCC to India 1939/40 (tour cancelled). *Tests* England (1947–50, 4 matches).
Career batting
436–717–66–24413–212–37.50–50–*ct* 291–*st* 13
Bowling 32–0
Test batting
4–7–0–72–37–10.28–0–*ct* 1
He also played for Berkshire (1930–33) and made his first-class debut for Minor Counties in 1933. He exceeded 1,000 runs in a season 15 times and completed 2,000 twice (best 2,084, av 47.36, in 1949). Both his double centuries were for Warwickshire, the higher being 212 v Leicestershire at Birmingham in 1952. He captained Warwickshire jointly in 1948 and alone 1949–55. He was Warwickshire coah 1956–69 and a Test selector 1957–58. A useful soccer player he appeared for Reading.

Dollery, Keith Robert
Professional. *b:* 9.12.1924, Cooroy, Queensland, Australia. Lower order right-hand batsman, right-arm fast medium bowler. *Teams* Queensland (1947/8, 2 matches); Auckland (1949/50); Tasmania (1950/51, 3 matches); Warwickshire (1951–56, 73 matches).
Career batting
80–107–27–958–41–11.97–0–*ct* 24
Bowling 6018–227–26.51–9–2–8/42

Dolman, Charles Eric
Amateur. *b:* 17.7.1903, Abertillery, Monmouthshire. *d:* 6.6.1969, Bristol. Lower order right-hand batsman, bowler. *Sch* Allhallows, Honiton. *Team* Wales (1926–28).
Career batting
2–2–0–46–35–23.00–0–*ct* 0
Bowling 85–2–42.50–0–0–1/22
His County cricket was for Monmouthshire (1922–34). He was Lord Mayor of Cardiff.

Dolphin, Arthur
Professional. *b:* 24.12.1885, Wilsden, Yorkshire. *d:* 23.10.1942, Lilycroft, Heaton, Bradford, Yorkshire. Lower order right-hand batsman, wicket-keeper. *Teams* Yorkshire (1905–27, 428 matches); Patiala (1926/7). *Tours* MCC to Australia 1920/1, to India 1926/7 (in emergency). *Test* England (1920/1, 1 match).
Career batting
449–465–164–3402–66–11.30–0–*ct* 609–*st* 273
Bowling 28–1–28.00–0–0–1/18
Test batting
1–2–0–1–1–0.50–0–*ct* 1
He umpired in first-class matches after retiring from County cricket (1930–39), standing in 6 Test matches (1933–37).

Dolphin, David Frederick
Cricketer. *b:* 13.5.1950, Pietermaritzburg, South Africa. Lower order right-hand batsman, slow left-arm bowler. *Team* Zimbabwe (1989/90 to 1990). *Tour* Zimbabwe to England 1990.
Career batting
4–4–2–40–25–20.00–0–*ct* 0
Bowling 286–5–57.20–0–0–3/59

Donald, Allan Anthony
Cricketer. *b:* 20.10.1966, Bloemfontein, South Africa. Lower order right-hand batsman, right-arm fast bowler. *Teams* Orange Free State (1985/6 to 1991/2); Warwickshire (1987–92, 95 matches). *Tours* South Africa to India 1991/2 (not first-class), to Australia and New Zealand (World Cup) 1991/2, to West Indies 1991/2. *Test* South Africa (1991/2, 1 match).
Career batting
151–178–69–1282–46*–11.76–0–*ct* 53

Donald, Peter Colligan Graham

Bowling 12586–546–23.05–30–3–8.37
Test batting
1–2–0–0–0–0.00–0–*ct* 0
Bowling 144–6–24.00–0–0–4/77

In 1989 he took 86 wickets at 16.25 and topped the first-class bowling averages.

Donald, Peter Colligan Graham
Cricketer. *b:* 8.8.1957, Bristol. Middle order left-hand batsman, right-arm medium pace or off break bowler. *Sch* Sherborne. *Team* Oxford U (1978).
Career batting
1–1–0–1–1–1.00–0–*ct* 0

His County cricket was for Wiltshire (1981–82).

Donald, William Alexander
Cricketer. *b:* 29.7.1953, Huntly, Aberdeenshire, Scotland. Opening right-hand batsman, right-arm medium pace bowler. *Team* Scotland (1978–86).
Career batting
8–13–2–221–45–20.09–0–*ct* 4
Bowling 164–5–32.80–0–0–3/17

Donaldson, Thomas Hubert
Amateur. *b:* 6.8.1882, Streatham, London. *d: circa* 1960, Transvaal, South Africa. Lower order batsman, bowler. *Team* Oxford U (1906).
Career batting
1–2–1–38–31*–38.00–0–*ct* 0
Bowling 26–0

Donaldson, William Patrick
Amateur. *b:* 4.3.1871, Anderston, Glasgow, Scotland. *d:* 27.3.1923, Dollar, Clackmannan, Scotland. Lower order batsman, left-arm fast medium bowler, good close field. *Sch* Loretto. *Team* Oxford U (1894).
Career batting
1–2–1–1–1*–1.00–0–*ct* 1

He represented Oxford at rugby and was a Scottish rugby international.

Donelan, Bradleigh Thomas Peter
Cricketer. *b:* 3.1.1968, Park Royal, Middlesex. Lower order right-hand batsman, off break bowler. *Team* Sussex (1989–92, 49 matches).
Career batting
49–62–20–1026–63*–24.42–0–*ct* 13
Bowling 4118–96–42.89–3–1–6/62

Donnan, Henry
Amateur. *b:* 12.11.1864, Liverpool, New South Wales, Australia. *d:* 13.8.1956, Bexley, Sydney, New South Wales, Australia. Brother-in-law of S. E. Gregory (New South Wales), son-in-law of E. J. Gregory (New South Wales). Defensive opening right-hand batsman, right-arm medium pace bowler. *Team* New South Wales (1887/8 to 1900/1, 58 matches). *Tour* Australia to England and North America 1896. *Tests* Australia (1891/2 to 1896, 5 matches).
Career batting
94–160–14–4262–167–29.19–6–*ct* 37
Bowling 1191–29–41.06–0–0–3/14
Test batting
5–10–1–75–15–8.33–0–*ct* 1
Bowling 22–0

He began his career mainly as a bowler and did not become noted as a batsman until the 1890s. He hit 1,009 runs, av 23.46, in 1896.

Donnellan, Rory Owen
Cricketer. *b:* 20.6.1941, Durban, South Africa. *d:* 15.1.1977, Drakensberg Mountains, South Africa, following a mountaineering accident. Opening right-hand batsman. *Team* Oxford U (1963).
Career batting
5–10–0–173–47–17.30–0–*ct* 3

Donnelly, J. A.
Amateur. Middle order batsman. *Team* Ireland (1914).
Career batting
1–2–0–65–59–32.50–0–*ct* 1

Donnelly, Martin Paterson
Amateur. *b:* 17.10.1917, Ngaruawahia, Auckland, New Zealand. Forcing middle order left-hand batsman, slow left-arm bowler, brilliant field. *Teams* Wellington (1936/7 to 1940/1); Canterbury (1938/9 to 1939/40); Middlesex (1946, 1 match); Oxford U (1946–47, blue both years); Warwickshire (1948–50, 20 matches). *Tours* New Zealand to England 1937, 1949, to Australia 1937/8. *Tests* New Zealand (1937–49, 7 matches).
Career batting
131–221–26–9250–208*–47.43–23–*ct* 75
Bowling 1683–43–39.13–0–0–4/32
Test batting
7–12–1–582–206–52.90–1–*ct* 7
Bowling 20–0

He scored 1,000 runs in a season five times, exceeding 2,000 once (2,287, av 61.81, in 1949). His highest innings was 208* for MCC v Yorkshire at Scarborough in 1948; his other double century was 206 for New Zealand v England at Lord's in 1949. He met with great success as a batsman in England, but in 1950 he took up a business appointment in Australia. He captained Oxford in 1947. His final first-class match was for Governor-General's XI in 1960/1. An excellent rugby player he appeared for Oxford U and England.

Donovan, E. J.
Amateur. Tail end batsman. *Team* Ireland (1907).
Career batting
1–2–1–5–3*–5.00–0–*ct* 0
Bowling 36–1–36.00–0–0–1/36

Donovan, Robert Leo
Amateur. *b:* 1899, Dublin, Ireland. *d:* 26.2.1932, Dublin, Ireland. Lower order left-hand batsman, left-arm medium pace bowler. *Team* Ireland (1921).

Career batting
1–1–0–3–3–3.00–0–*ct* 0

Dooland, Bruce
Professional. *b:* 1.11.1923, Cowandilla, Adelaide, South Australia. *d:* 8.9.1980, Adelaide, South Australia. Middle or lower order right-hand batsman, leg break and googly bowler, good field. *Teams* South Australia (1945/6 to 1957/8, 29 matches); Nottinghamshire (1953–57, 140 matches). *Tours* Australia to New Zealand 1945/6; Commonwealth to India and Ceylon 1950/1; Howard to India 1956/7. *Tests* Australia (1946/7 to 1947/8, 3 matches).
Career batting
214–326–33–7141–115*–24.37–4–*ct* 186
Bowling 22332–1016–21.98–84–23–8/20
Test batting
3–5–1–76–29–19.00–0–*ct* 3
Bowling 419–9–46.55–0–0–4/69
He took 100 wickets in a season five times (best 196, av 15.48, in 1954) and hit 1,000 runs twice (best 1,604, av 28.64 in 1957). He performed the 'double' in 1954 and 1957. His first match in England was for Commonwealth XI in 1951.

Dorey, Lewis Hugh John
Amateur. *b:* 23.10.1901, St Albans, Hertfordshire. Middle or lower order batsman. *Sch* Harrow. *Team* Hampshire (1925, 1 match).
Career batting
1–2–0–0–0–0.00–0–*ct* 1

Dorman, Rev Arthur William
Amateur. *b:* 24.10.1862, Sydenham, London. *d:* 7.1.1914, Hinton Charterhouse, Bath, Somerset. Lower order batsman, left-arm slow bowler. *Sch* Dulwich. *Team* Cambridge U (1886, blue).
Career batting
8–12–5–31–15–4.42–0–*ct* 6
Bowling 655–25–26.20–1–0–5/55
He was brother-in-law of the explorer Ernest Shackleton.

Dorrell, Philip George
Amateur. *b:* 6.12.1914, Worcester. Middle order right-hand batsman. *Sch* Bromsgrove. *Team* Worcestershire (1946, 1 match).
Career batting
1–1–0–1–1–1.00–0–*ct* 0

Dorrinton, William
Professional. *b:* 29.4.1809, West Malling, Kent. *d:* 8.11.1848, West Malling, Kent. Son of Thomas (Kent 1800), brother of Alban (Kent 1836). Lower order right-hand batsman, wicket-keeper. *Team* Kent (1836–48, 55 matches); Hampshire (1845, 2 matches).
Career batting
95–175–13–1440–65–8.88–0–*ct* 89–*st* 25
Bowling 2 wickets (no analyses)–0–0–1/?
He was an excellent wicket-keeper and earlier excelled as a long stop. He also played for Suffolk (1847).

Dorset, 3rd Duke of, John Frederick Sackville
(succeeded to title in 1769)
Amateur. *b:* 24.3.1745. *d:* 19.7.1799, Knole, Sevenoaks, Kent. Nephew of 2nd Duke (Kent 1734). Middle order batsman, bowler. *Sch* Harrow. *Team* Kent (1773–83).
He was one of the greatest supporters of the game and employed several of the most famous cricketers on his estate. He more or less gave up playing in 1784 when he was appointed ambassador to France. He was partially responsible for the proposed cricket tour to Paris in 1789 – the tour was abandoned due to the Revolution.

Doshi, Dilip Rasiklal
Cricketer. *b:* 22.12.1947, Rajkot, India. Tail end left-hand batsman, slow left-arm bowler. *Teams* Bengal (1968/9 to 1984/5); Nottinghamshire (1973–78, 44 matches); Warwickshire (1980–81, 43 matches); Saurashtra (1985/6). *Tours* Indian Universities to Ceylon 1970/1; India to Australia and New Zealand 1980/1, to England 1982, to Pakistan 1982/3; Rest of World to England 1985. *Tests* India (1979/80 to 1983/4, 33 matches).
Career batting
238–253–70–1442–44–7.87–0–*ct* 62
Bowling 23874–898–26.58–43–6–7/29
Test batting
33–38–10–129–20–4.60–0–*ct* 10
Bowling 3502–114–30.71–6–0–6/102
For Warwickshire in 1980 he took 101 wickets, av 26.73. On the 1982 tour to England he played in all three Tests and headed the Test bowling averages with 13 wickets, av 35.00. He also played for Hertfordshire (1976) and Northumberland (1979). His last first-class match was for D. B. Close's XI in 1986.

Doughty, David George
Professional. *b:* 9.11.1937, Chiswick, Middlesex. Lower order left-hand batsman, slow left-arm bowler. *Team* Somerset (1963–64, 17 matches).
Career batting
17–20–5–104–22–6.93–0–*ct* 6
Bowling 710–35–20.28–2–1–6/58

Doughty, Richard James
Cricketer. *b:* 17.11.1960, Bridlington, Yorkshire. Lower order right-hand batsman, right-arm fast medium bowler. *Teams* Gloucestershire (1981–84, 14 matches); Surrey (1985–87, 27 matches).
Career batting
41–52–11–845–65–20.60–0–*ct* 24
Bowling 2986–89–33.55–2–0–6/33

Doughty, Stephen
Professional. *b:* 16.10.1855, Staveley, Derbyshire. *d:* 11.11.1929, Halton East, Skipton, Yorkshire. Lower order right-hand batsman, right-arm medium pace off break bowler. *Team* Derbyshire (1880–86, 4 matches).
Career batting
4–7–1–40–13*–6.66–0–*ct* 1
Bowling 79–4–19.75–0–0–3/28

Douglas, Archibald Philip
Amateur. *b:* 7.6.1867, Norwood Green, Middlesex. *d:* 24.1.1953, Haines Hill, Taunton, Somerset. Brother of James (Middlesex), R. N. (Middlesex and Surrey) and Sholto (Middlesex), brother-in-law of F. J. C. Wyatt (Hampshire). Middle order right-hand batsman, good cover field. *Sch* Dulwich. *Teams* Surrey (1887, 1 match); Europeans (1898/9 to 1911/12); Middlesex (1902, 2 matches).
Career batting
9–14–1–328–91–25.23–0–*ct* 9
Bowling 48–8–6.00–1–0–6/34
Being stationed for many years in India, his County cricket was very restricted.

Douglas, Arthur Coates
Amateur. *b:* 16.8.1902, Belfast, Ireland. *d:* 27.6.1937, Stranmillis, Belfast, Ireland. Middle order right-hand batsman, right-arm fast medium bowler. *Sch* Royal Belfast Academical Institution. *Team* Ireland (1925–33).
Career batting
7–14–0–262–63–18.71–0–*ct* 4
Bowling 341–12–28.41–0–0–4/35
He was an Irish rugby international.

Douglas, Cecil Herbert
Amateur. *b:* 28.6.1886, Clapton, London. *d:* 30.9.1954, Frinton-on-Sea, Essex. Brother of J. W. H. T. (Essex). Middle order right-hand batsman, right-arm slow bowler. *Sch* Felsted. *Team* Essex (1912–19, 21 matches).
Career batting
21–27–0–326–78–12.07–0–*ct* 4
Bowling 350–6–58.33–0–0–3/46

Douglas, James
Amateur. *b:* 8.1.1870, Norwood Green, Middlesex. *d:* 8.2.1958, Cheltenham, Gloucestershire. Brother of A. P. (Surrey and Middlesex), R. N. (Surrey and Middlesex) and Sholto (Middlesex), brother-in-law of R. H. Juckes (Sussex). Opening right-hand batsman, slow left-arm bowler, excellent field. *Sch* Dulwich. *Teams* Cambridge U (1892–94, blue all three years); Middlesex (1893–1913, 164 matches).
Career batting
197–336–22–9099–204–28.97–15–*ct* 179
Bowling 1732–58–29.86–2–0–5/45
His only double century was 204 for Middlesex v Gloucestershire at Bristol in 1903. Being in the scholastic profession his County cricket was restricted mainly to the holidays.

Douglas, John William Henry Tyler
Amateur. *b:* 3.9.1882, Clapton, London. *d:* 19.12.1930, seven miles south of the Laeso Trindel Lightship, Denmark. He was drowned in a shipping accident. Brother of C. H. (Essex). Originally hard hitting, but later stolid, middle order right-hand batsman, right-arm fast medium bowler. *Sch* Felsted. *Teams* Essex (1901–28, 459 matches); London County (1903–04). *Tours* MCC to New Zealand 1906/7, to North America 1907, to Australia 1911/12, 1920/1, 1924/5, to South Africa 1913/14. *Tests* England (1911/12 to 1924/5, 23 matches).
Career batting
651–1035–156–24531–210*–27.90–26–*ct* 364
Bowling 44159–1893–23.32–113–23–9/47
Test batting
23–35–2–962–119–29.15–1–*ct* 9
Bowling 1486–45–33.02–1–0–5/46
An all-round sportsman, Douglas excelled at boxing, winning the Olympic middleweight title in 1908, at soccer, obtaining an England amateur international cap, and at cricket. He captained Essex from 1911 to 1928 and led England on two tours to Australia – in 1911/12, when he had the captaincy thrust upon him by Warner's illness, and in 1920/1. He also captained the MCC to South Africa in 1913/14. In all he led England in 18 Tests. He was a Test selector 1927–28.
His batting was of the stubborn variety and he was the ideal man to save a match. He hit 1,000 runs in a season 10 times with 1,547, av 37.73, in 1921 his best. Five times he completed the 'double' and seven times he completed 100 wickets in a season, his best being 147, av 21.38, in 1920. His highest score and only double hundred was 210* for Essex v Derbyshire at Leyton in 1921. His best bowling was 9/47 for Essex v Derbyshire at Leyton in 1921. His final first-class match was for MCC in 1930.
He died whilst attempting to save his father when the ship in which they were travelling, SS *Oberon*, was in collision with another in dense fog.

Douglas, Joseph Stanley
Professional. *b:* 4.4.1903, Bradford, Yorkshire. *d:* 27.12.1971, Paignton, Devon. Lower order left-hand batsman, left-arm medium fast bowler. *Team* Yorkshire (1925–34, 23 matches).
Career batting
23–26–8–125–19–6.94–0–*ct* 14
Bowling 1310–49–26.73–2–0–6/59

Douglas, Rev Robert Noel
Amateur. *b:* 9.11.1868, Norwood Green, Middlesex. *d:* 27.2.1957, Colyton, Devon. Brother of A. P. (Middlesex and Surrey), James (Middlesex) and Sholto (Middlesex). Middle order right-hand batsman. *Sch* Dulwich. *Teams* Cambridge U (1890–92, blue all

three years); Surrey (1890–91, 4 matches); Middlesex (1898–1905, 45 matches).
Career batting
75–122–7–2669–131–23.20–1–*ct* 48–*st* 3
Being in the scholastic profession, his first-class appearances were limited. A noted rugby player he was awarded his blue in 1891.

Douglas, Sholto
Amateur. *b:* 8.9.1873, Norwood Green, Middlesex. *d:* 28.1.1916, Cambrin, Arras, France. He was killed in action. Brother of A. P. (Middlesex and Surrey), James (Middlesex) and R. N. (Surrey and Middlesex). Middle order right-hand batsman. *Sch* Dulwich. *Team* Middlesex (1906, 1 match).
Career batting
1–2–0–30–16–15.00–0–*ct* 1

Douglas-Home, Sir Alec
(*see under* Dunglass, Lord)

Douglas-Home, Andrew
Cricketer. *b:* 14.5.1950, Galashiels, Selkirkshire, Scotland. Nephew of Sir Alec (Middlesex). Tail-end left-hand batsman, right-arm fast medium bowler. *Sch* Eton. *Team* Oxford U (1970).
Career batting
4–6–1–33–23–6.60–0–*ct* 1
Bowling 273–9–30.33–0–0–3/71

Douglas-Jones, Stanley Douglas
Amateur. *b:* 19.11.1885, Hendon, Middlesex. *d:* 12.10.1969, Rhos-yn-Wyst, Glyndyfrdwy, Merionethshire. Middle order batsman. *Team* MCC (1913–14).
Career batting
2–4–1–30–12–10.00–0–*ct* 0–*st* 1

Douglas-Pennant, Admiral Sir Cyril Eustace
Amateur. *b:* 7.4.1894, Westminster, London. *d:* 3.4.1961, Westminster, London. Uncle of Simon (Cambridge U). Middle order batsman. *Team* Royal Navy (1924–25).
Career batting
2–3–0–29–15–9.66–0–*ct* 0

Douglas-Pennant, Simon
Amateur. *b:* 28.6.1938, Jordanhill, Glasgow, Scotland. Nephew of C. E. (Royal Navy). Tail-end right-hand batsman, left-arm fast medium bowler. *Sch* Eton. *Team* Cambridge U (1959–61, blue 1959).
Career batting
35–53–31–101–14*–4.59–0–*ct* 6
Bowling 3031–83–36.51–3–1–7/56

Douthwaite, Harold
Amateur. *b:* 12.8.1900, Lancaster, Lancashire. *d:* 9.7.1972, Lancaster, Lancashire. Middle order right-hand batsman. *Sch* Lancaster GS. *Team* Lancashire (1920–21, 3 matches).
Career batting
3–5–0–85–29–17.00–0–*ct* 1
A prolific scorer in school cricket, he made over 1,000 runs for Lancaster GS in 1919 at an average of 112. He appeared in no first-class matches whilst at Cambridge U, but did win a blue for soccer and was an England amateur international.

Dove, Gregory (*see under* Gregory, D.)

Dovey, Raymond Randall
Professional. *b:* 18.7.1920, Chislehurst, Kent. *d:* 27.12.1974, Tunbridge Wells, Kent. Lower order left-hand batsman, off break bowler. *Sch* Eltham College. *Team* Kent (1938–54, 249 matches). *Tour* Commonwealth to India and Ceylon 1950/1.
Career batting
263–404–74–3841–65*–11.63–0–*ct* 79
Bowling 21391–777–27.53–25–2–8/23
He took 102 wickets, av 25.48, in 1950. After leaving Kent he played for Dorset (1955–59).

Dow, William David Fraser
Professional. *b:* 27.11.1933, Langside, Glasgow, Scotland. Lower order right-hand batsman, right-arm fast medium bowler. *Teams* Scotland (1956–67, 11 matches); Essex (1958–59, 2 matches).
Career batting
13–16–4–107–18–8.91–0–*ct* 2
Bowling 1015–38–26.71–2–1–6/56
He also played for Cumberland (1956–58).

Dowding, Alan Lorimer
Amateur. *b:* 4.4.1929, Unley, Adelaide, South Australia. Forcing middle order right-hand batsman, good field. *Team* Oxford U (1951–53, blue 1952–53).
Career batting
43–73–5–1950–105–28.67–2–*ct* 27
Bowling 116–1–116.00–0–0–1/4
His final first-class match was for MCC in 1956. He captained Oxford in 1953. He was awarded his soccer blue at Oxford.

Dowell, Alastair McQueen
Amateur. *b:* 17.5.1920, Kinross, Scotland. Lower order right-hand batsman, right-arm fast medium bowler. *Team* Scotland (1951–55).
Career batting
3–4–1–6–5–2.00–0–*ct* 0
Bowling 136–2–68.00–0–0–2/51

Dowen, Neville Thomas
Amateur. *b:* 18.8.1901, Bulwell, Nottinghamshire. *d:* 25.10.1964, Evington, Leicestershire. Middle order left-hand batsman, right-arm fast medium bowler. *Team* Leicestershire (1925–38, 7 matches).
Career batting
7–12–0–187–44–15.58–0–*ct* 3
Bowling 25–0
He was Leicestershire Hon Secretary 1940–46 and Treasurer 1947–64.

Dowling, Geoffrey Charles Walter
Amateur. *b:* 12.8.1891, Melbourne, Victoria, Australia. *d:* 30.7.1915, Hooge, Belgium. He was killed in action. Middle order batsman. *Sch* Charterhouse. *Team* Sussex (1911–13, 4 matches).
Career batting
4–8–0–123–48–15.37–0–*ct* 4
Bowling 19–1–19.00–0–0–1/19
Whilst at Cambridge he appeared in various trials, but no first-class matches for the University.

Dowling, Graham Thorne, OBE
Cricketer. *b:* 4.3.1937, Christchurch, New Zealand. Opening right-hand batsman, right-arm medium pace bowler. *Teams* Canterbury (1958/9 to 1971/2); Prime Minister's XI (in India) (1967/8). *Tours* New Zealand to England 1965, 1969, to South Africa 1961/2, to India and Pakistan 1964/5, 1969/70, to West Indies 1971/2, to Australia 1961/2, 1970/1. *Tests* New Zealand (1962/3 to 1971/2, 39 matches).
Career batting
158–282–13–9399–239–34.94–16–*ct* 111
Bowling 378–9–42.00–0–0–3/100
Test batting
39–77–3–2306–239–31.16–3–*ct* 23
Bowling 19–1–19.00–0–0–1/19
He played in all the Tests on his two tours to England, being captain in 1969, and was reasonably successful. He captained New Zealand in 19 Tests. In first-class matches he hit two double centuries, the higher being 239 for New Zealand v India at Christchurch in 1967/8.

Down, J. H.
Professional. Lower order left-hand batsman, slow left-arm bowler. *Team* Hampshire (1914, 2 matches).
Career batting
2–3–1–32–31*–16.00–0–*ct* 0
Bowling 53–1–53.00–0–0–1/33

Downend, Richard Hugh
Cricketer. *b:* 19.1.1945, Stoke-on-Trent, Staffordshire. Lower order right-hand batsman, right-arm medium pace bowler. *Team* Minor Counties (1972).
Career batting
1–2–0–6–5–3.00–0–*ct* 0
Bowling 71–1–71.00–0–0–1/71
His County cricket was for Staffordshire (1964–77).

Downer, Harry Rodney
Amateur. *b:* 19.10.1915, Southampton, Hampshire. Middle order right-hand batsman. *Team* Hampshire (1946, 2 matches).
Career batting
2–4–0–8–4–2.00–0–*ct* 0

Downes, Keith Drummond
Amateur. *b:* 12.6.1917, Mossley Hill, Liverpool, Lancashire. *d:* 18.2.1990, Fir Vale, Sheffield, Yorkshire. Middle or lower order right-hand batsman, wicket-keeper. *Sch* Rydal. *Team* Cambridge U (1939, blue).
Career batting
8–13–2–102–27–9.27–0–*ct* 6–*st* 1
His County cricket was for Denbighshire (1933). He also won a blue for rugby.

Downs, Alexander
Amateur. *b:* 28.5.1876, Uddingston, Lanarkshire, Scotland. *d:* 17.7.1924, Uddingston, Lanarkshire, Scotland. Lower order batsman, wicket-keeper. *Team* Scotland (1907).
Career batting
1–2–0–1–1–0.50–0–*ct* 0

Downton, George Charles
Amateur. *b:* 1.11.1928, Bexley, Kent. Father of P. R. (Kent and Middlesex). Lower order right-hand batsman, wicket-keeper. *Team* Kent (1948, 8 matches).
Career batting
10–15–5–88–20–8.80–0–*ct* 26–*st* 1
His final first-class match was for MCC in 1959.

Downton, Paul Rupert
Cricketer. *b:* 4.4.1957, Farnborough, Kent. Son of G. C. (Kent). Middle order right-hand batsman, occasional off break bowler, wicket-keeper. *Sch* Sevenoaks. *Teams* Kent (1977–79, 45 matches); Middlesex (1980–91, 219 matches). *Tours* England to Pakistan 1977/8, to New Zealand 1977/8, to West Indies 1980/1, 1985/6, to India and Sri Lanka 1984/5, to Australia 1984/5 (not first-class), to India and Pakistan (World Cup) 1987/8; Middlesex to Zimbabwe 1980/1. *Tests* England (1980/1 to 1988, 30 matches).
Career batting
314–405–76–8270–126*–25.13–6–*ct* 690–*st* 89
Bowling 9–1–9.00–0–0–1/4
Test batting
30–48–8–785–74–19.62–0–*ct* 70–*st* 5
The signing of Knott for Packer gave an early opportunity to Downton, who was chosen as England's reserve wicket-keeper for the 1977/8 twin tours, after only half a season in first-class cricket. The continuance of Knott's County career however meant that Downton had to move away in order to play first-class cricket. An eye injury in 1990 prematurely ended his cricket with Middlesex after a few matches in 1991. He hit 1,120 runs, av 37.33, in 1987.

Dowson, Edward
Amateur. *b:* 17.2.1838, Camberwell, London. *d:* 29.4.1922, Surbiton Hill, Surrey. Father of E. M. (Surrey). Middle order right-hand batsman, good deep field. *Sch* Shrewsbury. *Team* Surrey (1860–70, 54 matches).
Career batting
74–120–6–1927–94–16.90–0–*ct* 41
Bowling 13–0

His first-class debut was for Gentlemen of Surrey and Sussex in 1856. He was Surrey captain in 1866. He also played for Bedfordshire (1856), Buckinghamshire (1859) and Lincolnshire (1864–71).

Dowson, Edward Maurice
Amateur. *b:* 21.6.1880, Weybridge, Surrey. *d:* 22.7.1933, Hele House, Ashburton, Devon. Son of Edward (Surrey). Middle order right-hand batsman, slow left-arm bowler. *Sch* Harrow. *Teams* Cambridge U (1900–03, blue all four years); Surrey (1900–03, 44 matches). *Tours* Hawke to Australia and New Zealand 1902/3; Bosanquet to North America 1901; Bennett to West Indies 1901/2.
Career batting
113–187–14–5047–135–29.17–8–*ct* 61
Bowling 8544–357–23.93–23–3–8/21
He hit 1,000 runs in a season three times (best 1,343, av 34.43, in 1903). His last first-class match was for MCC in 1913, but he appeared in no other first-class matches after 1903. He captained Cambridge in 1903.

Draffan, Nigel Gordon Helm
Cricketer. *b:* 1.9.1950, Nakuru, Kenya. Opening or middle order right-hand batsman. *Sch* Malvern. *Team* Cambridge U (1971–72).
Career batting
4–7–1–35–29–5.83–0–*ct* 1

Drake, Alonzo
Professional. *b:* 16.4.1884, Parkgate, Rotherham, Yorkshire. *d:* 14.2.1919, Honley, Huddersfield, Yorkshire. Middle order left-hand batsman, left-arm slow medium bowler. *Team* Yorkshire (1909–14, 156 matches).
Career batting
157–246–24–4816–147*–21.69–3–*ct* 93
Bowling 8656–480–18.03–29–1–10/35
He took 100 wickets in a season twice (best 158, av 15.30, in 1914). His career was dogged by ill-health. His best bowling was 10/35 for Yorkshire v Somerset at Weston-super-Mare in 1914. He hit 1,000 runs in a season twice (best 1,487, av 30.97, in 1911) and completed the 'double' in 1913. He played soccer for Sheffield United.

Drake, Cyril Henry
Professional. *b:* 9.1.1922, Highfields, Leicester. Lower order right-hand batsman, right-arm fast bowler. *Team* Leicestershire (1939, 8 matches).
Career batting
8–11–3–43–13–5.37–0–*ct* 3
Bowling 605–19–31.84–1–0–5/21

Drake, Edward Joseph
Professional. *b:* 16.8.1912, Southampton, Hampshire. Middle order right-hand batsman. *Team* Hampshire (1931–36, 16 matches).
Career batting
16–27–0–219–45–8.11–0–*ct* 10
Bowling 171–4–42.75–0–0–2/37
One of the best known centre forwards of his day, Drake played soccer for Southampton, Arsenal and England, gaining five international caps.

Drake, Rev Edward Tyrwhitt
Amateur. *b:* 15.5.1832, Bucknell, Bicester, Oxfordshire. *d:* 20.6.1904, Amersham, Buckinghamshire. His niece married E. Mathews (Oxford U). Hard hitting right-hand batsman, right-hand lob bowler. *Sch* Westminster. *Team* Cambridge U (1852–54, blue all three years).
Career batting
55–102–8–1412–88–15.02–0–*ct* 41
Bowling 2007–154 + 43–13.03–19–8–8/61
His last first-class match was for MCC in 1871. He was regarded as one of the best lob bowlers, though at times very expensive. He entered the church in 1860 and rarely appeared in first-class matches after that – it was thought that the clergy should not take part in matches which involved betting. He also played for Oxfordshire (1853–61), Buckinghamshire (1865–70) and Hertfordshire (1869). He was a well-known steeplechase jockey, but in view of his occupation, he rode under the alias of Eckard.

Drake, John
Professional. *b:* 1.9.1893, Tong Park, Baildon, Yorkshire. *d:* 22.5.1967, Meanwood, Yorkshire. Lower order right-hand batsman, right-arm fast medium bowler. *Team* Yorkshire (1923–24, 3 matches).
Career batting
3–4–1–21–10–7.00–0–*ct* 2
Bowling 117–1–117.00–0–0–1/44

Drakes, Thomas Edwin
Amateur. *b:* 7.3.1908, Bardney, Lincolnshire. *d:* 10.5.1974, Hainault, Essex. Middle/lower order right-hand batsman, right-arm fast medium bowler. *Sch* Stamford. *Team* Cambridge U (1929).
Career batting
8–11–1–140–39*–14.00–0–*ct* 6
Bowling 648–20–32.40–1–0–5/70
His County cricket was for Lincolnshire (1926–33).

Draper, Robert William
Amateur. *b:* 20.1.1903, Calcutta, India. *d:* 29.8.1987, Cowie's Hill, Durban, South Africa. Lower order right-hand batsman, left-arm medium pace bowler. *Team* Somerset (1925–29, 3 matches).
Career batting
3–5–0–20–11–4.00–0–*ct* 2
Bowling 221–6–36.83–0–0–3/73

Draper, William
Professional. *b:* 12.11.1849, Penshurst, Kent. *d:* 13.3.1919, Tunbridge Wells, Kent. Brother of Henry (noted umpire). Lower order left-hand batsman, right-

arm medium pace bowler. *Team* Kent (1874–80, 9 matches).
Career batting
9–17–2–108–28–7.20–0–*ct* 3
Bowling 290–20–14.50–1–0–5/51
He was a first-class umpire (1897–98).

Dredge, Colin Herbert
Cricketer. *b:* 4.8.1954, Frome, Somerset. Lower order left-hand batsman, right-arm medium pace bowler, deep field. *Team* Somerset (1976–88, 194 matches).
Career batting
194–224–68–2182–56*–13.98–0–*ct* 84
Bowling 13338–443–30.10–12–0–6/37

Drew, Thomas Mitchell
Amateur. *b:* 9.6.1875, Kooringa, South Australia. *d:* 9.1.1928, Toowoomba, Queensland, Australia. Brother of C. F. (South Australia). Lower order left-hand batsman, bowler. *Teams* South Australia (1897/8, 3 matches); London County (1903).
Career batting
4–7–2–65–33*–13.00–0–*ct* 4
Bowling 33–0

Driffield, Lancelot Townshend
Amateur. *b:* 10.8.1880, Old, Northamptonshire. *d:* 9.10.1917, Leatherhead, Surrey. Lower order left-hand batsman, slow left-arm bowler. *Sch* St John's, Leatherhead. *Teams* Cambridge U (1900–02, blue 1902); Northamptonshire (1905–08, 40 matches).
Career batting
61–98–19–851–56–10.77–0–*ct* 32
Bowling 4102–137–29.94–6–1–7/7
A noted soccer player, he obtained his blue at Cambridge. He first played for Northamptonshire (pre first-class) in 1899.

Dring, Clive Frederick
Professional. *b:* 30.6.1934, Shooters Hill, London. Middle order right-hand batsman, right-arm medium pace bowler. *Team* Kent (1955, 1 match).
Career batting
1–2–0–8–8–4.00–0–*ct* 0

Drinnan, William Murdoch Ross
Amateur. *b:* 28.5.1883, St Quivox, Ayrshire, Scotland. *d:* 10.3.1948, Wallacetown, Ayr, Scotland. Lower order left-hand batsman, slow left-arm bowler. *Team* Scotland (1928).
Career batting
1–2–2–24–24*–no av–0–*ct* 0
Bowling 102–3–34.00–0–0–2/43

Driver, Jeremiah
Professional. *b:* 16.5.1861, Keighley, Yorkshire. *d:* 10.12.1946, Keighley, Yorkshire. Lower order right-hand batsman, wicket-keeper. *Team* Yorkshire (1889, 2 matches).
Career batting
2–4–1–24–8–8.00–0–*ct* 2

Druce, Eliot Albert Cross
Amateur. *b:* 20.6.1876, Weybridge, Surrey. *d:* 24.10.1934, Kensington, London. Cousin of W. G. (Cambridge U) and N. F. (Surrey). Middle order right-hand batsman, right-arm medium pace bowler. *Sch* Marlborough. *Teams* Cambridge U (1897–98); Kent (1898–1900, 3 matches).
Career batting
10–14–2–185–43–15.41–0–*ct* 6
Bowling 213–13–16.38–0–0–4/28
His final first-class match was for Free Foresters in 1913. He played hockey for Cambridge U in 1897/8.

Druce, Norman Frank
Amateur. *b:* 1.1.1875, Denmark Hill, London. *d:* 27.10.1954, Milford on Sea, Hampshire. Brother of W. G. (Cambridge U), cousin of E. A. C. (Kent). Middle order right-hand batsman. *Sch* Marlborough. *Teams* Cambridge U (1894–97, blue all four years); Surrey (1895–97, 12 matches). *Tours* Mitchell to North America 1895; Stoddart to Australia 1897/8. *Tests* England (1897/8, 5 matches).
Career batting
66–105–8–3416–227*–35.21–9–*ct* 66
Bowling 268–8–33.50–0–0–1/8
Test batting
5–9–0–252–64–28.00–0–*ct* 5
His double century was for Cambridge U v C. I. Thornton's XI at Cambridge in 1897. He captained Cambridge in 1897. After leaving Cambridge he appeared in very few first-class matches, but his final game was not until 1913, for Free Foresters.

Druce, Walter George
Amateur. *b:* 16.9.1872, Denmark Hill, London. *d:* 8.1.1963, Sherborne, Dorset. Brother of N. F. (Surrey), cousin of E. A. C. (Kent). Middle order right-hand batsman, good cover point, wicket-keeper. *Sch* Marlborough. *Team* Cambridge U (1894–95, blue both years).
Career batting
39–67–11–1568–129–28.00–3–*ct* 47–*st* 5
Bowling 18–0
His final first-class match was for MCC in 1913. He captained Cambridge in 1895. He also played rugby for Cambridge U.

Drummond, Alexander Victor
Amateur. *b:* 20.10.1888, Pimlico, Westminster, London. *d:* 29.4.1937, High Brooms, Tunbridge Wells, Kent. Brother of G. H. (Northamptonshire). Middle order batsman. *Sch* Harrow. *Team* MCC (1911–21). *Tour* MCC to Egypt 1909 (not first-class).
Career batting
8–15–1–182–30–13.00–0–*ct* 2
Bowling 157–3–52.33–0–0–2/44
His County cricket was for Buckinghamshire (1921). He married Pauline Chase, the actress.

Drummond, Duncan Weir
Amateur. *b:* 12.5.1923, Greenock, Renfrew, Scotland. *d:* 17.5.1985, Greenock, Renfrew, Scotland. Lower order right-hand batsman, right-arm medium pace bowler. *Sch* Merchiston. *Team* Scotland (1951–61).
Career batting
17–22–1–263–33–12.52–0–*ct* 3
Bowling 771–20–38.55–0–0–4/73

Drummond, George Henry
Amateur. *b:* 3.3.1883. Pimlico, Westminster, London. *d:* 12.10.1963, Kirk Braddan, Isle of Man. Brother of A. V. (MCC). Middle order right-hand batsman. *Sch* Harrow. *Team* Northamptonshire (1920–22, 4 matches). *Tours* MCC to Australia 1903/4 (he played in emergency); Brackley to West Indies 1904/5.
Career batting
15–27–1–186–34–7.15–0–*ct* 5
Bowling 21–0
Whilst at Cambridge he did not appear in first-class games. He made his first-class debut in England for MCC in 1906. He was Northamptonshire President 1924–28. He was High Sheriff of Northamptonshire.

Drury, John Joseph
Professional. *b:* 28.5.1874, Kimberley, Nottinghamshire. *d:* 16.10.1919, Dobcross, Yorkshire. Lower order right-hand batsman, right-arm fast bowler. *Team* Nottinghamshire (1899–1902, 4 matches).
Career batting
4–3–0–21–19–7.00–0–*ct* 0
Bowling 71–4–17.75–0–0–1/1

Drybrough, Colin David
Amateur. *b:* 31.8.1938, East Melbourne, Victoria, Australia. Lower order right-hand batsman, slow left-arm bowler, good close field. *Sch* Highgate. *Teams* Middlesex (1958–64, 92 matches); Oxford U (1960–62, blue all three years).
Career batting
133–161–41–1848–88–15.40–0–*ct* 98
Bowling 9270–319–29.05–10–1–7/35
He captained Oxford 1961–62 and Middlesex 1963–64. His final first-class match was for MCC in 1967. He also won a blue for soccer.

D'Souza, Antao
Cricketer. *b:* 17.1.1939, Goa, India. Brother of Marshall (Karachi) and V. P. (Karachi Schools). Lower order right-hand batsman, right-arm medium pace off break bowler. *Teams* Karachi (1956/7 to 1962/3); Peshawar (1959/60); PIA (1960/1 to 1966/7). *Tours* Pakistan to England 1962; Pakistan Eaglets to England 1963; PIA to East Africa 1964. *Tests* Pakistan (1958/9 to 1962, 6 matches).
Career batting
61–72–29–815–45–18.95–0–*ct* 20
Bowling 4947–190–26.03–12–1–7/33
Test batting
6–10–8–76–23*–38.00–0–*ct* 3
Bowling 745–17–43.82–1–0–5/112
On his only Test tour to England he took 58 wickets, av 34.79.

Dube, Langalibalele Ethan
Cricketer. *b:* 7.9.1970, Filabusi, Matabeleland, Rhodesia. Lower order right-hand batsman, right-arm fast medium bowler. *Team* Zimbabwe (1990 to 1990/1). *Tour* Zimbabwe to England 1990.
Career batting
4–4–1–4–2–1.33–0–*ct* 0
Bowling 324–5–64.80–0–0–2/39

Du Boulay, Arthur Houssemayne
Amateur. *b:* 18.6.1880, New Brompton, Chatham, Kent. *d:* 25.10.1918, Fillieres, France, of influenza. Uncle of H. E. Webb (Hampshire). Opening/middle order right-hand batsman, right-arm medium pace bowler. *Sch* Cheltenham. *Teams* Kent (1899, 5 matches); Gloucestershire (1908, 3 matches).
Career batting
9–14–3–303–58–27.54–0–*ct* 2
Bowling 177–3–59.00–0–0–1/4
His final first-class match was for MCC in 1910. He was a prolific scorer in military cricket, his most famous innings being 402* for School of Military Engineering v Royal Navy and Marines at Chatham in 1907.

Ducat, Andrew
Professional. *b:* 16.2.1886, Brixton, London. *d:* 23.7.1942, Lord's Cricket Ground, St John's Wood, London. He died of heart failure whilst batting. Sound middle order right-hand batsman, slow right-arm bowler. *Team* Surrey (1906–31, 422 matches). *Tour* MCC to Australia 1929/30 (in emergency). *Test* England (1921, 1 match).
Career batting
429–669–59–23373–306*–38.31–52–*ct* 206
Bowling 903–21–43.00–0–0–3/12
Test batting
1–2–0–5–3–2.50–0–*ct* 1
He hit 1,000 runs in a season 14 times, exceeding 2,000 once: 2,067, av 49.21, in 1930. He scored eight double centuries, all for Surrey, including one 300 – 306* v Oxford U at the Oval 1919. A noted soccer player he appeared for Aston Villa, Southend, Woolwich Arsenal and Fulham and was capped six times for England. He captained Aston Villa to win the FA Cup in 1920.

Duckfield, Richard George
Amateur in 1930, professional from 1931. *b:* 2.7.1907, Maesteg, Glamorgan. *d:* 30.12.1959, Bridgend, Glamorgan. Middle order right-hand batsman, right-arm medium pace bowler. *Team* Glamorgan (1930–38, 191 matches).
Career batting
192–302–39–7000–280*–26.61–10–*ct* 27
Bowling 255–0

He hit 1,000 runs in a season three times (best 1,343, av 37.30, in 1933). His only double century was 280* for Glamorgan v Surrey at the Oval in 1936. A useful rugby footballer, he appeared for Maesteg.

Duckworth, Christopher Anthony Russell
Amateur. *b:* 22.3.1933, Que Que, Rhodesia. Opening right-hand batsman, wicket-keeper. *Teams* Natal (1952/3 to 1953/4); Rhodesia (1954/5 to 1962/3). *Tours* South Africa to England 1955, 1960. *Tests* South Africa (1956/7, 2 matches).
Career batting
77–124–12–2572–158–22.96–3–*ct* 91–*st* 13
Test batting
2–4–0–28–13–7.00–0–*ct* 3
Selected as reserve wicket-keeper on his two visits to England, his opportunities were very limited.

Duckworth, George
Professional. *b:* 9.5.1901, Warrington, Lancashire. *d:* 5.1.1966, Warrington, Lancashire. Lower order right-hand batsman, wicket-keeper. *Team* Lancashire (1923–38, 424 matches). *Tours* MCC to Australia 1928/9, to South Africa 1930/1, to Australia and New Zealand 1932/3, 1936/7. *Tests* England (1924–36, 24 matches).
Career batting
504–545–206–4945–75–14.58–0–*ct* 753–*st* 343
Bowling 73–0
Test batting
24–28–12–234–39*–14.62–0–*ct* 45–*st* 15
He managed three Commonwealth teams to the Indian subcontinent: 1949/50, 1950/1 and 1953/4. One of the outstanding wicket-keepers of his day, he was small of stature but loud of voice. His final first-class match was for North v South in 1947. He also played for Cheshire (1939).

Dudhia, Maqbul Hussein Ebrahim Mahomed
Cricketer. *b:* 24.8.1954, Lusaka, Northern Rhodesia. Brother of Sadiq (Zimbabwe). Lower order right-hand batsman, right-arm medium pace bowler. *Team* Zimbabwe (1980/1 to 1982). *Tour* Zimbabwe to England 1982.
Career batting
2–1–0–0–0–0.00–0–*ct* 0
Bowling 71–5–14.20–0–0–2/13

Dudleston, Barry
Cricketer. *b:* 16.7.1945, Bebington, Cheshire. Sound opening or middle order right-hand batsman, slow left-arm bowler, occasional wicket-keeper. *Teams* Leicestershire (1966–80, 262 matches); Gloucestershire (1981–83, 9 matches); Rhodesia (1976/7 to 1979/80). *Tour* Robins to West Indies 1974/5 (not first-class).
Career batting
295–501–47–14747–202–32.48–32–*ct* 234–*st* 7
Bowling 1365–47–29.04–0–0–4/6
He hit 1,000 runs in a season eight times (best 1,374, av 31.22, in 1970). His only double century was 202 for Leicestershire v Derbyshire at Leicester in 1979. He was appointed coach to Gloucestershire in 1981 and then became a first-class umpire in 1989, standing in 2 Test matches (1991–92).

Dudley-Jones, Robert David Louis
Cricketer. *b:* 26.5.1952, Bridgend, Glamorgan. Lower order right-hand batsman, right-arm medium pace bowler. *Sch* Millfield. *Team* Glamorgan (1972–73, 5 matches).
Career batting
5–7–2–15–5–3.00–0–*ct* 1
Bowling 351–13–27.00–0–0–4/31
He played rugby for Cardiff and Bridgend.

Dudman, Leonard Charles
Amateur. *b:* 4.8.1933, Dundee, Angus, Scotland. Opening right-hand batsman. *Team* Scotland (1955–68).
Career batting
35–61–3–1286–161–22.17–1–*ct* 20
He played soccer for Falkirk and Forfar.

Dudney, William Hudson
Amateur. *b:* 8.1.1860, Portslade, Sussex. *d:* 16.6.1922, Aldrington, Hove, Sussex. Middle order right-hand batsman, wicket-keeper. *Sch* Cranleigh. *Teams* Canterbury (1883/4); Sussex (1887–93, 29 matches).
Career batting
36–67–4–912–97–14.47–0–*ct* 38–*st* 6

Duers, Kevin Gary
Cricketer. *b:* 30.6.1960, Lusaka, Northern Rhodesia. Lower order right-hand batsman, right-arm medium pace bowler. *Team* Zimbabwe (1984/5 to 1990/1). *Tours* Zimbabwe to England 1985, 1990, to Australia and New Zealand (World Cup) 1991/2.
Career batting
28–28–16–96–15*–8.00–0–*ct* 8
Bowling 2363–72–32.81–2–0–8/102

Duff, Alan Robert
Amateur. *b:* 12.1.1938, Dunsley, Kinver, Staffordshire. *d:* 28.6.1989, Malvern, Worcestershire. Lower order right-hand batsman, leg break and googly bowler. *Sch* Radley. *Teams* Oxford U (1959–61, blue 1960–61); Worcestershire (1960–61, 6 matches). *Tours* MCC to South America 1964/5, to Bangladesh 1976/7, 1978/9 (none of these first-class).
Career batting
36–57–16–676–55*–16.48–0–*ct* 33
Bowling 1396–54–25.85–0–0–4/24
His final first-class match was for MCC in 1968. An outstanding schoolboy cricketer, his County cricket was limited due to his scholastic duties at Malvern.

Duff, Reginald Alexander
Amateur. *b:* 17.8.1878, Botanic Gardens, Macquarie, Sydney, New South Wales, Australia. *d:* 13.12.1911, St Leonards, North Sydney, New South Wales, Australia, from alcoholism. Brother of W. S. (New South Wales). Opening right-hand batsman, right-arm medium pace bowler. *Team* New South Wales (1898/9 to 1907/8, 38 matches). *Tours* Australia to England 1902, 1905, to South Africa 1902/3, to New Zealand 1904/5. *Tests* Australia (1901/2 to 1905, 22 matches).
Career batting
121–197–9–6589–271–35.04–10–*ct* 73
Bowling 478–14–34.14–0–0–2/17
Test batting
22–40–3–1317–146–35.59–2–*ct* 14
Bowling 85–4–21.25–0–0–2/43

He hit 1,000 runs on both his tours to England (best 1,403, av 22.50, in 1902). His only double century was 271 for New South Wales v South Australia at Sydney in 1903/4. He scored a century in both his first and last Test match.

Duffield, John
Professional. *b:* 12.8.1917, Worthing, Sussex. *d:* 7.9.1956, Findon Valley, Worthing, Sussex. Lower order right-hand batsman, right-arm fast medium bowler. *Team* Sussex (1938–47, 16 matches).
Career batting
16–23–6–263–60*–15.47–0–*ct* 3
Bowling 1043–29–35.96–1–0–5/38

A noted soccer player, he appeared for Portsmouth.

Duffy, Gerald Andrew Anthony
Amateur. *b:* 4.11.1930, Dublin, Ireland. Middle order right-hand batsman, leg break bowler. *Team* Ireland (1953–73).
Career batting
16–27–6–317–55*–15.09–0–*ct* 12
Bowling 426–15–28.40–0–0–3/8

Dujon, Peter Jeffrey Leroy
Cricketer. *b:* 28.5.1956, Kingston, Jamaica. Son of L. V. (Jamaica). Middle order right-hand batsman, occasional right-arm medium pace bowler, wicket-keeper. *Team* Jamaica (1974/5 to 1991/2). *Tours* Young West Indies to Zimbabwe 1981/2; West Indies to Australia 1981/2, 1983/4 (not first-class), 1984/5, 1986/7 (not first-class), 1988/9, to India 1983/4, 1987/8, 1989/90 (not first-class), to England 1983 (World Cup), 1984, 1988, 1991, to Pakistan 1985/6 (not first-class), 1986/7, 1990/1, to Sharjah (not first-class) 1985/6, 1986/7, 1988/9, 1989/90, 1991/2, to New Zealand 1986/7, to India and Pakistan (World Cup) 1987/8; Rest of World to England 1987, 1989. *Tests* West Indies (1981/2 to 1991, 81 matches).
Career batting
194–289–45–9308–151*–38.14–19–*ct* 434–*st* 19
Bowling 45–1–45.00–0–0–1/43
Test batting
81–115–11–3322–139–31.94–5–*ct* 267–*st* 5

He became the regular West Indian wicket-keeper in 1981/2 and retained his position during three tours to England.

Duleepsinhji, Kumar Shri
(known in India as Jawansinhji Jadeja Duleepsinhji)
Amateur. *b:* 13.6.1905, Sarodar, India. *d:* 5.12.1959, Bombay, India, from a heart attack. Nephew of K. S. Ranjitsinhji (Sussex), uncle of K. S. Indrajitsinhji (India), Hanumant Singh (India) and Suryaveer Singh (Rajasthan). Middle order right-hand batsman, good slip field, leg break bowler. *Sch* Cheltenham. *Teams* Sussex (1924–32, 119 matches); Cambridge U (1925–28, blue 1925–26 and 1928); Hindus (1928/9). *Tour* MCC to Australia and New Zealand 1929/30. *Tests* England (1929–31, 12 matches).
Career batting
205–333–23–15485–333–49.95–50–*ct* 256
Bowling 1345–28–48.03–0–0–4/49
Test batting
12–19–2–995–173–58.52–3–*ct* 10
Bowling 7–0

He hit 1,000 runs in a season 7 times, going on to 2,000 three times (best 2,684, av 54.77, in 1931). His highest innings was 333 for Sussex v Northamptonshire at Hove in 1930 and he made three other scores over 200. He captained Sussex in 1931–32. Ill-health forced him to retire from first-class cricket in 1932. In the 1950s he was Indian High Commissioner in Australia and New Zealand. He also won a blue for rackets.

Dumbleton, Horatio Norris
Amateur. *b:* 23.10.1858, Ferozepore, India. *d:* 18.12.1935, Winchester, Hampshire. Middle order right-hand batsman, slow round-arm bowler. *Sch* Wimbledon. *Team* Hampshire (1884, 1 match).
Career batting
1–2–0–16–9–8.00–0–*ct* 0
Bowling 14–0

A noted cricketer in military matches, he hit 325 for the Royal Engineers v Royal Marines at Portsmouth in 1884. He designed the course at the Royal Hong Kong Golf Club.

Dumbrill, Richard
Cricketer. *b:* 19.11.1938, Wandsworth, London. Middle/lower order right-hand batsman, right-arm medium pace bowler. *Teams* Natal (1960/1 to 1966/7); Transvaal (1965/6 to 1967/8). *Tour* South Africa to England 1965. *Tests* South Africa (1965 to 1966/7, 5 matches).
Career batting
51–82–7–1761–94–23.48–0–*ct* 35
Bowling 2909–132–22.03–5–1–5/34
Test batting
5–10–0–153–36–15.30–0–*ct* 3

Bowling 336–9–37.33–0–0–4/30

He appeared in all three Tests on the 1965 tour to England and in all first-class matches hit 429 runs, av 22.57, and took 31 wickets, av 21.70.

Duminy, Jacobus Petrus
Amateur. *b:* 16.12.1897, Bellville, Cape Province, South Africa. *d:* 31.1.1980, Groot Schuur, Cape Town, South Africa. Middle order left-hand batsman, slow left-arm bowler. *Teams* Western Province (1919/20); Oxford U (1921); Transvaal (1927/8 to 1928/9). *Tour* South Africa to England 1929. *Tests* South Africa (1927/8 to 1929, 3 matches).
Career batting
13–23–4–557–168*–29.31–1–*ct* 11
Bowling 368–12–30.66–1–0–6/40
Test batting
3–6–0–30–12–5.00–0–*ct* 2
Bowling 39–1–39.00–0–0–1/17

He was on holiday in Switzerland when, due to injuries, he was co-opted into the 1929 South Africa team in England.

Dummer, William
Professional. *b:* 8.10.1847, Petworth, Sussex. *d:* 17.12.1909, Nichols Town, Southampton, Hampshire. Middle order right-hand batsman, right-hand fast round arm bowler. *Team* Sussex (1869, 3 matches).
Career batting
3–6–2–60–35*–15.00–0–*ct* 3
Bowling 43–0

Duncan, Adam Seymour Dickson
Amateur. *b:* 8.6.1852. *d:* 21.2.1940, Stanborough, Hatfield, Hertfordshire. Middle order batsman. *Sch* Eton. *Team* Cambridge U (1875).
Career batting
14–25–2–313–42–13.60–0–*ct* 5

His debut in first-class cricket was for MCC in 1873 and his final first-class match was for MCC in 1879.

Duncan, Alexander William
Amateur. *b:* 19.6.1881, Crichton, Midlothian, Scotland. *d:* 18.11.1934, Angmering-on-Sea, Sussex. Middle order right-hand batsman, right-arm fast bowler. *Sch* Merchiston. *Team* Scotland (1909).
Career batting
1–1–0–31–31–31.00–0–*ct* 0
Bowling 22–0

He was a Scottish rugby international.

Duncan, Anthony Arthur
Amateur. *b:* 10.12.1914, Cardiff, Glamorgan. Opening/middle order right-hand batsman. *Sch* Rugby. *Teams* Glamorgan (1934, 2 matches); Oxford U (1935).
Career batting
3–5–1–18–15*–4.50–0–*ct* 0

He was a well-known golfer, being runner-up in the 1939 Amateur Championship and Walker Cup Captain in 1953.

Duncan, Arthur James
Amateur. *b:* 21.11.1856, Southampton, Hampshire. *d:* 26.8.1936, Wandsworth, London. Brother of D. W. J. (Hampshire). Middle order batsman. *Team* Hampshire (1878–83, 2 matches).
Career batting
2–4–0–28–26–7.00–0–*ct* 0

Duncan, Dunbar Wilson Johnston
Amateur. *b:* 8.7.1852, Southampton, Hampshire. *d:* 12.12.1919, Regent's Park, London. Brother of A. J. (Hampshire). Middle order right-hand batsman. *Team* Hampshire (1875–85, 17 matches).
Career batting
17–29–3–581–87*–22.34–0–*ct* 5
Bowling 18–3–6.00–0–0–1/1

Dunglass, Lord Alexander Frederick
(later Sir Alexander Douglas-Home, then Lord Home of the Hirsel)
Amateur. *b:* 2.7.1903, Westminster, London. Uncle of Andrew (Oxford U), father-in-law of J. A. Wolfe-Murray (Oxford U). Lower order right-hand batsman, right-arm fast medium bowler. *Sch* Eton. *Teams* Middlesex (1924–25, 2 matches); Oxford U (1926). *Tour* MCC to South America 1926/7.
Career batting
10–15–6–147–37*–16.33–0–*ct* 9
Bowling 363–12–30.25–0–0–3/43

His final first-class match was for Harlequins in 1927. He was President of MCC 1966/7. He was Unionist MP for South Lanark 1931–45; Conservative MP for Lanark 1950–51; Secretary of State for Commonwealth Relations 1955–60; Lord President of the Council and Leader of the House of Lord's 1957–60; Secretary of State for Foreign Affairs 1960–63; Prime Minister 1963–64; Leader of the Opposition 1964–65; Secretary of State for Foreign and Commonwealth Affairs 1970–74. He disclaimed his peerage in 1963 and returned to the House of Commons as Conservative MP for Kinross and West Perthshire until 1974, when he was made a Life Peer. His brother, the playwright William Douglas-Home, married the niece of D. F. Brand (Cambridge U).

Dunham, Norman Leonard
Professional. *b:* 9.12.1925, Quorn, Leicestershire. Lower order right-hand batsman, right-arm medium pace bowler. *Team* Leicestershire (1949, 1 match).
Career batting
1–2–1–15–12*–15.00–0–*ct* 1
Bowling 60–0

Dunkels, Paul Renton
Cricketer. *b:* 26.11.1947, Marylebone, London. Lower order left-hand batsman, right-arm medium

pace bowler. *Sch* Harrow. *Teams* Warwickshire (1971, 1 match); Sussex (1972, 1 match).
Career batting
3–2–1–3–3*–3.00–0–*ct* 0
Bowling 253–3–84.33–0–0–2/60
He also played for Devon (1969–75). Standing 6 feet 9 inches, he was one of the tallest ever first-class cricketers.

Dunkley, Frederick John
Professional. *b:* 9.9.1862, Chelsea, London. *d:* 11.12.1901, Marylebone, London. Lower order left-hand batsman, left-arm fast bowler. *Team* Middlesex (1886–88, 15 matches).
Career batting
15–21–4–58–11–3.41–0–*ct* 13
Bowling 1170–49–23.87–4–0–6/42

Dunkley, Maurice Edward Frank
Professional. *b:* 19.2.1914, Kettering, Northamptonshire. *d:* 27.12.1989, Preston, Rutland. Middle order right-hand batsman. *Team* Northamptonshire (1937–39, 36 matches).
Career batting
36–64–4–904–70–15.06–0–*ct* 17
Bowling 12–0
He was a noted soccer player with Northampton Town and Manchester City.

Dunlop, Angus Richard
Cricketer. *b:* 17.3.1967, Dublin, Ireland. Middle order right-hand batsman, off break bowler. *Team* Ireland (1990–92).
Career batting
2–3–0–108–56–36.00–0–*ct* 1
Bowling 143–2–71.50–0–0–1/8

Dunlop, Charles Edward
Amateur. *b:* 25.6.1870, West End, Edinburgh, Scotland. *d:* 21.8.1911, Kensington, London. Middle order right-hand batsman, good field. *Sch* Merchiston. *Team* Somerset (1892–1905, 43 matches).
Career batting
43–77–6–1172–65–16.50–0–*ct* 20
Bowling 41–2–20.50–0–0–2/29
He played in several trials at Oxford, but no first-class matches.

Dunlop, George Colquhoun Hamilton
Amateur. *b:* 28.7.1846, Edinburgh, Scotland. *d:* 7.6.1929, Crichton, Dumfries, Scotland. Uncle of T. C. (Scotland). Opening right-hand batsman. *Sch* Edinburgh Academy. *Team* Lancashire (1868, 1 match).
Career batting
1–2–0–17–16–8.50–0–*ct* 0

Dunlop, Sir Thomas Charles
Amateur. *b:* 4.2.1878, Doonside, Ayr, Scotland. *d:* 13.8.1960, Doonside, Ayr, Scotland. Nephew of G. C. H. (Lancashire). Lower order right-hand batsman, wicket-keeper. *Sch* Eton. *Team* Scotland (1911).
Career batting
1–1–0–0–0–0.00–0–*ct* 0–*st* 2

Dunn, John
Amateur. *b:* 8.6.1862, Hobart, Tasmania, Australia. *d:* 10.10.1892, Sand Is, Pescadores, Formosa. He was drowned in a shipwreck on board SS *Bokhara*. Hard hitting middle order right-hand batsman, good field. *Sch* Harrow. *Team* Surrey (1881, 4 matches). *Tour* Gentlemen of Ireland to North America 1888 (not first-class).
Career batting
7–12–1–95–38*–8.63–0–*ct* 1
He was drowned with all except two of the Hong Kong Cricket Team, which was returning from their annual match with Shanghai, when the shipwreck occurred. His final first-class match was for Gentlemen of England in 1889. He played for Ireland (not first-class) in 1887–88.

Dunning, John Angus
Amateur. *b:* 6.2.1903, Omaha, Rodney, Auckland, New Zealand. *d:* 24.6.1971, Adelaide, South Australia. Lower order right-hand batsman, right-arm medium pace off break bowler. *Teams* Oxford U (1928); Otago (1923/4 to 1937/8); Auckland (1928/9). *Tour* New Zealand to England 1937. *Tests* New Zealand (1932/3 to 1937, 4 matches).
Career batting
60–95–14–1057–45–13.04–0–*ct* 34
Bowling 6290–228–27.58–15–2–6/42
Test batting
4–6–1–38–19–7.60–0–*ct* 2
Bowling 493–5–98.60–0–0–2/35
On the 1937 tour he took 83 wickets, av 30.10, but failed in the Tests.

Dunning, Michael Lindsay
Cricketer. *b:* 11.3.1941, Windsor, Berkshire. Middle order right-hand batsman, leg break bowler. *Sch* Eton. *Team* Combined Services (1962–64).
Career batting
2–4–0–134–85–33.50–0–*ct* 0
Bowling 22–0
His County cricket was for Dorset (1964).

Dunstan, Malcolm Stephen Thomas
Cricketer. *b:* 14.10.1950, Redruth, Cornwall. Middle order right-hand batsman, right-arm medium pace bowler. *Team* Gloucestershire (1971–74, 12 matches).
Career batting
12–20–3–283–52–16.64–0–*ct* 4
He played for Cornwall (1968–72) and returned to that County (1975–89) after appearing for Gloucestershire.

Durack, John Philip
Cricketer. *b:* 18.5.1956, Perth, Western Australia. Opening right-hand batsman, leg break bowler. *Team* Oxford U (1980).
Career batting
7–13–0–136–45–10.46–0–*ct* 3
Bowling 32–0

Durandu, Arthur
Amateur. *b:* 25.12.1860, Liverpool, Lancashire. *d:* 4.2.1903, Great Crosby, Liverpool, Lancashire. Middle order batsman. *Team* Lancashire (1887, 1 match).
Career batting
2–3–0–5–5–1.66–0–*ct* 2

Durden-Smith, Neil
Cricketer. *b:* 18.8.1933, Richmond, Surrey. Middle order right-hand batsman, off break bowler. *Sch* Aldenham. *Team* Combined Services (1961).
Career batting
4–6–1–111–50–22.20–0–*ct* 0
His last first-class match was for MCC in 1967. He is married to TV personality Judith Chalmers.

Durlacher, Patrick Neville
Amateur. *b:* 17.3.1903, Paddington, London. *d:* 26.2.1971, Ireland. He died suddenly whilst fishing. Opening right-hand batsman. *Sch* Wellington. *Team* Middlesex (1921–23, 5 matches).
Career batting
5–4–0–43–27–10.75–0–*ct* 3
He also played for Buckinghamshire (1920). He played no first-class matches whilst at Cambridge, but did represent the University at relay races and cross country.

Durley, Anthony William
Professional. *b:* 30.9.1933, Ilford, Essex. *d:* 1.1.1993, Luton, Bedfordshire. Lower order right-hand batsman, wicket-keeper. *Team* Essex (1957, 5 matches).
Career batting
5–8–0–38–16–4.75–0–*ct* 3
He also played for Bedfordshire (1960–76).

Durnell, Thomas Wilfred
Amateur. *b:* 17.6.1901, Cannon Hill, Birmingham. *d:* 10.4.1986, Hexham, Northumberland. Lower order left-hand batsman, right-arm fast bowler. *Team* Warwickshire (1921–30, 14 matches).
Career batting
14–13–3–21–5*–2.10–0–*ct* 7
Bowling 1190–42–28.33–3–1–7/29

Durose, Antony Jack
Cricketer. *b:* 5.10.1944, Dukinfield, Cheshire. Lower order right-hand batsman, right-arm fast medium bowler. *Team* Northamptonshire (1964–69, 70 matches).
Career batting
70–71–23–447–30–9.31–0–*ct* 24
Bowling 4035–150–26.90–2–1–7/23
He also played for Cheshire (1963–64) and Bedfordshire (1970–71).

Durston, Frederick John
Professional. *b:* 11.7.1893, Clophill, Bedfordshire. *d:* 8.4.1965, Norwood Green, Southall, Middlesex. Hard hitting lower order right-hand batsman, right-arm fast bowler, latterly medium pace. *Team* Middlesex (1919–33, 349 matches). *Tours* Cahn to Jamaica 1928/9; Brinckman to South America 1937/8 (no first-class matches). *Test* England (1921, 1 match).
Career batting
386–473–144–3918–92*–11.90–0–*ct* 257
Bowling 29279–1329–22.03–72–11–8/27
Test batting
1–2–1–8–6*–8.00–0–*ct* 0
Bowling 136–5–27.20–0–0–4/102
He took 100 wickets in a season six times (best 136, av 19.50, in 1921). He was a first-class umpire (1939). He kept goal for Brentford.

Dury, Guy Alexander Ingram
Amateur. *b:* 4.12.1895, Harrow-on-the-Hill, Middlesex. *d:* 10.8.1976, Eastbourne, Sussex. Son of T. S. (Yorkshire), he married the widow of F. S. G. Calthorpe (Sussex and Warwickshire). Middle order batsman, bowler. *Sch* Harrow. *Teams* Leveson-Gower's XI (1919); Army (1922); Free Foresters (1926).
Career batting
3–5–0–70–51–14.00–0–*ct* 0
Bowling 131–3–43.66–0–0–2/51

Dury, Theodore Seton
Amateur. *b:* 12.6.1854, Ripley, Yorkshire. *d:* 20.3.1932, Earl's Court, London. Father of G. A. I. (Army). Middle order right-hand batsman, right-hand medium pace round arm bowler. *Sch* Harrow. *Teams* Oxford U (1875–76, blue 1876); Yorkshire (1878–81, 13 matches).
Career batting
24–42–1–565–46–13.78–0–*ct* 8
Bowling 158–3–52.66–0–0–2/38
He also represented Oxford U at rackets, both singles and doubles.

Duthie, Arthur Murray
Amateur. *b:* 12.6.1881, Saharanpur, India. *d:* 3.6.1973, Chideock Court, Dorset. Lower order batsman, opening bowler. *Sch* Marlborough. *Team* Hampshire (1911, 1 match).
Career batting
1–2–0–6–5–3.00–0–*ct* 1
Bowling 141–5–28.20–0–0–3/85
He also played for Madras in Ceylon.

Duthie, Peter Gordon
Cricketer. *b:* 16.4.1959, Greenock, Renfrewshire, Scotland. Lower order right-hand batsman, right-arm medium pace bowler. *Team* Scotland (1984–91).

Career batting
5–6–1–122–54*–24.40–0–*ct* 5
Bowling 448–11–40.72–0–0–3/99

Dutnall, Frank
Professional. *b:* 30.3.1895, Canterbury, Kent. *d:* 24.10.1971, Burnley, Lancashire. Brother of William (Kent). Middle order right-hand batsman, right-arm medium pace bowler. *Team* Kent (1919–20, 4 matches).
Career batting
4–5–0–26–16–5.20–0–*ct* 1
Bowling 9–0

Dutnall, William
Amateur. *b:* 29.8.1888, Canterbury, Kent. *d:* 18.3.1960, Nunnery Fields, Canterbury, Kent. Brother of Frank (Kent). Middle order right-hand batsman, right-arm slow medium bowler. *Team* Kent (1923, 1 match).
Career batting
2–4–0–33–30–8.25–0–*ct* 0
Bowling 69–0
His first-class debut was for the Army in 1919. He and his brother frequently opened the batting for Kent Second Eleven – William playing as an amateur and his brother as a professional.

Dutton, Henry John
Amateur. *b:* 17.1.1847, Paddington, London. *d:* 1.1.1935, Hinton-Ampner House, Hampshire. Lower order batsman, change bowler. *Sch* Eton. *Team* Hampshire (1875, 1 match).
Career batting
1–2–2–7–7*–no av–0–*ct* 0
Bowling 8–0

Dutton, Richard Stuart
Cricketer. *b:* 24.11.1959, Liverpool, Lancashire. Lower order right-hand batsman, right-arm medium pace bowler. *Sch* Wrekin. *Team* Cambridge U (1981–82).
Career batting
6–6–4–7–7*–3.50–0–*ct* 2
Bowling 261–1–261.00–0–0–1/45

Dutton, Ronald Moore
Amateur. *b:* 24.11.1902, Chester, Cheshire. Middle order left-hand batsman, left-arm bowler. *Sch* Oakham. *Team* Minor Counties (1936–37).
Career batting
2–4–0–160–56–40.00–0–*ct* 1
Bowling 37–0
His County cricket was for Cheshire (1926–51).

Dwyer, John Elicius Benedict Bernard Placid Quirk Carrington
Professional. *b:* 3.5.1876, Redfern, Sydney, New South Wales, Australia. *d:* 19.10.1912, Crewe, Cheshire. Hard hitting lower order right-hand batsman, right-arm fast medium bowler. *Team* Sussex (1904–09, 61 matches).
Career batting
61–92–9–986–63*–11.87–0–*ct* 21
Bowling 5002–179–27.94–10–2–9/35
His best bowling was 9/35 for Sussex v Derbyshire at Hove in 1906. He was the great-grandson of Michael Dwyer, who was transported to Australia after the Irish insurrection of 1798.

Dyas, William George
Amateur. *b:* 6.11.1872, Madeley, Shropshire. *d:* 14.1.1940, Madeley, Shropshire. Middle order batsman, bowler. *Team* London County (1901–02).
Career batting
4–6–0–136–83–22.66–0–*ct* 0
Bowling 68–2–34.00–0–0–1/16
His County cricket was for Shropshire (1899–1900). He played hockey for England.

Dye, John Cooper James
Cricketer. *b:* 24.7.1942, Gillingham, Kent. Tail end right-hand batsman, left-arm fast medium bowler. *Teams* Kent (1962–71, 149 matches); Northamptonshire (1972–77, 112 matches); Eastern Province (1972/3).
Career batting
266–247–125–778–29*–6.37–0–*ct* 53
Bowling 17272–725–23.82–22–2–7/45
He also played for Bedfordshire (1978–79).

Dyer, Alan Willoughby
Cricketer. *b:* 8.7.1945, Winchester, Hampshire. Middle order right-hand batsman, wicket-keeper. *Sch* Mill Hill. *Team* Oxford U (1965–66, blue both years).
Career batting
25–41–9–765–67–23.90–0–*ct* 34–*st* 2

Dyer, David Dennis
Cricketer. *b:* 3.12.1946, Berea, Durban, South Africa. Son of D. V. (Natal), brother of G. D. (Western Province and Natal). Middle order right-hand batsman, slow right-arm bowler, wicket-keeper. *Teams* Natal (1967/8 to 1974/5); Transvaal (1975/6 to 1981/2). *Tour* South African Universities to England 1967.
Career batting
109–191–18–5651–196*–32.66–8–*ct* 149–*st* 8
Bowling 46–0
He made his first-class debut for South African Universities in 1965/6.

Dyer, Dennis Victor
Amateur. *b:* 2.5.1914, Berea, Durban, South Africa. *d:* 16.6.1990, Durban, South Africa. Father of D. D. (Natal and Transvaal) and G. D. (Western Province and Natal). Opening right-hand batsman, slow left-arm bowler. *Team* Natal (1939/40 to 1948/9). *Tour* South Africa to England 1947. *Tests* South Africa (1947, 3 matches).
Career batting
34–53–7–1725–185–37.50–3–*ct* 20

Bowling 16–0
Test batting
3–6–0–96–62–16.00–0–*ct* 0

He had a modest tour in 1947, being hampered by ill-health. He scored 185 on debut for Natal v Western Province at Pietermaritzburg in 1939/40.

Dyer, Geoffrey Barry Alexander
Cricketer. *b:* 14.5.1969, Glasgow, Scotland. Middle order right-hand batsman, off break bowler. *Sch* Glasgow Academy. *Team* Cambridge U (1990).
Career batting
4–8–2–107–23–17.83–0–*ct* 0

Dyer, Robin Ian Henry Benbow
Cricketer. *b:* 22.12.1958, Hertford. Middle order right-hand batsman, right-arm medium pace bowler. *Sch* Wellington. *Team* Warwickshire (1981–86, 65 matches).
Career batting
65–116–11–2843–109*–27.07–3–*ct* 39
Bowling 41–0

He hit 1,000 runs in a season twice (best 1,242, av 28.88, in 1985).

Dyke, Rev Canon Edwin Francis
Amateur. *b:* 27.9.1842, London. *d:* 26.8.1919, Maidstone, Kent. Nephew of J. D. (Kent), T. H. (Kent) and P. H. (Kent), cousin of W. H. (Gentlemen of Kent) and H. Jenner-Fust (Gloucestershire), nephew of H. Jenner (Kent), C. H. Jenner (Cambridge U) and H. L. Jenner (Cambridge U), brother-in-law of F. A. Currie (MCC). Lower order right-hand batsman, left-arm medium pace bowler, good field *Sch* Eton. *Team* Cambridge U (1864–65, blue 1865).
Career batting
6–11–2–132–46–14.66–0–*ct* 6
Bowling 248–19–13.05–1–1–6/14

His final first-class match was for MCC in 1866.

Dymock, Geoffrey
Cricketer. *b:* 21.7.1945, Maryborough, Queensland, Australia. Lower order left-hand batsman, left-arm fast medium bowler. *Team* Queensland (1971/2 to 1981/2, 87 matches). *Tours* Australia to New Zealand 1973/4, to England 1977, 1979 (World Cup), 1980, to Pakistan 1979/80, to India 1979/80. *Tests* Australia (1973/4 to 1979/80, 21 matches).
Career batting
126–159–54–1518–101*–14.45–1–*ct* 41
Bowling 11438–425–26.91–13–1–7/67
Test batting
21–32–7–236–31*–9.44–0–*ct* 1
Bowling 2116–78–27.12–5–1–7/67

He took only 15 wickets, av 31.20, on the 1977 tour to England and did not appear in the Tests. On the brief visit in 1980 he achieved little.

Dynes, Ernest Desmond
Amateur. *b:* 30.3.1903, Bedford. *d:* 21.6.1968, Ipswich, Suffolk. Middle order right-hand batsman, leg break bowler. *Sch* Bedford Modern. *Teams* Minor Counties (1928–30); Army (1929–31).
Career batting
9–17–2–410–127–27.33–1–*ct* 7
Bowling 511–34–15.02–2–0–5/31

His County cricket was for Bedfordshire (1921–37).

Dyson, Arnold Herbert
Professional. *b:* 10.7.1905, Halifax, Yorkshire. *d:* 7.6.1978, Goldsborough, Yorkshire. Sound opening right-hand batsman, excellent field. *Team* Glamorgan (1926–48, 412 matches). *Tour* Cahn to New Zealand 1938/9.
Career batting
413–697–37–17922–208–27.15–24–*ct* 243–*st* 1
Bowling 160–1–160.00–0–0–1/9

He hit 1,000 runs in a season ten times (best 1,884, av 40.95, in 1938). His only double century was 208 for Glamorgan v Surrey at the Oval in 1932.

Dyson, Edward Martin
Amateur. *b:* 21.10.1935, Sandal, Wakefield, Yorkshire. Opening right-hand batsman. *Team* Oxford U (1958–60, blue 1958).
Career batting
27–48–3–819–68*–18.20–0–*ct* 16
Bowling 8–0

His final first-class match was for MCC in 1968.

Dyson, Jack
Professional. *b:* 8.7.1934, Oldham, Lancashire. Opening right-hand batsman, off break bowler. *Team* Lancashire (1954–64, 150 matches).
Career batting
150–242–35–4433–118*–21.41–1–*ct* 55
Bowling 4447–161–27.62–8–1–7/83

He hit 1,087 runs in 1956, av 27.17. He also played for Staffordshire (1965). A noted soccer player he was inside left for Manchester City, scoring in their 1956 FA Cup final victory, and also played for Oldham.

Dyson, John
Cricketer. *b:* 11.6.1954, Kogarah, Sydney, New South Wales, Australia. Steady opening right-hand batsman, right arm slow medium bowler. *Team* New South Wales (1975/6 to 1988/9, 94 matches). *Tours* Australia to England 1980, 1981, to Sri Lanka 1980/1, to New Zealand 1981/2, to Pakistan 1982/3; Australian XI to South Africa 1985/6, 1986/7. *Tests* Australia (1977/8 to 1984/5, 30 matches).
Career batting
156–278–31–9935–241–40.22–19–*ct* 99
Bowling 66–2–33.00–0–0–1/0
Test batting
30–58–7–1359–127*–26.64–2–*ct* 10

On the 1981 tour to England he hit 582 runs, av 30.63, and appeared in five of the six Tests. His highest score was 241 for New South Wales v South Australia at Adelaide in 1983/4.

Dyson, John Humphrey
Amateur. *b:* 28.9.1913, Honley, Yorkshire. *d:* 16.7.1991, Wonford, Exeter, Devon. Lower order right-hand batsman, slow left-arm bowler. *Sch* Charterhouse. *Team* Oxford U (1933–36, blue 1936).
Career batting
26–40–12–211–35–7.53–0–*ct* 8
Bowling 2144–68–31.52–3–0–6/47

His last first-class match was for Free Foresters in 1938.

Dyson, William Lord
Professional. *b:* 11.12.1857, Halifax, Yorkshire. *d:* 1.5.1936, Brighouse, Yorkshire. Middle order right-hand batsman. *Team* Yorkshire (1887, 2 matches).
Career batting
2–4–0–8–6–2.00–0–*ct* 2

E

Eadie, John Thom Clarke
Amateur. *b:* 25.9.1861, Burton-on-Trent, Staffordshire. *d:* 19.8.1923, Aldershawe, Lichfield, Staffordshire. Brother of W. S. (Derbyshire), uncle of K. W. C. Dobson (Derbyshire and Warwickshire). Lower order batsman, bowler. *Team* Derbyshire (1882, 1 match).
Career batting
1–2–1–8–8*–8.00–0–*ct* 0
Bowling 6–1–6.00–0–0–1/6

He was Derbyshire President in 1899.

Eadie, William Stewart
Amateur. *b:* 27.11.1864, Burton-on-Trent, Staffordshire. *d:* 20.9.1914, Barrow-upon-Trent, Derbyshire. Brother of J. T. C. (Derbyshire), uncle of K. W. C. Dobson (Derbyshire and Warwickshire). Middle order right-hand batsman. *Sch* Dollar and Edinburgh Institution (later Melville College). *Team* Derbyshire (1885–99, 23 matches).
Career batting
23–41–3–399–62–10.50–0–*ct* 7
Bowling 13–0

Owing to business, his appearances were limited.

Eadon, Wilfred Myles
Amateur. *b:* 19.6.1915, Terry Hill, Milstead, Kent. Middle/lower order right-hand batsman, leg break and googly bowler. *Sch* Canford. *Team* Oxford U (1934).
Career batting
1–2–0–17–14–8.50–0–*ct* 0
Bowling 88–3–29.33–0–0–2/61

Eady, Charles John
Amateur. *b:* 29.10.1870, Hobart, Tasmania, Australia. *d:* 20.12.1945, Hobart, Tasmania, Australia. Middle order right-hand batsman, right-arm fast bowler. *Team* Tasmania (1889/90 to 1907/8, 20 matches). *Tour* Australia to England and North America 1896. *Tests* Australia (1896 to 1901/2, 2 matches).
Career batting
43–71–6–1490–116–22.92–3–*ct* 45
Bowling 3146–136–23.13–12–5–8/34
Test batting
2–4–1–20–10*–6.66–0–*ct* 2
Bowling 112–7–16.00–0–0–3/30

He achieved little on his tour of England. His most famous feat was an innings of 566 for Break o' Day v Wellington in March 1902. He was a member of the Tasmania Legislative Council.

Eagar, Edward Desmond Russell
Amateur. *b:* 8.12.1917, Cheltenham, Gloucestershire. *d:* 13.9.1977, Kingsbridge, Devon. Uncle of M. A. (Gloucestershire). Middle order right-hand batsman, slow left-arm bowler, excellent close field. *Sch* Cheltenham. *Teams* Gloucestershire (1935–39, 21 matches); Oxford U (1938–39, blue 1939); Hampshire (1946–57, 311 matches). *Tour* Norfolk to Jamaica 1956/7.
Career batting
363–599–42–12178–158*–21.86–10–*ct* 369
Bowling 1481–31–47.77–1–0–6/66

He hit 1,000 runs in a season 6 times (best 1,200, av 26.66, in 1949). He captained Hampshire 1946–57 and was Secretary to the County from 1946 to his death. He obtained his blue for hockey at Oxford.

He was an authority on the history of cricket. His son, Patrick, is a well-known cricket photographer.

Eagar, Michael Antony
Amateur. *b:* 20.3.1934, Kensington, London. Nephew of E. D. R. (Gloucestershire and Hampshire). Middle order right-hand batsman. *Sch* Rugby. *Teams* Oxford U (1956–59, blue all four years); Gloucestershire (1957–61, 6 matches).
Career batting
58–105–8–2465–125–25.41–1–*ct* 46
Bowling 4–0

He played for Ireland (not first-class) in 1957. A noted hockey player, he was awarded his blue and was capped for Ireland at right-wing.

Eaglestone, James Thomas
Professional. *b:* 24.7.1923, Paddington, London. Hard hitting middle order left-hand batsman. *Teams* Middlesex (1947, 9 matches); Glamorgan (1948–49, 50 matches).
Career batting
60–97–7–1420–77–15.77–0–*ct* 23

Ealham, Alan George Ernest
Cricketer. *b:* 30.8.1944, Willesborough, Ashford, Kent. Father of M. A. (Kent). Middle order right-hand batsman, off break bowler, good outfield. *Team* Kent (1966–82, 305 matches).
Career batting
305–466–68–10996–153–27.62–7–*ct* 175
Bowling 189–3–63.00–0–0–1/1
He hit 1,000 runs in a season three times (best 1,363, av 34.94, in 1971). From 1978 to 1980 he captained Kent, and since his retirement has captained Kent 2nd XI.

Ealham, Mark Alan
Cricketer. *b:* 27.8.1969, Willesborough, Ashford, Kent. Son of A. G. E. (Kent). Middle order right-hand batsman, right-arm medium fast bowler. *Team* Kent (1989–92, 25 matches).
Career batting
25–39–8–656–67*–21.16–0–*ct* 7
Bowling 1835–58–31.63–2–0–5/39

Eames, David George Roniel
Professional. *b:* 15.4.1937, London Colney, Hertfordshire. Middle order right-hand batsman, right-arm medium pace bowler. *Team* MCC (1958).
Career batting
1–2–0–21–14–10.50–0–*ct* 0
Bowling 9–0

Earl, George Burrill
(registered at death as G. B. Earle)
Professional. *b:* 7.8.1859, Melbourne, Derbyshire. *d:* 20.4.1933, Melbourne, Derbyshire. Middle order right-hand batsman, right-arm fast medium bowler. *Team* Derbyshire (1883, 1 match).
Career batting
1–1–0–4–4–4.00–0–*ct* 1
His last match for Derbyshire was in 1888 (not first-class).

Earl, Kenneth John
Amateur. *b:* 10.11.1925, Low Fell, Gateshead, Co Durham. *d:* 13.10.1986, Ryton, Co Durham. Lower order right-hand batsman, right-arm fast medium bowler. *Team* Minor Counties (1950).
Career batting
2–4–0–4–4–1.00–0–*ct* 2
Bowling 162–9–18.00–1–0–5/75
His County cricket was for Northumberland (1948–65).

Earle, Guy Fife
Amateur. *b:* 24.8.1891, Newcastle upon Tyne, Northumberland. *d:* 30.12.1966, Maperton, Wincanton, Somerset. Nephew of H. M. Grayson (Liverpool). His first wife later married M. D. Lyon (Somerset). Hard hitting middle order right-hand batsman, right-arm fast bowler. *Sch* Harrow. *Teams* Surrey (1911–21, 4 matches); Somerset (1922–31, 152 matches). *Tours* MCC to India, Burma and Ceylon 1926/7, to New Zealand and Australia 1929/30; Martineau to Egypt 1932, 1933 and 1934 (not first-class).
Career batting
188–295–7–5810–130–20.17–2–*ct* 112
Bowling 3107–104–29.87–1–0–5/137
He captained Harrow in the famous 1910 Fowler's Match. For Somerset v Gloucestershire at Taunton in 1929 he hit 59 in 15 minutes, and for MCC v Taranaki (not first-class) in 1929/30 his 98 came in 40 minutes. He was badly injured in a motor cycle accident in Egypt in 1932 and retired from first-class cricket.

Earls-Davis, Michael Richard Gratwicke
Amateur. *b:* 21.2.1921, Hampstead, London. Grandson of W. G. Heasman (Sussex). Lower order left-hand batsman, right-arm fast medium bowler. *Sch* Sherborne. *Teams* Cambridge U (1947); Somerset (1950, 1 match).
Career batting
6–7–1–14–4–2.33–0–*ct* 2
Bowling 361–12–30.08–0–0–4/87
He appeared for Cambridge U in 1940 in non first-class wartime matches, then returned to the University in 1947.

Earnshaw, George Russell Bell
Amateur. *b:* 5.5.1857, Clapham, London. *d:* 29.12.1894, Meran, Austria. Son of Alfred (Surrey 1847). Middle order right-hand batsman, good close field. *Sch* King's College. *Team* Surrey (1880, 2 matches).
Career batting
2–4–1–31–13*–10.33–0–*ct* 1
Bowling 4–0

Earnshaw, Richard Oliver
Amateur. *b:* 8.1.1939, Huddersfield, Yorkshire. *d:* 28.7.1963, Westminster, London. Lower order right-hand batsman, right-arm fast medium bowler. *Team* Combined Services (1960–61).
Career batting
2–3–1–11–9–5.50–0–*ct* 0
Bowling 211–0

Earnshaw, Wilson
Professional. *b:* 20.9.1867, Morley, Leeds, Yorkshire. *d:* 24.11.1941, Low Town, Pudsey, Yorkshire. Lower order right-hand batsman, wicket-keeper. *Team* Yorkshire (1893–96, 6 matches).
Career batting
6–7–3–44–23–11.00–0–*ct* 6–*st* 2

Easby, J.
Professional. Middle order batsman. *Team* Players of the North (1878).
Career batting
1–1–0–13–13–13.00–0–*ct* 2

Easby, Joseph William
Professional. *b:* 12.8.1867, Appleton-Wiske, Yorkshire. *d:* 7.2.1915, Dover, Kent. Sound middle order right-hand batsman, right-arm medium pace bower, wicket-keeper. *Team* Kent (1894–99, 62 matches).
Career batting
62–110–9–1851–73–18.32–0–*ct* 26–*st* 3
Bowling 424–13–32.61–0–0–2/8
A regular soldier, he showed so much promise in military matches that he was persuaded to resign and take the post of groundsman at St Lawrence, Canterbury in order to qualify for Kent. Though scoring brilliantly in club matches, he did little in first-class cricket, however. He also played for Hampshire in non first-class matches.

East, David Edward
Cricketer. *b:* 27.7.1959, Clapton, London. Lower order right-hand batsman, wicket-keeper. *Team* Essex (1981–89, 190 matches).
Career batting
190–254–32–4553–134–20.50–4–*ct* 480–*st* 53
Bowling 17–0
He caught the first eight batsmen to be dismissed in an innings for Essex v Somerset at Taunton in 1985. He recorded 83 dismissals (64 ct, 19 st) in 1986.

East, Raymond Eric
Cricketer. *b:* 20.6.1947, Manningtree, Essex. Lower order right-hand batsman, slow left-arm bowler, close field. *Team* Essex (1965–84, 405 matches). *Tours* Robins to South Africa 1973/4; Overseas XI to India 1980/1.
Career batting
410–517–112–7178–113–17.72–1–*ct* 256
Bowling 26210–1019–25.72–49–10–8/30
His best season was 1978 when he took 92 wickets, av 16.36. From 1984 to 1988 he was captain and manager of Essex 2nd XI. Although he played his cricket seriously, he was a natural clown and cheered up some otherwise dull moments. He also played for Suffolk (1991–92).

East, William
Professional. *b:* 29.8.1872, Northampton. *d:* 19.12.1926, Abington, Northampton. Middle or lower order right-hand batsman, right-arm medium pace bowler. *Team* Northamptonshire (1905–14, 157 matches).
Career batting
163–270–38–4012–86*–17.29–0–*ct* 77
Bowling 10431–499–20.90–28–4–7/71
He first appeared for Northamptonshire in 1894 and was a major force in gaining that County first-class status. His first-class debut was for MCC in 1902.

Easter, John Nicholas Cave
Cricketer. *b:* 17.12.1945, Shawford, Hampshire. Tail end right-hand batsman, right-arm medium pace bowler. *Sch* St Edwards, Oxford. *Team* Oxford U (1966–68, blue 1967–68).
Career batting
28–36–13–90–14–3.91–0–*ct* 8
Bowling 1940–58–33.44–1–0–5/62
He was a well-known squash player.

Eastman, George Frederick
Professional. *b:* 7.4.1903, Leyton, Essex. *d:* 15.3.1991, Eastbourne, Sussex. Brother of L. C. (Essex). Tail end right-hand batsman, wicket-keeper. *Team* Essex (1926–29, 48 matches).
Career batting
48–66–28–265–34*–6.97–0–*ct* 29–*st* 21
A useful soccer player, he appeared for Clapton Orient.

Eastman, Lawrence Charles
Amateur, but turned professional in 1927. *b:* 3.6.1897, Enfield Wash, Middlesex. *d:* 17.4.1941, Harefield, Middlesex, in hospital after an operation. Brother of G. F. (Essex). Middle or opening right-hand batsman, originally right-arm medium, later leg break bowler. *Teams* Essex (1920–39, 442 matches); Otago (1927/8 to 1928/9). *Tour* Brinckman to South America 1937/8.
Career batting
451–693–50–13385–161–20.81–7–*ct* 259
Bowling 26940–1006–26.77–30–3–7/28
He hit 1,000 runs in a season 5 times (best 1,338, av 32.63, in 1933). His best bowling season was 1935 when he took 99 wickets, av 19.58.

Eastwood, David
Professional. *b:* 30.3.1848, Lascelles Hall, Yorkshire. *d:* 17.5.1903, Sheepridge, Huddersfield, Yorkshire. Middle order right-hand batsman, right-hand slow round arm bowler. *Team* Yorkshire (1870–77, 29 matches).
Career batting
36–63–2–807–68–13.22–0–*ct* 20
Bowling 714–36–19.83–1–0–6/69
His final first-class match was for London United in 1879. He also played for Durham (pre first-class, 1874–75) and Northumberland (1875). He was a first-class umpire (1895).

Eato, Alwyne
Professional. *b:* 15.2.1929, Duckmanton, Derbyshire. Tail end right-hand batsman, right-arm fast medium bowler. *Team* Derbyshire (1950–55, 25 matches).
Career batting
25–28–5–220–44–9.56–0–*ct* 7
Bowling 1429–50–28.58–1–0–5/14

Eaton, Hubert Francis Joseph
Amateur. *b:* 19.1.1864, Westminster, London. *d:* 25.3.1910, Ketton, Rutland. Son of C. O. (MCC 1847), son-in-law of G. A. Campbell (Lancashire). Opening or middle order right-hand batsman. *Sch* Oratory. *Team* Cambridge U (1885).

Eaton, Vivian John

Career batting
8–14–2–173–64*–14.41–0–*ct* 4

His first-class debut was for C. I. Thornton's XI in 1884, and his last first-class match was for MCC in 1894. His County cricket was for Rutland (1883–85) and Lincolnshire (1890). He won a blue for royal tennis.

Eaton, Vivian John
Professional. *b:* 19.6.1902, Steyning, Sussex. *d:* 31.12.1972, Brighton, Sussex. Lower order right-hand batsman, wicket-keeper. *Team* Sussex (1926–46, 36 matches).
Career batting
36–52–8–465–44–10.56–0–*ct* 52–*st* 29
Bowling 5–0

Ebden, Charles Hotson Murray
Amateur. *b:* 29.6.1880, Westminster, London. *d:* 24.5.1949, Newton House, near Elvanfoot, Lanarkshire, Scotland. Brother-in-law of E. F. Penn (Cambridge U). Opening right-hand batsman. *Sch* Eton. *Teams* Cambridge U (1902–03, blue both years); Sussex (1904, 3 matches); Middlesex (1905, 2 matches); Scotland (1906). *Tour* Brackley to West Indies 1904/5.
Career batting
40–74–3–1465–137–20.63–1–*ct* 24
Bowling 89–2–44.50–0–0–1/15

His last first-class match was for MCC in 1909. He scored 137 on debut for Cambridge U v Leveson-Gower's XI at Cambridge in 1902. A noted hockey player, he represented both Cambridge and England.

Ebdon, Edward William
Amateur. *b:* 22.4.1870, Milverton, Somerset. *d:* 6.12.1950, Weston-super-Mare, Somerset. Brother of J. F. (Somerset) and P. J. (Somerset). Tail end right-hand batsman, wicket-keeper. *Team* Somerset (1891–98, 2 matches).
Career batting
2–4–1–9–5–3.00–0–*ct* 1–*st* 2

He first played for Somerset (pre first-class) in 1890. He played hockey for England.

Ebdon, John Francis
Amateur. *b:* 16.2.1876, Milverton, Somerset. *d:* 1.11.1952, Burley-in-Wharfedale, Yorkshire. Brother of E. W. (Somerset) and P. J. (Somerset). Tail end right-hand batsman, slow right-arm bowler. *Team* Somerset (1898, 1 match).
Career batting
1–2–0–2–1–1.00–0–*ct* 2
Bowling 73–0

He played hockey for England.

Ebdon, Percy John
Amateur. *b:* 16.3.1874, Milverton, Somerset. *d:* 16.2.1943, Wellington, Somerset. Brother of E. W. (Somerset) and J. F. (Somerset). Opening or middle order batsman. *Team* Somerset (1894, 2 matches).
Career batting
2–4–0–13–7–3.25–0–*ct* 1

He played rugby for England.

Ebeling, Hans Irvine, MBE
Amateur. *b:* 1.1.1905, Avoca, Victoria, Australia. *d:* 12.1.1980, East Bentleigh, Melbourne, Victoria, Australia. Lower order right-hand batsman, right-arm fast medium bowler. *Team* Victoria (1923/4 to 1937/8, 44 matches). *Tours* Australia to England 1934; Victoria to New Zealand 1924/5. *Test* Australia (1934, 1 match).
Career batting
73–83–12–1005–76–14.15–0–*ct* 38
Bowling 5768–217–26.58–7–2–7/33
Test batting
1–2–0–43–41–21.50–0–*ct* 0
Bowling 89–3–29.66–0–0–3/74

He performed usefully on his tour to England, but was always in the shadow of Grimmett and O'Reilly. He was the prime mover in the staging of the Centenary Test Match at Melbourne in 1977.

Eccles, Alexander
Amateur. *b:* 16.3.1876, Ashton-on-Ribble, Lancashire. *d:* 17.3.1919, Bilsborough Hall, Preston, Lancashire. He died suddenly whilst ploughing. Middle order right-hand batsman, good field. *Sch* Repton. *Teams* Oxford U (1896–99, blue last three years); Lancashire (1898–1907, 123 matches).
Career batting
152–244–23–5129–139–23.20–6–*ct* 95
Bowling 88–1–88.00–0–0–1/17

He hit 1,070 runs, av 26.09, in 1899.

Eccles, Charles Vernon
Amateur. *b:* 20.8.1843, Davenham, Cheshire. *d:* 21.2.1890, Bareilly, India. Brother of W. H. (MCC). Middle order right-hand batsman, slow lob bowler. *Sch* Cheltenham. *Team* Hampshire (1870–75, 2 matches).
Career batting
3–5–0–42–23–8.40–0–*ct* 0
Bowling 44–0

He also played for Devon (1868).

Eccles, Henry
Amateur. *b:* 4.3.1863, Huyton Park, Lancashire. *d:* 10.2.1931, Roby, Lancashire. Middle order right-hand batsman, right-arm fast bowler. *Sch* Uppingham. *Team* Lancashire (1885–86, 5 matches).
Career batting
6–9–1–40–14–5.00–0–*ct* 1
Bowling 5–0

His final first-class match was for Liverpool and District in 1889.

Eccles, Joseph
Amateur. *b:* 13.4.1863, Accrington, Lancashire. *d:* 2.9.1933, Barton, Preston, Lancashire. Middle order right-hand batsman. *Team* Lancashire (1886–89, 47 matches).
Career batting
49–79–6–1802–184–24.68–2–*ct* 17
Bowling 38–0

Eccles, William Hall
Amateur. *b:* 24.3.1838, Davenham, Cheshire. *d:* 18.4.1900, Folkestone, Kent. Brother of C. V. (Hampshire). Middle order right-hand batsman, good field. *Sch* Eton. *Team* MCC (1866–67).
Career batting
2–4–2–30–17–15.00–0–*ct* 0
He was Hon Sec of Hampshire CCC 1867–69, but never appeared in first-class matches for that County.

Eckersley, Peter Thorp
Amateur. *b:* 2.7.1904, Lowton, Newton-le-Willows, Lancashire. *d:* 13.8.1940. He was killed whilst serving in the RNVR in a flying accident from Eastleigh, Hampshire. Middle order right-hand batsman, good field. *Sch* Rugby. *Team* Lancashire (1923–35, 256 matches). *Tours* MCC to India, Burma and Ceylon 1926/7; Tennyson to Jamaica 1927/8; Cahn to Argentina 1929/30.
Career batting
292–339–51–5629–102*–19.54–1–*ct* 141
Bowling 348–7–49.71–0–0–2/21
He captained Lancashire 1929–35. In 1928 he gave up a political career for cricket, then in 1935 gave up cricket for politics, being Conservative MP for Manchester Exchange at his death. Whilst at Cambridge U he did not appear in first-class matches. His final first-class match was for an England XI in 1938.

Eckersley, Ronald
Amateur. *b:* 4.9.1925, Bingley, Yorkshire. Tail end right-hand batsman, left-arm medium fast bowler. *Team* Yorkshire (1945, 1 match).
Career batting
1–1–1–9–9*–no av–0–*ct* 0
Bowling 62–0
He appeared in wartime matches for Cambridge U.

Edbrooke, Roger Michael
Cricketer. *b:* 30.12.1960, Bristol. Middle order right-hand batsman. *Team* Oxford U (1982–84, blue 1984).
Career batting
11–20–2–591–84*–32.83–0–*ct* 5
He also won blues for hockey and soccer.

Eddie, William
Amateur. *b:* 19.12.1891, Brechin, Angus, Scotland. *d:* 3.9.1979, Brechin, Angus, Scotland. Lower order right-hand batsman, right-arm medium pace bowler. *Team* Scotland (1913).
Career batting
1–2–1–6–4–6.00–0–*ct* 1
Bowling 90–0

Eddington, Roderick Ian
Cricketer. *b:* 2.1.1950, Subiaco, Perth, Western Australia. Lower order left-hand batsman, slow left-arm bowler. *Team* Oxford U (1975–76).
Career batting
8–14–4–130–24–13.00–0–*ct* 4
Bowling 329–8–41.12–0–0–3/48

Eddis, Sir Basil Eden Garth
Amateur. *b:* 17.9.1881, Calcutta, India. *d:* 5.11.1971, Aldeburgh, Suffolk. Brother of B. L. (Army and Navy). Sound middle order right-hand batsman, useful change bowler. *Sch* Charterhouse. *Team* MCC (1908).
Career batting
1–2–0–62–40–31.00–0–*ct* 0

Eddis, Bruce Lindsay
Amateur. *b:* 17.8.1883, Calcutta, India. *d:* 12.5.1966, Maidenhead, Berkshire. Brother of B. E. G. (MCC). Middle order batsman. *Sch* Rugby. *Team* Army and Navy (1919).
Career batting
1–2–1–21–21*–21.00–0–*ct* 1

Ede, Edward Lee
Amateur. *b:* 22.2.1834, Itchen, Southampton, Hampshire. *d:* 7.7.1908, Southampton, Hampshire. Twin brother of G. M. (Hampshire), father of E. M. C. (Hampshire). Middle or lower order right-hand batsman, lob bowler. *Sch* Eton. *Team* Hampshire (1861–70, 17 matches).
Career batting
17–32–4–265–49–9.46–0–*ct* 6
Bowling 400–15–26.66–0–0–4/79

Ede, Edward Murray Charles
Amateur. *b:* 24.4.1881, Southampton, Hampshire. Son of E. L. (Hampshire), nephew of G. M. (Hampshire). Lower order left-hand batsman, slow left-arm bowler. *Sch* Eton. *Teams* Hampshire (1902–06, 14 matches).
Career batting
16–28–8–245–43–12.25–0–*ct* 11
Bowling 247–40–31.17–2–1–7/72
His last first-class match was for Hambledon in 1908.

Ede, George Matthew
Amateur. *b:* 22.2.1834, Itchen, Southampton, Hampshire. *d:* 13.3.1870, Sefton, Liverpool, Lancashire. Twin brother of E. L. (Hampshire), uncle of E. M. C. (Hampshire). Middle order right-hand batsman. *Sch* Eton. *Team* Hampshire (1864–69, 15 matches).
Career batting
15–29–2–257–52–9.51–0–*ct* 0
Bowling 2–1–22.00–0–0–1/22

Eden, Ernest

A well-known amateur jockey he was badly injured whilst riding at Aintree on Grand National day, and died later at Sefton. He was captain of Hampshire 1864–69.

Eden, Ernest
Professional. *b: circa* 1899, Blockley, Moreton-in-Marsh, Gloucestershire. Middle order batsman, right-arm fast medium bowler. *Teams* Gloucestershire (1921, 1 match); Worcestershire (1923, 1 match).
Career batting
2–4–1–30–18*–10.00–0–*ct* 0
He played soccer for Walsall.

Edgar, Bruce Adrian
Cricketer. *b:* 23.11.1956, Wellington, New Zealand. Son of A. J. (Wellington). Stylish opening left-hand batsman, occasional wicket-keeper. *Team* Wellington (1975/6 to 1989/90). *Tours* New Zealand to England 1978, 1979 (World Cup), 1983, 1986, to Australia 1980/1, 1985/6, to Sri Lanka 1983/4, 1984/5 (not first-class), to Pakistan 1984/5; Young New Zealand to Zimbabwe 1984/5. *Tests* New Zealand (1978–86, 39 matches).
Career batting
175–307–26–11304–203–40.22–24–*ct* 94–*st* 1
Bowling 92–2–46.00–0–0–1/0
Test batting
39–68–4–1958–161–30.59–3–*ct* 14
Bowling 3–0
Coming to England on three Test tours, he played in all the Test matches on each visit. He was most prolific on his first trip, hitting 823 runs, av 37.40. His highest score was 203 for Young New Zealand v Zimbabwe at Bulawayo in 1984/5.

Edgar, Samuel James
Amateur. *b:* 23.9.1913, Lisburn, Co Antrim, Ireland. *d:* 31.1.1937, Lisburn, Co Antrim, Ireland. Opening right-hand batsman, right-arm medium pace bowler. *Team* Ireland (1934).
Career batting
1–2–0–32–32–16.00–0–*ct* 0

Edge, Cyril Arthur
Professional. *b:* 14.12.1916, Ashton-under-Lyne, Lancashire. *d:* 5.10.1985, Ormskirk, Lancashire. Tail end right-hand batsman, right-arm fast medium bowler. *Team* Lancashire (1936–38, 8 matches).
Career batting
9–6–3–17–15*–5.66–0–*ct* 2
Bowling 873–29–30.10–0–0–4/71
His last first-class match was for Minor Counties in 1939.

Edge, Geoffrey Donald
Amateur. *b:* 8.9.1936, Eccles, Lancashire. *d:* 3.2.1989, Newport, Monmouthshire. Middle order right-hand batsman, off break bowler. *Sch* Manchester GS. *Team* Cambridge U (1957).
Career batting
2–4–0–55–33–13.75–0–*ct* 0
Bowling 2–0
He won a blue for soccer.

Edge, Harold Emerton
Professional. *b:* 8.6.1892, Market Drayton, Shropshire. *d:* 24.1.1944, Winsford, Middlewich, Cheshire. Tail end batsman, useful medium pace bowler. *Teams* Lancashire (1913, 1 match); Wales (1927–29).
Career batting
3–5–1–27–19*–6.75–0–*ct* 5
Bowling 276–4–69.00–0–0–4/115
He also played for Denbighshire (1930–31).

Edgson, Charles Leslie
Amateur. *b:* 22.8.1915, Morcott, Rutland. *d:* 28.6.1983, Brentwood, Essex. Middle order right-hand batsman. *Sch* Stamford. *Team* Leicestershire (1933–39, 14 matches).
Career batting
14–24–0–321–49–13.37–0–*ct* 4
He played in the Freshmen's match at Oxford in 1936, but no first-class matches. He was also a noted rugby and hockey player.

Edlmann, Herbert Gottlieb
Amateur. *b:* July 1840, Peckham, London. *d:* 2.3.1912, Wokingham, Berkshire. Brother-in-law of M. J. Hall (Gentlemen of South). Middle order batsman, change bowler. *Team* Gentlemen of Kent (1864).
Career batting
1–2–1–17–13*–17.00–0–*ct* 0
Bowling 8–0

Edmeades, Brian Ernest Arthur
Professional. *b:* 17.9.1941, Matlock, Derbyshire. Opening right-hand batsman, right-arm medium pace bowler. *Team* Essex (1961–76, 335 matches).
Career batting
335–555–69–12593–163–25.91–14–*ct* 105
Bowling 9688–374–25.90–10–1–7/37
He hit 1,000 runs in a season 5 times (best 1,620, av 35.21, in 1970) and took 100 wickets in a season once – 106, av 18.59, in 1966.

Edmeades, James Frederick
Amateur. *b:* 8.7.1843, Nurstead Court, Kent. *d:* 6.2.1917, Hazells, Northfleet, Kent. Middle order batsman, change bowler. *Sch* Harrow. *Team* Gentlemen of Kent (1866).
Career batting
1–2–0–26–24–13.00–0–*ct* 1
Bowling 17–0

Edmonds, James William
Cricketer. *b:* 4.6.1951, Smethwick, Staffordshire. Tail end right-hand batsman, left-arm fast medium bowler. *Team* Lancashire (1975, 1 match).

Career batting
1 match, did not bat–*ct* 0
Bowling 82–3–27.33–0–0–3/52

Edmonds, Philippe-Henri
Cricketer. *b:* 8.3.1951, Lusaka, Northern Rhodesia. Aggressive middle order right-hand batsman, slow left-arm bowler, good field. *Sch* Cranbrook. *Teams* Cambridge U (1971–73, blue all three years); Middlesex (1971–92, 257 matches); Eastern Province (1975/6). *Tours* England to Pakistan and New Zealand 1977/8, to Australia 1978/9, 1984/5 (not first-class), 1986/7, to India and Sri Lanka 1984/5, to Sharjah (not first-class) 1984/5, 1986/7, to West Indies 1985/6; International Wanderers to Rhodesia 1975/6. *Tests* England (1975–87, 51 matches).
Career batting
391–495–91–7651–142–18.93–3–*ct* 345
Bowling 31981–1246–25.66–47–9–8/53
Test batting
51–65–15–875–64–17.50–0–*ct* 42
Bowling 4273–125–34.18–2–0–7/66

The best orthodox left-arm spinner in England of his generation, his Test career, especially overseas, was irregular possibly as much due to his provocative nature as his bowling form. His best season was 1983 when he took 92 wickets, av 21.45, and his best bowling 8/53 for Middlesex v Hampshire at Bournemouth in 1984. At the close of the 1987 season he announced he was unable to spare the time for full-time County cricket, but would be available as an amateur for some matches. Middlesex rejected his offer, but he reappeared in one match in 1992. He is a member of the Middlesex CCC Committee. He captained Cambridge in 1973.

Edmonds, Roger Bertram
Professional. *b:* 2.3.1941, Moseley, Birmingham. Middle order right-hand batsman, right-arm medium pace off break bowler. *Team* Warwickshire (1962–67, 78 matches). *Tour* Warwickshire to East Africa 1967/8 (not first-class).
Career batting
78–100–31–1006–102*–14.57–1–*ct* 35
Bowling 3994–146–27.35–2–0–5/40

Edmunds, Richard Harold
Cricketer. *b:* 27.5.1970, Oakham, Rutland. *d:* 10.12.1989, Leicester. He died as a result of a road accident which occurred in Oakham on November 21, 1989. Lower order right-hand batsman, left-arm medium fast bowler. *Team* Leicestershire (1989, 2 matches).
Career batting
2–3–0–17–17–5.66–0–*ct* 0
Bowling 113–3–37.66–0–0–2/38

Edrich, Brian Robert
Professional. *b:* 18.8.1922, Cantley, Norfolk. Brother of W. J. (Middlesex), E. H. (Lancashire) and G. A. (Lancashire), cousin of J. H. (Surrey). Forcing middle order left-hand batsman, off break bowler, close field. *Teams* Kent (1947–53, 128 matches); Glamorgan (1954–56, 52 matches).
Career batting
181–302–25–5529–193*–19.96–4–*ct* 130
Bowling 4546–137–33.18–4–0–7/41

He also played for Oxfordshire (1966–71), and his last first-class match was for Minor Counties in 1967. He hit 1,267 runs, av 26.39, in 1951.

Edrich, Eric Harry
Amateur but turned professional in 1946. *b:* 27.3.1914, Lingwood, Norfolk. Brother of W. J. (Middlesex), G. A. (Lancashire) and B. R. (Kent and Glamorgan), cousin of J. H. (Surrey). Middle order right-hand batsman, wicket-keeper. *Team* Lancashire (1946–48, 33 matches).
Career batting
36–46–5–949–121–23.14–2–*ct* 38–*st* 15

He also played for Norfolk (1935–39 and 1949–51). His first-class debut was for Minor Counties in 1938.

Edrich, Geoffrey Arthur
Professional. *b:* 13.7.1918, Lingwood, Norfolk. Brother of B. R. (Kent and Glamorgan), E. H. (Lancashire) and W. J. (Middlesex), cousin of J. H. (Surrey). Middle order right-hand batsman, right-arm medium pace bowler, fine leg-slip. *Team* Lancashire (1946–58, 322 matches). *Tour* Commonwealth to India 1953/4.
Career batting
339–508–60–15600–167*–34.82–26–*ct* 331
Bowling 399–5–79.80–0–0–1/8

He hit 1,000 runs in a season eight times, exceeding 2,000 once: 2,067, av. 41.34, in 1952. He also played for Norfolk (1937–39) and Cumberland (1960–62).

Edrich, John Hugh, MBE
Professional. *b:* 21.6.1937, Blofield, Norfolk. Cousin of B. R. (Kent and Glamorgan), E. H. (Lancashire), G. A. (Lancashire) and W. J. (Middlesex). Opening left-hand batsman, right-arm medium pace bowler. *Team* Surrey (1958–78, 410 matches). *Tours* Surrey to Rhodesia 1959/60; MCC to India 1963/4, to Australia and New Zealand 1965/6, 1970/1, 1974/5, to West Indies 1967/8, to Ceylon and Pakistan 1968/9; Cavaliers to South Africa 1962/3; International Wanderers to Rhodesia 1972/3; Robins to South Africa 1973/4. *Tests* England (1963–76, 77 matches).
Career batting
564–979–104–39790–310*–45.47–103–*ct* 311
Bowling 53–0
Test batting
77–127–9–5138–310*–43.54–12–*ct* 43
Bowling 23–0

Commencing his County career with Norfolk in 1954, Edrich made his first-class debut for Combined Services in 1956 and his Surrey debut in 1958. The following season he began his long career as Surrey's opening batsman, and despite two injuries easily completed 1,000 runs – a feat he was to achieve 19 times plus twice more in overseas seasons. In six summers he went on to 2,000 runs; 1962, with 2,482, av. 51.70, being his most prolific. His highest innings came in 1965 when he made 310* for England v New Zealand at Headingley; the three other scores he made over 200 were all for Surrey.

For some 12 years he was in the England side and proved one of the most dependable of postwar Test openers. His runs were made generally by concentration and application and he kept his wicket by being rarely tempted into indiscretion – not for him the dazzling footwork and fluent strokes to which many batsmen aspire.

He captained Surrey from 1973 to 1977 and led England in one Test – at Sydney in 1974/5; he was vice-captain of the MCC touring party that winter. After leaving first-class cricket he returned to play for his native Norfolk (1979). He was a Test selector in 1981.

He was awarded the MBE in the 1977 Birthday Honours.

Edrich, William John
Professional, but turned amateur 1947. *b:* 26.3.1916, Lingwood, Norfolk. *d:* 24.4.1986, Whitehill Court, Chesham, Buckinghamshire. Brother of E. H. (Lancashire), G. A. (Lancashire) and B. R. (Kent and Glamorgan), cousin of J. H. (Surrey). Aggressive middle order right-hand batsman, right-arm fast medium bowler, also off breaks from about 1952. *Team* Middlesex (1937–58, 389 matches). *Tours* Tennyson to India 1937/8; MCC to South Africa 1938/9, to Australia and New Zealand 1946/7, 1954/5; Howard to India 1956/7. *Tests* England (1938 to 1954/5, 39 matches).
Career batting
571–964–92–36965–267*–42.39–86–*ct* 529–*st* 1
Bowling 15956–479–33.31–11–3–7/48
Test batting
39–63–2–2440–219–40.00–6–*ct* 39
Bowling 1693–41–41.29–0–0–4/68

After five successful seasons with his native Norfolk (1932–36), making his first-class debut for Minor Counties in 1934, Edrich qualified for Middlesex in 1937 and the following summer won his England cap. In each of his three pre-war seasons he hit over 2,000 runs, but his greatest year came in 1947, when his total reached 3,539, av 80.43, with 12 centuries, and he and Compton broke many records. In all he exceeded 1,000 runs in a season 15 times, going on to 2,000 nine times. Of his nine double centuries, eight were for Middlesex, with the highest 267* v Northamptonshire at Northampton in 1947. His other 200 was for England – 219 v South Africa at Durban in 1938/9. In 1938 he performed the great feat of reaching 1,000 runs before the end of May.

A most determined and courageous cricketer, his batting was none too elegant, relying mainly on pulls and hooks. His bowling was of the slinging variety and very fast for a few overs. In the field he excelled at slip. A somewhat controversial figure, he was several times dropped from the England side, only to be recalled when the Test team needed some gumption in the middle order, or even at the start.

He captained Middlesex from 1951 to 1957, the first two years being in harness with D. C. S. Compton. After retiring from Middlesex he returned to the Norfolk side for several more years of cricket (1959–71). He played soccer for Tottenham Hotspur. During the war he was awarded the DFC.

Edward, William Alfred
Amateur. *b:* 19.6.1916, Glasgow, Scotland. Middle order right-hand batsman, right-arm medium pace bowler. *Team* Scotland (1947–55).
Career batting
28–43–5–898–99–23.63–0–*ct* 10
Bowling 1475–38–38.81–0–0–4/51

Edwards, Aubrey Mansel Edward
Amateur. *b:* 4.7.1918, Penygraig, Glamorgan. Lower order right-hand batsman, right-arm medium pace bowler. *Team* Glamorgan (1947, 1 match).
Career batting
1–1–0–0–0–0.00–0–*ct* 0
Bowling 71–3–23.66–0–0–2/34

Edwards, Charles William
Amateur. *b:* 18.10.1884, Port Elizabeth, South Africa. *d:* 22.5.1938, Earl's Court, London. Middle order batsman. *Sch* Cheltenham. *Team* Gloucestershire (1911–12, 7 matches).
Career batting
7–14–0–184–42–13.14–0–*ct* 7
Bowling 28–0

Edwards, Sir Fleetwood Isham
Amateur. *b:* 21.4.1842, Thames Ditton, Surrey. *d:* 14.8.1910, Lindfield Manor, Sussex. Brother-in-law of W. A. Smith-Masters (Kent), son-in-law of A. Cowburn (Oxford U 1841). Middle order right-hand batsman. *Sch* Harrow and Uppingham. *Team* I Zingari (1866).
Career batting
1–2–1–39–27*–39.00–0–*ct* 0
Bowling 8–1–8.00–0–0–1/8

Edwards, Frank
Professional. *b:* 23.5.1885, Merstham, Surrey. *d:* 10.7.1970, Winscombe, Somerset. Lower order left-hand batsman, originally medium then slow left-arm bowler. *Team* Surrey (1909, 1 match).
Career batting
6–8–0–31–10–3.87–0–*ct* 1
Bowling 399–19–21.00–1–1–8/98

He joined Buckinghamshire in 1914 and from then until the Second World War was one of the leading Minor County bowlers. In all he took over 1,000 wickets for his adopted County. His final first-class match was for the Minor Counties in 1933.

Edwards, Gordon
Cricketer. *b:* 17.9.1947, Glapthorn, Northamptonshire. Lower order left-hand batsman, off break bowler. *Sch* Oundle. *Team* Nottinghamshire (1973, 9 matches).
Career batting
9–16–4–191–46*–15.91–0–*ct* 5
Bowling 224–12–18.66–1–0–5/44

Edwards, Graham Neil
Cricketer. *b:* 27.5.1955, Nelson, New Zealand. Attacking middle order right-hand batsman, wicket-keeper. *Team* Central Districts (1973/4 to 1984/5). *Tours* New Zealand to Australia 1974/5 (not first-class), to England 1978. *Tests* New Zealand (1976/7 to 1980/1, 8 matches).
Career batting
92–164–8–4589–177*–29.41–5–*ct* 126–*st* 16
Bowling 32–0
Test batting
8–15–0–377–55–25.13–0–*ct* 7
The main wicket-keeper on the 1978 tour to England, he played in the first two Tests, but was then dropped due to lack of form.

Edwards, Guy Janion
Amateur. *b:* 11.5.1881, Kensington, London. *d:* 30.9.1962, Rockcliff House, Upper Slaughter, Gloucestershire. Uncle of A. McCorquodale (Middlesex). Middle order right-hand batsman. *Sch* Eton. *Team* Essex (1907, 2 matches).
Career batting
2–3–0–45–21–15.00–0–*ct* 2

Edwards, Henry Richard
Amateur. *b:* 1861. *d:* 22.6.1921, Haywards Heath, Sussex. Middle order batsman. *Team* Sussex (1885, 1 match).
Career batting
1–2–0–0–0–0.00–0–*ct* 0

Edwards, Herbert Charles
Amateur. *b:* 3.12.1913, Colley Gate, Staffordshire. Middle order right-hand batsman, leg break bowler. *Team* Worcestershire (1946, 1 match).
Career batting
1–2–0–11–10–5.50–0–*ct* 1

Edwards, Herbert Ivor Powell
(also known as Powell-Edwards)
Amateur. *b:* 12.3.1884, Westminster, London. *d:* 24.9.1946, Cowes, Isle of Wight. Middle order right-hand batsman. *Sch* Winchester. *Team* Sussex (1908, 1 match).
Career batting
1–2–0–22–15–11.00–0–*ct* 0

Edwards, John Dunlop
Amateur. *b:* 12.6.1862, Prahran, Melbourne, Victoria, Australia. *d:* 31.7.1911, Hawksburn, Victoria, Australia. Steady middle order right-hand batsman, leg break bowler. *Team* Victoria (1880/1 to 1889/90, 9 matches). *Tour* Australia to England 1888. *Tests* Australia (1888, 3 matches).
Career batting
50–84–14–961–65–13.72–0–*ct* 19
Bowling 194–7–27.71–0–0–2/6
Test batting
3–6–1–48–26–9.60–0–*ct* 1
He achieved very little on his visit to England.

Edwards, Michael John
Professional. *b:* 1.3.1940, Balham, London. Opening right-hand batsman, off break bowler, excellent close field. *Sch* Alleyns. *Teams* Cambridge U (1960–62); Surrey (1961–74, 236 matches). *Tours* Commonwealth to Pakistan 1967/8; Norfolk to West Indies 1969/70.
Career batting
256–452–26–11378–137–26.70–12–*ct* 273
Bowling 179–2–89.50–0–0–2/53
He hit 1,000 runs in a season five times (best 1,428, av 36.61, in 1969).

Edwards, Patrick Gervase
Cricketer. *b:* 21.10.1965, Bradford-on-Avon, Wiltshire. Lower order right-hand batsman, slow left-arm bowler. *Sch* Canford. *Team* Oxford U (1987–89, blue all three years).
Career batting
19–22–12–83–10*–8.30–0–*ct* 6
Bowling 1726–40–43.15–0–0–4/93

Edwards, Philip George
Professional. *b:* 6.12.1906, Hoxton, London. *d:* 3.4.1987, Hampstead, London. Lower order right-hand batsman, slow left-arm bowler. *Team* Middlesex (1930–33, 4 matches).
Career batting
4–5–2–12–10–4.00–0–*ct* 1
Bowling 140–1–140.00–0–0–1/35

Edwards, Reginald Owen
Amateur. *b:* 17.10.1881, Great Yarmouth, Norfolk. *d:* 15.11.1925, Bishop's Stortford, Hertfordshire. Middle order right-hand batsman. *Sch* Christs Hospital. *Team* Rest of England (1922).
Career batting
1–2–1–1–1–1.00–0–*ct* 0
His County cricket was for Norfolk (1920) and Cambridgeshire (1921–22) and he went on several minor tours abroad with Incognti and MCC. During an expedition to Southern Russia just after the First

World War, he lost all his baggage save for his set of Wisdens which always travelled with him.

Edwards, Richard Martin
Cricketer. *b:* 3.6.1940, Garden Gap, Worthing, Christ Church, Barbados. Lower order right-hand batsman, right-arm fast bowler. *Team* Barbados (1961/2 to 1969/70). *Tours* Barbados to England 1969; West Indies to Australia and New Zealand 1968/9. *Tests* West Indies (1968/9, 5 matches).
Career batting
35–43–10–389–34–11.78–0–*ct* 15
Bowling 2831–78–36.29–3–0–6/45
Test batting
5–8–1–65–22–9.28–0–*ct* 0
Bowling 626–18–34.77–1–0–5/84

Edwards, Ross
Cricketer. *b:* 1.12.1942, Cottesloe, Perth, Western Australia. Son of E. K. (Western Australia). Middle order right-hand batsman, occasional wicket-keeper. *Teams* Western Australia (1964/5 to 1974/5, 71 matches); New South Wales (1979/80, 5 matches). *Tours* Australia to England 1972, 1975, to West Indies 1972/3. *Tests* Australia (1972–75, 20 matches).
Career batting
126–212–25–7345–170*–39.27–14–*ct* 111–*st* 11
Bowling 75–1–75.00–0–0–1/24
Test batting
20–32–3–1171–170*–40.37–2–*ct* 7
Bowling 20–0

Edwards, Timothy David Warneford
Cricketer. *b:* 6.12.1958, Merton, Surrey. Middle order left-hand batsman. *Sch* Sherborne. *Team* Cambridge U (1979–81, blue 1981).
Career batting
12–21–2–393–57–20.68–0–*ct* 5
Bowling 58–1–58.00–0–0–1/17

Edwards, William
Amateur. *b:* 27.6.1859, Bloomsbury, London. *d:* 21.8.1947, St Pancras, London. Middle order right-hand batsman, right-arm slow bowler. *Sch* Hurstpierpoint. *Team* Kent (1884, 2 matches).
Career batting
2–4–1–44–25–14.66–0–*ct* 0
Bowling 27–3–9.00–0–0–3/16
He broke his leg playing football in 1885 and this injury handicapped his cricket.

Eele, Peter James
Professional. *b:* 27.1.1935, Taunton, Somerset. Lower order left-hand batsman, wicket-keeper. *Sch* Taunton. *Team* Somerset (1958–65, 54 matches).
Career batting
54–70–20–612–103*–12.24–1–*ct* 87–*st* 19
He was a first-class umpire from 1981 until 1984, returning to the list in 1989. He also played for Devon (1966–72).

Eggar, John Drennan
Amateur. *b:* 1.12.1916, Nowshera, India. *d:* 3.5.1983, Hinton St George, Somerset, whilst playing tennis. Son-in-law of J. L. Crommelin-Brown (Derbyshire). Sound middle order right-hand batsman, right-arm bowler. *Sch* Winchester. *Teams* Oxford U (1938, blue); Hampshire (1938, 2 matches); Derbyshire (1946–54, 31 matches).
Career batting
41–64–6–1847–219–31.84–4–*ct* 20
Bowling 193–1–193.00–0–0–1/2
His only double century was 219 for Derbyshire v Yorkshire at Bradford in 1949. His County cricket was restricted due to his scholastic duties.

Eglington, Richard
Amateur. *b:* 1.4.1908, Esher, Surrey. *d:* 20.3.1979, Winchester, Hampshire. Middle order right-hand batsman. *Sch* Sherborne. *Team* Surrey (1938, 2 matches).
Career batting
3–4–0–82–34–20.50–0–*ct* 1
He captained Surrey 2nd XI in the Minor Counties Competition in 1938–39 and his last first-class match was for the Minor Counties in 1939. He played in trial matches at Oxford U, but not in first-class games.

Ehtesham-ud-din
Cricketer. *b:* 4.9.1950, Lahore, Pakistan. Lower order right-hand batsman, right-arm medium pace bowler. *Teams* Punjab Univ (1969/70); Lahore (1970/1 to 1974/5); PIA (1972/3); Punjab (1973/4); National Bank (1973/4 to 1981/2); United Bank (1982/3 to 1985/6). *Tours* Pakistan Under 25 to Sri Lanka 1973/4; Pakistan to India 1979/80, to England 1982. *Tests* Pakistan (1979/80 to 1982, 5 matches).
Career batting
134–145–52–1059–83–11.38–0–*ct* 39
Bowling 10414–507–20.54–37–8–9/124
Test batting
5–3–1–2–2–1.00–0–*ct* 2
Bowling 375–16–23.43–1–0–5/47
He was co-opted into the 1982 touring team and appeared in two matches, one of which was the third Test. His best bowling was 9/124 for United Bank v Muslim Commercial Bank at Lahore in 1984/5.

Elam, Frederick William
Amateur. *b:* 13.9.1871, Hunslet, Yorkshire. *d:* 19.3.1943, Headingley, Leeds, Yorkshire. Opening right-hand batsman, right-arm fast bowler. *Team* Yorkshire (1900–02, 2 matches).
Career batting
2–3–1–48–28–24.00–0–*ct* 0

Elder, John Watson George
Cricketer. *b:* 16.8.1949, Bangor, Co Down, Ireland. Lower order right-hand batsman, right-arm fast medium bowler. *Team* Ireland (1973–85).

Career batting
9–9–3–36–11*–6.00–0–*ct* 7
Bowling 337–14–24.07–0–0–3/56

Elderkin, Thomas
Amateur. *b:* 19.7.1909, Peterborough, Northamptonshire. *d:* 9.12.1961, Peterborough, Northamptonshire. Middle order right-hand batsman. *Team* Northamptonshire (1934, 1 match).
Career batting
1–2–0–13–13–6.50–0–*ct* 0

Elderton, Merrick Beaufoy
Amateur. *b:* 21.2.1884, Brentford, Middlesex. *d:* 11.12.1939, Sherborne, Dorset. Middle order right-hand batsman, wicket-keeper. *Sch* Merchant Taylors. *Team* Cambridge U (1907).
Career batting
5–6–0–74–24–12.33–0–*ct* 4–*st* 5
His County cricket was for Dorset (1921–38) and his final first-class match for the Minor Counties in 1931. He won a blue for lacrosse.

Elers, Charles George Carew
Amateur. *b:* 2.1.1867, Lyme Regis, Dorset. *d:* 11.12.1927, Maryfield, Antony, Torpoint, Cornwall. Attractive middle order batsman, wicket-keeper. *Team* West of England (1910).
Career batting
1–1–0–4–4–4.00–0–*ct* 5–*st* 1
His County cricket was for Devon (1896) and Glamorgan (pre first-class, 1910–11).

Elgie, Michael Kelsey
Amateur. *b:* 6.3.1933, Berea, Durban, South Africa. Middle order right-hand batsman, slow left-arm bowler. *Team* Natal (1957/8 to 1961/2). *Tour* SA Fezela to England 1961. *Tests* South Africa (1961/2, 3 matches).
Career batting
32–55–5–1834–162*–36.68–3–*ct* 25
Bowling 405–10–40.50–0–0–3/16
Test batting
3–6–0–75–56–12.50–0–*ct* 4
Bowling 46–0
An excellent rugby footballer, he represented Middlesex and Scotland.

Elgood, Bernard Cyril
Amateur. *b:* 10.3.1922, Hampstead, London. Middle order right-hand batsman, *Sch* Bradfield. *Teams* Cambridge U (1948, blue).
Career batting
14–21–2–631–127*–33.21–2–*ct* 5
His County cricket was for Berkshire (1949).

Eliot, Robin Francis
Amateur. *b:* 7.3.1942, Gloucester. Lower order left-hand batsman, left-arm medium pace bowler. *Sch* Radley. *Team* Oxford U (1961).
Career batting
2–4–2–55–30–27.50–0–*ct* 0
Bowling 140–1–140.00–0–0–1/70

Ellcock, Ricardo McDonald
Cricketer. *b:* 17.6.1965, Redmans Village, St Thomas, Barbados. Brother of D. E. (Barbados). Lower order right-hand batsman, right-arm fast bowler. *Sch* Malvern. *Teams* Worcestershire (1982–88, 31 matches); Barbados (1983/4); Middlesex (1989–91, 12 matches). *Tour* England to West Indies 1989/90 (returned home injured without playing a match).
Career batting
46–47–13–424–45*–12.47–0–*ct* 9
Bowling 3395–117–29.01–1–0–5/35
Having spent seven seasons on the fringes of the Worcestershire side, he joined Middlesex in 1989, but in 1990 was unavailable owing to a back injury, though he reappeared briefly in 1991, this effectively ended his career.

Elliot, Edgar William
Amateur. *b:* 9.7.1878, Roker, Sunderland, Co Durham. *d:* 23.3.1931, Vancouver, British Columbia, Canada. Attractive middle order right-hand batsman, right-arm medium fast bowler. *Sch* Wellington. *Team* Gentlemen of England (1907).
Career batting
2–4–2–30–15–15.00–0–*ct* 1
His County cricket was for Durham (pre first-class, 1897–1907). His most famous innings came for Borderers v Newcastle Garrison in 1905 when he hit 332 in 225 minutes. An excellent rugby player, he appeared for Durham and England as a three quarter. He was for some years manager of the soda mines in California.

Elliott, Charles Standish, MBE
Professional. *b:* 24.4.1912, Scarcliffe, Derbyshire. Nephew of Harry (Derbyshire). Opening right-hand batsman, off break bowler, good slip field. *Team* Derbyshire (1932–53, 275 matches).
Career batting
275–468–29–11965–215–27.25–9–*ct* 210–*st* 1
Bowling 526–11–47.81–0–0–2/25
His only double century was 215 for Derbyshire v Nottinghamshire at Trent Bridge in 1947. He hit 1,000 runs in a season 6 times (best 1,599, av 34.76, in 1952). He was later a first-class umpire (1956–74), standing in 42 Test matches (1957–74), including one in New Zealand. He was a Test selector from 1975 to 1981. He played soccer for Coventry City.

Elliott, George Frederick
Professional. *b:* 1.5.1850, Farnham, Surrey. *d:* 23.4.1913, Farnham, Surrey. Sound middle order right-hand batsman, right-arm fast bowler. *Teams* Kent (1874, 2 matches); Surrey (1875–80, 44 matches).

Elliott, Harold

Career batting
51–93–8–1163–53–13.68–0–*ct* 9
Bowling 485–8–60.62–0–0–1/2

Elliott, Harold
Professional. *b:* 15.6.1904, Hindley, Wigan, Lancashire. *d:* 15.4.1969, Hindley, Wigan, Lancashire. Tail end right-hand batsman, wicket-keeper. *Team* Lancashire (1930, 1 match).
Career batting
1–1–0–4–4–4.00–0–*ct* 2–*st* 1
He was a first-class umpire (1939–56), standing in 7 Test matches (1950–53).

Elliott, Harry
Professional. *b:* 2.11.1891, Scarcliffe, Derbyshire. *d:* 2.2.1976, Derby. Uncle of C. S. (Derbyshire). Lower order right-hand batsman, wicket-keeper. *Team* Derbyshire (1920–47, 520 matches). *Tours* MCC to South Africa 1927/8, to India 1933/4. *Tests* England (1927/8 to 1933/4, 4 matches).
Career batting
532–764–220–7580–94–13.93–0–*ct* 904–*st* 302
Bowling 5–0
Test batting
4–5–1–61–37*–15.25–0–*ct* 8–*st* 3
He was a first-class umpire (1946 and 1952–60) and Derbyshire coach (1947–51).

Elliott, Herbert Denis Edleston
Amateur. *b:* 30.3.1887, Newport, Shropshire. *d:* 26.4.1973, Bognor Regis, Sussex. Tail end batsman, bowler. *Team* Essex (1913, 2 matches).
Career batting
2–4–0–3–3–0.75–0–*ct* 1
Bowling 107–1–107.00–0–0–1/67

Elliott, John William
Cricketer. *b:* 12.2.1942, Diglis, Worcester. Lower order left-hand batsman, wicket-keeper. *Sch* Worcester RGS. *Team* Worcestershire (1959–65, 10 matches).
Career batting
10–11–3–66–18*–8.25–0–*ct* 18–*st* 8

Elliott, William
Professional. *b:* 15.11.1842, Bulwell, Nottinghamshire. Lower order right-hand batsman, right-arm fast bowler. *Team* Nottinghamshire (1871, 2 matches).
Career batting
3–4–0–12–5–3.00–0–*ct* 0
Bowling 73–2–36.50–0–0–1/18
His first-class debut was for R. Daft's XI in 1870. He also played for Durham (pre first-class, 1875).

Ellis, Charles Howard
Professional. *b:* 9.8.1830, Ditchling, Sussex. *d:* 17.1.1880, Brighton, Sussex. Hard hitting middle order right-hand batsman, wicket-keeper, lob bowler. *Team* Sussex (1856–68, 65 matches).
Career batting
80–136–10–1811–83–14.37–*ct* 97–*st* 36
Bowling 2108–100–21.08–5–1–8/96

Ellis, Francis Edward
Professional. *b:* 20.9.1889, Gloucester. Lower order batsman, right-arm fast medium bowler. *Team* Gloucestershire (1914–21, 26 matches).
Career batting
26–44–19–241–24*–9.64–0–*ct* 6
Bowling 2185–70–31.21–4–0–6/90

Ellis, Geoffrey Phillip
Cricketer. *b:* 24.5.1950, Llandudno, Caernarvonshire. Opening or middle order right-hand batsman, right-arm medium pace bowler. *Team* Glamorgan (1970–76, 75 matches).
Career batting
75–139–10–2673–116–20.72–1–*ct* 24
Bowling 1418–24–59.08–0–0–2/20
He also played for Wales in the ICC Trophy (1979) and the Minor Counties Championship (1988–89).

Ellis, Harold
Professional. *b:* 13.3.1883, Burnley, Lancashire. *d:* 31.12.1962, Stockport, Cheshire. Tail end right-hand batsman, wicket-keeper. *Team* Northamptonshire (1908–10, 18 matches).
Career batting
18–27–10–72–18–4.23–0–*ct* 27–*st* 7

Ellis, Henry Wilson
Amateur. *b:* 23.11.1840, Cambridge. *d:* 13.5.1902, Cambridge. Middle order batsman. *Team* Cambridgeshire (1864, 1 match).
Career batting
1–2–0–12–10–6.00–0–*ct* 1

Ellis, Jeremy
Professional. *b:* 15.2.1866, Walmersley-cum-Shuttleworth, Bury, Lancashire. *d:* 14.8.1943, Billington, Lancashire. Father of Stanley (Lancashire) and Walker (Lancashire). Lower order left-hand batsman, left-arm medium pace bowler. *Team* Lancashire (1892–98, 6 matches).
Career batting
6–9–1–56–26*–7.00–0–*ct* 5
Bowling 240–21–11.42–1–1–8/21

Ellis, John Ernest
Professional. *b:* 10.11.1864, Sheffield, Yorkshire. *d:* 1.12.1927, Walkley, Sheffield, Yorkshire. Tail end right-hand batsman, wicket-keeper. *Team* Yorkshire (1888–92, 11 matches).
Career batting
11–15–6–14–4*–1.55–0–*ct* 11–*st* 10

Ellis, John Leslie
Amateur. *b:* 9.5.1890, Malvern, Melbourne, Victoria, Australia. *d:* 26.7.1974, Glen Iris, Melbourne, Victoria, Australia. Lower order right-hand batsman,

wicket-keeper. *Team* Victoria (1918/9 to 1929/30, 72 matches). *Tours* Australia to England 1926, to India 1935/6; Victoria to New Zealand 1924/5.
Career batting
101–141–30–2351–119–21.18–2–*ct* 187–*st* 107
As the reserve wicket-keeper, he was not required for any of the Tests on his tour to England.

Ellis, Peter Michael
Professional. *b:* 25.9.1932, Ladywell, Lewisham, London. Father of R. G. P. (Middlesex and Gloucestershire). Lower order right-hand batsman, right-arm medium fast bowler. *Team* MCC (1953).
Career batting
1 match, did not bat–*ct* 0
Bowling 120–0

Ellis, Reginald Sidney
Amateur. *b:* 26.11.1917, Angaston, South Australia. Tail end left-hand batsman, slow left-arm bowler. *Team* South Australia (1945/6, 1 match). *Tours* Australian Services to England 1945, to Ceylon and India 1945/6.
Career batting
21–28–12–47–10*–2.93–0–*ct* 6
Bowling 2070–78–26.53–6–1–6/144

Ellis, Richard Gary Peter
Cricketer. *b:* 20.12.1960, Paddington, London. Son of P. M. (MCC). Middle order right-hand batsman, off break bowler. *Sch* Haileybury. *Tours* Oxford U (1981–83, blue all three years); Middlesex (1982–84, 11 matches); Gloucestershire (1985, 1 match).
Career batting
40–73–3–2020–105*–28.85–2–*ct* 21
Bowling 271–5–54.20–0–0–2/40
He captained Oxford in 1982. He also played for Cambridgeshire (1990).

Ellis, Robert
Cricketer. *b:* 19.5.1940, Kilmarnock, Ayr, Scotland. Middle order left-hand batsman, right-arm medium pace bowler. *Team* Scotland (1963–74).
Career batting
10–13–3–133–35–13.30–0–*ct* 6
Bowling 379–6–63.16–0–0–1/3

Ellis, Robert Thomas
Amateur. *b:* 16.9.1853, Burgess Hill, Sussex. *d:* 23.9.1937, Stone, Kent. Steady opening right-hand batsman, right-hand fast round arm bowler. *Sch* Brighton and Hurstpierpoint. *Teams* Sussex (1877–86, 65 matches).
Career batting
70–133–7–2356–103–18.69–2–*ct* 28
Bowling 70–0
In 1880 he was captain and manager of Sussex. Owing to ill-health he was obliged to retire early from first-class matches.

Ellis, S. E.
Amateur. Middle order batsman. *Team* Somerset (1902, 1 match).
Career batting
1–2–0–5–5–2.50–0–*ct* 0

Ellis, Samuel
Amateur. *b:* 23.11.1851, Dewsbury, Yorkshire. *d:* 28.10.1930, Milnthorpe, Sandal Magna, Wakefield, Yorkshire. Middle order right-hand batsman. *Team* Yorkshire (1880, 2 matches).
Career batting
3–5–0–16–9–3.20–0–*ct* 2
His debut in first-class matches was for An England Eleven at Dewsbury in 1878.

Ellis, Stanley
Professional. *b:* 12.2.1896, Ramsbottom, Lancashire. *d:* 14.2.1987, Wilpshire, Lancashire. Brother of Walker (Lancashire), son of Jeremy (Lancashire). Lower order left-hand batsman, off break bowler. *Team* Lancashire (1923–24, 8 matches).
Career batting
8–7–1–57–25–9.50–0–*ct* 0
Bowling 252–14–18.00–1–0–5/21
He also played for Durham (pre first-class, 1929–37).

Ellis, Walker
Professional. *b:* 27.1.1895, Summerseat, Lancashire. *d:* 25.11.1974, Eccleston, Lancashire. Brother of Stanley (Lancashire), son of Jeremy (Lancashire). Opening right-hand batsman. *Team* Lancashire (1920–23, 36 matches).
Career batting
36–55–4–846–138*–16.58–1–*ct* 14

Ellis, William
Professional. *b:* 28.8.1876, Whitwell, Derbyshire. *d:* 22.1.1931, Crimble Moor, Huddersfield, Yorkshire. Middle order batsman, change bowler. *Team* Derbyshire (1898–1906, 18 matches).
Career batting
18–32–2–361–58–12.03–0–*ct* 7
Bowling 120–0

Ellis, William
Professional. *b:* 15.8.1919, Rolleston, Nottinghamshire. Lower order right-hand batsman, right-arm fast medium bowler. *Team* Nottinghamshire (1948, 2 matches).
Career batting
2–1–0–29–29–29.00–0–*ct* 0
Bowling 77–1–77.00–0–0–1/49

Ellis, William Arnot
Amateur. *b:* 16.9.1923, Carriden, West Lothian, Scotland. Middle order right-hand batsman. *Team* Scotland (1954).
Career batting
1–1–0–6–6–6.00–0–*ct* 1

Ellison, Charles Christopher
Cricketer. *b:* 11.2.1962, Pembury, Kent. Brother of R. M. (Kent). Lower order right-hand batsman, right-arm medium pace bowler. *Sch* Tonbridge. *Team* Cambridge U (1982–86, blue 1982–83 and 1985–86).
Career batting
23–22–7–268–51*–17.86–0–*ct* 7
Bowling 1383–39–35.46–1–0–5/82
His County cricket was for Wiltshire (1984–88).

Ellison, Rev Henry Richard Nevile
Amateur. *b:* 16.7.1868, Blyth, Nottinghamshire. *d:* 7.10.1948, Truxford, Elstead, Surrey. Middle order batsman, change bowler. *Sch* Rugby. *Team* Nottinghamshire (1897, 1 match).
Career batting
1–2–0–5–3–2.50–0–*ct* 0
Bowling 5–0
He also played for Lincolnshire (1889–93) and Wiltshire (1901–05). From 1930 until 1942 he was Hon Sec of Derbyshire CCC.

Ellison, Michael Joseph
Amateur. *b:* 1.6.1817, Worksop, Nottinghamshire. *d:* 12.7.1898, Broomhill, Sheffield, Yorkshire. Middle order right-hand batsman. *Teams* Yorkshire (1849–55, 5 matches); Nottinghamshire (1852, 1 match).
Career batting
16–28–0–195–6.96–0–*ct* 1
Bowling 15–0+1–no av–0–0–1/?
He was the prime mover in the establishment of the County cricket ground at Bramall Lane, Sheffield, and was President of Yorkshire CCC from 1864 to his death, and Treasurer 1863–1893. His first first-class match was for Sheffield in 1846.

Ellison, Richard Mark
Cricketer. *b:* 21.9.1959, Willesborough, Ashford, Kent. Brother of C. C. (Cambridge U). Middle order left-hand batsman, right-arm medium fast bowler. *Sch* Tonbridge. *Teams* Kent (1981–92, 173 matches); Tasmania (1986/7, 9 matches). *Tours* England to India and Sri Lanka 1984/5, to Sharjah (not first-class) 1984/5, to Australia 1984/5 (not first-class), to West Indies 1985/6; England XI to South Africa 1989/90. *Tests* England (1984–86, 11 matches).
Career batting
204–280–71–4954–108–23.70–1–*ct* 85
Bowling 13604–471–28.88–18–2–7/33
Test batting
11–16–1–202–41–13.46–0–*ct* 2
Bowling 1048–35–29.94–3–1–6/77
In 1985 he topped the England bowling averages against Australia with 17 wickets, av 10.88, but lack of form and a serious injury then prevented him from becoming an automatic choice for England. He missed the whole of the 1987 season through injury. Returning in 1988 he took 71 wickets, av 21.90, which was his best season to date.

Elms, John Emmanuel
Professional. *b:* 24.12.1874, Pitsmoor, Sheffield, Yorkshire. *d:* 1.11.1951, Sheffield, Yorkshire. Lower order right-hand batsman, medium or slow bowler. *Team* Yorkshire (1905, 1 match).
Career batting
1–2–0–20–20–10.00–0–*ct* 1
Bowling 28–1–28.00–0–0–1/20

Elms, Richard Burtenshaw
Cricketer. *b:* 5.4.1949, Sutton, Surrey. Lower order right-hand batsman, left-arm fast medium bowler. *Teams* Kent (1970–76, 55 matches); Hampshire (1977–78, 17 matches).
Career batting
72–73–23–558–48–11.16–0–*ct* 17
Bowling 4606–116–39.70–4–0–5/38

Elsby, George
Professional. *b:* 6.6.1902, Tunstall, Staffordshire. *d:* 20.6.1953, Ipswich, Suffolk. Middle order right-hand batsman, right-arm medium pace bowler. *Team* Wales (1927).
Career batting
1–2–0–36–22–18.00–0–*ct* 0
Bowling 36–0
His County cricket was for Caernarvonshire (1929).

Elsdon, Harold
Professional. *b:* 19.2.1921, Lemington, Northumberland. Lower order right-hand batsman, right-arm fast bowler. *Team* Minor Counties (1949).
Career batting
1–2–1–12–12*–12.00–0–*ct* 1
Bowling 100–3–33.33–0–0–3/51
His County cricket was for Northumberland (1938–56).

Else, Robert
Professional. *b:* 17.11.1876, Leawood, Matlock, Derbyshire. *d:* 16.9.1955, Broomhill, Sheffield, Yorkshire. Middle order left-hand batsman. *Team* Derbyshire (1901–03, 5 matches).
Career batting
5–10–2–59–28–7.37–0–*ct* 3
Bowling 61–1–61.00–0–0–1/56

Elson, Geoffrey
Amateur. *b:* 19.3.1913, Coventry, Warwickshire. Tail end left-hand batsman, slow left-arm bowler. *Sch* Rydal. *Team* Warwickshire (1947, 1 match).
Career batting
1–2–1–7–4–7.00–0–*ct* 0
Bowling 116–1–116.00–0–0–1/99

Elstob, Eric Bramley
Amateur. *b:* 2.8.1885, Brentford, Middlesex. *d:* 15.5.1949, Little Fowlers. Hawkhurst, Kent. Middle order batsman. *Sch* Marlborough. *Team* Royal Navy (1913–23).

Career batting
2–4–1–23–14–7.66–0–*ct* 0
Bowling 46–2–23.00–0–0–1/5

Elviss, Richard William
Cricketer. *b:* 19.7.1945, Fulwood, Sheffield, Yorkshire. Lower order left-hand batsman, off break bowler. *Sch* Leeds GS. *Team* Oxford U (1966–67, blue both years).
Career batting
19–26–9–114–16–6.70–0–*ct* 4
Bowling 1718–65–26.43–4–0–5/83

Emburey, John Ernest
Cricketer. *b:* 20.8.1952, Peckham, London. Stubborn middle order right-hand batsman, off break bowler, excellent gully field. *Teams* Middlesex (1973–92, 329 matches); Western Province (1982/3 to 1983/4). *Tours* England to Australia 1978/9, 1979/80, 1986/7, 1987/8, to India 1979/80, 1981/2, 1988/9 (tour cancelled), to West Indies 1980/1, 1985/6, to Sri Lanka 1981/2, to Sharjah (not first-class) 1986/7, to Pakistan 1987/8, to New Zealand 1987/8; Robins to Sri Lanka 1977/8; Middlesex to Zimbabwe 1980/1; England XI to South Africa 1981/2, 1989/90. *Tests* England (1978–89, 60 matches).
Career batting
446–562–112–10316–133–22.92–5–*ct* 403
Bowling 35599–1366–26.06–63–9–7/27
Test batting
60–89–18–1540–75–21.69–0–*ct* 33
Bowling 5105–138–36.99–6–0–7/78
England's principal off spin bowler of the 1980s, his Test career has been broken twice by his decision to tour South Africa. He took 103 wickets, av 17.88, in 1983. He captained England in two Tests in 1988.

Emery, Kevin St John Dennis
Cricketer. *b:* 28.2.1960, Swindon, Wiltshire. Lower order right-hand batsman, right-arm fast medium bowler. *Team* Hampshire (1982–83, 30 matches).
Career batting
30–27–15–45–18–3.75–0–*ct* 3
Bowling 2231–88–25.35–3–1–6/51
He took 83 wickets, av 23.72, in 1982, his debut season. He also played for Wiltshire (1978–80 and 1985–88).

Emery, Sidney Hand
Amateur. *b:* 15.10.1885, Macdonald Town, Sydney, New South Wales, Australia. *d:* 7.1.1967, Petersham, Sydney, New South Wales, Australia. Lower order right-hand batsman, leg break and googly bowler. *Team* New South Wales (1908/9 to 1912/13, 20 matches). *Tours* Australia to England and North America 1912, to New Zealand 1909/10, to North America 1913. *Tests* Australia (1912, 4 matches).
Career batting
58–80–15–1192–80*–18.33–0–*ct* 30
Bowling 4355–183–23.79–11–3–7/28
Test batting
4–2–0–6–5–3.00–0–*ct* 2
Bowling 249–5–49.80–0–0–2/46
Although he bowled fairly well in the county matches, he proved ineffective in the Tests on his visit to England.

Emery, William
Professional. *b:* 25.8.1897, Pentrebach, Merthyr Tydfil, Glamorgan. *d:* 13.12.1962, Gowerton, Glamorgan. Lower order right-hand batsman, right-arm fast medium bowler. *Teams* Glamorgan (1922, 2 matches); Wales (1925).
Career batting
3–5–0–16–11–3.20–0–*ct* 0
Bowling 246–6–41.00–0–0–2/25

Emmett, Arthur
Professional. *b:* 18.8.1873, Halifax, Yorkshire. *d:* 12.11.1935, Evington, Leicester. Son of Thomas (Yorkshire). Lower order right-hand batsman, right-arm medium pace bowler. *Team* Leicestershire (1902, 3 matches).
Career batting
3–4–0–12–10–3.00–0–*ct* 0
Bowling 240–5–48.00–0–0–3/48
In a minor match in 1905 for Leicester v Oakham he bowled the first four batsmen with his first four deliveries.

Emmett, George Malcolm
Professional. *b:* 2.12.1912, Agra, India. *d:* 18.12.1976, Knowle, Somerset. Opening right-hand batsman, slow left-arm bowler, good field. *Team* Gloucestershire (1936–59, 454 matches). *Tours* Commonwealth to India and Ceylon 1950/1, to India 1953/4. *Test* England (1948, 1 match).
Career batting
509–865–50–25602–188–31.41–37–*ct* 296
Bowling 2641–60–44.01–2–0–6/137
Test batting
1–2–0–10–10–5.00–0–*ct* 0
He hit 1,000 runs in a season 13 times plus once overseas and went on to 2,000 runs three times (best 2,115, av 35.25, in 1953). He captained Gloucestershire 1955–58 and was county coach 1959–61. He also played for Devon (1932–35).

Emmett, Thomas
Professional. *b:* 3.9.1841, Halifax, Yorkshire. *d:* 30.6.1904, Leicester. Father of Arthur (Leicestershire). Middle order left-hand batsman, left-hand fast round-arm bowler. *Team* Yorkshire (1866–88, 298 matches). *Tours* Lillywhite to Australia 1876/7; Harris to Australia 1878/9; Daft to North America 1879 (not first-class); Lillywhite, Shaw and Shrewsbury to Australia 1881/2. *Tests* England (1876/7 to 1881/2, 7 matches).
Career batting
426–700–90–9053–104–14.84–1–*ct* 276

Bowling 21314–1571–13.56–121–29–9/23
Test batting
7–13–1–160–48–13.33–0–*ct* 9
Bowling 284–9–31.55–1–0–7/68

He took 100 wickets in a season on four occasions (best 124, av 12.83, in 1886). His best bowling was 9/23 for Yorkshire v Cambridgeshire at Hunslet in 1869. He captained Yorkshire 1878–82. He also played for Northamptonshire (pre first-class, 1870).

Emmitt, Herbert William
(known as H. W. Emmett)
Professional. *b:* 6.8.1857, The Meadows, Nottingham. *d:* 23.4.1901, Nottingham. Middle order batsman. *Team* Nottinghamshire (1888, 2 matches).
Career batting
3–5–1–6–4*–1.50–0–*ct* 2

He was a noted soccer player, appearing for both Notts County and Nottingham Forest. His first-class debut was for North v South in 1884.

Endean, William Russell
Amateur. *b:* 31.5.1924, Parkview, Johannesburg, South Africa. Middle order right-hand batsman, wicket-keeper, brilliant close field. *Team* Transvaal (1945/6 to 1960/1). *Tours* South Africa to England 1951, 1955, to Australia and New Zealand 1952/3. *Tests* South Africa (1951 to 1957/8, 28 matches).
Career batting
134–230–25–7757–247–37.83–15–*ct* 158–*st* 13
Bowling 73–2–36.50–0–0–1/1
Test batting
28–52–4–1630–162*–33.95–3–*ct* 41

He came to England in 1951 as the principal wicket-keeper, but found himself deposed by Waite, and had only a moderate season with the bat. In 1955 he hit 1,242 runs, av 34.50, and appeared in all five Tests as a batsman. His highest score was 247 for Transvaal v Eastern Province at Johannesburg in 1955/6 and for Transvaal against Orange Free State at Johannesburg in 1954/5 hit a record 197* runs before lunch, going on to 235. His final first-class match was for MCC in 1964. He played hockey for South Africa.

Enfield, Henry
Amateur. *b:* 12.9.1849, Hampstead, London. *d:* 19.9.1923, The Park, Nottingham. Middle order right-hand batsman, brilliant close field. *Sch* Brighton. *Team* Nottinghamshire (1869–72, 2 matches).
Career batting
2–4–0–6–4–1.50–0–*ct* 3

Engineer, Farokh Maneksha
Professional. *b:* 25.2.1938. Bombay, India. Brother of D. M. (Mysore). Opening/middle order right-hand batsman, wicket-keeper, leg break bowler. *Teams* Bombay (1959/60 to 1974/5); Lancashire (1968–76, 175 matches). *Tours* Indian Starlets to Pakistan 1959/60; India to West Indies 1961/2, to England 1967, 1974, 1975 (World Cup), to Australia and New Zealand 1967/8, to East Africa 1967; Rest of World to England 1970, to Pakistan 1970/1, to Australia 1971/2. *Tests* India (1961/2 to 1974/5, 46 matches).
Career batting
335–510–55–13436–192–29.52–13–*ct* 704–*st* 120
Bowling 117–1–117.00–0–0–1/40
Test batting
46–87–3–2611–121–31.08–2–*ct* 66–*st* 16

His first-class debut was for Combined Indian Universities 1958/9. He did not exceed 1,000 runs in a season in England, but made 1,050, av 47.72, in India in 1964/5.

England, Richard Michael
Amateur. *b:* 23.8.1918, Midgham, Berkshire. Lower order right-hand batsman, wicket-keeper. *Sch* Eton. *Team* Oxford U (1938–39).
Career batting
2–3–1–59–43*–29.50–0–*ct* 4

His County cricket was for Berkshire (1936–39).

English, Edward Apsey
Amateur. *b:* 1.1.1864, Dorking, Surrey. *d:* 5.9.1966, Ball, Tiverton, Devon. Middle order right-hand batsman. *Team* Hampshire (1898–1901, 18 matches).
Career batting
18–32–2–565–98–18.83–0–*ct* 5
Bowling 101–1–101.00–0–0–1/11

As far as is known he was the oldest English first-class cricketer, living to the age of 102. Only R. De Smidt (Western Province) of all first-class cricketers lived to a greater age.

English, Ernest Robert Maling
Amateur. *b:* 2.12.1874, Charlton Kings, Gloucestershire. *d:* 18.8.1941, South Kensington, London. Middle order right-hand batsman. *Sch* Wellington. *Team* Gloucestershire (1909, 1 match).
Career batting
1–2–0–2–2–1.00–0–*ct* 0

He also played for Shropshire (1907). When he retired from the Army in 1919, he became a stage and screen actor.

English, Winston
Cricketer. *b:* 1943, British Guiana. Lower order right-hand batsman, left-arm fast bowler. *Team* Guyana (1966/7 to 1969/70).
Career batting
12–16–5–479–112–43.54–1–*ct* 8
Bowling 916–27–33.92–0–0–4/111

His only first-class match in England was for D. H. Robins' XI in 1969.

Ennis, James Tench
Amateur. *b:* 27.2.1900, Naul Park, Co Dublin, Ireland. *d:* 15.10.1976, Dublin, Ireland. Lower order right-hand batsman. *Team* Dublin University (1926).

Career batting
1–2–0–0–0–0.00–0–*ct* 0

Ensor, Ernest
Amateur. *b:* 17.12.1870, Cheltenham, Gloucestershire. *d:* 13.8.1929, Bellevue Park, Cork, Ireland. Lower order right-hand batsman, right-arm fast medium bowler. *Team* Dublin University (1895).
Career batting
4–7–0–65–18–9.28–0–*ct* 1
Bowling 468–23–20.34–2–0–5/74
He played for Ireland (not first-class) in 1896.

Enthoven, Henry John
Amateur. *b:* 4.6.1903, Cartagena, Spain. *d:* 29.6.1975, Kensington, London. Middle order right-hand batsman, right-arm medium pace bowler. *Sch* Harrow. *Teams* Cambridge U (1923–26, blue all four years); Middlesex (1925–36, 123 matches). *Tour* MCC to Canada 1937 (not first-class).
Career batting
194–301–30–7362–139–27.16–9–*ct* 78
Bowling 8099–252–32.13–5–1–6/64
He captained Cambridge in 1926 and Middlesex jointly with N. E. Haig in 1933–34. He hit 1,129 runs, av 31.36, in 1926. His final first-class match was for MCC in 1948.

Entwistle, Robert
Cricketer. *b:* 20.10.1941, Burnley, Lancashire. Middle order right-hand batsman, good outfield. *Team* Lancashire (1962–66, 48 matches).
Career batting
49–81–4–1612–85–20.93–0–*ct* 16
He hit 1,030 runs, av 28.61, in 1964. He also played for Cumberland (1967–84), and his final first-class match was for Minor Counties in 1976.

Eskdaill, Lord (*see under* Earl of Dalkeith)

Estcourt, Noël Sidney Dudley
Amateur. *b:* 7.1.1929, Ralolia, Rhodesia. Middle order right-hand batsman, off break bowler. *Team* Cambridge U (1953–54, blue 1954).
Career batting
21–34–7–513–56*–19.00–0–*ct* 6
Bowling 1262–23–54.86–0–0–4/79
He also played for Devon. An excellent rugby footballer, he represented Cambridge and England.

Estridge, Edward
Amateur. *b:* 28.4.1843, Hounslow, Middlesex. *d:* 30.8.1919, Abingdon, Berkshire. Middle order batsman. *Sch* Tonbridge. *Team* Derbyshire (1874, 1 match).
Career batting
1–1–0–4–4–4.00–0–*ct* 0

Estridge, George Tyler
Amateur. *b:* 11.8.1835, Carshalton, Surrey. *d:* 26.6.1862, Belgaum, India. Brother of H. W. (Gentlemen of South). Sound middle order right-hand batsman, good field at point. *Team* Surrey (1859–60, 5 matches).
Career batting
8–13–2–168–47–15.27–0–*ct* 3
Bowling 105–7–15.00–1–0–6/44
His career in County cricket was brief as he joined the army in India in 1861.

Estridge, Henry Whatley
Amateur. *b:* 1837, Carshalton, Surrey. *d:* 15.1.1902, Hailey Manor, Oxfordshire. Brother of G. T. (Surrey). Middle order right-hand batsman, slow round arm bowler. *Team* Gentlemen of South (1868).
Career batting
1–2–0–14–14–7.00–0–*ct* 0
His County cricket was for Devon (1868–74).

Estwick, Roderick Orville
Cricketer. *b:* 28.6.1961, Christchurch, Christ Church, Barbados. Half-brother of S. T. Clarke (Surrey). Lower order right-hand batsman, right-arm fast medium bowler. *Teams* Barbados (1982/3 to 1986/7); Transvaal (1987/8 to 1989/90). *Tour* Young West Indies to Zimbabwe 1983/4.
Career batting
37–49–12–376–43*–10.16–0–*ct* 16
Bowling 3088–141–21.90–6–0–6/68
He played County cricket for Lincolnshire (1982–83). His only first-class match in England was for D. B. Close's XI in 1986.

Etheridge, Charles Robert
Professional. *b:* 5.7.1870, Horsham, Sussex. *d:* 14.2.1948, Oakhill, Horsham, Sussex. Lower order batsman, slow left-arm bowler. *Team* Sussex (1896–1901, 3 matches).
Career batting
3–5–2–22–17*–7.33–0–*ct* 1
Bowling 251–3–83.66–0–0–3/105

Etheridge, Robert James
Professional. *b:* 25.3.1934, Gloucester. *d:* 4.4.1988, Gloucester. Lower order right-hand batsman, wicket-keeper. *Team* Gloucestershire (1955–66, 39 matches).
Career batting
39–64–14–796–48–15.92–0–*ct* 33–*st* 8
He played soccer for Bristol City. He played bowls for Gloucestershire.

Etheridge, Sydney Graver
Amateur. *b:* 3.11.1882, Cockfosters, New Barnet, Hertfordshire. *d:* 3.9.1945, Barnet, Hertfordshire. Middle order right-hand batsman. *Sch* Aldenham. *Team* Middlesex (1908–10, 8 matches).
Career batting
8–12–2–81–22–8.10–0–*ct* 6
He also played for Hertfordshire (1902 and 1913–22).

Etherington, Maurice William
Professional. *b:* 24.8.1916, White City, North Hammersmith, London. Lower order right-hand batsman, right-arm fast bowler. *Teams* Middlesex (1946, 2 matches); Leicestershire (1948, 3 matches).
Career batting
5–9–2–64–27–9.14–0–*ct* 1
Bowling 292–8–36.50–0–0–3/23

Evans, Vice Admiral Sir Alfred Englefield
Amateur. *b:* 30.1.1884, South Africa. *d:* 29.12.1944, Cranbourne, Dorset. Brother of D. M. (Hampshire) and W. H. B. (Hampshire and Worcestershire), nephew of A. H. (Hampshire and Somerset), cousin of A. J. (Hampshire and Kent) and R. du B. (Hampshire). Lower order right-hand batsman, right-arm medium pace bowler. *Team* Hampshire (1919–20, 5 matches).
Career batting
13–22–0–310–77–14.09–0–*ct* 8
Bowling 841–23–36.56–0–0–4/74
Most of his first-class cricket was for the Royal Navy, making his debut in 1914 and playing his last match in 1925.

Evans, Alfred Henry
Amateur. *b:* 14.6.1858, Madras, India. *d:* 26.3.1934, Saunton, Devon. He died whilst playing golf. Father of A. J. (Hampshire and Kent) and R. du B. (Hampshire), uncle of A. E. (Hampshire), D. M. (Hampshire) and W. H. B. (Hampshire and Worcestershire). Middle order right-hand batsman, right-arm fast medium bowler. *Sch* Rossall and Clifton. *Teams* Oxford U (1878–81, blue all four years); Somerset (1882–84, 6 matches); Hampshire (1885, 3 matches).
Career batting
44–74–8–908–59*–13.75–0–*ct* 45
Bowling 3234–201 + 3–16.08–20–6–9/59
He was awarded his rugby blue at Oxford and was also a noted athlete. His best bowling was 9/59 for England XI v Daft's XI at Lord's in 1880. He captained Oxford in 1881. He first played for Somerset (pre first-class) in 1877 and last played for Hampshire (not first-class) in 1886.

Evans, Alfred John
Amateur. *b:* 1.5.1889, Newtown, Hampshire. *d:* 18.9.1960, Marylebone, London. Nephew of A. H. (Hampshire and Somerset), brother of R. du B. (Hampshire), cousin of A. E. (Hampshire), D. M. (Hampshire) and W. H. B. (Hampshire and Worcestershire). Middle order right-hand batsman, right-arm medium fast bowler. *Sch* Winchester. *Teams* Hampshire (1908–20, 7 matches); Oxford U (1909–12, blue all four years); Kent (1921–28, 36 matches). *Test* England (1921, 1 match).
Career batting
90–148–6–3499–143–24.64–6–*ct* 94
Bowling 3062–110–27.83–4–1–7/50
Test batting
1–2–0–18–14–9.00–0–*ct* 0
He captained Oxford in 1911 and Kent in 1927. He represented Oxford at rackets in 1910 and golf in 1909–10. During the First World War he won fame for his escapes from German prisoner-of-war camps.

Evans, Bertram Sutton
Amateur. *b:* 17.12.1872, Charterhouse, Godalming, Surrey. *d:* 2.3.1919, Paris, France. Middle order batsman. *Team* Hampshire (1900–09, 5 matches).
Career batting
5–8–2–67–18*–11.16–0–*ct* 2
His County cricket was very limited due to his naval career.

Evans, Charles
Professional. *b:* 19.2.1866, Whittington Moor, Derbyshire. *d:* 14.1.1956, Chesterfield, Derbyshire. Lower order right-hand batsman, right-arm fast medium bowler. *Team* Derbyshire (1894–95, 9 matches).
Career batting
9–14–2–157–31–13.08–0–*ct* 7
Bowling 526–19–27.68–0–0–4/46
He first played for Derbyshire (not first-class) in 1889.

Evans, Charles William Henry
Amateur. *b:* 19.8.1851, Guernsey. *d:* 2.11.1909, Bognor, Sussex. Middle order right-hand batsman. *Sch* Haileybury. *Team* Cambridge U (1871).
Career batting
3–6–1–33–8*–6.60–0–*ct* 2–*st* 2
His last first-class match was for Gentlemen of England in 1879.

Evans, David Gwilym Lloyd
Professional. *b:* 27.7.1933, Lambeth, London. *d:* 25.3.1990, Cwmpengraig, Drefach, Llandysul, Cardigan. Lower order right-hand batsman, wicket-keeper. *Team* Glamorgan (1956–69, 270 matches).
Career batting
270–364–91–2875–46*–10.53–0–*ct* 503–*st* 55
Bowling 12–0
He was awarded a Winston Churchill Scholarship in 1967–68 to travel around the world studying cricket coaching. He was a first-class umpire (1971–89), standing in 9 Test matches (1981–85).

Evans, David Linzee
Amateur. *b:* 13.4.1869, West Town, Somerset. *d:* 11.11.1907, West Town, Somerset. Aggressive middle order right-hand batsman, right-arm fast medium bowler. *Sch* Loretto. *Teams* Gloucestershire (1889–91, 7 matches); Somerset (1894–1902, 15 matches).
Career batting
22–42–3–382–60–9.79–0–*ct* 8
Bowling 51–1–51.00–0–0–1/7
He played for Gloucestershire whilst still at school.

Evans, Dudley MacNeil
Amateur. *b:* 11.12.1886, South Africa. *d:* 18.12.1972, Petersfield, Hampshire. Brother of A. E. (Hampshire) and W. H. B. (Hampshire and Worcestershire), nephew of A. H. (Hampshire and Somerset), cousin of A. J. (Hampshire and Kent) and R. du B. (Hampshire). Middle order right-hand batsman, right-arm fast medium bowler. *Sch* Winchester. *Team* Hampshire (1904–11, 15 matches).
Career batting
16–29–3–382–64–14.69–0–*ct* 17
Bowling 1449–55–26.34–4–0–6/81

Evans, Edward Noel
Amateur. *b:* 7.12.1911, Edmonton, Middlesex. *d:* 12.2.1964, Kensington, London. Middle order left-hand batsman, leg break and googly bowler. *Sch* Haileybury. *Team* Oxford U (1931–33, blue 1932).
Career batting
22–37–3–617–91–18.14–0–*ct* 5
Bowling 224–5–44.80–0–0–2/56
His final first-class match was for MCC in 1934.

Evans, Edwin
Amateur. *b:* 26.3.1849, Emu Plains, New South Wales, Australia. *d:* 2.7.1921, Walgett, New South Wales, Australia. Uncle of W. P. Howell (New South Wales). Lower order right-hand batsman, right-arm fast medium bowler. *Team* New South Wales (1874/5 to 1887/8, 27 matches). *Tour* Australia to England 1886. *Tests* Australia (1881/2 to 1886, 6 matches).
Career batting
65–105–23–1006–74*–12.26–0–*ct* 61
Bowling 3356–201–16.69–18–4–7/16
Test batting
6–10–2–82–33–10.25–0–*ct* 5
Bowling 332–7–47.42–0–0–3/64
He achieved very little on his visit to England.

Evans, Ernest Dering
Amateur. *b:* 21.8.1861, Clifton, Bristol. *d:* 4.11.1948, Clifton, Bristol. Lower order batsman. *Sch* Clifton. *Team* Somerset (1891, 1 match).
Career batting
1–1–0–0–0–0.00–0–*ct* 1

Evans, Canon Frederic Rawlins
Amateur. *b:* 1.6.1842, Griff, Warwickshire. *d:* 4.3.1927, Bedworth, Warwickshire. Middle order right-hand batsman, right-hand fast round arm bowler. *Sch* Cheltenham and Rugby. *Team* Oxford U (1863–65, blue all three years).
Career batting
12–17–1–302–43–18.87–0–*ct* 6
Bowling 177–12 + 1–14.75–1–0–5/32
His County cricket was for Warwickshire (pre first-class, 1862–80) and Worcestershire (pre first-class, 1866–76) and he was a leading member of the Free Foresters. In 1863 he was no-balled for having his hand above his shoulder and for this reason his bowling was not used as much as his ability warranted. He was a nephew of the author George Eliot (Mary Ann Evans).

Evans, George Herbert David
Amateur. *b:* 22.8.1928, Westbury-on-Trym, Bristol. *d:* 20.6.1991, Weston-super-Mare, Somerset. Middle order right-hand batsman, right-arm medium pace bowler. *Team* Somerset (1953, 8 matches).
Career batting
8–14–0–180–42–12.85–0–*ct* 5
Bowling 22–0
He played hockey for Wales.

Evans, Gwynn
Amateur. *b:* 13.8.1915, Bala, Merioneth. Middle order right-hand batsman, right-arm medium fast bowler. *Teams* Oxford U (1938–39, blue 1939); Glamorgan (1939, 7 matches); Leicestershire (1949, 10 matches).
Career batting
33–56–6–824–65*–16.48–0–*ct* 19
Bowling 2458–72–34.13–2–0–6/80
He also played for Denbighshire (1933–35).

Evans, Harold Ernest
Amateur. *b:* 20.10.1891. Hampstead, London. *d:* 24.9.1980, Crowthorne, Berkshire. Middle order batsman. *Team* Royal Navy (1920).
Career batting
1–2–0–5–3–2.50–0–*ct* 1

Evans, Henry
Amateur. *b:* 8.7.1857, Stoneyford, Codnor, Derbyshire. *d:* 30.7.1920, Spondon, Derbyshire. Brother of Thomas (Derbyshire). Lower/middle order right-hand batsman, right-arm fast medium bowler. *Team* Derbyshire (1878–82, 5 matches).
Career batting
5–10–0–41–10–4.10–0–*ct* 4
Bowling 252–19–13.26–2–0–7/47

Evans, Herbert Price
Amateur. *b:* 30.8.1894, Llandaff, Cardiff. *d:* 19.11.1982, Llandough, Penarth, Glamorgan. Middle order right-hand batsman. *Team* Glamorgan (1922, 1 match).
Career batting
1–2–0–9–9–4.50–0–*ct* 0
He first played for Glamorgan (pre first-class) in 1920. He played football for Cardiff City, Tranmere Rovers and Wales.

Evans, James
Professional. *b:* 9.11.1886, Shropshire. *d:* 26.8.1973, Lower Upham, Hampshire. Middle order right-hand batsman, slow right-arm bowler. *Team* Hampshire (1913–21, 15 matches).
Career batting
15–26–7–196–41–10.31–0–*ct* 10–*st* 1
Bowling 81–1–81.00–0–0–1/34

Evans, John Brian
Professional. *b:* 9.11.1936, Clydach, Glamorgan. Lower order right-hand batsman, right-arm fast medium bowler. *Team* Glamorgan (1958–63, 87 matches).
Career batting
88–131–19–1535–62*–13.70–0–*ct* 46
Bowling 6789–251–27.04–10–0–8/42
After leaving Glamorgan he played for Lincolnshire (1965–71) and his last first-class match was for Minor Counties in 1969.

Evans, Kevin Paul
Cricketer. *b:* 10.9.1963, Nottingham. Brother of R. J. (Nottinghamshire). Middle order right-hand batsman, right-arm medium fast bowler. *Team* Nottinghamshire (1984–92, 89 matches).
Career batting
89–123–30–2374–104–25.52–2–*ct* 69
Bowling 6405–182–35.19–3–0–5/27

Evans, Martin James
Amateur. *b:* 16.10.1904, Kingsclere, Hampshire. Tail end batsman, opening bowler. *Team* Royal Navy (1925).
Career batting
1–2–1–8–7*–8.00–0–*ct* 0
Bowling 42–0

Evans, Michael
Amateur. *b:* 3.5.1908, Leicester. *d:* 14.11.1974, Leicester. Tail end right-hand batsman, right-arm fast medium bowler. *Sch* Magdalen College School. *Team* Leicestershire (1946, 2 matches).
Career batting
2–4–1–26–14*–8.66–0–*ct* 0
Bowling 130–6–21.66–0–0–3/30

Evans, Nicholas John
Cricketer. *b:* 9.9.1954, Weston-super-Mare, Somerset. Lower order right-hand batsman, right-arm medium pace bowler. *Team* Somerset (1976, 1 match).
Career batting
1–1–0–0–0–0.00–0–*ct* 0
Bowling 62–0

Evans, Percy Stanbrook
Amateur. *b:* 20.7.1894, China. *d:* 17.1.1959, Bromley-by-Bow, London. Tail end batsman, slow left-arm bowler. *Team* Worcestershire (1928, 5 matches).
Career batting
5–9–3–15–5–2.50–0–*ct* 3
Bowling 199–3–66.33–0–0–3/84

Evans, Ralph Du Boulay
Amateur. *b:* 1.10.1891, Newtown, Hampshire. *d:* 27.7.1929, Wheelers Ridge, Los Angeles, California, USA. He was killed in a road accident. Brother of A. J. (Kent and Hampshire), son of A. H. (Hampshire and Somerset), cousin of A. E. (Hampshire), D. M. (Hampshire) and W. H. B. (Hampshire and Worcestershire). Tail end right-hand batsman, right-arm medium pace bowler. *Sch* Winchester. *Team* Hampshire (1912, 1 match); Cambridge U (1913).
Career batting
5–7–4–102–70–34.00–0–*ct* 1
Bowling 227–5–45.40–0–0–3/37
His last first-class match was for Free Foresters in 1914.

Evans, Robert Gordon
Amateur. *b:* 20.8.1899, Great Barton, Suffolk. *d:* 2.8.1981, Sidlesham, Sussex. Lower order left-hand batsman, right-arm fast medium bowler. *Sch* Bury St Edmunds. *Team* Cambridge U (1920–21, blue 1921).
Career batting
14–20–9–248–46*–22.54–0–*ct* 5
Bowling 1191–50–23.82–3–0–6/45
His last first-class match was for Free Foresters in 1923. His County cricket was for Berkshire (1935–36).

Evans, Ronald Ernest
Amateur. *b:* 22.7.1922, East Ham, Essex. Sound middle order right-hand batsman. *Team* Essex (1950–57, 17 matches).
Career batting
17–29–0–482–79–16.62–0–*ct* 8

Evans, Rupert Arnold
Cricketer. *b:* 24.2.1954, Kingston, Jamaica. Lower order right-hand batsman, off break bowler. *Team* Minor Counties (1990).
Career batting
1–1–1–4–4*–no av–0–*ct* 0
Bowling 147–2–73.50–0–0–2/147
His County cricket was for Oxfordshire (1973–92).

Evans, Russell John
Cricketer. *b:* 1.10.1965, Calverton, Nottinghamshire. Brother of K. P. (Nottinghamshire). Middle order right-hand batsman, right-arm medium pace bowler. *Team* Nottinghamshire (1987–90, 6 matches).
Career batting
6–9–3–112–50*–18.66–0–*ct* 4
Bowling 97–3–32.33–0–0–3/40

Evans, Talfryn
Professional. *b:* 10.6.1914, Sandy, Llanelly, Carmarthen. *d:* 31.3.1944, Llanelly, Carmarthen. Lower order left-hand batsman, slow left-arm bowler. *Team* Glamorgan (1934, 1 match).
Career batting
1–2–1–0–0*–0.00–0–*ct* 0
Bowling 25–0

Evans, Thomas
Amateur. *b:* 3.6.1852, Stoneyford, Codnor, Derbyshire. *d:* 2.12.1916, Heaton Moor, Lancashire. Brother of Henry (Derbyshire). Lower order right-hand batsman, right-arm slow medium bowler. *Team* Derbyshire (1883, 2 matches).

Career batting
4–7–0–91–35–13.00–0–*ct* 2
Bowling 150–6–25.00–0–0–2/27

He appeared in first-class matches for Liverpool and District in 1886 and 1889.

Evans, Thomas Godfrey, CBE
Professional. *b:* 18.8.1920, Finchley, Middlesex. Hard hitting lower order right-hand batsman, occasional leg break bowler, brilliant wicket-keeper. *Sch* Kent College, Canterbury. *Team* Kent (1939–67, 258 matches). *Tours* MCC to Australia and New Zealand 1946/7, 1950/1, 1954/5, 1958/9, to West Indies 1947/8, 1953/4, to South Africa 1948/9, 1956/7; Commonwealth to South Africa 1959/60; Cavaliers to Jamaica 1963/4, to West Indies 1964/5; Prime Minister's XI in India 1963/4. *Tests* England (1946–59, 91 matches).
Career batting
465–753–52–14882–144–21.22–7–*ct* 816–*st* 250
Bowling 245–2–122.50–0–0–2/50
Test batting
91–133–14–2439–104–20.49–2–*ct* 173–*st* 46

Though he appeared in a handful of Kent matches in 1939, Evans' regular County cricket began in 1946, and within twelve months he was recognised as the leading wicket-keeper in England. In contrast to most of his contemporaries behind the stumps, he was a very extrovert cricketer, relishing the acrobatics and flourishes that can be introduced into wicket-keeping, not that this showmanship detracted from his performances – he was the automatic choice for England both at home and overseas.

He hit 1,000 runs in a season four times with 1,613, av 28.80, in 1952 as his best, but ever keen to play to the gallery, he rarely treated the bowling seriously. To prove however that he could bat, he saved England from collapse on several occasions, including the famous 1946/7 Adelaide Test, when he was at the crease 95 minutes before scoring.

He retired from full-time first-class cricket in 1959, soon after being dropped as the England stumper, but he played his last first-class match for Cavaliers in 1969 and made fleeting reappearances in Charity matches much later.

Evans, Victor James
Professional. *b:* 4.3.1912, Woodford, Essex. *d:* 28.3.1975, Barking, Essex. Lower order right-hand batsman, right-arm medium pace off break bowler. *Team* Essex (1932–37, 62 matches).
Career batting
62–96–37–469–23*–7.94–0–*ct* 12
Bowling 3843–129–29.79–5–1–6/47

Evans, William Henry Brereton
Amateur. *b:* 29.1.1883, South Africa. *d:* 7.8.1913, Farnborough, Hampshire. Brother of A. E. (Hampshire) and D. M. (Hampshire), nephew of A. H. (Hampshire and Somerset), cousin of A. J. (Hampshire and Kent) and R. du B. (Hampshire). Middle order right-hand batsman, right-arm fast bowler. *Sch* Malvern. *Teams* Worcestershire (1901, 6 matches); Oxford U (1902–05, blue all four years); Hampshire (1902–10, 20 matches).
Career batting
66–114–5–3175–142–29.12–5–*ct* 61
Bowling 4550–175–26.00–12–2–7/41

Being in the Egyptian Civil Service, his County cricket was very limited, but it was thought that he would have represented England, had he been able to play regular first-class cricket. He captained Oxford in 1904. He was awarded his soccer blue 1902–05 and was also a noted rackets player. He was killed in a flying accident with the well known aviator Colonel Cody.

Evans, William Lewis
Amateur. *b:* 29.11.1897, Streatham, London. *d:* 25.4.1966, West Park, Horton, Epsom, Surrey. Middle order batsman, useful bowler. *Team* Civil Service (1927)
Career batting
1–2–1–23–15*–23.00–0–*ct* 1
Bowling 52–0

Evan-Thomas, Charles Marmaduke
Amateur. *b:* 5.11.1897, Caerwnon, Builth Wells, Brecon. *d:* 28.3.1953, Llwyn Madoc, Llanwrtyd Wells, Brecon. Brother-in-law of C. G. Stileman (Europeans). Middle or lower order batsman, opening bowler. *Teams* Royal Navy (1919–20); MCC (1929).
Career batting
3–6–0–45–19–7.50–0–*ct* 1
Bowling 59–1–59.00–0–0–1/16

Eve, Stanley Charles
Amateur. *b:* 18.12.1925, Stepney, London. *d:* 27.1.1990, Havering, Essex. Middle order right-hand batsman, right-arm medium pace bowler. *Team* Essex (1950–57, 32 matches).
Career batting
32–51–4–1041–120–22.14–1–*ct* 17

He did not appear for Essex in the years 1952–56 inclusive owing to business commitments.

Evelyn, Francis Lyndon
Amateur. *b:* 24.5.1859, Corton, Presteigne, Radnorshire. *d:* 8.12.1910, Kinsham Court, Herefordshire. Middle order right-hand batsman, good deep field. *Sch* Rugby. *Team* Oxford U (1880–81, blue 1880).
Career batting
5–10–0–33–10–3.30–0–*ct* 1

His County cricket was for Herefordshire (1879–91) and Radnorshire (1885). He also won a blue for rackets.

Everard, Sir William Lindsay
Amateur. *b:* 13.3.1891, Knighton, Leicester. *d:* 11.3.1949, Torquay, Devon. Brother-in-law of H. Logan (Leicestershire). Opening right-hand batsman. *Sch* Harrow. *Team* Leicestershire (1924, 1 match).
Career batting
1–2–0–3–3–1.50–0–*ct* 0
He was President of Leicestershire in 1936 and 1939. A pioneer of private flying, he had his own aerodrome near Ratcliffe Hall, Leicestershire. He was Unionist MP for Melton 1924–35.

Everett, Harold
Amateur. *b:* 13.11.1891, Kennington, London. *d:* 27.4.1979, East Preston, Sussex. Middle order right-hand batsman, right-arm slow medium bowler. *Team* Civil Service (1927).
Career batting
1–2–0–2–2–1.00–0–*ct* 0
Bowling 34–0

Everett, John
Cricketer. *b:* 12.9.1964, Kuala Belait, Brunei. Middle order left-hand batsman. *Team* Scotland (1992).
Career batting
1–2–0–53–33–26.50–0–*ct* 3

Everett, Samuel Charles
Amateur. *b:* 17.6.1901, Sydney, New South Wales, Australia. *d:* 10.10.1970, Wahroonga, Sydney, New South Wales, Australia. Tail end left-hand batsman, right-arm fast bowler. *Team* New South Wales (1921/2 to 1929/30, 28 matches). *Tours* Australia to England 1926; New South Wales to New Zealand 1923/4.
Career batting
45–51–9–617–77–14.69–0–*ct* 26
Bowling 3634–134–27.11–8–0–6/23
He accomplished very little on his tour to England.

Everitt, Russell Stanley
Amateur. *b:* 8.9.1881, Kings Heath, Birmingham. *d:* 11.5.1973, Kew Gardens, Surrey. Middle order right-hand batsman, wicket-keeper. *Sch* Malvern. *Teams* Worcestershire (1901, 1 match); Warwickshire (1909, 3 matches).
Career batting
4–7–1–63–38–10.50–0–*ct* 3

Evers, Ralph Denis Mark
Amateur. *b:* 11.8.1913, Pedmore, Stourbridge, Worcestershire. Middle order right-hand batsman. *Sch* Haileybury. *Team* Worcestershire (1936–38, 15 matches).
Career batting
15–26–1–383–60*–15.32–0–*ct* 7

Evershed, Edward
Amateur. *b:* 3.11.1867, Stapenhill, Burton-on-Trent, Staffordshire. *d:* 18.2.1957, Handsworth Wood, Birmingham. Brother of S. H. (Derbyshire) and Wallis (Derbyshire), cousin of G. F. Bell (Derbyshire). Middle order right-hand batsman. *Team* Derbyshire (1898, 1 match).
Career batting
1–1–0–1–1–1.00–0–*ct* 2
He played no first-class matches at Oxford U. He first played for Derbyshire (not first-class) in 1888. A noted rugby footballer, he appeared for Rosslyn Park.

Evershed, Sir Sydney Herbert
Amateur. *b:* 13.1.1861, Stapenhill, Burton-on-Trent, Staffordshire. *d:* 7.3.1937, Burton-on-Trent, Staffordshire. Brother of Edward (Derbyshire) and Wallis (Derbyshire), cousin of G. F. Bell (Derbyshire). Opening right-hand batsman, right-arm medium pace bowler. *Sch* Clifton. *Team* Derbyshire (1880–1901, 75 matches).
Career batting
76–129–2–3137–153–24.70–4–*ct* 35
Bowling 122–5–24.40–1–0–5/19
He captained Derbyshire 1891–98. He also played for Staffordshire (1878). He was President of Derbyshire 1905 and 1907–08. An excellent rugby footballer, he played for Midland Counties as half-back and was reserve for England.

Evershed, Wallis
(entered at Clifton as Wallis Emerond Evershed)
Amateur. *b:* 10.5.1863, Stapenhill, Burton-on-Trent, Staffordshire. *d:* 8.5.1911, Kendal, Westmorland. Brother of Edward (Derbyshire) and S. H. (Derbyshire), cousin of G. F. Bell (Derbyshire). Middle order right-hand batsman, right-arm medium pace bowler. *Sch* Clifton. *Team* Derbyshire (1882–84, 13 matches).
Career batting
13–24–0–357–92–14.87–0–*ct* 6
Bowling 8–3–2.66–0–0–3/8

Every, Trevor
Professional. *b:* 19.12.1909, Llanelly, Carmarthen. *d:* 20.1.1990, Newport, Monmouthshire. Lower order right-hand batsman, wicket-keeper. *Team* Glamorgan (1929–34, 128 matches).
Career batting
128–198–44–2518–116–16.35–1–*ct* 108–*st* 71
Bowling 49–0
Failing eyesight, which eventually led to total blindness, caused his retirement in 1934.

Evetts, Julian Arthur
Amateur. *b:* 24.11.1911, Tackley Park, Thame, Oxfordshire. Grandson of William (Oxford U). Opening right-hand batsman. *Sch* Westminster. *Team* Oxford U (1933).
Career batting
1–1–0–0–0–0.00–*ct* 0
His County cricket was for Oxfordshire (1930–34).

Evetts, William
Amateur. *b:* 30.6.1847, Tackley Park, Thame, Oxfordshire. *d:* 7.4.1936, Hill Court, Tackley, Thame, Oxfordshire. Grandfather of J. A. (Oxford U). Hard hitting middle order right-hand batsman, brilliant deep field. *Sch* Harrow. *Team* Oxford U (1868–69, blue both years).
Career batting
22–36–2–531–102–15.61–1–*ct* 4
His County cricket was for Buckinghamshire (1865–68). His last first-class match was for MCC in 1882.

Ewbank, Rev Christopher Cooper
Amateur. *b:* 10.3.1845, Cambridge. *d:* 9.7.1933, Langford, Bedfordshire. Brother of G. H. W. (Sussex 1855). Middle order right-hand batsman, wicket-keeper. *Sch* Brighton. *Team* Sussex (1867–79, 3 matches).
Career batting
4–8–0–95–31–11.87–0–*ct* 2
He was not in the Eleven whilst at Cambridge U. His first-class debut was for MCC in 1866. He also played for Bedfordshire (1868).

Ewens, Percival Charles
Amateur. *b:* 23.11.1882, Yeovil, Somerset. *d:* 21.7.1961, Galmington, Taunton, Somerset. Middle order right-hand batsman. *Team* Somerset (1923–26, 7 matches).
Career batting
7–11–4–114–27–16.28–0–*ct* 3

Exham, Percy George
Amateur. *b:* 26.6.1859, Cork, Ireland. *d:* 7.10.1922, Laurel Hill, Repton, Derbyshire. Middle order right-hand batsman, good cover field. *Sch* Repton. *Teams* Cambridge U (1880–81); Derbyshire (1883, 1 match).
Career batting
6–10–0–88–43–8.80–0–*ct* 3
He also played for Dorset (1884). He played soccer for Derby County.

Exton, Rodney Noel
Amateur. *b:* 28.12.1927, Boscombe, Bournemouth, Hampshire. Middle/lower order right-hand batsman, off break bowler. *Sch* Clifton. *Team* Hampshire (1946, 4 matches).
Career batting
4–5–1–39–24*–9.75–0–*ct* 1
Bowling 40–0

Eyre, Charles Howard
Amateur. *b:* 26.3.1883, Toxteth, Liverpool, Lancashire. *d:* 25.9.1915, near Loos, France. He was killed in action. Middle order right-hand batsman. *Sch* Harrow. *Team* Cambridge U (1903–06, blue 1904–06). *Tour* MCC to North America 1905.
Career batting
30–53–2–1092–153–21.41–1–*ct* 40
Bowling 50–2–25.00–0–0–1/9
He captained Cambridge in 1906.

Eyre, John
Amateur. *b:* 29.10.1859, Shaw, Berkshire. *d:* 24.11.1941, Bayswater, London. Middle order right-hand batsman. *Sch* Winchester. *Team* MCC (1887).
Career batting
1–1–0–9–9–9.00–0–*ct* 0
He did not appear in first-class matches whilst at Oxford U, but did win a soccer blue.

Eyre, John Arthur
Professional. *b:* 25.7.1885, North Wingfield, Derbyshire. *d:* 12.6.1964, Bolton-on-Dearne, Yorkshire. Middle order right-hand batsman. *Team* Derbyshire (1908, 1 match).
Career batting
1–2–1–2–1*–2.00–0–*ct* 0

Eyre, John Richard
Cricketer. *b:* 13.6.1944, Glossop, Derbyshire. Middle order right-hand batsman, right-arm medium pace bowler. *Team* Derbyshire (1963–67, 48 matches).
Career batting
48–84–4–1194–106–14.92–1–*ct* 17
Bowling 248–1–248.00–0–0–1/6

Eyre, Thomas John Peter
Professional. *b:* 17.10.1939, Brough, Derbyshire. Lower order left-hand batsman, right-arm fast medium bowler. *Team* Derbyshire (1959–72, 197 matches).
Career batting
197–264–49–3436–102–15.98–1–*ct* 83
Bowling 10305–359–28.70–8–0–8/65
In 1965 he was reported to MCC as having a suspect bowling action.

Ezekowitz, Raymond Alan Bryan
Cricketer. *b:* 19.1.1954, Durban, South Africa. Opening right-hand batsman. *Team* Oxford U (1980–81, blue both years).
Career batting
18–32–1–635–93–20.48–0–*ct* 13

F

Faber, Mark James Julian
Cricketer. *b:* 15.8.1950, Horsted Keynes, Sussex. *d:* 10.12.1991, Marylebone, London. Middle order right-hand batsman, right-arm medium pace bowler. *Sch* Eton. *Teams* Oxford U (1970–72, blue 1972); Sussex (1973–76, 57 matches). *Tour* Oxford and Cambridge U to Malaysia 1972/3 (not first-class).
Career batting
78–144–8–3009–176–22.12–3–*ct* 42
Bowling 66–1–66.00–0–0–1/11

He hit 1,060 runs, av 30.28, in 1975. He was grandson of the former Prime Minister Harold Macmillan.

Fabian, Aubrey Howard
Amateur. *b:* 20.3.1909, East Finchley, Middlesex. *d:* 26.9.1984, Cranbrook, Kent. Lower order right-hand batsman, right-arm medium pace bowler. *Sch* Highgate. *Team* Cambridge U (1929–31, blue all three years). *Tour* Oxford and Cambridge U to Jamaica 1938/9 (not first-class).
Career batting
35–51–22–763–76–26.31–0–*ct* 22
Bowling 2280–61–37.37–2–0–8/69
He also won blues for fives and soccer, and also played soccer for Derby County, and in amateur Internationals for England.

Fabling, Arthur Hugh
Amateur. *b:* 6.9.1889, Grandborough, Warwickshire. *d:* 13.10.1972, Grandborough, Warwickshire. Middle order right-hand batsman, wicket-keeper. *Sch* Wellingborough. *Team* Warwickshire (1921, 1 match).
Career batting
1–2–0–8–7–4.00–0–*ct* 0
A soccer player, he represented Northampton.

Fagg, Arthur Edward
Professional. *b:* 18.6.1915, Chartham, Kent. *d:* 13.9.1977, Tunbridge Wells, Kent. Opening right-hand batsman, right-arm medium pace bowler, occasional wicket-keeper. *Team* Kent (1932–57, 414 matches). *Tour* MCC to Australia 1936/7. *Tests* England (1936–39, 5 matches).
Career batting
435–803–46–27291–269*–36.05–58–*ct* 425–*st* 7
Bowling 47–0
Test batting
5–8–0–150–39–18.75–0–*ct* 5
Ill health reduced his opportunities in Test cricket, but he was very successful for Kent. He completed 1,000 runs 13 times, going on to 2,000 five times, his best being 2,456 (av 52.25) in 1938. He was the youngest ever player to reach 1,000 runs for a county in a season. In the same season he performed the unique feat of hitting a double century in both innings of the same match: 244 and 202* for Kent v Essex at Colchester. Of his six double centuries, the highest was 269* for Kent v Nottinghamshire at Trent Bridge in 1953. He was a county umpire from 1959 to his death and stood in 18 Test matches from 1967 to 1975.

Fagge, Rev John Frederick
Amateur. *b:* 5.10.1814, Chartham, Kent. *d:* 30.3.1884, Chartham, Kent. Brother-in-law of W. de C. Baker (Kent). Middle order right-hand batsman, right-hand medium pace round-arm bowler. *Teams* Oxford U (1834–35); Kent (1834–51, 14 matches).
Career batting
44–78–2–588–55–7.73–0–*ct* 26
Bowling 334–17 + 82–19.64–5–1–6/?
His first-class debut was for Gentlemen of Kent in 1833 and his last match was for Gentlemen of Kent in 1853. He also played for Norfolk (1844). He was twice married and had 18 children.

Fairbairn, Alan
Amateur. *b:* 25.1.1923, Winchmore Hill, Middlesex. Opening left-hand batsman. *Sch* Haileybury. *Team* Middlesex (1947–51, 20 matches).
Career batting
21–34–4–776–110*–25.86–2–*ct* 10
Bowling 2–0
He hit 108 on his first-class debut for Middlesex v Somerset at Taunton in 1947.

Fairbairn, Gordon Armytage
Amateur. *b:* 26.6.1892, Logan Downs, Queensland, Australia. *d:* 5.11.1973, Ocean Grove, Victoria, Australia. Brother of S. G. (MCC to West Indies 1912/13). Middle order left-hand batsman, leg break bowler. *Sch* Geelong GS, Australia. *Teams* Cambridge U (1912–19, blue 1913, 1914 and 1919); Middlesex (1919, 4 matches).
Career batting
32–52–9–971–112–22.58–1–*ct* 30
Bowling 2396–80–29.95–6–1–5/55
His final first-class match was for Free Foresters in 1924.

Fairbairn, Sir Robert Duncan
Amateur. *b:* 25.9.1910, Longhirst, Northumberland. *d:* 26.3.1988, Guildford, Surry. Middle order right-hand batsman. *Teams* Scotland (1938); Europeans (1944/5).
Career batting
2–4–0–19–13–4.75–0–*ct* 1
His County cricket was for Cheshire (1938–39). He played soccer for Corinthian Casuals, Queen's Park, St Johnstone and Partick Thistle.

Fairbanks, Walter
Amateur. *b:* 13.4.1852, Luton, Chatham, Kent. *d:* 25.8.1924, Guildford, Surrey. Middle order right-hand batsman, good point field. *Sch* Clifton. *Teams* Cambridge U (1875); Gloucestershire (1877–84, 24 matches).
Career batting
27–38–7–316–46–10.19–0–*ct* 21
He gained a rugby blue whilst at Cambridge.

Fairbanks-Smith, Cuthbert
Amateur. *b:* 18.3.1885, Lee, London. *d:* 25.5.1948, Middleton, Sussex. Tail end batsman. *Sch* Bradfield. *Team* Somerset (1921, 2 matches).
Career batting
2–3–1–6–6–3.00–0–*ct* 1

Fairbrother, Neil Harvey
Cricketer. *b:* 9.9.1963, Warrington, Lancashire. Middle order left-hand batsman, left-arm medium pace bowler. *Team* Lancashire (1982–92, 202 matches). *Tours* England to New Zealand 1987/8, 1991/2, to Pakistan 1987/8, to Australia 1987/8 (not first-class), to Australia and New Zealand (World Cup) 1991/2; England A to Pakistan and Sri Lanka 1990/1; Lancashire to Jamaica 1987/8. *Tests* England (1987–90, 7 matches).
Career batting
221–345–55–12177–366–41.98–26–*ct* 140
Bowling 423–5–84.60–0–0–2/91
Test batting
7–9–1–64–33*–8.00–0–*ct* 4
Bowling 9–0
He hit 1,000 runs in a season eight times (best 1,740, av 69.60, in 1990). His highest score was 366 for Lancashire v Surrey at the Oval in 1990. In this innings he scored 100 in each session and 311 in a single day. In 1992 he was appointed captain of Lancashire.

Fairclough, Peter Moss
Professional. *b:* 25.9.1887, Bickershaw, Lancashire. *d:* 16.11.1952, Stanley Park, Blackpool, Lancashire. Lower order right-hand batsman, slow left-arm bowler. *Team* Lancashire (1911–23, 20 matches).
Career batting
20–27–14–140–19–10.76–0–*ct* 9
Bowling 1158–52–22.26–2–0–7/27

Fairfax, Alan Geoffrey
Amateur. *b:* 16.6.1906, Summer Hill, Sydney, New South Wales, Australia. *d:* 17.5.1955, Kensington, London. Middle order right-hand batsman, right-arm fast medium bowler. *Team* New South Wales (1928/9 to 1931/2, 21 matches). *Tour* Australia to England 1930. *Tests* Australia (1928/9 to 1930/1, 10 matches).
Career batting
56–76–10–1910–104–28.93–1–*ct* 41
Bowling 3735–134–27.87–2–0–6/54
Test batting
10–12–4–410–65–51.25–0–*ct* 15
Bowling 645–21–30.71–0–0–4/31
He emigrated to England in 1932, running a cricket school and later joining the staff of a Sunday newspaper, and his final first-class match was for Gentlemen v Players in 1934.

Fairservice, Colin
Professional. *b:* 6.8.1909, Hadlow, Kent. Son of W. J. (Kent). Middle order right-hand batsman, off break bowler. *Teams* Kent (1929–33, 59 matches); Middlesex (1936, 6 matches).
Career batting
74–107–13–1650–110–17.55–1–*ct* 44
Bowling 694–18–38.55–0–0–3/49

Fairservice, William John
Professional. *b:* 16.5.1881, Nunhead, London. *d:* 26.6.1971, Canterbury, Kent. Father of Colin (Kent and Middlesex). Tail end right-hand batsman, right-arm medium pace off break bowler. *Team* Kent (1902–21, 301 matches).
Career batting
302–419–96–4939–61*–15.29–0–*ct* 164
Bowling 19419–859–22.60–39–7–7/44
He completed 100 wickets in a season once, in 1920: 113, av 17.46. He also played for Northumberland (1924–26).

Fairweather, James Henry Whitton
Cricketer. *b:* 16.7.1946, West End, Edinburgh, Scotland. Opening right-hand batsman. *Sch* Edinburgh Academy. *Team* Scotland (1971).
Career batting
2–4–0–23–9–5.75–0–*ct* 2

Fakir, S. A. U. (*see under* Aizazuddin, F. S.)

Falck, Ernest Dyson
Amateur. *b:* 21.10.1907, Huddersfield, Yorkshire. *d:* 19.2.1982, Bridport, Dorset. Middle order right-hand batsman. *Team* Somerset (1935–36, 4 matches).
Career batting
4–8–1–74–28–10.57–0–*ct* 2

Falcon, Joseph Henry
Amateur. *b:* 9.4.1892, Sprowston Hall, Norwich, Norfolk. *d:* 11.2.1950, Lowestoft, Suffolk. Brother of Michael (Cambridge U). Lower order right-hand batsman, right-arm fast medium bowler. *Sch* Harrow. *Team* Cambridge U (1914).
Career batting
2–1–1–3–3*–no av–0–*ct* 0
Bowling 165–5–33.00–0–0–3/72
His County cricket was for Norfolk (1910–22).

Falcon, Michael
Amateur. *b:* 21.7.1888, Sprowston Hall, Norwich, Norfolk. *d:* 27.2.1976, Norwich, Norfolk. Brother of J. H. (Cambridge U). Middle order right-hand batsman, right-arm fast medium bowler, fine field. *Sch* Harrow. *Team* Cambridge U (1908–11, blue all four years). *Tour* Incogniti to USA 1913 (not first-class).
Career batting
89–155–25–3282–134–25.24–4–*ct* 44
Bowling 5727–231–24.79–20–1–7/70
He played for Norfolk from 1906 to 1946, being captain from 1912 to 1946. One of the greatest of regular Minor Counties cricketers, he might have played for England if he had appeared more often in first-class cricket. His final first-class match was for Free Foresters in 1936. He captained Cambridge in 1910. He was MP for East Norfolk (1918–23).

Falconer, Roderick
Professional. *b:* 10.11.1886, Bank, Hampshire. *d:* 8.3.1966, Malvern, Worcestershire. Lower order

right-hand batsman, right-arm medium pace bowler. *Team* Northamptonshire (1907–10, 7 matches).
Career batting
7–12–4–29–12*–3.62–0–*ct* 1
Bowling 228–9–25.33–0–0–2/13

He also played for Norfolk (1912–14).

Falding, Sydney Wheatley
Professional. *b:* 5.5.1891, Kirkstall, Leeds, Yorkshire. *d:* 7.11.1959, Leeds, Yorkshire. Lower order left-hand batsman, left-arm opening bowler. *Team* Northamptonshire (1921, 1 match).
Career batting
2–3–0–8–8–2.66–0–*ct* 0
Bowling 168–3–56.00–0–0–2/49

He also played for Lincolnshire (1914) and Devon (1925–32). His final first-class match was for West of England in 1927.

Falkner, Nicholas James
Cricketer. *b:* 30.9.1962, Redhill, Surrey. Opening right-hand batsman, right-arm medium pace bowler. *Teams* Surrey (1984–87, 16 matches); Sussex (1988–89, 10 matches).
Career batting
26–42–3–1042–102–26.71–2–*ct* 14
Bowling 9–1–9.00–0–0–1/3

On his first-class debut he scored 101* for Surrey v Cambridge U at Banstead in 1984.

Fallows, John Armstrong
Amateur. *b:* 25.7.1907, Woodley, Cheshire. *d:* 20.1.1974, Macclesfield, Cheshire. Lower order right-hand batsman. *Sch* Worksop. *Team* Lancashire (1946, 25 matches).
Career batting
25–22–1–171–35–8.14–0–*ct* 10

He also played for Cheshire (1929–32). Appointed as Lancashire's captain in 1946, he played first-class County cricket for just that summer, but later served on the Lancashire Committee.

Fane, Frederick Luther
Amateur. *b:* 27.4.1875, Curragh Camp, Co Kildare, Ireland. *d:* 27.11.1960, Kelvedon Hatch, Brentwood, Essex. Son of F. J. (Essex, pre first-class). Opening right-hand batsman. *Sch* Charterhouse. *Teams* Essex (1895–1922, 292 matches); Oxford U (1896–98, blue 1897–98); London County (1901). *Tours* Bennett to West Indies 1901/2; Hawke to New Zealand and Australia 1902/3; MCC to South Africa 1905/6, 1909/10, to Australia 1907/8; Leveson-Gower to Rhodesia 1909/10. *Tests* England (1905/6 to 1909/10, 14 matches).
Career batting
417–721–44–18548–217–27.39–25–*ct* 194
Bowling 49–2–24.50–0–0–2/17
Test batting
14–27–1–682–143–26.23–1–*ct* 6

He captained Essex 1904–06 and England in five Tests – three in Australia in 1907/8 and two in South Africa in 1909/10; on both occasions he was the vice-captain of the MCC touring party. He hit 1,000 runs in a season five times (best 1,572, av 34.93, in 1906). His two double centuries were for Essex, the higher being 217 v Surrey at the Oval in 1911. His final first-class match was for H. D. G. Leveson-Gower's XI in 1924.

Fantham, William Edward
Professional. *b:* 14.5.1918, Birmingham. Middle order right-hand batsman, off break bowler. *Team* Warwickshire (1935–48, 63 matches).
Career batting
63–103–12–1168–51–12.83–0–*ct* 33
Bowling 2907–64–45.42–2–0–5/55

Faragher, Harold Alker
Amateur. *b:* 20.7.1917, Reddish, Lancashire. Middle order right-hand batsman, right-arm medium pace or leg break bowler. *Team* Essex (1949–50, 6 matches).
Career batting
6–9–2–274–85*–39.14–0–*ct* 4

Farbrace, Paul
Cricketer. *b:* 7.7.1967, Ash, Kent. Lower order right-hand batsman, wicket-keeper. *Teams* Kent (1987–89, 8 matches); Middlesex (1990–92, 30 matches).
Career batting
38–48–11–694–79–18.75–0–*ct* 86–*st* 12
Bowling 64–1–64.00–0–0–1/64

Farebrother, Michael Humphrey
Amateur. *b:* 28.2.1920, Chelsea, London. *d:* 27.9.1987, Seaford, Sussex. Lower order right-hand batsman, left-arm fast medium bowler. *Sch* Eton. *Team* Oxford U (1939).
Career batting
1–2–0–1–1–0.50–0–*ct* 2
Bowling 128–4–32.00–0–0–2/49

Fargus, Rev Archibald Hugh Conway
Amateur. *b:* 15.12.1878, Clifton, Bristol. *d:* 6.10.1963, Eastville, Bristol. Lower order right-hand batsman, right-arm fast bowler. *Sch* Clifton and Haileybury. *Teams* Cambridge U (1900–01, blue both years); Gloucestershire (1900–01, 15 matches).
Career batting
28–51–9–507–61–12.07–0–*ct* 19
Bowling 2048–60–34.13–2–1–7/55

He also played for Devon (1904). He was the son of a well-known Victorian novelist who wrote under the name Hugh Conway.

Farmer, Charles George Edgar
Amateur. *b:* 28.11.1885, Chelsea, London. *d:* 18.8.1916, Longueval, France. He was killed in action. Nephew of A. A. (Surrey) and W. P. Crawley (MCC), father-in-law of F. A. V. Parker (Hampshire). Middle order batsman. *Sch* Eton. *Team* MCC (1905–

06).
Career batting
2–3–0–78–55–26.00–0–*ct* 1
He appeared in the Freshmen's and Seniors' matches at Oxford, but no first-class games.

Farmer, John James Stewart
Amateur. *b:* 5.8.1934, Leatherhead, Surrey. Middle order right-hand batsman. *Sch* Eton. *Team* Oxford U (1958).
Career batting
2–4–0–10–6–2.50–0–*ct* 0

Farnes, Kenneth
Amateur. *b:* 8.7.1911, Leytonstone, Essex. *d:* 20.10.1941, Chipping-Warden, Oxfordshire. He was killed while flying on active service. Tail end right-hand batsman, right-arm fast bowler. *Teams* Essex (1930–39, 79 matches); Cambridge U (1931–33, blue all three years). *Tours* MCC to West Indies 1934/5, to Australia and New Zealand 1936/7, to South Africa 1938/9. *Tests* England (1934 to 1938/9, 15 matches).
Career batting
168–201–59–1182–97*–8.32–0–*ct* 84
Bowling 14804–690–21.45–44–8–8/38
Test batting
15–17–5–58–20–4.83–0–*ct* 1
Bowling 1719–60–28.65–3–1–6/96
Although the best amateur fast bowler of the 1930s, Farnes' County cricket was very restricted – after leaving Cambridge in 1933 he was a master at Worksop College. He twice took 100 wickets in a season (best 113, av 18.38, in 1933). He tragically died shortly after qualifying as a pilot in the RAF.

Farnfield, Geoffrey George
Amateur. *b:* 13.7.1897, West Ham, Essex. *d:* 22.3.1974, Leamington Spa, Warwickshire. Middle order right-hand batsman. *Team* Essex (1921, 12 matches).
Career batting
12–20–1–252–41–13.26–0–*ct* 5

Farnfield, Percy Hamilton
Amateur. *b:* 16.6.1881, Guildford, Surrey. *d:* 19.8.1962, Solihull, Warwickshire. Middle order right-hand batsman. *Team* Worcestershire (1925, 1 match).
Career batting
1–1–0–0–0–0.00–0–*ct* 0
He played no first-class cricket whilst at Cambridge U, but did win a blue for soccer.

Farnsworth, Andrew William
Professional. *b:* 14.1.1887, Newtown, Sydney, New South Wales, Australia. *d:* 30.10.1966, Sydney, New South Wales, Australia. Middle order right-hand batsman. *Teams* New South Wales (1908/9, 1 match); Lancashire (1919, 1 match).
Career batting
2–4–0–78–69–19.50–0–*ct* 0

Farooq Hamid
Cricketer. *b:* 3.3.1945, Lahore, India. Tail end right-hand batsman, right-arm fast medium bowler. *Teams* Lahore (1961/2 to 1968/9); PIA (1962/3 to 1969/70). *Tours* Pakistan Eaglets to England 1963; Pakistan to Australia and New Zealand 1964/5, to Ceylon 1964/5; PIA to East Africa 1964/5. *Test* Pakistan (1964/5, 1 match).
Career batting
43–54–12–546–38–13.00–0–*ct* 27
Bowling 2799–111–25.21–3–1–7/16
Test batting
1–2–0–3–3–1.50–0–*ct* 0
Bowling 107–1–107.00–0–0–1/82

Farquhar, John Stewart
Amateur. *b:* 8.4.1904, Cargill, Perthshire, Scotland. *d:* 7.3.1984, Dundee, Angus, Scotland. Lower order right-hand batsman, right-arm fast medium bowler. *Team* Scotland (1930–39).
Career batting
6–9–7–20–6*–10.00–0–*ct* 1
Bowling 422–22–19.18–0–0–4/13

Farr, Bryan Henry
Amateur. *b:* 16.3.1924, Nottingham. Middle or lower order right-hand batsman, right-arm medium pace bowler. *Sch* Harrow. *Team* Nottinghamshire (1949–51, 6 matches).
Career batting
7–12–2–143–37–14.30–0–*ct* 2
Bowling 538–10–53.80–1–0–5/96
He appeared for Cambridge U against Oxford in 1943. His final first-class match was for Free Foresters in 1952.

Farrands, Frank Henry
(registered as F. H. Farrand at death)
Professional. *b:* 28.3.1835, Sutton-in-Ashfield, Nottinghamshire. *d:* 22.9.1916, Sutton-in-Ashfield, Nottinghamshire. Lower order right-hand batsman, right-hand fast round-arm bowler. *Team* Nottinghamshire (1871, 2 matches).
Career batting
30–49–15–212–41–6.23–0–*ct* 13
Bowling 1925–127 + 1–15.15–12–4–6/23
His first-class debut was for MCC in 1868 and his final first-class match was for the same club in 1880. He was a first-class umpire (1883–88), standing in seven Test matches (1884–88).

Farrant, Percy Robert
Amateur. *b:* 25.4.1868, Llandudno, Caernarvonshire. *d:* 4.9.1921, at sea on board SS *Ortega*. Middle order right-hand batsman, right-arm fast bowler. *Sch* Repton. *Team* Oxford U (1890).

Farrar, Albert

Career batting
2–4–1–12–5*–4.00–0–*ct* 1
Bowling 30–1–30.00–0–0–1/20

His County cricket was for Worcestershire (pre first-class, 1890). He won a blue for soccer.

Farrar, Albert
Professional. *b:* 29.4.1883, Brighouse, Yorkshire. *d:* 25.12.1954, Salterhebble, Halifax, Yorkshire. Middle order batsman. *Team* Yorkshire (1906, 1 match).
Career batting
1–1–0–2–2–2.00–0–*ct* 1

A rugby league footballer, he appeared for Rochdale Hornets.

Farrar, Harry
Amateur. *b:* 14.3.1930, Radcliffe, Lancashire. Lower order left-hand batsman, left-arm fast medium bowler. *Team* Lancashire (1955, 1 match).
Career batting
1 match, did not bat–*ct* 0
Bowling 25–0

Farrar, Hubert Lister
Amateur. *b:* 2.4.1881, Broughton Park, Manchester, Lancashire. *d:* 4.7.1939, Bowdon, Cheshire. Middle order right-hand batsman. *Sch* Repton. *Team* Lancashire (1904, 1 match).
Career batting
1–2–0–28–25–14.00–0–*ct* 0

Farren, George Clement
Amateur. *b:* 25.6.1874, Rugby, Warwickshire. *d:* 2.11.1956, Coventry, Warwickshire. Middle order right-hand batsman. *Team* Warwickshire (1912, 1 match).
Career batting
1–1–0–0–0–0.00–0–*ct* 0

Farrimond, William
Professional. *b:* 23.5.1903, Daisy Hill, Lancashire. *d:* 15.11.1979, Westhoughton, Bolton, Lancashire. Middle order right-hand batsman, wicket-keeper. *Team* Lancashire (1924–45, 134 matches). *Tours* MCC to South Africa 1930/1, to West Indies 1934/5. *Tests* England (1930/1 to 1935, 4 matches).
Career batting
153–168–45–2908–174–23.64–1–*ct* 255–*st* 77
Bowling 16–0
Test batting
4–7–0–116–35–16.57–0–*ct* 5–*st* 2

Although selected to play for England in four matches, Farrimond did not at that time command a regular place in his County team, being deputy to Duckworth. His only full seasons in County cricket were 1938 and 1939.

Fasih-ud-din, Rashid
Cricketer. *b:* 28.12.1939, Quetta, India. Opening or middle order right-hand batsman, wicket-keeper. *Teams* Karachi (1957/8 to 1961/2); Quetta (1962/3 to 1974/5); Baluchistan (1972/3 to 1973/4). *Tour* Pakistan to England 1967.
Career batting
51–83–5–2286–237–29.30–6–*ct* 80–*st* 36

As reserve wicket-keeper to Wasim Bari on the 1967 Tour to England, he was required for only six matches. His only double century was for Quetta v East Pakistan at Karachi in 1962/3.

Fasken, David Kenneth
Amateur. *b:* 23.3.1932, Batu Gajah, Ipoh, Federated Malay States. Lower order right-hand batsman, right-arm medium fast bowler. *Sch* Wellington. *Team* Oxford U (1953–55, blue all three years).
Career batting
36–53–8–559–61–12.42–0–*ct* 21
Bowling 2862–71–40.59–1–0–5/108

His final first-class match was for Free Foresters in 1962. His County cricket was for Oxfordshire (1950–55).

Faulkner, George Aubrey
Amateur. *b:* 17.12.1881, Port Elizabeth, South Africa. *d:* 10.9.1930, Walham Green, London, of gas poisoning. Brilliant middle order right-hand batsman, googly bowler. *Teams* Transvaal 1902/03 to 1909/10); MCC (1912–20). *Tours* South Africa to England 1907, 1912, 1924 (1 match), to Australia 1910/11. *Tests* South Africa (1905/6 to 1924, 25 matches).
Career batting
118–197–23–6366–204–36.58–13–*ct* 94
Bowling 7826–449–17.42–33–8–7/26
Test batting
25–47–4–1754–204–40.79–4–*ct* 20
Bowling 2180–82–26.58–4–0–7/84

He was very successful on his two full tours to England, scoring over 1,000 runs on each (best 1,206, av 29.82, in 1907) and in 1912 taking 163 wickets, av 15.42. He also performed brilliantly in 1909/10 in the Tests against England in South Africa and in the following season in Australia. In 1913 he moved to England and after serving with distinction in the First World War opened an indoor cricket school in London, which became world famous. His last first-class match in South Africa was for South African XI in 1910/11. His highest score was 204 for South Africa v Australia at Melbourne in 1910/11.

Faulkner, William George
Amateur. *b:* 5.5.1923, Bromley-by-Bow, London. Lower order right-hand batsman, right-arm fast medium bowler. *Team* RAF (1946).
Career batting
1–2–0–23–18–11.50–1–*ct* 1
Bowling 56–0

Faviell, William Frederick Oliver
Amateur. *b:* 5.6.1882, Loughton, Essex. *d:* 14.2.1950, Nairobi, Kenya. Middle order right-hand batsman,

right-arm medium pace bowler. *Sch* Forest. *Teams* Europeans (1903/4 to 1909/10); Essex (1908, 7 matches).
Career batting
14–24–5–241–66*–12.68–0–*ct* 11
Bowling 261–10–26.10–0–0–3/40

Fawcett, Arthur Henry
Amateur. *b:* 16.9.1880, Sculcoates, Hull, Yorkshire. *d:* 11.1.1957, Stannington, Northumberland. Lower order batsman, wicket-keeper. *Teams* Europeans (1916/17 to 1918/19); Gentlemen (1922).
Career batting
6–8–3–29–9–5.80–0–*ct* 6–*st* 1

Fawcett, Edward Boyd
Amateur. *b:* 10.10.1839, Poona, India. *d:* 26.9.1884, Teignmouth, Devon. Middle order right-hand batsman, right-hand fast medium round-arm bowler. *Sch* Brighton. *Teams* Cambridge U (1859–61, blue 1959–60); Sussex (1860–63, 10 matches).
Career batting
21–37–0–326–53–8.81–0–*ct* 17
Bowling 528–28 + 29–18.84–4–1–6/56
He also played for Devon (1868) and Brecon (1868). He was the father of the well-known explorer Col Percy Fawcett (who played for Cornwall) who was lost in 1925 in the Mato Grosso area of Brazil.

Fawcett, George Walter
Amateur. *b:* 6.8.1929, Ardglass, Co Down, Ireland. Lower order right-hand batsman, wicket-keeper. *Team* Ireland (1956–59).
Career batting
6–9–2–56–21–8.00–0–*ct* 8–*st* 4

Fawcus, Charles Leslie Dinsdale
Amateur. *b:* 8.12.1898, Bromley, Kent. *d:* 8.12.1967, West Chiltington, Sussex. Opening left-hand batsman, left-arm medium pace bowler. *Sch* Bradfield. *Teams* Kent (1924, 1 match); Oxford U (1925–26); Worcestershire (1925, 1 match).
Career batting
7–13–0–202–70–15.53–0–*ct* 2
Bowling 21–0
He also played for Dorset (1933–34).

Fawcus, Ernest Augustus
Amateur. *b:* 10.11.1895, Newcastle upon Tyne, Northumberland. *d:* 30.6.1966, Halton, Wendover, Buckinghamshire. Middle order right-hand batsman, right-arm bowler. *Sch* Aldenham. *Team* RAF (1927–29).
Career batting
5–8–1–291–115–41.57–1–*ct* 4
Bowling 206–8–25.75–0–0–4/51
His County cricket was for Buckinghamshire (1925–28).

Fawcus, Lieut Gen Dr Sir Harold Ben
Amateur. *b:* 20.5.1876, South Charlton, Northumberland. *d:* 24.10.1947, Moorcroft, Hillingdon, Middlesex. Middle or lower order right-hand batsman, useful bowler. *Sch* Durham. *Teams* Orange Free State (1910/11); Army (1913–14).
Career batting
9–15–0–276–56–18.40–0–*ct* 6
Bowling 619–45–13.75–3–2–7/19
His County cricket was for Northumberland (1898–1906).

Fawkes, John
Amateur. *b:* 9.10.1933, Brompton, Chesterfield, Derbyshire. Middle order left-hand batsman, wicket-keeper. *Team* Combined Services (1959–60).
Career batting
4–6–0–117–41–19.50–0–*ct* 5–*st* 2

Fazal Mahmood
Amateur. *b:* 18.2.1927, Lahore, India. Son-in-law of Mohammed Saeed (Muslims), brother-in-law of Yawar Saeed (Somerset). Lower order right-hand batsman, right-arm fast medium bowler. *Teams* Northern India (1943/4 to 1946/7); Punjab (1951/2 to 1956/7); Lahore (1958/9). *Tours* Pakistan to England 1954, 1962, to West Indies 1957/8, to India 1952/3, 1960/1, to Ceylon 1948/9. *Tests* Pakistan (1952/3 to 1962, 34 matches).
Career batting
111–146–33–2602–100*–23.02–1–*ct* 38
Bowling 8792–460–19.11–38–8–9/43
Test batting
34–50–6–620–60–14.09–0–*ct* 11
Bowling 3434–139–24.70–13–4–7/42
Vice-captain of the first Pakistan Test team to tour England, Fazal proved to be the outstanding bowler of the visit, and mainly through his efforts Pakistan gained their first Test victory at the Oval. During the tour he took 77 wickets, av 17.53. However he was not very successful on his second tour in 1962. He played for MCC in England in 1962 and his last first-class match was for President's XI in Pakistan in 1963/4. His best bowling was 9/43 for Punjab v Services at Lahore in 1956/7. He captained Pakistan in 10 Tests.

Fear, Harold Percival
Amateur. *b:* 16.4.1908, Finchley, Middlesex. *d:* 13.5.1943, Bishop's Hull, Somerset. Middle order right-hand batsman. *Sch* Taunton. *Team* Somerset (1934, 2 matches).
Career batting
2–3–0–28–23–9.33–0–*ct* 0
Bowling 29–0

Fearnley, Charles Duncan
Professional. *b:* 12.4.1940, Pudsey, Yorkshire. Brother of M. C. (Yorkshire). Middle order left-hand batsman, off break bowler, close field. *Team* Worces-

tershire (1962–68, 97 matches).
Career batting
97–174–14–3294–112–20.58–1–*ct* 28
Bowling 37–1–37.00–0–0–1/37

He also played for Lincolnshire (1969–71). Since 1986 he has been Chairman of Worcestershire CCC. He runs a well-known firm of cricket outfitters.

Fearnley, Michael Carruthers
Cricketer. *b:* 21.8.1936, Horsforth, Leeds, Yorkshire. *d:* 7.7.1979, East Bierley, Yorkshire, whilst playing cricket. Brother of C. D. (Worcestershire). Lower order left-hand batsman, right-arm medium pace bowler. *Team* Yorkshire (1962–64, 3 matches).
Career batting
3–4–2–19–11*–9.50–0–*ct* 0
Bowling 133–6–22.16–0–0–3/56

Featherby, William Dixon
Professional. *b:* 18.8.1888, Goodmanham Lodge, Yorkshire. *d:* 20.11.1958, Goodmanham Lodge, Yorkshire. Lower order right-hand batsman, off break bowler. *Team* Yorkshire (1920, 2 matches).
Career batting
2 matches, did not bat–*ct* 0
Bowling 12–0

Featherstone, Norman George
Cricketer. *b:* 20.8.1949, Que Que, Rhodesia. Middle order right-hand batsman, off break bowler, slip field. *Teams* Transvaal (1967/8 to 1977/8); Middlesex (1968–79, 216 matches); Glamorgan (1980–81, 45 matches); Northern Transvaal (1981/2).
Career batting
329–528–54–13922–147–29.37–12–*ct* 277
Bowling 4986–181–27.54–4–0–5/32

He hit 1,000 runs in a season four times (best 1,156, av 35.03, in 1975).

Fee, Francis
Amateur. *b:* 14.5.1934, Belfast, Ireland. Lower order right-hand batsman, right-arm medium pace off break bowler. *Team* Ireland (1956–59).
Career batting
5–9–2–57–15*–8.14–0–*ct* 4
Bowling 356–37–9.62–3–2–9/26

On his first-class debut he took 14/100 for Ireland v MCC at Dublin in 1956. His best bowling was 9/26 for Ireland v Scotland at Dublin in 1957.

Felix, Nicholas
(real name N. Wanostrocht)
Amateur. *b:* 5.10.1804, Camberwell, London. *d:* 3.9.1876, Wimborne Minster, Dorset. Brother-in-law of H. T. Reed (MCC). Excellent middle order left-hand batsman, left-hand slow under-arm bowler, point field. *Teams* Kent (1834–52, 55 matches); Surrey (1846–52, 23 matches).
Career batting
148–264–13–4556–113–18.15–2–*ct* 112
Bowling 14–0 + 9–no av–0–0–3/?

One of the greatest players of his day, he did not become well known until the 1830s, and then appeared in most of the important matches until 1852. He invented the 'Catapulta' bowling machine and also tubular india rubber batting gloves. In his later years he was an artist and painted the likenesses of a number of cricketers. He expressed the wish that his biography should appear under his alias, when consulted by Arthur Haygarth. His debut in first-class matches was for MCC in 1830.

Fell, David John
Cricketer. *b:* 27.10.1964, Stafford. Middle order right-hand batsman, leg break bowler, occasional wicket-keeper. *Sch* John Lyon. *Team* Cambridge U (1985–87, blue all three years).
Career batting
27–47–5–974–114–23.19–2–*ct* 10

Fell, Desmond Robert
Amateur. *b:* 16.12.1912, Pietermaritzburg, South Africa. *d:* 22.1.1992, Durban, South Africa. Opening left-hand batsman, off break bowler. *Team* Natal (1931/2 to 1949/50).
Career batting
39–64–2–1958–161–31.58–5–*ct* 14
Bowling 1–0

His single appearance in first-class matches in England was for the Dominion side in 1945; he played some matches for Sussex (not first-class) in the same season. He umpired one Test match in South Africa in 1961/2.

Fell, Mark Andrew
Cricketer. *b:* 17.11.1960, Newark, Nottinghamshire. Middle order right-hand batsman, slow left-arm bowler. *Teams* Nottinghamshire (1982–83, 15 matches); Derbyshire (1985, 5 matches).
Career batting
20–35–0–506–108–14.45–1–*ct* 13
Bowling 157–1–157.00–0–0–1/20

He also played for Lincolnshire (1985–92).

Fellowes, Rev Edward Lyon
Amateur. *b:* 23.4.1845, Beighton, Lingwood, Norfolk. *d:* 23.7.1896, Papworth Everard, Cambridgeshire. Lower order right-hand batsman, right-hand fast round-arm bowler, slip field. *Sch* Marlborough. *Team* Oxford U (1865–68, blue 1865, 1866, and 1868).
Career batting
17–25–5–376–56–18.80–0–*ct* 18
Bowling 1009–71 + 14–14.21–6–1–7/46

In 1889 he was elected President of the resuscitated Cambridgeshire CCC. His final first-class match was for Gentlemen of England 1869. He captained Oxford in 1868. He also played for Norfolk (1863–72) and Huntingdonshire (1877–78).

Fellowes, James
Amateur. *b:* 25.8.1841, Cape of Good Hope, South Africa. *d:* 3.5.1916, Dedham, Essex. Father-in-law of W. C. Hedley (Somerset). Hard hitting lower order right-hand batsman, right-hand fast round-arm bowler. *Teams* Kent (1873–81, 9 matches); Hampshire (1883–85, 11 matches).
Career batting
23–41–6–432–32–12.34–0–*ct* 23
Bowling 1138–60–18.96–4–1–7/24

He made his first-class debut for MCC in 1870. Most of his cricket was for the Royal Engineers, but he also played for Devon (1869), being founder of the Devon Dumplings as well as the Hampshire Hogs. He was Secretary of Hampshire 1883–86, and last played for the county (not first-class) in 1887.

Fellows, Harvey Winson
Amateur. *b:* 11.4.1826, Rickmansworth, Hertfordshire. *d:* 13.1.1907, Rickmansworth, Hertfordshire. Brother of Walter (Oxford U 1854–57). Middle order right-hand batsman, right-hand fast round-arm bowler, good cover point. *Sch* Eton. *Team* MCC (1847–69).
Career batting
67–115–15–1019–61*–10.19–0–*ct* 32–*st* 8
Bowling 441–54 + 115–8.16–16–7–8/?

In 1848 and 1849 he was regarded as one of the fastest bowlers ever to appear, but after 1849 his pace was much reduced. His County cricket was for Hertfordshire (1855–72).

Fellows, John Pulteney
Amateur. *b:* 28.3.1881, Beeston Fields, Nottinghamshire. *d:* 3.2.1942, Hove, Sussex. Middle order batsman, change bowler. *Sch* Repton. *Team* Nottinghamshire (1904–05, 2 matches)
Career batting
2–3–1–23–18*–11.50–0–*ct* 1
Bowling 36–1–36.00–0–0–1/3

Fellows-Smith, Jonathan Payn
Amateur. *b:* 3.2.1932, Berea, Durban, South Africa. Son of Herbert (Natal). Aggressive middle order right-hand batsman, right-arm medium pace bowler. *Teams* Oxford U (1953–55, blue all three years); Northamptonshire (1957, 13 matches); Transvaal (1958/9 to 1959/60). *Tour* South Africa to England 1960. *Tests* South Africa (1960, 4 matches).
Career batting
94–157–21–3999–109*–29.40–5–*ct* 69
Bowling 4414–149–29.62–6–1–7/26
Test batting
4–8–2–166–35–27.66–0–*ct* 2
Bowling 61–0

He also won a rugby blue. His final first-class match in South Africa was for an Invitation XI in 1960/1. His final first-class match was for Free Foresters in 1964. He also played for Hertfordshire (1965–66).

Feltham, Mark Andrew
Cricketer. *b:* 26.6.1963, St John's Wood, London. Middle order right-hand batsman, right-arm medium fast bowler. *Sch* Tiffin. *Team* Surrey (1983–92, 114 matches).
Career batting
114–142–38–2526–101–24.28–1–*ct* 48
Bowling 9266–292–31.73–6–0–6/53

Feltham, Walter George
Professional. *b:* 23.4.1864, Ringwood, Hampshire. *d:* 23.9.1904, Ringwood, Hampshire. Tail end left-hand batsman, left-arm fast bowler. *Team* Hampshire (1884, 3 matches).
Career batting
3–5–1–1–1–0.25–0–*ct* 1
Bowling 254–12–21.16–0–0–4/54

Felton, Nigel Alfred
Cricketer. *b:* 24.10.1960, Guildford, Surrey. Opening left-hand batsman, off break bowler. *Sch* Millfield. *Teams* Somerset (1982–88, 108 matches); Northamptonshire (1989–92, 75 matches). *Tour* Northamptonshire to South Africa 1991/2.
Career batting
183–312–18–8771–173*–29.83–13–*ct* 101
Bowling 345–2–172.50–0–0–1/48

He hit 1,000 runs in a season four times (best 1,538, av 41.56, in 1990).

Felton, Robert
Amateur. *b:* 27.12.1909, Streatham, London. *d:* 4.10.1982, Ealing, Middlesex. Middle order right-hand batsman, right-arm fast medium bowler. *Sch* St Paul's. *Team* Middlesex (1935–48, 11 matches).
Career batting
13–22–0–558–171–25.36–1–*ct* 5
Bowling 152–2–76.00–0–0–1/4

Fender, Percy George Herbert
Amateur. *b:* 22.8.1892, Balham, London. *d:* 15.6.1985, Exeter, Devon. Nephew of P. Herbert (Gentlemen of South). Hard hitting middle order right-hand batsman, right-arm medium pace leg break bowler, brilliant slip field. *Sch* St George's, Weybridge and St Paul's. *Teams* Sussex (1910–13, 52 matches); Surrey (1914–35, 414 matches). *Tours* MCC to Australia 1920/1, to South Africa 1922/3; Tennyson to Jamaica 1926/7. *Tests* England (1920/1 to 1929, 13 matches).
Career batting
557–783–69–19034–185–26.65–21–*ct* 600
Bowling 47458–1894–25.05–100–16–8/24
Test batting
13–21–1–380–60–19.00–0–*ct* 14
Bowling 1185–29–40.86–2–0–5/90

Fenley, Stanley

His name is remembered for his famous century in 35 minutes made in the match between Surrey and Northamptonshire at Northampton in 1920 – he scored 113* in 42 minutes. He was, however, probably a greater bowler than batsman, though such was his all round ability that few cricketers can equal him, when his fielding and captaincy is added to his batting and bowling.

He initially played for Sussex and did not make much of a mark until he joined Surrey in 1914. In all he took 100 wickets in a season seven times (best 178, av 19.98, in 1923) and hit 1,000 runs nine times (best 1,625, av 33.16, in 1929). He completed the 'double' six times. He captained Surrey from 1920 to 1931, but was never invited to lead England, and in fact appeared in only five Tests in England, never commanding a regular place in the side. A noted writer on the game, he published books on four series between England and Australia. His last first-class match was for MCC in 1936. He played soccer for Casuals, Corinthians and Fulham.

Fenley, Stanley
Amateur to 1924, but professional from 1925. *b:* 4.1.1896, Kingston-upon-Thames, Surrey. *d:* 2.9.1972, Bournemouth, Hampshire. Tail end right-hand batsman, leg break bowler. *Teams* Surrey (1924–29, 116 matches); Hampshire (1935, 3 matches).
Career batting
119–117–45–421–26–5.84–0–*ct* 52
Bowling 10068–346–29.09–19–4–8/69

Fenner, Derek Alfred
Amateur. *b:* 17.9.1933, Woodford, Essex. Lower order right-hand batsman, slow left-arm bowler. *Sch* Epsom. *Team* Cambridge U (1954).
Career batting
1–1–0–21–21–21.00–0–*ct* 0
Bowling 63–2–31.50–0–0–2/33

Fenner, Francis Phillips
Professional. *b:* 1.3.1811, Cambridge. *d.* 22.5.1896, Bath, Somerset. Stylish middle order right-hand batsman, right-hand fast round-arm bowler, slip field. *Teams* Cambridge Town Club (1829–56); Hampshire (1843).
Career batting
55–97–8–1232–87*–13.84–0–*ct* 27–*st* 1
Bowling 19–1 + 182–19.00–14–4–9/?

A noted player for Cambridge Town his lasting memorial is the cricket ground at Cambridge, which he laid out in 1846. It was described soon after its opening as 'perhaps the smoothest ground in England – being in fact too easy, causing too much run getting.' He took 17 wickets in the match for Cambridge Town Club v Cambridge U at Cambridge in 1844.

Fenner, George David
Professional. *b:* 15.11.1896, Linton, Kent. *d:* 14.9.1971, Linton, Kent. Father of M. D. (Kent). Lower order right-hand batsman. *Team* Kent (1925–27, 2 matches).
Career batting
7–11–1–163–63–16.30–0–*ct* 2
Bowling 52–1–52.00–0–0–1/12

His final first-class match was for MCC in 1929. He was a noted coach and groundsman.

Fenner, Maurice David
Amateur. *b:* 16.2.1929, Linton, Kent. Son of G. D. (Kent). Middle order left-hand batsman, wicket-keeper. *Sch* Maidstone GS. *Team* Kent (1951–54, 14 matches).
Career batting
33–54–6–708–77–14.75–0–*ct* 47–*st* 13
Bowling 1–1–1.00–0–0–1/1

He was one of the leading cricketers in the RAF for some seasons, making his first-class debut for Combined Services in 1949 and playing his last first-class match for the same team in 1964. From 1977–82 he was Secretary of Kent CCC.

Fennex, William
Professional. *b: circa* 1764, Gerrards Cross, Buckinghamshire. *d:* 4.3.1838, Stepney, London. Elegant middle order right-hand batsman, right-hand fast under-arm bowler, good field. *Teams* Middlesex (1816); England (1802–06).
Career batting
9–18–3–90–44–6.00–0–*ct* 7
Bowling 16 wickets (no analyses)–1–0–7/?

He was best known as a single-wicket player, but was regularly picked for England in the 1780s and 1790s.

Fenton, Nigel Charles Windsor
Cricketer. *b:* 22.6.1965, Bradford, Yorkshire. Tail end right-hand batsman, right-arm fast medium bowler. *Sch* Rugby. *Team* Cambridge U (1988–91, blue 1988).
Career batting
8–10–4–11–7*–1.83–0–*ct* 1
Bowling 821–21–39.09–0–0–4/64

He reappeared in 1991 in emergency, having left the University in 1988.

Fereday, John Benjamin
Professional. *b:* 24.11.1873, Burnt Tree, Dudley, Worcestershire. *d:* 1.1.1958, Holy Cross, Worcestershire. Opening right-hand batsman, off break bowler. *Team* Worcestershire (1899–1901, 10 matches).
Career batting
10–19–0–211–37–11.10–0–*ct* 5
Bowling 103–2–51.50–0–0–1/27

He first played for Worcestershire (pre first-class) in 1895. He also played for Staffordshire (1902–11).

Ferguson, George William
Amateur. *b:* 17.9.1912, Buenos Aires, Argentina. Middle order right-hand batsman. *Team* Argentine (1929/30 to 1937/8). *Tour* South America to England 1932.
Career batting
12–23–0–445–85–19.34–0–*ct* 9
Bowling 1–0

Ferguson, Simon Alexander Ross
Cricketer. *b:* 13.5.1961, Lagos, Nigeria. Middle order right-hand batsman, right-arm medium pace bowler. *Sch* Framlingham. *Team* Somerset (1985, 1 match).
Career batting
1–1–0–8–8–8.00–0–*ct* 0
He also played for Suffolk (1983–84).

Ferguson, William Henry Noel
Amateur. *b:* 6.12.1927, Downpatrick, Co Down, Ireland. Lower order left-hand batsman, right-arm medium pace bowler. *Team* Ireland (1951–64).
Career batting
5–9–1–122–37–15.25–0–*ct* 3
Bowling 375–19–19.73–1–0–6/37

Fergusson, John Alexander
Amateur. *b:* 24.6.1882, Westminster, London. *d:* 28.4.1947, Muirton, Perth, Scotland. Middle order right-hand batsman, right-arm medium pace bowler. *Team* Scotland (1911–23).
Career batting
8–15–1–283–103*–20.21–1–*ct* 7
Bowling 226–9–25.11–1–0–5/36

Fernandes, Maurius Pacheco
Amateur. *b:* 12.8.1897, British Guiana. *d:* 8.5.1981, Georgetown, Guyana. Father of Leslie (British Guiana). Middle order right-hand batsman. *Team* British Guiana (1922/3 to 1931/2). *Tours* West Indies to England 1923, 1928. *Tests* West Indies (1928 to 1929/30, 2 matches).
Career batting
46–79–5–2087–141–28.20–4–*ct* 30
Bowling 183–5–36.60–0–0–2/29
Test batting
2–4–0–49–22–12.25–0–*ct* 0
He batted well on his first visit to England in 1923, being second in the averages (523 runs, av 34.86), but in 1928 quite failed to live up to his reputation. He captained West Indies in one Test.

Fernando, Edward Ranjit
Cricketer. *b:* 22.2.1944, Colombo, Ceylon. Middle order right-hand batsman, wicket-keeper. *Team* Sri Lanka (1964/5 to 1978/9). *Tours* Sri Lanka to India 1964/5, 1966/7, 1968/9, 1970/1, 1975/6, to Pakistan 1973/4, to England 1975.
Career batting
38–65–4–1349–81–22.11–0–*ct* 50–*st* 15
He played in one-day Internationals for Sri Lanka.

Fernando, Lantra Jayantha
Cricketer. *b:* 20.8.1956, Colombo, Ceylon. Lower order right-hand batsman, right-arm medium fast bowler. *Teams* Moratuwa (1988/9); Old Cambrians (1989/90 to 1991/2). *Tours* Sri Lanka to India 1980/1, to England 1981; Arosa Sri Lankan XI to South Africa 1982/3.
Career batting
20–25–1–326–53–13.58–0–*ct* 10
Bowling 1235–26–47.50–0–0–4/84
He played in only four first-class matches on the 1981 tour.

Fernie, Arthur Ernest
Amateur. *b:* 9.4.1877, Stone, Staffordshire. *d:* 24.7.1959, Bideford, Devon. Lower order right-hand batsman, slow left-arm bowler. *Sch* Wellingborough. *Team* Cambridge U (1897–1900, blue 1897 and 1900).
Career batting
22–32–16–121–24–7.56–0–*ct* 11
Bowling 1558–61–25.54–1–0–6/104
His County cricket was for Staffordshire (1898–1900) and Berkshire (1907). His final first-class match was for MCC in 1901.

Ferreira, Anthonie Michal
Cricketer. *b:* 13.4.1955, Pretoria, South Africa. Middle order right-hand batsman, right-arm medium pace bowler, good field. *Teams* Northern Transvaal (1974/5 to 1991/2); Warwickshire (1979–86, 138 matches).
Career batting
245–386–70–9064–133–28.68–5–*ct* 138
Bowling 17708–583–30.37–18–2–8/38
His best season in County cricket was 1984 when he took 79 wickets, av 27.94.

Ferris, George John Fitzgerald
Cricketer. *b:* 18.10.1964, Urlings Village, Antigua. Cousin of H. A. G. Anthony (Leeward Islands). Lower order right-hand batsman, right-arm fast bowler, deep field. *Teams* Leeward Islands (1982/3 to 1988/9); Leicestershire (1983–90, 71 matches). *Tours* Young West Indies to Zimbabwe 1983/4, 1986/7.
Career batting
94–105–44–745–36*–12.21–0–*ct* 13
Bowling 7355–286–25.71–9–1–7/42

Ferris, John James
Amateur. *b:* 21.5.1867, Sydney, New South Wales, Australia. *d:* 17.11.1900, Addington, Durban, South Africa, of enteric fever. Lower order left-hand batsman, slow or medium left-arm bowler. *Teams* New South Wales (1886/7 to 1897/8, 19 matches); Gloucestershire (1892–95, 63 matches); South Australia (1895/6, 1 match). *Tours* Australia to England 1888, 1890; Read to South Africa 1891/2. *Tests* Australia (1886/7 to 1890, 8 matches); England (1891/2, 1 match).

Ferris, Stewart Wesley

Career batting
198–328–56–4264–106–15.67–1–*ct* 90
Bowling 14250–812–17.54–63–11–8/41
Test batting
9–17–4–114–20*–8.76–0–*ct* 4
Bowling 775–61–12.70–6–1–7/37

He was outstandingly successful on his Australian tours to England, taking 199 wickets, av 14.74, in 1888 and 186, av 14.28, in 1890, but his skill deserted him as the 1890s progressed, so that he had dropped out of first-class cricket soon after he was 30. He hit 1,056 runs, av 22.46, in 1893.

Ferris, Stewart Wesley
Amateur. *b:* 2.5.1927, Lurgan, Co Armagh, Ireland. Tail end right-hand batsman, right-arm medium pace bowler. *Team* Ireland (1956).
Career batting
2–3–2–10–4*–10.00–0–*ct* 0
Bowling 144–4–36.00–0–0–4/106

Fetherstonhaugh, Charles Bateman Robert
Amateur. *b:* 17.11.1932, Tavistock, Devon. Nephew of H. Burgess (Leicestershire) and J. Burgess (Leicestershire and Northamptonshire). Middle or lower order right-hand batsman, wicket-keeper. *Sch* Bradfield. *Teams* MCC (1956); Free Foresters (1962–64). *Tour* Surridge to Bermuda 1961 (not first-class).
Career batting
4–8–2–59–20*–9.83–0–*ct* 4–*st* 1

His County cricket was for Devon (1953–63).

Few, Harry Gleaves
Amateur. *b:* 8.9.1848, Willingham, Cambridgeshire. *d:* 9.4.1931, Newnham, Cambridge. Lower order right-hand batsman, left-hand medium pace round-arm bowler. *Team* Cambridgeshire (1866, 2 matches).
Career batting
2–4–0–4–4–1.00–0–*ct* 1
Bowling 170–8–21.25–1–0–5/72

He also played for Huntingdonshire (1877–81).

Fewings, James
Amateur. *b:* 3.10.1849, Bristol. *d:* 20.8.1920, Banisters Park, Southampton, Hampshire. Lower order right-hand batsman, wicket-keeper. *Team* Gloucestershire (1872, 2 matches).
Career batting
2–4–1–4–3*–1.33–0–*ct* 0

Fewkes, Alfred
Amateur. *b:* 31.8.1837, Basford, Nottinghamshire. *d:* 1.4.1912, Sherwood Rise, Nottingham. Lower order batsman, wicket-keeper. *Team* Nottinghamshire (1864, 1 match).
Career batting
1–2–0–11–9–5.50–0–*ct* 2–*st* 2

Fiddian-Green, Charles Anderson Fiddian
Amateur. *b:* 22.12.1898, Handsworth, Birmingham. *d:* 5.9.1976, Malvern, Worcestershire. Middle order right-hand batsman, right-arm medium pace bowler. *Sch* The Leys. *Teams* Warwickshire (1920–28, 64 matches); Cambridge U (1921–22, blue both years); Worcestershire (1931–34, 24 matches).
Career batting
107–169–29–4350–120–31.07–4–*ct* 71–*st* 1
Bowling 372–6–62.00–0–0–1/6

He hit 1,000 runs in a season twice (best 1,079, av 31.73, in 1921). An excellent hockey player he represented both Cambridge and England; he also played golf for Cambridge.

Fiddling, Kenneth
Professional. *b:* 13.10.1917, Hebden Bridge, Yorkshire. *d:* 19.6.1992, Shaw Hill, Halifax, Yorkshire. Lower order right-hand batsman, wicket-keeper. *Teams* Yorkshire (1938–46, 18 matches); Northamptonshire (1947–53, 142 matches).
Career batting
160–191–73–1380–68–11.69–0–*ct* 226–*st* 76

Field, Edwin
Amateur. *b:* 18.12.1871, Hampstead, London. *d:* 9.1.1947, South Bromley, Kent. Opening or middle order right-hand batsman, right-arm medium pace bowler, good field. *Sch* Clifton. *Teams* Cambridge U (1893–94, blue 1894); Middlesex (1904–06, 6 matches).
Career batting
17–31–2–618–107*–21.31–1–*ct* 13
Bowling 48–0

He also played for Berkshire (1895). A noted rugby footballer, he was awarded his blue at Cambridge and went on to represent England in 1893.

Field, Ernest Frank
(known as Frank Ernest Field)
Professional. *b:* 23.9.1874, Weethley, Warwickshire. *d:* 25.8.1934, Droitwich, Worcestershire. Lower order right-hand batsman, right-arm fast bowler. *Teams* Warwickshire (1897–1920, 256 matches); London County (1900).
Career batting
264–352–104–1900–39–7.66–0–*ct* 108
Bowling 24091–1026–23.48–80–17–9/104

He took 100 wickets in a season three times (best 146, av 20.37, in 1911). He performed a most remarkable piece of bowling for Warwickshire v Worcestershire at Dudley in 1914. Going on with the total 85 for 4, he returned figures of 8.4–7–2–6, there being only one scoring stroke off him despite five no-balls. His best bowling was 9/104 for Warwickshire v Leicestershire at Leicester in 1899. He was a first-class umpire (1927–34).

Field, Frank
Professional. *b:* 29.2.1908, Langley, Worcestershire. *d:* 25.4.1981, Stourbridge, Worcestershire. Tail end right-hand batsman, right-arm fast medium bowler. *Team* Worcestershire (1928–31, 2 matches).

Career batting
3–6–2–26–12–6.50–0–*ct* 0
Bowling 194–4–48.50–0–0–4/60
His final first-class match was for MCC in 1932.

Field, George
Amateur. *b:* 30.9.1871, Anfield, Liverpool, Lancashire. *d:* 9.6.1942, Portreath, Cornwall. Lower order right-hand batsman, wicket-keeper. *Sch* Uppingham. *Team* Oxford U (1893).
Career batting
1–2–0–4–4–2.00–0–*ct* 0–*st* 1
His County cricket was for Shrophire (1902).

Field, Maxwell Nicholas
Cricketer. *b:* 23.3.1950, Coundon, Coventry, Warwickshire. Lower order right-hand batsman, right-arm medium pace bowler. *Sch* Bablake. *Teams* Cambridge U (1974, blue); Warwickshire (1974–75, 3 matches).
Career batting
11–15–5–122–39*–12.20–0–*ct* 1
Bowling 896–24–37.33–0–0–4/76

Field-Buss, Michael Gwyn
Cricketer. *b:* 23.9.1964, Imtarfa, Malta. Lower order right-hand batsman, off break bowler. *Teams* Essex (1987, 2 matches); Nottinghamshire (1989–92, 16 matches).
Career batting
18–18–4–136–34*–9.71–0–*ct* 7
Bowling 1004–22–45.63–0–0–4/33

Fielder, Albert Edward
Professional. *b:* 3.4.1889, Sarisbury Green, Hampshire. *d:* 29.4.1947, Bellevue, Southampton, Hampshire. Lower order right-hand batsman, right-arm fast medium bowler. *Team* Hampshire (1911–13, 3 matches).
Career batting
3–4–1–38–35–12.66–0–*ct* 4
Bowling 225–6–37.50–1–0–5/128

Fielder, Arthur
Professional. *b:* 19.7.1877, Plaxtol, Tonbridge, Kent. *d:* 30.8.1949, Lambeth, London. Lower order right-hand batsman, right-arm fast bowler. *Team* Kent (1900–14, 253 matches). *Tours* MCC to Australia 1903/4, 1907/8. *Tests* England (1903/4 to 1907/8, 6 matches).
Career batting
287–380–175–2320–112*–11.31–1–*ct* 119
Bowling 26852–1277–21.02–97–28–10/90
Test batting
6–12–5–78–20–11.14–0–*ct* 4
Bowling 711–26–27.34–1–0–6/82
He took 100 wickets in a season five times (best 186, av 20.19, in 1906). His most famous feat was performed in the Players v Gentlemen match of 1906, when he took all 10 wickets in an innings at Lord's (for 90 runs). Though not much of a batsman, he achieved the unusual distinction of hitting a century when coming in at number 11 for Kent v Worcestershire at Stourbridge in 1909. He and Woolley added 235 for the last wicket, a record in County cricket.

Fielder, Walter George
Professional. *b:* 6.3.1899, Fareham, Hampshire. *d:* 7.1.1968, Sarisbury Green, Hampshire. Lower order batsman, bowler. *Team* Hampshire (1923, 1 match).
Career batting
1–1–1–2–2*–no av–0–*ct* 0
Bowling 26–0

Fielding, Felix
Amateur. *b:* 24.2.1858, Lewisham, London. *d:* 4.2.1910, Surbiton, Surrey. Lower/middle order right-hand batsman, wicket-keeper. *Sch* Malvern. *Team* Surrey (1889, 2 matches).
Career batting
4–6–1–100–75–20.00–0–*ct* 4–*st* 3
His last first-class match was for the South in 1890.

Fieldwick, Edward
Amateur. *b:* 25.3.1868, Huyton, Lancashire. *d:* 22.12.1910, Huyton, Lancashire. Middle order batsman. *Team* Liverpool and District (1894).
Career batting
1–2–0–0–0–0.00–0–*ct* 2
Bowling 39–0

Figg, George
Professional. *b:* 13.6.1824, Horsham, Sussex. *d:* 20.7.1888, Horsham, Sussex. Lower order right-hand batsman, right-hand medium pace round-arm bowler. *Teams* Middlesex (1850, 1 match); Sussex (1865–66, 10 matches).
Career batting
11–19–7–77–26*–6.41–0–*ct* 7
Bowling 702–38–18.47–3–0–6/42
For about 10 years he managed a cricket ground in Norwich, commencing in or about 1851. He also played for Suffolk (1849) and Norfolk (1864–69).

Filgas, Frank Miroslav
Amateur. *b:* 3.11.1926, Carlow, Co Carlow, Ireland. Tail end right-hand batsman, wicket-keeper. *Team* Ireland (1948).
Career batting
1–2–0–3–3–1.50–0–*ct* 1

Filgate, Charles Roden
Amateur. *b:* 16.10.1849, Lisrenny, Ardee, Co Louth, Ireland. *d:* 1.9.1930, Grove House, Pinner, Middlesex. Middle order right-hand batsman, fine deep field. *Sch* Cheltenham. *Team* Gloucestershire (1870–77, 15 matches).
Career batting
25–41–5–563–93–15.63–0–*ct* 18
His first-class debut was for MCC in 1869. He played much cricket in Ireland, notably for County Louth, and played for Ireland (not first-class) in 1868.

Fillary, Edward William Joseph
Cricketer. *b:* 14.4.1944, Heathfield, Sussex. Opening right-hand batsman, leg break and googly bowler. *Sch* St Lawrence College, Ramsgate. *Teams* Oxford U (1963–65, blue all three years); Kent (1963–66, 13 matches).
Career batting
45–83–11–1371–75–19.04–0–*ct* 24
Bowling 2163–82–26.37–5–0–6/77

Fillery, Richard
Professional. *b:* 4.2.1842, Henfield, Sussex. *d:* 22.11.1881, Henfield, Sussex. Middle order right-hand batsman, right-hand medium pace round-arm bowler. *Team* Sussex (1862–79, 102 matches).
Career batting
123–210–28–2676–105–14.70–1–*ct* 87
Bowling 6104–318–19.19–28–4–7/24

Fillingham, George Henry
Amateur. *b:* 24.8.1841, Syerston Hall, Newark, Nottinghamshire. *d:* 17.1.1895, Syerston Hall, Newark, Nottinghamshire, following a shooting accident whilst hunting. Nephew of T. G. Blake (Sussex 1829). Middle order batsman, change bowler. *Sch* Harrow. *Team* Gentlemen of South (1870).
Career batting
1–1–0–0–0–0.00–0–*ct* 0
In his only first-class match he appeared for the Gentlemen of South in emergency, being in fact a prominent member of the Gentlemen of Nottinghamshire CC.

Finan, Nicholas Hugh
Cricketer. *b:* 3.7.1954, Knowle, Bristol. Lower order right-hand batsman, right-arm medium pace bowler. *Team* Gloucestershire (1975–79, 8 matches).
Career batting
8–4–2–26–18–13.00–0–*ct* 1
Bowling 313–4–78.25–0–0–2/57

Finch, Henry Randolph
Amateur. *b:* 18.10.1842, Paddington, London. *d:* 6.12.1935, Oakham, Rutland. Middle order batsman. *Sch* Harrow. *Team* MCC (1866).
Career batting
2–3–1–34–19–17.00–0–*ct* 0
He did not appear in first-class matches whilst at Oxford U, but was later a notable member of the Harlequins and Free Foresters. His first first-class match was for Southgate in 1864. He also played for Rutland (1859–85) and Northamptonshire (pre first-class, 1864).

Fincham, Anthony Leonard Rupert
Cricketer. *b:* 19.3.1955, Lambeth, London. Lower order right-hand batsman, right-arm medium pace bowler. *Sch* Tonbridge. *Team* Oxford U (1976).
Career batting
1–1–1–3–3*–no av–0–*ct* 0
Bowling 64–5–12.80–0–0–4/42

Findlay, Francis
Amateur. *b:* 4.2.1920, Rubislaw, Aberdeen, Scotland. *d:* 16.6.1963, Kilmarnock, Ayr, Scotland. Brother of T. A. (Scotland). Middle order right-hand batsman. *Team* Scotland (1948).
Career batting
2–3–0–9–6–3.00–0–*ct* 1

Findlay, Thaddeus Michael, MBE
Cricketer. *b:* 19.10.1943, Troumaca, St Vincent. Lower order right-hand batsman, wicket-keeper. *Team* Windward Islands (1964/5 to 1977/8). *Tours* West Indies to Australia and New Zealand 1968/9, to England 1969, 1976. *Tests* West Indies (1969 to 1972/3, 10 matches).
Career batting
110–170–25–2927–90–20.18–0–*ct* 209–*st* 43
Test batting
10–16–3–212–44*–16.30–0–*ct* 19–*st* 2
He appeared in two Tests on his 1969 tour of England, but in 1976 was reserve wicket-keeper to D. L. Murray and did not take part in any Tests.

Findlay, Thomas Alexander
Amateur. *b:* 22.3.1918, Rubislaw, Aberdeen, Scotland. Brother of Francis (Scotland). Middle order right-hand batsman. *Team* Scotland (1947).
Career batting
1–2–0–19–19–9.50–0–*ct* 1

Findlay, William
Amateur. *b:* 22.6.1880, Princes Park, Liverpool, Lancashire. *d:* 19.6.1953, Tenterden, Kent. Brother-in-law of J. R. Tylden (Kent). Steady middle order right-hand batsman, wicket-keeper. *Sch* Eton. *Teams* Oxford U (1901–03, blue all three years); Lancashire (1902–06, 58 matches). *Tour* MCC to Argentine 1911/12.
Career batting
88–131–29–1984–81–19.45–0–*ct* 140–*st* 27
Bowling 15–0
He captained Oxford in 1903. In 1907 he was appointed Secretary to Surrey CCC; in 1919 he became Assistant Secretary to MCC and then Secretary from 1926 to 1936. In 1937 he headed the 'Findlay Commission' into the problems of County Cricket Clubs. He was President of Lancashire 1947–48 and of MCC 1951/2.

Findlay, William Schreiner
Amateur. *b:* 2.1.1908, South Africa. Lower order batsman, bowler. *Team* Cambridge U (1930).
Career batting
1–1–1–30–30*–no av–0–*ct* 0
Bowling 102–4–25.50–0–0–3/53

Fingleton, John Henry Webb, OBE
Amateur. *b:* 28.4.1908, Waverley, Sydney, New South Wales, Australia. *d:* 22.11.1981, St Leonards, Killara, Sydney, New South Wales, Australia. Cousin of C. O'Brien (New South Wales). Opening right-hand batsman, excellent close field. *Team* New South Wales (1928/9 to 1939/40, 49 matches). *Tours* Australia to South Africa 1935/6, to England 1938. *Tests* Australia (1931/2 to 1938, 18 matches).
Career batting
108–166–13–6816–167–44.54–22–*ct* 81–*st* 4
Bowling 54–2–27.00–0–0–1/6
Test batting
18–29–1–1189–136–42.46–5–*ct* 13
He had only a moderate return on his 1938 tour of England with 1,141 runs, av 38.03, and appearing in four of the five Tests he could muster only 123 runs, av 20.50. A noted author and journalist, he wrote several major cricket books.

Finlay, Aubrey James
Amateur. *b:* 2.3.1938, Sion Mills, Co Tyrone, Ireland. Cousin of O. D. Colhoun (Ireland). Middle order right-hand batsman. *Team* Ireland (1957–65).
Career batting
9–16–1–170–30–11.33–0–*ct* 12

Finlay, Frank Dazell
Amateur. *b:* 31.8.1868, Belfast, Ireland. *d:* 21.1.1947, Biarritz, France. Opening right-hand batsman. *Sch* UCS. *Team* MCC (1902).
Career batting
1–1–0–19–19–19.00–0–*ct* 0
His County cricket was for Northumberland.

Finlay, Ian William
Cricketer. *b:* 14.5.1946, Woking, Surrey. Opening or middle order left-hand batsman, left-arm medium pace bowler, good field. *Teams* Surrey (1965–67, 23 matches); Transvaal (1967/8); Northern Transvaal (1968/9 to 1975/6).
Career batting
43–69–5–1640–150–25.62–2–*ct* 29
Bowling 691–18–38.38–0–0–3/17

Finney, Roger John
Cricketer. *b:* 2.8.1960, Darley Dale, Derbyshire. Middle order right-hand batsman, left-arm medium pace, later slow left-arm bowler. *Team* Derbyshire (1982–88, 114 matches).
Career batting
114–168–29–2856–82–20.54–0–*ct* 26
Bowling 6297–202–31.17–8–0–7/54
He also played for Norfolk (1989–92).

Finney, William
Professional. *b:* 13.8.1866, Newtown, Montgomery. *d:* 8.5.1927, Stamford, Lincolnshire. Sound middle or lower order right-hand batsman, right-arm medium fast, later slow, bowler. *Team* Leicestershire (1894, 3 matches).
Career batting
3–5–1–29–14*–7.25–0–*ct* 0
Bowling 123–3–41.00–0–0–1/7
His County career with Leicestershire began in 1890 (pre-first-class).

Firbank, Godfrey Christopher
Amateur. *b:* 19.6.1895, Aldwick Court, Wrington, Somerset. *d:* 8.7.1947, Hoplands, King's Somborne, Hampshire. Lower order batsman, slow left-arm bowler. *Sch* Cheltenham. *Teams* Services (1922); Army (1927).
Career batting
2–4–2–0–0*–0.00–0–*ct* 0
Bowling 177–5–35.40–0–0–3/67

Firth, Alfred
Amateur. *b:* 3.9.1847, Dewsbury, Yorkshire. *d:* 16.1.1927, Wyke, Bradford, Yorkshire. Middle order batsman. *Team* Yorkshire (1869, 1 match).
Career batting
1–1–0–4–4–4.00–0–*ct* 0

Firth, Rev Edgar Beckwith
Amateur. *b:* 11.4.1863, Malton, Yorkshire. *d:* 25.7.1905, Matjesfontein, Cape Province, South Africa. Middle order batsman. *Team* Yorkshire (1894, 1 match).
Career batting
1–1–0–1–1–1.00–0–*ct* 0

Firth, Edward Loxley
(also known as Loxley-Firth)
Amateur. *b:* 7.3.1886, Hope, Derbyshire. *d:* 8.1.1949, Syracuse, New York, USA. Middle order batsman. *Sch* Charterhouse. *Team* Yorkshire (1912, 2 matches).
Career batting
2–4–0–43–37–10.75–0–*ct* 1

Firth, Jack
Professional. *b:* 27.6.1917, Cottingley, Yorkshire. *d:* 7.9.1981, Cottingley, Yorkshire. Lower order right-hand batsman, wicket-keeper. *Teams* Yorkshire (1949–50, 8 matches); Leicestershire (1951–58, 223 matches).
Career batting
235–340–94–3588–90*–14.58–0–*ct* 373–*st* 95
He played soccer for York City.

Firth, Canon John D'Ewes Evelyn
Amateur. *b:* 21.2.1900, The Park, Nottingham. *d:* 21.9.1957, Winchester College, Hampshire. Lower order right-hand batsman, leg break bowler. *Sch* Winchester. *Teams* Oxford U (1919–20); Nottinghamshire (1919, 2 matches).
Career batting
4–4–1–22–19*–7.33–0–*ct* 2
Bowling 248–8–31.00–0–0–2/22

Firth, Timothy
Cricketer. *b:* 1.4.1964, Bristol. Lower order right-hand batsman, right-arm medium pace bowler. *Sch* Stockport GS. *Team* Oxford U (1987, blue).
Career batting
7–7–0–33–10–4.71–0–*ct* 1
Bowling 682–14–48.71–0–0–4/129

Fisher, Charles Dennis
Amateur. *b:* 19.6.1877, Blatchington Court, Sussex. *d:* 31.5.1916, aboard HMS *Invincible* at Jutland. Steady middle order right-hand batsman, right-arm medium pace off break bowler. *Sch* Westminster. *Teams* Sussex (1898–1903, 15 matches); Oxford U (1899–1900, blue 1900).
Career batting
21–33–1–429–80–13.40–0–*ct* 7
Bowling 242–8–30.25–0–0–2/8

Fisher, Horace
Professional. *b:* 3.8.1903, Featherstone, Yorkshire. *d:* 16.4.1974, Middlestown, Horbury, Yorkshire. Lower order left-hand batsman, slow left-arm bowler. *Team* Yorkshire (1928–36, 52 matches). *Tour* Yorkshire to Jamaica 1935/6.
Career batting
52–58–14–681–76*–15.47–0–*ct* 22
Bowling 2621–93–28.18–2–0–6/11

For Yorkshire v Somerset at Bramall Lane in 1932 he performed the hat trick by dismissing all three batsmen lbw.

Fisher, John
Professional. *b:* 4.8.1897, Hodthorpe, Derbyshire. *d:* 22.6.1954, Castleford, Yorkshire. Middle or lower order left-hand batsman, right-arm medium pace bowler. *Team* Derbyshire (1921–22, 3 matches).
Career batting
3–6–1–52–39*–10.40–0–*ct* 0
Bowling 15–0

He was a noted soccer player with Chesterfield, Burnley, Lincoln City and Mansfield.

Fisher, Paul Bernard
Cricketer. *b:* 19.12.1954, Edmonton, Middlesex. Lower order right-hand batsman, wicket-keeper. *Teams* Oxford U (1974–78, blue 1975–78); Middlesex (1979, 2 matches); Worcestershire (1980–81, 14 matches).
Career batting
57–85–14–654–42–9.21–0–*ct* 92–*st* 12

Fisher, Reginald Wordsworth Cecil
Amateur. *b:* 17.4.1872, Grantham, Lincolnshire. *d:* 31.12.1939, Hemel Hempstead, Hertfordshire. Middle order right-hand batsman, change bowler, good point. *Sch* Haileybury. *Team* Hampshire (1898, 1 match).
Career batting
1–1–0–3–3–3.00–0–*ct* 0

Fishlock, Laurence Barnard
Professional. *b:* 2.1.1907, Battersea, London. *d:* 25.6.1986, Sutton, Surrey. Opening left-hand batsman, slow left-arm bowler. *Team* Surrey (1931–52, 347 matches). *Tours* MCC to Australia and New Zealand 1936/7, 1946/7; Commonwealth to India and Ceylon 1950/1. *Tests* England (1936 to 1946/7, 4 matches).
Career batting
417–699–54–25376–253–39.34–56–*ct* 216
Bowling 504–11–45.81–0–0–4/62
Test batting
4–5–1–47–19*–11.75–0–*ct* 1

He hit 1,000 runs in a season 12 times plus once overseas and went on to exceed 2,000 runs in six seasons (best 2,426, av 45.77, in 1949). Both his double centuries were for Surrey, the higher being 253 v Leicestershire at Leicester in 1948. A noted soccer player he appeared for Crystal Palace, Millwall, Aldershot, Southampton and Gillingham as a forward, and he also obtained an amateur international cap for England.

Fishwick, Tom Silvester
Amateur. *b:* 24.7.1876, Stone, Staffordshire. *d:* 21.2.1950, Sandown, Isle of Wight. Middle order right-hand batsman, brilliant slip field. *Sch* Wellingborough. *Teams* Warwickshire (1896–1909, 206 matches); London County (1901).
Career batting
210–349–13–8833–140*–26.28–13–*ct* 231–*st* 2
Bowling 35–0

He hit 1,000 runs in a season twice (best 1,440, av 32.00, in 1905). He also played for Staffordshire (1892–94). He was joint Warwickshire captain in 1902 and 1907.

Fisk, Eric
Amateur. *b:* 27.3.1931, East Ardsley, Yorkshire. Lower order left-hand batsman, slow left-arm bowler. *Team* Combined Services (1950–51).
Career batting
3–5–0–37–16–7.40–0–*ct* 1
Bowling 123–2–61.50–0–0–1/19

He appeared for Yorkshire 2nd XI (1948–53).

Fitton, John Dexter
Cricketer. *b:* 24.8.1965, Littleborough, Lancashire. Middle order left-hand batsman, off break bowler. *Team* Lancashire (1987–92, 52 matches).
Career batting
52–61–15–872–60–18.95–0–*ct* 11
Bowling 4359–82–53.15–3–0–6/59

He took 14 wickets, av 103.35, in 1990 – the first bowler to average over 100 in a season for a minimum of 10 wickets.

Fitton, Thomas Edmond John
Amateur. *b:* 16.8.1911, Killarney, Co Kerry, Ireland. Lower order right-hand batsman, right-arm medium

fast bowler. *Sch* Trent. *Team* Oxford U (1932).
Career batting
1–2–2–7–4*–no av–0–*ct* 0
Bowling 76–2–38.00–0–0–2/76

Fitzgerald, Alfred William
Amateur. *b:* 1.12.1849, Shalstone Manor, Buckinghamshire. *d:* 30.7.1871, Shalstone Manor, Buckinghamshire. Brother of R. A. (Middlesex). Middle order batsman. *Sch* Eton. *Team* MCC (1868).
Career batting
1–2–0–3–3–1.50–0–*ct* 0
His County cricket was for Buckinghamshire (1866–68).

Fitzgerald, Francis John
Amateur. *b:* 4.7.1864, St Kilda, Melbourne, Victoria, Australia. *d:* 24.2.1939, Chelsea, London. Brother of P. D. (MCC). Lower order batsman, useful bowler. *Sch* Oscott College. *Team* MCC (1890).
Career batting
1–2–0–3–3–1.50–0–*ct* 0
Bowling 15–0

Fitzgerald, James Francis
Cricketer. *b:* 28.11.1945, Whitehouse Common, Sutton Coldfield, Warwickshire. Lower order right-hand batsman, slow left-arm bowler. *Team* Cambridge U (1966–68, blue 1968).
Career batting
15–24–11–147–27*–11.30–0–*ct* 4
Bowling 894–29–30.82–1–0–6/70
His County cricket was for Cambridgeshire (1974).

Fitzgerald, Maurice Noel Ryder Purcell
Amateur. *b:* 22.12.1835, Torquay, Devon. *d:* 17.12.1877, Boulge Hall, Woodbridge, Suffolk. Steady opening right-hand batsman. *Sch* Brighton. *Team* Sussex (1864, 1 match).
Career batting
2–2–0–8–8–4.00–0–*ct* 1
His final first-class match was for MCC in 1866. He also played for Suffolk.

Fitzgerald, Brig Gen Percy Desmond
Amateur. *b:* 17.4.1872, St Kilda, Melbourne, Victoria, Australia. *d:* 17.8.1933, Marylebone, London. Brother of F. J. (MCC). Middle order batsman. *Sch* Oscott College. *Team* MCC (1897).
Career batting
1–2–0–5–4–2.50–0–*ct* 0

Fitzgerald, Robert Allan
Amateur. *b:* 1.10.1834, Purley, Berkshire. *d:* 28.10.1881, Chorley Wood, Hertfordshire. Brother of A. W. (MCC). Middle order right-hand batsman, right-hand fast round-arm bowler. *Sch* Harrow. *Teams* Cambridge U (1854–56, blue 1854 and 1856); Middlesex (1864, 1 match). *Tour* Fitzgerald to North America 1872 (not first-class).
Career batting
46–79–7–1123–91*–15.59–0–*ct* 34
Bowling 112–4+3–28.00–0–0–3/23
He was Honorary Secretary of MCC 1863–76.
His final first-class match was for MCC in 1874. He also played for Berkshire (1858–59), Buckinghamshire (1864–69) and Hertfordshire (1869–75). He played for Ireland (not first-class) 1858–67.

Fitzherbert, Major Gen Edward Herbert
Amateur. *b:* 3.12.1885, Poona, India. *d:* 1.8.1979, Wandsworth, London. Middle order batsman. *Sch* Rossall. *Team* Army (1923).
Career batting
1–2–0–3–3–1.50–0–*ct* 0

Fitzmaurice, Desmond Michael John
Amateur. *b:* 16.10.1917, Carlton, Melbourne, Victoria, Australia. *d:* 19.1.1981, Prahran, Melbourne, Victoria, Australia. Brother of D. J. A. (Victoria). Lower order right-hand batsman, right-arm fast medium bowler. *Team* Victoria (1947/8, 2 matches). *Tour* Commonwealth to India, Pakistan and Ceylon 1949/50.
Career batting
17–18–2–272–45–17.00–0–*ct* 3
Bowling 798–28–28.50–0–0–3/29
His final first-class match, and only one in England, was for a Commonwealth XI in 1950.

Fitzroy, Hon John Maurice
(changed name to Fitzroy-Newdegate in 1936)
Amateur. *b:* 20.3.1897, Chelsea, London. *d:* 7.5.1976, Nuneaton, Warwickshire. Hard hitting middle order right-hand batsman, slip field. *Sch* Eton. *Team* Northamptonshire (1925–27, 56 matches).
Career batting
56–101–6–1373–50–14.45–0–*ct* 47
Bowling 82–6–13.66–0–0–4/14
He captained Northamptonshire 1925 to 1927 – a knee injury in the latter season ending his first-class cricket.

Flaherty, Kevin Frederick
Cricketer. *b:* 17.9.1939, Birmingham. Tail end right-hand batsman, off break bowler. *Team* Warwickshire (1969, 1 match).
Career batting
1 match, did not bat–*ct* 0
Bowling 107–4–26.75–0–0–3/38

Flamson, William Henry
Professional. *b:* 12.8.1904, Heather, Leicestershire. *d:* 9.1.1945, Heather, Leicestershire. Tail end right-hand batsman, right-arm medium fast bowler. *Team* Leicestershire (1934–39, 49 matches).
Career batting
49–67–20–351–50*–7.46–0–*ct* 24
Bowling 4971–151–32.92–7–0–7/46

Flanagan, John Patrick Douglas
Cricketer. *b:* 20.9.1947, Sandringham, Johannesburg, South Africa. Son of F. F. (Griqualand West and Transvaal). Middle/lower order right-hand batsman, right-arm medium pace bowler. *Team* Transvaal (1965/6 to 1977/8). *Tours* SA Universities to England 1967; Isaacs to England 1969 (not first-class).
Career batting
57–91–15–1835–98–24.14–0–*ct* 48
Bowling 3191–116–27.50–3–1–8/113

Flanagan, Michael
Professional. *b:* 15.3.1842, Glen Colombkill, Co Clare, Ireland. *d:* 14.1.1890, Paddington, London. Tail end right-hand batsman, right-hand fast round-arm bowler, slip field. *Team* Middlesex (1873–78, 15 matches).
Career batting
18–32–9–100–14–4.34–0–*ct* 7
Bowling 1094–68–16.08–3–1–9/78
His best bowling was 9/78 for MCC v Surrey at Lord's in 1876. He played for Ireland (not first-class) in 1863.

Flavell, John Alfred
Professional. *b:* 15.5.1929, Wall Heath, Staffordshire. Tail end left-hand batsman, right-arm fast medium bowler. *Team* Worcestershire (1949–67, 392 matches). *Tours* Worcestershire World Tour (Rhodesia first-class) 1964/5, to Jamaica 1965/6. *Tests* England (1961–64, 4 matches).
Career batting
401–453–141–2032–54–6.51–0–*ct* 129
Bowling 32847–1529–21.48–86–15–9/30
Test batting
4–6–2–31–14–7.75–0–*ct* 0
Bowling 367–7–52.42–0–0–2/65
He took 100 wickets in a season eight times (best 171, av 17.79, in 1961). His best bowling was 9/30 for Worcestershire v Kent at Dover in 1955. In 1963 he had the unusual distinction of dismissing three batsmen lbw with successive deliveries for Worcestershire v Lancashire at Old Trafford. He played soccer for Walsall.

Flaxington, Samuel
Professional. *b:* 14.10.1860, Otley, Yorkshire. *d:* 10.3.1895, Otley, Yorkshire. Middle order right-hand batsman, good field. *Team* Yorkshire (1882, 4 matches).
Career batting
4–8–0–121–57–15.12–0–*ct* 1

Fleetwood-Smith, Leslie O'Brien
Amateur. *b:* 30.3.1908, Stawell, Victoria, Australia. *d:* 16.3.1971, Fitzroy, Melbourne, Victoria, Australia. Lower order right-hand batsman, slow left-arm bowler with chinamen. *Team* Victoria (1931/2 to 1939/40, 51 matches). *Tours* Australia to England 1934, 1938, to South Africa 1935/6. *Tests* Australia (1935/6 to 1938, 10 matches).
Career batting
112–117–33–617–63–7.34–0–*ct* 42
Bowling 13519–597–22.64–57–18–9/36
Test batting
10–11–5–54–16*–9.00–0–*ct* 0
Bowling 1570–42–37.38–2–1–6/110
Due to his very moderate batting and fielding, Fleetwood-Smith did not appear in any of the Tests on his 1934 visit to England, but his bowling was most successful – 106 wkts, av 19.20 – and he was second to O'Reilly in the averages. He returned similar figures in 1938, but appeared in four Tests, when unfortunately his uncertain length and direction counter-balanced his well concealed spin. His best bowling was 9/36 for Victoria v Tasmania at Melbourne in 1932/3.

Fleming, Charles Barnett
Amateur. *b:* 28.2.1887, Derby. *d:* 22.9.1918, Grevillers, France. He was killed in action. Middle order right-hand batsman. *Team* Derbyshire (1907, 1 match).
Career batting
1–2–0–5–3–2.50–0–*ct* 0

Fleming, Damien William
Cricketer. *b:* 24.4.1970, Bentley, Perth, Western Australia. Lower order right-hand batsman, right-arm fast bowler. *Team* Victoria (1989/90 to 1991/2). *Tour* Victoria to England 1991.
Career batting
29–29–10–264–63*–13.89–0–*ct* 17
Bowling 2682–83–32.37–2–0–6/37

Fleming, David
Cricketer. *b:* 7.4.1964, Broxburn, West Lothian, Scotland. Lower order right-hand batsman, wicket-keeper. *Team* Scotland (1986).
Career batting
1 match, did not bat–*ct* 3

Fleming, Frank
Amateur. *b:* 6.10.1861, Edmonton, Middlesex. Lower order batsman. *Team* London County (1901).
Career batting
1–2–0–10–5–5.00–0–*ct* 0

Fleming, Ian Douglas Keith
Amateur. *b:* 21.8.1908, Georgetown, British Guiana. *d:* 4.7.1988, Pembury, Kent. Nephew of W. Weber (British Guiana). Middle order right-hand batsman, right-arm medium pace bowler. *Sch* Winchester. *Team* Kent (1934, 3 matches).
Career batting
5–8–2–183–66–30.50–0–*ct* 5
His last first-class match was for H. D. G. Leveson-Gower's XI in 1935.

Fleming, James Millar
Amateur. *b:* 5.9.1901, Philpstoun, West Lothian, Scotland. *d:* 4.9.1962, Murrayfield, Edinburgh, Scotland. Lower order right-hand batsman, wicket-keeper. *Team* Scotland (1926).
Career batting
1–1–1–51–51*–no av–0–*ct* 4–*st* 1

Fleming, Matthew Valentine
Cricketer. *b:* 12.12.1964, Macclesfield, Cheshire. Great-grandson of C. F. H. Leslie (Middlesex). Aggressive middle order right-hand batsman, right-arm medium pace bowler, brilliant field. *Sch* Eton. *Team* Kent (1989–92, 68 matches).
Career batting
68–108–14–2898–116–30.82–4–*ct* 34
Bowling 2786–68–40.97–0–0–4/63
He played representative cricket for the Army and Combined Services.

Fleming, Robert Christopher John
Cricketer. *b:* 20.7.1953, Woking, Surrey. Lower order right-hand batsman, off break bowler. *Sch* KCS, Wimbledon. *Team* Cambridge U (1974).
Career batting
9–15–7–60–13*–7.50–0–*ct* 5
Bowling 522–7–74.57–0–0–3/91

Fletcher, Barry Elyston
Professional. *b:* 7.3.1935, Birmingham. Middle order left-hand batsman, right-arm medium pace bowler, fine field. *Team* Warwickshire (1956–61, 49 matches).
Career batting
49–79–13–1511–102*–22.89–1–*ct* 39
Bowling 13–0
He was a Welsh badminton International.

Fletcher, Christopher David Bryan
Cricketer. *b:* 10.12.1957, Harrogate, Yorkshire. Lower order left-hand batsman, right-arm fast medium bowler. *Team* Sussex (1979, 1 match).
Career batting
1 match, did not bat–*ct* 0
Bowling 51–1–51.00–0–0–1/35

Fletcher, David George William
Professional. *b:* 6.7.1924, Sutton, Surrey. Stylish opening right-hand batsman, right-arm fast bowler. *Team* Surrey (1946–61, 300 matches). *Tours* Commonwealth to India 1953/4; Surrey to Rhodesia 1959/60.
Career batting
316–519–41–14461–194–30.25–22–*ct* 178
Bowling 0–0
He hit 1,000 runs in a season four times (best 1,960, av 37.69, in 1952). Illness and injury reduced his chances of further honours in the game.

Fletcher, Duncan Andrew Gwynne
Cricketer. *b:* 27.9.1948, Salisbury, Rhodesia. Brother of A. W. R. (Rhodesia). Middle order left-hand batsman, right-arm fast medium bowler. *Teams* Rhodesia/Zimbabwe (1969/70 to 1984/5); Western Province (1984/5). *Tours* Zimbabwe to England 1982, 1983 (World Cup).
Career batting
111–198–25–4097–93–23.68–0–*ct* 75
Bowling 6027–215–28.03–5–1–6/31
He captained the Zimbabwe team in the 1982 tour and the 1983 World Cup. In 1977 he played for Cambridgeshire.

Fletcher, Geoffrey Everingham
Amateur. *b:* 20.7.1919, Charterhouse, Godalming, Surrey. *d:* 27.3.1943, Djebel Saikra, Matmata, Tunisia. Middle order right-hand batsman. *Sch* Marlborough. *Teams* Oxford U (1939); Somerset (1939, 1 match).
Career batting
5–10–1–165–65–18.33–0–*ct* 4
Bowling 15–0

Fletcher, Henry
Professional. *b:* 25.7.1882, Clay Cross, Derbyshire. *d:* 27.10.1937, Chaddesden, Derby. Middle order batsman. *Team* Derbyshire (1907–08, 5 matches).
Career batting
5–10–2–17–4–2.12–0–*ct* 2

Fletcher, Iain
Cricketer. *b:* 31.8.1971, Sawbridgeworth, Hertfordshire. Middle order right-hand batsman, right-arm medium pace bowler. *Sch* Millfield. *Team* Somerset (1991, 1 match).
Career batting
1–2–1–58–56–58.00–0–*ct* 0
He also played for Hertfordshire (1990).

Fletcher, Keith William Robert, OBE
Professional. *b:* 20.5.1944, Worcester. Sound middle order right-hand batsman, leg break bowler, good slip field. *Team* Essex (1962–88, 574 matches). *Tours* MCC Under 25 to Pakistan 1966/7; MCC to Ceylon and Pakistan 1968/9, to Ceylon 1969/70, to Australia and New Zealand 1970/1, 1974/5, to India, Pakistan and Sri Lanka 1972/3, to West Indies 1973/4, to India, Sri Lanka and Australia 1976/7; England to India and Sri Lanka 1981/2; Cavaliers to West Indies 1964/5; International XI to India, Pakistan and Ceylon 1967/8. *Tests* England (1968 to 1981/2, 59 matches).
Career batting
730–1167–170–37665–228*–37.77–63–*ct* 644
Bowling 2296–51–45.01–1–0–5/41
Test batting
59–96–14–3272–216–39.90–7–*ct* 54
Bowling 193–2–96.50–0–0–1/6

He hit 1,000 runs in a season 20 times (best 1,890, av 41.08, in 1968). He scored two double centuries, 228* for Essex v Sussex at Hastings in 1968 and 216 for England v New Zealand at Auckland 1974/5. He captained Essex from 1974 to 1985 and in 1988; also he led England in seven Tests including the 1981/2 tour to India and Sri Lanka. He went with the England A side to Zimbabwe in 1989/90 as coach. After his retirement he remained with Essex captaining the 2nd XI until 1992 when he was appointed England Team Manager.

Fletcher, Stuart David
Cricketer. *b:* 8.6.1964, Keighley, Yorkshire. Lower order right-hand batsman, right-arm medium fast bowler. *Teams* Yorkshire (1983–91, 107 matches); Lancashire (1992, 6 matches).
Career batting
113–96–32–476–28*–7.43–0–*ct* 27
Bowling 8375–240–34.89–5–0–8/58

Fletcher, Thomas
Amateur. *b:* 15.6.1881, Heanor, Derbyshire. *d:* 29.9.1954, Markeaton, Derby. Middle order right-hand batsman, right-arm medium pace bowler. *Team* Derbyshire (1906, 1 match).
Career batting
1–1–0–28–28–28.00–0–*ct* 0
Bowling 3–0
A noted amateur soccer player, he appeared for Derby County and Leicester Fosse.

Fletcher, William
Professional. *b:* 16.2.1866, Leeds, Yorkshire. *d:* 1.6.1935, Knaresborough, Yorkshire. Middle or lower order right-hand batsman, right-arm fast bowler. *Teams* Yorkshire (1891–92, 6 matches).
Career batting
6–10–2–100–31*–12.50–0–*ct* 7
Bowling 222–9–24.66–0–0–4/45

Flick, Barry John
Cricketer. *b:* 5.3.1952, Coventry, Warwickshire. Tail end right-hand batsman, wicket-keeper. *Team* Warwickshire (1969–73, 16 matches).
Career batting
16–14–8–46–18–7.66–0–*ct* 17–*st* 4

Flint, Benjamin
Professional. *b:* 12.1.1893, Underwood, Nottinghamshire. *d:* 20.7.1959, Sherwood Rise, Nottingham. Brother of W. A. (Nottinghamshire), father of Derrick (Warwickshire). Lower order right-hand batsman, right-arm fast bowler. *Team* Nottinghamshire (1919–20, 13 matches).
Career batting
13–13–4–81–36–9.00–0–*ct* 5
Bowling 564–19–29.68–0–0–3/28
He was a first-class umpire (1946–50).

Flint, Derrick
Professional. *b:* 14.6.1924, Creswell, Derbyshire. Son of Benjamin (Nottinghamshire), nephew of W. A. (Nottinghamshire), husband of Rachael Heyhoe Flint (England Women). Tail end right-hand batsman, leg break and googly bowler. *Team* Warwickshire (1948–49, 10 matches).
Career batting
10–10–3–33–11–4.71–0–*ct* 5
Bowling 465–12–38.75–0–0–4/67

Flint, Joseph
Professional. *b:* 23.4.1840, Wirksworth, Derbyshire. *d:* 2.11.1912, Wirksworth, Derbyshire. Lower order right-hand batsman, right-hand slow round-arm bowler, good slip. *Team* Derbyshire (1872–79, 14 matches).
Career batting
14–24–3–143–24–6.80–0–*ct* 11
Bowling 601–44–13.65–2–0–6/28
His most famous bowling feat was to take 6 wickets for 7, when XVI of Derbyshire dismissed Nottinghamshire for 14 in 1873 (not first-class).

Flint, Louis Edward
Amateur. *b:* 10.1.1895, Ripley, Derbyshire. *d:* 3.4.1958, Kings Mill, Sutton-in-Ashfield, Nottinghamshire. Lower order left-hand batsman, right-arm fast medium bowler. *Team* Derbyshire (1919–20, 7 matches).
Career batting
7–11–0–100–35–9.09–0–*ct* 1
Bowling 291–8–36.37–0–0–3/30

Flint, William Arthur
Professional. *b:* 21.3.1890, Underwood, Nottinghamshire. *d:* 5.2.1955, West Bridgford, Nottingham. Brother of Benjamin (Nottinghamshire), uncle of Derrick (Warwickshire). Middle order right-hand batsman, right-arm medium pace bowler. *Team* Nottinghamshire (1919–29, 145 matches).
Career batting
145–195–22–3345–103–19.33–3–*ct* 77
Bowling 6965–236–29.51–6–1–6/23
A well-known soccer player, he appeared for Notts County as a half-back from 1908 to 1926.

Flockton, Raymond George
Amateur. *b:* 14.3.1930, Paddington, Sydney, New South Wales, Australia. Middle order right-hand batsman, right-arm medium pace bowler. *Team* New South Wales (1951/2 to 1962/3, 34 matches).
Career batting
35–50–9–1695–264*–41.34–2–*ct* 11
Bowling 1027–27–38.03–0–0–4/33
His only first-class match in England was for a Commonwealth XI in 1956. His highest score was 264* for New South Wales v South Australia at Sydney in 1959/60.

Flood, Dr John Wellesley
Amateur. *b:* 22.4.1884, Australia. *d:* 1934, Kokopo, New Britain, New Guinea. Lower order right-hand batsman, right-arm fast medium bowler. *Sch* Rossall. *Team* Ireland (1909).
Career batting
1–2–0–25–16–12.50–0–*ct* 0
Bowling 27–0

Flood, Raymond David
Professional. *b:* 20.11.1935, Northam, Southampton, Hampshire. Middle order right-hand batsman, off break bowler. *Team* Hampshire (1956–60, 24 matches).
Career batting
24–43–5–885–138*–23.28–1–*ct* 10
Bowling 9–0

Flower, Grant William
Cricketer. *b:* 20.12.1970, Salisbury, Rhodesia. Brother of Andrew (Zimbabwe). Middle order right-hand batsman, slow left-arm bowler. *Team* Zimbabwe (1989/90 to 1991/2). *Tour* Zimbabwe to England 1990.
Career batting
10–18–1–427–84–25.11–0–*ct* 10
Bowling 391–10–39.10–0–0–2/6

Flower, Russell William
Cricketer. *b:* 6.11.1942, Stone, Staffordshire. Tail end left-hand batsman, slow left-arm bowler. *Team* Warwickshire (1978, 9 matches).
Career batting
9–8–4–23–10*–5.75–0–*ct* 0
Bowling 554–10–55.40–0–0–3/45
He also played for Staffordshire (1964–88).

Flowers, John
Amateur. *b:* 5.10.1882, Shoreham-by-Sea, Sussex. *d:* 8.5.1968, Brighton, Sussex. Lower order batsman, bowler. *Team* Sussex (1905, 2 matches).
Career batting
2–3–0–9–5–3.00–0–*ct* 0
Bowling 59–0

Flowers, Thomas
(birth registered as T. Flower)
Professional. *b:* 25.10.1868, Daybrook, Nottinghamshire. *d:* 26.3.1939, Standard Hill, Nottingham. Cousin of Wilfred (Nottinghamshire). Lower order right-hand batsman, right-arm slow medium bowler. *Team* Nottinghamshire (1894, 1 match).
Career batting
1–2–0–16–11–8.00–0–*ct* 0
Bowling 10–0

Flowers, Wilfred
(birth registered as W. Flower)
Professional. *b:* 7.12.1856, Calverton, Nottinghamshire. *d:* 1.11.1926, Carlton, Nottingham. Cousin of Thomas (Nottinghamshire), uncle of Emmott Robinson (Yorkshire). Middle order right-hand batsman, off break bowler, good deep field. *Team* Nottinghamshire (1877–96, 281 matches). *Tours* Lillywhite, Shaw and Shrewsbury to Australia 1884/5, 1886/7. *Tests* England (1884/5 to 1893, 8 matches).
Career batting
442–696–54–12891–173–20.07–9–*ct* 222
Bowling 18887–1188–15.89–73–15–8/22
Test batting
8–14–0–254–56–18.14–0–*ct* 2
Bowling 296–14–21.14–1–0–5/46
He hit 1,000 runs in a season twice and took 100 wickets in a season twice, his best year with both bat and ball being 1883 when he achieved the 'double': 1,144 runs (av 24.86) and 113 wickets (av 15.03). He was a first-class umpire (1907–12).

Flynn, Vincent Anthony
Cricketer. *b:* 3.10.1955, Aylesbury, Buckinghamshire. Lower order right-hand batsman, wicket-keeper. *Team* Northamptonshire (1976–78, 3 matches).
Career batting
3–2–1–21–15–21.00–0–*ct* 4
He also played for Buckinghamshire (1980–82).

Foat, James Clive
Cricketer. *b:* 21.11.1952, Salford Priors, Warwickshire. Middle order right-hand batsman, right-arm medium pace bowler, brilliant field. *Sch* Millfield. *Team* Gloucestershire (1972–79, 91 matches).
Career batting
91–150–15–2512–126–18.60–5–*ct* 39
Bowling 40–0

Foley, Charles Windham
Amateur. *b:* 26.8.1856, Wadhurst, Sussex. *d:* 20.11.1933, Kensington, London. Lower order bat – originally left hand, but 'foolishly' changed to right, wicket-keeper. *Sch* Eton. *Team* Cambridge U (1880, blue).
Career batting
7–11–0–51–12–4.63–0–*ct* 7–*st* 12
He was awarded his soccer blue, playing against Oxford in 1880. His last first-class match was for MCC in 1891.

Foley, Cyril Pelham
Amateur. *b:* 1.11.1868, Westminster, London. *d:* 9.3.1936, Wimborne St Giles, Dorset. Defensive opening right-hand batsman, slow right-arm bowler, deep field. *Sch* Eton. *Teams* Cambridge U (1888–91, blue 1889–91); Middlesex (1893–1906, 57 matches). *Tour* Brackley to West Indies 1904/5.
Career batting
123–207–16–3175–117–16.62–2–*ct* 43
Bowling 26–1–26.00–0–0–1/14
He also played for Worcestershire (pre first-class, 1888). He took part in the Jameson Raid of 1895 and later fought in both the Boer War and First World

War. In 1909 he went on an expedition to Jerusalem in an attempt to discover the Ark of the Covenant.

Foley, Edward Francis Walwyn
Amateur. *b:* 6.10.1851, Derby. *d:* 21.10.1923, Kensington, London. Lower order right-hand batsman. *Sch* Repton. *Team* Derbyshire (1871, 1 match).
Career batting
1–2–0–0–0–0.00–0–*ct* 1
He did not appear in first-class matches whilst at Oxford U.

Foley, Henry Thomas Hamilton
Amateur. *b:* 25.4.1905, Stoke Edith Park, Hereford. *d:* 13.12.1959, Stoke Edith Park, Hereford. Son of P. H. (MCC), son-in-law of R. B. Pearson (Oxford U). Middle order left-hand batsman. *Sch* Eton. *Team* Worcestershire (1925, 1 match).
Career batting
1–2–1–6–6–6.00–0–*ct* 0
He also played for Monmouthshire (1932–34).

Foley, Dr James Henry
Amateur. *b:* 1.11.1898, Macroom, Co Cork, Ireland. *d:* 30.3.1969, Cork, Ireland. Lower order right-hand batsman. *Team* Ireland (1926).
Career batting
1–2–0–26–16–13.00–0–*ct* 0
Bowling 54–0

Foley, Paul Henry
Amateur. *b:* 19.3.1857, Westminster, London. *d:* 21.1.1928, Pimlico, Westminster, London. Father of H. T. H. (Worcestershire). Middle order left-hand batsman, right-hand slow under-arm bowler. *Sch* Eton. *Team* MCC (1891).
Career batting
1–2–0–21–13–10.50–0–*ct* 0
His County cricket was for Worcestershire (pre-first-class, 1878–96) and he was Honorary Secretary to the County Club until 1908.

Foljambe, Edmond Walter Savile
Amateur. *b:* 19.9.1890, Southwell, Nottinghamshire. *d:* 22.8.1960, Walkley, Sheffield, Yorkshire. Son of G. S. (Nottinghamshire), nephew of G. A. T. (MCC), great-nephew of A. B. S. Acheson (MCC) and E. A. B. Acheson (MCC). Opening or middle order batsman. *Sch* Eton. *Team* Oxford U (1912).
Career batting
3–6–1–91–38–18.20–0–*ct* 1
He won a blue for soccer.

Foljambe, George Savile
Amateur. *b:* 10.10.1856, Osberton Hall, Nottinghamshire. *d:* 13.9.1920, Kensington, London. Father of E. W. S. (Oxford U), brother of G. A. T. (MCC), nephew of A. B. S. Acheson (MCC) and E. A. B. Acheson (MCC), brother-in-law of W. Bury (Nottinghamshire). Middle order right-hand batsman, left-arm medium pace bowler. *Sch* Eton. *Team* Nottinghamshire (1879–81, 7 matches).
Career batting
24–38–2–297–99–8.25–0–*ct* 12
He did not appear in first-class cricket whilst at Oxford U, but did win a blue for royal tennis. His last first-class match was for MCC in 1882.

Foljambe, Godfrey Acheson Thornhagh
Amateur. *b:* 21.10.1869, Marylebone, London. *d:* 16.3.1942, The Lizard, Cornwall. Uncle of E. W. S. (Oxford U), brother of G. S. (Nottinghamshire), nephew of A. B. S. Acheson (MCC) and E. A. B. Acheson (MCC), brother-in-law of H. F. Wright (Derbyshire). Lower order batsman, left-arm medium pace bowler. *Sch* Eton. *Team* MCC (1892–93). *Tour* Hawke to India 1892/3.
Career batting
5–8–0–97–34–12.12–0–*ct* 2
Bowling 145–9–16.11–0–0–4/32
He appeared in the Cambridge Seniors' match of 1892, but no first-class matches for the University. His County cricket was for Cambridgeshire (1899).

Folkes, Castell
Cricketer. *b:* 29.7.1944, Kingston, Jamaica. Father of C. R. (Jamaica). Tail end right-hand batsman, right-arm fast medium bowler. *Team* Jamaica (1967/8 to 1970/1). *Tour* Jamaica to England 1970.
Career batting
13–9–1–36–9–4.50–0–*ct* 1
Bowling 745–25–29.80–2–0–5/22
He bowled well on his single tour to England.

Folland, Nicholas Arthur
Cricketer. *b:* 17.9.1963, Bristol. Middle order left-hand batsman, right-arm medium pace bowler. *Team* Somerset (1992, 1 match).
Career batting
2–4–1–212–82*–70.66–0–*ct* 1
He also played for Devon (1981–92) and made his first-class debut for Minor Counties in 1990.

Follett, Edward Charles
Amateur. *b:* 16.2.1842, Westminster, London. *d:* 6.6.1869, Birmingham. Middle order right-hand batsman, slow round-arm bowler. *Sch* Eton. *Team* MCC (1868).
Career batting
1–2–0–3–3–1.50–0–*ct* 0
He was at Oxford U, but not in the eleven. His County cricket was for Berkshire (1860).

Folley, Ian
Cricketer. *b:* 9.1.1963, Stoneyholme, Burnley, Lancashire. Lower order right-hand batsman, left-arm medium pace bowler, later changing to slow left-arm. *Teams* Lancashire (1982–90, 135 matches); Derbyshire (1991, 4 matches). *Tours* Lancashire to Jamaica 1986/7, 1987/8, to Zimbabwe 1988/9.

Career batting
140–163–50–1485–69–13.14–0–*ct* 60
Bowling 9359–287–32.60–10–1–7/15
His best season was 1987 when he took 74 wickets, av 25.20.

Foord, Charles William
Professional. *b:* 11.6.1924, Scarborough, Yorkshire. Lower order right-hand batsman, right-arm fast medium bowler. *Team* Yorkshire (1947–53, 51 matches).
Career batting
52–36–16–125–35–6.25–0–*ct* 19
Bowling 3469–128–27.10–5–0–6/63

Foord, E. A.
Amateur. Tail end batsman. *Team* W. G. Grace's XI (1871).
Career batting
1–1–0–0–0–0.00–0–*ct* 0
Foord played in emergency for Grace's XI against his own county, Kent.

Foord-Kelcey, John
(changed name from Foord in May 1872)
Amateur. *b:* 2.10.1860, Smeeth, Ashford, Kent. *d:* 10.1.1931, Gloucester. Brother of William (Kent), uncle of O. C. Mordaunt (Somerset). Middle order right-hand batsman, useful bowler. *Sch* Chatham House, Ramsgate. *Team* Oxford U (1883).
Career batting
2–3–0–36–23–12.00–0–*ct* 0
Bowling 125–11–11.36–1–0–6/58

Foord-Kelcey, William
(changed name from Foord in May 1872)
Amateur. *b:* 21.4.1854, Smeeth, Ashford, Kent. *d:* 3.1.1922, Woolwich, London. Brother of John (Oxford U), uncle of O. C. Mordaunt (Somerset). Middle order right-hand batsman, right-hand fast round-arm bowler, good field. *Sch* Chatham House, Ramsgate. *Team* Oxford U (1874–75, blue both years); Kent (1874–83, 64 matches).
Career batting
78–136–10–1798–105–14.26–1–*ct* 66
Bowling 4828–272–17.75–18–6–8/49

Forbes, Carlton
Professional. *b:* 9.8.1936, Cross Roads, Kingston, Jamaica. Lower order left-hand batsman, left-arm medium pace bowler. *Team* Nottinghamshire (1959–73, 244 matches).
Career batting
245–319–69–3597–86–14.38–0–*ct* 145
Bowling 17993–707–25.44–23–2–7/19
He hit 1,000 runs in a season once: 1,020 (av 20.40) in 1961 and took 100 wickets in a season three times (best 117, av 19.64, in 1965).

Forbes, Dudley Henry
Amateur. *b:* 13.1.1873, Forenaughts, Naas, Co Kildare, Ireland. *d:* 21.4.1901, Kroonstad, Orange Free State, South Africa, of enteric fever. Brother-in-law of A. G. Hotham (Hampshire), his niece married J. R. Tylden (Kent). Lower order right-hand batsman, right-arm fast bowler. *Sch* Eton. *Team* Oxford U (1894–95, blue 1894).
Career batting
12–21–3–83–25*–4.61–0–*ct* 9
Bowling 1121–44–25.47–3–0–6/86
His last first-class match was for Oxford U, Past and Present, in 1899.

Forbes, George Thomson
Amateur. *b:* 25.11.1906, Aberdeen, Scotland. *d:* 3.11.1984, Aberdeen, Scotland. Lower order right-hand batsman, right-arm fast medium bowler. *Team* Scotland (1936–38).
Career batting
4–8–0–122–29–15.25–0–*ct* 3
Bowling 173–11–15.72–0–0–3/25

Forbes, Walter Francis
Amateur. *b:* 20.1.1858, Malvern Link, Worcestershire. *d:* 29.3.1933, Marylebone, London. Brother-in-law of B. Lawley (I Zingari). Middle order right-hand batsman, right-hand fast round-arm bowler, good deep field. *Sch* Eton. *Teams* Gentlemen (1877–84); I Zingari (1878).
Career batting
11–18–0–382–80–21.22–0–*ct* 6
Bowling 679–31–21.90–2–0–6/32
He did not appear in first-class County cricket, most of his matches being for Yorkshire Gentlemen and I Zingari. In 1876 he threw the cricket ball 132 yards, though only 18 years old.

Forbes-Adam, Eric Graham
Amateur. *b:* 3.10.1888, Malabar Hill, Bombay, India. *d:* 7.7.1925, Constantinople, Turkey. Middle order batsman. *Sch* Eton. *Team* Cambridge U (1911).
Career batting
1–2–0–27–17–13.50–0–*ct* 1
He was First Secretary at the British Embassy in Constantinople at the time of his death.

Ford, Alexander Clark
Amateur. *b:* 8.11.1900, Uddingston, Lanarkshire, Scotland. *d:* 8.2.1986, Broxburn, West Lothian, Scotland. Father of J. M. C. (Scotland). Middle order, right-hand batsman, right-arm medium pace bowler. *Team* Scotland (1924–25).
Career batting
2–3–0–18–17–6.00–0–*ct* 0
Bowling 78–1–78.00–0–0–1/64

Ford, Augustus Frank Justice
Amateur. *b:* 12.9.1858, Paddington, London. *d:* 20.5.1931, Marylebone, London. Son of W. A. (MCC 1839), brother of F. G. J. (Middlesex) and W. J. (Middlesex), uncle of N. M. (Derbyshire and Middlesex), nephew of G. J. (Oxford U 1837). Lower order

right-hand batsman, right-hand medium pace round-arm bowler, good field. *Sch* Repton. *Teams* Cambridge U (1878–81, blue all four years); Middlesex (1879–82, 18 matches).
Career batting
51–77–8–983–102–14.24–1–*ct* 58
Bowling 2484–153–16.23–9–2–7/32
His final first-class match was for Cambridge U, Past and Present, in 1886. He was a noted billiards player, and represented Cambridge.

Ford, Cecil William
Amateur. *b:* 20.4.1913, Elstree, Hertfordshire. Middle order right-hand batsman, right-arm medium fast bowler. *Team* Minor Counties (1936).
Career batting
1–2–0–5–3–2.50–0–*ct* 1
Bowling 31–0
His County cricket was for Hertfordshire (1932–39) and Devon (1946–47).

Ford, Charles Richard
Professional. *b:* 8.8.1838, Bungay, Suffolk. Middle or lower order right-hand batsman, right-hand medium pace round-arm bowler, slip field. *Team* England (1874).
Career batting
1–2–0–7–5–3.50–0–*ct* 0
His County cricket was for Staffordshire (1873). A noted coach and umpire, he was engaged at Cambridge U for at least 15 years, commencing 1865.

Ford, Edgar Samuel
Amateur. *b:* 20.5.1876, Bradford-on-Avon, Wiltshire. *d:* 11.4.1943, Cranmore, Isle of Wight. Lower order batsman, wicket-keeper. *Team* London County (1902).
Career batting
1–1–1–0–0*–no av–0–*ct* 0–*st* 1
His County cricket was for Wiltshire (1899–1903).

Ford, Ernest Claudius Bramhall
Amateur. *b:* 23.7.1855, Cheltenham, Gloucestershire. *d:* 19.6.1900, Southend, Essex. Middle or lower order right-hand batsman, wicket-keeper. *Sch* Clifton. *Team* Gloucestershire (1874–75, 6 matches).
Career batting
6–9–2–75–32*–10.71–0–*ct* 3–*st* 1
He also played for Somerset (pre first-class) in 1877.

Ford, Francis Gilbertson Justice
Amateur. *b:* 14.12.1866, Paddington, London. *d:* 7.2.1940, Burwash, Sussex. Son of W. A. (MCC 1839), brother of A. F. J. (Middlesex) and W. J. (Middlesex), nephew of G. J. (Oxford U 1837), uncle of N. M. (Derbyshire and Middlesex), great-uncle of J. R. T. Barclay (Sussex). Attractive middle order left-hand batsman, slow left-arm bowler, slip field. *Sch* Repton. *Teams* Middlesex (1886–99, 102 matches); Cambridge U (1887–90, blue all four years). *Tour* Stoddart to Australia 1894/5. *Tests* England (1894/5, 5 matches).
Career batting
168–289–17–7359–191–27.05–14–*ct* 131
Bowling 4757–200–23.78–8–1–7/65
Test batting
5–9–0–168–48–18.66–0–*ct* 58
Bowling 129–1–129.00–0–0–1/47
His final first-class match was for an England XII in 1908. He hit 1,000 runs in a season twice (best 1,195, av 28.45, in 1899). He captained Cambridge in 1889. A noted goalkeeper, he was awarded his blue at Cambridge.

Ford, James Malcolm Clark
Amateur. *b:* 29.12.1936, Edinburgh, Scotland. *d:* 13.4.1987, Polbeth, Scotland. Son of A. C. (Scotland). Middle order left-hand batsman. *Team* Scotland (1960–66).
Career batting
10–17–4–235–50–18.07–0–*ct* 7

Ford, John Kenneth
Professional. *b:* 5.3.1934, Redland, Bristol. Tail end right-hand batsman, right-arm fast bowler. *Team* Gloucestershire (1951, 1 match).
Career batting
1–1–0–0–0–0.00–0–*ct* 0
Bowling 44–1–44.00–0–0–1/44

Ford, Neville Montague
Amateur. *b:* 18.11.1906, Repton, Derbyshire. Grandson of W. A. (MCC 1839), nephew of A. F. J. (Middlesex), F. G. J. (Middlesex) and W. J. (Middlesex). Middle order right-hand batsman. *Sch* Harrow. *Teams* Derbyshire (1926–34, 31 matches); Oxford U (1928–30, blue all three years); Middlesex (1932, 1 match). *Tour* MCC to Canada 1937 (not first-class).
Career batting
75–121–9–2925–183–26.11–5–*ct* 15
Bowling 117–1–117.00–0–0–1/19
He hit 1,096 runs, av 37.79, in 1930. His last first-class match was for Free Foresters in 1935. He represented Oxford U at fives.

Ford, Percy Hadley
Amateur. *b:* 5.7.1877, Wheatenhurst, Gloucestershire. *d:* 2.12.1920, Gloucester, of septic pneumonia. Lower order right-hand batsman, right-arm fast bowler. *Sch* Wycliffe. *Team* Gloucestershire (1906–08, 29 matches).
Career batting
29–51–9–419–36–9.97–0–*ct* 10
Bowling 2148–87–24.68–7–2–6/24
Business restricted his appearances in County cricket.

Ford, Reggie Gilbert
Professional. *b:* 5.3.1907, Bristol. *d:* 2.10.1981, Horfield, Bristol. Middle order right-hand batsman, right-arm medium pace bowler. *Team* Gloucestershire (1929–36, 51 matches).
Career batting
51–70–23–496–37*–10.55–0–*ct* 23
Bowling 493–10–49.30–0–0–2/11

Ford, Walter Ronald
Amateur. *b:* 19.10.1913, Teddington, Middlesex. Lower order left-hand batsman, wicket-keeper. *Team* Combined Services (1946–49).
Career batting
4–7–0–69–36–9.85–0–*ct* 7
He was Assistant Secretary (Admin) of MCC 1973–77.

Ford, William Justice
Amateur. *b:* 7.11.1853, Paddington, London. *d:* 3.4.1904, Kensington, London. Son of W. A. (MCC 1839), brother of A. F. J. (Middlesex) and F. G. J. (Middlesex), uncle of N. M. (Derbyshire and Middlesex), nephew of G. J. (Oxford U 1837). Very hard-hitting middle order right-hand batsman, right-hand slow round-arm bowler, good point. *Sch* Repton. *Teams* Cambridge U (1873–74, blue 1873); Middlesex (1879–94, 7 matches); Nelson (1886/7 to 1888/9).
Career batting
25–42–2–711–75–17.77–0–*ct* 19–*st* 2
Bowling 213–13–16.38–1–0–6/56
He was regarded second only to C. I. Thornton as a hitter. A noted writer on cricket, his works included Histories of Cambridge University CC and Middlesex CCC. His final first-class match was for MCC in 1896. He also played for Wiltshire (1882–83).

Fordham, Alan
Cricketer. *b:* 9.11.1964, Bedford. Opening right-hand batsman, right-arm medium pace bowler. *Sch* Bedford Modern. *Team* Northamptonshire (1986–92, 103 matches). *Tour* Northamptonshire to South Africa 1991/2.
Career batting
103–182–16–6759–206*–40.71–14–*ct* 65
Bowling 238–3–79.33–0–0–1/25
His highest score was 206* for Northamptonshire v Yorkshire at Headingley in 1990, putting on a County record 393 with A. J. Lamb for the 3rd wicket. He has reached 1,000 runs in a season three times (best 1,840, av 47.17, in 1991). He also played for Bedfordshire (1982–89).

Fordham, Cyril Bernard
Amateur. *b:* 22.9.1906, Puckeridge, Hertfordshire. *d:* 22.4.1988, Bath, Somerset. Middle order right-hand batsman, off break bowler. *Sch* Bishop's Stortford. *Team* Minor Counties (1931–37).
Career batting
5–10–2–414–140–51.75–2–*ct* 2
Bowling 91–2–45.50–0–0–2/34
His County cricket was for Hertfordshire (1924–39).

Fordham, James
Professional. *b:* 19.3.1839, Cambridge. *d:* 2.4.1901, Barnwell, Cambridge. Middle order right-hand batsman. *Team* Cambridgeshire (1865–69, 5 matches).
Career batting
5–9–1–27–10–3.37–0–*ct* 5
Bowling 11–1–11.00–0–0–1/11

Foreman, Denis Joseph
Professional. *b:* 1.2.1933, Athlone, Cape Town, South Africa. Middle/lower order right-hand batsman, off break bowler, slip field. *Teams* Western Province (1951/2); Sussex (1952–67, 125 matches).
Career batting
130–203–23–3277–104–18.20–1–*ct* 124
Bowling 273–9–30.33–0–0–4/64
He played soccer for Brighton and Hove Albion at outside left.

Forman, Rev Arthur Francis Emilius
Amateur. *b:* 26.7.1850, Gibraltar. *d:* 13.2.1905, Repton, Derbyshire. Father of Humphrey (Somerset). Middle order right-hand batsman, right-hand fast round-arm bowler, deep field. *Sch* Sherborne. *Team* Derbyshire (1877–82, 5 matches).
Career batting
5–7–0–90–36–12.85–0–*ct* 0
Bowling 3–0
He did not play in first-class matches whilst at Oxford U. His cricketing fame rests with his coaching when a master at Repton. He also played for Dorset (1870–77) and Somerset (pre first-class, 1871). His daughter married the Most Rev Geoffrey Fisher, the 99th Archbishop of Canterbury.

Forman, Frederick Gerald
Amateur. *b:* 30.8.1884, Chellaston, Derbyshire. *d:* 8.12.1960, Penzance, Cornwall. Middle/lower order batsman, change bowler. *Team* Derbyshire (1911, 1 match).
Career batting
1–2–0–3–3–1.50–0–*ct* 1
A well-known hockey player, he represented Derbyshire.

Forman, Humphrey
Amateur. *b:* 26.4.1888, Repton, Derbyshire. *d:* 21.5.1923, Bangkok, Siam. He died following an operation. Son of A. F. E. (Derbyshire). Middle order batsman, left-arm medium pace bowler. *Sch* Shrewsbury. *Teams* Cambridge U (1910); Somerset (1910, 1 match).
Career batting
2–4–0–13–8–3.25–0–*ct* 0
Bowling 159–5–31.80–0–0–4/62

Forman, Peter Ralph
Amateur. *b:* 9.3.1934, West Bridgford, Nottingham. Lower order right-hand batsman, slow left-arm bowler. *Sch* Oakham. *Team* Nottinghamshire (1959–62, 16 matches).
Career batting
16–25–8–180–26–10.58–0–*ct* 14
Bowling 1291–40–32.27–1–0–5/73

Formby, Miles Robert
Amateur. *b:* 14.2.1906, Kirklake Bank, Formby, Lancashire. *d:* 15.6.1989, Norwich, Norfolk. Lower order right-hand batsman, right-arm medium fast bowler. *Sch* Cheltenham. *Team* Cambridge U (1925).
Career batting
2–4–2–18–11–9.00–0–*ct* 0
Bowling 106–2–53.00–0–0–2/27
He won a blue for lacrosse.

Forrester, Alexander Roxburgh
Amateur. *b:* 26.10.1899, Glasgow, Scotland. *d:* 11.12.1976, Glasgow, Scotland. Lower order right-hand batsman, leg break and googly bowler. *Sch* Glasgow Academy. *Team* Scotland (1925–27).
Career batting
3–4–2–43–25*–21.50–0–*ct* 1
Bowling 290–17–17.05–1–0–5/66

Forrester, George Douglas
Amateur. *b:* 22.5.1890, Colinton, Edinburgh, Scotland. *d:* 6.5.1959, Burrabogie. Barwon Heads, Victoria, Australia. Middle order right-hand batsman. *Sch* Rugby. *Team* Oxford U (1912–13).
Career batting
6–11–0–235–82–21.36–0–*ct* 4
Bowling 17–0
He won a blue for golf.

Forrester, Thomas
(known as Forester)
Professional with Warwickshire, then amateur. *b:* 21.9.1873, Clay Cross, Derbyshire. *d:* 27.12.1927, Standard Hill, Nottingham. Lower order left-hand batsman, right-arm medium pace bowler. *Sch* Saltley College. *Teams* Warwickshire (1896–99, 26 matches); Derbyshire (1902–20, 105 matches).
Career batting
131–212–33–2829–87–15.80–0–*ct* 62
Bowling 8920–347–25.70–17–3–7/18
His bowling action was unusual in that he appeared to bowl off the wrong foot.

Forster, Grant
Cricketer. *b:* 27.5.1961, Seaham, Co Durham. Lower order left-hand batsman, off break bowler. *Teams* Northamptonshire (1980, 1 match); Leicestershire (1980/1 to 1982, 4 matches). *Tour* Leicestershire to Zimbabwe 1980/1.
Career batting
5–4–2–45–22*–22.50–0–*ct* 3
Bowling 275–4–68.75–0–0–2/30
He also played for Durham (pre first-class, 1983–86).

Forster, Harold Thomas
Amateur. *b:* 14.11.1878, Winchester, Hampshire. *d:* 29.5.1918, Bouleuse Ridge, near Ventalay, France. He was killed in action. Lower order left-hand batsman, left-arm medium slow bowler. *Team* Hampshire (1911, 5 matches).
Career batting
5–8–3–33–13–6.60–0–*ct* 3
Bowling 212–10–21.20–1–0–5/38
A Colour Sergeant in the Royal Berkshire Regiment, Forster created a great impression on his debut for Hampshire, taking 9/92 in the match, but did very little in his other first-class games.

Forster, Henry William
(created Lord Forster of Lepe in 1919)
Amateur. *b:* 31.1.1866, Southend Hall, Catford, London. *d:* 15.1.1936, Marylebone, London. His mother later married A. G. Renshaw (MCC). Middle order right-hand batsman, slow left-arm bowler, splendid field. *Sch* Eton. *Teams* Hampshire (1885–95, 5 matches); Oxford U (1886–89, blue 1887–89).
Career batting
43–75–6–807–60*–11.69–0–*ct* 43
Bowling 2923–135–21.65–7–2–8/119
He was President of MCC in 1919 and Kent in 1921. He was MP for Sevenoaks 1892–1919 and Governor-General of Australia 1919–25.

Forster, Ralph
Amateur. *b:* 21.7.1835, Springhill, Co Durham. *d:* 17.2.1879, Rome, Italy. Lower order right-hand batsman, excellent long stop. *Sch* Harrow. *Team* Cambridge U (1859).
Career batting
17–28–7–117–40*–5.57–0–*ct* 5
His final first-class match was for MCC in 1870 and his County cricket was for Buckinghamshire.

Forsyth, Harry Hollingsworth
Amateur. *b:* 18.12.1903, Dublin, Ireland. Middle order left-hand batsman, wicket-keeper. *Team* Dublin University (1926).
Career batting
1–2–0–49–43–24.50–0–*ct* 2–*st* 1

Fortescue, Rev Arthur Trosse
Amateur. *b:* 7.4.1848, Fallapit, Totnes, Devon. *d:* 21.11.1899, Marylebone, London. Opening right-hand batsman, deep field. *Sch* Marlborough. *Team* Oxford U (1868–70, blue all three years). *Tour* Sanders to North America 1886.
Career batting
19–32–0–480–68–15.00–0–*ct* 12
Bowling 291–15–19.40–0–0–4/28

His final first-class match in England was for the Gentlemen in 1872. He played county cricket for Devon (1865–74), Warwickshire (not first-class, 1878), Essex (not first-class, 1882) and Lincolnshire (1887–93).

Fortin, Richard Chalmers Gordon
Cricketer. *b:* 12.4.1941, Singapore. Nephew of D. J. W. Bridge (Northamptonshire). Opening right-hand batsman, wicket-keeper. *Sch* Wellington. *Team* Oxford U (1963).
Career batting
2–4–0–52–25–13.00–0–*ct* 0
His County cricket was for Berkshire (1965–70).

Fosh, Matthew Kailey
Cricketer. *b:* 26.9.1957, Epping, Essex. Middle order left-hand batsman, right-arm medium pace bowler. *Sch* Harrow. *Teams* Essex (1976–78, 14 matches); Cambridge U (1977–78, blue both years).
Career batting
30–48–2–1069–109–23.23–1–*ct* 9
He was awarded his rugby blue whilst at Cambridge. In 1975 he hit 161* for Harrow v Eton at Lord's, the third highest innings recorded to that date in this fixture.

Foster, Arthur Webster
Amateur. *b:* 12.8.1894, Deritend, Birmingham. *d:* 9.1.1954, Acocks Green, Birmingham. Brother of F. R. (Warwickshire). Lower order right-hand batsman, wicket-keeper. *Sch* Repton. *Team* Warwickshire (1914, 1 match).
Career batting
1–2–1–1–1*–1.00–0–*ct* 2

Foster, Basil Samuel
Amateur. *b:* 12.2.1882, Malvern, Worcestershire. *d:* 28.9.1959, Pield Heath, Hillingdon, Middlesex. Brother of H. K. (Worcestershire), M. K. (Worcestershire), N. J. A. (Worcestershire), R. E. (Worcestershire), G. N. (Worcestershire and Kent) and W. L. (Worcestershire), uncle of C. K. (Worcestershire), P. G. (Kent) and J. W. Greenstock (Worcestershire), brother-in-law of W. Greenstock (Worcestershire). Middle order right-hand batsman. *Sch* Malvern. *Teams* Worcestershire (1902–11, 7 matches); Middlesex (1912, 12 matches).
Career batting
34–52–1–753–86–14.76–0–*ct* 32
Bowling 50–0
He was a well-known actor on the London stage.

Foster, Christopher Knollys
Amateur. *b:* 27.9.1904, Tarrinton, Herefordshire. *d:* 4.12.1971, Kingsthorne, Hereford. Son of H. K. (Worcestershire), nephew of B. S. (Worcestershire and Middlesex), M. K. (Worcestershire), N. J. A. (Worcestershire), R. E. (Worcestershire), G. N. (Worcestershire and Kent) and W. L. (Worcestershire), cousin of P. G. (Kent) and J. W. Greenstock (Worcestershire), nephew of W. Greenstock (Worcestershire). Middle order right-hand batsman. *Sch* Malvern. *Team* Worcestershire (1927, 3 matches).
Career batting
3–5–2–34–16*–11.33–0–*ct* 0

Foster, Daren Joseph
Cricketer. *b:* 14.3.1966, Tottenham, Middlesex. Tail end right-hand batsman, right-arm fast medium bowler. *Teams* Somerset (1986–89, 28 matches); Glamorgan (1991–92, 17 matches).
Career batting
45–39–15–201–20–8.37–0–*ct* 8
Bowling 3844–96–40.04–2–0–6/84

Foster, David Charles Geoffrey
Cricketer. *b:* 19.9.1959, Holbeach, Lincolnshire. Middle order left-hand batsman, slow left-arm bowler. *Sch* Sutton Valence. *Team* Oxford U (1980).
Career batting
4–6–1–124–67–24.80–0–*ct* 0

Foster, Derek George
Amateur. *b:* 19.3.1907, Sutton Coldfield, Warwickshire. *d:* 13.10.1980, Chipping Campden, Gloucestershire. Lower order right-hand batsman, right-arm fast medium bowler. *Sch* Shrewsbury. *Team* Warwickshire (1928–34, 52 matches).
Career batting
58–79–7–757–70–10.51–0–*ct* 50
Bowling 4120–150–27.46–8–1–742

Foster, Ernest
Amateur. *b:* 23.11.1873, Bramley, Yorkshire. *d:* 16.4.1956, Moor Allerton, Leeds, Yorkshire. Lower order right-hand batsman, right-arm medium fast bowler. *Team* Yorkshire (1901, 1 match).
Career batting
1–1–0–2–2–2.00–0–*ct* 0
Bowling 27–0

Foster, Francis George
Amateur. *b:* 6.11.1848, Havant, Hampshire. Middle order right-hand batsman. *Team* Hampshire (1876, 1 match).
Career batting
1–2–0–12–10–6.00–0–*ct* 1

Foster, Frank Rowbotham
Amateur. *b:* 31.1.1889, Deritend, Birmingham. *d:* 3.5.1958, Northampton. Brother of A. W. (Warwickshire). Middle order right-hand batsman, left-arm fast medium bowler. *Sch* Solihull. *Team* Warwickshire (1908–14, 127 matches). *Tour* MCC to Australia 1911/12. *Tests* England (1911/12 to 1912, 11 matches).
Career batting
159–263–17–6548–305*–26.61–7–*ct* 121
Bowling 14879–717–20.75–53–8–9/118

Test batting
11–15–1–330–71–23.57–0–*ct* 11
Bowling 926–45–20.57–4–0–6/91

He hit 1,000 runs in a season twice (best 1,614, av 42.47, in 1911) and took 100 wickets in a season four times (best 141, av 20.31, in 1911). In 1911 and 1914 he performed the 'double'.

His highest score of 305* was for Warwickshire v Worcestershire at Dudley in 1914 and his only other double century was also for Warwickshire. His best bowling was 9/118 for Warwickshire v Yorkshire at Edgbaston in 1911.

He captained his County from 1911 to 1914. A motor cycle accident during the First World War ended any chance he had of resuming his first-class career in 1919.

He was one of the first bowlers to employ 'leg-theory'.

Foster, Geoffrey Norman
Amateur. *b:* 16.10.1884, Malvern, Worcesteshire. *d:* 11.8.1971, Westminster, London. Brother of B. S. (Worcestershire and Middlesex), H. K. (Worcestershire), M. K. (Worcestershire), N. J. A. (Worcestershire), R. E. (Worcestershire) and W. L. (Worcestershire), father of P. G. (Kent), uncle of C. K. (Worcestershire) and J. W. Greenstock (Worcestershire), father-in-law of F. G. H. Chalk (Kent), brother-in-law of H. E. W. Prest (Kent) and W. Greenstock (Worcestershire). Middle order right-hand batsman, excellent field. *Sch* Malvern. *Teams* Worcestershire (1903–14, 81 matches); Oxford U (1905–08, blue all four years); Kent (1921–22, 10 matches); Europeans (1909/10).
Career batting
141–249–16–6600–175–28.32–11–*ct* 160–*st* 1
Bowling 284–8–35.50–0–0–2/21

He hit 1,000 runs in a season three times (best 1,182, av 40.75, in 1907). His final first-class match was for MCC in 1931. He gained his soccer blue at Oxford and went on to win an amateur international cap for England. He also won blues for golf and rackets.

Foster, Henry Knollys
Amateur. *b:* 30.10.1873, Malvern, Worcestershire. *d:* 23.6.1950, Aconbury, Kingsthorne, Herefordshire. Brother of B. S. (Worcestershire and Middlesex), G. N. (Worcestershire and Kent), M. K. (Worcestershire), N. J. A. (Worcestershire), R. E. (Worcestershire), and W. L. (Worcestershire), father of C. K. (Worcestershire), uncle of P. G. (Kent) and J. W. Greenstock (Worcestershire), brother-in-law of W. Greenstock (Worcestershire). Opening or middle order right-hand batsman, right-arm fast medium bowler. *Sch* Malvern. *Teams* Oxford U (1894–96, blue all three years); Worcestershire (1899–1925, 246 matches).
Career batting
289–524–21–17154–216–34.10–29–*ct* 206
Bowling 444–15–29.60–0–0–3/63

He hit 1,000 runs in a season eight times (best 1,635, av 43.02, in 1904). Both his double centuries were for Worcestershire, the higher being 216 v Somerset at Worcester in 1903. He first played for Worcestershire (pre first-class) in 1891. He captained Worcestershire 1899–1900, 1902–10 and 1913. He was a Test selector in 1907, 1912 and 1921. A noted rackets player, he was the English Amateur Champion, and won a blue.

Foster, Jack Heygate Nedham
Amateur. *b:* 8.9.1905, Chatham, Kent. *d:* 16.11.1976, Bough Beech, Kent. Middle order right-hand batsman. *Sch* Harrow. *Team* Kent (1930, 2 matches).
Career batting
2–2–0–1–1–0.50–0–*ct* 0

Foster, James Bryan
(also known as J. B. Hone-Foster and J. B. Hone)
Professional. *b:* 9.3.1854, Ramsgate, Kent. *d:* 22.11.1914, Stirchley, Warwickshire. Middle/lower order right-hand batsman, right-arm medium pace bowler. *Team* Kent (1880–81, 2 matches).
Career batting
2–3–0–10–6–3.33–0–*ct* 2

He also played for Northamptonshire (pre first-class, 1887).

Foster, Maurice Kirshaw
Amateur. *b:* 1.1.1889, Malvern, Worcesteshire. *d:* 3.12.1940, Borrocop, Lichfield, Staffordshire. Brother of B. S. (Worcestershire and Middlesex), G. N. (Worcestershire and Kent), H. K. (Worcestershire), N. J. A. (Worcestershire), R. E. (Worcestershire), and W. L. (Worcestershire), uncle of C. K. (Worcestershire), P. G. (Kent) and J. W. Greenstock (Worcestershire), brother-in-law of W. Greenstock (Worcestershire). Middle order right-hand batsman, right-arm medium pace bowler. *Sch* Malvern. *Teams* Worcestershire (1908–34, 157 matches); Bengal Governor's XI (1917/18).
Career batting
170–301–12–8295–158–28.70–12–*ct* 139–*st* 4
Bowling 282–3–94.00–0–0–2/17

He hit 1,000 runs in five seasons (best 1,615, av 32.95, in 1926). He captained Worcestershire 1923 to 1925. His final first-class match was for MCC in 1936. He also played for Staffordshire (1933).

Foster, Maurice Linton Churchill
Cricketer. *b:* 9.5.1943, Retreat, St Mary, Jamaica. Middle order right-hand batsman, off break bowler. *Team* Jamaica (1963/4 to 1977/8). *Tours* West Indies to England 1969, 1973; Jamaica to England 1970. *Tests* West Indies (1969 to 1977/8, 14 matches).
Career batting
112–175–26–6731–234–45.17–17–*ct* 37

Bowling 4056–132–30.72–2–0–5/65
Test batting
14–24–5–580–125–30.52–1–*ct* 3
Bowling 600–9–66.66–0–0–2/41

In both 1969 and 1973 he appeared in only one Test, but in the latter year his batting in first-class matches was very successful – 828 runs, av 63.69. His highest score was 234 for Jamaica v Trinidad at Montego Bay in 1976/7. There was some criticism of his non-selection for all the 1973 Tests.

Foster, Neil Alan

Cricketer. *b:* 6.5.1962, Colchester, Essex. Lower order right-hand batsman, right-arm fast medium bowler, deep field. *Teams* Essex (1980–92, 174 matches); Transvaal (1991/2). *Tours* England to Pakistan 1983/4, 1987/8, to New Zealand 1983/4, 1987/8, to Sri Lanka 1984/5, to India 1984/5, 1988/9 (tour cancelled), to Australia 1984/5 (not first-class), 1986/7, 1987/8, to Sharjah (not first-class) 1984/5, 1986/7, to West Indies 1985/6, to India and Pakistan (World Cup) 1987/8; England XI to South Africa 1989/90. *Tests* England (1983–89, 28 matches).
Career batting
222–257–56–4108–107*–20.43–2–*ct* 115
Bowling 21473–896–23.96–49–8–8/99
Test batting
28–43–7–410–39–11.38–0–*ct* 7
Bowling 2797–88–31.78–5–1–8/107

A most promising fast bowler as a teenager, he suffered a serious back injury which meant an operation and missing the whole of the 1982 season. His recovery was so good that in 1983 he made his Test debut. His form, and selection, for England was erratic over the next few years, but in 1987 against Pakistan he topped England's bowling averages. Injury again affected his appearances in 1988. He played in three Tests for England against Australia in 1989, then chose to join the side going to South Africa. His best season in English cricket was 1986 when he took 105 wickets, av 22.37; he also captured more than 100 wickets in 1991.

Foster, Neville John Acland

Amateur. *b:* 28.9.1890, Malvern, Worcestershire. *d:* 8.1.1978, Malvern, Worcestershire. Brother of B. S. (Worcestershire and Middlesex), G. N. (Worcestershire and Kent), H. K. (Worcestershire), M. K. (Worcestershire), R. E. (Worcestershire), and W. L. (Worcestershire), uncle of C. K. (Worcestershire), P. G. (Kent) and J. W. Greenstock (Worcestershire), brother-in-law of W. Greenstock (Worcestershire). Middle order right-hand batsman. *Sch* Malvern. *Team* Worcestershire (1914–23, 8 matches).
Career batting
8–14–4–219–40*–21.90–0–*ct* 5

He spent most of his life in Malaya and captained the Federated Malay States side.

Foster, Peter Geoffrey

Amateur. *b:* 9.10.1916, Beckenham, Kent. Son of G. N. (Worcestershire and Kent), nephew of B. S. (Worcestershire and Middlesex), H. K. (Worcestershire), M. K. (Worcestershire), N. J. A. (Worcestershire), R. E. (Worcestershire), W. L. (Worcestershire), cousin of C. K. (Worcestershire) and J. W. Greenstock (Worcestershire), nephew of W. Greenstock (Worcestershire), brother-in-law of F. G. H. Chalk (Kent). Middle order right-hand batsman, left-arm bowler, excellent deep field. *Sch* Winchester. *Teams* Oxford U (1936–38); Kent (1939–46, 25 matches).
Career batting
30–50–2–882–107–18.37–1–*ct* 16
Bowling 7–0

He was President of Kent in 1991. He won a blue for golf.

Foster, Reginald Erskine

Amateur. *b:* 16.4.1878, Malvern, Worcestershire. *d:* 13.5.1914, Brompton, Kensington, London, of diabetes. Brother of B. S. (Worcestershire and Middlesex), G. N. (Worcestershire and Kent), H. K. (Worcestershire), M. K. (Worcestershire), N. J. A. (Worcestershire), and W. L. (Worcestershire), uncle of C. K. (Worcestershire), P. G. (Kent) and J. W. Greenstock (Worcestershire), brother-in-law of W. Greenstock (Worcestershire). Brilliant middle order right-hand batsman, right-arm fast bowler. *Sch* Malvern. *Teams* Oxford U (1897–1900, blue all four years); Worcestershire (1899–1912, 80 matches). *Tours* MCC to Australia 1903/4. *Tests* England (1903/4 to 1907, 8 matches).
Career batting
139–234–17–9076–287–41.82–22–*ct* 179
Bowling 1153–25–46.12–0–0–3/54
Test batting
8–14–1–602–287–46.30–1–*ct* 13

He could not afford the time for regular County cricket and in fact only had one full English season – 1901 – when he hit 2,128 runs, av 50.66. He also exceeded 1,000 runs in 1899 and 1900. His most famous innings was 287 for England v Australia in the Sydney Test of 1903/4, which was a record for the series for many years. He captained England in three Tests in 1907, Oxford in 1900 and Worcestershire in 1901.

A noted soccer player, he won his blue and went on to play for Corinthians and England. He also won blues for golf and rackets. He first played for Worcestershire (pre first-class) in 1895.

Foster, Thomas

Professional. *b:* 15.12.1848, Mill Town, Glossop, Derbyshire. *d:* 22.3.1929, East Glossop, Derbyshire. Middle order right-hand batsman, right-hand fast round-arm bowler, excellent field. *Team* Derbyshire (1873–84, 85 matches).

Foster, Thomas William

Career batting
90–167–6–2594–101–16.11–1–*ct* 64
Bowling 233–9–25.88–0–0–2/18
He was a first-class umpire (1892).

Foster, Thomas William
Professional. *b:* 12.11.1871, Birkdale, Lancashire. *d:* 31.1.1947, Dewsbury, Yorkshire. Lower order right-hand batsman, right-arm medium pace bowler. *Team* Yorkshire (1894–95, 14 matches).
Career batting
14–20–5–138–25–9.20–0–*ct* 6
Bowling 952–58–16.41–5–3–9/59
His best bowling was 9/59 for Yorkshire v MCC at Lord's in 1894.

Foster, Wilfrid Lionel
Amateur. *b:* 2.12.1874, Great Malvern, Worcestershire. *d:* 22.3.1958, Ryton Grove near Shifnal, Shropshire. Brother of B. S. (Worcestershire and Middlesex), G. N. (Worcestershire and Kent), H. K. (Worcestershire), M. K. (Worcestershire), N. J. A. (Worcestershire) and R. E. (Worcestershire), uncle of C. K. (Worcestershire), P. G. (Kent) and J. W. Greenstock (Worcestershire), brother-in-law of W. Greenstock (Worcestershire). Opening right-hand batsman. *Sch* Malvern. *Team* Worcestershire (1899–1911, 29 matches).
Career batting
38–67–2–1993–172*–30.66–3–*ct* 18
Bowling 13–0
Owing to his military duties his only season of regular first-class cricket was 1899. He hit 1,041 runs, av 34.70, that year. He was an excellent soccer player with Corinthians and a noted rackets player. He first played for Worcestershire (pre first-class) in 1891.

Foster, William
Professional. *b:* 8.6.1859, Beeston, Nottinghamshire. *d:* 1.11.1944, Arnold, Nottinghamshire. Middle order batsman. *Team* Nottinghamshire (1889, 1 match).
Career batting
1–2–0–0–0–0.00–0–*ct* 0

Foster, William John
Cricketer. *b:* 3.2.1934, Glasgow, Scotland. Opening right-hand batsman, slow left-arm bowler. *Sch* Harrow. *Team* Combined Services (1964).
Career batting
2–4–0–79–36–19.75–0–*ct* 1
Bowling 13–0

Fothergill, Andrew Robert
Cricketer. *b:* 10.2.1962, Newcastle upon Tyne, Northumberland. Lower order right-hand batsman, wicket-keeper. *Team* Durham (1992, 6 matches).
Career batting
7–9–1–74–23–9.25–0–*ct* 10–*st* 1
He first played for Durham (pre first-class) in 1982 and made his first-class debut for Minor Counties in 1990.

Fothergill, Arnold James
Amateur, then professional from 1877. *b:* 26.8.1854, Newcastle upon Tyne, Northumberland. *d:* 1.8.1932, Newcastle upon Tyne, Northumberland. Lower order left-hand batsman, left-arm medium fast bowler. *Team* Somerset (1882–84, 16 matches). *Tour* Warton to South Africa 1888/9. *Tests* England (1888/9, 2 matches).
Career batting
40–69–9–843–74–14.05–0–*ct* 15
Bowling 2164–119–18.18–6–1–6/43
Test batting
2–2–0–33–32–16.50–0–*ct* 0
Bowling 90–8–11.25–0–0–4/19
He was on the staff at Lord's commencing 1882 and much of his first-class cricket was for MCC. His final first-class match in England was for South of England in 1887. He also played for Northumberland (1874–75). His last match for Somerset (not first-class) was in 1890.

Foulds, Frederick George
Professional. *b:* 23.4.1935, West End, Leicester. Forcing middle order right-hand batsman. *Team* Leicestershire (1952–56, 2 matches).
Career batting
2–4–0–1–1–0.25–0–*ct* 0
He was on National Service in 1953 and 1954.

Foulke, William Henry
(registered at birth as Foulk and death as Foulkes)
Professional. *b:* 12.4.1874, Old Park, Dawley, Shropshire. *d:* 1.5.1916, Sheffield, Yorkshire. Middle order batsman. *Team* Derbyshire (1900, 4 matches).
Career batting
4–7–1–65–53–10.83–0–*ct* 2
Bowling 92–2–46.00–0–0–2/15
Famous as a goalkeeper, he represented Sheffield United (winning FA Cup winners medals in 1899 and 1902), Chelsea, Bradford City and England. In 1901 he weighed 21 stone, but was still very active.

Fowke, Gustavus Henry Spencer
Amateur. *b:* 14.10.1880, Brighton, Sussex. *d:* 24.6.1946, Bulwick Park, Wansford, Northamptonshire. Opening, later middle order, right-hand batsman, right-arm fast medium bowler, good slip. *Sch* Uppingham. *Team* Leicestershire (1899–1927, 159 matches).
Career batting
160–261–27–4438–113–18.96–2–*ct* 89
Bowling 738–13–56.76–0–0–2/13
After making his County debut in 1899, Fowke went to fight in the Boer War and then was stationed in India. His County cricket was very restricted until he was appointed County captain in 1922, a post he

held until 1927. He had the unusual misfortune to be a Prisoner of War both in the Boer War and the First World War.

Fowler, Archibald John Burgess
Professional. *b:* 1.4.1891, Marylebone, London. *d:* 7.5.1977, Basingstoke, Hampshire. Father-in-law of G. E. E. Lambert (Gloucestershire and Somerset). Lower order right-hand batsman, slow left-arm bowler. *Team* Middlesex (1921–30, 26 matches).
Career batting
30–39–15–167–21–6.95–0–*ct* 16
Bowling 1293–43–30.06–1–0–5/29
He was head coach at Lord's in the 1930s. He was a first-class umpire (1954–55).

Fowler, Gerald
Amateur. *b:* 27.7.1866, Whipps Cross, Leytonstone, Essex. *d:* 24.5.1916, Trull, Somerset, after an operation for appendicitis. Brother of W. H. (Somerset) and Howard (Oxford U). Lower order right-hand batsman, right-arm fast medium bowler. *Sch* Clifton. *Teams* Oxford U (1888–89, blue 1888); Somerset (1891–1903, 119 matches).
Career batting
132–231–19–3571–118–16.84–1–*ct* 66
Bowling 2855–92–31.03–4–0–6/50
He also played for Essex (pre first-class, 1884–89). From 1896 to his death he was Hon Treasurer of Somerset CCC and he was also Hon Secretary 1911–12. He first played for Somerset (not first-class) in 1890.

Fowler, Graeme
Cricketer. *b:* 20.4.1957, Accrington, Lancashire. Hard-hitting opening left-hand batsman, right-arm medium pace bowler, occasional wicket-keeper, good cover field. *Team* Lancashire (1979–92, 233 matches). *Tours* England to Australia 1982/3, 1984/5 (not first-class), to New Zealand 1982/3 (not first-class), 1983/4, to Pakistan 1983/4, to India and Sri Lanka 1984/5, to Sharjah (not first-class) 1984/5; International XI to Jamaica 1982/3; Lancashire to Zimbabwe 1988/9. *Tests* England (1982 to 1984/5, 21 matches).
Career batting
274–464–27–15803–226–36.16–35–*ct* 143–*st* 5
Bowling 366–10–36.60–0–0–2/34
Test batting
21–37–0–1307–201–35.32–3–*ct* 10
Bowling 11–0
He hit 1,000 runs in a season eight times (best 1,800, av 47.36, in 1987). His highest innings was 226 for Lancashire v Kent at Maidstone in 1984 and he scored 201 for England v India at Madras in 1984/5. After being a major figure in the Test series in 1984/5, his omission from the England side, after a single one-day international, in 1985, caused much press comment. Injury and lack of form meant that he was not chosen to tour with England in 1985/6 and his international career therefore came to an unexpectedly abrupt halt.

Fowler, Howard
Amateur. *b:* 20.10.1857, Tottenham, Middlesex. *d:* 6.5.1934, Burnham-on-Sea, Somerset. Brother of Gerald (Somerset) and W. H. (Somerset). Hard hitting middle order right-hand batsman, wicket-keeper. *Sch* Clifton. *Team* Oxford U (1877–80, blue 1877, 1879 and 1880).
Career batting
17–30–1–471–63–16.24–0–*ct* 13–*st* 7
His County cricket was for Essex (pre first-class, 1879–89) and Somerset (pre first-class, 1880). His final first-class match was for MCC in 1884. A noted rugby footballer, he represented both Oxford and England.

Fowler, Rev Richard Harold
Amateur. *b:* 5.3.1887, Islington, London. *d:* 27.10.1970, Clent, Worcestershire. Lower order right-hand batsman, right-arm fast medium bowler. *Team* Worcestershire (1921, 4 matches).
Career batting
4–7–1–72–35–12.00–0–*ct* 3
Bowling 105–7–15.00–1–0–5/33
Due to a doubtful bowling action, his County career was very short.

Fowler, Robert Henry
Amateur. *b:* 28.6.1857, Mellifont, Co Louth, Ireland. *d:* 11.5.1957, Rahinstown, Enfield, Co Meath, Ireland. Father of R. St L. (Hampshire). Middle order right-hand batsman. *Sch* Cheltenham. *Team* Cambridge U (1876).
Career batting
1–2–0–4–3–2.00–0–*ct* 0
He played for Ireland (not first-class) in 1880.

Fowler, Robert St Leger
Amateur. *b:* 7.4.1891, Rahinstown, Enfield, Co Meath, Ireland. *d:* 13.6.1925, Rahinstown, Enfield, Co Meath, Ireland. Son of R. H. (Cambridge U). Middle/lower order right-hand batsman, off break bowler. *Sch* Eton. *Team* Hampshire (1924, 3 matches). *Tours* Appointed captain of the MCC Team to West Indies 1924/25, but the tour was postponed until the following winter and Fowler died in June 1925.
Career batting
24–38–4–957–92*–28.14–0–*ct* 21
Bowling 1462–59–24.77–2–0–7/22
His most famous match was Eton v Harrow in 1910. Captain of Eton, he hit 64 to save an innings defeat and then with Harrow needing only 55 to win, Fowler took 8 wickets to achieve victory by 5 runs. The game is always referred to as 'Fowler's Match'. His military career prevented him from appearing in all but a handful of first-class matches, his first-class debut being in 1913 for MCC.

Fowler, Theodore Humphrey
Amateur. *b:* 25.9.1879, Cirencester, Gloucestershire. *d:* 17.8.1915, London County Hospital, Epsom, Surrey. Opening/middle order batsman, wicket-keeper. *Sch* Lancing. *Team* Gloucestershire (1901–14, 46 matches).
Career batting
46–78–4–1057–114–14.28–1–*ct* 35–*st* 1
Bowling 36–0

He was an excellent long distance runner. He twice declined a commission in the HAC whilst serving in the First World War. He also played for Dorset (1908–11).

Fowler, Thomas Frederick
Amateur. *b:* 12.3.1841, Kennington Park, London. *d:* 7.1.1915, Woolston, Hampshire. Middle/lower order right-hand batsman, right-hand fast round arm bowler, cover point. *Sch* Uppingham and Giggleswick. *Team* Cambridge U (1863–64, blue 1864).
Career batting
10–16–5–208–38*–18.90–0–*ct* 6
Bowling 98–9–10.88–1–0–5/37

His final first-class match was for MCC in 1867. He played for Huntingdonshire (1862–79), being Honorary Secretary and captain of that County club 1862 to 1868. He also played for Northamptonshire (pre first-class, 1865–66).

Fowler, William Herbert
Amateur. *b:* 28.5.1856, Tottenham, Middlesex. *d:* 13.4.1941, Chelsea, London. Brother of Gerald (Somerset) and Howard (Oxford U). Hard hitting middle order right-hand batsman, right-arm fast bowler. *Team* Somerset (1882–84, 15 matches).
Career batting
26–49–0–905–139–18.46–1–*ct* 6
Bowling 521–23–22.65–0–0–4/8

He also played for Essex (pre first-class, 1877). His debut in first-class matches in 1880 and his final first-class match in 1885 were both for MCC. His first match for Somerset (pre first-class) was in 1878 and his last in 1888 (not first-class).

Fowler, William Peter
Cricketer. *b:* 13.3.1959, St Helens, Lancashire. Middle order right-hand batsman, slow left-arm bowler. *Teams* Northern Districts (1979/80 to 1984/5); Auckland (1981/2 to 1989/90); Derbyshire (1983–85, 49 matches).
Career batting
77–125–17–2577–116–23.86–2–*ct* 49
Bowling 1775–44–40.34–1–0–6/41

He was educated in New Zealand and unexpectedly called up to play limited overs matches for Derbyshire in 1982, having to be registered on the morning of his debut.

Fox, Charles John Macdonald
Amateur. *b:* 5.12.1858, Dum Dum, India. *d:* 1.4.1901, Albury, New South Wales, Australia. He died from heart failure. Opening or middle order right-hand batsman, right-arm medium pace bowler, fine field. *Sch* Westminster. *Teams* Surrey (1876, 1 match); Kent (1888–93, 74 matches).
Career batting
80–135–10–2147–103–17.17–1–*ct* 40
Bowling 818–46–17.78–3–0–5/21

About 1890 he was a very prolific scorer in London Club cricket, mainly for the Crystal Palace club.

Fox, Frederick Isaac
Amateur. *b:* 7.11.1863, Nottingham. *d:* 21.8.1935, Beltinge, Kent. Middle order right-hand batsman, deep field. *Sch* Nottingham HS. *Team* Nottinghamshire (1890, 2 matches).
Career batting
2–4–2–34–23–17.00–0–*ct* 0

Fox, Henry
Amateur. *b:* 30.9.1856, Wellington, Somerset. *d:* on or after 30.8.1888, Georgia, Russia. *Team* Somerset (1882, 3 matches).
Career batting
3–6–0–16–6–2.66–0–*ct* 0

He was lost in the Caucasus Mountains.

Fox, Herbert Francis
Amateur. *b:* 1.8.1858, Brislington, Somerset. *d:* 20.1.1926, Denmark Hill, London. Sound middle order right-hand batsman, left-arm bowler. *Sch* Clifton. *Team* Somerset (1882–91, 10 matches).
Career batting
10–18–1–133–31–7.82–0–*ct* 5

He appeared in the Oxford Freshmen's match of 1878 and later for Oxfordshire (1902) and Suffolk (1904–08). His first match for Somerset (pre first-class) was in 1878.

Fox, John
Professional. *b:* 7.9.1904, Selly Park, Birmingham. *d:* 15.11.1961, Birmingham. He collapsed and died on a bus whilst on his way home from work. Lower order left-hand batsman, slow left-arm bowler. *Teams* Warwickshire (1922–28, 46 matches); Worcestershire (1929–33, 94 matches).
Career batting
140–209–35–2907–73–16.70–0–*ct* 30
Bowling 2193–46–47.67–0–0–4/27

Fox, John Charles Ker
Amateur. *b:* 10.3.1851, Castle Dillon, Co Armagh, Ireland. *d:* 10.8.1929, Brislington, Somerset. Middle order right-hand batsman. *Sch* Clifton. *Team* Gloucestershire (1872, 2 matches).
Career batting
2–3–1–13–11*–6.50–0–*ct* 1

He played for Ireland (not first-class) in 1873.

Fox, John George
Professional. *b:* 22.7.1929, Norton-on-Tees, Co Durham. Lower order right-hand batsman, wicket-keeper. *Team* Warwickshire (1959–61, 43 matches).
Career batting
43–54–6–515–52–10.72–0–*ct* 91–*st* 14
Bowling 0–0
He also played for Durham (pre first-class, 1950–64) and Devon (1968–69).

Fox, Raymond Wodehouse
Amateur. *b:* 11.7.1873, Frampton-Cotterell, Gloucestershire. *d:* 21.8.1948, Ticehurst House, Sussex. Tail end right-hand batsman, wicket-keeper. *Sch* Wellington. *Teams* Oxford U (1896–98, blue 1897–98); Sussex (1896–1900, 7 matches).
Career batting
27–38–18–106–20–5.30–0–*ct* 39–*st* 13
His final first-class match was for H. D. G. Leveson-Gower's XI in 1909.

Fox, Ronald Henry
Amateur. *b:* 23.1.1880, Caversham, New Zealand. *d:* 27.8.1952, Firs Hall, Bloxham, Oxfordshire. Tail end right-hand batsman, wicket-keeper. *Sch* Haileybury. *Team* MCC (1906–10). *Tours* MCC to New Zealand 1906/7; New Zealand to England 1927 (1 first-class match).
Career batting
19–32–6–407–54–15.65–0–*ct* 26–*st* 8
Bowling 51–2–25.50–0–0–1/17
His debut was for Gentlemen of England in 1904.

Fox, Dr Thomas Colcott
Amateur. *b:* 13.6.1849, Broughton, Hampshire. *d:* 11.4.1916, Westminster, London. Lower order batsman, bowler. *Sch* University College School. *Team* Hampshire (1875, 2 matches).
Career batting
2–4–0–10–7–2.50–0–*ct* 1
Bowling 26–0

Fox, Thomas Seely
Amateur. *b:* 23.8.1878, Upton, Essex. *d:* 3.4.1931, Bournemouth, Hampshire. Lower order batsman, wicket-keeper. *Team* Middlesex (1905, 1 match).
Career batting
1 match, did not bat–*ct* 0

Fox, William Victor
Professional. *b:* 8.1.1898, Middlesbrough, Yorkshire. *d:* 17.2.1949, Withington, Manchester, Lancashire. Middle order right-hand batsman. *Team* Worcestershire (1923–32, 163 matches).
Career batting
163–281–31–6654–198–26.61–11–*ct* 88
Bowling 137–2–68.50–0–0–1/13
He hit 1,000 runs in a season three times (best 1,457, av 31.00, in 1929). He began his cricket with Worcestershire in 1923, but it was found that he was not qualified and he had to wait for two years before being permitted to make any further appearances in the Championship.
He played soccer for Middlesborough, Wolves and Newport.

Foy, Frederick George
Professional. *b:* 11.4.1915, Maidstone, Kent. Middle order right-hand batsman, slow left-arm bowler. *Team* Kent (1937–38, 11 matches).
Career batting
11–17–1–153–25–9.56–0–*ct* 5
Bowling 18–0

Foy, Philip Arnold
Amateur. *b:* 16.10.1891, Axbridge, Somerset. *d:* 12.2.1957, Adrogue, Buenos Aires, Argentine. Middle/lower order right-hand batsman, right-arm fast medium bowler. *Sch* Bedford GS. *Teams* Somerset (1919–30, 21 matches); Argentine (1911/2 to 1929/30).
Career batting
25–40–4–504–72–14.00–0–*ct* 20
Bowling 1524–78–19.53–7–1–7/84
He was for some years one of the leading bowlers in Argentine cricket. He also played for Bedfordshire (1909).

Francis, Arthur Stopford
Amateur. *b:* 14.6.1854, Ramsden Hall, Upminster, Essex. *d:* January 1908. Brother of C. K. (Middlesex). Middle order right-hand batsman, right-hand medium pace round-arm bowler. *Sch* Rugby. *Team* Middlesex (1880, 2 matches).
Career batting
3–6–0–98–26–16.33–0–*ct* 1
His final first-class match was for South of England in 1887.

Francis, Bruce Colin
Cricketer. *b:* 18.2.1948, Mosman, Sydney, New South Wales, Australia. Opening right-hand batsman, right-arm medium pace bowler. *Teams* New South Wales (1968/9 to 1972/3, 32 matches); Essex (1971–73, 47 matches). *Tours* Australia to England 1972; International Wanderers to Rhodesia 1972/3; Robins to South Africa 1973/4, 1974/5. *Tests* Australia (1972, 3 matches).
Career batting
109–192–10–6183–210–33.97–13–*ct* 42
Bowling 15–1–15.00–0–0–1/10
Test batting
3–5–0–52–27–10.40–0–*ct* 1
He hit 1,000 runs in both his seasons with Essex (1971 and 1973), the best being 1,578, av 38.48, in 1971, but achieved little in 1972 with the Australian touring team, except his highest innings of 210 v Combined Universities at Oxford.

Francis, Charles King
Amateur. *b:* 3.2.1851, Ramsden Hall, Upminster, Essex. *d:* 28.10.1925, Crichel, Dorset. Brother of A. S. (Middlesex). Lower order right-hand batsman, right-hand fast round-arm bowler. *Sch* Rugby. *Teams* Oxford U (1870–73, blue all four years); Middlesex (1875–77, 9 matches). *Tour* Fitzgerald to North America 1872 (not first-class).
Career batting
47–75–10–717–45–11.03–0–*ct* 38
Bowling 2797–136+6–20.56–6–1–7/12

He gained a tremendous reputation in school cricket as a fast bowler, but after his first year at Oxford, proved a very moderate success. His final first-class match was for MCC in 1879. He also played for Essex (pre first-class, 1868).

Francis, Conway James
Amateur. *b:* 27.4.1870, Westbury, Clifton, Bristol. *d:* 15.4.1924, Staple Hill, Bristol. Brother of H. H. (Gloucestershire). Middle order right-hand batsman, right-arm fast bowler. *Sch* Blundell's. *Team* Gloucestershire (1895, 1 match).
Career batting
1–1–0–8–8–8.00–0–*ct* 0
Bowling 11–0

Francis, David Arthur
Cricketer. *b:* 29.11.1953, Clydach, Glamorgan. Middle order right-hand batsman, off break bowler, midwicket. *Team* Glamorgan (1973–84, 138 matches).
Career batting
138–237–36–4938–142*–24.56–3–*ct* 62
Bowling 31–0

His best season was 1982 with 1,076 runs, av 38.42. He also played for Wales in the Minor Counties Championship (1988–90).

Francis, Francis Philip
Amateur. *b:* 15.9.1852, Upminster, Essex. *d:* 18.1.1926, Claygate, Surrey. Lower order batsman, wicket-keeper. *Team* Middlesex (1881, 1 match).
Career batting
1–1–0–0–0–0.00–0–*ct* 0

He also played for Essex (pre first-class, 1883–93).

Francis, George Nathaniel
(birth registered as John Nathaniel Francis)
Professional. *b:* 11.12.1897, Trents, St James, Barbados. *d:* 12.1.1942, Black Rock, St Michael, Barbados. Lower order right-hand batsman, right-arm fast bowler. *Team* Barbados (1924/5 to 1929/30). *Tours* West Indies to England 1923, 1928, 1933, to Australia 1930/1. *Tests* West Indies (1928–33, 10 matches).
Career batting
62–91–23–874–61–12.85–0–*ct* 42
Bowling 5159–223–23.13–8–2–7/50
Test batting
10–18–4–81–19*–5.78–0–*ct* 7
Bowling 763–23–33.17–0–0–4/40

He was the outstanding success of the 1923 West Indian tour with 82 wickets, av 15.58, but in 1928 achieved only a modest return. In 1933 he was a professional with the Radcliffe Club and appeared for the West Indies only in the Lord's Test. His final first-class match in the West Indies was for C. A. Merry's XI in 1932/3.

Francis, Guy
Amateur. *b:* 16.8.1860, Maugersbury, Gloucestershire. *d:* 18.5.1948, Wynne's Parc, Denbigh. Middle order right-hand batsman, right-arm fast bowler. *Sch* Cheltenham. *Team* Gloucestershire (1884–88, 31 matches).
Career batting
32–57–7–670–89–13.40–0–*ct* 9
Bowling 23–1–23.00–0–0–1/16

Francis, Howard Henry
Amateur. *b:* 26.5.1868, Westbury, Clifton, Bristol. *d:* 7.1.1936, Sea Point, Cape Town, South Africa. Brother of C. J. (Gloucestershire). Middle order batsman. *Teams* Gloucestershire (1890–94, 18 matches); Western Province (1895/6 to 1902/3). *Tests* South Africa (1898/9, 2 matches).
Career batting
25–44–3–529–55–12.90–0–*ct* 13–*st* 1
Test batting
2–4–0–39–29–9.75–0–*ct* 1

Francis, Percy Thomas
Amateur. *b:* 6.5.1875, Badwell Ash, Suffolk. *d:* 8.9.1964, Branksome, Poole, Dorset. Opening right-hand batsman. *Team* Worcestershire (1901–02, 3 matches).
Career batting
3–5–1–95–66–23.75–0–*ct* 0

He also played for Suffolk (1904–05).

Francis, Thomas Egerton Seymour
Amateur. *b:* 21.11.1902, Uitenhage, Cape Province, South Africa. *d:* 24.2.1969, Bulawayo, Rhodesia. Opening right-hand batsman. *Sch* Tonbridge. *Teams* Somerset (1921–25, 16 matches); Cambridge U (1923–25, blue 1925); Eastern Province (1927/8).
Career batting
34–56–4–804–79–15.46–0–*ct* 14
Bowling 202–3–67.33–0–0–2/100

A noted rugby player, he gained a blue at Cambridge as stand-off half and was capped for England .

Francis, Dr William
Amateur. *b:* 21.3.1856, Little Waltham, Chelmsford, Essex. *d:* 28.4.1917, Upton, Forest Gate, Essex. Hard hitting middle order right-hand batsman, good deep field. *Team* Sussex (1877–79, 7 matches).
Career batting
7–13–1–83–17–6.91–0–*ct* 5

He also played for Essex (pre first-class, 1881–88).

Frank, Joseph
Amateur. *b:* 27.12.1857, Helmsley, Yorkshire. *d:* 22.10.1940, Helmsley, Yorkshire. Lower order left-hand batsman, very fast right-arm bowler. *Team* Yorkshire (1881, 1 match).
Career batting
7–13–1–198–46–16.50–0–*ct* 9
Bowling 258–9–28.66–0–0–3/70
His bowling action was very suspect, which probably limited his appearances in first-class cricket. His final first-class appearance was for A. J. Webbe's XI in 1887.

Frank, Robert Wilson
Amateur. *b:* 29.5.1864, Pickering, Yorkshire. *d:* 9.9.1950, Pickering, Yorkshire. Opening/middle order right-hand batsman, slow right-arm bowler, excellent deep field. *Team* Yorkshire (1889–1903, 19 matches).
Career batting
20–31–4–430–92–15.92–0–*ct* 9
Bowling 9–0
He captained Yorkshire 2nd XI 1900–14.

Franklin, Henry William Fernehough
Amateur. *b:* 30.6.1901, Ford End, Essex. *d:* 25.5.1985, Worthing, Sussex. Brother of R. C. (Essex). Middle/lower order right-hand batsman, leg break bowler. *Sch* Christ's Hospital. *Teams* Oxford U (1921–24, blue 1924); Surrey (1921, 1 match); Essex (1921–31, 73 matches). *Tour* Martineau to Egypt 1931 (not first-class).
Career batting
92–134–19–2212–106–19.23–2–*ct* 41
Bowling 2002–46–43.52–0–0–4/40
He also won a blue for rugby.

Franklin, Reginald Carey
Amateur. *b:* 30.4.1880, Radford, Coventry, Warwickshire. *d:* 25.6.1957, Saltdean, Brighton, Sussex. Middle order right-hand batsman, leg break bowler. *Sch* Repton. *Team* Warwickshire (1900, 1 match).
Career batting
1–1–0–0–0–0.00–0–*ct* 1

Franklin, Ronald Christian
Amateur. *b:* 9.9.1904, Ford End, Essex. *d:* 28.9.1982, Prestwood, Buckinghamshire. Brother of H. W. F. (Essex). Lower order right-hand batsman, right-arm medium pace bowler. *Sch* Christ's Hospital. *Team* Essex (1924, 1 match).
Career batting
1–2–0–1–1–0.50–0–*ct* 1
Bowling 41–1–41.00–0–0–1/20

Franklin, Trevor John
Cricketer. *b:* 15.3.1962, Mount Eden, Auckland, New Zealand. Opening right-hand batsman, right-arm medium pace bowler. *Team* Auckland (1980/1 to 1991/2). *Tours* New Zealand to Australia 1982/3 (not first-class), 1985/6, to England 1983, 1986, 1990, to India 1988/9, to Pakistan 1990/1; Young New Zealand to Zimbabwe 1984/5, 1988/9. *Tests* New Zealand (1983 to 1990/1, 21 matches).
Career batting
140–241–20–7484–181–33.86–15–*ct* 75
Bowling 51–1–51.00–0–0–1/21
Test batting
21–37–1–828–101–23.00–1–*ct* 8
Having played with modest success on his first visit to England in 1983, he was unfortunate to break a thumb on his second tour in 1986 and rarely looked in form thereafter. In 1990 he finally established himself, scoring most runs in both the Test and first-class matches for the tourists, his Test figures being 227 runs, av 56.75, and first-class 731, av 45.68.

Franklin, Walter Bell
Amateur. *b:* 16.8.1891, Upper Norwood, Surrey. *d:* 5.3.1968, Knodishall Place, Suffolk. Lower order right-hand batsman, wicket-keeper. *Sch* Repton. *Team* Cambridge U (1911–13, blue 1912).
Career batting
60–91–19–1362–77–18.91–0–*ct* 61–*st* 54
His County cricket was for Buckinghamshire (1911–46), captaining the County from 1919 to 1946. His final first-class match was for Minor Counties in 1937.

Franks, Jonathan Guy
Cricketer. *b:* 23.9.1962, Stamford, Lincolnshire. Middle order right-hand batsman, wicket-keeper. *Sch* Stamford. *Team* Oxford U (1983–85, blue 1984–85).
Career batting
16–24–3–339–42*–16.14–0–*ct* 14–*st* 2
His County cricket was for Lincolnshire (1980–89) and Hertfordshire (1990–92).

Frasat Ali Mughal
Cricketer. *b:* 31.7.1949, Lahore, Pakistan. Middle order right-hand batsman, right-arm medium pace bowler. *Tour* East Africa to England 1975.
Career batting
1–2–0–42–30–21.00–0–*ct* 0
Bowling 82–2–41.00–0–0–2/37

Fraser, Alan
Amateur. *b:* 13.7.1892, Perth, Scotland. *d:* 28.8.1962, Dundee, Angus, Scotland. Brother of W. L. (Scotland). Lower order right-hand batsman. *Sch* Merchiston. *Team* Scotland (1921).
Career batting
1–1–0–9–9–9.00–0–*ct* 1
Bowling 28–0

Fraser, Alastair Gregory James
Cricketer. *b:* 17.10.1967, Edgware, Middlesex. Brother of A. R. C. (Middlesex). Lower order right-hand batsman, right-arm fast medium bowler. *Sch* John Lyon. *Teams* Middlesex (1986–88, 5 matches);

Fraser, Angus Robert Charles

Essex (1991–92, 5 matches).
Career batting
10–10–5–137–52*–27.40–0–*ct* 1
Bowling 386–12–32.16–0–0–3/46

Fraser, Angus Robert Charles
Cricketer. *b:* 8.8.1965, Billinge, Lancashire. Brother of A. G. J. (Middlesex and Essex). Lower order right-hand batsman, right-arm fast medium bowler. *Team* Middlesex (1984–92, 102 matches). *Tours* England to India 1989/90 (not first-class), to West Indies 1989/90, to Australia 1990/1, to New Zealand 1990/1 (not first-class). *Tests* England (1989 to 1990/1, 11 matches).
Career batting
119–134–34–1240–92–12.40–0–*ct* 19
Bowling 9376–355–26.41–16–2–7/77
Test batting
11–14–1–88–29–6.76–0–*ct* 1
Bowling 1255–47–26.70–4–0–6/82
In 1989 he took 92 wickets (av 20.22) and appeared in three Tests during that season. In 1990 he played in three Tests against India and topped the Test bowling averages. In the series against Australia the following winter he again topped the England bowling averages, but missed nearly all of the 1991 season due to injury.

Fraser, David Dempster
Cricketer. *b:* 9.4.1943, Duddingston, Edinburgh, Scotland. Lower order right-hand batsman, right-arm fast medium bowler. *Sch* Royal High School, Edinburgh. *Team* Scotland (1967–69).
Career batting
4–2–2–0–0*–no av–0–*ct* 1
Bowling 363–8–45.37–0–0–3/29

Fraser, John Neville
Amateur. *b:* 6.8.1890, Toorak, Melbourne, Victoria, Australia. *d:* 23.1.1962, Lindfield, New South Wales, Australia. Lower order right-hand batsman, leg break and googly bowler. *Team* Oxford U (1912–14, blue 1912–13).
Career batting
17–28–11–195–33–11.47–0–*ct* 13
Bowling 1391–59–23.57–4–0–6/35

Fraser, Patrick Shaw
Amateur. *b:* 15.6.1892, Raipur, India. *d:* 1.3.1962, Everton, Lancashire. Brother of C. J. S. (Europeans). Opening/middle order left-hand batsman, leg break bowler. *Sch* Rugby. *Teams* Scotland (1911–13); MCC (1925–27).
Career batting
9–17–0–289–79–17.00–0–*ct* 4
Bowling 54–1–54.00–0–0–1/14
His County cricket was for Buckinghamshire (1919).

Fraser, Thomas William
Amateur. *b:* 26.6.1912, Natal, South Africa. Lower order right-hand batsman, slow left-arm bowler. *Teams* Cambridge U (1936–37, blue 1937); Orange Free State (1937/8 to 1946/7).
Career batting
22–37–11–249–61*–9.57–0–*ct* 11
Bowling 1834–58–31.62–3–0–8/71
His final first-class match was for Free Foresters in 1948.

Fraser, William Lovat
Amateur. *b:* 7.11.1884, Perth, Scotland. *d:* 21.11.1968, Scone, Perthshire, Scotland. Brother of Alan (Scotland). Lower order right-hand batsman, right-arm medium pace bowler. *Sch* Merchiston. *Team* Scotland (1909–13).
Career batting
3–5–1–53–44–13.25–0–*ct* 3
Bowling 278–15–18.53–1–0–5/50

Fraser-Darling, Callum David
Cricketer. *b:* 30.9.1963, Sheffield, Yorkshire. Middle order right-hand batsman, right-arm medium fast bowler. *Sch* Edinburgh Academy. *Team* Nottinghamshire (1984–88, 11 matches).
Career batting
11–12–2–242–61–24.20–0–*ct* 11
Bowling 876–17–51.52–1–0–5/84

Frazer, Charles Ewan
Amateur. *b:* 23.9.1905. *d:* 30.4.1971, Tenterden, Kent. Brother of J. E. (Sussex). Opening/middle order right-hand batsman, slow right-arm bowler, good field. *Sch* Winchester. *Team* Oxford U (1927–28).
Career batting
4–8–0–101–43–12.62–0–*ct* 2
He played billiards for Oxford U.

Frazer, John Ewan
Amateur. *b:* 2.4.1901, Lydney, Gloucestershire. *d:* 2.1.1927, Davos Platz, Switzerland, as the result of a ski-ing accident. Brother of C. E. (Oxford U). Middle order left-hand batsman, left-arm medium fast bowler, fine field. *Sch* Winchester. *Teams* Somerset (1921, 1 match); Sussex (1921–24, 23 matches); Oxford U (1924, blue).
Career batting
37–65–0–887–81–13.64–0–*ct* 13
He also gained his blue for soccer. In 1921 he appeared for both Somerset and Sussex, but for the former only against Oxford. His last first-class match was for Free Foresters in 1925.

Frearson, Raymond Eric
Amateur. *b:* 14.1.1904, Lincoln. *d:* 26.2.1991, Skegness, Lincolnshire. Middle order right-hand batsman, leg break bowler. *Sch* Eastbourne. *Teams* Minor Counties (1929–31).

Career batting
3–3–0–19–13–6.33–0–*ct* 1

His first-class debut was for East of England in 1927. His County cricket was for Lincolnshire (1924–32).

Frederick, Sir Edward Boscawen
Amateur. *b:* 29.6.1880, Loppington, Shropshire. *d:* 26.10.1956, St John's Wood, London. Nephew of J. St J. (Hampshire and Middlesex). Lower order right-hand batsman, slow right-arm bowler. *Sch* Eton. *Teams* Hampshire (1903–04, 5 matches); Europeans (1907/8).
Career batting
6–11–4–36–11–5.14–0–*ct* 12
Bowling 362–10–36.20–0–0–3/41

Frederick, John St John
Amateur. *b:* 6.1.1846, London. *d:* 10.9.1907, Camberley, Surrey. Uncle of E. B. (Hampshire). Hard hitting middle order right-hand batsman, very fast right-hand round-arm bowler, excellent deep field. *Sch* Eton. *Teams* Oxford U (1864–67, blue 1864 and 1867); Hampshire (1864–69, 5 matches); Middlesex (1864, 1 match).
Career batting
25–43–0–635–44–14.76–0–*ct* 15
Bowling 106–4–26.50–0–0–4/45

Though bowling very fast, his direction was rather erratic. A severe accident prevented him playing for Oxford in 1865. He was on the MCC Committee for several years.

Frederick, Michael Campbell
Amateur. *b:* 6.5.1927, Mile and a Quarter, St Peter, Barbados. Opening or middle order right-hand batsman, right-arm medium pace bowler, excellent field. *Teams* Barbados (1944/5); Derbyshire (1949, 2 matches); Jamaica (1953/4). *Test* West Indies (1953/4, 1 match).
Career batting
6–10–0–294–84–29.40–0–*ct* 3
Test batting
1–2–0–30–30–15.00–0–*ct* 0

Fredericks, Roy Clifton
Cricketer. *b:* 11.11.1942, Blairmont, Berbice, British Guiana. Opening left-hand batsman, slow left-arm bowler. *Teams* British Guiana/Guyana (1963/4 to 1982/3); Glamorgan (1971–73, 45 matches). *Tours* West Indies to Australia and New Zealand 1968/9, to England 1969, 1973, 1975 (World Cup), 1976, to India, Pakistan and Ceylon 1974/5, to Australia 1975/6. *Tests* West Indies (1968/9 to 1976/7, 59 matches).
Career batting
223–391–34–16384–250–45.89–40–*ct* 177
Bowling 2846–75–37.94–0–0–4/36
Test batting
59–109–7–4334–169–42.49–8–*ct* 62
Bowling 548–7–78.28–0–0–1/12

He was most successful on his three tours to England, scoring over 1,000 runs on each visit; he also made 1,000 runs for Glamorgan in 1971. His best English season was 1973 with 1,506 runs, av 43.02, but he completed 1,000 runs in 1968/9 and 1971/2. Of the four double centuries he scored the highest was 250 for Guyana v Barbados at Bridgetown in 1974/5 and the only one in England was 228* for Glamorgan v Northamptonshire at Swansea in 1972. He was a leading member of the World Series Cricket in Australia. He reappeared after three years in 1982/3 and scored 217 and 103 in his only two innings. He was Minister of Sport in the Guyana Government.

Freeland, General Sir Ian Henry
Amateur. *b:* 14.9.1912, Milton, Hampshire. *d:* 2.7.1979, Cambridge. Middle order right-hand batsman. *Sch* Wellington. *Teams* Army (1937); Europeans (1937/8).
Career batting
3–5–0–44–26–8.80–0–*ct* 1
Bowling 47–1–47.00–0–0–1/8

Freeman, Albert
Professional. *b:* 3.6.1844, Croydon, Surrey. *d:* 27.3.1920, Upper Holloway, London. Lower order right-hand batsman, right-arm medium pace bowler, good point field. *Team* Surrey (1871–75, 29 matches).
Career batting
30–56–5–419–32–8.21–0–*ct* 18
Bowling 478–11–43.45–0–0–3/20

He also played for Essex (pre first-class, 1887–91).

Freeman, Albert James
Professional. *b:* 19.7.1887, Kennington, London. *d:* 7.1.1945, Greenwich, London. Tail end right-hand batsman, right-arm medium fast bowler. *Team* Surrey (1919, 1 match).
Career batting
1–1–1–0–0*–no av–0–*ct* 0
Bowling 67–0

Freeman, Alfred James
Professional. *b:* 2.4.1892, Edmonton, Middlesex. *d:* 28.4.1972, Chelmsford, Essex. Tail end batsman, left-arm medium pace bowler. *Team* Essex (1920, 1 match).
Career batting
1–2–1–1–1–1.00–0–*ct* 0
Bowling 95–0

Freeman, Alfred Percy
Professional. *b:* 17.5.1888, Lewisham, London. *d:* 28.1.1965, Bearsted, Kent. Brother of J. R. (Essex), nephew of E. C. (Essex), cousin of E. J. (Essex), uncle of D. P. (Kent). Lower order right-hand batsman, leg break and googly bowler. *Team* Kent (1914–

36, 506 matches). *Tours* MCC to Australia and New Zealand 1922/3, to Australia 1924/5, 1928/9, to South Africa 1927/8. *Tests* England (1924/5 to 1929, 12 matches).
Career batting
592–716–194–4961–66–9.50–0–*ct* 238–*st* 1
Bowling 69577–3776–18.42–386–140–10/53
Test batting
12–16–5–154–50*–14.00–0–*ct* 4
Bowling 1707–66–25.86–5–3–7/71

The most consistent of all bowlers in County Championship cricket, Freeman is the only cricketer to capture over 300 wickets in a single summer: 304, av 18.05, in 1928. In the seven seasons following that record-breaking feat, he took over 200 wickets, thus acquiring a total of 2,090 wickets in eight English seasons. In all he took at least 100 wickets in a season 17 times.

Despite this prodigious success, Freeman proved only a moderate player in Test matches, appearing in little more than one tenth of the English Tests played during his career and, more surprisingly, during his really great County years from 1930 to 1935, he played no Test cricket at all. His bowling relied on a perfect length, which no doubt soon forced the ordinary County cricketer into indiscretion, but in Test cricket the more experienced batsmen just bided their time. His best bowling was 10/53 for Kent v Essex at Southend in 1930.

Freeman, Arthur Ernest Boden
Amateur. *b:* 15.10.1871, Iron Acton, Chipping Sodbury, Gloucestershire. *d:* 30.11.1948, Bath, Somerset. Lower order batsman, fast bowler. *Team* Somerset (1905, 1 match).
Career batting
1–1–0–3–3–3.00–0–*ct* 0

Freeman, Charles Redfern
Professional. *b:* 22.8.1887, Overseal, Derbyshire. *d:* 16.3.1956, Fulham, London. Middle order right-hand batsman. *Team* Derbyshire (1911, 1 match).
Career batting
1–2–0–7–4–3.50–0–*ct* 1

He played soccer for Chelsea.

Freeman, Douglas Percy
Professional. *b:* 21.7.1914, Sherborne, Dorset. Son of E. J. (Essex), grandson of E. C. (Essex), nephew of A. P. (Kent) and J. R. (Essex). Middle order left-hand batsman. *Team* Kent (1937, 1 match).
Career batting
1–2–0–10–6–5.00–0–*ct* 0

He also played for Dorset (1934–48).

Freeman, Edward Charles
Professional. *b:* 7.12.1860, Lewisham, London. *d:* 16.10.1939, Westbury, near Sherborne, Dorset. Father of E. J. (Essex), grandfather of D. P. (Kent), uncle of A. P. (Kent) and J. R. (Essex), father-in-law of W. Reeves (Essex). Middle order right-hand batsman. *Team* Essex (1894–96, 5 matches).
Career batting
5–9–0–95–35–10.55–0–*ct* 1
Bowling 40–0

Most of his cricket with Essex was played prior to that County being first-class, first appearing in 1887. He was for many years head groundsman at Leyton.

Freeman, Edward John
Professional. *b:* 16.10.1880, Ladywell, Lewisham, London. *d:* 22.2.1964, Sherborne, Dorset. Son of E. C. (Essex), father of D. P. (Kent), cousin of J. R. (Essex) and A. P. (Kent), brother-in-law of W. Reeves (Essex). Middle order batsman. *Team* Essex (1904–12, 55 matches).
Career batting
55–91–3–1280–84–14.54–0–*ct* 14
Bowling 50–1–50.00–0–0–1/6

He also played for Dorset (1913–20). A noted soccer player, he represented Essex.

Freeman, Edwin
Professional. *b:* 5.6.1886, Northampton. *d:* 7.12.1945, Northampton. Lower order right-hand batsman, right-arm medium pace bowler. *Team* Northamptonshire (1908–20, 16 matches).
Career batting
16–26–5–133–30–6.33–0–*ct* 4
Bowling 416–6–69.33–0–0–3/62

He was a noted soccer player with Northampton Town.

Freeman, Eric Walter
Cricketer. *b:* 13.7.1944, Semaphore, Adelaide, South Australia. Middle or lower order right-hand batsman, right-arm fast medium bowler, excellent field. *Team* South Australia (1964/5 to 1973/4, 44 matches). *Tours* Australia to England 1968, to South Africa 1969/70, to India 1969/70, to New Zealand 1966/7. *Tests* Australia (1967/8 to 1969/70, 11 matches).
Career batting
83–123–6–6–2244–116–19.17–1–*ct* 60
Bowling 6690–241–27.75–7–2–8/47
Test batting
11–18–0–345–76–19.16–0–*ct* 5
Bowling 1128–34–33.17–0–0–4/52

He appeared in two Tests on his 1968 tour to England, but did not do as well as expected.

Freeman, George
Professional until 1872, then amateur. *b:* 27.7.1843, Boroughbridge, Yorkshire. *d:* 18.11.1895, Sowerby Grange, near Thirsk, Yorkshire, of Bright's disease. Hard hitting middle order right-hand batsman, right-hand very fast round-arm bowler, good slip. *Team* Yorkshire (1865–80, 32 matches). *Tour* Willsher to North America 1868 (not first-class).
Career batting
44–70–3–918–53–13.70–0–*ct* 20

Bowling 2797–284 + 4–9.84–32–10–8/11

Regarded as the greatest fast bowler of his time – succeeding Jackson and Tarrant – Freeman's career was very short, for after five seasons (1867–1871) he virtually retired from first-class cricket to devote his time to business. He also played for Northumberland (1865).

Freeman, John Robert
Professional. *b:* 3.9.1883, Ladywell, Lewisham, London. *d:* 8.8.1958, Napsbury, Hertfordshire. Brother of A. P. (Kent), nephew of E. C. (Essex), cousin of E. J. (Essex), uncle of D. P. (Kent). Middle order right-hand batsman, right-arm medium pace bowler, wicket-keeper. *Team* Essex (1905–28, 336 matches).
Career batting
337–579–56–14602–286–27.91–26–*ct* 231–*st* 46
Bowling 365–10–36.50–0–0–3/31

He hit 1,000 runs in a season seven times (best 1,958, av 41.65, in 1926). His only double century was 286 for Essex v Northamptonshire at Northampton in 1921.

Freeman, Sidney Thomas
Amateur. *b:* 21.8.1888, Gloucester. *d:* 6.6.1971, Whitbourne, Hereford. Middle order batsman. *Team* Gloucestershire (1920–21, 3 matches).
Career batting
6–9–2–163–58–23.28–0–*ct* 4
Bowling 183–10–18.30–0–0–4/31

His first-class debut was for H. K. Foster's XI in 1919.

Freeman, Terence
Amateur. *b:* 21.10.1931, Finedon, Northamptonshire. Tail end right-hand batsman, right-arm fast medium bowler. *Team* Northamptonshire (1954, 1 match).
Career batting
1–1–0–4–4–4.00–0–*ct* 0
Bowling 90–1–90.00–0–0–1/43

Freeman-Thomas, F.
(*see under* Thomas, F. F.)

Freemantle, Andrew
Professional. *c:* 22.10.1768, Bishops Sutton, Hampshire. *d:* 19.1.1837, Easton, Hampshire. Brother of George (Hampshire). Steady middle order left-hand batsman, excellent field. *Team* Hampshire (1803–07).
Career batting
45–80–8–803–49–11.15–0–*ct* 23–*st* 1

His first-class debut was for England in 1801, although he had played in great matches in the 18th century, and his last match for England in 1810.

Freemantle, Frederick William
Professional. *b:* 27.6.1871, Binley, St Mary Bourne, Hampshire. *d:* 12.9.1943, Houghton, Stockbridge, Hampshire. Lower order batsman, opening bowler. *Team* Hampshire (1900, 2 matches).
Career batting
2–4–1–28–26–9.33–0–*ct* 0
Bowling 53–0

Freethy, Albert Edwin
Amateur. *b:* 27.4.1885, Swansea, Glamorgan. *d:* 17.7.1966, Cimla, Neath, Glamorgan. Opening batsman. *Team* Glamorgan (1921, 3 matches).
Career batting
3–4–1–79–31–26.33–0–*ct* 1

He was a well-known rugby referee. He first played for Glamorgan (pre first-class) in 1908.

French, Bruce Nicholas
Cricketer. *b:* 13.8.1959, Warsop, Nottinghamshire. Lower order right-hand batsman, wicket-keeper. *Team* Nottinghamshire (1976–92, 304 matches). *Tours* England to India 1984/5, to Sharjah (not first-class) 1984/5, to West Indies 1985/6, to Australia 1986/7, 1987/8, to New Zealand 1987/8, to Pakistan 1987/8; England XI to South Africa 1989/90. *Tests* England (1986 to 1987/8, 16 matches).
Career batting
340–444–88–6721–105*–18.87–1–*ct* 772–*st* 95
Bowling 70–1–70.00–0–0–1/37
Test batting
16–21–4–308–59–18.11–0–*ct* 38–*st* 1

A finger injury in 1988 caused him to miss most of that summer and to lose his place in the England side. Recovering in 1989 he then chose to tour South Africa. He made 87 dismissals (76 ct, 11 st) in 1985.

French, Hon Edward Gerald Fleming
Amateur. *b:* 11.12.1883, Woburn, Buckinghamshire. *d:* 17.9.1970, Hove, Sussex. Middle order left-hand batsman. *Sch* Wellington. *Team* MCC (1922–36).
Career batting
2–2–0–10–5–5.00–0–*ct* 0
Bowling 32–0

His County cricket was for Devon (1924–27) and he was a noted member of I Zingari for over 60 years.

French, Sir Edward Lee
Amateur. *b:* 22.7.1857, Worlingworth, Suffolk. *d:* 17.5.1916, Bath, Somerset. Lower order batsman, wicket-keeper. *Sch* Marlborough. *Teams* London County (1902); Gentlemen of India (1892/3).
Career batting
3–5–2–17–8*–5.66–0–*ct* 4–*st* 2

His County cricket was for Suffolk (1877).

French, John
Professional. *b:* 1834, Impington, Cambridgeshire. *d:* 15.5.1884, Impington, Cambridgeshire. Middle order batsman. *Team* Cambridgeshire (1864, 1 match).
Career batting
1–2–0–1–1–0.50–0–*ct* 0

Frere, Henry Tobias
Amateur. *b:* 27.9.1830, Odiham, Hampshire. *d:* 15.8.1881, Westbourne, Hampshire. Middle order

right-hand batsman, right-hand fast round-arm bowler, slip field. *Teams* Hampshire (1850–66, 7 matches); Sussex (1868, 1 match).
Career batting
13–24–6–177–26–9.83–0–*ct* 5–*st* 2
Bowling 647–24–26.95–1–0–5/20
He also played for Wiltshire (1859). He was also noted as a crack shot.

Frere, Lionel Robert Temple
Amateur. *b:* 10.12.1870, Marylebone, London. *d:* 15.3.1936, Kensington, London. Middle order right-hand batsman, wicket-keeper. *Sch* Haileybury. *Team* Cambridge U (1892).
Career batting
1–2–0–3–2–1.50–0–*ct* 2
His County cricket was for Norfolk (1894–95).

Friend, Major General Hon Sir Lovick Bransby
Amateur. *b:* 25.4.1856, Penhill, Half Way Street, Kent. *d:* 19.11.1944, West Kensington, London. Middle order right-hand batsman, wicket-keeper. *Sch* Cheltenham. *Team* Kent (1886–87, 3 matches).
Career batting
6–12–1–189–72–17.18–0–*ct* 2
He also played for Northumberland (1888), but was best known in military cricket, mainly for the Royal Engineers. His final first-class match was for MCC in 1891.

Frisby, Joseph Brankin
(registered at birth as Joseph Rankin Frisby)
Amateur. *b:* 26.2.1908, Stackley House, Carlton-Curlieu, Leicestershire. *d:* 2.11.1977, Leicester. Lower order right-hand batsman, wicket-keeper. *Sch* Harrow. *Team* Leicestershire (1938, 1 match).
Career batting
1–1–0–4–4–4.00–0–*ct* 3
He was Hon Secretary to Leicestershire CCC 1937–39.

Frith, William Frederick Lowndes
(also known as Lowndes-Frith and as Lowndes)
Amateur. *b:* 1.7.1871, Wandsworth, London. *d:* 6.10.1956, West Wittering, Sussex. Father of W. G. L. F. Lowndes (Hampshire). Lower order batsman, useful bowler. *Team* London County (1901–02).
Career batting
2–1–0–4–4–4.00–*ct* 0
Bowling 23–1–23.00–0–0–1/23
His County cricket was for Buckinghamshire (1907–13).

Frost, George
Professional. *b:* 16.10.1848, Wirksworth, Derbyshire. *d:* 12.2.1913, Wirksworth, Derbyshire. Brother of J. H. (Derbyshire). Opening/middle order right-hand batsman. *Team* Derbyshire (1872–80, 36 matches).
Career batting
37–67–4–771–52–12.23–0–*ct* 10

Frost, Graham
Cricketer. *b:* 15.1.1947, Old Basford, Nottinghamshire. Opening right-hand batsman, right-arm medium pace bowler. *Team* Nottinghamshire (1967–73, 102 matches).
Career batting
104–169–17–3439–107–22.62–2–*ct* 83
Bowling 680–15–45.33–0–0–3/33

Frost, John Henry
Professional. *b:* 30.1.1847, Wirksworth, Derbyshire. *d:* 1.11.1916, Ashover, Derbyshire. Brother of George (Derbyshire). Middle order batsman. *Team* Derbyshire (1874, 1 match).
Career batting
1–2–0–19–18–9.50–0–*ct* 2

Frost, Mark
Cricketer. *b:* 21.10.1962, Barking, Essex. Tail end right-hand batsman, right-arm medium fast bowler. *Teams* Surrey (1988–89, 13 matches); Glamorgan (1990–92, 49 matches). *Tour* Glamorgan to Zimbabwe 1990/1.
Career batting
62–48–16–87–12–2.71–0–*ct* 7
Bowling 5825–162–35.95–4–2–7/99
He also played for Staffordshire (1984–87).

Frost, Patrick David
Amateur. *b:* 3.10.1940, St John's, Antigua. Middle order right-hand batsman. *Team* Oxford U (1961).
Career batting
1 match, did not bat–*ct* 1

Fry, Charles Anthony
Amateur. *b:* 14.1.1940, Henley-in-Arden, Warwickshire. Son of Stephen (Hampshire), grandson of C. B. (Sussex and Hampshire). Middle order right-hand batsman, right-arm medium pace bowler, wicket-keeper. *Sch* Repton. *Teams* Oxford U (1959–61, blue all three years); Hampshire (1960, 5 matches); Northamptonshire (1962, 2 matches). *Tour* MCC to Bangladesh 1978/9 (not first-class).
Career batting
50–85–7–1952–103*–25.02–2–*ct* 38
Bowling 13–0
His last first-class match was for Free Foresters in 1968.

Fry, Charles Burgess
Amateur. *b:* 25.4.1872, West Croydon, Surrey. *d:* 7.9.1956, Child's Hill, Hampstead, London. Father of Stephen (Hampshire), grandfather of C. A. (Hampshire and Northamptonshire), cousin of K. R. B. (Sussex). Brilliant opening or middle order right-hand batsman, right-arm fast medium bowler, good field. *Sch* Repton. *Teams* Oxford U (1892–95, blue all four years); Sussex (1894–1908, 236 matches); London County (1900–02); Hampshire (1909–21, 44 matches); Europeans (1921/2). *Tour* Hawke to South

Africa 1895/6. *Tests* England (1895/6 to 1912, 26 matches).
Career batting
394–658–43–30886–258*–50.22–94–*ct* 240
Bowling 4872–166–29.34–9–2–6/78
Test batting
26–41–3–1223–144–32.18–2–*ct* 17
Bowling 3–0

Perhaps the most talented of all English athletes, C. B. Fry was a triple blue at Oxford – cricket, soccer and athletics – and would have been awarded his rugby blue, but for injury just before the University match. He played soccer for England (v Ireland in 1901) and for Southampton in the 1902 FA Cup Final, and held the world long jump record in addition to his career in English Test cricket. Although he made his Test debut in 1895/6, he did not really come to the forefront of English batsmen until 1898, when he averaged 54.18 with the bat. The following year he completed 2,000 runs for the first of six times and in 1901 reached 3,147 (av 78.67). In this season he hit six centuries in successive innings and had a total of 13 hundreds to his name. In all he completed 1,000 runs in a season 12 times. Early in his career the fairness of his bowling action was open to question, several times being no-balled for throwing.

He also played for Surrey in a non-first-class match in 1891. He missed nearly all of the 1906 season due to injury.

His appearances in Test cricket were restricted by the fact that he never toured Australia, although invited to do so at least twice.

He was a Test selector in 1909 and 1912 and he captained England in the six Tests of the 1912 Triangular Series and did not lose a match; he also led Oxford in 1894 and Sussex from 1904 to 1908. Of his 16 double centuries, 13 were for Sussex, two for Hampshire and one for the Gentlemen v Players at Lord's. His highest first-class innings was 258* for Hampshire v Gloucestershire at Southampton in 1911.

He stood for Parliament several times but failed to be elected and after the war acted as India's representative at the League of Nations. He was offered the Kingship of Albania, but declined.

A noted writer on cricket and other games, he published his own magazine for some years as well as his autobiography in 1939.

Fry, Kenneth Robert Burgess
Amateur. *b:* 15.3.1883, Surat, India. *d:* 21.6.1949, Chelsea, London. Cousin of C. B. (Sussex and Hampshire). Middle order right-hand batsman, wicket-keeper. *Sch* Cheltenham. *Teams* Sussex (1901–02, 4 matches); Cambridge U (1902–04, blue 1904).
Career batting
26–46–0–1036–129–22.52–2–*ct* 15–*st* 2

Fry, Stephen
Amateur. *b:* 23.5.1900, Portsmouth, Hampshire. *d:* 18.5.1979, Notting Hill, London. Son of C. B. (Sussex and Hampshire), father of C. A. (Hampshire and Northamptonshire). Lower order right-hand batsman, wicket-keeper. *Team* Hampshire (1922–31, 29 matches).
Career batting
29–50–2–508–78–10.58–0–*ct* 16–*st* 1

Fryer, Frederick Eustace Reade
Amateur. *b:* 7.1.1849, Holbrook House, Suffolk. *d:* 1.10.1917, Poplar, London. Brother-in-law of A. C. Lucas (Surrey and Middlesex). Middle order right-hand batsman, right-arm medium pace bowler. *Sch* Harrow. *Team* Cambridge U (1870–73, blue all four years).
Career batting
58–103–5–2149–91–21.92–0–*ct* 31
Bowling 1131–39–29.00–2–0–5/49

His County cricket was for Suffolk (1867–83). His first-class debut was for Gentlemen of the South in 1869 and his final match for Orleans Club in 1883. He captained Cambridge in 1873. In his later years he was a noted golfer.

Fryer, Philip Algernon
Amateur. *b:* 26.6.1870, Wymondham, Norfolk. *d:* 4.11.1950, Wilby, Northamptonshire. Opening right-hand batsman, lob bowler. *Sch* Wellingborough. *Team* Northamptonshire (1908, 2 matches).
Career batting
2–4–0–83–38–20.75–0–*ct* 1
Bowling 66–3–22.00–0–0–3/35

He did not appear for Cambridge whilst at the university, but missed his soccer blue only through injury. He also played for Norfolk (1890–1905).

Fryer, William Henry
Professional. *b:* 29.3.1829, Greenwich, London. *d:* 19.1.1919, Loose, Maidstone, Kent. Opening right-hand batsman, right-hand medium fast round-arm bowler, wicket-keeper. *Team* Kent (1852–72, 75 matches).
Career batting
88–161–9–1666–67–10.96–0–*ct* 73–*st* 25
Bowling 950–49–19.38–1–0–8/40

In September 1862 he was thrown out of a trap and lost the sight of one eye as a result of the accident, but continued to appear in County cricket, though he gave up keeping wicket.

Fulcher, Arthur William
Amateur. *b:* 7.5.1855, Pau, France. *d:* 17.5.1932, Bayswater, London. Father of E. J. (Kent). Middle order right-hand batsman, right-hand slow round-arm bowler, good deep field. *Sch* Westminster. *Team* Kent (1878–87, 7 matches).
Career batting
7–12–1–156–44*–14.18–0–*ct* 2

Fulcher, Eric Jesser
Amateur. *b:* 12.3.1890, Bearsted, Kent. *d:* 14.2.1923, Llandogo, Monmouth, as the result of a gun accident. Son of A. W. (Kent). Hard hitting middle order right-hand batsman, splendid field. *Sch* Radley. *Team* Kent (1919, 4 matches). *Tour* MCC to Argentine 1911/12.
Career batting
10–18–1–329–64–19.35–0–*ct* 9
Bowling 228–4–57.00–0–0–2/35
He played with success for Norfolk (1910–22). His first-class debut in England was for L. Robinson's Team in 1913 and his final first-class match for MCC in 1921.

Fuller, Edward Russell Henry
Amateur. *b:* 2.8.1931, Worcester, Cape Province, South Africa. Hard hitting lower order right-hand batsman, right-arm fast medium bowler, fine field. *Team* Western Province (1950/1 to 1957/8). *Tours* South Africa to Australia and New Zealand 1952/3, to England 1955. *Tests* South Africa (1952/3 to 1957/8, 7 matches).
Career batting
59–86–16–1062–69–15.10–0–*ct* 29
Bowling 5026–190–26.45–11–3–7/40
Test batting
7–9–1–64–17–8.00–0–*ct* 3
Bowling 668–22–30.36–1–0–5/66
Although he appeared in only two Tests during his one tour to England – he was competing with Heine and Adcock – he had a successful visit, taking 49 wickets (av 19.51). His final first-class match was for a Commonwealth XI in 1958. He also played for Cumberland (1965).

Fuller, Rev John Mee
Amateur. *b:* 4.12.1834, Westminster, London. *d:* 16.8.1893, Combe Martin, Devon. He died suddenly whilst travelling to Minehead, Somerset. Stylish middle order batsman, excellent long-stop. *Sch* Marlborough. *Teams* Cambridge U (1855–58); Cambridgeshire (1857–58, 3 matches).
Career batting
32–56–4–579–69–11.13–0–*ct* 17
His first-class debut was for MCC in 1854.

Fullerton, George Murray
Amateur. *b:* 8.12.1922, Kensington, Johannesburg, South Africa. Brother of I. R. (Transvaal). Middle order right-hand batsman, right-arm medium pace bowler, wicket-keeper. *Team* Transvaal (1945/6 to 1950/1). *Tours* South Africa to England 1947, 1951. *Tests* South Africa (1947–51, 7 matches).
Career batting
63–97–8–2768–167–31.10–3–*ct* 64–*st* 18
Bowling 107–3–35.66–0–0–2/41
Test batting
7–13–0–325–88–25.00–0–*ct* 10–*st* 2
In 1947 he came into the last two Tests as wicket-keeper, but in 1951 appeared in the first three Tests as a batsman. On the latter tour he hit 1,129 runs, av 31.36. His first-class debut was for the Rest of South Africa in 1942/3.

Fullerton, Ian Ramsay
Amateur. *b:* 24.9.1935, Kensington, Johannesburg, South Africa. Brother of G. M. (Transvaal). Opening right-hand batsman. *Team* Transvaal (1958/9 to 1965/6). *Tour* South African Fezela to England 1961.
Career batting
31–56–2–1853–145–34.31–5–*ct* 11
Bowling 8–0
He also played hockey for Transvaal.

Fulljames, Reginald Edgar Gilbert
Amateur. *b:* 13.11.1896, Southsea, Hampshire. *d:* 31.7.1985, Curdridge, Hampshire. Lower order left-hand batsman, slow left-arm bowler. *Sch* St Paul's. *Team* RAF (1927–32).
Career batting
8–14–2–173–47–14.41–0–*ct* 7
Bowling 795–38–20.92–5–1–7/25
He played in the trials at Cambridge U, but not in first-class matches.

Fullwood, Walter
Professional. *b:* 8.2.1907, Holmewood, Derbyshire. *d:* 4.1.1988, Hythe, Kent. Tail end right-hand batsman, wicket-keeper. *Team* Derbyshire (1946, 6 matches).
Career batting
6–10–1–41–13–4.55–0–*ct* 5–*st* 1

Fulton, David Paul
Cricketer. *b:* 15.11.1971, Lewisham, London. Middle order right-hand batsman. *Team* Kent (1992, 1 match).
Career batting
1–2–0–58–42–29.00–0–*ct* 2
He has played chess for England and table-tennis for Southern England.

Fulton, Herbert Angus
Amateur. *b:* 3.10.1872, Bangalore, India. *d:* 23.12.1951, Minehead, Somerset. Lower order batsman, wicket-keeper. *Sch* Bedford. *Team* Worcestershire (1914, 1 match).
Career batting
1–1–1–2–2*–no av–0–*ct* 0
He also played for Bedfordshire (1901).

Furley, John
Amateur. *b:* 24.3.1847, Oakham, Rutland. *d:* 30.6.1909, Oakham, Rutland. Middle order right-hand batsman, right-hand fast round arm bowler, slip field. *Sch* Oakham. *Teams* North (1875); England (1877).
Career batting
2–4–0–13–5–3.25–0–*ct* 0

He appeared in several matches under the alias 'A. Yorker'. His county cricket was for Lincolnshire (1871–74), Northamptonshire (pre first-class, 1873–82) and Rutland (1881–85).

Furniss, John Brian
Professional. *b:* 16.11.1934, Baslow, Derbyshire. Lower order right-hand batsman, right-arm fast medium bowler. *Team* Derbyshire (1955–56, 4 matches).
Career batting
4–5–1–9–6–2.25–0–*ct* 2
Bowling 259–7–37.00–0–0–3/52

Fursdon, Edward David
Cricketer. *b:* 20.12.1952, Bitchet Green, Seal, Kent. Middle or lower right-hand batsman, right-arm medium fast bowler. *Sch* Sherborne. *Teams* Oxford U (1973–75, blue 1974–75).
Career batting
17–29–6–484–112*–21.04–1–*ct* 2
Bowling 1428–43–33.20–1–0–6/60
His County cricket was for Devon (1981).

Fussell, Philip Hillier
Amateur. *b:* 12.2.1931, Rode, Bath. Lower order right-hand batsman, right-arm medium pace bowler, close field. *Sch* Monkton Combe. *Team* Somerset (1953–56, 2 matches).
Career batting
2–4–0–10–5–2.50–0–*ct* 1
Bowling 71–1–71.00–0–0–1/26

Fyfe, Douglas Munro
Amateur. *b:* 1824. *d:* 25.2.1871, Westminster, London. Middle order batsman. *Teams* Gentlemen of South (1866); MCC (1868–69).
Career batting
5–8–0–60–31–7.50–0–*ct* 2
His County cricket was for Devon (1851–53), Hampshire (pre first-class, 1853), Wiltshire (1858–59) and Monmouthshire (1858–59).

Fyffe, Alan Herbert
Amateur. *b:* 30.4.1884, Kensington, London. *d:* 5.3.1939, Minchinhampton, Gloucestershire. Lower order right-hand batsman, right-arm fast medium bowler. *Sch* Winchester. *Team* Oxford U (1906).
Career batting
13–24–4–130–39–6.50–0–*ct* 7
Bowling 1149–40–28.72–0–0–4/62
His final first-class match was for Harlequins in 1925. His County cricket was for Denbighshire (1910) and Cheshire (1911). He won a blue for athletics.

Fynn, Charles Garnet
Amateur. *b:* 24.4.1897, Marylebone, London. *d:* 26.8.1976, Bournemouth, Hampshire. Lower order right-hand batsman, right-arm slow bowler. *Team* Hampshire (1930–31, 9 matches).
Career batting
9–12–5–45–21–6.42–0–*ct* 2
Bowling 446–11–40.54–0–0–3/92

G

Gabe-Jones, A. R. (*see under* Jones, A. R. G.)

Gaddum, Frederick Ducange
Amateur. *b:* 28.6.1860, Didsbury, Manchester, Lancashire. *d:* 14.10.1900, Stockport, Cheshire, as the result of a bicycling accident. Tail end left-hand batsman, slow left-arm bowler, moderate field. *Sch* Uppingham and Rugby. *Teams* Cambridge U (1880–82, blue 1882); Lancashire (1884, 1 match).
Career batting
11–20–7–87–16–6.69–0–*ct* 9
Bowling 406–21–19.33–0–0–4/34

Gaekwad, Anshuman Dattajirao
Cricketer. *b:* 23.9.1952, Bombay, India. Son of D. K. (India). Opening right-hand batsman, off break bowler. *Team* Baroda (1969/70 to 1991/2). *Tours* India to England 1975 (World Cup), 1979, to New Zealand 1975/6, to West Indies 1975/6, 1982/3, to Australia 1977/8, to Pakistan 1978/9, 1984/5; Wadekar to Sri Lanka 1975/6. *Tests* India (1974/5 to 1984/5, 40 matches).
Career batting
206–326–34–12136–225–41.56–34–*ct* 160
Bowling 4587–143–32.07–3–0–6/49
Test batting
40–70–4–1985–201–30.07–2–*ct* 15
Bowling 187–2–93.50–0–0–1/4
He scored 574 runs, av 31.88, on his tour to England, playing in two Tests. His highest score was 225 for Baroda v Gujarat at Baroda in 1982/3.

Gaekwad, Dattajirao Krishnarao
Amateur. *b:* 27.10.1928, Baroda, India. Father of A. D. (India). Opening/middle order right hand batsman, right-arm medium pace or leg break bowler. *Team* Baroda (1947/8 to 1963/4). *Tours* India to England 1952, 1959, to West Indies 1952/3. *Tests* India (1952 to 1960/1, 11 matches).
Career batting
110–172–13–5788–249*–36.40–17–*ct* 49
Bowling 1016–25–40.64–0–0–4/117
Test batting
11–20–1–350–52–18.42–0–*ct* 5
Bowling 12–0
In 1952 he batted adequately in first-class matches, but was required for only one Test; in 1959, as captain, he hit 1,174 runs, av 34.52, and appeared in four Tests, but made little impact. He hit three double centuries, all for Baroda, his highest being 249* v Maharashtra at Poona in 1959/60. His first-class debut was for D. B. Deodhar's XII in 1943/44.

Gaekwad, Hiralal Ghasulal
Amateur. *b:* 29.8.1923, Nagpur, India. Lower order left-hand batsman, left-arm medium pace or slow spin bowler. *Teams* CP and Berar (1941/2); Holkar (1943/4 to 1954/5); Madhya Bharat (1955/6 to 1956/7); Madhya Pradesh (1957/8 to 1963/4). *Tours* India to England 1952; Holkar to Ceylon 1947/8. *Test* India (1952/3, 1 match).
Career batting
101–147–19–2487–164–19.42–2–*ct* 43
Bowling 8859–375–23.62–21–5–7/67
Test batting
1–2–0–22–14–11.00–0–*ct* 0
Bowling 47–0

Gaekwar, HH Prince Udayasinhrao Shivajirao
(later Maharajah of Baroda)
Amateur. *b:* 11.6.1918, Baroda, India. *d:* 11.8.1960, Baroda, India. Son of H. H. Baroda (Oxford U). Lower order right-hand batsman, right-arm fast medium bowler. *Team* Cambridge U (1939).
Career batting
4–5–3–16–13*–8.00–0–*ct* 0
Bowling 188–2–94.00–0–0–1/12

Gale, Henry
Amateur. *b:* 11.7.1836, Winchester, Hampshire. *d:* 3.3.1898, Westbourne, Bournemouth, Hampshire. Middle order right-hand batsman. *Sch* Marlborough. *Teams* Hampshire (1865–66, 5 matches).
Career batting
6–9–0–144–44–16.00–0–*ct* 2
He also played for Norfolk (1864–66).

Gale, Leslie Edward
Amateur. *b:* 11.11.1904, Solihull, Warwickshire. *d:* 22.1.1982, Dudley, Worcestershire. Middle order right-hand batsman. slow right-arm bowler. *Team* Worcestershire (1923–28, 14 matches).
Career batting
14–26–6–155–19–7.75–0–*ct* 5
Bowling 394–10–39.40–1–0–5/49
He also played for Staffordshire (1931–38).

Gale, Percival George
Amateur. *b:* 22.5.1865, Kensington, London. *d:* 7.9.1940, Croydon, Surrey. Middle order right-hand batsman. *Team* London County (1901–04).
Career batting
11–17–1–140–40–8.75–0–*ct* 5
Bowling 37–0
He was mainly associated with the Wanderers CC of London. His final first-class match was for W. G. Grace's XI in 1906.

Gale, Robert Alec
Professional. *b:* 10.12.1933, Old Warden, Bedfordshire. Opening left-hand batsman, right-arm medium pace, or leg break bowler. *Sch* Bedford Modern. *Team* Middlesex (1956–65, 219 matches). *Tours* Swanton to West Indies 1960/1; Brown to East Africa 1961/2 (not first-class); MCC to South America 1964/5 (not first-class).
Career batting
242–439–13–12505–200–29.35–15–*ct* 124
Bowling 1748–47–37.19–0–0–4/57
He hit 1,000 runs in a season six times (best 2,211, av 38.78, in 1962). His only double century was 200 for Middlesex v Glamorgan at Newport in 1962. His first-class debut was for Combined Services in 1955 and his final first-class match for Free Foresters in 1968. He also played for Bedfordshire (1950).

Gallacher, Thomas Nesbitt
Cricketer. *b:* 3.4.1936, Kilmarnock, Ayr, Scotland. Middle order right-hand batsman. *Team* Scotland (1965–66).
Career batting
4–5–0–126–73–25.20–0–*ct* 0

Gallaugher, Robert George
Amateur. *b:* 8.1.1923, Epsom, Auckland, New Zealand. Lower order left-hand batsman, slow left-arm bowler. *Tour* New Zealand Services to England 1945.
Career batting
1–1–0–2–2–2.00–0–*ct* 0
Bowling 27–0

Galley, James Martyn
Cricketer. *b:* 4.10.1944, Clifton, Bristol. Middle order right-hand batsman. *Team* Somerset (1969, 3 matches).
Career batting
3–6–1–27–17–5.40–0–*ct* 1
He also played for Wiltshire (1980–81). A noted rugby player, he appeared for Bath at scrum-half.

Gallian, Jason Edward Riche
Cricketer. *b:* 25.6.1971, Manly, Sydney, New South Wales, Australia. Opening right-hand batsman, right-arm medium pace bowler. *Teams* Lancashire (1990, 1 match); Oxford U (1992, blue).
Career batting
10–16–1–485–112–32.33–1–*ct* 6
Bowling 693–19–36.47–0–0–4/29
He scored two hundreds in a match three times in succession for Lancashire 2nd XI in 1992.

Gallichan, Norman
Amateur. *b:* 3.6.1906, Palmerston North, Wellington, New Zealand. *d:* 25.3.1969, Taupo, Auckland, New Zealand. Middle/lower order right-hand batsman, slow left-arm bowler. *Team* Wellington (1928/9 to 1938/9). *Tour* New Zealand to England 1937. *Test* New Zealand (1937, 1 match).
Career batting
31–43–8–636–62–18.17–0–*ct* 22
Bowling 2244–86–26.09–4–1–6/46
Test batting
1–2–0–32–30–16.00–0–*ct* 0

Bowling 113–3–37.66–0–0–3/99

Although only a last minute selection for the 1937 tour of England he bowled better than anticipated, taking 59 wickets, av 23.92, and earning a place in one Test. His first-class debut was for The Rest v New Zealand 1927/8.

Gallop, Henry George
Amateur. *b:* 21.8.1857, Redland, Bristol. *d:* 21.8.1940, Bitton, Gloucestershire. Lower order right-hand batsman, right-arm medium pace bowler. *Team* Gloucestershire (1877–83, 6 matches).
Career batting
6–10–2–43–16–5.37–0–*ct* 4
Bowling 104–5–20.80–0–0–3/47

Galpin, John George
Professional. *b:* 13.1.1843, Alverstoke, Gosport, Hampshire. *d:* 5.3.1917, Luton, Bedfordshire. Lower order right-hand batsman, right-hand fast round-arm bowler. *Team* Hampshire (1875–80, 7 matches).
Career batting
7–14–5–100–27–11.11–0–*ct* 4
Bowling 462–28–16.50–2–0–6/68

He also played for Buckinghamshire (1870–71) and Northamptonshire (pre first-class, 1871).

Gamble, Frederick Charles
Professional. *b:* 29.5.1905, Charing Cross, London. *d:* 15.5.1965, Lambeth, London. Lower order right-hand batsman, right-arm medium pace bowler. *Team* Surrey (1933–35, 19 matches).
Career batting
19–25–10–132–29–8.80–0–*ct* 10
Bowling 1555–40–38.87–0–0–4/82

He also played for Devon (1939). A well-known soccer player, he was a centre forward for West Ham, Aldershot and Reading.

Gamble, George Frederick
Professional. *b:* 24.10.1877, Leicester. *d:* 27.7.1949, Southfields, Leicester. Tail end right-hand batsman, left-arm bowler. *Teams* London County (1900–03); Surrey (1906, 8 matches).
Career batting
11–13–7–54–21*–9.00–0–*ct* 5
Bowling 691–26–26.57–1–0–5/78

Gamble, Neil Walton
Cricketer. *b:* 17.1.1943, Macclesfield, Cheshire. Lower order right-hand batsman, right-arm medium pace bowler. *Sch* Stockport GS. *Team* Oxford U (1967, blue).
Career batting
13–17–5–87–24–7.25–0–*ct* 8
Bowling 786–19–41.36–0–0–4/57

His County cricket was for Cheshire (1965–73).

Game, William Henry
Amateur. *b:* 2.10.1853, Stoke Newington, London. *d:* 11.8.1932, Brancaster, Norfolk. Hard hitting middle order right-hand batsman, right-arm slow bowler, brilliant outfield. *Sch* Sherborne. *Teams* Surrey (1871–83, 39 matches); Oxford U (1873–76, blue all four years).
Career batting
59–104–5–1862–141–18.80–2–*ct* 33
Bowling 308–5–61.60–0–0–1/5

He also played for Dorset (1871–75). He captained Oxford in 1876. He won his blue for rugby football.

Gamlin, Herbert Temlett
Professional. *b:* 12.2.1878, Wellington, Somerset. *d:* 12.7.1937, Pylford Bridge, North Cheam, Surrey. Tail end right-hand batsman, off-break bowler. *Team* Somerset (1895–96, 3 matches).
Career batting
3–6–0–7–5–1.16–0–*ct* 4
Bowling 207–2–103.50–0–0–2/100

A noted rugby footballer, he appeared for England at full-back.

Gamsy, Dennis
Amateur. *b:* 17.2.1940, Glenwood, Durban, South Africa. Opening right-hand batsman, wicket-keeper. *Team* Natal (1958/9 to 1972/3). *Tour* South Africa to England 1965. *Tests* South Africa (1969/70, 2 matches).
Career batting
93–145–14–3106–137–23.70–2–*ct* 278–*st* 33
Bowling 13–0
Test batting
2–3–1–39–30*–19.50–0–*ct* 5

He was reserve wicket-keeper on the 1965 tour to England and did not appear in any Tests.

Gandon, Nicholas John Charles
Cricketer. *b:* 7.7.1956, Leicester. Opening or middle order right-hand batsman, off break bowler. *Sch* Haileybury. *Team* Oxford U (1979).
Career batting
8–13–1–170–38–14.16–0–*ct* 6

His County cricket was for Hertfordshire (1975–88) and Lincolnshire (1989–92).

Gandy, Christopher Henry
Professional. *b:* 24.6.1867, Bethnal Green, London. *d:* 18.6.1907, Ingrave, Brentwood, Essex. Lower order batsman, left-arm opening bowler. *Team* Hampshire (1900, 2 matches).
Career batting
2–4–1–6–6*–2.00–0–*ct* 1
Bowling 117–3–39.00–0–0–2/84

Gange, Thomas Henry
Professional. *b:* 15.4.1891, Pietermaritzburg, South Africa. *d:* 11.7.1947, Swansea, Glamorgan. Lower order right-hand batsman, right-arm fast bowler. *Team* Gloucestershire (1913–20, 37 matches).
Career batting
37–64–7–571–39–10.01–0–*ct* 12

Bowling 3265–103–31.69–6–0–7/91

In Wisden's Almanack for 1950, Gange is given an obituary stating he died in March 1949, but this is incorrect. He also played for Wiltshire (1911).

Ganly, James Blandford
Amateur. *b:* 7.3.1904, Dublin, Ireland. *d:* 22.7.1976, Oughterard, Co Galway, Ireland. Middle order right-hand batsman, right-arm fast medium bowler. *Teams* Ireland (1921–37); Dublin University (1924).
Career batting
15–29–1–486–62*–17.35–0–*ct* 5
Bowling 177–7–25.28–0–0–2/22

He played rugby for Ireland.

Gannon, Jack Rose Compton
Amateur. *b:* 1.11.1882, Ireland. *d:* 25.4.1980, near Eastshaw, Midhurst, Sussex. Son-in-law of G. P. Robertson (Oxford U). Lower order batsman, wicket-keeper. *Sch* Sutton Valence. *Teams* MCC (1908–10); Europeans (1917/18).
Career batting
8–15–3–158–48–13.16–0–*ct* 10–*st* 3

Ganteaume, Andrew Gordon
Amateur. *b:* 22.1.1921, Belmont, Port of Spain, Trinidad. Opening right-hand batsman, wicket-keeper. *Team* Trinidad (1940/1 to 1962/3). *Tour* West Indies to England 1957. *Test* West Indies (1947/8, 1 match).
Career batting
50–85–5–2785–159–34.81–5–*ct* 34–*st* 3
Bowling 51–0
Test batting
1–1–0–112–112–112.00–1–*ct* 0

He was brought into the West Indies Test side as deputy for the injured Stollmeyer and hit a century on his Test debut. This proved to be his only Test. In 1957 he only had a modest tour of England.

Gard, Trevor
Cricketer. *b:* 2.6.1957, West Lambrook, Somerset. Lower order right-hand batsman, wicket-keeper. *Team* Somerset (1976–89, 112 matches).
Career batting
112–126–25–1389–51*–13.75–0–*ct* 178–*st* 39
Bowling 8–0

Gardiner, Peter Leitham
Amateur. *b:* 22.7.1896, Perth, Scotland. *d:* 15.6.1975, Perth, Scotland. Middle order right-hand batsman, right-arm medium pace bowler. *Team* Scotland (1925–31).
Career batting
2–4–0–67–42–16.75–0–*ct* 1
Bowling 136–3–45.33–0–0–2/7

Gardiner, Robert P.
Amateur. Opening right-hand batsman, wicket-keeper. *Team* Scotland (1909–14).
Career batting
3–5–0–130–72–26.00–0–*ct* 6

Gardiner, Stuart James
Cricketer. *b:* 19.3.1947, Bloemfontein, South Africa. Lower order left-hand batsman, left-arm medium pace bowler. *Teams* Cambridge U (1978, blue); Orange Free State (1967/8 to 1973/4).
Career batting
34–49–16–556–40*–16.84–0–*ct* 13
Bowling 2772–111–24.97–5–0–6/49

Gardiner-Hill, Peter Farquhar
Amateur. *b:* 22.10.1926, Westminster, London. Middle order right-hand batsman. *Sch* Eton. *Team* Oxford U(1949).
Career batting
2–2–0–78–50–39.00–0–*ct* 0

Gardner, Fred Charles
Amateur in 1947, professional from 1948. *b:* 4.6.1922, Bell Green, Coventry, Warwickshire. *d:* 12.1.1979, Coventry, Warwickshire. Opening right-hand batsman, fine slip field. *Team* Warwickshire (1947–61, 338 matches).
Career batting
340–597–66–17905–215*–33.71–29–*ct* 198
Bowling 99–0

He hit 1,000 runs in a season 10 times (best 1,911, av 45.50, in 1950). His only double century was 215* for Warwickshire v Somerset at Taunton in 1950. He was a first-class umpire (1962–65). He played soccer for Coventry City and Newport County.

Gardner, Harry
Amateur. *b:* 12.6.1890, City of London. *d:* 12.2.1939, Blackwell, East Grinstead, Sussex. Middle order batsman. *Sch* King's, Canterbury. *Team* Army (1914).
Career batting
2–4–0–42–17–10.50–0–*ct* 1

Gardner, Herbert Wilson
Amateur. *b:* 19.1.1852, Rugeley, Staffordshire. *d:* 5.12.1924, Armitage, Staffordshire. Middle order right-hand batsman, good cover point. *Sch* Rugby. *Team* MCC (1882).
Career batting
1–2–0–2–1–1.00–0–*ct* 0

His County cricket was for Staffordshire (1895–98).

Gardner, Leslie Robin
Professional. *b:* 23.2.1934, Ledbury, Herefordshire. Middle order right-hand batsman, right-arm medium pace bowler, good slip field. *Team* Leicestershire (1954–62, 126 matches).
Career batting
126–227–19–4119–102*–19.80–2–*ct* 63
Bowling 199–5–39.80–0–0–3/54

He hit 1,000 runs, av 27.77, in 1959. He also played for Hertfordshire (1964–65). A useful soccer player, he appeared as inside right for Hereford.

Gardom, Barrie Keith
Cricketer. *b:* 31.12.1952, Birmingham. Middle order right-hand batsman, leg break and googly bowler. *Team* Warwickshire (1973–74, 17 matches).
Career batting
17–25–2–427–79*–18.56–0–*ct* 6
Bowling 700–17–41.17–1–0–6/139

Garforth, William Henry
Amateur. *b:* 14.1.1855, Otherington, Yorkshire. *d:* 15.6.1931, Malton, Yorkshire. Lower order batsman, bowler. *Sch* Uppingham. *Team* I Zingari (1887).
Career batting
1–2–0–0–0–0.00–0–*ct* 1
Bowling 3–0

Garland-Wells, Herbert Montandon
Amateur. *b:* 14.11.1907, Brockley, London. Hard hitting middle order right-hand batsman, right-arm medium pace bowler. *Sch* St Paul's. *Teams* Oxford U (1927–30, blue 1928–30); Surrey (1928–39, 130 matches).
Career batting
190–283–23–6068–128–23.33–4–*ct* 141
Bowling 7617–185–41.17–2–0–5/25
He captained Surrey in 1939. He hit 1,270 runs, av 43.79, in 1928. A good soccer player, he played for Oxford U, Clapton Orient and England in an Amateur International as goalkeeper. He also won blues for soccer and Rugby fives.

Garlick, Paul Lawrence
Cricketer. *b:* 2.8.1964, Chiswick, Middlesex. Tail end right-hand batsman, right-arm fast medium bowler. *Sch* Sherborne. *Team* Cambridge U (1984, blue).
Career batting
10–15–6–13–6*–1.44–0–*ct* 1
Bowling 1092–12–91.00–0–0–2/69
His County cricket was for Dorset (1984–92). He failed to score in 9 consecutive innings for Cambridge.

Garlick, Richard Gordon
Professional. *b:* 11.4.1917, Kirkby Lonsdale, Westmorland. *d:* 16.5.1988, Blackpool, Lancashire. Lower order right-hand batsman, right-arm medium pace off break bowler, good field. *Teams* Lancashire (1938–47, 44 matches); Northamptonshire (1948–50, 77 matches).
Career batting
121–152–32–1664–62*–13.86–0–*ct* 39
Bowling 8670–332–26.11–10–1–6/27

Garlies, Lord Alan Plantagenet Stewart
(succeeded as 10th Earl of Galloway in 1873)
Amateur. *b:* 21.10.1835, London. *d:* 7.2.1901, Cumloden House, Newton Stewart, Kirkcudbrightshire, Scotland. Brother of R. H. Stewart (Gentlemen of England 1856), uncle of M. G. Tollemache (Cambridge U). Steady opening right-hand batsman, good deep field. *Sch* Harrow. *Team* MCC (1858–64).
Career batting
5–9–2–96–24–13.71–0–*ct* 1–*st* 2
He was President of MCC in 1858. His County cricket was for Rutland (1859). He was MP for Wigtownshire 1868–73.

Garne, William Henry
Amateur. *b:* 9.5.1861, Middle Aston, Oxfordshire. *d:* 24.5.1895, Wellingborough, Northamptonshire. Middle order right-hand batsman, right-arm medium pace bowler. *Sch* Framlingham. *Team* Gloucestershire (1884, 1 match).
Career batting
1–2–0–2–2–1.00–0–*ct* 0

Garner, Joel, MBE
Cricketer. *b:* 16.12.1952, Enterprise, Christ Church, Barbados. Hard hitting lower order right-hand batsman, right-arm fast bowler, gully field. *Teams* Barbados (1975/6 to 1987/8); Somerset (1977–86, 93 matches); South Australia (1982/3, 8 matches). *Tours* West Indies to England 1979 (World Cup), 1980, 1983 (World Cup), 1984, to Australia 1979/80, 1981/2, 1983/4 (not first-class), 1984/5, 1986/7, to New Zealand 1979/80, 1986/7, to Pakistan 1980/1, 1985/6 (not first-class), to Sharjah (not first-class) 1985/6. *Tests* West Indies (1976/7 to 1986/7, 58 matches).
Career batting
214–231–54–2964–104–16.74–1–*ct* 129
Bowling 16333–881–18.53–48–7–8/31
Test batting
58–68–14–672–60–12.44–0–*ct* 42
Bowling 5433–259–20.97–7–0–6/56
Six feet eight inches tall, he used his height to its best advantage and formed one of the formidable array of West Indian fast bowlers of his generation. On his first tour to England in 1980 he topped both Test and first-class bowling tables with 26 wickets, av 14.26, and 49 wickets, av 13.93, respectively. Returning in 1984 he was again very successful with 19 wickets, av 18.62, in the Tests. A major figure in taking Somerset to 'double' champions in 1979 and 1981, he topped the county's Championship averages in both years and in 1981 took 88 wickets, av 15.32. He was awarded an MBE in 1985.

Garnett, Harold Gwyer
Amateur. *b:* 19.11.1879, Aigburth, Liverpool, Lancashire. *d:* 3.12.1917, Marcoing, Cambrai, France. He was killed in action. Brother of F. M. (Europeans). Dashing opening left-hand batsman, slow left-arm bowler, wicket-keeper. *Sch* Clifton. *Teams* Lancashire (1899–1914, 144 matches); Argentine (1911/12). *Tours* MacLaren to Australia 1901/2.
Career batting
152–245–22–5798–139–26.00–5–*ct* 185–*st* 18
Bowling 224–8–28.00–0–0–2/18

He hit 1,000 runs in a season twice (best 1,758, av 35.87, in 1901). He was absent from England for several years, being in business in Argentina, but returned home in 1912.

Garnett, Rev Lionel
Amateur. *b:* 25.12.1843, Wyreside, Lancaster. *d:* 1.5.1912, Belfast, Ireland. Nephew of H. O. Nethercote (Oxford U 1839), brother-in-law of J. C. P. Thompson (Liverpool). Middle order batsman. *Sch* Eton. *Team* Southgate (1864).
Career batting
1–1–1–3–3*–no av–0–*ct* 0
His County cricket was for Cheshire (1862).

Garnett, Thomas Ronald
Amateur. *b:* 1.1.1915, Marple, Cheshire. Opening or middle order right-hand batsman, off break bowler. *Sch* Charterhouse. *Team* Somerset (1935–39, 5 matches).
Career batting
5–8–0–161–75–20.12–0–*ct* 6
He appeared in the Freshmen's match and Seniors' match at Cambridge, but no first-class games. He also played for Wiltshire (1953).

Garnham, Michael Anthony
Cricketer. *b:* 20.8.1960, Johannesburg, South Africa. Middle order right-hand batsman, wicket-keeper. *Teams* Gloucestershire (1979, 3 matches); Leicestershire (1980–88, 73 matches); Essex (1989–92, 95 matches).
Career batting
171–221–46–4956–123–28.32–4–*ct* 361–*st* 31
Bowling 39–0
He also played for Devon (1976–77) and Cambridgeshire (1986–88). He retired from first-class cricket at the end of the 1985 season, being disillusioned with it. In 1988 he played in one first-class game for Leicestershire, and joined Essex in 1989.

Garnier, Rev Edward Southwell
Amateur. *b:* 5.4.1850, Paddington, London. *d:* 8.8.1938, Shropham House, Norfolk. Son of Thomas (Oxford U 1832), brother of T. P. (Hampshire), nephew of John (Oxford U 1832). Opening right-hand batsman, right-hand medium pace round-arm bowler. *Sch* Marlborough. *Team* Oxford U (1871–73, blue 1873).
Career batting
10–18–2–187–66*–11.68–0–*ct* 3
Bowling 60–0
His County cricket was for Shropshire (1871) and Bedfordshire (1876). He was an excellent athlete, both as a hurdler and at throwing the hammer, winning his blue.

Garnier, Rev Thomas Parry
Amateur. *b:* 22.2.1841, Longford, Derbyshire. *d:* 18.3.1898, St Moritz, Switzerland. Son of Thomas (Oxford U 1832), brother of E. S. (Oxford U), nephew of John (Oxford U 1832). Opening or middle order right-hand batsman, good deep field. *Sch* Winchester. *Teams* Oxford U (1861–63, blue all three years); Hampshire (1864, 1 match).
Career batting
13–24–3–287–35–13.66–0–*ct* 4
He also played for Norfolk (1863) and Lincolnshire (1864).

Garofall, Alan Robert
Cricketer. *b:* 1.6.1946, Kingston-upon-Thames, Surrey. Middle order right-hand batsman, right-arm medium pace bowler. *Sch* Latymer Upper. *Team* Oxford U (1966–68, blue 1967–68).
Career batting
27–47–0–874–99–18.59–0–*ct* 19
Bowling 8–0
His County cricket was for Hertfordshire (1970–89). He also won a blue for soccer.

Garrat, William
Professional. *b:* 21.4.1805, Shrewsbury, Shropshire. Sound middle order right-hand batsman. *Team* Nottinghamshire (1835–45, 11 matches).
Career batting
32–58–2–543–41–9.69–0–*ct* 10
Bowling 5–0
His first-class debut was for Nottingham in 1832.

Garratt, Humphry Stone
Amateur. *b:* 12.1.1898, Kingston-upon-Thames, Surrey. *d:* 1.9.1974, Worplesden Hill, Surrey. Lower order batsman, wicket-keeper. *Sch* Haileybury. *Team* Worcestershire (1925–28, 5 matches).
Career batting
5–9–0–111–39–12.33–0–*ct* 3

Garrett, Charles Richard
Amateur. *b:* 3.3.1901, Puri, India. *d:* 16.2.1968, Kenya, in a car accident. Lower order batsman, useful bowler. *Team* Royal Navy (1926–29).
Career batting
4–7–1–70–23–11.66–0–*ct* 5
Bowling 240–7–34.28–0–0–3/124

Garrett, Hubert Frederic
Amateur. *b:* 13.11.1885, Melbourne, Victoria, Australia. *d:* 4.6.1915, near Achi Baba, Gallipoli, Turkey. He was killed in action. Son of T. W. (New South Wales). Lower order right-hand batsman, leg break bowler. *Team* Somerset (1913, 8 matches).
Career batting
11–21–3–220–37*–12.22–0–*ct* 4
Bowling 755–34–22.20–2–1–6/60
He did not appear for Cambridge whilst at the University. His final first-class match was for MCC in 1914.

Garrett, Thomas William
Amateur. *b:* 26.7.1858, Wollongong, New South Wales, Australia. *d:* 6.8.1943, Warrawee, Sydney, New South Wales, Australia. Father of H. F. (Somerset). Lower order right-hand batsman, right-arm fast medium bowler. *Team* New South Wales (1876/7 to 1897/8, 56 matches). *Tours* Australia to England 1878, 1882, 1886, to North America 1878. *Tests* Australia (1876/7 to 1887/8, 19 matches).
Career batting
160–256–29–3673–163–16.18–2–*ct* 81
Bowling 8352–446–18.72–29–4–7/38
Test batting
19–33–6–339–51*–12.55–0–*ct* 7
Bowling 970–36–26.94–2–0–6/78
Of his three tours to England, his most successful was 1882 when he took 118 wickets, av 14.35, in first-class matches. He was also a noted sprinter.

Garrett, William Thomas
Amateur. *b:* 9.1.1876, Camberwell, London. *d:* 16.2.1953, Buckhurst Hill, Essex. Middle order right-hand batsman, change bowler. *Team* Essex (1900–03, 15 matches).
Career batting
15–25–1–516–92–21.50–0–*ct* 4
Bowling 142–1–142.00–0–0–1/72

Garth, Jonathan Digby
Cricketer. *b:* 12.1.1965, Johannesburg, South Africa. Middle order right-hand batsman, right-arm medium pace bowler. *Team* Ireland (1986–89).
Career batting
3–6–0–34–11–5.66–0–*ct* 2
Bowling 68–0

Garthwaite, Clive Charlton
Amateur. *b:* 22.10.1909, Guisborough, Yorkshire. *d:* 20.1.1979, Aylesbury, Buckinghamshire. Twin brother of P. F. (Oxford U). Sound right-hand middle order batsman, right-arm medium pace bowler. *Sch* Wellington. *Team* Army (1930).
Career batting
1–2–0–7–7–3.50–0–*ct* 0
Bowling 22–0

Garthwaite, Peter Fawcitt
Amateur. *b:* 22.10.1909, Guisborough, Yorkshire. Twin brother of C. C. (Army). Lower order right-hand batsman, leg break bowler. *Sch* Wellington. *Team* Oxford U (1929–30, blue 1929).
Career batting
11–15–5–99–31–9.90–0–*ct* 7
Bowling 917–23–39.86–1–0–5/74
He also won a blue for hockey.

Gatacre, Admiral Galfry George Ormond
Amateur. *b:* 11.6.1907, Wooroolin, Queensland, Australia. *d:* 1985, Sydney, New South Wales, Australia. Lower order batsman, bowler. *Team* Royal Navy (1928).
Career batting
1–2–0–19–12–9.50–0–*ct* 0
Bowling 34–1–34.00–0–0–1/24

Gatehouse, Peter Warlow
Professional. *b:* 3.5.1936, Caerphilly, Glamorgan. Lower order right-hand batsman, left-arm fast medium bowler. *Team* Glamorgan (1957–62, 19 matches).
Career batting
19–23–8–85–20–5.66–0–*ct* 3
Bowling 1551–53–29.26–3–1–7/94
A well known rugby footballer, he played for Caerphilly.

Gatting, Michael William, OBE
Cricketer. *b:* 6.6.1957, Kingsbury, Middlesex. Aggressive middle order right-hand batsman, right-arm medium pace bowler, good close field. *Team* Middlesex (1975–92, 311 matches). *Tours* England to Pakistan 1977/8, 1983/4, 1987/8, to New Zealand 1977/8, 1983/4, 1987/8, to West Indies 1980/1, 1985/6, to India and Sri Lanka 1981/2, 1984/5, to Australia 1984/5 (not first-class), 1986/7, 1987/8, to India and Pakistan (World Cup) 1987/8; Middlesex to Zimbabwe 1980/1; England XI to South Africa 1989/90. *Tests* England (1977/8 to 1989, 68 matches).
Career batting
432–676–107–28512–258–50.10–72–*ct* 376
Bowling 4466–154–29.00–2–0–5/34
Test batting
68–117–14–3870–207–37.57–9–*ct* 51
Bowling 317–4–79.25–0–0–1/14
One of the outstanding batsmen of the 1980s, he was a prolific run-getter in County cricket almost from the outset of his first-class career, but after six years of Test cricket his record at the highest level was very moderate, 24 Tests, average 23.53. It was in 1984/5 in India that he finally proved himself at Test level, topping the England averages with 575 runs, av 95.83, and scoring over 1,000 runs on the tour. The following winter in West Indies his Test career was interrupted when his nose was broken batting against Marshall in the first one-day international. He recovered remarkably quickly and was chosen as England's captain for the Second Test of 1986 against India. Leading England against Australia in 1986/7 he had the satisfaction of securing the Ashes, but the following winter, when he led England in Pakistan and New Zealand, was marred by his open disagreement with a Pakistani umpire. However the selectors retained him as captain for the opening of the series against West Indies in 1988. Some unsavoury press attacks on his off the field activity during the First Test led to him being replaced as captain. In 1989/90 he was chosen as the captain of the English side to South Africa and thus banned from Test cricket; the ban ended in 1992.

In 1983 he was appointed captain of Middlesex, Brearley having retired, and has led the county for ten seasons. He has reached 1,000 runs in an English season 14 times, going on to 2,000 three times (best 2,257, av 68.39, in 1984). His highest first-class innings was 258 for Middlesex v Somerset at Bath in 1984 and in Test cricket 207 v India at Madras in 1984/5. To date he has captained England in 23 Tests. He was awarded an OBE in 1987.

Gaukrodger, George Warrington
Professional. *b:* 11.9.1877, Kirkburton, Yorkshire. *d:* 4.1.1938, Low Moor, Bradford, Yorkshire. Middle or lower order right-hand batsman, wicket-keeper. *Team* Worcestershire (1900–10, 114 matches).
Career batting
115–179–46–2241–91–16.84–0–*ct* 169–*st* 62
He played soccer for Ireland.

Gauld, Dr George Ogg
Amateur. *b:* 21.6.1873, Rubislaw, Aberdeen, Scotland. *d:* 16.6.1950, The Park, Nottingham. Lower order right-hand batsman, right-arm fast bowler. *Team* Nottinghamshire (1913–19, 14 matches).
Career batting
14–19–0–350–90–18.42–0–*ct* 9
Bowling 250–5–50.00–0–0–1/11
He captained Nottinghamshire in 1913 and 1914 in the absence through illness of A. O. Jones. He was Hon Secretary of Nottinghamshire 1922–35.

Gaunt, Rev Canon Howard Charles Adie
Amateur. *b:* 13.11.1902, Edgbaston, Warwickshire. *d:* 1.2.1983, Winchester, Hampshire. Middle order right-hand batsman. *Sch* Tonbridge and Charterhouse. *Team* Warwickshire (1919–22, 11 matches).
Career batting
11–20–1–147–32–7.73–0–*ct* 6
He played no first-class matches whilst at Cambridge U, but did win blues for hockey and lawn tennis.

Gaunt, Ronald Arthur
Amateur. *b:* 26.2.1934, York, Western Australia. Lower order left-hand batsman, right-arm fast bowler. *Teams* Western Australia (1955/6 to 1959/60, 29 matches); Victoria (1960/1 to 1963/4, 18 matches). *Tours* Australia to South Africa 1957/8, to New Zealand 1956/7, 1959/60, to England 1961. *Tests* Australia (1957/8 to 1963/4, 3 matches).
Career batting
85–92–33–616–32*–10.44–0–*ct* 31
Bowling 7143–266–26.85–10–0–7/104
Test batting
3–4–2–6–3–3.00–0–*ct* 1
Bowling 310–7–44.28–0–0–3/53
Though he headed the tourists' first-class bowling averages in 1961 with 40 wickets, av 21.12, he appeared in only one Test.

Gauntlett, Rev Gilbert Bernard
Amateur. *b:* 19.9.1936, Dolgelley, Merioneth. Lower order right-hand batsman, wicket-keeper. *Sch* Charterhouse. *Team* Oxford U (1957).
Career batting
1 match, did not bat–*ct* 3

Gavaskar, Sunil Manohar
Cricketer. *b:* 10.7.1949, Bombay, India. Nephew of M. K. Mantri (India), brother-in-law of G. R. Viswanath (India). Excellent opening right-hand batsman, leg break bowler, slip field. *Teams* Bombay (1967/8 to 1986/7); Somerset (1980, 15 matches). *Tours* Indian Universities to Ceylon 1970/1; India to West Indies 1970/1, 1975/6, 1982/3, to England 1971, 1974, 1975 (World Cup), 1979, 1982, 1983 (World Cup), 1986, to Ceylon 1973/4, 1985/6, to New Zealand 1975/6, 1980/1, to Australia 1977/8, 1980/1, 1984/5 (not first-class), 1985/6, to Pakistan 1978/9, 1982/3, 1984/5, to Sharjah (not first-class) 1983/4, 1984/5, 1985/6; Rest of World to Australia 1971/2, to England 1987. *Tests* India (1970/1 to 1986/7, 125 matches).
Career batting
348–563–61–25834–340–51.46–81–*ct* 293
Bowling 1240–22–56.36–0–0–3/43
Test batting
125–214–16–10122–236*–51.12–34–*ct* 108
Bowling 206–1–206.00–0–0–1/34
On his first tour to England in 1971 he hit 1,141 runs, av 43.88, and played in all three Tests. In 1974 his record was 993 runs, av 41.37, and he again appeared in all three Tests, hitting the only century for the Indians in the series at Old Trafford. His performances in 1979 improved even on his previous visits, with 1,062 runs, av 55.89, and an innings of 221 in the Test at the Oval. He captained India on the 1982 tour but was not very successful as a batsman. On his final tour to England in 1986 he played no big innings, but seemed content with what might be described as 'cameo' parts.

By the time he retired from Test cricket he had set records for the most appearances and most hundreds, as well as being the first player to reach 10,000 runs. He made 106 consecutive Test appearances, another record. His highest first-class innings was 340 for Bombay v Bengal at Bombay in 1981/2. The secret of his success was his careful building of each innings, confining himself to the strokes, mainly drives, in which he had most confidence until he had thoroughly mastered the attack. The power behind his shots was most formidable. He retired after the 1987/8 World Cup was played in India. He captained India in 47 Tests. His first-class debut was for Vazir Sultan Colts XI in 1966/7.

Gavin, Norman Leslie
Amateur. *b:* 5.9.1922, Camberwell, London. Tail end left-hand batsman, slow left-arm bowler. *Team* RAF

(1946).
Career batting
1–2–1–52–29–52.00–0–*ct* 1
Bowling 102–3–34.00–0–0–3/76

Gay, David William Maurice
Amateur. *b:* 2.4.1920, Kensington, London. Lower order right-hand batsman, right-arm medium pace bowler. *Sch* Shrewsbury. *Team* Sussex (1949, 2 matches).
Career batting
4–6–1–16–11–3.20–0–*ct* 1
Bowling 288–9–32.00–0–0–4/57

Gay, Leslie Hewitt
Amateur. *b:* 24.3.1871, Brighton, Sussex. *d:* 1.11.1949, Salcombe Hill, Sidmouth, Devon. Cousin of K. J. Key (Surrey). Lower order right-hand batsman, wicket-keeper. *Sch* Brighton and Marlborough. *Teams* Cambridge U (1891–93, blue 1892–93); Somerset (1894, 4 matches); Hampshire (1900, 9 matches). *Tour* Stoddart to Australia 1894/5. *Test* England (1894/5, 1 match).
Career batting
46–80–15–1005–60*–15.46–0–*ct* 69–*st* 20
Test batting
1–2–0–37–33–18.50–0–*ct* 3–*st* 1
His final first-class match was for MCC in 1904. A noted soccer player, he represented both Cambridge and England as goalkeeper.

Geary, Albert Charles Taylor
Professional. *b:* 11.9.1900, Croydon, Surrey. *d:* 23.1.1989, St Peter, Jersey. Lower order right-hand batsman, right-arm medium fast bowler. *Team* Surrey (1922–31, 90 matches).
Career batting
90–90–27–670–40–10.63–0–*ct* 33
Bowling 6068–198–30.64–6–1–6/50

Geary, Frederick William
Professional. *b:* 9.12.1887, Hinckley, Leicestershire. *d:* 8.1.1980, Hinckley, Leicestershire. Lower order batsman, bowler. *Team* Glamorgan (1923, 2 matches).
Career batting
2–4–0–3–2–0.75–0–*ct* 2
Bowling 24–0

Geary, George
Professional. *b:* 9.7.1893, Barwell, Leicestershire. *d:* 6.3.1981, Leicester. Lower order right-hand batsman, right-arm fast medium bowler, good slip field. *Team* Leicestershire (1912–38, 456 matches). *Tours* Joel to South Africa 1924/5; MCC to India, Burma and Ceylon 1926/7, to South Africa 1927/8, to Australia 1928/9; Tennyson to Jamaica 1931/2. *Tests* England (1924–34, 14 matches).
Career batting
549–820–138–13504–122–19.80–8–*ct* 451
Bowling 41339–2063–20.03–125–30–10/18
Test batting
14–20–4–249–66–15.56–0–*ct* 13
Bowling 1353–46–29.41–4–1–7/70
He took 100 wickets in a season 11 times (best 152, av 19.60, in 1929). His best bowling in an innings was 10/18 for Leicestershire v Glamorgan at Pontypridd in 1929.

Geeson, Frederic
Professional. *b:* 23.8.1862, Redmile, Leicestershire. *d:* 2.5.1920, Houghton, Johannesburg, South Africa. Lower order right-hand batsman, right-arm medium pace bowler, also leg breaks, slip field. *Team* Leicestershire (1895–1902, 135 matches).
Career batting
150–250–55–3694–104*–18.94–1–*ct* 138
Bowling 12199–472–25.85–28–7–8/110
His first-class debut was for MCC in 1892, his County cricket originally being for Lincolnshire to where he returned after leaving first-class cricket (1889–1913). In 1901 he took 125 wickets, av 26.64. His bowling action had been condemned in 1900 and as a result he switched to spin.

Gehrs, Donald Raeburn Algernon
Amateur. *b:* 29.11.1880, Port Victor, South Australia. *d:* 25.6.1953, King's Park, Adelaide, South Australia. Middle order right-hand batsman, right-arm slow bowler. *Team* South Australia (1902/3 to 1920/1, 49 matches). *Tours* Australia to New Zealand 1904/5, to England 1905. *Tests* Australia (1903/4 to 1910/11, 6 matches).
Career batting
83–142–12–4377–170–33.66–13–*ct* 71–*st* 4
Bowling 416–8–52.00–0–0–2/9
Test batting
6–11–0–221–67–20.09–0–*ct* 6
Bowling 4–0
He had a very moderate tour of England in 1905.

Gemmill, William Neilson
Amateur. *b:* 14.6.1900, Thio, New Caledonia. *d:* 18.9.1987, Kenfield, Canterbury, Kent. Middle order right-hand batsman, right-arm medium fast bowler. *Sch* King's, Taunton. *Teams* Glamorgan (1921–26, 47 matches); Wales (1923).
Career batting
48–89–2–1243–77–14.28–0–*ct* 31
Bowling 104–0
He first played for Glamorgan (pre first-class) in 1920. He played hockey for Wales.

Genders, William Roy
Amateur. *b:* 21.1.1913, Dore, Derbyshire. *d:* 28.9.1985, Worthing, Sussex. Middle order right-hand batsman, bowler. *Sch* King's School, Ely. *Teams* Derbyshire (1946, 3 matches); Worcestershire (1947–48, 5 matches); Somerset (1949, 2 matches).

Gentry, Jack Sydney Bates

Career batting
10–19–4–245–55*–16.33–0–*ct* 6
Bowling 98–3–32.66–0–0–2/43

He played in trials at Cambridge U, but no first-class games. He was the author of 'League Cricket in England' and books on gardening.

Gentry, Jack Sydney Bates
Amateur. *b:* 4.10.1899, Wanstead, Essex. *d:* 16.4.1978, Loxwood, Sussex. Lower order right-hand batsman, slow left-arm bowler. *Sch* Christ's Hospital. *Teams* Hampshire (1919, 1 match); Surrey (1922–23, 10 matches); Essex (1925, 1 match).
Career batting
12–12–4–68–13–8.50–0–*ct* 3
Bowling 794–36–22.05–0–0–4/36

George, Walter
Professional. *b:* 20.9.1847, Selling, Faversham, Kent. *d:* 2.11.1938, Bell Green, Sydenham, London. Tail end right-hand batsman, left-hand fast or medium round-arm bowler. *Team* Kent (1875, 5 matches).
Career batting
5–8–5–4–2*–1.33–0–*ct* 1
Bowling 315–22–14.31–2–0–7/86

George, William
Professional. *b:* 29.6.1874, Atcham, Shropshire. *d:* 4.12.1933, Selly Oak, Birmingham. Hard hitting middle order right-hand batsman. *Team* Warwickshire (1901–06, 13 matches).
Career batting
13–18–2–342–71–21.37–0–*ct* 8

He also played for Wiltshire (1899) and Shropshire (1900). A noted soccer player, he kept goal for Aston Villa and England.

Gerds, George Fortunato
Amateur. *b:* 27.1.1866, Uitenhage, Cape Province, South Africa. *d:* 26.9.1914, Cape Town, South Africa. Lower order right-hand batsman, wicket-keeper. *Sch* Clifton. *Team* Cambridge U (1887).
Career batting
1–1–0–0–0–0.00–0–*ct* 1–*st* 1

His County cricket was for Hampshire (not first-class, 1886–93). He was an athlete of some note and a useful rugby footballer.

German, Arthur Clive Johnson
Amateur. *b:* 28.6.1905, Ashby-de-la-Zouch, Leicestershire. *d:* 2.2.1968, Aberdeen, Scotland. Nephew of Harry (Leicestershire). Middle order right-hand batsman. *Sch* Repton. *Teams* Leicestershire (1923–24, 3 matches).
Career batting
3–6–0–73–36–12.16–0–*ct* 2

He appeared in the Freshmen's match at Oxford, but no first-class matches. A good soccer player, he captained Oxford in 1927 and appeared in the half back line for Corinthians and Nottingham Forest.

German, Harry
Amateur. *b:* 1.11.1865, Measham, Leicestershire. *d:* 14.6.1945, Charing Cross, London. Uncle of A. C. J. (Leicestershire). Lower order right-hand batsman, wicket-keeper. *Team* Leicestershire (1896–98, 5 matches).
Career batting
5–9–0–69–13–7.66–0–*ct* 0

Gerrans, Philip Simon
Cricketer. *b:* 14.10.1959, Melbourne, Victoria, Australia. Middle order right-hand batsman, right-arm medium pace bowler. *Team* Oxford U (1990–91, blue both years).
Career batting
12–12–1–137–39–12.45–0–*ct* 4
Bowling 1003–17–59.00–0–0–3/86

He was awarded a blue for golf.

Gerrard, Martin James
Cricketer. *b:* 19.5.1967, Southmead, Bristol. Lower order right-hand batsman, left-arm medium fast bowler. *Teams* Gloucestershire (1991–92, 12 matches); Western Transvaal (1991/2).
Career batting
16–19–7–81–42–6.75–0–*ct* 4
Bowling 1016–26–39.07–1–1–6/40

Gerrard, Ronald Anderson
Amateur. *b:* 26.1.1912, Hong Kong. *d:* 22.1.1943, near Tripoli, Libya. Middle order right-hand batsman. *Sch* Taunton. *Team* Somerset (1935, 3 matches).
Career batting
3–5–0–36–18–7.20–0–*ct* 1

He played rugby for England.

Gethin, Stanley John
Amateur. *b:* 16.2.1875, Kidderminster, Worcestershire. *d:* 17.2.1950, Kidderminster, Worcestershire. Brother of W. G. (Worcestershire). Middle order right-hand batsman, right-arm medium pace bowler. *Team* Worcestershire (1900–01, 4 matches).
Career batting
4–7–0–86–41–12.28–0–*ct* 0
Bowling 49–1–49.00–0–0–1/25

Gethin, William George
Amateur. *b:* 4.5.1877, Kidderminster, Worcestershire. *d:* 4.11.1939, Kidderminster, Worcestershire. Brother of S. J. (Worcestershire). Lower order right-hand batsman, right-arm medium pace bowler. *Team* Worcestershire (1921, 1 match).
Career batting
1–2–0–20–19–10.00–0–*ct* 2
Bowling 38–0

Ghavri, Karson Devjibhai
Cricketer. *b:* 28.2.1951, Rajkot, India. Lower order left-hand batsman, left-arm medium, or slow, bowler. *Teams* Saurashtra (1969/70 to 1984/5); Bombay (1973/4 to 1981/2). *Tours* India to Sri Lanka 1973/4,

to England 1975 (World Cup), 1979, to Australia 1977/8, to Pakistan 1978/9, to Australia and New Zealand 1980/1; CCI to Sri Lanka 1972/3; Wadekar to Sri Lanka 1975/6; International XI to Jamaica 1982/3. *Tests* India (1974/5 to 1980/1, 39 matches).
Career batting
159–205–48–4500–102–28.66–1–*ct* 60
Bowling 13117–452–29.01–20–2–7/34
Test batting
39–57–14–913–86–21.23–0–*ct* 16
Bowling 3656–109–33.54–4–0–5/33

He played in all four Tests on the 1979 tour to England, but his record in first-class matches was a modest one – 27 wickets, av 41.55.

Ghazali, Mohammad Ebrahim Zainuddin
Amateur. *b:* 15.6.1924, Gujarat, India. Middle or lower order right-hand batsman, off break bowler. *Teams* Maharashtra (1942/3 to 1947/8); Muslims (1943/4 to 1945/6); Services (1953/4 to 1954/5). *Tours* Pakistan to England 1954; Pakistan Services to Ceylon 1953/4. *Tests* Pakistan (1954, 2 matches).
Career batting
46–68–7–1569–160–25.72–2–*ct* 17
Bowling 2053–61–33.65–2–0–5/28
Test batting
2–4–0–32–18–8.00–0–*ct* 0
Bowling 18–0

Although he appeared in two Tests on the 1954 tour of England, he achieved little in first-class matches either with bat or ball. His first-class debut in Pakistan was in 1948/9.

Ghorpade, Jaysinghrao Mansinghrao
Amateur. *b:* 2.10.1930, Panchgani, Maharashtra, India. *d:* 29.3.1978, Baroda, India. Uncle of F. P. Gaekwad (Baroda), R. P. Gaekwad (Baroda) and S. P. Gaekwad (Baroda). Middle order right-hand batsman, leg break and googly bowler, brilliant deep field. *Team* Baroda (1948/9 to 1965/6). *Tours* India to West Indies 1952/3, to England 1959. *Tests* India (1952/3 to 1959, 8 matches).
Career batting
82–116–13–2631–123–25.54–2–*ct* 33
Bowling 3515–114–30.83–4–0–6/19
Test batting
8–15–0–229–41–15.26–0–*ct* 4
Bowling 131–0

He failed to do himself justice on his single tour to England. At the time of his death he was Chairman of the Indian Selection Committee.

Ghulam Abbas
Cricketer. *b:* 1.5.1947, Delhi, India. Middle order left-hand batsman, slow left-arm bowler. *Teams* Karachi (1962/3 to 1970/1); National Bank (1971/2 to 1972/3); PIA (1973/4 to 1984/5). *Tours* Pakistan to England 1967, to Australia and New Zealand 1964/5, to Ceylon 1964/5; PIA to Zimbabwe 1981/2. *Test* Pakistan (1967, 1 match).
Career batting
102–166–18–5271–276–35.61–9–*ct* 83
Bowling 229–7–32.71–0–0–2/9
Test batting
1–2–0–12–12–6.00–0–*ct* 0

He hit 871 runs, av 34.84, on his 1967 tour to England and appeared in one Test. His highest score was 276 for PIA v Punjab B at Karachi in 1975/6. He scored 1,069 runs, av 56.26, in Pakistan in 1975/6.

Ghulam Ahmed
Amateur. *b:* 4.7.1922, Hyderabad, India. Uncle of Asif Iqbal Razvi (Pakistan and Kent). Lower order right-hand batsman, off break bowler. *Teams* Hyderabad (1939/40 to 1958/9); Muslims (1945/6). *Tours* India to England 1952, to Pakistan 1954/5, to Ceylon 1956/7. *Tests* India (1948/9 to 1958/9, 22 matches).
Career batting
98–126–30–1379–90–14.36–0–*ct* 57
Bowling 9190–407–22.57–32–9–9/53
Test batting
22–31–9–192–50–8.72–0–*ct* 11
Bowling 2052–68–30.17–4–1–7/49

He was easily the most successful bowler on the 1952 tour of England, taking 15 wickets, av 24.73, in the Tests, and in all first-class matches 80 wickets, av 21.92. His best bowling was 9/53 for Hyderabad v Madras at Secunderabad in 1947/8. He captained India in three Tests.

Ghulam Mohammad
Amateur. *b:* 12.7.1898, India. *d:* 21.7.1966, Karachi, Pakistan. Lower order right-hand batsman, left-arm medium pace bowler. *Teams* Muslims (1924/5 to 1931/2); Sind (1934/5 to 1938/9). *Tours* India to England 1932; Vizianagram to Ceylon 1930/1.
Career batting
42–63–7–677–74–12.08–0–*ct* 18
Bowling 2548–99–25.73–1–0–5/114

Although effective on matting wickets in India, he proved useless in England in 1932, taking only three wickets on the tour.

Gibaut, Russel Philip
Cricketer. *b:* 5.3.1963, St Saviour, Jersey. Tail end right-hand batsman, right-arm medium pace bowler. *Team* Oxford U (1983).
Career batting
2–2–0–7–7–3.50–0–*ct* 0

Gibb, Frank
Professional. *b:* 18.1.1868, Wadhurst, Sussex. *d:* 23.3.1957, Hawkenbury, Tunbridge Wells, Kent. Lower order batsman, left-arm fast bowler. *Team* Sussex (1890, 10 matches).
Career batting
10–19–7–41–8–3.41–0–*ct* 2
Bowling 550–9–61.11–0–0–2/140

Gibb, Paul Antony
Amateur, turned professional in 1951. *b:* 11.7.1913, Brandsby, Yorkshire. *d:* 7.12.1977, Guildford, Surrey. Opening or middle order right-hand batsman, wicket-keeper. *Sch* St Edward's, Oxford. *Teams* Scotland (1934–38); Cambridge U (1935–38, blue all four years); Yorkshire (1935–46, 36 matches); Essex (1951–56, 145 matches). *Tours* Cahn to North America 1933 (not first-class); Yorkshire to Jamaica 1935/6; Tennyson to India 1937/8; MCC to South Africa 1938/9, to Australia 1946/7; Commonwealth to India 1953/4. *Tests* England (1938/9 to 1946/7, 8 matches).
Career batting
287–479–33–12520–204–28.07–19–*ct* 425–*st* 123
Bowling 161–5–32.20–0–0–2/40
Test batting
8–13–0–581–120–44.69–2–*ct* 3–*st* 1

His career is unusual in that he obtained a blue at Cambridge and later became a professional cricketer. He hit 1,000 runs in a season five times (best 1,658, av 48.76, in 1938). His only double century was 204 for Cambridge U v Free Foresters at Cambridge in 1938. After leaving County cricket he was on the first-class umpires' list for 10 years (1957–66). For some years before his death he had been a bus driver.

Gibb, Richard Carver
Amateur. *b:* 30.8.1917, Christchurch, Hampshire. Lower order right-hand batsman, left-arm bowler. *Team* Cambridge U (1938).
Career batting
3–4–0–28–17–7.00–0–*ct* 2
Bowling 280–6–46.66–0–0–2/52

Gibbon, Rev John Houghton
Amateur. *b:* 21.8.1847, Gateacre, Liverpool, Lancashire. *d:* 29.4.1883, Willersey, Gloucestershire. Steady middle order right-hand batsman. *Sch* Harrow. *Team* Oxford U (1869, blue).
Career batting
4–6–0–31–17–5.16–0–*ct* 2

He played for Cheshire (1868) and Warwickshire (pre first-class, 1873).

Gibbons, Harold Harry Ian Haywood
Professional. *b:* 8.10.1904, Devonport, Devon. *d:* 16.2.1973, Worcester. Sound opening right-hand batsman, right-arm bowler, fine field. *Team* Worcestershire (1927–46, 380 matches).
Career batting
383–671–57–21087–212*–34.34–44–*ct* 157
Bowling 737–7–105.28–0–0–2/27

He hit 1,000 runs in a season 12 times going on to 2,000 on three occasions (best 2,654, av 52.03, in 1934). His two double hundreds were both for Worcestershire, the higher being 212* v Northamptonshire at Dudley in 1939.

Gibbons, Herbert Gladstone Coe
Professional *b:* 12.3.1905, Langley Hill, Tilehurst, Berkshire. *d:* 13.1.1963, Shirley, Southampton, Hampshire. Lower order right-hand batsman, leg break and googly bowler. *Team* Hampshire (1925–28, 7 matches).
Career batting
7–8–1–70–27–10.00–0–*ct* 1
Bowling 92–0

Gibbs, Arthur Holland Dyer
Amateur. *b:* 15.4.1894, Weston-super-Mare, Somerset. *d:* 29.10.1963, Uphill, Weston-super-Mare, Somerset. Lower order batsman, wicket-keeper. *Team* Somerset (1919–20, 3 matches).
Career batting
3–5–0–66–41–13.20–0–*ct* 4–*st* 2

Gibbs, Joseph Arthur
Amateur. *b:* 25.11.1867, Westminster, London. *d:* 13.5.1899, Marylebone, London. Middle order right-hand batsman. *Sch* Eton. *Team* Somerset (1891–94, 5 matches). *Tour* Hawke to India 1892/3.
Career batting
10–18–1–162–75–9.52–0–*ct* 5

His first match for Somerset (not first-class) was in 1890. His final first-class match was for MCC in 1896. He was the author of a book on the care of cricket grounds.

Gibbs, Lancelot Richard
Professional. *b:* 29.9.1934, Queenstown, Georgetown, British Guiana. Cousin of C. H. Lloyd (Lancashire and West Indies). Lower order right-hand batsman, off break bowler. *Teams* British Guiana/Guyana (1953/4 to 1974/5); Warwickshire (1967–73, 109 matches); South Australia (1969/70, 8 matches). *Tours* West Indies to India and Pakistan 1958/9, 1974/5, to Australia 1960/1, 1975/6, to England 1963, 1966, 1969, 1973, 1975 (World Cup), to India and Ceylon 1966/7, to Australia and New Zealand 1968/9; West Indian XI to England 1964; Rest of World to England 1965, 1967, 1970. *Tests* West Indies (1957/8 to 1975/6, 79 matches).
Career batting
330–352–150–1729–43–8.55–0–*ct* 203
Bowling 27878–1024–27.22–50–10–8/37
Test batting
79–109–39–488–25–6.97–0–*ct* 52
Bowling 8989–309–29.09–18–2–8/38

One of the greatest off spin bowlers, Gibbs was most successful on his first two tours to England, but achieved only moderate figures on his later two visits. His best season with Warwickshire was 1971, when, in all first-class matches, he took 131 wickets, av 18.89. He created a new Test career record in his last Test (v Australia 1975/6) by capturing his 308th wicket. He played for USA v Canada in 1983. He was manager of the 1991 West Indies team to England.

Gibbs, Peter John Keith
Cricketer. *b:* 17.8.1944, Buglawton, Cheshire. Opening right-hand batsman, off break bowler. *Teams* Oxford U (1964–66, blue all three years); Derbyshire (1966–72, 145 matches).
Career batting
178–319–14–8885–138*–29.13–11–*ct* 96
Bowling 321–4–80.25–0–0–2/54
He also played for Staffordshire (1961–73). He hit 1,000 runs in a season five times (best 1,441, av 41.17, in 1970). He is a well-known radio and TV playwright.

Gibbs, Wyatt
Amateur. *b:* 5.5.1830, West Itchenor, Sussex. *d:* 25.5.1891, Bagshot, Surrey. Lower order left-hand batsman, right-hand fast round-arm bowler. *Team* Sussex (1864–65, 5 matches).
Career batting
5–7–3–42–18–10.50–0–*ct* 2
Bowling 180–7–25.71–0–0–3/49

Gibson, Alfred Leonard
Professional. *b:* 13.2.1912, Devon, Jamaica. Hard hitting middle order right-hand batsman. *Team* Leicestershire (1946, 2 matches).
Career batting
2–3–0–17–11–5.66–0–*ct* 0

Gibson, Archibald Lesley
Amateur. *b:* 4.9.1877, Kingsclere, Hampshire. *d:* 29.7.1943, Nakuru, Kenya. Middle order right-hand batsman, right-arm slow bowler, good field. *Sch* Winchester. *Teams* Essex (1895–1910, 23 matches); Up-Country XI, Ceylon (1926/7).
Career batting
25–39–3–504–71–14.00–0–*ct* 9
Bowling 18–0
He resided in Russia 1897–98 and afterwards was a tea planter in Ceylon; his County cricket was therefore very limited. His final first-class match in England was for P. F. Warner's XI in 1919.

Gibson, Arthur Buchwald Edgar
Amateur. *b:* 15.6.1863, Salford, Manchester, Lancashire. *d:* 11.3.1932, Cambridge. Middle order right-hand batsman, right-arm medium pace bowler. *Sch* Cheltenham. *Team* Lancashire (1887, 2 matches). *Tours* Vernon to India 1889/90 (not first-class); Hawke to India 1892/3.
Career batting
14–23–0–311–58–13.52–0–*ct* 4
Bowling 227–16–14.18–0–0–3/24
He emigrated to the colonies soon after his appearances for Lancashire. His final first-class match was for MCC in 1896.

Gibson, Arthur Cracroft
Amateur. *b:* 7.11.1863, Sittingbourne, Kent. *d:* 8.12.1895, Sittingbourne, Kent. Lower order right-hand batsman, right-arm medium pace bowler. *Team* Kent (1883–84, 5 matches).
Career batting
5–8–2–35–17*–5.83–0–*ct* 1
Bowling 50–0

Gibson, Arthur Kenneth
Amateur. *b:* 19.5.1889, Kensington, London. *d:* 28.1.1950, South Side, Edinburgh, Scotland. Middle order batsman. *Team* Somerset (1919, 1 match).
Career batting
5–9–0–139–36–15.44–0–*ct* 0
Bowling 11–0
His first-class debut was for the Royal Navy in 1914 and final first-class match for the same team in 1924. He also played for Hertfordshire (1911–12).

Gibson, Clement Herbert
Amateur. *b:* 23.8.1900, Entre Rios, Argentina. *d:* 31.12.1976, Buenos Aires, Argentina. Lower order right-hand batsman, right-arm fast medium bowler. *Sch* Eton. *Teams* Sussex (1919–26, 26 matches); Cambridge U (1920–21, blue both years); Argentina (1926/7 to 1937/8). *Tours* MCC to Australia and New Zealand 1922/3; South America to England 1932.
Career batting
84–125–34–1369–64–15.04–0–*ct* 53
Bowling 7109–249–28.55–8–2–8/57
Spending most of his life in the Argentine, his appearances in County cricket were very limited. His final first-class match was for MCC in 1939.

Gibson, David
Professional. *b:* 1.5.1936, Mitcham, Surrey. Middle or lower order right-hand batsman, right-arm fast medium bowler. *Team* Surrey (1957–69, 183 matches).
Career batting
185–211–45–3143–98–18.93–0–*ct* 76
Bowling 12266–552–22.22–26–1–7/26
He was also a useful rugby full back. He also played for Berkshire (1976–78). He was Surrey coach 1979–83.

Gibson, Dr Ian
Amateur. *b:* 15.8.1936, Glossop, Derbyshire. *d:* 3.5.1963, Bowdon, Cheshire. He died by his own hand. Middle order right-hand batsman, leg break and googly bowler, good field. *Sch* Manchester GS. *Teams* Oxford U (1955–58, blue all four years); Derbyshire (1957–61, 7 matches).
Career batting
51–92–7–1697–100*–19.96–1–*ct* 29
Bowling 1959–51–38.41–2–0–5/29

Gibson, James Forbes
Amateur. *b:* 14.4.1888, Coatbridge, Lanarkshire, Scotland. *d:* 21.5.1960, Mount Ephraim, Tunbridge Wells, Kent. Lower order batsman, wicket-keeper. *Teams* Scotland (1912); Rangoon Gymkhana

(1926/7); Burma (1926/7).
Career batting
3–6–1–30–21–6.00–0–*ct* 2
Bowling 11–0

Gibson, Sir Kenneth Lloyd
Amateur. *b:* 11.5.1888, Kensington, London. *d:* 14.5.1967, Marylebone, London. Middle order right-hand batsman, wicket-keeper. *Sch* Eton. *Team* Essex (1909–12, 36 matches). *Tour* MCC to Egypt 1909 (not first-class).
Career batting
42–63–6–959–75–16.82–0–*ct* 62–*st* 11
Bowling 9–1–9.00–0–0–1/9
His final first-class match was for the Army in 1920.

Giddins, Edward Simon Hunter
Cricketer. *b:* 20.7.1971, Eastbourne, Sussex. Tail end right-hand batsman, right-arm fast medium bowler. *Sch* Eastbourne. *Team* Sussex (1991–92, 13 matches).
Career batting
13–9–7–29–14*–14.50–0–*ct* 4
Bowling 1043–33–31.60–2–0–5/32

Gidley, Martyn Ian
Cricketer. *b:* 30.9.1968, Leicester. Middle order left-hand batsman, off break bowler. *Teams* Leicestershire (1989–92, 17 matches); Orange Free State (1990/1).
Career batting
21–32–7–559–80–22.36–0–*ct* 11
Bowling 1116–16–69.75–0–0–3/51

Gidney, Brian Bruce
Cricketer. *b:* 6.4.1938, Kingston-upon-Thames, Surrey. Opening right-hand batsman. *Sch* Kingston GS. *Team* Cambridge U (1963).
Career batting
1–2–0–16–9–8.00–0–*ct* 0
He won a blue for hockey.

Giffen, George
Amateur. *b:* 27.3.1859, Norwood, Adelaide, South Australia. *d:* 29.11.1927, Parkside, Adelaide, South Australia. Brother of W. F. (South Australia). Hard hitting middle order right-hand batsman, right-arm medium slow bowler. *Team* South Australia (1877/8 to 1903/4, 64 matches). *Tours* Australia to England 1882, 1884, 1886, 1893, 1896, to North America 1893, 1896. *Tests* Australia (1881/2 to 1896, 31 matches).
Career batting
251–421–23–11758–271–29.54–18–*ct* 194
Bowling 21785–1022–21.31–95–30–10/66
Test batting
31–53–0–1238–161–23.35–1–*ct* 24
Bowling 2791–103–27.09–7–1–7/117
He was most successful on his tours to England and on the last three performed the 'double', having his best record with both bat and ball in 1886–1,424 runs, av 26.86, and 154 wickets, av 17.36. He performed the unique feat in first-class matches of hitting 271 and taking 16 wickets (for 166) in the same match – South Australia v Victoria at Adelaide in 1891/2. His best bowling in an innings was 10/66 for Australian XI v Rest at Sydney in 1883/4. On nine occasions he performed the match 'double' of 100 runs and 10 wickets, though never in England. By many he was regarded as Australia's W. G. Grace. He captained Australia in 4 Tests.

Giffen, Walter Frank
Amateur. *b:* 20.9.1861, Norwood, Adelaide, South Australia. *d:* 28.6.1949, North Unley, Adelaide, South Australia. Brother of George (South Australia). Defensive right-hand batsman, good deep field. *Team* South Australia (1882/3 to 1901/2, 31 matches). *Tour* Australia to England and North America 1893. *Tests* Australia (1886/7 to 1891/2, 3 matches).
Career batting
47–80–6–1178–89–15.91–0–*ct* 23
Bowling 15–0
Test batting
3–6–0–11–3–1.83–0–*ct* 1
He did very little on his tour to England and was not required for the Tests.

Gifford, George Cooper
Amateur. *b:* 17.11.1891, Huntingdon. *d:* 16.9.1972, Huntingdon. Middle order right-hand batsman. *Team* Northamptonshire (1923–29, 14 matches).
Career batting
14–24–0–387–98–16.12–0–*ct* 5
He also played for Huntingdonshire (1927).

Gifford, James
Amateur. *b:* 10.1.1864, Buenos Aires, Argentina. *d:* 18.4.1931, Buenos Aires, Argentina. Middle order right-hand batsman. *Sch* Christ College, Brecon. *Team* MCC (1897–98).
Career batting
5–10–2–143–37–17.87–0–*ct* 0
He played in the North v South series in Argentina.

Gifford, Norman, MBE
Professional. *b:* 30.3.1940, Ulverston, Lancashire. Lower order left-hand batsman, slow left-arm bowler, gully field. *Teams* Worcestershire (1960–82, 541 matches); Warwickshire (1983–88, 139 matches). *Tours* International XI to Rhodesia and Pakistan 1961/2; Worcestershire World Tour (Rhodesia first-class) 1964/5; Commonwealth to Pakistan 1970/1; Rest of World to Australia 1971/2; International Wanderers to Rhodesia 1972/3; MCC to India, Pakistan and Sri Lanka 1972/3; England to Sharjah (not first-class) 1984/5; England B to Sri Lanka 1985/6. *Tests* England (1964–73, 15 matches).
Career batting
710–805–264–7048–89–13.02–0–*ct* 319

Bowling 48731–2068–23.56–93–14–8/28
Test batting
15–20–9–179–25*–16.27–0–*ct* 8
Bowling 1026–33–31.09–1–0–5/55

He took 100 wickets in a season four times (best 133, av 19.66, in 1961). From 1971 to 1980 he captained Worcestershire. He was appointed a Test selector in 1982. He captained Warwickshire 1985–87 and in 1989 was appointed coach to Sussex.

Gifkins, Charles John
Amateur. *b:* 19.2.1856, Thames Ditton, Surrey. Opening right-hand batsman, right-arm fast bowler. *Team* Yorkshire (1880, 2 matches).
Career batting
2–3–0–30–23–10.00–0–*ct* 1

Gilbert, Charles Arthur William
Amateur. *b:* 9.1.1855, Melton Mowbray, Leicestershire. *d:* 28.9.1937, St John's Wood, London. Middle order right-hand batsman, right-arm fast or slow bowler, good field. *Team* Surrey (1877–78, 2 matches).
Career batting
2–4–1–25–17*–8.33–0–*ct* 0

He did not appear in first-class cricket whilst at Oxford, but was a noted athlete, winning his blue. He also played for Wiltshire (1883) and Staffordshire (1894–95).

Gilbert, David Robert
Cricketer. *b:* 29.12.1960, Darlinghurst, Sydney, New South Wales, Australia. Lower order right-hand batsman, right-arm fast medium bowler. *Teams* New South Wales (1983/4 to 1987/8, 43 matches); Tasmania (1988/9 to 1991/2, 38 matches); Gloucestershire (1991, 22 matches). *Tours* Australia to England 1985, to New Zealand 1985/6, to India 1986/7; Young Australia to Zimbabwe 1985/6; New South Wales to Zimbabwe 1987/8. *Tests* Australia (1985 to 1986/7, 9 matches).
Career batting
127–149–53–1374–117–14.31–1–*ct* 34
Bowling 11469–354–32.39–11–1–8/55
Test batting
9–12–4–57–12–7.12–0–*ct* 0
Bowling 843–16–52.68–0–0–3/48

Coming to England with the 1985 Australians, he played in one Test, but was still developing his bowling skills. He was only moderately successful in 1991 for Gloucestershire, when he replaced C. A. Walsh as the County's overseas cricketer. He also played for Lincolnshire (1984).

Gilbert, George Henry Bailey
Amateur. *b:* 2.9.1829, Cheltenham, Gloucestershire. *d:* 16.6.1906, Summer Hill, Sydney, New South Wales, Australia. Half-brother of W. R. (Middlesex and Gloucestershire), cousin of the Graces. Lower order right-hand batsman, right-hand medium pace round-arm bowler. *Teams* Middlesex (1851, 2 matches); New South Wales (1855/6 to 1874/5, 12 matches).
Career batting
18–34–0–283–31–8.32–0–*ct* 13
Bowling 160–16 + 12–10.00–2–1–6/65

He captained New South Wales in the first ever match against Victoria in 1855/6.

Gilbert, Humphrey Adam
Amateur. *b:* 2.6.1886, Malabar Hill, Bombay, India. *d:* 19.7.1960, Bishopstone, Hereford. Lower order right-hand batsman, right-arm medium pace off break bowler. *Sch* Charterhouse. *Teams* Oxford U (1907–09, blue all three years); Worcestershire (1921–30, 72 matches).
Career batting
118–180–65–811–35*–7.05–0–*ct* 59
Bowling 11268–476–23.67–38–8–8/48

He also played for Monmouthshire (1913), Radnorshire and Wiltshire (1919).

Gilbert, John
Professional. *b:* 7.3.1816, Mansfield, Nottinghamshire. *d:* 22.11.1887, Mansfield, Nottinghamshire. Middle order right-hand batsman. *Team* Nottinghamshire (1843–48, 3 matches).
Career batting
4–7–2–115–91–23.00–0–*ct* 4

He scored 91 on his debut, but did little in the few other Nottinghamshire matches in which he played.

Gilbert, John
Professional. *c:* 17.10.1830, Buxted, Sussex. *d:* 28.11.1896, Newick, Sussex. Middle order batsman. *Team* Lord Sheffield's XI (1881).
Career batting
1–1–0–0–0–0.00–0–*ct* 0

He was aged 50 when he played in his only first-class match.

Gilbert, John Dudley Harwood
Amateur. *b:* 8.10.1910, Chellaston, Derbyshire. Opening/middle order right-hand batsman. *Sch* Repton. *Team* Derbyshire (1930–36, 11 matches).
Career batting
11–11–0–106–25–9.63–0–*ct* 2

Gilbert, Walter Raleigh
Amateur, professional in 1886. *b:* 16.9.1853, Strand, London. *d:* 26.7.1924, Calgary, Canada. Half-brother of G. H. B. (Middlesex and New South Wales), cousin of the Graces. Middle order right-hand batsman, right-hand slow round-arm bowler. *Teams* Middlesex (1873–74, 9 matches); Gloucestershire (1876–86, 108 matches). *Tour* Grace to Australia 1873/4 (not first-class).
Career batting
175–296–20–5290–205*–19.16–3–*ct* 160–*st* 6
Bowling 5291–295–17.93–15–1–7/28

In 1886 he emigrated to Canada, after a scandal involving some stealing from a dressing room. His double century was 205* for an England XI v Cambridge U at Fenner's in 1876. He also played for Worcestershire (pre first-class, 1869–70) and Northamptonshire (pre first-class, 1875).

Gilbert, William
Professional. *b:* 4.6.1856, Newick, Sussex. *d:* 4.1.1918, Holborn, London. Lower order right-hand batsman, right-hand fast round arm bowler, moderate field. *Team* Sussex (1879, 1 match).
Career batting
1–2–0–5–5–2.50–0–*ct* 1
Bowling 14–3–4.66–0–0–3/14

Gilby, William
Professional. *b:* 26.7.1834, Leamington Priors, Warwickshire. *d:* 19.3.1905, Wandsworth, London. Tail end right-hand batsman, lob bowler. *Team* Middlesex (1872, 1 match).
Career batting
1–2–1–9–5*–9.00–0–*ct* 0
Bowling 84–2–42.00–0–0–2/70

Gilchrist, Robert Selby Nesbit
Amateur. *b:* 1822. *d:* 9.2.1905, Berwick-on-Tweed, Northumberland. Lower order batsman, bowler. *Team* Gentlemen of Middlesex (1865).
Career batting
1–2–0–2–2–1.00–0–*ct* 0
Bowling 19–0
His County cricket was for Northumberland (1863).

Gilchrist, Roy
Amateur. *b:* 28.6.1934, Seaforth, Jamaica. Tail end right-hand batsman, right-arm fast bowler. *Teams* Jamaica (1956/7 to 1961/2); Hyderabad (1962/3). *Tours* West Indies to England 1957, to India 1958/9. *Tests* West Indies (1957 to 1958/9, 13 matches).
Career batting
42–43–10–258–43*–7.81–0–*ct* 10
Bowling 4342–167–26.00–7–1–6/16
Test batting
13–14–3–60–12–5.45–0–*ct* 4
Bowling 1521–57–26.68–1–0–6/55
He was at his fastest on the 1957 tour to England and noted for the venom of his bouncers, but his figures were not impressive, his 37 wickets costing 31.78 runs each.

Giles, Godwin Merryweather
Professional. *b:* 16.6.1876, Mere, Wiltshire. *d:* 1.6.1955, Sunbury-on-Thames, Middlesex. Middle order batsman, opening bowler. *Team* Gloucestershire (1903, 1 match).
Career batting
1–2–0–8–8–4.00–0–*ct* 1
Bowling 31–0

Giles, Ronald James
Professional. *b:* 17.10.1919, Chilwell, Nottinghamshire. Opening right-hand batsman, slow left-arm bowler. *Team* Nottinghamshire (1937–59, 195 matches).
Career batting
195–310–19–7639–142–26.25–9–*ct* 65
Bowling 1318–23–57.30–0–0–3/1
He hit 1,000 runs in a season three times (best 1,293, av 34.94, in 1955).

Gilfillan, Andrew Douglas
Cricketer. *b:* 21.8.1959, Johannesburg, South Africa. Lower order right-hand batsman, leg break bowler. *Team* Oxford U (1982).
Career batting
3–4–1–40–31–13.33–0–*ct* 0
Bowling 218–2–109.00–0–0–2/177

Gill, Alan
Professional. *b:* 5.8.1940, Underwood, Nottinghamshire. Middle order right-hand batsman, leg break bowler. *Team* Nottinghamshire (1960–65, 53 matches).
Career batting
53–98–7–1756–67–19.29–0–*ct* 18
Bowling 481–10–48.10–0–0–2/28

Gill, Ernest Harry
Professional. *b:* 24.8.1877, Mountsorrel, Leicestershire. *d:* 1.6.1950, Drypool, Hull, Yorkshire. Brother of G. C. (Leicestershire and Somerset). Lower order right-hand batsman, right-arm fast medium bowler. *Team* Leicestershire (1901, 5 matches).
Career batting
5–5–3–23–11*–11.50–0–*ct* 3
Bowling 413–12–34.41–0–0–3/61

Gill, Fairfax
Professional. *b:* 3.9.1883, Wakefield, Yorkshire. *d:* 1.11.1917, Wimereux, Boulogne, France. He died of wounds. Opening or middle order right-hand batsman. *Team* Yorkshire (1906, 2 matches).
Career batting
2–4–0–18–11–4.50–0–*ct* 0

Gill, George Cooper
Professional. *b:* 18.4.1876, Mountsorrel, Leicestershire. *d:* 21.8.1937, Leicester. Brother of E. H. (Leicestershire). Middle or lower order right-hand batsman, right-arm fast medium bowler. *Teams* Somerset (1897–1902, 93 matches); London County (1902–03); Leicestershire (1903–06, 71 matches).
Career batting
171–290–31–4160–100–16.06–1–*ct* 74
Bowling 11793–465–25.36–26–3–9/89
He also played for Staffordshire (1910). His best bowling was 9/89 for Leicestershire v Warwickshire at Edgbaston in 1905.

Gill, James Rupert
Amateur. *b:* 24.9.1911, Dublin, Ireland. Opening right-hand batsman. *Team* Ireland (1948).
Career batting
1–2–0–106–106–53.00–1–*ct* 0
He made a century (106) in his only first-class match v MCC at Dublin.

Gill, Paul
Cricketer. *b:* 31.5.1963, Greenfield, Lancashire. Lower order right-hand batsman, wicket-keeper. *Team* Leicestershire (1986, 8 matches).
Career batting
8–11–4–68–17–9.71–0–*ct* 24

Gill, Peter Nigel
Cricketer. *b:* 12.11.1947, Clayton, Newcastle-under-Lyme, Staffordshire. Middle order right-hand batsman, off break bowler. *Sch* Repton. *Team* Minor Counties (1976–79). *Tour* Minor Counties to Kenya 1977/8 (not first-class).
Career batting
2–4–0–64–20–16.00–0–*ct* 1
His County cricket was for Staffordshire (1966–85).

Gill, Roderick Ian
Amateur. *b:* 21.7.1919, Dublin, Ireland. *d:* 28.10.1983, Dublin, Ireland. Middle order right-hand batsman, right-arm medium pace bowler. *Team* Ireland (1947–50).
Career batting
3–6–1–72–37–14.40–0–*ct* 2
Bowling 128–3–42.66–0–0–2/19

Gillespie, Albert George
Amateur. *b:* 1912. *d:* 7.8.1938, Bury St Edmunds, Suffolk, in a flying accident. Middle order batsman, useful bowler. *Team* Combined Services (1937).
Career batting
1–2–0–11–10–5.50–0–*ct* 0
Bowling 48–1–48.00–0–0–1/33

Gillespie, Derek William
Amateur. *b:* 26.4.1917, Aberford, Leeds, Yorkshire. *d:* 21.8.1981, Oxton, Tadcaster, Yorkshire. Nephew of R. H. (Leveson-Gower's XI). Lower order right-hand batsman, right-arm fast bowler. *Sch* Uppingham. *Team* Cambridge U (1938–39, blue 1939).
Career batting
10–15–3–155–60–12.91–0–*ct* 2
Bowling 683–22–31.04–0–0–4/48

Gillespie, Francis Sydney
Amateur. *b:* 26.3.1889, Upper Norwood, Surrey. *d:* 18.6.1916, Ypres, Belgium. He died of wounds. Middle order left-hand batsman. *Sch* Dulwich. *Team* Surrey (1913, 6 matches).
Career batting
6–11–0–249–72–22.63–0–*ct* 2

Gillespie, Richard Henry
Amateur. *b:* 10.9.1878, Morpeth, Northumberland. *d:* 20.5.1952, Balham, London. Uncle of D. W. (Cambridge U). Lower order batsman, bowler. *Sch* Uppingham. *Team* Leveson-Gower's XI (1909–11).
Career batting
3–4–0–10–8–2.50–0–*ct* 2
Bowling 209–3–69.66–0–0–3/89
His County cricket was for Northumberland (1901–04).

Gillett, Charles Richard
Amateur. *b:* 24.8.1880, Compton, Surrey. *d:* 22.1.1964, Camberley, Surrey. Son of H. H. (Oxford U). Middle order batsman. *Sch* St Edward's, Oxford. *Team* MCC (1920).
Career batting
1–2–0–5–3–2.50–0–*ct* 1

Gillett, Rev Hugh Hodgson
Amateur. *b:* 19.6.1836, Waltham-on-the-Wolds, Melton Mowbray, Leicestershire. *d:* 22.1.1915, Thornbury, Gloucestershire. Father of C. R. (MCC). Opening/middle order right-hand batsman, right-hand medium pace round-arm bowler, deep field. *Sch* Winchester. *Team* Oxford U (1857–58, blue both years).
Career batting
6–7–0–117–53–16.71–0–*ct* 3
Bowling 205–17–12.05–2–0–6/22
His final first-class match was for MCC in 1868. His County cricket was for Leicestershire (pre first-class, 1855–73) and Northamptonshire (pre first-class, 1863–65).

Gillhouley, Keith
Professional. *b:* 8.8.1934, Crosland Moor, Huddersfield, Yorkshire. Lower order right-hand batsman, slow left-arm bowler. *Teams* Yorkshire (1961, 24 matches); Nottinghamshire (1963–66, 83 matches).
Career batting
108–166–28–2051–75*–14.86–0–*ct* 60
Bowling 6922–255–27.14–8–0–7/82

Gilliat, Ivor Algernon Walter
Amateur. *b:* 8.1.1903, Eton, Buckinghamshire. *d:* 22.7.1967, Oxford. Uncle of R. M. C. (Hampshire), brother-in-law of J. Leslie (Oxford U). Lower order right-hand batsman, wicket-keeper. *Sch* Charterhouse. *Team* Oxford U (1922–25, blue 1925).
Career batting
13–21–4–435–70–25.58–0–*ct* 28–*st* 7
Bowling 17–0
An excellent soccer player, he appeared for Oxford U at inside right.

Gilliat, Richard Michael Charles
Cricketer. *b:* 20.5.1944, Ware, Hertfordshire. Nephew of I. A. W. (Oxford U). Middle order left-hand batsman, leg break bowler. *Sch* Charterhouse. *Teams* Oxford U (1964–67, blue all four years);

Hampshire (1966–78, 220 matches). *Tour* MCC to Ceylon 1969/70 (no first-class matches).
Career batting
269–441–46–11589–223*–29.33–18–*ct* 221
Bowling 157–3–52.33–0–0–1/3

He captained Oxford in 1966 and Hampshire 1971 to 1978. He hit 1,000 runs in a season four times (best 1,386, av 39.60, in 1969). His only double hundred was 223* for Hampshire v Warwickshire at Southampton in 1969. A good soccer player he won his blue in 1964 and captained Oxford in 1966, thus having the unusual distinction of leading his University at both sports. He also played for Devon (1965).

Gilligan, Alfred Herbert Harold
Amateur. *b:* 29.6.1896, Denmark Hill, London. *d:* 5.5.1978, Stroud Common, Shamley Green, Surrey. Brother of A. E. R. (Surrey and Sussex) and F. W. (Essex), father-in-law of P. B. H. May (Surrey). Opening/middle order right-hand batsman, leg break bowler, good cover point. *Sch* Dulwich. *Team* Sussex (1919–31, 289 matches). *Tours* Joel to South Africa 1924/5; MCC to New Zealand and Australia 1929/30. *Tests* England (1929/30, 4 matches).
Career batting
321–525–31–8873–143–17.96–1–*ct* 123
Bowling 3872–115–33.66–0–0–4/13
Test batting
4–4–0–71–32–17.75–0–*ct* 0

He captained MCC and England on the tour of 1929/30 and Sussex in 1930. He hit 1,000 runs in a season three times (best 1,186, av 17.70, in 1923). In the same season he completed a record 70 innings.

Gilligan, Arthur Edward Robert
Amateur. *b:* 23.12.1894, Denmark Hill, London. *d:* 5.9.1976, Mare Hill, Pulborough, Sussex. Brother of A. H. H. (Sussex) and F. W. (Essex). Middle/lower order right-hand batsman, right-arm fast medium bowler, brilliant field. *Sch* Dulwich. *Teams* Cambridge U (1919–20, blue both years); Surrey (1919, 3 matches); Sussex (1920–32, 227 matches). *Tours* MCC to South Africa 1922/3, to Australia 1924/5, to India and Ceylon 1926/7. *Tests* England (1922/3 to 1924/5, 11 matches).
Career batting
337–510–55–9140–144–20.08–12–*ct* 180
Bowling 20141–868–23.20–42–4–8/25
Test batting
11–16–3–209–39*–16.07–0–*ct* 3
Bowling 1046–36–29.05–2–1–6/7

He hit 1,000 runs in a season twice (best 1,183, av 21.12, in 1923) and took 100 wickets three times (best 163, av 17.50, in 1923). He performed the 'double' once. He captained England in nine Tests and MCC on the 1924/5 and 1926/7 tours. He was a Test selector in 1926. From 1922 to 1929 he led Sussex. After retiring from first-class cricket, he remained a major figure in Sussex cricket, being Chairman of the County Club for many years and President 1974–75. In 1967/8 he was President of MCC.

Gilligan, Frank William
Amateur. *b:* 20.9.1893, Denmark Hill, London. *d:* 4.5.1960, Wanganui, Wellington, New Zealand. Brother of A. E. R. (Surrey and Sussex) and A. H. H. (Sussex). Middle order right-hand batsman, wicket-keeper. *Sch* Dulwich. *Teams* Oxford U (1919–20, blue both years); Essex (1919–29, 79 matches).
Career batting
129–174–46–3024–110–23.62–1–*ct* 153–*st* 68
Bowling 6–0

He emigrated to New Zealand and was headmaster of Wanganui Grammar School for 19 years. His final first-class match was for MCC in 1935. He captained Oxford in 1920.

Gillingham, Rev Canon Frank Hay
Amateur. *b:* 6.9.1875, Tokyo, Japan. *d:* 1.4.1953, Monaco. Middle order right-hand batsman, wicket-keeper. *Sch* Dulwich. *Team* Essex (1903–28, 181 matches). *Tour* Tennyson to Jamaica 1926/7.
Career batting
210–352–24–10050–201–30.64–19–*ct* 111–*st* 1
Bowling 13–0

His best season was 1908 when he made 1,033 runs, av 39.73. His only double century was 201 for Essex v Middlesex at Lord's in 1904. He was a noted preacher and after-dinner speaker. He commentated on some of the pre-1940 Tests on the wireless.

Gillott, Eric Kenneth
Cricketer. *b:* 15.4.1951, Waiuku, Auckland, New Zealand. Tail end right-hand batsman, slow left-arm bowler. *Team* Northern Districts (1971/2 to 1978/9). *Tour* New Zealand to England 1973.
Career batting
31–37–17–172–22–8.60–0–*ct* 9
Bowling 2493–81–30.77–2–0–6/79

His bowling was completely ineffective on his 1973 tour to England and he did not appear in the Tests. He played for Buckinghamshire in 1976.

Gilman, James
Amateur. *b:* 17.3.1879, Marylebone, London. *d:* 14.9.1976, Shoreham-by-Sea, Sussex. Middle order right-hand batsman, right-arm slow bowler, good field. *Sch* St Paul's. *Teams* Middlesex (1900–01, 5 matches); Cambridge U (1901–02, blue 1902); London County (1900–04).
Career batting
41–67–8–977–72*–16.55–0–*ct* 21
Bowling 138–3–46.00–0–0–2/74

He also played for Northumberland (1906–11). A good athlete, he represented Cambridge in the mile.

Gilmour, Gary John
Cricketer. *b:* 26.6.1951, Waratah, New South Wales, Australia. Middle order left-hand batsman, left-arm

fast medium bowler, excellent close field. *Team* New South Wales (1971/2 to 1979/80, 42 matches). *Tours* Australia to New Zealand 1973/4, 1976/7, to England 1975; International Wanderers to South Africa 1975/6. *Tests* Australia (1973/4 to 1976/7, 15 matches).
Career batting
75–120–18–3126–122–30.64–5–*ct* 68
Bowling 7345–233–31.52–6–0–6/85
Test batting
15–22–1–483–101–23.00–1–*ct* 8
Bowling 1406–54–26.03–3–0–6/85

Although he only appeared in one Test on the 1975 English tour, he performed usefully with both bat and ball. He scored 122 on debut for New South Wales v South Australia at Sydney in 1971/2.

Gilroy, George Bruce
Amateur. *b:* 16.9.1889, Clatto House, Cupar, Fife, Scotland. *d:* 15.7.1916, Corbie-sur-Somme, France. He was mortally wounded. Lower order batsman, wicket-keeper. *Sch* Winchester. *Team* Oxford U (1909).
Career batting
1–1–1–2–2*–no av–0–*ct* 0

Gilson, Ronald Louis Desormeaux
Amateur. *b:* 23.12.1907, Klip Rug, Kokstad, Cape Province, South Africa. *d:* 9.10.1973, Kokstad, Cape Province, South Africa. Lower order batsman, useful bowler. *Team* Cambridge U (1930).
Career batting
2–3–1–38–17*–19.00–0–*ct* 4

He won a blue for lacrosse.

Gimblett, Harold
Professional. *b:* 19.10.1914, Bicknoller, Somerset. *d:* 30.3.1978, Dewlands Park, Verwood, Dorset. He died by his own hand. Hard hitting opening right-hand batsman, right-arm medium pace bowler, good outfield. *Team* Somerset (1935–54, 329 matches). *Tours* MCC to India 1939/40 (tour cancelled); Commonwealth to India and Ceylon 1950/1. *Tests* England (1936–39, 3 matches).
Career batting
368–673–37–23007–310–36.17–50–*ct* 246–*st* 1
Bowling 2124–41–51.80–0–0–4/10
Test batting
3–5–1–129–67*–32.25–0–*ct* 1

He hit 1,000 runs in a season 12 times plus once overseas, and reached 2,000 twice (best 2,134, av 39.51, in 1952). His highest innings was 310 for Somerset v Sussex at Eastbourne in 1948 and he exceeded 200 on one other occasion. On his first-class debut for Somerset v Essex at Frome he made 123 in 80 minutes, reaching his 100 in 63 minutes. He also played for Dorset (1959).

Gimson, Christopher
Amateur. *b:* 24.12.1886, Leicester. *d:* 8.11.1975, Leicester. Middle order right-hand batsman. *Sch* Oundle and Stoneygate. *Teams* Cambridge U (1908); Leicestershire (1921, 8 matches).
Career batting
9–17–1–175–40–10.93–0–*ct* 4
Bowling 52–1–52.00–0–0–1/20

He spent much of his life in the Indian Civil Service.

Gittins, Albert Edward
(registered as A. E. Gittings at death)
Professional. *b:* 12.9.1897, Southport, Lancashire. *d:* 6.10.1977, Ladywood, Birmingham. Lower order right-hand batsman, right-arm medium pace bowler. *Team* Warwickshire (1919, 2 matches).
Career batting
2–3–0–2–2–0.66–0–*ct* 1
Bowling 67–4–16.75–0–0–2/17

He is in *Wisden* wrongly as A. E. Giddings.

Gladdon, Frederick
Professional. *b:* 9.6.1881. Lower order batsman, bowler. *Team* Hampshire (1905, 1 match).
Career batting
1–2–0–1–1–0.50–0–*ct* 0
Bowling 44–0

Gladwin, Christopher
Cricketer. *b:* 10.5.1962, East Ham, Essex. Opening left-hand batsman, right-arm medium pace bowler. *Teams* Essex (1981–87, 67 matches); Derbyshire (1989, 4 matches).
Career batting
71–122–7–3080–162–26.78–1–*ct* 33
Bowling 71–0

He scored 1,396 runs, av 33.23, in 1984. He also played for Suffolk (1988–90).

Gladwin, Clifford
Professional. *b:* 3.4.1916, Doe Lea, Derbyshire. *d:* 9.4.1988, Chesterfield, Derbyshire. Son of Joseph (Derbyshire). Lower order right-hand batsman, right-arm fast medium bowler. *Team* Derbyshire (1939–58, 332 matches). *Tour* MCC to South Africa 1948/9. *Tests* England (1947–49, 8 matches).
Career batting
374–510–148–6283–124*–17.35–1–*ct* 134
Bowling 30265–1653–18.30–101–18–9/41
Test batting
8–11–5–170–51*–28.33–0–*ct* 2
Bowling 571–15–38.06–0–0–3/21

He took 100 wickets in a season 12 times (best 152, av 19.19, in 1952). In 1949 he was only 86 runs short of performing the 'double'. His most famous match was the Durban Test of 1948/9 when he ran a leg bye off the final ball of the game to bring England victory.

Gladwin, Joseph
Professional. *b:* 6.9.1890, Doe Lea, Derbyshire. *d:* 8.9.1962, Chesterfield, Derbyshire. Father of Clifford (Derbyshire). Lower order right-hand batsman, right-arm fast medium bowler. *Team* Derbyshire (1914–19, 3 matches).
Career batting
3–5–2–8–5*–2.66–0–*ct* 3
Bowling 20–1–20.00–0–0–1/15

Glassford, John
Cricketer. *b:* 20.7.1946, Sunderland, Co Durham. Lower order right-hand batsman, right-arm fast medium bowler. *Team* Warwickshire (1969, 2 matches).
Career batting
2–1–0–0–0–0.00–0–*ct* 1
Bowling 161–5–32.20–0–0–2/9
He also played for Durham (pre first-class, 1968–74).

Gleeson, John William
Cricketer. *b:* 14.3.1938, Kyogle, New South Wales, Australia. Lower order right-hand batsman, leg break and googly bowler. *Teams* New South Wales (1966/7 to 1972/3, 35 matches); Eastern Province (1974/5). *Tours* Australia to New Zealand 1966/7, to England 1968, 1972, to Ceylon, India and South Africa 1969/70; Robins to South Africa 1973/4. *Tests* Australia (1967/8 to 1972, 29 matches).
Career batting
116–137–38–1095–59–11.06–0–*ct* 58
Bowling 10729–430–24.95–22–2–7/52
Test batting
29–46–8–395–45–10.39–0–*ct* 17
Bowling 3367–93–36.20–3–0–5/61
He did well in the first-class matches on the 1968 tour – 58 wickets, av 20.65, but managed little in the Tests. He was not so successful in 1972.

Glendenen, John David
Cricketer. *b:* 20.6.1965, Middlesbrough, Yorkshire. Opening right-hand batsman, right-arm medium pace bowler. *Team* Durham (1992, 17 matches).
Career batting
17–28–1–607–117–22.48–1–*ct* 5
He first played for Durham (pre first-class) in 1988 and hit 200* for Durham v Victoria in 1991. He scored 117 on first-class debut in Durham's initial first-class match v Oxford U at Oxford in 1992.

Glenister, Clement Edward
Amateur. *b:* 23.7.1897, Watford, Hertfordshire. *d:* 24.5.1968, Bovingdon, Hertfordshire. Lower order right-hand batsman, slow right-arm bowler. *Sch* Berkhamsted. *Team* Royal Navy (1924–29).
Career batting
5–9–0–104–49–11.55–0–*ct* 1
Bowling 245–9–27.22–0–0–2/39
He was an England amateur soccer international.

Glenn, Michael
Cricketer. *b:* 14.6.1956, Belper, Derbyshire. Lower order right-hand batsman, right-arm fast medium bowler. *Team* Derbyshire (1975–76, 7 matches).
Career batting
7–7–4–23–11*–7.66–0–*ct* 1
Bowling 398–6–66.33–0–0–3/36

Glennie, Mervin Stephen
Amateur. *b:* 23.10.1918, Tours, France. *d:* 16.1.1986, Hadley Common, Hertfordshire. Opening right-hand batsman, wicket-keeper. *Sch* Sherborne. *Team* Cambridge U (1939).
Career batting
3–5–0–19–11–3.80–0–*ct* 2–*st* 1
His final first-class match was for MCC in 1947.

Glennie, Rev Reginald Gerard
Amateur. *b:* 11.11.1864, Blore, Staffordshire. *d:* 24.10.1953, Worcester. Son of J. D. (Cambridge U 1848). Opening/middle order right-hand batsman. *Sch* King's, Canterbury. *Team* Oxford U (1886).
Career batting
2–4–0–5–2–1.25–0–*ct* 1
His County cricket was for Staffordshire (1885).

Glennon, Joseph Edward
Professional. *b:* 17.10.1889, Whitwick, Leicestershire. *d:* 26.6.1926, Moorhead, Sheffield, Yorkshire. Middle order batsman. *Team* Leicestershire (1921, 2 matches).
Career batting
2–4–0–12–7–3.00–0–*ct* 0
He played soccer for Sheffield U and Grimsby.

Glerum, Herman Wilhelm
Amateur. *b:* 28.8.1911, Amsterdam, Netherlands. Middle order right-hand batsman, right-arm medium pace off break bowler. *Team* Free Foresters (1957).
Career batting
1–2–0–1–1–0.50–0–*ct* 0
Bowling 32–3–10.66–0–0–2/16
He was a well-known cricketer in Holland.

Glover, Alfred Charles Stirrup
Amateur. *b:* 19.4.1872, Sideway, Longton, Stoke-on-Trent, Staffordshire. *d:* 22.5.1949, Kenilworth, Warwickshire. Middle order right-hand batsman, right-arm medium pace bowler. *Sch* Repton. *Team* Warwickshire (1895–1909, 149 matches).
Career batting
151–230–28–5187–124–25.67–7–*ct* 81
Bowling 1578–49–32.20–1–0–5/21
He also played for Staffordshire (1893–94). He first played for Warwickshire (pre first-class) in 1892. He hit 1,011 runs, av 40.44, in 1904. He captained Warwickshire in 1908 and 1909.

Glover, Edward Robert Kenneth
Amateur. *b:* 19.7.1911, Worcester. *d:* 23.3.1967, Cardiff, Glamorgan. Brother-in-law of M. J. L. Turnbull

(Glamorgan). Lower order right-hand batsman, fast medium bowler. *Sch* Sherborne. *Team* Glamorgan (1932–38, 47 matches).
Career batting
47–73–23–406–62–8.12–0–*ct* 18
Bowling 4284–118–36.30–3–0–5/79
He was a useful rugby footballer with Glamorgan Wanderers and later a well-known sports journalist.

Glover, Trevor Richardson
Cricketer. *b:* 26.11.1951, Lancaster, Lancashire. Opening right-hand batsman, off break bowler. *Sch* Lancaster RGS. *Team* Oxford U (1973–75, blue all three years).
Career batting
22–42–1–769–117–18.75–2–*ct* 13
Bowling 12–0
He captained Oxford in 1975.

Glynn, Brian Thomas
Professional. *b:* 27.4.1940, Birmingham. Middle order right-hand batsman, off break bowler. *Team* Warwickshire (1959–61, 2 matches).
Career batting
2–3–1–13–7–6.50–0–*ct* 0

Goatly, Edward Garnett
Professional. *b:* 3.12.1882, Twickenham, Middlesex. *d:* 12.2.1958, Brighton, Sussex. Middle order right-hand batsman, slow left-arm bowler, moderate field. *Team* Surrey (1901–14, 126 matches).
Career batting
126–198–21–4419–147*–24.96–3–*ct* 22
Bowling 733–19–38.57–0–0–4/48
He was the dressing room attendant at the Oval from 1919 to 1939.

Gobey, Stanley Clarke
Amateur. *b:* 18.6.1916, Doxey, Stafford. *d:* 20.11.1992, Harpole, Northampton. Lower order left-hand batsman, right-arm medium pace bowler. *Sch* Wycliffe. *Team* Warwickshire (1946, 2 matches).
Career batting
2–3–0–2–2–0.66–0–*ct* 0
Bowling 9–0

Godambe, Shankarrao Ramachandra
Amateur. *b:* 1.3.1899, Bombay, India. *d:* 6.12.1969, Bombay, India. Lower order right-hand batsman, right-arm medium pace bowler. *Teams* Bombay (1926/7 to 1939/40); Hindus (1920/1 to 1941/2); Gujarat (1934/5 to 1937/8). *Tours* India to England 1932; Bombay to Ceylon 1925/6; Vizianagram to Ceylon 1930/1.
Career batting
50–74–22–848–62–16.30–0–*ct* 49
Bowling 2355–103–22.80–4–1–6/32
He achieved almost nothing on his single tour to England.

Goddard, George Fergusson
Cricketer. *b:* 19.5.1938, Edinburgh, Scotland. Lower order right-hand batsman, off-break bowler. *Team* Scotland (1960–80).
Career batting
22–33–5–371–39–13.25–0–*ct* 8
Bowling 1094–41–26.68–2–1–8/34

Goddard, John Douglas Claude, OBE
Amateur. *b:* 21.4.1919, Fontabelle, St Michael, Barbados. *d:* 26.8.1987, Paddington, London. Middle order left-hand batsman, right-arm medium pace off break bowler, excellent short leg. *Team* Barbados (1936/7 to 1957/8). *Tours* West Indies to India, Pakistan and Ceylon 1948/9, to England 1950, 1957, to Australia and New Zealand 1951/2, to New Zealand 1955/6. *Tests* West Indies (1947/8 to 1957, 27 matches).
Career batting
111–145–32–3769–218*–33.35–5–*ct* 94
Bowling 3845–146–26.33–4–0–5/20
Test batting
27–39–11–859–83*–30.67–0–*ct* 22
Bowling 1050–33–31.81–1–0–5/31
Goddard captained West Indies on both the 1950 and 1957 tours of England – on both he was more important as captain than as all-rounder, but performed usefully with bat and ball when required. In all he led West Indies in 22 Tests. His only first-class double century was 218* for Barbados v Trinidad at Bridgetown in 1943/4.

Goddard, Thomas William John
Professional. *b:* 1.10.1900, Gloucester. *d:* 22.5.1966, Gloucester. Lower order right-hand batsman, right-arm fast bowler until 1927, then off break for the remainder of his career. *Team* Gloucestershire (1922–52, 558 matches). *Tours* MCC to South Africa 1930/1, 1938/9. *Tests* England (1930–39, 8 matches).
Career batting
593–775–217–5234–71–9.37–*ct* 312
Bowling 59116–2979–19.84–251–86–10/113
Test batting
8–5–3–13–8–6.50–0–*ct* 3
Bowling 588–22–26.72–1–0–6/29
He took 100 wickets in a season 16 times and on four occasions went on to exceed 200 (best 248, av 16.76, in 1937). His 238, av 17.30, in 1947, when he was 46 years old, should also be noted. His best bowling in an innings was 10/113 for Gloucestershire v Worcestershire at Cheltenham in 1937, and he took nine wickets in an innings an additional eight times (all for Gloucestershire).

Goddard, Trevor Leslie
Amateur. *b:* 1.8.1931, Durban, South Africa. Opening left-hand batsman, left-arm fast medium bowler. *Teams* Natal (1952/3 to 1969/70); North East Transvaal (1966/7 to 1967/8). *Tours* South Africa to Eng-

land 1955, 1960, to Australia and New Zealand 1963/4; Commonwealth to Rhodesia 1962/3. *Tests* South Africa (1955 to 1969/70, 41 matches).
Career batting
179–297–19–11279–222–40.57–26–*ct* 175
Bowling 11563–534–21.65–24–1–6/3
Test batting
41–78–5–2516–112–34.46–1–*ct* 48
Bowling 3226–123–26.22–5–0–6/53

On his 1955 tour of England he hit 1,163 runs, av 30.60, and took 60 wickets, av 21.90, and in 1960, 1,377 runs, av 37.21, and 73 wickets, av 19.71. Thus he was one of the leading all-rounders on both tours. He captained South Africa in 13 Tests and on the 1963/4 Tour. His final first-class match in England was for MCC in 1962.

Godfrey, Rev Charles John Melville
Amateur. *b:* 24.11.1862, Upper Clapton, London. *d:* 28.9.1941, Great Chesterford, Essex. Lower order right-hand batsman, right-arm fast bowler. *Sch* Magdalen College School. *Teams* Oxford U (1882–85); Sussex (1885–92, 10 matches).
Career batting
18–34–7–179–20–6.62–0–*ct* 8
Bowling 801–33–24.27–2–0–5/22

He was a leading figure in London Club cricket in the 1890s.

Godfrey, John Frederick
Professional. *b:* 18.8.1917, Garsington, Headington, Oxfordshire. Tail end right-hand batsman, right-arm fast medium bowler. *Team* Hampshire (1939–47, 12 matches).
Career batting
12–19–5–61–25*–4.35–0–*ct* 1
Bowling 753–15–50.20–0–0–4/116

He also played for Oxfordshire (1948–49) and Cambridgeshire (1950–56).

Godfrey, Lt Gen Sir William Wellington
Amateur. *b:* 2.4.1880, Newry, Co Down, Ireland. *d:* 18.5.1952, Tavistock, Devon. Opening right-hand batsman. *Sch* Dulwich. *Team* Royal Navy (1912).
Career batting
1–2–0–30–30–15.00–0–*ct* 2–*st* 1

Godsell, Richard Thomas
Amateur. *b:* 9.1.1880, Stratford Court, Stroud, Gloucestershire. *d:* 11.4.1954, Bromley, Kent. Opening right-hand batsman. *Sch* Clifton. *Teams* Cambridge U (1903–04, blue 1903); Gloucestershire (1903–10, 51 matches). *Tour* MCC to North America 1905.
Career batting
61–115–5–1492–111–13.56–1–*ct* 24
Bowling 8–0

Godwin, Cuthbert Blair
Amateur. *b:* 16.10.1891, Frenchay, Bristol. *d:* 23.10.1969, Clifton, Bristol. Lower order right-hand batsman, slow right-arm bowler. *Sch* Winchester. *Team* Somerset (1926, 2 matches).
Career batting
2–4–0–8–5–2.00–0–*ct* 1
Bowling 72–1–72.00–0–0–1/66

Gofton, Robert Paul
Cricketer. *b:* 10.9.1968, Scarborough, Yorkshire. Middle order right-hand batsman, right-arm medium pace bowler. *Team* Leicestershire (1992, 5 matches).
Career batting
5–8–1–142–75–20.28–0–*ct* 2
Bowling 348–6–58.00–0–0–4/81

Gold, Cecil Argo
Amateur. *b:* 3.6.1887, St Pancras, London. *d:* 3.7.1916, Ovillers, France. He was killed in action. Middle order batsman. *Sch* Eton. *Team* Middlesex (1907, 1 match).
Career batting
1–2–1–0–0*–0.00–0–*ct* 0

He appeared in the Freshmen's match at Oxford, but no first-class matches. He also played for Berkshire (1906).

Goldie, Christopher Frederick Evelyn
Cricketer. *b:* 2.11.1960, Johannesburg, South Africa. Lower order right-hand batsman, wicket-keeper. *Sch* St Pauls. *Teams* Cambridge U (1981–82, blue both years); Hampshire (1983–85, 3 matches). *Tour* MCC to North America 1982 (not first-class).
Career batting
23–24–3–302–77–14.38–0–*ct* 35–*st* 9

Goldie, Kenneth Oswald
Amateur. *b:* 19.9.1882, Toungoo, Burma. *d:* 14.1.1938, Madras, India. Middle order right-hand batsman, right-arm fast bowler, good outfield. *Sch* Wellington. *Teams* Sussex (1900–11, 64 matches); London County (1901); Europeans (1913/14 to 1920/1); Gentlemen of India (1902/3). *Tour* MCC to North America 1907.
Career batting
86–139–7–3114–140–23.59–4–*ct* 90–*st* 2
Bowling 2205–65–33.92–2–0–5/80

Being in the Indian Army, his County cricket was fairly limited. He was a noted polo player.

Golding, Andrew Kenneth
Cricketer. *b:* 5.10.1963, Colchester, Essex. Lower order right-hand batsman, slow left-arm bowler. *Teams* Essex (1983, 1 match); Cambridge U (1984–88, blue 1984 and 1986).
Career batting
17–27–6–403–47–19.19–0–*ct* 6
Bowling 1647–18–91.50–0–0–3/51

He also played for Suffolk (1990–92). He reappeared in emergency for the University in 1988, having left in 1986.

Goldney, G. H.
(*see under* Hone-Goldney, G. H.)

Goldring, Stephen
Cricketer. *b:* 18.11.1932, Portsmouth, Hampshire. Tail end right-hand batsman, right-arm fast bowler. *Team* Combined Services (1964).
Career batting
1–2–2–23–14*–no av–0–*ct* 0
Bowling 43–0

Goldsmith, George
Amateur. *b:* 7.8.1850, Brighton, Sussex. *d:* 5.4.1916, Hanwell, Middlesex. Lower order right-hand batsman, right-hand fast bowler. *Sch* Brighton GS. *Teams* Kent (1875, 1 match); Sussex (1878–79, 2 matches).
Career batting
3–6–4–9–3*–4.50–0–*ct* 2
Bowling 71–1–71.00–0–0–1/38
He was Secretary to Sussex CCC 1881–88.

Goldsmith, Steven Clive
Cricketer. *b:* 19.2.1964, Ashford, Kent. Middle order right-hand batsman, right-arm medium pace bowler. *Teams* Kent (1987, 2 matches); Derbyshire (1988–92, 73 matches).
Career batting
75–118–12–2646–127–24.96–2–*ct* 37
Bowling 1571–29–54.17–0–0–3/42
He scored 1,071 runs, av 30.60, in 1988.

Goldstein, Frederick Steven
Cricketer. *b:* 14.10.1944, Bulawayo, Rhodesia. Opening right-hand batsman, off break bowler. *Teams* Oxford U (1966–69, blue all four years); Northamptonshire (1969, 10 matches); Transvaal (1969/70 to 1970/1); Western Province (1971/2 to 1977/8).
Career batting
89–163–4–4810–155–30.25–2–*ct* 62
Bowling 53–1–53.00–0–0–1/3
He captained Oxford in 1968 and 1969.

Gomes, Hilary Angelo
Cricketer. *b:* 13.7.1953, Arima, Trinidad. Brother of S. A. (Trinidad) and Gregory (East Trinidad). Middle order left-hand batsman, right-arm medium pace or off break bowler, good field. *Teams* Trinidad (1971/2 to 1987/8); Middlesex (1973–76, 42 matches). *Tours* West Indies to England 1976, 1983 (World Cup), 1984, to India 1978/9, 1983/4, to Sri Lanka 1978/9, to Australia 1979/80, 1981/2, 1983/4 (not first-class), 1984/5, 1986/7, to New Zealand 1979/80, 1986/7, to Pakistan 1980/1, 1985/6 (not first-class), to Sharjah (not first-class) 1985/6, 1986/7. *Tests* West Indies (1976 to 1986/7, 60 matches).
Career batting
231–370–50–12982–200*–40.56–32–*ct* 77
Bowling 4208–107–39.32–0–0–4/22
Test batting
60–91–11–3171–143–39.63–9–*ct* 18
Bowling 930–15–62.00–0–0–2/20
On the 1976 tour to England he hit 1,393 runs, av 48.03, and played in two Tests (1,435, av 47.83, in all first-class matches). His highest score was 200* for West Indians v Queensland at Brisbane in 1981/2.

Gomez, Gerald Ethridge
Amateur. *b:* 10.10.1919, Belmont, Port of Spain, Trinidad. Son of J. E. (Trinidad), father of G. P. (North Trinidad). Middle order right-hand batsman, right-arm medium pace bowler. *Team* Trinidad (1937/8 to 1955/6). *Tours* West Indies to England 1939, 1950, to India, Pakistan and Ceylon 1948/9, to Australia and New Zealand 1951/2. *Tests* West Indies (1939 to 1953/4, 29 matches).
Career batting
126–182–27–6764–216*–43.63–14–*ct* 92
Bowling 5052–200–25.26–5–2–9/24
Test batting
29–46–5–1243–101–30.31–1–*ct* 18
Bowling 1590–58–27.41–1–1–7/55
He had a modest tour of England in 1939, but in 1950 was second only to Worrell as the all-rounder of the side and hit 1,116 runs, av 42.92, in addition to taking 55 wickets, av 25.58. His highest score was 216* for Trinidad v Barbados at Port of Spain in 1942/3 and his best bowling 9/24 for West Indies v South Zone at Madras in 1948/9. His final first-class match in England was for MCC in 1957. He captained West Indies in one Test. He was an active member of the West Indies Board of Control and also in emergency umpired in one Test. He played soccer for Trinidad.

Gomm, Brian Arthur
Amateur. *b:* 24.6.1918, Castle Cary, Somerset. Lower order right-hand batsman, left-arm medium pace bowler. *Team* Somerset (1939, 2 matches).
Career batting
2–3–0–7–5–2.33–0–*ct* 2
Bowling 21–0

Gooch, Graham Alan, OBE
Cricketer. *b:* 23.7.1953, Whipps Cross, Leytonstone, Essex. Cousin of G. J. Saville (Essex). Aggressive opening right-hand batsman, right-arm medium pace bowler, slip field. *Teams* Essex (1973–92, 322 matches); Western Province (1982/3 to 1983/4). *Tours* England to Australia 1978/9, 1979/80, 1990/1, to India 1979/80, 1981/2, 1988/9 (tour cancelled), 1989/90 (not first-class), to West Indies 1980/1, 1985/6, 1989/90, to Sri Lanka 1981/2, to India and Pakistan (World Cup) 1987/8, to Pakistan 1987/8, to New Zealand 1990/1 (not first-class), 1991/2, to Australia and New Zealand (World Cup) 1991/2; SAB England XI to South Africa 1981/2. *Tests* England

(1975–92, 99 matches).
Career batting
484–816–66–36126–333–48.16–99–*ct* 478
Bowling 8034–231–34.77–3–0–7/14
Test batting
99–179–6–7573–333–43.77–17–*ct* 96
Bowling 894–22–40.63–0–0–3/39

After two Tests against Australia in 1975, he gained a regular place in the England team during the summer of 1978 and topped the Test averages against New Zealand. The following winter's tour to Australia, in which he played in all six Tests, was one of promise rather than achievement, save in the final match. An attractive stroke-maker, who scores all round the wicket, his Test career came to a temporary halt when he agreed to tour South Africa in 1981/2. His rehabilitation came on the 1985/6 tour to West Indies, when like everyone, save Gower, he failed to come to terms with the fast bowlers. After Gower had lost the selectors' confidence and Gatting signed for South Africa, Gooch found himself captaining England to the West Indies in 1989/90. A broken hand allowed him to play in only two Tests; he had, however, enough time to surprise his critics and he has continued as England's captain for 28 Tests to the end of the 1992 English season. In 1990, playing in the six Tests (three each v New Zealand and India) he hit 1,058 runs, av 96.18, including 333 and 123 v India at Lord's.

He has scored 1,000 runs in an English season 16 times, going on to 2,000 four times (best 2,746, av 101.70, in 1990). In 1990 he also completed 12 nnings of 100 or more. He was appointed captain of Essex in 1986, resigning after the 1987 season because he felt his batting form was affected, but returning to the captaincy in 1988. In 1991 he was awarded an OBE.

Gooch, Peter Anthony
Cricketer. *b:* 2.5.1949, Timperley, Cheshire. Lower order left-hand batsman, right-arm fast medium bowler. *Sch* Wyggeston GS. *Teams* Lancashire (1970, 4 matches).
Career batting
4–3–1–0–0*–0.00–0–*ct* 3
Bowling 252–6–42.00–0–0–4/52

He also played for Cheshire (1971) and Buckinghamshire (1976–79).

Good, Antony John
Cricketer. *b:* 10.11.1952, Kumasi, Gold Coast. Tail end right-hand batsman, right-arm fast medium bowler. *Sch* Worksop. *Team* Lancashire (1973–76, 8 matches).
Career batting
8–8–2–10–6–1.66–0–*ct* 1
Bowling 482–17–28.35–1–0–5/62

He also played for Cheshire (1977–79).

Good, Bartholomew
Professional. *b:* 20.1.1812, Market Rasen, Lincolnshire. *d:* 12.3.1848, Kensington, London, of consumption. Middle order left-hand batsman, left-hand slow round-arm bowler. *Teams* Nottinghamshire (1831–43, 16 matches); Hampshire (1844, 1 match).
Career batting
68–124–14–1154–82–10.49–0–*ct* 26
Bowling 207–6+21–34.50–0–0–3/84

His final first-class match was for MCC in 1847.

Good, Dennis Cunliffe
Amateur. *b:* 29.8.1926, Leeds, Yorkshire. Lower order right-hand batsman, right-arm fast medium bowler. *Sch* Denstone. *Teams* Worcestershire (1946, 1 match); Glamorgan (1947, 3 matches).
Career batting
4–7–3–54–21–13.50–0–*ct* 1
Bowling 300–8–37.50–0–0–2/34

Goodacre, William Bennett
Amateur. *b:* 26.2.1873, Nottingham. *d:* 29.6.1948, Manor Farm, Sproxton, Leicestershire. Middle order right-hand batsman, useful bowler. *Team* Nottinghamshire (1898–1903, 43 matches).
Career batting
43–66–4–1169–104*–18.85–1–*ct* 27
Bowling 440–12–36.66–0–0–3/30

Goodall, Harry Hornby
Amateur. *b:* 17.1.1877, Nottingham. *d:* 20.2.1961, Beeston, Nottinghamshire. Middle order right-hand batsman. *Team* Nottinghamshire (1902–05, 5 matches).
Career batting
5–7–1–92–26–15.33–0–*ct* 1

An architect, he designed the Dixon Memorial Gates at Trent Bridge.

Goodall, John
Professional. *b:* 19.6.1863, Westminster, London. *d:* 20.5.1942, Watford North, Hertfordshire. Middle order batsman. *Team* Derbyshire (1895–96, 2 matches).
Career batting
2–3–0–38–32–12.66–0–*ct* 2

He also played for Hertfordshire (1905–07). He was a noted soccer player, appearing for England, Preston North End, Derby County, New Brighton and Glossop.

Goodden, Cecil Phelips
Amateur. *b:* 12.11.1879, Compton House, Sherborne, Dorset. *d:* 5.11.1969, Hays, Sedgehill, Wiltshire. Middle order right-hand batsman, moderate field. *Sch* Harrow. *Teams* MCC (1900–03).
Career batting
3–5–0–27–9–5.40–0–*ct* 1
Bowling 37–0

He did not appear in first-class cricket whilst at Cambridge. His County cricket was for Dorset (1903–22).

Gooder, Leonard Montague Harry
Professional. *b:* 11.2.1876, Paddington, London. *d:* 26.11.1928, Kilburn, London. Lower order right-hand batsman, slow right-arm bowler. *Team* Surrey (1901–05, 19 matches).
Career batting
19–29–2–312–35–11.55–0–*ct* 7
Bowling 1862–54–34.48–3–1–5/66

Goodfellow, Anthony
Amateur. *b:* 8.1.1940, Seale, Surrey. Middle order left-hand batsman, off break bowler. *Sch* Marlborough. *Team* Cambridge U (1960–62, blue 1961–62).
Career batting
21–42–1–941–81–22.95–0–*ct* 6
Bowling 4–0

Goodfellow, G.
Professional. Middle order batsman, change bowler. *Team* London United (1879).
Career batting
1–2–0–4–4–2.00–0–*ct* 0
Bowling 31–1–31.00–0–0–1/24

Goodhew, William
Professional. *b:* 24.5.1828, Chislehurst, Kent. *d:* 1.5.1897, Canterbury, Kent. Hard hitting middle order right-hand batsman, right-hand medium pace round-arm bowler. *Team* Kent (1854–66, 69 matches).
Career batting
86–160–19–1616–70–11.46–0–*ct* 40
Bowling 424–26–16.30–1–0–7/40

Goodland, Edward Stanley
Amateur. *b:* 22.9.1883, North Town, Taunton, Somerset. *d:* 12.1.1974, Bicknoller, Somerset. Middle order right-hand batsman. *Sch* Taunton. *Team* Somerset (1908–09, 4 matches).
Career batting
4–6–1–47–42*–9.40–0–*ct* 2

Goodliffe, Guy Vernon
Amateur. *b:* 17.9.1883, Kensington, London. *d:* 29.5.1963, Londonderry, Ireland. Lower order batsman, bowler. *Sch* Charterhouse. *Team* Oxford U (1904).
Career batting
1–1–0–0–0–0.00–0–*ct* 1
Bowling 21–2–10.50–0–0–1/0
His County cricket was for Berkshire (1901–07). He won a blue for soccer.

Goodman, Percy Arnold
Amateur. *b:* 3.10.1874, Sandford, St Philip, Barbados. *d:* 25.4.1935, Elbank, St Lawrence, Christ Church, Barbados. Brother of C. E. (Barbados), G. A. (Barbados) and W. E. (Barbados and British Guiana). Middle order right-hand batsman, right-arm medium pace bowler. *Team* Barbados (1891/2 to 1912/13). *Tours* West Indies to England 1900 (not first-class), 1906.
Career batting
40–66–7–1824–180–30.91–5–*ct* 47
Bowling 1155–85+3–13.58–5–1–7/18
He was the leading all-rounder in Barbados at the turn of the century and on the 1906 tour to England he headed the tourists first-class batting averages with 607 runs, av 31.94.

Goodreds, William Arthur
Amateur. *b:* 3.11.1920, Pensnett, Staffordshire. Lower order right-hand batsman, right-arm fast medium bowler. *Team* Worcestershire (1952, 1 match).
Career batting
1–1–1–4–4*–no av–0–*ct* 0
Bowling 48–0

Goodson, Donald
Amateur. *b:* 15.10.1932, Eastwell, Leicestershire. Lower order right-hand batsman, right-arm medium pace bowler. *Team* Leicestershire (1950–53, 9 matches).
Career batting
9–13–4–36–22*–4.00–0–*ct* 1
Bowling 394–7–56.28–0–0–3/43

Goodway, Cyril Clement
Amateur. *b:* 10.7.1909, Smethwick, Staffordshire. *d:* 22.5.1991, Birmingham. Lower order right-hand batsman, wicket-keeper. *Team* Warwickshire (1937–47, 40 matches). *Tours* Cahn to Ceylon 1936/7, to New Zealand 1938/9 (no first-class matches in either tour).
Career batting
40–66–12–434–37*–8.03–0–*ct* 43–*st* 22
He also played for Staffordshire (1932–36). He was chairman of Warwickshire CCC 1972–83.

Goodwin, Douglas Edward
Cricketer. *b:* 2.5.1938, Clontarf, Dublin, Ireland. Lower order right-hand batsman, right-arm fast medium bowler. *Team* Ireland (1965–73).
Career batting
11–16–2–188–39–13.42–0–*ct* 2
Bowling 583–20–29.15–1–0–5/46

Goodwin, Francis Herbert
Professional. *b:* 4.1.1866, Rainhill, Lancashire. *d:* 20.1.1931, Garston, Lancashire. Lower order left-hand batsman, slow left-arm bowler. *Team* Lancashire (1894, 3 matches).
Career batting
3–6–1–14–10–2.80–0–*ct* 0
Bowling 47–0

Goodwin, Fred
Professional. *b:* 28.6.1933, Heywood, Lancashire. Lower order right-hand batsman, right-arm fast med-

ium bowler. *Team* Lancashire (1955–56, 11 matches).
Career batting
11–10–4–47–21*–7.83–0–*ct* 7
Bowling 715–27–26.48–1–0–5/35

He played soccer for Manchester United, Leeds United and Scunthorpe at left half.

Goodwin, George William
Amateur. *b:* 7.9.1898, Chesterton, Staffordshire. Lower order batsman, slow left-arm bowler. *Sch* Rossall. *Team* Derbyshire (1921, 8 matches).
Career batting
8–16–1–224–53–14.93–0–*ct* 1
Bowling 205–7–29.28–0–0–4/23

Goodwin, Harold James
Amateur. *b:* 31.1.1886, Edgbaston, Warwickshire. *d:* 24.4.1917, Arras, France. He was killed in action. Middle order right-hand batsman, leg break bowler, excellent field. *Sch* Marlborough. *Teams* Cambridge U (1906–08, blue 1907–08); Warwickshire (1907–12, 19 matches).
Career batting
39–67–4–1255–101–19.92–1–*ct* 33
Bowling 2092–86–24.32–5–1–7/33

He captained Warwickshire in 1910. A noted hockey player, he appeared for Cambridge U and England.

Goodwin, Harry Smyth
Amateur. *b:* 30.9.1870, Merthyr Tydfil, Glamorgan. *d:* 13.11.1955, Christ's Hospital, Horsham, Sussex. Middle order right-hand batsman. *Sch* Rossall. *Team* Gloucestershire (1896–1907, 31 matches).
Career batting
31–50–6–546–46–12.40–*ct* 20

Goodwin, Keith
Cricketer. *b:* 25.6.1938, Oldham, Lancashire. Lower order right-hand batsman, wicket-keeper. *Team* Lancashire (1960–74, 122 matches). *Tour* Rest of World to Pakistan 1973/4.
Career batting
124–153–43–636–23–5.78–*ct* 229–*st* 28

Goodwin, Thomas Jeffrey
Professional. *b:* 22.1.1929, Bignall End, Staffordshire. Nephew of A. Lockett (Minor Counties). Lower order left-hand batsman, left-arm fast medium bowler, good close field. *Team* Leicestershire (1950–59, 136 matches).
Career batting
136–167–80–474–23*–5.44–0–*ct* 40
Bowling 10108–335–30.17–15–2–8/81

Goodwyn, Canon Frederick Wyldman
Amateur. *b:* 20.1.1850, Calicut, India. *d:* 23.4.1931, St Leonards-on-Sea, Sussex. Middle order right-hand batsman, excellent deep field. *Sch* Clifton. *Team* Gloucestershire (1871–73, 3 matches).
Career batting
3–3–0–69–38–23.00–0–*ct* 0

He did not appear in any first-class matches whilst at Oxford, but rowed for his College. He also played for Somerset (pre first-class, 1871).

Goonasekera, Yohan
Cricketer. *b:* 8.11.1957, Colombo, Ceylon. Middle order left-hand batsman, left-arm medium, or slow, bowler. *Team* Sri Lanka (1980/1 to 1986/7). *Tours* Sri Lanka to India 1980/1, to England 1981, to Australia and New Zealand 1982/3. *Tests* Sri Lanka (1982/3, 2 matches).
Career batting
12–17–2–445–79*–29.66–0–*ct* 12
Bowling 98–3–32.66–0–0–2/36
Test batting
2–4–0–48–23–12.00–0–*ct* 6

Goonatilleke, Hettiarachige Mahes
Cricketer. *b:* 16.8.1952, Kegalla, Ceylon. Solid opening right-hand batsman, wicket-keeper. *Team* Sri Lanka (1975/6 to 1982/3). *Tours* Sri Lanka to India 1975/6, 1976/7, 1982/3, to England 1981, to Pakistan 1981/2; Arosa Sri Lankan XI to South Africa 1982/3. *Tests* Sri Lanka (1981/2 to 1982/3, 5 matches).
Career batting
26–39–7–430–56–13.43–0–*ct* 36–*st* 18
Test batting
5–10–2–177–56–22.12–0–*ct* 10–*st* 3

Goonesena, Gamini
Professional, then amateur from 1954. *b:* 16.2.1931, Colombo, Ceylon. Middle order right-hand batsman, leg break bowler, good outfield. *Teams* Ceylon (1947/8 to 1961/2); Nottinghamshire (1952–64, 94 matches); Cambridge U (1954–57, blue all four years); New South Wales (1960/1 to 1963/4, 7 matches). *Tours* Ceylon to Pakistan 1949/50; Swanton to West Indies 1955/6; Cavaliers to West Indies 1964/5; International XI to India, Pakistan and Ceylon 1967/8.
Career batting
194–304–37–5751–211–21.53–3–*ct* 108
Bowling 16431–674–24.37–41–8–8/39

He hit 1,000 runs in a season twice (best 1,380, av 28.75, in 1955) and took 100 wickets in a season twice (best 134, av 21.05, in 1955). He achieved the 'double' twice. His only double century was for Cambridge U v Oxford U at Lord's in 1957. His final first-class match was for Free Foresters in 1968, when he took 10 for 87 in the match. He captained Cambridge in 1957.

Gopalan, Morappakam Joysam
Amateur. *b:* 6.6.1909, Morappakam, India. Middle/lower order right-hand batsman, right-arm fast medium bowler. *Teams* Madras (1926/7 to 1951/2); Hindus (1934/5). *Tour* India to England 1936. *Test* India (1933/4, 1 match).

Career batting
78–133–16–2916–101*–24.92–1–*ct* 49
Bowling 4695–194–24.20–9–3–7/57
Test batting
1–2–1–18–11*–18.00–0–*ct* 3
Bowling 39–1–39.00–0–0–1/39

Madras and Ceylon/Sri Lanka competed annually for the Gopalan Trophy which is named after him. He played hockey for India.

Gopinath, Coimbatarao Doraikannu
Amateur. *b:* 1.3.1930, Madras, India. Middle order right-hand batsman, right-arm medium pace off break bowler. *Team* Madras (1949/50 to 1962/3). *Tours* India to England 1952, to Pakistan 1954/5; Madras to Ceylon 1953/4, 1956/7, 1958/9. *Tests* India (1951/2 to 1959/60, 8 matches).
Career batting
83–119–18–4259–234–42.16–9–*ct* 50
Bowling 389–14–27.78–0–0–3/15
Test batting
8–12–1–242–50*–22.00–0–*ct* 2
Bowling 11–1–11.00–0–0–1/11

On his single tour to England he found conditions difficult and had a very modest return. His highest score was 234 for Madras v Mysore at Coimbatore in 1958/9.

Goram, Andrew Lewis
Cricketer. *b:* 13.4.1964, Bury, Lancashire. Middle order left-hand batsman, right-arm medium pace bowler. *Team* Scotland (1989–91).
Career batting
2–3–0–48–32–16.00–0–*ct* 3
Bowling 78–2–39.00–0–0–1/16

He played soccer as goalkeeper for Oldham Athletic, Hibernian, Glasgow Rangers and Scotland.

Gordon, Alan
Cricketer. *b:* 29.3.1944, Coventry, Warwickshire. Middle order right-hand batsman, right-arm slow medium bowler, good slip field. *Sch* King Henry VIII, Coventry. *Team* Warwickshire (1966–71, 34 matches).
Career batting
34–59–4–891–65–16.20–0–*ct* 35
Bowling 1–0

Gordon, Charles
Amateur. *b:* 25.12.1814, Finsbury, London. *d:* 27.7.1899, Bedford. Opening or middle order right-hand batsman, slow round-arm bowler, good field. *Team* Middlesex (1851–62, 3 matches).
Career batting
27–46–5–493–33*–12.02–0–*ct* 13
Bowling 1 wicket (no analysis)–0–0–1/?

He was a noted cricketer in London for some 20 years and the 'crack of the once-famous Clapton Club'. His first-class debut was for Gentlemen of England 1844.

Gordon, Brig-Gen Charles Steward
(later Gordon-Steward)
Amateur. *b:* 8.9.1849, Oakleaze, Gloucestershire. *d:* 24.3.1930, Nottington House, Dorset. Opening right-hand batsman, slow under-arm bowler. *Sch* Marlborough. *Teams* Victoria (1869/70, 1 match); Gloucestershire (1870–75, 13 matches).
Career batting
14–21–0–504–121–24.00–1–*ct* 8
Bowling 202–8–25.25–0–0–3/67

His single first-class match (in which he scored 121 v New South Wales at Melbourne) in Australia occurred when he was stationed there with his regiment. He also played for Dorset (1867–71).

Gordon, Herbert Pritchard
Amateur. *b:* 13.9.1898, Stanmore Hall, Bridgnorth, Shropshire. *d:* 17.10.1965, Elm Grove, Brighton, Sussex. Middle order right-hand batsman, right-arm medium pace bowler. *Sch* Malvern. *Team* Worcestershire (1923–24, 7 matches).
Career batting
7–13–1–157–68*–13.08–0–*ct* 6

He played in trials at Cambridge U, but not in first-class matches.

Gordon, John Harvey
Amateur. *b:* 15.6.1886, Reigate, Surrey. *d:* 23.4.1933, Charlottesville, Virginia, USA. Middle order right-hand batsman, change bowler. *Sch* Winchester. *Teams* Oxford U (1906–07, blue both years); Surrey (1906–07, 3 matches).
Career batting
21–39–1–796–117–20.94–1–*ct* 12
Bowling 117–2–58.50–0–0–2/8

He emigrated to the United States about 1908, and appeared for USA v Canada in 1911. He won a blue for golf.

Gordon-Lennox, Lord Bernard Charles
Amateur. *b:* 1.5.1878, Westminster, London. *d:* 10.11.1914, Kleinzillebeke, Belgium. He was killed in action. Third son of the Duke of Richmond, great-grandson of A. F. Greville (MCC), great-nephew of Lord Charles Lennox (MCC). Middle order batsman. *Sch* Eton. *Team* Middlesex (1903, 1 match). *Tour* I Zingari to Egypt 1914 (not first-class).
Career batting
1–1–0–0–0–0.00–0–*ct* 1

He scored many runs in military cricket.

Gordon-Walker, Rupert Adam
Cricketer. *b:* 10.8.1961, Moniaive, Dumfries, Scotland. Lower order left-hand batsman, wicket-keeper. *Team* Oxford U (1981).
Career batting
3–5–1–19–12–4.75–0–*ct* 3–*st* 2

Gore, Adrian Clements
Amateur. *b:* 14.5.1900, Dunoon, Argyll, Scotland. *d:* 7.6.1990, Sellinge, Kent. Lower order right-hand batsman, right-arm fast medium bowler. *Sch* Eton. *Team* Army (1921–32).
Career batting
16–20–5–142–32*–9.46–0–*ct* 11
Bowling 1139–52–21.90–3–0–8/46

Gore, Francis William George
Amateur. *b:* 22.6.1855, Newton St Loe, Somerset. *d:* 17.7.1938, Westminster, London. Brother-in-law of H. A. Milles (Kent) and Viscount Throwley (Kent). Middle order batsman. *Sch* Harrow. *Team* I Zingari (1881).
Career batting
1–2–1–0–0*–0.00–0–*ct* 2

Gore, Hugh Edmond Ivor
Cricketer. *b:* 18.6.1953, St John's, Antigua. Lower order right-hand batsman, left-arm fast medium bowler. *Teams* Leeward Islands (1972/3 to 1978/9); Somerset (1980, 11 matches).
Career batting
34–41–12–382–67–13.17–0–*ct* 14
Bowling 1917–57–33.63–1–0–5/66

Gore, Spencer William
Amateur. *b:* 10.3.1850, Wimbledon Common, Surrey. *d:* 19.4.1906, Ramsgate, Kent. Nephew of F. G. B. Ponsonby (Surrey), S. C. B. Ponsonby (Surrey and Middlesex) and J. G. B. Ponsonby (MCC), brother-in-law of W. A. Smith-Masters (Kent), son-in-law of A. Cowburn (Oxford U 1841). Middle order right-hand batsman, right-hand fast round-arm bowler, good cover point. *Sch* Harrow. *Team* Surrey (1874–75, 2 matches).
Career batting
5–9–1–75–36–9.37–0–*ct* 3
Bowling 93–1–93.00–0–0–1/9

His final first-class match was for Gentlemen of the South in 1879. He also played for Dorset (1871) and Wiltshire (1877). He was well-known as a lawn tennis player, being English Champion in 1877.

Gorell, Lord R. (*see under* Barnes, R. G.)

Gorman, Shaun Rodney
Cricketer. *b:* 28.4.1965, Middlesbrough, Yorkshire. Middle order right-hand batsman, off break bowler. *Sch* St Peter's, York. *Team* Cambridge U (1985–87, blue 1985 and 1987).
Career batting
22–35–9–370–43–14.23–0–*ct* 11
Bowling 649–5–129.80–0–0–1/27

Gornall, James Parrington
Amateur. *b:* 22.9.1899, Farnborough, Hampshire. *d:* 13.11.1983, Lower Froyle, Hampshire. Middle order right-hand batsman, right-arm medium pace bowler. *Sch* Christ's Hospital. *Team* Hampshire (1923, 1 match).
Career batting
4–8–0–149–33–18.62–0–*ct* 1
Bowling 16–0

He appeared in the Freshmen's match at Cambridge, but no first-class matches. His first-class debut was for the Royal Navy in 1921 and his last first-class match for the same team in 1924.

Gorringe, Allan Lindsay
Amateur. *b:* 20.1.1884, Eastbourne, Sussex. *d:* 22.11.1918, Repton, Derbyshire. Middle order batsman. *Team* Sussex (1905, 4 matches).
Career batting
4–6–0–46–16–7.66–0–*ct* 0

He also played for Cambridgeshire (1914). He played in trials at Cambridge U, but not in first-class matches.

Gorringe, Hubert Maurice
Amateur. *b:* 30.1.1886, Eastbourne, Sussex. *d:* 28.8.1958, Hove, Sussex. Middle order batsman. *Team* Sussex (1920, 2 matches).
Career batting
2–4–1–49–29–16.33–0–*ct* 1

Goschen, Sir William Edward
Amateur. *b:* 18.7.1847, Oberlosnitz, Saxony. *d:* 20.5.1924, Chelsea, London. Uncle of G. R. Wood (Somerset) and E. H. Hardcastle (Kent). Middle order right-hand batsman, wicket-keeper. *Sch* Rugby. *Team* Oxford U (1868–69).
Career batting
3–5–0–10–4–2.00–0–*ct* 1

He won a blue for royal tennis.

Gosling, Cecil Henry
Amateur. *b:* 22.2.1910, Barrington Hall, Hatfield-Broad Oak, Essex. *d:* 19.5.1974, Barrington Hall, Hatfield-Broad Oak, Essex. Nephew of R. C. (Essex). Middle order right-hand batsman. *Sch* Eton. *Teams* Oxford U (1929); Essex (1930, 2 matches).
Career batting
5–8–0–132–37–16.50–0–*ct* 3

He won a blue for fives. He was Deputy Lieutenant of Essex in 1949.

Gosling, Robert Cunliffe
Amateur. *b:* 15.6.1868, Hassobury, Farnham, Essex. *d:* 8.4.1922, Hassobury, Farnham, Essex. Uncle of C. H. (Essex), R. J. R. Remnant (Minor Counties) and P. F. Remnant (Minor Counties), nephew of G. J. Spencer-Smith (Hampshire) and O. Spencer-Smith (Hampshire). Stylish middle order right-hand batsman, right-arm slow bowler, good field. *Sch* Eton. *Teams* Cambridge U (1888–90, blue all three years); Essex (1894–96, 4 matches).
Career batting
26–48–5–584–61–13.58–0–*ct* 18
Bowling 11–0

He first played for Essex (pre first-class) in 1888. He was Essex President 1915–18. A noted all-round sportsman, he also won his blue for soccer and went on to play for England. He was donor of the Arthur Dunn Cup.

Gothard, Edward James
Amateur. *b:* 1.10.1904, Burton-on-Trent, Staffordshire. *d:* 17.1.1979, Birmingham. Lower order right-hand batsman, right-arm medium pace bowler. *Team* Derbyshire (1947–48, 45 matches).
Career batting
45–63–19–543–50–12.34–0–*ct* 10
Bowling 730–18–40.55–0–0–3/84
He captained Derbyshire in 1947 and 1948 and was later Hon Secretary (1960–62 and jointly 1972–73) and Hon Treasurer (1968–71) to the County Club. He also played for Staffordshire (1927).

Goudge, Rev William Henry
Amateur. *b:* 29.10.1877, Highworth, Wiltshire. *d:* 31.5.1967, Cheltenham, Gloucestershire. Opening right-hand batsman. *Sch* Bath College. *Team* Royal Navy (1919–23).
Career batting
5–10–0–191–58–19.10–0–*ct* 3
His County cricket was for Wiltshire (1897–99).

Gough, Darren
Cricketer. *b:* 18.9.1970, Barnsley, Yorkshire. Lower order right-hand batsman, right-arm medium fast bowler. *Team* Yorkshire (1989–92, 41 matches). *Tour* Yorkshire to South Africa 1991/2.
Career batting
41–47–14–532–72–16.12–0–*ct* 7
Bowling 3105–79–39.30–1–0–5/41

Gough-Calthorpe, Hon F. S.
(*see under* Calthorpe, Hon F. S. G.)

Gould, Anthony Victor Endersby
Cricketer. *b:* 22.2.1944, Windsor, Berkshire. Opening/middle order right-hand batsman, off break bowler. *Sch* Ardingly. *Team* Cambridge U (1964–66).
Career batting
13–24–0–241–38–10.04–0–*ct* 3
Bowling 16–1–16.00–0–0–1/10

Gould, Ian James
Cricketer. *b:* 19.8.1957, Taplow, Buckinghamshire. Middle order left-hand batsman, wicket-keeper. *Teams* Middlesex (1975 to 1980/1, 90 matches); Auckland (1979/80); Sussex (1981–90, 195 matches). *Tours* International XI to Pakistan 1980/1; Middlesex to Zimbabwe 1980/1; England to Australia 1982/3, to New Zealand 1982/3 (not first-class).
Career batting
297–399–63–8756–128–26.05–4–*ct* 536–*st* 67
Bowling 365–7–52.14–0–0–3/10
He captained Sussex in 1987. He played in 18 one-day Internationals for England.

Gould, Thomas
Professional. *b:* 26.9.1863, Brassington, Derbyshire. *d:* 30.3.1948, Burton-on-Trent, Staffordshire. Lower order batsman, change bowler. *Team* Derbyshire (1896–97, 7 matches).
Career batting
7–10–2–63–16*–7.87–0–*ct* 5
Bowling 225–9–25.00–0–0–4/45
He played soccer for Stockport County.

Goulder, Alfred
Professional. *b:* 16.8.1907, Attercliffe, Sheffield, Yorkshire. *d:* 11.6.1986, Sheffield, Yorkshire. Lower order left-hand batsman, slow left-arm bowler. *Team* Yorkshire (1929, 2 matches).
Career batting
2–1–0–3–3–3.00–0–*ct* 0
Bowling 90–3–30.00–0–0–2/21

Goulding, Sir William Basil
Amateur. *b:* 4.11.1909, Dublin, Ireland. *d:* 16.1.1982, Dargle, Enniskerry, Co Wicklow, Ireland. Son-in-law of W. T. Monckton (Combined U). Lower order right-hand batsman, wicket-keeper. *Sch* Winchester. *Team* Ireland (1934).
Career batting
1–2–1–0–0*–0.00–0–*ct* 0
An all-round sportsman, he represented Ireland at squash and won his blue for soccer at Oxford.

Gouldstone, Mark Roger
Cricketer. *b:* 3.2.1963, Bishop's Stortford, Hertfordshire. Middle order right-hand batsman, right-arm medium pace bowler. *Team* Northamptonshire (1986–88, 8 matches).
Career batting
8–13–1–274–71–22.83–0–*ct* 4
He also played for Hertfordshire (1984) and Bedfordshire (1989–92).

Gouldsworthy, William Robert
Amateur. *b:* 20.5.1892, Bristol. *d:* 4.2.1969, Westbourne, Bournemouth, Hampshire. Lower order right-hand batsman, right-arm medium pace bowler. *Team* Gloucestershire (1921–29, 26 matches).
Career batting
26–44–10–277–65*–8.14–0–*ct* 11
Bowling 1729–62–27.88–4–1–6/47

Govan, James Walter
Cricketer. *b:* 6.5.1966, Dunfermline, Fife, Scotland. Lower order right-hand batsman, off break bowler. *Teams* Scotland (1987–92); Northamptonshire (1989–90, 5 matches).
Career batting
10–13–1–87–17–7.25–0–*ct* 6
Bowling 846–35–24.17–2–0–6/70

Gover, Alfred Richard
Professional. *b:* 29.2.1908, Woodcote, Epsom, Surrey. Brother-in-law of E. A. Watts (Surrey). Lower

order right-hand batsman, right-arm fast bowler. *Team* Surrey (1928–47, 336 matches). *Tour* Tennyson to India 1937/8. *Tests* England (1936–46, 4 matches).
Career batting
362–414–167–2312–41*–9.36–0–*ct* 171
Bowling 36753–1555–23.63–95–17–8/34
Test batting
4–1–1–2–2*–no av–0–*ct* 1
Bowling 359–8–44.87–0–0–3/85

He took 100 wickets in a season eight times, going on to 200 in two seasons (best 201, av 18.98, in 1937). His final first-class match was for an England XI v Glamorgan in 1948. For many years he was proprietor of an Indoor Cricket School in South London. He also played for Bedfordshire (1948). He was President of Surrey in 1980. He was a noted goalkeeper in amateur football.

Govindraj, Devraj Devendraraj
Cricketer. *b:* 2.1.1947, Hyderabad, India. Nephew of C. K. Nayudu (India). Lower order right-hand batsman, right-arm fast medium bowler. *Team* Hyderabad (1964/5 to 1974/5). *Tours* Hyderabad Blues to Ceylon 1966/7; State Bank of India to Ceylon 1968/9; India to West Indies 1970/1, to England 1971.
Career batting
93–107–18–1202–72–13.50–0–*ct* 36
Bowling 5256–190–27.66–5–2–6/38

He achieved very little on his tour to England and did not appear in the Tests.

Gowans, James
Amateur. *b:* 23.4.1872, Westoe House, Co Durham. *d:* 14.3.1936, Rosherville, Johannesburg, South Africa. Lower order right-hand batsman, wicket-keeper. *Sch* Harrow. *Team* MCC (1891).
Career batting
1–1–0–40–40–40.00–0–*ct* 0

Whilst at Cambridge he appeared in the Freshmen's match, but no first-class matches. An excellent rugby footballer, he represented Cambridge and Scotland.

Gower, David Ivon, OBE
Cricketer. *b:* 1.4.1957, Tunbridge Wells, Kent. Excellent middle order left-hand batsman, off break bowler, good field. *Sch* King's, Canterbury. *Teams* Leicestershire (1975–89, 186 matches); Hampshire (1990–92, 57 matches). *Tours* England to Australia 1978/9, 1979/80, 1982/3, 1984/5 (not first-class), 1986/7, 1990/1, to India 1979/80, 1981/2, 1984/5, 1988/9 (tour cancelled), to West Indies 1980/1, 1985/6, 1989/90, to Sri Lanka 1981/2, 1984/5, to New Zealand 1982/3 (not first-class), 1983/4, 1990/1 (not first-class), to Pakistan 1983/4; Robins to Sri Lanka 1977/8. *Tests* England (1978–92, 117 matches).
Career batting
432–699–69–25203–228–40.00–49–*ct* 269–*st* 1
Bowling 227–4–56.75–0–0–3/47
Test batting
117–204–18–8231–215–44.25–18–*ct* 74
Bowling 20–1–20.00–0–0–1/1

No batsman in England over the last two decades timed the ball as well as Gower. The runs flowed sweetly and seemingly without effort from his bat. His success in Test cricket, after just one full season of County cricket, was instantaneous. His Test debut in 1978 resulted in 438 runs in six Tests, av 54.75. The winter which followed was spent in Australia where he topped the England Test batting averages with 420 runs, av 42.00. From then on, no England side was really complete without him, though the selectors had occasional aberrations. He took over as England's captain in 1983/4 and then led the Test side in the home series of 1984 and 1985, as well as the touring teams of 1984/5 to India and 1985/6 to West Indies. On the latter tour his leadership was criticised in some quarters, the influential report in *Wisden* commenting, 'instead of the strong leader England wanted, they had a dilettante'. After the First Test of 1986, Gower was unavailable due to injury, and though he returned to the side later, it was without the captaincy. He did, however, resume the role for the 1989 series against Australia, though the fact that, apparently, the England manager was against the appointment, tended to sour Gower's chances of success before he began. He not only lost the captaincy but was not chosen for the winter tour to West Indies. In the event he travelled with the press and was co-opted for one first-class game. On the following winter's tour to Australia he appeared in all six Tests and, apart from Gooch, was England's only consistent batsman. He hired an aeroplane during one match and flew low over the ground during play, which failed to amuse those in charge. Despite a successful series in 1992, during which he became England's leading run scorer in Tests, he was omitted, amid much controversy, from the 1992/3 England touring team.

He hit 1,000 runs in a season 12 times (best 1,530, av 46.36, in 1982). His highest score was 228 for Leicestershire v Glamorgan at Leicester in 1989 and his highest in Tests 215 v Australia at Edgbaston in 1985. Because he has played in well over 100 Tests and over 100 one-day internationals his appearances in county cricket have been restricted. He captained Leicestershire from 1984–86 and 1988–89, and captained England in 32 Tests.

Graburn, William Turbett
Amateur. *b:* 16.3.1865, Filey, Yorkshire. *d:* 13.12.1944, Kent Town, West Molesey, Surrey. Middle order right-hand batsman, slow right-arm bowler. *Sch* Repton. *Team* Surrey (1894, 1 match).
Career batting
2–3–0–63–39–21.00–0–*ct* 0

His debut in first-class matches was for the Hurst Park Club v Australians in 1890. He was Surrey coach 1892–1904.

Grace, Dr Alfred Henry
Amateur. *b:* 10.3.1866, Chipping Sodbury, Gloucestershire. *d:* 16.9.1929, Iron-Acton, Gloucestershire. Nephew of W. G. (Gloucestershire), E. M. (Gloucestershire), Henry (Gloucestershire) and G. F. (Gloucestershire), cousin of W. G. jun (Gloucestershire), C. B. (London County) and N. V. (Royal Navy). Hard hitting right-hand batsman, right-arm medium pace bowler. *Sch* Epsom. *Team* Gloucestershire (1886–91, 2 matches).
Career batting
2–3–0–5–4–1.66–0–*ct* 1
Bowling 42–1–42.00–0–0–1/42

Grace, Charles Butler
Amateur. *b:* 26.3.1882, Bristol. *d:* 6.6.1938, Bexhill, Sussex, whilst playing cricket. Son of W. G. (Gloucestershire), brother of W. G. jun (Gloucestershire), nephew of E. M. (Gloucestershire), Henry (Gloucestershire) and G. F. (Gloucestershire), cousin of A. H. (Gloucestershire) and N. V. (Royal Navy). Tail end right-hand batsman, lob bowler. *Sch* Clifton. *Team* London County (1900).
Career batting
4–5–0–42–36–8.40–0–*ct* 3
Bowling 92–3–30.66–0–0–3/62

His final first-class match was for W. G. Grace's XI in 1906.

Grace, Dr Edward Mills
Amateur. *b:* 28.11.1841, Downend, Bristol. *d:* 20.5.1911, Park House, Thornbury, Gloucestershire. Brother of G. F. (Gloucestershire), Henry (Gloucestershire) and W. G. (Gloucestershire), father of N. V. (Royal Navy), uncle of A. H. (Gloucestershire), W. G. jun (Gloucestershire) and C. B. (London County). Opening right-hand batsman, right-hand fast round-arm, later slow under-arm bowler, brilliant point. *Team* Gloucestershire (1870–96, 253 matches). *Tour* Parr to Australia 1863/4. *Test* England (1880, 1 match).
Career batting
314–555–18–10025–192*–18.66–5–*ct* 369–*st* 1
Bowling 6213–305–20.37–17–2–10/69
Test batting
1–2–0–36–36–18.00–0–*ct* 1

Although his first-class record does not match that of W. G., E. M. was a great cricketer in his own right and a formidable figure in local cricket – even in 1909 he took 119 wickets, though his batting was handicapped by his lameness. His greatest feat in first-class matches was to score 192* and take 10 wickets in an innings in the same match for MCC v Gentlemen of Kent at Canterbury in 1862. His first-class debut was for MCC in 1862. He also played for Monmouthshire (1860) and Carmarthenshire (1864). He was Hon Secretary of Gloucestershire 1873–1908.

Grace, George Frederick
Amateur. *b:* 13.12.1850, Downend, Bristol. *d:* 22.9.1880, Basingstoke, Hampshire, of congestion of the lungs. Brother of E. M. (Gloucestershire), Henry (Gloucestershire) and W. G. (Gloucestershire), uncle of A. H. (Gloucestershire), W. G. jun (Gloucestershire), C. B. (London County) and N. V. (Royal Navy). Middle order right-hand batsman, right-hand fast round-arm bowler, good field. *Team* Gloucestershire (1870–80, 85 matches). *Test* England (1880, 1 match).
Career batting
195–316–40–6906–189*–25.02–8–*ct* 170–*st* 3
Bowling 6600–329–20.06–17–5–8/43
Test batting
1–2–0–0–0–0.00–0–*ct* 2

He was only 15 years and 159 days old when he made his first-class debut for Gentlemen of England v Oxford U in 1866. He was taken ill and died whilst on his way to Winchester to play in a match.

Grace, Dr Henry
Amateur. *b:* 31.1.1833, Downend, Bristol. *d:* 13.11.1895, Honiton, Devon. Brother of E. M. (Gloucestershire), G. F. (Gloucestershire) and W. G. (Gloucestershire), uncle of A. H. (Gloucestershire), W. G. jun (Gloucestershire), C. B. (London County) and N. V. (Royal Navy). Middle order right-hand batsman, right-hand medium pace round-arm bowler. *Team* Gloucestershire (1871, 2 matches).
Career batting
3–3–0–4–4–1.33–0–*ct* 0
Bowling 85–3–28.33–0–0–3/48

He was the eldest of the five Grace brothers, most of his cricket being played before Gloucestershire became first-class.

Grace, Norman Vere
Amateur. *b:* 31.7.1894, Thornbury, Gloucestershire. *d:* 20.2.1975, Amberley, Gloucestershire. Son of E. M. (Gloucestershire), nephew of W. G. (Gloucestershire), Henry (Gloucestershire) and G. F. (Gloucestershire), cousin of A. H. (Gloucestershire), W. G. jun (Gloucestershire) and C. B. (London County). Middle order right-hand batsman, right-arm slow bowler. *Team* Royal Navy (1920–27).
Career batting
3–5–0–25–24–5.00–0–*ct* 1
Bowling 114–7–16.28–1–0–5/69

Grace, Dr William Gilbert
Amateur. *b:* 18.7.1848, Downend, Bristol. *d:* 23.10.1915, Mottingham, Kent. Brother of E. M. (Gloucestershire), G. F. (Gloucestershire) and Henry (Gloucestershire), father of W. G. jun (Gloucester-

shire) and C. B. (London County), uncle of A. H. (Gloucestershire) and N. V. (Royal Navy). Opening right-hand batsman, right-hand medium pace round-arm bowler, excellent field. *Teams* Gloucestershire (1870–99, 360 matches); Kent (1877, 1 match as given man); London County (1900–04). *Tours* Fitzgerald to North America 1872 (not first-class); Grace to Australia 1873/4 (not first-class); Sheffield to Australia 1891/2. *Tests* England (1880–99, 22 matches).
Career batting
869–1478–104–54211–344–39.45–124–*ct* 875–*st* 5
Bowling 50980–2809–18.14–240–64–10/49
Test batting
22–36–2–1098–170–32.29–2–*ct* 39
Bowling 236–9–26.22–0–0–2/12

The most famous of all cricketers, W. G. Grace dominated the game from 1871 until the turn of the century. With his brothers he made Gloucestershire a first-class cricketing county and was the captain from the beginning until 1899, when he resigned owing to a dispute. His final years were mainly at Crystal Palace where he played for London County.

During his long career he broke, or perhaps created would be a more appropriate description, many first-class records. He hit the first first-class triple century: 344 for MCC v Kent at Canterbury in 1876, and a few days later hit 318 for Gloucestershire v Yorkshire at Clifton. Despite these innings he was unable to match, in 1876, the formidable run aggregate he had compiled in 1871 with 2,739 runs (av 78.25) – this was the first time any player had reached 2,000 runs in a first-class season. In 1874 he became the first player to perform the 'double' and in 1876 the first to achieve 2,000 runs and 100 wickets in a single season.

In all he made 1,000 runs in 28 seasons, going on to 2,000 five times. In nine summers he reached 100 wickets (best 191, av 12.94, in 1875) and in seven seasons achieved the 'double'. Around 1890 he seemed to be losing his appetite for records, but in 1895, at the age of 47, he came back to hit 1,000 runs in the month of May, the first time this rare feat had been achieved. His best bowling was 10/49 for MCC v Oxford U at Oxford in 1886.

His career record both in terms of runs scored and centuries remained unbeaten for many years – he was the first to hit 100 first-class centuries.

His record in Test cricket spanned 20 seasons, but as he visited Australia with only one Test playing side, he appeared in just 22 Tests, being captain in 13. He hit the first English Test hundred and created another record with his 170 in 1886.

Altogether his was the most remarkable of all cricket careers. His first-class debut was for Gentlemen of South in 1865. His final first-class match was for Gentlemen of England in 1908. He also played for Suffolk (1865) and Worcestershire (pre first-class, 1870). He was Gloucestershire Secretary 1871–72 and a Test selector in 1899.

Grace, William Gilbert (jun)
Amateur. *b:* 6.7.1874, West Brompton, Kensington, London. *d:* 2.3.1905, East Cowes, Isle of Wight, after an appendicitis operation. Son of W. G. (Gloucestershire), brother of C. B. (London County), nephew of E. M. (Gloucestershire), Henry (Gloucestershire) and G. F. (Gloucestershire), cousin of A. H. (Gloucestershire) and N. V. (Royal Navy). Middle order right-hand batsman, right-arm fast medium bowler. *Sch* Clifton. *Teams* Gloucestershire (1893–98, 29 matches); Cambridge U (1894–96, blue 1895–96); London County (1900–03).
Career batting
57–91–4–1324–79–15.21–0–*ct* 43
Bowling 1657–42–39.45–1–0–6/79

Gracey, Peter Bosworth Kirkwood
Amateur. *b:* 12.12.1921, Bannu, India. Middle order right-hand batsman, leg break bowler. *Sch* Wellington. *Teams* Oxford U (1947–48); Europeans (1945/6).
Career batting
5–9–1–176–61–22.00–0–*ct* 7
Bowling 54–2–27.00–0–0–2/21

He played against Cambridge U in a war-time match (1941). He won blues for hockey and golf.

Graf, Shaun Francis
Cricketer. *b:* 19.5.1957, Somerville, Melbourne, Victoria, Australia. Lower order right-hand batsman, right-arm fast medium bowler. *Teams* Victoria (1979/80 to 1984/5, 29 matches); Hampshire (1980, 15 matches); Western Australia (1983/4, 11 matches).
Career batting
55–77–15–1559–100*–25.14–1–*ct* 30
Bowling 4206–124–33.91–1–0–5/95

He also played for Wiltshire (1979) and Cornwall (1983). He played for Australia in limited overs Internationals.

Graham, David
Amateur. *b:* 13.3.1922, Belfast, Ireland. Tail end right-hand batsman, right-arm fast medium bowler. *Team* Ireland (1948).
Career batting
1–2–0–13–7–6.50–0–*ct* 0
Bowling 20–1–20.00–0–0–1/13

Graham, Godfrey Richard
Amateur. *b:* 23.8.1936, Dublin, Ireland. Tail end right-hand batsman, leg break and googly bowler. *Team* Ireland (1954).
Career batting
1–1–1–1–1*–no av–0–*ct* 1
Bowling 100–2–50.00–0–0–2/100

Graham, Henry
Amateur. *b:* 22.11.1870, Carlton, Melbourne, Victoria, Australia. *d:* 7.2.1911, Dunedin, New Zealand.

Middle order right-hand batsman, leg break bowler, good field. *Teams* Victoria (1892/3 to 1902/3, 43 matches); Otago (1903/4 to 1906/7). *Tours* Australia to England and North America 1893, 1896. *Tests* Australia (1893–96, 6 matches).
Career batting
114–201–9–5054–124–26.32–7–*ct* 85
Bowling 258–6–43.00–0–0–4/39
Test batting
6–10–0–301–107–30.10–2–*ct* 3
He was successful on his 1893 tour of England, hitting 1,119 runs, av 24.87, and scoring 107 in the Lord's Test, but in 1896 was dogged by ill-health.

Graham, Henry Canning
Professional. *b:* 31.5.1914, Belfast, Ireland. *d:* 6.3.1982, Copthorne, Shrewsbury, Shropshire. Middle order right-hand batsman. *Team* Leicestershire (1936–37, 23 matches).
Career batting
23–38–4–589–75–17.32–0–*ct* 13
Bowling 37–1–37.00–0–0–1/9

Graham, James McGill
Amateur. *b:* 2.11.1874, Ayr, Scotland. *d: circa* 1955. Tail end right-hand batsman, leg break and googly bowler. *Team* Scotland (1924).
Career batting
1–2–1–3–3*–3.00–0–*ct* 1
Bowling 89–1–89.00–0–0–1/89

Graham, James Robert
Amateur. *b:* 1908, Dublin, Ireland. *d:* 14.1.1942, Dublin, Ireland. Tail end right-hand batsman, off break bowler. *Team* Ireland (1936–39).
Career batting
6–12–1–50–12*–4.54–0–*ct* 3
Bowling 389–13–29.92–0–0–3/76

Graham, John
Amateur. *b:* 10.10.1870, Notting Hill, London. *d:* 26.8.1893, Norway. He was drowned while on holiday. Lower order batsman, wicket-keeper. *Sch* Clifton. *Team* Cambridge U (1892).
Career batting
1–1–0–3–3–3.00–0–*ct* 0–*st* 1
He won a blue for hockey.

Graham, John Norman
Cricketer. *b:* 8.5.1943, Hexham, Northumberland. Tail end right-hand batsman, right-arm medium pace bowler. *Team* Kent (1964–77, 186 matches). *Tour* Kent to West Indies 1972/3 (not first-class).
Career batting
189–178–73–404–23–3.84–0–*ct* 40
Bowling 13722–614–22.34–26–3–8/20
He took 104 wickets, av 13.90, in 1967. He also played for Northumberland (1980–84).

Graham, Leonard
Professional. *b:* 20.8.1901, Leyton, Essex. *d:* 21.12.1962, Kensington, London. Middle order batsman. *Team* Essex (1926, 2 matches).
Career batting
2–3–1–14–12–7.00–0–*ct* 2
He played soccer for Millwall and England.

Graham, Ogilvie Blair
Amateur. *b:* 8.7.1891, Dunmurry, Co Antrim, Ireland. *d:* 30.5.1971, Quinton House, Lower Quinton, Warwickshire. Lower order batsman, bowler. *Sch* Harrow. *Teams* Free Foresters (1923); Europeans (1926/7).
Career batting
4–6–0–31–16–5.16–0–*ct* 2
Bowling 165–10–16.50–0–0–4/12
He played in trials at Oxford U, but not in first-class matches.

Graham, Peter Arthur Onslow
Amateur. *b:* 27.12.1920, Kurseong, Darjeeling, India. Lower order right-hand batsman, right-arm fast bowler. *Sch* Tonbridge. *Teams* Somerset (1948, 6 matches).
Career batting
6–11–2–82–33–9.11–0–*ct* 3
Bowling 316–7–45.14–0–0–3/47

Graham, Robert
Amateur. *b:* 16.9.1877, Grahamstown, South Africa. *d:* 21.4.1946, Upperton, Eastbourne, Sussex. Lower order right-hand batsman, right-arm medium pace bowler. *Team* Western Province (1897/8). *Tour* South Africa to England 1901. *Tests* South Africa (1898/9, 2 matches).
Career batting
18–33–9–260–63*–10.83–0–*ct* 22
Bowling 1406–61–23.04–5–1–8/90
Test batting
2–4–0–6–4–1.50–0–*ct* 2
Bowling 127–3–42.33–0–0–2/22

Graham, Samuel
(known as Uel Graham)
Cricketer. *b:* 9.1.1967, Lisburn, Co Antrim, Ireland. Middle order right-hand batsman, right-arm medium pace bowler. *Team* Ireland (1992).
Career batting
1–2–0–62–35–31.00–0–*ct* 0

Graham-Brown, James Martin Hilary
Cricketer. *b:* 11.7.1951, Thetford, Norfolk. Great-nephew of L. B. Blaxland (Derbyshire). Middle order right-hand batsman, right-arm medium pace bowler. *Sch* Sevenoaks. *Teams* Kent (1974–76, 13 matches); Derbyshire (1977–78, 17 matches).
Career batting
30–37–7–368–43–12.26–0–*ct* 8
Bowling 696–12–58.00–0–0–2/23

He also played for Cornwall (1981–84) and Dorset (1989–91).

Grainge, Clifford Marshall
Amateur. *b:* 21.7.1927, Heckmondwike, Yorkshire. *d:* 26.5.1989, Leeds, Yorkshire. Tail end right-hand batsman, right-arm fast medium bowler. *Team* Oxford U (1950–52).
Career batting
14–15–6–47–14*–5.22–0–*ct* 4
Bowling 1090–25–43.60–1–0–5/127

Grainger, Charles Edward
Amateur. *b:* 22.11.1858, South Kensington, London. *d:* 19.9.1934, Kensington, London. Middle order right-hand batsman. *Sch* Marlborough. *Team* Cambridge U (1879).
Career batting
1–2–1–2–2*–2.00–0–*ct* 2

Grainger, George
Professional. *b:* 11.11.1887, Morton, Derbyshire. *d:* 17.8.1977, Walton, Chesterfield, Derbyshire. Lower order left-hand batsman, left-arm slow or medium bowler. *Team* Derbyshire (1909–21, 5 matches).
Career batting
5–9–3–36–10*–6.00–0–*ct* 1
Bowling 348–7–49.71–0–0–4/91

Grant, Christopher Robert Wellesley
Cricketer. *b:* 19.12.1935, Lincoln. Middle order left-hand batsman. *Team* Nottinghamshire (1968, 3 matches).
Career batting
3–6–0–125–48–20.83–0–*ct* 0

Grant, Edward
Amateur. *b:* 16.6.1874, Stockbridge, Hampshire. *d:* 12.1.1953, Odd Down, Bath, Somerset. Lower order batsman, slow bowler. *Team* Somerset (1899–1901, 5 matches).
Career batting
5–8–2–66–14–11.00–0–*ct* 6
Bowling 144–4–36.00–0–0–2/19
He also played for Wiltshire (1903–12).

Grant, George Copeland
Amateur. *b:* 9.5.1907, Port of Spain, Trinidad. *d:* 26.10.1978, Cambridge. Brother of R. S. (West Indies) and F. G. (Trinidad). Lower order right-hand batsman, right-arm fast medium bowler. *Teams* Cambridge U (1928–30, blue 1929–30); Trinidad (1933/4 to 1934/5); Rhodesia (1931/2). *Tours* West Indies to Australia 1930/1, to England 1933. *Tests* West Indies (1930/1 to 1934/5, 12 matches).
Career batting
81–136–17–3831–115–32.19–4–*ct* 71
Bowling 969–19–51.00–0–0–3/24
Test batting
12–22–6–413–71*–25.81–0–*ct* 10
Bowling 18–0

He captained West Indies in all the Tests in which he played. His first-class debut in West Indies was for G. C. Grant's XI in 1932/3. He hit 1,195 runs, av 30.64, in 1933. He also won a soccer blue.

Grant, Rolph Stewart
Amateur. *b:* 15.12.1909, Port of Spain, Trinidad. *d:* 18.10.1977, Oakville, Ontario, Canada. Brother of G. C. (West Indies) and F. G. (Trinidad). Lower order right-hand batsman, off break bowler, brilliant close field. *Teams* Cambridge U (1932–33, blue 1933); Trinidad (1933/4 to 1938/9). *Tour* West Indies to England 1939. *Tests* West Indies (1934/5 to 1939, 7 matches).
Career batting
48–74–8–1883–152–28.53–1–*ct* 66
Bowling 1989–79–25.17–0–0–4/41
Test batting
7–11–1–220–77–22.00–0–*ct* 13
Bowling 353–11–32.09–0–0–3/68
He was awarded his blue at Cambridge mainly on account of his fielding. In 1939 he captained the West Indies tourists in England. He won an amateur international soccer cap for England.

Grant, Trevor John Duncan
Amateur. *b:* 24.5.1926, Charlwood, Surrey. *d:* 10.10.1957, Shotley Gate, Suffolk. He died by his own hand. Opening right-hand batsman. *Teams* Sussex (1946, 1 match).
Career batting
1–2–0–6–6–3.00–0–*ct* 1

Grant, William St Clair
Amateur. *b:* 8.9.1894, Bhagalpur, Bengal, India. *d:* 26.9.1918, near Passchendaele, Belgium. He was killed in action. Hard hitting batsman, medium pace bowler, fair field. *Sch* Clifton. *Team* Gloucestershire (1914, 4 matches).
Career batting
4–7–0–55–16–7.85–0–*ct* 1
Bowling 22–0

Grant-Asher, A. G.
(*see under* Asher, A. G. G.)

Granville, Richard St Leger
Amateur. *b:* 24.4.1907, King's Worthy, Hampshire. *d:* 8.8.1972, Banbury, Oxfordshire. Great-nephew of F. Compton (Hampshire). Middle order right-hand batsman. *Sch* Eton. *Team* Warwickshire (1934, 1 match).
Career batting
1–2–0–9–7–4.50–0–*ct* 0

Grasett, Geoffrey William
Amateur. *b:* 28.7.1890, Hereford. *d:* 31.10.1934, Cranham, Gloucestershire. Lower order batsman, bowler. *Team* Oxford U (1912).
Career batting
1–2–1–2–2*–2.00–0–*ct* 0

Bowling 35–2–17.50–0–0–2/19

His County cricket was for Herefordshire (1908). He won a blue for hockey.

Grass, Arthur Conrad
Amateur. *b:* 11.10.1897, Grove Park, Denmark Hill, London. Middle order right-hand batsman, right-arm medium pace bowler, good cover point. *Sch* City of London. *Tour* South Americans to England 1932.
Career batting
3–6–4–60–24*–30.00–0–*ct* 0

Graveney, David Anthony
Cricketer. *b:* 2.1.1953, Westbury-on-Trym, Bristol. Son of J. K. R. (Gloucestershire), nephew of T. W. (Gloucestershire and Worcestershire). Lower order right-hand batsman, slow left-arm bowler. *Sch* Millfield. *Teams* Gloucestershire (1972–90, 381 matches); Somerset (1991, 21 matches); Durham (1992, 21 matches). *Tours* Gloucestershire to Sri Lanka 1986/7; England XI to South Africa 1989/90.
Career batting
425–530–158–6501–119–17.47–2–*ct* 224
Bowling 27314–912–29.94–38–7–8/85

His best season was 1976 when he took 73 wickets, av 24.89. He captained Gloucestershire 1981–88 and was appointed the first captain for Durham in 1992 when Durham gained first-class status. In 1989/90 he acted as manager of the England XI to South Africa.

Graveney, John Kenneth Richard
Professional. *b:* 16.12.1924, Hexham, Northumberland. Brother of T. W. (Gloucestershire and Worcestershire), father of D. A. (Gloucestershire, Somerset and Durham). Lower order left-hand batsman, right-arm fast medium bowler. *Sch* Bristol GS. *Team* Gloucestershire (1947–64, 110 matches).
Career batting
111–167–26–2034–62–14.42–0–*ct* 52
Bowling 4819–173–27.86–6–1–10/66

He retired owing to a back injury in 1951, but returned to captain Gloucestershire in 1963 and 1964. His outstanding performance was taking all ten wickets (for 66) for Gloucestershire v Derbyshire at Chesterfield in 1949. He was Gloucestershire Chairman 1978–79 and President 1985.

Graveney, Thomas William, OBE
Professional. *b:* 16.6.1927, Riding Mill, Northumberland. Brother of J. K. R. (Gloucestershire), uncle of D. A. (Gloucestershire, Somerset and Durham). Brilliant middle order right-hand batsman, leg break bowler. *Sch* Bristol GS. *Teams* Gloucestershire (1948–60, 296 matches); Worcestershire (1961–70, 208 matches); Queensland (1969/70 to 1971/2, 7 matches). *Tours* MCC to Australia and New Zealand 1954/5, 1958/9, to Australia 1962/3, to West Indies 1953/4, 1967/8, to Ceylon, India and Pakistan 1951/2, to Ceylon and Pakistan 1968/9; Norfolk to West Indies 1956/7; Swanton to West Indies 1955/6; Cavaliers to West Indies 1963/4, to South Africa 1960/1; Commonwealth to South Africa 1959/60, to Pakistan 1963/4; Howard to India 1956/7; Worcestershire World Tour (Rhodesia first-class) 1964/5; Rest of World to Barbados 1966/7; International XI to Pakistan, New Zealand and Rhodesia 1961/2. *Tests* England (1951–69, 79 matches).
Career batting
732–1223–159–47793–258–44.91–122–*ct* 550–*st* 1
Bowling 3037–80–37.96–1–0–5/28
Test batting
79–123–13–4882–258–44.38–11–*ct* 80
Bowling 167–1–167.00–0–0–1/34

Scoring over 1,000 runs in an English season no fewer than 20 times and going on to 2,000 seven times, Graveney was the equal in consistency of any of his contemporaries in County cricket. His runs were made in a most attractive style and he appeared the complete batsman, yet for over half his career he was unable to command a regular place in the England side. It was not until he had left Gloucestershire – over a disagreement concerning the captaincy – and re-established himself in the Worcestershire side that he really matured as an international cricketer.

His greatest innings for England were both made late in his career: 96 at Lord's against the West Indies in 1966 and 118 at Port of Spain on the 1967/8 tour. The most runs he scored in a season were 2,397, av 49.93, in 1956. Of his seven double centuries, five were for Gloucestershire, one for MCC and the highest, 258, for England against West Indies at Trent Bridge in 1957. He captained Gloucestershire in 1959 and 1960, Worcestershire 1968–70 and England in one Test in 1968. He was banned from Test cricket in 1969, when he played in a benefit match on a Sunday in the middle of a Test match in which he was appearing.

After retiring from first-class cricket he became well-known as a commentator on the game. Apart from cricket he was a talented golfer.

Graves, Sir Cecil George
Amateur. *b:* 4.3.1892, Kensington, London. *d:* 12.1.1957, West Cults, Aberdeenshire. Lower order batsman, opening bowler. *Sch* Gresham's Holt and Wellington. *Team* MCC (1920).
Career batting
1–2–0–48–33–24.00–0–*ct* 0
Bowling 81–0

He was joint Director-General of the BBC in 1942–43.

Graves, Nelson Zwingluis
Amateur. *b:* 10.8.1880, Philadelphia, USA. *d:* 31.3.1918, Germantown, Philadelphia, USA. Opening/middle order right-hand batsman. *Team* Philadelphia (1898–1908). *Tours* Philadelphia to England 1903, 1908.

Graves, Peter John

Career batting
33–62–3–1133–103*–19.20–1–*ct* 21
Bowling 57–1–57.00–0–0–1/13

He was described as being of first-class County standard on the 1903 tour to England and came second in the tourists' batting averages, but in 1908 he failed to find his form. He appeared for USA v Canada, making a century on his debut in this series in 1898.

Graves, Peter John
Cricketer. *b:* 19.5.1946, Hove, Sussex. Middle order left-hand batsman, slow left-arm bowler. *Teams* Sussex (1965–80, 270 matches); Orange Free State (1969/70 to 1976/7).
Career batting
292–502–51–12076–145*–26.77–14–*ct* 223
Bowling 797–15–53.13–0–0–3/69

He hit 1,000 runs in a season five times (best 1,282, av 38.84, in 1974). He was also a useful soccer player.

Gravett, Mark
Professional. *b:* 11.2.1865, Milford, Surrey. *d:* 8.2.1938, Godalming, Surrey. Lower order batsman, slow left-arm bowler. *Team* Hampshire (1899–1900, 4 matches).
Career batting
4–7–1–41–17*–6.83–0–*ct* 4
Bowling 445–15–29.66–1–0–5/50

He also played for Wiltshire (1894) and Staffordshire (1901).

Gray, Anthony Hollis
Cricketer. *b:* 23.5.1963, Belmont, Port of Spain, Trinidad. Lower order right-hand batsman, right-arm fast bowler. *Teams* Trinidad (1983/4 to 1991/2); Surrey (1985–90, 48 matches). *Tours* West Indies to Pakistan 1985/6 (not first-class), 1986/7, to Sharjah (not first-class) 1986/7, to Australia 1986/7 (not first-class), to New Zealand 1986/7; Young West Indies to Zimbabwe 1989/90. *Tests* West Indies (1986/7, 5 matches).
Career batting
108–114–15–1304–58–13.17–0–*ct* 53
Bowling 9070–402–22.56–19–4–8/40
Test batting
5–8–2–48–12*–8.00–0–*ct* 6
Bowling 377–22–17.13–0–0–4/39

His best season for Surrey was 1985 when he took 79 wickets (av 22.98). He left the County after 1988 and was re-signed for 1990.

Gray, Cyril Douglas
Amateur. *b:* 26.4.1895, Hampstead, London. *d:* 20.2.1969, St Johns Hill, Woking, Surrey. Middle order right-hand batsman. *Sch* Harrow and Westminster. *Team* Middlesex (1925–27, 15 matches).
Career batting
15–25–1–563–81–23.45–0–*ct* 7
Bowling 0–2–15.00–0–0–2/7

A well known golfer, he represented England.

Gray, David Anthony Athelstan
Amateur. *b:* 19.6.1922, Kensington, London. Lower order right-hand batsman, slow left-arm bowler. *Sch* Winchester. *Teams* Cambridge U (1947); Essex (1947, 1 match).
Career batting
3–5–0–22–8–4.40–0–*ct* 1
Bowling 182–3–60.66–0–0–2/67

Gray, Evan John
Cricketer. *b:* 18.11.1954, Wellington, New Zealand. Middle order right-hand batsman, slow left-arm bowler. *Team* Wellington (1975/6 to 1991/2). *Tours* New Zealand to England 1983, 1986, to Pakistan 1984/5, to Sri Lanka 1984/5 (not first-class), 1985/6 (not first-class), 1986/7, to Sharjah (not first-class) 1985/6, to Australia 1987/8, to India 1988/9. *Tests* New Zealand (1983 to 1988/9, 10 matches).
Career batting
162–241–51–5472–128*–28.80–6–*ct* 138
Bowling 12522–444–28.20–16–3–8/37
Test batting
10–16–0–248–50–15.50–0–*ct* 6
Bowling 886–17–52.11–0–0–3/73

Having had modest results on his first tour to England in 1983, he played a key role on the 1986 tour as a stock bowler and useful batsman at number 6, though without returning any outstanding figures in either part.

Gray, Frank Davis
Amateur. *b:* 2.7.1873, Stoneygate, Leicester. *d:* 23.2.1947, Stoneygate, Leicester. Middle order batsman. *Sch* Mill Hill. *Teams* Leicestershire (1895, 1 match).
Career batting
1–2–0–17–9–8.50–0–*ct* 0

Gray, Rev Horace
Amateur. *b:* 29.11.1874, Chesterton, Cambridge. *d:* 21.1.1938, Bredfield, Suffolk. Lower order right-hand batsman, right-arm fast bowler. *Sch* Perse. *Team* Cambridge U (1894–96, blue 1894–95).
Career batting
18–27–11–97–10–6.06–0–*ct* 6
Bowling 2026–89–22.76–8–1–7/48

His County cricket was for Cambridgeshire (1893–1906) and Devon (1900).

Gray, James Roy
Professional. *b:* 19.5.1926, Portswood, Southampton, Hampshire. Opening right-hand batsman, right-arm medium pace bowler, brilliant field. *Sch* King Edward VI School, Southampton. *Team* Hampshire (1948–66, 453 matches).
Career batting
458–818–81–22650–213*–30.73–30–*ct* 352

Bowling 13719–457–30.01–11–1–7/52

He reached 1,000 runs in a season 13 times, going on to 2,000 on three occasions (best 2,224, av 40.43, in 1962). His only double century is 213* for Hampshire v Derbyshire at Portsmouth in 1962. He played soccer for Arsenal.

Gray, John Denis
Cricketer. *b:* 9.10.1948, Meriden, Coventry, Warwickshire. Lower order left-hand batsman, left-arm medium fast bowler. *Team* Warwickshire (1968–69, 7 matches).
Career batting
7–6–3–34–18–11.33–0–*ct* 1
Bowling 534–21–25.42–1–0–5/2

He took five wickets for two runs in the first innings of his debut match – Warwickshire v Scotland 1968. He was also a useful rugby footballer.

Gray, Lawrence Herbert
Professional. *b:* 15.12.1915, Tottenham, Middlesex. *d:* 3.1.1983, Langdon Hills, Essex. Lower order right-hand batsman, right-arm fast medium bowler. *Team* Middlesex (1934–51, 204 matches).
Career batting
219–252–130–901–35*–7.38–0–*ct* 125
Bowling 16014–637–25.13–26–3–8/59

He took 102 wickets, av 18.43, in 1946. He was a first-class umpire (1953–70), standing in 2 Test matches (1955–63).

Gray, Roger Ibbotson
Amateur. *b:* 16.6.1921, Headingley, Leeds, Yorkshire. *d:* 19.10.1992, Cheltenham, Gloucestershire. Lower order right-hand batsman, right-arm medium pace bowler. *Sch* Wycliffe. *Team* Oxford U (1947).
Career batting
1–2–0–11–11–5.50–0–*ct* 1
Bowling 57–0

He was a well-known barrister.

Gray, Walter (*see under* Bunting, W. H.)

Gray, William Johns
Amateur. *b:* 26.11.1864, Chelmsford, Essex. *d:* 18.12.1898, Chelmsford, Essex. Opening batsman. *Sch* Mill Hill. *Team* Essex (1894, 1 match).
Career batting
1–2–0–4–3–2.00–0–*ct* 0

His brother was the actor, Alfred Gray

Grayland, Albert Victor
Professional. *b:* 24.3.1900, Small Heath, Birmingham. *d:* 3.2.1963, Birmingham. Lower order right-hand batsman, right-arm fast medium bowler. *Team* Warwickshire (1922–30, 4 matches).
Career batting
4–6–1–15–6–3.00–0–*ct* 0
Bowling 204–2–102.00–0–0–1/23

Grayson, Adrian Paul
Cricketer. *b:* 31.3.1971, Ripon, Yorkshire. Middle order right-hand batsman, slow left-arm bowler. *Team* Yorkshire (1990–92, 14 matches). *Tour* Yorkshire to South Africa 1991/2.
Career batting
14–18–5–291–57–22.38–0–*ct* 7
Bowling 523–3–174.33–0–0–1/3

Grayson, Sir Henry Mulleneux
Amateur. *b:* 26.6.1865, Liverpool, Lancashire. *d:* 27.10.1951, Marylebone, London. Brother of J. H. F. (Liverpool and District), uncle of G. F. Earle (Surrey and Somerset). Middle order right-hand batsman, wicket-keeper. *Sch* Winchester. *Team* Liverpool and District (1889–90).
Career batting
2–4–0–66–42–16.50–0–*ct* 0

His County cricket was for Cheshire (1886–92). He was MP for Birkenhead 1918–22.

Grayson, John Hubert FitzHenry
Amateur. *b:* 17.6.1871, West Derby, Liverpool, Lancashire. *d:* 31.5.1936, Eastbourne, Sussex. Brother of H. M. (Liverpool and District). Middle order right-hand batsman, right-arm medium pace bowler. *Sch* Radley. *Team* Liverpool and District (1891–93).
Career batting
2–4–0–46–36–11.50–0–*ct* 0

His County cricket was for Cheshire (1892–93).

Greasley, Douglas George
Professional. *b:* 20.1.1926, East Hull, Yorkshire. Middle order right-hand batsman, slow left-arm bowler. *Team* Northamptonshire (1950–55, 58 matches).
Career batting
58–85–11–1659–104*–22.41–1–*ct* 22
Bowling 573–16–35.81–0–0–4/36

Greatbatch, Mark John
Cricketer. *b:* 11.12.1963, Auckland, New Zealand. Middle order left-hand batsman, occasional wicket-keeper. *Teams* Auckland (1982/3 to 1985/6); Central Districts (1986/7 to 1991/2). *Tours* New Zealand to Sharjah (not first-class) 1987/8, 1989/90, to India 1988/9, to Australia 1989/90, 1990/1 (not first-class), to England 1990, to Pakistan 1990/1; Young New Zealand to Zimbabwe 1988/9; Rest of World to England 1988, 1990, 1992. *Tests* New Zealand (1987/8 to 1991/2, 20 matches).
Career batting
104–179–22–5774–202*–36.77–12–*ct* 92
Bowling 65–0
Test batting
20–33–5–1116–146*–39.85–2–*ct* 14
Bowling 0–0

He batted with moderate success on the 1990 tour to England and played in all three Tests. His highest score was 202* for Central Districts v Otago at Palmerston North in 1988/9.

Greatorex, Joseph Edward Alfred
Amateur. *b:* 7.3.1863, Kensington, London. *d:* 16.12.1940, Uppingham, Rutland. Brother of Theophilus (Middlesex). Middle order right-hand batsman, slow bowler, good field. *Sch* Harrow. *Team* MCC (1882–84).
Career batting
2–3–0–18–12–6.00–0–*ct* 0

Greatorex, Rev Canon Theophilus
Amateur. *b:* 14.12.1864, Hyde Park, Westminster, London. *d:* 27.7.1933, Westminster, London. Brother of J. E. A. (MCC). Middle order right-hand batsman, right-arm medium pace bowler. *Sch* Harrow. *Team* Middlesex (1883–92, 6 matches); Cambridge U (1884–86).
Career batting
19–32–1–338–44*–10.90–0–*ct* 7
Bowling 61–6–10.16–0–0–3/4
A broken finger at Cambridge in 1884 possibly deprived him of his blue.

Green, Allan Michael
Cricketer. *b:* 28.5.1960, Pulborough, Sussex. Opening right-hand batsman, off break bowler. *Sch* Brighton. *Teams* Sussex (1980–89, 149 matches); Orange Free State (1984/5 to 1986/7).
Career batting
164–291–17–7932–179–28.94–9–*ct* 85
Bowling 2192–49–44.73–1–0–6/82
He hit 1,000 runs in a season three times (best 1,646, av 42.20, in 1985).

Green, Charles Ernest
Amateur. *b:* 26.8.1846, Walthamstow, Essex. *d:* 4.12.1916, Theydon Grove, Epping, Essex. Middle order right-hand batsman, right-hand fast round-arm bowler. *Sch* Uppingham. *Teams* Cambridge U (1865–68, blue all four years); Middlesex (1868–79, 33 matches); Sussex (1869, 1 match).
Career batting
94–162–15–2488–72–16.92–0–*ct* 46
Bowling 1358–65 + 1–20.89–2–0–8/66
He also played for Essex (1862–91) and was the leading spirit behind that county's cricket for many years, being captain 1883–88, Chairman 1886–1912 and President 1913. In 1905 he was President of MCC. A noted huntsman, he was Master of the Essex Hunt for many years. His final first-class match was for Over 30s in 1881. He captained Cambridge in 1868. He also won a blue for athletics.

Green, David John
Amateur. *b:* 18.12.1935, Burton-on-Trent, Staffordshire. Opening right-hand batsman. *Teams* Derbyshire (1953–60, 37 matches); Cambridge U (1957–59, blue all three years). *Tours* MCC to Canada 1959 (not first-class).
Career batting
87–152–7–2929–134–20.20–1–*ct* 61
Bowling 99–1–99.00–0–0–1/19
His final first-class match was for Free Foresters in 1961. He also played for Wiltshire (1963–67). He captained Cambridge in 1959.

Green, David Michael
Amateur. *b:* 10.11.1939, Llanengan, Caernarvon. Opening right-hand batsman, right-arm medium pace bowler. *Sch* Manchester GS. *Teams* Oxford U (1959–61, blue all three years); Lancashire (1959–67, 135 matches); Gloucestershire (1968–71, 81 matches). *Tour* International Wanderers to Rhodesia 1972/3.
Career batting
266–479–15–13381–233–28.83–14–*ct* 96
Bowling 4460–116–38.44–1–0–5/61
He hit 1,000 runs in a season seven times, going on to 2,000 twice (best 2,137, av 40.32, in 1968). In 1965 he reached 2,000 runs without the aid of a single hundred. His highest score was 233 for Gloucestershire v Sussex at Hove in 1968. He is a well-known cricket journalist.

Green, George
Professional. *b:* 13.4.1880, Hasland, Derbyshire. *d:* 25.11.1940, Clay Cross, Derbyshire. Lower order batsman, left-arm medium pace bowler. *Team* Derbyshire (1903–07, 6 matches).
Career batting
6–11–0–39–20–3.54–0–*ct* 2
Bowling 236–6–39.33–0–0–2/31

Green, John Herbert
Amateur. *b:* 9.5.1908, Kenilworth, Warwickshire. *d:* 13.9.1987, Hove, Sussex. Lower order right-hand batsman, slow left-arm bowler. *Sch* Brighton. *Team* Warwickshire (1927, 1 match).
Career batting
1–1–1–0–0*–no av–0–*ct* 0
Bowling 16–0

Green, John James
Professional. *b:* 31.12.1896, Marylebone, London. *d:* 25.10.1960, North Kensington, London. Tail end right-hand batsman, right-arm medium fast bowler. *Team* Middlesex (1919, 1 match).
Career batting
1–1–0–3–3–3.00–0–*ct* 1
Bowling 129–2–64.50–0–0–2/97

Green, Joseph Fletcher
Amateur. *b:* 28.4.1846, West Ham, Essex. *d:* 28.8.1923, Leeds, Yorkshire. Uncle of E. F. Penn (Cambridge U) and F. Penn jun (Kent), brother-in-law of A. Penn (Kent), F. Penn (Kent) and W. Penn (Kent). Middle order batsman, bowler, excellent field. *Sch* Rugby. *Team* MCC (1870).

Career batting
2–3–1–23–12–11.50–0–*ct* 1
He also played for the Gentlemen of the South in 1870.

Green, Leonard
Amateur. *b:* 1.2.1890, Whalley Manor, Lancashire. *d:* 2.3.1963, Whalley, Lancashire. Middle order right-hand batsman, good field. *Sch* Bromsgrove. *Team* Lancashire (1922–35, 152 matches). *Tours* Tennyson to Jamaica 1926/7; Cahn to Argentina 1929/30.
Career batting
160–185–29–3981–110*–25.51–2–*ct* 39
Bowling 406–12–33.83–0–0–2/2
He captained Lancashire 1926–28 – winning the Championship in each of the three seasons. He was President of Lancashire 1951–52. A good hockey and rugby player, he represented Lancashire at both sports.

Green, Michael Arthur
Amateur. *b:* 3.10.1891, Clifton, Bristol. *d:* 28.12.1971, Kensington, London. Middle order right-hand batsman. *Teams* Gloucestershire (1912–28, 91 matches); Europeans (1922/3): Essex (1930, 2 matches). *Tours* Manager of MCC to South Africa 1948/9 and joint-manager of MCC to Australia and New Zealand 1950/1.
Career batting
107–183–20–2629–127–16.12–1–*ct* 55
Bowling 65–0
He was Secretary of Worcestershire CCC 1945–51. His final first-class match was for Free Foresters in 1934. A noted footballer, he appeared for the Army and Surrey both at soccer and rugby.

Green, Neil Howard
Cricketer. *b:* 8.10.1957, South Norwood, Surrey. Middle order right-hand batsman, off break bowler. *Team* Oxford U (1988).
Career batting
1–1–0–9–9–9.00–0–*ct* 1

Green, Robert Lawrence Herbert
Amateur. *b:* 11.12.1894, Chippenham, Wiltshire. *d:* 13.9.1969, Pulverbatch, Shropshire. Middle order batsman. *Sch* Cheltenham. *Team* Gloucestershire (1924, 1 match).
Career batting
1–2–0–5–3–2.50–0–*ct* 0

Green, Russell Christopher
Cricketer. *b:* 30.7.1959, St Albans, Hertfordshire. Lower order right-hand batsman, right-arm fast medium bowler. *Team* Glamorgan (1984, 2 matches).
Career batting
2–1–1–3–3*–no av–0–*ct* 1
Bowling 92–2–46.00–0–0–2/65
He also played for Suffolk (1982–91).

Green, Simon James
Cricketer. *b:* 19.3.1970, Bloxwich, Staffordshire. Middle order right-hand batsman, left-arm medium pace bowler. *Team* Warwickshire (1988–91, 5 matches).
Career batting
5–8–1–168–77*–24.00–0–*ct* 2

Green, W.
Professional. Lower order batsman, right-arm medium pace bowler. *Team* Surrey (1883, 1 match).
Career batting
1–2–0–2–2–1.00–0–*ct* 1

Green, William Barham
Amateur. *b:* August 1852, St Kilda, Melbourne, Victoria, Australia. *d:* 18.1.1924, North Chailey, Sussex. Opening batsman. *Sch* Eton. *Team* MCC (1880–84).
Career batting
4–6–0–53–21–8.83–0–*ct* 0
His County cricket was for Hertfordshire (1875–82). He played soccer for Cambridge U.

Greene, Alan Douglas
Amateur. *b:* 15.4.1856, Brandeston, Suffolk. *d:* 18.6.1928, Calverley, Tunbridge Wells, Kent. Middle order right-hand batsman, lob bowler, good field. *Sch* Clifton. *Teams* Gloucestershire (1876–86, 21 matches); Oxford U (1877–80, blue all four years).
Career batting
40–69–6–661–93*–10.49–0–*ct* 24
Bowling 55–1–55.00–0–0–1/34
He also played for Somerset (pre first-class, 1877–78). He captained Oxford in 1880. A good rugby footballer, he represented Gloucestershire.

Greene, Frank Awl
Amateur. *b:* 14.3.1878, Philadelphia, USA. *d:* 20.4.1961, Philadelphia, USA. Lower order batsman, left-arm bowler. *Team* Philadelphia (1908–12). *Tour* Philadelphia to England 1908.
Career batting
9–17–4–160–49*–12.30–0–*ct* 4
Bowling 346–17–20.35–0–0–4/27
He did not achieve anything out of the ordinary on his tour to England in 1908 and the best performance of his career was his bowling for Germantown against the Australians in 1913, when he took 8 for 66 in the match (not first-class).

Greene, Robin Morton
Amateur. *b:* 1.11.1931, Berea, Durban, South Africa. Lower order right-hand batsman, right-arm fast bowler. *Teams* South African XI (1949/50); Gloucestershire (1951, 1 match).
Career batting
2–4–3–59–26*–59.00–0–*ct* 1
Bowling 79–1–79.00–0–0–1/56
He was forced to retire due to an elbow injury.

Greene, Victor Sylvester
Cricketer. *b:* 24.9.1960, Lodge Road, Christ Church, Barbados. Lower order right-hand batsman, right-arm medium fast bowler. *Teams* Barbados (1985/6 to 1987/8); Gloucestershire (1987–89, 16 matches). *Tour* Young West Indies to Zimbabwe 1986/7.
Career batting
28–35–8–332–62*–12.29–0–*ct* 11
Bowling 2273–93–24.44–4–1–7/96

Greenfield, Rev Frederick Francis John
Amateur. *b:* 10.5.1850, Gorakhpur, India. *d:* 25.10.1900, near Dundee, Natal, South Africa. Opening/middle order right-hand batsman, right-hand slow round-arm bowler *Sch* Hurstpierpoint. *Teams* Sussex (1873–83, 62 matches); Cambridge U (1873–76, blue 1874–76).
Career batting
85–155–3–2549–126–16.76–2–*ct* 81
Bowling 1979–110 + 1–17.99–4–1–7/26
He captained Cambridge 1876 and Sussex 1876–78 and 1881–82. He was also a noted athlete, being captain of Cambridge in 1876. He was taken prisoner by the Boers, 'robbed of everything,' and died of pleurisy.

Greenfield, George Price
Amateur. *b:* 24.1.1843, Weeke, Winchester, Hampshire. *d:* 3.9.1917, Ealing, Middlesex. Lower order right-hand batsman, right-hand fast round-arm bowler. *Teams* Surrey (1867–69, 3 matches); Hampshire (1875, 1 match).
Career batting
5–7–1–120–102–20.00–1–*ct* 0
Bowling 99–5–19.80–0–0–3/38
His first-class debut was for Gentlemen of the South in 1866.

Greenfield, Keith
Cricketer. *b:* 6.12.1968, Brighton, Sussex. Middle order right-hand batsman, right-arm medium pace bowler. *Team* Sussex (1987–92, 25 matches).
Career batting
25–42–5–995–127*–26.89–3–*ct* 27
Bowling 133–0

Greenhalgh, Eric Washington
Professional. *b:* 18.5.1910, Sale, Cheshire. Middle order right-hand batsman, right-arm medium bowler. *Team* Lancashire (1935–38, 14 matches).
Career batting
14–18–5–366–53*–28.15–0–*ct* 2
Bowling 282–3–94.00–0–0–2/75

Greenhill, Hubert Maclean
Amateur. *b:* 18.9.1881, Christchurch, Hampshire. *d:* 22.1.1926, near Bockhampton, Dorset. He was found dead in a wood. Lower order right-hand batsman, slow left-arm bowler. *Sch* Sherborne. *Team* Hampshire (1901, 2 matches).
Career batting
2–3–0–15–6–5.00–0–*ct* 0
Bowling 77–3–25.66–0–0–3/39
Most of his county cricket was for Dorset (1903–25); he was also well known in military matches.

Greenhill, Walter
Amateur. *b:* 19.6.1849, St John's Wood, London. *d:* 26.6.1913, Warsash, Hampshire. Middle order right-hand batsman. *Team* Sussex (1868, 2 matches).
Career batting
2–4–0–24–15–6.00–0–*ct* 2

Greenhough, Thomas
Professional. *b:* 9.11.1931, Cronkey Shaw, Rochdale, Lancashire. Lower order right-hand batsman, leg break and googly bowler. *Team* Lancashire (1951–66, 241 matches). *Tours* Norfolk to Jamaica 1956/7; MCC to West Indies 1959/60. *Tests* England (1959–60, 4 matches).
Career batting
255–313–85–1913–76*–8.39–0–*ct* 84
Bowling 16802–751–22.37–34–5–7/56
Test batting
4–4–1–4–2–1.33–0–*ct* 1
Bowling 357–16–22.31–1–0–5/35
He took 100 wickets in a season twice (best 122, av 22.37, in 1959).

Greenidge, Cuthbert Gordon, MBE
Cricketer. *b:* 1.5.1951, Black Bess, St Peter, Barbados. Aggressive opening right-hand batsman, right-arm medium or off break bowler, good slip field. *Teams* Hampshire (1970–87, 275 matches); Barbados (1972/3 to 1990/1). *Tours* West Indies to India 1974/5, 1983/4, 1987/8, to Pakistan 1974/5, 1980/1, 1986/7, 1990/1, to England 1975 (World Cup), 1976, 1979 (World Cup), 1980, 1983 (World Cup), 1984, 1988, 1991, to Australia 1975/6, 1979/80, 1981/2, 1984/5, 1986/7, 1988/9, to New Zealand 1979/80, 1986/7, to Sharjah (not first-class) 1986/7, 1988/9; Rest of World to England 1989, 1990, 1992. *Tests* West Indies (1974/5 to 1990/1, 108 matches).
Career batting
523–889–75–37354–273*–45.88–92–*ct* 516
Bowling 479–18–26.61–1–0–5/49
Test batting
108–185–16–7558–226–44.72–19–*ct* 96
Bowling 4–0
He hit 1,000 runs in an English season 15 times, going on to 2,000 once, 2,035, av 67.83, in 1986. His form in English limited overs cricket has been quite outstanding and he held three records simultaneously, namely the highest innings in the Gillette Cup – 177 v Glamorgan at Southampton in 1975, the highest innings in the John Player League – 163* v Warwickshire at Edgbaston in 1979 and the highest innings in the B & H Competition – 173* v Minor Counties South at Amersham in 1973, although all three

records have been subsequently beaten.

He toured England with West Indies five times, with excellent results, particularly in 1976 when he hit 1,952 runs, av 55.77, in first-class matches which included 592, av 65.77, in the Tests. On the 1984 tour he again reached 1,000 first-class runs and hit 572 runs, av 81.71, in the Tests. On this tour he also compiled his highest Test innings of 223 at Old Trafford. His 1991 tour was ended by injury. He captained West Indies in one Test. His highest score was 273* for D. H. Robins' XI v Pakistanis at Eastbourne in 1974. He played in limited overs matches for Scotland in 1990. He was awarded an MBE in 1985.

Greenidge, Geoffrey Alan
Cricketer. *b:* 26.5.1948, Fontabelle, St Michael, Barbados. Opening right-hand batsman, leg break and googly bowler. *Teams* Barbados (1966/7 to 1975/6); Sussex (1968–75, 152 matches). *Tours* Robins to South Africa 1974/5; International Wanderers to Rhodesia 1975/6. *Tests* West Indies (1971/2 to 1972/3, 5 matches).
Career batting
182–332–22–9112–205–29.39–16–*ct* 95
Bowling 948–13–72.92–1–0–7/124
Test batting
5–9–2–209–50–29.85–0–*ct* 3
Bowling 75–0

He hit 1,000 runs in a season five times (best 1,334, av 26.68, in 1971). His only double century was 205 for Barbados v Jamaica at Bridgetown in 1966/7.

Barbados were refused entry into Guyana in 1974/5 because the former included Greenidge, who had played in South Africa.

Greening, Thomas
Amateur. *b:* 1883, Scotland. *d:* 25.3.1956, Victoria Park, Leamington Spa, Warwickshire. Lower order right-hand batsman, off break bowler. *Team* Warwickshire (1912, 2 matches).
Career batting
2–2–1–26–14–26.00–0–*ct* 0
Bowling 91–1–91.00–0–0–1/35

Greenlees, Weir Loudon Greenlees
Amateur. *b:* 26.12.1882, Islington, London. *d:* 10.1.1975, Marylebone, London. Middle or lower order batsman, wicket-keeper. *Sch* Harrow. *Teams* Oxford U (1904); London County (1904).
Career batting
2–4–1–68–39*–22.66–0–*ct* 1

Green-Price, Rev Alfred Edward
(changed name from Price in 1861)
Amateur. *b:* 11.2.1860, Knighton, Radnor. *d:* 29.6.1940, Presteigne, Radnor. Uncle of H. C. Meredith (Foster's XI). Middle order right-hand batsman. *Sch* Repton and Clifton. *Team* H. K. Foster's XI (1919).
Career batting
1–2–0–10–10–5.00–0–*ct* 1

His County cricket was for Herefordshire (1881–82) and Radnorshire (1885). He was aged 59 when he played in his only first-class match. He won a blue for soccer at Cambridge U.

Greensmith, William Thomas
Professional. *b:* 16.8.1930, Middlesbrough, Yorkshire. Middle or lower order right-hand batsman, leg break and googly bowler. *Team* Essex (1947–63, 371 matches).
Career batting
379–566–151–8249–138*–19.87–1–*ct* 149
Bowling 21206–733–28.93–21–2–8/59

Greenstock, John Wilfrid
Amateur. *b:* 15.5.1905, Great Malvern, Worcestershire. *d:* 6.2.1992. Son of William (Worcestershire), nephew of B. S. Foster (Worcestershire and Middlesex), G. N. Foster (Worcestershire and Kent), H. K. Foster (Worcestershire), M. K. Foster (Worcestershire), N. J. A. Foster (Worcestershire), R. E. Foster (Worcestershire) and W. L. Foster (Worcestershire), cousin of C. K. Foster (Worcestershire) and P. G. Foster (Kent). Lower order right-hand batsman, slow left-arm bowler. *Sch* Malvern. *Teams* Worcestershire (1924–27, 13 matches); Oxford U (1925–27, blue all three years).
Career batting
46–68–14–507–43–9.38–0–*ct* 31
Bowling 3662–139–26.34–4–0–5/36

His final first-class match was for Leveson-Gower's XI in 1929. He also won a blue for soccer.

Greenstock, William
Amateur. *b:* 15.1.1865, Keiskama Hoek, Cape Province, South Africa. *d:* 13.11.1944, Pilcot, Dogmersfield, Hampshire. Father of J. W. (Worcestershire), brother-in-law of B. S. Foster (Worcestershire and Middlesex), G. N. Foster (Worcestershire and Kent), H. K. Foster (Worcestershire), M. K. Foster (Worcestershire), N. J. A. Foster (Worcestershire), R. E. Foster (Worcestershire) and W. L. Foster (Worcestershire), uncle of C. K. Foster (Worcestershire) and P. G. Foster (Kent). Middle order right-hand batsman, off break bowler. *Sch* Fettes. *Teams* Cambridge U (1886–87); Worcestershire (1899–1919, 4 matches).
Career batting
7–12–1–165–49–15.00–0–*ct* 3
Bowling 26–0

Greensword, Stephen
Cricketer. *b:* 6.9.1943, Gateshead, Co Durham. Middle order right-hand batsman, right-arm medium pace bowler. *Team* Leicestershire (1963–66, 39 matches).
Career batting
43–74–8–1095–84*–16.59–0–*ct* 30
Bowling 1002–29–34.55–0–0–3/22

He also played for Northumberland (1967–69, 1977 and 1991–92) and Durham (pre first-class, 1970–74 and 1978–90) and appeared in first-class cricket for the Minor Counties, his final match being in 1990.

Greenway, Charles Howard
Professional. *b:* 1862. *d:* 19.3.1949, St Pancras, London. Tail end batsman, opening bowler. *Team* Gloucestershire (1890–91, 3 matches).
Career batting
3–6–0–8–6–1.33–0–*ct* 1
Bowling 196–4–49.00–0–0–2/40

Greenway, Cleveland Edmund
Amateur. *b:* 29.10.1864. *d:* 17.6.1934, West Wickham, Kent. Opening or middle order right-hand batsman, good field. *Sch* Cheltenham. *Team* Somerset (1882, 1 match). *Tour* Incogniti to USA 1913 (not first-class).
Career batting
2–4–0–31–18–7.75–0–*ct* 0
His final first-class match was for MCC in 1895. He was stationed in India for some years and was a leading batsman with the Calcutta Club. He also played for Northumberland (1900–02).

Greenwood, Andrew
Professional. *b:* 20.8.1847, Cowmes, Huddersfield, Yorkshire. *d:* 12.2.1889, Huddersfield, Yorkshire. Nephew of Luke (Yorkshire). Opening/middle order right-hand batsman, good deep field. *Team* Yorkshire (1869–80, 94 matches). *Tours* Grace to Australia 1873/4 (not first-class); Lillywhite to Australia 1876/7. *Tests* England (1876/7, 2 matches).
Career batting
141–249–14–4307–111–18.32–1–*ct* 70
Bowling 9–0
Test batting
2–4–0–77–49–19.25–0–*ct* 2

Greenwood, Charles William
Amateur. *b:* 23.7.1847, Kensington, London. *d:* 14.9.1907, Westgate-on-Sea, Kent. Son of John (Cambridge U 1821), brother of G. G. (Hampshire). Middle order batsman. *Sch* Eton. *Team* MCC (1875).
Career batting
1–2–0–4–3–2.00–0–*ct* 0

Greenwood, Edward
Amateur. *b:* 19.1.1845, St John's Wood, London. *d:* 25.1.1899, Smithwood Common, Cranleigh, Surrey. Opening/middle order batsman. *Team* Kent (1873, 1 match).
Career batting
1–2–0–13–13–6.50–0–*ct* 0

Greenwood, Frank Edwards
Amateur. *b:* 28.9.1905, Birkby, Huddersfield, Yorkshire. *d:* 30.7.1963, Lindley, Huddersfield, Yorkshire. Middle order right-hand batsman, right-arm medium pace bowler. *Sch* Oundle. *Team* Yorkshire (1929–32, 57 matches).
Career batting
57–66–8–1558–104*–26.86–1–*ct* 37
Bowling 36–2–18.00–0–0–1/1
He captained Yorkshire in 1931 and 1932.

Greenwood, Sir Granville George
Amateur. *b:* 3.1.1850, Kensington, London. *d:* 27.10.1928, Notting Hill, London. Son of John (Cambridge U 1821), brother of C. W. (MCC). Batsman. *Sch* Eton. *Team* Hampshire (1875, 1 match).
Career batting
1–2–0–2–1–1.00–0–*ct* 1
He was MP for Peterborough 1906–18.

Greenwood, Henry William
Professional. *b:* 4.9.1909, East Preston, Sussex. *d:* 24.3.1979, Bromley, Kent. Opening right-hand batsman, right-arm slow bowler, wicket-keeper. *Teams* Sussex (1933–36, 19 matches); Northamptonshire (1938–46, 60 matches).
Career batting
79–133–4–2590–115–20.07–1–*ct* 55–*st* 13
Bowling 37–0
He also played for Durham (pre first-class, 1949). His obituary was incorrectly included in Wisden in 1984.

Greenwood, John Frederick
Professional. *b:* 10.3.1851, Epsom, Surrey. *d:* 31.8.1935, Lewes, Sussex. Middle order right-hand batsman, right-arm medium pace bowler. *Team* Surrey (1874, 3 matches).
Career batting
3–5–0–17–8–3.40–0–*ct* 3

Greenwood, Leonard Warwick
Amateur. *b:* 25.3.1899, Toxteth Park, Liverpool, Lancashire. *d:* 20.7.1982, Astley, Stourport, Worcestershire. Middle order right-hand batsman. *Sch* Winchester. *Teams* Oxford U (1919); Somerset (1920, 1 match); Worcestershire (1922–26, 3 matches).
Career batting
5–7–0–51–25–7.28–0–*ct* 2

Greenwood, Luke
Professional. *b:* 13.7.1834, Cowmes, Huddersfield, Yorkshire. *d:* 1.11.1909, Morley, Yorkshire. Uncle of Andrew (Yorkshire). Middle order right-hand batsman, right-hand fast round-arm bowler, good field. *Team* Yorkshire (1861–74, 50 matches).
Career batting
69–122–18–1244–83–11.96–0–*ct* 31
Bowling 2066–113–18.28–6–1–8/35
He was a noted umpire after retiring from first-class matches, standing in one Test match in 1882. His final first-class match was for United North in 1875.

Greenwood, Peter
Professional. *b:* 11.9.1924, Todmorden, Yorkshire. Middle order right-hand batsman, right-arm medium fast or off break bowler, good field. *Team* Lancashire (1948–52, 75 matches).
Career batting
75–92–15–1270–113–16.49–1–*ct* 21
Bowling 5090–208–24.47–9–1–6/35
He played soccer for Chester at wing half or inside forward.

Greetham, Christopher Herbert Millington
Professional. *b:* 28.8.1936, Wargrave, Berkshire. Middle order right-hand batsman, right-arm medium pace bowler. *Team* Somerset (1957–66, 205 matches).
Career batting
205–332–26–6723–151*–21.97–5–*ct* 96
Bowling 5529–195–28.35–5–1–7/56
He hit 1,000 runs in a season twice (best 1,186, av 28.23, in 1963). He also played for Devon (1968–69).

Gregg, Thomas
Professional. *b:* 18.11.1859, Wilford, Nottinghamshire. *d:* 25.3.1938, Gotham, Nottinghamshire. Lower order right-hand batsman, right-arm fast bowler. *Teams* Somerset (1883, 1 match); Gloucestershire (1884–89, 32 matches).
Career batting
35–59–4–494–62–8.98–0–*ct* 23
Bowling 1540–55–28.00–1–0–6/47

Gregory, Benjamin Bridge
Professional. *b:* 6.10.1863, Eastwood, Nottinghamshire. *d:* 27.1.1951, Kilton, Worksop, Nottinghamshire. Lower order batsman, right-arm medium pace bowler. *Team* Nottinghamshire (1895–97, 5 matches).
Career batting
5–8–3–9–4*–1.80–0–*ct* 6
Bowling 321–9–35.66–0–0–4/48
He always appeared, both for Nottinghamshire and during his pro engagements in Lancashire, under the surname Gregory, though registered at birth and death as Simpson.

Gregory, David William
Amateur. *b:* 15.4.1845, Fairy Meadow, New South Wales, Australia. *d:* 4.8.1919, Turramurra, Sydney, New South Wales, Australia. Brother of A. H. (New South Wales), E. J. (New South Wales), and C. S. (New South Wales), uncle of S. E. (New South Wales), C. W. (New South Wales) and J. M. (New South Wales). Middle order right-hand batsman, right-hand fast round-arm bowler. *Team* New South Wales (1866/7 to 1882/3, 19 matches). *Tour* Australia to England and North America 1878. *Tests* Australia (1876/7 to 1878/9, 3 matches).
Career batting
41–68–7–889–85–14.57–0–*ct* 35
Bowling 558–29–19.24–1–0–5/55
Test batting
3–5–2–60–43–20.00–0–*ct* 0
Bowling 9–0
He captained Australia in the first three Tests and also on the 1878 tour to England, but on the tour had little success with the bat.

Gregory, Dove
(real name Gregory Dove)
Professional. *b:* 9.2.1837, Sutton-in-Ashfield, Nottinghamshire. *d:* 21.5.1873, Derby. Lower order right-hand batsman, right-hand fast round-arm bowler, good slip field. *Team* Derbyshire (1871–72, 4 matches).
Career batting
4–7–3–19–10–4.75–0–*ct* 3
Bowling 255–25–10.20–3–0–6/9
His first-class career was very brief owing to the fact that Derbyshire did not enter first-class cricket until 1871, and he died tragically young in 1873.

Gregory, George Robert
Amateur. *b:* 27.8.1878, Pilsley, Derbyshire. *d:* 28.11.1958, Scarborough, Yorkshire. Opening or middle order right-hand batsman, leg break bowler. *Team* Derbyshire (1899–1910, 15 matches).
Career batting
15–22–2–174–23–8.70–0–*ct* 5
Bowling 267–12–22.25–0–0–4/70

Gregory, Henry Vernon
Professional. *b:* 18.1.1936, Manchester, Lancashire. Lower order right-hand batsman, leg-break bowler. *Team* Sussex (1960, 1 match).
Career batting
1–2–0–18–14–9.00–0–*ct* 0
Bowling 46–0
He also played for Cheshire (1957).

Gregory, Jack Morrison
Amateur. *b:* 14.8.1895, North Sydney, New South Wales, Australia. *d:* 7.8.1973, Bega, New South Wales, Australia. Son of C. S. (New South Wales), nephew of A. H. (New South Wales), D. W. (New South Wales) and E. J. (New South Wales), cousin of S. E. (New South Wales) and C. W. (New South Wales). Opening/middle order left-hand batsman, right-arm fast bowler. *Team* New South Wales (1920/1 to 1928/9, 17 matches). *Tours* Australia to England 1921, 1926, to South Africa 1921/2; AIF to England 1919, to South Africa 1919/20. *Tests* Australia (1920/1 to 1928/9, 24 matches).
Career batting
129–173–18–5659–152–36.50–13–*ct* 195
Bowling 10580–504–20.99–33–8–9/32
Test batting
24–34–3–1146–119–36.96–2–*ct* 37
Bowling 2648–85–31.15–4–0–7/69
His fast bowling partnership with McDonald on the 1921 tour of England was the equal of any pair of

Test opening bowlers. Gregory took 116 wickets, av 16.58, on that tour and on the AIF tour of 1919 took 131 wickets, av 18.19. He was at this period of his career Australia's leading all-rounder. In 1926 however his bowling was not so effective and during the 1928/9 series in Australia injury brought his career to a premature close. On the 1921 tour he hit 1,135 runs, av 36.61, thus performing the 'double'. His best bowling was 9/32 for AIF v Natal at Durban in 1919/20. He married Miss Australia in 1927.

Gregory, John Constable
Amateur. *b:* 17.8.1842, Marylebone, London. *d:* 28.6.1894, Weymouth, Dorset. Dashing middle order right-hand batsman, good field. *Teams* Middlesex (1865, 3 matches); Surrey (1870–71, 19 matches).
Career batting
23–42–5–760–70–20.54–0–*ct* 8
Bowling 12–0
Playing for Surrey v Sussex in 1871 he ruptured one of the arteries in his right leg and this ended his career in first-class matches. He captained Surrey in 1871. For several years he appeared in more matches than, perhaps, any other player in England and on some days played in no fewer than three matches, though of an inferior description. In 1868 it was stated that he belonged to 18 separate London cricket clubs!

Gregory, John Thomas
Professional. *b:* 22.4.1887, Eckington, Chesterfield, Derbyshire. *d:* 27.11.1914, near Zonnebeke, Belgium. He was killed in action. Lower order batsman, slow left-arm bowler. *Team* Hampshire (1913, 1 match).
Career batting
1–1–0–0–0–0.00–0–*ct* 0
Bowling 87–0

Gregory, Robert James
Professional. *b:* 26.8.1902, Selsdon. Surrey. *d:* 6.10.1973, Wandsworth, London. Opening/middle order right-hand batsman, leg break bowler. *Team* Surrey (1925–47, 413 matches). *Tour* MCC to India and Ceylon 1933/4.
Career batting
430–646–78–19495–243–34.32–39–*ct* 301
Bowling 14122–437–32.31–11–1–6/21
He hit 1,000 runs in a season nine times, going on to 2,000 twice (best 2,379, av 51.71, in 1934). His only double century was 243 for Surrey v Somerset at the Oval in 1938. A good soccer player, he appeared as full back for Norwich and Fulham.

Gregory, Sydney Edward
Amateur. *b:* 14.4.1870, Moore Park, Randwick, Sydney, New South Wales, Australia. *d:* 1.8.1929, Moore Park, Randwick, Sydney, New South Wales, Australia. Brother of C. W. (New South Wales), son of E. J. (New South Wales), nephew of A. H. (New South Wales), C. S. (New South Wales) and D. W. (New South Wales), cousin of J. M. (New South Wales), brother-in-law of H. Donnan (New South Wales). Middle order right-hand batsman, right-arm bowler, brilliant cover point. *Team* New South Wales (1889/90 to 1911/12, 81 matches). *Tours* Australia to England 1890, 1893, 1896, 1899, 1902, 1905, 1909, 1912, to South Africa 1902/3, to New Zealand 1904/5, to North America 1893, 1896, 1912. *Tests* Australia (1890–1912, 58 matches).
Career batting
369–587–55–15190–201–28.55–25–*ct* 174
Bowling 390–2–195.00–0–0–1/8
Test batting
58–100–7–2282–201–24.53–4–*ct* 25
Bowling 33–0
He hit over 1,000 runs on four of his tours to England, his best being 1,464, av 31.95, in 1896. He captained the 1912 team and altogether led Australia in six Tests. He hit two double centuries, the most noteworthy being 201 in the first Test of the 1894/5 series at Sydney.

Gregory, William Robert
Amateur. *b:* 20.5.1881, Coole Park, Gort, Co Galway, Ireland. *d:* 23.1.1918, near Grossa, Padua, Italy, when his plane was shot down. Lower order right-hand batsman, leg break and googly bowler. *Sch* Harrow. *Team* Ireland (1912).
Career batting
1–2–0–0–0–0.00–0–*ct* 0
Bowling 92–9–10.22–1–0–8/80

Gregson, William Russell
Professional. *b:* 5.8.1878, Lancaster, Lancashire. *d:* 18.6.1963, Lancaster Moor, Lancashire. Lower order right-hand batsman, right-arm fast bowler. *Team* Lancashire (1906, 5 matches).
Career batting
5–7–1–62–26–10.33–0–*ct* 0
Bowling 428–24–17.83–1–0–5/8
He had startling figures in his second first-class match 9.3–6–8–5 (for Lancashire v Leicestershire at Blackpool), including the hat-trick.

Greig, Anthony William
Cricketer. *b:* 6.10.1946, Queenstown, South Africa. Brother of I. A. (Sussex and Surrey), brother-in-law of R. P. Hodson (Cambridge U). Middle order right-hand batsman, right-arm medium pace or off break bowler. *Teams* Border (1965/6 to 1969/70); Sussex (1966–78, 209 matches); Eastern Province (1970/1 to 1971/2). *Tours* International XI to India, Pakistan and Ceylon 1967/8; Norfolk to West Indies 1969/70; Rest of World to Australia 1971/2; MCC to India, Pakistan and Sri Lanka 1972/3, to West Indies 1973/4, to Australia and New Zealand 1974/5, to India, Sri Lanka and Australia 1976/7; International Wanderers to Rhodesia 1972/3, to South Africa 1974/5. *Tests* England (1972–77, 58 matches).

Career batting
350–579–45–16660–226–31.19–26–*ct* 345
Bowling 24702–856–28.85–33–8–8/25
Test batting
58–93–4–3599–148–40.43–8–*ct* 87
Bowling 4541–141–32.20–6–2–8/86

Qualifying for Sussex in 1967 at the age of 20, Greig made an immediate impact with a century (v Lancashire) in his first Championship match. From this he went on to record 1,299 runs and take 67 wickets in the season. By 1970 he was in the England side for the unofficial Tests against the Rest of the World and his appointment as captain of Sussex in 1973 (until 1977) was followed by the England captaincy in 1975. He was by this time the leading all-round cricketer in England. In 1976/7 he led the MCC team to India with its final match as the Centenary Test in Melbourne in March 1977.

During this tour the scheme to create Kerry Packer's World Series cricket was evolved and Greig acted as the leader of the English players in league with Packer. Though the subsequent court case between the TCCB and Greig and his colleagues went in favour of the latter, Greig's involvement with World Series Cricket effectively ended his role in first-class and Test cricket and thus his short, but brilliant, career ceased soon after he was 30.

He hit 1,000 runs in a season seven times (best 1,699, av 47.19, in 1975) and captained England in 14 out of his 58 Tests. His only double century was 226 for Sussex v Warwickshire at Hastings in 1975. After 1978 he went to live permanently in Australia where he is a well-known commentator on cricket.

Greig, Rev Geoffrey George Fenner
Amateur. *b:* 15.8.1897, Southwold, Suffolk. *d:* 24.10.1960, Ewhurst, Surrey. Lower order right-hand batsman, right-arm fast bowler. *Sch* Westminster. *Teams* Oxford U (1920); Worcestershire (1920–25, 18 matches).
Career batting
20–38–8–238–37–7.93–0–*ct* 7
Bowling 1347–34–39.61–1–0–7/86

He won a blue for soccer.

Greig, Ian Alexander
Cricketer. *b:* 8.12.1955, Queenstown, South Africa. Brother of A. W. (Sussex), brother-in-law of R. P. Hodson (Cambridge U). Middle order right-hand batsman, right-arm medium pace bowler, slip field. *Teams* Border (1974/5 to 1979/80); Griqualand West (1975/6); Cambridge U (1977–79, blue all three years); Sussex (1980–85, 107 matches); Surrey (1987–91, 115 matches). *Tests* England (1982, 2 matches).
Career batting
253–339–50–8301–291–28.72–8–*ct* 152
Bowling 13023–419–31.08–10–2–7/43
Test batting
2–4–0–26–14–6.50–0–*ct* 0
Bowling 114–4–28.50–0–0–4/53

He hit 1,000 runs in a season twice (best 1,259, av 54.73, in 1990). His highest innings was 291 for Surrey v Lancashire at the Oval in 1990. He took 76 wickets, av 19.32, in 1981. He was released by Sussex due to lack of funds after 1985, and returned to County cricket as captain of Surrey (1987–91). He remained on the Surrey staff in 1992 but played in only limited overs matches. He captained Cambridge in 1979 and also won a blue for rugby.

Greig, Canon John Glennie
Amateur. *b:* 24.10.1871, Mhow, India. *d:* 24.5.1958, Milford-on-Sea, Hampshire. Opening right-hand batsman, slow right-arm bowler. *Sch* Downside. *Teams* Europeans (1893/4 to 1920/1); Hampshire (1901–22, 77 matches).
Career batting
125–219–17–7348–249*–36.37–15–*ct* 102
Bowling 3238–138–23.46–8–2–7/35

His first-class debut in England was for MCC in 1898. In the regular army stationed in India before the First World War, his County cricket was limited, though in 1901 he hit 1,277 runs, av 41.19. His highest score was 249* for Hampshire v Lancashire at Liverpool in 1901. He was secretary of Hampshire from 1921 to 1930 and President in 1945. In 1935 he was ordained in Rome as a Catholic priest.

Greive, John
Amateur. *b:* 26.6.1886, Howden, Selkirk, Scotland. *d:* 7.6.1971, Selkirk, Scotland. Brother of Walter (Scotland) and William (Scotland). Middle order right-hand batsman, right-arm medium pace bowler. *Team* Scotland (1911–26).
Career batting
5–9–1–208–58–26.00–0–*ct* 6
Bowling 22–0

Greive, Walter
Amateur. *b:* 10.2.1891, Selkirk, Scotland. *d:* 1.4.1917, France. He was killed in action. Brother of John (Scotland) and William (Scotland). Middle order right-hand batsman, right-arm medium pace bowler. *Team* Scotland (1912–14).
Career batting
2–4–0–28–18–7.00–0–*ct* 0
Bowling 73–0

Greive, William
Amateur. *b:* 1.3.1888, Howden, Selkirk, Scotland. *d:* 17.7.1916, Siege Farm, Kemmel, France. Brother of John (Scotland) and Walter (Scotland). Middle order right-hand batsman. *Team* Scotland (1910).
Career batting
1–2–0–6–6–3.00–0–*ct* 0
Bowling 21–0

Gresson, Francis Henry
Amateur. *b:* 18.2.1868, Worthing, Sussex. *d:* 31.1.1949, Eastbourne, Sussex. Nephew of E. B. Haygarth (Hampshire and Gloucestershire) and J. W. Haygarth (Oxford U). Opening left-hand batsman, left-arm fast medium bowler. *Sch* Winchester. *Teams* Oxford U (1887–89, blue all three years); Sussex (1887–1901, 21 matches).
Career batting
47–80–5–1241–114–16.54–1–*ct* 23
Bowling 839–30–27.96–1–0–5/50
A school master by profession, his County cricket was very limited, and between 1890 and 1899 he did not appear in the ranks of Sussex.

Greswell, Ernest Arthur
Amateur. *b:* 8.6.1885, Cuddalore, Madras, India. *d:* 15.1.1962, Minehead, Somerset. Brother of W. T. (Somerset), grandfather of S. R. Northcote-Green (Oxford U). Middle order right-hand batsman, right-arm slow bowler. *Sch* Repton. *Team* Somerset (1903–10, 12 matches).
Career batting
12–22–1–246–44–11.71–0–*ct* 4
Bowling 89–2–44.50–0–0–1/5
He played in trials at Oxford U, but not in first-class matches.

Greswell, William Territt
Amateur. *b:* 15.10.1889, Cuddalore, Madras, India. *d:* 12.2.1971, Wedcombe, Bicknoller, Somerset. Brother of E. A. (Somerset), great-uncle of S. R. Northcote-Green (Oxford U). Middle order right-hand batsman, right-arm slow medium bowler. *Sch* Repton. *Teams* Somerset (1908–30, 115 matches); Ceylon (1925/6); Europeans (1926/7).
Career batting
134–200–27–2580–100–14.91–1–*ct* 103
Bowling 11516–540–21.32–37–7–9/62
He took 132 wickets, av 17.78, in 1912, and his best bowling was 9/62 for Somerset v Hampshire at Weston-super-Mare in 1928. In 1909 he went out to Ceylon to work in the family business and his appearances in County cricket were therefore limited. He was regarded as the leading cricketer in Ceylon and he captained both the Ceylonese hockey and soccer teams. His final first-class match was for Free Foresters in 1933. He was Somerset President 1962–65.

Grevett, Robert Gordon
Amateur. *b:* 24.11.1914, Eastbourne, Sussex. Nephew of W. S. G. (Sussex). Middle order right-hand batsman, off break bowler. *Team* Sussex (1939, 1 match).
Career batting
1–2–0–0–0–0.00–0–*ct* 0

Grevett, William Sydney Gordon
Amateur. *b:* 25.10.1892, Eastbourne, Sussex. *d:* 26.7.1967, Eastbourne, Sussex. Uncle of R. G. (Sussex). Middle order batsman. *Team* Sussex (1922, 1 match).
Career batting
1–2–0–13–9–6.50–0–*ct* 0

Grewcock, George
Professional. *b:* 16.5.1862, Barwell, Leicestershire. *d:* 15.8.1922, Toxteth Park, Liverpool, Lancashire. Lower order left-hand batsman, left-arm fast medium bowler. *Team* Leicestershire (1899, 3 matches).
Career batting
3–6–0–4–1–0.66–0–*ct* 1
Bowling 308–8–38.50–0–0–4/93

Gribble, Herbert Willis Reginald
Amateur. *b:* 23.12.1860, Clifton, Gloucestershire. *d:* 12.6.1943, Teddington, Middlesex. Middle order right-hand batsman, good point. *Sch* Clifton. *Team* Gloucestershire (1878–82, 29 matches).
Career batting
29–40–7–342–37–10.36–0–*ct* 20

Grierson, Henry
Amateur. *b:* 26.8.1891, Chertsey, Surrey. *d:* 29.1.1972, Sunbury-on-Thames, Middlesex. Lower order batsman, left-arm medium pace bowler. *Sch* Bedford GS. *Team* Cambridge U (1911–12, blue 1911).
Career batting
11–18–5–89–24–6.84–0–*ct* 6
Bowling 500–21–23.80–0–0–4/27
His County cricket was for Bedfordshire (1909–21). He was a well-known writer and after-dinner speaker and founded the Forty Club in 1936. A good rugby footballer, he appeared for Bedford, Rosslyn Park and Leicester.

Grieve, Charles Frederick
Amateur. *b:* 1.10.1913, Manila, Philippines. Middle order right-hand batsman. *Team* Oxford U (1936).
Career batting
1–2–0–8–6–4.00–0–*ct* 1
Bowling 24–0
He played rugby for Scotland and toured South Africa with the British Lions.

Grieves, Kenneth James
Professional. *b:* 27.8.1925, Burwood, Sydney, New South Wales, Australia. *d:* 3.1.1992, Rawtenstall, Lancashire. Middle order right-hand batsman, leg break and googly bowler, brilliant slip field. *Teams* New South Wales (1945/6 to 1946/7, 10 matches); Lancashire (1949–64, 452 matches). *Tour* Commonwealth to India and Ceylon 1950/1
Career batting
490–746–79–22454–224–33.66–29–*ct* 608–*st* 4
Bowling 7209–242–29.78–8–0–6/60
He hit 1,000 runs in a season 13 times, plus once in India, and once went on to 2,000 –2,253, av 41.72, in 1959. His three double centuries were all for Lancashire, the highest being 224 v Cambridge U at

Fenner's in 1957. He captained Lancashire in 1963–64. A useful soccer player, he kept goal for Bury, Stockport County and Bolton Wanderers.

Griffin, Arthur Wilfrid Michael Stewart
Amateur. *b:* 19.2.1887, Iquique, Chile. *d:* 29.6.1962, Brook House, East Grinstead, Sussex. Lower order right-hand batsman, right-arm fast medium bowler. *Sch* Harrow. *Team* Cambridge U (1910); Middlesex (1910, 1 match).
Career batting
2–4–0–14–11–3.50–0–*ct* 1
Bowling 90–0
After leaving Cambridge he went to Northern Rhodesia as Commissioner.

Griffin, Geoffrey Merton
Amateur. *b:* 12.6.1939, Greytown, Natal, South Africa. Lower order right-hand batsman, right-arm fast bowler. *Teams* Natal (1957/8 to 1960/1); Rhodesia (1961/2 to 1962/3). *Tour* South Africa to England 1960. *Tests* South Africa (1960, 2 matches).
Career batting
42–58–8–895–73–17.90–0–*ct* 19
Bowling 2324–108–21.51–4–1–7/11
Test batting
2–4–0–25–14–6.25–0–*ct* 0
Bowling 192–8–24.00–0–0–4/87
He was no-balled for throwing 28 times on his tour to England – the first time in first-class cricket that a bowler touring England had been called. He achieved the hat-trick in the second Test, but was no-balled during the match and did not bowl in the remaining first-class matches on the tour.

Griffin, Gerard Sandiforth Featherstone
Amateur. *b:* 18.8.1882, Shepherd's Bush, London. *d:* 28.12.1950, Hyde Heath, Buckinghamshire. Middle order right-hand batsman, good field. *Team* Middlesex (1900–03, 15 matches).
Career batting
20–29–2–452–88*–16.74–0–*ct* 13

Griffin, Harry
Professional. *b:* 21.4.1873, Glastonbury, Somerset. *d:* 26.9.1938, Bristol. Middle/lower order left-hand batsman, slow left-arm bowler. *Team* Somerset (1898–99, 4 matches).
Career batting
4–7–0–69–23–9.85–0–*ct* 2
Bowling 217–14–15.50–1–0–6/40

Griffin, Neville Fetherstone
Cricketer. *b:* 17.12.1933, Croydon, Surrey. Middle order right-hand batsman, right-arm medium pace bowler. *Team* Surrey (1963, 1 match).
Career batting
1–2–1–90–83*–90.00–0–*ct* 0
Bowling 45–0

Griffith, Charles Christopher
Amateur. *b:* 14.12.1938, Pie Corner, St Lucy, Barbados. Tail end right-hand batsman, right-arm fast bowler. *Team* Barbados (1959/60 to 1965/6). *Tours* West Indies to England 1963, 1966, to Australia and New Zealand 1968/9, to India 1966/7; President's XI in India 1963/4; Commonwealth to Pakistan 1963/4; West Indian XI to England 1964; Rest of World to England 1965. *Tests* West Indies (1959/60 to 1968/9, 28 matches).
Career batting
96–119–32–1502–98–17.26–0–*ct* 39
Bowling 7172–332–21.60–17–1–8/23
Test batting
28–42–10–530–54–16.56–0–*ct* 16
Bowling 2683–94–28.54–5–0–6/36
He was the success of the 1963 tour to England taking 119 wickets, av 12.83, in first-class matches and 32 wickets, av 16.21, in the Tests. On his second tour in 1966, his bowling came in for much criticism and he was no-balled for throwing. This affected his form and he was nothing like as successful as in 1963, though he still headed the first-class averages for the tour. His final first-class match in West Indies was in 1967/8.

Griffith, Frank Alexander
Cricketer. *b:* 15.8.1968, Whipps Cross, Leytonstone, Essex. Lower order right-hand batsman, right-arm medium pace bowler. *Team* Derbyshire (1988–92, 20 matches).
Career batting
20–31–4–467–81–17.29–0–*ct* 12
Bowling 1017–33–30.81–0–0–4/33
He was a product of Haringey Cricket College.

Griffith, George
Professional. *b:* 20.12.1833, Ripley, Surrey. *d:* 3.5.1879, Stoke-next-Guildford, Surrey. He died by his own hand. Lower order left-hand batsman, left-hand fast round-arm, also (from 1862) slow under-arm bowler, brilliant field. *Team* Surrey (1856–71, 165 matches). *Tours* Stephenson to Australia 1861/2; Willsher to North America 1868 (not first-class).
Career batting
243–423–27–6314–142–15.94–2–*ct* 201–*st* 3
Bowling 11308–670–16.87–52–9–9/130
A brilliant hitter, he hit the ball out of the ground four times in succession at Hastings in 1864 for the United Eleven (not first-class). His best bowling was 9/130 for Surrey v Lancashire at the Oval in 1867.

Griffith, George Hugh Clarence
Amateur. *b:* 21.8.1929, New Orleans, Bridgetown, Barbados. Son of H. C. (West Indies), brother of H. L. V. (Barbados) and E. H. C. (Barbados and Jamaica). Tail end right-hand batsman, leg break bowler. *Team* Cambridge U (1949–51).

Griffith, Herman Clarence

Career batting
5–6–0–62–33–10.33–0–*ct* 3
Bowling 177–2–88.50–0–0–1/27

Griffith, Herman Clarence
Amateur. *b:* 1.12.1893, Arima, Trinidad. *d:* 18.3.1980, Bridgetown, Barbados. Father of G. H. C. (Cambridge U), E. H. C. (Barbados and Jamaica) and H. L. V. (Barbados). Lower order right-hand batsman, right-arm fast bowler. *Team* Barbados (1921/2 to 1940/1). *Tours* West Indies to England 1928, 1933, to Australia 1930/1. *Tests* West Indies (1928–33, 13 matches).
Career batting
79–108–28–1204–84–15.05–0–*ct* 36
Bowling 7294–258–28.27–12–2–7/38
Test batting
13–23–5–91–18–5.05–0–*ct* 4
Bowling 1243–44–28.25–2–0–6/103
He was the most successful bowler for West Indies in the 1928 Tests with 11 wickets, av 22.72, and in all first-class matches took 76 wickets, av 27.89. On the 1933 visit he was not so successful.

Griffith, Kevin
Cricketer. *b:* 17.1.1950, Warrington, Lancashire. Lower order right-hand batsman, off break bowler. *Sch* Worcester RGS. *Team* Worcestershire (1967–72, 44 matches).
Career batting
44–61–8–795–59–15.00–0–*ct* 17
Bowling 1753–50–35.06–1–0–7/41

Griffith, Mike Grenville
Cricketer. *b:* 25.11.1943, Beaconsfield, Buckinghamshire. Son of S. C. (Surrey and Sussex). Middle order right-hand batsman, wicket-keeper. *Sch* Marlborough. *Teams* Sussex (1962–74, 232 matches); Cambridge U (1963–65, blue all three years). *Tours* MCC to South America 1964/5 (not first class); Norfolk to West Indies 1969/70; Swanton to West Indies 1963/4; MCC to East Africa 1973/4.
Career batting
276–455–90–8890–158–24.35–5–*ct* 268–*st* 20
Bowling 28–1–28.00–0–0–1/4
He hit 1,144 runs, av 30.10, in 1964. He captained Sussex from 1968 to 1972. An excellent hockey player, he represented Cambridge and England and was also awarded his blue for rackets.

Griffith, Stewart Cathie, CBE
Amateur. *b:* 16.6.1914, Wandsworth, London. Father of M. G. (Sussex). Lower order right-hand batsman, wicket-keeper. *Sch* Dulwich. *Teams* Cambridge U (1934–36, blue 1935); Surrey (1934, 1 match); Sussex (1937–54, 122 matches). *Tours* MCC to Australia and New Zealand 1935/6, to India 1939/40 (cancelled), to West Indies 1947/8, to South Africa 1948/9, to East Africa 1958/9 (not first-class). *Tests* England (1947/8 to 1948/9, 3 matches).
Career batting
215–336–41–4846–140–16.42–3–*ct* 328–*st* 80
Bowling 23–0
Test batting
3–5–0–157–140–31.40–1–*ct* 5
He captained Sussex in 1946 and was Secretary to the County Club 1946–50 and President 1950. He was Assistant Secretary of MCC 1952–62, Secretary 1962–74 and President 1979/80.

Griffiths, Alan
Cricketer. *b:* 18.9.1957, Newcastle-under-Lyme, Staffordshire. Lower order right-hand batsman, wicket-keeper. *Team* Minor Counties (1981).
Career batting
1–1–0–26–26–26.00–0–*ct* 0
His County cricket was for Staffordshire (1979–89).

Griffiths, Algernon Sydney
Amateur. *b:* 23.5.1847, Marylebone, London. *d:* 18.4.1899, West Kensington, London. Brother of H. T. (MCC). Middle order right-hand batsman, good point field. *Sch* Wimbledon. *Team* Middlesex (1871–72, 2 matches).
Career batting
6–11–1–121–36–12.10–0–*ct* 0
His first-class debut was for Gentlemen of the South in 1867 and his final first-class match for Gentlemen of MCC in 1873.

Griffiths, Brian James
Cricketer. *b:* 13.6.1949, Wellingborough, Northamptonshire. Tail end right-hand batsman, right-arm medium pace bowler. *Team* Northamptonshire (1974–86, 177 matches).
Career batting
177–138–51–290–16–3.33–0–*ct* 36
Bowling 12899–444–29.05–13–0–8/50
He recorded ten consecutive first-class innings without a run. He took 70 wickets, av 26.35, in 1981. He also played for Lincolnshire (1987–88).

Griffiths, Colin
Amateur. *b:* 9.12.1930, Upminster, Essex. Middle order right-hand batsman, right-arm medium pace bowler. *Sch* Brentwood. *Team* Essex (1951–53, 27 matches).
Career batting
27–41–3–615–105–16.18–1–*ct* 4
Bowling 22–0

Griffiths, Edward Llewellyn
Amateur. *b:* 17.3.1862, Winchcombe, Gloucestershire. *d:* 20.4.1893, Cleeve, Cheltenham, Gloucestershire. Middle order right-hand batsman. *Sch* Rossall. *Teams* Gloucestershire (1885–89, 30 matches).
Career batting
30–52–9–499–40*–11.60–0–*ct* 14
Bowling 11–0

Griffiths, Gordon Craven
Amateur. *b:* 19.6.1905, King's Norton, Birmingham. Lower order right-hand batsman, wicket-keeper. *Sch* Malvern. *Team* Worcestershire (1932–35, 5 matches).
Career batting
5–10–0–42–16–4.20–0–*ct* 2–*st* 1

Griffiths, Dr Herbert Tyrrell
Amateur. *b:* 10.8.1853, Ryde, Isle of Wight. *d:* 3.11.1905, Preston-Candover, Hampshire. Brother of A. S. (Middlesex), son-in-law of R. Garth (Surrey). Middle order right-hand batsman, good deep field. *Sch* Eton. *Team* MCC (1876–78).
Career batting
2–3–1–84–68*–42.00–0–*ct* 1
He was not in the eleven whilst at Cambridge.

Griffiths, John Thomas
(registered at birth as James Griffiths)
Professional. *b:* 27.1.1863, Long Eaton, Derbyshire. Middle order batsman. *Team* Nottinghamshire (1891, 1 match).
Career batting
1 match, did not bat–*ct* 0

Griffiths, John Vesey Claude
Professional. *b:* 19.1.1931, Lee, London. *d:* 18.2.1982, Wedmore, Somerset. Tail end left-hand batsman, slow left-arm bowler. *Team* Gloucestershire (1952–57, 34 matches).
Career batting
34–53–10–396–32–9.20–0–*ct* 15
Bowling 1167–48–24.31–0–0–4/74
He was a first-class umpire (1979).

Griffiths, Peter David
Cricketer. *b:* 13.7.1961, Bulawayo, Rhodesia. Lower order right-hand batsman, slow left-arm bowler. *Sch* Charterhouse. *Team* Cambridge U (1982).
Career batting
1–2–0–1–1–0.50–0–*ct* 0
Bowling 39–0

Griffiths, Shirley Spencer
Professional. *b:* 11.7.1930, Marley Vale, Christ Church, Barbados. Lower order right-hand batsman, right-arm fast bowler. *Team* Warwickshire (1956–58, 27 matches).
Career batting
27–26–12–76–17*–5.42–0–*ct* 3
Bowling 1827–74–24.68–4–0–7/62

Griffiths, Sir William Hugh
Amateur. *b:* 26.9.1923, Marylebone, London. Tail end right-hand batsman, right-arm fast medium bowler. *Sch* Charterhouse. *Teams* Cambridge U (1946–48, blue all three years); Glamorgan (1946–48, 8 matches).
Career batting
38–48–13–137–19–3.91–0–*ct* 7
Bowling 3210–102–31.47–3–0–6/129
His final first-class match was for Free Foresters in 1949. He was President of MCC 1990/1.

Grimes, Alexander David Hugh
Cricketer. *b:* 8.1.1965, Beirut, Lebanon. Lower order right-hand batsman, right-arm medium pace bowler. *Sch* Tonbridge. *Team* Cambridge U (1984–85, blue 1984).
Career batting
13–14–3–101–22*–9.18–0–*ct* 3
Bowling 907–12–75.58–0–0–3/99

Grimmett, Clarence Victor
Amateur. *b:* 25.12.1891, Caversham, Dunedin, New Zealand. *d:* 2.5.1980, Kensington Park, Adelaide, South Australia. Lower order right-hand batsman, brilliant leg break and googly bowler. *Teams* Wellington (1911/12 to 1913/14); Victoria (1918/19 to 1923/4, 5 matches); South Australia (1924/5 to 1940/1, 105 matches). *Tours* Australia to England 1926, 1930, 1934, to New Zealand 1927/8, to South Africa 1935/6. *Tests* Australia (1924/5 to 1935/6, 37 matches).
Career batting
248–321–54–4720–71*–17.67–0–*ct* 139
Bowling 31738–1424–22.28–127–33–10/37
Test batting
37–50–10–557–50–13.92–0–*ct* 17
Bowling 5231–216–24.21–21–7–7/40
Taking over 100 wickets in first-class matches on each of his three tours to England (best 144, av 16.85, in 1930), Grimmett had three most successful trips. In 1930 he took all 10 wickets (for 37) in an innings v Yorkshire at Bramall Lane and was the first bowler to claim over 200 wickets in a Test career.

Grimsdell, Arthur
Amateur. *b:* 23.3.1894, Watford, Hertfordshire. *d:* 13.3.1963, Watford, Hertfordshire. Middle order right-hand batsman, wicket-keeper. *Team* East of England (1927).
Career batting
1–2–0–43–40–21.50–0–*ct* 1
His County cricket was for Hertfordshire (1922–47). A noted soccer player, he appeared at left half for Tottenham Hotspur and England.

Grimshaw, Charles Henry
Professional. *b:* 12.5.1880, Armley, Leeds, Yorkshire. *d:* 25.9.1947, Calverley, Yorkshire. Opening left-hand batsman, slow left-arm bowler. *Team* Yorkshire (1904–08, 54 matches).
Career batting
54–75–7–1219–85–17.92–0–*ct* 42
Bowling 221–7–31.57–0–0–2/23

Grimshaw, George Henry
Amateur. *b:* 26.1.1839, Ardenshaw, Lancashire. *d:* 21.1.1898, Grafton, Herefordshire. Middle order batsman. *Team* Lancashire (1868, 1 match).

Grimshaw, Irwin

Career batting
1–2–0–11–11–5.50–0–*ct* 0

Grimshaw, Irwin
Professional. *b:* 4.5.1857, Farsley, Leeds, Yorkshire. *d:* 18.1.1911, Farsley, Leeds, Yorkshire. Middle order right-hand batsman. *Team* Yorkshire (1880–87, 125 matches).
Career batting
138–216–17–3682–129*–18.50–4–*ct* 87–*st* 3
He also excelled at the game of knurr and spell.

Grimshaw, James William Travis
Amateur. *b:* 17.2.1912, Darlington, Co Durham. *d:* 26.9.1944, Nijmegen, Arnhem, Holland. Tail end right-hand batsman, slow left-arm bowler. *Sch* King William's, IOM. *Teams* Cambridge U (1932–35, blue 1934–35); Kent (1934, 2 matches).
Career batting
29–40–14–355–40–13.65–0–*ct* 20
Bowling 1760–65–27.02–1–0–5/92
His final first-class match was for MCC in 1936.

Grimshaw, Norman
Professional. *b:* 5.5.1912, Leeds, Yorkshire. Middle order right-hand batsman, right-arm slow bowler, good field. *Teams* Northamptonshire (1933–38, 78 matches).
Career batting
78–147–6–2445–92–17.34–0–*ct* 21
Bowling 427–6–71.16–0–0–2/60

Grimshaw, Vernon
Professional. *b:* 15.4.1916, Roundhay, Leeds, Yorkshire. *d:* 21.6.1989, Clifton, Bedfordshire. Opening right-hand batsman, leg break bowler. *Team* Worcestershire (1936–38, 19 matches).
Career batting
19–32–2–418–103–13.93–1–*ct* 8
Bowling 46–2–23.00–0–0–1/2
He also played for Bedfordshire (1955).

Grimston, Hon and Rev Edward Harbottle
Amateur. *b:* 2.4.1812, Mayfair, London. *d:* 4.5.1881, Pebmarsh, Essex. Brother of J. W. (Gentlemen), F. S. (Cambridge U) and Robert (Middlesex), father of W. E. (Southgate). Stylish opening right-hand batsman, under-arm medium pace bowler. *Sch* Harrow. *Team* Oxford U (1836, blue).
Career batting
30–54–5–669–74–13.65–0–*ct* 5
Bowling 10 wickets (no analyses)–1–0–8/?
One of the best amateur bats of his day, he gave up serious cricket on entering the Church in 1843. His first-class debut was for MCC in 1832 and his last match for MCC in 1849. His County cricket was for Hertfordshire (1836–45) and Essex (not first-class, 1854–58). He was MP for St Albans 1835–41.

Grimston, Hon and Rev Francis Sylvester
Amateur. *b:* 8.12.1822, Gorhambury, Hertfordshire. *d:* 28.10.1865, Wakes-Colne, Essex. Brother of J. W. (Gentlemen), E. H. (Oxford U) and Robert (Middlesex), uncle of W. E. (Southgate). Middle order batsman, wicket-keeper. *Sch* Harrow. *Team* Cambridge U (1843–45, blue all three years).
Career batting
18–30–1–172–20–5.93–0–*ct* 5–*st* 13
His final first-class match was for MCC in 1851 and his County cricket for Hertfordshire (1844–58); Essex (pre first-class, 1854–60).

Grimston, George Sylvester
Amateur. *b:* 2.4.1905, Rawalpindi, India. *d:* 18.9.1990, Brighton, Sussex. Lower order right-hand batsman, right-arm medium fast or leg break bowler. *Sch* Winchester. *Teams* Sussex (1924–30, 18 matches); South Punjab (1926/7).
Career batting
26–43–5–826–104–21.73–1–*ct* 9
Bowling 419–11–38.09–1–0–5/40
He was a notable figure in Army cricket in the 1930s and his final first-class match was for the Army in 1939. He was Secretary to Sussex CCC from 1950 to 1964.

Grimston, Viscount James Walter
(in 1845 succeeded as 2nd Earl of Verulam)
Amateur. *b:* 22.2.1809, Mayfair, London. *d:* 27.7.1895, Gorhambury House, Hertfordshire. Brother of E. H. (Oxford U), F. S. (Cambridge) and Robert (Middlesex), uncle of W. E. (Southgate). Opening right-hand batsman. *Sch* Harrow. *Teams* Gentlemen (1836–39); MCC (1830–43)
Career batting
21–37–2–377–48–10.74–0–*ct* 3
He was at Oxford 1828–30, but there being only one match of note by the University in those three years, he did not appear in recorded matches for Oxford. His final first-class match was for Married v Single in 1849. His County cricket was for Hertfordshire (1835). He was President of MCC 1867. He was MP for St Albans 1830–31, Newport, Cornwall 1831–32 and Hertfordshire 1832–45.

Grimston, Hon Robert
Amateur. *b:* 18.9.1816, Mayfair, London. *d:* 7.4.1884, Gorhambury House, Hertfordshire. Brother of J. W. (Gentlemen), E. H. (Oxford U) and F. S. (Cambridge U), uncle of W. E. (Southgate). Opening right-hand batsman, moderate field. *Sch* Harrow. *Teams* Oxford U (1838–40, blue 1838); Middlesex (1850–51, 3 matches).
Career batting
63–116–4–1124–76–10.03–0–*ct* 7
According to Haygarth, when playing in a match against A. Mynn's bowling, Grimston took two bats to the wicket, a larger one to face Mynn and a stand-

ard one for the other bowlers! His first-class debut was for MCC in 1836 and his last match for MCC in 1855. He was on the MCC Committee for many years and was President in 1883. He also played for Hertfordshire (1838–45). He was one of the pioneers of the electric telegraph.

Grimston, Walter Edward
Amateur. *b:* 16.5.1844, Pebmarsh, Essex. *d:* 28.7.1932, Colne Place, Earls Colne, Essex. Son of E. H. (Oxford U), nephew of J. W. (Gentlemen), F. S. (Cambridge U) and Robert (Middlesex). Hard hitting middle order right-hand batsman, wicket-keeper. *Sch* Harrow. *Team* Southgate (1868).
Career batting
1–2–0–8–5–4.00–0–*ct* 0

His County cricket was for Hertfordshire (1863–69), Suffolk (1865–66) and Essex (pre first-class, 1876).

Grimwood, Alfred Stanley
Professional. *b:* 8.9.1905, Walthamstow, Essex. *d:* 2.7.1986, Chingford, Essex. Middle order left-hand batsman, slow left-arm bowler. *Team* Essex (1925, 4 matches).
Career batting
4–6–0–26–15–4.33–0–*ct* 0
Bowling 5–0

Grinter, Trayton Golding
Amateur. *b:* 12.12.1885, Leytonstone, Essex. *d:* 21.4.1966, Frinton-on-Sea, Essex. Middle order right-hand batsman, right-arm fast medium bowler. *Team* Essex (1909–21, 8 matches).
Career batting
8–13–1–201–49*–16.75–0–*ct* 2

Despite being severely wounded in the left arm, he continued to play in good class cricket after the First World War, including some County matches, batting virtually one handed. It was estimated that he scored over 200 centuries in all.

Gripper, Raymond Arthur
Amateur. *b:* 7.7.1938, Salisbury, Rhodesia. Opening right-hand batsman, right-arm medium pace bowler. *Team* Rhodesia (1957/8 to 1971/2). *Tour* SA Fezela to England 1961.
Career batting
83–154–11–4353–279*–30.44–7–*ct* 58
Bowling 120–3–40.00–0–0–1/9

His highest score was 279* for Rhodesia v Orange Free State at Bloemfontein in 1967/8.

Grisewood, Frederick Henry
Amateur. *b:* 11.4.1888, Daylesford, Worcestershire. *d:* 15.11.1972, Hindhead, Surrey. Middle order right-hand batsman. *Sch* Radley. *Team* Worcestershire (1908, 1 match).
Career batting
1–2–1–7–6*–7.00–0–*ct* 0

He appeared in the Freshmen's match at Oxford, but no first-class matches. He became a well-known broadcaster and for many years chairman of the BBC Radio programme 'Any Questions?'

Groome, Jeremy Jonathan
Cricketer. *b:* 7.4.1955, Aldwick, Bognor Regis, Sussex. Middle order right-hand batsman, off break bowler. *Sch* Seaford. *Team* Sussex (1974–78, 40 matches).
Career batting
40–74–3–1120–86–15.77–0–*ct* 19
Bowling 0–0

Grose, Daniel Charles Evans
Amateur. *b:* 3.4.1903, South Stoneham, Hampshire. *d:* 14.11.1971, Tonbridge, Kent. Middle order right-hand batsman, wicket-keeper. *Sch* Felsted. *Team* Army (1925–27).
Career batting
4–8–0–113–35–14.12–0–*ct* 3

His County cricket was for Wiltshire (1923).

Gross, Frederick Albert
Amateur, turned professional in 1930. *b:* 17.9.1902, South Stoneham, Southampton, Hampshire. *d:* 11.3.1975, Birmingham. Lower order right-hand batsman, leg break and googly bowler. *Sch* King Edward VI School, Southampton. *Teams* Hampshire (1924–29, 34 matches); Warwickshire (1934, 1 match).
Career batting
35–45–17–202–32*–7.21–0–*ct* 18
Bowling 1926–51–37.76–1–0–5/53

Groube, Thomas Underwood
Amateur. *b:* 2.9.1857, Taranaki, New Zealand. *d:* 5.8.1927, Glenferrie, Melbourne, Victoria, Australia. Middle order right-hand batsman, right-arm medium pace bowler, excellent deep field. *Team* Victoria (1878/9 to 1881/2, 2 matches). *Tour* Australia to England 1880. *Test* Australia (1880, 1 match).
Career batting
13–23–2–179–61–8.52–0–*ct* 2
Test batting
1–2–0–11–11–5.50–0–*ct* 0

Considering that he played in all 37 matches on the 1880 tour to England his career in first-class cricket was remarkably brief and his fame rests with his batting for East Melbourne CC.

Grout, Arthur Theodore Wallace
Amateur. *b:* 20.3.1927, Mackay, Queensland, Australia. *d:* 9.11.1968, Wickham Terrace, Brisbane, Queensland, Australia. He died from heart failure, having had an earlier attack in 1964. Lower order right-hand batsman, wicket-keeper. *Team* Queensland (1946/7 to 1965/6, 94 matches). *Tours* Australia to South Africa 1957/8, to Pakistan and India 1959/60, 1964/5, to England 1961, 1964, to West Indies 1964/5; Rest of World to England 1965. *Tests* Austra-

lia (1957/8 to 1965/6, 51 matches).
Career batting
183–253–24–5168–119–22.56–4–*ct* 473–*st* 114
Bowling 115–3–38.33–0–0–1/22
Test batting
51–67–8–890–74–15.08–0–*ct* 163–*st* 24

In 1961 in England he played in all five Tests and by securing 23 victims behind the wicket set up a new record. In 1964 he again played in all five Tests and his ability behind the wicket was such that he was regarded as one of the greatest of all Australian wicket-keepers.

Grove, Charles William Collard
Professional. *b:* 16.12.1912, Aston, Birmingham. *d:* 15.2.1982, Solihull, Warwickshire. Lower order right-hand batsman, right-arm medium fast bowler. *Teams* Warwickshire (1938–53, 201 matches); Worcestershire (1954, 15 matches).
Career batting
217–310–37–3161–104*–11.57–1–*ct* 90
Bowling 16866–744–22.66–28–5–9/39

He took 100 wickets in a season twice (best 118, av 17.13, in 1952). His best bowling was 9/39 for Warwickshire v Sussex at Edgbaston in 1952. He was Warwickshire scorer 1974–81.

Grove, Lancelot Townley
Amateur. *b:* 22.8.1905, Satra, India. *d:* 9.2.1943, Newfoundland, Canada, in an air crash. Opening batsman. *Sch* Charterhouse. *Team* Army (1937–38).
Career batting
4–7–0–332–106–47.42–1–*ct* 1
Bowling 22–1–22.00–0–0–1/11

Grover, John Nelson
Amateur. *b:* 21.10.1915, Hexham, Northumberland. *d:* 17.12.1990, Waytown, Dorset. Middle order right-hand batsman, right-arm medium pace bowler. *Sch* Winchester. *Teams* Oxford U (1936–38, blue all three years).
Career batting
33–52–2–1188–121–23.96–3–*ct* 12
Bowling 9–0

His County cricket was for Northumberland (1935–50). He captained Oxford in 1938.

Groves, Charles
Amateur. *b:* 13.1.1896, Leith, Midlothian, Scotland. *d:* 14.12.1969, Danby, Whitby, Yorkshire. Middle order right-hand batsman, right-arm medium pace bowler. *Team* Scotland (1923–28).
Career batting
4–8–0–150–64–18.75–0–*ct* 1
Bowling 284–9–31.55–0–0–3/83

Groves, George Jasper
Amateur. *b:* 19.10.1868, Nottingham. *d:* 18.2.1941, Newmarket, Suffolk, as the result of an air-raid. Middle order right-hand batsman. *Team* Nottinghamshire (1899–1900, 17 matches).
Career batting
17–29–4–584–56*–23.36–0–*ct* 12
Bowling 6–0

His father was a well-known sporting journalist, G. T. Groves, editor of Whittam's 'Modern Cricket'.

Groves, Michael Godfrey Melvin
Amateur. *b:* 14.1.1943, Taihape, Wellington, New Zealand. Son of H. B. M. (Europeans), nephew of J. Heathcote-Amory (Oxford U). Middle order right-hand batsman, right-arm fast medium bowler. *Teams* Western Province (1960/1); Oxford U (1963–66, blue 1964–66); Somerset (1965, 7 matches).
Career batting
55–97–10–2541–86–29.20–0–*ct* 33
Bowling 374–7–53.42–0–0–3/33

His first first-class match in England was for Free Foresters in 1962, and his last for Free Foresters in 1968. He hit 1,048 runs, av 29.11, in 1965.

Grundy, George Graham Stewart
Amateur. *b:* 24.6.1859, Cheetham Hill, Manchester, Lancashire. *d:* 4.3.1945, Hunstanton, Norfolk. Middle order left-hand batsman, right-arm bowler. *Sch* Harrow. *Team* Sussex (1880, 2 matches).
Career batting
2–4–0–45–20–11.25–0–*ct* 0

Grundy, James
Professional. *b:* 5.3.1824, New Radford, Nottingham. *d:* 24.11.1873, Carrington, Nottingham. Father of John (An England XI), father-in-law of C. Clifton (Nottinghamshire). Middle order right-hand batsman, right-hand fast round-arm bowler, good field. *Team* Nottinghamshire (1851–67, 53 matches). *Tour* Parr to North America 1859 (not first-class).
Career batting
298–506–40–5898–95–12.65–0–*ct* 233–*st* 2
Bowling 11293–881 + 256–12.81–84–24–9/19

He took 114 wickets in 1851 and 103 in 1852. His first-class debut was for Under 35s in 1850 and his final first-class match for MCC in 1869. His best bowling was 9/19 for Nottinghamshire v Kent at Trent Bridge in 1864. He also played for Norfolk (1847–50) and Monmouthshire (1860). He played for Ireland (not first-class) in 1862.

Grundy, John
Professional. *b:* 25.6.1859, Carrington, Nottingham. *d:* 28.4.1909, Nottingham. Son of James (Nottinghamshire), brother-in-law of C. Clifton (Nottinghamshire). Lower order right-hand batsman, wicket-keeper. *Team* An England XI (1886).
Career batting
1–1–0–2–2–2.00–0–*ct* 0–*st* 2

His County cricket was for Warwickshire (pre first-class, 1886–87).

Guard, David Radclyffe
Amateur. *b:* 19.5.1928, Romsey, Hampshire. *d:* 12.12.1978, Hartfield, Sussex. Middle order right-hand batsman. *Sch* Winchester. *Team* Hampshire (1946–49, 15 matches).
Career batting
16–29–1–430–89–15.35–0–*ct* 8

Guest, Melville Richard John
Cricketer. *b:* 18.11.1943, Salisbury, Rhodesia. Middle order right-hand batsman, right-arm medium pace bowler. *Sch* Rugby. *Team* Oxford U (1964–66, blue all three years).
Career batting
23–37–3–576–77–16.94–0–*ct* 10
Bowling 882–22–40.09–0–0–2/25
His County cricket was for Wiltshire (1961–66).

Guggisberg, Brig Gen Sir Frederick Gordon
Amateur. *b:* 20.7.1869, Toronto, Ontario, Canada. *d:* 21.4.1930, Bexhill-on-Sea, Sussex. Middle order batsman. *Team* MCC (1905).
Career batting
1–1–0–0–0–0.00–0–*ct* 1
Bowling 8–0
He wrote several interesting pieces on cricket. From 1919 to 1927 he was Governor of the Gold Coast and afterwards Governor of British Guiana.

Guha, Subrata
Cricketer. *b:* 31.1.1946, Calcutta, India. Lower order right-hand batsman, right-arm medium fast bowler. *Team* Bengal (1965/6 to 1976/7). *Tours* India to England 1967; State Bank to Ceylon 1968/9. *Tests* India (1967 to 1969/70, 4 matches).
Career batting
85–102–18–1067–75–12.70–0–*ct* 45
Bowling 6068–299–20.29–18–4–7/18
Test batting
4–7–2–17–6–3.40–0–*ct* 2
Bowling 311–3–103.66–0–0–2/55
He had a very modest tour of England, but appeared in one Test.

Guise, James Louis Theodore
Amateur. *b:* 26.8.1910, Calcutta, India. Son of J. D. (Gentlemen of India), brother of J. L. (Middlesex), brother-in-law of P. J. Brett (Oxford U). Middle order right-hand batsman, slow left-arm bowler. *Sch* Winchester. *Team* Free Foresters (1937).
Career batting
1–2–0–18–11–9.00–0–*ct* 0
He did not appear in any first-class matches for the University whilst at Oxford.

Guise, John Lindsay
Amateur. *b:* 29.11.1903, Calcutta, India. *d:* 29.6.1991, Eastbourne, Sussex. Son of J. D. (Gentlemen of India), brother of J. L. T. (Free Foresters). Middle order right-hand batsman, right-arm medium pace bowler. *Sch* Winchester. *Teams* Middlesex (1922–34, 57 matches); Oxford U (1923–25, blue 1924–25); Europeans (1926/7 to 1927/8). *Tour* Martineau to Egypt 1934 (not first-class).
Career batting
94–156–12–3775–154*–26.21–4–*ct* 53
Bowling 1771–63–28.11–0–0–4/19
His most noteworthy innings was 278 for Winchester v Eton in 1921. He captained Oxford in 1925. From 1926 to 1929 he resided in India. He also played for Cornwall (1953).

Gul Mohammad
Amateur. *b:* 15.10.1921, Lahore, India. *d:* 8.5.1992, Lahore, Pakistan. Father of Firdaus Gul (Lahore). Middle order left-hand batsman, left-arm medium pace bowler, brilliant cover point. *Teams* Northern India (1938/9 to 1943/4); Muslims (1941/2 to 1944/5); Baroda (1943/4 to 1950/1); Hyderabad (1951/2 to 1954/5); Lahore (1955/6 to 1958/9). *Tours* India to England 1946, to Australia 1947/8. *Tests* India (1946 to 1952/3, 8 matches); Pakistan (1956/7, 1 match).
Career batting
118–187–21–5614–319–33.81–12–*ct* 60
Bowling 2911–107–27.20–3–0–6/60
Test batting
9–17–1–205–34–12.81–0–*ct* 3
Bowling 24–2–12.00–0–0–2/21
On his 1946 tour to England he was unable to come to terms with English wickets and had a moderate tour, appearing in only one Test. His most celebrated innings was 319 for Baroda v Holkar at Baroda in 1946/7, adding a record 577 for the 4th wicket with V. S. Hazare. His last first-class match in England was for a Commonwealth XI in 1954.

Gunary, William Charles
Amateur. *b:* 5.8.1895, Dagenham, Essex. *d:* 26.1.1969, Upminster, Essex. Tail end right-hand batsman, left-arm fast medium bowler. *Team* Essex (1929, 1 match).
Career batting
1–1–0–0–0–0.00–0–*ct* 1
Bowling 58–0

Gunasekara, Dr Churchill Hector
Amateur. *b:* 27.7.1894, Colombo, Ceylon. *d:* 16.5.1969, Mawala, Ceylon. Father of C. H. (Ceylon), uncle of L. D. S. (Ceylon), C. I. (Ceylon) and W. L. Mendis (Ceylon). Lower order right-hand batsman, right-arm medium pace bowler. *Teams* Middlesex (1919–22, 39 matches); Ceylon (1926/7 to 1932/3). *Tour* Ceylon to India 1932/3.
Career batting
51–74–13–957–88*–15.68–0–*ct* 32
Bowling 2875–90–31.94–4–0–5/15

Gunatilleke, Frederick Ranjan Manilal de Silva

One of the leading Sinhalese cricketers, he captained Ceylon 1930/1 to 1932/3. His final first-class match was for Indian University Occasionals in 1935/6.

Gunatilleke, Frederick Ranjan Manilal de Silva
Cricketer. *b:* 15.8.1951, Colombo, Ceylon. Lower order right-hand batsman, right-arm medium pace bowler. *Team* Sri Lanka (1973/4 to 1979). *Tours* Sri Lanka to India 1976/7, to England 1979.
Career batting
11–12–4–130–60*–16.25–0–*ct* 0
Bowling 688–16–43.00–1–0–5/79

He played for Sri Lanka in one-day Internationals.

Gunn, Brian George Herbert
Professional. *b:* 19.9.1921, Gravesend, Kent. Middle order right-hand batsman. *Team* Kent (1946, 4 matches).
Career batting
4–7–0–105–39–15.00–0–*ct* 7

Gunn, George
Professional. *b:* 13.6.1879, Hucknall Torkard, Nottinghamshire. *d:* 29.6.1958, Tylers Green, Cuckfield, Sussex. Brother of J. R. (Nottinghamshire), father of G. V. (Nottinghamshire), nephew of William (Nottinghamshire), brother-in-law of E. Stapleton (Derbyshire). Opening right-hand batsman, right-arm bowler, good slip field. *Team* Nottinghamshire (1902–32, 583 matches). *Tours* MCC to Australia 1907/8, 1911/12, to West Indies 1929/30. *Tests* England (1907/8 to 1929/30, 15 matches).
Career batting
643–1061–82–35208–220–35.96–62–*ct* 473
Bowling 2355–66–35.68–1–0–5/50
Test batting
15–29–1–1120–122*–40.00–2–*ct* 15
Bowling 8–0

He hit 1,000 runs in a season 20 times (best 1,933, av 40.27, in 1928). His only double century was 220 for Nottinghamshire v Derbyshire at Trent Bridge in 1923. He and W. W. Whysall hit 40 century first wicket partnerships for Nottinghamshire. Regarded by some as one of the greatest batsmen of his generation, his rather eccentric approach to the game meant that he only once appeared for England in England.

Gunn, George Vernon
Professional. *b:* 21.7.1905, West Bridgford, Nottingham. *d:* 15.10.1957, Shelton, Shrewsbury, Shropshire, following a motor cycle accident. Son of George (Nottinghamshire), nephew of J. R. (Nottinghamshire) and E. Stapleton (Derbyshire). Middle order right-hand batsman, leg break bowler. *Sch* Nottingham HS. *Team* Nottinghamshire (1928–50, 264 matches).
Career batting
266–395–43–10337–184–29.36–11–*ct* 115
Bowling 10026–281–35.67–9–1–7/44

He hit 1,000 runs in a season five times (best 1,763, av 44.07, in 1937). He was Worcestershire coach 1953–56.

Gunn, John Richmond
Professional. *b:* 19.7.1876, Hucknall Torkard, Nottinghamshire. *d:* 21.8.1963, Basford, Nottingham. Brother of George (Nottinghamshire), nephew of William (Nottinghamshire), uncle of G. V. (Nottinghamshire), brother-in-law of E. Stapleton (Derbyshire). Middle order left-hand batsman, left-arm medium or slow bowler. *Teams* Nottinghamshire (1896–1925, 489 matches); London County (1904). *Tours* MacLaren to Australia 1901/2; Cahn to Argentina 1929/30. *Tests* England (1901/2 to 1905, 6 matches).
Career batting
535–845–105–24557–294–33.18–40–*ct* 248
Bowling 30463–1242–24.52–82–17–8/65
Test batting
6–10–2–85–24–10.62–0–*ct* 3
Bowling 387–18–21.50–1–0–5/76

He hit 1,000 runs in a season 11 times (best 1,665, av 42.69, in 1903) and took 100 wickets in a season five times (best 123, av 25.27, in 1904). He performed the 'double' four times. His only double century was 294 for Nottinghamshire v Leicestershire at Trent Bridge in 1903. His last first-class match was for Sir Julien Cahn's XI in 1932.

Gunn, Lewis James Hamilton
Amateur. *b:* 14.5.1918, Corstorphine, Edinburgh, Scotland. Middle order right-hand batsman, right-arm medium pace bowler. *Team* Canada (1951–54). *Tour* Canada to England 1954.
Career batting
2–2–0–47–46–23.50–0–*ct* 1

Rain virtually washed out the only first-class match in which he appeared on the 1954 tour, but in fact he achieved very little in the minor matches of the visit.

Gunn, Terry
Professional. *b:* 27.9.1935, Barnsley, Yorkshire. Lower order right-hand batsman, wicket-keeper. *Team* Sussex (1961–67, 41 matches).
Career batting
41–54–19–179–19*–5.11–0–*ct* 109–*st* 4

Gunn, Thomas William
Professional. *b:* 10.7.1843, Croydon, Surrey. *d:* 4.5.1908, West Croydon, Surrey. Middle order right-hand batsman, right-hand slow round arm bowler. *Team* Surrey (1863–69, 6 matches).
Career batting
6–11–3–52–13–6.50–0–*ct* 1

According to Haygarth his height was 5ft 1½in only – one of the shortest men to appear in first-class cricket.

Gunn, William
Professional. *b:* 4.12.1858, St Anne's, Nottingham. *d:* 29.1.1921, Nottingham. Uncle of George (Nottinghamshire) and J. R. (Nottinghamshire). Middle order right-hand batsman, slow right-arm bowler, occasionally lobs. *Team* Nottinghamshire (1880–1904, 363 matches). *Tour* Shaw, Shrewsbury and Lillywhite to Australia 1886/7. *Tests* England (1886/7 to 1899, 11 matches).
Career batting
521–850–72–25691–273–33.02–48–*ct* 333–*st* 1
Bowling 1800–76–23.68–2–1–6/48
Test batting
11–20–2–392–102*–21.77–1–*ct* 5
He hit 1,000 runs in a season 12 times (best 2,057, av 42.85, in 1893). In all he hit eight double centuries, six for Nottinghamshire, one for MCC and one for Players v Gentlemen. His highest score was 273 for Nottinghamshire v Derbyshire at Derby in 1901. A noted soccer player, he appeared for Nottingham Forest and Notts County and at outside left for England. He was co-founder of the sports goods firm of Gunn and Moore.

Gunner, Charles Richards
Amateur. *b:* 7.1.1853, Bishops Waltham, Hampshire. *d:* 4.2.1934, Ridgemeade, Bishops Waltham, Hampshire. Father of J. H. (Hampshire). *Sch* Marlborough. *Teams* Hampshire (1878, 1 match).
Career batting
1 match, did not bat–*ct* 1
He played rugby for England.

Gunner, John Hugh
Amateur. *b:* 17.5.1884, Bishops Waltham, Hampshire. *d:* 9.8.1918, Kemmel, Belgium. He died of wounds. Son of C. R. (Hampshire). Middle order batsman. *Sch* Marlborough. *Team* Hampshire (1906–07, 6 matches).
Career batting
6–9–1–65–32–8.12–0–*ct* 4
He did not appear in first-class cricket at Oxford, but did win a blue for hockey.

Gupte, Chinmay Madhukar
Cricketer. *b:* 5.7.1972, Poona, India. Son of M. S. (Maharashtra). Middle order right-hand batsman, slow left-arm bowler. *Team* Oxford U (1991–92, blue 1991).
Career batting
13–15–2–236–55*–18.15–0–*ct* 3
Bowling 253–4–63.25–0–0–2/41

Gupte, Subhashchandra Pandharinath
Amateur. *b:* 11.12.1929, Bombay, India. Brother of B. P. (India). Lower order right-hand batsman, leg break and googly bowler. *Teams* Bombay (1948/9 to 1958/9); Bengal (1953/4 to 1957/8); Rajasthan (1960/1 to 1962/3); Trinidad (1963/4). *Tours* India to West Indies 1952/3, to Pakistan 1954/5, to England 1959; International XI to Pakistan and Rhodesia 1961/2. *Tests* India (1951/2 to 1961/2, 36 matches).
Career batting
115–125–32–761–47–8.18–0–*ct* 52
Bowling 12567–530–23.71–36–11–10/78
Test batting
36–42–13–183–21–6.31–0–*ct* 14
Bowling 4403–149–29.55–12–1–9/102
On his 1959 visit to England he took most wickets – 95, av 26.58, but was in fact not as successful as had been expected. For Bombay v Pakistan Services and Bahawalpur at Bombay in 1954/5 he took all 10 wickets in an innings for 78 runs. His debut in English first-class cricket was for a Commonwealth XI in 1957. He emigrated to the West Indies in 1963.

Gurney, Edward Richmond
Amateur. *b:* 16.4.1868, Wridden Hall, Kidderminster, Worcestershire. *d:* 17.6.1938, Hove, Sussex. Opening batsman. *Team* Gloucestershire (1911, 1 match).
Career batting
1–2–0–10–8–5.00–0–*ct* 0
He also played for Warwickshire in a non-first-class match in 1896.

Gurr, David Roberts
Cricketer. *b:* 27.3.1956, Whitchurch, Buckinghamshire. Lower order right-hand batsman, right-arm fast medium bowler. *Teams* Oxford U (1976–77, blue both years); Somerset (1976–79, 24 matches).
Career batting
41–48–23–410–46*–16.40–0–*ct* 9
Bowling 3079–110–27.99–5–0–6/82

Gurusinha, Asanka Pradeep
Cricketer. *b:* 16.9.1966, Colombo, Ceylon. Middle order left-hand batsman, right-arm medium pace bowler, occasional wicket-keeper. *Teams* Sinhalese SC (1988/9 to 1991/2); Nondescripts CC (1990/1). *Tours* Sri Lanka to Pakistan 1985/6, 1991/2, to Sharjah (not first-class) 1985/6, 1986/7, 1987/8, 1989/90, 1990/1, to India 1986/7, 1989/90 (not first-class), 1990/1, to Australia 1987/8, 1989/90, to India and Pakistan (World Cup) 1987/8, to England 1990, 1991, to New Zealand 1990/1, to Australia and New Zealand (World Cup) 1991/2. *Tests* Sri Lanka (1985/6 to 1991/2, 17 matches).
Career batting
70–103–13–3855–121–42.83–11–*ct* 53
Bowling 1182–57–20.73–1–0–5/54
Test batting
17–28–3–947–119–37.88–3–*ct* 13
Bowling 298–11–27.09–0–0–2/19
He batted successfully on his two tours to England, playing in the Test in 1991, when he also acted as vice-captain of the touring side. His first-class debut was for Sri Lanka Under 23 in 1984/5.

Guthrie, James Shields
Amateur. *b:* 14.12.1931, Kandy, Ceylon. Tail end right-hand batsman, off break bowler. *Sch* Eton. *Team* Cambridge U (1953).
Career batting
1–2–0–1–1–0.50–0–*ct* 0
Bowling 30–0

Gutteres, Rev George Gilbert
Amateur. *b:* 11.10.1859, Kensington, London. *d:* 2.3.1898, Algiers. Opening right-hand batsman, brilliant cover point. *Sch* Winchester. *Teams* Oxford U (1881); Hampshire (1882, 1 match).
Career batting
3–5–2–111–34*–37.00–0–*ct* 4
He also played for Devon (1878).

Guttridge, Frank Herbert
Professional. *b:* 12.4.1866, Nottingham. *d:* 13.6.1918, Nottingham. Lower order right-hand batsman, right-arm fast bowler. *Teams* Nottinghamshire (1889–1900, 58 matches); Sussex (1892–94, 49 matches).
Career batting
107–174–19–2190–114–14.12–1–*ct* 46
Bowling 5279–176–29.99–6–1–7/35
He played soccer for Notts County. His obituary was erroneously published in 1906. He was a first-class umpire (1912).

Guy, John Bernard
Amateur. *b:* 16.5.1916, Ramsgate, Kent. Opening right-hand batsman, left-arm medium pace bowler. *Sch* Chatham House, Ramsgate. *Teams* Oxford U (1938–39); Kent (1938, 1 match); Warwickshire (1950, 2 matches).
Career batting
9–16–0–130–45–8.12–0–*ct* 4

Guy, John Williams
Professional. *b:* 29.8.1934, Nelson, New Zealand. Attractive opening left-hand batsman, right-arm slow medium bowler. *Teams* Central Districts (1953/4 to 1962/3); Northamptonshire (1958, 2 matches); Canterbury (1957/8 to 1958/9); Otago (1959/60); Wellington (1960/1); Northern Districts (1964/5 to 1972/3). *Tours* New Zealand to India and Pakistan 1955/6, to Australia and South Africa 1961/2. *Tests* New Zealand (1955/6 to 1961/2, 12 matches).
Career batting
90–165–13–3923–115–25.80–3–*ct* 32
Bowling 82–1–82.00–0–0–1/0
Test batting
12–23–2–440–102–20.95–1–*ct* 2

Guy, Joseph
Professional. *b:* 30.7.1813, Nottingham. *d:* 15.4.1873, Nottingham. Middle order right-hand batsman, occasional wicket-keeper, good point. *Team* Nottinghamshire (1837–54, 32 matches).
Career batting
148–267–14–3395–98–13.41–0–*ct* 102–*st* 14
He was one of the leading batsmen of his day, noted for the elegance of his style.

Gwynn, Arthur Percival
Amateur. *b:* 11.6.1874, Ramelton, Co Donegal, Ireland. *d:* 14.2.1898, Rangoon, Burma. Brother of L. H. (Ireland), R. M. (Dublin U) and J. T. (Europeans), uncle of J. D. (Dublin U). Middle order right-hand batsman, wicket-keeper. *Team* Dublin University (1895).
Career batting
4–8–0–267–130–33.37–1–*ct* 5–*st* 1
He played for Ireland (not first-class, 1893–96). He played rugby for Ireland.

Gwynn, John David
Amateur. *b:* 13.7.1907, Clontarf, Co Dublin, Ireland. Nephew of A. P. (Dublin U), J. T. (Europeans), L. H. (Ireland) and R. M. (Dublin U). Tail end right-hand batsman. *Team* Dublin University (1926).
Career batting
1–2–1–11–11*–11.00–0–*ct* 0

Gwynn, Lucius Henry
Amateur. *b:* 5.5.1873, Ramelton, Co Donegal, Ireland. *d:* 23.12.1902, Davos Platz, Switzerland. Brother of A. P. (Dublin U), R. M. (Dublin U) and J. T. (Europeans), uncle of J. D. (Dublin U). Opening right-hand batsman. *Teams* Dublin University (1895); Gentlemen of England (1895–96); Ireland (1902).
Career batting
8–16–3–577–153*–44.38–2–*ct* 10
Bowling 410–18–22.77–0–0–4/81
He was regarded as a most accomplished batsman and would have played regularly in first-class County cricket if he had resided in England. A noted rugby footballer, he was a three quarter for Monkstown and Ireland.

Gwynn, Rev Robert Malcolm
Amateur. *b:* 26.4.1877, Ramelton, Co Donegal, Ireland. *d:* 2.6.1962, Dublin, Ireland. Brother of A. P. (Dublin U), L. H. (Ireland) and J. T. (Europeans), uncle of J. D. (Dublin U). Lower order right-hand batsman, right-arm slow bowler. *Team* Dublin University (1895).
Career batting
4–7–2–52–23*–10.40–0–*ct* 2
Bowling 274–8–34.25–0–0–3/21
He played for Ireland (not first-class) in 1901.

Gwynne, David Graham Pugsley
Amateur. *b:* 8.12.1904, Swansea, Glamorgan. *d:* 11.12.1934, Swansea, Glamorgan. Middle order right-hand batsman. *Sch* Llandovery College. *Team* Glamorgan (1922–23, 3 matches).
Career batting
3–6–0–20–12–3.33–0–*ct* 1

H

Habib, Aftab
Cricketer. *b:* 7.2.1972, Reading, Berkshire. Cousin of Z. A. Sadiq (Surrey and Derbyshire). Middle order right-hand batsman, right-arm medium fast bowler. *Sch* Millfield and Taunton. *Team* Middlesex (1992, 1 match).
Career batting
1–2–1–19–12–19.00–0–*ct* 0

Hack, Edward John
Amateur. *b:* 1.10.1913, Long Ashton, Somerset. *d:* 20.9.1987, Bath, Somerset. Middle order right-hand batsman. *Team* Somerset (1937, 1 match).
Career batting
1–1–0–6–6–6.00–0–*ct* 1

Hacker, Peter John
Cricketer. *b:* 16.7.1952, Lenton Abbey, Nottingham. Lower order right-hand batsman, left-arm fast medium bowler. *Teams* Nottinghamshire (1974–81, 61 matches); Orange Free State (1979/80); Derbyshire (1982, 8 matches).
Career batting
71–77–30–449–35–9.55–0–*ct* 16
Bowling 4792–153–31.32–4–0–6/35
He also played for Lincolnshire (1983) and Cheshire (1984–85).

Hacker, William Stamford
Professional. *b:* 8.12.1876, Chipping Sodbury, Gloucestershire. *d:* 8.12.1925, Bristol. Lower order right-hand batsman, right-arm fast medium bowler. *Teams* Gloucestershire (1899–1901, 3 matches); Glamorgan (1921–23, 21 matches).
Career batting
25–40–12–222–27–7.92–0–*ct* 8
Bowling 2110–91–23.18–4–1–7/84
He also played for Herefordshire (1904). He first played for Glamorgan (pre first-class) in 1908.

Hacking, John Kenneth
Amateur. *b:* 21.3.1909, Kenilworth, Warwickshire. *Sch* Warwick. Middle order right-hand batsman, right-arm medium pace bowler. *Team* Warwickshire (1946, 1 match).
Career batting
1–2–0–17–14–8.50–0–*ct* 2

Hadden, Sidney
Professional. *b:* 26.8.1877, Hastings, Sussex. *d:* 2.11.1934, Whipps Cross, Leytonstone, Essex. Lower order batsman, wicket-keeper. *Team* Essex (1912–20, 6 matches).
Career batting
6–5–2–29–17*–9.66–0–*ct* 5–*st* 1

Haden, J. V.
Professional. Opening/middle order batsman. *Team* Surrey (1882, 7 matches).
Career batting
7–10–0–42–22–4.20–0–*ct* 2

Hadfield, George Hugh
Amateur. *b:* 16.7.1880, Edmonton, Middlesex. *d:* 30.11.1935, Lambeth, London. Tail end right-hand batsman, right-arm medium pace bowler. *Team* Surrey (1903–04, 4 matches).
Career batting
5–6–2–53–27*–13.25–0–*ct* 3
Bowling 526–17–30.94–1–0–5/52
His final first-class match was for W. G. Grace's XI in 1906.

Hadi, Syed Mohammad
Amateur. *b:* 12.8.1899, India. *d:* 14.7.1971, Hyderabad, India. Brother of S. M. Hussain (Hyderabad). Middle order right-hand batsman. *Teams* Hyderabad (1930/1 to 1940/1); Madras (1933/4). *Tour* India to England 1936.
Career batting
24–42–10–1043–132*–32.59–2–*ct* 9
On the 1936 tour he appeared in emergency in two matches only. He was the first cricketer to score a century in the Ranji Trophy Competition. He played no first-class cricket at Cambridge U, but did win a blue for lawn tennis and he also played tennis for India.

Hadingham, Anthony Wallace Gwynne
Amateur. *b:* 1.3.1913, Mentone, France. *d:* 14.7.1986, Southbroom, Natal, South Africa. Nephew of H. Jones (Gloucestershire). Opening right-hand batsman. *Sch* St Paul's. *Teams* Cambridge U (1932–33, blue 1932); Surrey (1932, 1 match). *Tour* Martineau to Egypt 1935 (not first-class).
Career batting
19–32–1–554–80–17.87–0–*ct* 4
Bowling 6–0
He was a major figure in London club cricket until he emigrated to South Africa in 1946.

Hadlee, Dayle Robert
Cricketer. *b:* 6.1.1948, Riccarton, Christchurch, New Zealand. Son of W. A. (New Zealand), brother of R. J. (New Zealand) and B. G. (Canterbury). Lower order right-hand batsman, right-arm medium fast bowler. *Team* Canterbury (1969/70 to 1983/4). *Tours* New Zealand to England 1969, 1973, 1975 (World Cup), 1978, to Australia 1969/70, 1973/4, 1974/5 (not first-class), to India and Pakistan 1969/70. *Tests* New Zealand (1969 to 1977/8, 26 matches).
Career batting
111–152–39–2113–109*–18.69–1–*ct* 40
Bowling 8853–351–25.22–11–3–7/55
Test batting
26–42–5–530–56–14.32–0–*ct* 8

Bowling 2389–71–33.64–0–0–4/30

Only on the second of his three tours to England did he have much success. On the first visit his inexperience told against him and on the 1978 tour he broke down after one match. His first-class debut was for New Zealand Under 23 in 1966/7.

Hadlee, Sir Richard John

Cricketer. *b:* 3.7.1951, St Albans, Christchurch, New Zealand. Son of W. A. (New Zealand), brother of D. R. (New Zealand) and B. G. (Canterbury), husband of Karen (New Zealand Women). Aggressive middle order left-hand batsman, right-arm fast bowler. *Teams* Canterbury (1971/2 to 1988/9); Nottinghamshire (1978–87, 148 matches); Tasmania (1979/80, 6 matches). *Tours* New Zealand to Australia 1972/3, 1973/4, 1980/1, 1982/3 (not first-class), 1984/5 (not first-class), 1985/6, 1987/8, to England 1973, 1975 (World Cup), 1978, 1979 (World Cup), 1983, 1986, 1990, to India 1976/7, 1988/9, to Pakistan 1976/7, to Sri Lanka 1983/4, 1986/7, to West Indies 1984/5, to Sharjah (not first-class) 1987/8. *Tests* New Zealand (1972/3 to 1990, 86 matches).
Career batting
342–473–93–12052–210*–31.71–14–*ct* 198
Bowling 26998–1490–18.11–102–18–9/52
Test batting
86–134–19–3124–151*–27.16–2–*ct* 39
Bowling 9611–431–22.29–36–9–9/52

The greatest cricketer to represent New Zealand, he was the first bowler in the history of the game to capture 400 Test wickets, the landmark being achieved on his home ground of Christchurch against India in February 1990. This was only his 79th Test match which emphasises his incredible strike rate over such a long career.

Until 1980 he was one fast bowler among many, but the grind of County cricket made him adapt his bowling to reduce wear and tear. By shortening his run and concentrating on accuracy, as well as variation, he became the equal of any bowler in the world. Due to his ability, New Zealand, for the first time, beat both England and Australia in a Test series.

Apart from the 1973 tour to England, he was the major figure on all his other four visits. His best innings bowling analysis in Tests was 9 for 52 v Australia at Brisbane in 1985/6, and on 36 occasions he took five wickets in a Test innings and on nine took ten in a match. In his early days he was regarded as a useful lower order batsman, but by the middle of his career his batting was capable of making a major contribution to any innings.

His domination of English county batsmen was unique in post-war cricket. His record in the eight seasons from 1980 to 1987 is so impressive that it deserves to be recorded:

	Wkts	Avge	Place
1980	29	14.13	Top
1981	101	14.89	Top
1982	61	14.57	Top
1983	49	21.73	18th
1984	117	14.05	Top
1985	59	17.38	Second
1986	76	15.98	Second
1987	97	12.64	Top

In 1984 he completed the 'double', scoring 1,179 runs, av 51.26, being in the top ten in the first-class batting averages that year. In the same season he made his highest score of 210* for Nottinghamshire v Middlesex at Lord's. In 1987 he scored 1,111 runs, av 52.90, in addition to his 97 wickets. He was awarded the MBE in 1980 and made a KBE in 1990 during his final tour with New Zealand to England. His last first-class match in New Zealand was in the final Test in 1989/90.

Hadlee, Walter Arnold, CBE

Amateur. *b:* 4.6.1915, Lincoln, Canterbury, New Zealand. Father of D. R. (New Zealand), R. J. (New Zealand) and B. G. (Canterbury). Middle order right-hand batsman, right-arm medium pace bowler, good deep field. *Teams* Canterbury (1933/4 to 1951/2); Otago (1945/6 to 1946/7). *Tours* New Zealand to England 1937, 1949, to Australia 1937/8. *Tests* New Zealand (1937 to 1950/1, 11 matches).
Career batting
117–203–17–7523–198–40.44–18–*ct* 67
Bowling 293–6–48.83–0–0–3/14
Test batting
11–19–1–543–116–30.16–1–*ct* 6

He scored 1,225 runs, av 29.87, on the 1937 tour and 1,439, av 35.97, on the 1949 visit, being captain of the latter. In all he led New Zealand in eight Tests. Since retiring from first-class cricket he has been an important figure on the New Zealand Cricket Council.

Hadley, Dr Robert John

Cricketer. *b:* 22.10.1951, Neath, Glamorgan. Tail end right-hand batsman, left-arm fast medium bowler. *Teams* Cambridge U (1971–73, blue all three years); Glamorgan (1971, 2 matches). *Tour* Oxford and Cambridge U to Malaysia 1972/3 (not first-class).
Career batting
28–36–16–65–17–3.25–0–*ct* 8
Bowling 1647–56–29.41–3–0–5/31

Hadow, Alexander Astell

Amateur. *b:* 1.6.1853, Regent's Park, London. *d:* 1.6.1894, Bad Neuenahr, Rhenish Prussia, Germany. Brother of E. M. (Middlesex), P. F. (Middlesex) and W. H. (Middlesex). Middle order right-hand batsman, round-arm or under-arm medium pace bowler. *Sch* Harrow. *Team* Middlesex (1872, 1 match).
Career batting
1–2–0–27–18–13.50–0–*ct* 1

Bowling 24–2–12.00–0–0–2/24

He was also a noted rackets player. Business prevented him from playing in County matches regularly.

Hadow, Edward Maitland
Amateur. *b:* 13.3.1863, Sudbury Priory, Middlesex. *d:* 20.2.1895, Cannes, France. Brother of A. A. (Midlesex), P. F. (Middlesex) and W. H. (Middlesex). Hard hitting middle order batsman, right-arm fast bowler, good field. *Sch* Harrow. *Team* Middlesex (1883–93, 54 matches).
Career batting
77–133–10–1933–75–15.71–0–*ct* 38
Bowling 1189–50–23.78–0–0–4/24

He was also a good rackets player.

Hadow, Patrick Francis
Amateur. *b:* 24.1.1855, Regent's Park, London. *d:* 29.6.1946, Bridgwater, Somerset. Brother of A. A. (Middlesex), E. M. (Middlesex) and W. H. (Middlesex). Middle order right-hand batsman, good field. *Sch* Harrow. *Team* Middlesex (1873–74, 4 matches).
Career batting
7–13–1–134–37–11.16–0–*ct* 4

His cricket career was very limited as he became a planter in Ceylon. He was men's singles champion at Wimbledon in 1878 and also a noted rackets player.

Hadow, Walter Henry
Amateur. *b:* 25.9.1849, Regent's Park, London. *d:* 15.9.1898, Dupplin Castle, Perthshire, Scotland. Brother of A. A. (Middlesex), E. M. (Middlesex) and P. F. (Middlesex), son-in-law of Viscount Dupplin (MCC 1852). Hard hitting middle order right-hand batsman, right-hand slow round-arm bowler. *Sch* Harrow. *Teams* Oxford U (1869–72, blue 1870–72); Middlesex (1870–79, 37 matches). *Tour* Fitzgerald to North America 1872 (not first-class).
Career batting
97–168–11–3071–217–19.56–2–*ct* 84
Bowling 2327–138 + 1–16.86–9–3–8/35

His only double century was 217 for Middlesex v MCC at Lord's in 1871. He also played for Brecon (1868) and Shropshire (1869). His final first-class match was for MCC in 1884. He was a champion rackets player at Oxford, a good tennis player and rowed for his college.

Hafeez, A. (*see under* Kardar, A. H.)

Hagan, David Andrew
Cricketer, *b:* 25.6.1966, Wide Open, Northumberland. Opening right-hand batsman, off break bowler. *Team* Oxford U (1985–91, blue 1986, 1988–90).
Career batting
41–65–4–12.42–88–20.36–0–*ct* 18
Bowling 31–0

Haggas, Stell
Professional. *b:* 18.4.1856, Keighley, Yorkshire. *d:* 14.3.1926, Werneth, Oldham, Lancashire. Father of Walter (Lancashire). Middle order right-hand batsman, good long stop, occasional wicket-keeper. *Teams* Yorkshire (1878–82, 31 matches); Lancashire (1884–85, 3 matches).
Career batting
34–52–3–537–43–10.95–0–*ct* 10

Haggas, Walter
Professional. *b:* 1.4.1881, Werneth, Oldham, Lancashire. *d:* 14.11.1959, Macclesfield, Cheshire. Son of Stell (Yorkshire and Lancashire). Lower order batsman, wicket-keeper. *Team* Lancashire (1903, 2 matches).
Career batting
2–2–0–6–4–3.00–0–*ct* 3

Haggett, Norman Louis
Amateur. *b:* 8.7.1926, Lee, London. Opening right-hand batsman, right-arm slow bowler. *Team* Combined Services (1962–64).
Career batting
4–8–0–204–71–25.50–0–*ct* 4

Haggo, David John
Cricketer. *b:* 13.4.1964, Ayr, Scotland. Middle order right-hand batsman, wicket-keeper. *Team* Scotland (1983–91).
Career batting
5–7–0–140–45–20.00–0–*ct* 6–*st* 4

Haig, Nigel Esmé
(birth registered as Lionel Esmé Haig)
Amateur. *b:* 12.12.1887, Kensington, London. *d:* 27.10.1966, Eastbourne, Sussex. Nephew of Lord Harris (Kent). Middle order right-hand batsman, right-arm fast medium bowler, good field. *Sch* Eton. *Team* Middlesex (1912–34, 417 matches). *Tour* MCC to West Indies (1929/30). *Tests* England (1921 to 1929/30, 5 matches).
Career batting
513–779–51–15220–131–20.90–12–*ct* 221
Bowling 30698–1117–27.48–47–2–7/33
Test batting
5–9–0–126–47–14.00–0–*ct* 4
Bowling 448–13–34.46–0–0–3/73

He hit 1,000 runs in a season six times (best 1,552, av 25.02, in 1929) and took 100 wickets five times (best 129, av 24.17, in 1929). He performed the 'double' three times. From 1929 to 1934 he captained Middlesex (and was also Hon Secretary), in the last two years jointly with H. J. Enthoven. He also played tennis, rackets, squash and golf to a high standard. His final first-class match was for Leveson-Gower's XI in 1936. He was a Test selector in 1929.

Haigh, Charles Henry
Amateur. *b:* 26.9.1854, Rochdale, Lancashire. *d:* 15.3.1915, Bollington, Cheshire. Middle order right-hand batsman. *Sch* Bromsgrove. *Team* Lancashire (1879–87, 24 matches).
Career batting
24–33–3–435–80–14.50–0–*ct* 11

Haigh, Schofield
Professional. *b:* 19.3.1871, Berry Brow, Huddersfield, Yorkshire. *d:* 27.2.1921, Taylor Hill, Huddersfield, Yorkshire. Middle or lower order right-hand batsman, right-arm fast medium bowler. *Team* Yorkshire (1895–1913, 513 matches). *Tours* Hawke to South Africa 1898/9; MCC to South Africa 1905/06. *Tests* England (1898/9 to 1912, 11 matches).
Career batting
561–747–119–11713–159–18.65–4–*ct* 299
Bowling 32091–2012–15.94–135–30–9/25
Test batting
11–18–3–113–25–7.53–0–*ct* 8
Bowling 622–24–25.91–1–0–6/11

He once exceeded 1,000 runs in a season – 1,055, av 26.37, in 1904. He took 100 wickets in a season 11 times (best 174, av 14.59, in 1906). His best bowling was 9/25 for Yorkshire v Gloucestershire at Leeds in 1912. In 1904 he performed the 'double'. He never made his mark in Test cricket, but played with success in County cricket, his batting perhaps being underestimated.

Hailey, Henry
Amateur. *b:* 7.4.1851, Limehouse, London. *d:* 24.9.1932, Southend-on-Sea, Essex. Middle order right-hand batsman. *Team* Essex (1894–95, 13 matches).
Career batting
13–22–5–301–66*–17.70–0–*ct* 5

He first played for Essex (pre first-class) in 1891.

Haines, Alfred Hubert
Amateur. *b:* 27.8.1877, Long Sutton, Lincolnshire. *d:* 30.5.1935, Ashford, Kent. Father of C. V. G. (Glamorgan). Middle order right-hand batsman. *Sch* Merchant Taylors. *Team* Gloucestershire (1901–10, 7 matches).
Career batting
7–13–2–117–23–10.63–0–*ct* 4

Haines, Claude Vincent Godby
Amateur. *b:* 17.1.1906, Bristol. *d:* 28.1.1965, Lower Cwmtwrch, Glamorgan. Son of A. H. (Gloucestershire). Middle order right-hand batsman. *Sch* King's, Canterbury. *Team* Glamorgan (1933–34, 12 matches).
Career batting
12–20–2–350–59–19.44–0–*ct* 3
Bowling 33–1–33.00–0–0–1/15

He also played for Devon (1946).

Haines, Harold Atlee
Amateur. *b:* 17.11.1878, USA. *d:* 28.11.1970, Chestnut Hill, Pennsylvania, USA. Nephew of C. E. (USA). Hard hitting middle order batsman, excellent field. *Team* Philadelphia (1903–09). *Tour* Philadelphia to England 1903.
Career batting
9–14–1–136–58–10.46–0–*ct* 8
Bowling 45–0

He met with little success on his visit to England, but fared well for United States v Canada, appearing in four matches between 1901 and 1911.

Haines, John
Amateur. *c:* 1.7.1825, St Pancras, London. *d:* 27.5.1894, St Pancras, London. Middle order batsman. *Team* Middlesex (1865–67, 2 matches).
Career batting
2–4–0–13–5–3.25–0–*ct* 3

Hake, George John Gordon
Amateur. *b:* 24.8.1918, Sutton, Surrey. Middle order right-hand batsman, right-arm fast medium bowler. *Sch* Bromsgrove. *Team* Middlesex (1948, 1 match).
Career batting
1–1–0–2–2–2.00–0–*ct* 0
Bowling 84–1–84.00–0–0–1/84

Hake, Herbert Denys
Amateur. *b:* 8.11.1894, Christchurch, Hampshire. *d:* 12.4.1975, Sydney, New South Wales, Australia. Nephew of S. M. Toyne (Hampshire). Attractive middle order right-hand batsman, good field, occasional wicket-keeper. *Sch* Haileybury. *Teams* Hampshire (1920–25, 21 matches); Cambridge U (1920–21).
Career batting
26–38–3–557–94–15.91–0–*ct* 6–*st* 1
Bowling 24–0

He won blues for hockey and rackets.

Hale, Harold
Amateur. *b:* 27.3.1867, Perth, Western Australia. *d:* 2.8.1947, Melbourne, Victoria, Australia. Lower order right-hand batsman, right-arm medium pace off break bowler. *Teams* Gloucestershire (1886–89, 19 matches); Cambridge U (1887–90, blue 1887, 1889 and 1890); Tasmania (1883/4 to 1910/11, 13 matches). *Tour* Tasmania to New Zealand 1883/4.
Career batting
57–101–13–1067–53–12.12–0–*ct* 24
Bowling 2295–99–23.18–6–0–7/42

Hale, Ivor Edward
Amateur. *b:* 6.10.1922, Worcester. Middle order right-hand batsman, off break bowler. *Sch* Royal Grammar School, Worcester. *Teams* Sussex (1946, 3 matches); Gloucestershire (1947–48, 13 matches).
Career batting
16–28–3–314–61–12.56–0–*ct* 8
Bowling 65–2–32.50–0–0–1/18

Hale, John Hinde
Amateur. *b:* 16.9.1830, East Grinstead, Sussex. *d:* 11.7.1878, Notting Hill, London. Brother of T. W. (Oxford U 1851). Middle order right-hand batsman, good deep field. *Sch* Rugby. *Team* Sussex (1853–65, 35 matches).
Career batting
49–94–1–1242–61–13.35–0–*ct* 37–*st* 1
He was regarded as the fastest scoring batsman of his day, 'though not possessing an elegant style'. He was captain of Sussex 1863–64. For some years he was on the Committee of Sussex CCC. He also played for Buckinghamshire.

Hale, Percy William
Amateur. *b:* 7.2.1874, Kensington, London. *d:* 8.1.1933, Headstone, Harrow, Middlesex. Middle order batsman. *Sch* City of London. *Team* Middlesex (1900, 1 match).
Career batting
1–2–0–29–26–14.50–0–*ct* 2

Hale, Terrance Saville
Cricketer. *b:* 8.10.1936, Waterbeach, Cambridgeshire. Middle order left-hand batsman. *Team* Minor Counties (1965).
Career batting
1–2–0–8–8–4.00–0–*ct* 0
His County cricket was for Cambridgeshire (1960–79), being captain in 1977–78.

Hale, Walter Henry
Professional. *b:* 6.3.1870, West Bromwich, Staffordshire. *d:* 12.8.1956, Bishopston, Bristol. Middle order right-hand batsman, right-arm slow bowler. *Teams* Somerset (1892, 8 matches); Gloucestershire (1895–1909, 60 matches).
Career batting
69–119–7–2124–135–18.96–2–*ct* 39
Bowling 414–9–46.00–0–0–2/16
A noted rugby footballer he appeared for Bristol as well as Gloucestershire and Somerset.

Hale, Warren Stormes
Amateur. *b:* 22.7.1862, Bures, Suffolk. *d:* 5.2.1934, Highgate, Middlesex. Middle order batsman. *Team* Middlesex (1893, 4 matches).
Career batting
5–9–1–86–36–10.75–0–*ct* 1
He was a prolific scorer in London Club cricket, notably for Hampstead. His final first-class match was for MCC in 1897.

Hales, John
Amateur. *b:* 16.9.1833, Charmouth, Dorset. *d:* 25.1.1915, Bournemouth, Hampshire. Steady opening right-hand batsman, right-hand fast medium round-arm bowler. *Sch* Rugby. *Teams* Cambridge U (1855–59, blue 1855 and 1856); Surrey Club (1865).
Career batting
8–15–0–69–19–4.60–0–*ct* 5

Hales, Lloyd Archibald
Amateur. *b:* 27.6.1921, Leicester. *d:* 12.9.1984, Leicester. Middle order right-hand batsman, right-arm medium pace off break bowler. *Sch* Wyggeston and Bristol GS. *Team* Leicestershire (1947, 2 matches).
Career batting
2–4–0–76–62–19.00–0–*ct* 0
Bowling 38–0

Halford, John
Amateur. *b:* 21.4.1846, Redmarley D'Abitot, Worcestershire. *d:* 1.4.1901, Gloucester. Middle order right-hand batsman. *Team* Gloucestershire (1870–74, 10 matches).
Career batting
10–15–2–150–42–11.53–0–*ct* 8–*st* 1
Bowling 12–0

Halfyard, David John
Professional. *b:* 3.4.1931, Winchmore Hill, Middlesex. Lower order right-hand batsman, right-arm fast medium or medium bowler. *Teams* Kent (1956–64, 185 matches); Nottinghamshire (1968–70, 77 matches).
Career batting
264–348–51–3242–79–10.91–0–*ct* 113
Bowling 24822–963–25.77–55–13–9/39
In 1967, having retired from first-class cricket due to injury he was appointed to the first-class umpires' list, but after one year resumed County cricket with Nottinghamshire. He also played for Durham (pre first-class, 1971–72), Northumberland (1973) and Cornwall (1974–77 and 1982). He returned to the umpires' list (1977–81). He took 100 wickets in a season five times (best 135, av 20.39, in 1958). His best bowling was 9/39 for Kent v Glamorgan at Neath in 1957.

Hall, Alfred Ewart
Professional. *b:* 23.1.1896, Bolton, Lancashire. *d:* 1.1.1964, Hospital Hill, Johannesburg, South Africa. Tail end right-hand batsman, left-arm fast medium bowler. *Teams* Transvaal (1920/1 to 1930/1); Lancashire (1923–24, 9 matches). *Tests* South Africa (1922/3 to 1930/1, 7 matches).
Career batting
46–57–21–134–22–3.72–0–*ct* 13
Bowling 4501–234–19.23–21–6–8/80
Test batting
7–8–2–11–5–1.83–0–*ct* 4
Bowling 886–40–22.15–3–1–7/63

Hall, Bert
Professional. Middle order batsman. *Team* Derbyshire (1902, 1 match).

Hall, Brian

Career batting
1–2–0–10–7–5.00–0–*ct* 0

Hall, Brian
Professional. *b:* 16.9.1929, Morley, Yorkshire. *d:* 27.2.1989, Doncaster, Yorkshire. Tail end right-hand batsman, right-arm medium fast bowler. *Team* Yorkshire (1952, 1 match).
Career batting
1–2–0–14–10–7.00–0–*ct* 1
Bowling 55–1–55.00–0–0–1/55

Hall, Brian Charles
Professional. *b:* 2.3.1934, Marylebone, London. Lower order right-hand batsman, right-arm medium pace bowler. *Team* Worcestershire (1956–57, 3 matches).
Career batting
3–4–1–34–21–11.33–0–*ct* 1
Bowling 97–3–32.33–0–0–2/11

Hall, Charles
Professional. *b:* 16.10.1842, Islington, London. Lower order right-hand batsman, right-hand fast round-arm bowler. *Team* Middlesex (1867, 1 match).
Career batting
1–2–0–12–7–6.00–0–*ct* 0

Hall, Charles Henry
Professional. *b:* 5.4.1906, York. *d:* 11.12.1976, Upper Poppleton, Yorkshire. Lower order right-hand batsman, right-arm medium fast bowler. *Team* Yorkshire (1928–34, 23 matches).
Career batting
23–22–9–67–15*–5.15–0–*ct* 11
Bowling 1226–45–27.24–2–0–6/71

Hall, Charles John
Professional. *b:* 12.8.1848, Kingston-upon-Thames, Surrey. *d:* 18.11.1931, Heybridge, Essex. Middle or lower order right-hand batsman, right-hand fast round-arm bowler. *Team* Surrey (1868–73, 8 matches).
Career batting
8–13–1–71–15–5.91–0–*ct* 1
Bowling 13–1–13.00–0–0–1/4

Hall, Clifford Geoffrey
Amateur. *b:* 19.1.1902, Breamore, Hampshire. *d:* 9.7.1982, Breamore, Hampshire. Middle order right-hand batsman. *Team* Hampshire (1933–35, 5 matches).
Career batting
5–7–0–77–37–11.00–0–*ct* 1
He also played for Wiltshire (1938).

Hall, Derek
Professional. *b:* 21.2.1932, Bolsover, Derbyshire. *d:* 13.3.1983, San Jose, California, USA, in a car accident. Tail end right-hand batsman, right-arm fast medium bowler. *Team* Derbyshire (1955–58, 20 matches).
Career batting
20–29–16–43–10*–3.30–0–*ct* 6
Bowling 1386–48–28.87–0–0–4/57

Hall, E.
Amateur. Middle order right-hand batsman, wicket-keeper. *Team* Hampshire (1880–85, 11 matches).
Career batting
11–21–2–198–22–10.42–0–*ct* 11–*st* 3

Hall, Egerton Hawkesley
Amateur. *b:* 25.4.1861. *d:* 8.2.1919, Axbridge, Somerset. Lower order batsman, useful bowler. *Team* Somerset (1884–85, 3 matches).
Career batting
3–6–1–43–23–8.60–0–*ct* 1
Bowling 145–3–48.33–0–0–2/67

Hall, Frederick Harrison
Amateur. *b:* 15.8.1892, Blackrock, Co Cork, Ireland. *d:* 4.1.1947, Virginia Water, Surrey. Brother-in-law of J. A. Hussey (Royal Navy). Lower order right-hand batsman. *Sch* Dover. *Teams* Ireland (1925–26); Dublin U (1924).
Career batting
3–5–0–71–34–14.20–0–*ct* 2

Hall, Geoffrey Harold
Professional. *b:* 1.6.1941, Colne, Lancashire. Tail end right-hand batsman, right-arm fast bowler. *Team* Somerset (1961–65, 48 matches).
Career batting
48–51–26–90–12*–3.60–0–*ct* 9
Bowling 3425–111–30.85–2–0–6/60
He also played for Cumberland (1966).

Hall, Harold St Alban
Amateur. *b:* 1875. *d:* 17.5.1915, Farnham, Surrey. Middle order batsman. *Team* Northamptonshire (1907, 1 match).
Career batting
1–2–0–12–7–6.00–0–*ct* 0
He first played for Northamptonshire (pre first-class) in 1901.

Hall, Henry George Hamlet
Amateur. *b:* 24.12.1857, Bedminster, Somerset. *d:* 13.2.1934, Southmead, Bristol. Lower order batsman, useful bowler. *Team* Somerset (1882–85, 2 matches).
Career batting
2–4–1–2–2–0.66–0–*ct* 1
Bowling 57–1–57.00–0–0–1/47
His last match for Somerset (not first-class) was in 1887.

Hall, Ian William
Professional. *b:* 27.12.1939, Sutton Scarsdale, Derbyshire. Opening right-hand batsman, right-arm medium pace bowler, occasional wicket-keeper. *Team* Derbyshire (1959–72, 270 matches).

Career batting
270–483–32–11666–136*–25.86–9–*ct* 189
Bowling 23–0
He hit 1,000 runs in a season five times (best 1,449, av 33.69, in 1971). A well-known soccer player, he appeared for Derby County and Mansfield Town at inside right.

Hall, J. W. C.
(*see under* Cressy-Hall, J. W.)

Hall, James William
Cricketer. *b:* 30.3.1968, Chichester, Sussex. Opening right-hand batsman, off break bowler. *Team* Sussex (1990–92, 55 matches).
Career batting
55–97–9–2951–140*–33.53–4–*ct* 21
Bowling 14–0
He scored 1,140 runs, av 32.57, in 1990, his debut season in first-class cricket, and again completed 1,000 runs in 1992.

Hall, John
Professional. *b:* 11.11.1815, Nottingham. *d:* 17.4.1888, South Retford, Nottinghamshire. Middle order right-hand batsman, right-arm lob bowler. *Team* Yorkshire (1844–63, 4 matches).
Career batting
4–7–1–49–28*–8.16–0–*ct* 6
Bowling 37–9 + 3–4.11–1–0–5/18
He appeared for Leicester in 1839 and moving to Bradford in 1841 was for many years the leading batsman of that town.

Hall, John Bernard
Amateur. *b:* 17.6.1903, Worksop, Nottinghamshire. *d:* 27.5.1979, Retford, Nottinghamshire. Father of M. J. (Nottinghamshire). Lower order right-hand batsman, right-arm medium pace bowler. *Sch* Bloxham. *Team* Nottinghamshire (1935–46, 5 matches). *Tour* Cahn to Ceylon 1936/7.
Career batting
7–13–1–114–24–9.50–0–*ct* 3
Bowling 516–21–24.57–1–0–6/75

Hall, John Edwin
Cricketer. *b:* 5.1.1950, Maseru, Basutoland. Middle order right-hand batsman. *Sch* Ardingly. *Team* Cambridge U (1969–70, blue 1969).
Career batting
14–26–0–385–69–14.80–0–*ct* 3
His County cricket was for Suffolk (1968–71).

Hall, John Keith
Amateur. *b:* 29.7.1934, West Wickham, Kent. Lower order right-hand batsman, right-arm fast medium bowler. *Sch* Lancing. *Teams* Surrey (1958–62, 13 matches); Sussex (1960, 1 match). *Tours* Surridge to Bermuda 1961 (not first-class); Brown to East Africa 1961/2 (not first-class).
Career batting
21–22–6–57–22–3.56–0–*ct* 9
Bowling 1532–54–28.37–1–0–5/30
He was also a good middle distance runner.

Hall, John Peter
Professional. *b:* 20.8.1874, Worksop, Nottinghamshire. *d:* 9.11.1925, Worksop, Nottinghamshire. Lower order right-hand batsman, right-arm fast medium bowler. *Team* Derbyshire (1895–97, 4 matches).
Career batting
4–7–1–3–2–0.50–0–*ct* 3
Bowling 112–3–37.33–0–0–1/12

Hall, Louis
Professional. *b:* 1.11.1852, Batley, Yorkshire. *d:* 19.11.1915, Morecambe, Lancashire. Steady opening right-hand batsman, right-hand slow round-arm or lob bowler, brilliant close field. *Team* Yorkshire (1873–94, 279 matches).
Career batting
315–544–63–11095–160–23.06–12–*ct* 195
Bowling 927–22–42.13–0–0–4/51
He hit 1,000 runs in a season four times (best 1,240, av 38.75, in 1887). He carried his bat through a completed innings no less than 15 times and on many occasions batted with remarkable slowness; for Yorkshire v Kent at Canterbury in 1885 he lasted 165 minutes for 12. He captained Yorkshire often in the absence of Lord Hawke. He was a first-class umpire (1894–99 and 1904).

Hall, Maurice James
Amateur. *b:* 22.9.1849, Whatton Manor, Nottinghamshire. *d:* 24.7.1914, Middelburg, Cape Province, South Africa. Brother-in-law of H. G. Edlmann (Gentlemen of Kent). Middle order batsman. *Sch* Uppingham. *Team* Gentlemen of South (1870).
Career batting
1–1–0–9–9–9.00–0–*ct* 0
He appeared in emergency for Gentlemen of the South, being in fact a member of the Nottinghamshire Gentlemen's Club, on which ground his only first-class match was played.

Hall, Michael John
Professional. *b:* 29.5.1935, Worksop, Nottinghamshire. Son of J. B. (Nottinghamshire). Middle order right-hand batsman, good field. *Team* Nottinghamshire (1958–59, 17 matches).
Career batting
17–30–1–430–72–14.82–0–*ct* 17
He was a leading batsman in Bassetlaw League cricket for 25 years.

Hall, Patrick Martin
Amateur. *b:* 14.3.1894, Portsmouth, Hampshire. *d:* 5.8.1941, Fareham, Hampshire. Opening or middle order right-hand batsman. *Sch* Winchester. *Teams* Oxford U (1919); Hampshire (1919–26, 11 matches).

Hall, Peter James

Career batting
14–23–1–292–101–13.27–1–*ct* 3
He scored 101 on debut for Oxford U v Free Foresters at Oxford in 1919.

Hall, Peter James
Amateur. *b:* 4.12.1927, The Peak, Hong Kong. Middle or lower order right-hand batsman, right-arm medium pace bowler. *Teams* Cambridge U (1948–49, blue 1949); Otago (1955/6).
Career batting
12–14–3–235–49–21.36–0–*ct* 5
Bowling 1045–28–37.32–1–0–5/51

Hall, Thomas Auckland
Amateur. *b:* 19.8.1930, Darlington, Co Durham. *d:* 21.4.1984, Arlesey, Bedfordshire from a fall from a train. Lower order right-hand batsman, right-arm fast medium bowler. *Sch* Uppingham. *Teams* Derbyshire (1949–52, 28 matches); Somerset (1953–54, 23 matches).
Career batting
66–103–23–892–69*–11.15–0–*ct* 29
Bowling 5108–183–27.91–4–0–5/50
His final first-class match was for Free Foresters in 1958. He also played for Norfolk (1956–57).

Hall, Walter
Professional. *b:* 27.11.1861, Whitfield, Derbyshire. *d:* 19.11.1924, Sheffield, Yorkshire. Lower order right-hand batsman, right-arm medium pace bowler. *Team* Derbyshire (1882–86, 11 matches).
Career batting
11–17–4–146–43–11.23–0–*ct* 9
Bowling 376–14–26.85–1–0–6/47
He last played for Derbyshire (not first-class) in 1892.

Hall, Wesley Winfield
Amateur. *b:* 12.9.1937, Glebe Land, Station Hill, St Michael, Barbados. Hard hitting lower order right-hand batsman, right-arm fast bowler, good deep field, originally wicket-keeper. *Teams* Barbados (1955/6 to 1970/1); Trinidad (1966/7 to 1969/70); Queensland (1961/2 to 1962/3, 17 matches). *Tours* West Indies to England 1957, 1963, 1966, to India and Pakistan 1958/9, to India and Ceylon 1966/7, to Australia 1960/1, to Australia and New Zealand 1968/9; Commonwealth to Rhodesia 1962/3; West Indian XI to England 1964; Rest of the World to England 1965, 1968. *Tests* West Indies (1958/9 to 1968/9, 48 matches).
Career batting
170–215–38–2673–102*–15.10–1–*ct* 58
Bowling 14273–546–26.14–19–2–7/51
Test batting
48–66–14–818–50*–15.73–0–*ct* 11
Bowling 5066–192–26.38–9–1–7/69
Of his three Test tours to England, Hall achieved little in 1957, was at his peak in 1963 with 74 wickets, av 20.35, and in 1966 reserved his greatest efforts for the Tests. On the twin tour of India and Pakistan in 1958/9 he took no less than 48 wickets in the Tests. His bowling is chiefly associated with his partnership with C. C. Griffith, the pair being for a time the most feared fast bowling combination in the world. He was Minister for Sport in Barbados.

Hall, William
Professional. *b:* 7.4.1878, Bedworth, Warwickshire. *d: circa* 1930, Bedworth, Warwickshire. Lower order right-hand batsman, right-arm fast bowler. *Team* Warwickshire (1905, 2 matches).
Career batting
2–3–0–11–8–3.66–0–*ct* 2
Bowling 66–0

Hall, William Fletcher
Professional. *b:* 22.3.1853, Lindfield, Sussex. *d:* 1.11.1911, East Grinstead, Sussex. Lower order batsman, bowler. *Team* Sussex (1874, 1 match).
Career batting
1–2–0–19–18–9.50–0–*ct* 1
Bowling 57–1–57.00–0–0–1/57

Hallam, Albert William
Professional. *b:* 12.11.1869, East Leake, Nottinghamshire. *d:* 24.7.1940, Loughborough, Leicestershire. Lower order right-hand batsman, right-arm medium pace bowler. *Teams* Lancashire (1895–1900, 71 matches); Nottinghamshire (1901–10, 194 matches).
Career batting
273–365–100–2606–57–9.83–0–*ct* 171
Bowling 19255–1012–19.02–63–10–8/63
He took 100 wickets in a season three times (best 168, av 12.69, in 1907). He also played for Leicestershire (pre first-class, 1889–93).

Hallam, Maurice Raymond
Professional. *b:* 10.9.1931, Leicester. Opening right-hand batsman, good close field. *Team* Leicestershire (1950–70, 493 matches).
Career batting
504–905–56–24488–210*–28.84–32–*ct* 451
Bowling 142–4–35.50–0–0–1/12
He hit 1,000 runs in a season 13 times, going on to 2,000 in three seasons (best 2,262, av 39.68, in 1961). He made four double centuries, all for Leicestershire, the highest being 210* v Glamorgan at Leicester in 1959. In that match he also made a century, and against Sussex at Worthing in 1961 again performed the rare feat of 200 and 100 in the same match. He captained Leicestershire 1963–65 and in 1968.

Hallam, Thomas Haydn
Professional. *b:* 12.4.1881, Pilsley, Derbyshire. *d:* 24.11.1958, Christchurch, New Zealand. Opening or middle order right-hand batsman. *Team* Derbyshire

(1906–07, 10 matches).
Career batting
10–19–0–224–68–11.78–0–*ct* 5

Hallett, Jeremy Charles
Cricketer. *b:* 18.10.1970, Yeovil, Somerset. Lower order right-hand batsman, right-arm medium fast bowler. *Sch* Millfield. *Team* Somerset (1990–91, 11 matches).
Career batting
11–6–1–35–15–7.00–0–*ct* 4
Bowling 875–18–48.61–0–0–3/154

Halliday, Harry
Professional. *b:* 9.2.1920, Pudsey, Yorkshire. *d:* 27.8.1967, Stanley, Wakefield, Yorkshire. Stylish middle order right-hand batsman, off break bowler, good slip field. *Team* Yorkshire (1938–53, 182 matches).
Career batting
187–287–18–8556–144–31.80–12–*ct* 144
Bowling 3201–107–29.91–2–0–6/79

He hit 1,000 runs in a season four times (best 1,484, av 38.05, in 1950). He also played for Cumberland (1957–59).

Halliday, John Gordon
Amateur. *b:* 4.7.1915, Cockermouth, Cumberland. *d:* 3.12.1945, Rochefort, Pay du Dome, France. He was killed in an air crash. Opening right-hand batsman, right-arm medium pace bowler. *Sch* City of Oxford. *Team* Oxford U (1934–37, blue 1935).
Career batting
26–42–8–848–87–24.94–0–*ct* 8
Bowling 747–21–35.57–0–0–3/11

His County cricket was for Oxfordshire (1932–39), whom he captained in 1938.

Halliday, Michael
Cricketer. *b:* 20.8.1948, Harolds Cross, Dublin, Ireland. Lower order right-hand batsman, off break bowler. *Team* Ireland (1970–89).
Career batting
14–16–6–250–47–25.00–0–*ct* 5
Bowling 965–36–26.80–1–0–5/39

Halliday, Simon John
Cricketer. *b:* 13.7.1960, Haverfordwest, Pembroke. Middle order right-hand batsman. *Sch* Downside. *Team* Oxford U (1980–82, blue 1980).
Career batting
9–14–2–348–113*–29.00–1–*ct* 3

His County cricket was for Dorset (1979–87). He played rugby for Bath and England.

Halliday, Thomas Maxwell
Professional. *b:* 1.7.1904, Leyland, Lancashire. *d:* 28.2.1977, Leyland, Lancashire. Middle order right-hand batsman. *Team* Lancashire (1925–29, 41 matches).
Career batting
41–55–11–996–109*–22.63–1–*ct* 12
Bowling 16–0

Halliley, Charles
Professional. *b:* 5.12.1852, Earlsheaton, Dewsbury, Yorkshire. *d:* 23.3.1929, Ravensthorpe, Yorkshire. Middle order right-hand batsman, good field. *Team* Yorkshire (1872, 3 matches).
Career batting
3–5–0–27–17–5.40–0–*ct* 2

Halliwell, Ernest Austin
Amateur. *b:* 7.9.1864, Drayton Green, Ealing, Middlesex. *d:* 2.10.1919, Hillbrow, Johannesburg, South Africa. Son of R. B. (Middlesex). Middle order right-hand batsman, wicket-keeper. *Teams* Middlesex (1901, 1 match); London County (1901); Transvaal (1892/3 to 1908/9). *Tours* South Africa to England 1894 (not first-class), 1901, 1904. *Tests* South Africa (1891/2 to 1902/3, 8 matches).
Career batting
60–96–8–1702–92–19.34–0–*ct* 75–*st* 37
Bowling 175–3–58.33–0–0–2/49
Test batting
8–15–0–188–57–12.53–0–*ct* 9–*st* 2

His single appearance for Middlesex was made whilst he was a member of the 1901 South African touring team to England. He was the principal wicket-keeper on his three visits to England and also proved useful with the bat. Vice-captain of the 1904 side, he led South Africa in three Tests at home. He emigrated to the Gold Coast in 1882 and then moved to India, where he played much club cricket, before settling in South Africa in 1891.

Halliwell, Richard Bisset
Amateur. *b:* 30.11.1842, Bloomsbury, London. *d:* 9.11.1881, St Pancras, London. Father of E. A. (Middlesex and South Africa). Very hard hitting lower order right-hand batsman, wicket-keeper. *Team* Middlesex (1865–71, 20 matches).
Career batting
43–60–8–502–38*–9.65–0–*ct* 35–*st* 41

His final first-class match was Gentlemen v Players in 1873. He played most of his first-class cricket under various aliases.

Hallows, Charles
Professional. *b:* 4.4.1895, Little Lever, Lancashire. *d:* 10.11.1972, Bolton, Lancashire. Nephew of James (Lancashire). Opening left-hand batsman, slow left-arm bowler, good deep field. *Team* Lancashire, (1914–32, 370 matches). *Tests* England (1921–28, 2 matches)
Career batting
383–586–66–20926–233*–40.24–55–*ct* 140
Bowling 784–19–41.26–0–0–3/28
Test batting
2–2–1–42–26–42.00–0–*ct* 0

Hallows, James

He hit 1,000 runs in a season eleven times, going on to 2,000 on three occasions (best 2,645, av 64.51, in 1928). His three double centuries were all for Lancashire, the highest being 233* v Hampshire at Liverpool in 1927. In 1928 he hit exactly 1,000 runs (av 125.00) in the month of May. After retiring from first-class cricket he was chief coach at Worcester 1957–64 and then held the same post at Old Trafford 1965–67.

Hallows, James
Professional. *b:* 14.11.1873, Little Lever, Lancashire. *d:* 20.5.1910, Farnworth, Lancashire. Uncle of Charles (Lancashire). Middle order left-hand batsman, originally left-arm fast bowler, but changed to medium in 1897. *Team* Lancashire (1898–1907, 138 matches).
Career batting
139–203–27–5065–137*–28.77–8–*ct* 57
Bowling 6677–287–23.26–14–5–9/37

His great season was 1904 when he performed the 'double', taking 108 wickets, av 19.37, and scoring 1,071 runs, av 39.66. He hit 1,000 runs in a season twice (best 1,170, av 31.62, in 1901). His best bowling was 9/37 for Lancashire v Gloucestershire at Gloucester in 1904. He suffered from epilepsy and his career was marred by ill health.

Halsey, Sir Thomas Edgar
Amateur. *b:* 28.11.1898, South Mimms, Hertfordshire. *d:* 30.8.1970, Golden Parsonage, Gaddesden Row, Hemel Hempstead, Hertfordshire. Middle order right-hand batsman, right-arm fast bowler. *Sch* Eton. *Team* Cambridge U (1920).
Career batting
12–23–5–685–102*–38.05–1–*ct* 5
Bowling 388–7–55.42–0–0–2/78

His County cricket was for Hertfordshire (1921–32). His last first-class match was for Royal Navy in 1928.

Hamblin, Christopher Bryan
Cricketer. *b:* 14.4.1952, Bletchingley, Surrey. Lower order right-hand batsman, right-arm medium pace bowler. *Sch* King's, Canterbury. *Team* Oxford U (1971–73, blue all three years).
Career batting
29–45–10–693–123*–19.80–1–*ct* 13
Bowling 1696–38–44.63–0–0–4/32

He also won a blue for hockey.

Hambling, Montague Leslie
Amateur. *b:* 6.12.1893, Croydon, Surrey. *d:* 22.8.1960, Stoke Bishop, Gloucestershire. Middle order right-hand batsman, right-arm fast bowler. *Team* Somerset (1920–27, 18 matches).
Career batting
18–30–4–350–59–13.46–0–*ct* 16
Bowling 493–24–20.54–1–0–6/31

He was also a good soccer player and golfer.

Hamence, Ronald Arthur
Amateur. *b:* 25.11.1915, Hindmarsh, Adelaide, South Australia. Middle order right-hand batsman, right-arm medium pace bowler, good outfield. *Team* South Australia (1935/6 to 1950/1, 69 matches). *Tours* Australia to New Zealand 1945/6, to England 1948. *Tests* Australia (1946/7 to 1947/8, 3 matches).
Career batting
99–155–15–5285–173–37.75–11–*ct* 34
Bowling 239–8–29.87–0–0–2/13
Test batting
3–4–1–81–30*–27.00–0–*ct* 1

Owing to the success of the principal batsmen, Hamence had little opportunity to shine on his tour to England and was not required for the Tests. He scored 121 on debut for South Australia v Tasmania at Adelaide in 1935/6.

Hamer, Arnold
Professional. *b:* 8.12.1916, Primrose Hill, Huddersfield, Yorkshire. Sound opening right-hand batsman, off break bowler. *Teams* Yorkshire (1938, 2 matches); Derbyshire (1950–60, 290 matches).
Career batting
295–515–19–15465–227–31.17–19–*ct* 164
Bowling 2363–71–33.28–0–0–4/27

He hit 1,000 runs in a season 10 times (best 1,850, av 36.27, in 1959). His only double century was 227 for Derbyshire v Nottinghamshire at Trent Bridge in 1955. A useful soccer player, he appeared for York City.

Hamilton, Andrew Caradoc
Cricketer. *b:* 23.9.1953, Ardingly, Sussex. Opening left-hand batsman, slow left-arm bowler. *Sch* Charterhouse. *Team* Oxford U (1975–76, blue 1975).
Career batting
12–24–0–308–45–12.83–0–*ct* 2
Bowling 6–0

Hamilton, Blayney Balfour
Amateur. *b:* 13.6.1872, Mellifont, Collon, Co Louth, Ireland. *d:* 16.12.1946, Dublin, Ireland. Brother of W. D. (Oxford U). Middle order right-hand batsman, slow left-arm bowler. *Sch* Haileybury. *Team* Ireland (1907).
Career batting
1–2–0–4–4–2.00–0–*ct* 2
Bowling 21–0

He played badminton, hockey and tennis for Ireland.

Hamilton, Cyril Penn
Amateur. *b:* 12.8.1909, Adelaide, South Australia. *d:* 10.2.1941, Keren, Eritrea. His widow married P. M. Studd (Cambridge U). Opening right-hand batsman, right-arm slow bowler. *Sch* Wellington. *Teams* Army (1932–36); Kent (1935, 2 matches).
Career batting
8–13–1–475–121–39.58–2–*ct* 8

Bowling 203–6–33.83–1–0–5/83
He played hockey for Scotland.

Hamilton, Lord George Francis
Amateur. *b:* 17.12.1845, Brighton, Sussex. *d:* 22.9.1927, Marylebone, London. Brother-in-law of E. Turnour (Sussex). Lower order right-hand batsman, right-hand fast under-arm bowler, good field. *Sch* Harrow. *Team* MCC (1864).
Career batting
1–2–0–7–5–3.50–0–*ct* 0
Bowling 12–0
First Lord of the Admiralty for six years, then Secretary of State for India for eight years, he was MP for County of Middlesex 1868–85, and for Ealing Division 1885–1906. He was President of the MCC 1881, being a member for 64 years. He was President of Kent in 1911 and 1920.

Hamilton, Canon the Rev Hamilton Anne
(name changed to Douglas-Hamilton in 1875)
Amateur. *b:* 28.5.1853, Simla, India. *d:* 22.8.1929, Marlesford, Suffolk. Middle/lower order right-hand batsman, right-hand fast round-arm bowler, wicket-keeper. *Sch* Wellington. *Team* Cambridge U (1873–75, blue 1873, 1875).
Career batting
15–26–9–204–37–12.00–0–*ct* 12–*st* 7
Bowling 269–8–33.62–0–0–4/80
He also won a blue for rugby.

Hamilton, Leonard Alison Hall
Amateur. *b:* 23.12.1862, Mount Abu, Rajputana, India. *d:* 14.3.1957, Umberleigh Hall, Devon. Middle order right-hand batsman. *Sch* Tonbridge. *Team* Kent (1890–92, 20 matches).
Career batting
21–37–2–645–117*–18.42–1–*ct* 7
Bowling 50–2–25.00–0–0–2/24
His final first-class match was for MCC in 1893.

Hamilton, William Drummond
Amateur. *b:* 4.5.1859, Mellifont, Collon, Co Louth, Ireland. *d:* 4.3.1914, Park Town, Oxford. Brother of B. B. (Ireland). Middle order left-hand batsman. *Sch* Haileybury. *Team* Oxford U (1882, blue).
Career batting
9–17–2–310–54–20.66–0–*ct* 5
He was so nervous when appearing at Lord's in the University Match that when called for a run, he started off in the wrong direction! His final first-class match was for MCC in 1883. He played for Ireland (not first-class) in 1883–96. He also won a blue for athletics.

Hammersley, William Josiah
Amateur. *b:* 25.9.1826, Ash, Surrey. *d:* 15.11.1886, Fitzroy, Melbourne, Victoria, Australia. Lower order right-hand batsman, right-hand medium pace round-arm bowler. *Teams* Cambridge U (1847, blue); Surrey (1848–50, 4 matches); Cambridge Town Club (1848–49); Victoria (1856/7 to 1860/1, 5 matches).
Career batting
34–60–5–567–46–10.30–0–*ct* 23–*st* 1
Bowling 41–9 + 41–4.55–2–1–6/?
He was Editor of Cricketers' Register for Australia. His last first-class match in England was for Gentlemen in 1854. He also played for Essex (pre first-class, 1846) and Suffolk (1847).

Hammond, Charles James
Professional. *b:* 6.9.1818, Storrington, Sussex. *d:* 20.7.1901, Rackham, Sussex. Son of John (Sussex), uncle of Ernest (Sussex). Opening/middle order right-hand batsman. *Teams* Sussex (1841–54, 40 matches).
Career batting
49–89–8–1045–92–12.90–0–*ct* 19
Bowling 4–0 + 2-no av–0–0–2/?
A noted batsman, he made only restricted appearances in important matches due to poor fielding.

Hammond, Ernest
Professional. *b:* 29.7.1850, Storrington, Sussex. *d:* 31.7.1921, Storrington, Sussex. Nephew of C. J. (Sussex), grandson of John (Sussex). Middle order right-hand batsman, right-hand slow round-arm bowler. *Team* Sussex (1870, 5 matches).
Career batting
5–8–1–16–5–2.28–0–*ct* 2
Owing to ill-health his County cricket was very limited.

Hammond, Herbert Edward
Professional. *b:* 7.11.1907, Brighton, Sussex. *d:* 16.6.1985, Brighton, Sussex. Steady opening or middle order right-hand batsman, right-arm medium pace bowler. *Team* Sussex (1928–46, 196 matches).
Career batting
196–267–40–4251–103*–18.72–1–*ct* 170
Bowling 12290–428–28.73–16–1–8/76
He was a first-class umpire (1961–63). He was a noted inside forward with Fulham and won an amateur international cap for England.

Hammond, Jeffrey Roy
Cricketer. *b:* 19.4.1950, North Adelaide, South Australia. Lower order right-hand batsman, right-arm fast medium bowler. *Team* South Australia (1969/70 to 1980/1, 46 matches). *Tours* Australia to England 1972, to West Indies 1972/3. *Tests* Australia (1972/3, 5 matches).
Career batting
69–87–31–922–53–16.46–0–*ct* 36
Bowling 5315–184–28.88–8–0–6/15
Test batting
5–5–2–28–19–9.33–0–*ct* 2
Bowling 488–15–32.53–0–0–4/38
A strained back prevented him bowling at his best on his 1972 tour to England and he was not required for the Tests.

Hammond, John
Professional. *b:* 15.1.1769, Pulborough, Sussex. *d:* 15.10.1844, Storrington, Sussex. Father of C. J. (Sussex), grandfather of Ernest (Sussex). Hard hitting middle order left-hand batsman, right-hand slow semi-round-arm bowler, wicket-keeper. *Teams* Sussex (1790–1816); Kent (1806).
Career batting
51–90–6–1490–108–17.73–1–*ct* 47–*st* 62
Bowling 45 wickets (no analyses)–1–0–5/?

He was regarded as one of the best all-round cricketers of his day, though many of his best performances no doubt are unrecorded. His first first-class match (after 1800) was for England in 1801.

Hammond, Reginald Joseph Leslie
Amateur. *b:* 16.12.1909, Battersea, London. *d:* 3.1.1991, Chichester, Sussex. Opening right-hand batsman, wicket-keeper. *Team* Combined Services (1948).
Career batting
6–11–0–199–46–18.09–0–*ct* 6–*st* 3

Hammond, Walter Reginald
Professional, changed to amateur at start of 1938 season. *b:* 19.6.1903, Buckland, Dover, Kent. *d:* 1.7.1965, Kloof, Durban, South Africa. Great-uncle of R. E. Soule (Tasmania). Middle order right-hand batsman, right-arm medium fast bowler, brilliant close field. *Sch* Portsmouth GS. *Teams* Gloucestershire (1920–51, 405 matches); South African Air Force (1942/3). *Tours* MCC to West Indies 1925/6, 1934/5, to South Africa 1927/8, 1930/1, 1938/9, to Australia 1928/9, to Australia and New Zealand 1932/3, 1936/7, 1946/7. *Tests* England (1927/8 to 1946/7, 85 matches).
Career batting
634–1005–104–50551–336*–56.10–167–*ct* 819–*st* 3
Bowling 22389–732–30.58–22–3–9/23
Test batting
85–140–16–7249–336*–58.45–22–*ct* 110
Bowling 3138–83–37.80–2–0–5/36

The greatest English batsman of his generation, Hammond statistically dominated County cricket during the 1930s and his achievement of heading the first-class batting averages for eight successive summers (1933–46) has never been equalled. He completed 1,000 runs in 17 English seasons plus five overseas ones, on twelve occasions went on to top 2,000 and three times exceeded 3,000. His best year was 1933 with 3,323 runs, av 67.81. In no fewer than five seasons he hit over ten centuries and his tally of 36 double centuries in his career is a figure not remotely approached by another English cricketer. Of his triple centuries, three were for Gloucestershire, but the highest was 336* for England v New Zealand at Auckland in 1932/3, which created a Test record.

His career was rather slow to mature. First he was prevented from appearing in County Championship matches for Gloucestershire because he was not properly qualified, then in 1926 illness prevented him playing any first-class cricket. The following season however he had great success and being picked to go with MCC to South Africa won a place in the England team, which he held until his retirement from regular County cricket, after the 1946 season. He was to appear in a single match in 1950 and make a final appearance in 1951.

In 1928, for Gloucestershire v Surrey, he took ten catches, a first-class record except for wicket-keepers. In the same match he scored a century in each innings, a feat he performed seven times in all. His best bowling was 9/23 for Gloucestershire v Worcestershire at Cheltenham in 1928.

In 1938, when he became an amateur, he was chosen to captain England and led his country in 20 Tests and the MCC on two major overseas tours (1938/9 and 1946/7). He also captained Gloucestershire in 1939 and 1946. Apart from his batting he was a brilliant slip field and a very useful bowler. He played soccer for Bristol Rovers.

Hammond-Chambers-Borgnis, R. P.
(*see under* Borgnis, R. P.)

Hampshire, Alan Wesley
Cricketer. *b:* 18.10.1950, Rotherham, Yorkshire. Son of John (Yorkshire), brother of J. H. (Yorkshire and Derbyshire). Middle order right-hand batsman, right-arm medium pace bowler. *Team* Yorkshire (1975, 1 match).
Career batting
1–2–0–18–17–9.00–0–*ct* 1

Hampshire, John
Professional. *b:* 5.10.1913, Goldthorpe, Yorkshire. Father of A. W. (Yorkshire) and J. H. (Yorkshire and Derbyshire). Lower order right-hand batsman, right-arm fast bowler. *Team* Yorkshire (1937, 3 matches).
Career batting
3–2–0–5–5–2.50–0–*ct* 1
Bowling 109–5–21.80–0–0–2/22

He played soccer for Bristol City.

Hampshire, John Harry
Professional. *b:* 10.2.1941, Thurnscoe, Yorkshire. Son of John (Yorkshire), brother of A. W. (Yorkshire). Attacking middle order right-hand batsman, leg break bowler, good field. *Teams* Yorkshire (1961–81, 456 matches); Tasmania (1967/8 to 1978/9, 15 matches); Leicestershire (1980/1, 3 matches); Derbyshire (1982–84, 57 matches). *Tours* MCC to Ceylon 1969/70, to Australia and New Zealand 1970/1; Cavaliers to West Indies 1964/5; Commonwealth to Pakistan 1967/8; Robins to South Africa 1972/3, 1974/5, to West Indies 1974/5 (not first-class); Leicestershire to Zimbabwe 1980/1. *Tests* England (1969–75, 8 matches).

Career batting
577–924–112–28059–183*–34.55–43–*ct* 446
Bowling 1637–30–54.56–2–0–7/52
Test batting
8–16–1–403–107–26.86–1–*ct* 9

He hit 1,000 runs in a season 15 times (best 1,596, av 53.20, in 1978). In 1979 and 1980 he captained Yorkshire. He played for Leicestershire as a guest player on their tour of Zimbabwe. He became a first-class umpire in 1985, standing in 10 Test matches (1989–92), including four in Pakistan in 1989/90.

Hampson, Arthur Harry
Professional. *b:* 21.5.1878, Earl Shilton, Leicestershire. *d:* 24.11.1952, Earl Shilton, Leicestershire. Lower order right-hand batsman, wicket-keeper. *Team* Leicestershire (1905–06, 11 matches).
Career batting
11–18–4–100–23–7.14–0–*ct* 9–*st* 7

Hampson, James Frederick
Amateur. *b:* 19.12.1877, Altrincham, Cheshire. *d:* 26.1.1931, Withington, Lancashire. Lower order batsman, bowler. *Sch* Rugby. *Team* London County (1901).
Career batting
2–2–0–18–17–9.00–0–*ct* 1
Bowling 29–2–14.50–0–0–1/1

Hampton, Anthony Nicholas Seymour
Cricketer. *b:* 25.4.1967, Burton-on-Trent, Staffordshire. Middle order right-hand batsman, left-arm medium pace bowler. *Sch* Reading. *Team* Oxford U (1988–89, blue 1989).
Career batting
11–18–2–257–55–16.06–0–*ct* 8
Bowling 319–5–63.80–0–0–4/91

Hampton, William Marcus
Amateur. *b:* 20.1.1903, Bromsgrove, Worcestershire. *d:* 7.4.1964, Ogdens, Fordingbridge, Hampshire. Middle order right-hand batsman, off break bowler. *Sch* Clifton. *Teams* Warwickshire (1922, 1 match); Worcestershire (1925–26, 12 matches).
Career batting
13–25–1–332–57–13.83–0–*ct* 8
Bowling 26–1–26.00–0–0–1/11

He played in trials at Cambridge U, but not in first-class matches.

Hanbury, Edwin Charles
Amateur. *b:* 23.6.1848, Clapham Park, London. *d:* 29.9.1914, Ramsgate, Kent. Middle order right-hand batsman. *Team* Surrey (1871, 3 matches).
Career batting
3–6–2–44–17–11.00–0–*ct* 0

Hanbury, T. P.
Amateur. Lower order batsman. *Team* MCC (1882).
Career batting
1–1–1–0–0*–no av–0–*ct* 0

Hancock, Joseph William
Professional. *b:* 26.11.1876, Old Tupton, Derbyshire. *d:* 23.5.1939, Clifton, Rotherham, Yorkshire. Lower order left-hand batsman, left-arm medium pace bowler. *Teams* Derbyshire (1897–1900, 47 matches); Scotland (1906).
Career batting
48–77–19–459–43*–7.91–0–*ct* 21
Bowling 2795–94–29.73–1–0–5/61

Hancock, Leslie Frank
Amateur. *b:* 25.10.1899, Jamnagar, India. *d:* 12.7.1944, Normandy, France. Middle/lower order right-hand batsman, right-arm medium fast bowler. *Sch* Cheltenham. *Team* MCC (1926).
Career batting
2–2–0–24–23–12.00–0–*ct* 3
Bowling 24–1–24.00–0–0–1/4

He was married to the actress Ellen Pollock.

Hancock, Ralph Escott
Amateur. *b:* 20.12.1887, Llandaff, Cardiff, Glamorgan. *d:* 29.10.1914, Festubert, France. His widow married the brother of J. A. G. Kennard (Hampshire). Middle order right-hand batsman, change bowler. *Sch* Rugby. *Team* Somerset (1907–14, 9 matches).
Career batting
9–17–0–206–34–12.11–0–*ct* 0
Bowling 29–0

Hancock, Timothy Harold Coulter
Cricketer. *b:* 20.4.1972, Reading, Berkshire. Middle order right-hand batsman, right-arm medium pace bowler. *Sch* St Edward's, Oxford. *Team* Gloucestershire (1991–92, 15 matches).
Career batting
15–26–3–529–102–23.00–1–*ct* 15
Bowling 136–4–34.00–0–0–2/43

He also played for Oxfordshire (1990).

Hancock, Dr William Ilbert
Amateur. *b:* 10.4.1873, Wiveliscombe, Somerset. *d:* 26.1.1910, Marylebone, London. Brother-in-law of E. R. Sweet-Escott (Glamorgan). Middle order batsman. *Sch* Dulwich. *Team* Somerset (1892, 1 match).
Career batting
1–2–0–7–7–3.50–0–*ct* 0

Handford, Alick
Professional. *b:* 3.5.1869, Wilford, Nottinghamshire. *d:* 15.10.1935, Tavistock, Devon. Brother of Saunders (Players of USA). Lower order right-hand batsman, right-arm medium pace bowler. *Teams* Nottinghamshire (1894–98, 15 matches); Southland (1914/15).
Career batting
26–38–9–275–24*–9.48–0–*ct* 16
Bowling 1722–60–28.70–5–0–7/39

Handford, James

His first-class debut was for Players of USA in 1892. His final first-class match in England was for MCC in 1901.

Handford, James
Professional. *b:* 1.2.1890, Hayfield, Derbyshire. *d:* 14.8.1948, Stockport, Cheshire. Middle order right-hand batsman. *Team* Derbyshire (1910, 9 matches).
Career batting
9–17–3–137–23–9.78–0–*ct* 4
Bowling 31–0

Hands, Barry Onslow
Amateur. *b:* 26.9.1916, Moseley, Birmingham. *d:* 1.7.1984, Birmingham. Nephew of W. C. (Warwickshire). Lower order left-hand batsman, right-arm off break bowler. *Team* Warwickshire (1946–47, 3 matches).
Career batting
3–2–0–13–9–6.50–0–*ct* 0
Bowling 137–4–34.25–0–0–3/76

Hands, Kenneth Charles Myburgh
Amateur. *b:* 22.3.1892, Stellenbosch, Cape Province, South Africa. *d:* 18.11.1954, Parys, Orange Free State, South Africa. Brother of P. A. M. (South Africa) and R. H. M. (South Africa). Middle order right-hand batsman. *Teams* Oxford U (1912); Western Province (1921/2 to 1930/1).
Career batting
31–60–7–1543–171*–29.11–3–*ct* 12
Bowling 568–17–33.41–0–0–4/25
A noted rugby footballer, he was awarded his blue.

Hands, Philip Albert Myburgh
Amateur. *b:* 18.3.1890, Claremont, Cape Town, South Africa. *d:* 27.4.1951, Parys, Orange Free State, South Africa. Brother of K. C. M. (Oxford U) and R. H. M. (South Africa). Middle order right-hand batsman. *Team* Western Province (1906/7 to 1926/7). *Tour* South Africa to England 1924. *Tests* South Africa (1913/14 to 1924, 7 matches).
Career batting
52–86–5–2034–119–25.11–3–*ct* 20
Bowling 84–5–16.80–0–0–3/9
Test batting
7–12–0–300–83–25.00–0–*ct* 3
Bowling 18–0
He had a very moderate tour to England in 1924, appearing in only one Test. He played no first-class cricket at Oxford U, but did win a blue for rugby.

Hands, William Cecil
Amateur. *b:* 20.12.1886, Calthorpe Park, Edgbaston, Birmingham. *d:* 31.8.1974, Northwood, Middlesex. Uncle of B. O. (Warwickshire). Lower order right-hand batsman, right-arm medium fast bowler. *Sch* KES, Birmingham. *Team* Warwickshire (1909–20, 60 matches).
Career batting
60–91–23–856–63–12.58–0–*ct* 36
Bowling 3509–142–24.71–3–0–5/10
Business prevented him appearing regularly in County cricket.

Hanif Mohammad
Amateur. *b:* 21.12.1934, Junagadh, India. Brother of Wazir (Pakistan), Mushtaq (Pakistan), Sadiq (Pakistan) and Raees (Karachi), father of Shoaib (Pakistan), uncle of Shahid (PIA) and Asif (PIA). Steady opening right-hand batsman, off break bowler, occasional wicket-keeper. *Teams* Bahawalpur (1953/4); Karachi (1954/5 to 1968/9); PIA (1960/1 to 1975/6). *Tours* Pakistan to England 1954, 1962, 1967, to Australia and New Zealand 1964/5, to India 1952/3, 1960/1, to West Indies 1957/8; PIA to Ireland 1969 (not first-class); International XI to Rhodesia 1961/2; Rest of World to England 1965, 1966, 1968. *Tests* Pakistan (1952/3 to 1969/70, 55 matches).
Career batting
238–370–44–17059–499–52.32–55–*ct* 178–*st* 12
Bowling 1509–53–28.47–0–0–3/4
Test batting
55–97–8–3915–337–43.98–12–*ct* 40
Bowling 95–1–95.00–0–0–1/1
He scored over 1,000 runs in 1954 and 1962 in England (best 1,623, av 36.88, in 1954), but considering his reputation, he never really succeeded in England and in the five 1962 Tests was in fact a complete failure. He captained the 1967 tourists in England and altogether led Pakistan in 11 Tests. His highest score is the world record 499 for Karachi v Bahawalpur at Karachi in 1958/9 and his highest Test score 337 v West Indies at Bridgetown in 1957/8. None of his seven scores over 200 were made in England. His first-class debut was for Karachi and Bahawalpur in 1951/2.

Hankey, Reginald
Amateur. *b:* 3.11.1832, Marylebone, London. *d:* 25.8.1886, Brighton, Sussex. Middle order right-hand batsman, right-hand medium round-arm bowler. *Sch* Harrow. *Teams* Oxford U (1853–55, blue 1853 and 1855); Surrey (1855, 1 match).
Career batting
18–34–1–489–70–14.81–0–*ct* 9
Bowling 200–10 + 12–20.00–0–0–4/?
He was regarded as one of the best amateur batsmen of his day, but business restricted his appearances in important cricket. He also played for Oxfordshire. His final first-class match was for MCC in 1860. He captained Oxford in 1855.

Hanley, Robin
Cricketer. *b:* 5.1.1968, Tonbridge, Kent. Middle order right-hand batsman. *Team* Sussex (1990–92, 5 matches).

Career batting
5–7–0–52–28–7.42–0–*ct* 0

Hanley, Rupert William
Cricketer. *b:* 29.1.1952, Port Elizabeth, South Africa. Son of A. W. D. (Border). Tail end right-hand batsman, right-arm fast bowler. *Teams* Eastern Province (1970/1 to 1974/5); Orange Free State (1975/6); Transvaal (1976/7 to 1986/7); Northamptonshire (1984, 17 matches).
Career batting
113–99–44–320–33*–5.81–0–*ct* 39
Bowling 8491–408–20.81–23–3–7/31
His first appearance in English first-class cricket was for D. H. Robins' XI in 1974. Suffering no fewer than four injuries during his season with Northamptonshire in 1984, he had few days of success.

Hanna, Michael
Amateur. *b:* 6.6.1926, Camberwell, London. Lower order right-hand batsman, wicket-keeper. *Team* Somerset (1951–54, 2 matches).
Career batting
2–3–1–5–4*–2.50–0–*ct* 0
He also played for Wiltshire (1957–68). He was a noted rugby scrum-half with Bath and Somerset.

Hannay, Charles Scott
Amateur. *b:* 2.11.1879, West Derby, Liverpool, Lancashire. *d:* 27.6.1955, Grassendale, Aigburth, Liverpool, Lancashire. Middle order right-hand batsman, right-arm medium pace bowler, good field. *Sch* Rugby. *Team* Oxford U (1901).
Career batting
1–2–0–24–20–12.00–0–*ct* 0

Hansell, Thomas Michael Geoffrey
Cricketer. *b:* 24.8.1954, Sutton Coldfield, Warwickshire. Middle order left-hand batsman, slow left-arm bowler. *Sch* Millfield. *Team* Surrey (1975–77, 14 matches).
Career batting
14–26–5–319–54–15.19–0–*ct* 2
Bowling 0–0

Hansford, Alan Roderick
Cricketer. *b:* 1.10.1968, Cuckfield, Sussex. Lower order right-hand batsman, right-arm medium pace bowler. *Team* Sussex (1989–92, 10 matches).
Career batting
10–11–3–109–29–13.62–0–*ct* 3
Bowling 991–30–33.03–1–0–5/79

Hanson, Raymond Leslie
Cricketer. *b:* 12.4.1951, Chesterfield, Derbyshire. Lower order right-hand batsman, wicket-keeper. *Team* Derbyshire (1973, 1 match).
Career batting
1–1–1–1–1*–no av–0–*ct* 1

Hanumant Singh
(Maharajkumar of Banswara)
Amateur. *b:* 29.3.1939, Banswara, India. Brother of Suryaveer Singh (Rajasthan), nephew of K. S. Duleepsinhji (Sussex), cousin of K. S. Indrajitsinhji (India). Middle order right-hand batsman, leg break bowler. *Teams* Madhya Bharat (1956/7); Rajasthan (1957/8 to 1978/9). *Tour* India to England 1967. *Tests* India (1963/4 to 1969/70, 14 matches).
Career batting
207–331–50–12338–213*–43.90–29–*ct* 110
Bowling 2293–56–40.94–1–0–5/48
Test batting
14–24–2–686–105–31.18–1–*ct* 11
Bowling 51–0
He looked a better player than his figures with the bat (554, av 29.35) indicated on his single tour to England, and appeared in two Tests. His highest score was 213* for Rajasthan v Bombay at Bombay in 1966/7. He hit 1,000 runs in India in three seasons (best 1,586, av 68.95, in 1966/7).

Harben, Henry Eric Southey
Amateur. *b:* 1.8.1900, Ward Hill, Farnham, Surrey. *d:* 1.10.1971, Malta. Son-in-law of M. F. Ramsay (MCC). Middle order right-hand batsman, change bowler. *Sch* Eton. *Team* Sussex (1919, 4 matches).
Career batting
4–8–2–126–34–21.00–0–*ct* 1
Bowling 36–0

Harber, John
Professional. *b:* 12.11.1889, Malvern Wells, Worcestershire. *d:* 11.8.1962, Baughton Hill Farm, Hill Croome, Worcestershire. Lower order right-hand batsman, bowler. *Team* Worcestershire (1914, 1 match).
Career batting
1–2–0–3–3–1.50–0–*ct* 0
Bowling 46–3–15.33–0–0–2/24

Harbin, Dr Leonard
Amateur. *b:* 30.4.1915, Tunapuna, Trinidad. Lower order right-hand batsman, off break bowler. *Teams* Trinidad (1935/6 to 1940/1); Gloucestershire (1949–51, 4 matches).
Career batting
12–18–1–337–89–19.82–*ct* 11
Bowling 633–25–25.32–1–0–5/80

Harbinson, William Kenneth
Amateur. *b:* 11.7.1906, Larne, Co Antrim, Ireland. Steady middle order right-hand batsman, right-arm medium fast bowler, fine extra cover. *Sch* Marlborough. *Team* Cambridge U (1926–29, blue 1929).
Career batting
14–22–2–604–130–30.20–2–*ct* 6
Bowling 91–2–45.50–0–0–1/14
He also won a blue for hockey.

Harbord, William Edward
Amateur. *b:* 15.12.1908, Manton, Rutland. *d:* 28.7.1992, Harrogate, Yorkshire. Brother-in-law of J. C. Atkinson-Clark (Middlesex), uncle of Mike D'Abo, the musician. Opening or middle order right-hand batsman, right-arm slow medium bowler. *Sch* Eton. *Teams* Yorkshire (1929–35, 16 matches); Oxford U (1930). *Tours* Martineau to Egypt 1934 (not first-class); MCC to West Indies 1934/5.
Career batting
21–29–1–512–109–18.28–1–*ct* 9
Bowling 15–0
He was for many years on the Yorkshire CCC Committee.

Harbottle, Michael Neale
Amateur. *b:* 7.2.1917, Littlehampton, Sussex. Middle order left-hand batsman, slow left-arm bowler. *Sch* Marlborough. *Team* Army (1938).
Career batting
1–1–0–156–156–156.00–1–*ct* 0
His first-class career is noteworthy because he hit 156 in his only innings. His County cricket was for Dorset (1936–56).

Harcombe, John Dowie
Amateur. *b:* 1884, Cape Town, South Africa. *d:* 19.7.1954, North Town, Taunton, Somerset. Middle order right-hand batsman, right-arm slow bowler. *Sch* Taunton. *Team* Somerset (1905–19, 7 matches).
Career batting
7–12–2–76–29–7.60–0–*ct* 2
Bowling 132–3–44.00–0–0–3/51

Harcourt, Arthur Bryan
Amateur. *b:* 14.11.1917, Pietermaritzburg, Natal, South Africa. *d:* 12.8.1973, Pietermaritzburg, Natal, South Africa. Lower order right-hand batsman, wicket-keeper. *Team* Oxford U (1947).
Career batting
4–8–2–76–25*–12.66–0–*ct* 4–*st* 3

Harcourt, Aubrey
Amateur. *b:* 16.8.1852, Nuneham, Abingdon, Oxfordshire. *d:* 22.3.1904, Monte Carlo, Monaco. Nephew of Viscount Pevensey (Sussex). *Sch* Eton. *Team* Lord Sheffield's XI (1891).
Career batting
1–1–0–0–0–0.00–0–*ct* 0

Hardcastle, Ven Edward Hoare
Amateur. *b:* 6.3.1862, Manchester, Lancashire. *d:* 20.5.1945, Brighton, Sussex. Nephew of W. E. Goschen (Oxford U). Lower order left-hand batsman, left-arm fast bowler. *Sch* Winchester. *Team* Kent (1883–84, 2 matches).
Career batting
2–2–0–12–7–6.00–0–*ct* 4
Bowling 64–3–21.33–0–0–3/29
He also appeared for Worcestershire (not first-class), but whilst at Cambridge U did not play in the eleven.

Hardcastle, Frank
Amateur. *b:* 12.5.1844, Firwood, Bolton, Lancashire. *d:* 5.11.1908, Paddington, London. Middle order batsman. *Sch* Repton. *Team* Lancashire (1868–69, 2 matches).
Career batting
2–4–1–17–9–5.66–0–*ct* 1
He was MP for Westhoughton 1885–92.

Hardcastle, Walter Mitchel
Amateur. *b:* 10.2.1843, Great Bolton, Lancashire. *d:* 27.4.1901, Bolton, Lancashire. Middle order right-hand batsman, right-arm fast bowler. *Team* Lancashire (1869–74, 4 matches).
Career batting
4–7–0–33–11–4.71–0–*ct* 1

Harden, Richard John
Cricketer. *b:* 16.8.1965, Bridgwater, Somerset. Middle order right-hand batsman, slow left-arm bowler. *Sch* King's, Taunton. *Teams* Somerset (1985–92, 147 matches); Central Districts (1987/8).
Career batting
155–245–41–7902–187–38.73–15–*ct* 99
Bowling 952–19–50.10–0–0–2/7
He scored 1,000 runs in a season four times (best 1,460, av 60.83, in 1990).

Hardie, Brian Ross
Cricketer. *b:* 14.1.1950, Stenhousemuir, Stirlingshire, Scotland. Brother of K. M. (Scotland). Opening right-hand batsman, right-arm medium pace bowler, close field. *Teams* Scotland (1970–72); Essex (1973–90, 374 matches).
Career batting
378–608–79–18103–162–34.22–27–*ct* 349
Bowling 254–3–84.66–0–0–2/39
He hit 1,000 runs in a season 11 times (best 1,522, av 43.48, in 1975).

Hardie, J.
Amateur. Lower order batsman. *Team* Australians in England (in emergency) (1886).
Career batting
1–1–0–0–0–0.00–0–*ct* 0

Hardie, Keith Millar
Cricketer. *b:* 13.5.1947, Larbert, Stirlingshire, Scotland. Brother of B. R. (Essex). Lower order right-hand batsman, slow left-arm bowler. *Team* Scotland (1966–76).
Career batting
10–11–4–158–65*–22.57–0–*ct* 1
Bowling 626–35–17.88–0–0–4/23

Harding, Kenneth
Amateur. *b:* 12.2.1892, Greenwich, London. *d:* 30.11.1977, Eastbourne, Sussex. Middle order right-hand batsman. *Sch* St Edward's, Oxford. *Team* Sussex (1928, 3 matches).
Career batting
3–6–1–91–55*–18.20–0–*ct* 0
Despite losing part of his right hand in the First World War, he was a most successful batsman in Sussex Club cricket in the 1920s.

Harding, Norman Walter
Professional. *b:* 19.3.1916, Woolston, Hampshire. *d:* 25.9.1947, Abingdon, Berkshire. He died of infantile paralysis after a few days illness. Lower order right-hand batsman, right-arm fast bowler. *Sch* Reading. *Team* Kent (1937–47, 83 matches).
Career batting
84–123–22–966–71–9.56–0–*ct* 55
Bowling 6531–229–28.51–9–1–5/31
He played as an amateur for Berkshire (1934–36) before joining Kent. For Kent 2nd XI v Wiltshire at Swindon in 1936 he took 18 wickets for 100 (nine in each innings), a feat unique in Minor County Championship cricket.

Hardinge, Harold Thomas William
Professional. *b:* 25.2.1886, Greenwich, London. *d:* 8.5.1965, Tenison Road, Cambridge. Opening right-hand batsman, slow left-arm bowler. *Team* Kent (1902–33, 606 matches). *Test* England (1921, 1 match).
Career batting
623–1021–103–33519–263*–36.51–75–*ct* 297
Bowling 9825–371–26.48–8–1–7/64
Test batting
1–2–0–30–25–15.00–0–*ct* 0
He hit 1,000 runs in a season eighteen times, going on to 2,000 five times (best 2,446, av 59.65, in 1928). His four double centuries were all for Kent, his highest being 263* v Gloucestershire at Gloucester in 1928.
An inside-left, he was a noted soccer player with Newcastle United, Sheffield United and Arsenal, and was capped for England in 1910. He was employed for many years by the sports goods firm, John Wisden and Co.

Hardisty, Charles Henry
Professional. *b:* 10.12.1885, Horsforth, Yorkshire. *d:* 2.3.1968, Leeds, Yorkshire. Middle order right-hand batsman, moderate field. *Team* Yorkshire (1906–09, 38 matches).
Career batting
39–57–5–998–84–19.19–0–*ct* 20
He also played for Northumberland (1911–12), but not in Minor Counties Championship matches.

Hardstaff, Joseph (sen)
Professional. *b:* 9.11.1882, Kirkby-in-Ashfield, Nottinghamshire. *d:* 2.4.1947, Nuncargate, Nottinghamshire. Father of Joseph jun (Nottinghamshire), grandfather of Joseph (Free Foresters). Middle order right-hand batsman, right-arm fast medium bowler, excellent outfield. *Team* Nottinghamshire (1902–24, 340 matches). *Tour* MCC to Australia 1907/8. *Tests* England (1907/8, 5 matches).
Career batting
377–620–73–17146–213*–31.34–26–*ct* 187–*st* 2
Bowling 2244–58–38.68–1–0–5/133
Test batting
5–10–0–311–72–31.10–0–*ct* 1
He hit 1,000 runs in a season seven times plus once overseas (best 1,547, av 45.50, in 1911). His only double century was 213* for Nottinghamshire v Sussex at Hove in 1914. His final first-class match was for MCC in 1926. He became well-known as an umpire (1927–46), going with MCC to West Indies in that capacity in 1929/30, and officiated in 21 Test Matches (1928–35) until the inclusion of his son in the England side prevented this. He played soccer for Nottingham Forest.

Hardstaff, Joseph (jun)
Professional. *b:* 3.7.1911, Nuncargate, Nottinghamshire. *d:* 1.1.1990, Worksop, Nottinghamshire. Son of Joseph sen (Nottinghamshire), father of Joseph (Free Foresters). Middle order right-hand batsman, right-arm medium pace bowler, excellent outfield. *Teams* Nottinghamshire (1930–55, 408 matches); Services in India (1943/4 to 1944/5); Europeans (1944/5); Auckland (1948/9 to 1949/50). *Tours* MCC to Australia and New Zealand 1935/6, 1936/7, 1946/7, to West Indies 1947/8; Tennyson to India 1937/8; Cahn to New Zealand 1938/9. *Tests* England (1935–48, 23 matches).
Career batting
517–812–94–31847–266–44.35–83–*ct* 123
Bowling 2141–36–59.47–0–0–4/43
Test batting
23–38–3–1636–205*–46.74–4–*ct* 9
Regarded as the most elegant batsman of his generation, Hardstaff rarely failed in County cricket, scoring over 1,000 runs in an English season 13 times and going on to 2,000 four times. His highest season's aggregate was 2,540, av 57.72, in 1937, but his best year was 1949 when he was the leading batsman in the country with 2,251 runs, av 72.61. In all he hit ten double centuries, eight of which were for Nottinghamshire, including the highest – 266 v Leicestershire at Leicester in 1937. Of the other two, one was for England v India at Lord's in 1946 and the second for Lord Tennyson's Team in India in 1937/38.
He was a regular member of the England team in the three seasons before the Second World War, but failed to regain a permanent Test place after 1946.

His appearance for Auckland in 1949/50 caused some controversy, since it was claimed that in playing for Nottinghamshire and Auckland he was representing two 'counties' in the same year.

Hardstaff, Joseph
Amateur. *b:* 28.2.1935, Kirkby-in-Ashfield, Nottinghamshire. Grandson of Joseph sen (Nottinghamshire), son of Joseph jun (Nottinghamshire). Middle order right-hand batsman, right-arm medium pace bowler. *Team* Free Foresters (1961–62).
Career batting
2–4–0–57–36–14.25–0–*ct* 0
Bowling 32–1–32.00–0–0–1/32
A well-known player in Services cricket, he captained the RAF. He was appointed Secretary of Middlesex CCC in 1989.

Hardstaff, Richard Green
Professional. *b:* 12.1.1863, Selston, Nottinghamshire. *d:* 18.4.1932, Selston, Nottinghamshire. Lower order left-hand batsman, left-arm medium pace bowler. *Team* Nottinghamshire (1887–99, 30 matches).
Career batting
30–41–10–252–60–8.12–0–*ct* 17
Bowling 1988–100–19.88–8–3–8/53
His County career ended in 1899 when he was no-balled for throwing.

Hardy, David
Professional. *b:* 2.8.1877, Northampton. *d:* 22.1.1951, Northampton. Lower order right-hand batsman, right-arm medium pace bowler. *Team* Northamptonshire (1907–24, 37 matches).
Career batting
37–62–13–499–37–10.18–0–*ct* 15
Bowling 584–14–41.71–1–0–6/11
He first played for Northamptonshire (pre first-class) in 1904.

Hardy, Donald Wrightson
Cricketer. *b:* 24.3.1926, East Boldon, Co Durham. Middle order right-hand batsman, right-arm medium pace bowler. *Sch* Worksop. *Team* Minor Counties (1965).
Career batting
1–2–0–29–29–14.50–0–*ct* 1
His County cricket was for Durham (pre first-class, 1948–67).

Hardy, Evan Michael Pearce
Amateur. *b:* 13.11.1927, Meerut, India. Middle order right-hand batsman. *Sch* Ampleforth. *Team* Combined Services (1959).
Career batting
1–2–0–15–15–7.50–0–*ct* 1
An excellent rugby footballer he was capped for England.

Hardy, Frederick Percy
Professional. *b:* 26.6.1880, Blandford, Dorset. *d:* 9.3.1916, King's Cross, London. He died by his own hand. Middle order left-hand batsman, right-arm medium pace bowler. *Team* Somerset (1902–14, 99 matches).
Career batting
100–176–8–2743–91–16.32–0–*ct* 41
Bowling 3216–91–35.34–2–0–6/82
He also played for Dorset (1902).

Hardy, Jonathan James Ean
Cricketer. *b:* 2.10.1960, Nakuru, Kenya. Opening or middle order left-hand batsman. *Sch* Canford. *Teams* Hampshire (1984–85, 29 matches); Somerset (1986–90, 87 matches); Western Province (1987/8 to 1990/1); Gloucestershire (1991, 10 matches).
Career batting
142–236–31–6120–119–29.85–4–*ct* 80
Bowling 26–0
In 1987 he scored 1,089 runs, av 28.65. He also played for Dorset (1992).

Hardy, Michael John
Amateur. *b:* 30.7.1929, Hendon, Middlesex. Hard hitting middle order right-hand batsman, slow left-arm bowler. *Sch* Oundle. *Team* D. R. Jardine's XI (1958).
Career batting
1–2–0–15–15–7.50–0–*ct* 0
Bowling 35–1–35.00–0–0–1/35
His County cricket was for Buckinghamshire (1959–64).

Hardy, Norman
Amateur. *b:* 11.3.1892, Norton-Malreward, Somerset. *d:* 17.11.1923, Fishponds, Bristol. He died of heart failure whilst playing football. Lower order right-hand batsman, right-arm fast medium bowler. *Team* Somerset (1912–21, 11 matches).
Career batting
11–19–7–169–38–14.08–0–*ct* 6
Bowling 747–34–21.97–0–0–4/22

Hardy, Norman Whittaker
Amateur. *b:* 3.6.1907, Wakefield, Yorkshire. *d:* 2.6.1980. Lower order batsman, opening bowler. *Team* Leveson-Gower's XI (1932).
Career batting
1–2–1–14–8*–14.00–0–*ct* 2
Bowling 91–4–22.75–0–0–3/48

Hardy, Silas
Professional. *b:* 30.4.1867, Ilkeston, Derbyshire. *d:* 27.6.1905, Kimberley, Nottinghamshire. Lower order batsman, right-arm fast medium bowler. *Team* Nottinghamshire (1893–95, 5 matches).
Career batting
5–8–3–45–12*–9.00–0–*ct* 2
Bowling 274–4–68.50–0–0–2/100

He is not to be confused with Solomon Hardy (Derbyshire) although volume 15 of Scores and Biographies states, in error, that Silas Hardy played for both Nottinghamshire and Derbyshire.

Hardy, Solomon
Professional. *b:* 18.5.1863, Ilkeston, Derbyshire. *d:* 5.7.1931, Ilkeston, Derbyshire. Lower order right-hand batsman, wicket-keeper. *Team* Derbyshire (1898, 1 match).
Career batting
1–2–0–10–9–5.00–0–*ct* 2

Hare, John Hugh Montague
Amateur. *b:* 31.5.1857, Docking Hall, Norfolk. *d:* 1.8.1935, Docking Hall, Norfolk. Middle order right-hand batsman, right-arm medium pace bowler, good field. *Sch* Uppingham. *Team* Oxford U (1879–80, blue 1879).
Career batting
8–16–5–126–38*–11.45–0–*ct* 6
Bowling 12–1–12.00–0–0–1/5
His County cricket was for Norfolk (1876–88).

Hare, Peter Macduff Christian
Amateur. *b:* 12.3.1920, Wokingham, Berkshire. Lower order right-hand batsman, wicket-keeper. *Sch* Canford. *Team* Oxford U (1947).
Career batting
1–1–0–39–39–39.00–0–*ct* 2

Hare, Steriker Norman
Amateur. *b:* 31.3.1900, Tottenham, Middlesex. *d:* 30.9.1977, Meadle, Buckinghamshire. Middle order right-hand batsman. *Sch* Chigwell. *Team* Essex (1921, 3 matches).
Career batting
3–5–0–117–98–23.40–0–*ct* 1

Hare, Sir Thomas
Amateur. *b:* 27.7.1930, Westminster, London. *d:* 25.1.1993, Sandringham, Norfolk. He married the grand-daughter of I. F. W. Bligh (Kent). Middle order right-hand batsman, right-arm fast medium bowler. *Sch* Eton. *Team* Cambridge U (1953).
Career batting
10–17–1–218–47–13.62–0–*ct* 5
Bowling 754–19–39.68–1–0–5/35
His final first-class match was for Free Foresters in 1954 and his County cricket was for Norfolk (1947–54).

Hare, William Henry
Cricketer. *b:* 29.11.1952, Newark, Nottinghamshire. Middle order right-hand batsman, right-arm medium bowler. *Team* Nottinghamshire (1971–77, 10 matches).
Career batting
10–18–4–171–36–12.21–0–*ct* 5
Bowling 18–0

A well-known rugby full back, he has appeared for Newark, East Midlands, Leicester, Nottingham and England and toured New Zealand with the British Lions in 1983.

Harenc, Charles Joseph
Amateur. *b:* 3.8.1811, Foots Cray, Kent. *d:* 14.12.1877, Bedford. Brother of A. R. (Kent 1840), E. A. F. (Cambridge U 1837) and H. B. (Gentlemen of Kent 1842). Lower order right-hand batsman, right-hand fast under-arm bowler, later slow round-arm. *Sch* Harrow. *Teams* Oxford U (1832); Kent (1834–48, 14 matches).
Career batting
56–99–12–830–68–9.54–0–*ct* 34
Bowling 154–6 + 124–25.66–7–2–8/?
In the period 1830 to 1834 he was considered one of the best bowlers in England. His final first-class match was for Gentlemen of Kent in 1849, his debut being for the same team in 1830.

Harfield, Lewis
Professional. *b:* 16.8.1905, Cheriton, Hampshire. *d:* 19.11.1985, Winchester, Hampshire. Middle order right-hand batsman, right-arm medium pace bowler. *Team* Hampshire (1925–31, 80 matches).
Career batting
80–133–10–2460–89–20.00–0–*ct* 37
Bowling 649–14–46.35–0–0–3/35
He hit 1,216 runs, av 26.43, in 1929.

Harford, Noel Sherwin
Amateur. *b:* 30.8.1930, Winton, Otago, New Zealand. *d:* 30.3.1981, Auckland, New Zealand. He died by his own hand. Attractive middle order right-hand batsman, right-arm slow medium bowler. *Teams* Central Districts (1953/4 to 1958/9); Auckland (1963/4 to 1966/7). *Tours* New Zealand to India and Pakistan 1955/6, to England 1958. *Tests* New Zealand (1955/6 to 1958, 8 matches).
Career batting
74–122–8–3149–158–27.62–3–*ct* 39
Bowling 478–18–26.55–0–0–3/19
Test batting
8–15–0–229–93–15.26–0–*ct* 0
He appeared in four Tests on the 1958 tour, but in eight innings made only 41 runs. In first-class matches however he hit 1,067 runs, av 26.02.

Hargreave, Sam
Professional. *b:* 22.9.1875, Rusholme, Lancashire. *d:* 1.1.1929, Stratford-on-Avon, Warwickshire. Lower order left-hand batsman, left-arm slow medium bowler, good field. *Team* Warwickshire (1899–1909, 188 matches). *Tour* Hawke to Australia and New Zealand 1902/3.
Career batting
206–263–63–1932–45–9.66–0–*ct* 155
Bowling 20079–919–21.84–74–18–9/35

Injury prematurely ended his County cricket. He took 100 wickets in a season five times (best 134, av 14.02, in 1903). His best bowling was 9/35 for Warwickshire v Surrey at the Oval in 1903.

Hargreaves, Frederick William
Amateur. *b:* 16.8.1858, Brook House, Blackburn, Lancashire. *d:* 5.4.1897, Wilpshire, Blackburn, Lancashire. Middle order batsman. *Sch* Malvern. *Team* Lancashire (1881, 1 match).
Career batting
1–1–0–0–0–0.00–0–*ct* 2
He played soccer for England.

Hargreaves, Herbert Silvester
Professional. *b:* 22.3.1912, Cinder Hill, Shireoaks, Yorkshire. *d:* 29.9.1990, Bury St Edmunds, Suffolk. Lower order right-hand batsman, right-arm fast medium bowler. *Team* Yorkshire (1934–38, 18 matches).
Career batting
19–22–6–53–9–3.31–0–*ct* 5
Bowling 1251–59–21.20–1–0–5/93
He also played for Suffolk (1947–56). He was born 100 yards inside the Yorkshire border.

Hargreaves, James Henry
(played under the alias J. Smith)
Professional. *b:* 1859. *d:* 11.4.1922, Portsmouth, Hampshire. Middle order batsman. *Team* Hampshire (1884–85, 2 matches).
Career batting
2–4–0–15–14–3.75–0–*ct* 0

Hargreaves, Reginald Gervis
Amateur. *b:* 13.10.1852, Oakhill Park, Accrington, Lancashire. *d:* 13.2.1926, Cuffnell's, Lyndhurst, Hampshire. Brother-in-law of R. Henderson (Middlesex). Middle order right-hand batsman, lob bowler. *Sch* Eton. *Team* Hampshire (1875–85, 12 matches).
Career batting
25–47–8–544–46–13.94–0–*ct* 17
Bowling 426–15–28.40–0–0–4/55
He played no first-class matches whilst at Oxford U, but did win a blue for royal tennis. He married Alice Liddell, the inspiration for Lewis Carroll's 'Alice in Wonderland'.

Hargreaves, William Henry
Amateur. *b:* 6.9.1872, Baldock, Hertfordshire. *d:* 19.4.1948, Kings Farm, Gravesend, Kent. Middle order batsman, bowler. *Team* Kent (1893, 1 match).
Career batting
1–2–0–10–10–5.00–0–*ct* 1

Harilal Raishi Shah
Cricketer. *b:* 1943, Kenya. Middle order right-hand batsman, right-arm medium pace bowler. *Tour* East Africa to England 1975.
Career batting
1–2–0–92–59–46.00–0–*ct* 0
Bowling 7–0

Harington, Herbert Henry
Amateur. *b:* 14.8.1868, Chichester, Sussex. *d:* 1.1.1948, Tunbridge Wells, Kent. Middle order right-hand batsman. *Sch* Cheltenham. *Team* Kent (1897, 2 matches).
Career batting
2–4–0–49–34–12.25–0–*ct* 1
In 1893/4 he went with the Straits Settlements team on their tour of Ceylon.

Harkness, Donald Peter
Professional. *b:* 13.2.1931, Sydney, New South Wales, Australia. Middle order left-hand batsman, right-arm medium fast bowler. *Team* Worcestershire (1954, 13 matches).
Career batting
13–19–0–488–163–25.68–1–*ct* 9
Bowling 274–6–45.66–0–0–3/29

Harman, George Richard Uniacke
Amateur. *b:* 6.6.1874, Crosshaven, Co Cork, Ireland. *d:* 14.12.1975, Downderry, Torpoint, Cornwall. Brother of W. C. R. (Ireland). Tail end right-hand batsman. *Team* Dublin University (1895).
Career batting
1–2–1–2–2*–2.00–0–*ct* 0
He was an Irish rugby international.

Harman, Mark David
Cricketer. *b:* 30.6.1964, Aylesbury, Buckinghamshire. Lower order right-hand batsman, off break bowler. *Teams* Somerset 1986–87, 9 matches); Kent (1988–89, 14 matches).
Career batting
23–27–11–201–41–12.56–0–*ct* 16
Bowling 1359–43–31.60–3–0–5/55

Harman, Roger
Professional. *b:* 28.12.1941, Hersham, Surrey. Lower order right-hand batsman, slow left-arm bowler. *Team* Surrey (1961–68, 141 matches).
Career batting
144–147–52–947–34–9.96–0–*ct* 84
Bowling 8975–378–23.74–18–3–8/12
He took 136 wickets, av 21.01, in 1964.

Harman, William Crooke Ronayne
Amateur. *b:* 29.5.1869, Crosshaven, Co Cork, Ireland. *d:* 4.7.1962, Dunlea, Cobh, Co Cork, Ireland. Brother of G. R. U. (Dublin U). Middle order batsman. *Team* Ireland (1907).
Career batting
1–2–0–2–2–1.00–0–*ct* 1

Harold, Frederick Vere
Professional. *b:* 5.9.1888, Eling, Hampshire. *d:* 17.2.1964, Southall, Middlesex. Lower order batsman, bowler. *Team* Hampshire (1909–12, 2 matches).
Career batting
2–2–0–16–16–8.00–0–*ct* 1
Bowling 15–0

Haroon Rashid Dar
Cricketer. *b:* 25.3.1953, Karachi, Pakistan. Brother of Mahmood Rashid (United Bank), Umar Rashid (Karachi) and Tahir Rashid (Karachi). Attacking middle order right-hand batsman. *Teams* Karachi (1971/2 to 1983/4); National Bank (1972/3 to 1975/6); PIA (1976/7); United Bank (1977/8 to 1984/5). *Tours* Pakistan to Sri Lanka 1975/6, to West Indies 1976/7, to Australia 1976/7, to England 1978, 1979 (World Cup), 1982, to Australia and New Zealand 1978/9. *Tests* Pakistan (1976/7 to 1982/3, 23 matches).
Career batting
149–234–27–7500–153–36.23–15–*ct* 126
Bowling 255–8–31.87–0–0–3/34
Test batting
23–36–1–1217–153–34.77–3–*ct* 16
Bowling 3–0
He had a most disappointing tour to England in 1978, though he played in three Tests; in 1982 he had a better record in first-class matches, but scored only one run in his single Test innings.

Harper, George Minto
Amateur. *b:* 30.8.1865, Notting Hill, Kensington, London. Middle order right-hand batsman, right-arm medium pace bowler. *Sch* Rugby. *Team* Lancashire (1883, 1 match).
Career batting
1–1–0–1–1–1.00–0–*ct* 0

Harper, Herbert
Amateur. *b:* 1.2.1889, King's Heath, Birmingham. *d:* 6.8.1983, Birmingham. Middle order right-hand batsman, leg break bowler. *Team* Worcestershire (1920, 1 match).
Career batting
1–2–0–10–7–5.00–0–*ct* 0

Harper, Sir Kenneth Brand
Amateur. *b:* 8.8.1891, South Kensington, London. *d:* 21.1.1961, Hoe, Abinger Hammer, Surrey. Middle order right-hand batsman. *Sch* Uppingham. *Teams* Middlesex (1910, 3 matches); Bengal Governor's XI (1917/18).
Career batting
4–7–0–37–28–5.28–0–*ct* 1

Harper, Leonard Vyse
Amateur. *b:* 12.12.1880, Bedford Hill, Balham, London. *d:* 13.1.1924, Bedford Hill, Balham, London. Hard hitting middle order right-hand batsman, brilliant field. *Sch* Rossall. *Teams* Cambridge U (1901–03, blue all three years); Surrey (1904, 6 matches).
Career batting
34–61–2–988–84–16.74–0–*ct* 14
He also represented Cambridge at hockey.

Harper, Mark Anthony
Cricketer. *b:* 31.10.1957, Georgetown, British Guiana. Brother of R. A. (West Indies). Middle order right-hand batsman, right-arm medium pace bowler. *Team* Guyana (1975/6 to 1990/1).
Career batting
42–71–7–2156–149*–33.68–4–*ct* 42
Bowling 267–6–44.50–0–0–2/10
His only first-class match in England was for D. B. Close's XI in 1986. His first-class debut was for Demerara in 1974/5.

Harper, Nicholas John
Amateur. *b:* 11.4.1939, Forest Hill, London. Lower order left-hand batsman, left-arm medium pace bowler. *Sch* Caterham. *Team* Cambridge U (1961).
Career batting
1–1–0–1–1–1.00–0–*ct* 0
Bowling 39–1–39.00–0–0–1/39

Harper, Roger Andrew
Cricketer. *b:* 17.3.1963, Georgetown, British Guiana. Brother of M. A. (Guyana). Middle order right-hand batsman, off break bowler, brilliant field. *Teams* Guyana (1979/80 to 1991/2); Northamptonshire (1985–87, 54 matches) *Tours* West Indies to India 1983/4, 1987/8, to Australia 1983/4 (not first-class), 1984/5, 1986/7, 1988/9, 1991/2 (World Cup), to England 1984, 1988, 1991, to Pakistan 1985/6 (not first-class), 1986/7, to Sharjah (not first-class) 1985/6, 1986/7, 1988/9, to India and Pakistan (World Cup) 1987/8; Rest of World to England 1987, 1989, 1990, 1992. *Tests* West Indies (1983/4 to 1988/9, 24 matches).
Career batting
174–226–39–6113–234–32.68–8–*ct* 219
Bowling 13085–475–27.54–20–2–6/57
Test batting
24–31–3–532–74–19.00–0–*ct* 35
Bowling 1252–45–27.82–1–0–6/57
Effectively the only specialist spin bowler on the 1984 West Indies tour to England he bowled extremely well on the few occasions when he was given a reasonable opportunity and played in all five Tests. His bowling went to pieces during most of the 1988 tour, but he batted so well that he topped the first-class averages with 622 runs, av 77.75, and played in three Tests. He had an excellent all-round record for Northamptonshire; in 1986 he hit 933 runs, av 35.88, and took 62 wickets, av 27.41. His first first-class match in England was for D. B. Close's XI in 1983. His highest score was 234 Northamptonshire v Gloucestershire at Northampton in 1986.

Harpur, Thomas
Cricketer. *b:* 16.5.1944, Sion Mills, Co Tyrone, Ireland. Middle order right-hand batsman. *Team* Ireland (1980–81).
Career batting
2–2–0–10–6–5.00–0–*ct* 2
Bowling 5–0

Harragin, Alfred Ernest Albert
Amateur. *b:* 4.5.1877, Port of Spain, Trinidad. *d:* 21.5.1941, Port of Spain, Trinidad. Middle order right-hand batsman, good field. *Team* Trinidad (1896/7 to 1931/2). *Tour* West Indies to England 1906.
Career batting
39–67–3–1585–123–24.76–2–*ct* 32
He finished second in the first-class batting averages on his single visit to England with 412 runs, av 31.69.

Harries, Air Vice Marshal Sir Douglas
Amateur. *b:* 30.3.1893, Sidcup, Kent. *d:* 6.12.1972, Crondall, Hampshire. Middle order batsman. *Team* Free Foresters (1919–20).
Career batting
4–8–1–112–34–16.00–0–*ct* 3

Harrington, William
Amateur. *b:* 27.12.1869, Templeogue, Co Dublin, Ireland. *d:* 2.1.1940, Templeogue, Co Dublin, Ireland. Lower order right-hand batsman, off break bowler. *Team* Ireland (1902–21). *Tour* Ireland to North America 1909.
Career batting
15–25–5–153–28–7.65–0–*ct* 3
Bowling 1019–53–19.22–4–1–7/76

Harrington, William John Roy
Professional. *b:* 30.1.1915, St John's Wood, London. *d:* 23.1.1988, Blandford, Dorset. Lower order right-hand batsman, right-arm fast bowler. *Team* Middlesex (1946–48, 9 matches).
Career batting
12–19–2–143–45–8.41–0–*ct* 3
Bowling 376–16–23.50–1–0–6/57
His final first-class match was for MCC in 1951.

Harris
Professional. Lower order batsman, wicket-keeper. *Team* Essex (1905, 2 matches).
Career batting
2–3–1–0–0*–0.00–0–*ct* 4

Harris, Alwyn
Professional. *b:* 31.1.1936, Aberdylais, Glamorgan. Middle order left-hand batsman. *Team* Glamorgan (1960–64, 49 matches).
Career batting
49–91–3–1698–110–19.29–2–*ct* 19
Bowling 0–0
He hit 1,048 runs, av 23.81, in 1962.

Harris, Archibald John
Amateur. *b:* 22.12.1892, Rugby, Warwickshire. *d:* 10.4.1955, Lymington, Hampshire. Brother of W. H. (Warwickshire). Middle order right-hand batsman. *Sch* Rugby. *Team* Warwickshire (1919, 1 match).
Career batting
1–2–0–18–14–9.00–0–*ct* 1

Harris, Charles Bowmar
Professional. *b:* 6.12.1907, Underwood, Nottinghamshire. *d:* 8.8.1954, Standard Hill, Nottingham. Brother of G. J. (Glamorgan). Opening right-hand batsman, right-arm medium or slow bowler. *Team* Nottinghamshire (1928–51, 362 matches).
Career batting
362–601–64–18823–239*–35.05–30–*ct* 164
Bowling 8395–196–42.83–3–0–8/80
He hit 1,000 runs in a season eleven times (best 1,891, av 38.59, in 1934). His two double centuries were both for Nottinghamshire, the highest being 239* v Hampshire at Trent Bridge in 1950. With W. W. Keeton he shared in 46 century partnerships for the first wicket. He was a first-class umpire (1954).

Harris, Christopher Robin
Cricketer. *b:* 16.10.1942, Buckingham. Lower order right-hand batsman, right-arm fast medium bowler. *Team* Oxford U (1964–65, blue 1964).
Career batting
12–16–6–48–14–4.80–0–*ct* 5
Bowling 896–17–52.70–1–1–6/83
His County Cricket was for Buckinghamshire (1964–75).

Harris, David
Professional. *b:* 1755, Elvetham, Hampshire. *d:* 19.5.1803, Crookham, Hampshire. Lower order left-hand batsman, right-hand fast under-arm bowler, moderate field. *Team* Hampshire (1782–98).
The greatest bowler of the Hambledon Club, it is impossible to gauge his real success owing to lack of bowling analyses. During the latter part of his career he was much troubled by gout and used to arrive at the ground on crutches. His illness prevented him playing after 1798.

Harris, Dennis Frank
Amateur. *b:* 18.4.1911, Birmingham. *d:* 17.12.1959, Moseley, Birmingham. Middle order right-hand batsman. *Sch* KES, Birmingham. *Team* Warwickshire (1946, 1 match).
Career batting
1–1–0–2–2–2.00–0–*ct* 0

Harris, Earlston Joseph
Cricketer. *b:* 3.11.1952, Lodge Village, St Kitts. Lower order right-hand batsman, right-arm medium pace bowler. *Team* Warwickshire (1975, 4 matches).
Career batting
4–5–2–26–16–8.66–0–*ct* 3
Bowling 295–9–32.77–0–0–3/66

Harris, Edwin Lawson James
Amateur. *b:* 29.8.1891, Littlehampton, Sussex. *d:* 31.7.1961, East Preston, Sussex. Son of H. E. (Hampshire). Middle order right-hand batsman, right-arm medium pace bowler. *Team* Sussex (1922–24, 9

matches).
Career batting
9–15–1–208–51*–14.85–0–*ct* 3
Bowling 59–3–19.66–0–0–2/3

Harris, Frank Albert
Professional. *b:* 19.3.1907, Bristol. *d:* 21.2.1936, Greenbank, Bristol. Middle order right-hand batsman, change bowler. *Team* Gloucestershire (1929–31, 10 matches).
Career batting
10–13–1–68–33–5.66–0–*ct* 2
Bowling 33–0

Harris, George Cecil
Professional. *b:* 3.3.1906, Droitwich, Worcestershire. Lower order batsman, left-arm fast bowler. *Team* Worcestershire (1925, 4 matches).
Career batting
4–8–3–6–4–1.20–0–*ct* 1
Bowling 120–2–60.00–0–0–2/40

Harris, George Joseph
Amateur. *b:* 22.11.1904, Underwood, Nottinghamshire. *d:* 28.12.1988, Swansea, Glamorgan. Brother of C. B. (Nottinghamshire). Opening right-hand batsman, right-arm medium pace bowler, slip field. *Team* Glamorgan (1932, 1 match).
Career batting
1–1–0–0–0–0.00–0–*ct* 1

He was a professional until 1929, but on joining the police force played later as an amateur. A good soccer player, he appeared for Mansfield Town and Swansea as goalkeeper.

Harris, Hon George Robert Canning
(succeeded as 4th Lord Harris in 1872)
Amateur. *b:* 3.2.1851, St Anne's, Trinidad. *d:* 24.3.1932, Belmont, Faversham, Kent. Nephew of W. M. Jervis (Derbyshire), uncle of N. E. Haig (Middlesex). Middle order right-hand batsman, right-hand fast round-arm bowler, good field. *Sch* Eton. *Teams* Kent (1870–1911, 157 matches); Oxford U (1871–74, blue 1871, 1872 and 1874). *Tours* Fitzgerald to North America 1872 (not first-class); Harris to Australia 1878/9. *Tests* England (1878/9 to 1884, 4 matches).
Career batting
224–395–23–9990–176–26.85–11–*ct* 190
Bowling 1758–70 + 5–25.11–1–0–5/57
Test batting
4–6–1–145–52–29.00–0–*ct* 2
Bowling 29–0

One of the most influential personalities involved in cricket, Lord Harris virtually controlled the Kent County Club for a period of about 50 years. Being appointed captain of the County in 1871 he gradually improved its fortunes, which had been at a very low point for many years. Apart from the leadership, which he held until 1889, he was President of the County in 1875, Hon Secretary 1875 to 1880 and for most of his life a Committee member. He hit 1,417 runs, av 33.73, in 1884.

He held various offices with the MCC, generally on the financial side, being a Trustee from 1906 to 1916 and Hon Treasurer from 1916 to his death. He was President in 1895.

He was a great believer in the correct administration of the Laws of cricket and was the prime mover in the stamping out of the 'throwing' epidemic which plagued the game in the 1880s. Although he was noted for the fairness of his judgment in all matters, his hot temper made him a fearsome opponent. He captained England in all the four Tests in which he took part, including the first Test ever played in England, but various political offices restricted his first-class cricket after 1884. In the following year he was appointed Under-Secretary for India and later Under-Secretary for War. He spent five years in India as Governor of Bombay and assisted in the development of the game there.

Harris, George Woodrouffe
Amateur. *b:* 6.8.1880, Chelsea, London. *d:* 10.7.1954, Carpenters Wood, Chorley Wood, Hertfordshire. Sound middle order right-hand batsman, good field. *Sch* Uppingham. *Team* Hampshire (1899, 1 match).
Career batting
1–2–0–10–10–5.00–0–*ct* 0

He played in trials at Cambridge U, but not in first-class matches.

Harris, Gordon Andrew Robert
Cricketer. *b:* 11.1.1964, Tottenham, Middlesex. Lower order right-hand batsman, right-arm fast medium bowler. *Sch* Merchant Taylors. *Team* Leicestershire (1986, 1 match).
Career batting
1–2–1–6–6–6.00–0–*ct* 0
Bowling 34–0

He also played for Bedfordshire (1988–89) and Hertfordshire (1990–92).

Harris, Henry Edward
Amateur. *b:* 6.8.1854, Brighton, Sussex. *d:* 8.11.1923, Littlehampton, Sussex. Father of E. L. J. (Sussex). Middle order right-hand batsman, good field at point. *Team* Hampshire (1880, 3 matches).
Career batting
3–5–0–53–28–10.60–0–*ct* 1

Harris, John Henry
Professional. *b:* 13.2.1936, Taunton, Somerset. Lower order left-hand batsman, right-arm fast medium bowler. *Team* Somerset (1952–59, 15 matches).
Career batting
15–18–4–154–41–11.00–0–*ct* 6
Bowling 609–19–32.05–0–0–3/29

He also played for Suffolk (1960–63) and Devon (1975). He became a first-class umpire (1983).

Harris, Kenrick Henry
Professional. *b:* 15.11.1885, Newport, Monmouthshire. Middle order batsman, bowler. *Team* Wales (1925).
Career batting
1–1–0–14–14–14.00–0–*ct* 0
Bowling 135–6–22.50–1–0–6/112
His County cricket was for Glamorgan (pre first-class, 1913) and Monmouthshire (1921–31).

Harris, Leslie John
Amateur. *b:* 20.7.1915, St Fagans, Cardiff, Glamorgan. *d:* 28.10.1985, Beckenham, Kent. Brother of W. E. (Glamorgan). Lower order right-hand batsman, right-arm medium pace bowler. *Team* Glamorgan (1947, 3 matches).
Career batting
3–4–2–7–5–3.50–0–*ct* 1
Bowling 183–5–36.60–0–0–3/39
He was Secretary of the Primary Club.

Harris, Michael John
Cricketer. *b:* 25.5.1944, St Just-in-Roseland, Cornwall. Opening right-hand batsman, leg break bowler, wicket-keeper. *Teams* Middlesex (1964–68, 72 matches); Nottinghamshire (1969–82, 261 matches); Eastern Province (1971/2); Wellington (1975/6). *Tour* Robins to West Indies 1974/5 (not first-class).
Career batting
344–581–58–19196–201*–36.70–41–*ct* 288–*st* 14
Bowling 3459–79–43.78–0–0–4/16
He hit 1,000 runs in a season eleven times, going on to 2,000 once – 2,238, av 50.86, in 1971. His only double century was 201* for Nottinghamshire v Glamorgan at Trent Bridge in 1973.

Harris, Stanley Shute
Amateur. *b:* 19.7.1881, Sea Mills, Clifton, Bristol. *d:* 4.5.1926, Farnham, Surrey. Middle order right-hand batsman. *Sch* Westminster. *Teams* Cambridge U (1902–04); Gloucestershire (1902, 1 match); Surrey (1904, 1 match); London County (1904); Sussex (1919, 3 matches).
Career batting
16–28–2–375–76–14.42–0–*ct* 4
Bowling 25–0
An excellent soccer player he captained Cambridge and went on to appear for Corinthians and England.

Harris, Terence Anthony
Amateur. *b:* 27.8.1916, Kimberley, South Africa. Forcing right-hand middle order batsman, excellent field. *Teams* Griqualand West (1933/4 to 1934/5); Transvaal (1936/7 to 1948/9). *Tour* South Africa to England 1947. *Tests* South Africa (1947 to 1948/9, 3 matches).
Career batting
55–80–7–3028–191*–41.47–6–*ct* 52
Bowling 33–0
Test batting
3–5–1–100–60–25.00–0–*ct* 1
He performed only moderately on his tour of England, but appeared in two of the five Tests. He scored 114* on debut for Griqualand West v Orange Free State at Kimberley in 1933/4. A noted rugby fly-half, he represented South Africa.

Harris, Thomas
Amateur. *b:* 9.5.1845, Bellary, India. *d:* 28.3.1918, Bedford Park, Chiswick, Middlesex. Lower order right-hand batsman, right-hand round-arm bowler. *Team* Kent (1864, 1 match).
Career batting
2–4–0–4–3–1.00–0–*ct* 1
Bowling 184–10–18.40–1–0–6/81
He played for Ireland (not first-class) 1868–69.

Harris, Wilfred Ernest
Amateur. *b:* 24.4.1919, St Fagans, Cardiff, Glamorgan. Brother of L. J. (Glamorgan). Middle order right-hand batsman, right-arm medium pace bowler. *Team* Glamorgan (1938–47, 5 matches).
Career batting
5–8–0–59–25–7.37–0–*ct* 1
Bowling 43–0

Harris, William
Professional. *b:* 21.11.1861, Greasbrough, Yorkshire. *d:* 23.5.1923, Longsight, Manchester, Lancashire. Middle order left-hand batsman. *Team* Yorkshire (1884–87, 4 matches).
Career batting
4–8–2–45–25–7.50–0–*ct* 1
Bowling 18–0

Harris, William
Professional. *b:* 17.6.1864, Kimberley, Nottinghamshire. *d:* 18.6.1949, Crofton Park, London. Middle order right-hand batsman, off break bowler. *Team* Nottinghamshire (1886, 1 match).
Career batting
1–1–0–2–2–2.00–0–0–*ct* 0
He also played for Surrey (1889–91), but not in first-class matches. He was for many years groundsman at Guy's Hospital.

Harris, William Henry
Amateur. *b:* 30.12.1883, Rugby, Warwickshire. *d:* 14.10.1967, Shabani, Southern Rhodesia. Brother of A. J. (Warwickshire). Lower order right-hand batsman, wicket-keeper. *Team* Warwickshire (1904–19, 12 matches).
Career batting
12–18–1–204–42–12.00–0–*ct* 11–*st* 2
He played soccer for West Bromwich Albion.

Harrison, Aelfric Milton
Amateur. *b:* 28.7.1889, Blandford, Dorset. *d:* 2.6.1958, Clifton, Bristol. Middle order right-hand batsman, right-arm bowler. *Sch* Christ's Hospital.

Team Sussex (1913, 2 matches).
Career batting
3–5–0–32–14–6.40–0–*ct* 3
Bowling 33–1–33.00–0–0–1/33
He also played for Dorset (1908–46). His last first-class match was for the West of England in 1927. He played in trials at Cambridge U, but not in first-class matches.

Harrison, Bernard Reginald Stanhope
Professional. *b:* 28.9.1934, St Johns, Worcester. Opening right-hand batsman, right-arm medium pace bowler. *Team* Hampshire (1957–62, 14 matches).
Career batting
14–24–2–519–110–23.59–1–*ct* 8
Bowling 65–1–65.00–0–0–1/34
A useful soccer player, he appeared for Crystal Palace, Southampton and Exeter City.

Harrison, Rev Christopher
Amateur. *b:* 24.3.1847, Brandesburton Hall, Yorkshire. *d:* 23.2.1932, Bishop Norton, Lincolnshire. Middle order right-hand batsman, right-arm slow bowler, good field. *Sch* Shrewsbury. *Team* Nottinghamshire (1878, 1 match).
Career batting
1–2–0–3–3–1.50–0–*ct* 0
He did not appear in any first-class matches whilst at Cambridge U. He also played for Lincolnshire (1881–83).

Harrison, Cyril Stanley
Amateur. *b:* 11.11.1915, Droitwich, Worcestershire. Middle/lower order left-hand batsman, slow left-arm bowler. *Sch* Worcester RGS. *Team* Worcestershire (1934–35, 17 matches).
Career batting
17–29–2–166–28–6.14–0–*ct* 11
Bowling 1043–25–41.72–1–0–7/51

Harrison, Deryck William
Cricketer. *b:* 3.11.1943, Lurgan, Co Armagh, Ireland. Brother of G. D. (Ireland), James (Ireland) and Roy (Ireland), brother-in-law of E. A. Bushe (Ireland). Middle order right-hand batsman. *Team* Ireland (1978–79).
Career batting
2–1–0–0–0–0.00–0–*ct* 2

Harrison, Dominic Stephen
Cricketer. *b:* 15.1.1963, Tittensor, Staffordshire. Lower order right-hand batsman, wicket-keeper. *Sch* Ampleforth. *Team* Oxford U (1983–85).
Career batting
5–7–2–21–8–4.20–0–*ct* 5–*st* 2

Harrison, E. E. (*see under* Ward, E. E.)

Harrison, Edward Ernest
Amateur. *b:* 25.5.1910, Chichester, Sussex. Lower order right-hand batsman, right-arm fast medium bowler. *Sch* Harrow. *Team* Sussex (1946–47, 10 matches).
Career batting
10–17–5–120–23–10.00–0–*ct* 3
Bowling 498–17–29.29–0–0–2/28

Harrison, Frank
Professional. *b:* 1909. *d:* 9.6.1955, York. Lower order batsman, leg break bowler. *Team* Lancashire (1936, 3 matches).
Career batting
3–3–1–4–2*–2.00–0–*ct* 3
Bowling 118–4–29.50–0–0–2/30
He also played for Cornwall.

Harrison, Garfield David
Cricketer. *b:* 8.5.1961, Lurgan, Co Armagh, Ireland. Brother of D. W. (Ireland), James (Ireland) and Roy (Ireland), brother-in-law of E. A. Bushe (Ireland). Middle order left-hand batsman, off break bowler. *Team* Ireland (1983–91).
Career batting
9–15–1–413–86–29.50–0–*ct* 2
Bowling 474–19–24.94–2–0–9/113
His best bowling was 9/113 for Ireland v Scotland at Edinburgh in 1990.

Harrison, George Benjamin
Professional. *b:* 14.9.1895, Dalton, Ulverston, Lancashire. Middle order left-hand batsman. *Team* Glamorgan (1924–25, 9 matches).
Career batting
9–17–0–109–34–6.41–0–*ct* 2
Bowling 10–0

Harrison, George Crawford
Amateur. *b:* 27.6.1860, Maida Hill, London. *d:* 16.3.1900, Inverleith, Edinburgh, Scotland. Lower order right-hand batsman, slow right-arm bowler. *Sch* Malvern and Clifton. *Team* Oxford U (1880–81, blue both years).
Career batting
18–31–3–237–28–8.46–0–*ct* 18
Bowling 1230–64–19.21–4–0–7/69
His County cricket was for Herefordshire (1881).

Harrison, George Puckrin
Professional. *b:* 11.2.1862, Scarborough, Yorkshire. *d:* 14.9.1940, Scarborough, Yorkshire. Lower order right-hand batsman, right-arm very fast, but after 1884 medium fast bowler. *Team* Yorkshire (1883–92, 61 matches).
Career batting
67–100–28–484–28–6.72–0–*ct* 39
Bowling 3910–249–15.70–14–3–7/43
He took 100 wickets, av 13.26, in 1883, which was his debut season. He was a noted umpire after ceasing to play in first-class cricket (1907–24).

Harrison, Gerald Cartmell
Amateur. *b:* 8.10.1883. *d:* 10.8.1943, Spital, Blyth, Nottinghamshire. Middle order right-hand batsman. *Sch* Eton. *Team* Hampshire (1914–20, 22 matches).
Career batting
33–57–3–1401–111–25.94–1–*ct* 12
He also played for Devon (1907). His first-class debut was for Royal Navy in 1912.

Harrison, Harold
Professional. *b:* 24.1.1885, Horsforth, Yorkshire. *d:* 11.2.1962, Rawdon, Yorkshire. Tail end batsman, slow left-arm bowler. *Team* Yorkshire (1907, 2 matches).
Career batting
2–1–1–4–4*–no av–0–*ct* 1
Bowling 39–2–19.50–0–0–2/15

Harrison, Henry Starr
Professional. *b:* 12.4.1883, Cheam, Surrey. *d:* 8.12.1971, Bognor Regis, Sussex. Steady middle order right-hand batsman, slow right-arm bowler, good slip. *Team* Surrey (1909–23, 164 matches).
Career batting
165–255–33–5237–155*–23.59–2–*ct* 117
Bowling 726–20–36.30–0–0–2/14
He hit 1,293 runs, av 40.40, in 1913. He was a first-class umpire (1927).

Harrison, Hugh Robert Edward
Amateur. *b:* 16.4.1875, Caerhowel, Forden, Montgomeryshire. *d:* 19.5.1912, Folkestone, Kent. Lower order right-hand batsman, right-arm fast bowler. *Sch* Eton. *Team* MCC (1896–97).
Career batting
4–8–1–123–55–17.57–0–*ct* 1
Bowling 73–2–36.50–0–0–2/47
His County cricket was for Shropshire (1893).

Harrison, Isaac Marshall
Professional. *b:* 8.6.1880, Calverton, Nottinghamshire. *d:* 25.2.1909, Calverton, Nottinghamshire. Middle order batsman, excellent field. *Team* Nottinghamshire (1901, 7 matches).
Career batting
7–12–2–143–33–14.30–0–*ct* 1

Harrison, James
Cricketer. *b:* 3.5.1941, Lurgan, Co Armagh, Ireland. Brother of D. W. (Ireland), G. D. (Ireland) and Roy (Ireland), brother-in-law of E. A. Bushe (Ireland). Middle order right-hand batsman. *Team* Ireland (1969–77).
Career batting
8–15–1–309–100*–22.07–1–*ct* 3

Harrison, Leo
Professional. *b:* 5.6.1922, Mudeford, Hampshire. Middle order right-hand batsman, wicket-keeper. *Team* Hampshire (1939–66, 387 matches).
Career batting
396–606–100–8854–153–17.49–6–*ct* 579–*st* 103
Bowling 166–0
He hit 1,000 runs in a season twice (best 1,191, av 27.06, in 1952). He was Hampshire coach 1966–69.

Harrison, Nigel Sydney Augustine
Amateur. *b:* 29.11.1878, Maidstone, Kent. *d:* 13.11.1947, Norton, Stockton-on-Tees, Co Durham. Middle order right-hand batsman, right-arm fast medium bowler. *Sch* Haileybury. *Team* London County (1900).
Career batting
4–7–1–37–18–6.16–0–*ct* 3
His County cricket was for Durham (pre first-class, 1902–05).

Harrison, Percy
Professional. *b:* 15.10.1878, Mansfield Woodhouse, Nottinghamshire. *d:* 11.4.1935, Worksop, Nottinghamshire. Opening or middle order batsman, change bowler. *Team* Nottinghamshire (1899, 1 match).
Career batting
1–2–0–13–11–6.50–0–*ct* 0
Bowling 25–0

Harrison, Richard
Professional. *b:* 1881, Clitheroe, Lancashire. Middle order right-hand batsman, right-arm medium pace bowler. *Team* Minor Counties (1912).
Career batting
1–1–1–8–8*–no av–0–*ct* 0
His County cricket was for Durham (pre first-class, 1910–13).

Harrison, Roy
Cricketer. *b:* 30.8.1939, Lurgan, Co Armagh, Ireland. Brother of D. W. (Ireland), G. D. (Ireland) and James (Ireland), brother-in-law of E. A. Bushe (Ireland). Middle order right-hand batsman, right-arm medium pace bowler. *Team* Ireland (1968).
Career batting
1–2–0–16–12–8.00–0–*ct* 2

Harrison, Stuart Charles
Cricketer. *b:* 21.9.1951, Cwmbran, Monmouthshire. Lower order right-hand batsman, right-arm fast medium bowler. *Team* Glamorgan (1971–77, 5 matches).
Career batting
5–6–0–32–15–5.33–0–*ct* 1
Bowling 314–7–44.85–0–0–3/55

Harrison, Rev William Bealey
Amateur. *b:* 16.1.1838, Norton Hall, Staffordshire. *d:* 23.3.1912, Aldershaw, Wall, Lichfield, Staffordshire. Father of W. E. (Bosanquet to North America 1901), his granddaughter married C. M. Andreae (Cambridge U). Lower order batsman, useful bowler. *Sch* Rugby. *Team* Gentlemen of North (1861–62).

Career batting
2–4–0–6–5–1.50–0–*ct* 2
Bowling 60–1–60.00–0–0–1/31

Harrison, William Hendy
Professional. *b:* 27.5.1863, Shipley, Bradford, Yorkshire. *d:* 15.7.1939, Lister Hills, Bradford, Yorkshire. Middle order batsman, bowler. *Team* Yorkshire (1888, 3 matches).
Career batting
3–6–1–12–7–2.40–0–*ct* 0

Harrison, William Henry
Amateur. *b:* 1866, Nursling, Southampton, Hampshire. *d:* 23.12.1936, Salisbury, Wiltshire. Middle order batsman. *Team* Hampshire (1902, 1 match).
Career batting
1–2–1–12–12*–12.00–0–*ct* 0

Harrison, William Philip
Amateur. *b:* 13.11.1885, Church End, Finchley, Middlesex. *d:* 7.9.1964, Rudding Park, Harrogate, Yorkshire. Middle order right-hand batsman, leg break bowler. *Sch* Rugby. *Teams* Kent (1904–05, 7 matches); Cambridge U (1905–07, blue 1907); Middlesex (1906–11, 29 matches). *Tour* MCC to New Zealand 1906/7.
Career batting
56–90–10–1896–156–23.70–2–*ct* 29
Bowling 201–7–28.71–0–0–4/61
He was Treasurer of Middlesex 1923–35.

Harrold, James George William
Professional. *b:* 26.3.1892. *d:* 7.10.1950, Epsom, Surrey. Lower order right-hand batsman, off break bowler. *Team* Essex (1923–28, 11 matches).
Career batting
11–19–3–88–17–5.50–0–*ct* 13
Bowling 123–3–41.00–0–0–1/15
He played soccer for Leicester City and Millwall and won an amateur international cap for England.

Harron, Dawson Gascoigne
Professional. *b:* 12.9.1921, Langley Park, Co Durham. *d:* 21.7.1988, Coventry, Warwickshire. Opening right-hand batsman. *Team* Leicestershire (1951, 10 matches).
Career batting
10–14–2–186–53–15.50–0–*ct* 2
He also played for Durham (pre first-class, 1947–48).

Harrop, Douglas John
Cricketer. *b:* 16.4.1947, Cosby, Leicestershire. Lower order left-hand batsman, wicket-keeper. *Team* Leicestershire (1972, 1 match).
Career batting
1–2–1–11–11*–11.00–0–*ct* 3

Harrop, J.
Amateur. Lower order batsman, bowler. *Sch* Bramham College, Tadcaster. *Team* Lancashire (1874, 1 match).
Career batting
1–2–0–5–5–2.50–0–*ct* 0
Bowling 14–0

Harry, Frank
Professional, but became amateur from 1919. *b:* 22.12.1876, Torquay, Devon. *d:* 27.10.1925, Great Malvern, Worcestershire. Lower order right-hand batsman, right-arm medium pace bowler. *Teams* Lancashire (1903–08, 69 matches); Worcestershire (1919–20, 7 matches).
Career batting
76–117–11–1605–88–15.14–0–*ct* 40
Bowling 4089–215–19.01–14–1–9/44
His best bowling was 9/44 for Lancashire v Warwickshire at Old Trafford in 1906. He also played for Cheshire (1902) and Durham (pre first-class, 1912–14). A noted rugby footballer, he played for Broughton Rangers. He was a first-class umpire (1921).

Harry, John
Professional. *b:* 1.8.1857, Ballarat, Victoria, Australia. *d:* 27.10.1919, Canterbury, Melbourne, Victoria, Australia. Middle order right-hand batsman, off break bowler, wicket-keeper. *Teams* Victoria (1883/4 to 1897/8, 28 matches); MCC (1896). *Tests* Australia (1894/5, 1 match).
Career batting
32–60–3–1466–114–25.71–2–*ct* 18–*st* 3
Bowling 618–26–23.76–0–0–4/15
Test batting
1–2–0–8–6–4.00–0–*ct* 1

Hart, Eustace John Hewitt
Amateur. *b:* 14.11.1907, Poona, India. *d:* 4.2.1972, Swainswick, Bath, Somerset. Middle order right-hand batsman. *Sch* Monkton Combe. *Team* Somerset (1930, 3 matches).
Career batting
3–6–1–45–16–9.00–0–*ct* 1

Hart, George Edmead
Professional. *b:* 13.1.1902, Harlington, Middlesex. *d:* 11.4.1987, Raleigh Park, Barnstaple, Devon. Opening right-hand batsman, right-arm medium pace bowler. *Team* Middlesex (1926–39, 194 matches).
Career batting
198–309–31–5786–121–20.81–4–*ct* 60
Bowling 1082–21–51.52–0–0–3/64
He was also a useful soccer player.

Hart, Herbert William
Amateur. *b:* 21.9.1859, Hull, Yorkshire. *d:* 2.11.1895, Hull, Yorkshire. Lower order left-hand batsman, left-arm fast bowler. *Team* Yorkshire (1888,

1 match).
Career batting
1–2–0–6–6–3.00–0–*ct* 0
Bowling 32–2–16.00–0–0–2/19

Hart, Martin De Lisle
Amateur. *b:* 17.11.1927, Ealing, Middlesex. Lower order right-hand batsman, leg break bowler. *Sch* Sherborne. *Team* Oxford U (1951).
Career batting
4–5–0–8–4–1.60–0–*ct* 4
Bowling 330–6–55.00–0–0–2/77

Hart, Philip Richard
Cricketer. *b:* 12.1.1947, Seamer, Yorkshire. Brother-in-law of M. D. Moxon (Yorkshire). Lower order right-hand batsman, slow left-arm bowler. *Team* Yorkshire (1981, 3 matches).
Career batting
3–5–0–23–11–4.60–0–*ct* 1
Bowling 140–2–70.00–0–0–1/22

Hart, Richard Joseph
Cricketer. *b:* 7.12.1967, Beckenham, Kent. Lower order left-hand batsman, slow left-arm bowler. *Sch* Eltham College. *Team* Cambridge U (1987–88).
Career batting
9–14–2–53–12–4.41–0–*ct* 1
Bowling 708–13–54.46–0–0–4/66

Hart, Thomas Mure
Amateur. *b:* 1.3.1909, Langside, Glasgow, Scotland. Middle/lower order right-hand batsman, right-arm fast medium bowler, good field. *Sch* Strathallan. *Teams* Oxford U (1931–32, blue both years); Scotland (1933–34).
Career batting
12–19–3–318–57–19.87–0–*ct* 5
Bowling 465–9–51.66–0–0–3/26
He played rugby for Scotland.

Harte, Christopher Charles John
Cricketer. *b:* 23.2.1949, Belfast, Ireland. Middle order right-hand batsman. *Sch* Royal Belfast Academical Institution. *Team* Ireland (1973–81).
Career batting
2–3–0–82–40–27.33–0–*ct* 0

Hartigan, Gerald Patrick Desmond
Amateur. *b:* 30.12.1884, King William's Town, South Africa. *d:* 7.1.1955, Addington, Durban, South Africa. Brother of E. M. (Border). Middle order right-hand batsman, leg break bowler, good field. *Team* Border (1903/4 to 1926/7). *Tour* South Africa to England 1912. *Tests* South Africa (1912 to 1913/14, 5 matches).
Career batting
37–62–9–1544–176*–29.13–3–*ct* 19
Bowling 1940–92–21.08–4–0–7/44
Test batting
5–10–0–114–51–11.40–0–*ct* 0
Bowling 141–1–141.00–0–0–1/72
He was moderately successful on the 1912 tour of England, but called upon for only 12 matches. He played soccer for South Africa.

Hartigan, Roger Joseph
Amateur. *b:* 12.12.1879, Chatswood, Sydney, New South Wales, Australia. *d:* 7.6.1958, Brisbane, Queensland, Australia. Brother of T. J. (New South Wales). Opening right-hand batsman. *Teams* New South Wales (1903/4, 1 match); Queensland (1905/6 to 1920/1, 19 matches). *Tour* Australia to England 1909. *Tests* Australia (1907/8, 2 matches).
Career batting
45–80–4–1901–116–25.01–2–*ct* 36
Bowling 361–9–40.11–0–0–3/27
Test batting
2–4–0–170–116–42.50–1–*ct* 1
Bowling 7–0
He failed to find his form on the 1909 tour to England and was not selected for the Tests.

Hartill, William Norman
Amateur. *b:* 13.12.1911, Dudley, Worcestershire. *d:* 3.3.1971, Martley, Worcestershire. Middle order right-hand batsman. *Team* Worcestershire (1935, 1 match).
Career batting
1–1–0–2–2–2.00–0–*ct* 0

Hartington, Harry Edmondson
Professional. *b:* 18.9.1881, Dewsbury, Yorkshire. *d:* 16.2.1950, Pontefract, Yorkshire. Lower order right-hand batsman, right-arm fast medium bowler. *Team* Yorkshire (1910–11, 10 matches).
Career batting
10–10–4–51–16–8.50–0–*ct* 2
Bowling 764–23–33.21–1–0–5/81

Hartley, Alfred
Amateur. *b:* 11.4.1879, New Orleans, USA. *d:* 9.10.1918, near Maissemy, France. He was killed in action. Brother of C. R. (Lancashire), son of George (Lancashire). Defensive opening right-hand batsman. *Team* Lancashire (1907–14, 112 matches).
Career batting
116–191–9–5049–234–27.74–6–*ct* 39
Bowling 61–1–61.00–0–0–1/39
He hit 1,000 runs in a season three times (best 1,585, av 36.86, in 1910). His only double century was 234 for Lancashire v Somerset at Old Trafford in 1910.

Hartley, Charles Robert
Amateur. *b:* 13.2.1873, New Orleans, USA. *d:* 14.11.1927, Brooklands, Cheshire. Brother of Alfred (Lancashire), son of George (Lancashire). Sound middle order right-hand batsman. *Team* Lancashire (1897–1909, 106 matches).

Career batting
106–168–11–3729–139–23.75–4–*ct* 56
Bowling 53–0

His best season was 1900 when he hit 1,084 runs, av 30.11. He was a noted rugby footballer playing for Cheshire, as full back.

Hartley, Frank
Amateur. *b:* 20.7.1896, Shipton-under-Wychwood, Oxfordshire. *d:* 20.10.1965, Shipton-under-Wychwood, Oxfordshire. Middle order right-hand batsman, right-arm bowler. *Team* Minor Counties (1930).
Career batting
2–3–0–15–13–5.00–0–*ct* 2
Bowling 156–3–52.00–0–0–2/72

His County cricket was for Oxfordshire (1922–31). An excellent soccer player, he appeared in seven England amateur internationals, after having appeared in a full England international in 1923. He also played for Corinthians and Tottenham Hotspur. A good hockey player, he played in several trials for England.

Hartley, Fred
Amateur. *b:* 24.4.1906, Waterfoot, Bacup, Lancashire. *d:* 24.12.1976, Stacksteads, Bacup, Lancashire. Lower order right-hand batsman, slow left-arm bowler. *Team* Lancashire (1924–45, 2 matches).
Career batting
2–1–0–2–2–2.00–0–*ct* 0
Bowling 44–1–44.00–0–0–1/44

Hartley, George
Amateur. *b:* 17.3.1849, Heywood, Lancashire. *d:* 9.9.1909, Timperley, Cheshire. Father of Alfred and C. R. (Lancashire). Middle order right-hand batsman, wicket-keeper. *Sch* Rossall. *Team* Lancashire (1871–72, 3 matches).
Career batting
3–3–0–37–24–12.33–0–*ct* 2

Hartley, George Edward
Amateur. *b:* 23.7.1909, Walsden, Yorkshire. *d:* 25.8.1992, Guildford, Surrey. Middle order right-hand batsman, slow right-arm bowler. *Sch* Rydal. *Team* MCC (1946).
Career batting
1–2–0–6–3–3.00–0–*ct* 0

His County cricket was for Denbighshire (1931–35).

Hartley, John Cabourn
Amateur. *b:* 15.11.1874, Lincoln. *d:* 8.3.1963, Woodhall Spa, Lincolnshire. Middle or lower order right-hand batsman, leg break bowler, good field. *Sch* Tonbridge and Marlborough. *Teams* Oxford U (1895–97, blue 1896–97); Sussex (1895–98, 31 matches). *Tours* Mitchell to North America 1895; MCC to South Africa 1905/6, to Australia and New Zealand 1922/3. *Tests* England (1905/6, 2 matches).
Career batting
84–128–21–1380–84*–12.89–0–*ct* 53
Bowling 5767–227–25.40–12–4–8/161
Test batting
2–4–0–15–9–3.75–0–*ct* 2
Bowling 115–1–115.00–0–0–1/62

His final first-class match was for MCC in 1926. He also played for Devon (1909–10). He also won a blue for rugby.

Hartley, John D'Arcy
Amateur. *b:* 4.12.1855, Ashfield House, Otley, Yorkshire. *d:* 24.12.1936, Billesdon, Leicestershire. Middle order batsman. *Sch* Harrow. *Team* MCC (1878).
Career batting
1–2–0–6–6–3.00–0–*ct* 0

Hartley, Peter John
Cricketer. *b:* 18.4.1960, Keighley, Yorkshire. Lower order right-hand batsman, right-arm medium fast bowler. *Teams* Warwickshire (1982, 3 matches); Yorkshire (1985–92, 122 matches). *Tours* Yorkshire to Windward Islands 1986/7, to South Africa 1991/2.
Career batting
125–140–36–2279–127*–21.91–1–*ct* 43
Bowling 10863–318–34.16–12–0–8/111

Hartley, Stuart Neil
Cricketer. *b:* 18.3.1956, Shipley, Yorkshire. Middle order right-hand batsman, right-arm medium pace bowler. *Teams* Yorkshire (1978–88, 133 matches); Orange Free State (1981/2 to 1982/3).
Career batting
142–215–28–4667–114–24.95–4–*ct* 54
Bowling 2182–48–45.45–0–0–4/51

In the latter part of his career he played for Yorkshire more often in Sunday League matches than in first-class.

Hartley-Smith, Hartley
(changed name from Hartley Smith in March 1881)
Amateur. *b:* 30.7.1852, Hammersmith, London. *d:* 21.3.1905, Upwey, Dorset. Lower order batsman, wicket-keeper. *Teams* Surrey (1880, 1 match); Sussex (1889, 1 match).
Career batting
2–4–0–27–11–6.75–0–*ct* 2–*st* 1

Hartopp, Edward Samuel Evans
Amateur. *b:* 7.9.1820, Thurnby, Leicestershire. *d:* 5.10.1894, South Pickenham Hall, Swaffham, Norfolk. Defensive middle order batsman, brilliant longstop. *Sch* Eton. *Teams* Cambridge U (1841–42, blue both years); Nottinghamshire (1843, 1 match).
Career batting
69–120–16–442–22–4.25–0–*ct* 16
Bowling 1 wicket (no analyses)–0–0–1/?

He was a member of the MCC Committee and auditor to the Club from 1876 to his death. His final first-class match was for Gentlemen of England in 1857. He also played for Leicestershire (pre first-class, 1842–51).

Harvey, Edmund
Amateur. *b:* 3.11.1852, Islington, London. *d:* 23.2.1902, Falmouth, Cornwall. Lower order batsman, left-arm fast bowler. *Sch* Radley. *Teams* Middlesex (1872, 1 match); Cambridge U (1872).
Career batting
4–6–0–17–7–2.83–0–*ct* 3
Bowling 143–12–11.91–2–0–5/22

Harvey, Rev Frank Northam
Amateur. *b:* 19.12.1864, Southampton, Hampshire. *d:* 10.11.1939, Southampton, Hampshire. Father of G. T. B. (Europeans). Lower order right-hand batsman, wicket-keeper. *Team* Hampshire (1899–1900, 3 matches).
Career batting
3–4–0–20–7–5.00–0–*ct* 2–*st* 1
He also played under the alias of 'F. H. Northam'. His daughter was the first wife of Lord Denning, the Judge.

Harvey, John Frank
Professional. *b:* 27.9.1939, Barnwell, Cambridge. Middle order right-hand batsman, off break bowler. *Team* Derbyshire (1963–72, 204 matches).
Career batting
206–344–32–7538–168–24.16–4–*ct* 87
Bowling 21–1–21.00–0–0–1/0
He hit 1,000 runs in a season three times (best 1,226, av 32.26, in 1971). His first-class debut was for MCC in 1961. He also played for Cambridgeshire (1958–59 and 1973–77) and Berkshire (1978–87).

Harvey, Jonathan Robert William
Amateur. *b:* 3.2.1944, Yeovil, Somerset. Tail end right-hand batsman, right-arm fast medium bowler. *Sch* Marlborough. *Team* Cambridge U (1963–65, blue 1965).
Career batting
6–8–2–5–3–0.83–0–*ct* 1
Bowling 431–17–25.35–1–0–5/28
He won a blue for rugby.

Harvey, Peter Fairfield
Professional. *b:* 15.1.1923, Linby, Nottinghamshire. Lower order right-hand batsman, leg break and googly bowler, slip field. *Team* Nottinghamshire (1947–58, 173 matches).
Career batting
175–244–46–3645–150–18.40–2–*ct* 116
Bowling 11908–335–35.54–13–3–8/122

Harvey, Peter Vernon
Amateur. *b:* 6.1.1926, Wallington, Surrey. *d:* 27.10.1966, Galmington, Taunton, Somerset. Middle order left-hand batsman. *Sch* Epsom. *Team* Oxford U (1949).
Career batting
1–1–0–9–9–9.00–0–*ct* 0
He played against Cambridge U in the 1944 wartime match.

Harvey, Robert Neil, MBE
Amateur. *b:* 8.10.1928, Fitzroy, Melbourne, Victoria, Australia. Brother of C. E. (Victoria), M. R. (Victoria) and Raymond (Victoria). Brilliant middle order left-hand batsman, off break bowler, excellent field. *Teams* Victoria (1946/7 to 1956/7, 64 matches); New South Wales (1958/9 to 1962/3, 30 matches). *Tours* Australia to England 1948, 1953, 1956, 1961, to South Africa 1949/50, 1957/8, to West Indies 1954/5, to India and Pakistan 1956/7, 1959/60, to New Zealand 1956/7; Commonwealth to Ceylon 1951/2. *Tests* Australia (1947/8 to 1962/3, 79 matches).
Career batting
306–461–35–21699–231*–50.93–67–*ct* 228
Bowling 1106–30–36.86–0–0–4/8
Test batting
79–137–10–6149–205–48.41–21–*ct* 64
Bowling 120–3–40.00–0–0–1/8
He hit 1,000 runs on his 1948 and 1961 tours to England and 2,040, av 65.80, in 1953, which was easily his best tour. He also reached 1,000 runs in Australia four times and in South Africa once. Of his seven double centuries, two were hit in Tests – v South Africa and West Indies – and two in England. His highest score was 231* for New South Wales v South Australia at Sydney in 1962/3. He captained Australia in one Test.

Harvey, Ronald Charles
Professional. *b:* 7.5.1934, Ingatestone, Essex. Lower order left-hand batsman, right-arm fast medium bowler. *Team* Essex (1952, 1 match).
Career batting
1–2–2–12–12*–no av–0–*ct* 0
Bowling 88–3–29.33–0–0–3/88

Harvey, Rev Thomas Arnold
Amateur. *b:* 17.4.1878, Marsh's Library, Dublin, Ireland. *d:* 25.12.1966, Dublin, Ireland. Lower order right-hand batsman, right-arm medium pace bowler. *Sch* Ellesmere College. *Team* Ireland (1902).
Career batting
2–4–0–113–62–28.25–*ct* 1
Bowling 78–2–39.00–0–0–2/67
He played rugby for Ireland. He was later Bishop of Cashel.

Harvey, William Henry Tompkins
Amateur. *b:* 12.4.1896, Shirley, Southampton, Hampshire. *d:* *circa* 1970, South Africa. Middle order right-hand batsman, right-arm medium pace bowler. *Teams* Warwickshire (1927, 1 match); Border (1920/1).
Career batting
5–9–1–116–28–14.50–0–*ct* 3

Bowling 290–13–22.30–1–0–5/70

A noted soccer player, he appeared for England in amateur internationals, and for Sheffield Wednesday, Southend United and Birmingham City.

Harvey-Walker, Ashley John

Cricketer. *b:* 21.7.1944, East Ham, Essex. Middle order right-hand batsman, right-arm medium pace off break bowler. *Sch* Strathallan. *Team* Derbyshire (1971–78, 81 matches).

Career batting

81–143–10–3186–117–23.95–3–*ct* 31

Bowling 1150–34–33.82–1–1–7/35

He scored 110* in the second innings of his debut match for Derbyshire v Oxford U at Burton-on-Trent in 1971.

Harwood, Baron

Professional. *b:* 14.8.1852, Darwen, Lancashire. *d:* 16.12.1915, Moses Gate, Lancashire. Tail end right-hand batsman, right-arm fast bowler. *Team* Lancashire (1877, 1 match).

Career batting

1–2–2–0–0*–no av–0–*ct* 2

Bowling 16–1–16.00–0–0–1/16

Harwood, Frederick

Professional. *b:* 1.6.1827, Mitcham, Surrey. *d:* 11.12.1887, Mitcham, Surrey. Lower order right-hand batsman, right-hand fast round arm bowler. *Team* Surrey (1851–65, 4 matches).

Career batting

4–5–1–8–5–2.00–0–*ct* 3

Bowling 158–7–22.57–0–0–3/39

Hasan Jamil Alvi

Cricketer. *b:* 25.7.1952, Karachi, Pakistan. Middle order left-hand batsman, left-arm medium pace bowler. *Teams* Kalat (1969/70); Karachi (1969/70 to 1971/2); Universities (1972/3 to 1974/5); PIA (1975/6 to 1984/5). *Tours* Pakistan Under 25 to Sri Lanka 1973/4; Pakistan to Sri Lanka 1975/6, to England 1978; PIA to Zimbabwe 1981/2.

Career batting

120–175–33–4228–172–29.77–4–*ct* 57

Bowling 6239–204–30.58–7–0–5/38

He played in one first-class match on the 1978 tour to England in emergency. He played for Pakistan in one-day Internationals.

Haseeb Ahsan

Amateur. *b:* 15.7.1939, Peshawar, India. Lower order right-hand batsman, off break bowler. *Teams* Peshawar (1956/7 to 1959/60); PIA (1960/1 to 1962/3); Karachi (1961/2 to 1962/3). *Tours* Pakistan to England 1962, to West Indies 1957/8, to India 1960/1; Pakistan Eaglets to England 1963. *Tests* Pakistan (1957/8 to 1961/2, 12 matches).

Career batting

49–59–16–242–36–5.62–0–*ct* 9

Bowling 3935–142–27.71–13–2–8/23

Test batting

12–16–7–61–14–6.77–0–*ct* 1

Bowling 1330–27–49.25–2–0–6/202

Owing to injury he appeared in only three matches on the 1962 tour to England, but his bowling action was also suspect. He was manager of the 1987 tour to England.

Haskett-Smith, Algernon

Amateur. *b:* 4.7.1856, Marylebone, London. *d:* 21.11.1887, Paddington, London, from a gun accident. Opening right-hand batsman, good field. *Sch* Eton. *Team* Oxford U (1879, blue).

Career batting

5–8–1–114–38–16.28–0–*ct* 2

He also played for the Gentlemen of Kent in 1879. He also won a blue for athletics.

Haslip, Shearman Montague

Amateur. *b:* 13.5.1897, Twickenham, Middlesex. *d:* 4.7.1968, Weymouth, Dorset. Lower order right-hand batsman, right-arm fast medium bowler. *Sch* Rugby. *Team* Middlesex (1919, 5 matches).

Career batting

9–12–0–91–20–7.58–0–*ct* 4

Bowling 592–18–32.88–0–0–3/12

His final first-class match was for MCC in 1920.

Haslop, Peter

Amateur. *b:* 17.10.1941, Midhurst, Sussex. Lower order right-hand batsman, right-arm medium pace bowler, good field. *Team* Hampshire (1962, 1 match).

Career batting

1–1–1–2–2*–no av–0–*ct* 1

Bowling 82–2–41.00–0–0–2/82

He reappeared for Hampshire in a John Player League match in 1972.

Hassall, Frederick

Professional. *b:* 1868, Nantwich, Cheshire. *d:* 1945, Leicester. Hard hitting middle order right-hand batsman, right-arm medium pace bowler. *Team* Leicestershire (1894, 4 matches).

Career batting

4–7–0–57–20–8.14–0–*ct* 1

Bowling 25–0

He also played for Staffordshire (1898–1902). He first played for Leicestershire (pre first-class) in 1892.

Hassan, Frederick

Professional. *b: circa* 1860. *d:* 15.4.1940, Tooting Bec, London. Lower order batsman, bowler. *Team* Kent (1879, 1 match).

Career batting

1–2–0–0–0–0.00–0–*ct* 0

Bowling 12–1–12.00–0–0–1/5

Hassan, Sheikh Basharat
Cricketer. *b:* 24.3.1944, Nairobi, Kenya. Sound opening right-hand batsman, right-arm medium pace bowler, occasional wicket-keeper. *Teams* East Africa (1963/4 to 1964/5); Nottinghamshire (1966–85, 329 matches).
Career batting
332–549–54–14394–182*–29.07–15–*ct* 310–*st* 1
Bowling 407–6–67.83–0–0–3/33

He also played for Kenya. He hit 1,000 runs in a season five times (best 1,395, av 32.44, in 1970). He was a first-class umpire (1989–91). In 1991 he was appointed Commercial Manager to Nottinghamshire CCC. He was a useful hockey player.

Hassan, Syed Farooq Azim
Cricketer. *b:* 17.10.1941, Lahore, India. Lower order right-hand batsman, right-arm medium fast bowler. *Teams* Oxford U (1962–63); Pakistan Universities (1959/60).
Career batting
11–14–6–44–17–5.50–0–*ct* 3
Bowling 664–15–44.26–0–0–2/15

Hassett, Arthur Lindsay, MBE
Amateur. *b:* 28.8.1913, Geelong, Victoria, Australia. Brother of R. J. (Victoria), uncle of J. H. Shaw (Victoria). Middle order right-hand batsman, right-arm medium pace bowler. *Team* Victoria (1932/3 to 1952/3, 73 matches). *Tours* Australia to England 1938, 1948, 1953, to New Zealand 1945/6, to South Africa 1949/50; Australian Services to England, India and Ceylon 1945. *Tests* Australia (1938–53, 43 matches).
Career batting
216–322–32–16890–232–58.24–59–*ct* 169
Bowling 703–18–39.05–0–0–2/10
Test batting
43–69–3–3073–198*–46.56–10–*ct* 30
Bowling 78–0

He hit 1,000 runs on each of his three Test tours to England with 1,589, av 54.79, in 1938 and 1,563, av 74.42, in 1948, whilst in 1953, when he captained the side, he headed the Test batting averages. In all he led Australia in 24 Tests. He also hit 1,000 twice in a season in Australia. Of his eight double centuries, six, including his highest of 232 v MCC at Melbourne in 1950/51, were for Victoria and two were for the Australians in England. His final first-class match was for A. L. Hassett's XI in 1953/4.

Hastie, James Henderson
Amateur. *b:* 20.6.1920, Glasgow, Scotland. Middle order left-hand batsman, slow left-arm bowler. *Team* Minor Counties (1953).
Career batting
1–2–0–37–22–18.50–0–*ct* 0

His County cricket was for Buckinghamshire (1938–54).

Hastilow, Cyril Alexander Frederick
Amateur. *b:* 31.5.1895, Aston, Birmingham. *d:* 30.9.1975, Moseley, Birmingham. Father-in-law of A. H. Kardar (India and Pakistan). Lower order right-hand batsman, right-arm slow bowler. *Team* Warwickshire (1919, 2 matches).
Career batting
2–3–0–26–14–8.66–0–*ct* 0
Bowling 72–2–36.00–0–0–2/56

He was Hon Secretary and Chairman of Warwickshire 1948–62.

Hastings, Alfred Gardiner
Amateur. *b:* 29.10.1847, Deal, Kent. *d:* 26.12.1916, Brook Green, Hammersmith, London. Steady middle order right-hand batsman, good field. *Sch* Winchester. *Team* MCC (1869).
Career batting
1–2–0–1–1–0.50–0–*ct* 0

He did not appear in first-class cricket whilst at Oxford U. His County cricket was for Shropshire.

Hastings, Brian Frederick
Amateur. *b:* 23.3.1940, Island Bay, Wellington, New Zealand. Middle order right-hand batsman, leg break and googly bowler. *Teams* Wellington (1957/8); Central Districts (1960/1); Canterbury (1961/2 to 1976/7). *Tours* New Zealand to England 1969, 1973, 1975 (World Cup), to Australia 1969/70, 1973/4, 1974/5 (not first-class), to West Indies 1971/2, to India and Pakistan 1969/70. *Tests* New Zealand (1968/9 to 1975/6, 31 matches).
Career batting
163–273–32–7686–226–31.89–15–*ct* 112
Bowling 139–4–34.75–0–0–1/0
Test batting
31–56–6–1510–117*–30.20–4–*ct* 23
Bowling 9–0

He appeared in all three Tests on both his tours to England and was one of the leading batsmen, scoring in first-class matches 708 runs av 35.00, in 1969 and 662, av 38.94, in 1973. His highest score was 226 for Canterbury v New Zealand Under 23 at Christchurch in 1964/5.

Hatch, Peter George
Amateur. *b:* 3.7.1938, Kirkee, India. Hard hitting middle order right-hand batsman. *Sch* Malvern. *Teams* Combined Services (1960); Free Foresters (1961).
Career batting
5–7–0–60–15–8.57–0–*ct* 2

Hatfeild, Charles Eric
Amateur. *b:* 11.3.1887, Hartsdown, Margate, Kent. *d:* 21.9.1918, Cambrai, France. He was killed in action. Middle order batsman, slow left-arm bowler. *Sch* Eton. *Teams* Oxford U (1907–09, blue 1908); Kent (1910–14, 45 matches). *Tour* MCC to the Argentine 1911/12.

Career batting
65–101–8–1498–74–16.10–0–*ct* 45
Bowling 1475–64–23.04–2–0–5/48
He gained his place in the Eton Eleven as a bowler, but won his blue as a batsman.

Hathorn, Christopher Maitland Howard
Amateur. *b:* 7.4.1878, Pietermaritzburg, South Africa. *d:* 17.5.1920, Parktown West, Johannesburg, South Africa. He died from pneumonia. Middle order right-hand batsman. *Teams* Transvaal (1897/8 to 1906/7); London County (1901–04). *Tours* South Africa to England 1901, 1904, 1907, to Australia 1910/11. *Tests* South Africa (1902/3 to 1910/11, 12 matches).
Career batting
87–142–9–3541–239–26.62–9–*ct* 27
Bowling 52–1–52.00–0–0–1/16
Test batting
12–20–1–325–102–17.10–1–*ct* 5
He was most successful on his first two tours to England, heading the first-class batting averages in 1901 and in 1904 completing 1,000 runs –1,317, av 36.58. His 1907 tour was not so successful. His highest score was 239 for South Africans v Cambridge U at Cambridge in 1901. His final first-class match in South Africa was for Wanderers Club in 1908/9. He also played tennis for South Africa.

Hathurusingha, Upul Chandika
Cricketer. *b:* 13.9.1968, Colombo, Ceylon. Opening right-hand batsman, right-arm medium fast bowler. *Team* Tamil Union (1988/9 to 1991/2). *Tours* Sri Lanka B to Pakistan 1988/9; Sri Lanka to England 1990, 1991, to New Zealand 1990/1, to Pakistan 1991/2, to Australia and New Zealand (World Cup) 1991/2. *Tests* Sri Lanka (1990/1 to 1991/2, 6 matches).
Career batting
54–82–6–2645–136–34.80–4–*ct* 30
Bowling 1655–72–22.98–1–0–5/44
Test batting
6–10–0–375–81–37.50–0–*ct* 1
Bowling 68–1–68.00–0–0–1/40
He batted well on both his visits to England and played in the 1991 Test.

Hatteea, Saeed Ahmed
Cricketer. *b:* 2.2.1950, Bombay, India. Tail end right-hand batsman, right-arm fast-medium bowler. *Sch* City of London. *Teams* Bombay (1969/70 to 1970/1); Rest of World (1970).
Career batting
8–5–0–1–1–0.20–0–*ct* 6
Bowling 764–27–28.29–1–0–5/33
His County cricket was for Oxfordshire (1972).

Hattersley, G. P. (*see under* Pinder, G.)

Hattersley-Smith, Rev Percy
Amateur. *b:* 19.5.1847, Merton Hall, Cambridge. *d:* 19.1.1918, Cheltenham, Gloucestershire. Middle order batsman. *Sch* Perse, Cambridge. *Team* Gloucestershire (1878–79, 11 matches).
Career batting
11–15–2–198–56–15.23–0–*ct* 3
He also played for Cambridgeshire (1895–96).

Hatton, Anthony George
Professional. *b:* 25.3.1937, Whitkirk, Leeds, Yorkshire. Lower order left-hand batsman, right-arm fast bowler. *Team* Yorkshire (1960–61, 3 matches).
Career batting
3–1–1–4–4*–no av–0–*ct* 1
Bowling 202–6–33.66–0–0–2/27

Hatton, John
Amateur. *b:* 25.2.1858, West Dean, Gloucestershire. *d:* 25.4.1915, Gloucester. Middle order batsman, wicket-keeper. *Team* Gloucestershire (1884, 3 matches).
Career batting
3–6–1–28–11*–5.60–0–*ct* 1

Haughton, William Edward
Amateur. *b:* 31.10.1923, Bray, Co Wicklow, Ireland. Middle order right-hand batsman. *Team* Ireland (1953).
Career batting
1–2–0–0–0–0.00–0–*ct* 0
He played hockey for Ireland.

Hawes, George Howard
Amateur. *b:* 19.10.1881, Rothwell, Kettering, Northamptonshire. *d:* 26.10.1934, Desborough, Northamptonshire. Lower order right-hand batsman, right-arm medium pace bowler. *Team* Northamptonshire (1919, 2 matches).
Career batting
2–3–1–16–12*–8.00–0–*ct* 1
Bowling 87–1–87.00–0–0–1/43

Hawke, Dr Christopher Richard John
Amateur. *b:* 12.4.1934, North End, Portsmouth, Hampshire. Middle or lower order right-hand batsman, wicket-keeper. *Sch* Harrow. *Team* Oxford U (1953).
Career batting
1–2–1–31–23*–31.00–0–*ct* 1

Hawke, Hon Martin Bladen
(succeeded as 7th Baron Hawke in 1887)
Amateur. *b:* 16.8.1860, Willingham Rectory, Gainsborough, Lincolnshire. *d:* 10.10.1938, West End, Edinburgh, Scotland. Uncle of A.M. Tew (Oxford U) and J. E. Tew (Oxford U). Middle order right-hand batsman, good deep field. *Sch* Eton. *Teams* Yorkshire (1881–1911, 513 matches); Cam-

bridge U (1882–85, blue 1882, 1883 and 1885). *Tours* Vernon to Australia 1887/8, to India 1889/90 (not first-class); Hawke to North America 1891, to India 1892/3, to North America 1894, to South Africa 1895/6, to West Indies 1896/7, to South Africa 1898/9; MCC to Argentine 1911/12. *Tests* England (1895/6 to 1898/9, 5 matches).
Career batting
633–936–105–16749–166–20.15–13–*ct* 209
Bowling 16–0
Test batting
5–8–1–55–30–7.85–0–*ct* 3

He captained Yorkshire from 1883 to 1910, Cambridge in 1885 and England in four of the five Tests in which he played, as well as his various touring teams overseas. President of Yorkshire from 1898 to his death, he virtually controlled the County's affairs for most of those years. He is credited with introducing Winter Pay for professionals, and at the same time he weeded out players who belonged to the 'hard drinking' variety. Following his suggestion Test selectors were introduced for home internationals, Hawke himself being a selector 1899–1911, and all in all his influence was much in evidence in the modernisation of first-class cricket. He was MCC President 1914 and Treasurer 1932–37. He hit 1,078 runs, av 23.95, in 1895.

Hawke, Neil James Napier
Amateur. *b:* 27.6.1939, Cheltenham, Adelaide, South Australia. Lower order right-hand batsman, right-arm medium fast bowler. *Teams* Western Australia (1959/60, 7 matches); South Australia (1960/1 to 1967/8, 60 matches); Tasmania (1968/9, 2 matches). *Tours* Australia to England 1964, 1968, to India and Pakistan 1964/5, to West Indies 1964/5, to South Africa 1966/7; Commonwealth to Pakistan 1970/1; Rest of World to Barbados 1966/7; Cavaliers in England 1969. *Tests* Australia (1962/3 to 1968, 27 matches).
Career batting
145–198–57–3383–141*–23.99–1–*ct* 85
Bowling 12088–458–26.39–23–5–8/61
Test batting
27–37–15–365–45*–16.59–0–*ct* 9
Bowling 2677–91–29.41–6–1–7/105

He had a most successful tour of England in 1964 taking 83 wickets, av 19.80, including 18 in Tests, but in 1968 his bowling was of little account and he took only one Test wicket. His final first-class match in England was for Cavaliers in 1969.

Hawker, Sir Frank Cyril
Amateur. *b:* 21.7.1900, Epping, Essex. *d:* 22.2.1991, Hastings, Sussex. Grandson of John Bastow (Middlesex), brother-in-law of T. N. Pearce (Essex). Middle order right-hand batsman. *Sch* City of London. *Team* Essex (1937, 1 match).
Career batting
1–2–0–26–16–13.00–0–*ct* 0

He was President of MCC 1970/1.

Hawkes, Christopher James
Cricketer. *b:* 14.7.1972, Loughborough, Leicestershire. Lower order left-hand batsman, slow left-arm bowler. *Team* Leicestershire (1990-92, 4 matches).
Career batting
4–6–2–65–18–16.25–0–*ct* 2
Bowling 162–5–32.40–0–0–4/18

Hawkey, Richard Bladworth
Amateur. *b:* 7.8.1923, Teddington, Middlesex. *d:* 19.3.1991, Hillingdon, Middlesex. Opening right-hand batsman, right-arm medium pace bowler. *Sch* Merchant Taylors. *Team* Cambridge U (1949).
Career batting
3–6–0–42–13–7.00–0–*ct* 0
Bowling 139–1–139.00–0–0–1/40

His first-class debut was for Free Foresters in 1948. He played squash for England.

Hawkins, Charles
Professional. *b:* 20.6.1817, Cosham, Hampshire. *d:* 9.9.1846, Fittleworth, Petworth, Sussex. Middle order right-hand batsman, brilliant field. *Team* Sussex (1839–44, 25 matches).
Career batting
56–104–7–1198–95–12.35–0–*ct* 50–*st* 6
Bowling 1 wicket (no analyses)–0–0–1/?

Regarded as the best point field of his day and would have developed perhaps into the best bat if he had not died so young. 'He had a most curious way of taking guard. He would make his block, or guard, within about an inch only of the stumps; then, when the bowler advanced to deliver the ball, he too would come forward, raising his bat over his shoulder.' His final first-class match was for Petworth in 1845.

Hawkins, Christopher George
Professional. *b:* 31.8.1938, Slough, Buckinghamshire. Stylish middle order right-hand batsman, right-arm medium pace bowler, wicket-keeper. *Team* Warwickshire (1957, 4 matches).
Career batting
4–5–2–16–11*–5.33–0–*ct* 7–*st* 2

He also played for Buckinghamshire (1955 and 1965).

Hawkins, Derek Graham
Professional. *b:* 18.5.1935, Alveston, Gloucestershire. Middle order right-hand batsman, off break bowler. *Team* Gloucestershire (1952–62, 134 matches).
Career batting
134–220–14–3755–106–18.22–3–*ct* 78
Bowling 1153–38–30.34–1–0–6/81

He hit 1,021 runs, av 21.72, in 1961.

Hawkins, Frederick Albert
Amateur. *b:* 11.12.1888, Wandsworth, London. *d:* 12.9.1975, Elstead, Surrey. Middle order right-hand batsman, right-arm medium pace bowler. *Team* Middlesex (1927, 2 matches).
Career batting
2–2–1–19–19–19.00–0–*ct* 0

Hawkins, Henry
Amateur. *b:* 15.1.1876, Kegworth, Leicestershire. *d:* 12.8.1930, Everdon Hall, Daventry, Northamptonshire. Hard hitting lower order right-hand batsman, right-arm fast medium bowler. *Sch* Taunton. *Team* Northamptonshire (1905–09, 26 matches).
Career batting
26–44–9–350–33–10.00–0–*ct* 10
Bowling 767–24–31.95–0–0–2/12
He first played for Northamptonshire (pre first-class) in 1902.

Hawkins, Herbert Hervey Baines
Amateur. *b:* 9.1.1876, Streatham Hill, London. *d:* 1.1.1933, Trincomalee, Ceylon. He drowned whilst bathing. Middle order right-hand batsman, right-arm medium pace bowler. *Sch* Whitgift. *Team* Cambridge U (1896–99, blue 1898–99).
Career batting
20–31–11–159–15*–7.95–0–*ct* 14
Bowling 1143–48–23.81–2–0–7/45

Hawkins, Laurence Cyril
Amateur. *b:* 15.5.1907, Solihull, Warwickshire. Middle order right-hand batsman, leg break bowler. *Team* Somerset (1928–37, 46 matches).
Career batting
46–81–8–1252–96–17.15–0–*ct* 21
Bowling 1067–22–48.50–0–0–4/39

Hawkwood, Clifford
Professional. *b:* 16.11.1909, Nelson, Lancashire. *d:* 15.5.1960, Burnley, Lancashire. Middle order right-hand batsman. *Team* Lancashire (1931–35, 24 matches).
Career batting
24–26–5–596–113–28.38–1–*ct* 9
Bowling 92–1–92.00–0–0–1/63

Hawley, Frank
Professional. *b:* 19.7.1877, Nottingham. *d:* 23.8.1913, Sutton-in-Ashfield, Nottinghamshire. Lower order batsman, fast medium bowler. *Team* Nottinghamshire (1897, 1 match).
Career batting
1–1–0–1–1–1.00–0–*ct* 0
Bowling 67–1–67.00–0–0–1/31

Haworth, William Barratt
Amateur. *b:* 18.3.1884, Oldham, Lancashire. *d:* 27.1.1975, St Annes-on-Sea, Lancashire. Lower order right-hand batsman, leg break bowler, good close field. *Team* Gentlemen (1924).
Career batting
1–2–0–1–1–0.50–0–*ct* 0
Bowling 9–0
He was for many years the mainstay of the Blackpool Club.

Hawtin, Alfred Powell Rawlins
Amateur. *b:* 1.2.1883, Bugbrooke, Northamptonshire. *d:* 15.1.1975, Abington, Northampton. Brother of R. W. R. (Northamptonshire). Sound opening right-hand batsman. *Sch* Northampton GS. *Team* Northamptonshire (1908–30, 85 matches).
Career batting
86–151–5–3595–135–24.62–3–*ct* 31
During the Second World War he more or less single-handedly kept the Northamptonshire County Club in existence, and was the Club's Chairman 1945–53.

Hawtin, Roger William Rawlins
Amateur. *b:* 30.9.1880, Bugbrooke, Northamptonshire. *d:* 7.9.1917, Abington, Northampton. Brother of A. P. R. (Northamptonshire). Steady middle order right-hand batsman, right-arm medium pace bowler. *Sch* Northampton GS. *Team* Northamptonshire (1905–08, 19 matches).
Career batting
19–37–4–508–65–15.39–0–*ct* 11
Bowling 663–22–30.13–2–0–5/33

Hawtin, William Henry
Professional. *b:* 18.1.1908, Northampton. *d:* 27.3.1940, Hawkley Hall Explosive Works, Worsley, Mesnes, Pemberton, Wigan, Lancashire in an accident whilst working on munitions. Middle order right-hand batsman, right-arm medium pace bowler. *Team* Northamptonshire (1929–34, 4 matches).
Career batting
4–8–1–51–24–7.28–0–*ct* 4
Bowling 23–1–23.00–0–0–1/9

Hawtrey, Edward Montague
Amateur. *b:* 10.10.1847, Windsor, Berkshire. *d:* 14.8.1916, Westgate-on-Sea, Kent. Middle order batsman, bowler. *Sch* Eton. *Team* MCC (1880–82).
Career batting
2–4–0–1–1–0.25–0–*ct* 1
Bowling 64–2–32.00–0–0–2/50
He played no first-class cricket whilst at Cambridge U, but won a blue for athletics.

Hay, Sir David Osborne
Amateur. *b:* 29.11.1916, Corowa, New South Wales, Australia. Grandson of W. H. Moule (Australia). Hard hitting middle order right-hand batsman. *Team* Oxford U (1936–38).
Career batting
4–6–0–129–96–21.50–0–*ct* 1

Hay, George
Professional. *b:* 28.1.1851, Staveley, Derbyshire. *d:* 4.10.1913, Staveley, Derbyshire. Lower order right-hand batsman, right-hand fast medium round-arm bowler, good cover field. *Team* Derbyshire (1875–86, 47 matches).
Career batting
55–94–16–669–49–8.57–0–*ct* 34
Bowling 2444–148–16.51–8–1–6/16

His final first-class match was for the North in 1887. He joined the MCC Ground staff in 1882 and remained until 1912. He was a first-class umpire (1895–98).

Hay, Thomas Douglas Baird
Amateur. *b:* 31.8.1876, Auckland, New Zealand. *d:* 19.4.1967, Auckland, New Zealand. Brother of W. P. C. (Auckland), uncle of S. C. (Auckland). Middle order right-hand batsman, useful change bowler. *Team* Auckland (1893/4 to 1906/7). *Tour* New Zealand to England 1927.
Career batting
25–47–5–689–144–16.40–1–*ct* 9
Bowling 444–19–23.36–1–0–5/10

He was manager of the 1927 team to England, but appeared in one first-class match.

Hay, William Harrington
Amateur. *b:* 21.1.1849, London. *d:* 3.3.1925, Great Bowden Hall, Leicestershire. Middle order right-hand batsman, good longstop. *Sch* Eton. *Team* MCC (1877).
Career batting
3–5–1–67–26*–16.75–0–*ct* 4

His first-class debut was for Gentlemen of England in 1875. His County cricket was for Leicestershire (pre first-class, 1873–86).

Haycraft, James Samuel
Amateur. *b:* 11.9.1865, Islington, London. *d:* 26.3.1942, St Pancras, London. Opening right-hand batsman. *Sch* University College School. *Team* Middlesex (1885, 1 match).
Career batting
1–2–0–5–5–2.50–0–*ct* 0

A brilliant bat in London club cricket, notably for Stoics, Nondescripts and Pallingswick, he failed to do himself justice in his single County match.

Haye, William
Cricketer. *b:* 15.9.1948, St Catherine, Jamaica. Tail end right-hand batsman, right-arm fast medium bowler. *Team* Jamaica (1970 to 1971/2). *Tour* Jamaica to England 1970.
Career batting
7–8–0–198–60–24.75–0–*ct* 1
Bowling 287–6–47.83–0–0–1/8

He appeared in only one first-class match on the 1970 Jamaica tour to England.

Hayes, Ernest George
Professional before First World War, amateur 1919–23, professional from 1924. *b:* 6.11.1876, Peckham, London. *d:* 2.12.1953, West Dulwich, London. Excellent middle order right-hand batsman, leg break bowler, brilliant slip field. *Teams* Surrey (1896–1919, 500 matches); London County (1903); Leicestershire (1926, 5 matches). *Tours* Brackley to West Indies 1904/5; MCC to South Africa 1905/6, to Australia 1907/8. *Tests* England (1905/6 to 1912, 5 matches).
Career batting
560–896–48–27318–276–32.21–48–*ct* 608–*st* 2
Bowling 13754–515–26.70–12–2–8/22
Test batting
5–9–1–86–35–10.75–0–*ct* 2
Bowling 52–1–52.00–0–0–1/28

He hit 1,000 runs in a season six times, twice going on to 2,000 (best 2,309, av 45.27, in 1906). His four double centuries were all for Surrey with his highest being 276 v Hampshire at the Oval in 1909. He achieved very little for England and fared so poorly during the 1907/8 tour to Australia that he was not selected for any of the Tests in that series. He was chief coach at Leicester 1923–28 and at the Oval 1929–34.

Hayes, Frank Charles
Cricketer. *b:* 6.12.1946, Preston, Lancashire. Attractive middle order right-hand batsman, right-arm medium pace bowler, good cover field. *Team* Lancashire (1970–84, 228 matches). *Tours* MCC to West Indies 1973/4; Robins to South Africa 1972/3, 1974/5, 1975/6; International Wanderers to Rhodesia 1975/6; Overseas XI to India 1980/1; International XI to Pakistan 1981/2. *Tests* England (1973–76, 9 matches).
Career batting
272–421–58–13018–187–35.86–23–*ct* 176
Bowling 15–0
Test batting
9–17–1–244–106*–15.25–1–*ct* 7

He hit 1,000 runs in a season six times (1,311, av 35.43, in 1974). He hit 34 off one over from M. A. Nash, Lancashire v Glamorgan at Swansea in 1977. From 1978 to 1980 he captained Lancashire.

Hayes, John Arthur
Amateur. *b:* 11.1.1927, Auckland, New Zealand. Lower order right-hand batsman, right-arm fast bowler. *Teams* Auckland (1946/7 to 1958/9); Canterbury (1950/1 to 1954/5). *Tours* New Zealand to England 1949, 1958, to India and Pakistan 1955/6. *Tests* New Zealand (1950/1 to 1958, 15 matches).
Career batting
78–100–36–611–36–9.54–0–*ct* 29
Bowling 6759–292–23.14–12–3–7/28
Test batting
15–22–7–73–19–4.86–0–*ct* 3
Bowling 1217–30–40.56–0–0–4/36

Owing to illness he had a very moderate tour of England in 1949, but in 1958, though achieving little in the Tests, he headed the first-class bowling averages with 62 wickets, av 20.20. His final first-class match was Governor-General's XI v MCC in 1960/1.

Hayes, Kevin Anthony
Cricketer. *b:* 26.9.1962, Thurnscoe, Yorkshire. Middle order right-hand batsman, right-arm medium pace bowler. *Teams* Lancashire (1980–86, 18 matches); Oxford U (1981–84, blue all four years).
Career batting
44–71–4–1595–152–23.80–2–*ct* 15
Bowling 537–17–31.58–1–0–6/58
He also played for Cumberland (1988–91). He captained Oxford in 1984, and also won a blue for soccer.

Hayes, Peter James
Cricketer. *b:* 20.5.1954, Crowborough, Sussex. Lower order right-hand batsman, right-arm medium pace bowler. *Sch* Brighton. *Team* Cambridge U (1974–77, blue 1974, 1975 and 1977).
Career batting
27–44–11–343–56*–10.39–0–*ct* 19
Bowling 1832–51–35.92–1–0–5/48
His County cricket was for Suffolk (1981–90).

Haygarth, Arthur
Amateur. *b:* 4.8.1825, Hastings, Sussex. *d:* 1.5.1903, Pimlico, Westminster, London. Cousin of E. B. (Gloucestershire and Hampshire) and J. W. (Oxford U). Defensive opening/middle order right-hand batsman. *Sch* Harrow. *Teams* MCC (1844–61); Sussex (1848–60, 3 matches); Middlesex (1850–51, 3 matches).
Career batting
136–247–14–3042–97–13.05–0–*ct* 65
Bowling 145–19–7.63–3–1–6/36
He also played for Warwickshire (pre first-class, 1844). His lasting memorial is the set of 15 *Cricket Scores and Biographies* volumes, the first four published by F. Lillywhite and the remainder by MCC. This work contains the most comprehensive collection ever published of match scores and cricketers' biographies up to the year 1878.

Haygarth, Edward Brownlow
Amateur. *b:* 26.4.1854, Cirencester, Gloucestershire. *d:* 14.4.1915, Siddington Manor, Gloucestershire. Brother of J. W. (Oxford U), cousin of Arthur (Middlesex and Sussex), uncle of F. H. Gresson (Sussex). Lower order right-hand batsman, wicket-keeper, lob bowler. *Sch* Lancing. *Teams* Gloucestershire (1883, 2 matches); Hampshire (1875, 1 match).
Career batting
3–5–0–18–7–3.60–0–*ct* 0–*st* 1
He also played for Berkshire (1870). He played soccer for England.

Haygarth, John William
Amateur. *b:* 3.12.1842, Rodmarton, Gloucestershire. *d:* 30.3.1923, Boonah, Queensland, Australia. Brother of E. B. (Gloucestershire and Hampshire), cousin of Arthur (Middlesex and Sussex), uncle of F. H. Gresson (Sussex). Hard hitting lower order right-hand batsman, excellent wicket-keeper. *Sch* Winchester. *Team* Oxford U (1862–64, blue all three years).
Career batting
10–14–2–81–17–6.75–0–*ct* 12–*st* 12
He also played for Gloucestershire (pre first-class, 1858). He emigrated to Australia in 1865 and thus took no part in English cricket after leaving Oxford.

Hayhurst, Albert
Professional. *b:* 17.9.1905, Birdwell, Yorkshire. *d:* 8.11.1991, Reading, Berkshire. Lower order right-hand batsman, right-arm fast medium bowler. *Team* Warwickshire (1934–35, 7 matches).
Career batting
7–8–0–98–42–12.25–0–*ct* 2
Bowling 457–12–38.08–0–0–4/120
He also played for Buckinghamshire (1948–53). An excellent soccer player, he was centre half for Reading and Luton Town.

Hayhurst, Andrew Neil
Cricketer. *b:* 23.11.1962, Davyhulme, Manchester, Lancashire. Opening or middle order right-hand batsman, right-arm medium pace bowler. *Teams* Lancashire (1985–89, 42 matches); Somerset (1990–92, 64 matches). *Tours* Lancashire to Jamaica 1986/7, 1987/8, to Zimbabwe 1988/9.
Career batting
106–168–21–4851–172*–33.00–9–*ct* 31
Bowling 3918–86–45.55–0–0–4/27
He reached 1,000 runs in a season twice (best 1,559, av 57.74, in 1990).

Hayles, Basil Ratcliffe Marshall
Amateur. *b:* 29.10.1916, Andover, Hampshire. Lower order right-hand batsman, wicket-keeper. *Sch* Haileybury. *Teams* Army (1938–39); Combined Services (1947–49).
Career batting
7–10–1–69–40–7.66–0–*ct* 6–*st* 2
His County cricket was for Norfolk (1947).

Hayley, Harry
Professional. *b:* 22.2.1860, Heath, Wakefield, Yorkshire. *d:* 3.6.1922, St John's, Wakefield, Yorkshire. Middle or lower order right-hand batsman, right-arm medium pace bowler. *Team* Yorkshire (1884–98, 7 matches).
Career batting
7–12–1–122–24–11.09–0–*ct* 3
Bowling 48–0

Hayman, Rev Henry Telford
Amateur. *b:* 20.11.1853, West Malling, Kent. *d:* 8.2.1941, Cheltenham, Gloucestershire. Nephew of B. Norton (Kent), S. Norton (Kent) and W. S. Norton (Kent). Middle order right-hand batsman, good long-stop. *Sch* Bradfield. *Team* Kent (1873, 2 matches).
Career batting
2–4–0–37–29–9.25–0–*ct* 2
He was not in the Eleven whilst at Cambridge.

Hayman, Herbert Bailey
Amateur. *b:* 5.10.1873, Hendon, Middlesex. *d:* 31.7.1930, Winslow, Buckinghamshire. Hard hitting opening right-hand batsman, excellent outfield. *Team* Middlesex (1893–1901, 86 matches).
Career batting
105–191–15–4663–165–26.49–4–*ct* 46
Bowling 138–4–34.50–0–0–2/9
He was mainly connected with Hampstead CC, being a prolific scorer in London Club cricket.

Haynes, Carleton
Amateur. *b:* 7.2.1858, Newcastle, Barbados. *d:* 20.11.1945, Woodlands, Southampton, Hampshire. Nephew of H. H. (Barbados). Hard hitting lower order right-hand batsman, right-arm fast bowler, good field. *Sch* Clifton. *Team* Gloucestershire (1878–79, 5 matches).
Career batting
5–10–2–76–21–9.50–0–*ct* 3
Bowling 38–1–38.00–0–0–1/8

Haynes, Denis Marshall
Amateur. *b:* 29.12.1923, Stoke-on-Trent, Staffordshire. Middle order right-hand batsman, right-arm medium pace bowler. *Sch* Denstone. *Team* MCC (1956).
Career batting
1–2–0–8–8–4.00–0–*ct* 1
He played for Cambridge U v Oxford U in the 1944 and 1945 war-time matches. His County cricket was for Staffordshire (1946–57).

Haynes, Desmond Leo
Cricketer. *b:* 15.2.1956, Holders Hill, St James, Barbados. Opening right-hand batsman, right-arm leg break and googly bowler, good field. *Team* Barbados (1976/7 to 1991/2); Middlesex (1989–92, 63 matches). *Tours* West Indies to England 1979 (World Cup), 1980, 1983 (World Cup), 1984, 1988, 1991, to Australia 1979/80, 1981/2, 1983/4 (not first-class), 1984/5, 1986/7, 1988/9, 1991/2, to New Zealand 1979/80, 1986/7, to Pakistan 1980/1, 1985/6 (not first-class), 1986/7, 1990/1, to Sharjah (not first-class) 1985/6, 1986/7, 1988/9, 1989/90, to India 1983/4, 1987/8, 1989/90 (not first-class), to India and Pakistan (World Cup) 1987/8, to Australia and New Zealand (World Cup) 1991/2; Young West Indies to Zimbabwe 1981/2; Rest of World to England 1987. *Tests* West Indies (1977/8 to 1991/2, 103 matches).
Career batting
298–510–58–21176–255*–46.84–50–*ct* 162–*st* 1
Bowling 201–7–28.71–0–0–1/2
Test batting
103–180–21–6725–184–42.29–16–*ct* 59
Bowling 8–1–8.00–0–0–1/2
Of his four tours to England, the first, in 1980, was the most successful with 874 runs, av 46.00, in first-class matches and 308, av 51.33, in the Tests. In 1984 he had a lean time until the final Test when his innings of 125 won the match. A hamstring injury on the 1988 visit ended a run of 72 consecutive Test appearances and in 1991 he seemed content to give the innings a sound start and leave the high scoring to the more junior players. He reached 100 Tests during this last series, the fourth West Indian to achieve that milestone. He captained West Indies in 4 Tests. Coming to County cricket late in his career he had a brilliant record in 1990 hitting 2,346 runs (av 69.00) and making his highest innings to date of 255* v Sussex at Lord's. He also hit over 1,000 runs in 1989 and 1992 and 1,066, av 76.14, in West Indies in 1990/1. He played limited overs matches for Scotland in 1983.

Haynes, Gavin Richard
Cricketer. *b:* 29.9.1969, Wordsley, Stourbridge, Worcestershire. Middle order right-hand batsman, right-arm medium pace bowler. *Team* Worcestershire (1991–92, 13 matches).
Career batting
13–17–3–339–66–24.21–0–*ct* 5
Bowling 210–0

Haynes, John Perigoe
Amateur. *b:* 27.11.1926, Canterbury, Kent. Lower order right-hand batsman, right-arm medium pace bowler. *Sch* Dauntsey's. *Team* Cambridge U (1946).
Career batting
1–2–0–0–0–0.00–0–*ct* 1
Bowling 34–0

Haynes, Michael William
Professional. *b:* 19.5.1936, Sherwood, Nottingham. Middle order right-hand batsman. *Team* Nottinghamshire (1959–61, 9 matches).
Career batting
9–16–1–119–23–7.93–0–*ct* 6

Haynes, Richard William
Professional. *b:* 27.8.1913, Shipston-on-Stour, Warwickshire. *d:* 16.10.1976, Oxford. He died whilst playing golf. Opening right-hand batsman, slow left-arm bowler. *Team* Gloucestershire (1930–39, 74 matches).
Career batting
74–121–6–1673–89–14.54–0–*ct* 40
Bowling 815–15–54.33–0–0–4/76
He also played for Oxfordshire (1929–53). He was a useful hockey player.

Hays, David Leslie
Cricketer. *b:* 5.11.1944, Finchley, Middlesex. Middle order right-hand batsman, wicket-keeper. *Sch* Highgate. *Teams* Cambridge U (1965–68, blue 1966 and 1968); Scotland (1980).
Career batting
25–47–1–751–72–16.32–0–*ct* 26–*st* 2
Bowling 5–0

Haysman, Michael Donald
Cricketer. *b:* 22.4.1961, North Adelaide, South Australia. Middle order right-hand batsman, off break bowler. *Teams* South Australia (1982/3 to 1987/8, 35 matches); Leicestershire (1984, 5 matches); Northern Transvaal (1988/9 to 1991/2). *Tours* Young Australia to Zimbabwe 1982/3; Australian XI to South Africa 1985/6, 1986/7.
Career batting
88–156–21–5212–180–38.60–13–*ct* 122
Bowling 544–3–181.33–0–0–2/19
He hit 106 on his first-class debut for South Australia v Queensland at Adelaide in 1982/3, and a further century on his Leicestershire first-class debut v Cambridge U at Fenner's in 1984.

Hayter, E.
Professional. *b:* 8.9.1913, Southampton, Hampshire. Lower order right-hand batsman, leg break bowler. *Team* Hampshire (1935–37, 3 matches).
Career batting
3–6–1–36–17–7.20–0–*ct* 0
Bowling 29–0

Hayter, Montague William
Professional. *b:* 16.11.1871, Ringwood, Hampshire. *d:* 6.5.1948, Christchurch, Hampshire. Middle order right-hand batsman. *Team* Hampshire (1904, 7 matches).
Career batting
7–12–0–166–82–13.83–0–*ct* 3

Hayward, Arthur John
Professional. *b:* 12.9.1905, Christchurch, Hampshire. Lower order right-hand batsman, leg break and googly bowler. *Team* Hampshire (1925–26, 4 matches).
Career batting
4–4–0–17–10–4.25–0–*ct* 0

Hayward, Daniel (sen)
Professional. *b:* 25.8.1808, Mitcham, Surrey. *d:* 29.5.1852, Cambridge. Father of Daniel jun (Surrey and Cambridgeshire) and Thomas (Cambridgeshire), grandfather of T. W. (Surrey). Middle order right-hand batsman, wicket-keeper. *Teams* Cambridge Town Club (1832–51); Surrey (1839–47, 3 matches).
Career batting
24–42–4–420–53–11.05–0–*ct* 9–*st* 9
Bowling 5 wickets (no analyses)–0–0–2/?

Hayward, Daniel (jun)
Professional. *b:* 19.10.1832, Chatteris, Cambridgeshire. *d:* 30.5.1910, Cambridge. Son of Daniel sen (Surrey), father of T. W. (Surrey), brother of Thomas (Cambridgeshire). Middle order right-hand batsman, good long stop. *Teams* Cambridge Town Club (1852–61); Surrey (1854, 1 match); Cambridgeshire (1861–69, 31 matches).
Career batting
43–77–8–690–59–10.00–0–*ct* 18
His single appearance for Surrey was played under the mistaken impression that he was born in Mitcham.

Hayward, David Russell
Amateur. *b:* 7.6.1920, Australia. *d:* 21.4.1945, Lasham Hill, Hampshire. Lower order right-hand batsman, leg break and googly bowler. *Sch* Harrow. *Teams* Oxford U (1939); Middlesex (1939, 1 match).
Career batting
9–13–7–36–14–6.00–0–*ct* 2
Bowling 591–20–29.55–1–0–6/79

Hayward, James Gordon Rotherham
Professional. *b:* 31.12.1926, Bridlington, Yorkshire. Lower order left-hand batsman, right-arm fast medium bowler. *Team* Nottinghamshire (1951, 1 match).
Career batting
1 match, did not bat–*ct* 0
Bowling 78–2–39.00–0–0–2/78

Hayward, Richard Edward
Cricketer. *b:* 15.2.1954, Ickenham, Middlesex. Middle order left-hand batsman, left-arm medium pace bowler. *Sch* Latymer. *Teams* Hampshire (1981–82, 13 matches); Central Districts (1982/3 to 1985/6); Somerset (1985, 9 matches).
Career batting
50–80–14–1766–102–26.75–3–*ct* 27
Bowling 63–0
He also played for Buckinghamshire (1978–80 and 1983–89) and made his first-class debut for Minor Counties in 1979. He was captain of Central Districts in 1984/5.

Hayward, Thomas
Professional. *b:* 21.3.1835, Chatteris, Cambridgeshire. *d:* 21.7.1876, Cambridge. Son of Daniel sen (Surrey), brother of Daniel jun (Surrey and Cambridgeshire), uncle of T. W. (Surrey). Opening/middle order right-hand batsman, right-hand medium pace round-arm bowler, excellent cover point. *Teams* Cambridgeshire (1857–71, 35 matches), Cambridge Town Club (1854–61). *Tours* Parr to North America 1859 (not first-class), to Australia 1863/4.
Career batting
118–200–11–4789–132–25.33–6–*ct* 62
Bowling 3935–249 + 18–15.80–19–2–9/30
He was for a few years regarded as the equal of any batsman in England, but most of his famous feats

were performed for the AEE in odds matches. His final first-class match was for MCC in 1872. His best bowling was 9/30 for England v 16 of Kent at Lord's in 1860.

Hayward, Thomas Walter
Professional. *b:* 29.3.1871, Cambridge. *d:* 19.7.1939, Cambridge. Son of Daniel jun (Cambridgeshire and Surrey), grandson of Daniel sen (Surrey), nephew of Thomas (Cambridgeshire). Very sound opening right-hand batsman, right-arm medium pace bowler, good field. *Team* Surrey (1893–1914, 593 matches). *Tours* Hawke to South Africa 1895/96; Stoddart to Australia 1897/8; MCC to Australia 1901/02, 1903/04. *Tests* England (1895/6 to 1909, 35 matches).
Career batting
712–1138–96–43551–315*–41.79–104–*ct* 492
Bowling 11042–481–22.95–18–2–8/89
Test batting
35–60–2–1999–137–34.46–3–*ct* 19
Bowling 514–14–36.71–0–0–4/22

One of the most reliable of batsmen during the twenty years prior to the First World War, Hayward originally went in first wicket down for Surrey, but was promoted to open the innings about 1900, initially with R. Abel. Later he became associated with J. B. Hobbs and the pair produced a century stand for the first wicket on 40 occasions, with their highest partnership realising 352 runs against Warwickshire at the Oval in 1909. Hayward also assisted in six century first wicket stands for England.

For twenty successive seasons, commencing 1895, he reached 1,000 runs, going on to 2,000 in ten seasons and thence to 3,000 twice. His best year – 1906 – produced 3,518 runs, av 66.37, which created a new English first-class aggregate record that stood until 1947. In 1900 he reached the 1,000-run mark on the last day of May.

Eight times Hayward hit over 200 runs in an innings, his highest score being 315* for Surrey v Lancashire at the Oval in 1898.

In his early days he was a very useful bowler and in 1897 took 114 wickets, av 18.21, thus achieving the 'double' for the only time in his career. After 1904 he scarcely bowled at all.

All his tours to Australia were successful. In 1903/4 he topped the batting averages and in 1901/2 came second to A. C. MacLaren.

Hayward, William Irvine Dudley
Amateur. *b:* 15.4.1930, Glenelg, Adelaide, South Australia. Middle or lower order right-hand batsman, right-arm medium fast bowler, excellent field. *Team* Cambridge U (1950–53, blue 1950, 1951 and 1953).
Career batting
27–33–4–309–57–10.65–0–*ct* 23
Bowling 1948–68–28.64–4–0–6/89

His final first-class match was for MCC in 1954.

Haywood, David Charles
Cricketer. *b:* 20.3.1945, Hucknall, Nottinghamshire. Middle order left-hand batsman, leg break bowler. *Sch* Nottingham High School. *Team* Cambridge U (1968, blue).
Career batting
9–15–0–284–62–18.93–0–*ct* 5

He also won a blue for soccer.

Haywood, Esme Thomas Lancelot Reed
Amateur. *b:* 23.8.1900, East Preston, Sussex. *d:* 8.1.1985, Fownhope, Herefordshire. Middle order right-hand batsman. *Sch* Cheltenham. *Team* Somerset (1925–27, 8 matches).
Career batting
8–16–0–137–38–8.56–0–*ct* 1

He played no first-class cricket whilst at Cambridge U, but did win a blue for hockey.

Haywood, John William
Professional. *b:* 17.4.1878, Harby, Leicestershire. *d:* 2.2.1963, Oakham, Rutland. Lower order right-hand batsman, right-arm medium pace bowler. *Team* Leicestershire (1901–03, 3 matches).
Career batting
3–5–0–37–16–7.40–0–*ct* 1
Bowling 240–4–60.00–0–0–2/81

Haywood, Paul Raymond
Cricketer. *b:* 30.3.1947, Leicester. Middle order right-hand batsman, right-arm medium pace bowler, good cover point. *Sch* Wyggeston. *Team* Leicestershire (1969–73, 54 matches).
Career batting
54–82–8–1570–100*–21.21–1–*ct* 15
Bowling 324–9–36.00–0–0–4/60

He represented Leicestershire at hockey.

Haywood, Robert Allnutt
Professional. *b:* 16.9.1887, Eltham, London. *d:* 1.6.1942, Edinburgh, Scotland. Father of R. O. (Scotland), son of R. J. (Kent). Middle order right-hand batsman, right-arm medium pace bowler. *Team* Northamptonshire (1908–24, 172 matches).
Career batting
172–306–15–8373–198–28.77–20–*ct* 85
Bowling 1466–34–43.11–0–0–3/73

He hit 1,000 runs in a season three times (best 1,909, av 42.42, in 1921). After the 1921 season he demanded better financial remuneration from the Northamptonshire Club; his request being turned down, he went as coach to Fettes and henceforth only appeared in the school holidays – a great loss to the County.

Haywood, Robert John
Professional. *b:* 3.3.1858, Eltham, London. *d:* 9.5.1922, Eltham, London. Father of R. A. (Northamptonshire), grandfather of R. O. (Scotland). Lower order batsman, bowler. *Team* Kent (1878, 1 match).

Career batting
1–2–1–0–0*–0.00–0–*ct* 1
Bowling 15–0

Haywood, Robert Oliver
Amateur. *b:* 22.4.1917, Northampton. *d:* 21.12.1963, Edinburgh, Scotland. Son of R. A. (Northamptonshire), grandson of R. J. (Kent). Middle order right-hand batsman. *Team* Scotland (1949).
Career batting
1–2–0–12–12–6.00–0–*ct* 0

Haywood, William John
Professional. *b:* 25.2.1841, Upper Hallam, Sheffield, Yorkshire. *d:* 7.1.1912, Walkley, Sheffield, Yorkshire. Lower order right-hand batsman, right-arm fast medium bowler. *Team* Yorkshire (1878, 1 match).
Career batting
1–2–0–7–7–3.50–0–*ct* 0
Bowling 14–1–14.00–0–0–1/14

Hayzelden, Allan Frederick George
Amateur. *b:* 10.1.1904, Leytonstone, Essex. *d:* 10.4.1955, Harefield, Middlesex. Lower order right-hand batsman, right-arm fast bowler. *Sch* Merchant Taylors. *Team* Essex (1929–31, 2 matches).
Career batting
2–3–1–5–4*–2.50–0–*ct* 3
Bowling 110–6–18.33–0–0–3/30

Hazare, Vijay Samuel
Amateur. *b:* 11.3.1915, Sangli, Maharashtra, India. Brother of Vivekanand Samuel (Mysore), father of R. V. (Baroda), uncle of V. V. (Baroda) and S. S. (Baroda). Middle order right-hand batsman, right-arm medium pace bowler, good slip field. *Teams* Maharashtra (1934/5 to 1940/1); Central India (1935/6 to 1938/9); Baroda (1941/2 to 1960/1). *Tours* India to England 1946, 1952, to Australia 1947/8, to West Indies 1952/3, to Ceylon 1944/5. *Tests* India (1946 to 1952/3, 30 matches).
Career batting
238–367–46–18740–316*–58.38–60–*ct* 165
Bowling 14643–595–24.61–27–3–8/90
Test batting
30–52–6–2192–164*–47.65–7–*ct* 11
Bowling 1220–20–61.00–0–0–4/29

He hit 1,000 runs on both his tours of England (best 1,344, av 49.77, in 1946) and appeared in all the Tests on both visits, leading India on the 1952 tour. In all he captained India in 14 Tests. He hit 1,000 runs five times in a season in India (best 1,480, av 87.05, in 1949/50) and once in Australia. In all he hit 10 scores over 200, including two over 300, the higher being 316* for Maharashtra v Baroda at Poona in 1939/40. His highest innings in England was 244* v Yorkshire at Bramall Lane in 1946. His partnership of 577 with Gul Mahomed for the 4th wicket in the match Baroda v Holkar at Baroda in 1946/7 created a new world first-class record. His final first-class match was his benefit for President's XI v West Indies in 1966/7.

Hazell, Horace Leslie
Professional. *b:* 30.9.1909, Brislington, Somerset. *d:* 31.3.1990, Brislington, Somerset. Hard hitting lower order left-hand batsman, slow left-arm bowler, good close field. *Team* Somerset (1929–52, 350 matches).
Career batting
350–507–228–2280–43–8.17–0–*ct* 250
Bowling 22941–957–23.97–57–7–8/27

He took 100 wickets in a season twice (best 106, av 19.48, in 1949). For Somerset v Gloucestershire at Taunton in 1949 he bowled 105 balls (including 17 successive maidens) without conceding a run.

Hazelton, Edward Wyndham
Amateur. *b:* 8.5.1894, Buckingham. *d:* 13.3.1958, Great Dunmow, Essex. Middle or lower order right-hand batsman, right-arm medium or leg break bowler. *Sch* Wellingborough. *Team* Essex (1919, 1 match).
Career batting
8–16–4–77–43–6.41–0–*ct* 6
Bowling 621–23–27.00–2–1–6/45

He also played for Buckinghamshire (1912–31). His final first-class match was for MCC in 1930.

Hazelton, Brig Gen Edwin Hills
Amateur. *b:* 16.12.1861, Southampton, Hampshire. *d:* 25.7.1916, Simla, India. Middle order batsman. *Team* Hampshire (1883, 3 matches).
Career batting
3–5–0–83–50–16.60–0–*ct* 0

Hazlerigg, Sir Arthur Grey, Bart
(created 1st Baron Hazlerigg in 1945)
Amateur. *b:* 17.11.1878, Ayr, Scotland. *d:* 25.5.1949, Marylebone, London. Father of Lord A. G. Hazlerigg (Leicestershire). Lower order right-hand batsman, lob bowler. *Sch* Eton. *Team* Leicestershire (1907–10, 65 matches).
Career batting
65–108–28–866–55*–10.82–0–*ct* 36
Bowling 44–0

He captained Leicestershire 1907 to 1910 and was President of the County Club in 1930. Whilst at Cambridge U he did not appear in any first-class matches.

Hazlerigg, Sir Arthur Grey
(succeeded as 2nd Baron Hazlerigg in 1949)
Amateur. *b:* 24.2.1910, South Kensington, London. Son of Lord A. G. Hazlerigg (Leicestershire). Opening right-hand batsman, right-arm medium slow off break bowler, good slip field. *Sch* Eton. *Teams* Cambridge U (1930–32, blue all three years); Leicestershire (1930–34, 34 matches). *Tour* Martineau to Egypt 1935 (not first-class).
Career batting
66–106–9–2515–135–25.92–3–*ct* 75
Bowling 3476–112–31.03–1–0–6/27

Hazlitt, Gervys Rignold

He captained Cambridge U in 1932 and Leicestershire in 1934. He hit 1,010 runs, av 36.07, in 1932.

Hazlitt, Gervys Rignold
Amateur. *b:* 4.9.1888, Enfield, Sydney, New South Wales, Australia. *d:* 30.10.1915, Parramatta, New South Wales, Australia. He died from a heart attack. Lower order right-hand batsman, right-arm medium pace off break bowler. *Teams* Victoria (1905/6 to 1910/11, 16 matches); New South Wales (1911/12 to 1912/13, 6 matches). *Tours* Australia to England 1912; Waddy to Ceylon 1913/14 (not first-class). *Tests* Australia (1907/8 to 1912, 9 matches).
Career batting
57–83–14–876–82*–12.69–0–*ct* 33
Bowling 4906–188–26.09–8–0–7/25
Test batting
9–12–4–89–34*–11.12–0–*ct* 4
Bowling 623–23–27.08–1–0–7/25
He had a very successful tour of England, taking, in all matches, 101 wickets, av 18.96; though his bowling action came in for some criticism.

Head, Francis Somerville
Amateur. *b:* 30.6.1846, Kensington, London. *d:* 2.4.1941, Bushey Hall, Hertfordshire. Middle order batsman. *Sch* Marlborough. *Team* Lancashire (1868–69, 6 matches).
Career batting
7–12–0–80–24–6.66–0–*ct* 3
His final first-class match was for MCC in 1881.

Head, John Reginald
Amateur. *b:* 15.7.1868, Hackney, London. *d:* 15.5.1949, Folkestone, Kent. Brother-in-law of H. R. Bromley-Davenport (Middlesex) and M. G. Tollemache (Cambridge U). Middle order right-hand batsman, right-arm medium pace bowler. *Sch* Clifton. *Team* Middlesex (1892–98, 5 matches). *Tour* Warner to North America 1897.
Career batting
8–14–2–242–101–20.16–1–*ct* 3
Bowling 60–3–20.00–0–0–3/22
He also played for Suffolk (1909).

Head, Timothy John
Cricketer. *b:* 22.9.1957, Hammersmith, London. Lower order right-hand batsman, wicket-keeper. *Sch* Lancing. *Teams* Sussex (1976–81, 22 matches); Cambridge U (1986).
Career batting
25–31–7–397–52*–16.54–0–*ct* 55–*st* 6

Headlam, Cecil
Amateur. *b:* 19.9.1872, London. *d:* 12.8.1934, Charing, Kent. Lower order right-hand batsman, wicket-keeper. *Sch* Rugby. *Teams* Oxford U (1895); Middlesex (1902–06, 8 matches). *Tour* Oxford Univ Authentics to India 1902/3.
Career batting
23–35–7–287–44–10.25–0–*ct* 34–*st* 12
He also played for Oxfordshire (1893–1901). A noted author his major cricket work was a book on his 1902/3 tour of India 'Ten Thousand Miles through India and Burma'.

Headley, Dean Warren
Cricketer. *b:* 27.1.1970, Norton, Stourbridge, Worcestershire. Son of R. G. A. (Worcestershire), grandson of G. A. (West Indies). Lower order right-hand batsman, right-arm fast medium bowler. *Team* Middlesex (1991–92, 29 matches).
Career batting
29–29–4–472–91–18.88–0–*ct* 10
Bowling 2516–60–41.93–2–0–5/46

Headley, George Alphonso, MBE
Amateur. *b:* 30.5.1909, Colon, Panama. *d:* 30.11.1983, Meadowbridge, Kingston, Jamaica. Father of R. G. A. (Worcestershire and West Indies), grandfather of D. W. (Middlesex). Brilliant middle order right-hand batsman, leg break bowler, good field. *Team* Jamaica (1927/8 to 1953/4). *Tours* West Indies to Australia 1930/1, to England 1933, 1939, to India and Pakistan 1948/9. *Tests* West Indies (1929/30 to 1953/4, 22 matches).
Career batting
103–164–22–9921–344*–69.86–33–*ct* 76
Bowling 1842–51–36.11–1–0–5/33
Test batting
22–40–4–2190–270*–60.83–10–*ct* 14
Bowling 230–0
He was the outstanding batsman on both his tours to England, heading the first-class averages each year – 2,320, av 66.28, in 1933 and 1,745, av 72.70, in 1939. These successes merely confirmed that he was the outstanding West Indian batsman of the 1930s. He also scored 1,000 in an Australian season.
His highest innings was 344* for Jamaica v Lord Tennyson's XI at Kingston in 1931/2 and of his other scores over 200, two were in Tests against England – 223* at Kingston in 1929/30 and 270* at the same venue in 1934/5. He hit two double centuries on his 1933 visit to England and another two in 1939. His final first-class match was for a Commonwealth XI in 1954. He captained West Indies in one Test.

Headley, Ronald George Alphonso
Amateur in 1958, then professional. *b:* 29.6.1939, Mountain View, Vineyard Town, Kingston, Jamaica. Son of G. A. (West Indies), father of D. W. (Middlesex). Opening/middle order left-hand batsman, leg break bowler. *Teams* Jamaica (1965/6 to 1973/4); Worcestershire (1958–74, 403 matches). *Tours* West Indies to England 1973; Worcestershire World Tour (Rhodesia first-class) 1964/5, to Jamaica 1965/6; Commonwealth to Pakistan 1970/1; Cavaliers to West Indies 1964/5. *Tests* West Indies (1973, 2

matches).
Career batting
423–758–61–21695–187–31.12–32–*ct* 356
Bowling 588–12–49.00–0–0–4/40
Test batting
2–4–0–62–42–15.50–0–*ct* 2

He hit 1,000 runs in a season thirteen times, going on to 2,000 once – 2,040, av 31.87, in 1961. He played for Derbyshire in one-day matches only 1975–76.

Heal, Michael George
Cricketer. *b:* 7.9.1948, Bristol. Middle order right-hand batsman, right-arm medium pace bowler. *Team* Oxford U (1969–72, blue 1970 and 1972).
Career batting
22–41–1–637–124*–15.92–1–*ct* 10
Bowling 3–0

He was awarded his rugby blue.

Heale, Rev William Henry
Amateur. *b:* 27.4.1859, Highfield, Hemel Hempstead, Hertfordshire. *d:* 24.4.1907, Lambeth, London. Opening or middle order right-hand batsman, right-arm medium pace bowler. *Sch* Harrow. *Team* Oxford U (1881).
Career batting
1–2–0–10–9–5.00–0–*ct* 0

His County cricket was for Hertfordshire (1879–95).

Healey, Robert Dennis
Cricketer. *b:* 10.2.1934, Plymouth, Devon. Lower order right-hand batsman, right-arm fast medium bowler. *Team* Combined Services (1964).
Career batting
2–4–0–14–7–3.50–0–*ct* 0
Bowling 146–0

His County cricket was for Devon (1953–69).

Healing, John Alfred
Amateur. *b:* 14.6.1873, Southwick Park, Tewkesbury, Gloucestershire. *d:* 4.7.1933, Caister-on-Sea, Norfolk. Stylish middle order left-hand batsman. *Sch* Clifton. *Teams* Cambridge U (1894); Gloucestershire (1899–1906, 10 matches).
Career batting
12–20–0–195–37–9.75–0–*ct* 10

He also played for Bedfordshire (1894).

Healing, Percival
Amateur. *b:* 16.7.1878, Tewkesbury, Gloucestershire. *d:* 1.2.1915, Marylebone, London. Steady middle order right-hand batsman. *Sch* Cheltenham. *Team* Gloucestershire (1911, 1 match).
Career batting
1–2–0–38–30–19.00–0–*ct* 0

Healy, Ian Andrew
Cricketer. *b:* 30.4.1964, Spring Hill, Brisbane, Queensland, Australia. Brother of K. J. (Queensland). Middle order right-hand batsman, wicket-keeper. *Team* Queensland (1986/7 to 1991/2, 28 matches). *Tours* Australia to Pakistan 1988/9, to England 1989, to New Zealand 1989/90, 1991/2 (World Cup), to India 1989/90 (not first-class), to Sharjah (not first-class) 1989/90, to West Indies 1990/1. *Tests* Australia (1988/9 to 1991/2, 36 matches).
Career batting
79–113–20–2649–90–28.48–0–*ct* 246–*st* 12
Bowling 1–0
Test batting
36–52–2–1016–69–20.32–0–*ct* 108–*st* 2

He established himself as Australia's principal wicket-keeper in the 1988/89 overseas season and kept wicket in all six Tests on the 1989 tour to England.

Heane, George Frank Henry
Amateur. *b:* 2.1.1904, Worksop, Nottinghamshire. *d:* 24.10.1969, Skendleby, Lincolnshire. Middle order left-hand batsman, right-arm medium pace bowler. *Team* Nottinghamshire (1927–51, 172 matches). *Tours* Cahn to Argentina 1929/30, to New Zealand 1938/9.
Career batting
189–268–24–6183–138–25.34–9–*ct* 100
Bowling 7307–222–32.91–5–1–6/52

He captained Nottinghamshire 1935 to 1946, jointly with S. D. Rhodes in the first year. He hit 1,000 runs in a season three times (best 1,627, av 37.83, in 1939). He also played for Lincolnshire (1947–50). A useful soccer player, he represented Nottinghamshire.

Heap, James Sutcliffe
Professional. *b:* 12.8.1882, Lowerhouse, Burnley, Lancashire. *d:* 30.1.1951, Stoneclough, Bolton, Lancashire. Lower order left-hand batsman, slow left-arm bowler. *Team* Lancashire (1903–21, 210 matches).
Career batting
210–312–41–5146–132*–18.98–1–*ct* 76
Bowling 9513–412–23.08–25–5–9/43

His best bowling was 9/43 for Lancashire v Northamptonshire at Northampton in 1910.

Heap, John Garsden
Amateur. *b:* 5.1.1857, Higher Baxenden, Accrington, Lancashire. *d:* 20.4.1931, North Shore, Blackpool, Lancashire. Middle order batsman. *Team* Lancashire (1884, 2 matches).
Career batting
2–2–0–0–0–0.00–0–*ct* 2
Bowling 4–0

Heap, Russell
Cricketer. *b:* 6.12.1968, Leeds, Yorkshire. Opening right-hand batsman. *Sch* Ipswich. *Team* Cambridge U (1988–90, blue 1989–90).
Career batting
20–36–4–669–63–20.90–0–*ct* 11

His County cricket was for Suffolk (1988–89).

Heard, Hartley
Cricketer. *b:* 29.10.1947, Bristol. Tail end right-hand batsman, right-arm medium pace bowler. *Team* Oxford U (1967–70, blue 1969–70).
Career batting
30–45–14–273–31–8.80–0–*ct* 5
Bowling 2048–49–41.79–1–0–6/78

Hearn, Peter
Professional. *b:* 25.11.1925, Tunbridge Wells, Kent. Nephew of S. G. (Kent). Middle order left-hand batsman, slow left-arm bowler, good cover. *Team* Kent (1947–56, 196 matches).
Career batting
200–351–32–8138–172–25.51–7–*ct* 66
Bowling 1245–22–56.59–0–0–3/34
He hit 1,000 runs in a season three times (best 1,413, av 30.06, in 1954). He scored 124 on debut for Kent v Warwickshire at Gillingham in 1947.

Hearn, Sidney George
Professional. *b:* 28.7.1899, Harbledown, Kent. *d:* 23.8.1963, Chartham, Kent. Uncle of Peter (Kent). Middle order left-hand batsman, slow left-arm bowler. *Team* Kent (1922–26, 31 matches).
Career batting
32–44–7–465–54*–12.56–0–*ct* 20
Bowling 399–22–18.13–0–0–3/15

Hearn, William
Professional. *b:* 30.11.1849, Essendon, Hertfordshire. *d:* 30.1.1904, Barnet, Hertfordshire. Middle order right-hand batsman, right-hand medium pace round-arm bowler, excellent cover point. *Team* MCC (1878–91).
Career batting
41–72–5–806–91–12.02–0–*ct* 27
Bowling 57–0
He was on the ground staff at Lord's from 1878 until his death, and latterly was a well known umpire (1896–1903), standing in 4 Test matches (1898–1902). His County cricket was for Hertfordshire (1870–95).

Hearne, Alec
Professional. *b:* 22.7.1863, Ealing, Middlesex. *d:* 16.5.1952, Beckenham, Kent. Son of George (Middlesex), brother of G. G. (Kent) and Frank (Kent), nephew of Thomas (Middlesex), cousin of G. F. (MCC), uncle of G. A. L. (South Africa). Steady middle order right-hand batsman, right-arm slow bowler, good slip. *Team* Kent (1884–1906, 403 matches). *Tours* Read to South Africa 1891/2; Kent to North America 1903. *Test* England (1891/2, 1 match).
Career batting
488–833–78–16346–194–21.65–15–*ct* 404
Bowling 23120–1160–19.93–52–9–8/15
Test batting
1–1–0–9–9–9.00–0–*ct* 1
He hit 1,000 runs in a season four times (best 1,477, av 29.54, in 1895). His final first-class match was for MCC in 1910.

Hearne, Frank
Professional. *b:* 23.11.1858, Ealing, Middlesex. *d:* 14.7.1949, Mowbray, Cape Town, South Africa. Son of George (Middlesex), brother of G. G. (Kent) and Alec (Kent), father of G. A. L. (South Africa), nephew of Thomas (Middlesex), cousin of G. F. (MCC). Sound opening right-hand batsman, right-hand fast round-arm bowler, good cover point. *Teams* Kent (1879–89, 125 matches); Western Province (1889/90 to 1903/4). *Tours* Warton to South Africa 1888/9; South Africa to England 1894 (not first-class). *Tests* England (1888/9, 2 matches); South Africa (1891/2 to 1895/6, 4 matches).
Career batting
161–285–20–4760–144–17.96–4–*ct* 111
Bowling 1346–57–23.61–1–0–5/47
Test batting
6–10–0–168–30–16.80–0–*ct* 3
Bowling 40–2–20.00–0–0–2/40
He emigrated for his health to South Africa in 1889, opening a sports outfitters in Cape Town. He umpired 6 Test matches in South Africa (1898/9 to 1905/6). He also played for Huntingdonshire and for Ireland (not first-class) in 1883.

Hearne, George
Professional. *b:* 15.5.1829, Chalfont St Peter, Buckinghamshire. *d:* 9.12.1904, Rushey Green, Catford, London. Brother of Thomas (Middlesex), father of G. G. (Kent), Frank (Kent) and Alec (Kent), grandfather of G. A. L. (South Africa), uncle of G. F. (Middlesex). Hard hitting middle order right-hand batsman, longstop. *Team* Middlesex (1861–68, 18 matches).
Career batting
20–32–6–550–72–21.15–0–*ct* 15–*st* 2
He was groundsman at the Private Banks Ground at Catford Bridge for a period of some thirty years. He also played for Buckinghamshire (1864).

Hearne, George Alfred Lawrence
Amateur. *b:* 27.3.1888, Catford, London. *d:* 13.11.1978, Barberton, East Transvaal, South Africa. Son of Frank (Kent), grandson of George (Middlesex), nephew of Alec (Kent) and G. G. (Kent). Opening or middle order right-hand batsman, bowler. *Team* Western Province (1910/11 to 1926/7). *Tour* South Africa to England 1924. *Tests* South Africa (1922/3 to 1924, 3 matches).
Career batting
41–72–2–1981–138–28.30–2–*ct* 38–*st* 2
Bowling 401–14–28.64–0–0–3/9
Test batting
3–5–0–59–28–11.80–0–*ct* 3

He appeared in only one Test on the 1924 tour to England and his batting in first-class matches attained only modest success.

Hearne, George Francis
Professional. *b:* 18.10.1851, Stoke Poges, Buckinghamshire. *d:* 30.5.1931, Hill End, St Albans, Hertfordshire. Son of Thomas (Middlesex), father of T. J. (Middlesex), nephew of George (Middlesex), cousin of Alec (Kent), G. G. (Kent) and Frank (Kent). Lower order right-hand batsman, change bowler, longstop. *Team* MCC (1882).
Career batting
1–1–0–26–26–26.00–0–*ct* 0
Bowling 23–0

Hearne, George Gibbons
Professional. *b:* 7.7.1856, Ealing, Middlesex. *d:* 13.2.1932, Denmark Hill, London. Son of George (Middlesex), brother of Frank (Kent) and Alexander (Kent), nephew of Thomas (Middlesex), uncle of G. A. L. (South Africa). Middle/lower order left-hand batsman, left-hand medium pace round-arm bowler. *Team* Kent (1875–95, 252 matches). *Tour* Read to South Africa 1891/2. *Test* England (1891/2, 1 match).
Career batting
328–571–56–9022–126–17.51–5–*ct* 214
Bowling 11503–686–16.76–41–12–8/21
Test batting
1–1–0–0–0–0.00–0–*ct* 0
He hit 1,000 runs in 1886 (1,125, av 28.84) and took 100 wickets in a season twice (best 119, av 13.13, in 1878). His final first-class match was for MCC in 1903.

Hearne, Herbert
Professional. *b:* 15.3.1862, Chalfont St Giles, Buckinghamshire. *d:* 13.6.1906, Chalfont St Giles, Buckinghamshire. Brother of Walter (Kent) and J. T. (Middlesex). Lower order right-hand batsman, right-arm fast bowler, good field. *Team* Kent (1884–86, 25 matches).
Career batting
25–36–9–252–36–9.33–0–*ct* 16
Bowling 1415–57–24.82–3–0–5/27
He also played for Buckinghamshire (1891). He was forced to retire due to injury.

Hearne, John Thomas
Professional. *b:* 3.5.1867, Chalfont St Giles, Buckinghamshire. *d:* 17.4.1944, Chalfont St Giles, Buckinghamshire. Brother of Herbert (Kent) and Walter (Kent). Lower order right-hand batsman, right-arm medium pace off break bowler, slip field. *Team* Middlesex (1888–1923, 453 matches). *Tours* Read to South Africa 1891/2; Stoddart to Australia 1897/8. *Tests* England (1891/2 to 1899, 12 matches).
Career batting
639–919–318–7205–71–11.98–0–*ct* 426
Bowling 54352–3061–17.75–255–66–9/32
Test batting
12–18–4–126–40–9.00–0–*ct* 4
Bowling 1082–49–22.08–4–1–6/41
He took 100 wickets in a season fifteen times, going on to 200 on three occasions, (best 257, av 14.28, in 1896). He took nine wickets in an innings no fewer than eight times – five for MCC and three for Middlesex, his best figures being 9/32 for Middlesex v Nottinghamshire at Trent Bridge in 1891. For six winters he went to India as a coach, but did not appear in any first-class matches whilst there.

Hearne, John William
Professional. *b:* 11.2.1891, Hillingdon, Middlesex. *d:* 14.9.1965, West Drayton, Middlesex. He was not closely related to the Hearnes of Middlesex and Kent. Stylish middle order right-hand batsman, leg break and googly bowler. *Team* Middlesex (1909–36, 465 matches). *Tours* MCC to West Indies 1910/11, to Australia 1911/12, 1920/1, 1924/5, to South Africa 1913/14. *Tests* England (1911/12 to 1926, 24 matches).
Career batting
647–1025–116–37252–285*–40.98–96–*ct* 348
Bowling 44926–1839–24.42–107–23–9/61
Test batting
24–36–5–806–114–26.00–1–*ct* 13
Bowling 1462–30–48.73–1–0–5/49
One of the leading all-rounders of his day, J. W. Hearne achieved the 'double' five times and on three of those occasions had the added distinction of exceeding 2,000 runs. In all he hit 1,000 runs in a season nineteen times, going on to 2,000 four times with 2,151, av 43.89, in 1932 as his best aggregate. He took over 100 wickets in a season five times (best 142, av 17.83, in 1930).
All eleven of his double centuries were for Middlesex, the highest being 285* v Essex at Leyton in 1929. His best bowling was 9/61 for Middlesex v Derbyshire at Chesterfield in 1933.
He went to Australia with the MCC on three tours, but managed only a moderate record – the best opportunity he had was in 1920/1, when unfortunately he was taken ill in the early stages of the tour and was unable to appear in the majority of matches. In fact ill-health to some extent affected his career and made him a much more cautious batsman than he might otherwise have been. He was Middlesex coach 1946–60.

Hearne, Thomas
Professional. *b:* 4.9.1826, Chalfont St Peter, Buckinghamshire. *d:* 13.5.1900, Ealing, Middlesex. Brother of George (Middlesex), father of G. F. (MCC), grandfather of T. J. (Middlesex), uncle of Alec (Kent), G. G. (Kent) and Frank (Kent). Middle order right-hand batsman, right-hand medium pace round-arm bowler, good point. *Team* Middlesex (1859–75, 59 matches). *Tour* Stephenson to Australia 1861/2.

Hearne, Thomas John

Career batting
173–292–20–5048–146–18.55–4–*ct* 116–*st* 7
Bowling 3994–283 + 9–14.11–16–2–6/12

His first-class debut was for MCC in 1857 and his final first-class match was for the same club in 1876. He also played for Hertfordshire (1852), Buckinghamshire (1857–68) and Northamptonshire (pre first-class, 1870–73). From 1872 he was manager of the ground bowlers at Lord's, not resigning until 1897.

Hearne, Thomas John
Professional. *b:* 3.7.1887, Ealing, Middlesex. *d:* 25.5.1947, Poole, Dorset. Grandson of Thomas (Middlesex), son of G. F. (Middlesex). Lower order batsman, left-arm medium pace bowler. *Team* Middlesex (1908, 1 match).
Career batting
1 match, did not bat–*ct* 0

He also played for Berkshire (1922–23).

Hearne, Walter
Professional. *b:* 15.1.1864, Chalfont St Giles, Buckinghamshire. *d:* 2.4.1925, Canterbury, Kent. Brother of Herbert (Kent) and J. T. (Middlesex). Lower order right-hand batsman, right-arm fast, later medium, bowler. *Team* Kent (1887–96, 55 matches).
Career batting
55–92–19–553–34*–7.57–0–*ct* 23
Bowling 4349–273–15.93–28–10–8/40

He took 116 wickets, av 13.29, in 1894 and his career came to a sudden end in 1896 when he seriously injured his knee.

Hearsum, John
Amateur. *b:* 2.11.1852, Chelsea, London. *d:* 21.7.1931, Chelmsford, Essex. Middle order right-hand batsman, right-hand fast round arm bowler. *Team* Surrey (1871, 2 matches).
Career batting
2–4–0–43–25–10.75–0–*ct* 0
Bowling 59–0

Heartfield, James Henry
Professional. *b:* 19.1.1823, Mitcham, Surrey. *d:* 28.11.1891, Greenwich, London. Tail end right-hand batsman, right-hand fast round-arm bowler. *Team* Surrey (1860–67, 9 matches).
Career batting
10–14–2–29–10*–2.41–0–*ct* 5
Bowling 338–21–16.09–2–0–6/28

Heaslip, John Ganly
Amateur. *b:* 26.11.1899, Dublin, Ireland. *d:* 23.5.1966, St Margaret's, Twickenham, Middlesex. Middle order right-hand batsman, off break bowler. *Teams* Ireland (1920–29); Dublin U (1922–24).
Career batting
10–19–1–389–92*–21.61–0–*ct* 4
Bowling 610–25–24.40–2–0–5/67

Heasman, Dr William Gratwicke
Amateur. *b:* 9.12.1862, Angmering, Sussex. *d:* 25.1.1934, Upperton, Eastbourne, Sussex. Grandfather of M. R. G. Earls-Davis (Somerset). Middle order right-hand batsman, right-arm fast bowler, good point. *Team* Sussex (1885–95, 15 matches). *Tour* Philadelphians to Bermuda 1907 (not first-class).
Career batting
15–26–0–566–66–21.76–0–*ct* 7
Bowling 46–0

He also played for Norfolk (1890–91) and Berkshire (1896).

Heath, Allan Borman
Amateur. *b:* 19.1.1865, Falcombe Manor, East Woodhay, Hampshire. *d:* 21.6.1913, Cullompton, Devon. Stylish middle order right-hand batsman, right-arm fast medium bowler, good cover point. *Sch* Cheltenham. *Team* Hampshire (1883–85, 7 matches).
Career batting
7–14–0–132–42–9.42–0–*ct* 2
Bowling 28–2–14.00–0–0–2/28

He appeared for Hampshire with still a full year to go at school. His last match for Hampshire (not first-class) was in 1892.

Heath, Arthur Howard
Amateur. *b:* 29.5.1856, Titterton, Newcastle-under-Lyme, Staffordshire. *d:* 24.4.1930, Marylebone, London. Brother of Sir James (MCC), brother-in-law of W. T. Toynbee (MCC) and J. H. Savory (Oxford U), son-in-law of H. R. Peel (Oxford U 1855). Middle order right-hand batsman, right-hand fast round-arm, or lob bowler. *Sch* Clifton. *Teams* Gloucestershire (1875, 6 matches); Oxford U (1876–79, blue all four years); Middlesex (1878, 2 matches).
Career batting
44–77–4–969–71–13.27–0–*ct* 26
Bowling 381–26–14.65–1–0–6/11

His final first-class match was for MCC in 1894. He was chiefly associated with Staffordshire, playing for that County from 1879 to 1898, being captain 1884 to 1893, but he also played for Cheshire (1892). A noted rugby footballer, he played for Oxford and England. He was Conservative MP for Hanley 1900–06 and Leek in 1910.

Heath, David Michael William
Amateur. *b:* 14.12.1931, Hall Green, Birmingham. Opening right-hand batsman. *Team* Warwickshire (1949–53, 16 matches).
Career batting
19–28–1–580–149–21.48–1–*ct* 15

He batted well for Combined Services in 1951 and 1952. He was appointed Secretary of Warwickshire CCC in 1986.

Heath, Frederick Rhead
Amateur. *b:* 30.10.1894, Swadlincote, Derbyshire. *d:* 19.9.1967, Sutton, Seaford, Sussex. Brother of J. S.

(Derbyshire). Middle order batsman. *Team* Derbyshire (1924–25, 4 matches).
Career batting
4–6–1–72–17–14.40–0–*ct* 1
Bowling 47–3–15.66–0–0–2/4
He also played for Staffordshire (1913–21).

Heath, George Edward Mansell
Professional. *b:* 20.2.1913, The Peak, Hong Kong. Tail end right-hand batsman, right-arm fast medium bowler. *Team* Hampshire (1937–49, 132 matches).
Career batting
132–188–83–586–34*–5.58–0–*ct* 49
Bowling 11359–404–28.11–23–2–7/49
His best season was 1938 when he took 97 wickets, av 23.77.

Heath, Rev Henry Francis Trafford
Amateur. *b:* 19.12.1885, Kadina, South Australia. *d:* 9.9.1967, Edinburgh, Scotland. Lower order batsman, left-arm bowler. *Team* South Australia (1923/4, 2 matches). *Tour* AIF to England 1919.
Career batting
3–4–1–35–21–11.66–0–*ct* 3
Bowling 225–7–32.14–1–0–5/43

Heath, Sir James
Amateur. *b:* 26.1.1852, Titterton, Newcastle-under-Lyme, Staffordshire. *d:* 24.12.1942, Westminster, London. Brother of A. H. (Middlesex), brother-in-law of W. T. Toynbee (MCC). Middle order right-hand batsman, right-hand medium pace round-arm bowler. *Sch* Clifton. *Team* MCC (1882).
Career batting
1–1–0–16–16–16.00–0–*ct* 0
His County cricket was for Staffordshire (1871–72). He was MP for North West Staffordshire from 1892 to 1906.

Heath, Jeremy Richard Percy
Cricketer. *b:* 26.4.1959, Turner's Hill, Sussex. Middle order left-hand batsman. *Team* Sussex (1980–83, 17 matches).
Career batting
17–31–4–611–101*–22.62–1–*ct* 6
Bowling 58–0

Heath, John
Professional. *b:* 12.11.1807, Lambeth, London. *d:* 7.11.1878, City of London. Steady middle order right-hand batsman, brilliant longstop. *Team* Surrey (1846–54, 19 matches).
Career batting
25–46–5–294–35–7.17–0–*ct* 23
Owing to the paucity of Surrey matches in the 1830s, he had little opportunity to appear in County cricket. His first-class debut was for England in 1842.

Heath, John Stanley
Amateur. *b:* 30.8.1891, Swadlincote, Derbyshire. *d:* 1.9.1972, Trentham, Staffordshire. Brother of F. R. (Derbyshire). Middle order right-hand batsman, leg break bowler. *Team* Europeans (1918/19); Derbyshire (1924–25, 6 matches).
Career batting
11–19–2–214–34–12.58–0–*ct* 8
Bowling 832–30–27.73–3–0–5/33
His first-class debut in England was for Leveson-Gower's XI in 1921. He also played for Staffordshire (1911–35).

Heath, Malcolm Brewster
Professional. *b:* 9.3.1934, Ferndown, Dorset. Tail end left-hand batsman, right-arm fast medium bowler. *Team* Hampshire (1954–62, 143 matches).
Career batting
143–163–66–569–33–5.86–0–*ct* 42
Bowling 13237–527–25.11–18–5–8/43
He took 100 wickets in a season once – 126, av 16.42, in 1958.

Heath, Stephen David
Cricketer. *b:* 7.7.1967, Bristol. Middle order right-hand batsman, leg break bowler. *Sch* KES, Birmingham. *Team* Cambridge U (1986–88, blue 1988).
Career batting
10–17–2–170–33*–11.33–0–*ct* 2
Bowling 39–0

Heath, Thomas
Professional. *b:* 10.12.1806, Sutton-in-Ashfield, Nottinghamshire. *d:* 16.10.1872, Sutton-in-Ashfield, Nottinghamshire. Middle order right-hand batsman, good deep field. *Team* Nottinghamshire (1828–48, 18 matches).
Career batting
20–36–2–324–35–9.52–0–*ct* 7
He was a noted single-wicket player.

Heath, Walter
Amateur. *b:* 20.1.1860, Tewkesbury, Gloucestershire. *d:* 7.3.1937, Evesham, Worcestershire. Tail end batsman, wicket-keeper. *Team* Gloucestershire (1886, 1 match).
Career batting
1–1–0–0–0–0.00–0–*ct* 2

Heath, Walter Hodsoll Gordon
Amateur. *b:* 3.12.1897, Streatham, London. *d:* 4.12.1965, Kingswear, Devon. Middle/lower order batsman, wicket-keeper. *Sch* Haileybury. *Team* Surrey (1919, 3 matches).
Career batting
7–11–2–170–58*–18.88–0–*ct* 8–*st* 1
His final first-class match was for Leveson-Gower's XI in 1924. He also appeared in matches for the RAF.

Heathcoat-Amory, Sir John
(birth registered as J. Amory)
Amateur. *b:* 2.5.1894, Mayfair, Kensington, London. *d:* 22.11.1972, Knightshayes Court, Somerset. Uncle

of M. G. M. Groves (Somerset). Forcing middle order right-hand batsman, right-arm fast medium bowler. *Sch* Eton. *Team* Oxford U (1914).
Career batting
6–8–3–137–67*–27.40–0–*ct* 1
Bowling 357–15–23.80–0–0–4/52
His County cricket was for Devon (1914–32), whom he captained for seven years; his final first-class match was for Minor Counties in 1928. He married the well-known golfer Joyce Wethered.

Heathcoat-Amory, Ludovic
Amateur. *b:* 11.5.1881, Westminster, London. *d:* 25.8.1918, Bayonvillers, France. Nephew of H. T. Stanley (Somerset). Lower order right-hand batsman, right-arm fast bowler. *Sch* Eton. *Team* Oxford U (1902–03).
Career batting
6–11–0–76–26–6.90–0–*ct* 8
Bowling 165–9–18.33–0–0–4/55
His County cricket was for Devon (1902).

Heatley, Arthur Edward
Amateur. *b:* 25.10.1865, Kemp Town, Brighton, Sussex. *d:* 1.7.1941, Ingrave, Brentwood, Essex. Middle order batsman. *Team* Essex (1894, 1 match).
Career batting
1–2–1–20–13*–20.00–0–*ct* 4
Bowling 10–0

Heaven, Raymond Maurice
Professional. *b:* 8.10.1918, Shoreham-by-Sea, Sussex. Lower order right-hand batsman, leg break bowler. *Team* Essex (1939, 1 match).
Career batting
1–1–1–5–5*–no av–0–*ct* 4

Hebden, Geoffrey George Lockwood
Amateur. *b:* 14.7.1918, Chiswick, Middlesex. Son of G. L. (Middlesex). Middle/lower order right-hand batsman, right-arm fast medium bowler. *Sch* King's Bruton. *Team* Hampshire (1937–51, 6 matches).
Career batting
6–11–3–69–22*–8.62–0–*ct* 1
Bowling 172–3–57.33–0–0–1/11
He also played for Dorset (1952–60).

Hebden, George Lockwood
Amateur. *b:* 16.12.1879, Brentford, Middlesex. *d:* 11.6.1946, Winton, Bournemouth, Hampshire. Father of G. G. L. (Hampshire). Middle order right-hand batsman. *Team* Middlesex (1908–19, 28 matches).
Career batting
28–44–7–677–101–18.29–1–*ct* 13
Bowling 96–0

Hebert, Martyn Carthew
Amateur. *b:* 6.9.1841, Clapham, London. *d:* 5.7.1905, Hampstead, London. Middle order batsman, change bowler. *Sch* Rossall. *Team* Middlesex (1862, 1 match).
Career batting
1–2–0–14–14–7.00–0–*ct* 0
Bowling 35–3–11.66–0–0–2/25

Hector, Patrick Anthony
Cricketer. *b:* 29.7.1958, Islington, London. Lower order right-hand batsman, right-arm medium pace bowler. *Team* Essex (1977, 3 matches).
Career batting
3–5–1–75–40–18.75–0–*ct* 0
Bowling 190–7–27.14–0–0–3/56

Hedges, Bernard
Professional. *b:* 10.11.1927, Pontypridd, Glamorgan. Opening right-hand batsman, fine outfield. *Team* Glamorgan (1950–67, 422 matches).
Career batting
422–744–41–17733–182–25.22–21–*ct* 200
Bowling 260–3–86.66–0–0–1/16
He hit 1,000 runs in a season nine times, going on to 2,000 once – 2,026, av 32.15, in 1961. He was a noted rugby footballer with Pontypridd and Swansea.

Hedges, Lionel Paget
Amateur. *b:* 13.7.1900, Streatham, London. *d:* 12.1.1933, Naunton Park, Cheltenham, Gloucestershire. He died from septicaemia. Middle order right-hand batsman, fine cover point. *Sch* Tonbridge. *Teams* Kent (1919–24, 52 matches); Oxford U (1920–22, blue all three years); Gloucestershire (1926–29, 30 matches).
Career batting
120–196–6–4219–130–22.20–4–*ct* 69
Bowling 60–1–60.00–0–0–1/23
His best season in first-class cricket was 1921 when he hit 1,138 runs, av 34.48. However, he never fully realised the potential he had shown as a schoolboy – in 1919 he hit 1,038 runs, av 86.50, for Tonbridge.

Hedley, Sir Walter Coote
Amateur. *b:* 12.12.1865, Monkton, Heathfield, Taunton, Somerset. *d:* 27.12.1937, Sunningdale, Berkshire. Son-in-law of J. Fellowes (Hampshire and Kent), brother-in-law of A. E. Newton (Somerset). Middle order right-hand batsman, right-arm fast medium bowler. *Sch* Marlborough. *Teams* Kent (1888, 3 matches); Somerset (1892–1904, 84 matches); Hampshire (1905, 3 matches).
Career batting
103–181–17–2834–102–17.28–2–*ct* 76
Bowling 6628–343–19.32–23–5–8/18
In 1900 his bowling action was condemned by the Captains of the first-class Counties by eleven votes to one. He first played for Somerset (not first-class) in 1890. He also played for Devon (1902).

Hegg, Warren Kevin
Cricketer. *b:* 23.2.1968, Whitefield, Manchester, Lancashire. Middle order right-hand batsman, wicket-keeper. *Team* Lancashire (1986–92, 124 matches).

Tours Lancashire to Jamaica 1986/7, 1987/8, to Zimbabwe 1988/9; England A to Sri Lanka 1990/1.
Career batting
127–179–34–3698–130–25.50–2–*ct* 284–*st* 35
Bowling 7–0

He held 11 catches in the match for Lancashire v Derbyshire at Chesterfield in 1989.

Heggie, William Robert
Amateur. *b:* 10.8.1914, Cupar, Fife, Scotland. *d:* 10.8.1985, Paisley, Renfrewshire, Scotland. Middle order right-hand batsman. *Team* Scotland (1937–47).
Career batting
5–10–0–123–44–12.30–0–*ct* 3

Heighes, Bernard Roy
Cricketer. *b:* 16.1.1947, Chiswick, Middlesex. Lower order right-hand batsman, slow left-arm bowler. *Team* MCC (1967).
Career batting
1–1–1–6–6*–no av–0–*ct* 0
Bowling 61–2–30.50–0–0–1/27

Heine, Peter Samuel
Amateur. *b:* 28.6.1928, Winterton, Natal, South Africa. Lower order right-hand batsman, right-arm fast bowler. *Teams* North East Transvaal (1951/2 to 1952/3); Orange Free State (1953/4 to 1954/5); Transvaal (1955/6 to 1964/5). *Tour* South Africa to England 1955. *Tests* South Africa (1955 to 1961/2, 14 matches).
Career batting
61–97–14–1255–67–15.52–0–*ct* 34
Bowling 5924–277–21.38–20–4–8/92
Test batting
14–24–3–209–31–9.95–0–*ct* 8
Bowling 1455–58–25.08–4–0–6/58

The most hostile of the fast bowlers on the 1955 tour of England, he was surprisingly omitted from the first Test, but thereafter bowled extremely well – in first-class matches he took 74 wickets, av 19.82, and had 21 wickets av 23.52, in the Tests.

Hellard, John Alexander
Amateur. *b:* 20.3.1882, Stogumber, Somerset. *d:* 2.7.1916, near Beaumont Hamel, France. Middle order right-hand batsman, right-arm fast medium bowler. *Sch* King's Canterbury. *Team* Somerset (1907–10, 2 matches).
Career batting
2–3–0–18–15–6.00–0–*ct* 0

Hellawell, Michael Stephen
Amateur. *b:* 30.6.1938, Keighley, Yorkshire. Middle order right-hand batsman, right-arm medium pace bowler. *Team* Warwickshire (1962, 1 match).
Career batting
1–2–2–59–30*–no av–0–*ct* 0
Bowling 114–6–19.00–0–0–4/54

A good soccer player, he appeared at outside left for England, Birmingham City, QPR, Sunderland, Huddersfield and Peterborough.

Hellmuth, Leon
Professional. *b:* 14.8.1934, Blackheath, London. *d:* 29.12.1981, Sidcup, Kent. Lower order left-hand batsman, slow left-arm bowler. *Sch* Haberdashers Aske's School. *Team* Kent (1951–52, 7 matches).
Career batting
7–13–1–34–11–2.83–0–*ct* 8
Bowling 383–8–47.87–0–0–2/11

Helm, Dr George Frederick
Amateur. *b:* 11.1.1838, Findon, Worthing, Sussex. *d:* 31.3.1898. He died in his carriage travelling between Penzance and Marazion, Cormwall. Middle order right-hand batsman, left-hand medium pace round-arm bowler, short-slip. *Sch* Marlborough. *Teams* Sussex (1860, 2 matches); Cambridge U (1861–63, blue 1862 and 1863).
Career batting
5–6–1–21–11–4.20–0–*ct* 1
Bowling 76–5 + 8–15.20–1–0–6/?

He also played for Cambridgeshire (1856).

Hemingway, George Edward
Amateur. *b:* 29.1.1872, Foden Bank, Sutton, Macclesfield, Cheshire. *d:* 11.3.1907, Rangoon, Burma. Brother of R. E. (Nottinghamshire) and W. M. (Gloucestershire). Hard hitting middle order right-hand batsman, left-arm bowler. *Sch* Uppingham. *Team* Gloucestershire (1898, 1 match).
Career batting
1–2–0–0–0–0.00–0–*ct* 1

Hemingway, Ralph Eustace
Amateur. *b:* 15.12.1877, Foden Bank, Sutton, Macclesfield, Cheshire. *d:* 15.10.1915, Hohenzollern Redoubt, near Vermelles, France. He was killed in action. Brother of G. E. (Gloucestershire) and W. M. (Gloucestershire). Middle order right-hand batsman. *Sch* Rugby. *Team* Nottinghamshire (1903–05, 30 matches).
Career batting
32–50–2–976–85–20.33–0–*ct* 17
Bowling 6–0

He was also a noted rugby footballer.

Hemingway, William McGregor
Amateur. *b:* 12.11.1873, Foden Bank, Sutton, Macclesfield, Cheshire. *d:* 11.2.1967, Paignton, Devon. Brother of G. E. (Gloucestershire) and R. E. (Nottinghamshire). Middle order right-hand batsman. *Sch* Uppingham. *Teams* Gloucestershire (1893–1900, 48 matches); Cambridge U (1895–96, blue both years). *Tours* Mitchell to North America 1895; Warner to North America 1897.

Hemming, Sir Augustus William Lawson

Career batting
70–120–3–1999–104–17.08–1–*ct* 30
He also won a blue for athletics.

Hemming, Sir Augustus William Lawson
Amateur. *b:* 2.9.1841, Westminster, London. *d:* 27.3.1907, Cairo, Egypt. Lower order right-hand batsman, right-hand fast round-arm bowler, good field. *Sch* Epsom and Godolphin. *Team* MCC (1866–74).
Career batting
6–9–1–56–16–8.00–0–*ct* 3
Bowling 127–6–21.16–1–0–5/69
He was a founder member of the Incogniti and commencing 1871 the Hon Secretary of that Club. His last first-class match in England was for MCC in 1878 and his next and final first-class match for Jamaica and United Services in 1901/2 – 23 years separating the two games. In 1896 and 1897 he was Governor of British Guiana and from 1898 to 1904 Governor of Jamaica.

Hemming, Leonard Ernest Gerald
Amateur. *b:* 30.9.1916, Enfield, Middlesex. Middle order right-hand batsman, off break bowler. *Team* Minor Counties (1951).
Career batting
1–2–0–28–14–14.00–0–*ct* 0
Bowling 60–1–60.00–0–0–1/60
His County cricket was for Oxfordshire (1946–54).

Hemmings, Edward Ernest
Cricketer. *b:* 20.2.1949, Leamington Spa, Warwickshire. Lower order right-hand batsman, right-arm medium, later off break bowler. *Teams* Warwickshire (1966–78, 177 matches); Nottinghamshire (1979–92, 270 matches). *Tours* Robins to South Africa 1974/5; International XI to Pakistan 1981/2, to Jamaica 1982/3; England to Australia 1982/3, 1987/8, 1990/1, to New Zealand 1982/3 (not first-class), 1987/8, 1990/1 (not first-class), to Pakistan 1987/8, to India and Pakistan (World Cup) 1987/8, to India 1988/9 (tour cancelled), 1989/90 (not first-class), to West Indies 1989/90. *Tests* England (1982 to 1990/1, 16 matches).
Career batting
482–627–146–9297–127*–19.32–1–*ct* 196
Bowling 41461–1404–29.53–66–14–10/175
Test batting
16–21–4–383–95–22.52–0–*ct* 5
Bowling 1825–43–42.44–1–0–6/58
His best season was 1984 with 94 wickets, av 23.61. In Jamaica in 1982/3 he took 10 for 175 in an innings for an International XI v West Indian XI at Kingston. His career seemed to be in the doldrums when he changed counties in 1979, but this move restored his confidence and during the 1980s he competed with Emburey for the England off-spinner's place.

Hemp, David Lloyd
Cricketer. *b:* 8.11.1970, Hamilton, Bermuda. Middle order left-hand batsman, right-arm medium pace bowler. *Sch* Millfield. *Team* Glamorgan (1991–92, 13 matches).
Career batting
13–19–3–338–84*–21.12–0–*ct* 8
He also played for Wales in the Minor Counties Championship (1992).

Hemsley, Edward John Orton
Cricketer. *b:* 1.9.1943, Norton, Stoke-on-Trent, Staffordshire. Middle order right-hand batsman, right-arm medium pace bowler. *Team* Worcestershire (1963–82, 243 matches).
Career batting
243–389–57–9740–176*–29.33–8–*ct* 180
Bowling 2497–70–35.67–0–0–3/5
He hit 1,168 runs, av 38.93, in 1978. He also played for Shropshire (1961). A noted soccer player, he appeared for Shrewsbury, Sheffield United and Doncaster Rovers.

Hemsley, Philip David
Cricketer. *b:* 23.11.1959, Buxted, Sussex. Lower order right-hand batsman, right-arm medium pace bowler. *Team* Cambridge U (1980–81).
Career batting
3–5–2–26–12*–8.66–0–*ct* 1
Bowling 143–1–143.00–0–0–1/4

Hemsted, Edward
Amateur. *b:* 10.10.1846, Whitchurch, Hampshire. *d:* 12.3.1884, Weymouth, Dorset. Middle order right-hand batsman, right-hand fast round-arm bowler, slip field. *Sch* Lancing and Chatham House, Ramsgate. *Team* Hampshire (1866–69, 7 matches).
Career batting
8–15–1–220–39–15.71–0–*ct* 3
Bowling 139–10–13.90–1–0–5/14
His first-class debut was for Gentlemen of Kent in 1863.

Henderson, Andrew Arthur
Cricketer. *b:* 14.7.1941, Chadwell Heath, Essex. Lower order right-hand batsman, right-arm medium pace bowler. *Team* Sussex (1972, 1 match).
Career batting
1–2–0–11–9–5.50–0–*ct* 0
Bowling 132–5–26.40–0–0–3/65
He also played for Buckinghamshire (1964-65).

Henderson, Andrew William
Amateur. *b:* 23.1.1922, Selkirk, Scotland. Lower order right-hand batsman, right-arm medium pace bowler. *Team* Scotland (1953).
Career batting
1–1–0–2–2–2.00–0–*ct* 0
Bowling 10–0

Henderson, Derek
Amateur. *b:* 9.3.1926, Bexhill-on-Sea, Sussex. Father of S. P. (Worcestershire and Glamorgan). Lower order right-hand batsman, right-arm medium fast bowler. *Sch* St Edward's, Oxford. *Team* Oxford U (1949–50, blue 1950).
Career batting
16–20–8–131–21*–10.91–0–*ct* 3
Bowling 1039–34–30.55–0–0–4/39
His final first-class match was for Free Foresters in 1954.

Henderson, Iain Mark
Cricketer. *b:* 8.9.1967, Glapthorn, Northamptonshire. Lower order right-hand batsman, right-arm medium fast bowler. *Sch* Oundle. *Team* Oxford U (1987–90, blue 1987, 1989 and 1990).
Career batting
21–23–6–186–44–10.94–0–*ct* 5
Bowling 1547–25–61.88–0–0–3/48
His County cricket was for Bedfordshire (1991–92).

Henderson, James Douglas
Amateur. *b:* 13.10.1918, Kelso, Roxburgh, Scotland. Middle order left-hand batsman, left-arm medium pace bowler. *Team* Scotland (1946–56).
Career batting
14–22–3–429–121–22.57–1–*ct* 7
Bowling 650–29–22.41–1–0–5/27

Henderson, Matthew
Amateur. *b:* 2.8.1895, Auckland, New Zealand. *d:* 17.6.1970, Lower Hutt, Wellington, New Zealand. Lower order left-hand batsman, left-arm fast medium bowler. *Team* Wellington (1921/2 to 1931/2). *Tours* New Zealand to England 1927, to Australia 1927/8. *Test* New Zealand (1929/30, 1 match).
Career batting
41–57–22–495–47–14.14–0–*ct* 12
Bowling 3200–107–29.90–5–0–6/70
Test batting
1–2–1–8–6–8.00–0–*ct* 1
Bowling 64–2–32.00–0–0–2/38
He obtained only modest results on the 1927 tour of England, his bowling being somewhat wayward.

Henderson, Paul William
Cricketer. *b:* 22.10.1974, Stockton-on-Tees, Durham. Middle order right-hand batsman, right-arm fast medium bowler. *Team* Durham (1992, 5 matches).
Career batting
5–7–0–119–46–17.00–0–*ct* 1
Bowling 405–10–40.50–0–0–3/59
He first played for Durham (pre first-class) in 1991.

Henderson, Robert
Amateur. *b:* 3.5.1851, Fulham, London. *d:* 22.9.1895, Sedgewick Park, Horsham, Sussex. Brother-in-law of R. G. Hargreaves (Hampshire). Lower order right-hand batsman, right-hand slow round-arm bowler, point field. *Sch* Harrow. *Team* Middlesex (1872–78, 16 matches).
Career batting
24–41–5–349–42–9.69–0–*ct* 15
Bowling 2503–151–16.57–17–3–8/46

Henderson, Robert
Professional. *b:* 30.3.1865, Newport, Monmouthshire. *d:* 28.1.1931, Wallington, Surrey. Middle order right-hand batsman, slow right-arm bowler. *Team* Surrey (1883–96, 141 matches).
Career batting
148–230–30–3701–106–18.50–1–*ct* 88
Bowling 1278–60–21.30–1–0–6/17
Owing to ill-health he played very little in the three seasons 1884 to 1886 and was twice sent overseas at the expense of the Surrey Club for health reasons.

Henderson, Stephen Peter
Cricketer. *b:* 24.9.1958, Oxford. Son of Derek (Oxford U). Middle order left-hand batsman, right-arm medium pace bowler. *Sch* Downside. *Team* Worcestershire (1977–81, 24 matches); Cambridge U (1982–83, blue both years); Glamorgan (1983–85, 27 matches). *Tour* MCC to North America 1982 (not first-class).
Career batting
71–118–17–2628–209*–26.01–4–*ct* 47
Bowling 216–3–72.00–0–0–2/48
His highest innings was 209* for Cambridge U v Middlesex at Fenner's in 1982. He captained Cambridge in 1983. His last first-class match was for MCC in 1987. He also played for Shropshire (1982) and Hertfordshire (1987–89).

Henderson, Dr Thomas Bonhote
Amateur. *b:* 3.1.1875, Paddington, London. *d:* 19.4.1920, East Harnham, Wiltshire. Middle order right-hand batsman, right-arm fast medium bowler, good field. *Sch* Winchester. *Team* Oxford U (1897).
Career batting
8–13–1–220–49–18.33–0–*ct* 10
Bowling 207–7–29.57–0–0–3/39
His final first-class match was for MCC in 1901.

Hendren, Denis
Professional. *b:* 25.9.1882, Turnham Green, Middlesex. *d:* 29.5.1962, Paddington, London. Brother of E. H. (Middlesex). Middle order right-hand batsman, slow right-arm bowler. *Team* Middlesex (1905–19, 9 matches).
Career batting
9–16–2–109–23–7.78–0–*ct* 5
Bowling 104–3–34.66–0–0–1/19
His first-class cricket effectively ended in 1907 and he played for Durham (pre first-class) from 1910 to 1921; later he was on the first-class umpires' list (1931–49).

Hendren, Elias Henry
Professional. *b:* 5.2.1889, Turnham Green, Middlesex. *d:* 4.10.1962, Tooting Bec, London. Brother of Denis (Middlesex). Middle order right-hand batsman, slow right-arm bowler, excellent deep field. *Team* Middlesex (1907–37, 581 matches). *Tours* MCC to Australia 1920/1, 1924/5, 1928/9, to West Indies 1929/30, 1934/5, to South Africa 1930/1. *Tests* England (1920/1 to 1934/5, 51 matches).
Career batting
833–1300–166–57611–301*–50.80–170–*ct* 754
Bowling 2574–47–54.76–1–0–5/43
Test batting
51–83–9–3525–205*–47.63–7–*ct* 33
Bowling 31–1–31.00–0–0–1/27

The leading middle order batsman in English cricket during the 1920s, 'Patsy' Hendren was equally at home overseas and had tremendous success on all his MCC tours. His greatest triumph was the visit to West Indies in 1929/30. Hendren hit no fewer than four double centuries during the tour and a total of 1,765 runs, av 135.76 – a record which still stands. On each of his three trips to Australia he exceeded 1,000 runs with an average over 60.00 and he was almost as successful on his single tour to South Africa.

In English cricket he hit over 3,000 runs in a season three times, his highest aggregate being 3,311, av 70.44, in 1928. On twelve other occasions he exceeded 2,000 and on another six occasions he exceeded 1,000 runs. His highest innings was 301* for Middlesex v Worcestershire at Dudley in 1933. In all he hit 22 first-class innings of 200 or more – only W. R. Hammond and D. G. Bradman scored more. In Test cricket his highest innings was 205* v West Indies at Port of Spain in 1929/30 and of his contemporaries only J. B. Hobbs made more runs. No England team was representative if it lacked Hendren during the decade following the First World War.

His last first-class match was for an England XI in 1938. He was Sussex coach 1947–51 and Middlesex scorer 1953–59.

He was an excellent soccer player, appearing for Brentford, Queen's Park Rangers, Manchester City and Coventry as a wing forward.

Hendrick, Michael
Cricketer. *b:* 22.10.1948, Darley Dale, Derbyshire. Lower order right-hand batsman, right-arm fast medium bowler, slip field. *Teams* Derbyshire (1969–81, 167 matches); Nottinghamshire (1982–84, 34 matches). *Tours* MCC to West Indies 1973/4, to Australia and New Zealand 1974/5, to Pakistan and New Zealand 1977/8, to Australia 1978/9, 1979/80; Robins to South Africa 1975/6; SAB England XI to South Africa 1981/2. *Tests* England (1974–81, 30 matches).
Career batting
267–267–109–1601–46–10.13–0–*ct* 176
Bowling 15785–770–20.50–30–3–8/45
Test batting
30–35–15–128–15–6.40–0–*ct* 25
Bowling 2248–87–25.83–0–0–4/28

His best seasons were 1975 with 68 wickets, av 15.83, and 1977 with 67, av 15.94. His bowling, with its nagging accuracy, was particularly effective in limited overs cricket. He was appointed Nottinghamshire CCC Cricket Manager in 1992.

Hendricks, John Leslie
Amateur. *b:* 21.12.1933, St Andrew, Kingston, Jamaica. Lower order right-hand batsman, occasional right-arm slow bowler, wicket-keeper. *Team* Jamaica (1953/4 to 1966/7). *Tours* West Indies to India and Pakistan 1958/9, to India 1966/7, to Australia 1960/1, to Australia and New Zealand 1968/9, to England 1966, 1969. *Tests* West Indies (1961/2 to 1969, 20 matches).
Career batting
83–113–23–1568–82–17.42–0–*ct* 140–*st* 50
Bowling 61–0
Test batting
20–32–8–447–64–18.62–0–*ct* 42–*st* 5

After missing the first two Tests of the 1966 England tour due to injury, he was in fine form behind the wicket for the remainder of the tour. In 1969 however, though starting as the principal wicket-keeper, he lost his Test place to Findlay.

Hendry, Hunter Scott Thomas Laurie
Amateur. *b:* 24.5.1895, Double Bay, Sydney, New South Wales, Australia. *d:* 16.12.1988, Rose Bay, Sydney, New South Wales, Australia. Middle or lower order right-hand batsman, right-arm fast medium bowler. *Teams* New South Wales (1918/19 to 1923/4, 38 matches); Victoria (1924/5 to 1932/3, 41 matches). *Tours* Australia to England 1921, 1926, to South Africa 1921/2, to India and Ceylon 1935/6; New South Wales to New Zealand 1923/4. *Tests* Australia (1921 to 1928/9, 11 matches).
Career batting
140–206–25–6799–325*–37.56–14–*ct* 151
Bowling 6647–229–29.02–6–1–8/33
Test batting
11–18–2–335–112–20.93–1–*ct* 10
Bowling 640–16–40.00–0–0–3/36

He played in four of the five Tests in England in 1921, but batted very low in the order and bowled only in order to rest the main attack; in 1926 he was struck down with scarlet fever early on the tour and missed all the Tests. Thus his record in English cricket was very modest. In Australia however he proved a most accomplished all-rounder. His only innings over 200 was 325* for Victoria v New Zealanders at Melbourne in 1925/6.

Hendy, A. S.
Amateur. *b:* 1910. *d:* 1965, British Columbia, Canada. Lower order left-hand batsman, slow left-arm

bowler. *Team* Canada (1951–54). *Tour* Canada to England 1954.
Career batting
4–6–0–46–22–7.66–0–*ct* 2
Bowling 222–10–22.20–0–0–4/73

Henery, Perceval Jeffery Thornton
Amateur. *b:* 6.6.1859, London. *d:* 10.8.1938, Old Cleeve, Washford, Somerset. Hard hitting middle order right-hand batsman, right-hand slow round-arm bowler, brilliant field. *Sch* Harrow. *Teams* Middlesex (1879–94, 72 matches); Cambridge U (1881–83, blue 1882–83); British Guiana (1883/4).
Career batting
94–152–11–2229–138*–15.80–1–*ct* 53
Bowling 209–12–17.41–1–0–5/56

Henfrey, Arthur George
Amateur. *b:* 19.12.1867, Finedon, Northamptonshire. *d:* 17.10.1929, Finedon, Northamptonshire. Middle order right-hand batsman. *Sch* Wellingborough. *Team* Cambridge U (1890).
Career batting
1–2–0–17–11–8.50–0–*ct* 0
His County cricket was for Northamptonshire (pre first-class, 1886–99). He won a blue for soccer and also played for England.

Henley, Dr Anthony Alfred
Amateur. *b:* 7.11.1846, Sherborne, Dorset. *d:* 14.12.1916, Woodbridge, Suffolk. Brother of Robert (Hampshire), father of F. A. H. (Middlesex). Middle order batsman. *Sch* Sherborne. *Team* Hampshire (1866, 1 match).
Career batting
1–2–0–16–9–8.00–0–*ct* 0
He also played for Dorset (1863–72) and Somerset (pre first-class, 1865).

Henley, David Francis
(changed name to Henley-Welch in 1948)
Amateur. *b:* 21.7.1923, Melton, Suffolk. Nephew of F. A. H. (Middlesex). Lower order right-hand batsman, right-arm fast medium bowler. *Sch* Harrow. *Team* Oxford U (1946–48, blue 1947).
Career batting
17–30–4–558–58–21.46–0–*ct* 13
Bowling 931–23–40.47–0–0–3/28
His County cricket was for Suffolk (1946–57) and his final first-class match was for Minor Counties in 1949.

Henley, Francis Anthony Hoste
Amateur. *b:* 11.2.1884, Woodbridge, Suffolk. *d:* 26.6.1963, Wheathampstead, Hertfordshire. Son of A. A. (Hampshire), nephew of Robert (Hampshire), uncle of D. F. (Oxford U). Lower order right-hand batsman, right-arm fast bowler. *Sch* Forest. *Teams* Oxford U (1903–05, blue 1905); Middlesex (1908, 3 matches). *Tour* MCC to North America 1905.
Career batting
15–26–3–257–52*–11.17–0–*ct* 14
Bowling 1106–41–26.97–0–0–4/39
He also played for Suffolk (1904–07).

Henley, Robert
Amateur. *b:* 10.6.1851, Sherborne, Dorset. *d:* 21.3.1889, Ovington, Hampshire. Brother of A. A. (Hampshire), uncle of F. A. H. (Middlesex). Middle order batsman. *Sch* Sherborne. *Team* Hampshire (1875, 1 match).
Career batting
1–1–0–14–14–14.00–0–*ct* 0
Bowling 14–0
He also played for Dorset.

Henriksen, Soren
Cricketer. *b:* 1.12.1964, Rodoure, Copenhagen, Denmark. Lower order right-hand batsman, right-arm fast medium bowler. *Team* Lancashire (1985–86, 3 matches).
Career batting
3–4–3–17–10*–17.00–0–*ct* 2
Bowling 105–2–52.50–0–0–1/26
He played for Denmark in ICC Trophy 1986.

Henry, Denis Philip
Amateur. *b:* 7.7.1907, Stamford Hill, Middlesex. *d:* 27.3.1990, Chichester, Sussex. Lower order right-hand batsman, leg break bowler. *Team* Free Foresters (1948).
Career batting
1–1–0–1–1–1.00–0–*ct* 0
Bowling 16–0

Henry, F.
Professional. Tail end batsman, opening bowler. *Team* Middlesex (1882, 1 match).
Career batting
1–2–1–5–5*–5.00–0–*ct* 1
Bowling 52–2–26.00–0–0–2/16

Henry, Ian Clifford
Amateur. *b:* 23.10.1914, Kensington, London. Middle order right-hand batsman, leg break bowler. *Sch* Uppingham. *Team* Free Foresters (1937).
Career batting
1–2–0–84–80–42.00–0–*ct* 1

Henry, Omar
Cricketer. *b:* 23.1.1952, Stellenbosch, Cape Province, South Africa. Middle order left-hand batsman, slow left-arm bowler. *Teams* Western Province (1977/8 to 1983/4); Boland (1984/5 to 1988/9); Orange Free State (1989/90 to 1991/2); Scotland (1989–91). *Tours* South Africa to New Zealand (World Cup) 1991/2, to West Indies 1991/2.
Career batting
111–172–31–3946–125–27.98–4–*ct* 111
Bowling 9742–402–24.23–20–3–7/22

Henslow, Edward Lancelot Wall

A leading all-rounder in South African cricket, he played in two unofficial Tests v Australia in 1986/7. He has captained Scotland and Boland.

Henslow, Edward Lancelot Wall
Amateur. *b:* 19.3.1879, Mere, Wiltshire. *d:* 12.3.1947, Salisbury, Wiltshire. Middle order batsman, bowler. *Team* Army (1912).
Career batting
1–2–0–0–0–0.00–0–*ct* 0
Bowling 22–1–22.00–0–0–1/22
His County cricket was for Wiltshire (1914–23).

Henson, Richard
Professional. *b:* 10.10.1864, Ruddington, Nottinghamshire. *d:* 29.11.1930, Ruddington, Nottinghamshire. Lower order batsman, left-arm slow medium bowler. *Team* Liverpool and District (1894).
Career batting
1–2–0–19–17–9.50–0–*ct* 0
Bowling 5–2–2.50–0–0–2/5

Henson, William Walker
Professional. *b:* 7.12.1872, Lenton, Nottingham. *d:* 7.9.1922, Dumfries, Scotland. Lower order right-hand batsman, right-arm fast medium bowler. *Team* Nottinghamshire (1897–98, 13 matches).
Career batting
13–16–5–110–35*–10.00–0–*ct* 7
Bowling 835–24–34.79–0–0–4/82

Henty, Edward
Professional. *b:* 11.8.1839, Hawkhurst, Kent. *d:* 20.1.1900, Lewisham, London. Very steady lower order right-hand batsman, excellent wicket-keeper. *Team* Kent (1865–81, 116 matches).
Career batting
119–209–64–1154–72–7.95–0–*ct* 137–*st* 66
Bowling 10–1–10.00–0–0–1/3
He was a first-class umpire (1883–94).

Henwood, Pelham Peter
Cricketer. *b:* 22.5.1946, Berea, Pietermaritzburg, South Africa. Lower order right-hand batsman, slow left-arm bowler. *Teams* Orange Free State (1965/6); Natal (1966/7 to 1979/80). *Tour* South African Universities to England 1967; Isaacs to England 1969 (not first-class).
Career batting
79–102–22–769–46–9.61–0–*ct* 26
Bowling 5877–212–27.72–9–1–7/34

Heppel, Nicolas
Cricketer. *b:* 12.12.1967, Hampton Court, Middlesex. Lower order right-hand batsman, slow left-arm bowler. *Sch* Reading. *Team* Oxford U (1988).
Career batting
1–1–1–14–14*–no av–0–*ct* 0
Bowling 74–0

Hepworth, Peter Nash
Cricketer. *b:* 4.5.1967, Ackworth, Yorkshire. Middle order right-hand batsman, off break bowler. *Team* Leicestershire (1988–92, 46 matches).
Career batting
46–75–7–1672–115–24.58–2–*ct* 28
Bowling 902–19–47.47–0–0–3/51
He scored 1,119 runs, av 32.91, in 1991.

Herbert, Allen Henry William
Amateur. *b:* 20.10.1852, Hythe, Kent. *d:* 14.9.1897, Belgravia, London. Middle order right-hand batsman. *Teams* Kent (1874, 1 match); Middlesex (1875, 1 match).
Career batting
11–19–2–239–63–14.05–0–*ct* 6
His first-class debut in 1872 and his final first-class match in 1876 were both for MCC. He also played for Essex (not first-class, 1872) and Wiltshire (1877).

Herbert, Eric James
Professional. *b:* 12.8.1908, Higham Ferrers, Northamptonshire. *d:* 14.10.1963, Wellingborough, Northamptonshire. Steady lower order right-hand batsman, right-arm medium pace bowler. *Team* Northamptonshire (1937–39, 35 matches).
Career batting
35–57–24–291–20–8.81–0–*ct* 11
Bowling 2322–69–33.65–1–0–5/103

Herbert, Henry Moore Bungay
(birth registered as H. M. Bungey)
Amateur. *b:* 22.1.1863, Southwark, London. *d:* 30.11.1884, St Pancras, London. He died from tuberculosis. Lower order batsman. *Team* Middlesex (1883, 1 match).
Career batting
1–2–1–1–1–1.00–0–*ct* 1

Herbert, Hon Mervyn Robert Howard Molyneux
Amateur. *b:* 27.12.1882, Highclere Castle, Hampshire. *d:* 26.5.1929, Rome, Italy. Grandson of H. J. G. (MCC) and H. Howard (Sussex), his son married daughter of H. W. Hibbert (Northamptonshire). Opening or middle order right-hand batsman. *Sch* Eton. *Teams* Nottinghamshire (1901–02, 6 matches); Somerset (1903–24, 31 matches); Oxford U (1904).
Career batting
42–74–3–854–78–12.02–0–*ct* 18
Bowling 28–0
His niece married Evelyn Waugh, the writer.

Herbert, Percy
Amateur. *b:* 12.8.1878, Shoreham-by-Sea, Sussex. *d:* 24.1.1958, Hove, Sussex. Uncle of P. G. H. Fender (Surrey). Lower order batsman. *Team* Gentlemen of South (1920).
Career batting
1 match, did not bat–*ct* 0

Herbert, Reuben
Cricketer. *b:* 1.12.1957, Lansdown, Cape Town, South Africa. Middle order right-hand batsman, off break bowler. *Team* Essex (1976–80, 6 matches).
Career batting
8–12–1–138–43–12.54–0–*ct* 6
Bowling 262–6–43.66–0–0–3/64
He also played for Suffolk (1984–86) and Hertfordshire (1987) and his last first-class match was for Minor Counties in 1986.

Herkes, Robert
Cricketer. *b:* 30.6.1957, Lincoln. Tail end right-hand batsman, right-arm medium pace bowler. *Team* Middlesex (1978–79, 3 matches).
Career batting
3–5–3–0–0*–0.00–0–*ct* 0
Bowling 93–6–15.50–1–0–6/60
He also played for Lincolnshire (1977).

Herman, Oswald William
Professional. *b:* 18.9.1907, Horsepath, Oxfordshire. *d:* 24.6.1987, Southampton, Hampshire. Father of R. S. (Middlesex and Hampshire). Lower order right-hand batsman, right-arm fast medium bowler. *Team* Hampshire (1929–48, 321 matches).
Career batting
322–496–105–4336–92–11.08–0–*ct* 123
Bowling 28222–1045–27.00–58–6–8/49
He took 100 wickets in a season five times (best 142, av 22.07, in 1937). He also played for Wiltshire (1950–51). He was later on the first-class umpires' list (1963–71).

Herman, Robert Stephen
Cricketer. *b:* 30.11.1946, Shirley, Southampton, Hampshire. Son of O. W. (Hampshire). Lower order right-hand batsman, right-arm fast medium bowler. *Teams* Middlesex (1965–71, 92 matches); Hampshire (1972–77, 89 matches); Border (1972/3); Griqualand West (1974/5).
Career batting
189–189–49–1426–56–10.18–0–*ct* 74
Bowling 13348–506–26.37–14–0–8/42
He also played for Dorset (1978–79). He was a first-class umpire (1980–82).

Hermiston, William
Amateur. *b:* 4.2.1913, Makerston, Roxburghshire, Scotland. *d:* 17.1.1987, Edinburgh, Scotland. Middle order right-hand batsman, right-arm fast medium bowler. *Team* Scotland (1949).
Career batting
2–4–0–35–21–8.75–0–*ct* 1
Bowling 84–2–42.00–0–0–2/21

Heron, George Allen
Amateur. *b:* 19.2.1877, Marylebone, London. *d:* 22.7.1948, Pevensey Bay, Sussex. Middle order right-hand batsman, right-arm medium pace bowler. *Sch* Merchant Taylors and St Pauls. *Team* MCC (1899).
Career batting
1–2–0–37–31–18.50–0–*ct* 0

Heron, Jack Gunner
Cricketer. *b:* 8.11.1948, Salisbury, Rhodesia. Opening or middle order right-hand batsman. *Team* Rhodesia/Zimbabwe (1967/8 to 1982/3). *Tour* Zimbabwe to England 1982, 1983 (World Cup).
Career batting
60–113–5–2830–175–26.20–5–*ct* 39
Bowling 17–0
He also played for Lincolnshire (1977). He also represented Rhodesia at hockey.

Heroys, Nicholas
Amateur. *b:* 1.4.1937, Marylebone, London. Middle order right-hand batsman, right-arm medium pace bowler. *Sch* Tonbridge. *Team* Cambridge U (1960).
Career batting
1–2–0–10–10–5.00–0–*ct* 0
Bowling 35–0

Herring, Lt Gen Hon Sir Edmund Francis
Amateur. *b:* 2.9.1892, Maryborough, Victoria, Australia. *d:* 5.1.1982, Camberwell, Melbourne, Victoria, Australia. Brother of R. W. (Victoria), nephew of L. L. (Western Australia). Opening right-hand batsman. *Team* Oxford U (1913).
Career batting
2–4–0–65–21–16.25–0–*ct* 1
He won a blue for lawn tennis. He was Lieutenant Governor of Victoria 1945–72.

Herringshaw, John Percy
Professional. *b:* 22.5.1892, Derby. *d:* 13.11.1974, Yapton, Sussex. Lower order left-hand batsman, slow left-arm bowler. *Team* Essex (1921–22, 9 matches).
Career batting
9–14–5–94–18–10.44–0–*ct* 7
Bowling 498–9–55.33–0–0–2/48

Herriot, Dr Thomas Pearson
Amateur. *b:* 11.5.1887, Berwick-on-Tweed, Northumberland. *d:* 20.10.1949, Berwick-on-Tweed, Northumberland. Opening batsman. *Sch* Fettes. *Team* Scotland (1911).
Career batting
1–1–0–80–80–80.00–0–*ct* 1
His County cricket was for Northumberland (1911).

Herting, Frederick John
Professional. *b:* 25.2.1940, South Ruislip, Middlesex. Lower order right-hand batsman, left-arm fast medium bowler. *Sch* Millfield. *Team* Somerset (1960, 5 matches).
Career batting
5–7–2–44–16*–8.80–0–*ct* 1
Bowling 506–7–72.28–0–0–4/85

Hervey-Bathurst, Sir Frederick Hutchison
(changed name from Hervey in 1818)
Amateur. *b:* 6.6.1807. *d:* 29.10.1881, Clarendon Park, Wiltshire. Father of F. T. A. (Hampshire) and Lionel (Hampshire), great-grandfather of H. R. C. Tudway (Somerset). Slogging tail end right-hand batsman, right-hand fast round-arm bowler. *Sch* Winchester. *Team* Hampshire (1842–61).
Career batting
93–159–21–817–46–5.92–*ct* 41
Bowling 977–74 + 275–13.20–32–8–7/?

Regarded as one of the finest of all fast bowlers, he played regularly for the Gentlemen v Players between 1831 and 1854. His debut was for England in 1831. He also played for Devon and Wiltshire. He was on the Committee of MCC and President of the Club in 1857.

Hervey-Bathurst, Sir Frederick Thomas Arthur
Amateur. *b:* 13.3.1833, London. *d:* 20.5.1900, Westminster, London. Son of F. H. (Hampshire), half-brother of Lionel (Hampshire), grandfather of H. R. C. Tudway (Somerset). Hard-hitting lower order batsman, fast round-arm or slow under-arm bowler. *Sch* Eton. *Team* Hampshire (1865–66, 3 matches).
Career batting
13–24–2–187–49–8.50–0–*ct* 2
Bowling 44–2–22.00–0–0–1/17

His first-class debut was for MCC in 1852 and he also played County cricket for Devon (1852–66) and Wiltshire (1859–75). He was MP for South Wiltshire 1861–65 and he fought in the Crimean War.

Hervey-Bathurst, Lionel
(changed name to Paston-Cooper in October 1905)
Amateur. *b:* 7.7.1849, Clarendon, Wiltshire. *d:* 4.5.1908, The Lockers, Hemel Hempstead, Hertfordshire. Son of F. H. (Hampshire), half-brother of F. T. A. (Hampshire). Opening batsman, wicket-keeper. *Sch* Rugby. *Team* Hampshire (1875, 2 matches).
Career batting
2–4–0–30–14–7.50–0–*ct* 1–*st* 1
Bowling 8–0

Heseltine, Christopher
Amateur. *b:* 26.11.1869, South Kensington, London. *d:* 13.6.1944, Walhampton, Lymington, Hampshire. Lower order right-hand batsman, right-arm fast bowler. *Sch* Eton. *Team* Hampshire (1895–1904, 52 matches). *Tours* Hawke to India 1892/3, to South Africa 1895/6, to West Indies 1896/7. *Tests* England (1895/6, 2 matches).
Career batting
79–121–8–1390–77–12.30–0–*ct* 54
Bowling 4171–170–24.53–7–0–7/106
Test batting
2–2–0–18–18–9.00–0–*ct* 3
Bowling 84–5–16.80–1–0–5/38

He did not play first-class cricket whilst at Cambridge, but was awarded his soccer blue in 1891/2. His debut in first-class cricket was for MCC in 1892 and his final first-class match for MCC in 1914. His first match for Hampshire (not first-class) was in 1894. He was President of Hampshire 1924–26 and 1936–44.

Heseltine, Peter Anthony William
Cricketer. *b:* 5.4.1965, Barnsley, Yorkshire. Brother of P. J. (Oxford U). Lower order right-hand batsman, off break bowler. *Team* Sussex (1987–88, 20 matches)
Career batting
20–20–3–186–26–10.94–0–*ct* 3
Bowling 1069–22–48.59–0–0–3/33

He also played for Durham (pre first-class, 1991).

Heseltine, Phillip John
Cricketer. *b:* 21.6.1960, Skipton, Yorkshire. Brother of P. A. W. (Sussex). Middle order right-hand batsman, right-arm medium pace or off break bowler. *Team* Oxford U (1983, blue).
Career batting
6–10–1–176–40–19.55–0–*ct* 5

His County cricket was for Berkshire (1988–89) and Lincolnshire (1991).

Hesketh-Prichard, Hesketh Vernon
Amateur. *b:* 17.11.1876, Jhansi, India. *d:* 14.6.1922, Gorhambury, Hertfordshire. Lower order right-hand batsman, right-arm fast bowler. *Sch* Fettes. *Teams* Hampshire (1900–13, 60 matches); London County (1902–04). *Tours* Brackley to West Indies 1904/5; MCC to North America 1907.
Career batting
86–135–38–724–37–7.46–0–*ct* 44
Bowling 7586–339–22.37–25–5–8/32

In 1904 he took 106 wickets, av 21.92. He was a well-known traveller and writer, and an authority on moose-calling.

Heslop, Gerald Gwydyr
Amateur. *b:* 17.4.1879, Ditton Marsh, Thames Ditton, Surrey. *d:* 28.11.1913, Cringleford, Norwich, Norfolk. Opening batsman. *Sch* Norwich. *Team* Cambridge U (1898).
Career batting
2–4–0–19–14–4.75–0–*ct* 1

His County cricket was for Norfolk (1895–1901). He won a blue for billiards.

Hester, Edmund Dominic
Cricketer. *b:* 23.8.1967, Radcliffe, Lancashire. Lower order right-hand batsman, left-arm medium pace bowler. *Team* Oxford U (1989, blue).
Career batting
5–6–1–16–5–3.20–0–*ct* 0
Bowling 572–11–52.00–0–0–4/100

He played under the alias of E. D. H. Terse on first-class debut, in an attempt to deceive his tutor who had banned him from cricket.

Hettiaratchy, Nirmal Dilhan Peter
Cricketer. *b:* 30.9.1951, Colombo, Ceylon. Opening right-hand batsman, wicket-keeper. *Team* Ceylon/Sri Lanka (1970/1 to 1982/3). *Tours* Sri Lanka to India 1974/5, to England 1981; Arosa Sri Lankan XI to South Africa 1982/3.
Career batting
20–32–1–686–80–22.12–0–*ct* 14

Hever, Harold Lawrence
Professional. *b:* 23.6.1895, Southborough, Kent. *d:* 18.7.1958, Pembury, Kent. Lower order left-hand batsman, slow left-arm bowler. *Team* Kent (1921–25, 6 matches).
Career batting
7–11–6–25–11*–5.00–0–*ct* 4
Bowling 391–15–26.06–0–0–3/57

Hever, Norman George
Professional. *b:* 17.12.1924, Marylebone, London. *d:* 11.9.1987, Oxford. Tail end right-hand batsman, right-arm fast medium bowler. *Teams* Middlesex (1947, 9 matches); Glamorgan (1948–53, 133 matches).
Career batting
144–177–81–896–40–9.33–0–*ct* 64
Bowling 7901–333–23.72–12–0–7/55

Hewan, Gethyn Elliot
Amateur. *b:* 23.12.1916, Merchiston, Edinburgh, Scotland. *d:* 1.7.1988, Chertsey, Surrey. Middle order right-hand batsman, off break bowler. *Sch* Marlborough. *Team* Cambridge U (1938, blue).
Career batting
6–9–0–187–88–20.77–0–*ct* 2
Bowling 725–20–36.25–2–0–6/91
His County cricket was for Berkshire (1946). He also won a blue for hockey.

Hewetson, Edward Pearson
Amateur. *b:* 27.5.1902, Edgbaston, Birmingham. *d:* 26.12.1977, Bampton, Oxfordshire. Hard hitting lower order right-hand batsman, right-arm fast bowler. *Sch* Shrewsbury. *Teams* Warwickshire (1919–27, 29 matches); Oxford U (1922–25, blue 1923–25).
Career batting
66–94–10–1213–66–14.44–0–*ct* 41
Bowling 4169–163–25.58–6–1–5/16
His final first-class match was for Free Foresters in 1934. He appeared for Warwickshire in 1919 with two full years at school still to complete. He also won blues for athletics, relay races and hockey.

Hewetson, General Sir Reginald Hackett
Amateur. *b:* 4.8.1908, Shortlands, Kent. *d:* 19.1.1993. Middle order right-hand batsman. *Sch* Repton. *Teams* Army (1935–37); Europeans (1929/30).
Career batting
6–11–1–115–25–11.50–0–*ct* 3

Hewett, Herbert Tremenheere
Amateur. *b:* 25.5.1864, Norton Court, Somerset. *d:* 4.3.1921, Hove, Sussex. Hard hitting opening left-hand batsman, medium pace bowler. *Sch* Harrow. *Teams* Somerset (1884–93, 50 matches); Oxford U (1886–87, blue 1886). *Tours* Hawke to North America 1891, to South Africa 1895/6 (no first-class matches).
Career batting
104–182–8–5099–201–29.30–7–*ct* 49
Bowling 240–2–120.00–0–0–2/40
He captained Somerset from 1889 to 1893, in which year he resigned because he felt that his authority during the match against the Australians had been unwarrantably overruled. After that season he rarely appeared in first-class matches, this being a great loss to the game, since he was one of the most remarkable batsmen of his time. He hit 1,000 runs in a season twice (best 1,407, av 35.17, in 1892). His only double century was 201 for Somerset v Yorkshire at Taunton in 1892. His final first-class match was for MCC in 1896. He first played for Somerset (not first-class) in 1887.

Hewitson, Joseph
Professional. *b:* 27.10.1865, Little Bolton, Lancashire. *d:* 4.12.1925, Halliwell, Bolton, Lancashire. Lower order left-hand batsman, slow left-arm bowler. *Team* Lancashire (1890, 4 matches).
Career batting
4–5–0–99–56–19.80–0–*ct* 1
Bowling 235–14–16.78–1–1–6/57

Hewitt, Eric Joseph
Amateur. *b:* 19.12.1935, Erdington, Birmingham. Middle order right-hand batsman, leg break and googly bowler. *Team* Warwickshire (1954, 1 match).
Career batting
2–3–0–55–40–18.33–0–*ct* 1
Bowling 60–1–60.00–0–0–1/20
His final first-class match was for Combined Services in 1957.

Hewitt, Francis Stanley Arnot
Cricketer. *b:* 13.3.1936, Malone, Belfast, Ireland. Middle order right-hand batsman, right-arm fast medium or off break bowler. *Sch* Royal Belfast Academical Institution. *Team* Ireland (1966).
Career batting
1–2–0–53–36–26.50–0–*ct* 1
Bowling 44–0

Hewitt, Simon Mark
Cricketer. *b:* 30.7.1961, Radcliffe, Lancashire. Brother of S. G. P. (Cambridge U). Lower order right-hand batsman, right-arm medium pace bowler.

Hewitt, Steven Guy Paul

Team Oxford U (1984).
Career batting
4–6–1–60–22–12.00–0–*ct* 0
Bowling 232–4–58.00–0–0–2/52

He captained France in the 1992 European Cricketer Cup.

Hewitt, Steven Guy Paul
Cricketer. *b:* 6.4.1963, Radcliffe, Lancashire. Brother of S. M. (Oxford U). Tail end right-hand batsman, wicket-keeper. *Team* Cambridge U (1983–84, blue 1983).
Career batting
9–12–6–29–14*–4.83–0–*ct* 9–*st* 2

Hewitt, W.
Amateur. Lower order batsman, useful bowler. *Team* Gentlemen of North (1877).
Career batting
1–2–0–1–1–0.50–0–*ct* 0
Bowling 16–1–16.00–0–0–1/16

Hewlett, Reginald James
Amateur. *b:* 12.8.1885, Bristol. *d:* 7.5.1950, Bishopston, Bristol. Middle order right-hand batsman. *Team* Gloucestershire (1909–22, 5 matches).
Career batting
5–10–0–80–24–8.00–0–*ct* 2

Heygate, Harold John
Amateur. *b:* 4.8.1884, Wellingborough, Northamptonshire. *d:* 27.6.1937, Guildford, Surrey. Brother of R. B. (Sussex). Stylish opening right-hand batsman. *Sch* Epsom and Wellingborough. *Team* Sussex (1903–1919, 6 matches).
Career batting
6–11–1–250–80–25.00–0–*ct* 0

He appeared for Canada v United States in 1908. He also played for Cornwall. He was judged out by the umpire when he failed to appear at the wicket when the statutory two minutes had elapsed, the only example of such a dismissal in first-class cricket. The match was Sussex v Somerset at Taunton in 1919.

Heygate, Dr Reginald Beaumont
Amateur. *b:* 13.5.1883, Wellingborough, Northamptonshire. *d:* 24.4.1956, Crieff, Perthshire, Scotland. Brother of H. J. (Sussex). Middle order right-hand batsman, useful change bowler. *Sch* Epsom and Wellingborough. *Teams* Sussex (1902–11, 70 matches); London County (1903).
Career batting
73–111–12–2818–136–28.46–3–*ct* 38
Bowling 102–4–25.50–0–0–2/21

He hit 1,000 runs in a season twice (best 1,062, av 35.40, in 1909).

Heymann, William Goodall
Amateur. *b:* 26.10.1885, West Bridgford Hall, Nottingham. *d:* 27.11.1969, Long Clawson, Leicestershire. Lower order right-hand batsman, left-arm medium pace bowler. *Sch* Haileybury. *Team* Nottinghamshire (1905, 1 match).
Career batting
1 match, did not bat–*ct* 0
Bowling 48–2–24.00–0–0–2/37

Heys, William
Professional. *b:* 19.2.1931, Oswaldtwistle, Lancashire. Lower order right-hand batsman, wicket-keeper. *Team* Lancashire (1957, 5 matches).
Career batting
5–7–0–74–46–10.57–0–*ct* 5–*st* 3

Hibbard, Henry
Professional. *b:* 1854. *d:* 12.2.1902, St Michaels, Liverpool, Lancashire. Lower order batsman, bowler. *Team* Lancashire (1884, 1 match).
Career batting
1–2–0–7–4–3.50–0–*ct* 0
Bowling 54–2–27.00–0–0–2/35

Hibbard, John Arthur
Amateur. *b:* 7.9.1863, Chatham, Kent. *d:* 17.10.1905, Gillingham, Kent. Lower order batsman, wicket-keeper. *Team* Kent (1893, 4 matches).
Career batting
4–7–3–19–7–4.75–0–*ct* 10

Hibberd, George
Professional. *b:* 8.2.1845, Sheffield, Yorkshire. *d:* 24.8.1911, Todwick, Yorkshire. Tail end batsman, right-arm fast bowler. *Team* Lancashire (1867, 1 match).
Career batting
1–2–1–4–2*–4.00–0–*ct* 1
Bowling 37–0

Hibberd, H.
Amateur. Middle order batsman, wicket-keeper. *Team* Surrey Club (1866).
Career batting
1–1–0–0–0–0.00–0–*ct* 0

Hibbert, Hugh Washington
Amateur. *b:* 4.10.1911, Kensington, London. *d:* 12.3.1985, Salisbury, Wiltshire. His daughter married a son of M. R. H. M. Herbert (Nottinghamshire and Somerset). Middle order right-hand batsman. *Sch* Downside. *Team* Northamptonshire (1931, 1 match).
Career batting
1–2–0–11–10–5.50–0–*ct* 1

Hibbert, John Calvert
Amateur. *b:* 4.8.1853, Chalfont Lodge, Buckinghamshire. *d:* 23.3.1929, Valescure, St Raphael, France. Nephew of C. Calvert (Surrey). Middle order right-hand batsman, wicket-keeper. *Team* MCC (1881–82).
Career batting
2–3–0–0–0–0.00–0–*ct* 0

His County cricket was for Lincolnshire (1874).

Hibbert, William John
Professional. *b:* 11.7.1873, Nottingham. *d:* 6.6.1934, Lincoln. Middle order left-hand batsman, bowler. *Team* Lancashire (1900–01, 14 matches).
Career batting
14–22–4–445–79–24.72–0–*ct* 5
Bowling 116–3–38.66–0–0–2/41
He also played for Lincolnshire (1907–09).

Hichens, Andrew Lionel
Amateur. *b:* 24.8.1936, Westminster, London. Lower order right-hand batsman, right-arm fast medium bowler. *Sch* Winchester. *Team* Oxford U (1957–59).
Career batting
3–2–0–4–4–2.00–0–*ct* 0
Bowling 270–6–45.00–0–0–4/97
His County cricket was for Oxfordshire (1957–64).

Hick, Graeme Ashley
Cricketer. *b:* 23.5.1966, Salisbury, Rhodesia. Middle order right-hand batsman, off break bowler, brilliant slip field. *Teams* Zimbabwe (1983/4 to 1985/6); Worcestershire (1984–92, 160 matches); Northern Districts (1987/8 to 1988/9); Queensland (1990/91). *Tours* Zimbabwe to Sri Lanka 1983/4, to England 1985; Worcestershire to Zimbabwe 1990/1; England to New Zealand 1991/2, to Australia and New Zealand (World Cup) 1991/2. *Tests* England (1991–92, 11 matches).
Career batting
226–364–41–19083–405*–59.08–67–*ct* 271
Bowling 5575–142–39.26–4–1–5/37
Test batting
11–17–0–307–51–18.05–0–*ct* 22
Bowling 306–6–51.00–0–0–4/126
Regarded as the outstanding young batsman of the mid-1980s, Hick had to wait until 1991 to qualify for England by residence. Whilst waiting to appear in Test cricket, he reached 2,000 runs in a season three times (best 2,713, av 77.51, in 1988). In 1988 he also completed 1,000 runs before the end of May and hit 405* for Worcestershire v Somerset at Taunton. In 1986 he became the youngest batsman to score 2,000 runs in a season. He has scored 1,000 runs in a season eight times, and also 1,228, av 94.46, in New Zealand 1988/9. However his first two seasons in Test cricket have not been as successful as many critics predicted.

Hickey, Denis Jon
Cricketer. *b:* 31.12.1964, Mooroopna, Victoria, Australia. Lower order right-hand batsman, right-arm fast medium bowler. *Teams* Victoria (1985/6 to 1989/90, 13 matches); Glamorgan (1986, 13 matches); South Australia (1990/1 to 1991/2, 20 matches). *Tour* Australia B to Zimbabwe 1991/2.
Career batting
48–45–15–284–32–9.46–0–*ct* 11
Bowling 5257–136–38.65–6–1–7/81

Hickinbottom, Geoffrey Alfred
Professional. *b:* 15.11.1932, West End, Leicester. Tail end right-hand batsman, wicket-keeper. *Team* Leicestershire (1959, 5 matches).
Career batting
5–7–5–6–4*–3.00–0–*ct* 4–*st* 3

Hickley, Anthony North
Amateur. *b:* 10.3.1906, Marylebone, London. *d:* 5.9.1972, Glencalvie, Ross-shire, Scotland. Middle order batsman, slow left-arm bowler. *Sch* Winchester. *Team* Middlesex (1930, 1 match).
Career batting
1–2–0–27–22–13.50–0–*ct* 0

Hickley, Admiral Cecil Spencer
Amateur. *b:* 22.1.1865, Ashcott, Somerset. *d:* 1.5.1941, Kensington, London. Middle order batsman. *Teams* Western Province (1890/1); Somerset (1898–99, 5 matches).
Career batting
7–13–0–149–45–11.46–0–*ct* 0
He joined the Navy at the age of 13.

Hickley, Charles Lushington
Amateur. *b:* 19.11.1862, Lachmere, Ham Common, Surrey. *d:* 2.7.1935, Bayswater, London. Lower order right-hand batsman, right-arm fast medium bowler, moderate field. *Sch* Winchester. *Team* Oxford U (1883).
Career batting
1–2–0–29–15–14.50–0–*ct* 0
Bowling 25–0

Hickley, Frank
Amateur. *b:* 14.12.1895, Leicester. *d:* 28.10.1972, Leicester. Middle order right-hand batsman, change bowler. *Team* Leicestershire (1921, 2 matches).
Career batting
2–3–0–34–27–11.33–0–*ct* 0
Bowling 18–1–18.00–0–0–1/8

Hickman, George
Professional. *b:* 17.1.1909, Lanchester, Co Durham. *d:* 26.8.1978, Stranraer, Wigtown, Scotland. Middle order right-hand batsman. *Team* Warwickshire (1929, 2 matches).
Career batting
4–6–0–26–17–4.33–0–*ct* 2
He also played for Durham (pre first-class, 1933–36) and his final first-class match was for Minor Counties in 1935. A useful soccer player, he represented West Bromwich Albion and Halifax Town.

Hickman, Malcolm Francis
Professional. *b:* 30.6.1936, Market Harborough, Leicestershire. Middle order right-hand batsman, good deep field. *Team* Leicestershire (1954–57, 12 matches).
Career batting
12–22–2–232–40–11.60–0–*ct* 5

Hickmott, Edward
Professional. *b:* 20.3.1850, Maidstone, Kent. *d:* 7.1.1934, West Malling, Kent. Uncle of W. E. (Kent and Lancashire). Hard hitting lower order right-hand batsman, wicket-keeper. *Team* Kent (1875–88, 10 matches).
Career batting
10–15–2–85–44–6.53–0–*ct* 16–*st* 3

Hickmott, William Edward
Professional. *b:* 10.4.1893, Boxley, Kent. *d:* 16.1.1968, West Malling, Kent. Nephew of Edward (Kent). Lower order right-hand batsman, left-arm medium slow bowler. *Teams* Kent (1914–21, 3 matches); Lancashire (1923–24, 34 matches).
Career batting
37–40–11–301–31*–10.37–0–*ct* 25
Bowling 2360–92–25.65–2–0–5/20
He created a Central Lancashire League record by taking 140 wickets in a season for Rochdale in 1927. He was well-known as a breeder and trainer of golden retrievers.

Hicks, John
Professional. *b:* 10.12.1850, York. *d:* 10.6.1912, York. Middle order right-hand batsman, good field, right-arm fast bowler. *Team* Yorkshire (1872–76, 15 matches).
Career batting
21–36–4–423–66–13.21–0–*ct* 13
Bowling 70–3–23.33–0–0–2/53

Hickson, John Arnold Einem
Amateur. *b:* 22.12.1864, Hornsey, Middlesex. *d:* 2.1.1945, Surbiton, Surrey. Lower order batsman, wicket-keeper. *Teams* Transvaal (1889/90); Middlesex (1894–96, 3 matches).
Career batting
4–5–1–11–11–2.75–0–*ct* 8–*st* 1

Hickton, William
Professional. *b:* 14.12.1842, Hardstoft, Derbyshire. *d:* 25.2.1900, Lower Broughton, Manchester, Lancashire. Father of W. H. (Worcestershire). Lower order right-hand batsman, right-hand fast round-arm bowler, good slip. *Teams* Lancashire (1867–71, 24 matches); Derbyshire (1871–78, 34 matches).
Career batting
60–103–17–1054–63–12.25–0–*ct* 32
Bowling 4020–284–14.15–24–7–10/46
His feat of taking all 10 wickets in an innings (for 46) was for Lancashire v Hampshire at Old Trafford in 1870.

Hickton, William Henry
Professional. *b:* 28.8.1884, Lower Broughton, Manchester, Lancashire. *d:* 8.4.1942, Leeds, Yorkshire. Son of William (Lancashire and Derbyshire). Tail end right-hand batsman, slow left-arm bowler. *Team* Worcestershire (1909, 5 matches).
Career batting
5–9–0–41–17–4.55–0–*ct* 2
Bowling 104–2–52.00–0–0–1/9
He also played for Northumberland (1914).

Hiddleston, Douglas Stuart
Amateur. *b:* 2.3.1910, Johannesburg, South Africa. Lower order right-hand batsman, leg break and googly bowler. *Team* Scotland (1930–34).
Career batting
5–8–1–65–15–9.28–0–*ct* 0
Bowling 414–27–15.33–2–0–7/69

Hide, Arthur Bollard
Professional. *b:* 7.5.1860, Eastbourne, Sussex. *d:* 5.11.1933, Denmark Hill, London. Brother of J. B. (Sussex). Lower order left-hand batsman, left-arm medium pace bowler, good close field. *Team* Sussex (1882–90, 113 matches).
Career batting
115–196–40–1132–45–7.25–0–*ct* 73
Bowling 7736–403–19.19–20–1–7/44
He was a first-class umpire (1897–1901), standing in one Test match (1899).

Hide, Jesse Bollard
Professional. *b:* 12.3.1857, Eastbourne, Sussex. *d:* 19.3.1924, Edinburgh, Scotland. Brother of A. B. (Sussex). Middle order right-hand batsman, right-hand fast round-arm bowler. *Teams* Sussex (1876–93, 155 matches); South Australia (1880/1 to 1882/3, 4 matches).
Career batting
176–323–20–4824–173–15.92–4–*ct* 112
Bowling 9572–441–21.70–19–4–8/47
He went to South Australia for a three year engagement, his services being lost to Sussex during that period commencing 1878. He also played for Cornwall (1906). He was a first-class umpire (1912).

Higginbotham, Charles Ernest
Amateur. *b:* 4.7.1866, Charing Cross, Glasgow, Scotland. *d:* 11.3.1915, near Neuve Chapelle, France. Son-in-law of James Round (MCC), brother-in-law of C. J. Round (Essex). Middle order right-hand batsman. *Sch* Rugby. *Teams* Army (1912); Army in South Africa (1905/06).
Career batting
2–4–1–45–40*–15.00–0–*ct* 1
His County cricket was for Devon (1902).

Higgins, George Frederick
Amateur. *b:* 25.12.1868, Mile End, London. *d:* 19.8.1951, Woodford Green, Essex. Middle order right-hand batsman. *Team* Essex (1894–95, 9 matches).
Career batting
9–17–0–306–118–18.00–1–*ct* 2

Higgins, Harry Leslie
Amateur. *b:* 24.2.1894, Bournville, Warwickshire. *d:* 19.9.1979, Malvern, Worcestershire. Brother of J. B. (Worcestershire). Middle order right-hand batsman. *Sch* KES, Birmingham. *Team* Worcestershire (1920–27, 97 matches).
Career batting
98–181–13–3437–137*–20.45–4–*ct* 54
He hit 1,000 runs in a season twice (best 1,182, av 28.82, in 1921).

Higgins, James
Professional. *b:* 13.3.1877, Birstall, Yorkshire. *d:* 19.7.1954, Wibsey, Yorkshire. Lower order right-hand batsman, wicket-keeper. *Team* Yorkshire (1901–05, 9 matches).
Career batting
9–14–5–93–28*–10.33–0–*ct* 10–*st* 3

Higgins, John Bernard
Amateur. *b:* 31.12.1885, Harborne, Warwickshire. *d:* 3.1.1970, Malvern, Worcestershire. Brother of H. L. (Worcestershire). Middle order right-hand batsman, slow left-arm bowler. *Sch* KES Birmingham. *Teams* Worcestershire (1912–30, 111 matches); Europeans (1922/3 to 1928/9).
Career batting
121–223–11–4149–123–19.57–3–*ct* 59
Bowling 1604–30–53.46–1–0–5/72
He hit 1,041 runs, av 30.61, in 1928. He also played for Staffordshire (1909). He umpired one Test match in India (1933/4).

Higgins, William Charles
Amateur. *b:* 12.12.1850, Westminster, London. *d:* 8.4.1926, Chelsea, London. Lower order right-hand batsman, right-hand slow round-arm bowler, short-slip. *Sch* Eton. *Team* MCC (1870–73).
Career batting
6–10–2–66–20*–8.25–0–*ct* 2
He did not play any first-class cricket whilst at Oxford U.

Higginson, J. G.
Amateur. *b:* January 1885, Worcester. *d:* September 1940, Wolverhampton, Staffordshire. Lower order right-hand batsman, right-arm fast bowler. *Team* Worcestershire (1912, 1 match).
Career batting
1–1–1–0–0*–no av–0–*ct* 0
Bowling 20–0

Higginson, Thomas William
Amateur. *b:* 6.11.1936, Esher, Surrey. Lower order right-hand batsman, right-arm medium pace bowler. *Team* Middlesex (1960, 3 matches).
Career batting
4–4–2–50–20–25.00–0–*ct* 5
Bowling 24–1–24.00–0–0–1/24

Higgo, Justin Beresford
Cricketer. *b:* 28.9.1968, Cape Town, South Africa. Middle order right-hand batsman, off break bowler. *Sch* Lancing. *Team* Oxford U (1989).
Career batting
3–6–0–18–9–3.00–0–*ct* 2
He was awarded his blue for golf.

Higgs, James Donald
Cricketer. *b:* 11.7.1950, Kyabram, Victoria, Australia. Tail end right-hand batsman, leg break and googly bowler. *Team* Victoria (1970/1 to 1982/3, 83 matches). *Tours* Australia to England 1975, to West Indies 1977/8, to India 1979/80. *Tests* Australia (1977/8 to 1980/1, 22 matches).
Career batting
122–131–60–384–21–5.40–0–*ct* 43
Bowling 11838–399–29.66–19–3–8/66
Test batting
22–36–16–111–16–5.55–0–*ct* 3
Bowling 2057–66–31.16–2–0–7/143
Required for only eight first-class matches on the 1975 tour to England, he did not appear in any Tests and had a very modest bowling return in the other games. He was dismissed by the only ball he faced during the tour!

Higgs, Kenneth
Professional. *b:* 14.1.1937, Kidsgrove, Staffordshire. Tail end left-hand batsman, right-arm fast, later medium pace, bowler. *Teams* Lancashire (1958–69, 306 matches); Leicestershire (1972–86, 167 matches). *Tours* MCC to Australia and New Zealand 1965/6, to West Indies 1967/8. *Tests* England (1965–68, 15 matches).
Career batting
511–530–207–3648–98–11.29–0–*ct* 311
Bowling 36267–1536–23.61–50–5–7/19
Test batting
15–19–3–185–63–11.56–0–*ct* 4
Bowling 1473–71–20.74–2–0–20.74
He also played for Staffordshire (1957). He took 100 wickets in a season five times (best 132, av 19.42, in 1960). He captained Leicestershire in 1979. He was coach to Leicestershire 1981–90 and in 1986 he reappeared in two Championship matches for the county after a break of four years. With R. Illingworth he added 228 for the 10th wicket for Leicestershire v Northamptonshire at Leicester in 1977 and with J. A. Snow added 128 for the 10th wicket for England v West Indies at the Oval in 1966. A good soccer player, he appeared as half-back for Port Vale.

Higgs, Kenneth Alan
Amateur. *b:* 5.10.1886, Haywards Heath, Sussex. *d:* 21.1.1959, Haywards Heath, Sussex. Middle order right-hand batsman. *Team* Sussex (1920–27, 41 matches).

Career batting
41–69–3–1693–111–25.65–2–*ct* 21
Bowling 131–4–32.75–0–0–2/15
He scored 101 for Sussex v Worcestershire at Hove in 1920 on his first-class debut.

Higgs-Walker, James Arthur
Amateur. *b:* 31.7.1892, Wychbury House, Clent, Worcestershire. *d:* 3.9.1979, Midhurst, Sussex. Tail end right-hand batsman, right-arm fast bowler. *Sch* Repton. *Team* Worcestershire (1913–19, 2 matches).
Career batting
2–3–1–44–44–22.00–0–*ct* 0
Bowling 89–1–89.00–0–0–1/69
He played in trials at Oxford U, but not in first-class matches.

Highton, Edward Frederick William
Professional. *b:* 29.8.1924, Formby, Lancashire. *d:* 9.10.1985, Formby, Lancashire. Lower order right-hand batsman, right-arm fast medium bowler. *Team* Lancashire (1951, 1 match).
Career batting
2–3–0–34–26–11.33–0–*ct* 1
Bowling 162–7–23.14–0–0–4/87
His first-class debut was for Minor Counties in 1950.

Hignell, Alastair James
Cricketer. *b:* 4.9.1955, Cambridge. Son of A. F. (Gloucestershire). Middle order right-hand batsman, leg break bowler. *Sch* Denstone. *Teams* Gloucestershire (1974–83, 137 matches); Cambridge U (1975–78, blue for all four years).
Career batting
170–289–36–7459–149*–29.48–11–*ct* 150
Bowling 230–3–76.66–0–0–2/13
He hit 1,000 runs in a season three times (best 1,140, av 30.81, in 1976). He captained Cambridge in 1977–78. A noted rugby footballer, he played for Cambridge and England.

Hignell, Dr Antony Francis
Amateur. *b:* 6.7.1928, Kroonstad, Orange Free State, South Africa. Father of A. J. (Gloucestershire). Lower order right-hand batsman, right-arm medium pace bowler. *Sch* Denstone. *Team* Gloucestershire (1947, 1 match).
Career batting
1–1–0–7–7–7.00–0–*ct* 1
Bowling 48–0

Higson, Peter
Amateur. *b:* 1.12.1905, Bramhall, Cheshire. *d:* 19.4.1986, Hove, Sussex. Son of T. A. (Derbyshire and Lancashire), brother of T. A. jun (Derbyshire and Lancashire). Middle order right-hand batsman. *Team* Lancashire (1928–31, 3 matches).
Career batting
4–4–2–51–29–25.50–0–*ct* 2
Bowling 18–0
His final first-class match was for Minor Counties in 1933. He played in trials at Oxford U, but not in first-class matches. He was President of Lancashire CCC 1973–74.

Higson, Thomas Atkinson
Amateur. *b:* 18.11.1873, Stockport, Cheshire. *d:* 3.8.1949, Grange-over-Sands, Lancashire. Father of Peter (Lancashire) and T. A. jun (Lancashire and Derbyshire). Middle order right-hand batsman, off break bowler. *Sch* Rossall. *Teams* Oxford U (1892); Derbyshire (1899–1910, 21 matches); Lancashire (1905–23, 5 matches).
Career batting
29–50–4–584–46–12.69–0–*ct* 12
Bowling 1165–41–28.41–0–0–4/74
He also played for Cheshire (1892–1912). From 1931 to 1937 he was a member of the Test Selection Committee. For 49 years he was on the Lancashire CCC Committee, being for eight years Hon Treasurer (1925–32) and then Chairman. He was also a useful soccer and hockey player.

Higson, Thomas Atkinson (jun)
Amateur. *b:* 25.3.1911, Whaley Bridge, Derbyshire. *d:* 15.1.1993. Son of T. A. (Lancashire and Derbyshire), brother of Peter (Lancashire). Middle order left-hand batsman, right-arm medium pace bowler. *Sch* Cheltenham. *Teams* Derbyshire (1932–35, 6 matches); Lancashire (1936–46, 20 matches).
Career batting
26–32–1–326–51–10.51–0–*ct* 8
Bowling 302–6–50.33–0–0–1/14
He was President of Lancashire 1977–78.

Hilder, Alan Lake
Amateur. *b:* 8.10.1901, Beckenham, Kent. *d:* 2.5.1970, St Leonards-on-Sea, Sussex. Hard hitting middle order right-hand batsman. *Sch* Lancing. *Team* Kent (1924–29, 14 matches). *Tours* Tennyson to Jamaica 1926/7, 1927/8; Cahn to Jamaica 1928/9 (not first-class); Martineau to Egypt 1932 (not first-class).
Career batting
21–36–5–451–103*–14.54–1–*ct* 12
Bowling 536–13–41.23–0–0–3/77
He scored 103* for Kent v Essex at Gravesend in 1924 on his first-class debut. His final first-class match was for MCC in 1930.

Hilditch, Andrew Mark Jefferson
Cricketer. *b:* 20.5.1956, North Adelaide, South Australia. Opening right-hand batsman. *Teams* New South Wales (1976/7 to 1980/1, 21 matches); South Australia (1982/3 to 1991/2, 102 matches). *Tours* Australia to England 1979 (World Cup), 1985, to India 1979/80. *Tests* Australia (1978/9 to 1985/6, 18 matches).

Career batting
156–276–13–9984–230–37.96–20–*ct* 101
Bowling 197–4–49.25–0–0–1/5
Test batting
18–34–0–1073–119–31.55–2–*ct* 13

On the 1985 tour to England he hit 119 and 80 in the first Test at Headingley and, although he remained in the side for the rest of the series, achieved very little afterwards. His highest score was 230 for South Australia v Victoria at Melbourne in 1983/4.

Hilditch, Thomas Arthur
Amateur. *b:* 10.1.1885, Sandbach, Cheshire. *d:* 7.8.1957, Bermuda, Nuneaton, Warwickshire. Lower order right-hand batsman, right-arm fast medium bowler. *Team* Warwickshire (1907–13, 8 matches).
Career batting
8–11–1–42–17–4.20–0–*ct* 3
Bowling 319–9–35.44–0–0–3/41

He also played for Shropshire (1907) and Cheshire (1910). He played soccer for Aston Villa.

Hildyard, Rev Lyonel D'Arcy
Amateur. *b:* 5.2.1861, Bury, Lancashire. *d:* 22.4.1931, Rowley Rectory, Hull, Yorkshire. Great-nephew of H. S. (Oxford U 1832). Middle order right-hand batsman, good point field. *Teams* Somerset (1882–83, 7 matches); Oxford U (1884–87, blue 1884–86); Lancashire (1884–85, 8 matches).
Career batting
32–56–9–811–62*–17.25–0–*ct* 26
Bowling 24–0

His last match for Somerset (not first-class) was in 1890. He also played for Glamorgan (pre first-class, 1891).

Hill, Alan
Cricketer. *b:* 29.6.1950, Buxworth, Derbyshire. Opening right-hand batsman, off break bowler. *Teams* Derbyshire (1972–86, 253 matches); Orange Free State (1976/7).
Career batting
258–447–47–12356–172*–30.89–18–*ct* 97
Bowling 365–9–40.55–0–0–3/5

He hit 1,000 runs in a season five times (best 1,438, av 42.29, in 1986). He scored 103 for Orange Free State v Griqualand West at Bloemfontein in 1976/7 without a single boundary.

Hill, Alfred John Bostock
Amateur. *b:* 8.4.1887, Olton, Solihull, Warwickshire. *d:* 20.8.1959, Okehampton, Devon. Nephew of H. B. G. (Warwickshire) and J. E. (Warwickshire). Lower order batsman, right-arm bowler. *Team* Warwickshire (1920, 1 match).
Career batting
1–2–0–4–4–2.00–0–*ct* 0
Bowling 22–0

He played no first-clas cricket whilst at Cambridge U, but did win a blue for hockey. He was a judge of the Supreme Court of Malaya. He married the sister of Lord Mancroft, the politician.

Hill, Alfred William
Professional. *b:* 29.7.1865, Little Rissington, Gloucestershire. *d:* 27.5.1936, Bourton-on-the-Water, Gloucestershire. Lower order left-hand batsman, off break bowler. *Team* Gloucestershire (1904–05, 2 matches).
Career batting
2–2–1–30–29*–30.00–0–*ct* 0
Bowling 54–1–54.00–0–0–1/47

His son created 'Birdland' in Gloucestershire.

Hill, Allen
Professional. *b:* 14.11.1843, Newton, Kirkheaton, Huddersfield, Yorkshire. *d:* 28.8.1910, Leyland, Lancashire. Lower order right-hand batsman, right-hand fast round-arm bowler. *Team* Yorkshire (1871–82, 139 matches). *Tour* Lillywhite to Australia 1876/7. *Tests* England (1876/7, 2 matches).
Career batting
193–312–35–2478–49–8.94–0–*ct* 142
Bowling 10686–744 + 5–14.36–57–10–8/48
Test batting
2–4–2–101–49–50.50–0–*ct* 1
Bowling 130–7–18.57–0–0–4/27

He took 100 wickets in a season three times (best 116, av 15.45, in 1875). His final first-class match was for North v South in 1883. He took the first wicket in Test cricket. He umpired one Test match in 1890.

Hill, Anthony Ewart Ledger
Amateur. *b:* 14.7.1901, Sparsholt House, Hampshire. *d:* 25.10.1986, Winchester, Hampshire. Son of A. J. L. (Hampshire), cousin of R. K. Page (Army). Middle order right-hand batsman. *Sch* Marlborough. *Team* Hampshire (1920–30, 18 matches).
Career batting
19–29–2–204–24–7.55–0–*ct* 7

Hill, Arthur James Ledger
Amateur. *b:* 26.7.1871, Bassett, Hampshire. *d:* 6.9.1950, Sparsholt House, Hampshire. Father of A. E. L. (Hampshire), uncle of R. K. Page (Army). Middle order right-hand batsman, originally right-arm fast medium bowler, later lobs, good slip field. *Sch* Marlborough. *Teams* Cambridge U (1890–93, blue all four years); Hampshire (1895–1921, 161 matches). *Tours* Hawke to India 1892/3, to North America 1894, to South Africa 1895/6; MCC to Argentine 1911/12. *Tests* England (1895/6, 3 matches).
Career batting
221–396–26–10353–199–27.98–19–*ct* 143
Bowling 8537–305–27.99–4–1–7/36
Test batting
3–4–0–251–124–62.75–1–*ct* 1

Bowling 8–4–2.00–0–0–4/8

He also played for Wiltshire. A splendid all-round sportsman, he captained Hampshire at rugby football and hockey and was also well known as a rackets player and boxer.

Hill, Barrington Julian Warren
Amateur. *b:* 31.7.1915, Broadstairs, Kent. *d:* 7.8.1985, Sandwich, Kent. Lower order right-hand batsman, off break bowler. *Sch* St Lawrence College, Ramsgate. *Team* Oxford U (1935–37).
Career batting
4–5–0–46–28–9.20–0–*ct* 7
Bowling 129–5–25.80–0–0–2/48

Hill, Charles Merrin
Amateur. *b:* 18.7.1903, Dublin, Ireland. *d:* 7.7.1982, Dublin, Ireland. Lower order right-hand batsman. *Team* Ireland (1927).
Career batting
1–1–0–5–5–5.00–0–*ct* 0

Hill, Clement
Amateur. *b:* 18.3.1877, Hindmarsh, Adelaide, South Australia. *d:* 5.9.1945, Parkville, Melbourne, Victoria, Australia. He died from injuries received when he was thrown from a tram which was involved in a traffic accident. Brother of Arthur (South Australia), H. J. (South Australia), L. R. (South Australia), Percival (South Australia) and Stanley (South Australia and New South Wales), uncle of W. Hill-Smith (Western Australia). Excellent middle order left-hand batsman, leg break bowler. *Team* South Australia (1892/3 to 1922/3, 87 matches). *Tours* Australia to England 1896, 1899, 1902, 1905, to South Africa 1902/3, to North America 1896, to New Zealand 1904/5. *Tests* Australia (1896 to 1911/12, 49 matches).
Career batting
252–416–21–17213–365*–43.57–45–*ct* 168–*st* 1
Bowling 323–10–32.30–0–0–2/6
Test batting
49–89–2–3412–191–39.21–7–*ct* 33

He hit 1,000 runs on three of his English tours (best 1,722, av 38.26, in 1905) and on all four visits was most successful, though not so formidable as in Australia – all his four double centuries were scored for South Australia, the highest being 365* v New South Wales at Adelaide in 1900/1. His batting was more suited to hard wickets, but he was also very much a man for the big occasion and rarely failed in Tests. He also hit 1,000 runs twice in a season in Australia. His final first-class match was for an Australian XI in 1924/5. He captained Australia in 10 Tests.

Hill, Denys Vivian
Amateur. *b:* 13.4.1896, Edmonton, Middlesex. *d:* 15.5.1971, Barton-on-Sea, Hampshire. Lower order right-hand batsman, right-arm fast bowler. *Team* Worcestershire (1927–29, 28 matches).
Career batting
42–65–13–469–38–9.01–0–*ct* 23
Bowling 3487–130–26.82–6–0–6/59

He made his first-class debut for the Army in 1922. He also played for Oxfordshire (1935).

Hill, Eric
Professional. *b:* 9.7.1923, Taunton, Somerset. Stylish opening right-hand batsman, good outfield. *Sch* Taunton. *Team* Somerset (1947–51, 72 matches).
Career batting
72–138–5–2118–85–15.92–0–*ct* 26
Bowling 55–1–55.00–0–0–1/25

Hill, Eustace Tickell
Amateur. *b:* 13.4.1869, Rookwood, Llandaff, Glamorgan. *d:* 11.1.1933, Ruthin, Denbighshire. Brother of V. T. (Somerset) and P. M. T. (Glamorgan, pre first-class), uncle of E. V. L. (Somerset) and M. L. (Glamorgan and Somerset). Hard hitting right-hand batsman, useful change bowler. *Sch* Winchester. *Team* Somerset (1898–1901, 2 matches).
Career batting
2–4–0–70–31–17.50–0–*ct* 3

Hill, Evelyn Vernon Llewellyn
Amateur. *b:* 18.4.1907, Cyntwell, Cardiff, Glamorgan. *d:* 25.10.1953, Weston-super-Mare, Somerset. Son of V. T. (Somerset), brother of M. L. (Glamorgan and Somerset), nephew of E. T. (Somerset) and P. M. T. (Glamorgan, pre first-class). Lower order right-hand batsman, right-arm fast bowler. *Sch* Eton. *Team* Somerset (1926–29, 13 matches).
Career batting
13–16–8–134–32–16.75–0–*ct* 9
Bowling 1055–33–31.96–2–0–5/36

Hill, Francis John
Amateur. *b:* 1.10.1862, Timsbury, Bath, Somerset. *d: circa* 1935, Saskatoon, Saskatchewan, Canada. Brother of R. E. (Somerset). Middle order right-hand batsman. *Sch* Marlborough. *Team* Somerset (1882, 1 match).
Career batting
1–2–0–31–29–15.50–0–*ct* 0

Hill, Rev Frederick Henry
Amateur. *b:* 29.11.1847, Bradfield, Berkshire. *d:* 28.7.1913, Kempston, Bedfordshire. Lower order right-hand batsman, right-hand medium pace round-arm bowler. *Sch* Bradfield. *Team* Oxford U (1867–70, blue 1867, 1869 and 1870).
Career batting
11–19–2–360–73–21.17–0–*ct* 9
Bowling 270–9–30.00–0–0–2/2

His final first-class match was for MCC in 1871. His County cricket was for Northamptonshire (pre first-class, 1866), Buckinghamshire (1867), Bedfordshire (1868) and Worcestershire (pre first-class, 1873).

Hill, Geoffrey Harry
Professional. *b:* 17.9.1934, Hayley Green, Halesowen, Worcestershire. Lower order left-hand batsman, slow left-arm bowler. *Team* Warwickshire (1958–60, 41 matches).
Career batting
42–48–6–247–23–5.88–0–*ct* 26
Bowling 3195–108–29.58–3–0–8/70
His first-class debut was for Combined Services in 1957.

Hill, Gerald
Professional. *b:* 15.4.1913, Totton, Hampshire. Middle order right-hand batsman, off break bowler, fine outfield. *Team* Hampshire (1932–54, 371 matches).
Career batting
371–595–94–9085–161–18.13–4–*ct* 169
Bowling 18464–617–29.92–18–3–8/62
He hit 1,000 runs in a season twice (best 1,051, av 22.36, in 1946); in 1935 he took 93 wickets, av 24.49.

Hill, Henry
Amateur. *b:* 29.11.1858, Thornhill, Dewsbury, Yorkshire. *d:* 14.8.1935, Headingley, Leeds, Yorkshire. Hard hitting middle order right-hand batsman, excellent deep field. *Team* Yorkshire (1888–91, 14 matches).
Career batting
14–27–2–337–34–13.48–0–*ct* 10

Hill, Henry Barratt Grosvenor
Amateur. *b:* 23.7.1861, Old Square, Birmingham. *d:* 4.6.1913, Handsworth, Birmingham. Brother of J. E. (Warwickshire), uncle of A. J. B. (Warwickshire). Lower order right-hand batsman, slow left-arm bowler. *Sch* KES, Birmingham. *Team* Warwickshire (1894–1900, 5 matches).
Career batting
5–7–1–41–13–6.83–0–*ct* 3
Bowling 248–5–49.60–0–0–3/15
He was founder of the Birmingham and District League. He first played for Warwickshire (pre first-class) in 1888.

Hill, Henry James
Amateur. *b:* 8.4.1851, Edmonton, Middlesex. *d:* 7.5.1905, Bayswater, London. Opening right-hand batsman, right-hand medium pace round-arm bowler. *Team* MCC (1880–83).
Career batting
4–7–0–31–17–4.42–0–*ct* 1
He played in trials at Cambridge U, but not in first-class matches.

Hill, Herbert James
Amateur. *b:* 12.2.1867, Kingston-upon-Thames, Surrey. *d:* 27.2.1946, Sheringham, Norfolk. Brother-in-law of W. Law (Yorkshire). Middle order right-hand batsman. *Sch* Harrow. *Team* MCC (1900–01).
Career batting
2–4–0–90–54–22.50–0–*ct* 0
His County cricket was for Hertfordshire (1894–1903).

Hill, John Charles
Amateur. *b:* 25.6.1923, Murrumbeena, Melbourne, Victoria, Australia. *d:* 11.8.1974, Caulfield, Melbourne, Victoria, Australia. Lower order right-hand batsman, leg break and googly bowler. *Team* Victoria (1945/6 to 1955/6, 38 matches). *Tours* Australia to England 1953, to West Indies 1954/5. *Tests* Australia (1953 to 1954/5, 3 matches).
Career batting
69–78–24–867–51*–16.05–0–*ct* 63
Bowling 5040–218–23.11–9–1–7/51
Test batting
3–6–3–21–8*–7.00–0–*ct* 2
Bowling 273–8–34.12–0–0–3/35
He took 63 wickets, av 20.98, on the 1953 tour to England, but did not impress in the Tests.

Hill, John Ernest
Amateur. *b:* 27.9.1867, Handsworth, Warwickshire. *d:* 2.12.1963, Smethwick, Staffordshire. Brother of H. B. G. (Warwickshire), uncle of A. J. B. (Warwickshire). Middle order right-hand batsman, left-arm medium pace bowler. *Sch* KES, Birmingham. *Team* Warwickshire (1894–98, 25 matches).
Career batting
27–38–7–737–139*–23.77–1–*ct* 20
Bowling 14–0
He scored 139* on debut for Warwickshire v Nottinghamshire at Trent Bridge in 1894, Warwickshire's first first-class match. He first played for Warwickshire (pre first-class) in 1888. Being the Public Prosecutor for Birmingham, his County cricket was very restricted.

Hill, John William
Amateur. *b:* 10.6.1920, Coleraine, Co Londonderry, Ireland. *d:* 17.1.1984, Dublin, Ireland. Lower order right-hand batsman, off break bowler. *Team* Ireland (1946–51).
Career batting
7–12–7–82–18*–16.40–0–*ct* 1
Bowling 367–17–21.58–0–0–3/16

Hill, Lenard Winston
Cricketer. *b:* 14.4.1941, Caerleon, Monmouthshire. Middle order right-hand batsman, occasional wicket-keeper, good cover. *Team* Glamorgan (1964–76, 76 matches).
Career batting
76–130–20–2690–96*–24.45–0–*ct* 40–*st* 1
Bowling 44–0
He played soccer at right half for Newport County and Swansea.

Hill, Lewis Gordon
Amateur. *b:* 2.11.1860, Bradford, Yorkshire. *d:* 27.8.1940, Heaton, Yorkshire. Middle order right-hand batsman. *Team* Yorkshire (1882, 1 match).
Career batting
1–2–0–13–8–6.50–0–*ct* 1

Hill, Maurice
Professional. *b:* 14.9.1935, Scunthorpe, Lincolnshire. Attractive middle order right-hand batsman, leg break bowler, good deep field. *Teams* Nottinghamshire (1953–65, 237 matches); Derbyshire (1966–67, 32 matches); Somerset (1970–71, 22 matches).
Career batting
292–484–39–10722–137*–24.09–7–*ct* 151
Bowling 311–5–62.20–0–0–2/60
He hit 1,000 runs in a season six times (best 1,416, av 27.76, in 1964).

Hill, Mervyn Llewellyn
Amateur. *b:* 23.6.1902, Rookwood, Llandaff, Glamorgan. *d:* 27.2.1948, Westminster, London. Son of V. T. (Oxford U and Somerset), brother of E. V. L. (Somerset), nephew of E. T. (Somerset) and P. M. T. (Glamorgan, pre first-class). Lower order right-hand batsman, wicket-keeper. *Sch* Eton. *Teams* Somerset (1921–32, 42 matches); Cambridge U (1923–24); Glamorgan (1923, 3 matches) *Tour* MCC to India, Burma and Ceylon (1926/7).
Career batting
64–95–29–864–60–13.09–0–*ct* 58–*st* 31
His first-class debut was for Gentlemen of England in 1920. He also played for Devon (1935).

Hill, Michael John
Cricketer. *b:* 1.7.1951, Harwell, Berkshire. Lower order left-hand batsman, wicket-keeper. *Sch* Abingdon. *Team* Hampshire (1973–76, 6 matches).
Career batting
6–8–4–68–27*–17.00–0–0–*ct* 9

Hill, Norman Wilfred
Professional. *b:* 22.8.1935, Holbeck, Nottinghamshire. Opening left-hand batsman, leg break bowler, slip field. *Team* Nottinghamshire (1953–68, 280 matches).
Career batting
283–518–32–14303–201*–29.43–23–*ct* 224
Bowling 261–2–130.50–0–0–1/28
He hit 1,000 runs in a season eight times, going on to 2,000 twice (best 2,239, av 39.98, in 1961). His only double century was 201* for Nottinghamshire v Sussex at Shireoaks in 1961. He captained Nottinghamshire in 1966 and 1967.

Hill, Richard Ernest
Amateur. *b:* 12.8.1861, Timsbury, Bath, Somerset. *d:* 25.12.1924, Westminster, London. Brother of F. J. (Somerset). Lower order right-hand batsman, left-arm fast bowler. *Sch* Marlborough. *Team* Somerset (1882, 1 match).
Career batting
1–2–1–7–7*–7.00–0–*ct* 0
Bowling 21–1–21.00–0–0–1/21
He first played for Somerset (pre first-class) in 1881.

Hill, Richard Hamilton
Amateur. *b:* 28.11.1900, Kensington, London. *d:* 5.10.1959, Hosey Hill, Westerham, Kent. Opening right-hand batsman. *Sch* Winchester. *Team* Middlesex (1921–31, 42 matches).
Career batting
45–59–4–861–71–15.65–0–*ct* 16
He appeared in the Freshmen's and Seniors' matches at Cambridge but no first-class games; however he represented the University at royal tennis and rackets. For many years he reported both tennis and cricket for *The Times*.

Hill, Robert Gribben
Amateur. *b:* 15.7.1938, Kilmarnock, Ayr, Scotland. Middle order left-hand batsman. *Team* Scotland (1963–69).
Career batting
6–9–0–105–50–11.66–0–*ct* 2

Hill, Rowland Wright Davenport
(known as Davenport-Hill from 1877)
Amateur. *b:* 5.9.1851, Hajepoor, India. *d:* 29.8.1912, Gladesville, New South Wales, Australia. Middle order right-hand batsman, wicket-keeper. *Team* Lancashire (1871, 1 match).
Career batting
1–2–0–8–5–4.00–0–*ct* 1

Hill, Rupert Knight
Cricketer. *b:* 14.8.1954, Kingston, Jamaica. Tail end right-hand batsman, right-arm medium pace bowler. *Team* Glamorgan (1975, 1 match).
Career batting
1 match, did not bat–*ct* 0
Bowling 58–1–58.00–0–0–1/34

Hill, Vernon Tickell
Amateur. *b:* 30.1.1871, Rookwood, Llandaff, Glamorgan. *d:* 29.9.1932, Woodspring Priory, Somerset. Brother of E. T. (Somerset) and P. M. T. (Glamorgan, pre first-class), father of E. V. L. (Somerset) and M. L. (Somerset and Glamorgan). Hard hitting middle order left-hand batsman, right-arm fast medium bowler. *Sch* Winchester. *Teams* Somerset (1891–1912, 121 matches); Oxford U (1892–93, blue 1892). *Tours* Mitchell to North America 1895; Warner to North America 1898.
Career batting
140–240–8–4560–116–19.65–2–*ct* 126
Bowling 911–31–29.38–0–0–4/20

He first played for Somerset (not first-class) in 1890. He also played for Glamorgan (pre first-class, 1903–05). He was Somerset President in 1930.

Hill, W. H.
Amateur. Middle order batsman. *Team* Worcestershire (1900, 2 matches).
Career batting
2–4–1–46–13*–15.33–0–*ct* 0

Hill, William Aubrey
Amateur until 1930, then professional. *b:* 27.4.1910, Carmarthen. Sound opening right-hand batsman, right-arm medium pace bowler. *Team* Warwickshire (1929–48, 169 matches).
Career batting
169–279–22–6423–147*–24.99–6–*ct* 51
Bowling 27–1–27.00–0–0–1/9
He hit 1,000 runs in a season twice (best 1,197, av 24.42, in 1947).

Hillary, Anthony Aylmer
Amateur. *b:* 28.8.1926, Shenfield, Essex. *d:* 20.6.1991, Truro, Cornwall. Middle order right-hand batsman, off break bowler. *Sch* Brentwood. *Team* Cambridge U (1951).
Career batting
1–1–0–49–49–49.00–0–*ct* 0
His County cricket was for Berkshire (1954–62).

Hiller, Robert
Cricketer. *b:* 14.10.1942, Woking, Surrey. Lower order left-hand batsman, right-arm fast medium bowler. *Team* Oxford U (1966, blue).
Career batting
8–11–1–87–64–8.70–0–*ct* 6
Bowling 494–17–29.05–0–0–4/53
He played rugby for England at full back and toured with the British Lions.

Hillkirk, John Ritson
Amateur. *b:* 25.6.1845, Manchester, Lancashire. *d:* 8.10.1921, Cowes, Isle of Wight. Hard hitting middle order right-hand batsman, right-hand medium pace round-arm bowler. *Sch* Ardwick School. *Team* Lancashire (1871–77, 30 matches).
Career batting
31–48–4–607–56*–13.79–0–*ct* 18–*st* 1
He was also a noted athlete.

Hills, Harry Mountford
Professional. *b:* 28.9.1886, Mayland, Essex. Lower order right-hand batsman, leg break bowler. *Team* Essex (1912–19, 14 matches).
Career batting
14–21–4–139–26–8.17–0–*ct* 7
Bowling 738–15–49.20–1–0–5/63

Hills, Henry
Amateur. *b:* 1.6.1844, Leverington, Cambridgeshire. *d:* 22.5.1914, Cambridge. Lower order batsman, useful bowler. *Team* Cambridgeshire (1866–68, 5 matches).
Career batting
5–10–0–39–9–3.90–0–*ct* 3
Bowling 80–3–26.66–0–0–2/18

Hills, Joseph John
Professional. *b:* 14.10.1897, Plumstead, London. *d:* 21.9.1969, Westbourne, Bournemouth, Hampshire. Middle order right-hand batsman, good field, occasional wicket-keeper. *Team* Glamorgan (1926–31, 104 matches); Wales (1928–29).
Career batting
107–170–9–3474–166–21.57–7–*ct* 93–*st* 5
After retiring from first-class cricket he became a first-class umpire (1939–56), standing in one Test match (1947). A good soccer player, he was goalkeeper for Cardiff City, Swansea and Fulham.

Hills, Richard William
Cricketer. *b:* 8.1.1951, Borough Green, Kent. Lower order right-hand batsman, right-arm medium pace bowler. *Team* Kent (1973–80, 85 matches).
Career batting
85–95–25–995–45–14.21–0–*ct* 33
Bowling 4494–161–27.91–2–0–6/64

Hills, Robert Savi
Amateur. *b:* 8.5.1837, St Johns Wood, Middlesex. *d:* 5.1.1909, Manar, Inverurie, Aberdeenshire, Scotland. Father of J. Hills (Europeans). Middle order batsman. *Sch* Rugby. *Team* MCC (1867–76).
Career batting
2–4–0–17–8–4.25–0–*ct* 1

Hill-Wood, Sir Basil Samuel Hill
(changed name from Wood in 1910)
Amateur. *b:* 5.2.1900, Chelsea, London. *d:* 3.7.1954, Farley Hill, Berkshire. Son of S. H. (Derbyshire), brother of C. K. H. (Derbyshire), D. J. C. H. (Derbyshire) and W. W. H. (Derbyshire), uncle of P. D. (Free Foresters), brother-in-law of D. F. Brand (Cambridge U). Lower order right-hand batsman, right-arm fast medium bowler. *Sch* Eton. *Team* Derbyshire (1919–25, 22 matches). *Tour* MCC to Australia and New Zealand 1922/3 (not in first-class matches).
Career batting
22–35–4–505–61–16.29–0–*ct* 8
Bowling 1406–45–31.24–1–0–6/74
He did not appear in first-class matches whilst at Cambridge.

Hill-Wood, Charles Kerrison Hill
(changed name from Wood in 1910)
Amateur. *b:* 5.6.1907, Hoxne, Suffolk. *d:* 21.9.1988, Barton-le-Clay, Bedfordshire. Son of S. H. (Derbyshire), brother of B. S. H. (Derbyshire), D. J. C. H. (Derbyshire) and W. W. H. (Derbyshire), uncle of P. D. (Free Foresters). Lower order right-hand batsman, fast medium left-arm bowler. *Sch* Eton. *Teams*

Derbyshire (1928–30, 18 matches); Oxford U (1928–30, blue all three years); Europeans (1935/6). *Tours* Martineau to Egypt 1929, 1930 (not first-class).
Career batting
58–77–13–1256–72–19.62–0–*ct* 20
Bowling 5547–185–29.98–10–1–7/68

His final first-class match in England was for Free Foresters in 1932. He also won a blue for fives.

Hill-Wood, Denis John Charles Hill
(changed name from Wood in 1910)
Amateur. *b:* 25.6.1906, Hoxne, Suffolk. *d:* 4.5.1982, Hartley-Wintney, Hampshire. Son of S. H. (Derbyshire), brother of B. S. H. (Derbyshire), C. K. H. (Derbyshire) and W. W. H. (Derbyshire), father of P. D. (Free Foresters). Steady opening right-hand batsman, change bowler. *Sch* Eton. *Teams* Derbyshire (1928–29, 5 matches); Oxford U (1928, blue).
Career batting
12–21–1–453–85–22.65–0–*ct* 6
Bowling 123–3–41.00–0–0–1/4

He was a useful soccer player, obtaining his blue at Oxford; he was Chairman of Arsenal FC from 1959 until his death.

Hill-Wood, Peter Denis
Amateur. *b:* 25.2.1936, Kensington, London. Son of D. J. C. H. (Derbyshire), nephew of B. S. H. (Derbyshire), C. K. H. (Derbyshire) and W. W. H. (Derbyshire), grandson of S. H. (Derbyshire). Middle order right-hand batsman, right-arm medium pace bowler. *Sch* Eton. *Team* Free Foresters (1960).
Career batting
1–1–0–30–30–30.00–0–*ct* 1
Bowling 20–1–20.00–0–0–1/4

He has been Chairman of Arsenal FC since 1982.

Hill-Wood, S. H. (*see under* Wood, S. H.)

Hill-Wood, Sir Wilfred William Hill
(changed name from Wood in 1910)
Amateur. *b:* 8.9.1901, Chelsea, London. *d:* 10.10.1980, Kensington, London. Son of S. H. (Derbyshire), brother of B. S. H. (Derbyshire), C. K. H. (Derbyshire) and D. J. C. H. (Derbyshire), uncle of P. D. (Free Foresters), son-in-law of H. J. Wyld (Middlesex). Solid opening right-hand batsman, leg break bowler. *Sch* Eton. *Teams* Derbyshire (1919–36, 35 matches); Cambridge U (1921–22, blue 1922); Viceroy's XI (1932/3). *Tour* MCC to Australia and New Zealand 1922/3.
Career batting
63–107–4–2848–122*–27.65–3–*ct* 34
Bowling 2237–65–34.41–1–0–5/62

He hit 1,082 runs, av 36.06, in 1923. His final first-class match was for MCC in 1939.

Hillyard, George Whiteside
Amateur. *b:* 6.2.1864, Hanwell, Middlesex. *d:* 24.3.1943, Pulborough, Sussex. Lower order right-hand batsman, right-arm fast medium bowler. *Teams* Middlesex (1886, 3 matches); Leicestershire (1894–96, 32 matches). *Tours* Hawke to North America 1891, 1894.
Career batting
49–89–12–707–36–9.18–0–*ct* 63
Bowling 3144–145–21.68–9–1–6/74

He also played for Hertfordshire (1891). He first played for Leicestershire (pre first-class) in 1893. A noted lawn tennis player, he was Secretary of the All-England Club, Wimbledon, 1907–24, and in addition he excelled at golf and billiards. His wife (formerly Miss Bingley) won the ladies singles championship at Wimbledon six times.

Hillyer, Charles
Professional. *b:* 4.8.1845, Biddenden, Kent. *d:* 4.10.1872, Woodchurch, Kent. Middle order batsman, bowler. *Team* Kent (1868, 1 match).
Career batting
1–2–0–6–6–3.00–0–*ct* 1
Bowling 34–1–34.00–0–0–1/6

Hillyer, William Richard
Professional. *b:* 5.3.1813, Leybourne, Kent. *d:* 8.1.1861, Maidstone, Kent. Middle order right-hand batsman, right-hand medium fast round-arm bowler, excellent slip. *Teams* Kent (1835–53, 82 matches); Cambridge Town Club (1846); Surrey (1849, 2 matches as given man).
Career batting
230–411–68–2655–83–7.74–0–*ct* 203
Bowling 4148–376 + 1099–11.03–148–54–8/26

Described by some as 'the best of all bowlers', he was at his most brilliant about 1845. He took 100 wickets in a season seven times (best 174 in 1845). Owing to ill-health he was forced to give up cricket in 1855 and died aged 47 after a long and painful illness. He was the first cricketer known to have performed the match 'double' of 100 runs and 10 wickets in first-class cricket, when he scored 26 and 83 and took 7 and 6 wickets for MCC v Oxford U at Oxford in 1847. He also played for Buckinghamshire (1846) and Norfolk (1847).

Hilton, Albert Walter
Professional. *b:* 9.7.1862, Alfriston, Sussex. *d:* 4.9.1935, Brighton, Sussex. Lower order batsman, left-arm medium pace bowler. *Team* Sussex (1891–95, 29 matches).
Career batting
29–37–9–182–28–6.50–0–*ct* 17
Bowling 2284–89–25.66–4–1–7/47

Hilton, Colin
Professional. *b:* 26.9.1937, Atherton, Lancashire. Tail end right-hand batsman, right-arm fast bowler. *Teams* Lancashire (1957–63, 91 matches); Essex (1964, 24 matches)

Career batting
115–133–44–665–36–7.47–0–*ct* 40
Bowling 9038–321–28.15–8–1–6/38

His best season was 1962 when he took 92 wickets, av 26.62.

Hilton, Jim
Professional. *b:* 29.12.1930, Werneth, Oldham, Lancashire. Brother of M. J. (Lancashire). Lower order right-hand batsman, off break bowler, good outfield. *Teams* Lancashire (1952–53, 8 matches); Somerset (1954–57, 71 matches).
Career batting
79–129–29–1093–61*–10.93–0–*ct* 53
Bowling 3675–135–27.22–7–0–7/98

Hilton, John (jun)
Professional. *b:* 19.4.1838, Mansfield, Nottinghamshire. *d:* 8.5.1910, Stafford. Son of John sen (Nottinghamshire 1830). Opening batsman. *Team* Nottinghamshire (1865, 1 match).
Career batting
1–1–0–7–7–7.00–0–*ct* 0

Hilton, Malcolm Jameson
Professional. *b:* 2.8.1928, Chadderton, Lancashire. *d:* 8.7.1990, Oldham, Lancashire. Brother of Jim (Lancashire and Somerset). Lower order right-hand batsman, slow left-arm bowler. *Team* Lancashire (1946–61, 241 matches). *Tour* MCC to India, Pakistan and Ceylon 1951/2. *Tests* England (1950 to 1951/2, 4 matches).
Career batting
270–324–42–3416–100*–12.11–1–*ct* 202
Bowling 19542–1006–19.42–51–8–8/19
Test batting
4–6–1–37–15–7.40–0–*ct* 1
Bowling 477–14–34.07–1–0–5/61

He took 100 wickets in a season four times (best 158, av 13.96, in 1956).

Hilton, Philip
Amateur. *b:* 10.3.1840, Selling, Faversham, Kent. *d:* 26.5.1906, St Pancras, London. Middle order right-hand batsman, good deep field. *Sch* Cheltenham. *Team* Kent (1865–73, 26 matches).
Career batting
33–56–1–621–74–11.29–0–*ct* 19

He was Treasurer of Kent CCC 1867–1871. His final first-class match was for MCC in 1874. It is assumed that 'H. Peters', who played for Kent in one match, is an alias for Philip Hilton.

Hincks, R. H.
Amateur. Middle order batsman, change bowler. *Team* Leicestershire (1895, 2 matches).
Career batting
2–4–0–15–14–3.75–0–*ct* 1
Bowling 29–2–14.50–0–0–1/3

He first played for Leicestershire (pre first-class) in 1890.

Hind, Alfred Ernest
Amateur. *b:* 7.4.1878, Preston, Lancashire. *d:* 21.3.1947, Oadby, Leicestershire. Lower order right-hand batsman, right-arm medium pace bowler, slip field. *Sch* Uppingham. *Teams* Cambridge U (1898–1901, blue all four years); Nottinghamshire (1901, 1 match).
Career batting
37–62–14–681–54*–14.18–0–*ct* 37
Bowling 2148–80–26.85–3–0–7/30

An excellent rugby footballer, he won his blue and went on to represent England, and toured South Africa with the British Lions in 1903. He also won a blue for athletics.

Hind, Amos
Professional. *b:* 1.2.1849, Calverton, Nottinghamshire. *d:* 27.4.1931, Calverton, Nottinghamshire. Brother of Samuel (Nottinghamshire). Middle order right-hand batsman, right-hand medium pace round-arm bowler, deep field. *Team* Derbyshire (1876–77, 16 matches).
Career batting
16–30–0–392–77–13.06–0–*ct* 4
Bowling 419–24–17.45–0–0–4/9

Hind, Benjamin James
Amateur. *b:* 22.12.1882, Nottingham. *d:* 1.4.1974, Nottingham. Lower order right-hand batsman, leg break bowler. *Team* Nottinghamshire (1911, 1 match).
Career batting
1–2–0–28–23–14.00–0–*ct* 0
Bowling 42–0

Hind, Samuel
Professional. *b:* 14.12.1850, Calverton, Nottinghamshire. *d:* 28.3.1923, Calverton, Nottinghamshire. Brother of Amos (Derbyshire). Middle order right-hand batsman, left-hand fast round-arm bowler, good field. *Team* Nottinghamshire (1877–78, 6 matches).
Career batting
6–10–0–90–22–9.00–0–*ct* 2
Bowling 51–0

He also played for Worcestershire (pre first-class, 1881).

Hinde, Frank Langford
Amateur. *b:* 1869, Dublin, Ireland. *d:* 22.8.1931, Reigate, Surrey. Middle order right-hand batsman. *Team* Gloucestershire (1895, 1 match).
Career batting
1–2–0–5–3–2.50–0–*ct* 0

He played with success in the Cambridge Freshmen's Match of 1893, but in no first-class matches whilst at the University. He also played for Lincolnshire (1892–94).

Hinde, Harold Montague
Amateur. *b:* 24.8.1895, Southsea, Hampshire. *d:* 16.11.1965, Santa Margherita Liguse, Italy. Lower order right-hand batsman, right-arm fast bowler. *Sch* Wellington and Blundells. *Team* Minor Counties (1924).
Career batting
1–2–1–0–0*–0.00–0–*ct* 0
Bowling 138–9–15.33–1–0–8/77
His County cricket was for Berkshire (1921–32).

Hindlekar, Dattaram Dharmaji
Amateur. *b:* 1.1.1909, Bombay, India. *d:* 30.3.1949, Bombay, India. Uncle of V. L. Manjrekar (India). Originally opening, later lower order right-hand batsman, wicket-keeper. *Teams* Bombay (1934/5 to 1946/7); Hindus (1935/6 to 1945/6). *Tours* India to England 1936, 1946. *Tests* India (1936–46, 4 matches).
Career batting
96–151–8–2439–135–17.05–1–*ct* 128–*st* 59
Test batting
4–7–2–71–26–14.20–0–*ct* 3
Injury and blurred vision on the 1936 tour to England meant that he had very restricted opportunities. In 1946 he again was injured and in the absence of a competent deputy kept wicket when not fully fit.

Hindson, James Edward
Cricketer. *b:* 13.9.1973, Huddersfield, Yorkshire. Lower order right-hand batsman, slow left-arm bowler. *Team* Nottinghamshire (1992, 1 match).
Career batting
1 match, did not bat–*ct* 0
Bowling 74–8–9.25–1–0–5/42

Hine-Haycock, Rev Trevitt Reginald
(changed name from Haycock in 1878)
Amateur. *b:* 3.12.1861, Little Heath, Old Charlton, Kent. *d:* 2.11.1953, Bedford. He married the widow of W. A. Thornton (Oxford U). Steady opening right-hand batsman. *Sch* Wellington. *Teams* Oxford U (1882–84, blue 1883–84); Kent (1885–86, 6 matches). *Tours* Sanders to North America 1885, 1886.
Career batting
30–55–5–945–85–18.90–0–*ct* 23
Bowling 12–1–12.00–0–0–1/5
He also played for Devon (1882–88).

Hings, John Preston
Amateur. *b:* 22.12.1910, Leicester. Middle order right-hand batsman. *Team* Leicestershire (1934, 2 matches).
Career batting
2–4–0–18–10–4.50–0–*ct* 2
Bowling 4–0

Hinkly, Edmund
Professional. *b:* 12.1.1817, Benenden, Kent. *d:* 8.12.1880, Walworth, London. Tail end left-hand batsman, left-hand fast round-arm bowler, moderate field. *Teams* Kent (1846–58, 34 matches); Surrey (1848–53, 2 matches).
Career batting
43–77–27–318–24–6.36–0–*ct* 22
Bowling 1303–87 + 102–14.96–18–7–10/?
On his debut at Lord's, playing for Kent v England, he took all ten wickets in England's second innings (in addition to six in the first). His career was short but brilliant. He also played for Hampshire (not first-class, 1848), Northamptonshire (pre first-class, 1854), Rutland (1859) and Suffolk (1859).

Hinks, Simon Graham
Cricketer. *b:* 12.10.1960, Northfleet, Kent. Opening left-hand batsman, right-arm medium pace bowler, occasional wicket-keeper. *Teams* Kent (1982–91, 154 matches); Gloucestershire (1992, 10 matches).
Career batting
164–283–18–7971–234–30.07–11–*ct* 99
Bowling 381–8–47.62–0–0–2/18
He hit 1,000 runs in a season three times (best 1,588, av 36.93, in 1990). His highest score was 234 for Kent v Middlesex at Canterbury in 1990.

Hinwood, John William James
Amateur. *b:* 8.4.1894, Wilton, Wiltshire. *d:* 14.5.1971, Swansea, Glamorgan. Lower order right-hand batsman, right-arm fast medium bowler. *Team* Glamorgan (1923, 1 match).
Career batting
1–2–0–0–0–0.00–0–*ct* 0
Bowling 25–0
He first played for Glamorgan (pre first-class) in 1920.

Hipkin, Augustus Bernard
Professional. *b:* 8.8.1900, Brancaster, Norfolk. *d:* 11.2.1957, Carluke, Lanarkshire, Scotland. Lower order left-hand batsman, slow left-arm bowler, good field. *Team* Essex (1923–31, 231 matches).
Career batting
232–326–55–4239–108–15.64–2–*ct* 210
Bowling 13435–522–25.73–18–3–8/71
His best season was 1924 when he took 116 wickets, av 20.80. After leaving Essex he went to Scotland and appeared for Scotland in one non-first-class match. He played soccer for Charlton Athletic.

Hippisley, Harold Edwin
Amateur. *b:* 3.9.1890, Wells, Somerset. *d:* 23.10.1914, Langemarck, Belgium. He was killed in action. Middle order right-hand batsman. *Sch* Kings, Bruton. *Team* Somerset (1909–13, 7 matches).
Career batting
7–13–1–114–40*–9.50–0–*ct* 2
He was an excellent hockey player.

Hird, Sydney Francis
Professional. *b:* 7.1.1910, Balmain, Sydney, New South Wales, Australia. *d:* 20.12.1980, Bloemfontein, South Africa. Middle order right-hand batsman, leg break, later off break bowler. *Teams* New South Wales (1931/2 to 1932/3, 14 matches); Lancashire (1939, 1 match); Eastern Province (1945/6 to 1948/9); Border (1950/1).
Career batting
32–49–5–1453–130–33.02–5–*ct* 8
Bowling 1684–59–28.54–3–0–6/56
In 1934 he emigrated to England, becoming a professional in the Lancashire League – he neither batted or bowled in his single match for Lancashire, the game being ruined by rain. His first-class debut in England was for Sir L. Parkinson's XI in 1935.

Hirsch, John Gauntlett
Amateur. *b:* 20.2.1883, South Africa. *d:* 26.2.1958, Wynberg, Cape Town, South Africa. Middle order batsman, bowler. *Sch* Shrewsbury. *Teams* Cambridge U (1903–04); London County (1903–04).
Career batting
6–11–0–166–56–15.09–0–*ct* 4
Bowling 93–1–93.00–0–0–1/41
A noted rugby footballer, he toured England with the 1906 Springbok rugby team as centre three-quarter.

Hirst, Christopher Halliwell
Cricketer. *b:* 27.5.1947, Odsall, Bradford, Yorkshire. Opening right-hand batsman, off break bowler. *Sch* Merchant Taylors. *Team* Cambridge U (1967).
Career batting
1–2–1–8–6*–8.00–0–*ct* 0
His County cricket was for Buckinghamshire (1967–68).

Hirst, Edward Theodore
Amateur. *b:* 6.5.1857, New House, Deighton, Huddersfield, Yorkshire. *d:* 26.10.1914, Barnwood, Gloucestershire. Brother of E. W. (Yorkshire). Middle order right-hand batsman, good field. *Sch* Rugby. *Teams* Yorkshire (1877–88, 21 matches); Oxford U (1878–80, blue all three years).
Career batting
39–65–3–778–114–12.54–1–*ct* 17
An excellent rugby footballer, he gained his blue at Oxford.

Hirst, Ernest William
Amateur. *b:* 27.2.1855, New House, Deighton, Huddersfield, Yorkshire. *d:* 24.10.1933, Evershot, Dorchester, Dorset. Brother of E. T. (Yorkshire). Middle order right-hand batsman, right-arm fast medium bowler. *Team* Yorkshire (1881, 2 matches).
Career batting
2–3–0–33–28–11.00–0–*ct* 0
Bowling 3–0

Hirst, George Herbert
Professional. *b:* 7.9.1871, Kirkheaton, Yorkshire. *d:* 10.5.1954, Lindley, Huddersfield, Yorkshire. Aggressive middle order right-hand batsman, left-arm medium fast bowler, excellent field. *Teams* Yorkshire (1891–1929, 718 matches); Europeans (1921/2). *Tours* Stoddart to Australia 1897/8; MCC to Australia 1903/4. *Tests* England (1897/8 to 1909, 24 matches).
Career batting
826–1217–152–36356–341–34.13–60–*ct* 604
Bowling 51372–2742–18.73–184–40–9/23
Test batting
24–38–3–790–85–22.57–0–*ct* 18
Bowling 1770–59–30.00–3–0–5/48
Achieving the unique feat in English first-class cricket of scoring 2,000 runs and taking 200 wickets in the same season, Hirst must rank among the greatest of all cricketers. No fewer than 19 times did he hit 1,000 runs in a season, going on to 2,000 three times, with 2,501, av 54.36, in 1904 as his highest aggregate. In 15 seasons he topped 100 wickets and once exceeded 200 – 208, av 16.50, in 1906.
Apart from his 2,000 runs and 200 wickets in a season, he made 2,000 runs and took 100 wickets in two other years and in all performed the 'double' fourteen times.
His highest innings was 341 for Yorkshire v Leicestershire at Leicester in 1905, and his three other scores over 200 were also for Yorkshire. To him is attributed the perfection of seam and swing bowling – he possessed the knack of making the ball dip into the batsman very late in its flight. His match winning performances with both bat and ball for Yorkshire are numerous, yet curiously he achieved very little for England and was among the 'also-rans' on both his tours to Australia. His best bowling was 9/23 for Yorkshire v Lancashire at Headingley in 1910.
He appeared in County cricket until 1929, but after 1921, when he began his 18-year engagement at Eton College, his first-class matches were very few.

Hirst, Thomas Henry
Professional. *b:* 21.5.1865, Lockwood, Huddersfield, Yorkshire. *d:* 3.4.1927, Meltham, Huddersfield, Yorkshire. Opening right-hand batsman, right-arm fast medium bowler. *Teams* Yorkshire (1899, 1 match); Scotland (1905).
Career batting
2–3–1–66–33–33.00–0–*ct* 1
Bowling 44–0
In the Yorkshire v Somerset match of 1899 he was not part of the Yorkshire Eleven, but came on as substitute when C. E. M. Wilson was injured, and was allowed to both bat and bowl with the consent of the Somerset captain.

Hirwani, Narendra Deepchand
Cricketer. *b:* 18.10.1968, Gorakhpur, India. Lower order right-hand batsman, leg break and googly

bowler. *Team* Madhya Pradesh (1984/5 to 1991/2). *Tours* India to Sharjah (not first-class) 1987/8, 1988/9, to Bangladesh (not first-class) 1988/9, to West Indies 1988/9, to New Zealand 1989/90, to England 1990, to Australia 1991/2. *Tests* India (1987/8 to 1990/1, 14 matches).
Career batting
57–60–27–334–33–10.12–0–*ct* 24
Bowling 7175–227–31.60–17–3–8/61
Test batting
14–18–10–45–17–5.62–0–*ct* 5
Bowling 1799–58–31.01–3–1–8/61
He took 16 wickets in his Test debut v West Indies (Madras) 1987/8. He played in all three Tests in the 1990 tour to England and topped the tourists' first-class bowling averages with 31 wickets, av 41.29; his effectiveness was reduced by a badly injured spinning finger.

Hitch, John William
Professional. *b:* 7.5.1886, Radcliffe, Lancashire. *d:* 7.7.1965, Rumney, Cardiff, Glamorgan. Hard hitting lower order right-hand batsman, right-arm fast bowler, brilliant short-leg. *Team* Surrey (1907–25, 305 matches). *Tours* MCC to Australia 1911/12, 1920/1. *Tests* England (1911/12 to 1921, 7 matches).
Career batting
350–480–51–7643–107–17.81–3–*ct* 230
Bowling 29915–1387–21.56–101–24–8/38
Test batting
7–10–3–103–51*–14.71–0–*ct* 4
Bowling 325–7–46.42–0–0–2/31
He took 100 wickets in a season seven times (best 174, av 18.55, in 1913). A great bowler for Surrey, he achieved very little on his appearances in Tests or on either of his two tours to Australia. He hit 1,061 runs, av 31.20, in 1921. He was a first-class umpire (1932–36), standing in four Test matches (including three in India 1933/4).

Hitchcock, Lt Gen Sir Basil Ferguson Burnett
(also known as Burnett-Hitchcock)
Amateur. *b:* 3.3.1877, Chatham, Kent. *d:* 23.11.1938, Westminster, London. Son-in-law of J. Robertson (Middlesex). *Sch* Harrow and Brighton. *Team* Hampshire (1896, 2 matches).
Career batting
2–3–0–33–21–11.00–0–*ct* 0

Hitchcock, Raymond Edward
Professional, but amateur 1957–59. *b:* 28.11.1929, Christchurch, New Zealand. Middle order left-hand batsman, leg break and googly bowler. *Teams* Canterbury (1947/8); Warwickshire (1949–64, 319 matches).
Career batting
323–519–71–12473–153*–27.84–13–*ct* 113
Bowling 5845–196–29.82–7–1–7/76
He hit 1,000 runs in a season five times (best 1,840, av 34.07, in 1961). A good rugby scrum half, he appeared for Nuneaton.

Hoad, Edward Lisle Goldsworthy
Amateur. *b:* 29.1.1896, Richmond, St Michael, Barbados. *d:* 5.3.1986, Bridgetown, Barbados. Father of E. L. G. jun (Barbados), brother of J. J. S. (Barbados) and W. C. (Barbados and Trinidad), cousin of Edwin (Barbados). Opening right-hand batsman, leg break and googly bowler. *Team* Barbados (1921/2 to 1937/8). *Tours* West Indies to England 1928, 1933. *Tests* West Indies (1928 to 1933, 4 matches).
Career batting
63–104–13–3502–174*–38.48–8–*ct* 26
Bowling 1923–53–36.28–1–0–5/84
Test batting
4–8–0–98–36–12.25–0–*ct* 1
He topped the first-class batting averages for the 1928 tour (765 runs, av 36.42) but was not so successful in 1933 though he hit 1,083 runs, av 27.76, as he failed in both the Tests in which he took part. He captained West Indies in one Test.

Hoadley, Simon Peter
Cricketer. *b:* 16.8.1956, Eridge, Sussex. Brother of S. J. (Sussex). Middle order right-hand batsman, off break bowler. *Team* Sussex (1978–79, 12 matches).
Career batting
12–19–0–329–112–17.31–1–*ct* 5

Hoadley, Stephen John
Cricketer. *b:* 7.7.1955, Pembury, Kent. Brother of S. P. (Sussex). Middle order right-hand batsman, off break bowler. *Team* Sussex (1975–76, 7 matches).
Career batting
7–13–2–202–58–18.36–0–*ct* 3
Bowling 22–0

Hoar, Charles James
Amateur. *b:* 28.7.1862, Witley, Surrey. *d:* 25.6.1913, Ash Vale, Farnham, Surrey. Middle order right-hand batsman. *Team* Sussex (1885, 1 match).
Career batting
1–2–1–12–8–12.00–0–*ct* 0
Bowling 28–0

Hoare, Arthur
Amateur. *b:* 16.9.1840, Withyham, Sussex. *d:* 26.12.1896, Edenbridge, Kent. Middle order right-hand batsman, bowler. *Teams* Sussex (1869–73, 2 matches); Kent (1871, 1 match).
Career batting
3–6–0–87–39–14.50–0–*ct* 1
Bowling 37–1–37.00–0–0–1/37

Hoare, Rev Arthur Robertson
Amateur. *b:* 17.10.1871, Stibbard, Norfolk. *d:* 18.3.1941, Ashill, Thetford, Norfolk. Nephew of William (Gentlemen of Kent), son-in-law of J. Marsham (Kent), brother-in-law of W. J. Marsham (India).

Middle order right-hand batsman, right-arm medium pace bowler. *Sch* Eton. *Team* MCC (1903).
Career batting
1–2–0–45–41–22.50–0–*ct* 2
Bowling 19–0
His County cricket was for Norfolk (1890–1907). He played no first-class cricket whilst at Cambridge U, but did win a blue for soccer.

Hoare, Charles Arthur Richard
Amateur. *b:* 18.5.1847, Blackfriars, London. *d:* 22.5.1908, Hall Place, West Meon, Hampshire. Middle order right-hand batsman. *Team* Kent (1872, 1 match).
Career batting
1–2–0–18–14–9.00–0–*ct* 0
He was President of Hampshire 1905–08. He founded and maintained the training ship *Mercury* on the Hamble.

Hoare, Charles Hugh
Amateur. *b:* 24.10.1819, Mitcham, Surrey. *d:* 4.4.1869, Roke Abbey, Romsey, Hampshire. Son of G. M. (Surrey 1807), father of C. T. (Surrey and Middlesex), brother of H. W. (Oxford U). Hard hitting middle order right-hand batsman. *Sch* Rugby. *Team* Surrey (1846–53, 17 matches).
Career batting
36–59–5–507–58–9.38–0–*ct* 9
Bowling 2 wickets (no analyses)–0–0–2/?
His last first-class match was for Gentlemen of South in 1858. He also played for Devon (1851).

Hoare, Charles Twysden
Amateur. *b:* 10.11.1851, Mitcham, Surrey. *d:* 22.1.1935, Bignell Park, Bicester, Oxfordshire. Son of C. H. (Surrey), grandson of G. M. (Surrey 1807), nephew of H. J. (MCC 1835). Middle order right-hand batsman, excellent field. *Sch* Eton. *Teams* Surrey (1871–74, 4 matches); Middlesex (1875, 1 match).
Career batting
10–18–0–139–35–7.72–0–*ct* 4
He was not in the eleven whilst at Oxford. He also played for Devon (1869). His final first-class match was for MCC in 1878.

Hoare, Ernest Stanley
Amateur. *b:* 21.6.1903, Upper Clatford, Andover, Hampshire. Middle order right-hand batsman. *Sch* Dean Close. *Team* Gloucestershire (1929, 3 matches).
Career batting
3–4–0–16–10–4.00–0–*ct* 1
He played in no first-class cricket whilst at Cambridge U, but did win a blue for hockey and also played for England.

Hoare, Henry William
(changed name to Hamilton-Hoare in 1908)
Amateur. *b:* 1.4.1844, Oakfield Lodge, Three Bridges, Sussex. *d:* 7.9.1931, Pimlico, Westminster, London. Great-nephew of G. M. (Surrey 1807), brother of H. N. (Sussex 1853). Opening/middle order batsman. *Sch* Eton. *Team* Oxford U (1865).
Career batting
5–6–0–43–33–7.16–0–*ct* 0
His final first-class match was for MCC in 1867.

Hoare, Wilfred Norman Stewart
Amateur. *b:* 23.10.1909, Gloucester. Lower order right-hand batsman, wicket-keeper. *Team* Cambridge U (1931).
Career batting
1–2–1–15–11*–15.00–0–*ct* 1–*st* 1

Hoare, William
Amateur. *b:* 15.9.1847, Westminster, London. *d:* 22.7.1925, Benenden, Kent. Uncle of A. R. (MCC). Lower order batsman. *Sch* Eton. *Team* Gentlemen of Kent (1879).
Career batting
1–1–0–9–9–9.00–0–*ct* 3
He was President of Kent in 1900.

Hobbs, John Anthony David
Amateur. *b:* 30.11.1935, Aigburth, Liverpool, Lancashire. Opening right-hand batsman. *Sch* Liverpool College. *Team* Oxford U (1956–58, blue 1957).
Career batting
18–36–1–614–95–17.54–0–*ct* 18
He represented Lancashire at hockey.

Hobbs, Sir John Berry
Professional. *b:* 16.12.1882, Cambridge. *d:* 21.12.1963, Hove, Sussex. Brilliant opening right-hand batsman, right-arm medium pace bowler, excellent cover. *Team* Surrey (1905–34, 598 matches). *Tours* MCC to Australia 1907/8, 1911/12, 1920/1, 1924/5, 1928/9, to South Africa 1909/10, 1913/14; Vizianagram's XI to India and Ceylon 1930/1. *Tests* England (1907/8 to 1930, 61 matches).
Career batting
834–1325–107–61760–316*–50.70–199–*ct* 340
Bowling 2704–108–25.04–3–0–7/56
Test batting
61–102–7–5410–211–56.94–15–*ct* 17
Bowling 165–1–165.00–0–0–1/19
'The Master' certainly earned his sobriquet. Although his figures as a batsman were later dwarfed by Bradman's achievements, many still ranked Hobbs the better of the two, stating that Hobbs scored his runs in a more attractive manner and was more capable on difficult wickets. Certainly he was recognised as the finest English batsman of his generation and for most of his career an essential part of the England side. He holds the record for the most runs scored in a first-class career as well as the most centuries. In 24 English seasons he completed 1,000 runs, going on to 2,000 17 times and in 1925 reaching 3,000 for the only time – 3,024, av 70.32. In 1926 he averaged

77.60 and the following year 82.00. He also hit 1,000 in a season in South Africa twice.

His highest score was 316* for Surrey v Middlesex at Lord's in 1926, but he made 15 other scores of 200 or more.

As an opening batsman he was fortunate to be associated with three distinguished partners; with Hayward he added a century for the first wicket on 40 occasions, with Sandham on 66 occasions and with Sutcliffe for England on 11 occasions. In all he was involved in 166 first-wicket three-figure partnerships.

He rarely failed in Test cricket, being the first batsman to reach a Test aggregate of 5,000 runs, and he was equally successful on his five consecutive Test tours to Australia.

He was an active member of Surrey CCC Committee from his retirement to his death and was knighted for his services to the game in 1953. Before appearing for Surrey he played for Cambridgeshire (1901–04).

Hobbs, Norman Frederick Charles
Professional. *b:* 17.10.1900, Cheltenham, Gloucestershire. *d:* 6.4.1966, Weston, Bath, Somerset. Middle order batsman. *Team* Gloucestershire (1924, 6 matches).
Career batting
6–10–1–53–28–5.88–0–*ct* 5

Hobbs, Robin Nicholas Stuart
Professional. *b:* 8.5.1942, Chippenham, Wiltshire. Lower order right-hand batsman, leg break and googly bowler. *Teams* Essex (1961–75, 325 matches); Glamorgan (1979–81, 41 matches). *Tours* MCC to East Africa 1963/4, to South Africa 1964/5, to Pakistan 1966/7, 1968/9, to West Indies 1967/8; Cavaliers to Jamaica 1963/4; Norfolk to West Indies 1969/70; Robins to South Africa 1972/3; Commonwealth to Pakistan 1970/1; Rest of World to Pakistan 1973/4. *Tests* England (1967–71, 7 matches).
Career batting
440–546–138–4940–100–12.10–2–*ct* 295
Bowling 29776–1099–27.09–50–8–8/63
Test batting
7–8–3–34–15*–6.80–0–*ct* 8
Bowling 481–12–40.08–0–0–3/25

He took 100 wickets in a season twice (best 102, av 21.40, in 1970). For Essex v Australians at Chelmsford in 1975 he hit 100 in 44 minutes. In 1979 he captained Glamorgan. He also played for Suffolk (1976–78 and 1982).

Hobgen, Arthur
Amateur. *b:* 3.9.1849, Sidlesham, Chichester, Sussex. *d:* 26.3.1886, Appledram, Chichester, Sussex. Lower order left-hand batsman, right-hand slow round-arm bowler, good deep field. *Team* Sussex (1872–73, 3 matches).
Career batting
3–5–1–31–12–7.75–0–*ct* 1
Bowling 25–2–12.50–0–0–2/22

Hobson, Barry Sinton
Amateur. *b:* 22.11.1925, Dunmurry, Co Antrim, Ireland. Lower order right-hand batsman, right-arm medium pace bowler. *Sch* Taunton. *Team* Cambridge U (1946, blue).
Career batting
7–14–3–50–16*–4.54–0–*ct* 1
Bowling 460–10–46.00–0–0–3/60

His County cricket was for Wiltshire (1950–53).

Hockey, George William
Professional. *b:* 1.1.1905, Ipswich, Suffolk. Middle order right-hand batsman, right-arm medium pace bowler. *Sch* Ipswich. *Team* Essex (1928–31, 19 matches).
Career batting
19–33–5–305–23–10.89–0–*ct* 4
Bowling 20–0

He also played for Suffolk (1935–48).

Hodder, Francis Samuel
Amateur. *b:* 11.2.1906, Ringabella House, Carrigaline, Co Cork, Ireland. *d:* 6.9.1943. He was killed in action over Germany. Lower order right-hand batsman, right-arm bowler. *Team* RAF (1931).
Career batting
1–2–2–11–10*–no av–0–*ct* 1
Bowling 69–1–69.00–0–0–1/69

Hodge, Robert Stevenson
Amateur. *b:* 5.11.1914, Greenock, Renfrew, Scotland. Lower order right-hand batsman, right-arm fast medium bowler. *Team* Scotland (1938–51).
Career batting
10–16–0–178–38–11.12–0–*ct* 2
Bowling 817–30–27.23–1–0–5/82

He played with success for Under 33 v Over 33 at Lord's in 1945. He played badminton for Scotland.

Hodges, Albert Edward
Amateur. *b:* 29.1.1905, Newport, Monmouthshire. *d:* 23.9.1986, Maindee, Newport, Monmouthshire. Middle order right-hand batsman. *Teams* Wales (1930); Glamorgan (1936, 1 match).
Career batting
2–4–0–14–8–3.50–0–*ct* 0
Bowling 23–0

He also played for Monmouthshire (1926–32).

Hodges, Dr Aubrey Davis
Amateur. *b:* 3.2.1912, Kampala, Uganda. *d:* 27.5.1944, Minna, Nigeria. Opening right-hand batsman, good field. *Sch* Epsom. *Team* MCC (1936).
Career batting
1–2–0–44–34–22.00–*ct* 0

Hodges, Harold Augustus
Amateur. *b:* 22.1.1886, Mansfield Woodhouse, Nottinghamshire. *d:* 22.3.1918, near Mesnil, France. He was killed in action. Middle order batsman. *Sch* Sedbergh. *Team* Nottinghamshire (1911–12, 3 matches).
Career batting
3–4–1–141–62–47.00–0–*ct* 1
He did not appear in first-class cricket whilst at Oxford. A noted rugby footballer, he played for Oxford U and England.

Hodgkins, Henry Joseph Jordan
Amateur. *b:* 11.11.1868, Cheltenham, Gloucestershire. *d:* 24.6.1952, Dorchester, Dorset. Middle order left-hand batsman, left-arm medium pace bowler. *Sch* Trent College. *Team* Gloucestershire (1900–01, 10 matches).
Career batting
10–17–1–209–44–13.06–0–*ct* 4
Bowling 183–5–36.60–0–0–3/68
He also played for Bedfordshire (1904–06) and Berkshire (1911).

Hodgkins, John Seymour
Amateur. *b:* 2.1.1916, West Bridgford, Nottingham. *d;* 16.8.1988, Stanton-on-the-Wolds, Nottinghamshire. He died whilst playing golf. Middle or lower order right-hand batsman, right-arm fast medium bowler. *Sch* Nottingham High School. *Team* Nottinghamshire (1938–51, 3 matches).
Career batting
3–5–0–106–44–21.20–0–*ct* 0
Bowling 238–3–79.33–0–0–1/55

Hodgkinson, Canon George Langton
Amateur. *b:* 13.10.1837, Kentish Town, London. *d:* 16.2.1915, Wotton-under-Edge, Gloucestershire. Middle order right-hand batsman, good field. *Sch* Harrow. *Teams* Oxford U (1857–59, blue all three years); Middlesex (1861, 1 match).
Career batting
11–18–1–129–22–7.58–0–*ct* 4
Bowling 61–13–4.69–2–0–5/6

Hodgkinson, Gerard William
Amateur. *b:* 19.2.1883, Clifton, Bristol. *d:* 6.10.1960, Wookey Hole, Somerset. Grandson of R. S. Philpott (Victoria). Middle order right-hand batsman. *Sch* Eton. *Team* Somerset (1904–11, 19 matches).
Career batting
19–35–1–515–99*–15.14–0–*ct* 6

Hodgkinson, Gilbert Frank
Amateur. *b:* 19.2.1913, Derby. *d:* 7.1.1987, Mickleover, Derbyshire. Middle order right-hand batsman, good field. *Sch* Derby. *Team* Derbyshire (1935–46, 19 matches).
Career batting
19–32–0–472–44–14.75–0–*ct* 10
He captained Derbyshire in 1946.

Hodgkinson, J.
Professional. Lower order batsman, bowler. *Team* Derbyshire (1882, 1 match).
Career batting
1–2–0–5–5–2.50–0–*ct* 1
Bowling 83–1–83.00–0–0–1/83

Hodgson, Alan
Cricketer. *b:* 27.10.1951, Moorside, Consett, Co Durham. Lower order left-hand batsman, right-arm fast medium bowler. *Team* Northamptonshire (1970–79, 99 matches).
Career batting
99–118–24–909–41*–9.67–0–*ct* 31
Bowling 5964–206–28.95–2–0–5/30

Hodgson, Craig Andrew Thornton
Cricketer. *b:* 13.7.1955, East London, South Africa. Hard hitting middle order right-hand batsman. *Team* Zimbabwe (1979/80 to 1986/7). *Tour* Zimbabwe to England 1982.
Career batting
8–13–1–300–87–25.00–0–*ct* 6
Bowling 3–0

Hodgson, Geoffrey
Cricketer. *b:* 24.7.1938, Lepton, Huddersfield, Yorkshire. Lower order right-hand batsman, wicket-keeper. *Teams* Yorkshire (1964, 1 match); Lancashire (1965, 1 match).
Career batting
2–2–0–5–4–2.50–0–*ct* 3–*st* 2

Hodgson, Geoffrey Dean
Cricketer. *b:* 22.10.1966, Carlisle, Cumberland. Opening right-hand batsman. *Team* Gloucestershire (1989–92, 71 matches).
Career batting
71–119–7–3705–147–33.08–5–*ct* 30
Bowling 65–0
He also played for Cumberland (1984–88) and in Sunday League matches for Warwickshire in 1987. He reached 1,000 runs in a season three times (best 1,320, av 36.66, in 1990).

Hodgson, Gordon
Professional. *b:* 16.4.1904, Johannesburg, South Africa. *d:* 14.6.1951, Stoke-on-Trent, Staffordshire. Lower order right-hand batsman, right-arm fast bowler. *Team* Lancashire (1928–33, 56 matches).
Career batting
56–52–17–244–20–6.97–0–*ct* 37
Bowling 4107–148–27.75–4–0–6/77
A well-known soccer player, he appeared as a forward for Liverpool, Aston Villa and Leeds United, as well as for England. He toured England with the South African soccer team in 1924.

Hodgson, Herbert William
Amateur. *b:* 23.5.1891, Toxteth Park, Liverpool, Lancashire. *d:* 30.4.1964, Sewardstone, Chelmsford,

Hodgson, Isaac

Essex. Middle order right-hand batsman. *Team* Minor Counties (1924–27).
Career batting
2–4–0–79–45–19.75–0–*ct* 1
His County cricket was for Cheshire (1914–32).

Hodgson, Isaac
Professional. *b:* 15.11.1828, Bradford, Yorkshire. *d:* 24.11.1867, Bowling, Bradford, Yorkshire. Lower order right-hand batsman, left-hand slow round-arm bowler. *Team* Yorkshire (1852–66, 30 matches).
Career batting
39–65–21–329–32–7.47–0–*ct* 30
Bowling 2750–175–15.71–9–2–7/23
He also played for Northumberland (1860), Lincolnshire (1861–62) and Shropshire (1866). He was also a noted knurr and spell player.

Hodgson, Kenneth Ian
Cricketer. *b:* 24.2.1960, Port Elizabeth, South Africa. Lower order right-hand batsman, right-arm medium pace bowler. *Sch* Oundle. *Team* Cambridge U (1981–83, blue all three years).
Career batting
27–34–9–633–50–25.32–0–*ct* 4
Bowling 2093–55–38.05–1–1–8/68
His County cricket was for Buckinghamshire (1980–88). He also represented Cambridge at squash.

Hodgson, Philip
Professional. *b:* 21.9.1935, Todmorden, Yorkshire. Lower order right-hand batsman, right-arm fast medium bowler. *Team* Yorkshire (1954–56, 13 matches).
Career batting
17–11–4–65–26–9.28–0–*ct* 7
Bowling 946–39–24.25–1–0–5/41
His final first-class match was for Combined Services in 1957.

Hodgson, Rev Richard Greaves
Amateur. *b:* 9.3.1845, Manchester, Lancashire. *d:* 1.11.1931, Canterbury, Kent. Middle order right-hand batsman, point field. *Team* Kent (1871–74, 3 matches).
Career batting
3–6–0–77–47–12.83–0–*ct* 3

Hodson, James
Professional. *b:* 30.10.1808, Streat-Place, Ditchling, Sussex. *d:* 17.3.1879, Hunston Mill, Sussex. Hard-hitting right-hand batsman, right-hand medium pace round-arm bowler. *Team* Sussex (1838–54, 51 matches).
Career batting
54–95–16–620–44–7.84–0–*ct* 48
Bowling 454–29 + 66–15.65–3–0–8/?
One of the leading Sussex players of his day, he was no-balled for bowling with his arm above his shoulder at Lord's in 1839, one umpire considering his delivery fair, whilst the other not.

Hodson, Richard Phillip
Cricketer. *b:* 26.4.1951, Horbury, Wakefield, Yorkshire. Brother-in-law of A. W. Greig (Sussex) and I. A. Greig (Sussex and Surrey). Opening right-hand batsman, right-arm medium pace bowler. *Sch* Queen Elizabeth GS, Wakefield. *Team* Cambridge U (1971–73, blue 1972–73).
Career batting
19–36–3–687–111–20.81–1–*ct* 8
Bowling 766–29–26.41–0–0–4/54
He played rugby for Western Transvaal.

Hoey, Conor Joseph
Cricketer. *b:* 24.3.1968, Dublin, Ireland. Lower order right-hand batsman, leg break bowler. *Team* Ireland (1991–92).
Career batting
2–3–1–16–8–8.00–0–*ct* 0
Bowling 144–5–28.80–0–0–3/38

Hoffman, Dean Stuart
Cricketer. *b:* 13.1.1966, Erdington, Birmingham. Lower order right-hand batsman, right-arm medium fast bowler. *Teams* Warwickshire (1985, 17 matches); Northamptonshire (1988, 1 match).
Career batting
18–16–5–59–20*–5.36–0–*ct* 4
Bowling 1257–31–40.54–0–0–4/100
He also played for Cambridgeshire (1989).

Hoffman, Dr Myer
Amateur. *b:* 21.7.1902, Leeds, Yorkshire. *d:* 14.10.1959, Lourenco Marques, Mozambique. Tail end right-hand batsman, right-arm medium pace bowler. *Team* Dublin University (1925).
Career batting
1–2–1–6–6*–6.00–0–*ct* 0
Bowling 18–0

Hofmeyr, Murray Bernard
Amateur. *b:* 9.12.1925, Pretoria, South Africa. Sound opening right-hand batsman. *Teams* Oxford U (1949–51, blue all three years); North East Transvaal (1951/2 to 1953/4).
Career batting
44–81–10–3178–161–44.76–7–*ct* 29
Bowling 12–1–12.00–0–0–1/0
He hit 1,063 runs, av 55.94, in 1950. He captained Oxford in 1951. A noted rugby footballer, he obtained his blue and went on to represent England as full-back.

Hogan, Charles Ronald
Amateur. *b:* 10.1.1939, Paisley, Renfrew, Scotland. Lower order right-hand batsman, right-arm fast medium bowler. *Team* Scotland (1962–64).
Career batting
6–6–0–25–7–4.16–0–*ct* 2
Bowling 415–24–17.29–2–0–6/36

Hogan, Raymond P.
Professional. *b:* 8.5.1932, Temora, New South Wales, Australia. Hard-hitting right-hand batsman, right-arm fast medium bowler. *Team* Northamptonshire (1954–55, 3 matches).
Career batting
3–4–0–18–8–4.50–0–*ct* 2
Bowling 218–3–72.66–0–0–2/16
A rugby footballer, he played for Northampton.

Hogg, Arthur
Professional. *b:* 20.6.1877, Ripley, Derbyshire. *d:* 21.4.1956, Ripley, Derbyshire. Middle order right-hand batsman. *Team* Derbyshire (1905–06, 3 matches).
Career batting
3–6–0–5–4–0.83–0–*ct* 0

Hogg, Rodney Malcolm
Cricketer. *b:* 5.3.1951, Richmond, Melbourne, Victoria, Australia. Lower order right-hand batsman, right-arm fast bowler. *Teams* South Australia (1975/6 to 1983/4, 39 matches); Victoria (1984/5, 2 matches). *Tours* Australia to England 1979 (World Cup), 1981, 1983 (World Cup), to India 1979/80, 1984/5 (not first-class), to Sri Lanka 1980/1, 1982/3, to West Indies 1983/4; Australian XI to South Africa 1985/6, 1986/7. *Tests* Australia (1978/9 to 1984/5, 38 matches).
Career batting
107–141–28–1185–52–10.48–0–*ct* 25
Bowling 9211–378–24.36–20–4–7/53
Test batting
38–58–13–439–52–9.75–0–*ct* 7
Bowling 3503–123–28.47–6–2–6/74
In the 1978/9 series against England, when the leading Australian players were appearing in World Series Cricket, he created a sensation by taking a record 41 wickets, av 12.85, but on the 1981 tour to England he played in only two Tests and in first-class matches took 27 wickets, av 24.33.

Hogg, Vincent Richard
Cricketer. *b:* 3.7.1952, Salisbury, Rhodesia. Lower order right-hand batsman, right-arm fast medium bowler. *Team* Rhodesia/Zimbabwe (1971/2 to 1983/4). *Tours* Zimbabwe to England 1982, 1983 (World Cup).
Career batting
43–54–20–181–30–5.32–0–*ct* 12
Bowling 3234–123–26.29–3–0–6/26

Hogg, William
Cricketer. *b:* 12.7.1955, Ulverston, Lancashire. Son-in-law of S. Ramadhin (Lancashire and West Indies). Lower order right-hand batsman, right-arm fast bowler. *Teams* Lancashire (1976–80, 44 matches); Warwickshire (1981–83, 50 matches).
Career batting
96–90–25–394–31–6.06–0–*ct* 19
Bowling 6437–222–28.99–6–1–7/84

Hoggarth, Francis Harry
Amateur. *b:* 17.10.1876, Whitby, Yorkshire. *d:* 7.1.1961, Aberdeen, Scotland. Middle order batsman. *Team* Scotland (1906).
Career batting
1–2–0–38–22–19.00–0–*ct* 0

Hogsflesh, William
Professional. *b:* 1744. *d:* April 1818, Southwick, Hampshire. Lower order batsman, excellent bowler. *Team* Hampshire (1769–75).
He was one of the most famous bowlers connected with the Hambledon Club, but his career seems to have been a short one, ending when he was only 32 years of age.

Hohns, Trevor Victor
Cricketer. *b:* 23.1.1954, Nundah, Brisbane, Queensland, Australia. Middle order left-hand batsman, leg break bowler. *Team* Queensland (1972/3 to 1990/1, 120 matches). *Tours* Australian XI to South Africa 1985/6, 1986/7; Australia to England 1989. *Tests* Australia (1988/9 to 1989, 7 matches).
Career batting
152–232–40–5210–103–27.13–2–*ct* 86
Bowling 10701–288–37.15–11–1–6/56
Test batting
7–7–1–136–40–22.66–0–*ct* 3
Bowling 580–17–34.11–0–0–3/59
He appeared in five of the six 1989 Tests in England and bowled accurate leg breaks. After the tour he announced his retirement, and did not play in Australia in 1989/90, but the following Australian season he was appointed the Queensland captain.

Holbech, William Hugh
Amateur. *b:* 18.8.1882, Murray Bay, Canada. *d:* 1.11.1914, Kidbrooke, London. Nephew of W. H. Walrond (MCC). Middle order right-hand batsman. *Sch* Eton. *Team* Warwickshire (1910, 1 match).
Career batting
3–6–0–28–21–4.66–0–*ct* 1
His first-class debut was for MCC in 1908.

Holden, Cecil
Amateur. *b:* 1.6.1865, West Derby, Liverpool. *d:* 22.8.1928, Claughton, Cheshire. Hard-hitting middle order right-hand batsman, right-arm medium pace bowler, good slip. *Team* Lancashire (1890, 3 matches).
Career batting
8–14–1–136–45–10.46–0–*ct* 6
Bowling 63–1–63.00–0–0–1/29
Most of his County cricket was for Cheshire (1886–95) and he captained Birkenhead Park for 20 years. He also played for Liverpool and District (1886–91).

Holden, Stanley Mitton
Professional. *b:* 25.1.1886, Chesterfield, Derbyshire. *d:* 10.5.1971, Coventry, Warwickshire. Lower order right-hand batsman, left-arm fast medium bowler. *Team* Derbyshire (1910–20, 4 matches).
Career batting
4–6–2–13–6*–3.25–0–*ct* 1
Bowling 111–3–37.00–0–0–3/72

Holder, John Wakefield
Cricketer. *b:* 19.3.1945, Superlative, St George, Barbados. Lower order right-hand batsman, right-arm fast medium bowler. *Team* Hampshire (1968–72, 47 matches).
Career batting
47–49–14–374–33–10.68–0–*ct* 12
Bowling 3415–139–24.56–5–1–7/79
He joined the umpires' list in 1983, standing in 10 Test matches (including four in Pakistan) 1988–91.

Holder, Vanburn Alonzo
Cricketer. *b:* 10.10.1945, Deans Village, St Michael, Barbardos. Lower order right-hand batsman, right-arm fast medium bowler. *Teams* Barbardos (1966/7 to 1977/8); Worcestershire (1968–80, 181 matches); Orange Free State (1985/6). *Tours* West Indies to England 1969, 1973, 1975 (World Cup), 1976, to India, Sri Lanka and Pakistan 1974/5, to Australia 1975/6, to India and Sri Lanka 1978/9; Rest of World to Pakistan 1973/4. *Tests* West Indies (1969 to 1978/9, 40 matches).
Career batting
313–358–81–3593–122–12.97–1–*ct* 99
Bowling 23300–950–24.52–38–3–7/40
Test batting
40–59–11–682–42–14.20–0–*ct* 16
Bowling 3627–109–33.27–3–0–6/28
The most successful of his three tours to England was in 1976 when he took 52 wickets, av 19.30. He also played for Shropshire (1981). He became a first-class umpire in 1992.

Holding, Michael Anthony
Cricketer. *b:* 16.2.1954, Half Way Tree, Kingston, Jamaica. Lower order right-hand batsman, right-arm fast bowler. *Teams* Jamaica (1972/3 to 1988/9); Lancashire (1981, 7 matches); Tasmania (1982/3, 7 matches); Derbyshire (1983–89, 66 matches); Canterbury (1987/8). *Tours* West Indies to Australia 1975/6, 1979/80, 1981/2, 1983/4 (not first-class), 1984/5, 1986/7, to England 1976, 1979 (World Cup), 1980, 1983 (World Cup), 1984, to New Zealand 1979/80, 1986/7, to Pakistan 1980/1, 1985/6 (not first-class), to India 1983/4, to Sharjah (not first-class) 1985/6; International XI to Pakistan 1981/2. *Tests* West Indies (1975/6 to 1986/7, 60 matches).
Career batting
222–283–43–3600–80–15.00–0–*ct* 125
Bowling 18233–778–23.43–39–5–8/92
Test batting
60–76–10–910–73–13.78–0–*ct* 22
Bowling 5898–249–23.68–13–2–8/92
On his first tour to England in 1976 he headed the first-class and Test bowling averages with 55 wickets, av 14.38, and 28, av 12.71, respectively. In 1980 he again played in all the Tests, but proved more expensive, his record in the Tests being 20 wickets, av 31.60. On his final tour to England in 1984 he bowled off a shorter run, but still commanded respect and played in four Tests. His best season with Derbyshire was 1986 when he took 52 wickets, av 20.09.

Holdship, William Ernest Johnstone
Amateur. *b:* 15.2.1872, Auckland, New Zealand. Brother of A. R. (Wellington). Middle order batsman. *Sch* Cheltenham. *Team* Middlesex (1894, 3 matches).
Career batting
3–5–0–21–15–4.20–0–*ct* 2

Holdsworth, Romilly Lisle
Amateur. *b:* 25.2.1899, Mysore, India. *d:* 20.6.1976, Blagdon Hill, Somerset. Sound middle order right-hand batsman. *Sch* Repton. *Teams* Oxford U (1919–22, blue all four years); Warwickshire (1919–21, 30 matches); Sussex (1925–29, 36 matches); Northern India (1934/5); NWFP (1937/8 to 1941/2).
Career batting
109–197–17–4716–202–26.20–8–*ct* 51
Bowling 78–1–78.00–0–0–1/4
He hit 1,021 runs, av 26.17, in 1921. His only double century was 202 for Oxford U v Free Foresters at Oxford in 1921. Being in the scholastic profession his cricket after leaving Oxford was restricted and he later moved to India, where he was headmaster of Doon School, Dehra Dun. He also won a blue for relay races and soccer. He was botanist to the Mount Kamet Expedition, the first peak over 25,000 feet to be climbed.

Holdsworth, William Edgar Newman
Professional. *b:* 17.9.1928, Armley, Leeds, Yorkshire. Lower order right-hand batsman, right-arm fast medium bowler. *Team* Yorkshire (1952–53, 27 matches).
Career batting
27–26–12–111–22*–7.92–0–*ct* 7
Bowling 1598–53–30.15–2–0–6/58

Hole, Gilbert Lindsay Douglas
Amateur. *b:* 28.6.1882, Edinburgh, Scotland. *d:* 10.11.1967, Edinburgh, Scotland. Middle order right-hand batsman, right-arm medium pace bowler. *Sch* Edinburgh Academy. *Team* Scotland (1910–26).
Career batting
10–17–2–260–37–17.33–0–*ct* 2
Bowling 450–27–16.66–2–0–5/20

Hole, Graeme Blake
Amateur. *b:* 6.1.1931, Concord West, Sydney, New South Wales, Australia. *d:* 14.2.1990, Adelaide, South Australia. Middle order right-hand batsman, off break bowler. *Teams* New South Wales (1949/50, 1 match); South Australia (1950/1 to 1957/8, 51 matches); Commonwealth in Ceylon 1951/2. *Tour* Australia to England 1953. *Tests* Australia (1950/1 to 1954/5, 18 matches).
Career batting
98–166–12–5647–226–36.66–11–*ct* 82
Bowling 2686–61–44.03–1–0–5/109
Test batting
18–33–2–789–66–25.45–0–*ct* 21
Bowling 126–3–42.00–0–0–1/9
Although he played in all five Tests on the 1953 tour to England, he had only moderate success and in all first-class matches hit 1,118 runs, av 33.87. His highest score was 226 for South Australia v Queensland at Adelaide in 1953/4.

Holford, David Anthony Jerome
Cricketer. *b:* 16.4.1940, Upper Collymore Rock, St Michael, Barbados. Cousin of G. St. A. Sobers (West Indies and Nottinghamshire). Middle order right-hand batsman, leg break bowler. *Teams* Barbados (1960/1 to 1978/9); Trinidad (1962/3). *Tours* West Indies to England 1966, to India 1966/7, to Australia and New Zealand 1968/9; Barbados to England 1969. *Tests* West Indies (1966 to 1976/7, 24 matches).
Career batting
99–149–27–3821–111–31.31–3–*ct* 83
Bowling 8096–253–32.00–8–2–8/52
Test batting
24–39–5–768–105*–22.58–1–*ct* 18
Bowling 2009–51–39.39–1–0–5/23
He proved a most useful all-rounder on the 1966 tour to England and played in all five Tests – in first-class matches he hit 759 runs, av 37.95, and took 51 wickets, av 28.60. He was Assistant Manager of the 1991 West Indies team to England.

Holgate, Gideon
Professional. *b:* 23.6.1839, Sawley, Barnoldswick, Yorkshire. *d:* 11.7.1895, Accrington, Lancashire. Middle order right-hand batsman, wicket-keeper. *Teams* Yorkshire (1865–67, 12 matches); Lancashire (1866–67, 8 matches).
Career batting
20–34–1–455–65–13.78–0–*ct* 24–*st* 10

Holland, Frederick Charles
Professional. *b:* 10.2.1876, Battersea, London. *d:* 5.2.1957, Crystal Palace, London. Father-in-law of H. O. Bloomfield (Surrey). Middle order right-hand batsman, slow right-arm bowler. *Team* Surrey (1894–1908, 282 matches).
Career batting
284–429–29–10384–171–25.96–12–*ct* 232
Bowling 570–13–43.84–0–0–2/20
He hit 1,000 runs in a season four times (best 1,129, av 23.52, in 1903).

Holland, John
Professional. *b:* 7.4.1869, Nantwich, Cheshire. *d:* 22.8.1914, Bury, Lancashire. Middle order right-hand batsman. *Teams* Leicestershire (1894–96, 42 matches); Lancashire (1900–02, 12 matches).
Career batting
54–101–7–1650–65–17.55–0–*ct* 25
Bowling 54–0
He first played for Leicestershire (pre first-class) in 1889. He also played for Cheshire (1910–13).

Holland, Kenneth
Amateur. *b:* 29.3.1911, Rowley Fields, Leicester. *d:* 21.7.1986, Norwich, Norfolk. Lower order right-hand batsman, right-arm fast medium bowler. *Sch* Heriot's. *Team* Leicestershire (1935, 2 matches).
Career batting
2–2–0–2–2–1.00–0–*ct* 1
Bowling 146–3–48.66–0–0–1/9

Holland, Lawrence Edward
Amateur. *b:* 17.1.1887, Tinsley, Sheffield, Yorkshire. *d:* 3.7.1956, Desborough, Northamptonshire. Middle order right-hand batsman, slow right-arm bowler. *Team* Northamptonshire (1912–20, 10 matches).
Career batting
10–19–0–202–63–10.63–0–*ct* 1
Bowling 193–6–32.16–0–0–3/26

Holland, Robert George
Cricketer. *b:* 19.10.1946, Camperdown, Sydney, New South Wales, Australia. Lower order right-hand batsman, leg break bowler. *Teams* New South Wales (1978/9 to 1986/7, 68 matches); Wellington (1987/8). *Tours* Australia to England 1985; New South Wales to Zimbabwe 1985/6. *Tests* Australia (1984/5 to 1985/6, 11 matches).
Career batting
95–95–22–706–53–9.67–0–*ct* 54
Bowling 9857–316–31.16–14–3–9/83
Test batting
11–15–4–35–10–3.18–0–*ct* 5
Bowling 1352–34–39.76–3–2–6/54
He played in four Tests on the 1985 tour to England, but only in the Second Test at Lord's did his leg breaks prove of much value. He had taken ten wickets in the final Test of 1984/5 against the West Indies at Sydney, winning the match for Australia, and this proved to be the outstanding game of his international career.

Holland-Martin, Admiral Sir Deric Douglas Eric
(changed name from Holland in 1917)
Amateur. *b:* 10.4.1906, Kensington, London. *d:* 6.1.1977, Kemerton, Gloucestershire. Nephew of E. G. Bromley-Martin (Worcestershire) and G. E.

Bromley-Martin (Worcestershire). Lower order right-hand batsman, wicket-keeper. *Teams* Royal Navy (1928); Combined Services (1937).
Career batting
2–4–0–25–16–6.25–0–*ct* 7

Hollands, Frederick
Professional. *b:* 7.10.1822, Leeds, Kent. *d:* 30.6.1898, Broomfield, Kent. Opening left-hand batsman, slow left-hand round-arm bowler. *Team* Kent (1849–59, 29 matches).
Career batting
31–55–4–322–52–6.31–0–*ct* 25
Bowling 1258–100 + 24–12.58–11–0–6/15

Hollands, Sydney
Professional. *b:* 24.1.1866, East Grinstead, Sussex. *d:* 28.4.1949, Croydon, Surrey. Middle order batsman. *Team* Sussex (1887–93, 11 matches).
Career batting
11–21–0–154–21–7.33–0–*ct* 6

Hollick, Alexander Francis George Philip
Amateur. *b:* 13.2.1936, Cairo, Egypt. Middle order right-hand batsman. *Sch* Royal Belfast Academical Institution. *Team* Ireland (1957).
Career batting
1–2–0–0–0–0.00–0–*ct* 1

Holliday, David Charles
Cricketer. *b:* 20.12.1958, Cambridge. Lower order right-hand batsman, leg break bowler. *Sch* Oundle. *Team* Cambridge U (1979–81, blue all three years).
Career batting
29–37–8–522–76*–18.00–0–*ct* 15
Bowling 400–6–66.66–0–0–2/23
His County cricket was for Cambridgeshire (1979–87).

Hollies, William Eric
Professional. *b:* 5.6.1912, Old Hill, Staffordshire. *d:* 16.4.1981, Chinley, Derbyshire. Tail end right-hand batsman, leg break and googly bowler. *Team* Warwickshire (1932–57, 476 matches). *Tours* MCC to West Indies 1934/5, to Australia 1950/1. *Tests* England (1934/5 to 1950, 13 matches).
Career batting
515–616–282–1673–47–5.00–0–*ct* 179
Bowling 48656–2323–20.94–182–40–10/49
Test batting
13–15–8–37–18*–5.28–0–*ct* 2
Bowling 1332–44–30.27–5–0–7/50
He took 100 wickets in a season 14 times (best 184, av 15.60, in 1946); his outstanding analysis was for Warwickshire v Nottinghamshire at Edgbaston in 1946 when he took all ten wickets in the innings at a cost of 49 runs. His most famous wicket was that of Bradman, when the great Australian was making his final appearance in Test cricket at the Oval in 1948; Hollies bowled him before he had scored a run. He captained Warwickshire in 1956. He also played for Staffordshire (1958).

Hollingdale, Reginald Allen
Professional. *b:* 6.3.1906, Burgess Hill, Sussex. *d:* 3.8.1989, South Side, Edinburgh, Scotland. Lower order right-hand batsman, right-arm fast medium bowler. *Teams* Sussex (1925–30, 78 matches); Scotland (1938).
Career batting
79–115–35–1071–57–13.38–0–*ct* 38
Bowling 2644–84–31.47–2–0–5/23

Hollings, Herbert John Butler
Amateur. *b:* 18.6.1855, Manningham, Yorkshire. *d:* 6.3.1922, Bournemouth, Hampshire. Middle order right-hand batsman, off break bowler. *Sch* Winchester. *Team* Oxford U (1877).
Career batting
1–2–0–0–0–0.00–0–*ct* 0
He won a blue for rackets.

Hollington, Hugh Basil
Cricketer. *b:* 14.8.1949, Harpenden, Hertfordshire. Opening left-hand batsman. *Sch* Haileybury. *Team* Minor Counties (1972).
Career batting
1–2–0–21–15–10.50–0–*ct* 0
His County cricket was for Hertfordshire (1966–74).

Hollingworth, Thomas Vernon
Amateur. *b:* 27.7.1907, USA. *d:* 2.10.1973, Topsham, Devon. Middle order right-hand batsman, bowler. *Sch* Bromsgrove. *Teams* Hampshire (1929, 2 matches); Europeans (1932/3 to 1933/4).
Career batting
4–7–1–58–17–9.66–0–*ct* 0
Bowling 123–4–30.75–0–0–4/92
He also played for Devon (1933–48).

Hollins, Sir Arthur Meyrick
Amateur. *b:* 16.7.1876, Preston, Lancashire. *d:* 30.7.1938, Knot House, Walton-le-Dale, Lancashire. Brother of F. H. (Lancashire) and J. C. H. L. (Lancashire). Middle order right-hand batsman, excellent deep field. *Sch* Eton. *Team* Oxford U (1899–1900, blue 1899). *Tour* Bosanquet to North America 1901.
Career batting
12–20–2–389–63–21.61–0–*ct* 6
Bowling 249–3–83.00–0–0–1/19
A noted athlete, he ran in the 440 yards for Oxford in three seasons.

Hollins, Sir Frank Hubert
Amateur. *b:* 31.10.1877, Bowness-on-Windermere, Westmorland. *d:* 31.1.1963, Paddington, London. Brother of A. M. (Oxford U) and J. C. H. L. (Lancashire). Middle order right-hand batsman. *Sch* Eton. *Teams* Oxford U (1900–01, blue 1901); Lancashire (1902–04, 12 matches). *Tours* Bennett to West Indies

1901/2; Oxford U Authentics to India 1902/3.
Career batting
35–58–5–1114–114–21.01–1–*ct* 33
Bowling 87–3–29.00–0–0–2/39

He also played for Cumberland (1913). His first-class debut was for G. J. V. Weigall's XI in 1898 and his final first-class match for MCC in 1927. He was President of Lancashire 1919–20.

Hollins, John Chard Humphrey Lancelot
Amateur. *b:* 3.6.1890, Fulwood, Preston, Lancashire. *d:* 13.11.1938, Whittle-le-Woods, Lancashire. Brother of A. M. (Oxford U) and F. H. (Lancashire). Opening right-hand batsman. *Sch* Eton. *Team* Lancashire (1914–19, 20 matches).
Career batting
20–30–0–454–65–15.13–0–*ct* 8
Bowling 99–1–99.00–0–0–1/45

He appeared in the Freshmen's match at Oxford, but no first-class games.

Hollinshead, Cyril
Amateur. *b:* 26.5.1902, Timberland, Lincolnshire. Lower order left-hand batsman, left-arm fast medium bowler. *Team* Gloucestershire (1946, 1 match).
Career batting
1 match, did not bat –*ct* 0
Bowling 7–0

He also played for Lincolnshire (1931).

Holloway, Bernard Henry
Amateur. *b:* 13.1.1888, Burntwood Grange, Wandsworth Common, London. *d:* 27.9.1915, Loos, France. He was killed in action. Brother of N. J. (Sussex). Middle order right-hand batsman, right-arm fast medium bowler. *Sch* The Leys. *Team* Sussex (1911–14, 8 matches). *Tour* MCC to West Indies 1910/11.
Career batting
19–33–2–701–100–22.61–1–*ct* 13

He appeared in the Seniors' match at Cambridge but no first-class matches. He was a noted rugby footballer, appearing for Cambridge, and also excelled at lacrosse, appearing for both Cambridge and England.

Holloway, George James Warner Sinclair
Amateur. *b:* 26.4.1884, Stroud, Gloucestershire. *d:* 22.9.1966, Montpellier, Cheltenham, Gloucestershire. Middle order left-hand batsman. *Sch* Clifton. *Team* Gloucestershire (1908–11, 10 matches).
Career batting
10–20–1–187–34*–9.84–0–*ct* 4

Holloway, Norman James
Amateur. *b:* 11.11.1889, Burntwood Grange, Wandsworth Common, London. *d:* 17.8.1964, Walton-on-the-Hill, Surrey. Brother of B. H. (Sussex). Lower order right-hand batsman, right-arm fast bowler. *Sch* The Leys. *Teams* Cambridge U (1910–12, blue all three years); Sussex (1911–25, 67 matches).
Career batting
102–161–49–1227–55–10.95–0–*ct* 40
Bowling 8046–324–24.83–16–3–8/99

His final first-class match was for Free Foresters in 1928. He also won a blue for lacrosse.

Holloway, Piran Christopher Laity
Cricketer. *b:* 1.10.1970, Helston, Cornwall. Middle order left-hand batsman, wicket-keeper. *Sch* Millfield and Taunton. *Team* Warwickshire (1988–92, 11 matches).
Career batting
11–17–6–436–102*–39.63–1–*ct* 25–*st* 1

Holloway, Reginald Frederick Price
Amateur. *b:* 31.10.1904, Dursley, Gloucestershire. *d:* 12.2.1979, Bristol. Opening right-hand batsman. *Sch* Clifton. *Team* Gloucestershire (1923–26, 7 matches).
Career batting
7–12–3–108–28*–12.00–0–*ct* 4
Bowling 19–0

He appeared in the Freshmen's and Seniors' matches at Oxford, but no first-class games. He was President of Gloucestershire 1974–75. He represented England at bridge.

Holloway, William Octavius
Amateur. *b:* 15.9.1870, Ivy House, Charlbury, Oxfordshire. *d:* 2.12.1907, Farnborough, Hampshire. Tail end batsman, useful bowler. *Team* Sussex (1890, 1 match).
Career batting
4–5–2–36–18*–12.00–0–*ct* 1
Bowling 98–3–32.66–0–0–3/60

His final first-class match was for MCC in 1902.

Holman, John Charles
Amateur. *b:* 5.4.1938, Calcutta, India. Middle order right-hand batsman, wicket-keeper. *Sch* Tonbridge. *Team* Combined Services (1962–64).
Career batting
2–4–1–39–17–13.00–0–*ct* 3

Holmes, Albert John
Amateur. *b:* 30.6.1899, Thornton Heath, Surrey. *d:* 21.5.1950, Hollington, Hastings, Sussex. He died from a heart attack. Father of J. R. R. (Sussex). Middle order right-hand batsman. *Sch* Repton. *Team* Sussex (1922–39, 203 matches). *Tours* Manager of MCC to South Africa 1938/9; Proposed captain MCC to India 1939/40 (tour cancelled).
Career batting
208–320–24–6282–133*–21.22–6–*ct* 122
Bowling 425–8–53.12–0–0–1/2

He hit 1,000 runs in a season twice (best 1,134, av 24.65, in 1937). He was Chairman of the Test Match Selection Committee 1946 to 1949, and a member of the Committee in 1939. Serving in the RAF 1925–35, his important cricket was very restricted during this period. He captained Sussex 1936–39.

Holmes, Errol Reginald Thorold
Amateur. *b:* 21.8.1905, Calcutta, India. *d:* 16.8.1960, Marylebone, London. He died from a heart attack. Son-in-law of F. A. G. Leveson-Gower (Hampshire). Hard-hitting middle order right-hand batsman, right-arm fast, later medium pace bowler. *Sch* Malvern. *Teams* Surrey (1924–55, 198 matches); Oxford U (1925–27, blue all three years). *Tours* Tennyson to Jamaica 1926/7; MCC to West Indies 1934/5, to Australia and New Zealand 1935/6. *Tests* England (1934/5 to 1935, 5 matches).
Career batting
301–465–51–13598–236–32.84–24–*ct* 192
Bowling 9531–283–33.67–4–0–6/16
Test batting
5–9–2–114–85*–16.28–0–*ct* 4
Bowling 76–2–38.00–0–0–1/10
He hit 1,000 runs in a season six times (best 1,925, av 41.84, in 1935). Of his two double centuries, the higher was 236 for Oxford U v Free Foresters at Oxford in 1927 and the other for Surrey. He captained Oxford in 1927. He played very little important cricket from 1928 to 1933 owing to business, but in 1934 was appointed captain of Surrey, continuing until 1938 and again in 1947–48. He also led MCC on the 1935/6 tour of Australia and New Zealand. A good soccer player, he obtained his blue at Oxford as a Freshman.

Holmes, Geoffrey Clarke
Cricketer. *b:* 16.9.1958, Newcastle upon Tyne, Northumberland. Middle order right-hand batsman, right-arm medium pace bowler. *Teams* Glamorgan (1978–91, 203 matches); Border (1989/90).
Career batting
209–335–51–8092–182–28.49–11–*ct* 85
Bowling 3963–88–45.03–2–0–5/38
He hit 1,000 runs in a season three times (best 1,129, av 30.51, in 1985).

Holmes, Henry
Professional. *b:* 11.11.1833, Romsey, Hampshire. *d:* 6.1.1913, Freemantle, Southampton, Hampshire. Opening/middle order right-hand batsman, right-hand medium pace round-arm bowler. *Team* Hampshire (1861–78, 28 matches).
Career batting
32–58–4–798–77–14.77–0–*ct* 14–*st* 1
Bowling 762–28–27.21–2–0–5/57
He also played for Wiltshire (1859). He was a first-class umpire (1883–99).

Holmes, John Rodney Reay
Amateur. *b:* 24.4.1924, Hollington, Hastings, Sussex. *d:* 3.2.1980, Breuil-Cervinia, Italy. He was killed by an avalanche. Son of A. J. (Sussex). Lower order right-hand batsman, wicket-keeper. *Sch* Repton. *Team* Sussex (1950–51, 2 matches).
Career batting
3–4–0–41–24–10.25–0–*ct* 6–*st* 1
His first-class debut was for Free Foresters in 1949.

Holmes, John Trevor
Cricketer. *b:* 16.11.1939, Holmfirth, Yorkshire. Lower order right-hand batsman, wicket-keeper. *Team* Somerset (1969, 1 match).
Career batting
1–2–0–8–8–4.00–0–*ct* 1

Holmes, Percy
Professional. *b:* 25.11.1886, Oakes, Huddersfield, Yorkshire. *d:* 3.9.1971, Marsh, Huddersfield, Yorkshire. Very sound opening right-hand batsman, right-arm medium pace bowler, excellent field. *Team* Yorkshire (1913–33, 485 matches). *Tours* Joel to South Africa 1924/5; MCC to West Indies 1925/6, to South Africa 1927/8. *Tests* England (1921–32, 7 matches).
Career batting
555–810–84–30573–315*–42.11–67–*ct* 342
Bowling 185–2–92.50–0–0–1/5
Test batting
7–14–1–357–88–27.46–0–*ct* 3
He hit 1,000 runs in a season 14 times, going on to 2,000 seven times (best 2,453, av 57.04, in 1925). His highest innings was 315* for Yorkshire v Middlesex at Lord's in 1925; he hit a second triple hundred for his County in 1920 and ten other scores over 200. He was associated with H. Sutcliffe in 69 century partnerships for the first wicket, including the record 555 for Yorkshire v Essex at Leyton in 1932. He also hit 1,000 runs in a season in South Africa. His final first-class match was for Sir L. Parkinson's XI in 1935. He was a first-class umpire (1947).

Holmes, William
Professional. *b:* 29.10.1885, Eastwood, Nottinghamshire. *d:* 6.12.1951, Doncaster, Yorkshire. Lower order right-hand batsman, right-arm medium pace bowler, good deep field. *Team* Nottinghamshire (1919, 2 matches).
Career batting
2–2–0–33–19–16.50–0–*ct* 1
Bowling 105–4–26.25–0–0–2/50

Holroyd, Edwin
Amateur. *b:* 27.10.1855, Halifax, Yorkshire. *d:* 9.4.1914, Mitchell Hey, Rochdale, Lancashire. Middle order right-hand batsman, right-arm medium pace bowler, good field. *Team* Lancashire (1878, 1 match).
Career batting
1–2–0–6–4–3.00–0–*ct* 1

Holroyd, John
Professional. *b:* 15.4.1907, Oldham, Lancashire. *d:* 15.9.1975, St Bees, Cumberland. Tail end left-hand batsman, slow left-arm bowler. *Team* Lancashire (1927–33, 11 matches).

Career batting
11–9–5–33–18*–8.25–0–*ct* 2
Bowling 652–23–28.34–2–0–5/47

Holt, Alfred
Amateur. *b:* 2.3.1863, City of London. *d:* 3.2.1942, Battersea, London. Middle order left-hand batsman, left-arm fast bowler. *Team* MCC (1883).
Career batting
2–4–0–39–31–9.75–0–*ct* 0
His first-class debut was for Gentlemen of England in 1881. His County cricket was for Wiltshire (1888).

Holt, Arthur George
Professional. *b:* 8.4.1911, Bitterne Park, Southampton, Hampshire. Opening/middle order right-hand batsman, off break bowler. *Team* Hampshire (1935–48, 79 matches).
Career batting
79–140–13–2853–116–22.46–2–*ct* 32
Bowling 47–1–47.00–0–0–1/24
After retiring from first-class cricket he became coach to Hampshire CCC (1949–65). A noted soccer player, he captained Southampton.

Holt, Ernest Gerald
Amateur. *b:* 2.7.1904, Burnham Hall, Somerset. *d:* 27.8.1970, Brent Knoll, Somerset. Middle order right-hand batsman. *Sch* Marlborough. *Team* Somerset (1930, 2 matches).
Career batting
2–3–0–12–8–4.00–0–*ct* 0
Bowling 15–0

Holt, John Kenneth
Amateur. *b:* 10.1.1885, Trelawny Parish, Jamaica. *d:* 5.8.1968, Kingston, Jamaica. Father of J. K. C. (West Indies). Middle order right-hand batsman, right-arm medium bowler, occasional wicket-keeper. *Team* Jamaica (1905/6 to 1929/30). *Tour* West Indies to England 1923.
Career batting
36–60–2–1600–142–27.58–4–*ct* 25–*st* 1
Bowling 1054–26–40.53–0–0–3/34
He achieved very little on his tour of England.

Holt, Richard Anthony Appleby
Amateur. *b:* 11.3.1920, Kensington, London. Middle order right-hand batsman. *Sch* Harrow. *Team* Sussex (1938–39, 5 matches).
Career batting
6–9–1–60–30–7.50–0–*ct* 1
His final first-class match was for Free Foresters in 1947.

Holyoake, Ronald Hubert
Amateur. *b:* 17.2.1894, Droitwich, Worcestershire. *d:* 8.11.1966, Droitwich, Worcestershire. Middle order left-hand batsman. *Team* Worcestershire (1924, 3 matches).
Career batting
3–6–0–47–22–7.83–0–*ct* 0

Homer, Herbert Wesley Farmer
Amateur. *b:* 6.10.1895, Dudley, Worcestershire. *d:* 10.2.1977, Old Hill, Staffordshire. Opening right-hand batsman. *Team* Minor Counties (1928–31).
Career batting
4–6–0–185–71–30.83–0–*ct* 1
His County cricket was for Staffordshire (1922–35) and later he served on the Warwickshire CCC Committee for 25 years.

Hone, Sir Brian William
Amateur. *b:* 1.7.1907, Semaphore, Adelaide, South Australia. *d:* 28.5.1978, Paris, France. Brother of G. M. (South Australia), father of D. J. (Oxford U). Opening/middle order right-hand batsman. *Teams* South Australia (1928/9 to 1929/30, 11 matches); Oxford U (1931–33, blue all three years).
Career batting
44–75–6–2768–170–40.11–9–*ct* 25
Bowling 7–0
His County cricket was for Wiltshire (1936–39). He captained Oxford in 1933. He scored 137 on debut for South Australia v Victoria at Adelaide in 1928/9. A noted tennis player, he was awarded his blue.

Hone, David Jeremy
Cricketer. *b:* 30.6.1946, Melbourne, Victoria, Australia. Son of B. W. (South Australia), nephew of G. M. (South Australia). Tail end right-hand batsman, right-arm medium pace bowler. *Team* Oxford U (1970).
Career batting
3–5–0–26–13–5.20–0–*ct* 1
Bowling 284–1–284.00–0–0–1/82

Hone, Leland
Amateur. *b:* 30.1.1853, Dublin, Ireland. *d:* 31.12.1896, St Stephen's Green, Dublin, Ireland. Brother of William (MCC), uncle of W. P. (Ireland). Middle order right-hand batsman, occasional wicket-keeper. *Team* MCC (1878–80). *Tour* Harris to Australia 1878/9. *Test* England (1878/9, 1 match).
Career batting
8–13–1–85–27–7.08–0–*ct* 10–*st* 2
Test batting
1–2–0–13–7–6.50–0–*ct* 2
A noted figure in Irish cricket, he went on Lord Harris's 1878/9 tour to Australia and was pressed into service as a wicket-keeper – the team not possessing one! He played for Ireland (not first-class) 1874–78.

Hone, Nathaniel Thomas
Amateur. *b:* 21.6.1861, Yapton, Monkstown, Co Dublin, Ireland. *d:* 1.8.1881, Limerick, Ireland, from drinking carbolic acid in error whilst on a cricket tour. Lower order right-hand batsman, wicket-keeper. *Sch* Rugby. *Team* Cambridge U (1881, blue).

Hone, William

Career batting
3–5–3–2–1–1.00–0–*ct* 6–*st* 2

Hone, William
Amateur. *b:* 9.5.1842, Dublin, Ireland. *d:* 20.3.1919, Killiney, Dublin, Ireland. Brother of Leland (MCC), father of W. P. (Ireland). Middle order right-hand batsman. *Sch* Trinity College, Dublin. *Team* MCC (1864–77).
Career batting
9–15–2–266–76–20.46–0–*ct* 6
Bowling 64–3–21.33–0–0–3/41

Most of his cricket was played in Ireland, where he had considerable success. He played for Ireland (not first-class) 1861–78.

Hone, William Patrick
Amateur. *b:* 28.8.1886, Monkstown, Co Dublin, Ireland. *d:* 28.2.1976, Clondalkin, Co Dublin, Ireland. Son of William (MCC), nephew of Leland (MCC). Middle order right-hand batsman, wicket-keeper. *Sch* Wellington. *Team* Ireland (1910–28). *Tour* Ireland to North America 1909.
Career batting
6–12–0–162–92–13.50–0–*ct* 7

Hone-Foster, J. B. (*see under* Foster, J. B.)

Hone-Goldney, George Hone
(formerly Goldney)
Amateur. *b:* 24.1.1851, Southborough, Kent. *d:* 28.3.1921, Winchester, Hampshire. Son of George (Cambridge U 1838). Lower order right-hand batsman, right-arm medium pace bowler. *Sch* Eton. *Team* Cambridge U (1873, blue). *Tour* Vernon to India 1889/90 (not first-class).
Career batting
3–6–1–20–10–4.00–0–*ct* 2
Bowling 88–4–22.00–0–0–2/16

His final first-class match was for MCC in 1876.

Hood, Ernest Hugo Meggeson
Amateur. *b:* 27.8.1915, Pocklington, Yorkshire. *d:* 1.8.1968, Scarborough, Yorkshire. Lower order batsman, left-arm bowler. *Sch* Wellington. *Team* Somerset (1935, 1 match).
Career batting
1–2–0–6–4–3.00–0–*ct* 0
Bowling 43–0

He was a well-known player in military matches. He played in trials at Cambridge U, but not in first-class matches.

Hood, John Antony
Cricketer. *b:* 2.1.1952, Napier, Hawke's Bay, New Zealand. Middle order right-hand batsman, off break bowler. *Team* Oxford U (1977).
Career batting
2–3–0–9–7–3.00–0–*ct* 1

Hood, Rev John Shapland Elliott
(changed name to Cockburn-Hood in April 1866)
Amateur. *b:* 16.1.1844, Sydney, New South Wales, Australia. *d:* 30.8.1902, Catterick Bridge, Yorkshire, as the result of a bicycle accident. Hard-hitting middle order right-hand batsman, useful right-hand round-arm bowler, excellent deep field. *Sch* Rugby. *Team* Cambridge U (1864–67, blue 1865 and 1867).
Career batting
19–29–2–433–117–16.03–1–*ct* 6
Bowling 322–12–26.83–0–0–3/19

He played little cricket after leaving Cambridge, except for a few non-first-class matches for Free Foresters. His final first-class match was for Gentlemen of England in 1869. He also won a blue for athletics.

Hood, Hon William Nelson
Amateur. *b:* 6.1.1848, Westminster, London. *d:* 25.10.1921, Putney Bridge, Fulham, London. Middle order batsman. *Team* MCC (1875–80).
Career batting
2–4–0–13–6–3.25–0–*ct* 1

His County cricket was for Somerset (pre first-class, 1880).

Hook, Rev Arthur James
Amateur. *b:* 12.2.1877, Porlock, Somerset. *d:* 12.2.1957, Over Stowey, Bridgwater, Somerset. Nephew of C. S. Bere (Oxford U 1851). Middle order left-hand batsman. *Sch* Blundells. *Team* Somerset (1897–1906, 2 matches).
Career batting
2–4–1–43–15*–14.33–0–*ct* 1

He played in trials at Oxford U, but not in first-class matches.

Hook, John Stanley
Cricketer. *b:* 27.5.1954, Weston-super-Mare, Somerset. Lower order right-hand batsman, off break bowler. *Team* Somerset (1975, 1 match).
Career batting
1–2–1–7–4*–7.00–0–*ct* 0
Bowling 29–0

Hooker, Ronald William
Professional. *b:* 22.2.1935, Lower Clapton, London. Middle order right-hand batsman, right-arm medium pace bowler. *Team* Middlesex (1956–69, 300 matches).
Career batting
300–442–71–8222–137–22.16–5–*ct* 301
Bowling 13457–490–27.46–16–0–7/18

He hit 1,000 runs in a season twice (best 1,449, av 30.18, in 1959). He also played for Buckinghamshire (1970–76).

Hooker, William
Professional. *b:* 17.5.1796, Fernherst, Midhurst, Sussex. *d:* 27.12.1867, Midhurst, Sussex. Steady middle order right-hand batsman, wicket-keeper. *Team*

Sussex (1823–33).
Career batting
26–46–4–517–92–12.30–0–*ct* 15–*st* 1
Bowling 1 wicket (no analyses)–0–0–1/?

He was for a few seasons one of the leading batsmen in England, but did not play in great matches for long.

Hookes, David William
Cricketer. *b:* 3.5.1955, Mile End, Adelaide, South Australia. Attacking middle order left-hand batsman, left-arm medium, or slow, bowler. *Team* South Australia (1975/6 to 1991/2, 130 matches). *Tours* Australia to England 1977, 1983 (World Cup), to Pakistan 1979/80, to Sri Lanka 1982/3, to West Indies 1983/4. *Tests* Australia (1976/7 to 1985/6, 23 matches).
Career batting
178–304–16–12671–306*–43.99–32–*ct* 167
Bowling 2379–41–58.02–0–0–3/58
Test batting
23–41–3–1306–143*–34.36–1–*ct* 12
Bowling 41–1–41.00–0–0–1/4

On the 1977 tour to England he hit 804 runs, av 32.16, and played in all five Tests. When scoring 107 for South Australia v Victoria at Adelaide in 1982/3 he reached 100 in 34 balls, at the time the fastest century in terms of balls received ever scored in first-class cricket. He scored 1,000 runs in a season in Australia three times (best 1,424, av 64.72, in 1982/3). His highest score was 306* for South Australia v Tasmania at Adelaide in 1986/7 when he shared a partnership of 462* for 4th wicket with W. B. Phillips, then the highest partnership by any pair of Australian batsmen.

Hookey, Scott Gregory
Cricketer. *b:* 10.2.1967, Sydney, New South Wales, Australia. Opening left-hand batsman. *Team* New South Wales (1987/8, 1 match); Tasmania (1989/90, 7 matches). *Tour* Rest of World to England 1988.
Career batting
9–17–1–436–116*–27.25–1–*ct* 1
Bowling 1–0

Hool, Dr Nathan Bernard
Amateur. *b:* 28.1.1924, Dublin, Ireland. *d:* 10.10.1988, Belfast, Ireland. Lower order right-hand batsman, slow left-arm bowler. *Team* Ireland (1947–61).
Career batting
9–16–8–132–27–16.50–0–*ct* 4
Bowling 601–18–33.38–1–0–5/73

Hooman, Charles Victor Lisle
Amateur. *b:* 3.10.1887, Ditton, Kent. *d:* 20.11.1969, Palm Beach, Florida, USA. Middle order right-hand batsman, right-arm medium pace bowler. *Sch* Charterhouse. *Teams* Oxford U (1907–10, blue 1909–10); Kent (1910, 15 matches).
Career batting
38–64–2–1758–117–28.35–3–*ct* 33
Bowling 59–0

He also played for Devon (1906–09). He hit 1,070 runs, av 29.72, in 1910. A brilliant golfer, he gained his blue and went on the play for England in the Walker Cup. He also obtained his blue for rackets.

Hooper, Andrew James Mendez
Cricketer. *b:* 17.9.1945, Denmark Hill, London. Lower order right-hand batsman, slow left-arm bowler. *Team* Kent (1966–69, 13 matches).
Career batting
13–13–4–70–35–7.77–0–*ct* 7
Bowling 493–16–30.81–1–0–6/92

Hooper, Antony Mark
Cricketer. *b:* 5.9.1967, Perivale, Middlesex. Opening right-hand batsman, right-arm medium pace bowler. *Sch* Latymer Upper. *Team* Cambridge U (1987–92, blue 1987, 1991 and 1992).
Career batting
24–41–2–848–125–21.74–1–*ct* 2
Bowling 275–6–45.83–0–0–1/5

Hooper, Carl Llewellyn
Cricketer. *b:* 15.12.1966, Georgetown, Guyana. Middle order right-hand batsman, off break bowler. *Teams* Guyana (1984/5 to 1991/2); Kent (1992, 21 matches). *Tours* West Indies to New Zealand 1986/7, to India 1987/8, to England 1988, 1991, to Australia 1988/9, 1991/2, to Pakistan 1990/1, 1991/2 (not first-class), to India and Pakistan (World Cup) 1987/8, to Sharjah (not first-class) 1988/9, 1991/2, to Australia and New Zealand (World Cup) 1991/2; Young West Indies to Zimbabwe 1986/7, 1989/90. *Tests* West Indies (1987/8 to 1991/2, 32 matches).
Career batting
118–178–21–6528–196–41.57–15–*ct* 120
Bowling 6039–181–33.36–5–0–5/33
Test batting
32–54–4–1409–134–28.18–3–*ct* 29
Bowling 1247–15–83.13–0–0–2/28

On his first tour to England in 1988 he played in all five Tests, but failed to play a major part in the series. In 1991 he again played in every Test and hit 111 in the Second Test at Lord's; he scored 1,501 runs, av 93.81, for the season. Joining Kent in 1992 he scored 1,329 runs, av 47.46. His bowling was more than useful in 1991 and 1992. His first-class debut was for Demerara in 1983/4.

Hooper, John Michael Mackenzie
Cricketer. *b:* 23.4.1947, Milford, Surrey. Middle order right-hand batsman, right-arm medium pace bowler. *Sch* Charterhouse. *Team* Surrey (1967–71, 21 matches).
Career batting
21–36–10–406–41*–15.61–0–*ct* 14

Bowling 10–1–10.00–0–0–1/10

He was also a useful soccer player.

Hope, Arthur Oswald James
(later Baron Rankeillour)
Amateur. *b:* 7.5.1897, Westminster, London. *d:* 26.5.1958, Chelsea, London. Middle order batsman. *Sch* Oratory. *Team* Army (1926).
Career batting
1–2–0–25–23–12.50–0–*ct* 0

He was MP for Nuneaton 1924–29 and for Aston 1931–39.

Hope, Kenneth William
Amateur. *b:* 3.5.1939, Portarlington, Co Leix, Ireland. Lower order right-hand batsman, off break bowler. *Team* Ireland (1958–66).
Career batting
9–14–3–75–21–6.81–0–*ct* 5
Bowling 339–12–28.25–1–0–6/59

Hope, Philip Palmer
Amateur. *b:* 10.2.1889, Hartlepool, Co Durham. *d:* 19.5.1962, Clifton, Bristol. Middle order right-hand batsman, right-arm fast medium bowler. *Sch* Sedbergh and Sherborne. *Team* Somerset (1914–25, 41 matches).
Career batting
41–71–2–1048–77–15.18–0–*ct* 15
Bowling 145–1–145.00–0–0–1/17

He also played for Dorset (1911–13).

Hopkins, Albert John Young
Amateur. *b:* 3.5.1874, Young, New South Wales, Australia. *d:* 25.4.1931, North Sydney, New South Wales, Australia. Brother of C. C. (Otago), uncle of H. O. (Worcestershire). Opening/middle order right-hand batsman, right-arm fast medium bowler. *Team* New South Wales (1896/7 to 1914/15, 52 matches). *Tours* Australia to England 1902, 1905, 1909, to South Africa 1902/3, to New Zealand 1904/5, 1909/10. *Tests* Australia (1901/2 to 1909, 20 matches).
Career batting
162–240–21–5563–218–25.40–8–*ct* 87
Bowling 6612–271–24.39–10–0–7/10
Test batting
20–33–2–509–43–16.41–0–*ct* 11
Bowling 696–26–26.76–0–0–4/81

He produced his best form on his first visit to England scoring 1,100 runs, av 23.91, and taking 34 wickets. Although he appeared in 10 Tests in England he never really played up to his Australian reputation. His highest score was 218 for New South Wales v South Australia at Adelaide in 1908/9.

Hopkins, David Charles
Cricketer. *b:* 11.2.1957, Birmingham. Lower order right-hand batsman, right-arm medium pace bowler. *Team* Warwickshire (1977–81, 36 matches).
Career batting
36–44–12–332–34*–10.37–0–*ct* 8
Bowling 2021–53–38.13–1–0–6/67

He also played for Buckinghamshire (1982).

Hopkins, Frank Jesse
Professional. *b:* 30.6.1875, King's Norton, Birmingham. *d:* 15.1.1930, Bellevue, Southampton, Hampshire. Tail end batsman, left-arm medium pace bowler. *Teams* Warwickshire (1898–1903, 11 matches); Hampshire (1906–11, 3 matches).
Career batting
14–22–6–44–13–2.75–0–*ct* 3
Bowling 940–29–32.41–1–0–5/10

He was appointed groundsman at Southampton in 1904 and thus qualified for Hampshire.

Hopkins, Dr Herbert Oxley
Amateur. *b:* 6.7.1895, Adelaide, South Australia. *d:* 23.2.1972, Milverton, Somerset. Nephew of A. J. Y. (Australia) and C. C. (Otago). Middle order right-hand batsman. *Teams* Oxford U (1921–23, blue 1923); Worcestershire (1921–31, 63 matches).
Career batting
85–152–9–3204–142*–22.40–4–*ct* 28
Bowling 202–4–50.50–0–0–2/23

He went to the Malay States and thus appeared in little County cricket after 1924. He also won a blue for lacrosse.

Hopkins, Jeffris David
Cricketer. *b:* 23.8.1950, Bridgend, Glamorgan. Brother of J. A. (Glamorgan). Tail end right-batsman, wicket-keeper. *Team* Middlesex (1969–72, 4 matches).
Career batting
4–5–0–8–4–1.60–0–*ct* 9

He played for Wales in the ICC Trophy in 1979.

Hopkins, John Anthony
Cricketer. *b:* 16.6.1953, Maesteg, Glamorgan. Brother of J. D. (Middlesex). Opening right-hand batsman, occasional wicket-keeper. *Teams* Glamorgan (1970–88, 299 matches); Eastern Province (1981/2).
Career batting
305–535–32–13742–230–27.32–18–*ct* 213–*st* 1
Bowling 148–0

He hit 1,000 runs in a season seven times (best 1,500, av 33.33, in 1984). His highest score was 230 for Glamorgan v Worcestershire at Worcester in 1977.

Hopkins, Victor
Professional. *b:* 21.1.1911, Dumbleton, Gloucestershire. *d:* 6.8.1984, Dumbleton, Gloucestershire. Lower order right-hand batsman, wicket-keeper. *Team* Gloucestershire (1934–48, 139 matches).
Career batting
139–210–34–2608–83*–14.81–0–*ct* 138–*st* 44

Hopley, Frederick John Vanderbyl
Amateur. *b:* 27.8.1883, Grahamstown, South Africa. *d:* 16.8.1951, Marandellas, Rhodesia. Brother of G. W. V. (Cambridge U). Hard hitting middle order right-hand batsman, right-arm fast bowler. *Sch* Harrow. *Teams* Cambridge U (1904–06, blue 1904); Western Province (1909/10). *Tours* MCC to North America 1905; Leveson-Gower to Rhodesia 1909/10.
Career batting
27–47–5–599–55–14.26–0–*ct* 17
Bowling 1620–48–33.75–1–1–6/37
His final first-class match in England was for Leveson-Gower's XI in 1907. An excellent rugby footballer, he won his blue and went on to represent England; he was also regarded as the best amateur heavyweight boxer of his day.

Hopley, Geoffrey William Vanderbyl
Amateur. *b:* 9.9.1891, Kimberley, Griqualand West, South Africa. *d:* 12.5.1915, Boulogne, France. He died of wounds. Brother of F. J. V. (Cambridge U). Middle order right-hand batsman. *Sch* Harrow. *Team* Cambridge U (1911–14, blue 1912).
Career batting
15–29–4–309–42–12.36–0–*ct* 23
Bowling 21–1–21.00–0–0–1/21
In 1912 he won the heavyweight boxing title for Cambridge.

Hopwood, John Anthony
Amateur. *b:* 23.10.1926, Herne Bay, Kent. Opening right-hand batsman. *Sch* Dulwich. *Team* Free Foresters (1951).
Career batting
1–2–0–9–8–4.50–0–*ct* 1

Hopwood, John Leonard
Professional. *b:* 30.10.1903, Newton Hyde, Cheshire. *d:* 15.6.1985, Denton, Lancashire. Defensive opening/middle order right-hand batsman, left-arm medium pace bowler. *Team* Lancashire (1923–39, 397 matches). *Tests* England (1934, 2 matches).
Career batting
400–575–55–15548–220–29.90–27–*ct* 198
Bowling 15110–673–22.45–35–6–9/33
Test batting
2–3–1–12–8–6.00–0–*ct* 0
Bowling 155–0
He hit 1,000 runs in a season eight times (best 1,972, av 46.95, in 1933) and took 100 wickets twice (best 111, av 20.69, in 1934). He performed the 'double' in 1934 and 1935. His only double century was 220 for Lancashire v Gloucestershire at Bristol in 1934. His best bowling was 9/33 for Lancashire v Leicestershire at Old Trafford in 1933. He also played for Cheshire (1926–27). He was President of Lancashire 1981–82.

Hopwood, Reginald Arthur
Amateur. *b:* 5.7.1903, Marylebone, London. *d:* 3.6.1969, Tangier. Tail end batsman, opening bowler. *Sch* Eton. *Team* Gloucestershire (1924, 1 match).
Career batting
1–2–0–2–2–1.00–0–*ct* 0
Bowling 8–0

Horan, Thomas Patrick
Amateur. *b:* 8.3.1854, Midleton, Co Cork, Ireland. *d:* 16.4.1916, Malvern, Melbourne, Victoria, Australia. Father of J. F. (Victoria) and T. I. B. (Victoria). Defensive middle order right-hand batsman, right-hand fast medium round-arm bowler. *Team* Victoria (1874/5 to 1891/2, 42 matches). *Tours* Australia to England 1878, 1882, to North America 1878. *Tests* Australia (1876/7 to 1884/5, 15 matches).
Career batting
106–187–14–4027–141*–23.27–8–*ct* 39
Bowling 829–35–23.68–2–0–6/40
Test batting
15–27–2–471–124–18.84–1–*ct* 6
Bowling 143–11–13.00–1–0–6/40
He was most successful on his 1882 visit to England, scoring over 1,000 runs in all matches and coming second to Murdoch in the averages. He captained Australia in two Tests. He was a well-known cricket reporter.

Hordern, Dr Herbert Vivian
Amateur. *b:* 10.2.1883, North Sydney, New South Wales, Australia. *d:* 17.6.1938, Darlinghurst, Sydney, New South Wales, Australia. Brother-in-law of F. E. McElhone (New South Wales). Lower order right-hand batsman, leg break and googly bowler. *Teams* New South Wales (1905/6 to 1912/13, 10 matches); Philadelphia (1907 to 1909/10). *Tours* Philadelphia to England 1908, to Jamaica 1908/9. *Tests* Australia (1910/11 to 1911/12, 7 matches).
Career batting
35–55–9–781–64–16.97–0–*ct* 39
Bowling 3752–228–16.45–25–9–8/31
Test batting
7–13–2–254–50–23.09–0–*ct* 6
Bowling 1075–46–23.36–5–2–7/90
He was, after J. B. King, the principal bowler on the 1908 tour to England and in all matches took 74 wickets, av 17.09. The previous season he had visited England with the Pennsylvania University team and returned figures of 110 wickets, av 9.68 (not first-class).

Hore, Fraser Salter
Amateur. *c:* 6.6.1835, Dulwich, London. *d:* 7.7.1903, Westbourne, Bournemouth, Hampshire. Middle order right-hand batsman, right-hand medium pace round-arm bowler. *Sch* Tonbridge. *Team* Surrey (1861, 1 match).

Horlick, Sir James Nockells

Career batting
5–8–2–32–9–5.33–0–*ct* 1
His final first-class match was for MCC in 1866.

Horlick, Sir James Nockells
Amateur. *b:* 22.3.1886, Brooklyn, New York, USA. *d:* 31.12.1972, Achamore, Isle of Gigha, Argyll, Scotland. Lower order right-hand batsman, slow left-arm bowler. *Sch* Eton. *Teams* Oxford U (1906); Gloucestershire (1907–10, 2 matches).
Career batting
3–5–1–24–9–6.00–0–*ct* 2
Bowling 48–0
He was President of Gloucestershire 1925–26 and MP for Gloucester 1923–29.

Hornby, Albert Henry
Amateur. *b:* 29.7.1877, Parkfield, Wardle, Nantwich, Cheshire. *d:* 6.9.1952, North Kilworth, Leicestershire. Son of A. N. (Lancashire), nephew of C. L. (Lancashire) and E. K. (Gentlemen of North 1862). Middle order right-hand batsman. *Sch* Harrow. *Teams* Cambridge U (1898); Lancashire (1899–1914, 283 matches). *Tour* Oxford U Authentics to India 1902/3.
Career batting
292–439–41–9784–129–24.58–8–*ct* 217–*st* 2
Bowling 269–3–89.66–0–0–1/13
He hit 1,000 runs in a season once: 1,336, av 28.42, in 1913. From 1908 to 1914 he captained Lancashire.

Hornby, Albert Neilson
Amateur. *b:* 10.2.1847, Blackburn, Lancashire. *d:* 17.12.1925, Parkfield, Wardle, Nantwich, Cheshire. Father of A. H. (Lancashire), brother of C. L. (Lancashire) and E. K. (Gentlemen of North 1862). Opening right-hand batsman, bowled both right and left arm, brilliant cover point. *Sch* Harrow. *Team* Lancashire (1867–99, 292 matches). *Tours* Fitzgerald to North America 1872 (not first-class); Harris to Australia 1878/9. *Tests* England (1878/9 to 1884, 3 matches).
Career batting
437–710–41–16109–188–24.07–16–*ct* 313–*st* 3
Bowling 258–11–23.45–0–0–4/40
Test batting
3–6–0–21–9–3.50–0–*ct* 0
Bowling 0–1–0.00–0–0–1/0
He hit 1,000 runs in a season twice (best 1,534, av 40.36, in 1881). He captained Lancashire 1880–93 and 1897–98. His final first-class match was for an England XI in 1906. A noted rugby footballer, he was capped nine times for England. He also played for Cheshire (1864–76). He was President of Lancashire CCC 1894–1916.

Hornby, Cecil Lumsden
Amateur. *b:* 25.7.1843, Blackburn, Lancashire. *d:* 27.2.1896, Leamington Spa, Warwickshire. Brother of A. N. (Lancashire) and E. K. (Gentlemen of North 1862), uncle of A. H. (Lancashire). Opening right-hand batsman, good field. *Sch* Harrow. *Team* Lancashire (1877, 1 match).
Career batting
2–3–0–27–23–9.00–0–*ct* 0
Bowling 3–1–3.00–0–0–1/3
His cricket was confined mainly to military matches. He made his first-class debut for Gentlemen of England in 1874 and also played occasionally for Cheshire (1862–66) and Shropshire (1867).

Hornby, Edgar Christian
Amateur. *b:* 14.9.1863, Wavertree, Liverpool, Lancashire. *d:* 2.4.1922, Claygate, Surrey. Father of A. H. (Europeans), brother of G. F. (Oxford U). Middle order left-hand batsman, slow left-arm bowler. *Sch* Winchester. *Team* Lancashire (1885–87, 9 matches).
Career batting
13–20–1–360–82–18.94–0–*ct* 9
Bowling 177–6–29.50–0–0–2/23
He was principally connected with Liverpool CC and appeared in the Liverpool and District XI, his final first-class match being for that side in 1894.

Hornby, Gerald Frederick
Amateur. *b:* 9.6.1862, Aigburth, Liverpool, Lancashire. *d:* 9.2.1890, Tarporley, Cheshire. Brother of E. C. (Lancashire), uncle of A. H. (Europeans). Lower order right-hand batsman, right-arm fast bowler. *Sch* Winchester. *Team* Oxford U (1882).
Career batting
1–2–0–1–1–0.50–0–*ct* 0
Bowling 35–0
He won a blue for athletics.

Hornby, Thomas Whitfield
Professional. *b:* 2.10.1831, Stockton-on-Tees, Durham. *d:* 1.4.1900, Stockton-on-Tees, Durham. Middle order left-hand batsman. *Team* Yorkshire and Durham (1858–61).
Career batting
3–6–0–65–22–10.83–0–*ct* 1
His final first-class match was for an England XI in 1864. He also played for Durham (pre first-class, 1856).

Horncastle, William Allen
Amateur. *b:* 21.9.1864, Tottenham, Middlesex. *d:* 26.1.1917, Leyton, Essex. Lower order right-hand batsman, right-arm medium pace bowler. *Team* Middlesex (1883, 1 match).
Career batting
1–2–0–11–8–5.50–0–*ct* 1
Bowling 72–3–24.00–0–0–2/39

Horner, Charles Edward
Amateur. *b:* 9.4.1857, Dulwich Common, London. *d:* 4.9.1925, Regent's Park, London. Tail end right-hand batsman, right-arm fast medium bowler. *Sch* Cheltenham. *Teams* Oxford U (1877–80); Surrey (1882–86, 53 matches). *Tour* Sanders to North America (1885).

Career batting
65–103–31–546–37*–7.58–0–*ct* 22
Bowling 4470–252–17.73–15–3–8/35

He took 107 wickets, av 14.97, in 1884, which was easily his best season in first-class cricket. He was on the Surrey CCC Committee for many years. A noted amateur billiards player, he was a prominent member of the Billiards Control Club.

Horner, Sir John Francis Fortescue
Amateur. *b:* 28.12.1842, Mells Park, Somerset. *d:* 31.3.1927, Westminster, London. Brother-in-law of K. A. Muir-Mackenzie (Oxford U) and Q. Hogg (British Guiana). Lower order batsman, left-arm medium fast bowler. *Sch* Eton. *Team* MCC (1867).
Career batting
5–10–2–19–7–2.37–0–*ct* 4
Bowling 124–9–13.77–0–0–4/24

His first-class debut was for Southgate in 1866 and his final first-class match for Gentlemen of England in 1873. His County cricket was for Somerset (pre first-class, 1870).

Horner, Norman Frederick
Professional. *b:* 10.5.1926, Queensbury, Yorkshire. Sound opening right-hand batsman. *Teams* Yorkshire (1950, 2 matches); Warwickshire (1951–65, 357 matches).
Career batting
362–656–34–18533–203*–29.79–25–*ct* 130
Bowling 78–0

He hit 1,000 runs in a season 12 times (best 1,902, av 33.36, in 1960). His only double century was 203* for Warwickshire v Surrey at the Oval in 1960; with K. Ibadulla he created a record Warwickshire first-wicket partnership of 377* in the same match.

Hornibrook, Percival Mitchell
Amateur. *b:* 27.7.1899, Obi Obi, Queensland, Australia. *d:* 25.8.1976, Spring Hill, Brisbane, Queensland, Australia. Lower order left-hand batsman, left-arm medium or slow bowler. *Team* Queensland (1919/20 to 1933/4, 28 matches). *Tours* Australia to New Zealand 1920/1, to England 1930. *Tests* Australia (1928/9 to 1930, 6 matches).
Career batting
71–91–21–754–59*–10.77–0–*ct* 66
Bowling 6650–279–23.83–17–6–8/60
Test batting
6–7–1–60–26–10.00–0–*ct* 7
Bowling 664–17–39.05–1–0–7/92

He was considered unlucky not to be chosen for either the 1921 or 1926 Australian tours to England. In 1930, on his only visit, he took 96 wickets, av 18.79, in first-class matches but succeeded in only the fifth Test.

Hornsby, John Henry James
Amateur. *b:* 18.4.1860, Barrowby, Grantham, Lincolnshire. *d:* 9.7.1926, Cuckfield Park, Sussex. Lower order right-hand batsman, slow left-arm bowler, good field. *Sch* Fettes. *Team* Middlesex (1893, 1 match). *Tours* Vernon to India 1889/90 (not first-class); Hawke to North America 1891, to India 1892/3.
Career batting
31–54–4–678–56–13.56–0–*ct* 22
Bowling 891–52–17.13–3–2–8/40

His first-class debut was for the Gentlemen at Scarborough in 1887, and his final first-class match was for MCC in 1898.

Horrex, Graham Wade
Amateur. *b:* 27.12.1932, Goodmayes, Essex. Opening right-hand batsman. *Sch* Brentwood. *Team* Essex (1956–57, 7 matches).
Career batting
7–13–0–141–41–10.84–0–*ct* 0

A noted squash player, he represented Essex.

Horridge, Leonard
Professional. *b:* 18.8.1907, Adlington, Lancashire. *d:* 1.9.1976, Deepdale, Preston, Lancashire. Lower order right-hand batsman, off break bowler. *Team* Lancashire (1927–29, 3 matches).
Career batting
5–6–1–57–15–11.40–0–*ct* 4
Bowling 79–3–26.33–0–0–2/46

His final first-class match was for Minor Counties in 1930.

Horrocks, Richard
Professional. *b:* 29.8.1857, Church, Lancashire. *d:* 19.6.1926, Church, Lancashire. Middle order right-hand batsman, good field. *Team* Lancashire (1880–82, 6 matches).
Career batting
7–12–0–121–61–10.08–0–*ct* 1

Horrocks, William John
Professional. *b:* 18.6.1905, Warrington, Lancashire. *d:* 15.11.1985, Melbourne, Victoria, Australia. Middle order right-hand batsman. *Teams* Lancashire (1931–33, 15 matches); Western Australia (1926/7 to 1936/7, 11 matches).
Career batting
29–44–6–1255–148*–33.02–3–*ct* 9
Bowling 51–0

Horsey, Frank Lankester
Amateur. *b:* 22.1.1884, Woodbridge, Suffolk. *d:* 19.8.1956, Hyde Stile, Surrey. Middle order right-hand batsman, right-arm fast medium bowler. *Sch* King Edward, Southampton. *Team* Royal Navy (1914).
Career batting
1–2–0–23–15–11.50–0–*ct* 1
Bowling 17–2–8.50–0–0–2/17

Horsfall, Richard
Professional. *b:* 26.6.1920, Todmorden, Yorkshire. *d:* 25.8.1981, Halifax, Yorkshire. Middle order right-

hand batsman, good field. *Teams* Essex (1947–55, 207 matches); Glamorgan (1956, 5 matches).
Career batting
214–361–25–9777–206–29.09–17–*ct* 88
Bowling 41–1–41.00–0–0–1/4

He hit 1,000 runs in a season four times (best 1,731, av 37.63, in 1953). His only double century was 206 for Essex v Kent at Blackheath in 1951.

Horsley, Albert Beresford
Amateur. *b:* 2.1.1880, Hartlepool, Co Durham. *d:* 19.11.1923, West Hartlepool, Co Durham. He died by his own hand. Father of R. H. (Oxford U). Lower order batsman, useful bowler. *Sch* Leys. *Team* London County (1904).
Career batting
1–1–0–24–24–24.00–0–*ct* 0
Bowling 22–0

His County cricket was for Durham (pre first-class, 1897–1914).

Horsley, James
Professional. *b:* 4.1.1890, Melbourne, Derbyshire. *d:* 13.2.1976, Derby. Lower order right-hand batsman, right-arm fast medium bowler. *Teams* Nottinghamshire (1913, 3 matches); Derbyshire (1914–25, 84 matches).
Career batting
87–132–32–1367–66–13.67–0–*ct* 47
Bowling 5412–267–20.26–19–3–7/48

Horsley, Norman
Amateur. *b:* 20.8.1922, Spinney Hills, Leicester. Lower order right-hand batsman, right-arm fast bowler. *Team* Nottinghamshire (1947, 3 matches).
Career batting
3–1–0–0–0–0.00–0–*ct* 1
Bowling 249–6–41.50–0–0–2/27

Horsley, Rupert Harry
Amateur. *b:* 17.12.1905, West Hartlepool, Co Durham. *d:* 5.3.1988, Nether Wallop, Hampshire. Son of A. B. (London County). Lower order right-hand batsman, wicket-keeper. *Sch* Winchester. *Team* Oxford U (1927).
Career batting
3–5–1–78–25–19.50–0–*ct* 9–*st* 1

Horton, Henry
Amateur in 1946, then professional. *b:* 18.4.1923, Colwall Green, Herefordshire. Brother of Joseph (Worcestershire). Middle order right-hand batsman, slow left-arm bowler. *Teams* Worcestershire (1946–49, 11 matches); Hampshire (1953–67, 405 matches).
Career batting
417–744–84–21669–160*–32.83–32–*ct* 264
Bowling 194–3–64.66–0–0–2/0

He hit 1,000 runs in a season 12 times, going on to 2,000 in three seasons (best 2,428, av 47.60, in 1959). He was Worcestershire coach 1968–72 and 1977–79 and a first-class umpire (1973–76). A good soccer player, he appeared for Blackburn Rovers, Southampton and Bradford.

Horton, Joseph
Professional. *b:* 12.8.1915, Colwall Green, Herefordshire. Brother of Henry (Worcestershire and Hampshire). Middle order right-hand batsman, right-arm medium pace bowler. *Team* Worcestershire (1934–38, 62 matches).
Career batting
62–103–12–1258–70–13.82–0–*ct* 33
Bowling 362–5–72.40–0–0–2/3

He also played for Herefordshire (1952).

Horton, Martin John
Professional. *b:* 21.4.1934, Worcester. Opening right-hand batsman, off break bowler. *Teams* Worcestershire (1952–66, 376 matches); Northern Districts (1967/8 to 1970/1). *Tours* Worcestershire World Tour (Rhodesia first-class) 1964/5, to Jamaica 1965/6. *Tests* England (1959, 2 matches).
Career batting
410–724–49–19945–233–29.54–23–*ct* 166
Bowling 22226–825–26.94–40–7–9/56
Test batting
2–2–0–60–58–30.00–0–*ct* 2
Bowling 59–2–29.50–0–0–2/24

He hit 1,000 runs in a season 11 times, going on to 2,000 once: 2,468, av 44.87, in 1959. His two double centuries were both for Worcestershire, the higher being 233 v Somerset at Worcester in 1962. He took 100 wickets in a season twice (best 103, av 27.38, in 1955) and performed the 'double' twice. In 1967 he was appointed New Zealand national coach and therefore retired from County cricket. His best bowling was 9/56 for Worcestershire v South Africans at Worcester in 1955.

Horton, R.
Professional. Lower order batsman, slow left-arm bowler. *Team* Gloucestershire (1925, 3 matches).
Career batting
3–5–2–13–7–4.33–0–*ct* 1
Bowling 149–1–149.00–0–0–1/97

Horton, Thomas
Amateur. *b:* 16.5.1871, Edgbaston, Birmingham. *d:* 18.6.1932, Bilton House, Rugby, Warwickshire. Forcing right-hand middle order batsman, good field. *Sch* Repton. *Team* Northamptonshire (1905–06, 26 matches).
Career batting
29–55–7–581–53–12.10–10–0–*ct* 18
Bowling 4–0

He first played for Northamptonshire (pre first-class) in 1895, being captain 1896–1906. His first-class debut was for MCC in 1900. He was President of Northamptonshire 1922–23.

Horton, William Herbert Francis Kenneth
Amateur. *b:* 25.4.1906, Brentford, Middlesex. *d:* 31.10.1986, Hove, Sussex. Middle order right-hand batsman. *Sch* Stonyhurst. *Teams* Middlesex (1927, 2 matches); Europeans (1929/30 to 1934/5).
Career batting
4–7–0–59–38–8.42–0–*ct* 1

Horwood, Charles
Amateur. *b:* 8.12.1839, Berkhamsted, Hertfordshire. *d:* 7.1.1870, Manor House, Broadwater, Worthing, Sussex. Lower order right-hand batsman, right-hand round-arm bowler. *Sch* Highgate. *Team* Sussex (1864–65, 3 matches).
Career batting
3–4–1–23–12*–7.66–0–*ct* 3

Horwood, Stanley Ebden
Amateur. *b:* 22.7.1877, Port Elizabeth, South Africa. *d:* 15.8.1959, Plumstead, Cape Town, South Africa. Middle order right-hand batsman. *Team* Western Province (1903/4 to 1909/10). *Tour* South Africa to England 1904.
Career batting
22–35–1–484–74–14.23–0–*ct* 8
His single visit to England proved to be a very modest affair. His first-class debut was for Cape Colony in 1898/9. His son, Owen, was Minister of Finance in the South African government 1975.

Hosen, Roger Wills
Cricketer. *b:* 12.6.1933, Helston, Cornwall. Lower order right-hand batsman, right-arm fast medium bowler. *Team* Minor Counties (1965).
Career batting
1–2–0–2–2–1.00–0–*ct* 0
Bowling 73–1–73.00–0–0–1/55
His County cricket was for Cornwall (1955–69). He was an English rugby international.

Hosie, Alexander Lindsay
Amateur. *b:* 6.8.1890, Wenchow, China. *d:* 11.6.1957, Ashurst, Totton, Southampton, Hampshire. Hard-hitting middle order right-hand batsman, right-arm medium pace bowler. *Sch* St Lawrence College, Ramsgate. *Teams* Hampshire (1913–35, 80 matches); Oxford U (1913); Europeans (1921/2 to 1929/30); Bengal (1935/6 to 1937/8). *Tour* Tennyson to India (1937/8) – as an emergency.
Career batting
133–232–8–6195–200–27.65–8–*ct* 85
Bowling 500–11–45.45–0–0–4/35
He hit 1,000 runs in a season twice (best 1,331, av 30.25, in 1928). His only double century was 200 for Europeans v Hindus at Bombay in 1924/5. His first-class debut in India was for Bengal Governor's XI in 1917/18. His final first-class match was for MCC in 1938. He won blues for lawn tennis, hockey and soccer.

Hoskin, Worthington Wynn
Amateur. *b:* 8.5.1885, Cape Province, South Africa. *d:* 4.3.1956, East London, South Africa. Lower order batsman, useful bowler. *Teams* Oxford U (1907); Gloucestershire (1912, 5 matches).
Career batting
6–11–0–90–28–8.18–0–*ct* 7
Bowling 103–1–103.00–0–0–1/13
A noted rugby footballer, he played in the University match for four seasons.

Hoskyns, Sir John Chevallier
Amateur. *b:* 23.5.1926, Newnham, Cambridge. *d:* 12.4.1956, Powick, Worcestershire. Opening left-hand batsman. *Sch* Marlborough. *Team* Cambridge U (1949).
Career batting
2–4–1–63–42*–21.00–0–*ct* 0

Hossack, Anthony Henry
Amateur. *b:* 2.5.1867, Walsall, Staffordshire. *d:* 24.1.1925, Torquay, Devon. Lower order batsman, useful bowler. *Sch* Chigwell. *Team* Cambridge U (1889).
Career batting
1–1–0–3–3–3.00–0–*ct* 0
Bowling 14–0
His County cricket was for Essex (pre first-class, 1891). A noted soccer player, he obtained his blue at Cambridge and appeared for Corinthians and England at wing-half.

Hossell, John Johnson
Amateur. *b:* 25.5.1914, Handsworth, Birmingham. Middle order left-hand batsman, slow left-arm bowler. *Team* Warwickshire (1939–47, 35 matches).
Career batting
35–62–5–1217–83–21.35–0–*ct* 12
Bowling 370–7–52.85–0–0–3/24

Hotchkin, Neil Stafford
Amateur. *b:* 4.2.1914, Woodall Spa Manor, Lincolnshire. Opening right-hand batsman. *Sch* Eton. *Teams* Cambridge U (1934–35, blue 1935); Middlesex (1939–48, 6 matches); Services in India (1944/5); Europeans (1944/5).
Career batting
23–37–2–736–74–21.02–0–*ct* 4
Bowling 4–0
He also played for Lincolnshire (1934–37).

Hotham, Admiral Sir Alan Geoffrey
Amateur. *b:* 3.10.1876, Edinburgh, Scotland. *d:* 10.7.1965, Victoria, London. Brother-in-law of D. H. Forbes (Oxford U). Middle order right-hand batsman. *Team* Hampshire (1901, 1 match).
Career batting
1–2–0–16–11–8.00–0–*ct* 0
Bowling 6–0

He also played for Hertfordshire (1901) and Devon (1905).

Hotham, Rev Frederick William
Amateur. *b:* 17.1.1844, Bath, Somerset. *d:* 23.6.1908, Cricket-Malherbie, Somerset. Middle order right-hand batsman. *Sch* Eton. *Team* Somerset (1882, 1 match).
Career batting
2–4–0–18–7–4.50–0–*ct* 1
He also played for Hertfordshire (1876–77). His final first-class match was for MCC in 1883.

Hough, Charles Henry
Amateur. *b:* 14.3.1855, Cambridge. *d:* 15.10.1933, Victoria Park, Manchester, Lancashire. Middle order batsman. *Sch* Uppingham. *Team* MCC (1883).
Career batting
1–2–1–12–10–12.00–0–*ct* 0

Hough, Edwin John
Cricketer. *b:* 29.7.1957, Rusape, Rhodesia. Lower order right-hand batsman, right-arm fast-medium bowler. *Team* Zimbabwe (1981/2 to 1982/3). *Tour* Zimbabwe to England 1982.
Career batting
4–3–1–13–9–6.50–0–*ct* 0
Bowling 287–12–23.91–0–0–4/48

Hough, Gerald De Lisle
Amateur. *b:* 14.5.1894, Kensington, London. *d:* 29.9.1959, Canterbury, Kent. Hard-hitting middle order right-hand batsman, off break bowler. *Sch* Winchester. *Team* Kent (1919–20, 14 matches).
Career batting
15–20–5–444–87*–29.60–0–*ct* 5
Bowling 21–1–21.00–0–0–1/7
He was appointed manager of Kent in 1934 and secretary in 1936, resigning through ill-health in 1949.

Houghton, David Laud
Cricketer. *b:* 23.6.1957, Salisbury, Rhodesia. Brother of W. J. (Rhodesia). Middle order right-hand batsman, occasional off break bowler, wicket-keeper. *Team* Rhodesia/Zimbabwe (1978/9 to 1991/2). *Tours* Zimbabwe to England 1982, 1983 (World Cup), 1985, to Sri Lanka 1983/4, to India (World Cup) 1987/8, to Australia and New Zealand (World Cup) 1991/2.
Career batting
80–142–9–4545–202–34.17–8–*ct* 137–*st* 16
Bowling 31–0
He made a useful contribution as a wicket-keeper on both tours to England. His highest score was 202 for Zimbabwe v England A at Bulawayo in 1989/90.

Houghton, William Eric
Amateur. *b:* 29.6.1910, Billingborough, Lincolnshire. Middle order right-hand batsman, right-arm medium pace bowler. *Team* Warwickshire (1946–47, 7 matches).
Career batting
7–11–0–165–41–15.00–0–*ct* 2
He also played for Lincolnshire (1931–39). He played soccer for Aston Villa and Notts County, and played seven times for England.

Houldsworth, William Harry
Amateur. *b:* 6.4.1873, Levenshulme, Manchester, Lancashire. *d:* 19.4.1909, Barnfield, Flixton, Lancashire. Middle order batsman. *Team* Lancashire (1893–94, 10 matches).
Career batting
10–16–1–156–21–10.40–0–*ct* 2

Houlton, Gerard
Professional. *b:* 25.4.1939, St Helens, Lancashire. Middle order right-hand batsman, left-arm fast medium bowler. *Team* Lancashire (1961–63, 20 matches).
Career batting
20–33–2–688–86–22.19–0–*ct* 5
Bowling 6–0

Hounsfield, Thomas Douglas
Amateur. *b:* 29.4.1910, Hackenthorpe Farm, Yorkshire. Middle order right-hand batsman. *Team* Derbyshire (1938–39, 16 matches).
Career batting
16–24–3–274–56–13.04–0–*ct* 7

House, Biron Howe
Professional. *b:* 18.12.1884, Langport, Somerset. *d:* 3.6.1930, Langalier, Creech St Michael, Somerset. Tail end batsman, wicket-keeper. *Team* Somerset (1912–14, 3 matches).
Career batting
3–4–1–30–19*–10.00–0–*ct* 3

Houseman, Edward Outram
Professional. *b:* 19.3.1869, Dronfield, Derbyshire. *d:* 10.4.1942, Westhoughton, Lancashire. Middle order right-hand batsman. *Team* Derbyshire (1897, 1 match).
Career batting
1–2–0–4–4–2.00–0–*ct* 2

Houseman, Ian James
Cricketer. *b:* 12.10.1969, Harrogate, Yorkshire. Lower order right-hand batsman, right-arm fast medium bowler. *Team* Yorkshire (1989–91, 5 matches).
Career batting
5–2–1–18–18–18.00–0–*ct* 0
Bowling 311–3–103.66–0–0–2/26

Housley, Richard
Professional. *b:* 8.5.1849, Mansfield Woodhouse, Nottinghamshire. *d:* 23.4.1881, Mansfield Woodhouse, Nottinghamshire. Middle order right-hand batsman, good field. *Team* Nottinghamshire (1870, 1 match).

Career batting
1–2–0–3–2–1.50–0–*ct* 0

Howard, Alan Raymond
Professional. *b:* 11.12.1909, Clarendon Park, Leicester. Brother of Jack (Leicestershire), son of Arthur (Leicestershire). Middle order left-hand batsman, left-arm medium pace bowler. *Teams* Glamorgan (1928–33, 59 matches); Wales (1930).
Career batting
60–99–2–1181–63–12.17–0–0–*ct* 35
Bowling 70–0

Howard, Arthur
Amateur. *b:* 27.7.1882, Whitwick, Leicestershire. *d:* 5.8.1946, Belgrave, Leicester. Father of Jack (Leicestershire) and A. R. (Glamorgan). Middle order right-hand batsman. *Team* Leicestershire (1921, 3 matches).
Career batting
3–6–0–60–27–10.00–0–*ct* 0

Howard, Arthur Stanley
Amateur. *b:* 14.11.1936, Grahamstown, South Africa. Lower order right-hand batsman, off break bowler. *Team* Cambridge U (1961).
Career batting
3–2–0–0–0–0.00–0–*ct* 1
Bowling 352–8–44.00–0–0–3/100

Howard, Barry John
Amateur. *b:* 21.5.1926, Gee Cross, Hyde, Cheshire. Brother of N. D. (Lancashire), son of Rupert (Lancashire). Sound middle order right-hand batsman. *Sch* Rossall. *Team* Lancashire (1947–51, 32 matches).
Career batting
35–51–3–1232–114–25.66–3–*ct* 29
He was President of Lancashire 1987–88.

Howard, Cecil Geoffrey
Amateur. *b:* 14.2.1909, Hampstead Garden Suburb, London. Middle order right-hand batsman. *Team* Middlesex (1930, 3 matches).
Career batting
3–6–0–25–12–4.16–0–*ct* 2
He was Secretary of Lancashire CCC from 1949 to 1964 and of Surrey CCC from 1965 to 1975. He was manager of MCC tours to India 1951/2 and Australia 1954/5 appearing once in a non-first-class match in Australia.

Howard, Charles William Henry
Professional. *b:* 7.11.1904, Beckenham, Kent. Middle order right-hand batsman, right-arm medium pace bowler. *Sch* Tonbridge. *Team* Middlesex (1931, 9 matches).
Career batting
9–12–2–123–29–12.30–0–*ct* 2

Howard, Charlie
Professional. *b:* 27.9.1854, Chichester, Sussex. *d:* 20.5.1929, Chichester, Sussex. Middle order right-hand batsman. *Team* Sussex (1874–82, 22 matches).
Career batting
23–39–3–588–106–16.33–1–*ct* 6
Bowling 8–0

Howard, Jack
Professional. *b:* 24.11.1917, Belgrave, Leicester. Son of Arthur (Leicestershire), brother of A. R. (Glamorgan). Middle order left-hand batsman, wicket-keeper. *Team* Leicestershire (1946–48, 41 matches).
Career batting
41–66–14–589–38*–11.32–0–*ct* 17
Bowling 5–0

Howard, Joseph
Amateur. *b:* 12.1.1871, Epsom, Surrey. *d:* 25.1.1951, Evenlode, Gloucestershire. Middle order right-hand batsman. *Sch* Haileybury. *Team* Worcestershire (1900–01, 5 matches).
Career batting
5–10–0–85–28–8.50–0–*ct* 1
He first played for Worcestershire (pre first-class) in 1895.

Howard, Kenneth
Professional. *b:* 2.6.1941, Manchester, Lancashire. Lower order left-hand batsman, off break bowler. *Team* Lancashire (1960–66, 61 matches).
Career batting
61–82–35–395–23–8.40–0–*ct* 57
Bowling 3175–104–30.52–3–0–7/33

Howard, Nigel David
Amateur. *b:* 18.5.1925, Gee Cross, Hyde, Cheshire. *d:* 31.5.1979, Douglas, Isle of Man. Son of Rupert (Lancashire), brother of B. J. (Lancashire). Attractive right-hand batsman, fine cover field. *Sch* Rossall. *Team* Lancashire (1946–53, 170 matches). *Tour* MCC to India and Pakistan 1951/2. *Tests* England (1951/2, 4 matches).
Career batting
198–279–30–6152–145–24.70–3–*ct* 153
Bowling 52–1–52.00–0–0–1/14
Test batting
4–6–1–86–23–17.20–0–*ct* 4
He captained MCC on the tour in 1951/2 and England in his four Tests; also Lancashire 1949 to 1953. He hit 1,000 runs in a season once: 1,174, av 36.68, in 1950. His final first-class match was for MCC in 1954.

Howard, Rupert
Amateur. *b:* 17.4.1889, Ashton-under-Lyne, Lancashire. *d:* 10.9.1967, Manchester, Lancashire. Father of B. J. (Lancashire) and N. D. (Lancashire). Middle order right-hand batsman. *Team* Lancashire (1922–33, 8 matches). *Tours* Manager of MCC to Australia

and New Zealand 1936/7 and 1946/7 (he played in non-first-class matches on the former).
Career batting
8–9–2–166–88*–23.71–0–*ct* 4
Bowling 18–0
He was Secretary of Lancashire CCC 1932–48.

Howard, Thomas Charles
Professional. *b:* 19.7.1781, Hartley Wintney, Hampshire. *d:* 18.5.1864, Hartford Bridge, Hartley Row, Hampshire. Middle order right-hand batsman, right-hand fast under-arm bowler, wicket-keeper. *Team* Hampshire (1803–28).
Career batting
88–161–17–1539–54*–10.68–0–*ct* 73–*st* 64
Bowling 326 wickets (no analyses)–14–1–7/?
He was remarkable for excelling both as a bowler and a wicket-keeper. His final first-class match was for Players in 1829.

Howard-Smith, Gerald
Amateur. *b:* 21.1.1880, Kensington, London. *d:* 29.3.1916, Merville St Vaast, France. Middle order right-hand batsman, right-arm fast bowler. *Sch* Eton. *Team* Cambridge U (1901–03, blue 1903).
Career batting
20–33–16–189–23*–11.11–0–*ct* 15
Bowling 1279–29–44.10–1–0–6/23
His first-class debut was for MCC in 1900. He also played for Staffordshire (1908–10). He also won a blue for athletics.

Howarth, Geoffrey Philip, OBE
Cricketer. *b:* 29.3.1951, Auckland, New Zealand. Brother of H. J. (New Zealand). Attractive opening or middle order right-hand batsman, off break bowler, good field. *Teams* Surrey (1971–85, 188 matches); Auckland (1972/3 to 1973/4); Northern Districts (1974/5 to 1985/6). *Tours* New Zealand to Australia 1974/5 (not first-class), 1980/1, 1982/3, 1984/5 (not first-class), to England 1975 (World Cup), 1978, 1979 (World Cup), 1983, to India and Pakistan 1976/7, to Sri Lanka 1983/4, to West Indies 1984/5; Robins to South Africa 1975/6, to Sri Lanka 1977/8. *Tests* New Zealand (1974/5 to 1984/5, 47 matches).
Career batting
338–584–42–17294–183–31.90–32–*ct* 229
Bowling 3593–112–32.08–1–0–5/32
Test batting
47–83–5–2531–147–32.44–6–*ct* 29
Bowling 271–3–90.33–0–0–1/13
On the 1978 tour to England he headed both the Test and first-class batting averages with 296 runs, av 74.00, and 816 runs, av 45.33. He captained the 1983 side to England, but was not so successful in the Tests, though in the first-class matches he hit 697 runs, av 41.00. In all he hit 1,000 runs in an English season four times (best 1,554, av 37.90, in 1976). He captained New Zealand in 30 Tests and in 1984 and 1985 was captain of Surrey. In the latter season however he found himself playing in only two matches since Surrey could use just a single overseas cricketer and preferred A. H. Gray. His first-class debut was for New Zealand Under 23 in 1968/9. He was awarded an MBE in 1981 and OBE in 1984.

Howarth, Hedley John
Cricketer. *b:* 28.12.1943, Grey Lynn, Auckland, New Zealand. Brother of G. P. (New Zealand and Surrey). Lower order left-hand batsman, slow left-arm bowler. *Teams* Auckland (1963/4 to 1978/9). *Tours* New Zealand to England 1969, 1973, 1975 (World Cup), to Australia 1969/70, 1970/1, 1974/5 (not first-class), to India and Pakistan 1969/70, to West Indies 1971/2. *Tests* New Zealand (1969 to 1976/7, 30 matches).
Career batting
145–179–58–1668–61–13.78–0–*ct* 137
Bowling 13674–541–25.27–31–6–8/75
Test batting
30–42–18–291–61–12.12–0–*ct* 33
Bowling 3178–86–36.95–2–0–5/34
He headed the first-class bowling averages on the 1969 tour to England with 57 wickets, av 19.75, and played in all three Tests; on his 1973 tour he was not so successful. His first-class debut was for New Zealand Under 23 in 1962/3.

Howarth, John Stirling
Cricketer. *b:* 26.3.1945, Stockport, Cheshire. Lower order right-hand batsman, right-arm fast medium bowler. *Team* Nottinghamshire (1966–67, 13 matches).
Career batting
13–7–3–0–0*–0.00–0–*ct* 3
Bowling 642–19–33.78–0–0–3/30
He also played for Cheshire (1976–78).

Howarth, Thomas
Professional. *b:* 10.5.1845, Glossop, Derbyshire. *d:* 12.10.1897, Fylde, Lancashire. Middle order batsman. *Team* Derbyshire (1873, 1 match).
Career batting
1–2–0–7–5–3.50–0–*ct* 1

Howat, Michael Gerald
(birth registered as M. G. Henderson-Howat)
Cricketer. *b:* 2.3.1958, Tavistock, Devon. Lower order right-hand batsman, right-arm medium fast bowler. *Sch* Abingdon. *Team* Cambridge U (1977–80, blue 1977 and 1980).
Career batting
26–22–3–194–32–10.21–0–*ct* 7
Bowling 1560–26–60.00–0–0–3/39
His father, Gerald, is a well-known cricketer writer.

Howcroft, Albert
Professional. *b:* 27.12.1882, Cliffe, Yorkshire. *d:* 7.3.1955, Belper, Derbyshire. Middle order left-hand

batsman. *Team* Derbyshire (1908–10, 4 matches).
Career batting
4–8–0–46–19–5.75–0–*ct* 2

Howe, Richard
Amateur. *b:* 17.2.1853, Denton, Manchester, Lancashire. *d:* 21.1.1914, Alderley Edge, Cheshire. Hard-hitting middle order right-hand batsman, good cover point. *Team* Lancashire (1876–77, 3 matches).
Career batting
4–7–0–38–14–5.42–0–*ct* 4
Bowling 6–0

Howell, Albert Louis
Professional. *b:* 26.7.1898, Ladywood, Birmingham. *d:* 26.7.1958, Wingrove, Newcastle upon Tyne, Northumberland. Brother of Henry (Warwickshire). Lower order right-hand batsman, right-arm medium fast bowler. *Team* Warwickshire (1919–22, 34 matches).
Career batting
35–57–16–249–26–6.07–0–*ct* 14
Bowling 2019–56–36.05–1–0–5/65

He also played for Durham (pre first-class, 1926–36). His final first-class match was for Minor Counties in 1929.

Howell, Henry
Professional. *b:* 29.11.1890, Hockley, Birmingham. *d:* 9.7.1932, Selly Oak, Birmingham. Brother of A. L. (Warwickshire). Lower order right-hand batsman, right-arm fast bowler. *Team* Warwickshire (1913–28, 198 matches). *Tours* MCC to Australia 1920/1, 1924/5. *Tests* England (1920/1 to 1924, 5 matches).
Career batting
227–326–111–1679–36–7.80–0–*ct* 67
Bowling 20700–975–21.23–75–18–10/51
Test batting
5–8–6–15–5–7.50–0–*ct* 0
Bowling 559–7–79.85–0–0–4/115

He took 100 wickets in a season six times (best 161, av 17.91, in 1920). In 1923 he took all ten wickets in an innings (for 51 runs) for Warwickshire v Yorkshire at Edgbaston. A useful soccer player, he appeared for Wolverhampton Wanderers and Accrington Stanley.

Howell, Leonard Sidgwick
Amateur. *b:* 6.8.1848, Herne Hill, Dulwich, London. *d:* 7.9.1895, Lausanne, Switzerland. Middle order right-hand batsman. *Sch* Winchester. *Team* Surrey (1869–80, 13 matches).
Career batting
19–34–6–519–96–18.53–0–*ct* 9

An excellent soccer player for Wanderers and Surrey, he represented England in 1873, as well as appearing on the winning side in the FA Cup in the same season.

Howell, Miles
Amateur. *b:* 9.9.1893, Thames Ditton, Surrey. *d:* 23.2.1976, Worplesdon, Surrey. Son of Reginald (Surrey). Opening right-hand batsman, brilliant outfield. *Sch* Repton. *Teams* Oxford U (1914 and 1919, blue both years); Surrey (1919–25, 36 matches).
Career batting
97–162–17–4670–170–32.20–8–*ct* 32
Bowling 26–1–26.00–0–0–1/5

His final first-class match was for Free Foresters in 1939. He captained Oxford in 1919. He played for Combined Universities v Glamorgan in 1922 under the alias of W. G. Osborne. A noted soccer player, he captained Oxford in 1919, played also for the Corinthians and won several amateur international caps for England.

Howell, Reginald
Amateur. *b:* 16.4.1856, Streatham, London. *d:* 3.8.1912, Esher, Surrey. Father of Miles (Surrey). Middle order right-hand batsman, right-hand slow round-arm bowler, good cover field. *Sch* Tonbridge. *Team* Surrey (1878–79, 3 matches).
Career batting
3–5–1–31–10–7.75–0–*ct* 0

Howell, Robert George Dunnett
Amateur. *b:* 23.1.1877, Edmonton, Middlesex. *d:* 27.9.1942, Sydenham, London. Opening batsman. *Sch* Felsted. *Teams* Cambridge U (1898–99); Sussex (1900, 1 match).
Career batting
3–5–0–14–7–2.80–0–*ct* 0

Howell, William Peter
Amateur. *b:* 29.12.1869, Penrith, New South Wales, Australia. *d:* 14.7.1940, Castlereagh, Sydney, New South Wales, Australia. Father of W. H. (New South Wales), nephew of E. Evans (New South Wales). Lower order left-hand batsman, right-arm medium pace bowler. *Team* New South Wales (1894/5 to 1904/5, 48 matches). *Tours* Australia to England 1899, 1902, 1905, to South Africa 1902/3, to New Zealand 1904/5. *Tests* Australia (1897/8 to 1903/4, 18 matches).
Career batting
141–201–51–2227–128–14.84–1–*ct* 126
Bowling 11154–519–21.49–30–5–10/28
Test batting
18–27–6–158–35–7.52–0–*ct* 12
Bowling 1407–49–28.71–1–0–5/81

He was most successful on his first visit to England in 1899, playing in all five Tests, and against Surrey at the Oval taking all ten wickets for 28. Neither of his other tours to England proved as profitable, and in 1902 he appeared in only one Test, whilst in 1905 he was not required for any. He took 117 wickets, av 20.35, in 1899.

Howgego, James Alan
Cricketer. *b:* 3.8.1948, Folkestone, Kent. Middle order right-hand batsman, leg break bowler. *Team* Kent (1977, 1 match).
Career batting
1–2–0–91–52–45.50–0–*ct* 0

Howick, Nicholas Keith
Cricketer. *b:* 14.3.1954, St Peter Port, Guernsey. Middle order right-hand batsman, right-arm medium pace bowler. *Sch* Elizabeth College, Guernsey. *Team* Oxford U (1974).
Career batting
5–10–0–51–14–5.10–0–*ct* 1
He won a blue for hockey.

Howitt, George
Professional. *b:* 14.3.1843, Old Lenton, Nottinghamshire. *d:* 19.12.1881, Nottingham. Tail end left-hand batsman, left-hand fast round-arm bowler. *Teams* Nottinghamshire (1866–70, 8 matches); Middlesex (1865–76, 43 matches).
Career batting
79–129–29–483–49–4.83–0–*ct* 64
Bowling 5522–347 + 1–15.91–26–7–7/19
He also played for Lincolnshire (1875).

Howitt, Richard Holmes
Amateur. *b:* 21.7.1864, Farnsfield, Nottinghamshire. *d:* 10.1.1951, Farndon, Nottinghamshire. Middle order right-hand batsman, medium pace bowler, good field. *Team* Nottinghamshire (1893–1901, 28 matches).
Career batting
28–50–2–492–119–10.25–1–*ct* 17
Bowling 337–8–42.12–0–0–2/25
He was on the committee of Nottinghamshire CCC 1899 to 1934.

Howland, Christopher Burfield
Amateur. *b:* 6.2.1936, Whitstable, Kent. Brother of P. C. (Cambridge U). Middle/lower order right-hand batsman, wicket-keeper. *Sch* Dulwich. *Teams* Cambridge U (1958–60, blue all three years); Sussex (1960, 4 matches); Kent (1965, 2 matches). *Tours* MCC to South America 1958/9, to North America 1959 (neither first-class).
Career batting
64–104–8–1629–124–16.96–1–*ct* 130–*st* 21
Bowling 11–0
His first-class debut was for Combined Services in 1956 and his final first-class match for MCC in 1968. He captained Cambridge in 1960.

Howland, Peter Charles
Cricketer. *b:* 9.3.1947, Orpington, Kent. Brother of C. B. (Kent and Sussex). Middle order right-hand batsman, off break bowler. *Sch* Dulwich. *Team* Cambridge U (1969).
Career batting
6–11–1–104–21–10.40–0–*ct* 4
Bowling 7–0

Howlett, Bernard
Amateur. *b:* 18.12.1898, Stoke Newington, London. *d:* 29.11.1943, Santa Maria Imbaro, Italy. He was killed in action. Lower order right-hand batsman, right-arm fast bowler. *Sch* St Edmund's, Canterbury. *Teams* Kent (1922–28, 26 matches); Europeans (1925/6 to 1928/9); Bombay (1926/7).
Career batting
42–55–21–319–58–9.38–0–*ct* 23
Bowling 3156–108–29.22–3–0–6/35
He was a well-known player in military cricket and his final first-class match was for MCC in 1931.

Howman, John
Amateur. *b:* 26.4.1895, Stow-on-the-Wold, Gloucestershire. *d:* 4.4.1958, Oxford. Middle order right-hand batsman. *Team* Gloucestershire (1922–23, 13 matches).
Career batting
13–21–1–128–23–6.40–0–*ct* 4

Howorth, Richard
Professional. *b:* 26.4.1909, Bacup, Lancashire. *d:* 2.4.1980, Worcester. Middle/lower order left-hand batsman, slow left-arm bowler. *Teams* Worcestershire (1933–51, 348 matches); Europeans (1944/5). *Tour* MCC to West Indies 1947/8. *Tests* England (1947 to 1947/8, 5 matches).
Career batting
372–611–56–11479–114–20.68–4–*ct* 197
Bowling 29425–1345–21.87–74–7–7/18
Test batting
5–10–2–145–45*–18.12–0–*ct* 2
Bowling 635–19–33.42–1–0–6/124
He took 100 wickets in a season nine times (best 164, av 17.85, in 1947) and hit 1,000 runs in a season four times (best 1,510, av 26.03, in 1947), three times performing the 'double'.

Howsin, Dr Edward Arthur
Amateur. *b:* 26.7.1838, North Muskham, Nottinghamshire. *d:* 27.2.1921, Boscombe, Hampshire. Middle order right-hand batsman, medium pace bowler. *Team* Nottinghamshire (1863, 2 matches).
Career batting
4–8–1–114–48*–16.28–0–*ct* 3–*st* 2
Bowling 49–2–24.50–0–0–1/15
His first-class debut was for Gentlemen of the South in 1862.

Hoyer Millar, Gurth Christian
Amateur. *b:* 13.12.1929, Chelsea, London. Lower order right-hand batsman, wicket-keeper. *Sch* Harrow. *Team* Oxford U (1952).

Career batting
2–3–1–17–10–8.50–0–*ct* 4
He played rugby for Scotland.

Hoyle, Theodore Hind
Professional. *b:* 19.3.1884, Halifax, Yorkshire. *d:* 2.6.1953, Hull, Yorkshire. Lower order batsman, wicket-keeper. *Team* Yorkshire (1919, 1 match).
Career batting
1–2–0–7–7–3.50–0–*ct* 0–*st* 1

Huband, Ralph Croft
Amateur. *b:* 19.6.1902, Killiskey, Co Wicklow, Ireland. *d:* 7.11.1964, Lambeth, London. Brother-in-law of G. Ashton (Worcestershire). Opening/middle order right-hand batsman, wicket-keeper. *Sch* Winchester. *Team* Cambridge U (1923).
Career batting
2–4–2–64–61*–32.00–0–*ct* 0

Hubback, Theodore Rathbone
Amateur. *b:* 17.12.1872, Liverpool, Lancashire. *d:* 1942, Malaya. He was killed prior to the fall of Singapore. Middle order batsman, wicket-keeper. *Team* Lancashire (1892, 4 matches).
Career batting
6–10–1–140–67–15.55–0–*ct* 3–*st* 2
His final first-class match was for Liverpool and District in 1893.

Hubbard, George Cairns
Amateur. *b:* 23.11.1867, Benares, India. *d:* 18.12.1931, Eltham, Kent. Middle order right-hand batsman, right-arm medium pace bowler. *Sch* Tonbridge. *Team* Kent (1895, 3 matches).
Career batting
3–4–0–61–36–15.25–0–*ct* 4
Bowling 25–1–25.00–0–0–1/25
He played rugby for Blackheath and England.

Hubble, Harold John
Professional. *b:* 3.10.1904, Headcorn, Kent. *d:* 12.1.1989, Tenterden, Kent. Nephew of J. C. (Kent). Middle order right-hand batsman, leg break bowler. *Team* Kent (1929–31, 13 matches).
Career batting
13–21–3–285–50–15.83–0–*ct* 3
Bowling 33–1–33.00–0–0–1/5

Hubble, John Charlton
Professional. *b:* 10.2.1881, Wateringbury, Kent. *d:* 26.2.1965, St Leonards-on-Sea, Sussex. Uncle of H. J. (Kent). Middle/lower order right-hand batsman, wicket-keeper. *Team* Kent (1904–29, 343 matches). *Tours* MCC to South Africa 1927/8 (in emergency).
Career batting
360–528–64–10939–189–23.57–5–*ct* 437–*st* 221
Bowling 27–0
He hit 1,000 runs in a season once: 1,282, av 33.73, in 1914. He took over as the regular County wicket-keeper only after the First World War.

Hubble, William George
Amateur. *b:* 20.6.1898, Leyton, Essex. *d:* 14.12.1978, Bishops Waltham, Hampshire. Opening left-hand batsman, slow left-arm bowler. *Team* Essex (1923, 1 match).
Career batting
1–1–0–0–0–0.00–0–*ct* 0
Bowling 60–2–30.00–0–0–2/3

Huddleston, William
Professional. *b:* 27.2.1873, Earlestown, Lancashire. *d:* 21.5.1962, Warrington, Lancashire. Lower order right-hand batsman, right-arm medium pace off break bowler. *Team* Lancashire (1899–1914, 183 matches).
Career batting
185–258–32–2765–88–12.23–0–*ct* 149
Bowling 12042–685–17.57–42–14–9/36
He took 100 wickets in a season once: 113, av 19.68, in 1913. His best bowling was 9/36 for Lancashire v Nottinghamshire at Liverpool in 1906. He was a first-class umpire (1930).

Hudleston, Air Chief Marshal Sir Edmund Cuthbert
Amateur. *b:* 30.12.1908, St Albans, Perth, Western Australia. Opening right-hand batsman, wicket-keeper. *Team* RAF (1929–31).
Career batting
4–7–0–97–38–13.85–0–*ct* 1
He was Commander Allied Air Forces Central Europe 1964–67.

Hudson, Bennett
Professional. *b:* 29.6.1851, Sheffield, Yorkshire. *d:* 11.11.1901, Wortley, Yorkshire. Lower order right-hand batsman, right-arm fast bowler. *Teams* Yorkshire (1880, 3 matches); Lancashire (1886–88, 5 matches).
Career batting
8–10–0–220–98–22.00–0–*ct* 2
Bowling 59–3–19.66–0–0–2/14

Hudson, Eric Vaughan Hamilton
Amateur. *b:* 30.6.1900, Bihar, India. *d:* 6.2.1974, Churston-Ferrers, Devon. Brother of R. E. H. (Army). Lower order right-hand batsman, right-arm fast bowler. *Sch* Haileybury. *Team* Army (1930).
Career batting
1–2–0–7–7–3.50–0–*ct* 0
Bowling 86–4–21.50–0–0–3/55
His County cricket was for Hertfordshire (1933–34).

Hudson, Frederick John
Amateur. *b:* 22.11.1878, Bottesford, Leicestershire. *d:* 7.10.1966, Bottesford, Leicestershire. Middle order right-hand batsman, change bowler. *Team* Leicestershire (1901, 1 match).
Career batting
1–2–0–1–1–0.50–0–*ct* 0

Bowling 38–0

He also played for Lincolnshire (1903), but not in the Minor Counties Championship.

Hudson, George Neville
Amateur. *b:* 12.7.1905, Clitheroe, Lancashire. *d:* 24.11.1981, Preston, Lancashire. Lower order batsman, slow right-arm bowler. *Team* Lancashire (1936, 2 matches).
Career batting
2–2–1–1–1–1.00–0–*ct* 1
Bowling 82–0

Hudson, Gideon Dacre
Cricketer. *b:* 8.11.1944, Salisbury, Wiltshire. Lower order right-hand batsman, wicket-keeper. *Sch* St Edward's, Oxford. *Team* Oxford U (1964).
Career batting
1–2–0–6–6–3.00–0–*ct* 2

His County cricket was for Buckinghamshire (1964–75).

Hudson, Reginald Eustace Hamilton
Amateur. *b:* 22.8.1904, Bihar, India. Brother of E. V. H. (Army). Opening right-hand batsman, right-arm medium pace bowler. *Sch* Haileybury. *Teams* Army (1925–38); Europeans (1926/7 to 1929/30).
Career batting
27–49–4–1807–217–40.15–5–*ct* 7
Bowling 14–0

His highest score was 217 for Army v RAF at the Oval in 1932. His County cricket was for Devon (1928–32).

Huey, Samuel Scott Johnston
Amateur. *b:* 21.12.1923, Ture, Co Donegal, Ireland. Tail end right-hand batsman, slow left-arm bowler. *Team* Ireland (1951–66).
Career batting
20–30–4–135–23*–5.19–0–*ct* 14
Bowling 1203–66–18.22–5–1–8/48

He played badminton for Ireland.

Huggett, Arthur
Professional. *b:* 14.1.1861, Godstone, Surrey. *d:* 14.4.1945, High Brooms, Tunbridge Wells, Kent. Lower order batsman, bowler. *Team* Sussex (1883–85, 3 matches).
Career batting
3–5–1–14–5*–3.50–0–*ct* 1
Bowling 10–0

Huggins, Henry James
Professional. *b:* 15.3.1877, Headington, Oxfordshire. *d:* 20.11.1942, Stroud, Gloucestershire. Hard-hitting lower order right-hand batsman, right-arm fast medium bowler. *Team* Gloucestershire (1901–21, 200 matches).
Career batting
200–347–44–4375–92–14.43–0–*ct* 47
Bowling 16957–584–29.03–24–5–9/34

His best bowling was 9/34 for Gloucestershire v Sussex at Bristol in 1904.

Hughes, David Garfield
Amateur. *b:* 21.5.1934, Taunton, Somerset. Lower order right-hand batsman, wicket-keeper. *Sch* Taunton. *Team* Somerset (1955, 1 match).
Career batting
1–1–0–2–2–2.00–0–*ct* 1–*st* 1

He also played for Wiltshire (1965–68).

Hughes, David Paul
Cricketer. *b:* 13.5.1947, Newton-le-Willows, Lancashire. Hard hitting middle order right-hand batsman, slow left-arm bowler. *Teams* Lancashire (1967–91, 436 matches); Tasmania (1975/6 to 1976/7, 2 matches). *Tours* Robins to South Africa 1972/3; Lancashire to Jamaica 1986/7, 1987/8, to Zimbabwe 1988/9.
Career batting
447–587–109–10419–153–21.79–8–*ct* 325
Bowling 19858–655–30.31–20–2–7/24

He hit 1,000 runs in a season twice (best 1,303, av 48.25, in 1982) and took 82 wickets in 1970 and again in 1972. From 1987 to 1991 he captained Lancashire.

Hughes, David Wilfred
Amateur. *b:* 12.7.1910, Ebbw Vale, Monmouthshire. *d:* 21.4.1984, Sarisbury Green, Southampton, Hampshire. Lower order right-hand batsman, right-arm fast medium bowler. *Team* Glamorgan (1935–38, 22 matches).
Career batting
22–33–8–274–70*–10.96–0–*ct* 6
Bowling 1692–52–32.53–2–0–5/70

He also played for Monmouthshire (1933–34) and Dorset (1946–49).

Hughes, Gwyn
Cricketer. *b:* 26.3.1941, Mynachdy, Cardiff, Glamorgan. Lower order right-hand batsman, slow left-arm bowler, excellent short-leg. *Sch* Cardiff HS. *Teams* Glamorgan (1962–64, 17 matches); Cambridge U (1965, blue).
Career batting
27–41–4–457–92–12.35–0–*ct* 22
Bowling 1368–31–44.12–0–0–4/31

Hughes, John
Professional. *b:* 2.7.1825, Hertford. *d:* 29.1.1907, Hertford. Lower order right-hand batsman, right-hand slow round-arm bowler, close field. *Team* South (1874).
Career batting
1–2–0–8–8–4.00–0–*ct* 1
Bowling 94–9–10.44–1–0–7/46

His County cricket was for Hertfordshire (1855–79) being very successful for the county, and for Staffordshire (1873) and Essex (pre first-class, 1878).

Hughes, John Gareth
Cricketer. *b:* 3.5.1971, Wellingborough, Northamptonshire. Lower order right-hand batsman, right-arm medium pace bowler. *Team* Northamptonshire (1990 to 1991/2, 6 matches). *Tours* Northamptonshire to South Africa 1991/2.
Career batting
6–9–0–11–6–1.22–0–*ct* 1
Bowling 450–7–64.28–0–0–3/56

Hughes, Kimberley John
Cricketer. *b:* 26.1.1954, Margaret River, Western Australia. Brother of G. A. (Tasmania). Stylish middle order right-hand batsman, right-arm medium pace bowler. *Teams* Western Australia (1975/6 to 1988/9, 66 matches); Natal (1989/90 to 1990/1). *Tours* Australia to New Zealand 1976/7, 1981/2, to England 1977, 1979 (World Cup), 1980, 1981, 1983 (World Cup), to West Indies 1977/8, 1983/4, to India 1979/80, 1984/5 (not first-class), to Pakistan 1979/80, 1982/3, to Sri Lanka 1980/1, to Sharjah (not first-class) 1984/5; Australian XI to South Africa 1985/6, 1986/7. *Tests* Australia (1977 to 1984/5, 70 matches).
Career batting
216–368–20–12711–213–36.52–26–*ct* 155
Bowling 97–3–32.33–0–0–1/0
Test batting
70–124–6–4415–213–37.41–9–*ct* 50
Bowling 28–0

His 1977 tour to England produced modest results, and he played in only one Test. In the 1980 Centenary Test he hit 117 and 84, being the highest scorer in the match. He captained Australia on the 1981 tour, playing in all six Tests and scoring 300 runs, av 25.00. He led Australia in 28 Tests, and captained them in the 1983 World Cup. He scored 119 on debut for Western Australia v New South Wales at Perth in 1975/6. He scored 1,000 runs in a season in Australia twice (best 1,280, av 64.00, in 1982/3).

Hughes, Lewis Patrick
Cricketer. *b:* 10.4.1943, Blackrock, Co Dublin, Ireland. Lower order right-hand batsman, right-arm fast medium bowler. *Team* Ireland (1965–72).
Career batting
5–8–3–55–35–11.00–0–*ct* 6
Bowling 439–9–48.77–0–0–3/77

Hughes, Mervyn Gregory
Cricketer. *b:* 23.11.1961, Euroa, Victoria, Australia. Lower order right-hand batsman, right-arm fast medium bowler. *Teams* Victoria (1981/2 to 1991/2, 73 matches); Essex (1983, 1 match). *Tours* Australia to England 1989, to India 1989/90 (not first-class), to New Zealand 1989/90, to Sharjah (not first-class) 1989/90, to West Indies 1990/1; Victoria to England 1991. *Tests* Australia (1985/6 to 1991/2, 37 matches).
Career batting
125–149–33–1896–72*–16.34–0–*ct* 42
Bowling 13115–446–29.40–17–3–8/87
Test batting
37–49–5–688–72*–15.63–0–*ct* 17
Bowling 4154–144–28.84–5–1–8/87

On his only tour to England in 1989 he played in all six Test matches and proved a very useful back up to Alderman and Lawson as part of the seam attack, but produced no outstanding analyses.

Hughes, Noel
Professional. *b:* 6.4.1929, Sydney, New South Wales, Australia. Middle order right-hand batsman, off break bowler, occasional wicket-keeper. *Team* Worcestershire (1953–54, 21 matches).
Career batting
21–32–6–651–95–25.03–0–*ct* 13–*st* 3
Bowling 317–10–31.70–0–0–4/19

Hughes, Owen
Amateur. *b:* 7.7.1889, Wallfield, Reigate, Surrey. *d:* 4.6.1972, Beaumont, St Peter, Jersey. Middle order right-hand batsman. *Sch* Malvern. *Team* Cambridge U (1910, blue).
Career batting
6–9–1–168–65–21.00–0–*ct* 7

Hughes, Richard Clive
Professional. *b:* 30.9.1926, Watford, Hertfordshire. Lower order right-hand batsman, left-arm medium fast bowler. *Team* Worcestershire (1950–51, 11 matches).
Career batting
11–10–2–47–21–5.87–0–*ct* 2
Bowling 694–15–46.26–0–0–3/38

He also played for Hertfordshire (1953–59).

Hughes, Simon Peter
Cricketer. *b:* 20.12.1959, Kingston-upon-Thames, Surrey. Lower order right-hand batsman, right-arm fast medium bowler. *Sch* Latymer. *Teams* Middlesex (1980–91, 172 matches); Northern Transvaal (1982/3); Durham (1992, 20 matches). *Tours* Middlesex to Zimbabwe 1980/1; Overseas XI to India 1980/1.
Career batting
199–218–68–1738–53–11.58–0–*ct* 49
Bowling 14587–458–31.84–10–0–7/35

Hughes, Walter Laurence
Amateur. *b:* 9.9.1917, New Lambton, New South Wales, Australia. Lower order right-hand batsman, slow right-arm bowler. *Team* Oxford U (1947).
Career batting
1–1–0–3–3–3.00–0–*ct* 2
Bowling 28–0

Hughes-Hallett, Norton Montrésor
Amateur. *b:* 18.4.1895, Melbourne, Derbyshire. *d:* 26.3.1985, Tewkesbury, Gloucestershire. Brother-in-law of J. H. Pawle (Essex). Middle order right-hand batsman, leg break bowler. *Sch* Clifton and Hailey-

bury. *Teams* Derbyshire (1913–14, 6 matches); Europeans (1925/6 to 1926/7).
Career batting
10–17–1–255–67–15.93–0–*ct* 4
Bowling 312–17–18.35–2–1–8/81

Hugo, Stephanus Gideon
Cricketer. *b:* 20.7.1945, Caledon, Cape Province, South Africa. Lower order right-hand batsman, right-arm medium fast bowler. *Team* Western Province (1967/8 to 1977/8). *Tour* South African Universities to England 1967.
Career batting
22–29–6–584–68*–25.39–0–*ct* 12
Bowling 951–48–19.81–0–0–4/31

He achieved useful all-round figures on the 1967 tour and hit 57 in his only first-class innings as well as taking 5 wickets at moderate cost. His first-class debut was for South African Universities in 1966/7.

Hugonin, Francis Edgar
Amateur. *b:* 16.8.1897, Kensington, London. *d:* 5.3.1967, Stainton-in-Cleveland House, North Yorkshire. Lower order right-hand batsman, wicket-keeper. *Sch* Eastbourne. *Team* Essex (1927–28, 6 matches).
Career batting
14–19–6–167–44–12.84–*ct* 26–*st* 6

He appeared in many military matches and his final first-class match was for the Army in 1937. He also played for Berkshire (1935).

Huish, Francis Edward
Professional. *b:* 9.12.1867, Clapham, London. *d:* 1955, California, USA. Brother of F. H. (Kent). Middle order left-hand batsman, left-arm medium pace bowler. *Team* Kent (1895, 5 matches).
Career batting
5–8–4–32–12–8.00–0–*ct* 3
Bowling 433–11–39.36–1–0–5/52

He played for Surrey in 1888, but not in first-class matches.

Huish, Frederick Henry
Professional. *b:* 15.11.1869, Clapham, London. *d:* 16.3.1957, Northiam, Sussex. Brother of F. E. (Kent). Lower order right-hand batsman, wicket-keeper. *Teams* Kent (1895–1914, 469 matches); London County (1900). *Tour* Kent to North America 1903.
Career batting
497–726–139–7547–93–12.85–0–*ct* 933–*st* 377
Bowling 87–0

He exceeded 100 dismissals in a season once: 102 in 1913, and in 1911 obtained exactly 100.

Hull, Rear Admiral Dr Herbert Richard Barnes
Amateur. *b:* 27.10.1886, Chippenham, Wiltshire. *d:* 31.5.1970, Westminster, London. Tail end batsman, useful bowler. *Sch* Bath College. *Team* Royal Navy (1924).
Career batting
1–1–1–1–1*–no av–0–*ct* 0
Bowling 56–0

Hulls, Charles Henry
Amateur. *b:* 18.3.1861, Luton, Bedfordshire. *d:* 19.12.1912, Southend, Essex. Middle order batsman. *Team* Somerset (1885, 1 match).
Career batting
2–4–0–38–30–9.50–0–*ct* 1
Bowling 5–0

His final first-class match was for MCC in 1896. He also played for Warwickshire (pre first-class, 1882) and Oxfordshire (1896).

Hulme, John Joseph
Professional. *b:* 30.6.1862, Church Gresley, Derbyshire. *d:* 11.7.1940, Nelson, Lancashire. Lower order left-hand batsman, left-arm medium fast bowler. *Team* Derbyshire (1887–1903, 133 matches).
Career batting
142–229–32–2433–59–12.35–0–*ct* 80
Bowling 13364–557–23.99–34–9–9/27

His best bowling was 9/27 for Derbyshire v Yorkshire at Sheffield in 1894.

Hulme, Joseph Harold Anthony
Professional. *b:* 26.8.1904, Stafford. *d:* 27.9.1991, Winchmore Hill, Middlesex. Middle order right-hand batsman, right-arm medium bowler, good deep field. *Team* Middlesex (1929–39, 223 matches).
Career batting
225–350–45–8103–143–26.56–12–*ct* 110
Bowling 3240–89–36.40–0–0–4/44

He hit 1,000 runs in a season three times (best 1,258, av 34.94, in 1934). A well-known soccer player, he appeared for Blackburn Rovers, Arsenal, Huddersfield Town and England at outside right.

Hulse, Charles Westrow
Amateur. *b:* 25.11.1860, Breamore House, Hampshire. *d:* 4.6.1901, Braklaagte, South Africa. Middle order batsman. *Sch* Winchester and Radley. *Team* MCC (1885).
Career batting
1–1–0–22–22–22.00–0–*ct* 0

Hulton, Campbell Arthur Grey
Amateur. *b:* 16.3.1846, Manchester, Lancashire. *d:* 23.6.1919, Marylebone, London. Father of C. B. (MCC) and J. M. (MCC). Middle order batsman. *Sch* Rossall and Aldenham. *Team* Lancashire (1869–82, 8 matches).
Career batting
8–12–3–80–19–8.88–0–*ct* 6

He also played for Cheshire (1875).

Hulton, Rev Campbell Blethyn
(registered at birth as Campbell Grey Hulton)
Amateur. *b:* 30.5.1877, Whalley Range, Manchester, Lancashire. *d:* 10.4.1947, Mentmore, Bedfordshire.

Son of C. A. G. (Lancashire), brother of J. M. (MCC). Middle order batsman. *Sch* Charterhouse. *Team* MCC (1903).
Career batting
1–2–0–4–4–2.00–0–*ct* 2

Hulton, Harrington Arthur Harrop
Amateur. *b:* 9.11.1846, Bardsley, Ashton-under-Lyne, Lancashire. *d:* 28.1.1923, Lansdown, Cheltenham, Gloucestershire. Middle order batsman. *Sch* Rossall. *Team* Lancashire (1868, 2 matches).
Career batting
2–4–1–13–6–4.33–0–*ct* 0

Hulton, John Meredith
Amateur. *b:* 8.1.1882, Whalley Range, Manchester, Lancashire. *d:* 13.7.1942, Poole, Dorset. Son of C. A. G. (Lancashire), brother of C. B. (MCC). Middle order right-hand batsman. *Sch* Charterhouse. *Team* MCC (1903–05).
Career batting
3–5–0–127–65–25.40–0–*ct* 1
Bowling 36–0

Human, John Hanbury
Amateur. *b:* 13.1.1912, Gosforth, Newcastle upon Tyne, Northumberland. *d:* 22.7.1991, Sydney, New South Wales, Australia. Brother of R. H. C. (Worcestershire). Middle order right-hand batsman, leg break bowler. *Sch* Repton. *Teams* Cambridge U (1932–34, blue all three years); Middlesex (1935–38, 41 matches). *Tours* MCC to India and Ceylon 1933/4, to Australia and New Zealand 1935/6.
Career batting
105–161–14–5246–158*–35.68–15–*ct* 66
Bowling 2499–73–34.23–3–0–7/119
He hit 1,000 runs in a season twice (best 1,399, av 53.80, in 1934). He also played for Berkshire (1928–34). He scored 158* on debut for Cambridge U v Leveson-Gower's XI at Eastbourne in 1932. He captained Cambridge in 1934.

Human, Roger Henry Charles
Amateur. *b:* 11.5.1909, Gosforth, Newcastle upon Tyne, Northumberland. *d:* 21.11.1942, Bangalore, India. He died from a brain tumor. Brother of J. H. (Middlesex). Forcing middle order right-hand batsman, right-arm medium pace bowler. *Sch* Repton. *Teams* Cambridge (1930–31, blue both years); Worcestershire (1934–39, 39 matches). *Tour* MCC to India 1939/40 (tour cancelled).
Career batting
59–95–4–2236–81–24.57–0–*ct* 34
Bowling 1947–51–38.17–0–0–4/42
He also played for Berkshire (1926–34) and Oxfordshire (1932). He also won a blue for soccer.

Humble, Rev William John
(changed name to Humble-Crofts in May 1879)
Amateur. *b:* 9.12.1846, Sutton Scarsdale, Derbyshire. *d:* 1.7.1924, Waldron, Sussex. Uncle of A. W. White (Yorkshire). Middle order right-hand batsman, good cover field. *Team* Derbyshire (1873–77, 6 matches).
Career batting
6–10–1–77–19*–8.55–0–*ct* 6
He did not appear in first-class cricket whilst at Oxford.

Hume, Edward
Amateur. *b:* 25.9.1841, Scaldwell, Northamptonshire. *d:* 24.10.1921, Totland Bay, Isle of Wight. Middle order right-hand batsman. *Sch* Marlborough. *Team* Oxford U (1861–63, blue 1861–62).
Career batting
8–14–2–102–26*–8.50–0–*ct* 4
He was on the MCC Committee and his final first-class match was for an England Eleven in 1879. His County cricket was for Northamptonshire (pre first-class).

Humfrey, Dr Stuart Harold Guise
Amateur. *b:* 17.2.1894, Headington, Oxfordshire. *d:* 9.6.1975, Dallington, Northampton. Hard-hitting middle order right-hand batsman, right-arm medium pace bowler. *Sch* Oakham. *Team* Northamptonshire (1913–26, 21 matches).
Career batting
21–36–2–477–61*–14.02–0–*ct* 4
Bowling 135–1–135.00–0–0–1/40
He was also a noted rugby centre three quarter.

Humpage, Geoffrey William
Cricketer. *b:* 24.4.1954, Sparkhill, Birmingham. Middle order right-hand batsman, occasional right-arm medium pace bowler, wicket-keeper. *Teams* Warwickshire (1974–90, 345 matches); Orange Free State (1981/2). *Tour* SAB England XI to South Africa 1981/2.
Career batting
351–574–76–18098–254–36.34–29–*ct* 671–*st* 72
Bowling 553–13–42.53–0–0–2/13
He hit 1,000 runs in a season eleven times (best 1,891, av 48.48, in 1984). His highest score was 254 for Warwickshire v Lancashire at Southport in 1982, in the course of which he created with A. I. Kallicharran a new first-class English 4th wicket record partnership of 470. He appeared in one-day internationals for England, but no Test matches.

Humpherson, Victor William
Amateur. *b:* 15.7.1896, Bewdley on Severn, Worcestershire. *d:* 19.10.1978, Rowfant, Sussex. Lower order right-hand batsman, right-arm medium pace bowler. *Sch* Worcester RGS. *Team* Worcestershire (1921–23, 13 matches).
Career batting
13–25–5–154–16–7.70–0–*ct* 10
Bowling 500–16–31.25–1–0–5/50

Humphrey, Richard
Professional. *b:* 12.12.1848, Mitcham, Surrey. *d:* 24.2.1906, Westminster, London. He was drowned in the River Thames. Brother of Thomas (Surrey), John (Surrey 1862) and William (Surrey and Hampshire). Opening right-hand batsman. *Team* Surrey (1870–81, 145 matches). *Tour* Grace to Australia 1873/4 (not first-class).
Career batting
194–355–23–5614–116*–16.90–1–*ct* 106
He hit 1,072 runs, av 23.82, in 1872, which was his best season. At the time of his death he had been in very poor circumstances for some years. He was a first-class umpire (1885 and 1890).

Humphrey, Richard Geoffrey
Cricketer. *b:* 17.9.1936, Hampstead, London. Lower order right-hand batsman, wicket-keeper. *Team* Surrey (1964–70, 2 matches).
Career batting
2–2–1–63–58–63.00–0–*ct* 4–*st* 1
He also played for Buckinghamshire (1980–85).

Humphrey, Thomas
Professional. *b:* 16.1.1839, Mitcham, Surrey. *d:* 3.9.1878, Knaphill, Brookwood, Surrey. Brother of Richard (Surrey), John (Surrey 1862) and William (Surrey and Hampshire). Splendid opening right-hand batsman, right-hand slow round-arm bowler, excellent deep field. *Team* Surrey (1862–74, 159 matches). *Tour* Willsher to North America 1868 (not first-class).
Career batting
212–381–18–6687–144–18.42–4–*ct* 95
Bowling 2461–114 + 2–21.58–6–0–6/29
He hit 1,223 runs, av 29.82, in 1865 and about that time was regarded as one of the leading batsmen in England, being known as the 'Pocket Hercules'. His final first-class match was for the South of England in 1876. He also played for Northamptonshire (pre first-class, 1860) and Buckinghamshire (1866).

Humphrey, William
Professional. *b:* 15.9.1843, Mitcham, Surrey. *d:* 24.2.1918, Norwich, Norfolk. Brother of Thomas (Surrey), John (Surrey 1862) and Richard (Surrey). Lower order right-hand batsman, right-hand fast round-arm bowler. *Teams* Surrey (1864, 4 matches); Hampshire (1864, 4 matches).
Career batting
8–14–1–99–25–7.61–0–*ct* 1
Bowling 248–6–41.33–0–0–3/61
He also played for Norfolk (1865).

Humphreys, Edward
Professional. *b:* 24.8.1881, Ditton, Kent. *d:* 6.11.1949, Maidstone, Kent. Opening right-hand batsman, slow left-arm bowler. *Team* Kent (1899–1920, 366 matches); Canterbury (1908/9). *Tour* MCC to West Indies 1912/13.
Career batting
393–639–45–16603–208–27.95–22–*ct* 229
Bowling 9314–379–24.57–12–2–7/33
He hit 1,000 runs in a season eight times (best 1,777, av 40.38, in 1911). Both his double centuries were for Kent, his highest being 208 v Gloucestershire at Catford in 1909. He was Kent coach 1946–48.

Humphreys, George Thomas
Professional. *b:* 28.3.1845, Brighton, Sussex. *d:* 18.12.1894, Preston, Brighton, Sussex, as the result of breaking a blood vessel. Brother of W. A. sen (Sussex), uncle of W. A. jun (Sussex). Good middle order right-hand batsman, originally wicket-keeper, excellent field. *Team* Sussex (1869–86, 32 matches).
Career batting
32–60–7–545–58–10.28–0–*ct* 21–*st* 3

Humphreys, Walter Alexander (sen)
Professional. *b:* 28.10.1849, Southsea, Hampshire. *d:* 23.3.1924, Brighton, Sussex. Brother of G. T. (Sussex), father of W. A. jun (Sussex). Middle or lower order right-hand batsman, right-hand under-arm lob bowler, good field. *Teams* Sussex (1871–96, 248 matches); Hampshire (1900, 2 matches). *Tour* Stoddart to Australia (1894/5).
Career batting
273–485–96–6268–117–16.11–1–*ct* 213
Bowling 15456–718–21.52–51–8–8/83
He took 100 wickets in a season once: 150, av 17.32, in 1893. No lob bowler since has achieved such figures in first-class cricket. He was a first-class umpire (1896).

Humphreys, Walter Alexander (jun)
Professional. *b:* 28.6.1878, Brighton, Sussex. *d:* 1.1.1960, Hove, Sussex. Son of W. A. sen (Sussex and Hampshire), nephew of G. T. (Sussex). Lower order right-hand batsman, right-hand slow under-arm bowler. *Team* Sussex (1898–1900, 14 matches).
Career batting
14–20–6–81–27–5.78–0–*ct* 9
Bowling 1353–48–28.18–2–0–5/107

Humphries, Cedric Alfred
Amateur. *b:* 26.12.1913, Kidderminster, Worcestershire. *d:* 18.11.1944, near Brunssum, Holland. Brother of G. H. (Worcestershire) and N. H. (Worcestershire). Middle order right-hand batsman, right-arm medium pace bowler. *Team* Worcestershire (1934–35, 13 matches).
Career batting
13–24–3–328–44–15.61–*ct* 3
He played in trials at Cambridge U, but not in first-class matches.

Humphries, David John
Cricketer. *b:* 6.8.1953, Alveley, Shropshire. Middle order left-hand batsman, wicket-keeper. *Teams*

Leicestershire (1974–76, 5 matches); Worcestershire (1977–85, 170 matches).
Career batting
175–252–46–5116–133*–24.83–4–*ct* 293–*st* 60
He also played for Shropshire (1971–73).

Humphries, Gerald Harvey
Amateur. *b:* 8.12.1908, Kidderminster, Worcestershire *d:* 3.2.1983, Rock, near Kidderminster. Brother of C. A. (Worcestershire) and N. H. (Worcestershire). Middle order right-hand batsman, right-arm medium pace bowler. *Team* Worcestershire (1932–34, 2 matches).
Career batting
2–3–0–66–36–22.00–0–*ct* 0
Bowling 13–0

Humphries, Henry Hurl
Amateur. *b:* 8.9.1879, Warkworth, Ontario, Canada. *d:* 12.10.1964, Weston, Bath, Somerset. Middle order left-hand batsman. *Teams* Somerset (1906, 1 match); Combined USA/Canada (1913).
Career batting
2–3–0–56–49–18.66–0–*ct* 0
Bowling 32–0

Humphries, Joseph
Professional. *b:* 19.5.1876, Stonebroom, Derbyshire. *d:* 7.5.1946, Chesterfield, Derbyshire. Lower order right-hand batsman, wicket-keeper. *Teams* Derbyshire (1899–1914, 276 matches). *Tour* MCC to Australia 1907/8. *Tests* England (1907/8, 3 matches).
Career batting
302–514–129–5464–68–14.19–0–*ct* 564–*st* 110
Bowling 43–3–14.33–0–0–1/5
Test batting
3–6–1–44–16–8.80–0–*ct* 7
He was due to reappear for Derbyshire in 1920 in his benefit match but play was abandoned without a ball being bowled. He was a first-class umpire (1933).

Humphries, Norman Hampton
Amateur. *b:* 19.5.1917, Kidderminster, Worcestershire. Brother of C. A. (Worcestershire) and G. H. (Worcestershire). Middle order right-hand batsman, leg break bowler. *Team* Worcestershire (1946, 7 matches).
Career batting
7–11–1–137–22–13.70–0–*ct* 1
Bowling 52–0
He also played for Devon (1938–55).

Humphrys, Sir Francis Henry
Amateur. *b:* 24.4.1879, Oswestry, Shropshire. *d:* 28.8.1971, Hampstead-Marshall, Berkshire. Lower order right-hand batsman, right-arm fast bowler, good field. *Sch* Shrewsbury. *Team* Oxford U (1899–1900).
Career batting
4–5–1–18–12–4.50–0–*ct* 3
Bowling 253–13–19.46–0–0–4/16
He appeared frequently for Free Foresters, Harlequins and I Zingari. His County cricket was for Wiltshire (1895–1900).

Hunt, Alan Jeffrey
Cricketer. *b:* 28.12.1968, Birmingham. Middle order right-hand batsman. *Team* Gloucestershire (1991, 1 match).
Career batting
1–2–0–15–12–7.50–0–*ct* 1

Hunt, Alma Victor
Professional. *b:* 1.10.1910, Somerset, Bermuda. Middle order left-hand batsman, right-arm fast medium bowler. *Teams* Scotland (1938); G. C. Grant's XI (West Indies 1932/3).
Career batting
2–4–0–65–31–16.25–0–*ct* 3
Bowling 71–2–35.50–0–0–1/15
He was the leading cricketer in Bermuda and has continued as a major figure in the administration of cricket in Bermuda.

Hunt, Frederick
Professional. *b:* 13.9.1875, Aldworth, Berkshire. *d:* 31.3.1967, Worcester. Lower order right-hand batsman, right-arm medium pace bowler. *Teams* Kent (1897–98, 6 matches); Worcestershire (1900–22, 53 matches).
Career batting
59–97–21–806–40*–10.60–0–*ct* 17
Bowling 1635–51–32.05–0–0–4/36
He was the groundsman at Worcester for many years.

Hunt, George Edward
Professional. *b:* 30.9.1896, Pill, Somerset. *d:* 22.1.1959, Bristol. Brother of Hubert (Somerset). Middle order right-hand batsman, right-arm medium pace bowler, good short leg. *Team* Somerset (1921–31, 233 matches).
Career batting
233–381–60–4952–101–15.42–1–*ct* 197
Bowling 12691–386–32.87–11–1–7/61

Hunt, George Rupert
Amateur. *b:* 23.3.1873, Bath, Somerset. *d:* 22.8.1960, Old Bursledon, Hampshire. Father of Kenneth (Gloucestershire). Middle order right-hand batsman, right-arm medium pace bowler. *Sch* Sutton Valence. *Team* Somerset (1898, 1 match).
Career batting
1–2–0–4–3–2.00–0–*ct* 1

Hunt, Hubert
Amateur. *b:* 18.11.1911, Long Ashton, Somerset. *d:* 29.11.1985, Pill, Somerset. Brother of George (Somerset). Lower order right-hand batsman, off break bowler. *Team* Somerset (1936, 11 matches).

Hunt, J. H.

Career batting
11–16–3–100–22–7.69–0–*ct* 2
Bowling 285–15–19.00–1–0–7/49
He also played for Cornwall (1939–48).

Hunt, J. H.
(*see under* Husey-Hunt, J. H.)

Hunt, John Henry Sneyd
Amateur. *b:* 24.11.1874, Kensington, London. *d:* 16.9.1916, near Ginchy, France. Middle order right-hand batsman, right-arm medium pace bowler. *Sch* Winchester. *Team* Middlesex (1902–12, 44 matches).
Career batting
46–71–6–1393–128–21.43–1–*ct* 29
Bowling 2137–80–26.71–2–0–5/60

Hunt, Kenneth
Amateur. *b:* 4.12.1902, Clifton, Bristol. *d:* 16.3.1971, Hyde, Chalford, Stroud, Gloucestershire. Son of G. R. (Somerset). Middle order right-hand batsman. *Sch* Dover. *Teams* Royal Navy (1925); Gloucestershire (1926, 1 match).
Career batting
2–4–0–11–7–2.75–0–*ct* 2

Hunt, Louis Edward
Amateur. *b:* 9.11.1908, Prestatyn, Flintshire. Son-in-law of L. P. Collins (Oxford U). Lower order right-hand batsman, wicket-keeper. *Sch* Bradfield. *Teams* Cambridge U (1929); Bengal (1935/6); Europeans (1940/1).
Career batting
3–4–0–21–10–5.25–0–*ct* 2

Hunt, Robert Geoffrey
Amateur. *b:* 13.4.1915, Horsham, Sussex. Middle order right-hand batsman, off break bowler. *Sch* Aldenham. *Teams* Cambridge U (1935–37, blue 1937); Sussex (1936–47, 11 matches); Services (1943/4).
Career batting
26–46–4–831–117–19.78–1–*ct* 21
Bowling 959–31–30.93–2–0–5/51

Hunt, Robert Norman
Amateur. *b:* 24.9.1903, Worsley, Lancashire. *d:* 13.10.1983, Chichester, Sussex. Lower order right-hand batsman, right-arm fast medium bowler. *Team* Middlesex (1926–28, 8 matches).
Career batting
8–10–3–138–81*–19.71–0–*ct* 3
Bowling 453–5–90.60–0–0–3/32

Hunt, Samuel Walter
Professional. *b:* 9.1.1909, Doe Lea, Derbyshire. *d:* 2.8.1963, Rochdale, Lancashire. Middle order right-hand batsman, leg break bowler. *Team* Derbyshire (1936, 5 matches).
Career batting
5–5–0–48–17–9.60–0–*ct* 0
Bowling 3–0
He also played for Northumberland (1950). He played soccer for Lincoln City, Mansfield, Torquay, Rochdale, Stockport, Accrington and Carlisle.

Hunt, Thomas
Professional. *b:* 2.9.1819, Chesterfield, Derbyshire. *d:* 11.9.1858, Rochdale, Lancashire. He was run over by a train. Stylish opening right-hand batsman, right-hand fast round-arm bowler, wicket-keeper. *Teams* Yorkshire (1845–51, 9 matches); Lancashire (1849).
Career batting
39–66–5–922–102–15.11–1–*ct* 33–*st* 9
Bowling 234–18 + 49–13.00–5–1–7/?
One of the best batsmen in the North of England, he was also a noted single wicket player. His final first-class match was for Manchester in 1858. He also played for Derbyshire (pre first-class, 1848–58).

Hunte, Conrad Cleophas
Amateur. *b:* 9.5.1932, Greenland Plantation, Shorey's Village, St Andrew, Barbados. Sound right-hand opening batsman, right-arm medium bowler, brilliant outfield. *Team* Barbados (1950/1 to 1966/7). *Tours* West Indies to England 1963, 1966, to Australia 1960/1, to India and Pakistan 1958/9, to India 1966/7; Prime Minister's XI in India 1963/4; Rest of World to England 1965, 1967. *Tests* West Indies (1957/8 to 1966/7, 44 matches).
Career batting
132–222–19–8916–263–43.92–16–*ct* 68–*st* 1
Bowling 644–17–37.88–0–0–3/5
Test batting
44–78–6–3245–260–45.06–8–*ct* 16
Bowling 110–2–55.00–0–0–1/17
On his 1963 tour to England he hit 1,367 runs, av 44.09, and performed brilliantly in the five Tests, heading the batting averages; he was vice-captain of the tourists. Though not as prolific in 1966, he still appeared in all five Tests and only just missed scoring 1,000 runs in first-class matches. He hit 206 v Somerset at Taunton on the latter tour, his highest innings in England. His highest in all first-class matches was 263 for Barbados v Jamaica at Georgetown in 1961/2. He hit 1,000 in a season in India and Pakistan. His first first-class match in England was for a Commonwealth XI in 1956.

Hunter, C. V.
Amateur. Middle order right-hand batsman. *Team* British Guiana (1912/13 to 1922/3). *Tour* West Indies to England 1923.
Career batting
7–12–0–275–66–22.91–0–*ct* 0
Bowling 16–0
On the 1923 tour he was mainly confined to minor matches, playing only two first-class innings. His first-class debut was for a West Indian XI in 1910/11.

Hunter, Charles Herbert
Amateur. *b:* 18.4.1867, Lee, London. *d:* 2.4.1955, Budleigh Salterton, Devon. Hard-hitting lower order right-hand batsman, wicket-keeper. *Sch* Uppingham. *Teams* Cambridge U (1889); Kent (1895, 2 matches).
Career batting
3–5–1–29–16–7.25–0–*ct* 2–*st* 1

Hunter, Charles Michael Geoffrey
Cricketer. *b:* 11.9.1937, Windle, St Helens, Lancashire. Middle order right-hand batsman, right-arm medium pace bowler. *Sch* Malvern. *Team* Minor Counties (1971).
Career batting
1–2–1–50–41–50.00–0–*ct* 0
Bowling 52–0
His County cricket was for Dorset (1965–74).

Hunter, David
Professional. *b:* 23.2.1860, Scarborough, Yorkshire. *d:* 11.1.1927, Northstead, Scarborough, Yorkshire. Brother of Joseph (Yorkshire). Lower order right-hand batsman, wicket-keeper. *Team* Yorkshire (1888–1909, 521 matches).
Career batting
552–728–351–4538–58*–12.03–0–*ct* 913–*st* 350
Bowling 43–0

Hunter, Frederic Cecil
Amateur. *b:* 23.8.1886, Glossop, Derbyshire. *d:* 21.7.1926, Adelaide, South Australia. Middle or lower order right-hand batsman, leg break bowler. *Team* Derbyshire (1905–07, 28 matches).
Career batting
28–49–3–564–51–12.26–0–*ct* 8
Bowling 684–17–40.23–0–0–2/18
He also played for Cheshire (1910–12).

Hunter, Joseph
Professional. *b:* 3.8.1855, Scarborough, Yorkshire. *d:* 4.1.1891, Rotherham, Yorkshire. Brother of David (Yorkshire). Tail end right-hand batsman, wicket-keeper. *Team* Yorkshire (1878–88, 143 matches). *Tour* Lillywhite, Shaw and Shrewsbury to Australia 1884/5. *Tests* England (1884/5, 5 matches).
Career batting
162–240–71–1330–60*–7.86–0–*ct* 232–*st* 124
Test batting
5–7–2–93–39*–18.60–0–*ct* 8–*st* 3

Hunter, William Raymond
Amateur. *b:* 3.4.1938, Belfast, Ireland. Middle order right-hand batsman, right-arm medium pace bowler. *Team* Ireland (1958–65).
Career batting
11–18–0–201–39–11.16–0–*ct* 11
Bowling 445–19–23.42–1–0–5/22
He was an Irish rugby international and toured South Africa with the British Lions in 1962.

Hurd, Alan
Amateur. *b:* 7.9.1937, Ilford, Essex. Tail end left-hand batsman, off break bowler. *Sch* Chigwell. *Teams* Cambridge U (1958–60, blue all three years); Essex (1958–60, 35 matches).
Career batting
90–106–36–376–21–5.37–0–*ct* 16
Bowling 7671–249–30.80–13–1–6/15

Hurd, William Sydney
Amateur. *b:* 10.9.1908, Ashby-de-la-Zouch, Leicestershire. Lower order batsman, bowler. *Team* Leicestershire (1932–34, 3 matches).
Career batting
3–4–0–7–5–1.75–0–*ct* 0
Bowling 28–0

Hurst, Alan George
Cricketer. *b:* 15.7.1950, Altona, Melbourne, Victoria, Australia. Lower order right-hand batsman, right-arm fast bowler. *Team* Victoria (1972/3 to 1980/1, 50 matches). *Tours* Australia to England 1975, 1979 (World Cup), to New Zealand 1976/7, to India 1979/80; International Wanderers to South Africa 1975/6. *Tests* Australia (1973/4 to 1979/80, 12 matches).
Career batting
77–88–30–504–27*–8.68–0–*ct* 26
Bowling 7360–280–26.28–11–1–8/84
Test batting
12–20–3–102–26–6.00–0–*ct* 3
Bowling 1200–43–27.90–2–0–5/28
He took 21 wickets, av 31.38, on the 1975 tour to England and did not appear in the Tests.

Hurst, Christopher Salkeld
Amateur. *b:* 20.7.1886, Beckenham, Kent. *d:* 18.12.1963, Dorking, Surrey. Free scoring middle order right-hand batsman. *Sch* Uppingham. *Teams* Oxford U (1907–09, blue all three years); Kent (1908–27, 19 matches).
Career batting
47–82–6–1787–124–23.51–3–*ct* 41
Bowling 96–3–32.00–0–0–2/26
He captained Oxford in 1909. A noted hockey player, he represented Oxford.

Hurst, Geoffrey Charles
Professional. *b:* 8.12.1941, Ashton-under-Lyne, Lancashire. Lower order right-hand batsman, brilliant field, wicket-keeper. *Team* Essex (1962, 1 match).
Career batting
1–2–1–0–0*–0.00–0–*ct* 1
A well-known soccer player, he appeared as centre-forward for West Ham United, West Bromwich Albion, Stoke City and England, scoring a hat-trick in the World Cup Final of 1966.

Hurst, Gordon Thomas
Professional. *b:* 26.8.1920, Kenley, Surrey. Lower order right-hand batsman, off break bowler. *Team* Sussex (1947–49, 9 matches).
Career batting
9–13–4–27–9–3.00–0–*ct* 0
Bowling 760–28–27.14–2–0–6/80

Hurst, Robert Jack
Professional. *b:* 29.12.1933, Hampton Hill, Middlesex. Lower order right-hand batsman, slow left-arm bowler. *Team* Middlesex (1954–61, 100 matches).
Career batting
105–128–56–721–62–10.01–0–*ct* 56
Bowling 6189–255–24.27–6–1–8/65

Hurt, Colin Noel Bickley
Amateur. *b:* 16.12.1893, Darley Dale, Derbyshire. *d:* 31.12.1972, Little Common, Bexhill, Sussex. Middle order right-hand batsman, right-arm medium pace bowler. *Sch* Malvern. *Team* Derbyshire (1914, 3 matches).
Career batting
3–5–0–23–13–4.60–0–*ct* 1
Bowling 6–0
He played in trials at Oxford U, but not in first-class matches.

Hurwood, Alexander
Amateur. *b:* 17.6.1902, Kangaroo Point, Brisbane, Queensland, Australia. *d:* 26.9.1982, Coffs Harbour, New South Wales, Australia. Lower order right-hand batsman, right-arm medium pace off break bowler. *Team* Queensland (1925/6 to 1931/2, 18 matches). *Tour* Australia to England 1930. *Tests* Australia (1930/1, 2 matches).
Career batting
43–56–5–575–89–11.27–0–*ct* 29
Bowling 3132–113–27.62–5–1–6/80
Test batting
2–2–0–5–5–2.50–0–*ct* 2
Bowling 170–11–15.45–0–0–4/22
For some reason he was given very little opportunity on the 1930 tour and did not appear in any Tests – on the occasions when he did bowl he looked impressive and economical.

Husey-Hunt, James Hubert
(originally J. H. Senior)
Amateur. *b:* 20.4.1853, Compton-Pauncefoot, Castle Cary, Somerset. *d:* 13.5.1924, Hove, Sussex. Lower order right-hand batsman. *Sch* Marlborough. *Team* Gloucestershire (1880, 2 matches).
Career batting
3–5–0–20–6–4.00–0–*ct* 1
His first-class debut was for MCC in 1878.

Huskinson, Geoffrey Mark Clement
Amateur. *b:* 25.9.1935, Langar, Nottinghamshire. Son of G. N. B. (Nottinghamshire). Middle order right-hand batsman, leg break bowler. *Sch* Ampleforth. *Team* Free Foresters (1959).
Career batting
1–2–0–10–7–5.00–0–*ct* 0

Huskinson, Geoffrey Neville Bayley
Amateur. *b:* 1.2.1900, Locarno, Switzerland. *d:* 17.6.1982, Hinton-Waldrist, Berkshire. Father of G. M. C. (Free Foresters). Middle order right-hand batsman, leg break bowler. *Sch* Oundle. *Team* Nottinghamshire (1922, 2 matches). *Tour* Martineau to Egypt 1933 (not first-class).
Career batting
2–2–0–33–33–16.50–0–*ct* 0
He was on the Nottinghamshire CCC Committee 1943–58 and President 1959–60. Whilst at Oxford U he did not appear in any first-class matches. A noted rugby footballer, he played for Nottingham, East Midlands and Harlequins.

Hussain, Mehriyar
Cricketer. *b:* 17.10.1963, South Shields, Co Durham. Son of Javaid (Madras), brother of Nasser (Essex). Middle order right-hand batsman, off break bowler. *Team* Worcestershire (1985, 1 match).
Career batting
1–1–0–4–4–4.00–0–*ct* 0

Hussain, Nasser
Cricketer. *b:* 28.3.1968, Madras, India. Son of Javaid (Madras), brother of Mehriyar (Worcestershire). Middle order right-hand batsman, leg break bowler. *Team* Essex (1987–92, 85 matches). *Tours* England to India 1989/90 (not first-class), to West Indies 1989/90; England A to Pakistan and Sri Lanka 1990/1, to West Indies 1991/2. *Tests* England (1989/90, 3 matches).
Career batting
99–142–22–5163–197–43.02–10–*ct* 121
Bowling 198–1–198.00–0–0–1/38
Test batting
3–5–0–100–35–20.00–0–*ct* 1
He scored 1,354 runs, av 54.16, in 1991.

Hussain, Syed Mohammad
Amateur. *b:* 8.12.1909, India. *d:* 2.7.1982, Hyderabad, India. Brother of S. M. Hadi (India). Middle order batsman. *Teams* Madras (1926/7 to 1933/4); Hyderabad (1930/1 to 1942/3); Muslims (1927/8 to 1936/7). *Tour* India to England 1936.
Career batting
44–76–6–1724–94–24.62–0–*ct* 24
Bowling 115–3–38.33–0–0–2/35
He achieved modest success on the 1936 tour and did not appear in the Tests. His first-class debut was for Indians v Europeans in 1925/6.

Hussey, John Allen
Amateur. *b:* 17.4.1897, Axbridge, Somerset. *d:* 18.8.1969, Raynes Park, Surrey. Brother-in-law of F. H. Hall (Ireland). Middle order right-hand bats-

man. *Team* Royal Navy (1929).
Career batting
1–1–0–54–54–54.00–0–*ct* 1

Hutchings, Frederick Vaughan
Amateur. *b:* 3.6.1880, Southborough, Kent. *d:* 6.8.1934, Hamburg, Germany. Brother of K. L. (Kent) and W. E. C. (Kent and Worcestershire), nephew of E. L. Colebrooke (Oxford U). Sound middle order right-hand batsman, good cover point. *Sch* Tonbridge. *Team* Kent (1901–05, 3 matches).
Career batting
4–6–0–89–31–14.83–0–*ct* 0

Hutchings, Kenneth Lotherington
Amateur. *b:* 7.12.1882, Southborough, Kent. *d:* 3.9.1916, Ginchy, France. He was killed in action. Brother of F. V. (Kent) and W. E. C. (Kent and Worcestershire), nephew of E. L. Colebrooke (Oxford U). Excellent middle order right-hand batsman, right-arm fast bowler, brilliant field. *Sch* Tonbridge. *Team* Kent (1902–12, 163 matches). *Tours* Kent to North America 1903; MCC to Australia 1907/8. *Tests* England (1907/8 to 1909, 7 matches).
Career batting
207–311–12–10054–176–33.62–22–*ct* 179
Bowling 938–24–39.08–0–0–4/15
Test batting
7–12–0–341–126–28.41–1–*ct* 9
Bowling 81–1–81.00–0–0–1/5
He hit 1,000 runs in a season six times (best 1,697, av 36.10, in 1909). His most notable asset was his driving, the force with which he hit the ball being quite remarkable.

Hutchings, William Edward Colebrooke
Amateur. *b:* 31.5.1879, Southborough, Kent. *d:* 8.3.1948, Prees, near Whitchurch, Shropshire. Brother of F. V. (Kent) and K. L. (Kent), nephew of E. L. Colebrooke (Oxford U). Middle order right-hand batsman. *Sch* Tonbridge. *Teams* Kent (1899, 2 matches); Worcestershire (1905–06, 22 matches).
Career batting
24–42–3–845–21.66–0–*ct* 20
He also played for Berkshire (1901).

Hutchins, Gilbert William
Professional. *b:* 28.2.1858, Knebworth, Hertfordshire. *d:* 25.11.1902, Bedford. Lower order right-hand batsman, slow right-arm bowler. *Team* Middlesex (1890, 1 match).
Career batting
1–2–0–9–7–4.50–0–*ct* 0
Bowling 25–0
He also played for Bedfordshire (1879–82), Huntingdonshire (1884) and Hertfordshire (1885–86).

Hutchinson, Gordon Michael
Cricketer. *b:* 10.2.1969, Welshpool, Montgomeryshire. Brother of I. J. F. (Middlesex). Middle order right-hand batsman, right-arm medium pace bowler. *Sch* Shrewsbury. *Team* Cambridge U (1990).
Career batting
2–2–0–31–29–15.50–0–*ct* 0

Hutchinson, Ian James Frederick
Cricketer. *b:* 31.10.1964, Welshpool, Montgomeryshire. Brother of G. M. (Cambridge U). Aggressive opening right-hand batsman, right-arm medium fast bowler. *Sch* Shrewsbury. *Team* Middlesex (1988–91, 27 matches).
Career batting
27–46–4–1435–201*–34.16–5–*ct* 29
Bowling 29–1–29.00–0–0–1/18
He also played for Shropshire (1984–86). His highest score was 201* for Middlesex v Oxford U at Oxford in 1989.

Hutchinson, James Metcalf
Professional. *b:* 29.11.1896, New Tupton, Derbyshire. Middle order right-hand batsman, right-arm medium pace off break bowler, brilliant cover point. *Team* Derbyshire (1920–31, 255 matches).
Career batting
256–416–38–7055–143–18.66–5–*ct* 97–*st* 2
Bowling 1238–31–39.93–0–0–3/44
His best year was 1928 with 990 runs, av 22.50.

Hutchinson, Leonard Staughton
Professional. *b:* 16.4.1901, Anstey, Leicestershire. *d:* 2.10.1976, Glenfield, Leicester. Middle order right-hand batsman, bowler. *Team* Leicestershire (1923–25, 8 matches).
Career batting
8–15–1–65–14–4.64–0–*ct* 8
Bowling 64–1–64.00–0–0–1/9

Hutchinson, Major General William Francis Moore
Amateur. *b:* 3.2.1841, City of London. *d:* 22.4.1917, Eastbourne, Sussex. Middle order batsman. *Team* MCC (1869).
Career batting
1–1–0–1–1–1.00–0–*ct* 0
His County cricket was for Devon (1863–68) and Norfolk (1869).

Huth, Henry
Amateur. *b:* 14.2.1856, Huddersfield, Yorkshire. *d:* January 1930. Middle order batsman. *Team* Gentlemen of the North (1877).
Career batting
1–2–0–7–7–3.50–0–*ct* 0
An excellent rugby footballer, he was capped for England.

Hutson, Dr Andrew Massey
Cricketer. *b:* 18.3.1952, Tamworth, Staffordshire. Tail end right-hand batsman, right-arm medium pace bowler. *Sch* Kimbolton. *Team* Cambridge U (1972).

Hutson, Henry Wolseley

Career batting
1–1–1–0–0*–no av–0–*ct* 0
Bowling 54–0

Hutson, Henry Wolseley
Amateur. *b:* 1866, Demerara, British Guiana. *d:* 25.3.1916, Cottenham Park, Wimbledon, Surrey. Middle order batsman. *Team* Cambridge U (1886).
Career batting
1–2–0–20–20–10.00–0–*ct* 1
Bowling 4–0

His County cricket was for Berkshire (1899–1906).

Hutton, George
Amateur. *b:* 20.8.1942, Paisley, Renfrew, Scotland. Lower order right-hand batsman, right-arm fast medium bowler. *Team* Scotland (1966–67).
Career batting
2–2–1–0–0*–0.00–0–*ct* 1
Bowling 56–2–28.00–0–0–2/16

Hutton, Sir Leonard
Professional. *b:* 23.6.1916, Fulneck, Pudsey, Yorkshire. *d:* 6.9.1990, Norbiton, Kingston-upon-Thames, Surrey. Father of R. A. (Yorkshire) and J. L. (MCC in East Africa), brother-in-law of F. Dennis (Yorkshire), uncle of S. J. Dennis (Yorkshire and Glamorgan). Excellent opening right-hand batsman, leg break bowler, fine field. *Team* Yorkshire (1934–55, 341 matches). *Tours* Yorkshire to Jamaica 1935/6; MCC to South Africa 1938/9, 1948/9, to Australia and New Zealand 1946/7, 1950/1, 1954/5, to West Indies 1947/8, 1953/4. *Tests* England (1937 to 1954/5, 79 matches).
Career batting
513–814–91–40140–364–55.51–129–*ct* 400
Bowling 5106–173–29.51–4–1–6/76
Test batting
79–138–15–6971–364–56.67–19–*ct* 57
Bowling 232–3–77.33–0–0–1/2

Hutton succeeded Hobbs as the greatest opening batsman in England, and though forced in the second half of his career, especially for his country, to adopt a dour and unsmiling attitude to batting, he was also an attractive attacking player with a wide range of strokes. He placed himself above the ordinary by his innings of 364 for England against Australia at the Oval in 1938 and he remained for the rest of his career – nearly two decades – an outstanding player.

His best season in England was 1949 when he hit 3,429 runs, av 68.58. He exceeded 2,000 runs in a season in England eight other times and in all hit at least 1,000 runs 12 times, plus five times overseas.

Apart from his famous 364 he scored three double centuries for England – two being against the West Indies and one against New Zealand – and his total number of innings over 200 was 11.

His three MCC tours to Australia were all successes, in particular the 1950/1 visit when he carried the batting almost single handed. Called in emergency to reinforce the MCC in West Indies in 1947/8 midway through the tour, he ended by heading the batting averages.

Despite being a professional he was selected to captain England in 1953 and won back the Ashes; he then led England in the West Indies and managed to draw the series, two matches each, and on the 1954/5 tour to Australia won the series three matches to one. He retired from Test cricket after that series. He captained England in 23 Tests.

His post-war career was made that much more difficult by an accident to his arm during the war, which meant that his left arm was slightly shorter than his right. He was knighted for his services to cricket in 1956; and served as a Test selector in 1975 and 1976. His final first-class match was for MCC in 1960. He was President of Yorkshire 1990.

Hutton, Richard Anthony
Cricketer. *b:* 6.9.1942, Pudsey, Yorkshire. Son of Leonard (Yorkshire), brother of J. L. (MCC in East Africa), nephew of F. Dennis (Yorkshire), cousin of S. J. Dennis (Yorkshire and Glamorgan), son-in-law of B. G. Brocklehurst (Somerset). Middle order right-hand batsman, right-arm fast medium bowler. *Sch* Repton. *Teams* Yorkshire (1962–74, 208 matches); Cambridge U (1962–64, blue all three years); Transvaal (1975/6). *Tours* MCC to Pakistan 1966/7; Rest of World to Australia 1971/2; Swanton to India 1963/4. *Tests* England (1971, 5 matches).
Career batting
281–410–58–7561–189–21.48–5–*ct* 216
Bowling 15008–625–24.01–21–3–8/50
Test batting
5–8–2–219–81–36.50–0–*ct* 9
Bowling 257–9–28.55–0–0–3/72

He hit 1,000 runs in a season twice (best 1,122, av 27.36, in 1963). He was appointed editor of *The Cricketer* in 1991.

Hutton, Stewart
Cricketer. *b:* 30.11.1969, Stockton-on-Tees, Durham. Middle order left-hand batsman, right-arm medium pace bowler. *Team* Durham (1992, 8 matches).
Career batting
8–15–0–406–78–27.06–0–*ct* 3
Bowling 4–0

He first played for Durham (pre first-class) in 1991.

Hutton, Wilfred Noel Maxwell
Amateur. *b:* 5.6.1901, Summerhill, Dublin, Ireland. *d:* 12.9.1978, Carrigaline, Co Cork, Ireland. Middle order right-hand batsman. *Sch* Shrewsbury. *Team* Dublin University (1922).
Career batting
1–2–0–2–2–1.00–0–*ct* 0

He played for Ireland (not first-class) in 1927.

Huxford, Peter Nigel
Cricketer. *b:* 17.2.1960, Enfield, Middlesex. Tail end left-hand batsman, wicket-keeper. *Team* Oxford U (1980–81, blue 1981).
Career batting
7–9–4–27–10–5.40–0–*ct* 3–*st* 2

Huxter, Rupert James Alexander
Cricketer. *b:* 29.10.1959, Abingdon, Berkshire. Lower order right-hand batsman, right-arm medium pace bowler. *Sch* Magdalen College School. *Team* Cambridge U (1981, blue).
Career batting
4–5–0–34–20–6.80–0–*ct* 0
Bowling 224–5–44.80–0–0–2/49

Huyshe, Oliver Francis
Amateur. *b:* 26.7.1885, Wimborne Minster, Dorset. *d:* 23.8.1960, Exeter, Devon. Lower order batsman, wicket-keeper. *Sch* King's Canterbury. *Team* Oxford U (1907).
Career batting
1–1–1–0–0*–no av–0–*ct* 0
He also played for Dorset (1904–07). He won a blue for cross-country.

Hyde, Alfred Joseph
Professional. *b:* 1884. Lower order left-hand batsman, slow left-arm bowler. *Team* Warwickshire (1905–07, 2 matches).
Career batting
2–1–1–2–2*–no av–0–*ct* 0
Bowling 121–2–60.50–0–0–1/22

Hyde, Edward
Amateur. *b:* 18.3.1881, Earls Barton, Wellingborough, Northamptonshire. *d:* 9.10.1941, Cambridge. Lower order batsman. *Team* Northamptonshire (1907, 1 match).
Career batting
1–2–1–3–3*–3.00–0–*ct* 2

Hyde, Lord Edward Hyde Villiers
(succeeded as Earl of Clarendon in June 1870)
Amateur. *b:* 11.2.1846, Westminster, London. *d:* 2.10.1914, The Grove, near Watford, Hertfordshire. Middle order right-hand batsman, fast round-arm bowler. *Sch* Harrow. *Team* Cambridge U (1864).
Career batting
1–2–0–8–7–4.00–0–*ct* 1
His County cricket was for Hertfordshire and he was on the Committee both of MCC and the Prince's Club. He was President of the MCC 1871. He was MP for Brecon 1869–70.

Hyland, Frederick James
Professional. *b:* 16.12.1893, Battle, Sussex. *d:* 27.2.1964, Hartford, Cheshire. Lower order batsman. *Team* Hampshire (1924, 1 match).
Career batting
1 match, did not bat–*ct* 0

Hylton, Leslie George
Amateur. *b:* 29.3.1905, Kingston, Jamaica. *d:* 17.5.1955, Spanish Town, Jamaica. He was hanged for the murder of his wife. Lower order right-hand batsman, right-arm fast bowler. *Team* Jamaica (1926/7 to 1938/9). *Tour* West Indies to England 1939. *Tests* West Indies (1934/5 to 1939, 6 matches).
Career batting
40–54–9–843–80–18.73–0–*ct* 31
Bowling 3075–120–25.62–3–0–5/24
Test batting
6–8–2–70–19–11.66–0–*ct* 1
Bowling 418–16–26.12–0–0–4/27
Although he appeared in two Tests on the 1939 tour, he achieved very little and in all first-class matches took only 39 wickets, av 27.71.

Hylton-Stewart, Bruce De la Coeur
Amateur. *b:* 27.11.1891, New Brighton, Cheshire. *d:* 1.10.1972, Marlborough, Wiltshire. Hard-hitting middle order right-hand batsman, right-arm fast medium bowler. *Sch* Bath College. *Teams* Somerset (1912–14, 33 matches); Cambridge U (1912–14).
Career batting
36–63–6–1003–110–17.59–1–*ct* 17
Bowling 1665–58–28.70–2–0–5/3
He also played for Hertfordshire (1920–27).

Hyman, William
Amateur, changed to professional in 1902. *b:* 7.3.1875, Radstock, Bath, Somerset. *d:* 11.2.1959, Mount Charles, St Austell, Cornwall. Hard-hitting middle order batsman, right-arm medium pace bowler. *Team* Somerset (1900–14, 38 matches).
Career batting
38–68–4–1000–110–15.62–1–*ct* 10
He played an incredible innings of 359* for the Bath Cricket Association v Thornbury in 1902, including 32 sixes off the bowling of E. M. Grace. He was also a noted local soccer player.

Hyndman, Henry Mayers
Amateur. *b:* 7.3.1842, Paddington, London. *d:* 22.11.1921, Hampstead, London. Middle order right-hand batsman, good field. *Teams* Cambridge U (1864); Sussex (1864–65, 9 matches).
Career batting
13–20–1–309–62–16.26–0–*ct* 3
He was a well-known Socialist politician.

Hyndson, James Gerard Wyndham
Amateur. *b:* 25.4.1892, Cape Town, South Africa. *d:* 23.2.1935, Holborn, London. Brother of R. W. J. G. (Essex). Lower order right-hand batsman, left-arm fast medium bowler. *Sch* Worksop. *Team* Surrey (1927, 2 matches).
Career batting
13–19–6–224–33–17.23–0–*ct* 6
Bowling 953–35–27.22–4–1–5/25

His first-class debut was for the Army in 1921 and much of his cricket was for MCC or in military matches.

Hyndson, Robert Wilberforce James Gerard
Amateur. *b:* 1894, Cape Town, South Africa. *d:* 27.9.1943, Bradford, Yorkshire. Brother of J. G. W. (Surrey). Middle order batsman, change bowler. *Team* Essex (1919, 1 match).
Career batting
1–2–0–7–6–3.50–0–*ct* 0
Bowling 71–0

Hyslop, Hector Henry
Professional. *b:* 13.12.1840, Southampton, Hampshire. *d:* 11.9.1920, Cosham, Hampshire. He died by his own hand. Opening right-hand batsman, wicket-keeper. *Team* Hampshire (1876–77, 7 matches). *Tours* Australia to England 1878 (not first-class), 1886.
Career batting
9–16–1–121–34–8.06–0–*ct* 7–*st* 11
Bowling 31–2–15.50–0–0–2/12

He appeared in emergency for both the 1878 and 1886 Australians in England, it being thought that he was born in Australia.

I

I'Anson, John
Professional. *b:* 26.10.1868, Scorton, Yorkshire. *d:* 14.9.1936, Chester, Cheshire. Middle order right-hand batsman, right-arm fast medium pace bowler. *Team* Lancashire (1896–1908, 57 matches).
Career batting
57–76–9–986–110*–14.71–1–*ct* 29
Bowling 3072–148–20.75–7–2–7/31

Ibadulla, Kassem Ben Khalid
Cricketer. *b:* 13.10.1964, Birmingham. Son of Khalid (Warwickshire). Middle order right-hand batsman, off break bowler. *Teams* Otago (1982/3 to 1990/1); Gloucestershire (1987–88, 9 matches).
Career batting
31–50–8–1131–107–26.52–2–*ct* 14
Bowling 1290–29–44.48–1–0–5/22

He also played for Cheshire (1985).

Ibadulla, Khalid
Professional. *b:* 20.12.1935, Lahore, India. Father of K. B. K. (Gloucestershire). Opening right-hand batsman, right-arm medium pace off break bowler. *Teams* Punjab (1953/4); Warwickshire (1954–72, 377 matches); Otago (1964/5 to 1966/7); Tasmania (1970/1 to 1971/2, 4 matches). *Tours* Pakistan to India 1952/3, to New Zealand 1964/5, to England 1967; Commonwealth to Pakistan 1963/4; International XI to India, Pakistan and Ceylon 1967/8. *Tests* Pakistan (1964/5 to 1967, 4 matches).
Career batting
416–702–78–17039–171–27.30–22–*ct* 337
Bowling 14264–462–30.87–6–0–7/22
Test batting
4–8–0–253–166–31.62–1–*ct* 3
Bowling 99–1–99.00–0–0–1/42

He hit 1,000 runs in a season six times, going on to 2,000 once: best 2,098, av 33.83, in 1962. With N. F. Horner he created a new Warwickshire first wicket record partnership of 377* v Surrey at the Oval in 1960 and with R. B. Kanhai created a County fourth wicket record of 402 v Nottinghamshire at Trent Bridge in 1968. He was a first-class umpire (1982–83).

Iddison, Roger
Professional. *b:* 15.9.1834, Bedale, Yorkshire. *d:* 19.3.1890, York. Brother of W. H. (Lancashire). Middle order right-hand batsman, right-hand fast round-arm, later lob bowler, excellent point. *Teams* Yorkshire (1853–76, 72 matches); Lancashire (1865–70, 16 matches). *Tour* Stephenson to Australia 1861/2.
Career batting
134–232–30–3791–112–18.76–2–*ct* 133
Bowling 3498–210 + 2–16.65–11–2–7/30

For several seasons in the 1860s he was among the leading batsmen in England. He was the principal organiser of the United North of England Eleven, which began in 1869, and in 1874 was co-secretary of the newly formed Yorkshire United Eleven. He captained Yorkshire 1863–70. He also played for Cheshire (1872).

Iddison, William Holdsworth
(death registered as William Hallsworth Iddison)
Professional until 1866. *b:* 5.2.1840, Bedale, Yorkshire. *d:* 6.3.1898, Withington, Lancashire. Brother of Roger (Yorkshire and Lancashire). Middle order right-hand batsman. *Team* Lancashire (1867–68, 4 matches).
Career batting
4–8–0–46–19–5.75–0–*ct* 1
Bowling 95–1–95.00–0–0–1/33

Iddon, John
Professional. *b:* 8.1.1902, Mawdesley, Lancashire. *d:* 17.4.1946, Madeley, Staffordshire. He was killed in a car accident. Uncle of K. Bowling (Lancashire). Middle order right-hand batsman, slow left-arm bowler. *Team* Lancashire (1924–45, 483 matches). *Tours* Cahn to Jamaica 1928/9; MCC to West Indies 1934/5. *Tests* England (1934/5 to 1935, 5 matches).
Career batting
504–712–95–22681–222–36.76–46–*ct* 217
Bowling 14823–551–26.90–14–2–9/42
Test batting
5–7–1–170–73–28.33–0–*ct* 0

Bowling 27–0

He hit 1,000 runs in a season 13 times, once going on to 2,000: 2,381, av 52.91 in 1934. His five double centuries were all for Lancashire, the highest being 222 v Leicestershire at Liverpool in 1929. His best bowling was 9/42 for Lancashire v Yorkshire at Sheffield in 1937.

Igglesden, Alan Paul
Cricketer. *b:* 8.10.1964, Farnborough, Kent. Lower order right-hand batsman, right-arm fast medium bowler. *Teams* Kent (1986–92, 94 matches); Western Province (1987/8). *Tour* England A to Zimbabwe 1989/90. *Test* England (1989, 1 match).
Career batting
103–106–37–670–41–9.71–0–*ct* 29
Bowling 9275–328–28.27–14–2–6/34
Test batting
1–1–1–2–2*–no av–0–*ct* 1
Bowling 146–3–48.66–0–0–2/91

Ijaz Ahmed
Cricketer. *b:* 20.9.1968, Sialkot, Pakistan. Attacking middle order right-hand batsman, left-arm medium pace or slow bowler. *Teams* Gujranwala (1983/4 to 1985/6); PACO (1983/4 to 1985/6); Habib Bank (1987/8 to 1990/1). *Tours* Pakistan to Australia 1986/7 (not first-class), 1988/9, 1989/90, 1991/2, to India 1986/7, 1989/90 (not first-class), to Sharjah (not first-class) 1986/7, 1988/9, 1989/90, 1990/1, 1991/2, to England 1987, 1992, to West Indies 1987/8, to New Zealand 1988/89, to Bangladesh (not first-class) 1988/9, to Australia and New Zealand (World Cup) 1991/2; Pakistan B to Kenya 1986/7; Pakistan Under 23 to Sri Lanka 1984/5. *Tests* Pakistan (1986/7 to 1990/1, 19 matches).
Career batting
87–144–7–5351–201*–39.05–11–*ct* 70
Bowling 533–20–26.65–0–0–4/50
Test batting
19–25–0–743–122–29.72–2–*ct* 16
Bowling 18–1–18.00–0–0–1/9

Coming to England as a very promising young batsman in 1987, he played some useful innings and appeared in four Tests. He played in one match on the 1992 tour when called up as a replacement. His highest score was 201* for PACO v Karachi at Karachi in 1984/5, the youngest cricketer ever to score a first-class double hundred. He played for Durham in the NatWest Trophy in 1991.

Ijaz Butt, Mohammed
Amateur. *b:* 10.3.1938, Sialkot, India. Opening right-hand batsman, wicket-keeper. *Teams* Punjab (1955/6 to 1957/8); Universities (1958/9 to 1959/60); Lahore (1959/60 to 1967/8); Rawalpindi (1959/60 to 1961/2); Multan (1963/4). *Tours* Pakistan to England 1962, to West Indies 1957/8, to India 1960/1; PIA Eaglets to Ceylon 1960/1. *Tests* Pakistan (1958/9 to 1962, 8 matches).
Career batting
67–120–8–3842–161–34.30–7–*ct* 52–*st* 20
Bowling 148–3–49.33–0–0–1/21
Test batting
8–16–2–279–58–19.92–0–*ct* 5

He hit 1,016 runs, av 28.22, on the 1962 tour to England and, although the reserve wicket-keeper, gained a place in the Test side as a batsman – in the Oval Test, Pakistan's batting was opened in both innings by the two wicket-keepers, Imtiaz Ahmed and Ijaz Butt.

Ijaz Hussain
Cricketer. *b:* 7.4.1942, Bahawalpur, India. Opening right-hand batsman, right-arm medium pace or leg break bowler, wicket-keeper. *Teams* Bahawalpur (1956/7 to 1959/60); Multan (1961/2 to 1962/3); Railways (1963/4 to 1967/8); Karachi (1968/9); PWD (1968/9 to 1969/70); National Bank (1969/70 to 1975/6); Sind (1973/4). *Tour* Pakistan Eaglets to England 1963.
Career batting
82–141–6–4580–173–33.92–8–*ct* 122–*st* 38
Bowling 400–16–25.00–1–0–5/37

He appeared in only three first-class matches on the 1963 Eaglets tour to England.

Ikin, John Thomas
Professional. *b:* 7.3.1918, Bignall End, Staffordshire. *d:*15.9.1984, Bignall End, Staffordshire. Father of M. J. (Minor Counties). Middle order left-hand batsman, leg break and googly bowler, brilliant short leg. *Team* Lancashire (1939–57, 288 matches). *Tours* MCC to Australia and New Zealand 1946/7, to West Indies 1947/8; Commonwealth to India and Ceylon 1950/51. *Tests* England (1946–55, 18 matches).
Career batting
365–554–66–17968–192–36.81–27–*ct* 419
Bowling 10262–339–30.27–11–1–6/21
Test batting
18–31–2–606–60–20.89–0–*ct* 31
Bowling 354–3–118.00–0–0–1/38

He hit 1,000 runs in a season 10 times plus once overseas (best 1,912, av 45.52, in 1952). He also played for Staffordshire (1932–38 and 1958–68). His first-class debut was for Minor Counties in 1938 and his final first-class match was for MCC in 1964.

Ikin, Michael John
Cricketer. *b:* 31.12.1946, Bignall End, Staffordshire. Son of J. T. (Lancashire). Middle order left-hand batsman, off break bowler. *Team* Minor Counties (1972–79).
Career batting
2–3–0–40–31–13.33–0–*ct* 0
Bowling 112–0

His County cricket was for Staffordshire (1967–85).

Ikram Elahi
Amateur. *b:* 3.3.1933, Quetta, India. Hard-hitting lower order right-hand batsman, right-arm fast medium bowler. *Teams* Sind (1953/4); East Pakistan (1954/5); Karachi (1954/5 to 1961/2); PWD (1969/70). *Tours* Pakistan to England 1954, to West Indies 1957/8.
Career batting
47–59–5–1058–73–19.59–0–*ct* 19
Bowling 2400–107–22.42–4–0–6/25

He achieved little on his 1954 tour to England and did not appear in the Tests. His first-class debut was for Rest of Pakistan in 1952/3

Iles, John Henry
Amateur. *b:* 17.9.1871, Clifton, Bristol. *d:* 29.5.1951, Birchington, Kent. Lower order batsman, bowler. *Team* Gloucestershire (1890–91, 3 matches).
Career batting
3–6–1–13–7–2.60–0–*ct* 3
Bowling 152–3–50.66–0–0–3/79

Illingworth, Edward Arnold
Professional. *b:* 11.4.1896, Ossett, Yorkshire. *d:* 2.4.1924, Wilthorpe, Barnsley, Yorkshire. Lower order left-hand batsman, slow left-arm bowler. *Team* Warwickshire (1920, 6 matches).
Career batting
6–12–3–17–8*–1.88–0–*ct* 2
Bowling 312–8–39.00–0–0–2/18

Illingworth, Nigel John Bartle
Cricketer. *b:* 23.11.1960, Chesterfield, Derbyshire. Lower order right-hand batsman, right-arm medium pace bowler. *Sch* Denstone. *Team* Nottinghamshire (1981–83, 15 matches).
Career batting
15–20–5–207–49–13.80–0–*ct* 8
Bowling 694–16–43.37–1–0–5/89

He also played for Lincolnshire (1987–92).

Illingworth, Raymond, CBE
Professional. *b:* 8.6.1932, Pudsey, Yorkshire. Father-in-law of A. A. Metcalfe (Yorkshire). Solid middle order right-hand batsman, off break bowler. *Teams* Yorkshire (1951–83, 496 matches); Leicestershire (1969–78, 176 matches). *Tours* MCC to West Indies 1959/60, to Australia and New Zealand 1962/3, 1970/1; Cavaliers to South Africa 1960/1. *Tests* England (1958–73, 61 matches).
Career batting
787–1073–213–24134–162–28.06–22–*ct* 446
Bowling 42023–2072–20.28–104–11–9/42
Test batting
61–90–11–1836–113–23.24–2–*ct* 45
Bowling 3807–122–31.20–3–0–6/29

One of the most complete cricketers of his generation, his career is divided into three parts. From 1951 to 1968 he was a Yorkshire and England all rounder who completed the 'double' six times – 1957, 1959–62 and 1964. He appeared with success in 29 Tests, but only had a modest record on his major tour to Australia in 1962/3.

A difference between himself and the Yorkshire Club at the end of 1968 led to his appointment as captain of Leicestershire for 1969 and an injury to M. C. Cowdrey meant that he also captained England in the six Tests of 1969. In 1970 he continued to lead England in the series against the Rest of the World and the following winter was captain of the MCC team to Australia and New Zealand. In all he captained his country in 31 Tests ending in 1973. In 1975 he took Leicestershire to the top of the County Championship – in his initial season with his new County he headed both batting and bowling averages, but latterly went in very low down the order and concentrated more on captaincy and bowling.

The third phase of his career began in 1979 when he retired from first-class cricket and took over as manager of Yorkshire. The internal differences within that County Club continued to grow and midway through 1982 he returned to first-class cricket as Yorkshire's captain, a role from which he resigned at the close of 1983.

In all he hit 1,000 runs in a season eight times (best 1,726, av 46.64, in 1959) and took 100 wickets ten times (best 131, av 14.36, in 1968). His best innings analysis was 9/42 for Yorkshire v Worcestershire at Worcester in 1957. He was awarded the CBE in the 1973 New Year's Honours list. He is a well-known commentator.

Illingworth, Richard Keith
Cricketer. *b:* 23.8.1963, Greengates, Bradford, Yorkshire. Lower order right-hand batsman, slow left-arm bowler. *Teams* Worcestershire (1982–92, 225 matches); Natal (1988/9). *Tours* England A to Zimbabwe 1989/90, to Pakistan and Sri Lanka 1990/1; Worcestershire to Zimbabwe 1990/1; England to New Zealand 1991/2, to Australia and New Zealand (World Cup) 1991/2. *Tests* England (1991, 2 matches).
Career batting
243–264–70–4094–120*–21.10–3–*ct* 105
Bowling 16749–525–31.90–19–4–7/50
Test batting
2–4–2–31–13–15.50–0–*ct* 1
Bowling 213–4–53.25–0–0–3/110

His best season was 1990 when he took 75 wickets, av 28.29. In 1991 on his Test debut he dismissed P. V. Simmons with the first delivery he bowled, v West Indies at Trent Bridge.

Ilott, Mark Christopher
Cricketer. *b:* 27.8.1970, Watford, Hertfordshire. Lower order right-hand batsman, left-arm medium fast bowler. *Team* Essex (1988–92, 40 matches). *Tour* England A to Pakistan and Sri Lanka 1990/1.

Career batting
42–39–11–331–42*–11.82–0–*ct* 10
Bowling 3980–117–34.01–5–0–6/87
He also played for Hertfordshire (1987–88).

Ilsley, Stanley Thomas
Professional. *b:* 18.6.1938, Marylebone, London. Lower order left-hand batsman, slow left-arm bowler. *Team* MCC (1956).
Career batting
2–2–0–8–8–4.00–0–*ct* 0
Bowling 137–5–27.40–0–0–3/39

Imlay, Alan Durant
Amateur. *b:* 14.2.1885, Cotham, Bristol. *d:* 3.7.1959, Brent Knoll, Somerset. Lower order right-hand batsman, wicket-keeper. *Sch* Clifton. *Teams* Gloucestershire (1905–11, 7 matches); Cambridge U (1906–07, blue 1907).
Career batting
12–21–0–166–26–7.90–0–*ct* 16–*st* 1

Imran Khan Niazi
Cricketer. *b:* 25.11.1952, Lahore, Pakistan. Cousin of Majid Jahangir Khan (Pakistan), A. J. Khan (Oxford U), Humayun Zaman (Lahore), Javed Zaman (Lahore) and Javed Burki (Pakistan), nephew of M. Baqa Jilani (India) and M. Jahangir Khan (India). Attacking middle order right-hand batsman, right-arm fast bowler, excellent outfield. *Sch* Worcester RGS. *Teams* Lahore (1969/70 to 1970/1); Worcestershire (1971–76, 42 matches); Oxford U (1973–75, blue all three years); Dawood Club (1975/6); PIA (1975/6 to 1980/1); Sussex (1977–88, 131 matches); New South Wales (1984/5, 5 matches). *Tours* Pakistan to England 1971, 1974, 1975 (World Cup), 1979 (World Cup), 1982, 1983 (World Cup), 1987, to Sri Lanka 1975/6, 1985/6, to Australia 1976/7, 1978/9, 1981/2, 1983/4, 1984/5 (not first-class), 1986/7 (not first-class), 1988/9, 1989/90, 1991/2, to West Indies 1976/7, 1987/8, to New Zealand 1978/9, 1988/9, to India 1979/80, 1986/7, 1989/90 (not first-class), to Sharjah (not first-class) 1984/5, 1985/6, 1988/9, 1989/90, 1990/1, 1991/2, to Australia and New Zealand (World Cup) 1991/2; Rest of World to England 1987, 1988. *Tests* Pakistan (1971 to 1991/2, 88 matches).
Career batting
382–582–99–17771–170–36.79–30–*ct* 117
Bowling 28726–1287–22.32–70–13–8/34
Test batting
88–126–25–3807–136–37.69–6–*ct* 28
Bowling 8258–362–22.81–23–6–8/58
The outstanding personality of Pakistan cricket through the 1980s, he was the first Pakistani cricketer to take more than 300 wickets in Test cricket and with over 3,000 runs to his name, by far the leading all-rounder yet produced by his country. To these accomplishments must be added his captaincy. He seemed to be able to mould the differing factions of Pakistani cricket into a relatively harmonious whole. He toured England with four Test playing sides; in 1971, at the age of 18, he appeared in one Test; in 1974 he appeared after coming down from Oxford, where he was captain, but achieved little in the three Tests. In 1982 and 1987 he captained the tourists. On the first of these two visits he had an outstanding series with a batting average of 53.00 and a bowling average of 18.57. However 1987 was really his great year, since he led Pakistan to their first series win in England, as well as topping the Test bowling table with 21 wickets, av 21.66. His final success in international cricket was to take Pakistan to the World Cup and beat England in the final at Melbourne in March 1992. His optimism galvanised his side, when most critics had written them off. In all he captained Pakistan in 48 Tests.
Although he played County cricket from 1971 to 1986 his appearances in each season were generally restricted. However some idea of his impact when he did play can be gauged from the fact that in his final three years with Sussex, 1983, 1985 and 1986, he topped both the batting and bowling tables in each year. In all he hit 1,000 runs in a season in England four times (best 1,339, av 41.84, in 1978). His best English season with the ball was 1979 with 73 wickets, av 14.94. He missed all of the 1984 season due to injury. A fierce critic of Pakistan's domestic first-class structure he did not appear in Pakistan after 1980/1 except in international matches.

Imtiaz Ahmed
Amateur. *b:* 5.1.1928, Lahore, India. Sound opening right-hand batsman, wicket-keeper. *Teams* Northern India (1944/5 to 1946/7); Punjab (1947/8 to 1948/9); Services (1953/4 to 1964/5); PAF (1969/70 to 1972/3). *Tours* Pakistan to England 1954, 1962, to India 1952/3, 1960/1, to Ceylon 1948/9, 1964/5, to West Indies 1957/8; Services to India and Ceylon 1954/5. *Tests* Pakistan (1952/3 to 1962, 41 matches).
Career batting
179–309–32–10323–300*–37.26–22–*ct* 316–*st* 77
Bowling 166–4–41.50–0–0–2/12
Test batting
41–72–1–2079–209–29.28–3–*ct* 77–*st* 16
Bowling 0–0
The principal Pakistan wicket-keeper during the country's first years in Test cricket, he appeared in every one of the initial 39 Tests involving Pakistan. He was successful on both tours to England, hitting 1,105 runs, av 29.07, in 1954 and 1,140 runs, av 30.00, in 1962 in addition to being a splendid wicket-keeper. He captained Pakistan in four Tests, including three v England in 1961/2. His final first-class match was for NWFP XI in 1973/4. His highest score was 300* for Prime Minister's XI v Commonwealth at Bombay in 1950/1. He hit 1,142 runs, av 49.65, in Pakistan in 1961/2.

Ince, Harry Wakefield
Amateur. *b:* 9.4.1893, Aberdare, Christ Church, Barbados. *d:* 11.5.1978, Bayville, St Michael, Barbados. Middle order left-hand batsman, right-arm slow bowler. *Team* Barbados (1912/3 to 1929/30). *Tour* West Indies to England 1923.
Career batting
35–52–6–1352–167–29.39–3–*ct* 13
Bowling 242–5–48.40–0–0–3/34

Inchmore, John Darling
Cricketer. *b:* 22.2.1949, Ashington, Northumberland. Lower order right-hand batsman, right-arm fast medium bowler. *Teams* Worcestershire (1973–86, 216 matches); Northern Transvaal (1976/7).
Career batting
218–246–53–3137–113–16.25–1–*ct* 72
Bowling 14777–510–28.97–18–1–8/58
He also played for Northumberland (1970) and Wiltshire (1987).

Indrajitsinhji, Kumar Shri Madhavsinhji Jadeja
Amateur. *b:* 15.6.1937, Jamnagar, India. Nephew of K. S. Duleepsinhji (Sussex), cousin of Hanumant Singh (India) and Suryaveer Singh (Rajasthan). Lower order right-hand batsman, wicket-keeper. *Teams* Saurashtra (1954/5 to 1971/2); Delhi (1958/9 to 1960/1). *Tour* India to Australia and New Zealand 1967/8. *Tests* India (1964/5 to 1969/70, 4 matches).
Career batting
90–146–8–3694–124–26.76–5–*ct* 133–*st* 80
Bowling 61–0
Test batting
4–7–1–51–23–8.50–0–*ct* 6–*st* 3
His only first-class match in England was for L. C. Stevens' XI in 1960. His final first-class match was for UFoam in India in 1972/3.

Inge, William Walter
Amateur. *b:* 29.11.1907, Holmwood, Surrey. *d:* 18.3.1991, Rugby, Warwickshire. Great-nephew of F. G. (Oxford U 1861), J. W. (Gentlemen of Kent 1863) and William (Oxford U 1853). Middle/lower order right-hand batsman, wicket-keeper. *Sch* Winchester. *Team* Oxford U (1930).
Career batting
3–4–2–20–9*–10.00–0–*ct* 2–*st* 4
His County cricket was for Oxfordshire (1928–55).

Ingham, Peter Geoffrey
Cricketer. *b:* 28.9.1956, Beauchief, Sheffield, Yorkshire. Middle order right-hand batsman, off break bowler. *Team* Yorkshire (1979–81, 8 matches).
Career batting
8–14–0–290–64–20.71–0–*ct* 0
He also played for Northumberland (1984–86).

Ingle, Reginald Addington
Amateur. *b:* 5.11.1903, Bodmin, Cornwall. *d:* 19.12.1992, Bath, Somerset. Middle order right-hand batsman. *Sch* Oundle. *Teams* Somerset (1923–39, 309 matches); Cambridge U (1924–26)
Career batting
325–543–19–9829–119*–18.75–10–*ct* 129
Bowling 26–0
He hit 1,000 runs in a season twice (best 1,083, av 24.06, in 1932). From 1932 to 1937 he captained Somerset.

Ingleby, Charles Willis
Professional. *b:* 11.12.1870, Sheepscar, Leeds, Yorkshire. *d:* 15.11.1939, Eccleshill, Bradford, Yorkshire. Middle order batsman, useful bowler. *Team* Lancashire (1899, 1 match).
Career batting
1–2–1–40–29–40.00–0–*ct* 0
Bowling 17–0
He also played for Cumberland (1904).

Ingleby-Mackenzie, Alexander Colin David
Amateur. *b:* 15.9.1933, Dartmouth, Devon. Forcing middle order left-hand batsman, off break bowler, occasional wicket-keeper. *Sch* Eton. *Team* Hampshire (1951–65, 309 matches). *Tours* Swanton to West Indies 1955/6, to India 1963/4; Norfolk to Jamaica 1956/7, Commonwealth to South Africa 1959/60, to Rhodesia 1962/3; Cavaliers to Jamaica 1963/4, to West Indies 1964/5.
Career batting
343–574–64–12421–132*–24.35–11–*ct* 205–*st* 1
Bowling 35–0
He hit 1,000 runs in a season five times (best 1,613, av 25.68, in 1959). From 1958 to 1965 he captained Hampshire.

Inglis, Alfred Markham
Amateur. *b:* 24.9.1857, Rugby. *d:* 17.6.1919, French Street, Westerham, Kent. Brother of J. F. (Kent), uncle of C. T. Ashton (Essex), G. Ashton (Worcestershire), P. Ashton (Essex) and H. Ashton (Essex). Hard-hitting middle order right-hand batsman, fine field. *Sch* Rugby. *Team* Kent (1887, 1 match).
Career batting
2–4–0–35–12–8.75–0–*ct* 0
He did not appear in first-class matches whilst at Oxford U. His first-class debut was for MCC in 1885.

Inglis, John Frederic
Amateur. *b:* 16.7.1853, Peshawar, India. *d:* 27.2.1923, Littleham, Devon. Brother of A. M. (Kent), uncle of C. T. Ashton (Essex), G. Ashton (Worcestershire), P. Ashton (Essex), and H. Ashton (Essex). Middle order batsman. *Sch* Charterhouse. *Team* Kent (1883, 1 match).
Career batting
1–1–0–19–19–19.00–0–*ct* 0

Inglis, Russell
Cricketer. *b:* 13.6.1936, Crook Hall, Co Durham. *d:* 28.4.1982, Gosforth, Newcastle upon Tyne, North-

umberland. Sound right-hand batsman, right-arm medium pace bowler. *Team* Minor Counties (1965–69).
Career batting
3–6–1–91–43–18.20–0–*ct* 5
Bowling 24–2–12.00–0–0–2/2
His County cricket was for Durham (pre first-class, 1956–73).

Ingram, Edward
Amateur. *b:* 14.8.1910, Dublin, Ireland. *d:* 13.3.1973, Basingstoke, Hampshire. Lower order right-hand batsman, right-arm medium pace or leg break bowler. *Teams* Ireland (1928–53); Middlesex (1938–49, 12 matches).
Career batting
31–55–4–766–64–15.01–0–*ct* 14
Bowling 1896–79–24.00–1–0–5/48

Ingram, Isaac
Professional. *b:* 14.5.1855, Leigh, Tonbridge, Kent. *d:* 19.11.1947, Leigh, Tonbridge, Kent. Lower order right-hand batsman, wicket-keeper. *Team* Kent (1878–79, 12 matches).
Career batting
12–20–1–112–25–5.89–0–*ct* 8–*st* 7

Ingram, John Barkly
Amateur. *b:* 1857. *d:* 23.7.1924, Dewsbury, Yorkshire. Middle order batsman. *Team* England XI (1878).
Career batting
1–1–0–7–7–7.00–0–*ct* 0

Ingram, Dr Peter Robert
Amateur. *b:* 21.2.1869, Chapel of Garioch, Aberdeenshire, Scotland. *d:* 8.12.1955, Perranporth, Cornwall. Lower order left-hand batsman, slow left-arm bowler. *Team* Somerset (1910, 2 matches).
Career batting
2–4–0–16–7–4.00–0–*ct* 1
Bowling 69–0

Inman, Clive Clay
Professional. *b:* 29.1.1936, Colombo, Ceylon. Son of H. C. (Ceylon). Middle order left-hand batsman, off break bowler. *Teams* Ceylon (1956/7 to 1966/7); Leicestershire (1961–71, 242 matches). *Tours* Ceylon to Pakistan 1966/7, to India 1957/8.
Career batting
255–422–42–13112–178–34.50–21–*ct* 108
Bowling 89–1–89.00–0–0–1/30
He hit 1,000 runs in a season eight times (best 1,735, av 36.91, in 1968). He hit 51 in eight minutes for Leicestershire v Nottinghamshire at Trent Bridge in 1965, the fastest fifty in first-class cricket. He played for Derbyshire in Sunday League matches in 1973.

Innes, Andrew David
Amateur. *b:* 3.5.1905, Glasgow, Scotland. *d:* 23.2.1968, Milngavie, Dunbartonshire, Scotland. Middle order right-hand batsman, off break bowler. *Team* Scotland (1925–34).
Career batting
6–11–1–164–48–16.40–0–*ct* 6
Bowling 26–1–26.00–0–0–1/12

Inniss, Sir Clifford de Lisle
Amateur. *b:* 26.10.1910, Friendly Hall, St Michael, Barbados. Brother of B. de L. (Barbados). Middle order right-hand batsman, right-arm slow bowler. *Team* Barbados (1927/8 to 1938/9). *Tour* West Indies in England 1933.
Career batting
10–18–1–474–80–27.88–0–*ct* 4
Bowling 50–1–50.00–0–0–1/17
An undergraduate at Oxford he appeared in the Seniors' match of 1933 and then assisted the West Indian tourists in two first-class matches. He played for Oxfordshire (1933–34).

Inns, John Herbert
Professional. *b:* 30.3.1876, Writtle, Essex. *d:* 14.6.1905, Writtle, Essex. Lower order batsman, wicket-keeper. *Team* Essex (1898–1904, 10 matches).
Career batting
10–14–3–73–28–6.63–*ct* 8
Bowling 15–0

Insole, Douglas John, CBE
Amateur. *b:* 18.4.1926, Clapton, London. Sound middle order right-hand batsman, right-arm medium pace bowler, excellent all-round fielder, occasional wicket-keeper. *Teams* Cambridge U (1947–49, blue all three years); Essex (1947–63, 345 matches). *Tours* MCC to South Africa 1956/7; Manager of England to Australia 1978/9, 1982/3. *Tests* England (1950–57, 9 matches).
Career batting
450–743–72–25241–219*–37.61–54–*ct* 366–*st* 6
Bowling 4680–138–33.95–1–0–5/22
Test batting
9–17–2–408–110*–27.20–1–*ct* 8
He hit 1,000 runs in a season 13 times, going on to 2,000 three times (best 2,427, av 42.57, in 1955). His only double century is 219* for Essex v Yorkshire at Colchester in 1949. He captained Cambridge in 1949 and Essex 1950–60. He was appointed a Test Selector in 1959 and was Chairman of the TCCB 1975–78. Since 1984 he has been Chairman of Essex, having previously held the position 1976–78. He was awarded the CBE for his services to cricket. A noted soccer player, he won his blue and also played for Southend United and Corinthian Casuals, appearing in the FA Amateur Cup Final in 1955/6.

Intikhab Alam Khan
Amateur. *b:* 28.12.1941, Hoshiarpur, India. Brother of Aftab Alam (Karachi). Middle order right-hand batsman, leg break and googly bowler. *Teams* Karachi (1957/8 to 1970/1); PIA (1960/1 to 1974/5); PWD (1967/8 to 1969/70); Surrey (1969–81, 232 matches); Sind (1973/4); Punjab (1975/6). *Tours* Pakistan to India 1960/1, to England 1962, 1967, 1971, 1974, to Ceylon 1964, to Australia and New Zealand 1964/5, 1972/3, to Australia and West Indies 1976/7; Pakistan Eaglets to England 1963; PIA to East Africa 1964; Rest of World to England 1970, to Australia 1971/2. *Tests* Pakistan (1959/60 to 1976/7, 47 matches).
Career batting
489–725–78–14331–182–22.14–9–*ct* 227
Bowling 43474–1571–27.67–85–13–8/54
Test batting
47–77–10–1493–138–22.28–1–*ct* 20
Bowling 4494–125–35.95–5–2–7/52

He took 104 wickets, av 28.36, in 1971. He led Pakistan in 17 Tests and his most successful tour of England was as captain in 1974; he also captained the 1971 tour to England. He acted as manager on the 1982 and 1992 Pakistan tours to England. His last first-class match in Pakistan was for Pakistan in 1976/7 and last first-class match in England for D. B. Close's XI in 1982.

Intin, John Wilfred
Amateur. *b:* 8.7.1886, Hull, Yorkshire. *d:* 11.4.1970, Grangemouth, Stirlingshire, Scotland. Middle order right-hand batsman, right-arm medium pace bowler. *Team* Scotland (1920).
Career batting
1–1–0–14–14–14.00–0–*ct* 0
Bowling 42–2–21.00–0–0–2/25

Inverarity, Robert John
Cricketer. *b:* 31.1.1944, Subiaco, Perth, Western Australia. Son of Mervyn (Western Australia). Opening or middle order right-hand batsman, slow left-arm bowler, good slip. *Teams* Western Australia (1962/3 to 1978/9, 119 matches); South Australia (1979/80 to 1984/5, 53 matches). *Tours* Australia to England 1968, 1972, to New Zealand 1969/70. *Tests* Australia (1968–72, 6 matches).
Career batting
223–377–49–11777–187–35.90–26–*ct* 251
Bowling 6780–221–30.67–7–0–7/86
Test batting
6–11–1–174–56–17.40–0–*ct* 4
Bowling 93–4–23.25–0–0–3/26

Although he appeared in some Tests on both his tours to England, his first-class batting records were quite modest. On the 1968 tour he bowled only 8 overs, but in 1972 his spin bowling was used much more often.

Inzamam-ul-Haq
Cricketer. *b:* 3.3.1970, Multan, Pakistan. Middle order right-hand batsman, slow left-arm bowler. *Teams* Multan (1985/6 to 1991/2); United Bank (1988/9 to 1990/1). *Tours* Pakistan A to Sri Lanka 1990/1; Pakistan to Australia 1991/2, to Australia and New Zealand (World Cup) 1991/2, to England 1992. *Tests* Pakistan (1992, 4 matches).
Career batting
76–120–27–4701–201*–50.54–14–*ct* 61
Bowling 1217–37–32.89–2–0–5/80
Test batting
4–6–1–66–26–13.20–0–*ct* 4

He came to prominence in the World Cup final stages in 1991/2, and played in 4 Tests in 1992 but made little impression. His highest score was 201* for United Bank v PNSC at Karachi in 1988/9. He scored 1,000 runs in a season in Pakistan twice, best 1,645, av 60.92, in 1989/90, narrowly missing the national record.

Iqbal Qasim, Mohammad
Cricketer. *b:* 6.8.1953, Karachi, Pakistan. Lower order left-hand batsman, slow left-arm bowler, good close field. *Teams* Karachi (1971/2 to 1989/90); National Bank (1972/3 to 1991/2); Sind (1972/3). *Tours* Pakistan to Australia 1976/7, 1978/9, 1981/2, 1984/5, to West Indies 1976/7, to England 1978, 1982, 1987, to New Zealand 1978/9, 1984/5, to India 1979/80, 1983/4, 1986/7, to Bangladesh (not first-class) 1988/9. *Tests* Pakistan (1976/7 to 1988/9, 50 matches).
Career batting
244–230–63–2403–61–14.38–0–*ct* 166
Bowling 20348–998–20.38–68–14–9/80
Test batting
50–57–15–549–56–13.07–0–*ct* 42
Bowling 4807–171–28.11–8–2–7/49

Although he appeared in three Tests on the 1978 tour to England his record was very moderate. On the 1982 visit he did not play in the Tests. He was Assistant Manager on the 1987 tour to England and played in one first-class match. His best bowling was 9/80 for Pakistan v International XI at Lahore in 1981/2. He also played for Cheshire (1981).

Irani, Ronald Charles
Cricketer. *b:* 26.10.1971, Leigh, Lancashire. Middle order right-hand batsman, right-arm medium pace bowler. *Team* Lancashire (1990–92, 7 matches).
Career batting
7–7–1–99–31*–16.50–0–*ct* 4
Bowling 292–5–58.40–0–0–2/21

Iredale, Francis Adams
Amateur. *b:* 19.6.1867, Surry Hills, Sydney, New South Wales, Australia. *d:* 15.4.1926, Crows Nest, North Sydney, New South Wales, Australia. Nephew of F. Adams (New South Wales). Sound opening

right-hand batsman, good deep field. *Team* New South Wales (1888/9 to 1901/2, 56 matches). *Tours* Australia to England 1896, 1899, to North America 1896. *Tests* Australia (1894/5 to 1899, 14 matches).
Career batting
133–214–12–6795–196–33.63–12–*ct* 111
Bowling 211–6–35.16–0–0–3/1
Test batting
14–23–1–807–140–36.68–2–*ct* 16
Bowling 3–0

After a poor start, he batted well during the 1896 tour to England and hit 1,328 runs, av 27.66, including a century in the Old Trafford Test. In 1899 he did not fair quite so well – 1,039 runs, av 29.68 – and was left out of two Tests.

Ireland, Arthur
Amateur. *b:* 13.9.1850, Brighton, Sussex. *d:* 5.6.1895, Marylebone, London. Lower order batsman. *Team* MCC (1881).
Career batting
1–1–0–1–1–1.00–0–*ct* 1

Ireland, Frederick Schomberg
Amateur. *b:* 6.4.1860, Port Louis, Mauritius. *d:* 16.3.1937, Mentone, France. Uncle of J. F. (Cambridge U). Middle order right-hand batsman, roundarm fast right-hand bowler, close field. *Team* Kent (1878–87, 4 matches).
Career batting
4–8–1–125–87–17.85–0–*ct* 1
Bowling 54–3–18.00–0–0–3/37

Owing to his profession, as a solicitor, his appearances in first-class cricket were limited. He also played for Devon (1883). He was also a good golfer.

Ireland, John Frederick
Amateur. *b:* 12.8.1888, Port Louis, Mauritius. *d:* 21.10.1970, Uckfield, Sussex. Nephew of F. S. (Kent), brother-in-law of E. N. S. Crankshaw (Gloucestershire). Middle order right-hand batsman, right-arm medium pace bowler. *Sch* Marlborough. *Team* Cambridge U (1908–11, blue all four years).
Career batting
28–50–3–1355–123–28.82–3–*ct* 21
Bowling 787–37–21.27–2–0–5/25

A brilliant schoolboy batsman, he scarcely bowled until his final year at Cambridge, when he performed the hat-trick against Oxford. He captained Cambridge in 1911. His County cricket was for Suffolk (1906–11). His final first-class match was for MCC in 1912. He also represented Cambridge at golf and hockey.

Iremonger, Albert
Professional. *b:* 15.6.1884, Wilford, Nottinghamshire. *d:* 9.3.1958, Nottingham. Brother of James (Nottinghamshire). Lower order right-hand batsman, right-arm medium pace bowler. *Team* Nottinghamshire (1906–10, 14 matches).
Career batting
14–19–3–261–60*–16.31–0–*ct* 17
Bowling 296–10–29.60–1–0–5/83

A noted goalkeeper, he appeared for Notts County from 1905 to 1926, and for Lincoln City in 1926/7.

Iremonger, James
Professional. *b:* 5.3.1876, Norton, Yorkshire. *d:* 25.3.1956, West Bridgford, Nottingham. Brother of Albert (Nottinghamshire). Opening right-hand batsman, right-arm medium pace bowler. *Team* Nottinghamshire (1899–1914, 315 matches). *Tour* MCC to Australia 1911/12.
Career batting
334–534–60–16622–272–35.06–31–*ct* 191
Bowling 14224–619–22.97–35–8–8/21

He hit 1,000 runs in a season nine times (best 1,983, av 60.09, in 1904). All his four double centuries were for Nottinghamshire, the highest being 272 v Kent at Trent Bridge in 1904. He exceeded 100 wickets in a season once: 101, av 26.10, in 1911. He was Nottinghamshire CCC coach from 1921 to 1938. An excellent soccer player, he appeared as full back for Nottingham Forest from 1895 to 1909 and for England.

Irish, Arthur Frank
Professional. *b:* 23.11.1918, Dudley, Worcestershire. Middle order right-hand batsman, right-arm medium pace bowler. *Team* Somerset (1950, 16 matches).
Career batting
16–29–4–629–76–25.16–0–*ct* 5
Bowling 206–3–68.66–0–0–2/5

He also played for Devon (1937–53).

Irvin, Rev Arthur John Edward
Amateur. *b:* 10.3.1848, Hackness, Scarborough, Yorkshire. *d:* 22.7.1945, Old Basing, Hampshire. Lower order right-hand batsman, wicket-keeper. *Sch* Rossall. *Team* Oxford U (1868–71).
Career batting
2–3–1–18–12–9.00–0–*ct* 4–*st* 1

Irvine, Brian Lee
Cricketer. *b:* 9.3.1944, Durban, South Africa. Middle order left-hand batsman, right-arm medium pace bowler, wicket-keeper. *Teams* Essex (1968–69, 54 matches); Natal (1965/6 to 1968/9); Transvaal (1969/70 to 1976/7). *Tours* South Africa to England 1970 (tour cancelled), to Australia 1971/2 (tour cancelled). *Tests* South Africa (1969/70, 4 matches).
Career batting
157–271–26–9919–193–40.48–21–*ct* 240–*st* 7
Bowling 142–1–142.00–0–0–1/39
Test batting
4–7–0–353–102–50.42–1–*ct* 2

He scored over 1,000 runs in both his seasons in English first-class cricket (best 1,439, av 32.70, in 1968). His first class debut was for a Western Province Invitation XI in 1962/3.

Irvine, Dr Leonard George
Amateur. *b:* 11.1.1906, Bombay, India. *d:* 27.4.1973, Canterbury, Kent. Lower order right-hand batsman, slow leg break bowler. *Sch* Taunton. *Teams* Cambridge U (1926–28, blue 1926–27); Kent (1927, 1 match).
Career batting
28–35–16–154–14*–8.10–0–*ct* 13
Bowling 2287–98–23.33–7–2–7/79

Irwin, Philip Hastings
Amateur. *b:* 1.11.1884, Didsbury, Lancashire. *d:* 12.1.1958, St Peter Port, Guernsey. Grandson of F. B. Wright (Oxford U 1829). Opening right-hand batsman. *Sch* Forest. *Team* Royal Navy (1914–19).
Career batting
4–8–0–207–80–25.87–0–*ct* 0
His County cricket was for Cornwall (1921–25). His final first-class match was for MCC in 1924.

Isaac, Arthur Whitmore
Amateur. *b:* 4.10.1873, Powick Court, Worcestershire. *d:* 7.7.1916, Contalmaison, France. He was killed in action. Brother of J. E. V. (Worcestershire), father of H. W. (Worcestershire). Middle order right-hand batsman, excellent field. *Sch* Harrow. *Team* Worcestershire (1899–1911, 51 matches).
Career batting
52–87–5–1136–60–13.85–0–*ct* 9
He did not play in first-class cricket whilst at Oxford U. His final first-class match was for H. K. Foster's XII in 1913. He first played for Worcestershire (pre first-class) in 1895.

Isaac, Herbert Whitmore
Amateur. *b:* 11.12.1899, Hallow, Worcester. *d:* 26.4.1962, Chisekesi, Northern Rhodesia. Son of A. W. (Worcestershire), nephew of J. E. V. (Worcestershire). Lower order batsman, bowler. *Sch* Harrow. *Team* Worcestershire (1919, 3 matches).
Career batting
3–3–0–32–23–10.66–0–*ct* 0
Bowling 22–0

Isaac, John Edmund Valentine
Amateur. *b:* 14.2.1880, Powick Court, Worcestershire. *d:* 9.5.1915, Rouge Bancs, Fromelles Ridge, Armentieres, France. He was killed in action. Brother of A. W. (Worcestershire), uncle of H. W. (Worcestershire). Middle order right-hand batsman. *Sch* Harrow. *Teams* Worcestershire (1907–08, 5 matches); Orange Free State (1906/7).
Career batting
10–17–1–140–34*–8.75–0–*ct* 2
Bowling 0–0
His first-class debut was for the Army in South Africa in 1905/6. A well known gentleman jockey, he won the 1911 Cairo Grand National.

Isherwood, Francis William Ramsbottom
Amateur. *b:* 16.10.1852. *d:* 30.4.1888, Southsea, Hampshire. Middle or lower order right-hand batsman, right-hand fast medium round-arm bowler, good field. *Sch* Rugby. *Team* Oxford U (1872, blue).
Career batting
5–8–2–71–19*–11.83–0–*ct* 1
Bowling 221–7–31.57–0–0–4/52
His County cricket was for Essex (pre first-class, 1872). He played rugby for England.

Isherwood, Frederic
Professional. *b:* 13.8.1858, Over Darwen, Lancashire. *d:* 20.2.1927, Blackley, Manchester, Lancashire. Middle order batsman. *Team* Lancashire (1881, 1 match).
Career batting
1–1–0–0–0–0.00–0–*ct* 0

Isherwood, Lionel Charlie Ramsbottom
Amateur. *b:* 13.4.1891, Portsmouth, Hampshire. *d:* 30.9.1970, Merrow, Surrey. Middle order right-hand batsman, right-arm medium pace bowler. *Sch* Eton. *Teams* Hampshire (1919–23, 26 matches); Sussex (1925–27, 28 matches). *Tour* MCC to South America 1926/7.
Career batting
60–101–8–1529–75*–16.44–0–*ct* 25
Bowling 24–1–24.00–0–0–1/16
He also played for Buckinghamshire (1939).

Isles, Derek
Cricketer. *b:* 14.10.1943, Bradford, Yorkshire. Lower order batsman, wicket-keeper. *Team* Worcestershire (1967, 1 match).
Career batting
1–2–2–21–17*–no av–0–*ct* 1–*st* 1

Ives, George Cecil
Amateur. *b:* 1867. *d:* 4.6.1950, Hampstead, London. Tail end batsman. *Team* MCC (1902).
Career batting
1–2–0–9–7–4.50–0–*ct* 0
He was the adopted son of The Hon Mrs Emma Ives.

Ivey, Alfred Michael
Amateur. *b:* 11.7.1928, Leeds, Yorkshire. Opening right-hand batsman, right-arm medium pace bowler. *Sch* Leeds GS. *Team* Oxford U (1949–51).
Career batting
7–12–0–220–40–18.33–0–*ct* 11
Bowling 160–2–80.00–0–0–1/7

Izzard, Wilfred Cyril
Amateur. *b:* 25.2.1892, Northampton. *d:* 15.9.1977, Northampton. Opening right-hand batsman. *Team* Northamptonshire (1919–20, 12 matches).
Career batting
12–20–0–206–51–10.30–0–*ct* 8

J

Jack, Trevor Bernard
Cricketer. *b:* 16.7.1960, Perth, Western Australia. Middle order right-hand batsman, leg break bowler. *Team* Oxford U (1988, blue).
Career batting
2–3–0–57–29–19.00–0–*ct* 1

Jackman, Frederick
Professional. *b:* 15.5.1841, Fareham, Hampshire. *d:* 5.9.1891, Horndean, Hampshire. Middle/lower order right-hand batsman, right-hand fast round-arm bowler, slip field. *Team* Hampshire (1875–77, 2 matches).
Career batting
2–4–2–26–16–13.00–0–*ct* 0
Bowling 42–1–42.00–0–0–1/21

Jackman, Robin David
Cricketer. *b:* 13.8.1945, Simla, India. Lower order right-hand batsman, right-arm fast medium bowler. *Sch* St Edmund's, Canterbury. *Teams* Surrey (1966–82, 338 matches); Western Province (1971/2); Rhodesia (1972/3 to 1979/80). *Tours* England to West Indies 1980/1, to Australia 1982/3; Robins to South Africa 1972/3. *Tests* England (1980/1 to 1982, 4 matches).
Career batting
399–478–157–5681–92*–17.69–0–*ct* 177
Bowling 31978–1402–22.80–67–8–8/40
Test batting
4–6–0–42–17–7.00–0–*ct* 0
Bowling 445–14–31.78–0–0–4/110

He took 121 wickets, av 15.40, in 1980. His inclusion in the England team to tour West Indies in 1980/1 caused the abandonment of the Georgetown Test, because the Guyanan Government objected to Jackman's previous connections with South Africa. He is a nephew of Patrick Cargill, the actor.

Jackson, Albert Brian
Professional. *b:* 21.8.1933, Kettleshulme, Cheshire. Lower order right-hand batsman, right-arm fast medium bowler. *Team* Derbyshire (1963–68, 148 matches).
Career batting
149–160–83–647–27–8.40–0–*ct* 29
Bowling 8656–457–18.94–17–4–8/18

He took 120 wickets, av 12.42, in 1965. He also played for Cheshire (1956–59 and 1969–70).

Jackson, Alfred Louis Stewart
Amateur. *b:* 28.2.1904, Vina del Mar, Chile. *d:* 23.7.1982, Valparaiso, Chile. Brother of J. A. S. (Somerset). Opening right-hand batsman, wicket-keeper. *Sch* Cheltenham. *Team* Argentina (1937/8). *Tour* South Americans to England 1932.
Career batting
8–15–1–349–78–24.92–0–*ct* 3–*st* 1

He headed the batting averages, for all matches, on the 1932 tour.

Jackson, Sir Anthony Henry Mather
(also known as Mather-Jackson)
Amateur. *b:* 9.11.1899, Westminster, London. *d:* 11.10.1983, Kirklington, Nottinghamshire. Cousin of G. L. (Derbyshire) and G. R. (Derbyshire). Middle order right-hand batsman, right-arm fast medium bowler. *Sch* Harrow. *Team* Derbyshire (1920–27, 64 matches).
Career batting
64–96–15–1199–75–14.80–0–*ct* 15
Bowling 1311–44–29.79–1–0–5/84

Jackson, Archibald (Alexander)
Amateur. *b:* 5.9.1909, Rutherglen, Lanark, Scotland. *d:* 16.2.1933, Clayfields, Brisbane, Queensland, Australia, of tuberculosis. Brilliant middle order right-hand batsman, good deep field. *Team* New South Wales (1926/7 to 1930/1, 28 matches). *Tours* Australia to New Zealand 1927/8, to England 1930. *Tests* Australia (1928/9 to 1930/1, 8 matches).
Career batting
70–107–11–4383–182–45.65–11–*ct* 26
Bowling 49–0
Test batting
8–11–1–474–164–47.40–1–*ct* 7

On his single tour to England he hit 1,097 runs, av 34.28. He had arrived in England with a brilliant reputation as a batsman, but failed to live up to it. His final years were marred by ill-health.

Jackson, Arnold Kenneth
Amateur. *b:* 21.6.1903, Edgbaston, Birmingham. *d:* 31.5.1971, Halstenbeck, West Germany. Lower order right-hand batsman, right-arm fast medium bowler. *Team* Warwickshire (1928–31, 2 matches).
Career batting
2–3–2–5–3*–5.00–0–*ct* 0
Bowling 73–0

He was on the Warwickshire CCC Committee from 1959 to his death.

Jackson, Charles Henry
Amateur. *b:* 6.6.1839, Chatham, Kent. Middle order batsman. *Team* Gentlemen of Kent (1865).
Career batting
1–2–1–10–6–10.00–0–*ct* 0

Jackson, Edward
Amateur. *b:* 17.3.1849, Lancaster. *d:* 24.11.1926, Overton, Flint. Brother of J. W. (Lancashire). Tail end right-hand batsman, wicket-keeper. *Team* Lancashire (1871–85, 15 matches).
Career batting
15–23–4–105–11–5.52–0–*ct* 21–*st* 14

Jackson, Edward John Wycliffe
Cricketer. *b:* 26.3.1955, Kuala Lumpur, Malaya. Middle order right-hand batsman, left-arm medium fast bowler. *Sch* Winchester. *Team* Cambridge U (1974–76, blue all three years).
Career batting
28–51–6–762–63–16.93–0–*ct* 4
Bowling 2215–43–51.51–1–1–7/98
He also won a blue for soccer.

Jackson, Finlay William
Amateur. *b:* 21.11.1901, Belfast, Ireland. *d:* 13.3.1941, Belfast, Ireland. Brother of Harold (Ireland). Middle order right-hand batsman, leg break bowler. *Team* Ireland (1924–25).
Career batting
3–5–1–154–71–38.50–0–*ct* 0
He was an Irish rugby international.

Jackson, Rt Hon Sir Frank Stanley
(also known as Francis Stanley Jackson)
Amateur. *b:* 21.11.1870, Allerton Hall, Chapel Allerton, Leeds, Yorkshire. *d:* 9.3.1947, Knightsbridge, London. Uncle of J. M. Brocklebank (Lancashire) and T. A. L. Brocklebank (Cambridge U), brother-in-law of J. P. Wilson (Yorkshire). Stylish middle order right-hand batsman, right-arm fast medium bowler, good field. *Sch* Harrow. *Teams* Cambridge U (1890–93, blue all four years); Yorkshire (1890–1907, 207 matches). *Tour* Hawke to India 1892/3. *Tests* England (1893–1905, 20 matches).
Career batting
309–505–35–15901–160–33.83–31–*ct* 195
Bowling 15767–774–20.37–42–6–8/54
Test batting
20–33–4–1415–144*–48.79–5–*ct* 10
Bowling 799–24–33.29–1–0–5/52
The epitome of the 'Golden Age' of cricket – the Edwardian era – Jackson captained England in the 1905 series of Tests v Australia, which England won two matches to nil; he also played a major part in the 1902 series, but pressure of business prevented him from going on tour to Australia.
At his best he was a brilliant all rounder, though he only achieved the 'double' once – in 1898 – this lack of statistical success again being due to the fact that he rarely managed to play a full season of first-class cricket in England. In all he hit 1,000 runs in a season ten times, with his best year being 1899: 1,847 runs, av 45.04. He took 104 wickets, av 15.67, in 1898.
Although he had the unusual distinction of captaining Cambridge for two seasons (1892–93) and going on to lead England in five Tests, he did not captain his County. He was President of MCC in 1921 and of Yorkshire from 1939 until his death. He was a Test selector in 1934 and 1946.
He saw active service in the Boer War which meant his absence for two years from County cricket and later became a well-known politician, being MP for the Howdenshire Division of Yorkshire from 1915 to 1926, Financial Secretary to the War Office in 1922 and Chairman of the Unionist Party in 1923. Later he was appointed Governor of Bengal, where he narrowly escaped assassination.

Jackson, Geoffrey Laird
Amateur. *b:* 10.1.1894, Birkenhead, Cheshire. *d:* 9.4.1917, Faimpoux, Arras, Belgium. He was killed in action. Brother of G. R. (Derbyshire), cousin of A. H. M. (Derbyshire). Middle order right-hand batsman, right-arm medium pace bowler, good cover-point. *Sch* Harrow. *Teams* Derbyshire (1912–14, 4 matches); Oxford U (1914).
Career batting
7–12–0–150–50–12.50–0–*ct* 4
Bowling 238–10–23.80–0–0–3/52

Jackson, Guy Rolf
Amateur. *b:* 23.6.1896, Ankerbold House, Tupton, Derbyshire. *d:* 21.2.1966, Chesterfield, Derbyshire. Brother of G. L. (Derbyshire), cousin of A. H. M. (Derbyshire). Middle order left-hand batsman. *Sch* Harrow. *Team* Derbyshire (1919–36, 260 matches). *Tours* MCC to Argentine 1926/7; Selected to captain MCC to South Africa 1927/8, but forced to decline through ill health.
Career batting
280–468–22–10291–140–23.07–9–*ct* 110
Bowling 208–3–69.33–0–0–1/10
He hit 1,000 runs in a season four times (best 1,278, av 26.62, in 1925). From 1922 to 1930 he captained Derbyshire.

Jackson, Harold
Amateur. *b:* September 1888, Belfast, Ireland. *d:* 17.12.1979, Belfast, Ireland. Brother of F. W. (Ireland). Middle order left-hand batsman. *Team* Ireland (1923).
Career batting
1–2–1–65–62*–65.00–0–*ct* 0
Bowling 35–1–35.00–0–0–1/35

Jackson, Herbert Leslie
Professional. *b:* 5.4.1921, Whitwell, Derbyshire. Lower order right-hand batsman, right-arm fast bowler. *Team* Derbyshire (1947–63, 394 matches). *Tour* Commonwealth to India 1950/1. *Tests* England (1949–61, 2 matches).
Career batting
418–489–153–2083–39*–6.19–0–*ct* 136
Bowling 30101–1733–17.36–115–20–9/17
Test batting
2–2–1–15–8–15.00–0–*ct* 1
Bowling 155–7–22.14–0–0–2/26
He took 100 wickets in a season 10 times (best 160, av 13.61, in 1960). His best bowling performance in an innings was 9/17 for Derbyshire v Cambridge U at Fenner's in 1959.

Jackson, John
Professional. *b:* 21.5.1833, Bungay, Suffolk. *d:* 4.11.1901, Brownlow Hill, Liverpool, Lancashire. Hard-hitting right-hand batsman, right-hand fast round-arm bowler. *Teams* Nottinghamshire (1855–66, 33 matches); Kent (1858, 2 matches as given man). *Tours* Parr to North America 1859 (not first-class), to Australia 1863/4.
Career batting
115–191–33–1993–100–12.61–1–*ct* 106
Bowling 7490–650+5–11.52–59–20–9/27
He took 100 wickets in a season twice (best 109, av 9.20, in 1860). For several seasons he was regarded as the leading fast bowler in England. His best bowling was 9/27 for Kent v England at Lord's in 1858. His final first-class match was for the AEE in 1867. He was a first-class umpire (1884). In his later years he fell on very hard times and died in a Liverpool workhouse.

Jackson, John Alfred Stewart
Amateur. *b:* 27.12.1898, Valparaiso, Chile. *d:* 13.3.1958, Santiago, Chile. Brother of A. L. S. (South America). Middle order right-hand batsman, leg break bowler. *Sch* Cheltenham. *Teams* Cambridge U (1920); Somerset (1920, 14 matches).
Career batting
19–34–1–739–106–22.39–1–*ct* 1
Bowling 38–0

Jackson, John Frederick Cecil
Amateur. *b:* 8.5.1880, North Aylesford, Kent. *d:* 22.11.1968, Kidderminster, Worcestershire. Middle order right-hand batsman. *Sch* Tonbridge. *Team* Worcestershire (1907, 1 match).
Career batting
1–2–0–6–6–3.00–0–*ct* 0

Jackson, John Wilson
Amateur. *b:* 21.5.1841, Lancaster, Lancashire. *d:* 29.8.1906, Birmingham. Brother of Edward (Lancashire). *Team* Lancashire (1867, 1 match).
Career batting
1–2–0–6–3–3.00–0–*ct* 0

Jackson, Kenneth Leslie Tattersall
Amateur. *b:* 17.11.1913, Shanghai, China. *d:* 21.3.1982, Hinton St George, Somerset. Lower order right-hand batsman, right-arm fast medium bowler. *Sch* Rugby. *Team* Oxford U (1934–35, blue 1934).
Career batting
9–16–2–181–33–12.92–0–*ct* 4
Bowling 874–29–30.13–1–0–5/66
His County cricket was for Berkshire (1938–46). A noted rugby footballer, he was capped for Scotland.

Jackson, Leonard
Professional. *b:* 8.4.1848, Norton Woodseats, Yorkshire. *d:* 21.3.1887, Sheffield, Yorkshire. Lower order right-hand batsman, right-hand fast round-arm bowler, close field. *Team* Derbyshire (1877–82, 5 matches).
Career batting
6–12–1–109–28–9.90–0–*ct* 4
Bowling 198–10–19.80–0–0–3/9
His debut was for the North in 1875.

Jackson, Lionel
Amateur. *b:* 12.9.1877, Epsom, Surrey. *d:* 13.6.1949, Dorking, Surrey. Lower order batsman, wicket-keeper. *Sch* Dulwich. *Team* London County (1901).
Career batting
1–2–0–50–26–25.00–0–*ct* 0–*st* 3

Jackson, McIvor Tindall
Professional. *b:* 24.5.1880, Merton, Surrey. *d:* 15.6.1936, Southwark, London. Lower order left-hand batsman, left-arm medium pace bowler. *Team* Surrey (1903–07, 11 matches).
Career batting
11–17–8–21–9–2.33–0–*ct* 6
Bowling 660–33–20.00–3–0–7/96

Jackson, Paul Barry
Cricketer. *b:* 9.12.1959, Belfast, Ireland. Lower order right-hand batsman, wicket-keeper. *Team* Ireland (1981–90).
Career batting
10–14–3–244–59–22.18–0–*ct* 16–*st* 5

Jackson, Paul William
Cricketer. *b:* 1.11.1961, East Melbourne, Victoria, Australia. Lower order right-hand batsman, slow left-arm bowler. *Team* Victoria (1985/6 to 1991/2, 39 matches). *Tour* Victoria to England 1991.
Career batting
39–39–14–217–31–8.68–0–*ct* 13
Bowling 3549–98–36.21–1–0–6/55

Jackson, Percy Frederick
Professional. *b:* 11.5.1911, Aberfeldy, Perthshire, Scotland. Lower order right-hand batsman, right-arm medium pace off break bowler. *Team* Worcestershire (1929–50, 383 matches).
Career batting
385–549–208–2052–40–6.01–0–*ct* 194
Bowling 30501–1159–26.31–61–12–9/45
He took 100 wickets in a season four times (best 125, av 23.70, in 1947). His best bowling was 9/45 for Worcestershire v Somerset at Dudley in 1935.

Jackson, Robert Mark
Cricketer. *b:* 10.3.1968, Huddersfield, Yorkshire. Lower order right-hand batsman, right-arm medium pace bowler. *Team* Oxford U (1989).
Career batting
1 match, did not bat–*ct* 0
Bowling 87–0
He was awarded his blue for gymnastics.

Jackson, Roger Frank
Cricketer. *b:* 5.1.1939, Woolwich, London. Tail end right-hand batsman, right-arm fast bowler. *Team* Oxford U (1962).
Career batting
2–3–2–8–5*–8.00–0–*ct* 0
Bowling 126–0
He won a blue for soccer.

Jackson, Samuel Robinson
Amateur. *b:* 15.7.1859, Ecclesall, Sheffield, Yorkshire. *d:* 19.7.1941, Leeds, Yorkshire. Middle order right-hand batsman, right-arm fast bowler, good deep field. *Team* Yorkshire (1891, 1 match).
Career batting
1–2–0–9–9–4.50–0–*ct* 0

Jackson, Victor Edward
Professional. *b:* 25.10.1916, Sydney, New South Wales, Australia. *d:* 30.1.1965, near Manildra, New South Wales, Australia. He was killed in a level crossing accident. Hard-hitting middle order right-hand batsman, right-arm medium pace off break bowler, slip field. *Teams* New South Wales (1936/7 to 1940/1, 20 matches); Leicestershire (1938–56, 322 matches). *Tour* Cahn to New Zealand 1938/9.
Career batting
354–605–53–15698–170–28.43–21–*ct* 253
Bowling 23874–965–24.73–43–7–8/43
He hit 1,000 runs in a season 11 times (best 1,582, av 29.29, in 1955); took 100 wickets in a season once: 112, av 21.71, in 1955, achieving the 'double' that year. His final first-class match was for a Commonwealth XI in 1958.

Jacob, Norman Ernest
Amateur. *b:* 9.7.1901, Neath, Glamorgan. *d:* 12.3.1970, Grimsby, Lincolnshire. Opening or middle order right-hand batsman, right-arm medium pace bowler. *Sch* Tonbridge. *Team* Glamorgan (1922, 7 matches).
Career batting
7–13–0–79–19–6.07–0–*ct* 2
Bowling 42–0
He first played for Glamorgan (pre first-class) in 1920.

Jacobs, Arnold Leslie
Amateur. *b:* 12.11.1892, Buenos Aires, Argentina. *d:* 9.8.1974, Buenos Aires, Argentina. Tail end right-hand batsman, wicket-keeper. *Tour* South America to England 1932.
Career batting
2–3–0–19–10–6.33–0–*ct* 3

Jacobs, Jack
Amateur. *b:* 16.4.1909, Dunedin, New Zealand. Middle order right-hand batsman, occasional wicket-keeper. *Team* Canterbury (1927/8 to 1937/8). *Tour* New Zealand Services to England 1945.
Career batting
12–21–1–464–69–23.20–0–*ct* 5–*st* 1

Jacobson, Dr Louis Collins
Amateur. *b:* 26.1.1918, Dublin, Ireland. Opening right-hand batsman. *Team* Ireland (1948–52).
Career batting
4–7–2–153–101*–30.60–1–*ct* 1

Jacques, Thomas Alec
Amateur turning professional in 1928. *b:* 19.2.1905, Cliffe, Yorkshire. Lower order right-hand batsman, right-arm fast bowler. *Team* Yorkshire (1927–36, 28 matches).
Career batting
30–22–9–168–35*–12.92–0–*ct* 14
Bowling 1935–62–31.20–2–0–5/33

Jaffey, Dr Isaac Mervyn
(now known as Mervyn Jeffries)
Amateur. *b:* 9.9.1929, Dublin, Ireland. Lower order right-hand batsman, wicket-keeper. *Team* Ireland (1953).
Career batting
1 match, did not bat–*ct* 1–*st* 1

Jagger, Samuel Thornton
Amateur. *b:* 30.6.1904, Llangollen, Denbigh. *d:* 30.5.1964, Hove, Sussex. Lower order right-hand batsman, right-arm medium pace bowler. *Sch* Malvern. *Teams* Worcestershire (1922–23, 5 matches); Cambridge U (1923–26, blue 1925–26); Sussex (1931, 3 matches); Wales (1927–29).
Career batting
44–64–11–599–58–11.30–0–*ct* 38
Bowling 3040–90–33.77–4–0–5/24
He also played for Denbighshire (1930–34). He also represented Cambridge U at rugby fives.

Jahangir Khan, Dr Mohammad
Amateur. *b:* 1.2.1910, Basti Ghuzaar, Jullundur, India. *d:* 23.7.1988, Lahore, Pakistan. Father of Majid Jahangir Khan (Pakistan) and A. J. Khan (Oxford U), uncle of Javed Burki (Pakistan), Imran Khan (Pakistan), Humayan Zaman (Lahore) and Javed Zaman (Lahore), brother-in-law of M. Baqa Jilani (India). Fast scoring middle or lower order right-hand batsman, right-arm fast medium bowler. *Teams* Cambridge U (1933–36, blue all 4 years); Muslims (1928/9 to 1939/40); Northern India (1940/1 to 1945/6); South Punjab (1946/7); Punjab Governor's XI (1947/8); Punjab (1951/2). *Tours* India to England 1932, 1936. *Tests* India (1932–36, 4 matches).
Career batting
109–172–25–3280–133–22.31–4–*ct* 81
Bowling 8197–327–25.06–12–2–8/33
Test batting
4–7–0–39–13–5.57–0–*ct* 4
Bowling 255–4–63.75–0–0–4/60

He appeared in the Tests on both his tours to England, but his figures were only modest ones and his days of success infrequent. His final first-class match in England was for MCC in 1939. He scored 108 and took 7/42 on debut for Muslims v Hindus at Lahore in 1928/9.

Jai, Laxmidas Purshottamdas
Amateur. *b:* 1.4.1902, Bombay, India. *d:* 29.1.1968, Bombay, India. Middle order right-hand batsman. *Teams* Hindus (1920/1 to 1941/2); Bombay (1926/7 to 1941/2). *Tour* India to England 1936. *Test* India (1933/4, 1 match).
Career batting
67–108–7–3231–156–31.99–6–*ct* 26
Bowling 134–3–44.66–0–0–1/6
Test batting
1–2–0–19–19–9.50–0–*ct* 0
His general form in England in 1936 did not reflect the reputation he had acquired for himself in India.

Jaidka, Rattan Chand
Amateur. *b: circa* 1904, Malaya. Lower order batsman, bowler. *Team* Gloucestershire (1927, 2 matches).
Career batting
2–1–0–5–5–5.00–0–*ct* 1
Bowling 160–2–80.00–0–0–1/57
He played for Gloucestershire whilst at Bristol University.

Jaisimha, Motganhalli Laxmanarsu
Amateur. *b:* 3.3.1939, Secunderabad, India. Father of Vivek (Hyderabad). Opening/middle order right-hand batsman, right-arm medium off break bowler. brilliant field. *Team* Hyderabad (1954/5 to 1976/7). *Tours* India to England 1959, to West Indies 1961/2, 1970/1, to Australia and New Zealand 1967/8; Indian Starlets to Pakistan 1959/60; Hyderabad Blues to Ceylon 1966/7. *Tests* India (1959 to 1970/1, 39 matches).
Career batting
245–387–27–13515–259–37.54–33–*ct* 157
Bowling 12873–431–29.86–18–3–7/45
Test batting
39–71–4–2056–129–30.68–3–*ct* 17
Bowling 829–9–92.11–0–0–2/54
His only visit to England was very early in his career and though he showed much promise he accomplished very little and appeared in only one Test. His highest score was 259 for Hyderabad v Bengal at Hyderabad in 1964/5. He hit 1,000 runs in a season in India three times (best 1,293, av 41.70, in 1964/5).

Jakeman, Frederick
Professional. *b:* 10.1.1920, Holmfirth, Yorkshire. *d:* 17.5.1986, Huddersfield, Yorkshire. Father of R. S. (Northamptonshire). Aggressive middle order left-hand batsman, good outfield. *Teams* Yorkshire (1946–47, 10 matches); Northamptonshire (1949–54, 119 matches).
Career batting
134–205–19–5952–258*–32.00–11–*ct* 42
Bowling 162–5–32.40–0–0–2/8
He hit 1,000 runs in a season twice (best 1,989, av 56.82, in 1951). His only double century, 258* for Northamptonshire v Essex at Northampton in 1951, was a new county record. He was a first-class umpire (1961–72).

Jakeman, Ronald Stuart
Cricketer. *b:* 20.9.1943, Holmfirth, Yorkshire. Son of Frederick (Yorkshire and Northamptonshire). Middle order left-hand batsman. *Team* Northamptonshire (1962–63, 3 matches).
Career batting
3–4–0–31–20–7.75–0–*ct* 1
He also played for Cumberland (1965–66).

Jakobson, Tonu Robert
Amateur. *b:* 17.12.1937, Marylebone, London. Lower order right-hand batsman, right-arm fast medium bowler. *Sch* Charterhouse. *Team* Oxford U (1960–61, blue 1961).
Career batting
14–19–7–112–20–9.33–0–*ct* 10
Bowling 1184–37–32.00–1–0–5/61
His parents came from Estonia.

Jalal-ud-din
Cricketer. *b:* 12.6.1959, Karachi, Pakistan. Lower order right-hand batsman, right-arm fast-medium bowler. *Teams* Railways (1975/6); PWD (1977/8); Karachi (1978/9 to 1988/9); Industrial Development Bank (1979/80 to 1981/2); Allied Bank (1982/3 to 1984/5); Customs (1986/7). *Tours* Pakistan to England 1982; to India 1983/4 (not first-class). *Tests* Pakistan (1982/3 to 1985/6, 6 matches).
Career batting
73–86–27–696–45–11.79–0–*ct* 12
Bowling 6396–268–23.86–18–5–7/43
Test batting
6–3–2–3–2–3.00–0–*ct* 0
Bowling 537–11–48.81–0–0–3/77
He came to England as a replacement during the 1982 tour, but did not appear in the Tests.

James, Albert Edward
Professional. *b:* 7.8.1924, Newton Longville, Buckinghamshire. Lower order right-hand batsman, right-arm medium pace bowler. *Team* Sussex (1948–60, 299 matches).
Career batting
299–414–135–3411–63*–12.22–0–*ct* 111
Bowling 22841–843–27.09–27–2–9/60
He took 100 wickets in a season twice (best 111, av 21.31, in 1955). His best bowling in an innings was 9/60 for Sussex v Yorkshire at Hove in 1955. He also played for Buckinghamshire (1947).

James, Brian
Professional. *b:* 23.4.1934, Darfield, Barnsley, Yorkshire. Lower order right-hand batsman, left-arm fast medium, bowler. *Team* Yorkshire (1954, 4 matches).
Career batting
4–5–3–22–11*–11.00–0–*ct* 0
Bowling 228–8–28.50–0–0–4/54

James, Burnet George
Amateur. *b:* 26.10.1886, Durdham Down, Stoke Bishop, Bristol. *d:* 26.9.1915, Langemark, Belgium. Middle order left-hand batsman, slow left-arm bowler. *Sch* Charterhouse. *Team* Gloucestershire (1914, 3 matches).
Career batting
3–6–1–27–10–5.40–0–*ct* 1

James, Charles Cecil
Professional. *b:* 14.9.1885, New Basford, Nottinghamshire. *d:* 28.7.1950, Highbury Vale, Bulwell, Nottingham. Middle order right-hand batsman, right-arm medium pace bowler. *Team* Nottinghamshire (1906–21, 20 matches).
Career batting
20–34–3–355–43–11.45–0–*ct* 7
He also played for Northumberland (1911), but not in the Minor Counties Championship.

James, David Harry
Amateur. *b:* 3.3.1921, Briton Ferry, Glamorgan. Son of E. H. (Glamorgan). Lower order right-hand batsman, right-arm medium fast bowler. *Team* Glamorgan (1948, 1 match).
Career batting
1–1–0–17–17–17.00–0–*ct* 1
Bowling 59–1–59.00–0–0–1/59

James, David John Gwynne
(later D. J. Gwynne-James)
Amateur. *b:* 12.6.1937, Pembroke Dock, Pembroke. Middle order right-hand batsman, right-arm medium fast bowler. *Sch* Cheltenham. *Team* Free Foresters (1961).
Career batting
1–2–0–40–29–20.00–0–*ct* 0

James, Edward Hugh
Amateur. *b:* 14.4.1896, Briton-Ferry, Glamorgan. *d:* 15.3.1975, Briton-Ferry, Glamorgan. Father of D. H. (Glamorgan). Lower order left-hand batsman, slow left-arm bowler. *Team* Glamorgan (1922, 3 matches).
Career batting
3–6–0–13–4–2.16–0–*ct* 1
Bowling 209–7–29.85–0–0–4/79
He first played for Glamorgan (pre first-class) in 1920.

James, Evan Llewellyn
Amateur. *b:* 10.5.1918, Barry, Glamorgan. Middle order right-hand batsman, right-arm medium pace bowler. *Team* Glamorgan (1946–47, 9 matches).
Career batting
9–12–4–232–62*–29.00–0–*ct* 10
Bowling 45–1–45.00–0–0–1/8

James, F. W.
Amateur. Middle order batsman. *Team* Gentlemen of England (1905).
Career batting
1–1–1–11–11*–no av–0–*ct* 0

James, J.
Professional. Lower order batsman, useful bowler. *Team* Northamptonshire (1906, 2 matches).
Career batting
2–3–0–2–1–0.66–0–*ct* 0
Bowling 125–2–62.50–0–0–1/14

James, Kenneth Cecil
Amateur turned professional in 1935. *b:* 12.3.1904, Wellington, New Zealand. *d:* 21.8.1976, Palmerston North, Wellington, New Zealand. Middle or lower order right-hand batsman, wicket-keeper. *Teams* Wellington (1923/4 to 1946/7); Northamptonshire (1935–39, 101 matches). *Tours* New Zealand to Australia 1925/6, 1927/8, to England 1927, 1931; New Zealand Services to England 1945. *Tests* New Zealand (1929/30 to 1932/3, 11 matches).
Career batting
205–330–41–6413–109*–22.19–7–*ct* 311–*st* 112
Bowling 17–0
Test batting
11–13–2–52–14–4.72–0–*ct* 11–*st* 5
He hit 1,000 runs in a season once: 1,032, av 23.45, in 1938. On both tours with New Zealand to England, he was the visitors' outstanding wicket-keeper.

James, Kevan David
Cricketer. *b:* 18.3.1961, Lambeth, London. Lower order left-hand batsman, left-arm medium pace bowler. *Teams* Middlesex (1980–84, 13 matches); Wellington (1982/3 to 1984/5); Hampshire (1985–92, 119 matches).
Career batting
140–197–36–5379–162–33.40–8–*ct* 47
Bowling 7228–219–33.00–7–0–6/22
He hit 1,000 runs in a season twice (best 1,274, av 47.18, in 1991).

James, P.
Amateur. Middle order batsman. *Team* H. K. Foster's XI (1919).
Career batting
1–1–0–11–11–11.00–0–*ct* 0

James, Robert Michael
Amateur. *b:* 2.10.1934, Wokingham, Berkshire. Hard hitting middle order right-hand batsman, right-arm medium pace bowler. *Sch* St John's, Leatherhead. *Teams* Cambridge U (1956–58, blue all three years); Wellington (1964/5).

Career batting
51–90–10–2208–168–27.60–4–*ct* 16
Bowling 1356–38–35.68–0–0–4/5

His County cricket was for Berkshire (1954–70). His final first-class match in England was for MCC in 1961.

James, Stephen Peter
Cricketer. *b:* 7.9.1967, Lydney, Gloucestershire. Opening right-hand batsman. *Sch* Monmouth. *Teams* Glamorgan (1985–92, 57 matches); Cambridge U (1989–90, blue both years). *Tour* Glamorgan to Zimbabwe 1990/1.
Career batting
77–131–11–4067–152*–33.89–10–*ct* 53

He reached 1,000 runs in a season twice (best 1,376, av 39.31, in 1992).

James, Wayne Robert
Cricketer. *b:* 27.8.1965, Bulawayo, Rhodesia. Middle order right-hand batsman, wicket-keeper. *Team* Zimbabwe (1986/7 to 1990/1). *Tour* Zimbabwe to England 1990, to Australia and New Zealand (World Cup) 1991/2.
Career batting
10–18–2–392–61–24.50–0–*ct* 12

James, William
Professional. Middle order batsman. *Team* Kent (1881, 1 match).
Career batting
1–2–0–0–0–0.00–0–*ct* 0

Jameson, Harold Gordon
Amateur. *b:* 25.1.1918, Dundrum, Co Dublin, Ireland. *d:* 26.8.1940, Fort Cumberland, Eastney, Hampshire. Tail end right-hand batsman, right-arm fast medium bowler. *Sch* Monkton Combe. *Team* Cambridge U (1938).
Career batting
2–4–1–7–4–2.33–0–*ct* 0
Bowling 204–2–102.00–0–0–2/68

Jameson, John Alexander
Professional. *b:* 30.6.1941, Byculla, Bombay, India. Brother of T. E. N. (Warwickshire). Forcing opening right-hand batsman, right-arm medium pace off break bowler, occasional wicket-keeper, good cover point. *Sch* Taunton. *Team* Warwickshire (1960–76, 345 matches). *Tours* Warwickshire to East Africa 1967/8 (not first-class); MCC to West Indies 1973/4; Robins to West Indies 1974/5 (not first-class); International Wanderers to Rhodesia 1972/3. *Tests* England (1971 to 1973/4, 4 matches).
Career batting
361–611–43–18941–240*–33.34–33–*ct* 255–*st* 1
Bowling 3782–89–42.49–0–0–4/22
Test batting
4–8–0–214–82–26.75–0–*ct* 0
Bowling 17–1–17.00–0–0–1/17

He hit 1,000 runs in a season 11 times (best 1,948, av 48.70 in 1973). Both his double centuries were for Warwickshire, the higher being 240* v Gloucestershire at Edgbaston in 1974; during the course of this innings he added 465* for the 2nd wicket with R. B. Kanhai, creating a new first-class world record, since beaten. He was a first-class umpire (1984–87), coach to Sussex CCC (1988) and since 1989 has been Assistant Secretary of MCC.

Jameson, Thomas Edward Neville
Cricketer. *b:* 23.7.1946, Fort, Bombay, India. Brother of J. A. (Warwickshire). Lower order left-hand batsman, right-arm medium pace bowler. *Sch* Taunton. *Teams* Cambridge U (1970, blue); Warwickshire (1970, 1 match).
Career batting
10–17–2–181–32–12.06–0–*ct* 12
Bowling 531–10–53.10–0–0–2/21

He also won a blue for hockey.

Jameson, Thomas George Cairnes
Amateur. *b:* 6.4.1908, Bihar, India. *d:* 18.1.1987, Henley-on-Thames, Oxfordshire. Middle order right-hand batsman, right-arm medium pace or leg break bowler. *Team* Hampshire (1930–31, 3 matches).
Career batting
5–7–1–55–23*–9.16–0–*ct* 0
Bowling 25–0

His first-class debut was for the Royal Navy in 1929.

Jameson, Tom Ormsby
Amateur. *b:* 4.4.1892, Clonsilla, Co Dublin, Ireland. *d:* 6.2.1965, Dun Laoghaire, Co Dublin, Ireland. Middle order right-hand batsman, leg break and googly bowler, good slip field. *Sch* Harrow. *Teams* Hampshire (1919–32, 53 matches); Ireland (1926–28). *Tours* Joel to South Africa 1924/5; MCC to West Indies 1925/6, to South America 1926/7; Tennyson to India 1937/8.
Career batting
124–198–22–4675–133–26.56–5–*ct* 102
Bowling 6057–252–24.03–11–2–7/92

A fine rackets player, he won the Army singles Championship three times and he also won the Amateur Squash Championship twice.

Jaques, Arthur
Amateur. *b:* 7.3.1888, Shanghai, China. *d:* 27.9.1915, Bois Hugo, Loos, France. He was killed in action. Lower order right-hand batsman, right-arm medium pace or leg break bowler. *Sch* Aldenham. *Team* Hampshire (1913–14, 49 matches). *Tour* MCC to West Indies 1912/13.
Career batting
60–99–22–982–68–12.75–0–*ct* 40
Bowling 3835–175–21.91–10–3–8/21

He took 117 wickets, av 18.69, in 1914. Whilst at Cambridge he played in the Freshmen's and Seniors' matches, but no first-class games.

Jaques, Peter Heath
Amateur. *b:* 20.11.1919, Aylestone, Leicester. Middle order right-hand batsman. *Sch* Wyggeston GS. *Team* Leicestershire (1949, 1 match).
Career batting
1–2–0–69–55–34.50–0–*ct* 0

Jaques, Tom
Professional. *b:* 9.11.1911, Auckland, Co Durham. *d:* 13.8.1976, Denbigh. Lower order right-hand batsman, right-arm medium pace bowler. *Team* Lancashire (1937, 2 matches).
Career batting
2–2–0–4–2–2.00–0–*ct* 1
Bowling 70–1–70.00–0–0–1/45

Jardine, Douglas Robert
Amateur. *b:* 23.10.1900, Malabar Hill, Bombay, India. *d:* 18.6.1958, Montreux, Switzerland. He died from tick fever caught in Rhodesia. Son of M. R. (Middlesex). Middle order right-hand batsman, leg break bowler. *Sch* Winchester. *Teams* Oxford U (1920–23, blue 1920, 1921 and 1923); Surrey (1921–33, 141 matches). *Tours* MCC to Australia 1928/9, to Australia and New Zealand 1932/3, to India and Ceylon 1933/4. *Tests* England (1928 to 1933/4, 22 matches).
Career batting
262–378–61–14848–214–46.83–35–*ct* 188
Bowling 1493–48–31.10–1–0–6/28
Test batting
22–33–6–1296–127–48.00–1–*ct* 26
Bowling 10–0

Captain of England on the 1932/3 tour to Australia, Jardine employed the controversial leg-theory bowling tactics in conjunction with Larwood and Voce. His captaincy caused much ill-feeling between England and Australia, but he proved successful, winning the series by four matches to one. After taking the 1933/4 MCC team to India, Jardine retired from regular first-class cricket, though still at the height of his powers.

A determined batsman, he hit 1,000 runs in a season eight times, plus once overseas. His highest aggregate was 1,473, av 46.03, in 1926, but his best seasons were 1927 and 1928 when he headed the first-class averages with figures of 91.09 and 87.15 respectively. His only double century was 214 for MCC v Tasmania at Launceston in 1928/9. He led England in 15 Tests in all, losing only once, and also captained Surrey in 1932 and 1933.

His final first-class match was for England XI v Glamorgan in 1948. He wrote a book on the 1932/3 tour and various other articles and commentaries on the game. He also won a blue for royal tennis.

Jardine, James
Amateur. *b:* 6.6.1846, Dunstable Park, Bedfordshire. *d:* 6.1.1909, St Moritz, Switzerland. Opening right-hand batsman. *Sch* Dunstable. *Team* MCC (1870–74).
Career batting
4–7–0–53–21–7.57–0–*ct* 0

His County cricket was for Northumberland.

Jardine, Malcolm Robert
Amateur. *b:* 8.6.1869, Simla, India. *d:* 16.1.1947, South Kensington, London. Father of D. R. (Surrey). Middle order right-hand batsman, right-arm fast medium bowler, good deep field. *Sch* Fettes. *Teams* Oxford U (1889–92, blue all four years); Middlesex (1892, 6 matches); Europeans (1894/5 to 1902/03).
Career batting
46–84–3–1439–140–17.76–1–*ct* 42
Bowling 216–15–14.40–1–0–5/78

He spent most of his working life in India, rising to become Advocate-General of Bombay. His final first-class match in England was for MCC in 1897. He captained Oxford in 1891.

Jarman, Barrington Noel
Amateur. *b:* 17.2.1936, Hindmarsh, Adelaide, South Australia. Middle order right-hand batsman, wicket-keeper. *Team* South Australia (1955/6 to 1968/9, 94 matches). *Tours* Australia to New Zealand 1956/7, 1966/7, to South Africa 1957/8, to India and Pakistan 1959/60, 1964/5, to England 1961, 1964, 1968, to West Indies 1964/5. *Tests* Australia (1959/60 to 1968/9, 19 matches).
Career batting
191–284–37–5615–196–22.73–5–*ct* 431–*st* 129
Bowling 98-3–32.66–0–0–1/17
Test batting
19–30–3–400–78–14.81–0–*ct* 50–*st* 4

In 1961 and 1964 in England he acted as reserve wicket-keeper to Grout and was not required for the Tests, but in 1968 he was principal wicket-keeper as well as being vice-captain of the touring party, and played in four Tests, one as captain.

Jarman, Harold James
Professional. *b:* 4.5.1939, Kingsdown, Bristol. Middle order right-hand batsman, right-arm medium pace bowler. *Team* Gloucestershire (1961–71, 45 matches).
Career batting
45–74–18–1041–67*–18.58–0–*ct* 20
Bowling 131–0

A noted soccer player, he appeared for Bristol Rovers and Newport County.

Jarrett, David William
Cricketer. *b:* 19.4.1952, Lowes Hill, Bromsgrove, Worcestershire. Middle order right-hand batsman, right-arm medium pace bowler. *Sch* Wellington. *Teams* Oxford U (1974–75, blue 1975): Cambridge U (1976, blue).

Career batting
21–41–0–678–62–16.53–0–*ct* 12
Bowling 7–0

In 1976 he became the first cricketer ever to gain a blue at both Oxford and Cambridge. His County cricket was for Bedfordshire (1978–81). He also won a blue for hockey at Cambridge.

Jarrett, Graham Maurice
Cricketer. *b:* 9.2.1937, Bedford. Tail end right-hand batsman, leg break bowler. *Sch* Bedford Modern. *Team* Minor Counties (1971–74).
Career batting
3–4–2–32–24*–16.00–0–*ct* 0
Bowling 260–2–130.00–0–0–2/83

His County cricket was for Bedfordshire (1954–77).

Jarrett, Harold Harvey
(also known as Harold Herman Jarrett)
Professional. *b:* 23.9.1907, Johannesburg, South Africa. *d:* 17.3.1983, Pontypool, Monmouthshire. Father of K. S. (Glamorgan). Lower order right-hand batsman, leg break and googly bowler. *Sch* Highgate. *Teams* Warwickshire (1932–33, 14 matches); Glamorgan (1938, 1 match).
Career batting
15–16–1–228–45–15.20–0–*ct* 6
Bowling 1650–51–32.35–2–0–8/187

Jarrett, Keith Stanley
Cricketer. *b:* 18.5.1948, Newport, Monmouth. Son of H. H. (Warwickshire and Glamorgan). Middle order right-hand batsman, right-arm medium pace bowler, good outfield. *Sch* Monmouth. *Team* Glamorgan (1967, 2 matches).
Career batting
2–3–1–27–18*–13.50–0–*ct* 0
Bowling 76–0

An excellent rugby full back or three quarter he played for Newport and Wales, and toured South Africa with the British Lions in 1968. He later played rugby league for Barrow and Wales.

Jarrett, Michael Eugene Dominic
Cricketer. *b:* 18.9.1972, Lambeth, London. Middle order right-hand batsman, right-arm medium pace bowler. *Sch* Harrow. *Team* Cambridge U (1992, blue).
Career batting
9–13–2–106–27–9.63–0–*ct* 2

Jarvis, Arthur Harwood
Amateur. *b:* 19.10.1860, Hindmarsh, Adelaide, South Australia. *d:* 15.11.1933, Hindmarsh, Adelaide, South Australia. Brother of Alfred (South Australia), father of H. S. C. (South Australia). Steady middle/lower order right-hand batsman. *Team* South Australia (1877/8 to 1900/1, 42 matches). *Tours* Australia to England 1880, 1886, 1888, 1893. *Tests* Australia (1884/5 to 1894/5, 11 matches).
Career batting
141–226–23–3161–98*–15.57–0–*ct* 115–*st* 82
Bowling 63–1–63.00–0–0–1/9
Test batting
11–21–3–303–82–16.83–0–*ct* 9–*st* 9

Since his career ran almost parallel to that of Blackham, he was always Australia's second choice wicket-keeper and his opportunities were therefore, in Test cricket, very limited, though his career with South Australia spanned over 20 years.

Jarvis, George
Professional. *b:* 24.6.1800, Radford, Nottinghamshire. *d:* 27.3.1880, Nottingham. Brother of Charles (Nottinghamshire). Excellent middle order right-hand batsman, right-hand fast under-arm bowler. *Team* Nottinghamshire (1835–41, 6 matches).
Career batting
37–68–4–814–59–12.71–0–*ct* 13
Bowling 16–0 + 9–no av–0–0–2/?

His first-class debut was for Nottingham in 1826.

Jarvis, James Edward Frisby
Amateur. *b:* 21.1.1875, Leicester. *d:* 24.1.1962, Knighton Park, Leicester. Lower order right-hand batsman, wicket-keeper. *Team* Leicestershire (1900, 1 match).
Career batting
1–2–1–0–0*–0.00–0–*ct* 1–*st* 1

Jarvis, Kevin Bertram Sidney
Cricketer. *b:* 23.4.1953, Dartford, Kent. Tail end right-hand batsman, right-arm fast medium bowler. *Teams* Kent (1975–87, 237 matches); Gloucestershire (1988–90, 18 matches). *Tours* Robins to Sri Lanka 1977/8; International XI to Jamaica 1982/3.
Career batting
260–199–87–403–32–3.59–0–*ct* 59
Bowling 19998–674–29.67–20–3–8/97

His best season was 1981 when he took 81 wickets, av 23.27. During the early part of his career he was looked upon as a possible Test cricketer, once being picked in the England twelve, but his final years were marred by injury. Few players have attained such a poor batting record.

Jarvis, Lewis Kerrison
Amateur. *b:* 3.8.1857, Tower End. Middleton Towers, Norfolk. *d:* 16.5.1938, Kensington, London. Excellent opening or middle order right-hand batsman, slow under-arm bowler, good deep field. *Sch* Harrow. *Team* Cambridge U (1877–79, blue all 3 years).
Career batting
23–35–2–504–47–15.27–0–*ct* 7
Bowling 49–4–12.25–0–0–2/7

His County cricket was for Norfolk (1878–90) and together with his two brothers, he played a major role in Norfolk cricket. Whilst at Cambridge he was a triple blue, representing the University at soccer and the hurdles as well as cricket. His final first-class match was for Cambridge University, Past and Present, in 1886.

Jarvis, Malcolm Peter
Cricketer. *b:* 6.12.1955, Fort Victoria, Rhodesia. Lower order right-hand batsman, left-arm fast medium bowler. *Team* Zimbabwe (1979/80 to 1991/2). *Tours* Zimbabwe to Sri Lanka 1983/4, to England 1985, 1990, to India (World Cup) 1987/8, to Australia and New Zealand (World Cup) 1991/2.
Career batting
30–42–11–298–33–9.61–0–*ct* 8
Bowling 2679–82–32.67–4–1–7/86

Jarvis, Paul William
Cricketer. *b:* 29.6.1965, Redcar, Yorkshire. Lower order right-hand batsman, right-arm fast medium bowler. *Team* Yorkshire (1981–92, 130 matches). *Tours* Yorkshire to Windward Islands 1986/7; England to Pakistan 1987/8, to New Zealand 1987/8, to Australia 1987/8 (not first-class); England XI to South Africa 1989/90. *Tests* England (1987/8 to 1989, 6 matches).
Career batting
143–162–51–1896–80–17.08–0–*ct* 36
Bowling 12571–457–27.50–18–3–7/55
Test batting
6–9–2–109–29*–15.57–0–*ct* 0
Bowling 708–14–50.57–0–0–4/107

Aged 16 years 75 days he was the youngest player to make his first-class debut for Yorkshire. He took 81 wickets, av 24.58, in 1987.

Jarvis, Terrence Wayne
Cricketer. *b:* 29.7.1944, Auckland, New Zealand. Steady right-hand opening batsman, slip field. *Teams* Auckland (1964/5 to 1976/7); Canterbury (1969/70 to 1970/1). *Tours* New Zealand to England 1965, to India and Pakistan 1964/5, to Australia 1967/8, to West Indies 1971/2. *Tests* New Zealand (1964/5 to 1972/3, 13 matches).
Career batting
97–167–8–4666–182–29.34–6–*ct* 102
Bowling 89–0
Test batting
13–22–1–625–182–29.76–1–*ct* 3

Unfortunately he contracted an illness in India, just prior to the 1965 tour of England and was not really fit. He did not play in any of the Tests.

Jarvis, Victor Edmund
Amateur. *b:* 30.9.1898, Hampstead, London. *d:* 30.4.1975, Stokenchurch, Buckinghamshire. Middle order right-hand batsman, slow left-arm bowler. *Team* Essex (1925, 2 matches).
Career batting
2–4–0–44–37–11.00–0–*ct* 0
Bowling 23–0

Javed Akhtar
Amateur. *b:* 21.11.1940, Delhi, India. Lower order right-hand batsman, off break bowler. *Teams* Rawalpindi (1959/60 to 1975/6); Services (1962/3 to 1963/4). *Tour* Pakistan to England 1962. *Test* Pakistan (1962, 1 match).
Career batting
51–63–10–835–88–15.75–0–*ct* 38
Bowling 3407–187–18.21–12–3–7/56
Test batting
1–2–1–4–2*–4.00–0–*ct* 0
Bowling 52–0

He was flown to England midway through the 1962 tour to replace the injured Haseeb Ahsan, appearing in seven matches, including the third Test. He umpired in 9 Test matches in Pakistan (1979/80 to 1983/4).

Javed Burki (*see under* Burki, J.)

Javed Miandad Khan
Cricketer. *b:* 12.6.1957, Karachi, Pakistan. Brother of Anwar (Karachi), Bashir (Karachi) and Sohail (PNSC). Aggressive middle order right-hand batsman, leg break and googly bowler, good deep field. *Teams* Karachi (1973/4 to 1975/6); Sind (1973/4 to 1975/6); Sussex (1976–79, 40 matches); Habib Bank (1976/7 to 1990/1); Glamorgan (1980–85, 82 matches). *Tours* Pakistan to England 1975 (World Cup), 1978, 1979 (World Cup), 1982, 1983 (World Cup), 1987, 1992, to Sri Lanka 1975/6, 1985/6, to Australia 1976/7, 1978/9, 1981/2, 1983/4, 1984/5 (not first-class), 1986/7 (not first-class), 1988/9 (not first-class), 1989/90, to West Indies 1976/7, 1987/8, to New Zealand 1978/9, 1984/5, 1988/9, to India 1979/80, 1983/4, 1986/7, 1989/90 (not first-class), to Sharjah (not first-class) 1983/4, 1984/5, 1985/6, 1986/7, 1988/9, 1989/90, 1990/1, 1991/2, to Bangladesh (not first-class) 1988/9, to Australia and New Zealand (World Cup) 1991/2; Rest of World to England 1987, 1991. *Tests* Pakistan (1976/7 to 1991/2, 117 matches).
Career batting
394–618–94–28248–311–53.90–80–*ct* 337–*st* 3
Bowling 6395–191–33.48–6–0–7/39
Test batting
117–177–21–8465–280*–54.26–23–*ct* 93–*st* 1
Bowling 682–17–40.11–0–0–3/74

One of the most exciting batsmen of his day, his career has been peppered with controversial incidents. He toured England on four occasions and appeared in all 16 Tests during those tours. Results on his visits in 1978 and 1982 did not match up to the reputation he had gained both in County cricket and Test matches overseas, but in 1987 and 1992 he had outstanding tours. In 1987 he hit 360 Test runs, av 72.00, and in 1992 364, av 60.66. He joined Sussex in 1976, though appearing in only a handful of matches that year; in 1977 he hit over 1,000 runs and in 1978, with appearances restricted due to the Pakistan tour, made 586 runs, av 58.60. In 1979 Sussex found themselves with too many overseas players, Miandad was released and from 1980 to 1985 batted with outstanding brilliance for Glamorgan. In 1981 he broke several Glamorgan records, scoring 2,083 runs, av 69.43 and hitting 8 centuries. He came second in the overall first-class batting averages that summer. In 1982, 1983 and 1984 his appearances for Glamorgan were restricted due to commitments to Pakistan and injury. In 1985 he scored 1,441 runs, av 62.65. For unexplained reasons he failed to report at Cardiff for the start of the 1986 season, thus breaking his contract and ending his county career.

Non-cricketing matters have always played a part in the Pakistani captaincy; the retirement and reinstatement of Imran Khan has not made the leadership problem any more straitforward, but after captaining Pakistan on and off for several years, Javed led the 1992 tour to England and proved an effective captain. His highest first-class score was 311 for Karachi Whites v National Bank at Karachi in 1974/5; his highest Test innings 280* v India at Hyderabad in 1982/3, when he equalled the then Test partnership record of 451 with Mudassar Nazar, and his highest score in England 260 for Pakistan in the Oval Test of 1987. Apart from leading Pakistan in 33 Tests, he also captained Glamorgan in 1982. Among his other feats was 163 on his Test debut v New Zealand in 1976/7. He is the first Pakistani Test player to appear in more than 100 Tests and has at the present time scored over 3,000 more Test runs than any of his compatriots. He scored 1,000 runs in a season in Pakistan four times (best 1,353, av 75.16, in 1977/8).

Jawahir Shah
Cricketer. *b:* 1942, Kenya. Middle order right-hand batsman. *Team* East Africa (1967/8 to 1975). *Tour* East Africa to England 1975.
Career batting
3–6–0–141–50–23.50–0–*ct* 2
Bowling 13–0

Jayantilal, Hirji Kenia
Cricketer. *b:* 13.1.1948, Hyderabad, India. Opening right-hand batsman. *Team* Hyderabad (1968/9 to 1978/9). *Tours* India to West Indies 1970/1, to England 1971; Indian Universities to Ceylon 1970/1. *Test* India (1970/1, 1 match).
Career batting
91–154–25–4687–197–36.33–8–*ct* 66
Bowling 311–6–51.83–0–0–3/47
Test batting
1–1–0–5–5–5.00–0–*ct* 0

He was most disappointing on the 1971 tour to England and did not appear in the Tests. His first-class debut was for Hyderabad Blues in 1967/8.

Jayaram, Bangalore
Amateur. *b:* 23.4.1872, Bangalore, India. *d:* 4.12.1936, Bangalore, India. Middle order right-hand batsman, slow right-arm bowler. *Team* London County (1903–04). *Tour* India to England 1911.
Career batting
12–23–0–340–57–14.78–0–*ct* 5
Bowling 35–0

He did not appear in first-class matches in India.

Jayasekera, Rohan Stanley Amarasiriwardene
Cricketer. *b:* 7.12.1957, Colombo, Ceylon. Aggressive opening right-hand batsman, wicket-keeper. *Team* Sri Lanka (1979 to 1981/2). *Tours* Sri Lanka to England 1979, to India 1980/1, to Pakistan 1981/2. *Test* Sri Lanka (1981/2, 1 match).
Career batting
8–13–1–356–79*–29.66–0–*ct* 6–*st* 2
Bowling 8–0
Test batting
1–2–0–2–2–1.00–0–*ct* 0

Jayasinghe, Stanley
Professional. *b:* 19.1.1931, Badulla, Ceylon. Middle order right-hand batsman, off break bowler. *Team* Ceylon (1949/50 to 1968/9); Leicestershire (1961–65, 112 matches). *Tours* Ceylon to Pakistan 1949/50, 1966/7, to India 1964/5.
Career batting
144–254–10–6811–135–27.91–6–*ct* 109
Bowling 1197–34–35.20–1–0–6/38

He hit 1,000 runs in a season four times (best 1,499, av 29.39 in 1962).

Jayasinghe, Sunil Asoka
Cricketer. *b:* 15.7.1955, Matugama, Ceylon. Middle order right-hand batsman, wicket-keeper. *Team* Sri Lanka (1979). *Tour* Sri Lanka to England 1979.
Career batting
6–7–1–183–64–30.50–0–*ct* 10–*st* 4

He appeared for Sri Lanka in limited overs internationals.

Jayasuriya, Sanath Teran
Cricketer. *b:* 30.6.1969, Matara, Ceylon. Middle order left-hand batsman, slow left-arm bowler. *Team* Colombo CC (1988/9 to 1991/2). *Tours* Sri Lanka B to Pakistan 1988/9; Sri Lanka to Australia 1989/90, to India (not first-class) 1989/90, 1990/1, to England 1990, 1991, to New Zealand 1990/1, to Sharjah (not first-class) 1990/1, to Pakistan 1991/2, to Australia and New Zealand (World Cup) 1991/2. *Tests* Sri Lanka (1990/1 to 1991/2, 6 matches).
Career batting
61–85–15–3025–207*–43.21–6–*ct* 26
Bowling 820–21–39.04–0–0–2/6
Test batting
6–9–2–380–81–54.28–0–*ct* 2
Bowling 19–0

Jayes, Thomas

He headed the batting averages on the 1991 tour to England with 483 runs, av 53.55. His highest score was 207* for Sri Lanka B v Pakistan B at Karachi in 1988/9. He scored 1,137 runs, av 54.14, in Sri Lanka and Pakistan in 1988/9, his debut season.

Jayes, Thomas
Professional. *b:* 17.4.1877, Ratby, Leicestershire. *d:* 16.4.1913, Ratby, Leicestershire, of consumption. Uncle of W. E. Astill (Leicestershire). Hard hitting lower order right-hand batsman, right-arm fast bowler. *Team* Leicestershire (1903–11, 124 matches).
Career batting
128–210–20–2764–100–14.54–1–*ct* 116
Bowling 12832–535–23.98–41–9–9/78

He took 100 wickets in a season three times (best 109, av 20.61, in 1909). His best bowling was 9/78 for Leicestershire v Derbyshire at Leicester in 1905. He was selected to play for England v Australia in 1909, but dropped from the final eleven. His health broke down in 1911 and though Leicestershire CCC paid for him to go to Switzerland, he never recovered.

Jeacocke, Alfred
Amateur. *b:* 1.12.1892, Islington, London. *d:* 26.9.1961, Ladywell, Lewisham, London. Opening right-hand batsman, off break bowler, good slip. *Team* Surrey (1920–34, 132 matches).
Career batting
148–233–17–6228–201*–28.83–8–*ct* 111
Bowling 576–14–41.14–0–0–2/24

He hit 1,056 runs, av 42.24, in 1921 and his only double century was 201* for Surrey v Sussex at the Oval in 1922. In the same season Kent objected that he was unqualified for Surrey, the house in which he lived being in Kent, but the houses on the opposite side of the road were in Surrey! However he resumed playing for Surrey in 1923.

Jean-Jacques, Martin
Cricketer. *b:* 2.7.1960, Soufriere, Dominica. Lower order right-hand batsman, right-arm medium fast bowler. *Team* Derbyshire (1986–92, 53 matches).
Career batting
53–66–14–587–73–11.28–0–*ct* 13
Bowling 4091–115–35.57–2–1–8/77

He also played for Buckinghamshire (1983–88). On his debut he scored 73 batting at number 11 and shared a 10th wicket partnership of 132 with A. Hill, v Yorkshire at Sheffield, a county record.

Jeavons, Enoch Percy
Amateur. *b:* 12.1.1893, Dudley, Worcestershire. *d:* 29.7.1967, Kates Hill, Dudley, Worcestershire. Middle order right-hand batsman. *Team* Worcestershire (1924, 1 match).
Career batting
1–2–1–1–1*–1.00–0–*ct* 2

Jeeves, Percy
Professional. *b:* 5.3.1888, Earlsheaton, Yorkshire. *d:* 22.7.1916, High Wood, Montauban, France. He was killed in action. Punishing lower order right-hand batsman, right-arm medium fast bowler. *Team* Warwickshire (1912–14, 49 matches).
Career batting
50–81–6–1204–86*–16.05–0–*ct* 49
Bowling 3987–199–20.03–12–1–7/34

He took 106 wickets, av 20.88, in 1913 and at the outbreak of war was regarded as one of the most promising young cricketers in England. His name was taken by P. G. Wodehouse, who saw him play in 1913, when Wodehouse wrote his first stories about the famous butler three years later.

Jeffares, Alfred Shaun
Amateur. *b:* 14.8.1906, Korngha, South Africa. Middle order left-hand batsman, right-arm medium pace bowler. *Team* Dublin University (1926).
Career batting
1–2–0–15–13–7.50–0–*ct* 0
Bowling 72–2–36.00–0–0–2/72

Jefferies, Stephen Thomas
Cricketer. *b:* 8.12.1959, Cape Town, South Africa. Middle or lower order left-hand batsman, left-arm fast medium bowler. *Teams* Western Province (1978/9 to 1991/2); Derbyshire (1982, 1 match); Lancashire (1983–85, 32 matches); Hampshire (1988–89, 22 matches).
Career batting
139–184–37–3735–93–25.40–0–*ct* 54
Bowling 13028–469–27.77–19–4–10/59

His impact in County cricket was mainly in the limited overs matches. He played regularly for South Africa from 1981/2 onwards. His best innings analysis was 10/59 for Western Province v Orange Free State at Cape Town in 1987/8.

Jefferson, Julian
Amateur. *b:* 18.7.1899, Ripon, Yorkshire. *d:* 18.6.1966, Marylebone, London. Middle order batsman. *Sch* Gresham's Holt. *Teams* Army (1919); Combined Services (1922).
Career batting
2–4–0–84–26–21.00–0–*ct* 1
Bowling 168–5–33.60–0–0–4/129

Jefferson, Richard Ingleby
Amateur. *b:* 15.8.1941, Frimley Green, Surrey. Middle/lower order right-hand batsman, right-arm fast medium bowler. *Sch* Winchester. *Teams* Cambridge U (1961, blue); Surrey (1961–66, 76 matches). *Tours* Brown to East Africa 1961/2 (not first-class); MCC to South America 1964/5 (not first-class).
Career batting
94–137–31–2094–136–19.75–2–*ct* 32
Bowling 7250–263–27.56–10–1–6/25

He also played for Norfolk (1968–71) and his final first-class match was for Minor Counties in 1969. He played soccer for Corinthian Casuals.

Jeffery, George Ernest
Amateur. *b:* 9.2.1853, Eastbourne, Sussex. *d:* 8.4.1891, Streatham Common, London. Middle order right-hand batsman, slow round-arm bowler, good deep field. *Sch* Rugby. *Teams* Cambridge U (1872–74, blue 1873–74); Sussex (1872–74, 14 matches).
Career batting
31–55–5–808–127–16.16–1–*ct* 30
Bowling 1018–61+7–16.68–6–0–8/44

Jeffery, Howard William James
Cricketer. *b:* 5.5.1944, Workington, Cumberland. Lower order right-hand batsman, right-arm fast medium bowler. *Team* Leicestershire (1964, 2 matches).
Career batting
2–3–1–6–6–3.00–0–*ct* 1
Bowling 103–2–51.50–0–0–2/77
He also played for Cumberland (1963 and 1969–74).

Jeffrey, Alan Samuel
Cricketer. *b:* 18.10.1963, Londonderry, Ireland. Lower order left-hand batsman, left-arm medium pace bowler. *Team* Ireland (1989).
Career batting
1–1–1–12–12*–no av–0–*ct* 0
Bowling 61–4–15.25–0–0–3/22

Jeffreys, Arthur Frederick
Amateur. *b:* 7.4.1848, London. *d:* 14.2.1906, Burkham House, Lasham, Hampshire. Father-in-law of C. B. W. Magnay (Middlesex). Middle order right-hand batsman, good cover point. *Sch* Eton. *Teams* New South Wales (1872/3, 1 match); Hampshire (1876–78, 10 matches).
Career batting
26–44–3–587–60–14.31–0–*ct* 9–*st* 1
He played no first-class matches whilst at Oxford U, but did win a blue for athletics. His first-class debut was for MCC in 1872 and his final match for MCC in 1879. He was MP for Northern Division, Hampshire from 1887 until his death.

Jeffries, W.
Professional. Lower order batsman, bowler. *Teams* Gloucestershire (1919, 2 matches).
Career batting
2–4–1–0–0*–0.00–0–*ct* 0
Bowling 93–5–18.60–0–0–3/38

Jeganathan, Sridharan
Cricketer. *b:* 11.7.1951, Colombo, Ceylon. Middle order right-hand batsman, slow left-arm bowler. *Team* Sri Lanka (1973/4 to 1987/8). *Tours* Sri Lanka to Pakistan 1973/4, to England 1979, to Australia and New Zealand 1982/3, to Zimbabwe 1982/3, to India and Pakistan (World Cup) 1987/8, to Australia 1987/8. *Tests* Sri Lanka (1982/3, 2 matches).
Career batting
29–38–6–437–74–13.65–0–*ct* 14
Bowling 1549–49–31.61–1–0–5/34
Test batting
2–4–0–19–8–4.75–0–*ct* 0
Bowling 12–0

Jeh, Michael Pradeep Williams
Cricketer. *b:* 21.4.1968, Colombo, Ceylon. Lower order right-hand batsman, right-arm medium pace bowler. *Team* Oxford U (1992, blue).
Career batting
9–11–2–81–23–9.00–0–*ct* 3
Bowling 846–17–49.76–0–0–3/44

Jelf, Hector Gordon
Amateur. *b:* 6.5.1917, Putney, London. Lower order right-hand batsman, wicket-keeper. *Sch* Marlborough. *Team* Oxford U (1938).
Career batting
2–3–0–48–35–16.00–0–*ct* 5–*st* 1
He won a blue for hockey.

Jelf, Henry Francis Donhoff
Amateur. *b:* 27.8.1877, Aldershot, Hampshire. *d:* 18.4.1944, Southport, Lancashire. Brother of W. W. (Leicestershire). Middle order batsman. *Team* Derbyshire (1910–11, 10 matches).
Career batting
10–20–0–220–37–11.00–0–*ct* 3

Jelf, Wilfrid Wykeham
Amateur. *b:* 22.7.1880, Halifax, Nova Scotia, Canada. *d:* 17.10.1933, Bawdrip, Bridgwater, Somerset. Brother of H. F. D. (Derbyshire). Middle order right-hand batsman. *Sch* Eton. *Team* Leicestershire (1911, 3 matches).
Career batting
3–6–0–6–6–1.00–0–*ct* 3

Jellicoe, Rev Frederick Gilbert Gardiner
Amateur. *b:* 24.2.1858, Bellevue, Southampton, Hampshire. *d:* 29.7.1927, Southwark, London. Lower order right-hand batsman, left-hand medium slow round-arm bowler. *Sch* Haileybury. *Teams* Oxford U (1877–79, blue 1877 and 1879); Hampshire (1877–80, 4 matches).
Career batting
18–29–9–58–12–2.90–0–*ct* 8
Bowling 1164–78–14.92–5–1–8/36

Jellie, J. P. S.
(*see under* Stephenson-Jellie, J. P.)

Jenkins, Huw
Cricketer. *b:* 24.10.1944, Swansea, Glamorgan. Middle order left-hand batsman, right-arm medium pace bowler. *Team* Glamorgan (1970, 1 match).
Career batting
1–2–1–81–65–81.00–0–*ct* 1

Jenkins, Roland Oliver
Professional. *b:* 24.11.1918, Rainbow Hill, Worcester. Uncle of P. J. Robinson (Worcestershire and Somerset). Sound middle/lower order right-hand batsman, leg break and googly bowler. *Team* Worcestershire (1938–58, 352 matches). *Tour* MCC to South Africa 1948/9. *Tests* England (1948/9 to 1952, 9 matches).
Career batting
386–573–120–10073–109–22.23–1–*ct* 213
Bowling 30945–1309–23.64–92–20–8/62
Test batting
9–12–1–198–39–18.00–0–*ct* 4
Bowling 1098–32–34.31–1–0–5/116

He hit 1,000 runs in a season four times (best 1,356, av 27.12) and took 100 wickets in a season five times (best 183, av 21.19, in 1949). He performed the 'double' in 1949 and 1952.

Jenkins, Rory Harry John
Cricketer. *b:* 29.6.1970, Leicester. Lower order right-hand batsman, right-arm medium pace bowler. *Sch* Oundle. *Team* Cambridge U (1990–92, blue 1990–91).
Career batting
17–21–6–123–20–8.20–0–*ct* 4
Bowling 1610–24–67.08–1–0–5/100

His County cricket was for Devon (1990). He also won blues for athletics and rugby.

Jenkins, Vivian Gordon James
Amateur. *b:* 2.11.1911, Aberavon, Port Talbot, Glamorgan. Lower order right-hand batsman, right-arm medium pace bowler, wicket-keeper. *Sch* Llandovery College. *Teams* Glamorgan (1931–37, 44 matches); Oxford U (1933, blue).
Career batting
53–84–10–1328–69–17.94–0–*ct* 17–*st* 7
Bowling 54–2–27.00–0–0–1/13

He was awarded his rugby blue and went on to appear for Wales as full back and three quarter, touring South Africa with the British Lions in 1938. He became well-known as a sports commentator.

Jenkins, Wyndham Leslie Trevor
Amateur. *b:* 26.8.1898, Newport, Monmouth. *d:* 14.6.1971, Penarth, Glamorgan. Lower order right-hand batsman, wicket-keeper. *Sch* Malvern. *Team* Glamorgan (1921, 10 matches).
Career batting
10–20–1–155–39–8.15–0–*ct* 8–*st* 2

Jenkinson, Cecil Victor
Amateur. *b:* 15.5.1891, Ilford, Essex. *d:* 6.11.1980, Pembury, Kent. Lower order right-hand batsman, wicket-keeper. *Team* Essex (1922–23, 5 matches).
Career batting
5–6–2–9–8–2.25–0–*ct* 4–*st* 4

Jenner, Felix Donovan
Professional. *b:* 15.11.1892, Hastings, Sussex. *d:* 31.3.1953, New End, Hampstead, London. Middle order right-hand batsman. *Team* Sussex (1919–21, 28 matches).
Career batting
28–50–1–595–55–12.14–0–*ct* 9
Bowling 66–2–33.00–0–0–2/34

He also played for Durham (pre first-class, 1924).

Jenner, Herbert
(changed name to Jenner-Fust in 1864)
Amateur. *b:* 23.2.1806, Mayfair, London. *d:* 30.7.1904, Hill Court, Falfield, Gloucestershire. Brother of C. H. (Cambridge U 1826) and H. L. (Cambridge U 1839), father of H. Jenner-Fust (Gloucestershire), great-uncle of E. A. Nepean (Middlesex). Opening right-hand batsman, wicket-keeper, right-hand semi-under-arm bowler. *Sch* Eton. *Teams* Cambridge U (1825–27, blue 1827); Kent (1828–36).
Career batting
36–63–3–842–75–14.03–0–*ct* 24–*st* 17
Bowling 75 wickets (no analyses)–5–0–7/?

He was one of the best wicket-keepers of his day, but owing to his profession, a barrister, retired from serious cricket in 1836. He took a great interest in the game all his life, but 'he never took the trouble to see W. G. Grace play.' His final match was for Gentlemen of Kent in 1838. He captained Cambridge in 1827 and was President of MCC in 1833.

Jenner-Fust, Herbert
(changed name from Jenner in 1864)
Amateur. *b:* 14.8.1841, Beckenham, Kent. *d:* 11.11.1940, Hill Court, Falfield, Gloucestershire. Son of H. Jenner (Kent), nephew of C. H. Jenner (Cambridge U 1826) and H. L. Jenner (Cambridge U 1839), uncle of E. A. Nepean (Middlesex), brother-in-law of J. D. Dyke (Kent), P. H. Dyke (Kent)and T. H. Dyke (Kent), cousin of E. F. Dyke (Cambridge U). Lower order batsman. *Sch* Eton. *Team* Gloucestershire (1875, 1 match).
Career batting
1–2–1–1–1–1.00–0–*ct* 0

Jennings, Claude Barrows
Amateur. *b:* 5.6.1884, East St Kilda, Melbourne, Victoria, Australia. *d:* 20.6.1950, North Adelaide, South Australia. Opening right-hand batsman. *Teams* South Australia (1902/3 to 1907/8, 21 matches): Queensland (1910/11 to 1911/12, 5 matches). *Tour* Australia to England 1912. *Tests* Australia (1912, 6 matches).
Career batting
60–103–7–2453–123–25.55–1–*ct* 38–*st* 3
Bowling 17–0
Test batting
6–8–2–107–32–17.83–0–*ct* 5

He hit 1,037 runs, av 22.54, on his 1912 tour to England and played some useful innings, despite the fact that the wet pitches told against him.

Jennings, David William
Professional. *b:* 4.6.1889, Kentish Town, London. *d:* 6.8.1918, Tunbridge Wells, Kent, after illness due to shell-shock. Brother of G. A. (Warwickshire), L. F. (RAF) and T. S. (Surrey). Middle order right-hand batsman. *Team* Kent (1909–14, 35 matches).
Career batting
35–48–4–1064–106–24.18–3–*ct* 28
Bowling 80–1–80.00–0–0–1/13

Jennings, F. L.
Amateur. Middle order batsman. *Team* Somerset (1895, 1 match).
Career batting
1–2–0–7–7–3.50–0–*ct* 0

Jennings, George Adolphus
Professional. *b:* 14.1.1895, Tiverton, Devon. *d:* 12.7.1959, Marlborough, Wiltshire. Brother of D. W. (Kent), L. F. (RAF) and T. S. (Surrey). Lower order right-hand batsman, slow left-arm bowler. *Team* Warwickshire (1923–25, 20 matches).
Career batting
20–27–5–243–41–11.04–0–*ct* 8
Bowling 916–23–39.82–1–0–5/92
He also played for Devon (1923–25), and was coach at Marlborough College for over 30 years.

Jennings, Keith Francis
Cricketer. *b:* 5.10.1953, Wellington, Somerset. Lower order right-hand batsman, right-arm medium pace bowler. *Team* Somerset (1975–81, 68 matches).
Career batting
68–73–24–521–49–10.63–0–*ct* 47
Bowling 3403–96–35.44–1–0–5/18

Jennings, Leonard Frank
Amateur, *b:* 5.11.1903, Marlborough, Wiltshire. *d:* 28.3.1977, Battle, Sussex. Brother of D. W. (Kent), G. A. (Warwickshire) and T. S. (Surrey). Middle order batsman, change bowler. *Team* Royal Air Force (1929).
Career batting
2–3–1–55–45*–27.50–0–*ct* 1
Bowling 22–0

Jennings, Thomas Shepherd
Professional. *b:* 3.11.1896, Tiverton, Devon. *d:* 7.9.1972, Tiverton, Devon. Brother of D. W. (Kent), G. A. (Warwickshire) and L. F. (RAF). Lower order left-hand batsman, slow left-arm bowler. *Team* Surrey (1921–24, 18 matches).
Career batting
18–17–3–194–37*–13.85–0–*ct* 4
Bowling 1094–37–29.56–3–1–6/51
He also played for Devon (1926–33).

Jephson, Digby Loder Armroid
Amateur. *b:* 23.2.1871, Brixton, London. *d:* 19.1.1926, Cambridge. Opening/middle order right-hand batsman, right-arm fast bowler, changing to under-arm lobs about 1892. *Teams* Cambridge U (1890–92, blue all three years); Surrey (1894–1904, 165 matches).
Career batting
207–313–53–7973–213–30.66–11–*ct* 104
Bowling 7457–297–25.10–14–2–7/51
He hit 1,000 runs in a season four times (best 1,952, av 41.53, in 1900). His only double century was 213 for Surrey v Derbyshire at the Oval in 1900. From 1900 to 1902 he captained Surrey.

Jephson, Selwyn Victor
Amateur. *b:* 24.5.1900, Beaminster, Dorset. *d:* 6.11.1978, Salisbury, Wiltshire. Son of W. V. (Hampshire). Lower order right-hand batsman, right-arm fast medium bowler. *Team* Royal Navy (1924–28).
Career batting
4–7–0–49–14–7.00–0–*ct* 2
Bowling 421–6–70.16–0–0–2/73
His County cricket was for Dorset (1920–31).

Jephson, Rev William Vincent
Amateur. *b:* 6.10.1873, Ayot St Peter, Hertfordshire. *d:* 12.11.1956, Waterhouse, Monkton Combe, Bath, Somerset. Father of S. V. (Royal Navy). Hard hitting right-hand batsman, wicket-keeper or slip. *Sch* Haileybury. *Team* Hampshire (1903–19, 57 matches).
Career batting
62–109–7–1791–114*–17.55–1–*ct* 39–*st* 1
Bowling 13–1–13.00–0–0–1/13
He also played for Hertfordshire (1892) and Dorset (1920–25). His final first-class match was for MCC in 1920.

Jepson, Arthur
Professional. *b:* 12.7.1915, Selston, Nottinghamshire. Hard hitting lower order right-hand batsman, right-arm fast medium bowler. *Team* Nottinghamshire (1938–59, 390 matches).
Career batting
392–534–89–6369–130–14.31–1–*ct* 201
Bowling 30567–1051–29.08–40–6–8/45
He took 100 wickets in a season once: 115, av 27.78, in 1947. A noted soccer player, he appeared in goal for Port Vale, Stoke City and Lincoln City. He was a first-class umpire (1960–84), standing in 4 Test matches (1966–69).

Jerman, Lindsey Crawford Stapleton
Amateur. *b:* 23.4.1915, Old Fletton, Huntingdonshire. Lower order right-hand batsman, right-arm fast medium bowler. *Team* Essex (1950–51, 3 matches).
Career batting
3–2–0–8–8–4.00–0–*ct* 2
Bowling 222–1–222.00–0–0–1/39
He also played for Cambridgeshire (1955–56).

Jerram, Dr Nigel Martyn
Amateur. *b:* 9.3.1900, Weymouth, Dorset. *d:* 19.12.1968, Trescoll, Roche, Cornwall. Middle order right-hand batsman. *Sch* Marlborough. *Team* Royal Air Force (1930).
Career batting
1–2–1–78–43*–78.00–0–*ct* 1
His County cricket was for Oxfordshire (1923). He played no first-class cricket whilst at Cambridge U, but did win a blue for hockey.

Jervis, Hon William Monk
Amateur. *b:* 25.1.1827, Marylebone, London. *d:* 25.3.1909, Quarndon, Derbyshire. Uncle of Lord Harris (Kent). Middle order right-hand batsman. *Sch* Eton. *Teams* Oxford U (1848); Derbyshire (1873, 1 match).
Career batting
5–8–3–34–17–6.80–0–*ct* 3
He also played for Staffordshire (1852), Warwickshire (pre first-class, 1852) and Herefordshire (1854–55). He assisted in the establishment of Derbyshire CCC and was President of the County Club, 1871 to 1886, and Hon Secretary 1887.

Jervis, William Swynfen
Amateur. *b:* 18.11.1840, Stafford. *d:* 3.4.1920, Southsea, Hampshire. Middle order batsman, useful bowler. *Team* Lancashire (1874, 1 match).
Career batting
2–4–0–27–13–6.75–0–*ct* 0
Bowling 91–8–11.37–1–0–6/30
He also played for Cheshire (1873–76) and Warwickshire (not first-class, 1880–84). His first-class debut was for Gentlemen of Kent in 1865. He was Hon Treasurer of Warwickshire 1884.

Jesson, Robert Wilfred Fairey
Amateur. *b:* 17.6.1886, Southampton, Hampshire. *d:* 22.2.1917, near Kut, Mesopotamia. Lower order right-hand batsman, leg break bowler. *Sch* Sherborne. *Teams* Hampshire (1907–10, 14 matches). Oxford U (1908).
Career batting
15–28–4–198–38–8.25–0–*ct* 8
Bowling 528–21–25.14–1–0–5/42

Jessop, Gilbert Laird
Amateur. *b:* 19.5.1874, Cheltenham, Gloucestershire. *d:* 11.5.1955, Fordington, Dorset. Father of G. L. O. (Hampshire), brother of O. W. T. (Gloucestershire). Brilliant middle order right-hand batsman, right-arm fast bowler, excellent deep field. *Teams* Gloucestershire (1894–1914, 345 matches); Cambridge U (1896–99, blue all four years); London County (1900–03). *Tours* Warner to USA 1897; Ranjitsinhji to North America 1899; MacLaren to Australia 1901/02. *Tests* England (1899–1912, 18 matches).
Career batting
493–855–37–26698–286–32.63–53–*ct* 463
Bowling 19904–873–22.79–41–4–8/29
Test batting
18–26–0–569–104–21.88–1–*ct* 11
Bowling 354–10–35.40–0–0–4/68
The most consistent of all fast scoring batsmen in first-class cricket, Jessop was known as 'The Croucher' from his stance at the wicket. Very quick on his feet and having a wonderful eye, he was able to come out to even the fastest bowlers and either straight drive them or pull them with incredible certainty. A few players have been able to hit the ball harder, but none excelled him in his all-round hitting. Inevitably he would sometimes fail due to his determination to hit out almost from the start of an innings, but on many occasions his batting quickly turned the course of a match. His fielding at extra mid off was almost worth a place in a County side for the number of runs he saved and he was a notable fast bowler.
In all he hit 1,000 runs in a season 14 times, going on to 2,000 twice, with 2,323, av 40.75, in 1901 his best aggregate. Of his five double centuries, the highest was 286 for Gloucestershire v Sussex at Hove in 1903. In that innings he reached the 200 mark in 120 minutes – a record in first-class cricket (since beaten), and three of his other double centuries came up in less than 2½ hours, a record totally without parallel. He took 100 wickets in a season twice (best 116, av 85, in 1897) and performed the 'double' twice, once including 2,000 runs.
His most famous innings came in the fifth Test against Australia at the Oval in 1902, when he scored 104 of 139 in 77 minutes, allowing England to recover from 48 for 5 and win by one wicket. His name in fact dominates the 'Fast Scoring Record' section of the cricket press. Twice he reached fifty in 15 minutes and his fastest century came in 40 minutes, closely followed by another 42 minutes. He captained Cambridge 1899 and Gloucestershire 1900–12. He was Hon Secretary of Gloucestershire 1909–12 and an England selector in 1911.

Jessop, Rev Gilbert Laird Osborne
Amateur. *b:* 6.9.1906, Kensington, London. *d:* 16.1.1990, Lambeth, London. Son of G. L. (Gloucestershire), nephew of O. W. T. (Gloucestershire). Middle order right-hand batsman, off break bowler. *Sch* Weymouth. *Team* Hampshire (1933, 3 matches).
Career batting
4–7–0–86–29–12.28–0–*ct* 2
Bowling 67–1–67.00–0–0–1/16
His debut in first-class matches was for MCC in 1929. He also played for Cambridgeshire (1936) and Dorset (1939–54).

Jessop, Hylton
Amateur. *b:* 12.2.1868, Cheltenham, Gloucestershire. *d:* 19.7.1924, Montpellier, Cheltenham, Gloucestershire. Father of W. H. (Gloucestershire). Hard hitting

middle order batsman, slow bowler. *Team* Gloucestershire (1896, 3 matches).
Career batting
3–6–0–75–41–12.50–0–*ct* 5
Bowling 29–1–29.00–0–0–1/12

Jessop, Osman Walter Temple
Amateur. *b:* 3.1.1878, Cheltenham, Gloucestershire. *d:* 25.5.1941, Northwood, Middlesex. Brother of G. L. (Gloucestershire), uncle of G. L. O. (Hampshire). Middle order batsman. *Team* Gloucestershire (1901–11, 2 matches).
Career batting
2–4–1–61–29–20.33–0–*ct* 1

Jessop, Walter Hylton
Amateur. *b:* 22.3.1899, Cheltenham, Gloucestershire. *d:* 25.12.1960, Charlton Kings, Gloucestershire. Son of Hylton (Gloucestershire). Middle order right-hand batsman. *Sch* Cheltenham. *Team* Gloucestershire (1920–21, 5 matches).
Career batting
5–10–1–118–25–13.11–0–*ct* 1

Jessopp, Neville Augustus
Amateur. *b:* 31.7.1898, South Leasingham, Sleaford, Lincolnshire. *d:* 13.7.1977, Claremont, Cape Province, South Africa. Lower order batsman, left-arm fast medium bowler. *Sch* Harrow. *Team* MCC (1919).
Career batting
2–3–1–2–2–1.00–0–*ct* 2
Bowling 150–7–21.42–0–0–3/64

His County cricket was for Norfolk (1914–20), but he then emigrated to British East Africa.

Jessup, Anthony
Amateur. *b:* 31.8.1928, Blindley Heath, Surrey. Lower order left-hand batsman, slow left-arm bowler. *Sch* Caterham. *Team* Oxford U (1950–51).
Career batting
7–10–7–18–7*–6.00–0–*ct* 4
Bowling 432–19–22.73–3–1–5/30

Jesty, Trevor Edward
Cricketer. *b:* 2.6.1948, Gosport, Hampshire. Middle order right-hand batsman, right-arm medium pace bowler. *Teams* Hampshire (1966–84, 340 matches); Border (1973/4); Griqualand West (1974/5 to 1980/1); Canterbury (1979/80); Surrey (1985–87, 68 matches); Lancashire (1987/8 to 1991, 56 matches). *Tours* England to Australia and New Zealand 1982/3 (not first-class); International XI to West Indies 1982/3; Lancashire to Jamaica 1987/8, to Zimbabwe 1988/9.
Career batting
490–777–107–21916–248–32.71–35–*ct* 265–*st* 1
Bowling 16075–585–27.47–19–0–7/75

He hit 1,000 runs in a season ten times (best 1,645, av 58.75, in 1982). His highest score was 248 for Hampshire v Cambridge U at Fenner's in 1984. He played for England in one-day internationals, but no Tests.

Jewell, Arthur North
Amateur. *b:* 1888, Iquique, Chile. *d:* 8.9.1922, Selsey, Sussex. Brother of M. F. S. (Worcestershire and Sussex) and J. E. (Orange Free State), uncle of J. M. H. (Worcestershire). Attractive middle order right-hand batsman, wicket-keeper. *Sch* Felsted. *Teams* Orange Free State (1910/11); Worcestershire (1919–20, 22 matches).
Career batting
29–56–0–946–128–16.89–3–*ct* 21–*st* 10

Jewell, Guy Alonzo Frederick William
Amateur. *b:* 6.10.1916, Axford Hampshire. *d:* 23.12.1965, Basingstoke, Hampshire. Left-hand batsman, slow left-arm bowler. *Team* Hampshire (1952, 1 match).
Career batting
1–2–0–1–1–0.50–0–*ct* 2
Bowling 52–1–52.00–0–0–1/38

He also played for Berkshire (1938).

Jewell, John Mark Herbert
Amateur. *b:* 3.5.1917, Bloemfontein, South Africa. *d:* 29.10.1946, Durban, South Africa. Son of J. E. (Orange Free State), nephew of A. N. (Worcestershire) and M. F. S. (Worcestershire and Sussex). Middle order right-hand batsman. *Sch* Felsted. *Team* Worcestershire (1939, 2 matches).
Career batting
2–4–0–30–24–7.50–0–*ct* 2

Jewell, Maurice Frederick Stewart
Amateur. *b:* 15.9.1885, Iquique, Chile. *d:* 28.5.1978, Whiteleaf, Buckinghamshire. Brother of A. N. (Worcestershire) and J. E. (Orange Free State), uncle of J. M. H. (Worcestershire), brother-in-law of W. H. Taylor (Worcestershire). Attacking middle order right-hand batsman, slow left-arm bowler. *Sch* Marlborough. *Teams* Worcestershire (1909–33, 121 matches); Sussex (1914–19, 6 matches). *Tour* MCC to South America 1926/7.
Career batting
133–239–15–4114–125–18.36–2–*ct* 67
Bowling 3448–104–33.15–2–0–7/56

He appeared for both Sussex and Worcestershire in 1919, one of the few 20th century players to represent two first-class Counties in a single season. He captained Worcestershire 1920–21, 1926, 1928 and 1929 and was for many years one of the major figures behind the scenes at Worcester, ending as President from 1950 to 1956.

Jewell, William John
Amateur. *b:* 1.1.1855, Wendron, Helston, Cornwall. *d:* 3.3.1927, Taunton. Opening batsman. *Team* Somerset (1884, 1 match).

Career batting
1–2–0–10–9–5.00–0–*ct* 0
Bowling 14–0

Jeyarajasingham, V. J. B.
(*see under* John, V.)

Jilani, Mohammad Baqa Khan
(*see under* Baqa Jilani, M.)

Jobson, Edward Percy
Amateur. *b:* 20.3.1855, Wall Heath, Staffordshire. *d:* 20.4.1909, Holbeche House, Wall Heath, Staffordshire. He died following an operaton for appendicitis. Middle order right-hand batsman, right-hand medium pace round-arm bowler, cover point. *Team* Worcestershire (1900–03, 7 matches).
Career batting
8–14–0–208–43–14.85–0–*ct* 1
Bowling 8–0
His first-class debut was for MCC in 1891 and most of his County cricket was played for Worcestershire before that side became first-class, from 1881.

Joginder Singh
Amateur. *b:* 7.7.1904, Manakmasra, India. *d:* 1940, India. Attacking middle order right-hand batsman. *Teams* Sikhs (1925/6); Southern Punjab (1926/7 to 1938/9). *Tour* India to England 1932.
Career batting
23–41–6–521–79–14.88–0–*ct* 16–*st* 1
Bowling 101–2–50.50–0–0–2/101
He performed very modestly on his visit to England. He was known in India as Capt. Joginder Singh to avoid confusion with another player of the same name.

John, George
Amateur. *b: circa* 1883, St Vincent. *d:* 14.1.1944, Port of Spain, Trinidad. Lower order right-hand batsman, right-arm fast medium bowler. *Team* Trinidad (1909/10 to 1925/6). *Tour* West Indies to England 1923.
Career batting
29–42–9–466–111–14.12–1–*ct* 16
Bowling 2559–133–19.24–7–1–7/52
On his 1923 tour to England he headed the bowling averages of all matches, but was not quite so successful in strictly first-class games, taking 49 wickets, av 19.51. His final first-class match was for Trinidad and Barbados in 1927/8. He was the father of Errol John, the actor.

John, Henry Celestin Robert
Amateur. *b:* 26.5.1862, Agra, India. *d:* 24.6.1941, Oxford. Lower order right-hand batsman, right-arm fast medium bowler. *Sch* Stonyhurst. *Teams* Lancashire (1881, 1 match); Europeans (1893/4 to 1903/4).
Career batting
6–9–5–65–15*–16.25–0–*ct* 8
Bowling 380–19–20.00–1–0–5/53

John, Vinothen
(real name Vinothen John Bede Jeyarajasingham)
Cricketer. *b:* 27.5.1960, Colombo, Ceylon. Lower order right-hand batsman, right-arm fast medium bowler. *Team* Sri Lanka (1981/2 to 1986/7). *Tours* Sri Lanka to Zimbabwe 1982/3, to India 1982/3 (not first-class), to Australia 1982/3, 1984/5, to New Zealand 1982/3, to England 1983 (World Cup), 1984, to Sharjah (not first-class) 1983/4, to Pakistan 1985/6 (not first-class), to India and Pakistan (World Cup) 1987/8. *Tests* Sri Lanka (1982/3 to 1984, 6 matches).
Career batting
21–23–9–127–27*–9.07–0–*ct* 4
Bowling 1875–74–25.33–6–0–6/58
Test batting
6–10–5–53–27*–10.60–0–*ct* 2
Bowling 614–28–21.92–2–0–5/60
He headed the Sri Lankan first-class bowling averages on the 1984 tour to England with 26 wickets, av 23.19, and was the most successful bowler in the Test match.

Johns, Alfred Edward
Amateur. *b:* 22.1.1868, Hawthorn, Melbourne, Victoria, Australia. *d:* 13.2.1934, Melbourne, Victoria, Australia. Lower order left-hand batsman, wicket-keeper. *Team* Victoria (1894/5 to 1898/9, 16 matches). *Tours* Australia to England 1896, 1899.
Career batting
37–54–16–429–57–11.28–0–*ct* 58–*st* 26
On both his visits to England he was the reserve wicket-keeper and did not appear in any Tests.

Johns, David Frank Victor
Amateur. *b:* 27.6.1921, Paddington, London. *d:* 20.11.1979, High Wycombe, Buckinghamshire. Middle order left-hand batsman, slow left-arm bowler. *Team* Minor Counties (1952).
Career batting
1–2–0–4–4–2.00–0–*ct* 1
Bowling 55–1–55.00–0–0–1/55
His County cricket was for Buckinghamshire (1950–66), being captain for three seasons.

Johns, John
Amateur. *b:* 15.10.1885, Briton Ferry, Glamorgan. *d:* 10.1.1956, Neath, Glamorgan. Lower order right-hand batsman, right-arm fast medium bowler. *Team* Glamorgan (1922, 1 match).
Career batting
1–2–1–4–3–4.00–0–*ct* 0
Bowling 62–2–31.00–0–0–2/29
He first played for Glamorgan (pre first-class) in 1920.

Johns, Robert Leslie
(known as Robin Leslie Johns)
Cricketer. *b:* 30.6.1946, Southampton, Hampshire. Middle order right-hand batsman, off break bowler. *Sch* St Albans. *Teams* Oxford U (1970, blue); North-

amptonshire (1971, 6 matches).
Career batting
14–22–2–335–61*–16.75–0–*ct* 9
Bowling 730–17–42.94–0–0–4/76
He also played for Hertfordshire (1975–86).

Johnson, Anthony Alexander
Cricketer. *b:* 30.3.1944, Loughborough, Leicestershire. Lower order right-hand batsman, right-arm fast medium bowler. *Teams* Nottinghamshire (1963–66, 26 matches).
Career batting
27–37–4–289–45–8.75–0–*ct* 24
Bowling 1717–49–35.04–0–0–4/13
He also played for Northumberland (1968–71 and 1974–77) and Durham (pre first-class, 1972–73). His final first-class match was for Minor Counties in 1974.

Johnson, Colin
Cricketer. *b:* 5.9.1947, Pocklington, Yorkshire. Middle order right-hand batsman, off break bowler. *Sch* Pocklington. *Team* Yorkshire (1969–79, 100 matches).
Career batting
100–152–14–2960–107–21.44–2–*ct* 50
Bowling 265–4–66.25–0–0–2/22

Johnson, Air Vice Marshal Frank Sidney Roland
Amateur. *b:* 4.8.1917, Simla, India. Middle order right-hand batsman. *Teams* Sind (1941/2); Delhi (1942/3); Combined Services (1947).
Career batting
5–9–0–142–39–15.77–0–*ct* 0

Johnson, Frederick
Professional. *b:* 14.3.1851, Rolvenden, Kent. *d:* 24.11.1923, Lambeth, London. Lower order left-hand batsman, left-arm fast medium bowler. *Team* Surrey (1878–83, 20 matches).
Career batting
20–32–8–158–21*–6.58–0–*ct* 14
Bowling 1302–51–25.52–4–1–6/42

Johnson, George Henry
Amateur. *b:* 16.12.1894, Middlesbrough, Yorkshire. *d:* 20.1.1965, Uppingham, Rutland. Lower order right-hand batsman, wicket-keeper. *Team* Northamptonshire (1922–32, 18 matches).
Career batting
18–28–14–142–43*–10.14–0–*ct* 14–*st* 6
He served on Northamptonshire CCC Committee from 1926 to 1939.

Johnson, George James
Professional. *b:* 23.12.1907, Loddington, Northamptonshire. *d:* 9.6.1986, Market Harborough, Leicestershire. Lower order right-hand batsman, right-arm fast bowler. *Team* Northamptonshire (1929–35, 5 matches).
Career batting
5–8–1–49–28*–7.00–0–*ct* 1
Bowling 349–5–69.80–0–0–2/41

Johnson, Graham William
Cricketer. *b:* 8.11.1946, Beckenham, Kent. Brother-in-law of G. R. Dilley (Kent and Worcestershire). Opening or middle order right-hand batsman, off break bowler, good slip field. *Teams* Kent (1965–85, 376 matches); Transvaal (1981/2 to 1984/5). *Tours* Kent to West Indies 1972/3 (not first-class); Robins to South Africa 1973/4, to West Indies 1974/5 (not first-class).
Career batting
390–605–78–12922–168–24.51–11–*ct* 315
Bowling 17601–567–31.04–23–3–7/76
He hit 1,000 runs in a season three times (best 1,438, av 31.26, in 1973 and 1,438, av 35.95, in 1975).

Johnson, Hophnie Hobah Hines
Amateur. *b:* 13.7.1910, Kingston, Jamaica. *d:* 24.6.1987, Miami, Florida, USA. Vigorous tail end right-hand batsman, right-arm fast bowler, good slip. *Team* Jamaica (1934/5 to 1950/1). *Tour* West Indies to England 1950. *Tests* West Indies (1947/8 to 1950, 3 matches).
Career batting
28–30–12–316–39*–17.55–0–*ct* 13
Bowling 1589–68–23.36–5–1–5/33
Test batting
3–4–0–38–22–9.50–0–*ct* 0
Bowling 238–13–18.30–2–1–5/41
Not fully fit during the 1950 tour to England, he appeared in only two Tests and returned a modest record.

Johnson, Hubert Laurence
Amateur until 1950, professional from 1955. *b:* 8.11.1927, Pine Hill, St Michael, Barbados. Middle order right-hand batsman, off break bowler, fine cover field, occasional wicket-keeper. *Team* Derbyshire (1949–66, 350 matches).
Career batting
351–606–65–14286–154–26.40–16–*ct* 217–*st* 2
Bowling 822–21–39.14–0–0–3/12
He hit 1,000 runs in a season six times (best 1,872, av 37.44, in 1960). He did not play first-class cricket from 1951 to 1954.

Johnson, Ian William, OBE
Amateur. *b:* 8.12.1917, North Melbourne, Victoria, Australia. Son of W. J. (Victoria), son-in-law of R. L. Park (Victoria). Lower order right-hand batsman, off break bowler. *Team* Victoria (1935/6 to 1955/6, 77 matches). *Tours* Australia to England 1948, 1956, to South Africa 1949/50, to West Indies 1954/5, to India and Pakistan 1956/7, to New Zealand 1945/6. *Tests* Australia (1945/6 to 1956/7, 45 matches).

Johnson, Ivan Nicholas

Career batting
189–243–29–4905–132*–22.92–2–*ct* 137
Bowling 14423–619–23.30–27–4–7/42
Test batting
45–66–12–1000–77–18.51–0–*ct* 30
Bowling 3182–109–29.19–3–0–7/44

On his 1948 tour to England he took 85 wickets, av 18.37, in first-class matches, but proved ineffective in the Tests; in 1956 he was less successful, but as captain of the side proved an effective leader. He captained Australia in 17 Tests. He was awarded the MBE in 1956 and the OBE in 1977.

Johnson, Ivan Nicholas
Cricketer. *b:* 27.6.1953, Nassau, Bahamas. Middle order left-hand batsman, slow left-arm bowler. *Sch* Malvern. *Team* Worcestershire (1972–75, 33 matches).
Career batting
33–43–10–716–69–21.69–0–*ct* 13
Bowling 1533–37–41.43–1–0–5/74

Johnson, Dr John Inchbald
Amateur. *b:* 10.7.1871, Aldwarke Bridge, Yorkshire. *d:* 20.10.1930, Culworth, Northamptonshire. Middle order batsman. *Team* Northamptonshire (1907, 1 match).
Career batting
1–1–0–0–0–0.00–0–*ct* 1

Johnson, John Stephen
Cricketer. *b:* 7.7.1944, Belle Vue, Doncaster, Yorkshire. Opening right-hand batsman. *Team* Minor Counties (1979).
Career batting
1–2–1–170–146*–170.00–1–*ct* 0

He hit a century in his only first-class match v Indians at Wellington in 1979. His County cricket was for Shropshire (1967–91).

Johnson, Joseph
Professional. *b:* 16.5.1916, South Kirkby, Yorkshire. Lower order right-hand batsman, slow left-arm bowler. *Team* Yorkshire (1936–39, 3 matches).
Career batting
3–3–2–5–4*–5.00–0–*ct* 1
Bowling 27–5–5.40–1–0–5/16

He played soccer for Doncaster Rovers and Southport.

Johnson, Laurence Allen
Professional. *b:* 12.8.1936, West Horsley, Surrey. Lower order right-hand batsman, occasional leg break bowler, wicket-keeper. *Team* Northamptonshire (1958–72, 153 matches). *Tour* MCC to East Africa 1963/4.
Career batting
156–189–40–1573–50–10.55–0–*ct* 262–*st* 67
Bowling 61–1–61.00–0–0–1/60

Johnson, Mark
Cricketer. *b:* 23.4.1958, Gleadless, Sheffield, Yorkshire. Middle order right-hand batsman, right-arm medium pace or off break bowler. *Sch* Pocklington. *Team* Yorkshire (1981, 4 matches).
Career batting
4–4–2–2–2–1.00–0–*ct* 1
Bowling 301–7–43.00–0–0–4/48

Johnson, Paul
Cricketer. *b:* 24.4.1965, Newark, Nottinghamshire. Stylish middle order right-hand batsman, right-arm medium pace bowler. *Team* Nottinghamshire (1982–92, 209 matches). *Tour* England A to West Indies 1991/2.
Career batting
215–353–37–11467–165*–36.28–22–*ct* 144–*st* 1
Bowling 510–5–102.00–0–0–1/9

He hit 1,000 runs in a season six times (best 1,518, av 37.95, in 1990).

Johnson, Peter David
Cricketer. *b:* 12.11.1949, Sherwood, Nottingham. Middle order right-hand batsman, leg break and googly bowler. *Sch* Nottingham High School. *Teams* Cambridge U (1970–72, blue all three years); Nottinghamshire (1970–77, 58 matches) *Tour* Minor Counties to East Africa 1982/3 (not first-class).
Career batting
89–149–14–3363–106*–24.91–2–*ct* 33
Bowling 972–11–88.36–0–0–3/34

His first-class debut was for D. H. Robins' XI in 1969. He hit 1,063 runs, av 32.21, in 1975. He also played for Lincolnshire (1978–87), and for Cambridgeshire (in one-day matches only) in 1983. His final first-class match was for Minor Counties in 1982.

Johnson, Peter Lovell
Amateur. *b:* 22.8.1926, Huyton, Liverpool, Lancashire. Middle order right-hand batsman, right-arm medium pace bowler. *Sch* Liverpool College. *Teams* Cambridge U (1947); Combined Services (1950).
Career batting
2–3–0–61–40–20.33–0–*ct* 1

Johnson, Peter Michael
Cricketer. *b:* 21.12.1947, Brixton, London. Tail end right-hand batsman, wicket-keeper. *Sch* Bec. *Team* Oxford U (1971).
Career batting
1–2–0–2–2–1.00–0–*ct* 0–*st* 1

Johnson, Peter Randall
Amateur. *b:* 5.8.1880, Wellington, New Zealand. *d:* 1.7.1959, Sidmouth, Devon. Son of G. R. (Cambridge U 1854), nephew of R. C. (Cambridge U 1850). Stylish right-hand opening batsman, right-arm fast bowler. *Sch* Eton. *Teams* Cambridge U (1900–01, blue 1901); Somerset (1901–27, 229 matches). *Tours*

Bosanquet to North America 1901; Hawke to Australia and New Zealand 1902/3; MCC to New Zealand 1906/7.
Career batting
275–488–24–11931–164–25.71–18–*ct* 176
Bowling 777–20–38.85–0–0–4/99

He hit 1,000 runs in a season once: 1,012, av 28.91, in 1921. He also played for Devon (1900).

Johnson, Richard Leonard
Cricketer. *b:* 29.12.1974, Chertsey, Surrey. Lower order right-hand batsman, right-arm medium pace bowler. *Team* Middlesex (1992, 1 match).
Career batting
1–1–0–1–1–1.00–0–*ct* 1
Bowling 71–1–71.00–0–0–1/25

Johnson, Simon Wolseley
Cricketer. *b:* 29.1.1970, Newcastle upon Tyne, Northumberland. Lower order right-hand batsman, right-arm medium fast bowler. *Sch* Newcastle RGS. *Team* Cambridge U (1990–92, blue all three years).
Career batting
22–27–9–321–50–17.83–0–*ct* 9
Bowling 1601–16–100.06–0–0–3/62

Johnson, Tyrell Fabian
Amateur. *b:* 10.1.1917, Tunapuna, Trinidad. *d:* 5.4.1985, Couva, Trinidad. Lower order left-hand batsman, left-arm fast bowler. *Team* Trinidad (1935/6 to 1938/9). *Tour* West Indies to England 1939. *Test* West Indies (1939, 1 match).
Career batting
18–21–11–90–27–9.00–0–*ct* 8
Bowling 1075–50–21.50–1–0–6/41
Test batting
1–1–1–9–9*–no av–0–*ct* 1
Bowling 129–3–43.00–0–0–2/53

He looked a better bowler than his modest record in England showed, his physique being unable to stand the strain of constant first-class cricket.

Johnston, Alexander Colin
Amateur. *b:* 26.1.1884, Derby. *d:* 27.12.1952, Littlewick, Knaphill, Woking, Surrey. Son of D. A. (Derbyshire). Opening right-hand batsman, leg break bowler. *Sch* Winchester. *Team* Hampshire (1902–19, 108 matches). *Tour* Martineau to Egypt 1930 (not first-class).
Career batting
116–206–13–5966–175–30.91–10–*ct* 58–*st* 1
Bowling 805–18–44.72–0–0–4/21

A noted all-round sportsman, he played soccer and hockey for the Army and also was well known on the polo field. A permanent limp due to wounds received in the First World War did not prevent him from continuing to play cricket. He hit 1,000 runs in a season twice (best 1,158, av 36.18, in 1910). His final first-class match was for Gentlemen of England in 1920.

Johnston, Andrew
Amateur. *b:* 26.2.1916, Linlithgow, West Lothian, Scotland. Middle order right-hand batsman, off break bowler. *Team* Scotland (1947–51).
Career batting
2–4–1–82–50*–27.33–0–*ct* 2
Bowling 47–1–47.00–0–0–1/47

Johnston, Arthur Sannox
Amateur. *b:* 16.3.1863, Hornsey, Middlesex. *d:* 8.8.1929, Well Hall, Eltham, London. Middle order right-hand batsman, right-arm medium pace bowler. *Sch* Mill Hill. *Teams* Middlesex (1886–87, 3 matches); Essex (1894–96, 7 matches).
Career batting
10–18–2–259–63–16.18–0–*ct* 5

He first played for Essex (pre first-class) in 1889. He was Amateur Golf Champion in 1895.

Johnston, Donald Clark
Amateur. *b:* 2.12.1894, Shanghai, China. *d:* 13.9.1918, Beugneux, France. He died of wounds. Tail end batsman, bowler. *Sch* Malvern. *Team* Oxford U (1914).
Career batting
2–2–1–6–6–6.00–0–*ct* 2
Bowling 71–2–35.50–0–0–2/27

Johnston, Sir Duncan Alexander
Amateur. *b:* 25.6.1847, Edinburgh, Scotland. *d:* 22.10.1931, West End, Edinburgh, Scotland. Father of A. C. (Hampshire). Opening right-hand batsman. *Sch* Glenalmond. *Team* Derbyshire (1882, 4 matches).
Career batting
4–8–0–65–31–8.12–0–*ct* 0

Johnston, Harry Grant Forsyth
Cricketer. *b:* 24.12.1949, Kirkwall, Orkney, Scotland. Lower order left-hand batsman, slow left-arm bowler. *Team* Scotland (1975–81).
Career batting
2–3–0–24–12–8.00–0–*ct* 0
Bowling 86–3–28.66–0–0–2/60

He played football for Montrose, Partick Thistle and Stenhousemuir.

Johnston, Robert Herbert
Amateur. *b:* 1.5.1865, Edinburgh, Scotland. *d:* 15.2.1910, Edinburgh, Scotland. Lower order right-hand batsman, wicket-keeper. *Sch* Edinburgh Academy and Clifton. *Team* Scotland (1905).
Career batting
1–2–0–13–13–6.50–0–*ct* 2

Johnston, Robert Ian
Cricketer. *b:* 1.7.1948, Woodvale, Belfast, Ireland. Middle order right-hand batsman, right-arm medium pace bowler. *Sch* Royal Belfast Academical Institution. *Team* Ireland (1979–83).

Career batting
3–5–2–86–34–28.66–0–*ct* 3
Bowling 3–0

Johnston, William Arras
Amateur. *b:* 26.2.1922, Beeac, Victoria, Australia. Father of D. A. (South Australia). Lower order left-hand batsman, left-arm fast medium bowler or slow spin bowler. *Team* Victoria (1945/6 to 1954/5, 56 matches). *Tours* Australia to England 1948, 1953, to South Africa 1949/50, to West Indies 1954/5. *Tests* Australia (1947/8 to 1954/5, 40 matches).
Career batting
142–162–73–1129–38–12.68–0–*ct* 52
Bowling 12936–554–23.35–29–6–8/52
Test batting
40–49–25–273–29–11.37–0–*ct* 16
Bowling 3826–160–23.91–7–0–6/44
He had a most successful tour to England in 1948 taking 102 wickets, av 16.42, in first-class matches and 27 wickets in the Tests. In 1953 he was injured in a preliminary practice match and was never really fit, a fact that was reflected in his figures; he did however obtain a batting average of 102.00, by dint of being dismissed only once in 17 innings.

Johnstone, Conrad Powell, CBE
Amateur. *b:* 19.8.1895, Sydenham, London. *d:* 23.6.1974, Eastry, Kent. Opening left-hand batsman, right-arm medium pace bowler. *Sch* Rugby. *Teams* Cambridge U (1919–20, blue both years); Kent (1919–33, 36 matches); Europeans (1926/7 to 1947/8); Madras (1934/5 to 1944/5).
Career batting
110–190–11–5482–135–30.62–6–*ct* 106
Bowling 2798–102 + 1–27.43–3–0–6/28
He spent much of his life in India and was awarded the CBE for his efforts on behalf of cricket in Madras. His last first-class matches in England were for Free Foresters and for MCC in 1939. He was President of Kent in 1966. A noted golfer, he captained Cambridge in 1920.

Jolley, William Turner
Amateur. *b:* 3.8.1923, Smallthorne, Stoke-on-Trent, Staffordshire. Lower order right-hand batsman, right-arm fast bowler. *Team* Lancashire (1947, 2 matches).
Career batting
2–2–1–21–13–21.00–0–*ct* 5
Bowling 132–5–26.40–0–0–4/31
He also played for Staffordshire (1949–56).

Jolliffe, Henry James
Amateur. *b:* 1867. *d:* 11.2.1909, Northam, Southampton, Hampshire. Middle order batsman. *Team* Hampshire (1902, 1 match).
Career batting
1–2–0–1–1–0.50–0–*ct* 1

Jolly, Norman William
Amateur. *b:* 5.8.1882, Mintaro, South Australia. *d:* 18.5.1954, Adelaide, South Australia. Lower order batsman, wicket-keeper. *Team* Worcestershire (1907, 1 match).
Career batting
1–2–1–9–8–9.00–0–*ct* 3
He played in trials at Oxford U, but not in first-class matches.

Jones, Adrian Nicholas
Cricketer. *b:* 22.7.1961, Woking, Surrey. Lower order left-hand batsman, right-arm fast medium bowler. *Teams* Sussex (1981–92, 80 matches); Border (1981/2); Somerset (1987–90, 88 matches).
Career batting
170–147–61–998–43*–11.60–0–*ct* 42
Bowling 13143–408–32.21–12–1–7/30
His best season was 1989 when he took 71 wickets, av 28.36.

Jones, Alan, MBE
Professional. *b:* 4.11.1938, Velindre, Glamorgan. Brother of E. W. (Glamorgan). Sound opening left-hand batsman, off break bowler. *Teams* Glamorgan (1957–83, 610 matches); Western Australia (1963/4, 9 matches); Northern Transvaal (1975/6); Natal (1976/7). *Tours* Glamorgan to West Indies 1969/70; MCC to Ceylon 1969/70.
Career batting
645–1168–72–36049–204*–32.89–56–*ct* 288
Bowling 333–3–111.00–0–0–1/24
He hit 1,000 runs in a season 23 times (best 1,865, av 34.53, in 1966). His only double century was 204* for Glamorgan v Hampshire at Basingstoke in 1980. He appeared for England v Rest of the World in 1970. From 1976 to 1978 he captained Glamorgan. He scored more runs in first-class cricket than any other non-Test player. He was appointed coach to Glamorgan CCC in 1984.

Jones, Alan Keith Colin
Cricketer. *b:* 20.4.1951, Solihull, Warwickshire. Opening right-hand batsman, right-arm medium pace bowler. *Sch* Solihull. *Teams* Warwickshire (1969–73, 4 matches); Oxford U (1971–73, blue all three years).
Career batting
35–65–1–1403–111–21.92–1–*ct* 13
Bowling 7–0
He appeared for Warwickshire in one match in 1969, then not again until 1973. He captained Oxford in 1973.

Jones, Alan Lewis
Cricketer. *b:* 1.6.1957, Alltwen, Glamorgan. Opening or middle order left-hand batsman. *Team* Glamorgan (1973–86, 160 matches). *Tour* Robins to New Zealand 1979/80 (not first-class).
Career batting
160–278–24–6548–132–25.77–5–*ct* 104

Bowling 152–1–152.00–0–0–1/60

He hit 1,000 runs in a season twice (best 1,811, av 36.95, in 1984). He also played for Wales in the Minor Counties Championship (1988).

Jones, Alfred William
Amateur. *b:* 6.8.1900, Tewkesbury, Gloucestershire. *d:* 7.8.1986, Orton Longueville, Cambridgeshire. Middle order left-hand batsman, right-arm medium pace bowler. *Team* Northamptonshire (1933, 1 match).
Career batting
1–2–0–13–12–6.50–0–*ct* 0

Jones, Allan Arthur
Cricketer. *b:* 9.12.1947, Horley, Surrey. Tail end right-hand batsman, right-arm fast medium bowler. *Sch* St John's, Horsham. *Teams* Sussex (1966–69, 18 matches); Somerset (1970–75, 118 matches); Northern Transvaal (1972/3); Middlesex (1976–79, 52 matches); Orange Free State (1976/7); Glamorgan (1980–81, 19 matches).
Career batting
214–216–68–799–33–5.39–0–*ct* 50
Bowling 15414–549–28.07–23–3–9/51

He was the first player since the rules governing County qualifications were introduced in 1873 to appear for four first-class Counties. His best bowling was 9/51 for Somerset v Sussex at Hove in 1972. He became a first-class umpire in 1985.

Jones, Andrew Howard
Cricketer. *b:* 9.5.1959, Wellington, New Zealand. Middle order right-hand batsman, off break bowler. *Teams* Otago (1979/80 to 1984/5); Wellington (1985/6 to 1991/2). *Tours* New Zealand to Sri Lanka 1986/7, to Sharjah (not first-class) 1987/8, 1989/90, to Australia 1987/8, 1989/90, 1990/1 (not first-class), to India 1987/8 (World Cup), 1988/9, to England 1990; Wellington to Australia 1990/1. *Tests* New Zealand (1986/7 to 1991/2, 23 matches).
Career batting
110–189–28–6950–186–43.16–14–*ct* 72
Bowling 1260–31–40.64–0–0–4/28
Test batting
23–42–5–1929–186–52.13–6–*ct* 16
Bowling 126–1–126.00–0–0–1/40

He scored 692 runs, av 53.23, on the 1990 tour to England and played in all three Tests, but was not very successful in the latter. He shared the Test record partnership of 467 (for 3rd wicket) with M. D. Crowe v Sri Lanka at Wellington in 1990/1.

Jones, Andrew Paul
Cricketer. *b:* 22.9.1964, Southampton, Hampshire. Tail end right-hand batsman, right-arm medium fast bowler. *Team* Somerset (1985, 3 matches).
Career batting
3–4–2–3–1*–1.50–0–*ct* 1
Bowling 142–3–47.33–0–0–1/9

Jones, Archibald Trevor Maxwell
Amateur. *b:* 9.4.1920, Wells, Somerset. Middle order right-hand batsman, leg break bowler. *Team* Somerset (1938–48, 21 matches).
Career batting
21–35–0–399–106–11.40–1–*ct* 16
Bowling 132–3–44.00–0–0–1/3

Jones, Arthur Owen
Amateur. *b:* 16.8.1872, Shelton, Nottinghamshire. *d:* 21.12.1914, Dunstable, Bedfordshire. He died of tuberculosis. Opening right-hand batsman, leg break bowler, brilliant close field. *Sch* Bedford Modern. *Teams* Cambridge U (1892–93, blue 1893); Nottinghamshire (1892–1914, 397 matches); London County (1901). *Tours* MacLaren to Australia 1901/2; MCC to Australia 1907/8. *Tests* England (1899–1909, 12 matches).
Career batting
472–774–47–22935–296–31.54–34–*ct* 577–*st* 2
Bowling 10929–333–32.81–8–1–8/71
Test batting
12–21–0–291–34–13.85–0–*ct* 15
Bowling 133–3–44.33–0–0–3/73

He hit 1,000 runs in a season nine times, going on to 2,000 once: 2,292, av 46.77, in 1901. His four double centuries were all for Nottinghamshire, the highest being 296 v Gloucestershire at Trent Bridge in 1903, a new County record. He captained Nottinghamshire from 1900 to 1914, though missing many matches in the last two years due to illness. He also led MCC to Australia in 1907/8 and captained England in two Tests. He also played for Bedfordshire (1891). A noted rugby footballer, he played as a three quarter for Leicester and later became a well-known referee.

Jones, Arthur Royston Gabe
(also known as Gabe-Jones)
Amateur. *b:* 25.11.1906, Clydach Vale, Glamorgan. *d:* 26.2.1965, Cardiff, Glamorgan. Middle order batsman, useful bowler. *Sch* Blundell's. *Team* Glamorgan (1922, 1 match).
Career batting
1–1–1–6–6*–no av–0–*ct* 0

He was only 15 years and 9 months old on his appearance for Glamorgan v Leicestershire at Cardiff in 1922, with still two seasons in front of him at school.

Jones, Barry John Richardson
Cricketer. *b:* 2.11.1955, Shrewsbury, Shropshire. Opening left-hand batsman, right-arm medium pace bowler. *Sch* Wrekin College. *Team* Worcestershire (1976–80, 46 matches).
Career batting
46–81–3–1076–65–13.79–0–*ct* 19

He also played for Shropshire (1981).

Jones, Charles Ian McMillan
Amateur. *b:* 11.10.1934, Woodhouse, Leeds, Yorkshire. Middle order right-hand batsman batsman, right-arm medium pace bowler. *Sch* Bishops Stortford. *Team* Cambridge U (1959).
Career batting
2–3–0–44–44–14.66–0–*ct* 1
His County cricket was for Hertfordshire (1959–69). He played hockey for England and took part in the 1960 and 1964 Olympic Games.

Jones, Charles Langton
Amateur. *b:* 27.11.1853, Sefton, Liverpool, Lancashire. *d:* 2.4.1904, Toxteth Park, Liverpool, Lancashire. Brother of F. J. (Liverpool). Opening right-hand batsman, useful bowler. *Team* Lancashire (1876–88, 5 matches).
Career batting
11–22–1–165–36–7.85–0–*ct* 0
Bowling 6–1–6.00–0–0–1/6
He was a noted player for Sefton and in Liverpool and District matches, his final first-class match being for Liverpool and District in 1890.

Jones, Christopher David Parry
Cricketer. *b:* 30.4.1971, Maidstone, Kent. Middle order right-hand batsman, right-arm medium pace bowler. *Team* Oxford U (1991).
Career batting
1–2–0–27–23–13.50–0–*ct* 0
He won a blue for hockey.

Jones, David
Professional. *b:* 9.4.1914, Hodthorpe, Derbyshire. Middle order right-hand batsman. *Team* Nottinghamshire (1935–39, 24 matches).
Career batting
24–38–5–594–60–18.00–0–*ct* 15
Bowling 7–1–7.00–0–0–1/7
A good soccer player, he appeared at right half for Bury.

Jones, David Alfred
Amateur. *b:* 9.3.1920, Aberkenfig, Glamorgan. *d:* 18.4.1990, Pen-y-Fai, Bridgend, Glamorgan. Lower order right-hand batsman, right-arm medium pace bowler. *Sch* King's College, Taunton. *Team* Glamorgan (1938, 1 match).
Career batting
1–1–0–6–6–6.00–0–*ct* 0
Bowling 43–2–21.50–0–0–2/22

Jones, Dean Mervyn
Cricketer. *b:* 24.3.1961, Coburg, Melbourne, Victoria, Australia. Powerful middle order right-hand batsman, right-arm medium pace bowler. *Teams* Victoria (1981/2 to 1991/2, 70 matches); Durham (1992, 14 matches). *Tours* Australia to West Indies 1983/4, 1990/1, to Sharjah (not first-class) 1984/5, 1985/6, 1989/90, to India 1986/7, 1989/90 (not first-class), to India and Pakistan (World Cup) 1987/8, to Pakistan 1988/9, to England 1989, to New Zealand 1989/90, 1991/2 (World Cup); Young Australia to Zimbabwe 1985/6; Rest of World to England 1987; Victoria to England 1991. *Tests* Australia (1983/4 to 1991/2, 49 matches).
Career batting
157–255–28–11790–248–51.93–34–*ct* 119
Bowling 966–15–64.40–0–0–1/0
Test batting
49–83–10–3355–216–45.95–10–*ct* 32
Bowling 64–1–64.00–0–0–1/5
A very competitive batsman, attacking the bowling on every possible occasion and a remarkable runner between the wickets, Jones topped the batting averages on the 1989 tour to England with 1,510 runs, av 88.82, and was just as successful with Durham in 1992 when he hit 1,179 runs, av 73.68. His highest score was 248 for the Australians v Warwickshire at Edgbaston in 1989. He scored 1,248 runs, av 96.00, in Australia 1991/2.

Jones, Edward Cyril
Amateur. *b:* 11.3.1896, Cardiff, Glamorgan. *d:* 23.12.1978, Cardiff, Glamorgan. Middle order batsman. *Team* Glamorgan (1926, 1 match).
Career batting
1 match, did not bat–*ct* 1

Jones, Eifion Wyn
Professional. *b:* 25.6.1942, Velindre, Glamorgan. Brother of Alan (Glamorgan). Lower order right-hand batsman, wicket-keeper. *Team* Glamorgan (1961–83, 405 matches). *Tour* Glamorgan to West Indies 1969/70.
Career batting
405–591–119–8341–146*–17.67–3–*ct* 840–*st* 93
Bowling 5–0

Jones, Emrys Closs
Amateur, turned professional in 1937 season. *b:* 14.12.1911, Briton Ferry, Glamorgan. *d:* 14.4.1989, Briton Ferry, Glamorgan. Lower order right-hand batsman, off break bowler. *Team* Glamorgan (1934–46, 100 matches).
Career batting
101–142–30–2016–132–18.00–2–*ct* 44
Bowling 3345–103–32.47–6–1–7/79

Jones, Ernest
Amateur. *b:* 30.9.1869, Auburn, South Australia. *d:* 23.11.1943, Norwood, Adelaide, South Australia. Uncle of A. F. Richter (South Australia). Hard hitting lower order right-hand batsman, right-arm fast bowler, excellent mid off. *Teams* South Australia (1892/3 to 1902/3, 47 matches): Western Australia (1906/7 to 1907/8, 3 matches). *Tours* Australia to England 1896, 1899, 1902, to South Africa 1902/3. *Tests* Australia (1894/5 to 1902/3, 19 matches).

Career batting
144–209–27–2390–82–13.13–0–*ct* 107
Bowling 14638–641–22.83–47–9–8/39
Test batting
19–26–1–126–20–5.04–0–*ct* 21
Bowling 1857–64–29.01–3–1–7/88

His great tour was in 1896 when he took 121 wickets, av 16.03; in 1899 he took 135 wickets, but his average increased to 21.10, whilst in 1902 he was definitely past his best. On his first visit his bowling action came in for considerable criticism, but later he modified his style. His deadliness with the ball came from his ability to make short-pitched deliveries rear up in a most alarming manner and at his height he was regarded by many as the greatest of all Australian fast bowlers.

Jones, F. M.
(*see under* Meyrick-Jones, F. M.)

Jones, Fred Alan
Amateur. *b:* 23.2.1927, Macclesfield, Cheshire. Middle order right-hand batsman, wicket-keeper. *Sch* King's, Macclesfield. *Teams* Oxford U (1951–52); Scotland (1954–61); Hyderabad (1962/3 to 1963/4).
Career batting
16–31–0–618–88–19.93–0–*ct* 11–*st* 3
Bowling 1–0

In the scholastic profession, he was teaching in Hyderabad when he appeared in Pakistan first-class cricket. His County cricket was for Cheshire (1954–60).

Jones, Frederic John
Amateur. *b:* 2.11.1850, West Derby, Liverpool, Lancashire. *d:* 9.6.1921. Liverpool, Lancashire. Brother of C. L. (Lancashire). Tail end batsman, right-arm fast bowler. *Team* Liverpool and District (1889).
Career batting
1–2–0–13–12–6.50–0–*ct* 0
Bowling 71–4–17.75–0–0–4/71

Jones, Garri Wyn
Cricketer. *b:* 1.5.1970, Birmingham. Opening left-hand batsman, off break bowler. *Sch* King's, Chester. *Team* Cambridge U (1991–92, blue 1992).
Career batting
9–17–1–268–44–16.75–0–*ct* 1

Jones, George Gregory
Professional. *b:* 8.1.1856, Mitcham, Surrey. *d:* 1.4.1936, Watford, Hertfordshire. Hard hitting lower order right-hand batsman, right-hand fast round-arm bowler, good mid off. *Team* Surrey (1875–88, 98 matches).
Career batting
102–162–23–1199–63–8.62–0–*ct* 61
Bowling 5569–323–17.24–15–2–7/20

Jones, George Leonard
Amateur. *b:* 11.2.1909, Lockerbie, Dumfries, Scotland. *d:* 6.6.1944, Normandy, France. Middle order right-hand batsman. *Team* Hampshire (1937, 9 matches).
Career batting
9–16–4–169–37*–14.08–0–*ct* 3

He also played for Dorset (1925–34).

Jones, Harry Ogwyn
Amateur. *b:* 6.10.1922, Llangennech, Carmarthen. Lower order right-hand batsman, right-arm medium pace bowler. *Team* Glamorgan (1946, 2 matches).
Career batting
2–3–3–10–7*–no av–0–*ct* 0
Bowling 53–0

Jones, Hugh
Amateur. *b:* 1889, Nass House, Lydney, Gloucestershire. *d:* 10.11.1918, Chatham, Kent, of pneumonia. Uncle of A. W. G. Hadingham (Surrey). Middle order batsman. *Sch* Wycliffe. *Team* Gloucestershire (1914, 1 match).
Career batting
1–2–0–11–11–5.50–0–*ct* 0

Jones, Ivor Jeffrey
Professional. *b:* 10.12.1941, Dafen, Carmarthenshire. Tail end right-hand batsman, left-arm fast medium bowler. *Team* Glamorgan (1960–68, 157 matches). *Tours* MCC to East Africa 1963/4, to India 1963/4, to Australia and New Zealand 1965/6, to West Indies 1967/8. *Tests* England (1963/4 to 1967/8, 15 matches).
Career batting
198–213–84–513–21–3.97–0–*ct* 46
Bowling 13278–511–25.98–18–0–8/11
Test batting
15–17–9–38–16–4.75–0–*ct* 4
Bowling 1769–44–40.20–1–0–6/118

He took 100 wickets, av 19.49, in 1967. A serious injury to his arm ended his first-class career in 1968.

Jones, James Bruce
Amateur. *b:* 19.8.1910, Larbert, Stirlingshire, Scotland. *d:* 29.4.1943, near Enfidaville, Tunisia. Cousin of J. F. (Scotland). Opening right-hand batsman. *Sch* Charterhouse. *Team* Scotland (1936–37).
Career batting
2–4–0–91–47–22.75–0–*ct* 0

Jones, James Forbes
Amateur. *b:* 9.1.1911, Larbert, Stirlingshire, Scotland. *d:* 14.12.1980, Kilchrenen-by-Taynuilt, Argyllshire, Scotland. Cousin of J. B. (Scotland). Opening right-hand batsman, right-arm medium pace bowler. *Sch* Fettes. *Team* Scotland (1930–39).
Career batting
10–18–1–404–91–23.76–0–*ct* 11
Bowling 38–1–38.00–0–0–1/38

Jones, James Lindley
Amateur. *b:* 1876, Liverpool, Lancashire. Lower order batsman, wicket-keeper. *Sch* Liverpool College. *Team* Lancashire (1910, 4 matches).
Career batting
4–5–4–10–7*–10.00–0–*ct* 5
He also played for Cheshire (1909–12).

Jones, James M.
Professional. Opening or middle order left-hand batsman, wicket-keeper. *Teams* Somerset (1922–23, 17 matches); Glamorgan (1928–29, 8 matches); Wales (1929).
Career batting
27–48–3–846–75–18.80–0–*ct* 23–*st* 13

Jones, John
Professional. *b:* 18.9.1858, Birmingham. *d:* 18.9.1937, Chalfont St Giles, Buckinghamshire. Middle order right-hand batsman, right-arm medium pace bowler, good deep field. *Team* South (1884).
Career batting
3–4–0–173–125–43.25–1–*ct* 1
His County cricket was for Essex (pre first-class, 1884–89) and his final first-class match for Players of the South in 1885.

Jones, Keith Vaughan
Cricketer. *b:* 28.3.1942, Park Royal, Middlesex. Lower order right-hand batsman, right-arm medium pace bowler. *Team* Middlesex (1967–74, 117 matches).
Career batting
118–157–37–2064–57*–17.20–0–*ct* 49
Bowling 6603–242–27.28–7–0–7/52
He also played for Bedfordshire (1975–89), his last first-class match being for Minor Counties in 1976.

Jones, Leslie Norman
Amateur. *b:* 13.7.1891, Tattenhall, Chester, Cheshire. *d:* 8.1.1962, Chester, Cheshire. Middle order right-hand batsman, right-arm bowler. *Team* Minor Counties (1937).
Career batting
1–2–1–13–9*–13.00–0–*ct* 0
Bowling 22–7–3.14–1–0–5/8
His County cricket was for Cheshire (1910–38) as a leading all-rounder – his brother, W. E. Jones, and his two sons, also represented the County.

Jones, Peter Charles Howard
Cricketer. *b:* 19.8.1948, Rhodesia. Middle order right-hand batsman, leg break bowler. *Team* Oxford U (1971–72, blue both years).
Career batting
26–45–8–521–67–14.08–0–*ct* 13
Bowling 525–13–40.38–0–0–3/51
He captained Oxford in 1972.

Jones, Peter Henry
Professional. *b:* 19.6.1935, Woolwich, London. Middle order left-hand batsman, slow left-arm bowler. *Team* Kent (1953–67, 140 matches).
Career batting
141–232–32–4196–132–20.98–2–*ct* 99
Bowling 6549–231–28.35–6–1–6/41
He hit 1,000 runs in a season twice (best 1,262, av 26.85, in 1961). He also played for Suffolk (1971–81). He played soccer for Hastings United.

Jones, Prior Erskine Waverley
Amateur. *b:* 6.6.1917, Princes Town, Trinidad. *d:* 21.11.1991, Port of Spain, Trinidad. Lower order right-hand batsman, right-arm fast bowler, fine slip. *Team* Trinidad (1940/1 to 1950/1). *Tours* West Indies to India, Pakistan and Ceylon 1948/9, to England 1950, to Australia and New Zealand 1951/2. *Tests* West Indies (1947/8 to 1951/2, 9 matches).
Career batting
61–71–16–775–60*–14.09–0–*ct* 33
Bowling 4531–169–26.81–6–1–7/29
Test batting
9–11–2–47–10*–5.22–0–*ct* 4
Bowling 751–25–30.04–1–0–5/85
He had a very modest tour of England in 1950. He played soccer for Trinidad.

Jones, Richard Henry
(later R. H. Cartwright-Jones)
Amateur. *b:* 3.11.1916, Redditch, Worcestershire. Opening left-hand batsman, right-arm medium pace bowler. *Team* Warwickshire (1946, 1 match).
Career batting
1–2–0–32–23–16.00–0–*ct* 1
Bowling 27–0

Jones, Richard Stoakes
Amateur. *b:* 14.3.1857, Dymchurch, Kent. *d:* 9.5.1935, Dymchurch, Kent. Stylish middle order right-hand batsman, good deep field. *Sch* Chatham House, Ramsgate. *Teams* Kent (1877–86, 49 matches); Cambridge U (1877–80, blue 1879–80).
Career batting
69–116–6–1887–124–17.15–1–*ct* 46

Jones, Richard Tyrrell
Amateur. *b:* 28.6.1871, Derwen, Oswestry, Shropshire. *d:* 31.8.1940, Knolton Bryn, Flintshire. Steady middle order right-hand batsman, right-arm medium pace bowler. *Sch* Eton. *Teams* Oxford U (1890–92, blue 1892).
Career batting
10–20–0–310–63–15.50–0–*ct* 2
Bowling 13–0
His County cricket was for Shropshire (1891) and Staffordshire (1898).

Jones, Ronald
Amateur. *b:* 9.9.1938, Tettenhall, Wolverhampton, Staffordshire. Middle order right-hand batsman, good cover point. *Team* Worcestershire (1955, 1 match).
Career batting
1–2–0–25–23–12.50–0–*ct* 0

Jones, Samuel Percy
Amateur. *b:* 1.8.1861, Sydney, New South Wales, Australia. *d:* 14.7.1951, Auckland, New Zealand. Opening/middle order right-hand batsman, right-arm fast medium bowler, brilliant field. *Teams* New South Wales (1880/1 to 1894/5, 31 matches); Queensland (1896/7 to 1899/1900, 8 matches); Auckland (1904/5 to 1908/9). *Tours* Australia to England 1882, 1886, 1888, 1890; Queensland to New Zealand 1896/7. *Tests* Australia (1881/2 to 1887/8, 12 matches).
Career batting
151–259–13–5189–151–21.09–5–*ct* 81
Bowling 1844–55–33.52–1–0–5/54
Test batting
12–24–4–428–87–21.40–0–*ct* 12
Bowling 112–6–18.66–0–0–4/47

His most successful tour to England was in 1886 when he hit 1,497 runs, av 24.95. On the 1888 tour he unfortunately contracted smallpox and missed over half the tour – the nature of his illness was not revealed in case it caused the tour to be cut short.

Jones, Thomas Babington
Amateur. *b:* 20.1.1851, Maesteg, Bridgend, Glamorgan. *d:* 6.8.1890, Brislington, Somerset. Lower order left-hand batsman, right-hand medium pace round-arm bowler, mid off. *Sch* Christ College, Brecon. *Team* Oxford U (1874, blue).
Career batting
6–10–1–146–40–16.22–0–*ct* 6
Bowling 267–19–14.05–1–1–6/26

His County cricket was for Breconshire (1872–76).

Jones, Thomas Charles
Amateur. *b:* 1.4.1901, Pontypool, Monmouthshire. *d:* 19.7.1935, Westminster, London. Opening/middle order batsman, good cover point. *Sch* Shrewsbury. *Team* Glamorgan (1925–28, 3 matches).
Career batting
3–6–0–36–21–6.00–0–*ct* 0

Jones, Watkin Edward
Professional. *b:* 6.7.1917, Gwaun-cae-Gurwen, Glamorgan. Lower order right-hand batsman, right-arm fast medium bowler. *Team* Glamorgan (1946–47, 5 matches).
Career batting
5–1–0–0–0–0.00–0–*ct* 1
Bowling 342–13–26.30–1–0–7/92

Jones, Wilfred Edward
Professional. *b:* 2.2.1912, Pontardawe, Glamorgan. Lower order left-hand batsman, slow left-arm bowler. *Team* Glamorgan (1929–33, 50 matches).
Career batting
50–73–30–300–27–6.97–0–*ct* 21
Bowling 2754–77–35.76–3–0–6/93

Jones, William Edward
Amateur turned professional 1946. *b:* 31.10.1916, Carmarthen. Attractive middle order left-hand batsman, slow left-arm bowler, brilliant deep field. *Team* Glamorgan (1937–58, 340 matches).
Career batting
345–563–64–13536–212*–27.12–11–*ct* 120
Bowling 5782–192–30.11–3–0–5/50

He hit 1,000 runs in a season seven times (best 1,656, av 40.39, in 1948). Both his double centuries were for Glamorgan, the higher being 212* v Essex at Brentwood in 1948. A noted rugby fly-half for Gloucester, he appeared for Wales in war-time internationals.

Jones, William Maxwell
Amateur. *b:* 11.2.1911, Alltwen, Glamorgan. *d:* December 1941, Denbigh. Middle order right-hand batsman, bowler. *Team* Glamorgan (1933–38, 11 matches).
Career batting
11–15–3–116–51*–9.66–0–*ct* 1
Bowling 214–6–35.66–0–0–3/11

Jones-Davies, Henry Mydrian Orford
(also known as H. M. O. J. Davies)
Amateur. *b:* 21.10.1911, Portsmouth, Hampshire. *d:* 30.10.1976, Fairford, Gloucestershire. Lower order right-hand batsman, right-arm fast medium bowler. *Sch* St John's Leatherhead. *Team* Oxford U (1932).
Career batting
1–2–1–4–4*–4.00–0–*ct* 1
Bowling 38–0

Jordan, Henry Guy Bowen
Amateur. *b:* 10.6.1898, Buxton, Derbyshire. *d:* 5.10.1981, Tonbridge, Kent. Middle order right-hand batsman. *Sch* Marlborough. *Team* Derbyshire (1926, 1 match).
Career batting
1–2–0–0–0–0.00–0–*ct* 0

Jordan, John
Professional. *b:* 7.2.1932, Clough Fold, Rossendale, Lancashire. Lower order right-hand batsman, wicket-keeper. *Team* Lancashire (1955–57, 62 matches).
Career batting
62–75–7–754–39–11.08–0–*ct* 104–*st* 24

Jordan, Thomas
Professional. *b:* 15.10.1843, Stoke Newington, London. Son of David (Groundkeeper at Lord's, 1864–74). Lower order right-hand batsman, right-hand medium pace round-arm bowler, wicket-keeper or longstop. *Team* Players (1867).

Jordan, Thomas Carrick

Career batting
1–1–0–0–0–0.00–0–*ct* 0

Jordan, Thomas Carrick
Amateur. *b:* 10.2.1877, Philadelphia, USA. *d:* 28.3.1925, USA. Lower order right-hand batsman, wicket-keeper. *Team* Philadephia (1901–13). *Tours* Philadelphia to England 1903, 1908.
Career batting
23–40–15–257–24*–10.28–0–*ct* 30–*st* 10

He is regarded as the best of all American wicket-keepers and was a great asset to the Philadelphians on his two tours to England, being able to cope with the bowling of J. B. King. He represented USA v Canada in four matches commencing 1897.

Jorden, Anthony Mervyn
Cricketer. *b:* 28.1.1947, Radlett, Hertfordshire. Lower order right-hand batsman, right-arm fast medium bowler. *Sch* Monmouth. *Teams* Essex (1966–70, 60 matches); Cambridge U (1968–70, blue all three years).
Career batting
89–130–31–1112–67*–11.23–0–*ct* 47
Bowling 5347–176–30.38–1–0–5/95

He also played for Bedfordshire (1975–77). He captained Cambridge 1969–70. A noted rugby footballer, he won his blue and also played for Blackheath and England as full back.

Jose, Dr Anthony Douglas
Amateur. *b:* 17.2.1929, Adelaide, South Australia. *d:* 3.2.1972, Los Angeles, California, USA. He died by his own hand. Son of G. E. (South Australia). Lower order right-hand batsman, right-arm fast medium bowler. *Teams* South Australia (1947/8, 3 matches); Oxford U (1950–51, blue both years); Kent (1951–52, 5 matches).
Career batting
29–44–8–269–39–7.47–0–*ct* 11
Bowling 2293–75–30.57–1–0–6/45

His final first-class match was for Free Foresters in 1953.

Joseph, Arthur Frederick
Amateur. *b:* 13.3.1919, Neath Abbey, Glamorgan. Middle order right-hand batsman, leg break and googly bowler. *Team* Glamorgan (1946, 1 match).
Career batting
1–2–0–8–8–4.00–0–*ct* 1

Joseph, Linden Anthony
Cricketer. *b:* 8.1.1969, Georgetown, Guyana. Lower order right-hand batsman, right-arm fast bowler. *Team* Guyana (1986/7 to 1991/2); Hampshire (1990, 6 matches). *Tour* Young West Indies to Zimbabwe 1989/90.
Career batting
32–37–7–612–69*–20.40–0–*ct* 8
Bowling 2529–88–28.73–2–0–6/51

Joseph, Ray Fitzpatrick
Cricketer. *b:* 12.2.1961, Belladrum, British Guiana. Lower order right-hand batsman, right-arm fast medium bowler. *Teams* Guyana (1979/80 to 1985/6); Northamptonshire (1985, 2 matches).
Career batting
28–40–21–137–26*–7.21–0–*ct* 5
Bowling 2187–49–44.63–1–0–6/114

Josephs, John Michael
Amateur. *b:* 16.1.1924, Hendon, Middlesex. Lower order right-hand batsman, slow left-arm bowler. *Sch* Clifton. *Teams* Leicestershire (1946–53, 9 matches).
Career batting
9–14–2–116–25*–9.66–0–*ct* 1
Bowling 86–1–86.00–0–0–1/21

Joshi, Padmanabh Govind
Amateur. *b:* 27.10.1926, Baroda, India. *d:* 8.1.1987, Pune, India. Middle order right-hand batsman, wicket-keeper. *Team* Maharashtra (1946/7 to 1964/5). *Tours* India to West India 1952/3, to England 1959. *Tests* India (1951/2 to 1960/1, 12 matches).
Career batting
78–111–10–1724–100*–17.06–1–*ct* 120–*st* 61
Bowling 13–0
Test batting
12–20–1–207–52*–10.89–0–*ct* 18–*st* 9

He was completely unable to find his batting form on his 1959 tour of England and in the last two Tests lost his place to the reserve wicket-keeper.

Joshi, Udaykumar Chaganlal
Cricketer. *b:* 23.12.1944, Rajkot, India. Lower order right-hand batsman, off break bowler. *Teams* Saurashtra (1965/6 to 1982/3); Railways (1967/8); Gujarat (1968/9 to 1979/80); Sussex (1970–74, 76 matches).
Career batting
186–238–55–2287–100*–12.49–1–*ct* 79
Bowling 16203–557–29.08–34–3–6/33

Joslin, Leslie Ronald
Cricketer. *b:* 13.12.1947, Yarraville, Melbourne, Victoria, Australia. Middle order left-hand batsman, left-arm medium pace bowler. *Team* Victoria (1966/7 to 1969/70, 30 matches). *Tour* Australia to England 1968. *Test* Australia (1967/8, 1 match).
Career batting
44–67–6–1816–126–29.77–2–*ct* 27
Bowling 73–1–73.00–0–0–1/14
Test batting
1–2–0–9–7–4.50–0–*ct* 0

He had a very moderate tour of England in 1968 and was not required for the Tests.

Jowett, David Colin Patrick Robert
Amateur. *b:* 24.1.1931, Clifton Park, Bristol. Lower order left-hand batsman, off break bowler. *Sch* Sherborne. *Team* Oxford U (1952–55, blue all four years).

Career batting
50–73–25–578–57–12.04–0–*ct* 15
Bowling 4074–125–32.59–3–0–7/132

His County cricket was for Dorset (1952–60). His final first-class match was for MCC in 1958.

Jowett, George Edwin
Amateur. *b:* 20.8.1863, Roby, Prescot, Lancashire. *d:* 19.5.1928, Eccles, Lancashire. Middle order right-hand batsman, right-arm fast bowler. *Sch* King William's College, Isle of Man. *Team* Lancashire (1885–89, 19 matches).
Career batting
19–32–2–507–58–16.90–0–*ct* 11
Bowling 55–0

He was no-balled for throwing whilst playing for Lancashire.

Jowett, Dr Richard Lund
Amateur. *b:* 29.4.1937, Rawdon, Yorkshire. Middle order right-hand batsman, off break bowler. *Sch* Bradford GS. *Team* Oxford U (1957–60, blue 1957–59).
Career batting
43–78–5–1499–122–20.53–2–*ct* 44
Bowling 802–20–40.10–0–0–4/67

He also won a blue for golf.

Joy, Frank Douglas Howarth
Amateur. *b:* 26.9.1880, Hessle, Yorkshire. *d:* 17.2.1966, Winchester, Hampshire. Lower order right-hand batsman, left-arm fast medium bowler. *Sch* Winchester. *Teams* Europeans (1908/9); Somerset (1909–12, 11 matches).
Career batting
14–26–4–189–24–8.59–0–*ct* 9
Bowling 1353–57–23.73–4–2–7/24

He appeared in the Freshmen's match at Oxford, but no first-class matches. He won a blue for athletics. His daughter, Nancy Joy, wrote a history of women's cricket entitled 'Maiden Over'.

Joy, Jonathan
Professional. *b:* 29.12.1826, Preston Bottoms, Knaresborough, Yorkshire. *d:* 27.9.1889, Middlesbrough, Yorkshire. Middle order right-hand batsman, right-hand fast round-arm bowler, good point. *Team* Yorkshire (1849–67, 7 matches).
Career batting
11–20–0–283–74–14.15–0–*ct* 10
Bowling 56–1–56.00–0–0–1/16

He also played for Durham (pre first-class, 1849–56).

Joy, Ronald Cecil Graham
Amateur. *b:* 30.7.1898, Colchester, Essex. *d:* 12.12.1974, Holly Hill House, Ditchingham, Norfolk. Son-in-law of F. Penn (Kent). Lower order right-hand batsman, right-arm fast medium bowler. *Sch* Winchester. *Teams* Essex (1922–28, 13 matches); Europeans (1929/30); Hyderabad (1931/2).
Career batting
21–29–4–315–36–12.60–0–*ct* 14
Bowling 916–41–22.34–1–0–5/70

Joyce, Francis Matthew
Amateur. *b:* 16.12.1886, Blackfordby, Leicestershire. *d:* 23.9.1958, Earl's Court, London. Brother of J. H. (Leicestershire) and Ralph (Leicestershire). Middle order right-hand batsman, right-arm fast medium bowler. *Sch* Bedford GS. *Team* Leicestershire (1911–20, 16 matches).
Career batting
16–27–1–431–73–16.57–0–*ct* 7
Bowling 684–17–40.23–1–0–5/117

Joyce, Dr John Hall
Amateur. *b:* 5.12.1868, Blackfordby, Leicestershire. *d:* 17.4.1938, Vence, Nice, France. Brother of F. M. (Leicestershire) and Ralph (Leicestershire). Middle order right-hand batsman, right-arm fast medium bowler. *Team* Leicestershire (1894, 1 match).
Career batting
1–1–0–18–18–18.00–0–*ct* 2
Bowling 47–2–23.50–0–0–2/33

He also played for Bedfordshire (1914–21). He first played for Leicestershire (pre first-class) in 1890. He played in trials at Cambridge U, but not in first-class matches.

Joyce, Ralph
Amateur. *b:* 28.8.1878, Blackfordby, Leicestershire. *d:* 12.3.1908, Ashbourne, Derbyshire. Brother of F. M. (Leicestershire) and J. H. (Leicestershire). Stylish middle order right-hand batsman, right-arm slow bowler. *Sch* Bedford Grammar School. *Team* Leicestershire (1896–1907, 48 matches).
Career batting
48–88–4–1586–102–18.88–1–*ct* 17
Bowling 590–11–53.63–0–0–2/36

He appeared in the Freshmen's match and Seniors' match at Oxford, but no first-class games.

Joynson, William Reginald Hamborough
Amateur. *b:* 18.5.1917, Bickley, Kent. Middle order right-hand batsman. *Sch* Harrow. *Team* Oxford U (1939).
Career batting
2–4–0–30–11–7.50–0–*ct* 0

Joynt, Henry Walter
Amateur. *b:* 1.7.1931, St Giles, Devon. Middle order right-hand batsman, right-arm medium pace bowler. *Sch* Bradfield. *Teams* Oxford U (1952–53); Madras (1957/8).
Career batting
12–23–4–280–42*–14.73–0–*ct* 9
Bowling 879–18–48.83–0–0–4/36

His County cricket was for Dorset (1954–59). He won a blue for soccer.

Juckes, Richard Humphrey
Amateur. *b:* 21.1.1902, Horsham, Sussex. *d:* 21.1.1981, Tredington, Gloucestershire. Brother-in-law of J. Douglas (Middlesex). Middle order right-hand batsman. *Sch* King's, Canterbury. *Team* Sussex (1924, 1 match).
Career batting
1–1–0–1–1–1.00–0–*ct* 0

Judd, Arthur Kenneth
Amateur. *b:* 1.1.1904, Sunbury-on-Thames, Middlesex. *d:* 15.2.1988, Carse Mill, Abbotskerswell, Newton Abbot, Devon. Middle order right-hand batsman, leg break bowler, good field. *Sch* St Paul's. *Team* Hampshire (1925–35, 64 matches); Cambridge U (1927, blue). *Tour* Tennyson to Jamaica 1927/8.
Career batting
84–141–18–2624–124–21.33–2–*ct* 31
Bowling 1036–30–34.53–1–0–6/65
His appearances for Hampshire were restricted due to his posting in Nigeria during the 1930s.

Judd, Peter
Professional. *b:* 29.4.1938, Balham, London. Lower order right-hand batsman, off break bowler. *Team* Surrey (1960, 1 match).
Career batting
1 match, did not bat–*ct* 1
Bowling 14–0

Judd, William George
Amateur. *b:* 23.10.1845, New Forest, Hampshire. *d:* 12.3.1925, Boscombe, Hampshire. Lower order batsman, bowler. *Team* Hampshire (1878, 1 match).
Career batting
1–2–0–8–7–4.00–0–*ct* 0
Bowling 50–1–50.00–0–0–1/22

Judge, Peter Francis
Amateur for Middlesex, professional for Glamorgan. *b:* 23.5.1916, Cricklewood, Middlesex. *d:* 4.3.1992, London. Lower order right-hand batsman, right-arm fast medium bowler. *Sch* St Pauls. *Teams* Middlesex (1933–34, 8 matches); Glamorgan (1939–47, 54 matches); Bengal (1944/5 to 1945/6); Europeans (1944/5).
Career batting
68–90–31–454–40–7.69–0–*ct* 33
Bowling 4676–173–27.02–5–0–8/75

Judson, Albert
Professional. *b:* 10.7.1885, Cullingworth, Keighley, Yorkshire. *d:* 8.4.1975, Bingley, Yorkshire. Lower order right-hand batsman, right-arm fast medium bowler. *Team* Yorkshire (1920, 1 match).
Career batting
1 match, did not bat–*ct* 0
Bowling 5–0

Julian, Raymond
Professional. *b:* 23.8.1936, Cosby, Leicestershire. Lower order right-hand batsman, wicket-keeper. *Team* Leicestershire (1953–71, 192 matches).
Career batting
192–288–23–2581–51–9.73–0–*ct* 381–*st* 40
He joined the first-class umpires' list in 1972.

Julien, Bernard Denis
Cricketer. *b:* 13.3.1950, Carenage Village, Trinidad. Attacking middle order right-hand batsman, left-arm fast medium, or slow, bowler. *Teams* Trinidad (1968/9 to 1981/2); Kent (1970–77, 80 matches). *Tours* West Indies to England 1973, 1975 (World Cup), 1976, to India, Sri Lanka and Pakistan 1974/5, to Australia 1975/6; West Indian XI to South Africa 1982/3 (no first-class matches), 1983/4. *Tests* West Indies (1973 to 1976/7, 24 matches).
Career batting
195–273–36–5792–127–24.43–3–*ct* 126
Bowling 13871–483–28.71–15–1–9/97
Test batting
24–34–6–866–121–30.92–2–*ct* 14
Bowling 1868–50–37.36–1–0–5/57
He proved a useful all-rounder on the 1973 tour to England and appeared in all three Tests. On his second tour in 1976 he played well in the first-class matches but achieved little in the Tests. His best bowling was 9/97 for Trinidad v Jamaica at Port of Spain in 1981/2. His first-class debut was for North Trinidad in 1967/8.

Jumadeen, Raphick Rasif
Cricketer. *b:* 12.4.1948, Harmony Hall, Gasparillo, Trinidad. Brother of Shamshuddin (Trinidad), uncle of Ashmead (Trinidad). Lower order right-hand batsman, slow left-arm bowler. *Team* Trinidad (1970/1 to 1980/1). *Tours* West Indies to England 1976, to India and Sri Lanka 1978/9. *Tests* West Indies (1971/2 to 1978/9, 12 matches).
Career batting
99–119–48–604–56–8.50–0–*ct* 45
Bowling 9686–347–27.91–16–3–6/30
Test batting
12–14–10–84–56–21.00–0–*ct* 4
Bowling 1141–29–39.34–0–0–4/72
He took 58 wickets, av 30.00, on the 1976 tour to England and played in one Test. His first-class debut was for South Trinidad in 1967/8.

Juniper, John William
Professional. *b:* 6.2.1862, Southwick, Sussex. *d:* 20.6.1885, Southwick, Sussex, of typhoid. Lower order batsman, left-arm fast bowler. *Team* Sussex (1880–85, 57 matches).
Career batting
57–97–24–490–31–6.71–0–*ct* 20
Bowling 3623–184–19.69–6–0–7/24

He suffered from the disability of having sight in only one eye. His death occurred just a few days after his final first-class match for Sussex.

Jupp, George Harman
Amateur. *b:* 26.2.1845, Brentford, Middlesex. *d:* 24.2.1930, West Ealing, Middlesex. Hard hitting middle order right-hand batsman, slow round-arm bowler, good long stop. *Team* Middlesex (1867–68, 7 matches).
Career batting
8–14–0–181–49–12.92–0–*ct* 1
Bowling 49–2–24.50–0–0–2/49
He was also a noted athlete, especially excelling at the hurdles and 100 yards.

Jupp, George William
Amateur. *b:* 30.10.1875, Axbridge, Somerset. *d:* 6.7.1938, Longniddry, East Lothian, Scotland. Middle order right-hand batsman, bowler. *Teams* Somerset (1901–07, 5 matches); Scotland (1905–12).
Career batting
11–17–0–209–56–12.29–0–*ct* 6
Bowling 244–6–40.66–0–0–3/36

Jupp, Henry
Professional. *b:* 19.11.1841, Dorking, Surrey. *d:* 8.4.1889, Bermondsey, London. Cousin of W. T. (Surrey). Excellent opening right-hand batsman, right-hand fast round-arm bowler, wicket-keeper, good deep field. *Team* Surrey (1862–81, 252 matches). *Tours* Willsher to North America 1868 (not first-class); Grace to Australia 1873/4 (not first-class); Lillywhite to Australia 1876/7. *Tests* England (1876/7, 2 matches)
Career batting
378–692–48–15319–165–23.78–12–*ct* 228–*st* 19
Bowling 316–7–45.14–0–0–3/75
Test batting
2–4–0–68–63–17.00–0–*ct* 2
He hit 1,000 runs in a season eight times (best 1,275, av 36.42, in 1874). He was one of the most prolific batsmen of his day and owing to his great defensive powers known as ‘Young Stonewall’. He also played for Buckinghamshire (1866). He was a first-class umpire (1883–88).

Jupp, Vallance William Crisp
Professional, turned amateur in 1919. *b:* 27.3.1891, Burgess Hill, Sussex. *d:* 9.7.1960, Spratton, Northamptonshire. Middle order right-hand batsman, right-arm medium fast bowler, changed to off break in 1919, good cover field. *Teams* Sussex (1909–22, 173 matches); Northamptonshire (1923–38, 280 matches). *Tour* MCC to South Africa 1922/3. *Tests* England (1921–28, 8 matches).
Career batting
529–876–84–23296–217*–29.41–30–*ct* 222
Bowling 38166–1658–23.01–111–18–10/127
Test batting
8–13–1–208–38–17.33–0–*ct* 5
Bowling 616–28–22.00–0–0–4/37
He hit 1,000 runs in a season 13 times, going on to 2,000 once: 2,169, av 38.73, in 1921. His only double century was 217* for Sussex v Worcestershire at Worcester in 1914. He took 100 wickets in a season 10 times (best 166, av 20.15, in 1928) and achieved the ‘double’ in each of those 10 seasons – twice whilst a Sussex player and eight times with Northamptonshire. From 1922 until 1932 he was Secretary to Northamptonshire CCC and captained the County 1927 to 1931. He took all 10 wickets (for 127) in an innings for Northamptonshire v Kent at Tunbridge Wells in 1932.

Jupp, William Thomas
Professional. *b:* 11.11.1851, Dorking, Surrey. *d:* 3.8.1878, Chertsey, Surrey. Cousin of Henry (Surrey). Middle order right-hand batsman, right-hand fast round-arm bowler. *Team* Surrey (1876, 2 matches).
Career batting
3–5–1–27–11–6.75–0–*ct* 2
Bowling 57–0

K

Kalaugher, Wilfrid George
Amateur. *b:* 26.11.1904, Winchester, Canterbury, New Zealand. Lower order left-hand batsman, right-arm fast medium bowler. *Team* Oxford U (1928–31).
Career batting
8–10–3–27–10–3.85–0–*ct* 4
Bowling 641–20–32.05–1–0–5/87
His County cricket was for Oxfordshire (1931–32). He won blues for relay races and athletics.

Kallicharran, Alvin Isaac
Cricketer. *b:* 21.3.1949, Paidama, British Guiana. Brother of D. I. (Guyana). Attractive middle order left-hand batsman, slow right-arm bowler, good deep field. *Teams* Guyana (1966/7 to 1980/1); Warwickshire (1971–90, 285 matches); Queensland (1977/8, 7 matches); Transvaal (1981/2 to 1983/4); Orange Free State (1984/5 to 1987/8). *Tours* West Indies to England 1973, 1975 (World Cup), 1976, 1979 (World Cup), 1980, to India, Sri Lanka and Pakistan 1974/5, to Australia 1975/6, to India and Sri Lanka 1978/9, to Australia and New Zealand 1979/80, to Pakistan 1980/1; Rest of World to Pakistan 1973/4; West Indian XI to South Africa 1982/3, 1983/4. *Tests* West Indies (1971/2 to 1980/1, 66 matches).
Career batting
505–834–86–32650–243*–43.64–87–*ct* 323
Bowling 4030–84–47.97–1–0–5/45

Kaluperuma, Lalith Vasantha Silva

Test batting
66–109–10–4399–187–44.43–12–*ct* 51
Bowling 158–4–39.50–0–0–2/16

On the 1973 tour to England he hit 889 runs, av 46.78, in first-class matches and played in all three Tests. In 1976 he was not so successful and appeared in three out of the five Tests; in 1980, although playing in all five Tests, his form was again disappointing. He captained West Indies in nine Tests, but none in England. His Test career ended when he agreed to tour South Africa. He hit 1,000 runs in an English season twelve times going on to 2,000 twice (best 2,301, av 52.59, in 1984). He missed the 1987 season, but in 1988 was registered as an English qualified player, therby continuing his county career for three more years, but with limited success. His highest score was 243* for Warwickshire v Glamorgan at Edgbaston in 1983. He also played for Shropshire (1992).

Kaluperuma, Lalith Vasantha Silva
Cricketer. *b:* 25.6.1949, Colombo, Ceylon. Brother of S. M. S. (Sri Lanka). Lower order right-hand batsman, off break bowler. *Team* Ceylon/Sri Lanka (1970/1 to 1982/3). *Tours* Sri Lanka to India 1970/1, 1975/6, 1976/7, to Pakistan 1973/4, 1981/2, to England 1975; Arosa Sri Lankan XI to South Africa 1982/3. *Tests* Sri Lanka (1981/2, 2 matches).
Career batting
57–81–22–1023–96–17.33–0–*ct* 48
Bowling 3931–129–30.47–7–1–8/43
Test batting
2–4–1–12–11*–4.00–0–*ct* 2
Bowling 93–0

Kaluwitharana, Romesh Shantha
Cricketer. *b:* 24.11.1969, Colombo, Ceylon. Middle order right-hand batsman, wicket-keeper. *Teams* Western Province Suburbs (1990/1), Western Province South (1991/2). *Tours* Sri Lanka to New Zealand 1990/1, to India 1990/1 (not first-class), to England 1991.
Career batting
15–22–2–485–63–24.25–0–*ct* 27–*st* 3

He came to England in 1991 as the Sri Lankan reserve wicket-keeper and played in three first-class matches. His first-class debut was for Sri Lanka Youth XI in 1988/9.

Kamm, Anthony
Amateur. *b:* 2.3.1931, Hampstead, London. Lower order right-hand batsman, wicket-keeper. *Sch* Charterhouse. *Teams* Oxford U (1952–55, blue 1954); Middlesex (1952, 2 matches).
Career batting
9–11–4–154–59*–22.00–0–*ct* 10–*st* 5

His final first-class match was for Free Foresters in 1956.

Kanga, Dr Hormasji Dorabji
Amateur. *b:* 9.4.1880, Bombay, India. *d:* 29.12.1945, Bombay, India. Brother of M. D. (Parsis) and D. D. (Parsis). Opening right-hand batsman, right-arm medium pace bowler. *Team* Parsis (1899/1900 to 1921/2). *Tour* India to England 1911.
Career batting
43–77–6–1905–233–26.83–3–*ct* 31–*st* 4
Bowling 761–37–20.56–1–0–8/14

He was one of the more successful batsmen on the 1911 tour of England and scored 163 v Leicestershire to give the Indians their first ever win in a first-class match in England. His highest score was 233 for Parsis v Europeans at Poona in 1905/6. His first-class debut in England was for Leveson-Gower's XI in 1909.

Kanhai, Rohan Bholalall
Professional. *b:* 26.12.1935, Port Mourant, British Guiana. Uncle of Romain Etwaroo (Guyana), Reginald Etwaroo (Berbice) and T. R. Etwaroo (Guyana). Attacking middle order right-hand batsman, right-arm medium pace bowler, wicket-keeper during the early part of his career. *Teams* British Guiana/Guyana (1954/5 to 1973/4); Western Australia (1961/2, 8 matches); Trinidad (1964/5); Warwickshire (1968–77, 173 matches); Tasmania (1969/70, 2 matches). *Tours* West Indies to England 1957, 1963, 1966, 1973, 1975 (World Cup), to India and Pakistan 1958/9, to Australia 1960/1, to India and Ceylon 1966/7, to Australia and New Zealand 1968/9; Commonwealth to Rhodesia 1962/3; West Indian XI to England 1964; Rest of World to England 1965, 1967, 1970, to Pakistan 1970/1, 1973/4, to Australia 1971/2; International XI to Pakistan 1981/2. *Tests* West Indies (1957 to 1973/4, 79 matches).
Career batting
416–669–82–28774–256–49.01–83–*ct* 319–*st* 7
Bowling 1009–18–56.05–0–0–2/5
Test batting
79–137–6–6227–256–47.53–15–*ct* 50
Bowling 85–0

He hit 1,000 runs in a season 10 times (best 1,894, av 57.39, in 1970). He also hit 1,000 in a season once in Australia and once in India and Pakistan. Of his seven double centuries the highest is 256 for West Indies v India at Calcutta in 1958/9; he scored another in Test cricket – 217 v Pakistan at Lahore in 1958/9; of the three he made for Warwickshire the highest is 253 v Nottinghamshire at Trent Bridge in 1968. He created a new first-class world record, since beaten, with J. A. Jameson when they added 465* for the 2nd wicket for Warwickshire v Gloucestershire at Edgbaston in 1974. He captained West Indies in 13 Tests including the tour of England in 1973.

Kapadia, Bahadur Edulji
Amateur. *b:* 9.4.1900, Bombay, India. *d:* 1.1.1973, Bombay, India. Brother of F. E. (Parsis and Bombay),

cousin of D. K. (Parsis). Defensive lower order right-hand batsman, wicket-keeper. *Teams* Bombay (1925/6 to 1929/30); Parsis (1920/1 to 1929/30). *Tours* India to England 1932; Bombay to Ceylon 1925/6, 1929/30.

Career batting
30–44–6–522–59–13.73–0–*ct* 47–*st* 24

Travelling to England in 1932 as the reserve wicket-keeper, he appeared in only seven first-class matches. His final first-class match was for Vizianagram's XI in 1935/6.

Kapil Dev Ramlal Nikhanj
Cricketer. *b:* 6.1.1959, Chandigarh, India. Attacking middle order right-hand batsman, right-arm fast medium bowler, good outfield. *Teams* Haryana (1975/6 to 1991/2); Northamptonshire (1981–83, 16 matches); Worcestershire (1984–85, 24 matches). *Tours* India to Pakistan 1978/9, 1982/3, 1984/5, 1989/90, to England 1979, 1982, 1983 (World Cup), 1986, 1990, to Australia 1980/1, 1984/5 (not first-class), 1985/6, 1991/2, to New Zealand 1980/1, 1989/90, to West Indies 1982/3, 1988/9, to Sharjah (not first-class) 1984/5, 1985/6, 1986/7, 1987/8, 1988/9, 1989/90, 1991/2, to Sri Lanka 1985/6, to Bangladesh (not first-class) 1988/9, to Australia and New Zealand (World Cup) 1991/2; Rest of World to England 1987, 1991. *Tests* India (1978/9 to 1991/2, 115 matches).

Career batting
255–365–37–10765–193–32.82–17–*ct* 183
Bowling 21559–798–27.01–39–3–9/83
Test batting
115–168–13–4690–163–30.25–7–*ct* 58
Bowling 11894–401–29.66–23–2–9/83

On the 1979 tour to England he played in all four Tests and headed the Test bowling averages with 16 wickets, av 30.93. He appeared in all three Tests on the 1982 tour and as well as taking 10 wickets he hit 292 runs, av 73.00. He was the youngest player to take 100 Test wickets – 21 years 25 days – beating the record held by I. T. Botham. As captain of the 1986 Indian team to England, Kapil Dev deserves credit for the success of that side both in the Test series and one-day internationals. His all-round ability was a major factor in the victories, but he produced no outstanding performances at Test level. His fourth tour to England was in 1990 when he was no longer captain. In the Lord's Test he hit four consecutive balls from E. E. Hemmings for six to save the follow-on, but his only hundred on the tour was a brilliant 110 in the Third Test at The Oval. By this time his all-round Test record exceeded both 4,000 runs and 300 wickets. He captained India in 34 Tests. Although he played County cricket from 1981 to 1985 he never appeared in many more than half the county first-class matches in any one season, so did not complete 1,000 runs or take 50 wickets in a season. His best bowling was 9/83 for India v West Indies at Ahmedabad in 1983/4.

Kardar, Abdul Hafeez
(played as Abdul Hafeez until 1947)
Amateur. *b:* 17.1.1925, Lahore, India. Father of Shahid (Lahore), son-in-law of C. A. F. Hastilow (Warwickshire), brother-in-law of Zulfiqar Ahmed (Pakistan). Attacking middle left-hand batsman, slow left-arm bowler. *Teams* Northern India (1943/4 to 1945/6); Muslims (1944/5); Services (1953/4 to 1954/5); Oxford U (1947–49, blue all three years); Warwickshire (1948–50, 45 matches). *Tours* India to England 1946; Pakistan to England 1954, to India 1952/3, to West Indies 1957/8; Services to India and Ceylon 1954/5. *Tests* India (1946, 3 matches); Pakistan (1952/3 to 1957/8, 23 matches).

Career batting
174–262–33–6832–173–29.83–8–*ct* 110
Bowling 8448–344–24.55–19–4–7/25
Test batting
26–42–3–927–93–23.76–0–*ct* 16
Bowling 954–21–45.42–0–0–3/35

His best playing season in England was 1949 when he took 92 wickets, av 19.31. He captained Pakistan in the country's first 23 Test matches. His last first-class match was for Punjab Governor's XI 1965/6. After retiring from first-class cricket, he was President of the Pakistan Board of Control and a major force in the re-organisation of cricket in Pakistan.

Kasippillai, Mahendra
Amateur. *b:* 21.9.1927, Colombo, Ceylon. Middle order left-hand batsman, slow left-arm bowler. *Teams* Cambridge U (1956–57); Ceylon (1948/9 to 1951/2).

Career batting
11–21–2–277–62*–14.57–0–*ct* 4
Bowling 130–3–43.33–0–0–2/36

His County cricket was for Cambridgeshire (1954–55).

Katinakis, George Demetrius
Amateur. *b:* 25.7.1873, Bayswater, London. *d:* 15.5.1943, Southwold, Suffolk. He died in an air-raid. Opening batsman. *Team* Hampshire (1904–05, 4 matches).

Career batting
4–6–1–46–16*–9.20–0–*ct* 1
Bowling 27–0

Kay, Henry George
Amateur. *b:* 3.10.1851, Havant, Hampshire. *d:* 8.9.1922, Tottenham, Middlesex. Lower order right-hand batsman, wicket-keeper. *Sch* Cheltenham. *Team* Hampshire (1882, 2 matches).

Career batting
2–2–0–0–0–0.00–0–*ct* 0
Bowling 20–0

He was father of Anton Dolin, the ballet dancer and director.

Kaye, Harold Swift
Amateur. *b:* 9.5.1882, Mirfield, Yorkshire. *d:* 6.11.1953, St John's, Wakefield, Yorkshire. Father of M. A. C. P. (Cambridge U). Middle order right-hand batsman, useful bowler. *Sch* Harrow. *Team* Yorkshire (1907–08, 18 matches). *Tour* Leveson-Gower to Rhodesia 1909/10.
Career batting
21–29–2–262–37–9.70–0–*ct* 9
Bowling 0–0
He appeared with much success for the Yorkshire Gentlemen; later he was for several years a member of Yorkshire CCC Committee.

Kaye, Haven
Professional. *b:* 11.6.1846, Huddersfield, Yorkshire. *d:* 24.1.1892, Halifax, Yorkshire. Middle order right-hand batsman, right-hand fast round-arm bowler. *Team* Yorkshire (1872–73, 8 matches).
Career batting
8–14–0–117–33–8.35–0–*ct* 3

Kaye, Dr Henry Wynyard
Amateur. *b:* 21.5.1875, Hyde Park, London. *d:* 21.4.1922, Hatfield-Peverel, Essex. He died from pneumonia. Brother of J. L. (Hampshire), brother-in-law of C. Wigram (MCC) and K. Wigram (Europeans). Opening or middle order right-hand batsman, good cover point. *Sch* Winchester. *Team* Middlesex (1900, 3 matches).
Career batting
3–5–0–117–76–23.40–0–*ct* 0
He appeared in the Freshmen's match at Oxford, but no first-class matches.

Kaye, James Levett
Amateur. *b:* 27.12.1861, Potters Bar, Hertfordshire. *d:* 17.11.1917, Chelsea, London. Brother of H. W. (Middlesex). Lower order right-hand batsman, wicket-keeper. *Sch* Winchester. *Team* Hampshire (1881, 1 match).
Career batting
1–2–0–14–11–7.00–0–*ct* 0–*st* 1
He was for many years serving in India, being latterly in the Political Dept of the Government of India.

Kaye, Joseph Lowther
Professional. *b:* 21.6.1846, Honley, Huddersfield, Yorkshire. *d:* 12.10.1882, Kirkham, Whitefield, Bury, Lancashire. Middle order right-hand batsman, right-arm fast bowler. *Team* Lancashire (1867, 1 match).
Career batting
1–2–0–21–20–10.50–0–*ct* 0
Bowling 16–0

Kaye, Michael Arthur Chadwick Porter
Amateur. *b:* 11.1.1916, Kensington, London. Son of H. S. (Yorkshire). Hard hitting lower order right-hand batsman, right-arm medium fast bowler. *Sch* Harrow. *Team* Cambridge U (1937–38, blue 1938). *Tour* Oxford and Cambridge to Jamaica 1938/9.
Career batting
17–28–6–395–78–17.95–0–*ct* 11
Bowling 1244–31–40.12–1–0–5/89
His final first-class match was for Free Foresters in 1949.

Kayum, Donald Amrul
Cricketer. *b:* 13.10.1955, La Penitence, British Guiana. Middle order right-hand batsman, off break bowler. *Team* Oxford U (1977–78, blue both years).
Career batting
12–18–1–423–57–24.88–0–*ct* 8

Keate, Robert William
Amateur. *b:* 16.6.1814, Westminster, London. *d:* 17.3.1873, Cape Coast Castle, Gold Coast. Middle order batsman. *Sch* Eton. *Team* Oxford U (1833–35).
Career batting
39–69–6–387–30–6.14–0–*ct* 8
Bowling 2 wickets (no analyses)–0–0–2/?
His first-class debut was for Gentlemen in 1832, and his last match for Gentlemen of England in 1853. He was Governor and Commander-in-Chief of Trinidad in 1860.

Keay, George Alexander
Amateur. *b:* 14.3.1897, Broughty Ferry, Dundee, Angus, Scotland. *d:* 8.8.1981, Swanage, Dorset. Lower order right-hand batsman, off break bowler. *Sch* Whitgift. *Team* Oxford U (1919–20).
Career batting
3–4–1–26–15–8.66–0–*ct* 3
Bowling 94–3–31.33–0–0–3/11

Kedward, Philip Morris
Amateur. *b:* 26.7.1909, Hull, Yorkshire. Middle order right-hand batsman, right-arm medium pace bowler. *Sch* Kingswood, Bath. *Team* Leveson-Gower's XI (1935).
Career batting
1–1–0–0–0–0.00–0–*ct* 0

Keeble, George
Professional. *b:* 26.9.1849, Southfleet, Kent. *d:* 26.5.1923, Dartford, Kent. Lower order right-hand batsman, right-hand fast round-arm bowler. *Team* Kent (1876, 1 match).
Career batting
1–2–1–8–6*–8.00–0–*ct* 0
Bowling 37–1–37.00–0–0–1/21

Keech, Matthew
Cricketer. *b:* 21.10.1970, Hampstead, London. Middle order right-hand batsman, right-arm medium pace bowler. *Team* Middlesex (1991, 15 matches).
Career batting
15–24–3–420–58*–20.00–0–*ct* 4
Bowling 36–0

Keeler, John George
Professional. *b:* 2.5.1924, South Moor, Co Durham. Opening right-hand batsman, right-arm medium pace bowler. *Team* Minor Counties (1953).
Career batting
1–2–0–11–10–5.50–0–*ct* 0
His County cricket was for Durham (pre first-class, 1949–57).

Keeling, Harry Walter
Amateur. *b:* 8.11.1873, Hove, Sussex. *d:* 19.2.1898, Marylebone, London. Lower order right-hand batsman, off break bowler. *Sch* Hurstpierpoint. *Team* Kent (1893, 2 matches).
Career batting
2–3–0–40–24–13.33–0–*ct* 0
Bowling 48–0

Keeling, Michael Edward Allis
Amateur. *b:* 6.11.1925, Westminster, London. Opening right-hand batsman. *Sch* Eton. *Team* Oxford U (1948–49).
Career batting
5–6–0–75–40–12.50–0–*ct* 1
Bowling 5–0
He played against Cambridge U in a 1944 wartime match.

Keen, Frederick Francis
Amateur. *b:* 14.7.1898, Larida, Argentine. Lower order left-hand batsman, left-arm fast medium bowler. *Team* Argentine (1926/7). *Tour* South America to England 1932.
Career batting
7–10–2–115–23–14.37–0–*ct* 2
Bowling 505–13–38.84–0–0–3/31

Keene, John William
Professional. *b:* 25.4.1873, Mitcham, Surrey. *d:* 3.1.1931, Crichton, Midlothian, Scotland. Lower order left-hand batsman, left-arm slow medium bowler. *Teams* Surrey (1897, 2 matches); Worcestershire 1903–05, 24 matches); Scotland (1907).
Career batting
27–36–11–115–12–4.60–0–*ct* 12
Bowling 1580–66–23.93–5–1–6/22

Keeton, Frederick William
Professional. *b:* 26.10.1855, Mosbrough, Derbyshire. *d:* 27.11.1911, Bolton, Lancashire. Middle order right-hand batsman, right-hand medium pace round-arm bowler. *Team* Derbyshire (1876–80, 3 matches).
Career batting
3–6–0–33–9–5.50–0–*ct* 1

Keeton, William Walter
Professional. *b:* 30.4.1905, Shirebrook, Derbyshire. *d:* 10.10.1980, Forest Town, Nottinghamshire. Attractive opening right-hand batsman, good deep field. *Team* Nottinghamshire (1926–52, 382 matches). *Tests* England (1934–39, 2 matches).
Career batting
397–657–43–24276–312*–39.53–54–*ct* 76
Bowling 103–2–51.50–0–0–2/16
Test batting
2–4–0–57–25–14.25–0–*ct* 0
He hit 1,000 runs in a season 12 times, going on to 2,000 six times (best 2,258, av 42.60, in 1933). His highest score was 312* for Nottinghamshire v Middlesex at the Oval in 1939, a county record. He hit six other double centuries all for Nottinghamshire. With C. B. Harris he recorded century partnerships for the first wicket on 46 occasions. A good inside right, he played soccer for Sunderland and Nottingham Forest.

Keey, Christopher Leyton
Cricketer. *b:* 27.12.1969, Johannesburg, South Africa. Middle order right-hand batsman, off break bowler. *Sch* Harrow. *Team* Oxford U (1992, blue).
Career batting
8–13–1–308–64–25.66–0–*ct* 1

Keighley, William Geoffrey
Amateur. *b:* 10.1.1925, Nice, France. Sound opening right-hand batsman, right-arm medium pace bowler. *Sch* Eton. *Teams* Oxford U (1947–48, blue both years); Yorkshire (1947–51, 35 matches). *Tour* MCC to Canada 1951.
Career batting
65–102–8–2539–110–27.01–2–*ct* 16
Bowling 79–0

Keigwin, Henry David
Amateur. *b:* 14.5.1881, Lexden, Colchester, Essex. *d:* 20.9.1916, near Thiepval, France. He was killed in action. Brother of R. P. (Essex and Gloucestershire) and H. S. (Cambridge U). Middle order right-hand batsman, left-arm medium pace bowler. *Sch* St Paul's. *Teams* Essex (1906–07, 4 matches); Scotland (1907–09).
Career batting
11–18–0–351–77–19.50–0–*ct* 3
Bowling 472–15–31.46–1–0–5/83
His first-class debut was for Gentlemen of England in 1905. He played in trials at Cambridge U, but not in first-class matches.

Keigwin, Herbert Stanley
Amateur. *b:* 4.5.1878, Capel, Colchester, Essex. *d:* 11.3.1962, Amalinda, East London, South Africa. Brother of H. D. (Essex) and R. P. (Essex and Gloucestershire). Middle order right-hand batsman. *Sch* St Paul's. *Teams* Cambridge U (1901); London County (1901); Rhodesia (1909/10).
Career batting
8–15–1–296–111–21.14–1–*ct* 5

Keigwin, Richard Prescott
Amateur. *b:* 8.4.1883, Lexden, Colchester, Essex. *d:* 26.11.1972, Polstead, Suffolk. Brother of H. D. (Essex) and H. S. (Cambridge U). Middle order right-

hand batsman, slow right-arm bowler. *Sch* Clifton. *Teams* Cambridge U (1903–06, blue all four years); Essex (1903–19, 20 matches); Gloucestershire (1921–23, 9 matches).
Career batting
74–129–12–2316–116–19.79–1–*ct* 41
Bowling 2614–87–30.04–3–1–8/79
A noted all-round sportsman, he gained his blue for soccer, hockey and rackets and represented Essex at hockey as well as England. He was a recognised authority on the works of Hans Christian Andersen.

Keith, Geoffrey Leyden
Professional. *b:* 19.11.1937, Winchester, Hampshire. *d:* 26.12.1975, Southampton, Hampshire. Middle order right-hand batsman, off break bowler, good slip. *Teams* Hampshire (1962–67, 60 matches); Somerset (1959–61, 15 matches); Western Province (1968/9).
Career batting
77–124–14–2108–101*–19.16–1–*ct* 79
Bowling 561–13–43.15–0–0–4/49
He was Hampshire coach 1973–75.

Keith, Headley James
Amateur. *b:* 25.10.1927, Dundee, South Africa. Forcing middle order left-hand batsman, slow left-arm bowler. *Team* Natal (1950/1 to 1957/8). *Tours* South Africa to Australia and New Zealand 1952/3, to England 1955. *Tests* South Africa (1952/3 to 1956/7, 8 matches).
Career batting
74–113–8–3203–193–30.50–8–*ct* 61
Bowling 2174–79–27.51–2–0–5/27
Test batting
8–16–1–318–73–21.20–0–*ct* 9
Bowling 63–0
Although he appeared in four Tests on the 1955 tour of England, his record was only a modest one.

Kelland, Peter Alban
Amateur. *b:* 20.9.1926, Pinner, Middlesex. Tail end right-hand batsman, right-arm fast medium bowler. *Sch* Repton. *Teams* Cambridge U (1949–50, blue 1950); Sussex (1951–52, 3 matches).
Career batting
15–15–7–72–25–9.00–0–*ct* 4
Bowling 1053–27–39.00–0–0–3/24

Kelleher, Daniel John Michael
Cricketer. *b:* 5.5.1966, Southwark, London. Nephew of H. R. A. (Surrey and Northamptonshire). Lower order right-hand batsman, right-arm medium fast bowler. *Team* Kent (1987–91, 34 matches).
Career batting
34–43–6–565–53*–15.27–0–*ct* 8
Bowling 2533–77–32.89–2–0–6/109

Kelleher, Henry Robert Albert
Professional. *b:* 3.3.1929, Bermondsey, London. Uncle of D. J. M. (Kent). Lower order left-hand batsman, right-arm fast medium bowler. *Teams* Surrey (1955, 3 matches); Northamptonshire (1956–58, 52 matches).
Career batting
55–51–17–256–25–7.52–0–*ct* 45
Bowling 3097–112–27.65–4–1–5/23

Kellett, Simon Andrew
Cricketer. *b:* 16.10.1967, Mirfield, Yorkshire. Opening right-hand batsman, right-arm fast medium bowler. *Teams* Yorkshire (1989–92, 65 matches); Wellington (1991/2). *Tours* Yorkshire to South Africa 1991/2.
Career batting
66–111–9–3422–125*–33.54–2–*ct* 57
Bowling 19–0
He hit 1,000 runs in a season twice (best 1,326, av 37.88, in 1992).

Kelleway, Charles
Amateur. *b:* 25.4.1886, Lismore, New South Wales, Australia. *d:* 16.11.1944, Lindfield, Sydney, New South Wales, Australia. Sound opening right-hand batsman, right-arm fast medium bowler. *Team* New South Wales (1907/8 to 1928/9, 57 matches). *Tours* Australia to England and North America 1912, to New Zealand 1909/10, to South Africa 1914/15 (tour cancelled); AIF to England 1919. *Tests* Australia (1910/11 to 1928/9, 26 matches).
Career batting
132–205–23–6389–168–35.10–15–*ct* 102
Bowling 8927–339–26.33–10–1–7/35
Test batting
26–42–4–1422–147–37.42–3–*ct* 24
Bowling 1683–52–32.36–1–0–5/33
He hit 1,281 runs, av 31.24, on his 1912 tour to England – his very defensive batting earning the comment 'one Kelleway in a side is well enough, two or three would be almost unbearable'. He captained the AIF 1919 Team in England for the first few matches, then, for some unexplained reason, left the side.

Kelly, Acheson William Blake
Amateur. *b:* 5.8.1903, Dublin, Ireland. *d:* 6.10.1961, Combe Down, Bath, Somerset. Son of G. W. F. B. (Oxford U and Ireland), brother of G. N. B. (Ireland), nephew of A. D. Comyn (Ireland). Middle order right-hand batsman, right-arm medium pace bowler. *Sch* Stonyhurst. *Teams* Dublin University (1924–26); Ireland (1926).
Career batting
4–8–0–92–35–11.50–0–*ct* 1
Bowling 59–3–19.66–0–0–3/29

Kelly, Augustine Patrick
Amateur. *b: circa* 1894, Dublin, Ireland. *d:* 12.5.1960, Hackney, London. Middle order right-hand batsman, wicket-keeper. *Sch* Ampleforth College. *Teams* Ireland (1920–30); Dublin University (1922).
Career batting
14–25–1–505–98–21.04–0–*ct* 17–*st* 6

Kelly, Edward Arthur
Professional. *b:* 26.11.1932, Bootle, Lancashire. Lower order right-hand batsman, right-arm bowler. *Team* Lancashire (1957, 4 matches).
Career batting
4–6–2–38–16*–9.50–0–*ct* 1
Bowling 248–4–62.00–0–0–3/77

Kelly, Gustavus Noel Blake
Amateur. *b:* 26.12.1901, Dublin, Ireland. *d:* 14.3.1980, Castlebar, Co Mayo, Ireland. Son of G. W. F. B. (Oxford U and Ireland), brother of A. W. B. (Ireland), nephew of A. D. Comyn (Ireland). Middle order right-hand batsman, right-arm fast medium bowler. *Sch* Stonyhurst. *Teams* Dublin University (1922–26); Ireland (1922–26).
Career batting
7–14–5–275–76*–30.55–0–*ct* 5
Bowling 397–17–23.35–2–0–6/62

Kelly, Gustavus William Francis Blake
Amateur. *b:* 2.4.1877, Dublin, Ireland. *d:* 16.8.1951, Dundermott, Ballymoe, Co Roscommon, Ireland. Father of A. W. B. and G. N. B. (Ireland), brother-in-law of A. D. Comyn (Ireland). Lower order right-hand batsman, right-arm fast bowler. *Sch* Stonyhurst. *Teams* Oxford (1901–02, blue both years); Ireland (1907–14).
Career batting
26–43–6–614–52–16.59–0–*ct* 10
Bowling 1257–55–22.85–2–0–5/32
He was a noted athlete, winning the long jump in the inter-University sports.

Kelly, James Joseph
Amateur. *b:* 10.5.1867, Port Melbourne, Victoria, Australia. *d:* 14.8.1938, Bellevue Hill, New South Wales, Australia. His sister-in-law married V. T. Trumper (New South Wales). Lower order right-hand batsman, wicket-keeper. *Team* New South Wales (1894/5 to 1904/5, 53 matches). *Tours* Australia to England 1896, 1899, 1902, 1905, to South Africa 1902/3, to New Zealand 1904/5, to North America 1896. *Tests* Australia (1896–1905, 36 matches).
Career batting
185–266–60–4108–108–19.94–3–*ct* 244–*st* 112
Bowling 16–0
Test batting
36–56–17–664–46*–17.02–0–*ct* 43–*st* 20
He was the principal wicket-keeper for the tourists on all his four visits to England – injury received during the 1905 tour compelled him to retire from first-class cricket. His final first-class match was for Rest of Australia in 1906/7.

Kelly, John
Professional. *b:* 15.9.1930, Conisbrough, Yorkshire. Middle order left-hand batsman, slow left-arm bowler. *Team* Nottinghamshire (1953–57, 51 matches).
Career batting
51–72–11–1303–113–21.36–1–*ct* 29
Bowling 1844–38–48.52–0–0–4/25
He also played for Devon (1960–62).

Kelly, John Martin
Professional. *b:* 19.3.1922, Bacup, Lancashire. *d:* 13.11.1979, Rochdale, Lancashire. Stylish opening right-hand batsman. *Teams* Lancashire (1947–49, 6 matches); Derbyshire (1950–60, 253 matches).
Career batting
259–437–29–9614–131–23.56–9–*ct* 121
Bowling 103–1–103.00–0–0–1/21
He hit 1,000 runs in a season five times (best 1,535, av 30.70, in 1957).

Kelsall, Robert Stuart
Cricketer. *b:* 29.6.1946, Stockport, Cheshire. Middle order right-hand batsman, off break bowler. *Teams* Nottinghamshire (1969, 1 match).
Career batting
1–1–1–8–8*–no av–0–*ct* 1
Bowling 6–1–6.00–0–0–1/6
He also played for Cheshire (1970–79).

Kelsey, John Heneage
Amateur. *b:* 30.3.1867, Tunbridge Wells, Kent. *d:* 21.10.1945, Kilndown, Wadhurst, Sussex. Middle order right-hand batsman. *Sch* Repton. *Team* Sussex (1902, 1 match).
Career batting
1–1–0–1–1–1.00–0–*ct* 0
He also played for Warwickshire (pre first-class, 1889).

Kelson, George Mortimer
Amateur. *b:* 8.12.1835, Sevenoaks, Kent. *d:* 29.3.1920, Kingston-upon-Thames, Surrey. Son of George (Kent 1828). Fine middle order right-hand batsman, right-hand fast round-arm bowler, occasional wicket-keeper, good deep field. *Team* Kent (1859–73, 69 matches).
Career batting
90–163–7–2240–122–14.35–1–*ct* 57–*st* 2
Bowling 1586–75 + 1–21.14–2–0–6/22
He also played for Buckinghamshire (1869). He was a well-known writer on fishing.

Kember, Owen David
Amateur. *b:* 23.1.1943, Bombers Farm, near Crowhurst, Surrey. Lower order left-hand batsman, wicket-keeper. *Sch* Shrewsbury. *Teams* Surrey

(1962–63, 4 matches); Cambridge U (1963).
Career batting
6–9–2–61–19*–8.71–0–*ct* 6–*st* 3

Kemble, Arthur Twiss
Amateur. *b:* 3.2.1862, Sebergham, Carlisle, Cumberland. *d:* 13.3.1925, Crawley Down, Sussex. Middle/lower order right-hand batsman, wicket-keeper. *Team* Lancashire (1885–94, 76 matches).
Career batting
95–144–23–1347–50–11.13–0–*ct* 122–*st* 54

He also played for Cumberland (1889), and was for several years Secretary of Liverpool CC. His final first-class match was for West of England in 1896. An excellent rugby footballer, he represented Lancashire and England.

Kemmey, William
Professional. *b:* 21.7.1912, Atcham, Shropshire. *d:* 18.6.1987, Shrewsbury, Shropshire. Lower order right-hand batsman, wicket-keeper. *Team* Northamptonshire (1939, 5 matches).
Career batting
5–9–1–55–18–6.87–0–*ct* 4–*st* 2

Kemp, Arthur Fitch
Amateur. *b:* 1.8.1863, Forest Hill, Sydenham, London. *d:* 14.2.1940, Wentworth, Virginia Water, Surrey. Brother of C. W. M. (Kent) and M. C. (Kent). Lower order right-hand batsman, right-arm slow bowler. *Sch* Harrow. *Team* Kent (1884, 3 matches).
Career batting
5–9–1–40–13–5.00–0–*ct* 2
Bowling 54–1–54.00–0–0–1/26

His first-class debut was for an Oxford and Cambridge XI in 1883 and his final match for MCC in 1885.

Kemp, Arthur Lock
Amateur. *b:* 15.12.1868, Kentish Town, London. *d:* 1.3.1929, Monken Hadley, Hertfordshire. Middle or lower order batsman, bowler. *Sch* Denstone. *Team* Middlesex (1890–94, 2 matches).
Career batting
2–3–0–10–6–3.33–0–*ct* 0
Bowling 13–0

Kemp, Charles William Middleton
Amateur. *b:* 26.4.1856, Forest Hill, Sydenham, London. *d:* 15.5.1933, Copthall, Ightham, Kent. Brother of A. F. (Kent) and M. C. (Kent). Middle order right-hand batsman, right-hand slow round-arm bowler, cover point. *Sch* Harrow. *Teams* Oxford U (1878, blue); Kent (1878, 1 match).
Career batting
4–7–2–58–17–11.60–0–*ct* 7
Bowling 8–0

He represented Oxford against Cambridge in the Athletics Meetings of 1878 and 1879, being victorious in the long jump.

Kemp, Sir George
(created Baron Rochdale in 1913)
Amateur. *b:* 9.6.1866, Beechwood, Rochdale, Lancashire. *d:* 24.3.1945, Lingholm, Keswick, Cumberland. Brother-in-law of Lord Brackley (MCC). Stylish middle order right-hand batsman, slow right-arm bowler, good mid off. *Sch* Mill Hill and Shrewsbury. *Teams* Cambridge U (1885–88, blue 1885, 1886 and 1888); Lancashire (1885–92, 18 matches).
Career batting
51–92–4–1641–125–18.64–3–*ct* 17
Bowling 3–0

His final first-class match was for A. J. Webbe's XI in 1899. He also represented Cambridge at lawn tennis. He was MP for the Heywood Division of Lancashire 1895–1906 and for North West Division of Manchester 1910–12, both as a Liberal.

Kemp, Sir Kenneth Hagar
Amateur. *b:* 21.4.1853, Erpingham, Norfolk. *d:* 22.4.1936, Sheringham, Norfolk. Useful right-hand middle order batsman. *Sch* Clergy Orphan School, Canterbury. *Team* Cambridge U (1873).
Career batting
4–7–1–105–41–17.50–0–*ct* 1
Bowling 7–0

His first-class debut was for MCC in 1872. His County cricket was for Norfolk (1882–85) and Suffolk (1882), and he was for some years Hon Secretary of the former County.

Kemp, Manley Colchester
Amateur. *b:* 7.9.1861, Forest Hill, Sydenham, London. *d:* 30.6.1951, Aylesbury, Buckinghamshire. Brother of A. F. (Kent) and C. W. M. (Kent). Middle order right-hand batsman, wicket-keeper. *Sch* Harrow. *Teams* Kent (1880–95, 88 matches); Oxford U (1881–84, blue all four years).
Career batting
134–226–34–3040–175–15.83–1–*ct* 172–*st* 73

He captained Oxford in 1883 and 1884, which was unusual. His first-class debut was for Gentlemen of the South in 1879. An all-round sportsman, he also excellded at rackets, soccer (winning blues) and athletics.

Kemp, Nicholas John
Cricketer. *b:* 16.12.1956, Bromley, Kent. Lower order right-hand batsman, right-arm fast medium bowler. *Sch* Tonbridge. *Teams* Kent (1977–81, 13 matches); Middlesex (1982, 5 matches).
Career batting
18–19–4–210–46*–14.00–0–*ct* 8
Bowling 801–16–50.06–1–0–6/119

Kemp, Percival Hepworth
Amateur. *b:* 2.7.1888, Luton, Bedfordshire. *d:* 14.2.1974, Islington, London. Middle order batsman. *Team* Middlesex (1919, 1 match).

Career batting
1–2–0–43–38–21.50–0–*ct* 1

Kemp, Trevor Rodney
Cricketer. *b:* 22.9.1971, Colchester, Essex. Lower order right-hand batsman, off break bowler. *Team* Cambridge U (1992).
Career batting
2–1–0–0–0–0.00–0–*ct* 1
Bowling 128–1–128.00–0–0–1/35

Kempe, Cuthbert Reeves
(birth registered as C. R. Kemp)
Amateur. *b:* 10.2.1856, Long Ashton, Somerset. *d:* 18.4.1953, Weston-super-Mare, Somerset. Middle order batsman. *Team* Gloucestershire (1877, 2 matches).
Career batting
2–3–0–28–15–9.33–0–*ct* 1

Kempe, Rev Wilfrid Noel
Amateur. *b:* 10.10.1887, Long Ashton, Somerset. *d:* 17.10.1958, Frenchay, Gloucestershire. His mother was half-sister of A. G. Richardson (Somerset and Gloucestershire). Lower order batsman, wicket-keeper. *Sch* King's, Canterbury. *Team* Somerset (1919, 1 match).
Career batting
1–2–1–9–9–9.00–0–*ct* 0–*st* 1

Kempson, Simon Matthews Edwin
Amateur. *b:* 3.5.1831, Castle Bromwich, Birmingham. *d:* 20.6.1894, Stoutshill, Uley, Gloucestershire. Brother of W. J. (Cambridge U 1855). Hard hitting lower order right-hand batsman, right-hand medium pace round-arm bowler. *Sch* Cheltenham. *Team* Cambridge U (1851–56, blue 1851, and 1853).
Career batting
11–19–0–206–48–10.84–0–*ct* 11
Bowling 166–19 + 47–8.73–7–3–7/?

Illness prevented him playing against Oxford U in 1852. He played little cricket after 1856 as he was in India until 1878. His final first-class match was for MCC in 1865.

Kempster, James Francis
Amateur. *b:* 15.10.1892, Galway, Co Galway, Ireland. *d:* 21.4.1975, Kilternan, Co Dublin, Ireland. Middle order right-hand batsman, right-arm medium pace bowler. *Team* Ireland (1920–22).
Career batting
2–4–0–55–33–13.75–0–*ct* 0
Bowling 18–0

Kemp-Welch, George Durant
Amateur. *b:* 4.8.1907, Chelsea, London. *d:* 18.6.1944, Chelsea, London. He died as a result of an air-raid on the Guards Chapel. Attractive opening right-hand batsman, right-arm fast medium bowler. *Sch* Charterhouse. *Teams* Warwickshire (1927–35, 57 matches); Cambridge U (1929–31, blue all three years). *Tours* Tennyson to Jamaica 1927/8, 1931/2.
Career batting
114–182–14–4170–186–24.82–6–*ct* 50
Bowling 1716–41–41.85–0–0–4/41

He hit 1,561 runs, av 37.16, in 1931, the only season he exceeded 1,000 runs. His final first-class match was for Free Foresters in 1936. He captained Cambridge in 1931. He also won a blue for soccer. He was son-in-law of Stanley Baldwin, the Prime Minister and his sister Betty Kenward is a well-known diarist.

Kemsley, Jeremy Neil
Amateur. *b:* 28.9.1933, Melbourne, Victoria, Australia. Middle order right-hand batsman. *Team* Scotland (1955–57).
Career batting
8–14–0–285–103–20.35–1–*ct* 2

Kendall, Francis James
Professional. *b:* 25.7.1908, Hardingstone, Northamptonshire. *d:* 10.9.1966, Abington, Northampton. Tail end left-hand batsman, left-arm medium pace bowler. *Team* Northamptonshire (1930, 3 matches).
Career batting
3–6–1–1–1*–0.20–0–*ct* 0–*ct* 2
Bowling 172–6–28.66–0–0–2/26

His first-class batting record contains five consecutive ducks.

Kendall, John Thomas
Professional. *b:* 31.3.1921, Hawkesbury, Coventry, Warwickshire. Lower order right-hand batsman, wicket-keeper. *Team* Warwickshire (1948–49, 4 matches).
Career batting
4–4–1–26–18*–8.66–0–*ct* 5–*st* 4

He played soccer for Coventry City.

Kendall, Michael Philip
Cricketer. *b:* 10.11.1949, Canterbury, Kent. Lower order right-hand batsman, left-arm medium pace bowler. *Team* Cambridge U (1971–72, blue 1972).
Career batting
12–16–4–60–13–5.00–0–*ct* 2
Bowling 852–23–37.04–1–0–6/43

Kenderdine, Derek Charles
Amateur. *b:* 28.10.1897, Chislehurst, Kent. *d:* 28.8.1947, Cambridge. Tail end right-hand batsman, right-arm medium fast bowler. *Team* Royal Navy (1921–22).
Career batting
2–4–1–7–6–2.33–0–*ct* 1
Bowling 121–2–60.50–0–0–1/46

Kendle, Charles Edward Compton
Amateur. *b:* 10.2.1875, Amesbury, Wiltshire. *d:* 3.1.1954, Hellingly, Sussex. Lower order right-hand batsman, wicket-keeper. *Team* Hampshire (1899, 2 matches).

Kendle, Rev William James

Career batting
2–4–1–27–11–9.00–0–*ct* 2–*st* 1
He also played for Wiltshire (1911–14).

Kendle, Rev William James
Amateur. *b:* 9.4.1847, Broadlands, Romsey, Hampshire. *d:* 30.1.1920, Woodsford, Dorset. Useful middle order right-hand batsman. *Sch* Sherborne. *Team* Hampshire (1869–78, 5 matches).
Career batting
5–9–0–66–29–7.33–0–*ct* 1
He appeared in the Cambridge Freshmen's match of 1867, but no first-class matches whilst at the University.

Kendrick, Neil Michael
Cricketer. *b:* 11.11.1967, Bromley, Kent. Lower order right-hand batsman, slow left-arm bowler. *Team* Surrey (1988–92, 36 matches).
Career batting
36–41–12–513–55–17.68–0–*ct* 35
Bowling 3259–95–34.30–5–1–6/61

Kennard, John Adam Gaskell
Amateur. *b:* 8.11.1884, Chelsea, London. *d:* 6.4.1949, Hove, Sussex. His brother married the widow of R. E. Hancock (Somerset). Middle order batsman. *Sch* Harrow. *Team* Hampshire (1919, 2 matches).
Career batting
2–3–1–46–18–23.00–0–*ct* 0
Bowling 17–0
He also played for Oxfordshire (1922–23).

Kennedy, Alexander Stuart
Professional. *b:* 24.1.1891, Edinburgh, Scotland. *d:* 15.11.1959, Langdown, Hythe, Southampton, Hampshire. Sound opening or middle order batsman, right-arm medium pace inswing bowler. *Team* Hampshire (1907–36, 596 matches). *Tours* MCC to South Africa 1922/3; Joel to South Africa 1924/5. *Tests* England (1922/3, 5 matches).
Career batting
677–1025–130–16586–163*–18.53–10–*ct* 530
Bowling 61034–2874–21.23–225–45–10/37
Test batting
5–8–2–93–41*–15.50–0–*ct* 5
Bowling 599–31–19.32–2–0–5/76
He hit 1,000 runs in a season five times (best 1,437, av 26.61, in 1928) and took 100 wickets in a season 15 times, going on to 200 once: 205, av 16.80, in 1922. He performed the 'double' five times. His best bowling was 10/37 for Players v Gentlemen at the Oval in 1927.

Kennedy, Andrew
Cricketer. *b:* 4.11.1949, Billinge End, Blackburn, Lancashire. Opening left-hand batsman, right-arm medium pace bowler. *Team* Lancashire (1970–82, 149 matches). *Tour* Robins to South Africa 1975/6.
Career batting
150–243–20–6298–180–28.24–6–*ct* 85
Bowling 398–10–39.80–0–0–3/58
He hit 1,000 runs in a season three times (best 1,194, av 34.11, in 1980). He also played for Dorset (1983–87).

Kennedy, Charles Marshall
Amateur. *b:* 15.12.1849, Brighton, Sussex. *d:* 31.1.1906, Tunbridge Wells, Kent. Middle order right-hand batsman, wicket-keeper. *Sch* Brighton. *Team* Sussex (1872–78, 21 matches).
Career batting
23–43–7–284–37–7.88–0–*ct* 8–*st* 1
He did not play in any first-class matches whilst at Cambridge U, but did win a blue for rugby.

Kennedy, David
Amateur. *b:* 10.7.1890, Uddingston, Lanark, Scotland. *d:* 1.7.1916, The Somme, France. Lower order right-hand batsman, wicket-keeper. *Team* Scotland (1914).
Career batting
1–2–0–11–10–5.50–0–*ct* 0

Kennedy, Sir Derrick Edward de Vere
Amateur. *b:* 5.6.1904, Dublin, Ireland. *d:* 27.6.1976, Johnstown, Rathcoole, Co Dublin, Ireland. Tail end right-hand batsman, right-arm fast medium bowler. *Sch* Clifton. *Teams* Dublin University (1924); Ireland (1924).
Career batting
2–3–1–23–15*–11.50–0–*ct* 1
Bowling 89–1–89.00–0–0–1/65

Kennedy, Iain George
Cricketer. *b:* 29.5.1960, Paisley, Renfrewshire, Scotland. Opening right-hand batsman. *Team* Scotland (1983).
Career batting
1–2–0–15–12–7.50–0–*ct* 0

Kennedy, Dr James Henry
Cricketer. *b:* 23.4.1949, Langside, Glasgow, Scotland. Tail end right-hand batsman, left-arm fast medium bowler. *Team* Scotland (1970–71).
Career batting
2–2–1–7–6*–7.00–0–*ct* 0
Bowling 99–1–99.00–0–0–1/17

Kennedy, John Maxwell
Professional. *b:* 15.12.1931, Barton-upon-Irwell, Manchester, Lancashire. Middle order right-hand batsman. *Team* Warwickshire (1960–62, 31 matches).
Career batting
31–55–9–1188–94–25.82–0–*ct* 17
Bowling 1–2–0.50–0–0–2/1
He also played for Staffordshire (1964).

Kenney, Edward Maxwell
(changed name to Kenney-Herbert in July 1875)
Amateur. *b:* 10.12.1845, Bourton-on-Dunsmore, Warwickshire. *d:* 24.1.1916, Ealing, Middlesex. Free hitting lower order right-hand batsman, left-hand fast round-arm bowler. *Sch* Rugby. *Team* Oxford U (1865–68, blue 1866–68).
Career batting
17–25–3–204–64–9.27–0–*ct* 9
Bowling 903–60 + 6–15.05–5–1–8/68
His County cricket was for Warwickshire (pre first-class, 1864–69) and Buckinghamshire (1869). He was also a noted rackets player.

Kennie, George
Professional. *b:* 17.5.1904, Bradford, Yorkshire. Middle order right-hand batsman. *Team* Yorkshire (1927, 1 match).
Career batting
1–2–0–6–6–3.00–0–*ct* 1
He also played for Cumberland. He played soccer for Bradford Park Avenue.

Kenny, Charles John Michael
Amateur. *b:* 19.5.1929, Wallington, Surrey. Tail end right-hand batsman, right-arm fast medium bowler. *Sch* Ampleforth. *Teams* Essex (1950–53, 18 matches); Cambridge U (1952, blue); Ireland (1952–55).
Career batting
40–38–16–75–16–3.40–0–*ct* 17
Bowling 3348–117–28.61–6–1–7/45
His final first-class match was for Free Foresters in 1962.

Kenrick, Jarvis
Amateur. *b:* 13.11.1852, Chichester, Sussex. *d:* 29.1.1949, Blatchington, Sussex. Brother-in-law of F. H. Birley (Lancashire and Surrey). Lower order right-hand batsman, left-arm medium pace bowler, slip field. *Sch* Lancing. *Team* Surrey (1876, 1 match).
Career batting
1–1–0–11–11–11.00–0–*ct* 0
Bowling 44–1–44.00–0–0–1/26

Kent, Humphrey Neild
Amateur. *b:* 2.11.1893, Watford, Hertfordshire. *d:* 19.4.1972, Upper Norwood, London. Lower order batsman, bowler. *Sch* Clifton. *Team* Middlesex (1920, 2 matches).
Career batting
4–5–0–45–36–9.00–0–*ct* 2
Bowling 75–3–25.00–0–0–2/14
His final first-class match was for MCC in 1927. He also played for Hertfordshire (1919).

Kent, Kenneth Gwynne
Amateur. *b:* 10.12.1901, Sparkhill, Birmingham. *d:* 29.12.1974, Fife, Scotland. Lower order right-hand batsman, right-arm fast medium bowler. *Sch* KES, Birmingham. *Team* Warwickshire (1927–31, 9 matches).
Career batting
9–10–1–40–23*–4.44–0–*ct* 2
Bowling 639–10–63.90–0–0–3/91

Kent, Martin Francis
Cricketer. *b:* 23.11.1953, Mossman, Queensland, Australia. Opening or middle order right-hand batsman. *Team* Queensland (1974/5 to 1981/2, 49 matches). *Tours* Australia to Sri Lanka 1980/1, to England 1981; International Wanderers to South Africa 1975/6. *Tests* Australia (1981, 3 matches).
Career batting
64–110–11–3567–171–36.03–7–*ct* 60
Bowling 3–0
Test batting
3–6–0–171–54–28.50–0–*ct* 6
He hit 347 runs, av 23.13, on the 1981 tour and appeared in three of the six Tests. He scored 140 on debut for Queensland v New South Wales at Brisbane in 1974/5.

Kent, Terence
Professional. *b:* 21.10.1939, Battersea, London. Lower order right-hand batsman, slow left-arm bowler. *Team* Essex (1960–62, 10 matches).
Career batting
10–10–4–74–23*–12.33–0–*ct* 5
Bowling 561–15–37.40–0–0–4/54
He played soccer for Southend United.

Kentfield, Richard William
Amateur. *b:* 25.5.1862, Bognor, Sussex. *d:* On or after 16.10.1904, his body being found in the River Ouse, Bedford. Lower order batsman, left-arm medium pace bowler. *Team* Lancashire (1888, 2 matches); Sussex (1894–96, 2 matches).
Career batting
4–8–0–49–18–6.12–0–*ct* 0
Bowling 232–10–23.20–1–0–6/45

Kentish, Esmond Seymour Maurice
Amateur. *b:* 21.11.1916, Cornwall Mountain, Westmoreland, Jamaica. Tail end right-hand batsman, right-arm fast medium bowler. *Teams* Jamaica (1947/8 to 1956/7); Oxford U (1956, blue). *Tests* West Indies (1947/8 to 1953/4, 2 matches).
Career batting
27–29–21–109–15*–13.62–0–*ct* 6
Bowling 2084–78–26.71–4–0–5/36
Test batting
2–2–1–1–1*–1.00–0–*ct* 1
Bowling 178–8–22.25–1–0–5/49
He acted as manager of the West Indies team in England in 1973. He is the oldest cricketer to be awarded his blue.

Kenward, Charles
Amateur. *b:* 7.9.1877, Rye, Sussex. *d:* 14.11.1948, Watlands, Rye, Sussex. Brother of Richard (Derbyshire and Sussex). Middle order batsman. *Sch* Eastbourne. *Team* Gentlemen of England (1905).
Career batting
1–2–0–47–43–23.50–0–*ct* 2

Kenward, Richard
Amateur. *b:* 23.5.1875, Hastings, Sussex. *d:* 24.12.1957, Croydon, Surrey. Brother of Charles (Gentlemen of England). Middle order right-hand batsman. *Sch* Hurstpierpoint. *Teams* Derbyshire (1899, 11 matches): Sussex (1902, 4 matches); London County (1902).
Career batting
17–27–0–387–56–14.33–0–*ct* 4
His final first-class match was for Gentlemen of England in 1905.

Kenyon, Donald, MBE
Professional. *b:* 15.5.1924, Wordsley, Staffordshire. Sound opening right-hand batsman, right-arm medium pace bowler, excellent field. *Team* Worcestershire (1946–67, 589 matches). *Tours* MCC to India, Pakistan and Ceylon 1951/52; Worcestershire World Tour (Rhodesia first-class) 1964/5, to Jamaica 1965/6. *Tests* England (1951/2 to 1955, 8 matches).
Career batting
643–1159–59–37002–259–33.63–74–*ct* 327
Bowling 187–1–187.00–0–0–1/8
Test batting
8–15–0–192–87–12.80–0–*ct* 5
He hit 1,000 runs in a season 19 times, going on to 2,000 seven times (best 2,636, av 51.68, in 1954). His double centuries were all for Worcestershire, the highest being 259 v Yorkshire at Kidderminster in 1956. He captained Worcestershire 1959–67 and was a Test selector 1965–72. He was President of Worcestershire 1986–89.

Kenyon, Myles Noel
Amateur. *b:* 25.12.1886, Walshaw Hall, Bury, Lancashire. *d:* 21.11.1960, Birdham, Sussex. His daughter married the brother of E. W. Dawson (Leicestershire). Middle/lower order right-hand batsman. *Sch* Eton. *Team* Lancashire (1919–25, 91 matches).
Career batting
91–127–30–1435–61*–14.79–0–*ct* 20
He captained Lancashire 1919 to 1922 and was President of the County Club 1936 and 1937.

Kenyon-Slaney, Rt Hon William Slaney
Amateur. *b:* 24.8.1847, Rajkot, India. *d:* 24.4.1908, Hatton Grange, Shifnal, Shropshire. Middle order right-hand batsman, good cover point. *Sch* Eton. *Team* MCC (1869–80).
Career batting
11–17–3–145–34–10.35–0–*ct* 2
He did not appear in any first-class matches whilst at Oxford U. His County cricket was for Shropshire (1866–78) and he served on the MCC Committee for eight years. He played soccer for England. At the time of his death he was Unionist MP for the Newport Division of Shropshire, having represented that constituency since 1886.

Ker, Andrew Burgher Michael
Cricketer. *b:* 16.10.1954, Kelso, Roxburghshire, Scotland. Brother of J. E. (Scotland). Middle order right-hand batsman. *Team* Scotland (1981–84).
Career batting
4–7–1–178–65–29.66–0–*ct* 4
He played rugby for Scotland.

Ker, John Edward
Cricketer. *b:* 17.10.1952, Kelso, Roxburghshire, Scotland. Brother of A. B. M. (Scotland). Lower order right-hand batsman, right-arm medium pace bowler. *Team* Scotland (1977–88).
Career batting
12–16–7–189–50–21.00–0–*ct* 3
Bowling 482–19–25.36–0–0–4/54

Kermode, Alexander
Professional. *b:* 15.5.1876, Sydney, New South Wales, Australia. *d:* 17.7.1934, Balmain, Sydney, New South Wales, Australia. Lower order right-hand batsman, right-arm fast medium bowler. *Teams* New South Wales (1901/2, 2 matches); Lancashire (1902–08, 76 matches); London County (1903).
Career batting
80–109–24–680–64*–8.00–0–*ct* 33
Bowling 7825–340–23.01–21–3–7/44
He took 100 wickets in a season once: 113, av 21.60, in 1905. He came to England at the invitation of A. C. MacLaren specifically to qualify for Lancashire – a move that was severely criticised at the time by the traditionalists. He also played for Cheshire (1902).

Kerr, James Reid
Amateur. *b:* 4.12.1883, Greenock, Renfrew, Scotland. *d:* 19.8.1963, Greenock, Renfrew, Scotland. Middle order right-hand batsman. *Team* Scotland (1921).
Career batting
1–2–0–15–14–7.50–0–*ct* 2
He played rugby for Scotland and toured South Africa in 1910 with the British Lions.

Kerr, John
Amateur. *b:* 8.4.1885, Greenock, Renfrew, Scotland. *d:* 27.12.1972, Greenock, Renfrew, Scotland. Opening right-hand batsman, right-arm slow bowler, brilliant slip field. *Team* Scotland (1908–33).
Career batting
32–59–6–1975–178*–37.26–4–*ct* 31
Bowling 252–7–36.00–0–0–2/48

Regarded as one of Scotland's greatest cricketers, he hit 147 against the 1921 Australians at Edinburgh (not first-class).

Kerr, John Lambert
Amateur. *b:* 28.12.1910, Dannevirke, Hawkes Bay, New Zealand. Opening or middle order right-hand batsman, right-arm medium pace bowler, good field. *Team* Canterbury (1929/30 to 1939/40). *Tours* New Zealand to England 1931, 1937, to Australia 1937/8. *Tests* New Zealand (1931–37, 7 matches).
Career batting
89–157–7–4829–196–32.19–8–*ct* 28
Bowling 46–2–23.00–0–0–2/32
Test batting
7–12–1–212–59–19.27–0–*ct* 4
After a modest tour in 1931, he was one of the leading batsmen on the 1937 visit, scoring 1,205 runs, av 31.71. His final first-class match was for New Zealand Army XI in 1942/3.

Kerr, Kevin John
Cricketer. *b:* 11.9.1961, Airdrie, Lanarkshire, Scotland. Lower order right-hand batsman, off break bowler. *Teams* Transvaal (1978/9 to 1989/90); Warwickshire (1986, 14 matches).
Career batting
83–89–25–1040–74–16.25–0–*ct* 64
Bowling 5674–211–26.89–8–1–6/37

Kerrigan, Michael
Amateur. *b:* 8.11.1931, Perth, Scotland. Lower order left-hand batsman, slow left-arm bowler. *Team* Scotland (1954–61).
Career batting
12–18–4–84–18*–6.00–0–*ct* 4
Bowling 892–39–22.87–2–1–7/84

Kersey, Graham James
Cricketer. *b:* 19.5.1971, Plumstead, London. Middle order right-hand batsman, wicket-keeper. *Team* Kent (1991–92, 4 matches).
Career batting
4–3–2–69–27*–69.00–0–*ct* 14–*st* 1

Kershaw, John Edward
Amateur. *b:* 12.1.1854, Heywood, Lancashire. *d:* 29.11.1903, Burnley, Lancashire, of consumption. Useful middle order right-hand batsman, wicket-keeper. *Team* Lancashire (1877–85, 33 matches).
Career batting
35–57–3–582–66–10.77–0–*ct* 15–*st* 1

Kerslake, Roy Cosmo
Amateur. *b:* 26.12.1942, Paignton, Devon. Lower order right-hand batsman, off break bowler, excellent field. *Sch* Kingswood. *Teams* Cambridge U (1962–64, blue 1963–64): Somerset (1962–68, 52 matches). *Tour* MCC to South America 1964/5 (not first-class).
Career batting
85–132–14–1939–80–16.43–0–*ct* 64
Bowling 2617–114–22.95–4–0–6/77
His final first-class match was for Minor Counties in 1976. He captained Somerset in 1968. He was Somerset Chairman in 1979.

Kersley, Tom
Professional. *b:* 9.2.1879, Surbiton, Surrey. *d:* 4.12.1927, Folkestone, Kent. Lower order batsman, opening bowler. *Team* Surrey (1899, 3 matches).
Career batting
3–4–1–23–15*–7.66–0–*ct* 1
Bowling 145–7–20.71–0–0–3/36

Kesteven, John
Professional. *b:* 8.7.1849, Sutton-in-Ashfield, Nottinghamshire. Middle order right-hand batsman, right-hand medium pace round-arm bowler. *Team* Nottinghamshire (1876, 3 matches).
Career batting
3–4–0–24–12–6.00–0–*ct* 1

Kettle, Michael Keith
Cricketer. *b:* 18.3.1944, Stamford, Lincolnshire. Lower order right-hand batsman, left-arm medium pace bowler. *Team* Northamptonshire (1963–70, 88 matches).
Career batting
88–105–20–1117–88–13.14–0–*ct* 63
Bowling 4800–179–26.81–5–0–6/67
He played for Rhodesia in limited overs cricket in 1974/5.

Kettlewell, Henry Wildman
Amateur. *b:* 20.7.1876, Harptree Court, East Harptree, Bath, Somerset. *d:* 28.4.1963, Harptree Court, East Harptree, Bath, Somerset. Middle order right-hand batsman, right-arm fast bowler. *Sch* Eton. *Team* Somerset (1899, 1 match).
Career batting
1–2–1–7–6*–7.00–0–*ct* 0
Bowling 30–0

Kevan, Joseph Henry
Amateur. *b:* 13.9.1855, Bolton, Lancashire. *d:* 9.12.1891, Queens Park, Bolton, Lancashire. Lower order batsman. *Team* Lancashire (1875, 2 matches).
Career batting
2–4–0–12–12–3.00–0–*ct* 0

Kewley, Edward
Amateur. *b:* 20.6.1852, Eton, Buckinghamshire. *d:* 17.4.1940, Winchester, Hampshire. Middle order right-hand batsman. *Sch* Marlborough. *Team* Lancashire (1875, 1 match).
Career batting
1–2–0–3–3–1.50–0–*ct* 1
He played rugby for England.

Key, Sir Kingsmill James
Amateur. *b:* 11.10.1864, Streatham, London. *d:* 9.8.1932, Wittersham, Kent, from blood poisoning

after an insect bite. Cousin of L. H. Gay (Hampshire and Somerset). Attacking middle order right-hand batsman, off break bowler. *Sch* Clifton. *Teams* Surrey (1882–1904, 288 matches); Oxford U (1884–87, blue all four years). *Tours* Sanders to North America 1886; Hawke to North America 1891; Oxford Univ Authentics to India 1902/3.
Career batting
368–567–71–13008–281–26.22–13–*ct* 113
Bowling 337–12–28.08–0–0–2/32

He hit 1,000 runs in a season three times (best 1,684, av 43.17, in 1887). His only double century was 281 for Oxford U v Middlesex at Chiswick Park in 1887. He led Surrey from 1894 to 1899 – 'a man of most original views, an always philosophic cricketer and an imperturbable captain'. His final first-class match was in 1909 for Leveson-Gower's XI. A noted rugby footballer, he gained his blue at Oxford.

Key, Laurence Henry
Amateur. *b:* 5.5.1895, Lincoln. *d:* 18.4.1971, Taunton, Somerset. Lower order left-hand batsman, slow left-arm bowler. *Sch* Taunton. *Team* Somerset (1919–22, 8 matches).
Career batting
8–12–2–80–30–8.00–0–*ct* 5
Bowling 58–2–29.00–0–0–2/50

Key, Richard Leigh Troward
Amateur. *b:* 13.1.1844, Camden Town, London. *d:* 23.7.1875, Moorcroft, Hillingdon, Middlesex. Middle order batsman. *Team* MCC (1866).
Career batting
1–2–0–5–5–2.50–0–*ct* 0

Khalid Hassan
Amateur. *b:* 14.7.1937, Peshawar, India. Lower order right-hand batsman, leg break and googly bowler. *Teams* Punjab (1953/4); Lahore (1958/9). *Tour* Pakistan to England 1954. *Test* Pakistan (1954, 1 match).
Career batting
17–16–6–113–30–11.30–0–*ct* 2
Bowling 1071–28–38.25–0–0–3/27
Test batting
1–2–1–17–10–17.00–0–*ct* 0
Bowling 116–2–58.00–0–0–2/116

He was, according to his published birth date, only 16 years and 352 days old when making his Test debut in the second Test of 1954; he achieved however only moderate results on the 1954 tour.

Khalid Ibadulla
(*see under* Ibadulla, K.)

Khalid Wazir Ali
Amateur. *b:* 27.4.1936, Jullundur, India. Son of S. Wazir Ali (India), nephew of S. Nazir Ali (India). Middle order right-hand batsman, right-arm fast medium bowler. *Teams* Rest (1952/3); Hasan Mahmood's XI (1953/4). *Tour* Pakistan to England 1954. *Tests* Pakistan (1954, 2 matches).
Career batting
18–23–5–271–53–15.05–0–*ct* 12
Bowling 746–14–53.28–0–0–3/82
Test batting
2–3–1–14–9*–7.00–0–*ct* 0

He had very little success on his single tour to England, though appearing in two Tests. After the 1954 tour he settled in England.

Khan Mohammad
Professional. *b:* 1.1.1928, Lahore, India. Lower order right-hand batsman, right-arm fast medium bowler, good short leg. *Teams* Northern India (1946/7); Punjab Univ (1947/8 to 1948/9); Somerset (1951, 1 match); Bahawalpur (1953/4); Karachi (1956/7); Lahore (1960/1). *Tours* Pakistan to Ceylon 1948/9, to India 1952/3, 1954/5, to England 1954, to West Indies 1957/8. *Tests* Pakistan (1952/3 to 1957/8, 13 matches).
Career batting
53–64–18–524–93–11.39–0–*ct* 20
Bowling 4939–212–23.29–16–1–7/56
Test batting
13–17–7–100–26*–10.00–0–*ct* 4
Bowling 1292–54–23.92–4–0–6/21

Playing in the Lancashire League, he was drafted into the 1954 Pakistan touring team to England for five first-class matches, including two Tests. He played for Commonwealth teams in England 1950, 1951, 1955 and 1957.

Khan, Asad Jahangir
Cricketer. *b:* 25.12.1945, Campbellpur, India. Brother of Majid Jahangir (Pakistan), son of M. Jahangir Khan (India), cousin of Javed Burki (Pakistan), Imran Khan (Pakistan), Humayun Zaman (Lahore) and Javed Zaman (Lahore), nephew of M. Baqa Jilani (India). Middle order right-hand batsman, off break bowler. *Teams* Oxford U (1967–69, blue 1968–69); Lahore (1964/5 to 1970/1); Punjab Univ (1965/6).
Career batting
40–64–5–1154–92–19.55–0–*ct* 43
Bowling 2030–53–38.30–2–0–7/84

Khan, M. J. (*see under* Majid J. Khan)

Khanna, Bharat Chand
Amateur. *b:* 22.6.1914, India. Middle order right-hand batsman, right-arm medium fast bowler. *Teams* Hyderabad (1932/3 to 1952/3); Madras (1933/4); Cambridge U (1937, blue).
Career batting
39–70–13–1398–83*–24.52–0–*ct* 10
Bowling 2661–100–26.61–3–0–5/61

Khanna, Surinder Chamanlal
Cricketer. *b:* 3.6.1956, Delhi, India. Opening right-hand batsman, wicket-keeper. *Team* Delhi (1976/7 to 1987/8). *Tours* India to England 1979, to Sharjah (not

first-class) 1983/4, to Pakistan 1984/5 (not first-class).
Career batting
106–141–18–5337–220*–43.39–17–*ct* 181–*st* 52
Bowling 51–0
The reserve wicket-keeper on the 1979 tour to England, he was not required for the Tests. He played for India in one-day internationals. His highest score was 220* for Delhi v Himachal Pradesh at Delhi in 1987/8.

Kibble, George Herbert
Professional. *b:* 9.10.1865, Greenwich, London. *d:* 4.1.1923, Camberwell, London. Middle order batsman. *Team* Kent (1889, 1 match).
Career batting
1–2–0–9–6–4.50–0–*ct* 0

Kidd, Eric Leslie
Amateur. *b:* 18.10.1889, Westminster, London. *d:* 2.7.1984, Dun Laoghaire, Co Dublin, Ireland. Son of P. M. (Kent). Attractive middle order right-hand batsman, leg break bowler, excellent field. *Sch* Wellington. *Teams* Cambridge U (1910–13, blue all four years); Middlesex (1910–28, 77 matches); Ireland (1921–28).
Career batting
147–218–13–5113–167–24.94–6–*ct* 129
Bowling 4581–186–24.62–8–1–8/49
His final first-class match was for Free Foresters in 1930. His best season was 1913 when he hit 1,041 runs, av 49.57. He captained Cambridge in 1912.

Kidd, Dr Percy Marmaduke
Amateur. *b:* 13.2.1851, Blackheath, London. *d:* 21.1.1942, Chalfont St Giles, Buckinghamshire. Father of E. L. (Middlesex). Middle order right-hand batsman, right-arm medium pace bowler. *Sch* Uppingham *Team* Kent (1874, 1 match).
Career batting
1–2–0–0–0–0.00–0–*ct* 0
Bowling 36–0

Kidman, Edward Arnold
Amateur. *b:* 9.10.1875, Edmonton, Middlesex. *d:* 30.4.1917, Calcutta, India. Opening/middle order batsman. *Sch* Liverpool College. *Team* Cambridge U (1897).
Career batting
1–2–0–25–23–12.50–0–*ct* 0

Kilbee, John Richard
Cricketer. *b:* 24.7.1947, Victoria, Hong Kong. Middle order right-hand batsman, right-arm medium pace bowler. *Sch* King's Canterbury. *Team* Oxford U (1968–69).
Career batting
8–12–4–70–18*–8.75–0–*ct* 4
Bowling 270–8–33.75–0–0–4/96

Kilborn, Michael John
Cricketer. *b:* 20.9.1962, Gunnedah, New South Wales, Australia. Middle order right-hand batsman, right-arm medium pace bowler. *Team* Oxford U (1986–90, blue 1986–88).
Career batting
31–49–4–1275–95–28.33–0–*ct* 23
Bowling 312–6–52.00–0–0–3/37
He captained Oxford in 1988.

Kilburn, Sam
Professional. *b:* 16.10.1868, Dalton, Huddersfield, Yorkshire. *d:* 25.9.1940, Crossland Moor, Huddersfield, Yorkshire. Middle order right-hand batsman. *Team* Yorkshire (1896, 1 match).
Career batting
1–1–0–8–8–8.00–0–*ct* 0

Killick, Anthony
Professional. *b:* 1829. *d:* 8.12.1881, Uckfield, Sussex. Brother of Harry (Sussex), uncle of E. H. (Sussex). Lower order batsman. *Team* Sussex (1866, 1 match).
Career batting
1–1–0–0–0–0.00–0–*ct* 0

Killick, Rev Edgar Thomas
Amateur. *b:* 9.5.1907, Fulham, London. *d:* 18.5.1953, Northampton, whilst playing in a diocesan cricket match. Stylish opening right-hand batsman, good deep field. *Sch* St Paul's. *Teams* Middlesex (1926–39, 47 matches); Cambridge U (1927–30, blue 1928, 1929 and 1930). *Tests* England (1929, 2 matches).
Career batting
92–153–11–5730–206–40.35–15–*ct* 50
Bowling 229–3–76.33–0–0–1/20
Test batting
2–4–0–81–31–20.25–0–*ct* 2
He hit 1,000 runs in a season twice (best 1,384, av 44.64, in 1929). He scored two double centuries for Cambridge, but his highest score was his only double century for Middlesex – 206 v Warwickshire at Lord's in 1931, curiously the only County Championship innings he played that season. His final first-class match was for Free Foresters in 1946. Owing to his calling he played little first-class cricket after leaving Cambridge. He was also a good rugby footballer.

Killick, Ernest Harry
Professional. *b:* 17.1.1875, Horsham, Sussex. *d:* 29.9.1948, Hove, Sussex. Nephew of Anthony (Sussex) and Harry (Sussex). Free scoring middle order left-hand batsman, right-arm medium or slow bowler. *Team* Sussex (1893–1913, 450 matches).
Career batting
461–770–53–18768–200–26.17–22–*ct* 188
Bowling 19903–729–27.30–25–1–7/10
He hit 1,000 runs in a season 11 times (best 1,767, av 36.06, in 1906) and took 100 wickets once – 108, av 21.93, in 1905 – performing the 'double' that sea-

son. He had the misfortune to be hit for 34 off one over (including two no balls) when playing for Sussex v Nottinghamshire at Hove in 1911; the batsman was E. B. Alletson. His highest score was 200 for Sussex v Yorkshire at Hove in 1901. After retiring from County cricket he was Sussex scorer 1919–39.

Killick, Harry
Professional. *b:* 13.7.1837, Crabtree, Horsham, Sussex. *d:* 22.11.1877, Brighton, Sussex. He dropped down dead having broken a blood vessel. Brother of Anthony (Sussex), uncle of E. H. (Sussex). Opening or middle order left-hand batsman, right-hand medium pace round-arm bowler, wicket-keeper. *Team* Sussex (1866–75, 40 matches).
Career batting
44–80–5–1097–78–14.62–0–*ct* 25
Bowling 219–6–36.50–0–0–3/37

Killick, William
Professional. *b:* 14.5.1855, Reigate, Surrey. *d:* 2.4.1938, Horley, Surrey. Middle order right-hand batsman, good field. *Team* Surrey (1876, 1 match).
Career batting
1–2–0–3–3–1.50–0–*ct* 0

Kilner, Norman
Professional. *b:* 21.7.1895, Low Valley, Wombwell, Yorkshire. *d:* 28.4.1979, Alum Rock, Birmingham. Brother of Roy (Yorkshire), nephew of W. A. I. Washington (Yorkshire). Sound opening/middle order right-hand batsman, right-arm medium pace bowler. *Teams* Yorkshire (1919–23, 69 matches); Warwickshire (1924–37, 330 matches).
Career batting
403–619–42–17522–228–30.36–25–*ct* 184
Bowling 166–2–83.00–0–0–1/19

He hit 1,000 runs in a season 12 times, going on to 2,000 once – 2,159, av 44.97, in 1933. His only double century was 228 for Warwickshire v Worcestershire at Worcester in 1935. After retiring he became coach and then groundsman at Edgbaston. He was a first-class umpire (1938–47).

Kilner, Roy
Professional. *b:* 17.10.1890, Low Valley, Wombwell, Yorkshire. *d:* 5.4.1928, Kendray, Barnsley, Yorkshire, of enteric fever. Brother of Norman (Yorkshire and Warwickshire), nephew of W. A. I. Washington (Yorkshire). Aggressive middle order left-hand batsman, slow left-arm bowler, good field. *Teams* Yorkshire (1911–27, 365 matches); Europeans (1922/3). *Tours* MCC to Australia 1924/5, to West Indies 1925/6. *Tests* England (1924–26, 9 matches).
Career batting
416–546–56–14707–206*–30.01–18–*ct* 266
Bowling 18516–1003–18.46–48–10–8/26
Test batting
9–8–1–233–74–33.28–0–*ct* 6
Bowling 734–24–30.58–0–0–4/51

He hit 1,000 runs in a season 10 times (best 1,586, av 34.47, in 1913). His only double century was 206* for Yorkshire v Derbyshire at Bramall Lane in 1920. He took 100 wickets in a season five times (best 158, av 12.91, in 1923) and achieved the 'double' four times – 1922, 1923, 1925 and 1926.

Kimbell, Rev Ralph Raymond
Amateur. *b:* 12.6.1884, Boughton, Brixworth, Northamptonshire. *d:* 4.8.1964, Ledbury, Herefordshire. Lower order batsman, bowler. *Team* Northamptonshire (1908, 1 match).
Career batting
1–2–0–4–4–2.00–0–*ct* 0
Bowling 45–2–22.50–0–0–2/45

He also played for Oxfordshire (1925).

Kimber, Simon Julian Spencer
Cricketer. *b:* 6.10.1963, Ormskirk, Lancashire. Lower order right-hand batsman, right-arm medium fast bowler. *Teams* Worcestershire (1985, 2 matches); Natal (1986/7 to 1991/2); Sussex (1987–89, 14 matches).
Career batting
35–48–13–581–54–16.60–0–*ct* 14
Bowling 2609–86–30.33–1–0–5/63

Kimish, Arthur Edwards
Amateur. *b:* 5.7.1917, Southampton, Hampshire. Lower order right-hand batsman, wicket-keeper. *Team* Hampshire (1946, 3 matches).
Career batting
3–4–1–18–12*–6.00–0–*ct* 3–*st* 3

Kimmins, Simon Edward Anthony
Amateur. *b:* 26.5.1930, Belgravia, London. Middle order right-hand batsman, right-arm medium pace bowler, good coverpoint. *Sch* Charterhouse. *Teams* Kent (1950–51, 12 matches).
Career batting
16–29–3–563–81–21.65–0–*ct* 13
Bowling 996–24–41.50–1–0–5/42

His final first-class match was for Free Foresters in 1959. He is the son of Anthony Kimmins, the film director.

Kimpton, Roger Charles MacDonald
Amateur. *b:* 21.9.1916, Toorak, Melbourne, Victoria, Australia. Brother of S. M. (Oxford U). Middle order right-hand batsman, wicket-keeper. *Teams* Oxford U (1935–38, blue 1935, 1937 and 1938); Worcestershire (1937–49, 14 matches). *Tours* Oxford and Cambridge U to Jamaica 1938/9; Swanton to West Indies 1955/6.
Career batting
62–109–8–3562–160–35.26–8–*ct* 57–*st* 14
Bowling 1336–28–47.71–0–0–4/42

He hit 1,568 runs, av 34.84, in 1937, the only season he exceeded 1,000 runs.

Kimpton, Stephen MacDonald
Amateur. *b:* 5.3.1914, Toorak, Melbourne, Victoria, Australia. Brother of R. C. M. (Worcestershire). Middle order left-hand batsman, slow right-arm bowler. *Team* Oxford U (1935).
Career batting
4–7–1–112–31–18.66–0–*ct* 1
Bowling 384–9–42.66–0–0–4/65

Kindermann, Frederick Louis
Amateur. *b:* 1.5.1840, Liverpool, Lancashire. *d:* 5.7.1918, Aberfeldy, Perthshire, Scotland. Middle order batsman. *Team* Gentlemen of North (1867).
Career batting
1–2–0–10–9–5.00–0–*ct* 1

King, Anthony Mountain
Professional. *b:* 8.10.1932, Laughton-en-le-Morthern, Sheffield, Yorkshire. Middle order right-hand batsman. *Sch* Bradford GS. *Team* Yorkshire (1955, 1 match).
Career batting
1–1–0–12–12–12.00–0–*ct* 0
He played as stand-off half for Bradford RUFC.

King, Benjamin Philip
Professional. *b:* 22.4.1915, Leeds, Yorkshire. *d:* 31.3.1970, Bradford, Yorkshire. Aggressive middle order right-hand batsman, wicket-keeper. *Teams* Worcestershire (1935–39, 80 matches); Lancashire (1946–47, 37 matches).
Career batting
117–196–9–4124–145–22.05–6–*ct* 53–*st* 6
Bowling 4–0
He hit 1,000 runs in a season twice (best 1,177, av 22.63, in 1938). In 1946 he offered to play for Worcester without payment until he had reached 1,000 runs and to be paid £1 per run thereafter. The County turned down the offer and he joined Lancashire. He later became a well-known sporting journalist.

King, Collis Llewellyn
Cricketer. *b:* 11.6.1951, Fairview, Christ Church, Barbados. Hard hitting middle order right-hand batsman, right-arm medium pace bowler. *Teams* Barbados (1972/3 to 1981/2); Glamorgan (1977, 16 matches); Worcestershire (1983, 2 matches); Natal (1984/5 to 1986/7). *Tours* West Indies to England 1976, 1979 (World Cup), 1980, to Australia and New Zealand 1979/80; International XI to Pakistan 1981/2; West Indian XI to South Africa 1982/3, 1983/4. *Tests* West Indies (1976 to 1980/1, 9 matches).
Career batting
125–202–25–6770–163–38.24–14–*ct* 98
Bowling 4380–128–34.21–1–0–5/91
Test batting
9–16–3–418–100*–32.15–1–*ct* 5
Bowling 282–3–94.00–0–0–1/30
On the 1976 tour he hit 1,320 runs, av 55.00, and played in three of the five Tests; in 1980 he was quite out of form and appeared in only one Test. His last first-class match in England was for D. B. Close's XI in 1986.

King, Edmund Hugh
Amateur. *b:* 26.3.1906, Edgbaston, Birmingham *d:* 25.11.1981, Cropthorne, Worcestershire. He was killed in a road accident. Middle order right-hand batsman, off break bowler. *Sch* Ampleforth. *Team* Warwickshire (1928–32, 7 matches).
Career batting
7–10–0–84–24–8.40–0–*ct* 3
Bowling 15–0
He was Hon Treasurer of Warwickshire 1959 to 1962 and Chairman 1962 to 1972, and a key figure in the formation of the TCCB, being Chairman of the TCCB Finance sub-committee from 1968 to 1980.

King, Edmund Poole
Amateur. *b:* 21.1.1907, Avondale, Clifton, Bristol. *d:* 11.9.1990, Wonham, Bampton, Devon. Middle order right-hand batsman. *Sch* Winchester *Team* Gloucestershire (1927, 3 matches).
Career batting
3–4–0–14–6–3.50–0–*ct* 1

King, Edwin
Professional. *b:* 1884. *d:* 7.7.1952, Braunstone, Leicester. Lower order right-hand batsman, wicket-keeper. *Team* Leicestershire (1925, 2 matches).
Career batting
2–4–1–33–31*–11.00–0–*ct* 5–*st* 1
He also played soccer for Leicester City.

King, Frank
Amateur. *b:* 6.4.1911, Lewisham, London. Lower order right-hand batsman, right-arm fast medium bowler. *Sch* Dulwich. *Team* Cambridge U (1934–35, blue 1934).
Career batting
10–15–5–68–16*–6.80–0–*ct* 7
Bowling 615–22–27.95–2–0–6/64
His County cricket was for Dorset (1937–54).

King, Frederick
Amateur. *b:* 12.11.1850, Harbledown, Kent. *d:* 16.6.1893, Hammersmith, London. Opening batsman. *Team* Kent (1871, 1 match).
Career batting
1–2–0–11–6–5.50–0–*ct* 0
Bowling 15–0

King, George Lionel
Amateur. *b:* 6.4.1857, Brighton, Sussex. *d:* 29.6.1944, Kemp Town, Brighton, Sussex. Son of G. W. (Sussex), nephew of H. P. Tamplin (Sussex 1827). Middle order right-hand batsman, wicket-keeper. *Sch* Rugby. *Team* Sussex (1880–81, 6 matches).

King, George William

Career batting
6–10–0–112–29–11.20–0–*ct* 2

He appeared in the Freshmen's and Seniors' matches at Cambridge, but no first-class matches. He also played for Devon.

King, George William
Amateur. *b:* 15.6.1822, Rottingdean, Sussex. *d:* 22.12.1881, Brighton, Sussex. Father of G. L. (Sussex), brother-in-law of H. P. Tamplin (Sussex 1827). Defensive middle order left-hand batsman, good longstop. *Sch* Eton. *Teams* Sussex (1842–64, 18 matches); Cambridge U (1843).
Career batting
19–31–5–166–25–6.38–0–*ct* 4

He was Secretary of Sussex CCC 1848–56 and 1870–80.

King, Harry
Amateur. *b:* 6.11.1881, Leicester. *d:* 30.6.1947, South Knighton, Leicester. Middle order right-hand batsman, right-arm medium pace bowler. *Team* Leicestershire (1912–20, 3 matches).
Career batting
3–6–1–29–11–5.80–0–*ct* 0
Bowling 64–0

King, Sir Henry Clark
Amateur. *b:* 20.6.1857, Durham. *d:* 23.7.1920, Hove, Sussex. Son of C. W. (Oxford U 1852). Steady middle order right-hand batsman, right-arm medium pace bowler. *Sch* Durham and Marlborough. *Team* MCC (1895).
Career batting
1–1–0–0–0–0.00–0–*ct* 0

He lived in India for some years and appeared for Madras (not first-class). His County cricket was for Warwickshire (pre first-class, 1877). A noted rugby footballer, he represented Midland Counties.

King, Horace David
Amateur. *b:* 10.2.1915, Brentford, Middlesex. *d:* 7.3.1974, Worthing, Sussex. Lower order right-hand batsman, wicket-keeper. *Sch* Taunton. *Teams* Europeans (1934/5); Middlesex (1936–46, 7 matches); Services (1943/4).
Career batting
9–13–4–104–26–11.55–0–*ct* 7–*st* 8

King, Ian Metcalfe
Professional. *b:* 10.11.1931, Leeds, Yorkshire. Lower order left-hand batsman, slow left-arm bowler. *Teams* Warwickshire (1952–55, 53 matches); Essex (1957, 28 matches).
Career batting
81–96–39–476–33–8.35–0–*ct* 60
Bowling 3706–129–28.72–1–0–5/59

King, J.
Professional. Lower order left-hand batsman, left-arm fast bowler. *Teams* Kent (1881, 2 matches); Hampshire (1882, 1 match).
Career batting
3–5–1–39–16*–9.75–0–*ct* 3
Bowling 223–10–22.30–0–0–4/64

King, James
Professional. *b:* 3.5.1869, Lutterworth, Leicestershire. *d:* 8.3.1948, The Park, Wisbech, Cambridgeshire. Brother of J. H. (Leicestershire), father of J. W. (Leicestershire and Worcestershire). Sound middle order right-hand batsman, useful change bowler. *Team* Leicestershire (1899–1905, 7 matches).
Career batting
7–10–2–83–24*–10.37–0–*ct* 2
Bowling 146–2–73.00–0–0–2/71

He was also a good local rugby footballer.

King, James Morris Roy
Cricketer. *b:* 15.9.1942, Bristol. Middle order right-hand batsman, right-arm medium pace or leg break bowler. *Team* Gloucestershire (1966, 3 matches).
Career batting
3–5–0–47–28–9.40–0–*ct* 2

King, John
Professional. *b:* 2.8.1845, Cambridge. Middle order batsman. *Teams* Cambridgeshire (1861–64, 4 matches); Cambridge Town Club (1861).
Career batting
4–8–1–26–10*–3.71–0–*ct* 1

He made his first-class debut aged 15 years 298 days.

King, John Barton
Amateur. *b:* 19.10.1873, Philadelphia, USA. *d:* 17.10.1965, Philadelphia, USA. Middle order right-hand batsman, right-arm fast bowler. *Team* Philadelphia (1893–1912). *Tours* Philadelphia to England 1897, 1903, 1908.
Career batting
65–114–10–2134–113*–20.51–1–*ct* 67
Bowling 6502–415–15.66–38–11–10/53

Regarded as the greatest bowler produced by Philadelphia, he proved his ability in 1908 when he took 87 wickets, av 11.01, in first-class matches and was the leading bowler in England that year. His best bowling was 10/53 for Philadelphia v Ireland at Haverford in 1909.

King, John Herbert
Professional. *b:* 16.4.1871, Lutterworth, Leicestershire. *d:* 18.11.1946, Denbigh. Brother of James (Leicestershire), uncle of J. W. (Leicestershire and Worcestershire). Excellent middle order left-hand batsman, left-arm medium pace bowler, good slip field. *Team* Leicestershire (1895–1925, 502 matches). *Test* England (1909, 1 match).
Career batting
552–988–69–25122–227*–27.33–34–*ct* 340
Bowling 30312–1204–25.17–69–11–8/17

Test batting
1–2–0–64–60–32.00–0–*ct* 0
Bowling 99–1–99.00–0–0–1/99

He hit 1,000 runs in a season 14 times (best 1,788, av 38.04, in 1904) and took 100 wickets in a season twice (best 130, av 17.63, in 1912). He completed the 'double' in 1912. Both his double centuries were for Leicestershire, the highest being 227* v Worcestershire at Coalville in 1914 and the other being remarkable for the fact that it was scored in 1923, when King was aged 52 (205 v Hampshire at Leicester). He was a first-class umpire (1926–32).

King, John William
Professional. *b:* 21.1.1908, Leicester. *d:* 25.3.1953, Narborough, Leicestershire. Son of James (Leicestershire), nephew of J. H. (Leicestershire). Sound right-hand batsman. *Teams* Worcestershire (1927–28, 40 matches); Leicestershire (1929, 8 matches).
Career batting
48–88–14–1169–91–15.79–0–*ct* 13

King, Kenneth Charles William
Amateur, turned professional midway through 1936 season. *b:* 4.12.1915, Beddington, Surrey. Lower order left-hand batsman, slow left-arm bowler. *Sch* KCS Wimbledon. *Team* Surrey (1936–38, 31 matches).
Career batting
32–40–8–361–64–11.28–0–*ct* 18
Bowling 1201–34–35.32–0–0–4/38

His final first-class match was for D. R. Jardine's XI in 1955.

King, Lester Anthony
Amateur. *b:* 27.2.1939, St Catherine Parish, Jamaica. Lower order right-hand batsman, right-arm fast bowler, good deep field. *Teams* Jamaica (1961/2 to 1967/8); Bengal (1962/3). *Tours* West Indies to England 1963, to India and Ceylon 1966/7, to Australia and New Zealand 1968/9; West Indian XI to England 1964. *Tests* West Indies (1961/2 to 1967/8, 2 matches).
Career batting
62–87–19–1404–89–20.64–0–*ct* 38
Bowling 4463–142–31.42–3–0–5/46
Test batting
2–4–0–41–20–10.25–0–*ct* 2
Bowling 154–9–17.11–1–0–5/46

He was overshadowed by W. W. Hall and C. C. Griffith on the 1963 tour to England and was not required for the Tests.

King, Percival
Professional. *b:* 9.12.1835, Stockwell, London. *d:* 29.10.1910, Edinburgh, Scotland. Lower order right-hand batsman, right-hand round-arm bowler, either fast or slow, wicket-keeper. *Team* Surrey (1871, 1 match).
Career batting
1–2–0–16–13–8.00–0–*ct* 1
Bowling 18–0

He was prominently identified with cricket in Scotland, captaining the Players of Scotland against the Gentlemen, and was Editor of the 'Scottish Cricketers Guide' 1870/1 to 1887/8.

King, Robert Jasper Stuart
(also known as Stuart-King)
Amateur. *b:* 10.5.1909, Leigh-on-Sea, Essex. *d:* 11.5.1992, Westcliff-on-Sea, Essex. Lower order right-hand batsman, leg break bowler. *Sch* Felsted. *Team* Essex (1928, 1 match).
Career batting
1–1–0–3–3–3.00–0–*ct* 0
Bowling 20–0

King, Rev Robert Turner
Amateur. *b:* 14.7.1824, Melton Mowbray, Leicestershire. *d:* 12.5.1884, Bootle, Lancashire. Powerful middle order batsman, medium fast round-arm bowler, excellent field at point. *Sch* Oakham. *Teams* Cambridge U (1846–49, blue all four years); Cambridge Town Club (1847).
Career batting
45–77–5–935–50*–12.98–0–*ct* 61
Bowling 32 wickets (no analyses)–3–1–6/?

He captained Cambridge in 1849. His last first-class match was for Gentlemen in 1851, and he played little after leaving Cambridge. His County cricket was for Leicestershire (pre first-class, 1849), Warwickshire (pre first-class, 1849), Staffordshire (1852) and Rutland (1859).

King, Sidney
Amateur. *b:* 1885, Rushden, Northamptonshire. *d:* 1972, Rushden, Northamptonshire. Middle order batsman. *Team* Northamptonshire (1907–08, 4 matches).
Career batting
4–7–2–47–23–9.40–0–*ct* 2

King, William Robert
Amateur. *b:* 16.12.1902, Clonlea, Kilkishen, Co Clare, Ireland. Lower order left-hand batsman, slow left-arm bowler. *Team* Dublin University (1922).
Career batting
1–2–0–15–8–7.50–0–*ct* 1
Bowling 36–0

Kingscote, Henry Bloomfield
Amateur. *b:* 28.2.1843, Kingscote Park, Gloucestershire. *d:* 1.8.1915, Belgravia, London. Nephew of H. R. (Surrey, Hampshire and Sussex), cousin of A. F. (MCC 1858). His former wife married C. F. Buller (Middlesex). Hard hitting middle order right-hand batsman, wicket-keeper. *Teams* Kent (1867, 1 match); Gloucestershire (1877, 3 matches).

Kingscote, Henry Robert

Career batting
12–18–2–91–44*–5.68–0–*ct* 12–*st* 8

His final first-class match was for MCC in 1878. He was principally connected with Army cricket, being a member of the Royal Artillery team from 1864 to 1881; from 1882 to 1889 he was stationed in India taking part in many matches there, and latterly selected the Army team to play the Bar in the annual match at Lord's.

Kingscote, Henry Robert
Amateur. *b:* 25.5.1802, Kingscote Park, Gloucestershire. *d:* 13.7.1882, Westminster, London. Father of A. F. (MCC 1858), uncle of H. B. (Kent and Gloucestershire). Middle order right-hand batsman. *Sch* Harrow. *Teams* Surrey (1828–31); Hampshire (1828); Sussex (1832).
Career batting
33–62–2–593–38–9.88–0–*ct* 13

His first-class debut was for MCC in 1825, and his last match for West of England in 1844. President of MCC in 1827, he promoted the games between Sussex and England that season.

Kingsford, Robert Kennett
Amateur. *b:* 23.12.1849, Sydenham Hill, London. *d:* 14.10.1895, Adelaide, South Australia. Free hitting middle order right-hand batsman, good deep field, occasional wicket-keeper. *Sch* Marlborough. *Team* Surrey (1872–74, 3 matches).
Career batting
3–5–0–80–30–16.00–0–*ct* 2

He played soccer for England.

Kingsley, Sir Patrick Graham Toler
Amateur. *b:* 26.5.1908, Calcutta, India. Opening or middle order right-hand batsman, excellent slip field. *Sch* Winchester. *Team* Oxford (1928–30, blue all three years).
Career batting
47–78–2–2270–176–29.86–2–*ct* 41
Bowling 218–4–54.50–0–0–2/46

His County cricket was for Hertfordshire (1926–48) and Devon (1931); his final first-class match being for Free Foresters in 1938. He captained Oxford in 1930. He also won a blue for soccer.

Kingston, Rev Frederick William
Amateur. *b:* 24.12.1855, Oundle, Northamptonshire. *d:* 30.1.1933, Willington, Bedfordshire. Brother of J. P. (Warwickshire), H. E. (Northamptonshire), W. H. (Northamptonshire), and C. A. (British Guiana). Lower order right-hand batsman, wicket-keeper. *Team* Cambridge U (1878, blue).
Career batting
6–9–0–141–61–15.66–0–*ct* 7–*st* 3

His final first-class match was for Cambridge University Past and Present in 1886. His County cricket was for Northamptonshire (pre first-class, 1874–94).

Kingston, Graham Charles
Cricketer. *b:* 1.11.1950, Newport, Monmouthshire. Middle order right-hand batsman, right-arm medium pace bowler. *Team* Glamorgan (1967–71, 9 matches). *Tours* Glamorgan to West Indies 1969/70.
Career batting
9–15–2–161–26–12.38–0–*ct* 4
Bowling 210–4–52.50–0–0–2/18

He was also a good soccer and rugby footballer.

Kingston, Hubert Ernest
Amateur. *b:* 15.8.1876, Northampton. *d:* 9.6.1955, Long Buckby, Northamptonshire. Brother of W. H. (Northamptonshire), F. W. (Cambridge U), J. P. (Warwickshire) and C. A. (British Guiana). Steady right-hand middle order batsman, right-arm slow bowler. *Sch* Blair Lodge. *Team* Northamptonshire (1905–06, 13 matches).
Career batting
13–25–4–335–68–15.95–0–*ct* 7
Bowling 246–6–41.00–0–0–2/8

He first played for Northamptonshire (pre first-class) in 1904.

Kingston, James Phillips
Amateur. *b:* 8.7.1857, Hardingstone, Northampton. *d:* 14.3.1929, Italy. Brother of F. W. (Cambridge U), H. E. (Northamptonshire), W. H. (Northamptonshire) and C. A. (British Guiana). Opening right-hand batsman, leg break bowler, excellent point. *Team* Warwickshire (1894, 1 match).
Career batting
1–1–0–24–24–24.00–0–*ct* 0

Most of his County cricket was for Northamptonshire (1875–92) before that side became first-class. He was captain from 1877 to 1887 and in 1891, in which year he was also appointed Secretary.

Kingston, William Harold
Amateur. *b:* 12.8.1874, Northampton. *d:* 17.2.1956, Northampton. Brother of H. E. (Northamptonshire), F. W. (Cambridge U), J. P. (Warwickshire) and C. A. (British Guiana). Sound right-hand opening batsman. *Team* Northamptonshire (1905–09, 77 matches).
Career batting
78–141–2–2599–83–18.69–0–*ct* 44
Bowling 25–2–12.50–0–0–2/5

His first-class debut was for the Gentlemen in 1904. He first played for Northamptonshire (pre first-class) in 1894.

Kingston, William Miles Nairne
Amateur. *b:* 24.9.1838, Clifton, Bristol. *d:* 21.4.1898, Montreux, Switzerland. Brother of P. O. (Victoria), father of W. M. (Europeans). Middle order right-hand batsman. *Sch* Harrow. *Team* Gloucestershire (1875–76, 2 matches).
Career batting
4–6–0–53–17–8.83–0–*ct* 0

He also played for Monmouthshire (1858). His first-class debut was for Manchester in 1858.

King-Turner, Dr Charles John
Amateur. *b:* 13.12.1904, Cirencester, Gloucestershire. *d:* 4.4.1972, Cirencester, Gloucestershire. Good middle order right-hand batsman but too impatient, excellent cover point. *Sch* Cheltenham. *Team* Gloucestershire (1922, 6 matches).
Career batting
6–9–0–29–10–3.22–0–*ct* 3
He played in trials at Oxford U, but not in first-class matches.

Kinkead-Weekes, Roderick Calder
Cricketer. *b:* 15.3.1951, East London, South Africa. Lower order right-hand batsman, wicket-keeper. *Sch* Eton. *Teams* Oxford U (1972, blue); Middlesex (1976, 2 matches).
Career batting
6–9–2–76–25*–10.85–0–*ct* 7–*st* 3

Kinneir, Septimus Paul
Professional. *b:* 13.5.1871, Corsham, Wiltshire. *d:* 16.10.1928, Birmingham. He was found lying across his motor cycle in Lakey Lane, Hall Green and was declared dead on arrival at Birmingham Hospital. Stylish opening left-hand batsman, slow left-arm bowler. *Team* Warwickshire (1898–1914, 302 matches). *Tour* MCC to Australia 1911/12. *Test* England (1911/12, 1 match).
Career batting
312–525–47–15641–268*–32.72–26–*ct* 181
Bowling 1492–48–31.08–0–0–3/13
Test batting
1–2–0–52–30–26.00–0–*ct* 0
He hit 1,000 runs in a season eight times (best 1,629, av 49.36, in 1911). Both his double centuries were for Warwickshire, the higher being 268* v Hampshire at Edgbaston in 1911. He also played for Wiltshire (1894–97).

Kinnersley, Kenneth Charles
Amateur. *b:* 13.3.1914, Apia, Samoa. *d:* 30.6.1984, Clifton, Bristol. Opening right-hand batsman, right-arm medium slow bowler. *Sch* Clifton. *Team* Somerset (1932–38, 10 matches).
Career batting
10–18–3–143–25*–9.53–0–*ct* 8
Bowling 436–17–25.64–0–0–3/40
He also played for Devon (1947–55).

Kippax, Alan Falconer
Amateur. *b:* 25.5.1897, Paddington, Sydney, New South Wales, Australia. *d:* 5.9.1972, Bellevue Hill, Sydney, New South Wales, Australia. Stylish right-hand middle order batsman, leg break bowler. *Team* New South Wales (1918/19 to 1935/6, 87 matches). *Tours* Australia to New Zealand 1920/1, 1927/8, to England 1930, 1934; New South Wales to New Zealand 1923/4. *Tests* Australia (1924/5 to 1934, 22 matches).
Career batting
175–256–33–12762–315*–57.22–43–*ct* 72
Bowling 1099–21–52.33–0–0–4/66
Test batting
22–34–1–1192–146–36.12–2–*ct* 13
Bowling 19–0
He was most successful on the 1930 tour to England with 1,451 runs, av 58.04, but in 1934 he suffered from illness and appeared in only one Test. His triple century was 315* for New South Wales v Queensland at Sydney in 1927/8; of his other scores over 200, the only one hit in England was 250 v Sussex at Hove in 1934. He was considered unlucky not to have been chosen for the Australian 1926 tour to England. He hit 1,000 runs in a season in Australia twice.

Kippax, Peter John
Professional. *b:* 15.10.1940, Huddersfield, Yorkshire. Middle order right-hand batsman, leg break and googly bowler. *Sch* Bedford Modern. *Team* Yorkshire (1961–62, 4 matches). *Tour* Minor Counties to Kenya 1977/8 (not first-class).
Career batting
5–8–2–40–9–6.66–0–*ct* 1
Bowling 396–12–33.00–1–0–5/74
He also played for Northumberland (1975–77) and Durham (pre first-class, 1978–90). His last first-class match was for MCC in 1987, 25 years after his previous game. He is well-known as a bat maker.

Kirby, David
Amateur. *b:* 18.1.1939, Darlington, Co Durham. Opening/middle order right-hand batsman, off break bowler. *Sch* St Peter's, York. *Teams* Cambridge U (1959–61, blue all three years); Leicestershire (1959–64, 63 matches).
Career batting
117–218–9–4105–118–19.64–3–*ct* 51
Bowling 4251–113–37.61–1–0–5/76
He hit 1,000 runs in a season three times (best 1,158, av 23.63, in 1961). He captained Cambridge in 1961 and Leicestershire in 1962. He also played for Durham (pre first-class, 1956–58).

Kirby, Geoffrey Norman George
Professional. *b:* 6.11.1923, Reading, Berkshire. Lower order right-hand batsman, wicket-keeper. *Team* Surrey (1948–53, 19 matches).
Career batting
23–21–8–168–32–12.92–0–*ct* 43–*st* 10
He made his first-class debut for South v North in 1947. He also played for Berkshire (1954).

Kirby, Henry Richard
Amateur. *b:* 19.3.1889, Patrixbourne, Kent. *d:* 20.7.1976, Mayfield, Sussex. Middle order batsman. *Sch* Malvern. *Team* Sussex (1911, 1 match).

Kirby, John Edward Weston

Career batting
1–2–0–9–7–4.50–0–*ct* 0

Kirby, John Edward Weston
Amateur. *b:* 4.2.1936, Low Fell, Gateshead, Co Durham. Opening right-hand batsman, right-arm medium pace bowler. *Sch* Ampleforth. *Team* Oxford U (1956).
Career batting
3–6–0–78–28–13.00–0–*ct* 4

Kirk, Edwin
Amateur. *b:* 6.5.1866, Coventry, Warwickshire. *d:* 10.3.1957, Coventry, Warwickshire. Middle order right-hand batsman. *Team* Warwickshire (1898, 1 match).
Career batting
1–1–0–0–0–0.00–0–*ct* 1

Kirk, Ernest Charles
Amateur. *b:* 21.3.1884, Clapham, London. *d:* 19.12.1932, Fulham, London, after an operation for appendicitis. Lower order left-hand batsman, left-arm medium fast bowler. *Team* Surrey (1906–21, 36 matches).
Career batting
40–57–8–495–43–10.10–0–*ct* 12
Bowling 3445–143–24.09–7–1–7/130

He was unable to find the time to appear regularly in County cricket, though worth his place in the Surrey Eleven. His first-class debut was for Gentlemen of the South in 1905.

Kirk, John Alexander Wright
Amateur. *b:* 2.12.1888, Coatbridge, Lanarkshire, Scotland. *d:* 21.10.1961, Coatbridge, Lanarkshire, Scotland. Lower order right-hand batsman, right-arm medium pace bowler. *Team* Scotland (1920–23).
Career batting
3–4–0–15–11–3.75–0–*ct* 3
Bowling 345–11–31.36–0–0–4/80

Kirk, Lionel
Amateur. *b:* 1.11.1884, Sheffield, Yorkshire. *d:* 27.2.1953, Nottingham. Middle order right-hand batsman. *Sch* Oakham. *Team* Nottinghamshire (1920–29, 14 matches).
Career batting
14–22–2–358–86–17.90–0–*ct* 6
Bowling 1–0

He was a member of Nottinghamshire CCC Committee (1923–52) and President of the County Club in 1951. A good rugby footballer, he represented Nottinghamshire.

Kirk, William Naylor
Professional. *b:* 18.1.1866, Radford, Nottinghamshire. Middle order batsman. *Team* Nottinghamshire (1888, 1 match).
Career batting
1–1–0–4–4–4.00–0–*ct* 0

Kirkman, Frederick
Amateur. *b:* 13.7.1849, Croft, Lancashire. *d:* 8.12.1879, Croft, Lancashire. Lower order batsman, opening bowler. *Sch* Rossall. *Team* Cambridge U (1870).
Career batting
1–1–0–5–5–5.00–0–*ct* 0
Bowling 58–0

His County cricket was for Cheshire (1867).

Kirkman, Michael
Cricketer. *b:* 11.2.1942, Bodmin, Cornwall. Tail end right-hand batsman, leg break bowler. *Sch* Dulwich. *Team* Cambridge U (1963, blue).
Career batting
10–15–11–28–7*–7.00–0–*ct* 2
Bowling 741–14–52.92–0–0–3/32

Kirkpatrick, Alexander Kennedy
Cricketer. *b:* 25.7.1938, Woodvale, Belfast, Ireland. Lower order left-hand batsman, off break bowler. *Team* Ireland (1962).
Career batting
1–2–1–31–30–31.00–0–*ct* 1
Bowling 46–0

Kirkpatrick, Sir James
Amateur. *b:* 22.3.1841, Closeburn, Dumfries, Scotland. *d:* 10.11.1899, Forest Hill, London. Nephew of James (Gentlemen of Kent). Lower order right-hand batsman, right-arm fast bowler. *Team* Gentlemen of South (1867).
Career batting
1–2–1–10–10*–10.00–0–*ct* 2
Bowling 48–3–16.00–0–0–3/36

A well-known soccer player, he captained Scotland in the first international against England in 1870.

Kirkwood, Euan MacMillan
Amateur. *b:* 7.12.1934, Ferguslie, Paisley, Renfrewshire, Scotland. Middle order right-hand batsman. *Sch* Merchiston. *Team* Scotland (1958).
Career batting
3–5–0–17–10–3.40–0–*ct* 5

Kirkwood, Henry Raphael
Amateur. *b:* 12.10.1886, Hartley Wintney, Hampshire. *d:* 14.4.1954, Folkestone, Kent. Lower order batsman, leg break bowler. *Team* Army (1923–28).
Career batting
5–9–1–127–50–15.87–0–*ct* 3
Bowling 362–12–30.16–1–0–5/100

Kirmani, Syed Mujtaba Hussein
Cricketer. *b:* 29.12.1949, Madras, India. Attacking middle order right-hand batsman, occasional off break bowler, wicket-keeper. *Team* Mysore/Karnataka (1967/8 to 1991/2); Railways (1988/9 to 1989/90). *Tours* India to England 1971, 1974, 1982, 1983 (World Cup), to West Indies 1975/6, 1982/3, to New Zealand 1975/6, 1980/1, to Australia 1977/8,

1980/1, 1985/6, to Pakistan 1978/9, 1982/3, 1984/5, to Sharjah (not first-class) 1985/6; Wadekar to Sri Lanka 1975/6. *Tests* India (1975/6 to 1985/6, 88 matches).
Career batting
262–365–63–8971–161–29.70–12–*ct* 357–*st* 112
Bowling 114–1–114.00–0–0–1/9
Test batting
88–124–22–2759–102–27.04–2–*ct* 160–*st* 38
Bowling 13–1–13.00–0–0–1/9

He did not appear in any Tests in the 1971 and 1974 tours to England, but in 1982 played in all three.

Kirnon, Samuel
Cricketer. *b:* 25.12.1962, Fulwood, Preston, Lancashire. Lower order right-hand batsman, right-arm medium fast bowler. *Team* Glamorgan (1992, 1 match).
Career batting
1 match, did not bat–*ct* 0
Bowling 21–1–21.00–0–0–1/14

Kirsten, Peter Noel
Cricketer. *b:* 14.5.1955, Pietermaritzburg, South Africa. Son of Noel (Border), brother of A. M. (Western Province) and Gary (Western Province). Middle order right-hand batsman, off break bowler. *Teams* Western Province (1973/4 to 1989/90); Sussex (1975, 1 match); Derbyshire (1978–82, 106 matches); Border (1990/1 to 1991/2). *Tours* South Africa to India 1991/2 (not first-class), to Australia and New Zealand (World Cup) 1991/2, to West Indies 1991/2. *Test* South Africa (1991/2, 1 match).
Career batting
271–472–51–18862–228–44.80–48–*ct* 166
Bowling 4367–111–39.34–2–0–6/48
Test batting
1–2–0–63–52–31.50–0–*ct* 2

He hit 1,000 runs in a season five times (best 1,941, av 64.70, in 1982). He also hit 1,074 runs, av 76.71, in South Africa in 1976/7 including six centuries in seven innings. His highest innings was 228 for Derbyshire v Somerset at Taunton in 1981. He played in 4 unofficial Tests for South Africa in 1982/3, captaining the team in each game.

Kirti Azad (*see under* Azad, K. B. J.)

Kirton, Harold Osborne
Amateur. *b:* 4.1.1894, Paddington, London. *d:* 9.5.1974, Holland-on-Sea, Essex. Middle order right-hand batsman, right-arm medium pace bowler. *Team* Warwickshire (1925–29, 2 matches).
Career batting
2–3–0–82–52–27.33–0–*ct* 0

Kirwan, Rev John Henry
Amateur. *b:* 25.12.1816, Beaumaris, Anglesey. *d:* 13.6.1899, St Johns, near Antony, Cornwall. Brother of E. D. G. M. (Cambridge U 1834), George (Sussex 1853) and Richard (Gentlemen of England 1853). Lower order batsman, right-hand fast round-arm bowler. *Sch* Eton. *Teams* Cambridge U (1836–42, blue 1839); Cambridge Town Club (1840).
Career batting
19–36–1–330–41–9.42–0–*ct* 3
Bowling 111 wickets (no analyses)–11–3–9/?

His most notable bowling feat was to take 9 wickets in an innings, all bowled, (15, all bowled, in the match) for Cambridge U v Cambridge Town Club in 1836, though in the previous season he took all ten wickets for Eton v MCC at Lord's. His County cricket was for Somerset (pre first-class, 1845) and Cornwall (1858).

Kitcat, Sidney Austyn Paul
Amateur. *b:* 20.7.1868, Charlton, Tetbury, Gloucestershire. *d:* 17.6.1942, Esher, Surrey. Middle order right-hand batsman, right-arm medium pace bowler. *Sch* Marlborough. *Team* Gloucestershire (1892–1904, 50 matches).
Career batting
54–97–10–1899–95*–21.82–0–*ct* 38
Bowling 481–14–34.35–0–0–2/0

Owing to business his County cricket was restricted. His first-class debut was for MCC in 1890. A talented hockey player, he represented Middlesex, Surrey and England.

Kitchen, Mervyn John
Professional. *b:* 1.8.1940, Nailsea, Somerset. Opening left-hand batsman, right-arm medium pace bowler. *Team* Somerset (1960–79, 352 matches). *Tour* International Wanderers to Rhodesia 1972/3.
Career batting
354–612–32–15230–189–26.25–17–*ct* 157
Bowling 109–2–54.50–0–0–1/4

He hit 1,000 runs in a season seven times (best 1,730, av 36.04, in 1968). He was appointed to the first-class umpires' list in 1982, standing in 5 Test matches (1990–92).

Kitchener, Frederick George
Professional. *b:* 2.7.1871, Hartley Row, Hampshire. *d:* 25.5.1948, East Boldon, Co Durham. Tail end right-hand batsman, right-arm fast medium bowler. *Team* Hampshire (1896–1903, 13 matches).
Career batting
13–19–3–80–16–5.00–0–*ct* 6
Bowling 630–28–22.50–2–0–6/59

Kitching, Ernest William
Amateur. *b:* 1851. *d:* 8.12.1902, Winson Green, Birmingham. Lower order batsman. *Team* Gentlemen of North (1877).
Career batting
1–1–0–0–0–0.00–0–*ct* 1

He appeared as a substitute in his only first-class match and was allowed to bat in the second innings.

Kitson, David Lees
Professional. *b:* 13.9.1925, Batley, Yorkshire. Opening right-hand batsman. *Team* Somerset (1952–54, 32 matches).
Career batting
32–60–3–886–69–15.54–0–*ct* 3

Kitson, Frederick
Professional. *b:* 20.5.1893, Marylebone, London. *d:* 25.1.1925, Northampton. Tail end batsman, slow left-arm bowler. *Team* Northamptonshire (1919–20, 4 matches).
Career batting
4–6–3–31–13–10.33–0–*ct* 2
Bowling 192–3–64.00–0–0–3/63

Kline, Lindsay Francis
Amateur. *b:* 29.9.1934, Camberwell, Melbourne, Victoria, Australia. Lower order left-hand batsman, slow left-arm bowler. *Team* Victoria (1955/6 to 1961/2, 31 matches). *Tours* Australia to South Africa 1957/8, to India and Pakistan 1959/60, to England 1961, to New Zealand 1956/7. *Tests* Australia (1957/8 to 1960/1, 13 matches).
Career batting
88–96–31–559–37*–8.60–0–*ct* 55
Bowling 7562–276–27.39–11–0–7/75
Test batting
13–16–9–58–15*–8.28–0–*ct* 9
Bowling 776–34–22.82–1–0–7/75
He only had a moderate tour to England in 1961 and was not required to appear in any of the Tests.

Knapp, Dr Edward Michael Molineux
Amateur. *b:* 28.4.1848, Bath, Somerset. *d:* 24.11.1903, Croydon, Surrey. Free hitting lower order right-hand batsman, right-hand fast round-arm bowler, good deep field. *Sch* Stonyhurst. *Team* Gloucestershire (1871–80, 12 matches).
Career batting
12–17–3–216–90*–15.42–0–*ct* 4
Bowling 48–2–24.00–0–0–2/27
He also played for Herefordshire (1883).

Knapp, John Walter
Amateur. *b:* 8.3.1841, Paddington, London. *d:* 22.6.1881, St Leonards-on-Sea, Sussex. Lower order batsman, right-arm fast bowler. *Sch* Merchant Taylors. *Team* Middlesex (1864, 1 match).
Career batting
1–1–0–3–3–3.00–0–*ct* 0
He also played for Dorset (1864) and Cornwall (1864).

Knatchbull, Rev Henry Edward
Amateur. *b:* 30.8.1808, Mersham Hatch, Kent. *d:* 31.8.1876, Campsey Ash, Suffolk. Fine free-hitting right-hand batsman, occasional wicket-keeper. *Sch* Winchester. *Teams* Oxford U (1827–29, blue 1827 and 1829); Kent (1827–48); Norfolk (1834–36); Cambridge U (1837).
Career batting
41–72–2–736–72–10.51–0–*ct* 31–*st* 5
Having taken holy orders he played often under the name of 'Edwards'. His last first-class match was for MCC in 1849. He played in emergency for Cambridge U in 1837, being on the ground when the team arrived one short. He also played for Suffolk (1829).

Knatchbull-Hugessen, Hon Cecil Marcus
(succeeded to the title 4th Lord Brabourne in 1915)
Amateur. *b:* 27.11.1863, Chelsea, London. *d:* 15.2.1933, at sea on SS *Caernarvon Castle* en route Cape Town to London. Nephew of W. W. (Kent). Middle order right-hand batsman, wicket-keeper. *Sch* Eton. *Teams* Cambridge U (1884–86, blue 1886); Kent (1884, 1 match).
Career batting
12–22–3–192–32–10.10–0–*ct* 10–*st* 1

Kneller, Arthur Harry
Amateur. *b:* 28.4.1894, Kingsclere, Hampshire. *d:* 19.7.1969, Chichester, Sussex. Middle order right-hand batsman. *Sch* Ardingly. *Team* Hampshire (1924–26, 8 matches).
Career batting
8–11–2–76–25*–8.44–0–*ct* 1
He spent many years in East Africa.

Knew, George Alan
Cricketer. *b:* 5.3.1954, Leicester. Son of G. F. (Leicestershire). Middle order right-hand batsman. *Sch* Wyggeston GS. *Team* Leicestershire (1972–73, 4 matches).
Career batting
4–6–1–59–25–11.80–0–*ct* 0

Knew, George Frank
Professional. *b:* 13.10.1920, Wigston, Leicester. Father of G. A. (Leicestershire). Stylish middle order right-hand batsman. *Team* Leicestershire (1939, 5 matches).
Career batting
5–8–0–78–42–9.75–0–*ct* 2
Bowling 100–1–100.00–0–0–1/58

Knight, Albert Ernest
Professional. *b:* 8.10.1872, Leicester. *d:* 25.4.1946, Edmonton, Middlesex. Sound middle order right-hand batsman, excellent cover point. *Teams* Leicestershire (1895–1912, 367 matches); London County (1903–04). *Tour* MCC to Australia 1903/4. *Tests* England (1903/4, 3 matches).
Career batting
391–702–40–19357–229*–29.24–34–*ct* 132
Bowling 117–4–29.25–0–0–2/34
Test batting
3–6–1–81–70*–16.20–0–*ct* 1
He hit 1,000 runs in a season 10 times (best 1,834, av 45.85, in 1903). Both his double centuries were for

Leicestershire, the highest being 229* v Worcestershire at Worcester 1903. He was the author of a notable book on the game entitled 'The Complete Cricketer' published in 1906.

Knight, Arthur Egerton
Amateur. *b:* 7.9.1887, Godalming, Surrey. *d:* 10.3.1956, Milton, Hampshire. Opening batsman. *Team* Hampshire (1913–23, 4 matches).
Career batting
4–7–0–41–29–5.85–0–*ct* 2
Bowling 17–1–17.00–0–0–1/17
He played soccer for Portsmouth and England.

Knight, Barry Rolfe
Professional. *b:* 18.2.1938, Chesterfield, Derbyshire. Middle order right-hand batsman, right-arm fast medium bowler. *Teams* Essex (1955–66, 239 matches); Leicestershire (1967–69, 46 matches). *Tours* MCC to Pakistan, India and Ceylon 1961/2, to Australia and New Zealand 1962/3, 1965/6, to India 1963/4; Cavaliers to West Indies 1964/5; Commonwealth to India 1964/5. *Tests* England (1961/2 to 1969, 29 matches).
Career batting
379–602–83–13336–165–25.69–12–*ct* 263
Bowling 26205–1089–24.06–45–8–8/69
Test batting
29–38–7–812–127–26.19–2–*ct* 14
Bowling 2223–70–31.75–0–0–4/38
He hit 1,000 runs in a season five times (best 1,689, av 34.46, in 1962) and took 100 wickets in a season five times (best 140, av 21.72, in 1963). He achieved the 'double' in four seasons, 1962 to 1965 inclusive. For Essex v Warwickshire at Edgbaston in 1962 he hit no fewer than 21 fours in an innings total of 88.

Knight, Donald John
Amateur. *b:* 12.5.1894, Sutton, Surrey. *d:* 5.1.1960, Marylebone, London. Stylish opening right-hand batsman, good close field. *Sch* Malvern. *Teams* Surrey (1911–37, 107 matches); Oxford U (1914 and 1919, blue both years). *Tests* England (1921, 2 matches).
Career batting
139–215–13–6231–156*–30.84–13–*ct* 74
Bowling 25–3–8.33–0–0–2/0
Test batting
2–4–0–54–38–13.50–0–*ct* 1
He hit 1,000 runs in a season twice (best 1,588, av 45.37, in 1919). Being in the scholastic profession limited his County cricket after he left Oxford.

Knight, George
Professional. *b:* 28.3.1835, Petworth, Sussex. *d:* 8.1.1901, Petworth, Sussex. Lower order right-hand batsman, slow under-arm bowler, wicket-keeper. *Team* Sussex (1860–74, 13 matches).
Career batting
13–24–4–125–21–6.25–0–*ct* 8–*st* 11
Bowling 43–1–43.00–0–0–1/25

Knight, George Thomas
(changed name from Austen in November 1812)
Amateur. *b:* 22.11.1795, Goodnestone Park, Kent. *d:* 25.8.1867, Moorfields, Hereford. Brother of Edward (Kent and Hampshire), Henry (Sussex) and B. J. (Kent), uncle of P. H. (Cambridge U) and W. W. (Kent). Attacking lower order right-hand batsman, right-hand fast round-arm bowler. *Teams* Hampshire (1820–25); Kent (1827–28).
Career batting
23–43–2–282–36–6.87–0–*ct* 5–*st* 6
Bowling 22 wickets (no analyses)–0–0–4/?
He was one of the first bowlers to defy the Law by bowling 'round-arm' and wrote strongly in favour of the new style of bowling. His final match was for Gentlemen in 1837. He was the nephew of Jane Austen, the novelist.

Knight, John Mark
Cricketer. *b:* 16.3.1958, Oundle, Northamptonshire. Lower order right-hand batsman, right-arm fast medium bowler. *Sch* Oundle. *Team* Oxford U (1978–81, blue 1979).
Career batting
23–35–3–318–41*–9.93–0–*ct* 3
Bowling 1431–33–43.36–0–0–4/69
His County cricket was for Wiltshire (1977–82).

Knight, Joseph William
Amateur. *b:* 20.9.1896, Highworth, Wiltshire. *d:* 3.3.1974, Childrey, Oxfordshire. Lower order batsman, opening bowler. *Team* Cambridge U (1921).
Career batting
1–2–0–1–1–0.50–0–*ct* 0
Bowling 53–0
His County cricket was for Wiltshire (1920–22).

Knight, Nicholas Verity
Cricketer. *b:* 28.11.1969, Watford, Hertfordshire. Middle order left-hand batsman. *Sch* Felsted. *Team* Essex (1991–92, 27 matches).
Career batting
27–40–7–1215–109–36.81–3–*ct* 22
Bowling 32–0
He played hockey for Essex and Young England.

Knight, Norman Spencer
Amateur. *b:* 30.3.1914, Eltham, London. Lower order left-hand batsman, wicket-keeper. *Sch* Uppingham. *Team* Oxford U (1933–35, blue 1934).
Career batting
11–15–1–189–87–13.50–0–*ct* 18–*st* 5

Knight, Philip Henry
Amateur. *b:* 25.8.1835, Chawton House, Alton, Hampshire. *d:* 4.1.1882, Chawton House, Alton, Hampshire. Brother of W. W. (Kent), son of Edward (Hampshire and Kent), nephew of G. T. (Hampshire and Kent), Henry (Sussex) and B. J. (Kent). Opening/middle order batsman. *Sch* Harrow. *Team* Cam-

bridge U (1854).
Career batting
8–15–0–159–38–10.60–0–*ct* 4

His first first-class match was for Gentlemen of Kent in 1853 and his last was in 1864 for the same team.

Knight, Rev Richard
Amateur. *b:* 8.5.1892, South Molton, Devon. *d:* 9.1.1960, Kewstroke, Weston-super-Mare, Somerset. Opening right-hand batsman. *Sch* St John's Leatherhead. *Team* Cambridge U (1912).
Career batting
4–7–1–101–66–16.83–0–*ct* 2
Bowling 177–8–22.12–0–0–4/23

His County cricket was for Devon (1910–13).

Knight, Robert Frank
Amateur. *b:* 10.8.1879, Rushden, Northamptonshire. *d:* 9.1.1955, Kettering, Northamptonshire. Middle order right-hand batsman, leg break bowler. *Sch* Wellingborough. *Team* Northamptonshire (1905–21, 22 matches).
Career batting
22–37–3–408–67–12.00–0–*ct* 13
Bowling 667–21–31.76–1–0–6/90

He first played for Northamptonshire (pre first-class) in 1900.

Knight, Robert Lougher
Amateur. *b:* 21.4.1858, St Bride's Major, Glamorgan. *d:* 22.5.1938, Tythegston Court, Glamorgan. Nephew of F. E. Stacey (Cambridge U 1850), father-in-law of L. E. W. Williams (Glamorgan). Lower order right-hand batsman, left-hand medium pace round-arm bowler, good close field. *Sch* Clifton. *Team* Oxford U (1878–80, blue 1878).
Career batting
8–14–2–100–36*–8.33–0–*ct* 6
Bowling 436–30–14.53–2–1–7/39

A good rugby footballer, he appeared for Oxford in 1880.

Knight, Roger David Verdon
Cricketer. *b:* 6.9.1946, Streatham, London. Middle order left-hand batsman, right-arm medium pace bowler. *Sch* Dulwich. *Teams* Cambridge U (1967–70, blue all four years); Surrey (1968–84, 174 matches); Gloucestershire (1971–75, 105 matches); Sussex (1976–77, 43 matches). *Tours* Robins to South Africa 1972/3; MCC to West Africa 1975/6 (not first-class); MCC to East Africa 1973/4; Overseas XI to India 1980/1.
Career batting
387–672–61–19558–165*–32.00–31–*ct* 295
Bowling 13335–369–36.13–4–0–6/44

He hit 1,000 runs in a season thirteen times (best 1,350, av 38.57, in 1974). From 1978 to 1983 he captained Surrey. His last first-class match was for MCC in 1989. He also played for Bedfordshire (1987–88).

Knight, Ronald
Professional. *b:* 12.5.1913, Northampton. Middle order right-hand batsman, right-arm fast bowler. *Team* Northamptonshire (1933–34, 10 matches).
Career batting
10–20–3–182–50–10.70–0–*ct* 4
Bowling 348–10–34.80–1–0–5/108

Knightley-Smith, William
Amateur. *b:* 1.8.1932, West Smithfield, London. *d:* 31.7.1962, Edinburgh, Scotland. He collapsed and died while playing tennis. Opening/middle order left-hand batsman. *Sch* Highgate. *Teams* Cambridge U (1953–55, blue 1953); Middlesex (1952, 26 matches); Gloucestershire (1955–57, 29 matches).
Career batting
87–155–10–2530–95–17.44–0–*ct* 28
Bowling 72–0

His final first-class match was for Free Foresters in 1961. A good soccer player, he received his blue at Cambridge.

Knott, Alan Philip Eric
Cricketer. *b:* 9.4.1946, Belvedere, Kent. Middle order right-hand batsman, wicket-keeper, occasional off break bowler. *Teams* Kent (1964–85, 349 matches); Tasmania (1969/70, 2 matches). *Tours* MCC Under 25 to Pakistan 1966/7; MCC to West Indies 1967/8, 1973/4, to Ceylon and Pakistan 1968/9, to Australia and New Zealand 1970/1, 1974/5, to India, Sri Lanka and Pakistan 1972/3, to India, Sri Lanka and Australia 1976/7; Cavaliers to West Indies 1964/5; SAB England XI to South Africa 1981/2. *Tests* England (1967–81, 95 matches).
Career batting
511–745–134–18105–156–29.63–17–*ct* 1211–*st* 133
Bowling 87–2–43.50–0–0–1/5
Test batting
95–149–15–4389–135–32.75–5–*ct* 250–*st* 19

He hit 1,000 runs in a season twice (best 1,209, av 41.68, in 1971). His best season as wicket-keeper was 1967 with 98 victims (90 ct, 8 st). For ten years he was regarded as the best wicket-keeper in England and commanded an automatic place in the Test side, but in 1977 he joined Packer's World Series Cricket and though he regained his England place after the agreement between Packer and the Australian Board, Knott later went on the SAB tour to South Africa and was banned from Test cricket for three years.

Knott, Charles Harold
Amateur. *b:* 20.3.1901, Tunbridge Wells, Kent. *d:* 18.6.1988, Tonbridge, Kent. Brother of F. H. (Kent). Attacking middle order right-hand batsman, leg break bowler, excellent cover point. *Sch* Tonbridge. *Teams* Kent (1921–39, 104 matches); Oxford U (1922–24, blue all 3 years). *Tours* Martineau to Egypt 1929, 1930, 1931, 1933, 1934, 1936 (not first-class).

Career batting
136–206–27–5633–261*–31.46–9–*ct* 66
Bowling 660–24–27.50–0–0–4/24

His only double century was 261* for Harlequins v West Indians at Eastbourne in 1928. He captained Oxford in 1924.

Knott, Charles James
Amateur. *b:* 26.11.1914, Southampton, Hampshire. Lower order right-hand batsman, right-arm medium pace or off break bowler. *Team* Hampshire (1938–54, 166 matches).
Career batting
173–245–98–1023–27–6.95–0–*ct* 57
Bowling 15771–676–23.32–47–8–8/26

He took 100 wickets in a season four times (best 122, av 18.47, in 1946). His final first-class match was for MCC in 1957.

Knott, Frederick Hammett
Amateur. *b:* 30.10.1891, Tunbridge Wells, Kent. *d:* 10.2.1972, Horsell Birch, Woking, Surrey. Brother of C. H. (Kent). Middle order right-hand batsman, slow medium leg break and googly bowler, cover point. *Sch* Tonbridge. *Teams* Kent (1910–14, 11 matches); Oxford U (1911–14, blue 1912–14); Sussex (1926, 1 match).
Career batting
44–77–7–1800–116–25.71–3–*ct* 32–*st* 1
Bowling 103–4–25.75–0–0–3/65

A brilliant schoolboy cricketer, he was later handicapped by eye-trouble, which considerably affected his career in County cricket. He captained Oxford in 1914. A good rugby player, he represented Oxford as a half-back.

Knowles, Arthur
Amateur. *b:* 10.4.1858, Pendlebury, Manchester, Lancashire. *d:* 10.7.1929, Alvaston Hall, Cheshire. Middle order right-hand batsman, right-arm medium pace bowler. *Sch* Rugby. *Team* Lancashire (1888, 1 match).
Career batting
5–10–0–83–16–8.30–0–*ct* 2

His final first-class match was for MCC in 1896.

Knowles, Joseph
Professional. *b:* 25.3.1910, Nottingham. Middle order right-hand batsman, right-arm slow bowler. *Team* Nottinghamshire (1935–46, 125 matches).
Career batting
125–188–18–4194–114–24.67–2–*ct* 39
Bowling 1441–34–42.38–0–0–3/55

He hit 1,179 runs, av 25.08, in 1938.

Knowles, William Lancelot
Amateur. *b:* 27.11.1870, Twineham Grange, Henfield, Sussex. *d:* 1.12.1943, Ditchling, Sussex. Middle order right-hand batsman, good cover point. *Sch* Hurstpierpoint. *Teams* Kent (1892–1903, 34 matches); Sussex (1905, 1 match).
Career batting
37–65–2–1439–127–22.84–2–*ct* 13

He was Secretary of Sussex CCC 1922–43, resigning shortly before his death. For several years he was Master of the Brighton foot beagles.

Knox, Frank Pery
Amateur. *b:* 23.1.1880, Clapham, London. *d:* 1.2.1960, Hove, Sussex. Brother of N. A. (Surrey). Very patient opening left-hand batsman, right-arm medium pace bowler. *Sch* Dulwich. *Teams* Oxford U (1899–1901, blue all three years); Surrey (1899–1902, 7 matches).
Career batting
31–50–9–1281–198–31.24–2–*ct* 19
Bowling 2414–87–27.74–1–0–5/73

He captained Oxford in 1901.

Knox, Gerald Keith
Cricketer. *b:* 22.4.1937, North Shields, Northumberland. Opening right-hand batsman, right-arm medium pace bowler, cover point. *Sch* Newcastle GS. *Team* Lancashire (1964–67, 52 matches).
Career batting
52–92–3–1698–108–19.07–3–*ct* 38
Bowling 161–2–80.50–0–0–1/10

He also played for Northumberland (1957–63).

Knox, John
Amateur. *b:* 4.10.1904, Buenos Aires, Argentina. *d:* 10.4.1966, Buenos Aires, Argentina. Middle order right-hand batsman, good field. *Sch* Malvern. *Team* Argentine (1926/7 to 1937/8). *Tour* South America to England 1932.
Career batting
12–22–4–575–110*–31.94–1–*ct* 9
Bowling 87–1–87.00–0–0–1/46

Knox, Neville Alexander
Amateur. *b:* 10.10.1884, Clapham, London. *d:* 3.3.1935, Southborough, Surbiton, Surrey. Brother of F. P. (Surrey), brother-in-law of C. Palmer (Middlesex). Lower order right-hand batsman, right-arm fast bowler. *Sch* Dulwich. *Team* Surrey (1904–10, 73 matches). *Tests* England (1907, 2 matches).
Career batting
88–129–40–905–45*–10.16–0–*ct* 32
Bowling 8860–411–21.55–38–9–8/48
Test batting
2–4–1–24–8*–8.00–0–*ct* 0
Bowling 105–3–35.00–0–0–2/39

He took 100 wickets in a season twice (best 144, av 19.63, in 1906). His career was brief but brilliant, his bowling being regarded as the equal of any fast bowler in England, but lameness ended his County cricket in 1910. His final first-class match was for the Army in 1919.

Knox, William
Amateur. *b:* 20.11.1903, Paisley, Renfrewshire, Scotland. *d:* 11.6.1954, Paisley, Renfrewshire, Scotland. Middle order right-hand batsman. *Team* Scotland (1938).
Career batting
1–2–0–0–0–0.00–0–*ct* 1

Knutton, Herbert John
Professional. *b:* 14.6.1867, Coventry, Warwickshire. *d:* 12.12.1946, Heaton, Bradford, Yorkshire. Lower order right-hand batsman, right-arm fast bowler. *Team* Warwickshire (1894, 1 match).
Career batting
2–3–0–17–8–5.66–0–*ct* 0
Bowling 178–10–17.80–1–1–9/100
Although a talented bowler he preferred League cricket to the first-class game and made just one first-class County appearance; in 1902 however he created a small sensation by taking 9 for 100 in the first innings of a match between an Eleven of England and the Australians at Bradford – it was his final first-class match.

Kok, Myron
Amateur. *b:* 7.12.1932, Houghton, Johannesburg, South Africa. Tail end right-hand batsman, right-arm medium pace bowler. *Sch* Harrow. *Team* Cambridge U (1953).
Career batting
2–2–0–14–8–7.00–0–*ct* 2
Bowling 68–2–34.00–0–0–2/38

Konig, Peter Hans
Amateur. *b:* 16.10.1931, Vienna, Austria. Lower order right-hand batsman, wicket-keeper. *Team* Leicestershire (1949, 1 match).
Career batting
1–1–0–3–3–3.00–0–*ct* 1–*st* 1

Kortright, Charles Jesse
Amateur. *b:* 9.1.1871, Furze Hall, Fryerning, Ingatestone, Essex. *d:* 12.12.1952, Brookstreet, South Weald, Essex. Punishing middle order right-hand batsman, right-arm fast bowler. *Sch* Brentwood and Tonbridge. *Team* Essex (1894–1907, 160 matches).
Career batting
170–271–21–4404–131–17.61–2–*ct* 176
Bowling 10294–489–21.05–39–8–8/57
His debut in first-class matches was for MCC in 1893. Regarded as the fastest bowler of his day, and by some as the fastest ever to appear in first-class County cricket, his best season was 1895 when he took 76 wickets, av 15.83, though in 1898 he took 96 wickets, but at an average of 19.19. He first played for Essex (pre first-class) in 1889 and captained the county in 1903.

Kotze, Johannes Jacobus
Amateur. *b:* 7.8.1879, Hopefield, Cape Province, South Africa. *d:* 7.7.1931, Rondebosch, Cape Town, South Africa. Tail end right-hand batsman, right-arm fast bowler, poor field. *Teams* Transvaal (1902/3); Western Province (1903/4 to 1910/11); London County (1904). *Tours* South Africa to England 1901, 1904, 1907. *Tests* South Africa (1902/3 to 1907, 3 matches).
Career batting
72–105–25–688–60–8.60–0–*ct* 31
Bowling 6217–348–17.86–30–9–8/18
Test batting
3–5–0–2–2–0.40–0–*ct* 3
Bowling 243–6–40.50–0–0–3/64
Of his three visits to England, his most successful in first-class matches was 1904 when he took 104 wickets, av 20.50 – on that tour he also appeared for London County and in all first-class matches took 121, av 19.85. He was regarded as the fastest bowler ever to appear in first-class cricket in South Africa.

Krikken, Brian Egbert
Cricketer. *b:* 26.8.1946, Horwich, Lancashire. Father of K. M. (Derbyshire). Lower order left-hand batsman, wicket-keeper. *Teams* Lancashire (1966–67, 2 matches); Worcestershire (1969, 1 match).
Career batting
3–3–0–8–4–2.66–0–*ct* 7

Krikken, Karl Matthew
Cricketer. *b:* 9.4.1969, Bolton, Lancashire. Son of B. E. (Lancashire and Worcestershire). Middle order right-hand batsman, wicket-keeper. *Teams* Griqualand West (1988/9); Derbyshire (1989–92, 73 matches).
Career batting
74–104–16–1676–77*–19.04–0–*ct* 175–*st* 12
Bowling 40–0

Kripal Singh, Amritsar Govindsingh
Amateur. *b:* 6.8.1933, Madras, India. *d:* 22.7.1987, Madras, India. He died from a heart attack. Son of A. G. Ram Singh (Madras), brother of A. G. Milka Singh (India), A. G. Satwender Singh (Madras) and A. G. Harjinder Singh (Tamil Nadu), father of Swaran (Tamil Nadu) and Arjun (Tamil Nadu). Middle order right-hand batsman, off break bowler, moderate field. *Teams* Madras (1950/1 to 1964/5); Hyderabad (1965/6). *Tours* India to Ceylon 1956/7, to England 1959; Madras to Ceylon 1953/4, 1956/7, 1958/9, 1960/1, 1963/4. *Tests* India (1955/6 to 1964/5, 14 matches).
Career batting
96–142–21–4939–208–40.81–10–*ct* 57
Bowling 5029–177–28.41–3–1–6/14
Test batting
14–20–5–422–100*–28.13–1–*ct* 4
Bowling 584–10–58.40–0–0–3/43

Owing to injury he performed only moderately on his single tour to England, appearing in one Test. His highest score was 208 for Madras v Travancore-Cochin at Ernakulam in 1954/5.

Krishnamurthy, Pochiah
Cricketer. *b:* 12.7.1947, Hyderabad, India. Lower order right-hand batsman, occasional leg break bowler, wicket-keeper. *Team* Hyderabad (1967/8 to 1978/9). *Tours* India to West Indies 1970/71, to England 1971, to Ceylon 1973/4, to New Zealand and West Indies 1975/6; Hyderabad Blues to Ceylon 1966/7. *Tests* India (1970/1, 5 matches).
Career batting
108–130–25–1559–82–14.84–0–*ct* 150–*st* 68
Bowling 32–0
Test batting
5–6–0–33–20–5.50–0–*ct* 7–*st* 1

He was almost superfluous during the 1971 tour to England, since F. M. Engineer was co-opted into the team as wicket-keeper for the Tests and S. M. H. Kirmani was also on the tour. His first-class debut was for Indian Starlets in 1966/7.

Kuiper, Adrian Paul
Cricketer. *b:* 24.8.1959, Johannesburg, South Africa. Brother of J. L. (South African Univ). Middle order right-hand batsman, right-arm medium fast bowler. *Teams* Western Province (1977/8 to 1991/2); Derbyshire (1990, 12 matches). *Tours* South Africa to India (not first-class) 1991/2, to Australia and New Zealand (World Cup) 1991/2; to West Indies 1991/2. *Test* South Africa (1991/2, 1 match).
Career batting
124–200–25–5680–161*–32.45–6–*ct* 84
Bowling 4742–173–27.41–4–0–6/55
Test batting
1–2–0–34–34–17.00–0–*ct* 1

He met with little success during his season in English cricket, arriving with the reputation of one of the hardest hitters in the game.

Kumble, Anil Radhakrishna
Cricketer. *b:* 17.10.1970, Bangalore, India. Middle order right-hand batsman, leg break and googly bowler. *Team* Karnataka (1989/90 to 1991/2). *Tours* India to Sharjah (not first-class) 1989/90, 1991/2, to England 1990. *Test* India (1990, 1 match).
Career batting
26–34–11–1013–154*–44.04–3–*ct* 9
Bowling 2667–105–25.40–7–1–6/41
Test batting
1–1–0–2–2–2.00–0–*ct* 0
Bowling 170–3–56.66–0–0–3/105

He played in one Test on the 1990 tour to England, his leg breaks proving very expensive.

Kumleben, John Michael
Amateur. *b:* 26.5.1933, Waverley, Bloemfontein, South Africa. Middle order right-hand batsman. *Teams* Oxford U (1956–57); Orange Free State (1957/8 to 1960/1).
Career batting
29–50–2–955–100–19.89–1–*ct* 16

He won a hockey blue and also represented South Africa.

Kunderan, Budhisagar Krishnappa
(changed name from Kunderam in 1964)
Amateur. *b:* 2.10.1939, Mulki, Mangalore, India. Attractive right-hand opening batsman, right-arm medium pace bowler, wicket-keeper. *Teams* Railways (1959/60 to 1964/5); Mysore (1965/6 to 1969/70). *Tours* India to West Indies 1961/2, to England 1967, to East Africa 1967; International Wanderers to Rhodesia 1975/6; State Bank of India to Ceylon 1966/7, 1968/9. *Tests* India (1959/60 to 1967, 18 matches).
Career batting
129–217–20–5708–205–28.97–12–*ct* 175–*st* 86
Bowling 160–3–53.33–0–0–2/15
Test batting
18–34–4–981–192–32.70–2–*ct* 23–*st* 7
Bowling 13–0

Although going to England as reserve wicket-keeper to F. M. Engineer, Kunderan gained a place in two of the three Tests as a batsman and seemed equally at home either opening the innings or going lower down. His highest score was 205 for Railways v Jammu and Kashmir at Delhi in 1959/60. He hit 1,079 runs, av 38.53, in 1963/4 in India. His first-class debut was for Cricket Club of India in 1958/9. He represented Scotland in limited-overs matches.

Kuruppu, Don Sardha Brendon Priyantha
Cricketer. *b:* 5.1.1962, Colombo, Ceylon. Opening right-hand batsman, wicket-keeper. *Team* Burgher RC (1988/9 to 1989/90). *Tours* Sri Lanka to England 1983 (World Cup), 1984, 1988, 1990, 1991, to Australia 1984/5, 1987/8, 1989/90, to Sharjah (not first-class) 1983/4, 1986/7, 1987/8, 1988/9, 1989/90, to India and Pakistan (World Cup) 1987/8, to India 1989/90 (not first-class), to Bangladesh (not first-class) 1988/9; Sri Lanka Under 23 to Pakistan 1983/4. *Tests* Sri Lanka (1986/7 to 1991, 4 matches).
Career batting
48–79–7–2671–201*–37.09–5–*ct* 47–*st* 10
Test batting
4–7–1–320–201*–53.33–1–*ct* 1

He scored 201* in 777 minutes for Sri Lanka v New Zealand at Colombo in 1986/7 on his Test debut, the slowest double century in the history of the game. He achieved little on his three tours to England, though he played in the 1991 Test. His first-class debut was for Sri Lanka Board President's XI in 1982/3.

Kynaston, Roger
Amateur. *b:* 5.11.1805, Marylebone, London. *d:* 21.6.1874, Marylebone, London. Middle order right-

hand batsman, excellent longstop. *Sch* Eton. *Teams* MCC (1830–54); Middlesex (1850, 2 matches).
Career batting
167–304–18–2618–54–9.15–0–*ct* 42

He also played for Norfolk (1833). 'When in position for batting he stood with his legs as far away from the wicket as possible'. He was Secretary of MCC from 1842 to 1858 and Treasurer until 1866.

L

Labrooy, Graeme Fredrick
Cricketer. *b:* 7.6.1964, Colombo, Ceylon. Lower order right-hand batsman, right-arm fast medium bowler. *Team* Colombo CC (1988/9 to 1991/2). *Tours* Sri Lanka to India 1986/7, 1989/90 (not first-class), 1990/1, to Australia 1987/8, 1989/90, 1991/2 (World Cup), to Sharjah (not first-class) 1986/7, 1987/8, 1988/9, 1990/1, to England 1988, 1990, to Bangladesh (not first-class) 1988/9, to New Zealand 1990/1, to Pakistan 1991/2 (not first-class). *Tests* Sri Lanka (1986/7 to 1990/1, 9 matches).
Career batting
40–39–7–677–70*–21.15–0–*ct* 12
Bowling 3458–104–33.25–5–0–7/71
Test batting
9–14–3–158–70*–14.36–0–*ct* 3
Bowling 1194–27–44.22–1–0–5/133

He bowled well on his two tours to England, but in 1990 was troubled by injury.

Lacey, Sir Francis Eden
Amateur. *b:* 19.10.1859, Wareham, Dorset. *d:* 26.5.1946, Sutton-Veny House, Wiltshire. Middle order right-hand batsman, right-hand slow round-arm bowler, good field. *Sch* Sherborne. *Teams* Hampshire (1880–97, 33 matches); Cambridge U (1882, blue).
Career batting
50–89–10–2589–211–32.77–4–*ct* 34
Bowling 1123–52–21.59–3–1–7/149

His only double century was 211 for Hampshire v Kent at Southampton in 1884. He hit 323* for Hampshire v Norfolk in 1887 – the record score for a Minor County. In 1878 he played for Dorset. He also won a blue for soccer. For 28 years commencing 1898, he was Secretary to MCC; in 1926 he was knighted for his services to the game. He was President of Hampshire 1927–28.

Lacy-Scott, David Geffrey
Amateur. *b:* 18.8.1920, Calcutta, India. Opening right-hand batsman, right-arm fast medium bowler. *Sch* Marlborough. *Teams* Cambridge U (1946, blue); Kent (1946, 1 match).
Career batting
11–21–0–294–36–14.00–0–*ct* 0
Bowling 268–9–29.77–1–0–5/35

His final first-class match was for Free Foresters in 1948.

Lagden, Reginald Bousfield
Amateur. *b:* 15.4.1893, Maseru, Basutoland. *d:* 20.10.1944, Karachi, India. He was killed in an air crash. Son of G. Y. (MCC in South Africa), brother of R. O. (Oxford U). Middle order right-hand batsman, off break bowler. *Sch* Marlborough. *Teams* Cambridge U (1912–14, blue all three years); Surrey (1912, 1 match); Europeans (1926/7).
Career batting
32–56–1–1751–153–31.83–6–*ct* 18
Bowling 343–11–31.18–0–0–2/22

A good half back, he played hockey for Cambridge U and England. After the First World War he moved to India where he played both cricket and hockey extensively.

Lagden, Ronald Owen
Amateur. *b:* 21.11.1889, Maseru, Basutoland. *d:* 1.3.1915, St Eloi, Belgium. He was killed in action. Son of G. Y. (MCC in South Africa), brother of R. B. (Surrey). Hard hitting middle order right-hand batsman, right-arm fast bowler. *Sch* Marlborough. *Team* Oxford U (1909–12, blue all four years).
Career batting
31–54–7–1197–99*–25.46–0–*ct* 18
Bowling 1406–56–25.10–1–0–6/57

An all-round sportsman, he represented Oxford at rugby football, rackets and hockey, later gaining an England cap for rugby.

Laidlaw, William Kennedy
Amateur. *b:* 26.8.1912, Edinburgh, Scotland. Lower order right-hand batsman, leg break and googly bowler. *Teams* Scotland (1938–53); Minor Counties (1950).
Career batting
17–27–9–132–25–7.33–0–*ct* 8
Bowling 1225–42–29.16–2–0–7/70

His County cricket was for Durham (pre first-class, 1948–52).

Laidlay, William James
Amateur. *b:* 12.8.1846, Calcutta, India. *d:* 25.10.1912, Freshwater, Isle of Wight. Lower order batsman, useful bowler. *Sch* Loretto. *Team* North (1875).
Career batting
1–2–0–14–11–7.00–0–*ct* 0
Bowling 105–3–35.00–0–0–2/85

He was a well-known artist.

Laing, Dean Ralph
Cricketer. *b:* 18.9.1970, Durban, South Africa. Middle order right-hand batsman, right-arm medium pace bowler. *Teams* Transvaal (1989/90 to 1991/2); Nottinghamshire (1990, 1 match).

Career batting
24–37–4–830–101*–25.15–1–*ct* 12
Bowling 1464–40–36.60–0–0–3/34

Laing, James Gordon Brodie
Cricketer. *b:* 10.1.1938, Meigle, Perthshire, Scotland. Brother of J. R. (Scotland). Middle order right-hand batsman. *Team* Scotland (1964–74).
Career batting
19–32–4–655–93–23.39–0–*ct* 11

Laing, John Ralph
Cricketer. *b:* 27.8.1942, Meigle, Perthshire, Scotland. Brother of J. G. B. (Scotland). Middle order left-hand batsman. *Team* Scotland (1969–79).
Career batting
8–15–1–301–127*–21.50–1–*ct* 6

Laird, Bruce Malcolm
Cricketer. *b:* 21.11.1950, Mount Lawley, Perth, Western Australia. Opening right-hand batsman. *Team* Western Australia (1972/3 to 1983/4, 64 matches). *Tours* Australia to England 1975, 1980, to Pakistan 1979/80, 1982/3, to New Zealand 1981/2. *Tests* Australia (1979/80 to 1982/3, 21 matches).
Career batting
103–186–14–6085–171–35.37–8–*ct* 86
Bowling 69–0
Test batting
21–40–2–1341–92–35.28–0–*ct* 16
Bowling 12–0

He played in only nine first-class matches on the 1975 tour to England and was not required for the Tests. On the brief 1980 Centenary tour he appeared in the only Test, but was unfit for selection for the 1981 visit to England.

Laitt, David James
Amateur. *b:* 3.5.1931, Oxford. Lower order right-hand batsman, right-arm medium pace bowler. *Sch* Magdalen College School, Oxford. *Team* Minor Counties (1959–60).
Career batting
2–3–1–25–10–12.50–0–*ct* 2
Bowling 186–6–31.00–0–0–4/58

His County cricket was for Oxfordshire (1952–72).

Lake, Graham Johnson
Professional. *b:* 13.4.1935, Croydon, Surrey. Lower order right-hand batsman, right-arm fast medium bowler. *Team* Gloucestershire (1956–58, 13 matches).
Career batting
13–18–4–106–18–7.57–0–*ct* 6
Bowling 464–17–27.29–0–0–4/39

He also played for Hertfordshire (1952–59).

Lake, Ronald Dewé
Amateur. *b:* 9.5.1891, Bury St Edmunds, Suffolk. *d:* 28.7.1950, Winkton, Hampshire. Middle order right-hand batsman. *Sch* Uppingham. *Team* Northamptonshire (1922, 2 matches).
Career batting
2–4–1–48–30–16.00–0–*ct* 1

He also played for Suffolk (1913).

Laker, James Charles
Professional for Surrey, amateur for Essex in 1962. *b:* 9.2.1922, Frizinghall, Bradford, Yorkshire. *d:* 23.4.1986, Putney, London. Lower order right-hand batsman, accurate off break bowler. *Teams* Surrey (1946–59, 309 matches); Auckland (1951/2); Essex (1962–64, 30 matches). *Tours* MCC to West Indies 1947/8, 1953/4, to South Africa 1956/7, to Australia and New Zealand 1958/9; Commonwealth to India 1950/1; Cavaliers to Jamaica 1963/4, to West Indies 1964/5. *Tests* England (1947/8 to 1958/9, 46 matches).
Career batting
450–548–108–7304–113–16.60–2–*ct* 270
Bowling 35791–1944–18.41–127–32–10/53
Test batting
46–63–15–676–63–14.08–0–*ct* 12
Bowling 4101–193–21.24–9–3–10/53

The most accomplished English off spin bowler of his generation, Laker was one of the principal architects of Surrey's great team which won the County Championship in seven successive seasons 1952 to 1958. He first played for England in the West Indies in 1947/8 and was the most successful bowler on the tour, in both the Tests and first-class games. The English Test selectors nonetheless showed little faith in him during the next eight years and he was never sure of a place in the England side. In 1956 however he completely demoralised the Australians, taking no fewer than 46 wickets in the series at a cost of 9.60 and at Old Trafford creating a unique record with 19 wickets for 90 runs. He caused controversy by at first declining a place in the team to tour Australia in 1958/9, although he later accepted. In 1960 he wrote his book 'Over to Me', which caused some ill-feeling. He had retired from Surrey at the close of the 1959 season, but reappeared for Essex from 1962 to 1964. In all he took 100 wickets in a season 11 times, his best total being 166 wickets, av 15.32, in 1950. Twice he achieved the feat of all 10 wickets in an innings, once for England (for 53 runs) in the 1956 Manchester Test noted previously, and once for Surrey, in the same year, also v Australians (for 88 runs at the Oval). After leaving first-class cricket, he was well-known as a commentator on the game.

Laker, Peter Guy
Professional. *b:* 5.12.1926, Hurstpierpoint, Sussex. Lower order right-hand batsman, leg break bowler. *Team* Sussex (1948–49, 2 matches).
Career batting
2–2–1–14–8*–14.00–0–*ct* 1
Bowling 70–0

He was a well-known sports journalist.

Lall Singh
Amateur. *b:* 16.12.1909, Kuala Lumpur, Malaya. *d:* 19.11.1985, Kuala Lumpur, Malaya. Dashing middle order right-hand batsman, right-arm slow medium bowler, brilliant field. *Teams* Southern Punjab (1933/4 to 1935/6); Hindus (1934/5 to 1935/6). *Tour* India to England 1932. *Test* India (1932, 1 match).
Career batting
32–51–6–1123–107*–24.95–1–*ct* 23
Bowling 59–1–59.00–0–0–1/9
Test batting
1–2–0–44–29–22.00–0–*ct* 1

The most noteworthy feature of his cricket on the 1932 tour was his fielding. His first-class debut was in the Indian Trial matches of 1931/2.

Lamason, John Rider
Amateur. *b:* 29.10.1905, Wellington, New Zealand. *d:* 25.6.1961, Wellington, New Zealand. Middle order right-hand batsman, right-arm bowler. *Team* Wellington (1927/8 to 1946/7). *Tours* New Zealand to England 1937, to Australia 1937/8.
Career batting
60–106–7–2065–127–20.85–2–*ct* 61
Bowling 1476–45–32.80–1–0–5/67

He quite failed to reproduce his New Zealand form when visiting England in 1937 and was not required for the Tests.

Lamb, Allan Joseph
Cricketer. *b:* 20.6.1954, Langebaanweg, Cape Province, South Africa. Middle order right-hand batsman, right-arm medium pace bowler. *Teams* Western Province (1972/3 to 1981/2); Northamptonshire (1978–92, 234 matches); Orange Free State (1987/8). *Tours* England to Australia 1982/3, 1984/5 (not first-class), 1986/7, 1990/1, to New Zealand 1982/3 (not first-class), 1983/4, 1990/1 (not first-class), 1991/2, to Pakistan 1983/4, to India 1984/5, 1988/9 (tour cancelled), 1989/90 (not first-class), to Sri Lanka 1984/5, to West Indies 1985/6, 1989/90, to India and Pakistan (World Cup) 1987/8, to Australia and New Zealand (World Cup) 1991/2. *Tests* England (1982–92, 79 matches).
Career batting
412–684–101–28495–294–48.87–79–*ct* 320
Bowling 199–8–24.87–0–0–2/29
Test batting
79–139–10–4656–142–36.09–14–*ct* 75
Bowling 23–1–23.00–0–0–1/6

A batsman who is unhappy unless he is on the attack, he made an almost immediate impact on English cricket when he arrived to play for Northamptonshire in 1978. By 1980 he was regarded as one of the best batsmen in England and as soon as he qualified as an English player he was drafted into the Test side. As with his success in county cricket he soon settled to a permanent England place. In 1983 against New Zealand he topped the England Test batting averages with 392 runs, av 65.33, and the following season against the West Indies was again the leading English batsman (one of the few not overawed by the fast bowlers). In 1985 he played in all six Tests against Australia, but poor results in 1986 led to his exclusion from the 1987 England side. Injuries in 1988 and 1989 restricted his cricket, though he regained his Test place. More recently his Test form has been erratic, though since 1988 he has consistently headed the Northamptonshire batting averages. In 1992 he played in only two Tests. It should however be noted that his impact in one-day internationals has perhaps been greater than that in Test cricket: his one-day international career average is several runs higher than his Test record. He was appointed Northamptonshire captain in 1989 and has captained England in three Tests.

He hit 1,000 runs in a season eleven times going on to 2,000 once: 2,049, av 60.26, in 1981. His highest score was 294 for Orange Free State v Eastern Province at Bloemfontein in 1987/8 and his highest in England 235 for Northamptonshire v Yorkshire at Headingley in 1990.

Lamb, Arthur
Amateur. *b:* 17.12.1868, Cheltenham, Gloucestershire. *d:* 26.7.1908, Cliftonville, Margate, Kent. Lower order batsman, useful bowler. *Team* Gloucestershire (1895–96, 2 matches).
Career batting
2–4–0–24–10–6.00–0–*ct* 0
Bowling 32–0

Lamb, Bruce
Amateur. *b:* 25.8.1878, Andover, Hampshire. *d:* 21.3.1932, Andover, Hampshire. Middle order batsman. *Sch* Marlborough. *Team* Hampshire (1898–1901, 4 matches).
Career batting
4–7–0–29–8–4.14–0–*ct* 2

Lamb, Henry John Hey
Amateur. *b:* 3.5.1912, Warkton, Kettering, Northamptonshire. Hard hitting middle order right-hand batsman, wicket-keeper. *Sch* Winchester. *Team* Northamptonshire (1934–38, 38 matches).
Career batting
38–69–5–1085–91*–16.95–0–*ct* 23–*st* 1

Lamb, Hon Timothy Michael
Cricketer. *b:* 24.3.1953, Hartford, Cheshire. Lower order right-hand batsman, right-arm medium pace bowler. *Sch* Shrewsbury. *Teams* Oxford U (1973–74, blue both years); Middlesex (1974–77, 36 matches); Northamptonshire (1978–83, 108 matches).
Career batting
160–163–61–1274–77–12.49–0–*ct* 40
Bowling 10459–361–28.97–10–0–7/56

He was Middlesex Secretary 1984–87 and has been Cricket Secretary to the TCCB since 1987.

Lamba, Raman
Cricketer. *b:* 2.1.1960, Meerut, India. Opening right-hand batsman, right-arm medium pace bowler. *Team* Delhi (1978/9 to 1991/2). *Tours* India to England 1986, to Sharjah (not first-class) 1986/7, 1989/90, to Pakistan 1989/90. *Tests* India (1986/7 to 1987/8, 4 matches).
Career batting
93–133–12–6507–320–53.77–24–*ct* 51
Bowling 394–6–65.66–0–0–2/9
Test batting
4–5–0–102–53–20.40–0–*ct* 5
Although he did not play in any Tests on the 1986 tour to England, he showed great batting potential in County matches. He hit 320 for North Zone v West Zone at Bhilai in 1987/8. In 1990 he appeared for Ireland in the NatWest Trophy.

Lambert, Clayton Benjamin
Cricketer. *b:* 10.2.1962, New Amsterdam, British Guiana. Opening left-hand batsman, off break bowler. *Team* Guyana (1983/4 to 1991/2). *Tours* Young West Indies to Zimbabwe 1989/90; West Indies to England 1991, to Sharjah (not first-class) 1991/2. *Test* West Indies (1991, 1 match).
Career batting
63–109–10–4460–219–45.05–11–*ct* 93
Bowling 104–4–26.00–0–0–2/33
Test batting
1–2–0–53–29–26.50–0–*ct* 2
Bowling 4–1–4.00–0–0–1/4
He batted well in the County matches on his 1992 tour to England, but found a place in the Test side only for the final match of the series. His highest score was 219 for Young West Indies v Zimbabwe at Harare in 1989/90.

Lambert, George Ernest Edward
Professional. *b:* 11.5.1919, Paddington, London. *d:* 30.10.1991, Bristol. Son-in-law of A. J. B. Fowler (Middlesex), father-in-law of D. J. Constant (Kent and Leicestershire). Aggressive lower order right-hand batsman, right-arm fast medium bowler. *Teams* Gloucestershire (1938–57, 334 matches); Somerset (1960, 3 matches).
Career batting
340–489–61–6375–100*–14.89–1–*ct* 194
Bowling 26189–917–28.55–37–5–8/35
He took 100 wickets in a season once: 113, av 22.75, in 1952. About 1949 he was regarded as the fastest bowler in English County cricket. He was Somerset coach 1959–63.

Lambert, Noel Hamilton
Amateur. *b:* 5.6.1910, Dublin, Ireland. Son of R. J. H. (Ireland), nephew of S. D. (Ireland). Middle order right-hand batsman. *Sch* Rossall. *Team* Ireland (1932–47).
Career batting
9–17–2–213–69*–14.20–0–*ct* 5
He played rugby for Ireland.

Lambert, Reginald Everitt
Amateur. *b:* 25.9.1882, Telham Court, Sussex. *d:* 23.1.1968, Shaftesbury, Dorset. Middle order batsman, right-arm medium pace bowler. *Sch* Harrow. *Teams* Cambridge U (1903–04); Sussex (1904, 1 match).
Career batting
4–6–0–72–30–12.00–0–*ct* 1
Bowling 164–3–54.66–0–0–3/53

Lambert, Robert James Hamilton
Amateur. *b:* 18.7.1874, Rathmines, Dublin, Ireland. *d:* 24.3.1956, Rathfarnham, Dublin, Ireland. Brother of S. D. (Ireland), father of N. H. (Ireland). Middle order right-hand batsman, off break bowler. *Teams* Ireland (1902–28); London County (1903).
Career batting
25–45–6–1121–103*–28.74–1–*ct* 19
Bowling 1686–70–24.08–4–1–7/11
He was regarded as Ireland's greatest all-round cricketer and in three successive seasons achieved the feat of scoring over 2,000 runs and taking over 200 wickets. He captained Ireland in 13 matches and was for many years a selector of Irish teams, being in addition President of the Irish Cricket Union twice. A noted badminton player, he represented Ireland.

Lambert, Septimus Drummond
Amateur. *b:* 3.8.1876, Rathmines, Dublin, Ireland. *d:* 21.4.1959, Dublin, Ireland. Brother of R. J. H. (Ireland), uncle of N. H. (Ireland). Middle order right-hand batsman, wicket-keeper. *Team* Ireland (1902–21).
Career batting
7–10–2–184–60*–23.00–0–*ct* 3

Lambert, William
Professional. *b:* 1779, Burstow, Surrey. *d:* 19.4.1851, Nutfield, Surrey. Excellent middle order right-hand batsman, slow under-arm bowler. *Teams* Surrey (1801–17); Kent (1806); Hampshire (1806–07); Sussex (1816–17).
Career batting
64–114–5–3013–157–27.64–4–*ct* 62–*st* 26
Bowling 187 wickets (no analyses)–2–0–6/?
He was regarded as one of the best all-round cricketers of his day and was an excellent single-wicket player. He was the first batsman to hit a century in both innings of an important match, scoring 107* and 157 for Sussex v Epsom at Lord's in 1817. He did not appear in matches at Lord's after 1817 because, it is said, that he 'sold' the England v Nottingham match of that year.

Lambert, William
Professional. *b:* 19.4.1843, Hatfield, Hertfordshire. *d:* 4.3.1927, St Fagan's, Cardiff, Glamorgan. Middle order right-hand batsman, right-hand medium pace round-arm bowler, slip field. *Team* Middlesex (1874–77, 7 matches).
Career batting
7–14–3–112–34*–10.18–0–*ct* 9
Bowling 54–1–54.00–0–0–1/14
He also played for Hertfordshire (1875) and Glamorgan (pre first-class, 1897–98). His brother was George Lambert, the Tennis Master at Lord's, who was regarded as the leading player in England between 1871 and 1885.

Lampard, Albert Wallis
Amateur. *b:* 3.7.1885, Richmond, Melbourne, Victoria, Australia. *d:* 11.1.1984, Armadale, Melbourne, Victoria, Australia. Middle order right-hand batsman, leg break and googly bowler, wicket-keeper. *Team* Victoria (1908/9 to 1921/2, 18 matches). *Tours* AIF to England 1919, to South Africa 1919/20; Australia to New Zealand 1920/1.
Career batting
63–96–12–2597–132–30.91–3–*ct* 30–*st* 4
Bowling 3492–134–26.05–7–1–9/42
Without doing anything outstanding, he was a distinctly useful all-rounder on the 1919 tour of England. His best bowling was 9/42 for AIF v Lancashire at Old Trafford in 1919.

Lampitt, Stuart Richard
Cricketer. *b:* 29.7.1966, Wolverhampton, Staffordshire. Middle order right-hand batsman, right-arm medium pace bowler. *Team* Worcestershire (1985–92, 88 matches). *Tour* Worcestershire to Zimbabwe 1990/1.
Career batting
89–99–22–1665–93–21.62–0–*ct* 35
Bowling 5673–186–30.50–8–0–5/32

Lanaway, Charles
Professional. *b:* 16.3.1793, Henfield, Sussex. *d:* 6.2.1870, Brighton, Sussex. Middle order right-hand batsman, under-arm bowler. *Team* Sussex (1825–38, 34 matches).
Career batting
36–70–6–393–31–6.14–0–*ct* 21
Bowling 29–2 + 7–14.50–0–0–3/?

Lancashire, Oswald Philip
Amateur. *b:* 10.12.1857, Newton Heath, Manchester, Lancashire. *d:* 23.7.1934, Fielden Park, West Didsbury, Manchester, Lancashire. Hard hitting middle order right-hand batsman, good field. *Sch* Lancing. *Teams* Cambridge U (1878–81, blue 1880); Lancashire (1878–88, 97 matches).
Career batting
122–197–18–2349–76*–13.12–0–*ct* 45
He was President of Lancashire CCC 1923–24. A noted soccer player, he appeared three times for Cambridge v Oxford.

Lancashire, Walter
Amateur. *b:* 28.10.1903, Hemsworth, Yorkshire. *d:* 7.6.1981, Dorchester, Dorset. Lower order right-hand batsman, right-arm medium pace bowler. *Sch* Taunton. *Team* Hampshire (1935–37, 18 matches).
Career batting
18–29–1–471–66–16.82–0–*ct* 7
Bowling 357–7–51.00–0–0–2/49
He also played for Dorset (1946–50).

Lancaster, Thomas
Professional. *b:* 11.2.1863, Dalton, Huddersfield, Yorkshire. *d:* 12.12.1935, Blackburn, Lancashire. Brother of W. W. (Yorkshire). Lower order left-hand batsman, slow left-arm bowler. *Team* Lancashire (1894–99, 27 matches).
Career batting
27–40–11–554–66–19.10–0–*ct* 6
Bowling 1456–66–22.06–5–0–7/25
He played for Yorkshire in a non-first-class match in 1891.

Lancaster, William Whiteley
Professional. *b:* 4.2.1873, Scholes, Huddersfield, Yorkshire. *d:* 30.12.1938, Marsh, Huddersfield, Yorkshire. Brother of Thomas (Lancashire). Middle order right-hand batsman, right-hand fast round-arm bowler. *Team* Yorkshire (1895, 7 matches).
Career batting
7–10–0–163–51–16.30–0–*ct* 1
Bowling 29–0

Lance, Herbert Roy
Amateur. *b:* 6.6.1940, Pretoria, South Africa. Son of W. P. (North East Transvaal), brother of A. P. (Northern Transvaal). Opening or middle order right-hand batsman, right-arm medium pace bowler. *Teams* North East Transvaal (1958/9 to 1960/1); Transvaal (1961/2 to 1970/1); Northern Transvaal (1971/2). *Tours* South Africa to England 1965, 1970 (tour cancelled). *Tests* South Africa (1961/2 to 1969/70, 13 matches).
Career batting
103–171–18–5336–169–34.87–11–*ct* 101
Bowling 4284–167–25.65–2–0–6/55
Test batting
13–22–1–591–70–28.14–0–*ct* 7
Bowling 479–12–39.91–0–0–3/30
He played in all three Tests on the 1965 tour, but prospered more when not opening the batting in the latter half of the visit.

Lanchbury, Robert John
Cricketer. *b:* 11.2.1950, Evesham, Worcestershire. Middle order right-hand batsman. *Teams* Gloucestershire (1971, 5 matches); Worcestershire (1973–74, 8

matches).
Career batting
14–23–3–357–50*–17.85–0–*ct* 2
Bowling 6–0
He also played for Wiltshire (1984–88). His last first-class match was for Minor Counties in 1985.

Landon, Charles Whittington
Amateur. *b:* 30.5.1850, Bromley, Kent. *d:* 5.3.1903, Ledston Hall, Yorkshire. Middle order right-hand batsman, right-hand medium pace round-arm bowler, excellent cover point. *Sch* Bromsgrove. *Teams* Lancashire (1874–75, 6 matches); Yorkshire (1878–82, 9 matches).
Career batting
15–23–0–172–47–7.47–0–*ct* 8
Bowling 143–2–71.50–0–0–1/10
He was the leading figure in the Yorkshire Gentlemen's side for many years.

Lane, Albert Frederick
Amateur. *b:* 29.8.1885, Rowley Regis, Staffordshire. *d:* 29.1.1948, Upper Fulbrook, Warwickshire. Middle order right-hand batsman, off break bowler. *Teams* Worcestershire (1914–32, 45 matches); Warwickshire (1919–25, 12 matches).
Career batting
57–97–11–1422–76–16.53–0–*ct* 27
Bowling 1892–46–41.13–0–0–4/56
He also played for Staffordshire (1909–12).

Lane, Rev Charlton George
Amateur. *b:* 11.6.1836, Kennington, London. *d:* 2.11.1892, Little Gaddesden, Hertfordshire. Brother of W. W. C. (Surrey), brother-in-law of C. E. Boyle (Oxford U). Hard hitting middle order right-hand batsman, good outfield. *Sch* Westminster. *Teams* Oxford U (1856–60, blue 1856, 1858–60); Surrey (1856–61, 18 matches).
Career batting
46–82–4–1021–72–13.08–0–*ct* 14
Bowling 63–3–21.00–0–0–3/31
His first-class debut was for Gentlemen of England in 1854 and his final first-class match for Gentlemen of Surrey and Sussex in 1867. He also played for Worcestershire (1863), Buckinghamshire (1864–67) and Hertfordshire (1870–77). He captained Oxford in 1859 and 1860. He was a rowing blue in 1858 and 1859.

Lane, George
Professional. *b:* 25.7.1852, Kimberley, Nottinghamshire. *d:* 31.7.1917, Haverford, Philadelphia, USA. Lower order left-hand batsman, left-arm medium pace bowler. *Teams* Nottinghamshire (1881, 3 matches); Players of USA (1883–94).
Career batting
14–22–5–119–19*–7.00–0–*ct* 9
Bowling 801–58–13.81–4–2–8/62
For some years he was one of the leading professional cricketers in Philadelphia where his first-class debut was for English Residents in 1880.

Lane, Sivell
Amateur. *b:* 21.8.1881, Ledbury, Herefordshire. *d:* 10.2.1961, Toronto, Ontario, Canada. Lower order batsman, useful bowler. *Team* Gloucestershire (1901, 3 matches).
Career batting
3–5–1–16–8–4.00–0–*ct* 2
Bowling 296–7–42.28–1–0–5/139
He also played for Herefordshire (1900).

Lane, William Ward Claypon
(assumed the name Lane-Claypon in 1875)
Amateur. *b:* 1.8.1845, Kennington, London. *d:* 31.3.1939, Wheathampstead, Hertfordshire. Brother of C. G. (Surrey), brother-in-law of M. H. Stow (Cambridge U). Lower order right-hand batsman, right-hand slow round-arm bowler. *Sch* Westminster. *Teams* Cambridge U (1866–67); Surrey (1868–70, 2 matches).
Career batting
5–9–0–69–36–7.66–0–*ct* 0
Bowling 37–1–37.00–0–0–1/23
He also played for Lincolnshire (1873).

Lang, Arthur Horace
Amateur. *b:* 25.10.1890, Malabar Hill, Bombay, India. *d:* 25.1.1915, Cuinchy, France. He was posted missing, believed killed in action. Sound middle order right-hand batsman, wicket-keeper. *Sch* Harrow. *Teams* Sussex (1911–13, 13 matches); Cambridge U (1912–13, blue 1913).
Career batting
22–40–3–830–141–22.43–2–*ct* 17–*st* 16
His final first-class match was for L. Robinson's XI in 1914. He also played for Suffolk (1907–11). He also won a blue for rackets.

Lang, J. M.
Professional. Lower order left-hand batsman, slow left-arm bowler. *Team* Worcestershire (1923–24, 8 matches).
Career batting
8–14–8–27–9*–4.50–0–*ct* 4
Bowling 412–8–51.50–0–0–2/21
He also played for Northumberland (1928), but not in the Minor Counties Championship.

Lang, Thomas William
Amateur. *b:* 22.6.1854, Selkirk, Scotland. *d:* 30.5.1902, Virginia Water, Surrey. Opening or middle order right-hand batsman, right-hand medium pace round-arm bowler. *Sch* Clifton. *Teams* Gloucestershire (1872–74, 8 matches); Oxford U (1874–75, blue both years).
Career batting
18–26–3–303–54–13.17–0–*ct* 9

Bowling 1104–76–14.52–5–1–6/27

He also played for Northumberland (1882). His brother was Andrew Lang, the well-known writer.

Langdale, George Richmond
Amateur. *b:* 11.3.1916, Thornaby-on-Tees, Yorkshire. Forcing middle order left-hand batsman, off break bowler. *Teams* Derbyshire (1936–37, 4 matches); Somerset (1946–49, 20 matches).
Career batting
25–42–3–709–146–18.17–1–*ct* 7
Bowling 939–23–40.82–1–0–5/30

His final first-class match was for Minor Counties in 1953. He also played for Norfolk (1939) and Berkshire (1952–63) and in 1953 took all 10 wickets (for 25) for Berkshire v Dorset at Reading.

Langdon, Rev George Leopold
Amateur. *b:* 11.2.1818, Winchester, Hampshire. *d:* 2.1.1894, St Paul's Cray, Kent. Middle order left-hand batsman. *Team* Sussex (1839–42, 8 matches).
Career batting
15–29–1–224–38–8.00–0–*ct* 9

He was regarded as one of the most promising players of his day, but retired from important matches on entering the Church. He was Hon Secretary of Sussex CCC 1839–42.

Langdon, Thomas
Professional. *b:* 8.1.1879, Brighton, Sussex. *d:* 30.11.1944, Nuneaton, Warwickshire. Steady opening right-hand batsman, slow left-arm bowler. *Team* Gloucestershire (1900–14, 279 matches).
Career batting
282–519–14–10723–156–21.23–6–*ct* 207–*st* 3
Bowling 839–22–38.13–0–0–3/4

He hit 1,000 runs in a season three times (best 1,369, av 30.42, in 1907).

Langford, Brian Anthony
Professional. *b:* 17.12.1935, Birmingham. Lower order right-hand batsman, off break bowler. *Team* Somerset (1953–74, 504 matches).
Career batting
510–720–162–7588–68*–13.59–0–*ct* 229
Bowling 34964–1410–24.79–83–16–9/26

He took 100 wickets in a season five times (best 116, av 18.28, in 1958); his best bowling was 9/26 for Somerset v Lancashire at Weston-super-Mare in 1958. He created a sensation when he first appeared for Somerset, by taking 26 wickets for 308 runs in his first three matches. From 1969 to 1971 he captained Somerset. For Somerset in the John Player League he bowled eight overs in a match without conceding a run – a record for the competition.

Langford, William Thomas
Professional. *b:* 5.10.1875, New Forest, Hampshire. *d:* 20.2.1957, Ospringe, Faversham, Kent. Lower order right-hand batsman, right-arm fast medium bowler. *Team* Hampshire (1902–08, 93 matches).
Career batting
93–153–25–1663–62*–12.99–0–*ct* 67
Bowling 5781–215–26.88–5–2–8/82

Langhorne, Alfred Robert Maskell
Amateur. *b:* 20.12.1845. *d:* 4.6.1930, Watford, Hertfordshire. Middle order batsman. *Sch* Rugby. *Team* MCC (1880).
Career batting
1–2–0–16–15–8.00–*ct* 0

Langley, Colin Kendall
Amateur. *b:* 11.7.1888, Narborough, Leicestershire. *d:* 26.6.1948, Hatton, Warwick. Lower order right-hand batsman, right-arm fast medium bowler. *Sch* Radley. *Team* Warwickshire (1908–14, 33 matches).
Career batting
33–52–4–455–61*–9.47–0–*ct* 12
Bowling 1391–54–25.75–3–0–8/29

He played in the Seniors' match at Oxford, but no first-class matches. At the time of his death he was Hon Secretary and Chairman of Warwickshire CCC, having held both offices since 1943.

Langley, Gilbert Roche Andrews
Amateur. *b:* 14.9.1919, North Adelaide, South Australia. Uncle of J. N. (Queensland and South Australia). Stolid lower order right-hand batsman, wicket-keeper. *Team* South Australia (1945/6 to 1956/7, 55 matches). *Tours* Australia to England 1953, 1956, to West Indies 1954/5, to Pakistan and India 1956/7, to South Africa 1949/50. *Tests* Australia (1951/2 to 1956/7, 26 matches).
Career batting
122–165–39–3236–160*–25.68–4–*ct* 292–*st* 77
Bowling 2–0
Test batting
26–37–12–374–53–14.96–0–*ct* 83–*st* 15

He appeared in four out of the five Tests on the 1953 tour of England and three out of five in 1956 – in the latter Test series he dismissed 19 of the 44 batsmen to fall whilst he was wicket-keeper. He dismissed nine batsmen (8 ct, 1 st) for Australia v England at Lord's in 1956, a Test record at the time.

Langley, Henry Fitzroy James
Amateur. *b:* 8.12.1846, Westminster, London. *d:* 20.11.1884, Buenos Aires, Argentina. Middle order batsman. *Sch* Eton. *Team* I Zingari (1866).
Career batting
2–4–2–4–4–2.00–0–*ct* 1

Langley, John Douglas Algernon
Amateur. *b:* 25.4.1918, Northwood, Middlesex. Middle order right-hand batsman. *Sch* Stowe. *Teams* Middlesex (1937, 1 match); Cambridge U (1938–39, blue 1938).
Career batting
14–22–0–442–119–20.09–1–*ct* 9

Langridge, James
Professional. *b:* 10.7.1906, Chailey, Sussex. *d:* 10.9.1966, Withdean, Brighton, Sussex. Brother of J. G. (Sussex), father of R. J. (Sussex). Middle order left-hand batsman, slow left-arm bowler, safe field. *Teams* Sussex (1924–53, 622 matches); Auckland (1927/8). *Tours* MCC to India and Ceylon 1933/4, Australia and New Zealand 1935/6, 1946/7; Tennyson to India 1937/8. *Tests* England (1933–46, 8 matches).
Career batting
695–1058–157–31716–167–35.20–42–*ct* 384
Bowling 34524–1530–22.56–91–14–9/34
Test batting
8–9–0–242–70–26.88–0–*ct* 6
Bowling 413–19–21.73–2–0–7/56
He hit 1,000 runs in a season 20 times, going on to 2,000 once: 2,082, av 40.82, in 1937. He took 100 wickets in a season six times in the 1930s (best 158, av 16.56, in 1933) and performed the 'double' on each occasion. His best bowling was 9/34 for Sussex v Yorkshire at Sheffield in 1934. From 1950 to 1952 he captained Sussex, and from 1953 to 1960 was County coach.

Langridge, John George, MBE
Professional. *b:* 10.2.1910, Chailey, Sussex. Brother of James (Sussex), uncle of R. J. (Sussex). Fine opening right-hand batsman, right-arm medium pace bowler, excellent slip field. *Team* Sussex (1928–55, 567 matches). *Tour* MCC to India 1939/40 (tour cancelled).
Career batting
574–984–66–34380–250*–37.45–76–*ct* 784
Bowling 1848–44–42.00–0–0–3/15
He hit 1,000 runs in a season 17 times going on to 2,000 11 times (best 2,914, av 60.70, in 1949). All his eight double centuries were for Sussex, the highest being 250* v Glamorgan at Hove in 1933. With E. H. Bowley he added 490 for the first wicket for Sussex v Middlesex at Hove in 1933. After retiring, he became a first-class umpire (1956–80), standing in 7 Test matches (1960–63) and was awarded the MBE for his services to cricket in 1979.

Langridge, Richard James
Professional. *b:* 13.4.1939, Brighton, Sussex. Son of James (Sussex), nephew of J. G. (Sussex). Middle order left-hand batsman, off break bowler. *Team* Sussex (1957–71, 207 matches). *Tour* MCC to East Africa 1963/4.
Career batting
212–391–28–8310–137*–22.89–5–*ct* 188
Bowling 91–0
He hit 1,000 runs in a season four times (best 1,885, av 30.90, in 1962). He did not play regularly after 1966 (except in 1970) in County cricket.

Langridge, William
Amateur. Lower order batsman. *Team* Hambledon XII (1908).
Career batting
1–1–0–2–2–2.00–0–*ct* 0
Bowling 42–1–42.00–0–0–1/42

Langton, Arthur Chudleigh Beaumont
Amateur. *b:* 2.3.1912, Pietermaritzburg, Natal. *d:* 27.11.1942, Accra, Gold Coast. He was killed in an air accident. Lower order right-hand batsman, right-arm fast medium or medium pace bowler. *Team* Transvaal (1931/2 to 1941/2). *Tour* South Africa to England 1935. *Tests* South Africa (1935 to 1938/9, 15 matches).
Career batting
52–74–13–1218–73*–19.96–0–*ct* 41
Bowling 4969–193–25.74–9–2–6/53
Test batting
15–23–4–298–73*–15.68–0–*ct* 8
Bowling 1827–40–45.67–1–0–5/58
He was most effective on his single tour to England, taking 115 wickets, av 21.16.

Langton, Samuel Thomas
Professional. *b:* 24.1.1886, Parkgate, Rotherham, Yorkshire. *d:* 10.7.1918, Bentley, Doncaster, Yorkshire. Middle order right-hand batsman, change bowler. *Team* Derbyshire (1909–10, 3 matches).
Career batting
3–5–0–14–6–2.80–0–*ct* 1
Bowling 42–0

Lapham, Arthur William Edwards
Amateur. *b:* 1879. *d:* 9.2.1964, Portsmouth, Hampshire. Middle order batsman, useful bowler. *Team* Essex (1921, 3 matches).
Career batting
3–5–0–31–16–6.20–0–*ct* 0
Bowling 90–5–18.00–0–0–2/25
He also played for Wiltshire (1906–13).

Lara, Brian Charles
Cricketer. *b:* 2.5.1969, Santa Cruz, Trinidad. Middle order left-hand batsman, leg break and googly bowler. *Team* Trinidad (1987/8 to 1991/2). *Tours* Young West Indies to Zimbabwe 1989/90; West Indies to Pakistan 1990/1, 1991/2 (not first-class), to England 1991, to Sharjah (not first-class) 1991/2, to Australia 1991/2, to Australia and New Zealand (World Cup) 1991/2. *Tests* West Indies (1990/1 to 1991/2, 2 matches).
Career batting
44–70–2–2921–182–42.95–7–*ct* 53
Bowling 77–0
Test batting
2–4–0–130–64–32.50–0–*ct* 6
He played some useful innings on the 1991 tour to England and might have gained Test selection late in the summer, but for injury.

Larkham, William Trevor
Amateur. *b:* 10.11.1929, Kidderminster, Worcestershire. Lower order right-hand batsman, leg break bowler, good field. *Team* Worcestershire (1952, 1 match).
Career batting
1–2–0–13–13–6.50–0–*ct* 0
Bowling 64–1–64.00–0–0–1/64

Larking, John Gordon
Amateur. *b:* 4.11.1921, Loose, Maidstone, Kent. Middle order right-hand batsman. *Sch* Charterhouse. *Team* Kent (1946, 3 matches).
Career batting
3–6–1–15–8–3.00–0–*ct* 2

Larkins, Wayne
Cricketer. *b:* 22.11.1953, Roxton, Bedfordshire. Attractive opening right-hand batsman, right-arm medium pace bowler, fine field. *Teams* Northamptonshire (1972–91, 363 matches); Eastern Province (1982/3 to 1983/4); Durham (1992, 22 matches). *Tours* England to Australia 1979/80, 1990/1, to India 1979/80, 1989/90 (not first-class), to West Indies 1989/90; SAB England XI to South Africa 1981/2; Overseas XI to India 1980/1. *Tests* England (1979/80 to 1990/1, 13 matches).
Career batting
436–762–48–24384–252–34.15–53–*ct* 260
Bowling 1858–42–44.23–1–0–5/59
Test batting
13–25–1–493–64–20.54–0–*ct* 8

He hit 1,000 runs in a season twelve times (best 1,863, av 45.43, in 1982). His highest score was 252 for Northamptonshire v Glamorgan at Cardiff in 1983. A prolific scorer for Northamptonshire in both first-class and limited overs cricket, he did not prosper at the highest level. His decision to tour South Africa reduced his opportunities for England.

Larmour, Sir Edward Noel
Amateur. *b:* 25.12.1916, Milltown, Belfast, Ireland. Opening right-hand batsman. *Sch* Royal Belfast Academical Institution. *Team* Ireland (1938).
Career batting
1–2–0–45–34–22.50–0–*ct* 0

Larter, John David Frederick
Professional. *b:* 24.4.1940, Inverness, Scotland. Tail end right-hand batsman, right-arm fast medium bowler. *Sch* Framlingham. *Team* Northamptonshire (1960–69, 134 matches). *Tours* MCC to New Zealand 1960/1, to Australia and New Zealand 1962/3, 1965/6, to East Africa 1963/4, to India 1963/4; International XI to Rhodesia and Pakistan 1961/2. *Tests* England (1962–65, 10 matches).
Career batting
182–162–57–639–51*–6.08–0–*ct* 56
Bowling 13013–666–19.53–27–5–8/28
Test batting
10–7–2–16–10–3.20–0–*ct* 5
Bowling 941–37–25.43–2–0–5/57

He took 100 wickets in a season twice (best 121, av 16.76, in 1963). His promising career was marred by injury. He also played for Suffolk (1958).

Larwood, Harold
Professional. *b:* 14.11.1904, Nuncargate, Nottinghamshire. Hard hitting lower order right-hand batsman, devastating right-arm fast bowler. *Teams* Nottinghamshire (1924–38, 300 matches); Europeans (1936/7). *Tours* MCC to Australia 1928/9, 1932/3. *Tests* England (1926 to 1932/3, 21 matches).
Career batting
361–438–72–7289–102*–19.91–3–*ct* 234
Bowling 24994–1427–17.51–98–20–9/41
Test batting
21–28–3–485–98–19.40–0–*ct* 15
Bowling 2212–78–28.35–4–1–6/32

Controversy and ill-feeling reduced the Test career of Larwood, regarded as the greatest fast bowler of the inter-war period, to just over six years. His name is inevitably linked with the English 1932/3 tour to Australia, when the 'Bodyline' battle was at its height. In all first-class matches on that tour he took 49 wickets, av 16.66, and in the Tests alone 33 wickets, av 19.51, being the leading bowler in both. England won the series by four matches to one, but the outcome was that Larwood never again played for England and the subsequent rows in 1934–35 caused much heated argument in Nottingham.

Larwood took 100 wickets in a season eight times, with 162 wickets, av 12.86, in 1932 as his best year. His best bowling in an innings was 9/41 for Nottinghamshire v Kent at Trent Bridge in 1931 and five times, in 1927, 1928, 1931, 1932 and 1936, he headed the season's first-class bowling averages.

Owing to injury, he retired from County cricket in 1938 and in 1949 emigrated to Australia. His memoirs were published in 1933, 'Bodyline?' and again in 1965, 'The Larwood Story'.

Lashbrooke, Albert Edward
Professional. *b:* 30.11.1883, West Ham, Essex. *d:* 2.10.1963, West Hulme, Oldham, Lancashire. Lower order batsman, opening bowler. *Team* Essex (1908, 1 match).
Career batting
1–2–0–9–9–4.50–0–*ct* 0
Bowling 61–1–61.00–0–0–1/26

Lashley, Patrick Douglas
(known as Peter Lashley)
Amateur. *b:* 11.2.1937, St Matthias Gap, Christ Church, Barbados. Steady middle order left-hand batsman, right-arm medium pace bowler, good field. *Team* Barbados (1957/8 to 1974/5). *Tours* West Indies to Australia 1960/1, to England 1966; Bar-

bados to England 1969. *Tests* West Indies (1960/1 to 1966, 4 matches).
Career batting
85–132–13–4932–204–41.44–8–*ct* 66
Bowling 958–27–35.48–0–0–3/15
Test batting
4–7–0–159–49–22.71–0–*ct* 4
Bowling 1–1–1.00–0–0–1/1

On the 1966 tour to England he appeared in two Tests, but in all first-class matches had only a modest return with 647 runs, av 29.40. His highest score was 204 for Barbados v Guyana at Georgetown in 1966/7.

Latchford, John Richard
Professional. *b:* 16.6.1909, Delph, Yorkshire. *d:* 30.4.1980, Omagh, Co Tyrone, Ireland. Middle order right-hand batsman, right-arm medium pace bowler. *Team* Lancashire (1930–32, 7 matches).
Career batting
7–10–0–154–63–15.40–0–*ct* 4
Bowling 181–4–45.25–0–1/6

He also played for Durham (pre first-class, 1935–39).

Latchman, Amritt Harrichand
(known as Harry Chand Latchman)
Cricketer. *b:* 26.7.1943, Kingston, Jamaica. Lower order right-hand batsman, leg break and googly bowler. *Teams* Middlesex (1965–73, 170 matches); Nottinghamshire (1974–76, 40 matches). *Tour* International XI to Ceylon and India 1967/8.
Career batting
213–240–64–2333–96–13.25–0–*ct* 107
Bowling 13588–487–27.90–22–1–7/65

He also played for Cambridgeshire (1977–78).

Latham, Geoffrey Chitty
Amateur. *b:* 15.3.1887, Shanghai, China. *d:* 23.9.1980, Waverley Abbey House, Farnham, Surrey. Son of Thomas (Cambridge U). Middle order right-hand batsman. *Sch* Winchester. *Team* Oxford U (1907).
Career batting
1–2–0–25–22–12.50–0–*ct* 1

He won a blue for hockey.

Latham, Hubert Joseph
Amateur. *b:* 13.9.1932, Winson Green, Birmingham. Lower order right-hand batsman, right-arm fast bowler. *Team* Warwickshire (1955–59, 10 matches).
Career batting
10–13–2–129–26–11.72–0–*ct* 2
Bowling 751–27–27.81–1–0–6/49

Latham, Michael Edward
Professional. *b:* 14.1.1939, Birmingham. Lower order right-hand batsman, right-arm fast medium bowler. *Team* Somerset (1961–62, 18 matches).
Career batting
18–21–12–133–21*–14.77–0–*ct* 10
Bowling 888–29–30.62–2–0–5/20

He also played for Northumberland (1963–72).

Latham, Percy Holland
Amateur. *b:* 3.2.1873, Llandudno, Caernarvonshire. *d:* 22.6.1922, Haileybury School, Hertfordshire. Attacking middle order right-hand batsman, right-arm slow bowler, good cover point. *Sch* Malvern. *Teams* Cambridge U (1892–94, blue all three years); Sussex (1898–1906, 40 matches).
Career batting
63–106–7–2580–172–26.06–4–*ct* 31
Bowling 99–2–49.50–0–0–1/0

He also played for Worcestershire (pre first-class, 1891–95). He captained Cambridge in 1894.

Latham, Richard Lockhart
Amateur. *b:* 5.1.1908, Sao Paulo, Brazil. *d:* 4.2.1953, Sao Paulo, Brazil. Sound middle order right-hand batsman, wicket-keeper. *Sch* Repton. *Tour* South America to England 1932.
Career batting
5–9–1–120–58–15.00–0–*ct* 6

He was one of the leading cricketers in Brazil.

Latham, Roger Done
Amateur. *b:* 1.1.1900, Chelsea, London. *d:* 24.11.1971, Onchan, Isle of Man. Tail end batsman. *Sch* Wellington. *Team* MCC (1920).
Career batting
1–2–2–16–16*–no av–0–*ct* 0

He was a well-known actor under the stage name 'Roger Maxwell'.

Latham, Thomas
Amateur. *b:* 22.6.1847, St Pancras, London. *d:* 13.1.1926, West Folkestone, Kent. Father of G. C. (Oxford U). Stylish middle order right-hand batsman, good deep field. *Sch* Winchester and Highgate. *Team* Cambridge U (1873–74, blue both years).
Career batting
9–17–1–293–48–18.31–0–*ct* 5

His County cricket was for Cheshire (1878).

Lathwell, Mark Nicholas
Cricketer. *b:* 26.12.1971, Bletchley, Buckinghamshire. Opening right-hand batsman, right-arm medium pace bowler. *Team* Somerset (1991–92, 21 matches).
Career batting
21–36–1–1239–114–35.40–1–*ct* 14
Bowling 323–5–64.60–0–0–1/9

He scored 1,176 runs, av 36.75, in 1992.

Laver, Frank Jonas
Amateur. *b:* 7.12.1869, Castlemaine, Victoria, Australia. *d:* 24.9.1919, East Melbourne, Victoria, Australia. Uncle of J. F. L. (Tasmania). Middle order right-hand bat with ungainly style, right-arm medium pace bowler, splendid point. *Team* Victoria (1891/2 to 1911/12, 78 matches). *Tours* Australia to England

1899, 1905, 1909, to New Zealand 1904/5, 1913/14. *Tests* Australia (1899–1909, 15 matches).
Career batting
163–255–38–5430–164–25.02–6–*ct* 147
Bowling 9990–404–24.72–19–5–8/31
Test batting
15–23–6–196–45–11.52–0–*ct* 8
Bowling 964–37–26.05–2–0–8/31

He was most successful as a bowler on the tour of 1905 and 1909, heading the first-class averages for each tour and in 1905 taking 115 wickets, av 18.19. He acted as player-manager of the 1905 and 1909 visits to England, as well as the two tours to New Zealand. He was author of 'An Australian Cricketer on Tour' published in 1905. His death was hastened through privations sustained whilst exploring the interior of Australia.

Lavers, Alan Braden
Amateur. *b:* 6.9.1912, Melbourne, Victoria, Australia. Middle order right-hand batsman, off break bowler. *Sch* Chigwell. *Teams* Essex (1937–53, 25 matches).
Career batting
26–46–3–734–42*–17.06–0–*ct* 6
Bowling 497–13–38.23–0–0–4/68

Lavis, George
Professional. *b:* 17.8.1908, Sebastopol, Monmouth. *d:* 29.7.1956, Pontypool, Monmouth. Steady middle order right-hand batsman, right-arm medium fast bowler. *Team* Glamorgan (1928–49, 206 matches).
Career batting
206–312–43–4957–154–18.42–3–*ct* 71
Bowling 7768–156–49.79–0–0–4/55

He was coach to Glamorgan from 1946 until shortly before his death.

Law, Alexander Patrick
Amateur. *b:* 14.1.1832, Northrepps, Norfolk. *d:* 30.10.1895, Richmond, Surrey. Stylish middle order right-hand batsman, right-hand medium pace round-arm bowler. *Sch* Rugby and Cheltenham. *Teams* Oxford U (1855–57, blue 1857).
Career batting
19–35–4–488–59–15.74–0–*ct* 6
Bowling 516–19–27.15–1–0–5/72

He usually played under the name of 'Infelix'. His first-class debut was for Gentlemen of England in 1851 and his final match for MCC in 1866. His County cricket was for Norfolk (1854–66) and Warwickshire (pre first-class, 1864).

Law, Alfred
Professional. *b:* 16.12.1862, Birmingham. *d:* 19.5.1919, Handsworth, Birmingham. Sound middle order right-hand batsman, good deep field. *Team* Warwickshire (1894–99, 52 matches).
Career batting
52–81–5–1459–89–19.19–0–*ct* 21

He first played for Warwickshire (pre first-class) in 1885. He was a first-class umpire (1908).

Law, George
Amateur. *b:* 17.4.1846, Rochdale, Lancashire. *d:* 30.7.1911, Marylebone, London. Brother of William (Yorkshire). Middle order right-hand batsman, right-hand fast medium round-arm bowler. *Sch* Radley. *Team* Middlesex (1881, 3 matches).
Career batting
11–16–1–160–54–10.66–0–*ct* 6

His first-class debut was for Gentlemen of England in 1871. He also played for Essex (pre first-class, 1870) and Norfolk (1877).

Law, John Alexander Gordon Charles
Amateur. *b:* 25.3.1923, Bangalore, India. Middle order right-hand batsman, wicket-keeper. *Sch* Edinburgh Academy. *Teams* Madras (1940/1 to 1941/2); Europeans (1944/5); Oxford U (1949).
Career batting
9–17–0–194–35–11.41–0–*ct* 16–*st* 3

Law, Rev William
Amateur. *b:* 9.4.1851, Rochdale, Lancashire. *d:* 20.12.1892, Rotherham, Yorkshire, of pleurisy. Brother of George (Middlesex), brother-in-law of H. J. Hill (MCC 1900). Hard hitting middle order right-hand batsman, right-arm fast bowler, brilliant cover point. *Sch* Harrow. *Teams* Oxford U (1871–74, blue all four years); Yorkshire (1871–73, 4 matches).
Career batting
28–47–0–501–39–10.65–0–*ct* 17
Bowling 353–14–25.21–0–0–4/83

His last first-class match was for Gentlemen of England in 1883. He was also a good footballer.

Lawley, Rt Hon Beilby
(succeeded to the title 3rd Lord Wenlock in 1880)
Amateur. *b:* 12.5.1849, Westminster, London. *d:* 15.1.1912, Marylebone, London. Brother-in-law of W. F. Forbes (I Zingari). Opening batsman. *Sch* Eton. *Team* I Zingari (1880).
Career batting
1–1–0–3–3–3.00–0–*ct* 1

He played no first-class matches at Cambridge U. In 1885 he was President of MCC. He was appointed Governor of Madras in 1890 and took an active interest in the development of cricket in India. He was MP for Chester, April to July, 1880, when he was unseated.

Lawlor, Peter John
Cricketer. *b:* 8.5.1960, Gowerton, Glamorgan. Lower order right-hand batsman, off break bowler. *Team* Glamorgan (1981, 1 match).
Career batting
1–2–0–8–8–4.00–0–*ct* 1
Bowling 50–1–50.00–0–0–1/36

Lawrence, Anthony Sackville
Amateur. *b:* 25.3.1911, Mayfair, Westminster, London. *d:* 17.3.1939, Westminster, London. Sound middle order right-hand batsman, left-arm medium pace bowler, good cover. *Sch* Harrow. *Team* Cambridge U (1932–33, blue 1933).
Career batting
14–24–2–575–80–26.13–0–*ct* 7
Bowling 527–9–58.55–0–0–3/33
His final first-class match was for the Army in 1935.

Lawrence, Arthur Alfred Kenneth
Professional. *b:* 3.11.1930, Marlborough, Wiltshire. Middle order right-hand batsman, leg break bowler. *Team* Sussex (1952–56, 28 matches).
Career batting
28–44–7–632–63*–17.08–0–*ct* 28
Bowling 40–1–40.00–0–0–1/14

Lawrence, C.
Amateur. Lower order batsman. *Team* MCC (1898).
Career batting
1 match, did not bat–*ct* 0

Lawrence, Charles
Professional. *b:* 16.12.1828, Hoxton, London. *d:* 20.12.1916, Canterbury, Melbourne, Victoria, Australia. Middle order right-hand batsman, right-hand medium pace round-arm bowler. *Teams* Surrey (1854–57, 2 matches); Middlesex (1861, 1 match); New South Wales (1862/3 to 1869/70, 5 matches). *Tours* Stephenson to Australia 1861/2; Australian Aboriginals to England 1868 (not first-class).
Career batting
9–15–0–227–78–15.13–0–*ct* 7
Bowling 416–38–10.94–4–2–7/25
Having travelled to Australia with the 1861/2 English Team, he remained in that country when the tour ended and as a coach was largely responsible for the improvement of cricket in Australia in the 1860s. He played for Ireland (not first-class) 1856–61.

Lawrence, David Valentine
(birth registered as Dave Valentine Lawrence)
Cricketer. *b:* 28.1.1964, Gloucester. Lower order right-hand batsman, right-arm fast bowler. *Team* Gloucestershire (1981–91, 166 matches). *Tours* England B to Sri Lanka 1985/6; Gloucestershire to Sri Lanka 1986/7; England to India 1988/9 (tour cancelled), to New Zealand 1991/2; England A to Zimbabwe 1989/90 (not first-class). *Tests* England (1988 to 1991/2, 5 matches).
Career batting
181–205–35–1819–66–10.70–0–*ct* 44
Bowling 16162–507–31.87–21–1–7/47
Test batting
5–6–0–60–34–10.00–0–*ct* 0
Bowling 676–18–37.55–1–0–5/106
He took 85 wickets, av 24.62, in 1985. His international career looked assured for some years when he was selected for the 1991/2 tour to New Zealand and England's World Cup squad in Australia, but he fractured his left knee cap whilst bowling in the Third Test at Wellington in 1991/2 and thus missed the whole of the World Cup competition and the 1992 English season.

Lawrence, Douglas Rosyth
Amateur. *b:* 20.10.1929, Portobello, Edinburgh, Scotland. Lower order right-hand batsman, right-arm fast medium bowler. *Team* Scotland (1956–58).
Career batting
7–12–4–32–10–4.00–0–*ct* 1
Bowling 491–12–40.91–0–0–4/56

Lawrence, Hervey Major
Amateur. *b:* 24.3.1881, Hadlow, Kent. *d:* 17.9.1975, Ely, Cambridgeshire. Lower order right-hand batsman, right-arm fast medium bowler, good slip. *Team* Kent (1899, 4 matches).
Career batting
7–12–4–49–23–6.12–0–*ct* 1
Bowling 539–13–41.46–0–0–4/37
His final first-class match was Army in 1914. He also played for Suffolk (1913).

Lawrence, John
Professional. *b:* 29.3.1911, Carlton, Leeds, Yorkshire. *d:* 10.12.1988, Toulston, Tadcaster, Yorkshire. Father of J. M. (Somerset). Middle order right-hand batsman, leg break and googly bowler. *Team* Somerset (1946–55, 281 matches).
Career batting
283–500–52–9183–122–20.49–3–*ct* 262
Bowling 19927–798–24.97–40–4–8/41
He hit 1,000 runs in a season three times (best 1,128, av 22.11, in 1955) and took 100 wickets twice (best 115, av 18.90, in 1950). He also played for Lincolnshire (1958–67).

Lawrence, John Fortune
Amateur. *b:* 9.9.1904, Dublin, Ireland. *d:* 13.8.1984, Eastbourne, Sussex. Opening right-hand batsman. *Team* Dublin University (1926).
Career batting
1–2–0–7–6–3.50–0–*ct* 0

Lawrence, John Miles
Professional. *b:* 7.11.1940, Rothwell, Yorkshire. *d:* 16.4.1989, Toulston, Tadcaster, Yorkshire. Son of John (Somerset). Middle order right-hand batsman, leg break bowler. *Sch* Millfield. *Team* Somerset (1959–61, 18 matches).
Career batting
18–33–9–372–41–15.50–0–*ct* 7
Bowling 363–9–40.33–0–0–3/44

Lawrence, Mark Philip
Cricketer. *b:* 6.5.1962, Warrington, Lancashire. Lower order left-hand batsman, slow left-arm bowler. *Sch* Manchester GS. *Team* Oxford U (1982–86, blue 1984–86).
Career batting
30–35–10–101–18–4.04–0–*ct* 9
Bowling 2979–42–70.92–0–0–3/79

Lawrence, Patrick J.
Cricketer. *b:* 3.10.1942, Roseau, Dominica. Lower order right-hand batsman, right-arm fast medium bowler. *Team* Middlesex (1964, 4 matches).
Career batting
4–4–1–19–14*–6.33–0–*ct* 0
Bowling 186–6–31.00–0–0–3/52
He was no-balled for throwing during the match between Middlesex and Sussex at Lord's in 1964 and did not play again in first-class cricket.

Lawrence, Terence Patrick
Amateur. *b:* 26.4.1910, Waltham Abbey, Essex. Middle order right-hand batsman, leg break bowler. *Sch* Uppingham. *Team* Essex (1933–35, 7 matches).
Career batting
7–14–0–133–39–9.50–0–*ct* 3
He played in the Freshmen's and Seniors' matches at Cambridge but no first-class games. He also played for Hertfordshire (1929–31) and Berkshire (1947).

Lawrence, Walter Nicholas Murray
Amateur. *b:* 8.2.1935, Marylebone, London. Opening right-hand batsman. *Sch* Winchester. *Team* Oxford U (1954).
Career batting
3–3–0–2–1–0.66–0–*ct* 3

Lawrie, Percy Edward
Amateur. *b:* 12.12.1902, Kensington, London. *d:* 7.2.1988, Teignmouth, Devon. Middle order right-hand batsman. *Sch* Eton. *Teams* Hampshire (1921–28, 28 matches); Oxford U (1922–24).
Career batting
33–53–2–1084–107–21.25–1–*ct* 13

Lawry, William Justus
Cricketer. *b:* 24.4.1940, St Just, Cornwall. Lower order left-hand batsman, wicket-keeper. *Team* Minor Counties (1965–69).
Career batting
3–4–3–13–9–13.00–0–*ct* 8
His County cricket was for Cornwall (1958–80).

Lawry, William Morris
Amateur. *b:* 11.2.1937, Thornbury, Melbourne, Victoria, Australia. Very sound left-hand opening batsman, left-arm medium pace bowler. *Team* Victoria (1955/6 to 1971/2, 99 matches). *Tours* Australia to England 1961, 1964, 1968, to India and Pakistan 1964/5, to South Africa 1966/7, 1969/70, to West Indies 1964/5, to India and Sri Lanka 1969/70; Rest of World to Barbados 1966/7. *Tests* Australia (1961 to 1970/1, 67 matches).
Career batting
249–417–49–18734–266–50.90–50–*ct* 121
Bowling 188–5–37.60–0–0–1/3
Test batting
67–123–12–5234–210–47.15–13–*ct* 30
Bowling 6–0
His greatest success in England came on his first visit in 1961, when he topped both first-class and Test batting averages with figures of 2,019, av 61.18, and 420, av 52.50; he exceeded 1,000 runs in first-class matches on the 1964 tour, but a broken finger in 1968, when he captained the side, forced him to miss a number of games and his aggregate did not reach four figures. None of his four double centuries was made in England, where his highest innings was 165 v Surrey at the Oval in 1961. He captained Australia in 25 Tests, including 9 against England. His highest score was 266 for Victoria v New South Wales at Sydney in 1960/1. He hit 1,000 runs in an Australian season four times (best 1,445, av 72.25, in 1965/6).

Laws, Michael Lutener
Amateur. *b:* 12.8.1926, Finchley, Middlesex. Lower order right-hand batsman, wicket-keeper. *Sch* Highgate. *Team* Middlesex (1948–50, 5 matches).
Career batting
8–8–3–19–12–3.80–0–*ct* 10–*st* 5
His first-class debut was for Combined Services in 1946.

Lawson, Geoffrey Francis
Cricketer. *b:* 7.12.1957, Wagga Wagga, New South Wales, Australia. Lower order right-hand batsman, right-arm fast bowler. *Teams* New South Wales (1977/8 to 1991/2, 115 matches); Lancashire (1979, 1 match). *Tours* Australia to India 1979/80, 1984/5 (not first-class), 1989/90 (not first-class), to Pakistan 1979/80, 1982/3, to Sri Lanka 1980/1, to England 1981, 1983 (World Cup), 1985, 1989, to West Indies 1983/4; New South Wales to Zimbabwe 1987/8; Rest of World to England 1988. *Tests* Australia (1980/1 to 1989/90, 46 matches).
Career batting
191–225–44–2683–74–14.82–0–*ct* 75
Bowling 16564–666–24.87–28–2–8/112
Test batting
46–68–12–894–74–15.96–0–*ct* 10
Bowling 5501–180–30.56–11–2–8/112
His first tour to England was marred by injury which meant that he appeared in only three Tests, but on his two subsequent tours, in 1985 and 1989, he played a major part in the Test series, appearing in all 12 Tests. In 1985 he took 22 Test wickets, av 37.72, and in 1989 29 wickets, av 27.27. His seam bowling has been of major importance to New South Wales cricket and at the present time he holds the record for the most wickets in a first-class career for that state.

Lawson, Howard Maurice
Amateur. *b:* 22.5.1914, Bournemouth, Hampshire. Son of M. B. (Hampshire). Lower order right-hand batsman, right-arm fast medium bowler. *Team* Hampshire (1935–37, 45 matches).
Career batting
46–70–14–560–53–10.00–0–*ct* 18
Bowling 2573–71–36.23–2–0–5/91

Lawson, Joseph Frank
Amateur. *b:* 13.11.1893, Stroud, Gloucestershire. *d:* 1970, Wellington, New Zealand. Middle order batsman. *Sch* Wycliffe. *Team* Gloucestershire (1914, 1 match).
Career batting
1–2–0–4–3–2.00–0–*ct* 0

Lawson, Maurice Bertie
Amateur. *b:* 28.2.1885, Christchurch, Hampshire. *d:* 8.8.1961, Alton, Hampshire. Father of H. M. (Hampshire). Lower order right-hand batsman, right-arm fast medium bowler. *Team* Hampshire (1907–19, 7 matches).
Career batting
7–11–1–122–36–12.20–0–*ct* 2
Bowling 170–5–34.00–0–0–2/45

Lawson, Thomas Morrison
Amateur. *b:* 16.9.1890, Penrith, Cumberland. *d:* 8.2.1967, Church Village, Glamorgan. Middle order right-hand batsman. *Team* Scotland (1923–24).
Career batting
3–6–0–59–22–9.83–0–*ct* 0

Lawton, Albert Edward
Amateur. *b:* 31.3.1879, Dukinfield, Cheshire. *d:* 25.12.1955, Manchester, Lancashire. Hard hitting middle order right-hand batsman, right-arm medium slow bowler, occasional wicket-keeper. *Sch* Rugby. *Teams* Derbyshire (1900–10, 131 matches); London County (1901–03); Lancashire (1912–14, 12 matches).
Career batting
182–314–11–7509–168–24.78–11–*ct* 125–*st* 1
Bowling 3607–113–31.92–0–0–4/19
He hit 1,000 runs in a season twice (best 1,064, av 22.63, in 1901). He was captain of Derbyshire 1902–03 and 1909, and joint captain 1904–06 and 1908. He also played for Cheshire (1919).

Lawton, William
Professional. *b:* 4.6.1920, Pitses, Ashton-under-Lyne, Lancashire. Lower order right-hand batsman, right-arm medium pace bowler. *Team* Lancashire (1948, 2 matches).
Career batting
2–2–0–3–3–1.50–0–*ct* 1
Bowling 64–1–64.00–0–0–1/0
He also played for Cumberland (1955–56). A good soccer player, he appeared for Oldham Athletic and Chester. His wife is Dora Bryan, the actress.

Laxton, William John
Professional. *b:* 17.8.1849, Cambridge. *d:* 26.8.1882, Cambridge. Lower order right-hand batsman, right-hand fast round-arm bowler. *Team* All England Eleven (1872–73).
Career batting
2–3–1–49–36–24.50–0–*ct* 0
Bowling 69–2–34.50–0–0–2/49
His County cricket was for Wiltshire (1877).

Laycock, David Allen
Cricketer. *b:* 2.9.1947, Woolwich, London. Opening right-hand batsman. *Team* Kent (1969–73, 10 matches).
Career batting
10–16–2–266–58–19.00–0–*ct* 2

Layman, Alfred Richard
Amateur. *b:* 24.4.1858, Norwood, Surrey. *d:* 8.11.1940, Beckenham, Kent. Lower order right-hand batsman, wicket-keeper. *Sch* Hurstpierpoint. *Team* Kent (1893, 1 match).
Career batting
1–2–0–1–1–0.50–0–*ct* 1

Layne, Oliver Hoffran
Professional. *b:* 3.7.1876, Brittons Hill, St Michael, Barbados. *d:* 16.8.1932, Ballevne, New York, USA. Middle order right-hand batsman, right-arm medium pace bowler. *Team* Barbados (1901/2 to 1904/5); British Guiana (1909/10 to 1912/13). *Tour* West Indies to England 1906.
Career batting
27–48–2–1023–106–22.23–1–*ct* 19
Bowling 2035–91–22.36–6–2–9/19
He proved a useful all-rounder on the 1906 tour to England. His best bowling was 9/19 for British Guiana v Shepherd's XI at Georgetown in 1909/10.

Lea, Antony Edward
Cricketer. *b:* 29.9.1962, Wolverhampton, Staffordshire. Opening right-hand batsman, leg break bowler. *Team* Cambridge U (1984–86, blue all three years).
Career batting
22–41–2–772–119–19.79–1–*ct* 11
Bowling 292–8–36.50–0–0–3/61
His County cricket was for Staffordshire (1988).

Leach, Clive William
Professional. *b:* 4.12.1934, Almudabad, Bombay, India. Middle order right-hand batsman, slow left-arm bowler. *Team* Warwickshire (1955–58, 39 matches).
Career batting
39–64–6–1025–67–17.67–0–*ct* 28
Bowling 657–26–25.26–0–0–3/19

He also played for Durham (pre first-class, 1959–65) and Buckinghamshire (1966–71). He was also a noted local soccer player.

Leach, Edward Leach Cecil
Professional. *b:* 28.11.1896, Featherstall, Lancashire. *d:* 4.1.1973, Nailsea, Somerset. Middle order batsman. *Teams* Lancashire (1923–24, 12 matches); Somerset (1924–28, 8 matches).
Career batting
20–29–1–250–79–8.92–0–*ct* 6
Bowling 87–1–87.00–0–0–1/62
He appeared for both Lancashire and Somerset in 1924, but not in a County Championship match for the latter.

Leach, George
Professional. *b:* 18.7.1881, Malta. *d:* 10.1.1945, Rawtenstall, Lancashire. Free hitting middle order right-hand batsman, right-arm fast bowler. *Team* Sussex (1903–14, 225 matches).
Career batting
226–352–42–5870–113*–18.93–2–*ct* 106
Bowling 11543–413–27.94–19–1–8/48
He hit 1,016 runs, av 24.78, in 1906 and in 1909 took 106 wickets, av 20.06.

Leach, Harold
Amateur. *b:* 13.3.1862, Lower Fold, Rochdale, Lancashire. *d:* 15.2.1928, Widcombe, Bath, Somerset. Brother of John (Lancashire), Robert (Lancashire), R. C. (Lancashire) and W. E. (Lancashire). Middle order right-hand batsman, slow right-arm bowler, good field. *Team* Lancashire (1881, 1 match).
Career batting
3–5–1–101–46–25.25–0–*ct* 2
Bowling 4–0
His final first-class match was for Liverpool and District XI in 1891.

Leach, John
Amateur. *b:* 17.10.1846, Lower Fold, Rochdale, Lancashire. *d:* 1.2.1893, Lower Fold, Rochdale, Lancashire. Brother of Harold (Lancashire), Robert (Lancashire), R. C. (Lancashire) and W. E. (Lancashire). Opening right-hand batsman. *Sch* Marlborough. *Team* Lancashire (1866–77, 5 matches).
Career batting
5–9–0–103–34–11.44–0–*ct* 1

Leach, Rev Robert
Amateur. *b:* 18.12.1849, Lower Fold, Rochdale, Lancashire. *d:* 10.9.1939, Westbury, Newport Pagnell, Buckinghamshire. Brother of Harold (Lancashire), John (Lancashire), R. C. (Lancashire) and W. E. (Lancashire). Middle order right-hand batsman. *Sch* Marlborough. *Team* Lancashire (1868–76, 3 matches).
Career batting
3–5–0–35–14–7.00–0–*ct* 0

Leach, Roger Chadwick
Amateur. *b:* 21.9.1853, Lower Fold, Rochdale, Lancashire. *d:* 21.4.1889, Salta, Argentine. Brother of Harold (Lancashire), John (Lancashire), Robert (Lancashire) and W. E. (Lancashire), great-grandfather of N. M. K. Smith (Warwickshire). Middle order right-hand batsman. *Sch* Marlborough. *Team* Lancashire (1885, 1 match).
Career batting
1–2–0–49–39–24.50–0–*ct* 0

Leach, William Edmund
Amateur. *b:* 7.11.1851, Lower Fold, Rochdale, Lancashire. *d:* 30.11.1932, Ivinghoe, Buckinghamshire. Brother of Harold (Lancashire), John (Lancashire), Robert (Lancashire) and R. C. (Lancashire). Middle order right-hand batsman, right-hand under-arm bowler, good field. *Sch* Marlborough. *Teams* Lancashire (1885, 5 matches); Canterbury (1876/7).
Career batting
6–11–1–235–56–23.50–0–*ct* 1
Bowling 11–0
He played in the North v South series in Argentina.

Leach, William Robert Ronald
Amateur. *b:* 3.4.1883, Kensington, London. *d:* 1.11.1969, Eastbourne, Sussex. Lower order right-hand batsman, slow left-arm bowler. *Team* Royal Navy (1913).
Career batting
1–2–0–13–12–6.50–0–*ct* 1
Bowling 61–3–20.33–0–0–3/61

Leadbeater, Barrie
Cricketer. *b:* 14.8.1943, Harehills, Leeds, Yorkshire. Sound opening right-hand batsman, right-arm medium pace bowler. *Team* Yorkshire (1966–79, 144 matches). *Tour* Norfolk to West Indies 1969/70.
Career batting
147–241–29–5373–140*–25.34–1–*ct* 82
Bowling 5–1–5.00–0–0–1/1
He was appointed to the first-class umpires' list in 1981.

Leadbeater, Edric
Professional. *b:* 15.8.1927, Lockwood, Huddersfield, Yorkshire. Lower order right-hand batsman, leg break and googly bowler. *Teams* Yorkshire (1949–56, 81 matches); Warwickshire (1957–58, 27 matches). *Tour* MCC to India and Ceylon 1951/2. *Tests* England (1951/2, 2 matches).
Career batting
118–138–36–1548–116–15.17–1–*ct* 74
Bowling 7947–289–27.49–11–2–8/83
Test batting
2–2–0–40–38–20.00–0–*ct* 3
Bowling 218–2–109.00–0–0–1/38

Leadbeater, Harry
Amateur. *b:* 31.12.1863, Scarborough, Yorkshire. *d:* 9.10.1928, Scarborough, Yorkshire. Attacking middle order left-hand batsman, left-arm medium pace bowler. *Team* Yorkshire (1884–90, 6 matches).
Career batting
10–15–2–218–65–16.76–0–*ct* 11
Bowling 93–3–31.00–0–0–2/42

Leadbetter, Stanley Austin
Amateur. *b:* 22.5.1937, Stanion, Northamptonshire. Middle order right-hand batsman, right-arm medium pace bowler. *Team* Combined Services (1956–57).
Career batting
3–6–1–112–46–22.40–*ct* 0
Bowling 15–0

Leaf, Henry Meredith
Amateur. *b:* 18.10.1862, Scarborough, Yorkshire. *d:* 23.4.1931, Charing Cross, Westminster, London. He died as the result of a street accident. Middle order right-hand batsman, off break bowler, good point field. *Sch* Marlborough and Clifton. *Teams* MCC (1884); G. J. V. Weigall's XI (1904).
Career batting
2–3–0–17–10–5.66–0–*ct* 1
His County cricket was for Essex (pre first-class, 1887). Whilst at Cambridge he did not play in any first-class matches, but he did win blues for rackets and royal tennis.

Leaf, Herbert
Amateur. *b:* 10.10.1854, Norwood, Surrey. *d:* 13.2.1936, The Green, Marlborough, Wiltshire. Middle order right-hand batsman, good deep field. *Sch* Harrow. *Teams* Cambridge U (1876); Surrey (1877, 1 match).
Career batting
5–8–1–60–18–8.57–0–*ct* 3
He also played for Wiltshire (1883). A noted royal tennis player, he represented Cambridge U. He was Mayor of Marlborough in 1906.

Leaf, James Gordon
Amateur. *b:* 18.10.1900, Honington, Shipston-on-Stour, Warwickshire. *d:* 8.12.1972, Osmaston, Ashbourne, Derbyshire. Son-in-law of H. F. Wright (Derbyshire). Middle order batsman. *Sch* Harrow. *Team* Army (1937).
Career batting
1–2–0–5–4–2.50–0–*ct* 0

Leaney, Edwin
Professional. *b:* 3.6.1860, Woolwich, London. *d:* 1.9.1904, Greenwich, London, as the result of an operation. Lower order right-hand batsman, wicket-keeper. *Team* Kent (1892, 6 matches). *Tour* Read to South Africa 1891/2 (he did not appear in first-class matches).
Career batting
6–11–3–76–33*–9.50–0–*ct* 4–*st* 1
His brother James umpired the Test in South Africa 1891/2.

Learmond, George Cyril
Amateur. *b:* 4.7.1875, Demerara, British Guiana. *d:* 2.3. 1918, St Vincent. Father of Arnold (British Guiana), grandfather of G. S. Camacho (West Indies), father-in-law of G. A. Camacho (British Guiana). Opening right-hand batsman. *Teams* Barbados (1894/5 to 1895/6); British Guiana (1896/7 to 1899/1900); Trinidad (1900/1 to 1906/7). *Tours* West Indies to England 1900 (not first-class), 1906.
Career batting
45–78–3–1700–120–22.66–1–*ct* 27–*st* 2
Bowling 69–2–34.50–0–0–1/4
Although successful in the West Indies, he was totally unable to make runs in England on either of his visits.

Leary, Stuart Edward
Professional. *b:* 30.4.1933, Green Point, Cape Town, South Africa. *d:* 21.8.1988, Table Mountain, Cape Town, South Africa. His body was found on 23rd and he was thought to have died two days earlier. Middle order right-hand batsman, leg break bowler, good close field. *Team* Kent (1951–71, 381 matches).
Career batting
387–627–96–16517–158–31.10–18–*ct* 362
Bowling 4935–146–33.80–2–0–5/22
He hit 1,000 runs in a season nine times (best 1,440, av 38.91, in 1961). A noted soccer player, he appeared as centre forward for Charlton Athletic and Queen's Park Rangers.

Leat, Charles William
Professional. *b:* 6.12.1855, Ringwood, Hampshire. *d:* 18.12.1937, Winkton Common, Christchurch, Hampshire. Lower order right-hand batsman, right-hand fast round-arm bowler, wicket-keeper. *Team* Hampshire (1878–85, 16 matches).
Career batting
16–29–1–323–63–11.53–0–*ct* 21–*st* 1
Bowling 49–2–24.50–0–0–2/10
He last played for Hampshire (not first-class) in 1887.

Leat, Edwin John
Amateur. *b:* 24.4.1885, Wellington, Somerset. *d:* 8.6.1918, near Beaumont Hamel, France. He was killed in action. Middle order batsman. *Team* Somerset (1908–10, 2 matches).
Career batting
2–3–0–18–11–6.00–0–*ct* 3
He also played for Buckinghamshire (1908–11).

Leatham, Albert Edward
Amateur. *b:* 9.8.1859, Heath, Wakefield, Yorkshire. *d:* 13.7.1948, Christchurch, New Zealand. Cousin of

Leatham, Gerald Arthur Buxton

G. A. B. (Yorkshire). Lower order right-hand batsman, left-arm medium slow bowler. *Sch* Eton. *Teams* Gloucestershire (1883–84, 7 matches); Cambridge U (1885). *Tours* Vernon to India and Ceylon 1889/90 (not first-class); Hawke to India 1892/3, to West Indies 1896/7, to New Zealand 1902/3.
Career batting
53–84–17–672–52–10.02–0–*ct* 22
Bowling 1104–47–23.48–2–0–7/54
His final first-class match in England was for MCC in 1897.

Leatham, Gerald Arthur Buxton
Amateur. *b:* 30.4.1851, Hemsworth Hall, Pontefract, Yorkshire. *d:* 19.6.1932, Dinas, Padstow, Cornwall. Uncle of H. W. (Weigall's XI), cousin of A. E. (Gloucestershire). Lower order right-hand batsman, wicket-keeper. *Sch* Uppingham. *Team* Yorkshire (1874–86, 12 matches).
Career batting
32–51–18–172–20–5.21–0–*ct* 47–*st* 20
Bowling 0–0
His final first-class match was for A. J. Webbe's XI in 1887. He was also an excellent golfer.

Leatham, Dr Hugh William
Amateur. *b:* 14.6.1891, Wentbridge, Pontefract, Yorkshire. *d:* 22.12.1973, Hurstmore, Godalming, Surrey. Nephew of G. A. B. (Yorkshire). Lower order batsman, right-hand slow under-arm bowler. *Sch* Charterhouse. *Team* G. J. V. Weigall's XI (1914).
Career batting
1–2–0–0–0–0.00–0–*ct* 1
Bowling 31–1–31.00–0–0–1/31
He was the last boy to be chosen for the Public Schools Match at Lord's purely on the strength of his 'lob' bowling. He played in the Freshmen's and Seniors' matches at Cambridge, and won blues for rackets and royal tennis.

Leather, Roland Sutcliffe
Amateur. *b:* 17.8.1880, Wyther, Kirkstall, Leeds, Yorkshire. *d:* 3.1.1913, Heliopolis, Egypt. Middle order right-hand batsman, good field. *Sch* Marlborough. *Team* Yorkshire (1906, 1 match).
Career batting
1–2–0–19–14–9.50–0–*ct* 0
He did not play in first-class cricket whilst at Oxford U.

Leatherdale, David Antony
Cricketer. *b:* 26.11.1967, Dirk Hill, Bradford, Yorkshire. Middle order right-hand batsman, right-arm medium pace bowler. *Team* Worcestershire (1988–92, 49 matches).
Career batting
49–75–6–1864–157–27.01–2–*ct* 38
Bowling 59–1–59.00–0–0–1/12

Le Bas, Reginald Vincent
Amateur. *b:* 26.7.1856, Barnet, Hertfordshire. *d:* 7.7.1938, Winsford, Somerset. Uncle of M. B. Burrows (Surrey). Middle order batsman. *Sch* Charterhouse. *Team* MCC (1882).
Career batting
1–2–0–0–0–0.00–0–*ct* 0

Le Couteur, Philip Ridgeway
Amateur. *b:* 26.6.1885, Kyneton, Victoria, Australia. *d:* 30.6.1958, Gunnedah, New South Wales, Australia. Attacking middle order right-hand batsman, leg break and googly bowler. *Team* Oxford U (1909–11, blue all three years); Victoria (1918/9, 3 matches).
Career batting
30–50–4–982–160–21.34–1–*ct* 31
Bowling 2633–138–19.07–10–4–8/99

Ledden, Peter Robert Varville
Professional. *b:* 12.7.1943, Scarborough, Yorkshire. Middle order left-hand batsman, right-arm medium pace bowler. *Team* Sussex (1961–67, 35 matches).
Career batting
35–56–6–756–98–15.12–0–*ct* 18
Bowling 338–8–42.25–1–0–5/43

Lee, Rev Arthur George
Amateur. *b:* 31.8.1849, Chelsea, London. *d:* 11.7.1925, Paddington, London. Middle order right-hand batsman, wicket-keeper. *Sch* Westminster. *Team* Oxford U (1868–71).
Career batting
4–6–1–22–16*–4.40–0–*ct* 6
His County cricket was for Berkshire (1869–70), Worcestershire (pre-first-class, 1875–76) and Suffolk (1877–85).

Lee, Arthur Michael
Amateur. *b:* 22.8.1913, Fowley, Liphook, Hampshire. *d:* 14.1.1983, Midhurst, Sussex. Son of E. C. (Hampshire). Middle order right-hand batsman, slow left-arm bowler. *Sch* Winchester. *Teams* Hampshire (1933, 1 match); Oxford U (1934–35).
Career batting
4–6–0–64–24–10.66–0–*ct* 1

Lee, Charles
Professional. *b:* 17.3.1924, Eastwood, Rotherham, Yorkshire. Opening right-hand batsman, right-arm medium pace bowler. *Teams* Yorkshire (1952, 2 matches); Derbyshire (1954–64, 268 matches).
Career batting
271–472–16–12129–150–26.59–8–*ct* 202
Bowling 721–21–34.33–0–0–2/9
He hit 1,000 runs in a season eight times (best 1,503, av 37.57, in 1962). He captained Derbyshire in 1963 and 1964.

Lee, Edward Cornwall
Amateur. *b:* 18.6.1877, Torquay, Devon. *d:* 16.6.1942, Petersfield, Hampshire. Father of A. M.

(Hampshire). Lower order right-hand batsman, right-arm fast medium bowler. *Sch* Winchester. *Teams* Hampshire (1896–1909, 46 matches); Oxford U (1897–1900, blue 1898). *Tours* Warner to North America 1898 (no first-class matches); Bennett to West Indies 1901/2.

Career batting

85–138–14–1764–66*–14.22–0–*ct* 59

Bowling 1254–39–32.15–2–0–6/42

He played both golf and ice hockey for Oxford U v Cambridge U.

Lee, Frank Stanley

Professional. *b:* 24.7.1905, St John's Wood, London. *d:* 30.3.1982, Westminster, London. Brother of H. W. (Middlesex) and J. W. (Middlesex and Somerset). Solid opening left-hand batsman, right-arm medium pace bowler. *Teams* Middlesex (1925, 2 matches); Somerset (1929–47, 328 matches).

Career batting

331–586–38–15310–169–27.93–23–*ct* 158–*st* 12

Bowling 862–25–34.48–1–0–5/53

He hit 1,000 runs in a season eight times, going on to 2,000 once: 2,019, av 44.86, in 1938. From 1948 to 1963 he was a first-class umpire and stood in 29 Tests (1949–62) – his most notable decision being to no-ball Griffin, the fast bowler of the 1960 South African Touring Team to England.

Lee, Frederick

Amateur. *b:* 11.8.1840, Finsbury, London. *d:* 13.11.1922, Streatham, London. Half-brother of J. M. (Surrey). Lively middle order right-hand batsman, excellent field. *Sch* Rugby. *Teams* Cambridge U (1860–62, blue 1860); Surrey (1861, 1 match); Middlesex (1863–68, 4 matches).

Career batting

17–26–1–357–35–14.28–0–*ct* 9

Bowling 140–5–28.00–0–0–2/26

He was a member of the Committee of Surrey CCC for many years, resigning shortly before his death; he also served two terms on the MCC Committee.

Lee, Frederick

Professional. *b:* 18.11.1856, Baildon, Bradford, Yorkshire. *d:* 13.9.1896, Baildon, Bradford, Yorkshire. Middle order right-hand batsman, point field, occasional wicket-keeper. *Team* Yorkshire (1882–90, 106 matches).

Career batting

114–195–10–3953–165–21.36–3–*ct* 58–*st* 1

Lee, Frederick George

Professional. *b:* 24.5.1905, Chard, Somerset. *d:* 19.11.1977, Taunton, Somerset. Lower order batsman, bowler. *Team* Somerset (1925–27, 10 matches).

Career batting

10–13–6–21–8–3.00–0–*ct* 7

Bowling 439–11–39.90–0–0–3/103

Lee, Frederick Marshall

Amateur. *b:* 8.1.1871, Kensington, London. *d:* 18.11.1914, Wonford, Devon. Middle order right-hand batsman, slow left-arm bowler. *Sch* Uppingham. *Teams* Kent (1895, 2 matches); Somerset (1902–07, 77 matches).

Career batting

79–136–20–2253–83–19.42–0–*ct* 58

Bowling 190–4–47.50–0–0–3/17

Lee, Garnet Morley

Professional. *b:* 7.6.1887, Calverton, Nottinghamshire. *d:* 29.2.1976, Hawtonville, Newark, Nottinghamshire. Opening/middle order right-hand batsman, leg break and googly bowler. *Teams* Nottinghamshire (1910–22, 140 matches); Derbyshire (1925–33, 229 matches). *Tour* Tennyson to Jamaica 1927/8.

Career batting

373–624–47–14858–200*–25.75–22–*ct* 156

Bowling 11133–397–28.04–19–1–7/67

He hit 1,000 runs in a season seven times (best 1,279, av 28.42, in 1928). His only double century was 200* for Nottinghamshire v Leicestershire at Trent Bridge in 1913. He was a first-class umpire (1935–49). A useful soccer player, he appeared for Notts County.

Lee, George Henry

Professional. *b:* 24.8.1854, Scarr, Almondbury, Yorkshire. *d:* 4.10.1919, Lockwood, Yorkshire. Brother of Herbert (Yorkshire). Opening batsman. *Team* Yorkshire (1879, 1 match).

Career batting

1–2–0–13–9–6.50–0–*ct* 0

Lee, Henry William

Professional. *b:* 26.10.1890, Marylebone, London. *d:* 21.4.1981, Westminster, London. Brother of F. S. (Middlesex and Somerset) and J. W. (Middlesex and Somerset). Solid opening right-hand batsman, right-arm slow medium off break bowler. *Teams* Middlesex (1911–34, 401 matches); Cooch-Behar's XI (1917/18); England (in India) (1918/19). *Tour* MCC to South Africa 1930/1 (co-opted, whilst coaching in South Africa). *Test* England (1930/1, 1 match).

Career batting

437–722–49–20158–243*–29.95–38–*ct* 181

Bowling 12278–401–30.61–12–3–8/39

Test batting

1–2–0–19–18–9.50–0–*ct* 0

He hit 1,000 runs in a season 13 times (best 1,995, av 37.64, in 1929). His four double centuries were all for Middlesex, the highest being 243* v Nottinghamshire at Lord's in 1921. He was a first-class umpire (1935–46).

Lee, Herbert

Professional. *b:* 2.7.1856, Taylor Hill, Huddersfield, Yorkshire. *d:* 4.2.1908, Lockwood, Yorkshire. Brother of G. H. (Yorkshire). Middle order right-

hand batsman. *Team* Yorkshire (1885, 5 matches).
Career batting
5–6–0–20–12–3.33–0–*ct* 2

Lee, Horace Cedric
Amateur. *b:* 14.3.1909, North Shields, Northumberland. *d:* 14.7.1981, Wallsend, Northumberland. Middle order right-hand batsman. *Team* Minor Counties (1936–37).
Career batting
2–4–0–112–61–28.00–0–*ct* 1

His County cricket was for Northumberland (1928–47).

Lee, Jack
Amateur. *b:* 4.11.1920, Sileby, Leicestershire. Lower order right-hand batsman, right-arm medium pace bowler. *Team* Leicestershire (1947, 1 match).
Career batting
1–2–0–3–3–1.50–0–*ct* 2
Bowling 13–1–13.00–0–0–1/13

The only wicket he took in first-class cricket was obtained with the first ball he bowled. He played soccer for England, Leicester City, Derby County and Coventry City.

Lee, James Edward
Amateur. *b:* 23.3.1838, Soothill, Dewsbury, Yorkshire. *d:* 2.4.1880, Earlsheaton, Dewsbury, Yorkshire. Middle order batsman. *Team* Yorkshire (1867, 2 matches).
Career batting
2–3–0–9–6–3.00–0–*ct* 0

Lee, Canon John Morley
Amateur. *b:* 12.10.1825, Chelsea, London. *d:* 20.1.1903, Botley, Hampshire. Half-brother of Frederick (Surrey and Middlesex). Middle order right-hand batsman, right-hand medium fast round-arm bowler, good field. *Sch* Oundle. *Teams* Cambridge U (1845–49, blue 1846–48); Surrey (1847–50, 7 matches); Cambridge Town Club (1847).
Career batting
36–57–6–678–110–13.29–1–*ct* 24
Bowling 25–3+94–8.33–7–3–7/?

Lee, John William
Professional. *b:* 1.2.1902, Marylebone, London. *d:* 20.6.1944, near Bazenville, Normandy, France. He was killed in action. Brother of F. S. (Middlesex and Somerset) and H. W. (Middlesex). Opening right-hand batsman, leg break bowler. *Teams* Middlesex (1923, 1 match); Somerset (1925–36, 241 matches).
Career batting
243–418–44–7856–193*–21.00–6–*ct* 123
Bowling 14723–495–29.74–19–2–7/45

He hit 1,000 runs in a season three times (best 1,465, av 31.37, in 1934). He played soccer for Arsenal, Chesterfield and Aldershot.

Lee, Nevill Bernard
Professional. *b:* 13.8.1898, Barlestone, Leicestershire. *d:* 21.7.1978, Blackpool, Lancashire. Nephew of H. Whitehead (Leicestershire). Middle order right-hand batsman. *Team* Leicestershire (1922–24, 8 matches).
Career batting
8–12–1–117–62–10.63–0–*ct* 4
Bowling 6–0

Lee, Peter Granville
Cricketer. *b:* 27.8.1945, Arthingworth, Northamptonshire. Lower order right-hand batsman, right-arm fast medium bowler. *Teams* Northamptonshire (1967–71, 44 matches); Lancashire (1972–82, 152 matches). *Tours* Robins to South Africa 1973/4, 1975/6.
Career batting
202–164–68–779–26–8.11–0–*ct* 29
Bowling 15339–599–25.60–29–7–8/34

He took 100 wickets in a season twice (best 112, av 18.45, in 1975). His best innings analysis was 8 for 34 for Lancashire v Oxford U at Oxford in 1980. He also played for Durham (pre first-class, 1983).

Lee, Richard John
Cricketer. *b:* 6.3.1950, Ryde, Sydney, New South Wales, Australia. Attacking opening right-hand batsman, right-arm medium pace bowler. *Team* Oxford U (1972–74, blue all three years).
Career batting
24–45–1–951–130–21.61–1–*ct* 14
Bowling 1081–29–37.27–0–0–4/56

Lee, Dr Ronald Outram
Amateur. *b:* 26.12.1876, Thame, Oxfordshire. *d:* 12.3.1940, Oxford. Tail end right-hand batsman, right-arm fast bowler. *Sch* Haileybury. *Team* Cambridge U (1899).
Career batting
1–1–0–0–0–0.00–0–*ct* 1
Bowling 79–3–26.33–0–0–2/59

His County cricket was for Oxfordshire (1899–1901).

Leech, Andrew David
Cricketer. *b:* 9.3.1952, Farnworth, Lancashire. Lower order right-hand batsman, right-arm medium pace bowler. *Team* Oxford U (1972).
Career batting
9–11–4–24–8*–3.42–0–*ct* 3
Bowling 521–12–43.41–0–0–3/40

Leech, Colin
Amateur. *b:* 30.8.1889, Hayfield, Derbyshire. *d:* 6.3.1961, Frome, Somerset. Middle order right-hand batsman. *Team* Derbyshire (1922, 1 match).
Career batting
1–2–0–38–36–19.00–0–*ct* 1

Lees, Geoffrey William
Amateur. *b:* 1.7.1920, Chorlton, Manchester, Lancashire. Middle order right-hand batsman, leg break bowler. *Sch* King's, Rochester. *Teams* Cambridge U (1947); Sussex (1951, 1 match).
Career batting
3–5–0–28–15–5.60–0–*ct* 1

Lees, John
Amateur. *b:* 5.9.1861, Ashton-under-Lyne, Lancashire. *d:* 20.12.1934, The Knowle, Brenchley, Kent. Sound opening right-hand batsman, slow right-arm bowler. *Sch* Uppingham. *Team* Cambridge U (1881). *Tour* West Indies to USA 1886 (not first-class).
Career batting
1–2–0–15–9–7.50–0–*ct* 0
Bowling 10–0
His County cricket was for Cambridgeshire (1897–99). He later appeared for Jamaica in non-first-class matches. An excellent rugby footballer he represented Cambridge U.

Lees, Robin Douglas
Cricketer. *b:* 19.5.1949, Cranleigh, Surrey. Lower order right-hand batsman, right-arm medium bowler. *Sch* Gresham's, Holt. *Team* Oxford U (1970).
Career batting
3–6–2–29–17*–7.25–0–*ct* 0
Bowling 144–1–144.00–0–0–1/53
He won a blue for athletics.

Lees, Walter Scott
Professional. *b:* 25.12.1875, Sowerby Bridge, Yorkshire. *d:* 10.9.1924, West Hartlepool, Co Durham. He died from pneumonia. Free hitting lower order right-hand batsman, right-arm medium fast bowler. *Teams* Surrey (1896–1911, 343 matches); London County (1903). *Tour* MCC to South Africa 1905/6. *Tests* England (1905/6, 5 matches).
Career batting
364–522–76–7642–137–17.13–2–*ct* 125
Bowling 30008–1402–21.40–97–20–9/81
Test batting
5–9–3–66–25 *–11.00–0–*ct* 2
Bowling 467–26–17.96–2–0–6/78
He took 100 wickets in a season seven times (best 193, av 18.01, in 1905); his best bowling in an innings was 9 for 81 for Surrey v Sussex at Eastbourne in 1905.

Lees, Warren Kenneth, MBE
Cricketer. *b:* 19.3.1952, Dunedin, New Zealand. Middle order right-hand batsman, wicket-keeper. *Team* Otago (1972/3 to 1987/8). *Tours* New Zealand to India and Pakistan 1976/7, to England 1979 (World Cup), 1983, to Australia 1980/1, 1982/3. *Tests* New Zealand (1976/7 to 1983, 21 matches).
Career batting
146–243–43–4932–152–24.66–5–*ct* 304–*st* 44
Bowling 109–2–54.50–0–0–1/34
Test batting
21–37–4–778–152–23.57–1–*ct* 57–*st* 7
Bowling 4–0
He played in two Tests on the 1983 tour of England. His first-class debut was for New Zealand Under 23 in 1970/1.

Leese, Charles Philip
Amateur. *b:* 22.5.1889, Eccles, Manchester, Lancashire. *d:* 19.1.1947, Hope Court, Hope-Bagot, Shropshire. Son of Ernest (Lancashire), nephew of J. F. (Lancashire), cousin of W. H. (MCC), V. F. (Cambridge U) and Neville (MCC). Opening right-hand batsman. *Sch* Wellington. *Teams* Oxford U (1908–10); Lancashire (1911, 1 match).
Career batting
16–29–1–341–48–12.17–0–*ct* 3
He won blues for golf and hockey, also playing hockey for England.

Leese, Ernest
Amateur. *b:* 30.11.1854, Bowdon, Cheshire. *d:* 15.11.1913, Southport, Lancashire. Brother of J. F. (Lancashire), father of C. P. (Lancashire), uncle of W. H. (MCC), V. F. (Cambridge U) and Neville (MCC). Middle order right-hand batsman, good field. *Sch* Cheltenham. *Team* Lancashire (1880–84, 8 matches).
Career batting
8–11–1–146–62–14.60–0–*ct* 1

Leese, Sir Joseph Francis
Amateur. *b:* 28.2.1845, Chorlton, Manchester, Lancashire. *d:* 29.7.1914, Sutton Park, Guildford, Surrey. Brother of Ernest (Lancashire), father of W. H. (MCC), V. F. (Cambridge U) and Neville (MCC), uncle of C. P. (Lancashire). Hard hitting middle order right-hand batsman, good point. *Team* Lancashire (1865–81, 24 matches).
Career batting
25–44–1–561–44–13.04–0–*ct* 14
Bowling 94–5–18.80–0–0–3/49
He was MP for Accrington from 1892 to 1909.

Leese, Neville
Amateur. *b:* 23.3.1872, Preston, Lancashire. *d:* 22.6.1948, Zeals, Wiltshire. Son of J. F. (Lancashire), brother of W. H. (MCC) and V. F. (Cambridge U), nephew of Ernest (Lancashire), cousin of C. P. (Lancashire). Middle order batsman. *Sch* Winchester. *Team* MCC (1895).
Career batting
6–12–0–226–59–18.83–0–*ct* 3

Leese, Vernon Francis
Amateur. *b:* 20.2.1870, Kensington, London. *d:* 3.8.1927, Alassio, Italy. Son of J. F. (Lancashire), brother of W. H. (MCC) and Neville (MCC), nephew of Ernest (Lancashire), cousin of C. P. (Lancashire). Middle order batsman. *Sch* Winchester. *Team* Cam-

bridge U (1892).
Career batting
7–12–0–171–44–14.25–0–*ct* 3
His final first-class match was for MCC in 1897. His County cricket was for Devon (1894).

Leese, Sir William Hargreaves
Amateur. *b:* 24.8.1868, Sendholme, Send, Woking, Surrey. *d:* 17.1.1937, Sidmouth, Devon. Son of J. F. (Lancashire), brother of V. F. (Cambridge U) and Neville (MCC), nephew of Ernest (Lancashire), cousin of C. P. (Lancashire). Middle order right-hand batsman. *Sch* Winchester. *Team* MCC (1889–90).
Career batting
2–4–0–57–35–14.25–0–*ct* 3
He played in the Seniors' match at Cambridge.

Leeson, Patrick George
Amateur. *b:* 17.7.1915, Darjeeling, India. Middle order right-hand batsman, off break bowler. *Sch* Malvern. *Team* Worcestershire (1936, 1 match).
Career batting
1–2–0–7–7–3.50–0–*ct* 1
He played in trials at Cambridge U, but not in first-class matches.

Leeston-Smith, F. A.
(*see under* Smith, F. A. L.)

Lefebvre, Roland Philippe
Cricketer. *b:* 7.2.1963, Rotterdam, Holland. Lower order right-hand batsman, right-arm medium fast bowler. *Teams* Somerset (1990–92, 36 matches); Canterbury (1990/1).
Career batting
43–44–10–715–100–21.02–1–*ct* 20
Bowling 2945–74–39.79–2–0–6/53
He played for Holland 1983 to 1990, including the ICC Trophy competitions of 1986 and 1990.

Le Fleming, John
Amateur. *b:* 23.10.1865, Tonbridge, Kent. *d:* 7.10.1942, Montreux, Switzerland. Brother of L. J. (Kent). Stylish middle order right-hand batsman, slow right-arm bowler, good deep field. *Sch* Tonbridge. *Team* Kent (1889–99, 40 matches).
Career batting
40–65–2–1201–134–19.06–1–*ct* 25
Bowling 120–3–40.00–0–0–2/44
He did not appear in any first-class matches whilst at Cambridge U. A well-known rugby footballer he played for Cambridge, Blackheath and England as a three-quarter; he also won the hurdles for Cambridge and was English Champion. His other achievements were in skating, winning various championships.

Le Fleming, Lawrence Julius
Amateur. *b:* 3.6.1879, Tonbridge, Kent. *d:* 21.3.1918, Maissemy, France. He was killed in action. Brother of John (Kent). Middle order right-hand batsman. *Sch* Tonbridge. *Team* Kent (1897–99, 12 matches).
Career batting
13–18–0–240–40–13.33–0–*ct* 3
Bowling 20–0
His final first-class match was for the Army in 1912.

Legard, Alfred Digby
Amateur. *b:* 19.6.1878, Scarborough, Yorkshire. *d:* 15.8.1939, Pentire, Newquay, Cornwall. Opening right-hand batsman, slow right-arm bowler. *Sch* Eton. *Team* Yorkshire (1910, 4 matches).
Career batting
6–8–1–68–27–9.71–0–*ct* 1
Bowling 33–0
His first-class debut was for MCC in 1904.

Legard, Antony Ronald
Amateur. *b:* 17.1.1912, Sialkot, India. Lower order right-hand batsman, right-arm medium pace bowler. *Sch* Winchester. *Teams* Oxford U (1932–35, blue 1932 and 1935); Worcestershire (1935, 1 match); Europeans (1943/4).
Career batting
36–52–10–234–38–5.57–0–*ct* 17
Bowling 2793–93–30.03–3–0–7/36
His final first-class match was for MCC in 1952.

Legard, Edwin
Professional. *b:* 23.8.1935, Barnsley, Yorkshire. Lower order right-hand batsman, wicket-keeper. *Team* Warwickshire (1962–68, 20 matches).
Career batting
20–24–11–144–21–11.07–0–*ct* 33–*st* 9
He played for Yorkshire in 1957 in a non-first-class match.

Leggat, Logie Colin
Amateur. *b:* 24.9.1894, St John's Hill, Bangalore, India. *d:* 31.7.1917, Pilckem Ridge, Belgium. He was killed in action. Opening right-hand batsman, leg break bowler. *Sch* Eton. *Team* Cambridge U (1914).
Career batting
1–2–0–9–6–4.50–0–*ct* 0

Leggatt, William Murray
Amateur. *b:* 2.9.1900, Crail, Fife, Scotland. *d:* 13.8.1946, Westminster, London. Middle order right-hand batsman, right-arm fast bowler. *Sch* Winchester. *Team* Kent (1926, 5 matches).
Career batting
11–16–0–479–92–29.93–0–*ct* 9
He played in many military matches and in India for South Punjab (not first-class); his final first-class match was for the Army in 1933.

Legge, Geoffrey Bevington
Amateur. *b:* 26.1.1903, Bromley, Kent. *d:* 21.11.1940, Brampford Speke, Devon. He was killed whilst flying with the Fleet Air Arm. Brother-in-law of J. V. Richardson (Essex). Stylish middle order right-hand batsman, leg break bowler, good slip field.

Sch Malvern. *Teams* Kent (1924–31, 114 matches); Oxford U (1925–26, blue both years). *Tours* MCC to South Africa 1927/8, to Australia and New Zealand 1929/30. *Tests* England (1927/8 to 1929/30, 5 matches).
Career batting
147–210–11–4955–196–24.89–7–*ct* 122
Bowling 181–8–22.62–0–0–3/23
Test batting
5–7–1–299–196–49.83–1–*ct* 1
Bowling 34–0
His highest score was 196 for England v New Zealand at Auckland in 1929/30. He captained Oxford in 1926 and Kent 1928–30.

Le Gros, Philip Walter
Amateur. *b:* 3.10.1892, Reigate, Surrey. *d:* 27.2.1980, Richmond, Surrey. Attacking middle order right-hand batsman, right-arm fast bowler. *Sch* Rugby. *Team* MCC (1921–22).
Career batting
4–7–1–94–51–15.66–0–*ct* 1
Bowling 24–0
His first-class debut was for the Gentlemen in 1920 and his final first-class match for Minor Counties in 1924. His County cricket was for Buckinghamshire (1911–30).

Lehmann, Darren Scott
Cricketer. *b:* 5.2.1970, Gawler, South Australia. Dashing middle order left-hand batsman, slow left-arm bowler. *Teams* South Australia (1987/8 to 1989/90, 20 matches); Victoria (1990/1 to 1991/2, 21 matches). *Tour* Victoria to England 1991.
Career batting
42–72–5–3125–228–46.64–10–*ct* 25
Bowling 126–3–42.00–0–0–2/15
In 1989/90 he hit 1,000 runs (1,142 runs, av 57.10) in Australian first-class cricket, the youngest ever to achieve the feat. His highest score was 228 for South Australia v New South Wales at Adelaide in 1989/90.

Leigh, James
Amateur. *b:* December 1862, West Leigh, Lancashire. *d:* 25.9.1925, Shepperton-on-Thames, Middlesex. Stylish middle order right-hand batsman, good field. *Sch* Uppingham. *Team* Lancashire (1887, 1 match). *Tour* Priestley to West Indies 1896/7.
Career batting
10–16–0–157–26–9.81–0–*ct* 5
Bowling 14–0
His final first-class match was for MCC in 1900.

Leigh, Spencer Austen
Amateur. *b:* 17.2.1834, Speen, Newbury, Berkshire. *d:* 9.12.1913, Frog-Firle, Alfriston, Sussex. Brother of C. E. A. (MCC 1862), C. A. (MCC 1862), E. C. (Oxford U 1852) and A. H. A. (Gentlemen of England 1857). Hard hitting right-hand batsman, good deep field. *Sch* Harrow. *Team* Sussex (1862–66, 10 matches).
Career batting
13–21–2–209–42–11.00–0–*ct* 4
Bowling 14–1–14.00–0–0–1/9
He also played for Berkshire (1853–59). His first-class debut was for Gentlemen of England in 1857. His four brothers were all notable cricketers, but played mainly for Berkshire.

Leiper, John Morton
Amateur. *b:* 17.2.1921, Woodford Green, Essex. Father of R. J. (Essex). Attacking lower order left-hand batsman, right-arm fast medium bowler, occasional wicket-keeper. *Sch* Chigwell. *Team* Essex (1950, 2 matches).
Career batting
2–4–0–50–44–12.50–0–*ct* 1
Bowling 79–1–79.00–0–0–1/38

Leiper, Robert James
Cricketer. *b:* 30.8.1961, Woodford Green, Essex. Son of J. M. (Essex). Middle order left-hand batsman, right-arm medium pace bowler. *Sch* Chigwell. *Team* Essex (1981–82, 2 matches).
Career batting
2–4–0–53–49–13.25–0–*ct* 2

Lemmy, Brian Allan
Professional. *b:* 6.1.1937, Isleworth, Middlesex. Lower order right-hand batsman, right-arm fast medium bowler. *Team* MCC (1958).
Career batting
1–2–2–12–7*–no av–0–*ct* 1
Bowling 117–3–39.00–0–0–2/92
His County cricket was for Staffordshire (1961–62).

Leney, Frederick Barcham
Amateur. *b:* 29,11.1876, Wateringbury, Maidstone, Kent. *d:* 25.7.1921, Galway, Ireland. Nephew of Herbert (Kent). Middle order right-hand batsman, right-arm medium fast bowler. *Sch* Bradfield. *Team* Kent (1905, 1 match).
Career batting
1–2–0–39–30–19.50–0–*ct* 1
Bowling 23–1–23.00–0–0–1/0

Leney, Herbert
Amateur. *b:* 8.9.1850, Wateringbury, Kent. *d:* 18.11.1915, Smiths Hall, West Farleigh, Kent. Uncle of F. B. (Kent). Middle order right-hand batsman, right-hand fast round-arm bowler, good mid-off. *Sch* Chatham House. *Team* Kent (1873–77, 4 matches).
Career batting
4–6–1–58–33–11.60–0–*ct* 0
Bowling 7–0
He was not in the Eleven whilst at Oxford U.

Leng, Denis
Cricketer. *b:* 26.11.1934, Pudsey, Yorkshire. Lower order right-hand batsman, right-arm fast medium

bowler. *Team* Ireland (1966).
Career batting
1–2–1–1–1–1.00–0–*ct* 1
Bowling 36–1–36.00–0–0–1/36

Lenham, Leslie John
Professional. *b:* 24.5.1936, Worthing, Sussex. Father of N. J. (Sussex). Opening right-hand batsman, off break bowler. *Team* Sussex (1956–70, 300 matches).
Career batting
300–539–50–12796–191*–26.16–7–*ct* 110
Bowling 306–6–51.00–0–0–2/24

He hit 1,000 runs in a season six times, going on to 2,000 once: 2,016, av 32.51, in 1961. After his first-class career ended he was coach to Sussex CCC (1970–76).

Lenham, Neil John
Cricketer. *b:* 17.12.1965, Worthing, Sussex. Son of L. J. (Sussex). Opening right-hand batsman, right-arm medium fast bowler. *Sch* Brighton. *Team* Sussex (1984–92, 122 matches).
Career batting
128–218–21–6467–222*–32.82–13–*ct* 53
Bowling 1395–29–48.10–0–0–4/85

He reached 1,000 runs three times (best 1,663, av 41.57, in 1990). His highest score was 222* for Sussex v Kent at Hove in 1992.

Lennox, Hon Charles
(succeeded as Duke of Richmond in 1806)
Amateur. *b:* 9.9.1764, Gordon Castle, Banff, Scotland. *d:* 28.8.1819, near Perth, Ontario, Canada, of hydrophobia, having been bitten by a fox. Middle order right-hand batsman, wicket-keeper. *Team* Surrey (1802).
Career batting
1–2–0–6–5–3.00–0–*ct* 0

One of the leading amateur cricketers of his day, he was a great patron of all athletic sports. In 1789 he fought a notorious duel with the Duke of York (brother of King George III) on Wimbledon Common. At the time of his death he was Governor-General of Canada.

Le Peton, Howard Guerin
Amateur. *b:* 19.1.1895, Pwllheli, Caernarvonshire. *d:* 19.9.1981, The Park, Wisbech, Cambridgeshire. Lower order right-hand batsman. *Team* Ireland (1921).
Career batting
1–1–0–16–16–16.00–0–*ct* 0

Le Roux, Garth Stirling
Cricketer. *b:* 4.9.1955, Kenilworth, Cape Town, South Africa. Lower order right-hand batsman, right-arm fast bowler. *Teams* Western Province (1975/6 to 1988/9); Sussex (1978–87, 137 matches).
Career batting
239–290–79–5425–86–25.71–0–*ct* 80
Bowling 17800–838–21.24–35–3–8/107

A major figure in South African cricket, he appeared in 15 unofficial Tests for South Africa between 1981/2 and 1986/7. His best season in England was 1981, with 81 wickets, av 19.53.

Leroy, Philip Newbold
Amateur. *b:* 25.9.1880. *d: circa* 1950. Lower order batsman, bowler. *Team* Philadelphia (1901 to 1909/10). *Tours* Philadelphia to England 1903, to Jamaica 1908/9.
Career batting
14–24–2–241–42–10.95–0–*ct* 11
Bowling 377–10–37.70–0–0–4/62

He had very little success on his tour to England.

Leslie, Charles Frederick Henry
Amateur. *b:* 8.12.1861, Westminster, London. *d:* 12.2.1921, Mayfair, Westminster, London. Father of John (Oxford U), great-grandfather of M. V. Fleming (Kent), father-in-law of H. C. Pilkington (Middlesex). Hard hitting middle order right-hand batsman, right-arm fast bowler, good cover point. *Sch* Rugby. *Teams* Oxford U (1881–83, blue all three years); Middlesex (1881–86, 20 matches). *Tour* Bligh to Australia 1882/3. *Tests* England (1882/3, 4 matches).
Career batting
48–86–5–1860–144–22.96–4–*ct* 18
Bowling 165–8–20.62–0–0–3/31
Test batting
4–7–0–106–54–15.14–0–*ct* 1
Bowling 44–4–11.00–0–0–3/31

His final first-class match was for Oxford University (Past and Present) v Australians in 1888. He also played for Shropshire (1879–82). He scored 111* on debut for Oxford U v MCC at Oxford in 1881. He excelled at rackets and rugby, representing Oxford at both sports.

Leslie, John
Amateur. *b:* 26.8.1888, Westminster, London. *d:* 1.10.1965, Brancaster, Norfolk. Son of C. F. H. (Middlesex), brother-in-law of H. C. Pilkington (Middlesex) and I. A. W. Gilliat (Oxford U). Opening/middle order right-hand batsman, right-arm slow bowler. *Sch* Winchester. *Team* Oxford U (1908).
Career batting
3–5–0–42–23–8.40–0–*ct* 4
Bowling 42–0

Lester, Edward
Professional. Lower order right-hand batsman, right-arm medium pace bowler. *Team* Middlesex (1929–30, 7 matches).
Career batting
7–11–4–41–13–5.85–0–*ct* 0
Bowling 10–0

Lester, Edward Ibson
Amateur, turned professional in 1948. *b:* 18.2.1923, Scarborough, Yorkshire. Aggressive middle order right-hand batsman, off break bowler. *Team* Yorkshire (1945–56, 228 matches).
Career batting
232–347–28–10912–186–34.20–25–*ct* 108
Bowling 160–3–53.33–0–0–1/7
He hit 1,000 runs in a season six times (best 1,801, av 37.52, in 1949). He was the Yorkshire scorer 1962–92. He played in a Gillette Cup match in 1964 in emergency.

Lester, Gerald
Professional. *b:* 27.12.1915, Long Whatton, Leicestershire. Sound opening or middle order right-hand batsman, leg break and googly bowler. *Team* Leicestershire (1937–58, 373 matches).
Career batting
373–649–54–12857–143–21.60–9–*ct* 159
Bowling 10882–307–35.44–7–1–6/42
He hit 1,000 runs in a season five times (best 1,599, av 33.31, in 1949). He was coach to Leicestershire 1962–66.

Lester, John Ashby
Amateur. *b:* 1.8.1871, Penrith, Cumberland. *d:* 3.9.1969, Haverford, Philadelphia, USA. Middle order right-hand batsman, right-arm slow bowler, good slip. *Sch* Haverford College. *Team* Philadelphia (1896–08). *Tours* Philadelphia to England, 1897, 1903, 1908.
Career batting
47–84–7–2552–126*–33.14–2–*ct* 15
Bowling 1267–57–22.22–3–1–7/33
He headed the batting averages for both the 1897 and 1903 tours to England and was regarded for some years as the best batsman in the United States, playing for United States v Canada in 1901 and 1906.

Lester, Timothy Adam
Cricketer. *b:* 25.3.1964, Hampstead, London. Middle order right-hand batsman. *Sch* Stowe. *Team* Minor Counties (1990).
Career batting
1–1–0–4–4–4.00–0–*ct* 0
His County cricket was for Oxfordshire (1984–92).

L'Estrange, Michael Gerard
Cricketer. *b:* 12.10.1952, North Sydney, New South Wales, Australia. Middle order left-hand batsman, occasional right-arm medium pace bowler. *Team* Oxford U (1977–79, blue 1977 and 1979).
Career batting
23–37–3–521–63–15.32–0–*ct* 18
He also won a blue for rugby.

Lethbridge, Christopher
Cricketer. *b:* 23.6.1961, Castleford, Yorkshire. Middle order right-hand batsman, right-arm medium pace bowler. *Team* Warwickshire (1981–85, 50 matches).
Career batting
50–58–13–1033–87*–22.95–0–*ct* 16
Bowling 2996–77–38.90–1–0–5/68
He dismissed G. Boycott with his first delivery in first-class cricket. He also played for Cambridgeshire (1986–91).

Leventon, Edwin Charles
Amateur. *b:* 1845. *d:* 21.8.1909, Roby, Lancashire. Lower order batsman, useful bowler. *Team* Lancashire (1867, 1 match).
Career batting
1–2–0–6–6–3.00–0–*ct* 0
Bowling 24–2–12.00–0–0–2/24

Lever, Colin
Cricketer. *b:* 4.8.1939, Todmorden, Yorkshire. Brother of Peter (Lancashire). Middle order right-hand batsman, right-arm medium pace bowler. *Team* Minor Counties (1965).
Career batting
1–2–0–20–12–10.00–0–*ct* 0
Bowling 23–2–11.50–0–0–1/5
His County cricket was for Buckinghamshire (1962–78).

Lever, John Kenneth, MBE
Cricketer. *b:* 24.2.1949, Stepney, London. Lower order right-hand batsman, left-arm fast medium bowler. *Teams* Essex (1967–89, 443 matches); Natal (1982/3 to 1984/5). *Tours* MCC to India, Sri Lanka and Australia 1976/7; England to Pakistan and New Zealand 1977/8, to Australia 1978/9, to Australia and India 1979/80, to India and Sri Lanka 1981/2; Robins to South Africa 1972/3, 1973/4, to Sri Lanka 1977/8; Overseas XI to India 1980/1; SAB England XI to South Africa 1981/2. *Tests* England (1976/7 to 1986, 21 matches).
Career batting
529–541–192–3678–91–10.53–0–*ct* 187
Bowling 41772–1722–24.25–85–12–8/37
Test batting
21–31–5–306–53–11.76–0–*ct* 11
Bowling 1951–73–26.72–3–1–7/46
A very effective seam bowler in both Championship and limited overs county cricket, he currently holds the record for most wickets in a career in the Sunday League (386, av 19.37) and in the Benson & Hedges Competition (149, av 18.71). He took 100 wickets in a season four times: 106, av 15.18, in 1978, 106, av 17.30, in 1979, 106, av 16.28, in 1983 and 116, av 21.98, in 1984. This record, since 1969, has only been beaten by D. L. Underwood. His career with England was cut short when he chose to tour South Africa and after that he appeared in just one Test. He also played for Cambridgeshire (1990–91).

Lever, Peter
Professional. *b:* 17.9.1940, Todmorden, Yorkshire. Brother of Colin (Minor Counties). Lower order right-hand batsman, right-arm fast medium bowler. *Teams* Lancashire (1960–76, 268 matches); Tasmania (1971/2, 1 match). *Tours* MCC to Australia and New Zealand 1970/1, 1974/5. *Tests* England (1970/1 to 1975, 17 matches).
Career batting
301–314–66–3534–88*–14.25–0–*ct* 106
Bowling 20377–796–25.59–28–2–7/70
Test batting
17–18–2–350–88*–21.87–0–*ct* 11
Bowling 1509–41–36.80–2–0–6/38
In 1974/5 when playing for England v New Zealand, one of his deliveries hit the New Zealand tailender, Chatfield, in the face. The batsman was taken unconscious to hospital and for some time his life was in danger. Happily, Chatfield fully recovered. Lever was later joint Lancashire coach.

Leveson-Gower, Rev Frederick Archibald Gresham
Amateur. *b:* 20.2.1871, Titsey Place, Surrey. *d:* 3.10.1946, Folkestone, Kent. Brother of H. D. G. (Surrey), nephew of E. C. Leigh (Oxford U 1852) and J. W. Leigh (MCC 1861), father-in-law of E. R. T. Holmes (Surrey). Middle order right-hand batsman, wicket-keeper. *Sch* Winchester. *Teams* Oxford U (1894); Hampshire (1899–1900, 2 matches).
Career batting
16–30–3–424–86–15.70–0–*ct* 11–*st* 1
Bowling 53–0
His final first-class match was for H. D. G. Leveson-Gower's XI in 1909.

Leveson-Gower, Sir Henry Dudley Gresham
Amateur. *b:* 8.5.1873, Titsey Place, Surrey. *d:* 1.2.1954, Kensington, London. Brother of F. A. G. (Hampshire), nephew of E. C. Leigh (Oxford U 1852) and J. W. Leigh (MCC 1861). Middle order right-hand batsman, leg break bowler, cover field. *Sch* Winchester. *Teams* Oxford U (1893–96, blue all four years); Surrey (1895–1920, 122 matches). *Tours* Hawke to West Indies 1896/7; Warner to North America 1897; MCC to South Africa 1905/6, 1909/10; Leveson-Gower to Rhodesia 1909/10. *Tests* England (1909/10, 3 matches).
Career batting
277–400–78–7638–155–23.72–4–*ct* 103
Bowling 1378–46–29.95–3–0–6/49
Test batting
3–6–2–95–31–23.75–0–*ct* 1
His final first-class match was for his own Team v Cambridge U in 1931. He captained Oxford in 1896, Surrey 1908 to 1910, and the MCC Team to South Africa 1909/10, leading England in three Tests on that tour. A noted cricket administrator, he joined the Test Selection Committee for 1909 and was Chairman 1924 and 1927–30. He was also on the Committees of MCC and Surrey and was Surrey President 1929–39. In 1953 he was knighted for his services to cricket.

Levett, William Howard Vincent
Amateur. *b:* 25.1.1908, Goudhurst, Kent. Lower order right-hand batsman, wicket-keeper. *Sch* Brighton. *Team* Kent (1930–47, 142 matches). *Tour* MCC to India and Ceylon 1933/4. *Test* England (1933/4, 1 match).
Career batting
175–264–58–2524–76–12.25–0–*ct* 283–*st* 195
Bowling 6–0
Test batting
1–2–1–7–5–7.00–0–*ct* 3
He was President of Kent in 1974.

Levick, Deryck Cyril
Amateur. *b:* 27.5.1929, Ealing, Middlesex. Aggressive middle order right-hand batsman, good field. *Team* Essex (1950–51, 3 matches).
Career batting
3–6–0–14–6–2.33–0–*ct* 1

Levy, Solomon
Professional. *b:* 18.5.1886, Stroud, Gloucestershire. Lower order right-hand batsman, off break bowler. *Team* Gloucestershire (1910–11, 4 matches).
Career batting
4–8–2–43–22–7.16–0–*ct* 0
Bowling 147–4–36.75–0–0–2/41

Lewin, Rear Admiral Charles la Primaudaye
Amateur. *b:* 22.8.1874, Greenwich, London. *d:* 14.9.1952, St Helier, Jersey. Opening batsman. *Team* Royal Navy (1920).
Career batting
1–2–0–52–37–26.00–0–*ct* 0
His County cricket was for Devon (1920).

Lewington, Peter John
Cricketer. *b:* 30.1.1950, Finchampstead, Berkshire. Lower order right-hand batsman, off break bowler. *Team* Warwickshire (1970–82, 69 matches). *Tours* Robins to South Africa 1972/3; MCC to Bangladesh 1978/9 (not first-class).
Career batting
72–73–21–383–34–7.36–0–*ct* 31
Bowling 5705–191–29.86–6–0–7/52
He also played for Berkshire (1967–92). He did not play for Warwickshire, 1977 to 1981.

Lewis, Albert Edward
Professional. *b:* 20.1.1877, Bedminster, Somerset. *d:* 22.2.1956, Southmead, Bristol. Middle order right-hand batsman, right-arm fast medium bowler. *Team* Somerset (1899–1914, 208 matches).
Career batting
210–388–27–7745–201*–21.45–9–*ct* 106
Bowling 12091–522–23.16–39–5–8/103

He went out to India as coach in 1920, but did not play in any first-class matches. An excellent soccer player he appeared as goalkeeper for Sunderland, Sheffield United, West Bromwich, Leicester Fosse and Bristol City. His highest score was 201* for Somerset v Kent at Taunton in 1909.

Lewis, Dr Anthony Charles Wilson
Amateur. *b:* 29.9.1932, Newcastle-under-Lyme, Staffordshire. Middle order right-hand batsman. *Sch* Repton. *Team* Cambridge U (1952–53).
Career batting
6–9–0–83–55–9.22–0–*ct* 0
His County cricket was for Staffordshire (1950–53). He was an excellent tennis player.

Lewis, Anthony Robert
Amateur. *b:* 6.7.1938, Uplands, Swansea, Glamorgan. Middle order right-hand batsman, leg break bowler. *Teams* Glamorgan (1955–74, 315 matches); Cambridge U (1960–62, blue all three years). *Tours* MCC to South America 1964/5 (not first-class), to Ceylon 1969/70, to India, Pakistan and Sri Lanka 1972/3; Glamorgan to West Indies 1969/70. *Tests* England (1972/3 to 1973, 9 matches).
Career batting
409–708–76–20495–223–32.42–30–*ct* 193
Bowling 432–6–72.00–0–0–3/18
Test batting
9–16–2–457–125–32.64–1–*ct* 0
He hit 1,000 runs in a season 11 times, going on to 2,000 twice (best 2,190, av 41.32, in 1966). His only double century was 223 for Glamorgan v Kent at Gravesend in 1966. He captained MCC on the 1972/3 tour, including eight Tests, and also led Cambridge in 1962 and Glamorgan from 1967 to 1972. He has been Glamorgan Chairman since 1988. Since retiring from first-class cricket he has become a well-known writer and commentator on the game. He also won a blue for rugby.

Lewis, Arthur Hamilton
Amateur. *b:* 16.9.1901, Maseru, Basutoland. *d:* 23.8.1980, Heavitree, Devon. Hard hitting middle order right-hand batsman, brilliant cover point. *Sch* King William's College, IOM. *Team* Hampshire (1929, 1 match).
Career batting
1–1–0–20–20–20.00–0–*ct* 1
He also played for Berkshire (1931–37). He played in trials at Cambridge U, but not in first-class matches.

Lewis, Brian
Cricketer. *b:* 18.7.1945, Maesteg, Glamorgan. Lower order right-hand batsman, off break bowler. *Team* Glamorgan (1965–68, 37 matches).
Career batting
37–45–5–333–38–8.32–0–*ct* 29
Bowling 2001–82–24.40–6–1–7/28

Lewis, Charles Prytherch
Amateur. *b:* 20.8.1853, Llwyncelyn, Llangadog, Carmarthenshire. *d:* 28.5.1923, Llandingat, Llandovery, Carmarthenshire. Lower order right-hand batsman, right-arm fast bowler. *Sch* Llandovery College. *Team* Oxford U (1876, blue).
Career batting
5–7–0–76–33–10.85–0–*ct* 2
Bowling 501–17–29.47–1–0–7/35
A noted rugby footballer, he represented Wales. He also won a blue for athletics. He was Mayor of Llandovery 1894/5 and 1904/5.

Lewis, Clairmonte Christopher
Cricketer. *b:* 14.2.1968, Georgetown, Guyana. Middle order right-hand batsman, right-arm fast medium bowler. *Teams* Leicestershire (1987–91, 59 matches); Nottinghamshire (1992, 12 matches). *Tours* England to West Indies 1989/90, to Australia 1990/1, to New Zealand 1991/2, to Australia and New Zealand (World Cup) 1991/2. *Tests* England (1990–92, 14 matches).
Career batting
91–132–17–3282–189*–28.53–3–*ct* 65
Bowling 7757–271–28.62–13–3–6/22
Test batting
14–19–1–446–70–24.77–0–*ct* 13
Bowling 1520–42–36.19–2–0–6/111
Regarded as one of the most promising all-rounders in English cricket, he played in all five Tests in England in 1992, having had a successful tour to Australia and New Zealand in the previous winter.

Lewis, Claude
Professional. *b:* 27.7.1908, Sittingbourne, Kent. Lower order left-hand batsman, slow left-arm bowler. *Team* Kent (1933–53, 128 matches).
Career batting
128–187–72–738–27–6.41–0–*ct* 61
Bowling 8198–301–27.23–14–4–8/58
In 1988 he retired as scorer to Kent CCC, having been connected with the County Club for 60 years, as player, coach (1949–62) and scorer (1959–88).

Lewis, David Alan
Cricketer. *b:* 1.6.1964, Cork, Ireland. Middle order right-hand batsman, right-arm medium pace bowler. *Team* Ireland (1988–92).
Career batting
5–9–1–260–122*–32.50–1–*ct* 1
Bowling 232–4–58.00–0–0–2/39

Lewis, David John
Amateur. *b:* 27.7.1927, Bulawayo, Rhodesia. Middle order right-hand batsman, off break bowler. *Team* Rhodesia (1945/6 to 1963/4); Oxford U (1949–51, blue 1951).
Career batting
88–146–16–3662–170*–28.16–8–*ct* 39
Bowling 457–11–41.54–0–0–2/19

His County cricket was for Oxfordshire (1950). He also won a rugby blue and played for Rhodesia.

Lewis, David Wyndham
Amateur. *b:* 18.12.1940, Roath, Cardiff. Lower order right-hand batsman, leg break bowler. *Sch* Wycliffe College. *Teams* Glamorgan (1960–69, 12 matches); Transvaal (1972/3).
Career batting
14–20–7–122–29*–9.38–0–*ct* 3
Bowling 958–21–45.61–0–0–4/42
He did not appear in first-class County cricket 1963 to 1967 inclusive.

Lewis, Desmond Michael
Cricketer. *b:* 21.2.1946, Kingston, Jamaica. Middle order right-hand batsman, wicket-keeper. *Team* Jamaica (1970 to 1975/6). *Tour* Jamaica to England 1970. *Tests* West Indies (1970/1, 3 matches).
Career batting
36–56–5–1623–96–31.82–0–*ct* 67–*st* 11
Test batting
3–5–2–259–88–86.33–0–*ct* 8

Lewis, Esmond Burman
Amateur. *b:* 5.1.1918, Shirley, Solihull, Warwickshire. *d:* 19.10.1983, Dorridge, Solihull, Warwickshire. Lower order right-hand batsman, wicket-keeper. *Team* Warwickshire (1949–58, 43 matches).
Career batting
47–56–12–553–51–12.56–0–*ct* 93–*st* 26
He was a member of the Warwickshire Committee.

Lewis, Euros John
Professional. *b:* 31.1.1942, Llanelly, Carmarthenshire. Middle order left-hand batsman, off break bowler. *Teams* Glamorgan (1961–66, 95 matches); Sussex (1967–69, 86 matches).
Career batting
182–276–28–3487–80–14.06–0–*ct* 131
Bowling 9286–341–27.23–13–2–8/89

Lewis, Frederick Stafford
Amateur. *b:* 17.4.1879. Edmonton, Middlesex. *d:* 22.5.1967, Dunsfold, Chiddingfold, Surrey. Middle order right-hand batsman, right-arm medium pace bowler. *Sch* Marlborough. *Team* MCC (1903).
Career batting
1–1–0–1–1–1.00–0–*ct* 0

Lewis, Jonathan James Benjamin
Cricketer. *b:* 21.5.1970, Isleworth, Middlesex. Middle order right-hand batsman, right-arm medium pace bowler. *Team* Essex (1990–92, 16 matches).
Career batting
16–23–5–935–133–51.94–2–*ct* 5
He scored 116* on his first-class debut for Essex v Surrey at the Oval in 1990.

Lewis, Kenneth Humphrey
Professional. *b:* 10.11.1928, Penygladdfa, Newtown, Montgomeryshire. Lower order right-hand batsman, right-arm fast medium bowler. *Team* Glamorgan (1950–56, 36 matches).
Career batting
36–48–14–312–34–9.17–0–*ct* 15
Bowling 2044–55–37.16–0–0–4/25

Lewis, Leslie Keith
Amateur. *b:* 25.9.1929, East Finchley, Middlesex. Middle order right-hand batsman, off break bowler, cover field. *Sch* Taunton. *Team* Cambridge U (1952–53, blue 1953).
Career batting
6–11–1–155–53*–15.50–0–*ct* 2
An excellent hockey player, he appeared for Cambridge U.

Lewis, Reginald Chester Vale
Amateur. *b:* 4.10.1927, Cape Town, South Africa. *d:* 1.8.1981, Cape Town, South Africa. Lower order right-hand batsman, leg break bowler. *Team* Oxford U (1949–50).
Career batting
4–6–2–65–34–16.25–0–*ct* 0
Bowling 222–8–27.75–0–0–3/31
His County cricket was for Oxfordshire (1949).

Lewis, Richard Percy
Amateur. *b:* 10.3.1874, Kensington, London. *d:* 7.9.1917, Ypres, Belgium. He died of wounds received in battle. Lower order right-hand batsman, wicket-keeper. *Sch* Winchester. *Teams* Oxford U (1894–96, blue all three years); Middlesex (1898, 2 matches). *Tour* Priestley to West Indies 1896/7.
Career batting
36–58–21–134–27*–3.62–0–*ct* 55–*st* 21
His final first-class match was for MCC in 1907. He was a notable figure in military cricket, both in England and overseas. In 1892 he played for Surrey, but not in first-class matches.

Lewis, Richard Victor
Cricketer. *b:* 6.8.1947, Winchester, Hampshire. Middle order right-hand batsman, leg break bowler. *Team* Hampshire (1967–76, 103 matches).
Career batting
105–190–14–3471–136–19.72–2–*ct* 65
Bowling 104–1–104.00–0–0–1/59
He also played for Dorset (1977–89) and his final first-class match was for the Minor Counties in 1981.

Lewis, Roy Markham
Cricketer. *b:* 29.6.1948, Bromley, Kent. Middle order right-hand batsman, right-arm medium pace bowler. *Team* Surrey (1968–73, 38 matches).
Career batting
38–68–9–1746–87–29.59–0–*ct* 26
Bowling 7–0

Lewis, William Ian
Amateur. *b:* 29.9.1935, Dublin, Ireland. Middle order right-hand batsman. *Team* Ireland (1956–72).
Career batting
5–10–0–67–20–6.70–0–*ct* 2

Lewis-Barclay, Harry Samuel
(changed name from H. S. Lewis)
Amateur. *b:* 7.11.1892, Shoreditch, London. *d:* 20.4.1956, Barnet, Hertfordshire. Lower order left-hand batsman, slow bowler. *Teams* Southern Punjab (1926/7); Army (1928).
Career batting
4–6–3–32–14*–10.66–0–*ct* 1
Bowling 316–9–35.11–0–0–3/75

Lewisham, Viscount William Heneage Legge
(succeeded as 6th Earl of Dartmouth in 1891)
Amateur. *b:* 6.5.1851, Westminster, London. *d:* 11.3.1936, Patshull House, Staffordshire. Son-in-law of Earl of Leicester (MCC 1851). Lower order right-hand batsman, right-hand slow round-arm bowler, long stop. *Sch* Eton. *Team* MCC (1877).
Career batting
1–2–2–29–24*–no av–0–*ct* 0

He was not in the Eleven whilst at Oxford. He held office as President of Kent (1888), of MCC (1893) and for 40 years of Staffordshire. In 1878 he was elected MP for West Kent and 1885–91 for Lewisham. His County cricket was for Shropshire (1869) and Staffordshire (1871–77).

Leycester, George
Amateur. *b:* 1768, Toft Hall, Knutsford, Cheshire. *d:* 5.7.1827, Westminster, London. Middle order batsman, wicket-keeper. *Teams* Surrey (1801–08); Hampshire (1807).
Career batting
30–55–2–508–49–9.58–0–*ct* 15–*st* 4

Leyland, Morris
(known as Maurice Leyland)
Professional. *b:* 20.7.1900, New Park, Harrogate, Yorkshire. *d:* 1.1.1967, Scotton Banks, Harrogate, Yorkshire. Brilliant middle order left-hand batsman, slow left-arm bowler. *Teams* Yorkshire (1920–47, 548 matches); Patiala (1926/7). *Tours* MCC to India 1926/7 (in emergency), to Australia and New Zealand 1928/9, 1932/3, 1936/7, to South Africa 1930/1, to West Indies 1934/5; Yorkshire to Jamaica 1935/6. *Tests* England (1928–38, 41 matches).
Career batting
686–932–101–33660–263–40.50–80–*ct* 246
Bowling 13659–466–29.31–11–1–8/63
Test batting
41–65–5–2764–187–46.06–9–*ct* 13
Bowling 585–6–97.50–0–0–3/91

One of the greatest of Yorkshire's batsmen, he hit over 1,000 runs for the County each season from 1923 to 1939, but had to wait until his eighth season in first-class cricket before winning a Test cap. Having however gained an England place he remained a major force in international cricket for eight seasons. He had three successful tours to Australia, his batting average exceeding 40 on each tour, and of the regular England players of his time only Hammond and Sutcliffe can boast better Test batting records.

In all he hit 1,000 runs in a season 17 times, going on to 2,000 three times, with his best 2,317, av 50.36, in 1933. All his five double centuries were for Yorkshire, the highest being 263 v Essex at Hull in 1936. He helped to break no fewer than three Yorkshire partnership records: 346 for the 2nd wicket with W. Barber v Middlesex at Bramall Lane in 1932; 323 for the 3rd wicket with H. Sutcliffe v Glamorgan at Huddersfield in 1928 and 276 for the 6th wicket with E. Robinson v Glamorgan at Swansea in 1926.

His slow bowling was at times most effective and he is reputed to have invented the term 'Chinaman' to denote his left-arm off breaks. He was a brilliant fielder in the deep.

His final first-class match was for an England XI in 1948. After retiring from first-class cricket he was coach to Yorkshire for 12 seasons until 1963.

Liaqat Ali Khan
Cricketer. *b:* 21.5.1955, Karachi, Pakistan. Lower order right-hand batsman, left-arm medium pace bowler. *Teams* Karachi (1970/1 to 1974/5); Sind (1974/5); Habib Bank (1975/6 to 1990/1); PIA (1981/2). *Tours* Pakistan to England 1978; PIA to Zimbabwe 1981/2. *Tests* Pakistan (1974/5 to 1978, 5 matches).
Career batting
172–173–76–737–51–7.59–0–*ct* 63
Bowling 12431–485–25.63–24–2–8/44
Test batting
5–7–3–28–12–7.00–0–*ct* 1
Bowling 359–6–59.83–0–0–3/80

On the 1978 tour to England he took 18 wickets, av 28.33, in first-class matches and appeared in two Tests.

Liddell, Alan William George
Amateur. *b:* 8.8.1930, Northampton. *d:* 9.2.1972, Duston, Northamptonshire. Son of A. G. (Northamptonshire). Lower order right-hand batsman, right-arm medium pace bowler. *Team* Northamptonshire (1951–55, 18 matches).
Career batting
18–20–6–201–38*–14.35–0–*ct* 4
Bowling 1399–24–58.29–0–0–3/62

Liddell, Allan Graham
Professional. *b:* 2.5.1908, Northampton. *d:* 17.2.1970, Northampton. Father of A. W. G. (Northamptonshire). Stylish middle order right-hand batsman, slow right-arm bowler. *Team* Northamptonshire (1927–34, 91 matches).

Liebenrood, Fitzhardinge Hancock

Career batting
91–161–7–2355–120–15.29–3–*ct* 66
Bowling 563–9–62.55–0–0–4/59

Liebenrood, Fitzhardinge Hancock
(changed name to Fitzhardinge Hancock in 1921)
Amateur. *b:* 14.9.1885, Half Way Street, Eltham, Kent. *d:* 11.5.1969, Poole, Dorset. Father-in-law of H. E. Scott (Sussex). Middle order batsman. *Sch* Wellington. *Team* MCC (1905–07).
Career batting
7–12–1–125–26–11.36–0–*ct* 6
Bowling 44–2–22.00–0–0–1/9

Ligertwood, David George Coutts
Cricketer. *b:* 16.5.1969, Oxford. Opening right-hand batsman, wicket-keeper. *Team* Surrey (1992, 4 matches).
Career batting
4–7–0–63–28–9.00–0–*ct* 7–*st* 1
He also played for Hertfordshire (1990–92).

Light, Elisha Edward
Professional. *b:* 1.9.1873, Winchester, Hampshire. *d:* 12.3.1952, Llanelly, Carmarthenshire. Brother of W. F. (Hampshire). Lower order left-hand batsman, slow left-arm bowler. *Team* Hampshire (1898–1900, 13 matches).
Career batting
13–22–6–168–35–10.50–0–*ct* 6
Bowling 263–5–52.60–0–0–2/22
He also played for Carmarthenshire (1908). He first played for Hampshire (not first-class) in 1894.

Light, William Frederick
Professional. *b:* 1.3.1878, St Faiths, Hampshire. *d:* 10.11.1930, St James Park, Exeter, Devon. Brother of E. E. (Hampshire). Lower order left-hand batsman, left-arm medium pace bowler. *Team* Hampshire (1897–98, 12 matches).
Career batting
12–19–2–101–41–5.94–0–*ct* 9
Bowling 343–10–34.30–0–0–3/32
He also played for Devon (1901–28).

Lightfoot, Albert
Professional. *b:* 8.1.1936, Woore, Shropshire. Middle order left-hand batsman, right-arm medium pace bowler. *Team* Northamptonshire (1953–70, 290 matches).
Career batting
294–495–61–12000–174*–27.64–12–*ct* 161
Bowling 6192–172–36.00–4–0–7/25
He hit 1,000 runs in a season four times (best 1,878, av 41.73, in 1962). With R. Subba Row he created a new Northamptonshire partnership record by adding 376 for the 6th wicket v Surrey at the Oval in 1958.

Lilford, Lord John
(born John Powys, succeeded as 5th Baron in 1882)
Amateur. *b:* 12.1.1863, Lilford Hall, Lilford-cum-Wigsthorpe, Northamptonshire. *d:* 17.12.1945, Kettering, Northamptonshire. Nephew of A. W. Crichton (MCC 1856). Tail end batsman. *Sch* Harrow. *Team* Northamptonshire (1911, 1 match).
Career batting
1–1–0–4–4–4.00–0–*ct* 0
President of Northamptonshire CCC from 1904 to 1921 and a member of the County Committee until 1936, Lord Lilford was the major benefactor of the County Club in its early years in first-class cricket. Although a very moderate player himself he was invited to play for Northamptonshire v Indians in 1911, in appreciation of his work for the County.

Lillee, Dennis Keith, MBE
Cricketer. *b:* 18.7.1949, Subiaco, Perth, Western Australia. Lower order right-hand batsman, right-arm fast bowler. *Teams* Western Australia (1969/70 to 1983/4, 76 matches); Tasmania (1987/8, 6 matches); Northamptonshire (1988, 7 matches). *Tours* Australia to New Zealand 1969/70, 1976/7, 1981/2, to England 1972, 1975, 1980, 1981, 1983 (World Cup), to West Indies 1972/3, to Pakistan 1979/80, to Sri Lanka 1982/3; International Wanderers to South Africa 1975/6; Rest of World to England 1988. *Tests* Australia (1970/1 to 1983/4, 70 matches).
Career batting
198–241–70–2377–73*–13.90–0–*ct* 67
Bowling 20695–882–23.46–50–13–8/29
Test batting
70–90–24–905–73*–13.71–0–*ct* 23
Bowling 8493–355–23.92–23–7–7/83
The outstanding fast bowler of his generation, his tally of 355 Test wickets was a record until overtaken by Botham in August 1986. He missed several Test series when he joined Packer's World Series Cricket, otherwise his total might have exceeded 400. He headed the Test bowling averages on his first tour to England in 1972 with 31 wickets, av 17.67, and also took most wickets in first-class matches: 53, av 22.58. In 1975 he was again the principal wicket taker with 21, av 21.90, in Tests and 41, av 21.60, in all first-class matches. On his 1981 visit he took 39 wickets, av 22.30, in the Tests and 47, av 21.87, in first-class matches. He signed for Northamptonshire in 1988, but an injury to his ankle restricted his appearances.

Lilley, Alan William
Cricketer. *b:* 8.5.1959, Ilford, Essex. Middle order right-hand batsman, right-arm medium pace bowler, occasional wicket-keeper. *Team* Essex (1978–90, 120 matches).
Career batting
120–190–15–4495–113*–25.68–3–*ct* 67
Bowling 565–8–70.62–0–0–3/116
He scored 100* in the second innings on his first-class debut for Essex v Nottinghamshire at Trent Bridge in 1978.

Lilley, Arthur Frederick Augustus
Professional. *b:* 28.11.1866, Holloway Head, Birmingham. *d:* 17.11.1929, Sandy Park, Brislington, Bristol. Middle order right-hand batsman, wicket-keeper, occasional right-arm medium pace bowler. *Teams* Warwickshire (1894–1911, 321 matches); London County (1900–01). *Tours* MacLaren to Australia 1901/2; MCC to Australia 1903/4. *Tests* England (1896–1909, 35 matches).
Career batting
416–639–46–15597–171–26.30–16–*ct* 716–*st* 195
Bowling 1485–41–36.21–1–0–6/46
Test batting
35–52–8–903–84–20.52–0–*ct* 70–*st* 22
Bowling 23–1–23.00–0–0–1/23
He hit 1,000 runs in a season three times (best 1,399, av 34.97, in 1895). His first-class debut was for North v South at Edgbaston in 1891. He was for some ten years regarded as the best wicket-keeper in England. He first played for Warwickshire (pre first-class) in 1888.

Lilley, Ben
Professional. *b:* 11.2.1894, Kimberley, Nottinghamshire. *d:* 4.8.1950, Forest Fields, Nottingham. Middle order right-hand batsman, wicket-keeper. *Team* Nottinghamshire (1921–37, 369 matches). *Tour* Cahn to Jamaica 1928/9.
Career batting
373–513–79–10496–124–24.18–7–*ct* 657–*st* 132
Bowling 27–0
He hit 1,000 runs in a season twice (best 1,074, av 27.53, in 1928).

Lillington, George Godfrey
Amateur. *b:* 31.10.1843, Bedminster, Somerset. *d:* 25.8.1914, Brislington, Somerset. Lower order batsman, wicket-keeper. *Team* Somerset (1883–85, 2 matches).
Career batting
2–3–1–2–1*–1.00–0–*ct* 3–*st* 3

Lillywhite, Frederick William
Professional. *b:* 13.6.1792, Westhampnett, Sussex. *d:* 21.8.1854, Islington, London. He died of cholera. Father of Frederick (cricket reporter), John (Middlesex and Sussex) and James (Middlesex and Sussex), uncle of James, jun (Sussex). Lower order right-hand batsman, right-hand slow medium round-arm bowler. *Teams* Sussex (1825–53, 70 matches); Surrey (1829, 2 matches as given man); Cambridge Town Club (1841); Hampshire (1842–45, 3 matches as given man); Middlesex (1850–51, 3 matches).
Career batting
237–416–93–2352–44*–7.28–0–*ct* 140
Bowling 2342–215+1355–10.89–155–54–10/?
He was regarded as one of the leading bowlers of his day, though he did not appear in important matches until he was over 30. He took 100 wickets in a season four times (best 115 wickets, in 1844). He took ten wickets in an innings for Players v 18 Gentlemen at Lord's in 1837.

Lillywhite, James (sen)
Professional. *b:* 29.10.1825, Hove, Sussex. *d:* 24.11.1882, Cheltenham, Gloucestershire. Son of F. W. (Sussex and Middlesex), brother of John (Sussex and Middlesex), cousin of James jun (Sussex). Lower order right-hand batsman, right-hand medium pace round-arm bowler. *Teams* Sussex (1850–60, 18 matches); Middlesex (1851, 2 matches).
Career batting
20–33–6–169–33–6.25–0–*ct* 11
Bowling 324–21+10–15.42–0–0–3/11
He also played for Essex (pre first-class, 1846), Leicestershire (pre first-class, 1856), Suffolk (1859), Monmouthshire (1860) and Buckinghamshire (1866). He was the senior partner in the London sporting firm of James Lillywhite, Frowd and Co of the Haymarket.

Lillywhite, James (jun)
Professional. *b:* 23.2.1842, Westhampnett, Sussex. *d:* 25.10.1929, Westerton, Chichester, Sussex. Nephew of F. W. (Middlesex and Sussex), cousin of James (Sussex) and John (Sussex and Middlesex). Lower order left-hand batsman, slow medium left-arm bowler. *Teams* Sussex (1862–83, 157 matches). *Tours* Willsher to North America 1868 (non-first-class); Grace to Australia 1873/4 (non-first-class); Lillywhite to Australia 1876/7; Lillywhite, Shaw and Shrewsbury to Australia 1881/2, 1884/5, 1886/7 (did not play in first-class matches on these 3 tours). *Tests* England (1876/7, 2 matches).
Career batting
256–445–59–5523–126*–14.30–2–*ct* 109
Bowling 18433–1210–15.23–96–22–10/129
Test batting
2–3–1–16–10–8.00–0–*ct* 1
Bowling 126–8–15.75–0–0–4/70
He took 100 wickets in a season once: 110, av 13.34, in 1873. He took 10 wickets in an innings (for 129) for South v North at Canterbury in 1872. He also took 9 for 29 on his first-class debut for Sussex v MCC at Lord's in 1862. He captained England in the first two Test matches. His final first-class match was for Lord Sheffield's XI in 1885. He was a first-class umpire (1883–1901), standing in 6 Test matches, all in Australia except one in 1899.

Lillywhite, John
Professional. *b:* 10.11.1826, Hove, Sussex. *d:* 27.10.1874, St Pancras, London. Son of F. W. (Sussex and Middlesex), brother of James sen (Sussex and Middlesex), cousin of James jun (Sussex). Middle order right-hand batsman, originally right-hand fast round-arm, but latterly slow bowler. *Teams* Sussex (1850–69, 100 matches); Middlesex (1851–64, 6 matches).

Limb, Thomas

Career batting
185–323–29–5127–138–17.43–2–*ct* 94
Bowling 2402–210 + 13–11.43–12–2–8/54

His first-class debut was for Manchester in 1848 and his final first-class match was for W. G. Grace's XI v Kent in 1873.

Limb, Thomas
Professional. *b:* 25.2.1850, Eastwood, Nottinghamshire. *d:* 21.2.1901, Eastwood, Nottinghamshire. Lower order right-hand batsman, right-hand medium pace round-arm bowler. *Team* Derbyshire (1878, 1 match).
Career batting
1–2–0–0–0–0.00–0–*ct* 0

Limbdi, Kumar Shri Ghanshyamshinhji Daulatsinhji Jhalla
Amateur. *b:* 23.10.1902, Limbdi, India. *d:* 10.11.1964, Bhavnagar, India. Brother-in-law of Maharaja of Porbandar (India). Middle order right-hand batsman. *Sch* The Leys. *Team* Western Indian States (1932/3 to 1942/3). *Tour* India to England 1932.
Career batting
19–31–2–505–57–17.41–0–*ct* 11

He was vice-captain of the 1932 Indian touring team, but found batting in England not easy. His first-class debut was for Rest of India in 1930/1.

Linaker, Lewis
Professional. *b:* 8.4.1885, Paddock, Huddersfield, Yorkshire. *d:* 17.11.1961, Paddock, Huddersfield, Yorkshire. Lower order right-hand batsman, left-arm medium fast bowler. *Team* Yorkshire (1909, 1 match).
Career batting
1–2–0–0–0–0.00–0–*ct* 0
Bowling 28–1–28.00–0–0–1/28

Linathan, Douglas Valentine
Professional. *b:* 29.5.1885, Woodhouse, Sheffield, Yorkshire. *d:* 17.12.1932, Derby. Middle/lower order left-hand batsman, slow left-arm bowler. *Team* Derbyshire (1920, 3 matches).
Career batting
3–6–1–35–14*–7.00–0–*ct* 2
Bowling 78–1–78.00–0–0–1/15

Lindley, Leonard Oscroft
Amateur. *b:* 22.2.1861, Nottingham. *d:* 3.5.1915, King's Norton, Warwickshire. Brother of Tinsley (Nottinghamshire). Middle order batsman. *Sch* Nottingham High School. *Team* North (1884).
Career batting
2–3–0–28–22–9.33–0–*ct* 2

Lindley, Tinsley
Amateur. *b:* 27.10.1865, Nottingham. *d:* 31.3.1940, The Park, Nottingham. Brother of L. O. (North). Middle order right-hand batsman, right-arm slow medium bowler. *Sch* The Leys and Nottingham High School. *Teams* Cambridge U (1885–88); Nottinghamshire (1888, 4 matches).
Career batting
10–16–1–150–40–10.00–0–*ct* 6
Bowling 220–9–24.44–0–0–3/44

His final first-class match was for Oxford and Cambridge (Past and Present) v Australians in 1893. A noted soccer player, he appeared as centre forward for Nottingham Forest, Cambridge U, and England. He also represented Nottinghamshire at rugby.

Lindo, Cleveland Vincent
Professional. *b:* 6.6.1936, Bigwoods, St Elizabeth, Jamaica. Lower order right-hand batsman, right-arm fast bowler. *Teams* Nottinghamshire (1960, 1 match); Somerset (1963, 1 match).
Career batting
2–3–1–65–24–32.50–0–*ct* 0
Bowling 162–8–20.25–1–0–8/88

He also played for Staffordshire (1965–66).

Lindop, Hubert Harry
Amateur. *b:* 21.8.1907, Walsall, Staffordshire. *d:* 30.5.1982, Stafford. Opening/middle order batsman. *Sch* Rossall. *Team* MCC (1936).
Career batting
1–2–1–25–19*–25.00–0–*ct* 0

His County cricket was for Staffordshire (1932–34).

Lindsay, Alexander
Amateur. *b:* 13.2.1883, Broughty Ferry, Angus, Scotland. *d:* 26.1.1941, Dundee, Angus, Scotland. Middle order right-hand batsman, leg break and googly bowler. *Sch* Fettes. *Team* Scotland (1909).
Career batting
1–2–0–7–7–3.50–0–*ct* 1
Bowling 6–0

Lindsay, Denis Thomson
Amateur. *b:* 4.9.1939, Benoni, Transvaal, South Africa. Son of J. D. (South Africa), great-nephew of N. V. (South Africa). Middle order right-hand batsman, wicket-keeper. *Teams* North East Transvaal (1958/9 to 1973/4); Transvaal (1964/5). *Tours* SA Fezela to England 1961; South Africa to England 1965, 1970 (tour cancelled), to Australia and New Zealand 1963/4, to Australia 1971/2 (tour cancelled); Rest of World to England 1967, 1968. *Tests* South Africa (1963/4 to 1969/70, 19 matches).
Career batting
124–214–15–7074–216–35.54–12–*ct* 292–*st* 41
Bowling 14–0
Test batting
19–31–1–1130–182–37.66–3–*ct* 57–*st* 2

The principal wicket-keeper on the 1965 tour to England, he appeared in all three of the Tests. In the match between Fezela XI and Essex at Chelmsford in 1961 he hit five sixes off consecutive balls to end the match. His highest score was 216 for North East Transvaal v Transvaal B at Johannesburg in 1966/7. He hit 1,014 runs, av 72.42, in South Africa in 1966/7.

Lindsay, John Dixon
Amateur. *b:* 8.9.1908, Barkly East, Cape Province, South Africa. *d:* 31.8.1990, Benoni, Transvaal, South Africa. Nephew of N. V. (South Africa), father of D. T. (South Africa). Lower order right-hand batsman, wicket-keeper. *Teams* Transvaal (1933/4 to 1936/7); North East Transvaal (1937/8 to 1948/9). *Tour* South Africa to England 1947. *Tests* South Africa (1947, 3 matches).
Career batting
29–45–14–346–51–11.16–0–*ct* 39–*st* 16
Test batting
3–5–2–21–9*–7.00–0–*ct* 4–*st* 1

He began the 1947 tour as the principal wicket-keeper but lost his place after the third Test to Fullerton. He played soccer for Huddersfield Town and Transvaal, and also played hockey for Transvaal.

Lindsay, William
Amateur. *b:* 3.8.1847, India. *d:* 15.2.1923, Rochester, Kent. Stylish middle order right-hand batsman, excellent cover field. *Sch* Winchester. *Team* Surrey (1876–82, 33 matches).
Career batting
33–62–5–987–74–17.31–0–*ct* 17

He also played for Devon. An excellent soccer player, he represented England as full back and was in the winning FA Cup side three years in succession for Wanderers.

Lindsay, Sir William O'Brien
Amateur. *b:* 8.10.1909, Canterbury, Kent. *d:* 20.10.1975, Nairobi, Kenya. Determined opening right-hand batsman, wicket-keeper. *Sch* Harrow. *Teams* Oxford U (1929–32, blue 1931); Kent (1931, 2 matches); Scotland (1929).
Career batting
17–28–1–531–63–19.66–0–*ct* 10–*st* 2
Bowling 18–0

He had a distinguished career in the Sudan, becoming Chief Justice.

Lindsey, Peter John
Professional. *b:* 29.5.1944, Matlock, Derbyshire. Tail end right-hand batsman, off break bowler, outfield. *Team* Essex (1964, 1 match).
Career batting
1–1–1–7–7*–no av–0–*ct* 0
Bowling 50–1–50.00–0–0–1/8

Lindwall, Raymond Russell, MBE
Amateur. *b:* 3.10.1921, Mascot, Sydney, New South Wales, Australia. Hard hitting lower order right-hand batsman, brilliant right-arm fast bowler. *Teams* New South Wales (1941/2 to 1953/4, 50 matches); Queensland (1954/5 to 1959/60, 34 matches). *Tours* Australia to England 1948, 1953, 1956, to South Africa 1949/50, to West Indies 1954/5, to New Zealand 1945/6, to Pakistan and India 1956/7, 1959/60; Swanton to West Indies 1960/1; International XI to Rhodesia, India and Pakistan 1961/2. *Tests* Australia (1945/6 to 1959/60, 61 matches)
Career batting
228–270–39–5042–134*–21.82–5–*ct* 123
Bowling 16956–794–21.35–34–2–7/20
Test batting
61–84–13–1502–118–21.15–2–*ct* 26
Bowling 5251–228–23.03–12–0–7/38

The outstanding fast bowler of the decade immediately following the Second World War, he headed both the Test and first-class bowling averages on both the 1948 and 1953 tours to England. In 1948 he took 86 wickets, av 15.68, and in 1953, 85 wickets, av 16.40, his figures in the two Test series being 27, av 19.62, and 26, av 18.84, respectively. He captained Australia in one Test v India in 1956/7. He played rugby league for St George in Australia.

Lineham, Edwin
Amateur. *b:* 28.4.1879, Landport, Portsmouth, Hampshire. *d:* 12.8.1949, Fratton, Portsmouth, Hampshire. Middle order batsman. *Team* Hampshire (1898, 1 match).
Career batting
1–2–1–0–0*–0.00–0–*ct* 0

His name was incorrectly given as 'Lynam' in the printed scores of his only first-class match.

Linehan, Alphonsus James
Cricketer. *b:* 20.4.1940, Dublin, Ireland. Middle order right-hand batsman. *Team* Ireland (1972–74).
Career batting
2–4–0–29–16–7.25–0–*ct* 2

Lines, Steven John
Cricketer. *b:* 16.3.1963, Luton, Bedfordshire. Middle order right-hand batsman, right-arm medium pace bowler. *Team* Northamptonshire (1983, 1 match). *Tour* Minor Counties to East Africa 1982/3 (not first-class).
Career batting
1–1–0–29–29–29.00–0–*ct* 1

He also played for Bedfordshire (1980–90).

Ling, Anthony John Patrick
Amateur. *b:* 10.8.1910, Skewen, Glamorgan. *d:* 12.1.1987, Eastbourne, Sussex. Middle order left-hand batsman. *Sch* Stowe. *Teams* Glamorgan (1934–36, 9 matches); Somerset (1939, 5 matches).
Career batting
14–19–3–256–41*–16.00–0–*ct* 2
Bowling 12–0

He also played for Wiltshire (1929–32).

Ling, David John
Cricketer. *b:* 2.7.1946, Enfield, Middlesex. Middle order right-hand batsman, right-arm medium pace bowler. *Team* Middlesex (1966–68, 14 matches).
Career batting
14–15–3–174–40–14.50–0–*ct* 6
Bowling 386–7–55.14–0–0–3/24
He also played for Suffolk (1963–65 and 1971).

Linnell, Herbert James
Amateur. *b:* 7.3.1909, Paddington, London. *d:* 8.2.1968, Canterbury, Kent. Aggressive middle order right-hand batsman, right-arm fast bowler. *Sch* St Lawrence, Ramsgate. *Team* Oxford U (1929–32).
Career batting
4–6–0–34–11–5.66–0–*ct* 3
Bowling 310–8–38.75–0–0–4/57
He won a blue for hockey.

Linnell, Michael Gerald
Amateur. *b:* 13.1.1876, Reigate, Surrey. *d:* 2.8.1959, Salisbury, Rhodesia. Lower order right-hand batsman, right-arm medium fast bowler. *Sch* St Lawrence, Ramsgate. *Teams* Rhodesia (1904/5); H. D. G. Leveson-Gower's XI (1909).
Career batting
2–4–1–36–15–12.00–0–*ct* 1
Bowling 33–0

Linney, Charles Keith
Professional. *b:* 26.8.1912, Hobart, Tasmania, Australia. *d:* September 1992, Tunbridge Wells, Kent. Son of G. F. (Tasmania). Middle order left-hand batsman, left-arm medium pace bowler. *Team* Somerset (1931–37, 32 matches).
Career batting
32–49–9–576–60–14.40–0–*ct* 9
Bowling 119–2–59.50–0–0–1/9

Linton, James Edward Fryer
Amateur. *b:* 7.5.1909, Llandaff, Glamorgan. *d:* 27.12.1989, Cozumel Island, Mexico. Middle order right-hand batsman, right-arm medium fast bowler. *Sch* Charterhouse. *Team* Glamorgan (1932, 2 matches).
Career batting
2–4–0–3–2–0.75–0–*ct* 0
Bowling 82–1–82.00–0–0–1/34

Lipscomb, Francis Wallis
Amateur. *b:* 20.7.1834. *d:* 3.10.1906, Southsea, Hampshire. Middle order right-hand batsman, slow round-arm bowler. *Team* Hampshire (1881–82, 3 matches).
Career batting
5–9–1–121–53–15.12–0–*ct* 2
Bowling 103–2–51.50–0–0–2/46
His first first-class match was for Gentlemen of England in 1857.

Lipscomb, Frank
Amateur. *b:* 13.3.1863, East Peckham, Kent. *d:* 25.9.1951, Randwick, Sydney, New South Wales, Australia. Son of Robert (Kent). Hard hitting lower order right-hand batsman, right-arm fast bowler. *Team* Kent (1882–84, 16 matches).
Career batting
18–31–5–158–28–6.07–0–*ct* 8
Bowling 1178–52–22.65–1–0–5/19
He emigrated to Australia after the 1884 season and therefore did not again appear in County cricket.

Lipscomb, Robert
Amateur. *b:* 28.2.1837, Penshurst, Kent. *d:* 8.1.1895, Sherenden, Capel, Kent. Father of Frank (Kent). Lower order right-hand batsman, right-hand fast round-arm bowler, good slip. *Team* Kent (1862–73, 48 matches).
Career batting
60–105–19–428–22–4.97–0–*ct* 23
Bowling 4611–271–17.01–19–3–9/88
His best bowling was 9/88 for Kent v MCC at Lord's in 1871.

Lipscomb, William Henry
Amateur. *b:* 20.11.1846, Weeke, Winchester, Hampshire. *d:* 9.4.1918, Clapham, London. Lower order right-hand batsman, right-hand medium pace round-arm bowler, good close field. *Sch* Marlborough. *Teams* Hampshire (1866–67, 4 matches); Oxford U (1868, blue).
Career batting
7–13–2–154–34–14.00–0–*ct* 3
Bowling 100–3–33.33–0–0–2/26
He was a noted oarsman.

Lister, Benjamin
Professional. *b:* 9.12.1850, Birkenshaw, Yorkshire. *d:* 3.12.1919, Bradford, Yorkshire. Lower order right-hand batsman, wicket-keeper. *Team* Yorkshire (1874–78, 6 matches).
Career batting
7–12–2–46–19*–4.60–0–*ct* 2
Although paid to play in County cricket, he did not accept engagements as a professional.

Lister, Derek John
Amateur. *b:* 25.8.1930, Norwood, Surrey. *d:* 27.11.1980, Northampton. Middle order right-hand batsman. *Sch* Cranleigh. *Team* Cambridge U (1954).
Career batting
1–2–0–35–31–17.50–0–*ct* 0
His County cricket was for Wiltshire (1951).

Lister, John Wilton
Cricketer. *b:* 1.4.1959, Darlington, Co Durham. Opening right-hand batsman. *Team* Derbyshire (1978–79, 5 matches).

Career batting
5–10–0–205–48–20.50–0–*ct* 1
He also played for Durham (pre first-class, 1983–88).

Lister, Joseph
Amateur. *b:* 14.5.1930, Thirsk, Yorkshire. *d:* 28.1.1991, Granby, Harrogate, Yorkshire. Nephew of G. G. Macaulay (Yorkshire). Middle order right-hand batsman. *Sch* Cheltenham. *Teams* Yorkshire (1954, 2 matches); Worcestershire (1954–59, 21 matches).
Career batting
24–43–4–796–99–20.41–0–*ct* 14
His first-class debut was for Combined Services in 1951. He appeared for both Yorkshire and Worcestershire in 1954. He was Secretary of Worcestershire CCC 1956–71 and Yorkshire CCC from 1972 until he died. He also played hockey for Yorkshire.

Lister, William Hubert Lionel
Amateur. *b:* 11.10.1911, Freshfield, Formby, Lancashire. Middle order right-hand batsman. *Sch* Malvern. *Teams* Cambridge U (1933); Lancashire (1933–39, 158 matches).
Career batting
162–218–17–3709–104*–18.45–2–*ct* 73–*st* 2
Bowling 87–1–87.00–0–0–1/10
He captained Lancashire from 1936 to 1939. He was President of Lancashire 1969–70. A noted soccer half back, he appeared for Cambridge and for England in Amateur Internationals.

Lister-Kaye, Sir Kenelm Arthur
Amateur. *b:* 27.3.1892, Kensington, London. *d:* 28.2.1955, Tamboerskloof, Cape Town, South Africa. Lower order right-hand batsman, left-arm medium pace bowler. *Sch* Eton. *Teams* Oxford U (1912); Yorkshire (1928, 2 matches); Europeans (1920/1 to 1922/3).
Career batting
12–18–5–149–35–11.46–0–*ct* 8
Bowling 966–37–26.10–2–1–7/118

Lithgow, William Samuel Plenderleath
Amateur. *b:* 18.2.1920, Westminster, London. Sound middle order right-hand batsman, off break bowler, good field. *Sch* Harrow. *Team* Oxford U (1939).
Career batting
3–5–1–69–27–17.25–0–*ct* 2
His County cricket was for Oxfordshire (1937–49).

Litteljohn, Dr Arthur Rieusett
Amateur. *b:* 1.4.1881, Hanwell, Middlesex. *d:* 8.12.1919, Marylebone, London. Brother of E. S. (Middlesex). Middle order right-hand batsman, right-arm slow medium leg break bowler. *Sch* St Paul's. *Team* Middlesex (1905–14, 31 matches).
Career batting
33–45–8–683–76*–18.45–0–*ct* 15
Bowling 1798–86–20.90–7–2–8/69

Owing to his profession his first-class cricket was very limited.

Litteljohn, Dr Edward Salterne
Amateur. *b:* 24.9.1878, Hanwell, Middlesex. *d:* 22.1.1955, Beaconsfield, Buckinghamshire. Brother of A. R. (Middlesex). Middle order right-hand batsman. *Sch* St Paul's. *Team* Middlesex (1900–14, 74 matches).
Career batting
74–120–9–2832–141*–25.51–5–*ct* 34
Bowling 25–1–25.00–0–0–1/11

Little, Charles William
Amateur. *b:* 22.5.1870, Tonbridge, Kent. *d:* 20.5.1922, Southgate, Winchester, Hampshire. Lower order right-hand batsman, wicket-keeper. *Sch* Winchester. *Teams* Oxford U (1890); Kent (1893, 5 matches).
Career batting
11–16–1–160–28–10.66–0–*ct* 16–*st* 2
He also played for Shropshire (1900).

Littlehales, Rev Charles Gough
Amateur. *b:* 20.5.1871, Bulphan, Essex. *d:* 28.8.1945, Wickham Bishops, Essex. Lower order right-hand batsman, wicket-keeper. *Sch* Forest School. *Teams* Essex (1896–1904, 6 matches).
Career batting
6–10–1–109–23–12.11–0–*ct* 4–*st* 1
He did not play in any first-class matches whilst at Oxford U.

Littlewood, David John
Cricketer. *b:* 28.10.1955, Holloway, London. Lower order right-hand batsman, wicket-keeper. *Sch* Enfield GS. *Team* Cambridge U (1977–78, blue 1978).
Career batting
10–10–3–95–51–13.57–0–*ct* 12–*st* 6

Littlewood, George Hubert
Professional. *b:* 12.5.1882, Friarmere, Yorkshire. *d:* 20.12.1917, Oldham, Lancashire. Son of G. W. (Lancashire), brother of Jesse (Essex). Lower order batsman, slow left-arm bowler. *Team* Lancashire (1902–04, 14 matches).
Career batting
14–19–5–129–42–9.21–0–*ct* 12
Bowling 1123–58–19.36–5–1–7/49

Littlewood, George William
Professional. *b:* 10.5.1857, Holmfirth, Huddersfield, Yorkshire. *d:* 5.3.1928, Watersheddings, Oldham, Lancashire. Father of G. H. (Lancashire) and Jesse (Essex). Lower order right-hand batsman, wicket-keeper. *Team* Lancashire (1885, 3 matches).
Career batting
3–6–1–28–8*–5.60–0–*ct* 4–*st* 3
He also played for Essex (pre first-class, 1887–92).

Littlewood, Herbert Dell
(changed name to Littlewood-Clarke in 1894)
Amateur. *b:* 18.12.1858, Islington, London. *b:* 31.12.1925, Pegwell, Ramsgate, Kent. Middle order right-hand batsman, deep field. *Team* MCC (1887–96).
Career batting
5–10–1–86–35–9.55–0–*ct* 1
His County cricket was for Cheshire (1888–93).

Littlewood, Jesse
Professional. *b:* 8.4.1878, Holmfirth, Huddersfield, Yorkshire. *d:* 27.10.1942, Kidderminster, Worcestershire. Son of G. W. (Lancashire), brother of G. H. (Lancashire). Tail end batsman, bowler. *Team* Essex (1905, 1 match).
Career batting
1–1–1–5–5*–no av–0–*ct* 1
Bowling 36–0

Littlewood, John
Professional. *b:* 12.5.1852, Scissett, Huddersfield, Yorkshire. *d:* 22.3.1932, Harrogate, Yorkshire. Lower order left-hand batsman, slow left-arm bowler. *Team* An England XI (1888).
Career batting
1–2–2–2–2*–no av–0–*ct* 1
Bowling 14–0
He played for Yorkshire in 1887 in a non-first-class match. He was a first-class umpire (1896).

Livesay, Brig-Gen Robert O'Hara
Amateur. *b:* 27.6.1876, Old Brompton, Gillingham, Kent. *d:* 23.3.1946, Magham Down, Sussex. Attractive middle order right-hand batsman, right-hand medium bowler, good field. *Sch* Wellington. *Team* Kent (1895–1904, 26 matches).
Career batting
26–46–3–986–78–22.93–0–*ct* 8
Bowling 7–0
A noted rugby footballer, he appeared as a half back for Blackheath and England.

Livingston, Leonard
Professional. *b:* 3.5.1920, Hurlswood Park, Canterbury, Sydney, New South Wales, Australia. Forcing middle order left-hand batsman, slow left-arm bowler, occasional wicket-keeper, excellent cover field. *Teams* New South Wales (1941/2 to 1946/7, 5 matches); Northamptonshire (1950–57, 198 matches). *Tours* Commonwealth to India, Pakistan and Ceylon 1949/50; Howard to India 1956/7.
Career batting
236–384–45–15260–210–45.01–34–*ct* 148–*st* 23
Bowling 50–4–12.50–0–0–2/22
He hit 1,000 runs in a season seven times, going on to 2,000 three times (best 2,269, av 55.34, in 1954). He also hit 1,000 on the 1949/50 tour. His four double centuries were all for Northamptonshire, the highest being 210 v Somerset at Weston-super-Mare in 1951. His final first-class match was for MCC in 1964.

Livingstone, Daintes Abbia
Professional. *b:* 21.9.1933, St John's, Antigua. *d:* 8.9.1988, St John's, Antigua. Middle order left-hand batsman, right-arm medium pace bowler, good slip field. *Team* Hampshire (1959–72, 299 matches).
Career batting
301–519–63–12722–200–27.89–16–*ct* 243–*st* 2
Bowling 93–1–93.00–0–0–1/31
He hit 1,000 runs in a season six times (best 1,817, av 37.08, in 1962); his only double century was 200 for Hampshire v Surrey at Southampton in 1962, when he shared in a County 9th wicket record partnership of 230 with A. T. Castell.

Livingstone, David
Amateur. *b:* 23.2.1927, Crosshill, Glasgow, Scotland. Lower order right-hand batsman, off break bowler. *Team* Scotland (1957–66).
Career batting
18–26–10–102–16*–6.37–0–*ct* 5
Bowling 1255–50–25.10–4–1–6/33

Livock, Gerald Edward
Amateur. *b:* 11.7.1897, Newmarket, Suffolk. *d:* 27.1.1989, Blandford Forum, Dorset. Lower order right-hand batsman, wicket-keeper. *Sch* Cheltenham. *Team* Middlesex (1925–27, 5 matches). *Tour* Martineau to Egypt 1934 (not first-class).
Career batting
13–20–4–403–65–25.18–0–*ct* 19–*st* 5
His first-class debut was for Lord Cowdray's XI at Hastings in 1923 and his final first-class match for Gentlemen of England in 1934. He also played for Cambridgeshire (1921).

Livock, Michael Denzil
Amateur. *b:* 26.7.1936, Surbiton, Surrey. Lower order right-hand batsman, right-arm fast bowler. *Sch* Charterhouse. *Team* Free Foresters (1960).
Career batting
2–2–0–21–12–10.50–0–*ct* 1
Bowling 235–8–29.37–0–0–4/71

Livsey, Walter Herbert
(birth registered as W. H. Livesey)
Professional. *b:* 23.9.1893, Todmorden, Yorkshire. *d:* 12.9.1978, Merton Park, Surrey. Lower order right-hand batsman, wicket-keeper. *Teams* Hampshire (1913–29, 309 matches); England XI in India (1915/6 to 1918/19); Cooch Behar's XI (1917/18). *Tour* MCC to South Africa 1922/3 (he did not play in any first-class matches owing to injury).
Career batting
320–455–137–4940–110*–15.53–2–*ct* 384–*st* 265
He was to a large extent responsible for the incredible recovery by Hampshire against Warwickshire at Edgbaston in 1922. Hampshire were dismissed for 15

in their first innings and were 186 for 6 having followed on. Livsey came in at number ten and hit 110*, adding 177 for the 9th wicket and then 70 for the 10th wicket; eventually Hampshire won the game by 155 runs.

Llewellyn, Charles Bennett
Professional. *b:* 26.9.1876, Pietermaritzburg, South Africa. *d:* 7.6.1964, Chertsey, Surrey. Attacking middle order left-hand batsman, left-arm slow medium bowler, excellent mid off. *Teams* Natal (1894/5 to 1897/8); Hampshire (1899–1910, 196 matches); London County (1901–03). *Tours* South Africa to England 1904, 1912, to Australia 1910/11; Ranjitsinhji to North America 1899. *Tests* South Africa (1895/6 to 1912, 15 matches).
Career batting
267–461–34–11425–216–26.75–18–*ct* 175
Bowling 23715–1013–23.41–82–20–9/55
Test batting
15–28–1–544–90–20.14–0–*ct* 7
Bowling 1421–48–29.60–4–1–6/92

He hit 1,000 runs in a season six times (best 1,347, av 28.06, in 1908) and took 100 wickets in a season four times (best 170, av 18.61, in 1902). In 1901, 1908 and 1910 he achieved the 'double'.

His only double century was 216 for Hampshire v South Africans at Southampton in 1901. His best bowling was 9/55 for London County v Cambridge U at Crystal Palace in 1902.

He left Hampshire due to a disagreement over terms and after touring Australia with the 1910/11 South Africans came back to play League cricket in England. He was co-opted into the South African side in England in 1912, playing in five Tests and one other first-class match.

He played soccer for Accrington Stanley.

Llewellyn, Michael John
Cricketer. *b:* 27.11.1953, Clydach, Glamorgan. Hard hitting middle order left-hand batsman, off break bowler. *Team* Glamorgan (1970–82, 136 matches).
Career batting
136–215–30–4288–129*–23.17–3–*ct* 87
Bowling 615–23–26.73–0–0–4/35

He also played for Wiltshire (1983).

Llewelyn, William Dillwyn
(also known as Dillwyn-Llewelyn)
Amateur. *b:* 1.4.1868, Ynisygerwn, Glamorgan. *d:* 24.8.1893, Penllergaer, Swansea, Glamorgan. He died as the result of a shooting accident. Middle order right-hand batsman, right-arm fast medium bowler. *Sch* Eton. *Team* Oxford U (1890–91, blue both years).
Career batting
20–39–2–834–116–22.54–1–*ct* 15
Bowling 44–0

His County cricket was for Glamorgan (pre first-class, 1889–93). His final first-class match was for MCC in 1893. He was Treasurer of Glamorgan 1893.

Llong, Nigel James
Cricketer. *b:* 11.2.1969, Ashford, Kent. Middle order left-hand batsman, off break bowler. *Team* Kent (1990–92, 9 matches).
Career batting
9–12–2–200–92–20.00–0–*ct* 9
Bowling 264–7–37.71–0–0–3/50

Lloyd, Barry John
Cricketer. *b:* 6.9.1953, Neath, Glamorgan. Lower order right-hand batsman, off break bowler. *Team* Glamorgan (1972–83, 147 matches).
Career batting
147–184–47–1631–48–11.90–0–*ct* 87
Bowling 10133–247–41.02–3–0–8/70

He also played for Wales in Minor Counties Championship (1988–92). He captained Glamorgan in the second half of 1982 after Javed Miandad had joined the Pakistan tourists.

Lloyd, Clive Hubert, OBE
Cricketer. *b:* 31.8.1944, Queenstown, Georgetown, British Guiana. Cousin of L. R. Gibbs (West Indies). Excellent middle order left-hand batsman, right-arm medium pace bowler, good outfield. *Teams* British Guiana/Guyana (1963/4 to 1982/3); Lancashire (1968–86, 268 matches). *Tours* West Indies to India 1966/7, 1974/5, 1983/4, to Sri Lanka 1966/7, 1974/5, to Australia 1968/9, 1975/6, 1981/2, 1983/4 (not first-class), 1984/5, to New Zealand 1968/9, 1979/80, to England 1969, 1973, 1975 (World Cup), 1976, 1979 (World Cup), 1980, 1983 (World Cup), 1984, to Pakistan 1974/5, 1980/1; Rest of World to England 1967, 1968, 1970, to Pakistan 1970/1, 1973/4, to Australia 1971/2. *Tests* West Indies (1966/7 to 1984/5, 110 matches).
Career batting
490–730–96–31232–242*–49.26–79–*ct* 377
Bowling 4104–114–36.00–0–0–4/48
Test batting
110–175–14–7515–242*–46.67–19–*ct* 90
Bowling 622–10–62.20–0–0–2/13

A hard-hitting, fast scoring left-hand batsman, he led West Indies in 74 Tests of which 36 ended in victory. Both these figures created new records. Under his command the West Indies reached their greatest strength. His final Test tour to England in 1984 produced the ultimate result when he led West Indies to victory in all five Tests. His four previous tours had all seen him in excellent form, his best record being on the 1976 tour with 1,363 runs, av 61.95. He appeared in every Test on all his visits, except in 1980 when he missed one match through injury. He captained West Indies in 1976 and 1980, as well as in 1984. On his Test debuts against both England

(1966/7) and Australia (1968/9) he scored centuries. A leading member of Packer's World Series Cricket, he was at odds with the West Indian Board of Control in 1977/8 and missed several Tests as a consequence.

In all he has hit 1,000 runs in an English season ten times, his best being 1,603, av 47.14, in 1970; in addition he reached 1,000 runs in four overseas seasons. His highest innings was 242* for West Indies v India at Bombay in 1974/5 and his highest in England 217* for Lancashire v Warwickshire at Old Trafford in 1971. He reached 200 in 120 minutes for West Indies v Glamorgan at Swansea in 1976 which equalled the record set by G. L. Jessop. He captained Lancashire in 1981–83 and in 1986. Also very successful in limited overs cricket, he hit 102 in the first World Cup Final at Lord's in 1975 when West Indies beat Australia.

Lloyd, David
Cricketer. *b:* 18.3.1947, Accrington, Lancashire. Father of G. D. (Lancashire). Stylish opening or middle order left-hand batsman, slow left-arm bowler, excellent short leg field. *Team* Lancashire (1965–83, 370 matches). *Tours* MCC to Australia 1974/5; Robins to South Africa 1975/6. *Tests* England (1974 to 1974/5, 9 matches).
Career batting
407–652–74–19269–214*–33.33–38–*ct* 334
Bowling 7172–237–30.26–5–1–7/38
Test batting
9–15–2–552–214*–42.46–1–*ct* 11
Bowling 17–0

He hit 1,000 runs in a season eleven times (best 1,510, av 47.18, in 1972). His highest innings was 214* for England v India at Edgbaston in 1974. He was captain of Lancashire, 1973–77. He also played for Cumberland (1984–89). He was a first-class umpire (1987). He is well-known as a speaker and commentator on the game.

Lloyd, Edward Wynell Mayow
Amateur. *b:* 19.3.1845, Benares, India. *d:* 27.9.1928, Hartford Bridge, Hampshire. Middle order right-hand batsman. *Sch* Rugby. *Team* Cambridge U (1866–68).
Career batting
4–6–2–63–20*–15.75–0–*ct* 1

His County cricket was for Shropshire (1868) and Somerset (pre first-class, 1868–77).

Lloyd, Graham David
Cricketer. *b:* 1.7.1969, Accrington, Lancashire. Son of David (Lancashire). Middle order right-hand batsman, right-arm medium pace bowler. *Team* Lancashire (1988–92, 63 matches).
Career batting
63–101–13–3478–132–39.52–7–*ct* 44
Bowling 186–1–186.00–0–0–1/57

He scored 1,389 runs, av 51.44, in 1992.

Lloyd, Henry James
Amateur. *b:* 2.2.1794, Marylebone, London. *d:* 3.9.1853, Brighton, Sussex. Brother of C. S. (MCC). Middle order batsman. *Sch* Harrow. *Team* MCC (1816–28).
Career batting
34–59–3–386–37–6.89–0–*ct* 20

His first-class debut was for Epsom in 1815 and his last match for Gentlemen in 1830. He was President of MCC in 1822.

Lloyd, J. G.
Amateur. Middle order batsman. *Team* W. G. Grace's XI (1871).
Career batting
1–1–0–4–4–4.00–0–*ct* 1

Lloyd, John Maurice Edward
Amateur. *b:* 7.5.1844, Llanmerewig, Abermule, Montgomery. *d:* 21.1.1910, Montgomery. Middle order batsman. *Sch* Marlborough. *Team* Oxford U (1866).
Career batting
1–1–0–6–6–6.00–0–*ct* 1

Lloyd, Martyn Frederick Dafydd
Cricketer. *b:* 6.6.1954, Headington, Oxford. Middle order right-hand batsman, occasional right-arm medium pace bowler. *Sch* Magdalen College School. *Team* Oxford U (1974–75, blue 1974).
Career batting
6–11–0–74–36–6.72–0–*ct* 2

His County cricket was for Oxfordshire, (1974–77) and Dorset (1981).

Lloyd, Richard Averill
Amateur. *b:* 4.8.1891, Tamnamore, Moy, Dungannon, Co Tyrone, Ireland. *d:* 23.12.1950, Belfast, Ireland. Middle order right-hand batsman. *Teams* Ireland (1911–12); Lancashire (1921–22, 3 matches).
Career batting
6–10–0–202–51–20.20–0–*ct* 5

He also played for Denbighshire (1930–35). A noted rugby footballer, he appeared at half back for Lancashire, Ulster and Ireland.

Lloyd, Timothy Andrew
Cricketer. *b:* 5.11.1956, Oswestry, Shropshire. Middle order left-hand batsman, right-arm medium pace bowler. *Teams* Warwickshire (1977–92, 299 matches); Orange Free State (1978/9 to 1979/80). *Tours* English Counties to Zimbabwe 1984/5; Warwickshire to South Africa 1991/2. *Test* England (1984, 1 match).
Career batting
312–547–45–17211–208*–34.28–29–*ct* 147
Bowling 1682–23–73.13–0–0–3/7
Test batting
1–1–1–10–10*–no av–0–*ct* 0

He hit 1,000 runs in a season nine times (best 1,673, av 45.21, in 1983). His highest score was 208* for Warwickshire v Gloucestershire at Edgbaston in 1983. He captained Warwickshire 1988–92. He was unfortunate in that he was forced to retire injured whilst batting on his Test debut and failed to be selected again for England. He also played for Shropshire (1975).

Lloyds, Jeremy William
Cricketer. *b:* 17.11.1954, Penang, Malaya. Middle order left-hand batsman, off break bowler. *Sch* Blundell's. *Teams* Somerset (1979–84, 100 matches); Orange Free State (1983/4 to 1987/8); Gloucestershire (1985–91, 162 matches). *Tour* Gloucestershire to Sri Lanka 1986/7.
Career batting
267–408–64–10679–132*–31.04–10–*ct* 229
Bowling 12943–333–38.86–13–1–7/88

He hit 1,000 runs in a season three times (best 1,295, av 43.16, in 1986).

Loader, Peter James
Professional. *b:* 25.10.1929, Wallington, Surrey. Lower order right-hand batsman, right-arm fast bowler. *Teams* Surrey (1951–63, 298 matches); Western Australia (1963/4, 1 match). *Tours* MCC to Australia and New Zealand 1954/5, 1958/9, to South Africa 1956/7; Commonwealth to India 1953/4, to Rhodesia 1962/3; Surrey to Rhodesia 1959/60; Brown to East Africa 1961/2 (not first-class). *Tests* England (1954 to 1958/9, 13 matches).
Career batting
371–382–110–2314–81–8.50–0–*ct* 120
Bowling 25260–1326–19.04–70–13–9/17
Test batting
13–19–6–76–17–5.84–0–*ct* 2
Bowling 878–39–22.51–1–0–6/36

He took 100 wickets in a season seven times (best 133, av 15.47, in 1957). Twice he obtained nine wickets in an innings, his best being 9/17 for Surrey v Warwickshire at the Oval in 1958. He performed the hat-trick in the Headingley Test against the West Indies in 1957.

Lobb, Bryan
Professional. *b:* 11.1.1931, Bournville, Birmingham. Tail end right-hand batsman, right-arm fast medium bowler. *Sch* KES, Birmingham. *Teams* Warwickshire (1953, 1 match); Somerset (1955–69, 115 matches).
Career batting
116–170–50–624–42–5.20–0–*ct* 24
Bowling 8760–370–23.67–15–2–7/43

He took 110 wickets, av 19.48, in 1957. After 1958 he ceased to appear regularly in first-class cricket, having gone into the scholastic profession.

Lobban, Hartley W.
Amateur in 1952, then professional. *b:* 9.5.1922, Jamaica. Lower order right-hand batsman, right-arm fast bowler. *Team* Worcestershire (1952–54, 17 matches).
Career batting
17–23–11–81–18–6.75–0–*ct* 4
Bowling 1452–47–30.89–4–0–6/51

Lock, Bernard Henry
Amateur. *b:* 8.6.1915, Exeter, Devon. Middle order right-hand batsman, slip field. *Sch* Sherborne. *Team* Kent (1952, 1 match).
Career batting
2–4–0–69–57–17.25–0–*ct* 1

He also played for Devon (1934–57). His last first-class match was for MCC in 1955. A good rugby footballer, he represented Exeter and Ulster.

Lock, Edward John
Amateur. *b:* 21.11.1868, Taunton, Somerset. *d:* 3.5.1949, North Town, Taunton, Somerset. Middle order batsman. *Team* Somerset (1891–93, 2 matches).
Career batting
2–4–1–16–10–5.33–0–*ct* 0

He first played for Somerset (not first-class) in 1890.

Lock, Graham Anthony Richard
Professional. *b:* 5.7.1929, Limpsfield, Surrey. Lower order right-hand batsman, brilliant slow medium left-arm bowler, excellent close field. *Teams* Surrey (1946–63, 385 matches); Leicestershire (1965–67, 65 matches); Western Australia (1962/3 to 1970/1, 74 matches). *Tours* MCC to West Indies 1953/4, 1967/8, to Pakistan 1955/6, to South Africa 1956/7, to Australia and New Zealand 1958/9, to India, Pakistan and Ceylon 1961/2; Surrey to Rhodesia 1959/60. *Tests* England (1952 to 1967/8, 49 matches).
Career batting
654–812–161–10342–89–15.88–0–*ct* 830
Bowling 54709–2844–19.23–196–50–10/54
Test batting
49–63–9–742–89–13.74–0–*ct* 59
Bowling 4451–174–25.58–9–3–7/35

The epitome of ebullience, Lock found great success with each of the four major sides for whom he played: England, Surrey, Western Australia and Leicestershire. Initially a slow bowler, he developed into almost medium pace about 1950, but this faster delivery led to his being called for 'throwing' and throughout the 1950s he was on the borderline between bowling and throwing, being no-balled several times by various umpires. He then reverted to his former slower style and during the last ten years of his first-class career was free from criticism.

He took 100 wickets in a season 14 times, going on to 200 twice, his best year being 1955 with 216 wickets, av 14.39. His outstanding bowling performance was taking all ten wickets in an innings (for 54) for Surrey v Kent at Blackheath in 1956.

In 1962/3, when he was surprisingly omitted from the MCC team to tour Australia, he went to that country and played for Western Australia. In the opinion of many, his nine years with that State were the best of his career and he led them to the Sheffield Shield title. In 1965 he appeared for Leicestershire and the following two seasons captained that County, taking them to second place in the County Championship in 1967, the best season they had ever enjoyed to that date.

Lock, Herbert Christmas
Professional. *b:* 8.5.1903, East Molesey, Surrey. *d:* 19.5.1978, Honor Oak, London. Lower order right-hand batsman, right-arm medium pace bowler. *Team* Surrey (1926–32, 32 matches). *Tour* Tennyson to Jamaica 1926/7.
Career batting
35–31–9–93–20*–4.22–0–*ct* 10
Bowling 2658–81–32.81–0–0–4/34
After leaving the Surrey staff he played for Devon (1934–39) and his final first-class appearance was for the Minor Counties in 1935. He was in later years the head groundsman at the Oval and Official Inspector of pitches for the TCCB.

Lock, Norman William
Professional. *b:* 13.3.1912, Ham Common, Surrey. Lower order right-hand batsman, right-arm medium pace bowler. *Team* Surrey (1934, 1 match).
Career batting
1–2–1–1–1–1.00–0–*ct* 0
Selected as scorer for Surrey, he played in emergency due to Sandham being taken ill just prior to the match.

Lock, Walter George
Amateur. *b:* 11.10.1907, Bristol. *d:* 10.3.1980, Taunton, Somerset. Middle order batsman. *Sch* Taunton. *Team* Somerset (1928, 1 match).
Career batting
1–1–0–2–2–2.00–0–*ct* 0

Locker, William
Professional. *b:* 16.2.1866, Long Eaton, Derbyshire. *d:* 15.8.1952, California, Derby. Opening right-hand batsman. *Team* Derbyshire (1894–1903, 16 matches).
Career batting
16–30–0–511–76–17.03–0–*ct* 4
A noted soccer player, he appeared for Notts County, taking part in the FA Cup final of 1891.

Lockett, Aaron
Professional. *b:* 1.12.1892, Audley, Newcastle-under-Lyme, Staffordshire. *d:* 10.2.1965, Bignall End, Staffordshire. Uncle of T. J. Goodwin (Leicestershire). Middle order right-hand batsman, right-arm bowler. *Team* Minor Counties (1928–29).
Career batting
2–4–1–197–154–65.66–1–*ct* 2
Bowling 71–2–35.50–0–0–1/14
His County cricket was for Staffordshire (1920–39), but he was also a noted figure in the Central Lancashire League, appearing for Oldham for 12 years. His first-class debut was for Minor Counties v West Indies at Exeter in 1928. The Minor Counties were made to follow on, being 181 behind on the first innings. Lockett hit a brilliant 154 in the second innings and Minor Counties went on to win the match. He was a first-class umpire (1948–50). An excellent inside forward, he played soccer for Port Vale and Stoke City.

Lockhart, J. H. B.
(*see under* Bruce-Lockhart, J. H.)

Lockhart, R. B. B.
(*see under* Bruce-Lockhart, R. B.)

Locks, George Melbourne
Amateur. *b:* 24.5.1889, Leytonstone, Essex. *d:* 17.9.1965, Redbridge, Essex. Lower order batsman, useful bowler. *Team* Essex (1928, 2 matches).
Career batting
2–4–2–5–3*–2.50–0–*ct* 0
Bowling 227–3–75.66–0–0–2/86

Lockton, John Henry
Amateur. *b:* 22.5.1892, Peckham, London. *d:* 29.6.1972, Thornton Heath, Surrey. Attacking lower order right-hand batsman, right-arm fast medium bowler. *Sch* Dulwich. *Team* Surrey (1919–26, 32 matches).
Career batting
32–34–9–409–77*–16.36–0–*ct* 26
Bowling 2071–78–26.55–1–0–5/80
He represented London University at both cricket and soccer and went on to play soccer as inside forward for Nottingham Forest and Crystal Palace; later he became a noted soccer referee.

Lockwood, Arthur Leslie
Amateur. *b:* 1.4.1903, Romiley, Cheshire. *d:* 8.11.1933, Llandudno, Caernarvonshire. Lower order right-hand batsman, right-arm bowler. *Team* Wales (1926).
Career batting
1–1–0–5–5–5.00–0–*ct* 1
Bowling 84–1–84.00–0–0–1/34
His County cricket was for Carmarthenshire (1927) and Denbighshire (1930–33).

Lockwood, Ephraim
Professional. *b:* 4.4.1845, Lascelles Hall, Huddersfield, Yorkshire. *d:* 19.12.1921, Tandem, Lascelles Hall, Huddersfield, Yorkshire. Brother of Henry (Yorkshire), nephew of John Thewlis (Yorkshire). Sound opening or middle order right-hand batsman, right-hand slow medium round-arm bowler. *Team* Yorkshire (1868–84, 213 matches). *Tour* Daft to North America 1879 (not first-class).

Career batting
328–569–39–12512–208–23.60–8–*ct* 232–*st* 3
Bowling 3458–206 + 1–16.78–7–1–7/35

He hit 1,000 runs in a season four times (best 1,261, av 32.33, in 1876). His only double century was 208 for Yorkshire v Kent at Gravesend in 1883. In 1876 and 1877 he captained Yorkshire.

Lockwood, Henry
Professional. *b:* 20.10.1855, Lascelles Hall, Huddersfield, Yorkshire. *d:* 18.2.1930, Lepton, Huddersfield, Yorkshire. Brother of Ephraim (Yorkshire), nephew of John Thewlis (Yorkshire). Middle order right-hand batsman, right-hand fast round-arm bowler. *Team* Yorkshire (1877–82, 16 matches).
Career batting
16–27–2–408–90–16.32–0–*ct* 8
Bowling 37–0

Lockwood, William Henry
Professional. *b:* 25.3.1868, Old Radford, Nottinghamshire. *d:* 26.4.1932, Old Radford, Nottinghamshire. Middle/lower order right-hand batsman, right-arm fast bowler. *Teams* Nottinghamshire (1886–87, 5 matches); Surrey (1889–1904, 305 matches). *Tour* Stoddart to Australia 1894/5. *Tests* England (1893–1902, 12 matches).
Career batting
362–531–45–10673–165–21.96–15–*ct* 140
Bowling 25246–1376–18.34–121–29–9/59
Test batting
12–16–3–231–52*–17.76–0–*ct* 4
Bowling 883–43–20.53–5–1–7/71

Regarded as one of the most effective fast bowlers of his day, Lockwood's particular asset was the ability to bowl a slower ball without a noticeable change in his action. In the early 1890s he was a major force in English cricket, but he failed on the 1894/5 tour to Australia, and within a couple of years looked likely to drop out of County cricket. In 1898, however, not only did his bowling form return but his batting improved, and in both 1899 and 1900 he performed the 'double'. His best Test series came in 1902, when he took 11 for 76 in the fourth Test.

He took 100 wickets in a season seven times (best 151, av 13.60, in 1892), and hit 1,000 runs twice (best 1,367, av 32.54, in 1900). His best bowling was 9/59 for Surrey v Essex at Leyton in 1902.

Lockyer, Thomas
Professional. *b:* 1.11.1826, Old Town, Croydon, Surrey. *d:* 22.12.1869, Croydon, Surrey. He died of consumption. Middle order right-hand batsman, right-hand fast medium round-arm bowler, excellent wicket-keeper. *Team* Surrey (1849–66, 124 matches). *Tours* Parr to North America 1859 (not first-class), to Australia 1863/4.
Career batting
223–361–51–4917–108*–15.86–1–*ct* 301–*st* 123
Bowling 1986–99 + 20–20.06–10–1–6/33

He was regarded as the equal of any wicket-keeper in England about 1860.

Lodge, Joe Thomas
Professional. *b:* 16.4.1921, Skelmanthorpe, Huddersfield, Yorkshire. Middle order right-hand batsman, right-arm medium fast bowler. *Team* Yorkshire (1948, 2 matches).
Career batting
2–3–0–48–30–16.00–0–*ct* 0
Bowling 17–0

He played soccer for Huddersfield.

Lodge, Lewis Vaughan
Amateur. *b:* 21.12.1872, Aycliffe, Co Durham. *d:* 21.10.1916, Burbage, Derbyshire. He was found drowned in a pond. Middle order right-hand batsman. *Sch* Durham. *Team* Hampshire (1900, 3 matches).
Career batting
3–4–0–6–4–1.50–0–*ct* 0
Bowling 6–0

He also played for Durham (pre first-class, 1893–1902). Whilst at Cambridge he played in the Freshmen's and Seniors' matches, but no first-class games. A noted soccer player, he won his blue and went on to represent England, and played (once) for Birmingham City.

Logan, Hugh
Amateur. *b:* 10.5.1885, East Langton Grange, Market Harborough, Leicestershire. *d:* 24.2.1919, Tournai, Belgium. Brother-in-law of W. L. Everard (Leicestershire). Middle order right-hand batsman, brilliant deep field. *Sch* Westminster. *Team* Leicestershire (1903, 1 match).
Career batting
1–2–0–13–12–6.50–0–*ct* 0

He appeared in the Freshmen's match at Cambridge, but no first-class games.

Logan, James Douglas (jun)
Amateur. *b:* 24.6.1880, Cape Town, South Africa. *d:* 3.1.1960, Matjesfontein, South Africa. Middle order batsman. *Sch* Blair Lodge. *Tour* South Africa to England 1901.
Career batting
4–8–0–100–35–12.50–0–*ct* 3
Bowling 20–0

His father, the Hon J. D. Logan, financed the 1901 tour to England. He never appeared in first-class cricket in South Africa.

Logan, William Ross
Amateur. *b:* 24.11.1909, Edinburgh, Scotland. Lower order batsman, wicket-keeper. *Sch* Merchiston. *Team* Scotland (1932).
Career batting
1–1–0–1–1–1.00–0–*ct* 5

He played rugby for Scotland.

Logie, Augustine Lawrence
Cricketer. *b:* 28.9.1960, Sobo, Trinidad. Middle order right-hand batsman, off break bowler. *Team* Trinidad (1978/9 to 1991/2). *Tours* West Indies to Australia 1981/2, 1983/4 (not first-class), 1984/5, 1986/7, 1988/9, to England 1983 (World Cup), 1984, 1988, 1991, to India 1983/4, 1987/8, 1989/90 (not first-class), to Pakistan 1985/6 (not first-class), 1986/7, 1990/1, to Sharjah (not first-class) 1985/6, 1986/7, 1988/9, 1989/90, 1991/2, to New Zealand 1986/7, to India and Pakistan (World Cup) 1987/8, to Australia and New Zealand (World Cup) 1991/2; Young West Indies to Zimbabwe 1981/2. *Tests* West Indies (1982/3 to 1991, 52 matches).
Career batting
154–239–25–7514–171–35.11–13–*ct* 103–*st* 1
Bowling 128–3–42.66–0–0–1/2
Test batting
52–78–9–2470–130–35.79–2–*ct* 57
Bowling 4–0

Although he came second in the first-class batting averages on the 1984 tour to England he was unable to force his way into the Test side. In 1988 he batted in his usual attacking style and topped the Test batting table with 364 runs, av 72.80. In 1991 however he was nothing like as successful and his form was not helped by injury, which lost him his Test place. His first-class debut was for South Trinidad in 1977/8.

Lohmann, George Alfred
Professional. *b:* 2.6.1865, Campden Hill, Kensington, London. *d:* 1.12.1901, Worcester, Cape Province, South Africa. Lower order right-hand batsman, right-arm medium fast bowler, excellent slip. *Teams* Surrey (1884–96, 186 matches); Western Province (1894/5 to 1896/7). *Tours* Lillywhite, Shaw and Shrewsbury to Australia 1886/7, 1887/8; Sheffield to Australia 1891/2; Hawke to South Africa 1895/6. *Tests* England (1886–96, 18 matches).
Career batting
293–427–39–7247–115–18.67–3–*ct* 337
Bowling 25295–1841–13.73–176–57–9/28
Test batting
18–26–2–213–62*–8.87–0–*ct* 28
Bowling 1205–112–10.75–9–5–9/28

The leading wicket-taker in England for several successive seasons, Lohmann had much to do with the rise in Surrey's fortunes in the 1880s. He was equally successful in Australia on each of his three tours and in 1887/8 took 63 wickets in first-class matches at a cost of 11.98 runs each. On his tour to South Africa he proved altogether too much for the opposition and produced some startling performances in the Tests, including 9 for 28 at Johannesburg, which was the best innings analysis of his career. His best in England was 9 for 67 for Surrey v Essex at Hove in 1889. He took 100 wickets in a season eight times and went on to 200 three times with 220, av 13.62, in 1890 as his best.

Owing to ill-health his career was relatively short and he emigrated to South Africa in the hope that the climate might benefit him. His final first-class match was for A. Bailey's XI in South Africa in 1897/8. In 1901 he came back to England as assistant manager of the South African team, but died of consumption later in the same year.

Lomas, John Millington
Amateur. *b:* 12.12.1917, Ashtead, Surrey. *d:* 4.12.1945, Westminster, London. Opening right-hand batsman. *Sch* Charterhouse. *Team* Oxford U (1938–39, blue both years).
Career batting
23–43–1–1460–138–34.76–2–*ct* 10

Lomax, Ian Raymond
Amateur. *b:* 30.7.1931, Fulham, London. Stylish middle order right-hand batsman, right-arm fast medium bowler. *Sch* Eton. *Team* Somerset (1962, 6 matches). *Tour* Surridge to Bermuda 1961 (not first-class).
Career batting
12–21–1–370–83–18.50–0–*ct* 6
Bowling 229–4–57.25–0–0–2/45

His first-class debut was for Free Foresters in 1952 and his final first-class match for MCC in 1965. Most of his County cricket was for Wiltshire (1950–70) although he also played for Buckinghamshire (1949).

Lomax, James Geoffrey
Professional. *b:* 20.5.1925, Rochdale, Lancashire. *d:* 21.5.1992, Frenchay, Bristol. Middle order right-hand batsman, right-arm fast medium bowler. *Teams* Lancashire (1949–53, 57 matches); Somerset (1954–62, 211 matches).
Career batting
269–463–23–8672–104*–19.70–2–*ct* 238
Bowling 10773–316–34.09–4–0–6/75

He hit 1,000 runs in a season twice (best 1,298, av 24.96, in 1959). He also played for Devon (1966–68).

Loney, Escott Frith
Amateur. *b:* 21.7.1903, Bristol. *d:* 19.6.1982, Toronto, Ontario, Canada. Middle/lower order left-hand batsman, right-arm medium fast bowler. *Sch* Derby School. *Team* Derbyshire (1925–27, 25 matches).
Career batting
25–37–7–511–39*–17.03–0–*ct* 18
Bowling 650–20–32.50–0–0–4/27

He also appeared for Canada in non-first-class matches.

Loney, Joseph Kevin
Cricketer. *b:* 30.8.1951, Lurgan, Co Armagh, Ireland. Middle order left-hand batsman, occasional right-arm medium pace bowler. *Team* Cambridge U (1974).
Career batting
2–2–0–4–2–2.00–0–*ct* 0

Long, Arnold
Professional. *b:* 18.12.1940, Cheam, Surrey. Lower order left-hand batsman, wicket-keeper. *Teams* Surrey (1960–75, 352 matches); Sussex (1976–80, 97 matches). *Tour* Robins to South Africa 1972/3.
Career batting
452–537–131–6801–92–16.75–0–*ct* 922–*st* 124
Bowling 2–0
He created a first-class record by taking 11 catches in the match for Surrey v Sussex at Hove in 1964. From 1978 to 1980 he captained Sussex. An excellent soccer player, he appeared for Corinthian Casuals.

Long, Edmund James
Amateur. *b:* 28.3.1883, Darlinghurst, Sydney, New South Wales, Australia. *d:* 8.12.1947, Leichhardt, Sydney, New South Wales, Australia. Lower order right-hand batsman, wicket-keeper. *Team* New South Wales (1911/12, 1 match). *Tours* AIF to England 1919, to South Africa 1919/20; Waddy to Ceylon 1913/4 (not first-class).
Career batting
18–22–10–135–24–11.25–0–*ct* 20–*st* 12

Long, Rev Henry James
Amateur. *b:* 14.8.1859, Henlow, Bedfordshire. *d:* 18.6.1902, Marylebone, London. Middle order batsman. *Sch* King's, Canterbury. *Team* MCC (1880).
Career batting
1–2–0–8–5–4.00–0–*ct* 0

Long, Robert
Professional. *b:* 9.11.1846, Richmond, Surrey. *d:* 6.8.1924, Enfield, Middlesex. Lower order right-hand batsman, right-arm fast bowler. *Team* Surrey (1870, 2 matches).
Career batting
2–4–0–0–0–0.00–0–*ct* 0
Bowling 20–0

Longcroft, Okeover Butler
Amateur. *b:* 6.3.1850, Hall Place, Havant, Hampshire. *d:* 7.9.1871, Hall Place, Havant, Hampshire. Opening right-hand batsman, wicket-keeper. *Sch* Bradfield. *Team* Hampshire (1869–70, 2 matches).
Career batting
2–4–0–28–12–7.00–0–*ct* 1–*st* 1
Bowling 75–8–9.37–0–0–3/15

Longdon, Albert
Professional. *b:* 1.11.1865, Watnall Greasley, Nottinghamshire. *d:* 13.5.1937, Bentley, Doncaster, Yorkshire. Middle order right-hand batsman, right-arm medium pace bowler. *Team* Nottinghamshire (1895, 2 matches).
Career batting
2–4–1–28–20*–9.33–0–*ct* 1

Longfield, Geoffrey Phelps
Amateur. *b:* 4.12.1909, High Halstow, Kent. *d:* 25.2.1943, Rennes, France. He was killed during air operations. Brother of T. C. (Kent). Middle order right-hand batsman, right-arm bowler. *Sch* Aldenham. *Team* RAF (1931–32).
Career batting
2–4–0–36–26–9.00–0–*ct* 0
Bowling 138–2–69.00–0–0–2/51

Longfield, Thomas Cuthbert
Amateur. *b:* 12.5.1906, High Halstow, Kent. *d:* 21.12.1981, Ealing, Middlesex. Brother of G. P. (RAF), father-in-law of E. R. Dexter (Sussex). Middle order right-hand batsman, right-arm medium pace bowler, good field. *Sch* Aldenham. *Teams* Cambridge U (1927–28, blue both years); Kent (1927–39, 30 matches); Europeans (1929/30 to 1944/5); Bengal (1935/6 to 1938/9).
Career batting
82–127–18–2446–120–22.44–2–*ct* 49
Bowling 6416–195–32.90–7–0–6/12
Going to India after leaving Cambridge, he could play for Kent very infrequently. His final first-class match was for Free Foresters in 1951.

Longland, Harry
Amateur. *b:* 3.5.1881, Leicester. *d:* 20.9.1911, Fenny Stratford, Buckinghamshire. Middle order batsman. *Team* Northamptonshire (1907, 1 match).
Career batting
1 match, did not bat–*ct* 0

Longley, Jonathan Ian
Cricketer. *b:* 12.4.1969, New Brunswick, New Jersey, USA. Middle order right-hand batsman. *Sch* Tonbridge. *Team* Kent (1989–92, 7 matches).
Career batting
7–12–0–211–110–17.58–1–*ct* 4

Longman, George Henry
Amateur. *b:* 3.8.1852, Farnborough Hill, Hampshire. *d:* 19.8.1938, Wimbledon Common, Surrey. Father of H. K. (Surrey and Middlesex). Stylish opening right-hand batsman, brilliant deep field. *Sch* Eton. *Teams* Cambridge U (1872–75, blue all four years); Hampshire (1875–85, 27 matches).
Career batting
68–121–2–2448–98–20.57–0–*ct* 41–*st* 4
Bowling 180–3–60.00–0–0–1/1
He captained Cambridge in 1874 and 1875. He was President of Surrey CCC 1926–28 and Hon Treasurer from 1929 to his death. A good footballer, he represented Middlesex.

Longman, Henry Kerr
Amateur. *b:* 8.3.1881, Kensington, London. *d:* 7.10.1958, Pyrford, Surrey. Son of G. H. (Hampshire). Opening right-hand batsman, good field. *Sch* Eton. *Teams* Cambridge U (1901, blue); Surrey (1901–08, 5 matches); Middlesex (1919–20, 11 matches).

Career batting
32–58–2–1148–150–20.50–1–*ct* 24
Bowling 50–0

His final first-class match was for H. D. G. Leveson-Gower's XI in 1921.

Longmore, Andrew Nigel Murray
Cricketer. *b:* 24.9.1953, Woolwich, London. Lower order right-hand batsman, wicket-keeper. *Sch* Winchester. *Team* Oxford U (1973–75).
Career batting
2–4–1–28–15–9.33–0–*ct* 3

He was the Assistant Editor of *The Cricketer* magazine (1982–87).

Longrigg, Edmund Fallowfield
Amateur. *b:* 16.4.1906, Batheaston, Bath, Somerset. *d:* 23.7.1974, Widcombe Hill, Bath, Somerset. Sound middle order left-hand batsman, right-arm slow bowler, good close field. *Sch* Rugby. *Teams* Somerset (1925–47, 219 matches); Cambridge U (1926–28, blue 1927 and 1928).
Career batting
248–407–25–9416–205–24.64–10–*ct* 143
Bowling 100–1–100.00–0–0–1/7

He hit 1,000 runs in a season twice (best 1,567, av 30.72, in 1930); his only double century was 205 for Somerset v Leicestershire at Taunton in 1930. From 1938 to 1946 he captained Somerset. Being in the legal profession his appearances in first-class cricket were limited and he played little between 1931 and 1937. He was President of Somerset 1968–70 and Chairman 1960–69. Also a noted hockey player, he represented Somerset.

Lord, Albert
(real name Albert Callington)
Professional. *b:* 28.8.1888, Barwell, Leicestershire. *d:* 29.3.1969, Barwell, Leicestershire. Sound opening right-hand batsman, right-arm medium pace bowler. *Team* Leicestershire (1910–26, 130 matches).
Career batting
130–235–12–3864–102–17.32–1–*ct* 73
Bowling 1060–39–27.17–2–0–5/40

He always appeared for Leicestershire under his 'cricketing name' of A. Lord. The story behind his pseudonym is that he arrived on the Leicestershire staff to find one cricketer called 'King' and another called 'Knight', so thought he should also join the aristocracy.

Lord, Gordon John
Cricketer. *b:* 25.4.1961, Edgbaston, Birmingham. Nephew of C. G. Watts (Leicestershire). Opening left-hand batsman, slow left-arm bowler. *Sch* Warwick. *Teams* Warwickshire (1983–86, 18 matches); Worcestershire (1987–91, 67 matches). *Tour* Worcestershire to Zimbabwe 1990/1.
Career batting
85–137–10–3406–199–26.81–5–*ct* 22
Bowling 61–0

He scored 1,003 runs, av 45.59, in 1990. He also played for Herefordshire (1992).

Lord, John Carr
Amateur. *b:* 17.8.1844, Hobart, Tasmania, Australia. *d:* 25.5.1911, Antill Ponds, Tasmania, Australia. Middle order right-hand batsman. *Teams* Hampshire (1864, 1 match); Tasmania (1872/3, 1 match).
Career batting
2–4–1–29–11–9.66–0–*ct* 1

Lord, Reginald Arthur
Amateur. *b:* 29.1.1905, Beckenham, Kent. Opening right-hand batsman, slow left-arm bowler. *Sch* Marlborough. *Team* Oxford U (1924).
Career batting
3–6–0–57–21–9.50–0–*ct* 0

His final first-class match was for H. D. G. Leveson-Gower's XI in 1926.

Lord, Thomas
Professional *b:* 23.11.1755, Thirsk, Yorkshire. *d:* 13.1.1832, West Meon, Hampshire. Father of Thomas jun (Surrey and Middlesex). Lower order right-hand slow under-arm bowler. *Teams* Middlesex (1801); Epsom (1815).
Career batting
2–2–1–12–10*–12.00–0–*ct* 0
Bowling 1 wicket (no analyses)–0–0–1/?

His memorial is Lord's Cricket Ground, which he originally laid out where Dorset Square now stands in 1787. He moved to North Bank, Regent's Park and in 1813/14 to the present site in St John's Wood, Marylebone.

Lord, Timothy Michael
Cricketer. *b:* 10.2.1966, Cambridge. Middle order right-hand batsman. *Sch* Bedford Modern. *Team* Cambridge U (1986).
Career batting
2–4–0–31–23–7.75–0–*ct* 0

He was awarded his blue for rugby.

Lord, Wilfrid Fraser
Amateur. *b:* 1.8.1888, Kolhapur, India. *d:* 19.9.1960, Hove, Sussex. Tail end right-hand batsman, right-arm fast bowler. *Sch* Tonbridge. *Teams* Oxford U (1911–12); Middlesex (1919, 2 matches).
Career batting
9–15–5–121–44*–12.10–0–*ct* 4
Bowling 543–12–45.25–0–0–4/107

Lord, William Alston
Professional. *b:* 8.8.1873, Washwood Heath, Birmingham. *d:* 16.6.1906, Gravelly Hill North, Erdington, Birmingham. Lower order left-hand batsman, left-arm fast medium bowler. *Team* Warwickshire (1897–99, 13 matches).

Career batting
13–18–8–69–10*–6.90–0–*ct* 4
Bowling 811–26–31.19–1–0–5/73

Lorimer, James
Amateur. *b:* 10.9.1860, Toorak, Melbourne, Victoria, Australia. Lower order batsman, bowler. *Team* Oxford U (1883).
Career batting
1–2–2–7–4*–no av–0–*ct* 0
Bowling 22–0

Lorrimer, Alexander
Amateur. *b:* 9.1.1859, Aylestone, Leicester. *d:* 2.2.1947, Oadby, Leicestershire. Brother of David (Leicestershire). Middle order right-hand batsman. *Team* Leicestershire (1894–96, 6 matches).
Career batting
6–12–0–174–46–14.50–0–*ct* 3
He hit a century on his debut for Leicestershire (v Surrey in 1890) – not a first-class match.

Lorrimer, David
Amateur. *b:* 16.1.1865, Aylestone, Leicester. *d:* 12.11.1925, Boscombe, Hampshire. Brother of Alexander (Leicestershire). Middle order right-hand batsman, good point. *Team* Leicestershire (1894–95, 9 matches).
Career batting
9–16–0–194–46–12.12–0–*ct* 6
He first played for Leicestershire (pre first-class) in 1890.

Louden, George Marshall
Amateur. *b:* 6.9.1885, Forest Gate, Essex. *d:* 28.12.1972, Amersham, Buckinghamshire. Lower order right-hand batsman, right-arm fast medium bowler. *Team* Essex (1912–27, 82 matches).
Career batting
94–140–39–931–74–9.21–0–*ct* 62
Bowling 10081–451–22.35–36–5–8/36

Loudon, William David Grafton
Cricketer. *b:* 22.5.1954, Lanark, Scotland. Middle order right-hand batsman, right-arm medium pace bowler. *Sch* Edinburgh Acadamy. *Team* Scotland (1982).
Career batting
1–1–0–21–21–21.00–0–*ct* 1
Bowling 11–3–3.66–0–0–3/4

Loughery, William Gordon Ridley
Amateur. *b:* 1.11.1907, Belfast, Ireland. *d:* 1.8.1977, Abbey Dore, Herefordshire. Lower order right-hand batsman. *Sch* Campbell College. *Team* Ireland (1929–33).
Career batting
2–4–1–34–18*–11.33–0–*ct* 1

Love, Geoffrey Robert Stuart
Amateur. *b:* 19.4.1889, Islington, London. *d:* 6.2.1978, Balquhidder, Perthshire, Scotland. Lower order left-hand batsman, slow left-arm bowler. *Team* Middlesex (1920, 1 match).
Career batting
1–2–0–2–2–1.00–0–*ct* 0
Bowling 39–0

Love, Hampden Stanley Bray
Amateur. *b:* 10.8.1895, Lilyfield, Sydney, New South Wales, Australia. *d:* 22.7.1969, Mosman, Sydney, New South Wales, Australia. Uncle of A. G. Cheetham (New South Wales). Middle order right-hand batsman, wicket-keeper. *Teams* New South Wales (1920/1 to 1932/3, 21 matches); Victoria (1922/3 to 1926/7, 16 matches). *Tours* AIF to England 1919; Australia to India 1935/6. *Test* Australia (1932/3, 1 match).
Career batting
54–90–7–2906–192–35.01–7–*ct* 73–*st* 29
Bowling 19–0
Test batting
1–2–0–8–5–4.00–0–*ct* 3
He appeared in only one match for AIF in England.

Love, Harry
Professional. *b:* 30.5.1871, Hastings, Sussex. *d:* 26.3.1942, Ore, Hastings, Sussex. Opening right-hand batsman, right-arm slow medium bowler. *Team* Sussex (1892–94, 5 matches).
Career batting
5–10–1–110–30–12.22–0–*ct* 3
Bowling 7–0

Love, James Derek
Cricketer. *b:* 22.4.1955, Headingley, Leeds, Yorkshire. Middle order right-arm batsman, right-arm medium pace bowler. *Team* Yorkshire (1975–89, 247 matches). *Tour* Yorkshire to Windward Islands 1986/7.
Career batting
249–391–59–10327–170*–31.10–13–*ct* 125
Bowling 835–12–69.58–0–0–2/0
He hit 1,000 runs in a season twice (best 1,203, av 33.41, in 1983). He represented England in one-day internationals, but no Tests. He also played for Lincolnshire (1990–92).

Love, Raymond Henry Arnold Davison
Amateur. *b:* 11.5.1888, Chatham, Kent. *d:* 12.10.1962, Pyrford, Woking, Surrey. Lower order right-hand batsman, right-arm medium pace bowler. *Sch* Marlborough. *Team* Hampshire (1923, 2 matches).
Career batting
2–3–1–15–13*–7.50–0–*ct* 2
Bowling 6–0

Loveday, Francis Alfred
Professional. *b:* 14.9.1892, Hackney, London. *d:* 18.10.1954, Bluebell Common, North Walsham, Norfolk. Middle order left-hand batsman. *Sch* City of London. *Teams* Essex (1921–23, 7 matches).
Career batting
7–14–0–321–81–22.92–0–*ct* 2
He also played for Cambridgeshire (1914).

Loveitt, Frank Russell
Amateur. *b:* 24.4.1871, Easenhall, Rugby, Warwickshire. *d:* 1.9.1939, Coventry, Warwickshire. Middle order right-hand batsman. *Team* Warwickshire (1898–1905, 25 matches).
Career batting
25–42–6–846–110–23.50–1–*ct* 7
He was a noted rugby footballer with Coventry.

Lovell, Geoffrey Bruce Tasman
Cricketer. *b:* 11.7.1966, Sydney, New South Wales, Australia. Middle order right-hand batsman, right-arm medium pace bowler. *Team* Oxford U (1991–92, blue both years).
Career batting
18–26–4–672–110*–30.54–1–*ct* 13
Bowling 141–1–141.00–0–0–1/13
He captained Oxford in 1992.

Lovell-Hewitt, William
Amateur. *b:* 7.11.1901, Trowbridge, Wiltshire. *d:* 5.10.1984, Woodcote Park, Coulsdon, Surrey. Lower order right-hand batsman, right-arm medium pace bowler. *Sch* King's, Bruton. *Team* Minor Counties (1938–39).
Career batting
3–5–0–175–92–35.00–0–*ct* 1
Bowling 55–0
His County cricket was for Wiltshire (1920–39).

Lowe, Charles
Professional. *b:* 23.6.1890, Whitwell, Derbyshire. *d:* 11.5.1953, Worksop, Nottinghamshire. Tail end batsman, right-arm fast medium bowler. *Team* Derbyshire (1909–12, 5 matches).
Career batting
5–8–2–25–17–4.16–0–*ct* 0
Bowling 90–2–45.00–0–0–1/20

Lowe, George
Amateur. *b:* 25.5.1915, Mastin Moor, Derbyshire. Middle order right-hand batsman. *Team* Derbyshire (1949–53, 2 matches).
Career batting
2–3–0–43–22–14.33–0–*ct* 3
He played soccer for Chesterfield.

Lowe, George Emmanuel
(birth registered as G. E. Low)
Professional. *b:* 12.1.1877, Guisborough, Yorkshire. *d:* 15.8.1932, Middlesbrough. Lower order batsman, wicket-keeper. *Team* Yorkshire (1902, 1 match).
Career batting
1–1–1–5–5*–no av–0–*ct* 1

Lowe, H. F.
Amateur. Middle order batsman. *Team* Hampshire (1882, 1 match).
Career batting
1–1–0–0–0–0.00–0–*ct* 0

Lowe, John Claude Malcolm
Amateur. *b:* 21.2.1888, Edgbaston, Birmingham. *d:* 27.7.1970, Hastings, Sussex. Lower order right-hand batsman, right-arm fast medium bowler. *Sch* Uppingham. *Teams* Oxford U (1907–10, blue 1907–09), Warwickshire (1907, 1 match).
Career batting
35–59–20–300–46–7.69–0–*ct* 33
Bowling 2767–106–26.10–7–0–8/144
He was also a good hockey player, obtaining his blue at Oxford.

Lowe, Peter John
Cricketer. *b:* 7.1.1935, Sutton Coldfield, Warwickshire. *d:* 4.8.1988, Avon Gorge, Durdham Down, Bristol. Lower order right-hand batsman, wicket-keeper. *Team* Warwickshire (1964, 1 match).
Career batting
1 match, did not bat–*ct* 2

Lowe, Richard
Professional. *b:* 18.6.1869, Kirkby-in-Ashfield, Nottinghamshire. *d:* 3.7.1946, Kirkby-in-Ashfield, Nottinghamshire. Brother of Tom (Nottinghamshire) and Sam (Nottinghamshire). Lower order right-hand batsman, left-arm medium pace bowler. *Team* Sussex (1893–94, 14 matches).
Career batting
15–25–8–183–34*–10.76–0–*ct* 5
Bowling 578–22–26.27–0–0–4/26
He played in one non-first-class match for Nottinghamshire in 1891 and from 1896 to 1901 for Glamorgan (pre first-class). His first-class debut was for Lord Sheffield's XI in 1891.

Lowe, Richard Geoffrey Harvey
Amateur. *b:* 11.6.1904, Wimbledon, Surrey. *d:* 5.7.1986, Tunbridge Wells, Kent. Middle order left-hand batsman, right-arm fast medium bowler. *Sch* Westminster. *Teams* Cambridge U (1925–27, blue all three years); Kent (1926, 2 matches).
Career batting
33–44–7–697–83–18.83–0–*ct* 16
Bowling 1837–70–26.24–3–0–5/31
He also won a soccer blue and played one amateur International for England.

Lowe, Ronald Francis
Professional. *b:* 28.7.1905, Shepherd's Bush, London. *d:* 29.8.1960, Colchester, Essex. Tail end right-hand batsman, slow left-arm bowler. *Team* Surrey (1923, 10 matches).

Career batting
10–11–3–15–7–1.87–0–*ct* 3
Bowling 557–26–21.42–1–0–5/15

Lowe, Sam
Professional. *b:* 19.7.1867, Kirkby-in-Ashfield, Nottinghamshire. *d:* 29.3.1947, Kirkby-in-Ashfield, Nottinghamshire. Brother of Richard (Sussex) and Tom (Nottinghamshire). Lower order right-hand batsman, right-arm fast bowler. *Team* Nottinghamshire (1894, 1 match).
Career batting
1–2–0–8–8–4.00–0–*ct* 0
Bowling 9–0
He also played for Glamorgan (pre first-class, 1895–1902).

Lowe, Tom
Professional. *b:* 25.7.1859, Kirkby-in-Ashfield, Nottinghamshire. *d:* 29.8.1934, Kirkby-in-Ashfield, Nottinghamshire. Brother of Richard (Sussex) and Sam (Nottinghamshire). Lower order right-hand batsman, right-arm medium pace bowler. *Team* Nottinghamshire (1894, 1 match).
Career batting
1–1–1–0–0*–no av–0–*ct* 0
Bowling 41–0
He also played for Northamptonshire (pre first-class, 1886–87).

Lowe, Walter George Hassall
Amateur. *b:* 26.8.1870, Bretby, Derbyshire. *d: circa* 1935, California, USA. Middle order batsman. *Team* Nottinghamshire (1895, 1 match).
Career batting
1–2–1–29–15*–29.00–0–*ct* 1
He emigrated to USA about 1910 and became a fruit farmer.

Lowe, William Walter
Amateur. *b:* 17.11.1873, Stamford, Lincolnshire. *d:* 26.5.1945, Hartley Wintney, Hampshire. Lower order right-hand batsman, right-arm fast bowler. *Sch* Malvern. *Teams* Cambridge U (1895–96, blue 1895); Worcestershire (1899–1911, 39 matches). *Tour* Mitchell to North America 1895.
Career batting
54–90–11–1713–154–21.68–4–*ct* 18
Bowling 2167–77–28.14–4–0–6/15
He first played for Worcestershire (pre first-class) in 1898. A noted soccer player, he played for Cambridge U and Corinthians.

Lowles, George William
(birth registered as G. W. Lowls)
Professional. *b:* 27.7.1865, Aldgate, Whitechapel, London. *d:* 12.1.1940, Lambeth, London. Lower order batsman, wicket-keeper. *Teams* Surrey (1887, 1 match); Middlesex (1889, 1 match).
Career batting
2–4–1–4–3–1.33–0–*ct* 0

Lowndes, William Geoffrey Lowndes Frith
(formerly W. G. L. Frith)
Amateur. *b:* 24.1.1898, Wandsworth, London. *d:* 23.5.1982, Newbury, Berkshire. Son of W. F. L. Frith (London County). Fast scoring middle order right-hand batsman, right-arm medium fast bowler, good close field. *Sch* Eton. *Teams* Oxford U (1921, blue); Hampshire (1924–35, 41 matches). *Tours* Martineau to Egypt 1930, 1931 and 1932 (not first-class).
Career batting
79–139–4–3244–216–24.02–5–*ct* 38
Bowling 3003–78–38.50–0–0–3/5
His only double century was 216 for Oxford U v H. D. G. Leveson-Gower's XI in 1921 at Eastbourne. His final first-class match was for Free Foresters in 1936. He captained Hampshire 1934–35.

Lowrey, Mark John
Cricketer. *b:* 13.9.1971, Hampstead, London. Middle order right-hand batsman, off break bowler. *Sch* Radley. *Team* Cambridge U (1990–91, blue both years).
Career batting
20–34–4–597–72–19.90–0–*ct* 3
Bowling 979–19–51.52–0–0–3/31

Lowry, Thomas Coleman
Amateur. *b:* 17.2.1898, Fernhill, Napier, New Zealand. *d:* 20.7.1976, Okawa, Hastings, New Zealand. Son of T. H. (Hawke's Bay), brother-in-law of A. P. F. Chapman (Kent) and R. H. B. Bettington (New South Wales). Attacking right-hand batsman, right-arm slow medium bowler, wicket-keeper. *Teams* Auckland (1917/18); Cambridge U (1921–24, blue 1923–24); Somerset (1921–24, 46 matches); Wellington (1926/7 to 1932/3). *Tours* MCC to Australia and New Zealand 1922/3; New Zealand to England 1927, 1931, 1937, to Australia 1937/8. *Tests* New Zealand (1929/30 to 1931, 7 matches).
Career batting
198–322–20–9421–181–31.19–18–*ct* 188–*st* 49
Bowling 1323–49–27.00–0–0–4/14
Test batting
7–8–0–223–80–27.87–0–*ct* 8
Bowling 5–0
His first-class debut in England was for Leveson-Gower's XI in 1919. He hit 1,000 runs in a season three times (best 1,564, av 35.54, in 1923). He captained Cambridge in 1924 and the New Zealand tourists on their 1927 and 1931 tours to England and was manager of the 1937 tour; he also led New Zealand in seven Tests.

Lowson, Frank Anderson
Professional. *b:* 1.7.1925, Bradford, Yorkshire. *d:* 8.9.1984, Pool-in-Wharfedale, Yorkshire. Sound opening right-hand batsman, off break bowler, good

outfield. *Sch* Bradford GS. *Team* Yorkshire (1949–58, 252 matches). *Tour* MCC to India, Pakistan and Ceylon 1951/2. *Tests* England (1951–55, 7 matches).
Career batting
277–449–37–15321–259*–37.18–31–*ct* 190
Bowling 31–0
Test batting
7–13–0–245–68–18.84–0–*ct* 5

He hit 1,000 runs in a season eight times, going on to 2,000 once: 2,152, av 42.19, in 1950. His only double century was 259* for Yorkshire v Worcestershire at Worcester in 1953. He also hit 1,000 runs on the 1951/2 tour.

Lowther, Hon Henry Cecil
Amateur. *b:* 27.7.1790, Lowther Castle, Westmorland. *d:* 6.12.1867, Barleythorpe Hall, Rutland. Steady middle order right-hand batsman, slow right-arm bowler. *Sch* Westminster. *Teams* Hampshire (1819); Surrey (1839, 1 match).
Career batting
47–75–2–387–34–5.30–0–*ct* 11
Bowling 7 wickets (no analyses)–0–0–3/?

Most of his cricket was played for MCC. He was MP for Westmorland for 55 years and Father of the House of Commons when he died.

Loxley-Firth, E. (*see under* Firth, E. L.)

Loxton, Colin Cameron
Amateur. *b:* 1.1.1914, Brisbane, Queensland, Australia. Father of J. F. C. (Queensland). Lower order right-hand batsman, right-arm fast medium bowler. *Teams* Cambridge U (1935); Queensland (1937/8, 4 matches).
Career batting
5–10–1–100–36*–11.11–0–*ct* 4
Bowling 299–8–37.37–0–0–2/27

Loxton, Samuel John Everett
Amateur. *b:* 29.3.1921, Albert Park, Melbourne, Victoria, Australia. Fine driving middle order right-hand batsman, right-arm fast medium bowler, good field. *Team* Victoria (1946/7 to 1957/8, 77 matches). *Tours* Australia to England 1948, to South Africa 1949/50; Commonwealth to India 1953/4; Australia to India and Pakistan 1959/60 (manager, but played in one match). *Tests* Australia (1947/8 to 1950/1, 12 matches).
Career batting
140–192–23–6249–232*–36.97–13–*ct* 83
Bowling 5971–232–25.73–3–0–6/49
Test batting
12–15–0–554–101–36.93–1–*ct* 7
Bowling 349–8–43.62–0–0–3/55

Although hitting 973 runs, av 57.23, in first-class matches during the 1948 Australian tour to England, he could find a place in only three of the five Tests. His highest score was 232* (on debut) for Victoria v Queensland at Melbourne in 1946/7.

Loyd, General Sir Henry Charles
Amateur. *b:* 21.2.1891, Belgravia, Westminster, London. *d:* 11.11.1973, Mettingham, Bungay, Suffolk. Middle order batsman, wicket-keeper. *Sch* Eton. *Team* Army (1914–20).
Career batting
3–5–1–100–63*–25.00–0–*ct* 2–*st* 1

Loye, Malachy Bernard
Cricketer. *b:* 27.9.1972, Northampton. Middle order right-hand batsman, off break bowler. *Team* Northamptonshire (1991–92, 11 matches).
Career batting
11–15–2–198–46–15.23–0–*ct* 8

Luard, Arthur John Hamilton
Amateur. *b:* 3.9.1861, Waltair, India. *d:* 22.5.1944, Guildford, Surrey. Hard hitting middle order right-hand batsman, excellent cover point. *Sch* Denstone and Cheltenham. *Teams* Gloucestershire (1892–1907, 45 matches); Hampshire (1897, 5 matches).
Career batting
52–92–2–1218–75*–13.53–0–*ct* 29

He was stationed in India from 1882 to 1890 and therefore not available for County cricket.

Lubbock, Alfred
Amateur. *b:* 31.10.1845, London. *d:* 17.7.1916, Kilmarth Manor, Par, Cornwall. Brother of Nevile (Kent) and Edgar (Kent), great-uncle of C. W. S. (Northamptonshire), brother-in-law of C. A. Wallroth (Kent and Derbyshire). Excellent free hitting middle order right-hand batsman, good deep field. *Sch* Eton. *Team* Kent (1863–75, 4 matches). *Tour* Fitzgerald to North America 1872 (not first-class).
Career batting
28–51–7–1043–129–23.70–2–*ct* 14
Bowling 92–4–23.00–0–0–2/62

He was regarded as one of the most promising of young players, but owing to his profession as a banker he played little County cricket.

Lubbock, Christopher William Stuart
Amateur. *b:* 4.1.1920, London. Great-nephew of Alfred (Kent), Edgar (Kent) and Nevile (Kent), brother-in-law of C. G. S. Shuckburgh (Warwickshire). Middle order right-hand batsman, right-arm medium or leg break bowler. *Sch* Charterhouse. *Teams* Northamptonshire (1938–39, 6 matches); Oxford U (1939).
Career batting
9–15–1–189–69–13.50–0–*ct* 1
Bowling 372–25–14.88–0–0–4/44

He also played for Suffolk (1952–54).

Lubbock, Edgar
Amateur. *b:* 22.2.1847, London. *d:* 9.9.1907, Chelsea, London. Brother of Alfred (Kent) and Nevile (Kent), great-uncle of C. W. S. (Northamptonshire), brother-in-law of H. O. Peacock (MCC). Middle

order right-hand batsman, right-hand fast under-arm bowler. *Sch* Eton. *Team* Kent (1871, 1 match). *Tour* Fitzgerald to North America 1872 (not first-class).
Career batting
3–5–0–77–54–15.40–0–*ct* 1
Bowling 27–1–27.00–0–0–1/4
His first-class debut was for Gentlemen of Kent in 1866.

Lubbock, Sir Nevile
Amateur. *b:* 31.3.1839, Pimlico, London. *d:* 12.9.1914, Oakley House, Bromley Common, Kent. Brother of Alfred (Kent) and Edgar (Kent), great-uncle of C. W. S. (Northamptonshire). Steady middle order right-hand batsman, good close field. *Sch* Eton. *Team* Kent (1860, 2 matches).
Career batting
6–10–1–135–42–15.00–0–*ct* 2
His first-class debut was for Gentlemen of Kent in 1858.

Lucas, Alfred George
Amateur. *b:* 26.10.1854, Wandsworth, London. *d:* 4.5.1941, Hove, Sussex. Brother of C. J. (Sussex), F. M. (Sussex) and M. P. (Sussex), uncle of C. E. (Sussex). Middle order batsman. *Team* MCC (1879).
Career batting
1–1–0–46–46–46.00–0–*ct* 0
His County cricket was for Suffolk (1878–79) and Hertfordshire (1894).

Lucas, Alfred Perry
Amateur. *b:* 20.2.1857, Westminster, London. *d:* 12.10.1923, Great Waltham, Essex. Cousin of C. F. (Hampshire). Stylish opening right-hand batsman, right-hand slow round-arm bowler, good field. *Sch* Uppingham. *Teams* Surrey (1874–82, 41 matches); Cambridge U (1875–78, blue all four years); Middlesex (1883–88, 11 matches); Essex (1894–1907, 98 matches). *Tour* Harris to Australia 1878/9. *Tests* England (1878/9 to 1884, 5 matches).
Career batting
256–435–46–10263–145–26.38–8–*ct* 152
Bowling 2849–155–18.38–4–0–6/10
Test batting
5–9–1–157–55–19.62–0–*ct* 1
Bowling 54–0
He first played for Essex (pre first-class) in 1889, and was captain 1892 to 1894 and jointly in 1901, but his County cricket was fairly limited throughout his long career.

Lucas, Sir Arthur Charles
Amateur. *b:* 22.5.1853, Lowestoft, Suffolk. *d:* 14.6.1915, Marylebone, London. Brother-in-law of F. E. R. Fryer (Cambridge U) and W. Penn (Kent). Stylish opening or middle order right-hand batsman, good point. *Sch* Harrow. *Teams* Surrey (1874, 1 match); Middlesex (1877, 2 matches).
Career batting
5–9–0–140–29–15.55–0–*ct* 4
His final first-class match was for Gentlemen of England in 1879.

Lucas, Charles Eric
Amateur. *b:* 16.4.1885, Westminster, London. *d:* 4.4.1967, Broom Hall, Warnham, Sussex. Son of C. J. (Middlesex and Sussex), nephew of A. G. (MCC), F. M. (Sussex) and M. P. (Sussex). Middle order right-hand batsman, right-arm slow bowler. *Sch* Eton. *Teams* Sussex (1906–08, 3 matches); Cambridge U (1908).
Career batting
5–8–1–78–22–11.14–0–*ct* 3
Bowling 197–11–17.90–2–1–5/74

Lucas, Charles Frank
Amateur. *b:* 25.11.1843, Stowe, Staffordshire. *d:* 27.9.1919, Carshalton, Surrey. Cousin of A. P. (Surrey, Middlesex and Essex). Middle order right-hand batsman, excellent long stop. *Team* Hampshire (1864–80, 14 matches).
Career batting
17–31–1–650–135–21.66–1–*ct* 10

Lucas, Charles James
Amateur. *b:* 25.2.1853, Clapham Common, London. *d:* 17.4.1928, Pimlico, Westminster, London. Brother of A. G. (MCC), F. M. (Sussex) and M. P. (Sussex), father of C. E. (Sussex). Lower order right-hand batsman, right-hand fast round-arm bowler. *Sch* Harrow. *Teams* Middlesex (1876–77, 3 matches); Sussex (1880–82, 8 matches).
Career batting
12–23–3–237–38–11.85–0–*ct* 7
Bowling 165–7–23.57–0–0–3/17
He was President of Sussex in 1907.

Lucas, Frederick Charles
Professional. *b:* 29.9.1933, Slade Green, Kent. Middle order right-hand batsman, off break bowler. *Team* Kent (1954, 2 matches).
Career batting
2–4–0–62–38–15.50–0–*ct* 1
Bowling 17–0
He played football for Charlton Athletic and Crystal Palace.

Lucas, Frederick Murray
Amateur. *b:* 3.2.1860, Clapham Common, London. *d:* 7.11.1887, Surat, India. He died of choleraic diarrhoea. Brother of A. G. (MCC), C. J. (Middlesex and Sussex) and M. P. (Sussex), uncle of C. E. (Sussex). Hard hitting middle order left-hand batsman, medium pace bowler, good deep field. *Sch* Marlborough. *Teams* Sussex (1880–87, 18 matches); Cambridge U (1881–82).
Career batting
28–45–3–1291–215*–30.73–2–*ct* 10

Bowling 32–0

He captained Sussex in 1886. He hit 215* for Sussex v Gloucestershire at Hove in 1885. He also played for Suffolk (1879). A noted rackets player, he represented Cambridge U.

Lucas, John Herman
Amateur. *b:* 12.6.1922, Weymouth, St Michael, Barbados. Middle order right-hand batsman, off break bowler. Brother of N. S. (Barbados). *Teams* Barbados (1945/6 to 1949/50); Canada (1951/2 to 1954). *Tour* Canada to England 1954.
Career batting
15–25–5–1074–216*–53.70–2–*ct* 11
Bowling 484–15–32.26–0–0–4/88

He achieved very little on the 1954 visit to England. His highest score was 216* for Barbados v Trinidad at Bridgetown in 1948/9.

Lucas, Morton Peto
Amateur. *b:* 24.11.1856, Clapham Common, London. *d:* 9.7.1921, St James Park, Westminster, London. Brother of A. G. (MCC), C. J. (Middlesex and Sussex) and F. M. (Sussex), uncle of C. E. (Sussex). Middle order right-hand batsman, right-hand fast round-arm bowler, good cover point. *Sch* Harrow. *Team* Sussex (1877–90, 23 matches).
Career batting
27–49–2–940–131–20.00–1–*ct* 18
Bowling 263–7–37.57–0–0–3/35

He also played for Warwickshire (pre first-class, 1879).

Lucas, Robert Slade
Amateur. *b:* 17.7.1867, Teddington, Middlesex. *d:* 5.1.1942, Franklands Village, Haywards Heath, Sussex. Middle order right-hand batsman, right-arm medium pace bowler. *Sch* Merchant Taylors. *Team* Middlesex (1891–1900, 73 matches). *Tours* Hawke to North America 1894; Lucas to West Indies 1894/5.
Career batting
93–153–9–2685–185–18.64–1–*ct* 42
Bowling 366–6–61.00–0–0–2/44

He was also a well-known hockey player, being captain of Teddington for many years.

Luce, Frank Mowbray
Amateur. *b:* 26.4.1878, Gloucester. *d:* 9.9.1962, Reading, Berkshire. Middle order right-hand batsman, left-arm bowler. *Sch* Cheltenham. *Team.* Gloucestershire (1901–11, 25 matches).
Career batting
25–46–5–754–57–18.39–0–*ct* 19
Bowling 20–0

He played no first-class matches whilst at Oxford U, but did win a blue for rugby.

Luck, Arthur
Professional. *b:* 9.9.1914, Northampton. *d:* 3.5.1989, Abington, Northampton. Lower order right-hand batsman, right-arm medium pace bowler. *Team* Northamptonshire (1937–38, 2 matches).
Career batting
2–4–0–52–18–13.00–0–*ct* 0
Bowling 155–2–77.50–0–0–1/34

Luckes, Walter Thomas
Professional. *b:* 1.1.1901, Lambeth, London. *d:* 27.10.1982, Bridgwater, Somerset. Lower order right-hand batsman, wicket-keeper. *Team* Somerset (1924–49, 365 matches).
Career batting
365–564–212–5710–121*–16.22–1–*ct* 585–*st* 241

Owing to ill health he played little during the three seasons 1929 to 1931.

Luckhurst, Brian William
Professional. *b:* 5.2.1939, Sittingbourne, Kent. Solid opening right-hand batsman, slow left-arm bowler. *Team* Kent (1958–85, 336 matches). *Tours* MCC to Australia and New Zealand 1970/1, 1974/5; Commonwealth to Pakistan 1967/8; Cavaliers to West Indies 1969/70; Kent to West Indies 1972/3 (not first-class). *Tests* England (1970/1 to 1974/5, 21 matches).
Career batting
389–662–77–22303–215–38.12–48–*ct* 391
Bowling 2744–64–42.87–0–0–4/32
Test batting
21–41–5–1298–131–36.05–4–*ct* 14
Bowling 32–1–32.00–0–0–1/9

He hit 1,000 runs in a season 14 times (best 1,914, av 47.85, in 1969); both his double centuries were for Kent, the higher being 215 v Derbyshire at Derby in 1973. He was Cricket Manager to Kent CCC 1981–86 and since then has held the post of Cricket Administrator with the club. In 1985 he reappeared in one first-class match in emergency, Kent v Australians, his previous match for Kent being in 1976.

Luckin, Roger Alfred Geoffrey
Amateur. *b:* 25.11.1939, High Easter, Pleshey, Essex. Middle order left-hand batsman, moderate field. *Sch* Felsted. *Team* Essex (1962–63, 29 matches).
Career batting
29–46–3–735–82–17.09–0–*ct* 8

He also played for Cambridgeshire (1969–72).

Luckin, Verner Valentine
Professional. *b:* 14.2.1892, Maybury Hill, Woking, Surrey. *d:* 28.11.1931, High Cross, Froxfield, Hampshire. Lower order left-hand batsman, leg break and googly bowler. *Teams* Hampshire (1910–12, 10 matches); Warwickshire (1919, 9 matches).
Career batting
19–28–14–212–59*–15.14–0–*ct* 9
Bowling 845–24–35.20–0–0–3/19

Luddington, Henry Tansley
Amateur. *b:* 9.12.1854, Littleport, Cambridgeshire. *d:* 14.4.1922, Walton's Park, Ashdon, Essex. Tail end

right-hand batsman, right-hand fast round-arm bowler. *Sch* Uppingham. *Team* Cambridge U (1876–77, blue both years).
Career batting
11–15–4–76–25–6.90–0–*ct* 4
Bowling 832–42–19.80–3–0–5/28
His County cricket was for Norfolk (1881–83) and Cambridgeshire (1892–93). His final first-class match was for Gentlemen of England in 1878.

Luddington, Richard Simon
Cricketer. *b:* 8.4.1960, Kingston-upon-Thames, Surrey. Lower order right-hand batsman, wicket-keeper. *Sch* KCS, Wimbledon. *Team* Oxford U (1982, blue).
Career batting
10–14–1–290–65–22.30–0–*ct* 5–*st* 1
An all-round sportsman, he also gained blues for rugby football and hockey.

Luff, Alfred
Professional. *b:* 5.4.1846, Kew, Surrey. *d:* 26.12.1925, Horsham, Sussex. Stylish middle order right-hand batsman, right-hand fast round-arm bowler. *Team* Surrey (1867, 3 matches).
Career batting
3–6–1–25–8–5.00–0–*ct* 0
Bowling 111–2–55.50–0–0–1/25
He was a noted coursing slipper.

Lulham, Edwin Percy Habberton
Amateur. *b:* 7.4.1865, Norwich, Norfolk. *d:* 27.6.1940, Hurstpierpoint, Sussex. Lower order batsman, useful bowler. *Team* Sussex (1894, 1 match).
Career batting
1–2–0–6–5–3.00–0–*ct* 0
Bowling 25–3–8.33–0–0–3/25

Lumb, Edward
Amateur. *b:* 12.9.1852, Dalton, Huddersfield, Yorkshire. *d:* 5.4.1891, Westminster, London. He died of pleurisy. Very steady opening right-hand batsman, cover point. *Team* Yorkshire (1872–86, 14 matches).
Career batting
17–28–5–356–70*–15.47–0–*ct* 7
Owing to illness he was unable to appear in County cricket as often as his ability merited, missing the whole of 1884 and 1885 seasons for that reason.

Lumb, Richard Graham
Cricketer. *b:* 27.2.1950, Doncaster, Yorkshire. Brother-in-law of A. J. S. Smith (Natal). Opening right-hand batsman, right-arm medium pace bowler. *Team* Yorkshire (1970–84, 239 matches).
Career batting
245–406–30–11723–165*–31.17–22–*ct* 131
Bowling 5–0
He hit 1,000 runs in a season five times (best 1,532, av 41.40, in 1975).

Lumsden, Ian James Michael
Amateur. *b:* 6.4.1923, Bruntisfield, Edinburgh, Scotland. Middle order right-hand batsman. *Sch* George Watson's College. *Teams* Scotland (1946–48); Combined Services (1948–49).
Career batting
7–14–0–379–66–27.07–0–*ct* 3
An excellent rugby footballer, he was capped for Scotland.

Lumsden, Vincent Roy
Amateur. *b:* 19.7.1930, Buff Bay, Jamaica. Hard hitting middle order right-hand batsman, off break bowler, occasional wicket-keeper. *Teams* Jamaica (1949/50 to 1959/60); Cambridge U (1953–56, blue 1953–55).
Career batting
57–102–5–2699–107–27.82–1–*ct* 36
Bowling 355–11–32.27–0–0–4/20
His County cricket was for Cambridgeshire (1955).

Lund, Edward Victor
Amateur. *b:* 28.4.1902, Eton, Buckinghamshire. *d:* 20.2.1971, Cippenham, Buckinghamshire. Lower order right-hand batsman, right-arm medium pace bowler. *Team* Minor Counties (1937).
Career batting
1–2–0–5–4–2.50–0–*ct* 0
Bowling 94–3–31.33–0–0–2/78
His County cricket was for Buckinghamshire (1929–47). He was also a useful soccer player.

Lunn, Peter Daniel
Cricketer. *b:* 16.4.1970, Oxford. Middle order right-hand batsman, leg break bowler. *Sch* Abingdon. *Team* Oxford U (1989–90, blue both years).
Career batting
16–21–5–431–61–26.93–0–*ct* 2
Bowling 383–3–127.66–0–0–1/34

Lupton, Arthur William
Amateur. *b:* 23.2.1879, Bradford, Yorkshire. *d:* 14.4.1944, Carlton Manor, Guiseley, Yorkshire. Hard hitting lower order left-hand batsman, right-arm fast medium bowler. *Sch* Sedbergh. *Team* Yorkshire (1908–27, 104 matches).
Career batting
109–88–18–724–43*–10.34–0–*ct* 30
Bowling 455–14–32.50–0–0–4/109
Although he made his Yorkshire debut in 1908, his first-class career was to all intents and purposes confined to the three seasons 1925 to 1927, when he captained the County.

Lush, John Grantley
Amateur. *b:* 14.10.1913, Prahran, Melbourne, Victoria, Australia. *d:* 23.8.1985, Sydney, New South Wales, Australia. Lower order right-hand batsman, right-arm fast bowler. *Team* New South Wales (1933/4 to 1946/7, 18 matches). *Tour* Cahn to New

Zealand 1938/9 (no first-class matches).
Career batting
20–33–5–554–54–19.78–0–*ct* 10
Bowling 1346–50–26.92–3–1–7/72
His only first-class match in England was for Sir Julien Cahn's XI in 1938.

Lushington, Algernon Hay
Amateur. *b:* 29.9.1847, Lyndhurst, Hampshire. *d:* 13.9.1930, Shanklin, Isle of Wight. Great-nephew of S. (Surrey 1799). Middle order right-hand batsman. *Sch* Rugby. *Team* Hampshire (1870–77, 3 matches).
Career batting
3–6–0–48–21–8.00–0–*ct* 1
Bowling 98–3–32.66–0–0–2/48

Luther, Alan Charles Grenville
Amateur. *b:* 17.9.1880, Kensington, London. *d:* 23.6.1961, Staplemead, Curland, Somerset. Middle order right-hand batsman, good point field. *Sch* Rugby. *Team* Sussex (1908, 9 matches). *Tour* MCC to Egypt 1909 (not first-class).
Career batting
17–26–3–383–42–16.65–0–*ct* 7
His final first-class match was for MCC in 1911. He was a noted cricketer in military matches. He also played for Berkshire (1926–27) and later became Secretary to Berkshire CCC. Also a well-known rackets player, he was runner-up in the Amateur Singles Championship of 1907.

Lutterlock, Edward
Professional. *b:* 26.2.1852, Stockwell, London. *d:* 30.7.1938, Hill End, St Albans, Hertfordshire. Free hitting middle order right-hand batsman, right-hand fast round-arm bowler, long stop. *Team* Surrey (1874, 3 matches).
Career batting
3–6–0–23–8–3.83–0–*ct* 0

Luxton, Rev Charles Henry
Amateur. *b:* 19.1.1861, Bondleigh, Okehampton, Devon. *d:* 17.10.1918, St Pancras, London. Tail end batsman, useful bowler. *Team* Cambridge U (1881–82).
Career batting
2–4–0–10–9–2.50–0–*ct* 0
Bowling 94–4–23.50–0–0–2/60
His County cricket was for Devon (1882–85).

Luyt, Sir Richard Edmonds
Amateur. *b:* 8.11.1915, Cape Town, South Africa. Son of R. R. (Western Province), nephew of F. P. (Western Province). Middle order right-hand batsman, wicket-keeper. *Team* Oxford U (1938).
Career batting
3–5–1–71–32–17.75–0–*ct* 9–*st* 4

Lyall, Charles Ross
Amateur. *b:* 3.10.1880, Calcutta, India. *d:* 4.6.1950, Basingstoke, Hampshire. Middle order right-hand batsman. *Sch* Edinburgh Academy. *Team* Somerset (1911, 2 matches).
Career batting
2–4–2–55–21*–27.50–0–*ct* 0

Lyle, Sir Archibald Moir Park
Amateur. *b:* 5.2.1884, Greenock, Renfrewshire, Scotland. *d:* 4.12.1946, Marylebone, London. Middle order batsman. *Sch* Fettes. *Teams* Oxford U (1904–06); Scotland (1912).
Career batting
3–6–0–77–27–12.83–0–*ct* 2
Bowling 30–0
An all-round sportsman, he represented Oxford against Cambridge in the 120 yards hurdles and putting the weight, as well as being in the rugby XV for three seasons.

Lynas, George Goulton
Professional. *b:* 7.9.1832, Coatham, Redcar, Yorkshire. *d:* 8.12.1896, Skelton-in-Cleveland, Yorkshire. Lower order right-hand batsman, wicket-keeper, occasional right-hand fast round-arm bowler. *Team* Yorkshire (1867, 2 matches).
Career batting
2–3–1–4–4*–2.00–0–*ct* 2

Lynch, Monte Alan
Cricketer. *b:* 21.5.1958, Georgetown, British Guiana. Middle order right-hand batsman, off break bowler. *Teams* Surrey (1977–92, 283 matches); Guyana (1982/3). *Tours* International XI to Pakistan 1981/2; West Indian XI to South Africa 1983/4.
Career batting
300–483–58–15377–172*–36.18–34–*ct* 289
Bowling 1360–26–52.30–0–0–3/6
He hit 1,000 runs in a season eight times (best 1,714, av 53.56, in 1985). Educated in England, he therefore qualified as an English player, and played in one-day internationals in 1988.

Lynch, Ronald Victor
Amateur. *b:* 22.5.1923, Stratford, Essex. Tail end right-hand batsman, slow left-arm bowler. *Sch* St Paul's. *Team* Essex (1954, 3 matches).
Career batting
3–3–2–7–6*–7.00–0–*ct* 2
Bowling 107–4–26.75–0–0–4/64

Lynes, John
Professional. *b:* 6.6.1872, Coleshill, Warwickshire. Lower order right-hand batsman, right-arm fast medium bowler. *Team* Warwickshire (1897–1905, 8 matches).
Career batting
8–8–0–79–26–9.87–0–*ct* 6
Bowling 576–15–38.40–0–0–3/54

Lyness, George Edward Given
Amateur. *b:* 16.12.1937, Dunmurry, Belfast, Ireland. Lower order right-hand batsman, off break bowler.

Team Ireland (1961).
Career batting
1–2–0–12–9–6.00–0–*ct* 2
Bowling 90–8–11.25–1–0–6/39

Lynn, George Henry
Professional. *b:* 31.3.1848, East Grinstead, Sussex. *d:* 21.9.1921, East Grinstead, Sussex. Free hitting right-hand middle order batsman, deep field. *Team* Sussex (1872–73, 8 matches).
Career batting
8–13–0–128–25–9.84–0–*ct* 1
Bowling 8–1–8.00–0–0–1/8

Lynn, Joseph
Professional. *b:* 15.2.1856, Newington, London. *d:* 2.2.1927, Southampton, Hampshire. Lower order batsman, fair bowler. *Team* Hampshire (1875, 1 match).
Career batting
1–2–1–4–4*–4.00–0–*ct* 1
Bowling 34–2–17.00–0–0–2/25

Lyon, Beverley Hamilton
Amateur. *b:* 19.1.1902, Caterham, Surrey. *d:* 22.6.1970, Balcombe, Sussex. Brother of M. D. (Somerset). Hard hitting middle order right-hand batsman, excellent close field. *Sch* Rugby. *Teams* Gloucestershire (1921–47, 238 matches); Oxford U (1922–23, blue both years); Europeans (1924/5 to 1945/6). *Tour* Cahn to Ceylon 1936/7 (no first-class matches).
Career batting
267–448–20–10694–189–24.98–16–*ct* 263
Bowling 2341–52–45.02–1–0–5/72

He hit 1,000 runs in a season four times (best 1,576, av 38.43, in 1930). From 1929 to 1934 he captained Gloucestershire and in 1931 was the instigator of the 'freak' declaration, whereby a County declared their first innings closed, after a nominal single ball, when rain had reduced the playing time, in order to have the chance of gaining maximum points. He was also among the first to advocate County cricket on Sunday. His final first-class match was for West v East in the 1948 Kingston Festival. He also played for Wiltshire (1920).

Lyon, Brigadier-General Charles Harry
Amateur. *b:* 18.3.1878, Woodseat, Rocester, Staffordshire. *d:* 3.12.1959, Ightfield, Shropshire. Nephew of W. J. (Cambridge U 1861). Middle order right-hand batsman. *Sch* Newton College. *Team* Derbyshire (1902, 2 matches).
Career batting
2–2–0–6–4–3.00–0–*ct* 0
Bowling 6–0

Lyon, Admiral Sir George Hamilton D'Oyly
Amateur. *b:* 3.10.1883, Bankipore, India. *d:* 19.8.1947, Eastshaw, Midhurst, Sussex. Middle order right-hand batsman, right-arm pace bowler. *Sch* King's School, Bruton. *Teams* Hampshire (1907, 2 matches); Royal Navy (1911–22).
Career batting
4–7–0–185–90–26.42–0–*ct* 4
Bowling 140–7–20.00–0–0–4/51

An excellent rugby full back, he represented Surrey and England.

Lyon, Gordon William Francis
Amateur. *b:* 22.5.1905, Bradford-on-Avon, Wiltshire. *d:* 22.12.1932, Steyning, Sussex. Opening right-hand batsman. *Sch* Brighton. *Team* Oxford U (1925–27, blue 1925).
Career batting
9–17–1–262–52–16.37–0–*ct* 7
Bowling 5–1–5.00–0–0–1/5

Lyon, Herbert
Amateur. *b:* 29.4.1867, Valparaiso, Chile. *d:* 7.12.1951, Woking, Surrey. Attacking lower order right-hand batsman, wicket-keeper. *Sch* Winchester. *Team* Oxford U (1887–90).
Career batting
3–6–2–13–9*–3.25–0–*ct* 1

Lyon, John
Cricketer. *b:* 17.5.1951, St Helens, Lancashire. Lower order right-hand batsman, wicket-keeper. *Team* Lancashire (1973–79, 84 matches). *Tour* Robins to South Africa 1974/5.
Career batting
86–91–18–1016–123–13.91–1–*ct* 159–*st* 12

Lyon, Malcolm Douglas
Amateur. *b:* 22.4.1898, Caterham, Surrey. *d:* 17.2.1964, St Helens, St Leonards-on-Sea, Sussex. Brother of B. H. (Gloucestershire), he married the former wife of G. F. Earle (Surrey and Somerset). Forcing middle order right-hand batsman, wicket-keeper. *Sch* Rugby. *Teams* Somerset (1920–38, 123 matches); Cambridge U (1920–22, blue 1921–22).
Career batting
158–265–16–7294–219–29.29–14–*ct* 149–*st* 43
Bowling 574–8–71.75–0–0–3/43

He hit 1,000 runs in a season twice (best 1,298, av 34.15, in 1923); both his double centuries were for Somerset, the higher being 219 v Derbyshire at Burton-on-Trent in 1924. He was regarded as one of the best batsmen not to be capped by England; the fact that he was rather a controversial cricketer perhaps swayed the selectors. His County cricket virtually ended in 1932 when he was appointed a magistrate in Gambia; from 1948 to 1957 he was Chief Justice in the Seychelles and later Puisne Judge in Uganda. He also played for Wiltshire (1919).

Lyons, Godfrey Louis
Amateur. *b:* 23.5.1853, Fleetwood, Lancashire. *d:* 30.3.1931, Brighton, Sussex. Middle order right-hand

batsman, deep field. *Team* Surrey (1880, 1 match).
Career batting
1–2–0–8–8–4.00–0–*ct* 0

Lyons, John James
Amateur. *b:* 21.5.1863, Gawler, South Australia. *d:* 21.7.1927, Magill, Adelaide, South Australia. Fine attacking opening right-hand batsman, right-arm medium pace bowler. *Team* South Australia (1894/5 to 1899/1900, 47 matches). *Tours* Australia to England 1888, 1890, 1893, to North America 1893. *Tests* Australia (1886/7 to 1897/8, 14 matches).
Career batting
153–275–11–6753–149–25.57–11–*ct* 60
Bowling 3225–107–30.14–5–0–6/38
Test batting
14–27–0–731–134–27.07–1–*ct* 3
Bowling 149–6–24.83–1–0–5/30

He hit 1,000 runs on the tours of 1890 and 1893, being seen at his best in the latter season with 1,377 runs, av 28.10.

Lyons, Kevin James
Cricketer. *b:* 18.12.1946, Cardiff, Glamorgan. Middle order right-hand batsman, right-arm medium pace bowler. *Team* Glamorgan (1967–77, 62 matches). *Tour* Glamorgan to West Indies 1969/70.
Career batting
62–99–14–1673–92–19.68–0–*ct* 27
Bowling 252–2–126.00–0–0–1/36

He was a first-class umpire (1985–91). He was caoch to Glamorgan CCC 1972–84 and Worcestershire CCC from 1992.

Lyons, Reginald William
Amateur. *b:* 12.7.1922, Dublin, Ireland. *d:* 12.9.1976, Worthing, Sussex. Lower order right-hand batsman, wicket-keeper. *Team* Ireland (1947).
Career batting
1–1–1–0–0*–no av–0–*ct* 0–*st* 4

Lyons, Russell John
Cricketer. *b:* 6.12.1967, Johannesburg, South Africa. Middle order right-hand batsman, leg break bowler. *Team* Cambridge U (1991).
Career batting
1–2–0–38–20–19.00–0–*ct* 0
Bowling 26–1–26.00–0–0–1/26

Lyttelton, Hon Alfred
Amateur. *b:* 7.2.1857, Westminster, London. *d:* 5.7.1913, Marylebone, London. He died following an operation. Son of 4th Lord Lyttelton (Cambridge U 1836), brother of Edward (Middlesex), C. G. (Cambridge U), R. H. (MCC), A. T. (MCC) and G. W. S. (Cambridge U), uncle of J. C. (Worcestershire), C. F. (Worcestershire) and N. S. Talbot (Oxford U), son-in-law of A. Balfour (MCC). Fine middle order right-hand batsman, wicket-keeper, occasional right-hand under-arm bowler. *Sch* Eton. *Teams* Cambridge U (1876–79, blue all four years); Middlesex (1877–87, 35 matches). *Tests* England (1880–84, 4 matches).
Career batting
101–171–12–4429–181–27.85–7–*ct* 134–*st* 70
Bowling 172–4–43.00–0–0–4/19
Test batting
4–7–1–94–31–15.66–0–*ct* 2
Bowling 19–4–4.75–0–0–4/19

He was President of MCC in 1898 and a member of the Committee 1881–85 and 1899–1903. He also played for Worcestershire (pre first-class, 1874–85). Owing to his work at the Bar, he gave up first-class cricket in 1887. He captained Cambridge in 1879. An excellent soccer player, he represented Cambridge, England in 1877 and the Old Etonians in the FA Cup Final of 1876. He also represented Cambridge at royal tennis, rackets and athletics. From 1895 to 1906 he was MP for Warwick and from 1906 to his death MP for St George's, Hanover Square.

Lyttelton, Right Rev the Hon Arthur Temple
Amateur. *b:* 7.1.1852, Westminster, London. *d:* 19.2.1903, Petersfield, Hampshire. Son of 4th Lord Lyttelton (Cambridge U 1836), brother of Alfred (Middlesex), C. G. (Cambridge U), Edward (Middlesex), R. H. (MCC) and G. W. S. (Cambridge U), uncle of J. C. (Worcestershire), C. F. (Worcestershire) and N. S. Talbot (Oxford U). Middle order right-hand batsman, good deep field. *Sch* Eton. *Team* MCC (1872).
Career batting
1–2–0–4–4–2.00–0–*ct* 0

At the time of his death he was Bishop of Southampton. He was not in the Eleven whilst at Cambridge.

Lyttelton, Rev Hon Charles Frederick
Amateur. *b:* 26.1.1887, Marylebone, London. *d:* 3.10.1931, Paddington, London. Grandson of 4th Lord Lyttelton (Cambridge U 1836), son of C. G. (Cambridge U), nephew of Alfred (Middlesex), A. T. (MCC), Edward (Middlesex), R. H. (MCC) and G. W. S. (Cambridge U), brother of J. C. (Worcestershire), uncle of C. J. (Worcestershire), brother-in-law of G. R. R. Colman (Essex) and D. G. Wigan (Oxford U). Lower order right-hand batsman, right-arm fast bowler. *Sch* Eton. *Teams* Worcestershire (1906–10, 9 matches); Cambridge U (1907–09, blue 1908–09).
Career batting
31–48–15–304–25*–9.21–0–*ct* 16
Bowling 2155–86–25.05–2–0–5/33

Curiously he was unable to find a place in the eleven at Eton, but still won his blue at Cambridge. He also played for Flintshire (1925).

Lyttelton, Hon Charles George
(succeeded as 8th Viscount Cobham in 1888)
Amateur. *b:* 27.10.1842, Hagley Hall, Stourbridge, Worcestershire. *d:* 9.6.1922, Hagley Hall, Stour-

bridge, Worcestershire. Son of 4th Lord Lyttelton (Cambridge U 1836), brother of Alfred (Middlesex), Edward (Middlesex), R. H. (MCC), A. T. (MCC) and G. W. S. (Cambridge U), father of J. C. (Worcestershire) and C. F. (Worcestershire), grandfather of C. J. (Worcestershire), uncle of N. S. Talbot (Oxford U). Hard hitting middle order right-hand batsman, right-hand fast medium round-arm bowler, also under-arm lobs, occasional wicket-keeper. *Sch* Eton. *Teams* Cambridge U (1861–64, blue all four years).
Career batting
35–54–1–1439–129–27.15–2–*ct*–35–*st* 3
Bowling 547–28 + 1–19.53–0–0–4/19

His County cricket was for Worcestershire (pre first-class, 1865–73). His final first-class match was for Southgate in 1867. He was President of Worcestershire 1909–10. He also won a blue for royal tennis. He was MP for East Worcestershire 1868–74.

Lyttelton, Hon Charles John
(succeeded as 10th Viscount Cobham in 1949)
Amateur. *b:* 8.8.1909, Kensington, London. *d:* 20.3.1977, Marylebone, London. Son of J. C. (Worcestershire), grandson of C. G. (Cambridge U), great-grandson of 4th Lord Lyttelton (Cambridge U 1836), nephew of C. F. (Worcestershire). Hard hitting middle order right-hand batsman, right-arm medium pace bowler. *Sch* Eton. *Team* Worcestershire (1932–39, 93 matches). *Tours* MCC to Australia and New Zealand 1935/6; Norfolk to Jamaica 1956/7 (he did not play in first-class matches).
Career batting
104–171–14–3181–162–20.26–1–*ct* 52
Bowling 1318–32–41.18–0–0–4/83

His final first-class match was for Governor-General's XI v MCC in New Zealand in 1960/1 – he was Governor-General from 1957 to 1962. In 1954 he was President of MCC and Treasurer in 1963–64. From 1936 to 1939 he captained Worcestershire.

Lyttelton, Rev the Hon Edward
Amateur. *b:* 23.7.1855, Westminster, London. *d:* 26.1.1942, Lincoln. Son of 4th Lord Lyttelton (Cambridge U 1836), brother of Alfred (Middlesex), C. G. (Cambridge U), R. H. (MCC), A. T. (MCC) and G. W. S. (Cambridge U), uncle of J. C. (Worcestershire), C. F. (Worcestershire) and N. S. Talbot (Oxford U). Middle order right-hand batsman, good deep field. *Sch* Eton. *Teams* Cambridge U (1875–78, blue all four years); Middlesex (1878–82, 13 matches).
Career batting
57–95–5–2013–113–22.36–1–*ct* 43
Bowling 50–1–50.00–0–0–1/4

He also played for Worcestershire (pre first-class, 1871–76), and Hertfordshire (1873). He captained Cambridge in 1878. He excelled at soccer (playing for England), fives and athletics. From 1905 to 1916 he was Headmaster of Eton.

Lyttelton, Hon George William Spencer
Amateur. *b:* 12.6.1847, Westminster, London. *d:* 5.12.1913, Westminster, London. Son of 4th Lord Lyttelton (Cambridge U 1836), brother of Alfred (Middlesex), A. T. (MCC), C. G. (Cambridge U), Edward (Middlesex) and R. H. (MCC), uncle of J. C. (Worcestershire), C. F. (Worcestershire) and N. S. Talbot (Oxford U), brother-in-law of F. R. Spofforth (Australia). Middle order right-hand batsman, right-hand fast round-arm bowler, good field. *Sch* Eton. *Team* Cambridge U (1866–67, blue both years).
Career batting
18–29–1–581–114–20.75–1–*ct* 11–*st* 6
Bowling 781–33–23.66–2–1–7/33

His final first-class match was for Gentlemen of England in 1872. His County cricket was for Worcestershire (pre first-class 1865–78), Shropshire (1865) and Northamptonshire (pre first-class, 1866–67). He was chief private secretary to the Prime Minister, W. E. Gladstone, 1892–94.

Lyttelton, Hon J. C.
(*see under* Cobham, 9th Viscount)

Lyttelton, Hon Robert Henry
Amateur. *b:* 18.1.1854, Westminster, London. *d:* 7.11.1939, North Berwick, East Lothian, Scotland. Son of 4th Lord Lyttelton (Cambridge U 1836), brother of Alfred (Middlesex), C. G. (Cambridge U), Edward (Middlesex), A. T. (MCC) and G. W. S. (Cambridge U), uncle of J. C. (Worcestershire), C. F. (Worcestershire) and N. S. Talbot (Oxford U). Middle order right-hand batsman, slow under-arm bowler. *Sch* Eton. *Team* MCC (1873).
Career batting
7–12–1–67–27–6.09–0–*ct* 2
Bowling 31–1–31.00–0–0–1/27

His County cricket was for Worcestershire (pre first-class, 1880–81). He was not in the eleven whilst at Cambridge, but represented the University at royal tennis. Although not a famous cricketer, he was a noted student and critic of the game, contributing several well-known essays on various aspects of cricket. His final first-class match was for I Zingari in 1880.

Lywood, Lewis William
Professional. *b:* 23.12.1906, Walthamstow, Essex. *d:* 31.10.1971, Caterham, Surrey. Lower order right-hand batsman, right-arm fast medium bowler. *Teams* Surrey (1927–28, 2 matches); Essex (1930, 2 matches).
Career batting
4–5–0–19–7–3.80–0–*ct* 0
Bowling 260–3–86.66–0–0–1/7

He was for many years a noted club cricketer in South London.

M

Maartensz, Sydney Gratien Adair
Amateur. *b:* 14.4.1882, Colombo, Ceylon. *d:* 10.9.1967, Pyrford, Surrey. Lower order right-hand batsman, wicket-keeper. *Team* Hampshire (1919, 12 matches).
Career batting
12–17–2–283–60–18.86–0–*ct* 21–*st* 4

Maazullah Khan
Cricketer. *b:* 1.9.1947, Peshawar, Pakistan. Lower order right-hand batsman, off break bowler. *Teams* Peshawar (1965/6 to 1984/5); Railways (1971/2). *Tour* Pakistan to England 1974.
Career batting
45–73–9–1272–130–19.87–2–*ct* 22
Bowling 2701–107–25.24–3–1–8/97
He played in only four first-class matches on the 1974 tour.

McAdam, Dr Keith Paul William James
Cricketer. *b:* 13.8.1945, Edinburgh, Scotland. Opening left-hand batsman, right-arm bowler. *Sch* Millfield. *Team* Cambridge U (1965–66, blue both years).
Career batting
21–39–0–815–63–20.89–0–*ct* 10
Bowling 2–0
His final first-class match was for MCC in 1967. His County cricket was for Buckinghamshire (1966–68).

McAdam, William James
Cricketer. *b:* 3.10.1944, Springs, Transvaal, South Africa. Brother of S. J. (Eastern Province), grandson of S. J. Snooke (South Africa). Middle order right-hand batsman. *Teams* Western Province (1966/7 to 1968/9); Eastern Province (1971/2). *Tour* South African Universities to England 1967.
Career batting
19–30–1–668–129–23.03–1–*ct* 7
Bowling 3–0
His first-class debut was for South African Universities in 1966/7.

McAlister, Peter Alexander
Amateur. *b:* 11.7.1869, Williamstown, Melbourne, Victoria, Australia. *d:* 10.5.1938, Richmond, Melbourne, Victoria, Australia. Stylish opening right-hand batsman. *Team* Victoria (1898/9 to 1910/11, 53 matches). *Tour* Australia to England 1909. *Tests* Australia (1903/4 to 1909, 8 matches).
Career batting
85–148–9–4552–224–32.74–9–*ct* 91
Bowling 56–3–18.66–0–0–1/0
Test batting
8–16–1–252–41–16.80–0–*ct* 10
A good batsman, he came to England too late in his career and it was unfortunate for him that the selectors made a controversial decision in choosing him as vice-captain of the tourists over the heads of Trumper and Armstrong. His highest score was 224 for Victoria v New Zealand at Melbourne in 1898/9.

McAllister, Alexander Eric
Amateur. *b:* 19.12.1920, Paisley, Renfrewshire, Scotland. Middle order right-hand batsman. *Team* Scotland (1950).
Career batting
1–2–0–13–9–6.50–0–*ct* 1

McAlpine, Kenneth
Amateur. *b:* 11.4.1858, Leamington, Warwickshire. *d:* 10.2.1923, Loose, Maidstone, Kent. Opening right-hand batsman. *Sch* Haileybury. *Team* Kent (1885–86, 3 matches). *Tours* Hawke to North America 1891, 1894 (he did not play in first-class matches).
Career batting
4–7–1–30–10–5.00–0–*ct* 2
He was a great supporter of Kent cricket and President of the County Club in 1922.

Macan, George
Amateur. *b:* 9.9.1853, Greenmount, Castle Bellingham, Co Louth, Ireland. *d:* 2.11.1943, Wimbledon Common, Surrey. Lower order right-hand batsman, right-hand slow round-arm bowler. *Sch* Harrow. *Team* Cambridge U (1872–75, blue 1874–75).
Career batting
18–33–6–391–57–14.48–0–*ct* 6

Macartney, Charles George
Amateur. *b:* 27.6.1886, West Maitland, New South Wales, Australia. *d:* 9.9.1958, Little Bay, Sydney, New South Wales, Australia. Grandson of G. Moore (New South Wales), nephew of L. Moore (New South Wales) and W. H. Moore (New South Wales and Western Australia). Attacking middle order right-hand batsman, slow left-arm bowler, fine field. *Team* New South Wales (1905/6 to 1926/7, 81 matches). *Tours* Australia to England 1909, 1912, 1921, 1926, to South Africa 1914/15 (tour cancelled), 1921/2, to North America 1913, to India and Ceylon 1935/6. *Tests* Australia (1907/8 to 1926, 35 matches).
Career batting
249–360–32–15019–345–45.78–49–*ct* 102
Bowling 8781–419–20.95–17–1–7/58
Test batting
35–55–4–2131–170–41.78–7–*ct* 17
Bowling 1240–45–27.55–2–1–7/58
His outstanding tour to England was in 1921 when he hit 2,317 runs, av 59.42, but he also scored over 2,000 runs in 1912 when in addition he headed the bowling averages; in 1926 he easily topped 1,000 runs. On his first visit he was regarded more as a bowler than a batsman, taking 64 wickets, av 17.85. His most famous innings was 345 against Nottinghamshire at Trent Bridge in 1921 – the entire innings was completed on the first day, a record in first-class

cricket. He hit three other double centuries, including one v Essex in 1912.

Macaulay, George Gibson
Professional. *b:* 7.12.1897, Thirsk, Yorkshire. *d:* 13.12.1940, Sullom Voe, Shetland Islands. He died from pneumonia. Uncle of J. Lister (Yorkshire and Worcestershire). Lower order right-hand batsman, originally right-arm fast, but in 1921 altered to medium pace bowler, brilliant close field. *Sch* Barnard Castle. *Team* Yorkshire (1920–35, 445 matches). *Tours* MCC to South Africa 1922/3). *Tests* England (1922/3 to 1933, 8 matches).
Career batting
468–460–125–6056–125*–18.07–3–*ct* 373
Bowling 32440–1837–17.65–126–31–8/21
Test batting
8–10–4–112–76–18.66–0–*ct* 5
Bowling 662–24–27.58–1–0–5/64
He took 100 wickets in a season ten times including over 200 once – 211, av 15.48, in 1925. An injury to his finger in 1934 caused him to retire from first-class cricket earlier than would otherwise have been the case.

Macaulay, Michael John
Amateur. *b:* 19.4.1939, Durban, South Africa. Lower order right-hand batsman, left-arm medium pace bowler. *Teams* Transvaal (1957/8 to 1965/6); Western Province (1960/1); Orange Free State (1963/4 to 1964/5); North East Transvaal (1966/7 to 1968/9); Eastern Province (1977/8 to 1978/9). *Tour* South Africa to England 1965. *Test* South Africa (1964/65, 1 match).
Career batting
69–91–23–888–59–13.05–0–*ct* 45
Bowling 5357–234–22.89–16–4–7/49
Test batting
1–2–0–33–21–16.50–0–*ct* 0
Bowling 73–2–36.50–0–0–1/10
Although he bowled usefully on the 1965 tour to England, he was not required for any of the Tests.

McBride, Walter Nelson
Amateur. *b:* 27.11.1904, East Croydon, Surrey. *d:* 30.1.1974, South Ealing, Middlesex. Lower order left-hand batsman, right-arm medium pace bowler. *Sch* Westminster. *Teams* Hampshire (1925–29, 31 matches); Oxford U (1925–27, blue 1926).
Career batting
47–67–16–656–51–12.86–0–*ct* 31
Bowling 1791–56–31.98–2–0–5/57
He also played for Dorset (1938). A good goalkeeper, he obtained his soccer blue in 1927.

McBrine, Alexander
Cricketer. *b:* 16.9.1963, Omagh, Co Tyrone, Ireland. Twin brother of James (Ireland). Lower order right-hand batsman, slow left-arm bowler. *Team* Ireland (1985–92).
Career batting
4–6–0–155–102–25.83–1–*ct* 1
Bowling 221–6–36.83–0–0–3/64

McBrine, James
Cricketer. *b:* 16.9.1963, Omagh, Co Tyrone, Ireland. Twin brother of Alexander (Ireland). Lower order right-hand batsman, right-arm medium pace bowler. *Team* Ireland (1986).
Career batting
1–2–2–29–27*–no av–0–*ct* 1
Bowling 67–0

MacBryan, John Crawford William
Amateur. *b:* 22.7.1892, Box, Wiltshire. *d:* 14.7.1983, Cambridge. Stylish middle order right-hand batsman. *Sch* Cheltenham and Exeter. *Teams* Somerset (1911–31, 156 matches); Cambridge U (1919–20, blue 1920). *Tour* Joel to South Africa 1924/5. *Test* England (1924, 1 match).
Career batting
206–362–12–10322–164–29.49–18–*ct* 128
Bowling 61–0
Test batting
1 match, did not bat–*ct* 0
He hit 1,000 runs in a season four times (best 1,831, av 35.90, in 1923). His final first-class match was for MCC in 1936.

McCabe, Stanley Joseph
Amateur. *b:* 16.7.1910, Grenfell, New South Wales, Australia. *d:* 25.8.1968, Beauty Point, Mosman, Sydney, New South Wales, Australia. He died following an accidental fall over a cliff near his home. Brilliant middle order right-hand batsman, right-arm medium pace bowler. *Team* New South Wales (1928/9 to 1941/2, 55 matches). *Tours* Australia to England 1930, 1934, 1938, to South Africa 1935/6. *Tests* Australia (1930–38, 39 matches).
Career batting
182–262–20–11951–240–49.38–29–*ct* 139
Bowling 5362–159–33.72–1–0–5/36
Test batting
39–62–5–2748–232–48.21–6–*ct* 41
Bowling 1543–36–42.86–0–0–4/13
His greatest innings in England was his 232 in the Trent Bridge Test of 1938 – regarded by many as one of the all time exhibitions of batsmanship. Curiously he had a very moderate tour otherwise and scored only 1,124 runs. In 1934 he hit 2,078, av 69.26, and in 1930, 1,012, av 32.64, so that in terms of figures 1934 was easily his most rewarding visit. His highest score was 240 for Australians v Surrey at the Oval in 1934.

McCague, Martin John
Cricketer. *b:* 24.5.1969, Larne, Co Antrim, Ireland. Lower order right-hand batsman, right-arm fast bowler. *Teams* Western Australia (1990/1 to 1991/2, 11 matches); Kent (1991–92, 24 matches).

McCall, Barney Ernest Willford

Career batting
35–41–10–386–34–12.45–0–*ct* 20
Bowling 2997–101–29.67–7–1–8/26
He emigrated with his parents to Australia at the age of one.

McCall, Barney Ernest Willford
Amateur. *b:* 13.5.1913, Clifton, Bristol. *d:* 31.3.1991, Heath Park, Cardiff, Glamorgan. Middle order right-hand batsman, right-arm bowler. *Sch* Weymouth. *Teams* Army (1936); Minor Counties (1937); Combined Services (1948).
Career batting
3–6–0–56–31–9.33–0–*ct* 4
Bowling 35–1–35.00–0–0–1/34
His County cricket was for Dorset (1931–36). A noted rugby footballer, he was capped for Wales. The man who died in 1982, whose death was noted in the first edition of this book from the cricket press, was another cricketer of the same name.

McCall, Hugh Con
Cricketer. *b:* 29.3.1940, Holywood, Co Down, Ireland. Middle order right-hand batsman, slow left-arm bowler. *Sch* Campbell College. *Team* Ireland (1964–68).
Career batting
7–14–1–308–81–23.69–0–*ct* 3
Bowling 1–0

McCanlis, George
Professional. *b:* 3.12.1847, Landguard, Suffolk. *d:* 18.10.1937, Upper Norwood, London. Brother of William (Kent). Middle order right-hand batsman, right-hand medium pace round-arm bowler. *Team* Kent (1873–78, 17 matches).
Career batting
17–31–2–364–60–12.55–0–*ct* 8
Bowling 117–3–39.00–0–0–1/9

McCanlis, Maurice Alfred
Amateur. *b:* 17.6.1906, Quetta, India. *d:* 27.9.1991, Pershore, Worcestershire. Middle order right-hand batsman, right-hand medium pace bowler. *Sch* Cranleigh. *Teams* Oxford U (1926–28, blue all three years); Surrey (1926–27, 2 matches); Gloucestershire (1929, 1 match); Rajputana (1938/9 to 1939/40).
Career batting
30–45–13–493–40*–15.40–0–*ct* 19
Bowling 2642–82–32.21–4–0–5/42
He captained Oxford in 1928. A noted rugby footballer, he won his blue and was capped for England.

McCanlis, William
Professional. *b:* 30.10.1840, Woolwich, London. *d:* 19.11.1925, Westcombe Park, London. Brother of George (Kent). Hard hitting middle order right-hand batsman. *Team* Kent (1862–77, 45 matches).
Career batting
45–86–4–1113–67–13.57–0–*ct* 19
Bowling 496–18–27.55–0–0–4/67
He appeared in some matches under the alias of 'Willis'.

McCarthy, Charles Henry Florence D'Arcy
Amateur. *b:* 29.6.1899, Coimbatore, India. *d:* 24.7.1977, Lyford Cay, New Providence, Bahamas. Sound middle order right-hand batsman, leg break bowler, good field. *Sch* Rugby. *Teams* Army (1921); Burma/Rangoon (1926/7).
Career batting
3–6–1–75–48–15.00–0–*ct* 0
Bowling 33–1–33.00–0–0–1/33
His County cricket was for Devon (1929–31).

McCarthy, Cuan Neil
Amateur. *b:* 24.3.1929, Pietermaritzburg, South Africa. Tail end right-hand batsman, right-arm fast bowler. *Teams* Natal (1947/8 to 1950/1); Cambridge U (1952, blue). *Tour* South Africa to England 1951. *Tests* South Africa (1948/9 to 1951, 15 matches).
Career batting
60–68–35–141–23*–4.27–0–*ct* 23
Bowling 4551–176–25.85–8–1–8/36
Test batting
15–24–15–28–5–3.11–0–*ct* 6
Bowling 1510–36–41.94–2–0–6/43
He was not too successful on the 1951 tour to England, taking 59 wickets, av 23.96, in first-class matches, but he appeared in all five Tests. In 1952 he easily headed the Cambridge University bowling averages, but was no-balled for throwing, and he did not appear in first-class cricket after 1952. He played County cricket for Dorset (1958–59). A good boxer, he was awarded his blue whilst at Cambridge.

MacCarthy-Morrogh, Dr William Charles Frederick
Amateur. *b:* 19.11.1870, Kerry, Ireland. *d:* 15.9.1939, Falmouth, Cornwall. Lower order left-hand batsman, slow left-arm bowler. *Sch* Stonyhurst. *Team* Dublin U (1895).
Career batting
1–2–0–3–2–1.50–0–*ct* 1
Bowling 50–0

McCaskie, Norman
Amateur. *b:* 23.3.1911, Kensington, London. *d:* 1.7.1968, Theale, Berkshire. Nephew of R. M. Thorburn (Scotland). Middle order left-hand batsman, left-arm medium pace bowler. *Sch* Winchester. *Teams* Middlesex (1931–32, 3 matches); Oxford U (1932).
Career batting
4–6–0–55–26–9.16–0–*ct* 1
Bowling 22–0
He won blues for rackets and squash.

McCaughey, Samuel
Amateur. *b:* 27.11.1892, Coree Station, Deniliquin, New South Wales, Australia. *d:* 29.1.1955, Manly,

Sydney, New South Wales, Australia. Lower order batsman, right-arm medium and leg break bowler. *Sch* Haileybury. *Team* Cambridge U (1913).
Career batting
2–3–0–10–9–3.33–0–*ct* 3
Bowling 123–9–13.66–1–0–7/46

McCausland, Dr Charles Edward
Amateur. *b:* 4.10.1898, Dublin, Ireland. *d:* 12.11.1965, Folkestone, Kent. Middle order right-hand batsman, right-arm fast medium bowler. *Sch* Winchester. *Teams* Dublin U (1922–25); Ireland (1922–24).
Career batting
5–10–0–139–26–13.90–0–*ct* 4
Bowling 175–3–58.33–0–0–2/38

McCay, David Laurence Cornelius
Cricketer. *b:* 18.11.1943, De Aar, Cape Province, South Africa. Lower order right-hand batsman, right-arm medium pace bowler. *Team* Western Province (1966/7 to 1973/4). *Tour* South African Universities to England 1967.
Career batting
17–25–3–345–82–15.68–0–*ct* 12
Bowling 1071–49–21.85–2–1–8/76

McClintock, William Kerr
Amateur. *b:* 7.3.1896, Jesmond, Newcastle upon Tyne, Northumberland. *d:* 30.3.1946, Bow, London. Middle order right-hand batsman. *Sch* Harrow. *Team* Gloucestershire (1920–21, 8 matches).
Career batting
8–13–0–98–24–7.53–0–*ct* 4

McCloughin, Kenelm Rees
Amateur. *b:* 18.8.1884, Bombay, India. *d:* 26.9.1915, Hohenzollern Redoubt, near Cambrin, France. Opening or middle order batsman. *Sch* Dulwich. *Teams* Europeans (1909/10); Army (1914); L. Robinson's XI (1914); Free Foresters (1914).
Career batting
5–9–0–158–57–17.55–0–*ct* 2
Bowling 52–1–52.00–0–0–1/4

McCloy, Thomas
Amateur. *b:* 31.8.1927, Lambeg, Co Antrim, Ireland. Middle order right-hand batsman, right-arm medium pace bowler. *Team* Ireland (1952–65).
Career batting
12–24–0–374–53–15.58–0–*ct* 6
Bowling 15–0

MacColl, René
Amateur. *b:* 12.1.1905, Brentford, Middlesex. *d:* 20.5.1971, Crowborough, Sussex. Opening or middle order batsman, change bowler. *Sch* University College School. *Team* Oxford U (1924).
Career batting
1–2–0–4–4–2.00–0–*ct* 0

He was a well-known journalist and broadcaster.

McConnon, James Edward
Professional. *b:* 21.6.1922, Burnopfield, Co Durham. Lower order right-hand batsman, off break bowler. *Team* Glamorgan (1950–61, 243 matches). *Tours* MCC to Australia 1954/5; Commonwealth to India 1953/4. *Tests* England (1954, 2 matches).
Career batting
256–366–42–4661–95–14.38–0–*ct* 151
Bowling 16285–819–19.88–49–12–8/36
Test batting
2–3–1–18–11–9.00–0–*ct* 4
Bowling 74–4–18.50–0–0–3/19

He took 100 wickets in a season three times (best 136, av 16.07, in 1951). His best innings analysis was 8/36 for Glamorgan v Nottinghamshire at Trent Bridge in 1953. He also played for Cheshire (1962–67). A good soccer player, he was centre half for Aston Villa.

McCool, Colin Leslie
Professional. *b:* 9.12.1915, Paddington, Sydney, New South Wales, Australia. *d:* 5.4.1986, Concord, Sydney, New South Wales, Australia. Father of R. J. (Somerset). Middle order right-hand batsman, leg break bowler, good slip field. *Teams* New South Wales (1939/40 to 1940/1, 7 matches); Queensland (1945/6 to 1952/3, 47 matches); Somerset (1956–60, 138 matches). *Tours* Australia to England 1948, to South Africa 1949/50, to New Zealand 1945/6; Howard to India 1956/7. *Tests* Australia (1945/6 to 1949/50, 14 matches).
Career batting
251–412–34–12421–172–32.85–18–*ct* 263–*st* 2
Bowling 16542–602–27.47–34–2–8/74
Test batting
14–17–4–459–104*–35.30–1–*ct* 14
Bowling 958–36–26.61–3–0–5/41

Although he was a useful all-rounder he did not appear in any of the Tests on the 1948 tour – as a bowler he took 57 wickets, av 17.82. During his seasons with Somerset he hit 1,000 runs four times (best 1,967, av 37.82, in 1956).

McCool, Russell John
Cricketer. *b:* 4.12.1959, Taunton, Somerset. Son of C. L. (New South Wales, Queensland and Somerset). Lower order right-hand batsman, leg break and googly bowler. *Team* Somerset (1982, 1 match).
Career batting
1–2–0–19–12–9.50–0–*ct* 1
Bowling 63–0

McCorkell, Neil Thomas
Professional. *b:* 23.3.1912, Portsmouth, Hampshire. Opening right-hand batsman, wicket-keeper. *Team* Hampshire (1932–51, 383 matches). *Tour* Tennyson to India 1937/8.
Career batting
396–696–67–16107–203–25.60–17–*ct* 532–*st* 184

Bowling 117–1–117.00–0–0–1/73

He hit 1,000 runs in a season nine times (best 1,871, av 38.18, in 1949). His only double century was 203 for Hampshire v Gloucestershire at Gloucester in 1951.

McCormick, Edward James
Amateur. *b:* 1.11.1862, Hastings, Sussex. *d:* 31.12.1941, Templemore, Co Tipperary, Ireland. Middle order right-hand batsman, right-arm medium pace bowler, good deep field. *Team* Sussex (1880–90, 46 matches).
Career batting
50–91–4–1346–73–15.47–0–*ct* 26
Bowling 338–9–37.55–0–0–2/36

He was for many years a noted figure in Hastings cricket, but owing to his profession (he was a banker), was unable to appear often in County matches.

McCormick, Ernest Leslie
Amateur. *b:* 16.5.1906, North Carlton, Melbourne, Victoria, Australia. *d:* 28.6.1991, Tweed Heads, New South Wales, Australia. Tail end left-hand batsman, right-arm fast bowler. *Team* Victoria (1929/30 to 1938/9, 43 matches). *Tours* Australia to South Africa 1935/6, to England 1938. *Tests* Australia (1935/6 to 1938, 12 matches).
Career batting
85–98–31–582–77*–8.68–0–*ct* 46
Bowling 6686–241–27.74–6–1–9/40
Test batting
12–14–5–54–17*–6.00–0–*ct* 8
Bowling 1079–36–29.97–0–0–4/101

Described at the time as the most over-rated bowler ever to tour England, he tried to bowl too fast and suffered from being no-balled for overstepping the crease on many occasions. His results were very moderate, with 34 wickets, av 33.41, in first-class matches. His best bowling was 9/40 for Victoria v South Australia at Adelaide in 1936/7.

McCormick, Rev Canon Joseph
Amateur. *b:* 29.10.1834, Liverpool, Lancashire. *d:* 9.4.1914, Westminster, London. Father of W. P. G. (MCC). Fine punishing middle order right-hand batsman, right-hand slow round-arm bowler. *Sch* Liverpool College. *Team* Cambridge U (1854–56, blue 1854 and 1856).
Career batting
19–35–0–561–137–16.82–1–*ct* 11–*st* 1
Bowling 490–35+31–14.00–5–1–7/?

He played little important cricket after leaving Cambridge. His final first-class match was for MCC in 1868. He played for Ireland (not first-class) 1855–58). He captained Cambridge in 1856. He was in the Cambridge boat in 1856 and was also a noted boxer.

McCormick, Rev William Patrick Glyn
Amateur. *b:* 14.6.1877, Hull, Yorkshire. *d:* 16.10.1940, Westminster, London. Son of Joseph (Cambridge U). Middle order right-hand batsman, slow left-arm bowler. *Sch* Exeter. *Team* MCC (1907).
Career batting
1–2–0–17–17–8.50–0–*ct* 0
Bowling 5–0

His County cricket was for Devon (1896). He played in trials at Cambridge U, but not in first-class matches. He played rugby for Transvaal.

McCorquodale, Alastair
Amateur. *b:* 5.12.1925, Hillhead, Glasgow, Scotland. Nephew of G. J. Edwards (Essex). Lower order left-hand batsman, right-arm fast bowler. *Sch* Harrow. *Team* Middlesex (1951, 3 matches). *Tour* MCC to Canada 1951 (not first-class).
Career batting
5–6–2–34–21–8.50–0–*ct* 1
Bowling 399–4–99.75–0–0–2/62

His first-class debut was for MCC in 1948. A noted athlete, he came fourth in the 100 metres in the 1948 Olympic Games and won a silver medal in the sprint relay.

McCorquodale, Edmund George
Amateur. *b:* 23.7.1881, Weybridge, Surrey. *d:* 24.5.1904, Tulchan Lodge, Morayshire, Scotland. He died of appendicitis. Lower order right-hand batsman, right-arm medium pace bowler, moderate field. *Sch* Harrow. *Team* Cambridge U (1901).
Career batting
2–1–1–3–3*–no av–0–*ct* 1
Bowling 82–1–82.00–0–0–1/27

His County cricket was for Hertfordshire (1899).

McCosker, Richard Bede
Cricketer. *b:* 11.12.1946, Inverell, New South Wales, Australia. Sound opening right-hand batsman. *Team* New South Wales (1973/4 to 1983/4, 86 matches). *Tours* Australia to England 1975, 1977, to New Zealand 1976/7. *Tests* Australia (1974/5 to 1979/80, 25 matches).
Career batting
127–228–24–8983–168–44.03–27–*ct* 144
Bowling 177–2–88.50–0–0–2/28
Test batting
25–46–5–1622–127–39.56–4–*ct* 21

His great match of the 1977 tour to England was the third Test, when he hit 51 and 107. He played in all the other Tests, but with little success, nor did he score many runs in the other first-class matches.

McCray, Ewan
Cricketer. *b:* 29.10.1964, Altrincham, Cheshire. Lower order right-hand batsman, off break bowler. *Team* Derbyshire (1991, 2 matches).
Career batting
2–2–0–68–37–34.00–0–*ct* 1

Bowling 87–0

He also played for Cheshire (1989–90). He played lacrosse for Lancashire and England Under 25.

McCrum, Charles
Cricketer. *b:* 8.12.1964, Belfast, Ireland. Brother of Paul (Ireland). Lower order right-hand batsman, right-arm medium pace bowler. *Team* Ireland (1992).
Career batting
1–2–0–109–70–54.50–0–*ct* 0
Bowling 97–3–32.33–0–0–3/57

McCrum, Paul
Cricketer. *b:* 11.8.1962, Waringstown, Co Armagh, Ireland. Brother of Charles (Ireland). Lower order right-hand batsman, right-arm fast medium bowler. *Team* Ireland (1990–92).
Career batting
2–3–1–0–0*–0.00–0–*ct* 0
Bowling 173–1–173.00–0–0–1/80

McCulloch, John Wyndham Hamilton
Amateur. *b:* 4.12.1894, Calcutta, India. *d:* 21.10.1915, Bailleul, Lille, France. He died of wounds. Middle order right-hand batsman. *Sch* Westminster. *Team* Middlesex (1914, 2 matches).
Career batting
2–3–0–18–14–6.00–0–*ct* 0

He was also a talented soccer player.

McCurdy, Rodney John
Cricketer. *b:* 30.12.1959, Melbourne, Victoria, Australia. Lower order right-hand batsman, right-arm fast medium bowler. *Teams* Derbyshire (1979, 1 match); Tasmania (1980/1, 7 matches); Victoria (1981/2 to 1983/4, 24 matches); South Australia (1984/5, 9 matches); Eastern Province (1986/7 to 1990/1); Natal (1991/2). *Tours* Young Australia to Zimbabwe 1982/3; Australia to Sharjah (not first-class) 1984/5; Australian XI to South Africa 1985/6, 1986/7.
Career batting
80–90–28–659–55–10.62–0–*ct* 24
Bowling 8593–290–29.63–15–0–7/55

He also played for Shropshire (1979). He played for Australia in one-day international matches.

McDermott, Craig John
Cricketer. *b:* 14.4.1965, Ipswich, Queensland, Australia. Lower order right-hand batsman, right-arm fast bowler. *Team* Queensland (1983/4 to 1991/2, 63 matches). *Tours* Australia to Sharjah (not first-class) 1984/5, 1985/6, to England 1985, to New Zealand 1985/6, 1991/2 (World Cup), to India 1986/7, to India and Pakistan (World Cup) 1987/8, to Pakistan 1988/9, to West Indies 1990/1. *Tests* Australia (1984/5 to 1991/2, 36 matches).
Career batting
118–146–24–2018–74–16.54–0–*ct* 34
Bowling 12761–481–26.53–30–4–8/44
Test batting
36–50–5–501–42*–11.13–0–*ct* 9
Bowling 4329–153–28.29–9–2–8/97

The outstanding bowler of the Australian visit to England in 1985, he took 30 Test wickets, av 30.03, and 51 first-class wickets, av 31.54, topping both bowling tables. His Test career since that tour has not been one of continuous success and he was omitted from the Test side for more than one series. He was signed as Yorkshire's first overseas cricketer for 1992, but then withdrew due to injury.

McDermott, Enda Anthony
Cricketer. *b:* 1.12.1945, Dublin, Ireland. Opening left-hand batsman. *Team* Ireland (1982).
Career batting
1–2–0–18–18–9.00–0–*ct* 1

MacDonagh, Samuel Wilfred
Amateur. *b:* 8.8.1899, Armagh, Ireland. *d:* 1983, Bangor, Co Down, Ireland. Opening right-hand batsman, wicket-keeper. *Team* Ireland (1930).
Career batting
1–2–0–61–48–30.50–0–*ct* 0

McDonald, Colin Campbell
Amateur. *b:* 17.11.1928, Glen Iris, Melbourne, Victoria, Australia. Brother of I. H. (Victoria), cousin of K. E. Rigg (Australia). Sound opening right-hand batsman. *Team* Victoria (1947/8 to 1962/3, 60 matches). *Tours* Australia to England 1953, 1956, 1961, to South Africa 1957/8, to West Indies 1954/5, to India and Pakistan 1956/7, 1959/60; International XI to Rhodesia and Pakistan 1961/2. *Tests* Australia (1951/2 to 1961, 47 matches).
Career batting
192–307–26–11375–229–40.48–24–*ct* 55–*st* 2
Bowling 192–3–64.00–0–0–1/10
Test batting
47–83–4–3107–170–39.32–5–*ct* 14
Bowling 3–0

In 1953 he had a very modest tour and did not appear in the Tests, but in 1956 he hit 1,202 runs, av 34.34, and was the main opening bat. His last tour to England was not a success and after a poor start he was handicapped by injury. His highest score was 229 for Victoria v South Australia at Adelaide in 1953/4.

McDonald, Donald
Amateur. *b:* 22.2.1887, Chard, Somerset. *d:* 29.6.1961, Southbourne, Hampshire. Lower order batsman, slow left-arm bowler. *Sch* Taunton. *Team* Scotland (1913).
Career batting
1–1–0–6–6–6.00–0–*ct* 1
Bowling 148–6–24.66–1–0–5/51

McDonald, Edgar Arthur
Professional. *b:* 6.1.1891, Launceston, Tasmania, Australia. *d:* 22.7.1937, Blackrod, Bolton, Lancashire. He was killed in a road accident. Lower order right-hand batsman, right-arm fast bowler. *Teams* Lancashire (1924–31, 217 matches); Tasmania (1909/10 to 1910/11, 2 matches); Victoria (1911/12 to 1921/2, 22 matches). *Tours* Australia to England 1921, to South Africa 1921/2. *Tests* Australia (1920/1 to 1921/2, 11 matches).
Career batting
281–302–47–2663–100*–10.44–1–*ct* 98
Bowling 28966–1395–20.76–119–31–8/41
Test batting
11–12–5–116–36–16.57–0–*ct* 3
Bowling 1431–43–33.27–2–0–5/32

Coming to England with the 1921 Australians, he proved to be the outstanding bowler of the tour, heading the Test averages and in first-class matches taking 138 wickets, av 16.55. He later returned to England to qualify for Lancashire and in 1925 took 205 wickets, av 18.66 – the only time he exceeded 200 wickets in a season, though he achieved over 100 seven times. His final first-class match was for Sir L. Parkinson's XI in 1935. In Australia he was also a noted footballer, both rugby and association.

MacDonald, Harry Lindsay Somerled
Amateur. *b:* 2.8.1861, Westminster, London. *d:* 15.8.1936, Bathford, Somerset. Middle order batsman. *Sch* Charterhouse. *Team* Somerset (1896, 1 match).
Career batting
1–2–1–22–22*–22.00–0–*ct* 2

MacDonald, James
Amateur. *b:* 17.9.1906, Comber, Co Down, Ireland. *d:* 8.3.1969, Bangor, Co Down, Ireland. Brother of T. J. (Ireland). Middle order left-hand batsman, slow left-arm bowler. *Team* Ireland (1926–39).
Career batting
14–27–1–622–108*–23.92–1–*ct* 5
Bowling 891–35–25.45–1–0–5/33

McDonald, John Archibald
Amateur. *b:* 29.5.1882, Belper, Derbyshire. *d:* 4.6.1961, Brownhill, Blackburn, Lancashire. Middle order right-hand batsman. *Team* Derbyshire (1905–06, 3 matches).
Career batting
3–6–0–57–21–9.50–0–*ct* 0

MacDonald, Robert
Amateur. *b:* 14.2.1870, Clunes, Melbourne, Victoria, Australia. *d:* May 1945, Victoria, British Columbia, Canada. Middle order right-hand batsman, leg break bowler. *Teams* Queensland (1893/4 to 1903/4, 14 matches); Leicestershire (1899–1902, 33 matches). *Tour* Queensland to New Zealand 1896/7.
Career batting
48–80–15–2069–147*–31.83–4–*ct* 34
Bowling 181–3–60.33–0–0–3/49

He was Hon Secretary of Leicestershire 1922–29 and 1937–39.

Macdonald, Robert Hepburn
Cricketer. 18.7.1965, Cape Town, South Africa. Lower order right-hand batsman, right-arm medium fast bowler. *Team* Oxford U (1991–92, blue both years).
Career batting
10–9–4–54–20–10.80–0–*ct* 0
Bowling 645–15–43.00–0–0–3/66

He was awarded a blue for squash in 1990.

MacDonald, Thomas John
Amateur. *b:* 27.12.1908, Comber, Co Down, Ireland. Brother of James (Ireland). Opening right-hand batsman, leg break bowler. *Teams* Ireland (1928–36); Cambridge U (1930).
Career batting
7–14–0–291–132–20.78–1–*ct* 4
Bowling 32–0

His County cricket was for Lincolnshire (1934–36).

MacDonald-Watson, Alastair
Amateur. *b:* 29.1.1909, Croydon, Surrey. *d:* 19.11.1987, Alverstoke, Hampshire. Tail end right-hand batsman, right-arm fast bowler. *Team* Somerset (1932–33, 4 matches).
Career batting
4–6–1–2–1–0.40–0–*ct* 1
Bowling 219–8–27.37–1–0–5/27

McDonell, Harold Clark
Amateur. *b:* 19.9.1882, Wimbledon, Surrey. *d:* 23.7.1965, Onich, Fort William, Inverness, Scotland. Brother of J. F. (Europeans). Lower order right-hand batsman, leg break bowler, good field. *Sch* Winchester. *Teams* Surrey (1901–04, 13 matches); Cambridge U (1902–05, blue 1903–05); Hampshire (1908–21, 78 matches). *Tour* MCC to North America 1905.
Career batting
129–210–19–3005–78–15.73–0–*ct* 124
Bowling 9710–443–21.91–22–3–8/83

He also won a blue for golf.

McDonnell, Guy Francis Henry
Cricketer. *b:* 24.1.1963, Lytham, Lancashire. Middle order left-hand batsman, off break bowler. *Team* Cambridge U (1984).
Career batting
2–4–0–7–5–1.75–0–*ct* 0

MacDonnell, James Edward
Amateur. *b:* 23.4.1841, Ireland. *d:* 26.11.1891, Brighton, Sussex. Middle order batsman. *Team* Gloucestershire (1881, 1 match).
Career batting
1–1–0–0–0–0.00–0–*ct* 0

McDonnell, Percy Stanislaus
Amateur. *b:* 13.11.1858, Kennington, London. *d:* 24.9.1896, South Brisbane, Queensland, Australia. He died of heart disease. Fine attacking opening right-hand batsman, brilliant slip. *Teams* Victoria (1877/8 to 1884/5, 14 matches); New South Wales (1885/6 to 1891/2, 17 matches); Queensland (1894/5 to 1895/6, 3 matches). *Tours* Australia to England 1880, 1882, 1884, 1888. *Tests* Australia (1880–88, 19 matches).
Career batting
166–285–10–6474–239–23.54–7–*ct* 98
Bowling 247–2–123.50–0–0–1/7
Test batting
19–34–1–955–147–28.93–3–*ct* 6
Bowling 53–0
He was most successful on the 1888 tour to England, hitting 1,331 runs, av 23.35. He captained the side on this visit. He led Australia in six Tests, but was on the losing side in five of them. His only double century was 239 for New South Wales v Victoria at Melbourne in 1886/7.

McDougall, John Robson
Amateur. *b:* 2.3.1886, Galashiels, Selkirkshire, Scotland. *d:* 1.4.1971, Ayr, Scotland. Lower order right-hand batsman, wicket-keeper. *Team* Scotland (1912).
Career batting
1–2–0–15–12–7.50–0–*ct* 1

McDowall, James Ian
Cricketer. *b:* 9.12.1947, Sutton Coldfield, Warwickshire. Opening/middle order right-hand batsman, wicket-keeper. *Sch* Rugby. *Teams* Cambridge U (1969–70, blue 1969); Warwickshire (1969–73, 12 matches).
Career batting
29–53–5–811–89–16.89–0–*ct* 50–*st* 3
His father was Hon Treasurer of Warwickshire CCC 1962–79.

McEntyre, Kenneth Brinsley
Cricketer. *b:* 24.3.1944, Chester, Cheshire. Middle order right-hand batsman, good field. *Team* Surrey (1965–66, 3 matches).
Career batting
3–3–0–33–15–11.00–0–*ct* 0
He also played for Cheshire (1962–68).

McEvoy, Michael Stephen Anthony
Cricketer. *b:* 25.1.1956, Jorhat, Assam, India. Opening right-hand batsman, right-arm medium pace bowler. *Teams* Essex (1976–81, 43 matches); Worcestershire (1983–84, 26 matches). *Tour* Minor Counties to East Africa 1982/3 (not first-class).
Career batting
69–113–2–2128–103–19.17–1–*ct* 70
Bowling 103–3–34.33–0–0–3/20
He also played for Cambridgeshire (1982) and Suffolk (1985–92).

McEwan, Kenneth Scott
Cricketer. *b:* 16.7.1952, Bedford, Cape Province, South Africa. Middle order right-hand batsman, off break bowler, occasional wicket-keeper. *Teams* Eastern Province (1972/3 to 1989/90); Essex (1974–85, 282 matches); Western Australia (1979/80 to 1980/1, 18 matches); Western Province (1981/2 to 1987/8); Border (1991/2).
Career batting
428–705–67–26628–218–41.73–74–*ct* 359–*st* 7
Bowling 309–4–77.25–0–0–1/0
His first-class debut in England was for T. N. Pearce's XI in 1973. He hit 1,000 runs in a season twelve times, going on to 2,000 once – 2,176, av 64.00, in 1983. His highest score was 218 for Essex v Sussex at Chelmsford in 1977. He played unofficial Tests for South Africa against West Indies in 1983/4.

McEwan, Steven Michael
Cricketer. *b:* 5.5.1962, Worcester. Lower order right-hand batsman, right-arm fast medium bowler. *Sch* Worcester RGS. *Teams* Worcestershire (1985–90, 55 matches); Durham (1992, 10 matches).
Career batting
65–48–17–407–54–13.12–0–*ct* 24
Bowling 4869–156–31.21–3–0–6/34

McEwen, John William
Amateur. *b:* 25.11.1862, Dalston, London. *d:* 16.2.1902, Stepney, London. Lower order right-hand batsman, right-arm fast bowler. *Team* Middlesex (1884, 3 matches).
Career batting
3–5–0–13–8–2.60–0–*ct* 1
Bowling 126–4–31.50–0–0–3/37

MacFadyen, Air Marshal Sir Douglas
Amateur. *b:* 8.8.1902, Newcastle upon Tyne, Northumberland. *d:* 26.7.1968, Shurlock Row, Berkshire. Lower order batsman, useful bowler. *Sch* RGS, Newcastle. *Team* RAF (1929–31).
Career batting
2–4–0–11–9–2.75–0–*ct* 0
Bowling 63–2–31.50–0–0–2/59
His County cricket was for Northumberland (1919–20).

McFarlane, Andrew
Amateur. *b:* 21.6.1899, Sion Mills, Co Tyrone, Ireland. *d:* 14.6.1972, Londonderry, Ireland. Middle order right-hand batsman, off break bowler. *Team* Ireland (1937).
Career batting
1–2–0–23–23–11.50–0–*ct* 1

McFarlane, Leslie Leopold
Cricketer. *b:* 19.8.1952, Skibo, Portland, Jamaica. Tail end right-hand batsman, right-arm medium pace bowler. *Teams* Northamptonshire (1979, 8 matches); Lancashire (1982–84, 35 matches); Glamorgan

(1985, 13 matches).
Career batting
56–42–20–127–15*–5.77–0–*ct* 13
Bowling 4140–102–40.58–1–0–6/59

He also played for Bedfordshire (1981 and 1986) and Staffordshire (1989).

MacFarlane, Robert
Amateur. *b:* 29.4.1908, Uddingston, Lanarkshire, Scotland. *d:* 13.2.1986, Uddingston, Lanarkshire, Scotland. Middle order right-hand batsman, right-arm medium pace bowler. *Team* Scotland (1939).
Career batting
1–2–0–70–48–35.00–0–*ct* 0

McGahey, Charles Percy
Amateur. *b:* 12.2.1871, Hackney, London. *d:* 10.1.1935, Whipps Cross, Leytonstone, Essex. He died of septic poisoning. Attacking middle order right-hand batsman, leg break bowler. *Teams* Essex (1894–1921, 400 matches); London County (1901–04). *Tour* MacLaren to Australia 1901/2. *Tests* England (1901/2, 2 matches).
Career batting
437–751–65–20723–277–30.20–31–*ct* 151
Bowling 10300–330–31.21–12–3–7/27
Test batting
2–4–0–38–18–9.50–0–*ct* 1

He hit 1,000 runs in a season ten times (best 1,838, av 48.36, in 1901). His three double centuries were all for Essex, the highest being 277 v Derbyshire at Leyton in 1905. He captained Essex 1907 to 1910 and was for several years Assistant Secretary. From 1930 he was the County Scorer. He first played for Essex (pre first-class) in 1893. A good full-back he played soccer for Tottenham Hotspur, Clapton Orient, Arsenal and Sheffield United, as well as captaining representative teams of London and Middlesex.

McGaw, Alfred Joseph Thoburn
Amateur. *b:* 1.4.1900, Haslemere, Surrey. *d:* 8.2.1984, St Helier, Jersey, Channel Islands. Lower order right-hand batsman, slow right-arm bowler. *Sch* Charterhouse. *Teams* Sussex (1928, 2 matches); Punjab Governor's XI (1929/30).
Career batting
7–11–1–170–52–17.00–0–*ct* 3
Bowling 274–8–34.25–0–0–4/17

His final first-class match was for the Army in 1932, and he was a noted figure in military cricket in the 1930s.

MacGibbon, Anthony Roy
Amateur. *b:* 28.8.1924, Christchurch, New Zealand. Lower order right-hand batsman, right-arm fast medium bowler. *Team* Canterbury (1947/8 to 1961/2). *Tours* New Zealand to Australia and South Africa 1953/4, to India and Pakistan 1955/6, to England 1958. *Tests* New Zealand (1950/1 to 1958, 26 matches).
Career batting
124–206–20–3639–94–19.56–0–*ct* 82
Bowling 9301–356–26.12–8–0–7/56
Test batting
26–46–5–814–66–19.85–0–*ct* 13
Bowling 2160–70–30.85–1–0–5/64

He was easily the best bowler on the 1958 tour to England, taking 20 wickets, av 19.45, in the Tests – no other New Zealand bowler captured more than six wickets. In all first-class matches his record was 73, av 21.35.

McGibbon, Charles Edward
Amateur. *b:* 21.4.1880, Portsmouth, Hampshire. *d:* 2.4.1954, Hamble, Hampshire. Lower order batsman, useful bowler. *Team* Hampshire (1919, 1 match).
Career batting
1–2–1–1–1*–1.00–0–*ct* 0
Bowling 10–0

McGibbon, Lewis
Professional. *b:* 8.10.1931, Byker, Newcastle upon Tyne, Northumberland. Lower order right-hand batsman, right-arm medium pace in-swing bowler. *Team* Northamptonshire (1957–59, 13 matches).
Career batting
13–11–5–17–4–2.83–0–*ct* 2
Bowling 858–33–26.00–0–0–4/42

He also played for Northumberland (1950–57).

MacGinty, Raphael Joseph Anthony
Amateur. *b:* 22.3.1927, Croydon, Surrey. Tail end right-hand batsman, off break bowler. *Team* Cambridge U (1952).
Career batting
6–8–1–32–18–4.57–0–*ct* 4
Bowling 504–17–29.64–0–0–4/58

His County cricket was for Cambridgeshire (1951–52).

McGirr, Herbert Mendelson
Amateur. *b:* 5.11.1891, Wellington, New Zealand. *d:* 14.4.1964, Nelson, New Zealand. Son of W. P. (Wellington). Middle order right-hand batsman, right-arm medium pace bowler. *Team* Wellington (1913/14 to 1932/3). *Tours* New Zealand to England 1927, to Australia 1927/8. *Tests* New Zealand (1929/30, 2 matches).
Career batting
88–146–7–3992–141–28.71–5–*ct* 54
Bowling 6571–239–27.49–9–1–7/45
Test batting
2–1–0–51–51–51.00–0–*ct* 0
Bowling 115–1–115.00–0–0–1/65

On his visit to England he took 49 wickets, av 27.67, and scored 737 runs.

McGlew, Derrick John
Amateur. *b:* 11.3.1929, Pietermaritzburg, South Africa. Stubborn opening right-hand batsman, leg

break and googly bowler, brilliant cover field. *Team* Natal (1947/8 to 1966/7). *Tours* South Africa to England 1951, 1955, 1960, to Australia and New Zealand 1952/3. *Tests* South Africa (1951 to 1961/2, 34 matches).
Career batting
190–299–34–12170–255*–45.92–27–*ct* 103
Bowling 932–35–26.62–0–0–2/4
Test batting
34–64–6–2440–255*–42.06–7–*ct* 18
Bowling 23–0

He topped 1,000 runs in each of his three tours to England (best 1,871, av 58.46, in 1955). In 1955 he also headed the Test batting averages. He was vice-captain of the 1955 tourists and captain in 1960. In all he captained South Africa in 14 Tests.

He holds a curious record. During the Natal v Transvaal match at Durban in 1963/4, he performed a hat-trick, with two wickets in one innings and another in the other, yet at no time in his career did he capture more than two wickets in a single innings. His highest score was 255* for South Africa v New Zealand at Wellington in 1952/3.

McGrady, John Ewart
Cricketer. *b:* 30.4.1968, Ryton, Co Durham. Lower order right-hand batsman, wicket-keeper. *Team* Oxford U (1990).
Career batting
6–2–0–15–14–7.50–0–*ct* 0–*st* 2

MacGregor, Gregor
Amateur. *b:* 31.8.1869, Merchiston, Edinburgh, Scotland. *d:* 20.8.1919, Marylebone, London. Lower order right-hand batsman, wicket-keeper. *Sch* Uppingham. *Teams* Cambridge U (1888–91, blue all four years); Middlesex (1892–1907, 184 matches); Scotland (1905). *Tours* Sheffield to Australia 1891/2; MCC to North America 1907. *Tests* England (1890–93, 8 matches).
Career batting
265–412–58–6381–141–18.02–3–*ct* 411–*st* 148
Test batting
8–11–3–96–31–12.00–0–*ct* 14–*st* 3

He captained Cambridge in 1891 and Middlesex from 1899 to 1907. He was Middlesex Treasurer from 1916 until his death and a Test selector in 1902. A brilliant rugby footballer, he represented Cambridge and Scotland.

McGurk, Gordon Benedict John
Cricketer. *b:* 5.9.1965, Edinburgh, Scotland. Opening right-hand batsman. *Team* Scotland (1988).
Career batting
1–1–0–63–63–63.00–0–*ct* 3

Machin, Reginald Stanley
Amateur. *b:* 16.4.1904, Oatlands Park, Weybridge, Surrey. *d:* 3.11.1968, Wellingborough, Northamptonshire. Lower order right-hand batsman, wicket-keeper. *Sch* Lancing. *Teams* Cambridge U (1926–27, blue 1927); Surrey (1927–30, 8 matches).
Career batting
32–33–6–300–57–11.11–0–*ct* 57–*st* 14

His final first-class match was for Gentlemen in 1934.

McHugh, Francis Prest
Professional. *b:* 15.11.1925, Burmantofts, Leeds, Yorkshire. Lower order right-hand batsman, right-arm fast medium bowler. *Teams* Yorkshire (1949, 3 matches); Gloucestershire (1952–56, 92 matches).
Career batting
95–111–43–179–18–2.63–0–*ct* 24
Bowling 6857–276–24.84–15–4–7/32

His best season was 1954 when he took 92 wickets, av 20.00.

McIlwaine, Richard Johnston
Cricketer. *b:* 16.3.1950, Milton, Portsmouth, Hampshire. Lower order right-hand batsman, right-arm medium pace bowler. *Team* Hampshire (1969–70, 4 matches).
Career batting
4–3–1–29–17–14.50–0–0–*ct* 1
Bowling 273–4–68.25–0–0–2/40

McIlwraith, John
Amateur. *b:* 7.9.1857, Collingwood, Melbourne, Victoria, Australia. *d:* 5.7.1938, Camberwell, Melbourne, Victoria, Australia. Attacking middle order right-hand batsman. *Team* Victoria (1884/5 to 1889/90, 13 matches). *Tour* Australia to England 1886. *Test* Australia (1886, 1 match).
Career batting
44–68–7–1468–133–24.06–2–*ct* 24
Test batting
1–2–0–9–7–4.50–0–*ct* 1

He achieved very little on his tour to England.

Macindoe, David Henry
Amateur. *b:* 1.9.1917, Eton, Buckinghamshire. *d:* 3.3.1986, Eton, Buckinghamshire. Lower order right-hand batsman, right-arm medium fast bowler. *Sch* Eton. *Team* Oxford U (1937–39 and 1946, blue all four years).
Career batting
42–64–12–747–51–14.36–0–*ct* 38
Bowling 4339–152–28.54–5–1–6/61

His County cricket was for Buckinghamshire (1937–47). He captained Oxford in 1946.

McInerny, James Jeremy
Amateur. *b:* 12.4.1933, Paddington, London. Middle order right-hand batsman. *Sch* Christs Hospital. *Team* Oxford U (1955–56).
Career batting
2–3–0–25–22–8.33–0–*ct* 1

McIntosh, Robert Ian Fanshawe
Amateur. *b:* 19.8.1907, Darjeeling, India. *d:* 21.3.1988, Budleigh Salterton, Devon. Tail end right-hand batsman, right-arm medium fast bowler. *Sch* Uppingham. *Teams* Oxford U (1927–29, blue 1927–28); Madras (1933/4).
Career batting
24–32–18–161–23–11.50–0–*ct* 9
Bowling 2273–69–32.94–2–0–5/52
His County cricket was for Devon (1927).

McIntyre, Arthur John William
Professional. *b:* 14.5.1918, Kennington, London. Middle or lower order right-hand batsman, leg break bowler, wicket-keeper. *Team* Surrey (1938–63, 376 matches). *Tours* MCC to Australia and New Zealand 1950/1; Surrey to Rhodesia 1959/60. *Tests* England (1950–55, 3 matches).
Career batting
390–567–79–11145–143*–22.83–7–*ct* 639–*st* 156
Bowling 180–4–45.00–0–0–1/10
Test batting
3–6–0–19–7–3.16–0–*ct* 8
He hit 1,000 runs in a season three times (best 1,200, av 24.48, in 1949). He was appointed County coach to Surrey after the 1958 season, but continued to appear in first-class matches occasionally until 1963. He continued to coach, being latterly Cricket Manager, until 1979.

McIntyre, Arthur Seymour
Amateur. *b:* 29.5.1889, Hartley Wintney, Hampshire. *d:* 14.3.1945, Nottingham. Middle order right-hand batsman. *Sch* Blundells. *Team* Hampshire (1920–23, 28 matches).
Career batting
28–45–2–493–55–11.46–0–*ct* 15
Bowling 36–0

McIntyre, Euan James
Cricketer. *b:* 16.12.1951, Edinburgh, Scotland. Lower order right-hand batsman, off break bowler. *Team* Scotland (1981–83).
Career batting
2–3–1–7–6–3.50–0–*ct* 1
Bowling 39–0

McIntyre, Hugh
Professional. *b:* 16.1.1857, Milton, Glasgow, Scotland. *d:* 25.6.1905, Westminster, London. Lower order batsman, wicket-keeper. *Team* Lancashire (1884, 1 match).
Career batting
1–1–1–1–1*–no av–0–*ct* 1–*st* 2
A noted soccer player, he represented Glasgow Rangers and Scotland.

McIntyre, John McLachlan
Cricketer. *b:* 4.7.1944, Auckland, New Zealand. Lower order left-hand batsman, slow left-arm bowler. *Teams* Auckland (1961/2 to 1982/3); Canterbury (1965/6 to 1968/9). *Tour* New Zealand to England 1978.
Career batting
113–148–55–1668–87*–17.93–0–*ct* 46
Bowling 7917–336–23.56–10–1–6/84
He achieved only modest results on the 1978 tour of England and did not appear in the Tests.

McIntyre, Martin
Professional. *b:* 15.8.1847, Eastwood, Nottinghamshire. *d:* 28.2.1885, Moor Green, Nottinghamshire, Brother of Michael (Nottinghamshire) and William (Nottinghamshire and Lancashire). Middle order right-hand batsman, right-hand fast round-arm bowler. *Team* Nottinghamshire (1868–77, 45 matches). *Tour* Grace to Australia 1873/74 (not first-class).
Career batting
77–127–5–1992–88*–16.32–0–*ct* 33
Bowling 3374–194–17.39–12–2–9/33
His final first-class match was for an England XI v Cambridge U in 1878. He took 9/33 for Nottinghamshire v Surrey at the Oval in 1872.

McIntyre, Michael
Professional. *b:* 13.11.1839, St Anns, Nottingham. *d:* 9.10.1888, Basford, Nottinghamshire. Brother of Martin (Nottinghamshire) and William (Nottinghamshire and Lancashire). Lower order batsman, useful bowler. *Team* Nottinghamshire (1864, 1 match).
Career batting
3–5–1–44–23–11.00–0–*ct* 0
Bowling 78–4–19.50–0–0–2/30
His first-class debut was for the North v Surrey in 1863.

McIntyre, Terence Frank
Amateur. *b:* 2.7.1930, Hendon, Middlesex. Lower order right-hand batsman, wicket-keeper. *Team* Combined Services (1959–64).
Career batting
5–9–0–87–36–9.66–0–*ct* 5–*st* 2
His County cricket was for Bedfordshire (1957–60).

McIntyre, William
Professional. *b:* 24.5.1844, Eastwood, Nottinghamshire. *d:* 13.9.1892, Prestwich, Lancashire. Brother of Martin (Nottinghamshire) and Michael (Nottinghamshire). Lower order right-hand batsman, right-arm fast bowler. *Teams* Nottinghamshire (1869–71, 14 matches); Lancashire (1872–80, 72 matches).
Career batting
97–151–24–1323–99–10.41–0–*ct* 69
Bowling 6436–510–12.61–53–14–8/31

He headed the first-class bowling averages for three seasons – 1872, 41 wickets, av 5.65; 1873, 63, av 8.38; 1876, 89, av 11.41, being for a few years one of the best bowlers in England. He also played for Northamptonshire (pre first-class, 1869).

McIver, Colin Donald
Amateur. *b:* 23.1.1881, Hong Kong. *d:* 13.5.1954, Worcester College, Oxford, whilst on a visit. Middle order right-hand batsman, slow right-arm bowler, wicket-keeper. *Sch* Forest. *Teams* Essex (1902–22, 59 matches); Oxford U (1903–04, blue both years).
Career batting
134–227–18–4651–134–22.25–5–*ct* 98–*st* 24
Bowling 40–1–40.00–0–0–1/4

He hit 1,197 runs, av 30.69, in 1914. His final first-class match was for MCC in 1934; he continued to play in club matches for MCC until over 60. A good soccer player he was centre-forward for Essex and won his blue and an England amateur international cap.

Mack, Andrew James
Cricketer. *b:* 14.1.1956, Aylsham, Norfolk. Lower order left-hand batsman, left-arm medium pace bowler. *Teams* Surrey (1976–77, 10 matches); Glamorgan (1978–80, 21 matches).
Career batting
31–32–10–102–18–4.63–0–*ct* 4
Bowling 1889–44–42.93–0–0–4/28

He also played for Norfolk (1989–91).

Mackay, Claude Lysaght
Amateur. *b:* 29.10.1894, Satara, India. *d:* 7.6.1915, Boulogne, France. He died of wounds received in action. Middle order right-hand batsman, right-arm fast medium bowler. *Sch* Clifton. *Team* Gloucestershire (1914, 1 match).
Career batting
1–2–0–28–15–14.00–0–*ct* 1
Bowling 24–0

He played in trials at Cambridge U, but not in first-class matches. He was a noted athlete and represented the public schools as a heavyweight boxer.

Mackay, Daniel Alexander
Amateur. *b:* 12.3.1894, Glasgow, Scotland. *d:* 13.5.1951, Pollockshaws, Glasgow, Scotland. Middle order right-hand batsman, right-arm medium pace bowler. *Team* Scotland (1923–30).
Career batting
8–14–0–203–68–14.50–0–*ct* 2
Bowling 40–3–13.33–0–0–3/35

Mackay, Kenneth Donald, MBE
Amateur. *b:* 24.10.1925, Windsor, Queensland, Australia. *d:* 13.6.1982, Point Lookout, Stradbroke Island, Queensland, Australia. Very stubborn middle order left-hand batsman, right-arm medium pace bowler. *Team* Queensland (1946/7 to 1963/4, 109 matches). *Tours* Australia to England 1956, 1961, to South Africa 1957/8, to India 1956/7, to India and Pakistan 1959/60. *Tests* Australia (1956 to 1962/3, 37 matches).
Career batting
201–294–46–10823–223–43.64–23–*ct* 84
Bowling 8363–251–33.31–7–0–6/42
Test batting
37–52–7–1507–89–33.48–0–*ct* 16
Bowling 1721–50–34.42–2–0–6/42

On his 1956 tour to England he headed the first-class batting averages, 1,103 runs, av 52.52, but failed utterly in the Tests. He had only a modest tour in 1961, though appearing in all five Tests. His highest score was 223 for Queensland v Victoria at Brisbane in 1953/4.

Mackay, William Gilfellon
Amateur. *b:* 1892. *d:* 8.8.1962, High Heaton, Newcastle upon Tyne, Northumberland. Middle order right-hand batsman. *Team* Minor Counties (1929).
Career batting
1 match, did not bat–*ct* 0

His County cricket was for Northumberland (1920–39).

McKee, William D.
Amateur. *b:* 27.8.1923, Belfast, Ireland. *d:* September 1986. Tail end right-hand batsman, right-arm fast medium bowler. *Team* Ireland (1946).
Career batting
1–1–0–16–16–16.00–0–*ct* 2
Bowling 57–0

He played rugby for Ireland.

McKelvey, Dr James Moorhead
Amateur. *b:* 2.4.1933, Belfast, Ireland. Middle order left-hand batsman. *Sch* Campbell College. *Team* Ireland (1954).
Career batting
2–4–0–25–9–6.25–0–*ct* 1

A noted rugby union footballer, he was capped for Ireland.

McKelvey, Patrick George
Professional. *b:* 25.12.1935, Barnet, Hertfordshire. Lower order right-hand batsman, slow left-arm bowler. *Team* Surrey (1959–60, 2 matches).
Career batting
2 matches, did not bat–*ct* 1
Bowling 19–1–19.00–0–0–1/7

McKelvie, Robert Douglas
Amateur. *b:* 1.7.1912, Blofield, Norfolk. Lower order right-hand batsman, wicket-keeper. *Sch* Malvern. *Team* Free Foresters (1948).
Career batting
1–2–0–22–12–11.00–0–*ct* 1

His County cricket was for Buckinghamshire (1947).

Mackenna, Robert Ogilvie
Amateur. *b:* 21.3.1913, Paisley, Renfrewshire, Scotland. Lower order right-hand batsman, right-arm fast medium bowler. *Team* Scotland (1938–46).
Career batting
2–4–1–8–4*–2.66–0–*ct* 0
Bowling 129–2–64.50–0–0–1/20

MacKenzie, Lord Charles Kincaid
Amateur. *b:* 9.3.1857, Edinburgh, Scotland. *d:* 1.4.1938, New Town, Edinburgh, Scotland. Father of M. K. (Oxford U). Lower order right-hand batsman, useful bowler. *Sch* Repton. *Team* Oxford U (1876).
Career batting
1–2–1–10–8*–10.00–0–*ct* 0
Bowling 3–0
He won a blue for golf.

MacKenzie, Frederick Finch
Amateur. *b:* 14.7.1849, Kensington, London. *d:* 17.7.1934, Hove, Sussex. Middle order right-hand batsman, right-hand medium round-arm bowler. *Sch* Wellington. *Team* Kent (1880, 2 matches).
Career batting
2–3–0–6–4–2.00–0–*ct* 2
He did not play in first-class matches whilst at Oxford U. He also played for Shropshire (1871).

McKenzie, Graham Douglas
Amateur. *b:* 24.6.1941, Cottesloe, Perth, Western Australia. Son of E. N. (Western Australia), nephew of D. C. (Western Australia). Lower order right-hand batsman, right-arm medium fast bowler. *Teams* Western Australia (1959/60 to 1973/4, 81 matches); Leicestershire (1969–75, 151 matches). *Tours* Australia to England 1961, 1964, 1968, to South Africa 1966/7, 1969/70, to West Indies 1964/5, to India and Pakistan 1964/5, to Ceylon and India 1969/70; Rest of World to West Indies 1966/7, to England 1966, 1967, 1968, 1970; Cavaliers to India and South Africa 1962/3; International Wanderers to Rhodesia 1972/3, to South Africa 1974/5. *Tests* Australia (1961 to 1970/1, 60 matches).
Career batting
383–471–109–5662–76–15.64–0–*ct* 201
Bowling 32868–1219–26.96–49–5–8/71
Test batting
60–89–12–945–76–12.27–0–*ct* 34
Bowling 7328–246–29.78–16–3–8/71
Of his three tours to England easily his best was in 1964 when he took 88 wickets, av 22.45, in first-class matches and headed the Test averages with 29 wickets, av 22.55. He was at the time the youngest player ever to achieve the milestones of 100, 150 and 200 Test wickets in a career. He played for Transvaal in 1979/80 in limited overs matches.

Mackenzie, K. A. M.
(*see under* Muir-Mackenzie, K. A.)

MacKenzie, Mark Kincaid
Amateur. *b:* 22.8.1888, New Town, Edinburgh, Scotland. *d:* 25.9.1914, Soupir, Soissons, France. He was killed in action. Son of C. K. (Oxford U). Lower order batsman, left-arm fast medium bowler. *Sch* Winchester. *Team* Oxford U (1910).
Career batting
3–5–1–65–48*–16.25–0–*ct* 3
Bowling 185–6–30.83–0–0–2/65

MacKenzie, Percy Alec
Professional. *b:* 5.10.1918, Canterbury, Kent. *d:* 1.1.1989, Rye, Sussex. Middle order right-hand batsman, leg break and googly bowler. *Team* Hampshire (1938–39, 22 matches).
Career batting
22–36–3–652–76–19.75–0–*ct* 11
Bowling 605–17–35.58–0–0–4/34
He also played for Berkshire (1947–48).

Mackenzie, Robert Theodore Hope
Amateur. *b:* 8.10.1886, Poona, India. *d:* 20.3.1934, New Delhi, India. Forcing middle order right-hand batsman, right-arm fast bowler. *Sch* Cheltenham. *Teams* Gloucestershire (1907, 2 matches); Cambridge U (1907–08).
Career batting
4–7–0–38–21–5.42–0–*ct* 2
Bowling 84–3–28.00–0–0–2/30
He also played for Devon (1905–06).

MacKenzie, William Forbes
Amateur. *b:* 5.6.1907, Salisbury, Rhodesia. *d:* 1.8.1980, Salisbury, Zimbabwe. Tail end right-hand batsman, right-arm fast medium bowler. *Sch* Merchiston. *Team* Cambridge U (1927).
Career batting
1–1–0–1–1–1.00–0–*ct* 0
Bowling 150–9–16.66–1–0–5/50

Mackeson, William James
Amateur. *b:* 7.12.1856, Kensington, London. *d:* 21.7.1925, Atcham, Shropshire. Middle order batsman. *Sch* Harrow. *Team* MCC (1883).
Career batting
1–2–0–8–7–4.00–0–*ct* 0
His County cricket was for Shropshire (1907).

Mackessack, Douglas
Amateur. *b:* 7.10.1903, Alves, Morayshire, Scotland. *d:* 28.10.1987, Inverugie, Morayshire, Scotland. Brother of Kenneth (Army). Middle order right-hand batsman, useful bowler. *Sch* Rugby. *Team* Scotland (1927).
Career batting
1–2–0–27–14–13.50–0–*ct* 2
Bowling 51–0

Mackessack, Kenneth
Amateur. *b:* 24.10.1902, Alves, Morayshire, Scotland. *d:* 18.10.1982, Elgin, Morayshire, Scotland.

Brother of Douglas (Scotland). Tail end batsman, good bowler. *Sch* Rugby. *Teams* Army (1926); Northern Punjab (1926/7); Europeans (1927/8).
Career batting
4–5–2–34–20*–11.33–0–*ct* 2
Bowling 200–8–25.00–0–0–3/42

McKibbin, David Gordon Robinson
Amateur. *b:* 16.6.1912, Comber, Co Down, Ireland. Opening right-hand batsman, leg break bowler. *Team* Ireland (1937).
Career batting
1–2–0–46–31–23.00–0–*ct* 0

McKibbin, Thomas Robert
Amateur. *b:* 10.12.1870, Raglan, Bathurst, New South Wales, Australia. *d:* 15.12.1939, Macquarie Plains Homestead, Bathurst, New South Wales, Australia. Lower order left-hand batsman, right-arm medium pace or off break bowler, good slip field. *Team* New South Wales (1894/5 to 1898/9, 25 matches). *Tour* Australia to England and North America 1896. *Tests* Australia (1894/5 to 1897/8, 5 matches).
Career batting
57–92–24–682–75–10.02–0–*ct* 46
Bowling 6297–320–19.67–28–11–9/68
Test batting
5–8–2–88–28–14.66–0–*ct* 4
Bowling 496–17–29.17–0–0–3/35
He was the leading bowler on the 1896 tour to England, taking 101 wickets, av 14.26, but the fairness of his delivery was questioned by some.
His best bowling was 9/68 for New South Wales v Queensland at Brisbane in 1894/5.

McKiddie, Gavin Thomson
Cricketer. *b:* 17.5.1940, Forfar, Angus, Scotland. Tail end right-hand batsman, off break bowler. *Team* Scotland (1977).
Career batting
1–2–0–10–8–5.00–0–*ct* 1
Bowling 41–2–20.50–0–0–1/3

McKinna, Gordon Hayden
Amateur. *b:* 2.8.1930, Sale, Cheshire. Lower order right-hand batsman, right-arm medium pace bowler. *Sch* Manchester GS. *Team* Oxford U (1951–53, blue 1953).
Career batting
6–8–2–40–18–6.66–0–*ct* 1
Bowling 391–17–23.00–0–0–4/39
His final first-class match was for Combined Services in 1955. His County cricket was for Cheshire (1949–53). He also won a blue for soccer.

McKinnon, Atholl Henry
Amateur. *b:* 20.8.1932, Port Elizabeth, South Africa. *d:* 1.12.1983, Durban, South Africa. Father of G. P. (Eastern Province). Lower order right-hand batsman, slow left-arm bowler. *Teams* Eastern Province (1952/3 to 1962/3); Transvaal (1963/4 to 1968/9). *Tours* South Africa to England 1960, 1965. *Tests* South Africa (1960 to 1966/67, 8 matches).
Career batting
111–152–39–1687–62–14.92–0–*ct* 32
Bowling 9937–470–21.14–38–9–7/37
Test batting
8–13–7–107–27–17.83–0–*ct* 1
Bowling 925–26–35.57–0–0–4/128
On the 1960 tour, he appeared in one Test and ought to have been given more opportunities early in the season; he took 53 wickets, av 20.88, in first-class matches. On the short tour of 1965 he appeared in two Tests and proved to be most effective.

MacKinnon, Donald William
Amateur. *b:* 3.3.1842, Bangalore, India. *d:* 19.11.1931, Stakes, Waterlooville, Hampshire. Middle order batsman, useful bowler. *Team* Lancashire (1870–71, 3 matches).
Career batting
4–7–0–112–42–16.00–0–*ct* 4
Bowling 132–7–18.85–0–0–3/13

MacKinnon of MacKinnon, Francis Alexander
Amateur. *b:* 9.4.1848, Paddington, London. *d:* 27.2.1947, Drumduan, Forres, Morayshire, Scotland. Steady middle order right-hand batsman. *Sch* Harrow. *Teams* Cambridge U (1870, blue); Kent (1875–85, 78 matches). *Tour* Harris to Australia 1878/9. *Test* England (1878/9, 1 match).
Career batting
88–162–15–2310–115–15.71–2–*ct* 38
Test batting
1–2–0–5–5–2.50–0–*ct* 0
He was President of Kent in 1889.

MacKinnon, James Curdie
Amateur. *b:* 10.1.1865, Terang, Melbourne, Victoria, Australia. *d:* 4.7.1957, Melbourne, Victoria, Australia. Lower order right-hand batsman, slow left-arm bowler. *Team* Cambridge U (1886–88).
Career batting
5–8–2–31–11*–5.16–0–*ct* 3
Bowling 236–4–59.00–0–0–2/39

Mackinnon, Malcolm
Amateur. *b:* 11.5.1891, Toward Point, Argyll, Scotland. *d:* 13.2.1975, Sunningdale, Berkshire. Middle order right-hand batsman, off break bowler. *Teams* Essex (1927, 3 matches); Europeans (1927/8 to 1934/5).
Career batting
6–10–0–122–31–12.20–0–*ct* 3
He did not appear in first-class cricket whilst at Oxford.

Mackintosh, Dr David Stewart
Cricketer. *b:* 18.2.1947, Paisley, Renfrewshire, Scotland. Opening right-hand batsman. *Team* Scotland

(1972).
Career batting
1–2–0–66–57–33.00–0–*ct* 0
His County cricket was for Buckinghamshire (1971–76).

Mackintosh, Kevin Scott
Cricketer. *b:* 30.8.1957, Surbiton, Surrey. Lower order right-hand batsman, right-arm fast medium bowler. *Sch* Kingston GS. *Teams* Nottinghamshire (1978–80, 19 matches); Surrey (1981–83, 14 matches).
Career batting
33–33–17–303–31–18.93–0–*ct* 14
Bowling 2092–59–35.45–1–0–6/61

McKnight, Craig Thomas
Cricketer. *b:* 6.9.1969, Bellshill, Lanarkshire, Scotland. Lower order left-hand batsman, slow left-arm bowler. *Team* Scotland (1990).
Career batting
1–1–0–0–0–0.00–0–*ct* 1
Bowling 72–3–24.00–0–0–3/48

MacLachlan, Andrew
Amateur. *b:* 27.2.1941, Trearrdur Bay, Anglesey. Lower order right-hand batsman, right-arm medium pace bowler. *Sch* St Edwards, Oxford. *Team* Oxford U (1962).
Career batting
5–10–3–99–28–14.14–0–*ct* 1
Bowling 239–3–79.66–0–0–1/49

McLachlan, Angus Alexander
Cricketer. *b:* 11.11.1944, North Adelaide, South Australia. Brother of I. M. (South Australia and Cambridge U). Lower order right-hand batsman, leg break and googly bowler. *Team* Cambridge U (1964–65, blue both years).
Career batting
17–28–3–232–27–9.28–0–*ct* 8
Bowling 1198–32–37.43–0–0–4/36

McLachlan, Ian Murray
Amateur. *b:* 2.10.1936, Norh Adelaide, South Australia. Brother of A. A. (Cambridge U). Opening right-hand batsman, leg break bowler. *Teams* Cambridge U (1956–58, blue 1957 and 1958); South Australia (1960/1 to 1963/4, 31 matches). *Tour* Swanton to West Indies 1960/1.
Career batting
72–128–10–3743–188*–31.72–9–*ct* 41
Bowling 382–6–63.66–0–0–2/33

MacLachlan, Norman
Amateur. *b:* 12.10.1858, Darlington, Co Durham. *d:* 18.2.1928, Torquay, Devon. Tail end right-hand batsman, right-arm fast medium bowler, good deep field. *Sch* Loretto. *Team* Oxford U (1879–82, blue all four years).
Career batting
20–34–4–252–27–8.40–0–*ct* 15
Bowling 675–38–17.76–1–0–6/40
His County cricket was for Cheshire (1884). He captained Oxford in 1882. He was also a noted rugby footballer, being awarded his blue as a back.

MacLaren, Archibald Campbell
Amateur. *b:* 1.12.1871, Whalley Range, Manchester, Lancashrie. *d:* 17.11.1944, Warfield Park, Bracknell, Berkshire. Brother of J. A. (Lancashire) and G. (Lancashire), son-in-law of R. Power (Victoria), his mother married A. B. Rowley (Lancashire) in 1901. Attacking opening right-hand batsman, right-arm fast bowler, good slip field. *Sch* Harrow. *Team* Lancashire (1890–1914, 308 matches). *Tours* Stoddart to Australia 1894/5, 1897/8; MacLaren to Australia 1901/2; Ranjitsinhji to North America 1899; MCC to South America 1911/12, to New Zealand and Australia 1922/3. *Tests* England (1894/5 to 1909, 35 matches).
Career batting
424–703–52–22236–424–34.15–47–*ct* 453
Bowling 267–1–267.00–0–0–1/44
Test batting
35–61–4–1931–140–33.87–5–*ct* 29
Holder of the highest innings record in first-class English cricket with 424 for Lancashire against Somerset at Taunton in 1895, MacLaren is also regarded by some contemporaries as England's best captain. Everyone is agreed that he was a great tactical expert, but whilst he led his country in 22 Tests he was criticised for his part in the selection of some of the England teams. At the end of his career however he silenced his critics by choosing a side to meet the strong 1921 Australian team and, against all odds, beating them when everyone else had failed.

On his three tours to Australia – he captained the 1897/8 and 1901/2 Test sides there – he batted quite brilliantly, but in England the damper climate aggravated his lumbago, so that he was not such a prolific scorer. In spite of this he hit 1,000 runs in a season eight times, the best year being 1903 with 1,886 runs, av 42.86. Apart from his 424 he hit three other scores above 200 for Lancashire and one each in Australia and New Zealand. He also hit 1,000 runs in an Australian season. He score 108 on debut for Lancashire v Sussex at Hove in 1890.

From 1894 to 1896 and from 1899 to 1907 he captained Lancashire. At the end of its life he managed the weekly magazine *Cricket*, which ceased publication in 1914. His final first-class match in England was for England XI in 1921.

MacLaren, Frederic Grahame
Amateur. *b:* 5.11.1875, Worsley, Manchester, Lancashire. *d:* 10.5.1952, Bowdon, Cheshire. Middle order batsman, useful bowler, good slip field. *Sch* Fettes. *Team* Lancashire (1903, 1 match).

Career batting
1–2–0–19–19–9.50–0–*ct* 0
Bowling 7–0
He also played for Cheshire (1909–10).

McLaren, Frederick Albert
Amateur. *b:* 19.8.1874, Farnham, Surrey. *d:* 23.9.1952, Dartford, Kent. Lower order batsman, useful bowler. *Team* Hampshire (1908, 2 matches).
Career batting
2–3–0–4–4–1.33–0–0–*ct* 1
Bowling 114–4–28.50–0–0–2/30

MacLaren, Geoffrey
Amateur. *b:* 28.2.1883, Whalley Range, Manchester, Lancashire. *d:* 14.9.1966, Bexhill-on-Sea, Sussex. Brother of A. C. (Lancashire) and J. A. (Lancashire), his mother married A. B. Rowley (Lancashire) in 1901. Lower order batsman, useful bowler. *Sch* Harrow. *Team* Lancashire (1902, 2 matches).
Career batting
2–4–0–7–3–1.75–0–*ct* 0
Bowling 13–2–6.50–0–0–1/5

MacLaren, Dr James Alexander
Amateur. *b:* 4.1.1870, Whalley Range, Manchester, Lancashire. *d:* 8.7.1952, Odstock, Salisbury, Wiltshire. Brother of A. C. (Lancashire) and Geoffrey (Lancashire), his mother married A. B. Rowley (Lancashire) in 1901. Hard hitting middle order right-hand batsman, slip field. *Sch* Harrow. *Team* Lancashire (1891–94, 4 matches).
Career batting
4–4–0–9–6–2.25–0–*ct* 4

McLaren, John William
Amateur. *b:* 22.12.1886, Toowong, Brisbane, Queensland, Australia. *d:* 17.11.1921, Highgate Hill, Brisbane, Queensland, Australia. He died from diabetes. Lower order right-hand batsman, right-arm fast bowler. *Team* Queensland (1906/7 to 1914/15, 18 matches). *Tour* Australia to England and North America 1912. *Test* Australia (1911/12, 1 match).
Career batting
34–59–14–564–43*–12.53–0–*ct* 8
Bowling 2862–107–26.74–3–0–5/55
Test batting
1–2–2–0–0*–no av–0–*ct* 0
Bowling 70–1–70.00–0–0–1/23
He was very much one of the reserves on the 1912 tour of England, his record in first-class matches being a modest one.

McLaren, Robert Stewart
Amateur. *b:* 10.5.1919, Perth, Scotland. Lower order right-hand batsman, wicket-keeper. *Team* Scotland (1947–49).
Career batting
6–10–2–23–7–2.87–0–*ct* 6–*st* 7

MacLarnon, Patrick Craig
Cricketer. *b:* 24.9.1963, Nottingham. Lower order right-hand batsman, right-arm medium pace bowler. *Team* Oxford U (1985–86, blue 1985).
Career batting
11–15–2–177–56–13.61–0–*ct* 3
Bowling 318–3–106.00–0–0–2/25

MacLaurin, Neil Ralph Charter
Cricketer. *b:* 22.3.1966, Welwyn Garden City, Hertfordshire. Middle order right-hand batsman, right-arm medium pace bowler. *Sch* Malvern. *Team* Middlesex (1988, 1 match).
Career batting
1–2–0–37–35–18.50–0–*ct* 0
Bowling 4–0
He also played for Hertfordshire (1989–92).

McLean, Douglas Hamilton
Amateur. *b:* 18.3.1863, Westbrook, Darling Downs, Queensland, Australia. *d:* 5.2.1901, Johannesburg, South Africa. He died from colitis. Middle order batsman. *Sch* Eton. *Team* Somerset (1896, 1 match).
Career batting
1–2–1–13–9*–13.00–0–*ct* 0
He played no first-class cricket whilst at Oxford U, but won five rowing blues (1883–87).

MacLean, John Francis
Amateur. *b:* 1.3.1901, Morwick Hill, Acklington, Northumberland. *d:* 9.3.1986, Ross-on-Wye, Herefordshire. Son of M. F. (MCC). Middle order right-hand batsman, wicket-keeper. *Sch* Eton. *Teams* Worcestershire (1922–24, 45 matches); Gloucestershire (1930–32, 6 matches). *Tour* MCC to Australia and New Zealand 1922/3.
Career batting
69–113–15–1812–121–18.48–1–*ct* 60–*st* 43
His first-class debut was in 1919 for H. K. Foster's XI.

McLean, Leslie Eric
Amateur. *b:* 19.4.1918, Lynton, Devon. *d:* 16.12.1987, Guildford, Surrey. Opening right-hand batsman. *Sch* Bishop's Stortford. *Team* Oxford U (1939).
Career batting
3–6–0–79–51–13.16–0–*ct* 3
His County cricket was for Hertfordshire (1936–39).

MacLean, Montague Francis
Amateur. *b:* 12.9.1870, Kensington, London. *d:* 14.1.1951, Ross-on-Wye, Herefordshire. Father of J. F. (Worcestershire and Gloucestershire). Middle order batsman, change bowler. *Sch* Eton. *Team* MCC (1893). *Tour* Hawke to India 1892/3.
Career batting
5–8–5–65–25–21.66–0–*ct* 3
Bowling 31–0

McLean, Roy Alastair
Amateur. *b:* 9.7.1930, Pietermaritzburg, South Africa. Aggressive middle order right-hand batsman, right-arm slow bowler. *Team* Natal (1949/50 to 1965/6). *Tours* South Africa to England 1951, 1955, 1960, to Australia and New Zealand 1952/3; SA Fezela to England 1961; Commonwealth to New Zealand 1961/2. *Tests* South Africa (1951 to 1964/5, 40 matches).
Career batting
200–318–19–10969–207–36.68–22–*ct* 132
Bowling 122–2–61.00–0–0–2/22
Test batting
40–73–3–2120–142–30.28–5–*ct* 23
Bowling 1–0
He hit 1,000 runs on both the 1955 and 1960 visits (best 1,516, av 37.90, in 1960). Possibly his most noteworthy innings in England was 142 in the Lord's Test of 1955, the runs being hit out of 196. His highest score was 207 for South Africans v Worcestershire at Worcester in 1960.

MacLeay, Kenneth Hervey
Cricketer. *b:* 2.4.1959, Bradford-on-Avon, Wiltshire. Middle order right-hand batsman, right-arm medium pace bowler. *Teams* Western Australia (1981/2 to 1991/2, 100 matches); Somerset (1991–92, 27 matches). *Tours* Young Australia to Zimbabwe 1982/3; Australia to England 1983 (World Cup); Western Australia to India 1989/90.
Career batting
129–173–34–3750–114*–26.97–3–*ct* 79
Bowling 9080–300–30.26–6–0–6/93
He played in one-day internationals for Australia, thus losing his English qualification until 1991.

McLellan, Alan James
Cricketer. *b:* 2.9.1958, Ashton-under-Lyne, Lancashire. Lower order right-hand batsman, wicket-keeper. *Team* Derbyshire (1978–79, 26 matches).
Career batting
26–24–8–99–41–6.18–0–*ct* 41–*st* 2

MacLeod, Alister
Amateur. *b:* 12.11.1894, Kensington, London. *d:* 24.4.1982, Broomfield, Essex. Middle order right-hand batsman. *Sch* Felsted. *Team* Hampshire (1914–38, 12 matches).
Career batting
12–18–0–271–87–15.05–0–*ct* 5
He was Secretary of Hampshire 1936–39.

McLeod, Charles Edward
Amateur. *b:* 24.10.1869, Sandridge (now Port Melbourne), Victoria, Australia. *d:* 26.11.1918, Toorak, Melbourne, Victoria, Australia. Brother of R. W. (Victoria) and D. H. (Victoria). Opening right-hand batsman, right-arm medium pace bowler. *Team* Victoria (1893/4 to 1903/4, 41 matches). *Tours* Australia to England 1899, 1905, to New Zealand 1904/5. *Tests* Australia (1894/5 to 1905, 17 matches).
Career batting
114–179–23–3321–112–21.28–2–*ct* 61
Bowling 8124–335–24.25–22–4–7/34
Test batting
17–29–5–573–112–23.87–1–*ct* 9
Bowling 1325–33–40.15–2–0–5/65
He put in some useful performances on both tours to England, but achieved nothing outstanding.

MacLeod, Kenneth Grant
Amateur. *b:* 2.2.1888, Liverpool, Lancashire. *d:* 7.3.1967, St James, Cape Province, South Africa. Middle/lower order right-hand batsman, right-arm fast bowler. *Sch* Fettes. *Teams* Cambridge U (1908–09, blue both years); Lancashire (1908–13, 75 matches).
Career batting
94–161–16–3458–131–23.84–6–*ct* 107
Bowling 2748–103–26.67–2–1–6/29
He hit 1,361 runs, av 28.95, in 1911. His final first-class match was for Free Foresters in 1914. A noted rugby footballer, he represented both Cambridge and Scotland as a wing threequarter; he also appeared for his University as a 100 yards sprinter and in the long jump.

MacLeod, Kenneth Walcott
Cricketer. *b:* 18.3.1964, Fyffes Pen, Jamaica. Lower order right-hand batsman, left-arm fast medium bowler. *Teams* Jamaica 1983/4 to 1987/8); Lancashire (1987, 6 matches).
Career batting
13–17–1–128–31–8.00–0–*ct* 4
Bowling 897–28–32.03–2–0–5/8

McLeod, Robert William
Amateur. *b:* 19.1.1868, Sandridge (now Port Melbourne), Victoria, Australia. *d:* 14.6.1907, Middle Park, Melbourne, Victoria, Australia. Brother of C. E. (Victoria) and D. H. (Victoria). Correct middle order left-hand batsman, right-arm medium pace bowler. *Team* Victoria (1889/90 to 1899/1900, 26 matches). *Tour* Australia to England and North America 1893. *Tests* Australia (1891/2 to 1893, 6 matches).
Career batting
57–95–19–1701–101–22.38–1–*ct* 39
Bowling 3204–141–22.72–7–2–7/24
Test batting
6–11–0–146–31–13.27–0–*ct* 3
Bowling 382–12–31.83–1–0–5/55
He achieved modest success on the 1893 tour, and appeared in all three Tests.

McMahon, John William Joseph
Professional. *b:* 28.12.1917, Balaklava, South Australia. Lower order left-hand batsman, slow left-arm bowler. *Teams* Surrey (1947–53, 84 matches); Somerset (1954–57, 115 matches).

Career batting
201–285–125–989–24–6.18–0–*ct* 109
Bowling 16289–590–27.60–30–2–8/46

His best season was 1956 when he took 103 wickets, av 25.57, and twice he took 8 for 46 in an innings – for Surrey v Northamptonshire at the Oval in 1948 and for Somerset v Kent at Yeovil in 1955.

McMahon, Dr William John Alexander
Amateur. *b:* 13.7.1894, Richhill, Co Armagh, Ireland. *d:* December 1974, Dublin, Ireland. Lower order batsman, useful bowler. *Team* Dublin U (1925–26).
Career batting
3–6–1–23–18–4.60–0–*ct* 4
Bowling 178–2–89.00–0–0–2/92

McMaster, Michael
Amateur. *b:* 11.5.1896, Minehead, Somerset. *d:* 29.3.1965, Brook, Isle of Wight. Lower order batsman, useful bowler. *Team* Royal Navy (1920).
Career batting
1–2–1–13–7*–13.00–0–*ct* 1
Bowling 73–1–73.00–0–0–1/55

McMillan, Brian Mervin
Cricketer. *b:* 22.12.1963, Welkom, Orange Free State, South Africa. Middle order right-hand batsman, right-arm medium fast bowler. *Teams* Transvaal (1984/5 to 1988/9); Warwickshire (1986, 12 matches); Western Province (1989/90 to 1991/2). *Tours* South Africa to India 1991/2 (not first-class), to Australia and New Zealand (World Cup) 1991/2.
Career batting
66–108–18–3377–136–37.52–5–*ct* 61
Bowling 4165–159–26.19–3–0–5/39

Although engaged as a fast bowler by Warwickshire in 1986, he made a greater impact as a batsman, hitting 999 runs, av 58.76, and finishing fifth in the overall first-class averages. He played for South Africa in unofficial Tests.

McMillan, Quintin
Amateur. *b:* 23.6.1904, Germiston, Transvaal, South Africa. *d:* 3.7.1948, Randfontein, Transvaal, South Africa. He died from heart disease and nephritis. Hard hitting right-hand batsman, leg break and googly bowler. *Team* Transvaal (1928/9 to 1929/30). *Tours* South Africa to England 1929, to Australia and New Zealand 1931/2. *Tests* South Africa (1929 to 1931/2, 13 matches).
Career batting
50–76–16–1607–185*–26.78–1–*ct* 30
Bowling 5033–189–26.62–12–2–9/53
Test batting
13–21–4–306–50*–18.00–0–*ct* 8
Bowling 1243–36–34.52–2–0–5/66

On the 1929 tour he took most first-class wickets – 91, av 25.45 – but was ineffective in the Tests. He retired from important cricket early for business reasons, his final first-class match in South Africa being in 1930/1. His best bowling was 9/53 for South Africans v South Australians at Adelaide in 1931/2.

McMillan, Stuart Thomas
Professional. *b:* 17.9.1896, Leicester. *d:* 27.9.1963, Ashbourne, Derbyshire. Lower order right-hand batsman, right-arm medium fast bowler. *Team* Derbyshire (1922–24, 4 matches).
Career batting
4–6–2–30–24–7.50–0–*ct* 0
Bowling 14–0

A noted soccer player, he appeared for Derby County, Gillingham, Wolverhampton Wanderers, Bradford City, Chelsea, Nottingham Forest and Clapton Orient.

McMorris, Easton Dudley Ashton St John
Amateur. *b:* 4.4.1935, St Andrew, Kingston, Jamaica. Sound opening right-hand batsman, off break bowler. *Team* Jamaica (1956/7 to 1971/2). *Tours* West Indies to England 1963, 1966; Jamaica to England 1970. *Tests* West Indies (1957/8 to 1966, 13 matches).
Career batting
95–158–18–5906–218–42.18–18–*ct* 36
Bowling 107–0
Test batting
13–21–0–564–125–26.85–1–*ct* 5

Apart from an innings of 190* v Middlesex, he achieved very little on the 1963 tour, though he appeared in two Tests. His experience in 1966 was curiously similar, he again doing little in the two Tests for which he was selected. His highest score was 218 for Jamaica v Guyana at Georgetown in 1966/7.

McMurray, Alfred
Amateur. *b:* 4.11.1914, Belfast, Ireland. Brother of Thomas (Surrey). Lower order right-hand batsman. *Team* Ireland (1939).
Career batting
1–2–0–9–5–4.50–0–*ct* 1

McMurray, Thomas
Professional. *b:* 24.7.1911, Belfast, Ireland. *d:* 24.3.1964, Belfast, Ireland. Brother of Alfred (Ireland). Middle order right-hand batsman, wicket-keeper. *Team* Surrey (1933–39, 33 matches).
Career batting
33–54–6–892–62–18.58–0–*ct* 14
Bowling 23–1–23.00–0–0–1/3

He played for Ireland (not first-class) in 1938. He was only 5ft 2in tall. He was a noted soccer forward, appearing for Tranmere Rovers, Millwall and Rochdale.

McNab, Alexander
Amateur. *b:* 11.1.1887, Uddingston, Lanarkshire, Scotland. *d: circa* 1925, Philadelphia, USA. Tail end right-hand batsman, right-arm medium pace bowler. *Team* Scotland (1910).

MacNab, Maurice Ronald

Career batting
1–2–1–0–0*–0.00–0–*ct* 0
Bowling 43–0

MacNab, Maurice Ronald
Amateur. *b:* 6.5.1902, Hythe, Kent. *d:* 12.4.1962, Parciau, Marianglas, Anglesey. Lower order left-hand batsman, left-arm bowler. *Sch* Malvern and St Edward's, Oxford. *Team* Wales (1930).
Career batting
1–2–0–3–2–1.50–0–*ct* 0
Bowling 16–1–16.00–0–0–1/16
His County cricket was for Denbighshire (1934–35).

McNab, William
Amateur. *b:* 2.10.1916, Morningside, Edinburgh, Scotland. Lower order right-hand batsman, wicket-keeper. *Sch* George Watson's College. *Team* Scotland (1947).
Career batting
1–2–0–10–10–5.00–0–*ct* 2

MacNairy, Roy
Professional. *b:* 11.2.1904, Barrow-in-Furness, Lancashire. *d:* 5.9.1962, Bradley, Huddersfield, Yorkshire. Lower order batsman, useful bowler. *Team* Lancashire (1925, 1 match).
Career batting
1–1–1–4–4*–no av–0–*ct* 0
Bowling 73–1–73.00–0–0–1/23

McNamara, Francis Knyvett
Amateur. *b:* 30.4.1912, Missouri, India. Opening right-hand batsman, left-arm medium pace bowler. *Sch* Marlborough. *Team* Free Foresters (1952).
Career batting
1–2–0–18–16–9.00–0–*ct* 0

McNamara, N. F.
Amateur. Middle order batsman, useful bowler. *Team* Ireland (1913).
Career batting
1–2–1–54–30–54.00–0–*ct* 1
Bowling 49–0

McNeil, Alastair Simpson Bell
Amateur. *b:* 28.6.1915, Edinburgh, Scotland. *d:* 26.1.1944, Anzio, Italy. Middle order batsman, slow left-arm bowler. *Sch* George Watson's College. *Team* Scotland (1937).
Career batting
1–2–0–28–23–14.00–0–*ct* 0
He played rugby football for Scotland.

McNeill, Rt Hon Ronald John
(created Baron Cushendun in 1927)
Amateur. *b:* 30.4.1861, Crays, Belfast, Ireland. *d:* 12.10.1934, Cushendun House, Knocknacarry, Co Antrim, Ireland. Brother-in-law of W. E. T. Bolitho (Oxford U). Tail end right-hand batsman, useful under-arm bowler, brilliant field. *Sch* Harrow. *Team* MCC (1885).
Career batting
1–1–0–2–2–2.00–0–*ct* 0
He was at both Cambridge and Oxford, but in the eleven at neither. In 1911 he became MP for East Kent and from 1918 to 1927 for Canterbury. In 1922 and 1924 he was Under-Secretary of State for Foreign Affairs.

McNiven, Edward
Amateur. *b:* 21.6.1827, Offley, Hertfordshire. *d:* 4.1.1858, Perrysfield, Godstone, Surrey. He was killed when his dog-cart overturned. Hard hitting middle order right-hand batsman. *Sch* Eton. *Teams* Cambridge U (1846–48, blue 1846); Surrey (1851, 1 match).
Career batting
12–21–4–407–88*–23.94–0–*ct* 6
Bowling 2 wickets, no analyses
An excellent oarsman, he was in the eight at Eton and Cambridge.

McPate, William Adamson
Cricketer. *b:* 22.7.1951, Baillieston, Lanarkshire, Scotland. Tail end right-hand batsman, right-arm fast medium bowler. *Team* Scotland (1983–85).
Career batting
3–4–2–31–14–15.50–0–*ct* 0
Bowling 153–3–51.00–0–0–2/70

McPhail, Angus William
Cricketer. *b:* 25.5.1956, Ipswich, Suffolk. Lower order right-hand batsman, wicket-keeper. *Sch* Abingdon. *Team* Oxford U (1977).
Career batting
4–8–1–63–37–9.00–0–*ct* 6

Macpherson, Moray Charles Livingstone
Cricketer. *b:* 4.11.1959, Barton-on-Sea, Hampshire. Nephew of H. E. Webb (Hampshire). Lower order right-hand batsman, wicket-keeper. *Sch* Winchester. *Team* Oxford U (1980).
Career batting
5–10–1–52–22–5.77–0–*ct* 8–*st* 1

McPherson, Thomas Ian
Cricketer. *b:* 14.10.1942, Scone, Perthshire, Scotland. Lower order right-hand batsman, slow left-arm bowler. *Team* Scotland (1977–79).
Career batting
5–7–3–83–28–20.75–0–*ct* 0
Bowling 230–10–23.00–0–0–4/74

Macpherson, William Douglas Lawson
Amateur. *b:* 1841, Cheltenham, Gloucestershire. *d:* 24.2.1920, Silverton, Devon. Useful right-hand batsman, wicket-keeper. *Team* Gloucestershire (1870–71, 3 matches).
Career batting
3–4–1–7–5–2.33–0–*ct* 0

McQuilken, Archibald Lynn
Amateur. *b:* 30.9.1933, Muckamore, Co Antrim, Ireland. *d:* 16.10.1983, Belfast, Ireland. He died when knocked down by a motor cycle. Middle order right-hand batsman, leg break and googly bowler. *Team* Ireland (1962).
Career batting
2–4–0–140–42–35.00–0–*ct* 0
Bowling 60–5–12.00–1–0–5/37
He played amateur soccer for Northern Ireland.

McRae, Dr Foster Moverley
Amateur. *b:* 12.2.1916, Buenos Aires, Argentine. *d:* 25.2.1944. He died aboard HMS *Mahratta* in the Barents Sea. Middle order right-hand batsman. *Sch* Christ's Hospital. *Team* Somerset (1936–39, 25 matches).
Career batting
25–45–5–972–107–24.30–1–*ct* 9

McTavish, Alastair Kenneth
Amateur. *b:* 22.12.1904, Rothiemay, Banff, Scotland. *d:* 23.3.1961, Newton-Mearns, Renfrewshire, Scotland. Middle order right-hand batsman, wicket-keeper. *Team* Scotland (1929–39).
Career batting
15–26–0–675–109–25.96–1–*ct* 9–*st* 4

McVeagh, Trevor George Brooke
Amateur. *b:* 14.9.1906, Drewstown, Athboy, Co Meath, Ireland. *d:* 5.6.1968, Dublin, Ireland. Uncle of D. M. M. Pratt (Ireland). Sound opening or middle order left-hand batsman. *Teams* Dublin U (1925–26); Ireland (1926–34).
Career batting
12–23–2–814–109–38.76–2–*ct* 11
He played hockey, tennis and squash for Ireland.

MacVicar, Dr Angus David Lees
Cricketer. *b:* 25.8.1955, Sheffield, Yorkshire. Lower order right-hand batsman, right-arm fast medium bowler. *Sch* Rugby. *Team* Cambridge U (1977).
Career batting
1 match, did not bat–*ct* 0
Bowling 141–2–70.50–0–0–2/82

McVicker, Norman Michael
Cricketer. *b:* 4.11.1940, Whitefield, Radcliffe, Lancashire. Lower order right-hand batsman, right-arm fast medium bowler. *Teams* Warwickshire (1969–72, 104 matches); Leicestershire (1974–76, 67 matches).
Career batting
173–210–53–3108–83*–19.79–0–*ct* 48
Bowling 11567–453–25.53–19–0–7/29
He also played for Lincolnshire (1963–68) and made his first-class debut for Minor Counties in 1965.

McVittie, Charles Arthur Blake
Amateur. *b:* 30.7.1908, Rugeley, Staffordshire. *d:* 4.9.1973, Stowting Common, Kent. Middle order right-hand batsman, wicket-keeper. *Sch* Bedford. *Teams* Cambridge U (1929); Kent (1929, 1 match).
Career batting
4–4–2–58–30–29.00–0–*ct* 3–*st* 2

Madan Lal Udhouram Sharma
Cricketer. *b:* 20.3.1951, Amritsar, India. Attractive middle order right-hand batsman, right-arm medium-fast bowler. *Teams* Punjab (1968/9 to 1971/2); Delhi (1972/3 to 1989/90). *Tours* India to Sri Lanka 1973/4, to England 1974, 1975 (World Cup), 1983 (World Cup), 1986, to New Zealand 1975/6, to West Indies 1975/6, 1982/3, to Australia 1977/8, 1984/5 (not first-class), to Pakistan 1982/3, 1984/5, to Sharjah (not first-class) 1983/4, 1984/5, 1985/6, 1986/7; Rest of World to England 1991. *Tests* India (1974/5 to 1986, 39 matches).
Career batting
232–327–89–10204–223–42.87–22–*ct* 142
Bowling 15938–625–25.50–27–5–9/31
Test batting
39–62–16–1042–74–22.65–0–*ct* 15
Bowling 2846–71–40.08–4–0–5/23
He had very modest figures on the 1974 tour to England, though he appeared in two Tests. In 1982 he showed greatly improved form, hitting 309 runs, av 61.80, and taking 22 wickets, av 34.68, and played in all three Tests. In 1986 he was playing in the Central Lancashire League, but co-opted into the Indian touring side for the Second Test. In this match his bowling made a substantial contribution to the Indian victory. His highest score was 223 for Delhi v Rajasthan at Delhi in 1977/8 and his best bowling was 9/31 for Delhi v Haryana at Delhi in 1979/80.

Madden, John Charles Pengelley
(also known as Madden-Gaskell)
Amateur. *b:* 1.3.1896, Pontypool, Monmouthshire. *d:* 4.2.1975, Lowertown, Helston, Cornwall. Middle order right-hand batsman. *Sch* Haileybury. *Teams* Glamorgan (1922, 1 match); Somerset (1928–30, 9 matches).
Career batting
10–19–0–300–63–15.78–0–*ct* 5
Bowling 8–0

Maddocks, Leonard Victor
Amateur. *b:* 24.5.1926, Beaconsfield, Melbourne, Victoria, Australia. Brother of R. I. (Victoria), father of I. L. (Victoria). Middle order right-hand batsman, wicket-keeper. *Teams* Victoria (1946/7 to 1961/2, 66 matches); Tasmania (1962/3 to 1967/8, 6 matches). *Tours* Australia to England 1956, to West Indies 1954/5, to India 1956/7, to New Zealand 1959/60; Cavaliers to South Africa 1960/1. *Tests* Australia (1954/5 to 1956/7, 7 matches).
Career batting
112–158–33–4106–122*–32.84–6–*ct* 209–*st* 68
Bowling 4–1–4.00–0–0–1/4

Test batting
7–12–2–177–69–17.70–0–*ct* 19–*st* 1

He played in two Tests on the 1956 tour to England, standing in for the injured Langley. He was manager of the 1977 Australian team to England.

Madugalle, Ranjan Senerath
Cricketer. *b:* 22.4.1959, Kandy, Ceylon. Middle order right-hand batsman, off break bowler, good field. *Team* Nondescripts CC (1988/9). *Tours* Sri Lanka to England 1979, 1983 (World Cup), 1984, 1988, to India 1980/1, 1982/3, 1986/7, to Pakistan 1981/2, 1985/6, to Australia 1982/3, 1984/5 (not first-class), 1987/8, to New Zealand 1982/3, to Zimbabwe 1982/3, to Sharjah (not first-class) 1983/4, 1987/8, to India and Pakistan (World Cup) 1987/8, to Bangladesh (not first-class) 1988/9. *Tests* Sri Lanka (1981/2 to 1988, 21 matches).
Career batting
81–118–15–3301–142*–32.04–2–*ct* 42
Bowling 159–2–79.50–0–0–1/18
Test batting
21–39–4–1029–103–29.40–1–*ct* 9
Bowling 38–0

On the 1984 tour to England he hit 336 runs, av 42.00. Returning as captain in 1988 his total was 403, av 44.77. He played in the single Test on each visit. He captained Sri Lanka in 2 Tests.

Madurasinghe, Madurasinghe Arachchige Wijayasiri Ranjith
Cricketer. *b:* 30.1.1961, Kurunegala, Ceylon. Lower order left-hand batsman, off break bowler. *Team* Kurunegala (1991/2). *Tours* Sri Lanka to England 1988, 1990, 1991, to Bangladesh (not first-class) 1988/9, to Sharjah (not first-class) 1989/90, to Australia 1989/90, to India 1989/90 (not first-class), 1990/1, to New Zealand 1990/1, to Pakistan 1991/2; Sri Lanka B to Zimbabwe 1987/8 (not first-class), to Pakistan 1988/9. *Tests* Sri Lanka (1988 to 1990/1, 2 matches).
Career batting
47–57–16–728–83*–17.75–0–*ct* 24
Bowling 3358–125–26.86–4–1–5/19
Test batting
2–4–0–19–11–4.75–0–*ct* 0
Bowling 101–3–33.66–0–0–3/60

Although he played in the Test on the 1988 England tour, his record in first-class matches was modest. On the 1990 tour he was the leading wicket-taker, but the following summer he made little impression.

Magee, Brian Robert Boyd
Amateur. *b:* 4.5.1918, Toronto, Ontario, Canada. Lower order left-hand batsman, left-arm medium pace bowler. *Sch* Radley. *Team* Canada to England 1954.
Career batting
1–2–0–16–13–8.00–0–*ct* 0
Bowling 40–1–40.00–0–0–1/22

Magee, James Mary
Amateur. *b:* 1874, Rathmines, Co Dublin, Ireland. *d:* February 1949, Greystones, Co Wicklow, Ireland. Opening right-hand batsman. *Team* Ireland (1907). *Tour* Ireland to North America 1909.
Career batting
3–6–0–54–16–9.00–0–*ct* 1

He was a noted rugby footballer

Magill, Michael Desmond Ponsonby
Amateur. *b:* 28.9.1915, Sevenoaks, Kent. *d:* 5.9.1940, Filey, Yorkshire. Middle order right-hand batsman, right-arm fast medium bowler. *Sch* Eton. *Teams* Oxford U (1938); Army (1939). *Tour* Oxford and Cambridge to Jamaica 1938/9.
Career batting
6–9–2–160–80–22.85–0–*ct* 3
Bowling 291–7–41.57–1–0–5/57

His County cricket was for Berkshire (1939).

Magnay, Sir Christopher Boyd William
Amateur. *b:* 27.3.1884, Marylebone, London. *d:* 4.9.1960, Saxham Hall, Great Saxham, Suffolk. Son-in-law of A. F. Jeffreys (Hampshire). Middle order right-hand batsman. *Sch* Harrow. *Teams* Cambridge U (1904); Middlesex (1906–11, 3 matches).
Career batting
12–21–0–308–73–14.66–0–*ct* 5
Bowling 2–0

His County cricket was for Suffolk (1914). He won a blue for soccer.

Maguire, John Norman
Cricketer. *b:* 15.9.1956, Murwillumbah, New South Wales, Australia. Lower order right-hand batsman, right-arm fast medium bowler. *Teams* Queensland (1977/8 to 1988/9, 68 matches); Eastern Province (1989/90 to 1990/1); Leicestershire (1991, 24 matches). *Tours* Australia to West Indies 1983/4; Australian XI to South Africa 1985/6, 1986/7. *Tests* Australia (1983/4, 3 matches).
Career batting
134–152–46–1162–65*–10.96–0–*ct* 43
Bowling 12851–463–27.75–26–3–7/46
Test batting
3–5–1–28–15*–7.00–0–*ct* 2
Bowling 323–10–32.30–0–0–4/57

He performed steadily for Leicestershire taking 77 wickets, av 31.64.

Maguire, Keith Robert
Cricketer. *b:* 20.3.1961, Marston Green, Birmingham. Tail end right-hand batsman, right-arm medium pace bowler. *Team* Warwickshire (1982, 3 matches).

Career batting
3–3–0–3–2–1.00–0–*ct* 0
Bowling 123–1–123.00–0–0–1/32
He also played for Staffordshire (1984–86).

Mahaffy, John Pentland
Amateur. *b:* 18.6.1906, Suva, Fiji. *d:* 8.12.1937, Mundesley-on-Sea, Norfolk. Middle order batsman. *Team* MCC (1934).
Career batting
1–1–0–8–8–8.00–0–*ct* 0

Mahanama, Roshan Siriwardene
Cricketer. *b:* 31.5.1966, Colombo, Ceylon. Opening right-hand batsman. *Team* Colombo CC (1988/9 to 1991/2). *Tours* Sri Lanka to Sharjah (not first-class) 1985/6, 1986/7, 1987/8, 1988/9, 1990/1, to India 1986/7, 1989/90 (not first-class), 1990/1, to India and Pakistan (World Cup) 1987/8, to Australia 1987/8, 1989/90, to England 1988, 1990, 1991, to Bangladesh (not first-class) 1988/9, to New Zealand 1990/1, to Pakistan 1991/2, to Australia and New Zealand (World Cup) 1991/2. *Tests* Sri Lanka (1985/6 to 1991/2, 11 matches).
Career batting
63–93–12–2617–114–32.30–2–*ct* 56
Bowling 3–0
Test batting
11–16–0–375–85–23.43–0–*ct* 6
Bowling 3–0
The most successful of his three tours to England was the 1990 visit, though he did appear in the Test match in 1991. His first-class debut was for Sri Lanka President's XI in 1984/5.

Maher, Bernard Joseph Michael
Cricketer. *b:* 11.2.1958, Hillingdon, Middlesex. Opening or lower order right-hand batsman, wicket-keeper. *Team* Derbyshire (1981–91, 128 matches).
Career batting
128–200–35–3667–126–22.22–4–*ct* 280–*st* 14
Bowling 234–4–58.50–0–0–2/69

Mahmood Hussain
Amateur. *b:* 2.4.1932, Lahore, India. *d:* 25.12.1991, Northwick Park, Middlesex. Lower order right-hand batsman, right-arm fast medium bowler. *Teams* Universities (1949/50); West Punjab (1951/2); Karachi (1953/4 to 1961/2); East Pakistan (1955/6). *Tours* Pakistan to India 1952/3, 1960/1, to England 1954, 1962, to West Indies 1957/8. *Tests* Pakistan (1952/3 to 1962, 27 matches).
Career batting
95–115–12–1107–50–10.74–0–*ct* 29
Bowling 8071–322–25.06–19–3–8/95
Test batting
27–39–6–336–35–10.18–0–*ct* 5
Bowling 2628–68–38.64–2–0–6/67
On his 1954 visit to England he took 72 wickets, av 21.30, and though not so successful in 1962 he headed the first-class averages with 44 wickets, av 23.45. His final first-class match was for the National Tyre and Rubber Co in 1968/9.

Mahmood, Muzaffar
Cricketer. *b:* 13.6.1963, Lahore, Pakistan. Tail end right-hand batsman, off break bowler. *Team* Scotland (1990).
Career batting
1–1–0–3–3–3.00–0–*ct* 1
Bowling 103–4–25.75–0–0–3/63

Mahmoodul Hasan
Cricketer. *b:* 11.11.1938, Lucknow, India. Middle order batsman, useful bowler. *Teams* Karachi (1959/60 to 1970/1); PWD (1964/5 to 1971/2); Dacca (1964/5 to 1965/6); East Pakistan (1967/8). *Tour* Pakistan Eaglets to England 1963.
Career batting
63–95–7–3199–196–36.35–6–*ct* 40
Bowling 337–4–84.25–0–0–1/1

Mahony, Noel Cameron
Amateur. *b:* 15.1.1913, Fermoy, Co Cork, Ireland. Opening right-hand batsman. *Team* Ireland (1948–53).
Career batting
5–10–0–116–29–11.60–0–*ct* 3

Maidlow, William John
Cricketer. *b:* 15.7.1949, Southmead, Bristol. Opening right-hand batsman. *Sch* Malvern. *Team* Oxford U (1972).
Career batting
2–4–0–53–45–13.25–0–*ct* 2

Mailey, Arthur Alfred
Amateur. *b:* 3.1.1886, Zetland, Waterloo, Sydney, New South Wales, Australia. *d:* 31.12.1967, Kirrawee, Sydney, New South Wales, Australia. Lower order right-hand batsman, leg break and googly bowler. *Team* New South Wales (1912/13 to 1929/30, 67 matches). *Tours* Australia to England 1921, 1926, to South Africa 1921/2, to New Zealand 1913/14, to North America 1913; New South Wales to New Zealand 1923/4. *Tests* Australia (1920/1 to 1926, 21 matches).
Career batting
158–186–62–1530–66–12.33–0–*ct* 157
Bowling 18772–779–24.09–61–16–10/66
Test batting
21–29–9–222–46*–11.10–0–*ct* 14
Bowling 3358–99–33.91–6–2–9/121
On his first visit to England in 1921 he took 134 wickets, av 19.36, and in 1926, 126, av 19.34. His bowling was much more difficult to master than it appeared. His outstanding success was to take 10 for 66 v Gloucestershire at Cheltenham in 1921, but he also took 9 for 121 against England in the Test at Melbourne in 1920/1. His final first-class match was

for the Rest of Australia in 1930/1. He was a talented writer and cartoonist.

Mainprice, Humphrey
Amateur. *b:* 27.11.1882, Ashley, Cheshire. *d:* 24.11.1958, Penmere, Cornwall. Lower order right-hand batsman, leg break bowler. *Sch* Blundell's. *Teams* Gloucestershire (1905, 1 match); Cambridge U (1905–06, blue 1906).
Career batting
15–23–2–381–60–18.14–0–*ct* 9
Bowling 686–21–32.66–0–0–4/34

He also played for Cheshire (1903). He also won a blue for rugby.

Mains, Geoffrey
Professional. *b:* 24.1.1934, Mangotsfield, Gloucestershire. Lower order right-hand batsman, right-arm fast medium bowler. *Team* Gloucestershire (1951–54, 6 matches).
Career batting
6–10–1–19–8–2.11–0–*ct* 2
Bowling 305–6–50.83–0–0–2/42

Mair, Norman George Robertson
Amateur. *b:* 7.10.1928, Edinburgh, Scotland. Middle order left-hand batsman, slow left-arm bowler. *Sch* Merchiston. *Team* Scotland (1952).
Career batting
1–1–1–4–4*–no av–0–*ct* 0

An excellent rugby player, he represented Scotland.

Maitland, Reginald Paynter
Amateur. *b:* 6.3.1851, Southsea, Hampshire. *d:* 10.4.1926, Bartley Manor, Hampshire. Middle order batsman. *Team* MCC (1885).
Career batting
1–1–0–0–0–0.00–0–*ct* 0

Maitland, William Fuller
(also known as Fuller-Maitland)
Amateur. *b:* 6.5.1844, Stansted Hall, Essex. *d:* 15.11.1932, Kemp Town, Brighton, Sussex. Grandfather of A. M. Byng (Hampshire). Hard hitting lower order right-hand batsman, right-arm slow bowler. *Sch* Harrow. *Team* Oxford U (1864–67, blue all four years).
Career batting
38–62–5–790–61–13.85–0–*ct* 28
Bowling 1667–106 + 17–15.72–9–3–8/48

He was able to get an exceptional amount of spin on the ball and often obtained wickets with deliveries which the batsman regarded as too wide to be dangerous. His County cricket was for Oxfordshire (1864) and Essex (pre first-class, 1866–68). His final first-class match was for MCC in 1870. He captained Oxford in 1867. A noted athlete, he represented Oxford in both the high and the long jump as well as rackets. He was MP for Breconshire 1875–95.

Maitland, William James
Amateur. *b:* 22.7.1847, Edinburgh, Scotland. *d:* 8.5.1919, Covent Garden, Westminster, London. Middle order right-hand batsman, deep field. *Sch* Edinburgh Academy. *Team* MCC (1868–69).
Career batting
3–3–0–71–57–23.66–0–*ct* 2

He lived for many years in India, where he took a prominent part in cricket. His County cricket was for Devon (1870).

Majendie, Nicholas Lionel
Amateur. *b:* 9.6.1942, Cheltenham, Gloucestershire. Lower order right-hand batsman, wicket-keeper. *Sch* Winchester. *Teams* Oxford U (1961–63, blue 1962–63); Surrey (1963, 8 matches).
Career batting
26–33–6–313–54–11.59–0–*ct* 64–*st* 4

Majendie, Major-Gen Vivian Henry Bruce
Amateur. *b:* 20.4.1886, Ipplepen, Devon. *d:* 13.1.1960, North Watford, Hertfordshire. Son of H. W. (Oxford U 1860). Middle order right-hand batsman, wicket-keeper. *Sch* Winchester. *Team* Somerset (1907–10, 2 matches).
Career batting
2–4–0–55–28–13.75–0–*ct* 2–*st* 4

He also played for Devon (1908).

Majid Jahangir Khan
Cricketer. *b:* 28.9.1946, Ludhiana, India. Son of M. Jahangir Khan (India), brother of A. J. Khan (Oxford U), cousin of Imran Khan (Pakistan), Javed Burki (Pakistan), Humayun Zaman (Lahore) and Javed Zaman (Lahore), nephew of M. Baqa Jilani (India). Attacking middle order, later opening, right-hand batsman, right-arm medium pace or off break bowler, good close field. *Teams* Lahore (1961/2 to 1982/3); Punjab (1964/5 to 1967/8); PIA (1968/9 to 1980/1); Glamorgan (1968–76, 154 matches); Cambridge U (1970–72, blue all three years); Queensland (1973/4, 9 matches); Rawalpindi (1984/5). *Tours* Pakistan to England 1967, 1971, 1974, 1975 (World Cup), 1979 (World Cup), 1982, to Australia, New Zealand and Ceylon 1972/3, to Australia and New Zealand 1978/9, to Australia 1976/7, 1981/2, to West Indies 1976/7, to India 1979/80; Pakistan Eaglets to England 1963. *Tests* Pakistan (1964/5 to 1982/3, 63 matches).
Career batting
410–700–62–27444–241–43.01–73–*ct* 410
Bowling 7168–223–32.14–4–0–6/67
Test batting
63–106–5–3931–167–38.92–8–*ct* 70
Bowling 1456–27–53.92–0–0–4/45

Of his four tours to England the most successful was 1974 when he hit 1,000 runs, av 50.00, in first-class matches and 262, av 43.66, in the Tests. On the 1971 tour he appeared in just two games, both Tests, whilst in 1982 his form was such that he played in only one Test. In all he hit 1,000 runs in an English season eight times, going on to 2,000 once: 2,074, av 61.00, in 1972. His highest innings in England was 204 for Glamorgan v Surrey at the Oval in 1972 and his other English double century was for Cambridge in the 1970 University match. His highest score was 241 for Lahore Greens v Bahawalpur at Lahore in 1965/6. He scored 111* and took 6 for 67 on debut for Lahore B v Khairpur at Lahore in 1961/2. He captained Cambridge 1971–72, Glamorgan 1973–76 and Pakistan in 3 Tests.

Major, John
Professional. *b:* 6.2.1861, Seaford, Sussex. *d:* 30.12.1930, Wakefield, Yorkshire. Middle order right-hand batsman, right-arm medium pace bowler. *Team* Sussex (1888–89, 11 matches).
Career batting
12–23–2–363–106–17.28–1–*ct* 2
Bowling 53–3–17.66–0–0–2/10
He also played for Warwickshire (pre-first-class, 1892). A good soccer player, he played for West Bromwich Albion.

Major, Lionel Hugh
Amateur. *b:* 21.4.1883, Wembdon, Somerset. *d:* 25.6.1965, Exmouth, Devon. Lower order batsman, useful bowler. *Team* Somerset (1903, 1 match).
Career batting
1–2–0–17–11–8.50–*ct* 0
Bowling 5–1–5.00–0–0–1/5

Makepeace, Joseph William Henry
Professional. *b:* 22.8.1881, Middlesbrough, Yorkshire. *d:* 19.12.1952, Spital, Bebington, Cheshire. Stubborn opening right-hand batsman, slow leg break bowler, excellent cover point. *Team* Lancashire (1906–30, 487 matches). *Tour* MCC to Australia 1920/1. *Tests* England (1920/1, 4 matches).
Career batting
499–778–66–25799–203–36.23–43–*ct* 194
Bowling 1971–42–46.92–0–0–4/33
Test batting
4–8–0–279–117–34.87–1–*ct* 0
He hit 1,000 runs in a season thirteen times, going on to 2,000 twice (best 2,340, av 48.75, in 1926). Both his double centuries were for Lancashire, the highest being 203 v Worcestershire at Worcester in 1923. For 20 years up to 1951, he was chief coach at Old Trafford. A noted soccer player, he appeared as right half for Everton and England, thus being a double international.

Makinson, David John
Cricketer. *b:* 12.1.1961, Eccleston, Lancashire. Lower order right-hand batsman, left-arm fast medium bowler. *Team* Lancashire (1984–88, 35 matches).
Career batting
35–39–17–486–58*–22.09–0–*ct* 10
Bowling 2486–70–35.51–1–0–5/60
He also played for Cumberland (1989–92). He missed all of the 1987 season because of a back injury.

Makinson, Joseph
Amateur. *b:* 25.8.1836, Higher Broughton, Lancashire. *d:* 14.3.1914, Roundthorn, Sale, Cheshire. Brother of Charles (Victoria). Attacking middle order right-hand batsman, right-hand medium pace round-arm bowler, good field. *Teams* Cambridge U (1856–58, blue all three years); Cambridgeshire (1857–58, 3 matches); Lancashire (1865–73, 5 matches).
Career batting
27–50–2–862–66–17.95–0–*ct* 23–*st* 2
Bowling 566–39+7–14.51–2–1–7/38
He was for some years Chairman of Lancashire CCC.

Malalasekera, Vijaya Prasanna
Cricketer. *b:* 8.8.1945, Colombo, Ceylon. Middle order right-hand batsman. *Team* Cambridge U (1966–68, blue 1966–67).
Career batting
27–50–1–699–80–14.26–0–*ct* 11
Bowling 9–0

Malcolm, Devon Eugene
Cricketer. *b:* 22.2.1963, Kingston, Jamaica. Lower order right-hand batsman, right-arm fast bowler. *Team* Derbyshire (1984–92, 97 matches). *Tours* England to West Indies 1989/90, to Australia 1990/1; England A to West Indies 1991/2. *Tests* England (1989–92, 21 matches).
Career batting
130–143–39–826–51–7.94–0–*ct* 25
Bowling 12500–394–31.72–10–1–7/74
Test batting
21–29–8–105–15*–5.00–0–*ct* 3
Bowling 2673–74–36.12–4–1–6/77
Regarded as one of the most hostile bowlers in English Test cricket, his form has been very variable. His best wicket aggregate to date is 56, av 29.92, in 1988.

Malcolm, Henry John James
Amateur. *b:* 4.7.1914, Richmond, Surrey. Middle order right-hand batsman, right-hand fast medium bowler. *Team* Middlesex (1948, 4 matches).
Career batting
4–6–1–139–76*–27.80–0–*ct* 1
Bowling 6–0

Malden, Ernest
Amateur. *b:* 10.10.1870, Sheldwich, Kent. *d:* 13.9.1955, Salisbury, Rhodesia. Cousin of Eustace (Kent). Fast scoring middle order right-hand batsman, right-arm medium pace bowler, close field. *Sch* Clergy School, Canterbury. *Team* Kent (1893, 1 match).

Malden, Rev Eustace

Career batting
1–2–0–22–22–11.00–0–*ct* 1
Bowling 15–0

Malden, Rev Eustace
Amateur. *b:* 19.8.1863, Brighton, Sussex. *d:* 3.12.1947, Ovingdean, Rottingdean, Sussex. Cousin of Ernest (Kent), father of W. J. (Sussex). Lower order right-hand batsman, wicket-keeper. *Sch* Haileybury. *Team* Kent (1892–93, 12 matches).
Career batting
13–21–1–133–27–6.65–0–*ct* 7–*st* 5
He also played for Hertfordshire (1887–88).

Malden, William Jack
Amateur. *b:* 14.5.1899, Ticehurst, Sussex. *d:* 23.11.1963, Kingston Warren, Newbury, Berkshire. Son of Eustace (Kent). Opening or middle order right-hand batsman, fine field. *Sch* Haileybury. *Teams* Sussex (1920–22, 23 matches); Cambridge U (1921).
Career batting
24–36–1–624–100–17.82–1–*ct* 12

Malet, Alexander George William
Amateur. *b:* 25.10.1845, Portsmouth, Hampshire. *d:* 11.1.1922, Marylebone, London. Steady middle order right-hand batsman, wicket-keeper. *Sch* Cheltenham. *Team* Gentlemen of England (1865).
Career batting
1–2–0–23–12–11.50–0–*ct* 1
His County cricket was for Dorset (1862) and Cheshire (1866).

Malhotra, Ashok
Cricketer. *b:* 26.1.1957, Amritsar, India. Attractive middle order right-hand batsman, right-arm medium pace bowler. *Teams* Haryana (1973/4 to 1986/7); Bengal (1987/8 to 1991/2). *Tours* India to England 1982, to West Indies 1982/3, to Australia 1984/5. *Tests* India (1981/2 to 1984/5, 7 matches).
Career batting
138–204–31–8841–258*–51.10–21–*ct* 65
Bowling 326–1–326.00–0–0–1/37
Test batting
7–10–1–226–72*–25.11–0–*ct* 2
Bowling 3–0
He hit 462 runs, av 33.00, on the 1982 tour to England and played in one Test. His highest score was 258* for Bengal v Hyderabad at Secunderabad in 1989/90.

Malik, Hardit Singh
Amateur. *b:* 23.11.1894, Rawalpindi, India. *d:* 31.10.1985, Delhi, India. Middle order right-hand batsman. *Sch* Eastbourne. *Teams* Sussex (1914–21, 9 matches); Oxford U (1921); Sikhs (1922/3 to 1928/9); Hindus (1929/30).
Career batting
18–32–0–636–106–19.87–2–*ct* 8
Bowling 151–3+1–50.33–0–0–2/92
He won a blue for golf.

Malik, Hasnain Sadiq
Cricketer. *b:* 1.12.1971, Harrow, Middlesex. Middle order left-hand batsman, off break bowler. *Team* Oxford U (1992).
Career batting
1–1–0–4–4–4.00–0–*ct* 0
Bowling 88–0

Mallalieu, Albert Edward
Amateur. *b:* 13.1.1904, Delph, Yorkshire. Opening right-hand batsman. *Sch* Leys. *Team* Wales (1924–30).
Career batting
6–8–0–137–66–17.12–0–*ct* 2
His County cricket was for Caernarvonshire (1928).

Mallam, Charles George Cave
Amateur. *b:* 4.8.1859, Oxford. *d:* 8.12.1950, Brentwood, Essex. Lower order right-hand batsman, right-arm slow bowler. *Sch* Uppingham. *Team* Oxford U (1882).
Career batting
1–2–1–4–2*–4.00–0–*ct* 2
Bowling 39–0
His County cricket was for Rutland (1886), Oxfordshire (1892) and Devon.

Mallender, Neil Alan
Cricketer. *b:* 13.8.1961, Kirk Sandall, Yorkshire. Lower order right-hand batsman, right-arm fast medium bowler. *Teams* Northamptonshire (1980–86, 134 matches); Otago (1983/4 to 1991/2); Somerset (1987–92, 97 matches). *Tests* England (1992, 2 matches).
Career batting
307–343–107–3868–100*–16.38–1–*ct* 103
Bowling 22368–842–26.56–33–5–7/27
Test batting
2–3–0–8–4–2.66–0–*ct* 0
Bowling 215–10–21.50–1–0–5/50
On his Test debut for England at Headingley in 1992 he took 3 for 72 and 5 for 50 against Pakistan.

Mallett, Anthony William Haward
Amateur. *b:* 29.8.1924, Dulwich, London. Father of N. V. H. (Oxford U). Attacking middle order right-hand batsman, right-arm fast medium bowler. *Sch* Dulwich. *Teams* Kent (1946–53, 33 matches); Oxford U (1947–48, blue both years). *Tour* MCC to Canada 1951.
Career batting
75–108–14–1764–97–18.76–0–*ct* 61
Bowling 5748–213–26.98–9–0–6/42
His first-class debut was for the Under 33 XI in 1945 at Lord's.

Mallett, Ashley Alexander
Cricketer. *b:* 13.7.1945, Chatswood, Sydney, New South Wales, Australia. Lower order right-hand batsman, off break bowler. *Team* South Australia (1967/8 to 1980/1, 91 matches). *Tours* Australia to England 1968, 1972, 1975, 1980, to Ceylon and India 1969/70, to South Africa 1969/70, to New Zealand 1973/4; International Wanderers to South Africa 1975/6. *Tests* Australia (1968/9 to 1980, 38 matches).
Career batting
183–230–59–2326–92–13.60–0–*ct* 105
Bowling 18208–693–26.27–33–5–8/59
Test batting
38–50–13–430–43*–11.62–0–*ct* 30
Bowling 3940–132–29.84–6–1–8/59
He appeared in some Tests on all his major tours to England, but achieved only modest results.

Mallett, Nicholas Vivian Haward
Cricketer. *b:* 30.10.1956, Haileybury, Hertfordshire. Son of A. W. H. (Kent). Lower order right-hand batsman, right-arm medium pace bowler. *Team* Oxford U (1980–81, blue 1981).
Career batting
11–20–2–237–52–13.16–0–*ct* 3
Bowling 841–19–44.26–1–0–5/52

Mallett, Richard Henry
Amateur. *b:* 14.10.1858, Louth, Lincolnshire. *d:* 29.11.1939, Ickenham, Middlesex. Opening right-hand batsman, right-arm medium pace bowler. *Team* MCC (1901).
Career batting
1–1–0–8–8–8.00–0–*ct* 0
Bowling 28–0
His County cricket was for Durham (pre first-class, 1884–1906). He took a leading part in the formation of the Minor Counties Cricket Association in 1895 and was the Hon Secretary from 1897 to 1907, afterwards becoming Chairman and President. He managed the 1906, 1923 and 1928 West Indian teams to England and was well-known for his work for touring teams.

Malone, Michael Francis
Cricketer. *b:* 9.10.1950, Scarborough, Perth, Western Australia. Lower order right-hand batsman, right-arm fast medium bowler. *Teams* Western Australia (1974/5 to 1981/2, 45 matches); Lancashire (1979–80, 19 matches). *Tours* Australia to England 1977, to Pakistan 1979/80. *Test* Australia (1977, 1 match).
Career batting
73–79–22–914–46–16.03–0–*ct* 30
Bowling 6441–260–24.77–13–1–7/88
Test batting
1–1–0–46–46–46.00–0–*ct* 0
Bowling 77–6–12.83–1–0–5/63
He took 32 wickets, av 26.15, on the 1977 tour of England and made a successful Test debut on that tour, but his signing for World Series Cricket ended a possibly fruitful Test career. He played Australian Rules football professionally.

Malone, Steven John
Cricketer. *b:* 19.10.1953, Chelmsford, Essex. Lower order right-hand batsman, right-arm medium pace bowler. *Sch* King's School, Ely. *Teams* Essex (1975–78, 2 matches); Hampshire (1980–84, 46 matches); Glamorgan (1985, 9 matches).
Career batting
57–46–15–182–23–5.87–0–*ct* 13
Bowling 4236–118–35.89–3–1–7/55
He also played for Durham (pre first-class, 1986), Dorset (1987) and Wiltshire (1990–92).

Maltby, George
Professional. *b:* 1.10.1876, South Normanton, Derbyshire. *d:* 30.7.1924, Huthwaite, Nottinghamshire. Middle order right-hand batsman. *Team* Derbyshire (1905, 3 matches).
Career batting
3–6–1–22–7*–4.40–0–*ct* 1
Bowling 20–0

Maltby, Norman
Cricketer. *b:* 16.7.1951, Marske-by-the-Sea, Yorkshire. Lower order left-hand batsman, right-arm medium pace bowler. *Team* Northamptonshire (1972–74, 9 matches).
Career batting
9–14–4–185–59–18.50–0–*ct* 2
Bowling 97–2–48.50–0–0–2/43

Malthouse, Samuel
Professional. *b:* 13.10.1857, Whitwell, Derbyshire. *d:* 7.2.1931, Whitwell, Derbyshire. Father of W. N. (Derbyshire). Lower order left-hand batsman, right-arm medium pace off break bowler. *Team* Derbyshire (1894–95, 9 matches).
Career batting
9–12–2–118–38–11.80–0–*ct* 3
Bowling 67–0
He first played for Derbyshire (not first-class) in 1890.

Malthouse, William Norman
Professional. *b:* 16.12.1890, Whitwell, Derbyshire. *d:* 10.5.1961, South Kirkby, Yorkshire. Son of Samuel (Derbyshire). Middle order right-hand batsman, off break bowler. *Team* Derbyshire (1919–20, 7 matches).
Career batting
7–13–1–116–30–9.66–0–*ct* 2
Bowling 69–0

Manasseh, Maurice
Amateur. *b:* 12.1.1943, Calcutta, India. Middle order right-hand batsman, right-arm medium pace off break bowler. *Sch* Epsom. *Teams* Oxford U (1962–64, blue 1964); Middlesex (1964–67, 7 matches).

Maninder Singh

Career batting
42–73–11–1607–129*–25.91–2–*ct* 19
Bowling 2557–61–41.91–2–0–5/51

Maninder Singh
Cricketer. *b:* 13.6.1965, Poona, India. Lower order right-hand batsman, slow left-arm bowler. *Team* Delhi (1980/1 to 1991/2). *Tours* India to West Indies 1982/3, to Pakistan 1982/3, 1984/5, 1989/90, to Sri Lanka 1985/6, to Sharjah (not first-class) 1985/6, 1986/7, 1988/9, to England 1986, to Bangladesh (not first-class) 1988/9; Young Indians to Zimbabwe 1983/4; Rest of World to England 1987, 1988, 1989, 1991. *Tests* India (1982/3 to 1989/90, 34 matches).
Career batting
126–118–51–896–78–13.37–*ct* 51
Bowling 12887–531–24.26–40–12–8/48
Test batting
34–38–12–99–15–3.80–0–*ct* 9
Bowling 3143–81–38.80–3–2–7/27

To the surprise of some critics, he played in all three Tests on the 1986 tour and topped the Test bowling averages with 12 wickets, av 15.58. He also played for Shropshire (1986).

Manjrekar, Sanjay Vijay
Cricketer. *b:* 12.7.1965, Mangalore, India. Middle order right-hand batsman, off break bowler. *Team* Bombay (1984/5 to 1990/1). *Tours* India to West Indies 1988/9, to Pakistan 1989/90, to New Zealand 1989/90, to Sharjah (not first-class) 1989/90, 1991/2, to England 1990, to Australia 1991/2, to Australia and New Zealand (World Cup) 1991/2; Rest of World to England 1991. *Tests* India (1987/8 to 1991/2, 21 matches).
Career batting
74–111–16–5338–377–56.18–16–*ct* 37–*st* 1
Bowling 217–3–72.33–0–0–1/4
Test batting
21–34–2–1303–218–40.71–3–*ct* 12
Bowling 11–0

He proved a dependable batsman on the 1990 tour of England and appeared in all three Tests. For Bombay v Hyderabad at Bombay in 1990/1 he hit 377 and for India v Pakistan at Lahore in 1989/90 he made 218.

Manjrekar, Vijay Laxman
Amateur. *b:* 26.9.1931, Bombay, India. *d:* 18.10.1983, Madras, India. Father of S. V. (India), nephew of D. D. Hindlekar (India). Stylish middle order right-hand batsman, off break bowler, excellent field. *Teams* Bombay (1949/50 to 1955/6); Bengal (1953/4); Andhra (1956/7); Uttar Pradesh (1957/8); Rajasthan (1958/9 to 1965/6); Maharashtra (1966/7 to 1967/8). *Tours* India to England 1952, 1959, to West Indies 1952/3, 1961/2, to Pakistan 1954/5, to Ceylon 1956/7. *Tests* India (1951/2 to 1964/5, 55 matches).
Career batting
198–295–38–12832–283–49.92–38–*ct* 72–*st* 6
Bowling 657–20–32.85–0–0–4/21
Test batting
55–92–10–3208–189*–39.12–7–*ct* 19–*st* 2
Bowling 44–1–44.00–0–0–1/16

On the 1952 tour to England he hit 1,059 runs, av 39.22, his highest score of 133 coming in the first Test at Headingley. In 1959 he was much handicapped by injury, but batted well when available. His final first-class match was for Kerala Chief Minister's XI in 1972/3. His highest score was 283 for Vizianagram's XI v Tata SC at Hyderabad in 1963/4. He hit 1,077 runs, av 56.68, in the 1963/4 Indian season.

Mankad, Ashok Mulvantrai
(known as Ashok Vinoo Mankad)
Cricketer. *b:* 12.10.1946, Bombay, India. Son of M. H. (India), brother of Rahul (Bombay) and Atul (Saurashtra). Opening or middle order right-hand batsman, right-arm medium pace bowler. *Team* Bombay (1963/4 to 1982/3). *Tours* India to West Indies 1970/1, to England 1971, 1974, to Sri Lanka 1973/4, to Australia 1977/8; CCI to Sri Lanka 1972/3. *Tests* India (1969/70 to 1977/8, 22 matches).
Career batting
218–326–71–12980–265–50.90–31–*ct* 126
Bowling 3276–72–45.50–2–0–5/21
Test batting
22–42–3–991–97–25.41–0–*ct* 12
Bowling 43–0

On his 1971 tour to England he hit 795 runs, av 41.84, and played in all three Tests, though with no success. In 1974 he played in only one Test and in first-class matches hit 611 runs, av 38.18. His highest score was 265 for Bombay v Delhi at Bombay in 1980/1.

Mankad, Mulvantrai Himmatlal
(known as Vinoo Mankad)
Amateur. *b:* 12.4.1917, Jamnagar, India. *d:* 21.8.1978, Bombay, India. Father of Ashok (India), Rahul (Bombay) and Atul (Saurashtra). Talented opening right-hand batsman, slow left-arm bowler. *Teams* Western India (1935/6); Nawanagar (1936/7 to 1941/2); Hindus (1936/7 to 1945/6); Maharashtra (1943/4); Gujarat (1944/5 to 1950/1); Bengal (1948/9); Bombay (1951/2 to 1955/6); Rajasthan (1956/7 to 1961/2). *Tours* India to Ceylon 1944/5, to England 1946, 1952, to Australia 1947/8, to West Indies 1952/3, to Pakistan 1954/5. *Tests* India (1946 to 1958/9, 44 matches).
Career batting
233–361–27–11591–231–34.70–26–*ct* 190
Bowling 19183–782–24.53–38–9–8/35
Test batting
44–72–5–2109–231–31.47–5–*ct* 33
Bowling 5236–162–32.32–8–2–8/52

The leading Indian all-rounder of his generation, he performed the 'double' on his 1946 tour to England, hitting 1,120 runs, av 28.00, and taking 129 wickets, av 20.76. In 1952 he was engaged by a League Club and released only for the Tests. Between 1950 and 1958 he appeared for a Commonwealth XI in several Festival matches in England. His highest score was 231 for India v New Zealand at Bombay in 1955/6. His last first-class match was for Maharashtra Governor's XI in 1963/4. He captained India in six Tests.

Mann, Eric William
Amateur. *b:* 4.3.1882, Sidcup, Kent. *d:* 15.2.1954, Rye, Kent. Hard hitting middle order right-hand batsman, right-hand fast medium bowler. *Sch* Harrow. *Teams* Kent (1902–03, 6 matches); Cambridge U (1903–05, blue all three years). *Tour* MCC to North America, 1905.
Career batting
43–81–4–1932–157–25.09–2–*ct* 43
Bowling 744–19–39.15–0–0–4/25
He captained Cambridge in 1905.

Mann, Francis George, CBE
Amateur. *b:* 6.9.1917, Byfleet, Surrey. Son of F. T. (Middlesex), brother of J. P. (Middlesex), uncle of E. J. Cunningham (Gloucestershire). Middle order right-hand batsman. *Sch* Eton. *Teams* Middlesex (1937–54, 54 matches); Cambridge U (1938–39, blue both years). *Tour* MCC to South Africa 1948/9. *Tests* England (1948/9 to 1949, 7 matches).
Career batting
166–262–17–6350–136*–25.91–7–*ct* 72
Bowling 389–3–129.66–0–0–2/16
Test batting
7–12–2–376–136*–37.60–1–*ct* 3
He hit 1,000 runs in a season three times (best 1,311, av 24.73, in 1949). He captained MCC in South Africa in 1948/9 and England in all the seven Tests in which he played. In 1948 and 1949 he was captain of Middlesex. His final first-class match was for Free Foresters in 1958. He was Middlesex Hon Secretary 1951–65, Chairman 1980–83 and President 1983–90, Chairman of the TCCB 1978–83 and MCC President 1984/5.

Mann, Francis Thomas
Amateur. *b:* 3.3.1888, Winchmore Hill, Middlesex. *d:* 6.10.1964, Milton-Lilbourne, Wiltshire. Father of F. G. (Middlesex) and J. P. (Middlesex), great-uncle of E. J. Cunningham (Gloucestershire). Attacking middle order right-hand batsman, slow right-arm bowler, brilliant outfield. *Sch* Malvern. *Teams* Cambridge U (1908–11, blue 1909–11); Middlesex (1909–31, 314 matches). *Tour* MCC to South Africa 1922/3. *Tests* England (1922/3, 5 matches).
Career batting
398–612–47–13235–194–23.42–9–*ct* 174
Bowling 249–3–83.00–0–0–1/7
Test batting
5–9–1–281–84–35.12–0–*ct* 4
He captained Middlesex in 1921–28, MCC in South Africa 1922/3 and England in all five matches on the tour. In 1930 he was a Test selector. He hit 1,000 runs in a season three times (best 1,343, av 26.33, in 1923). His final first-class match was for H. D. G. Leveson-Gower's XI in 1933. He was Middlesex Hon Secretary 1923–38 and President 1947–49.

Mann, Sir Horatio
Amateur. *b:* 2.2.1744, Egerton, Kent. *d:* 2.4.1814, Margate, Kent. *Sch* Charterhouse. *Team* Kent (1773–82).
One of the greatest patrons of the game, his last recorded match was in 1782 and the details of most of his cricket have been lost. He was MP for Maidstone 1774–84 and for Sandwich from 1790 to 1807, but 'his life was rather dedicated to pleasure than business.' A number of great matches were staged at his estate at Dandelion, near Margate, and at Bourne House, Bishopsbourne, near Canterbury.

Mann, Ian Rutherford
Amateur. *b:* 4.5.1906, Melbourne, Victoria, Australia. Middle order right-hand batsman. *Team* Cambridge U (1927).
Career batting
1–1–0–26–26–26.00–0–*ct* 0
He won blues for relay races and athletics.

Mann, James Elliot Furneaux
Amateur. *b:* 2.12.1903, Melbourne, Victoria, Australia. *d:* 25.6.1984, Victoria, Australia. Middle order right-hand batsman. *Team* Cambridge U (1924, blue).
Career batting
6–10–1–219–114–24.33–1–*ct* 6

Mann, John Pelham
Amateur. *b:* 13.6.1919, Byfleet, Surrey. Brother of F. G. (Middlesex), son of F. T. (Middlesex), uncle of E. J. Cunningham (Gloucestershire). Middle order right-hand batsman, leg break bowler. *Sch* Eton. *Teams* Middlesex (1939–47, 15 matches); Cambridge U (1939).
Career batting
21–32–3–608–77–20.96–0–*ct* 18
Bowling 366–6–61.00–0–0–3/71

Mann, Noah
Professional. *b:* 15.11.1756, North Chapel, Sussex. *d:* December 1789, North Chapel, Sussex. Whilst sleeping in front of a fire his clothes caught alight and he died of burns. Father of Noah jun (MCC). Hard hitting left-hand batsman, left-hand under-arm bowler, good field. *Team* Hampshire (1777–89).
For about 10 years he was one of the principal cricketers of the Hambledon Club.

Mann, Norman Bertram Fleetwood
Amateur. *b:* 28.12.1920, Benoni, Transvaal, South Africa. *d:* 31.7.1952, Hillbrow, Johannesburg, South Africa. Hard hitting lower order right-hand batsman, slow left-arm bowler. *Teams* Natal (1939/40 to 1945/6); Eastern Province (1946/7 to 1950/1). *Tours* South Africa to England 1947, 1951. *Tests* South Africa (1947–51, 19 matches).
Career batting
73–99–16–1446–97–17.42–0–*ct* 25
Bowling 5952–251–23.71–14–3–8/59
Test batting
19–31–1–400–52–13.33–0–*ct* 3
Bowling 1920–58–33.10–1–0–6/59

Although at Cambridge, he was not tried in any first-class matches for the University and instead gained a golfing blue. On the 1947 tour he appeared in all five Tests and headed the Test bowling averages. In 1951 he repeated this feat, but his form was already being affected by the illness from which he died only a year later.

Mann, William Horace
Amateur. *b:* 28.7.1878, Highfield, Trowbridge, Wiltshire. *d:* 24.2.1938, Canford Cliffs, Dorset. Middle order right-hand batsman. *Sch* Marlborough. *Team* Worcestershire (1924, 1 match).
Career batting
1–2–0–7–4–3.50–0–*ct* 0

Manners, Dunlop Crawford John
Amateur. *b:* 24.8.1916, Kuala Lumpur, Malaya. Lower order right-hand batsman, right-arm fast bowler. *Sch* Lancing. *Team* Army (1939).
Career batting
1–1–1–33–33*–no av–0–*ct* 1
Bowling 83–1–83.00–0–0–1/83

Manners, Herbert Cecil
Amateur. *b:* 16.4.1877, Hartley Wintney, Hampshire. *d:* 30.12.1955, West Worthing, Sussex. Lower order right-hand batsman, wicket-keeper. *Sch* Cheltenham. *Team* Gloucestershire (1902–11, 5 matches).
Career batting
5–8–0–60–32–7.50–0–*ct* 1

Manners, John Errol
Amateur. *b:* 25.9.1914, Exeter, Devon. Aggressive middle order right-hand batsman. *Team* Hampshire (1936–48, 7 matches).
Career batting
21–37–0–1162–147–31.40–4–*ct* 4
Bowling 16–0

His final first-class match was for the Combined Services in 1953 and his County cricket was restricted due to his being an officer in the Royal Navy.

Mannes, Charles Turnbull
Amateur. *b:* 25.10.1863, Glasgow, Scotland. *d:* 29.12.1937, Airdrie, Lanarkshire, Scotland. Opening right-hand batsman, right-arm medium pace bowler. *Team* Scotland (1906–08).
Career batting
3–6–0–129–62–21.50–0–*ct* 1

Manning, John Stephen
Professional. *b:* 11.6.1923, Semaphore, Adelaide, South Australia. *d:* 5.5.1988, Adelaide, South Australia. Lower order left-hand batsman, left-arm slow bowler. *Teams* South Australia (1951/2 to 1953/4, 19 matches); Northamptonshire (1954–60, 117 matches).
Career batting
146–207–31–2766–132–15.71–1–*ct* 77
Bowling 11662–513–22.73–25–4–8/43

He took 100 wickets in a season three times (best 116, av 20.68, in 1956).

Manning, Thomas Edgar
Amateur. *b:* 2.9.1884, Northampton. *d:* 22.11.1975, Dallington, Northamptonshire. Middle order right-hand batsman, wicket-keeper. *Sch* Wellingborough. *Team* Northamptonshire (1906–22, 53 matches).
Career batting
53–93–15–1026–57–13.15–0–*ct* 29–*st* 3

He appeared in the Seniors match whilst at Cambridge, but no first-class matches. He first played for Northamptonshire (pre first-class) in 1903. He captained Northamptonshire from 1908 to 1910 and was President from 1948 to 1955.

Mannings, Dr George
Amateur. *b:* 13.10.1843, Downton, Wiltshire. *d:* 28.11.1876, Downton, Wiltshire. Middle order batsman. *Sch* Marlborough. *Team* Hampshire (1864, 1 match).
Career batting
1–2–0–7–5–3.50–0–*ct* 1

He also played for Wiltshire (1863).

Mansell, Alan William
Cricketer. *b:* 19.5.1951, Redhill, Surrey. Middle order right-hand batsman, wicket-keeper. *Team* Sussex (1969–75, 58 matches).
Career batting
58–93–21–1098–72*–15.25–0–*ct* 108–*st* 7

Mansell, Percy Neville Frank, MBE
Amateur. *b:* 16.3.1920, St George's, Shropshire. Brother of A. J. M. (Rhodesia). Middle order right-hand batsman, leg break or right-arm medium pace bowler. *Team* Rhodesia (1936/7 to 1959/60). *Tours* South Africa to England 1951, 1955, to Australia and New Zealand 1952/3. *Tests* South Africa (1951–55, 13 matches).
Career batting
113–172–17–4598–154–29.66–5–*ct* 156
Bowling 7798–299–26.08–21–5–7/43

Test batting
13–22–2–355–90–17.75–0–*ct* 15
Bowling 736–11–66.90–0–0–3/58

Without achieving anything of real note, he proved a useful all-rounder on both tours to England – curiously none of his 13 Tests took place at home. His last first-class match was for Rhodesia Invitation XI in 1961/2.

Manser, Robert Marsack
Amateur. *b:* 10.10.1880, Tonbridge, Kent. *d:* 15.2.1955, Parkstone, Dorset. Middle order right-hand batsman. *Sch* Tonbridge. *Team* Hampshire (1904, 1 match).
Career batting
1–2–0–1–1–0.50–0–*ct* 1

He also played for Dorset (1909–29).

Mansfield, Hon James William
Amateur. *b:* 12.2.1862, Poona, India. *d:* 17.6.1932, Westminster, London. Middle order right-hand batsman. *Sch* Winchester. *Team* Cambridge U (1883–84, blue both years).
Career batting
17–31–2–437–117–15.06–1–*ct* 10
Bowling 17–0

His County cricket was for Norfolk (1882). His first-class debut was for England XI in 1882 and his final match for MCC in 1888.

Mansoor Akhtar
Cricketer. *b:* 25.12.1957, Karachi, Pakistan. Opening or middle order right-hand batsman, right-arm medium pace bowler, excellent outfield. *Teams* Karachi (1974/5 to 1990/1); Sind (1976/7 to 1977/8); United Bank (1977/8 to 1991/2). *Tours* Pakistan to Australia 1981/2, 1983/4, 1989/90, to England 1982, 1987. *Tests* Pakistan (1980/1 to 1989/90, 19 matches).
Career batting
194–329–31–11680–224*–39.19–25–*ct* 136–*st* 2
Bowling 1000–27–37.03–0–0–3/24
Test batting
19–29–3–655–111–25.19–1–*ct* 9

In 1976/7, with Waheed Mirza, he created a new first-class first wicket record partnership of 561 for Karachi Whites v Quetta at Karachi. On the 1982 tour to England he scored 595 runs, av 39.66, and played in all three Tests. Returning to England in 1987 he played in all five Tests, scoring 152 runs, av 30.40, and in first-class matches hit 1,156, av 55.04, being the only tourist to top 1,000 runs. He scored 1,503 runs, av 48.48, in Pakistan in 1986/7.

Mansur Ali Khan
(*see under* Pataudi, Nawab of, Mansur Ali Khan)

Mantell, David Norman
Professional. *b:* 22.7.1934, Acton, Middlesex. Lower order right-hand batsman, wicket-keeper. *Team* Sussex (1954–58, 26 matches).
Career batting
26–31–6–150–34–6.00–0–*ct* 28–*st* 2

Mantle, Thomas Allen
Professional. *b:* 31.1.1840, Kates Hill, Worcestershire. *d:* 29.4.1884, Wandsworth Common, London. Lower order right-hand batsman, right-arm medium pace bowler. *Team* Middlesex (1864–72, 22 matches).
Career batting
27–48–3–503–46–11.17–0–*ct* 13
Bowling 651–29–22.44–0–0–4/30

His final first-class match was for Players of the South in 1873.

Manton, Joseph
Amateur. *b:* 4.12.1871, West Bromwich, Staffordshire. *d:* 9.12.1958, Henham, Essex. Middle order right-hand batsman, right-arm fast bowler. *Sch* KES, Birmingham. *Team* Warwickshire (1898, 1 match).
Career batting
1–2–0–5–5–2.50–0–*ct* 0
Bowling 51–1–51.00–0–0–1/51

He also played for Bedfordshire (1895) and Staffordshire (1904). He captained Warwickshire in his only first-class match.

Mantri, Madhav Krishnaji
Amateur. *b:* 1.9.1921, Nasik, India. Uncle of S. M. Gavaskar (India). Opening right-hand batsman, wicket-keeper. *Teams* Bombay (1941/2 to 1956/7); Maharashtra (1942/3). *Tours* India to England 1952, to Pakistan 1954/5; ACC to Pakistan 1961/2. *Tests* India (1951/2 to 1954/5, 4 matches).
Career batting
95–141–11–4403–200–33.86–7–*ct* 136–*st* 56
Bowling 121–3–40.33–0–0–2/38
Test batting
4–8–1–67–39–9.57–0–*ct* 8–*st* 1

He appeared in two Tests on the 1952 tour to England, but achieved little with the bat. His only double century was 200 for Bombay v Maharashtra at Poona in 1948/9. His final first-class match was for Goa Chief Minister's XI in 1967/8.

Manville, David Walter
Professional. *b:* 18.8.1934, Hollingbury, Brighton, Sussex. Lower order right-hand batsman, wicket-keeper. *Team* Sussex (1956, 3 matches).
Career batting
3–5–0–13–8–2.60–0–*ct* 1

Manzoor Elahi
Cricketer. *b:* 15.4.1963, Sahiwal, Pakistan. Middle order right-hand batsman, right-arm fast medium bowler. *Teams* Multan (1983/4 to 1991/2); Railways (1983/4 to 1984/5); ADBP (1985/6 to 1991/2). *Tours* Pakistan Under 23 to Sri Lanka 1984/5; Pakistan to Sri Lanka 1985/6 (not first-class), to Sharjah (not first-class) 1984/5, 1985/6, 1986/7, 1988/9, to Austra-

lia 1986/7 (not first-class), to India 1986/7, to England 1987, to Bangladesh (not first-class) 1988/9; Pakistan B to Kenya 1986/7. *Tests* Pakistan (1984/5 to 1986/7, 4 matches).
Career batting
109–168–15–5377–163*–35.14–8–*ct* 93
Bowling 5441–154–35.33–1–0–5/37
Test batting
4–6–1–109–52–21.80–0–*ct* 5
Bowling 84–2–42.00–0–0–1/8

He had little opportunity on the 1987 tour to England, but he hit the headlines when he made six sixes off an over in a Charity Match at West Bromwich. His first-class debut was for BCCP XI in 1982/3.

Maqsood Ahmed
Amateur. *b:* 26.3.1925, Amritsar, India. Middle order right-hand batsman, right-arm medium pace bowler. *Teams* Southern Punjab (1944/5 to 1946/7); Bahawalpur (1953/4); Karachi (1956/7); Rawalpindi (1960/1 to 1963/4). *Tours* Pakistan to India 1952/3, to England 1954. *Tests* Pakistan (1952/3 to 1955/6, 16 matches).
Career batting
81–125–9–3716–144–32.03–6–*ct* 46
Bowling 3412–120–28.43–6–1–7/39
Test batting
16–27–1–507–99–19.50–0–*ct* 13
Bowling 191–3–63.66–0–0–2/12

He hit 1,314 runs, av 34.57, in first-class matches on the 1954 tour to England and appeared in all four Tests. His first-class debut in Pakistan was for Punjab Governor's XI in 1947/8; he first played in England for a Commonwealth XI in 1952. He scored 144 on debut for Southern Punjab v Northern India at Lahore in 1944/5.

Marchant, Francis
Amateur. *b:* 22.5.1864, Matfield House, Kent. *d:* 13.4.1946, Roehampton, London. Stylish middle order right-hand batsman. *Sch* Eton and Rugby. *Teams* Kent (1883–1905, 226 matches); Cambridge U (1884–87, blue all four years).
Career batting
267–451–16–9124–176–20.97–8–*ct* 130
Bowling 609–20–30.45–0–0–2/11

He captained Cambridge in 1887 and Kent 1890–97, jointly in the first four years. He was President of Kent in 1934. He also won a blue for soccer.

Marchbank, Walter James
Professional. *b:* 2.11.1838, Preston, Lancashire. *d:* 9.8.1893, Walton-le-Dale, Preston, Lancashire. Lower order batsman, wicket-keeper. *Team* Lancashire (1869–70, 4 matches).
Career batting
4–7–1–20–15–3.33–0–*ct* 1–*st* 2

Mardall, James Henry Thrale
Amateur. *b:* 7.11.1899, Harpenden, Hertfordshire. *d:* 10.7.1988, Colchester, Essex. Middle order right-hand batsman, slow right-arm bowler. *Sch* Aldenham. *Team* Army (1931).
Career batting
1–2–0–1–1–0.50–0–*ct* 2

His County cricket was for Hertfordshire (1931–32).

Mare, John Matthew
Amateur. *b:* 22.2.1854, Paddington, London. *d:* 11.12.1909. Hard hitting middle order right-hand batsman. *Team* Sussex (1870–78, 26 matches).
Career batting
26–47–3–616–97–14.00–0–*ct* 9

Margrett, Charles Henry
Amateur. *b:* 10.8.1862, Cheltenham, Gloucestershire. *d:* 22.11.1941, Sandford, Cheltenham, Gloucestershire. Lower order batsman. *Team* Gloucestershire (1886, 1 match).
Career batting
1–2–0–14–14–7.00–0–*ct* 0

He played in emergency for Gloucestershire in the absence of W. R. Gilbert.

Marie, Gregory Vincent
Cricketer. *b:* 17.2.1945, Subiaco, Perth, Western Australia. Lower order right-hand batsman, right-arm medium pace bowler. *Team* Oxford U (1978–79, blue 1978).
Career batting
10–13–2–104–27–9.45–0–*ct* 1
Bowling 666–20–33.30–1–0–5/46

Appointed captain of Oxford in 1979, injury prevented him playing against Cambridge.

Mariner, Edward Charles
Amateur. *b:* 3.1.1877, Winchester, Hampshire. *d:* 10.5.1949, Fratton, Portsmouth, Hampshire. Lower order batsman, useful bowler. *Sch* Cranleigh. *Team* Hampshire (1896, 1 match).
Career batting
1–2–0–0–0–0.00–0–*ct* 0
Bowling 20–0

Marks, Alfred Edwin
Amateur. *b:* 15.5.1924, Knock, Belfast, Ireland. Tail end right-hand batsman, wicket-keeper. *Team* Ireland (1953–55).
Career batting
3–6–0–35–17–5.83–0–*ct* 5–*st* 2

Marks, Christopher Peter
Cricketer. *b:* 17.7.1946, Hanley, Staffordshire. Lower order right-hand batsman, right-arm medium pace bowler. *Sch* Worksop. *Team* Derbyshire (1967–69, 14 matches).

Career batting
14–21–2–216–39–11.36–0–*ct* 6
He also played for Staffordshire (1970–73).

Marks, Frederick David
Amateur. *b:* 5.2.1867, Mount Wise, Plymouth, Devon. Lower order right-hand batsman, right-arm fast bowler. *Team* Somerset (1884, 1 match).
Career batting
1–2–1–2–2–2.00–0–*ct* 0
Bowling 3–0
He also played for Wiltshire (1888–99).

Marks, Geoffrey
Amateur. *b:* 15.11.1864, Thornton Heath, Croydon, Surrey. *d:* 25.8.1938, Nately-Scures, Hampshire. Brother of Oliver (MCC), son-in-law of J. H. Bridges (Surrey). Lower order batsman, wicket-keeper. *Sch* Whitgift. *Team* Middlesex (1894–95, 2 matches).
Career batting
2–4–2–31–17–15.50–0–*ct* 3

Marks, M.
Amateur. Middle order batsman. *Team* W. G. Grace's XI (1873).
Career batting
1–1–0–1–1–1.00–0–*ct* 0

Marks, Oliver
Amateur. *b:* 10.9.1866, Thornton Heath, Croydon, Surrey. *d:* 24.5.1940, Brompton, Kensington, London. Brother of Geoffrey (Middlesex). Lower order batsman, useful bowler. *Sch* Whitgift. *Team* MCC (1901).
Career batting
1–1–0–1–1–1.00–0–*ct* 0
Bowling 36–0

Marks, Victor James
Cricketer. *b:* 25.6.1955, Middle Chinnock, Somerset. Middle order right-hand batsman, off break bowler. *Sch* Blundell's. *Teams* Oxford U (1975–78, blue all four years); Somerset (1975–89, 275 matches); Western Australia (1986/7, 11 matches). *Tours* England to Australia 1982/3, 1984/5 (not first-class), to New Zealand 1982/3 (not first-class), 1983/4, to Pakistan 1983/4, to India 1984/5. *Tests* England (1982 to 1983/4, 6 matches).
Career batting
342–500–90–12419–134–30.29–5–*ct* 144
Bowling 28591–859–33.28–40–5–8/17
Test batting
6–10–1–249–83–27.66–0–*ct* 0
Bowling 484–11–44.00–0–0–3/78
He hit 1,000 runs in a season twice (best 1,262, av 52.58, in 1984). He took 86 wickets, av 25.96, in 1984. Considering his record in County cricket it is surprising that he was not selected more often for England. After retiring he took up cricket journalism. He captained Oxford 1976–77 and Somerset 1989. He also represented Oxford at rugby fives.

Marlar, Robin Geoffrey
Amateur. *b:* 2.1.1931, Eastbourne, Sussex. Lower order right-hand batsman, off break bowler. *Sch* Harrow. *Teams* Cambridge U (1951–53, blue all three years); Sussex (1951–68, 223 matches). *Tour* Swanton to West Indies 1955/6.
Career batting
289–379–67–3033–64–9.72–0–*ct* 136
Bowling 24469–970–25.22–66–15–9/46
He took 100 wickets in a season four times (best 139, av 21.55, in 1955). His best bowling in an innings was 9/46 for Sussex v Lancashire at Hove in 1955. He captained Cambridge in 1953 and Sussex 1955–59. After 1959 he played very little first-class cricket. He is a well-known writer and commentator on the game.

Marlow, Christopher Roderick James
Cricketer. *b:* 30.9.1949, Bexhill-on-Sea, Sussex. Middle order left-hand batsman, right-arm medium pace bowler. *Sch* Uppingham. *Team* Cambridge U (1973).
Career batting
3–6–1–29–15–5.80–0–*ct* 2
Bowling 7–1–7.00–0–0–1/7

Marlow, Francis William
Professional. *b:* 8.10.1867, Tamworth, Staffordshire. *d:* 7.8.1952, Hove, Sussex. Stylish opening right-hand batsman, right-arm medium bowler, brilliant field. *Team* Sussex (1891–1904, 212 matches).
Career batting
219–379–23–7890–155–22.16–7–*ct* 58
Bowling 196–4–49.00–0–0–2/18
He also played for Staffordshire (1887–90). His first-class debut was for an England XI in 1890. He hit 1,054 runs, av 25.09, in 1895. He was a first-class umpire (1905–08 and 1914–21).

Marlow, Joseph
Professional. *b:* 12.12.1854, Bulwell, Nottinghamshire. *d:* 8.6.1923, Bulwell, Nottinghamshire. Middle order right-hand batsman, right-arm medium pace bowler. *Team* Derbyshire (1879–86, 24 matches).
Career batting
24–45–5–317–25–7.92–0–*ct* 23
Bowling 1237–60–20.61–5–1–7/46
He last played for Derbyshire (not first-class) in 1890.

Marlow, Thomas
Professional. *b:* 15.12.1878, Rothley, Leicestershire. *d:* 13.8.1954, Southfields, Leicester. Lower order left-hand batsman, slow medium left-arm bowler. *Team* Leicestershire (1900–03, 15 matches).
Career batting
15–22–8–46–10*–3.28–0–*ct* 7
Bowling 846–31–27.29–2–0–6/50

Marlow, William Henry
Professional. *b:* 13.2.1900, Wigston, Leicestershire. *d:* 16.12.1975, Leicester. Lower order left-hand batsman, left-arm medium pace bowler. *Team* Leicestershire (1931–36, 109 matches).
Career batting
109–158–33–1117–64–8.93–0–*ct* 77
Bowling 7615–261–29.17–12–2–7/90

Marner, Peter Thomas
Professional. *b:* 31.3.1936, Greenacres, Oldham, Lancashire. Middle order right-hand batsman, right-arm medium pace bowler. *Teams* Lancashire (1952–64, 236 matches); Leicestershire (1965–70, 165 matches). *Tour* Commonwealth to Pakistan 1967/8.
Career batting
414–680–62–17513–142*–28.33–18–*ct* 379
Bowling 11385–360–31.62–13–1–7/29
He hit 1,000 runs in a season twelve times (best 1,685, av 38.29, in 1958).

Marple, George Smith
Amateur. *b:* 14.8.1868, Chester, Cheshire. *d:* 12.8.1932, Ecclesall, Sheffield, Yorkshire. Lower order batsman. *Team* Derbyshire (1901, 1 match).
Career batting
1–1–0–6–6–6.00–0–*ct* 0
Bowling 17–1–17.00–0–0–1/17

Marples, Christopher
Cricketer. *b:* 3.8.1964, Chesterfield, Derbyshire. Middle order right-hand batsman, occasional off break bowler, wicket-keeper. *Team* Derbyshire (1985–86, 26 matches).
Career batting
26–39–8–580–57–18.70–0–*ct* 54–*st* 5
Bowling 48–0
He played soccer for Chesterfield, Stockport, York and Scunthorpe as goalkeeper.

Marples, George Holmes
Professional. *b:* 30.5.1883, Attercliffe, Yorkshire. *d:* 30.12.1947, Chesterfield, Derbyshire. Tail end batsman, left-arm medium fast bowler. *Team* Derbyshire (1905, 2 matches).
Career batting
2–4–0–11–6–2.75–0–*ct* 1
Bowling 116–1–116.00–0–0–1/53

Marriott, Charles
Amateur. *b:* 14.10.1848, Cotesbach, Leicestershire. *d:* 9.7.1918, Cotesbach, Leicestershire. Brother of G. S. (Oxford U), grandfather of P. M. R. Scott (Oxford U) and R. S. G. Scott (Sussex). Middle order right-hand batsman, slow right-arm bowler. *Sch* Bradfield and Winchester. *Team* Oxford U (1870–71, blue 1871).
Career batting
31–50–6–628–48–14.27–0–*ct* 23
Bowling 57–0 + 1–no av–0–0–1/?
His final first-class match was for I Zingari in 1882. He was a major figure in Leicestershire cricket (1873–93) before the County was raised to first-class status and County captain 1879–84. He was Leicestershire President 1890–93 and 1903–04. He was also on the MCC Committee. He also played for Warwickshire (pre first-class, 1868–69).

Marriott, Charles Stowell
(birth registered as Charlie Stowell Marriott)
Amateur. *b:* 14.9.1895, Heaton Moor, Lancashire. *d:* 13.10.1966, Dollis Hill, Middlesex. Tail end right-hand batsman, leg break and googly bowler. *Sch* St Columba's. *Teams* Lancashire (1919–21, 12 matches); Cambridge U (1920–21, blue both years); Kent (1924–37, 101 matches). *Tours* Joel to South Africa 1924/5; MCC to India and Ceylon 1933/4. *Test* England (1933, 1 match).
Career batting
159–178–48–574–21–4.41–0–*ct* 47
Bowling 14304–711–20.11–48–10–8/98
Test batting
1–1–0–0–0–0.00–0–*ct* 1
Bowling 96–11–8.72–2–1–6/59
Throughout the 1920s and early 1930s he was one of the leading bowlers in first-class County cricket, but being a master at Dulwich College most of his appearances were in August. His best season was 1931 with 76 wickets, av 14.61. His final first-class match was for Free Foresters in 1938.

Marriott, Dennis Alston
Cricketer. *b:* 29.11.1939, Amity Hall, St Thomas, Jamaica. Lower order right-hand batsman, left-arm fast medium bowler. *Teams* Surrey (1965–67, 19 matches); Middlesex (1972–74, 11 matches).
Career batting
30–26–13–139–24*–10.69–0–*ct* 5
Bowling 1990–67–29.70–1–0–5/71

Marriott, Rev George Strickland
Amateur. *b:* 7.10.1855, Cotesbach, Leicestershire. *d:* 21.10.1905, Sigglesthorne, Yorkshire. Brother of Charles (Oxford U). Middle order right-hand batsman, right-hand fast round-arm bowler. *Sch* Winchester. *Team* Oxford U (1878, blue).
Career batting
3–6–0–21–11–3.50–0–*ct* 0
Bowling 87–0
His County cricket was for Leicestershire (pre first-class, 1874–85).

Marriott, Harold Henry
Amateur. *b:* 20.1.1875, Oadby, Leicester. *d:* 15.11.1949, Kensington, London. Middle order right-hand batsman, right-arm medium pace bowler. *Sch* Malvern. *Teams* Leicestershire (1894–1902, 40 matches); Cambridge U (1895–98, blue all four years). *Tours* Mitchell to North America 1895 (he did not play in first-class matches); Warner to North

America 1897.
Career batting
87–151–4–3266–146*–22.21–5–*ct* 65
Bowling 296–8–37.00–0–0–4/60
His final first-class match was for MCC in 1919. He also won a blue for golf.

Marriott, William
Professional. *b:* 6.1.1850, Hucknall-under-Huthwaite, Nottinghamshire. *d:* 28.8.1887, Huyton, Lancashire. Middle order right-hand batsman, useful bowler. *Team* Nottinghamshire (1880–81, 2 matches).
Career batting
2–3–0–27–14–9.00–0–*ct* 0
Bowling 10–2–5.00–0–0–2/10

Marrison, Fernley
Amateur. *b:* 16.10.1891, Medway, Kent. *d:* 13.2.1967, South Farnborough, Hampshire. Lower order right-hand batsman, right-arm fast bowler. *Teams* Army (1914–20); Europeans (1925/6).
Career batting
8–11–3–85–20*–10.62–0–*ct* 6
Bowling 537–16–33.56–1–0–6/44
His final first-class match in England was for H. D. G. Leveson-Gower's XI in 1925.

Marsden, Arthur
Amateur. *b:* 28.10.1880, Buxton, Derbyshire. *d:* 31.7.1916, St Pancras, London. He died of wounds received on the Somme. Opening right-hand batsman. *Sch* Cheethams School, Manchester. *Team* Derbyshire (1910, 1 match).
Career batting
1–2–0–6–6–3.00–0–*ct* 1

Marsden, Edmund
Amateur. *b:* 18.4.1881, Madras, India. *d:* 26.5.1915, Myitkina, Burma. He died of malarial fever. Middle order batsman. *Sch* Cheltenham. *Team* Gloucestershire (1909, 2 matches).
Career batting
2–4–0–79–38–19.75–0–*ct* 0

Marsden, Edward Leverson
Amateur. *b:* 25.7.1870, Hampstead, London. *d:* 2.7.1946, New End, Hampstead, London. Lower order left-hand batsman, left-arm fast bowler. *Team* Middlesex (1897, 1 match).
Career batting
1–1–0–3–3–3.00–0–*ct* 0
Bowling 68–1–68.00–0–0–1/45

Marsden, George Allen
Amateur. *b:* 28.6.1869, Wirksworth, Derbyshire. *d:* 7.1.1938, Diep River, Cape Province, South Africa. Middle order right-hand batsman, leg break bowler. *Sch* Denstone College. *Team* Derbyshire (1894–98, 30 matches).
Career batting
30–46–6–417–37–10.42–0–*ct* 12

Marsden, Keith
Amateur. *b:* 24.7.1931, Carlisle, Cumberland. Lower order right-hand batsman, right-arm medium pace bowler. *Sch* Lancaster RGS. *Team* Cambridge U (1952).
Career batting
1 match, did not bat–*ct* 0
Bowling 56–0
An athletics blue, he also represented England.

Marsden, Robert
Cricketer. *b:* 2.4.1959, Hammersmith, London. Middle order right-hand batsman, off break bowler. *Sch* Merchant Taylors. *Team* Oxford U (1979–82, blue 1982).
Career batting
13–23–1–507–60–23.04–0–*ct* 6

Marsden, Thomas
Professional. *c:* 11.6.1805, Sheffield, Yorkshire. *d:* 27.2.1843, Sheffield, Yorkshire. Attacking middle order left-hand batsman, left-hand fast under-arm or slow round-arm bowler. *Teams* Sheffield (1827–30); Yorkshire (1833–35, 4 matches).
Career batting
55–99–3–1724–227–17.95–2–*ct* 44
Bowling 138–4 + 92–34.50–3–1–7/?
His most famous innings was 227 for the combined Sheffield and Leicester eleven v Nottingham at Darnall, Sheffield in 1826, being his debut. His final match was for MCC in 1841.

Marsh, Edward Caldecot
Amateur. *b:* 7.5.1865, Belgaum, Bombay, India. *d:* 27.11.1926, Kendal, Westmorland. Middle order right-hand batsman. *Sch* Malvern. *Team* Somerset (1885, 2 matches).
Career batting
2–4–0–18–15–4.50–0–*ct* 1
He also played for Devon (1887–88).

Marsh, Eric
Amateur. *b:* 30.5.1940, Greenwich, London. Middle order right-hand batsman, leg break bowler. *Sch* St Dunstan's. *Team* Oxford U (1962).
Career batting
10–20–3–419–50–24.64–0–*ct* 4
His County cricket was for Shropshire (1964–76).

Marsh, Frederick Eric
Professional. *b:* 17.7.1920, Bolsover, Derbyshire. Nephew of T. S. Worthington (Derbyshire). Lower order left-hand batsman, slow left-arm bowler. *Team* Derbyshire (1946–49, 66 matches).
Career batting
66–109–20–1627–86–18.28–0–*ct* 32
Bowling 1698–44–38.59–1–0–6/37

Marsh, Geoffrey Robert
Cricketer. *b:* 31.12.1958, Northam, Western Australia. Sound opening right-hand batsman. *Team* West-

ern Australia (1977/8 to 1991/2, 90 matches). *Tours* Australia to New Zealand 1985/6, 1989/90, 1991/2 (World Cup), to Sharjah (not first-class) 1985/6, 1986/7, 1989/90, to India 1986/7, 1989/90 (not first-class), to India and Pakistan (World Cup) 1987/8, to Pakistan 1988/9, to England 1989. *Tests* Australia (1985/6 to 1991/2, 50 matches).
Career batting
162–283–23–10240–355*–39.38–27–*ct* 127
Bowling 8–1–8.00–0–0–1/1
Test batting
50–93–7–2854–138–33.18–4–*ct* 38

He played in all six Tests on the 1989 tour to England and created a new first wicket record for England v Australia matches at Trent Bridge when with M. A. Taylor he batted through the whole of the first day, the pair eventually adding 329. His highest score was 355* for Western Australia v South Australia at Perth in 1989/90. He scored 1,000 runs in a season in Australia three times (best 1,200, av 48.00, in 1986/7).

Marsh, Rev James William
Amateur. *b:* 16.10.1870, Thame, Oxfordshire. *d:* 26.3.1930, Ludlow, Shropshire. Brother of J. F. (Cambridge U). Middle order right-hand batsman, wicket-keeper. *Sch* Amersham Hall. *Team* Cambridge U (1901).
Career batting
8–15–2–145–29*–11.15–0–*ct* 5–*st* 5

His final first-class match was for J. Bamford's XI in 1907. His County cricket was for Oxfordshire (1901–06).

Marsh, John Frederick
Amateur. *b:* 11.5.1875, Thame, Oxfordshire. *d:* 30.10.1927, Higham-on-the-Hill, Leicestershire. Brother of J. W. (Cambridge U). Stubborn opening right-hand batsman. *Sch* Amersham Hall. *Team* Cambridge U (1901–04, blue 1904).
Career batting
8–16–3–548–172*–42.15–2–*ct* 7
Bowling 18–0

His score of 172* in the 1904 University match was a record at the time. His County cricket was for Oxfordshire (1892–1906) and at one time he captained the County.

Marsh, Paul
Cricketer. *b:* 5.12.1939, Johannesburg, South Africa. Middle order right-hand batsman, off break bowler. *Team* Cambridge U (1965).
Career batting
1–2–0–25–23–12.50–0–*ct* 1
Bowling 22–0

His County cricket was for Cambridgeshire (1965).

Marsh, Reginald Bert
Professional. *b:* 11.8.1897, Wells, Somerset. *d:* 25.4.1969, Bristol. Lower order right-hand batsman, right-arm medium pace bowler. *Team* Somerset (1928–34, 4 matches).
Career batting
4–5–1–42–24*–10.50–0–*ct* 1
Bowling 197–2–98.50–0–0–2/121

Marsh, Rodney William, MBE
Cricketer. *b:* 11.11.1947, Armadale, Perth, Western Australia. Attacking middle order left-hand batsman, occasional off break bowler, wicket-keeper. *Team* Western Australia (1968/9 to 1983/4, 97 matches). *Tours* Australia to England 1972, 1975, 1977, 1980, 1981, 1983 (World Cup), to West Indies 1972/3, to New Zealand 1973/4, 1976/7, 1981/2, to Pakistan 1979/80, 1982/3. *Tests* Australia (1970/1 to 1983/4, 96 matches).
Career batting
257–396–41–11067–236–31.17–12–*ct* 803–*st* 66
Bowling 84–1–84.00–0–0–1/0
Test batting
96–150–13–3633–132–26.51–3–*ct* 343–*st* 12
Bowling 54–0

Apart from the period which he spent with World Series Cricket, he was Australia's principal wicket-keeper throughout his career and did not miss a single Test on his five tours to England. He holds the record for the most Test victims by a wicket-keeper. He scored 104 on debut for Western Australia v West Indians at Perth in 1968/9. His highest score was 236 for Western Australia v Pakistanis at Perth in 1972/3.

Marsh, Steven Andrew
Cricketer. *b:* 27.1.1961, Westminster, London. Son-in-law of R. C. Wilson (Kent). Middle order right-hand batsman, wicket-keeper. *Team* Kent (1982–92, 172 matches),
Career batting
172–240–45–5492–125–28.16–6–*ct* 368–*st* 31
Bowling 227–2–113.50–0–0–2/20

In 1991 he held eight catches in an innings and scored a hundred for Kent v Middlesex at Lord's. This wicket-keeping and batting combination created a new first-class record.

Marsh, William (Edward)
Amateur. *b:* 10.9.1917, Newbridge, Monmouthshire. *d:* 6.2.1978, Newbridge, Monmouthshire. Lower order batsman, right-arm fast medium bowler. *Team* Glamorgan (1947, 4 matches).
Career batting
4–6–1–39–13–7.80–0–*ct* 2
Bowling 290–8–36.25–0–0–3/70

Marshal, Alan
Amateur, turned professional in 1906. *b:* 12.6.1883, Warwick, Queensland, Australia. *d:* 23.7.1915, Imtarfa, Malta. He died of enteric fever. Hard hitting middle order right-hand batsman, right-arm fast medium bowler, brilliant catcher, excellent all-round field. *Teams* Queensland (1903/4 to 1913/14, 11

matches); Surrey (1907–10, 98 matches).
Career batting
119–198–13–5177–176–27.98–8–*ct* 114
Bowling 2718–119–22.84–7–1–7/41

He hit 1,000 runs in a season three times (best 1,931, av 40.22, in 1908). He came to England in 1904 and qualified by residence for Surrey. After two successful seasons, he was suspended in 1909 by the Surrey Committee and in 1910 returned to Australia. His first-class debut in England was for Gentlemen of England in 1905.

Marshal, Henry Worgan
Amateur. *b:* 27.6.1900, Santa Maria, Colombia. *d:* 6.1.1970, Ullesthorpe, Leicestershire. Opening right-hand batsman, wicket-keeper. *Sch* Oundle. *Team* Argentine (1926/7 to 1929/30). *Tour* South America to England 1932.
Career batting
10–18–1–487–153–28.64–2–*ct* 11

He was expected to be the outstanding batsman of the 1932 tour and in the first first-class match – v Oxford U – hit an excellent 153, but he achieved very little in the later first-class matches.

Marshall, Alan George
Amateur. *b:* 17.4.1895, Tripatur, Madras, India. *d:* 14.5.1973, Pettistree, Woodbridge, Suffolk. Brother of L. P. (Somerset). Lower order right-hand batsman, slow right-arm bowler, wicket-keeper. *Sch* Taunton. *Team* Somerset (1914–31, 45 matches).
Career batting
45–67–9–592–37–10.20–*ct* 34–*st* 9
Bowling 333–10–33.30–0–0–3/51

He played no first-class matches whilst at Oxford U, but did win a blue for lacrosse.

Marshall, Alexander
Amateur. *b:* 31.10.1820, Broadwater, Godalming, Surrey. *d:* 28.9.1871, Godalming, Surrey. Brother of Frederic (MCC) and Henry (Surrey). Very steady middle order right-hand batsman. *Team* Surrey (1849–57, 14 matches).
Career batting
26–43–6–221–23*–5.97–0–*ct* 13

His final first-class match was in 1860 for Gentlemen of the South.

Marshall, Amos
Professional. *b:* 10.7.1849, Yeadon, Yorkshire. *d:* 3.8.1891, Yeadon, Yorkshire. Lower order right-hand batsman, left-arm medium pace bowler, slip field. *Team* Yorkshire (1874, 1 match).
Career batting
2–4–1–18–13–6.00–0–*ct* 0
Bowling 18–1–18.00–0–0–1/7

His final first-class match was for the North in 1875. He also played for Northumberland (1875).

Marshall, Anthony Granville
Professional. *b:* 10.9.1932, Isleworth, Middlesex. *d:* 5.12.1988, Bristol. Lower order right-hand batsman, right-arm medium fast bowler. *Sch* Chatham House, Ramsgate. *Team* Kent (1950–54, 5 matches).
Career batting
6–11–1–37–7–3.70–0–*ct* 1
Bowling 399–13–30.69–1–0–6/53

He also played for Wiltshire (1955–70). His final first-class match was for Minor Counties in 1967.

Marshall, Bertie
Professional. *b:* 5.5.1902, Sutton-in-Ashfield, Nottinghamshire. *d:* 5.2.1991, Durham City. Lower order right-hand batsman, right-arm fast bowler. *Team* Nottinghamshire (1923–29, 4 matches).
Career batting
4–5–1–61–36–15.25–0–*ct* 3
Bowling 203–5–40.60–0–0–2/39

He played for Perthshire from 1927 to 1937 and appeared for Scotland but not in first-class matches. In 1939 he played as an amateur for Staffordshire.

Marshall, Charles
Amateur. *b:* 20.2.1843, Cricklewood, Middlesex. *d:* 25.2.1904, East Putney, London. Middle order right-hand batsman, right-arm medium pace bowler. *Sch* Rugby. *Teams* Middlesex (1866, 2 matches); Cambridgeshire (1866, 4 matches).
Career batting
6–9–0–178–50–19.77–0–*ct* 3

He also played for Norfolk (1865) and Huntingdonshire (1867–82).

Marshall, Charles
Professional. *b:* 1.10.1863, Woodville, Leicestershire. *d:* 20.11.1948, Birmingham. Lower order right-hand batsman, wicket-keeper. *Team* Surrey (1893–99, 43 matches).
Career batting
43–60–13–341–42–7.25–0–*ct* 82–*st* 15

He also played for Leicestershire (pre first-class, 1889–90). He was a first-class umpire (1919 and 1924–25).

Marshall, Charles James
Amateur. *b:* 17.10.1842, Cambridge. *d:* 11.2.1925. Brother of J. H. (Cambridgeshire) and J. W. (Cambridgeshire). Middle order batsman. *Sch* Repton. *Team* Cambridgeshire (1868, 1 match).
Career batting
1–2–0–31–28–15.50–0–*ct* 0

He also played for Warwickshire (pre first-class), Worcestershire (pre first-class) and Shropshire.

Marshall, David Alexander Cadman
Amateur. *b:* 29.12.1935, Dore, Sheffield, Yorkshire. Brother of J. C. (Oxford U). Middle order right-hand batsman, leg break bowler. *Sch* Rugby. *Team* Oxford U (1957).

Marshall, Edwin Alfred

Career batting
1–2–2–68–54*–no av–0–*ct* 1

Marshall, Edwin Alfred
Amateur. *b:* 21.8.1904, Nottingham. *d:* 28.1.1970, Nottingham. Lower order right-hand batsman, right-arm fast bowler. *Sch* Nottingham HS. *Team* Nottinghamshire (1937–38, 4 matches).
Career batting
4–5–0–19–13–3.80–0–*ct* 4
Bowling 167–3–0–55.66–0–0–2/43
He collapsed and died during the 1970 Nottinghamshire CCC AGM, being a member of the County Committee from 1942 and President in 1964–65.

Marshall, Francis William
Amateur. *b:* 30.1.1888, Rugby, Warwickshire. *d:* 24.5.1955, Kensington, London. Middle order right-hand batsman. *Team* Warwickshire (1922, 2 matches).
Career batting
2–2–0–14–10–7.00–0–*ct* 0
He also played for Montgomeryshire.

Marshall, Lt-Gen Sir Frederic
Amateur. *b:* 26.7.1829, Broadwater, Godalming, Surrey. *d:* 8.6.1900, Westminster, London. Brother of Alexander (Surrey) and Henry (Surrey). Middle order right-hand batsman. *Sch* Eton. *Team* MCC (1854–65).
Career batting
21–35–4–244–31–7.87–0–*ct* 12
He played for Surrey in 1857 in a non-first-class match. He was President of Surrey 1867–78.

Marshall, Gordon Alex
Amateur. *b:* 12.3.1935, Birmingham. Lower order right-hand batsman, right-arm fast medium bowler. *Sch* King's Norton GS. *Team* Warwickshire (1961–63, 4 matches).
Career batting
4–5–3–24–18*–12.00–0–*ct* 3
Bowling 221–9–24.55–1–0–5/22

Marshall, Henry
Amateur. *b:* 22.4.1831, Broadwater, Godalming, Surrey. *d:* 30.4.1914, Ipswich, Suffolk. Brother of Alexander (Surrey) and Frederic (MCC). Middle order right-hand batsman. *Sch* Winchester. *Team* Surrey (1853–54, 2 matches).
Career batting
17–31–1–200–33–6.66–0–*ct* 10
His final first-class match was for MCC in 1863. He was President of Surrey 1856–66.

Marshall, Herbert Menzies
Amateur. *b:* 1.8.1841, Outwood Hall, Leeds, Yorkshire. *d:* 2.3.1913, South Kensington, London. Middle order right-hand batsman, brilliant long stop. *Sch* Westminster. *Team* Cambridge U (1861–64, blue all four years).
Career batting
15–25–2–317–76*–13.78–0–*ct* 9
He was a well-known artist, being especially noted as a water-colourist.

Marshall, Hugh Dykes Ferguson
Cricketer. *b:* 11.1.1942, Ashford, Kent. Middle order right-hand batsman, right-arm medium pace bowler. *Team* Oxford U (1966).
Career batting
3–5–0–86–48–17.20–0–*ct* 1
He played hockey for Scotland.

Marshall, John Campbell
Amateur *b:* 30.1.1929, Dore, Sheffield, Yorkshire. Brother of D. A. C. (Oxford U). Opening right-hand batsman. *Sch* Rugby. *Team* Oxford U (1951–53, blue 1953).
Career batting
16–27–0–710–111–26.29–1–*ct* 10
He played rugby for Scotland.

Marshall, Rev John Hannah
Amateur. *b:* 1.10.1837, Cambridge. *d:* 2.2.1879, Kaiteriteri, Riwaka, Nelson, New Zealand. Brother of J. W. (Cambridgeshire) and C. J. (Cambridgeshire). Middle order right-hand batsman, good deep field. *Sch* KES, Birmingham. *Teams* Cambridge Town Club (1857); Cambridge U (1859, blue); Cambridgeshire (1861–67, 7 matches).
Career batting
12–20–4–240–47*–15.00–0–*ct* 9
Bowling 5–0
He also played for Suffolk (1863–70) and he represented Cambridge at rackets.

Marshall, John Maurice Alex
Amateur. *b:* 26.10.1916, Castle Green, Kenilworth, Warwickshire. Middle order right-hand batsman, leg break bowler. *Sch* Warwick. *Team* Warwickshire (1946–50, 28 matches).
Career batting
29–51–4–812–47–17.27–0–*ct* 14
Bowling 1604–47–34.12–2–0–5/65
A master at Warwick School, his first-class County cricket was very restricted. His final first-class match was for MCC in 1956.

Marshall, Joseph
Professional. *b:* 25.7.1862, Mosbrough, Yorkshire. *d:* 15.1.1913, Derby. Middle order right-hand batsman. *Team* Derbyshire (1887, 2 matches).
Career batting
2–4–0–50–31–12.50–0–*ct* 1
A useful soccer player, he appeared for Derby County.

Marshall, Kenneth Walker
Amateur. *b:* 23.7.1911, Kimberley, South Africa. *d:* October 1992, Cape Town, South Africa. Opening right-hand batsman. *Sch* Edinburgh Academy. *Team*

Scotland (1931–32), Europeans (1943/4).
Career batting
3–6–0–59–19–9.83–0–*ct* 2
Bowling 68–0

An excellent rugby union footballer, he represented Scotland.

Marshall, Dr Leslie Phillips
Amateur. *b:* 25.1.1894, Tripatur, Madras, India. *d:* 28.2.1978, Taunton, Somerset. Brother of A. G. (Somerset). Middle order right-hand batsman. *Sch* Taunton. *Team* Somerset (1913–31, 11 matches).
Career batting
11–20–1–162–37–8.52–0–*ct* 6
Bowling 16–1–16.00–0–0–1/7

Marshall, Malcolm Denzil
Cricketer. *b:* 18.4.1958, Bridgetown, Barbados. Middle order right-hand batsman, right-arm fast bowler. *Teams* Barbados (1977/8 to 1990/1); Hampshire (1979–92, 197 matches). *Tours* West Indies to India 1978/9, 1983/4, 1989/90 (not first-class), to Sri Lanka 1978/9, to Australia 1979/80, 1981/2, 1983/4 (not first-class), 1984/5, 1986/7 (not first-class), 1988/9, 1991/2 (not first-class), to New Zealand 1979/80, 1986/7, to England 1980, 1983 (World Cup), 1984, 1988, 1991, to Pakistan 1980/1, 1985/6 (not first-class), 1986/7, 1990/1, 1991/2 (not first-class), to Sharjah (not first-class) 1985/6, 1986/7, 1989/90, to Australia and New Zealand (World Cup) 1991/2; Young West Indies to Zimbabwe 1981/2. *Tests* West Indies (1978/9 to 1991, 81 matches).
Career batting
366–464–62–9863–117–24.53–6–*ct* 131
Bowling 28511–1524–18.70–83–13–8/71
Test batting
81–107–11–1810–92–18.85–0–*ct* 25
Bowling 7876–376–20.94–22–4–7/22

On his first tour to England in 1980 he played in four Tests taking 15 wickets, av 29.06, and was regarded as a very fast bowler with a bright future. Returning in 1984 he was labelled the world's fastest bowler and took 24 Test wickets, av 18.21, again missing one Test through injury. His third tour to England came in 1988 when he completely outshone his famous fellow West Indian quick bowlers, not due to an increase in speed, but because of his ability to move the ball late either way. He captured 35 wickets at 12.65 runs each. His fourth tour brought a further 20 Test wickets at 22.10. By this time he had overtaken L. R. Gibbs as the leading West Indian Test wicket-taker and become the first West Indian to top 350 wickets. His best Test analysis was 7 for 22 v England at Old Trafford in 1988.

His long service with Hampshire meant that he was a major figure in County cricket throughout the 1980s. He has taken fifty wickets in an English season eight times going on to a hundred twice: 134, av 15.73, in 1982 and 100, av 15.08, in 1986.

Marshall, Nariman Darabsha
Amateur. *b:* 3.1.1905, Bombay, India. *d:* 29.8.1979, Jaipur, India. Stylish middle order right-hand batsman, right-arm medium slow bowler, occasional wicket-keeper. *Teams* Parsis (1928/9 to 1934/5); Western India (1933/4 to 1934/5); Nawanagar (1936/7 to 1937/8). *Tour* India to England 1932.
Career batting
27–48–4–1006–120–22.58–2–*ct* 12
Bowling 335–12–27.91–0–0–3/17

He appeared in only six first-class matches on the 1932 tour, scoring 268 runs, av 26.80.

Marshall, Roger Philip Twells
Cricketer. *b:* 28.2.1952, Horsham, Sussex. Lower order right-hand batsman, left-arm fast medium bowler. *Sch* Charterhouse. *Team* Sussex (1973–78, 24 matches).
Career batting
24–37–15–315–37–14.31–0–*ct* 6
Bowling 1927–49–39.32–0–0–4/37

Marshall, Roy Edwin
Professional. *b:* 25.4.1930, Farmers Plantation, St Thomas, Barbados. *d:* 27.10.1992, Taunton, Somerset. Brother of N. E. (West Indies). Attractive opening right-hand batsman, off break bowler. *Teams* Barbados (1945/6 to 1951/2); Hampshire (1953–72, 504 matches). *Tours* West Indies to England 1950, to Australia and New Zealand 1951/2; Commonwealth to India 1953/4, to South Africa 1959/60, to Rhodesia 1962/3; Norfolk to Jamaica 1956/7; Brown to East Africa 1961/2 (not first-class); International XI to Pakistan, New Zealand and Rhodesia 1961/2; Cavaliers to Jamaica 1963/4, to West Indies 1964/5; West Indian XI to England 1964; Rest of World to England 1968. *Tests* West Indies (1951/2, 4 matches).
Career batting
602–1053–59–35725–228*–35.94–68–*ct* 294
Bowling 5092–176–28.93–5–0–6/36
Test batting
4–7–0–143–30–20.42–0–*ct* 1
Bowling 15–0

He scored 1,000 runs in a season eighteen times, going on to 2,000 six times (best 2,607, av 43.45, in 1961). His three double centuries were all for Hampshire, the highest being 228* v Pakistan at Bournemouth in 1962. On his 1950 tour to England he hit 1,117 runs, av 39.89, but was not selected for any Test matches. He captained Hampshire 1966 to 1970.

Marshall, Thomas Roger
Amateur. *b:* 26.6.1849, Chatton Park, Northumberland. *d:* 27.6.1913, Kingfield, Penton, Carlisle, Cumberland. Opening right-hand batsman. *Sch* Edinburgh Academy. *Team* MCC (1884–86).
Career batting
5–9–2–250–80–35.71–0–*ct* 2

Marshall, Walter

His County cricket was for Northumberland (1882). A noted rugby footballer, he represented Scotland.

Marshall, Walter
Professional. *b:* 27.10.1853, Hyson Green, Nottingham. *d:* 15.1.1943, West Bridgford, Nottingham. Middle order batsman, left-arm medium pace bowler. *Team* Nottinghamshire (1889–91, 3 matches).
Career batting
3–4–0–42–26–10.50–0–*ct* 1

He was appointed coach to Nottinghamshire CCC in 1897 and continued as groundsman 1922–36.

Marsham, Algernon James Bullock
Amateur. *b:* 14.8.1919, Chart Sutton, Kent. Son of C. H. B. (Kent), grandson of C. D. B. (Oxford U), nephew of F. W. B. (MCC). Lower order left-hand batsman, leg break bowler. *Sch* Eton. *Teams* Oxford U (1939, blue); Kent (1946–47, 6 matches).
Career batting
17–26–4–362–74*–16.45–0–*ct* 6
Bowling 1381–35–39.45–1–0–5/136

Marsham, Charles Jacob Bullock
Amateur. *b:* 18.1.1829, Merton College, Oxford. *d:* 20.8.1901, Westminster, London. Brother of C. D. B. (Oxford U) and R. H. B. (Oxford U), uncle of C. H. B. (Kent) and F. W. B. (MCC). Attacking middle order right-hand batsman, slip field. *Team* Oxford U (1851–52, blue 1851).
Career batting
38–70–5–782–50–12.03–0–*ct* 10
Bowling 6 wickets (no analyses)–0–0–4/?

His final first-class match was for MCC in 1867. His County cricket was for Northamptonshire (pre first-class, 1854), Oxfordshire (1860–64) and Buckinghamshire (1864).

Marsham, Rev Cloudesley Dewar Bullock
Amateur. *b:* 30.1.1835, Merton College, Oxford. *d:* 23.3.1915, Harrietsham, Maidstone, Kent. Brother of C. J. B. (Oxford U) and R. H. B. (Oxford U), father of C. H. B. (Kent) and F. W. B. (MCC), grandfather of A. J. B. (Kent), brother-in-law of George (Kent). Lower order right-hand batsman, right-hand medium fast round-arm bowler. *Team* Oxford U (1854–58, blue all five years).
Career batting
34–61–9–602–39*–11.57–0–*ct* 26
Bowling 2095–171+9–12.25–14–4–9/64

His best bowling was 9/64 for Gentlemen of England v Gentlemen of MCC at Lord's in 1855. He was regarded as the best amateur bowler of his day, appearing ten times for the Gentlemen against Players at Lord's. After 1862 he rarely played in important matches, but occasionally for Oxfordshire (1852–64), Northamptonshire (pre first-class, 1854) and Buckinghamshire (1864–69). His final first-class match was for Gentlemen of England in 1866. He captained Oxford in 1857 and 1858.

Marsham, Cloudesley Henry Bullock
Amateur. *b:* 10.2.1879, Stoke-Lyne, Bicester, Oxfordshire. *d:* 19.7.1928, Wrotham Heath, Kent. Son of C. D. B. (Oxford U), nephew of C. J. B. (Oxford U), R. H. B. (Oxford U) and George (Kent), brother of F. W. B. (MCC), father of A. J. B. (Kent). Sound middle order batsman. *Sch* Eton. *Teams* Oxford U (1900–02, blue all three years); Kent (1900–22, 141 matches).
Career batting
175–283–23–5879–161*–22.61–7–*ct* 88
Bowling 175–2–87.50–0–0–1/0

He captained Oxford in 1902 and Kent from 1904 to 1908, but after 1908 played only occasionally for the County. He hit 1,000 runs in a season twice (best 1,070, av 28.91, in 1904). He also played for Shropshire (1909). He was a Test selector in 1907.

Marsham, Francis William Bullock
Amateur. *b:* 13.7.1883, Stoke-Lyne, Bicester, Oxfordshire. *d:* 22.12.1971, Salen, Isle of Mull, Scotland. Son of C. D. B. (Oxford U), nephew of C. J. B. (Oxford U), R. H. B. (Oxford U) and George (Kent), brother of C. H. B. (Kent), uncle of A. J. B. (Kent). Middle order batsman. *Sch* Eton. *Team* MCC (1905).
Career batting
1–2–0–9–6–4.50–0–*ct* 0

Marsham, George
Amateur. *b:* 10.4.1849, Allington, Kent. *d:* 2.12.1927, Hayle Place, Maidstone, Kent. Uncle of C. H. B. (Kent) and F. W. B. (MCC), brother-in-law of C. D. (Oxford U). Lower order right-hand batsman, slow under-arm bowler, wicket-keeper. *Sch* Eton. *Team* Kent (1876–77, 3 matches).
Career batting
3–5–2–36–20–12.00–0–*ct* 2–*st* 2

He was President of Kent CCC in 1886.

Marsham, Rev Hon John
Amateur. *b:* 25.7.1842, Boxley, Kent. *d:* 16.9.1926, Roehampton, London. Father of W. J. (India), father-in-law of A. R. Hoare (MCC). Lower order right-hand batsman, right-hand fast round-arm bowler. *Sch* Eton. *Team* Kent (1873, 2 matches).
Career batting
2–4–0–5–3–1.25–0–*ct* 1

He was not in the eleven whilst at Oxford. He played occasionally for Northamptonshire (pre first-class, 1870).

Marsham, Robert Henry Bullock
Amateur. *b:* 3.9.1833, Merton College, Oxford. *d:* 5.4.1913, Bifrons, Canterbury, Kent. Brother of C. D. B. (Oxford U) and C. J. B. (Oxford U), uncle of C. H. B. (Kent) and F. W. B. (MCC), brother-in-law of G. H. Field (Kent). Opening right-hand batsman, right-hand medium slow round-arm bowler. *Team* Oxford U (1854–56, blue 1856).

Career batting
15–28–4–253–42–10.54–0–*ct* 8
Bowling 284–35–8.11–2–2–8/27

He appeared for Oxfordshire (1853), Northamptonshire (pre first-class, 1854), and Buckinghamshire (1864–67). His final first-class match was for MCC in 1863.

Marsland, Geoffrey Peter
Amateur. *b:* 17.5.1932, Ashton-under-Lyne, Lancashire. Opening/middle order right-hand batsman, off break bowler, good outfield. *Sch* Rossall. *Team* Oxford U (1953–54, blue 1954).
Career batting
17–31–3–448–74–16.00–0–*ct* 7
Bowling 138–2–69.00–0–0–2/68

Marson, Lionel Frederick
Amateur. *b:* 15.6.1895, Wandsworth, London. *d:* 31.3.1960, Ravenswood, Melrose, Roxburghshire, Scotland. Middle order right-hand batsman. *Sch* Haileybury *Team* Army (1930).
Career batting
1–2–0–56–53–28.00–0–*ct* 1

His County cricket was for Wiltshire (1926–27). He was an announcer for the BBC.

Marston, John William
Amateur. *b:* 25.10.1893, Rosario, Argentina. *d:* 9.7.1938, Lambeth, London. Lower order right-hand batsman, leg break and googly bowler. *Sch* Haileybury. *Team* Essex (1923–24, 2 matches).
Career batting
2–4–1–12–6–4.00–0–*ct* 1
Bowling 112–2–56.00–0–0–2/47

Marten, George Nisbet
Amateur. *b:* 20.6.1840, Ghazeepoor, Bengal, India. *d:* 25.8.1905, Crowborough, Sussex. Nephew of G. N. (Cambridge U 1821). Middle order right-hand batsman. *Sch* Harrow. *Team* MCC (1864–69).
Career batting
4–6–1–50–26–10.00–0–*ct* 2

His County cricket was for Hertfordshire (1863–78).

Marten, William George
Professional. *b:* 5.9.1845, Tunbridge Wells, Kent. *d:* 25.11.1907, Stoke Newington, London. Lower order right-hand batsman, right-hand fast round-arm bowler, good slip. *Teams* Kent (1865–71, 15 matches); Surrey (1871–72, 24 matches).
Career batting
45–80–23–312–27*–5.47–0–*ct* 27
Bowling 2543–114–22.30–4–2–6/11

He also played for Essex (pre first-class, 1878).

Martin, Arthur Dalby
Amateur. *b:* 9.11.1888, Hackney, London. *d:* 12.7.1958, Northwood, Middlesex. Lower order batsman, useful bowler. *Team* Essex (1920–21, 3 matches).
Career batting
3–3–0–0–0–0.00–0–*ct* 1
Bowling 210–5–42.00–0–0–3/43

Martin, Barry Robert
Cricketer. *b:* 18.7.1950, Hampton Court, Middlesex. Lower order right-hand batsman, right-arm medium fast bowler. *Sch* Kingston GS. *Team* Cambridge U (1971–73).
Career batting
6–10–1–36–14–4.00–0–*ct* 2
Bowling 400–9–44.44–0–0–2/42

Martin, Charles
Professional. *b:* 6.8.1836, Breamore, Hampshire. *d:* 28.3.1878, Cosham, Hampshire. Tail end left-hand batsman, left-hand fast round-arm bowler, slip field. *Team* Hampshire (1869–70, 4 matches).
Career batting
5–10–1–11–3–1.22–0–*ct* 3
Bowling 168–9–18.66–0–0–3/38

Martin, E. George
Amateur. Lower order batsman, useful bowler. *Team* Glamorgan (1921, 1 match).
Career batting
1–2–0–2–2–1.00–0–*ct* 1
Bowling 77–1–77.00–0–0–1/77

He first played for Glamorgan (pre first-class) in 1913.

Martin, Edward
Professional. *b:* 24.11.1814, Brenchley, Kent. *d:* 31.10.1869, Barcombe, Sussex. He died due to a fall from his horse whilst returning from a hunt. Hard hitting middle order right-hand batsman. *Teams* Hampshire (1843–45); Kent (1845–51, 31 matches).
Career batting
41–76–3–682–60–9.34–0–*ct* 20
Bowling 106–6 + 15–17.66–1–0–5/?

He also played for Dorset (1845) and Oxfordshire (1854).

Martin, Eric
Amateur. *b:* 20.5.1894, Barnet, Hertfordshire. *d:* 2.5.1924, Duxford, Cambridgeshire. He was killed in a flying accident. Middle order batsman. *Team* Middlesex (1919–23, 16 matches).
Career batting
17–26–4–325–64–14.77–*ct* 16

Martin, Eric Gordon
Amateur. *b:* 4.2.1907, Rock Ferry, Cheshire. *d:* 27.1.1978, Chelsea, London. Middle order right-hand batsman, right-arm medium pace bowler. *Sch* Birkenhead. *Team* Essex (1928, 2 matches).
Career batting
2–4–0–25–13–6.25–0–*ct* 1
Bowling 140–2–70.00–0–0–1/63

Martin, Eric James
Professional. *b:* 17.8.1925, Lambley, Nottinghamshire. Middle order right-hand batsman. *Team* Nottinghamshire (1949–59, 125 matches).
Career batting
125–199–20–4086–133*–22.82–3–*ct* 53
His best season was 1954 with 977 runs, av 30.53.

Martin, Evelyn George
Amateur. *b:* 22.3.1881, Upton-on-Severn, Worcestershire. *d:* 27.4.1945, Hadleigh, Suffolk. Lower order right-hand batsman, right-arm fast bowler. *Sch* Eton. *Teams* Oxford U (1903–06, blue all four years); Worcestershire (1903–07, 3 matches).
Career batting
29–51–10–519–56–12.65–0–*ct* 10
Bowling 2516–107–23.51–5–0–7/81

Martin, Frank Reginald
Amateur. *b:* 12.10.1893, Kingston, Jamaica. *d:* 23.11.1967, Kingston, Jamaica. Opening or middle order left-hand batsman, slow left-arm bowler. *Team* Jamaica (1924/5 to 1929/30). *Tours* West Indies to England 1928 and 1933, to Australia 1930/1. *Tests* West Indies (1928 to 1930/1, 9 matches).
Career batting
65–108–13–3589–204*–37.77–6–*ct* 19
Bowling 3149–74–42.55–1–0–5/90
Test batting
9–18–1–486–123*–28.58–1–*ct* 2
Bowling 619–8–77.37–0–0–3/91
On his 1928 visit to England he hit 1,370 runs, av 32.61, and headed the Test batting averages – his was a very difficult wicket to obtain. In 1933 he was injured after playing in six matches and the strain proved so serious that he did not play again on the tour. His highest score was 204* for Jamaica v L. H. Tennyson's XI at Kingston in 1926/7. He scored 194 on debut for Jamaica v Barbados at Bridgetown in 1924/5.

Martin, Frederick
Professional. *b:* 12.10.1861, Dartford, Kent. *d:* 13.12.1921, Dartford, Kent. Half-brother of A. Blackman (Surrey, Sussex and Kent). Lower order left-hand batsman, left-arm medium pace bowler. *Team* Kent (1885–99, 229 matches). *Tour* Read to South Africa 1891/2. *Tests* England (1890 to 1891/2, 2 matches).
Career batting
317–492–118–4545–90–12.15–0–*ct* 120
Bowling 22901–1317–17.38–95–23–8/45
Test batting
2–2–0–14–13–7.00–0–*ct* 2
Bowling 141–14–10.07–2–1–6/50
He took 100 wickets in a season six times (best 190, av 13.05, in 1890). His final first-class match was for MCC in 1900. He was a first-class umpire (1902–03 and 1919).

Martin, George
Professional. *b:* 29.11.1875, Tail end batsman, useful bowler. *Team* Hampshire (1898–99, 4 matches).
Career batting
4–7–5–19–6*–9.50–0–0–*ct* 3
Bowling 321–8–40.12–0–0–3/64

Martin, George Need
Professional. *b:* 25.7.1845, Nottingham. *d:* 2.9.1900, Nottingham. Lower order right-hand batsman, wicket-keeper. *Team* Nottinghamshire (1870, 1 match).
Career batting
2–4–0–15–14–3.75–0–*ct* 0
His final first-class match was for the All England XI in 1874.

Martin, Herbert
Amateur. *b:* 4.5.1927, Lisburn, Co Antrim, Ireland. Brother of Thomas (Ireland). Middle order right-hand batsman. *Sch* Royal Belfast Academical Institution. *Team* Ireland (1949–68).
Career batting
19–38–3–671–88–19.17–0–*ct* 17

Martin, J.
Professional. Tail end batsman. *Team* Hampshire (1904, 1 match).
Career batting
1–2–0–66–39–33.00–0–*ct* 3
Bowling 166–5–33.20–0–0–4/100
His career in first-class County cricket is a curiosity in that he batted at No. 11 in his only match, adding 76 for the 10th wicket in the first innings and 48 for the 10th wicket in the second innings.

Martin, James David
Amateur. *b:* 1.7.1901, South Edinburgh, Scotland. Middle order right-hand batsman. *Sch* George Watson's College. *Team* Scotland (1926–29).
Career batting
3–4–0–101–88–25.25–0–*ct* 1

Martin, John Donald
Cricketer. *b:* 23.12.1941, Oxford. Tail end right-hand batsman, right-arm fast medium bowler. *Sch* Magdalen College School. *Teams* Oxford U (1962–65, blue 1962, 1963 and 1965); Somerset (1964–65, 2 matches). *Tour* MCC to South America 1964/5 (not first-class).
Career batting
40–52–14–148–14*–3.89–0–*ct* 13
Bowling 2701–93–29.04–4–0–7/26
He also played for Oxfordshire (1959–61) and Berkshire (1972). He captained Oxford in 1965. He also won a blue for hockey and represented Wales.

Martin, John Newton
Amateur. *b:* 3.7.1867, St Austell, Cornwall. *d:* 31.8.1942, Lawes Bridge, Torquay, Devon. Middle order batsman. *Team* MCC (1891).

Career batting
1–2–1–30–29*–30.00–0–*ct* 0
His County cricket was for Devon (1901–03).

Martin, John Stapleton
Amateur. *b:* 15.3.1846, Holborn, London. *d:* 26.9.1922, The Firs, Norton juxta Kempsey, Worcestershire. Middle order right-hand batsman, good field. *Sch* Wimbledon. *Team* MCC (1871).
Career batting
3–5–2–107–51*–35.66–0–*ct* 1
He did not play in any first-class matches whilst at Cambridge U.

Martin, John Wesley
Amateur. *b:* 28.7.1931, Wingham, New South Wales, Australia. *d:* 16.7.1992, Burrell Creek, New South Wales, Australia, Lower order left-hand batsman, slow left-arm bowler. *Teams* New South Wales (1956/7 to 1967/8, 78 matches); South Australia (1958/9, 9 matches). *Tours* Australia to England 1964, to Pakistan and India 1964/5, to South Africa 1966/7, to New Zealand 1956/7, 1959/60; Cavaliers to India and South Africa 1962/3. *Tests* Australia (1960/1 to 1966/7, 8 matches).
Career batting
135–193–26–3970–101–23.77–1–*ct* 114
Bowling 13872–445–31.17–17–1–8/97
Test batting
8–13–1–214–55–17.83–0–*ct* 5
Bowling 832–17–48.94–0–0–3/56
He had little success in England in 1964 and did not appear in the Tests.

Martin, John William
Amateur. *b:* 16.2.1917, Catford, London. *d:* 4.1.1987, Woolwich, London. Lower order right-hand batsman, right-arm fast bowler. *Team* Kent (1939–53, 33 matches). *Test* England (1947, 1 match).
Career batting
44–69–15–623–40–11.53–0–*ct* 32
Bowling 3888–162–24.00–8–1–7/53
Test batting
1–2–0–26–26–13.00–0–*ct* 0
Bowling 129–1–129.00–0–0–1/111
A noted figure in London Club cricket, he could not afford the time for regular County matches and appeared in only a handful each season.

Martin, Marcus Trevelyan
Amateur. *b:* 29.4.1842, Barrackpore, Calcutta, India. *d:* 5.6.1908, Marylebone, London. He died of appendicitis. Middle order right-hand batsman, wicket-keeper. *Sch* Rugby. *Teams* Cambridge U (1862–64, blue 1862 and 1864); Middlesex (1870, 1 match).
Career batting
9–12–1–208–63–18.90–0–*ct* 8–*st* 6
His first-class debut was for Gentlemen of the North in 1861. He also played for Warwickshire (pre first-class, 1863–68) and Huntingdonshire (1869).

Martin, Peter James
Cricketer. *b:* 15.11.1968, Accrington, Lancashire. Lower order right-hand batsman, right-arm fast medium bowler. *Team* Lancashire (1989–92, 50 matches).
Career batting
50–46–17–641–133–22.10–1–*ct* 15
Bowling 3814–96–39.72–0–0–4/30

Martin, Robert Harold
Amateur. *b:* 7.10.1918, Liverpool, Lancashire. *d:* 30.6.1985, St Albans, Hertfordshire. Lower order right-hand batsman, right-arm medium pace bowler. *Sch* Oundle. *Team* Combined Services (1951).
Career batting
1–2–0–4–4–2.00–0–*ct* 0
Bowling 91–1–91.00–0–0–1/29

Martin, Sidney Hugh
Professional. *b:* 11.1.1909, Durban, South Africa. *d:* February 1988, Melbourne, Victoria, Australia. Father of Hugh (Transvaal and New South Wales), uncle of A. Tayfield (Transvaal), C. Tayfield (Transvaal and Griqualand West) and H. J. Tayfield (South Africa). Middle order right-hand batsman, right-arm medium pace bowler. *Teams* Natal (1925/6 to 1946/7); Worcestershire (1931–39, 236 matches); Rhodesia (1947/8 to 1949/50).
Career batting
267–457–31–11511–191*–27.02–13–*ct* 159
Bowling 15063–532–28.31–21–6–8/24
He hit 1,000 runs in a season seven times (best 1,705, av 31.57, in 1935). His first-class debut in England was for MCC in 1929. He took 100 wickets in a season twice (best 114, av 20.25, in 1937) and achieved the 'double' in 1937 and 1939. He was Secretary of the Transvaal Cricket Union and South African Cricket Association (1969–72).

Martin, Thomas
Amateur. *b:* 31.8.1909, Hamburg, Germany. Lower order right-hand batsman, wicket-keeper. *Sch* Cheltenham. *Team* Cambridge U (1928).
Career batting
2–4–0–5–2–1.25–0–*ct* 1–*st* 1

Martin, Thomas
Amateur. *b:* 15.1.1911, Lisburn, Co Antrim, Ireland. *d:* 7.12.1937, Lisburn, Co Antrim, Ireland. Brother of Herbert (Ireland). Tail end right-hand batsman, right-arm fast medium bowler. *Team* Ireland (1934).
Career batting
1–2–1–7–7–7.00–0–*ct* 0
Bowling 49–0

Martin, William
Professional. *b:* 19.2.1944, Nursling, Southampton, Hampshire. *d:* 27.5.1871, Southampton, Hampshire. Middle order right-hand batsman, right-arm medium pace bowler. *Team* Hampshire (1867, 1 match).

Martindale, Duncan John Richardson

Career batting
1–2–0–2–1–1.00–0–*ct* 0

Martindale, Duncan John Richardson
Cricketer. *b:* 13.12.1963, Harrogate, Yorkshire. Middle order right-hand batsman, off break bowler. *Team* Nottinghamshire (1985–91, 55 matches).
Career batting
55–85–10–1861–138–24.81–4–*ct* 23
Bowling 8–0
He also played for Herefordshire (1992).

Martindale, Emmanuel Alfred
Amateur. *b:* 25.11.1909, St Lucy, Barbados. *d:* 17.3.1972, St Joseph Hospital, near Ashton Hall, St Peter, Barbados. Hard hitting lower order right-hand batsman, attacking right-arm fast bowler. *Team* Barbados (1929/30 to 1935/6). *Tours* West Indies to England 1933, 1939. *Tests* West Indies (1933–39, 10 matches).
Career batting
59–84–20–972–134–15.18–1–*ct* 29
Bowling 5205–203–25.64–11–1–8/32
Test batting
10–14–3–58–22–5.27–0–*ct* 5
Bowling 804–37–21.72–3–0–5/22
The outstanding bowler of the 1933 tour – he took 103 wickets, av 20.98 – he was the only regular bowler to average less than 30.00 and in the Tests the only bowler to achieve respectable figures. He was however criticised for employing leg-theory bowling in the Tests. He totally failed to find his form on the 1939 tour.

Martineau, Alfred
Amateur. *b:* 11.11.1868, Littleworth, Esher, Surrey. *d:* 2.2.1940, Rubislaw, Aberdeen, Scotland. Lower order right-hand batsman, right-arm slow bowler, good slip field. *Sch* Uppingham. *Team* Cambridge U (1889).
Career batting
2–3–0–4–2–1.33–0–*ct* 0
Bowling 65–1–65.00–0–0–1/65

Martineau, Hubert Melville
Amateur. *b:* 24.10.1891, Westminster, London. *d:* 11.9.1976, Westminster, London. Son of P. H. (MCC), cousin of Lionel (Surrey). Lower order right-hand batsman, slow left-arm bowler. *Sch* Eton. *Team* Leveson-Gower's XI (1931–32). *Tours* He managed and captained his own team to Egypt for eleven successive years, 1929–39 (not first-class).
Career batting
3–6–2–44–19*–11.00–0–*ct* 0
Bowling 95–0
From 1924 to 1939 he ran his own team from his country house, Holyport Lodge, near Maidenhead.

Martineau, Lionel
Amateur. *b:* 19.2.1867, Esher, Surrey. *d:* 17.11.1906, Esher, Surrey. Cousin of H. M. (Leveson-Gower's XI) and P. H. (MCC). Middle order right-hand batsman, right-arm slow bowler, fine field. *Sch* Uppingham. *Team* Cambridge U (1887–88, blue 1887).
Career batting
11–19–5–277–109–19.78–1–*ct* 8
Bowling 542–17–31.88–0–0–4/59

Martineau, Sir Philip Hubert
Amateur. *b:* 28.10.1862, St Pancras, London. *d:* 7.10.1944, Sunningdale, Berkshire. Father of H. M. (Leveson-Gower's XI), uncle of Lionel (Cambridge U). Lower order batsman, left-arm fast medium bowler, good field. *Sch* Harrow. *Team* MCC (1883).
Career batting
2–4–0–27–14–6.75–0–*ct* 0
He did not appear in any first-class matches whilst at Cambridge. His County cricket was for Berkshire (1905).

Martingell, William
Professional. *b:* 20.8.1818, Nutfield, Surrey. *d:* 29.9.1897, Eton Wick, Buckinghamshire. Son of Russell (Surrey 1828). Hard hitting middle or lower order right-hand batsman, right-hand medium pace round-arm bowler. *Teams* Surrey (1839–59, 51 matches); Kent (1841–52, 49 matches); Hampshire (1845, 1 match as given man).
Career batting
182–308–46–2401–49–9.16–0–*ct* 129
Bowling 3852–333 + 196–11.56–37–4–8/37
His final first-class match was in 1860 for MCC. One of the great bowlers of his day he appeared for the Players v Gentlemen from 1844 to 1858 and in the 1853 match took 7 for 19 – possibly the best performance of his career. He also played (pre first-class) for Somerset (1845), Worcestershire (1849) and Warwickshire (1853).

Martyn, Damien Richard
Cricketer. *b:* 21.10.1971, Darwin, Northern Territories, Australia. Middle order right-hand batsman, right-arm medium pace bowler. *Teams* Western Australia (1990/1 to 1991/2, 17 matches); Leicestershire (1991, 1 match).
Career batting
18–32–6–1175–110–45.19–2–*ct* 11–*st* 1
Bowling 162–3–54.00–0–0–1/10

Martyn, Henry
Amateur. *b:* 16.7.1877, Lifton, Devon. *d:* 8.8.1928, Dawlish, Devon. Middle/lower order right-hand batsman, wicket-keeper. *Sch* Exeter. *Teams* Oxford U (1899–1900, blue both years); Somerset (1901–08, 74 matches).
Career batting
97–158–6–3740,196130*–24.60–1–*ct* 113–*st* 48
Bowling 143–2–71.50–0–0–1/19

He hit 1,005 runs, av 31.40, in 1906. he also played for Devon (1896) and Cornwall (1898). Regarded as one of the best wicket-keepers of his day, he was unfortunate not to represent England.

Martyn, Oswald
Amateur. *b:* 10.1.1887, Clapham, London. *d:* 14.9.1959, Patcham, Sussex. Middle order batsman. *Team* Essex (1922, 1 match).
Career batting
1–1–0–0–0–0.00–0–*ct* 1

Maru, Rajesh Jamandass Govind
Cricketer. *b:* 28.10.1962, Nairobi, Kenya. Lower order right-hand batsman, slow left-arm bowler. *Team* Middlesex (1980–82, 16 matches); Hampshire (1984–92, 184 matches). *Tour* Middlesex to Zimbabwe 1980/1.
Career batting
200–190–46–2353–74–16.34–0–*ct* 210
Bowling 15538–479–32.43–15–1–8/41
He took 73 wickets, av 26.34, in 1985.

Maslin, Martin
Cricketer. *b:* 14.3.1942, Grimsby, Lincolnshire. Opening right-hand batsman, right-arm medium pace or occasional leg break bowler. *Sch* Haileybury. *Team* Minor Counties (1967–74).
Career batting
5–10–1–274–66*–30.44–0–*ct* 2
Bowling 44–0
His County cricket was for Lincolnshire (1959–80).

Mason, Allan
Professional. *b:* 2.5.1921, Addingham, Yorkshire. Lower order right-hand batsman, slow left-arm bowler. *Team* Yorkshire (1947–50, 18 matches).
Career batting
18–19–3–205–22–6.56–0–*ct* 6
Bowling 1473–51–28.88–1–0–5/56

Mason, Andrew Lindsey
Cricketer. *b:* 22.9.1943, Birmingham. Lower order right-hand batsman, wicket-keeper. *Sch* Lancaster RGS. *Team* Oxford U (1963–65).
Career batting
15–23–4–213–47–11.21–0–*ct* 12–*st* 5

Mason, Charles Eagleton Stuart
Amateur. *b:* 6.6.1871, Woolwich, London. *d:* 19.4.1945, Kidbrooke, London. Middle order batsman. *Team* MCC (1896).
Career batting
1–2–0–8–8–4.00–0–*ct* 0

Mason, Henry
Amateur. *b:* 14.5.1840, Waterbeach, Cambridgeshire. *d:* 14.10.1902, Cambridge. Middle order batsman, bowler. *Team* Cambridgeshire (1869–71, 2 matches).
Career batting
2–4–0,19619–12–4.75–0–*ct* 0
Bowling 60–5–12.00–0–0–3/48

Mason, James Ernest
Amateur. *b:* 29.10.1876, Blackheath, Kent. *d:* 8.2.1938, South Beddington, Wallington, Surrey. Brother of J. R. (Kent). Middle order right-hand batsman, good cover field. *Sch* Tonbridge. *Team* Kent (1900, 1 match).
Career batting
1–1–0–1–1–1.00–0–*ct* 0
He also played for Berkshire (1905).

Mason, John Richard
Amateur. *b:* 26.3.1874, Blackheath, Kent. *d:* 15.10.1958, Cooden Beach, Sussex. Brother of J. E. (Kent). Stylish middle order right-hand batsman, right-arm fast medium bowler, good slip field. *Sch* Winchester. *Team* Kent (1893–1914, 300 matches). *Tours* Stoddart to Australia 1897/8; Kent to North America 1903. *Tests* England (1897/8, 5 matches).
Career batting
339–557–36–17337–183–33.27–34–*ct* 390
Bowling 18989–848–22.39–35–9–8/29
Test batting
5–10–0–129–32–12.90–0–*ct* 3
Bowling 149–2–74.50–0–0–1/8
He hit 1,000 runs in a season eight times (best 1,561, av 36.30, in 1901). In the same season he took 100 wickets for the only time – 118, av 20.44, thus completing the 'double'. His final first-class match was for L. Robinson's XII in 1919. He captained Kent in 1898–1902 and was President in 1939.

Mason, Percy
Professional. *b:* 19.11.1873, East Bridgford, Nottinghamshire. *d:* 27.11.1952, Gunthorpe, Nottinghamshire. Lower order right-hand batsman, right-arm fast bowler. *Team* Nottinghamshire (1896–1901, 43 matches).
Career batting
43–64–10–879–80–16.27–0–*ct* 7
Bowling 402–10–40.20–0–0–2/20
He also played for Cheshire (1909–12).

Masood Iqbal Qureshi
Cricketer. *b:* 17.4.1952, Lahore, Pakistan. Lower order right-hand batsman, wicket-keeper. *Teams* Lahore (1969/70 to 1985/6); Punjab U (1971/2); Punjab (1973/4 to 1975/6); Habib Bank (1976/7 to 1986/7). *Tours* Pakistan to Australia and New Zealand 1972/3, to England 1978.
Career batting
150–222–33–2665–69–14.10–0–*ct* 312–*st* 54
Bowling 134–3–44.66–0–0–1/12
He appeared in only one first-class match on the 1978 tour. He played for Pakistan in one-day international matches.

Masood, Mohammad Afzal
Cricketer. *b:* 2.5.1952, Lahore, Pakistan. Middle order right-hand batsman, right-arm medium pace bowler. *Teams* Lahore (1967/8 to 1971/2); Sargodha (1968/9 to 1969/70); Punjab U (1968/9 to 1970/1); PIA (1970/1 to 1972/3); Ireland (1986–87).
Career batting
25–43–3–1101–114–27.52–1–*ct* 19
Bowling 72–2–36.00–0–0–1/4

Massey, John Alfred
Amateur. *b:* 26.4.1899, Harrow, Middlesex. *d:* 23.6.1963, Ray Channel, West Mersea, Colchester, Essex. He was accidentally drowned. Middle order batsman. *Team* Middlesex (1927, 1 match).
Career batting
1–1–0–17–17–17.00–0–*ct* 0

Massey, Joseph
Amateur. Middle order right-hand batsman. *Team* Sir L. Parkinson's XI (1933–35).
Career batting
2–4–0–65–25–16.25–0–*ct* 0

Massey, William Morton
Amateur. *b:* 11.4.1846, Scotland. *d:* 19.4.1899, New York, USA. Middle order batsman. *Teams* Somerset (1882, 1 match); Lancashire (1883, 1 match).
Career batting
2–4–0–10–5–2.50–0–*ct* 1
He also played for Devon (1875–77). He first played for Somerset (pre first-class) in 1877.

Massie, Hugh Hamon
Amateur. *b:* 11.4.1854, near Belfast (now Point Fairy), Victoria, Australia. *d:* 12.10.1938, Point Piper, New South Wales, Australia. Father of R. J. A. (New South Wales). Opening right-hand batsman, good field. *Team* New South Wales (1877/8 to 1887/8, 17 matches). *Tour* Australia to England 1882. *Tests* Australia (1881/2 to 1884/5, 9 matches).
Career batting
64–113–5–2485–206–23.00–1–*ct* 35
Bowling 60–2–30.00–0–0–2/39
Test batting
9–16–0–249–55–15.56–0–*ct* 5
He had a successful tour to England in 1882, hitting 1,360 runs, av 25.66, in first-class matches, including 206 v Oxford U at Oxford, which was his only double century. His final first-class matches were in England in 1895 for MCC and for Gentlemen of England. Business commitments prevented him appearing more often in important matches. He captained Australia in one Test.

Massie, Robert Arnold Lockyer
Cricketer. *b:* 14.4.1947, Subiaco, Perth, Western Australia. Lower order left-hand batsman, right-arm medium fast bowler. *Teams* Western Australia (1965/6 to 1974/5, 28 matches); Ranji's XI in India 1972/3. *Tours* Australia to England 1972, to West Indies 1972/3. *Tests* Australia (1972 to 1972/3, 6 matches).
Career batting
52–54–14–385–42–9.62–0–*ct* 8
Bowling 4446–179–24.83–6–2–8/53
Test batting
6–8–1–78–42–11.14–0–*ct* 1
Bowling 647–31–20.87–2–1–8/53
He was an outstanding success on his tour to England, taking 23 wickets, av 17.78, in the Tests and 50 wickets, av 17.02, in first-class matches, including 16 in his first Test match (at Lord's). His exceptional ability to swing the ball in humid conditions accounted for his success, but he found that this knack faded and he soon dropped out of first-class cricket.

Master, A. W. C.
(*see under* Chester-Master, A. W.)

Master, E. C.
(*see under* Chester-Master, E.)

Masterman, Sir John Cecil
Amateur. *b:* 12.1.1891, Kingston Hill, Surrey. *d:* 6.6.1977, Oxford. Sound middle order left-hand batsman, right-arm medium pace bowler. *Teams* Leveson-Gower's XI (1926); Harlequins (1927); Free Foresters (1927–30). *Tours* Free Foresters to Canada 1923 (not first-class); Martineau to Egypt 1930, 1931 (not first-class); MCC to Canada 1937 (not first-class).
Career batting
4–6–2–77–36*–19.25–0–*ct* 7
Bowling 236–4–59.00–0–0–2/124
His County cricket was for Oxfordshire (1922–25). For many years he was on the Committees of I Zingari and Free Foresters. He wrote several delightful pieces on cricket. A noted all-round games player, he represented Oxford and England at hockey and lawn tennis, as well as winning the University high jump.

Masters, Kevin David
Cricketer. *b:* 19.5.1961, Chatham, Kent. Tail end left-hand batsman, right-arm medium fast bowler. *Team* Kent (1983–84, 4 matches).
Career batting
4–7–1–1–1–0.16–0–*ct* 2
Bowling 294–6–49.00–0–0–2/26

Masterson, Albert Edward George William
Professional. *b:* 19.5.1843, Cambridge. *d:* 14.12.1887, Great Parndon, Essex. Brother of John (Cambridge Town Club). Lower order batsman, bowler. *Team* Cambridgeshire (1867–71, 3 matches).
Career batting
3–5–1–13–5–3.25–0–*ct* 1

Matheson, Alexander Malcolm
Amateur. *b:* 27.2.1906, Omaha, Auckland, New Zealand. *d:* 31.12.1985, Auckland, New Zealand. Lower

order right-hand batsman, right-arm medium pace bowler. *Teams* Auckland (1926/7 to 1939/40); Wellington (1944/5 to 1946/7). *Tour* New Zealand to England 1931. *Tests* New Zealand (1929/30 to 1931, 2 matches).
Career batting
69–97–19–1844–112–23.64–1–*ct* 44
Bowling 5534–194–28.52–2–0–5/50
Test batting
2–1–0–7–7–7.00–0–*ct* 2
Bowling 136–2–68.00–0–0–2/7
His 44 wickets on the 1931 tour of England cost 23.81 runs each and he appeared in only one of three Tests.

Matheson, Edward
Amateur. *b:* 14.6.1865, Charlton, London. *d:* 26.2.1945, Uffculme, Tiverton, Devon. Middle order right-hand batsman, right-arm bowler. *Sch* Clergy Orphan School, Canterbury. *Team* Warwickshire (1899, 1 match).
Career batting
2–4–0–21–9–5.25–0–*ct* 1
His first-class debut was for the South of England in 1886.

Matheson, Dr John Alexander
Cricketer. *b:* 26.10.1950, Dunedin, New Zealand. Lower order right-hand batsman, wicket-keeper. *Team* Oxford U (1977).
Career batting
1 match, did not bat–*ct* 0

Mathews, Ernest
Amateur. *b:* 17.5.1847, Islington, London. *d:* 25.11.1930, Amersham, Buckinghamshire. He married a niece of E. T. Drake (Oxford U), his daughter married brother of A. H. J. Cochrane (Oxford U). Lower order right-hand batsman, right-hand slow round-arm bowler. *Sch* Harrow. *Team* Oxford U (1867–69, blue 1868–69).
Career batting
11–18–0–179–44–9.94–0–*ct* 9
Bowling 167–7–23.85–0–0–3/57
His County cricket was for Hertfordshire (1882).

Mathews, Frederick John
Professional. *b:* 7.3.1861, Thames Ditton, Surrey. *d:* 9.2.1950, Surbiton, Surrey. Brother-in-law of G. J. Carver (Surrey). Middle order batsman. *Team* Surrey (1883, 2 matches).
Career batting
2–3–0–14–9–4.66–0–*ct* 0

Mathews, John Kenneth
Amateur. *b:* 6.2.1884, Harlow, Essex. *d:* 6.4.1962, Worthing, Sussex. Father of K. P. A. (Sussex). Forcing middle order right-hand batsman. *Sch* Felsted. *Team* Sussex (1909–30, 40 matches).
Career batting
40–61–4–778–78–13.64–0–*ct* 11
Bowling 98–0
He also played for Wiltshire (1902–05). A noted hockey player, he represented England.

Mathews, Kenneth Patrick Arthur
Amateur. *b:* 10.5.1926, Worthing, Sussex. Son of J. K. (Sussex). Sound opening right-hand batsman, right-arm medium pace bowler. *Sch* Felsted. *Teams* Sussex (1950–51, 6 matches); Cambridge U (1951, blue).
Career batting
21–30–1–796–77–27.44–0–*ct* 7
Bowling 19–0
His final first-class match was for Free Foresters in 1956. He also was awarded his blue for golf and hockey, and appeared for Sussex and England at the latter sport.

Mathews, Leslie Henry Staverton
Amateur. *b:* 1.3.1875, Kensington, London. *d:* 7.4.1946, Fulham, London. Lower order batsman, wicket-keeper. *Sch* St Paul's. *Team* Oxford U (1897).
Career batting
2–3–0–9–9–3.00–0–*ct* 1
He represented Oxford as a heavyweight boxer.

Mathews, Michael John Anderson
Amateur. *b:* 6.1.1934, Durban, South Africa. Lower order right-hand batsman, leg break bowler. *Team* Oxford U (1957).
Career batting
2–4–0–9–5–2.25–0–*ct* 1
Bowling 77–6–12.83–1–0–5/58

Mathews, William
Professional. *b:* 23.3.1793, Crondall, Hampshire. *d:* 20.8.1858, Woodbridge, Suffolk. Lower order batsman, right-hand slow round-arm bowler. *Teams* Surrey (1828–29); Hampshire (1829).
Career batting
31–55–2–329–33–6.20–0–*ct* 26
Bowling 79 wickets (no analyses)–3–0–7/?
During his short career in great matches, he was one of the best bowlers in England. His debut was for Godalming in 1821 and his final match for Suffolk in 1830.

Mathias, Frederick William
Amateur. *b:* 7.8.1898, Abercynon, Radyr, Glamorgan. *d:* 19.4.1955, Radyr, Glamorgan. Middle order right-hand batsman, slow right-arm bowler. *Sch* Clifton. *Teams* Glamorgan (1922–30, 28 matches); Wales (1926).
Career batting
29–47–5–522–65–12.42–0–*ct* 8
Bowling 126–3–42.00–0–0–2/23

Mathie-Morton, Alexander Fullarton
Amateur. *b:* 7.6.1880, Belmont, Ayr, Scotland. *d:* 16.1.1965, Ayr, Scotland. Middle order right-hand batsman. *Sch* Blair Lodge. *Team* Scotland (1922).
Career batting
1–2–0–16–9–8.00–0–*ct* 0

Mathwin, Henry
Amateur. *b:* 23.8.1852, Bolton-le-Moors, Lancashire. *d:* 31.12.1911, Birkdale, Lancashire. Middle order batsman. *Team* Cambridge U (1874).
Career batting
1–2–1–18–17–18.00–0–*ct* 2

Matthews, Alan Ivor
Professional. *b:* 3.5.1913, Keynsham, Somerset. Lower order right-hand batsman, right-arm fast medium bowler. *Team* Gloucestershire (1933–38, 16 matches).
Career batting
16–25–6–185–51–9.73–0–*ct* 10
Bowling 980–14–70.00–0–0–4/81
He also played for Wiltshire (1948).

Matthews, Albert John
Cricketer. *b:* 29.4.1944, Fearn, Inverness, Scotland. Lower order right-hand batsman, off break bowler. *Team* Leicestershire (1965–68, 16 matches).
Career batting
16–20–3–167–32–9.82–0–*ct* 8
Bowling 786–24–32.75–0–0–4/87

Matthews, Austin David George
Professional, but amateur from 1946. *b:* 3.5.1904, Penarth, Glamorgan. *d:* 29.7.1977, Penrhyn Bay, Llandudno, Caernarvonshire. Lower order right-hand batsman, right-arm fast medium bowler. *Sch* St David's, Lampeter. *Teams* Northamptonshire (1927–36, 224 matches); Glamorgan (1937–47, 51 matches). *Test* England (1937, 1 match).
Career batting
281–447–70–5919–116–15.70–2–*ct* 124
Bowling 19099–816–23.40–45–6–7/57
Test batting
1–1–1–2–2*–no av–0–*ct* 1
Bowling 65–2–32.50–0–0–1/13
His best season was 1946 when he took 93 wickets, av 14.29. He was appointed Assistant Secretary of Glamorgan in 1946 and so became an amateur. A noted rugby footballer, he played for Northampton, Penarth, East Midlands and had a trial for Wales. He also represented Wales at table tennis.

Matthews, Christopher Darrell
Cricketer. *b:* 22.9.1962, Cunderdin, Perth, Western Australia. Lower order left-hand batsman, left-arm fast bowler. *Teams* Western Australia (1984/5 to 1990/1, 52 matches); Lancashire (1988, 3 matches); Tasmania (1991/2, 11 matches). *Tours* Western Australia to India 1989/90. *Tests* Australia (1986/7 to 1988/9, 3 matches).
Career batting
71–92–10–1693–71–20.64–0–*ct* 24
Bowling 7167–299–23.97–21–0–8/101
Test batting
3–5–0–54–32–10.80–0–*ct* 1
Bowling 313–6–52.16–0–0–3/95
He appeared briefly for Lancashire in 1988, acting as a stand-in for Wasim Akram.

Matthews, Colin Stuart
(birth registered as S. C. Matthews)
Professional. *b:* 17.10.1931, Worksop, Nottinghamshire. *d:* 15.3.1990, Kilton Hill, Worksop, Nottinghamshire. Tail end right-hand batsman, left-arm medium pace bowler. *Team* Nottinghamshire (1950–59, 84 matches).
Career batting
85–103–36–493–41–7.35–0–*ct* 38
Bowling 5433–147–36.95–4–0–6/65

Matthews, Dudley Muir
Amateur. *b:* 11.9.1916, Rainhill, Lancashire. *d:* 3.12.1968, Bangkok, Thailand. Brother of J. D. (Scotland). Middle order left-hand batsman. *Sch* Felsted. *Team* Lancashire (1936–38, 7 matches).
Career batting
7–8–0–130–46–16.25–0–*ct* 1

Matthews, Frank Cyril Leonard
Professional. *b:* 15.8.1892, Willoughby-on-the-Wolds, Nottinghamshire. *d:* 11.1.1961, Standard Hill, Nottingham. Tail end right-hand batsman, right-arm fast bowler. *Team* Nottinghamshire (1920–27, 82 matches).
Career batting
82–94–24–500–34–7.14–0–*ct* 42
Bowling 5331–261–20.42–14–2–9/50
His great season was 1923 when he took 115 wickets, av 15.30, and against Northamptonshire at Trent Bridge he took 17 wickets for 89, a County record.

Matthews, Gregory Richard John
Cricketer. *b:* 15.12.1959, Newcastle, New South Wales, Australia. Middle order left-hand batsman, off break bowler. *Team* New South Wales (1982/3 to 1991/2, 90 matches). *Tours* Australia to West Indies 1983/4, 1990/1, to England 1985, to New Zealand 1985/6, to Sharjah (not first-class) 1984/5, 1985/6, 1986/7, to India 1986/7, 1989/90 (not first-class); New South Wales to Zimbabwe 1987/8. *Tests* Australia (1983/4 to 1990/1, 28 matches).
Career batting
139–201–36–6440–184–39.03–12–*ct* 105
Bowling 11341–352–32.21–15–4–7/50
Test batting
28–44–8–1411–130–39.19–4–*ct* 14
Bowling 2402–49–49.02–2–1–5/103
He played in one Test on the 1985 tour to England, and did little in the County matches. Although picked

for Australia as an off break bowler, he has achieved as much fame with the bat as the ball.

Matthews, Dr John Duncan
Amateur. *b:* 19.9.1921, Rainhill, Lancashire. Brother of D. M. (Lancashire). Middle order left-hand batsman. *Sch* Shrewsbury. *Team* Scotland (1951–55).
Career batting
5–7–0–81–29–11.57–0–*ct* 0
He played for Cambridge U v Oxford U 1941 and 1942 in war-time matches.

Matthews, John Leonard
Amateur. *b:* 2.8.1847, Clifton, Bristol, Gloucestershire. *d:* 25.9.1912, Maidenhead, Berkshire. Brother of T. G. (Gloucestershire). *Sch* Cheltenham. *Team* Gloucestershire (1872, 1 match).
Career batting
1 match, did not bat–*ct* 0
The only match in which he appeared for Gloucestershire was almost completely washed out by rain.

Matthews, Michael Harrington
Amateur. *b:* 26.4.1914, Wandsworth, London. *d:* 29.5.1940, Dunkirk, France. He was killed in action on a destroyer off the coast. Attacking lower order right-hand batsman, wicket-keeper. *Sch* Westminster. *Team* Oxford U (1934–37, blue 1936–37).
Career batting
23–33–3–393–68–13.10–0–*ct* 32–*st* 6
He also achieved success as a sprinter and as a boxer whilst at Oxford.

Matthews, Robin Birkby
Cricketer. *b:* 30.1.1944, Stockton-on-Tees, Co Durham. Lower order right-hand batsman, right-arm medium pace bowler. *Team* Leicestershire (1971–73, 25 matches).
Career batting
25–18–8–89–16*–8.90–0–*ct* 8
Bowling 1338–48–27.87–1–0–7/51
He also played for Oxfordshire (1964–69).

Matthews, Thomas Gadd
Amateur. *b:* 9.12.1845, Clifton, Bristol, Gloucestershire. *d:* 5.1.1932, Newport, Gloucestershire. Brother of J. L. (Gloucestershire). Hard hitting opening right-hand batsman. *Team* Gloucestershire (1870–78, 29 matches).
Career batting
29–47–0–769–201–16.36–1–*ct* 13
His only double century was 201 for Gloucestershire v Surrey at Clifton in 1871 – he being the first cricketer to perform such a feat for Gloucestershire.

Matthews, Thomas James
Amateur. *b:* 3.4.1884, Williamstown, Melbourne, Victoria, Australia. *d:* 14.10.1943, Caulfield, Melbourne, Victoria, Australia. Stubborn lower order right-hand batsman, leg break bowler. *Team* Victoria (1906/7 to 1914/15, 32 matches). *Tour* Australia to England and North America 1912. *Tests* Australia (1911/12 to 1912, 8 matches).
Career batting
67–99–13–2149–93–24.98–0–*ct* 56
Bowling 4507–177–25.46–8–1–7/46
Test batting
8–10–1–153–53–17.00–0–*ct* 7
Bowling 419–16–26.18–0–0–4/29
At Old Trafford for Australia v South Africa in 1912 he performed one hat-trick in each innings – the only time such a feat has been achieved in Test matches. Although his performances on the rest of the tour did not match this, he was a very useful bowler.

Mattocks, Douglas Eric
Cricketer. *b:* 5.7.1944, Norwich, Norfolk. Lower order right-hand batsman, wicket-keeper. *Team* Minor Counties (1985).
Career batting
1–1–1–1–1*–no av–0–*ct* 4
His County cricket was for Norfolk (1961–91).

Matts, Alfred Shipley
Professional. *b:* 2.4.1893, Barrow-on-Soar, Leicesterhsire. *d:* 20.6.1970, Anstey, Leicestershire. Lower order left-hand batsman, left-arm bowler. *Team* Leicestershire (1921, 1 match).
Career batting
1–2–0–3–3–1.50–0–*ct* 0
Bowling 54–1–54.00–0–0–1/54

Maturin, Dr Henry
Amateur. *b:* 5.4.1842, Fanetglebe, Clondevaddock, Co Donegal, Ireland. *d:* 24.2.1920, Hartley Wintney, Hampshire. Lower order right-hand batsman, right-hand fast round-arm bowler. *Sch* Marlborough. *Teams* Middlesex (1863, 1 match); Hampshire (1864–82, 9 matches).
Career batting
12–19–1–178–28–9.88–0–*ct* 7
Bowling 201–6 + 2–33.50–0–0–4/68

Maude, Edmund
Amateur. *b:* 31.12.1839, Middleton, Leeds, Yorkshire. *d:* 2.7.1876, Headingley, Leeds, Yorkshire. Middle order batsman. *Team* Yorkshire (1866, 2 matches).
Career batting
2–2–0–17–16–8.50–0–*ct* 0

Maude, Frederick William
Amateur. *b:* 28.2.1857, Plumstead, London. *d:* 9.2.1923, St Pancras, London. Right-hand batsman, right-arm medium pace bowler, good slip. *Team* Middlesex (1890–96, 2 matches).
Career batting
13–26–0–323–60–12.42–0–*ct* 8
Bowling 325–9–36.11–1–0–6/90
His first-class debut was for MCC in 1883 and his final first-class match was for MCC in 1897. He

stood four times for Parliament but was not returned. He was a Baron of Cinque Ports.

Maude, John
Amateur. *b:* 17.3.1850, Millfield Road, Horbury, Yorkshire. *d:* 17.11.1934, Oberhofen, Switzerland. Lower order batsman, left-arm medium pace bowler. *Sch* Eton. *Team* Oxford U (1873, blue).
Career batting
5–7–3–25–12*–6.25–0–*ct* 2
Bowling 255–23–11.08–2–0–6/14
His County cricket was for Warwickshire (pre first-class, 1870).

Maudsley, Ronald Harling
Amateur. *b:* 8.4.1918, Lostock-Gralam, Cheshire. *d:* 29.9.1981, San Diego, California, USA. Sound middle order right-hand batsman, right-arm medium pace bowler. *Sch* Malvern. *Teams* Oxford U (1946–47, blue both years); Warwickshire (1946–51, 45 matches).
Career batting
67–116–5–2676–130–24.10–4–*ct* 48
Bowling 1470–52–28.26–2–0–6/54
He was joint captain of Warwickshire in 1948.

Maul, Rev John Broughton
Amateur. *b:* 28.11.1857, Newport Pagnell, Buckinghamshire. *d:* 5.11.1931, Banbury, Oxfordshire. Middle order right-hand batsman, right-hand slow round-arm bowler, excellent field. *Sch* Uppingham. *Team* Cambridge U (1878).
Career batting
1–1–0–0–0–0.00–0–*ct* 0
Bowling 8–1–8.00–0–0–1/8

Maundrell, Rev William Herbert
Amateur. *b:* 5.11.1876, Nagasaki, Japan. *d:* 17.6.1958, Deal, Kent. Middle order right-hand batsman. *Sch* King's, Canterbury. *Team* Hampshire (1900, 1 match).
Career batting
1–1–0–0–0–0.00–0–*ct* 0
He played no first-class matches whilst at Cambridge U, but did win an athletics blue.

Maw, Michael Trentham
Amateur *b:* 29.9.1912, Nutfield, Reigate, Surrey. *d:* 13.8.1944, on air operations over Germany. Tail end right-hand batsman, right-arm medium pace bowler. *Sch* Oundle. *Team* Cambridge U (1933–34).
Career batting
3–5–2–19–9–6.33–0–*ct* 0
Bowling 141–3–47.00–0–0–1/15

Mawle, Henry Edward
Professional. *b:* 14.1.1871, Bexhill-on-Sea, Sussex. *d:* 13.11.1943, Ugborough, Ivybridge, Devon. Lower order batsman, wicket-keeper. *Team* Sussex (1896, 1 match).
Career batting
1–1–0–0–0–0.00–0–*ct* 0
He also played for Devon (1901).

Maxwell, Cecil Reginald Napp
Amateur *b:* 21.5.1913, Paddington, London. *d:* 25.9.1973, Taunton, Somerset. Hard hitting middle order right-hand batsman, wicket-keeper. *Sch* Brighton. *Teams* Nottinghamshire (1936–39, 16 matches); Middlesex (1946, 4 matches); Worcestershire (1948–51, 7 matches). *Tours* Cahn to North America 1933 (not first-class), to Ceylon 1936/7, to New Zealand 1938/9.
Career batting
44–67–7–1564–268–26.06–1–*ct* 70–*st* 25
His first-class debut was for Sir J. Cahn's XI in 1932, and his most notable innings was 268 for the same team v Leicestershire at Loughborough Road, West Bridgford, in 1935. Whilst at Brighton he was regarded as the outstanding schoolboy batsman-wicketkeeper of his generation.

Maxwell, James
Professional. *b:* 13.1.1883, Taunton, Somerset. *d:* 27.12.1967, Taunton, Somerset. Lower order right-hand batsman, right-arm fast medium bowler. *Team* Somerset (1906–08, 10 matches).
Career batting
11–18–5–218–67*–16.76–0–*ct* 6
Bowling 917–24–38.20–1–0–5/63
He also played for Glamorgan (pre first-class, 1909–14). His final first-class match was for South Wales in 1912.

Maxwell, Lawrence Evan
Cricketer. *b:* 17.1.1941, Bayfield, St Philip, Barbados. Tail end right-hand batsman, off break bowler. *Team* Barbados (1968/9 to 1978/9). *Tour* Barbados to England 1969.
Career batting
16–23–11–90–19–7.50–0–*ct* 2
Bowling 1261–34–37.08–1–0–5/73

Maxwell, Dr Patrick Arthur
Amateur. *b:* 10.7.1869, Dublin, Ireland. Middle order batsman. *Team* Dublin U (1895).
Career batting
4–8–0–105–39–13.12–0–*ct* 1

Maxwell, Thomas Stanislaus Alfred Charles Joseph
Amateur. *b:* 15.3.1903, Westminster, London. *d:* 27.3.1970, Camberwell, London. Middle order right-hand batsman, right-arm medium fast bowler. *Team* Minor Counties (1937–38).
Career batting
2–4–2–79–78*–39.50–0–*ct* 0
Bowling 108–2–54.00–0–0–1/11
He played for Surrey 2nd XI.

Maxwell, W.
Amateur. Lower order batsman. *Team* MCC (1890).
Career batting
1–1–0–0–0–0.00–0–*ct* 0

Maxwell-Heron, John Heron
Amateur. *b:* 5.9.1836, Port Louis, Mauritius. *d:* 26.1.1899, Westminster, London. Great-uncle of P. V. F. Cazalet (Kent). Middle order batsman, left-hand round-arm bowler. *Sch* Harrow. *Team* Gentlemen of England (1865).
Career batting
1–1–0–3–3–3.00–0–*ct* 1
Bowling 44–2–22.00–0–0–2/32
He was MP for Kirkcudbright 1880–85.

May, Barry
Cricketer. *b:* 1.11.1944, Johannesburg, South Africa. Middle order right-hand batsman. *Team* Oxford U (1970–72, blue all three years).
Career batting
22–40–1–703–103–18.02–1–*ct* 12
He captained Oxford in 1971.

May, Frank Boyd
Amateur. *b:* 24.10.1862, Westminster, London. *d:* 1.6.1907, Hurley, Marlow, Buckinghamshire. He died by his own hand having been declared a defaulter on the Stock Exchange. Middle order batsman. *Sch* Clifton. *Team* MCC (1898–1906).
Career batting
4–7–1–12–7–2.00–0–*ct* 2

May, John
Professional. *b:* 26.9.1845, Southampton, Hampshire. Lower order right-hand batsman, right-arm fast bowler. *Team* Hampshire (1867–70, 4 matches).
Career batting
4–8–2–71–28–11.83–0–*ct* 0
Bowling 165–6–27.50–0–0–4/80

May, Percy Robert
Amateur. *b:* 13.3.1884, Chertsey, Surrey. *d:* 6.12.1965, Moor Green, Eastleigh, Hampshire. Lower order right-hand batsman, right-arm fast bowler. *Teams* Surrey (1902–09, 12 matches); London County (1902–04); Cambridge U (1903–06, blue 1905–06). *Tour* MCC to New Zealand 1906/7.
Career batting
72–112–39–1037–51*–14.20–0–*ct* 36
Bowling 6094–247–24.67–14–3–7/41
His final first-class match was in 1926 for Free Foresters. He was for some years well-known in Ceylon cricket. He also obtained his soccer blue at Cambridge.

May, Peter Barker Howard, CBE
Amateur. *b:* 31.12.1929, The Mount, Reading, Berkshire. Son-in-law of A. H. H. Gilligan (Sussex). Polished middle order right-hand batsman. *Sch* Charterhouse. *Teams* Surrey (1950–63, 208 matches); Cambridge U (1950–52, blue all three years). *Tours* MCC to West Indies 1953/4, 1959/60, to Australia and New Zealand 1954/5, 1958/9, to South Africa 1956/7. *Tests* England (1951–61, 66 matches).
Career batting
388–618–77–27592–285*–51.00–85–*ct* 282
Bowling 49–0
Test batting
66–106–9–4537–285*–46.77–13–*ct* 42
The most talented English batsman of his generation, May first came to the public eye whilst at Charterhouse, where he was in the Eleven for four years – heading the school's batting averages at the age of 14. In 1946 he represented Berkshire and at the age of 17 hit a brilliant 146 for the Public Schools against Combined Services at Lord's. His first-class debut was for Combined Services in 1948, and having ended his National Service he went up to Cambridge, where he had an outstanding three years. In the vacation of 1950 he made his Surrey debut and the following season celebrated his England debut with an innings of 138 v South Africa at Headingley; in the same year he topped the first-class averages, completing 2,000 runs for the first of five times. In all he exceeded 1,000 runs in an English season eleven times (best 2,554, av 51.08, in 1953). He also hit 1,000 runs in a season once in Australia and once in South Africa.
He remained an automatic choice for England until the demands of business coupled with ill health forced him to retire from regular first-class cricket after the 1961 season. He was appointed captain of Surrey in 1957, a post he held until 1962, and led England in 41 Tests commencing in 1955, and including the MCC tours to South Africa 1956/7, Australia and New Zealand 1958/9 and West Indies 1959/60. On the last named tour ill health forced him to return to England after the third Test.
Of his five double centuries the highest was 285* for England v West Indies at Edgbaston in 1957. He hit two double centuries for Surrey, one for Cambridge and one for MCC in Rhodesia.
He was Chairman of the English Test Selection Committee 1982–88, having previously been on the panel 1965–68. He was President of MCC 1980/1.

May, Timothy Brian Alexander
Cricketer. *b:* 26.1.1962, North Adelaide, South Australia. Lower order right-hand batsman, off break bowler. *Team* South Australia (1984/5 to 1991/2, 65 matches). *Tours* Australia to India and Pakistan (World Cup) 1987/8, to Pakistan 1988/9, to England 1989, to India 1989/90 (not first-class). *Tests* Australia (1987/8 to 1988/9, 7 matches).
Career batting
83–109–29–1365–128–17.06–1–*ct* 25
Bowling 9492–255–37.22–9–0–7/93
Test batting
7–10–4–90–24–15.00–0–*ct* 1

Bowling 895–25–35.80–0–0–4/97

He did not appear in any Tests on the 1989 tour to England, his form being affected by an injury which kept him out of some first-class matches.

Mayall, James
Professional. *b:* 8.1.1856, Oldham, Lancashire. *d:* 13.9.1916, Oldham, Lancashire. Lower order batsman, wicket-keeper. *Team* Lancashire (1885, 1 match).
Career batting
1–1–0–0–0–0.00–0–*ct* 1–*st* 2

Mayer, Joseph Herbert
Professional. *b:* 2.3.1902, Audley, Staffordshire. *d:* 6.9.1981, Kingsbury, Warwickshire. Useful lower order right-hand batsman, right-arm fast medium bowler. *Team* Warwickshire (1926–39, 332 matches).
Career batting
333–409–115–2839–74*–9.65–0–*ct* 184
Bowling 25404–1144–22.20–71–9–8/62

He took 100 wickets in a season twice (best 126, av 22.35, in 1929). He also played for Staffordshire (1921).

Mayes, Richard
Professional. *b:* 7.10.1922, Littlebourne, Kent. Stylish middle order right-hand batsman, good cover field. *Team* Kent (1947–53, 80 matches).
Career batting
80–144–7–2689–134–19.62–4–*ct* 28
Bowling 46–0

He also played for Suffolk (1957–63).

Mayes, T.
Professional. Lower order batsman, wicket-keeper. *Team* Sussex (1889, 7 matches).
Career batting
7–12–3–51–15–5.66–0–*ct* 11–*st* 3

He also played for Monmouthshire (1902–04).

Mayes, William Henry James
Amateur. *b:* 17.7.1885, Marylebone, London. *d:* 5.2.1946, Esher, Surrey. Lower order right-hand batsman, right-arm fast bowler. *Team* Essex (1914, 1 match).
Career batting
1–2–0–2–2–1.00–0–*ct* 0
Bowling 69–0

Mayhew, John Francis Nicholas
Amateur. *b:* 6.12.1909, Mungumbankum, India. Lower order right-hand batsman, wicket-keeper. *Sch* Eton. *Team* Oxford U (1929–31, blue 1930).
Career batting
14–21–9–115–26*–9.58–0–*ct* 8–*st* 4

His County cricket was for Buckinghamshire (1947–48).

Maynard, Christopher
Cricketer. *b:* 8.4.1958, Haslemere, Surrey. Middle order right-hand batsman, wicket-keeper. *Teams* Warwickshire (1978–82, 24 matches); Lancashire (1982–86, 91 matches). *Tour* Robins to New Zealand 1979/80.
Career batting
117–150–27–2541–132*–20.65–1–*ct* 186–*st* 28
Bowling 8–0

He appeared for both Warwickshire and Lancashire in 1982. He career ended due to injury in 1986.

Maynard, Edmund Anthony Jefferson
Amateur. *b:* 10.2.1861, Chesterfield, Derbyshire. *d:* 10.1.1931, Hoon, Hilton, Derbyshire. Middle order right-hand batsman, slow right-arm bowler. *Sch* Harrow. *Teams* Derbyshire (1880–87, 37 matches); Cambridge U (1881–83).
Career batting
47–85–4–720–84–8.88–0–*ct* 18
Bowling 53–2–26.50–0–0–2/34

He was captain of Derbyshire from 1885–87.

Maynard, Matthew Peter
Cricketer. *b:* 21.3.1966, Oldham, Lancashire. Attacking middle order right-hand batsman, right-arm medium pace bowler. *Teams* Glamorgan (1985–92, 159 matches); Northern Districts (1990/1 to 1991/2). *Tours* England XI to South Africa 1989/90. *Tests* England (1988, 1 match).
Career batting
188–306–36–11362–243–42.08–25–*ct* 161–*st* 2
Bowling 566–5–113.20–0–0–3/21
Test batting
1–2–0–13–10–6.50–0–*ct* 0

He scored 102 for Glamorgan v Yorkshire at Swansea on his first-class debut in 1985, reaching his hundred with three successive sixes. His best season was 1991, with 1,803 runs, av 60.10; he has reached 1,000 runs in a season seven times. His highest score was 243 for Glamorgan v Hampshire at Southampton in 1991.

Mayne, Richard Edgar
Amateur. *b:* 2.7.1882, Jamestown, South Australia. *d:* 26.10.1961, Carrum, Victoria, Australia. Opening right-hand batsman. *Teams* South Australia (1906/7 to 1914/15, 37 matches); Victoria (1918/19 to 1925/6, 43 matches). *Tours* Australia to England 1912, 1921, to New Zealand 1909/10, to North America 1912, 1913, to South Africa 1914/15 (tour cancelled); Victoria to New Zealand 1924/5. *Tests* Australia (1912 to 1921/2, 4 matches).
Career batting
141–243–10–7624–209–32.72–14–*ct* 80
Bowling 440–13–33.84–0–0–3/6
Test batting
4–4–1–64–25*–21.33–0–*ct* 2
Bowling 1–0

He achieved little on his two tours to England – in 1921 his opportunities were very limited and he did not appear in the Tests. His highest score was 209 for Victoria v Queensland at Melbourne in 1923/4.

Mayo, Charles Thomas Worsfold
Amateur. *b:* 5.2.1903, Victoria, British Columbia, Canada. *d:* 10.4.1943, near Alexandria, Egypt. He was killed in action. Middle order right-hand batsman. *Sch* Eton. *Team* Somerset (1928, 6 matches).
Career batting
6–9–0–193–60–21.44–0–*ct* 3

Mayo, Henry Edward
Amateur. *b:* 13.11.1847, South Lambeth, London. *d:* 30.10.1891, North Brixton, London. Middle order right-hand batsman, right-hand fast round-arm bowler. *Team* Surrey (1868–70, 14 matches).
Career batting
14–27–1–246–53–9.46–0–*ct* 8
Bowling 112–4–28.00–0–0–2/13

Mays, Christopher Sean
Cricketer. *b:* 11.5.1966, Brighton, Sussex. Lower order right-hand batsman, off break bowler. *Sch* Lancing. *Teams* Sussex (1986, 8 matches); Surrey (1987–88, 4 matches).
Career batting
12–9–4–39–13*–7.80–0–*ct* 5
Bowling 1009–16–63.06–0–0–3/77

Mead, Charles Philip
Professional. *b:* 9.3.1887, Battersea, London. *d:* 26.3.1958, Boscombe, Hampshire. Sound middle order left-hand batsman, slow left-arm bowler. *Team* Hampshire (1905–36, 700 matches). *Tours* MCC to Australia 1911/12, 1928/9, to South Africa 1913/14, 1922/3; Tennyson to Jamaica (1927/8. *Tests* England (1911/12 to 1928/9, 17 matches).
Career batting
814–1340–185–55061–280*–47.67–153–*ct* 671
Bowling 9613–277–34.70–5–0–7/18
Test batting
17–26–2–1185–182*–49.37–4–*ct* 4

He hit 1,000 runs in a season 27 times, going on 2,000 nine times and 3,000 twice (best 3,179, av 69.10, in 1921). He scored 13 double centuries, 11 of them for Hampshire, the highest being 280* v Nottinghamshire at Southampton in 1921. In the opinion of many he was unlucky not to obtain a regular place in the England team. He also played for Suffolk in 1938 and 1939. Though blind for the last ten years of his life he continued to attend Hampshire matches.

Mead, Harold
Professional. *b:* 13.6.1895, Walthamstow, Essex. *d:* 13.4.1921, Bell Common, Essex. He died from tuberculosis. Son of Walter (Essex). Tail end right-hand batsman, slow left-arm bowler. *Team* Essex (1913–14, 4 matches).
Career batting
4–8–2–19–8*–3.16–0–*ct* 3
Bowling 194–3–64.66–0–0–2/84

Mead, Walter
Professional. *b:* 1.4.1868, Clapton, London. *d:* 18.3.1954, Shelley, Ongar, Essex. Father of Harold (Essex). Lower right-hand batsman, slow medium off break, and occasional leg break bowler. *Teams* Essex (1894–1913, 332 matches); London County (1904). *Test* England (1899, 1 match).
Career batting
429–618–148–4991–119–10.61–1–*ct* 194
Bowling 36388–1916–18.99–152–39–9/40
Test batting
1–2–0–7–7–3.50–0–*ct* 1
Bowling 91–1–91.00–0–0–1/91

He took 100 wickets in a season ten times (best 179, av 14.55, in 1895); three times he took nine wickets in an innings for Essex, his best analysis being 9 for 40 v Hampshire at Southampton in 1900. His first-class debut was for MCC in 1892. He first played for Essex (pre first-class) in 1890.

Mead-Briggs, Richard
Amateur. *b:* 25.3.1902, St Dunstan, Canterbury, Kent. *d:* 15.5.1956, Harborne, Birmingham. Middle order right-hand batsman, right-arm medium fast bowler. *Sch* King's, Canterbury. *Team* Warwickshire (1946, 2 matches).
Career batting
2–2–1–46–44*–46.00–0–*ct* 3
Bowling 96–1–96.00–0–0–1/44

He was a noted all-rounder in Midlands Club cricket for over 30 years.

Meaden, H. J. B.
Amateur. Middle order batsman. *Team* Hampshire (1881, 3 matches).
Career batting
3–6–1–20–9*–4.00–0–0–*ct* 2

Meads, Eric Alfred
Professional. *b:* 17.8.1916, Carrington, Nottingham. Tail end right-hand batsman, wicket-keeper. *Team* Nottinghamshire (1939–53, 205 matches).
Career batting
205–240–90–1475–56*–9.83–0–*ct* 364–*st* 83
Bowling 5–0

Meads, James Wilford
(known as James Wilfred Meads)
Professional. *b:* 28.10.1877, Calverton, Nottinghamshire. *d:* 3.11.1957, Calverton, Nottinghamshire. Lower order batsman, slow right-arm bowler. *Team* Surrey (1905, 3 matches).
Career batting
3–4–0–9–4–2.25–0–*ct* 0
Bowling 135–7–19.28–0–0–4/36

Meakin, Bernard
Amateur. *b:* 5.3.1885, Darlaston Hall, Stone, Staffordshire. *d:* 17.2.1964, Dunsfold, Surrey. Middle order left-hand batsman, leg break bowler. *Sch* Clifton. *Teams* Gloucestershire (1906, 1 match); Cambridge U (1906–07).
Career batting
8–13–2–109–60–9.90–0–*ct* 4
He was a leading cricketer for Staffordshire (1904–22), captaining the County from 1911–21 and President from 1946–56. His final first-class match was for Free Foresters in 1922.

Meakin, Douglas
Amateur. *b:* 28.3.1929, Swadlincote, Derbyshire. Lower order right-hand batsman, right-arm fast bowler. *Team* Combined Services (1959–62).
Career batting
4–6–3–55–16–18.33–0–*ct* 0
Bowling 206–10–20.60–0–0–4/56
His County cricket was for Bedfordshire (1952–62).

Meale, Trevor
Amateur. *b:* 11.11.1928, Papatoetoe, Auckland, New Zealand. Opening left-hand batsman, right-arm medium pace bowler. *Team* Wellington (1951/2 to 1953/4). *Tour* New Zealand to England 1958. *Tests* New Zealand (1958, 2 matches).
Career batting
32–54–5–1352–130–27.59–2–*ct* 17
Bowling 3–0
Test batting
2–4–0–21–10–5.25–0–*ct* 0
He was a surprise choice for the 1958 tour to England, and though appearing in two Tests achieved very little. His final first-class match in New Zealand was for an Eleven of New Zealand in 1957/8.

Meares, George Brooke
Amateur. *b:* 26.10.1841, Glandovey Castle, Cardiganshire. *d:* 21.8.1894, Kneller Hall, Twickenham, Middlesex. Middle order right-hand batsman, good bowler. *Sch* Bedford GS. *Team* MCC (1874–76).
Career batting
4–7–1–52–23–8.66–0–*ct* 5
Bowling 163–7–23.28–0–0–4/18
He appeared for Hampshire (pre first-class) and Essex (pre first-class, 1876). For some considerable time he was stationed in India.

Mechen, William
Professional. *b:* 8.1.1852, Southwick, Sussex. *d:* 10.3.1880, Southwick Green, Sussex. Middle order right-hand batsman. *Team* Sussex (1876–79, 4 matches).
Career batting
4–8–0–43–20–5.37–0–*ct* 7

Medhurst, Robert Henry
Professional. *b:* 29.4.1922, Sydenham, London. Tail end right-hand batsman, right-arm fast medium bowler. *Team* Sussex (1948, 3 matches).
Career batting
3–3–2–17–15*–17.00–0–*ct* 1
Bowling 233–3–77.66–0–0–1/11
He also played for Cambridgeshire (1950–52).

Medlicott, Walter Sandfield
Amateur. *b:* 28.8.1879, Potterne, Wiltshire. *d:* 24.6.1970, Old Fodderlie, Hawick, Roxburghshire, Scotland. Steady middle order right-hand batsman, good field. *Sch* Harrow. *Team* Oxford U (1901–02, blue 1902).
Career batting
13–20–2–423–81–23.50–0–*ct* 13
His County cricket was for Wiltshire (1898–1912). His final first-class match for MCC in 1911.

Medlycott, Keith Thomas
Cricketer. *b:* 12.5.1965, Whitechapel, London. Middle order right-hand batsman, slow left-arm bowler. *Teams* Surrey (1984–91, 135 matches); Northern Transvaal (1988/9). *Tours* England to West Indies 1989/90; England A to Sri Lanka 1990/1 (not first-class).
Career batting
141–180–38–3684–153–25.94–3–*ct* 90
Bowling 11517–357–32.26–18–6–8/52
He scored 117* on his first-class debut for Surrey v Cambridge U at Banstead in 1984. He appeared in only three first-class matches on the 1989/90 West Indian tour.

Mee, Adrian Alexander Graham
Cricketer. *b:* 29.5.1963, Johannesburg, South Africa. Middle order right-hand batsman. *Sch* Merchant Taylors. *Team* Oxford U (1984–87, blue 1986).
Career batting
10–16–1–191–51–12.73–0–*ct* 4

Mee, Robert John
Professional. *b:* 25.9.1867, Shelford, Nottinghamshire. *d:* 6.2.1941, Shelford, Nottinghamshire. Lower order right-hand batsman, right-arm fast bowler. *Team* Nottinghamshire (1887–96, 37 matches).
Career batting
41–66–20–366–35–7.95–0–*ct* 25
Bowling 3207–133–24.11–4–1–9/54
His best bowling was 9/54 for Nottinghamshire v Sussex at Trent Bridge in 1893. He also played for Monmouthshire (1891) and Staffordshire (1905–09).

Mee, Steven Robert
Cricketer. *b:* 6.4.1965, Nottingham, Lower order right-hand batsman, right-arm medium pace bowler. *Team* Nottinghamshire (1984, 1 match).

Career batting
1 match, did not bat–*ct* 0
Bowling 63–2–31.50–0–0–2/44

Meek, Henry Edgar
Amateur. *b:* 8.10.1857, Devizes, Wiltshire. *d:* 23.6.1920, Gullane, East Lothian, Scotland. Middle order right-hand batsman. *Sch* Harrow. *Team* MCC (1878).
Career batting
1–1–0–0–0–0.00–0–*ct* 1

Meers, William Simmonds Meers
Amateur. *b:* 27.3.1844, Stoke, Kent. *d:* 12.7.1902, Horsham, Sussex. Middle order batsman. *Sch* Chatham House, Ramsgate. *Team* Kent (1866, 1 match).
Career batting
1–1–0–11–11–11.00–0–*ct* 0

Meeson, Martin Stewart
Amateur. *b:* 6.11.1933, Marylebone, London. Middle order left-hand batsman. *Sch* Bedford. *Team* Cambridge U (1957).
Career batting
1–2–0–25–21–12.50–0–*ct* 0
His County cricket was for Bedfordshire (1952–63).

Meggitt, Frank Claxton
Amateur. *b:* 17.2.1901, Barry, Glamorgan. *d:* 9.10.1945, Radyr, Glamorgan. Lower order right-hand batsman, wicket-keeper. *Sch* Mill Hill. *Team* Glamorgan (1923, 1 match).
Career batting
1–2–0–4–4–2.00–0–*ct* 0
He played no first-class cricket whilst at Cambridge U, but did win a hockey blue. He played hockey and golf for Wales.

Meherhomji, Khershed Rustomji
Amateur. *b:* 9.8.1911, Bombay, India. *d:* 10.2.1982, Bombay, India. Nephew of R. P. (India). Tail end right-hand batsman, wicket-keeper. *Teams* Bombay (1933/4); Western India (1934/5 to 1935/6); Parsis (1933/4 to 1945/6). *Tour* India to England 1936. *Test* India (1936, 1 match).
Career batting
30–46–4–656–71–15.61–0–*ct* 61–*st* 10
Test batting
1–1–1–0–0*–no av–0–*ct* 1
He was the reserve wicket-keeper on the 1936 tour.

Meherhomji, Rustomji Perozsha
Amateur. *b:* 4.3.1877, Bombay, India. *d:* 14.11.1943, Bombay, India. Uncle of K. R. (Bombay). Opening right-hand batsman, right-arm fast bowler. *Team* Parsis (1901/2 to 1916/17). *Tour* India to England 1911.
Career batting
39–69–1–1777–102–26.13–2–*ct* 9
Bowling 10–0
On the 1911 tour, he was the only batsman to complete 1,000 runs in all matches, and in first-class matches hit 684, av 24.42.

Mehta, Praful Swantilal
Cricketer. *b:* 1941, Dar-es-Salaam, Tanganyika. Opening left-hand batsman, wicket-keeper. *Team* East Africa (1975). *Tour* East Africa to England 1975.
Career batting
1–2–0–29–17–14.50–0–*ct* 4

Meintjes, Douglas James
Amateur. *b:* 9.6.1890, Pretoria, South Africa. *d:* 17.7.1979, Johannesburg, South Africa. Lower order right-hand batsman, right-arm fast medium bowler. *Team* Transvaal (1910/11 to 1925/6). *Tour* South Africa to England 1924. *Tests* South Africa (1922/3, 2 matches).
Career batting
52–78–7–1146–87–16.14–0–*ct* 25
Bowling 2698–91–29.64–1–1–8/63
Test batting
2–3–0–43–21–14.33–0–*ct* 3
Bowling 115–6–19.16–0–0–3/38
He had little success on his single visit to England and was not required for the Tests.

Meldon, Dr George Edward Pugin
Amateur. *b:* 12.9.1875, Dublin, Ireland. *d:* 2.7.1950, Dublin, Ireland. Middle order right-hand batsman. *Team* Dublin University (1895).
Career batting
4–8–2–93–33–15.50–0–*ct* 2

Meldon, Dr George James
Amateur. *b:* 18.1.1885, Dublin, Ireland. *d:* 27.11.1951, Stourbridge, Worcestershire. Brother of L. A. (Ireland). Middle order right-hand batsman. *Sch* Stonyhurst. *Team* Ireland (1907–12).
Career batting
10–18–0–263–41–14.61–0–*ct* 4
He played hockey for Ireland.

Meldon, John Michael
Amateur. *b:* 29.9.1869, Dublin, Ireland. *d:* 12.12.1954, Tunbridge Wells, Kent. Middle order right-hand batsman, right-arm bowler. *Sch* Beaumont. *Team* Ireland (1902–10).
Career batting
5–10–1–55–14–6.11–0–*ct* 1

Meldon, Louis Albert
Amateur. *b:* 10.10.1886, Dublin, Ireland. *d:* 21.2.1956, Ranelagh, Co Dublin, Ireland. Brother of G. J. (Ireland). Middle order right-hand batsman, right-arm medium pace bowler. *Sch* Stonyhurst. *Team* Ireland (1909–12).
Career batting
4–6–0–151–47–25.16–0–*ct* 3

Bowling 15–1–15.00–0–0–1/4
He played tennis for Ireland.

Meldon, Philip Albert
Amateur. *b:* 18.12.1874, Dublin, Ireland. *d:* 8.4.1942, Marylebone, London. Brother of W. W. (Warwickshire). Lower order batsman, bowler. *Sch* Beaumont. *Team* MCC (1911).
Career batting
2–3–0–14–7–4.66–0–*ct* 1
Bowling 83–3–27.66–0–0–2/83
He played for Ireland from 1899 to 1905, but not in a first-class match.
A brilliant soccer player, he represented Ireland.

Meldon, William Waltrude
Amateur. *b:* 9.4.1879, Dublin, Ireland. *d:* 23.5.1957, Putney, London. Brother of P. A. (MCC). Middle order right-hand batsman, right-arm fast medium bowler. *Sch* Beaumont College. *Teams* Warwickshire (1909–10, 5 matches); Ireland (1911–14).
Career batting
8–14–1–208–44–16.00–0–*ct* 4
Bowling 338–14–24.14–1–0–5/53
He also played for Northumberland (1912–14) and Devon (1924).

Melhuish, Francis
Amateur. *b:* 17.5.1857, Claughton, Birkenhead, Cheshire. Middle order right-hand batsman. *Sch* Marlborough. *Team* Lancashire (1877, 3 matches).
Career batting
3–6–0–32–13–5.33–0–*ct* 0

Melle, Dr Basil George von Brandis
Amateur. *b:* 31.3.1891, Somerset West, Cape Province, South Africa. *d:* 8.1.1966, Orchards, Johannesburg, South Africa. Father of M. G. (South Africa). Middle order right-hand batsman, right-arm medium pace, later leg break, bowler, good field. *Teams* Western Province (1908/9 to 1910/11); Oxford U (1913–14, blue, both years); Hampshire (1914–21, 27 matches); Transvaal (1923/4). *Tour* Incogniti to USA 1913 (not first-class).
Career batting
62–101–9–2535–145–27.55–3–*ct* 33
Bowling 2931–114–25.71–9–1–7/48
His best season as a bowler was 1913 with 55 wickets, av 15.90 – a broken finger the following year deprived his bowling of its bite and he was played more for his batting. He hit 1,021 runs, av 35.20, in 1919.

Melle, Michael George
Amateur. *b:* 3.6.1930, Forest Town, Johannesburg, South Africa. Son of B. G. von B. (Hampshire). Lower order right-hand batsman, right-arm fast bowler. *Teams* Transvaal (1948/9 to 1951/2); Western Province (1953/4). *Tours* South Africa to England 1951, to Australia and New Zealand 1952/3. *Tests* South Africa (1949/50 to 1952/3, 7 matches).
Career batting
52–68–20–544–59–11.33–0–*ct* 22
Bowling 3990–160–24.93–6–2–9/22
Test batting
7–12–4–68–17–8.50–0–*ct* 4
Bowling 851–26–32.73–2–0–6/71
He headed the first-class bowling averages on the 1951 tour (50 wkts, av 20.28), but injury forced him to miss many matches. Bowling for Transvaal v Griqualand West at Johannesburg in 1950/1 he took 8 for 8. His best bowling was 9/22 for South Africans v Tasmania at Launceston in 1952/3.

Mellin, Eric Lawrence
Amateur. *b:* 27.7.1886, Wickham Hall, West Wickham, Kent. *d:* 8.9.1968, Maresfield Park, Sussex. Hard hitting opening or middle order batsman, useful bowler. *Sch* Malvern. *Team* Cambridge U (1907).
Career batting
1–1–0–13–13–13.00–0–*ct* 0

Melling, John
Professional. *b:* 6.4.1848, Enfield, Clayton-le-Moors, Lancashire. *d:* 31.1.1881, Keighley Green, Burnley, Lancashire. Lower order right-hand batsman. *Team* Lancashire (1874–76, 3 matches).
Career batting
3–5–0–39–20–7.80–0–*ct* 4
Bowling 16–0

Mellon, Charles William
Amateur. *b:* 9.2.1915, Dublin, Ireland. *d:* 1990, Dublin, Ireland. Middle order right-hand batsman, right-arm medium pace bowler. *Team* Ireland (1937–38).
Career batting
2–4–0–48–30–12.00–0–*ct* 1
Bowling 2–0

Mellor, Alan John
Cricketer. *b:* 4.7.1959, Horninglow, Staffordshire. Tail end right-hand batsman, slow left-arm bowler. *Team* Derbyshire (1978–80, 13 matches).
Career batting
13–15–6–26–10*–2.88–0–*ct* 4
Bowling 653–17–38.41–1–0–5/52
He also played for Staffordshire (1981–86).

Mellor, Francis Hamilton
Amateur. *b:* 13.5.1854, Bloomsbury, London. *d:* 26.4.1925, Paris, France. Brother of Horace (Lancashire). Stylish middle order right-hand batsman, slow under-arm bowler, good outfield. *Sch* Cheltenham. *Teams* Cambridge U (1874–77, blue 1877); Kent (1877–78, 4 matches).
Career batting
12–22–1–211–46–10.04–0–*ct* 7

Mellor, Horace
Amateur. *b:* 21.2.1851, Paddington, London. *d:* 27.2.1942, Castletown, Isle of Man. Brother of F. H.

(Kent). Middle order right-hand batsman. *Sch* Cheltenham. *Team* Lancashire (1874–75, 2 matches).
Career batting
2–4–0–28–17–7.00–0–*ct* 0

Mellor, Dr James Philip
Cricketer. *b:* 19.1.1953, Oxford. Middle order right-hand batsman, slow left-arm bowler. *Sch* Rydal. *Team* Cambridge U (1973).
Career batting
3–5–0–27–22–5.40–0–*ct* 1

Melluish, Gordon Christopher
Amateur. *b:* 25.8.1906, Marylebone, London. *d:* 14.4.1977, Little Bushey, Hertfordshire. Tail end right-hand batsman, slow left-arm bowler. *Sch* Haberdashers' Aske's. *Team* Essex (1926, 4 matches).
Career batting
4–3–1–18–16*–9.00–0–*ct* 0
Bowling 115–3–38.33–0–0–1/17

Melluish, Michael Edward Lovelace
Amateur. *b:* 13.6.1932, Westcliff-on-Sea, Essex. Lower order right-hand batsman, wicket-keeper. *Sch* Rossall. *Teams* Cambridge U (1954–56, blue all three years); Middlesex (1957, 1 match).
Career batting
49–67–17–524–36–10.48–0–*ct* 80–*st* 35
His final first-class match was for MCC in 1959. He captained Cambridge in 1956. He was President of MCC 1991/2.

Melsome, Robert George William
Amateur. *b:* 16.1.1906, Sopley, Christchurch, Hampshire. *d:* 3.11.1991, South Harting, Sussex. Lower order right-hand batsman, right-arm medium pace bowler. *Sch* Lancing. *Team* Gloucestershire (1925–34, 16 matches).
Career batting
27–42–4–500–60–13.15–0–*ct* 22
Bowling 1098–45–24.40–3–0–8/103
His final first-class match was for the Army in 1938.

Melville, Alan
Amateur. *b:* 19.5.1910, Carnarvon, Cape Province, South Africa. *d:* 18.4.1983, Sabie, Transvaal, South Africa. Brother of C. M. (Oxford U), uncle of C. D. M. (Oxford U), cousin of B. L. Cumming (Sussex). Fluent stroke making opening right-hand batsman, leg break and googly, later off break bowler. *Teams* Natal (1928/9 to 1929/30); Oxford U (1930–33, blue all four years); Sussex (1932–36, 86 matches); Transvaal (1936/7 to 1948/9). *Tour* South Africa to England 1947. *Tests* South Africa 1938/9 to 1948/9, 11 matches).
Career batting
190–295–15–10598–189–37.85–25–*ct* 156
Bowling 3959–132–29.99–7–0–5/17
Test batting
11–19–2–894–189–52.58–4–*ct* 8
He captained Oxford U in 1931 and 1932, Sussex in 1934 and 1935, and South Africa in 10 Tests as well as on the 1947 tour to England. He hit 1,000 runs in a season three times (best 1,904, av 40.51, in 1935).

Melville, Dr Charles
Amateur. *b:* 9.4.1896, Falkirk, Stirlingshire, Scotland. *d:* 25.3.1954, Dumfries, Scotland. Middle order right-hand batsman, useful bowler. *Team* Scotland (1928–29).
Career batting
3–5–0–50–24–10.00–0–*ct* 0
Bowling 150–3–50.00–0–0–2/72

Melville, Christopher Duncan McLean
Amateur. *b:* 4.10.1935, Pietermaritzburg, South Africa. Son of C. M. (Oxford U), nephew of Alan (South Africa). Middle order right-hand batsman, right-hand medium bowler. *Team* Oxford U (1956–57, blue 1957).
Career batting
12–22–3–758–142–39.89–2–*ct* 10
Bowling 368–6–61.33–0–0–1/19

Melville, Colin McLean
Amateur. *b:* 13.7.1903, Carnarvon, Cape Province, South Africa. *d:* 12.6.1984, Johannesburg, South Africa. Father of C. D. M. (Oxford U), brother of Alan (South Africa), cousin of B. L. Cumming (Sussex). Middle order right-hand batsman. *Team* Oxford U (1928).
Career batting
1–2–0–29–28–14.50–0–*ct* 1

Melville, James
Amateur. *b:* 15.3.1909, Barrow-in-Furness, Lancashire. *d:* 2.8.1961, Coventry, Warwickshire. Lower order right-hand batsman, slow left-arm bowler. *Team* Warwickshire (1946, 2 matches).
Career batting
2–3–0–14–13–4.66–0–*ct* 1
Bowling 84–5–16.80–0–0–3/34
He played soccer for Blackburn Rovers, Hull City and Northampton.

Melville, James Edward
Cricketer. *b:* 3.3.1936, Streatham, London. Lower order right-hand batsman, right-arm fast medium bowler. *Sch* Beaumont. *Team* Kent (1962–63, 6 matches).
Career batting
6–8–4–20–6–5.00–0–*ct* 4
Bowling 422–14–30.14–0–0–4/78

Melville, John Hutchison
Amateur. *b:* 19.6.1895, Cowdenbeath, Fife, Scotland. *d:* 22.9.1951, Aylesbury, Buckinghamshire. Tail end right-hand batsman, slow left-arm bowler. *Team* Scotland (1932–37).

Mence, Michael David

Career batting
6–11–3–21–9*–2.62–0–*ct* 4
Bowling 559–33–16.93–3–0–6/32

He played for Buckinghamshire (1937).

Mence, Michael David
Cricketer. *b:* 13.4.1944, Newbury, Berkshire. Middle order left-hand batsman, right-arm medium pace bowler. *Sch* Bradfield. *Teams* Warwickshire (1962–65, 31 matches); Gloucestershire (1966–67, 22 matches). *Tours* MCC to West Africa 1975/6, to Bangladesh 1976/7 (neither first-class).
Career batting
54–78–15–949–78–15.06–0–*ct* 23
Bowling 3050–86–35.46–2–0–5/26

He played for Berkshire in 1961 and again after retiring from first-class cricket (1967–82). He was Assistant Secretary of MCC with responsibility for ICC in 1987.

Mendis, Gehan Dixon
Cricketer. *b:* 24.4.1955, Colombo, Ceylon. Opening right-hand batsman, occasional wicket-keeper. *Teams* Sussex (1974–85, 201 matches); Lancashire (1986–92, 142 matches). *Tours* International XI to Pakistan 1981/2, to Jamaica 1982/3; Lancashire to Jamaica 1986/7, 1987/8, to Zimbabwe 1988/9.
Career batting
348–609–61–20337–209*–37.11–40–*ct* 140–*st* 1
Bowling 158–1–158.00–0–0–1/65

He hit 1,000 runs in a season twelve times (best 1,756, av 47.45, in 1985). His highest score was 209* for Sussex v Somerset at Hove in 1984.

Mendis, Louis Rohan Duleep
Cricketer. *b:* 25.8.1952, Moratuwa, Ceylon. Middle order right-hand batsman, right-arm medium pace bowler, occasional wicket-keeper. *Team* Sinhalese SC (1988/9 to 1990/1). *Tours* Sri Lanka to India 1972/3, 1974/5, 1975/6, 1976/7, 1982/3, 1986/7, to Pakistan 1973/4, 1981/2, 1985/6, to England 1975, 1979, 1981, 1983 (World Cup), 1984, 1988, to Australia 1982/3, 1984/5, to New Zealand 1982/3, to Zimbabwe 1982/3, to Sharjah (not first-class) 1983/4, 1985/6, to India and Pakistan (World Cup) 1987/8. *Tests* Sri Lanka (1981/2 to 1988, 24 matches).
Career batting
121–190–16–6233–194–35.82–12–*ct* 49–*st* 1
Bowling 52–1–52.00–0–0–1/4
Test batting
24–43–1–1329–124–31.64–4–*ct* 9

He captained the Sri Lankans to England in 1984 and, leading his country in its first Test at Lord's, scored 111 and 94, the outstanding feat of the visit. In 1988 he also played in the single Test, but not as captain. In all he captained Sri Lanka in 19 Tests. His first-class debut was for Ceylon in 1971/2.

Mendl, Derek Francis
Amateur. *b:* 1.8.1914, Hurlingham, Argentine. Brother of J. F. (Scotland). Middle order right-hand batsman, wicket-keeper. *Sch* Repton. *Teams* Free Foresters (1951); MCC (1951).
Career batting
2–4–0–59–26–14.75–0–*ct* 2

Mendl, Jack Francis
Amateur. *b:* 6.12.1911, Hurlingham, Argentine. Brother of D. F. (MCC). Opening right-hand batsman. *Sch* Repton. *Teams* Minor Counties (1949); Scotland (1953–55); MCC (1957).
Career batting
7–13–2–269–65–24.45–0–*ct* 0

His County cricket was for Oxfordshire (1939–55).

Menzies, Dr Henry
Amateur. *b:* 28.3.1867, Lambeth, London. *d:* 7.3.1936, North Farnborough, Hampshire. Lower order right-hand batsman, wicket-keeper. *Sch* St Pauls. *Team* Middlesex (1891–93, 5 matches).
Career batting
5–7–3–47–18*–11.75–0–*ct* 6–*st* 2

He played in trials at Cambridge U, but not in first-class matches.

Mercer, Charles Frederick
Amateur. *b:* 28.8.1896, Hackney, London. *d:* 20.11.1965, Basildon, Essex. Middle order left-hand batsman. *Team* Essex (1929, 2 matches).
Career batting
2–4–0–26–8–6.50–0–*ct* 0

Mercer, Ian Pickford
Cricketer. *b:* 30.5.1930, Oldham, Lancashire. Middle order right-hand batsman, right-arm medium pace bowler. *Team* Minor Counties (1965).
Career batting
1–2–0–1–1–0.50–0–*ct* 1

His County cricket was for Norfolk (1964–72).

Mercer, John
Professional. *b:* 22.4.1893, Southwick, Sussex. *d:* 31.8.1987, Westminster, London. Lower order right-hand batsman, right-arm fast medium bowler. *Teams* Sussex (1919–21, 12 matches); Glamorgan (1922–39, 412 matches); Wales (1923–30); Northamptonshire (1947, 1 match). *Tours* MCC to India, Burma and Ceylon 1926/7; Cahn to Jamaica 1928/9.
Career batting
457–628–112–6076–72–11.77–0–*ct* 144
Bowling 37210–1591–23.38–104–17–10/51

He took 100 wickets in a season nine times (best 145, av 20.88, in 1929); his best bowling in an innings was 10/51 for Glamorgan v Worcestershire at Worcester in 1936. He was Northamptonshire coach 1946–60 and scorer 1963–81.

Mercer, William Norman
Amateur. *b:* 30.5.1922, Prescot, Lancashire. *d:* 11.4.1989, Brighton, Sussex. Lower order right-hand batsman, leg break and googly bowler. *Teams* Sussex (1948–56, 2 matches); South African Air Force (1942/3).
Career batting
3–4–1–40–24–13.33–0–*ct* 2
Bowling 103–6–17.16–0–0–3/31

Merchant, Vijaysingh Madhavji
(real name V. M. Thackersey)
Amateur. *b:* 12.10.1911, Bombay, India. *d:* 27.10.1987, Bombay, India. Brother of U. M. (Bombay). Stylish opening right-hand batsman, right-arm medium pace bowler. *Teams* Hindus (1929/30 to 1945/6); Bombay (1933/4 to 1950/1). *Tours* Indian University Occasionals to Ceylon 1935/6; India to England 1936, 1946, to Ceylon 1944/5. *Tests* India (1933/4 to 1951/2, 10 matches).
Career batting
150–234–46–13470–359*–71.64–45–*ct* 115
Bowling 2088–65–32.12–1–0–5/73
Test batting
10–18–0–859–154–47.72–3–*ct* 7
Bowling 40–0
He was the most accomplished batsman of the 1936 tour, heading the averages with 1,745 runs, av 51.32. In 1946 he was even more successful with 2,385 runs, av 74.53. His highest innings was 359* for Bombay v Maharastra at Bombay in 1943/4 and of his other 10 scores over 200, two were made in England, the highest being 242* v Lancashire at Old Trafford in 1946. He also hit 1,000 runs in a season in India. In the 1951/2 series of Tests in India, a shoulder injury ended his career. After retiring he became well-known as an administrator of cricket in India.

Meredith, Henry Chase
Amateur. *b:* 8.10.1881, Richmond, Surrey. *d:* 21.9.1957, Ludlow, Shropshire. Nephew of A. E. Green-Price (Foster's XI). Lower order batsman, useful bowler. *Sch* Eton. *Team* H. K. Foster's XI (1919).
Career batting
2–3–0–35–34–11.66–0–*ct* 2
Bowling 28–0
His County cricket was for Shropshire.

Mermagen, Patrick Hassell Frederick
Amateur. *b:* 8.5.1911, Colyton, Devon. *d:* 20.12.1984, Ipswich, Suffolk. Middle order right-hand batsman, right-arm fast medium bowler. *Sch* Sherborne. *Team* Somerset (1930, 8 matches).
Career batting
8–10–0–114–35–11.40–0–*ct* 4
Bowling 26–0
He played in trials at Cambridge U, but not in first-class matches.

Merrall, John Edwin
Amateur. *b:* 7.1.1909, Shipley, Yorkshire. Lower order right-hand batsman, right-arm fast medium bowler. *Team* Surrey (1932–33, 2 matches).
Career batting
3–2–0–10–5–5.00–0–*ct* 3
Bowling 202–6–33.66–0–0–3/24
His final first-class match was for Minor Counties in 1934.

Merrick, Horace
Amateur. *b:* 21.12.1887, Clifton, Bristol. *d:* 16.8.1961, Clifton, Bristol. Middle order right-hand batsman. *Sch* Bristol GS. *Team* Gloucestershire (1909–11, 12 matches).
Career batting
12–23–5–257–58–14.27–0–*ct* 4

Merrick, Tyrone Anthony
Cricketer. *b:* 10.6.1963, St John's, Antigua. Lower order right-hand batsman, right-arm fast medium bowler. *Teams* Leeward Islands (1982/3 to 1988/9); Warwickshire (1987–89, 34 matches); Kent (1990–91, 26 matches). *Tours* Young West Indies to Zimbabwe 1986/7.
Career batting
88–111–23–1265–74*–14.37–0–*ct* 30
Bowling 7918–311–25.45–15–2–7/45
His best season in English cricket was 1988 when he took 65 wickets, av 22.10.

Merritt, William Edward
Professional. *b:* 18.8.1908, Sumner, Christchurch, New Zealand. *d:* 9.6.1977, Christchurch, New Zealand. Lower order right-hand batsman, leg break and googly bowler. *Teams* Canterbury (1926/7 to 1935/6); Northamptonshire (1938–46, 41 matches). *Tours* New Zealand to England 1927, 1931, to Australia 1927/8. *Tests* New Zealand (1929/30 to 1931, 6 matches).
Career batting
125–191–33–3147–87–19.91–0–*ct* 58
Bowling 13669–536–25.50–37–8–8/41
Test batting
6–8–1–73–19–10.42–0–*ct* 2
Bowling 617–12–51.41–0–0–4/104
On the 1927 tour to England he was the most successful bowler taking 107 wickets, av 23.64, and in 1931 he took 99 wickets, av 26.48. He played in the Lancashire League as a professional and qualified for Northamptonshire in 1939. He played rugby league for Wigan and Halifax.

Merry, Cyril Arthur
Amateur. *b:* 20.1.1911, Scarborough, Tobago. *d:* 19.4.1964, St Clair, Port of Spain, Trinidad. Brother of David (Trinidad). Middle order right-hand batsman, useful bowler. *Team* Trinidad (1929/30 to 1938/9). *Tour* West Indies to England 1933. *Tests* West Indies (1933, 2 matches).

Merry, William Gerald

Career batting
37–64–7–1547–146–27.14–1–*ct* 33
Bowling 746–33–22.60–0–0–3/13
Test batting
2–4–0–34–13–8.50–0–*ct* 1

Although playing in two Tests on the 1933 tour, he only achieved modest results on the visit – 856 runs, av 28.53; 13 wickets, av 32.30.

Merry, William Gerald
Cricketer. *b:* 8.8.1955, Newbury, Berkshire. Lower order right-hand batsman, right-arm medium pace bowler. *Team* Middlesex (1979–82, 26 matches). *Tours* MCC to Bangladesh 1978/9, to East Africa 1981/2, to North America 1982 (none first-class); Robins to New Zealand 1979/80; Middlesex to Zimbabwe 1980/1.
Career batting
29–19–11–50–14*–6.25–0–*ct* 6
Bowling 1724–52–33.15–0–0–4/24

He also played for Hertfordshire (1976–78 and 1983–91) and his last first-class match was for Minor Counties in 1986.

Merson, Dr Ronald David
Amateur. *b:* 25.7.1925, Stockton-on-Tees, Co Durham. Middle order right-hand batsman. *Sch* Merchiston. *Team* Scotland (1947).
Career batting
1–2–0–16–15–8.00–0–*ct* 0

Meston, Alexander Hubert
Professional. *b:* 1.6.1898, Leyton, Essex. *d:* 1.3.1980, Illogan North, Redruth, Cornwall. Brother of S. P. (Essex and Gloucestershire). Lower order right-hand batsman. *Team* Essex (1926–27, 12 matches).
Career batting
12–17–4–143–41–11.00–0–*ct* 9
Bowling 352–4–88.00–0–0–2/18

Meston, Samuel Paul
Amateur. *b:* 19.11.1882, Islington, London. *d:* 9.1.1960, Vancouver, British Columbia, Canada. Brother of A. H. (Essex). Middle order right-hand batsman, right-hand medium bowler. *Teams* Gloucestershire (1906, 3 matches); Essex (1907–08, 17 matches).
Career batting
20–35–2–516–130–15.63–1–*ct* 11
Bowling 65–1–65.00–0–0–1/10

Metcalfe, Ashley Anthony
Cricketer. *b:* 25.12.1963, Horsforth, Yorkshire. Son-in-law of R. Illingworth (Yorkshire and Leicestershire). Opening right-hand batsman, off break bowler. *Sch* Bradford GS. *Teams* Yorkshire (1983–92, 167 matches); Orange Free State (1988/9). *Tours* Yorkshire to Windward Islands 1986/7, to South Africa 1991/2.
Career batting
177–307–18–10163–216*–35.16–23–*ct* 66
Bowling 316–4–79.00–0–0–2/18

He scored 122 on his first-class debut for Yorkshire v Nottinghamshire at Bradford in 1983. His highest score was 216* for Yorkshire v Middlesex at Headingley 1988. He hit 1,000 runs in a season six times, going on to 2,000 once: 2,047, av 51.17, in 1990.

Metcalfe, Stanley Gordon
Amateur. *b:* 20.6.1932, Horsforth, Yorkshire. Middle order right-hand batsman, off break bowler, good deep field. *Sch* Leeds GS. *Team* Oxford U (1954–56, blue 1956).
Career batting
27–50–3–1200–153*–25.53–2–*ct* 11
Bowling 352–9–39.11–0–0–2/32

He appeared regularly for Free Foresters, his final first-class match being for that side in 1968.

Metcalfe, Vivian Alderson
Amateur. *b:* 5.3.1906, Saltburn, Yorkshire. *d:* 28.12.1967, Addlestone, Surrey. Middle order right-hand batsman. *Teams* Wales (1928); Ireland (1936).
Career batting
4–7–0–81–36–11.57–0–*ct* 0

His County cricket was for Carmarthenshire.

Metson, Colin Peter
Cricketer. *b:* 2.7.1963, Goff's Oak, Hertfordshire. Lower order right-hand batsman, wicket-keeper. *Teams* Middlesex (1981–86, 24 matches); Glamorgan (1987–92, 142 matches).
Career batting
166–212–46–3001–96–18.07–0–*ct* 387–*st* 30
Bowling 0–0

Meunier, James Brown
Professional. *b:* 1885, Poynton, Stockport, Cheshire. *d:* 30.9.1957, Loughborough, Leicestershire. Lower order batsman, right-arm fast bowler. *Team* Warwickshire (1920, 2 matches).
Career batting
2–3–0–12–9–4.00–0–*ct* 1
Bowling 38–0

He also played for Lincolnshire (1914). A good soccer player, he appeared for Everton and Lincoln City.

Meyer, Barrie John
Professional. *b:* 21.8.1932, Bournemouth, Hampshire. Lower order right-hand batsman, leg break bowler, wicket-keeper. *Team* Gloucestershire (1957–71, 406 matches). *Tour* Gloucestershire to Bermuda, 1962 (not first-class).
Career batting
406–569–191–5367–63–14.19–0–*ct* 709–*st* 118
Bowling 28–0

He was appointed a first-class umpire in 1973 and has umpired in 24 Test matches since 1978. A noted soccer player, he appeared as inside left for Bristol Rovers, Plymouth Argyle, Newport County and Bristol City.

Meyer, Rollo John Oliver
Amateur. *b:* 15.3.1905, Clophill, Bedfordshire. *d:* 9.3.1991, Kingsdown, Bristol. Attacking middle order right-hand batsman, right-arm slow medium bowler. *Sch* Haileybury. *Teams* Cambridge U (1924–26, blue all three years); Western India (1930/1 to 1934/5); Bombay (1926/7); Somerset (1936–49, 65 matches); Europeans (1926/7 to 1934/5).
Career batting
127–210–15–4621–202*–23.69–2–*ct* 85
Bowling 10328–408–25.31–25–3–9/160
His final first-class match was for MCC in 1950. His only double century was 202* for Somerset v Lancashire at Taunton in 1936 and his best bowling was 9/160 for Europeans v Muslims at Bombay in 1927/8. He captained Somerset in 1947. He also played for Hertfordshire (1923–29) and Bedfordshire (1949–50). He also won a blue for rackets. He was founder and headmaster of Millfield School.

Meyer, William Eustace
Amateur. *b:* 12.1.1883, Redland, Bristol. *d:* 1.10.1953, Falmouth, Cornwall. Middle order right-hand batsman, right-arm fast medium bowler. *Team* Gloucestershire (1909–10, 9 matches).
Career batting
9–16–0–136–43–8.50–0–*ct* 5

Meyrick-Jones, Rev Frederic Meyrick
(changed name from Jones in 1893)
Amateur. *b:* 14.1.1867, Blackheath, Kent. *d:* 25.10.1950, Shaftesbury, Dorset. Hard hitting middle order right-hand batsman, slow right-arm bowler, good deep field or wicket-keeper. *Sch* Marlborough. *Team* Cambridge U (1887–88, blue 1888); Kent (1893–96, 6 matches).
Career batting
18–32–5–512–67–18.96–0–*ct* 9–*st* 2
Bowling 87–2–43.50–0–0–1/3
He also played for Hampshire (not first-class, 1886–90) and Norfolk (1909).

Michell, Charles
Amateur. *b:* 17.2.1849, York. *d:* 25.1.1900, Forcett, Yorkshire. Brother of E. J. (Hampshire). Lower order right-hand batsman, wicket-keeper. *Sch* Haileybury. *Team* MCC (1875).
Career batting
1–1–0–1–1–1.00–0–*ct* 1
He was 'The first boy to enter Haileybury School'.

Michell, Edward John
Amateur. *b:* 15.6.1853, Steyning, Sussex. *d:* 5.5.1900, New Zealand. Brother of Charles (MCC). Middle order right-hand batsman. *Sch* Harrow and Haileybury. *Team* Hampshire (1880, 1 match).
Career batting
1–1–0–7–7–7.00–0–*ct* 1

Micklem, Leonard
Amateur. *b:* 12.3.1845, Henley-on-Thames, Oxfordshire. *d:* 7.7.1919, Elstree, Hertfordshire. Middle order right-hand batsman, excellent deep field. *Sch* Eton. *Team* MCC (1869).
Career batting
1–1–0–9–9–9.00–0–*ct* 0
He did not appear in first-class matches whilst at Oxford. His County cricket was for Berkshire (1870).

Micklethwait, William Henry
Amateur. *b:* 12.11.1885, Rotherham, Yorkshire. *d:* 7.10.1947, Broom Hall, Rotherham, Yorkshire. Middle order left-hand batsman. *Team* Yorkshire (1911, 1 match).
Career batting
1–1–0–44–44–44.00–0–*ct* 0

Middlebrook, Willie
Professional. *b:* 23.5.1858, Middlethorpe, Morley, Yorkshire. *d:* 26.4.1919, Morley, Yorkshire. Lower order right-hand batsman, right-arm fast bowler. *Team* Yorkshire (1888–89, 17 matches).
Career batting
19–29–7–96–19*–4.36–0–*ct* 20
Bowling 1071–54–19.83–1–0–5/59
His final first-class match was for L. Hall's XI in 1891.

Middlemost, Livingston
Amateur. *b:* 1.4.1839, Westoe, South Shields, Co Durham. *d:* 28.10.1897, Sedgefield, Huddersfield, Yorkshire. Middle order batsman. *Teams* North (1860); Players of the North (1877).
Career batting
2–3–0–21–17–7.00–0–*ct* 1
Although an amateur, he appeared for the Players in 1877.

Middleton, Cecil
Amateur. *b:* 26.5.1911, Leeds, Yorkshire. *d:* 3.9.1984, South End, Campbeltown, Argyll, Scotland. Middle order right-hand batsman, right-arm medium pace bowler. *Sch* Charterhouse. *Team* Oxford U (1933).
Career batting
4–6–0–128–44–21.33–0–*ct* 1
Bowling 201–4–50.25–0–0–3/60

Middleton, Charles
Professional. *b:* 21.12.1868, Leeds, Yorkshire. *d:* 5.2.1938, Queen's Park, Chesterfield, Derbyshire. Middle order right-hand batsman, leg break bowler. *Team* Derbyshire (1896–1903, 4 matches).
Career batting
4–8–1–47–21–6.71–0–*ct* 0
Bowling 21–0

Middleton, James
Professional. *b:* 30.9.1865, Chester-le-Street, Co Durham. *d:* 23.12.1913, Newlands, Cape Town, South Africa. Father of Thomas (Western Province) and R. E. (Western Province). Attacking lower order batsman, left-arm slow medium bowler. *Team* Western Province (1890/1 to 1903/4). *Tours* South Africa to England 1894 (not first-class), 1904. *Tests* South Africa (1895/6 to 1902/03, 6 matches).
Career batting
31–50–21–176–32–6.06–0–*ct* 14
Bowling 2523–140–18.02–10–4–7/64
Test batting
6–12–5–52–22–7.42–0–*ct* 1
Bowling 442–24–18.41–2–0–5/51
He took 83 wickets, av 15.79, in the non first-class tour of 1894, but was not very effective in 1904. He was bought out of the Army by Cape Town CC in order to become their professional.

Middleton, John William
Professional. *b:* 26.10.1890, Stoney Stanton, Leicestershire. *d:* 16.9.1966, Stoney Stanton, Leicestershire. Opening right-hand batsman. *Team* Leicestershire (1914–21, 24 matches).
Career batting
24–45–0–478–37–10.62–0–*ct* 7
Bowling 60–0

Middleton, Mark Ross
Cricketer. *b:* 15.7.1968, Guildford, Surrey. Lower order right-hand batsman, slow left-arm bowler. *Sch* Harrow. *Team* Cambridge U (1987, blue).
Career batting
2–1–0–6–6–6.00–0–*ct* 0
Bowling 119–1–119.00–0–0–1/72

Middleton, Samuel Henry Windrush
Amateur. *b:* 27.9.1901, Greystones, Co Wicklow, Ireland. *d:* 6.1.1949, Dublin, Ireland. Lower order right-hand batsman, off break bowler. *Team* Dublin University (1922).
Career batting
1–2–1–0–0*–0.00–0–*ct* 0
Bowling 22–0
He played for Ireland (not first-class) in 1921.

Middleton, Tony Charles
Cricketer. *b:* 1.2.1964, Winchester, Hampshire. Opening right-hand batsman, slow left-arm bowler. *Team* Hampshire (1984–92, 78 matches).
Career batting
78–130–13–4522–221–38.64–12–*ct* 56
Bowling 237–5–47.40–0–0–2/41
He reached 1,000 runs in a season twice (best 1,780, av 49.44, in 1992) and scored 221 for Hampshire v Surrey at Southampton in 1992.

Middleton, William George
Amateur. *b:* 16.4.1846. *d:* 9.4.1892, Kineton, Warwickshire. His neck was broken in a fall during a point-to-point race. Grandfather of P. M. Borwick (Northamptonshire). Middle order batsman, useful bowler. *Team* MCC (1870–78).
Career batting
12–20–1–123–22–6.47–0–*ct* 3
Bowling 92–3–30.66–0–0–2/39
His final first-class match was for I Zingari in 1882. His County cricket was for Cheshire (1874).

Midgley, Charles Augustus
Amateur. *b:* 13.11.1877, Wetherby, Yorkshire. *d:* 24.6.1942, Bradford, Yorkshire. Lower order right-hand batsman, right-arm fast bowler. *Team* Yorkshire (1906, 4 matches).
Career batting
4–6–2–115–59*–28.75–0–*ct* 3
Bowling 149–8–18.62–0–0–2/13

Midwinter, William Evans
Professional. *b:* 19.6.1851, St Briavels, Gloucestershire. *d:* 3.12.1890, Yarra Bend, Kew, Melbourne, Victoria, Australia. In June 1890 he became insane and was confined to Kew Asylum, the loss of his wife and two children having unhinged his mind. Excellent middle order right-hand batsman, right-hand medium pace round-arm bowler, good deep field. *Teams* Victoria (1874/5 to 1886/7, 13 matches); Gloucestershire (1877–82, 58 matches). *Tours* Australia to England 1878, 1884; Lillywhite, Shaw and Shrewsbury to Australia 1881/2. *Tests* Australia (1876/7 to 1886/7, 8 matches); England (1881/2, 4 matches).
Career batting
160–264–27–4534–137*–19.13–3–*ct* 122
Bowling 7298–419–17.41–27–3–7/27
Test batting
12–21–1–269–37–13.45–0–*ct* 10
Bowling 605–24–25.20–1–0–5/78
Halfway through the 1878 tour of England, he was persuaded by W. G. Grace to leave the touring party and appear for Gloucestershire for whom he had played the season before.
He is the only cricketer to represent England in Australia and Australia in England.

Mignon, Edward
Professional. *b:* 1.11.1885, Kilburn, Middlesex. *d:* 14.5.1925, Southwark, London. He died of pneumonia. Lower order right-hand batsman, right-arm fast bowler with ungainly action. *Team* Middlesex (1905–13, 140 matches).
Career batting
149–200–78–1080–34–8.85–0–*ct* 83
Bowling 11471–439–26.12–27–8–7/28
His final first-class match was for MCC in 1914.

Mike, Gregory Wentworth
Cricketer. *b:* 14.7.1966, Nottingham. Hard hitting middle order right-hand batsman, right-arm fast medium bowler. *Team* Nottinghamshire (1989–92, 10 matches).
Career batting
10–13–4–246–61*–27.33–0–*ct* 6
Bowling 684–14–48.85–0–0–3/48

Milbank, Sir Mark Vane
Amateur. *b:* 11.1.1907, Kington, Herefordshire. *d:* 4.4.1984, Barningham Park, Richmond, Yorkshire. He married the widow of C. L. Crawley (Essex). Lower order right-hand batsman, left-arm medium slow bowler. *Sch* Eton. *Team* Army (1930).
Career batting
1–1–0–1–1–1.00–0–*ct* 1
Bowling 40–1–40.00–0–0–1/8

Milburn, Barry Douglas
Cricketer. *b:* 24.11.1943, Maori Hill, Dunedin, New Zealand. Lower order right-hand batsman, wicket-keeper. *Team* Otago (1963/4 to 1982/3). *Tours* New Zealand to England 1969, to India and Pakistan 1969/70. *Tests* New Zealand (1968/9, 3 matches).
Career batting
75–97–33–737–103–11.51–1–*ct* 176–*st* 19
Test batting
3–3–2–8–4*–8.00–0–*ct* 6–*st* 2
The reserve wicket-keeper on the 1969 tour of England, he appeared in only eight matches.

Milburn, Colin
Professional. *b:* 23.10.1941, Burnopfield, Co Durham. *d:* 28.2.1990, Newton Aycliffe, Co Durham. He died from a heart attack. Attacking opening right-hand batsman, right-arm medium pace bowler. *Teams* Northamptonshire (1960–74, 196 matches); Western Australia (1966/7 to 1968/9, 17 matches). *Tours* MCC to East Africa 1963/4, to West Indies 1967/8, to Pakistan 1968/9. *Tests* England (1966 to 1968/9, 9 matches).
Career batting
255–435–34–13262–243–33.07–23–*ct* 224
Bowling 3171–99–32.03–1–0–6/59
Test batting
9–16–2–654–139–46.71–2–*ct* 7
He hit 1,000 runs in a season six times (best 1,861, av 48.97, in 1966). His highest innings was 243 for Western Australia v Queensland at Brisbane in 1968/9 and his only other double century was for Northamptonshire.
He tragically lost an eye in a road accident on 23 May 1969 and this more or less ended his career in first-class cricket, although he reappeared for Northamptonshire in 1973/74. He also played for Durham (pre first-class, 1959 and 1976).

Milburn, Edward Thomas
Cricketer. *b:* 15.9.1967, Nuneaton, Warwickshire. Middle order right-hand batsman, right-arm medium pace bowler. *Teams* Warwickshire (1987, 3 matches); Gloucestershire (1990–91, 3 matches).
Career batting
6–8–4–86–35–21.50–0–*ct* 2
Bowling 307–5–61.40–0–0–3/43

Milburn, Stuart Mark
Cricketer. *b:* 29.9.1972, Harrogate, Yorkshire. Lower order right-hand batsman, right-arm fast medium bowler. *Team* Yorkshire (1992, 1 match).
Career batting
1–2–1–7–5–7.00–0–*ct* 0
Bowling 115–1–115.00–0–0–1/54

Mildmay, Sir Henry Paulet St John
Amateur. *b:* 28.4.1853, Westminster, London. *d:* 24.4.1916, Dogmersfield Park, Hampshire. Middle order right-hand batsman, useful bowler. *Sch* Eton. *Team* Hampshire (1881–84, 7 matches).
Career batting
7–13–1–137–26–11.41–0–*ct* 4
Bowling 51–1–51.00–0–0–1/26

Miles, Audley Charles
Amateur. *b:* 6.9.1855, Clifton, Bristol. *d:* 6.9.1919, Polmaise, Stirling, Scotland. Brother of C. N. (MCC). Middle order right-hand batsman, good field. *Sch* Eton. *Team* MCC (1876).
Career batting
1–1–0–0–0–0.00–0–*ct* 0
He did not appear in any first-class matches whilst at Oxford, but did win a blue for polo.

Miles, Charles Napier
Amateur. *b:* 9.4.1854, Clifton, Bristol. *d:* 25.5.1918, Inglebourne Manor, Malmesbury, Wiltshire. Brother of A. C. (MCC). Middle order right-hand batsman. *Sch* Eton. *Team* MCC (1874).
Career batting
1–1–0–8–8–8.00–0–*ct* 0
He was a well-known figure in military cricket.

Miles, Harold Philip
Amateur. *b:* 31.1.1899, Rosario, Santa Fe, Argentine. *d:* 21.7.1957, Raleigh Park, Barnstaple, Devon. Middle order right-hand batsman, off break bowler. *Sch* Shrewsbury. *Teams* Army (1920–31); Minor Counties (1928); Free Foresters (1930–36); Europeans (1937/8). *Tour* MCC to South America 1926/7.
Career batting
23–32–4–613–107–21.89–1–*ct* 8
Bowling 1180–38–31.05–2–0–5/74
His County cricket was for Devon (1927–33).

Miles, Othneil
Cricketer. *b:* 23.9.1939, Clarendon Parish, Jamaica. *d:* February 1982, Kingston, Jamaica. Lower order right-hand batsman, off break bowler. *Team* Jamaica

(1967/8 to 1975/6). *Tour* Jamaica to England 1970.
Career batting
21–22–6–214–43*–13.37–0–*ct* 15
Bowling 1588–58–27.37–2–0–7/71

Miles, Philip William Herbert
Amateur. *b:* 7.1.1848, Bingham, Nottinghamshire. *d:* 4.12.1933, Bude, Cornwall. Brother of R. F. (Gloucestershire). Middle order right-hand batsman, right-hand fast round-arm bowler, slip field. *Sch* Marlborough. *Team* Nottinghamshire (1868–77, 3 matches).
Career batting
3–6–0–65–23–10.83–0–*ct* 0
Bowling 16–1–16.00–0–0–1/11

Miles, Robert Fenton
Amateur. *b:* 24.1.1846, Bingham, Nottinghamshire. *d:* 26.2.1930, Clifton, Bristol. Brother of P. W. H. (Nottinghamshire). Tail end right-hand batsman, slow left-arm bowler. *Sch* Marlborough. *Teams* Oxford U (1867–69, blue all three years); Gloucestershire (1870–79, 59 matches).
Career batting
69–96–23–577–79–7.90–0–*ct* 28
Bowling 3335–217–15.36–15–2–7/38
He also played for Worcestershire (pre first-class, 1870).

Millard, David Edward Shaxson
Cricketer. *b:* 3.4.1931, Rondebosch, Cape Town, South Africa. *d:* 30.1.1978, Cape Town, South Africa. He died by his own hand. Middle order right-hand batsman, off break bowler. *Teams* Western Province (1951/2 to 1954/5); Eastern Province (1952/3 to 1953/4); Oxford U (1965).
Career batting
14–26–2–497–73–20.70–0–*ct* 4
Bowling 448–15–29.86–1–0–6/68

Millard, William Henry
Professional. *b:* 25.5.1856, New Swindon, Wiltshire. *d:* 20.7.1923, Tenby, Pembrokeshire. Middle order right-hand batsman, bowler, good deep field. *Team* Sussex (1879–80, 5 matches).
Career batting
5–8–0–54–26–6.75–0–*ct* 3
Bowling 44–2–22.00–0–0–2/32
He also played for Wiltshire (1874–85). He played under a handicap, having only one eye.

Millener, David John
Cricketer. *b:* 2.5.1944, Epsom, Auckland, New Zealand. Tail end right-hand batsman, right-arm medium fast bowler. *Team* Auckland (1964/5 to 1967/8); Oxford U (1969/70, blue both years).
Career batting
26–30–12–176–24–9.77–0–*ct* 9
Bowling 1958–57–34.35–0–0–4/97
He played for USA in ICC Trophy (1982).

Miller, Andrew John Trevor
Cricketer. *b:* 30.5.1963, Chesham, Buckinghamshire. Opening left-hand batsman. *Sch* Haileybury. *Teams* Oxford U (1982–85, blue 1983–85); Middlesex (1983–87, 44 matches).
Career batting
69–113–14–3131–128*–31.62–3–*ct* 20
Bowling 14–1–14.00–0–0–1/4
He scored 128* for Oxford U v Cambridge U at Lord's in 1984 and captained his university in 1985. He hit 1,003 runs, av 43.56, in 1983. He also played for Hertfordshire (1988–89).

Miller, Audley Montague
(death registered as Audley Montagu Miller)
Amateur. *b:* 19.10.1869, Brentry, Westbury-on-Trym, Gloucestershire. *d:* 26.6.1959, Clifton, Bristol. Middle order right-hand batsman, right-arm medium fast bowler. *Sch* Eton. *Team* MCC (1896–1903). *Tour* Hawke to South Africa 1895/6. *Test* England (1895/6, 1 match).
Career batting
5–9–2–105–36–15.00–0–*ct* 0
Bowling 49–1–49.00–0–0–1/1
Test batting
1–2–2–24–20*–no av–0–*ct* 0
His County cricket was for Wiltshire (1894–1920), which side he captained for 25 years, also being Hon Secretary. His first-class debut was for England v South Africa in 1895/6, standing as umpire in the other two Tests in the series.

Miller, E.
Professional. Lower order left-hand batsman, left-arm fast bowler. *Team* Sussex (1878, 1 match).
Career batting
1–2–0–2–1–1.00–0–*ct* 0
Bowling 7–0

Miller, Francis Samuel
Amateur. *b:* 24.6.1850, Ayr, Scotland. Brother of W. H. (MCC). Middle order right-hand batsman. *Team* MCC (1877).
Career batting
2–3–0–12–8–4.00–0–*ct* 2

Miller, Frank Joseph
Amateur. *b:* 2.10.1916, Cork, Ireland. Lower order right-hand batsman, wicket-keeper. *Team* Ireland (1949–54).
Career batting
7–11–6–44–18*–8.80–0–*ct* 8–*st* 7

Miller, Frank Noble
Amateur. *b:* 8.4.1880, South Africa. Opening batsman. *Sch* Manchester GS. *Teams* Lancashire (1904, 1 match); Natal (1909/10).
Career batting
2–4–0–64–37–16.00–0–*ct* 2

Miller, Frederick Peel
Amateur. *b:* 29.7.1828, Clapham, London. *d:* 22.11.1875, Chilworthy, Ilminster, Somerset. Brother of W. H. (MCC 1851). Attacking right-hand opening batsman, right-hand medium pace round-arm, also slow under-arm, bowler, good deep field. *Team* Surrey (1851–67, 80 matches).
Career batting
137–235–20–3117–133–14.49–2–*ct* 86
Bowling 4859–237 + 19–20.50–6–0–6/36
He captained Surrey from 1851 to 1857 and his final first-class match was for Gentlemen of the South in 1868. He also played for Bedfordshire (1856), Herefordshire (1857) and Leicestershire (pre first-class, 1860).
He was responsible for the retailing of Volumes 3 and 4 of *Scores and Biographies* and when sales were poor, he burnt all the copies still in stock.

Miller, Geoffrey
Cricketer. *b:* 8.9.1952, Chesterfield, Derbyshire. Middle order right-hand batsman, off break bowler. *Teams* Derbyshire (1973–90, 254 matches); Natal (1983/4); Essex (1987–89, 52 matches). *Tours* England to India, Sri Lanka and Australia 1976/7, to Pakistan and New Zealand 1977/8, to Australia 1978/9, 1979/80, to West Indies 1980/1, to Australia and New Zealand (New Zealand not first-class) 1982/3. *Tests* England (1976–84, 34 matches).
Career batting
383–548–94–12027–130–26.49–2–*ct* 309
Bowling 24854–888–27.98–39–7–8/70
Test batting
34–51–4–1213–98*–25.80–0–*ct* 17
Bowling 1859–60–30.98–1–0–5/44
He captained Derbyshire 1979 to 1981. He took 87 wickets in 1977, av 17.82, and 1984, av 25.70. Although he returned no outstanding figures in Test cricket, his determined batting and accurate bowling were very useful assets to England. He also played for Cheshire (1991–92). He has represented Derbyshire at table tennis.

Miller, George
Amateur. *b:* 19.8.1929, Edinburgh, Scotland. Tail end left-hand batsman, right-arm fast medium bowler. *Team* Scotland (1955).
Career batting
1–2–1–8–6*–8.00–0–*ct* 0
Bowling 50–0

Miller, Hamish David Sneddon
Cricketer. *b:* 20.4.1943, Blackpool, Lancashire. Lower order right-hand batsman, right-arm medium fast bowler. *Teams* Western Province (1962/3); Glamorgan (1963–66, 27 matches); Orange Free State (1969/70 to 1970/1).
Career batting
38–58–7–589–81–11.54–0–*ct* 23
Bowling 2200–76–28.94–1–0–7/48
He was also a useful rugby full back.

Miller, Harry Rayment
Amateur. *b:* 22.2.1907, Gravesend, Kent. *d:* 1.9.1966, Inverness, Scotland. Lower order batsman, right-arm medium pace bowler. *Sch* Solihull. *Team* Warwickshire (1928, 1 match).
Career batting
1–1–0–8–8–8.00–0–*ct* 1
Bowling 38–1–38.00–0–0–1/15

Miller, Henry
Amateur. *b:* 18.9.1859, Liverpool, Lancashire. *d:* 11.4.1927, Walton-on-Thames, Surrey. Lower order right-hand batsman, right-arm fast bowler. *Sch* Uppingham. *Team* Lancashire (1880–81, 5 matches).
Career batting
5–8–0–84–27–10.50–0–*ct* 1
Bowling 202–10–20.20–1–0–5/46

Miller, Keith Ross, MBE
Amateur. *b:* 28.11.1919, Sunshine, Melbourne, Victoria, Australia. Attacking middle order right-hand batsman, right-arm fast bowler. *Teams* Victoria (1937/8 to 1946/7, 18 matches); New South Wales (1947/8 to 1955/6, 50 matches); Nottinghamshire (1959, 1 match). *Tours* Australia to England 1948, 1953, 1956, to South Africa 1949/50, to West Indies 1954/5, to New Zealand 1945/6, to Pakistan 1956/7; Australian Services to England 1945, to India and Ceylon 1945/6. *Tests* Australia (1945/6 to 1956/7, 55 matches).
Career batting
226–326–36–14183–281*–48.90–41–*ct* 136
Bowling 11087–497–22.30–16–1–7/12
Test batting
55–87–7–2958–147–36.97–7–*ct* 38
Bowling 3906–170–22.97–7–1–7/60
A brilliant all-rounder of the immediate post-war period, he hit 1,000 runs on the 1948 and 1953 tours to England (best 1,433, av 51.17, in 1953). He also hit 1,000 runs in an Australian season twice. In 1956 he topped the bowling averages for the tour with 50 wickets, av 19.60. Four of his double centuries were scored in England, included the highest: 281* v Leicestershire at Leicester in 1956. He hit a century on his single appearance for Nottinghamshire in 1959. He scored 181 on debut for Victoria v Tasmania at Melbourne in 1937/8. After retiring from first-class cricket he became a well-known journalist.

Miller, Lawrence Somerville Martin
Amateur. *b:* 31.3.1923, New Plymouth, Taranaki, New Zealand. Hard hitting opening left-hand batsman, left-arm slow medium bowler. *Teams* Central Districts (1950/1 to 1952/3); Wellington (1954/5 to 1959/60). *Tours* New Zealand to South Africa and Australia 1953/4, to England 1958. *Tests* New Zealand (1952/3 to 1958).

Career batting
82–142–15–4777–144–37.61–5–*ct* 33
Bowling 75–3–25.00–0–0–1/7
Test batting
13–25–0–346–47–13.84–0–*ct* 1
Bowling 1–0
On his tour to England he hit 1,148 runs, av 30.21, playing in four Tests.

Miller, Martin Ellis
Cricketer. *b:* 15.12.1940, Lytham, Lancashire. Lower order right-hand batsman, off break bowler. *Team* Cambridge U (1963, blue).
Career batting
12–15–5–48–21*–4.80–0–*ct* 4
Bowling 770–33–23.33–2–0–6/89

Miller, Neville
Amateur. *b:* 27.8.1874, Shanghai, China. *d:* 3.3.1967, Tooting Graveney, London. Opening right-hand batsman, useful bowler. *Sch* Dulwich. *Team* Surrey (1899–1903, 9 matches).
Career batting
9–12–1–346–124–31.45–1–*ct* 1
Bowling 114–1–114.00–0–0–1/28
He scored 124 on his debut for Surrey v Sussex (Hove) in 1899. He was for many years a notable figure in London Club cricket and played for Streatham for 42 years.

Miller, Robert Alexander Tamplin
Amateur. *b:* 12.11.1895, Lockwood, Travancore, India. *d:* 10.7.1941, near Maala, South Yemen. Lower order right-hand batsman, wicket-keeper. *Sch* Uppingham. *Team* Sussex (1919, 12 matches).
Career batting
12–22–2–191–39–9.55–0–*ct* 10–*st* 10

Miller, Roger
Amateur. *b:* 20.4.1857, Reading, Berkshire. *d:* 13.7.1912, Lowestoft, Suffolk. Middle order right-hand batsman, right-arm medium pace bowler. *Sch* Somerset College and Uppingham. *Team* Cambridge U (1881).
Career batting
7–12–1–261–73–23.72–0–*ct* 2
Bowling 24–0
His final first-class match was for MCC in 1884.

Miller, Roger Simon
Amateur. *b:* 16.2.1938, Seaford, Sussex. Tail end left-hand batsman, right-arm fast medium bowler. *Sch* Harrow. *Team* MCC (1959).
Career batting
1–2–2–1–1*–no av–0–*ct* 1
Bowling 91–5–18.20–0–0–3/41
His County cricket was for Dorset (1963–69).

Miller, Roland
Professional. *b:* 6.1.1941, Philadelphia, Co Durham. Lower order right-hand batsman, slow left-arm bowler. *Team* Warwickshire (1961–68, 133 matches).
Career batting
133–166–34–1658–72–12.56–0–*ct* 144
Bowling 7289–241–30.24–6–0–6/28
He also played for Durham (pre first-class, 1960).

Miller, Thomas
Amateur. *b:* 8.3.1883, St Vicente, Cape Verde Islands. *d:* 20.10.1962, Goring, Oxfordshire. Lower order right-hand batsman, right-arm fast bowler. *Sch* Clifton. *Team* Gloucestershire (1902–14, 18 matches).
Career batting
18–32–1–406–35–13.09–0–*ct* 8
Bowling 253–4–63.25–0–0–2/5

Miller, William Henry
Amateur. *b:* 14.5.1848, Ayr, Scotland. *d:* 12.12.1909, West Ealing, Middlesex. Brother of F. S. (MCC). Opening right-hand batsman, good close field. *Team* MCC (1876).
Career batting
1–2–1–11–8*–11.00–0–*ct* 0

Milles, Hon Henry Augustus
(changed name to Milles-Lade in 1900)
Amateur. *b:* 24.11.1867, Lees Court, Faversham, Kent. *d:* 30.7.1937, Nash Court, Faversham. Son of G. W. (Gentlemen of Kent), brother of Viscount Throwley (Kent), brother-in-law of F. W. G. Gore (I Zingari). Middle order right-hand batsman, off break bowler. *Sch* Eton. *Team* Kent (1888–97, 2 matches). *Tour* Hawke to North America 1891.
Career batting
4–5–0–24–11–4.80–0–*ct* 1
Bowling 99–3–33.00–0–0–1/16
He was at Cambridge, but not in the eleven.

Millett, Frederick William
Amateur. *b:* 30.3.1928, Macclesfield, Cheshire. *d:* 30.4.1991, Macclesfield, Cheshire. Opening right-hand batsman, off break bowler. *Sch* Kings, Macclesfield. *Team* Minor Counties (1960–73).
Career batting
7–13–3–312–102*–31.20–1–*ct* 2
Bowling 106–2–53.00–0–0–1/4
His County cricket was for Cheshire (1946–73).

Milligan, Frank William
Amateur. *b:* 19.3.1870, Farnborough, Hampshire. *d:* 31.3.1900, Ramathlabama, South Africa. He fell in action whilst with the forces trying to relieve Mafeking. Hard hitting middle/lower order right-hand batsman, right-arm fast bowler, good field. *Sch* Eton. *Team* Yorkshire (1894–98, 81 matches). *Tours* Mitchell to North America 1895; Hawke to South Africa 1898/9. *Tests* England (1898/9, 2 matches).
Career batting
95–135–10–2232–74–17.85–0–*ct* 52
Bowling 3390–144–23.54–6–2–7/61

Test batting
2–4–0–58–38–14.50–0–*ct* 1
Bowling 29–0
He also played for Staffordshire (1891).

Milligan, William Laidlaw
Amateur. *b:* 2.12.1906, Scotland. *d:* 31.3.1977, Edinburgh, Scotland. Lower order batsman, slow left-arm bowler. *Sch* Merchiston. *Team* Cambridge U (1928).
Career batting
3–2–2–3–3*–no av–0–*ct* 3
Bowling 191–4–47.75–0–0–2/55

Milling, David Alexander Hyndman
Amateur. *b:* 8.10.1872, Comber, Co Down, Ireland. *d:* 26.4.1929, Upper Rathmines, Co Dublin, Ireland. Lower order right-hand batsman, wicket-keeper. *Team* Ireland (1912–14).
Career batting
2–4–1–17–8–5.66–0–*ct* 1–*st* 2

Milling, Hugh
Cricketer. *b:* 4.9.1962, Carrickfergus, Co Antrim, Ireland. Lower order right-hand batsman, right-arm fast medium bowler. *Team* Ireland (1987).
Career batting
1–2–1–6–4*–6.00–0–*ct* 1
Bowling 98–6–16.33–0–0–4/81

Millman, Geoffrey
Professional. *b:* 2.10.1934, Bedford. Opening or middle order right-hand batsman, occasional off break bowler, wicket-keeper. *Sch* Bedford Modern. *Team* Nottinghamshire (1957–65, 257 matches). *Tours* MCC to India and Pakistan 1961/2. *Tests* England (1961/2 to 1962, 6 matches).
Career batting
282–471–59–7771–131*–18.86–3–*ct* 559–*st* 97
Bowling 32–0
Test batting
6–7–2–60–32*–12.00–0–*ct* 13–*st* 2
His first-class debut was for Combined Services in 1956. He hit 1,000 runs in a season twice (best 1,350, av 22.50 in 1961). From 1963 to 1965 he captained Nottinghamshire. He also played for Bedfordshire (1954–56 and 1966–68).

Millmow, Jonathan Paul
Cricketer. *b:* 22.9.1967, Wellington, New Zealand. Lower order right-hand batsman, right-arm fast medium bowler. *Team* Wellington (1986/7 to 1991/2). *Tours* Young New Zealand to Zimbabwe 1988/9; New Zealand to Sharjah (not first-class) 1989/90, to England 1990.
Career batting
37–29–13–129–16*–8.06–0–*ct* 10
Bowling 2789–99–28.17–4–1–6/13
He played in only five first-class matches on the 1990 tour to England and no Tests. He has played in one-day international matches for New Zealand.

Millner, David
Professional. *b:* 24.7.1938, Dove Holes, Derbyshire. Middle order right-hand batsman, off break bowler. *Team* Derbyshire (1960–63, 31 matches).
Career batting
31–56–1–701–80–12.74–0–*ct* 6
Bowling 27–0

Millns, David James
Cricketer. *b:* 27.2.1965, Clipstone, Nottinghamshire. Brother-in-law of R. A. Pick (Nottinghamshire). Lower order left-hand batsman, right-arm fast medium bowler. *Teams* Nottinghamshire (1988–89, 15 matches); Leicestershire (1990–92, 48 matches).
Career batting
63–68–28–509–44–12.72–0–*ct* 30
Bowling 5227–195–26.80–11–2–9/37
Having moved to Leicestershire in 1990, Millns' success as a fast bowler has gathered momentum over the last three seasons, culminating in 74 wickets, av 20.62, in 1992. His best bowling was 9/37 for Leicestershire v Derbyshire at Derby in 1991.

Mills, Anthony Oliver Henry
Professional. *b:* 12.2.1920, Sherston, Wiltshire. Lower order right-hand batsman, right-arm medium pace or off break bowler. *Team* Gloucestershire (1939–48, 4 matches).
Career batting
4–5–0–81–39–16.20–0–*ct* 1
Bowling 62–3–20.66–0–0–2/28
He also played for Wiltshire (1939 and 1954–61).

Mills, Charles Henry
Professional. *b:* 26.11.1867, Peckham, London. *d:* 26.7.1948, Southwark, London. Lower order right-hand batsman, right-arm medium pace bowler. *Teams* Surrey (1888, 2 matches); Kimberley (1889/90); Western Province (1892/3 to 1894/5). *Tour* South Africa to England 1894 (not first-class). *Test* South Africa (1891/2, 1 match).
Career batting
8–13–0–160–31–12.30–0–*ct* 11
Bowling 451–29–15.55–3–0–5/36
Test batting
1–2–0–25–21–12.50–0–*ct* 2
Bowling 83–2–41.50–0–0–2/83
He went out to South Africa as coach to the Cape Town Club.

Mills, David Cecil
Amateur. *b:* 23.4.1937, Camborne, Cornwall. Opening right-hand batsman, right-arm medium pace bowler. *Sch* Clifton. *Team* Gloucestershire (1958, 1 match).
Career batting
2–2–0–19–17–9.50–0–*ct* 1
Bowling 25–0
His final first-class match was for Free Foresters in 1960. He did not appear in any first-class matches for

Cambridge U, but was awarded his blue for rugby and represented Cornwall and the Harlequins.

Mills, Edwin
Professional. *b:* 6.3.1857, Coddington, Nottinghamshire. *d:* 25.1.1899, Cossall, Nottinghamshire. Brother of John (Nottinghamshire). Lower order left-hand batsman, left-arm fast bowler. *Teams* Nottinghamshire (1878–84, 29 matches); Surrey (1885–87, 7 matches).
Career batting
43–68–8–919–74–15.31–0–*ct* 31
Bowling 1768–87–20.32–4–1–7/97

Mills, Frederick
Professional. *b:* 10.7.1898, Leicester. *d:* 4.11.1929, Southfields, Leicester. Middle order left-hand batsman, slow left-arm bowler. *Team* Leicestershire (1921–23, 5 matches).
Career batting
5–7–2–69–30*–13.80–0–*ct* 0

Mills, George Thomas
Amateur. *b:* 12.9.1923, Redditch, Worcestershire. *d:* 15.9.1983, Bromsgrove, Worcestershire. Lower order right-hand batsman, wicket-keeper. *Team* Worcestershire (1953, 2 matches).
Career batting
2–4–0–46–23–11.50–0–*ct* 5–*st* 4

Mills, Henry Maynard
Amateur. *b:* 18.8.1847, Paddington, London. *d:* 13.4.1915, Buenos Aires, Argentine. Lower order batsman, wicket-keeper. *Sch* St Pauls. *Team* Middlesex (1881, 1 match).
Career batting
4–7–0–27–10–3.85–0–*ct* 4–*st* 1
His first-class debut was for the Gentlemen of England in 1879. He also played in the North v South series in the Argentine.

Mills, John
Amateur. *b:* 1848. *d:* 14.4.1935, Oberwil, Basle, Switzerland. Middle order batsman. *Team* Gloucestershire (1870, 1 match).
Career batting
1–2–0–17–15–8.50–0–*ct* 1

Mills, John
Professional. *b:* 28.1.1855, Coddington, Nottinghamshire. *d:* 27.6.1932, Ilkeston, Derbyshire. He died whilst watching Nottinghamshire playing Derbyshire. Brother of Edwin (Nottinghamshire and Surrey). Middle order right-hand batsman, right-hand fast round-arm bowler. *Team* Nottinghamshire (1875–81, 11 matches).
Career batting
13–19–2–140–24–8.23–0–*ct* 12
Bowling 7–0
His final first-class match was for the Hon M. B. Hawke's XI in 1885.

Mills, John Ernest
Amateur. *b:* 3.9.1905, Carisbrook, Dunedin, New Zealand. *d:* 11.12.1972, Hamilton, Auckland, New Zealand. Son of George (Auckland), nephew of Edward (Auckland), Isaac (Auckland) and William (Auckland). Attractive opening left-hand batsman. *Team* Auckland (1924/5 to 1937/8). *Tours* New Zealand to England 1927, 1931, to Australia 1927/8. *Tests* New Zealand (1929/30 to 1932/3, 7 matches).
Career batting
97–161–8–5025–185–32.84–11–*ct* 30
Bowling 123–4–30.75–0–0–2/57
Test batting
7–10–1–241–117–26.77–1–*ct* 1
He batted well on both his tours to England, scoring 1,251 runs, 37.90, in 1927 and 1,368, av 31.81, in 1931.

Mills, John Michael
Amateur. *b:* 27.7.1921, Edgbaston, Birmingham. Father of J. P. C. (Northamptonshire). Lower order right-hand batsman, leg break and googly bowler. *Sch* Oundle. *Teams* Cambridge U (1946–48, blue all three years); Warwickshire (1946, 4 matches).
Career batting
38–60–10–743–44–14.86–0–*ct* 13
Bowling 2743–95–28.87–5–0–7/69
He captained Cambridge in 1948.

Mills, John Peter Crispin
Cricketer. *b:* 6.12.1958, Kettering, Northamptonshire. Son of J. M. (Warwickshire). Opening/middle order right-hand batsman, right-arm medium pace bowler. *Sch* Oundle. *Teams* Cambridge U (1979–82, blue all four years); Northamptonshire (1981, 3 matches).
Career batting
41–68–2–1585–111–24.01–1–*ct* 14
Bowling 5–0
He captained Cambridge U in the 1982 University match when the elected captain, D. R. Pringle, chose to play for England on the same dates. He also played for Cambridgeshire (1980–84).

Mills, Josiah
Professional. *b:* 25.10.1862, Oldham, Lancashire. *d:* 23.11.1929, Oldham, Lancashire. Tail end right-hand batsman, wicket-keeper. *Team* Lancashire (1889, 1 match).
Career batting
1–1–0–1–1–1.00–0–*ct* 1–*st* 1

Mills, Percy Thomas
Professional. *b:* 7.5.1879, Cheltenham, Gloucestershire. *d:* 8.12.1950, Abingdon, Berkshire. Lower order right-hand batsman, right-arm medium pace bowler. *Team* Gloucestershire (1902–29, 346 matches).
Career batting
347–548–117–5051–95–11.71–0–*ct* 186
Bowling 20764–825–25.16–39–5–7/30

He took 100 wickets in a season once: 101, av 23.55, in 1926. In the Gloucestershire v Somerset match at Bristol in 1928 he returned the remarkable analysis of 6.4–6–0–5. He also played for Berkshire (1931). He was a first-class umpire (1947–48).

Mills, Richard
Professional. *b:* 16.2.1798, Pump Farm, Benenden, Kent. *d:* 25.1.1882, Rolvenden, Kent. Powerful middle order left-hand batsman, left-hand medium pace round-arm bowler. *Team* Kent (1825–43, 17 matches).
Career batting
47–85–2–792–94–9.54–0–*ct* 29
Bowling 17–0 + 13–no av–0–0–3/?

Mills, Walter George
Amateur. *b:* 2.6.1852, Dalston, London. *d:* 6.1.1902, Chorlton-cum-Hardy, Manchester, Lancashire. Lower order right-hand batsman, right-hand fast round-arm bowler. *Team* Lancashire (1871–77, 6 matches).
Career batting
6–11–1–57–26–5.70–0–*ct* 4
Bowling 97–6–16.16–0–0–3/52

Millward, Arthur
Professional. *b:* 4.7.1858, Kidderminster, Worcestershire. *d:* 21.1.1933, Eastbourne, Sussex. Middle order right-hand batsman, off break bowler. *Team* North (1900).
Career batting
1–2–1–19–19*–19.00–0–*ct* 0
Bowling 32–0
His County cricket was for Worcestershire (pre first-class, 1881–97) and Cheshire (1884–87). He was a first-class umpire (1895–1921, but missed some years), standing in two Test matches (1907–21).

Millyard, George
Professional. *b:* 12.11.1814, Petworth, Sussex. *d:* 20.7.1848, Petworth, Sussex. Middle order left-hand batsman, right-hand medium pace round-arm bowler. *Team* Sussex (1835–42, 38 matches).
Career batting
50–96–5–707–37–7.76–0–*ct* 18–*st* 1
Bowling 99–6 + 38–16.50–2–0–5/?
Epilepsy ended his cricket career in about 1842.

Milman, Sir Dermot Lionel Kennedy
Amateur. *b:* 24.10.1912, Eltham, Kent. *d:* 13.1.1990, Warlingham, Surrey. Son of L. C. P. (Europeans), great-nephew of G. A. (MCC). Lower order right-hand batsman, slow left-arm bowler, excellent close field. *Sch* Uppingham and Bedford. *Team* Cambridge U (1932–33).
Career batting
2–4–2–15–7*–7.50–0–*ct* 0
Bowling 142–4–35.50–0–0–3/55
His County cricket was for Bedfordshire (1931–36). He played rugby for Cambridge and England.

Milman, George Alderson
Amateur. *b:* 11.10.1830, Westminster, London. *d:* 29.12.1898, Heavitree, Devon. Uncle of L. C. P. (Europeans), great-uncle of D. L. K. (Cambridge U). Opening or middle order right-hand batsman, right-hand medium pace round-arm bowler, slip field. *Team* MCC (1863–69).
Career batting
3–5–0–48–31–9.60–0–*ct* 2
Bowling 144–15–9.60–2–1–7/65
Whilst serving in Ceylon, he was accidently shot in the shoulder during an elephant hunt, but returning to England in 1858 he continued to play cricket, batting in military matches with much success, using a small bat with his good arm.

Milne, George Taylor
Professional. *b:* 18.1.1877, Westgate, Newcastle upon Tyne, Northumberland. *d:* 3.11.1968, Newcastle upon Tyne, Northumberland. Middle order left-hand batsman, left-arm bowler. *Team* Minor Counties (1912).
Career batting
1–1–1–9–9*–no av–0–*ct* 0
His County cricket was for Northumberland (1901–28).

Milne, Robert Oswald
Amateur. *b:* 10.9.1852, Manchester, Lancashire. *d:* 6.9.1927, Leamington Spa, Warwickshire. Middle order batsman. *Sch* Rugby. *Team* Lancashire (1882, 1 match).
Career batting
1–1–1–7–7*–no av–0–*ct* 0
He also played for Warwickshire (pre first-class, 1871–79). He played no first-class cricket whilst at Oxford U, but did win a blue for rackets.

Milner, Joseph
Professional. *b:* 22.8.1937, Johannesburg, South Africa. Forcing middle order right-hand batsman. *Team* Essex (1957–61, 66 matches).
Career batting
67–119–12–2767–135–25.85–3–*ct* 57
Bowling 14–0
He hit 1,387 runs, av 28.49, in 1961.

Milner, Marcus Henry
Amateur. *b:* 16.4.1864, West Retford House, Nottinghamshire. *d:* 16.1.1939, Liverpool, Lancashire. Uncle of S. R. D. H. Beresford (Middlesex). Lower order left-hand batsman, left-arm medium pace bowler. *Sch* Wellington. *Team* Cambridge U (1884).
Career batting
2–4–0–28–20–7.00–0–*ct* 0
Bowling 161–5–32.20–0–0–3/79
His County cricket was for Cambridgeshire (1892–93).

Milton, Clement Arthur
Professional. *b:* 10.3.1928, Bedminster, Somerset. Attractive opening right-hand batsman, right-arm medium pace bowler, good close field. *Team* Gloucestershire (1948–74, 585 matches). *Tours* MCC to Australia 1958/9; Gloucestershire to Bermuda 1962 (not first-class), to Zambia 1971/72 (not first-class). *Tests* England (1958–59, 6 matches).
Career batting
620–1078–125–32150–170–33.73–56–*ct* 758
Bowling 3630–79–45.94–1–0–5/64
Test batting
6–9–1–204–104*–25.50–1–*ct* 5
Bowling 12–0
He hit 1,000 runs in a season 16 times, going on to 2,000 once: 2,089, av 46.42, in 1967. In 1956 he held 63 catches in the field. He captained Gloucestershire in 1968. A well-known soccer player, he appeared at outside right for Arsenal and Bristol City and was capped for England in 1951/2.

Milton, Harold Aubrey
Amateur. *b:* 15.1.1882, Hackney Downs, London. *d:* 14.3.1970, Islington, London. Middle order right-hand batsman. *Sch* University College, London. *Team* Middlesex (1907, 3 matches).
Career batting
3–5–0–52–45–10.40–0–*ct* 4
He played no first-class matches at Cambridge U, but did win a soccer blue.

Minnett, Dr Roy Baldwin
Amateur. *b:* 13.6.1888, St Leonards, Sydney, New South Wales, Australia. *d:* 21.10.1955, Manly, Sydney, New South Wales, Australia. Brother of L. A. (New South Wales) and R. V. (New South Wales). Middle order right-hand batsman, right-arm fast medium bowler. *Team* New South Wales (1906/7 to 1914/15, 19 matches). *Tours* Australia to England 1912; Waddy to Ceylon 1913/14 (not first-class). *Tests* Australia (1911/12 to 1912, 9 matches).
Career batting
54–83–9–2142–216*–28.94–2–*ct* 17
Bowling 2152–86–25.02–3–1–8/50
Test batting
9–15–0–391–90–26.06–0–*ct* 0
Bowling 290–11–26.36–0–0–4/34
He had a disappointing tour of England in 1912, the wet wickets being totally against his style of batting. His highest score was 216* for New South Wales v Victoria at Sydney in 1911/12.

Minnett, Rupert Villiers
Amateur. *b:* 2.9.1884, St Leonards, Sydney, New South Wales, Australia. *d:* 24.6.1974, Cremorne, Sydney, New South Wales, Australia. Brother of L. A. (New South Wales) and R. B. (New South Wales). Middle order right-hand batsman. *Team* New South Wales (1909/10 to 1914/15, 5 matches).
Career batting
6–10–1–331–169–36.77–1–*ct* 4
His single match in England was for L. Robinson's XI in 1912.

Minney, John Harry
Amateur. *b:* 25.4.1939, Finedon, Northamptonshire. Middle order right-hand batsman, right-arm medium pace bowler. *Sch* Oundle. *Teams* Cambridge U (1959–61); Northamptonshire (1961–67, 5 matches).
Career batting
19–33–3–572–58–19.06–0–*ct* 10
Bowling 7–0
He did not appear in any first-class matches from 1962 to 1966.

Minnis, Arnold
Amateur. *b:* 26.10.1891, Oughty Bridge, Sheffield, Yorkshire. *d:* 26.9.1972, Cirencester, Gloucestershire. Tail end right-hand batsman, slow left-arm bowler. *Team* Army (1930–32).
Career batting
4–5–2–10–5*–3.33–0–*ct* 0
Bowling 348–23–15.13–1–0–7/48

Minns, Robert Ernest Frederick
Amateur. *b:* 18.11.1940, Penang, Malaya. Middle order right-hand batsman. *Sch* King's School, Canterbury. *Teams* Kent (1959–63, 2 matches); Oxford U (1962–63, blue both years).
Career batting
20–38–3–947–81–27.05–0–*ct* 12

Minshull, John
Professional. *b:* 1741. *d:* October 1793. Excellent middle order batsman. *Teams* Kent (1773); Surrey (1779).
For the Duke of Dorset's XI v Wrotham on 31 August 1769 he scored 107 – the first recorded instance of a player making a century, although in the detailed score of the match he is shown as Minchin.

Minton, Robert Samuel
Amateur. *b:* 4.1.1899, Kensington, London. *d:* 3.8.1928, near Three Bridges, Sussex. He died by his own hand. Middle order batsman. *Team* Sussex (1919, 1 match).
Career batting
1–2–0–24–24–12.00–0–*ct* 0

Mirehouse, George Tiernay
Amateur. *b:* 11.5.1863, St George's Hill, Easton-in-Gordano, Somerset. *d:* 5.3.1923, Turramurra, Sydney, New South Wales, Australia. Tail end right-hand batsman, right-arm medium fast bowler. *Sch* Westminster. *Teams* Cambridge U (1884–86); Somerset (1884–85, 4 matches).
Career batting
13–22–4–74–20–4.11–0–*ct* 4
Bowling 606–22–27.54–0–0–4/51
His final first-class match was for MCC in 1896.

Mirehouse, William Edward
Amateur. *b:* 29.10.1844, Hambrook Grove, Bristol. *d:* 16.6.1925, Hambrook, Bristol. Sound middle order right-hand batsman, useful bowler, good deep field. *Sch* Harrow. *Team* Gloucestershire (1872, 1 match).
Career batting
1 match, did not bat–*ct* 0
He played for Cambridge University in non-first-class matches only in 1864.

Mischler, Norman Martin
Amateur. *b:* 9.10.1920, Paddington, London. Lower order right-hand batsman, wicket-keeper. *Sch* St Paul's. *Teams* Europeans (1941/2 to 1943/4); Cambridge U (1946–47, blue both years).
Career batting
24–38–1–568–76–15.35–0–*ct* 35–*st* 10
His final first-class match was for Free Foresters in 1951.

Misselbrook, Henry
Professional. *b:* 16.12.1832, Otterbourne, Hampshire. *d:* 11.7.1895, Winchester, Hampshire. Middle order batsman, useful bowler. *Team* Hampshire (1869, 1 match).
Career batting
1–2–0–3–3–1.50–0–*ct* 0
Bowling 39–6–6.50–0–0–4/18

Missen, Edward Sebley
Amateur. *b:* 2.2.1875, Cambridge. *d:* 17.11.1927, Colchester, Essex. Middle order batsman, right-arm medium pace bowler. *Team* Essex (1921, 1 match).
Career batting
1–2–0–20–12–10.00–0–*ct* 0
He also played for Cambridgeshire (1904).

Misson, Francis Michael
Amateur. *b:* 19.11.1938, Darlinghurst, Sydney, New South Wales, Australia. Lower order right-hand batsman, right-arm fast medium bowler. *Team* New South Wales (1958/9 to 1963/4, 42 matches). *Tours* Australia to New Zealand 1959/60, to England 1961. *Tests* Australia (1960/1 to 1961, 5 matches).
Career batting
71–77–17–1052–51*–17.53–0–*ct* 58
Bowling 5511–177–31.13–1–0–6/75
Test batting
5–5–3–38–25*–19.00–0–*ct* 6
Bowling 616–16–38.50–0–0–4/58
He played in two Tests on the 1961 tour of England, but his returns were only modest.

Mistry, Kekhashru Maneksha
Amateur. *b:* 7.11.1874, Bombay, India. *d:* 22.7.1959, Bombay, India. Opening or middle order left-hand batsman, left-arm medium pace bowler. *Teams* Parsis (1893/4 to 1927/8); South Punjab (1926/7). *Tour* India to England 1911.
Career batting
39–69–1–1600–95–23.52–0–*ct* 34
Bowling 1370–104–13.17–6–2–8/70
Owing to other duties he was only available to play in three first-class matches on the 1911 tour – a great loss to the team.

Mitchell, Arthur
Professional. *b:* 13.9.1902, Baildon Green, Yorkshire. *d:* 25.12.1976, Bradford, Yorkshire. Steady middle order right-hand batsman, slow right-arm bowler, excellent close field. *Team* Yorkshire (1922–45, 401 matches). *Tours* MCC to India and Ceylon 1933/4; Yorkshire to Jamaica 1935/6. *Tests* England (1933/4 to 1936, 6 matches).
Career batting
426–593–72–19523–189–37.47–44–*ct* 438
Bowling 327–7–46.71–0–0–3/49
Test batting
6–10–0–298–72–29.80–0–*ct* 9
Bowling 4–0
He hit 1,000 runs in a season 10 times (2,300 av 58.97, in 1933 was the only time he exceeded 2,000). From 1945 to 1971 he was Yorkshire County Coach. His final first-class match was for the North in 1947.

Mitchell, Bruce
Amateur. *b:* 8.1.1909, Ferrierer Deep Gold Mine, Johannesburg, South Africa. Stylish opening right-hand batsman, leg break bowler, slip field. *Team* Transvaal (1925/6 to 1949/50). *Tours* South Africa to England 1929, 1935, 1947, to Australia and New Zealand 1931/2. *Tests* South Africa (1929 to 1948/9, 42 matches).
Career batting
173–281–30–11395–195–45.39–30–*ct* 228
Bowling 6382–249–25.63–15–2–6/33
Test batting
42–80–9–3471–189*–48.88–8–*ct* 56
Bowling 1380–27–51.11–1–0–5/87
He was most successful on all three of his tours to England with first-class aggregates of 1,615, av 32.95, in 1929; 1,451, av 45.34, in 1935; and 2,014, av 61.03, in 1947. In 1935 he topped the Test averages with 488 runs, av 69.71.

Mitchell, Clement
Amateur. *b:* 20.2.1862, Cambridge. *d:* 6.10.1937, Aldrington, Hove, Sussex. Dangerous middle order left-hand batsman, fine field. *Sch* Felsted. *Team* Kent (1890–92, 8 matches).
Career batting
8–14–1–126–38*–9.69–0–*ct* 6
He was a noted cricketer in Calcutta in the 1880s. He played soccer for England.

Mitchell, Colin Gerald
Amateur. *b:* 27.1.1929, Brislington, Somerset. Lower order right-hand batsman, right-arm fast medium bowler. *Team* Somerset (1952–54, 30 matches).

Mitchell, Frank

Career batting
30–45–20–186–26*–7.44–0–*ct* 9
Bowling 2035–53–38.39–2–1–6/62

A soccer player, he represented Gloucestershire.

Mitchell, Frank
Amateur. *b:* 13.8.1872, Market Weighton, Yorkshire. *d:* 11.10.1935, Blackheath, Kent. Father of T. F. (Kent). Attacking middle order right-hand batsman, right-arm medium pace bowler. *Sch* St Peter's, York. *Teams* Cambridge U (1894–97, blue all four years); Yorkshire (1894–1904, 83 matches); London County (1901); Transvaal (1902/3 to 1903/4). *Tours* Mitchell to North America 1895; Warner to North America 1898; Hawke to South Africa 1898/9; Bosanquet to North America 1901; South Africa to England 1904, 1912. *Tests* England (1898/9, 2 matches); South Africa (1912, 3 matches).
Career batting
199–306–19–9176–194–31.97–17–*ct* 148–*st* 2
Bowling 834–36–23.16–1–0–5/57
Test batting
5–10–0–116–41–11.60–0–*ct* 2

In 1899 he hit 1,748 runs, av 31.78 – then after serving in the Boer War he returned in 1901 to score 1,807 runs, av 44.07, these being the only two seasons he had as a regular County cricketer. He also reached 1,000 runs in 1904. He captained Cambridge in 1896, both the 1904 and 1912 South African tourists and led South Africa in three Tests. His final first-class match was for MCC in 1914. A brilliant all-round sportsman he also gained his blues for rugby football (later gaining six England caps) and putting the weight. He also played soccer, keeping goal for Sussex. Later he was a noted sports writer.

Mitchell, Sir Frank Herbert
Amateur. *b:* 13.6.1878, Eton, Buckinghamshire. *d:* 27.11.1951, Forest House, Crowborough Warren, Sussex. Son of R. A. H. (Oxford U). Middle order right-hand batsman, right-hand slow round-arm or under-arm bowler. *Sch* Eton. *Team* Oxford U (1898).
Career batting
3–4–0–23–9–5.75–0–*ct* 0
Bowling 114–5–22.80–1–0–5/32

His County cricket was for Buckinghamshire (1897–1905). A noted golfer, he represented Oxford and England. He was for some time Assistant Private Secretary to George VI.

Mitchell, Frank Rollason
Professional. *b:* 3.6.1922, Goulburn, New South Wales, Australia. *d:* 4.4.1984, Myton Hamlet, Warwickshire. Lower order right-hand batsman, right-arm medium pace off break bowler. *Team* Warwickshire (1946–48, 17 matches).
Career batting
17–29–2–224–43–8.29–0–*ct* 7
Bowling 856–22–38.90–0–0–4/69

He also played for Cornwall (1951). A noted half-back, he played soccer for Birmingham City, Chelsea and Watford.

Mitchell, George Frederick
Professional. *b:* 18.2.1897, Canning Town, Essex. Tail end left-hand batsman, useful bowler. *Team* Essex (1926, 1 match).
Career batting
1–1–0–4–4–4.00–0–*ct* 0
Bowling 45–1–45.00–0–0–1/25

Mitchell, Horace
Professional. *b:* 19.1.1858, West Tarring, Worthing, Sussex. *d:* 4.1.1951, West Tarring, Worthing, Sussex. Lower order right-hand batsman, right-arm medium fast bowler, slip field. *Team* Sussex (1882–91, 8 matches).
Career batting
8–14–3–44–9–4.00–0–*ct* 0
Bowling 355–19–18.68–1–0–5/35

He appeared for Sussex in 1882 and 1891, but not in the intervening years.

Mitchell, Ian Norman
Amateur. *b:* 17.4.1925, Henbury, Bristol, Gloucestershire. Middle order right-hand batsman. *Sch* Harrow. *Teams* Gloucestershire (1950–52, 9 matches); Cambridge U (1949).
Career batting
11–19–1–160–27–8.88–0–*ct* 5

Mitchell, James Stanley Lyons
Cricketer. *b:* 19.10.1946, Cullion, Dunamanagh, Co Tyrone, Ireland. Middle order left-hand batsman. *Team* Ireland (1974).
Career batting
1–2–0–29–27–14.50–0–*ct* 1

Mitchell, Kenneth James
Amateur. *b:* 5.12.1924, Old Hill, Staffordshire. Middle order left-hand batsman. *Team* Worcestershire (1946, 1 match).
Career batting
1–2–0–10–10–5.00–0–*ct* 1

Mitchell, Richard Arthur Henry
Amateur. *b:* 22.1.1843, Enderby Hall, Leicester. *d:* 19.4.1905, Mayford, Woking, Surrey. Father of F. H. (Oxford U). Fine powerful middle order right-hand batsman, right-hand medium pace round-arm bowler, good point field. *Sch* Eton. *Team* Oxford U (1862–65, blue all four years).
Career batting
57–90–6–2517–125*–29.96–2–*ct* 36–*st* 10
Bowling 403–15+7–26.86–0–0–4/30

His first-class debut was for Gentlemen of the North in 1861, and his final first-class match was for MCC in 1883. He also played for Leicestershire (pre first-class, 1860–74), Warwickshire (pre first-class, 1865–68) and Buckinghamshire (1867–68). He captained Oxford against Cambridge for three successive matches 1863–65. He also won a blue for rackets. An assistant master at Eton from 1866, his appearances in first-class cricket were very limited, though he was regarded as one of the best batsman of his day.

Mitchell, Richard William Gordon Lewis
Amateur. *b:* 27.2.1913, Grenada, Windward Islands. *d:* 13.1.1988, Port of Spain, Trinidad. Middle order right-hand batsman, right-arm fast medium bowler. *Teams* Oxford U (1935); R. S. Grant's XI (1938/9).
Career batting
3–4–2–58–30*–29.00–0–*ct* 0

Mitchell, Thomas Bignall
Professional. *b:* 4.9.1902, Creswell, Derbyshire. Lower order right-hand batsman, leg break and googly bowler. *Team* Derbyshire (1928–39, 303 matches). *Tour* MCC to Australia and New Zealand 1932/3. *Tests* England (1932/3 to 1935, 5 matches).
Career batting
328–412–107–2431–57–7.97–0–*ct* 132
Bowling 30543–1483–20.59–118–30–10/64
Test batting
5–6–2–20–9–5.00–0–*ct* 1
Bowling 498–8–62.25–0–0–2/49
He took 100 wickets in a season 10 times (best 171, av 20.16, in 1935). His best bowling in an innings was 10 for 64 for Derbyshire v Leicestershire at Leicester in 1935. He was known as the 'merry-hearted' cricketer.

Mitchell, Thomas Frank
Amateur. *b:* 22.10.1907, Johannesburg, South Africa. *d:* 20.5.1960, St John's Wood, London. Son of Frank (Yorkshire). Steady middle order right-hand batsman, off break bowler. *Sch* Tonbridge. *Team* Kent (1928–34, 24 matches).
Career batting
31–50–3–711–64–15.12–0–*ct* 15
Bowling 247–2–123.50–0–0–1/48

Mitchell, William Henry
Amateur. *b:* 20.1.1859, Arundel, Sussex. *d:* 16.11.1929, Southwater, Horsham, Sussex. Middle order batsman. *Team* Sussex (1886, 2 matches).
Career batting
2–4–0–8–4–2.00–0–*ct* 0

Mitchell, William MacFarlane
Amateur. *b:* 15.8.1929, Lewisham, London. Middle/lower order right-hand batsman, leg break and googly bowler. *Sch* Dulwich. *Team* Oxford U (1951–53, blue 1951 and 1952).
Career batting
26–40–8–480–48–15.00–0–*ct* 12
Bowling 1998–35–57.08–1–0–5/107

Mitchell-Innes, Norman Stewart
Amateur. *b:* 7.9.1914, Calcutta, India. Stylish middle order right-hand batsman, right-arm fast, later medium, bowler. *Sch* Sedbergh. *Teams* Somerset (1931–49, 69 matches); Oxford U (1934–37, blue all four years); Scotland (1937). *Tour* MCC to Australia and New Zealand 1935/6. *Test* England (1935, 1 match).
Career batting
132–239–18–6944–207–31.42–13–*ct* 152
Bowling 2846–82–34.70–0–0–4/65
Test batting
1–1–0–5–5–5.00–0–*ct* 0
He hit 1,000 runs in a season three times (best 1,438, av 44.93, in 1936). After leaving University he joined the Sudan Civil Service, thus restricting his appearances in first-class cricket. He captained Oxford in 1936 and in 1948 he was joint-captain of Somerset. His highest score was 207 for Oxford U v Leveson-Gower's XI at Reigate in 1936. He also won a blue for golf.

Mitra, Avijit
Cricketer. *b:* 6.7.1953, Bhowanipore, Calcutta, India. Opening right-hand batsman, off break bowler. *Sch* KES, Birmingham. *Team* Oxford U (1974–75).
Career batting
6–12–0–157–30–13.08–0–*ct* 2

Mitten, John
Professional. *b:* 30.3.1941, Davyhulme, Manchester, Lancashire. Lower order right-hand batsman, wicket-keeper. *Team* Leicestershire (1961–63, 14 matches).
Career batting
14–23–2–259–50*–12.33–0–*ct* 23
A noted soccer player, he appeared for Mansfield, Newcastle United, Leicester City, Coventry, Plymouth and Exeter.

Mitton, John
Professional. *b:* 7.11.1895, Todmorden, Yorkshire. *d:* 5.8.1983, Burnham Market, Norfolk. Tail end right-hand batsman, bowler. *Team* Somerset (1920, 2 matches).
Career batting
2–3–2–15–6–15.00–0–*ct* 0
Bowling 100–1–100.00–0–0–1/47
He played soccer for Exeter City, Sunderland and Wolverhampton.

Moan, Raymond
Cricketer. *b:* 12.1.1951, Carrigullen, Strabane, Co Tyrone, Ireland. Lower order left-hand batsman, off break bowler. *Team* Ireland (1970).
Career batting
1–1–1–0–0*–no av–0–*ct* 0
Bowling 58–1–58.00–0–0–1/58

Moberly, John Cornelius
Amateur. *b:* 22.4.1848, Winchester, Hampshire. *d:* 29.1.1928, Bassett, Hampshire. Uncle of R. W. Awdry (Oxford U). Middle order right-hand batsman, right-arm medium pace bowler. *Sch* Winchester. *Team* Hampshire (1877, 1 match).

Moberly, William Octavius

Career batting
1–2–0–31–27–15.50–0–*ct* 0

He played in the Oxford Freshmen's match of 1867. He was President of Hampshire 1913–18.

Moberly, William Octavius
Amateur. *b:* 14.11.1850, Shoreham-by-Sea, Sussex. *d:* 2.2.1914, Pulurrian, Mullion, Cornwall. Middle order right-hand batsman, wicket-keeper. *Sch* Rugby. *Teams* Oxford U (1870); Gloucestershire (1876–87, 64 matches).
Career batting
66–105–7–2104–121–21.46–3–*ct* 48–*st* 16

He also played for Warwickshire (pre first-class, 1869–72) and Leicestershire (pre first-class, 1872). A noted rugby footballer, he obtained his blue and went on to represent England.

Mobey, Gerald Spencer
Professional. *b:* 5.3.1904, Surbiton, Surrey. *d:* 2.3.1979, Woking, Surrey. Lower order right-hand batsman, wicket-keeper. *Sch* Tiffin. *Team* Surrey (1930–48, 77 matches). *Tour* MCC to India 1939/40 (tour cancelled).
Career batting
81–112–19–1684–75–18.10–0–*ct* 130–*st* 11

He was a first-class umpire (1950–55).

Mocatta, John Edward Abraham
Amateur. *b:* 6.5.1936, St John's Wood, London. Middle order right-hand batsman, leg break bowler. *Sch* Clifton. *Team* Oxford U (1958).
Career batting
4–8–0–106–37–13.25–0–*ct* 2

Modi, Rusi Sheriyar
Amateur. *b:* 11.11.1924, Bombay, India. Sound middle order right-hand batsman, right-arm medium pace bowler. *Teams* Parsis (1941/2 to 1945/6); Bombay (1943/4 to 1959/60). *Tours* India to Ceylon 1944/5, to England 1946; ACC to Pakistan 1961/2. *Tests* India (1946 to 1952/3, 10 matches).
Career batting
105–154–12–7529–245*–53.02–20–*ct* 29
Bowling 1226–32–38.31–1–0–5/25
Test batting
10–17–1–736–112–46.00–1–*ct* 3
Bowling 14–0

A consistent batsman on the 1946 tour with 1,196 runs, av 37.37, he was a prolific scorer in India. Three of his four double centuries were hit in the 1944/5 season, when he scored 1,386 runs, av 115.50. His highest score was 245* for Bombay v Baroda at Baroda in 1944/5. He scored 144 on debut for Parsis v Europeans at Bombay in 1941/2.

Moeller, David
Amateur. *b:* 2.3.1941, Marshfield, Monmouthshire. Middle order right-hand batsman. *Sch* Haileybury. *Team* Oxford U (1961).
Career batting
1–2–0–25–24–12.50–0–*ct* 0

Moffat, Douglas
Amateur. *b:* 31.7.1843, Cawnpore, India. *d:* 27.3.1922, Notting Hill, Kensington, London. Father of N. J. D. (Middlesex). Lower order right-hand batsman, bowler. *Team* Middlesex (1864, 1 match).
Career batting
2–3–0–31–25–10.33–0–*ct* 0

He made his first-class debut in 1863 for MCC. He also played for Northumberland (1870). Whilst at Oxford he did not play in the Eleven, but represented the University as a boxer.

Moffat, Norman John Douglas
Amateur. *b:* 13.9.1883, Edenhall, Roxburgh, Scotland. *d:* 11.10.1972, Dartford, Kent. Son of Douglas (Middlesex). Middle order right-hand batsman. *Team* Middlesex (1921–25, 11 matches).
Career batting
16–26–4–552–92–25.09–0–*ct* 8

His final first-class match was for MCC in 1926.

Moffatt, Rev Neil Thomas
Cricketer. *b:* 10.5.1946, Headington, Oxford. Middle order left-hand batsman. *Team* Cambridge U (1969).
Career batting
1–2–0–6–4–3.00–0–*ct* 1

Mohamed, Timur
Cricketer. *b:* 7.6.1957, Georgetown, British Guiana. Son of Edwin (British Guiana). Middle order left-hand batsman, leg break bowler. *Team* Guyana (1975/6 to 1986/7). *Tours* West Indies to England 1980; Young West Indies to Zimbabwe 1981/2, 1983/4.
Career batting
47–78–8–2526–200*–36.08–5–*ct* 21
Bowling 98–2–49.00–0–0–1/16

His County cricket was for Suffolk (1979–81) and he was co-opted into the 1980 West Indian touring team for two matches. His highest score was 200* for Guyana v Windward Islands at Berbice in 1985/6.

Mohammad Aslam Khokhar
Amateur. *b:* 5.1.1920, Lahore, India. Middle order right-hand batsman, leg break bowler, good outfield. *Teams* Muslims (1938/9); Northern India (1941/2 to 1946/7); Railways (1953/4 to 1963/4). *Tour* Pakistan to England 1954. *Test* Pakistan (1954, 1 match).
Career batting
44–72–8–1689–103–26.39–1–*ct* 18
Bowling 567–20–28.35–1–0–6/26
Test batting
1–2–0–34–18–17.00–0–*ct* 0

He had a modest tour of England in 1954, playing in only 12 first-class matches and one Test. He umpired in 3 Test matches in Pakistan (1972/3 to 1977/8).

Mohammad Farooq
Amateur. *b:* 8.4.1938, Junagadh, India. Hard hitting tail end right-hand batsman, right-arm fast medium bowler. *Team* Karachi (1959/60 to 1964/5). *Tours* Pakistan to India 1960/1, to England 1962. *Tests* Pakistan (1960/1 to 1964/5, 7 matches).
Career batting
33–31–17–173–47–12.35–0–*ct* 7
Bowling 3319–123–26.98–5–1–6/87
Test batting
7–9–4–85–47–17.00–0–*ct* 1
Bowling 682–21–32.47–0–0–4/70
Although perhaps the best of the seam bowlers on the 1962 tour of England, he achieved only modest results.

Mohammad Ilyas
Cricketer. *b:* 19.3.1946, Lahore, India. Attacking opening right-hand batsman, leg break and googly bowler. *Teams* Lahore (1961/2 to 1963/4); Punjab Univ (1964/5); PIA (1966/7 to 1971/2). *Tours* Pakistan to Australia and New Zealand 1964/5, to England 1967, to Ceylon and Australia 1972/3; International Wanderers to Rhodesia 1975/6. *Tests* Pakistan (1964/5 to 1968/9, 10 matches).
Career batting
82–139–10–4607–154–35.71–12–*ct* 48
Bowling 1643–53–31.00–3–0–6/66
Test batting
10–19–0–441–126–23.21–1–*ct* 6
Bowling 63–0
His Test career ended on a controversial note during the 1972/3 tour to Australia and he remained in Australia after the season ended.

Mohammad Munaf
Amateur. *b:* 2.11.1935, Bombay, India. Lower order right-hand batsman, right-arm fast medium bowler. *Teams* Sind (1953/4 to 1955/6); Karachi (1956/7 to 1963/4); PIA (1961/2 to 1970/1). *Tours* Pakistan Eaglets to England 1963; Pakistan to West Indies 1957/8, to India 1960/1; PIA to Ireland 1969 (not first-class). *Tests* Pakistan (1959/60 to 1961/2, 4 matches).
Career batting
71–90–13–1356–76–17.61–0–*ct* 47
Bowling 4360–180–24.22–6–1–8/84
Test batting
4–7–2–63–19–12.60–0–*ct* 0
Bowling 341–11–31.00–0–0–4/42

Mohammad Nazir
Cricketer. *b:* 8.3.1946, Rawalpindi, India. Brother of Mohammad Bashir (Railways) and Mohammad Arif sen (Rawalpindi). Lower order right-hand batsman, off break bowler. *Teams* Railways (1964/5 to 1987/8); Punjab U (1970/1). *Tours* Pakistan to England 1971, 1974, to India 1983/4, to Australia 1983/4. *Tests* Pakistan (1969/70 to 1983/4, 14 matches).
Career batting
180–255–66–4211–113*–22.28–2–*ct* 84
Bowling 15972–829–19.26–63–16–8/99
Test batting
14–18–10–144–29*–18.00–0–*ct* 4
Bowling 1124–34–33.05–3–0–7/99
He was a late replacement on the 1971 tour of England, but headed the first-class bowling averages with 20 wickets, av 19.80. On his return in 1974 he achieved very little. He did not appear in any Tests in England.

Mohammad Saeed
Professional. *b:* 31.8.1910, Lahore, India. *d:* 23.8.1979, Lahore, Pakistan. Father of Yawar Saeed (Somerset), father-in-law of Fazal Mahmood (Pakistan). Middle order right-hand batsman. *Teams* Muslims (1929/30 to 1934/5); Patiala (1932/3); Southern Punjab (1933/4 to 1945/6); Northern India (1944/5 to 1946/7); Punjab (1953/4 to 1954/5). *Tour* Pakistan to Ceylon 1948/9.
Career batting
51–81–2–2338–175–29.59–3–*ct* 31
Bowling 268–5–53.60–0–0–1/6
His only match in England was for a Commonwealth XI in 1952.

Mohammad Younis
(*see under* Younis Ahmed)

Mohan, Keith Frederick
Professional. *b:* 11.6.1935, Glossop, Derbyshire. Middle order right-hand batsman, leg break and googly bowler. *Team* Derbyshire (1957–58, 10 matches).
Career batting
10–17–2–163–49–10.86–0–*ct* 4
Bowling 23–0

Mohol, Sadanand Namdeo
Amateur. *b:* 6.10.1938, Bassein, Thana, India. Brother of A. N. (Maharashtra). Lower order right-hand batsman, right-arm medium fast bowler. *Team* Maharashtra (1959/60 to 1970/1). *Tour* India to England and East Africa 1967.
Career batting
47–54–11–549–40–12.76–0–*ct* 21
Bowling 3594–168–21.37–9–2–8/42
He appeared in only seven matches on the 1967 tour owing to injury.

Mohsin Hasan Khan
Cricketer. *b:* 15.3.1955, Karachi, Pakistan. Elegant opening right-hand batsman, right-arm medium pace bowler. *Teams* Railways (1970/1 to 1971/2); Karachi (1972/3 to 1974/5); Universities (1973/4); Sind (1974/5 to 1975/6); Habib Bank (1975/6 to 1985/6). *Tours* Pakistan to West Indies 1976/7, to England 1978, 1982, 1983 (World Cup), to Australia 1978/79, 1981/2, 1983/4, 1984/5 (not first-class), to New Zea-

land 1978/9, 1984/5, to India 1979/80, 1983/4, to Sharjah (not first-class) 1983/4, 1984/5, 1985/6, 1986/7, to Sri Lanka 1985/6. *Tests* Pakistan (1977/8 to 1986/7, 48 matches).

Career batting
191–320–31–11254–246–38.94–31–*ct* 135
Bowling 546–14–39.00–0–0–2/13
Test batting
48–79–6–2709–200–37.10–7–*ct* 34
Bowling 30–0

He played in all three Tests on the 1978 tour to England, but had only a modest first-class record; in 1982 however he hit 1,248 runs, av 73.41, and headed the Test batting averages with 310 runs, av 62.00, including 200 v England in the Second Test at Lord's. He also scored 203* v Leicestershire at Leicester. His highest score was 246 for Habib Bank v PIA at Karachi in 1976/7.

Mohsin Kamal
Cricketer. *b:* 16.6.1963, Lyallpur, Pakistan. Lower order right-hand batsman, right-arm fast medium bowler. *Teams* Lahore (1980/1 to 1985/6); Allied Bank (1983/4); PNSC (1986/7 to 1991/2). *Tours* Pakistan to New Zealand 1984/5, to Sri Lanka 1985/6, to Sharjah (not first-class) 1985/6, to England 1987, to Australia 1988/9 (not first-class); Pakistan Under 23 to Sri Lanka 1984/5; Pakistan B to Zimbabwe 1986/7, to Kenya 1986/7. *Tests* Pakistan (1983/4 to 1987, 7 matches).

Career batting
97–110–28–934–44–11.39–0–*ct* 24
Bowling 7228–221–32.70–5–0–7/87
Test batting
7–7–5–31–13*–15.50–0–*ct* 2
Bowling 597–17–35.11–0–0–4/127

On the 1987 tour to England he improved as the season progressed, played in four Tests and in first-class matches took 36 wickets, av 29.05.

Moin Khan
Cricketer. *b:* 23.9.1971, Rawalpindi, Pakistan. Middle order right-hand batsman, wicket-keeper. *Team* Karachi (1986/7 to 1990/1). *Tours* Pakistan B to Zimbabwe 1990/1; Pakistan A to Sri Lanka 1990/1; Pakistan to Sharjah (not first-class) 1991/2, to Australia 1991/2, to Australia and New Zealand (World Cup) 1991/2, to England 1992. *Tests* Pakistan (1990/1 to 1992, 9 matches).

Career batting
43–54–9–1110–129–24.66–1–*ct* 108–*st* 7
Bowling 3–0
Test batting
9–11–2–134–32–14.88–0–*ct* 17–*st* 1

He played in the first four Tests on the 1992 tour to England, but made little impression and lost his place in the final game.

Moir, Alexander McKenzie
Amateur. *b:* 17.7.1919, Dunedin North, New Zealand. Attacking lower order right-hand batsman, leg break and googly bowler. *Team* Otago (1949/50 to 1961/2). *Tours* New Zealand to India and Pakistan 1955/6, to England 1958. *Tests* New Zealand (1950/1 to 1958/9, 17 matches).

Career batting
97–150–22–2102–70–16.42–0–*ct* 44
Bowling 9040–368–24.56–25–5–8/37
Test batting
17–30–8–327–41*–14.86–0–*ct* 2
Bowling 1418–28–50.64–2–0–6/155

He showed modest returns on his 1958 tour to England, but played in the last two Tests.

Moir, Dallas Gordon
Cricketer. *b:* 13.4.1957, Imtarfa, Malta. Twin brother of J. D. (Scotland). Lower order right-hand batsman, slow left-arm bowler. *Teams* Scotland (1980–86); Derbyshire (1981–85, 71 matches).

Career batting
73–87–11–1172–107–15.42–1–*ct* 64
Bowling 6795–206–32.98–9–1–6/60

He took 76 wickets, av 27.31, in 1982.

Moir, Jeremy David
Cricketer. *b:* 13.4.1957, Imtarfa, Malta. Twin brother of D. G. (Derbyshire). Lower order right-hand batsman, right-arm medium pace bowler. *Team* Scotland (1989–90).

Career batting
2–3–1–28–15–14.00–0–*ct* 1
Bowling 139–3–46.33–0–0–2/47

Mold, Arthur Webb
Professional. *b:* 27.5.1863, Middleton Cheney, Northamptonshire. *d:* 29.4.1921, Middleton Cheney, Northamptonshire. Tail end right-hand batsman, right-arm fast bowler. *Team* Lancashire (1889–1901, 260 matches). *Tests* England (1893, 3 matches).

Career batting
287–389–130–1850–57–7.14–0–*ct* 111
Bowling 26010–1673–15.54–152–56–9/29
Test batting
3–3–1–0–0*–0.00–0–*ct* 1
Bowling 234–7–33.42–0–0–3/44

He took 100 wickets in a season nine times, going on to 200 twice (best 213, av 15.96, in 1895). He captured nine wickets in an innings four times, his best being 9/29 for Lancashire v Kent at Tonbridge in 1892. Throughout his career the fairness of his delivery was questioned, but not until 1900 was he no-balled for throwing. He was again no-balled in 1901 and this ended his County career. He also played for Northamptonshire (pre first-class, 1887–88 and 1903).

Moles, Andrew James
Cricketer. *b:* 12.2.1961, Solihull, Warwickshire. Opening right-hand batsman, right-arm medium pace bowler. *Teams* Warwickshire (1986–92, 145 matches); Griqualand West (1986/7 to 1988/9). *Tour* Warwickshire to South Africa 1991/2.
Career batting
164–296–31–10814–230*–40.80–22–*ct* 117
Bowling 1763–36–48.97–0–0–3/21

He has scored 1,000 runs in a season five times (best 1,854, av 48.78, in 1990). His highest score was 230* for Griqualand West v Northern Transvaal B at Verwoerdburg in 1988/9.

Moline, Charles Harry
Amateur. *b:* June 1863, Laibach, Austria (now Ljubljana, Yugoslavia). *d:* 23.5.1927, Weston-super-Mare, Somerset. Brother of E. R. (Gloucestershire). Lower order right-hand batsman, slow right-arm bowler. *Sch* Bristol GS. *Team* Cambridge U (1886).
Career batting
2–3–1–22–16–11.00–0–*ct* 2
Bowling 76–1–76.00–0–0–1/15

Moline, Edgar Robert
Amateur. *b:* 2.1.1855, Austria. *d:* 16.12.1943, Lynton, Devon. Brother of C. H. (Cambridge U). Middle order right-hand batsman, right-arm medium pace, or slow under-arm, bowler. *Sch* Bristol GS. *Team* Gloucestershire (1878, 2 matches).
Career batting
2–3–0–31–28–10.33–0–*ct* 0

Molineux, George King
Amateur. *b:* 15.4.1887, Meads, Eastbourne, Sussex. *d:* 5.5.1915, near Frenzenberg, Belgium. He was killed in action. Lower order right-hand batsman, slow bowler. *Sch* Winchester. *Team* Oxford U (1907).
Career batting
4–7–1–127–78*–21.16–0–*ct* 2
Bowling 308–11–28.00–0–0–4/62

His final first-class match was for Gentlemen of England in 1908.

Moloney, Denis Andrew Robert
Amateur. *b:* 11.8.1910, Dunedin, New Zealand. *d:* 15.7.1942, Ruwelsat Ridge, El Alamein, Egypt. Middle order right-hand batsman, leg break bowler. *Teams* Otago (1927/8 to 1939/40); Wellington (1935/6 to 1937/8); Canterbury (1940/1). *Tours* New Zealand to England 1937, to Australia 1937/8. *Tests* New Zealand (1937, 3 matches).
Career batting
64–119–7–3219–190–28.74–2–*ct* 35
Bowling 3151–95–33.16–3–0–5/23
Test batting
3–6–0–156–64–26.00–0–*ct* 3
Bowling 9–0

He hit 1,463 runs, av 34.83, on the 1937 tour to England and appeared in all three Tests.

Molony, Trevor James
Amateur. *b:* 6.7.1897, Kensington, London. *d:* 3.9.1962, Cannes, France. Lower order right-hand batsman, right-hand slow under-arm bowler. *Sch* Repton. *Team* Surrey (1921, 3 matches).
Career batting
3–4–0–2–2–0.50–0–*ct* 0
Bowling 89–4–22.25–0–0–3/11

He appeared in the Cambridge Freshmen's match of 1920, but no first-class matches for the University. It is believed that he was the last player to be chosen for a County Championship match purely on his merits as an under-arm bowler.

Molyneux, Paul Seymour Morthier
Amateur. *b:* 12.1.1906, Wells, Somerset. Middle order right-hand batsman, off break bowler. *Sch* Allhallows. *Team* Somerset (1937, 6 matches).
Career batting
6–10–0–94–25–9.40–0–*ct* 2

Monckton, Walter Turner
(created Viscount Monckton of Brenchley in 1957)
Amateur. *b:* 17.1.1891, Ightham Warren, Plaxtol, Kent. *d:* 9.1.1965, Folkington, Sussex. Father-in-law of W. B. Goulding (Ireland). Lower order batsman, wicket-keeper. *Sch* Harrow. *Team* Combined Oxford and Cambridge U (1911).
Career batting
1–2–1–72–43–72.00–0–*ct* 1–*st* 1

He appeared in the Freshmen's and Seniors' matches at Oxford but no first-class matches. In 1956/7 he was President of MCC and from 1950 to 1952, and 1959 to 1965, President of Surrey. After a distinguished career as a barrister, he was Attorney-General (at the time of the abdication of Edward VIII), Solicitor-General, Minister of Defence, Paymaster-General and Minister of Labour. He was MP for Bristol West 1951–57.

Money, David Charles
Amateur. *b:* 5.10.1918, Oxford. Lower order right-hand batsman, wicket-keeper. *Team* Oxford U (1947).
Career batting
1–1–1–27–27*–no av–0–*ct* 1–*st* 1

His County cricket was for Oxfordshire (1938–46) and Bedfordshire (1950–52).

Money, Rev Walter Baptist
Amateur. *b:* 27.7.1848, Sternfield, Suffolk. *d:* 1.3.1924, Edgbaston, Warwickshire. Middle order right-hand batsman, slow left-hand under-arm lob bowler, good field. *Sch* Harrow. *Teams* Kent (1867, 1 match); Cambridge U (1868–71, blue all four years); Surrey (1869, 2 matches).

Mongia, Nayan Ramlal

Career batting
29–52–4–1154–134–24.04–2–*ct* 34
Bowling 1452–82–17.70–8–2–6/24

His first-class debut was for Gentlemen of Kent in 1866, when he had the unusual distinction of bowling unchanged through the first innings, taking 5 for 35. He also played for Suffolk (1868). After entering the Church in 1871, he gave up serious cricket. A noted rackets player, he represented Cambridge.

Mongia, Nayan Ramlal
Cricketer. *b:* 19.12.1969, Baroda, India. Middle order right-hand batsman, wicket-keeper. *Team* Baroda (1989/90 to 1991/2). *Tour* India to England 1990.
Career batting
25–40–9–1327–165–42.80–3–*ct* 61–*st* 6

He came to England on the 1990 tour as reserve wicket-keeper and did not play in any Tests, but batted usefully in County matches.

Monkhouse, Graham
Cricketer. *b:* 26.4.1954, Langwathby, Carlisle, Cumberland. Lower order right-hand batsman, right-arm medium pace bowler. *Team* Surrey (1981–86, 74 matches). *Tour* English Counties to Zimbabwe 1984/5.
Career batting
75–86–33–1158–100*–21.84–1–*ct* 35
Bowling 4682–173–27.06–2–0–7/51

He also played for Cumberland (1972–79 and 1987). A good soccer player, he appeared for Carlisle United and Workington.

Monkhouse, Steven
Cricketer. *b:* 24.11.1962, Bury, Lancashire. Lower order right-hand batsman, left-arm fast medium bowler. *Teams* Warwickshire (1985–86, 2 matches); Glamorgan (1987–88, 9 matches).
Career batting
11–12–5–30–15–4.28–0–*ct* 2
Bowling 576–18–32.00–0–0–3/37

He also played for Staffordshire (1989).

Monkland, Francis George
Amateur. *b:* 8.10.1854, Trichinopoly, India. *d:* 15.1.1915, Regent's Park, London. Middle order right-hand batsman, right-hand slow under-arm bowler, good deep field. *Sch* Repton. *Team* Gloucestershire (1874–79, 26 matches).
Career batting
31–45–6–534–59–13.69–0–*ct* 11
Bowling 30–0

Monks, Clifford Ivon
Amateur, but turned professional in 1936. *b:* 4.3.1912, Keynsham, Somerset. *d:* 23.1.1974, Coalpit Heath, Bristol. Sound middle order right-hand batsman, right-arm medium pace bowler, good deep field. *Team* Gloucestershire (1935–52, 65 matches).
Career batting
65–101–17–1589–120–18.91–1–*ct* 31
Bowling 1629–36–45.25–0–0–4/70

Monks, George Derek
Professional. *b:* 3.9.1929, Sheffield, Yorkshire. Lower order right-hand batsman, wicket-keeper. *Team* Yorkshire (1952, 1 match).
Career batting
1–1–0–3–3–3.00–0–*ct* 1

Montagu, Admiral Sir Victor Alexander
Amateur. *b:* 20.4.1841. *d:* 30.1.1915, Brompton, Westminster, London. Son of Earl of Sandwich (Cambridge U 1832), brother-in-law of W. H. Dyke (Gentlemen of Kent 1863). Middle order batsman. *Team* MCC (1868–69).
Career batting
2–3–0–4–3–1.33–0–*ct* 0

His County cricket was for Huntingdonshire (1867–70) and Dorset (1876). He joined the Navy at the age of 12.

Monteith, James Dermott
Cricketer. *b:* 2.6.1943, Lisburn, Co Antrim, Ireland. Middle order right-hand batsman, slow left-arm bowler. *Sch* Royal Belfast Academical Institution. *Teams* Ireland (1965–84); Middlesex (1981–82, 9 matches).
Career batting
28–39–5–530–95–15.58–0–*ct* 23
Bowling 1941–94–20.64–7–1–7/38

Montgomerie, Richard Robert
Cricketer. *b:* 3.7.1971, Rugby, Warwickshire. Opening right-hand batsman, off break bowler. *Sch* Rugby. *Teams* Oxford U (1991–92, blue both years); Northamptonshire (1991, 1 match).
Career batting
18–28–5–786–103*–34.17–1–*ct* 12
Bowling 31–0

He also won a blue for rackets.

Montgomerie, Robert David
Amateur. *b:* 26.9.1937, Watford, Hertfordshire. Middle order right-hand batsman, leg break bowler. *Sch* Merchant Taylors. *Team* Free Foresters (1960).
Career batting
1–2–0–16–15–8.00–0–*ct* 0

His County cricket was for Hertfordshire (1956–61) and Oxfordshire (1963–72).

Montgomery, Rt Rev Bishop Henry Hutchinson
Amateur. *b:* 3.10.1847, Cawnpore, India. *d:* 25.11.1932, Old Park, Moville, Co Donegal, Ireland. Opening right-hand batsman, excellent point field. *Sch* Harrow. *Team* Cambridge U (1867–69).
Career batting
5–9–1–112–43*–14.00–0–*ct* 1

He played for Ireland (not first-class) 1867–68. He was Bishop of Tasmania 1889–1907. He was the father of Field Marshal Lord Montgomery of Alamein.

Montgomery, Hugh Ferguson
Amateur. *b:* 6.5.1880, Umbala, Bengal, India. *d:* 10.12.1920, Bray, Co Dublin, Ireland. Middle order right-hand batsman, good field. *Sch* Marlborough. *Team* Somerset (1901–09, 12 matches).
Career batting
17–30–0–416–50–13.86–0–*ct* 10
Bowling 267–5–53.40–0–0–2/17
His final first-class match was for the Navy in 1912.

Montgomery, Stanley William
Amateur. *b:* 7.7.1920, West Ham, Essex. Sound middle order right-hand batsman. *Team* Glamorgan (1949–53, 29 matches).
Career batting
29–43–2–763–117–18.60–1–*ct* 9
Bowling 99–6–16.50–0–0–3/29
A useful soccer player he appeared at centre half for Cardiff City, Southend, Newport and Hull City.

Montgomery, William
Professional. *b:* 4.3.1878, Staines, Middlesex. *d:* 14.11.1952, Peterborough, Northamptonshire. Lower order right-hand batsman, right-arm fast bowler. *Teams* Surrey (1901–04, 14 matches); Somerset (1905–07, 10 matches).
Career batting
24–39–4–234–50–6.68–0–*ct* 13
Bowling 687–25–27.48–0–0–4/17
He also played for Wiltshire, Cheshire (1911) and Hertfordshire (1913).

Montresor, Welby Francis
Amateur. *b:* 3.10.1849, Krishnagar, India. *d:* 27.1.1909, Kensington, London. Middle order batsman. *Sch* Eton. *Team* MCC (1880).
Career batting
2–4–0–22–7–5.50–0–*ct* 0

Moody, Thomas Masson
Cricketer. *b:* 2.10.1965, Adelaide, South Australia. Aggressive opening or middle order right-hand batsman, right-arm medium pace bowler. *Teams* Western Australia (1985/6 to 1991/2, 67 matches); Warwickshire (1990, 9 matches); Worcestershire (1991–92, 33 matches). *Tours* Australia to India 1987/8 (World Cup), 1989/90 (not first-class), to England 1989, to New Zealand (World Cup) 1991/2; Western Australia to India 1989/90; Australia B to Zimbabwe 1991/2. *Tests* Australia (1989/90 to 1991/2, 5 matches).
Career batting
130–213–18–9424–210–48.32–31–*ct* 103
Bowling 2365–73–32.39–1–1–7/43
Test batting
5–8–0–385–106–48.12–2–*ct* 6
Bowling 68–1–68.00–0–0–1/23
He failed to obtain a Test place on the 1989 tour to England, but joining Warwickshire the following summer, though his appearances were limited, he was a great success. He completed 1,000 runs in 12 innings and hit a hundred off 36 balls in 26 minutes (a record) v Glamorgan at Swansea. In 1991 he played for Worcestershire, scoring 1,887 runs, av 62.90, including 210 v Warwickshire at Worcester.

Moon, Sir Cecil Ernest
Amateur. *b:* 2.9.1867, Cassio Bridge, Hertfordshire. *d:* 22.2.1951, Buxton, Derbyshire. Son-in-law of B. S. Darbyshire (Oxford U). Middle order batsman. *Sch* Uppingham. *Team* London County (1900).
Career batting
1–2–0–29–17–14.50–0–*ct* 0

Moon, Leonard James
Amateur. *b:* 9.2.1878, Kensington, London. *d:* 23.11.1916, near Karasouli, Salonica, Greece. He died of wounds. Brother of W. R. (Middlesex). Forcing opening right-hand batsman, wicket-keeper. *Sch* Westminster. *Teams* Cambridge U (1897–1900, blue 1899 and 1900); Middlesex (1899–1909, 63 matches). *Tours* MCC to North America 1905, to South Africa 1905/6. *Tests* England (1905/6, 4 matches).
Career batting
96–163–8–4166–162–26.87–7–*ct* 72–*st* 13
Bowling 55–1–55.00–0–0–1/5
Test batting
4–8–0–182–36–22.75–0–*ct* 4
His final first-class match was for L. Robinson's XI in 1913. He also won a blue for soccer and played for Corinthians.

Moon, William Robert
Amateur. *b:* 7.6.1868, Maida Vale, London. *d:* 9.1.1943, Hendon, Middlesex. Brother of L. J. (Middlesex). Hard hitting middle order right-hand batsman, wicket-keeper. *Sch* Westminster. *Team* Middlesex (1891, 2 matches).
Career batting
2–1–1–17–17*–no av–0–*ct* 2
A well-known soccer player, he kept goal for Corinthians and England.

Mooney, Francis Leonard Hugh
Amateur. *b:* 26.5.1921, Wellington, New Zealand. Opening right-hand batsman, wicket-keeper. *Team* Wellington (1941/2 to 1954/5). *Tours* New Zealand to England 1949, to South Africa and Australia 1953/4. *Tests* New Zealand (1949 to 1953/4, 14 matches).
Career batting
91–150–14–3143–180–23.11–2–*ct* 168–*st* 53
Bowling 0–0

Mooney, William McCartan

Test batting
14–22–2–343–46–17.15–0–*ct* 22–*st* 8
Bowling 0–0

Going in fairly low down the order during the 1949 tour of England, he batted soundly and kept wicket in three Tests.

Mooney, William McCartan
Amateur. *b:* 5.10.1890, Blanchardstown, Co Dublin, Ireland. *d:* 1968, Ballsbridge, Co Dublin, Ireland. Middle order right-hand batsman. *Sch* Beaumont. *Team* Ireland (1912). *Tour* Ireland to North America 1909.
Career batting
3–6–1–25–23*–5.00–0–*ct* 3

Moor, David Child
Amateur. *b:* 18.12.1934, Faversham, Kent. Middle order left-hand batsman. *Sch* King's, Canterbury. *Team* Oxford U (1956).
Career batting
3–6–1–42–22–8.40–0–*ct* 0

Moorcroft, William
Amateur. Lower order batsman, good bowler. *Team* Hampshire (1911, 1 match).
Career batting
1 match, did not bat–*ct* 0
Bowling 68–0

Moore, Denis Neville
Amateur. *b:* 26.9.1910, Stanton House, Tewkesbury, Gloucestershire. Opening right-hand batsman, off break bowler. *Sch* Shrewsbury. *Teams* Oxford U (1930–31, blue 1930): Gloucestershire (1930–36, 31 matches).
Career batting
51–77–6–2307–206–32.49–4–*ct* 22
Bowling 252–6–42.00–0–0–3/39

He hit 1,000 runs in a season once: 1,317, av 41.15, in 1930. His only double century was 206 made on his debut for Gloucestershire – v Oxford U at Oxford in 1930. In 1931 he was captain of Oxford, but could not play in the University match due to illness.

Moore, Frederic James Stevenson
Amateur. *b:* 26.2.1873, Leominster, Herefordshire. *d:* 1.3.1947, Sherborne, Dorset. Opening or middle order right-hand batsman, slow left-arm bowler. *Sch* St George's, Harpenden. *Team* Cambridge U (1896).
Career batting
1–1–0–61–61–61.00–0–*ct* 2

His County cricket was for Herefordshire (1892) and Dorset (1902–03).

Moore, Frederick
Professional. *b:* 17.1.1931, Rochdale, Lancashire. Lower order right-hand batsman, right-arm medium pace bowler. *Team* Lancashire (1954–58, 24 matches).
Career batting
24–26–7–151–18–7.94–0–*ct* 11
Bowling 1516–54–28.07–2–1–6/45

Moore, Harry Ian
Cricketer. *b:* 28.2.1941, Sleaford, Lincolnshire. Middle order right-hand batsman, right-arm medium pace bowler. *Team* Nottinghamshire (1962–69, 176 matches).
Career batting
177–299–29–6765–206*–25.05–7–*ct* 106
Bowling 144–5–28.80–0–0–2/37

He hit 1,000 runs in a season three times (best 1,188, av 24.75, in 1965). His only double century was 206* for Nottinghamshire v Indians at Trent Bridge in 1967. He also played for Lincolnshire (1959–61 and 1970–77) and his final first-class match was for Minor Counties in 1973.

Moore, John William Spearink
Professional. *b:* 29.4.1891, Winchfield, Hampshire. *d:* 23.6.1980, Basingstoke, Hampshire. Middle order right-hand batsman, right-arm medium pace bowler. *Team* Hampshire (1910–13, 15 matches).
Career batting
15–25–6–256–30–13.47–0–*ct* 4
Bowling 72–0

Moore, Kenneth Francis
Professional. *b:* 4.1.1940, Croydon, Surrey. Tail end right-hand batsman, left-arm medium fast bowler. *Team* Essex (1961, 1 match).
Career batting
1–1–0–2–2–2.00–0–*ct* 2
Bowling 43–4–10.75–0–0–4/21

Moore, Nigel Harold
Amateur. *b:* 20.4.1930, Norwich, Norfolk. Middle order right-hand batsman, right-arm fast medium bowler. *Sch* Norwich. *Team* Cambridge U (1952).
Career batting
4–6–0–139–59–23.16–0–*ct* 2

His County cricket was for Norfolk (1947–64), and his final first-class match for Minor Counties in 1960.

Moore, Paul David
Cricketer. *b:* 10.6.1961, Bangor, Co Down, Ireland. Lower order right-hand batsman, wicket-keeper. *Team* Ireland (1992).
Career batting
1–1–1–0–0*–no av–0–*ct* 2

Moore, Richard Henry
Amateur. *b:* 14.11.1913, Charminster, Dorset. Opening right-hand batsman, right-arm medium pace bowler. *Team* Hampshire (1931–39, 129 matches).
Career batting
137–239–8–6026–316–26.08–10–*ct* 116
Bowling 978–25–39.12–0–0–3/46

He hit 1,000 runs in a season three times (best 1,569, av 30.17, in 1934). His only score over 200 was 316 for Hampshire v Warwickshire at Bournemouth in 1937. He captained Hampshire 1936–37. He also played for Denbighshire (1947).

Moore, Robert William
Amateur. *b:* 15.8.1905, Brooklands, USA. *d:* 27.10.1945, Sudden, Rochdale, Lancashire. Middle order right-hand batsman, slow left-arm bowler. *Team* Ireland (1926).
Career batting
2–3–0–51–22–17.00–0–*ct* 0
Bowling 17–0

Moore, William Frederic Powell
(also known as Powell-Moore)
Amateur. *b:* 23.3.1846, Westminster, London. *d:* 23.2.1919, Holborn, London. Lower order batsman, wicket-keeper. *Team* MCC (1870).
Career batting
2–4–1–21–19*–7.00–0–*ct* 2
His final first-class match was for Gentlemen of England in 1879.

Moore-Gwyn, Howell Gwyn
(changed name from H. G. Moore)
Amateur. *b:* 7.7.1886, Dyffryn Clydach, Neath, Glamorgan. *d:* 31.7.1956, Eastbourne, Sussex. Middle order right-hand batsman. *Sch* Winchester. *Teams* Army (1923); Punjab Governor's XI (1929/30).
Career batting
2–4–1–91–58–30.33–0–*ct* 1
Bowling 67–0
His County cricket was for Glamorgan (pre first-class, 1903–12).

Moores, Peter
Cricketer. *b:* 18.12.1962, Macclesfield, Cheshire. Lower order right-hand batsman, wicket-keeper. *Sch* King's, Macclesfield. *Teams* Worcestershire (1983–84, 11 matches); Sussex (1985–92, 124 matches); Orange Free State (1988/9).
Career batting
136–188–25–3933–116–24.12–4–*ct* 270–*st* 34
Bowling 16–0

Moorhouse, Edward
Amateur. *b:* 11.4.1851, Shaw Clough, Haslingden, Lancashire. *d:* 10.3.1927, Chorlton-cum-Medlock, Lancashire. Lower order batsman, wicket-keeper. *Team* Lancashire (1873–75, 5 matches).
Career batting
5–9–3–75–34–12.50–0–*ct* 8–*st* 3

Moorhouse, Fred
Professional. *b:* 25.3.1880, Berry Brow, Huddersfield, Yorkshire. *d:* 7.4.1933, Dudley, Worcestershire. Brother of Robert (Yorkshire). Lower order right-hand batsman, right-arm medium pace bowler. *Team* Warwickshire (1900–08, 117 matches).
Career batting
117–154–37–1549–75–13.23–0–*ct* 54
Bowling 6232–260–23.96–8–2–7/53
He also played for Cheshire (1910–11).

Moorhouse, Sir Harry Claude
Amateur. *b:* 30.1.1872, Bandora, Bombay, India. *d:* 16.12.1934, Newbury, Berkshire. Middle order batsman. *Sch* Brighton. *Team* MCC (1901–07).
Career batting
4–6–0–77–44–12.83–0–*ct* 1

Moorhouse, Robert
Professional. *b:* 7.9.1866, Berry Brow, Huddersfield, Yorkshire. *d:* 7.1.1921, Taylor Hill, Huddersfield, Yorkshire. Brother of Fred (Warwickshire). Middle/lower order right-hand batsman, right-arm medium pace bowler, good field. *Team* Yorkshire (1888–99, 209 matches).
Career batting
217–331–46–5337–113–18.72–3–*ct* 93
Bowling 1376–49–28.08–0–0–4/40
He hit 1,096 runs, av 32.23, in 1895. His final first-class match was for MCC in 1900.

Moorsom, Lewis Henry
Amateur. *b:* 1835. *d:* 10.3.1914, Moordown, Bournemouth, Hampshire. Middle order batsman, useful bowler. *Teams* Lancashire (1865, 1 match); Trinidad (1868/9).
Career batting
3–6–0–41–15–6.83–0–*ct* 1
Bowling 22–0

Morant, Edward John Harry Eden
Amateur. *b:* 29.1.1868, Westminster, London. *d:* 20.1.1910, Brockenhurst Park, Hampshire. Lower order batsman, bowler. *Sch* Westminster. *Team* MCC (1895).
Career batting
1–2–2–3–3*–no av–0–*ct* 0
Bowling 34–2–17.00–0–0–2/34

Morby-Smith, Lynton
Amateur. *b:* 27.5.1936, Durban, South Africa. Brother of Grahame (Natal). Middle order right-hand batsman, off break bowler. *Teams* Natal (1958/9 to 1960/1); Western Province (1963/4 to 1966/7). *Tour* SA Fezela to England 1961.
Career batting
35–55–4–1743–127–34.17–2–*ct* 19
Bowling 33–2–16.50–0–0–1/0

Morcom, Dr Alfred Farr
Amateur. *b:* 16.2.1885, Dunstable, Beds. *d:* 12.2.1952, Westminster, London. Lower order right-hand batsman, right-arm fast medium bowler. *Sch* Repton. *Team* Cambridge U (1905–07, blue all three years).
Career batting
23–36–14–257–29–11.68–0–*ct* 10
Bowling 2322–97–23.93–5–1–7/76

His County cricket was for Bedfordshire (1904–14). His final first-class match was for MCC in 1911.

Mordaunt, David John
Amateur. *b:* 24.8.1937, Chelsea, London. Grandson of G. J. (Kent), great-grandson of J. M. (MCC 1863). Middle/lower order right-hand batsman, right-arm medium fast bowler. *Sch* Wellington. *Team* Sussex (1958–60, 19 matches). *Tours* MCC to North America 1959 (not first-class), to South America 1964/5 (not first-class).
Career batting
20–29–3–599–96–23.03–0–*ct* 15
Bowling 601–24–25.04–1–0–5/42
His final first-class match was for MCC in 1964. He also played for Berkshire (1964–74).

Mordaunt, Eustace Charles
Amateur. *b:* 6.9.1870, Wellesbourne, Warwickshire. *d:* 21.6.1938, Marylebone, London. Son of J. M. (MCC 1863), brother of H. J. (Hampshire and Middlesex) and G. J. (Kent), nephew of Osbert (MCC), father-in-law of C. E. Awdry (Oxford U), son-in-law of H. Tubb (MCC). Lower order right-hand batsman, right-arm fast bowler. *Sch* Wellington. *Teams* Middlesex (1891–94, 4 matches); Kent (1896–97, 6 matches).
Career batting
11–18–0–132–21–7.33–0–*ct* 3
Bowling 136–4–34.00–0–0–1/4
He also played for Hampshire (not first-class, 1887). His final first-class match was for I Zingari in 1904.

Mordaunt, Gerald John
Amateur. *b:* 20.1.1873, Wellesbourne, Warwickshire. *d:* 5.3.1959, Westfield, Hayling Island, Hampshire. Son of J. M. (MCC 1863), brother of H. J. (Hampshire and Middlesex) and E. C. (Middlesex and Kent), grandfather of D. J. (Sussex), nephew of Osbert (MCC). Middle order right-hand batsman, slow ambidextrous under-arm bowler. *Sch* Wellington. *Teams* Oxford U (1893–96, blue all four years); Kent (1895–97, 16 matches). *Tour* Hawke to North America 1894.
Career batting
60–107–5–2675–264*–26.22–2–*ct* 72
Bowling 13–0
His highest score was 264* for Oxford U v Sussex at Hove in 1895. His final first-class match was for Gentlemen of England in 1904. He captained Oxford in 1895. A noted athlete, he represented Oxford in the long-jump.

Mordaunt, Sir Henry John
Amateur. *b:* 12.7.1867, Westminster, London. *d:* 15.1.1939, Westminster, London. Son of J. M. (MCC), brother of E. C. (Middlesex and Kent) and G. J. (Kent), nephew of Osbert (MCC). Middle order right-hand batsman, right-arm fast, later slow, bowler. *Sch* Eton. *Teams* Hampshire (1885, 1 match); Cambridge U (1888–89, blue both years); Middlesex (1889–93, 7 matches).
Career batting
27–48–1–729–127–15.51–1–*ct* 13
Bowling 1037–49–21.16–1–0–5/17
His final first-class match was for MCC in 1896. He last played for Hampshire (not first-class) in 1887.

Mordaunt, Canon Osbert
Amateur. *b:* 4.12.1842, Walton, Warwickshire. *d:* 25.9.1923, Hampton Lucy, Warwickshire. Brother of J. M. (MCC), uncle of H. J. (Hampshire and Middlesex), E. C. (Middlesex and Kent), G. J. (Kent) and F. J. Portman (Somerset), son-in-law of H. Snow (Cambridge U 1830). Middle order right-hand batsman, lob bowler, delivering with either hand, good close field. *Sch* Eton. *Team* MCC (1866).
Career batting
1–2–0–11–6–5.50–0–*ct* 0
His County cricket was for Warwickshire (pre first-class, 1864–81), Shropshire (1867) and Staffordshire (1892–93). He played no first-class cricket at Oxford U, but did win a blue for royal tennis.

Mordaunt, Osbert Cautley
Amateur. *b:* 26.5.1876, Flax Bourton, Somerset. *d:* 20.10.1949, Bells Yew Green, Sussex. Nephew of W. Foord-Kelcey (Kent) and J. Foord-Kelcey (Oxford U). Lower order right-hand batsman, right-arm slow bowler. *Team* Somerset (1905–10, 14 matches).
Career batting
17–30–8–148–23–6.72–0–*ct* 12
Bowling 1115–42–26.54–1–0–5/68
His final first-class match was for L. Robinson's XI in 1914.

More, Hamish Keith
Cricketer. *b:* 30.5.1940, Abbeyhill, Edinburgh, Scotland. Opening or middle order right-hand batsman, wicket-keeper. *Team* Scotland (1966–76).
Career batting
18–36–2–639–89–18.79–0–*ct* 29–*st* 2
He played his final first-class match for T. N. Pearce's XI in 1976.

More, Kiran Shankar
Cricketer. *b:* 4.9.1962, Baroda, India. Middle order right-hand batsman, wicket-keeper. *Team* Baroda (1980/1 to 1988/9). *Tours* India to West Indies 1982/3, 1988/9, to Australia 1985/6, 1991/2, to England 1986, 1990, to Sharjah (not first-class) 1987/8, 1988/9, 1989/90, 1991/2, to Bangladesh (not first-class) 1988/9, to Pakistan 1989/90, to New Zealand 1989/90, to Australia and New Zealand (World Cup) 1991/2. *Tests* India (1986 to 1991/2, 38 matches).
Career batting
101–134–29–3132–181*–29.82–3–*ct* 200–*st* 46
Bowling 96–0

Test batting
38–53–12–1104–73–26.92–0–*ct* 82–*st* 16
Bowling 12–0
He had a very successful tour to England in 1986, but was not so successful in 1990. He kept wicket in all three Tests on both tours.

More, Richard Edwardes
Amateur. *b:* 3.1.1879, Linley Hall, Bishop's Castle, Shropshire. *d:* 24.11.1936, Cairo, Egypt. Attacking middle order right-hand batsman, right-arm medium pace bowler. *Sch* Westminster. *Teams* Oxford U (1898–1901, blue last two years); Middlesex (1901–10, 36 matches). *Tour* Bosanquet to North America 1901.
Career batting
57–92–12–1671–133–20.88–3–*ct* 38
Bowling 3430–124–27.66–4–2–6/28
His final first-class match was for G. J. V. Weigall's XI in 1914. He also played for Shropshire (1897–1900). Being in the Egyptian Civil Service limited his opportunities for County cricket.

Morfee, Percival Ernest
Professional. *b:* 2.5.1886, Ashford, Kent. *d:* 12.2.1945, Darlington, Co Durham. Lower order right-hand batsman, right-arm fast bowler. *Team* Kent (1910–12, 11 matches).
Career batting
11–17–7–132–32–13.20–0–*ct* 12
Bowling 934–28–33.35–1–0–5/47
He played for Scotland in a non-first-class match in 1913.

Morgan, Andrew Howard
Cricketer. *b:* 30.11.1945, Ore, Hastings, Sussex. Middle order left-hand batsman, wicket-keeper. *Team* Oxford U (1966–69, blue 1969).
Career batting
11–20–4–381–59*–23.81–0–*ct* 9

Morgan, Aubrey Niel
Amateur. *b:* 30.1.1904, Cyncoed, Llandaff, Glamorgan. *d:* 14.9.1985, Ridgfield, Washington, USA. Brother of J. T. (Glamorgan). Lower order right-hand batsman, right-arm medium fast bowler. *Sch* Charterhouse. *Teams* Glamorgan (1928–29, 5 matches); Wales (1929).
Career batting
6–11–0–95–35–8.63–0–*ct* 1
Bowling 336–6–56.00–0–0–2/37
He married the sister of Charles Lindbergh, the aviator.

Morgan, Bertie Francis
Professional. *b:* 6.12.1885, Finsbury Park, Middlesex. *d:* 25.2.1959, Billingham, Co Durham. Lower order right-hand batsman, left-arm bowler. *Team* Somerset (1909–10, 6 matches).
Career batting
6–11–0–63–23–5.72–0–*ct* 3
Bowling 175–2–87.50–0–0–1/19
He also played for Staffordshire (1913–24).

Morgan, Charles
Amateur. *b:* 29.1.1839, Greenwich, London. *d:* 17.7.1904, Clapham, London. Father of C. L. (Surrey, non-first-class). Lower order right-hand batsman, left-hand fast round-arm bowler. *Team* Surrey (1871, 4 matches).
Career batting
5–8–0–60–29–7.50–0–*ct* 2
Bowling 220–4–55.00–0–0–1/22
His first-class debut was for the Gentlemen of England in 1865.

Morgan, Charles
Professional. *b:* 7.2.1917, Clay Cross, Derbyshire. Lower order right-hand batsman, off break bowler. *Team* Nottinghamshire (1946, 1 match).
Career batting
1–2–0–13–13–6.50–0–*ct* 0
Bowling 94–0

Morgan, Derek Clifton
Professional. *b:* 26.2.1929, Muswell Hill, Middlesex. Middle order right-hand batsman, right-arm fast medium bowler, good close field. *Sch* Berkhamsted. *Team* Derbyshire (1950–69, 540 matches).
Career batting
556–882–146–18356–147–24.94–9–*ct* 573
Bowling 31302–1248–25.08–35–5–7/33
He hit 1,000 runs in a season eight times (best 1,669, av 46.36, in 1962). His best season with the ball was 1957 with 94 wickets, av 23.04. He captained Derbyshire from 1965 to 1969.

Morgan, Donald Lindsay
Amateur. *b:* 5.11.1888, Tientsin, China. *d:* 22.1.1969, Pasadena, California, USA. Middle order batsman. *Sch* Clifton and Mill Hill. *Team* Gloucestershire (1907, 2 matches).
Career batting
2–4–0–3–2–0.75–0–*ct* 6

Morgan, Edward Noel
Amateur. *b:* 22.12.1905, Garnant, Carmarthenshire. *d:* 27.8.1975, Cardiff, Glamorgan. Brother of W. G. (Glamorgan). Middle order right-hand batsman. *Sch* Brecon. *Team* Glamorgan (1934, 1 match).
Career batting
1–1–0–1–1–1.00–0–*ct* 0

Morgan, Henry Randolph
Amateur. *b:* 6.7.1907, Ballynafeigh, Belfast, Ireland. Lower order right-hand batsman, right-arm fast medium bowler. *Team* Ireland (1931–38).
Career batting
4–8–3–54–21–10.80–0–*ct* 2

Bowling 187–18–10.38–1–1–7/41
He played soccer for Linfield.

Morgan, Howard William
Professional. *b:* 29.6.1931, Maesteg, Glamorgan. Lower order right-hand batsman, off break bowler. *Team* Glamorgan (1958, 2 matches).
Career batting
2–3–1–11–5–5.50–0–*ct* 0
Bowling 58–2–29.00–0–0–1/27

Morgan, John Trevil
Amateur. *b:* 7.5.1907, Cyncoed, Llandaff, Glamorgan. *d:* 18.12.1976, Leigh Woods, Clifton, Bristol. Brother of A. N. (Glamorgan). Middle order left-hand batsman, right-arm medium pace bowler, wicket-keeper. *Sch* Charterhouse. *Teams* Glamorgan (1925–34, 39 matches); Cambridge U (1927–30, blue last three years); Wales (1928).
Career batting
83–124–13–2339–149–21.07–4–*ct* 60–*st* 12
Bowling 1343–26–51.65–0–0–3/16
He captained Cambridge in 1930.

Morgan, Michael
Professional. *b:* 21.5.1936, Ynyshir, Glamorgan. Lower order right-hand batsman, off break bowler. *Team* Nottinghamshire (1957–61, 61 matches).
Career batting
61–86–16–488–56*–6.97–0–*ct* 24
Bowling 5287–146–36.21–3–0–6/50

Morgan, Dr Michael Naunton
Amateur. *b:* 15.5.1932, Marylebone, London. Lower order right-hand batsman, right-arm fast medium bowler. *Sch* Marlborough. *Team* Cambridge U (1951–54, blue 1954).
Career batting
14–14–9–49–11*–9.80–0–*ct* 4
Bowling 1062–30–35.40–1–0–5/58
His final first-class match was for MCC in 1957. His County cricket was for Berkshire (1950–59).

Morgan, Rev Philip Richard Llewelyn
Amateur. *b:* 11.3.1927, Derby. Lower order right-hand batsman, leg break bowler. *Sch* St John's, Leatherhead. *Team* Oxford U (1946).
Career batting
1–1–0–1–1–1.00–0–*ct* 0
Bowling 38–0
He was an international athlete.

Morgan, Ross Winston
Cricketer. *b:* 12.2.1941, Auckland, New Zealand. Middle order right-hand batsman, off break bowler. *Team* Auckland (1957/8 to 1976/7). *Tours* New Zealand to India and Pakistan 1964/5, to England 1965, to Australia 1969/70, 1970/1, to West Indies 1971/2. *Tests* New Zealand (1964/5 to 1971/2, 20 matches).
Career batting
136–229–13–5940–166–27.50–8–*ct* 85–*st* 1
Bowling 3558–108–32.94–4–0–6/40
Test batting
20–34–1–734–97–22.24–0–*ct* 12
Bowling 609–5–121.80–0–0–1/16
He played in all three Tests on the 1965 tour and in first-class matches scored 645 runs, av 23.88.

Morgan, Rurie Tranton
Amateur. *b:* 30.7.1912, Wellington, New Zealand. *d:* 4.1.1980, Wellington, New Zealand. Middle order right-hand batsman, right-arm slow medium bowler. *Team* Wellington (1932/3 to 1940/1). *Tour* New Zealand Services to England 1945.
Career batting
11–20–2–374–81–20.77–0–*ct* 12
Bowling 384–12–32.00–0–0–2/34

Morgan, Samuel Augustus
Cricketer. *b:* 7.8.1950, Half Way Tree, Kingston, Jamaica. Middle order right-hand batsman. *Team* Jamaica (1969/70 to 1973/4). *Tour* Jamaica to England 1970.
Career batting
22–35–3–998–126–31.18–1–*ct* 10
Bowling 82–1–82.00–0–0–1/16

Morgan, Tom Rees
(registered at death as Thomas Rhys Morgan)
Amateur. *b:* 11.4.1893, Porth, Glamorgan. *d:* 6.4.1975, Aberkenfig, Glamorgan. Middle order right-hand batsman, off break bowler. *Sch* Monmouth. *Team* Glamorgan (1921–25, 39 matches).
Career batting
39–73–5–1044–87*–15.35–0–*ct* 5
Bowling 10–0
He first played for Glamorgan (pre first-class) in 1913.

Morgan, W. A.
Amateur. Middle order batsman. *Team* Liverpool and District (1889).
Career batting
1–2–0–2–2–1.00–0–*ct* 0

Morgan, William
Amateur. *b:* 1862, Nantgarw, Glamorgan. *d:* 22.10.1914, Porthleven, Cornwall. Middle order batsman, useful bowler. *Team* West of England (1892–94).
Career batting
2–3–0–32–24–10.66–0–*ct* 2
Bowling 32–3–10.66–0–0–2/21
His County cricket was for Glamorgan (pre first-class, 1889–1901).

Morgan, William Guy
(later Stewart-Morgan, by marriage in 1941)
Amateur. *b:* 26.12.1907, Garnant, Carmarthenshire. *d:* 29.7.1973, Carmarthen. Brother of E. N. (Glamorgan). Middle order right-hand batsman, right-arm medium pace bowler. *Sch* Brecon. *Teams* Glamorgan

(1925–38, 45 matches); Cambridge U (1927–29); Wales (1929).
Career batting
49–73–12–1071–91*–17.55–0–*ct* 8
Bowling 257–3–85.66–0–0–1/15
A noted rugby footballer, he played for Swansea, Cambridge and Wales.

Morgan, William Percival
Amateur. *b:* 1.1.1905, Abercrave, Brecon. *d:* 3.3.1983, Neath, Glamorgan. Middle order right-hand batsman, right-arm medium pace bowler. *Sch* Brecon. *Team* Glamorgan (1925, 1 match).
Career batting
1–2–0–4–4–2.00–0–*ct* 0
Bowling 0–0

Morkel, Denijs Paul Beck
Amateur. *b:* 25.1.1906, Plumstead, Cape Town, South Africa. *d:* 6.10.1980, Nottingham. Brother of R. K. B. (Western Province and Orange Free State). Attacking middle order right-hand batsman, right-arm fast medium bowler, slip field. *Team* Western Province (1924/5 to 1929/30). *Tours* South Africa to England 1929, to Australia and New Zealand 1931/32; Cahn to North America 1933 (not first-class), to Ceylon 1936/7. *Tests* South Africa (1927/8 to 1931/2, 16 matches).
Career batting
86–143–12–4494–251–34.30–8–*ct* 67
Bowling 4973–174–28.58–6–0–8/13
Test batting
16–28–1–663–88–24.55–0–*ct* 13
Bowling 821–18–45.61–0–0–4/93
He showed excellent all-round form on his 1929 tour to England, hitting 1,443 runs, av 34.35, and taking 69 wickets, av 26.01, in first-class matches and coming second in both the batting and bowling tables in the Tests. His highest innings was 251 for Cahn's XI v South Americans at Nottingham in 1932, his other double century being for Western Province. He emigrated to England and appeared regularly for Sir J. Cahn's XI from 1932 to 1939. He also played for Bedfordshire (1931). His last first-class match was for Sir J. Cahn's XI in 1938.

Morley, Frederick
(birth registered as Frederic Morley)
Professional. *b:* 16.12.1850, Sutton-in-Ashfield, Nottinghamshire. *d:* 28.9.1884, Sutton-in-Ashfield, Nottinghamshire. Cousin of Thomas (Nottinghamshire). Tail end left-hand batsman, left-arm fast bowler. *Team* Nottinghamshire (1872–83, 113 matches). *Tour* Bligh to Australia 1882/3. *Tests* England (1880 to 1882/3, 4 matches).
Career batting
232–355–95–1404–31–5.40–0–*ct* 107
Bowling 17103–1273+1–13.43–119–36–8/26
Test batting
4–6–2–6–2*–1.50–0–*ct* 4
Bowling 296–16–18.50–1–0–5/56
He took 100 wickets in a season seven times (best 197, av 12.11, in 1878). On the sea voyage to Australia with Bligh's Team he was seriously injured when the ship was in collision with another and he never fully recovered from the accident. His first-class debut was for the United North in 1871.

Morley, Henry
Professional. *b:* 2.3.1785, Amberley, Sussex. *d:* 6.12.1857, Brighton, Sussex. Middle order right-hand batsman. *Team* Sussex (1815–38, 29 matches).
Career batting
30–57–2–285–18–5.18–0–*ct* 7

Morley, Henry
Professional. *c:* 16.11.1852, Edwinstowe, Nottinghamshire. *d:* 16.8.1924, Edwinstowe, Nottinghamshire. Lower order batsman, right-arm fast bowler. *Team* Nottinghamshire (1884, 1 match).
Career batting
1–1–0–0–0–0.00–0–*ct* 0
Bowling 29–2–14.50–0–0–1/9

Morley, James Henry
Amateur. *b:* 20.12.1835, The Lodge, Herne Hill, London. *d:* 7.4.1904, Hove, Sussex. Lower order batsman, wicket-keeper. *Sch* Merchant Taylors'. *Team* Middlesex (1865, 1 match).
Career batting
1–2–1–25–19–25.00–0–*ct* 1–*st* 2

Morley, Jeremy Dennis
Cricketer. *b:* 20.10.1950, Newmarket, Suffolk. Middle order left-hand batsman, right-arm medium pace bowler. *Team* Sussex (1971–76, 72 matches).
Career batting
72–131–12–2752–127–23.12–2–*ct* 26–*st* 1
Bowling 2–0
He also played for Cambridgeshire (1969–70).

Morley, Thomas
Professional. *b:* 10.3.1863, Sutton-in-Ashfield, Nottinghamshire. *d:* 28.10.1919, Thorpe St Andrew, Norwich, Norfolk. Cousin of Frederick (Nottinghamshire). Stylish middle/lower order right-hand batsman, right-arm fast bowler. *Team* Nottinghamshire (1887, 1 match).
Career batting
1–2–0–17–12–8.50–0–*ct* 0
Bowling 5–0
He also played for Norfolk (1888–1900). A useful soccer player, he represented Norfolk as a goalkeeper.

Mornement, Dr Robert Harry
Amateur. *b:* 15.8.1873, Roudham Hall, Norfolk. *d:* 16.4.1948, Chatham, Kent. Opening right-hand batsman, right-arm medium pace bowler. *Team* Hamp-

shire (1906, 3 matches).
Career batting
5–8–0–121–73–15.12–0–*ct* 4
Bowling 259–9–28.77–0–0–3/62

He played for the Combined Army and Navy Team in 1910 and 1911. He also played for Norfolk (1892–95).

Morres, Hugh Frederick Michael
Amateur. *b:* 8.7.1876, Wokingham, Berkshire. *d:* 28.1.1934, Swanage, Dorset. Middle order right-hand batsman, right-arm fast medium bowler. *Sch* Winchester. *Team* Oxford U (1898).
Career batting
2–3–0–29–28–9.66–0–*ct* 1
Bowling 10–0

His County cricket was for Berkshire (1897–1921) and Dorset (1903–05).

Morrill, Nicholas David
Cricketer. *b:* 9.12.1957, Ryde, Isle of Wight. Middle/lower order right-hand batsman, off break bowler. *Sch* Millfield. *Team* Oxford U (1978–79, blue 1979).
Career batting
14–21–3–241–45–13.38–0–*ct* 5
Bowling 741–12–61.75–0–0–3/53

He also won a blue for soccer.

Morris, Alan
Cricketer. *b:* 23.8.1953, Staveley, Derbyshire. Middle order right-hand batsman, leg break bowler. *Teams* Derbyshire (1974–78, 47 matches); Griqualand West (1979/80).
Career batting
49–81–5–1188–74–15.63–0–*ct* 31
Bowling 118–0

Morris, Alfred
Professional. *b:* 20.7.1873, Yarm, Stockton-on-Tees, Co Durham. *d:* 29.3.1961, Lancaster Moor, Lancashire. Lower order batsman, right-arm medium pace bowler. *Team* Minor Counties (1912).
Career batting
2–2–0–7–4–3.50–0–*ct* 0
Bowling 80–10–8.00–0–0–4/50

His County cricket was for Durham (pre first-class, 1905–14).

Morris, Arthur Robert, MBE
Amateur. *b:* 19.1.1922, Bondi, Sydney, New South Wales, Australia. Excellent opening left-hand batsman, slow left-arm bowler. *Team* New South Wales (1940/1 to 1954/5, 50 matches). *Tours* Australia to England 1948, 1953, to South Africa 1949/50, to West Indies 1954/5; Cavaliers to India and South Africa 1962/3; President's XI (Defence Fund Match) in India 1963/4. *Tests* Australia (1946/7 to 1954/5, 46 matches).
Career batting
162–250–15–12614–290–53.67–46–*ct* 73
Bowling 592–12–49.33–0–0–3/36
Test batting
46–79–3–3533–206–46.48–12–*ct* 15
Bowling 50–2–25.00–0–0–1/5

He had a splendid first tour of England in 1948, topping the Test batting averages with 696 runs, av 87.00, and in all first-class matches hitting 1,922 runs, av 71.18, including his highest innings of 290 v Gloucestershire at Bristol. He was not so successful in 1953, but in first-class matches hit 1,303 runs, av 38.29. He hit 1,000 runs in an Australian season three times and once in South Africa.

His most outstanding record was the scoring of a century in each innings of his first-class debut match: 148 and 111 for New South Wales v Queensland at Sydney in 1940/1. He captained Australia in two Tests.

Morris, Charles Antony
Amateur. *b:* 9.5.1939, Newnham, Cambridge. *d:* 17.11.1990, Wilmslow, Cheshire. Middle order left-hand batsman, leg break and googly bowler. *Sch* Marlborough. *Team* Cambridge U (1960).
Career batting
4–6–1–23–8–4.60–0–*ct* 3
Bowling 47–0

His County cricket was for for Cambridgeshire (1956–63). A useful rugby footballer, he appeared at scrum half for Rosslyn Park.

Morris, Charles Christopher
Amateur. *b:* 30.6.1882, USA. *d:* 17.6.1971, Villanova, Pennsylvania, USA. Middle order right-hand batsman, leg break and googly bowler, good close field. *Team* Philadelphia (1901–13). *Tours* Philadelphians to England 1903, 1908.
Career batting
36–63–2–1253–164–20.54–1–*ct* 22

Although he hit the highest score on the 1903 tour, his batting was on the whole disappointing. In 1908 his batting was again not up to the standard he displayed at home. He represented USA v Canada in 5 matches. The cricket library at Haverford College was named in his honour.

Morris, Charles Richard
Amateur. *b:* 26.8.1880, Nottingham. *d:* 10.8.1947, Hampstead, London. Middle order right-hand batsman. *Sch* Oakham. *Team* Nottinghamshire (1902–04, 5 matches).
Career batting
5–8–1–63–24*–9.00–0–*ct* 5

Morris, Edward Silvester
Amateur. *b:* 6.4.1849, Bedminster, Somerset. *d:* 14.11.1928, Rochdale, Lancashire. Useful batsman. *Team* Gloucestershire (1870, 2 matches).
Career batting
2–2–0–30–17–15.00–0–*ct* 0

Morris, Harold Marsh
Amateur. *b:* 16.4.1898, Wanstead, Essex. *d:* 18.11.1984, Brighton, Sussex. Middle order right-hand batsman, right-arm medium pace bowler. *Sch* Repton. *Teams* Essex (1919–32, 240 matches); Cambridge U (1919). *Tour* Tennyson to Jamaica 1926/7.
Career batting
246–393–30–7086–166–19.52–3–*ct* 80
Bowling 885–16–55.31–0–0–2/16
He captained Essex 1929 to 1932.

Morris, Hugh
Cricketer. *b:* 5.10.1963, Canton, Cardiff, Glamorgan. Opening left-hand batsman, right-arm medium pace bowler. *Sch* Blundell's. *Team* Glamorgan (1981–92, 201 matches). *Tours* England A to Sri Lanka 1990/1, to West Indies 1991/2; England to Australia 1990/1 (not first-class). *Tests* England (1991, 3 matches).
Career batting
216–367–38–12579–160*–38.23–31–*ct* 126
Bowling 380–2–190.00–0–0–1/6
Test batting
3–6–0–115–44–19.16–0–*ct* 3
He hit 1,000 runs in a season six times, going on to 2,000 once: 2,276, av 55.51, in 1990. This aggregate was a Glamorgan record and included ten hundreds, another county record. He captained Glamorgan from 1986 to 1989. He captained the England A team to Sri Lanka in 1990/1 and briefly formed a part of the senior side that winter to Australia, when he was brought in as a 'reinforcement' but appeared in only two minor matches.

Morris, Huson
Amateur. *b:* 22.5.1848, Kensington, London. *d:* 14.2.1924, St Jean de Luz, France. Middle order right-hand batsman, right-hand fast medium round-arm bowler. *Sch* Lancing and Dulwich. *Team* MCC (1868).
Career batting
1–1–0–0–0–0.00–0–*ct* 1

Morris, Ian
Cricketer. *b:* 27.6.1946, Maesteg, Glamorgan. Middle order right-hand batsman, slow left-arm bowler, close field. *Team* Glamorgan (1966–68, 14 matches).
Career batting
14–25–2–253–38–11.00–0–*ct* 15
Bowling 141–4–35.25–0–0–2/30

Morris, James George
Cricketer. *b:* 4.2.1967, Nottingham. Middle order right-hand batsman. *Sch* Nottingham HS. *Team* Oxford U (1991).
Career batting
3–5–0–63–28–12.60–0–*ct* 3

Morris, John Edward
Cricketer. *b:* 1.4.1964, Crewe, Cheshire. Middle order right-hand batsman, right-arm medium pace bowler. *Teams* Derbyshire (1982–92, 201 matches); Griqualand West (1988/9). *Tours* England to Australia 1990/1. *Tests* England (1990, 3 matches).
Career batting
218–359–26–12806–191–38.45–29–*ct* 92
Bowling 753–5–150.60–0–0–1/13
Test batting
3–5–2–71–32–23.66–0–*ct* 3
He hit 1,000 runs in a season seven times (best 1,739, av 47.00, in 1986).

Morris, John Frederick
Amateur. *b:* 14.10.1880, Ampthill, Bedfordshire. *d:* 23.3.1960, Earlham, Norfolk. Lower order right-hand batsman, slow right-arm bowler. *Sch* Wellingborough. *Team* Cambridge U (1902).
Career batting
1–2–2–9–7*–no av–0–*ct* 0
His County cricket was for Bedfordshire (1900–02).

Morris, Leonard John
Amateur. *b:* 26.9.1898, Aston, Birmingham. *d:* 9.3.1984, Dorridge, Warwickshire. Middle order left-hand batsman, right-arm medium pace bowler. *Sch* KES, Birmingham. *Team* Warwickshire (1925–26, 7 matches).
Career batting
7–11–0–262–76–23.81–0–*ct* 4
Bowling 70–3–23.33–0–0–2/41

Morris, Michael John
Cricketer. *b:* 8.3.1969, Melbourne, Victoria, Australia. Middle order right-hand batsman. *Team* Cambridge U (1989–91, blue 1991).
Career batting
25–39–5–452–60–13.29–0–*ct* 10
Bowling 15–0

Morris, Norman
Amateur. *b:* 1849, Peckham, London. *d:* 20.1.1874, Ford, Lingfield, Surrey. Middle order right-hand batsman, wicket-keeper. *Sch* Tonbridge. *Teams* Kent (1870–72, 10 matches); Surrey (1873, 5 matches).
Career batting
17–33–0–473–64–14.33–0–*ct* 7–*st* 4
Bowling 14–0

Morris, P. J.
Amateur. Middle order right-hand batsman. *Team* Worcestershire (1914, 1 match).
Career batting
1–2–0–74–71–37.00–0–*ct* 1
Bowling 13–0
He also played hockey for Worcestershire.

Morris, Philip Edward
Amateur. *b:* 26.11.1877, Kennington, London. *d:* 6.7.1945, Hove, Sussex. Lower order batsman, leg break bowler. *Sch* Mill Hill and Bancrofts. *Team* Essex (1909–24, 28 matches).

Morris, Raymond

Career batting
28–43–5–418–55*–11.00–0–*ct* 13
Bowling 1848–83–22.26–6–1–8/106

Morris, Raymond
Amateur. *b:* 20.6.1929, Hartlebury, Worcestershire. Lower order right-hand batsman, wicket-keeper. *Team* Worcestershire (1958, 2 matches).
Career batting
2–3–0–7–7–2.33–0–*ct* 8

Morris, Robert John
Amateur. *b:* 27.11.1926, Penllergaer, Swansea, Glamorgan. Son of V. L. (Glamorgan). Sound opening right-hand batsman, off break bowler. *Sch* Blundell's. *Teams* Cambridge U (1949–51, blue 1949); Kent (1950, 2 matches).
Career batting
22–36–2–778–96–22.88–0–*ct* 7
Bowling 192–2–96.00–0–0–1/38

Morris, Robert Sean Millner
Cricketer. *b:* 10.9.1968, Great Horwood, Buckinghamshire. Opening right-hand batsman, off break bowler. *Sch* Stowe. *Team* Hampshire (1992, 5 matches).
Career batting
5–9–1–209–74–26.12–0–*ct* 7

Morris, Russell Edward
Cricketer. *b:* 8.6.1967, St Asaph, Flintshire. Opening right-hand batsman, right-arm medium pace bowler. *Team* Oxford U (1987–91, blue 1987, 1989–91).
Career batting
35–52–4–1109–96–23.10–0–*ct* 8
Bowling 145–2–72.50–0–0–2/82
He captained Oxford in 1990. He was awarded a blue for soccer. He played for Wales in the Minor Counties Championship (1990–91).

Morris, Vernon Leslie
Amateur. *b:* 13.6.1894, Briton Ferry, Neath, Glamorgan. *d:* 11.1.1973, Exmouth, Devon. Father of R. J. (Kent). Opening right-hand batsman. *Sch* Brecon. *Team* Glamorgan (1921–29, 18 matches).
Career batting
18–33–1–407–42–12.71–0–*ct* 9

Morris, William
Amateur. *b:* 23.11.1873, Lee, London. *d:* 6.5.1945, Kensington, London. Steady middle order right-hand batsman. *Team* Kent (1896, 2 matches).
Career batting
2–4–0–14–6–3.50–0–*ct* 0

Morris, William Bancroft
Professional. *b:* 28.5.1917, Kingston, Jamaica. Middle order right-hand batsman, slow leg break bowler. *Team* Essex (1946–50, 48 matches).
Career batting
48–78–10–1219–68–17.92–0–*ct* 18
Bowling 1975–43–45.93–0–0–4/90
He also played for Cambridgeshire (1951–58).

Morris, William Percy
Amateur. *b:* 19.6.1881, Swansea, Glamorgan. *d:* 30.7.1975, Swansea, Glamorgan. Opening or middle order right-hand batsman, right-arm medium pace bowler. *Team* Glamorgan (1921–25, 8 matches).
Career batting
9–18–1–159–30–9.35–0–*ct* 6
Bowling 99–2–49.50–0–0–1/11
He first played for Glamorgan (pre first-class) in 1906. His first-class debut was for South Wales in 1912.

Morrison, Charles Stuart
Amateur. *b:* 27.5.1883, Jamaica. *d:* 25.11.1948, Kingston, Jamaica. Lower order right-hand batsman, right-arm slow medium bowler. *Team* Jamaica (1904/5 to 1925/6). *Tour* West Indies to England 1906.
Career batting
25–44–10–396–54–11.64–0–*ct* 13
Bowling 1236–60–20.60–2–1–7/44
Although quite effective in the minor matches of the 1906 tour, his bowling return was modest in first-class matches.

Morrison, Daniel Kyle
Cricketer. *b:* 3.2.1966, Auckland, New Zealand. Lower order right-hand batsman, right-arm fast medium bowler. *Teams* Auckland (1985/6 to 1991/2); Lancashire (1992, 14 matches). *Tours* New Zealand to Sri Lanka 1986/7, to Australia 1987/8, 1989/90, 1990/1 (not first-class), to Sharjah (not first-class) 1987/8, 1989/90, to India 1987/8 (World Cup), 1988/9, to England 1990, to Pakistan 1990/1; Young New Zealand to Zimbabwe 1988/9; Rest of World to England 1991. *Tests* New Zealand (1987/8 to 1991/2, 25 matches).
Career batting
93–90–28–495–36–7.98–0–*ct* 33
Bowling 8795–266–33.06–9–0–7/82
Test batting
25–35–10–146–27*–5.84–0–*ct* 7
Bowling 3011–78–38.60–5–0–5/69
Although he appeared in all three Tests on the 1990 tour of England, his fast bowling rarely troubled the batsmen. He topped the Lancashire bowling averages in 1992, his 36 wickets costing 33.58 runs each.

Morrison, Ewart Gladstone
Amateur. *b:* 7.10.1899, Kotagala, Ceylon. *d:* 12.5.1985, Lewes, Sussex. Middle order left-hand batsman, left-arm medium pace bowler. *Team* Gloucestershire (1926–33, 20 matches).
Career batting
20–34–1–340–59–10.30–0–*ct* 12
Bowling 209–3–69.66–0–0–1/30

Morrison, George Charles
Amateur. *b:* 27.6.1915, Downpatrick, Co Down, Ireland. Opening right-hand batsman. *Team* Ireland (1947).
Career batting
2–4–0–48–16–12.00–0–*ct* 0
Bowling 32–0

Morrison, John Stanton Fleming
Amateur. *b:* 17.4.1892, West Jesmond, Newcastle upon Tyne, Northumberland. *d:* 28.1.1961, Farnham, Surrey. Middle order right-hand batsman, wicket-keeper. *Sch* Charterhouse. *Teams* Cambridge U (1912–19, blue 1912, 1914 and 1919); Somerset (1920, 1 match).
Career batting
38–67–2–1982–233*–30.49–4–*ct* 21–*st* 4
Bowling 6–1–6.00–0–0–1/6
His final first-class match was for Combined Universities in 1922. He also played for Northumberland (1913–21). His highest score was 233* for Cambridge U v MCC at Cambridge in 1914. He captained Cambridge in 1919. A useful soccer player he played for Sunderland, and won amateur international caps for England. He also won blues for soccer and golf. He was a well-known designer of golf courses.

Morrogh, W. C. F. M.
(*see under* MacCarthy-Morrogh, W. C. F.)

Morrow, George Alexander
Amateur. *b:* 1877, Ireland. *d:* 15.11.1914, Ranelagh, Dublin, Ireland. Middle order right-hand batsman. *Team* Ireland (1907–12). *Tour* Ireland to North America 1909.
Career batting
8–14–1–271–50*–20.84–0–*ct* 4
Bowling 70–5–14.00–0–0–4/42
A noted badminton player, he represented Ireland.

Morse, Charles
Amateur. *b:* 20.8.1820, Catton Park, Norwich, Norfolk. *d:* 25.3.1883, Dresden, Saxony. Middle order right-hand batsman. *Team* Cambridge U (1842–44, blue all three years).
Career batting
40–68–6–561–82–9.04–0–*ct* 26
He was a leading member of the I Zingari in its early days. His last first-class match was for MCC in 1862. His County cricket was for Norfolk (1842).

Mortensen, Ole Henrik
Cricketer. *b:* 29.1.1958, Vejle, Jutland, Denmark. Lower order right hand batsman, right-arm fast medium bowler. *Team* Derbyshire (1983–92, 145 matches).
Career batting
145–159–89–639–74*–9.12–0–*ct* 43
Bowling 9673–411–23.53–15–1–6/27
He represented Denmark commencing 1975, appearing in the ICC Trophy in 1979 and 1986.

Morter, Frank William
Amateur. *b:* 14.8.1897, Down, Kent. *d:* 20.12.1958, Five Ways, Birmingham, after a road accident. Lower order right-hand batsman, right-arm medium fast bowler. *Team* Warwickshire (1922, 3 matches).
Career batting
3–5–2–13–8–4.33–0–*ct* 0
Bowling 138–3–46.00–0–0–2/5

Mortimer, Harry
Professional. *b:* 23.11.1872, Sculcoates, Yorkshire. *d:* 18.7.1953, King's Norton, Birmingham. Lower order batsman, wicket-keeper. *Team* Worcestershire (1904, 1 match).
Career batting
1–2–0–11–7–5.50–0–*ct* 0

Mortimer, John
Amateur. *b:* 13.1.1911, Peterculter, Aberdeenshire, Scotland. *d:* 22.3.1967, Aberdeen, Scotland. Lower order right-hand batsman, off break bowler. *Team* Scotland (1932–33).
Career batting
2–3–0–20–18–6.66–0–*ct* 3
Bowling 154–8–19.25–0–0–3/67

Mortimer, Sir Ralph George Elphinstone
Amateur. *b:* 7.7.1869, Newcastle upon Tyne, Northumberland. *d:* 3.5.1955, Milbourne Hall, Northumberland. Middle order right-hand batsman. *Sch* Harrow. *Team* Lancashire (1891, 1 match).
Career batting
1–1–1–22–22*–no av–0–*ct* 0
He did not appear in any first-class matches whilst at Cambridge. He also played for Northumberland (1893–1906).

Mortimore, John Brian
Professional. *b:* 14.5.1933, Southmead, Bristol. Lower order right-hand batsman, off break bowler. *Team* Gloucestershire (1950–75, 594 matches). *Tours* MCC to Australia and New Zealand 1958/9, to India 1963/4, to East Africa 1963/4; Brown to East Africa 1961/2 (not first-class); Gloucestershire to Bermuda 1962 (not first-class). *Tests* England (1958/9 to 1964, 9 matches).
Career batting
640–989–122–15891–149–18.32–4–*ct* 348
Bowling 41904–1807–23.18–75–8–8/59
Test batting
9–12–2–243–73*–24.30–0–*ct* 3
Bowling 733–13–56.38–0–0–3/36
He hit 1,000 runs in a season five times (best 1,425, av 26.88, in 1963) and took 100 wickets in a season three times (best 113, av 18.28, in 1959). He achieved the 'double' in three seasons. He captained Gloucestershire 1965 to 1967.

Mortlock, Harry Clive
Amateur. *b:* 13.10.1892, Hackney, London. *d:* 29.3.1963, Brentwood, Essex. Lower order batsman, slow left-arm bowler. *Sch* Brentwood and Felsted. *Team* Essex (1912–21, 4 matches).
Career batting
4–4–0–32–26–8.00–0–*ct* 6
Bowling 380–7–54.28–1–0–5/104

Mortlock, William
Professional. *b:* 18.7.1832, Kennington, London. *d:* 23.1.1884, Brixton, London. Opening or middle order right-hand batsman, right-arm medium pace, later lob, bowler, long stop. *Team* Surrey (1851–70, 138 matches). *Tour* Stephenson to Australia 1861/2.
Career batting
191–330–35–5528–106–18.73–3–*ct* 85
Bowling 2615–147–17–78–7–2–7/42
He also played for Buckinghamshire (1866).

Morton, A. F. M. (*see under* Mathie-Morton, A. F.)

Morton, Arthur
Professional. *b:* 27.3.1882, Salford, Lancashire. *d:* 21.2.1970, Sheffield, Yorkshire. Lower order right-hand batsman, right-arm fast medium bowler. *Team* Derbyshire (1901, 1 match).
Career batting
1–2–0–0–0–0.00–0–*ct* 0
Bowling 14–0

Morton, Arthur
Professional. *b:* 7.5.1883, Mellor, Derbyshire. *d:* 19.12.1935, Mellor, Derbyshire. Middle order right-hand batsman, right-arm medium pace off break bowler. *Team* Derbyshire (1903–26, 350 matches).
Career batting
357–623–56–10957–131–19.32–6–*ct* 128
Bowling 22352–981–22.78–63–11–9/71
He hit 1,000 runs in a season once: 1,089, av 25.32, in 1914 and took 100 wickets in a season twice (best 116, av 22.67, in 1910). His best bowling was 9/71 for Derbyshire v Nottinghamshire at Blackwell in 1911. After leaving County cricket he umpired in first-class matches (1927–35) and in one Test match in 1928.

Morton, Geoffrey Dalgleish
Professional. *b:* 27.7.1922, Acton, Middlesex. Lower order right-hand batsman, right-arm medium fast bowler. *Team* Middlesex (1950, 2 matches).
Career batting
3–3–2–1–1–1.00–0–*ct* 3
Bowling 146–0
His final first-class match was for MCC in 1952. An excellent soccer player, he kept goal for Watford, Exeter City and Southend.

Morton, John
Amateur. *b:* 17.8.1895, Drapers Field, Coventry, Warwickshire. *d:* 28.5.1966, Leamington Spa, Warwickshire. Middle order right-hand batsman. *Sch* King Henry VIII, Coventry. *Team* Warwickshire (1929–30, 9 matches).
Career batting
9–14–0–162–38–11.57–0–*ct* 4

Morton, Malcolm James Henry
Amateur. *b:* 13.5.1910, West Southbourne, Hampshire. Opening/middle order right-hand batsman, slow left-arm bowler. *Sch* Marlborough. *Team* Cambridge U (1931).
Career batting
1–2–0–3–2–1.50–0–*ct* 0

Morton, Philip Howard
Amateur. *b:* 20.6.1857, Tatterford, Norfolk. *d:* 13.5.1925, Boscombe, Hampshire. Lower order right-hand batsman, right-arm fast bowler, good close field. *Sch* Rossall. *Teams* Cambridge U (1877–80, blue 1878, 1879 and 1880); Surrey (1884, 2 matches).
Career batting
31–45–18–346–39*–12.81–0–*ct* 14
Bowling 2019–139–14.52–14–2–7/45
His final first-class match was for Cambridge University Past and Present in 1886. He also played for Norfolk (1881–83). Being in the scholastic profession limited his appearances in first-class matches after leaving Cambridge.

Morton, William
Cricketer. *b:* 21.4.1961, Stirling, Scotland. Lower order left-hand batsman, slow left-arm bowler. *Teams* Scotland (1982–88); Warwickshire (1984–85, 10 matches).
Career batting
13–12–2–57–13*–5.70–0–*ct* 11
Bowling 1003–29–34.58–0–0–4/40

Moseley, Ezra Alphonsa
Cricketer. *b:* 5.1.1958, Waldrons Village, Christ Church, Barbados. Lower order right-hand batsman, right-arm fast medium bowler. *Teams* Glamorgan (1980–86, 35 matches); Barbados (1981/2 to 1990/1); Eastern Province (1984/5); Northern Transvaal (1991/2). *Tours* West Indian XI to South Africa 1982/3, 1983/4; West Indies to Pakistan 1990/1; Rest of World to England 1990. *Tests* West Indies (1989/90, 2 matches).
Career batting
76–100–18–1431–70*–17.45–0–*ct* 21
Bowling 6506–279–23.31–11–1–6/23
Test batting
2–4–0–35–26–8.75–0–*ct* 1
Bowling 261–6–43.50–0–0–2/70
A back injury forced him to leave County cricket after 1981, but he soon recovered. He returned briefly to play for Glamorgan in 1986, when Javed Miandad was injured.

Moseley, Hallam Reynold
Cricketer. *b:* 28.5.1948, Providence, Christ Church, Barbados. Lower order right-hand batsman, right-arm fast medium bowler. *Teams* Barbados (1969 to 1971/2); Somerset (1971–82, 205 matches). *Tour* Barbados to England 1969.
Career batting
213–217–94–1533–67–12.46–0–*ct* 78
Bowling 13668–557–24.53–16–1–6/34

Moses, Eric Claude
(changed name to Murray)
Amateur. *b:* 18.7.1893, Johannesburg, South Africa. *d:* 10.7.1971, Durban, South Africa. Middle order right-hand batsman, off break bowler. *Sch* Repton. *Teams* Derbyshire (1911, 3 matches); Transvaal (1912/3 to 1922/3).
Career batting
11–18–1–125–31–7.35–0–*ct* 10
Bowling 291–17–17.11–0–0–4/32
He played for Derbyshire with still another season ahead of him at Repton.

Moses, Geoffrey Haydn
Cricketer. *b:* 24.9.1952, Mountain Ash, Glamorgan. Tail end left-hand batsman, right-arm fast medium bowler. *Team* Cambridge U (1974, blue).
Career batting
3–4–2–37–24*–18.50–0–*ct* 0
Bowling 176–9–19.55–1–0–5/31

Mosey, Stuart David Houlden
Amateur. *b:* 28.11.1937, Keighley, Yorkshire. Lower order right-hand batsman, right-arm fast medium bowler. *Team* Cambridge U (1959).
Career batting
2–2–1–17–17*–17.00–0–*ct* 0
Bowling 203–1–203.00–0–0–1/42
He is the brother of Don Mosey, the radio commentator and author.

Mosley, Henry
Professional. *b:* 8.3.1850, Kildwick, Skipton, Yorkshire. *d:* 29.11.1933, Crossland Moor, Huddersfield, Yorkshire. Lower order right-hand batsman, left-arm fast bowler. *Team* Yorkshire (1881, two matches).
Career batting
3–5–1–1–1–0.25–0–*ct* 1
Bowling 65–4–16.25–0–0–3/12

Moss, Alan Edward
Professional. *b:* 14.11.1930, Tottenham, Middlesex. Tail end right-hand batsman, right-arm fast medium bowler. *Team* Middlesex (1950–63, 307 matches). *Tours* MCC to West Indies 1953/4, 1959/60, to Pakistan 1955/6; Norfolk to Jamaica 1956/7; Howard to India 1956/7; Cavaliers to South Africa 1960/1. *Tests* England (1953/4 to 1960, 9 matches).
Career batting
382–410–171–1671–40–6.99–0–*ct* 143
Bowling 27035–1301–20.78–65–13–8/31
Test batting
9–7–1–61–26–10.16–0–*ct* 1
Bowling 626–21–29.80–0–0–4/35
He took 100 wickets in a season five times (best 136, av 13.72, in 1960). His final first-class match was for Free Foresters in 1968.

Moss, Edward Henry
Amateur. *b:* 25.5.1911, Godden Green, Kent. *d:* 31.3.1944. Rimbach, Fulda, Germany. Brother of R. F. (Europeans). Attacking middle order right-hand batsman, good field. *Sch* Malvern. *Team* Oxford U (1933–34).
Career batting
5–10–0–206–50–20.60–0–*ct* 2
His County cricket was for Berkshire (1938–39). He represented Oxford at golf.

Moss, Ernest
Professional. *b:* 25.11.1894, Mountain Ash, Glamorgan. Lower order right-hand batsman, right-arm fast bowler. *Team* Glamorgan (1923, 1 match).
Career batting
1–2–0–15–10–7.50–0–*ct* 1
Bowling 70–2–35.00–0–0–2/70

Moss, John
Professional. *b:* 7.2.1864, Clifton, Nottinghamshire. *d:* 10.7.1950, Keyworth, Nottinghamshire. Brother-in-law of J. Butler (Nottinghamshire). Middle order right-hand batsman, right-arm medium pace bowler. *Team* Nottinghamshire (1892, 1 match). *Tours* Brackley to West Indies 1904/5 (as umpire); MCC to New Zealand 1906/7 (as umpire).
Career batting
1–2–0–2–1–1.00–0–*ct* 0
He was a first-class umpire (1899–1929), standing in 11 Test matches (1902–21).

Moss, Rev Reginald Heber
Amateur. *b:* 24.2.1868, Huyton, Lancashire. *d:* 19.3.1956, Bridport, Dorset. Lower order right-hand batsman, right-arm fast, later medium pace, bowler. *Sch* Radley. *Teams* Oxford U (1887–89, blue 1889); Worcestershire (1925, 1 match).
Career batting
16–28–10–123–18*–6.83–0–*ct* 11
Bowling 886–25–35.44–0–0–4/9
His first-class career is a curiosity – his final match was for Worcestershire v Gloucestershire in May 1925, but his penultimate game had taken place in August 1893 – Liverpool and District v Australians. He also played for Bedfordshire (1901–09) and Herefordshire (1907). He also won a blue for athletics.

Motley, Arthur
Amateur. *b:* 5.2.1858, Osmondthorpe Hall, Yorkshire. *d:* 28.9.1897, Canning Town, Essex. Middle or lower order right-hand batsman, right-arm fast

bowler. *Teams* Yorkshire (1879, 2 matches); Wellington (1886/7 to 1888/9).
Career batting
7–10–2–106–58*–13.25–0–*ct* 1
Bowling 135–7–19.28–0–0–4/48

He was regarded as one of the fastest bowlers in England, but by some his bowling was looked upon as a pure throw. He emigrated to Australia in the autumn of 1879 and later to New Zealand.

Mottram, Thomas James
Cricketer. *b:* 7.9.1945, Liverpool, Lancashire. Tail end right-hand batsman, right-arm medium pace bowler. *Team* Hampshire (1972–76, 35 matches).
Career batting
35–35–18–95–15*–5.58–0–*ct* 11
Bowling 2677–111–24.11–4–0–6/63

Motz, Richard Charles
Amateur. *b:* 12.1.1940, Christchurch, New Zealand. Aggressive lower order right-hand batsman, right-arm fast bowler. *Team* Canterbury (1957/8 to 1968/9). *Tours* New Zealand to South Africa 1961/2, to Australia 1961/2, 1967/8 to England 1965, 1969, to India and Pakistan 1964/5. *Tests* New Zealand (1961/2 to 1969, 32 matches).
Career batting
142–225–21–3494–103*–17.12–1–*ct* 41
Bowling 11767–518–22.71–24–4–8/61
Test batting
32–56–3–612–60–11.54–0–*ct* 9
Bowling 3148–100–31.48–5–0–6/63

On his first tour of England in 1965, he headed the Test bowling averages and took most wickets in first-class matches – 54, av 22.98; in 1969 he was suffering from a displaced vertebra and although appearing in all three Tests, achieved little. His injury resulted in his retirement from first-class cricket after the tour.

Moulder, John Hardie
Professional. *b:* 29.9.1881, Richmond, Surrey. *d:* 13.10.1933, Johannesburg, South Africa. Middle order right-hand batsman, off break bowler. *Teams* Surrey (1902–06, 24 matches); London County (1904); Transvaal (1909/10 to 1912/13).
Career batting
36–52–6–757–70–16.45–0–*ct* 13
Bowling 413–14–29.50–0–0–3/33

Moulding, Roger Peter
Cricketer. *b:* 3.1.1958, Enfield, Middlesex. Middle order right-hand batsman, leg break bowler. *Sch* Haberdashers' Aske's. *Teams* Middlesex (1977, 1 match); Oxford U (1978–83, blue all six years).
Career batting
47–79–9–1344–80*–19.20–0–*ct* 17
Bowling 22–0

He captained Oxford in 1981. No other player has appeared in the University match six times, there being an agreed restriction until recent times.

Moule, Alfred Samuel
Professional. *b:* 31.7.1894, West Ham, Essex. *d:* 5.2.1973, Shoreham-by-Sea, Sussex. Middle order right-hand batsman. *Team* Essex (1921–24, 17 matches).
Career batting
17–31–5–317–64–12.19–0–*ct* 5
Bowling 6–0

He also played for Devon (1931–37). A good soccer player, he appeared for Millwall, Norwich City and Watford.

Moule, Harry George
Amateur. *b:* 23.12.1921, Brinton Park, Kidderminster, Worcestershire. Attractive opening right-hand batsman. *Team* Worcestershire (1952, 1 match).
Career batting
1–2–0–102–57–51.00–0–*ct* 0

Moule, Judge William Henry
Amateur. *b:* 31.1.1858, Brighton, Melbourne, Victoria, Australia. *d:* 24.8.1939, St Kilda, Melbourne, Victoria, Australia. Grandfather of D. O. Hay (Oxford U). Lower order right-hand batsman, right-arm medium pace bowler, good deep field. *Team* Victoria (1878/9 to 1885/6, 4 matches). *Tour* Australia to England 1880. *Test* Australia (1880, 1 match).
Career batting
9–15–3–137–34–11.41–0–*ct* 7
Bowling 106–5–21.20–0–0–3/23
Test batting
1–2–0–40–34–20.00–0–*ct* 1
Bowling 23–3–7.66–0–0–3/23

Although he played very little first-class cricket, he batted and bowled well in the Oval Test of 1880.

Mounsey, Joseph Thomas
Professional. *b:* 30.8.1871, Heeley, Sheffield, Yorkshire. *d:* 6.4.1949, Ockford Ridge, Godalming, Surrey. Steady middle order right-hand batsman, right-arm medium pace bowler. *Team* Yorkshire (1891–97, 95 matches).
Career batting
95–147–21–1963–64–15.57–0–*ct* 47
Bowling 476–13–36.61–0–0–3/58

Mounteney, Arthur
Professional. *b:* 11.2.1883, Loughborough, Leicestershire. *d:* 1.6.1933, Leicester. Son of Arthur sen (Leicestershire, pre first-class). Attractive middle order right-hand batsman. *Team* Leicestershire (1911–24, 144 matches).
Career batting
144–267–12–5306–153–20.80–6–*ct* 53
Bowling 504–17–29.64–0–0–3/38

A noted soccer player, he appeared for Leicester Fosse, Birmingham City, Preston North End and Grimsby Town.

Mountford, Peter Neville George
Amateur. *b:* 21.6.1940, Birmingham. Lower order right-hand batsman, right-arm medium fast bowler. *Sch* Bromsgrove. *Team* Oxford U (1962–63, blue 1963).
Career batting
18–27–11–111–22*–6.93–0–*ct* 5
Bowling 1606–40–40.15–1–0–7/47

Moxon, Howard
Amateur. *b:* 23.3.1940, Elsecar, Yorkshire. Middle order right-hand batsman, right-arm medium pace bowler. *Team* Cambridge U (1960).
Career batting
1–2–0–24–23–12.00–0–*ct* 0
He won a blue for soccer.

Moxon, Martyn Douglas
Cricketer. *b:* 4.5.1960, Stairfoot, Barnsley, Yorkshire. Brother-in-law of P. R. Hart (Yorkshire). Opening right-hand batsman, right-arm medium pace bowler. *Teams* Yorkshire (1981–92, 201 matches); Griqualand West (1982/3 to 1983/4). *Tours* England to West Indies 1984/5, to Australia 1984/5 (not first-class), 1987/8 (not first-class), to Sharjah (not first-class) 1984/5, to New Zealand 1987/8; England B to Sri Lanka 1985/6; England A to West Indies 1991/2 (not first-class); Yorkshire to Windward Islands 1986/7. *Tests* England (1986–89, 10 matches).
Career batting
236–401–28–15234–218*–40.84–33–*ct* 185
Bowling 1474–28–52.64–0–0–3/24
Test batting
10–17–1–455–99–28.43–0–*ct* 10
Bowling 30–0
He hit 1,000 runs in a season eight times (best 1,669, av 46.26, in 1991). His highest score was 218* for Yorkshire v Sussex at Eastbourne in 1990. He was appointed captain of Yorkshire in 1990. He was captain of England A in 1991/2 but broke his thumb before any of the main fixtures of the tour took place. He scored 116 in the second innings of his first-class debut, Yorkshire v Essex at Headingley in 1981.

Moylan, Adrian Charles David
Cricketer. *b:* 26.6.1955, Weston-super-Mare, Somerset. Opening left-hand batsman, slow left-arm bowler. *Sch* Clifton. *Team* Cambridge U (1976–77, blue 1977).
Career batting
5–9–0–176–29–19.55–0–*ct* 1
Bowling 3–0

Moylan-Jones, Admiral Roger Charles
Cricketer. *b:* 18.4.1940, Torquay, Devon. Middle order right-hand batsman, off break bowler. *Team* Combined Services (1964).
Career batting
1–2–0–34–31–17.00–0–*ct* 0
Bowling 36–2–18.00–0–0–2/36
His County cricket was for Devon (1959–75).

Mubarak, Aziz Mohamed
Cricketer. *b:* 4.7.1951, Colombo, Ceylon. Opening right-hand batsman, right-arm medium off break bowler. *Team* Cambridge U (1978–80, blue all three years).
Career batting
24–38–2–765–105–21.25–1–*ct* 14
Bowling 6–0

Mucklow, Peter
Cricketer. *b:* 5.11.1949, Edgbaston, Birmingham. Middle order right-hand batsman, wicket-keeper. *Sch* Shrewsbury. *Team* Oxford U (1970).
Career batting
2–4–0–48–32–12.00–0–*ct* 1
His County cricket was for Shropshire (1968–69).

Mudassar Nazar
Cricketer. *b:* 6.4.1956, Lahore, Pakistan. Son of Nazar Mohammad (Pakistan), brother of Mubashir Nazar (Lahore). Sound opening right-hand batsman, right-arm medium pace bowler. *Teams* Lahore (1971/2 to 1974/5); Universities (1974/5); Habib Bank (1975/6); PIA (1975/6 to 1977/8); United Bank (1978/9 to 1987/8). *Tours* Pakistan to Sri Lanka 1975/6, 1985/6, to Australia 1976/7, 1978/9, 1981/2, 1983/4, 1984/5 (not first-class), 1986/7 (not first-class), 1988/9, to England 1978, 1979 (World Cup), 1982, 1983 (World Cup), 1987, to New Zealand 1978/9, 1984/5, 1988/9, to India 1983/4, 1986/7, to Sharjah (not first-class) 1983/4, 1984/5, 1985/6, 1986/7, 1988/9, to West Indies 1987/8; Rest of World to England 1988, 1989, 1990, 1991, 1992. *Tests* Pakistan (1976/7 to 1988/9, 76 matches).
Career batting
219–354–33–14078–241–43.85–42–*ct* 141
Bowling 5221–152–34.34–2–0–6/32
Test batting
76–116–8–4114–231–38.09–10–*ct* 48
Bowling 2532–66–38.36–1–0–6/32
On his first tour to England in 1978 he hit 677 runs, av 33.85, in first-class matches and appeared in all three Tests, though not being successful in these. This pattern was repeated in 1982 when he topped the first-class averages with 825 runs, av 82.50, but scored few runs in the Tests; in the second Test however he took 6 wickets for 32 in the second innings and with ten wickets in the series headed the bowling table. His final tour to England was in 1987 when he proved very successful as a batsman, with 231 Test runs, av 57.75, but bowled less. He hit 1,000 in a season in Pakistan three times (best 1,110, av 85.38, in 1982/3). He scored the slowest 100 in first-class cricket (557 minutes) for Pakistan v England at Lahore in 1977/8. He also played for Cheshire (1980–88). His highest score was 241 for United Bank v

Rawalpindi at Lahore in 1981/2, and in Tests 231 v India at Hyderabad in 1982/3 when he shared a partnership of 451 with Javed Miandad which equalled the record Test partnership (since beaten).

Muddiah, Venatappa Musandra
Amateur. *b:* 8.6.1929, Bangalore, India. Tail end right-hand batsman, right-arm medium pace off break bowler. *Teams* Services (1949/50 to 1960/1); Mysore (1951/2); Hyderabad (1953/4). *Tour* India to England 1959. *Tests* India (1959/60 to 1960/1, 2 matches).
Career batting
61–71–13–805–67–13.87–0–*ct* 62
Bowling 4159–175–23.76–10–1–8/54
Test batting
2–3–1–11–11–5.50–0–*ct* 0
Bowling 134–3–44.66–0–0–2/40
He achieved very little on his tour to England, being unable to adapt to turf wickets and also missing many matches through illness. His final first-class match was for Indian Air Force in 1962/3.

Mudge, Harold
Professional. *b:* 14.2.1914, Stanmore, Sydney, New South Wales, Australia. Middle order right-hand batsman, leg break and googly bowler. *Teams* New South Wales (1935/6 to 1939/40, 14 matches); Leicestershire (1937, 1 match). *Tours* Cahn to Ceylon 1936/7, to New Zealand 1938/9 (not in first-class matches).
Career batting
18–34–2–1060–118–33.12–1–*ct* 15
Bowling 1106–25–44.24–2–0–6/42
His last first-class match in England was for Sir J. Cahn's XI in 1938.

Mudie, William
Professional. *b:* 26.4.1836, Kennington, London. *d:* 25.1.1871, Vauxhall, London. He died of paralysis of the brain. Steady middle order right-hand batsman, right-hand slow round-arm or under-arm bowler. *Team* Surrey (1856–65, 37 matches). *Tour* Stephenson to Australia 1861/2.
Career batting
41–64–11–666–79–12.56–0–*ct* 28
Bowling 760–47+1–16.17–3–0–7/61

Mugliston, Francis Hugh
Amateur. *b:* 7.6.1886, Singapore. *d:* 3.10.1932, Westminster, London. Lower order right-hand batsman, right-arm slow medium bowler. *Sch* Rossall. *Teams* Lancashire (1906–08, 7 matches); Cambridge U (1906–08, blue last two years).
Career batting
33–55–1–874–109–16.18–1–*ct* 16
Bowling 301–4–75.25–0–0–3/32
His final first-class match was for H. D. G. Leveson-Gower's XI in 1911. A noted soccer player, he appeared as left back for Cambridge and the Corinthians. He also represented Cambridge at golf.

Muir-Mackenzie, Sir Kenneth Augustus
Amateur. *b:* 26.6.1845, Delvine, Perthshire, Scotland. *d:* 22.5.1930, Regent's Park, London. Brother-in-law of J. F. F. Horner (Gentlemen of England) and Q. Hogg (British Guiana). Middle order batsman. *Sch* Charterhouse. *Team* MCC (1870).
Career batting
1–2–0–21–17–10.50–0–*ct* 0

Mulholland, Hon Godfrey John Arthur Murray Lyle
Amateur. *b:* 3.10.1892, Ballyscunion Park, Bellaghy, Co Londonderry, Ireland. *d:* 1.3.1948, St Pancras, London. Brother of H. G. H. (Cambridge U). Middle order batsman. *Sch* Eton. *Team* Cambridge U (1912).
Career batting
1–2–1–9–6–9.00–0–*ct* 1

Mulholland, Hon Sir Henry George Hill
Amateur. *b:* 20.12.1888, Ballyscunion Park, Bellaghy, Co Londonderry, Ireland. *d:* 5.3.1971, Bellaghy, Co Londonderry, Ireland. Brother of G. J. A. M. L. (Cambridge U). Middle order right-hand batsman, slow right-arm bowler. *Sch* Eton. *Teams* Cambridge U (1911–14, blue 1911–13); Ireland (1911). *Tour* Incogniti to USA 1913 (not first-class).
Career batting
32–55–1–1642–153–30.40–4–*ct* 37
Bowling 1217–51–23.86–2–0–5/9
He captained Cambridge in 1913. It was intended that he should play in the 1914 University Match, but in deference to an agreement of some 50 years previous he stood down. He was MP for Co Down 1921–29 and Ards Div 1929–45 and Speaker of the Northern Ireland House of Commons from 1929 to 1945.

Mulla, Hormasji Furdunji
Amateur. *b:* 4.5.1885, Bombay, India. Middle order right-hand batsman, wicket-keeper. *Team* Parsis (1907/8 to 1915/16). *Tour* India to England 1911.
Career batting
28–46–1–781–151–17.35–1–*ct* 26–*st* 13
He achieved very little on his visit to England.

Mullally, Alan David
Cricketer. *b:* 12.7.1969, Southend-on-Sea, Essex. Lower order right-hand batsman, left-arm fast medium bowler. *Teams* Western Australia (1987/8 to 1989/90, 15 matches); Hampshire (1988, 1 match); Leicestershire (1990–92, 40 matches); Victoria (1990/1, 1 match); *Tour* Western Australia to India 1989/90.
Career batting
57–55–17–314–34–8.26–0–*ct* 13
Bowling 4701–119–39.50–1–0–5/119
He lived in Australia during his schooldays, thus qualifying for Western Australia by residence.

Mullins, Mark Francis
Cricketer. *b:* 15.11.1966, Gravesend, Kent. Lower order right-hand batsman, right-arm medium pace bowler. *Team* Cambridge U (1989).
Career batting
6–4–1–3–3–1.00–0–*ct* 1
Bowling 438–10–43.80–1–0–5/77

Mumford, George
Professional. *b:* 1.2.1845, Ealing, Middlesex. *d:* 12.11.1877, Ealing, Middlesex. He died of consumption. Lower order right-hand batsman, left-hand fast round-arm bowler. *Team* Middlesex (1867–72, 2 matches).
Career batting
4–7–1–12–4*–2.00–0–*ct* 1
Bowling 39–1–39.00–0–0–1/6

Muncer, Bernard Leonard
Professional. *b:* 23.10.1913, Hampstead, London. *d:* 18.1.1982, Camden Town, London. Aggressive middle order right-hand batsman, leg break and googly bowler, changed to off breaks about 1947, good slip. *Teams* Middlesex (1933–46, 82 matches); Glamorgan (1947–54, 224 matches).
Career batting
317–478–64–8646–135–20.88–4–*ct* 144
Bowling 15783–755–20.90–44–8–9/62
He hit 1,000 runs in a season once – 1,097, av 24.37, in 1952, in which year he also completed the 'double'. He took 100 wickets in a season five times (best 159, av 17.27, in 1948). His final first-class match was for MCC in 1957. His best bowling was 9/62 for Glamorgan v Essex at Brentwood at 1948. After retiring from first-class cricket he became Head Coach at Lord's.

Muncey, George
Professional. *b:* 27.12.1835, Mildenhall, Suffolk. *d:* 14.3.1883, Cambridge. Middle order right-hand batsman, right-hand slow under-arm bowler, long stop. *Team* Cambridge Town Club (1860–61); Cambridgeshire (1861–66, 8 matches).
Career batting
11–20–1–197–37–10.36–0–*ct* 1
Bowling 174–9+1–19.33–0–0–4/27

Munden, Donald Francis Xavier
Professional. *b:* 17.10.1934, Leicester. Brother of P. A. (Leicestershire) and V. S. (Leicestershire). Lower order right-hand batsman, leg break bowler. *Team* Leicestershire (1960–61, 7 matches).
Career batting
7–13–0–98–34–7.53–0–*ct* 2
Bowling 13–0

Munden, Marwood Mintern
Amateur. *b:* 13.6.1885, Ilminster, Somerset. *d:* 8.3.1952, Eastcombe, Gloucestershire. Middle order batsman. *Sch* Weymouth. *Team* Somerset (1908, 3 matches).
Career batting
3–5–0–31–11–6.20–0–*ct* 0

Munden, Paul Anthony
Professional. *b:* 5.11.1938, Barrow-upon-Soar, Leicester. Brother of D. F. X. (Leicestershire) and V. S. (Leicestershire). Lower order left-hand batsman, off break bowler. *Team* Leicestershire (1957–64, 47 matches).
Career batting
47–85–6–1193–77–15.10–0–*ct* 17

Munden, Victor Stanislaus
Professional. *b:* 2.1.1928, Leicester. Brother of P. A. (Leicestershire) and D. F. X. (Leicestershire). Middle order left-hand batsman, slow left-arm bowler. *Team* Leicestershire (1946–57, 228 matches).
Career batting
232–376–43–5786–102–17.37–2–*ct* 82
Bowling 10603–371–28.57–14–1–6/33
He hit 1,259 runs, av 29.97, in 1952. Between 1951 and 1956 he appeared in 159 consecutive matches for Leicestershire.

Munds, Arthur Edward
Professional. *b:* 20.1.1870, Lydd, Kent. *d:* 19.7.1940, High Wycombe, Buckinghamshire. Brother of Raymond (Kent). Lower order left-hand batsman, left-arm medium pace bowler. *Team* Kent (1896, 1 match).
Career batting
1–2–0–10–9–5.00–0–*ct* 0
Bowling 16–0

Munds, Raymond
Professional. *b:* 28.12.1882, Lydd, Kent. *d:* 29.7.1962, Radnor Park, Folkestone, Kent. Brother of A. E. (Kent). Lower order left-hand batsman, right-arm slow bowler, wicket-keeper. *Team* Kent (1902–08, 7 matches).
Career batting
7–11–1–121–29–12.10–0–*ct* 3

Mungrue, Altaff Ali
Cricketer. *b:* 25.8.1934, Port of Spain, Trinidad. Middle order right-hand batsman, right-arm medium pace or off break bowler. *Team* Combined Services (1964).
Career batting
2–4–0–102–51–25.50–0–*ct* 0
Bowling 129–8–16.12–0–0–4/58

Munir Malik
Amateur. *b:* 10.7.1934, Leih, India. Lower order right-hand batsman, right-arm fast medium bowler. *Teams* Punjab (1956/7 to 1957/8); Rawalpindi (1958/9 to 1964/5); Services (1962/3 to 1963/4); Karachi (1965/6). *Tours* Pakistan Eaglets to Ceylon 1960/1; Pakistan to England 1962. *Tests* Pakistan (1959/60 to 1962, 3 matches).

Munn, John Shannon

Career batting
49–71–10–675–72–11.06–0–*ct* 23
Bowling 4285–197–21.75–14–4–8/154
Test batting
3–4–1–7–4–2.33–0–*ct* 1
Bowling 358–9–39.77–1–0–5/128

Although he appeared in two Tests on the 1962 tour, his bowling achieved only modest results – in first-class matches 43 wickets, av 39.93.

Munn, John Shannon
Amateur. *b:* 6.6.1880, Harbour Grace, St John's, Newfoundland, Canada. *d:* 24.2.1918. He was lost on board SS *Florizel* wrecked 7 miles from Cape Race en route between Newfoundland and New York. Lower order batsman, left-arm bowler. *Sch* Forest School. *Team* Oxford U (1900–01, blue 1901).
Career batting
10–13–7–55–13*–9.16–0–*ct* 2
Bowling 711–24–29.62–0–0–4/39

Munn, Reginald George
Amateur. *b:* 20.8.1869, Madresfield, Worcestershire. *d:* 12.4.1947, Virginia Water, Surrey. Middle order right-hand batsman. *Sch* Haileybury and St Edwards, Oxford. *Team* Worcestershire (1900, 1 match).
Career batting
1–1–0–2–2–2.00–0–*ct* 0

Munnion, Henry
Professional. *b:* 23.1.1849, Ardingly, Sussex. *d:* 24.6.1904, Ardingly, Sussex. Lower order right-hand batsman, left-arm medium pace bowler. *Team* Sussex (1877–80, 2 matches).
Career batting
2–3–0–0–0–0.00–0–*ct* 1
Bowling 28–2–14.00–0–0–2/15

Munro, Hector Campbell
Amateur. *b:* 24.10.1920, Calcutta, India. Middle order right-hand batsman, leg break bowler. *Sch* Rugby. *Team* Oxford U (1947).
Career batting
1–2–0–0–0–0.00–0–*ct* 1

Munro, Michael John
Cricketer. *b:* 15.3.1969, Clifton, Bristol. Lower order right-hand batsman, left-arm medium pace bowler. *Sch* Clifton. *Team* Oxford U (1989).
Career batting
1–1–1–12–12*–no av–0–*ct* 0
Bowling 21–1–21.00–0–0–1/15

Munt, Harry Raymond
Amateur. *b:* 31.10.1902, Paddington, London. *d:* 27.12.1965, Derby. He died following a road accident. Middle order right-hand batsman, right-arm fast bowler. *Sch* Westminster. *Team* Middlesex (1923, 1 match). *Tours* Cahn to Argentine 1929/30, to North America 1933 (not first-class).
Career batting
2–1–0–0–0–0.00–0–*ct* 0
Bowling 64–1–64.00–0–0–1/28

He was on the Committee of Nottinghamshire CCC 1941–62.

Munton, Timothy Alan
Cricketer. *b:* 30.7.1965, Melton Mowbray, Leicestershire. Lower order right-hand batsman, right-arm medium fast bowler. *Team* Warwickshire (1985–92, 135 matches). *Tours* England A to Pakistan and Sri Lanka 1990/91, to West Indies 1991/2. *Tests* England (1992, 2 matches).
Career batting
147–150–58–892–47–9.69–0–*ct* 52
Bowling 10839–392–27.65–15–3–8/89
Test batting
2–2–1–25–25*–25.00–0–*ct* 0
Bowling 200–4–50.00–0–0–2/22

He took 78 wickets, av 28.89, in 1990.

Muralitharan, Muttiah
Cricketer. *b:* 17.4.1972, Kandy, Ceylon. Lower order right-hand batsman, off break bowler. *Team* Tamil Union (1991/2). *Tour* Sri Lanka to England 1991.
Career batting
16–17–5–103–24*–8.58–0–*ct* 11
Bowling 1191–49–24.30–3–0–6/52

He achieved little success in the three first-class matches in which he played during the 1991 tour to England. His first-class debut was for Central Province in 1989/90.

Murch, Stewart Nigel Clifford
Cricketer. *b:* 27.6.1944, Warrnambool, Victoria, Australia. Lower order right-hand batsman, right-arm fast bowler. *Teams* Victoria (1966/7 to 1969/70, 9 matches); Northamptonshire (1968, 1 match).
Career batting
10–15–3–215–64–17.91–0–*ct* 5
Bowling 868–17–51.05–0–0–3/49

Murch, William Henry
Professional. *b:* 18.11.1867, Bristol, Gloucestershire. *d:* 1.5.1928, Bristol, Gloucestershire. Lower order right-hand batsman, right-arm medium pace bowler, good deep field. *Teams* Gloucestershire (1889–03, 77 matches); London County (1901–04).
Career batting
88–147–14–1337–58–10.05–0–*ct* 40–*st* 1
Bowling 5103–207–24.65–11–4–8/68

His final first-class match was for W. G. Grace's XI in 1906. He also played for Wiltshire (1895).

Murdin, John Vernon
Professional. *b:* 16.8.1891, Wollaston, Northamptonshire. *d:* 11.4.1971, Stonehouse, Gloucestershire. Tail end right-hand batsman, right-arm fast bowler. *Team* Northamptonshire (1913–27, 171 matches).

Career batting
173–279–69–1800–90*–8.57–0–*ct* 111
Bowling 12324–455–27.08–28–4–8/81

Murdoch, William Lloyd
Amateur. *b:* 18.10.1854, Sandhurst, Australia. *d:* 18.2.1911, Melbourne, Victoria, Australia. He was seized with apoplexy whilst attending a Test match between Australia and South Africa. Stylish middle order right-hand batsman, wicket-keeper. *Teams* New South Wales (1875/6 to 1893/4, 19 matches); Sussex (1893–99, 137 matches); London County (1901–04). *Tours* Australia to England 1878, 1880, 1882, 1884, 1890, to North America 1878; Read to South Africa 1891/2. *Tests* Australia (1876/7 to 1890, 18 matches); England (1891/2, 1 match).
Career batting
391–679–48–16953–321–26.86–19–*ct* 219–*st* 24
Bowling 430–10–43.00–0–0–2/11
Test batting
19–34–5–908–211–31.31–2–*ct* 14–*st* 1

He was most successful on his tours to England, being the equal of any of the batsmen on each tour and three times exceeding 1,000 runs (best 1,582, av 31.64, in 1882). In all he exceeded 1,000 runs in an English season seven times. His highest score in England was 286* for Australians v Sussex 1882, but he hit 211 for Australia in the Oval Test of 1884 and his highest score of 321 for New South Wales v Victoria at Sydney in 1881/2.

He captained the Australians on the tours of 1880, 1882, 1884 and 1890 and led Australia in 16 Tests. He captained Sussex from 1893 to 1899, dropping out of the side midway through the last season.

Murdoch-Cozens, Alan James
(changed name from Murdoch)
Amateur. *b:* 17.9.1893, Wallingford, Berkshire. *d:* 23.7.1970, Malvern, Worcestershire. Middle order right-hand batsman. *Sch* Brighton. *Team* Sussex (1919, 4 matches).
Career batting
4–7–0–124–56–17.71–0–*ct* 0

He also played for Berkshire (1911–13).

Murdock, Ernest George
Amateur. *b:* 14.11.1864, Keynsham, Somerset. *d:* 18.5.1926, Bower Ashton, Somerset. He died whilst waiting to bat in a local club match. Middle or lower order right-hand batsman, occasional bowler, wicket-keeper. *Teams* Somerset (1885, 2 matches); Gloucestershire (1889, 3 matches).
Career batting
5–10–1–40–14–4.44–0–*ct* 4
Bowling 11–1–11.00–0–0–1/11

He last played for Somerset (not first-class) in 1888.

Murgatroyd, Henry
Professional. *b:* 19.9.1853, New Swindon, Wiltshire. *d:* 15.3.1905, Portsmouth, Hampshire. Lower order right-hand batsman, right-arm fast bowler. *Team* Hampshire (1883, 1 match).
Career batting
1–2–1–2–1*–2.00–0–*ct* 0
Bowling 7–0

Murley, Anthony Jonathan
Cricketer. *b:* 7.8.1957, Radlett, Hertfordshire. Middle order right-hand batsman, right-arm medium pace bowler. *Sch* Oundle. *Team* Cambridge U (1981).
Career batting
6–11–0–152–48–13.81–0–*ct* 2
Bowling 1–0

He represented Cambridge at golf and rugby fives.

Murphy, Anthony John
Cricketer. *b:* 6.8.1962, Withington, Manchester, Lancashire. Tail end right-hand batsman, right-arm medium fast bowler. *Teams* Lancashire (1985–88, 13 matches); Central Districts (1985/6); Surrey (1989–92, 55 matches). *Tours* Lancashire to Jamaica 1986/7, 1987/8.
Career batting
72–71–28–225–38–5.23–0–*ct* 12
Bowling 6841–174–39.31–5–0–6/97

He also played for Cheshire (1984–88). He took 65 wickets, av 30.89, in 1989.

Murphy, Desmond James
Amateur. *b:* 6.7.1896, Armagh, Ireland. *d:* 30.1.1982, Cabinteely, Co Dublin, Ireland. Lower order right-hand batsman, leg break and googly bowler. *Team* Ireland (1920).
Career batting
1–2–0–0–0–0.00–0–*ct* 0
Bowling 49–0

Murphy, Dr Edward Gordon
Amateur. *b:* 6.12.1921, Sheffield, Yorkshire. Middle order right-hand batsman, right-arm medium pace bowler. *Team* Combined Services (1948).
Career batting
2–4–0–24–11–6.00–0–*ct* 1

Murphy, Patrick
Amateur. *d: circa* 1935, Dublin, Ireland. Lower order right-hand batsman, right-arm medium pace bowler. *Team* Ireland (1909–12).
Career batting
2–4–2–26–10–13.00–0–*ct* 1
Bowling 117–4–29.25–0–0–2/92

Murray, Anton Ronald Andrew
Amateur. *b:* 30.4.1922, Grahamstown, South Africa. Middle order right-hand batsman, right-arm slow medium bowler. *Team* Eastern Province (1947/8 to 1955/6). *Tours* South Africa to Australia and New Zealand 1952/3, to England 1955. *Tests* South Africa

(1952/3 to 1953/4, 10 matches).
Career batting
64–100–10–2685–133–29.83–4–*ct* 31
Bowling 4683–188–24.90–8–2–7/30
Test batting
10–14–1–289–109–22.23–1–*ct* 3
Bowling 710–18–39.44–0–0–4/169

He bowled usefully on his 1955 tour to England, but had limited opportunities and did not appear in the Tests.

Murray, Athol Leslie
Amateur. *b:* 29.6.1901, Mill Hill, Middlesex. *d:* 10.1.1981, Grasmere, Westmorland. Middle order right-hand batsman, right-arm medium fast bowler. *Sch* St Georges, Harpenden. *Team* Warwickshire (1922, 11 matches).
Career batting
11–17–0–161–33–9.47–0–*ct* 3
Bowling 49–2–24.50–0–0–2/29

He appeared in the Seniors' match whilst at Oxford, but no first-class matches. An excellent golfer, he represented the University.

Murray, Bruce Alexander Grenfell
Amateur. *b:* 18.9.1940, Johnsonville, Wellington, New Zealand. Sound opening right-hand batsman, leg break bowler, good field. *Team* Wellington (1958/9 to 1972/3). *Tours* New Zealand to Australia 1967/8, to England 1969, to India and Pakistan 1969/70. *Tests* New Zealand (1967/8 to 1970/1, 13 matches).
Career batting
102–187–11–6257–213–35.55–6–*ct* 124
Bowling 868–30–28.93–0–0–4/43
Test batting
13–26–1–598–90–23.92–0–*ct* 21
Bowling 0–1–0.00–0–0–1/0

He topped the first-class batting averages on the 1969 tour with 800 runs, av 40.00, but achieved little in the Tests. His highest score was 213 for Wellington v Otago at Dunedin in 1968/9.

Murray, David Anthony
Cricketer. *b:* 29.5.1950, Murray's Gap, Westbury Road, St Michael, Bridgetown, Barbados. Father of R. L. Hoyte (Barbados). Middle order right-hand batsman, wicket-keeper. *Team* Barbados (1970/1 to 1981/2). *Tours* West Indies to England 1973, 1980, to India, Pakistan and Sri Lanka 1974/5, to Australia 1975/6, 1979/80, 1981/2, to Pakistan 1980/1, to New Zealand 1979/80, to India and Sri Lanka 1978/9; West Indian XI to South Africa 1982/3, 1983/4. *Tests* West Indies (1977/8 to 1981/2, 19 matches).
Career batting
114–176–30–4503–206*–30.84–7–*ct* 292–*st* 31
Bowling 11–0
Test batting
19–31–3–601–84–21.46–0–*ct* 57–*st* 5

He came to England in 1973 as reserve wicket-keeper and did not play in any Tests; in 1980 he came in the same capacity and played in only six first-class matches and no Tests. His highest score was 206* for West Indies v East Zone at Jamshedpur in 1978/9.

Murray, Deryck Lance
Amateur. *b:* 20.5.1943, Port of Spain, Trinidad. Son of L. H. (Trinidad), cousin of C. E. (Trinidad). Sound middle order right-hand batsman, occasional leg break bowler, wicket-keeper. *Teams* Trinidad (1960/1 to 1980/1); Cambridge U (1965–66, blue both years); Nottinghamshire (1966–69, 97 matches); Warwickshire (1972–75, 58 matches). *Tours* West Indies to England 1963, 1973, 1975 (World Cup), 1976, 1979 (World Cup), 1980, to India and Ceylon 1966/7, to India, Pakistan and Sri Lanka 1974/5, to Australia 1975/6, 1979/80, to New Zealand 1979/80; West Indian XI to England 1964; Rest of World to England 1970. *Tests* West Indies (1963–80, 62 matches).
Career batting
367–554–85–13291–166*–28.33–10–*ct* 740–*st* 108
Bowling 367–5–73.40–0–0–2/50
Test batting
62–96–9–1993–91–22.90–0–*ct* 181–*st* 8

He hit 1,000 runs in a season three times (best 1,358, av 30.17, in 1966). He appeared in all the Tests on each of his four tours to England, being the principal wicket-keeper – he batted usefully on each visit but played no major innings. He captained Cambridge in 1966 and West Indies in one Test. He was the first Secretary of the West Indian Cricketers Association and an influential figure at the time of Packer's World Series Cricket. He also won a blue for soccer.

Murray, E. C. (*see under* Moses, E. C.)

Murray, John Congreve
Amateur. *b:* 21.8.1882, Edinburgh, Scotland. *d:* 23.9.1917, near Poelcappelle, Belgium. Middle order batsman. *Sch* Edinburgh Academy. *Team* Scotland (1909–13).
Career batting
3–5–0–78–34–15.60–0–*ct* 2

Murray, John Matthew
Amateur. *b:* 23.6.1873, Aberdeen, Scotland. *d:* 31.5.1916, aboard HMS *Queen Mary* at the Battle of Jutland. Middle order right-hand batsman, right-arm fast bowler. *Team* Royal Navy (1913).
Career batting
1–2–0–29–29–14.50–0–*ct* 0

Murray, John Thomas, MBE
Professional. *b:* 1.4.1935, North Kensington, London. Lower order right-hand batsman, right-arm medium pace bowler, wicket-keeper. *Team* Middlesex (1952–75, 508 matches). *Tours* MCC to New Zealand 1960/1, to India and Pakistan 1961/2, to Australia and

New Zealand 1962/3, 1965/6, to South Africa 1964/5, to Ceylon and Pakistan 1968/9; Cavaliers to Jamaica 1963/4, 1969/70; Rest of World to Barbados 1966/7; Robins to South Africa 1972/3, 1973/4. *Tests* England (1961–67, 21 matches).
Career batting
635–936–136–18872–142–23.59–16-*ct* 1270-*st* 257
Bowling 243–6–40.50–0–0–2/10
Test batting
21–28–5–506–112–22.00–1–*ct* 52–*st* 3

He hit 1,000 runs in a season six times (best 1,160, av 28.29, in 1965). In 1957 he took 104 dismissals as a wicket-keeper thus completing the 'double' of 1,000 runs and 100 dismissals in a season. He also exceeded 100 dismissals in 1960. On his retirement he held the record for the most dismissals in first-class cricket. He was an England selector 1977–78.

Murray, John Tinline
Amateur. *b:* 1.12.1892, Norwood, Adelaide, South Australia. *d:* 19.9.1974, Stirling, South Australia. Middle order right-hand batsman, right-arm medium pace bowler. *Team* South Australia (1911/12 to 1925/6, 17 matches). *Tours* AIF to England 1919, to South Africa 1919/20.
Career batting
48–79–5–1964–152–26.54–4–*ct* 38
Bowling 695–12–57.91–0–0–2/63

He hit 793 runs, av 24.03, during 1919 with the Australian Forces.

Murray, Michael Patrick
Amateur. *b:* 14.5.1930, Westminster, London. Sound opening right-hand batsman. *Team* Middlesex (1952–53, 5 matches).
Career batting
10–19–1–216–44–12.00–0–*ct* 7
Bowling 3–0

His first-class debut was for Combined Services in 1949 and his final first-class match was for MCC in 1963. The Chairman of the TCCB Finance Committee since 1989, he chaired a TCCB Working Party into the state of first-class cricket in England. The Working Party's recommendations were ratified in 1992, resulting in major changes for the 1993 season. He has been Chairman of Middlesex CCC since 1984.

Murray-Willis, Peter Earnshaw
Amateur. *b:* 14.7.1910, Castle Bromwich, Warwickshire. Opening/middle order right-hand batsman. *Sch* St Georges, Harpenden. *Teams* Worcestershire (1935–36, 7 matches); Northamptonshire (1938–46, 22 matches).
Career batting
29–47–2–467–54–10.37–0–*ct* 3

He captained Northamptonshire in 1946.

Murray-Wood, William
Amateur. *b:* 30.6.1917, Dartford, Kent. *d:* 21.12.1968, Southwark, London. Hard hitting middle order right-hand batsman, leg break bowler. *Sch* Mill Hill. *Teams* Oxford U (1936–38, blue 1936); Kent (1936–53, 77 matches). *Tours* Combined Oxford and Cambridge Team to Jamaica 1938/9; Surridge to Bermuda 1961 (not first-class).
Career batting
106–177–15–2262–107–13.96–3–*ct* 45
Bowling 3850–100–38.50–2–0–6/29

He captained Kent in 1952 and 1953. His last first-class match was for MCC in 1956. He scored 106* on debut for Oxford U v Gloucestershire at Oxford in 1936.

Murrell, Harry Robert
Professional. *b:* 19.11.1879, Hounslow, Middlesex. *d:* 15.8.1952, West Wickham, Kent. Lower order right-hand batsman, left-arm bowler, wicket-keeper. *Teams* Kent (1899–1905, 27 matches); Middlesex (1905–26, 342 matches).
Career batting
378–528–62–6663–96*–14.29–0–*ct* 565–*st* 269
Bowling 174–0

He was Middlesex scorer 1946–52. A noted soccer player, he appeared for Arsenal.

Murrills, Timothy James
Cricketer. *b:* 22.12.1953, Ecclesall, Sheffield, Yorkshire. Middle order right-hand batsman, right-arm medium pace bowler, wicket-keeper. *Sch* The Leys. *Team* Cambridge U (1973–76, blue 1973, 1974 and 1976).
Career batting
37–69–4–996–67–15.32–0–*ct* 18
Bowling 4–0

His County cricket was for Dorset (1974–81). He captained Cambridge in 1976.

Murtagh, Andrew Joseph
Cricketer. *b:* 6.5.1949, Dublin, Ireland. Lower order right-hand batsman, right-arm medium pace bowler. *Teams* Hampshire (1973–77, 26 matches); Eastern Province (1973/4).
Career batting
27–47–5–640–65–15.23–0–*ct* 9
Bowling 489–6–81.50–0–0–2/46

Musgrave, John Musgrave
(also known as Tattersall-Musgrave)
Amateur. *b:* 13.2.1845, Armley, Yorkshire. *d:* 12.3.1885, Beverley, Yorkshire. Lower order right-hand batsman, right-hand fast round-arm bowler. *Sch* Pocklington. *Team* Cambridge U (1868).
Career batting
1–1–0–0–0–0.00–0–*ct* 2
Bowling 19–1–19.00–0–0–1/19

Musgrove, Henry Alfred
Amateur. *b:* 27.11.1858, Surbiton, Surrey. *d:* 2.11.1931, Darlinghurst, Sydney, New South Wales, Australia. Middle order right-hand batsman. *Team* Victoria (1881/2 to 1887/8, 3 matches). *Tours* Australia to England 1896 (acting as manager, but he played in 2 matches). *Test* Australia (1884/5, 1 match).
Career batting
7–12–0–99–62–8.25–0–*ct* 3
Bowling 18–0
Test batting
1–2–0–13–9–6.50–0–*ct* 0

Mushet, John
Amateur. *b:* 10.10.1875, Edinburgh, Scotland. *d:* 10.3.1965, Edinburgh, Scotland. Lower order batsman. *Team* Scotland (1912).
Career batting
1–2–0–3–2–1.50–0–*ct* 0

Mushtaq Ahmed
Cricketer. *b:* 28.6.1970, Sahiwal, Pakistan. Lower order right-hand batsman, leg break and googly bowler. *Teams* Multan (1986/7 to 1990/1); United Bank (1987/8 to 1990/1). *Tours* Pakistan to Sharjah (not first-class) 1988/9, 1989/90, 1990/1, 1991/2, to India 1989/90 (not first-class), to Australia 1989/90, 1991/2, to Australia and New Zealand (World Cup) 1991/2, to England 1992. *Tests* Pakistan (1989/90 to 1992, 8 matches).
Career batting
53–58–9–537–75–10.95–0–*ct* 30
Bowling 4896–197–24.85–11–2–9/93
Test batting
8–11–2–49–11–5.44–0–*ct* 1
Bowling 716–19–37.68–0–0–3/32
He had a successful first tour to England in 1992, appearing in all five Tests, and his leg breaks proved a very effective contrast to the swing bowling of Wasim and Waqar. His best bowling was 9/93 for Multan v Peshawar at Sahiwal in 1990/1.

Mushtaq Ali, Syed
Amateur. *b:* 17.12.1914, Indore, India. Brother of S. Ishtiaq Ali (Holkar), father of S. Gulrez Ali (Madhya Pradesh). Opening or middle order right-hand batsman, slow left-arm bowler. *Teams* Central India (1934/5 to 1939/40); Muslims (1935/6 to 1944/5); Maharashtra (1940/1); Gujarat (1940/1); Holkar (1941/2 to 1954/5); Madhya Bharat (1955/6); Uttar Pradesh (1956/7); Madhya Pradesh (1957/8); *Tours* Vizianagram to India and Ceylon 1930/1; India to England 1936, 1946, to Ceylon 1944/5; Holkar to Ceylon 1947/8. *Tests* India (1933/4 to 1951/2, 11 matches).
Career batting
226–384–16–13213–233–35.90–30–*ct* 160
Bowling 4754–162–29.34–6–2–7/108
Test batting
11–20–1–612–112–32.21–2–*ct* 7
Bowling 202–3–67.33–0–0–1/45
On the 1936 tour he hit 1,078 runs, av 25.06, and in 1946 673 runs, av 24.03. A brilliant batsman on his day, he was very inconsistent in England – his 1936 aggregate contained four centuries, including one in the second Test. His highest score was 233 for Holkar v United Provinces at Indore in 1947/8. His first-class debut was for Indians v Europeans in Madras in 1930/1 and his final match for Bombay Chief Minister's XI in 1963/4.

Mushtaq Mohammad
Amateur. *b:* 22.11.1943, Junagadh, India. Brother of Hanif (Pakistan), Sadiq (Pakistan), Wazir (Pakistan) and Raees (Karachi), uncle of Shoaib (Pakistan), Asif (PIA) and Shahid (PIA). Versatile middle order right-hand batsman, leg break and googly bowler. *Teams* Karachi (1956/7 to 1967/8); PIA (1960/1 to 1979/80); Northamptonshire (1964–77, 262 matches). *Tours* Pakistan to India 1960/1, to England 1962, 1967, 1971, 1974, 1975 (World Cup), to Ceylon 1972/3, to Australia and New Zealand 1972/3, 1978/9, to Australia and West Indies 1976/7; Pakistan Eaglets to England 1963; Commonwealth to India 1964/5; Rest of World to England 1966, 1970, 1985, to Barbados 1966/7; Cavaliers to West Indies 1969/70; PIA to Zimbabwe 1981/2. *Tests* Pakistan (1958/9 to 1978/9, 57 matches).
Career batting
502–843–104–31091–303*–42.07–72–*ct* 349
Bowling 22789–936–24.34–39–2–7/18
Test batting
57–100–7–3643–201–39.17–10–*ct* 42
Bowling 2309–79–29.22–3–0–5/28
Of his four Test tours to England the outstanding one was his first in 1962, when he headed both Test and first-class averages with 401 runs, av 44.55, and 1,614 runs, av 41.38. In both 1967 and 1971 his appearances were virtually confined to the Tests, since he remained with Northamptonshire for each season. In all he hit 1,000 runs in a season in England 12 times (best 1,949, av 59.06, in 1972) as well as three times overseas. His highest score was 303* for Karachi Blues v Karachi University at Karachi in 1967/8 and of his four double centuries the only one in England was 204* for Northamptonshire v Hampshire at Northampton in 1976. If his published date of birth is correct, he was the youngest Test cricketer at 15 years 124 days in 1958/9. He captained Northamptonshire from 1975 to 1977 and Pakistan in 19 Tests, but none in England. He also played for Northumberland (1980), Staffordshire (1982–83) and Shropshire (1984–85).

Musson, Major-General Alfred Henry
Amateur. *b:* 14.8.1900, Clitheroe, Lancashire. Brother of F. W. (Lancashire) and R. G. (Combined

Services). Middle order right-hand batsman, right-arm medium pace bowler. *Sch* Tonbridge. *Team* Army (1925).
Career batting
1–2–0–51–27–25.50–0–*ct* 0
Bowling 42–0

Musson, Francis William
Amateur. *b:* 31.5.1894, Clitheroe, Lancashire. *d:* 2.1.1962, Chatham, Kent. Brother of A. H. (Army) and R. G. (Combined Services). Middle order right-hand batsman, wicket-keeper. *Sch* Tonbridge. *Team* Lancashire (1914–21, 16 matches).
Career batting
19–31–1–539–75–17.96–0–*ct* 13–*st* 4
Bowling 57–0
He played in the Cambridge Freshmen's match of 1914. His final first-class match was for Civil Service in 1927.

Musson, Rowland Gascoigne
Amateur. *b:* 7.2.1912, Clitheroe, Lancashire. *d:* 24.8.1943, Clovely, Devon. He was killed whilst serving with Coastal Command. Brother of A. H. (Army) and F. W. (Lancashire). Middle order batsman, useful bowler. *Sch* Tonbridge. *Team* Combined Services (1937).
Career batting
1–1–0–24–24–24.00–0–*ct* 0
He appeared for Lancashire in some non-first-class wartime matches and in the 1930s in service matches in Egypt. A well-known pilot, he made several world record flights.

Muzzell, Robert Kendal
Cricketer. *b:* 23.12.1945, Stutterheim, Cape Province, South Africa. Son of Kendal (Border), brother of P. J. (Border). Lower order right-hand batsman, leg break bowler. *Teams* Western Province (1964/5 to 1967/8); Transvaal (1968/9 to 1977/8); Eastern Province (1974/5). *Tour* South African Universities to England 1967.
Career batting
75–128–12–4052–238*–34.93–7–*ct* 49
Bowling 2028–61–33.24–1–0–6/69
His highest score was 238* for Transvaal B v Natal B at Johannesburg in 1969/70.

Myburgh, Claude John
Amateur. *b:* 4.7.1911, Cheltenham, Gloucestershire. *d:* 10.10.1987, Inholmes Court, Hartley Wintney, Hampshire. Lower order right-hand batsman, right-arm fast medium bowler. *Sch* St Lawrence College, Ramsgate. *Team* Army (1933).
Career batting
1–1–1–13–13*–no av–0–*ct* 1
Bowling 70–1–70.00–0–0–1/12
His County cricket was for Devon (1933–34).

Mycroft, Frank
Professional. *b:* 30.6.1873, Furnace, Shirland, Derbyshire. *d:* 26.9.1900, Leicester. Tail end left-hand batsman, wicket-keeper. *Team* Derbyshire (1894–95, 2 matches).
Career batting
2–4–0–7–4–1.75–0–*ct* 4
He first played for Derbyshire (not first-class) in 1893.

Mycroft, Thomas
Professional. *b:* 28.3.1848, Brimington, Derbyshire. *d:* 13.8.1911, Mickleover, Derbyshire. Half brother of William (Derbyshire). Lower order left-hand batsman, right-arm medium pace bowler, wicket-keeper. *Team* Derbyshire (1877–85, 16 matches).
Career batting
24–46–14–249–24*–7.78–0–*ct* 43–*st* 16
Bowling 16–0
He was on the ground staff at Lord's for 22 years, his last first-class match being for MCC in 1887. He umpired in many first-class matches (1897–1905), standing in two Test matches (1899–1902).

Mycroft, William
Professional. *b:* 1.2.1841, Brimington, Derbyshire. *d:* 19.6.1894, Derby. Half brother of Thomas (Derbyshire). Lower order right-hand batsman, left-arm fast bowler. *Team* Derbyshire (1873–85, 78 matches).
Career batting
138–234–86–791–44*–5.34–0–*ct* 94
Bowling 10441–863–12.09–87–28–9/25
He took 100 wickets in a season twice (157, av 12.27, in 1877 being his highest aggregate). His best season was 1875 when he topped the bowling averages with 90 wickets, av 7.37. By some his action was regarded as doubtful, especially when he bowled his fast yorker, which gained him many wickets. His best bowling was 9/25 for Derbyshire v Hampshire at Southampton in 1876. His final first-class match was for MCC in 1886. He umpired in first-class matches after retiring from County cricket.

Myers, Dr Arthur Thomas
Amateur. *b:* 16.4.1851, Keswick, Cumberland. *d:* 10.1.1894, Marylebone, London. Middle order right-hand batsman. *Sch* Cheltenham. *Team* Cambridge U (1870).
Career batting
1–2–0–13–7–6.50–0–*ct* 0
He won a blue for royal tennis.

Myers, Edwin Bertram
Professional. *b:* 5.7.1888, Blackheath, Kent. *d:* 15.9.1916, near Adanac, France. He was killed in action. Middle order right-hand batsman, slow left-arm bowler. *Team* Surrey (1910–14, 11 matches).
Career batting
11–17–1–217–40–13.56–0–*ct* 3
Bowling 211–3–70.33–0–0–1/10

Myers, Hubert
Professional. *b:* 2.1.1875, Yeadon, Yorkshire. *d:* 12.6.1944, Hobart, Tasmania, Australia. Lower order right-hand batsman, right-arm medium pace bowler. *Teams* Yorkshire (1901–10, 201 matches); Tasmania (1913/4 to 1924/5, 4 matches).
Career batting
210–304–48–4753–91–18.56–0–*ct* 110
Bowling 7664–303–25.29–13–1–8/81
After losing his place in the Yorkshire side he emigrated to Tasmania and was for many years coach to the Tasmanian Cricket Association.

Myers, Matthew
Professional. *b:* 12.4.1847, Yeadon, Yorkshire. *d:* 8.12.1919, Yeadon, Yorkshire. Middle order right-hand batsman, right-hand fast or slow round-arm bowler, deep field. *Team* Yorkshire (1876–78, 21 matches).
Career batting
24–44–6–600–49–15.78–0–*ct* 11
Bowling 20–0

Myles, Simon David
Cricketer. *b:* 2.6.1966, Mansfield, Nottinghamshire. Middle order right-hand batsman, right-arm medium pace bowler. *Teams* Sussex (1987, 2 matches); Warwickshire (1988, 4 matches).
Career batting
6–10–1–130–39–14.44–0–*ct* 1
Bowling 93–0
He represented Hong Kong in the ICC Trophy competition in 1986. He also played for Cumberland (1990) and Staffordshire (1992).

Mynn, Alfred
Amateur. *b:* 19.1.1807, Twisden, Goudhurst, Kent. *d:* 1.11.1861, Southwark, London. Brother of W. P. (Kent). Fine, powerful right-hand middle order batsman, right-hand fast round-arm bowler. *Teams* Kent (1834–59, 90 matches); Sussex (1839–47, 4 matches as given man); Hampshire (1844, 1 match as given man).
Career batting
212–395–26–4955–125*–13.42–1–*ct* 125
Bowling 2989–292+741–10.23–92–33–9/?
The greatest all-rounder of his day 'it was considered one of the grandest sights at cricket to see Mynn advance and deliver the ball' (*Scores and Biographies*). He appeared for the Gentlemen against the Players in twenty matches, being for many years the mainstay of the former team. His best bowling was 9 wickets in an innings for Gentlemen of Kent v Gentlemen of England at Lord's in 1842.
His first-class debut was for Gentlemen of Kent in 1832. He also played for Essex (pre first-class, 1846) and Suffolk (1847).

Mynn, Walter Parker
Amateur. *b:* 24.11.1805, Twisden, Goudhurst, Kent. *d:* 17.10.1878, Peckham, London. Brother of Alfred (Kent). Steady opening right-hand batsman, good long stop. *Team* Kent (1835–48, 45 matches).
Career batting
76–141–9–1107–41–8.38–0–*ct* 29
Bowling 17–1 + 1–17.00–0–0–1/17
His final first-class match was for Gentlemen of Kent in 1852, his debut having been for the same team in 1833.

N

Naden, James Rupert
Amateur. *b:* 13.7.1889, Tipton, Staffordshire. *d:* 14.6.1963, Turls Hill, Sedgley, Staffordshire. Lower order right-hand batsman, right-arm fast medium bowler. *Team* Worcestershire (1922, 2 matches).
Career batting
2–3–2–23–16*–23.00–0–*ct* 2
Bowling 136–2–68.00–0–0–2/111

Nadkarni, Rameshchandra Gangaram
Amateur. *b:* 4.4.1933, Nasik, India. Middle order left-hand batsman, slow left-arm bowler, good close field. *Teams* Maharashtra (1951/2 to 1959/60); Bombay (1960/1 to 1967/8). *Tours* India to Ceylon 1956/7, to England 1959, to West Indies 1961/2, to Australia and New Zealand 1967/8; ACC to Pakistan 1961/2; Rest of World to England 1966. *Tests* India (1955/6 to 1967/8, 41 matches).
Career batting
191–266–46–8880–283*–40.36–14–*ct* 140
Bowling 10686–500–21.37–19–1–6/17
Test batting
41–67–12–1414–122*–25.70–1–*ct* 22
Bowling 2559–88–29.07–4–1–6/43
He proved a useful all-rounder of the 1959 tour, appearing in four Tests, and in first-class matches hitting 945 runs, av 23.62, and taking 55 wickets, av 28.41. His three double centuries were all scored in India, the highest being 283* for Bombay v Delhi at Bombay in 1960/1. His final first-class match was for ACC in 1971/2. He hit 1,190 runs, av 70.00, in India in 1962/3.

Naeem Ahmed
Cricketer. *b:* 20.9.1952, Karachi, Pakistan. Middle order right-hand batsman, slow left-arm bowler. *Teams* Karachi (1969/70 to 1971/2); Universities (1972/3 to 1974/5); National Bank (1974/5); PIA (1975/6 to 1986/7); United Bank (1977/8). *Tours* Pakistan to Sri Lanka 1975/6, to England 1978; PIA to Zimbabwe 1981/2.
Career batting
129–167–42–3653–127–29.22–3–*ct* 60

Bowling 9957–359–27.73–20–3–8/49

He played in only two first-class matches on the 1978 tour to England. He played for Pakistan in one-day international matches.

Nagenda, John
Cricketer. *b:* 25.4.1938, Gahim, Ruanda Urundi. Lower order right-hand batsman, right-arm fast medium bowler. *Team* East Africa (1975). *Tour* East Africa to England 1975.
Career batting
1–2–2–5–5*–no av–0–*ct* 1
Bowling 91–3–30.33–0–0–2/17

Naik, Sudhir Sakharam
Cricketer. *b:* 21.2.1945, Bombay, India. Cousin of A. D. (Bombay). Steady opening or middle order right-hand batsman. *Team* Bombay (1966/7 to 1977/8). *Tours* India to England 1974; CCI to Ceylon 1972/3. *Tests* India (1974 to 1974/5, 3 matches).
Career batting
85–139–15–4376–200*–35.29–7–*ct* 42
Bowling 52–3–17.33–0–0–1/0
Test batting
3–6–0–141–77–23.50–0–*ct* 0

He hit 730 runs, av 40.55, on the 1974 tour to England, but played in only one Test. His highest score was 200* for Bombay v Baroda at Bombay in 1973/4.

Nana, P. G.
Cricketer. *b:* 1933, Northern Rhodesia. Lower order right-hand batsman, slow left-arm bowler. *Team* East Africa (1973/4 to 1975). *Tour* East Africa to England 1975.
Career batting
2–4–0–21–16–5.25–0–*ct* 1
Bowling 170–4–42.50–0–0–3/61

Nanan, Nirmal
Cricketer. *b:* 19.8.1951, Preysal Village, Couva, Trinidad. Uncle of Rangy (West Indies). Middle order right-hand batsman, leg break and googly bowler. *Teams* South Trinidad (1969/70 to 1983/4); Nottinghamshire (1971–80, 32 matches); Central Trinidad (1972/3).
Career batting
35–64–5–925–72–15.67–0–*ct* 22
Bowling 322–9–35.77–0–0–3/12

Naoomal Jaoomal Makhija
Amateur. *b:* 17.4.1904, Karachi, India. *d:* 28.7.1980, Bombay, India. Father of Hari Naoomal (Karachi). Steady opening right-hand batsman, leg break bowler. *Teams* Northern India (1926/7); Hindus (1927/8 to 1936/7); Sind (1932/3 to 1944/5). *Tours* India to England 1932; Vizianagram's XI to India and Ceylon 1930/1. *Tests* India (1932 to 1933/4, 3 matches).
Career batting
84–143–16–4140–203*–32.44–7–*ct* 43
Bowling 2975–108–27.54–6–0–5/18
Test batting
3–5–1–108–43–27.00–0–*ct* 0
Bowling 68–2–34.00–0–0–1/4

He batted well on his 1932 visit to England scoring 1,297 runs, av 30.88. His only double century was 203* for Sind v Nawanagar at Karachi in 1938/9. After the partition of India he was appointed National Coach to Pakistan.

Napier, Duncan Robertson
Amateur. *b:* 6.10.1871, Croydon, Surrey. *d:* 24.10.1898, Kensington, London. He died from injuries received whilst serving on the Indian frontier. Middle order left-hand batsman, slow left-arm bowler, good deep field. *Sch* Harrow. *Team* MCC (1892).
Career batting
2–3–0–50–33–16.66–0–*ct* 1

Napier, Guy Greville
Amateur. *b:* 26.1.1884, City of London. *d:* 25.9.1915, Loos, France. He died of wounds. Tail end right-hand batsman, right-arm medium pace bowler. *Sch* Marlborough. *Teams* Cambridge U (1904–07, blue all four years); Middlesex (1904–13, 21 matches); Europeans (1907–10). *Tour* MCC to North America 1905.
Career batting
81–127–29–854–59–8.71–0–*ct* 84
Bowling 7787–365–21.33–23–5–9/17

He had a splendid record in the University match, taking 31 wickets, av 17.55, in his four appearances. After leaving Cambridge he took up a Government appointment in Quetta, India and his County cricket was therefore very restricted. His best bowling was 9/17 for Europeans v Parsis at Poona in 1909/10.

Napier, Rev John Russell
Amateur. *b:* 5.1.1859, Preston, Lancashire. *d:* 12.3.1939, Sidley, Sussex. Lower order right-hand batsman, right-hand fast round-arm bowler, good mid off. *Sch* Marlborough. *Teams* Cambridge U (1881); Lancashire (1888, 2 matches).
Career batting
4–5–1–72–37–18.00–0–*ct* 1
Bowling 245–17–14.41–0–0–4/0

Injury prevented him from obtaining his blue at Cambridge and later he would probably have achieved much in County cricket, had he been able to afford the time.

Napier, Ronald Stuart
Amateur. *b:* 23.10.1935, Cape Town, South Africa. Lower order right-hand batsman, leg break bowler. *Team* Oxford U (1956)
Career batting
1–1–0–0–0–0.00–0–*ct* 1
Bowling 18–0

Napper, Edwin
Amateur. *b:* 26.1.1815, Sparr Farm, Wisborough Green, Sussex. *d:* 8.3.1895, Tismans House, Rudgwick, Sussex. Brother of William (Sussex). Attacking middle order left-hand batsman, right-hand medium pace round-arm bowler. *Team* Sussex (1839–62, 92 matches).
Career batting
128–242–8–2645–83*–11.30–0–*ct* 48
Bowling 330–21+18–15.71–1–0–6/27

He was on the Committees of both Sussex and Surrey Cricket Clubs. He captained Sussex, 1847–62.

Napper, William
Amateur. *b:* 25.8.1816, Sparr Farm, Wisborough Green, Sussex. *d:* 13.7.1897, Brighton, Sussex. Brother of Edwin (Sussex). Middle order left-hand batsman, right-hand slow round-arm bowler. *Team* Sussex (1842–60, 53 matches).
Career batting
63–114–5–945–67–8.66–0–*ct* 34
Bowling 431–24+9–17.95–1–0–5/19

Napper, William Henry
Amateur. *b:* 5.11.1880, Co Wexford, Ireland. *d:* August 1967, Ganges Harbour, Salt Spring Island, British Columbia, Canada. Lower order batsman, slow left-arm bowler. *Sch* Shrewsbury. *Team* Ireland (1908–09). *Tour* Ireland to North America 1909.
Career batting
5–10–1–19–10–2.11–0–*ct* 2
Bowling 225–7–32.14–0–0–4/74

Narayan, Prince Kumar Hitendra Singh
Amateur. *b:* 1.7.1890, Cooch Behar, India. *d:* 7.11.1920, Darjeeling, India. He died of influenza. Son of HH the Maharajah of Cooch Behar (Cooch Behar's XI). Middle order right-hand batsman. *Sch* Eton. *Teams* Somerset (1909–10, 4 matches); Cooch Behar's XI (1918/19).
Career batting
7–11–2–60–16–6.66–0–*ct* 2
Bowling 50–0

He did not appear in any first-class matches whilst at Cambridge.

Naseer Malik
Cricketer. *b:* 1.2.1950, Lyallpur, Pakistan. Lower order right-hand batsman, right-arm fast medium bowler. *Teams* Khairpur (1969/70 to 1972/3); Sind (1972/3 to 1973/4); Karachi (1973/4); National Bank (1974/5 to 1981/2). *Tours* Pakistan to England 1974, 1975 (World Cup); Pakistan Under 25 to Sri Lanka 1973/4.
Career batting
72–81–12–765–55–11.08–0–*ct* 46
Bowling 5053–203–24.89–15–0–8/49

He played in only seven matches on the 1974 tour of England, taking 20 wickets, av 26.90. He played for Pakistan in one-day internationals.

Nash, Albert
(known as Jack Nash)
Professional. *b:* 18.9.1873, Blean, Kent. *d:* 6.12.1956, Battersea, London. Lower order right-hand batsman, off break bowler. *Team* Glamorgan (1921–22, 36 matches).
Career batting
36–65–9–315–28–5.62–0–*ct* 6
Bowling 2901–133–21.81–11–2–9/93

He was easily the best bowler for Glamorgan on their debut in the County Championship in 1921, taking 91 wickets, av 18.57; most of his cricket however was played before the County became first-class, making his debut in 1900. His best bowling was 9/93 for Glamorgan v Sussex at Swansea in 1922. He was a first-class umpire (1926–30).

Nash, Edward Montague
Amateur. *b:* 12.4.1902, Gorse Hill, Swindon, Wiltshire. *d:* 9.5.1985, Swindon, Wiltshire. Lower order right-hand batsman, wicket-keeper. *Team* Minor Counties (1936–37).
Career batting
2–4–3–62–45*–62.00–0–*ct* 3

His County cricket was for Wiltshire (1923–50). He played soccer for Swindon and Brentford.

Nash, George
Professional. *b:* 1.4.1850, Oving, Aylesbury, Buckinghamshire. *d:* 13.11.1903, Aylesbury, Buckinghamshire. He died from paralysis. Tail end right-hand batsman, slow left-arm bowler, slip field. *Team* Lancashire (1879–85, 54 matches).
Career batting
58–88–28–347–30–5.78–0–*ct* 37
Bowling 2868–232–12.36–17–5–8/14

He achieved very good bowling figures for Lancashire from 1880 to 1883 (best 62 wickets, av 10.58, in 1882), but his delivery was considered illegal by some and he dropped out of first-class County cricket in 1885, though he later played for Buckinghamshire (1894–1903).

Nash, Malcolm Andrew
Cricketer. *b:* 9.5.1945, Abergavenny, Monmouth. Lower order left-hand batsman, left-arm medium pace bowler. *Team* Glamorgan (1966–83, 335 matches). *Tour* Glamorgan to West Indies 1969/70.
Career batting
336–469–67–7129–130–17.73–2–*ct* 148
Bowling 25698–993–25.87–45–5–9/56

He captained Glamorgan in 1980 and 1981. He suffered the misfortune of being hit for 36 off a single six-ball over, the batsman being G. St A. Sobers for Nottinghamshire v Glamorgan at Swansea in 1968. His best innings analysis was 9/56 for Glamorgan v Hampshire at Basingstoke in 1975. He also played for Shropshire (1984–85).

Nash, Philip Geoffrey Elwin
Amateur. *b:* 20.9.1906, Accrington, Lancashire. *d:* 8.12.1982, Old Basing, Hampshire. Middle order right-hand batsman, right-arm medium pace bowler. *Sch* St Paul's. *Team* Oxford U (1928).
Career batting
1–2–0–16–14–8.00–0–*ct* 0
Bowling 39–0
His County cricket was for Berkshire (1926–30). He won a blue for rugby fives.

Nash, Rev William Wallace Hayward
Amateur. *b:* 22.9.1884, Quedgeley, Gloucester. *d:* 24.7.1971, Minchinhampton, Gloucestershire. Middle order batsman. *Sch* King's, Bruton. *Team* Gloucestershire (1905–06, 3 matches).
Career batting
3–6–1–81–34–16.20–0–*ct* 0
He appeared in the Freshmen's and Seniors' matches at Cambridge, but no first-class games.

Nasim-ul-Ghani
Amateur. *b:* 14.5.1941, Delhi, India. Brother of Anis-ul-Ghani (Karachi) and Tehzib-ul-Ghani (Commercial Bank). Steady middle order left-hand batsman, left-arm medium or slow bowler. *Teams* Karachi (1956/7 to 1972/3); Universities (1958/9); Dacca (1965/6); East Pakistan (1966/7 to 1967/8); PWD (1966/7 to 1971/2); National Bank (1973/4 to 1974/5). *Tours* Pakistan to England 1962, 1967, to Australia and New Zealand 1964/5, to West Indies 1957/8, to India 1960/1, to Australia 1972/3. *Tests* Pakistan (1957/8 to 1972/3, 29 matches).
Career batting
117–175–17–4490–139–28.41–7–*ct* 104
Bowling 8628–343–25.15–23–3–6/24
Test batting
29–50–5–747–101–16.60–1–*ct* 11
Bowling 1959–52–37.67–2–0–6/67
Although appearing in all five Tests on the 1962 tour of England, his returns were modest, his one day of real success being his 101 in the Lord's Test. On the 1967 tour he was not a member of the main touring party, but, being engaged in League cricket in England, he appeared in three matches, including two Tests. If his published date of birth is correct, he made his first-class debut at 15 and his Test debut at 16. He has also played for Staffordshire (1968–78) and played in a first-class match for Minor Counties in 1972. He reappeared for Karachi in 1981/2 in limited overs matches.

Nasir Zaidi, Syed Mohammad
Cricketer. *b:* 25.3.1961, Karachi, Pakistan. Lower order right-hand batsman, leg break bowler. *Team* Lancashire (1983–84, 19 matches).
Career batting
19–22–9–313–51–24.07–0–*ct* 15
Bowling 827–19–43.52–0–0–3/27
He also played for Norfolk (1985–86). He played for Karachi in 1980/1 in limited overs cricket.

Nasiruddin, Shaikh Mohammed
Amateur. *b:* 9.8.1916, Mangrol, India. Son of Abdul Khaliq (Western India), uncle of K. S. Zahid (Saurashtra). Stylish middle order right-hand batsman. *Teams* Northamptonshire (1938–39, 5 matches); Western Indian States (1940/1 to 1941/2); Muslims (1940/1).
Career batting
9–15–1–263–64–18.78–0–*ct* 0
Bowling 7–0
He did not appear in any first-class matches whilst at Cambridge U. He played with his father in the Ranji Trophy, believed to be the first time this had occured in Indian first-class cricket.

Nason, John William Washington
Amateur. *b:* 4.8.1889, Corse Grange, Tewkesbury, Gloucestershire. *d:* 26.12.1916, near Vlamertinghe, Belgium. Opening/middle order right-hand batsman, slow right-arm bowler. *Teams* Sussex (1906–10, 22 matches); Cambridge U (1909–10, blue both years); Gloucestershire (1913–14, 19 matches).
Career batting
57–98–6–1649–139–17.92–1–*ct* 35
Bowling 395–10–39.50–0–0–2/24
He first represented Sussex with two seasons at school still ahead of him – on his first-class debut v Warwickshire at Hastings in 1906, he came into the side as a substitute, but was allowed to bat.

Naumann, Charles Cecil
Amateur. *b:* 27.8.1897, Croydon, Surrey. *d:* 16.12.1946, St Pancras, London. Brother of F. C. G. (Surrey) and J. H. (Sussex). Middle order right-hand batsman. *Sch* Malvern. *Team* Cambridge U (1919).
Career batting
1–1–0–5–5–5.00–0–*ct* 0

Naumann, Frank Charles Gordon
Amateur. *b:* 9.4.1892, Lewisham, London. *d:* 30.10.1947, Cranleigh, Surrey. Brother of C. C. (Cambridge U) and J. H. (Sussex). Middle order right-hand batsman, right-arm medium pace bowler. *Sch* Malvern. *Teams* Oxford U (1912–19, blue 1914 and 1919); Surrey (1919–21, 11 matches).
Career batting
51–84–8–1454–118*–19.13–2–*ct* 22
Bowling 2804–85–32.98–4–1–6/81
In the 1919 University match he appeared for Oxford whilst his brother played for Cambridge. His final first-class match was for H. D. G. Leveson-Gower's XI in 1926.

Naumann, John Harold
Amateur. *b:* 9.9.1893, Lewisham, London. *d:* 6.12.1964, New York, USA. Brother of C. C. (Cambridge U) and F. C. G. (Surrey). Middle order right-

hand batsman, left-arm slow medium bowler. *Sch* Malvern. *Teams* Cambridge U (1913–19, blue 1913 and 1919); Sussex (1925, 17 matches).
Career batting
44–73–8–1391–134*–21.40–1–*ct* 23
Bowling 1142–36–31.72–0–0–4/37

His brother F. C. G. Naumann was opposed to him in the 1919 University match. His final first-class match was for H. D. G. Leveson-Gower's XI in 1928.

Naushad Ali Rizvi
Amateur. *b:* 1.10.1943, Gwalior, India. Opening right-hand batsman, wicket-keeper. *Teams* Karachi (1960/1 to 1974/5); East Pakistan (1966/7 to 1967/8); Rawalpindi (1967/8 to 1969/70); Peshawar (1967/8 to 1972/3); Punjab (1976/7); Services (1976/7 to 1978/9). *Tours* Pakistan Eaglets to England 1963; Pakistan to Australia and New Zealand 1964/5, to England 1971. *Tests* Pakistan (1964/5, 6 matches).
Career batting
83–133–16–4310–158–36.83–9–*ct* 136–*st* 34
Bowling 5–0
Test batting
6–11–0–156–39–14.18–0–*ct* 9

As reserve wicket-keeper on the 1971 tour of England he was required for only eight matches.

Naved Anjum
Cricketer. *b:* 27.7.1963, Lahore, Pakistan. Middle order right-hand batsman, right-arm fast medium bowler. *Teams* Railways (1979/80 to 1983/4); Lahore (1983/4 to 1985/6); United Bank (1984/5 to 1986/7); Habib Bank (1987/8 to 1991/2). *Tours* Pakistan to West Indies 1987/8, to Bangladesh (not first-class) 1988/9, to England 1992. *Tests* Pakistan (1989/90 to 1990/1, 2 matches).
Career batting
116–184–18–4737–159–28.53–6–*ct* 55
Bowling 6595–304–21.69–17–1–9/45
Test batting
2–3–0–44–22–14.66–0–*ct* 0
Bowling 162–4–40.50–0–0–2/57

He appeared in only five first-class matches on the 1992 tour to England and was not required for the Tests. His best bowling was 9/45 for Habib Bank v National Bank at Lahore in 1991/2.

Navle, Janardan Gyanoba
Amateur. *b:* 7.12.1902, Fulgaon, India. *d:* 7.9.1979, Pune, India. Opening or middle order right-hand batsman, wicket-keeper. *Teams* Hindus (1918/9 to 1934/5); Rajputana (1926/7); Central India (1935/6); Holkar (1942/3); Gwalior (1943/4). *Tour* India to England 1932. *Tests* India (1932 to 1933/4, 3 matches).
Career batting
65–107–4–1976–96–19.18–0–*ct* 101–*st* 36
Test batting
2–4–0–42–13–10.50–0–*ct* 1

He was highly praised for his wicket-keeping on the 1932 tour of England and appeared in the single Test.

Nayak, Surendra Vithal
Cricketer. *b:* 20.10.1954, Bombay, India. Stylish middle order left-hand batsman, right-arm medium pace or leg break bowler, good cover point. *Team* Bombay (1976/7 to 1988/9). *Tour* India to England 1982. *Tests* India (1982, 2 matches).
Career batting
68–85–21–1799–100*–28.10–2–*ct* 38
Bowling 4718–133–35.47–4–1–6/65
Test batting
2–3–1–19–11–9.50–0–*ct* 1
Bowling 132–1–132.00–0–0–1/16

He had a modest tour of England in 1982, but appeared in two Tests.

Naylor, John Edward
Professional. *b:* 11.12.1930, Thurcroft, Yorkshire. Lower order right-hand batsman, slow left-arm bowler. *Team* Yorkshire (1953, 1 match).
Career batting
1 match, did not bat–*ct* 1
Bowling 88–0

Naylor, W.
Professional. Lower order batsman, wicket-keeper. *Team* Essex (1906, 1 match).
Career batting
1–2–0–2–2–1.00–0–*ct* 2

Nayudu, Cottari Kanakaiya
Amateur. *b:* 31.10.1895, Nagpur, India. *d:* 14.11.1967, Indore, India. Brother of C. S. (India), C. L. (Hindus) and C. R. (Vizianagram's XI), father of Prakash (Madhya Pradesh), grandfather of V. K. (Madhya Pradesh), uncle of D. D. Govindraj (Hyderabad). Hard hitting middle order right-hand batsman, right-arm medium slow bowler, good field. *Teams* Hindus (1916/7 to 1939/40); Rajputana (1926/7); Hyderabad (1931/2); CP and Berar (1932/3 to 1933/4); Central India (1934/5 to 1937/8); Holkar (1941/2 to 1952/3); Andhra (1953/4); United Provinces (1956/7). *Tours* India to England 1932, 1936; Vizianagram to India and Ceylon 1930/1; Bombay to Ceylon 1925/6; Holkar to Ceylon 1947/8. *Tests* India (1932–36, 7 matches).
Career batting
207–344–15–11825–200–35.94–26–*ct* 171–*st* 1
Bowling 12038–411–29.28–12–2–7/44
Test batting
7–14–0–350–81–25.00–0–*ct* 4
Bowling 386–9–42.88–0–0–3/40

He hit 1,000 runs on both tours to England (best 1,618, av 40.45, in 1932), and led India in their first Test match (at Lord's in 1932) – he captained India in four Tests in all. His highest score was 200 for Holkar v Baroda at Indore in 1945/6. He was later an

Indian Test Selector and Vice-President of the Indian Cricket Board of Control. His final first-class match was for Maharashtra Governor's XI in 1963/4 when he was aged 68. He was also a noted soccer and hockey player.

Nayudu, Cottari Subbanna
Amateur. *b:* 18.4.1914, Nagpur, India. Brother of C. K. (India), C. L. (Hindus) and C. R. (Vizianagram's XI), uncle of Prakash (Madhya Pradesh). Lower order right-hand batsman, leg break and googly bowler, good deep field. *Teams* Central Provinces & Berar (1932/3 to 1933/4); Central India (1934/5 to 1935/6); Hindus (1934/5 to 1944/5); Baroda (1939/40 to 1943/4); Holkar (1944/5 to 1949/50); Bengal (1950/1 to 1951/2); Andhra (1953/4 to 1959/60); Uttar Pradesh (1956/7 to 1958/9); Madhya Pradesh (1960/1). *Tours* India to England 1936, 1946, to Australia 1947/8, to Ceylon 1944/5; Holkar to Ceylon 1947/8. *Tests* India (1933/4 to 1951/2, 11 matches).
Career batting
174–267–25–5786–127–23.90–4–*ct* 144
Bowling 17174–647–26.54–50–13–8/93
Test batting
11–19–3–147–36–9.18–0–*ct* 3
Bowling 359–2–179.50–0–0–1/19

In 1936 he joined the side in June as a late reinforcement, but achieved little. On the 1946 tour, he appeared in two Tests, but was too erratic to be very economical. His first-class debut was in a Trial Match in 1931/2. He also played for Durham (pre first-class, 1956).

Nazir Ali, Syed
Amateur. *b:* 8.6.1906, Jullundur, India. *d:* 18.2.1975, Lahore, Pakistan. Brother of S. Wazir Ali (India), uncle of Khalid Wazir (Pakistan). Attacking opening right-hand batsman, right-hand fast medium bowler. *Teams* Muslims (1923/4 to 1939/40); Southern Punjab (1926/7 to 1941/2); Sussex (1927, 1 match); Patiala (1932/3). *Tour* India to England 1932. *Tests* India (1932 to 1933/4, 2 matches).
Career batting
75–122–8–3440–197–30.17–7–*ct* 48
Bowling 4028–158–25.49–6–0–7/93
Test batting
2–4–0–30–13–7.50–0–*ct* 0
Bowling 83–4–20.75–0–0–4/83

He resided in England for several years commencing 1927 and played much club cricket in the London area. He batted successfully on the 1932 tour to England hitting 1,020 runs, av 31.87, but his bowling was ineffective in first-class matches. His final first-class matches were in Pakistan for Punjab Governor's XI in 1947/8 and Hasan Mahmood's XI in 1953/4.

Neal, John Howard
Amateur. *b:* 18.10.1926, Ditchling, Sussex. Lower order right-hand batsman, wicket-keeper. *Sch* Hurstpierpoint. *Team* Sussex (1951, 1 match).
Career batting
1–2–0–28–23–14.00–0–*ct* 0

Neal, Reginald George
Amateur. *b:* 12.6.1901, Bedminster, Somerset. *d:* 2.10.1964, Boscombe, Hampshire. Middle order batsman, useful bowler. *Team* Gloucestershire (1922, 1 match).
Career batting
1–1–1–2–2*–no av–0–*ct* 0

Neale, George Henry
Amateur. *b:* 31.1.1869, Reigate, Surrey. *d:* 28.9.1915, near Loos, France. He was killed in action. Stylish middle order batsman. *Sch* Lancing. *Team* MCC (1902).
Career batting
1–2–0–0–0–0.00–0–*ct* 0

He was for some years stationed in India and took part in many matches there; in 1902/3 he hit 55 and 124* for Peshawar v Oxford Authentics touring team.

Neale, Maurice West
Amateur. *b:* 5.3.1849, Hardham, Sussex. *d:* 11.3.1935, Cheam, Surrey. Middle order batsman. *Team* W. G. Grace's XI (1871).
Career batting
1–1–0–0–0–0.00–0–*ct* 1

Neale, Phillip Anthony
Cricketer. *b:* 5.6.1954, Scunthorpe, Lincolnshire. Middle order right-hand batsman, right-arm medium pace bowler. *Team* Worcestershire (1975–92, 353 matches). *Tour* Worcestershire to Zimbabwe 1990/1.
Career batting
354–571–93–17445–167–36.49–28–*ct* 134
Bowling 369–2–184.50–0–0–1/15

He hit 1,000 runs in a season eight times (best 1,706, av 47.38, in 1984). He captained Worcestershire 1982–91. He also played for Lincolnshire (1972–74). A useful soccer player, he appeared for Lincoln City as a full back from 1974 to 1985.

Neale, William Legge
Amateur to 1928, then professional. *b:* 3.3.1904, Berkeley, Gloucestershire. *d:* 26.10.1955, Gloucester. Sound middle order right-hand batsman, slow right-arm bowler, good deep field. *Team* Gloucestershire (1923–48, 452 matches).
Career batting
452–700–79–14752–145*–23.75–14–*ct* 227
Bowling 3970–100–39.70–1–0–6/9

He hit 1,000 runs in a season six times (best 1,488, av 29.76, in 1938).

Neame, Arthur Rex Beale
Amateur. *b:* 14.6.1936, Faversham, Kent. Middle order right-hand batsman, off break bowler. *Sch* Harrow. *Team* Kent (1956–57, 4 matches).
Career batting
10–18–0–234–69–13.00–0–*ct* 8
Bowling 170–4–42.50–0–0–2/4
His final first-class match was for D. R. Jardine's XI in 1958.

Neate, Francis Webb
Amateur. *b:* 13.5.1940, Newbury, Berkshire. Brother of P. W. (Oxford U). Middle order right-hand batsman. *Sch* St Paul's. *Team* Oxford U (1960–62, blue 1961–62).
Career batting
17–30–6–914–112–38.08–1–*ct* 7
His County cricket was for Berkshire (1958–79), being captain from 1971 to 1975.

Neate, Patrick Whistler
Cricketer. *b:* 2.5.1946, Newbury, Berkshire. Brother of F. W. (Oxford U). Lower order left-hand batsman, right-arm medium pace bowler. *Sch* St Paul's. *Team* Oxford U (1966).
Career batting
1–1–0–3–3–3.00–0–*ct* 2
Bowling 53–0
His County cricket was for Berkshire (1964–79).

Neblett, James Montague
Amateur. *b:* 13.11.1901, Taylors Land, St Michael, Barbados. *d:* 28.3.1959, Mackenzie, British Guiana. Middle order right-hand batsman, leg break bowler. *Team* British Guiana (1925/6 to 1938/9). *Tour* West Indies to England 1928. *Test* West Indies (1934/5, 1 match).
Career batting
20–33–5–526–61–18.78–0–*ct* 16
Bowling 1205–29–41.55–0–0–4/82
Test batting
1–2–1–16–11*–16.00–0–*ct* 0
Bowling 75–1–75.00–0–0–1/44
He had a very modest tour of England in 1928 and appeared in only eight first-class matches. He represented 'Barbados-born' in 1927/8, but never played for the full Barbados team in a first-class match.

Needham, Andrew
Cricketer. *b:* 23.3.1957, Calow, Derbyshire. Middle order right-hand batsman, off break bowler. *Teams* Surrey (1977–86, 91 matches); Middlesex (1987–88, 18 matches).
Career batting
109–156–23–3077–138–23.13–4–*ct* 50
Bowling 5373–124–43.33–6–0–6/30
He scored 1,223 runs, av 38.21, in 1985. He also played for Hertfordshire (1989–92).

Needham, Ernest
Professional. *b:* 21.1.1873, Newbold Moor, Chesterfield, Derbyshire. *d:* 8.3.1936, Chesterfield, Derbyshire. Sound opening left-hand batsman, right-arm medium pace bowler, occasional wicket-keeper. *Team* Derbyshire (1901–12, 186 matches).
Career batting
186–340–15–6550–159–20.15–7–*ct* 135–*st* 1
Bowling 82–0
His best season was 1908 when he hit 1,178 runs, av 28.73. A notable soccer player, he appeared as half back for Sheffield United and England, gaining 16 caps.

Needham, Frank
Professional. *b:* 27.8.1861, Arnold, Nottinghamshire. *d:* 15.10.1923, Arnold, Nottinghamshire. Tail end batsman, left-arm slow medium bowler. *Team* Nottinghamshire (1890–91, 5 matches).
Career batting
8–15–3–49–13–4.08–0–*ct* 4
Bowling 442–24–18.41–1–0–5/44
His final first-class match was for MCC in 1901 – he was on the staff at Lord's from 1891 until his death in 1923.

Needham, Joseph
Professional. *b:* 9.1.1862, Flagg, Derbyshire. *d:* 30.8.1889, Taddington, Derbyshire. Middle order right-hand batsman. *Team* Derbyshire (1883, 1 match).
Career batting
1–2–1–9–6*–9.00–0–*ct* 0

Needham, Patrick John Easthope
Cricketer. *b:* 6.12.1951, Canton, Cardiff, Glamorgan. Middle order left-hand batsman, right-arm medium pace bowler, wicket-keeper. *Sch* Harrow. *Team* Glamorgan (1975, 1 match).
Career batting
1–1–0–4–4–4.00–0–*ct* 1
Bowling 105–2–52.50–0–0–1/49

Needham, Rowland
Professional. *b:* 10.11.1878, Huncote, Leicestershire. *d:* 28.4.1963, Victoria Park, Leicester. Lower order left-hand batsman, left-arm medium pace bowler. *Team* Leicestershire (1911, 1 match).
Career batting
1–2–1–31–16–31.00–0–*ct* 0
Bowling 75–2–37.50–0–0–2/75

Nelson, Alan Norris
Cricketer. *b:* 22.11.1965, Banbridge, Co Down, Ireland. Brother of Noel (Ireland). Lower order right-hand batsman, right-arm fast medium bowler. *Team* Ireland (1988–91).
Career batting
4–5–2–56–23*–18.66–0–*ct* 2
Bowling 316–14–22.57–1–0–5/27

Nelson, Alfred Leonard
Amateur. *b:* 13.11.1871, Crackley, Kenilworth, Warwickshire. *d:* 2.5.1927, Holly Green, Worcestershire. Nephew of G. M. B. (Warwickshire). Middle order right-hand batsman, wicket-keeper, change bowler. *Sch* Radley. *Team* Warwickshire (1895, 1 match).
Career batting
1–2–0–0–0–0.00–0–*ct* 0
He hit a century in the Oxford Freshmen's match of 1891, but never appeared in any first-class matches for the University.

Nelson, Guy Montague Blyth
Amateur. *b:* 8.8.1900, Coten End, Warwick. *d:* 13.1.1969, Great Bourton, Banbury, Oxfordshire. Nephew of A. L. (Warwickshire). Lower order right-hand batsman, right-arm fast medium bowler. *Sch* Rugby. *Team* Warwickshire (1921–22, 13 matches).
Career batting
13–21–8–97–23–7.46–0–*ct* 2
Bowling 746–22–33.90–0–0–4/53

Nelson, John
Amateur. *b:* 28.10.1891, Marton, Blackpool, Lancashire. *d:* 12.8.1917, near Pilckem, France. He was killed in action. Middle order batsman. *Team* Lancashire (1913, 1 match).
Career batting
1–2–0–7–5–3.50–0–*ct* 0

Nelson, Noel
Cricketer. *b:* 13.4.1967, Banbridge, Co Down, Ireland. Brother of A. N. (Ireland). Lower order right-hand batsman, right-arm medium pace bowler. *Team* Ireland (1990).
Career batting
1–1–0–0–0–0.00–0–*ct* 1
Bowling 51–0

Nelson, Peter John Mytton
Amateur. *b:* 16.5.1918, Finchley, Middlesex. *d:* 17.1.1992, Canterbury, Kent. Middle order left-hand batsman, right-arm medium pace bowler. *Sch* St George's, Harpenden. *Teams* Northamptonshire (1938, 1 match); Kent (1946, 1 match).
Career batting
2–4–1–55–32–18.33–0–*ct* 0
Bowling 51–2–25.50–0–0–1/9

Nelson, Peter Maurice
Amateur. *b:* 22.3.1913, Bradfield, Berkshire. Stylish middle order right-hand batsman, off break bowler. *Sch* Marlborough. *Team* Army (1939).
Career batting
1–1–0–62–62–62.00–0–*ct* 2
Bowling 63–1–63.00–0–0–1/63
His County cricket was for Oxfordshire (1931).

Nelson, Robert Prynne
Amateur. *b:* 7.8.1912, Fulham, London. *d:* 29.10.1940, Deal, Kent. He was killed while serving with the Royal Marines. Opening/middle order right-hand batsman, slow left-arm bowler. *Sch* St Albans and St George's, Harpenden. *Teams* Middlesex (1932–33, 9 matches); Cambridge U (1934–36, blue 1936); Northamptonshire (1937–39, 50 matches).
Career batting
77–136–12–3394–123*–27.37–2–*ct* 35
Bowling 2208–62–35.61–0–0–3/7
He hit 1,000 runs in a season twice (best 1,264, av 26.89, in 1938). In 1938 and 1939 he captained Northamptonshire. He also played for Hertfordshire (1931–34).

Nepean, Augustus Adolphus St John Marriott
Amateur. *b:* 24.6.1849, Westminster, London. *d:* 24.1.1933, Westminster, London. Brother of C. E. B. (Middlesex), uncle of E. A. (Middlesex). Middle order left-hand batsman, right-hand fast round-arm bowler. *Team* Middlesex (1876–77, 3 matches).
Career batting
7–11–3–187–51–23.37–0–*ct* 3
Bowling 66–2–33.00–0–0–1/13

Nepean, Rev Charles Edward Burroughs
Amateur. *b:* 5.2.1851, Mayfair, London. *d:* 26.3.1903, Lenham, Kent. Brother of A. A. St J. M. (Middlesex), uncle of E. A. (Middlesex). Middle order right-hand batsman, slow under-arm bowler, wicket-keeper. *Sch* Charterhouse. *Teams* Oxford U (1870–73, blue 1873); Middlesex (1873–74, 2 matches).
Career batting
10–17–1–290–50–18.12–0–*ct* 7–*st* 6
He also played for Dorset (1871–73) and was later on the Committee of Kent CCC. He also won a blue for soccer and played for England.

Nepean, Evan Alcock
Amateur. *b:* 13.9.1865, Mitcham, Surrey. *d:* 20.1.1906, Windsor, Berkshire. Nephew of C. E. B. (Middlesex), A. A. St J. M. (Middlesex) and H. Jenner-Fust (Gloucestershire), great-nephew of M. H. (MCC 1805) and H. Jenner (Kent). Middle order right-hand batsman, right-arm fast, later leg break, bowler. *Sch* Sherborne. *Teams* Oxford U (1887–88, blue both years); Middlesex (1887–95, 45 matches).
Career batting
89–152–21–2439–71–18.61–0–*ct* 28
Bowling 5307–264–20.10–12–1–8/48
His final first-class match was for MCC in 1902. He also played for Dorset (1883).

Nesbitt, Arnold Stearns
Amateur. *b:* 16.10.1878, Park House, Oatlands Park, Weybridge, Surrey. *d:* 7.11.1914, Ploegsteert Wood, Belgium. He was killed in action. Lower order right-hand batsman, wicket-keeper. *Sch* Bradfield. *Team* Worcestershire (1914, 1 match).
Career batting
1–2–1–5–3–5.00–0–*ct* 1

Neser, Justice Vivian Herbert
Amateur. *b:* 16.6.1894, Klerksdorp, Transvaal, South Africa. *d:* 22.12.1956, Pretoria, South Africa. Middle order right-hand batsman, wicket-keeper. *Teams* Oxford U (1919–21, blue 1921); Transvaal (1921/2 to 1924/5).
Career batting
18–29–2–743–90–27.51–0–*ct* 28–*st* 15
He was also awarded his blue for rugby football, which he played for South Africa.

Nesfield, Edward Roy
Amateur. *b:* 7.3.1900, Armthorpe, Yorkshire. *d:* 1.7.1987, Bridgetown, Somerset. Lower order right-hand batsman, off break bowler. *Sch* King's, Worcester. *Team* Worcestershire (1919–20, 3 matches).
Career batting
3–4–0–27–16–6.75–0–*ct* 0
Bowling 10–0

Neve, John Tanner
Amateur. *b:* 2.10.1902, Cranbrook, Kent. *d:* 7.7.1976, Woodcutts, Dorset. Hard-hitting lower order right-hand batsman, right-arm medium pace bowler. *Sch* Cheltenham. *Team* MCC (1936). *Tour* MCC to Canada 1937 (not first-class).
Career batting
1–2–0–14–9–7.00–0–*ct* 1
Bowling 66–2–33.00–0–0–1/32

Nevell, William Thomas
Professional. *b:* 13.6.1916, Balham, London. *d:* 25.8.1978, Worthing, Sussex. Hard-hitting lower order right-hand batsman, right-arm medium fast bowler. *Teams* Middlesex (1936–38, 13 matches); Surrey (1939, 1 match); Northamptonshire (1946–47, 36 matches).
Career batting
51–81–9–671–55*–9.31–0–*ct* 18
Bowling 3488–105–33.21–0–0–4/11

Nevile, Bernard Philip
Amateur. *b:* 1.8.1888, Wellingore Hall, Lincolnshire. *d:* 11.2.1916, near Ypres, Belgium. He was killed in action. Middle/lower order batsman, right-arm fast bowler. *Sch* Downside. *Team* Worcestershire (1913, 5 matches).
Career batting
6–10–2–65–17*–8.12–0–*ct* 1
Bowling 149–7–21.28–0–0–4/53
He appeared in the Freshmen's and Seniors' matches at Cambridge, but no first-class matches. His first-class debut was for Free Foresters in 1912. He also played for Lincolnshire (1911–14). A good golfer, he was awarded his blue. He also won a blue for hockey.

Neville, Patrick Augustine
Amateur. *b:* 22.6.1920, Donabate, Co Dublin, Ireland. *d:* 16.11.1977, Dublin, Ireland. Middle order right-hand batsman. *Team* Ireland (1956–60).
Career batting
4–8–0–143–38–17.87–0–*ct* 4
He played hockey for Ireland.

Nevin, Michael Robert Spencer
Cricketer. *b:* 5.4.1950, Marylebone, London. Lower order right-hand batsman, right-arm fast medium bowler. *Sch* Winchester. *Team* Cambridge U (1969, blue).
Career batting
8–12–8–34–14*–8.50–0–*ct* 1
Bowling 407–5–81.40–0–0–2/50

Nevinson, John Harcourt
Amateur. *b:* 2.11.1910, Lausanne, Switzerland. *d:* 22.8.1987, Lambeth, London. Tail end right-hand batsman, right-arm fast medium bowler. *Sch* Eton. *Teams* Oxford U (1929–31); Middlesex (1933, 6 matches).
Career batting
15–18–10–56–20*–7.00–0–*ct* 8
Bowling 1113–21–53.00–0–0–4/15
His final first-class match was for Free Foresters in 1935.

New, Frank Chandler
Amateur. *b:* 25.12.1859, Southwick, Sussex. *d:* 25.3.1924, Southwick, Sussex. Very steady middle order right-hand batsman, right-arm medium pace bowler. *Team* Sussex (1890, 3 matches).
Career batting
3–6–0–63–43–10.50–0–*ct* 1

Newbery, Arthur Leonard
Amateur. *b:* 6.1.1905, Battle, Sussex. *d:* 17.12.1976, Ightham, Kent. Middle order right-hand batsman. *Team* Sussex (1925, 3 matches).
Career batting
3–6–1–58–50*–11.60–0–*ct* 0
He was a director of John Wisden and Co and manager of Gray-Nicolls, manufacturers of cricket equipment.

Newbolt, Robert Henry
Amateur. *b:* 29.4.1833, Brentwood, Essex. *d:* 10.8.1885, Dresden, Germany. Middle order batsman. *Team* Gentlemen of England (1865).
Career batting
1–1–0–10–10–10.00–0–*ct* 0

Newburn, Thomas
Amateur. *b:* 10.8.1918, Belfast, Ireland. Lower order batsman, right-arm fast medium bowler. *Team* Ireland (1949).
Career batting
1–2–0–12–8–6.00–0–*ct* 1
Bowling 31–3–10.33–0–0–3/23

Newcomb, Alfred Edwin
Professional. *b:* 20.11.1873, Market Harborough, Leicestershire. *d:* 4.2.1932, Market Harborough, Leicestershire. Lower order right-hand batsman, right-arm fast medium, later slow, bowler. *Team* Leicestershire (1911, 1 match).
Career batting
1–2–0–1–1–0.50–0–*ct* 0
Bowling 74–1–74.00–0–0–1/26

Newcombe, Charles Niel
Amateur. *b:* 16.3.1891, Great Yarmouth, Norfolk. *d:* 27.12.1915, Fleuraix, France. He was killed in action. Lower order right-hand batsman, left-arm slow medium bowler. *Team* Derbyshire (1910, 1 match).
Career batting
1–2–0–1–1–0.50–0–*ct* 0
Bowling 32–0

Newell, Michael
Cricketer. *b:* 25.2.1965, Blackburn Lancashire. Opening or middle order right-hand batsman, leg break bowler, occasional wicket-keeper. *Team* Nottinghamshire (1984–92, 102 matches).
Career batting
102–178–26–4636–203*–30.50–6–*ct* 93–*st* 1
Bowling 282–7–40.28–0–0–2/38
He hit 203* for Nottinghamshire v Derbyshire at Derby in 1987, when he also scored 1,054 runs, av 39.03.

Newhall, William Price
Amateur. *b:* 30.1.1883, Philadelphia, USA. *d:* 3.1.1950, Philadelphia, USA. Son of G. M. (Philadelphia), nephew of R. S. (Philadelphia), D. S. (Philadelphia) and C. A. (Philadelphia). Middle order batsman, good cover. *Teams* Philadelphia (1908–12); US and Canada (1913). *Tours* Philadelphia to England 1908, to Jamaica 1908/9.
Career batting
7–12–0–235–57–19.58–0–*ct* 4
Bowling 63–2–31.50–0–0–2/30
He played in only two first-class matches on the 1908 tour and in 1912 represented the United States v Canada. He was the son of one of several brothers who played a prominent part in Philadelphian cricket.

Newham, William
Amateur. *b:* 12.12.1860, Shrewsbury, Shropshire. *d:* 26.6.1944, Portslade, Brighton, Sussex. Attractive fast scoring middle order right-hand batsman. *Sch* Ardingly. *Team* Sussex (1881–1905, 334 matches). *Tour* Lillywhite, Shaw and Shrewsbury to Australia 1887/8. *Test* England (1887/8, 1 match).
Career batting
368–643–43–14657–201*–24.42–19–*ct* 183
Bowling 615–10–61.50–0–0–3/57
Test batting
1–2–0–26–17–13.00–0–*ct* 0
He hit 1,000 runs in a season four times (best 1,183, av 31.97, in 1896). His only double century was 201* for Sussex v Somerset at Hove in 1896. He captained Sussex in 1889 and 1891–92 and was Secretary to the County Club 1889–1908, as well as being the manager. After resigning as Secretary, he became Assistant Secretary, a position he retained until his death.

Newland, Frederick
Professional. *b:* 14.1.1850, Henfield, Sussex. *d:* 10.8.1921, Kingston-by-Sea, Sussex. Lower order right-hand batsman, right-hand fast round-arm bowler. *Team* Sussex (1875–79, 3 matches).
Career batting
3–4–1–11–7*–3.66–0–*ct* 1
Bowling 79–2–39.50–0–0–2/46

Newland, Philip Mesmer
Amateur. *b:* 2.2.1875, Adelaide, South Australia. *d:* 11.8.1916, Westbury, Tasmania, Australia. Lower order batsman, wicket-keeper. *Team* South Australia (1899/1900 to 1905/6, 16 matches). *Tours* Australia to New Zealand 1904/5, to England 1905.
Career batting
28–46–13–599–77–18.15–0–*ct* 30–*st* 18
He came to England in 1905 as reserve wicket-keeper, and did not appear in any Tests.

Newland, Richard
Amateur. *c:* 2.3.1718, Slindon, Sussex. *d:* 29.5.1791, Bath, Somerset. Uncle of R. Nyren (Hampshire). Middle order left-hand batsman. *Team* Slindon.
His most famous innings was 88 for England v Kent in 1745 – most of his records are lost, but he was regarded as the finest batsman in England.

Newman, Arthur William
Professional. *b:* 15.9.1883, Westbury, Wiltshire. *d:* 16.3.1966, Melksham, Wiltshire. Middle order batsman, useful bowler. *Team* MCC (1907–19).
Career batting
5–6–1–39–15*–7.80–0–*ct* 4
Bowling 57–2–28.50–0–0–1/12
His County cricket was for Wiltshire (1900–30). His final first-class match was for West of England in 1927.

Newman, Charles
Professional. *b:* 7.8.1839, Cambridge. *d:* 23.4.1883, Cambridge. Hard-hitting middle order right-hand batsman. *Team* Cambridge Town Club (1860); Cambridgeshire (1861–69, 15 matches).
Career batting
17–32–2–195–32–6.50–0–*ct* 8

Newman, Douglas Leonard
Amateur. *b:* 25.6.1920, Harringay, Middlesex. *d:* 10.9.1959, St Pancras, London. Middle order right-hand batsman. *Team* Middlesex (1948–51, 11 matches).

Career batting
12–19–1–256–29–14.22–0–*ct* 5

His final first-class match was for MCC in 1953. A noted club cricketer in London, he captained Winchmore Hill.

Newman, Frederick Charles William
Amateur. *b:* 2.2.1896, Luton, Bedfordshire. *d:* 1.1.1966, Malpas, Truro, Cornwall. Middle order right-hand batsman. *Sch* Bedford Modern. *Team* Surrey (1919–21, 5 matches). *Tours* Cahn to Jamaica 1928/9 (did not play in first-class matches), to Argentine 1929/30.
Career batting
13–20–1–442–101–23.26–1–*ct* 4
Bowling 80–1–80.00–0–0–1/31

He was appointed Private Secretary to Julien Cahn in 1926, a post he retained until Cahn's death, and he was responsible for arranging Cahn's tours overseas. His final first-class match was for Sir Julien Cahn's XI in 1936. He also played for Bedfordshire (1911–23).

Newman, George Christopher
Amateur. *b:* 26.4.1904, Paddington, London. *d:* 13.10.1982, Braintree, Essex. Middle order right-hand batsman, right-arm medium pace bowler. *Sch* Eton. *Teams* Oxford U (1926–27, blue both years); Middlesex (1929–36, 50 matches). *Tour* MCC to Canada 1937 (not first-class).
Career batting
73–116–10–2742–112–25.86–3–*ct* 27
Bowling 670–17–39.41–0–0–3/48

He was President of Middlesex 1963–76. A noted athlete, he represented Oxford in the high jump, hurdles and relay races. He also won a blue for squash.

Newman, H. J.
Amateur. Middle order batsman. *Team* Northamptonshire (1905, 1 match).
Career batting
1–2–0–5–5–2.50–0–*ct* 0

Newman, John Alfred
Professional. *b:* 12.11.1884, Southsea, Hampshire. *d:* 21.12.1973, Groote Schuur, Cape Town, South Africa. Opening or middle order right-hand batsman, right-arm fast medium bowler. *Teams* Hampshire (1906–30, 506 matches); England XI in India (1915/16); Cooch Behar's XI (1917/18 to 1918/19); Canterbury (1927/8 to 1928/9).
Career batting
541–841–129–15364–166*–21.57–10–*ct* 320
Bowling 51397–2054–25.02–134–35–9/131

He hit 1,000 runs in a season six times (best 1,474, av 29.48, in 1928) and took 100 wickets nine times (best 177, av 21.56, in 1921). In all he achieved the 'double' five times. His best bowling in an innings was 9/131 for Hampshire v Essex at Bournemouth in 1921. During the Hampshire v Nottinghamshire match at Trent Bridge in 1922 he kicked down the stumps and was ordered off the field for indiscipline by his captain, Lord Tennyson.

Newman, Paul Geoffrey
Cricketer. *b:* 10.1.1959, Evington, Leicester. Lower order right-hand batsman, right-arm fast medium bowler. *Team* Derbyshire (1980–89, 130 matches). *Tour* English Counties to Zimbabwe 1984/5.
Career batting
134–170–33–2152–115–15.70–1–*ct* 37
Bowling 9736–312–31.20–6–0–8/29

Regarded as a very promising young cricketer, injury at vital stages in his career meant he did not achieve his full potential. He also played for Durham (pre first-class, 1990) and Staffordshire (1991–92).

Newman, Roger Grant
Amateur. *b:* 23.12.1933, Clifton, Bristol. Great-nephew of C. P. Wilson (Cambridge U). Attractive middle order right-hand batsman. *Sch* Clifton. *Team* Cambridge U (1955–57).
Career batting
4–7–0–133–44–19.00–0–*ct* 1

Newman, William
Amateur. *b:* 1837, Cambridge. Lower order batsman, bowler. *Team* Cambridgeshire (1867–71, 5 matches).
Career batting
5–10–0–34–9–3.40–0–*ct* 0
Bowling 124–6–20.66–0–0–3/19

Newnham, Arthur Tristram Herbert
Amateur. *b:* 17.1.1861, Dharwar, India. *d:* 29.12.1941, Wolborough, Devon. Middle/lower order right-hand batsman, right-arm fast bowler. *Sch* Malvern. *Teams* Gloucestershire (1887–94, 16 matches); Europeans (1892/3 to 1898/9).
Career batting
23–37–5–337–56–10.53–0–*ct* 11
Bowling 1127–59 + 1–19.10–4–0–6/64

Commencing in 1883 he was stationed in India, which restricted his opportunities in County cricket.

Newnham, Stanley William
Amateur. *b:* 7.4.1910, New Cross, London. *d:* 2.12.1985, Rhuddlan, Flint. Middle order right-hand batsman, slow left-arm bowler. *Sch* St Dunstan's. *Team* Surrey (1932, 1 match).
Career batting
1–1–0–4–4–4.00–0–*ct* 1
Bowling 13–2–6.50–0–0–2/13

He also played for Denbighshire (1948).

Newport, George Bernard
Amateur. *b:* 29.3.1876, Muttum, India. *d:* 12.7.1953, Exeter, Devon. Lower order right-hand batsman, wicket-keeper. *Sch* Bishop's Stortford. *Team* Somerset (1902–04, 2 matches).
Career batting
2–4–0–27–16–6.75–0–*ct* 4

Newport, Philip John
Cricketer. *b:* 11.10.1962, High Wycombe, Buckinghamshire. Lower order right-hand batsman, right-arm fast medium bowler. *Teams* Worcestershire (1982–92, 180 matches); Boland (1987/8). *Tours* England A to Pakistan and Sri Lanka 1990/1; England to India 1988/9 (tour cancelled), to Australia 1990/1. *Tests* England (1988 to 1990/1, 3 matches).
Career batting
194–212–66–3720–98–25.47–0–*ct* 55
Bowling 15757–568–27.74–27–3–8/52
Test batting
3–5–1–110–40*–27.50–0–*ct* 1
Bowling 417–10–41.70–0–0–4/87
He took 93 wickets, av 19.82, in 1988. He was borrowed from the England A team in Sri Lanka three days before the final England v Australia Test of the 1990/1 series and therefore made one first-class appearance in Australia. He also played for Buckinghamshire (1981–82).

Newsom, David John
Amateur. *b:* 5.10.1937, Plymouth, Devon. Opening right-hand batsman. *Sch* Haileybury. *Team* Combined Services (1960–61).
Career batting
2–2–0–33–23–16.50–0–*ct* 2

Newstead, John Thomas
Professional. *b:* 8.9.1877, Marton-in-Cleveland, Yorkshire. *d:* 25.3.1952, Blackburn, Lancashire. Steady middle order right-hand batsman, right-arm medium off break bowler. *Team* Yorkshire (1903–13, 96 matches).
Career batting
109–150–20–2104–100*–16.18–1–*ct* 83
Bowling 5947–310–19.18–14–4–7/10
He took 140 wickets, av 16.50, in 1908.

Newton, Arthur Edward
Amateur. *b:* 12.9.1862, Barton Grange, near Taunton, Somerset. *d:* 15.9.1952, Dipford House, Trull, Somerset. Brother-in-law of W. C. Hedley (Kent, Somerset and Hampshire). Free hitting lower order right-hand batsman, excellent wicket-keeper. *Sch* Eton. *Teams* Oxford U (1885, blue); Somerset (1891–1914, 197 matches). *Tours* Sanders to North America 1885; Vernon to Australia 1887/8.
Career batting
217–360–73–3614–77–12.59–0–*ct* 319–*st* 128
Bowling 4–0
He played club cricket until he was 81. Having made his debut for Somerset in 1880 (before the County were first-class), his career for that side lasted 35 seasons. He was President of Somerset in 1923.

Newton, Edward
Professional. *b:* 31.10.1871. *d:* 9.5.1906, Edinburgh, Scotland. He died of pneumonia. Middle order batsman, brilliant field. *Team* Hampshire (1900, 17 matches).
Career batting
17–32–1–568–69–18.32–0–*ct* 8
He first played for Hampshire (not first-class) in 1891.

Newton, Frederick Arthur
Professional. *b:* 16.9.1890, Denaby Main, Yorkshire. *d:* 8.8.1924, Warsop Main Colliery, Nottinghamshire. He was killed in a colliery accident. Middle order right-hand batsman, leg break bowler, good field. *Team* Derbyshire (1909–19, 20 matches).
Career batting
20–37–6–422–87–13.61–0–*ct* 7
Bowling 21–0

Newton, Harold Maurice
Amateur. *b:* 5.9.1918, Overstone, Northamptonshire. Middle order right-hand batsman. *Sch* Gresham's Holt. *Team* Northamptonshire (1938, 1 match).
Career batting
1–2–0–2–2–1.00–0–*ct* 0

Newton, Harry
Cricketer. *b:* 2.5.1935, Little Lever, Bolton, Lancashire. Lower order right-hand batsman, right-arm fast medium bowler. *Team* Sussex (1966, 2 matches).
Career batting
2–4–2–16–16*–8.00–0–*ct* 0
Bowling 141–6–23.50–1–0–5/54

Newton, Stephen Cox
Amateur. *b:* 21.4.1853, Nailsea, Somerset. *d:* 16.8.1916, Ipswich, Suffolk. Attacking middle order right-hand batsman, brilliant cover point. *Sch* Victoria College, Jersey. *Teams* Cambridge U (1876, blue); Somerset (1882–84, 16 matches); Middlesex (1885, 3 matches).
Career batting
33–59–3–1137–86–20.30–0–*ct* 20
Bowling 185–2–92.50–0–0–2/54
His final first-class match was for MCC in 1890. His first match for Somerset (pre first-class) was in 1878 and his last match for Somerset (not first-class) was in 1890. He captained Somerset 1882–84. He also played for Huntingdonshire (1868–71) and Suffolk (1905).

Newton-Thompson, Christopher Lawton
Amateur. *b:* 14.2.1919, Kensington, London. Brother of J. O. (Oxford U). Middle order right-hand batsman, wicket-keeper. *Team* Cambridge U (1939).
Career batting
1–2–0–16–8–8.00–0–*ct* 1
He won a blue for rugby.

Newton-Thompson, John Oswald
Amateur. *b:* 2.12.1920, Paddington, London. *d:* 3.4.1974, near Luderitz, South West Africa. He was killed in an air crash. Brother of C. L. (Cambridge U). Middle order right-hand batsman, right-arm slow

bowler. *Teams* Oxford U (1946, blue); Western Province (1948/9).
Career batting
9–18–1–281–78–16.52–0–*ct* 6
Bowling 125–0

A noted rugby footballer, he was awarded his blue and went on to play for England in 1947. He entered the South African Parliament in 1961, as a member of the United Party.

Niaz Ahmed
Cricketer. *b:* 11.11.1945, Benares, India. Lower order right-hand batsman, right-arm fast medium bowler. *Teams* Dacca (1965/6); PWD (1965/6 to 1973/4); East Pakistan (1967/8 to 1968/9); Railways (1970/1). *Tour* Pakistan to England 1967. *Tests* Pakistan (1967 to 1968/9, 2 matches).
Career batting
39–48–16–466–71*–14.56–0–*ct* 31
Bowling 2384–62–38.45–1–0–5/86
Test batting
2–3–3–17–16*–no av–0–*ct* 1
Bowling 94–3–31.33–0–0–2/72

He appeared in one Test on the 1967 tour of England, but his performances were very moderate.

Nice, Ernest Herbert Leonard
Professional. *b:* 1.8.1875, Earlswood, Surrey. *d:* 6.6.1946, Redhill, Surrey. Lower order right-hand batsman, right-arm fast medium bowler. *Team* Surrey (1895–1905, 69 matches).
Career batting
69–96–10–1247–66–14.50–0–*ct* 34
Bowling 4394–174–25.25–5–1–8/83

Nichol, David
Amateur. *b:* 25.8.1914, Galashiels, Selkirkshire, Scotland. Brother of R. J. (Scotland) and William (Scotland). Lower order right-hand batsman, slow left-arm bowler. *Team* Scotland (1952).
Career batting
1–2–0–6–4–3.00–0–*ct* 1
Bowling 1–2–30.50–0–0–2/61

Nichol, Maurice
Professional. *b:* 10.9.1904, Hetton, Co Durham. *d:* 21.5.1934, Chelmsford, Essex. Stylish middle order right-hand batsman. *Team* Worcestershire (1928–34, 135 matches).
Career batting
136–234–16–7484–262*–34.33–17–*ct* 64
Bowling 1281–21–61.00–0–0–2/6

He hit 1,000 runs in a season four times, going on to 2,000 once: 2,154, av 43.95, in 1933. His only double century was 262* for Worcestershire v Hampshire at Bournemouth in 1930. He also played for Durham (pre first-class, 1923–28). On the second morning of the Worcestershire v Essex match at Chelmsford in 1934, in which he was playing, he was found dead in bed. He had not enjoyed the best of health for several years, but his end was very unexpected. He scored 104 on debut for Worcestershire v West Indians at Worcester in 1928.

Nichol, Robert John
Amateur. *b:* 14.3.1924, Galashiels, Selkirkshire, Scotland. Brother of David (Scotland) and William (Scotland). Lower order right-hand batsman, right-arm fast medium bowler. *Team* Scotland (1951–55).
Career batting
7–10–2–67–19–8.37–0–*ct* 5
Bowling 505–12–42.08–1–0–5/87

Nichol, William
Amateur. *b:* 3.12.1912, Galashiels, Selkirkshire, Scotland. *d:* 1.6.1973, Paisley, Renfrewshire, Scotland. Brother of David (Scotland) and R. J. (Scotland). Middle order left-hand batsman, slow left-arm bowler. *Team* Scotland (1938–56).
Career batting
26–43–3–931–139*–23.27–2–*ct* 13
Bowling 1395–55–25.36–3–1–7/39

Nicholas, Frederick William Herbert
Amateur. *b:* 25.7.1893, Federated Malay States. *d:* 20.10.1962, Kensington, London. Grandfather of M. C. J. (Hampshire). Middle order right-hand batsman, wicket-keeper. *Sch* Forest. *Team* Essex (1912–29, 63 matches). *Tours* Joel to South Africa 1924/5; Cahn to Jamaica 1928/9, to Argentine 1929/30.
Career batting
76–122–5–2634–140–22.51–1–*ct* 51–*st* 16

He appeared in the Oxford Freshmen's match of 1913, but no first-class matches for the University. He won blues for athletics and soccer. From 1927 to 1931 he was a regular cricketer with Sir Julien Cahn's XI and in 1929 scored over 2,000 runs for that side. He also played for Bedfordshire (1913).

Nicholas, Mark Charles Jefford
Cricketer. *b:* 29.9.1957, Westminster, London. Grandson of F. W. H. (Essex). Middle order right-hand batsman, right-arm medium pace bowler. *Sch* Bradfield. *Team* Hampshire (1978–92, 305 matches). *Tours* English Counties to Zimbabwe 1984/5; England B to Sri Lanka 1985/6; England A to Zimbabwe 1989/90.
Career batting
321–526–76–14952–206*–33.22–29–*ct* 195
Bowling 3208–72–44.55–2–0–6/37

He hit 1,000 runs in a season eight times (best 1,559, av 33.89, in 1984). His highest innings was 206* for Hampshire v Oxford U at The Parks in 1982. He captained Hampshire from 1985 to 1992 and was also captain on his two later tours.

Nicholl, Kenneth Iltyd
Amateur. *b:* 13.2.1885, Marylebone, London. *d:* 2.3.1952, Famagusta, Cyprus. Grandson of F. I. (Cambridge U 1835). Stylish opening right-hand

batsman. *Sch* Eton. *Team* Middlesex (1904, 2 matches).
Career batting
6–11–0–254–62–23.09–0–*ct* 2
He did not appear in any first-class matches whilst at Oxford, but played some County cricket with Berkshire (1920–21). His final first-class match was for Free Foresters in 1921.

Nicholls, Benjamin Ernest
Amateur. *b:* 4.10.1864, Byfleet, Surrey. *d:* 6.6.1945, Brownings, Kirdford, Sussex. Hard-hitting lower order right-hand batsman, right-arm slow bowler, excellent slip field. *Sch* Winchester. *Teams* Sussex (1883–88, 4 matches); Oxford U (1884–85, blue 1884).
Career batting
16–25–6–192–44–10.10–0–*ct* 23
Bowling 666–31–21.40–1–0–5/46
His final first-class match was for MCC in 1901. From 1889 until 1900 he was farming at Lake Hindmarsh Station, Victoria, Australia.

Nicholls, Cecil Burleigh
Amateur. *b:* 21.12.1880. *d:* 1.6.1943, Folkestone, Kent. Lower order batsman, bowler. *Sch* Chigwell. *Team* W. G. Grace's XI (1906).
Career batting
1–2–0–20–19–10.00–0–*ct* 0
Bowling 42–0

Nicholls, David
Professional. *b:* 8.12.1943, East Dereham, Norfolk. Attacking opening left-hand batsman, off break bowler, often wicket-keeper in later years of his career. *Team* Kent (1960–77, 201 matches).
Career batting
202–342–24–7072–211–22.23–2–*ct* 326–*st* 13
Bowling 23–2–11.50–0–0–1/0
He hit 1,000 runs, av 32.25 in 1971. His only double century was 211 for Kent v Derbyshire at Folkestone in 1963.

Nicholls, Richard William
Amateur. *b:* 23.7.1875, Crouch End, Middlesex. *d:* 22.1.1948, Eastbourne, Sussex. Middle order right-hand batsman, good field. *Sch* Rugby. *Team* Middlesex (1896–1904, 65 matches).
Career batting
72–113–10–1732–154–16.81–1–*ct* 31
With W. Roche he added 230 for the last Middlesex wicket v Kent at Lord's in 1899, creating a new record.

Nicholls, Ronald Bernard
Professional. *b:* 4.12.1933, Sharpness, Gloucestershire. Sound opening right-hand batsman, off break bowler, good cover field, occasional wicket-keeper. *Team* Gloucestershire (1951–75, 534 matches).
Career batting
534–954–52–23607–217–26.17–18–*ct* 283–*st* 1
Bowling 719–11–65.36–0–0–2/19
He hit 1,000 runs in a season 15 times, going on to 2,000 once: 2,059, av 36.76, in 1962. His only double century was 217 for Gloucestershire v Oxford U at Oxford in 1962, during which innings he set up a County record 1st wicket partnership of 395 with D. M. Young. A well-known soccer player, he kept goal for Bristol Rovers, Cardiff City, Fulham and Bristol City.

Nichols, George Benjamin
Amateur for Gloucestershire, but professional for Somerset. *b:* 14.6.1862, Fishponds, Bristol. *d:* 19.2.1911, Dublin, Ireland. He died of pneumonia. Lower order right-hand batsman, right-arm fast medium bowler, good slip. *Teams* Gloucestershire (1883–85, 5 matches); Somerset (1891–99, 134 matches).
Career batting
143–248–31–2958–74*–13.63–0–*ct* 65
Bowling 7138–299–23.87–7–0–6/75
He first played for Somerset (not first-class) in 1887. He also played for Devon (1900–03). He was a first-class umpire (1903). He was also a playwright of some note.

Nichols, Dr John Bowes
Amateur. *b:* 1.1.1931, Latchford, Cheshire. Lower order right-hand batsman, slow left-arm bowler. *Sch* Wrekin. *Team* Cambridge U (1953).
Career batting
5–5–0–33–16–6.60–0–*ct* 0
Bowling 81–0

Nichols, John Ernest
Professional. *b:* 20.4.1878, Acle, Norwich, Norfolk. *d:* 29.2.1952, Thorpe, Norwich, Norfolk. Middle order batsman. *Team* Worcestershire (1902–04, 5 matches).
Career batting
6–10–1–45–13–5.00–0–*ct* 3
Bowling 13–0
He also played for Norfolk (1898 and 1921–31) and Staffordshire (1907–14). His final first-class match was for Minor Counties in 1912.

Nichols, Morris Stanley
Professional. *b:* 6.10.1900, Stondon Massey, Essex. *d:* 26.1.1961, Newark, Nottinghamshire. Attacking middle order left-hand batsman, right-arm fast bowler. *Team* Essex (1924–39, 418 matches). *Tours* Cahn to Jamaica 1928/9; MCC to Australia and New Zealand 1929/30, to India and Ceylon 1933/4; Tennyson to Jamaica 1931/2; selected for MCC to India 1939/40 (cancelled because of war). *Tests* England (1929/30 to 1939, 14 matches).
Career batting
483–756–85–17827–205–26.56–20–*ct* 326
Bowling 39666–1833–21.63–118–23–9/32

Nichols, Thomas

Test batting
14–19–7–355–78*–29.58–0–*ct* 11
Bowling 1152–41–28.09–2–0–6/35

One of the leading all-round cricketers of his day, he performed the 'double' eight times, including five seasons in succession. In all he hit 1,000 runs in a season nine times (best 1,460, av 30.41, in 1933) and took 100 wickets eleven times (best 171, av 19.92, in 1938). His only double century was 205 for Essex v Hampshire at Southend in 1936. His best bowling was 9/32 for Essex v Nottinghamshire at Trent Bridge in 1936. A useful soccer player, he kept goal for Queen's Park Rangers.

Nichols, Thomas
Professional. *b:* 25.5.1844, Dorking, Surrey. Lower order right-hand batsman, right-hand fast medium round-arm bowler. *Team* Players (1867).
Career batting
1–1–0–0–0–0.00–0–*ct* 0

Nichols, Rev Thomas Bartrup
Amateur. *b:* 25.5.1848, Cambridge. *d:* 7.3.1915, Kineton, Warwickshire. Middle order batsman. *Team* Cambridgeshire (1868, 1 match).
Career batting
1–2–1–16–15*–16.00–0–*ct* 0

He also played for Staffordshire (1873).

Nicholson, Anthony George
Professional. *b:* 25.6.1938, Dewsbury, Yorkshire. *d:* 4.11.1985, Harrogate, Yorkshire. Lower order right-hand batsman, right-arm medium pace bowler. *Team* Yorkshire (1962–75, 282 matches). *Tour* English Counties XI to West Indies 1974/5 (not first-class).
Career batting
283–268–126–1669–50–11.75–0–*ct* 85
Bowling 17371–879–19.76–40–3–9/62

He took 100 wickets in a season twice (best 113, av 15.50, in 1966). His best bowling in an innings was 9/62 for Yorkshire v Sussex at Eastbourne in 1967. He was chosen to tour South Africa with MCC in 1964/5, but prevented from going due to injury.

Nicholson, John Simmonds
(birth registered as John Nicholson Simmonds)
Professional. *b:* 30.4.1903, Irthlingborough, Northamptonshire. *d:* 18.3.1950, St John's, Bedford. Lower order right-hand batsman, right-arm medium pace bowler. *Team* Northamptonshire (1924–28, 63 matches).
Career batting
64–103–19–778–45–9.26–0–*ct* 54
Bowling 3221–93–34.63–3–0–5/40

Nicholson, Neil George
Cricketer. *b:* 17.10.1963, Danby, Yorkshire. Middle order left-hand batsman, right-arm medium pace bowler. *Team* Yorkshire (1988–89, 5 matches).
Career batting
5–8–3–134–56*–26.80–0–*ct* 8
Bowling 25–0

Nicholson, Thomas Brinsley
Amateur. *b:* 15.3.1876, Madras, India. *d:* 3.10.1939, Cambridge. Hard-hitting middle order right-hand batsman, good deep field. *Sch* Clifton. *Teams* London County (1904); Jamaica (1908/9 to 1910/11).
Career batting
12–22–2–470–73*–23.50–0–*ct* 10

Nicholson, William
Amateur. *b:* 2.9.1824, Upper Holloway, London. *d:* 25.7.1909, Westminster, London. Brother of John (Cambridge U), R. C. (Gentlemen) and R. P. (Gentlemen), his daughter was stepmother of E. R. Bradford (Hampshire). Attacking middle order right-hand batsman, wicket-keeper. *Sch* Harrow. *Team* Middlesex (1850–65, 5 matches).
Career batting
148–261–11–3447–86–13.78–0–*ct* 110–*st* 90

His first-class debut was for Gentlemen of England in 1845 and his final match for MCC in 1869. He also played for Berkshire (1858). In 1866 his financial support saved Lord's from the builders. He was on the MCC Committee and President of the Club in 1879. He was Middlesex Treasurer 1869–96. From 1866 to 1874 he was Liberal MP for Petersfield and from 1880 to 1885 Conservative for the same constituency.

Nicholson, William
Amateur. *b:* 7.5.1909, Kirn, Argyllshire, Scotland. Middle order right-hand batsman. *Sch* Loretto. *Team* Scotland (1929–33).
Career batting
10–18–2–396–101–24.75–1–*ct* 6

He scored 101 on debut for Scotland v Ireland at Dublin in 1929.

Nicoll, Henry Russell
Amateur. *b:* 27.2.1883, Mains, Angus, Scotland. *d:* 25.9.1948, Dundee, Angus, Scotland. Lower order batsman, good bowler. *Team* Scotland (1914).
Career batting
1–2–1–0–0*–0.00–0–*ct* 0
Bowling 144–8–18.00–1–0–7/64

Nicolson, John Fairless William
Amateur. *b:* 19.7.1899, Durban, South Africa. *d:* 13.12.1935, Mourne Grange, Kilkeel, Co Down, Ireland. Sound opening left-hand batsman. *Teams* Oxford U (1923); Natal (1923/4 to 1929/30). *Tests* South Africa (1927/8, 3 matches).
Career batting
28–44–3–1543–252*–37.63–3–*ct* 8
Bowling 205–3–68.33–0–0–2/36
Test batting
3–5–0–179–78–35.80–0–*ct* 0

Bowling 17–0

His most noteworthy innings was 252* for Natal v Orange Free State at Bloemfontein in 1926/7, when, with I. J. Siedle, he set up a new record of 424 for the 1st wicket. In 1932 he moved to Ireland where he took up a scholastic post.

Nightingale, James
Professional. *b:* 10.8.1840, Reigate, Surrey. *d:* 9.2.1917, Reigate, Surrey. Lower order batsman, useful bowler. *Team* Surrey (1868, 1 match).
Career batting
1–1–1–2–2*–no av–0–*ct* 1
Bowling 8–0

Nimbalkar, Raosaheb Babasaheb
Amateur. *b:* 1.12.1915, Kolhapur, India. *d:* 1.6.1965, Jalna, India. Brother of B. B. (Baroda), uncle of S. B. (Maharashtra). Middle order right-hand batsman, leg break bowler, wicket-keeper. *Teams* Maharashtra (1934/5 to 1940/1); Hindus (1938/9); Baroda (1938/9 to 1952/3). *Tours* India to Ceylon 1944/5, to England 1946.
Career batting
63–94–5–2687–132–30.19–4–*ct* 82–*st* 41
Bowling 179–3–59.66–0–0–1/8

Owing to a fractured thumb he appeared in just seven first-class matches on the 1946 tour to England and no Tests.

Nissar, Mohammad
Amateur. *b:* 1.8.1910, Hoshiarpur, India. *d:* 11.3.1963, Lahore, Pakistan. Tail end right-hand batsman, right-arm fast medium bowler. *Teams* Muslims (1928/9 to 1939/40); Patiala (1932/3 to 1933/4); Southern Punjab (1933/4 to 1940/1); Uttar Pradesh (1945/6); Railways (1953/4). *Tours* India to England 1932, 1936. *Tests* India (1932–36, 6 matches).
Career batting
93–136–34–1120–49–10.98–0–*ct* 65
Bowling 7010–396–17.70–32–3–6/17
Test batting
6–11–3–55–14–6.87–0–*ct* 2
Bowling 707–25–28.28–3–0–5/90

In 1932 he headed the tourists' first-class bowling averages with 71 wickets, av 18.09, and in 1936 took most wickets: 66, av 25.13. His first first-class match in Pakistan was for the Commander-in-Chief's XI in 1949/50.

Niven, Robert Andrew
Cricketer. *b:* 28.4.1948, Felixstowe, Suffolk. Lower order right-hand batsman, left-arm medium pace bowler. *Sch* Berkhamsted. *Team* Oxford U (1968–69 and 1973, blue all three years).
Career batting
25–31–14–182–24*–10.70–0–*ct* 6
Bowling 1806–53–34.07–2–0–5/60

His County cricket was for Hertfordshire (1968).

Nixon, George Tait St Aubyn
Amateur. *b:* 11.8.1850, Neermuck, Rajputana, India. *d:* February 1913, Lintlaw, Saskatchewan, Canada. Middle order right-hand batsman, right-hand slow round-arm bowler, wicket-keeper. *Sch* Rossall. *Teams* Middlesex (1868–70, 3 matches); Cambridge U (1870).
Career batting
6–10–0–113–54–11.30–0–*ct* 5–*st* 6

Nixon, Harry
Professional. *b:* 8.1.1878, Nottingham. *d:* 14.10.1935, Rutherglen, Glasgow, Scotland. Son of T. H. (MCC), grandson of Thomas (Nottinghamshire). Middle order batsman, left-arm bowler. *Team* Scotland (1906).
Career batting
1–2–0–53–41–26.50–0–*ct* 1
Bowling 195–5–39.00–0–0–3/106

Nixon, Henry
Professional. *b:* 1.5.1852, Cambridge. *d:* 30.1.1915, Cambridge. Lower order right-hand batsman, right-hand medium pace round-arm bowler. *Team* MCC (1873).
Career batting
1–1–1–15–15*–no av–0–*ct* 0

He was generally given the initial 'G' to distinguish him from T. H. Nixon in match scores. His County cricket was for Huntingdonshire (1871) and Shropshire (1872), but he was best known as an umpire.

Nixon, Paul Andrew
Cricketer. *b:* 21.10.1970, Carlisle, Cumberland. Middle order left-hand batsman, wicket-keeper. *Team* Leicestershire (1989–92, 45 matches).
Career batting
45–59–19–1081–107*–27.02–1–*ct* 109–*st* 9

He also played for Cumberland (1987).

Nixon, Thomas
Professional. *b:* 4.6.1815, Nottingham. *d:* 20.7.1877, Chelford, Cheshire. Father of T. H. (MCC), grandfather of Harry (Scotland). Tail end right-hand batsman, right-hand slow round-arm bowler. *Team* Nottinghamshire (1841–54, 7 matches).
Career batting
54–88–18–338–34–4.82–0–*ct* 22
Bowling 1290–129 + 135–10.00–23–7–9/?

He was on the staff at Lord's 1851 to 1859 and at that time one of the leading bowlers in England. He took 9 wickets in an innings for MCC v Middlesex at Lord's in 1851. He also played for Worcestershire (pre first-class, 1848–49), Devon (1851–52), Leicestershire (pre first-class, 1851–56), Oxfordshire (1856–57) and Cheshire. He invented cork pads in 1841, open pads and cane-handled bats in 1853, also about 1862 a mechanical round-arm bowling machine. His final first-class match was for MCC in 1859.

Nixon, Thomas Henry
Professional. *b:* 24.4.1843, Sneinton, Nottinghamshire. *d:* 23.1.1907, Hillingdon Heath, Middlesex. Son of Thomas (Nottinghamshire), father of Harry (Scotland). Lower order right-hand batsman, right-hand slow medium round-arm bowler, slip field. *Team* MCC (1862–67).
Career batting
2–3–0–15–9–5.00–0–*ct* 0
Bowling 76–4–19.00–0–0–2/26
He was engaged by MCC for 12 seasons and was best known as an umpire.

Noble, Charles
Amateur. *b:* 9.2.1850, Kennington, London. *d:* 8.3.1927, Trowbridge, Wiltshire. Brother of J. W. (Surrey). Middle order right-hand batsman, right-hand slow round-arm bowler, deep field. *Team* Surrey (1868, 4 matches).
Career batting
5–9–0–72–17–8.00–0–*ct* 3
His first-class debut was for Gentlemen of the South in 1867, when he replaced his brother who was injured.

Noble, John Wilson
Amateur. *b:* 4.8.1845, Kennington, London. *d:* 20.4.1889. Chelsea, London. Brother of Charles (Surrey). Lower order right-hand batsman, right-hand slow under-arm bowler, deep field. *Team* Surrey (1866–69, 26 matches).
Career batting
31–51–2–554–71–11.30–0–*ct* 5
Bowling 392–17–23.05–0–0–4/36

Noble, Montague Alfred
Amateur. *b:* 28.1.1873, Dixon Street, Chinatown, Sydney, New South Wales, Australia. *d:* 22.6.1940, Randwick, Sydney, New South Wales, Australia. Brother of E. G. (New South Wales), brother-in-law of W. Ferguson, the well-known scorer. Defensive right-hand middle order batsman, right-arm medium pace off break bowler, brilliant point field. *Team* New South Wales (1893/4 to 1919/20, 77 matches). *Tours* Australia to England 1899, 1902, 1905, 1909, to South Africa 1902/3, to New Zealand 1904/5, 1913/14; New South Wales to New Zealand 1893/4. *Tests* Australia (1897/8 to 1909, 42 matches).
Career batting
248–377–34–13975–284–40.74–37–*ct* 190
Bowling 14443–624–23.14–33–7–8/48
Test batting
42–73–7–1997–133–30.25–1–*ct* 26
Bowling 3025–121–25.00–9–2–7/17
He hit 1,000 runs on all four of his tours to England, going on to 2,000 once: 2,053, av 46.65, in 1905. Of his seven double centuries the highest was 284 for Australians v Sussex at Hove in 1896. His bowling proved effective on his first two visits to England, but latterly he bowled little. He captained the 1909 Team and led Australia in a total of 15 Tests. He also hit 1,000 in an Australian season once. He was the author of several notable books on cricket.

Noble, Norman Doncaster
Amateur. *b:* 2.3.1881, Lucknow, India. *d:* 21.9.1955, Hartlip, Kent. Middle order batsman. *Sch* Edinburgh Academy. *Team* Scotland (1922).
Career batting
1–2–0–53–38–26.50–0–*ct* 2
Bowling 8–0

Noblet, Geffery
Amateur. *b:* 14.9.1916, Parside, Adelaide, South Australia. Lower order right-hand batsman, right-arm medium pace bowler. *Team* South Australia (1945/6 to 1952/3, 49 matches). *Tour* Australia to South Africa 1949/50. *Tests* Australia (1949/50 to 1952/3, 3 matches).
Career batting
71–99–29–975–55*–13.92–0–*ct* 44
Bowling 5432–282–19.26–13–2–7/29
Test batting
3–4–1–22–13*–7.33–0–*ct* 1
Bowling 183–7–26.14–0–0–3/21
His only first-class match in England was for a Commonwealth XI in 1956.

Nolan, Geoffrey John
Cricketer. *b:* 6.10.1937, Colchester, Essex. Middle order right-hand batsman. *Team* Essex (1968, 1 match).
Career batting
1–2–0–14–11–7.00–0–*ct* 0
He was also a useful hockey player.

Noon, Wayne Michael
Cricketer. *b:* 5.2.1971, Grimsby, Lincolnshire. Middle order right-hand batsman, wicket-keeper. *Team* Northamptonshire (1989–92, 12 matches). *Tour* Northamptonshire to South Africa 1991/2.
Career batting
12–16–2–150–37–10.71–0–*ct* 23–*st* 3

Norbury, Duncan Victor
Professional. *b:* 3.8.1887, Bartley, Hampshire. *d:* 23.10.1972, Sutton, Surrey. Brother-in-law of H. G. Smoker (Hampshire). Hard-hitting middle order right-hand batsman, slow right-arm bowler. *Teams* Hampshire (1905–06, 11 matches); Lancashire (1919–22, 14 matches).
Career batting
26–44–2–806–100–19.19–1–*ct* 8
Bowling 996–30–33.20–0–0–4/28
His last first-class match was for Sir L. Parkinson's XI in 1935. He also played for Northumberland (1910–13).

Norley, Frederick
Professional. *b:* 23.2.1845, Canterbury, Kent. Brother of James (Kent and Gloucestershire). Lower order right-hand batsman, right-hand fast medium round-arm bowler. *Team* Kent (1864–65, 7 matches).
Career batting
8–15–4–69–12–6.27–0–*ct* 2
Bowling 233–10–23.30–1–0–5/52

Norley, James
Professional. *b:* 5.1.1847, Canterbury, Kent. *d:* 24.10.1900, Eastville, Bristol. Brother of Frederick (Kent). Middle/lower order right-hand batsman, right-hand medium pace round-arm bowler. *Teams* Kent (1870–71, 8 matches); Gloucestershire (1877, 1 match).
Career batting
9–17–3–60–21*–4.28–0–*ct* 8
Bowling 108–3–36.00–0–0–1/16

Norman, Charles Loyd
Amateur. *b:* 10.3.1833, Bromley Common, Kent. *d:* 17.2.1889, San Remo, Italy. Son of G. W. (Kent), brother of F. H. (Kent) and Philip (Gentlemen of Kent), nephew of Henry (Kent 1827), uncle of M. Bonham-Carter (Kent). Middle order right-hand batsman. *Sch* Eton. *Teams* Cambridge U (1852–53, blue both years); Kent (1853, 1 match).
Career batting
13–24–2–200–34–9.09–0–*ct* 4
His final first-class match was for Gentlemen of Kent in 1854.

Norman, Frederick Henry
Amateur. *b:* 23.1.1839, Bromley Common, Kent. *d:* 6.10.1916, Mayfair, London. Son of G. W. (Kent) and brother of C. L. (Kent) and Philip (Gentlemen of Kent), nephew of Henry (Kent 1827). Stylish middle order right-hand batsman, good deep field. *Sch* Eton. *Teams* Cambridge U (1858–60, blue all three years); Kent (1858–64, 10 matches); Cambridgeshire (1858, 1 match).
Career batting
26–44–2–782–103–18.61–2–*ct* 11
His final first-class match was for R. D. Walker's XI in 1866. He captained Cambridge in 1860. He served on the Committees of both MCC and Kent CCC.

Norman, George
Amateur. *b:* 23.8.1890, Westminster, London. *d:* 24.11.1964, Virginia Water, Surrey. Middle order batsman. *Sch* Bancroft's. *Team* Essex (1920, 4 matches).
Career batting
4–5–1–44–21–11.00–0–*ct* 1
Bowling 18–0

Norman, John William
Amateur. *b:* 22.8.1936, Maidstone, Kent. Lower order right-hand batsman, wicket-keeper. *Sch* Millfield and Downside. *Team* Cambridge U (1957).
Career batting
2–3–0–12–9–4.00–0–*ct* 3
His County cricket was for Berkshire (1966).

Norman, Michael Eric John Charles
Professional. *b:* 19.1.1933, Kingsley, Northampton. Opening right-hand batsman, right-arm leg break bowler. *Teams* Northamptonshire (1952–65, 202 matches); Leicestershire (1966–75, 151 matches). *Tour* MCC to Bangladesh 1976/7 (not first-class).
Career batting
363–640–44–17441–221*–29.26–24–*ct* 161
Bowling 164–2–82.00–0–0–2/0
He hit 1,000 runs in a season eight times (best 1,964, av 33.86, in 1960). His only double century was 221* for Leicestershire v Cambridge U at Fenner's in 1967. After the 1969 season he became a teacher and his County cricket was restricted.

Norman, Newman Frederick
Amateur. *b:* 2.2.1884, Camberwell, London. *d:* 28.8.1954, Westcliff-on-Sea, Essex. Brother-in-law of H. W. Barnes (Barbados). Middle order right-hand batsman. *Sch* City of London. *Teams* London County (1902–03); Northamptonshire (1905–09, 11 matches).
Career batting
18–32–1–258–32–8.32–0–*ct* 8
He first played for Northamptonshire (pre first-class) in 1903. He played in trials at Cambridge U, but not in first-class matches.

Norman, Philip
Amateur. *b:* 9.7.1842, Bromley Common, Kent. *d:* 17.5.1931, South Kensington, London. Son of G. W. (Kent), brother of C. L. (Kent) and F. H. (Kent), nephew of Henry (Kent 1827). Middle order right-hand batsman. *Sch* Eton. *Team* Gentlemen of Kent (1865).
Career batting
1–2–0–1–1–0.50–0–*ct* 2
He published many books on antiquarian and topographical subjects and also wrote two cricket books.

Norman, Dr Ralph Oliver Geoffrey
Amateur. *b:* 30.7.1911, Southend, Essex. *d:* 26.7.1983, Thorpe Bay, Essex. Middle order right-hand batsman, left-arm medium pace bowler. *Sch* Rugby. *Team* Essex (1932, 1 match).
Career batting
1–2–0–20–10–10.00–0–*ct* 0
He played in the Cambridge Seniors' match of 1932, but no first-class matches for the University.

Nornable, Charles Ernest
Professional. *b:* 25.12.1886, Norton, Derbyshire. *d:* 21.4.1970, Sheffield, Yorkshire. Lower order right-hand batsman, right-arm fast medium bowler. *Team* Derbyshire (1909, 1 match).
Career batting
1–1–0–8–8–8.00–0–*ct* 0
Bowling 72–5–14.40–0–0–3/24

Norris, David William Worsley
Cricketer. *b:* 1.5.1946, Hampstead, London. Middle order right-hand batsman, wicket-keeper. *Sch* Harrow. *Team* Cambridge U (1967–68, blue both years).
Career batting
20–33–2–307–43–9.90–0–*ct* 21–*st* 3

Norris, Graham Walter
Amateur. *b:* 17.10.1905, Steane Park, Brackley, Northamptonshire. *d:* 6.12.1933, Easington, Banbury, Oxfordshire. He was killed riding in a steeplechase. Lower order right-hand batsman, right-arm medium slow bowler. *Sch* Eton. *Team* Northamptonshire (1925–26, 5 matches).
Career batting
5–8–0–38–16–4.75–0–*ct* 3
Bowling 154–7–22.00–0–0–3/48
He did not play in any first-class matches whilst at Oxford.

Norris, Oswald Thomas
Amateur. *b:* 1.7.1883, Longshaw, Chipstead, Surrey. *d:* 22.3.1973, Tilgate Forest Lodge, Sussex. Father-in-law of M. J. C. Allom (Surrey). Sound middle order right-hand batsman, slow right-arm bowler. *Sch* Charterhouse. *Team* Oxford U (1904–05).
Career batting
11–20–0–413–87–20.65–0–*ct* 7
Bowling 272–4–68.00–0–0–2/109
He was in the Eleven selected to play Cambridge in 1904, but forced to stand down due to injury. A useful soccer player, he captained Oxford.

North, Albert Edward Charles
Professional. *b:* 20.12.1877, Bedminster, Somerset. *d:* 4.6.1933, Bristol. Lower order batsman, right-arm fast bowler. *Teams* Somerset (1903–09, 15 matches); Gloucestershire (1912, 2 matches).
Career batting
17–26–11–182–30*–12.13–0–*ct* 6
Bowling 929–25–37.16–0–0–4/47

North, Ernest Joseph
Professional. *b:* 23.9.1895, Burton-on-Trent, Staffordshire. *d:* 24.8.1955, Havant, Hampshire. Tail end right-hand batsman, right-arm slow medium bowler. *Team* Middlesex (1923–27, 24 matches).
Career batting
27–34–9–247–80–9.88–0–*ct* 10
Bowling 1414–49–28.85–0–0–4/18
He was a noted soccer player, appearing for Arsenal, Reading, Gillingham, Norwich and Watford.

North, John Andrew
Cricketer. *b:* 19.11.1970, Slindon, Sussex. Lower order right-hand batsman, right-arm medium pace bowler. *Team* Sussex (1990–92, 16 matches).
Career batting
16–20–3–285–63*–16.76–0–*ct* 2
Bowling 1164–37–31.45–0–0–4/47

North, Philip David
Cricketer. *b:* 16.5.1965, Newport, Monmouthshire. Lower order right-hand batsman, slow left-arm bowler. *Team* Glamorgan (1985–89, 22 matches).
Career batting
22–25–7–200–41*–11.11–0–*ct* 7
Bowling 1009–24–42.04–0–0–4/43
He played for Wales in the Minor Counties Championship (1990).

Northcote, Dr Percy
Amateur. *b:* 18.9.1866, Islington, London. *d:* 3.3.1934, Marylebone, London. Free scoring middle order right-hand batsman, slow left-arm bowler. *Sch* Cranbrook. *Teams* Middlesex (1888, 2 matches); Kent (1889–95, 3 matches).
Career batting
7–12–3–105–27*–11.66–0–*ct* 3
Bowling 156–2–78.00–0–0–1/31
His final first-class match was for MCC in 1903.

Northcote-Green, Simon Roger
Cricketer. *b:* 30.5.1954, Worksop, Nottinghamshire. Grandson of E. A. Greswell (Somerset), great-nephew of W. T. (Somerset). Opening/middle order right-hand batsman, right-arm medium pace bowler. *Sch* St Edward's, Oxford. *Team* Oxford U (1974 and 1979).
Career batting
9–16–2–138–38*–9.85–0–*ct* 3

Northway, Edward George
Amateur. *b:* 30.10.1901, Ceylon. *d:* 4.8.1966, Marylebone, London. Brother of R. P. (Somerset and Northamptonshire). Middle order batsman. *Team* Somerset (1925–26, 8 matches).
Career batting
11–18–4–265–83–18.92–0–*ct* 4
His final first-class match was for the RAF in 1928.

Northway, Reginald Philip
Amateur. *b:* 14.8.1906, Ceylon. *d:* 26.8.1936, Kibworth, Leicestershire. He was killed in a road accident. Brother of E. G. (Somerset). Steady opening right-hand batsman, brilliant deep field. *Sch* Oratory. *Teams* Somerset (1929–33, 17 matches); Northamptonshire (1936, 17 matches).
Career batting
34–57–5–806–75*–15.50–0–*ct* 5

Norton, Bradbury
Amateur. *b:* 23.8.1834, Town Malling, Kent. *d:* 21.2.1917, Porta de Taltal, Chile. Brother of W. S. (Kent) and Selby (Kent), cousin of W. O. J. (Kent), uncle of H. T. Hayman (Kent). Middle order right-hand batsman. *Team* Kent (1858–66, 10 matches).
Career batting
10–18–2–181–56–11.31–0–*ct* 7

Norton, Ernest Willmott
(birth registered as E. Willmott)
Amateur. *b:* 19.6.1889, Sparkhill, Birmingham. *d:* 14.3.1972, Five Ways, Birmingham. Lower order right-hand batsman, leg break and googly bowler. *Sch* KES, Birmingham. *Teams* Warwickshire (1920, 2 matches); Worcestershire (1922–23, 6 matches).
Career batting
8–11–4–108–26*–15.42–0–*ct* 2
Bowling 357–7–51.00–0–0–3/74

Norton, Gerald Ivor Desmond
Amateur. *b:* 19.5.1919, Earl Shilton, Leicestershire. Middle order right-hand batsman, slow left-arm bowler. *Sch* Malvern. *Team* MCC (1958–60).
Career batting
2–3–2–4–2*–4.00–0–*ct* 3
Bowling 133–17–7.82–2–0–6/57

Norton, Ian David
Amateur. *b:* 21.10.1937, Stamford, Lincolnshire. Middle order right-hand batsman. *Sch* Stamford. *Team* Oxford U (1959).
Career batting
1–1–0–30–30–30.00–0–*ct* 2

Norton, William South
Amateur. *b:* 8.6.1831, Town Malling, Kent. *d:* 19.3.1916, Charterhouse, London. Brother of Bradbury (Kent) and Selby (Kent), cousin of W. O. J. (Kent), uncle of H. T. Hayman (Kent). Very steady middle order right-hand batsman, right-hand medium pace round-arm bowler, point field. *Team* Kent (1849–70, 62 matches).
Career batting
87–161–16–2010–120*–13.86–1–*ct* 63
Bowling 1052–63 + 21–16.69–6–0–7/57
He was Hon Secretary and captain of Kent CCC 1859–70.

Notley, Bernarr
Amateur. *b:* 31.8.1918, Mapperley, Nottingham. Lower order right-hand batsman, off break bowler. *Team* Nottinghamshire (1949, 1 match).
Career batting
1–1–0–0–0–0.00–0–*ct* 0
Bowling 90–1–90.00–0–0–1/90

Nott, Arthur Samuel
Professional. *b:* 13.8.1881, Westbury-on-Trym, Bristol. *d:* 28.12.1959, Exhall, Warwickshire. Lower order right-hand batsman, wicket-keeper. *Team* Gloucestershire (1903–12, 15 matches).
Career batting
15–25–3–182–44*–8.27–0–*ct* 9–*st* 4
Bowling 77–0

Nourse, Arthur Dudley
Amateur. *b:* 12.11.1910, Durban, South Africa. *d:* 14.8.1981, Durban, South Africa. He died on the way to Durban Hospital. Son of A. W. (South Africa). Sound middle order right-hand batsman, excellent field. *Team* Natal (1931/2 to 1952/3). *Tours* South Africa to England 1935, 1947, 1951. *Tests* South Africa (1935–51, 34 matches).
Career batting
175–269–27–12472–260*–51.53–41–*ct* 135
Bowling 124–0
Test batting
34–62–7–2960–231–53.81–9–*ct* 12
Bowling 9–0
He hit 1,681 runs, av 41.00, on the 1935 tour, and 1,453, av 42.73, in 1947, but did not reach 1,000 runs in 1951 owing to a broken thumb. Two of his six double centuries were scored in England, the higher being 208 in the Trent Bridge Test of 1951. His highest score was 260* for Natal v Transvaal at Johannesburg in 1936/7. He was vice-captain of the 1947 tourists and captain in 1951; in all he led South Africa in 15 Tests.

Nourse, Arthur William
(known as Arthur David Nourse)
Amateur. *b:* 26.1.1879, Thornton Heath, Surrey. *d:* 8.7.1948, Port Elizabeth, South Africa. Father of A. D. (South Africa). Steady middle order left-hand batsman, left-arm medium or slow bowler, good slip field. *Teams* Natal (1896/7 to 1924/5); Transvaal (1925/6 to 1926/7); Western Province (1927/8 to 1935/6). *Tours* South Africa to England 1907, 1912, 1924, to Australia 1910/11. *Tests* South Africa (1902/3 to 1924, 45 matches).
Career batting
228–371–39–14216–304*–42.81–38–*ct* 171
Bowling 7125–305–23.36–13–1–6/33
Test batting
45–83–8–2234–111–29.78–1–*ct* 43
Bowling 1553–41–37.87–0–0–4/25
He hit 1,000 runs on each of his three visits to England (best 1,928, av 39.34, in 1924). His only double century in England was 213* v Hampshire at Bournemouth in 1912; his triple century was 304* for Natal v Transvaal at Johannesburg in 1919/20. He also hit 1,000 runs in an Australian season. He went to South Africa with the Army in 1895 and settled there. Spanning forty seasons – 1896/7 to 1935/6 – his first-class career was one of the longest on record and he was familiarly known as the 'Grand Old Man' of South African cricket.

Noyes, Francis
Amateur. *b:* 1817. Stylish middle order batsman. *Team* Nottinghamshire (1842–48, 9 matches).
Career batting
21–40–3–402–50–10.86–0–*ct* 11

He was allowed to bat twice in each innings for Nottinghamshire v Hampshire at Southampton in 1843 – one of the Nottinghamshire eleven having been injured on the journey from Nottingham. It is believed he emigrated to the USA in 1850.

Noyes, Stephen James
Cricketer. *b:* 17.9.1963, High Wycombe, Buckinghamshire. Middle order right-hand batsman, slow left-arm bowler. *Team* Cambridge U (1988, blue).
Career batting
8–14–1–170–38–13.07–0–*ct* 0

Nugent, Brig-General Frank Henry
(changed name to Burnell-Nugent)
Amateur. *b:* 5.9.1880, Vyne Park, Basingstoke, Hampshire. *d:* 12.3.1942, Kingsclere, Hampshire. Lower order right-hand batsman, wicket-keeper. *Sch* Winchester. *Team* Hampshire (1904, 1 match).
Career batting
1–2–0–0–0–0.00–0–*ct* 1

Nulty, Mark Alexander Fabian
Cricketer. *b:* 9.10.1967, Dublin, Ireland. Middle order right-hand batsman. *Team* Ireland (1989).
Career batting
1–2–0–60–43–30.00–0–*ct* 0

Nunes, Robert Karl
Amateur. *b:* 7.6.1894, Kingston, Jamaica. *d:* 23.7.1958, Paddington, London. Opening/middle order left-hand batsman, wicket-keeper. *Sch* Dulwich. *Team* Jamaica (1924/5 to 1931/2). *Tours* West Indies to England 1923, 1928. *Tests* West Indies (1928 to 1929/30, 4 matches).
Career batting
61–94–8–2695–200*–31.33–6–*ct* 31–*st* 8
Bowling 83–3–27.66–0–0–2/49
Test batting
4–8–0–245–92–30.62–0–*ct* 2

He was vice-captain of the 1923 tourists and captain in 1928, leading West Indies in that team's first four Tests. His highest score was 200* for Jamaica v Tennyson's XI at Kingston in 1926/7. He was a founder member of the Jamaican Cricket Board of Control and President of the West Indies Board of Control from 1945 to 1952.

Nunley, Harold
Professional. *b:* 12.1.1912, Raunds, Northamptonshire. Lower order left-hand batsman, slow left-arm bowler. *Team* Northamptonshire (1931, 3 matches).
Career batting
3–5–2–20–12–6.66–0–*ct* 0
Bowling 92–0

Nunn, Dr John Ayscough
Amateur. *b:* 19.3.1906, Hadley, Hertfordshire. *d:* 6.4.1987, Colintraive, Argyll, Scotland. Middle order right-hand batsman, right-arm fast bowler, excellent field. *Sch* Sherborne. *Teams* Oxford U (1926–28, blue 1926–27); Middlesex (1926, 3 matches).
Career batting
22–36–2–641–98–18.85–0–*ct* 10

His final first-class match was for Free Foresters in 1946. He also won a blue for rugby.

Nupen, Eiulf Peter
Amateur. *b:* 1.1.1902, Johannesburg, South Africa. *d:* 29.1.1977, Hospital Hill, Durban, South Africa. Cousin of N. R. P. (Transvaal). Lower order right-hand batsman, right-arm fast medium bowler. *Team* Transvaal (1920/1 to 1936/7). *Tour* South Africa to England 1924. *Tests* South Africa (1921/2 to 1935/6, 17 matches).
Career batting
74–105–14–1635–89–17.96–0–*ct* 34
Bowling 6077–334–18.19–33–12–9/48
Test batting
17–31–7–348–69–14.50–0–*ct* 9
Bowling 1788–50–35.76–5–1–6/46

On his tour to England he found himself unable to adapt to turf wickets and though appearing in two Tests, achieved very little. His best bowling was 9/48 for Transvaal v Griqualand West at Johannesburg in 1931/2. He captained South Africa in one Test. He lost an eye in an accident when four years old.

Nurse, Seymour MacDonald
Amateur. *b:* 10.11.1933, Jack-my-Nanny Gap, Black Rock, St Michael, Barbados. Middle order right-hand batsman, off break bowler, excellent close field. *Team* Barbados (1958/9 to 1971/2). *Tours* West Indies to Australia 1960/1, to England 1963, 1966, to India and Sri Lanka 1966/7, to Australia and New Zealand 1968/9; Commonwealth to Pakistan 1963/4; West Indian XI to England 1964; Rest of World to England 1967, 1968; Barbados to England 1969. *Tests* West Indies (1959/60 to 1968/9, 29 matches).
Career batting
141–235–19–9489–258–43.93–26–*ct* 116
Bowling 389–12–32.41–0–0–3/36
Test batting
29–54–1–2523–258–47.60–6–*ct* 21
Bowling 7–0

He was most successful on his 1966 tour to England, scoring 1,105 runs, av 44.20, in first-class matches and 501, av 62.62, in the five Tests, including two centuries. Three of his four double centuries were scored in West Indies, but the highest, 258, was made for West Indies v New Zealand at Christchurch in 1968/9. On his 1963 tour to England he achieved little due to an injury early on.

Nuttall, Henry
Professional. *b:* 6.2.1855, Erith, Kent. *d:* 8.10.1945, Bedgebury, Goudhurst, Kent. Lower order right-hand batsman, wicket-keeper. *Team* Kent (1889–94, 14 matches).
Career batting
14–19–6–39–8–3.00–0–*ct* 12–*st* 6

Nuttall, John Daniel
Cricketer. *b:* 29.12.1967, Fulford, Yorkshire. Middle order right-hand batsman, left-arm medium pace bowler. *Sch* Pocklington. *Team* Oxford U (1987–89, blue 1988–89).
Career batting
9–11–3–77–35–9.62–0–*ct* 3
Bowling 733–12–61.08–0–0–2/64

Nutter, Albert Edward
Professional. *b:* 28.6.1913, Burnley, Lancashire. Sound middle/lower order right-hand batsman, right-arm medium fast bowler, good slip. *Teams* Lancashire (1935–45, 70 matches); Northamptonshire (1948–53, 145 matches).
Career batting
224–294–47–4828–109*–19.54–1–*ct* 161
Bowling 15739–600–26.23–29–2–7/52

His best season was 1938, when he hit 1,156 runs, av 32.11, and took 91 wickets, av 24.64. He exceeded 100 wickets in a season once: 105, av 22.88, in 1948.

Nutter, Ezra
Professional. *b:* 21.11.1858, Marsden, Colne, Lancashire. *d:* 17.11.1903, Nelson, Lancashire. Middle order batsman. *Team* Lancashire (1885, 1 match).
Career batting
1–1–0–18–18–18.00–0–*ct* 0

Nye, John Kent
Professional. *b:* 23.5.1914, Isfield, Sussex. Lower order right-hand batsman, left-arm fast medium bowler. *Team* Sussex (1934–47, 99 matches).
Career batting
99–136–33–885–51–8.59–0–*ct* 35
Bowling 10407–304–34.23–10–0–6/95

He took 110 wickets, av 30.60, in 1939. He had emigrated to Australia in 1926 and spent several years there, before returning to Sussex. He emigrated to Kenya in 1947, but now lives in Sussex.

Nyren, John
Professional. *b:* 15.12.1764, Hambledon, Hampshire. *d:* 30.6.1837, Bromley-by-Bow, London. Son of Richard (Hampshire). Middle order left-hand batsman. *Teams* England (1802–05).
Career batting
12–20–1–159–50*–8.36–0–*ct* 7

His final first-class match was for F. Beauclerk's XI in 1817. Although a useful cricketer in his day, he is remembered principally as the author of 'The Young Cricketer's Tutor' published in 1833. The book was edited by C. C. Clarke and contained an account of the Hambledon Club and its players.

Nyren, Richard
Professional. *b:* 1734 or 1735. *d:* 25.4.1797, Lee or Leigh, Kent. Father of John (England), nephew of R. Newland (Slindon). Hard-hitting left-hand batsman, left-hand under-arm bowler. *Team* Hampshire (1772–84).

He was landlord of the Bat and Ball Inn at Hambledon and later the George Inn, Hambledon, and looked after the cricket grounds used by the Hambledon Club, being perhaps the major figure of the Club.

O

Oakden, Robert Patrick
Professional. *b:* 9.5.1938, Kirkby-in-Ashfield, Nottinghamshire. Tail end right-hand batsman, right-arm fast medium bowler. *Team* Nottinghamshire (1960–61, 8 matches).
Career batting
8–10–3–68–24–9.71–0–*ct* 4
Bowling 728–17–42.82–0–0–4/78

He also represented Nottinghamshire at golf.

Oakes, Charles
Professional. *b:* 10.8.1912, Horsham, Sussex. Brother of J. Y. (Sussex). Forceful middle order right-hand batsman, leg break and googly bowler. *Team* Sussex (1935–54, 285 matches).
Career batting
288–474–40–10893–160–25.09–14–*ct* 160
Bowling 14326–458–31.27–16–0–8/147

He hit 1,000 runs in a season five times (best 1,607, av 29.21, in 1949).

Oakes, Dennis Raymond
Cricketer. *b:* 10.4.1946, Bedworth, Warwickshire. Middle order right-hand batsman, leg break bowler, close field. *Team* Warwickshire (1965, 5 matches).
Career batting
5–8–1–81–33–11.57–0–*ct* 7
Bowling 1–0

A useful soccer player, he appeared for Notts County and Peterborough.

Oakes, John Ypres
Professional. *b:* 29.3.1916, Horsham, Sussex. Brother of Charles (Sussex). Hard-hitting middle order right-hand batsman, off break bowler. *Team* Sussex (1937–51, 128 matches).
Career batting
128–218–19–4410–151–22.16–2–*ct* 84
Bowling 6508–166–39.20–6–0–7/64

He hit 1,157 runs, av 22.68, in 1950. He also played for Northumberland (1954–65).

Oakley, Leonard
Professional. *b:* 11.1.1916, Stourbridge, Worcestershire. Lower order left-hand batsman, slow left-arm bowler. *Team* Worcestershire (1935–48, 8 matches).
Career batting
8–13–4–43–11–4.77–0–*ct* 2
Bowling 393–12–32.75–1–0–6/64

Oakley, William
Professional. *b:* 6.5.1868, Shrewsbury, Shropshire. Lower order batsman, left-arm medium pace bowler. *Team* Lancashire (1893–94, 20 matches).
Career batting
24–38–10–144–24–5.14–0–*ct* 21
Bowling 973–55–17.69–5–1–6/50
His first-class debut was for Liverpool and District XI in 1892. He also played for Shropshire.

Oakman, Alan Stanley Myles
Professional. *b:* 20.4.1930, Hastings, Sussex. Father-in-law of K. D. Smith (Warwickshire). Middle order right-hand batsman, off break bowler, excellent close fielder. *Team* Sussex (1947–68, 497 matches). *Tours* Swanton to West Indies 1955/6; MCC to South Africa 1956/7. *Tests* England (1956, 2 matches).
Career batting
538–912–79–21800–229*–26.17–22–*ct* 594
Bowling 20343–736–27.63–31–2–7/39
Test batting
2–2–0–14–10–7.00–0–*ct* 7
Bowling 21–0
He hit 1,000 runs in a season nine times, going on to 2,000 twice (best 2,307, av 36.61, in 1961). He took 99 wickets, av 20.97, in 1954. His only double century was 229* for Sussex v Nottinghamshire at Worksop in 1961. After retiring from first-class cricket he was a first-class umpire (1969) and then he took up an appointment as coach to Warwickshire CCC retiring in 1987. A useful soccer player, he kept goal for Hastings United.

Oates, Archer Williamson
Professional. *b:* 9.12.1908, Doncaster, Yorkshire. *d:* 31.12.1968, Nottingham. Nephew of T. W. (Nottinghamshire). Lower order right-hand batsman, right-arm fast medium bowler. *Team* Nottinghamshire (1931–33, 7 matches).
Career batting
7–7–2–21–12–4.20–0–*ct* 3
Bowling 465–8–58.12–0–0–2/38

Oates, Thomas William
Professional. *b:* 9.8.1875, Eastwood, Nottinghamshire. *d:* 18.6.1949, Eastwood, Nottinghamshire. Uncle of A. W. (Nottinghamshire). Lower order right-hand batsman, wicket-keeper. *Teams* Nottinghamshire (1897–1925, 420 matches); London County (1900).
Career batting
434–577–111–5976–88–12.82–0–*ct* 758–*st* 235
Bowling 20–0
He was a first-class umpire (1928–38), standing in five Test matches (1928–30).

Oates, William
Professional. *b:* 2.1.1852, Stud Lodge, Wentworth Park, Yorkshire. *d:* 9.12.1940, Clifton Park, Rotherham, Yorkshire. Lower order right-hand batsman, wicket-keeper. *Team* Yorkshire (1874–75, 7 matches).
Career batting
7–13–7–34–14*–5.66–0–*ct* 5–*st* 1

Oates, William Coape
Amateur. *b:* 7.7.1862, Besthorpe Hall, Nottinghamshire. *d:* 20.2.1942, Lincoln. He married the adopted daughter of J. T. Woolley (North). Opening/middle order right-hand batsman. *Sch* Harrow. *Team* Nottinghamshire (1881–82, 4 matches).
Career batting
5–8–0–124–39–15.50–0–*ct* 4
His final first-class match was for MCC in 1895. His chief claim to cricketing fame rests with his innings of 313 not out for the 1st Royal Munster Fusiliers v Army Service Corps at the Curragh in 1895, when, with F. Fitzgerald, he added 623 for the 2nd wicket – the match was described as 'a farce'.

Oates, William Farrand
Professional. *b:* 11.6.1929, Aston, Sheffield, Yorkshire. Attacking middle order right-hand batsman, right-arm medium pace off break bowler. *Teams* Yorkshire (1956, 3 matches); Derbyshire (1959–65, 121 matches).
Career batting
124–214–14–4588–148*–22.94–2–*ct* 54
Bowling 577–13–44.38–1–0–6/47
He hit 1,000 runs in a season twice (best 1,288, av 33.02, in 1961).

O'Bree, Arthur
Amateur. *b:* 31.5.1886, Poona, India. *d:* 27.12.1943, Baragwanath, Johannesburg, South Africa. Middle order right-hand batsman, right-arm medium pace bowler. *Team* Glamorgan (1921–23, 18 matches).
Career batting
18–34–1–431–42*–13.06–0–*ct* 9
He first played for Glamorgan (pre first-class) in 1920.

O'Brien, Brendan Anthony
Cricketer. *b:* 2.9.1942, Galway, Ireland. Middle order right-hand batsman. *Team* Ireland (1966–81).
Career batting
11–17–1–319–45–19.93–0–*ct* 6

O'Brien, Hon Donough
Amateur. *b:* 29.8.1879, Holyhead, Anglesey. *d:* 23.9.1953, Ras-el-Soda, Alexandria, Egypt. Cousin of A. P. (Dublin U), R. M. (Dublin U), and L. H. Gwynn (Ireland), uncle of L. R. White (Middlesex). Middle

order right-hand batsman. *Sch* Winchester. *Teams* Ireland (1902); MCC (1906–07).
Career batting
3–6–1–77–57–15.40–0–*ct* 1
He played in trials at Oxford U, but not in first-class matches.

O'Brien, Francis Patrick
Professional. *b:* 11.2.1911, Christchurch, New Zealand. *d:* 22.10.1991, Christchurch, New Zealand. Attacking middle order right-hand batsman, right-arm medium pace bowler. *Teams* Canterbury (1932/3 to 1945/6); Northamptonshire (1938–39, 40 matches).
Career batting
66–113–5–2649–164–24.52–4–*ct* 34
Bowling 655–14–46.78–0–0–2/14

O'Brien, Gerard Peter
Cricketer. *b:* 12.11.1942, Dublin, Ireland. Middle order right-hand batsman. *Team* Ireland (1976–77).
Career batting
2–4–0–22–11–5.50–0–*ct* 3

O'Brien, John George
Amateur. *b:* 10.1.1866, Dublin, Ireland. *d:* 15.8.1920, Dublin, Ireland. Brother of T. C. (Middlesex). Lower order batsman. *Team* Ireland (1910).
Career batting
1–2–0–7–4–3.50–0–*ct* 1
He also played for Herefordshire (1891).

O'Brien, Neil Terence
Cricketer. *b:* 9.3.1945, Heaton Moor, Lancashire. Middle order right-hand batsman, right-arm medium pace bowler. *Team* Minor Counties (1979–81).
Career batting
2–2–0–27–14–13.50–0–*ct* 1
Bowling 101–1–101.00–0–0–1/23
His County cricket was for Cheshire (1970–91).

O'Brien, Robin
Amateur. *b:* 20.11.1932, Shillong, India. *d:* 26.8.1959, Biddenden, Kent. Opening right-hand batsman, off break bowler. *Sch* Wellington. *Teams* Cambridge U (1954–56, blue 1955–56); Ireland (1954–58).
Career batting
40–74–3–1609–146–22.66–2–*ct* 10
Bowling 4–0
He was also awarded his blue for golf.

O'Brien, Sir Timothy Carew
Amateur. *b:* 5.11.1861, Dublin, Ireland. *d:* 9.12.1948, Ramsey, Isle of Man. Brother of J. G. (Ireland), brother-in-law of C. E. de Trafford (Warwickshire and Leicestershire). Attractive middle order right-hand batsman, left-arm bowler. *Sch* Downside. *Teams* Middlesex (1881–98, 156 matches); Oxford U (1884–85, blue both years); Ireland (1902–07). *Tours* Vernon to Australia 1887/8; Hawke to South Africa 1895/6. *Tests* England (1884 to 1895/6, 5 matches).
Career batting
266–452–30–11397–202–27.00–15–*ct* 173–*st* 2
Bowling 340–4–85.00–0–0–1/10
Test batting
5–8–0–59–20–7.37–0–*ct* 4
He hit 1,000 runs in a season three times (best 1,150, av 27.38, in 1884). His only double century was 202 for Middlesex v Sussex at Hove in 1895. He captained England in one Test. His final first-class match was for L. Robinson's XI in 1914, when he had the satisfaction of scoring 90 and 111.

O'Brien-Butler, Paget Terence
Amateur. *b:* 1.8.1911, Vanowrie, India. *d:* 22.6.1952, Ballynure, Co Wicklow, Ireland. Middle order batsman. *Sch* Clifton. *Team* Ireland (1936).
Career batting
1–2–0–33–18–16.50–0–*ct* 0

O'Byrne, William Francis Thomas
Amateur. *b:* 30.4.1908, Bromley, Kent. *d:* 23.10.1951, Baldslow, St Leonards-on-Sea, Sussex. Middle order right-hand batsman. *Team* Sussex (1935, 1 match).
Career batting
1–2–0–34–26–17.00–0–*ct* 1

Ochse, Arthur Lennox
Amateur. *b:* 11.10.1899, Graaff-Reinet, Cape Province, South Africa. *d:* 5.5.1949, Middelburg, Cape Province, South Africa. Lower order right-hand batsman, right-arm fast bowler. *Team* Eastern Province (1921/2 to 1937/8). *Tour* South Africa to England 1929. *Tests* South Africa (1927/8 to 1929, 3 matches).
Career batting
45–66–12–564–41–10.44–0–*ct* 20
Bowling 3967–140–28.33–7–1–6/37
Test batting
3–4–1–11–4*–3.66–0–*ct* 1
Bowling 362–10–36.20–0–0–4/79
Although the best of the fast bowlers on the 1929 tour to England, he returned only moderate figures, topping the Test averages with 10 wickets, av 31.70. He was very erratic in some of the County matches.

O'Connor, Jack
Professional. *b:* 6.11.1897, Cambridge. *d:* 22.2.1977, Buckhurst Hill, Essex. Son of John (Derbyshire), nephew of H. A. Carpenter (Essex). Middle order right-hand batsman, leg break and off break bowler. *Team* Essex (1921–39, 516 matches). *Tours* Tennyson to Jamaica 1926/7; Cahn to Jamaica 1928/9; MCC to West Indies 1929/30. *Tests* England (1929 to 1929/30, 4 matches).
Career batting
540–903–79–28764–248–34.90–72–*ct* 226–*st* 1
Bowling 18325–557–32.89–18–2–7/52
Test batting
4–7–0–153–51–21.85–0–*ct* 2

Bowling 72–1–72.00–0–0–1/31

He hit 1,000 runs in a season 16 times going on to 2,000 four times (best 2,350, av 55.95, in 1934). Both his double centuries were for Essex, the highest being 248 v Surrey at Brentwood 1934. He also played for Buckinghamshire (1946–47). He was Essex coach 1946–48.

O'Connor, John
Professional. *b:* 23.2.1867, Pinxton, Derbyshire. *d:* 13.7.1936, Cambridge. Father of Jack (Essex), brother-in-law of H. A. Carpenter (Essex). Tail end right-hand batsman, right-arm medium pace off break bowler. *Team* Derbyshire (1900, 9 matches).
Career batting
9–14–5–55–17–6.11–0–*ct* 4
Bowling 619–24–25.79–2–1–5/56
He also played for Cambridgeshire (1892–1912).

O'Connor, John Denis Alphonsus
Amateur. *b:* 9.9.1875, Burrowa, Sydney, New South Wales, Australia. *d:* 23.8.1941, Lewisham, Sydney, New South Wales, Australia. Lower order left-hand batsman, right-arm medium pace bowler. *Teams* New South Wales (1904/5 to 1905/6, 8 matches); South Australia (1906/7 to 1909/10, 15 matches). *Tour* Australia to England 1909. *Tests* Australia (1907/8 to 1909, 4 matches).
Career batting
50–77–18–695–54–11.77–0–*ct* 32
Bowling 5255–224–23.45–18–5–7/36
Test batting
4–8–1–86–20–12.28–0–*ct* 3
Bowling 340–13–26.15–1–0–5/40
Regarded as one of the principal bowlers of the 1909 touring team, he took a long time to adapt to English wickets and played in only one Test.

O'Connor, Valentine Rickard
Amateur. *b:* 1878, Ireland. *d:* 23.6.1956, Paddington, London. Middle order right-hand batsman, slow right-arm bowler. *Sch* Prior Park College. *Team* Middlesex (1908–09, 3 matches).
Career batting
3–4–0–40–30–10.00–0–*ct* 2
Bowling 62–1–62.00–0–0–1/62

O'Daly, G. N. (*see under* Daly, G. N.)

Odams, Frederick Williams
Professional. *b:* 5.1.1843, Cambridge. *d:* 30.1.1879, Cambridge. Lower order right-hand batsman, right-hand slow round-arm bowler, wicket-keeper. *Team* Cambridgeshire (1867, 2 matches).
Career batting
2–4–0–3–3–0.75–0–*ct* 0

Odell, Edwin Freame
Amateur. *b:* 2.12.1883, Leicester. *d:* 11.3.1960, Northfield, Birmingham. Brother of W. W. (Leicestershire). Lower order left-hand batsman, left-arm medium pace bowler. *Team* Leicestershire (1912, 1 match).
Career batting
1–1–0–0–0–0.00–0–*ct* 0
Bowling 42–2–21.00–0–0–2/42

Odell, William Ward
Amateur. *b:* 5.11.1881, Leicester. *d:* 4.10.1917, near Passchendaele, Belgium. He was killed in action. Brother of E. F. (Leicestershire). Lower order right-hand batsman, right-arm medium pace bowler. *Sch* KES, Birmingham. *Teams* Leicestershire (1901–14, 172 matches); London County (1902–04).
Career batting
193–299–53–3368–75–13.69–0–*ct* 88
Bowling 17416–737–23.63–45–6–8/20
He took 100 wickets in a season four times (best 112, av 25.08, in 1904).

Odendaal, André
Cricketer. *b:* 4.5.1954, Queenstown, Cape Province, South Africa. Middle order right-hand batsman, off break bowler. *Teams* Cambridge U (1980–83, blue 1980); Boland (1980/1 to 1981/2).
Career batting
22–37–3–659–61–19.38–0–*ct* 16
He was a well known writer on cricket.

O'Donnell, Simon Patrick
Cricketer. *b:* 26.1.1963, Deniliquin, New South Wales, Australia. Middle order right-hand batsman, right-arm fast medium bowler. *Team* Victoria (1983/4 to 1991/2, 61 matches). *Tours* Australia to Sharjah (not first-class) 1984/5, 1986/7, 1989/90, to England 1985, to India and Pakistan (World Cup) 1987/8, to New Zealand 1989/90, to India 1989/90 (not first-class); Rest of World to England 1989; Victoria to England 1991. *Tests* Australia (1985 to 1985/6, 6 matches).
Career batting
74–118–16–3948–130–38.70–7–*ct* 55
Bowling 5185–138–37.57–2–0–6/54
Test batting
6–10–3–206–48–29.42–0–*ct* 4
Bowling 504–6–84.00–0–0–3/37
He came to England as a young promising all-rounder in 1985 and began the tour well, but faded in the later stages and, after playing in the first five Tests, was dropped for the sixth. Since then he has gained a reputation as an ideal one-day international cricketer. In Sharjah in 1989/90 he hit 50 off 18 balls to create a new one-day record. He played for Northumberland in 1989, when he failed to gain selection for the Australian side to England. He missed the 1987/8 season due to cancer, but fully recovered by the following year.

Ogilvy, Geoffrey Littlejohn
Amateur. *b:* 25.1.1906, Lewisham, London. *d:* 20.1.1962, Dreekskerry, Maughold, Isle of Man. Mid-

dle order right-hand batsman. *Sch* St Bees. *Team* Somerset (1936, 2 matches).
Career batting
2–3–0–44–29–14.66–0–*ct* 1
He also played for Dorset (1931–32).

O'Gorman, Joseph George
Amateur. *b:* 24.7.1890, Walworth, London. *d:* 26.8.1974, Weybridge, Surrey. Grandfather of T. J. G. (Derbyshire). Lower order right-hand batsman, right-arm slow medium bowler. *Team* Surrey (1927, 3 matches).
Career batting
3–4–3–106–42*–106.00–0–*ct* 1
Bowling 167–4–41.75–0–0–2/49
With his brother, Dave, he formed a famous comedy act and his theatrical engagements prevented him from appearing in much County cricket.

O'Gorman, Timothy Joseph Gerard
Cricketer. *b:* 15.5.1967, Woking, Surrey. Grandson of J. G. (Surrey). Middle order right-hand batsman, off break bowler. *Sch* St George's College, Weybridge. *Team* Derbyshire (1987–92, 71 matches).
Career batting
71–120–16–3228–148–31.03–5–*ct* 45
Bowling 207–3–69.00–0–0–1/7
He hit 1,000 runs in a season twice (best 1,116, av 27.90, in 1991).

O'Halloran, James Patrick
Professional. *b:* 12.1.1872, Richmond, Melbourne, Victoria, Australia. *d:* 28.4.1943, East Melbourne, Victoria, Australia. Middle order right-hand batsman, right-arm medium pace bowler. *Teams* Victoria (1896/7, 3 matches); MCC (1897–98).
Career batting
9–15–3–243–128*–20.25–1–*ct* 4
Bowling 523–11–47.54–0–0–3/92
He scored 128* on debut for Victoria v South Australia at Melbourne in 1896/7.

O'Keeffe, Kerry James
Cricketer. *b:* 25.11.1949, Hurstville, Sydney, New South Wales, Australia. Lower order right-hand batsman, leg break and googly bowler. *Teams* New South Wales (1968/9 to 1979/80, 65 matches); Somerset (1971–72, 46 matches). *Tours* Australia to England 1977, to West Indies 1972/3, to New Zealand 1969/70, 1973/4, 1976/7. *Tests* Australia (1970/1 to 1977, 24 matches).
Career batting
169–233–73–4169–99*–26.05–0–*ct* 112
Bowling 13382–476–28.11–24–5–7/38
Test batting
24–34–9–644–85–25.76–0–*ct* 15
Bowling 2018–53–38.07–1–0–5/101
Although he played in three Tests on the 1977 tour of England his bowling record was a modest one – 36 wickets, av 28.75, in all first-class matches. His best season in England was 1972 when he took 77 wickets, av 23.57.

Old, Alan Gerald Bernard
Cricketer. *b:* 23.9.1945, Middlesbrough, Yorkshire. Brother of C. M. (Yorkshire and Warwickshire). Middle order right-hand batsman, right-arm fast medium bowler. *Team* Warwickshire (1969, 1 match).
Career batting
1–1–0–34–34–34.00–0–*ct* 1
Bowling 93–1–93.00–0–0–1/64
He also played for Durham (pre first-class, 1968–78). An excellent rugby footballer, he has represented England and the British Lions at fly-half and on one occasion was playing rugby for England on the same day as his brother represented England in a Test.

Old, Christopher Middleton
Cricketer. *b:* 22.12.1948, Middlesbrough, Yorkshire. Brother of A. G. B. (Warwickshire). Hard-hitting lower order left-hand batsman, right-arm fast medium bowler. *Teams* Yorkshire (1966–82, 222 matches); Northern Transvaal (1981/2 to 1982/3); Warwickshire (1983–85, 47 matches). *Tours* Norfolk to West Indies 1969/70; MCC to India and Pakistan 1972/3, to West Indies 1973/4, 1980/1, to Australia and New Zealand 1974/5, to India and Australia 1976/7; England to Pakistan and New Zealand 1977/8, to Australia 1978/9; International Wanderers to Rhodesia 1975/6; SAB England XI to South Africa 1981/2. *Tests* England (1972/3 to 1981, 46 matches).
Career batting
379–463–91–7756–116–20.84–6–*ct* 214
Bowling 25127–1070–23.48–39–2–7/20
Test batting
46–66–9–845–65–14.82–0–*ct* 22
Bowling 4020–143–28.11–4–0–7/50
Originally coming to Yorkshire as a batsman who could bowl, Old found himself succeeding Trueman as the County's principal opening bowler. So successful was he that he gained a regular place in the England team in 1973, despite the fact that serious knee injuries had necessitated operations both in 1970 and 1971. In 1972 he took 54 wickets, av 17.24, and in 1974, 72 wickets, av 18.97. In 1976, however, he was once again dogged by knee trouble, which meant that he played little first-class cricket at all that season. He proved his fitness in a dramatic manner in 1977 by hitting a century in 37 minutes for Yorkshire v Warwickshire at Edgbaston and the following summer was perhaps the best of his career. In the Tests v Pakistan his 13 wickets cost 14.69 runs each and in the Edgbaston Test he took four wickets in five balls. His first-class record for the year was 64 wickets, av 17.31, and his best all-round performance came in the Roses match at Old Trafford, when he not only took 9 wickets but hit a century.
In 1981 he was appointed captain of the troubled Yorkshire side, but in the middle of the following

year was dismissed and in rather acrimonious circumstances left the County at the end of 1982. He made his debut for Warwickshire in 1983, taking 62 wickets, av 29.41, in that season. His last first-class match was for D. B. Close's XI in 1986. He also played for Northumberland (1986–87).

Oldfield, Christopher Campbell
Amateur. *b:* 30.10.1838, Patna, India. *d:* 14.5.1916, Westminster, London. Tail end batsman, good bowler. *Sch* Eton. *Team* Gentlemen of Kent (1864).
Career batting
4–7–2–24–19–4.80–0–*ct* 1
Bowling 137–9–15.22–0–0–4/45

His final first-class match was for MCC in 1873.

Oldfield, Norman
Professional. *b:* 5.5.1911, Dukinfield, Cheshire. Stylish opening right-hand batsman, good field at gully. *Teams* Lancashire (1935–39, 151 matches); Northamptonshire (1948–54, 159 matches). *Tours* Cahn to New Zealand 1938/9; Commonwealth to India, Pakistan and Ceylon 1949/50. *Test* England (1939, 1 match).
Career batting
332–521–51–17811–168–37.89–38–*ct* 96
Bowling 121–2–60.50–0–0–1/0
Test batting
1–2–0–99–80–49.50–0–*ct* 0

He hit 1,000 runs in a season 11 times going on to 2,000 once: 2,192, av 49.81, in 1949. He was a first-class umpire (1955–65), standing in two Test matches (1960–62), and Lancashire coach 1968–72.

Oldfield, Peter Carlton
Amateur. *b:* 27.2.1911, Headingley, Leeds, Yorkshire. Lower order right-hand batsman, wicket-keeper. *Sch* Repton. *Team* Oxford U (1931–33, blue 1932–33).
Career batting
24–31–7–237–36–9.87–0–*ct* 26–*st* 33

His final first-class match was for MCC in 1934.

Oldfield, William Albert Stanley, MBE
Amateur. *b:* 9.9.1894, Alexandria, Sydney, New South Wales, Australia. *d:* 10.8.1976, Killara, Sydney, New South Wales, Australia. Lower order right-hand batsman, brilliant wicket-keeper. *Team* New South Wales (1919/20 to 1937/8, 82 matches). *Tours* AIF to England 1919, to South Africa 1919/20; Australia to England 1921, 1926, 1930, 1934, to South Africa 1921/2, 1935/6, to New Zealand 1927/8; New South Wales to New Zealand 1923/4. *Tests* Australia (1920/1 to 1936/7, 54 matches).
Career batting
245–315–57–6135–137–23.77–6–*ct* 400–*st* 262
Test batting
54–80–17–1427–65*–22.65–0–*ct* 78–*st* 52

On the 1921 tour to England he was the reserve wicket-keeper and appeared in only one Test, but on his three subsequent visits he appeared in all fifteen Tests and built up a reputation as one of the greatest of all wicket-keepers and the best of his generation.

Oldham, Stephen
Cricketer. *b:* 26.7.1948, High Green, Sheffield, Yorkshire. Tail end right-hand batsman, right-arm fast medium bowler. *Teams* Yorkshire (1974–85, 59 matches); Derbyshire (1980–83, 70 matches).
Career batting
129–98–41–648–50–11.36–0–*ct* 38
Bowling 8919–273–32.67–4–0–7/78

He was appointed Cricket Manager to Yorkshire CCC in 1990, having previously held a coaching position with the club. He reappeared for Yorkshire in 1989 in limited overs matches.

Oldknow, James
Professional. *b:* 12.3.1873, Denby, Derbyshire. *d:* 10.9.1944, Belper, Derbyshire. Tail end right-hand batsman, right-arm medium pace bowler. *Team* Derbyshire (1901, 2 matches).
Career batting
2–4–1–7–4*–2.33–0–*ct* 2
Bowling 162–4–40.50–0–0–3/123

Oldroyd, Edgar
Professional. *b:* 1.10.1888, Healey, Batley, Yorkshire. *d:* 27.12.1964, Truro, Cornwall. Sound middle order right-hand batsman, right-arm medium pace off break bowler. *Team* Yorkshire (1910–31, 383 matches).
Career batting
384–511–58–15925–194–35.15–36–*ct* 203
Bowling 1658–42–39.47–0–0–4/14

He hit 1,000 runs in a season ten times (best 1,690, av 43.33, in 1922).

O'Linn, Sidney
(birth registered as S. O'Linsky)
Professional. *b:* 5.5.1927, Oudtshoorn, Cape Province, South Africa. Middle order left-hand batsman, wicket-keeper, excellent field. *Teams* Western Province (1945/6 to 1946/7); Kent (1951–54, 26 matches); Transvaal (1957/8 to 1965/6). *Tours* South Africa to England 1960. *Tests* South Africa (1960 to 1961/2, 7 matches).
Career batting
92–156–29–4525–120*–35.62–4–*ct* 97–*st* 6
Bowling 119–2–59.50–0–0–2/14
Test batting
7–12–1–297–98–27.00–0–*ct* 4

He hit 1,000 runs in a season twice – once for Kent in 1952 and once for the South African tourists in 1960 (best 1,080, av 29.18, in 1952). On the 1960 tour he proved one of the most reliable batsmen, playing in all five Tests. He played soccer for Charlton Athletic, and for South Africa on tour to Australia in 1947.

Oliphant, Patrick James
Amateur. *b:* 19.3.1914, Edinburgh, Scotland. *d:* 1.1.1979, Edinburgh, Scotland. Middle order right-hand batsman. *Sch* Edinburgh Academy. *Team* Scotland (1937).
Career batting
1–2–0–15–15–7.50–0–*ct* 0

Oliphant-Callum, Ralph David
Cricketer. *b:* 26.9.1971, Twickenham, Middlesex. Lower order right-hand batsman, wicket-keeper. *Team* Oxford U (1992).
Career batting
3–2–0–28–19–14.00–0–*ct* 1

Olive, Martin
Cricketer. *b:* 18.4.1958, Watford, Hertfordshire. Middle order right-hand batsman, right-arm medium pace bowler. *Sch* Millfield. *Team* Somerset (1977–81, 17 matches).
Career batting
17–32–2–467–50–15.56–0–*ct* 9
He also played for Devon (1982–87).

Oliver, Charles Joshua
Amateur. *b:* 1.11.1905, Wanganui, Wellington, New Zealand. *d:* 25.9.1977, Brisbane, Queensland, Australia. Hard-hitting middle order right-hand batsman, good outfield. *Team* Canterbury (1923/4 to 1935/6). *Tours* New Zealand to Australia 1925/6, 1927/8, to England 1927.
Career batting
35–61–5–1301–91–23.23–0–*ct* 20
Bowling 169–1–169.00–0–0–1/35
He had very little success on the 1927 tour to England. His final first-class match was for NZ Air Force XI in 1942/3. A noted rugby footballer, he represented New Zealand, being vice captain of the 1935 All Blacks in England.

Oliver, Frederick William
Amateur. *b:* 4.1.1836, Mayfair, London. *d:* 7.7.1899, Earl's Court, London. Opening/middle order right-hand batsman, right-hand fast medium round-arm bowler, slip field. *Sch* Westminster. *Teams* Surrey (1855–56, 2 matches); Oxford U (1856–57, blue both years).
Career batting
10–19–0–247–32–13.00–0–*ct* 5–*st* 2
Bowling 77–3–25.66–0–0–3/43
He was the mainstay of the Wimbledon Club for many years.

Oliver, John Archibald Ralph
Amateur. *b:* 25.11.1918, Whitwell, Hertfordshire. *d:* 24.2.1992. Opening right-hand batsmam, right-arm medium fast or off break bowler. *Sch* Aldenham. *Team* Minor Counties (1951).
Career batting
1–2–1–93–84*–93.00–0–*ct* 0
His County cricket was for Bedfordshire (1935–61). He played soccer for Corinthian Casuals and hockey for Bedfordshire.

Oliver, Leonard
Amateur. *b:* 18.10.1886, Glossop, Derbyshire. *d:* 22.1.1948, Glossop, Derbyshire. Opening left-hand batsman, right-arm medium pace bowler. *Sch* Manchester GS. *Team* Derbyshire (1908–24, 174 matches).
Career batting
174–322–13–6303–170–20.39–6–*ct* 69
Bowling 328–5–65.60–0–0–2/20
He was joint captain of Derbyshire in 1920.

Oliver, Philip Robert
Cricketer. *b:* 9.5.1956, West Bromwich, Staffordshire. Middle order right-hand batsman, off break bowler. *Team* Warwickshire (1975–82, 89 matches).
Career batting
89–128–20–2679–171*–24.80–2–*ct* 46
Bowling 2115–27–78.33–0–0–2/28
He also played for Shropshire (1972–74 and 1985) and Staffordshire (1987–91).

Olivier, Eric
Amateur. *b:* 24.11.1888, Oudtshoorn, Cape Province, South Africa. *d:* 1.6.1928, Cape Town, South Africa. Tail end right-hand batsman, right-arm fast medium bowler. *Sch* Repton. *Teams* Cambridge U (1908–09, blue both years); Hampshire (1911, 7 matches).
Career batting
22–38–11–302–43–11.18–0–*ct* 9
Bowling 2036–90–22.62–8–4–8/51
He played in South Africa against MCC in 1913/14, but not in first-class matches.

Olivier, Sidney Richard
Amateur. *b:* 1.3.1870, Wilton, Wiltshire. *d:* 21.1.1932, Horton, Dorset. Nephew of F. M. Eden (Oxford U 1849), brother-in-law of L. P. Collins (Oxford U). Middle order batsman. *Team* Hampshire (1895, 1 match).
Career batting
1–1–0–0–0–0.00–0–*ct* 3
He also played for Wiltshire (1891). He was the uncle of Sir Laurence Olivier, the actor.

Olley, Martin William Charles
Cricketer. *b:* 27.11.1963, Romford, Essex. Lower order right-hand batsman, wicket-keeper. *Sch* Felsted. *Teams* Northamptonshire (1983, 1 match); Middlesex (1988, 4 matches).
Career batting
5–6–1–77–27*–15.40–0–*ct* 12
He also played for Hertfordshire (1984–90) and Cambridgeshire (1991–92).

Ollis, Richard Leslie
Cricketer. *b:* 14.1.1961, Clifton, Bristol. Middle order left-hand batsman, right-arm medium pace bowler.

Ollivant, Alfred

Team Somerset (1981–85, 37 matches).
Career batting
37–60–4–1016–99*–18.14–0–*ct* 19
Bowling 10–0

Ollivant, Alfred
Amateur. *b:* 4.1.1839, Stretford, Lancashire. *d:* 26.5.1906, Bowdon, Cheshire. Middle order batsman. *Team* Lancashire (1873–74, 2 matches).
Career batting
2–3–1–36–24*–18.00–0–*ct* 0

Ollivierre, Charles Augustus
Amateur. *b:* 20.7.1876, Kingstown, St Vincent. *d:* 25.3.1949, Pontefract, Yorkshire. Brother of Helon (Trinidad) and R. C. (West Indies). Attractive opening right-hand batsman, good field. *Teams* Trinidad (1894/5); Derbyshire (1901–07, 110 matches). *Tour* West Indies to England 1900 (not first-class).
Career batting
114–209–4–4830–229–23.56–3–*ct* 109
Bowling 664–29–22.89–3–1–6/51

After the 1900 tour of England, he remained behind in order to qualify for Derbyshire. He hit 1,268, av 34.27, in 1904; this included his only double century – 229 for Derbyshire v Essex at Chesterfield. His final first-class match in the West Indies was for A. B. St Hill's XII in 1898/9.

Ollivierre, Richard Cordice
Amateur. *b:* 1880, Kingstown, St Vincent. *d:* 5.6.1937, New York, USA. Brother of C. A. (Derbyshire) and Helon (Trinidad). Middle or lower order right-hand batsman, right-arm fast bowler. *Teams* A. B. St Hill's XII (1898/9 to 1900/1); W. C. Shepherd's XI (1909/10). *Tour* West Indies to England 1906.
Career batting
25–49–0–878–67–17.91–0–*ct* 22–*st* 2
Bowling 1867–88–21.21–4–1–7/23

He proved to be a useful all-rounder on the 1906 tour. His final first-class match was for a West Indies XI in 1912/13.

Olton, Michael Francis
Cricketer. *b:* 20.6.1938, San Fernando, Trinidad. Middle order right-hand batsman, off break bowler. *Teams* Trinidad (1959/60); Kent (1962, 1 match).
Career batting
3–6–1–98–28–19.60–0–*ct* 0
Bowling 199–2–99.50–0–0–2/86

O'Maille, Ciaran
Amateur. *b:* 14.6.1925, Dublin, Ireland. *d:* 4.3.1977, Dublin, Ireland. Opening right-hand batsman. *Team* Ireland (1953–60).
Career batting
2–3–1–10–5–5.00–0–*ct* 2

He played hockey for Ireland.

Omarshah, Ali Hassimshah
(known as A. H. Shah)
Cricketer. *b:* 7.8.1959, Salisbury, Rhodesia. Middle order left-hand batsman, right-arm medium pace bowler. *Team* Zimbabwe (1979/80 to 1991/2). *Tours* Zimbabwe to England 1983 (World Cup), 1985, 1990, to Sri Lanka 1983/4, to India (World Cup) 1987/8, to Australia and New Zealand (World Cup) 1991/2.
Career batting
33–55–4–1189–185–23.31–2–*ct* 13
Bowling 1040–18–57.77–0–0–4/113

He proved a useful all-rounder on the tours to England.

O'Meara, Joseph Anthony
Cricketer. *b:* 24.6.1943, Dublin, Ireland. Middle order right-hand batsman, off break bowler. *Team* Ireland (1963).
Career batting
1–2–0–0–0–0.00–0–*ct* 3
Bowling 14–1–14.00–0–0–1/14

He played hockey for Ireland.

O'Neill, Norman Clifford
Amateur. *b:* 19.2.1937, Carlton, Sydney, New South Wales, Australia. Father of M. D. (Western Australia and New South Wales). Attacking middle order right-hand batsman, right-arm medium, or leg break, bowler, excellent deep field. *Team* New South Wales (1955/6 to 1966/7, 70 matches). *Tours* Australia to England 1961, 1964, to West Indies 1964/5, to New Zealand 1956/7, 1966/7, to India and Pakistan 1959/60; Cavaliers to South Africa 1960/1, to India and South Africa 1962/3. *Tests* Australia (1958/9 to 1964/5, 42 matches).
Career batting
188–306–34–13859–284–50.95–45–*ct* 104
Bowling 4060–99–41.01–0–0–4/40
Test batting
42–69–8–2779–181–45.55–6–*ct* 21
Bowling 667–17–39.23–0–0–4/41

Coming to England in 1961 with a big reputation, he took some time to master English wickets, but latterly was most successful and in first-class matches hit 1,981 runs, av 60.03. He played in all five Tests hitting 117 in the fifth match at the Oval. A knee injury affected his form on the 1964 tour, but in first-class matches he made 1,369 runs, av 45.63; he appeared in four of the five Tests, failing to reach 50 in any of his six innings. His highest score was 284 for Australians v President's XI at Ahmedabad in 1959/60 and he twice hit 1,000 runs in an Australian season (best 1,288, av 53.66, in 1960/1). His final first-class match was for the Prime Minister's XI in the Koyna Relief Fund Match in India in 1967/8.

Onslow, Denzil Roberts
Amateur. *b:* 12.6.1839, Chittore, Madras, India. *d:* 21.3.1908, Westminster, London. Grandson of Denzil (Kent, Surrey and Hampshire). Attacking middle order right-hand batsman, right-arm fast bowler. *Sch* Brighton. *Teams* Cambridge U (1859–61, blue 1860–61); Sussex (1860–69, 6 matches).
Career batting
23–40–0–428–53–10.70–0–*ct* 6
Bowling 257–14 + 6–18.35–2–0–6/?
His final first-class match was for MCC in 1873. He was in India for some years, being Private Secretary to the Finance Minister and played for Calcutta. Commencing 1874 he was MP for Guildford until the borough was disenfranchised in 1885.

Ontong, Rodney Craig
Cricketer. *b:* 9.9.1955, Johannesburg, South Africa. Son-in-law of J. S. Pressdee (Glamorgan). Middle order right-hand batsman, right-arm fast medium, later off break bowler. *Teams* Border (1972/3 to 1984/5); Glamorgan (1975–89, 257 matches); Transvaal (1976/7 to 1977/8); Northern Transvaal (1978/9 to 1989/90).
Career batting
362–596–86–15071–204*–29.55–20–*ct* 178
Bowling 25972–836–31.06–33–4–8/67
He hit 1,000 runs in a season five times (best 1,320, av 35.66, in 1984). His highest score was 204* for Glamorgan v Middlesex at Swansea in 1984. In the match between Glamorgan and Nottinghamshire at Trent Bridge in 1985 he took 13 for 106 and scored 130 runs. He captained Glamorgan from 1985 to 1986. In 1988 he badly injured a knee in a road accident and this ended his career in county cricket, though he subsequently reappeared in first-class cricket in South Africa briefly.

Opatha, Antony Ralph Marinon
Cricketer. *b:* 5.8.1947, Colombo, Ceylon. Lower order right-hand batsman, right-arm medium pace bowler. *Team* Ceylon/Sri Lanka (1969/70 to 1982/3). *Tours* Sri Lanka to Pakistan 1973/4, to England 1975, 1979, to India 1975/6; Arosa Sri Lankan XI to South Africa 1982/3.
Career batting
39–53–7–790–65–17.17–0–*ct* 24
Bowling 3413–111–30.74–2–0–6/91
He acted as a manager on the 1982/3 tour to South Africa. He played for Sri Lanka in one-day international matches.

Openshaw, William Edward
Amateur. *b:* 5.2.1852. *d:* 7.2.1915, Haydock, Newton-le-Willows, Lancashire. Sound middle order right-hand batsman. *Sch* Harrow. *Team* Lancashire (1879–82, 4 matches).
Career batting
4–5–0–29–16–5.80–0–*ct* 1
He also played for Cheshire (1872–78). A noted rugby footballer, he represented England.

Oppenheimer, Jonathan Maximillian Ernest
Cricketer. *b:* 18.11.1969, Johannesburg, South Africa. Lower order right-hand batsman, right-arm medium pace bowler. *Sch* Harrow. *Team* Oxford U (1989–91, blue 1991).
Career batting
10–7–2–7–7–1.40–0–*ct* 2
Bowling 928–13–71.38–0–0–3/51

Ord, James Simpson
Professional. *b:* 12.7.1912, Backworth, Northumberland. Brother of J. D. (Minor Counties). Middle order right-hand batsman, right-arm medium pace bowler, excellent outfield. *Team* Warwickshire (1933–53, 273 matches).
Career batting
273–459–35–11788–187*–27.80–16–*ct* 78
Bowling 244–2–122.00–0–0–1/0
He hit 1,000 runs in a season six times (best 1,577, av 39.42, in 1948). He also played for Northumberland (1930).

Ord, John Douglas
Professional. *b:* 1.2.1907, Backworth, Northumberland. *d:* 3.1.1991, Earlsdon, Coventry, Warwickshire. Brother of J. S. (Warwickshire). Middle order left-hand batsman, slow left-arm bowler. *Team* Minor Counties (1934).
Career batting
1–2–0–42–35–21.00–0–*ct* 0
His County cricket was for Northumberland (1927–36).

Orders, Jonathan Oliver Darcy
Cricketer. *b:* 12.8.1957, Kent House, Beckenham, Kent. Middle order left-hand batsman, left-arm medium pace bowler. *Sch* Winchester. *Team* Oxford U (1978–81, blue all four years).
Career batting
27–49–3–1072–79–23.30–0–*ct* 9
Bowling 656–11–59.63–0–0–2/16

O'Reilly, Peter Mark
Cricketer. *b:* 23.7.1964, Dublin, Ireland. Tail end right-hand batsman, right-arm fast bowler. *Team* Ireland (1982–84).
Career batting
2–3–2–1–1*–1.00–0–*ct* 0
Bowling 81–5–16.20–0–0–3/43
He was on the Warwickshire staff but played no first-class matches for the county.

O'Reilly, William Joseph
Amateur. *b:* 20.12.1905, White Cliffs, New South Wales, Australia. *d:* 6.10.1992, Sutherland, Sydney, New South Wales, Australia. Lower order left-hand batsman, leg break and googly bowler. *Team* New South Wales (1927/8 to 1945/6, 54 matches). *Tours*

Australia to England 1934, 1938, to South Africa 1935/6, to New Zealand 1945/6. *Tests* Australia (1931/2 to 1945/6, 27 matches).
Career batting
135–167–41–1655–56*–13.13–0–*ct* 65
Bowling 12850–774–16.60–63–17–9/38
Test batting
27–39–7–410–56*–12.81–0–*ct* 7
Bowling 3254–144–22.59–11–3–7/54

The outstanding success of the 1934 tour to England, he headed the first-class averages with 109 wickets, av 17.04, and the Test averages with 28, av 24.92. His ability to vary his pace and turn the ball either way, plus the knack he had of making the ball lift unexpectedly, proved the downfall of many leading English batsmen. He was just as deadly in 1938 with 104 wickets, av 16.59, in first-class matches and 22, av 27.72, in Tests, again heading both tables. By the end of the 1938 visit he was described as one of the greatest bowlers of all time. His best bowling was 9/38 for Australians v Somerset at Taunton in 1934. After retiring he became a well-known cricket writer.

Orford, Lewis Alfred
Amateur. *b:* 12.3.1865, Cheetham Hill, Manchester, Lancashire. *d:* 18.1.1948, Crumpsall, Manchester, Lancashire. Lower order right-hand batsman, wicket-keeper. *Sch* Uppingham. *Team* Cambridge U (1886–87, blue both years).
Career batting
7–12–1–205–76–18.63–0–*ct* 13–*st* 3

O'Riordan, Alec John
Amateur. *b:* 26.7.1940, Rathmines, Co Dublin, Ireland. Middle order right-hand batsman, left-arm fast medium bowler. *Team* Ireland (1958–77).
Career batting
25–44–5–614–117–15.74–1–*ct* 19
Bowling 1604–75–21.38–2–0–6/35

Orman, Charles Edward Linton
Amateur. *b:* 6.9.1859, Roorkee, India. *d:* 11.2.1927, Epping, Essex. Middle order batsman. *Sch* Felsted. *Team* Essex (1896, 2 matches).
Career batting
2–2–0–16–12–8.00–0–*ct* 1

He also played for Bedfordshire (1891–1900).

Ormerod, Sir Cyril Berkeley
Amateur. *b:* 3.10.1897, Edmonton, Middlesex. *d:* 1.11.1983, Westminster, London. Lower order batsman, bowler. *Sch* St Pauls. *Team* MCC (1927).
Career batting
1–1–1–1–1*–no av–0–*ct* 0
Bowling 101–3–33.66–0–0–2/56

His County cricket was for Oxfordshire (1924).

Ormrod, Joseph Alan
Cricketer. *b:* 22.12.1942, Ramsbottom, Lancashire. Opening or middle order right-hand batsman, off break bowler. *Teams* Worcestershire (1962–83, 465 matches); Lancashire (1984–85, 27 matches). *Tours* Worcestershire to Jamaica 1965/6; MCC Under 25 to Pakistan 1966/7.
Career batting
500–846–95–23206–204*–30.89–32–*ct* 400
Bowling 1094–25–43.76–1–0–5/27

He hit 1,000 runs in a season 13 times (best 1,535, av 45.14, in 1978). Both his double centuries were for Worcestershire, the higher being 204* v Kent at Dartford in 1973. He was Cricket Manager to Lancashire CCC 1986–91.

O'Rourke, Christopher
Cricketer. *b:* 13.3.1945, Widnes, Lancashire. Lower order right-hand batsman, wicket-keeper. *Team* Warwickshire (1968, 1 match).
Career batting
1–1–1–23–23*–no av–0–*ct* 3

Orr, Donald Anderson
Cricketer. *b:* 11.6.1967, Glasgow, Scotland. Middle order right-hand batsman, wicket-keeper. *Team* Scotland (1992).
Career batting
1–1–1–23–23*–no av–0–*ct* 1–*st* 1

Orr, Frank William
Amateur. *b:* 6.3.1879, Marylebone, London. *d:* 18.6.1967, Wandsworth, London. Opening right-hand batsman, leg break bowler. *Sch* Tonbridge. *Team* P. F. Warner's XI (1903).
Career batting
1–2–0–30–28–15.00–0–*ct* 0

Orr, Herbert Richard
Amateur. *b:* 3.2.1865, Kensington, London. *d:* 22.5.1940, St John's, Sevenoaks, Kent. Stylish middle order right-hand batsman, right-arm slow bowler, good field. *Sch* Bedford Grammar. *Teams* Cambridge U (1886–87); Western Australia (1892/3, 2 matches).
Career batting
4–8–0–98–44–12.25–0–*ct* 2
Bowling 56–0

His County cricket was for Bedfordshire (1882–1921) and Northamptonshire (pre first-class, 1887).

Orr, Hugh James
Amateur. *b:* 21.1.1878, Deniliquin, New South Wales, Australia. *d:* 19.4.1946, Putney Common, London. Lower order batsman, good bowler. *Team* Hampshire (1902–07, 6 matches).
Career batting
7–14–2–85–13–7.08–0–*ct* 2
Bowling 468–19–24.63–1–0–7/74

His final first-class match was for the Royal Navy in 1912.

Orr, James Harper
Amateur. *b:* 18.10.1878, Glasgow, Scotland. *d:* 19.3.1956, Hay Park, Old Polmont, Stirlingshire,

Scotland. Middle order batsman. *Sch* Loretto. *Team* Scotland (1912–13).
Career batting
3–5–1–91–34–22.75–0–*ct* 0

Orrell, Timothy Michael
Cricketer. *b:* 25.11.1967, Prestwich, Manchester, Lancashire. Middle order right-hand batsman, right-arm medium pace bowler. *Team* Lancashire (1991, 1 match).
Career batting
1–2–0–21–16–10.50–0–*ct* 0

Orton, Charles Talbot
Amateur. *b:* 9.8.1910, Farnham, Surrey. *d:* 28.5.1940, Dunkirk, France. Lower order batsman, slow left-arm bowler. *Sch* Tonbridge. *Teams* Army (1937); Europeans (1938/9).
Career batting
4–8–6–55–20*–27.50–0–*ct* 1
Bowling 318–12–26.50–1–0–7/51

Osbaldeston, George
Amateur. *b:* 26.12.1786, Westminster, London. *d:* 1.8.1866, St John's Wood, London. Hard-hitting middle order right-hand batsman, right-hand fast under-arm bowler. *Sch* Eton. *Teams* MCC (1808–30); Surrey (1815–17); Sussex (1815–17).
Career batting
33–61–8–1002–112–18.90–2–*ct* 16–*st* 5
Bowling 45 wickets (no analyses)–1–0–5/?

A controversial figure, he was one of the best all-rounders of his day, but at the height of his career, in 1818, he resigned from the MCC on a matter of principle and scarcely played again in important matches. He was a crack shot and a famous rider. He was MP for East Retford 1812–18. He fought a duel with Lord George Bentinck in 1831.

Osborn, Frederick
Professional. *b:* 10.11.1889, Leicester. *d:* 11.10.1954, North Evington, Leicester. Middle order batsman. *Team* Leicestershire (1911–13, 2 matches).
Career batting
2–3–0–14–14–4.66–0–*ct* 2

A good soccer player, he appeared for Leicester Fosse and Preston North End.

Osborn, George Newland
Professional. *b:* 18.12.1850, Romford, Essex. *d:* 3.3.1913, Westminster, London. Lower order right-hand batsman, right-arm fast bowler. *Team* Middlesex (1881, 3 matches).
Career batting
3–4–1–9–6–3.00–0–*ct* 0
Bowling 105–4–26.25–0–0–2/32

Osborne, David Robert
Amateur. *b:* 29.9.1879, Perth, Western Australia. *d:* 1954, Bahamas, West Indies. Lower order batsman, right-arm medium pace bowler. *Teams* Cambridge U (1905); Middlesex (1911, 1 match).
Career batting
4–6–1–62–35*–12.40–0–*ct* 0
Bowling 225–5–45.00–0–0–2/79

His final first-class match was for MCC in 1914. He also played for Buckinghamshire (1913). He won a blue for boxing.

Osborne, Ernest Charles
Amateur. *b:* 24.4.1873, Elsternwick, Melbourne, Victoria, Australia. *d:* 25.3.1926, Cardinia, Victoria, Australia. Lower order batsman, opening bowler. *Team* Cambridge U (1894).
Career batting
3–5–0–6–5–1.20–0–*ct* 1
Bowling 227–5–45.40–0–0–3/46

Osborne, George
Professional. Middle order batsman, bowler. *Team* Derbyshire (1879–83, 7 matches).
Career batting
8–15–1–60–14–4.28–0–*ct* 3
Bowling 39–1–39.00–0–0–1/23

His first-class debut was for Players of the North in 1877.

Osborne, Michael John
Amateur. *b:* 9.4.1932, Southend-on-Sea, Essex. Middle order right-hand batsman, off break bowler. *Team* Combined Services (1961–62).
Career batting
3–6–0–155–60–25.83–0–*ct* 3
Bowling 81–2–40.50–0–0–2/65

His County cricket was for Devon (1968).

Osborne, W. G.
(*see under* Howell, M.)

Oscroft, Donald Straker
Amateur. *b:* 12.4.1908, St Pancras, London. *d:* 19.2.1944, Milltimber, Aberdeenshire, Scotland. Son of P. W. (Nottinghamshire). Opening/middle order right-hand batsman, right-arm medium pace bowler. *Sch* Uppingham. *Teams* Leicestershire (1928, 4 matches); Cambridge U (1929).
Career batting
5–9–1–105–50–13.12–0–*ct* 0

He also played for Hertfordshire (1934). He won a blue for rugby fives.

Oscroft, Eric
Professional. *b:* 20.4.1933, Sutton-in-Ashfield, Nottinghamshire. Tail end right-hand batsman, left-arm fast medium bowler. *Team* Nottinghamshire (1950–51, 9 matches).
Career batting
9–8–3–8–7*–1.60–0–*ct* 1
Bowling 707–13–54.38–0–0–4/88

Oscroft, John Thomas
Professional. *b:* 24.3.1846, Arnold, Nottinghamshire. *d:* 15.6.1885, Arnold, Nottinghamshire. Brother of William (Nottinghamshire). Hard-hitting middle order right-hand batsman, right-hand fast round-arm bowler. *Team* Nottinghamshire (1867–74, 14 matches).
Career batting
18–31–0–244–51–7.87–0–*ct* 10
Bowling 160–3–53.33–0–0–1/6
He also played for Northamptonshire (pre first-class, 1870).

Oscroft, Percy William
Amateur. *b:* 27.11.1872, Nottingham. *d:* 8.12.1933, St John's Wood, London. Father of D. S. (Leicestershire). Steady middle order right-hand batsman, left-arm medium pace bowler, excellent slip. *Sch* Nottingham HS. *Team* Nottinghamshire (1894–1900, 18 matches).
Career batting
18–31–2–409–40–14.10–0–*ct* 9
Bowling 37–2–18.50–0–0–1/10
He did not appear in any first-class matches whilst at Cambridge.

Oscroft, William
Professional. *b:* 16.12.1843, Arnold, Nottinghamshire. *d:* 10.10.1905, Nottingham. Brother of J. T. (Nottinghamshire). Excellent opening right-hand batsman, right-hand fast round-arm bowler, good field. *Team* Nottinghamshire (1864–82, 167 matches). *Tours* Grace to Australia 1873/4; Daft to North America 1879 (neither first-class).
Career batting
244–419–21–7596–140–19.08–2–*ct* 169–*st* 1
Bowling 1588–76–20.89–2–0–5/34
He was for some years one of the leading batsmen in England and in 1865 topped the first-class batting averages with 518 runs, av 43.16. He captained Nottinghamshire in 1881 and 1882.

O'Shaughnessy, Edward
Professional. *b:* 16.11.1860, Canterbury, Kent. *d:* 6.8.1885, Marylebone, London. He died of rapid consumption. Hard-hitting middle order batsman, right-hand slow round-arm bowler, good field. *Team* Kent (1879–85, 59 matches).
Career batting
62–109–9–1193–98–11.93–0–*ct* 47
Bowling 1607–80–20.08–5–1–7/16

O'Shaughnessy, Steven Joseph
Cricketer. *b:* 9.9.1961, Bury, Lancashire. Hard-hitting opening right-hand batsman, right-arm medium pace bowler. *Teams* Lancashire (1980–87, 100 matches); Worcestershire (1988–89, 12 matches).
Career batting
112–181–28–3720–159*–24.31–5–*ct* 57
Bowling 4108–114–36.03–0–0–4/66
For Lancashire v Leicestershire at Old Trafford in 1983 he hit 101* in 35 minutes (105 in all) to equal the fastest time for a century in first-class cricket (since beaten) – the innings was made in farcical conditions. He hit 1,167 runs, av 34.32, in 1984. He also played for Northumberland (1990).

Osman, Wayne Miles
Cricketer. *b:* 19.8.1950, Athens, Greece. Middle order left-hand batsman, left-arm medium pace bowler. *Team* Northamptonshire (1970–71, 9 matches).
Career batting
9–16–0–287–60–17.93–0–*ct* 6
He also played for Hertfordshire (1972–86).

Ostler, Dominic Piers
Cricketer. *b:* 15.7.1970, Solihull, Warwickshire. Middle order right-hand batsman, right-arm medium pace bowler. *Team* Warwickshire (1990–92, 55 matches).
Career batting
55–96–9–3019–192–34.70–4–*ct* 49
Bowling 90–0
He scored 1,000 runs in a season twice (best 1,284, av 36.68, in 1991).

O'Sullivan, David Robert
Cricketer. *b:* 16.11.1944, Palmerston North, Wellington, New Zealand. Lower order right-hand batsman, slow left-arm bowler. *Teams* Hampshire (1971–73, 26 matches); Central Districts (1972/3 to 1984/5). *Tours* New Zealand to Australia 1972/3, 1973/4, to England 1975 (World Cup), to India and Pakistan 1976/7. *Tests* New Zealand (1972/3 to 1976/7, 11 matches).
Career batting
136–187–46–2174–70*–15.41–0–*ct* 46
Bowling 13554–523–25.91–28–4–6/26
Test batting
11–21–4–158–23*–9.29–0–*ct* 2
Bowling 1221–18–67.83–1–0–5/148
He also played for Durham (pre first-class, 1974–77).

Oswald, Denis Geoffrey
Amateur. *b:* 12.11.1910, Port Stanley, Falkland Islands. Opening/middle order right-hand batsman. *Sch* St Lawrence College. *Team* Oxford U (1931).
Career batting
2–2–1–21–16–21.00–0–*ct* 0
His County cricket was for Hertfordshire (1931–32). He won a blue for hockey.

Ottaway, Cuthbert John
Amateur. *b:* 19.7.1850, Dover, Kent. *d:* 2.4.1878, Westminster, London. Sound middle order right-hand batsman, wicket-keeper. *Sch* Eton. *Teams* Kent (1869–70, 2 matches); Oxford U (1870–73, blue all four years); Middlesex (1874–76, 7 matches). *Tour* Fitzgerald to North America 1872 (not first-class).

Career batting
37–67–5–1691–112–27.27–2–*ct* 22–*st* 1

He was one of the best amateur batsmen of his day, but retired on being called to the bar. He captained Oxford in 1873. An all-round sportsman, he represented Oxford at athletics, rackets and royal tennis as well as receiving his soccer blue. A good forward, he appeared for England in two International soccer matches.

Ottley, David George
Cricketer. *b:* 23.6.1944, Worcester Park, Surrey. Middle order right-hand batsman. *Sch* Tiffin. *Team* Middlesex (1967, 7 matches).
Career batting
8–10–1–156–47–17.33–0–*ct* 3
Bowling 1–0

He also played for Hertfordshire (1975–86) and played his last first-class match for Minor Counties in 1985.

Outschoorn, Ladislaus
Professional. *b:* 26.9.1918, Colombo, Ceylon. Stylish middle order right-hand batsman, right-arm medium pace bowler. *Team* Worcestershire (1946–59, 341 matches).
Career batting
346–595–53–15496–215*–28.59–25–*ct* 278
Bowling 2030–33–61.51–0–0–2/15

He hit 1,000 runs in a season nine times (best 1,761, av 35.93, in 1951). Both his double centuries were for Worcestershire, the higher being 215* v Northamptonshire at Worcester in 1949.

Ovenstone, Douglas MacPherson
Amateur. *b:* 31.7.1921, Sea Point, Cape Town, South Africa. Middle order right-hand batsman, wicket-keeper. *Team* Western Province (1946/7 to 1947/8). *Tour* South Africa to England 1947.
Career batting
20–32–2–437–52–14.56–0–*ct* 40–*st* 15

South Africa's decision to include three wicket-keepers in the 1947 touring party meant that he would have few opportunities to prove his ability; as it was a broken finger prevented him for playing for half the season and he was not selected for any Tests. His first-class debut was for 1st South African Division XI in 1942/3.

Overton, William
Professional. *b:* 28.3.1873, Swindon, Wiltshire. *d:* 6.8.1949, Paddington, London. Lower order right-hand batsman, slow right-arm bowler. *Team* MCC (1898–1908).
Career batting
8–12–4–63–19–7.87–0–*ct* 5
Bowling 340–21–16.19–0–0–4/22

His County cricket was for Wiltshire (1896–1922).

Owen, Hugh Glendwr Palmer
Amateur. *b:* 19.5.1859, Bath, Somerset. *d:* 20.10.1912, Landwick, Dengie, Essex. Sound opening right-hand batsman, right-arm medium pace bowler. *Teams* Cambridge U (1882); Essex (1894–1902, 133 matches).
Career batting
136–228–17–4510–134–21.37–3–*ct* 38
Bowling 332–9–36.88–0–0–2/37

His career with Essex began in 1880 and most of his best batting for the County was performed during its pre-first-class period. He captained Essex from 1895 to 1902. He played soccer for Notts County.

Owen, Joseph Glyn
Professional for Surrey, but amateur for Bedfordshire. *b:* 23.1.1909, Llanelly, Glamorgan. *d:* 17.2.1978, Eastbourne, Sussex. Middle order left-hand batsman, slow left-arm bowler. *Team* Surrey (1930–33, 15 matches).
Career batting
18–19–3–361–57–22.56–0–*ct* 8
Bowling 837–16–52.31–0–0–3/15

He also played for Bedfordshire (1939–57) and his final first-class match was for Minor Counties in 1951.

Owen, Norman William
Professional. *b:* 16.3.1915, Shepherds Bush, London. *d:* 9.9.1977, Newton Aycliffe, Co Durham. Lower order right-hand batsman, right-arm medium fast or off break bowler. *Team* Minor Counties (1951).
Career batting
1–2–0–26–14–13.00–0–*ct* 0
Bowling 33–1–33.00–0–0–1/33

His County cricket was for Durham (pre first-class, 1947–55).

Owen, Paul Andrew
Cricketer. *b:* 9.6.1969, Regina, Saskatchewan, Canada. Lower order right-hand batsman, slow left-arm bowler. *Sch* Bedford Modern. *Team* Gloucestershire (1990, 3 matches).
Career batting
3–2–0–2–1–1.00–0–*ct* 0
Bowling 239–4–59.75–0–0–2/37

He also played for Bedfordshire (1989–92).

Owen-Smith, Dr Harold Geoffrey Owen
Amateur. *b:* 18.2.1909, Rondebosch, Cape Town, South Africa. *d:* 27.2.1990, Rosebank, Cape Town, South Africa. Adventurous middle order right-hand batsman, slow leg break bowler, brilliant outfield. *Teams* Western Province (1927/8 to 1949/50); Oxford U (1931–33, blue all three years); Middlesex (1935–37, 28 matches). *Tour* South Africa to England 1929. *Tests* South Africa (1929, 5 matches).
Career batting
101–162–11–4059–168*–26.88–3–*ct* 93
Bowling 7410–319–23.22–20–3–7/153

Owen-Thomas, Dudley Richard

Test batting
5–8–2–252–129–42.00–1–*ct* 4
Bowling 113–0

He was most successful on the 1929 tour to England, hitting 1,168 runs, av 35.39, and taking 30 wickets, av 25.80. An all-round sportsman, he was awarded his blue for rugby and boxing and went on the captain England at the former.

Owen-Thomas, Dudley Richard
Cricketer. *b:* 20.9.1948, Mombasa, Kenya. Middle order right-hand batsman, off break bowler. *Sch* KCS, Wimbledon. *Teams* Cambridge U (1969–72, blue all four years); Surrey (1970–75, 73 matches). *Tours* MCC to East Africa 1973/4, to Bangladesh 1976/7 (not first-class).
Career batting
112–188–20–4891–182*–29.11–8–*ct* 48
Bowling 798–20–39.90–0–0–3/20

He hit 1,065 runs, av 34.35, in 1971.

Oxley, John Haywood
Amateur. *b:* 16.2.1850, Kimberworth, Yorkshire. *d:* 4.7.1917, Sunbury-on-Thames, Middlesex. He died following an accident, his bicycle colliding with a cab. Lower order batsman, wicket-keeper. *Team* Middlesex (1883, 2 matches).
Career batting
2–4–0–10–5–2.50–0–*ct* 2–*st* 2

Oyston, Charles
Professional. *b:* 12.5.1869, Armley, Leeds, Yorkshire. *d:* 15.7.1942, Leeds, Yorkshire. Lower order left-hand batsman, slow left-arm bowler. *Team* Yorkshire (1900–09, 15 matches).
Career batting
15–21–8–96–22–7.38–0–*ct* 3
Bowling 872–31–28.12–0–0–3/30

P

Packe, Charles William Christopher
Amateur. *b:* 2.5.1909, Pietermaritzburg, South Africa. *d:* 1.7.1944, near Caen, Normandy, France. He was killed in action. Brother of M. St J. (Leicestershire) and R. J. (Leicestershire). Forcing middle order right-hand batsman, right-arm medium pace bowler, brilliant field. *Sch* Eton. *Team* Leicestershire (1929–34, 21 matches).
Career batting
26–41–0–1013–176–24.70–2–*ct* 17
Bowling 75–3–25.00–0–0–2/33

His final first-class match was for the Army in 1939 and military service very much restricted his appearances in County cricket. He captained Leicestershire in 1932.

Packe, Michael St John
Amateur. *b:* 21.8.1916, Upperton, Eastbourne, Sussex. *d:* 20.12.1978, St Anne, Alderney. Brother of C. W. C. (Leicestershire) and R. J. (Leicestershire). Forcing middle order right-hand batsman. *Sch* Wellington. *Teams* Cambridge U (1936–38); Leicestershire (1936–39, 35 matches).
Career batting
41–64–3–1151–118–18.86–1–*ct* 30
Bowling 14–1–14.00–0–0–1/0

He captained Leicestershire in 1939.

Packe, Robert Julian
Amateur. *b:* 8.7.1913, Hounslow, Middlesex. *d:* 24.10.1935, Ahmednagar, India. He died of dysentery. Brother of C. W. C. (Leicestershire) and M. St J. (Leicestershire). Lower order right-hand batsman, slow left-arm bowler. *Sch* Stowe. *Team* Leicestershire (1933, 3 matches).
Career batting
3–5–2–25–12–8.33–0–*ct* 2
Bowling 68–1–68.00–0–0–1/31

Packer, Admiral Sir Herbert Annesley
Amateur. *b:* 9.10.1894, Cressage, Shropshire. *d:* 23.9.1962, Bishopscourt, Wynberg, South Africa. Lower order batsman, wicket-keeper. *Team* Royal Navy (1920).
Career batting
1–2–0–3–3–1.50–0–*ct* 2

Padgett, Douglas Ernest Vernon
Professional. *b:* 20.7.1934, Dirk Hill, Bradford, Yorkshire. Opening or middle order right-hand batsman, right-arm medium pace bowler. *Team* Yorkshire (1951–71, 487 matches). *Tours* MCC to New Zealand 1960/1; Yorkshire to North America 1964 (not first-class). *Tests* England (1960, 2 matches).
Career batting
506–806–67–21124–161*–28.58–32–*ct* 261
Bowling 216–6–36.00–0–0–1/2
Test batting
2–4–0–51–31–12.75–0–*ct* 0
Bowling 8–0

He hit 1,000 runs in a season twelve times, going on to 2,000 once: 2,181, av 41.15, in 1959. He has been Yorkshire coach since 1972.

Padgett, George Hubert
Professional. *b:* 9.10.1931, Silkstone, Barnsley, Yorkshire. Forcing middle order right-hand batsman, right-arm medium pace bowler, good field. *Team* Yorkshire (1952, 6 matches).
Career batting
6–7–4–56–32*–18.66–0–*ct* 5
Bowling 336–4–84.00–0–0–2/37

Padgett, John
Professional. *b:* 21.11.1860, Scarborough, Yorkshire. Middle order right-hand batsman. *Team* Yorkshire

(1882–89, 6 matches).
Career batting
7–11–0–130–25–11.81–0–*ct* 2

Padley, William
Professional. *b:* 11.4.1842, Moor Green, Nottinghamshire. *d:* 21.7.1904, Bagthorpe, Nottinghamshire. Lower order right-hand batsman, right-hand medium pace round-arm bowler, wicket-keeper. *Team* Nottinghamshire (1876, 1 match).
Career batting
1–2–1–15–10–15.00–0–*ct* 0

Padmore, Albert Leroy
Cricketer. *b:* 17.12.1946, Halls Village, St James, Barbados. Lower order right-hand batsman, off break bowler. *Team* Barbados (1972/3 to 1981/2). *Tours* West Indies to India, Pakistan and Sri Lanka 1974/5, to Australia 1975/6, to England 1976; West Indian XI to South Africa 1983/4. *Tests* West Indies (1975/6 to 1976, 2 matches).
Career batting
68–66–23–562–79–13.06–0–*ct* 29
Bowling 5780–193–29.94–8–2–6/69
Test batting
2–2–1–8–8*–8.00–0–*ct* 0
Bowling 135–1–135.00–0–0–1/36
He took 59 wickets, av 23.40, on the 1976 tour to England, appearing in one Test, the fast bowlers dominating the series. He was manager of the West Indies teams to South Africa in 1982/3 and 1983/4.

Padmore, Hal Dacosta
Amateur. *b:* 12.11.1927, Barbados. Lower order right-hand batsman, right-arm medium pace bowler. *Team* Canada (1951–54). *Tour* Canada to England 1954.
Career batting
3–5–1–34–15*–8.50–0–*ct* 1
Bowling 312–14–22.28–1–0–5/47
He proved quite effective on the 1954 visit.

Page, Sir Arthur
Amateur. *b:* 9.3.1876, Westminster, London. *d:* 1.9.1958, Hildenborough, Kent. Brother-in-law of F. Symes-Thompson (Oxford U) and H. E. Symes-Thompson (Cambridge U). Opening or middle order right-hand batsman, good deep field. *Sch* Harrow. *Team* Oxford U (1899).
Career batting
9–13–2–180–45–16.36–0–*ct* 4
He was in India for some years and later became Chief Justice of Burma. He played for MCC between 1898 and 1904. He won a blue for royal tennis, and also appeared in the 1908 Olympics.

Page, Charles Carew
Amateur. *b:* 25.4.1884, Barnet, Hertfordshire. *d:* 10.4.1921, Hook Heath, Woking, Surrey. Opening or middle order right-hand batsman, good outfield. *Sch* Malvern. *Teams* Cambridge U (1905–06, blue both years); Middlesex (1905–09, 36 matches). *Tour* MCC to New Zealand 1906/7.
Career batting
71–115–4–2919–164*–26.29–2–*ct* 30
Bowling 53–1–53.00–0–0–1/25
A noted soccer player, he gained his blue and also appeared for the Corinthians.

Page, Dallas Alexander Chancellor
Amateur. *b:* 11.4.1911, Montpellier, Cheltenham, Gloucestershire. *d:* 2.9.1936, Cirencester, Gloucestershire. He died as the result of a road accident. Son of H. V. (Gloucestershire). Hard hitting middle order right-hand batsman, brilliant cover point. *Sch* Cheltenham. *Team* Gloucestershire (1933–36, 106 matches).
Career batting
106–167–7–2993–116–18.70–1–*ct* 75
Bowling 45–0
He hit 1,059 runs, av 20.36, in 1935. In 1935 and 1936 he captained Gloucestershire and was travelling home from the County's match with Nottinghamshire when the fatal accident occurred.

Page, E. W.
Amateur. Lower order batsman, useful bowler. *Team* Somerset (1885, 1 match).
Career batting
1–2–1–1–1*–1.00–0–*ct* 0
Bowling 67–0

Page, Edgar Wells
Amateur. *b:* 31.12.1884, Wolverhampton, Staffordshire. *d:* 12.5.1956, Park Dale, Wolverhampton, Staffordshire. Middle order right-hand batsman. *Sch* Repton. *Team* Minor Counties (1924).
Career batting
1–2–0–26–26–13.00–0–*ct* 0
His County cricket was for Staffordshire (1905–28). A noted hockey player, he represented England.

Page, Herbert Vivian
Amateur. *b:* 30.10.1862, Lancaster, Lancashire. *d:* 1.8.1927, Montpellier, Cheltenham, Gloucestershire. Father of D. A. C. (Gloucestershire). Sound middle order right-hand batsman, right-arm medium pace off break bowler. *Sch* Cheltenham. *Teams* Oxford U (1883–86, blue all four years); Gloucestershire (1883–95, 102 matches).
Career batting
146–247–22–4005–116–17.80–1–*ct* 111–*st* 14
Bowling 4928–212–23.24–5–0–6/28
He captained Oxford in 1885 and 1886. An all-round sportsman, he was awarded his blue for rugby and also played for Gloucestershire. He captained East Gloucestershire Hockey Club for 22 years.

Page, Hugh Ashton
Cricketer. *b:* 3.7.1962, Salisbury, Rhodesia. Lower order left-hand batsman, right-arm fast medium bowler. *Teams* Transvaal (1981/2 to 1990/1); Essex (1987, 15 matches).
Career batting
83–110–23–1688–60–20.58–0–*ct* 21
Bowling 6316–257–24.57–5–0–7/38

Despite his success in South Africa, he had a very moderate season with Essex in 1987 and his hopes were finally dashed by a knee injury, which curtailed his appearances. He appeared for South Africa in unofficial Tests commencing 1985/6. He also played for Staffordshire (1985).

Page, John Colin Theodore
Professional. *b:* 20.5.1930, Mereworth, Kent. *d:* 14.12.1990, Tunbridge Wells, Kent. Tail end right-hand batsman, right-arm medium pace, later off break bowler. *Team* Kent (1950–63, 198 matches).
Career batting
198–273–124–818–23–5.48–0–*ct* 74
Bowling 14967–521–28.72–22–2–8/117

After retiring he became manager of Kent (1975–81) and had been closely involved with coaching the county from 1963 until his death.

Page, Julian Thomas
Cricketer. *b:* 1.5.1954, Clifton, Bristol. Lower order left-hand batsman, left-arm medium pace bowler. *Team* Cambridge U (1974).
Career batting
2–4–0–31–11–7.75–0–*ct* 0
Bowling 95–1–95.00–0–0–1/14

He appeared for Gloucestershire in one John Player League match.

Page, Michael Harry
Cricketer. *b:* 17.6.1941, Blackpool, Lancashire. Middle order right-hand batsman, off break bowler. *Team* Derbyshire (1964–75, 254 matches).
Career batting
254–451–47–11538–162–28.55–9–*ct* 248
Bowling 527–7–75.28–0–0–1/0

He hit 1,000 runs in a season six times (best 1,344, av 40.72, in 1970).

Page, Milford Laurenson
Amateur. *b:* 8.5.1902, Lyttelton, Christchurch, New Zealand. *d:* 13.2.1987, Christchurch, New Zealand. Steady middle order right-hand batsman, right-arm slow bowler, good slip field. *Team* Canterbury (1920/1 to 1936/7). *Tours* New Zealand to England 1927, 1931, 1937, to Australia 1927/8, 1937/8. *Tests* New Zealand (1929/30 to 1937, 14 matches).
Career batting
132–213–17–5857–206–29.88–9–*ct* 117
Bowling 2365–73–32.39–0–0–4/10
Test batting
14–20–0–492–104–24.60–1–*ct* 6
Bowling 231–5–46.20–0–0–2/21

He exceeded 1,000 runs only on the 1927 tour to England: 1,154, av 34.96. Captain of New Zealand in seven Tests, he led the 1937 touring party. His final first-class match was for New Zealand Army XI in 1942/3. His highest score was 206 for Canterbury v Wellington at Wellington in 1931/2. He also played rugby for New Zealand.

Page, Richard Kennett
Amateur. *b:* 24.1.1910, Bursledon, Hampshire. Nephew of A. J. L. Hill (Hampshire), cousin of A. E. L. Hill (Hampshire). Middle order right-hand batsman, leg break bowler. *Sch* Marlborough. *Team* Army (1937).
Career batting
1–2–0–12–12–6.00–0–*ct* 0
Bowling 25–0

Page, Thomas Howard
Amateur. *b:* 28.5.1872, Dover, Kent. *d:* 7.12.1953, Swanage, Dorset. Lower order batsman, bowler. *Sch* St Edward's, Oxford. *Team* Hampshire (1900, 2 matches).
Career batting
2–4–1–77–61*–25.66–0–*ct* 3
Bowling 198–4–49.50–0–0–4/115

Page, William
Professional. *b:* 29.4.1847, Caverswall, Staffordshire. *d:* 27.9.1904, Rose Hill, Derby. Middle order right-hand batsman. *Team* Derbyshire (1881–82, 3 matches).
Career batting
3–6–0–50–19–8.33–0–*ct* 0

An accident which deprived him of the sight of one eye prematurely ended his cricket career.

Pai, Mukundrao Damodar
Amateur. *b:* 21.6.1883, Bombay, India. *d:* 5.8.1948, Bombay, India. Middle order right-hand batsman. *Team* Hindus (1906/7 to 1920/1). *Tour* India to England 1911.
Career batting
22–37–3–640–107–18.82–1–*ct* 14

He achieved very little on the 1911 tour to England. He scored 107 on debut for Hindus v Europeans at Bombay in 1906/7.

Pain, Edwin Llewellyn
Amateur. *b:* 2.6.1891, Swansea, Glamorgan. *d:* 14.7.1947, Mount Wise, Plymouth, Devon. Tail-end right-hand batsman, right-arm medium pace bowler. *Team* Royal Navy (1926).
Career batting
1–2–0–18–17–9.00–0–*ct* 2
Bowling 99–3–33.00–0–0–3/90

His County cricket was for Devon (1932).

Paine, George Alfred Edward
Professional. *b:* 11.6.1908, Paddington, London. *d:* 30.3.1978, Solihull, Warwickshire. Lower order right-hand batsman, slow left-arm bowler, good slip field. *Teams* Middlesex (1926, 5 matches); Warwickshire (1929–47, 240 matches). *Tour* MCC to West Indies 1934/5. *Tests* England (1934/5, 4 matches).
Career batting
258–349–62–3430–79–11.95–0–*ct* 160
Bowling 23334–1021–22.85–74–13–8/43
Test batting
4–7–1–97–49–16.16–0–*ct* 5
Bowling 467–17–27.47–1–0–5/168
He took 100 wickets in a season five times (best 156, av 17.07, in 1934). Rheumatism hampered his bowling from 1936 and a disagreement over terms in 1938 virtually ended his County cricket.

Paine, Dr John Gosling
Amateur. *b:* 10.11.1829, Brighton, Sussex. *d:* 1.11.1859, Brighton, Sussex. He died suddenly of apoplexy. Hard hitting middle order right-hand batsman, wicket-keeper. *Team* Sussex (1851–59, 5 matches).
Career batting
13–22–2–224–47–11.20–0–*ct* 7–*st* 3
A most promising cricketer, he died before he could fulfil expectations.

Painter, John Richard
Professional. *b:* 11.11.1856, Bourton-on-the-Water, Gloucestershire. *d:* 16.9.1900, Bourton-on-the-Water, Gloucestershire. Middle order right-hand batsman, right-arm fast bowler, good field. *Team* Gloucestershire (1881–97, 192 matches).
Career batting
198–353–16–5927–150–17.58–5–*ct* 151
Bowling 1232–46–26.78–2–1–8/67
His best season was 1890 when he scored 683 runs, av 25.29. He was a first-class umpire (1898–99).

Pairaudeau, Bruce Hamilton
Professional. *b:* 14.4.1931, Georgetown, British Guiana. Stylish opening right-hand batsman, leg break and googly bowler. *Teams* British Guiana (1946/7 to 1957/8); Northern Districts (1958/9 to 1966/7). *Tours* West Indies to New Zealand 1955/6, to England 1957. *Tests* West Indies (1952/3 to 1957, 13 matches).
Career batting
89–159–5–4930–163–32.01–11–*ct* 64
Bowling 82–0
Test batting
13–21–0–454–115–21.61–1–*ct* 6
Bowling 3–0
His debut in English first-class cricket was for a Commonwealth XI in 1950. Although he appeared in two Tests on the 1957 tour to England, his figures in first-class matches were very modest. He emigrated to New Zealand in 1958.

Paish, Arthur James
Professional. *b:* 5.4.1874, Gloucester. *d:* 16.8.1948, Parton, Gloucester. Tail end batsman, slow left-arm bowler. *Team* Gloucestershire (1898–1903, 79 matches).
Career batting
79–123–38–967–66–11.37–0–*ct* 79
Bowling 8610–354–24.32–27–7–8/68
His best season was 1899 when he took 137 wickets, av 18.54.

Palairet, Henry Hamilton
Amateur. *b:* 8.1.1845, Bradford-on-Avon, Wiltshire. *d:* 20.3.1923, Cattistock Lodge, Dorset. Father of L. C. H. (Somerset) and R. C. N. (Somerset). Middle order batsman. *Sch* Eton. *Team* MCC (1868–69).
Career batting
2–4–1–28–14*–9.33–0–*ct* 2
He was for many years the Champion Archer of England.

Palairet, Lionel Charles Hamilton
Amateur. *b:* 27.5.1870, Broughton East, Grange-over-Sands, Lancashire. *d:* 27.3.1933, Exmouth, Devon. Son of H. H. (MCC), brother of R. C. N. (Somerset). Stylish opening right-hand batsman, right-arm medium pace bowler and occasionally under-arm lobs. *Sch* Repton. *Teams* Oxford U (1890–93, blue all four years); Somerset (1891–1909, 222 matches). *Tests* England (1902, 2 matches).
Career batting
267–488–19–15777–292–33.63–27–*ct* 248–*st* 15
Bowling 4849–143–33.90–2–0–6/84
Test batting
2–4–0–49–20–12.25–0–*ct* 2
He hit 1,000 runs in a season seven times (best 1,906, av 57.75, in 1901). Both his double centuries were for Somerset, the higher being 292 v Hampshire at Southampton in 1896. He captained Oxford in 1892 and 1893, Somerset in 1907 and was President of Somerset CCC in 1929. He first played for Somerset (not first-class) in 1889. An all-round sportsman he played soccer for the Corinthians and represented Oxford in the three miles.

Palairet, Richard Cameron North
Amateur. *b:* 25.6.1871, Broughton East, Grange-over-Sands, Lancashire. *d:* 11.2.1955, Knowle, Budleigh Salterton, Devon. Son of H. H. (MCC), brother of L. C. H. (Somerset). Graceful opening right-hand batsman, good field. *Sch* Repton. *Teams* Oxford U (1891–94, blue 1893–94); Somerset (1891–1902, 85 matches). *Tour* Priestley to West Indies 1896/7.
Career batting
112–198–9–4000–156–21.16–2–*ct* 108
Bowling 167–3–55.66–0–0–1/19

He first played for Somerset (not first-class) in 1890. He was Secretary of Surrey CCC from 1921 to 1932 and in 1932/3 was joint-manager of the MCC Team to Australia. From 1937 to 1946 he was President of Somerset. He was awarded his soccer blue as an inside-forward.

Palfreman, Anthony Brian
Cricketer. *b:* 27.8.1946, Ravenshead, Nottinghamshire. Lower order right-hand batsman, right-arm fast medium bowler. *Sch* Nottingham HS. *Team* Cambridge U (1966–68, blue 1966).
Career batting
16–31–3–432–67–15.42–0–*ct* 11
Bowling 1158–31–37.35–1–0–5/63
He also won a blue for soccer.

Palia, Phiroze Edulji
Amateur. *b:* 5.9.1910, Bombay, India. *d:* 9.9.1981, Bangalore, India. Attractive middle order left-hand batsman, slow left-arm bowler, good field. *Teams* Parsis (1928/9 to 1945/6); Madras (1933/4); United Provinces (1934/5 to 1942/3); Bombay (1937/8); Mysore (1944/5 to 1953/4); Bengal (1948/9). *Tours* India to England 1932, 1936; Vizianagram's XI to India and Ceylon 1930/1; Indian University Occasionals to Ceylon 1935/6. *Tests* India (1932–36, 2 matches).
Career batting
100–162–22–4536–216–32.40–8–*ct* 40
Bowling 5005–208–24.06–7–0–7/109
Test batting
2–4–1–29–16–9.66–0–*ct* 0
Bowling 13–0
Although he appeared in a Test on each of the tours to England, his success in terms of figures was very modest. His only double century was 216 for the United Provinces v Maharashtra at Poona in 1939/40.

Paling, George
Professional. *b:* 29.11.1836, Nottingham. *d:* 18.12.1879, Nottingham. Hard hitting middle order right-hand batsman, right-hand medium pace round-arm bowler, good deep field. *Team* Nottinghamshire (1865–67, 7 matches).
Career batting
8–14–3–148–41*–13.45–0–*ct* 3

Pallett, Henry James
Professional. *b:* 2.1.1863, Birchfield, Staffordshire. *d:* 18.6.1917, Aston, Birmingham. Steady lower order right-hand batsman, right-arm slow bowler. *Team* Warwickshire (1894–98, 73 matches).
Career batting
77–104–21–929–55*–11.19–0–*ct* 21
Bowling 6580–305–21.57–21–7–9/55
His debut for Warwickshire was in 1883 and his best seasons for the County occurred before they became first-class. His first-class debut was for an Eleven of England v Australians in 1886. His best bowling was 9/55 for Warwickshire v Essex at Leyton in 1894. He also played for Staffordshire (1903).

Palmer, Cecil Howard
Amateur. *b:* 14.7.1873, Eastbourne, Sussex. *d:* 26.7.1915, near Hill Q, Gallipoli, Turkey. He was killed in action. Middle order right-hand batsman, excellent field. *Sch* Radley and Eastbourne. *Teams* Hampshire (1899–1907, 8 matches); Worcestershire (1904, 1 match).
Career batting
9–18–2–380–75*–23.75–0–*ct* 2
A regular soldier, his County cricket was very restricted, but in 1904 he had the curious experience of appearing both for Hampshire and Worcestershire in first-class matches. He also played for Barbados (not first-class).

Palmer, Charles Henry, CBE
Amateur. *b:* 15.5.1919, Old Hill, Staffordshire. Sound middle order right-hand batsman, right-arm medium, or very slow, bowler. *Teams* Worcestershire (1938–49, 66 matches); Leicestershire (1950–59, 231 matches); Europeans (1945/6). *Tours* MCC to South Africa 1948/9, to West Indies 1953/4. *Test* England (1953/4, 1 match).
Career batting
336–588–38–17458–201–31.74–33–*ct* 147
Bowling 9183–365–25.15–5–0–8/7
Test batting
1–2–0–22–22–11.00–0–*ct* 0
Bowling 15–0
He hit 1,000 runs in a season eight times going on to 2,000 once: 2,071, av 39.82, in 1952. His only double century was 201 for Leicestershire v Northamptonshire at Northampton in 1953. He returned the remarkable analysis of 14–12–7–8 for Leicestershire v Surrey at Grace Road, Leicester in 1955. From 1950 to 1957 he was captain of Leicestershire, also acting as Secretary to the County.He was then Hon Secretary 1958–86 and has been President since 1987. He was President of MCC 1978/9, Chairman of the Cricket Council 1979–85 and Chairman of TCCB 1983–85. In 1985/6 he chaired an enquiry into the standard of English cricket which resulted in the Palmer Report.

Palmer, Clayton
Amateur. *b:* 14.7.1885, Westminster, London. *d:* 11.4.1956, Blackwell, East Grinstead, Sussex. Brother-in-law of N. A. Knox (Surrey). Middle order right-hand batsman. *Sch* Uppingham. *Teams* Middlesex (1904–12, 19 matches); Cambridge U (1905–07, blue 1907).
Career batting
35–58–6–767–55*–14.75–0–*ct* 12

Palmer, Eric John
Amateur. *b:* 16.6.1931, Romford, Essex. Tail end left-hand batsman, right-arm fast medium bowler.

Team Essex (1957, 4 matches).
Career batting
4–6–5–39–11*–39.00–0–*ct* 1
Bowling 225–7–32.14–0–0–2/35

Palmer, Gary Vincent
Cricketer. *b:* 15.11.1965, Taunton, Somerset. Son of K. E. (Somerset), nephew of Roy (Somerset). Lower order right-hand batsman, right-arm medium pace bowler. *Sch* Queens, Taunton. *Team* Somerset (1982–88, 54 matches).
Career batting
54–70–11–903–78–15.30–0–*ct* 30
Bowling 4107–92–44.64–1–0–5/38
He also played for Bedfordshire (1990).

Palmer, George Arthur
Amateur. *b:* 5.6.1897, Hopsford, Withybrook, Warwickshire. *d:* 1.6.1962, Higham-on-the-Hill, Leicestershire. Lower order right-hand batsman, right-arm fast medium bowler. *Team* Warwickshire (1928, 9 matches).
Career batting
9–12–2–87–20–8.70–0–*ct* 7
Bowling 450–8–56.25–0–0–2/21

Palmer, George Eugene
Amateur. *b:* 22.2.1859, Mulwala, Corowa, New South Wales, Australia. *d:* 22.8.1910, Baddaginnie, Victoria, Australia. Brother-in-law of J. M. Blackham (Australia). Lower order right-hand batsman, right-arm medium off break bowler. *Teams* Victoria (1878/9 to 1894/5, 19 matches); Tasmania (1896/7, 1 match). *Tours* Australia to England 1880, 1882, 1884, 1886. *Tests* Australia (1880–86, 17 matches).
Career batting
133–200–31–2728–113–16.14–1–*ct* 107
Bowling 10520–594–17.71–54–16–8/48
Test batting
17–25–4–296–48–14.09–0–*ct* 13
Bowling 1678–78–21.51–6–2–7/65
He took 100 wickets in a season on three of his four tours to England (best 132, av 16.43, in 1884). With less matches in 1880 he took 66 wickets, av 11.69.

Palmer, George Harry
Amateur. *b:* 24.10.1917, Ibstock, Leicestershire. Son of John (Leicestershire). Lower order right-hand batsman, right-arm medium pace bowler. *Team* Leicestershire (1938–39, 5 matches).
Career batting
5–6–1–31–14*–6.20–0–*ct* 3
Bowling 320–12–26.66–0–0–3/36

Palmer, Harold James
Amateur. *b:* 30.8.1890, Epping, Essex. *d:* 12.2.1967, Bexhill-on-Sea, Sussex. Tail end right-hand batsman, right-arm fast medium or leg break bowler. *Team* Essex (1924–32, 53 matches).
Career batting
58–74–27–278–25*–5.91–0–*ct* 21
Bowling 4053–160–25.33–7–0–6/68
His final first-class match was for MCC in 1936.

Palmer, John
Professional. *b:* 29.3.1881, Ibstock, Leicestershire. *d:* 14.6.1928, Ibstock, Leicestershire. Father of G. H. (Leicestershire). Lower order right-hand batsman, right-arm medium pace bowler. *Team* Leicestershire (1906, 3 matches).
Career batting
3–6–1–27–13–5.40–0–*ct* 2
Bowling 209–8–26.12–0–0–3/14

Palmer, Kenneth Ernest
Professional. *b:* 22.4.1937, Winchester, Hampshire. Brother of Roy (Somerset), father of G. V. (Somerset). Middle order right-hand batsman, right-arm fast medium bowler. *Team* Somerset (1955–69, 302 matches). *Tours* MCC to South Africa 1964/5 – in an emergency (he was coaching there); Commonwealth to Pakistan 1963/4; Cavaliers to West Indies 1963/4. *Test* England (1964/5, 1 match).
Career batting
314–481–106–7771–125*–20.72–2–*ct* 158
Bowling 18485–866–21.34–47–5–9/57
Test batting
1–1–0–10–10–10.00–0–*ct* 0
Bowling 189–1–189.00–0–0–1/113
He took 100 wickets in a season four times (best 139, av 16.07, in 1963) and in 1961 hit 1,036 runs, av 25.90, achieving the 'double' that season. His best bowling was 9/57 for Somerset v Nottinghamshire at Trent Bridge in 1963. Appointed to the first class umpires' list in 1972, he has officiated in 20 Test matches (1978–92).

Palmer, Richard
Professional. *b:* 13.9.1848, Hadlow, Kent. *d:* 2.3.1939, Lower Halstow, Kent. Lower order right-hand batsman, right-hand medium pace round-arm bowler, wicket-keeper. *Team* Kent (1873–82, 13 matches).
Career batting
13–25–6–104–20–5.47–0–*ct* 5–*st* 7
Bowling 20–0
He also played for Staffordshire (1886).

Palmer, Robert William Michael
Cricketer. *b:* 4.6.1960, Hong Kong. Tail end right-hand batsman, left-arm medium pace bowler. *Sch* Bedford School. *Team* Cambridge U (1981–83, blue 1982).
Career batting
11–9–5–20–12–5.00–0–*ct* 4
Bowling 954–16–59.62–0–0–4/96
His County cricket was for Buckinghamshire (1986).

Palmer, Rodney Howell
Amateur. *b:* 24.11.1907, Sherfield-on-Loddon, Hampshire. *d:* 24.4.1987, Newbury, Berkshire. Tail end right-hand batsman, right-arm fast bowler. *Sch* Harrow. *Teams* Cambridge U (1929); Hampshire (1930–33, 3 matches).
Career batting
4–2–0–0–0–0.00–0–*ct* 1
Bowling 292–9–32.44–1–0–5/93
He also played for Berkshire (1928–29).

Palmer, Roy
Cricketer. *b:* 12.7.1942, Devizes, Wiltshire. Brother of K. E. (Somerset), uncle of G. V. (Somerset). Lower order right-hand batsman, right-arm fast medium bowler. *Team* Somerset (1965–70, 74 matches).
Career batting
74–110–32–1037–84–13.29–0–*ct* 25
Bowling 5439–172–31.62–4–0–6/45
He joined the first-class umpires' list in 1980 and umpired in one Test match in 1992.

Palmer, Septimus
Amateur. *b:* 23.8.1858, Collingwood, Melbourne, Victoria, Australia. *d:* 14.12.1935, Kensington, London. Middle order batsman. *Sch* Stonyhurst. *Team* Lancashire (1879–80, 6 matches).
Career batting
6–9–0–28–8–3.11–0–*ct* 4
Bowling 11–0

Palmer, Stephen Leonard
Cricketer. *b:* 31.3.1968, Brighton, Sussex. Lower order right-hand batsman, right-arm medium pace bowler. *Team* Cambridge U (1987).
Career batting
1–1–0–18–18–18.00–0–*ct* 0
Bowling 57–1–57.00–0–0–1/41
He won a blue for soccer.

Palmer, William Thomas
Professional. *b:* 5.1.1847, Canterbury, Kent. *d:* 2.9.1906, Southfields, London. Hard hitting middle order right-hand batsman, right-hand medium pace round-arm bowler, good deep field. *Teams* Kent (1867–70, 17 matches); Surrey (1872–76, 19 matches).
Career batting
39–72–1–654–54–9.21–0–*ct* 15
Bowling 29–1–29.00–0–0–1/8
His final first-class match was for the South v North in 1877.

Palmes, Manfred Jerome
Amateur. *b:* 5.2.1887, Naburn Hall, York. *d:* 5.5.1968, Murdoch Valley, Simonstown, Cape Province, South Africa. Lower order batsman, useful bowler. *Team* Royal Navy (1919–20).
Career batting
2–4–1–10–6–3.33–0–*ct* 0
Bowling 97–0

Pandit, Chandrakant Sitaram
Cricketer. *b:* 30.9.1961, Bombay, India. Middle order right-hand batsman, wicket-keeper. *Team* Bombay (1979/80 to 1990/1). *Tours* India to Sharjah (not first-class) 1985/6, 1986/7, 1988/9, to England 1986, to Bangladesh (not first-class) 1988/9, to Australia 1991/2. *Tests* India (1986 to 1991/2, 5 matches).
Career batting
76–108–21–4499–157–51.71–12–*ct* 188–*st* 26
Bowling 48–1–48.00–0–0–1/26
Test batting
5–8–1–171–39–24.42–0–*ct* 14–*st* 2
Although taken to England in 1986 as the reserve wicket-keeper, he batted well enough to play in one Test as a specialist batsman.

Pank, Dr Philip Esmond Durrell
Amateur. *b:* 22.4.1892, Jaypore, India. *d:* 15.2.1966, Colchester, Essex. Middle order batsman, slow left-arm bowler. *Sch* Wellington. *Teams* Europeans (1918/19); Army (1925).
Career batting
4–8–2–79–29–13.16–0–*ct* 3
Bowling 113–9–12.55–1–0–7/12

Pape, Arthur Albert Brinkley
Amateur. *b:* 30.7.1890, Fairford, Cirencester, Gloucestershire. *d:* 11.8.1945, Hartlepool, Co Durham. Middle order batsman. *Team* Somerset (1912, 1 match).
Career batting
1–2–0–0–0–0.00–0–*ct* 0
He also played for Durham (pre first-class, 1921).

Papillon, Godfrey Keppel
Amateur. *b:* 24.9.1867, Lexden Manor, Essex. *d:* 14.8.1942, Hexham, Northumberland. Grandson of T. Garnier (Oxford U 1832), brother-in-law of H. C. L. Tindall (Kent). Middle order right-hand batsman, wicket-keeper. *Sch* Marlborough. *Team* Gentlemen (1892).
Career batting
1–1–0–10–10–10.00–0–*ct* 1
He played for Northamptonshire (pre first-class, 1901–03).

Parfitt, Judge James John Alexander
Amateur. *b:* 23.12.1857, Bwlch, Breconshire. *d:* 17.5.1926, Wimbledon, Surrey. Lower order right-hand batsman, right-arm fast medium bowler, slip field. *Sch* Prior Park College. *Teams* Surrey (1881–82, 8 matches); Somerset (1883–85, 6 matches).
Career batting
14–27–3–222–41*–9.25–0–*ct* 4
Bowling 932–38–24.52–1–1–7/33

He appeared for Warwickshire in 1886 (pre first-class). In the legal profession he became a County Court Judge.

Parfitt, Peter Howard
Professional. *b:* 8.12.1936, Billingford, Fakenham, Norfolk. Sound middle order left-hand batsman, off break bowler, excellent slip field. *Team* Middlesex (1956–72, 387 matches). *Tours* MCC to India, Pakistan and Ceylon 1961/2, to Australia and New Zealand 1962/3, 1965/6, to East Africa 1963/4, 1973/4, to India 1963/4, to South Africa 1964/5; President's XI in India 1963/4. *Tests* England (1961/2 to 1972, 37 matches).
Career batting
498–845–104–26924–200*–36.33–58–*ct* 564
Bowling 8401–277–30.32–5–0–6/45
Test batting
37–52–6–1882–131*–40.91–7–*ct* 42
Bowling 574–12–47.83–0–0–2/5

One of the leading batsman in England in the 1960s, he played in 37 Test matches, but never managed to secure an unassailable position in the England side. Coming to the top in 1961 with over 2,000 runs, he gained a place in the MCC side to India that winter and in 1962 not only headed the Test batting averages, but hit 2,121 runs (av 45.12) in first-class matches – in all he completed 1,000 runs in a season fourteen times, plus once overseas and went on to 2,000 three times. A poor tour in Australia in 1962/3 however lost him his Test place and although he was to be given several other opportunities in the England team, he never made many runs. His final Test appearances came in his last summer with Middlesex, when he was batting well, but once more at Test level he could show only moderate form. He captained Middlesex 1968–70.

His only double century was 200* for Middlesex v Nottinghamshire at Trent Bridge in 1964. Before appearing for Middlesex he played for Norfolk (1953–55). A useful soccer player, he appeared for Norwich City.

Paris, Alexander
Amateur. *b:* 29.8.1908, Torphichen, West Lothian, Scotland. Lower order right-hand batsman, right-arm medium pace bowler. *Team* Scotland (1937–38).
Career batting
3–6–1–40–24–8.00–0–*ct* 2
Bowling 210–12–17.50–1–0–6/35

Paris, Cecil Gerard Alexander
Amateur. *b:* 20.8.1911, Kirkee, India. Middle order right-hand batsman, right-arm slow bowler. *Sch* King's Canterbury. *Team* Hampshire (1933–48, 98 matches).
Career batting
100–172–9–3730–134*–22.88–2–*ct* 75
Bowling 216–4–54.00–0–0–1/10

He hit 1,058, av 23.51, in 1938. He captained Hampshire in 1938 and was President of the County Club 1984–89. An important figure in cricket administration he was Chairman of the TCCB in 1974 and President of MCC 1975/6.

Paris, William
Professional. *b:* 29.4.1838, Old Alresford, Hampshire. *d:* 12.1.1915, Winchester, Hampshire. Attacking lower order right-hand batsman, right-hand round-arm bowler. *Team* Hampshire (1875–81, 6 matches).
Career batting
6–11–1–81–51*–8.10–0–*ct* 0
Bowling 52–5–10.40–0–0–3/28

Parkar, Ghulam Ahmed
Cricketer. *b:* 25.10.1955, Kaluste, India. Brother of Zulfiqar (Bombay). Opening right-hand batsman, right-arm medium pace bowler. *Team* Bombay (1978/9 to 1985/6). *Tours* India to England 1982, to Sharjah (not first-class) 1983/4, to Australia 1984/5 (not first-class). *Test* India (1982, 1 match).
Career batting
66–109–10–4167–170*–42.09–11–*ct* 46–*st* 1
Bowling 131–2–65.50–0–0–1/5
Test batting
1–2–0–7–6–3.50–0–*ct* 1

He hit 433 runs, av 36.08, on the 1982 tour to England and played in one Test.

Parke, Elliot Anderson
Amateur. *b:* 19.7.1850, Belgravia, Westminster, London. *d:* 22.6.1923, South Kensington, London. Middle order right-hand batsman, right-hand fast round-arm bowler, deep field. *Sch* Harrow. *Team* Kent (1874, 1 match).
Career batting
8–13–2–110–47–10.00–0–*ct* 4
Bowling 33–1–33.00–0–0–1/30

He did not appear in any first-class matches whilst at Oxford. Much of his cricket was for MCC and his final first-class match was for that Club in 1884.

Parke, Walter Evelyn
Amateur. *b:* 27.7.1891, Wimborne, Dorset. *d:* 13.10.1914, Hazebrouck, France. Middle order left-hand batsman. *Sch* Winchester. *Team* Army (1914).
Career batting
1–2–0–18–11–9.00–0–*ct* 1

His County cricket was for Dorset (1913).

Parker, Bradley
Cricketer. *b:* 23.6.1970, Mirfield, Yorkshire. Opening right-hand batsman, right-arm medium pace bowler. *Team* Yorkshire (1992, 1 match).
Career batting
1–2–0–37–30–18.50–0–*ct* 1

Parker, Charles Warrington Leonard
Professional. *b:* 14.10.1882, Prestbury, Gloucestershire. *d:* 11.7.1959, Cranleigh, Surrey. Lower order right-hand batsman, slow left-arm bowler. *Team* Gloucestershire (1903–35, 602 matches). *Tour* Joel to South Africa 1924/5. *Test* England (1921, 1 match).
Career batting
635–954–195–7951–82–10.47–0–*ct* 247
Bowling 63817–3278–19.46–277–91–10/79
Test batting
1–1–1–3–3*–no av–0–*ct* 0
Bowling 32–2–16.00–0–0–2/32

He took 100 wickets in a season sixteen times, going on to 200 five times (best 222, av 14.91, in 1925). His best bowling in an innings was 10 for 79 for Gloucestershire v Somerset at Bristol in 1920; in addition he took nine wickets in an innings on eight other occasions. For Gloucestershire v Yorkshire at Bristol in 1922 (his benefit match) he hit the stumps with five consecutive deliveries – unfortunately the second was a no-ball. He was a first-class umpire (1936–38) and Gloucestershire coach 1946–49. He was also an excellent golfer.

Parker, Cyril Brien Dennis
Amateur. *b:* 6.5.1897, Rathgar, Dublin, Ireland. *d:* 21.12.1962, Blackrock, Dublin, Ireland. Lower order right-hand batsman. *Team* Dublin U (1922).
Career batting
1–2–0–42–29–21.00–0–*ct* 0

Parker, Frederick Anthony Vivian
Amateur. *b:* 11.2.1913, Westminster, London. *d:* 26.5.1988, Plymouth, Devon. Son of W. M. (Army), son-in-law of C. G. E. Farmer (MCC). Opening or middle order right-hand batsman, right-arm medium pace bowler. *Sch* Winchester. *Team* Hampshire (1946, 2 matches).
Career batting
5–9–0–147–116–16.33–1–*ct* 2

He also played for Devon (1949).

Parker, Geoffrey Ross
Cricketer. *b:* 31.3.1968, Malvern, Melbourne, Victoria, Australia. Middle order right-hand batsman, right-arm medium pace bowler. *Team* Victoria (1985/6 to 1991/2, 18 matches). *Tour* Victoria to England 1991.
Career batting
18–31–3–639–76*–22.82–0–*ct* 17
Bowling 121–4–30.25–0–0–2/30

Parker, George Macdonald
Professional. *b:* 27.5.1899, Cape Town, South Africa. *d:* 1.5.1969, Thredbo, New South Wales, Australia. Lower order right-hand batsman, right-arm fast bowler. *Team* South Africa (1924). *Tour* South Africa to England 1924. *Tests* South Africa (1924, 2 matches).
Career batting
3–4–2–3–2*–1.50–0–*ct* 0
Bowling 307–12–25.58–1–0–6/152
Test batting
2–4–2–3–2*–1.50–0–*ct* 0
Bowling 273–8–34.12–1–0–6/152

A professional in the Bradford League he was co-opted into the 1924 team for two Tests only, and one other first-class game. He never appeared in first-class matches in South Africa.

Parker, Grahame Wilshaw
Amateur. *b:* 11.2.1912, Gloucester. Sound opening right-hand batsman, bowler, excellent field. *Teams* Gloucestershire (1932–50, 70 matches); Cambridge U (1934–35, blue both years).
Career batting
89–147–12–2956–210–21.89–5–*ct* 73
Bowling 2291–57–40.19–2–0–5/57

He hit 210 for Gloucestershire v Kent at Dover in 1937. He captained Cambridge in 1935. He was Secretary-Manager of Gloucestershire CCC 1968–76 and President 1986–87. He also played for Devon (1953–56). A noted rugby footballer, he appeared as full back for Cambridge and England.

Parker, Irvine Theodore
Amateur. *b:* 26.3.1890, Newton-on-Ayr, Ayrshire, Scotland. *d:* 14.5.1961, Kilmarnock, Ayrshire, Scotland. Opening right-hand batsman. *Team* Scotland (1920–26).
Career batting
2–2–0–62–62–31.00–0–*ct* 1

Parker, J. E.
Amateur. *b:* 2.7.1872. Tail end batsman, slow bowler. *Team* British Guiana (1905/6 to 1909/10). *Tour* West Indies to England 1906.
Career batting
8–15–1–61–15–4.35–0–*ct* 4
Bowling 281–5–56.20–0–0–2/28

He played in only five first-class matches on the 1906 visit to England, achieving very little.

Parker, John Frederick
Professional. *b:* 23.4.1913, Battersea, London. *d:* 26.1.1983, Bromley, Kent. Attacking middle order right-hand batsman, right-arm medium pace bowler, good slip field. *Team* Surrey (1932–52, 334 matches). *Tour* MCC to India 1939/40 (tour cancelled).
Career batting
340–523–71–14272–255–31.57–20–*ct* 331
Bowling 15677–543–28.87–8–0–6/34

He hit 1,000 runs in a season nine times (best 1,789, av 40.65 in 1949). Both his double centuries were for Surrey, the higher being 255 v New Zealanders at the Oval in 1949.

Parker, John Morton
Cricketer. *b:* 21.2.1951, Dannevirke, Hawke's Bay, New Zealand. Brother of N. M. (New Zealand) and K. J. (Auckland). Determined opening or middle order right-hand batsman, leg break and googly bowler, occasional wicket-keeper, good field. *Teams* Worcestershire (1971–75, 61 matches); Northern Districts (1972/3 to 1983/4). *Tours* New Zealand to England 1973, 1975 (World Cup), 1978, to Australia 1973/4, 1974/5 (not first-class), 1980/1, to India and Pakistan 1976/7. *Tests* New Zealand (1972/3 to 1980/1, 36 matches).
Career batting
207–362–39–11254–195–34.82–21–*ct* 177–*st* 5
Bowling 681–14–48.64–0–0–3/26
Test batting
36–63–2–1498–121–24.55–3–*ct* 30
Bowling 24–1–24.00–0–0–1/24
He hit 1,000 runs in a season twice (best 1,182, av 32.83, in 1973). On his 1973 tour to England he was very disappointing; playing in all three Tests he scored only 23 runs, av 4.60. On the 1978 tour he showed little improvement in the Tests, but hit 549 runs, av 36.60, in all first-class matches. He captained New Zealand in one Test v Pakistan in 1976/7.

Parker, John Palmer
Amateur. *b:* 29.11.1902, Portsmouth, Hampshire. *d:* 9.8.1984, Warblington, Hampshire. Middle order right-hand batsman. *Team* Hampshire (1926–33, 44 matches). *Tour* Tennyson to Jamaica 1926/7.
Career batting
47–72–8–1117–156–17.45–1–*ct* 22
Bowling 258–6–43.00–0–0–2/14

Parker, Paul William Giles
Cricketer. *b:* 15.1.1956, Bulawayo, Rhodesia. Middle order right-hand batsman, right-arm medium pace or leg break bowler, brilliant field. *Teams* Cambridge U (1976–78, blue all three years); Sussex (1976–91, 289 matches); Natal (1980/1); Durham (1992, 20 matches). *Test* England (1981, 1 match).
Career batting
352–601–78–18495–215–35.36–44–*ct* 244
Bowling 699–11–63.54–0–0–2/21
Test batting
1–2–0–13–13–6.50–0–*ct* 0
He hit 1,000 runs in a season nine times (best 1,692, av 47.00, in 1984). His highest score was 215 for Cambridge U v Essex at Fenner's in 1976. He captained Sussex from 1988 to 1991. Injuries in 1989, 1990 and 1991 meant that he missed a number of matches. At the end of 1991 he was asked to resign as Sussex captain but remain as a player but decided to move to Durham. A good rugby footballer, he was chosen for Cambridge but withdrew due to injury.

Parker, Roland John
Amateur. *b:* 19.7.1925, Pudsey, Yorkshire. Middle order right-hand batsman, off break bowler. *Sch* Uppingham. *Team* Combined Services (1947).
Career batting
2–3–0–36–18–12.00–0–*ct* 0

Parker, Wilfred
Amateur. Middle order batsman, opening bowler. *Team* Lancashire (1904, 2 matches).
Career batting
2–3–0–66–40–22.00–0–*ct* 0
Bowling 175–4–43.75–0–0–2/47

Parker, William Mackworth
Amateur. *b:* 1.9.1886, Belgaum, India. *d:* 30.7.1915, Hooge, Belgium. He was killed in action. Father of F. A. V. (Hampshire). Stylish middle order right-hand batsman, bowler. *Sch* Winchester. *Teams* MCC (1913); Army (1914).
Career batting
2–4–0–34–11–8.50–0–*ct* 2
Bowling 81–4–20.25–0–0–3/64
From 1906 when he was in the Sandhurst XI he was considered one of the best military batsmen.

Parkes, Howard Roderick
Amateur. *b:* 31.5.1877, Erdington, Birmingham. *d:* 28.5.1920, Studland, Dorset. Brother-in-law of T. L. Taylor (Yorkshire). Stylish opening or middle order right-hand batsman, excellent cover point. *Sch* Uppingham. *Teams* Warwickshire (1898, 1 match); London County (1900).
Career batting
7–10–0–79–21–7.90–0–*ct* 3
He appeared in the Freshmen's and Seniors' matches at Oxford, but no first-class games. He won a blue for athletics.

Parkes, John Leonard
Amateur. *b:* 23.6.1938, Leamington Spa, Warwickshire. Lower order left-hand batsman, leg break bowler. *Sch* Warwick. *Team* Free Foresters (1960).
Career batting
1–2–0–0–0–0.00–0–*ct* 0
Bowling 61–1–61.00–0–0–1/61

Parkhouse, Richard John
Amateur. *b:* 2.3.1910, Clydach, Neath, Glamorgan. Middle order right-hand batsman. *Team* Glamorgan (1939, 2 matches).
Career batting
2–1–0–0–0–0.00–0–*ct* 0

Parkhouse, William Gilbert Anthony
Professional. *b:* 12.10.1925, Swansea, Glamorgan. Stylish opening right-hand batsman, right arm medium pace bowler, good close field. *Sch* Wycliffe. *Team* Glamorgan (1948–64, 435 matches). *Tour* MCC to Australia and New Zealand 1950/1. *Tests* England (1950–59, 7 matches).

Parkin, Cecil Harry

Career batting
455–791–49–23508–201–31.68–32–*ct* 324
Bowling 125–2–62.50–0–0–1/4
Test batting
7–13–0–373–78–28.69–0–*ct* 3

He hit 1,000 runs in a season fifteen times, going on to 2,000 once: 2,243, av 48.76, in 1959. His only double century was 201 for Glamorgan v Kent at Swansea in 1956.

Parkin, Cecil Harry
Professional. *b:* 18.2.1886, Eaglescliffe, Co Durham. *d:* 15.6.1943, Cheetham Hill, Manchester, Lancashire. Father of R. H. (Lancashire). Useful lower order right-hand batsman, right-arm slow bowler, off break and leg break. *Teams* Yorkshire (1906, 1 match); Lancashire (1914–26, 157 matches). *Tour* MCC to Australia 1920/1. *Tests* England (1920/1 to 1924, 10 matches).
Career batting
197–239–33–2425–57–11.77–0–*ct* 126
Bowling 18434–1048–17.58–93–27–9/32
Test batting
10–16–3–160–36–12.30–0–*ct* 3
Bowling 1128–32–35.25–2–0–5/38

He took 100 wickets in a season four times, going on to 200 twice (best 209, av 16.94, in 1923). His best bowling in an innings was 9/32 for Lancashire v Leicestershire at Ashby-de-la-Zouch in 1924. Following a single appearance for Yorkshire it was discovered that he was not qualified to represent the County, being born 20 yards over the border. Most of his cricket was in the Leagues and his relatively brief career with Lancashire was brought to a premature close due to a disagreement with the Committee. He also played for Durham (pre first-class, 1907 and 1913). His non-stop humour earned him the title of 'Cricket's comedian'.

Parkin, John Maurice
Cricketer. *b:* 16.10.1944, Kimberley, Nottinghamshire. Middle order right-hand batsman. *Team* Nottinghamshire (1966–68, 28 matches).
Career batting
28–39–8–349–53–11.25–0–*ct* 9

Parkin, Reginald Henry
Professional. *b:* 25.7.1909, Tunstall, Staffordshire. Son of C. H. (Lancashire and Yorkshire). Middle order right-hand batsman, off break bowler. *Team* Lancashire (1931–39, 20 matches).
Career batting
21–19–4–286–60–19.06–0–*ct* 4
Bowling 880–23–38.26–0–0–3/52

He also played for Staffordshire (1935).

Parkins, William Richard
Amateur. *b:* 20.8.1925, Glenfield, Leicester. *d:* 1.11.1969, Leicester. Aggressive middle order right-hand batsman. *Sch* Wyggeston GS. *Team* Leicestershire (1950, 5 matches).
Career batting
5–10–0–125–39–12.50–0–*ct* 2

Parkinson, Ernest William
Amateur. *b:* 28.4.1894, Sileby, Leicestershire. *d:* 14.4.1978, Leicester. Lower order right-hand batsman, useful bowler. *Team* Leicestershire (1920, 2 matches).
Career batting
2–4–0–26–18–6.50–0–*ct* 0
Bowling 100–0

Parkinson, Herbert Black
Professional. *b:* 11.9.1892, Barrow-in-Furness, Lancashire. *d:* 27.4.1947, Barrow-in-Furness, Lancashire. Tail end right-hand batsman, wicket-keeper. *Team* Lancashire (1922–23, 15 matches).
Career batting
15–18–5–34–8–2.61–0–*ct* 14–*st* 3

Parkinson, Leonard Wright
Professional. *b:* 15.9.1908, Salford, Manchester, Lancashire. *d:* 16.3.1969, Manchester, Lancashire. Attacking middle or lower order right-hand batsman, leg break bowler, good field. *Team* Lancashire (1932–36, 88 matches).
Career batting
88–112–13–2132–93–21.53–0–*ct* 45
Bowling 5654–192–29.44–7–0–6/112

He also played for Cheshire (1938–39).

Parks, Henry William
Professional. *b:* 18.7.1906, Haywards Heath, Sussex. *d:* 7.5.1984, Taunton, Somerset. Brother of J. H. (Sussex), uncle of J. M. (Sussex and Somerset). Sound opening or middle order right-hand batsman, right-arm medium pace bowler. *Team* Sussex (1926–48, 480 matches). *Tour* Commonwealth to India 1949/50 (1 match).
Career batting
483–745–98–21725–200*–33.57–42–*ct* 196
Bowling 705–13–54.23–0–0–2/37

He hit 1,000 runs in a season fourteen times going on to 2,000 once: 2,122, av 38.58, in 1947. His only double century was 200* for Sussex v Essex at Chelmsford in 1931. He was a first-class umpire (1949–50). He was Somerset coach 1951–54.

Parks, James Horace
Professional. *b:* 12.5.1903, Haywards Heath, Sussex. *d:* 21.11.1980, Cuckfield, Sussex. Brother of H. W. (Sussex), father of J. M. (Sussex and Somerset), grandfather of R. J. (Hampshire). Sound opening or middle order right-hand batsman, right-arm slow medium bowler. *Teams* Sussex (1924–39, 434 matches); Canterbury (1946/7). *Tours* MCC to Australia and New Zealand 1935/6; Tennyson to India 1937/8. *Test* England (1937, 1 match).

Career batting
468–758–63–21369–197–30.74–41–*ct* 325
Bowling 22789–852–26.74–24–1–7/17
Test batting
1–2–0–29–22–14.50–0–*ct* 0
Bowling 36–3–12.00–0–0–2/26

He hit 1,000 runs in a season twelve times and in the only summer he exceeded 2,000, actually reached 3,003, av 50.89. In that same season, 1937, he took 101 wickets, av 25.83, thus achieving an unique 'double'. He reached 100 wickets in one other season, 103, av 19.57, in 1935. His last first-class match was for Commonwealth XI in 1952. He was a first-class umpire (1957–62). He was Nottinghamshire coach 1953–57 and Sussex coach 1965–69.

Parks, James Michael
Professional. *b:* 21.10.1931, Haywards Heath, Sussex. Son of J. H. (Sussex), father of R. J. (Hampshire), nephew of H. W. (Sussex). Attacking middle order right-hand batsman, leg break bowler, wicket-keeper, good cover point. *Teams* Sussex (1949–72, 563 matches); Somerset (1973–76, 47 matches). *Tours* MCC to Pakistan 1955/6, to South Africa 1956/7, 1964/5, to West Indies 1959/60, 1967/8, to New Zealand 1960/1, to India 1963/4, to Australia and New Zealand 1965/6; International Wanderers to Rhodesia 1972/3. *Tests* England (1954 to 1967/8, 46 matches).
Career batting
739–1227–172–36673–205*–34.76–51-*ct* 1088-*st* 9
Bowling 2235–51–43.82–0–0–3/23
Test batting
46–68–7–1962–108*–32.16–2–*ct* 103–*st* 11
Bowling 51–1–51.00–0–0–1/43

Although remembered as a wicket-keeper batsman, Parks played County cricket for almost ten years as a batsman and brilliant cover point and had been capped by England and had travelled on two MCC tours before he was made the regular Sussex wicket-keeper midway through the 1958 season. His first full year behind the stumps – 1959 – was one of continuous success. He hit 2,313 runs – one run fewer than in 1955, but with an average of 51.40 compared with 42.07 – and claimed 93 victims behind the wicket. Joining the 1959/60 MCC side in the West Indies following the illness of P. B. H. May, he was most successful and it looked as if his future as England's wicket-keeper was secure, but illness and lack of form meant that over the next few seasons he shared the Test wicket-keeping place with J. T. Murray.

In all he hit 1,000 runs in a season twenty times, going on to 2,000 three times. His only double century was 205* for Sussex v Somerset at Hove in 1955. He was made captain of Sussex in 1967, but resigned midway through the following summer and at the close of the 1972 season left Sussex for Somerset under controversial circumstances. He was joint Sussex coach in 1987.

Parks, Robert James
Cricketer. *b:* 15.6.1959, Cuckfield, Sussex. Grandson of J. H. (Sussex), son of J. M. (Sussex and Somerset). Lower order right-hand batsman, wicket-keeper. *Team* Hampshire (1980–92, 253 matches). *Tour* English Counties to Zimbabwe 1984/5.
Career batting
255–284–82–3944–89–19.52–0–*ct* 638–*st* 72
Bowling 166–0

Parnaby, Alan Herring
Amateur.*b:*2.9.1916, Sunderland, Co Durham. *d:* 25.11.1974, Westminster, London. Attractive opening right-hand batsman. *Teams* Minor Counties (1939); Combined Services (1949–53).
Career batting
8–16–0–433–101–27.06–1–*ct* 3
Bowling 10–0

His County cricket was for Durham (pre first-class, 1936–39) and he was for some years one of the leading cricketers in the Army side. He scored 101 on debut for Minor Counties v Oxford U at Oxford in 1939.

Parnell, William Henry
Amateur. *b:* 7.10.1837, Marylebone, London. *d:* 4.5.1879, Westminster, London. Attacking lower order right-hand batsman, right-hand fast round-arm bowler. *Sch* Rugby. *Team* MCC (1859–70).
Career batting
17–28–2–144–26–5.53–0–*ct* 10
Bowling 199–13–15.30–1–0–5/42

He was elected to the Committee of MCC in 1874.

Parnham, John Thomas
Professional. *b:* 6.9.1856, Bottesford, Leicestershire. *d:* 18.2.1908, Church, Lancashire. Lower order batsman, slow left-arm bowler, slip field. *Team* MCC (1883–89).
Career batting
8–11–2–178–90*–19.77–0–*ct* 3
Bowling 294–16–18.37–2–1–7/25

His first-class debut was for the United Eleven v Australians in 1882 when he created a sensation by taking 12 wickets for 126 in the match. In the North v South match in 1886 he added 157 runs for the last wicket with J. White. His County cricket was for Leicestershire (pre first-class, 1879–86) and Caernarvonshire (1882). After retiring he became a County umpire.

Parore, Adam Craig
Cricketer. *b:* 23.1.1971, Auckland, New Zealand. Middle order right-hand batsman, wicket-keeper. *Team* Auckland (1988/9 to 1991/2). *Tours* New Zealand to England 1990, to Pakistan 1990/1; Rest of World to England 1992. *Tests* New Zealand (1990 to 1991/2).
Career batting
31–37–8–1062–155*–36.62–1–*ct* 63–*st* 9

Test batting
2–4–1–47–20–15.66–0–*ct* 10–*st* 1
He played in one Test on the 1990 tour to England.

Parr, Butler
Professional. *b:* 9.11.1810, Marton, Lincolnshire. *d:* 16.3.1872, Radcliffe-on-Trent, Nottinghamshire. Father-in-law of Richard Daft (Nottinghamshire). Middle order right-hand batman, wicket-keeper. *Team* Nottinghamshire (1835–54, 18 matches).
Career batting
23–40–2–418–61*–11.00–0–*ct* 14–*st* 6
He was on the Nottinghamshire CCC Committee from 1865 until his death.

Parr, Francis David
Professional. *b:* 1.6.1928, Wallasey, Cheshire. Lower order left-hand batsman, wicket-keeper. *Team* Lancashire (1951–54, 48 matches).
Career batting
49–53–11–507–42–12.07–0–*ct* 71–*st* 20

Parr, George
Professional. *b:* 22.5.1826, Radcliffe-on-Trent, Nottinghamshire. *d:* 23.6.1891, Radcliffe-on-Trent, Nottinghamshire. Brother of H. J. (Nottinghamshire) and Samuel (Nottinghamshire). Excellent middle order right-hand batsman, right-hand under-arm lob bowler, good field. *Teams* Nottinghamshire (1845–70, 54 matches); Surrey (1852, 1 match as given man); Sussex (1853–54, 2 matches as given man); Kent (1854–58, 3 matches as given man). *Tours* Parr to North America 1859 (not first-class), to Australia and New Zealand 1863/4.
Career batting
207–358–30–6626–130–20.20–1–*ct* 126
Bowling 445–29–15.34–1–0–6/42
About 1860 he was regarded as the best batsman in England. From 1856 to 1870 he captained Nottinghamshire and also was captain and manager of the All England Eleven. He led the pioneering touring team to North America and the second touring team to Australia, having declined to go on the first. His first-class debut was for Players of Nottinghamshire in 1844. He also played for Warwickshire (pre first-class, 1852).

Parr, Henry Bingham
Amateur. *b:* 6.6.1845, Grappenhall Hayes, Lancashire. *d:* 24.3.1930, Liverpool, Lancashire. Stubborn middle order right-hand batsman, deep field. *Sch* Cheltenham. *Team* Lancashire (1872–76, 10 matches).
Career batting
11–16–0–180–61–11.25–0–*ct* 4
He also played for Cheshire (1874–78).

Parr, Henry John
Professional. *b:* 7.1.1838, Radcliffe-on-Trent, Nottinghamshire. *d:* 24.4.1863, Radcliffe-on-Trent, Nottinghamshire. Brother of George (Nottinghamshire) and Samuel (Nottinghamshire). Middle order right-hand batsman. *Team* Nottinghamshire (1856–58, 3 matches).
Career batting
3–6–1–55–13–11.00–0–*ct* 2

Parr, Percivall Chase
Amateur. *b:* 2.12.1859, Bromley, Kent. *d:* 3.9.1912, Widmore, Bromley, Kent. Lower order right-hand batsman, right-arm fast bowler. *Sch* Winchester. *Team* Gentlemen of Kent (1880).
Career batting
1–1–1–0–0*–no av–0–*ct* 0
Bowling 71–1–71.00–0–0–1/71
He played no first-class cricket matches at Oxford U, but did win a blue for soccer, and also played for England.

Parr, Samuel
Professional. *b:* 2.5.1820, Radcliffe-on-Trent, Nottinghamshire. *d:* 12.5.1873, Nottingham. Brother of George (Nottinghamshire) and H. J. (Nottinghamshire). Middle order right-hand batsman, good deep field. *Team* Nottinghamshire (1840–55, 17 matches).
Career batting
25–44–4–533–53–13.32–0–*ct* 16
Bowling 18–1–18.00–0–0–1/18
He achieved notoriety amongst his fellow cricketers due to his practical jokes.

Parratt, John
Professional. *b:* 24.3.1859, Morley, Yorkshire. *d:* 6.5.1905, Morley, Yorkshire. Lower order batsman, useful bowler. *Team* Yorkshire (1888–90, 2 matches).
Career batting
2–2–0–11–11–5.50–0–*ct* 4
Bowling 75–1–75.00–0–0–1/12

Parrington, William Ferguson
Amateur. *b:* 1.11.1889, Carley Hill, Sunderland, Co Durham. *d:* 7.5.1980, Northallerton, Yorkshire. Middle order right-hand batsman, right-arm medium pace bowler. *Sch* Rossall. *Team* Derbyshire (1926, 6 matches).
Career batting
6–11–1–148–47–14.80–0–*ct* 1
He also played for Durham (pre first-class, 1914). He played no first-class cricket matches at Cambridge U.

Parris, Frederick
Professional. *b:* 20.9.1867, Ringmer, Sussex. *d:* 17.1.1941, Cuckfield, Sussex. Lower order left-hand batsman, right-arm slow medium bowler. *Team* Sussex (1890–1901, 105 matches).
Career batting
105–177–24–2222–77–14.52–0–*ct* 59
Bowling 7539–291–25.90–20–5–8/28

After retiring he was a first-class umpire (1908–28), standing in one Test match (1909).

Parry, Cecil Wynne
Amateur. *b:* 6.8.1866, Clifton, Bristol. *d:* 4.1.1901, York. Stylish middle order right-hand batsman, right-arm medium pace bowler. *Sch* Charterhouse. *Team* Cambridge U (1889).
Career batting
1–2–0–16–9–8.00–0–*ct* 0
Bowling 25–0
His County cricket was for Buckinghamshire (1891).

Parry, Derick Recaldo
Cricketer. *b:* 22.12.1954, Cotton Ground, Nevis. Middle order right-hand batsman, off break bowler. *Team* Leeward Islands (1975/6 to 1981/2). *Tours* West Indies to India and Sri Lanka 1978/9, to Australia and New Zealand 1979/80, to England 1980, to Pakistan 1980/1; West Indian XI to South Africa 1982/3, 1983/4. *Tests* West Indies (1977/8 to 1979/80, 12 matches).
Career batting
77–119–24–2552–96–26.86–0–*ct* 50
Bowling 7268–251–28.95–12–1–9/76
Test batting
12–20–3–381–65–22.41–0–*ct* 4
Bowling 936–23–40.69–1–0–5/15
He did not play in any Tests on the 1980 tour to England. His best bowling was 9/76 for Combined Islands v Jamaica at Kingston in 1979/80. He also played for Cambridgeshire (1979–85).

Parry, Donald Morris
Amateur. *b:* 8.2.1911, Hatch End, Middlesex. Middle order right-hand batsman, right-arm medium pace bowler. *Sch* Merchant Taylors. *Team* Cambridge U (1931–32, blue 1931).
Career batting
17–31–5–574–87*–22.07–0–*ct* 6

Parry, Matthew Croose
Amateur. *b:* 11.12.1885, Birley, Herefordshire. *d:* 5.2.1931, Carrigrohane, Co Cork, Ireland. Middle order right-hand batsman. *Sch* Hereford and KES, Birmingham. *Teams* Warwickshire (1908–10, 2 matches); Ireland (1925).
Career batting
4–7–0–211–124–30.14–1–*ct* 2
Bowling 71–2–35.50–0–0–2/31
He also played for Herefordshire (1905).

Parslow, Leonard Frederick
Amateur. *b:* 11.11.1909, Islington, London. *d:* 6.8.1963, Rochford, Essex. Middle order right-hand batsman. *Team* Essex (1946, 1 match).
Career batting
1–2–0–9–5–4.50–0–*ct* 0

Parsons, Arthur Brian Douglas
Amateur, turned professional on joining Surrey staff in 1958. *b:* 20.9.1933, Guildford, Surrey. Steady opening or middle order right-hand batsman, leg break bowler. *Sch* Brighton. *Teams* Cambridge U (1954–55, blue both years); Surrey (1958–63, 119 matches).
Career batting
152–263–22–6376–125–26.45–3–*ct* 69
Bowling 23–0
He hit 1,000 runs in a season three times (best 1,415, av 32.15, in 1961).

Parsons, Austin Edward Werring
Cricketer. *b:* 9.1.1949, Glasgow, Scotland. Sound middle order right-hand batsman, leg break bowler. *Teams* Auckland (1973/4 to 1982/3); Sussex (1974–75, 21 matches).
Career batting
82–156–10–3847–141–26.34–4–*ct* 44
Bowling 183–2–91.50–0–0–1/26
His first-class debut was for New Zealand Under 23s XI in 1971/2. In 1975 for Sussex he hit 977 runs, av 25.71.

Parsons, David Joseph
Cricketer. *b:* 28.10.1954, Accrington, Lancashire. Lower order right-hand batsman, left-arm medium fast bowler. *Team* Minor Counties (1981).
Career batting
1–1–0–1–1–1.00–0–*ct* 0
Bowling 53–1–53.00–0–0–1/53
His County cricket was for Cumberland (1981–84).

Parsons, Gordon James
Cricketer. *b:* 17.10.1959, Slough, Buckinghamshire. Brother-in-law of W. J. Cronje (Orange Free State). Lower order left-hand batsman, right-arm medium pace bowler. *Teams* Leicestershire (1978–92, 164 matches); Boland (1983/4 to 1984/5); Griqualand West (1985/6 to 1986/7); Warwickshire (1986–88, 47 matches); Orange Free State (1988/9 to 1990/1). *Tours* Robins to New Zealand 1979/80 (not first-class); Leicestershire to Zimbabwe 1980/1.
Career batting
260–341–77–4929–76–18.67–0–*ct* 78
Bowling 18436–606–30.42–18–1–9/72
His best bowling was 9/72 for Boland v Transvaal at Johannesburg in 1984/5. He also played for Buckinghamshire (1977).

Parsons, Canon John Henry
Professional to 1914; amateur 1919 to 1923; professional 1924 to 1928; then amateur from 1929 onwards. *b:* 30.5.1890, Headington, Oxford. *d:* 2.2.1981, Plymouth, Devon. Attacking middle order right-hand batsman, right-arm medium pace bowler, slip field. *Sch* Bablake. *Teams* Warwickshire (1910–34, 312 matches); Europeans (1919/20 to 1921/2). *Tour* MCC to India, Burma and Ceylon 1926/7.

Career batting
355–555–52–17969–225–35.72–38–*ct* 260
Bowling 2405–83–28.97–3–1–7/41

He hit 1,000 runs in a season in England ten times (best 1,700, av 50.00, in 1927). His only double century was 225 for Warwickshire v Glamorgan at Edgbaston in 1927. His final first-class match was for MCC in 1936. He also hit 1,000 runs in India in 1926/7.

Parsons, Keith Alan
Cricketer. *b:* 2.5.1973, Taunton, Somerset. Lower order right-hand batsman, right-arm medium pace bowler. *Team* Somerset (1992, 1 match).
Career batting
1–2–0–1–1–0.50–0–*ct* 0

His twin brother, Kevin, joined the Somerset staff in 1992, and played in one Sunday League match.

Parsons, Walter Dyett
Professional. *b:* 26.6.1861, Southampton, Hampshire. *d:* 24.12.1939, East Wellow, Hampshire. Lower order batsman, useful bowler. *Team* Hampshire (1882, 2 matches).
Career batting
2–4–2–31–12*–15.50–0–*ct* 1
Bowling 72–1–72.00–0–0–1/23

Parthasarathi, Gopalaswami
Amateur. *b:* 7.7.1912, Madras, India. Middle order right-hand batsman, leg break and googly bowler. *Teams* Oxford U (1933–35); Madras (1936/7 to 1943/4); Indians (1929/30 to 1947/8).
Career batting
25–43–2–879–87–21.43–0–*ct* 17
Bowling 1473–62–23.75–2–1–6/49

Parton, John Wesley
Professional. *b:* 31.1.1863, Wellington, Shropshire. *d:* 30.1.1906, Rotherham, Yorkshire. Lower order batsman, useful bowler. *Team* Yorkshire (1889, 1 match).
Career batting
1–2–0–16–14–8.00–0–*ct* 0
Bowling 4–1–4.00–0–0–1/4

He also played for Shropshire.

Partridge, Brian John Macpherson
Cricketer. *b:* 21.1.1956, Haddington, East Lothian, Scotland. Tail end right-hand batsman, right-arm medium fast bowler. *Sch* Loretto. *Team* Oxford U (1977).
Career batting
4–6–4–5–4–2.50–0–*ct* 0
Bowling 170–4–42.50–0–0–2/38

Partridge, Cyril
Amateur. *b:* 2.8.1896, Higham Ferrers, Wellingborough, Northamptonshire. *d:* 23.2.1945, Hanscombe End, Shillington, Bedfordshire. He died in a motor accident. Middle order right-hand batsman. *Sch* Wellingborough. *Team* Northamptonshire (1921, 1 match).
Career batting
1–2–0–1–1–0.50–0–*ct* 0

Partridge, Martin David
Cricketer. *b:* 25.10.1954, Birdlip, Gloucestershire. Middle or lower order left-hand batsman, right-arm medium pace bowler. *Team* Gloucestershire (1976–80, 46 matches).
Career batting
46–66–21–1202–90–26.71–0–*ct* 16
Bowling 2076–41–50.63–1–0–5/29

Partridge, Norman Ernest
Amateur. *b:* 10.8.1900, Great Barr, Staffordshire. *d:* 10.3.1982, Aberystwyth, Cardigan. Middle order right-hand batsman, right-arm medium fast bowler. *Sch* Malvern. *Teams* Cambridge U (1920, blue); Warwickshire (1921–37, 100 matches).
Career batting
112–164–18–2719–102–18.62–1–*ct* 109
Bowling 9047–393–23.02–19–2–7/66

An outstanding schoolboy cricketer, he was invited to play for the Gentlemen in 1919, his final summer at Malvern, but the school authorities would not grant permission.

Partridge, Reginald Joseph
Professional. *b:* 11.2.1912, Wollaston, Northamptonshire. Defensive opening or middle order right-hand batsman, right-arm medium, later off break or leg break bowler. *Team* Northamptonshire (1929–48, 277 matches).
Career batting
280–462–122–3922–70–11.53–0–*ct* 105
Bowling 19946–638–31.26–22–2–9/66

His best season was 1938 with 94 wickets, av 25.70, and his best bowling was 9/66 for Northamptonshire v Warwickshire at Kettering in 1934.

Parvez Jamil Mir
Cricketer. *b:* 24.9.1953, Sutrapur, Dacca, Pakistan. Brother of Shahid Mir (Lahore). Middle order right-hand batsman, right-arm medium fast bowler. *Teams* Rawalpindi (1970/1); Lahore (1971/2 to 1984/5); Punjab (1972/3 to 1975/6); Universities (1973/4 to 1974/5); Derbyshire (1975, 1 match); Habib Bank (1975/6 to 1980/1); Glamorgan (1979, 1 match). *Tours* Pakistan to England 1975 (World Cup), to Sri Lanka 1975/6.
Career batting
80–139–14–3972–155–31.77–5–*ct* 70
Bowling 4939–191–25.85–12–1–6/31

He also played for Norfolk (1981–85) winning in consecutive seasons the Minor Counties leading batsman and bowler awards. He played for Pakistan in one-day international matches.

Parvin, Alfred William
Amateur. *b:* 31.12.1859, Southampton, Hampshire. *d:* 12.7.1916, Brighton, Sussex. Middle order batsman. *Sch* Ipswich. *Team* Hampshire (1885, 1 match).
Career batting
1–2–0–11–11–5.50–0–*ct* 1

Pascall, Victor S.
Amateur. *b:* 1886, Diego Martin, Trinidad. *d:* 7.7.1930, Port of Spain, Trinidad. Uncle of L. N. Constantine (West Indies), brother-in-law of L. S. Constantine (West Indies). Lower order left-hand batsman, slow left-arm bowler. *Team* Trinidad (1905/6 to 1926/7). *Tour* West Indies to England 1923.
Career batting
49–77–14–859–92–13.63–0–*ct* 31
Bowling 3435–171–20.08–6–1–6/26
In first-class matches on the 1923 tour he took 52 wickets, av 24.28. His final first-class match was a trial match in West Indies in 1927/8.

Pascoe, Charles Henry
Professional. *b:* 23.12.1876, Haggerston, London. *d:* 26.1.1957, Walthamstow, Essex. Tail end batsman, slow left-arm bowler. *Team* Essex (1909, 1 match).
Career batting
1–1–1–3–3*–no av–0–*ct* 0
Bowling 16–0

Pascoe, Leonard Stephen
(changed name from Durtanovich)
Cricketer. *b:* 13.2.1950, Bridgetown North, Western Australia. Lower order right-hand batsman, right-arm fast bowler. *Team* New South Wales (1974/5 to 1983/4, 54 matches). *Tours* Australia to England 1977, 1980, to New Zealand 1981/2. *Tests* Australia (1977 to 1981/2, 14 matches).
Career batting
80–81–25–502–51*–8.96–0–*ct* 23
Bowling 7913–309–25.60–12–2–8/41
Test batting
14–19–9–106–30*–10.60–0–*ct* 2
Bowling 1668–64–26.06–1–0–5/59
On the 1977 tour he took 41 wickets, av 21.78, and played in three Tests. On the brief 1980 visit he took 17 wickets, av 26.17, and bowled well in the Centenary Test.

Pasqual, Sudath Prajiv
Cricketer. *b:* 15.10.1961, Colombo, Ceylon. Middle order left-hand batsman, right-arm medium pace bowler. *Team* Sri Lanka (1979). *Tour* Sri Lanka to England 1979.
Career batting
7–9–2–250–101*–35.71–1–*ct* 3
Bowling 144–2–72.00–0–0–1/22
His only first-class cricket was in England in 1979, when he proved a useful all-rounder. He played for Sri Lanka in one-day international matches.

Passey, Michael Francis William
Amateur. *b:* 6.6.1937, Crossway Green, Worcestershire. Lower order right-hand batsman, off break bowler. *Team* Worcestershire (1953, 1 match).
Career batting
1–1–0–1–1–1.00–0–*ct* 0
Bowling 57–1–57.00–0–0–1/57

Passmore, George
Professional. *b:* 5.8.1852, Yealmpton, Devon. *d:* 8.2.1935, Oreston, Plymstock, Devon. Tail end batsman, wicket-keeper. *Team* Hampshire (1896, 1 match).
Career batting
1–1–0–0–0–0.00–*ct* 2–*st* 1
He first played for Hampshire (not first-class) in 1893.

Pataudi, Nawab of, Iftikhar Ali Khan
Amateur. *b:* 16.3.1910, Pataudi, India. *d:* 5.1.1952, New Delhi, India. He died of a heart attack while playing polo. Father of Nawab of Pataudi (India and Sussex). Attractive middle order right-hand batsman. *Teams* Oxford U (1928–31, blue 1929–31); Patiala (1931/2); Worcestershire (1932–38, 37 matches); Western India States (1943/4); Southern Punjab (1945/6). *Tours* MCC to Australia 1932/3; India to England 1946. *Tests* England (1932/3 to 1934, 3 matches); India (1946, 3 matches).
Career batting
127–204–24–8750–238*–48.61–29–*ct* 58
Bowling 529–15–35.26–1–0–6/111
Test batting
6–10–0–199–102–19.90–1–*ct* 0
He had three outstanding seasons in English first-class cricket. In 1934 he headed the first-class averages with 945 runs, av 78.75; in 1931 he came second with 1,454 runs, av 69.23, and 1933 was his most prolific season with 1,754 runs, av 48.72. His 238* for Oxford U v Cambridge U at Lord's in 1931 was a new record for the University match; his other three double centuries were all for Worcestershire. He captained the Indian touring team to England in 1946 and led the side in the three Tests. He also won blues for hockey and billiards.

Pataudi, Nawab of, Mansur Ali Khan
Amateur. *b:* 5.1.1941, Bhopal, India. Son of Nawab of Pataudi (Worcestershire and India), uncle of S. B. Jung (Hyderabad and Haryana). Attacking middle order right-hand batsman, right-arm medium pace bowler, good field. *Sch* Winchester. *Teams* Sussex (1957–70, 88 matches); Oxford U (1960–63, blue 1960 and 1963); Delhi (1960/1 to 1964/5); Hyderabad (1965/6 to 1975/6). *Tours* India to West Indies 1961/2, to England 1967, to Australia and New Zealand 1967/8, to East Africa 1967; Swanton to West Indies 1960/1; Rest of World to England 1966, 1968. *Tests* India (1961/2 to 1974/5, 46 matches).

Career batting
310–499–41–15425–203*–33.67–33–*ct* 208
Bowling 776–10–77.60–0–0–1/0
Test batting
46–83–3–2793–203*–34.91–6–*ct* 27
Bowling 88–1–88.00–0–0–1/10

He hit 1,000 runs in a season in England four times (best 1,290, av 32.25, in 1963) and twice in India (best 1,415, av 58.95, in 1964/5). Both his double centuries were made in India, the higher being 203* for India v England at Delhi in 1963/4. He captained Oxford in 1963, Sussex in 1966 and India in 40 Tests, including the 1967 tour of England. In 1961 he was seriously injured in a road accident, which damaged his eyesight and caused him to miss the 1961 University match, when he would have captained Oxford.

Patel, Ashok Sitaram
Cricketer. *b:* 23.9.1956, Nairobi, Kenya. Middle or lower order left-hand batsman, slow left-arm bowler. *Team* Middlesex (1978, 2 matches).
Career batting
3–5–1–93–30–23.25–0–*ct* 2
Bowling 96–2–48.00–0–0–2/55

He also played for Durham (pre first-class, 1981–91) and his last first-class match was for Minor Counties in 1986.

Patel, Brijesh Pursuram
Cricketer. *b:* 24.11.1952, Baroda, India. Nephew of B. R. (Mysore), K. R. (Mysore and Hyderabad), M. R. (Mysore and Hyderabad), cousin of Y. B. (Mysore). Stylish middle order right-hand batsman, off break bowler. *Teams* Mysore/Karnataka (1969/70 to 1987/8). *Tours* India to England 1974, 1975 (World Cup), 1979, to West Indies 1975/6, to New Zealand 1975/6, to Sri Lanka 1973/4, to Australia 1977/8. *Tests* India (1974 to 1977/8, 21 matches).
Career batting
203–311–50–11911–216–45.63–37–*ct* 86
Bowling 215–7–30.71–0–0–1/0
Test batting
21–38–5–972–115*–29.45–1–*ct* 17

He appeared in two Tests on the 1974 tour but none in 1979, and his record in England was a modest one. His highest score was 216 for Karnataka v Baroda at Bangalore in 1978/9. He hit 1,000 runs in a season in India three times (best 1,345, av 53.80, in 1976/7).

Patel, Dipak Narshibhai
Cricketer. *b:* 25.10.1958, Nairobi, Kenya. Cousin of H. V. (Worcestershire). Middle order right-hand batsman, off break bowler. *Teams* Worcestershire (1976–86, 236 matches); Auckland (1985/6 to 1991/2). *Tours* Robins to New Zealand 1979/80; New Zealand to Sri Lanka 1986/7, to India 1987/8 (World Cup), to Australia 1987/8, 1989/90, to Sharjah (not first-class) 1987/8, to Pakistan 1990/1; Rest of World to England 1992. *Tests* New Zealand (1986/7 to 1991/2, 16 matches).
Career batting
314–489–44–13951–204–31.35–26–*ct* 165
Bowling 18111–534–33.91–19–2–7/46
Test batting
16–31–2–598–99–20.62–0–*ct* 3
Bowling 961–15–64.06–0–0–4/87

He hit 1,000 runs in a season six times (best 1,615, av 38.45, in 1983). He emigrated to England in 1967. He qualified for New Zealand in 1986 since he had married a New Zealander and was permanently resident in New Zealand. He was the youngest player to score a first-class hundred for a County. His highest score was 204 for Auckland v Northern Districts at Auckland in 1991/2, also taking ten wickets in the same match. He also played for Staffordshire (1987).

Patel, Harshad Vallabhbha
Cricketer. *b:* 29.1.1964, Nairobi, Kenya. Cousin of D. N. (Worcestershire). Opening right-hand batsman. *Team* Worcestershire (1985, 1 match).
Career batting
1–1–0–39–39–39.00–0–*ct* 0

He also played for Staffordshire (1988–89) and Herefordshire (1992).

Patel, Minal Mahesh
Cricketer. *b:* 7.7.1970, Bombay, India. Lower order right-hand batsman, slow left-arm bowler. *Team* Kent (1989–91, 15 matches).
Career batting
15–20–7–183–43–14.07–0–*ct* 5
Bowling 1328–34–39.05–2–1–6/57

Patel, Tikendra
Cricketer. *b:* 9.10.1965, Ahmedabad, India. Middle order right-hand batsman, off break bowler. *Team* Oxford U (1985–86).
Career batting
15–25–4–222–47–10.57–0–*ct* 6
Bowling 12–0

His County cricket was for Bedfordshire (1983–85).

Paterson, Arthur William Sibbald
Amateur. *b:* 28.2.1878, Weston-super-Mare, Somerset. *d:* 13.11.1937, Burnham, Somerset. Middle order batsman. *Sch* Malvern. *Team* Somerset (1903, 2 matches).
Career batting
2–3–0–38–19–12.66–0–*ct* 1

Paterson, Charles Strathern
Amateur. *b:* 18.11.1882, Edinburgh, Scotland. *d:* 23.7.1973, Edinburgh, Scotland. Middle order right-hand batsman, right-arm medium pace bowler. *Team* Scotland (1913–27).
Career batting
7–10–3–188–49–26.85–0–*ct* 2
Bowling 244–10–24.40–0–0–4/33

Paterson, Grant Andrew
Cricketer. *b:* 9.6.1960, Salisbury, Rhodesia. Opening right-hand batsman. *Team* Zimbabwe (1981/2 to 1990/1). *Tours* Zimbabwe to England 1983 (World Cup), 1985, to Sri Lanka 1983/4, to India (World Cup) 1987/8.
Career batting
34–59–3–1154–93–20.60–0–*ct* 11
He batted well on the 1985 tour to England, usually giving the tourists a sound start to their innings.

Paterson, Joseph
Amateur. *b:* 27.12.1923, Coatbridge, Lanarkshire, Scotland. Middle order right-hand batsman, right-arm medium pace bowler. *Team* Scotland (1956).
Career batting
1–2–0–1–1–0.50–0–*ct* 0

Paterson, Robert Fraser Troutbeck
Amateur. *b:* 8.9.1916, Stansted, Essex. *d:* 29.5.1980, Edinburgh, Scotland. Middle order right-hand batsman, right-arm medium pace bowler, occasional wicket-keeper. *Sch* Brighton. *Team* Essex (1946, 25 matches).
Career batting
28–45–5–884–88–22.10–0–*ct* 16–*st* 3
Bowling 464–13–35.69–0–0–4/98
His final first-class match was for MCC in 1958. From 1947 to 1950 he was Secretary to Essex CCC.

Pathmanathan, Gajanand
Cricketer. *b:* 23.1.1954, Colombo, Ceylon. Hard hitting middle order right-hand batsman, leg break bowler. *Teams* Sri Lanka (1972/3 to 1978/9); Oxford U (1975–78, blue all four years); Cambridge U (1983, blue). *Tours* Sri Lanka to India 1972/3; to Pakistan 1973/4.
Career batting
44–77–3–1553–82–20.98–0–*ct* 35
Bowling 26–0

Patiala, Maharaja of, HH Sir Bhupendrasingh Rajindersingh
Amateur. *b:* 12.10.1891, Patiala, India. *d:* 23.3.1938, Patiala, India. Father of Yuvraj (later Maharaja) of Patiala (India) and M. K. B. Singh (Cambridge U). Hard hitting middle order right-hand batsman, good field. *Teams* Hindus (1915/6 to 1921/2); Sikhs (1922/3 to 1924/5); Northern India (1926/7); Patiala (1931/2 to 1937/8); Southern Punjab (1933/4 to 1934/5). *Tours* India to England 1911; MCC to India 1926/7 (co-opted); Australia to India 1935/6 (co-opted).
Career batting
27–40–3–643–83–17.37–0–*ct* 4
Bowling 60–2–30.00–0–0–2/40
A very keen patron of cricket in India, poor health limited his own participation in first-class matches. He was President of the Cricket Club of India at the time of his death.

Patil, Sandeep Madhusudan
Cricketer. *b:* 18.8.1956, Bombay, India. Son of M. S. (Bombay). Middle order right hand batsman, right-arm medium pace bowler. *Teams* Bombay (1976/7 to 1986/7); Madhya Pradesh (1988/9 to 1991/2). *Tours* India to Australia 1980/1, to New Zealand 1980/1, to England 1982, 1983 (World Cup), 1986, to Pakistan 1982/3, 1984/5, to Sharjah (not first-class) 1983/4, 1985/6; Wadekar to Sri Lanka 1975/6. *Tests* India (1979/80 to 1984/5, 29 matches).
Career batting
124–191–13–7726–210–43.40–20–*ct* 65
Bowling 2679–83–32.27–4–0–6/20
Test batting
29–47–4–1588–174–36.93–4–*ct* 12
Bowling 240–9–26.66–0–0–2/28
On his first visit to England in 1982, he played the innings of the season at Old Trafford in the Second Test, scoring 129*, but achieved little else. Returning in 1986 he failed to find any form and was not required for the Tests. His highest score was 210 for Bombay v Saurashtra at Bombay in 1979/80. He appeared in films in India.

Paton, J.
Amateur. Lower order batsman, good bowler. *Team* Scotland (1914).
Career batting
1–2–0–2–2–1.00–0–*ct* 1
Bowling 88–5–17.60–0–0–4/48

Patten, Mark
Amateur. *b:* 28.7.1901, West End, Edinburgh, Scotland. Lower order right-hand batsman, wicket-keeper. *Sch* Winchester. *Teams* Oxford U (1922–23, blue both years); Scotland (1922–25).
Career batting
27–41–7–407–58–11.97–0–*ct* 36–*st* 3
His final first-class match was for Free Foresters in 1929.

Pattenden, Edward Peter
Professional. *b:* 31.10.1842, Brighton, Sussex. *d:* 3.6.1879, Brighton, Sussex. Lower order right-hand batsman, useful bowler. *Team* Sussex (1874–75, 4 matches).
Career batting
4–5–1–6–3*–1.50–0–*ct* 1
Bowling 33–0

Patterson, Balfour Patrick
Cricketer. *b:* 15.9.1961, Happy Grove, Williamsfield, Jamaica. Tail end right-hand batsman, right-arm fast bowler. *Teams* Jamaica (1982/3 to 1991/2); Lancashire (1984–90, 70 matches); Tasmania (1984/5, 10 matches). *Tours* West Indies to Pakistan 1986/7, 1991/2 (not first-class), to New Zealand 1986/7, to India 1987/8, to India and Pakistan (World Cup) 1987/8, to England 1988, 1991, to Australia 1988/9, 1991/2, to Sharjah (not first-class) 1988/9, 1991/2.

Patterson, Bruce Mathew Winston

Tests (1985/6 to 1991/2, 27 matches).
Career batting
158–161–58–612–29–5.94–0–*ct* 32
Bowling 13259–487–27.72–25–2–7/24
Test batting
27–37–16–145–21*–6.90–0–*ct* 5
Bowling 2746–92–29.84–5–0–5/24

He appeared in only two Tests on the 1988 West Indian tour and in three on the 1991 tour when he was greatly improved so far as accuracy was concerned, considering his pace. In 1989 his season with Lancashire was marred by injury, but in 1990 he proved very useful.

Patterson, Bruce Mathew Winston
Cricketer. *b:* 29.1.1965, Ayr, Scotland. Opening right-hand batsman. *Team* Scotland (1988–92).
Career batting
5–8–0–462–108–57.75–2–*ct* 8

He scored 100 on his first-class debut v Ireland at Dumfries in 1988.

Patterson, George Stuart
Amateur. *b:* 10.10.1868, Philadelphia, USA. *d:* 7.5.1943, Philadelphia, USA. Stylish opening right-hand batsman, right-arm medium pace bowler. *Sch* Haverford College. *Team* Philadelphia (1885–97). *Tours* Philadelphia to England 1889 (not first-class), 1897.
Career batting
35–57–6–2051–271–40.21–5–*ct* 14
Bowling 1569–74–21.20–2–1–5/22

He was one of the principal batsmen in the United States and captained the 1897 team to England, when, despite injury, he came second in the batting averages. His highest score was 271 for G. S. Patterson's XI v A. M. Wood's XI at Elmwood in 1894.

Patterson, Rev John Irwin
Amateur. *b:* 11.3.1860, Sandhurst, Berkshire. *d:* 22.9.1943, Woking, Surrey. Brother of W. H. (Kent). Defensive lower order right-hand batsman, slow left-arm bowler, good field. *Sch* Chatham House School. *Teams* Kent (1881–82, 6 matches); Oxford U (1882, blue).
Career batting
7–11–3–38–9–4.75–0–*ct* 7
Bowling 197–12–16.41–1–0–5/12

In a minor match for St Lawrence v Dover in 1880 he took seven wickets in seven consecutive balls.

Patterson, Thomas James Taylor
Cricketer. *b:* 25.12.1959, Downpatrick, Co Down, Ireland. Middle order left-hand batsman, left-arm medium pace bowler. *Team* Ireland (1984–92).
Career batting
4–6–1–211–84–42.20–0–*ct* 3
Bowling 96–3–32.00–0–0–2/54

Patterson, William Harry
Amateur. *b:* 11.3.1859, Sandhurst, Berkshire. *d:* 3.5.1946, Hove, Sussex. Brother of J. I. (Kent). Sound opening or middle order right-hand batsman, right-hand medium or slow round-arm bowler, good field, occasional wicket-keeper. *Sch* Harrow. *Teams* Oxford U (1878–81, blue 1880–81); Kent (1880–1900, 152 matches).
Career batting
176–311–23–7570–181–26.28–10–*ct* 122
Bowling 1043–31–33.64–0–0–4/13

He was joint captain of Kent 1890 to 1893, but owing to his profession of solicitor was unable to play regularly in County cricket. His final first-class match was for G. J. V. Weigall's XI in 1904. He was President of Kent CCC in 1923 and served on the MCC Committee.

Patterson, William Seeds
Amateur. *b:* 19.3.1854, Mossley Hill, Liverpool, Lancashire. *d:* 20.10.1939, Hook Heath, Woking, Surrey. Attractive middle order right-hand batsman, right-arm slow bowler. *Sch* Uppingham. *Teams* Cambridge U (1874–77, blue last three years); Lancashire (1874–82, 7 matches).
Career batting
41–66–5–1114–105*–18.26–1–*ct* 20
Bowling 2330–158 + 5–14.74–17–5–7/30

He captained Cambridge in 1877. He appeared in American cricket for English Residents in 1880 and 1881.

Patteson, Canon Charles
Amateur. *b:* 11.11.1891, Upper Norwood, London. *d:* 9.12.1957, Howden, Yorkshire. Opening right-hand batsman. *Sch* Marlborough. *Team* Cambridge U (1912).
Career batting
5–9–2–157–57–22.42–0–*ct* 5
Bowling 36–1–36.00–0–0–1/12

His County cricket was for Wiltshire (1920–22). He won a blue for hockey, and played for England.

Pattisson, Hoel Carlos
Amateur. *b:* 5.9.1905, West Byfleet, Surrey. *d:* 10.7.1979, Playden, Rye, Sussex. Attacking middle order batsman. *Sch* Rugby. *Team* Free Foresters (1937).
Career batting
1–2–0–20–20–10.00–0–*ct* 0

Pattisson, Walter Badeley
Amateur. *b:* 27.8.1854, Witham, Essex. *d:* 6.11.1913, Beckenham, Kent. Middle order right-hand batsman, good deep field. *Sch* Tonbridge. *Team* Kent (1876–87, 12 matches).
Career batting
13–22–1–230–38–10.95–0–*ct* 6

He served on the Committee of Kent CCC for several years. A noted rugby footballer, he appeared as a three-quarter in some England trials.

Paul, Arthur George
Professional. *b:* 24.7.1864, Belfast, Ireland. *d:* 14.1.1947, Didsbury, Lancashire. Middle order right-hand batsman, right-arm slow bowler, occasional wicket-keeper. *Sch* Victoria College, Isle of Man. *Team* Lancashire (1889–1900, 95 matches).
Career batting
96–152–15–2976–177–21.72–4–*ct* 73–*st* 1
Bowling 146–2–73.00–0–0–1/7
After retiring from first-class cricket due to ill-health he became coach at Old Trafford. A good all-round sportsman, he toured Australia with the 1888 English rugby football team and as a soccer player kept goal for Blackburn Rovers.

Paul, Edmund Parris
Amateur. *b:* 4.2.1882, Taunton, Somerset. *d:* 26.4.1966, North Town, Taunton, Somerset. Lower order right-hand batsman, wicket-keeper. *Team* Somerset (1907–10, 4 matches).
Career batting
4–8–0–37–12–4.62–0–*ct* 2

Paul, James Hugh
Amateur. *b:* 10.2.1888. *d:*27.2.1937, Earlswood, Surrey. Middle order right-hand batsman. *Sch* Malvern. *Teams* Leveson-Gower's XI (1934–35); Argentine (1926/7 to 1929/30). *Tour* South America to England 1932.
Career batting
9–15–0–272–39–18.13–0–*ct* 2
Bowling 315–9–35.00–0–0–2/23

Paul, Nigel Aldridge
Amateur. *b:* 31.3.1933, Surbiton, Surrey. Forcing middle order right-hand batsman, left-arm fast medium bowler. *Sch* Cranleigh. *Team* Warwickshire (1954–55, 4 matches).
Career batting
7–10–0–157–40–15.70–0–*ct* 6
Bowling 196–3–65.33–0–0–1/5
His final first-class match was for D. R. Jardine's XI in 1958.

Pauline, Duncan Brian
Cricketer. *b:* 15.12.1960, Aberdeen, Scotland. Middle order right-hand batsman, right-arm medium pace bowler. *Teams* Surrey (1979–85, 49 matches); Glamorgan (1986, 12 matches).
Career batting
61–96–6–2258–115–25.08–1–*ct* 22
Bowling 662–18–36.77–1–0–5/52
Retiring from County cricket at the end of 1986, he moved back to Scotland and appeared in limited overs matches for his native country in 1987 and 1988.

Paull, Richard Kenyon
Cricketer. *b:* 20.2.1944, Bridgwater, Somerset. Middle order right-hand batsman, leg break bowler. *Sch* Millfield. *Teams* Somerset (1963–64, 6 matches); Cambridge U (1967, blue).
Career batting
13–20–1–257–37–13.52–0–*ct* 3
Bowling 104–1–104.00–0–0–1/12

Pauncefote, Bernard
Amateur. *b:* 28.6.1848, Cuddalore, India. *d:* 24.9.1882, Blackheath, Kent. Stylish middle order right-hand batsman, right-hand medium pace round-arm bowler, good deep field. *Sch* Rugby. *Teams* Oxford U (1868–71, blue all four years); Middlesex (1868–72, 8 matches).
Career batting
32–55–3–1141–123–21.94–2–*ct* 21
Bowling 322–18–17.88–1–0–5/43
He captained Oxford in 1869 and 1870. He went to China in 1872 and then to Ceylon, where he was in business. His County career was therefore very brief.

Paver, Kenneth Edwin
Amateur. *b:* 4.10.1903, Dover, Kent. *d:* 20.11.1975, Ringwood, Hampshire. Middle order batsman. *Team* Hampshire (1925–26, 2 matches).
Career batting
2–4–0–52–26–13.00–0–*ct* 2

Paver, Roland George Lyall
Cricketer. *b:* 4.4.1950, Johannesburg, South Africa. Lower order right-hand batsman, wicket-keeper. *Team* Oxford U (1972–74, blue 1973–74).
Career batting
16–26–2–290–34–12.08–0–*ct* 33–*st* 5

Pavey, Clement Star
Amateur. *b:* 7.5.1859, Cheddar, Somerset. *d:* 13.11.1925, Taunton, Somerset. Tail end batsman. *Team* MCC (1882).
Career batting
1–1–0–2–2–2.00–0–*ct* 0

Pavri, Dr Mehallasha Edulji
Amateur. *b:* 10.10.1866, Navsari, Surat, India. *d:* 19.4.1946, Bombay, India. Opening or middle order right-hand batsman, right-arm fast bowler. *Teams* Parsis (1892/3 to 1912/3); Middlesex (1895, 1 match). *Tour* Parsis to England 1888 (not first-class).
Career batting
26–39–1–589–69–15.50–0–*ct* 19
Bowling 891–44–20.25–2–0–6/36
He was most successful on the 1888 Parsi tour to England taking in all matches 170 wickets, and was all in all the greatest of the 19th century Parsi cricketers. Later he wrote an interesting book on Indian cricket.

Pawle, John Hanbury
Amateur. *b:* 18.5.1915, Widford, Hertfordshire. Brother-in-law of W. A. Anderson (Free Foresters) and N. M. Hughes-Hallett (Derbyshire). Middle order right-hand batsman. *Sch* Harrow. *Teams* Cambridge U (1935–37, blue 1936–37); Essex (1935–38, 6 matches).
Career batting
34–59–4–1544–125–28.07–3–*ct* 14
Bowling 13–0
His final first-class match was for Free Foresters in 1947. He also played for Hertfordshire (1933).

Pawley, Tom Edward
Amateur. *b:* 21.1.1859, Farningham, Kent. *d:* 3.8.1923, Canterbury, Kent. Middle order right-hand batsman, right-arm fast, later lob, bowler. *Sch* Tonbridge. *Team* Kent (1880–87, 4 matches).
Career batting
4–7–1–23–10–3.83–0–*ct* 1
Bowling 11–3–3.66–0–0–3/11
He was manager of the Kent team 1899–1923 and in 1903 acted in that capacity for the Kent tour to America, and in 1911/12 for the MCC tour to Australia. He died very suddenly whilst making arrangements for the 1923 Canterbury Cricket Festival.

Pawling, Sydney Southgate
Amateur. *b:* 6.2.1862, Wallingford, Berkshire. *d:* 23.12.1922, Eastbourne, Sussex. Lower order right-hand batsman, right-arm fast bowler. *Sch* Mill Hill. *Team* Middlesex (1894, 3 matches).
Career batting
3–4–1–5–3–1.66–0–*ct* 1
Bowling 219–9–24.33–1–0–5/60
He was a noted figure in North London Club cricket for many years. From 1919 to his death he was Hon Treasurer of Middlesex CCC.

Pawson, Albert Guy
Amateur. *b:* 30.5.1888, Bramley, Leeds, Yorkshire. *d:* 25.2.1986, Lamerton, Devon. Brother of A. C. (Oxford U), father of H. A. (Kent). Lower order right-hand batsman, wicket-keeper. *Sch* Winchester. *Teams* Oxford U (1908–11, blue all four years); Worcestershire (1908, 1 match).
Career batting
28–50–13–448–41*–12.10–0–*ct* 30–*st* 16
He captained Oxford in 1910.

Pawson, Arthur Clive
Amateur. *b:* 5.1.1882, Bramley, Leeds, Yorkshire. *d:* 14.8.1969, Nynehead, Wellington, Somerset. Brother of A. G. (Worcestershire), uncle of H. A. (Kent), step-father of A. J. E. Sealy (Oxford U). Sound middle order right-hand batsman, good field. *Sch* Winchester. *Team* Oxford U (1903, blue).
Career batting
7–13–1–177–51–14.75–0–*ct* 5

Pawson, Henry Anthony
Amateur. *b:* 22.8.1921, Chertsey, Surrey. Son of A. G. (Worcestershire), nephew of A. C. (Oxford U). Stylish middle order right-hand batsman, off break bowler, good outfield. *Sch* Winchester. *Teams* Kent (1946–53, 43 matches); Oxford U (1947–48, blue both years).
Career batting
69–113–11–3807–150–37.32–7–*ct* 36
Bowling 280–7–40.00–0–0–2/26
He hit 1,000 runs in a season twice (best 1,312, av 38.58, in 1947). He captained Oxford in 1948. A good soccer player, he was awarded his blue and later played for Charlton Athletic. He was also noted in fishing circles, and was awarded the OBE for services to angling.

Payn, Leslie William
Amateur. *b:* 6.5.1915, Umzinto, Natal, South Africa. *d:* 2.5.1992, Scottburgh, Natal, South Africa. Great-uncle of James (Natal). Lower order left-hand batsman, left-arm slow medium bowler. *Team* Natal (1936/7 to 1952/3). *Tour* South Africa to England 1947.
Career batting
51–51–5–657–103–14.28–1–*ct* 30
Bowling 3893–151–25.78–4–2–8/89
He achieved very little on the 1947 tour and did not appear in the Tests.

Payne, Alan Undy
Amateur. *b:* 28.1.1903, Witney, Oxfordshire. *d:* 16.8.1977, Braintree, Essex. Middle order right-hand batsman, right-arm medium fast bowler, good field. *Sch* St Edmund's, Canterbury. *Team* Cambridge U (1925, blue).
Career batting
7–9–1–86–27*–10.75–0–*ct* 2
Bowling 63–1–63.00–0–0–1/36
His County cricket was for Buckinghamshire (1923–29). He was awarded his blue at Cambridge on account of his fielding, a decision which was much criticised at the time.

Payne, Albert
Professional. *b:* 26.6.1885, Leicester. *d:* 7.5.1908, Leicester. He died of consumption. Tail end right-hand batsman, wicket-keeper. *Team* Leicestershire (1906–07, 5 matches).
Career batting
5–9–3–15–7*–2.50–0–*ct* 6–*st* 1

Payne, Rev Alfred
Amateur. *b:* 7.12.1831, Leicester. *d:* 25.6.1874, Westminster, London. Twin brother of A. F. (Oxford U). Lower order left-hand batsman, left-hand round-arm bowler. *Team* Oxford U (1852–56, blue 1852 and 1854–56).
Career batting
25–44–8–479–40–13.30–0–*ct* 17

Bowling 1024–84 + 27–12.19–8–1–7/42

His final first-class match was for Gentlemen in 1864. His County cricket was for Leicestershire (pre first-class, 1851–60), Oxfordshire (1852–53) and Staffordshire (1872). He captained Oxford in 1856.

Payne, Alfred
Professional. *b:* 28.4.1858, East Grinstead, Sussex. *d:* 23.7.1943, Uckfield, Sussex. Brother of William (Sussex), nephew of Charles (Sussex and Kent), J. S. (Sussex and Kent) and Richard (Sussex). Sound, steady middle order right-hand batsman, wicket-keeper. *Team* Sussex (1880–86, 17 matches).
Career batting
18–34–4–275–42–9.16–0–*ct* 8–*st* 1
Bowling 18–0

Payne, Rev Alfred Ernest
Amateur. *b:* 29.12.1849, Pentre Ucha, Oswestry, Shropshire. *d:* 30.6.1927, Pen-y-Nant, Ruabon, Denbighshire. Middle order batsman. *Team* MCC (1883–84).
Career batting
8–15–1–75–16–5.35–0–*ct* 2
Bowling 2–0

His County cricket was for Shropshire (1880–1900).

Payne, Andrew
Cricketer. *b:* 20.10.1973, Rossendale, Lancashire. Middle order right-hand batsman, right-arm medium pace bowler. *Team* Somerset (1992, 1 match).
Career batting
1–1–1–51–51*–no av–0–*ct* 0
Bowling 71–1–71.00–0–0–1/71

Payne, Arnold Cyril
Amateur. *b:* 3.10.1897, Northampton. *d:* 13.2.1973, Northampton. Lower order right-hand batsman, wicket-keeper. *Sch* Wycliffe. *Team* Northamptonshire (1931–34, 3 matches).
Career batting
3–5–1–27–22*–6.75–0–*ct* 6–*st* 4

He was President of Northamptonshire 1969–70.

Payne, Arthur Frederick
Amateur. *b:* 7.12.1831, Leicester. *d:* 23.7.1910, Brighton, Sussex. Twin brother of Alfred (Oxford U). Middle order right-hand batsman. *Team* Oxford U (1854–55, blue 1855).
Career batting
10–18–1–102–21–6.00–0–*ct* 5

His final first-class match was for MCC in 1867. His County cricket was for Leicestershire (pre first-class, 1851).

Payne, Cecil Arthur Lynch
Amateur. *b:* 30.8.1885, Dacca, India. *d:* 21.3.1976, Vancouver, Canada. Cousin of M. W. (Middlesex). Opening or middle order right-hand batsman, right-arm medium pace bowler. *Sch* Charterhouse. *Teams* Middlesex (1905–09, 13 matches); Oxford U (1906–07, blue both years).
Career batting
29–49–0–1001–101–20.42–1–*ct* 10
Bowling 59–0

His first-class debut was for MCC v Derbyshire at Lord's in 1905, when he hit 101. About 1910 he emigrated to Canada, thus ending his County cricket. He was a noted golfer and billiards player, winning his blue for billiards.

Payne, Charles
Professional. *b:* 12.5.1832, East Grinstead, Sussex. *d:* 18.2.1909, Tonbridge, Kent. Brother of J. S. (Sussex and Kent) and Richard (Sussex), uncle of Alfred (Sussex) and William (Sussex). Fine middle order right-hand batsman, good close field. *Teams* Sussex (1857–70, 50 matches); Kent (1863–70, 26 matches).
Career batting
88–162–20–2702–137–19.02–2–*ct* 69
Bowling 223–7–31.85–0–0–3/13

His final first-class match was for the North in 1875. He also umpired in first-class matches (1883–89).

Payne, Christopher John
Cricketer. *b:* 30.12.1947, Hatfield, Hertfordshire. Middle order right-hand batsman, occasional wicket-keeper. *Team* Middlesex (1968–70, 5 matches).
Career batting
5–8–0–40–22–5.00–0–*ct* 0

He also played for Hertfordshire (1974).

Payne, George Spencer
Professional. *b:* 25.3.1850, East Grinstead, Sussex. *d:* 17.7.1892, East Grinstead, Sussex. Lower order batsman, bowler. *Team* Sussex (1869, 1 match).
Career batting
1–2–0–4–4–2.00–0–*ct* 1
Bowling 7–0

Payne, Ian Roger
Cricketer. *b:* 9.5.1958, Kennington, London. Middle or lower order right-hand batsman, right-arm medium pace bowler. *Sch* Emanuel. *Teams* Surrey (1977–84, 29 matches); Gloucestershire (1985–86, 18 matches).
Career batting
47–55–10–550–43–12.22–0–*ct* 41
Bowling 1917–45–42.60–1–0–5/13

Payne, James
Professional. Lower order batsman, useful bowler. *Team* Lancashire (1898, 1 match).
Career batting
1–2–0–0–0–0.00–0–*ct* 0
Bowling 48–0

Payne, John Henry
Amateur. *b:* 19.3.1858, Broughton, Lancashire. *d:* 24.1.1942, Victoria Park, Manchester, Lancashire. Son of J. B. (Gentlemen of North 1860). Middle order

right-hand batsman, wicket-keeper. *Sch* Cheltenham. *Teams* Cambridge U (1880); Lancashire (1883, 9 matches).
Career batting
11–19–3–166–33–10.37–0–*ct* 7–*st* 4
A noted rugby footballer, he won his blue and played for England.

Payne, Joseph Spencer
Professional. *b:* 29.4.1829, East Grinstead, Sussex. *d:* 12.4.1880, Greenwich, London. Brother of Charles (Sussex and Kent) and Richard (Sussex), uncle of Alfred (Sussex) and William (Sussex). Lower order right-hand batsman, left-hand medium pace round-arm bowler. *Teams* Sussex (1861, 2 matches); Kent (1864, 1 match).
Career batting
3–6–1–35–32–7.00–0–*ct* 3
Bowling 150–13–11.53–1–0–8/73

Payne, Meyrick Whitmore
Amateur. *b:* 10.5.1885, Fulham, London. *d:* 2.6.1963, Little Easton, Essex. Cousin of C. A. L. (Middlesex), father-in-law of R. C. Brooks (Cambridge U). Attacking opening right-hand batsman, right-arm fast bowler, wicket-keeper. *Sch* Wellington. *Teams* Cambridge U (1904–07, blue all four years); Middlesex (1904–09, 25 matches). *Tour* MCC to North America 1905.
Career batting
86–152–9–3547–178–24.80–5–*ct* 116–*st* 33
Bowling 130–3–43.33–0–0–2/27
His final first-class match was for Free Foresters in 1929. He captained Cambridge in 1909.

Payne, Richard
Professional. *b:* 9.6.1827, East Grinstead, Sussex. *d:* 11.4.1906, Tonbridge, Kent. Brother of Charles (Sussex and Kent) and J. S. (Sussex and Kent), uncle of Alfred (Sussex) and William (Sussex). Lower order right-hand batsman, right-hand medium round-arm, or under-arm, bowler. *Team* Sussex (1853–66, 7 matches).
Career batting
7–12–0–81–28–6.75–0–*ct* 4
Bowling 50–3–16.66–0–0–2/23

Payne, Richard Bethune Tripp Selwyn
Amateur. *b:* 18.9.1885, Rangoon, Burma. *d:* 1.2.1949, Exmouth, Devon. Middle order batsman. *Sch* Malvern. *Team* Somerset (1906, 1 match).
Career batting
1–1–0–15–15–15.00–0–*ct* 0

Payne, Thelston Rodney O'Neale
Cricketer. *b:* 13.2.1957, Foul Bay, St Philip, Barbados. Middle order left-hand batsman, wicket-keeper. *Team* Barbados (1978/9 to 1989/90). *Tours* Young West Indies to Zimbabwe 1983/4; West Indies to England 1984, to Australia 1984/5, 1986/7, to Pakistan 1986/7, to New Zealand 1986/7. *Test* West Indies (1985/6, 1 match).
Career batting
68–106–14–3391–140–36.85–6–*ct* 103–*st* 8
Test batting
1–1–0–5–5–5.00–0–*ct* 5
He came to England in 1984 as the West Indies reserve wicket-keeper and was not required for the Tests.

Payne, William
Professional. *b:* 6.8.1854, East Grinstead, Sussex. *d:* 25.6.1909, East Grinstead, Sussex. Brother of Alfred (Sussex), nephew of Charles (Sussex and Kent), J. S. (Sussex and Kent) and Richard (Sussex). Lower order right-hand batsman, right-arm medium pace bowler, good cover point. *Team* Sussex (1877–83, 17 matches).
Career batting
18–33–7–189–39*–7.26–0–*ct* 9
Bowling 490–25–19.60–0–0–3/34

Payne-Gallwey, William Thomas
Amateur. *b:* 25.3.1881, Blackrock, Co Dublin, Ireland. *d:* 14.9.1914, Vendresse, Troyon, France. He was killed in action. Tail end batsman, right-arm fast bowler. *Sch* Eton. *Teams* Army (1912); MCC (1912).
Career batting
2–4–2–37–16–18.50–0–*ct* 1
Bowling 55–2–27.50–0–0–1/10

Paynter, Edward
Professional. *b:* 5.11.1901, Oswaldtwistle, Lancashire. *d:* 5.2.1979, Keighley, Yorkshire. Attacking opening or middle order left-hand batsman, right-arm medium pace bowler, brilliant outfield. *Team* Lancashire (1926–45, 293 matches). *Tours* MCC to Australia and New Zealand 1932/3, to South Africa 1938/9; Commonwealth to India 1950/1. *Tests* England (1931–39, 20 matches).
Career batting
352–533–58–20075–322–42.26–45–*ct* 160
Bowling 1371–30–45.70–0–0–3/13
Test batting
20–31–5–1540–243–59.23–4–*ct* 7
Playing in seven Tests for England v Australia, he hit 591 runs, average 84.42, a quite remarkable statistic, and his overall record in Tests is equalled by few. His Test career and indeed his first-class career were relatively brief, for he did not gain a regular place in the Lancashire side until 1931, the year of his England debut, and the outbreak of the Second World War effectively ended his first-class career.
He hit 1,000 runs in a season nine times, going on to 2,000 four times, his best year being 1937 with 2,904 runs, average 53.77. His highest score was 322 for Lancashire v Sussex at Hove in 1937; of his six other scores over 200, four were for his County and two for England. His best remembered innings came

in the fourth Test of the 1932/3 series, when he left his hospital bed – being laid low with tonsilitis – and scored 83 in four hours.

Although he lost the top joints of two fingers in an accident early in life, he was a brilliant fieldsman and actually kept wicket most efficiently in one innings of the 1938 Lord's Test. His final first-class matches in England came in the 1947 Harrogate Festival, when he had innings of 154, 73 and 127, though he had played in only one first-class match since 1939. He was a first-class umpire (1951).

Payton, Albert Ivan
Professional. *b:* 20.1.1898, Stapleford, Nottinghamshire. *d:* 27.9.1967, Sandiacre, Derbyshire. Brother of W. R. D. (Nottinghamshire), uncle of W. E. G. (Nottinghamshire and Derbyshire). Middle order right-hand batsman, right-arm medium pace bowler. *Team* Nottinghamshire (1922, 1 match).
Career batting
1–2–0–16–15–8.00–0–*ct* 0

Payton, Ven Wilfred Ernest Granville
Amateur. *b:* 27.12.1913, Beeston, Nottinghamshire. *d:* 4.9.1989, Ladder Hill, Nailsworth, Gloucestershire. Son of W. R. D. (Nottinghamshire), nephew of A. I. (Nottinghamshire). Sound opening right-hand batsman, good deep field. *Sch* Nottingham HS. *Teams* Nottinghamshire (1935, 1 match); Cambridge U (1937, blue); Derbyshire (1949, 2 matches).
Career batting
27–52–4–995–98–20.72–0–*ct* 11

Most of his cricket was for the RAF, and his final first-class match was for Combined Services in 1953.

Payton, Wilfred Richard Daniel
Professional. *b:* 13.2.1882, Stapleford, Nottinghamshire. *d:* 2.5.1943, Beeston Fields, Nottinghamshire. Brother of A. I. (Nottinghamshire), father of W. E. G. (Nottinghamshire and Derbyshire). Middle order right-hand batsman, good outfield. *Team* Nottinghamshire (1905–31, 489 matches).
Career batting
491–770–126–22132–169–34.36–39–*ct* 147
Bowling 68–1–68.00–0–0–1/18

He hit 1,000 runs in a season nine times (best 1,864, av 47.79, in 1926).

Peacey, Rev Canon John Raphael
Amateur. *b:* 16.7.1896, Hove, Sussex. *d:* 31.10.1971, Hurstpierpoint, Sussex. Middle order batsman. *Sch* St Edmund's School, Canterbury. *Team* Sussex (1920–22, 4 matches).
Career batting
4–7–1–54–26–9.00–0–*ct* 0

He played in trials at Cambridge U, but not in first-class matches.

Peach, Charles William
Professional. *b:* 3.1.1900, Cale Hill, Kent. *d:* 27.2.1977, Coxheath, Maidstone, Kent. Lower order right-hand batsman, right-arm medium fast bowler. *Team* Kent (1930–31, 19 matches).
Career batting
19–25–10–108–20–7.20–0–*ct* 9
Bowling 830–30–27.66–0–0–4/38

Owing to some doubts as to the fairness of his bowling action, he did not have an extended trial in County cricket.

Peach, Frederick George
Amateur. *b:* 2.11.1882, Repton, Derbyshire. *d:* 15.1.1965, Stapenhill, Staffordshire. Middle order right-hand batsman, leg break bowler, occasional wicket-keeper. *Team* Derbyshire (1907–25, 12 matches).
Career batting
12–24–1–258–61*–11.21–0–*ct* 3
Bowling 170–4–42.50–0–0–3/50

Peach, Herbert Alan
Professional. *b:* 6.10.1890, Maidstone, Kent. *d:* 8.10.1961, North End, Newbury, Hampshire. Middle or lower order right-hand batsman, right-arm medium pace bowler, good field. *Team* Surrey (1919–31, 324 matches). *Tour* Cahn to Jamaica 1928/9.
Career batting
338–428–51–8940–200*–23.71–4–*ct* 182
Bowling 21136–795–26.58–30–1–8/60

For Surrey v Sussex at the Oval in 1924 he took 4 wickets in 4 balls. His only double century was 200* for Surrey v Northamptonshire at Northampton in 1920. He also played for Berkshire (1933–34). From 1935 to 1939 he was coach to Surrey CCC.

Peach, Roy Alan
Amateur. *b:* 19.10.1937, St Pancras, London. Lower order right-hand batsman, right-arm medium pace bowler. *Team* Combined Services (1960).
Career batting
2–1–1–6–6*–no av–0–*ct* 2
Bowling 13–0

Peach, William
Professional. *b:* 6.5.1875, Timberland Fen, Lincolnshire. *d:* 29.1.1959, Stonegravels, Chesterfield, Derbyshire. Lower order right-hand batsman, right-arm fast medium bowler. *Team* Derbyshire (1905, 1 match).
Career batting
1–2–0–10–10–5.00–0–*ct* 1
Bowling 46–4–11.50–0–0–4/46

He also played for Lincolnshire (1908–14).

Peacock, Horace Ogilvie
Amateur. *b:* 26.9.1869, St Neots, Huntingdonshire. *d:* 5.6.1940, Harston, Leicestershire. Brother-in-law of W. Boden (Derbyshire) and E. Lubbock (Kent). Mid-

dle order right-hand batsman. *Sch* Harrow. *Team* MCC (1896–99).
Career batting
6–10–0–124–38–12.40–0–*ct* 5
His County cricket was for Lincolnshire (1892–95).

Peacocke, Joseph Reginald Hyde
Amateur. *b:* 23.3.1904, Dublin, Ireland. *d:* December 1961, Umtali, Southern Rhodesia. Middle order right-hand batsman. *Sch* Rossall. *Teams* Dublin U (1925); Ireland (1926).
Career batting
2–4–0–86–48–21.50–0–*ct* 0

Peake, Rev Edward
Amateur. *b:* 29.3.1860, Tideham, Monmouthshire. *d:* 3.1.1945, Huntingdon. Tail end right-hand batsman, right-arm fast bowler, close field. *Sch* Marlborough. *Teams* Oxford U (1880–83, blue 1881–83); Gloucestershire (1881–89, 26 matches).
Career batting
46–80–11–902–53–13.07–0–*ct* 27
Bowling 2554–116–22.01–6–1–7/39
He also played for Berkshire (1898–1906). He played rugby for Wales. He also won a blue for athletics.

Peake, Rev George Eden Frederick
Amateur. *b:* 6.3.1846, Taunton, Somerset. *d:* 24.6.1901, Newquay, Cornwall. Middle order batsman. *Team* Somerset (1885, 1 match).
Career batting
1–2–0–6–6–3.00–0–*ct* 0
He first played for Somerset (pre first-class) in 1875.

Peake, Kenneth George
Amateur. *b:* 24.7.1920, Newfoundpool, Leicester. Lower order right-hand batsman, right-arm fast medium bowler. *Team* Leicestershire (1946, 1 match).
Career batting
1–2–1–2–1*–2.00–0–*ct* 0
Bowling 52–0

Pearce, George Smart
Professional. *b:* 27.10.1908, Horsham, Sussex. *d:* 16.6.1986, Horsham, Sussex. Lower order right-hand batsman, right-arm medium pace bowler. *Team* Sussex (1928–36, 54 matches).
Career batting
54–79–10–1295–80–18.76–0–*ct* 23
Bowling 2588–89–29.07–3–0–5/34

Pearce, Harold Edgar
Amateur. *b:* 1.4.1884, Barnet, Hertfordshire. *d:* 19.5.1939, Chichester, Sussex. Middle order batsman. *Team* Middlesex (1905–07, 5 matches).
Career batting
5–9–1–169–46*–21.12–0–*ct* 4
Bowling 16–0
He was a well-known actor.

Pearce, Jonathan Peter
Cricketer. *b:* 18.4.1957, Newcastle upon Tyne, Northumberland. Lower order right-hand batsman, slow left-arm bowler. *Sch* Ampleforth. *Team* Oxford U (1978–79, blue 1979).
Career batting
7–11–5–22–8*–3.66–0–*ct* 2
Bowling 501–11–45.54–0–0–4/94

Pearce, Stanley Herbert Hicks
Amateur. *b:* 21.9.1863, Lopperwood, Totton, Hampshire. *d:* 5.4.1929, Oswestry, Shropshire. Middle order batsman. *Sch* Winchester. *Team* Hampshire (1885, 1 match).
Career batting
1–2–0–18–18–9.00–0–*ct* 0

Pearce, Thomas Albert
Professional. *b:* 11.5.1847, Essendon, Hertfordshire. *d:* 20.8.1898, St Albans, Hertfordshire. Lower order right-hand batsman, wicket-keeper, occasional right-hand slow round-arm bowler. *Team* MCC (1874–76).
Career batting
5–8–0–35–21–4.37–0–*ct* 4
His first-class debut was for the South of England in 1872 and his County cricket for Hertfordshire (1867–91).

Pearce, Thomas Alexander
Amateur. *b:* 18.12.1910, Hong Kong. *d:* 11.8.1982, Tunbridge Wells, Kent. Middle order right-hand batsman, off break bowler, brilliant field. *Sch* Charterhouse. *Team* Kent (1930–46, 52 matches).
Career batting
55–82–8–1213–106–16.39–1–*ct* 23
Bowling 22–1–22.00–0–0–1/22
In 1933 he left England to return to Hong Kong and his appearances in County cricket were therefore very sparse. After coming back to England in 1946 he served on the Kent CCC Committee and was President of the Club in 1978.

Pearce, Thomas Neill
Amateur. *b:* 3.11.1905, Stoke Newington, London. Brother-in-law of F. C. Hawker (Essex). Very sound middle order right-hand batsman, right-arm medium pace bowler. *Sch* Christ's Hospital. *Team* Essex (1929–50, 231 matches). *Tour* Martineau to Egypt 1939 (not first-class).
Career batting
250–406–54–12061–211*–34.26–22–*ct* 153
Bowling 927–15–61.80–0–0–4/12
He hit 1,000 runs in a season six times (best 1,826, av 49.35, in 1948). His only double century was 211* for Essex v Leicestershire at Westcliff in 1948. He was joint-captain of Essex 1933 to 1938 and 1950, and sole captain 1946 to 1949. He was Essex Chairman 1952–72 and has been President since 1970. In 1949 and 1950 he was a Test Selector. His final first-

class match was for a Commonwealth XI in 1952. For many years he selected a team to play in the Scarborough Festival each September. A noted rugby referee, he officiated in international matches.

Pearce, Walter Kennedy
Amateur. *b:* 2.4.1893, Bassett, Hampshire. *d:* 31.7.1960, Romsey, Hampshire. Middle order right-hand batsman. *Sch* Malvern. *Team* Hampshire (1923–26, 9 matches).
Career batting
9–10–3–127–63–18.14–0–*ct* 1

Pearce, Sir William
Amateur. *b:* 18.3.1853, Poplar, London. *d:* 24.8.1932, Walmer, Kent. Middle order right-hand batsman. *Team* Kent (1878, 3 matches).
Career batting
3–6–0–50–14–8.33–0–*ct* 2
Bowling 88–6–14.66–0–0–3/16
He also played for Essex (pre first-class, 1879). He was MP for Limehouse 1906–22.

Peare, William George
Professional, but amateur after 1926. *b:* 25.6.1905, Waterford, Ireland. *d:* 16.11.1979, St Luke's, Cork, Ireland. Lower order right-hand batsman, right-arm medium fast bowler. *Team* Warwickshire (1926, 7 matches).
Career batting
8–11–7–19–12*–4.75–0–*ct* 3
Bowling 213–8–26.62–0–0–3/45
His final first-class match was for MCC in 1936.

Pearman, Hugh
Cricketer. *b:* 1.6.1945, Edgbaston, Birmingham. Brother of Roger (Middlesex). Opening right-hand batsman, slow left-arm bowler. *Teams* Cambridge U (1969, blue); Middlesex (1969–72, 5 matches).
Career batting
12–17–1–294–61–18.37–0–*ct* 7
Bowling 578–16–36.12–0–0–4/56

Pearman, Roger
Amateur. *b:* 13.2.1943, Lichfield, Staffordshire. Brother of Hugh (Middlesex). Middle order right-hand batsman, off break bowler, close field. *Team* Middlesex (1962–64, 8 matches).
Career batting
8–13–3–264–72*–26.40–*ct* 4
He also played for Bedfordshire (1972–73) and Cheshire (1974–77). He was Chief Executive of Derbyshire CCC 1981–87.

Pearsall, Richard Devenish
Amateur. *b:* 15.1.1921, Kenilworth, Warwickshire. Lower order right-hand batsman, right-arm medium pace bowler. *Sch* Oundle. *Team* Cambridge U (1947–48).
Career batting
15–19–4–230–80*–15.33–0–*ct* 12
Bowling 982–27–36.37–0–0–4/51
He won a blue for hockey.

Pearse, Allan Arthur
Amateur. *b:* 22.4.1915, Watchet, Somerset. *d:* 14.6.1981, Watchet, Somerset. Middle order right-hand batsman, good field. *Team* Somerset (1936–38, 9 matches).
Career batting
9–15–1–81–20–5.78–0–*ct* 1
Bowling 3–0

Pearse, Gerald Vyvyan
Amateur. *b:* 7.9.1891, Pietermaritzburg, Natal, South Africa. *d:* 19.12.1956, Marylebone, London. Brother of C. O. C. (Natal) and D. K. (Natal). Middle order right-hand batsman, right-arm bowler. *Teams* Natal (1910/11); Oxford U (1919).
Career batting
14–23–5–413–67*–22.94–0–*ct* 12
Bowling 932–27–34.51–0–0–4/57
His final first-class match was for Free Foresters in 1927.

Pearson, Alexander Gillespie
Amateur. *b:* 21.1.1856, Edinburgh, Scotland. *d:* 24.1.1931, Locarno, Switzerland. Opening or middle order right-hand batsman, right-hand medium pace round-arm bowler, good field. *Sch* Rugby and Loretto. *Team* Oxford U (1876–77, blue both years).
Career batting
12–21–1–163–35–8.15–0–*ct* 5
Bowling 289–16–18.06–0–0–3/10
He also played for Scotland (not first-class). He also won a blue for golf.

Pearson, Dr Anthony John Grayhurst
Amateur. *b:* 30.12.1941, Pinner, Middlesex. Tail end right-hand batsman, right-arm fast medium bowler. *Sch* Millfield and Downside. *Teams* Cambridge U (1961–63, blue all three years); Somerset (1961–63, 6 matches).
Career batting
42–51–11–355–30–8.87–0–*ct* 29
Bowling 3918–139–28.18–2–1–10/78
He took 10 wickets in a single innings (for 78), for Cambridge U v Leicestershire at Loughborough in 1961.

Pearson, Dr Cecil Joseph Herbert
Amateur. *b:* 22.1.1888, Poplar, London. *d:* 14.9.1971, Porthcawl, Glamorgan. Middle order right-hand batsman, slow right-arm bowler. *Team* Glamorgan (1922, 1 match).
Career batting
1–2–0–9–9–4.50–0–*ct* 0
Bowling 12–0
He also played for Devon (1933–36).

Pearson, Derek Brooke
Professional. *b:* 29.3.1937, Kingswinford, Worcestershire. Lower order right-hand batsman, right-arm fast medium bowler. *Team* Worcestershire (1954–61, 74 matches).
Career batting
76–107–21–734–49–8.53–0–*ct* 35
Bowling 5540–210–26.38–9–1–6/70
He was no-balled for throwing in 1959 and 1960.

Pearson, Frederick Albert
Professional. *b:* 23.9.1880, Brixton, London. *d:* 10.11.1963, Newland, Droitwich, Worcestershire. Opening right-hand batsman, right-arm slow bowler. *Teams* Worcestershire (1900–26, 445 matches); Auckland (1910/11).
Career batting
454–811–38–18735–167–24.23–22–*ct* 162
Bowling 24716–853–28.97–38–4–9/41
He hit 1,000 runs in a season eight times (best 1,498, av 36.53, in 1921) and in 1923 took 111 wickets, av 22.89, completing the 'double' for the only time in his career. His best bowling was 9/41 for H. K. Foster's XI v Oxford U at Oxford in 1914.

Pearson, George Timothy
Amateur. *b:* 21.7.1921, Kensington, London. *d:* 24.7.1983, Cuxham, Oxfordshire. Lower order right-hand batsman, wicket-keeper. *Sch* Radley. *Team* Free Foresters (1948–59).
Career batting
2–3–2–54–28–54.00–0–*ct* 3

Pearson, Harry Eyre
Professional. *b:* 7.8.1851, Attercliffe, Sheffield, Yorkshire. *d:* 8.7.1903, Nether Edge, Sheffield, Yorkshire. Tail end right-hand batsman, right-hand fast, later slow, round-arm bowler, deep field. *Team* Yorkshire (1878–80, 4 matches).
Career batting
4–7–5–31–10*–15.50–0–*ct* 1
Bowling 90–5–18.00–0–0–3/37

Pearson, James W.
Professional. Tail end left-hand batsman, left-arm bowler. *Team* Northamptonshire (1932, 1 match).
Career batting
1–2–1–1–1–1*–1.00–0–*ct* 0
Bowling 43–0

Pearson, John Henry
Professional. *b:* 14.5.1915, Scarborough, Yorkshire. Hard hitting opening right-hand batsman. *Team* Yorkshire (1934–36, 3 matches).
Career batting
3–3–0–54–44–18.00–0–*ct* 0

Pearson, Joseph Garside
Professional. *b:* 26.3.1860, Worksop, Nottinghamshire. *d:* 18.1.1892, Boughton, Nottinghamshire. Middle order batsman. *Team* Nottinghamshire (1883, 1 match).
Career batting
1–1–0–1–1–1.00–0–*ct* 0
Bowling 1–3–0.33–0–0–3/1
His curious bowling record can be regarded as a fluke, since he played purely as a batsman, and even in local cricket, very rarely bowled.

Pearson, Kenneth
Cricketer. *b:* 30.8.1951, Bedlington, Northumberland. Sound opening right-hand batsman. *Team* Minor Counties (1976).
Career batting
1–2–0–13–9–6.50–0–*ct* 1
His County cricket was for Northumberland (1972–89).

Pearson, Kenneth R.
Professional. Lower order batsman, slow bowler. *Team* MCC (1946).
Career batting
1–2–0–26–17–13.00–0–*ct* 0
Bowling 74–2–37.00–0–0–2/42

Pearson, Lawrence Ivor
Professional. *b:* 25.1.1922, Darnall, Sheffield, Yorkshire. Middle order left-hand batsman. *Team* Derbyshire (1946, 2 matches).
Career batting
2–4–0–24–18–6.00–0–*ct* 0

Pearson, Richard Michael
Cricketer. *b:* 27.1.1972, Batley, Yorkshire. Lower order right-hand batsman, off break bowler. *Team* Cambridge U (1991–92, blue both years); Northamptonshire (1992, 1 match).
Career batting
21–25–6–166–33*–8.73–0–*ct* 6
Bowling 2369–35–67.68–1–0–5/108

Pearson, Sir Robert Barclay
Amateur. *b:* 20.11.1871, Johnston Lodge, Laurencekirk, Kirkcudbright, Scotland. *d:* 12.2.1954, Marylebone, London. Father-in-law of H. T. H. Foley (Worcestershire). Neat lower order right-hand batsman, right-arm slow bowler. *Sch* Loretto. *Team* Oxford U (1894).
Career batting
1–2–0–48–44–24.00–0–*ct* 0
Bowling 35–0
A noted all-round sportsman, he represented Oxford at rugby football and golf, as well as having a trial in the rowing eight. He was for many years Chairman of the London Stock Exchange.

Pearson, Thomas Sherwin
(changed name to Pearson-Gregory in 1892)
Amateur. *b:* 20.6.1851, Barwell, Leicestershire. *d:* 25.11.1935, Harlaxton Manor, Lincolnshire. Father of P. J. S. Pearson-Gregory (Nottinghamshire). Attacking middle order right-hand batsman, right-arm slow

bowler, wicket-keeper. *Sch* Rugby. *Teams* Oxford U (1872); Middlesex (1878–85, 66 matches).
Career batting
122–202–14–3347–121–17.80–1–*ct* 130–*st* 5
Bowling 1008–38–26.52–1–0–5/36

He also played for Bedfordshire (1871–76), Warwickshire (pre first-class, 1877) and Leicestershire (pre first-class, 1890–91). His final first-class match was for Gentlemen of England in 1891. In 1902 he was President of Nottinghamshire CCC. He represented Oxford at royal tennis and rackets.

Pearson-Gregory, Philip John Sherwin
(changed name from Pearson in 1892)
Amateur. *b:* 26.3.1888, Harlaxton Manor, Lincolnshire. *d:* 12.6.1955, St Pancras, London. Son of T. S. Pearson (Middlesex), son-in-law of A. W. Ridley (Hampshire and Middlesex). Middle order right-hand batsman, slip field. *Sch* Eton. *Team* Nottinghamshire (1910–14, 3 matches).
Career batting
3–2–0–119–71–59.50–0–*ct* 3

He appeared in the Freshmen's and Seniors' matches at Oxford, but no first-class games.

Peat, Charles Urie
Amateur. *b:* 28.2.1892, Edmonton, Middlesex. *d:* 27.10.1979, Wycliffe Hall, Barnard Castle, Co Durham. Lower order right-hand batsman, right-arm fast bowler. *Sch* Sedbergh. *Teams* Oxford U (1913, blue); Middlesex (1914, 6 matches).
Career batting
23–35–12–186–30–8.08–0–*ct* 8
Bowling 1696–54–31.40–2–0–6/51

His final first-class match was for Free Foresters in 1922. He was Conservative MP for Darlington 1931 to 1945.

Peate, Edmund
(birth registered as E. Peat)
Professional. *b:* 2.3.1855, Holbeck, Leeds, Yorkshire. *d:* 11.3.1900, Newlay, Horsforth, Yorkshire. He died from pneumonia. Tail end left-hand batsman, slow left-arm bowler. *Team* Yorkshire (1879–87, 154 matches). *Tour* Lillywhite, Shaw and Shrewsbury to Australia 1881/2. *Tests* England (1881/2 to 1886, 9 matches).
Career batting
209–312–88–2384–95–10.64–0–*ct* 132
Bowling 14517–1076–13.49–94–27–8/5
Test batting
9–14–8–70–13–11.66–0–*ct* 2
Bowling 683–31–22.03–2–0–6/85

He took 100 wickets in a season six times, going on to 200 once: 214, av 11.52, in 1882. His sudden departure from County cricket whilst in his prime was caused by Lord Hawke's determination to rid the Yorkshire team of its more unruly elements. His final first-class match was for the North in 1890.

Peatfield, Albert Edward
Amateur. *b:* 13.4.1874, Retford, Nottinghamshire. *d:* 12.12.1953, Retford, Nottinghamshire. Middle order right-hand batsman. *Team* England XI (1906).
Career batting
1–2–1–18–16–18.00–0–*ct* 0

His County cricket was for Glamorgan (pre first-class, 1903).

Peck, David Arthur
Amateur. *b:* 3.5.1940, Rushden, Northamptonshire. Brother of R. L. (Combined Services). Lower order right-hand batsman, wicket-keeper. *Sch* Wellingborough. *Team* Cambridge U (1960).
Career batting
1–1–0–0–0–0.00–0–*ct* 2

Peck, Ian George
Cricketer. *b:* 18.10.1957, Great Staughton, Huntingdonshire. Opening right-hand batsman, wicket-keeper. *Sch* Bedford School. *Teams* Cambridge U (1978–84, blue 1980 and 1981); Northamptonshire (1980–81, 2 matches).
Career batting
29–43–5–507–49*–13.34–0–*ct* 14–*st* 1

He also played for Bedfordshire (1976–79 and 1982–85). He captained Cambridge in 1980 and 1981, and reappeared as captain in 1984, though no longer at the University, when the appointed captain, A. J. Pollock, was unable to play due to his studies. An excellent rugby footballer, he was awarded his blue and toured with England.

Peck, Maj-Gen Richard Leslie
Amateur. *b:* 27.5.1937, Rushden, Northamptonshire. Brother of D. A. (Cambridge U). Middle order right-hand batsman, off break bowler. *Sch* Wellingborough. *Team* Combined Services (1960).
Career batting
2–2–0–24–19–12.00–0–*ct* 1
Bowling 1–2–0.50–0–0–2/1

His County cricket was for Berkshire (1969).

Pedder, Guy Richard
Amateur. *b:* 7.7.1892, Brandiston, Norwich, Norfolk. *d:* 6.4.1964, Park House, Hoxne, Suffolk. Brother-in-law of H. S. R. Critchley-Salmonson (Somerset). Tail end right-hand batsman, wicket-keeper. *Sch* Repton. *Team* Gloucestershire (1925, 1 match).
Career batting
5–5–1–120–82–30.00–0–*ct* 7–*st* 2

Most of his County cricket was for Norfolk (1913–31) and his first-class debut was in 1924 for the Minor Counties. His last first-class match was in 1931 for Free Foresters. He played in trials at Oxford U, but not in first-class matches.

Peden, David Murray
Cricketer. *b:* 4.11.1946, Edinburgh, Scotland. *d:* 12.3.1978, Dunfermline, Fife, Scotland. Middle order

right-hand batsman, right-arm medium pace bowler. *Team* Scotland (1973–76).
Career batting
3–5–0–108–45–21.60–0–*ct* 0
Bowling 74–2–37.00–0–0–2/53

Pedley, William Everard
Amateur. *b:* 16.6.1858, Stubbing Court, Wingerworth, Derbyshire *d:* 9.7.1920, Riverside, California, USA. Lower order right-hand batsman, right-arm medium pace bowler. *Sch* Eastbourne. *Team* Sussex (1879, 2 matches).
Career batting
2–4–1–45–16*–15.00–0–*ct* 0
Bowling 138–10–13.80–1–0–7/36

He appeared for Derbyshire in non-first-class matches in 1888. An engineer, he spent many years in India and thus was not afforded much opportunity for County cricket.

Peebles, Ian Alexander Ross
Amateur. *b:* 20.1.1908, Aberdeen, Scotland. *d:* 27.2.1980, Speen, Buckinghamshire. Lower order right-hand batsman, leg break and googly bowler. *Sch* Glasgow Academy. *Teams* Middlesex (1928–48, 165 matches); Oxford U (1930, blue); Scotland (1937). *Tours* MCC to South Africa 1927/8, 1930/1; Cahn to Ceylon 1936/7 (he did not play in first-class matches); Tennyson to India 1937/8. *Tests* England (1927/8 to 1931, 13 matches).
Career batting
251–330–101–2213–58–9.66–0–*ct* 172
Bowling 19738–923–21.38–62–15–8/24
Test batting
13–17–8–98–26–10.88–0–*ct* 5
Bowling 1391–45–30.91–3–0–6/63

He took 100 wickets in a season three times (best 139, av 18.51, in 1931). In 1939 he captained Middlesex. His first-class debut was for the Gentlemen in 1927. The loss of an eye in an air-raid during the Second World War more or less ended his first-class career. He later became a well-known cricket writer and journalist.

Peel, Bertram Lennox
Amateur. *b:* 19.4.1881, Wavertree, Liverpool, Lancashire. *d:* 19.1.1945, Colinton, Edinburgh, Scotland. Brother of D. H. (Oxford U). Opening or middle order right-hand batsman, slow right-arm bowler. *Sch* Bedford Grammar School. *Teams* Oxford U (1903); Scotland (1905–12).
Career batting
10–18–0–288–74–16.00–0–*ct* 4
Bowling 249–10–24.90–0–0–4/123

His County cricket was for Bedfordshire (1901–13).

Peel, Denis Heywood
Amateur. *b:* 1.2.1886, Wavertree, Liverpool, Lancashire. *d:* 25.10.1927, Montana, Switzerland. Brother of B. L. (Scotland). Lower order batsman, bowler. *Sch* Bedford Grammar School. *Team* Oxford U (1907).
Career batting
3–5–0–9–6–1.80–0–*ct* 1
Bowling 161–3–53.66–0–0–1/32

His County cricket was for Bedfordshire (1906–13).

Peel, Robert
Professional. *b:* 12.2.1857, Churwell, Leeds, Yorkshire. *d:* 12.8.1941, Morley, Leeds, Yorkshire. Middle or lower order left-hand batsman, slow left-arm bowler. *Team* Yorkshire (1882–97, 321 matches). *Tours* Lillywhite, Shaw and Shrewsbury to Australia 1884/5; Vernon to Australia 1887/8; Sheffield to Australia 1891/2; Stoddart to Australia 1894/5. *Tests* England (1884/5 to 1896, 20 matches).
Career batting
436–693–66–12191–210*–19.44–7–*ct* 214
Bowling 28758–1775–16.20–123–33–9/22
Test batting
20–33–4–427–83–14.72–0–*ct* 17
Bowling 1715–101–16.98–5–1–7/31

He took 100 wickets in a season eight times, (best 180, av 14.97, in 1895) and hit 1,000 runs once: 1,206, av 30.15, in 1896, completing the 'double' in the same summer. His only double century was 210* for Yorkshire v Warwickshire at Edgbaston in 1896, and his best bowling was 9/22 for Yorkshire v Somerset at Headingley in 1895. Regarded as the best bowler of his type in England, his County career came to a premature end when Lord Hawke dismissed him because of his inebriate habits. His final first-class match was for an England XI in 1899.

Pegler, Sidney James
Amateur. *b:* 28.7.1888, Durban, South Africa. *d:* 10.9.1972, Plumstead, Cape Town, South Africa. Uncle of J. W. Bristow (Natal, Western Province and Griqualand West) and K. L. Bristow (Orange Free State). Lower order right-hand batsman, right-arm medium pace leg break bowler. *Team* Transvaal (1908/9 to 1912/13). *Tours* South Africa to Australia 1910/11, to England 1912, 1924. *Tests* South Africa (1909/10 to 1924, 16 matches).
Career batting
103–150–18–1677–79–12.70–0–*ct* 56
Bowling 8324–425–19.58–32–5–8/54
Test batting
16–28–5–356–35*–15.47–0–*ct* 5
Bowling 1572–47–33.44–2–0–7/65

He was the outstanding success of the 1912 South African tour, taking 189 wickets, av 15.26, heading both Test and first-class averages. On his 1924 tour he again took over 100 wickets. He spent a number of summers in England and appeared in a few first-class matches, the final one being for MCC in 1930. A South African Test selector after the Second World

War, he was Manager of the 1951 touring team. He was a District Commissioner in the British Colonial Service.

Pelham, Anthony George
Amateur. *b:* 4.9.1911, Minehead, Somerset. *d:* 10.3.1969, Dorking, Surrey. Grandson of F. G. (Sussex). Lower order right-hand batsman, right-arm medium pace bowler. *Sch* Eton. *Teams* Sussex (1930–33, 10 matches); Cambridge U (1931–34, blue 1934); Somerset (1933, 2 matches).
Career batting
35–47–16–339–40*–10.93–0–*ct* 19
Bowling 2610–84–31.07–2–0–5/37

Pelham, Rev Hon Francis Godolphin
(succeeded as the 5th Earl of Chichester in 1901)
Amateur. *b:* 18.10.1844, Stanmer Park, Lewes, Sussex. *d:* 21.4.1905, Stanmer Park, Lewes, Sussex. Cousin of Sidney (Oxford U), grandfather of A. G. (Sussex), uncle of I. F. W. Bligh (Kent) and Lord Clifton (Kent). Middle order right-hand batsman, right-hand slow round-arm bowler, slip field. *Sch* Eton. *Teams* Cambridge U (1864–67, blue all four years); Sussex (1865–68, 8 matches).
Career batting
25–47–5–637–78–15.16–0–*ct* 24
Bowling 1731–88 + 4–19.67–7–0–7/26
He also played for Devon (1874–75). He captained Cambridge in 1866 and 1867. He was also a noted athlete, winning many races whilst at Cambridge, and winning his blue.

Pelham, Ven Archdeacon Sidney
Amateur. *b:* 16.5.1849, Brighton, Sussex. *d:* 14.7.1926, Norwich, Norfolk. Cousin of F. G. (Sussex). Lower order right-hand batsman, right-hand slow round-arm bowler. *Sch* Harrow. *Team* Oxford U (1871–72, blue 1871).
Career batting
7–9–4–24–14*–4.80–0–*ct* 6
Bowling 314–20 + 1–15.70–1–0–6/51
His County cricket was for Norfolk (1871).

Pell, Godfrey Arnold
Amateur. *b:* 11.3.1928, Sunderland, Co Durham. Lower order right-hand batsman, leg break and googly bowler. *Sch* KES, Birmingham. *Team* Warwickshire (1947, 1 match).
Career batting
1–2–1–24–16*–24.00–0–*ct* 1
Bowling 31–4–7.75–0–0–2/9

Pell, Oliver Claude
Amateur. *b:* 3.9.1826, Pinner Hill, Middlesex. *d:* 17.10.1891, Wilburton Manor, Ely, Cambridgeshire. Fine middle order right-hand batsman, excellent field. *Sch* Rugby. *Teams* Cambridge U (1844–48, blue 1844–47); Cambridge Town Club (1847–48).
Career batting
39–67–4–706–54–11.20–0–*ct* 6
An excellent shot, he represented England in rifle shooting. Owing to his career in the law his cricket in major matches was very restricted. He captained Cambridge in 1847.

Pellew, Clarence Everard
Amateur. *b:* 21.9.1893, Port Pirie, South Australia. *d:* 9.5.1981, Adelaide, South Australia. Brother of L. V. (South Australia), cousin of J. H. (South Australia) and A. H. (South Australia). Attacking middle order right-hand batsman, right-arm medium pace bowler, brilliant outfield. *Team* South Australia (1913/14 to 1928/9, 23 matches). *Tours* AIF to England 1919, to South Africa 1919/20; Australia to England 1921, to South Africa 1921/2. *Tests* Australia (1920/1 to 1921/2, 10 matches).
Career batting
91–147–12–4536–271–33.60–9–*ct* 43
Bowling 849–12–70.75–0–0–3/119
Test batting
10–14–1–484–116–37.23–2–*ct* 4
Bowling 34–0
He hit 1,260 runs, av 38.18, in 1919, but was not so successful in 1921, though he played in all five Tests due in part to his outstanding fielding. His highest score was 271 for South Australia v Victoria at Adelaide in 1919/20.

Pelly, John Noel
Amateur. *b:* 15.6.1888, Ware, Hertfordshire. *d:* 6.6.1945, Hove, Sussex. Middle or lower order batsman. *Sch* Bradfield. *Team* Royal Navy (1926).
Career batting
1–2–0–5–5–2.50–0–*ct* 0

Pember, Francis William
Amateur. *b:* 16.8.1862, Hatfield, Hertfordshire. *d:* 19.1.1954, Newnham, Cambridge. Middle order right-hand batsman. *Sch* Harrow. *Team* Hampshire (1885, 2 matches).
Career batting
5–9–2–112–47*–16.00–0–*ct* 5
He played in the 1881 Freshmen's match at Oxford, but no first-class matches for the University. His first-class debut was for MCC in 1882.

Pember, John Devereaux Dubricious
Amateur. *b:* 8.6.1940, Creaton, Northamptonshire. Tail end left-hand batsman, right-arm fast medium bowler. *Sch* Wellingborough. *Team* Leicestershire (1968–71, 24 matches).
Career batting
24–25–10–271–53–18.06–0–*ct* 11
Bowling 1370–43–31.86–1–0–5/45
He played rugby football for Northampton.

Pemberton, Ralph Hylton
Amateur. *b:* 17.7.1864, Barnes, Sunderland, Co Durham. *d:* 11.1.1931, Hookhams, Lurgashall, Sussex. Opening right-hand batsman. *Sch* Eton. *Team* Oxford U (1885).
Career batting
3–5–0–65–40–13.00–0–*ct* 0
His County cricket was for Durham (pre first-class, 1884–85).

Pemberton, William Cecil
Amateur. *b:* 15.11.1898, Dublin, Ireland. *d:* 25.12.1978, Dublin, Ireland. Lower order right-hand batsman, left-arm fast medium bowler. *Team* Ireland (1923–28).
Career batting
4–7–3–55–31–13.75–0–*ct* 1
Bowling 263–5–52.60–0–0–3/40

Penberthy, Anthony Leonard
Cricketer. *b:* 1.9.1969, Troon, Cornwall. Middle order left-hand batsman, right-arm medium pace bowler. *Team* Northamptonshire (1989–92, 39 matches). *Tour* Northamptonshire to South Africa 1991/2.
Career batting
39–56–7–905–101*–18.46–1–*ct* 25
Bowling 1909–50–38.18–0–0–4/91
He also played for Cornwall (1987–89). He took the wicket of M. A. Taylor with his first ball in first-class cricket for Northamptonshire v Australians at Northampton in 1989.

Penduck, Arthur Edward
Professional. *b:* 1885. *d:* 5.12.1924, Kingsdown, Bristol. Lower order right-hand batsman, right-arm fast bowler. *Team* Gloucestershire (1908–09, 5 matches).
Career batting
5–8–2–18–8–3.00–0–*ct* 0
Bowling 294–6–49.00–0–0–3/98

Penfold, Alexander George
Amateur. *b:* 14.5.1901, Kenley, Surrey. *d:* 28.9.1982, Isfield, Sussex. Lower order right-hand batsman, right-arm fast medium bowler. *Teams* Europeans (1924/5 to 1929/30); Madras (1926/7); Surrey (1929, 3 matches).
Career batting
12–19–7–78–17*–6.50–0–*ct* 2
Bowling 1007–62–16.24–3–1–8/43
Being employed by the Bank of India, his opportunities for County cricket were very limited.

Penn, Alfred
Amateur. *b:* 6.1.1855, Lewisham, London. *d:* 18.10.1889, Lee, London. Brother of Frank sen (Kent) and William (Kent), uncle of E. F. (Cambridge U) and Frank jun (Kent), brother-in-law of J. F. Green (MCC) and F. Stokes (Kent). Lower order left-hand batsman, left-hand slow round-arm bowler. *Team* Kent (1875–84, 41 matches).
Career batting
48–82–13–539–66–7.81–0–*ct* 21
Bowling 3568–222–16.07–20–3–8/34

Penn, Christopher
Cricketer. *b:* 19.6.1963, Dover, Kent. Lower order left-hand batsman, right-arm fast medium bowler. *Team* Kent (1982–92, 123 matches).
Career batting
123–141–36–1985–115–18.90–1–*ct* 54
Bowling 9493–283–33.54–12–0–7/70
He took 81 wickets, av 24.55, in 1988.

Penn, Eric Frank
Amateur. *b:* 17.4.1878, Westminster, London. *d:* 18.10.1915, Hohenzollern, Loos, France. He was killed in action. Son of William (Kent), nephew of Frank sen (Kent) and Alfred (Kent), cousin of Frank jun (Kent), nephew of J. F. Green (MCC) and F. Stokes (Kent), brother-in-law of C. H. M. Ebden (Sussex and Middlesex). Middle order right-hand batsman, right-arm slow bowler. *Sch* Eton. *Team* Cambridge U (1898–1902, blue 1899 and 1902). *Tour* Warner to North America 1898 (he did not play in first-class matches).
Career batting
22–36–6–449–51*–14.96–0–*ct* 13
Bowling 1076–34–31.64–1–0–5/47
In 1899 he left Cambridge in order to serve in the Boer War, resuming his place at the University in 1901. His final first-class match was for MCC in 1903. His County cricket was for Norfolk (1898–1906).

Penn, Frank (sen)
Amateur. *b:* 7.3.1851, Lewisham, London. *d:* 26.12.1916, Bifrons, Patrixbourne, Kent. Brother of Alfred (Kent) and William (Kent), father of Frank jun (Kent), uncle of E. F. (Cambridge U), brother-in-law of J. F. Green (MCC) and F. Stokes (Kent). Attacking middle order right-hand batsman, right-hand slow round-arm bowler, deep field. *Team* Kent (1875–81, 62 matches). *Tour* Harris to Australia 1878/9. *Test* England (1880, 1 match).
Career batting
98–172–14–4291–160–27.15–6–*ct* 49
Bowling 371–10–37.10–0–0–3/36
Test batting
1–2–1–50–27*–50.00–0–*ct* 0
Bowling 2–0
Regarded as one of the most brilliant batsman of his day, he was forced to retire from important cricket in 1881 on medical advice. He was President of Kent in 1905.

Penn, Frank (jun)
Amateur. *b:* 18.8.1884, Owsden, Suffolk. *d:* 23.4.1961, Bawdsey Hall, Woodbridge, Suffolk. Son

of Frank sen (Kent), nephew of Alfred (Kent), William (Kent), J. F. Green (MCC) and F. Stokes (Kent), cousin of E. F. (Cambridge U). Middle order right-hand batsman. *Team* Kent (1904–05, 5 matches).
Career batting
5–9–0–130–43–14.44–0–*ct* 3
He made a name for himself in military matches.

Penn, William
Amateur. *b:* 29.8.1849, Lewisham, London. *d:* 15.8.1921, Belgravia, Westminster, London. Brother of Alfred (Kent) and Frank sen (Kent), father of E. F. (Cambridge U), uncle of Frank jun (Kent), brother-in-law of A. C. Lucas (Surrey and Middlesex), J. F. Green (MCC) and F. Stokes (Kent). Opening right-hand batsman, right-hand fast round-arm bowler, good deep field. *Sch* Harrow. *Team* Kent (1870–78, 18 matches).
Career batting
22–37–1–402–39–11.16–0–*ct* 12

Pennett, David Barrington
Cricketer. *b:* 26.10.1969, Leeds, Yorkshire. Lower order right-hand batsman, right-arm fast medium bowler. *Team* Nottinghamshire (1992, 12 matches).
Career batting
12–11–1–69–29–6.90–0–*ct* 3
Bowling 981–26–37.73–0–0–4/58

Penney, Trevor Lionel
Cricketer. *b:* 12.6.1968, Salisbury, Rhodesia. Middle order right-hand batsman, leg break bowler. *Teams* Zimbabwe (1986/7 to 1987/8); Boland (1991/2); Warwickshire (1991/2 to 1992, 17 matches). *Tour* Warwickshire to South Africa 1991/2.
Career batting
22–33–10–1146–151–49.82–3–*ct* 6
Bowling 39–0
He played hockey for Zimbabwe.

Pennington, George Arthur Adam Septimus Carter Trenchard Sale
Amateur. *b:* 28.4.1899, Cote Brook, Cheshire. *d:* 15.9.1933, Armthorpe, Doncaster, Yorkshire. He was killed in a flying accident. Middle order right-hand batsman, useful bowler. *Team* Northamptonshire (1927, 12 matches).
Career batting
12–19–0–259–47–13.63–0–*ct* 6
Bowling 8–0
He was the pilot of a plane which took off from Armthorpe Aerodrome and crashed in an adjoining field – amongst the survivors were the jockey, Gordon Richards, and the Gloucestershire cricketer and racehorse trainer, Herbert Blagrave.

Pennington, Harry
Professional. *b:* 21.4.1880, Salford, Manchester, Lancashire. *d:* 17.3.1961, Moston, Lancashire. Lower order batsman, wicket-keeper. *Team* Lancashire (1900, 4 matches).
Career batting
4–5–1–41–29*–10.25–0–*ct* 2–*st* 3
He played soccer for Notts County.

Pennington, John Henry
Professional. *b:* 24.6.1881, Sutton-on-Trent, Nottinghamshire. *d:* 2.1.1942, Newark, Nottinghamshire. Lower order batsman, left-arm medium pace bowler. *Team* Nottinghamshire (1902–05, 18 matches).
Career batting
18–24–8–89–18–5.56–0–*ct* 8
Bowling 1345–41–32.80–3–0–7/223

Penny, Joshua Hudson
Professional. *b:* 29.9.1856, Yeadon, Yorkshire. *d:* 29.7.1902, Savile Town, Dewsbury, Yorkshire. Lower order left-hand batsman, slow left-arm bowler. *Team* Yorkshire (1891, 1 match).
Career batting
1–1–1–8–8*–no av–0–*ct* 1
Bowling 31–2–15.50–0–0–1/7

Penny, Thomas Simpson
Amateur. *b:* 15.7.1929, Bristol. *d:* 26.7.1983, Casterton, Westmorland. Sound middle order right-hand batsman, off break bowler. *Sch* Clifton. *Team* Oxford U (1951–52).
Career batting
5–5–2–73–34–24.33–0–*ct* 1
Bowling 400–11–36.36–0–0–4/75

Pennycuick, John
Amateur. *b:* 15.1.1841, Poona, India. *d:* 9.3.1911, Camberley, Surrey. Middle order right-hand batsman, right-arm medium pace bowler. *Sch* Cheltenham. *Team* MCC (1883).
Career batting
1–2–2–21–20*–no av–0–*ct* 0
He spent most of his life in India and was a major figure in the promotion of cricket there.

Pentecost, John
Professional. *b:* 15.10.1857, Brighton, Sussex. *d:* 23.2.1902, St John's Wood, London. Lower order right-hand batsman, wicket-keeper. *Team* Kent (1882–90, 63 matches).
Career batting
66–102–26–572–38–7.52–0–*ct* 95–*st* 32
Bowling 20–1–20.00–0–0–1/19
Failing eyesight forced him to retire from County cricket earlier than would otherwise have been the case.

Pepall, George
Professional. *b:* 29.2.1876, Stow-on-the-Wold, Gloucestershire. *d:* 8.1.1953, Bourton-on-the-Water, Gloucestershire. Tail end right-hand batsman, right-arm fast bowler. *Team* Gloucestershire (1896–1904, 14 matches).

Pepper, Cecil George

Career batting
14–24–7–99–45–5.82–0–*ct* 8
Bowling 725–20–36.25–1–0–5/63

Pepper, Cecil George
Professional. *b:* 15.9.1918, Forbes, New South Wales, Australia. Middle order right-hand batsman, leg break and googly bowler. *Team* New South Wales (1938/9 to 1940/1, 16 matches). *Tours* Australian Services to England 1945, to India and Ceylon 1945/6; Commonwealth to India and Pakistan 1949/50.
Career batting
44–72–7–1927–168–29.64–1–*ct* 41
Bowling 5019–171–29.35–7–0–6/33
His last first-class match was for a Commonwealth XI in 1957. From 1964 to 1979 he was on the English first-class umpires' list.

Pepper, Charles
Professional. *b:* 1875, Ireland. *d:* 13.9.1917, near La Clytte, Belgium. Defensive middle order right-hand batsman, right-arm medium pace bowler. *Team* Nottinghamshire (1900–01, 7 matches).
Career batting
7–12–3–162–40*–18.00–0–*ct* 2
Bowling 72–3–24.00–0–0–3/23
He also played for Bedfordshire (1903).

Pepper, John
Amateur. *b:* 21.10.1922, Wimbledon Park, London. Middle order right-hand batsman, good field. *Sch* The Leys. *Team* Cambridge U (1946–48, blue all three years).
Career batting
29–49–1–1108–185–23.08–1–*ct* 5
His County cricket was for Denbighshire (1959).

Pepys, Rev John Alfred
Amateur. *b:* 16.4.1838, Marylebone, London. *d:* 22.3.1924, Bexhill-on-Sea, Sussex. Forceful middle order right-hand batsman, good cover point. *Sch* Eton. *Teams* Kent (1859–69, 13 matches); Oxford (1861, blue).
Career batting
30–50–1–592–55–12.08–0–*ct* 19
Bowling 25–1–25.00–0–0–1/25
He also won a blue for royal tennis.

Percival, John Douglas
Amateur. *b:* 5.8.1902, Kensington, London. *d:* 5.3.1983, Roehampton, London. Hard hitting opening right-hand batsman. *Sch* Westminster and Radley. *Teams* Oxford U (1922); Gloucestershire (1923, 1 match).
Career batting
3–6–0–38–17–6.33–0–*ct* 0

Percival, W. Alan
Amateur. *b:* 1923, Canada. Middle order right-hand batsman, wicket-keeper. *Team* Canada (1951–54). *Tour* Canada to England 1954.
Career batting
5–7–0–61–23–8.71–0–*ct* 9–*st* 1

Pereira, Aloysius Stanislaus
Amateur. *b:* 30.12.1859, Calcutta, India. *d:* 11.11.1935, Dehra Dun, India. Lower order batsman, bowler. *Sch* Stonyhurst. *Team* Cambridge U (1880).
Career batting
1–2–0–10–7–5.00–0–*ct* 2
Bowling 44–1–44.00–0–0–1/44

Pereira, Rev Edward Thomas
Amateur. *b:* 26.9.1866, Wolseley Hall, Colwich, Staffordshire. *d:* 25.2.1939, Edgbaston, Birmingham. Forcing middle order right-hand batsman, right-arm fast bowler, excellent field. *Sch* Oratory. *Team* Warwickshire (1895–96, 5 matches).
Career batting
7–12–1–177–34–16.09–0–*ct* 4
Bowling 13–0
His Warwickshire debut was in 1886, but he did not appear again for the County until 1895. His final first-class match was for MCC in 1900.

Pereira, Eustace Lorenz
Amateur. *b:* 4.7.1939, Colombo, Ceylon. Middle order left-hand batsman, off break bowler. *Team* Cambridge U (1962–63).
Career batting
2–2–1–11–8*–11.00–0–*ct* 0

Perkins, Arthur Lionel Bertie
Amateur. *b:* 19.10.1905, Swansea, Glamorgan. *d:* 6.5.1992, Durban, South Africa. Middle order right-hand batsman. *Sch* Bromsgrove. *Team* Glamorgan (1925–33, 6 matches).
Career batting
6–10–3–102–26*–14.57–0–*ct* 4

Perkins, Charles Meigh
Amateur. *b:* 10.5.1854, Sowe, Warwickshire. *d:* 26.4.1912, Hove, Sussex. Middle order right-hand batsman. *Team* Sussex (1884, 1 match).
Career batting
1–2–1–12–11–12.00–0–*ct* 0

Perkins, George
(also known as William Carter)
Professional. *b:* 1864, Ealing, Middlesex. *d:* 4.7.1933, Isleworth, Middlesex. Middle order right-hand batsman, right-arm medium pace bowler. *Team* Middlesex (1884, 1 match).
Career batting
1–2–0–0–0–0.00–0–*ct* 0

Perkins, George Cyril
Professional. *b:* 4.6.1911, Wollaston, Northamptonshire. Middle order right-hand batsman, left-arm medium, later slow, bowler. *Team* Northamptonshire (1934–37, 56 matches).

Career batting
57–95–23–589–29–8.18–0–*ct* 30
Bowling 3359–93–36.11–5–0–6/54

He also played for Suffolk (1939–67). His final first-class match was for Minor Counties in 1951.

Perkins, Henry
Amateur. *b:* 10.12.1832, Sawston, Cambridgeshire. *d:* 6.5.1916, New Barnet, Hertfordshire. Brother of John (Cambridgeshire). Hard slashing middle order right-hand batsman, right-hand slow under-arm bowler, good mid wicket. *Sch* Bury St Edmunds. *Teams* Cambridge U (1854, blue); Cambridgeshire (1857–66, 9 matches).
Career batting
28–48–8–370–36–9.25–0–*ct* 15
Bowling 488–27 + 3–18.07–2–0–5/48

He also played for Hertfordshire (1868). His final first-class match was for MCC in 1868. He was Secretary of MCC from October 1876 to December 1897 – an easy-going autocrat.

Perkins, Hubert George
Professional. *b:* 18.6.1907, Attleborough, Warwickshire. *d:* 4.5.1935, Nuneaton, Warwickshire. Tail end left-hand batsman, slow left-arm bowler. *Team* Warwickshire (1926–27, 4 matches).
Career batting
4–5–2–10–6*–3.33–0–*ct* 1
Bowling 55–1–55.00–0–0–1/30

Perkins, John
Amateur. *b:* 17.5.1837, Sawston, Cambridgeshire. *d:* 30.4.1901, East Hatley, Cambridgeshire. He died from a gunshot wound. Brother of Henry (Cambridgeshire). Steady middle order right-hand batsman, deep field. *Sch* Bury St Edmunds. *Team* Cambridgeshire (1861–67, 11 matches).
Career batting
15–25–1–440–67–18.33–0–*ct* 5

He appeared occasionally for Cambridge U, but not in first-class matches. In 1866 he was appointed Hon Secretary to Cambridgeshire CCC. His final first-class match was for MCC in 1868.

Perkins, Thomas Tosswill Norwood
Amateur. *b:* 19.12.1870, Strood, Kent. *d:* 26.7.1946, Stone, Tonbridge, Kent. Sound middle order right-hand batsman, right-arm fast bowler, good deep field. *Sch* St John's, Leatherhead. *Teams* Cambridge U (1893–94, blue both years); Kent (1893–1900, 25 matches).
Career batting
46–77–6–1675–109–23.59–1–*ct* 27
Bowling 198–2–99.00–0–0–1/15

He also played for Essex (pre first-class, 1889), Hertfordshire (1892) and Wiltshire (1904–11), but had little time for serious cricket on taking up a scholastic appointment. A good soccer player, he was awarded his blue.

Perks, Reginald Thomas David
Professional. *b:* 4.10.1911, Hereford. *d:* 22.11.1977, Worcester. Son of Thomas (MCC). Hard hitting lower order left-hand batsman, right-arm fast medium bowler. *Team* Worcestershire (1930–55, 561 matches). *Tour* MCC to South Africa 1938/9. *Tests* England (1938/9 to 1939, 2 matches).
Career batting
595–884–150–8956–75–12.20–0–*ct* 240
Bowling 53770–2233–24.07–143–24–9/40
Test batting
2–2–2–3–2*–no av–0–*ct* 1
Bowling 355–11–32.27–2–0–5/100

He also played for Herefordshire (1926) and Monmouthshire (1928–29). He took 100 wickets in a season sixteen times (best 159, av 19.22, in 1939). Twice he had nine wickets in an innings, his best being 9/40 for Worcestershire v Glamorgan at Stourbridge in 1939. He captained Worcestershire in 1955. After retiring he was elected to the Committee of Worcestershire CCC remaining until shortly before his death.

Perks, Thomas
Professional. *b:* 2.10.1883, Worcester. *d:* 15.1.1953, Ledbury, Herefordshire. Father of R. T. D. (Worcestershire). Lower order batsman, wicket-keeper. *Team* MCC (1902).
Career batting
1–2–0–16–11–8.00–0–*ct* 1–*st* 3
Bowling 31–0

Perrin, Percival Albert
Amateur. *b:* 26.5.1876, Abney Park, Stoke Newington, London. *d:* 20.11.1945, Hickling, Norfolk. Sound middle order right-hand batsman, slow right-arm bowler, moderate field. *Teams* Essex (1896–1928, 525 matches); London County (1902).
Career batting
538–918–91–29709–343*–35.92–66–*ct* 293
Bowling 753–16–47.06–0–0–3/13

He hit 1,000 runs in a season eighteen times (best 1,893, av 47.32, in 1906). His highest innings was 343* for Essex v Derbyshire at Chesterfield in 1904 (Essex lost) and he scored two double centuries for the County. He was a Test Selector in 1926 and again from 1931 to 1939, being Chairman of the Selectors in 1939.

Perry, Ernest Harvey
Amateur. *b:* 16.1.1908, Chaddesley Corbett, Worcestershire. Lower order right-hand batsman, right-arm fast bowler. *Team* Worcestershire (1933–46, 10 matches).
Career batting
10–16–0–148–46–9.25–0–*ct* 3
Bowling 732–22–33.27–1–0–5/42

He also played for Staffordshire (1926 and 1946).

Perry, Harry
Amateur. *b:* 7.3.1895, Old Swinford, Stourbridge, Worcestershire. *d:* 28.2.1961, Stourbridge, Worcestershire. Middle or lower order right-hand batsman, right-arm medium pace bowler. *Team* Worcestershire (1927–28, 5 matches).
Career batting
5–8–1–109–40–15.57–0–*ct* 0
Bowling 46–1–46.00–0–0–1/38

Perry, Horace Thomas
Professional. *b:* 29.11.1905, Bedminster, Somerset. *d:* 25.12.1962, Kingsdown, Bristol. Middle order right-hand batsman, right-arm fast bowler. *Team* Somerset (1927, 1 match).
Career batting
1–2–0–9–9–4.50–0–*ct* 0

Perry, Jonathan Nicholas
Cricketer. *b:* 29.12.1965, Frimley, Surrey. Great-grandson of J. F. Byrne (Warwickshire). Lower order right-hand batsman, right-arm medium pace bowler. *Sch* Ampleforth. *Team* Cambridge U (1987–88, blue both years).
Career batting
11–12–1–104–26–9.45–0–*ct* 4
Bowling 836–18–46.44–0–0–3/56

Perry, Neil James
Cricketer. *b:* 27.5.1958, Sutton, Surrey. Tail end right-hand batsman, slow left-arm bowler. *Team* Glamorgan (1979–81, 13 matches).
Career batting
13–12–4–19–6–2.37–0–*ct* 9
Bowling 920–21–43.80–0–0–3/51

Perry, William
Professional. *b:* 12.8.1830, Oxford. *d:* 15.3.1913, Thatcham, Berkshire. Lower order batsman, good bowler. *Team* Lancashire (1865, 1 match).
Career batting
2–3–1–27–16–13.50–0–*ct* 3–*st* 1
Bowling 29–0
He also played for Berkshire (1849) and Oxfordshire (1850–56). His first-class debut was for the North of England in 1856.

Perryman, Stephen Peter
Cricketer. *b:* 22.10.1955, Yardley, Birmingham. Lower order right-hand batsman, right-arm medium pace bowler. *Teams* Warwickshire (1974–81, 130 matches); Worcestershire (1982–83, 26 matches).
Career batting
156–162–68–872–43–9.27–0–*ct* 58
Bowling 11337–358–31.66–19–3–7/49
He also played for Staffordshire (1988).

Pershke, William Jack
Amateur. *b:* 8.8.1918, Richmond, Surrey. *d:* 21.1.1944. He died on active service. Lower order right-hand batsman, right-arm fast medium bowler. *Sch* Uppingham. *Team* Oxford U (1938, blue).
Career batting
8–10–5–57–17*–11.40–0–*ct* 5
Bowling 752–28–26.85–3–0–6/46

Persse, Henry Wilfred
Amateur. *b:* 19.9.1885, Portswood, Southampton, Hampshire. *d:* 28.6.1918, near St Omer, France. He died of wounds. Lower order right-hand batsman, right-arm fast bowler. *Team* Hampshire (1905–09, 51 matches).
Career batting
51–84–8–889–71–11.69–0–*ct* 40
Bowling 3813–127–30.02–3–0–6/64
His County cricket ended in 1909 when he was posted abroad.

Pervez Sajjad Hassan
Cricketer. *b:* 30.8.1942, Lahore, India. Brother of Waqar Hassan (Pakistan). Tail end right-hand batsman, slow left-arm bowler. *Teams* Lahore (1961/2 to 1967/8); PIA (1967/8 to 1973/4); Karachi (1968/9). *Tours* Pakistan Eaglets to England 1963; Pakistan to England 1967, 1971, to Australia and New Zealand 1964/5, to Ceylon 1964/5, to Ceylon, Australia and New Zealand 1972/3; PIA to Ireland 1969 (not first-class). *Tests* Pakistan (1964/5 to 1972/3, 19 matches).
Career batting
133–128–53–786–56*–10.48–0–*ct* 57
Bowling 10750–493–21.80–28–6–8/89
Test batting
19–20–11–123–24–13.66–0–*ct* 9
Bowling 1410–59–23.89–3–0–7/74
He did not appear in any Tests on the 1967 tour to England, and when more was expected of him in 1971, he unfortunately missed several matches through injury, though playing in all three Tests.

Pestell, Kenneth Frederick
Amateur. *b:* 7.5.1931, Edmonton, Middlesex. Middle order right-hand batsman, right-arm medium pace bowler. *Team* D. R. Jardine's XI (1957).
Career batting
1–2–0–37–21–18.50–0–*ct* 0
Bowling 17–0

Petchey, Michael David
Cricketer. *b:* 16.12.1958, Ealing, Middlesex. Tail end right-hand batsman, right-arm medium pace bowler. *Sch* Latymer Upper. *Team* Oxford U (1983–84, blue 1983).
Career batting
7–6–0–21–18–3.50–0–*ct* 3
Bowling 886–16–55.37–0–0–4/65

Peters, Nicholas Howard
Cricketer. *b:* 21.2.1968, Guildford, Surrey. Lower order right-hand batsman, right-arm fast medium bowler. *Sch* Sherborne. *Team* Surrey (1988–89, 16 matches).

Career batting
16–18–8–101–25*–10.10–0–*ct* 7
Bowling 1246–40–31.15–1–1–6/31

Peters, Richard Charles
Amateur. *b:* 12.9.1911, Chew Magna, Somerset. *d:* 26.10.1989, Weston-super-Mare, Somerset. Tail end right-hand batsman, right-arm fast bowler. *Team* Somerset (1946, 1 match).
Career batting
1–2–1–5–3–5.00–0–*ct* 0
Bowling 18–0

Pether, Stewart
Amateur. *b:* 15.10.1916, Oxford. Lower order right-hand batsman, right-arm medium fast bowler. *Sch* Magdalen College School, Oxford. *Team* Oxford U (1939, blue).
Career batting
10–14–2–103–20*–8.58–0–*ct* 3
Bowling 622–31–20.06–2–0–5/7
His County cricket was for Oxfordshire (1936–48).

Petrie, Eric Charlton
Amateur. *b:* 22.5.1927, Ngaruawahia, Auckland, New Zealand. Opening or middle order right-hand batsman, occasional leg break bowler, wicket-keeper. *Teams* Auckland (1950/1 to 1955/6); Northern Districts (1956/7 to 1966/7); Gentlemen (1958). *Tours* New Zealand to England 1958, to India and Pakistan 1955/6. *Tests* New Zealand (1955/6 to 1965/6, 14 matches).
Career batting
115–189–34–2788–151–17.98–2–*ct* 197–*st* 37
Bowling 16–0
Test batting
14–25–5–258–55–12.90–0–*ct* 25
He was most successful on the 1958 tour to England, playing in all five Tests and appearing for the Gentlemen v Players.

Pettiford, John
Professional. *b:* 29.11.1919, Freshwater, Sydney, New South Wales, Australia. *d:* 11.10.1964, North Sydney, New South Wales, Australia. Middle order right-hand batsman, leg break and googly bowler. *Teams* New South Wales (1946/7 to 1947/8, 16 matches); Kent (1954–59, 153 matches). *Tours* Australian Services to England 1945, to India and Ceylon 1945/6; Commonwealth to India and Pakistan 1949/50.
Career batting
201–324–48–7077–133–25.64–4–*ct* 99
Bowling 9259–295–31.38–7–1–6/134
He hit 1,000 runs in a season twice (best 1,336, av 28.42, in 1955).

Pettit, David William
Amateur. *b:* 24.3.1937, Canterbury, Kent. *d:* 28.5.1990, Greta West, Victoria, Australia. Tail end right-hand batsman, right-arm fast medium bowler. *Sch* St Edmund's, Canterbury. *Team* Oxford U (1958–59).
Career batting
5–7–4–33–22–11.00–0–*ct* 0
Bowling 432–6–72.00–0–0–2/72

Pevensey, Viscount, Henry North Holroyd
(later 3rd Earl of Sheffield)
Amateur. *b:* 18.1.1832, Marylebone, London. *d:* 21.4.1909, Beaulieu, France. Uncle of A. Harcourt (Sheffield's XI). Middle order batsman. *Sch* Eton. *Team* Sussex (1854, 1 match).
Career batting
1–2–0–0–0–0.00–0–*ct* 0
He was the greatest patron Sussex cricket ever had, being President of the County Club from 1879 to 1896 and 1904. In 1891/2 he financed the English tour to Australia and opened his private ground at Sheffield Park in 1864. The Sheffield Shield was named after him. He was MP for East Sussex, 1857 to 1865.

Pewtress, Alfred William
Amateur. *b:* 27.8.1891, Rawtenstall, Lancashire. *d:* 21.9.1960, Brighton, Sussex. Middle order right-hand batsman, bowler. *Sch* Christ's Hospital and Manchester GS. *Team* Lancashire (1919–25, 50 matches).
Career batting
50–73–5–1483–89–21.80–0–*ct* 16
Bowling 10–1–10.00–0–0–1/10

Pfaff, David Brian
Cricketer. *b:* 26.6.1965, Cape Town, South Africa. Brother of M. W. (Northern Transvaal), son of B. D. (Western Province). Middle order left-hand batsman, right-arm medium pace bowler. *Team* Oxford U (1991, blue).
Career batting
8–7–2–231–50–46.20–0–*ct* 4
Bowling 6–0
He played hockey for South Africa.

Phadkar, Dattatraya Gajanan
Professional. *b:* 12.12.1925, Kolhapur, Poona, India. *d:* 17.3.1985, Madras, India. Attacking middle order right-hand batsman, right-arm fast medium or off break bowler. *Teams* Maharashtra (1942/3 to 1943/4); Bombay (1944/5 to 1951/2); Hindus (1944/5 to 1945/6); Bengal (1954/5 to 1957/8); Railways (1958/9 to 1959/60); Combined XI in Ceylon 1949/50. *Tours* India to Australia 1947/8, to England 1952, to West Indies 1952/3, to Pakistan 1954/5. *Tests* India (1947/8 to 1958/9, 31 matches).
Career batting
133–178–29–5377–217–36.08–8–*ct* 92
Bowling 10272–466–22.04–31–3–7/26
Test batting
31–45–7–1229–123–32.34–2–*ct* 21
Bowling 2285–62–36.85–3–0–7/159

Pheasant, Steven Thomas

Although he played in all four Tests on the 1952 tour of England, his all-round record was a modest one. His only double century was 217 for Bombay v Maharashtra at Bombay in 1950/1. His final first-class match in England was for a Commonwealth XI in 1957.

Pheasant, Steven Thomas
Cricketer. *b:* 25.6.1951, Borough, London. Lower order right-hand batsman, left-arm medium pace bowler. *Team* Sussex (1971, 1 match).
Career batting
1–2–1–2–2*–2.00–0–*ct* 2
Bowling 121–4–30.25–0–0–4/88

Phebey, Arthur Henry
Professional. *b:* 1.10.1924, Catford, Kent. Stylish opening right-hand batsman, good field. *Team* Kent (1946–61, 320 matches).
Career batting
327–599–34–14643–157–25.91–13–*ct* 205
Bowling 4–0

He hit 1,000 runs in a season nine times (best 1,800, av 33.33, in 1959). His final first-class match was for MCC in 1964. He was a member of Kent CCC Committee 1983–91. A good soccer player, he appeared at inside right for Dulwich Hamlet and Hendon and was a schoolboy international.

Phelan, Patrick John
Professional. *b:* 9.2.1938, Chingford, Essex. Lower order left-hand batsman, off break bowler. *Team* Essex (1958–65, 154 matches).
Career batting
160–199–71–1693–63–13.22–0–*ct* 67
Bowling 9006–314–28.68–17–2–8/109

He also played for Cambridgeshire (1986), making his debut aged 48.

Phelps, Peter Horsley
Amateur. *b:* 5.2.1909, Malvern, Worcestershire. *d:* 5.10.1986, Earlswood, Redhill, Surrey. Lower order right-hand batsman, right-arm medium pace bowler. *Sch* Felsted. *Team* Worcestershire (1931–32, 3 matches).
Career batting
3–4–0–25–11–6.25–0–*ct* 1

Philip, Iain Lindsay
Cricketer. *b:* 9.6.1958, Falkirk, Stirlingshire, Scotland. Opening right-hand batsman, slow left-arm bowler, wicket-keeper. *Team* Scotland (1986–92).
Career batting
7–11–1–574–145–57.40–3–*ct* 7

He scored 145 on his first-class debut v Ireland at Glasgow in 1986.

Philips, Stanley Ian
Amateur. *b:* 4.2.1920, Tunbridge Wells, Kent. Stylish middle order right-hand batsman, right-arm medium pace bowler. *Sch* Brighton. *Teams* Northamptonshire (1938–39, 6 matches); Europeans (1941/2).
Career batting
7–14–3–156–42–14.18–0–*ct* 3
Bowling 15–0

He appeared in wartime matches for Oxford University. On his first-class debut for Northamptonshire he still had another year at school to complete.

Philipson, Hylton
(birth registered as Hilton Philipson)
Amateur. *b:* 8.6.1866, Tynemouth, Northumberland. *d:* 4.12.1935, Westminster, London. Uncle of M. Woosnam (Cambridge U). Middle or lower order right-hand batsman, wicket-keeper. *Sch* Eton. *Teams* Oxford U (1887–89, blue all three years); Middlesex (1895–98, 10 matches). *Tours* Vernon to Ceylon and India 1889/90 (not first-class); Sheffield to Australia 1891/2; Stoddart to Australia 1894/5. *Tests* England (1891/2 to 1894/5, 5 matches).
Career batting
85–139–27–1951–150–17.41–2–*ct* 103–*st* 47
Test batting
5–8–1–63–30–9.00–0–*ct* 8–*st* 3

His final first-class match was for A. J. Webbe's XI in 1899. He also played for Northumberland (1884–93). He captained Oxford in 1889. An all-round sportsman, he represented Oxford at rackets, royal tennis and soccer, being a full back in 1889.

Phillip, Norbert
Cricketer. *b:* 12.6.1948, Bioche, Dominica. Hard hitting middle order right-hand batsman, right-arm fast medium bowler. *Teams* Windward Islands (1969/70 to 1984/5); Essex (1978–85, 144 matches). *Tour* West Indies to India and Sri Lanka 1978/9. *Tests* West Indies (1977/8 to 1978/9, 9 matches).
Career batting
230–334–37–7013–134–23.61–1–*ct* 75
Bowling 17032–688–24.75–30–2–7/33
Test batting
9–15–5–297–47–29.70–0–*ct* 5
Bowling 1041–28–37.17–0–0–4/48

His best season was 1982 with 82 wickets, av 22.46.

Phillips, Alan Geoffrey
Amateur. *b:* 27.3.1931, Blackburn, Lancashire. Middle order right-hand batsman, leg break bowler. *Sch* Shrewsbury. *Team* Oxford U (1953–54).
Career batting
3–5–0–71–31–14.20–0–*ct* 1

His County cricket was for Shropshire (1960).

Phillips, Edmund Frederick
Professional. *b:* 12.1.1932, Bridgnorth, Shropshire. Middle order right-hand batsman. *Team* Leicestershire (1957–59, 32 matches).
Career batting
32–54–7–629–55–13.38–0–*ct* 10

Phillips, Edward Stone
Amateur. *b:* 18.1.1883, Ffrwd Vale, Newport, Monmouthshire. *d:* 8.5.1915, near Ypres, Belgium. Brother of G. C. (Europeans). Middle order right-hand batsman. *Sch* Marlborough. *Team* Cambridge U (1903–04, blue 1904).
Career batting
10–18–0–422–107–23.44–1–*ct* 3
His County cricket was for Monmouthshire (1901–14).

Phillips, Francis Ashley
Amateur. *b:* 11.4.1873, Crumlin Hall, Monmouthshire. *d:* 5.3.1955, Kingsland, Herefordshire. Brother of N. C. (MCC). Free-scoring middle order right-hand batsman, right-arm medium pace bowler, fine deep field. *Sch* Rossall. *Teams* Oxford U (1892–95, blue 1892, 1894 and 1895); Somerset (1897–1911, 67 matches). *Tour* Mitchell to North America 1895.
Career batting
108–193–7–4310–163–23.17–4–*ct* 65–*st* 2
Bowling 390–7–55.71–0–0–2/8
He also played for Essex (pre first-class, 1892), Monmouthshire (1894) and Brecon (1911). His final first-class match was for H. K. Foster's XI in 1919.

Phillips, Henry
Professional. *b:* 14.10.1844, Hastings, Sussex. *d:* 3.7.1919, Clive Vale, Hastings, Sussex. Brother of James (Sussex). Middle order right-hand batsman, left-hand slow round-arm bowler, excellent wicket-keeper. *Team* Sussex (1868–91, 195 matches).
Career batting
216–366–75–2998–111–10.30–1–*ct* 341–*st* 194
Bowling 283–14–20.21–0–0–4/33

Phillips, Howard William
Professional. *b:* 20.4.1872, Isle of Wight. *d:* 17.3.1960, East London, South Africa. Opening batsman, useful bowler. *Teams* Hampshire (1899–1902, 5 matches); Border (1906/7 to 1913/14).
Career batting
17–31–2–276–47–9.51–0–*ct* 12
Bowling 162–2–81.00–0–0–1/10

Phillips, Hugh Raymond
Amateur. *b:* 8.4.1929, Kuala Lumpur, Malaya. Middle order right-hand batsman. *Sch* Wellingborough. *Team* Warwickshire (1951, 1 match).
Career batting
1–1–0–3–3–3.00–0–*ct* 0

Phillips, James
Professional. *b:* 26.9.1849, Hastings, Sussex. *d:* 31.1.1905, Old Town, Hastings, Sussex. Brother of Henry (Sussex). Middle order right-hand batsman, good field. *Team* Sussex (1871–86, 64 matches).
Career batting
73–137–6–1931–89–14.74–0–*ct* 67
His final first-class match was for an England XI in 1888.

Phillips, James
Professional. *b:* 1.9.1860. Pleasant Creek, South Australia. *d:* 21.4.1930, Burnaby, Vancouver, British Columbia, Canada. Lower order right-hand batsman, right-arm medium pace bowler, good cover point. *Teams* Victoria (1885/6 to 1895/6, 17 matches); Middlesex (1890–98, 90 matches); Canterbury (1898/9).
Career batting
124–203–58–1827–110*–12.60–1–*ct* 50
Bowling 7102–355–20.00–30–7–8/69
He was best known as an umpire and due to his actions, above all, the prevalence of 'throwing' among bowlers in the 1890s was stamped out – notably he no-balled the Australian, Ernest Jones, for throwing in 1897/8 and later, in England, A. W. Mold of Lancashire. He was a first-class umpire until 1905, standing in 29 Test matches in three countries.

Phillips, John Burton
Amateur. *b:* 19.11.1933, Canterbury, Kent. Tail end right-hand batsman, right-arm fast medium bowler. *Sch* King's, Canterbury. *Teams* Oxford U (1955–57, blue 1955); Kent (1955, 4 matches).
Career batting
32–43–15–151–25–5.39–0–*ct* 9
Bowling 2567–72–35.65–1–0–5/62

Phillips, Dr Joseph Evelyn
Amateur. *b:* 28.7.1891, Kendal Plantation, St John, Barbados. *d:* 10.12.1958, Edinburgh, Scotland. Middle order right-hand batsman, right-arm medium pace bowler. *Teams* Barbados (1919/20); Scotland (1923).
Career batting
4–6–0–52–25–8.66–0–*ct* 4
Bowling 118–2–59.00–0–0–1/15

Phillips, Joseph Herbert
Amateur. *b:* 2.12.1881, Ansley Hall, Warwickshire. *d:* 15.1.1951, Oldbury Grange, Nuneaton, Warwickshire. Lower order right-hand batsman, right-arm fast bowler. *Team* Warwickshire (1904–11, 6 matches).
Career batting
6–7–0–35–16–5.00–0–*ct* 5
Bowling 159–1–159.00–0–0–1/30
His grandson is Mark Phillips, former husband of HRH The Princess Royal.

Phillips, Leslie Jack
Amateur. *b:* 20.1.1899, Leyton, Essex. *d:* 22.4.1979, Woodford Wells, Essex. Middle order right-hand batsman, slow left-arm bowler. *Sch* Forest. *Team* Essex (1919–22, 4 matches).
Career batting
4–5–1–38–19–9.50–0–*ct* 0
Bowling 31–0

Phillips, Noel Clive
Amateur. *b:* 30.7.1883, Maindee, Newport, Monmouthshire. *d:* 15.8.1961, Colwall, Herefordshire. Brother of F. A. (Somerset). Attacking middle order right-hand batsman. *Sch* Marlborough. *Teams* MCC (1908); South Wales (1912).
Career batting
6–11–0–188–62–17.09–0–*ct* 4
His final first-class match was for Free Foresters in 1921. His County cricket was for Monmouthshire (1901–24).

Phillips, Raymond Berry
Cricketer. *b:* 23.5.1954, Paddington, Sydney, New South Wales, Australia. Middle order right-hand batsman, wicket-keeper. *Teams* New South Wales (1978/9, 3 matches); Queensland (1979/80 to 1985/6, 78 matches). *Tour* Australia to England 1985.
Career batting
89–129–28–2925–111*–28.96–1–*ct* 271–*st* 15
Bowling 11–0
He came to England on the 1985 tour as the reserve wicket-keeper and was the only tourist not selected for a Test.

Phillips, Raymond L.
Amateur. *b: circa* 1900, Jamaica. *d: circa* 1970, Jamaica. Lower order right-hand batsman, slow right-arm bowler. *Team* Jamaica (1925/6 to 1927/8). *Tour* West Indies to England 1923.
Career batting
7–5–1–69–38–17.25–0–*ct* 3
Bowling 622–24–25.91–1–0–5/68
Owing to injury he played in only one first-class match on the 1923 tour.

Phillips, Reginald Maurice
Amateur. *b:* 19.10.1897, Newport, Monmouthshire. *d:* 7.6.1963, Granary, Budleigh Salterton, Devon. *Sch* Shrewsbury. *Team* Wales (1925).
Career batting
1–2–0–13–11–6.50–0–*ct* 0
His County cricket was for Monmouthshire (1914–34).

Phillips, Roy Wycliffe
Cricketer. *b:* 8.4.1941, Holders Hill, St James, Barbados. Middle order right-hand batsman, leg break bowler. *Teams* Barbados (1966/7); Gloucestershire (1968–70, 16 matches).
Career batting
18–28–0–529–92–18.89–0–*ct* 11
Bowling 6–0

Phillips, Walter
Amateur. *b:* 1.4.1881, West Malling, Kent. *d:* 21.6.1948, Mereworth, Kent. Middle order batsman. *Sch* Eastbourne. *Team* Kent (1903, 1 match).
Career batting
2–4–0–83–55–20.75–0–*ct* 2
His final first-class match was for H. D. G. Leveson-Gower's XI in 1912.

Phillips, Wayne Bentley
Cricketer. *b:* 1.3.1958, Adelaide, South Australia. Middle order left-hand batsman, wicket-keeper. *Team* South Australia (1977/8 to 1990/1, 69 matches). *Tours* Australia to Pakistan 1982/3, to West Indies 1983/4, to India 1984/5 (not first-class), to England 1985, to New Zealand 1985/6; Young Australians to Zimbabwe 1982/3. *Tests* Australia (1983/4 to 1985/6, 27 matches).
Career batting
114–199–16–6907–260–37.74–13–*ct* 154–*st* 7
Bowling 13–0
Test batting
27–48–2–1485–159–32.28–2–*ct* 52
The principal wicket-keeper on the 1985 tour to England, he played in all six Tests. As well as proving effective behind the wicket, he also batted well. His highest score was 260 for South Australia v Queensland at Adelaide in 1981/2. He shared a partnership of 462* for the 4th wicket with D. W. Hookes for South Australia v Tasmania at Adelaide in 1986/7, at the time the highest ever partnership in Australian first-class cricket.

Phillips, Wayne Norman
Cricketer. *b:* 7.11.1962, Geelong, Victoria, Australia. Opening right-hand batsman, off break bowler. *Team* Victoria (1988/9 to 1991/2, 37 matches). *Tour* Victoria to England 1991. *Tests* Australia (1991/2, 1 match).
Career batting
39–68–7–2433–134–39.88–5–*ct* 17
Bowling 124–1–124.00–0–0–1/59
Test batting
1–2–0–22–14–11.00–0–*ct* 0
He scored 111 on his first-class debut for Victoria v West Indians at Melbourne in 1988/9.

Phillips, William
Professional. *b:* 15.12.1876, Pendleton, Lancashire. Lower order batsman, wicket-keeper. *Team* Lancashire (1904–08, 10 matches).
Career batting
10–18–3–109–18–7.26–0–*ct* 17–*st* 2
He also played for Cheshire (1902). He was a first-class umpire (1913–30), standing in two Test matches (1921).

Phillipson, Christopher Paul
Cricketer. *b:* 10.2.1952, Vrindaban, India. Tail end, originally, but from about 1975 middle order right-hand batsman, right-arm medium pace bowler. *Sch* Ardingly. *Team* Sussex (1970–86, 168 matches).
Career batting
168–226–61–3052–87–18.49–0–*ct* 137
Bowling 5213–153–34.07–4–0–6/56

Phillipson, William Edward
Professional. *b:* 3.12.1910, North Reddish, Cheshire. *d:* 25.8.1991, Trafford, Lancashire. Middle order right-hand batsman, right-arm fast medium bowler. *Team* Lancashire (1933–48, 158 matches). *Tour* Cahn to New Zealand 1938/9.
Career batting
162–208–49–4096–113–25.76–2–*ct* 82
Bowling 13722–555–24.72–29–6–8/100
He took 100 wickets in a season twice (best 133, av 22.33, in 1939). He also played for Northumberland (1950–52). He was a first-class umpire (1956–78), standing in 12 Test matches (1958–65).

Phipps, Douglas David
Cricketer. *b:* 27.7.1934, Edmonton, Middlesex. Middle order right-hand batsman, right-arm fast medium bowler. *Sch* Mill Hill. *Team* Combined Services (1964).
Career batting
1–2–0–15–15–7.50–0–*ct* 1
Bowling 53–1–53.00–0–0–1/53
His County cricket was for Buckinghamshire (1952–53) and Norfolk (1956–57).

Phipps, Herbert Gould
Amateur. *b:* 8.8.1845, Shepton Mallet, Somerset. *d:* 19.10.1899, Tientsin, China. Twin brother of W. T. (Southgate). Lower order right-hand batsman, right-hand slow medium round-arm bowler, excellent deep field. *Sch* Harrow. *Team* MCC (1865).
Career batting
2–3–1–9–6*–4.50–0–*ct* 0
A merchant in Foochow, China, from about 1870 he had no opportunities to appear in first-class cricket. The brothers were related to Joyce Grenfell, the entertainer.

Phipps, Walter Tudway
Amateur. *b:* 8.8.1845, Shepton Mallet, Somerset. *d:* 28.4.1902, Shanghai, China. Twin brother of H. G. (MCC). Middle order right-hand batsman, right-hand slow round-arm or fast under-arm bowler. *Sch* Harrow. *Team* Southgate (1867–68).
Career batting
2–3–1–44–30–22.00–0–*ct* 1
He did not appear in any first-class matches whilst at Oxford U, but did win a blue for rackets.

Piachaud, James Daniel
Amateur. *b:* 1.3.1937, Colombo, Ceylon. Lower order right-hand batsman, off break bowler, good close field. *Teams* Oxford U (1958–61, blue all four years); Hampshire (1960, 12 matches); Ceylon (1968/9). *Tours* MCC to North America 1959 (non-first-class), to Bangladesh 1976/7 (non-first-class); Swanton to India 1963/4.
Career batting
71–103–18–1037–40–12.20–0–*ct* 53
Bowling 5070–205–24.73–8–1–8/72

Pick, Robert Andrew
Cricketer. *b:* 19.11.1963, Nottingham. Brother-in-law of D. J. Millns (Nottinghamshire and Leicestershire). Lower order left-hand batsman, right-arm fast medium bowler. *Teams* Nottinghamshire (1983–92, 129 matches); Wellington (1989/90). *Tours* England A to Sri Lanka 1990/1, to West Indies 1991/2.
Career batting
138–135–39–1430–63–14.89–0–*ct* 32
Bowling 11521–352–32.73–11–3–7/128

Pickeman, Douglas C.
Amateur. *b: circa* 1900, Ireland. *d:* June 1945, Ireland. Middle order right-hand batsman, leg break bowler. *Team* Ireland (1926).
Career batting
1–2–0–2–2–1.00–0–*ct* 1

Pickering, Arthur
Amateur. *b:* 1878. *d:* 15.12.1939, Cotham, Bristol. Middle order batsman. *Teams* London County (1901); Gloucestershire (1908, 1 match).
Career batting
2–4–0–10–4–2.50–0–*ct* 0
Bowling 20–0

Pickering, Rev Edward Hayes
Amateur. *b:* 21.5.1807, Clapham, London. *d:* 19.5.1852, Eton, Buckinghamshire. Brother of W. P. (Surrey), uncle of F. P. U. (Sussex). Stylish middle order right-hand batsman. *Sch* Eton. *Teams* Cambridge U (1827–29, blue 1827 and 1829); Surrey (1844, 1 match).
Career batting
15–26–3–274–72*–11.91–0–*ct* 4
Bowling 15 wickets (no analyses)–1–0–5/?
A schoolmaster at Eton College, he was unable to spare the time for much cricket after leaving Cambridge. He captained Cambridge in 1829.

Pickering, Francis Percy Umfreville
Amateur. *b:* 4.8.1851, Shipton, York. *d:* 11.3.1879, West Chiltington, Sussex. Nephew of E. H. (Surrey) and W. P. (Surrey). Middle order right-hand batsman, right-hand fast under-arm bowler. *Sch* Eton. *Teams* Oxford U (1873); Sussex (1874–75, 3 matches). *Tour* Fitzgerald to North America 1872 (not first-class).
Career batting
5–7–0–87–24–12.42–0–*ct* 7
Bowling 64–8–8.00–0–0–4/16

Pickering, Harry Gordon
Amateur. *b:* 18.1.1917, Hackney, London. *d:* 4.3.1984, Seaford, Sussex. Middle order right-hand batsman, slow right-arm bowler. *Teams* Essex (1938, 3 matches); Leicestershire (1947, 5 matches).
Career batting
8–16–0–297–79–18.56–0–*ct* 0

Pickering, Peter Barlow
Professional. *b:* 24.3.1926, York. Middle order right-hand batsman, good close field. *Team* Northamptonshire (1953, 1 match).
Career batting
1–2–0–59–37–29.50–0–*ct* 0
He became a first-class umpire in South Africa. A well-known soccer player, he kept goal for Chelsea, York City and Northampton.

Pickering, William Percival
Amateur. *b:* 25.10.1819, Clapham, London. *d:* 16.8.1905, Vancouver, British Columbia, Canada. Brother of E. H. (Cambridge U and Surrey), uncle of F. P. U. (Sussex). Middle order right-hand batsman, left-hand medium pace round-arm bowler, brillant cover point. *Sch* Eton. *Teams* Cambridge U (1840–42, blue 1840 and 1842); Cambridge Town Club (1843); Surrey (1844–48, 3 matches).
Career batting
30–53–6–544–76*–11.57–0–*ct* 17
Bowling 35–0 + 7–no av–0–0–3/?
He could throw in with either hand. He emigrated to Montreal in 1852 and was chief organiser of the 1859 pioneering tour by the English side to Canada.

Pickett, Christopher Arthur
Amateur. *b:* 26.8.1926, Hedgerley, Buckinghamshire. Lower order left-hand batsman, left-arm fast, or slow, bowler. *Team* Minor Counties (1953).
Career batting
1–2–1–10–7*–10.00–0–*ct* 0
Bowling 54–0
His County cricket was for Buckinghamshire (1949–71).

Pickett, Henry
Professional. *b:* 26.3.1862, Stratford, Essex. *d:* 3.10.1907, Aberavon, Glamorgan. He disappeared from his home on September 27th and his body was found on the beach but not identified until December. Lower order right-hand batsman, right-arm fast bowler. *Team* Essex (1894–97, 52 matches).
Career batting
62–94–38–450–35–8.03–0–*ct* 25
Bowling 3269–134–24.39–4–1–10/32
His career with Essex began in 1881 and he made his first-class debut in 1884 for MCC. His best bowling in an innings was 10/32 for Essex v Leicestershire at Leyton in 1895. He was a first-class umpire (1899–1901).

Pickles, Christopher Stephen
Cricketer. *b:* 30.1.1966, Mirfield, Yorkshire. Middle order right-hand batsman, right-arm medium pace bowler. *Team* Yorkshire (1985–92, 58 matches).
Career batting
58–76–21–1336–66–24.29–0–*ct* 24
Bowling 3638–83–43.83–0–0–4/40

Pickles, David
Professional. *b:* 16.11.1935, Halifax, Yorkshire. Lower order right-hand batsman, right-arm fast medium bowler. *Team* Yorkshire (1957–60, 41 matches).
Career batting
41–40–20–74–12–3.70–0–*ct* 10
Bowling 2062–96–21.47–4–1–7/61

Pickles, Lewis
Professional. *b:* 17.9.1932, Wakefield, Yorkshire. Opening right-hand batsman, off break bowler, close field. *Team* Somerset (1955–58, 47 matches).
Career batting
47–88–5–1702–87–20.50–0–*ct* 21
Bowling 65–1–65.00–0–0–1/22
He hit 1,136 runs, av 24.69, in 1956.

Picknell, George
Professional. *b:* 29.11.1813, Chalvington, Sussex. *d:* 26.2.1863, Chalvington, Sussex. He died following the amputation of his leg. Brother of Robert (Sussex). Powerful middle order right-hand batsman, right-hand fast round-arm bowler. *Team* Sussex (1836–54, 63 matches).
Career batting
81–146–16–1661–79–12.77–0–*ct* 48
Bowling 498–33 + 35–15.09–4–0–6/?

Picknell, Robert
Professional. *b:* 2.6.1816, Chalvington, Sussex. *d:* 7.2.1869, Eastbourne, Sussex. Brother of George (Sussex). Middle order right-hand batsman, excellent cover point. *Team* Sussex (1837–45, 18 matches).
Career batting
18–34–1–182–23–5.51–0–*ct* 5

Pickthall, Harold
Professional. *b:* 31.7.1896, Burnley, Lancashire. *d:* 8.8.1965, Fulwood, Preston, Lancashire. Lower order batsman, good bowler. *Team* MCC (1928–35).
Career batting
12–16–6–109–29*–10.90–0–*ct* 3
Bowling 772–25–30.88–0–0–4/30
His County cricket was for Monmouthshire (1926–29).

Pickup, James Kenneth
Cricketer. *b:* 25.9.1952, Stalybridge, Cheshire. Middle order right-hand batsman, wicket-keeper. *Sch* Kings, Macclesfield. *Team* Oxford U (1973–75).
Career batting
3–6–0–19–14–3.16–0–*ct* 1
His County cricket was for Cheshire (1972–85).

Pidcock, Charles Alexander
Amateur. *b:* 27.8.1850, Bareilly, India. *d:* 28.10.1901, Hastings, Sussex. Lower order right-hand batsman, wicket-keeper. *Sch* Harrow. *Team* An England XI (1872).
Career batting
1–1–0–12–12–12.00–0–*ct* 0

He was for some years a Civil Commissioner in Matabeleland, Rhodesia.

Pienaar, Roy Francois
Cricketer. *b:* 17.7.1961, Johannesburg, South Africa. Middle order right-hand batsman, right-arm medium fast bowler. *Teams* Transvaal (1977/8 to 1991/2); Western Province (1981/2 to 1984/5); Northern Transvaal (1985/6 to 1987/8); Kent (1987–89, 45 matches).
Career batting
155–266–21–8777–153–35.82–17–*ct* 66
Bowling 4854–146–33.24–3–0–5/24
He was engaged by Kent mid-way through 1987 when Baptiste suffered a serious injury. His only two full seasons in English cricket were 1988 and 1989 when he scored 1,228 runs, av 37.21, and 1,321 runs, av 52.84, respectively. A knee operation restricted his bowling in 1989. He appeared for South Africa in unofficial Tests. He scored 1,010 runs, av 63.12, in South Africa 1989/90.

Pieris, Percival Ian
Amateur. *b:* 14.3.1933, Colombo, Ceylon. Middle order right-hand batsman, right-arm medium pace bowler. *Teams* Cambridge U (1956–58, blue 1957–58); Ceylon (1964/5 to 1966/7). *Tours* Ceylon to India 1966/7, to Pakistan 1966/7.
Career batting
44–66–13–917–55*–17.30–0–*ct* 14
Bowling 3530–101–34.95–4–1–6/30

Pierpoint, Frederick George
Professional. *b:* 24.4.1915, Walworth, London. Lower order right-hand batsman, right-arm fast medium bowler. *Team* Surrey (1936–46, 8 matches).
Career batting
8–11–7–15–4–3.75–0–*ct* 3
Bowling 592–13–45.53–0–0–3/60
He also played for Norfolk (1947–49) and Devon (1951).

Pierre, Lancelot Richard
Amateur. *b:* 5.6.1921, Woodbrook, Port of Spain, Trinidad. *d:* 14.4.1989, Port of Spain, Trinidad. Tail end right-hand batsman, right-arm fast medium bowler. *Team* Trinidad (1940/1 to 1949/50). *Tour* West Indies to England 1950. *Test* West Indies (1947/8, 1 match).
Career batting
35–35–14–131–23–6.23–0–*ct* 14
Bowling 2522–102–24.72–4–0–8/51
Test batting
1 match, did not bat – *ct* 0
Bowling 28–0
Due to injury he played only 12 first-class matches on the 1950 tour and no Tests.

Pierson, Adrian Roger Kirshaw
Cricketer. *b:* 21.7.1963, Enfield, Middlesex. Lower order right-hand batsman, off break bowler. *Team* Warwickshire (1985–91, 57 matches).
Career batting
57–64–29–427–42*–12.20–0–*ct* 17
Bowling 3753–85–44.15–3–0–6/82
He also played for Cambridgeshire (1992).

Pigg, Charles
Amateur. *b:* 4.9.1856, Buntingford, Hertfordshire. *d:* 28.2.1929, Lansdown, Cheltenham, Gloucestershire. Twin brother of Herbert (Cambridge U). Free hitting lower order right-hand batsman, right-hand slow round-arm bowler. *Team* Cambridge U (1877–79).
Career batting
17–27–5–300–48–13.63–0–*ct* 10
Bowling 151–6–25.16–0–0–1/0
His first-class debut was for An England XI in 1876, and his last first-class match was for MCC in 1901. For Hertfordshire v Northamptonshire in 1880 he took all ten wickets (for 13). His County cricket was for Northamptonshire (pre first-class, 1874–82), Hertfordshire (1877–1901) and Cambridgeshire (1903–11). He also won a blue for golf.

Pigg, Herbert
Amateur. *b:* 4.9.1856, Buntingford, Hertforshire. *d:* 8.6.1913, Manitoba, Canada. Twin brother of Charles (Cambridge U). Lower order right-hand batsman, right-arm fast round-arm bowler. *Team* Cambridge U (1877–78, blue 1877).
Career batting
15–29–4–363–59–14.52–0–*ct* 8
Bowling 579–28–20.67–1–1–7/55
His County cricket was for Northamptonshire (pre first-class, 1874–82) and Hertfordshire (1876–97). His final first-class match was for the Gentlemen in 1891. The brothers were generally known as Hot and Cold Pigg.

Piggott, Julian Ito
Amateur. *b:* 25.3.1888, Tokyo, Japan. *d:* 23.1.1965, Coldharbour, Dorking, Surrey. Middle order right-hand batsman. *Sch* Cheltenham. *Team* Surrey (1910–13, 3 matches).
Career batting
3–5–1–153–84–38.25–0–*ct* 5
He appeared in the Freshmen's and Seniors' matches at Cambridge but no first-class games.

Pigot, David Richard (sen)
Amateur. *b:* 14.1.1900, Dublin, Ireland. *d:* 10.8.1965, Sandymount, Dublin, Ireland. Brother of J. P. M. (Dublin University), father of D. R. jun (Ireland). Opening right-hand batsman, right-arm fast medium bowler. *Teams* Dublin University (1922–26); Ireland (1922–39).

Pigot, David Richard (jun)

Career batting
11–22–0–338–51–15.36–0–*ct* 4
Bowling 29–0

Pigot, David Richard (jun)
Cricketer. *b:* 18.7.1929, Dublin, Ireland. Son of D. R. sen (Ireland), nephew of J. P. M. (Dublin University). Opening right-hand batsman. *Team* Ireland (1966–75).
Career batting
11–21–0–406–88–19.33–0–*ct* 8

Pigot, James Poole Maunsell
Amateur. *b:* 31.1.1901, Dublin, Ireland. *d:* 20.7.1980, Glengeary, Dublin, Ireland. Brother of D. R. sen (Ireland), uncle of D. R. jun (Ireland). Lower order right-hand batsman, leg break and googly bowler. *Teams* Dublin University (1924–25); Europeans (1925/6 to 1929/30).
Career batting
5–9–1–67–50–8.37–0–*ct* 3
Bowling 184–4–46.00–0–0–3/71

Pigott, Anthony Charles Shackleton
Cricketer. *b:* 4.6.1958, Fulham, London. Lower order right-hand batsman, right-arm fast medium bowler. *Sch* Harrow. *Teams* Sussex (1978–92, 220 matches); Wellington (1982/3 to 1983/4). *Tours* Robins to New Zealand 1979/80; England to New Zealand 1983/4. *Test* England (1983/4, 1 match).
Career batting
234–282–63–4452–104*–20.32–1–*ct* 115
Bowling 18426–600–30.71–23–1–7/74
Test batting
1–2–1–12–8*–12.00–0–*ct* 0
Bowling 75–2–37.50–0–0–2/75

He took 74 wickets, av 28.08, in 1988. He was playing domestic cricket in New Zealand in 1983/4 when the touring English side was badly affected by injury and was co-opted into the team for the Second Test, having to postpone his wedding to play.

Pike, Arthur
Professional. *b:* 25.12.1862, Keyworth, Nottinghamshire. *d:* 15.11.1907, Keyworth, Nottinghamshire. Lower order right-hand batsman, wicket-keeper. *Team* Nottinghamshire (1894–99, 65 matches).
Career batting
66–101–20–1128–66–13.92–0–*ct* 102–*st* 30

His final first-class match was for MCC in 1901. From 1902 to 1906 he was on the first-class umpires' list, but then was compelled by ill-health to retire.

Pilch, Fuller
Professional. *b:* 17.3.1804, Horningtoft, Norfolk. *d:* 1.5.1870, Canterbury, Kent. Brother of Nathaniel (Norfolk) and William (Norfolk), uncle of William (Kent). Brilliant middle order right-hand batsman, right-hand slow round-arm bowler. *Teams* Norfolk (1820–36); Surrey (1830–44, 2 matches as given man); Cambridge Town Club (1832); Kent (1836–54, 84 matches); Sussex (1837–42, 5 matches as given man); Hampshire (1842–45, 5 matches as given man).
Career batting
229–416–32–7147–153*–18.61–3–*ct* 121
Bowling 184–9 + 133–20.44–3–0–7/?

For a period of about 15 years commencing in the early 1830s, Pilch was the premier batsman in England. Haygarth, writing in 1862, described Pilch as 'the best batsman that has ever yet appeared'. Haygarth went on: 'his style of batting was very commanding, extremely forward, and he seemed to crush the best bowling by his long forward plunge before it had time to shoot, or rise, or do mischief by catches.' He also played for Suffolk (1847).

Pilch, William
Professional. *b:* 18.6.1820, Brinton, Norfolk. *d:* 11.1.1882, Canterbury, Kent. Son of Nathaniel (Norfolk), nephew of Fuller (Kent) and William (Norfolk). Middle order right-hand batsman, useful bowler, excellent long-stop. *Team* Kent (1840–54, 44 matches).
Career batting
52–100–11–718–38–8.06–0–*ct* 33
Bowling 32–5 + 12–6.40–0–0–3/7

He won his place in the County side mainly due to his long-stopping. His final first-class match was in 1857 for Kent and Sussex. He also played for Norfolk (1842–44).

Pilkington, Alfred Frederick
Professional. *b:* 22.4.1901, Camberwell, London. *d:* 27.8.1986, Epsom, Surrey. Tail end batsman, right-arm medium pace bowler. *Team* Surrey (1926, 1 match).
Career batting
1–1–0–4–4–4.00–0–*ct* 0
Bowling 29–1–29.00–0–0–1/29

He played soccer for Fulham and won an Amateur Cup winners medal with Dulwich Hamlet in 1920.

Pilkington, Charles Carlisle
Amateur. *b:* 13.12.1876, Woolton, Liverpool, Lancashire. *d:* 8.1.1950, South Warnborough Manor, Hampshire. Brother of H. C. (Middlesex), father of T. A. (MCC to South America). Stylish middle order right-hand batsman, right-arm medium pace bowler. *Sch* Eton. *Teams* Lancashire (1895, 2 matches); Oxford U (1896, blue); Middlesex (1903, 2 matches).
Career batting
13–20–1–468–86–24.63–0–*ct* 6
Bowling 370–9–41.11–0–0–3/70

Regarded as a most gifted all-rounder, he played very rarely in first-class cricket. His final first-class match was for Gentlemen of England in 1919.

Pilkington, Hubert Carlisle
Amateur. *b:* 23.10.1879, Woolton, Liverpool, Lancashire. *d:* 17.6.1942, Letchworth, Hertfordshire. Brother of C. C. (Lancashire and Middlesex), uncle of T. A. (MCC to South America), son-in-law of C. F. H. Leslie (Middlesex), brother-in-law of J. Leslie (Oxford U). Stylish middle order right-hand batsman, right-arm slow bowler, good field. *Sch* Eton. *Teams* Oxford U (1899–1900, blue both years); Middlesex (1903–04, 4 matches).
Career batting
20–30–2–688–93–24.57–0–*ct* 7
Bowling 16–0

Pillans, Albert Alexander
Amateur. *b:* 25.2.1869, Dickoya, Ceylon. *d:* 28.11.1901, Maskeliya, Ceylon. He died of peritonitis. Middle/lower order batsman, good bowler, moderate field. *Team* Hampshire (1896, 3 matches).
Career batting
3–6–2–82–32*–20.50–0–*ct* 0
Bowling 151–6–25.16–0–0–2/31

Pilling, Harry
Cricketer. *b:* 23.2.1943, Ashton-under-Lyne, Lancashire. Sound middle order right-hand batsman, off break bowler. *Team* Lancashire (1962–80, 323 matches). *Tours* Robins to Sri Lanka 1977/8; Commonwealth to Pakistan 1970/1; Rest of World to Pakistan 1973/4.
Career batting
333–542–68–15279–149*–32.23–25–*ct* 89
Bowling 195–1–195.00–0–0–1/42
He hit 1,000 runs in a season eight times (best 1,606 runs, av 36.50, in 1967). He is only 5ft 3in tall.

Pilling, Richard
Professional. *b:* 11.8.1855, Old Warden, Bedfordshire. *d:* 28.3.1891, Old Trafford, Manchester, Lancashire. Brother of William (Lancashire). Lower order right-hand batsman, splendid wicket-keeper. *Team* Lancashire (1877–89, 177 matches). *Tours* Lillywhite, Shaw and Shrewsbury to Australia 1881/2, 1887/8. *Tests* England (1881/2 to 1888, 8 matches).
Career batting
250–372–111–2572–78–9.85–0–*ct* 459–*st* 208
Test batting
8–13–1–91–23–7.58–0–*ct* 10–*st* 4
He was regarded for several years as the equal of any wicket-keeper in England; his career was brought to an early end when he had inflammation of the lungs following a football match in 1889/90. He was sent to Australia at the expense of Lancashire CCC during the winter of 1890/1, but died six days after returning home.

Pilling, William
Professional. *b:* 5.11.1857, Church, Lancashire. *d:* 27.3.1924, Trafford Park, Stretford, Manchester, Lancashire. Brother of Richard (Lancashire). Lower order batsman, wicket-keeper. *Team* Lancashire (1891, 1 match).
Career batting
1–1–1–9–9*–no av–0–*ct* 1–*st* 1

Pinch, Francis Brewster
Amateur. *b:* 24.2.1891, Bodmin, Cornwall. *d:* 8.10.1961, Ashford, Kent. Middle order right-hand batsman, right-arm medium pace bowler. *Teams* Glamorgan (1921–26, 41 matches); Wales (1924).
Career batting
42–73–5–1082–138*–15.91–1–*ct* 25
Bowling 1265–39–32.43–0–0–4/48
On his first-class debut, for Glamorgan v Worcestershire at Swansea in 1921, he hit 138*. He first played for Glamorgan (pre first-class) in 1920.

Pinder, George
(real name George Pinder Hattersley)
Professional. *b:* 15.7.1841, Ecclesfield, Sheffield, Yorkshire. *d:* 15.1.1903, Hickleton, Yorkshire. Hard hitting lower order right-hand batsman, slow underarm bowler, wicket-keeper. *Team* Yorkshire (1867–80, 124 matches). *Tour* Daft to North America 1879 (not first-class).
Career batting
179–286–66–2415–78–10.97–0–*ct* 221–*st* 136
Bowling 481–23–20.91–0–0–4/56
His final first-class match was for T. Emmett's XI in 1881.

Pinfield, Reginald Gordon Cecil
Amateur. *b:* 31.12.1894, Chippenham, Wiltshire. *d:* 2.2.1972, Branksome, Dorset. Middle order batsman. *Team* Sussex (1922, 4 matches).
Career batting
4–7–1–97–42*–16.16–0–*ct* 6
He also played for Wiltshire (1911–20).

Pink, Alfred
Professional. *b:* 1.6.1853, Fratton Bridge, Portsmouth, Hampshire. *d:* 12.1.1931, Portsmouth, Hampshire. Middle or lower order right-hand batsman, right-arm medium pace bowler, close field. *Team* Hampshire (1885, 1 match).
Career batting
1–2–0–54–39–27.00–0–*ct* 0
Bowling 15–1–15.00–0–0–1/15

Pink, Hubert Selwyn
Amateur. *b:* 12.11.1878, Chapel-en-le-Frith, Derbyshire. *d:* 25.11.1946, Chapel-en-le-Frith, Derbyshire. Middle order right-hand batsman. *Sch* St Edmunds, Canterbury. *Team* Derbyshire (1900, 3 matches).
Career batting
3–5–0–24–11–4.80–0–*ct* 0
Bowling 33–0
He played no first-class matches at Cambridge U.

Pinner, William Gladstone
Amateur. *b:* 26.9.1877, Wednesbury, Staffordshire. *d:* 6.7.1944, Wednesbury, Staffordshire. Lower order batsman, useful bowler. *Team* Northamptonshire (1908, 1 match).
Career batting
1–2–1–26–24–26.00–0–*ct* 0
Bowling 17–0
He first played for Northamptonshire (pre first-class) in 1900.

Pinnock, Renford Augustus
Cricketer. *b:* 26.9.1937, Spanish Town, Jamaica. Middle order right-hand batsman, wicket-keeper. *Team* Jamaica (1963/4 to 1974/5). *Tour* Jamaica to England 1970.
Career batting
44–71–5–2662–176–40.33–6–*ct* 26–*st* 5
Bowling 52–1–52.00–0–0–1/25
He was most successful on the 1970 tour with 321 runs, av 80.25.

Piper, Keith John
Cricketer. *b:* 18.12.1969, Leicester. Lower order right-hand batsman, wicket-keeper. *Team* Warwickshire (1989–92, 64 matches). *Tour* Warwickshire to South Africa 1991/2.
Career batting
64–85–14–1388–111–19.54–1–*ct* 158–*st* 9
Bowling 57–1–57.00–0–0–1/57

Pitcher, Christopher Michael
Cricketer. *b:* 26.8.1973, Croydon, Surrey. Lower order right-hand batsman, right-arm medium pace bowler. *Sch* St Edward's, Oxford. *Team* Cambridge U (1992, blue).
Career batting
6–8–3–62–32*–12.40–0–*ct* 0
Bowling 453–3–151.00–0–0–1/35

Pitchford, Harry
Professional. *b:* 11.2.1891, Wing, Buckinghamshire. *d:* 11.7.1965, Aylesbury, Buckinghamshire. Brother of Leonard (Glamorgan). Middle order right-hand batsman, right-arm slow bowler. *Team* Minor Counties (1928).
Career batting
1–2–0–36–24–18.00–0–*ct* 0
Bowling 9–0
His County cricket was for Buckinghamshire (1913–29).

Pitchford, Leonard
Professional. *b:* 4.12.1900, Wing, Buckinghamshire. *d:* 10.5.1992, Clydach, Glamorgan. Brother of Harry (Minor Counties). Middle order right-hand batsman. *Team* Glamorgan (1935, 2 matches).
Career batting
2–3–1–24–14*–12.00–0–*ct* 0
Bowling 4–0
He also played for Monmouthshire (1933–34).

Pithey, Anthony John
Amateur. *b:* 17.7.1933, Umtali, Rhodesia. Brother of D. B. (Northamptonshire and South Africa). Sound opening right-hand batsman. *Teams* Rhodesia (1950/1 to 1968/9); Western Province (1955/6 to 1957/8). *Tours* South Africa to England 1960, to Australia and New Zealand 1963/4. *Tests* South Africa (1956/7 to 1964/5, 17 matches).
Career batting
124–213–16–7073–170–35.90–13–*ct* 59
Bowling 17–0
Test batting
17–27–1–819–154–31.50–1–*ct* 3
Bowling 5–0
He appeared in two Tests on the 1960 tour to England and in first-class matches scored 614 runs, av 27.90.

Pithey, David Bartlett
Amateur. *b:* 4.10.1936, Salisbury, Rhodesia. Brother of A. J. (South Africa). Forceful opening or middle order right-hand batsman, off break bowler. *Teams* Rhodesia (1956/7 to 1965/6); Western Province (1957/8); Oxford U (1960–62, blue 1961 and 1962); Northamptonshire (1962, 3 matches); Natal (1966/7); Transvaal (1967/8). *Tour* South Africa to Australia and New Zealand 1963/4. *Tests* South Africa (1963/4 to 1966/7, 8 matches).
Career batting
99–160–13–3420–166–23.26–3–*ct* 55
Bowling 7388–240–30.78–13–1–7/47
Test batting
8–12–1–138–55–12.54–0–*ct* 6
Bowling 577–12–48.08–1–0–6/58
His best season in England was 1961 with 824 runs, av 26.58.

Pitman, Raymond Walter Charles
Professional. *b:* 21.2.1933, Bartley, Hampshire. Middle order right-hand batsman, right-arm medium fast bowler. *Team* Hampshire (1954–59, 50 matches).
Career batting
50–76–8–926–77–13.61–0–*ct* 42
Bowling 68–1–68.00–0–0–1/4

Pitt, John Anthony
Amateur. *b:* 30.1.1939, Dewsbury, Yorkshire. Middle order right-hand batsman, right-arm medium pace bowler. *Team* Combined Services (1957).
Career batting
1–2–1–36–26*–36.00–0–*ct* 1
Bowling 4–0

Pitt, Thomas Alfred
Amateur. *b:* 19.9.1892, Hardingstone, Northamptonshire. *d:* 22.4.1957, Far Cotton, Northampton. Lower order right-hand batsman, right-arm medium pace

bowler. *Team* Northamptonshire (1932–35, 25 matches).
Career batting
25–43–14–207–31*–7.13–0–*ct* 6
Bowling 1563–43–36.34–0–0–4/65

Pitts, George James Stuart
Amateur. *b:* 6.10.1878, St John's, Newfoundland, Canada. *d:* 27.7.1939, Westbrook, Margate, Kent. Tail end right-hand batsman, right-arm fast bowler. *Sch* Merchant Taylors. *Team* Middlesex (1914, 2 matches).
Career batting
2–2–1–14–14–14.00–0–*ct* 0
Bowling 165–6–27.50–0–0–3/36

Place, Winston
Professional. *b:* 7.12.1914, Rawtenstall, Lancashire. Sound opening, later middle order, batsman, right-arm slow bowler, good field. *Team* Lancashire (1937–55, 298 matches). *Tours* MCC to West Indies 1947/8; Commonwealth to India, Pakistan and Ceylon 1949/50. *Tests* England (1947/8, 3 matches).
Career batting
324–487–49–15609–266*–35.63–36–*ct* 190
Bowling 42–1–42.00–0–0–1/2
Test batting
3–6–1–144–107–28.80–1–*ct* 0

He hit 1,000 runs in a season eight times, going on to 2,000 once: 2,501, av 62.52, in 1947. His three double centuries were all for Lancashire, the highest being 266* v Oxford U at Oxford in 1947. He was a first-class umpire (1957).

Platt, George John William
Professional. *b:* 9.6.1881, Richmond, Surrey. *d:* 14.4.1955, Old Hill, Staffordshire. Tail end right-hand batsman, right-arm medium, later off break, bowler. *Team* Surrey (1906–14, 33 matches).
Career batting
35–53–9–421–49–9.56–0–*ct* 28
Bowling 2253–111–20.29–6–1–6/61

For Surrey 2nd XI v Dorset at Dorchester in 1908 he created a Minor Counties Competition record by taking all 10 wickets in a single innings for 15 runs. He also played for Staffordshire (1923–27). He was Worcestershire coach 1946–52.

Platt, Robert Kenworthy
Professional. *b:* 26.12.1932, Holmfirth, Yorkshire. Lower order right-hand batsman, right-arm medium pace bowler. *Teams* Yorkshire (1955–63, 96 matches); Northamptonshire (1964, 2 matches).
Career batting
101–107–49–424–57*–7.31–0–*ct* 38
Bowling 6798–301–22.58–10–3–7/40

Platts, John Thomas Brown Dumelow
Professional. *b:* 23.11.1848, Chellaston, Derbyshire. *d:* 6.8.1898, Derby. Middle order left-hand batsman, right-hand fast, later slow, round-arm bowler. *Team* Derbyshire (1871–84, 90 matches).
Career batting
97–180–6–2237–115–12.85–1–*ct* 56
Bowling 3673–195–18.83–7–0–6/39

His first-class debut was for MCC in 1870 v Nottinghamshire at Lord's and during this match a delivery from Platts hit Summers on the head. The batsman subsequently died from the accident and Platts was so affected by the tragedy that he changed from fast bowler to slow. He was a County umpire (1885–96).

Playle, William Rodger
Amateur. *b:* 1.12.1938, Palmerston North, Wellington, New Zealand. Nephew of C. G. Crawford (Canterbury). Stylish middle order right-hand batsman, off break bowler. *Teams* Auckland (1956/7 to 1963/4); Western Australia (1965/6 to 1967/8, 17 matches). *Tour* New Zealand to England 1958. *Tests* New Zealand (1958 to 1962/3, 8 matches).
Career batting
85–145–13–2888–122–21.87–4–*ct* 82
Bowling 94–1–94.00–0–0–1/11
Test batting
8–15–0–151–65–10.06–0–*ct* 4

Although he played in all five Tests on the 1958 tour, he achieved very little.

Pleass, James Edward
Amateur in 1947, turned professional 1948. *b:* 21.5.1923, Cardiff, Glamorgan. Sound middle order right-hand batsman, fine outfield. *Team* Glamorgan (1947–56, 171 matches).
Career batting
171–253–31–4293–102*–19.33–1–*ct* 77
Bowling 15–0

Plimsoll, Jack Bruce
Amateur. *b:* 27.10.1917, Kalk Bay, Cape Town, South Africa. Father of J. B. jun (South African Universities). Tail end right-hand batsman, left-arm medium fast bowler. *Teams* Western Province (1939/40 to 1947/8); Natal (1948/9 to 1949/50). *Tour* South Africa to England 1947. *Test* South Africa (1947, 1 match).
Career batting
39–47–13–386–51–11.35–0–*ct* 9
Bowling 3581–155–23.10–9–3–7/35
Test batting
1–2–1–16–8*–16.00–0–*ct* 0
Bowling 143–3–47.66–0–0–3/128

He took 68 wickets, av 23.32, in first-class matches on the 1947 tour, but was only effective on pitches which suited him and appeared in just a single Test.

Plowden, Sir Henry Meredyth
Amateur. *b:* 26.9.1840, Sylhet, India. *d:* 8.1.1920, Sunninghill, Berkshire. Stylish middle or lower order right-hand batsman, right-hand slow off break round-

arm bowler. *Sch* Harrow. *Teams* Cambridge U (1860–63, blue all four years); Hampshire (1865, 1 match).
Career batting
15–25–6–248–69*–13.05–0–*ct* 10
Bowling 552–43 + 13–12.83–5–0–7/25
He went to India and from 1877 to 1894 was Judge of the Chief Court in the Punjab; his first-class cricket career was therefore very brief. He captained Cambridge in 1862 and 1863. His final first-class match was for MCC in 1866. He was also a noted rackets player, winning his blue.

Plowright, Arthur Vincent
Amateur. *b:* 6.10.1916, Edinburgh, Scotland. *d:* 29.11.1992, Guildford, Surrey. Middle order right-hand batsman. *Team* Scotland (1937).
Career batting
1–2–0–36–29–18.00–0–*ct* 1

Plumb, Stephen George
Cricketer. *b:* 17.1.1954, Wimbish, Essex. Middle order right-hand batsman, right-arm medium pace bowler. *Sch* Cranleigh. *Team* Essex (1975–77, 2 matches). *Tour* MCC to Bangladesh 1980/1 (not first-class).
Career batting
5–8–1–216–69–30.85–0–*ct* 2
Bowling 124–3–41.33–0–0–2/47
He also played for Norfolk (1978–92) and his final first-class match was for Minor Counties in 1986.

Plumb, Thomas
Professional. *b:* 26.7.1833, Aylesbury, Buckinghamshire. *d:* 29.3.1905, Northampton. Middle or lower order right-hand batsman, right-hand medium pace bowler, wicket-keeper. *Teams* North (1866–74); South (1879).
Career batting
26–47–10–474–67–12.81–0–*ct* 27–*st* 15
Bowling 35–3–11.66–0–0–3/35
His County cricket was for Northamptonshire (pre first-class, 1850–84) and occasionally for Bedfordshire (1860) and Buckinghamshire (1865–68). He died in very poor circumstances.

Plummer, Peter John
Cricketer. *b:* 28.1.1947, Nottingham. Lower order right-hand batsman, slow left-arm bowler. *Team* Nottinghamshire (1969–72, 33 matches).
Career batting
33–37–7–386–46–12.86–0–*ct* 16
Bowling 2016–63–32.00–2–0–7/71
He also played for Buckinghamshire (1973–77).

Pocknee, John
Professional. *b:* 3.1.1860, Brighton, Sussex. *d:* 18.6.1938, Paddington, London. Lower order batsman, wicket-keeper. *Team* Middlesex (1884, 1 match).
Career batting
1–2–0–8–5–4.00–0–*ct* 1

Pocock, Howard John
Amateur. *b:* 8.4.1921. Maidstone, Kent. Middle order right-hand batsman. *Team* Kent (1947–49, 7 matches).
Career batting
7–11–1–118–34–11.80–0–*ct* 3
Bowling 70–1–70.00–0–0–1/53
He was Chairman of Kent CCC 1978–85 and President 1988.

Pocock, Nicholas Edward Julian
Cricketer. *b:* 15.12.1951, Maracaibo, Venezuela. Middle order right-hand batsman, left-arm medium pace bowler. *Sch* Shrewsbury. *Team* Hampshire (1976–84, 127 matches). *Tours* MCC to Far East 1981, to United States 1982 (neither first-class).
Career batting
127–186–22–3790–164–23.10–2–*ct* 124
Bowling 396–4–99.00–0–0–1/4
He was captain of Hampshire (1980–84).

Pocock, Patrick Ian
Cricketer. *b:* 24.9.1946, Bangor, Caernarvonshire. Lower order right-hand batsman, off break bowler. *Teams* Surrey (1964–86, 485 matches); Northern Transvaal (1971/2). *Tours* MCC Under 25 to Pakistan 1966/7; MCC to West Indies 1967/8, 1973/4, to Ceylon and Pakistan 1968/9, to Ceylon 1969/70, to India, Pakistan and Sri Lanka 1972/3; England to India and Sri Lanka 1984/5, to Sharjah (not first-class) 1984/5; Rest of World to Pakistan 1970/1. *Tests* England (1967/8 to 1984/5, 25 matches).
Career batting
554–585–156–4867–75*–11.34–0–*ct* 186
Bowling 42648–1607–26.53–60–7–9/57
Test batting
25–37–4–206–33–6.24–0–*ct* 15
Bowling 2976–67–44.41–3–0–6/79
He took 112 wickets, av 18.22, in 1967. His best bowling was 9/57 for Surrey v Glamorgan at Sophia Gardens, Cardiff in 1979. He created a sensation during the Surrey v Sussex match at Eastbourne in 1972 by taking four wickets in four balls, then five in six, six in nine and finally seven wickets in eleven balls. He was captain of Surrey 1986. He was surprisingly recalled into the England team for the Fourth Test at Old Trafford v West Indies in 1984, having last appeared eight years previously. He held his place for the remaining two Tests of 1984 and then played in all five Tests on the subsequent winter tour to India.

Poidevin, Dr Leslie Oswald Sheridan
Amateur. *b:* 5.11.1876, Merrilla, New South Wales, Australia. *d:* 18.11.1931, Bondi, Sydney, New South Wales, Australia. Defensive middle order right-hand batsman, right-arm slow bowler, good field. *Teams* New South Wales (1895/6 to 1904/5, 13 matches);

London County (1902–04); Lancashire (1904–08, 105 matches). *Tour* New South Wales to New Zealand 1895/6.
Career batting
149–234–21–7022–179–32.96–14–*ct* 163
Bowling 1927–46–41.89–2–0–8/66
He hit 1,000 runs in a season twice (best 1,433, av 39.80, in 1905). Latterly he was a noted cricket writer. He played tennis for Australia in the Davis Cup.

Pointer, Graham Alan
Cricketer. *b:* 2.5.1967, Lewisham, London. Lower order right-hand batsman, left-arm medium fast bowler. *Sch* St Dunstan's. *Team* Cambridge U (1987–90, blue 1987–88).
Career batting
16–25–5–234–33–11.70–0–*ct* 1
Bowling 1298–17–76.35–0–0–3/31

Poland, Rev Frederick William
Amateur. *b:* 10.10.1858, Shepherd's Bush, London. *d:* 1940, Mount Royal, Montreal, Canada. Middle order right-hand batsman, wicket-keeper. *Sch* Newton College. *Team* Cambridge U (1881).
Career batting
1–1–1–4–4*–no av–0–*ct* 2–*st* 3
His County cricket was for Devon (1883) and Hertfordshire (1898–99).

Polkinghorne, David Andrew
Cricketer. *b:* 20.4.1964, Durban, South Africa. Middle order right-hand batsman, off break bowler. *Team* Oxford U (1988).
Career batting
3–4–1–72–45*–24.00–0–*ct* 2

Pollard, David
Professional. *b:* 7.8.1835, Cowmes, Lepton, Huddersfield, Yorkshire. *d:* 26.3.1909, Lepton, Yorkshire. He was found dead in bed. Lower order right-hand batsman, right-arm medium pace bowler, slip field. *Team* Yorkshire (1865, 1 match).
Career batting
2–3–0–6–3–2.00–0–*ct* 1
Bowling 124–2–62.00–0–0–2/75
His final first-class match was for An England XI in 1872.

Pollard, Paul Raymond
Cricketer. *b:* 24.9.1968, Nottingham. Opening left-hand batsman, right-arm medium pace bowler. *Team* Nottinghamshire (1987–92, 81 matches).
Career batting
81–143–7–4056–153–29.82–6–*ct* 75
Bowling 113–1–113.00–0–0–1/46
He reached 1,000 runs twice (best 1,255, av 33.02, in 1991).

Pollard, Richard
Professional. *b:* 19.6.1912, Westhoughton, Lancashire. *d:* 16.12.1985, Westhoughton, Lancashire. Hard hitting lower order right-hand batsman, right-arm fast medium bowler. *Team* Lancashire (1933–50, 266 matches). *Tour* MCC to Australia and New Zealand 1946/7. *Tests* England (1946–48, 4 matches).
Career batting
298–328–63–3522–63–13.29–0–*ct* 225
Bowling 25314–1122–22.56–60–10–8/33
Test batting
4–3–2–13–10*–13.00–0–*ct* 3
Bowling 378–15–25.20–1–0–5/24
He took 100 wickets in a season seven times (best 149, av 21.58, in 1938). His final first-class match was for a Commonwealth XI in 1952.

Pollard, Victor
Cricketer. *b:* 7.9.1945, Burnley, Lancashire. Middle order right-hand batsman, off break bowler. *Teams* Central Districts (1964/5 to 1968/9); Canterbury (1969/70 to 1974/5). *Tours* New Zealand to England 1965, 1969, 1973, to India and Pakistan 1964/5, 1969/70, to Australia 1967/8. *Tests* New Zealand (1964/5 to 1973, 32 matches).
Career batting
130–207–33–5314–146–30.54–6–*ct* 81
Bowling 6931–224–30.94–6–1–7/65
Test batting
32–59–7–1266–116–24.34–2–*ct* 19
Bowling 1853–40–46.32–0–0–3/3
After two modest tours to England in 1965 and 1969, he was most successful in 1973, and with two Test centuries headed the Test batting averages with 302 runs, av 100.66.

Polley, Vivian Ralph
Amateur. *b:* 22.12.1880, Fulham, London. *d:* 12.2.1967, Elm Grove, Brighton, Sussex. Lower order right-hand batsman, right-arm fast bowler. *Team* Middlesex (1913, 5 matches).
Career batting
5–8–4–18–5–4.50–0–*ct* 2
Bowling 382–10–38.20–0–0–3/49

Pollitt, George
Professional. *b:* 3.6.1874, Chickenley, Yorkshire. Middle order batsman. *Team* Yorkshire (1899, 1 match).
Career batting
1–1–0–51–51–51.00–0–*ct* 1
He also played for Bedfordshire (1900–07).

Pollitt, Tom Urquhart
Amateur. *b:* 14.7.1900, Farnham, Surrey. *d:* 13.8.1979, Ely, Cambridgeshire. Opening left-hand batsman. *Team* RAF (1931).
Career batting
1–2–0–20–14–10.00–0–*ct* 2

Pollock, Angus John
Cricketer. *b:* 19.4.1962, Liversedge, Yorkshire. Lower order right-hand batsman, right-arm medium pace bowler. *Sch* Shrewsbury. *Team* Cambridge U (1982–84, blue all three years).
Career batting
23–26–4–198–32–9.00–0–*ct* 7
Bowling 1853–49–37.81–2–0–5/107

He captained Cambridge in 1984. He also won a blue for soccer.

Pollock, John Stuart
Amateur. *b:* 5.6.1920, Ballynafeigh, Belfast, Ireland. Son of William (Ireland). Middle order right-hand batsman, off break bowler. *Sch* Campbell College. *Team* Ireland (1939–57).
Career batting
23–43–2–1036–129–25.26–1–*ct* 17
Bowling 2–0

His final first-class match was for Free Foresters in 1958. He represented Ireland at squash.

Pollock, Peter Maclean
Amateur. *b:* 30.6.1941, Pietermaritzburg, Natal, South Africa. Son of A. M. (Orange Free State), brother of R. G. (Eastern Province), father of S. M. (Natal), uncle of G. A. (Transvaal) and A. G. (Transvaal). Lower order right-hand batsman, right-arm fast bowler. *Team* Eastern Province (1958/9 to 1971/2). *Tours* SA Fezela to England 1961; South Africa to England 1965, 1970 (tour cancelled), to Australia and New Zealand 1963/4, to Australia 1971/2 (tour cancelled); Rest of World to England 1966, 1967, 1968, 1970, to Australia 1971/2. *Tests* South Africa (1961/2 to 1969/70, 28 matches).
Career batting
127–177–43–3028–79–22.59–0–*ct* 54
Bowling 10620–485–21.89–27–2–7/19
Test batting
28–41–13–607–75*–21.67–0–*ct* 9
Bowling 2806–116–24.18–9–1–6/38

The most successful bowler on the 1965 tour of England he headed both the Test and first-class averages and played in all three Tests.

Pollock, Robert Graeme
Cricketer. *b:* 27.2.1944, Durban, Natal, South Africa. Son of A. M. (Orange Free State), brother of P. M. (Eastern Province), father of G. A. (Transvaal) and A. G. (Transvaal), uncle of S. M. (Natal). Attacking middle order left-hand batsman, leg break bowler. *Teams* Eastern Province (1960/1 to 1977/8); Transvaal (1978/9 to 1986/7). *Tours* South Africa to England 1965, 1970 (tour cancelled), to Australia and New Zealand 1963/4, to Australia 1971/2 (tour cancelled); Rest of World to England 1966, 1967, 1968, 1970, to Australia 1971/2; Isaacs to England 1969 (not first-class); International Cavaliers to England 1969; International Wanderers to South Africa 1974/5. *Tests* South Africa (1963/4 to 1969/70, 23 matches).
Career batting
262–437–54–20940–274–54.67–64–*ct* 248
Bowling 2062–43–47.95–0–0–3/46
Test batting
23–41–4–2256–274–60.97–7–*ct* 17
Bowling 204–4–51.00–0–0–2/50

Most successful on the 1965 tour to England, he headed both Test and first-class batting averages, in the latter scoring 1,147 runs, av 57.35. He also hit 1,000 runs in a South African season four times (best 1,126, av 78.37, in 1974/5) and once in Australia. Regarded by many as the equal of any batsman in the world during the 1970s, his first-class cricket has been almost entirely confined to domestic matches in South Africa. His highest score was 274 for South Africa v Australia at Durban in 1969/70.

Pollock, William
Amateur. *b:* 28.8.1886, Holywood, Co Down, Ireland. *d:* 24.11.1972, Belfast, Ireland. Father of J. S. (Ireland). Middle order right-hand batsman, right-arm fast bowler. *Sch* Campbell College, Belfast. *Team* Ireland (1909–23).
Career batting
5–9–0–312–144–34.66–1–*ct* 0
Bowling 200–9–22.22–0–0–3/42

Pomfret, Rear Admiral Dr Arnold Ashworth
Amateur. *b:* 1.6.1900, Blackpool, Lancashire. *d:* 3.4.1984, Taunton, Somerset. Tail end right-hand batsman, right-arm fast medium bowler. *Team* Royal Navy (1929).
Career batting
3–5–1–5–5–1.25–0–*ct* 1
Bowling 291–12–24.25–1–0–6/39

Ponniah, Charles Edward Manoharan
Cricketer. *b:* 3.5.1943, Kalutara, Ceylon. Sound opening right-hand batsman, leg break bowler. *Teams* Cambridge U (1967–69, blue all three years); Ceylon (1963/4 to 1964/5). *Tour* Ceylon to India 1964/5.
Career batting
45–87–8–1978–101*–25.03–1–*ct* 12
Bowling 82–6–13.66–1–0–5/20

Ponsford, William Harold, MBE
Amateur. *b:* 19.10.1900, North Fitzroy, Melbourne, Victoria, Australia. *d:* 6.4.1991, Kyneton, Victoria, Australia. Sound opening right-hand batsman, right-arm medium pace bowler. *Team* Victoria (1920/1 to 1933/4, 55 matches). *Tours* Australia to England 1926, 1930, 1934, to New Zealand 1927/8. *Tests* Australia (1924/5 to 1934, 29 matches).
Career batting
162–235–23–13819–437–65.18–47–*ct* 71
Bowling 41–0
Test batting
29–48–4–2122–266–48.22–7–*ct* 21

A record-breaking batsman with 13 innings over 200 to his name, including two triple centuries and two over 400, his highest being 437 for Victoria v Queensland at Melbourne in 1927/8, he was relatively unsuccessful on two of his three visits to England. In 1926 tonsilitis laid him low, in 1930 he hit 1,425 runs, av 49.13, and only in 1934 did he really demonstrate his full talents with 1,784 runs, av 77.56, including 266 for Australia v England at the Oval. He twice hit 1,000 runs in an Australian season. His final first-class match was for W. M. Woodfull's XI in 1934/5.

Ponsonby, Cecil Brabazon
Amateur. *b:* 26.12.1889, Gravesend, Kent. *d:* 11.5.1945, St John's Wood, London. Great-nephew of F. G. B. (Surrey), S. C. B (Surrey and Middlesex) and J. G. B. (MCC). Lower order right-hand batsman, wicket-keeper. *Sch* Eton. *Team* Worcestershire (1911–28, 74 matches).
Career batting
76–131–26–844–50*–8.03–0–*ct* 73–*st* 11

He played in the Oxford Freshmen's match of 1912, but no first-class matches for the University. In 1927 he captained Worcestershire.

Ponsonby, Hon Frederick George Brabazon
(succeeded as 6th Earl of Bessborough in 1880)
Amateur. *b:* 11.9.1815, Marylebone, London. *d:* 11.3.1895, Mayfair, London. Brother of J. G. B. (MCC) and S. C. B. (Surrey and Middlesex), uncle of J. H. (MCC). Fine middle order right-hand batsman, good field at long stop or mid-wicket. *Sch* Harrow. *Teams* Cambridge U (1834–39, blue 1836); Surrey (1839, 1 match); Cambridge Town Club (1840).
Career batting
67–117–14–1129–74–10.96–0–*ct* 31–*st* 3
Bowling 1 wicket (no analyses)–0–0–1/?

Owing to an injury to his arm, as well as his work in the legal profession he did not play in great matches after 1845. With his brother and J. L. Baldwin he founded the I Zingari in 1845. In 1849 he became the first Life Member of Surrey CCC, thus helping to save the club which was in financial difficulties. He regularly went to Harrow to instruct the boys and the success of Harrow in the 1860s and 1870s was attributed largely to his efforts. His last first-class match was for MCC in 1856.

Ponsonby, John Henry
(changed name to Ponsonby Fane in 1875)
Amateur. *b:* 21.7.1848, Westminster, London. *d:* 11.9.1916, Brympton D'Evercy, Somerset. Son of S. C. B. (Surrey and Middlesex), father of R. A. B. (MCC in South Africa), nephew of F. G. B (Surrey) and J. G. B. (MCC). Steady lower order right-hand batsman, right-hand slow under-arm bowler, wicket-keeper. *Sch* Harrow. *Team* MCC (1870).
Career batting
7–9–1–161–53–20.12–0–*ct* 9–*st* 2
Bowling 209–13–16.07–1–0–5/51

Playing for I Zingari v School of Gunnery at Shoeburyness in 1874 he took 19 of the 22 wickets (the match being 12 a side).

Ponsonby, Rt Hon Sir Spencer Cecil Brabazon
(changed name to Ponsonby Fane in 1875)
Amateur. *b:* 14.3.1824, Mayfair, Westminster, London. *d:* 1.12.1915, Brympton D'Evercy, Yeovil. Brother of F. G. B. (Surrey) and J. G. B. (MCC), father of J. H. (MCC), uncle of S. W. Gore (Surrey), father-in-law of A. De Grey (I Zingari). Lively opening or middle order right-hand batsman, good deep field. *Teams* Surrey (1844–53, 3 matches); Middlesex (1862, 1 match).
Career batting
62–117–3–1359–108–11.92–1–*ct* 30–*st* 2
Bowling 48–2 + 12–24.00–1–0–5/?

His first first-class match was in 1841 and his last in 1864 (both for MCC). He was on the MCC Committee 1866–68, 1870–73, 1875–78, Treasurer 1879 to his death and Trustee from 1900; he was a founder member of the Surrey Committee and President of Somerset CCC from 1890 until his death. With his brother and J. L. Baldwin he founded I Zingari in 1845 and was Hon Secretary and Governor of the Club. He played for Ireland (not first-class) in 1858–62.

Apart from his cricket connections he held many important posts including Private Secretary to Lord Palmerston, the Earl of Clarendon and Earl Granville, also Comptroller of the Lord Chamberlain's Office, Gentleman Usher of the Sword and Bath King of Arms.

Pont, Ian Leslie
Cricketer. *b:* 28.8.1961, Brentwood, Essex. Brother of K. R. (Essex). Middle order right-hand batsman, right-arm medium pace bowler. *Sch* Brentwood. *Teams* Nottinghamshire (1982, 4 matches); Essex (1985–88, 23 matches); Natal (1985/6).
Career batting
28–35–10–404–68–16.16–0–*ct* 5
Bowling 2705–70–35.78–3–0–5/73

He also played for Buckinghamshire (1983–84), Northumberland (1989) and Lincolnshire (1990–91). He went to America to have trials as a baseball pitcher.

Pont, Keith Rupert
Cricketer. *b:* 16.1.1953, Wanstead, Essex. Brother of I. L. (Nottinghamshire and Essex). Middle order right-hand batsman, right-arm medium pace bowler. *Team* Essex (1970–86, 198 matches).
Career batting
198–305–44–6558–125*–25.12–7–*ct* 92
Bowling 3189–96–33.21–2–0–5/17

Pontifex, Rev Alfred
Amateur. *b:* 17.3.1842, London. *d:* 25.8.1930, Weston, Bath, Somerset. Middle order batsman. *Team* Gloucestershire (1871, 1 match).
Career batting
1–2–1–12–6–1–12.00–0–*ct* 1
Whilst at Cambridge he appeared in some trial matches, but no first-class contests. He also played for Somerset (pre-first-class, 1877), Norfolk (1878–86) and Suffolk (1880).

Pontifex, Dudley David
Amateur. *b:* 12.2.1855, Weston, Bath, Somerset. *d:* 27.9.1934, West Dulwich, London. Opening or middle order right-hand batsman. *Sch* Bath College. *Teams* Surrey (1881, 9 matches); Somerset (1882, 1 match).
Career batting
17–27–1–357–89–13.73–0–*ct* 3
Bowling 13–0
He played in the 1875 Freshmen's match at Cambridge, but no first-class games whilst at the University. His first-class debut was for the Gentlemen of England in 1878 and his final appearance for MCC in 1896. He first played for Somerset (pre first-class) in 1879. He won a blue for billiards.

Pook, Neil Robert
Cricketer. *b:* 9.2.1967, Rainham, Essex. Middle order right-hand batsman, right-arm medium pace bowler. *Teams* Essex (1988, 1 match); Glamorgan (1990, 1 match).
Career batting
2–3–1–6–6–3.00–0–*ct* 3
Bowling 19–0

Pool, Charles James Tomlin
Amateur. *b:* 21.1.1876, Northampton. *d:* 13.10.1954, Epsom, Surrey. Attractive middle order right-hand batsman. *Sch* Northampton GS. *Team* Northamptonshire (1905–10, 94 matches).
Career batting
94–177–6–4350–166–25.43–4–*ct* 51
Bowling 227–5–45.40–0–0–4/53
He made his debut for Northamptonshire (pre first-class) in 1893 and spent three years in Australia at the turn of the century. A good hockey player he represented Northamptonshire.

Poole, Arthur Bertram
Amateur. *b:* 30.6.1907, Bedford. *d:* 22.11.1979, Hammersmith, London. Hard hitting middle order right-hand batsman. *Sch* Bedford Modern. *Team* Minor Counties (1936).
Career batting
1–2–1–92–91*–92.00–0–*ct* 0
His County cricket was for Bedfordshire (1925–51), being captain from 1946 to 1951 and later Chairman and President of the County Club.

Poole, Cyril John
Professional. *b:* 13.3.1921, Forest Town, Mansfield, Nottinghamshire. Attacking middle order left-hand batsman, left-arm medium pace bowler, excellent deep field, occasional wicket-keeper. *Team* Nottinghamshire (1948–62, 366 matches). *Tour* MCC to India and Ceylon 1951/2. *Tests* England (1951/2, 3 matches).
Career batting
383–637–42–19364–222*–32.54–24–*ct* 224–*st* 5
Bowling 347–4–86.75–0–0–1/8
Test batting
3–5–1–161–69*–40.25–0–*ct* 1
Bowling 9–0
He hit 1,000 runs in a season twelve times (best 1,860, av 33.21, in 1961). Both his double centuries were for Nottinghamshire, the highest being 222* v Indians at Trent Bridge in 1952. A good soccer player, he appeared for Gillingham and Mansfield Town.

Poole, Kenneth John
Professional. *b:* 27.4.1934, Thurgarton, Nottinghamshire. Middle order right-hand batsman, right-arm medium fast bowler. *Team* Nottinghamshire (1955–57, 26 matches).
Career batting
26–44–5–612–58–15.69–0–*ct* 21
Bowling 1361–21–64.80–0–0–2/10
A farming accident in October 1957, which resulted in him losing three fingers of his right hand, ended his career in County cricket. He played football for Northampton Town.

Pooley, Edward
Professional. *b:* 13.2.1838, Richmond, Surrey. *d:* 18.7.1907, Lambeth, London. Brother of F. W. (Surrey). Hard hitting middle order right-hand batsman, occasional right-arm slow bowler, wicket-keeper. *Teams* Surrey (1861–83, 256 matches); Middlesex (1864–65, 7 matches). *Tours* Willsher to North America 1868 (not first-class); Lillywhite to Australia and New Zealand 1876/7 (not first-class in New Zealand).
Career batting
370–645–56–9345–125–15.86–1–*ct* 496–*st* 358
Bowling 390–6–65.00–0–0–2/39
One of the greatest wicket-keepers of his day, especially to slow bowling, his record of 12 dismissals in a match (ct 8, st 4 for Surrey v Sussex at the Oval in 1868) still stands unchallenged in English first-class cricket. He hit 1,084 runs, av 23.06, in 1870. Faults of a personal nature marred his otherwise brilliant career and he ended his days in the workhouse.

Pooley, Frederick William
Professional. *b:* 7.4.1852, Richmond, Surrey. *d:* 14.9.1905, West Ham, Essex. Brother of Edward (Surrey and Middlesex). Middle order right-hand

batsman, wicket-keeper. *Team* Surrey (1876–77, 3 matches).
Career batting
4–6–0–16–11–2.66–0–*ct* 5

Pooley, James Calvin
Cricketer. *b:* 8.8.1969, Hammersmith, London. Opening left-hand batsman, off break bowler. *Teams* Middlesex (1989–92, 17 matches)
Career batting
17–30–2–628–88–22.42–0–*ct* 9
Bowling 11–0

Pooley, Malcolm William
Cricketer. *b:* 27.7.1969, Truro, Cornwall. Lower order right-hand batsman, right-arm medium pace bowler. *Team* Gloucestershire (1988–90, 12 matches)
Career batting
12–16–6–155–38–15.50–0–*ct* 4
Bowling 564–15–37.60–0–0–4/80
He also played for Cornwall (1986–87).

Poore, Brigadier-General Robert Montagu
Amateur. *b:* 20.3.1866, Carysfort House, Dublin, Ireland. *d:* 14.7.1938, Boscombe, Hampshire. Attacking middle order right-hand batsman, right-arm slow bowler, fine field. *Teams* Europeans (1892/3 to 1913/14); South Africa (1895/6); Hampshire (1898–1906, 36 matches). *Tests* South Africa (1895/6, 3 matches).
Career batting
55–98–9–3441–304–38.66–11–*ct* 38
Bowling 252–13–19.38–0–0–2/0
Test batting
3–6–0–76–20–12.66–0–*ct* 3
Bowling 4–1–4.00–0–0–1/4
He created a sensation in 1899, the only English season in which he appeared regularly in County cricket, by hitting 1,551 runs, av 91.23, including 304 for Hampshire v Somerset at Taunton. He was easily the leading batsman of the summer. He also played for Wiltshire (1888). He was a prolific batsman in India in the early 1890s and appeared in non-first-class matches for Natal with such success that he gained a place in the South African team. A noted all-round sportsman he was a fine swordsman, a first-rate polo player and a good tennis player.

Pope, Alfred Vardy
Professional. *b:* 15.8.1909, Tibshelf, Derbyshire. Brother of G. H. (Derbyshire) and Harold (Derbyshire). Hard hitting lower order right-hand batsman, right-arm fast medium or off break bowler. *Team* Derbyshire (1930–39, 211 matches).
Career batting
214–316–46–4963–103–18.38–1–*ct* 98
Bowling 12512–555–22.54–22–3–7/84
His best season was 1936, when he took 99 wickets, av 18.13.

Pope, Andrew Noble
Amateur. *b:* 14.11.1881, Clifton, Bristol. *d:* 18.4.1942, Lansdown, Cheltenham, Gloucesterhire. Middle order batsman. *Sch* Harrow. *Team* Gloucestershire (1911, 2 matches).
Career batting
2–4–0–46–29–11.50–0–*ct* 1

Pope, Charles George
Amateur. *b:* 21.1.1872, Sandy Park, Bedfordshire. *d:* 31.1.1959, Bashley Lodge, New Milton, Hampshire. Lower order right-hand batsman, right-arm medium fast bowler. *Sch* Harrow. *Team* Cambridge U (1892–95, blue 1894).
Career batting
11–18–5–136–26*–10.46–0–*ct* 8
Bowling 497–20–24.85–1–0–5/39
His County cricket was for Bedfordshire (1892–1901).

Pope, Dudley Fairbridge
Professional. *b:* 28.10.1906, Barnes, Surrey. *d:* 8.9.1934, Writtle, Essex. He was killed in a road accident. Defensive opening right-hand batsman, excellent deep field. *Teams* Gloucestershire (1925–27, 11 matches); Essex (1928–34, 148 matches).
Career batting
159–268–19–6557–161–26.33–7–*ct* 37
Bowling 272–4–68.00–0–0–1/11
He hit 1,000 runs in a season four times (best 1,750, av 34.31, in 1934); his final first-class innings was 108 for Essex v Gloucestershire at Gloucester.

Pope, George Henry
Professional. *b:* 27.1.1911, Tibshelf, Derbyshire. Brother of A. V. (Derbyshire) and Harold (Derbyshire). Middle order right-hand batsman, right-arm fast medium bowler. *Team* Derbyshire (1933–48, 169 matches). *Tours* Tennyson to India 1937/8; Commonwealth to India, Pakistan and Ceylon 1949/50; MCC to India 1939/40 (tour cancelled). *Test* England (1947, 1 match).
Career batting
205–312–44–7518–207*–28.05–8–*ct* 157
Bowling 13488–677–19.92–40–7–8/38
Test batting
1–1–1–8–8*–no av–0–*ct* 0
Bowling 85–1–85.00–0–0–1/49
He hit 1,000 runs in a season four times (best 1,464, av 31.82, in 1939), and took 100 wickets three times (best 114, av 18.38, in 1947). In 1938 and 1948 he completed the 'double'. His highest score was 207* for Derbyshire v Hampshire at Portsmouth in 1948. He retired from County cricket after the 1948 season owing to the health of his wife, and was later a first-class umpire (1966–74).

Pope, Harold
Professional. *b:* 10.5.1919, Chesterfield, Derbyshire. Brother of A. V. (Derbyshire) and G. H. (Derby-

shire). Lower order right-hand batsman, leg break bowler. *Team* Derbyshire (1939–46, 10 matches).
Career batting
10–16–3–81–24*–6.23–0–*ct* 3
Bowling 599–15–39.93–0–0–3/80

Pope, Dr Roland James
Amateur. *b:* 18.2.1864, Sydney, New South Wales, Australia. *d:* 27.7.1952, Manly, Sydney, New South Wales, Australia. Neat middle order right-hand batsman, right-hand slow under-arm bowler, good deep field. *Teams* New South Wales (1884/5, 3 matches); MCC (1889–91). *Tours* Assisted the Australians in England 1886, 1890, 1902. *Test* Australia (1884/5, 1 match).
Career batting
20–33–7–318–47–12.23–0–*ct* 13
Bowling 19–0
Test batting
1–2–0–3–3–1.50–0–*ct* 0
He came to Britain to study medicine and remained for some years.

Popham, Reginald Francis
Amateur. *b:* 8.1.1892, Kensington, London. *d:* 9.9.1975, Old Manor, Warnham, Sussex. Steady middle order right-hand batsman. *Sch* Repton. *Team* MCC (1919).
Career batting
5–6–1–151–52*–30.20–0–*ct* 0
Bowling 10–0
His County cricket was for Norfolk (1910–21). A noted soccer player, he captained Oxford and went on to win three amateur caps for England.

Popplewell, Nigel Francis Mark
Cricketer. *b:* 8.8.1957, Chislehurst, Kent. Son of O. B. (Cambridge U). Attacking middle order right-hand batsman, right-arm medium pace bowler. *Sch* Radley. *Teams* Cambridge U (1977–79, blue all three years); Somerset (1979–85, 118 matches). *Tour* MCC to Bangladesh 1976/7 (not first-class).
Career batting
143–214–27–5070–172–27.11–4–*ct* 110
Bowling 4441–103–43.11–1–0–5/33
He hit 1,000 runs in a season twice (best 1,116, av 32.82, in 1984). He also played for Buckinghamshire (1975–78).

Popplewell, Sir Oliver Bury
Amateur. *b:* 15.8.1927, Northwood, Middlesex. Father of N. F. M. (Somerset). Lower order right-hand batsman, wicket-keeper. *Sch* Charterhouse. *Team* Cambridge U (1949–51), blue all three years).
Career batting
41–56–13–881–74*–20.48–0–*ct* 63–*st* 16
Bowling 10–0
His final first-class match was for Free Foresters in 1960.

Porbandar, HH the Maharaja of, Rana Saheb Shri Sir Natwarsinhji Bhavsinhji
Amateur. *b:* 30.6.1901, Porbandar, India. *d:* 4.10.1979, Porbandar, India. Brother-in-law of K. S. Limbdi (Western India States). Steady middle order right-hand batsman. *Teams* Roshanara Club (1931/2); Viceroys's XI (1932/3). *Tour* India to England 1932.
Career batting
6–7–0–42–22–6.00–0–*ct* 0
He came forward to captain the 1932 touring team, when the Maharaja of Patiala was forced to stand down. His abilities as a batsman were not up to first-class cricket and he played in very few matches on the tour and did not appear in the Test match.

Porch, Robert Bagehot
Amateur. *b:* 3.4.1875, Weston-super-Mare, Somerset. *d:* 29.10.1962, Great Malvern, Worcestershire. Middle order right-hand batsman, leg break bowler, excellent field. *Sch* Malvern. *Team* Somerset (1895–1910, 27 matches).
Career batting
27–50–7–665–85*–15.46–0–*ct* 10
Bowling 61–0
He appeared in the Seniors match at Oxford but no first-class matches – a schoolmaster, his opportunities for County cricket were limited.

Portal, Sir Gerald Herbert
Amateur. *b:* 13.3.1858, Laverstoke Park, Hampshire. *d:* 25.1.1894, Westminster, London. He died of typhoid fever. Nephew of B. J. Knight (Kent), E. Knight (Kent and Hampshire), H. Knight (Sussex) and G. T. Knight (Kent and Hampshire). Middle order right-hand batsman, left-arm fast bowler. *Sch* Eton. *Team* I Zingari (1885).
Career batting
1–1–0–6–6–6.00–0–*ct* 1
Bowling 55–4–13.75–0–0–4/55
At the time of his death he was Consul General at Zanzibar and was preparing an official report on Uganda, having been on a special mission to that country.

Porteous, Thomas Wilkie
Cricketer. *b:* 22.1.1948, Dennistoun, Glasgow, Scotland. Middle order right-hand batsman. *Team* Scotland (1973–74).
Career batting
2–4–0–18–18–4.50–0–*ct* 5

Porter, Rev Albert Lavington
Amateur. *b:* 20.1.1864, Croydon, Surrey. *d:* 14.12.1937, Tiverton, Devon. Middle order batsman. *Sch* Marlborough. *Teams* Somerset (1883, 2 matches); Hampshire (1895, 1 match).
Career batting
4–5–0–19–7–3.80–0–*ct* 3
Bowling 20–0

He appeared in the Cambridge Freshmen's match, but no first-class matches whilst at the University.

Porter, Andrew Marshall
Amateur. *b:* 6.1.1874, Donnycarney House, Dublin, Ireland. *d:* 5.6.1900, Ladywood, Lindley, Orange Free State, South Africa. Middle order right-hand batsman, wicket-keeper. *Sch* Harrow. *Team* Dublin University (1895).
Career batting
4–8–0–87–44–10.87–0–*ct* 2
Bowling 9–0
He played for Ireland (not first-class) in 1896.

Porter, Arthur
Amateur. *b:* 25.3.1914, Clayton-le-Moors, Lancashire. Steady middle order right-hand batsman, right-arm medium pace or off break bowler. *Team* Glamorgan (1936–49, 38 matches).
Career batting
38–64–7–1292–105–22.66–2–*ct* 16
Bowling 480–16–30.00–0–0–4/25

Porter, Edward Horatio
Amateur. *b:* 13.10.1846, Liverpool, Lancashire. *d:* 31.10.1918, Hooton, Cheshire. Hard hitting middle order right-hand batsman, right-hand medium pace round-arm bowler. *Team* Lancashire (1874–82, 17 matches).
Career batting
20–34–1–374–61–11.33–0–*ct* 13
Bowling 48–3–16.00–0–0–3/28
His final first-class match was for a combined Lancashire and Yorkshire XI in 1883.

Porter, George
Professional. *b:* 3.12.1861, Kilburn, Derbyshire. *d:* 15.7.1908, Spondon, Derbyshire. He died of sunstroke. Lower order right-hand batsman, right-arm fast medium bowler, moderate field. *Team* Derbyshire (1881–96, 36 matches).
Career batting
37–56–15–386–93–9.41–0–*ct* 26
Bowling 2795–130–21.50–8–1–7/49
His career ended abruptly due to a back injury in 1896; he afterwards umpired in County matches (1899–1903).

Porter, Dr Hugh Lachlan
Amateur. *b:* 25.1.1911, Kensington, London. *d:* 8.1.1982, Ealing, Middlesex. Middle order right-hand batsman, right-arm slow bowler. *Sch* Winchester. *Team* Minor Counties (1935).
Career batting
2–2–0–42–38–21.00–0–*ct* 0
His County cricket was for Suffolk (1934–49).

Porter, Simon Robert
Cricketer. *b:* 9.8.1950, Cowley, Oxford. Lower order right-hand batsman, off break bowler. *Team* Oxford U (1973, blue). *Tour* Minor Counties to East Africa 1982/3 (not first-class).
Career batting
7–12–2–76–20–7.60–0–*ct* 2
Bowling 600–18–33.33–0–0–4/26
His County cricket was for Oxfordshire (1971–88).

Porthouse, Stanley Clive
Amateur. *b:* 14.8.1910, Redditch, Worcestershire. Middle order right-hand batsman. *Team* Worcestershire (1934–35, 5 matches).
Career batting
5–8–1–70–27–10.00–0–*ct* 0
Bowling 4–0

Portman, Francis John
Amateur. *b:* 24.3.1878, Corton Denham, Somerset. *d:* 2.5.1905, Ajmer, India. He died of typhoid. Nephew of O. Mordaunt (MCC). Middle or lower order right-hand batsman, right-arm fast medium bowler. *Sch* Radley. *Team* Somerset (1897–99, 2 matches).
Career batting
2–4–1–12–8–4.00–0–*ct* 2
Bowling 68–3–22.66–0–0–2/38
He appeared in the Oxford Freshmen's match of 1897. He also played for Berkshire (1896).

Posnett, Charles Edward
Amateur. *b:* 29.5.1914, Woodvale, Belfast, Ireland. Middle order right-hand batsman. *Team* Ireland (1947).
Career batting
1–2–0–46–26–23.00–0–*ct* 1

Posno, Bernard Maurice
Amateur. *b:* 9.8.1850, Finchley, Middlesex. *d:* 24.2.1901, Paris, France. Middle order batsman. *Team* An England XI (1878–79).
Career batting
2–4–0–5–2–1.25–0–*ct* 0

Posthuma, Carst Jan
Amateur. *b:* 11.1.1868, Haarlem, Holland. *d:* 21.12.1939, near Haarlem, Holland. Middle order left-hand batsman, left-arm fast bowler. *Team* London County (1903).
Career batting
5–6–0–45–29–7.50–0–*ct* 1
Bowling 346–23–15.04–2–1–7/68
He was regarded as the 'W. G. Grace' of Dutch cricket.

Potbury, Frederick John
Amateur. *b:* 7.11.1862, Ottery St Mary, Devon. *d:* 4.4.1943, Sidmouth, Devon. Brother of J. A. (British Guiana). Middle order batsman. *Team* Somerset (1882, 1 match).
Career batting
1–2–0–0–0–0.00–0–*ct* 0

Pothecary, Arthur Ernest
Professional. *b:* 1.3.1906, Southampton, Hampshire. *d:* 21.5.1991, Iver, Buckinghamshire. Nephew of S. G. (Hampshire). Sound middle or lower order left-hand batsman, slow left-arm bowler. *Team* Hampshire (1927–46, 271 matches).
Career batting
271–445–39–9477–130–23.34–9–*ct* 146
Bowling 2140–52–41.15–0–0–4/47

He hit 1,000 runs in a season four times (1,357, av 27.14, in 1938 best). He was a first-class umpire (1949–58).

Pothecary, James Edward
Amateur. *b:* 6.12.1933, Cape Town, South Africa. Lower order right-hand batsman, right-arm medium pace bowler. *Team* Western Province (1954/5 to 1964/5). *Tour* South Africa to England 1960. *Tests* South Africa (1960, 3 matches).
Career batting
54–77–11–1039–81*–15.74–0–*ct* 42
Bowling 4054–143–28.34–2–0–5/29
Test batting
3–4–0–26–12–6.50–0–*ct* 2
Bowling 354–9–39.33–0–0–4/58

He played in three Tests on the 1960 tour and in first-class matches took 53 wickets, av 29.52 – a disappointing return.

Pothecary, Sidney George
Professional. *b:* 26.9.1886, Southampton, Hampshire. *d:* 31.10.1976, Fleming Park, Eastleigh, Hampshire. Uncle of A. E. (Hampshire). Lower order left-hand batsman, left-arm medium pace bowler. *Team* Hampshire (1912–20, 12 matches).
Career batting
12–16–6–103–22*–10.30–0–*ct* 5
Bowling 257–4–64.25–0–0–3/43

Potter, Charles Warren
Professional in 1869, but amateur from 1870. *b:* 18.4.1851, Albury, Surrey. *d:* 6.6.1895, Shamley Green, Surrey. Steady middle order right-hand batsman, good deep field. *Team* Surrey (1869–71, 17 matches).
Career batting
17–31–3–385–31–13.75–0–*ct* 3
Bowling 17–1–17.00–0–0–1/17

Potter, George
Amateur. *b:* 3.10.1878, Oldham, Lancashire. Middle order right-hand batsman. *Team* Lancashire (1902, 10 matches).
Career batting
10–17–1–449–86–28.06–0–*ct* 3

He also played for Cheshire (1910).

Potter, Gordon
Professional. *b:* 26.10.1931, Dormans Land, Surrey. Middle order right-hand batsman, leg break bowler. *Team* Sussex (1949–57, 55 matches).
Career batting
55–84–11–1313–88–17.98–0–*ct* 34
Bowling 863–19–44.89–0–0–3/29

Potter, Ian Caesar
Amateur. *b:* 2.9.1938, Woking, Surrey. Tail end right-hand batsman, right-arm medium pace bowler. *Sch* King's, Canterbury. *Teams* Kent (1959–61, 3 matches); Oxford U (1960–62, blue 1961–62).
Career batting
19–24–10–124–34–8.85–0–*ct* 11
Bowling 1300–45–28.88–2–0–6/74

Potter, Jack
Amateur. *b:* 13.4.1938, Coburg, Melbourne, Victoria, Australia. Attacking middle order right-hand batsman, leg break and googly bowler. *Team* Victoria (1956/7 to 1967/8, 81 matches). *Tours* Australia to England 1964, to New Zealand 1959/60.
Career batting
104–169–20–6142–221–41.22–14–*ct* 85
Bowling 1287–31–41.51–0–0–4/20

He hit 751 runs, av 31.29, on the 1964 tour of England, but was not required for any of the Tests. His highest score was 221 for Victoria v New South Wales at Melbourne 1965/6.

Potter, Joseph
Professional. *b:* 13.1.1839, Northampton. *d:* 2.6.1906, Northampton. Lower order right-hand batsman, right-arm medium pace bowler. *Teams* Kent (1871, 2 matches); Surrey (1875–81, 35 matches).
Career batting
38–68–14–357–27*–6.61–0–*ct* 32
Bowling 2111–100–21.11–7–3–7/31

He also played for Northamptonshire (pre first-class, 1860–88) and Wiltshire (1886). He became a first-class umpire (1891–97).

Potter, Laurie
Cricketer. *b:* 7.11.1962, Bexleyheath, Kent. Opening right-hand batsman, left-arm medium pace, later slow left-arm bowler. *Teams* Kent (1981–85, 47 matches); Griqualand West (1984/5 to 1985/6); Leicestershire (1986–92, 151 matches); Orange Free State (1987/8).
Career batting
211–337–40–8623–165*–29.03–7–*ct* 178
Bowling 6121–153–40.00–0–0–4/52

He played for both Young Australia and Young England. He hit 1,000 runs in a season three times (best 1,093, av 32.14, in 1989).

Potter, Thomas Owen
Amateur. *b:* 10.9.1844, Calcutta, India. *d:* 27.4.1909, Hoylake, Cheshire. Brother of W. H. (Lancashire). Middle order batsman. *Team* Lancashire (1866, 1 match).
Career batting
1–2–0–39–39–19.50–0–*ct* 0

Potter, Wilfred
Professional. *b:* 2.5.1910, Swinecliffe, Harrogate, Yorkshire. Lower order right-hand batsman, leg break bowler. *Team* Warwickshire (1932, 1 match).
Career batting
1–2–0–0–0–0.00–0–*ct* 1
Bowling 31–1–31.00–0–0–1/19

Potter, William Henry
Amateur. *b:* 20.8.1847, Gufsey, India. *d:* 10.4.1920, Boreham Wood, Hertfordshire. Brother of T. O. (Lancashire). Middle order batsman. *Team* Lancashire (1870, 1 match).
Career batting
1–2–0–23–12–11.50–0–*ct* 0
He also played for Herefordshire (1870–71).

Potts, Henry James
Amateur. *b:* 23.1.1925, Carlisle, Cumberland. Middle order right-hand batsman. *Team* Oxford U (1949–50, blue 1950).
Career batting
9–14–1–290–50–22.30–0–*ct* 6
He played football for Northampton Town.

Pougher, Arthur Dick
Professional. *b:* 19.4.1865, Leicester. *d:* 20.5.1926, Aylestone Park, Leicester. Middle order right-hand batsman, right-arm fast medium bowler, good field. *Team* Leicestershire (1894–1901, 88 matches). *Tours* Lillywhite, Shaw and Shrewsbury to Australia 1887/8; Read to South Africa 1891/2. *Test* England (1891/2, 1 match).
Career batting
164–275–30–4555–114–18.59–5–*ct* 98
Bowling 10179–535–19.02–31–7–9/34
Test batting
1–1–0–17–17–17.00–0–*ct* 2
Bowling 26–3–8.66–0–0–3/26
His first-class debut was for North v South at Lord's in 1886. He had made his debut for Leicestershire in 1885 and in 1887 became a member of the Lord's groundstaff, remaining there 20 years. His last first-class match was for MCC in 1902. He hit 1,121 runs, av 29.50, in 1896 and the previous year took 112 wickets, av 19.39. His best bowling was 9/34 for an England XI v Surrey at the Oval in 1895. He was a first-class umpire (1905).

Poulet, Dr Roger John
Cricketer. *b:* 18.7.1942, Richmond, Surrey. Middle order right-hand batsman. *Team* Cambridge U (1968).
Career batting
1–2–0–6–6–3.00–0–*ct* 2

Poulter, Stephen John
Cricketer. *b:* 9.9.1956, Hornsey, Middlesex. Middle order right-hand batsman. *Team* Middlesex (1978, 3 matches).
Career batting
3–3–0–47–36–15.66–0–*ct* 0
He also played for Buckinghamshire (1984).

Pountain, Francis Reginald
Professional. *b:* 23.4.1941, Eastleigh, Hampshire. Middle or lower order right-hand batsman, right-arm medium pace bowler. *Team* Sussex (1960–65, 76 matches).
Career batting
76–119–16–1920–96–18.64–0–*ct* 43
Bowling 3054–86–35.51–1–0–5/91

Povey, Arthur
Professional. *b:* 16.5.1886, West Bromwich, Staffordshire. *d:* 13.2.1946, Tonbridge, Kent. He died by his own hand. Tail end right-hand batsman, wicket-keeper. *Team* Kent (1921–22, 5 matches).
Career batting
5–8–4–64–21*–16.00–0–*ct* 5–*st* 1

Powell, Adam Gordon
Amateur. *b:* 17.8.1912, Boxted, Essex. *d:* 7.6.1982, Sandwich, Kent. Lower order right-hand batsman, wicket-keeper. *Sch* Charterhouse. *Teams* Essex (1932–37, 23 matches); Cambridge U (1933–34, blue 1934). *Tours* MCC to Australia and New Zealand 1935/6, to Canada (not first-class) 1937, 1951; Martineau to Egypt (not first-class) 1937, 1938, 1939.
Career batting
53–82–12–1149–79–16.41–0–*ct* 75–*st* 19
His final first-class match was for Free Foresters in 1957. He also played for Suffolk (1938–53).

Powell, Albert James
Amateur. *b:* 8.12.1893, Presteigne, Radnorshire, Wales. *d:* 15.2.1979, Liskeard, Cornwall. Lower order right-hand batsman, right-arm medium pace bowler. *Team* Worcestershire (1921, 1 match).
Career batting
1–2–0–10–9–5.00–0–*ct* 0
Bowling 8–0

Powell, Alfred Peter
Amateur. *b:* 19.8.1908, Hampstead, London. *d:* 21.4.1985, St Audry's, Melton, Suffolk. Lower order batsman. *Sch* Mill Hill. *Team* Middlesex (1927, 1 match).
Career batting
1–2–0–0–0–0.00–0–*ct* 1
He also played for Buckinghamshire (1932–37).

Powell, Ernest Ormsby
Amateur. *b:* 19.1.1861, Liverpool, Lancashire. *d:* 29.3.1928, Stafford. Sound middle order right-hand batsman, good cover point. *Sch* Charterhouse *Teams* Surrey (1882, 4 matches); Cambridge U (1883–84); Hampshire (1884–85, 11 matches).
Career batting
21–39–2–1024–140–27.67–1–*ct* 10

Powell, James Alfred

His final first-class match was for MCC in 1895. He last played for Hampshire (not first-class) in 1888.

Powell, James Alfred
Professional. *b:* 5.5.1899, Bloomsbury, London. *d:* 8.3.1973, Brompton, Kensington, London. Lower order right-hand batsman, leg break and googly bowler. *Team* Middlesex (1926–30, 29 matches).
Career batting
32–37–13–97–8*–4.04–0–*ct* 9
Bowling 2150–77–27.92–3–0–8/72
His final first-class match was for MCC in 1931.

Powell, Louis St Vincent
Amateur. *b:* 13.11.1902, Kingstown, St Vincent. Lower order right-hand batsman, right-arm fast bowler. *Team* Somerset (1927–38, 10 matches).
Career batting
10–15–1–153–52–10.92–0–*ct* 5
Bowling 376–5–75.20–0–0–3/63

Powell, Tyrone Lyndon
Cricketer. *b:* 17.6.1953, Bargoed, Glamorgan. Opening right-hand batsman, off break bowler. *Teams* New Zealand Under 23 (1971/2); Glamorgan (1976, 1 match).
Career batting
2–4–0–24–14–6.00–0–*ct* 0
He also played for Norfolk (1982–85).

Powell, William Allan
Amateur. *b:* 19.1.1885, Blundellsands, Lancashire. *d:* 1.1.1954, Earl's Court, London. Middle order right-hand batsman, right-arm slow bowler. *Team* Kent (1912–21, 12 matches).
Career batting
15–20–3–187–48–11.00–0–*ct* 8
Bowling 559–19–29.42–1–0–5/40
His first-class debut was for H. D. G. Leveson-Gower's XI in 1909.

Powell-Moore, W. F.
(*see under* Moore, W. F. P.)

Powell-Williams, R.
(*see under* Williams, R. P.)

Power, Dr George Edward
Amateur. *b:* 16.5.1849, Witchford, Cambridgeshire. *d:* 29.10.1904, Hucknall Torkard, Nottinghamshire. Middle order right-hand batsman. *Team* Nottinghamshire (1876, 1 match).
Career batting
1–1–0–3–3–3.00–0–*ct* 1
A spectator in the Nottinghamshire v Surrey match at Trent Bridge in 1876, he went on the field as a substitute for the injured Tolley and was subsequently allowed to bat.

Power, Dr Richard Wood
Amateur. *b:* 2.2.1896, Dublin, Ireland. *d:* 3.3.1978, Fownhope, Herefordshire. Middle order right-hand batsman, wicket-keeper. *Team* Ireland (1920–26).
Career batting
4–6–0–78–30–13.00–0–*ct* 1

Powers, John
Amateur. *b:* 30.9.1868, Barwell, Leicestershire. *d:* 9.11.1939, Leicester Forest East. Powerful middle order right-hand batsman. *Team* Leicestershire (1895–96, 9 matches).
Career batting
9–17–1–195–25–12.18–0–*ct* 4
He first played for Leicestershire (pre first-class) in 1890.

Powys, Walter Norman
Amateur. *b:* 28.7.1849, Titchmarsh, Northamptonshire. *d:* 7.1.1892, Nottingham. Brother of A. L. (Canterbury) and R. A. N. (Canterbury), nephew of A. W. Crichton (MCC 1856). Tail end left-hand batsman, left-hand fast round-arm bowler, slip field. *Teams* Cambridge U (1871–74, blue 1871, 1872 and 1874); Hampshire (1877–78, 2 matches).
Career batting
27–42–7–244–30–6.97–0–*ct* 9
Bowling 1372–95– + 3–14.44–6–3–9/42
He did not appear for Cambridge in 1873, being in the United States. His final first-class match was for MCC in 1879. His best bowling was on his debut, 9/42 for Cambridge U v MCC at Cambridge in 1871.

Powys-Keck, Horatio James
Amateur. *b:* 7.3.1873, Hyères, France. *d:* 30.1.1952, Kensington, London. Great-nephew of A. W. Crichton (MCC 1856). Tail end batsman, left-arm fast bowler. *Sch* Malvern and Monkton Combe. *Team* Worcestershire (1903–07, 3 matches). *Tours* Oxford Univ Authentics to India 1902/3; Brackley to West Indies 1904/5.
Career batting
9–14–5–69–25*–7.66–0–*ct* 0
Bowling 439–23–19.08–1–0–5/27
His greatest success came on the Authentics tour of India when, in all matches, he took 69 wickets, av 11.03. He did not appear in any trials at Oxford.

Powys-Maurice, Canon Lionel Selwyn
(changed name from L. S. Maurice)
Amateur. *b:* 7.5.1899, Brighton, Sussex. *d:* 8.1.1991, Buckden, Huntingdonshire. Middle order right-hand batsman. *Sch* Haileybury. *Team* Northamptonshire (1922–23, 11 matches).
Career batting
11–19–0–156–65–8.21–0–*ct* 1

Poynder, Charles Eustace Hadden
Amateur. *b:* 15.7.1910, Barnstaple, Devon. Middle order right-hand batsman. *Sch* Newton College. *Team*

Minor Counties (1937).
Career batting
1–2–0–6–3–3.00–0–*ct* 0
His County cricket was for Devon (1928–46).

Poynton, Dr Frederic John
Amateur. *b:* 26.6.1869, Kelston, Somerset. *d:* 29.10.1943, Weston, Bath, Somerset. Brother-in-law of H. S. Williams (Middlesex). Stylish middle order right-hand batsman, good field. *Sch* Marlborough. *Team* Somerset (1891–96, 25 matches).
Career batting
25–48–6–575–57–13.69–0–*ct* 7
Bowling 38–2–19.00–0–0–1/6
His profession restricted his County cricket.

Poyntz, Edward Stephen Massey
Amateur. *b:* 27.10.1883, Springfield, Chelmsford, Essex. *d:* 26.12.1934, Minehead, Somerset. Brother of H. S. (Somerset). Hard hitting middle order right-hand batsman, good field. *Sch* Haileybury. *Team* Somerset (1905–19, 102 matches).
Career batting
105–190–7–3127–114–17.08–1–*ct* 95
Bowling 317–8–39.62–1–0–5/36
He captained Somerset in 1913 and 1914.

Poyntz, Hugh Stainton
Amateur. *b:* 17.9.1877, The Park, Nottingham. *d:* 22.6.1955, Harestock, Hampshire. Brother of E. S. M. (Somerset). Middle order right-hand batsman, leg break bowler. *Sch* Eastbourne. *Teams* Somerset (1904–21, 37 matches); Orange Free State (1912/13).
Career batting
40–70–3–1288–85–19.22–0–*ct* 27
Bowling 182–5–36.40–0–0–3/37
A regular army officer, his County cricket was very restricted. He was also a good soccer player and captained the Army in 1907.

Prahakar, Manoj
Cricketer. *b:* 15.4.1963, Ghaziabad, India. Middle order right-hand batsman, right-arm medium pace bowler. *Team* Delhi (1982/3 to 1991/2). *Tours* Young Indians to Zimbabwe 1983/4; India to England 1986, 1990, to Sharjah (not first-class) 1983/4, 1986/7, 1989/90, 1991/2, to Pakistan 1989/90, to New Zealand 1989/90, to Australia 1991/2, to Australia and New Zealand (World Cup) 1991/2. *Tests* India (1984/5 to 1991/2, 18 matches).
Career batting
90–121–25–4391–229*–45.73–12–*ct* 30
Bowling 6886–230–29.93–9–1–6/36
Test batting
18–30–7–687–95–38.08–0–*ct* 6
Bowling 2331–53–43.98–3–0–6/132
He had little success on his two visits to England, though in 1990 he played in all three Tests. His highest score was 229* for Delhi v Himachal Pradesh at Delhi in 1988/9.

Prasanna, Erapalli Anatharao Srinivas
Amateur. *b:* 22.5.1940, Bangalore, India. Lower order right-hand batsman, off break bowler. *Team* Mysore/Karnataka (1961/2 to 1978/9). *Tours* India to West Indies 1961/2, 1970/1, 1975/6, to England 1967, 1971, 1974, to Australia and New Zealand 1967/8, to Australia 1977/8, to New Zealand 1975/6, to Pakistan 1978/9, to East Africa 1967/8. *Tests* India (1961/2 to 1978/9, 49 matches).
Career batting
235–275–67–2476–81–11.90–0–*ct* 127
Bowling 22442–957–23.45–56–9–8/50
Test batting
49–84–20–735–37–11.48–0–*ct* 18
Bowling 5742–189–30.38–10–2–8/76
His results on the three tours to England did not match his ability and he was overshadowed by India's three other slow bowlers. He appeared in all three Tests on the 1967 tour, none in 1971 and two in 1974.

Pratt, David
Professional. *b:* 20.7.1938, Watford, Hertfordshire. Tail end right-hand batsman, slow left-arm bowler. *Teams* Worcestershire (1959, 8 matches); Nottinghamshire (1962, 7 matches).
Career batting
18–23–7–50–14–3.12–0–*ct* 4
Bowling 1141–23–49.60–1–0–5/54
He also played for Hertfordshire (1957).

Pratt, Derek Edward
Professional. *b:* 31.10.1925, Balham, London. Brother of R. E. C. (Surrey). Sound middle order right-hand batsman, leg break bowler. *Team* Surrey (1954–57, 9 matches).
Career batting
9–12–4–171–33–21.37–0–*ct* 4
Bowling 392–13–30.15–1–0–6/119
He also played for Bedfordshire (1958–63).

Pratt, Donald Montague McVeagh
Amateur. *b:* 9.7.1935, Dublin, Ireland. Nephew of T. G. B. McVeagh (Ireland). Middle order left-hand batsman. *Team* Ireland (1963–66).
Career batting
6–12–0–171–58–14.25–0–*ct* 0

Pratt, John
Professional. *b:* 4.2.1834, Mitcham, Surrey. *d:* 6.6.1886, Phipps Bridge, Merton, Surrey. Brother-in-law of J. Southerton (Surrey). Lower order right-hand batsman, right-hand medium pace round-arm bowler, slip field. *Team* Surrey (1868, 1 match).
Career batting
1–2–0–10–9–5.00–0–*ct* 2
Bowling 12–0

Pratt, Richard
Professional. *b:* 23.6.1896, Lower Broughton, Manchester, Lancashire. *d:* 10.10.1982, Alvaston, Derby. Lower order right-hand batsman, wicket-keeper. *Team* Derbyshire (1923–24, 5 matches).
Career batting
5–10–1–73–17*–8.11–0–*ct* 3

Pratt, Rodney Lynes
Professional. *b:* 15.11.1938, Stoney Stanton, Leicestershire. Lower order right-hand batsman, right-arm fast medium bowler. *Team* Leicestershire (1955–64, 99 matches).
Career batting
102–158–22–1824–80–13.41–0–*ct* 69
Bowling 6726–259–25.96–11–2–7/47

Pratt, Ronald Ernest Charles
Professional. *b:* 5.5.1928, Balham, London. *d:* 1.6.1977, Woodcote, Epsom, Surrey. Brother of D. E. (Surrey). Stylish middle order left-hand batsman, off break bowler, good slip. *Team* Surrey (1952–59, 69 matches).
Career batting
69–102–14–1900–120–21.59–1–*ct* 53
Bowling 138–3–46.00–0–0–1/8

He hit over 1,000 runs for Surrey 2nd XI in the Minor Counties Competition in 1952, but never was able to command a regular place in the full County side.

Pratt, William Ewart
Amateur. *b:* 2.7.1895, Hinckley, Leicestershire. *d:* 27.5.1974, Leicester. Middle order right-hand batsman. *Team* Leicestershire (1920–30, 9 matches).
Career batting
9–17–1–166–29*–10.37–0–*ct* 2
Bowling 52–0

Pratten, Frederick Lewis
(birth registered as Fred Lewis Pratten)
Professional. *b:* 13.2.1904, Weston-super-Mare, Somerset. *d:* 23.2.1967, Midsomer-Norton, Somerset. Lower order right-hand batsman, wicket-keeper. *Team* Somerset (1930–31, 12 matches).
Career batting
12–18–9–71–16–7.88–0–*ct* 6–*st* 5

Preece, Charles Richard
Professional. *b:* 15.12.1888, Broadheath, Worcestershire. *d:* 5.2.1976, Oldbury, Worcestershire. Lower order right-hand batsman, right-arm medium pace bowler. *Team* Worcestershire (1920–29, 88 matches).
Career batting
89–161–23–1601–69–11.60–0–*ct* 53
Bowling 4174–140–29.81–5–0–7/35

His first-class debut was for H. K. Foster's XI in 1919. His obituary was incorrectly published in Wisden ten years prior to his actual demise.

Preece, Henry Charles
Amateur. *b:* 27.10.1867, Weobley, Herefordshire. *d:* 17.9.1937, Highgate, Middlesex. Middle order batsman. *Team* Essex (1895, 2 matches).
Career batting
2–4–0–74–49–18.50–0–*ct* 0

He also played for Cheshire (1893). He lost his sight relatively early in life, but continued his profession as a lecturer at King's College, London.

Preece, Trevor
Professional. *b:* 13.10.1882, Cowbridge, Glamorgan. *d:* 21.9.1965, Whitchurch, Cardiff, Glamorgan. Opening batsman. *Team* Glamorgan (1923, 1 match).
Career batting
1–2–0–8–4–4.00–0–*ct* 1

He first played for Glamorgan (pre first-class) in 1902.

Prentice, Christopher Norman Russell
Cricketer. *b:* 5.9.1954, Borough, London. Middle order right-hand batsman, right-arm medium pace off break bowler. *Sch* Shrewsbury. *Team* Oxford U (1974).
Career batting
1–2–0–23–19–11.50–0–*ct* 0

Prentice, Francis Thomas
Professional until 1950, amateur 1951. *b:* 22.4.1912, Knaresborough, Yorkshire. *d:* 10.7.1978, Headingley, Leeds, Yorkshire. Consistent middle order right-hand batsman, off break bowler. *Team* Leicestershire (1934–51, 241 matches).
Career batting
241–421–24–10997–191–27.70–17–*ct* 75
Bowling 5847–117–49.97–2–0–5/46

He hit 1,000 runs in a season five times (best 1,742, av 38.71, in 1949). After the 1949 season he retired from regular County cricket to concentrate on his business interests.

Prentice, Leslie Roff Vincent
Amateur. *b:* 1887, Fitzroy, Melbourne, Victoria, Australia. *d:* 13.8.1928, Harrold, Bedfordshire. He died in a motor accident. Lower order right-hand batsman, slow right-arm bowler. *Team* Middlesex (1920–23, 12 matches).
Career batting
18–24–1–147–42*–6.39–0–*ct* 9
Bowling 1032–31–33.29–1–0–6/95

Presland, Edward Robert
Professional. *b:* 27.3.1943, High Beech, Essex. Lower order right-hand batsman, right-arm medium pace off break bowler. *Team* Essex (1962–70, 30 matches).
Career batting
30–41–4–625–51–16.89–0–*ct* 24
Bowling 761–13–58.53–0–0–2/19

A noted soccer player, he has appeared for West Ham United, Crystal Palace and Colchester.

Pressdee, James Stuart
Professional. *b:* 19.6.1933, Mumbles, Glamorgan. Father-in-law of R. C. Ontong (Glamorgan). Middle order right-hand batsman, slow left-arm bowler, good close field. *Teams* Glamorgan (1949–65, 322 matches); North East Transvaal (1965/6 to 1969/70).
Career batting
347–583–88–14267–150*–28.82–13–*ct* 371
Bowling 10666–481–22.17–21–5–9/43
He hit 1,000 runs in a season six times (best 1,911, av 34.74, in 1962) and took 100 wickets in a season twice (best 106, av 21.62, in 1963). In 1963 and 1964 he performed the 'double'. His best bowling was 9/43 for Glamorgan v Yorkshire at Swansea in 1965. He emigrated to South Africa in the autumn of 1965. A good soccer player, he was a schoolboy international and appeared at left back for Swansea Town.

Prest, Charles Henry
Amateur. *b:* 9.12.1841, York. *d:* 4.3.1875, Gateshead, Co Durham. Brother of William (Yorkshire). Attacking opening or middle order right-hand batsman, good field. *Sch* St Peter's, York. *Teams* Yorkshire (1864, 2 matches); Middlesex (1870, 1 match).
Career batting
5–10–0–132–57–13.20–0–*ct* 3
His first-class debut was for Gentlemen of the North in 1861. A noted amateur actor he appeared on the London stage under the name of 'Mr Peveril'.

Prest, Harold Edward Westray
Amateur. *b:* 9.1.1890, Beckenham, Kent. *d:* 5.1.1955, Shalford, Surrey. Brother-in-law of G. N. Foster (Worcestershire and Kent). Stylish middle order right-hand batsman, good field. *Sch* Malvern. *Teams* Cambridge U (1909–11, blue 1909 and 1911); Kent (1909–22, 19 matches).
Career batting
32–45–4–1156–133*–28.19–1–*ct* 22
Bowling 4–1–4.00–0–0–1/4
He also was awarded his blue for soccer and golf.

Preston, Benjamin
Amateur. *b:* 20.4.1846, Lowestoft, Suffolk. *d:* 1.6.1914, North End, Lowestoft, Suffolk. Stylish opening right-hand batsman, deep field. *Sch* Westminster. *Team* Cambridge U (1869–70, blue 1869).
Career batting
8–14–2–124–28–10.33–0–*ct* 4
His County cricket was for Suffolk (1867–85) and Norfolk (1869–72).

Preston, Derek John
Amateur. *b:* 12.1.1936, Leyton, Essex. Middle order right-hand batsman, slow left-arm bowler. *Sch* Bancrofts. *Team* Sussex (1959, 12 matches).
Career batting
12–15–2–154–54–11.84–0–*ct* 8
Bowling 562–13–43.23–0–0–3/45

Preston, Henry John Berridge
Professional. *b:* 25.10.1883, Bareilly, India. *d:* 23.4.1964, Hastings, Sussex. Lower order right-hand batsman, right-arm medium pace bowler. *Team* Kent (1907–13, 19 matches).
Career batting
19–27–14–84–18–6.46–0–*ct* 4
Bowling 865–43–20.11–1–0–5/23
He appeared for Scotland in a representative non-first-class match in 1936. His career in club cricket was a long one and would have been even more extensive if he had not lost an arm in an accident with a mowing machine.

Preston, Joseph Merritt
Professional. *b:* 23.8.1864, Yeadon, Yorkshire. *d:* 26.11.1890, Windhill, Yorkshire. He died of a chill. Stylish middle or lower order right-hand batsman, off break bowler. *Team* Yorkshire (1885–89, 80 matches). *Tour* Lillywhite, Shaw and Shrewsbury to Australia 1887/8.
Career batting
95–157–14–2131–93–14.90–0–*ct* 43
Bowling 3763–211–17.83–9–5–9/28
His best season was 1887 with 52 wickets, av 18.73. His best bowling was 9/28 for Yorkshire v MCC at Scarborough in 1888.

Preston, Kenneth Charles
Professional. *b:* 22.8.1925, Goodmayes, Essex. Lower order right-hand batsman, right-arm fast medium bowler. *Team* Essex (1948–64, 391 matches).
Career batting
397–468–169–3053–70–10.21–0–*ct* 350
Bowling 30533–1160–26.32–37–2–7/55
He took 140 wickets, av 20.35, in 1957.

Preston, Stephen
Professional. *b:* 11.8.1905, Heywood, Lancashire. Lower order right-hand batsman, right-arm medium pace bowler. *Team* Lancashire (1928–30, 5 matches).
Career batting
5–4–2–46–33–23.00–0–*ct* 1
Bowling 212–6–35.33–0–0–2/42

Pretlove, John Frederick
Amateur. *b:* 23.11.1932, Camberwell, London. Determined middle order left-hand batsman, slow left-arm bowler. *Sch* Alleyns. *Teams* Cambridge U (1954–56, blue all three years); Kent (1955–59, 85 matches). *Tour* MCC to North America 1959 (not first-class).
Career batting
124–212–21–5115–137–26.78–10–*ct* 70–*st* 2
Bowling 1319–43–30.67–1–0–5/55
He hit 1,191 runs, av 25.89, in 1957. He was Assistant Secretary to Kent CCC, 1955 to 1957. His final

first-class match was for MCC in 1968. An all-round sportsman, he won blues for soccer and rugby fives.

Pretty, Dr Harold Cooper
Amateur. *b:* 23.10.1875, Fressingfield, Suffolk. *d:* 30.5.1952, Kettering, Northamptonshire. Punishing middle order right-hand batsman, off break bowler. *Sch* Epsom. *Teams* Surrey (1899, 8 matches); Northamptonshire (1906–07, 8 matches).
Career batting
16–26–0–696–200–26.76–2–*ct* 9
Bowling 138–5–27.60–0–0–3/39
He hit 124 for Surrey v Nottinghamshire at the Oval in 1899 on his first-class debut and his only other three-figure innings was 200 for Northamptonshire v Derbyshire at Chesterfield in 1906.

Price, Alfred
Professional. *b:* 5.1.1862, Ruddington, Nottinghamshire. *d:* 21.3.1942, Mumps, Oldham, Lancashire. Son of Walter (Nottinghamshire), brother of William (Liverpool) and Frederick (North). Defensive middle order right-hand batsman. *Teams* Lancashire (1885, 1 match); Nottinghamshire (1887, 3 matches).
Career batting
7–12–0–110–37–9.16–0–*ct* 7
His first-class debut was for North v South at Lord's in 1884.

Price, Charles Frederick Thomas
Amateur. *b:* 17.2.1917, Sydney, New South Wales, Australia. Lower order left-hand batsman, slow left-arm bowler. *Team* Australian Services (1945 to 1945/6). *Tours* Australian Services to England 1945, to India and Ceylon 1945/6.
Career batting
14–20–3–327–55–19.23–0–*ct* 11
Bowling 643–24–26.79–0–0–4/33

Price, Charley James
Amateur. *b:* 16.3.1890, South Hamlet, Gloucestershire. *d:* 7.6.1967, High Orchard, Gloucester. Middle order batsman. *Team* Gloucestershire (1919, 1 match).
Career batting
1–2–0–19–13–9.50–0–*ct* 0

Price, David Gregory
Cricketer. *b:* 7.2.1965, Luton, Bedfordshire. Middle order right-hand batsman, off break bowler. *Sch* Haberdashers' Aske's. *Team* Cambridge U (1984–87, blue all four years).
Career batting
29–47–3–785–60–17.84–0–*ct* 8
Bowling 42–1–42.00–0–0–1/18
He captained Cambridge in 1986 and 1987. His County cricket was for Hertfordshire (1986–90).

Price, David Howe
Cricketer. *b:* 25.7.1955, Gloucester. Middle order right-hand batsman, right-arm medium pace bowler. *Sch* Malvern. *Team* Oxford U (1975–78).
Career batting
5–10–0–104–27–10.40–0–*ct* 4
Bowling 174–2–87.00–0–0–1/22
He won a blue for soccer.

Price, Eric James
Professional. *b:* 27.10.1918, Middleton, Lancashire. Lower order left-hand batsman, slow left-arm bowler. *Teams* Lancashire (1946–47, 35 matches); Essex (1948–49, 43 matches).
Career batting
80–95–31–558–54–8.71–0–*ct* 40
Bowling 5722–215–26.61–10–2–8/125

Price, Frederic Richard
Amateur. *b:* 2.2.1840, Llewes Hall, Denbigh. *d:* 26.12.1894, at sea in the English Channel on board SS *Teutonic* sailing between USA and Britain. Middle order right-hand batsman, slow under-arm bowler, point field. *Sch* Cheltenham. *Teams* Oxford U (1861); Gloucestershire (1872, 2 matches).
Career batting
6–10–2–90–33–11.25–0–*ct* 8–*st* 3
Bowling 99–6–16.50–0–0–3/33
His first-class debut was for Gentlemen of the North in 1859. He also played for Monmouth (1860), Cheshire (1862), Shropshire (1865) and Denbigh (1865). He emigrated to the United States, becoming a farmer in Iowa and Colorado.

Price, Rev Frederic William Stephen
Amateur. *b:* 26.2.1852, Lutterworth, Leicestershire. *d:* 22.12.1937, Shoreham-by-Sea, Sussex. Middle order right-hand batsman, right-arm medium pace bowler. *Team* Cambridge U (1873).
Career batting
4–7–1–13–5–2.16–0–*ct* 3
Bowling 37–1–37.00–0–0–1/10
His final first-class match was for An England XI in 1874. His County cricket was for Berkshire (1870).

Price, Frederick
Professional. *b:* 24.12.1857, Ruddington, Nottinghamshire. *d:* 19.1.1927, Nottingham. Son of Walter (Nottinghamshire), brother of Alfred (Lancashire and Nottinghamshire) and William (Liverpool). Lower order batsman, right-arm medium pace bowler. *Team* North (1887).
Career batting
1–1–1–9–9*–no av –0–*ct* 0

Price, Herbert Leo
Amateur. *b:* 21.6.1899, Sutton, Surrey. *d:* 18.7.1943, Victoria Park, Manchester, Lancashire. He died following an operation. Brother of V. R. (Surrey). Middle order right-hand batsman. *Sch* Bishop's Stortford. *Team* Oxford U (1920–22).
Career batting
2–4–1–46–32*–15.33–0–*ct* 1

An all-round sportsman, he represented Oxford at rugby football, hockey and water polo, going on to be capped for England as a rugby wing forward and a hockey centre-half.

Price, John
Amateur. *b:* 6.7.1908, Shrub Hill, Worcester. Brother of W. H. (Worcestershire), nephew of E. G. Arnold (Worcestershire). Lower order right-hand batsman, right-arm fast medium bowler. *Team* Worcestershire (1927–29, 11 matches).
Career batting
11–18–4–81–33–5.78–0–*ct* 4
Bowling 611–12–50.91–0–0–2/35

Price, John Sidney Ernest
Professional. *b:* 22.7.1937, Harrow, Middlesex. Lower order left-hand batsman, right-arm fast medium bowler. *Team* Middlesex (1961–75, 242 matches). *Tours* MCC to India 1963/4, to South Africa 1964/5. *Tests* England (1963/4 to 1972, 15 matches).
Career batting
279–223–91–1108–53*–8.39–0–*ct* 103
Bowling 19221–817–23.52–26–4–8/48
Test batting
15–15–6–66–32–7.33–0–*ct* 7
Bowling 1401–40–35.02–1–0–5/73
His best season was 1966 with 94 wickets, av 18.74. Injury restricted his cricket during several seasons.

Price, Mark Richard
Cricketer. *b:* 20.4.1960, Liverpool, Lancashire. Lower order right-hand batsman, slow left-arm bowler. *Team* Glamorgan (1984–85, 17 matches).
Career batting
17–13–4–144–36–16.00–0–*ct* 2
Bowling 806–19–42.42–0–0–4/97

Price, Vincent Rains
(death registered as Vincent Ramo Price)
Amateur. *b:* 22.5.1895, Sutton, Surrey. *d:* 29.5.1973, Bexhill-on-Sea, Sussex. Brother of H. L. (Oxford U). Lower order right-hand batsman, right-arm fast medium bowler. *Sch* Bishop Stortford. *Teams* Oxford U (1919–22, blue all four years); Surrey (1919, 1 match).
Career batting
38–59–12–745–76*–15.85–0–*ct* 24
Bowling 3394–131–25.90–7–1–8/30
He created a stir by taking 14 wickets for 112 for Oxford U v Gentlemen in the first first-class match played after the 1914–18 war, but he scarcely lived up to expectations in his later appearances. His final first-class match was for Leveson-Gower's XI in 1924. He captained Oxford in 1921. A good rugby footballer, he appeared for Oxford three times.

Price, Walter
Professional. *b:* 9.10.1834, Ruddington, Nottinghamshire. *d:* 4.9.1894, Ruddington, Nottinghamshire. Father of Alfred (Lancashire and Nottinghamshire), Frederick (North) and William (Liverpool). Middle order right-hand batsman, right-hand medium pace round-arm bowler. *Team* Nottinghamshire (1869–70, 5 matches).
Career batting
33–56–5–625–57–12.25–0–*ct* 14
Bowling 301–15–20.06–1–0–5/66
His first-class debut was for MCC in 1868 and his final first-class match for the same Club in 1882. He was a first-class umpire for many years, being on the staff at Lord's until his death. He also played for Devon (1867).

Price, Walter Longsdon
Amateur. *b:* 2.2.1886, Toxteth Park, Liverpool, Lancashire. *d:* 26.12.1943, Lechlade, Gloucestershire. Lower order left-hand batsman, left-arm medium pace bowler. *Sch* Repton. *Team* Worcestershire (1904, 3 matches).
Career batting
3–3–0–12–7–4.00–0–*ct* 1
Bowling 284–8–35.50–0–0–4/86
He appeared for Canada v USA in 1912.

Price, Wilfred Frederick Frank
Professional. *b:* 25.4.1902, Westminster, London. *d:* 13.1.1969, Hendon, Middlesex. Sound opening or middle order right-hand batsman, wicket-keeper. *Team* Middlesex (1926–47, 382 matches). *Tours* MCC to West Indies 1929/30; Brinckman to Argentine 1937/8. *Test* England (1938, 1 match).
Career batting
402–590–97–9035–111–18.32–3–*ct* 666–*st* 321
Test batting
1–2–0–6–6–3.00–0–*ct* 2
He hit 1,000 runs in a season once: 1,298, av 25.96, in 1934. From 1949 to 1967 he was a first-class umpire and caused a sensation by no-balling G. A. R. Lock for throwing. He umpired 8 Test matches (1964–67).

Price, William
Professional. *b:* 4.12.1859, Ruddington, Nottinghamshire. Son of Walter (Nottinghamshire), brother of Alfred (Lancashire and Nottinghamshire) and Frederick (North). *Team* Liverpool and District (1889).
Career batting
2–4–2–28–26*–14.00–0–*ct* 1
Bowling 113–10–11.30–1–0–6/51

Price, William Harry
Amateur. *b:* 28.5.1900, Shrub Hill, Worcester. *d:* 15.4.1982, Worcester. Brother of John (Worcestershire), nephew of E. G. Arnold (Worcestershire). Lower order right-hand batsman, right-arm fast med-

ium bowler. *Sch* Royal Grammar School, Worcester. *Team* Worcestershire (1923, 1 match).
Career batting
1–1–1–0–0*–no av–0–*ct* 0
Bowling 12–0

Price, William Leslie
Amateur. *b:* 19.3.1881, Taunton, Somerset. *d:* 6.2.1958, North Town, Taunton, Somerset. Lower order batsman, wicket-keeper. *Team* Somerset (1901, 1 match).
Career batting
1–2–0–10–10–5.00–0–*ct* 0

Prichard, Hubert Cecil
(also known as Collins-Prichard)
Amateur. *b:* 6.2.1865, Clifton, Bristol. *d:* 12.11.1942, Pwllywrach, Cowbridge, Glamorgan. Brother-in-law of C. G. Carnegy (Europeans). Middle order batsman. *Sch* Clifton. *Team* Gloucestershire (1896, 2 matches).
Career batting
2–4–0–46–23–11.50–0–*ct* 1
He also played for Glamorgan (pre first-class, 1899–1900).

Prichard, Paul John
Cricketer. *b:* 7.1.1965, Billericay, Essex. Middle order right-hand batsman. *Team* Essex (1984–92, 194 matches).
Career batting
194–306–38–9610–245–35.85–16–*ct* 125
Bowling 409–1–409.00–0–0–1/28
He scored 1,000 runs in a season five times (best 1,485, av 43.67, in 1992). In 1990 he hit 245 for Essex v Leicestershire at Chelmsford, adding 405 for the second wicket with G. A. Gooch.

Priddy, James
Amateur. *b:* 3.12.1909, Chard, Somerset. Lower order batsman, useful bowler. *Team* Somerset (1933–39, 7 matches).
Career batting
7–10–2–104–27–13.00–0–*ct* 3
Bowling 241–4–60.25–0–0–2/114

Pride, Thomas
Professional. *b:* 23.7.1864, York. *d:* 16.2.1919, Canonbie, Dumfries, Scotland. Lower order right-hand batsman, wicket-keeper. *Team* Yorkshire (1887, 1 match).
Career batting
1–1–0–1–1–1.00–0–*ct* 4–*st* 3

Prideaux, Roger Malcolm
Amateur. *b:* 31.7.1939, Chelsea, London. Sound right-hand opening batsman, right-arm medium pace bowler. *Sch* Tonbridge. *Teams* Cambridge U (1958–60, blue all three years); Kent (1960–61, 33 matches); Northamptonshire (1962–70, 234 matches); Sussex (1971–73, 65 matches); Orange Free State (1971/2 to 1974/5). *Tours* MCC to North America 1959 (not first-class), to New Zealand 1960/1, to Ceylon and Pakistan 1968/9; Commonwealth to Pakistan 1967/8. *Tests* England (1968 to 1968/9, 3 matches).
Career batting
446–808–75–25136–202*–34.29–41–*ct* 303
Bowling 176–3–58.66–0–0–2/13
Test batting
3–6–1–102–64–20.40–0–*ct* 0
Bowling 0–0
He hit 1,000 runs in a season thirteen times (best 1,993, av 41.52, in 1968). His only double century was 202* for Northamptonshire v Oxford U at Oxford in 1963. In 1961 he hit a century in 52 minutes for North v South at Blackpool. From 1967 to 1970 he captained Northamptonshire.

Pridgeon, Alan Paul
Cricketer. *b:* 22.2.1954, Wall Heath, Staffordshire. Lower order right-hand batsman, right-arm medium pace bowler. *Team* Worcestershire (1972–89, 240 matches).
Career batting
240–221–84–1188–67–8.67–0–*ct* 82
Bowling 17367–530–32.76–10–1–7/35
He took 72 wickets, av 27.47, in 1983. He also played for Shropshire (1991–92).

Pridmore, Reginald George
Amateur. *b:* 29.4.1886, Edgbaston, Birmingham. *d:* 13.3.1918, near Piave River, north of Venice, Italy. He was killed in action. Middle order batsman. *Sch* Bedford County. *Team* Warwickshire (1909–12, 14 matches).
Career batting
14–26–1–315–49–12.60–0–*ct* 7
He also played for Hertfordshire (1902–03). He won a gold medal playing hockey for England in the 1908 Olympic Games.

Priest, Mark Wellings
Cricketer. *b:* 12.8.1961, Greymouth, Westland, New Zealand. Middle order left-hand batsman, slow left-arm bowler. *Team* Canterbury (1984/5 to 1991/2). *Tours* Young New Zealand to Zimbabwe 1988/9; New Zealand to Sharjah (not first-class) 1989/90, to England 1990, to Pakistan 1990/1. *Test* New Zealand (1990, 1 match).
Career batting
61–86–13–2304–119–31.56–3–*ct* 35
Bowling 5683–158–35.96–6–2–9/95
Test batting
1–1–0–26–26–26.00–0–*ct* 0
Bowling 26–1–26.00–0–0–1/26
On the 1990 tour to England he proved an all-rounder of promise and was unfortunate not to play in more than one Test. His best bowling was 9/95 for Canterbury v Otago at Dunedin in 1989/90.

Priestley, Sir Arthur Alexander
Amateur. *b:* 9.11.1865, Kensington, London. *d:* 10.4.1933, Monaco. Middle order right-hand batsman. *Team* MCC (1895). *Tours* Lucas to West Indies 1894/5; Priestley to West Indies 1896/7; Ranjitsinhji to North America 1899 (he did not play in first-class matches); Bosanquet to North America 1901 (he did not play in first-class matches).
Career batting
18–27–2–183–36–7.32–0–*ct* 11
He was MP for Grantham from 1900 to 1918.

Priestley, Donald Lacey
Amateur. *b:* 28.7.1887, Tewkesbury, Gloucestershire. *d:* 30.10.1917, Passchendale, Belgium. He was killed in action. Middle order right-hand batsman, right-arm medium pace bowler. *Team* Gloucestershire (1909–10, 7 matches).
Career batting
7–13–1–154–51–12.83–0–*ct* 2

Priestley, Hugh William
Amateur. *b:* 19.9.1887, Marylebone, London. *d:* 6.1.1932, Marylebone, London. Father of R. H. (Free Foresters). Opening right-hand batsman, right-arm medium pace bowler. *Sch* Uppingham. *Team* MCC (1911).
Career batting
1–2–0–33–31–16.50–0–*ct* 0
Bowling 16–1–16.00–0–0–1/16
He appeared in the Cambridge Freshmen's match of 1907, but no first-class matches for the University. His County cricket was for Buckinghamshire (1907).

Priestley, Iain Martin
Cricketer. *b:* 25.9.1967, Horsforth, Yorkshire. Lower order right-hand batsman, right-arm medium fast bowler. *Team* Yorkshire (1989, 2 matches).
Career batting
2–4–2–25–23–12.50–0–*ct* 1
Bowling 119–4–29.75–0–0–4/27

Priestley, Neil
Cricketer. *b:* 23.6.1961, Blyborough, Lincolnshire. Lower order right-hand batsman, wicket-keeper. *Team* Northamptonshire (1981, 1 match).
Career batting
1–1–1–20–20*–no av–0–*ct* 1–*st* 2
He also played for Lincolnshire (1983–90).

Priestley, Robert Hugh
Amateur. *b:* 23.11.1911, Maida Vale, London. Son of H. W. (MCC). Opening right-hand batsman, off break bowler. *Sch* Winchester. *Team* Free Foresters (1932).
Career batting
1–2–0–16–16–8.00–0–*ct* 0

Prince, Charles Frederick Henry
Amateur. *b:* 11.9.1874, Boshof, Orange Free State, South Africa. *d:* 2.2.1949, Wynberg, Cape Town, South Africa. Middle order right-hand batsman, wicket-keeper. *Teams* Western Province (1894/5 to 1904/5); Border (1897/8); Eastern Province (1902/3 to 1903/4); London County (1901). *Tour* South Africa to England 1901. *Test* South Africa (1898/9, 1 match).
Career batting
24–41–0–730–61–17.80–0–*ct* 14–*st* 14
Bowling 28–0
Test batting
1–2–0–6–5–3.00–0–*ct* 0
He played in few matches on the 1901 tour, but made a fleeting appearance for London County.

Prince, William
Professional. *b:* 28.3.1868, Somercotes, Derbyshire. *d:* 1.6.1948, New Ollerton, Nottinghamshire. Lower order right-hand batsman, right-arm medium fast bowler. *Team* Derbyshire (1898, 1 match).
Career batting
1–1–1–2–2*–no av–0–*ct* 0
Bowling 38–0

Pringle, Christopher
Cricketer. *b:* 26.1.1968, Auckland, New Zealand. Lower order right-hand batsman, right-arm fast medium bowler. *Team* Auckland (1989/90 to 1991/2). *Tours* New Zealand to England 1990, to Pakistan 1990/1, to Australia 1990/1 (not first-class); Rest of World to England 1990, 1992. *Tests* New Zealand (1990/1 to 1991/2, 6 matches).
Career batting
30–34–8–321–33–12.34–0–*ct* 10
Bowling 3003–93–32.29–2–1–7/52
Test batting
6–10–2–80–24*–10.00–0–*ct* 0
Bowling 695–18–38.61–1–1–7/52
He was co-opted into the 1990 New Zealand touring party to England, whilst engaged in the Bradford League, but played in only four first-class matches and no Tests.

Pringle, Derek Raymond
Cricketer. *b:* 18.9.1958, Nairobi, Kenya. Son of Don (East Africa in World Cup). Middle order right-hand batsman, right-arm medium pace bowler. *Sch* Felsted. *Teams* Essex (1978–92, 199 matches); Cambridge U (1979–82, blue 1979–81). *Tours* England to Australia 1982/3, to Sharjah (not first-class) 1984/5, to Pakistan (World Cup) 1987/8, to India 1989/90 (not first-class), to New Zealand 1991/2, to Australia and New Zealand (World Cup) 1991/2; England B to Sri Lanka 1985/6; England A to Zimbabwe 1989/90. *Tests* England (1982–92, 30 matches).
Career batting
281–383–74–8633–128–27.93–10–*ct* 142
Bowling 19189–732–26.21–25–3–7/18
Test batting
30–50–4–695–63–15.10–0–*ct* 10
Bowling 2518–70–35.97–3–0–5/95

In 1982 he took the unprecedented step of standing down from the University match, having been chosen as captain, in order to play for England. Having toured Australia with England immediately after leaving Cambridge, it would have seemed that he was set for a long Test career, but his international matches have been spasmodic. In 1989 he took 94 wickets, av 18.64, easily his best aggregate, however 1990 saw him beset by injury. Recovery in 1991 meant another return to Test cricket. He appeared in three Tests against Pakistan in 1992, with very modest results. He is also a journalist writing mainly for the *Daily Telegraph*.

Pringle, Meyrick Wayne
Cricketer. *b:* 22.6.1966, Adelaide, Cape Province, South Africa. Lower order right-hand batsman, right-arm fast medium bowler. *Teams* Orange Free State (1985/6); Sussex (1987–88, 6 matches); Eastern Province (1987/8 to 1988/9); Western Province (1989/90 to 1991/2). *Tours* South Africa to Australia and New Zealand (World Cup) 1991/2, to West Indies 1991/2. *Test* South Africa (1991/2, 1 match).
Career batting
48–66–10–831–53–14.83–0–*ct* 14
Bowling 4219–164–25.72–6–1–7/60
Test batting
1–2–0–19–15–9.50–0–*ct* 0
Bowling 105–2–52.50–0–0–2/62
His last first-class match in England was for MCC in 1989.

Pringle, Nicholas John
Cricketer. *b:* 20.9.1966, Weymouth, Dorset. Middle order right-hand batsman, right-arm medium fast bowler. *Sch* Taunton. *Team* Somerset (1986–91, 27 matches).
Career batting
27–48–6–707–79–16.83–0–*ct* 15
Bowling 551–5–110.20–0–0–2/35

Prior, Ian David
Cricketer. *b:* 26.7.1930, Battersea, London. Middle order right-hand batsman, wicket-keeper. *Team* Minor Counties (1967).
Career batting
1–2–0–21–21–10.50–0–*ct* 3
His County cricket was for Suffolk (1956–68).

Prior, John Andrew
Cricketer. *b:* 14.6.1960, Dublin, Ireland. Middle order right-hand batsman, right-arm medium pace bowler. *Team* Ireland (1981–86).
Career batting
6–10–1–232–87–25.77–0–*ct* 3
Bowling 119–3–39.66–0–0–2/7

Pritchard, Graham Charles
Cricketer. *b:* 14.1.1942, Farnborough, Hampshire. Lower order right-hand batsman, right-arm fast medium bowler. *Sch* King's, Canterbury. *Teams* Cambridge U (1962–64, blue 1964); Essex (1965–66, 10 matches).
Career batting
35–42–15–111–18–4.11–0–*ct* 13
Bowling 2058–56–36.75–2–0–6/51

Pritchard, Jack Mervyn
Amateur. *b:* 19.5.1895. *d:* 17.11.1936, South Kensington, London. Lower order batsman, good bowler. *Sch* Charterhouse. *Team* Oxford U (1919).
Career batting
2–3–1–36–22*–18.00–0–*ct* 2
Bowling 177–7–25.28–0–0–4/45

Pritchard, Thomas Leslie
Professional, but amateur in 1956. *b:* 10.3.1917, Kaupokonui, Taranaki, New Zealand. Fierce hitting lower order right-hand batsman, right-arm fast, later fast medium, bowler. *Teams* Wellington (1937/8 to 1940/1); Warwickshire (1946–55, 170 matches); Kent (1956, 4 matches).
Career batting
200–293–41–3363–81–13.34–0–*ct* 82
Bowling 19062–818–23.30–48–11–8/20
He took 100 wickets in a season four times (best 172, av 18.75, in 1948). His final first-class match in New Zealand was for North Island Army in 1942/3.

Procter, Michael John
Cricketer. *b:* 15.9.1946, Durban, South Africa. Son of W. C. (Eastern Province), brother of A. W. (Natal). Attacking middle order right-hand batsman, right-arm fast or off break bowler. *Teams* Gloucestershire (1965–81, 259 matches); Natal (1965/6 to 1988/9); Western Province (1969/70); Rhodesia (1970/1 to 1975/6); Orange Free State (1987/8). *Tours* South Africa to England 1970 (tour cancelled), to Australia 1971/2 (tour cancelled); Rest of World to England 1970. *Tests* South Africa (1966/7 to 1969/70, 7 matches).
Career batting
401–667–58–21936–254–36.01–48–*ct* 325
Bowling 27679–1417–19.53–70–15–9/71
Test batting
7–10–1–226–48–25.11–0–*ct* 4
Bowling 616–41–15.02–1–0–6/73
One of the most dynamic cricketers of the 1970s, he captained Gloucestershire from 1977 to 1981, but was forced to retire from County cricket in 1981 due to a knee injury. He hit 1,000 runs in a season nine times (best 1,786, av 45.79, in 1971) and took 100 wickets in a season twice (best 109, av 18.04, in 1977). His highest score in England was 203 for Gloucestershire v Essex at Gloucester in 1978. In 1970/1 he hit six hundreds in six consecutive innings for Rhodesia. His highest score was 254 for Rhodesia v Western Province at Salisbury in 1970/1; his best bowling was 9/71 for Rhodesia v Transvaal at

Bulawayo in 1972/3. He was cricket manager of Northamptonshire 1990–91, resigning when he took up a similar position with the South African national team.

Prodger, John Michael
Professional. *b:* 1.9.1935, Forest Hill, London. Opening right-hand batsman, excellent slip field. *Team* Kent (1956–67, 151 matches).
Career batting
151–259–22–4831–170*–20.38–3–*ct* 170
Bowling 14–1–14.00–0–0–1/14

Proffitt, Stanley
Professional. *b:* 8.10.1910, Oldham, Lancashire. Opening left-hand batsman, slow left-arm bowler. *Team* Essex (1937, 7 matches).
Career batting
7–14–0–170–39–12.14–0–*ct* 1
Bowling 32–0
He was English table tennis champion.

Prosser, William Henry
Amateur. *b:* 16.7.1870, Devauden Green, Monmouthshire. *d:* 30.6.1952, Heacham, Norfolk. Lower order batsman, right-arm fast medium bowler. *Team* Cambridge U (1893).
Career batting
1–1–0–0–0–0.00–0–*ct* 1
Bowling 32–0
His County cricket was for Monmouthshire (1891).

Prothero, Rowland Edmund
(birth registered as Roland Edmund Prothero; created 1st Lord Ernle in 1919)
Amateur. *b:* 6.9.1851, Clifton-upon-Teme, Worcestershire. *d:* 1.7.1937, Ginge, Berkshire. Son of George (Oxford U 1839). Middle order right-hand batsman, right-arm medium bowler. *Sch* Marlborough. *Team* Hampshire (1875–83, 4 matches).
Career batting
6–10–4–190–110–31.66–1–*ct* 7
Bowling 181–10–18.10–1–0–5/34
His first-class debut was for Gentlemen of England in 1872. He was MP for Oxford University 1904–19.

Proud, Roland Barton
Amateur. *b:* 29.9.1919, Bishop Auckland, Co Durham. *d:* 27.10.1961, Bishop Auckland, Co Durham. Dashing middle order right-hand batsman, right-arm medium pace bowler. *Sch* Winchester. *Teams* Hampshire (1938–39, 7 matches); Oxford U (1939, blue).
Career batting
18–33–1–681–87–21.28–0–*ct* 7
He also played for Durham (pre first-class, 1946–55) being captain for several years, and his last first-class match was for the Minor Counties in 1950.

Prouton, Ralph Oliver
Professional. *b:* 1.3.1926, Southampton, Hampshire. Sound opening or middle order right-hand batsman, wicket-keeper. *Team* Hampshire (1949–54, 52 matches).
Career batting
52–79–11–982–90–14.44–0–*ct* 84–*st* 13
He played football for Swindon Town.

Pruett, Harry George
Amateur. *b:* 1890. *d:* 22.1.1948, Clifton, Bristol. Tail end batsman, left-arm bowler. *Team* Somerset (1921–26, 2 matches).
Career batting
2–4–0–7–5–1.75–0–*ct* 0
Bowling 49–0

Pryer, Barry James Keith
Amateur. *b:* 1.2.1925, Plumstead, London. Lower order right-hand batsman, leg break bowler. *Sch* City of London. *Teams* Kent (1947–49, 2 matches); Cambridge U (1948–49, blue 1948).
Career batting
27–37–10–252–75*–9.33–0–*ct* 9
Bowling 1888–48–39.33–0–0–4/25
His first-class debut was for Combined Services in 1946 and his final first-class match for Free Foresters in 1950.

Pryor, Charles
Professional. *b:* 15.2.1815, Cambridge. Father of F. C. (Cambridgeshire). Free hitting middle order right-hand batsman. *Team* Cambridge Town Club (1833–59).
Career batting
32–55–5–595–103–11.90–1–*ct* 4
Bowling 1 wicket (no analyses)–0–0–1/?

Pryor, Frederick Charles
Professional. *b:* 10.11.1844, Cambridge. Son of Charles (Cambridge Town Club). Hard hitting middle order right-hand batsman, right-hand fast round-arm bowler, wicket-keeper. *Teams* Cambridge Town Club (1861); Cambridgeshire (1863–71, 22 matches).
Career batting
25–46–2–486–69–11.04–0–*ct* 16–*st* 3

Pryor, Ronald McDonell
Amateur. *b:* 1901, Brazil. *d:* 24.12.1977, Brazil. Tail end batsman, slow left-arm bowler. *Sch* Tonbridge. *Team* South America (1932). *Tour* South America to England 1932.
Career batting
1–2–0–0–0–0.00–0–*ct* 0
Bowling 13–0
He had little success on the 1932 tour and appeared in only a single first-class match.

Puckridge, Anthony
Cricketer. *b:* 5.4.1943, Bickley, Kent. Lower order right-hand batsman, wicket-keeper. *Sch* Malvern. *Team* Oxford U (1963).
Career batting
1–1–0–1–1–1.00–0–*ct* 2

Puddefoot, Sydney Charles
Professional. *b:* 17.10.1894, Limehouse, London. *d:* 2.10.1972, Rochford, Essex. Lower order right-hand batsman, left-arm medium pace bowler. *Team* Essex (1922–23, 8 matches).
Career batting
8–8–2–101–42–16.83–0–*ct* 2
Bowling 105–1–105.00–0–0–1/34
An excellent soccer player, he was inside right for West Ham United, Falkirk, Blackburn Rovers and appeared twice for England. When transferred from West Ham to Falkirk in 1922 he became the first player to be sold for £5,000.

Pugh, Charles Thomas Michael
Amateur. *b:* 13.3.1937, Marylebone, London. Nephew of J. G. (Warwickshire). Steady opening right-hand batsman, right arm slow bowler. *Sch* Eton. *Team* Gloucestershire (1959–62, 76 matches).
Career batting
80–142–9–2469–137–18.56–1–*ct* 42
Bowling 30–1–30.00–0–0–1/12
He hit 1,011 runs, av 21.51, in 1960. He captained Gloucestershire in 1961 and 1962.

Pugh, John Geoffrey
Amateur. *b:* 22.1.1904, Radford, Coventry, Warwickshire. *d:* 14.2.1964, Marine Gardens, Hastings, Barbados. Uncle of C. T. M. (Gloucestershire). Attacking middle order right-hand batsman, bowler. *Sch* Rugby. *Team* Warwickshire (1922–27, 9 matches).
Career batting
9–9–0–82–41–9.11–0–*ct* 3
Bowling 206–6–34.33–0–0–4/100

Pullan, Cecil Douglas Ayrton
Amateur. *b:* 26.7.1910, Mahoba, India. *d:* 24.6.1970, Tongaat Beach, Natal, South Africa. Middle order right-hand batsman, right-arm medium fast bowler. *Sch* Malvern. *Teams* Oxford U (1932); Worcestershire (1935–38, 25 matches).
Career batting
33–58–9–1049–84–21.40–0–*ct* 20
Bowling 357–8–44.62–0–0–2/26
He captained the Oxford U boxing team.

Pullan, David Anthony
Cricketer. *b:* 1.5.1944, Farsley, Yorkshire. Lower order right-hand batsman, wicket-keeper. *Team* Nottinghamshire (1970–74, 95 matches).
Career batting
95–106–36–613–34–8.75–0–*ct* 206–*st* 28
He was General Manager of Nottinghamshire CCC 1980 to 1982 and is Commercial Manager of Nottingham Forest FC.

Pullan, Peter
Professional. *b:* 29.3.1857, Guiseley, Yorkshire. *d:* 3.3.1901, Menston, Yorkshire. Lower order right-hand batsman, right-arm slow bowler. *Team* Yorkshire (1884, 1 match).
Career batting
1–1–0–14–14–14.00–0–*ct* 1
Bowling 5–0

Pullar, Geoffrey
Amateur, turned professional in 1956. *b:* 1.8.1935, Swinton, Lancashire. Stylish opening left-hand batsman, leg break bowler, good outfield. *Teams* Lancashire (1954–68, 312 matches); Gloucestershire (1969–70, 25 matches). *Tours* MCC to West Indies 1959/60, to India, Pakistan and Ceylon 1961/2, to Australia 1962/3; Cavaliers to South Africa 1960/1. *Tests* England (1959 to 1962/3, 28 matches).
Career batting
400–672–63–21528–175–35.34–41–*ct* 125
Bowling 387–10–38.70–0–0–3/91
Test batting
28–49–4–1974–175–43.86–4–*ct* 2
Bowling 37–1–37.00–0–0–1/1
Originally a middle order batsman, Pullar was promoted to open the innings in order to fulfil the needs of England, and with M. C. Cowdrey formed a splendid partnership on the 1959/60 tour to West Indies. A wrist injury hampered him in 1960, but again in 1961 and on the Indian sub-continent in 1961/2 he proved most reliable. On his visit to Australia, however, he came home early due to an injured knee and for the remainder of his career he never really was able to avoid injury for long – arthritis finally forced him to retire in 1970.
He hit 1,000 runs in a season nine times (plus once overseas) and went on to 2,000 twice, his best summer being 1959 with 2,647 runs, av 55.14. His highest innings was only 175 for England v South Africa at the Oval in 1960, but the keynote to his batsmanship was reliability, as can be seen by the fact that his Test batting average is 43.86, despite having only four Test hundreds to his name.

Pullen, William Wade Fitzherbert
Amateur. *b:* 24.6.1866, Itchington, Gloucestershire. *d:* 9.8.1937, West End, Southampton, Hampshire. Attacking middle order right-hand batsman, good field, occasional wicket-keeper. *Team* Gloucestershire (1882–92, 91 matches).
Career batting
94–167–8–2765–161–17.38–1–*ct* 63–*st* 4
Bowling 93–3–31.00–0–0–1/11
He made his County debut for Somerset (pre first-class) v Hampshire in 1881, being only 15 years and 2 months old, and made his first-class debut for Gloucestershire the following year. He also played for Glamorgan (pre first-class, 1895).

Pullinger, George Richard
Amateur. *b:* 14.3.1920, Islington, London. *d:* 4.8.1982, Thurrock, Essex. Lower order right-hand batsman, right-arm fast medium bowler. *Team* Essex

(1949–50, 18 matches).
Career batting
18–20–11–53–14*–5.88–0–*ct* 14
Bowling 1557–41–37.97–1–0–5/54

Pulman, Rev William Walker
Amateur. *b:* 14.11.1852, Wellington, Somerset. *d:* 22.8.1936, Wellington, Somerset. Hard hitting middle order right-hand batsman, good field. *Sch* Marlborough. *Team* Oxford U (1874–75, blue both years).
Career batting
10–17–2–271–46–18.06–0–*ct* 4
His County cricket was for Somerset (pre first-class, 1875) and Worcestershire (pre first-class, 1879).

Purchase, Richard
Professional. *b:* 24.9.1756, Liss, Hampshire. *d:* 1.4.1837, Liss, Hampshire. Opening or middle order right-hand batsman, medium pace under-arm bowler. *Team* Hampshire (1773–1803).
Career batting
1–1–0–0–0–0.00–0–*ct* 1
Bowling 2 wickets (no analyses)–0–0–2/?
In a minor match (details lost), he and William Harding hit up 200 runs for the first wicket, the first time a double century partnership had been recorded (*circa* 1780).

Purdy, Henry Fox
(birth registered as H. Fox)
Professional. *b:* 17.1.1883, Brimington, Derbyshire. *d:* 21.2.1943, Chesterfield, Derbyshire. Nephew of J. H. (Derbyshire). Lower order right-hand batsman, right-arm fast medium bowler. *Team* Derbyshire (1906–19, 16 matches).
Career batting
16–30–4–170–21–6.53–0–*ct* 5
Bowling 661–26–25.42–1–0–6/84

Purdy, John Henry
(also known as Purdew)
Professional. *b:* 23.9.1871, Brimington, Derbyshire. *d:* 19.5.1938, Ravensdale, Mansfield, Nottinghamshire. Uncle of H. F. (Derbyshire). Lower order right-hand batsman, right-arm fast medium bowler. *Team* Derbyshire (1896–1906, 9 matches).
Career batting
9–13–4–39–10–4.33–0–*ct* 4
Bowling 310–9–34.44–0–0–3/53

Purves, James Hamilton
Amateur. *b:* 4.12.1937, Hemel Hempstead, Hertfordshire. Middle order left-hand batsman, right-arm medium pace bowler. *Sch* Uppingham. *Team* Essex (1960–61, 5 matches).
Career batting
11–19–0–474–74–24.94–0–*ct* 5
His final first-class match was for Free Foresters in 1964.

Putner, Frank William
Professional. *b:* 26.9.1912, Greenwich, London. Middle order right-hand batsman, leg break bowler. *Team* Middlesex (1933–34, 11 matches).
Career batting
13–19–2–192–80–11.29–0–*ct* 4
Bowling 96–2–48.00–0–0–2/42
His final first-class match was for MCC in 1938.

Puttock, Eric Clarence
Amateur. *b:* 2.3.1900, Billingshurst, Sussex. *d:* 14.12.1969, Slinfold, Sussex. Middle order batsman. *Sch* Dover. *Team* Sussex (1921, 2 matches).
Career batting
2–4–0–9–5–2.25–0–*ct* 1

Pycroft, Andrew John
Cricketer. *b:* 6.6.1956, Salisbury, Rhodesia. Middle order right-hand batsman, off break bowler. *Teams* Western Province (1975/6 to 1978/9); Zimbabwe (1979/80 to 1991/2). *Tours* Zimbabwe to England 1982, 1983 (World Cup), 1985, 1990, to Sri Lanka 1983/4, to India 1987/8 (World Cup), to Australia and New Zealand 1991/2 (World Cup).
Career batting
69–124–14–4222–133–38.38–5–*ct* 61
Bowling 52–1–52.00–0–0–1/0
He was captain of the 1985 tour to England, but returned home early due to the birth of his first child.

Pyemont, Christopher Patrick
Cricketer. *b:* 17.1.1948, Etchingham, Sussex. Middle order right-hand batsman, slow left-arm bowler. *Sch* Marlborough. *Team* Cambridge U (1967, blue).
Career batting
14–25–2–516–61–22.43–0–*ct* 1
Bowling 83–3–27.66–0–0–2/7
A good hockey player, he represented Cambridge.

Pye-Smith, Dr Edward John
Amateur. *b:* 24.2.1901, Sheffield, Yorkshire. *d:* 6.3.1983, Bishop Monkton, Harrogate, Yorkshire. Middle order right-hand batsman, right-arm medium pace bowler. *Sch* Cheltenham. *Team* Cambridge U (1922).
Career batting
1–1–0–32–32–32.00–0–*ct* 1

Pyman, Richard Anthony
Cricketer. *b:* 17.4.1968, Changi, Singapore. Lower order right-hand batsman, right-arm medium pace bowler. *Sch* Harrow. *Team* Cambridge U (1988–91, blue 1989–90).
Career batting
23–31–6–340–69–13.60–0–*ct* 7
Bowling 1753–32–54.78–1–0–5/43
His County cricket was for Dorset (1990–92). He also represented the University at Eton fives.

Q

Quaife, Bernard William
Amateur. *b:* 24.11.1899, Olton, Warwickshire. *d:* 27.11.1984, Bridport, Dorset. Son of William (Warwickshire), nephew of Walter (Sussex and Warwickshire). Stolid middle order right-hand batsman, wicket-keeper. *Sch* Solihull. *Teams* Warwickshire (1920–26, 48 matches); Worcestershire (1928–37, 271 matches).
Career batting
319–528–49–9594–136*–20.02–3–*ct* 186–*st* 54
Bowling 297–9–33.00–0–0–2/5
He hit 1,000 runs in a season twice (best 1,167, av 26.52, in 1935).

Quaife, Frank Cyril
Professional. *b:* 5.4.1905, Hastings, Sussex. *d:* 27.8.1968, Eastbourne, Sussex. Lower order left-hand batsman, slow left-arm bowler. *Team* Sussex (1928, 2 matches).
Career batting
2–1–0–0–0–0.00–0–*ct* 0
Bowling 47–1–47.00–0–0–1/19

Quaife, Walter
Professional. *b:* 1.4.1864, Newhaven, Sussex. *d:* 18.1.1943, Norwood, Surrey. Brother of William (Warwickshire), uncle of B. W. (Warwickshire and Worcestershire). Stylish opening right-hand batsman, right-arm medium pace bowler. *Teams* Sussex (1884–91, 90 matches); Warwickshire (1894–1901, 121 matches).
Career batting
224–396–23–8536–156*–22.88–10–*ct* 80
Bowling 463–15–30.86–0–0–4/35
He hit 1,219 runs, av 34.82, in 1895. He also played for Suffolk (1905–09). He first played for Warwickshire (pre first-class) in 1893.

Quaife, William (George)
Professional. *b:* 17.3.1872, Newhaven, Sussex. *d:* 13.10.1951, Edgbaston, Birmingham. Brother of Walter (Sussex and Warwickshire), father of B. W. (Warwickshire and Worcestershire). Sound middle order right-hand batsman, right-arm medium pace or leg break bowler, excellent cover point. *Teams* Warwickshire (1894–1928, 665 matches); London County (1900–03); Griqualand West (1912/13). *Tours* MacLaren to Australia 1901/2. *Tests* England (1899 to 1901/2, 7 matches).
Career batting
719–1203–185–36012–255*–35.37–72–*ct* 354–*st* 1
Bowling 25443–931–27.32–32–2–7/76
Test batting
7–13–1–228–68–19.00–0–*ct* 4
Bowling 6–0
He hit 1,000 runs in a season 24 times, going on to 2,000 once: 2,060, av 54.21, in 1905. His four double centuries were all for Warwickshire, the highest being 255* v Surrey at the Oval in 1905. He played for Sussex in one non-first-class match in 1891 and first played for Warwickshire (pre first-class) in 1893.

Quentin, Rev George Augustus Frederick
Amateur. *b:* 3.11.1848, Kirkee, India. *d:* 6.5.1928, St Leonards-on-Sea, Sussex. Middle order right-hand batsman, right-hand fast round-arm bowler. *Sch* Shrewsbury. *Team* Gloucestershire (1874, 1 match).
Career batting
1–1–0–22–22–22.00–0–*ct* 0
He did not play in first-class matches whilst at Oxford U, being handicapped by ill-health.

Quick, Arnold Bertram
Amateur. *b:* 10.2.1915, Clacton-on-Sea, Essex. *d:* 17.7.1990, Frinton-on-Sea, Essex. Middle order right-hand batsman, off break bowler. *Team* Essex (1936–52, 19 matches).
Career batting
20–33–1–439–57–13.71–0–*ct* 13
Bowling 10–0
He also played for Suffolk (1936). He was Essex Chairman 1972–76.

Quick, Ian William
Amateur. *b:* 5.11.1933, Geelong, Victoria, Australia. Aggressive tail end right-hand batsman, slow left-arm bowler. *Team* Victoria (1956/7 to 1961/2, 34 matches). *Tours* Australia to England 1961, to New Zealand 1959/60.
Career batting
63–71–13–816–61*–14.06–0–*ct* 32
Bowling 5922–195–30.36–7–1–7/20
He had only modest success on the 1961 tour of England and failed to gain a place in the Test side.

Quin, Stanley Edgar Vivian
Amateur. *b:* 3.4.1896, Bishops Glen, Orange Free State, South Africa. *d:* 9.4.1970, Bishops Glen, Orange Free State, South Africa. Middle order right-hand batsman, right-arm medium pace off break bowler. *Teams* Essex (1924, 1 match); Orange Free State (1931/2).
Career batting
3–5–0–3–3–0.60–0–*ct* 0
Bowling 60–0

Quinlan, Dr Bernard Gerald
Amateur. *b: circa* 1885, Perth, Western Australia. *d: circa* 1950, Perth, Western Australia. Brother of P. F. (Ireland). Lower order right-hand batsman, leg break and googly bowler. *Team* Ireland (1911).
Career batting
1 match, did not bat – *ct* 0
Bowling 49–3–16.33–0–0–2/36

Quinlan, Jeremy David
Cricketer. *b:* 18.4.1965, Watford, Hertfordshire. Lower order right-hand batsman, right-arm medium pace bowler. *Sch* Sherborne. *Team* Oxford U (1985–86, blue 1985).
Career batting
12–11–3–80–24*–10.00–0–*ct* 3
Bowling 1004–14–71.71–0–0–4/76
His County cricket was for Wiltshire (1985).

Quinlan, Patrick Francis
Amateur. *b:* 17.3.1891, Perth, Western Australia. *d:* 15.8.1935, Perth, Western Australia. Brother of B. G. (Ireland). Opening right-hand batsman, right-arm medium pace bowler. *Teams* Ireland (1912–14); Western Australia (1925/6 to 1928/9, 8 matches).
Career batting
13–22–2–530–80–26.50–0–*ct* 8
Bowling 530–10–53.00–0–0–2/38

Quinn, Francis Michael
Amateur. *b:* 8.12.1915, Gort, Co Galway, Ireland. Brother of G. J. (Ireland) and K. J. (Ireland). Middle order right-hand batsman, right-arm medium pace bowler. *Team* Ireland (1936–48).
Career batting
7–14–0–227–140–16.21–1–*ct* 6
Bowling 22–0

Quinn, Gerard Joseph
Amateur. *b:* 10.9.1917, Gort, Co Galway, Ireland. *d:* 20.11.1968, Dublin, Ireland. Brother of F. M. (Ireland) and K. J. (Ireland). Lower order right-hand batsman. *Team* Ireland (1937).
Career batting
1–2–0–14–12–7.00–0–*ct* 1

Quinn, Kevin Joseph
Amateur. *b:* 14.3.1923, Gort, Co Galway, Ireland. Brother of F. M. (Ireland) and G. J. (Ireland). Opening right-hand batsman, slow left-arm bowler. *Team* Ireland (1957–59).
Career batting
3–5–0–49–25–9.80–0–*ct* 0
Bowling 14–0
He played rugby for Ireland.

Quinn, Neville Anthony
Amateur. *b:* 21.2.1908, Tweefontein, Orange Free State, South Africa. *d:* 5.8.1934, Kenilworth, Kimberley, South Africa. He died of heart disease. Brother of M. H. (Rhodesia). Lower order right-hand batsman, left-arm medium fast bowler. *Teams* Griqualand West (1927/8 to 1932/3); Transvaal (1933/4). *Tours* South Africa to England 1929, to Australia and New Zealand 1931/2. *Tests* South Africa (1929 to 1931/2, 12 matches).
Career batting
51–63–15–438–32–9.12–0–*ct* 10
Bowling 3866–186–20.78–12–3–8/37
Test batting
12–18–3–90–28–6.00–0–*ct* 1
Bowling 1145–35–32.71–1–0–6/92
On his 1929 tour to England he headed the first-class bowling averages with 65 wickets, av 23.89.

Quinney, David Henry
Cricketer. *b:* 28.7.1950, Basford, Nottinghamshire. Middle order right-hand batsman. *Sch* Nottingham HS. *Team* Cambridge U (1971).
Career batting
1–2–0–4–4–2.00–0–*ct* 1

Quinton, Brig-Gen Francis William Drummond
Amateur. *b:* 27.12.1865, Fyzabad, India. *d:* 5.11.1926, Marylebone, London. Brother of J. M. (Hampshire). Hard hitting middle order right-hand batsman, slow under-arm bowler, good outfield. *Sch* Marlborough. *Team* Hampshire (1895–1900, 45 matches).
Career batting
51–94–8–2393–178–27.82–2–*ct* 46
Bowling 855–30–28.50–1–0–5/93
His first-class debut was for C. I. Thornton's XI in 1885. He also played for Devon (1882–83). He first played for Hampshire (not first-class) in 1893.

Quinton, James Maurice
Amateur. *b:* 12.5.1874, Simla, India. *d:* 22.12.1922, Reading, Berkshire. Brother of F. W. D. (Hampshire). Attacking middle order right-hand batsman, right-arm fast bowler, good field. *Sch* Cheltenham. *Teams* Hampshire (1895–99, 4 matches); Oxford U (1895–96).
Career batting
6–10–2–79–22–9.87–0–*ct* 4
Bowling 111–1–111.00–0–0–1/14
He shot himself (through unnecessary worry) in a Great Western Railway express. He first played for Hampshire (not first-class) in 1894.

Quintrell, Robert N.
Amateur. *b:* 1931, Australia. Opening right-hand batsman. *Team* Canada (1954). *Tour* Canada to England 1954.
Career batting
4–6–0–76–29–12.66–0–*ct* 2
Bowling 43–0

R

Rabone, Geoffrey Osbourne
Amateur. *b:* 6.11.1921, Gore, Otago, New Zealand. Free scoring middle order right-hand batsman, off break, or leg break bowler. *Teams* Wellington (1945/6 to 1950/1); Auckland (1951/2 to 1959/60). *Tours* New Zealand to England 1949, to South Africa 1953/4. *Tests* New Zealand (1949 to 1954/5, 12

matches).
Career batting
82–135–14–3425–125–28.30–3–*ct* 76
Bowling 4835–173–27.94–9–0–8/66
Test batting
12–20–2–562–107–31.22–1–*ct* 5
Bowling 635–16–39.68–1–0–6/68

He hit 1,021 runs, av 32.93, and took 50 wickets, av 35.70, on the 1949 tour, appearing in all four Tests. His final first-class match was for the Governor-General's XI in 1960/1 in New Zealand. He captained New Zealand in five Tests.

Racionzer, Terence Beverley
Cricketer. *b:* 18.12.1943, Maidenhead, Berkshire. Middle order right-hand batsman, off break bowler. *Teams* Scotland (1965–84); Sussex (1967–69, 26 matches).
Career batting
45–80–9–1552–115–21.85–1–*ct* 35
Bowling 71–2–35.50–0–0–2/11

Rackemann, Carl Gray
Cricketer. *b:* 3.6.1960, Wondai, Brisbane, Queensland, Australia. Lower order right-hand batsman, right-arm fast bowler. *Team* Queensland (1979/80 to 1991/2, 81 matches). *Tours* Australia to West Indies 1983/4, to England 1989, to New Zealand 1989/90, to Sharjah (not first-class) 1989/90; Australian XI to South Africa 1985/6, 1986/7. *Tests* Australia (1982/3 to 1990/1, 12 matches).
Career batting
119–127–44–542–31*–6.53–0–*ct* 28
Bowling 11557–433–26.69–17–3–8/84
Test batting
12–14–4–53–15*–5.30–0–*ct* 2
Bowling 1137–39–29.15–3–1–6/86

His tours to South Africa restricted his appearances in official Tests, but he toured England in 1989 only to be injured and therefore unable to command a place in the Test team that season.

Radcliffe, Sir Everard Joseph Reginald Henry
Amateur. *b:* 27.1.1884, Hensleigh House, Tiverton, Devon. *d:* 23.11.1969, St Trinians Hall, Richmond, Yorkshire. Lower order right-hand batsman, useful bowler. *Sch* Downside. *Team* Yorkshire (1909–11, 64 matches).
Career batting
64–89–13–826–54–10.86–0–*ct* 21
Bowling 134–2–67.00–0–0–1/15

He captained Yorkshire in 1911, having acted as Lord Hawke's deputy in 1909 and 1910. He also played for Shropshire (1903). He played no first-class cricket whilst at Oxford U.

Radcliffe, George
Professional. *b:* 25.9.1877, Ormskirk, Lancashire. *d:* 27.10.1951, Dukinfield, Cheshire. Opening right-hand batsman. *Team* Lancashire (1903–06, 7 matches).
Career batting
7–11–0–171–60–15.54–0–*ct* 2

He also played for Cheshire (1895). Although a professional when playing for Lancashire he played in the Central Lancashire League as an amateur for Stalybridge.

Radcliffe, Lees
Professional. *b:* 23.11.1865, Smithy Bridge, Rochdale, Lancashire. *d:* 22.1.1928, Crumpsall, Manchester, Lancashire. Lower order right-hand batsman, wicket-keeper. *Team* Lancashire (1897–1905, 50 matches).
Career batting
50–67–22–275–25–6.11–0–*ct* 69–*st* 34

He also played for Durham (pre first-class, 1911).

Radcliffe, Octavius Goldney
Amateur. *b:* 20.10.1859, North Newnton, Wiltshire. *d:* 13.4.1940, Cherhill, Calne, Wiltshire. Steady opening right-hand batsman, off break bowler. *Teams* Somerset (1885, 5 matches); Gloucestershire (1886–93, 119 matches). *Tour* Sheffield to Australia 1891/2.
Career batting
144–264–7–5406–117–21.03–5–*ct* 60
Bowling 3050–103–29.61–2–0–5/43

He also played for Wiltshire (1884–1901).

Radcliffe, Stephen Tempest Adair
Amateur. *b:* 24.8.1904, Ballybrittas, Queen's County, Ireland. *d:* 25.4.1982, Netherbury, Dorset. Lower order right-hand batsman, right-arm medium pace bowler. *Sch* Oratory. *Team* Dublin University (1925–26).
Career batting
2–4–0–28–14–7.00–0–*ct* 1
Bowling 11–1–11.00–0–0–1/11

Radford, Henry William
Amateur. *b:* 19.6.1896, Derby. *d:* 29.11.1972, Banbury, Oxfordshire. Uncle of A. G. Baxter (Nottinghamshire). Tail end batsman, left-arm medium pace bowler. *Team* Derbyshire (1920, 3 matches).
Career batting
3–6–2–23–14–5.75–0–*ct* 0
Bowling 86–4–21.50–0–0–2/18

Radford, Neal Victor
Cricketer. *b:* 7.6.1957, Luanshya, Northern Rhodesia. Brother of W. R. (Orange Free State) and Glen (Eastern Transvaal). Lower order right-hand batsman, right-arm fast medium bowler. *Teams* Transvaal (1978/9 to 1988/9); Lancashire (1980–84, 24 matches); Worcestershire (1985–92, 153 matches). *Tours* England to New Zealand 1987/8, to Australia 1987/8 (not first-class); Worcestershire to Zimbabwe 1990/1. *Tests* England (1986 to 1987/8, 3 matches).
Career batting
257–253–62–3140–76*–16.43–0–*ct* 121

Bowling 23469–900–26.07–45–7–9/70
Test batting
3–4–1–21–12*–7.00–0–*ct* 0
Bowling 351–4–87.75–0–0–2/131

After five modestly successful seasons with Lancashire, he found immediate fame at Worcester, being the leading wicket-taker in English first-class cricket in 1985 with 101 wickets, av 25.68. In 1986 he played in two Tests without much reward, but continued to succeed in county cricket, taking 9 for 70 v Somerset at Worcester, the best innings analysis of the season. In 1987 he captured 109 wickets, av 20.81, again being the leading wicket-taker in first-class cricket. However a second opportunity for England on the 1987/8 winter tour produced no outstanding performances.

Radley, Clive Thornton
Cricketer. *b:* 13.5.1944, Hertford. Middle order right-hand batsman, leg break bowler, good close field. *Team* Middlesex (1964–87, 520 matches). *Tours* Robins to South Africa 1972/3, 1974/5; England to Pakistan and New Zealand 1977/8, to Australia 1978/9; Middlesex to Zimbabwe 1980/1. *Tests* England (1977/8 to 1978, 8 matches).
Career batting
559–880–134–26441–200–35.44–46–*ct* 517
Bowling 160–8–20.00–0–0–2/38
Test batting
8–10–0–481–158–48.10–2–*ct* 4

He hit 1,000 runs in a season 16 times (best 1,491, av 57.34, in 1980). His highest score was 200 for Middlesex v Northamptonshire at Uxbridge in 1985. A reliable batsman in county cricket his weakness against pace meant that his career in Test cricket was brief. He also played for Norfolk (1961) and for Auckland in a limited overs match in 1984/5.

Rae, Allan Fitzroy
Amateur. *b:* 30.9.1922, Rollington Town, Kingston, Jamaica. Son of E. A. (West Indies). Steady opening left-hand batsman. *Team* Jamaica (1946/7 to 1959/60). *Tours* West Indies to India, Pakistan and Ceylon 1948/9, to England 1950, to Australia and New Zealand 1951/2. *Tests* West Indies (1948/9 to 1952/3, 15 matches).
Career batting
80–128–7–4798–179–39.65–17–*ct* 42
Bowling 26–0
Test batting
15–24–2–1016–109–46.18–4–*ct* 10

He hit 1,330 runs, av 39.11, in first-class matches on the 1950 tour and 377, av 62.83, in the four Tests. He also hit 1,000 runs in a season on the Indian subcontinent. From 1981 to 1988 he was President of the West Indies Cricket Board of Control.

Rae, Ernest Allan
Amateur. *b:* 8.11.1897, Cross Roads, Kingston, Jamaica. *d:* 28.6.1969, Mona, Kingston, Jamaica. Father of A. F. (West Indies). Hard hitting middle order right-hand batsman, leg break bowler, good deep field. *Team* Jamaica (1924/5 to 1935/6). *Tour* West Indies to England 1928.
Career batting
29–43–6–1118–121–30.21–1–*ct* 27
Bowling 368–10–36.80–0–0–4/50

He achieved nothing of note on the 1928 tour.

Rae, Robert Burns
Professional. *b:* 23.7.1912, Littleborough, Lancashire. Middle order right-hand batsman, right-arm fast bowler. *Team* Lancashire (1945, 1 match).
Career batting
1–1–0–74–74–74.00–0–*ct* 0
Bowling 29–0

Raffety, Cairns Vezey
Amateur. *b:* 9.8.1906, Orpington, Kent. *d:* 28.9.1991, Eastbourne, Sussex. Middle order left-hand batsman, slow left-arm bowler. *Sch* Cranleigh. *Team* Minor Counties (1931).
Career batting
1–1–0–16–16–16.00–0–*ct* 1

His County cricket was for Buckinghamshire (1924–32).

Raikes, Douglas Charles Gordon
Amateur. *b:* 26.1.1910, Clifton, Bristol, Gloucestershire. Lower order right-hand batsman, wicket-keeper. *Sch* Shrewsbury. *Teams* Oxford U (1931, blue); Gloucestershire (1932, 5 matches); Kent (1948, 2 matches).
Career batting
12–12–2–76–37–7.60–0–*ct* 21–*st* 8

Raikes, Rev George Barkley
Amateur. *b:* 14.3.1873, Carleton-Forehoe, Norfolk. *d:* 18.12.1966, Lamyat, Shepton Mallet, Somerset. Brother of E. B. (Europeans), uncle of T. B. (Oxford U). Lower order right-hand batsman, right-arm medium pace bowler. *Sch* Shrewsbury. *Teams* Oxford U (1893–95, blue 1894–95); Hampshire (1900–02, 9 matches).
Career batting
30–53–5–816–77–17.00–0–*ct* 30
Bowling 1733–71–24.40–2–0–6/62

He also played for Norfolk (1890–1913). His final first-class match was for an England XI in 1912. An excellent goalkeeper, he gained his blue at Oxford and went on to play for England.

Raikes, Kenneth Cochrane
Amateur. *b:* 9.5.1889, Malpas, Newport, Monmouthshire. *d:* 29.11.1973, Digswell, Welwyn, Hertfordshire. Middle order right-hand batsman, good bowler. *Sch* Shrewsbury. *Team* Wales (1925–29).

Career batting
6–8–0–135–50–16.87–0–*ct* 5
Bowling 502–18–27.88–1–0–7/28

His County cricket was for Monmouthshire (1908–34). He played in trials at Oxford U, but not in first-class matches. He played hockey for Wales.

Raikes, Thomas Barkley
Amateur. *b:* 16.12.1902, Malabar Hill, Bombay, India. *d:* 2.3.1984, Rickinghall Superior, Suffolk. Son of E. B. (Europeans), nephew of G. B. (Hampshire). Middle order right-hand batsman, right-arm medium-fast bowler. *Sch* Winchester. *Team* Oxford U (1922–25, blue 1922–24).
Career batting
38–58–15–554–44–12.88–0–*ct* 24
Bowling 3305–132–25.03–7–2–9/38

His County cricket was for Norfolk (1920–23). His best bowling was 9/38 for Oxford U v Army at Oxford in 1924.

Raison, Maxwell
Amateur. *b:* 7.11.1901, Wanstead, Essex. *d:* 26.7.1988, Theberton, Suffolk. Middle order right-hand batsman, right-arm medium pace bowler. *Sch* Forest. *Team* Essex (1928–30, 17 matches).
Career batting
17–27–2–451–57–18.04–0–*ct* 6
Bowling 575–14–41.07–1–0–5/104

He was a well-known figure in magazine publishing.

Rait-Kerr, Rowan Scrope
Amateur. *b:* 13.4.1891, Bray, Co Wicklow, Ireland. *d:* 7.4.1961, Constantine Bay, Cornwall. Middle order right-hand batsman. *Sch* Rugby. *Teams* Army (1931); Europeans (1913/14 to 1920/1).
Career batting
6–12–0–89–24–7.41–0 –*ct* 3

He was Secretary of MCC from 1936 to 1952 and mainly responsible for the revised code of Laws of Cricket in 1947, after which he published a book tracing the history of the Laws. His daughter, Miss Diana Rait-Kerr, was for many years the Librarian at Lord's.

Rajadurai, Brian Eric Anton
Cricketer. *b:* 24.8.1965, Colombo, Ceylon. Lower order right-hand batsman, leg break and googly bowler. *Team* Sinhalese SC (1988/9 to 1990/1). *Tours* Sri Lanka to England 1988; Sri Lanka B to Pakistan 1988/9.
Career batting
31–31–7–381–65–15.87–0–*ct* 25
Bowling 1234–56–22.03–3–0–5/53

He played in only two first-class matches on the 1988 tour to England.

Rajkot, Thakore Saheb Sir Lakhaji Raj Bawaji Raj
(played cricket in England as Prince Chakorsab)
Amateur. *b:* 17.12.1885, India. *d:* 2.2.1930, India. Nephew of K. S. Ranjitsinhji (Sussex). Lower order right-hand batsman, fast bowler. *Teams* Gentlemen of England (1908); Hindus (1912/13); Combined Hindus and Muslims XI (1922/3).
Career batting
3–6–0–41–14–6.83–0–*ct* 2
Bowling 187–4–46.75–0–0–3/77

Ralph, Louis Henry Roy
Amateur, turned professional in 1958. *b:* 22.5.1920, Upton Park, East Ham, Essex. Lower order right-hand batsman, right-arm medium pace bowler. *Team* Essex (1953–61, 174 matches).
Career batting
174–262–39–3763–73–16.87–0–*ct* 143
Bowling 11053–460–24.02–19–3–7/42

His best season was 1957 with 102 wickets, av 22.00.

Ralston, Francis William
Amateur. *b:* 7.6.1867, Philadelphia, USA. *d:* 7.10.1920, Charleston, USA. Lower order right-hand batsman, wicket-keeper. *Team* Philadelphia (1886–97). *Tour* Philadelphia to England 1897.
Career batting
28–46–5–553–53–13.48–0–*ct* 34–*st* 1

He proved an excellent wicket-keeper on the 1897 tour to England, but did little with the bat.

Ramadhin, Sonny
Professional. *b:* 1.5.1929, Esperance Village, Trinidad. Father-in-law of W. Hogg (Lancashire and Warwickshire). Tail end right-hand batsman, off break bowler. *Teams* Trinidad (1949/50 to 1952/3); Lancashire (1964–65, 33 matches). *Tours* West Indies to England 1950, 1957, to Australia and New Zealand 1951/2, to New Zealand 1955/6, to Australia 1960/1, to India and Pakistan 1958/9; International XI to India, Pakistan, Rhodesia and New Zealand 1961/2; Commonwealth to India and Ceylon 1950/1, to India 1953/4. *Tests* West Indies (1950 to 1960/1, 43 matches).
Career batting
184–191–65–1092–44–8.66–0–*ct* 38
Bowling 15345–758–20.24–51–15–8/15
Test batting
43–58–14–361–44–8.20–0–*ct* 9
Bowling 4579–158–28.98–10–1–7/49

Coming to England in 1950 as a totally unknown cricketer he created a sensation by playing a major role in winning the rubber for West Indies. He headed the first-class bowling averages with 135 wickets, av 14.88, and took 26 wickets, av 23.23, in the Tests. In 1957 he again headed the first-class averages with 119 wickets, av 13.98, but was not so effective in the Tests.

He was fairly successful for Lancashire in 1964, but in 1965 lost his place in the County side. He also played for Lincolnshire (1968–72).

Ramage, Alan
Cricketer. *b:* 29.11.1957, Guisborough, Yorkshire. Lower order left-hand batsman, right-arm fast medium bowler. *Team* Yorkshire (1979–83, 23 matches).
Career batting
23–22–9–219–52–16.84–0–*ct* 1
Bowling 1649–44–37.47–1–0–5/65
He played soccer for Middlesbrough and Derby County.

Ramage, Paul Frederick
Amateur. *b:* 13.3.1940, Leamington Spa, Warwickshire. Lower order left-hand batsman, slow left-arm bowler. *Sch* Warwick. *Team* Cambridge U (1962–63).
Career batting
13–22–7–252–50–16.80–0–*ct* 5
Bowling 613–17–36.05–0–0–4/65
His County cricket was for Buckinghamshire (1970–72).

Raman, Wookeri Venkat
Cricketer. *b:* 23.5.1965, Madras, India. Opening left-hand batsman, slow left-arm bowler. *Team* Tamil Nadu (1982/3 to 1991/2). *Tours* India to Sharjah (not first-class) 1987/8, 1989/90, 1991/2, to West Indies 1988/9, to New Zealand 1989/90, to Pakistan 1989/90, to England 1990; Tamil Nadu to Australia 1988/9. *Tests* India (1987/8 to 1989/90, 6 matches).
Career batting
72–108–15–5108–313–54.92–13–*ct* 55
Bowling 2833–80–35.41–4–1–6/29
Test batting
6–10–1–303–96–33.66–0–*ct* 3
Bowling 66–2–33.00–0–0–1/7
He batted well in the county matches, but was not required for any of the Tests on the 1990 tour to England. His highest score was 313 for Tamil Nadu v Goa at Panaji in 1988/9, when uniquely A. Kripal Singh also made a triple hundred. He scored 1,000 runs in a season in India twice (best 1,159, av 105.36, in 1988/9).

Ramanayake, Champaka Priyadarshana Hewage
Cricketer. *b:* 8.1.1965, Colombo, Ceylon. Lower order right-hand batsman, right-arm fast medium bowler. *Team* Tamil Union (1988/9 to 1991/2). *Tours* Sri Lanka to Sharjah (not first-class) 1987/8, 1989/90, 1990/1, to Australia 1987/8, 1989/90, to England 1988, 1990, 1991, to Bangladesh (not first-class) 1988/9, to New Zealand 1990/1, to India 1990/1 (not first-class), to Pakistan 1991/2, to Australia and New Zealand (World Cup) 1991/2; Sri Lanka B to Pakistan 1988/9. *Tests* Sri Lanka (1987/8 to 1991/2, 10 matches).
Career batting
62–70–17–1084–69–20.45–0–*ct* 16
Bowling 5041–170–29.65–6–0–7/21
Test batting
10–15–5–100–34*–10.00–0–*ct* 3
Bowling 1116–19–58.73–0–0–2/39
He proved a useful bowler on his three tours to England and played in the two Tests of 1988 and 1991. His first-class debut was for Sri Lanka Colts in 1985/6.

Ramaswami, Cotar
Amateur. *b:* 16.6.1896, Madras, India. Brother of M. Baliah (Madras) and M. V. Ramanjulu (Madras), father of C. Ramaswaroop (Andhra), uncle of M. M. Kumar (Madras) and M. Suryanarayan (Madras). Sound middle order left-hand batsman, right-arm bowler. *Teams* Indians (1915/6 to 1939/40); Madras (1926/7 to 1941/2). *Tour* India to England 1936. *Tests* India (1936, 2 matches).
Career batting
53–92–9–2400–127*–28.91–2–*ct* 33
Bowling 992–30–33.06–0–0–4/29
Test batting
2–4–1–170–60–56.66–0–*ct* 0
After an uncertain start, he proved one of the most reliable batsmen on the 1936 tour, heading the Test averages, and in first-class matches scoring 737 runs, av 30.70. He played no first-class matches whilst at Cambridge U, but did win a blue for lawn tennis and represented India in the Davis Cup.

Ramchand, Gulabrai Sipahimalani
Professional. *b:* 26.7.1927, Karachi, India. Aggressive middle order right-hand batsman, right-arm medium fast bowler. *Teams* Sind (1945/6 to 1946/7); Bombay (1948/9 to 1965/6). *Tours* India to England 1952, to West Indies 1952/3, to Pakistan 1954/5, to Ceylon 1956/7. *Tests* India (1952 to 1959/60, 33 matches).
Career batting
145–202–36–6026–230*–36.30–16–*ct* 105
Bowling 7518–255–29.48–9–0–8/12
Test batting
33–53–5–1180–109–24.58–2–*ct* 20
Bowling 1899–41–46.31–1–0–6/49
He hit 644 runs, av 24.76, and took 64 wickets, av 25.85, on the 1952 tour to England, but failed to make any impression in the Tests, though playing in all four. He also played in England for a Commonwealth XI in 1953, 1954 and 1957. His highest score was 230* for Bombay v Maharashtra at Bombay in 1950/1. His final first-class match was for Dungarpur XI in India in 1967/8. He captained India in five Tests.

Rameez Raja
Cricketer. *b:* 14.8.1962, Lyallpur, Pakistan. Brother of Wasim Raja (Pakistan) and Zaeem Raja (National Bank), son of Raja Saleem Akhtar (Sargodha), cousin of Atif Rauf (ADBP). Opening right-hand batsman,

leg break bowler. *Teams* Servis Industries (1977/8); Punjab (1978/9); Lahore (1978/9 to 1985/6); Allied Bank (1983/4); PNSC (1987/8 to 1990/1). *Tours* Pakistan to New Zealand 1984/5, 1988/9, to Australia 1984/5 (not first-class), 1986/7 (not first-class), 1988/9, 1989/90, 1991/2, to Sharjah (not first-class) 1984/5, 1985/6, 1986/7, 1988/9, 1989/90, 1991/2, to Sri Lanka 1985/6, to India 1986/7, 1989/90 (not first-class), to England 1987, 1992, to West Indies 1987/8, to Bangladesh (not first-class) 1988/9, to Australia and New Zealand (World Cup) 1991/2; Pakistan Under 23 to Sri Lanka 1984/5. *Tests* Pakistan (1983/4 to 1992, 44 matches).
Career batting
141–234–19–8001–172–37.21–15–*ct* 75
Bowling 158–2–79.00–0–0–1/9
Test batting
44–71–5–2149–122–32.56–2–*ct* 27

He did not enjoy much success on the 1987 tour to England, but in 1992 he appeared in all five Tests and hit 1,036 first-class runs, av 43.16.

Rammell, Arthur William
Amateur. *b:* 21.9.1868, Sturry, Canterbury, Kent. *d:* 10.3.1956, Meads, Eastbourne, Sussex. Middle order batsman. *Team* MCC (1896).
Career batting
1–2–0–5–5–2.50–0–*ct* 0

His County cricket was for Essex (pre first-class, 1893).

Ramnarace, Randolph
Cricketer. *b:* 25.7.1941, Berbice, British Guiana. Lower order right-hand batsman, right-arm medium pace bowler. *Team* British Guiana (1965/6 to 1972/3). *Tour* Rest of World to England 1968.
Career batting
28–46–3–972–71–22.60–0–*ct* 15
Bowling 2336–75–31.14–1–0–6/101

His first-class debut was for Berbice in 1960/1 and his final match for the same side in 1973/4.

Ramprakash, Mark Ravin
Cricketer. *b:* 5.9.1969, Bushey, Hertfordshire. Middle order right-hand batsman, off break bowler. *Team* Middlesex (1987–92, 93 matches). *Tours* England A to Pakistan and Sri Lanka 1990/1, to West Indies 1991/2; England to New Zealand 1991/2. *Tests* England (1991–92, 9 matches).
Career batting
117–193–32–6327–233–39.29–12–*ct* 48
Bowling 583–6–97.16–0–0–1/0
Test batting
9–15–1–241–29–17.21–0–*ct* 5
Bowling 8–0

He hit 1,000 runs in a season four times (best 1,541, av 48.15, in 1990). His highest score was 233 for Middlesex v Surrey at the Oval in 1992.

Ramsamooj, Donald
Professional. *b:* 5.7.1932, San Fernando, Trinidad. Middle order right-hand batsman, right-arm off break bowler. *Teams* Trinidad (1952/3 to 1956/7); Northamptonshire (1958–64, 71 matches).
Career batting
79–143–9–2755–132–20.55–4–*ct* 36
Bowling 178–3–59.33–0–0–1/28

Ramsay, Marmaduke Francis
Amateur. *b:* 8.12.1860, Cheltenham, Gloucestershire. *d:* 31.12.1947, Lee, Canterbury, Kent. Brother of R. C. (Somerset), father-in-law of H. E. S. Harben (Sussex). Lower order right-hand batsman, right-arm medium pace bowler, good point field. *Sch* Harrow. *Teams* MCC (1894); Queensland (1892/3 to 1899/1900, 3 matches).
Career batting
4–8–0–170–58–21.25–0–*ct* 3
Bowling 182–9–20.22–0–0–4/61

He was for some years a sheep farmer in Australia. He also played for Somerset (pre first-class, 1880). He played in trials at Cambridge U, but not in first-class matches.

Ramsay, Robert Christian
Amateur. *b:* 20.12.1861, Cheltenham, Gloucestershire. *d:* 25.6.1957, Howletts, Bekesbourne, Kent. Brother of M. F. (Queensland). Lower order right-hand batsman, leg break bowler. *Sch* Harrow. *Teams* Cambridge U (1881–82, blue 1882); Somerset (1882, 4 matches).
Career batting
15–26–4–303–71–13.77–0–*ct* 11
Bowling 1230–69–17.82–5–2–7/22

Whilst bowling for Cambridge U v Lancashire at Old Trafford in 1882 he had the mortifying experience of seeing the batsman dropped off every ball of one four-ball over. He first played for Somerset (pre first-class) in 1881. In the 1880s he emigrated to Australia and spent most of his adult life there. He played for Queensland but not in first-class matches.

Ramsbotham, Wilfrid Hubert
Amateur. *b:* 20.12.1888, Well Place, Ipsden, Oxfordshire. *d:* 7.11.1978, Kensington, London. Middle order right-hand batsman. *Sch* Uppingham. *Teams* Cambridge U (1908–09); Sussex (1908–10, 7 matches).
Career batting
9–15–0–245–56–16.33–0–*ct* 2

Ramsbottom, Henry John
Professional. *b:* 21.10.1846, Enfield, Lancashire. *d:* 9.4.1905, Clayton-le-Moors, Lancashire. Opening right-hand batsman, right-arm medium pace bowler. *Team* Lancashire (1868, 1 match).
Career batting
1–2–0–1–1–0.50–0–*ct* 0
Bowling 11–0

Ramsden, Frederick William
Amateur. *b:* 11.1.1911, Leeds, Yorkshire. Opening right-hand batsman. *Team* Scotland (1937–39).
Career batting
4–8–0–108–29–13.50–0–*ct* 1

Ramshaw, Darrin Joseph
Cricketer. *b:* 29.11.1965, Subiaco, Perth, Western Australia. Opening right-hand batsman. *Teams* Western Australia (1989/90, 3 matches); Victoria (1990/1 to 1991/2, 11 matches). *Tour* Victoria to England 1991.
Career batting
14–25–2–551–60–23.95–0–*ct* 19

Ranasinghe, Anura Nandana
Cricketer. *b:* 13.10.1956, Kalutara, Ceylon. Attacking middle order right-hand batsman, left-arm medium, or slow, bowler. *Team* Burgher RC (1988/9 to 1989/90). *Tours* Sri Lanka to India 1974/5, 1975/6, 1980/1, 1982/3, to England 1981, to Pakistan 1981/2; Arosa Sri Lankan XI to South Africa 1982/3. *Tests* Sri Lanka (1981/2 to 1982/3, 2 matches).
Career batting
43–76–6–1664–77–23.77–0–*ct* 26
Bowling 1663–39–42.64–1–0–5/65
Test batting
2–4–0–88–77–22.00–0–*ct* 0
Bowling 9–1–69.00–0–0–1/23

Ranatunga, Arjuna
Cricketer. *b:* 1.12.1963, Colombo, Ceylon. Brother of Dammika (Sinhalese SC), Sanjeeva (Sinhalese SC) and Nishantha (Moratuwa). Middle order left-hand batsman, right-arm medium pace bowler. *Team* Sinhalese SC (1988/9 to 1991/2). *Tours* Sri Lanka to Pakistan 1981/2, 1985/6, 1991/2, to Zimbabwe 1982/3, to India 1982/3, 1986/7, 1989/90 (not first-class), 1990/1, to England 1983 (World Cup), 1984, 1988, to Australia 1984/5, 1987/8, 1989/90, to Sharjah (not first-class) 1983/4, 1985/6, 1986/7, 1987/8, 1988/9, 1989/90, 1990/1, to Bangladesh (not first-class) 1988/9, to New Zealand 1990/1, to India and Pakistan (World Cup) 1987/8, to Australia and New Zealand (World Cup) 1991/2; Sri Lanka Under 23 to Pakistan 1983/4. *Tests* Sri Lanka (1981/2 to 1991/2, 33 matches).
Career batting
94–132–13–4662–200*–39.17–8–*ct* 53
Bowling 2437–72–33.84–0–0–4/29
Test batting
33–57–3–1830–135*–33.88–2–*ct* 15
Bowling 811–14–57.92–0–0–2/17

He has been one of the mainstays of the Sri Lanka batting throughout the 1980s and performed well in England in 1984 and 1988, playing in the single Test on each tour. He captained Sri Lanka in six Test matches. His highest score was 200* for Sinhalese SC v Sebastianities SC at Columbo in 1991/2.

Randall, Derek William
Cricketer. *b:* 24.2.1951, Retford, Nottinghamshire. Attacking middle order right-hand batsman, right-arm medium pace bowler, brilliant cover field. *Team* Nottinghamshire (1972–92, 388 matches). *Tours* English Counties XI to West Indies 1974/5 (not first-class); Robins to South Africa 1975/6; MCC to India, Sri Lanka and Australia 1976/7; England to Pakistan and New Zealand 1977/8, 1983/4, to Australia 1978/9, 1979/80, 1982/3, to Sharjah (not first-class) 1984/5; England B to Sri Lanka 1985/6. *Tests* England (1976/7 to 1984, 47 matches).
Career batting
483–817–81–28176–237–38.28–52–*ct* 355
Bowling 413–13–31.76–0–0–3/15
Test batting
47–79–5–2470–174–33.37–7–*ct* 31
Bowling 3–0

He hit 1,000 runs in a season 13 times, going on to 2,000 once: 2,151, av 53.77, in 1985. His highest score was 237 for Nottinghamshire v Derbyshire at Trent Bridge in 1988. For Nottinghamshire against Middlesex at Trent Bridge in 1979 he hit 209 and 146. His most famous innings was 174 in the Centenary Test match at Melbourne in 1976/7. Regarded as the best fielder in England for several years, his rapport with spectators made him, perhaps, the most popular of English cricketers in the 1980s.

Randall, James
Amateur. *b:* 9.5.1876, Kensington, London. *d:* 8.9.1954, Guethary, Basses Pyrenees, France. Lower order batsman, useful bowler. *Sch* Sedbergh. *Team* MCC (1904).
Career batting
1–2–0–0–0–0.00–0–*ct* 0
Bowling 40–0

Randhir Singh
Cricketer. *b:* 16.8.1957, Delhi, India. Tail end right-hand batsman, right-arm fast medium bowler. *Teams* Orissa (1978/9 to 1979/80); Bihar (1980/1 to 1988/9). *Tour* India to England 1982.
Career batting
65–72–22–647–45*–12.94–0–*ct* 12
Bowling 5388–146–36.90–5–0–6/95

He achieved very little on the 1982 tour to England. He played for India in one-day international matches.

Randolph, Bernard Montgomery
Amateur. *b:* 10.4.1834, Much Hadham, Hertfordshire. *d:* 3.7.1857, Christ Church College, Oxford. He died from a fever. Brother of L. C. (Oxford U 1845). Middle order batsman. *Sch* Charterhouse. *Teams* Oxford U (1855–57, blue 1855 and 1856); Sussex (1856, 1 match).
Career batting
7–13–0–207–61–15.92–0–*ct* 4
Bowling 20–1–20.00–0–0–1/6

He also played for Cheshire (1855) and Herefordshire (1856). He appeared for Oxford U v MCC on 18 and 19 June 1857, was too ill to play in the University match the following week and died on 3 July.

Randolph, Rev John
Amateur. *b:* 15.5.1821, Sanderstead, Surrey. *d:* 11.7.1881, Sanderstead Court, Surrey. He died by his own hand. Lower order right-hand batsman, useful bowler, good long stop. *Sch* Westminster. *Team* Oxford U (1842–44, blue 1843).
Career batting
11–22–3–45–10–2.36–0–*ct* 8
Bowling 19–1–19.00–0–0–1/19

His final first-class match was for MCC in 1864. His County cricket was for Northamptonshire (pre first-class, 1852–66), Buckinghamshire (1859–69) and Bedfordshire (1860). From 1875 to his death he was Auditor to the MCC.

Randon, Frederick
Professional. *b:* 24.6.1845, Stapleford, Nottinghamshire. *d:* 17.2.1883, Hathern, Leicestershire. Father of F. J. (Leicestershire). Lower order right-hand batsman, right-hand fast round-arm bowler. *Team* MCC (1874–76).
Career batting
15–26–10–104–23*–6.50–0–*ct* 6
Bowling 655–37–17.70–2–0–6/54

His County cricket was for Leicestershire (pre first-class, 1873–89) and he also played for Nottinghamshire in a non-first-class match in 1871.

Randon, Frederick John
Professional. *b:* 18.11.1873, Hathern, Leicestershire. *d:* 15.1.1949, Hathern, Leicestershire. Son of Frederick (MCC). Lower order left-hand batsman, left-arm medium pace bowler. *Team* Leicestershire (1894, 3 matches).
Career batting
3–5–2–5–5–1.66–0–*ct* 1
Bowling 128–4–32.00–0–0–3/20

Ranjitsinhji, Kumar Shri
(later H. H. Shri Sir Ranjitsinhji Vibhaji, Jam Sahib of Nawanagar)
Amateur. *b:* 10.9.1872, Sarodar, Kathiawar, India. *d:* 2.4.1933, Jamnagar, India. Uncle of K. S. Digvijaysinhji (Western India), K. S. Duleepsinhji (Sussex), K. S. Himmatsinhji (Rajputana), T. S. Rajkot (Hindus) and M. S. Samarsinhji (Nawanagar). Fine middle order right-hand batsman, slow right-arm bowler. *Teams* Cambridge U (1893–94, blue 1893); Sussex (1895–1920, 211 matches); London County (1901–04). *Tours* Stoddart to Australia 1897/8; Ranjitsinhji to North America 1899. *Tests* England (1896–1902, 15 matches).
Career batting
307–500–62–24692–285*–56.37–72–*ct* 233
Bowling 4601–133–34.59–4–0–6/53
Test batting
15–26–4–989–175–44.95–2–*ct* 13
Bowling 39–1–39.00–0–0–1/23

After a modest career at Cambridge, Ranjitsinhji developed quickly into one of the foremost batsman in England – in fact in terms of statistics he was the best from 1899 to 1904. He hit 3,159 runs, av 63.18, in 1899 and the following year 3,065, av 87.57. These were his most prolific years, but he exceeded 2,000 runs in three other seasons and over 1,000 on six other occasions, also once in Australia. Fourteen times he compiled double centuries, all of which were for Sussex, the highest being 285* v Somerset at Taunton in 1901. He appeared in four Test series against Australia and was successful in all but the 1902 Tests.

He captained Sussex from 1899 to 1903 and left England in 1904 to return to India. Thereafter his appearances in County cricket were limited. He played in the summer of 1908 and again in 1912, in both years exceeding 1,000 runs. A shooting accident resulted in his losing one eye and this virtually ended his first-class career, though he played a little in 1920. He also played for Cambridgeshire (1892–93). He was President of Sussex in 1930.

In 1907 he became the Maharaja Jam Sahib of Nawanagar and was increasingly involved in the administration of his State. He was also a delegate to the League of Nations after the First World War.

Ransford, Vernon Seymour
Amateur. *b:* 20.3.1885, South Yarra, Melbourne, Victoria, Australia. *d:* 19.3.1958, Brighton, Melbourne, Victoria, Australia. Brother-in-law of W. R. F. Macrow (Victoria). Sound middle order left-hand batsman, slow left-arm bowler, good deep field. *Team* Victoria (1903/4 to 1927/8, 76 matches). *Tours* Australia to England 1909, to New Zealand 1913/14, 1920/1; Victoria to New Zealand 1924/5. *Tests* Australia (1907/8 to 1911/12, 20 matches).
Career batting
142–219–24–8268–190–42.40–25–*ct* 74
Bowling 888–29–30.62–1–0–6/38
Test batting
20–38–6–1211–143*–37.84–1–*ct* 10
Bowling 28–1–28.00–0–0–1/9

He was very successful on his only tour to England, hitting 1,736 runs, av 43.40. He appeared in all five Tests and easily topped the batting with 353, av 58.83.

Ransom, Victor Joseph
Amateur. *b:* 17.5.1917, New Malden, Surrey. Hard hitting lower order right-hand batsman, right-arm fast medium bowler. *Teams* Hampshire (1947–50, 34 matches); Surrey (1951–55, 2 matches).
Career batting
40–58–11–455–58–9.68–0–*ct* 22
Bowling 3469–98–35.39–3–0–5/50

Raper, James Rhodes Stanley
Amateur. *b:* 9.8.1909, Bradford, Yorkshire. Lower order right-hand batsman, right-arm medium pace bowler. *Sch* Leys. *Team* Yorkshire (1936–47, 3 matches). *Tour* Yorkshire to Jamaica 1935/6 (he did not play in first-class matches).
Career batting
3–4–0–24–15–6.00–0–*ct* 0

Raphael, Geoffrey Lewis
Amateur. *b:* 10.1.1910, Mayfair, Westminster, London. *d:* 12.6.1986, Kensington, London. Lower order right-hand batsman, right-arm medium pace bowler. *Sch* Harrow. *Team* Middlesex (1928, 1 match).
Career batting
1–1–0–1–1–1.00–0–*ct* 0
Bowling 36–0

Raphael, John Edward
Amateur. *b:* 30.4.1882, Brussels, Belgium. *d:* 11.6.1917, Remy, Belgium, He died of wounds. Attacking middle order right-hand batsman, slow medium right-arm bowler. *Sch* Merchant Taylors. *Teams* London County (1901–02); Oxford U (1903–05, blue all three years); Surrey (1903–09, 39 matches).
Career batting
77–128–8–3717–201–30.97–5–*ct* 36
Bowling 411–3–137.00–0–0–1/34

He hit 1,695 runs, av 39.41, in 1904 and in the same year hit 201 for Oxford U v Yorkshire at Oxford. His final first-class match was for MCC in 1913. An excellent three-quarter back he obtained his blue and was capped nine times for England. He also won blues for swimming and water polo. He stood as Liberal candidate for Croydon but was not elected.

Raphael, Richard Henry
Amateur. *b:* 29.8.1872, Steyning, Sussex. *d:* 23.1.1910, Westminster, London. Middle order right-hand batsman. *Sch* Wellington. *Team* G. J. V. Weigall's XI (1904). *Tour* Oxford University Authentics to India 1902/3.
Career batting
4–8–1–246–111–35.14–1–*ct* 0
Bowling 18–0

He played in trials at Oxford U, but not in first-class matches.

Rashid Latif
Cricketer. *b:* 14.10.1968, Karachi, Pakistan. Lower order right-hand batsman, occasional leg break bowler, wicket-keeper. *Teams* Karachi (1986/7 to 1991/2); United Bank (1990/1 to 1991/2). *Tour* Pakistan to England 1992. *Test* Pakistan (1992, 1 match).
Career batting
37–50–13–929–54*–25.10–0–*ct* 99–*st* 18
Bowling 37–3–12.33–0–0–2/17
Test batting
1–1–0–50–50–50.00–0–*ct* 2–*st* 1

His great enthusiasm on the 1992 England tour gained him a Test cap in the final game of the series.

Rashleigh, Canon William
Amateur. *b:* 7.3.1867, Farningham Manor, Kent. *d:* 13.2.1937, Balcombe, Sussex. Son of W. B. (Gentlemen of Kent 1851), nephew of C. E. (Gentlemen of Kent 1847). Stylish opening right-hand batsman, slow right-arm bowler. *Sch* Tonbridge. *Teams* Kent (1885–1901, 96 matches); Oxford U (1886–89, blue all four years).
Career batting
127–220–6–5379–163–25.13–9–*ct* 56
Bowling 29–0

He captained Oxford in 1888. A useful rugby footballer, he played as full back against Cambridge in 1887 and 1888.

Raspin, Peter Hugh
Cricketer. *b:* 26.11.1951, Farnworth, Bolton, Lancashire. Lower order left-hand batsman, slow left-arm bowler. *Sch* Birkenhead. *Team* Oxford U (1973).
Career batting
2–2–1–15–10–15.00–0–*ct* 0
Bowling 117–3–39.00–0–0–2/69

Ratcliff, John
Amateur. *b:* 31.12.1848, Richmond, Surrey. *d:* 11.8.1925, Twickenham, Middlesex. Lower order right-hand batsman, wicket-keeper. *Team* Surrey (1876, 4 matches).
Career batting
4–8–0–69–27–8.62–0–*ct* 1

Ratcliffe, Alan
Amateur. *b:* 31.3.1909, Dulwich, Surrey. *d:* 21.8.1967, Toronto, Ontario, Canada. Opening right-hand batsman. *Sch* Rydal. *Teams* Wales (1928–30); Cambridge U (1930–32, blue all three years); Surrey (1932–33, 7 matches).
Career batting
49–82–7–1969–201–26.25–5–*ct* 40
Bowling 22–0

He created a new University record by scoring 201 for Cambridge in 1931 – he was chosen for the match only at the last moment due to the injury of J. G. W. Davies. He also played for Denbighshire (1930–31) and Buckinghamshire (1937–39). His final first-class match was for Over 33 in 1945.

Ratcliffe, David Philip
Professional. *b:* 11.5.1939, Hall Green, Birmingham. Father of J. D. (Warwickshire). Opening right-hand batsman. *Team* Warwickshire (1957–68, 20 matches).
Career batting
20–33–2–603–79–19.45–0–*ct* 18

Ratcliffe, Edgar
Amateur. *b:* 19.1.1863, Liverpool, Lancashire. *d:* 29.7.1915, Aston, Birmingham. Middle order batsman. *Team* Lancashire (1884, 1 match).

Career batting
4–7–0–67–28–9.57–0–*ct* 2
Bowling 43–1–43.00–0–0–1/10

His final first-class match was for Liverpool and District in 1889.

Ratcliffe, George
Amateur. *b:* 1856, Ilkeston, Derbyshire. *d:* 7.3.1928, Nottingham. Attacking middle order left-hand batsman. *Team* Derbyshire (1887, 5 matches).
Career batting
5–10–0–145–64–14.50–0–*ct* 0
Bowling 8–0

He last played for Derbyshire (not first-class) in 1889. He also played for Nottinghamshire in non-first-class matches (1896).

Ratcliffe, George
Professional. *b:* 9.11.1882, Derby. *d:* 31.12.1949, Ollerton, Nottinghamshire. Tail end right-hand batsman, good bowler. *Team* Derbyshire (1919, 1 match).
Career batting
1–2–1–8–5*–8.00–0–*ct* 2
Bowling 10–1–10.00–0–0–1/10

Ratcliffe, Jason David
Cricketer. *b:* 19.6.1969, Solihull, Warwickshire. Son of D. P. (Warwickshire). Opening right-hand batsman, right-arm medium pace bowler. *Team* Warwickshire (1988–92, 54 matches). *Tour* Warwickshire to South Africa 1991/2.
Career batting
54–102–8–2715–127*–28.88–2–*ct* 33
Bowling 96–1–96.00–0–0–1/15

Ratcliffe, Robert Malcolm
Cricketer. *b:* 29.11.1951, Accrington, Lancashire. Lower order right-hand batsman, right-arm medium pace bowler. *Team* Lancashire (1972–80, 82 matches).
Career batting
82–84–22–1022–101*–16.48–1–*ct* 23
Bowling 5411–205–26.39–15–2–7/58

He also played for Cumberland (1981–86).

Ratliff, Thomas
Amateur. *b:* 31.3.1836, Camberwell, London. Middle order right-hand batsman, right-hand slow under-arm bowler, good cover point. *Team* Middlesex (1869–73, 3 matches).
Career batting
4–6–1–50–18–10.00–0–*ct* 0
Bowling 29–3–9.66–0–0–3/21

His first-class debut was for Gentlemen of the North in 1862. He also played for Warwickshire (pre first-class, 1863–76). He was Secretary of Essex 1886–87.

Ratnayake, Rumesh Joseph
Cricketer. *b:* 2.1.1964, Colombo, Ceylon. Lower order right-hand batsman, right-arm fast medium bowler. *Team* Nondescripts CC (1988/9 to 1991/2). *Tours* Sri Lanka to New Zealand 1982/3, 1990/1, to Australia 1982/3, 1984/5, 1989/90, to Zimbabwe 1982/3, to Pakistan 1985/6, 1991/2, to Sharjah (not first-class) 1985/6, 1986/7, 1989/90, 1990/1, to India 1982/3 (not first-class), 1986/7, 1990/1, to India and Pakistan (World Cup) 1987/8, to England 1991; Sri Lanka Under 23 to Pakistan 1983/4. *Tests* Sri Lanka (1982/3 to 1991/2, 23 matches).
Career batting
53–70–15–925–68*–16.81–0–*ct* 16
Bowling 4763–174–27.37–11–0–6/57
Test batting
23–36–6–433–56–14.43–0–*ct* 9
Bowling 2563–73–35.10–5–0–6/66

He was the most successful cricketer in the 1991 tour to England and topped the first-class bowling averages, as well as performing usefully with the bat.

Ratnayeke, Joseph Ravindran
Cricketer. *b:* 2.5.1960, Colombo, Ceylon. Occasional opening or middle order left-hand batsman, right-arm fast medium bowler. *Team* Nondescripts CC (1988/9). *Tours* Sri Lanka to India 1980/1, 1982/3, 1986/7, 1989/90 (not first-class), to England 1981, 1984, 1988, to Pakistan 1981/2, 1985/6, to Zimbabwe 1982/3, to Australia 1982/3, 1984/5, 1987/8, 1989/90, to New Zealand 1982/3, to Sharjah (not first-class) 1983/4, 1985/6, 1986/7, 1987/8, 1988/9, 1989/90, to India and Pakistan (World Cup) 1987/8, to Bangladesh (not first-class) 1988/9; Rest of World to England 1987. *Tests* Sri Lanka (1981/2 to 1989/90, 22 matches).
Career batting
71–103–25–2225–107–28.52–1–*ct* 18
Bowling 4891–133–36.77–5–0–8/83
Test batting
22–38–6–807–93–25.21–0–*ct* 1
Bowling 1972–56–35.21–4–0–8/83

He headed the first-class batting averages on the 1988 tour with 311 runs, av 62.20. He also played for Lincolnshire (1985). He emigrated to Australia after the tour in 1989/90, his last appearance in Sri Lanka being for Central Province that season.

Rattenbury, Gilbert Leach
Amateur. *b:* 28.2.1878, Cardiff, Glamorgan. *d:* 14.8.1958, Penarth, Glamorgan. Middle order right-hand batsman, right-arm fast bowler. *Team* Gloucestershire (1902–09, 2 matches).
Career batting
2–4–0–7–7–1.75–0–*ct* 0
Bowling 129–1–129.00–0–0–1/54

He also played for Glamorgan (pre first-class, 1905–12).

Rattigan, Cyril Stanley
Amateur. *b:* 5.8.1884, Camberwell, London. *d:* 13.11.1916, near Beaucourt, France. He was killed in

action. Middle order right-hand batsman, right-arm medium pace bowler. *Sch* Harrow. *Team* Cambridge U (1906–07).
Career batting
7–11–2–183–42–20.33–0–*ct* 3
Bowling 217–5–43.40–0–0–3/61
His final first-class match was for MCC in 1908.

Raven, John Earle Reynolds
Amateur. *b:* 23.2.1851, Broughton Astley, Leicestershire. *d:* 3.4.1940, Nutfield, Surrey. Tail end right-hand batsman, right-arm fast medium bowler. *Sch* Lancing. *Team* Sussex (1874, 1 match).
Career batting
1–2–0–14–10–7.00–0–*ct* 0
Bowling 37–0

Raven, Reginald Owen
Amateur. *b:* 26.11.1884, Baldock, Hertfordshire. *d:* 4.4.1936, Eastbourne, Sussex. Lower order right-hand batsman, bowler. *Sch* Wellingborough. *Team* Northamptonshire (1905–21, 31 matches).
Career batting
31–58–2–766–59–13.67–0–*ct* 10
Bowling 59–1–59.00–0–0–1/15
He captained Northamptonshire in 1920–21. He also represented Northamptonshire at hockey.

Ravenhill, Edward Harry Goring
Amateur. *b:* 11.11.1845, Leominster, Littlehampton, Sussex. *d:* 1.3.1924, Brentwood, Essex. Brother of F. H. H. (Sussex), brother-in-law of A. G. Chapman (Sussex). Middle order batsman. *Team* MCC (1882).
Career batting
1–2–0–9–6–4.50–0–*ct* 0

Ravenhill, Frederick Henry Harvey
Amateur. *b:* 25.7.1837, Leominster, Littlehampton, Sussex. *d:* 4.8.1897, Hove, Sussex. Brother of E. H. G. (MCC), brother-in-law of A. G. Chapman (Sussex). Middle order right-hand batsman. *Sch* Brighton. *Team* Sussex (1863–67, 2 matches).
Career batting
2–3–0–10–7–3.33–0–*ct* 1
He did not appear in first-class matches whilst at Oxford.

Ravenscroft, Joseph
Amateur. *b:* 19.3.1858, Birkenhead, Cheshire. *d:* 28.4.1913, North Birkenhead, Cheshire. Middle order right-hand batsman. *Sch* Rugby. *Team* Liverpool and District (1888–94).
Career batting
2–4–0–0–0–0.00–0–*ct* 1
His County cricket was for Cheshire (1884–95).

Raw, George David
Cricketer. *b:* 14.11.1944, Ossett, Yorkshire. Middle order right-hand batsman. *Sch* Tiffin. *Team* Cambridge U (1967–68).
Career batting
6–10–0–82–21–8.20–0–*ct* 0
His County cricket was for Cambridgeshire (1968).

Raw, Rowland
Amateur. *b:* 16.7.1884, Pietermaritzburg, Natal, South Africa. *d:* 7.8.1915, Suvla Bay, Gallipoli, Turkey. Middle order batsman. *Sch* Clifton. *Team* Gentlemen of England (1905).
Career batting
2–2–0–48–47–24.00–0–*ct* 0

Rawlence, John Rooke
Amateur. *b:* 23.9.1915, Brockenhurst, Hampshire. *d:* 17.1.1983, Ascot, Berkshire. Middle order right-hand batsman. *Sch* Wellington. *Team* Hampshire (1934, 2 matches).
Career batting
5–6–0–87–38–14.50–0–*ct* 3
His final first-class match was for Combined Services in 1950. He played no first-class cricket at Cambridge U, but did win a blue for rugby.

Rawlin, Eric Raymond
Professional. *b:* 4.10.1897, Rotherham, Yorkshire. *d:* 11.1.1943, Rotherham, Yorkshire. Son of J. T. (Yorkshire and Middlesex). Lower order left-hand batsman, right-hand fast medium bowler. *Team* Yorkshire (1927–36, 8 matches).
Career batting
8–10–1–72–35–8.00–0–*ct* 2
Bowling 498–21–23.71–0–0–3/28

Rawlin, John Thomas
Professional. *b:* 10.11.1856, Greasbrough, Rotherham, Yorkshire. *d:* 19.1.1924, Greasbrough, Rotherham, Yorkshire. Father of E. R. (Yorkshire). Lower order right-hand batsman, right-arm fast medium bowler. *Teams* Yorkshire (1880–85, 27 matches); Middlesex (1889–1909, 229 matches). *Tour* Vernon to Australia 1887/8.
Career batting
315–493–44–7651–122*–17.04–2–*ct* 201
Bowling 16689–811–20.57–46–12–8/29
He took 104 wickets, av 14.53, in 1894.

Rawlins, Frederick
Amateur. *b:* 28.9.1907, Biggleswade, Bedfordshire. *d:* 27.12.1968, Biddenham, Bedfordshire. Middle order right-hand batsman. *Sch* Wellingborough. *Team* Minor Counties (1930–34).
Career batting
2–3–0–110–74–36.66–0–*ct* 0
His County cricket was for Bedfordshire (1926–35).

Rawlinson, Elisha Barker
Professional. *b:* 10.4.1837, Yeadon, Yorkshire. *d:* 17.2.1892, Sydney, New South Wales, Australia. He died of jaundice. Middle order right-hand batsman, right-hand fast round-arm bowler, cover point. *Teams*

Yorkshire (1867–75, 37 matches); Lancashire (1867, 1 match).
Career batting
45–80–7–1120–55–15.34–0–*ct* 23
Bowling 79–8–9.87–0–0–4/41

His County cricket ended in 1875 as in April 1876 he emigrated to Australia.

Rawlinson, Henry Thomas
Cricketer. *b:* 21.1.1963, Edgware, Middlesex. Brother of J. L. (Oxford U). Lower order right-hand batsman, right-arm medium pace bowler. *Sch* Eton. *Team* Oxford U (1982–84, blue 1983–84).
Career batting
16–21–3–156–24–8.66–0–*ct* 5
Bowling 1407–23–61.17–1–0–5/123

Rawlinson, John Baldwin
Amateur. *b:* 1.5.1867, Whitehaven, Cumberland. *d:* 12.5.1945, Kensington, London. Lower order right-hand batsman, right-arm fast bowler. *Sch* Malvern. *Team* Oxford U (1887).
Career batting
1–1–0–0–0–0.00–0–*ct* 1
Bowling 45–1–45.00–0–0–1/45

Rawlinson, John Lawrence
Cricketer. *b:* 4.8.1959, Edgware, Middlesex. Brother of H. T. (Oxford U). Middle order right-hand batsman. *Sch* Eton. *Team* Oxford U (1979–80).
Career batting
9–16–2–112–19–8.00–0–*ct* 5

Rawlinson, William
Professional. *b:* 5.9.1850, Burnley, Lancashire. *d:* 12.5.1919, Burnley, Lancashire. Middle order batsman. *Team* Lancashire (1870–71, 3 matches).
Career batting
3–6–0–24–10–4.00–0–*ct* 1

Rawson, Major General Geoffrey Grahame
Amateur. *b:* 2.12.1887, Shirmadavy, India. *d:* 14.1.1979, Kensington, London. Opening right-hand batsman. *Sch* Cheltenham. *Team* Army (1921).
Career batting
3–5–0–69–39–13.80–0–*ct* 5

Rawson, Herbert Edward
Amateur. *b:* 3.9.1852, Port Louis, Mauritius. *d:* 18.10.1924, Westminster, London. Lower order right-hand batsman, wicket-keeper. *Sch* Westminster. *Team* Kent (1873, 1 match).
Career batting
1–2–0–0–0–0.00–0–*ct* 1–*st* 3

In 1874 he was posted overseas and therefore had no opportunity for County cricket. He played soccer for England.

Rawson, Peter Walter Edward
Cricketer. *b:* 25.5.1957, Salisbury, Rhodesia. Lower order right-hand batsman, right-arm fast medium bowler. *Teams* Zimbabwe (1982 to 1988/9); Natal (1989/90 to 1991/2). *Tours* Zimbabwe to England 1982, 1983 (World Cup), to Sri Lanka 1983/4, to India (World Cup) 1987/8.
Career batting
59–93–15–1655–95–21.21–0–*ct* 34
Bowling 5257–218–24.11–12–3–7/30

He played for Suffolk (1984).

Rawstorne, George Streynsham
Amateur. *b:* 22.1.1895, Croston, Lancashire. *d:* 15.7.1962, Rovie, Rogart, Sutherland, Scotland. Middle order batsman. *Sch* Eton. *Team* Lancashire (1919, 1 match).
Career batting
1–1–0–2–2–2.00–0–*ct* 0

Ray, Donald William Garnham
Amateur. *b:* 2.7.1903, Stoneleigh, Wimborne, Dorset. *d:* 12.7.1944, on board a hospital ship near Southampton, Hampshire. Lower order batsman, wicket-keeper. *Sch* Wellington. *Team* MCC (1931).
Career batting
1–2–0–2–2–1.00–0–*ct* 1–*st* 2

Raybould, John Griffith
Amateur. *b:* 26.7.1934, Normanby, Middlesbrough, Yorkshire. Lower order left-hand batsman, leg break and googly bowler. *Sch* Leeds GS. *Team* Oxford U (1957–59, blue 1959).
Career batting
18–32–10–281–81*–12.77–0–*ct* 8
Bowling 1302–34–38.29–0–0–4/31

His final first-class match was for Free Foresters in 1962.

Rayment, Alan William Harrington
Professional. *b:* 29.5.1928, Finchley, Middlesex. Middle order right-hand batsman. *Team* Hampshire (1949–58, 198 matches).
Career batting
199–340–28–6338–126–20.31–4–*ct* 86
Bowling 772–19–40.63–0–0–4/75

He hit 1,000 runs in a season twice (best 1,056, av 23.46, in 1952). His first-class debut was for Combined Services in 1947.

Raynbird, Robert
Amateur. *b:* 29.6.1851, Whitchurch, Hampshire. *d:* 26.12.1920, Basingstoke, Hampshire. Brother of Walter (Hampshire). Lower order batsman, bowler. *Sch* Framlingham. *Team* Hampshire (1878, 1 match).
Career batting
1–2–0–0–0–0.00–0–*ct* 0
Bowling 15–0

Raynbird, Walter
Amateur. *b:* 1.6.1854, Basingstoke, Hampshire. *d:* 6.5.1891, Hackwood Park, Hampshire. Brother of Robert (Hampshire). Middle order batsman. *Team* Hampshire (1880–81, 2 matches).

Career batting
2–4–1–25–13–8.33–0–*ct* 0
Bowling 14–0

Rayner, Dr Howard Luscombe
Amateur. *b:* 12.3.1896, Glenelg, Adelaide, South Australia. *d:* 13.6.1975, Twickenham, Middlesex. Middle order batsman. *Team* P. F. Warner's XI (1919).
Career batting
1–2–1–23–21*–23.00–0–*ct* 1

Raynes, Thomas Arthur
Amateur. *b:* 18.7.1835, Ripe, Sussex. *d:* 6.3.1914, Cockington, Torquay, Devon. Attacking middle order right-hand batsman, good point field. *Sch* Marlborough. *Team* Sussex (1854–64, 7 matches).
Career batting
10–19–2–207–59–12.17–0–*ct* 5

Raynor, Rev George Sydney
Amateur. *b:* 9.10.1852, Sandsend, Lythe, Yorkshire. *d:* 1.9.1887, West Wickham, Kent. Lower order right-hand batsman, right-arm fast bowler. *Sch* Winchester. *Team* Cambridge U (1872–73, blue 1872).
Career batting
7–10–1–66–37*–7.33–0–*ct* 5
Bowling 370–17–21.76–1–0–5/44
His County cricket was for Essex (pre first-class, 1872).

Raynor, Kenneth
Amateur. *b:* 23.5.1886, Wellington, Berkshire. *d:* 15.4.1973, Greendale, Rhodesia. Middle order right-hand batsman, leg break and googly bowler. *Sch* Ipswich. *Teams* Oxford U (1906–08); Leicestershire (1923, 1 match).
Career batting
7–14–1–125–31–9.61–0–*ct* 4
Bowling 12–1–12.00–0–0–1/12
He also played for Suffolk (1904–11). He won blues for hockey and soccer.

Razzall, Edward Timothy
Cricketer. *b:* 12.6.1943, Ealing, Middlesex. Lower order right-hand batsman, right-arm medium pace off break bowler. *Sch* St Paul's. *Team* Oxford U (1964).
Career batting
6–9–4–57–25*–11.40–0–*ct* 3
Bowling 396–13–30.46–0–0–3/44

Rea, Michael Peter
Cricketer. *b:* 19.2.1966, Bangor, Co Down, Ireland. Middle order right-hand batsman. *Team* Ireland (1985–92).
Career batting
6–12–1–307–89–27.90–0–*ct* 1

Read, Arnold Holcombe
Amateur. *b:* 24.1.1880, Snaresbrook, Essex. *d:* 20.5.1957, Englefield Green, Surrey. Father of H. D. (Surrey and Essex). Lower order right-hand batsman, right-arm slow medium bowler. *Sch* Winchester. *Team* Essex (1904–10, 22 matches).
Career batting
22–30–6–419–70–17.45–0–*ct* 7
Bowling 1192–38–31.36–1–0–7/75

Read, Ernest George
Amateur. *b:* 8.10.1873, Portsmouth, Hampshire. *d:* 21.3.1921, Wandsworth, London. Nephew of H. W. R. Bencraft (Hampshire). Middle order right-hand batsman, wicket-keeper. *Sch* St Edward's, Oxford. *Teams* Hampshire (1903, 3 matches); Sussex (1904–06, 4 matches).
Career batting
7–11–0–113–44–10.27–0–*ct* 7
He first played for Hampshire (not first-class) in 1893.

Read, Frederick Hurrell
Professional. *b:* 26.12.1855, Thames Ditton, Surrey. *d:* 4.5.1933, Hounslow, Middlesex. Brother of J. M. (Surrey), nephew of H. H. Stephenson (Surrey). Middle order batsman. *Team* Surrey (1881, 1 match).
Career batting
1–1–0–4–4–4.00–0–*ct* 0

Read, Henry Marvelle
Amateur. *b:* 8.11.1888, Roscrea, Co Tipperary, Ireland. *d:* 6.12.1972, Dalkey, Co Dublin, Ireland. Middle order right-hand batsman. *Team* Ireland (1912). *Tour* Ireland to North America 1909.
Career batting
3–6–0–48–19–8.00–0–*ct* 1
He played rugby for Ireland.

Read, Holcombe Douglas
Amateur. *b:* 28.1.1910, Woodford Green, Essex. Son of A. H. (Essex). Tail end right-hand batsman, right-arm fast bowler. *Sch* Winchester. *Teams* Essex (1933–35, 32 matches); Surrey (1933, 2 matches). *Tours* Martineau to Egypt 1933 (not first-class); MCC to Australia and New Zealand 1935/6. *Test* England (1935, 1 match).
Career batting
54–70–27–158–25*–3.67–0–*ct* 21
Bowling 5023–219–22.93–13–2–7/35
Test batting
1 match, did not bat–*ct* 0
Bowling 200–6–33.33–0–0–4/136
In 1935 he took 97 wickets, av 22.16. His final first-class match was for MCC in 1948. He played for both Surrey and Essex in 1933.

Read, John Maurice
Professional. *b:* 9.2.1859, Thames Ditton, Surrey. *d:* 17.2.1929, Winchester, Hampshire. Brother of F. H. (Surrey), nephew of H. H. Stephenson (Surrey). Middle order right-hand batsman, right-arm fast medium bowler. *Team* Surrey (1880–95, 278 matches). *Tours*

Lillywhite, Shaw and Shrewsbury to Australia 1884/5, 1886/7, 1887/8; Warton to South Africa 1888/9; Sheffield to Australia 1891/2. *Tests* England (1882–93, 17 matches).
Career batting
380–611–43–14008–186*–24.66–11–*ct* 214
Bowling 1807–73–24.75–1–0–6/41
Test batting
17–29–2–461–57–17.07–0–*ct* 8

He hit 1,000 runs in a season three times (best 1,364, av 34.97, in 1886). He retired whilst still worth his place in the County side, in order to take up an appointment on the Tichborne estate.

Read, Walter William
Amateur. *b:* 23.11.1855, Reigate, Surrey. *d:* 6.1.1907, Bingham Road, Addiscombe Park, Surrey. Excellent middle order right-hand batsman, right-hand fast round-arm, later slow under-arm bowler, excellent point field. *Team* Surrey (1873–97, 366 matches). *Tours* Bligh to Australia 1882/3; Vernon to Australia 1887/8; W. W. Read to South Africa 1891/2. *Tests* England (1882/3 to 1893, 18 matches).
Career batting
467–749–52–22349–338–32.06–38–*ct* 381–*st* 20
Bowling 3483–108–32.25–1–0–6/24
Test batting
18–27–1–720–117–27.69–1–*ct* 16
Bowling 63–0

He hit 1,000 runs in a season nine times (best 1,880, av 44.76, in 1885). His highest innings was 338 for Surrey v Oxford U at the Oval in 1880; he also made two other double centuries for Surrey. He was regarded as one of the best batsman in England during the 1880s, his most famous innings being 117 for England v Australia at the Oval in 1884, when he went in at number 10 and saved the match for his side. He captained England in two Tests. He was Surrey coach from 1905 until his death.

Reader-Blackton, Walter
(changed name from Reader)
Professional in 1914, amateur in 1920 and 1921. *b:* 4.7.1895, Shirland, Derbyshire. *d:* 1.1.1976, Derby. Middle order right-hand batsman, right-arm medium pace bowler. *Team* Derbyshire (1914–21, 8 matches).
Career batting
8–15–1–107–31*–7.64–0–*ct* 6
Bowling 81–5–16.20–0–0–3/40

Reading, Maj-Gen Arnold Hughes Eagleton
Amateur. *b:* 3.4.1896, Heilbron, Orange Free State, South Africa. *d:* 4.1.1975, Sellicks Green, Taunton, Somerset. Middle order batsman. *Sch* Cranleigh. *Team* Royal Navy (1929).
Career batting
1–2–0–19–12–9.50–0–*ct* 0

Reason, David Jordan
Amateur. *b:* 14.4.1897, Cadoxton, Neath, Glamorgan. *d:* 17.2.1955, Blackheath, London. Middle order right-hand batsman, occasional off break bowler, wicket-keeper. *Team* Glamorgan (1921–22, 2 matches).
Career batting
2–3–0–3–2–1.00–0–*ct* 3–*st* 1

He first played for Glamorgan (pre first-class) in 1920. He played rugby for London Welsh.

Reason, Dr Thomas Francis
Amateur. *b:* 4.7.1890, Cadoxton, Neath, Glamorgan. *d:* 15.2.1935, Skewen, Glamorgan. Lower order right-hand batsman, right-arm medium pace bowler. *Team* Glamorgan (1923, 1 match).
Career batting
1–2–0–13–10–6.50–0–*ct* 0
Bowling 34–0

He first played for Glamorgan (pre first-class) in 1914.

Reay, Gilbert Martin
Amateur. *b:* 24.1.1887, Wallington, Surrey. *d:* 31.1.1967, Croydon, Surrey. Brother of W. F. (Gentlemen). Hard hitting lower order right-hand batsman, right-arm fast bowler. *Team* Surrey (1913–23, 28 matches).
Career batting
29–36–4–423–54–13.21–0–*ct* 13
Bowling 1961–91–21.54–3–0–5/22

He played for Beddington CC for 42 years.

Reay, Wilfrid Francis
Amateur. *b:* 12.6.1891, Wallington, Surrey. *d:* 8.10.1915, near Thiepval, France. Brother of G. M. (Surrey). Tail end batsman, excellent fast medium bowler. *Team* Gentlemen of England (1910).
Career batting
1–2–2–5–5*–no av–0–*ct* 0
Bowling 51–1–51.00–0–0–1/51

Recordon, Lionel Walther
Amateur. *b:* 25.2.1907, Anerley, Kent. *d:* 6.10.1988, Godalming, Surrey. Middle order right-hand batsman, leg break and googly bowler. *Sch* Brighton. *Team* Kent (1927–29, 11 matches).
Career batting
11–16–3–242–64*–18.61–0–*ct* 9
Bowling 86–0

Reddick, Tom Bokenham
Amateur, but professional 1946–47. *b:* 17.2.1912, Shanghai, China. *d:* 1.6.1982, Newlands, Cape Town, South Africa. Middle order right-hand batsman, leg break bowler. *Sch* KCS Wimbledon. *Teams* Middlesex (1931, 2 matches); Nottinghamshire (1946–47, 50 matches); Western Province (1950/1). *Tours* Cahn to North America and Bermuda 1933 (not first-class), Ceylon 1936/7.

Career batting
62–99–11–2688–139–30.54–2–*ct* 15
Bowling 468–6–78.00–0–0–1/4

He hit 1,231 runs, av 35.17, in 1947. After being coach to Nottinghamshire CCC in 1946 and 1947, he took a similar post in Cape Town and remained in South Africa for most of the rest of his life, although he was Lancashire coach 1963–64.

Reddish, John
Professional. *b:* 22.12.1904, Nottingham. *d:* 18.10.1989, Manchester, Lancashire. Middle order right-hand batsman, leg break and googly bowler. *Team* Nottinghamshire (1930, 1 match).
Career batting
1–1–1–2–2*–no av–0–*ct* 1
Bowling 125–0

A noted soccer player, he was full back for Tottenham Hotspur and Lincoln City.

Reddy, Bharath
Cricketer. *b:* 12.11.1954, Madras, India. Lower order right-hand batsman, wicket-keeper. *Team* Tamil Nadu (1973/4 to 1985/6). *Tours* India to Sri Lanka 1973/4, to Australia 1977/8, to Pakistan 1978/9, to England 1979, to Australia and New Zealand 1981/2; Tamil Nadu to Sri Lanka 1975/6, 1982/3. *Tests* India (1979, 4 matches).
Career batting
95–117–19–1743–88–17.78–0–*ct* 171–*st* 49
Test batting
4–5–1–38–21–9.50–0–*ct* 9–*st* 2

The principal wicket-keeper on the 1979 tour to England, he played in all four Tests.

Reddy, Francis James Anthony
Amateur. *b:* 15.6.1906, Harolds Cross, Dublin, Ireland. Middle order right-hand batsman. *Team* Ireland (1931–39).
Career batting
7–14–2–202–50*–16.83–0–*ct* 11

Reddy, Nayini Santosh Kumar
(known in India as Santosh Reddy)
Amateur. *b:* 22.10.1938, Madras, India. Middle order left-hand batsman. *Teams* Cambridge U (1959–61, blue all three years); Hyderabad (1966/7 to 1970/1).
Career batting
61–102–8–2284–113*–24.29–2–*ct* 37
Bowling 306–5–61.20–0–0–3/26

Redfearn, Joseph
(birth registered as Joah Redfearn)
Professional. *b:* 13.5.1862, Lascelles Hall, Yorkshire. *d:* 14.1.1931, Lepton, Yorkshire. Middle order left-hand batsman. *Team* Yorkshire (1890, 1 match).
Career batting
1–1–0–5–5–5.00–0–*ct* 0

Redgate, Oliver
Amateur. *b:* 16.2.1863, Nottingham. *d:* 11.2.1913, Sherwood, Nottingham. Middle order right-hand batsman, bowler. *Team* Nottinghamshire (1889–94, 8 matches).
Career batting
12–20–2–205–37–11.38–0–*ct* 6
Bowling 130–7–18.57–0–0–3/8

Redgate, Samuel
Professional. *b:* 27.7.1810, Arnold, Nottinghamshire. *d:* 13.4.1851, Old Radford, Nottinghamshire. Lower order right-hand batsman, right-hand fast round-arm bowler. *Teams* Nottinghamshire (1830–45, 24 matches); Cambridge Town Club (1839).
Career batting
78–138–22–1011–41–8.71–0–*ct* 60–*st* 2
Bowling 800–67 + 357–11.94–30–11–8/?

For a few years he was regarded as one of the best round-arm bowlers, his bowling being 'very fast and ripping', but he was obliged to give up important cricket in 1846 owing to ill-health. His final first-class match was for the North in 1846. He also played for Somerset (pre first-class, 1845).

Redgewell, Louis John
Professional. *b:* 13.10.1894, Battersea, London. *d:* 17.2.1966, Wandsworth Common, London. Lower order right-hand batsman, wicket-keeper. *Team* Surrey (1922–23, 3 matches).
Career batting
3–4–2–5–4–2.50–0–*ct* 4–*st* 1

He was for many years chauffeur to the Mayor of Battersea.

Redhouse
Professional. Lower order batsman, useful bowler. *Team* Hampshire (1900, 1 match).
Career batting
1–2–0–4–4–2.00–0–*ct* 1
Bowling 13–0

Redman, James
Amateur in 1948, then professional. *b:* 1.3.1926, Walcot, Bath, Somerset. *d:* 24.9.1981, Salisbury, Wiltshire. Lower order right-hand batsman, right-arm fast medium bowler. *Team* Somerset (1948–53, 65 matches).
Career batting
65–105–23–1012–45–12.34–0–*ct* 19
Bowling 4169–117–35.63–4–0–7/23

He also played for Wiltshire (1958–64).

Redmond, Rodney Ernest
Cricketer. *b:* 29.12.1944, Whangarei, Auckland, New Zealand. Aggressive opening left-hand batsman, slow left-arm bowler. *Teams* Wellington (1966/7 to 1967/8); Auckland (1969/70 to 1975/6). *Tours* New Zealand to Australia 1972/3, to England 1973. *Tests* New Zealand (1972/3, 1 match).

Redpath, Ian

Career batting
53–100–7–3134–141–33.69–5–*ct* 31
Bowling 481–17–28.29–1–1–6/56
Test batting
1–2–0–163–107–81.50–1–*ct* 0

He hit 483 runs, av 28.41, on the 1973 tour, not playing in any Tests. His first-class debut was for New Zealand Under 23 in 1963/4. He had the unusual distinction of scoring a century in his only Test match.

Redpath, Ian
Cricketer. *b:* 12.9.1965, Basildon, Essex. Middle order right-hand batsman, right-arm medium pace or leg break bowler. *Teams* Essex (1987, 7 matches); Derbyshire (1989, 3 matches).
Career batting
10–18–3–216–46–14.40–0–*ct* 2
Bowling 11–0

Redpath, Ian Ritchie, MBE
Amateur. *b:* 11.5.1941, Geelong, Victoria, Australia. Sound opening right-hand batsman, right-arm medium pace bowler, good short leg field. *Team* Victoria (1961/2 to 1975/6, 92 matches). *Tours* Australia to England 1964, 1968, to South Africa 1966/7, 1969/70, to West Indies 1972/3, to India and Pakistan 1964/5, to India and Ceylon 1969/70, to New Zealand 1973/4. *Tests* Australia (1963/4 to 1975/6, 66 matches).
Career batting
226–391–34–14993–261–41.99–32–*ct* 211
Bowling 466–13–35.84–0–0–3/24
Test batting
66–120–11–4737–171–43.45–8–*ct* 83
Bowling 41–0

On the 1964 tour to England he hit 1,075 runs, av 32.57, and played in all five Tests; in 1968 he hit 1,474 runs, av 43.35 and again appeared in all five Tests, scoring his runs much more fluently than on his first visit. His highest score was 261 for Victoria v Queensland at Melbourne in 1962/3. He hit 1,150 runs, av 41.07, in Australia in 1974/5.

Reece, Courtenay Walton
Amateur. *b:* 4.12.1899, Selman's, St Thomas, Barbados. *d:* 16.4.1984, Hong Kong. Lower order right-hand batsman, right-arm medium pace bowler. *Teams* Oxford U (1925); Barbados (1926/7 to 1929/30).
Career batting
4–5–1–4–3–1.00–0–*ct* 4
Bowling 433–13–33.30–0–0–4/72

His County cricket was for Oxfordshire (1924–33). He umpired a Test match in West Indies in 1934/5.

Reed, Albert Adams
Professional. *b:* 16.11.1846, Sompting, Sussex. *d:* 8.5.1931, Lyminster, Littlehampton, Sussex. Brother of W. B. (Sussex) Middle order right-hand batsman, right-hand medium pace round-arm bowler, mid off. *Team* Sussex (1867–73, 25 matches).
Career batting
27–47–5–620–70*–14.76–0–*ct* 17
Bowling 389–23–16.91–1–0–5/28

Reed, Barry Lindsay
Amateur. *b:* 17.9.1937, Southsea, Hampshire. Opening right-hand batsman, right-arm slow bowler. *Sch* Winchester. *Team* Hampshire (1958–70, 122 matches). *Tour* MCC to Bangladesh 1978/9 (not first-class).
Career batting
123–215–11–4962–138–24.32–2–*ct* 61
Bowling 0–0

He hit 1,000 runs in a season three times (best 1,136, av 24.17, in 1967).

Reed, Basil Duck
Amateur. *b:* 8.11.1895, Malmesbury, Wiltshire. *d:* 12.10.1968, Wroughton, Wiltshire. Lower order right-hand batsman, right-arm medium pace bowler. *Team* Royal Navy (1921).
Career batting
1–2–1–8–8*–8.00–0–*ct* 1
Bowling 83–1–83.00–0–0–1/56

His County cricket was for Wiltshire (1921–23).

Reed, Rev Francis
Amateur. *b:* 24.10.1850, Ottery St Mary, Devon. *d:* 30.4.1912, Whitechapel, London. Middle order right-hand batsman, right-arm medium pace bowler, slip field. *Team* Somerset (1882–84, 10 matches).
Career batting
10–18–1–198–57*–11.64–0–*ct* 4
Bowling 380–12–31.66–0–0–4/35

He did not appear in any first-class matches whilst at Oxford University. He first played for Somerset (pre first-class) in 1875.

Reed, George Henry
Professional. *b:* 8.8.1906, St Fagans, Cardiff, Glamorgan. *d:* 11.12.1988, Whitchurch, Cardiff, Glamorgan. Tail end right-hand batsman, left-arm fast medium bowler. *Team* Glamorgan (1934–38, 25 matches).
Career batting
25–25–12–65–11–5.00–0–*ct* 6
Bowling 1941–62–31.30–1–0–5/30

Reed, H. F.
Amateur. Middle order right-hand batsman, good field. *Team* Somerset (1882–85, 7 matches).
Career batting
8–15–1–161–33–11.50–0–*ct* 4
Bowling 61–2–30.50–0–0–1/6

Reed, Henry Albert
Amateur. *b:* 17.5.1892, Bristol. *d:* 3.5.1963, Redland, Bristol. Middle order batsman. *Team* Gloucestershire (1921–23, 6 matches).

Career batting
6–12–0–110–45–9.16–0–*ct* 1

Reed, Walter Bartlett
Professional. *b:* 4.2.1839, Sompting, Sussex. *d:* 17.3.1880, Storrington, Sussex. Brother of A. A. (Sussex). Middle order right-hand batsman, left-hand fast round-arm bowler. *Team* Sussex (1860, 6 matches).
Career batting
6–10–1–38–10*–4.22–0–*ct* 0
Bowling 103–2–51.50–0–0–1/8

Rees, Alan
Professional. *b:* 17.2.1938, Port Talbot, Glamorgan. Middle order right-hand batsman, right-arm medium pace bowler, fine field. *Team* Glamorgan (1955–68, 216 matches).
Career batting
216–372–53–7681–111*–24.07–2–*ct* 113
Bowling 398–6–66.33–0–0–3/68

He hit 1,000 runs in a season four times (best 1,206, av 30.15, in 1964). A noted rugby footballer, he was capped for Wales in 1961/2 and then turned professional for Leeds in the Rugby League.

Rees-Davies, William Rupert
Amateur. *b:* 19.11.1916, Hong Kong. *d:* 12.1.1992, Monkton, Kent. Lower order right-hand batsman, right-arm fast medium bowler. *Sch* Eton. *Team* Cambridge U (1936–38, blue 1938).
Career batting
15–23–12–37–7–3.36–0–*ct* 6
Bowling 1433–33–43.42–0–0–4/21

He was Conservative MP for the Isle of Thanet from 1953 to 1983.

Reese, Daniel
Amateur. *b:* 27.1.1879, Christchurch, New Zealand. *d:* 12.6.1953, Christchurch, New Zealand. Brother of T. W. (Canterbury) and J. B. (Canterbury), uncle of D. W. (Canterbury). Forcing middle order left-hand batsman, left-arm slow medium bowler. *Teams* Essex (1906, 8 matches); Canterbury (1895/6 to 1920/1); London County (1903). *Tours* New Zealand to Australia 1898/9, 1913/14.
Career batting
72–134–8–3182–148–25.25–4–*ct* 36
Bowling 3893–196–19.86–11–1–7/53

He captained the New Zealand touring team in Australia and also Canterbury. He was later President of the New Zealand Cricket Council and wrote his memoirs 'Was it all Cricket?' in 1948.

Reeve, Dermot Alexander
Cricketer. *b:* 2.4.1963, Kowloon, Hong Kong. Middle order right-hand batsman, right-arm medium pace bowler. *Teams* Sussex (1983–87, 91 matches); Warwickshire (1988–92, 91 matches). *Tours* England to New Zealand 1991/2, to Australia and New Zealand (World Cup) 1991/2. *Tests* England (1991/2, 3 matches).
Career batting
189–248–63–6492–202*–35.09–5–*ct* 129
Bowling 10424–373–27.94–6–0–7/37
Test batting
3–5–0–124–59–24.80–0–*ct* 1
Bowling 60–2–30.00–0–0–1/4

He hit 1,000 runs in a season twice (best 1,412, av 54.30, in 1990). His highest score was 202* for Warwickshire v Northamptonshire at Northampton in 1990. He played for Hong Kong in the 1982 ICC Trophy.

Reeves, Edmund
Amateur. *c:* 27.11.1821, Lambeth, London. *d:* 10.12.1906, Wimbledon, Surrey. Stylish middle order right-hand batsman, right-arm medium fast bowler. *Teams* Surrey (1848–52, 9 matches); Middlesex (1851, 1 match).
Career batting
21–35–3–368–57–11.50–0–*ct* 2
Bowling 6 wickets (no analyses)–0–0–3/?

He played for the Gentlemen and was one of the best cricketers of his time, but his career in important matches was very brief.

Reeves, William
Professional. *b:* 22.6.1875, Cambridge. *d:* 22.3.1944, Hammersmith, London. Son-in-law of E. C. Freeman (Essex), brother-in-law of E. J. Freeman (Essex). Lower order right-hand batsman, right-arm medium pace bowler. *Team* Essex (1897–1921, 271 matches).
Career batting
280–436–35–6656–135–16.59–3–*ct* 121
Bowling 16526–601–27.49–38–5–7/33

He hit 1,174 runs, av 29.35, in 1905 and took 106 wickets, av 26.16, in 1904. After retiring from County cricket he was a first-class umpire (1922–39), standing in five Test matches (1924–39).

Regan, Charles
Professional. *b:* 11.5.1842, Barnsley, Yorkshire. *d:* 17.5.1921, Southend-on-Sea, Essex. Lower order right-hand batsman, wicket-keeper. Team, Derbyshire (1877, 5 matches).
Career batting
5–10–0–90–22–9.00–0–*ct* 1

He also played for Essex (pre first-class, 1884).

Reid, Allan
Amateur. *b:* 1.10.1877, Cape Town, South Africa. *d:* 31.10.1948, Rosebank, Cape Town, South Africa. Brother of Norman (South Africa) and Frank (Western Province). Middle order right-hand batsman. *Team* Western Province (1896/7 to 1908/9). *Tour* South Africa to England 1901.
Career batting
32–54–4–894–101*–17.88–1–*ct* 13

He was moderately successful on the 1901 tour.

Reid, Bruce Anthony
Cricketer. *b:* 14.3.1963, Osborne Park, Perth, Western Australia. Tail end left-hand batsman, left-arm fast medium bowler. *Team* Western Australia (1984/5 to 1991/2, 35 matches). *Tours* Young Australia to Zimbabwe 1985/6; Australia to New Zealand 1985/6, to Sharjah (not first-class) 1985/6, 1986/7, to India 1986/7, to Pakistan 1988/9, to West Indies 1990/1, to India and Pakistan (World Cup) 1987/8, to New Zealand (World Cup) 1991/2; Rest of World to England 1987. *Tests* Australia (1985/6 to 1991/2, 26 matches).
Career batting
74–81–32–451–30–9.20–0–*ct* 16
Bowling 7367–277–26.59–9–3–7/51
Test batting
26–32–13–91–13–4.78–0–*ct* 5
Bowling 2633–106–24.84–4–2–7/51

After missing the whole of the 1989/90 season due to a serious back injury, he recovered in 1990/1 to become Australia's principal bowler in the series v England, taking 27 wickets, av 16.00. Immediately after that series Australia went to West Indies, but Reid was a pale shadow of the man who had crushed England.

Reid, John Richard, OBE
Amateur. *b:* 3.6.1928, Auckland, New Zealand. Father of R. B. (Wellington and Transvaal). Attacking middle order right-hand batsman, right-arm fast medium, later off break bowler, good close field, occasional wicket-keeper. *Teams* Wellington (1947/8 to 1964/5); Otago (1956/7 to 1957/8). *Tours* New Zealand to England 1949, 1958, 1965, to South Africa and Australia 1953/4, 1961/2, to India and Pakistan 1955/6, 1964/5; Cavaliers to South Africa 1962/3; Rest of World to England 1965. *Tests* New Zealand (1949–65, 58 matches).
Career batting
246–418–28–16128–296–41.35–39–*ct* 240–*st* 7
Bowling 10535–466–22.60–15–1–7/20
Test batting
58–108–5–3428–142–33.28–6–*ct* 43–*st* 1
Bowling 2835–85–33.35–1–0–6/60

On his 1949 visit to England he developed into the most useful all-rounder of the party and hit 1,488 runs, av 41.33, and played in the last two Tests. In 1958 he topped the batting averages with 1,429 runs, av 39.69, but in 1965, coming as captain, he could only score 799 runs, av 31.96, but was handicapped by a knee injury. He led New Zealand in all three Tests in 1965 and on 34 occasions in all. For Wellington v Northern Districts at Wellington in 1962/3, he created a new first-class record by hitting 15 sixes in his innings of 296. None of his four double centuries was made in England. In the 1961/2 season, playing in Australia, New Zealand and South Africa, he hit 2,188 runs, av 57.57.

Reid, Keith Patrick
Cricketer. *b:* 24.7.1951, Newton Park, Port Elizabeth, South Africa. Brother of T. B. (Eastern Province). Middle order right-hand batsman, right-arm medium pace bowler. *Teams* Eastern Province (1970/1 to 1980/1); Northamptonshire (1973, 1 match).
Career batting
57–97–20–1518–109–19.71–1–*ct* 28
Bowling 2335–78–29.93–3–0–7/50

Reid, Leonard John
Amateur. *b:* 14.1.1888, Chesterton, Cambridgeshire. *d:* 25.10.1938, New York, USA. Middle order batsman. *Sch* Aldenham. *Team* MCC (1913).
Career batting
1–2–0–10–6–5.00–0–*ct* 1

His County cricket was for Cambridgeshire (1906–14) and Hertfordshire (1920–31). He was for some time City Editor of the *Daily Telegraph*.

Reid, Robert Threshie
(created 1st Earl Loreburn in 1906)
Amateur. *b:* 3.4.1846, Kerkira, Corfu, Ionian Isles. *d:* 30.11.1923, Walmer, Dover, Kent. Lower order right-hand batsman, wicket-keeper. *Sch* Cheltenham. *Team* Oxford U (1865–68, blue 1866–68).
Career batting
15–23–4–97–23–5.10–0–*ct* 17–*st* 5

He represented Oxford at rackets in 1865 and 1867. In 1907 he was President of the MCC and also of Kent. He was MP for Hereford 1880–85 and for Dumfries from 1886 to 1906. In 1894 he became Solicitor-General, then Attorney-General, and from 1906 to 1912 he was Lord Chancellor.

Reid, William Hamilton
Amateur. *b:* 25.7.1893, Uddingston, Lanarkshire, Scotland. *d:* 17.1.1949, Pollokshields, Glasgow, Scotland. Lower order right-hand batsman, off break bowler. *Team* Scotland (1923).
Career batting
1–2–1–0–0*–0.00–0–*ct* 0
Bowling 52–4–13.00–0–0–4/29

Reid-Kerr, J. (*see under* Kerr, J. R.)

Reidy, Bernard Wilfrid
Cricketer. *b:* 18.9.1953, Bramley Meade, Whalley, Lancashire. Middle order left-hand batsman, left-arm medium pace bowler. *Sch* St Mary's College, Blackburn. *Team* Lancashire (1973–82, 107 matches).
Career batting
107–162–26–3641–131*–26.77–2–*ct* 65
Bowling 2508–60–41.80–1–0–5/61

He also played for Cumberland (1983–92).

Reifer, Elvis Leroy
Cricketer. *b:* 21.3.1961, Airy Hill, St George, Barbados. Twin brother of G. N. (Barbados), brother of L. N. (Barbados). Lower order left-hand batsman, left-arm fast medium bowler. *Teams* Hampshire

(1984, 20 matches); Barbados (1985/6).
Career batting
21–27–9–408–51*–22.66–0–*ct* 6
Bowling 1811–49–36.95–0–0–4/43

Reiner, Charles Frederick
Amateur. *b:* 15.2.1884, Sutton, Surrey. *d:* 9.1.1947, Maida Vale, London. Brother of G. V. (Europeans). Opening batsman. *Sch* Dulwich. *Team* Surrey (1906, 1 match).
Career batting
2–4–0–82–26–20.50–0–*ct* 0

Reith, Michael Stevens
Cricketer. *b:* 2.5.1948, Lurgan, Co Armagh, Ireland. Opening left-hand batsman, right-arm medium pace bowler. *Team* Ireland (1970–80).
Career batting
9–16–0–346–82–21.62–0–*ct* 5
Bowling 56–1–56.00–0–0–1/24

Relf, Albert Edward
Professional. *b:* 26.6.1874, Burwash, Sussex. *d:* 26.3.1937, Wellington College, Crowthorne, Berkshire. He shot himself in a fit of depression. Brother of E. H. (Sussex) and R. R. (Sussex). Middle order right-hand batsman, right-arm medium pace off break bowler, excellent slip field. *Teams* Sussex (1900–21, 448 matches); London County (1904); Auckland (1907/8 to 1909/10). *Tours* MCC to Australia 1903/4, to South Africa 1905/6, 1913/4, to West Indies 1912/13. *Tests* England (1903/4 to 1913/14, 13 matches).
Career batting
565–900–70–22238–189*–26.79–26–*ct* 537
Bowling 39726–1897–20.94–114–23–9/95
Test batting
13–21–3–416–63–23.11–0–*ct* 14
Bowling 624–25–24.96–1–0–5/85

He hit 1,000 runs in a season 11 times (best 1,846, av 31.82, in 1913) and took 100 wickets in a season 11 times (best 158, av 19.67, in 1910). He achieved the 'double' eight times. Before appearing for Sussex he played for Berkshire (1895) and Norfolk (1898–99). His best bowling was 9/95 for Sussex v Warwickshire at Hove in 1910.

Relf, Ernest Herbert
Professional. *b:* 19.11.1888, Sandhurst, Berkshire. *d:* 27.7.1918, Evington, Leicester. Brother of A. E. (Sussex) and R. R. (Sussex). Lower order right-hand batsman, right-arm medium pace bowler. *Team* Sussex (1912–14, 12 matches).
Career batting
12–23–3–232–36–11.60–0–*ct* 5
Bowling 212–8–26.50–0–0–2/24

Relf, Robert Richard
Professional. *b:* 1.9.1883, Sandhurst, Berkshire. *d:* 28.4.1965, Reading, Berkshire. Brother of A. E. (Sussex) and E. H. (Sussex). Solid right-hand opening batsman, right-arm fast medium bowler. *Teams* Sussex (1905–24, 283 matches); P. W. Sherwell's XI (1913/14). *Tour* MCC to South Africa 1913/14 (he was co-opted).
Career batting
302–529–18–14522–272*–28.41–24–*ct* 300
Bowling 8715–317–27.49–12–2–8/79

He hit 1,000 runs in a season six times (best 1,804, av 32.21, in 1912). His three double centuries were all for Sussex, the highest being 272* v Worcestershire at Eastbourne in 1909. He played for Berkshire (1900–03) before appearing for Sussex and in 1923 reappeared for his native County. In 1924 he began to play in the Sussex v Surrey match at the Oval, but was objected to by the Surrey captain, as not qualified. Relf withdrew from the match, rejoined Berkshire and was instrumental in that County winning the Minor Counties Championship the same year. He played for Berkshire until 1946. His final first-class match was for Minor Counties in 1933.

Remnant, Ernest Richard
Professional. *b:* 1.5.1881, Croydon, Surrey. *d:* 18.3.1969, Harrow, Middlesex. Son of G. H. (Kent). Lower order right-hand batsman, slow left-arm bowler. *Teams* Hampshire (1908–22, 121 matches); England XI in India (1915/16); Europeans (1916/17).
Career batting
124–200–32–2877–115*–17.12–1–*ct* 60
Bowling 4701–172–27.33–7–0–8/61

Remnant, George Henry
Professional. *b:* 20.11.1846, Rochester, Kent. *d:* 24.2.1941, Higham, Rochester, Kent. Father of E. R. (Hampshire). Middle order right-hand batsman, right-hand fast round-arm bowler. *Team* Kent (1868–78, 42 matches).
Career batting
42–79–8–564–62–7.94–0–*ct* 23
Bowling 325–19–17.10–1–0–5/24

He was a first-class umpire (1896–98).

Remnant, Hon Peter Farquharson
Amateur. *b:* 21.9.1897, Paddington, London. *d:* 31.1.1968, Oxford. Brother of R. J. F. (Minor Counties), nephew of R. C. Gosling (Essex). Opening right-hand batsman. *Sch* Eton. *Team* Minor Counties (1929).
Career batting
1–2–0–62–62–31.00–0–*ct* 0

He did not appear in any first-class matches whilst at Oxford. His County cricket was for Berkshire (1920–38). From 1950 to 1959 he was Conservative MP for Wokingham.

Remnant, Hon Robert John Farquharson
(succeeded to the title 2nd Baron Remnant in 1933)
Amateur. *b:* 29.3.1895, Westminster, London. *d:* 4.6.1967, Bear Place, Twyford, Berkshire. Brother of

P. F. (Minor Counties), nephew of R. C. Gosling (Essex). Middle order right-hand batsman, right-arm medium fast bowler. *Sch* Eton. *Team* Minor Counties (1931–36).
Career batting
3–5–1–113–47–28.25–0–*ct* 1
Bowling 189–5–37.80–0–0–3/80
His County cricket was for Berkshire (1920–35).

Remy, Carlos Charles
Cricketer. *b:* 24.7.1968, Castries, St Lucia. Middle order right-hand batsman, right-arm medium pace bowler. *Team* Sussex (1989–92, 10 matches).
Career batting
10–11–1–196–47–19.60–0–*ct* 2
Bowling 593–12–49.61–0–0–4/63

Render, George William Armitage
Professional. *b:* 5.1.1887, Dewsbury, Yorkshire. *d:* 17.9.1922, Hanging-Heaton, Yorkshire. Middle order right-hand batsman, right-arm medium fast bowler. *Team* Yorkshire (1919, 1 match).
Career batting
1–1–0–5–5–5.00–0–*ct* 0

Renneberg, David Alexander
Cricketer. *b:* 23.9.1942, Paddington, Sydney, New South Wales, Australia. Tail end right-hand batsman, right-arm fast bowler. *Team* New South Wales (1964/5 to 1970/1, 54 matches). *Tours* Australia to England 1968, to South Africa 1966/7, to New Zealand 1969/70. *Tests* Australia (1966/7 to 1967/8, 8 matches).
Career batting
90–109–43–466–26–7.06–0–*ct* 35
Bowling 8527–291–29.30–13–1–8/72
Test batting
8–13–7–22–9–3.66–0–*ct* 2
Bowling 830–23–36.08–2–0–5/39
Although he bowled with some success in the first-class matches, he was not chosen for any Tests in the 1968 tour to England.

Renny-Tailyour, Henry Waugh
Amateur. *b:* 9.10.1849, Missouri, North West Provinces, India. *d:* 15.6.1920, Newmanswalls, Montrose, Scotland. Hard hitting middle order right-hand batsman, right-hand fast round-arm bowler, good cover point. *Sch* Cheltenham. *Team* Kent (1873–83, 19 matches).
Career batting
28–48–5–818–124–19.02–1–*ct* 16
Bowling 87–5–17.40–0–0–2/28
He was a noted batsman in military matches, and among his many large innings for the Royal Engineers was 331* in 330 minutes v Civil Service in 1880. An excellent soccer player he represented Scotland and played in three of the first four FA Cup finals for the Royal Engineers including the victory in 1875. He also played rugby for Scotland in 1872..

Renshaw, Alfred George
Amateur. *b:* 8.9.1844, Islington, Middlesex. *d:* 14.7.1897, Svenningdal, Nordland, Norway. Brother-in-law of T. L. Rolph (Cambridge U), he married the mother of H. W. Forster (Hampshire). Middle order batsman. *Team* MCC (1871).
Career batting
1–1–0–0–0–0.00–0–*ct* 0

Reoch, Earl Clark
Cricketer. *b:* 5.3.1942, Monifieth, Angus, Scotland. *d:* 1.12.1989, Dundee, Angus, Scotland. Middle order right-hand batsman, slow left-arm bowler. *Team* Scotland (1973).
Career batting
1–2–0–7–7–3.50–0–*ct* 1

Reunert, Clive
Amateur. *b:* 7.12.1887, Hillbrow, Johannesburg, South Africa. *d:* 11.4.1953, Johannesburg, South Africa. Brother of John (Cambridge U). Opening batsman, bowler. *Sch* Harrow. *Team* Cambridge U (1908).
Career batting
3–6–1–60–28*–12.00–0–*ct* 1
Bowling 138–4–34.50–0–0–3/89

Reunert, John
Amateur. *b:* 1.4.1886, Hillbrow, Johannesburg, South Africa. *d:* 25.7.1946, Johannesburg, South Africa. Brother of Clive (Cambridge U). Lower order left-hand batsman, left-arm fast bowler. *Sch* Harrow. *Team* Cambridge U (1908).
Career batting
5–9–1–65–19–8.12–0–*ct* 3
Bowling 393–9–43.66–1–0–5/100

Revill, Alan Chambers
Professional. *b:* 27.3.1923, Sheffield, Yorkshire. Son of T. F. (Derbyshire). Middle order right-hand batsman, off break bowler, brilliant short leg. *Team* Derbyshire (1946–57, 321 matches); Leicestershire (1958–60, 64 matches). *Tour* Surridge to Bermuda 1961 (not first-class).
Career batting
387–654–53–15917–156*–26.48–16–*ct* 396
Bowling 1924–49–39.26–0–0–3/12
He hit 1,000 runs in a season nine times (best 1,643, av 35.71, in 1950). He also played for Berkshire (1962–68)

Revill, Thomas Frederick
Professional. *b:* 9.5.1892, Bolsover, Derbyshire. *d:* 29.3.1979, Mansfield, Nottinghamshire. Father of A. C. (Derbyshire and Leicestershire). Middle order left-hand batsman, leg break and googly bowler. *Team* Derbyshire (1913–20, 11 matches).
Career batting
11–20–4–231–65*–14.43–0–*ct* 6
He played soccer for Chesterfield and Stoke City.

Reynolds, Alan Boyd
Amateur. *b:* 12.3.1879, Islington, London. *d:* 2.6.1940, Marylebone, London. Lower order right-hand batsman, wicket-keeper. *Sch* Westminster. *Team* Oxford U (1900).
Career batting
4–4–0–34–21–8.50–0–*ct* 0
His final first-class match was for MCC in 1903. His County cricket was for Hertfordshire (1898–1906).

Reynolds, Brian Leonard
Professional. *b:* 10.6.1932, Kettering, Northamptonshire. Middle order right-hand batsman, off break bowler, wicket-keeper. *Team* Northamptonshire (1950–70, 426 matches).
Career batting
429–737–65–18824–169–28.01–21–*ct* 302–*st* 20
Bowling 284–4–71.00–0–0–1/0
He hit 1,000 runs in a season ten times (best 1,843, av 35.44, in 1962). After retiring he was coach to the County from 1974 and since 1986 the county's Cricket Development Officer. A useful soccer player, he appeared for Kettering Town.

Reynolds, Frederick Reginald
Professional. *b:* 7.8.1833, Bottisham, Cambridgeshire. *d:* 18.4.1915, Chorlton-cum-Hardy, Lancashire. Brother of T. P. (Cambridge Town Club). Hard hitting tail end right-hand batsman, right-hand fast round-arm, later slow under-arm bowler. *Teams* Cambridge Town Club (1854–60); Cambridgeshire (1857–67, 16 matches); Lancashire (1865–74, 38 matches).
Career batting
65–106–26–444–34*–5.55–0–*ct* 52
Bowling 3025–172 + 36–17.58–11–0–6/58
From 1860 to 1908 he was manager of Old Trafford cricket ground.

Reynolds, Giles Denys
Cricketer. *b:* 13.7.1967, Monchengladbach, West Germany. Middle order right-hand batsman, wicket-keeper. *Sch* Wellington. *Team* Oxford U (1988–89, blue both years).
Career batting
12–17–2–294–59–19.60–0–*ct* 10–*st* 2
His County cricket was for Dorset (1989–92). He was awarded a half-blue for Eton fives.

Reynolds, Graham Edward Arthur
Cricketer. *b:* 23.9.1937, Newport, Monmouthshire. Lower order left-hand batsman, right-arm medium pace bowler. *Team* Glamorgan (1970–71, 2 matches).
Career batting
2–3–2–37–23*–37.00–0–*ct* 0
Bowling 75–2–37.50–0–0–2/24
He played soccer for Newport County.

Reynolds, Henry Smith
Professional. *b:* 6.1.1844, Ollerton, Nottinghamshire. *d:* 21.4.1894, Burnley, Lancashire. He died of dropsy. Middle order right-hand batsman, right-arm fast bowler, good mid off. *Team* Nottinghamshire (1872–75, 13 matches).
Career batting
17–26–4–319–70*–14.50–0–*ct* 8
Bowling 65–1–65.00–0–0–1/30
His final first-class match was for An Eleven of England in 1876.

Reynolds, James Francis
Amateur. *b:* 2.5.1866, Tonbridge, Kent. *d:* 6.9.1950, Malling Place, Kent. Lower order right-hand batsman, right-arm medium pace bowler. *Team* Kent (1890–97, 2 matches).
Career batting
2–2–0–21–13–10.50–0–*ct* 1
Bowling 63–3–21.00–0–0–3/63

Rhind, Peter Alan
Cricketer. *b:* 20.6.1945, Dundee, Angus, Scotland. Lower order right-hand batsman, right-arm fast medium bowler. *Team* Scotland (1968–82).
Career batting
6–7–4–23–10–7.66–0–*ct* 3
Bowling 332–6–55.33–0–0–3/62

Rhodes, Albert
Amateur. *b:* 9.4.1889, Saddleworth, Yorkshire. *d:* 10.3.1970, Blackpool, Lancashire. Middle order right-hand batsman, right-arm slow medium bowler. *Team* Lancashire (1922–24, 17 matches).
Career batting
17–25–3–382–70–17.36–0–*ct* 9
Bowling 475–15–31.66–0–0–2/24

Rhodes, Albert Ennion Groucott
Professional. *b:* 10.10.1916, Tintwistle, Cheshire. *d:* 17.10.1983, Barlow, Derbyshire. Father of H. J. (Derbyshire). Middle order right-hand batsman, right-arm fast medium or leg break bowler. *Team* Derbyshire (1937–54, 267 matches). *Tour* MCC to India 1951/2.
Career batting
275–422–34–7363–127–18.97–4–*ct* 85
Bowling 18660–661–28.22–29–4–8/162
He hit 1,156 runs, av 25.68, in 1949 and took 130 wickets, av 22.19, in 1950. Owing to injury he played in only three matches on the tour of India. He was a first-class umpire (1959–79), standing in eight Test matches (1963–73).

Rhodes, Arthur Cecil
Professional. *b:* 14.10.1906, Headingley, Leeds, Yorkshire. *d:* 21.5.1957, Headingley, Leeds, Yorkshire. Lower order right-hand batsman, right-arm fast medium pace bowler. *Team* Yorkshire (1932–34, 61 matches).

Rhodes, Cecil

Career batting
61–70–19–917–64*–17.98–0–*ct* 45
Bowling 3026–107–28.28–5–0–6/19

Rhodes, Cecil
Amateur, turned professional in 1938. *b:* 12.8.1906. Tail end batsman, slow left-arm bowler. *Team* Lancashire (1937–38, 8 matches).
Career batting
8–10–4–11–6–1.83–0–*ct* 1
Bowling 619–22–28.13–0–0–4/37
He also played for Berkshire (1948).

Rhodes, Harold James
Professional. *b:* 22.7.1936, Hadfield, Glossop, Derbyshire. Son of A. E. G. (Derbyshire). Tail end right-hand batsman, right-arm fast bowler. *Team* Derbyshire (1953–75, 288 matches). *Tours* International XI to Rhodesia, New Zealand, India and Pakistan 1961/2, to India, Pakistan and Ceylon 1967/8; Commonwealth to South Africa 1959/60; Swanton to West Indies 1960/1. *Tests* England (1959, 2 matches).
Career batting
322–399–143–2427–48–9.48–0–*ct* 86
Bowling 21145–1073–19.70–42–4–7/38
Test batting
2–1–1–0–0*–no av–0–*ct* 0
Bowling 244–9–27.11–0–0–4/50
He took 100 wickets in a season three times (best 119, av 11.04, in 1965). In 1960, 1961 and 1965 he was no-balled for throwing, but in 1966 the MCC sub-committee ruled that his action was fair. In spite of this he was again reported as having a suspect action. The TCCB in December 1968 reconsidered his case and after deliberation decided his bowling to be legal. In 1970 he appeared for Nottinghamshire in Sunday League matches.

Rhodes, Herbert Edward
Amateur. *b:* 11.1.1852, Hennerton, Berkshire. *d:* 10.9.1889, Dover, Kent. Stylish right-hand middle order batsman, wicket-keeper. *Sch* Eton. *Team* Yorkshire (1878–83, 10 matches).
Career batting
25–40–3–424–64–11.45–0–*ct* 14–*st* 2
He did not appear in first-class matches for the University whilst at Cambridge, but was in the University Eight for four years. He was among the players down to go on Vernon's tour to India in 1889/90, but died suddenly in September 1889, from the effects of a fall from a horse. He also played for Staffordshire.

Rhodes, James
Amateur. *b:* 27.7.1866, Aston, Birmingham. *d:* 26.8.1939, Solihull, Warwickshire. Middle order right-hand batsman. *Team* Warwickshire (1895, 3 matches).
Career batting
3–6–0–89–64–14.83–0–*ct* 2
He first played for Warwickshire (pre first-class) in 1891.

Rhodes, Steven John
Cricketer. *b:* 17.6.1964, Dirk Hill, Bradford, Yorkshire. Son of W. E. (Nottinghamshire). Lower order right-hand batsman, wicket-keeper. *Teams* Yorkshire (1981–84, 3 matches); Worcestershire (1985–92, 190 matches). *Tours* England B to Sri Lanka 1985/6; England to India 1988/9 (tour cancelled); England A to Zimbabwe 1989/90, to Sri Lanka 1990/1, to West Indies 1991/2; Worcestershire to Zimbabwe 1990/1.
Career batting
213–277–87–5939–116*–31.25–3–*ct* 504–*st* 62
Bowling 30–0
He appeared in one-day internationals for England in 1989 but no Tests.

Rhodes, Stuart Denzil
Amateur. *b:* 24.3.1910, Sneinton, Nottingham. *d:* 7.1.1989, Stamford, Lincolnshire. Middle order right-hand batsman, right-arm medium pace bowler. *Sch* Dean Close. *Team* Nottinghamshire (1930–35, 19 matches). *Tours* Cahn to the Argentine 1929/30, to North America and Bermuda 1933 (not first-class), to Ceylon 1936/7.
Career batting
24–32–3–599–70–20.65–0–*ct* 7
Bowling 57–0
He was joint-captain of Nottinghamshire in 1935. In 1946 he appeared in the Hertfordshire side. His final first-class match in England was for J. Cahn's XI in 1936. A useful hockey player, he represented Nottinghamshire at left back.

Rhodes, Dr Thomas Basil
Amateur. *b:* 13.8.1874, Uttoxeter, Staffordshire. *d:* 26.5.1936, Rustington, Sussex. Lower order right-hand batsman, wicket-keeper. *Sch* Malvern. *Team* Warwickshire (1899, 4 matches).
Career batting
4–7–1–105–55–17.50–0–*ct* 3
He also played for Worcestershire (pre first-class, 1892–96).

Rhodes, Wilfred
Professional. *b:* 29.10.1877, Kirkheaton, Yorkshire. *d:* 8.7.1973, Branksome Park, Dorset. Excellent right-hand batsman, slow left-arm bowler. *Teams* Yorkshire (1898–1930, 883 matches); Patiala (1926/7); Europeans (1921/2 to 1922/3). *Tours* MCC to Australia 1903/4, 1907/8, 1911/12, 1920/1, to South Africa 1909/10, 1913/14, to West Indies 1929/30. *Tests* England (1899 to 1929/30, 58 matches).
Career batting
1110–1534–237–39969–267*–30.81–58–*ct* 765
Bowling 70322–4204–16.72–287–68–9/24
Test batting
58–98–21–2325–179–30.19–2–*ct* 60
Bowling 3425–127–26.96–6–1–8/68

The sudden departure of Peel from the Yorkshire side created a vacancy for a slow left-arm bowler in 1898. Rhodes played in the opening match, took six for 63, and by the end of the summer had captured 154 wickets and stood second in the first-class averages, an astonishing opening to a record-breaking career. The following summer he was capped for England. No fewer than 23 times he was to take 100 wickets in a season – easily a record – and three times he went to 200, with 261, av 13.81, in 1900 his best. His tally of 4,204 wickets, av 16.72, stands alone, no one else having topped 4,000.

These bowling details place him among the greatest of all bowlers, but this was only one side of his talent. Although he began as a lower order batsman, within a few seasons he had developed into one of the principal batsmen in England. Twenty times he exceeded 1,000 runs in a season – plus once in Australia – and twice he went on to 2,000, with 2,261, av 38.32, in 1911 his best. In sixteen seasons he achieved the 'double' – another record unlikely to be beaten.

His highest innings was 267* for Yorkshire v Leicestershire at Headingley in 1921 and of his two other double centuries, one was for Yorkshire and the other for MCC. His best bowling was 9/24 for C. I. Thornton's XI v Australians at Scarborough in 1899.

On retiring from first-class cricket he became coach at Harrow School. After the Second World War when his sight failed, he still regularly attended important matches, and he took a keen interest in the game until the end.

Rhodes, William
Professional. *b:* 4.3.1883, Bradford, Yorkshire. *d:* 5.8.1941, Bradford, Yorkshire. Tail end right-hand batsman, right-arm fast bowler. *Team* Yorkshire (1911, 1 match).
Career batting
1–1–1–1–1*–no av–0–*ct* 0
Bowling 40–0

Rhodes, William Ernest
Professional. *b:* 5.8.1936, Five Lane Ends, Bradford, Yorkshire. Father of S. J. (Yorkshire and Worcestershire). Middle order right-hand batsman, wicket-keeper. *Team* Nottinghamshire (1961–64, 36 matches).
Career batting
36–66–6–1207–132–20.11–1–*ct* 41–*st* 1
Bowling 0-0

Rhys, Hubert Ralph John
Amateur. *b:* 31.8.1897, Aberdare, Glamorgan. *d:* 18.3.1970, Llandaff, Glamorgan. Sound middle order right-hand batsman. *Sch* Shrewsbury. *Teams* Glamorgan (1929–30, 7 matches); Wales (1930).
Career batting
10–19–1–383–149–21.27–1–*ct* 5

His first-class debut was for Free Foresters v Cambridge U at Fenner's in 1929, when he hit 149.

Riaz-ur-Rehman
Amateur. *b:* 1940, India. *d:* 10.7.1966, Loughborough, Leicestershire. He was killed in a road accident. Middle order right-hand batsman, occasional wicket-keeper. *Teams* Lahore (1958/9); Rawalpindi (1959/60 to 1960/1); Karachi (1961/2); Leicestershire (1966, 1 match).
Career batting
8–14–0–354–70–25.28–0–*ct* 3–*st* 1
Bowling 10–0

Rice, Alan Sedgwick
Amateur. *b:* 29.8.1929, West End, Leicester. Middle order left-hand batsman, right-arm fast medium bowler. *Sch* Wyggeston GS. *Team* Leicester (1954, 3 matches).
Career batting
3–2–0–15–13–7.50–0–*ct* 1
Bowling 269–8–33.62–0–0–3/34

He was also a useful rugby full back.

Rice, Clive Edward Butler
Cricketer. *b:* 23.7.1949, Johannesburg, South Africa. Grandson of P. S. S. Bower (Oxford U). Attacking middle order right-hand batsman, right-arm fast medium bowler. *Teams* Transvaal (1969/70 to 1991/2); Nottinghamshire (1975–87, 283 matches). *Tours* South Africa to Australia 1971/2 (tour cancelled), to India 1991/2 (not first-class).
Career batting
474–753–122–26045–246–41.27–48–*ct* 394
Bowling 20558–915–22.46–22–1–7/62

He hit 1,000 runs in a season 13 times (best 1,871, av 66.82, in 1978). His highest score was 246 for Nottinghamshire v Sussex at Hove in 1976. His first-class debut in England was for D. H. Robins' XI in 1973. He was appointed captain of Nottinghamshire for 1978, but then signed a contract for Packer's World Series Cricket and his appointment was cancelled; he was reappointed County captain in July 1979 and continued until 1987. He played in unofficial Tests for South Africa from 1981/2 and captained South Africa from 1983/4. When South Africa was re-admitted to the ICC he led his country to India for a series of one-day internationals, but did not retain his place for the World Cup. He played for Scotland in limited overs matches in 1988–89.

Rice, Dr David
Amateur. *b:* 8.4.1914, Low Hellesdon, Norfolk. Brother of H. M. (Europeans). Lower order right-hand batsman, right-arm medium pace bowler. *Sch* Lancing. *Team* L. C. Stevens' XI (1960–61).
Career batting
2–3–1–32–23–16.00–0–*ct* 2
Bowling 84–1–84.00–0–0–1/37

His County cricket was for Norfolk (1946).

Rice, John Michael
Cricketer. *b:* 23.10.1949, Chandlers Ford, Hampshire. Opening right-hand batsman, right-arm medium pace bowler. *Team* Hampshire (1971–82, 168 matches).
Career batting
168–271–22–5091–161*–20.44–2–*ct* 153
Bowling 7707–230–33.50–3–0–7/48
He also played for Wiltshire (1983–88).

Rice, Reginald William
Amateur. *b:* 14.11.1868, Tewkesbury, Gloucestershire. *d:* 11.2.1938, Bedford. Steady opening right-hand batsman, right-arm slow bowler. *Teams* Gloucestershire (1890–1903, 123 matches); Oxford U (1892–94, blue 1893).
Career batting
135–237–19–4376–111–20.07–2–*ct* 67
Bowling 4–0
He also played for Bedfordshire (1904–09).

Rice, Father William Ignatius
Amateur. *b:* 15.3.1883, Birmingham. *d:* 22.4.1955, Douai Abbey, Woolhampton, Reading, Berkshire. Middle order right-hand batsman, right-arm medium pace bowler. *Team* Warwickshire (1920, 2 matches).
Career batting
2–4–0–15–9–3.75–0–*ct* 1
Headmaster of Douai School from 1915 to 1952, he was a member of the Order of St Benedict and perhaps the only monk to play County Championship cricket.

Richards, Arthur Carew
Amateur. *b:* 20.2.1865, Grays, Essex. *d:* 29.11.1930, Nottingham. Son of W. H. (MCC). Hard hitting middle order right-hand batsman, slow right-arm bowler, good slip field. *Sch* Eton. *Team* Hampshire (1884–1904, 4 matches).
Career batting
4–6–0–104–47–17.33–0–*ct* 2
Bowling 112–3–37.33–0–0–3/45
In a minor military match in South Africa he scored 101* and 185 out of a combined total for the two innings of 311, no other batsman exceeding 6!

Richards, Barry Anderson
Cricketer. *b:* 21.7.1945, Morningside, Durban, South Africa. Brilliant opening right-hand batsman, off break bowler. *Teams* Natal (1964/5 to 1982/3); Gloucestershire (1965, 1 match); Hampshire (1968–78, 204 matches); South Australia (1970/1, 10 matches); Transvaal (1970/1). *Tours* Rest of World to England 1968, 1970; International Wanderers to South Africa 1974/5; South Africa to England 1970 (tour cancelled), to Australia 1971/2 (tour cancelled). *Tests* South Africa (1969/70, 4 matches).
Career batting
339–576–58–28358–356–54.74–80–*ct* 367
Bowling 2886–77–37.48–1–0–7/63
Test batting
4–7–0–508–140–72.57–2–*ct* 3
Bowling 26–1–26.00–0–0–1/12
He hit 1,000 runs in a season in England nine times, going on to 2,000 once: 2,395, av 47.90, in 1968. He scored three double centuries for Hampshire, the highest being 240 v Warwickshire at Coventry in 1973, but his most famous innings was 356 for South Australia v Western Australia at Perth in 1970/1, when he made 325* on the opening day of the match. He appeared in all five matches for the Rest of the World v England in 1970. He also hit 1,000 in a South African season five times (best 1,285, av 80.28, in 1973/4) and in Australia once. One of the outstanding batsmen of the 1970s, he was very successful in World Series Cricket in Australia.

Richards, Charles Herbert
Amateur. *b:* 20.8.1873, Caerynwch, Dolgelley, Merioneth. *d:* 21.9.1925, Ruthin, Denbigh. Middle order batsman. *Sch* Winchester. *Team* London County (1903).
Career batting
2–3–0–12–8–4.00–0–*ct* 3
Bowling 28–0

Richards, Clifton James
Cricketer. *b:* 10.8.1958, Penzance, Cornwall. Lower order right-hand batsman, occasional right-arm medium pace bowler, wicket-keeper. *Teams* Surrey (1976–88, 256 matches); Orange Free State (1983/4). *Tours* Robins to New Zealand 1979/80; England to India and Sri Lanka 1981/2, to Australia 1986/7, 1987/8 (not first-class), to Sharjah (not first-class) 1986/7, to New Zealand 1987/8; International XI to Jamaica 1982/3. *Tests* England (1986/7 to 1988, 8 matches).
Career batting
286–371–87–8012–172*–28.21–8–*ct* 604–*st* 72
Bowling 224–5–44.80–0–0–2/42
Test batting
8–13–0–285–133–21.92–1–*ct* 20–*st* 1
He hit 1,006 runs, av 40.24, in 1986. At the end of the 1988 season he was released from his contract with Surrey on the recommendation of the cricket sub-committee.

Richards, Cyril James Ridding
Amateur. *b:* 14.7.1870, Andover, Hampshire. *d:* 27.10.1933, Cluny, Aberdeenshire, Scotland. Middle order left-hand batsman, left-arm fast bowler, good field. *Sch* Lancing. *Team* Hampshire (1895, 1 match).
Career batting
1–2–0–48–43–24.00–0–0–*ct* 0
Whilst at Oxford he played in some trials but no first-class matches. He first played for Hampshire (not first-class) in 1892. He also played for Shropshire (1907).

Richards, Dick Stanley
Professional. *b:* 10.9.1908, Bognor Regis, Sussex. Middle order right-hand batsman, slow left-arm bowler. *Team* Sussex (1927–35, 18 matches).
Career batting
18–27–5–220–23–10.00–0–*ct* 7
Bowling 205–1–205.00–0–0–1/8

Richards, Gwyn
Cricketer. *b:* 29.11.1951, Maesteg, Glamorgan. Middle order right-hand batsman, off break bowler. *Team* Glamorgan (1971–79, 107 matches).
Career batting
107–174–26–3370–102*–22.77–1–*ct* 36
Bowling 2257–48–47.02–1–0–5/55

Richards, Ian Michael
Cricketer. *b:* 9.12.1957, Stockton-on-Tees, Co Durham. Middle order left-hand batsman, right-arm medium pace bowler. *Team* Northamptonshire (1976–79, 23 matches).
Career batting
23–25–4–467–50–22.23–0–*ct* 5
Bowling 201–7–28.71–0–0–4/57

He also played for Durham (pre first-class, 1981–82).

Richards, Isaac Vivian Alexander
Cricketer. *b:* 7.3.1952, St John's, Antigua. Son of M. R. (Antigua, not first-class), brother of Donald (Leeward Islands) and Mervin (Leeward Islands). Brilliant middle order right-hand batsman, right-arm medium pace or off break bowler. *Teams* Leeward Islands (1971/2 to 1990/1); Somerset (1974–86, 191 matches); Queensland (1976/7, 5 matches); Glamorgan (1990–92, 32 matches). *Tours* West Indies to India 1974/5, 1983/4, 1987/8, 1989/90 (not first-class), to Pakistan 1974/5, 1980/1, 1985/6 (not first-class), 1986/7, to Sri Lanka 1974/5, to England 1975 (World Cup), 1976, 1979 (World Cup), 1980, 1983 (World Cup), 1984, 1988, 1991, to Australia 1975/6, 1979/80, 1981/2, 1983/4 (not first-class), 1984/5, 1986/7 (not first-class), 1988/9, to Sharjah (not first-class) 1985/6, 1986/7, 1989/90, to New Zealand 1986/7, to India and Pakistan (World Cup) 1987/8. *Tests* West Indies (1974/5 to 1991, 121 matches).
Career batting
490–764–56–34977–322–49.40–112–*ct* 447–*st* 1
Bowling 9835–219–44.90–1–0–5/88
Test batting
121–182–12–8540–291–50.23–24–*ct* 122
Bowling 1964–32–61.37–0–0–2/17

At the height of his powers he was a batsman who could destroy any bowling attack. He came to England with the 1976 West Indian side with two full summers in County cricket behind him, and was the outstanding figure on that tour. He topped the first-class averages with 1,724 runs, av 71.83, and the Test averages with 829 runs, av 118.42. His second English tour in 1980 was no less of a triumph, again heading both sets of averages; 911 runs, av 56.93, and 379 runs, av 63.16. He captained West Indies in one Test on that visit. In 1984 he made a brilliant start but faded in the second half of the programme. He was captain on his fourth tour. There had been some criticism of his leadership ever since he succeeded Lloyd in 1985, but in 1988 he was certainly in command. His batting, however, showed only brief glimpses of his true form. Coming to England in 1991 again as captain, after an unhappy series in the Caribbean in 1989/90, both his leadership and batting were cloaked by the mantle of elder statesmanship. He announced his retirement from Test cricket during the Fifth Test at the Oval. It was his 50th as captain. He stepped down holding the record for the most Test runs by a West Indian batsman, as well as most Test appearances. He was also the first West Indian to hit 100 centuries in first-class cricket.

On the county scene his ability was always evident, but bowlers realised that there was hope because he lived dangerously. He completed 1,000 runs in a season twelve times, going on to 2,000 once: 2,161, av 65.48, in 1977. He has also reached 1,000 runs in an overseas season three times. His highest innings was 322 for Somerset v Warwickshire at Taunton in 1985, the highest ever score for the county, and he scored more than 200 on five other occasions for the county. His highest Test score was 291 v England at the Oval in 1976. His career with Somerset ended with some acrimony, then after a break he returned to county cricket with Glamorgan and topped the Glamorgan averages in 1990; in his second season of 1992, however, he missed many games through injury.

Richards, James Henry
Professional. *b:* 3.1.1855, Brixton, London. *d:* 24.8.1923, Tulse Hill, Brixton, London. Lower order batsman, useful bowler. *Team* Surrey (1881, 2 matches).
Career batting
2–4–0–9–8–2.25–0–*ct* 0
Bowling 89–2–0–44.50–0–0–2/40

Richards, John Lawson
Amateur. *b: circa* 1920, Australia. Tail end batsman, useful bowler. *Sch* Monmouth. *Team* Cambridge U (1939).
Career batting
1–2–0–0–0–0.00–0–*ct* 0
Bowling 50–0

Richards, Robert John
Cricketer. *b:* 5.6.1934, Winchester, Hampshire. Lower order right-hand batsman, wicket-keeper. *Team* Essex (1970, 1 match).
Career batting
1 match, did not bat–*ct* 0

Richards, Walter
Professional. *b:* 28.9.1863, Balsall Heath, Worcestershire. *d:* 14.10.1917, Highgate, Birmingham. Stylish middle order right-hand batsman, right-arm off break bowler, good field. *Team* Warwickshire (1895–96, 7 matches).
Career batting
7–11–1–112–61*–11.20–0–*ct* 4
He made his debut for Warwickshire in 1883; thus most of his County career took place before Warwickshire became first-class. He was a first-class umpire (1897–1914), standing in ten Test matches (1899–1912).

Richards, Rev William Henry
Amateur. *b:* 26.6.1833, Keevil, Wiltshire. *d:* 22.9.1912, St Helens, Isle of Wight. Father of A. C. (Hampshire). Middle order batsman. *Team* MCC (1866).
Career batting
2–3–1–39–20*–19.50–0–*ct* 0
His County cricket was for Essex (pre first-class, 1868–70).

Richardson, Alastair William
Cricketer. *b:* 23.10.1972, Derby. Grandson of A. W. (Derbyshire), son of G. W. (Derbyshire). Lower order right-hand batsman, right-arm fast medium bowler. *Sch* Oundle. *Team* Derbyshire (1992, 1 match).
Career batting
1–1–0–5–5–5.00–0–*ct* 0
Bowling 38–2–19.00–0–0–2/38

Richardson, Alfred Graham
Amateur. *b:* 24.7.1875, Sandy, Bedfordshire. *d:* 17.12.1935, Umtata, Cape Province, South Africa. His half-sister was mother of W. N. Kempe (Somerset). Opening or middle order right-hand batsman. *Sch* King's, Canterbury. *Teams* Somerset (1895, 1 match); Cambridge U (1895–97); Gloucestershire (1897–1901, 20 matches); Orange Free State (1906/7 to 1913/14).
Career batting
29–48–1–698–89–14.85–0–*ct* 10
Bowling 112–2–56.00–0–0–1/23
He also played for Bedfordshire (1895).

Richardson, Allan
Professional. *b:* 28.10.1926, Woodbeck, Nottinghamshire. Tail end right-hand batsman, right-arm fast medium bowler. *Team* Nottinghamshire (1949–51, 28 matches).
Career batting
28–31–16–73–7*–4.86–0–*ct* 10
Bowling 1819–40–45.47–0–0–4/24

Richardson, Arthur John
Amateur. *b:* 24.7.1888, Sevenhill, Clare, South Australia. *d:* 23.12.1973, Semaphore, Adelaide, South Australia. Brother-in-law of E. L. Bowley (South Australia). Opening right-hand batsman, right-arm medium pace off break bowler. *Teams* South Australia (1918/9 to 1926/7, 45 matches); Western Australia (1927/8 to 1929/30, 4 matches). *Tour* Australia to England 1926. *Tests* Australia (1924/5 to 1926, 9 matches).
Career batting
86–139–13–5238–280–41.57–13–*ct* 34
Bowling 6555–209–31.36–7–1–6/28
Test batting
9–13–0–403–100–31.00–1–*ct* 1
Bowling 521–12–43.41–0–0–2/20
He was a useful all-rounder on the 1926 tour hitting 728 runs, av 33.09, and taking 49 wickets, av 19.71. He played in all five Tests. His final first-class match was for Sir L. Parkinson's XI in 1933. His highest score was 280 for South Australia v MCC at Adelaide in 1922/3. He umpired two Test matches in 1934/5 in West Indies.

Richardson, Arthur Walker
Amateur. *b:* 4.3.1907, Quarndon, Derbyshire. *d:* 29.7.1983, Ednaston, Derbyshire. Father of G. W. (Derbyshire), grandfather of A. W. (Derbyshire). Middle order right-hand batsman. *Sch* Winchester. *Team* Derbyshire (1928–36, 159 matches).
Career batting
159–239–30–3982–90–19.05–0–*ct* 58
Bowling 34–0
He hit 1,258 runs, av 29.95, in 1932. He captained Derbyshire from 1931 to 1936.

Richardson, Bertram Harold
Professional. *b:* 12.3.1932, Ashton-under-Lyne, Lancashire. Lower order left-hand batsman, slow left-arm bowler, good outfield. *Team* Derbyshire (1950–53, 27 matches).
Career batting
27–36–11–279–29–11.16–0–*ct* 14
Bowling 1003–33–30.39–0–0–4/39

Richardson, Bryan Anthony
Cricketer. *b:* 24.2.1944, Kenilworth, Warwickshire. Brother of D. W. (Worcestershire) and P. E. (Worcestershire and Kent). Opening left-hand batsman, leg break bowler. *Sch* Malvern. *Team* Warwickshire (1963–67, 40 matches).
Career batting
40–72–4–1323–126–19.45–2–*ct* 28
Bowling 157–1–157.00–0–0–1/32

Richardson, Charles Stewart
Amateur. *b:* 23.3.1885, Terling, Essex. *d:* 5.4.1948, Great Totham, Essex. Middle order left-hand batsman. *Team* Essex (1914, 1 match).
Career batting
1–1–0–15–15–15.00–0–*ct* 1
He was Essex Chairman 1928–45.

Richardson, Derek Walter
Amateur, turned professional from 1956 season. *b:* 3.11.1934, Hereford. Brother of B. A. (Warwickshire) and P. E. (Worcestershire and Kent). Middle order left-hand batsman, left-arm medium pace bowler, good close field. *Sch* Hereford GS. *Team* Worcestershire (1952–67, 371 matches). *Tours* Worcestershire World Tour (Rhodesia first-class) 1964/5, to Jamaica 1965/6. *Test* England (1957, 1 match).
Career batting
383–660–65–16303–169–27.40–16–*ct* 422
Bowling 354–8–44.25–0–0–2/11
Test batting
1–1–0–33–33–33.00–0–*ct* 1
He hit 1,000 runs in a season nine times (best 1,830, av 32.67, in 1957).

Richardson, George William
Amateur. *b:* 26.4.1938, Marylebone, London. Son of A. W. (Derbyshire), father of A. W. (Derbyshire). Middle order right-hand batsman, left-arm fast medium bowler. *Sch* Winchester. *Team* Derbyshire (1959–65, 62 matches).
Career batting
69–107–15–1460–91–15.86–0–*ct* 12
Bowling 4072–147–27.70–5–2–8/54

Richardson, Harold Bamford
Amateur. *b:* 10.3.1873. Middle order right-hand batsman, slow right-arm bowler. *Sch* Clifton. *Team* Surrey (1899, 22 matches).
Career batting
22–31–5–585–72–22.50–0–*ct* 8
Bowling 1–0
He was in business in San Francisco until 1906 when his name can be found in street directories – after the earthquake there is no further trace of him and he may therefore have been killed in the 1906 earthquake.

Richardson, Henry
Professional. *b:* 4.10.1857, Bulwell, Nottinghamshire. *d:* 20.3.1940, Bulwell, Nottinghamshire. Lower order right-hand batsman, right-arm medium pace bowler. *Team* Nottinghamshire (1887–90, 53 matches).
Career batting
65–91–14–664–55–8.62–0–*ct* 44
Bowling 2545–185–13.75–10–1–7/24
His final first-class match was for MCC in 1894. He also played for Liverpool and District (1889).

Richardson, Henry Adair
Amateur. *b:* 31.7.1846, Bayswater, London. *d:* 17.9.1921, Hastings, Sussex. Forceful middle order right-hand batsman, wicket-keeper. *Sch* Tonbridge. *Teams* Cambridge U (1866–69, blue 1867–69); Kent (1866–68, 11 matches); Middlesex (1868–69, 2 matches).
Career batting
37–63–7–1166–143–20.82–1–*ct* 26–*st* 13
Bowling 65–4–16.25–0–0–2/19
His best season was 1868 when he hit 431 runs, av 28.73, coming fourth in the first-class averages. His last first-class match was for the Gentlemen of the South in 1871. An excellent billiards player he represented Cambridge in 1868, 1869 and 1870.

Richardson, James Vere
Amateur. *b:* 16.12.1903, Prenton, Cheshire. Brother-in-law of G. B. Legge (Kent). Middle order right-hand batsman, right-arm medium bowler. *Sch* Uppingham. *Teams* Essex (1924–26, 14 matches); Oxford U (1924–25, blue 1925).
Career batting
35–53–9–1038–89–23.59–0–*ct* 21
Bowling 838–27–31.03–0–0–3/25
A noted rugby footballer he was awarded his blue at Oxford and went on to be capped for England.

Richardson, John
Professional. *b:* 17.3.1856, Duckmanton, Derbyshire. *d:* 19.2.1940, Brimington, Derbyshire. Tail end right-hand batsman, right-arm fast bowler. *Team* Derbyshire (1878–83, 11 matches).
Career batting
11–21–4–117–18–6.88–0–*ct* 9
Bowling 517–32–16.15–1–0–7/76

Richardson, John Allan
Amateur. *b:* 4.8.1908, Sleights, Yorkshire. *d:* 2.4.1985, Scarborough, Yorkshire. Stylish middle order right-hand batsman, off break bowler. *Team* Yorkshire (1936–47, 7 matches).
Career batting
8–14–3–343–61–31.18–0–*ct* 4
Bowling 108–2–54.00–0–0–2/23
He was a major force in Yorkshire Council cricket. His first-class debut was for the Gentlemen in 1934.

Richardson, John Charles
Amateur. *b:* 5.12.1912, Carron, Morayshire, Scotland. Opening right-hand batsman, right-arm medium pace bowler. *Team* Scotland (1953).
Career batting
2–3–0–32–24–10.66–0–*ct* 1

Richardson, John Maunsell
Amateur. *b:* 12.6.1846, Great Limber, Caistor, Lincolnshire. *d:* 22.1.1912, Westminster, London. Son-in-law of H. G. Southwell (Cambridge U 1852). Middle order right-hand batsman, right-hand slow round-arm bowler, good deep field. *Sch* Harrow. *Team* Cambridge U (1866–68, blue all three years).
Career batting
18–31–1–347–58–11.56–0–*ct* 10
Bowling 35–1–35.00–0–0–1/21
His final first-class match was for MCC in 1874 and his County cricket was for Cheshire, Devon and

Lincolnshire (1867–68). A famous amateur jockey, he won the Grand National in 1873 and 1874 and was regarded as the leading amateur rider of his day. He was MP for Brigg in 1894 and 1895.

Richardson, Michael Sloan
Cricketer. *b:* 20.8.1969, Glasgow, Scotland. Lower order right-hand batsman, right-arm medium pace bowler. *Teams* Scotland (1992).
Career batting
1 match, did not bat–*ct* 1
Bowling 64–2–32.00–0–0–2/49

Richardson, Percy John
Amateur. *b:* 2.4.1891, Herman Hill, Snaresbrook, Essex. *d:* 23.3.1964, Wray Park, Reigate, Surrey. Middle order batsman. *Sch* Clifton. *Teams* Essex (1912, 2 matches); Cambridge U (1912).
Career batting
3–4–0–44–21–11.00–0–*ct* 2
Bowling 12–0

Richardson, Peter Edward
Amateur for Worcestershire, professional for Kent. *b:* 4.7.1931, Hereford. Brother of D. W. (Worcestershire) and B. A. (Warwickshire). Forceful opening left-hand batsman, excellent cover point. *Sch* Cathedral School, Hereford. *Teams* Worcestershire (1949–58, 161 matches); Kent (1959–65, 162 matches). *Tours* MCC to Pakistan 1955/6, to South Africa 1956/7, to East Africa 1957/8 (not first-class), to Australia and New Zealand 1958/9, to India, Pakistan and Ceylon 1961/2; Cavaliers to Jamaica 1963/4; Commonwealth to Pakistan 1963/4, to India 1964/5. *Tests* England (1956–63, 34 matches).
Career batting
454–794–41–26055–185–34.60–44–*ct* 220
Bowling 499–11–45.36–0–0–2/10
Test batting
34–56–1–2061–126–37.47–5–*ct* 6
Bowling 48–3–16.00–0–0–2/10

In his second full season of first-class County cricket, he hit 2,294 runs, av 39.55, and although he was to reach over 2,000 runs in three other seasons and in all top 1,000 runs eleven times in England, he never improved on his 2,294 of 1953. He also hit 1,000 runs on the 1961/2 tour. In 1956 he made his England debut, playing in all five Tests against the Australians and opening the innings with Cowdrey in each match. Richardson was also successful the following winter in South Africa and in the 1957 series against the West Indies. His place in the England side looked firmly established, but he failed completely on the 1958/9 tour to Australia, perhaps due to the problems he encountered when captain of Worcestershire 1956–58. He left the County in controversial circumstances after the 1958 season and was forced to spend an idle summer qualifying for Kent.

For several seasons he was back at his best with his new County, but apart from the 1961/2 tour to India and Pakistan, received only one further England cap – v West Indies in 1963. He retired from County cricket at the close of the 1965 season.

Richardson, Philip Charles
Cricketer. *b:* 12.6.1965, Paddington, London. Lower order right-hand batsman, off break bowler. *Team* Cambridge U (1984).
Career batting
1–1–0–7–7–7.00–0–*ct* 0
Bowling 122–1–122.00–0–0–1/92

Richardson, Richard Benjamin
Cricketer. *b:* 12.1.1962, Five Islands Village, Antigua. Attacking middle order right-hand batsman, right-arm medium pace bowler. *Team* Leeward Islands (1981/2 to 1991/2). *Tours* West Indies to India 1983/4, 1987/8, 1989/90 (not first-class), to Australia 1983/4 (not first-class), 1984/5, 1986/7, 1988/9, 1991/2 (not first-class), to England 1984, 1988, 1991, to Pakistan 1985/6 (not first-class), 1986/7, 1990/1, 1991/2 (not first-class), to Sharjah (not first-class) 1985/6, 1986/7, 1988/9, 1989/90, 1991/2, to New Zealand 1986/7, to India and Pakistan (World Cup) 1987/8, to Australia and New Zealand (World Cup) 1991/2; Rest of World to England 1990, 1992. *Tests* West Indies (1983/4 to 1991/2, 63 matches).
Career batting
151–250–22–9863–194–43.25–29–*ct* 144
Bowling 204–5–40.80–1–0–5/40
Test batting
63–109–10–4693–194–47.40–14–*ct* 70
Bowling 14–0

He failed to do himself justice on his first two tours to England, though he did play in three Tests on the 1988 tour. In 1991 however he finally mastered the slower English wickets and topped the Test batting table with 495 runs, av 55.00. In all first-class matches he hit 1,403 runs, av 66.60. On the harder wickets in West Indies and Australia, he had been successful for much of his career and is regarded as the leading West Indian batsman of his generation. He captained West Indies in the inaugural Test against South Africa 1991/2.

Richardson, Richard Taswell
Amateur. *b:* 9.8.1852, Broughton, Hampshire. *d:* 16.5.1930, Capenhurst Hall, near Chester, Cheshire. Middle order right-hand batsman. *Sch* Marlborough. *Team* MCC (1876–77).
Career batting
5–7–0–160–48–22.85–0–*ct* 0

Richardson, Samuel
Amateur. *b:* 24.5.1844, Derby. *d:* 18.1.1938, Madrid, Spain. Middle order right-hand batsman, wicket-keeper. *Team* Derbyshire (1871–78, 14 matches).

Career batting
15–27–0–202–25–7.48–0–*ct* 8–*st* 1
Bowling 43–1–43.00–0–0–1/43

He captained Derbyshire from 1871 to 1875 and was assistant secretary to the County club until 1890, when he absconded with about £1,000 of the Club's money and went to live under an assumed name in Spain where he is said to have become barber to the King.

Richardson, Stanley Hugh
Amateur. *b:* 2.7.1890, Marston Green, Warwickshire. *d:* 24.1.1958, Cambridge. Middle order right-hand batsman. *Teams* Warwickshire (1920, 2 matches); Nottinghamshire (1925, 1 match).
Career batting
3–5–1–22–8*–5.50–0–*ct* 0

Richardson, Thomas
Professional. *b:* 11.8.1870, Byfleet, Surrey. *d:* 2.7.1912, St Jean d'Arvey, Savoie, France. He died of congestion of the brain. His body was discovered above the Bout du Monde Cascade. Lower order right-hand batsman, right-arm fast bowler. *Teams* Surrey (1892–1904, 305 matches); London County (1904); Somerset (1905, 1 match). *Tours* Stoddart to Australia 1894/5, 1897/8. *Tests* England (1893 to 1897/8, 14 matches).
Career batting
358–479–124–3424–69–9.64–0–*ct* 126
Bowling 38794–2104–18.43–200–72–10/45
Test batting
14–24–8–177–25*–11.06–0–*ct* 5
Bowling 2220–88–25.22–11–4–8/94

He was regarded as the greatest English fast bowler of his generation, though his period at the very peak of his form lasted just five seasons. He made his Surrey debut in 1892 and the following year gained his England cap, taking 174 wickets, av 15.40, in first-class matches. In 1894 he was the leading bowler in England with 196 wickets, av 10.32. Going to Australia that winter he topped the bowling averages for the tour, and returning home exceeded 200 wickets for the first of three times – 290, av 14.37. In all he took 100 wickets in a season 10 times. His best bowling was 10/45 for Surrey v Essex at the Oval in 1894 and he took nine wickets in an innings on three other occasions.

After his second visit to Australia his increasing weight gradually reduced his effectiveness and he lost his place in the Surrey side in 1904.

Richardson, Thomas Geoffrey
Amateur. *b:* 7.3.1907, Worsley, Manchester, Lancashire. *d:* 13.7.1928, Worsley, Manchester, Lancashire. Middle order batsman, wicket-keeper. *Sch* Manchester GS. *Team* Oxford U (1927).
Career batting
1–2–1–4–4*–4.00–0–*ct* 0–*st* 1

Richardson, Thomas Haden
Amateur. *b:* 4.7.1865, Tutbury, Staffordshire. *d:* 10.12.1923, Tutbury, Staffordshire. Middle order right-hand batsman. *Team* Derbyshire (1895, 3 matches).
Career batting
4–7–0–49–15–7.00–0–*ct* 5

His first-class debut was for an England XI in 1888. He also played for Staffordshire (1888–92).

Richardson, Victor York
Amateur. *b:* 7.9.1894, Parkside, Unley, Adelaide, South Australia. *d:* 30.10.1969, Fullarton Park, Adelaide, South Australia. Grandfather of G. S. Chappell (Australia), I. M. Chappell (Australia) and T. M. Chappell (Australia). Forceful middle order right-hand batsman, excellent field. *Team* South Australia (1918/9 to 1937/8, 104 matches). *Tours* Australia to England 1930, to South Africa 1935/6, to New Zealand 1920/1, 1927/8. *Tests* Australia (1924/5 to 1935/6, 19 matches).
Career batting
184–297–12–10727–231–37.63–27–*ct* 211–*st* 4
Bowling 545–8–68.12–0–0–3/22
Test batting
19–30–0–706–138–23.53–1–*ct* 24

His batting was very disappointing on the 1930 tour to England. He was vice-captain of the side and later captained Australia in five Tests, all against South Africa. His highest score was 231 for South Australia v MCC at Adelaide in 1928/9. An all-round sportsman he also excelled at tennis, lacrosse and basketball. After retiring he became a well-known radio commentator.

Richardson, William Ethelbert
Amateur. *b:* 23.12.1894, St Helens, Lancashire. *d:* 5.11.1971, Hartlebury, Worcestershire. Lower order right-hand batsman, right-arm fast bowler. *Sch* Liverpool College. *Team* Worcestershire (1920–28, 30 matches).
Career batting
30–57–17–269–24–6.72–0–*ct* 9
Bowling 1865–44–42.38–1–0–6/48

A good rugby footballer he appeared for Moseley, Kidderminster and Bromsgrove.

Richardson, William Percival
Amateur. *b:* 25.2.1861, Great Barford, Bedfordshire. *d:* 13.6.1933, Littlestone-on-Sea, Kent. Lower order right-hand batsman, wicket-keeper. *Sch* Clifton. *Team* Cambridge U (1882).
Career batting
1–2–0–8–8–4.00–0–*ct* 1

He won a blue for rugby.

Riches, John Dansey Hurry
Amateur. *b:* 30.12.1920, Cathays, Cardiff, Glamorgan. Son of N. V. H. (Glamorgan). Middle order right-hand batsman, slow left-arm bowler. *Sch* Rep-

ton. *Team* Glamorgan (1947, 1 match).
Career batting
1–2–0–5–4–2.50–0–*çt* 0

Riches, Norman Vaughan Hurry
Amateur. *b:* 9.6.1883, Tredegarville, Cardiff, Glamorgan. *d:* 6.11.1975, Whitchurch, Cardiff, Glamorgan. Father of J. D. H. (Glamorgan). Sound opening right-hand batsman, right-arm medium pace bowler, occasional wicket-keeper. *Teams* Glamorgan (1921–34, 82 matches); Wales (1923–30).
Career batting
104–175–12–5750–239*–35.27–9–*ct* 49–*st* 6
Bowling 112–4–28.00–0–0–4/21

His debut for Glamorgan (pre fist-class) was in 1900. He captained the County in 1921 and jointly in 1929. After retiring he was for many years on the Committee and at one time President. He hit 1,080 runs, av 43.20, in 1921, which was his only full season in first-class cricket. His only double century was 239* for Wales v Ireland at Belfast in 1926. His first-class debut was for South Wales in 1912.

Richmond, Sir Bruce Lyttelton
Amateur. *b:* 12.1.1871, Kensington, London. *d:* 1,10.1964, Islip, Oxfordshire. Opening or middle order right-hand batsman. *Sch* Winchester. *Team* Oxford U (1892).
Career batting
2–3–0–12–11–4.00–0–*ct* 0

He edited the *Times Literary Supplement* 1902–37.

Richmond, Thomas Leonard
Professional. *b:* 23.6.1890, Radcliffe-on-Trent, Nottinghamshire. *d:* 29.12.1957, Saxondale, Nottinghamshire. Tail end right-hand batsman, leg break and googly bowler. *Team* Nottinghamshire (1912–28, 245 matches). *Tour* Cahn to South America 1929/30. *Test* England (1921, 1 match).
Career batting
252–281–116–1644–70–9.96–0–*ct* 39
Bowling 24959–1176–21.22–90–19–9/21
Test batting
1–2–0–6–4–3.00–0–*ct* 0
Bowling 86–2–43.00–0–0–2/69

He took 100 wickets in a season seven times (best 169, av 13.48, in 1922); his best bowling in an innings was 9/21 for Nottinghamshire v Hampshire at Trent Bridge in 1922. His final first-class match was for Sir Julien Cahn's XI in 1932.

Richmond, William
Professional. *b:* 1.12.1843, Keightley Green, Burnley, Lancashire. *d:* 11.11.1912, Burnley, Lancashire. Middle order batsman, wicket-keeper. *Team* Lancashire (1868, 1 match).
Career batting
1–2–0–1–1–0.50–0–*ct* 0

Rickards, Kenneth Roy
Amateur. *b:* 22.8.1923, Rollington Town, Kingston, Jamaica. Attractive middle order right-hand batsman, leg break bowler. *Teams* Essex (1953, 1 match); Jamaica (1945/6 to 1958/9). *Tours* West Indies to India, Pakistan and Ceylon 1948/9, to Australia and New Zealand 1951/2. *Tests* West Indies (1947/8 to 1951/2, 2 matches).
Career batting
37–60–7–2065–195–38.96–2–*ct* 10
Bowling 128–1–128.00–0–0–1/66
Test batting
2–3–0–104–67–34.66–0–*ct* 0

His English first-class debut was for a Commonwealth XI in 1952.

Ricketts, Arthur James
Professional. *b:* 27.8.1913, Farmborough, Somerset. Lower order left-hand batsman, slow left-arm bowler. *Team* Somerset (1936, 1 match).
Career batting
1 match, did not bat–*ct* 0

Ricketts, Courtney Ian Oswald
Cricketer. *b:* 26.4.1965, Kennington, London. Lower order right-hand batsman, slow left-arm bowler. *Team* Sussex (1987, 3 matches).
Career batting
3–1–0–29–29–29.00–0–*ct* 1
Bowling 253–5–50.60–0–0–2/40

Ricketts, George William
Amateur. *b:* 2.6.1864, Allahabad, India. *d:* 16.6.1927, South Kensington, London. He married the widow of E. H. Buckland (Middlesex and Hampshire). Aggressive middle order right-hand batsman, right-arm medium bowler, good point field. *Sch* Winchester. *Teams* Oxford U (1887, blue); Surrey (1887, 3 matches). *Tour* Hawke to North America 1891.
Career batting
13–21–1–385–92–19.25–0–*ct* 5
Bowling 79–3–26.33–0–0–2/21

He was for several years on the MCC Committee. His final first-class match was for MCC in 1902. Twice in 1910 he stood unsuccessfully as Liberal candidate for Winchester.

Ricketts, James
Professional. *b:* 9.2.1842, Manchester, Lancashire. *d:* 3.6.1894, Sale, Cheshire. Fine opening right-hand batsman, right-hand slow round-arm bowler, short leg. *Team* Lancashire (1867–77, 34 matches).
Career batting
42–79–5–1226–195*–16.56–1–*ct* 28–*st* 1
Bowling 284–12–23.66–0–0–4/40

He had a remarkable debut in first-class cricket, scoring 195 not out for Lancashire v Surrey at the Oval in 1867 and carrying his bat through the completed Lancashire innings. He was a first-class umpire (1884).

Ricketts, Michael Rodney
Amateur. *b:* 29.9.1923, Edgbaston, Birmingham. Middle order right-hand batsman. *Sch* Sherborne. *Team* Free Foresters (1948).
Career batting
1–1–0–1–1–1.00–0–*ct* 0
His County cricket was for Suffolk (1947–54).

Rickman, Reginald Binns
Amateur. *b:* 6.5.1881, Doncaster, Yorkshire. *d:* 22.11.1940, Chelsea, London. Lower order right-hand batsman, right-arm medium pace bowler. *Sch* Sherborne. *Team* Derbyshire (1906–11, 65 matches).
Career batting
65–118–8–1262–68–11.47–0–*ct* 7
Bowling 1967–62–31.72–1–0–5/80
He also played for Devon (1903). He was joint captain of Derbyshire in 1908. In later life he fell on very hard times.

Rickman, William
Amateur. *b:* 1849, South Yarra, Melbourne, Victoria, Australia. *d:* 6.6.1911, Frankston, Victoria, Australia. Middle order right-hand batsman, right-arm fast bowler. *Teams* Lancashire (1876, 1 match); Victoria (1880/1, 1 match).
Career batting
2–3–0–29–19–9.66–0–*ct* 1
Bowling 7–0

Riddell, David Adams
Amateur. *b:* 30.9.1899, Glasgow, Scotland. *d:* 3.4.1957, Fitzroy, Melbourne, Victoria, Australia. Middle order right-hand batsman. *Sch* Fettes. *Team* Scotland (1921–22).
Career batting
3–5–0–56–32–11.20–0–*ct* 2
He played in trials at Cambridge U, but not in first-class matches.

Riddell, Edward Mitford Hutton
Amateur. *b:* 31.10.1845, Carlton-on-Trent, Nottinghamshire. *d:* 22.10.1898, Lincoln. Lower order right-hand batsman, right-arm medium fast bowler. *Sch* Uppingham. *Team* MCC (1870–71).
Career batting
4–8–1–89–36–12.71–0–*ct* 2
Bowling 125–2–62.50–0–0–1/33
He played for Nottinghamshire in one non-first-class match in 1873, most of his major cricket being for the Gentlemen of that County.

Riddell, Neil Anthony
Cricketer. *b:* 16.7.1947, Staindrop, Co Durham. Middle order left-hand batsman, right-arm medium pace bowler. *Sch* Barnard Castle. *Team* Minor Counties (1976–86). *Tour* Minor Counties to Kenya 1977/8 (not first-class).
Career batting
3–5–0–84–23–16.80–0–*ct* 4
Bowling 5–0
His County cricket was for Durham (pre first-class, 1972–90) and he made a record number (218) of appearances for that county.

Riddell, Dr Victor Horsley Hume
Amateur. *b:* 23.7.1905, Hermeston Hall, Rotherham, Yorkshire. *d:* 9.8.1976, Stratford-on-Avon, Warwickshire. Lower order right-hand batsman, wicket-keeper. *Sch* Clifton. *Team* Cambridge U (1926, blue).
Career batting
5–8–2–48–13*–8.00–0–*ct* 3–*st* 3
His County cricket was for Devon (1924).

Ridding, Rev Charles Henry
Amateur. *b:* 26.11.1825, Winchester, Hampshire. *d:* 13.3.1905, Funtley, Fareham, Hampshire. Brother of William (Hampshire) and Arthur (Oxford U). Steady middle order right-hand batsman, excellent long stop. *Sch* Winchester. *Teams* Oxford U (1845–49, blue all five years); Hampshire (1861–64, 3 matches).
Career batting
29–50–9–492–33–12.00–0–*ct* 11
Bowling 1 wicket (no analyses)–0–0–1/?
He also played for Wiltshire (1849), Oxfordshire (1851–64) and Monmouthshire (1859).

Ridding, Rev William
Amateur. *b:* 23.11.1830, Winchester, Hampshire. *d:* 1.5.1900, Upper Clapton, London. Brother of C. H. (Hampshire) and Arthur (Oxford U). Attacking right-hand batsman, wicket-keeper. *Sch* Winchester. *Teams* Oxford U (1849–53, blue 1849, 1850, 1852 and 1853); Hampshire (1861, 1 match).
Career batting
17–25–4–326–53–15.52–0–*ct* 10–*st* 17
He also played for Oxfordshire (1849–53), Wiltshire (1859) and Monmouthshire (1859). He captained Oxford in 1852.

Riddington, Anthony
Professional. *b* 22.12.1911, Countesthorpe, Leicester. Opening or middle order left-hand batsman, left-arm slow medium, or medium bowler. *Team* Leicestershire (1931–50, 128 matches).
Career batting
128–214–17–3650–104*–18.52–1–*ct* 53
Bowling 3232–83–38.93–1–0–5/34

Ridge, Stuart Peter
Cricketer. *b:* 23.11.1961, Beaconsfield, Bucks. Lower order right-hand batsman, right-arm medium pace bowler. *Team* Oxford U (1981–82).
Career batting
11–15–6–71–22–7.88–0–*ct* 3
Bowling 894–14–63.85–0–0–4/128
His County cricket was for Buckinghamshire (1980–82). He won a blue for soccer.

Ridgway, Frederick
Professional. *b:* 10.8.1923, Stockport, Cheshire. Lower order right-hand batsman, right-arm fast medium bowler. *Team* Kent (1946–61, 298 matches). *Tours* Commonwealth to India and Ceylon 1950/1; MCC to India, Pakistan and Ceylon 1951/2. *Tests* England (1951/2, 5 matches).
Career batting
341–486–115–4081–94–11.00–0–*ct* 234
Bowling 25381–1069–23.74–41–6–8/39
Test batting
5–6–0–49–24–8.16–0–*ct* 3
Bowling 379–7–54.14–0–0–4/83
He took 105 wickets, av 23.32, in 1949.

Riding, Henry Wadsworth
Amateur. *b:* 19.9.1899, Epping, Essex. *d:* 21.5.1923, Forest Side, Chingford, Essex. Middle order batsman. *Sch* Bancrofts. *Team* Essex (1921, 1 match).
Career batting
1–2–0–23–16–11.50–0–*ct* 0

Ridland, James David
Amateur. *b:* 17.1.1923, New Plymouth, Taranaki, New Zealand. *d:* 4.2.1978, New Plymouth, Taranaki, New Zealand. Middle order left-hand batsman, wicket-keeper. *Tour* New Zealand Services to England 1945.
Career batting
1–2–0–62–44–31.00–0–*ct* 1
He did not appear in first-class matches in New Zealand.

Ridley, Alfred Bayley
Amateur. *b:* 14.12.1859, Hollington House, Hampshire. *d:* 26.3.1898, Lambeth, London. Brother of A. W. (Hampshire and Middlesex). Lower order right-hand batsman, right-hand fast round-arm bowler. *Sch* Eton. *Team* Hampshire (1884–85, 2 matches).
Career batting
2–4–0–43–41–10.75–0–*ct* 1
Bowling 35–2–17.50–0–0–2/30

Ridley, Arthur William
Amateur. *b:* 11.9.1852, Hollington House, Hampshire. *d:* 10.8.1916, Westminster, London. Brother of A. B. (Hampshire), father-in-law of P. J. S. Pearson-Gregory (Nottinghamshire). Stylish middle order right-hand batsman, excellent lob bowler. *Sch* Eton. *Teams* Oxford U (1872–75, blue all four years); Hampshire (1875–78, 10 matches); Middlesex (1882–85, 16 matches); Kent (1877, 1 match as given man).
Career batting
96–167–11–3150–136–20.19–4–*ct* 79–*st* 2
Bowling 3375–224–15.06–19–5–7/21
He captained Oxford in 1875.

Ridley, Christopher Jonathan Ben
Cricketer. *b:* 17.6.1946, Bulawayo, Rhodesia. Brother of G. N. S. (Kent). Lower order right-hand batsman, right-arm medium fast bowler. *Team* Oxford U (1971).
Career batting
6–10–2–88–23–11.00–0–*ct* 4
Bowling 356–3–118.66–0–0–2/70

Ridley, Gerald Vernon Newport
Amateur. *b:* 23.10.1897, Felsted, Essex. *d:* 12.11.1953, Chignal St James, Essex. Middle order right-hand batsman, right-arm medium bowler. *Sch* Marlborough. *Team* Essex (1922–26, 6 matches).
Career batting
6–11–0–113–54–10.27–0–*ct* 3
From 1929 to his death he was on the Committee of Essex CCC.

Ridley, Giles Nicholas Spencer
Cricketer. *b:* 27.11.1944, Bulawayo, Rhodesia. Brother of C. J. B. (Oxford U). Lower order right-hand batsman, slow left-arm bowler. *Teams* Kent (1965, 1 match); Oxford U (1965–68, blue all four years).
Career batting
45–68–8–889–50*–14.81–0–*ct* 40
Bowling 3051–123–24.80–2–0–7/110
He also played for Oxfordshire (1969–72), and his final first-class match was for Minor Counties in 1972. He captained Oxford in 1967.

Ridley, Robert Michael
Cricketer. *b:* 8.1.1947, Oxford. Opening right-hand batsman, right-arm medium pace bowler. *Sch* Clifton. *Teams* Oxford U (1967–70, blue 1968–70); Ireland (1968).
Career batting
23–42–1–994–79–24.24–0–*ct* 9
Bowling 0–0
His County cricket was for Berkshire (1972–73).

Ridley, Rev Thomas Glynn
Amateur. *b:* 20.7.1858, Cullencoats, Northumberland. *d:* 30.6.1945, Sea Point, Cape Town, South Africa. Opening or middle order right-hand batsman, right-hand slow round-arm bowler. *Sch* Uppingham. *Team* Gentlemen of England (1881).
Career batting
1–2–0–33–32–16.50–0–*ct* 0
He appeared in the Freshmen's and Seniors' matches at Oxford. His County cricket was for Northumberland (1880–86).

Righton, Edward Grantham (sen)
Amateur. *b:* 23.11.1884, Evesham, Worcestershire. *d:* 3.1.1964, Evesham, Worcestershire. Father of E. G. jun (Worcestershire). Middle order right-hand batsman, right-arm medium pace bowler. *Sch* Dean Close. *Team* Worcestershire (1911–13, 4 matches).

Career batting
4–4–0–60–48–15.00–0–*ct* 1
Bowling 21–1–21.00–0–0–1/21

Righton, Edward Grantham (jun)
Amateur. *b:* 24.9.1912, Evesham, Worcestershire. *d:* 2.5.1986, Evesham, Worcestershire. Son of E. G. sen (Worcestershire). Opening right-hand batsman. *Sch* Dean Close. *Team* Worcestershire (1934–36, 4 matches).
Career batting
4–7–0–27–19–3.85–0–*ct* 1

Rigley, William
Professional. *b:* 24.3.1852, Eastwood, Nottinghamshire. *d:* 15.3.1897, Nottingham. Opening or middle order right-hand batsman, right-arm medium pace bowler. *Teams* Derbyshire (1873–82, 57 matches); Players of USA (1893–94).
Career batting
66–121–1–1510–69–12.58–0–*ct* 25
Bowling 50–5–10.00–0–0–2/10
He was a first-class umpire (1883–84).

Riley, Edwin
Professional. *b:* 21.3.1867, Stoney Stanton, Leicestershire. *d:* 4.5.1936, Stoney Stanton, Leicestershire. Father of Harold (Leicestershire) Lower order batsman, bowler. *Team* Leicestershire (1895, 2 matches).
Career batting
2–3–1–13–8*–6.50–0–*ct* 0
Bowling 7–0
He first played for Leicestershire (pre first-class) in 1892.

Riley, Harold
Professional. *b:* 3.10.1902, Stoney Stanton, Leicestershire. *d:* 24.1.1989, Southfields, Leicester. Son of Edwin (Leicestershire). Middle order right-hand batsman, off break bowler, good cover point. *Team* Leicestershire (1928–37, 94 matches).
Career batting
94–147–11–2346–101–17.25–1–*ct* 30
Bowling 173–5–34.60–0–0–2/32
He was a useful soccer inside forward.

Riley, Harry
Professional. *b:* 17.8.1875, Thackley, Yorkshire. *d:* 6.11.1922, Bradford, Yorkshire. Lower order batsman, left-arm medium pace bowler. *Team* Yorkshire (1895–1900, 4 matches).
Career batting
4–5–1–36–25*–9.00–0–*ct* 1
Bowling 54–1–54.00–0–0–1/17

Riley, Jack
Professional. *b:* 27.4.1927, Accrington, Lancashire. Lower order right-hand batsman, slow left-arm bowler. *Team* Worcestershire (1953, 1 match).
Career batting
1–1–0–1–1–1.00–0–*ct* 1
Bowling 48–3–16.00–0–0–3/25

Riley, James
Professional. *b:* 11.12.1860, Kirkby-in-Ashfield, Nottinghamshire. *d:* 8.11.1937, Derby. Lower order right-hand batsman, right-arm medium pace bowler. *Team* Nottinghamshire (1898, 2 matches).
Career batting
2–1–0–3–3–3.00–0–*ct* 1
Bowling 49–0

Riley, John Christopher William
Amateur. *b:* 6.4.1934, Esher, Surrey. Tail end right-hand batsman, wicket-keeper. *Sch* Uppingham. *Team* Cambridge U (1955–56).
Career batting
2–3–1–0–0*–0.00–0–*ct* 3–*st* 1
He won a blue for hockey.

Riley, Martin
Amateur. *b:* 5.4.1851, Cleckheaton, Yorkshire. *d:* 1.6.1899, Harrogate, Yorkshire. Hard hitting middle order right-hand batsman, right-hand fast round-arm bowler. *Team* Yorkshire (1878–82, 17 matches).
Career batting
20–34–1–381–92–11.54–0–*ct* 5
Bowling 10–0
His final first-class match was for A. Shaw's Australian XI at Harrogate in 1885.

Riley, Terence Michael Noel
Cricketer. *b:* 25.12.1939, Birmingham. Opening right-hand batsman, leg break bowler. *Teams* Warwickshire (1961–64, 12 matches); Gloucestershire (1964, 11 matches).
Career batting
23–43–2–678–84–16.53–0–*ct* 5
Bowling 15–0
He played for both Gloucestershire and Warwickshire in 1964.

Riley, William
Professional. *b:* 11.8.1888, Newstead Colliery, Nottinghamshire. *d:* 9.8.1917, near Coxyde, Belgium. He was killed by a shell splinter. Tail end left-hand batsman, slow left-arm medium bowler. *Team* Nottinghamshire (1909–14, 80 matches).
Career batting
80–110–24–740–48–8.60–0–*ct* 69
Bowling 5497–235–23.39–10–2–7/80

Riley, William Nairn
Amateur. *b:* 24.11.1892, Appleby Magna, Leicestershire. *d:* 20.11.1955, Hove, Sussex. Middle order right-hand batsman, right-arm fast medium bowler. *Sch* Worcester RGS. *Teams* Leicestershire (1911–14, 32 matches); Cambridge U (1912–14, blue 1912).
Career batting
55–91–1–1620–121–18.00–2–*ct* 31

Rilstone, Thomas Melville

Bowling 314–7–44.85–0–0–2/12

He also won a blue for hockey, and played for England.

Rilstone, Thomas Melville
Amateur. *b:* 12.1.1918, Wallaroo, South Australia. Lower order left-hand batsman, right-arm leg break and googly bowler. *Team* Canada (1951–54). *Tour* Canada to England 1954.
Career batting
3–3–0–54–38–18.00–0–*ct* 0
Bowling 150–0

Rimbault, Geoffrey Acworth
Amateur. *b:* 17.4.1908, Braxted Park, Streatham, London. *d:* 20.10.1991, Bovey Tracey, Devon. Middle order right-hand batsman. *Sch* Dulwich. *Teams* Europeans (1934/5); Army (1938).
Career batting
2–3–0–31–16–10.33–0–*ct* 0

He was President of Surrey in 1982.

Rimell, Anthony Geoffrey Jordan
Amateur. *b:* 29.8.1928, Kasauli, India. Stylish middle order left-hand batsman, off break bowler. *Sch* Charterhouse. *Teams* Hampshire (1946–50, 2 matches); Cambridge U (1949–50, blue both years).
Career batting
23–35–5–854–160–28.46–1–*ct* 13
Bowling 1445–40–36.12–1–0–6/100

Rimmer, Joseph
Professional. *b:* 26.1.1925, Langwith, Derbyshire. Tail end right-hand batsman, right-arm medium pace bowler. *Team* Derbyshire (1949, 3 matches).
Career batting
3–3–2–1–1*–1.00–0–*ct* 0
Bowling 264–5–52.80–0–0–2/71

He retired due to an accident at work.

Ring, Douglas Thomas
Amateur. *b:* 14.10.1918, Hobart, Tasmania, Australia. Lower order right-hand batsman, leg break and googly bowler. *Team* Victoria (1938/9 to 1952/3, 67 matches). *Tours* Australia to England 1948, 1953, to New Zealand 1949/50. *Tests* Australia (1947/8 to 1953, 13 matches).
Career batting
129–169–22–3418–145–23.25–1–*ct* 93
Bowling 12847–451–28.48–21–2–7/88
Test batting
13–21–2–426–67–22.42–0–*ct* 5
Bowling 1305–35–37.28–2–0–6/72

Although he played little part in the Tests either in 1948 or 1953, he proved useful in the other first-class matches.

Ring, John
Professional. *b:* 1758, Darenth, Kent. *d:* 25.10.1800, Bridge, Kent. He died following an injury while playing cricket. Brother of George (England 1796). Steady middle order right-hand batsman, good cover point. *Team* Kent (1782–96).

He was for sometime regarded as the 'crack' batsman in Kent – his play being scientific. Beldham stated that Ring was partially responsible for the passing of the lbw law, since he was 'shabby enough' to use his legs to defend his wicket, but Beldham was in error, since the lbw law was passed before Ring played for Kent.

Ringrose, William
Professional. *b:* 2.9.1871, Ganton, Yorkshire. *d:* 14.9.1943, Manston, Cross Gates, Leeds, Yorkshire. Tail end left-hand batsman, right-arm fast medium bowler. *Teams* Yorkshire (1901–06, 57 matches); Scotland (1908–12).
Career batting
61–74–11–377–23–5.98–0–*ct* 27
Bowling 3568–175–20.38–11–2–9/76

He was Yorkshire scorer from 1923 to 1939. His best bowling was 9/76 for Yorkshire v Australians at Bradford in 1905.

Ripley, David
Cricketer. *b:* 13.9.1966, Leeds, Yorkshire. Middle order right-hand batsman, wicket-keeper. *Team* Northamptonshire (1984–92, 177 matches). *Tour* Northamptonshire to South Africa 1991/2.
Career batting
178–229–57–4268–134*–24.81–6–*ct* 372–*st* 55
Bowling 103–2–51.50–0–0–2/89

He made 87 dismissals (80 ct, 7 st) in 1988.

Ripley, Roderic George
Amateur. *b:* 16.5.1900, Weekley, Kettering, Northamptonshire. *d:* 19.1.1932, Compton, Kimberley, South Africa. Middle order right-hand batsman. *Teams* Northamptonshire (1922, 4 matches); Eastern Province (1928/9).
Career batting
6–11–1–94–23–9.40–0–*ct* 1
Bowling 25–0

Rippon, Albert Dudley Eric
Amateur. *b:* 29.4.1892, Kensington, London. *d:* 16.4.1963, Cholsey, Wallingford, Berkshire. Twin brother of A. E. S. (Somerset). Solid opening right-hand batsman, right-arm medium pace bowler. *Sch* King's College, Taunton. *Team* Somerset (1914–20, 31 matches).
Career batting
31–56–4–1043–134–20.05–2–*ct* 30
Bowling 1110–37–30.00–1–0–5/107

Soon after the First World War he was compelled to retire from County cricket owing to ill-health.

Rippon, Arthur Ernest Sydney
Amateur. *b:* 29.4.1892, Kensington, London. *d:* 13.4.1966, Berrylands, Surbiton, Surrey. Twin brother of A. D. E. (Somerset). Opening right-hand

batsman, right-arm slow bowler. *Sch* King's College, Taunton. *Team* Somerset (1914–37, 102 matches).
Career batting
104–185–8–3823–133–21.59–6–*ct* 44
Bowling 121–3–40.33–0–0–1/6

Rippon, Thomas John
Professional. *b:* 6.7.1918, Swansea, Glamorgan. Lower order right-hand batsman, wicket-keeper. *Team* Glamorgan (1947–48, 3 matches).
Career batting
3–4–2–45–30–22.50–0–*ct* 0–*st* 3

Rist, Frank Henry
Professional. *b:* 30.3.1914, Wandsworth, London. Middle order right-hand batsman, right-arm medium bowler, wicket-keeper. *Team* Essex (1934–53, 65 matches).
Career batting
65–108–9–1496–62–15.11–0–*ct* 35–*st* 5
Bowling 8–1–8.00–0–0–1/8

He was appointed coach to Essex CCC in 1949. A good soccer player, he appeared at centre half for Charlton Athletic.

Ritchie, David Mawdsley
Amateur. *b:* 12.8.1892, Toxteth Park, Liverpool, Lancashire. *d:* 10.9.1974, Stevenage, Hertfordshire. Lower order right-hand batsman, right-arm fast bowler. *Sch* Loretto. *Team* Lancashire (1924, 1 match).
Career batting
4–5–1–27–12–6.75–0–*ct* 4
Bowling 252–9–28.00–0–0–3/44

His first-class debut was for Free Foresters in 1922, and his final first-class match for the same club in 1926.

Ritchie, Gregory Michael
Cricketer. *b:* 23.1.1960, Stanthorpe, Queensland, Australia. Stylish middle order right-hand batsman, right-arm medium pace bowler. *Team* Queensland (1980/1 to 1991/2, 106 matches). *Tours* Australia to Pakistan 1982/3, to West Indies 1983/4, to England 1985, to New Zealand 1985/6, to Sharjah (not first-class) 1985/6, 1986/7, to India 1984/5 (not first-class), 1986/7; Young Australians to Zimbabwe 1982/3. *Tests* Australia (1982/3 to 1986/7, 30 matches).
Career batting
159–254–24–10170–213*–44.21–24–*ct* 115
Bowling 247–5–49.40–0–0–1/2
Test batting
30–53–5–1690–146–35.20–3–*ct* 14
Bowling 10–0

He was one of the few successes on the 1985 tour to England, scoring 422 runs, av 42.20, in the Tests and 1,097 runs, av 54.85, in all first-class matches. He played for Buckinghamshire in 1989.

Rivett-Carnac, Ernest Henry
Amateur. *b:* 30.6.1857, Steyning, Sussex. *d:* 4.9.1940, Beaulieu, Hampshire. His niece married R. H. D. Bolton (Hampshire). Middle order batsman. *Sch* Harrow. *Team* MCC (1900).
Career batting
1–1–0–10–10–10.00–0–*ct* 0

Rix, David William
Cricketer. *b:* 7.12.1939, Bulawayo, Rhodesia. Lower order right-hand batsman, left-arm fast medium bowler. *Team* Oxford U (1964).
Career batting
1–2–0–0–0–0.00–0–*ct* 1
Bowling 90–3–30.00–0–0–3/90

Rixon, Stephen John
Cricketer. *b:* 25.2.1954, Albury, New South Wales, Australia. Lower order right-hand batsman, wicket-keeper. *Team* New South Wales (1974/5 to 1987/8, 107 matches). *Tours* Australia to West Indies 1977/8, to England 1981, to Sri Lanka 1980/1, to Sharjah (not first-class) 1984/5; Australian XI to South Africa 1985/6, 1986/7. *Tests* Australia (1977/8 to 1984/5, 13 matches).
Career batting
151–221–35–4303–128–23.13–6–*ct* 394–*st* 66
Bowling 20–0
Test batting
13–24–3–394–54–18.76–0–*ct* 42–*st* 5

He went to England on the 1981 tour as a reserve wicket-keeper and had few opportunities, not playing in any Tests.

Roach, Clifford Archibald
Amateur. *b:* 13.3.1904, Port of Spain, Trinidad. *d:* 16.4.1988, Port of Spain, Trinidad. Attractive opening right-hand batsman, leg break bowler, excellent cover point. *Team* Trinidad (1923/4 to 1937/8). *Tours* West Indies to England 1928, 1933, to Australia 1930/1. *Tests* West Indies (1928 to 1934/5, 16 matches).
Career batting
98–177–4–4851–209–28.04–5–*ct* 43
Bowling 526–5–105.20–0–0–1/18
Test batting
16–32–1–952–209–30.70–2–*ct* 5
Bowling 103–2–51.50–0–0–1/18

In 1928 he played in all three Tests and in first-class matches hit 1,222 runs, av 26.56. On his second English tour he hit 1,286 runs, av 25.72, the highlight being his 180 v Surrey at the Oval which was regarded as the innings of the visit. His highest score was 209 for West Indies v England at Georgetown in 1929/30.

Robathan, George Lionel
Amateur. *b:* 18.7.1878, Brighton, Sussex. *d:* 3.8.1951, Farnham, Surrey. Father of R. D. B. (Europeans). Middle order right-hand batsman. *Sch* Epsom

and Cranbrook. *Team* Gloucestershire (1922, 3 matches).
Career batting
3–6–0–118–42–19.66–0–*ct* 1

He also played for Glamorgan (pre first-class, 1910–11) and Monmouthshire (1928).

Roberson, Benjamin
Professional. *b:* 12.9.1832, Ware, Hertfordshire. *d:* 6.4.1874, Upper Holloway, London. Middle order right-hand batsman. *Team* Middlesex (1865–66, 2 matches).
Career batting
2–3–0–19–13–6.33–0–*ct* 1–*st* 1

He also played occasionally for Hertfordshire.

Roberts, Albert William
Amateur. *b:* 20.8.1909, Christchurch, New Zealand. *d:* 13.5.1978, Clyde, Otago, New Zealand. Steady middle order right-hand batsman, right-arm medium pace bowler, good slip. *Teams* Canterbury (1927/8 to 1940/1); Otago (1944/5 to 1950/1). *Tours* New Zealand to England 1937, to Australia 1937/8. *Tests* New Zealand (1929/30 to 1937, 5 matches).
Career batting
84–135–17–3645–181–30.88–3–*ct* 78
Bowling 4762–167–28.51–3–0–5/47
Test batting
5–10–1–248–66*–27.55–0–*ct* 4
Bowling 209–7–29.85–0–0–4/101

He was a useful all-round cricketer on the 1937 tour with 510 runs, av 25.50, and 62 wickets, av 26.20.

Roberts, Allen Christian
Amateur. *b:* 16.12.1922, Sandringham, Auckland, New Zealand. Lower order right-hand batsman, right-arm medium pace bowler. *Team* Auckland (1947/8). *Tour* New Zealand Services to England 1945.
Career batting
2–3–1–26–12–13.00–0–*ct* 0
Bowling 182–4–45.50–0–0–3/83

Roberts, Anderson Montgomery Everton, CBE
Cricketer. *b:* 29.1.1951, Urlings Village, Antigua. Lower order right-hand batsman, right-arm fast bowler. *Teams* Leeward Islands (1969/70 to 1983/4); Hampshire (1973–78, 58 matches); New South Wales (1976/7, 2 matches); Leicestershire (1981–84, 36 matches). *Tours* West Indies to India, Pakistan and Sri Lanka 1974/5, to England 1975 (World Cup), 1976, 1979 (World Cup), 1980, 1983 (World Cup), to Australia 1975/6, 1979/80, 1981/2, to New Zealand 1979/80, to India 1983/4. *Tests* West Indies (1973/4 to 1983/4, 47 matches).
Career batting
228–291–67–3516–89–15.69–0–*ct* 52
Bowling 18679–889–21.01–47–7–8/47
Test batting
47–62–11–762–68–14.94–0–*ct* 9
Bowling 5174–202–25.61–11–2–7/54

On the 1976 tour to England he took 28 wickets, av 19.17, in the five Tests and 44 wickets, av 24.75, in first-class matches. In 1980 he was handicapped by injury and appeared in three of the five Tests, but only nine first-class matches altogether. He was dogged by injury during the 1983 World Cup and though he went to India in 1983/4 he was fit to play in only two of the six Tests. In 1984 he turned out for Leicestershire only when the county was struggling to find enough fit players – rather ironic considering his injury problems over the previous few years. At his peak he was ranked among the best fast bowlers of his generation. His best season in England was 1974 when he took 119 wickets, av 13.62.

Roberts, Andrew Richard
Cricketer. *b:* 16.4.1971, Kettering, Northamptonshire. Lower order right-hand batsman, leg break bowler. *Team* Northamptonshire (1989–92, 33 matches). *Tour* Northamptonshire to South Africa 1991/2.
Career batting
33–42–13–577–62–19.89–0–*ct* 15
Bowling 2571–61–42.14–1–0–6/72

Roberts, Arthur Wilson
Amateur. *b:* 23.9.1874, Malegaon, India. *d:* 27.6.1961, Hastings, Sussex. Brother of F. B. (Gloucestershire). Middle order right-hand batsman, right-arm fast medium bowler. *Sch* Rossall. *Team* Gloucestershire (1908–13, 28 matches).
Career batting
29–46–3–807–90–18.76–0–*ct* 17
Bowling 05–12–33.75–0–0–2/20

He also played for Oxfordshire (1897) and Buckinghamshire (1902).

Roberts, Bruce
Cricketer. *b:* 30.5.1962, Lusaka, Northern Rhodesia. Middle order right-hand batsman, right-arm medium pace bowler, occasional wicket-keeper. *Teams* Transvaal (1982/3 to 1988/9); Derbyshire (1984–91, 156 matches).
Career batting
205–333–34–9182–184–30.70–13–*ct* 166–*st* 1
Bowling 2948–89–33.12–1–0–5/68

He scored 1,000 runs in a season three times (best 1,643 runs, av 43.23, in 1987).

Roberts, Christopher Paul
Cricketer. *b:* 12.10.1951, Cleethorpes, Lincolnshire. *d:* 9.6.1977, Raven Crag, Coombe Ghyl, Borrowdale, Cumberland. He was killed in a climbing accident. Tail end right-hand batsman, right-arm medium pace bowler. *Team* Worcestershire (1974, 1 match).
Career batting
1–1–1–0–0*–no av–0–*ct* 0
Bowling 40–1–40.00–0–0–1/34

He also played for Lincolnshire (1971–72).

Roberts, David John
Cricketer. *b:* 1.10.1942, Harpenden, Hertfordshire. Son of E. A. (MCC). Middle order left-hand batsman, right-arm fast medium bowler. *Team* MCC (1963).
Career batting
1–1–0–6–6–6.00–0–*ct* 0
His County cricket was for Hertfordshire (1964).

Roberts, Desmond
Amateur. *b:* 5.2.1894, Hampstead, London. *d:* 11.1.1968, Eastbourne, Sussex. Middle order left-hand batsman, right-arm medium pace bowler. *Sch* St Bees. *Team* Surrey (1921, 1 match).
Career batting
12–19–2–255–56–15.00–0–*ct* 3
Bowling 438–9–48.66–0–0–3/49
His first-class debut was for Leveson-Gower's XI in 1920 and his final first-class match for MCC in 1936. He was a well-known actor.

Roberts, Edward Allen
Professional. *b:* 12.7.1907, Harpenden, Hertfordshire. *d:* 9.3.1986, St Albans, Hertfordshire. Father of D. J. (MCC). Lower order right-hand batsman, slow left-arm bowler. *Teams* MCC (1931–39); Minor Counties (1936–39).
Career batting
9–15–5–82–32–8.20–0–*ct* 4
Bowling 577–15–38.46–0–0–3/36
His County cricket was for Hertfordshire (1926–50). He was a first-class umpire (1953–56).

Roberts, Edward Stanley
Amateur. *b:* 6.5.1890, Oswestry, Shropshire. *d:* September 1964, Rhodesia. Middle order batsman. *Team* Worcestershire (1925, 3 matches).
Career batting
3–6–0–23–12–3.83–0–*ct* 2

Roberts, Francis Bernard
Amateur. *b:* 20.5.1882, Anjini Hill, Nasik, India. *d:* 8.2.1916, St Julien, Ypres, Belgium. He was killed in action. Brother of A. W. (Gloucestershire). Middle order right-hand batsman, right-arm fast bowler. *Sch* Rossall. *Teams* Cambridge U (1903–04, blue 1903); Gloucestershire (1906–14, 67 matches).
Career batting
80–138–12–2566–157–20.36–5–*ct* 66
Bowling 3005–88–34.14–1–0–5/69
He also played for Oxfordshire (1901–03). He also obtained his blue for hockey.

Roberts, Frederick
Professional. *b:* 24.9.1848, Kennington, London. *d:* 13.7.1903, Rotherhithe, London. Lower order right-hand batsman, right-hand fast round-arm bowler. *Team* Surrey (1867–68, 4 matches).
Career batting
4–7–2–20–7–4.00–0–*ct* 1
Bowling 159–9–17.66–1–0–7/72

Roberts, Frederick Charles
Amateur. *b:* 5.6.1881, Edington, Bridgwater, Somerset. Lower order batsman, bowler. *Team* Somerset (1899, 1 match).
Career batting
1–1–0–3–3–3.00–0–*ct* 0
Bowling 11–0

Roberts, Frederick George
Professional. *b:* 1.4.1862, Mickleton, Gloucestershire. *d:* 7.4.1936, Bristol. Tail end left-hand batsman, left-arm fast bowler. *Team* Gloucestershire (1887–1905, 260 matches).
Career batting
261–412–151–1927–38–7.38–0–*ct* 98
Bowling 21303–970–21.96–62–8–8/40
He took 119 wickets, av 22.70, in 1901. From 1906 to 1919 he stood as a first-class umpire.

Roberts, Harley James
Professional, changed to amateur in 1935. *b:* 24.5.1912, Bearwood, Staffordshire. *d:* 17.2.1989, Romsley, Worcestershire. Middle order right-hand batsman, right-arm medium pace bowler. *Team* Warwickshire (1932–37, 17 matches).
Career batting
17–27–4–348–61–15.13–0–*ct* 11
Bowling 407–9–45.22–0–0–3/6

Roberts, Harry Edmund
Professional. *b:* 5.6.1924, Earlsdon, Coventry. Opening left-hand batsman, right-arm medium pace bowler. *Sch* Bablake. *Team* Warwickshire (1949–50, 5 matches).
Career batting
5–8–0–52–30–6.50–0–*ct* 3

Roberts, Henry Edmund
Professional. *b:* 8.2.1888, East Preston, Sussex. *d:* 28.6.1963, Farnborough, Hampshire. Lower order right-hand batsman, right-arm medium pace bowler. *Team* Sussex (1911–25, 157 matches).
Career batting
157–249–76–2302–124*–13.30–1–*ct* 70
Bowling 8267–342–24.17–18–2–7/32
He also played for Devon (1932).

Roberts, James Brown
Amateur. *b:* 11.10.1933, Dundee, Angus, Scotland. Lower order right-hand batsman, right-arm fast medium bowler. *Team* Scotland (1956–59).
Career batting
10–17–5–154–31*–12.83–0–*ct* 4
Bowling 434–13–33.38–0–0–3/70

Roberts, James Harry
Amateur. *b:* 1.7.1864, Walton, Liverpool, Lancashire. *d:* 11.8.1911, Bexhill-on-Sea, Sussex. Attacking middle order left-hand batsman, bowler, good field. *Sch* Uppingham. *Team* Middlesex (1892, 1 match). *Tour* Warton to South Africa 1888/9 (he did not play in

first-class matches).
Career batting
1–1–0–35–35–35.00–0–*ct* 1
He also played for Buckinghamshire (1890–91).

Roberts, John Francis Esdale
Professional. *b:* 4.3.1933, Kearsley, Bolton, Lancashire. Lower order right-hand batsman, right-arm medium fast bowler. *Team* Lancashire (1957, 2 matches).
Career batting
2–4–2–5–5–2.50–0–*ct* 0
Bowling 90–0

Roberts, Air Vice Marshal John Frederick
Amateur. *b:* 24.2.1913, Pontardawe, Glamorgan. Middle order left-hand batsman. *Team* Glamorgan (1934–36, 5 matches).
Career batting
8–11–1–204–52–20.40–0–*ct* 7
His final first-class match was for Combined Services in 1949.

Roberts, John Kelvin
Cricketer. *b:* 9.10.1949, Liverpool, Lancashire. Tail end right-hand batsman, left-arm medium pace bowler. *Team* Somerset (1969–70, 8 matches).
Career batting
8–9–6–3–2*–1.00–0–*ct* 2
Bowling 485–15–32.33–0–0–4/38

Roberts, Lambert Lloyd
Amateur. *b:* 13.3.1878, St Margarets, Twickenham, Middlesex. *d:* 26.6.1919, Sekondi, Gold Coast. Middle order batsman. *Sch* Harrow. *Team* Gloucestershire (1900, 2 matches).
Career batting
2–3–0–4–4–1.33–0–*ct* 2

Roberts, Malcolm John
Cricketer. *b:* 18.2.1960, Bromley, Kent. Opening right-hand batsman, right-arm medium pace bowler. *Team* Minor Counties (1990).
Career batting
1–2–0–86–85–43.00–0–*ct* 0
His County cricket was for Buckinghamshire (1987–92).

Roberts, Martin Leonard
Cricketer. *b:* 12.4.1966, Mullion, Cornwall. Lower order right-hand batsman, wicket-keeper. *Team* Glamorgan (1985–91, 10 matches). *Tour* Glamorgan to Zimbabwe 1990/1.
Career batting
10–10–2–100–25–12.50–0–*ct* 16–*st* 4
He also played for Cornwall (1983–84). His uncle Graham Roberts played soccer for Chelsea and Tottenham Hotspur.

Roberts, General Sir Ouvry Lindfield
Amateur. *b:* 3.4.1898, Eltoffs Estate, near Bogawantalawa, Ceylon. *d:* 16.3.1986, Iffley, Oxford. Brother of H. P. L. (Ceylon). Middle order right-hand batsman, wicket-keeper. *Sch* Cheltenham. *Team* Cambridge U (1925).
Career batting
3–6–0–38–10–6.33–0–*ct* 4–*st* 1
His final first-class match was for Free Foresters in 1926. He won a blue for hockey and also played for Wales.

Roberts, Pascall Ronald
Amateur. *b:* 15.12.1937, Port of Spain, Trinidad. Lower order right-hand batsman, left-arm fast, later slow, bowler. *Team* Trinidad (1960/1 to 1971/2). *Tour* West Indies to England 1969.
Career batting
67–83–20–871–105*–13.82–1–*ct* 32
Bowling 5286–211–25.05–7–1–6/17
He achieved very little on the 1969 tour and did not appear in the Tests; earlier his bowling action had been criticised and he was no-balled for throwing in the West Indies in 1966/7. His final first-class match was for North Trinidad in 1978/9.

Roberts, R.
Amateur. Middle order batsman, wicket-keeper. *Team* Lancashire (1872–74, 10 matches).
Career batting
10–16–0–100–20–6.25–0–*ct* 9–*st* 5

Roberts, Simon Nicholas
Amateur. *b:* 11.9.1926, Durban, South Africa. Opening or middle order right-hand batsman, leg break bowler. *Team* Cambridge U (1947–49).
Career batting
6–11–1–158–49*–15.80–0–*ct* 0
Bowling 21–0
His County cricket was for Cambridgeshire (1947).

Roberts, William Braithwaite
Professional. *b:* 27.9.1914, Kirkham, Lancashire. *d:* 23.8.1951, Bangor, Caernarvonshire. Tail end right-hand batsman, slow left-arm bowler. *Team* Lancashire (1939–49, 114 matches).
Career batting
119–120–39–865–51–10.67–0–*ct* 61
Bowling 8296–392–21.16–25–3–8/50
He took 123 wickets, av 19.34, in 1946.

Robertson, Colin Michael
Cricketer. *b:* 4.5.1963, Gatooma, Rhodesia. Middle order right-hand batsman. *Team* Zimbabwe (1982/3 to 1990). *Tours* Zimbabwe to Sri Lanka 1983/4, to England 1990.
Career batting
18–32–1–433–125–13.96–1–*ct* 8

Robertson, Frank
Cricketer. *b:* 25.2.1944, Stocket Hill, Aberdeen, Scotland. Lower order right-hand batsman, right-arm fast medium bowler. *Team* Scotland (1971–81).
Career batting
12–17–1–163–51–10.18–0–*ct* 3
Bowling 743–36–20.63–2–0–6/58

Robertson, Frederick Marrant
Amateur. *b:* 1843, Friendship, Jamaica. *d:* 28.3.1920, Kensington, London. Lower order batsman, right-arm medium pace bowler. *Sch* Rossall. *Team* Surrey (1877, 1 match).
Career batting
1–2–1–7–4–7.00–0–*ct* 0
Bowling 49–2–0–24.50–0–0–2/32

Robertson, George André
Amateur. *b:* 8.9.1928, St Jean-de-Luz, France. Lower order right-hand batsman, right-arm medium pace bowler. *Sch* Ampleforth. *Team* Cambridge U (1950).
Career batting
2–2–1–7–7*–7.00–0–*ct* 0
Bowling 106–3–35.33–0–0–2/53

Robertson, George Pringle
Amateur. *b:* 22.8.1842, Hobart, Tasmania, Australia. *d:* 23.6.1895, Colac, Melbourne, Victoria, Australia. Father-in-law of J. R. C. Gannon (MCC). Middle order right-hand batsman. *Sch* Rugby *Teams* Oxford U (1866, blue); Victoria (1866/7 to 1871/2, 4 matches).
Career batting
9–14–1–234–53–18.00–0–*ct* 2
His County cricket was for Warwickshire (pre first-class, 1864–65).

Robertson, James
(changed name to Robertson-Walker in 1893)
Amateur. *b:* 10.11.1850, Wardieburn, Edinburgh, Scotland. *d:* 21.3.1927, Kensington, London. Father-in-law of B. F. B. Hitchcock (Hampshire). Lower order right-hand batsman, right-arm fast bowler, good slip. *Sch* Edinburgh Academy. *Team* Middlesex (1878–91, 102 matches).
Career batting
156–247–42–2102–62–10.25–0–*ct* 110
Bowling 9065–405–22.38–19–2–8/48
His first-class debut was for an England Eleven in 1877 and his final first-class match for MCC in 1892. Whilst at Oxford University he did not appear in any first-class matches. He was on the MCC Committee.

Robertson, James Richard
Amateur. *b:* 18.6.1844, Hollingbourne, Kent. *d:* 6.8.1877, Folkestone, Kent. Son of J. C. (Oxford U 1829). *Sch* Cheltenham. *Team* Gentlemen of Kent (1863–64).
Career batting
2–4–1–39–13*–13.00–0–*ct* 1
Bowling 43–0

Robertson, John David Benbow
Professional. *b:* 22.2.1917, Chiswick, Middlesex. Stylish opening right-hand batsman, off break bowler, good field. *Team* Middlesex (1937–59, 423 matches). *Tours* MCC to West Indies 1947/8, to India, Pakistan and Ceylon 1951/2. *Tests* England (1947 to 1951/2, 11 matches).
Career batting
509–897–46–31914–331*–37.50–67–*ct* 350
Bowling 2536–73–34.73–0–0–4/37
Test batting
11–21–2–881–133–46.36–2–*ct* 6
Bowling 58–2–29.00–0–0–2/17
He hit 1,000 runs in a season 14 times in England and once overseas, going on to 2,000 runs nine times (best 2,917, av 56.09, in 1951). His highest score was 331* for Middlesex v Worcestershire at Worcester in 1949 and he made three double centuries, all for his county. He was Middlesex coach 1958–68.

Robertson, L. G.
Amateur. Tail end batsman, bowler. *Team* D. R. Jardine's XI (1955).
Career batting
1–1–1–2–2*–no av–0–*ct* 2
Bowling 60–5–12.00–0–0–4/44

Robertson, William Parish
Amateur. *b:* 5.9.1879, Lima, Peru. *d:* 7.5.1950, Debden, Essex. Middle order right-hand batsman, wicket-keeper. *Sch* Harrow. *Teams* Middlesex (1900–19, 99 matches); Cambridge U (1901, blue). *Tour* Ranjitsinhji to North America 1899.
Career batting
116–187–13–4510–130–25.91–4–*ct* 61–*st* 15
Bowling 27–0
He hit 1,102 runs, av 27.55, in 1901. His first-class debut was for A. J. Webbe's XI in 1899.

Robertson-Glasgow, Raymond Charles
Amateur. *b:* 15.7.1901, Murrayfield, Edinburgh, Scotland. *d:* 4.3.1965, Buckhold, Berkshire. He died by his own hand. Opening, later lower order, right-hand batsman, right-arm fast medium bowler. *Sch* Charterhouse. *Teams* Oxford U (1920–23, blue all four years); Somerset (1920–35, 77 matches).
Career batting
144–223–64–2102–80–13.22–0–*ct* 88
Bowling 11959–464–25.77–28–6–9/38
His final first-class match was for Free Foresters in 1937. He took 108 wickets, av 17.40, in 1923; his best bowling was 9/38 for Somerset v Middlesex at Lord's in 1924. He was one of the most distinguished of cricket writers, both as a journalist for *The Morning Post* and other English newspapers and as an author of some notable books on the game.

Robins, Derrick Harold
Amateur. *b:* 27.6.1914, Bexleyheath, Kent. Lower order right-hand batsman, wicket-keeper. *Team* Warwickshire (1947, 2 matches).
Career batting
5–7–3–70–29*–17.50–0–*ct* 4
His final first-class match was for his own XI v Indians in 1971. He played no first-class cricket after 1947 until 1969. A great patron of cricket, he took teams of English cricketers regularly on overseas tours, including each winter from 1972/3 to 1979/80.

Robins, Glen Lello
Amateur. *b:* 23.10.1922, Kingston-upon-Thames, Surrey. Lower order batsman, slow left-arm bowler. *Sch* Merchant Taylors. *Team* Cambridge U (1947).
Career batting
1–2–1–0–0*–0.00–0–*ct* 0
Bowling 104–2–52.00–0–0–2/60

Robins, Robert Victor Charles
Amateur. *b:* 13.3.1935, Burnham, Buckinghamshire. Son of R. W. V. (Middlesex), nephew of W. V. H. (Army), brother-in-law of K. C. Came (Free Foresters). Lower order right-hand batsman, leg break and googly bowler. *Sch* Eton. *Team* Middlesex (1953–60, 44 matches). *Tours* MCC to East Africa 1957/8, to South America 1958/9; McAlpine to South Africa 1968/9 (none of these tours was first-class).
Career batting
60–92–9–1055–49–12.72–0–*ct* 19
Bowling 3597–107–33.61–3–0–7/78
His final first-class match was for MCC in 1962. He also played for Buckinghamshire (1950–51).

Robins, Robert Walter Vivian
Amateur. *b:* 3.6.1906, Stafford. *d:* 12.12.1968, Marylebone, London. Father of R. V. C. (Middlesex), brother of W. V. H. (Army), father-in-law of K. C. Came (Free Foresters). Middle order right-hand batsman, leg break bowler. *Sch* Highgate. *Teams* Middlesex (1925–51, 258 matches); Cambridge U (1926–28, blue all three years). *Tours* Cahn to Argentine 1929/30, to North America and Bermuda 1933 (not first-class); MCC to Australia 1936/7, to Canada 1951. *Tests* England (1929–37, 19 matches).
Career batting
379–565–39–13884–140–26.39–11–*ct* 221
Bowling 22580–969–23.30–54–4–8/69
Test batting
19–27–4–612–108–26.60–1–*ct* 12
Bowling 1758–64–27.46–1–0–6/32
He hit 1,000 runs in a season four times (best 1,397, av 31.04, in 1946) and in 1929 took 162 wickets, av 21.53, achieving the 'double' that season. He captained Middlesex from 1935 to 1938, 1946, 1947 and 1950, England in three Tests and was a Test Selector 1946–49, 1954, 1962–64, being Chairman in the last three years. He captained the MCC side to Canada in 1951 and was manager of the 1959/60 side to West Indies. His last first-class match was for MCC in 1958. He was Hon Secretary of Middlesex 1935–50. A good soccer player, he was inside left for Cambridge and Nottingham Forest.

Robins, William Vernon Harry
Amateur. *b:* 29.5.1907, Stafford. *d:* 26.6.1990, Congleton, Cheshire. Brother of R. W. V. (Middlesex), uncle of R. V. C. (Middlesex). Middle order left-hand batsman, leg break and googly bowler. *Sch* University College School, London. *Teams* Army (1931–37); Madras (1937/8 to 1938/9).
Career batting
8–13–1–207–60–17.25–0–*ct* 3
Bowling 563–15–37.53–0–0–4/36
His County cricket was for Staffordshire (1931).

Robinson, A. W.
Amateur. Middle order batsman. *Team* Worcestershire (1920–26, 6 matches).
Career batting
6–11–1–95–37–9.50–0–*ct* 2

Robinson, Albert George
Professional. *b:* 22.3.1917, Leicester. Lower order right-hand batsman, right-arm fast medium pace bowler. *Sch* Wyggeston GS. *Team* Northamptonshire (1937–46, 24 matches).
Career batting
24–37–12–167–32–6.68–0–*ct* 13
Bowling 1464–35–41.82–1–0–5/37
He also played for Cambridgeshire (1948–49) and Berkshire (1951–55).

Robinson, Arthur
Amateur. *b:* 1855. *d:* 24.2.1913, Lawrence Weston, Gloucestershire. Father of D. C. (Gloucestershire and Essex) and V. J. (Gloucestershire). Lower order right-hand batsman, right-arm slow bowler. *Team* Gloucestershire (1878, 3 matches).
Career batting
3–4–3–38–34*–38.00–0–*ct* 2

Robinson, Arthur Joseph Herbert
Amateur. *b: circa* 1896, Dublin, Ireland. *d:* 1937, Monkstown, Co Dublin, Ireland. Opening or middle order right-hand batsman. *Teams* Ireland (1924–29); Dublin University (1924).
Career batting
7–12–0–155–32–12.91–0–*ct* 3

Robinson, Arthur Leslie
Cricketer. *b:* 17.8.1946, Brompton, Yorkshire. Tail end left-hand batsman, left-arm fast medium bowler. *Team* Yorkshire (1971–77, 84 matches).
Career batting
84–69–31–365–30*–9.60–0–*ct* 46
Bowling 4927–196–25.13–7–0–6/61

Robinson, Crescens James
Amateur. *b:* 21.5.1864, Gloucester. *d:* 8.6.1941, Chelsea, London. Brother of Theodore (Somerset). Middle order right-hand batsman. *Sch* Mill Hill. *Team* Somerset (1885–96, 31 matches).
Career batting
32–51–8–547–55–12.72–0–*ct* 19
Bowling 3–0
He also played for Suffolk (1881).

Robinson, Canon Cyril Deason
Amateur. *b:* 18.7.1873, Durban, South Africa. *d:* 26.8.1948, Kearsney, Natal, South Africa. Brother of A. W. (Natal). Lower order right-hand batsman, wicket-keeper. *Teams* Cambridge U (1895–96); Natal (1905/6 to 1910/11). *Tours* Mitchell to North America 1895; South Africa to England 1907.
Career batting
30–51–8–542–41–12.60–0–*ct* 36–*st* 18
He played in only six first-class matches on the 1907 tour, being the reserve wicket-keeper. He played County cricket for Buckinghamshire (1894–1907).

Robinson, Douglas Charles
Amateur. *b:* 20.4.1884, Lawrence Weston, Bristol. *d:* 29.7.1963, Ham Court, Charlton Kings, Gloucestershire. Son of Arthur (Gloucestershire), brother of V. J. (Gloucestershire). Lower order right-hand batsman, wicket-keeper. *Sch* Marlborough. *Teams* Gloucestershire (1905–26, 124 matches); Essex (1908, 7 matches). *Tour* Tennyson to Jamaica 1927/8 (he did not play in first-class matches).
Career batting
155–267–14–4376–150*–17.29–1–*ct* 123–*st* 39
He captained Gloucestershire from 1924 to 1926.

Robinson, Edward
Amateur. *b:* 27.12.1862, Honley, Yorkshire. *d:* 3.9.1942, Clifton, Bristol. Middle order right-hand batsman. *Team* Yorkshire (1887, 1 match).
Career batting
1–2–1–23–23*–23.00–0–*ct* 0

Robinson, Ellis Pembroke
Professional. *b:* 10.8.1911, Denaby Main, Yorkshire. Nephew of G. L. (Nottinghamshire). Attacking lower order left-hand batsman, off break bowler, excellent close field. *Teams* Yorkshire (1934–49, 208 matches); Somerset (1950–52, 89 matches). *Tour* Yorkshire to Jamaica 1935/6.
Career batting
301–388–71–3492–75*–11.01–0–*ct* 265
Bowling 22784–1009–22.58–61–12–8/35
He took 100 wickets in a season five times (best 167, av 14.95, in 1946).

Robinson, Emmott
Professional. *b:* 16.11.1883, Keighley, Yorkshire. *d:* 17.11.1969, Hinckley, Leicestershire. Nephew of W. Flowers (Nottinghamshire). Middle order right-hand batsman, right-arm fast medium bowler, good cover point. *Team* Yorkshire (1919–31, 413 matches).
Career batting
416–460–78–9744–135*–25.50–7–*ct* 321
Bowling 19890–902–22.05–36–5–9/36
He hit 1,000 runs in a season twice (best 1,104, av 29.83, in 1921) and took 100 wickets once: 113, av 22.83, in 1928. His best bowling was 9 for 36 for Yorkshire v Lancashire at Bradford in 1920. He was a first-class umpire (1937–51), standing in one Test match (1938). He was Leicestershire coach 1946–48.

Robinson, Sir Foster Gotch
Amateur. *b:* 19.9.1880, Sneyd Park, Bristol. *d:* 31.10.1967, Eastwood Manor, East Harptree, Somerset. Brother of P. G. (Gloucestershire), father of J. F. (Gloucestershire). Middle order right-hand batsman, wicket-keeper. *Sch* Clifton. *Teams* London County (1900); Gloucestershire (1903–23, 68 matches).
Career batting
71–122–2–2121–144–17.67–2–*ct* 47–*st* 28
He appeared in the Oxford Freshmen's match in 1900. From 1919 to 1921 he captained Gloucestershire. He was President of Gloucestershire 1931–32. A member of the Jockey Club, he was a noted owner-breeder.

Robinson, Geoffrey
Cricketer. *b:* 13.1.1944, Bridlington, Yorkshire. Attacking middle order left-hand batsman, slow left-arm bowler, wicket-keeper. *Team* Minor Counties (1971–72).
Career batting
2–4–0–100–36–25.00–0–*ct* 0
His County cricket was for Lincolnshire (1965–86).

Robinson, George Adrian
Cricketer. *b:* 3.11.1949, Preston, Lancashire. Steady opening left-hand batsman, wicket-keeper. *Team* Oxford U (1970–71, blue 1971).
Career batting
14–25–0–573–62–22.92–0–*ct* 19–*st* 1

Robinson, George Edward
Amateur. *b:* 13.3.1861, Deytheur, Oswestry, Shropshire. *d:* 30.11.1944, Acton, Staffordshire. Lower order batsman, left-arm fast bowler. *Team* Oxford U (1881–83, blue all three years).
Career batting
17–30–11–168–28–8.84–0–*ct* 7
Bowling 1373–80–17.16–4–0–7/47
His County cricket was for Shropshire (1881–83).

Robinson, George Lutha
(known as George Luther Robinson)
Professional. *b:* 22.2.1873, Ruddington, Nottinghamshire. *d:* 23.3.1930, Burcroft, Conisbrough, Yorkshire. Uncle of E. P. (Yorkshire and Somerset). Lower order right-hand batsman, leg break bowler.

Robinson, George William

Team Nottinghamshire (1896, 5 matches).
Career batting
5–9–2–58–17–8.28–0–*ct* 2
Bowling 24–1–24.00–0–0–1/14

Robinson, George William
Professional until 1935, amateur in 1936. *b:* 15.2.1908, Kirkby-in-Ashfield, Nottinghamshire. *d:* 16.7.1967, Derby. Lower order right-hand batsman, slow left-arm bowler. *Team* Nottinghamshire (1930–36, 21 matches).
Career batting
21–20–7–39–10–3.00–0–*ct* 4
Bowling 1196–46–26.00–0–0–4/54
A useful soccer player he appeared for Mansfield Town.

Robinson, Henry
Professional. *b:* 12.5.1858, Yorkshire. *d:* 14.12.1909. Lower order batsman, useful bowler. *Team* Yorkshire (1879, 1 match).
Career batting
1–2–0–5–4–2.50–0–*ct* 0
Bowling 20–1–20.00–0–0–1/20

Robinson, Henry
Professional. *b:* 13.11.1863, Nottingham. Middle order batsman. *Team* Nottinghamshire (1889, 1 match).
Career batting
1–2–0–0–0–0.00–0–*ct* 0

Robinson, Henry Basil Oswin
Amateur. *b:* 3.3.1919, Eastbourne, Sussex. Lower order right-hand batsman, off break bowler. *Teams* Oxford U (1947–48, blue both years); Canada (1951–54). *Tour* Canada to England 1954.
Career batting
24–31–7–325–51–13.54–0–*ct* 16
Bowling 1442–53–27.20–3–0–6/55
He captained the 1954 Canadian touring team to England.

Robinson, Jethro Frederick
Amateur. *b:* 10.11.1914, Eastbourne, Sussex. Brother of M. T. (Sussex). Lower order batsman, slow left-arm bowler. *Sch* King's, Canterbury. *Teams* Sussex (1935–36, 2 matches); Cambridge U (1936).
Career batting
3–4–0–11–5–2.75–0–*ct* 3
Bowling 166–8–20.75–1–0–5/47

Robinson, John Foster
Amateur. *b:* 2.2.1909, Goldney House, Clifton, Bristol, Gloucestershire. *d:* 28.9.1988, Bristol. Son of F. G. (Gloucestershire), nephew of P. G. (Gloucestershire). Lower order right-hand batsman, leg break and googly bowler. *Sch* Harrow. *Team* Gloucestershire (1929, 1 match).
Career batting
1 match, did not bat–*ct* 0
Bowling 50–0
He did not appear in any first-class matches for the University whilst at Oxford.

Robinson, John James
Amateur. *b:* 28.6.1872, Burton-on-Trent, Staffordshire. *d:* 3.1.1959, Headingley, Leeds, Yorkshire. Middle order right-hand batsman, right-arm bowler. *Team* Cambridge U (1894, blue).
Career batting
10–18–6–173–29–14.41–0–*ct* 6
Bowling 690–28–24.64–2–0–7/93
His first-class debut was for MCC in 1893. An excellent rugby footballer, he played for Cambridge and England.

Robinson, John Sandford
Amateur. *b:* 5.2.1868, Arnold, Nottinghamshire. *d:* 21.4.1898, Worksop Manor, Nottinghamshire. He died after a fall from his horse. Middle order right-hand batsman, wicket-keeper. *Sch* Harrow. *Teams* Nottinghamshire (1888–96, 35 matches); Cambridge U (1888). *Tours* Hawke to India 1892/3, to North America 1894.
Career batting
48–74–6–751–72–11.04–0–*ct* 41–*st* 2
Bowling 3–0

Robinson, Jonathan David
Cricketer. *b:* 3.8.1966, Epsom, Surrey. Son of P. M. H. (L. C. Stevens' XI). Middle order left-hand batsman, right-arm medium pace bowler. *Sch* Lancing. *Team* Surrey (1988–92, 31 matches).
Career batting
31–49–10–898–79–23.02–0–*ct* 12
Bowling 1152–28–41.14–0–0–3/22

Robinson, Keith
Amateur. *b:* 17.12.1933, Thirsk, Yorkshire. Middle order batsman. *Team* Combined Services (1961).
Career batting
1–1–0–18–18–18.00–0–*ct* 0

Robinson, Kenneth Mark Lefebvre
Amateur. *b:* 16.2.1897, South Stoneham, Hampshire. *d:* 9.1.1963, Alverstoke, Hampshire. Middle order right-hand batsman, right-arm medium pace bowler. *Team* Royal Navy (1927).
Career batting
1–2–0–14–13–7.00–0–*ct* 0

Robinson, Lancelot Charles Digby
Amateur. *b:* 23.10.1905. *d:* 31.5.1935, Quetta, India. He was killed with his wife by an earthquake, which almost destroyed Quetta. Steady middle order right-hand batsman, right-arm slow bowler, good field. *Sch* Bedford. *Team* MCC (1934).
Career batting
1–1–0–39–39–39.00–0–*ct* 0
His County cricket was for Bedfordshire (1924–31).

Robinson, Mark Andrew
Cricketer. *b:* 23.11.1966, Hull, Yorkshire. Tail end right-hand batsman, right-arm fast medium bowler. *Teams* Northamptonshire (1987–90, 59 matches); Canterbury (1988/9); Yorkshire (1991–92, 35 matches). *Tour* Yorkshire to South Africa 1991/2.
Career batting
100–95–42–126–19*–2.37–0–*ct* 22
Bowling 7624–227–33.58–3–1–6/57
He failed to score in 12 successive first-class innings in 1990, a record in first-class cricket.

Robinson, Martin John
Cricketer. *b:* 12.9.1962, Tholthorpe, Yorkshire. Middle order left-hand batsman, right-arm fast medium bowler. *Team* MCC (1988–89).
Career batting
2–3–0–20–19–6.66–0–*ct* 0

Robinson, Maurice
Amateur. *b:* 16.7.1921, Lisburn, Co Antrim, Ireland. Sound middle order right-hand batsman, right-arm fast medium bowler. *Teams* Europeans (1942/3 to 1944/5); Hyderabad (1943/4); Madras (1944/5); Glamorgan (1946–50, 66 matches); Warwickshire (1951–52, 8 matches).
Career batting
83–134–11–2719–190–22.10–2–*ct* 22
Bowling 870–34–25.58–2–0–7/51

Robinson, Miles Trevor
Amateur. *b:* 13.12.1929, Eastbourne, Sussex. Brother of J. F. (Sussex). Lower order left-hand batsman, right-arm medium fast bowler. *Sch* Shrewsbury. *Team* Sussex (1947, 2 matches).
Career batting
2–2–0–4–4–2.00–0–*ct* 0
Bowling 157–0
He played in no first-class matches whilst at Oxford U, but did win blues for soccer.

Robinson, Paul Andrew
Cricketer. *b:* 16.7.1956, Boksburg, Transvaal, South Africa. Lower order right-hand batsman, right-arm fast medium bowler. *Teams* Northern Transvaal (1977/8 to 1987/8); Lancashire (1979, 1 match).
Career batting
34–51–13–567–49–14.92–0–*ct* 10
Bowling 2536–86–29.48–2–0–6/46
He also played for Cheshire (1978).

Robinson, Percy Gotch
Amateur. *b:* 2.11.1881, Sneyd Park, Bristol, Gloucestershire. *d:* 29.1.1951, Queen Charlton Manor, Somerset. Brother of F. G. (Gloucestershire), uncle of J. F. (Gloucestershire). Middle order right-hand batsman. *Sch* Clifton. *Team* Gloucestershire (1904–21, 26 matches).
Career batting
28–50–1–899–66–18.34–0–*ct* 23
Bowling 799–17–47.00–1–0–5/60

Robinson, Peter James
Cricketer. *b:* 9.2.1943, St John's, Worcester. Nephew of R. O. Jenkins (Worcestershire). Opening or middle order left-hand batsman, slow left-arm bowler. *Teams* Worcestershire (1963–64, 5 matches); Somerset (1965–77, 180 matches).
Career batting
185–287–55–4936–140–21.27–3–*ct* 170
Bowling 8101–297–27.27–10–1–7/10
He hit 1,158 runs, av 26.93, in 1970. He has been Somerset coach since 1981. A useful soccer player, he appeared for Worcester City.

Robinson, Peter Michael Heasty
Amateur. *b:* 14.10.1929, Port of Spain, Trinidad. Father of J. D. (Surrey). Middle order right-hand batsman, right-arm medium pace off break bowler. *Sch* Lancing. *Team* L. C. Stevens' XI (1961).
Career batting
1–2–0–19–12–9.50–0–*ct* 0
Bowling 41–0

Robinson, Phillip Edward
Cricketer. *b:* 3.8.1963, Keighley, Yorkshire. Middle order right-hand batsman, left-arm medium pace bowler. *Teams* Yorkshire (1984–91, 132 matches); Leicestershire (1992, 1 match).
Career batting
133–219–31–6687–189–35.56–7–*ct* 96
Bowling 238–1–238.00–0–0–1/10
He hit 1,000 runs in a season three times (best 1,402, av 43.81, in 1990). He also played for Cumberland (1992).

Robinson, Ralf Hubert
Amateur. *b:* 28.6.1885, Stratford, Essex. *d:* 23.8.1917, Westhoek Ridge, Ypres, Belgium. Lower order batsman, wicket-keeper. *Team* Essex (1912, 4 matches).
Career batting
4–7–2–25–11*–5.00–0–*ct* 9–*st* 4

Robinson, Raymond Thomas
Cricketer. *b:* 15.9.1940, Charmouth, Dorset. Middle order right-hand batsman. *Team* Somerset (1964, 1 match).
Career batting
1–2–0–0–0–0.00–0–*ct* 0

Robinson, Richard Daryl
Cricketer. *b:* 8.6.1946, East Melbourne, Victoria, Australia. Opening or middle order right-hand batsman, wicket-keeper. *Team* Victoria (1971/2 to 1981/2, 76 matches). *Tours* Australia to England 1975, 1977. *Tests* Australia (1977, 3 matches).
Career batting
97–153–33–4776–185–39.80–7–*ct* 289–*st* 40

Bowling 6-0
Test batting
3–6–0–100–34–16.66–0–*ct* 4

Coming to England in 1975 as reserve wicket-keeper, he was given few opportunities; in 1977 he was drafted into the Test side as a batsman, due to various injuries, but made little impact on the series.

Robinson, Robert
Professional. *b:* 1765, Ash, Surrey. *d:* 2.9.1822 or 2.10.1822, Ash, Surrey. Hard hitting middle order left-hand batsman. *Teams* Hampshire (1792–1816); Surrey (1794–1810); Kent (1795); Middlesex (1815).
Career batting
59–113–9–2168–93–20.84–0–*ct* 11
Bowling 22 wickets (no analyses)–0–0–3/?

Early in life he damaged the fingers of one hand in a fire and had the handle of his bat especially grooved to fit the injured hand. He made himself 'pads' of two thin angled boards to protect his legs, but being laughed at dispensed with them. Another of his innovations was a spiked shoe. His final first-class match was for Players in 1819.

Robinson, Robert Geoffrey
Professional. *b:* 23.9.1924, Wellingborough, Northamptonshire. *d:* 21.12.1973, Wellingborough, Northamptonshire. Middle order right-hand batsman, slow left-arm bowler. *Team* Northamptonshire (1946, 4 matches).
Career batting
4–8–1–85–53–12.14–0–*ct* 0
Bowling 90–0

Robinson, Robert Timothy
Cricketer. *b:* 21.11.1958, Skegby, Sutton-in-Ashfield, Nottinghamshire. Opening right-hand batsman, changed to middle order in 1988, right-arm medium pace bowler. *Team* Nottinghamshire (1978–92, 261 matches). *Tours* England to India 1984/5, 1988/9 (tour cancelled), to Sri Lanka 1984/5, to Sharjah (not first-class) 1984/5, to West Indies 1985/6, to Pakistan 1987/8, to New Zealand 1987/8, to Australia 1987/8, to India and Pakistan (World Cup) 1987/8; England XI to South Africa 1989/90. *Tests* England (1984/5 to 1989, 29 matches).
Career batting
312–544–71–20209–220*–42.72–46–*ct* 199
Bowling 254–3–84.66–0–0–1/22
Test batting
29–49–5–1601–175–36.38–4–*ct* 8
Bowling 0–0

He hit 1,000 runs in a season ten times, going on to 2,000 once: 2,032, av 50.80, in 1984. His highest score was 220* for Nottinghamshire v Yorkshire at Trent Bridge in 1990. After a successful Test series in 1985, he had little success during the following winter in West Indies. His Test career ended when he decided to tour South Africa. From 1988 to 1992 he captained Nottinghamshire.

Robinson, Sir Roy Lister
(created 1st Baron Robinson in 1947)
Amateur. *b:* 8.3.1883, Macclesfield, Adelaide, South Australia. *d:* 5.9.1952, Ottawa, Ontario, Canada. Lower order right-hand batsman, right-arm fast bowler. *Team* Oxford U (1908–09, blue both years).
Career batting
13–22–1–256–51–12.19–0–*ct* 7
Bowling 998–44–22.68–4–0–6/90

His final first-class match was for Gentlemen of England in 1910. He also represented the University at athletics and lacrosse. He died of pneumonia whilst leading the British Delegation to a Conference on Forestry.

Robinson, Theodore
Amateur. *b:* 16.2.1866, Beaminster, Dorset. *d:* 4.10.1959, West Town, Somerset. Brother of C. J. (Somerset). Middle order batsman, bowler. *Team* Somerset (1884–94, 10 matches).
Career batting
10–18–0–152–57–8.44–0–*ct* 3
Bowling 86–2–43.00–0–0–2/20

He was a member of the well-known family who fielded a complete team for some years. He also played for Glamorgan (pre first-class, 1889–91).

Robinson, Thomas Lloyd
Amateur. *b:* 21.12.1912, Sketty, Swansea, Glamorgan. Lower order right-hand batsman, right-arm medium fast bowler. *Sch* Wycliffe. *Team* Warwickshire (1946, 4 matches).
Career batting
4–7–1–27–13*–4.50–0–*ct* 0
Bowling 277–6–46.16–0–0–2/74

Robinson, Vivian John
Amateur. *b:* 16.5.1897, Lawrence Weston, Bristol, Gloucestershire. *d:* 28.2.1979, Warminster, Wiltshire. Son of Arthur (Gloucestershire), brother of D. C. (Gloucestershire and Essex). Lower order right-hand batsman, right-arm fast medium bowler. *Team* Gloucestershire (1923, 1 match).
Career batting
1–2–0–2–2–1.00–0–*ct* 1

Robinson, Walter
Professional. *b:* 29.11.1851, Greetland, Yorkshire. *d:* 14.8.1919. Hard hitting middle order right-hand batsman, right-hand medium pace round-arm bowler, cover point. *Teams* Yorkshire (1876–77, 7 matches); Lancashire (1880–88, 115 matches).
Career batting
129–213–11–3902–154–19.31–4–*ct* 52
Bowling 61–0

Robotham, Reginald
Amateur. *b:* 14.7.1911, Bidford-on-Avon, Warwickshire. *d:* 31.1.1978, Hastings, Sussex. Middle order right-hand batsman, occasional wicket-keeper. *Team* Sussex (1946, 1 match).
Career batting
1–2–0–31–21–15.50–0–*ct* 1

Robson, Andrew George
Cricketer. *b:* 27.4.1971, East Boldon, Co Durham. Tail end right-hand batsman, right-arm medium pace bowler. *Teams* Surrey (1991, 2 matches); Sussex (1992, 5 matches).
Career batting
7–7–3–3–3–0.75–0–*ct* 1
Bowling 508–9–56.44–0–0–4/37

Robson, Charles
Amateur. *b:* 20.6.1859, Kilburn, Middlesex. *d:* 27.9.1943, South Moor, Abingdon, Berkshire. Lower order right-hand batsman, slow right-arm bowler, wicket-keeper. *Teams* Middlesex (1881–83, 12 matches); Hampshire (1895–1906, 129 matches); London County (1903–04). *Tours* Ranjitsihji to North America 1899; MacLaren to Australia 1901/2.
Career batting
160–278–26–3840–101–15.23–1–*ct* 201–*st* 45
Bowling 165–2–82.50–0–0–1/2

He captained Hampshire 1900 to 1902. He first played for Hampshire (not first-class) in 1891.

Robson, Clayton Graeme Wynne
Amateur. *b:* 3.7.1901, Bareilly, India. *d:* 26.2.1989, Long Melford, Suffolk. Middle order right-hand batsman. *Sch* Malvern. *Teams* Worcestershire (1921, 2 matches); Middlesex (1926, 4 matches).
Career batting
6–10–1–136–46–15.11–0–*ct* 2

Robson, Ernest
Professional. *b:* 1.5.1870, Chapel Allerton, Leeds, Yorkshire. *d:* 23.5.1924, Bristol. He died following an operation. Middle order right-hand batsman, right-arm fast medium bowler. *Teams* Somerset (1895–1923, 424 matches); London County (1900).
Career batting
432–761–45–12620–163*–17.62–5–*ct* 258
Bowling 30337–1147–26.44–58–5–8/35

He hit 1,048 runs, av 31.75, in 1899. He also played for Cheshire (1891–93).

Robson, Henry
Professional. *b:* 1.8.1904, Chester-le-Street, Co Durham. *d:* 31.8.1968, Chester-le-Street, Co Durham. Lower order left-hand batsman, slow left-arm bowler. *Team* Minor Counties (1939).
Career batting
1–1–0–3–3–3.00–0–*ct* 0
Bowling 124–4–31.00–0–0–4/80

His County cricket was for Durham (pre first-class, 1928) and Northumberland (1932–47).

Roche, William
Professional. *b:* 20.7.1871, South Australia. *d:* 2.1.1950, East Brunswick, Melbourne, Victoria, Australia. Lower order right-hand batsman, off break bowler. *Teams* Victoria (1894/5 to 1897/8, 13 matches); Middlesex (1899–1900, 28 matches).
Career batting
62–96–33–924–77–14.66–0–*ct* 30
Bowling 4520–181–24.97–13–1–8/66

His first-class debut in England was for MCC in 1897.

Rochford, Peter
Professional. *b:* 27.8.1928, Halifax, Yorkshire. *d:* 18.6.1992, Stroud, Gloucestershire. Lower order right-hand batsman, wicket-keeper. *Team* Gloucestershire (1952–57, 80 matches).
Career batting
80–113–22–479–31*–5.26–0–*ct* 118–*st* 34

He was a first-class umpire (1975–77).

Rock, Claude William
Amateur. *b:* 9.6.1863, Deloraine, Tasmania, Australia. *d:* 27.7.1950, Longford, Tasmania, Australia. Brother of N. V. (Tasmania), father of H. O. (New South Wales). Steady middle order right-hand batsman, right-hand medium pace round-arm bowler. *Teams* Cambridge U (1884–86, blue all three years); Tasmania (1888/9 to 1892/3, 3 matches).
Career batting
31–55–5–809–102–16.18–1–*ct* 38
Bowling 2350–142–16.54–13–5–8/36

His County cricket was for Warwickshire (pre first-class, 1885–86).

Rock, David John
Cricketer. *b:* 20.4.1957, Southsea, Hampshire. Opening or middle order right-hand batsman, right-arm medium pace bowler. *Team* Hampshire (1976–79, 37 matches).
Career batting
37–65–1–1227–114–19.17–3–*ct* 19
Bowling 0–0

Rodger, Sir John Pickersgill
Amateur. *b:* 12.2.1851, Marylebone, London. *d:* 19.9.1910, Mayfair, Westminster, London. Brother of W. W. (Kent). Sound middle order right-hand batsman. *Sch* Eton. *Team* Kent (1870, 1 match).
Career batting
1–2–0–7–4–3.50–0–*ct* 0

He played in one or two trials at Oxford, but no first-class matches. For seven years he was Governor of the Gold Coast, retiring a few days before his death.

Rodger, Richard Gordon
Cricketer. *b:* 1.10.1947, Norwich, Norfolk. Middle order right-hand batsman, slow left-arm bowler. *Team* Scotland (1975).
Career batting
1–2–0–2–2–1.00–0–*ct* 0
Bowling 38–0
His County cricket as for Cheshire (1972–82).

Rodger, William Wallace
(changed his name to Rodger-Cunliffe in 1887)
Amateur. *b:* 13.1.1847, Marylebone, London. *d:* 23.10.1888, Barming Heath, Kent. Brother of J. F. (Kent). Middle order right-hand batsman. *Sch* Eton. *Team* Kent (1867–73, 17 matches).
Career batting
19–35–2–304–32–9.21–0–*ct* 3
Bowling 20–0
He did not play in any first-class matches whilst at Oxford University. His first-class debut was for Gentlemen of Kent in 1865. One of the leading billiards players of his day, he won the Champion Cue at Oxford and represented Oxford against Cambridge three times, afterwards playing in several notable contests.

Rodriguez, Chevalier Epifanio
Amateur. *b:* 1855, Spain. *d:* 20.11.1912, Westminster, London. Middle order batsman. *Team* MCC (1900).
Career batting
1–2–1–1–1*–1.00–0–*ct* 0

Rodriguez, William Vicente
Amateur. *b:* 25.6.1934, St Clair, Port of Spain, Trinidad. Middle order right-hand batsman, leg break and googly bowler. *Team* Trinidad (1953/4 to 1969/70). *Tours* West Indies to India and Pakistan 1958/9, to England 1963. *Tests* West Indies (1961/2 to 1967/8, 5 matches).
Career batting
64–98–15–2061–105–24.83–1–*ct* 36
Bowling 3342–119–28.08–8–0–7/90
Test batting
5–7–0–96–50–13.71–0–*ct* 3
Bowling 374–7–53.42–0–0–3/51
He played in one Test on the 1963 tour, but his opportunities were restricted due to cartilage trouble. He played soccer for Trinidad.

Rodwell, William Hunter
Amateur. *b:* 18.4.1850, Marylebone, London. *d:* 3.8.1929, Amersham, Buckinghamshire. Brother-in-law of H. G. Ruggles-Brise (Oxford U). Middle order batsman. *Sch* Harrow. *Team* MCC (1882).
Career batting
1–2–0–32–31–16.00–0–*ct* 1
His County cricket was for Suffolk (1868–76) and Essex (pre first-class, 1878).

Roe, Brian
Professional. *b:* 27.1.1939, Cleethorpes, Lincolnshire. Opening right-hand batsman. *Team* Somerset (1957–66, 131 matches).
Career batting
136–234–9–5010–128–22.26–4–*ct* 44
Bowling 104–2–52.00–0–0–1/43
He hit 1,000 runs in a season three times (best 1,552, av 26.30, in 1962). He also played for Devon (1972–74).

Roe, William Nichols
Amateur. *b:* 21.3.1861, Closworth, Somerset. *d:* 11.10.1937, Marylebone, London. Stylish middle order right-hand batsman, right-arm medium pace off break bowler, good deep field. *Sch* Clergy School, Canterbury. *Teams* Cambridge U (1882–83, blue 1883); Somerset (1882–99, 66 matches).
Career batting
83–141–8–2690–132–20.22–4–*ct* 35
Bowling 1005–32–31.40–0–0–3/17
He hit 415 not out for the Emmanuel Long Vacation Club v Caius Long Vacation Club in 1881. He first played for Somerset (pre first-class) in 1877.

Roebuck, Paul Gerrard Peter
Cricketer. *b:* 13.10.1963, Bath, Somerset. Brother of P. M. (Somerset). Lower order left-hand batsman, right-arm medium fast bowler. *Sch* Millfield. *Team* Cambridge U (1983–85, blue 1984–85); Gloucestershire (1984, 1 match); Glamorgan (1988, 2 matches).
Career batting
22–38–8–771–82–25.70–0–*ct* 8
Bowling 269–6–44.83–0–0–2/44

Roebuck, Peter Michael
Cricketer. *b:* 6.3.1956, Oxford. Brother of P. G. P. (Gloucestershire and Glamorgan). Opening right-hand batsman, off break bowler. *Sch* Millfield. *Teams* Somerset (1974–91, 306 matches); Cambridge U (1975–77, blue all three years).
Career batting
335–552–81–17552–221*–37.26–33–*ct* 162
Bowling 3540–72–49.16–1–0–6/50
He hit 1,000 runs in a season nine times (best 1,702, av 47.27, in 1984). His highest score was 221* for Somerset v Nottinghamshire at Trent Bridge in 1986. His determination and dedication helped his county recover from the traumatic events which led to the departure of Botham, Richards and Garner. He captained Somerset from 1986 to 1988. After retirement he became a fulltime journalist. He also played for Devon (1992).

Rogers, Basil Leonard
Professional. *b:* 20.6.1896, Bedford. *d:* 9.10.1975, Pateley Bridge, Yorkshire. Middle order batsman, useful bowler. *Team* Glamorgan (1923, 2 matches).
Career batting
2–4–1–46–16*–15.33–0–*ct* 0

Bowling 33–1–33.00–0–0–1/22

He also played for Bedfordshire (1911–24) and Oxfordshire (1932–35).

Rogers, Francis Galpin
Amateur. *b:* 7.4.1897, Bristol. *d:* 28.7.1967, Maumbury, Dorchester, Dorset. Forcing middle order right-hand batsman. *Teams* Gloucestershire (1924–31, 26 matches); Europeans (1924/5 to 1932/3); Madras (1933/4).
Career batting
37–63–4–1309–154–22.18–1–*ct* 22

Rogers, George Howard
Professional. *b:* 4.4.1905, Illogan North, Redruth, Cornwall. *d:* 24.2.1958, Camborne, Cornwall. Middle order right-hand batsman. *Team* Minor Counties (1939).
Career batting
1–2–0–8–8–4.00–0–*ct* 0

His County cricket was for Cornwall (1924–39).

Rogers, George John
Professional. *b:* 1.5.1815, Hackney, London. *d:* 2.9.1870, Holloway, London. Middle order right-hand batsman. *Team* Middlesex (1850–51, 3 matches).
Career batting
9–14–0–116–36–8.28–0–*ct* 9

His final first-class match was for the Surrey Club in 1854.

Rogers, George Russell
Amateur. *b:* 20.4.1847, West Brixton, London. *d:* 14.12.1905, Kensington, London. Middle order right-hand batsman. *Team* Surrey (1870, 5 matches).
Career batting
5–10–1–34–18–3.77–0–*ct* 2

Rogers, Harry Oliver
Professional. *b:* 21.1.1889, Hednesford, Staffordshire. *d:* 4.7.1956, Northwick, Worcester. Lower order left-hand batsman, right-arm medium pace bowler. *Team* Worcestershire (1923–28, 86 matches).
Career batting
86–146–31–1683–118*–14.63–1–*ct* 32
Bowling 3705–138–26.84–5–1–8/85

Rogers, Herbert James
Professional. *b:* 6.3.1893, Frimley, Surrey. Middle order left-hand batsman, off break bowler. *Team* Hampshire (1912–14, 7 matches).
Career batting
7–12–0–69–18–5.75–0–*ct* 0
Bowling 62–1–62.00–0–0–1/26

The Hampshire Year Book for many years carried a 'Roll of Honour' for the First World War which included Rogers – there are however a number of people of this name in the War Death records and it has not been possible to identify him.

Rogers, James Julian
Cricketer. *b:* 20.8.1958, Kendal, Westmorland. Middle order right-hand batsman, right-arm slow bowler. *Sch* Sedbergh. *Team* Oxford U (1979–81, blue all three years).
Career batting
26–45–3–693–54–16.50–0–*ct* 7
Bowling 39–1–39.00–0–0–1/24

His County cricket was for Cumberland (1979).

Rogers, John Hickling
Amateur. *b:* 7.8.1910, Birkenhead, Cheshire. Middle order right-hand batsman. *Sch* Birkenhead. *Team* Oxford U (1932).
Career batting
3–5–0–26–9–5.20–0–*ct* 2

His County cricket was for Cheshire (1930–34).

Rogers, John Philips
Amateur. *b:* 30.10.1860, Hackney, London. Lower order batsman, wicket-keeper. *Team* Middlesex (1891, 1 match).
Career batting
1–2–1–7–7*–7.00–0–*ct* 1

Rogers, Joseph Alfred
Professional. *b:* 1.2.1908, Oxford. *d:* 28.8.1968, Bath, Somerset. Lower order right-hand batsman, right-arm fast bowler. *Team* Gloucestershire (1929–33, 46 matches).
Career batting
46–56–2–461–59–8.53–0–*ct* 22
Bowling 1644–45–36.53–0–0–4/50

He also played for Oxfordshire (1928–35).

Rogers, Neville Hamilton
Professional. *b:* 9.3.1918, Cowley, Oxford. Sound opening right-hand batsman, excellent field. *Team* Hampshire (1946–55, 285 matches).
Career batting
298–529–28–16056–186–32.04–28–*ct* 197
Bowling 37–0

He hit 1,000 runs in a season nine times, going on to 2,000 once: 2,244, av 40.80, in 1952. He also played for Oxfordshire (1938).

Rogers, Peter James
Cricketer. *b:* 28.12.1928, Swansea, Glamorgan. Lower order right-hand batsman, off break or leg break bowler. *Team* MCC (1967).
Career batting
1–2–1–24–24*–24.00–0–*ct* 0
Bowling 95–0

Rogers, Rupert Ashby Cave
(known as Cave-Rogers)
Amateur. *b:* 27.5.1902, Cannock, Staffordshire. *d:* 2.5.1976, Eastbourne, Sussex. Opening right-hand batsman. *Sch* Malvern. *Team* Worcestershire (1919, 1 match).

Rogers, Stuart Scott

Career batting
1–1–0–3–3–3.00–0–*ct* 1
Bowling 25–0

Rogers, Stuart Scott
Amateur. *b:* 18.3.1923, Muswell Hill, Middlesex. *d:* 6.11.1969, Chartridge, Buckinghamshire. Attacking middle order right-hand batsman, excellent field. *Sch* Highgate. *Teams* Europeans (1946/7); Somerset (1948–53, 118 matches).
Career batting
119–202–11–3608–107*–18.89–3–*ct* 46
Bowling 145–2–72.50–0–0–2/13

He played for Cambridge U against Oxford in 1942 (not first-class). From 1950 to 1952 he was captain and secretary of Somerset. He hit 1,127 runs, av 25.61, in 1950.

Rogerson, George Henry
Amateur. *b:* 13.3.1896, Monks Coppenhall, Nantwich, Cheshire. *d:* 29.5.1961, Crewe, Cheshire. Middle order right-hand batsman. *Team* Lancashire (1923, 12 matches).
Career batting
12–20–1–340–47*–17.89–0–*ct* 3

Roll, Henry Trevor
Professional. *b:* 18.3.1905, Alloa, Clackmannan, Scotland. *d:* 25.5.1967, Downend, Gloucestershire. Grandfather of L. M. (Gloucestershire). Middle order right-hand batsman, right-arm medium pace bowler. *Team* Warwickshire (1927, 1 match).
Career batting
1–1–0–0–0–0.00–0–*ct* 1
Bowling 40–0

He was a noted batsman in London Club cricket for some years.

Roll, Lawson Macgregor
Cricketer. *b:* 8.3.1965, Thornbury, Gloucestershire. Grandson of H. T. (Warwickshire). Lower order right-hand batsman, off break bowler. *Team* Gloucestershire (1984, 1 match).
Career batting
1 match, did not bat–*ct* 0
Bowling 49–0

Roller, Charles Trevor
Amateur. *b:* 28.2.1865, Clapham Common, London. *d:* 15.11.1912, Eastbourne, Sussex. Brother of W. E. (Surrey). Middle order right-hand batsman, right-arm medium pace bowler, third man. *Sch* Westminster. *Team* Surrey (1886, 1 match).
Career batting
1–2–0–15–14–7.50–0–*ct* 0

Roller, William Eyton
Amateur. *b:* 1.2.1858, Clapham Common, London. *d:* 27.8.1949, Bayswater, London. Brother of C. T. (Surrey). Forceful middle order right-hand batsman, right-arm medium pace bowler, good field, occasional wicket-keeper. *Sch* Westminster. *Team* Surrey (1881–90, 102 matches). *Tours* Sanders to North America 1885, 1886.
Career batting
120–193–12–3820–204–21.10–7–*ct* 75
Bowling 3728–190–19.62–4–0–6/44

He did not appear in any first-class matches whilst at Cambridge – one of the best cricketers who was not awarded a blue. His highest score was 204 for Surrey v Sussex at the Oval in 1885. He was also a noted golfer.

Rollins, Herbert
Amateur. *b:* 29.12.1899, Dublin, Ireland. *d:* 17.6.1921, Dublin, Ireland. Opening right-hand batsman. *Team* Ireland (1920).
Career batting
1–2–0–11–8–5.50–0–*ct* 1

Rollins, Robert John
Cricketer. *b:* 30.1.1974, Plaistow, Essex. Lower order right-hand batsman, wicket-keeper. *Team* Essex (1992, 1 match).
Career batting
1–2–0–19–13–9.50–0–*ct* 2

Romaines, Paul William
Cricketer. *b:* 25.12.1955, Bishop Auckland, Co Durham. Opening or middle order right-hand batsman, off break bowler. *Teams* Northamptonshire (1975–76, 6 matches); Gloucestershire (1982–91, 161 matches); Griqualand West (1984/5). *Tour* Gloucestershire to Sri Lanka 1986/7.
Career batting
173–309–23–8120–186–28.39–13–*ct* 68
Bowling 247–4–61.75–0–0–3/42

He also played for Durham (pre first-class, 1977–81). He hit 1,000 runs in a season three times (best 1,844 runs, av 35.46, in 1984).

Romans, George
Amateur. *b:* 30.11.1876, Gloucester. *d:* 2.1.1946, Bedminster, Somerset. Middle order right-hand batsman. *Team* Gloucestershire (1899–1903, 11 matches).
Career batting
11–19–3–218–62–13.62–0–*ct* 4

A good rugby footballer, he played full back for Gloucestershire.

Rome, David Audley Moberley
Amateur. *b:* 14.4.1910, Marylebone, London. *d:* 20.5.1970, Kennington, London. He died as the result of a fall at the Oval. Middle order right-hand batsman, right-arm medium pace bowler. *Sch* Harrow. *Team* Middlesex (1930–33, 4 matches). *Tours* Martineau to Egypt 1935, 1936 and 1937 (not first-class).
Career batting
4–6–0–56–32–9.33–0–*ct* 1
Bowling 11–0

He appeared in the Freshmen's and Seniors' matches at Cambridge and was later a major figure in the Free Foresters and I Zingari. For many years he was a member of Surrey CCC Committee.

Romney, Francis William
Amateur. *b:* 25.11.1873, Tewkesbury, Gloucestershire. *d:* 28.1.1963, Malvern, Worcestershire. Middle order right-hand batsman. *Sch* Malvern. *Team* Worcestershire. (1900, 4 matches).
Career batting
4–7–3–39–20*–9.75–0–*ct* 0
He first played for Worcestershire (pre first-class) in 1895.

Rooney, E. A.
Amateur. Middle order batsman. *Team* Ireland (1913–14).
Career batting
2–3–1–34–12*–17.00–0–*ct* 1

Roope, Graham Richard James
Cricketer. *b:* 12.7.1946, Fareham, Hampshire. Middle order right-hand batsman, right-arm medium pace bowler, brilliant slip field. *Sch* Bradfield. *Teams* Surrey (1964–82, 342 matches); Griqualand West (1973/4). *Tours* MCC to Ceylon and Far East 1969/70, to Pakistan, India and Sri Lanka 1972/3; Robins to South Africa 1973/4; England to Pakistan and New Zealand 1977/8; International Wanderers to South Africa 1974/5, to Rhodesia 1975/6. *Tests* England (1972/3 to 1978, 21 matches).
Career batting
403–647–129–19116–171–36.90–26–*ct* 602–*st* 2
Bowling 8404–225–37.35–4–0–5/14
Test batting
21–32–4–860–77–30.71–0–*ct* 35
Bowling 76–0
He hit 1,000 runs in a season eight times (best 1,641, av 44.35, in 1971). He appeared for Berkshire in 1963 and returned to that County after leaving Surrey (1983–88). His last first-class match was for Minor Counties in 1986. A useful soccer player, he kept goal for Corinthian Casuals.

Roopnaraine, Rupert
Cricketer. *b:* 31.1.1943, Georgetown, British Guiana. Lower order right-hand batsman, off break bowler. *Team* Cambridge U (1964–66, blue 1965–66).
Career batting
29–52–14–302–50*–7.94–0–*ct* 7
Bowling 2119–58–36.53–2–0–8/88
His County cricket was for Cambridgeshire (1967).

Root, Charles Frederick
Professional. *b:* 16.4.1890, Somercotes, Derbyshire. *d:* 20.1.1954, Wolverhampton, Staffordshire. Hard hitting lower order right-hand batsman, right-arm fast medium pace bowler. *Teams* Derbyshire (1910–20, 57 matches); Worcestershire (1921–32, 284 matches). *Tour* MCC to West Indies 1925/6. *Tests* England (1926, 3 matches).
Career batting
365–586–51–7911–107–14.78–1–*ct* 244
Bowling 31933–1512–21.11–125–33–9/23
Test batting
3 matches, did not bat–*ct* 1
Bowling 194–8–24.25–0–0–4/84
He took 100 wickets in a season nine times, going on to 200 once: 219, av 17.21, in 1925. In 1928 he hit 1,044 runs, av 20.88, and achieved the 'double' for the only time in his career. Three times he captured nine wickets in an innings, his best analysis being 9/23 for Worcestershire v Lancashire at Worcester in 1931. His last first-class match was for Sir L. Parkinson's XI in 1933. He was a first-class umpire (1947–48) and Leicestershire coach (1949–50). After retiring from first-class cricket he became well-known as a sporting journalist.

Roper, Arthur William
Amateur. *b:* 20.2.1917, Petersham, Sydney, New South Wales, Australia. *d:* 4.9.1972, Woy Woy, New South Wales, Australia. Lower order right-hand batsman, right-arm fast medium bowler. *Team* New South Wales (1939/40, 2 matches). *Tours* Australian Services to England 1945, to India and Ceylon 1945/6.
Career batting
11–15–0–102–28–6.80–0–*ct* 11
Bowling 503–13–38.69–0–0–2/9

Roper, Arthur William Frederick
Amateur. *b:* 12.1.1890, Bedminster, Somerset. *d:* 21.6.1956, Marylebone, London. Middle order batsman. *Team* Gloucestershire (1920–21, 13 matches).
Career batting
13–21–2–226–55–11.89–0–*ct* 7
Bowling 7–0

Roper, Colin
Professional. *b:* 25.7.1936, Litton Cheney, Bridport, Dorset. Lower order right-hand batsman, wicket-keeper. *Team* Hampshire (1957, 1 match).
Career batting
1–1–0–7–7–7.00–0–*ct* 1
He also played for Dorset (1959–69).

Roper, Donald George Beaumont
Amateur. *b:* 14.12.1922, Botley, Hampshire. Middle order batsman. *Team* Hampshire (1947, 1 match).
Career batting
1–2–0–30–30–15.00–0–*ct* 0
A well-known soccer player, he appeared for Southampton and Arsenal.

Roper, Edward
Amateur. *b:* 8.4.1851, Richmond, Yorkshire. *d:* 27.4.1921, South Liverpool, Lancashire. He died after an appendicitis operation. Middle order right-hand

batsman. *Sch* Clifton. *Teams* Lancashire (1876–86, 28 matches); Yorkshire (1878–80, 5 matches).
Career batting
36–59–3–715–68–12.76–0–*ct* 9
Bowling 6–1–6.00–0–0–1/6

His final first-class match was for Liverpool and District in 1893. He was for many years involved in the organisation of cricket in the Liverpool area.

Rose, Alfred
Professional. *b:* 15.2.1894, Glossop, Derbyshire. *d:* 21.6.1985, Kilton, Worksop, Nottinghamshire. Middle order right-hand batsman. *Team* Derbyshire (1924, 1 match).
Career batting
1–1–0–0–0–0.00–0–*ct* 0

Rose, Brian Charles
Cricketer. *b:* 4.6.1950, Dartford, Kent. Opening left-hand batsman, left-arm medium pace bowler. *Team* Somerset (1969–87, 214 matches). *Tours* England to Pakistan and New Zealand 1977/8, to West Indies 1980/1. *Tests* England (1977/8 to 1980/1, 9 matches).
Career batting
270–448–50–13236–205–33.25–25–*ct* 124
Bowling 289–8–36.12–0–0–3/9
Test batting
9–16–2–358–70–25.57–0–*ct* 4

He hit 1,000 runs in a season eight times (best 1,624, av 46.40, in 1976). His only double century was 205 for Somerset v Northamptonshire at Weston-super-Mare in 1977. He captained Somerset from 1978 to 1983. He was Cricket Manager to Somerset but resigned at the end of the 1988 season.

Rose, Edward McQueen
Amateur. *b:* 2.9.1936, Oxted, Surrey. Middle order left-hand batsman, off break bowler. *Sch* Rugby. *Team* Cambridge U (1958–60).
Career batting
24–47–2–700–57–15.55–0–*ct* 8
Bowling 19–1–19.00–0–0–1/9

Rose, Graham David
Cricketer. *b:* 12.4.1964, Tottenham, Middlesex. Middle order right-hand batsman, right-arm medium pace bowler. *Teams* Middlesex (1985–86, 7 matches); Somerset (1987–92, 115 matches).
Career batting
122–159–36–3726–132–30.29–3–*ct* 57
Bowling 8340–264–31.59–4–0–6/41

He hit 1,000 runs, av 55.55, in 1990.

Rose, John
Professional. *b:* 24.12.1853, Warwick. *d:* 6.11.1920, Tiddington, Warwickshire. Lower order right-hand batsman, slow right-arm bowler, wicket-keeper. *Team* Surrey (1878, 1 match).
Career batting
1–2–0–0–0–0.00–0–*ct* 0
Bowling 2–1–2.00–0–0–1/2

He also played for Warwickshire (pre first-class, 1873–85).

Rose, Michael Harrison
Cricketer. *b:* 8.4.1942, Hereford. Middle order right-hand batsman, excellent outfield. *Sch* Pocklington. *Teams* Cambridge U (1962–64, blue 1963–64); Leicestershire (1963–64, 4 matches).
Career batting
31–52–4–808–86–16.83–0–*ct* 11
Bowling 0–0

Rose, Thomas Ginnever
Professional. *b:* 16.3.1901, Ilkeston, Derbyshire. *d:* 8.8.1979, St Ives, Cornwall. Lower order left-hand batsman, slow left-arm bowler. *Team* Worcestershire (1922, 6 matches).
Career batting
6–10–1–47–15–5.22–0–*ct* 1
Bowling 219–7–31.28–0–0–3/68

Rose, William Molyneux
Amateur. *b:* 20.9.1842, Wolston Grange, Warwickshire. *d:* 13.1.1917, Wolston Grange, Warwickshire. Lower order right-hand batsman, right-hand slow under-arm bowler. *Sch* Eton. *Team* MCC (1867–71). *Tour* Fitzgerald to North America 1872 (not first-class).
Career batting
7–10–2–35–12–4.37–0–*ct* 10
Bowling 219–23–9.52–2–1–8/71

His County cricket was for Buckinghamshire (1866–68).

Roseberry, Andrew
Cricketer. *b:* 2.4.1971, Sunderland, Co Durham. Brother of M. A. (Middlesex). Middle order right-hand batsman, right-arm medium pace bowler. *Sch* Durham. *Team* Leicestershire (1992, 1 match).
Career batting
1–2–0–14–14–7.00–0–*ct* 0

Roseberry, Michael Anthony
Cricketer. *b:* 28.11.1966, Houghton-le-Spring, Co Durham. Brother of Andrew (Leicestershire). Opening right-hand batsman, right-arm medium pace bowler. *Sch* Durham. *Team* Middlesex (1986–92, 120 matches).
Career batting
120–201–25–6782–173–38.53–15–*ct* 83
Bowling 382–4–95.50–0–0–1/1

He hit 1,000 runs in a season three times going on to 2,000 in 1992, when his record was 2,044, av 56.77. He also played for Durham (pre first-class, 1984).

Ross, Alexander
Amateur. *b:* 3.1.1895, Arbroath, Angus, Scotland. *d:* 12.12.1972, Gosport, Hampshire. Tail end right-hand batsman, wicket-keeper. *Team* Civil Service (1927).

Career batting
1–2–1–1–1–1.00–0–*ct* 0

Ross, Arthur Annesley Somerset Luce
Amateur. *b:* 13.7.1869, Bathampton, Somerset. *d:* 9.4.1947, Hove, Sussex. Opening or middle order batsman. *Sch* Bath College. *Team* Cambridge U (1889).
Career batting
2–3–0–24–17–8.00–0–*ct* 0
His County cricket was for Somerset (pre first-class, 1889).

Ross, Arthur Patrick Aloysius
Amateur. *b:* 21.1.1872, Dublin, Ireland. Middle order batsman. *Sch* Downside. *Team* Dublin University (1895).
Career batting
2–4–0–22–11–5.50–0–*ct* 0

Ross, Charles Hoadley Ashe
Amateur. *b:* 22.7.1852, Bath, Somerset. *d:* 5.2.1911, Hove, Sussex. Brother of Hamilton (Middlesex and Somerset). Attacking opening right-hand batsman, right-arm fast bowler, wicket-keeper. *Team* Middlesex (1875, 2 matches).
Career batting
3–6–1–19–10–3.80–*ct* 2

Ross, Christopher Jonathan
Cricketer. *b:* 24.6.1954, Warri, Nigeria. Tail end right-hand batsman, right-arm medium pace bowler. *Teams* Wellington (1975/6); Oxford U (1978–80, blue all three years).
Career batting
31–41–13–132–23*–4.71–0–*ct* 8
Bowling 1938–55–35.23–0–0–4/34
He captained Oxford in 1980.

Ross, Hamilton
Amateur. *b:* 26.8.1849, Grenada, Windard Islands. *d:* 29.3.1938, Grenada, Windward Islands. Brother of C. H. A. (Middlesex). Middle order right-hand batsman, wicket-keeper. *Teams* Middlesex (1876, 1 match); Somerset (1883–91, 5 matches).
Career batting
20–35–1–337–91–9.91–0–*ct* 9–*st* 2
His first-class debut was for the Gentlemen in 1874. He first played for Somerset (pre first-class) in 1878.

Ross, Nicholas Peter Gilbert
Cricketer. *b:* 2.10.1947, West End, Edinburgh, Scotland. Lower order left-hand batsman, leg break and googly bowler. *Sch* Marlborough. *Team* Cambridge U (1969–70, blue 1969).
Career batting
8–14–6–224–68–28.00–0–*ct* 5
Bowling 261–9–29.00–0–0–2/22
His County cricket was for Cambridgeshire (1979).

Ross, Nigel Douglas Carne
Amateur. *b:* 21.12.1882, Penzance, Cornwall. *d:* 27.1.1933, Manchester, Lancashire. Middle order batsman. *Sch* Uppingham. *Team* Cambridge U (1905).
Career batting
1–2–0–38–26–19.00–0–*ct* 2
His County cricket was for Buckinghamshire (1910–12). He won a blue for lacrosse.

Ross, Nigel Patrick Dorai
Cricketer. *b:* 5.4.1953, Chelsea, London. Middle order right-hand batsman, right-arm medium pace bowler, wicket-keeper. *Team* Middlesex (1973–77, 25 matches).
Career batting
25–36–3–506–53–15.33–0–*ct* 21
Bowling 13–0

Ross, P. C.
Amateur. Lower order right-hand batsman, useful bowler. *Team* Ireland (1912).
Career batting
1–2–0–29–26–14.50–0–*ct* 0
Bowling 99–2–49.50–0–0–2/99

Ross, Thomas Couland
Amateur. *b:* 14.2.1872, Belfast, Ireland. *d:* 2.1.1947, Foxrock, Co Dublin, Ireland. Middle order right-hand batsman, off break bowler. *Team* Ireland (1902–10).
Career batting
10–19–3–320–89–20.00–0–*ct* 8
Bowling 901–46–19.58–5–0–7/82

Rotherham, Gerard Alexander
Amateur. *b:* 28.5.1899, Allesley, Coventry, Warwickshire. *d:* 31.1.1985, Bakewell, Derbyshire. Nephew of Hugh (Warwickshire). Lower order right-hand batsman, right-arm medium pace bowler. *Sch* Rugby. *Teams* Cambridge U (1919–20, blue 1919); Warwickshire (1919–21, 44 matches); Wellington (1928/9).
Career batting
65–107–11–1801–84*–18.76–0–*ct* 48
Bowling 5105–180–28.36–8–0–7/69

Rotherham, Hugh
Amateur. *b:* 16.3.1861, Allesley, Coventry, Warwickshire. *d:* 24.2.1939, Coventry, Warwickshire. Uncle of G. A. (Warwickshire). Lower order right-hand batsman, right-hand fast round-arm bowler, wicket-keeper. *Sch* Uppingham. *Team* Warwickshire (1903, 1 match). *Tour* Sanders to North America 1886.
Career batting
23–32–7–179–33–7.16–0–*ct* 21
Bowling 2007–101–19.87–8–2–8/57
His first-class debut was for An England XII in 1880. For several years in the 1880s he lived in Australia. A noted rugby three-quarter, he played for Coventry. He first played for Warwickshire (pre first-class) in 1883.

Rothery, James William
Professional. *b:* 5.9.1876, Staincliffe, Yorkshire. *d:* 2.6.1919, Beckett Park, Leeds, Yorkshire. He died as the result of wounds received in the war. Stylish middle order right-hand batsman. *Team* Yorkshire (1903–10, 150 matches).
Career batting
151–238–18–4619–161–20.99–3–*ct* 45
Bowling 44–2–22.00–0–0–1/18
He also played for Durham (pre first-class, 1913).

Rothschild, Lord Nathaniel Mayer Victor
Amateur. *b:* 31.10.1910, Kensington, London. *d:* 20.3.1990, Westminster, London. Stylish opening right-hand batsman, leg break bowler, good slip. *Sch* Harrow. *Teams* Northamptonshire (1929–31, 10 matches); Cambridge U (1930).
Career batting
11–19–1–282–63–15.66–0–*ct* 8
Bowling 53–0
During the Second World War he served in Military Intelligence and was awarded the George Medal 'for dangerous work in hazardous circumstances'.

Rought-Rought, Basil William
Amateur. *b:* 15.9.1904, Brandon, Suffolk. Brother of D. C. (Cambridge U) and R. C. (Cambridge U). Middle order left-hand batsman. *Team* Minor Counties (1937–38).
Career batting
4–8–0–229–61–28.62–0–*ct* 3
His County cricket was for Norfolk (1926–48). His first-class debut was for H. D. G. Leveson-Gower's XI in 1933.

Rought-Rought, Desmond Charles
Amateur. *b:* 3.5.1912, Brandon, Suffolk. *d:* 7.1.1970, Cambridge. He died following a road accident. Brother of B. W. (Minor Counties) and R. C. (Cambridge U). Attacking middle order right-hand batsman, right-arm fast medium bowler. *Team* Cambridge U (1934–37, blue 1937).
Career batting
24–39–5–739–92–21.73–0–*ct* 16
Bowling 2129–74–28.77–3–1–7/100
His County cricket was for Norfolk (1931–47) and his final first-class match for Free Foresters in 1947.

Rought-Rought, Rodney Charles
Amateur. *b:* 17.2.1908, Brandon, Suffolk. *d:* 5.5.1979, Fulham, London. He died following an accident. Brother of D. C. (Cambridge U) and B. W. (Minor Counties). Hard hitting lower order right-hand batsman, fast medium bowler. *Team* Cambridge U (1930–32, blue 1930 and 1932).
Career batting
34–51–18–457–52–13.84–0–*ct* 17
Bowling 2892–122–23.70–6–2–7/36
His County cricket was for Norfolk (1926–47) and his final first-class match for Free Foresters in 1937.

Round, Charles James
Amateur. *b:* 3.9.1885, Kensington, London. *d:* 6.10.1945, Birch Hall, Essex. Son of James (Oxford U), brother-in-law of H. W. De Zoete (Essex) and C. E. Higginbotham (Army). Lower order batsman, bowler. *Sch* Eton and Winchester. *Team* Essex (1921, 2 matches).
Career batting
2–4–0–9–8–2.25–0–*ct* 0
Bowling 62–1–62.00–0–0–1/49

Round, Rt Hon James
Amateur. *b:* 6.4.1842, Colchester, Essex. *d:* 24.12.1916, Birch Hall, Essex. Father of C. J. (Essex), father-in-law of C. E. Higginbotham (Army). Defensive lower order right-hand batsman, right-hand under-arm bowler, wicket-keeper. *Sch* Eton. *Team* Oxford U (1864).
Career batting
22–34–6–472–142–16.85–1–*ct* 20–*st* 14
His County cricket was for Essex (pre first-class, 1876–82) as captain as well as being Chairman of the Club. His final first-class match was for MCC in 1869. For 38 years he represented East and North East Essex in the House of Commons.

Roundell, James
Cricketer. *b:* 23.10.1951, Nantwich, Cheshire. Tail end left-hand batsman, right-arm medium fast bowler. *Sch* Winchester. *Team* Cambridge U (1973, blue).
Career batting
10–14–9–36–10*–7.20–0–*ct* 1
Bowling 509–9–56.55–0–0–3/12

Rouse, Stephen John
Cricketer. *b:* 20.1.1949, Merthyr Tydfil, Glamorgan. Lower order left-hand batsman, left-arm medium pace bowler. *Team* Warwickshire (1970–81, 124 matches). *Tours* Robins to South Africa 1974/5, West Indies 1974/5 (not first-class).
Career batting
127–156–34–1924–93–15.77–0–*ct* 55
Bowling 8312–270–30.78–5–0–6/34

Routledge, Reginald
Professional. *b:* 12.6.1920, North Kensington, London. Aggressive middle order right-hand batsman, right-arm medium pace bowler. *Team* Middlesex (1946–54, 64 matches).
Career batting
65–98–18–1331–121–16.63–2–*ct* 38
Bowling 1604–38–42.21–0–0–4/29
He played for Devon in 1947.

Rowan, Athol Matthew Burchell
Amateur. *b:* 7.2.1921, Kensington, Johannesburg, South Africa. Brother of E. A. B. (South Africa). Lower order right-hand batsman, off break bowler, good field. *Team* Transvaal (1939/40 to 1949/50).

Tours South Africa to England 1947, 1951. *Tests* South Africa (1947–51, 15 matches).
Career batting
58–82–20–1492–100*–24.06–1–*ct* 25
Bowling 6408–273–23.47–20–7–9/19
Test batting
15–23–6–290–41–17.05–0–*ct* 7
Bowling 2084–54–38.59–4–0–5/68

He was the only tourist to take 100 wickets on the 1947 tour: 102, av 24.97, but was expensive in the Tests. In 1951 he was troubled with a knee injury and bowled less, though being more effective in the Tests. His best bowling was 9/19 for Transvaal v Australians at Johannesburg in 1949/50.

Rowan, Eric Alfred Burchell
Amateur. *b:* 20.7.1909, Johannesburg, South Africa. Brother of A. M. B. (South Africa). Sound opening right-hand batsman, right-arm medium pace bowler. *Teams* Transvaal (1929/30 to 1953/4); Eastern Province (1945/6). *Tours* South Africa to England 1935, 1951. *Tests* South Africa (1935–51, 26 matches).
Career batting
157–258–17–11710–306*–48.58–30–*ct* 83
Bowling 168–4–42.00–0–0–3/11
Test batting
26–50–5–1965–236–43.66–3–*ct* 14
Bowling 7–0

He scored more runs than any of his colleagues on the 1935 tour with 1,948, av 44.27, but was not so successful in the Tests. In 1951 he repeated his record with 1,852 runs, av 50.05, and also headed the Test averages with 515 runs, av 57.22. He hit two double centuries on the 1951 tour, including 236 v England at Headingley. His highest score was 306* for Transvaal v Natal at Johannesburg in 1939/40.

Rowbotham, Joseph
Professional. *b:* 8.7.1831, Highfield, Sheffield, Yorkshire. *d:* 22.12.1899, Morecambe, Lancashire. Fine middle order right-hand batsman. *Team* Yorkshire (1861–76, 100 matches). *Tours* Willsher to North America 1868 (not first-class).
Career batting
141–247–15–3694–113–15.92–3–*ct* 70–*st* 5
Bowling 37–3–12.33–0–0–3/37

His first-class debut was for Sheffield in 1854. He captained Yorkshire 1871–75. He umpired one Test match in 1884.

Rowden, George Henry
Amateur. *b:* 6.10.1914, Midsomer Norton, Somerset. Middle order right-hand batsman, off break bowler. *Team* Somerset (1936, 1 match).
Career batting
1–2–0–11–9–5.50–0–*ct* 0

Rowe, Charles James Castell
Cricketer. *b:* 27.11.1951, Hong Kong. Opening or middle order right-hand batsman, right-arm off break bowler. *Sch* King's School, Canterbury. *Teams* Kent (1974–81, 122 matches); Glamorgan (1982–84, 53 matches).
Career batting
175–277–43–6173–147*–26.38–6–*ct* 63
Bowling 5127–128–40.05–3–1–6/46

He hit 1,000 runs in a season twice (best 1,071, av 32.45, in 1982).

Rowe, Edmund John
Professional. *b:* 21.7.1920, Netherfield, Nottinghamshire. *d:* 17.12.1989, Bridlington, Yorkshire. Tail end right-hand batsman, wicket-keeper. *Team* Nottinghamshire (1949–57, 103 matches).
Career batting
103–122–68–295–16–5.46–0–*ct* 152–*st* 52

He was a first-class umpire (1971).

Rowe, Francis Coryndon Carpenter
Amateur. *b:* 27.7.1859, Colombo, Ceylon. *d:* 5.4.1897, at sea on board SS *Oruba* on a voyage from Australia to England. Middle order left-hand batsman, wicket-keeper. *Sch* Harrow. *Team* Cambridge U (1880–81, blue 1881).
Career batting
6–10–0–155–38–15.50–0–*ct* 3

Rowe, Francis Erskine
Amateur. *b:* 30.11.1864, Hartford End, Essex. *d:* 17.5.1928, Littlehampton, Sussex. Son of A. W. (Cambridge U 1859). Sound middle order right-hand batsman, occasional wicket-keeper. *Sch* Marlborough. *Team* Essex (1894–95, 3 matches).
Career batting
4–7–1–53–19–8.83–0–*ct* 2

He first played for Essex (pre first-class) in 1886. He did not appear in any first-class matches whilst at Cambridge U. He also played for Berkshire (1900–11). His first-class debut was for Cambridge University, Past and Present in 1890.

Rowe, George Alexander
Amateur. *b:* 15.6.1874, Grahamstown, South Africa. *d:* 8.1.1950, Pinelands, Cape Town, South Africa. Tail end right-hand batsman, slow left-arm bowler. *Team* Western Province (1893/4 to 1906/7). *Tours* South Africa to England 1894 (not first-class), 1901. *Tests* South Africa (1895/6 to 1902/3, 5 matches).
Career batting
36–62–19–303–21*–7.04–0–*ct* 22
Bowling 3592–170–21.12–13–5–8/25
Test batting
5–9–3–26–13*–4.33–0–*ct* 4
Bowling 456–15–30.40–1–0–5/115

He was easily the most successful bowler on the non-first-class 1894 tour with 136 wickets, av 12.89. He repeated his success in 1901 with 136, av 18.54, and in first-class matches took 70 wickets, 25.00.

Rowe, Lawrence George
Cricketer. *b:* 8.1.1949, Whitfield Town, Kingston, Jamaica. Attacking opening or middle order right-hand batsman, left-arm fast medium bowler. *Teams* Jamaica (1968/9 to 1981/2). Derbyshire (1974, 17 matches). *Tours* International Cavaliers to England 1969; West Indies to England 1973, 1976, 1980, to India 1974/5, to Australia and New Zealand 1979/80; Jamaica to England 1970; West Indian XI to South Africa 1982/3, 1983/4. *Tests* West Indies (1971/2 to 1979/80, 30 matches).
Career batting
149–245–12–8755–302–37.57–18–*ct* 118
Bowling 224–2–112.00–0–0–1/19
Test batting
30–49–2–2047–302–43.55–7–*ct* 17
Bowling 44–0

In 1974 he hit 1,059 runs, av 36.51; but on the 1976 tour to England he failed to reach 1,000 runs and appeared in only two Tests. On the tours of 1973 and 1980, he was dogged by injury and played little, missing all the Tests.

His principal claim to fame is his feat of scoring 214 and 100* for West Indies v New Zealand in 1971/2 on his Test debut. His highest innings is 302 for West Indies v England at Bridgetown in 1973/4. He captained the West Indian teams on the controversial tours to South Africa.

Rowe, Leonard Charles
Amateur. *b:* 23.1.1938, Northampton. Opening right-hand batsman. *Sch* Northampton GS. *Team* Oxford U (1958).
Career batting
5–10–2–61–35–7.62–0–*ct* 5

His County cricket was for Durham (pre first-class, 1963–66). He played rugby for Northampton.

Rowell, William Irvine
Amateur. *b:* 19.6.1869, Singapore. *d:* 17.12.1916, Stansted, Essex. Opening right-hand batsman. *Sch* Marlborough. *Team* Cambridge U (1888–91, blue 1891).
Career batting
11–21–0–261–53–12.42–0–*ct* 3

He also won a blue for rugby.

Rowland, Cyril Arthur
Amateur. *b:* 9.6.1905, Llandrillo-yn-Rhos, Colwyn Bay, Denbighshire. *d:* 30.6.1971, Great Horkesley, Essex. Brother of W. H. (Wales). Middle order right-hand batsman. *Sch* Westminster. *Team* Wales (1924–30). *Tour* Cahn to the Argentine 1929/30 (not in first-class matches).
Career batting
14–22–2–330–52*–16.50–0–*ct* 3

His County cricket was for Denbighshire (1930–34).

Rowland, Daniel
Professional. *b:* 1826, Bury, Lancashire. *d:* 1.10.1891, Lower Chesham, Bury, Lancashire. Middle order batsman, useful bowler. *Team* Lancashire (1849–68, 2 matches).
Career batting
2–4–0–9–9–2.25–0–*ct* 0
Bowling 23–0

Rowland, William Harold
Amateur. *b:* 24.2.1904, Llandrillo-yn-Rhos, Colwyn Bay, Denbighshire. *d:* 12.4.1942, Wilford, Nottinghamshire. He was found dead in a field suffering from exposure. Brother of C. A. (Wales). Middle order batsman. *Team* Wales (1925–30).
Career batting
6–9–4–25–11*–5.00–0–*ct* 4–*st* 1

His County cricket was for Denbighshire (1930).

Rowlands, Frank
Amateur. *b:* 26.7.1889, Bristol, Gloucestershire. *d:* 6.9.1975, Sydenham, London. Brother of W. H. (Gloucestershire). Middle order right-hand batsman. *Team* Gloucestershire (1920–22, 11 matches).
Career batting
11–21–0–308–50–14.66–0–*ct* 9

Rowlands, Leslie Samuel
Professional. *b:* 29.8.1880, Aston, Birmingham. *d:* 1.10.1947, Clapham Common, London. Lower order right-hand batsman, right-arm medium pace bowler. *Team* Lancashire (1903–10, 6 matches).
Career batting
7–11–4–33–9–4.71–0–*ct* 2
Bowling 357–18–19.83–0–0–4/29

He also played for Cheshire (1902).

Rowlands, William Henry
Amateur. *b:* 30.7.1883, Bristol. *d:* 29.6.1948, Kingsdown, Bristol. Brother of Frank (Gloucestershire). Middle order right-hand batsman. *Team* Gloucestershire (1901–28, 138 matches).
Career batting
138–207–14–3248–113–16.82–2–*ct* 100
Bowling 280–10–28.00–0–0–1/0

He hit 1,014 runs, av 22.04, in 1921. In 1927 and 1928 he captained Gloucestershire.

Rowley, Alexander Butler
Amateur. *b:* 3.10.1837, Manchester, Lancashire. *d:* 9.1.1911, Dover, Kent. Brother of E. B. (Lancashire) and J. C. (Lancashire 1851), uncle of E. B. jun (Lancashire), he married in 1901 the mother of A. C. MacLaren (Lancashire), G. MacLaren (Lancashire) and J. A. MacLaren (Lancashire). Forcing middle order right-hand batsman, left-hand slow medium round-arm bowler, short leg. *Sch* Rossall. *Team* Lancashire (1865–71, 12 matches).
Career batting
31–58–11–967–63*–20.57–0–*ct* 19

Bowling 1670–78–21.41–4–2–6/21

His first-class debut was for Manchester in 1854. He took a prominent part in the formation of Lancashire County Cricket Club and was President from 1874 to 1879. He also played for Cheshire (1869).

Rowley, Charles Robert

Amateur. *b:* 29.12.1849, Marylebone, London. *d:* 5.4.1933, Kensington., London Middle order right-hand batsman, right-hand slow under-arm bowler, wicket-keeper. *Sch* Harrow. *Team* Middlesex (1872, 1 match).

Career batting

9–17–3–177–49*–12.64–0–*ct* 5–*st* 2

His first-class debut was for MCC in 1870 and his final first-class match for the same Club in 1879. He also played for Devon (1866) and Suffolk (1878).

Rowley, Edmund Butler

Amateur. *b:* 4.5.1842, Manchester, Lancashire. *d:* 8.2.1905, Chorlton-cum-Medlock, Lancashire. Father of E. B. jun (Lancashire), brother of A. B. (Lancashire) and J. C. (Lancashire 1851). Hard hitting middle order right-hand batsman, slip field. *Sch* Rossall. *Team* Lancashire (1865–80, 81 matches).

Career batting

89–145–8–1853–78–13.52–0–*ct* 25–*st* 1

Bowling 31–1–31.00–0–0–1/14

His first-class debut was for Gentlemen of the North in 1860. He captained Lancashire from 1866 to 1879 and was afterwards on the County Committee until his death.

Rowley, Ernest Butler

Amateur. *b:* 15.1.1870, Kersal, Manchester, Lancashire. *d:* 4.10.1962, Manchester, Lancashire. Son of E. B. (Lancashire), nephew of A. B. (Lancashire) and J. C. (Lancashire 1851). Middle order right-hand batsman. *Sch* Clifton. *Team* Lancashire (1893–98, 16 matches).

Career batting

17–27–4–586–65–25.47–0–*ct* 4

Rowley, Sir George William

Amateur. *b:* 10.5.1896, Brabourne, Kent. *d:* 8.8.1953, Newlyn, Cornwall. Middle order right-hand batsman. *Sch* Repton. *Teams* Essex (1926, 5 matches); Central Provinces and Berar (1932/3).

Career batting

6–9–1–73–23–9.12–0–*ct* 0

Bowling 29–0

Rowley, John Vincent D'Alessio

Amateur. *b:* 12.9.1907, Graaff-Reinet, Cape Province, South Africa. Lower order right-hand batsman, wicket-keeper. *Team* Oxford U (1927).

Career batting

2–3–1–4–2*–2.00–0–*ct* 1–*st* 1

He won a blue for rugby.

Roy, Pankaj Lal

Amateur. *b:* 31.5.1928, Calcutta, India. Brother of N. L. (Bengal), uncle of Ambar (India), father of Pranab (India). Defiant opening right-hand batsman, right-arm medium pace bowler. *Team* Bengal (1946/7 to 1967/8). *Tours* India to England 1952, 1959, to West Indies 1952/3, to Pakistan 1954/5, to Ceylon 1956/7. *Tests* India (1951/2 to 1960/1, 43 matches).

Career batting

185–298–18–11868–202*–42.38–33–*ct* 74

Bowling 648–21–30.85–1–0–5/53

Test batting

43–79–4–2442–173–32.56–5–*ct* 16

Bowling 66–1–66.00–0–0–1/6

A successful batsman in India he was a complete failure on the 1952 tour to England, playing in all four Tests, but scoring only 54 runs. He was vice-captain of the 1959 side, but again failed in the Tests, though hitting 1,207 runs, av 28.73, in first-class matches. He captained India in one Test. He hit 112* for Bengal v United Provinces at Calcutta on his first-class debut in 1946/7. His highest score was 202* for Bengal v Orissa at Cuttack in 1963/4.

Roy, Pranab

Cricketer. *b:* 10.2.1957, Calcutta, India. Son of Pankaj (India), nephew of N. L. (Bengal), cousin of Ambar (India). Opening right-hand batsman, right-arm medium pace bowler. *Team* Bengal (1978/9 to 1991/2). *Tour* India to England 1982. *Tests* India (1981/2, 2 matches).

Career batting

72–114–15–4056–230*–40.96–13–*ct* 42

Bowling 134–1–134.00–0–0–1/3

Test batting

2–3–1–71–60*–35.50–0–*ct* 1

He hit 105 for Bengal v Assam at Dibrugarh on his first-class debut in 1978/9. On the 1982 tour to England he had a very modest record and did not appear in the Tests. His highest score was 230* for Bengal v Delhi at Calcutta in 1986/7.

Royle, George Murray

Amateur. *b:* 9.1.1843, Nottingham. *d:* 26.2.1910, Sherwood Rise, Nottingham. Middle order right-hand batsman, slow right-arm bowler, good deep field. *Team* Nottinghamshire (1871–81, 3 matches).

Career batting

3–5–0–52–45–10.40–0–*ct* 2

Owing to business he was unable to play regularly in County cricket.

Royle, Rev Vernon Peter Fanshawe Archer

Amateur. *b:* 29.1.1854, Brooklands, Cheshire. *d:* 21.5.1929, Stanmore Park, Middlesex. Fine middle order right-hand batsman, right-hand slow round-arm bowler, brilliant cover point. *Sch* Rossall. *Teams* Lancashire (1873–91, 74 matches); Oxford U (1875–76, blue both years). *Tours* Harris to Australia 1878/9.

Test England (1878/9, 1 match).
Career batting
102–165–15–2322–81–15.48–0–*ct* 69
Bowling 376–15–25.06–0–0–4/51
Test batting
1–2–0–21–18–10.50–0–*ct* 2
Bowling 6–0
He also played for Cheshire (1873–94), and in 1929 was President of Lancashire CCC.

Roynon, Gavin Devonald
Amateur. *b:* 26.4.1936, Sutton, Surrey. Middle order right-hand batsman, leg break bowler. *Sch* Charterhouse. *Team* Oxford U (1958).
Career batting
9–15–2–188–58–14.46–0–*ct* 10
Bowling 6–0
His County cricket was for Oxfordshire (1954–58).

Royston, Henry
Professional. *b:* 12.8.1819, Harrow-on-the-Hill, Middlesex. *d:* 30.9.1873, St John's Wood, London. Lower order right-hand batsman, right-hand slow round-arm bowler, good field. *Team* Middlesex (1850–62, 4 matches).
Career batting
68–121–19–1065–60–10.44–0–*ct* 28
Bowling 658–55 + 55–11.96–6–1–8/44
His first-class debut was for MCC in 1843. He also played for Berkshire (1849).

Ruane, John Davison
Amateur. *b:* 11.7.1919, Ely, Cambridgeshire. *d:* 3.11.1983, Bury St Edmunds, Suffolk. Lower order left-hand batsman, left-arm medium fast bowler. *Sch* Beaumont. *Team* Cambridge U (1938–39).
Career batting
2–3–0–27–19–9.00–0–*ct* 0
Bowling 166–3–55.33–0–0–2/41

Rubie, Claude Blake
Amateur. *b:* 25.3.1888, Lewes, Sussex. *d:* 3.11.1939, Hove, Sussex. He died following an operation. Lower order right-hand batsman, wicket-keeper. *Sch* Lancing. *Teams* Europeans (1919/20 to 1926/7); Northern India (1926/7); Sussex (1930, 4 matches).
Career batting
10–18–8–245–84–24.50–0–*ct* 16–*st* 7
Three months before his death he had been appointed Manager of the 1939/40 MCC team to India – war caused the tour to be abandoned.

Rucker, Charles Edward Sigismund
Amateur. *b:* 4.9.1894, Chislehurst, Kent. *d:* 24.11.1965, Blandford Forum, Dorset. Brother of P. W. (Oxford U). Lower order right-hand batsman, right-arm fast bowler. *Sch* Charterhouse. *Team* Oxford U (1914, blue).
Career batting
5–8–3–66–26*–13.20–0–*ct* 1
Bowling 289–13–22.23–2–0–6/69
The loss of a leg during the First World War ended his cricket career, but he was Secretary at Oxford in 1919, in which year his younger brother P. W. Rucker, played against Cambridge.

Rucker, Patrick William
Amateur. *b:* 5.5.1900, Chislehurst, Kent. *d:* 20.5.1940, Amiens, France. Brother of C. E. S. (Oxford U). Lower order batsman, left-arm medium pace bowler. *Sch* Charterhouse. *Team* Oxford U (1919, blue).
Career batting
7–10–4–48–17–8.00–0–*ct* 2
Bowling 462–11–42.00–0–0–4/107

Rudd, Charles John Lockhart
Amateur. *b:* 12.3.1873, Cape Town, South Africa. *d:* 1.4.1950, Kingston-upon-Thames, Surrey. Lower order left-hand batsman, left-arm fast bowler. *Sch* Harrow. *Team* Cambridge U (1894).
Career batting
1–1–1–1–1*–no av–0–*ct* 0
Bowling 29–0

Rudd, Christopher Francis Baines Paul
Cricketer. *b:* 9.12.1963, Sutton Coldfield, Warwickshire. Lower order right-hand batsman, off break bowler. *Sch* Douai. *Team* Derbyshire (1986–87, 4 matches).
Career batting
4–5–1–14–9–3.50–0–*ct* 1
Bowling 249–5–49.80–0–0–3/27
He also played for Devon (1984–86).

Rudd, Clifford Robin David
Amateur. *b:* 25.3.1929, Kenilworth, Cape Province, South Africa. Father of P. S. B. (Griqualand West). Stylish middle order right-hand batsman. *Sch* Eton. *Team* Oxford U (1949–51, blue 1949). *Tour* MCC to Canada 1951.
Career batting
21–40–4–604–70–16.77–0–*ct* 11
His final first-class match was for MCC in 1960.

Rudd, George Boyd Franklin
Amateur. *b:* 3.7.1894, Clarendon Park, Leicester. *d:* 4.2.1957, Evington, Leicester. Son of G. F. (Leicestershire). Forcing middle order right-hand batsman, right-arm medium bowler, occasional wicket-keeper. *Sch* Westminster. *Team* Leicestershire (1913–32, 88 matches).
Career batting
88–159–7–2916–114–19.18–1–*ct* 37
Bowling 713–18–39.61–0–0–3/38
He did not appear in first-class matches whilst at Oxford, but did win a blue for soccer. From 1947 to 1950 he was Hon Secretary of Leicestershire CCC.

Rudd, George Edward
Amateur. *b:* 14.1.1866, York. *d:* 16.9.1921, Southfields, Leicester. Father of G. B. F. (Leicestershire). Middle order right-hand batsman, slow left-arm bowler. *Team* Leicestershire (1894–1901, 22 matches).
Career batting
22–36–6–379–47–12.63–0–*ct* 11
Bowling 537–12–44.75–1–0–5/118
He did not play in any first-class matches whilst at Oxford. He first played for Leicestershire (pre first-class) in 1893. From 1907 to 1921 he was Hon Secretary of Leicestershire CCC.

Rudd, William James
Professional. *b:* 29.6.1880, Little Amwell, Hertfordshire. *d:* 27.3.1971, Ipswich, Suffolk. Tail end left-hand batsman, left-arm medium pace bowler. *Team* Surrey (1904, 1 match).
Career batting
1–2–0–4–4–2.00–0–*ct* 0
He also played for Hertfordshire (1901–03).

Ruddle, Marcus Poole
Amateur. *b:* 16.1.1905, Lansdowne, Dublin, Ireland. *d:* March 1986, Dublin, Ireland. Lower order right-hand batsman, right-arm medium pace bowler. *Team* Ireland (1937).
Career batting
1–2–1–0–0*–0.00–0–*ct* 0
Bowling 17–0

Rudge, Lloyd Maurice
Amateur. *b:* 11.2.1934, Walsall, Staffordshire. *d:* 15.10.1990, Worcester. Hard hitting lower order right-hand batsman, right-arm fast bowler. *Team* Worcestershire (1952, 1 match).
Career batting
1–1–0–1–1–1.00–*ct* 0
Bowling 36–0

Rudston, Horace
Professional. *b:* 22.11.1878, Hessle, Yorkshire. *d:* 14.4.1962, Hessle, Yorkshire. Opening or middle order right-hand batsman. *Team* Yorkshire (1902–07, 21 matches).
Career batting
22–31–0–631–164–20.35–1–*ct* 5

Ruggles-Brise, Major General Sir Harold Goodeve
Amateur. *b:* 17.3.1864, Spains Hall, Finchingfield, Essex. *d:* 24.6.1927, Marylebone, London. He died of pneumonia contracted while playing tennis. Brother-in-law of W. H. Rodwell (MCC), nephew of W. Bowyer-Smijth (MCC 1845). Middle order right-hand batsman, right-arm medium pace bowler. *Sch* Winchester. *Team* Oxford U (1883, blue).
Career batting
8–15–0–278–73–18.53–0–*ct* 6
Bowling 32–1–32.00–0–0–1/11
His County cricket was for Essex (pre first-class, 1883–88), but he played mainly in military matches. His final first-class match was for MCC in 1884.

Rumbold, Sir Jack Seddon
Amateur. *b:* 5.3.1920, Reefton, Nelson, New Zealand. Opening right-hand batsman. *Team* Oxford U (1946–47, blue 1946).
Career batting
7–14–0–175–25–12.50–0–*ct* 6

Rumsey, Frederick Edward
Professional. *b:* 4.12.1935, Stepney, London. Tail end right-hand batsman, left-hand fast medium bowler. *Teams* Worcestershire (1960–62, 13 matches); Somerset (1963–68, 153 matches); Derbyshire (1970, 1 match). *Tests* England (1964–65, 5 matches).
Career batting
180–204–84–1015–45–8.45–0–*ct* 91
Bowling 11773–580–20.29–30–5–8/26
Test batting
5–5–3–30–21*–15.00–0–0–*ct* 0
Bowling 461–17–27.11–0–0–4/25
He took 100 wickets in a season three times (best 119, av 16.18, in 1965). He joined Derbyshire CCC as the Public Relations Officer, remaining two years, and played chiefly for the County in limited overs matches.

Rumsey, Robert Edwin
Professional. *b:* 17.2.1844, Greenwich, London. *d:* 12.6.1884, Greenwich, London. Lower order right-hand batsman, right-hand fast round-arm bowler, slip field. *Team* Kent (1875, 3 matches).
Career batting
3–5–1–20–13–5.00–0–*ct* 2
Bowling 140–7–20.00–1–0–5/48

Rushby, Thomas
Professional. *b:* 6.9.1880, Cobham, Surrey. *d:* 13.7.1962, Ewell, Surrey. Tail end right-hand batsman, right-arm fast medium bowler. *Team* Surrey (1903–21, 228 matches).
Career batting
229–289–129–1192–58*–7.45–0–*ct* 64
Bowling 19640–954–20.58–58–9–10/43
He took 100 wickets in a season four times (best 132, av 21.71, in 1911). His best bowling in an innings was 10/43 for Surrey v Somerset at Taunton in 1921.

Rushmere, Colin George
Amateur. *b:* 16.4.1937, Summerstrand, Port Elizabeth, South Africa. Father of M. W. (Eastern Province). brother of J. W. (Western Province). Middle order right-hand batsman, right-arm medium pace bowler. *Teams* Eastern Province (1956/7 to 1965/6), Western Province (1957/8 to 1960/1). *Tour* SA Fezela to England 1961.

Rushton, Frank

Career batting
33–58–4–1245–153–23.05–2–*ct* 19
Bowling 576–20–28.80–0–0–4/29

Rushton, Frank
Professional. *b:* 21.4.1906, Bolton, Lancashire. *d:* 15.10.1975, Queen's Park, Bolton, Lancashire. Lower order right-hand batsman, right-arm fast medium bowler. *Team* Lancashire (1928–29, 6 matches).
Career batting
6–5–0–59–28–11.80–0–*ct* 2
Bowling 362–10–36.20–0–0–4/30

Rushton, Thomas Henry
Amateur. *b:* 14.5.1845, Horwich, Lancashire. *d:* 1.7.1903, Barnacre, Garstang, Lancashire. Middle order batsman. *Team* Lancashire (1870, 1 match).
Career batting
1–1–0–7–7–7.00–0–*ct* 0

Rushworth, William Robert
Amateur. *b:* 4.11.1914, Dulwich, London. *d:* 19.1.1966, St John's, Bedford. Tail end batsman, opening bowler. *Sch* Alleyns. *Team* Surrey (1946, 1 match).
Career batting
1–1–0–0–0–0.00–0–*ct* 3
Bowling 86–2–43.00–0–0–1/15

Russel, John Somerville
Amateur. *b:* 19.3.1849, Edinburgh, Scotland. *d:* 12.9.1902, Blackhall Castle, Banchory, Kincardine, Scotland. Brother of Patrick (MCC). Opening right-hand batsman, good point field. *Sch* Royal High School, Edinburgh. *Team* MCC (1875–91).
Career batting
79–134–7–1641–83–12.92–0–*ct* 32
Bowling 14–0
His County cricket was for Northumberland (1871–82). He played for Ireland (not first-class) in 1869 and Scotland (not first-class).

Russel, Patrick
Amateur. *b:* 16.10.1857, Edinburgh, Scotland. *d:* 12.10.1917, City of London. Brother of J. S. (MCC). Middle order batsman. *Sch* Fettes and Edinburgh Academy. *Team* MCC (1894).
Career batting
1–2–1–25–25*–25.00–0–*ct* 0

Russell, Alexander Bruce
Cricketer. *b:* 18.1.1958, Stirling, Scotland. Middle order right-hand batsman, right-arm medium pace bowler. *Team* Scotland (1985–92).
Career batting
6–8–1–200–51–28.57–0–*ct* 10
Bowling 98–3–32.66–0–0–2/27

Russell, Alfred Edward
Professional. *b:* 9.1.1875, Lewisham, London. *d:* 8.9.1940, Whipps Cross, Essex. Brother of T. M. (Essex), uncle of C. A. G. (Essex). Lower order left-hand batsman, wicket-keeper. *Team* Essex (1898–1910, 130 matches).
Career batting
130–196–42–2025–100–13.14–1–*ct* 163–*st* 44

Russell, Charles Albert George
(also known as Albert Charles Russell)
Professional. *b:* 7.10.1887, Leyton, Essex. *d:* 23.3.1961, Whipps Cross, Leytonstone, Essex. Son of T. M. (Essex), nephew of A. E. (Essex). Sound opening right-hand batsman, right-arm slow medium bowler, good slip field. *Team* Essex (1908–30, 379 matches). *Tours* MCC to Australia 1920/1, to South Africa 1922/3, Joel to South Africa 1924/5. *Tests* England (1920/1 to 1922/3, 10 matches).
Career batting
437–717–59–27358–273–41.57–71–*ct* 314
Bowling 7637–283–26.98–5–0–5/25
Test batting
10–18–2–910–140–56.87–5–*ct* 8
He hit 1,000 runs in a season 13 times, going on to 2,000 five times (best 2,575, av 54.78, in 1922). His highest innings was 273 for Essex v Northamptonshire at Leyton in 1921; his only other double century being for MCC in Australia. In the series between England and South Africa in 1922/3, he became the first English batsman to hit a century in each innings in a Test. He was a first-class umpire (1938–39).

Russell, David Francis
Amateur. *b:* 29.10.1936, Hackney, London. Lower order right-hand batsman, off break bowler. *Sch* St John's, Leatherhead. *Team* Oxford U (1959).
Career batting
5–6–2–57–22–14.25–0–*ct* 3
Bowling 344–11–31.27–0–0–3/53

Russell, David Paul
Cricketer. *b:* 4.6.1951, Haresfinch, St Helens, Lancashire. Middle order right-hand batsman, right-arm medium pace bowler. *Team* Cambridge U (1974–75, blue both years).
Career batting
16–30–4–514–56*–19.76–0–*ct* 7
Bowling 952–16–59.50–0–0–3/60
His County cricket was for Cambridgeshire (1976–77).

Russell, Denis Leslie
Amateur. *b:* 2.7.1909, Paddington, London. *d:* 29.12.1986, Merrow, Surrey. Lower order right-hand batsman, slow left-arm bowler. *Sch* Beaumont. *Teams* Middlesex (1928–32, 25 matches); Oxford U (1930–31).
Career batting
34–53–5–666–92–13.87–0–*ct* 11
Bowling 527–17–31.00–1–0–7/43

Russell, H. F.
Amateur. Middle order batsman. *Team* Hampshire (1884, 1 match).
Career batting
1–2–0–11–10–5.50–0–0–*ct* 0

Russell, John
Amateur. *b:* 8.4.1887, Liff, Angus, Scotland. *d:* 20.6.1965, Dundee, Angus, Scotland. Middle order right-hand batsman. *Team* Scotland (1923).
Career batting
1–2–0–58–29–29.00–0–*ct* 1

Russell, John Bernard
Amateur. *b:* 2.10.1883, Rushall, Walsall, Staffordshire. *d:* 17.8.1965, Lichfield, Staffordshire. Lower order right-hand batsman, wicket-keeper. *Sch* Bromsgrove. *Team* Warwickshire (1920, 1 match).
Career batting
1–2–0–31–23–15.50–0–*ct* 1–*st* 1
He also played for Staffordshire (1907–27).

Russell, Mark John
Cricketer. *b:* 18.11.1970, Lincoln. Middle order right-hand batsman, right-arm slow medium bowler. *Team* Oxford U (1990–91).
Career batting
7–9–0–101–30–11.22–0–*ct* 1
Bowling 31–4–7.75–0–0–4/31

Russell, Philip Edgar
Cricketer. *b:* 9.5.1944, Ilkeston, Derbyshire. Lower order right-hand batsman, right-arm medium pace off break bowler. *Team* Derbyshire (1965–85, 170 matches).
Career batting
170–210–46–2020–72–12.31–0–*ct* 124
Bowling 10351–339–30.53–5–0–7/46
He was Derbyshire coach in 1976–92 and reappeared in 1985 in three Championship and three Sunday League matches, having not played since 1979.

Russell, Robert Charles
Cricketer. *b:* 15.8.1963, Stroud, Gloucestershire. Middle order left-hand batsman, occasional leg break bowler, wicket-keeper. *Team* Gloucestershire (1981–92, 203 matches). *Tours* Gloucestershire to Sri Lanka 1986/7; England to Pakistan 1987/8, to India 1988/9 (tour cancelled), 1989/90 (not first-class), to West Indies 1989/90, to Australia 1990/1, to New Zealand 1990/1 (not first-class), 1991/2. *Tests* England (1988–92, 31 matches).
Career batting
251–351–80–7334–128*–27.06–4–*ct* 567–*st* 84
Bowling 38–1–38.00–0–0–1/4
Test batting
31–49–10–1060–128*–27.17–1–*ct* 80–*st* 8
Ranked as the equal of any wicket-keeper in England during the last few seasons his opportunities at the highest level have depended on the policies of the England Test selectors as to whether a specialist wicket-keeper rather than a batsman who can keep wicket should be used.

Russell, Sidney Edward James
Professional. *b:* 4.10.1937, Feltham, Middlesex. Middle order right-hand batsman, right-arm medium pace bowler. *Teams* Middlesex (1960–64, 61 matches); Gloucestershire (1965–68, 80 matches).
Career batting
142–248–19–5464–130–23.86–4–*ct* 41
Bowling 121–2–60.50–0–0–1/8
He hit 1,000 runs in a season twice (best 1,256, av 25.12, in 1965). A useful soccer player, he played for Brentford.

Russell, Stephen George
Cricketer. *b:* 13.3.1945, Sutton, Surrey. Tail end right-hand batsman, right-arm fast medium bowler. *Sch* Tiffin. *Teams* Cambridge U (1965–67, blue all three years); Surrey (1967, 1 match).
Career batting
35–58–21–203–21*–5.48–0–*ct* 12
Bowling 2480–76–32.63–4–0–5/41
He captained Cambridge in 1967.

Russell, Thomas Marychurch
Professional. *b:* 6.7.1868, Lewisham, London. *d:* 28.2.1927, Leyton, Essex. Father of C. A. G. (Essex), brother of A. E. (Essex). Lower order right-hand batsman, wicket-keeper. *Team* Essex (1894–1905, 162 matches).
Career batting
170–260–46–3273–139–15.29–3–*ct* 251–*st* 89
He first played for Essex (pre first-class) in 1888. He was a first-class umpire (1920–26).

Russell, William Cecil
Amateur. *b:* 25.4.1866, Rokewood, Victoria, Australia. *d:* 9.5.1929, Haremere, Etchingham, Sussex. Middle order batsman. *Sch* Eton. *Team* Hampshire (1898, 1 match).
Career batting
1–2–0–7–5–3.50–*ct* 0

Russell, William Eric
Professional. *b:* 3.7.1936, Dumbarton, Scotland. Opening right-hand batsman, right-arm medium pace bowler. *Team* Middlesex (1956–72, 400 matches). *Tours* MCC to New Zealand 1960/1, to India and Pakistan 1961/2, to Australia and New Zealand 1965/6. *Tests* England (1961/2 to 1967, 10 matches).
Career batting
448–796–64–25525–193–34.87–41–*ct* 304
Bowling 993–22–45.13–0–0–3/20
Test batting
10–18–1–362–70–21.29–0–*ct* 4
Bowling 44–0

He hit 1,000 runs in a season 13 times, going on to 2,000 three times (best 2,342, av 45.92, in 1964). He also played for Berkshire (1976–77).

Russom, Neil
Cricketer. *b:* 3.12.1958, Finchley, Middlesex. Middle order right-hand batsman, right-arm medium bowler. *Teams* Cambridge U (1979–81, blue 1980–81); Somerset (1980–83, 4 matches).
Career batting
25–34–14–641–79*–32.05–0–*ct* 6
Bowling 1744–42–41.52–0–0–4/84

Rust, Thomas Henry
Amateur. *b:* 3.3.1881, Gloucester. *d:* 9.8.1962, Tredworth, Gloucester. Middle order right-hand batsman. *Team* Gloucestershire (1914, 1 match).
Career batting
1–2–0–2–2–1.00–0–*ct* 0

Rutherford, Arnold Page
Amateur. *b:* 2.9.1892, Highclere, Hampshire. *d:* 23.7.1980, Weybridge, Surrey. Brother of J. S. (Hampshire). Middle order right-hand batsman, right-arm medium pace bowler. *Sch* Repton. *Team* Hampshire (1912, 1 match).
Career batting
1–1–0–18–18–18.00–0–*ct* 0

Rutherford, Ian Alexander
Cricketer. *b:* 30.6.1957, Dunedin, New Zealand. Brother of K. R. (Otago). Opening or middle order right-hand batsman, right-arm medium pace, off break bowler. *Teams* Otago (1974/5 to 1983/4); Worcestershire (1976, 2 matches); Central Districts (1977/8).
Career batting
79–144–4–3794–222–27.10–5–*ct* 50
Bowling 56–2–28.00–0–0–1/8
His highest score was 222 for Otago v Central Districts at New Plymouth in 1978/9.

Rutherford, John Robert Fulton
Amateur. *b:* 3.9.1935, Hawkhurst, Kent. Lower order right-hand batsman, right-arm medium pace bowler. *Sch* Nottingham HS. *Team* Cambridge U (1957–58).
Career batting
11–21–5–105–37*–6.56–0–*ct* 3
Bowling 555–10–55.50–0–0–3/53

Rutherford, John Seymour
Amateur. *b:* 27.2.1890, Highclere, Hampshire. *d:* 14.4.1943, Oxford. Brother of A. P. (Hampshire). Lower order right-hand batsman, right-arm medium pace bowler. *Sch* Repton. *Team* Hampshire (1913, 8 matches).
Career batting
8–15–1–128–33*–9.14–0–*ct* 1
Bowling 110–3–36.66–0–0–1/4

Rutherford, John Walter
Amateur. *b:* 25.9.1929, Bruce Rock, Western Australia. Opening right-hand batsman, leg break bowler. *Team* Western Australia (1952/3 to 1960/1, 38 matches). *Tours* Australia to England 1956, to India 1956/7. *Test* Australia (1956/7, 1 match).
Career batting
67–115–9–3367–167–31.76–6–*ct* 53
Bowling 1313–29–45.27–0–0–3/12
Test batting
1–1–0–30–30–30.00–0–*ct* 0
Bowling 15–1–15.00–0–0–1/11
He had a modest tour of England in 1956 and did not appear in the Tests.

Rutherford, Kenneth Robert
Cricketer. *b:* 26.10.1965, Dunedin, New Zealand. Brother of I. A. (Otago). Middle order right-hand batsman, right-arm medium pace bowler. *Team* Otago (1982/3 to 1991/2). *Tours* Young New Zealand to Zimbabwe 1984/5, 1988/9; New Zealand to West Indies 1984/5, to Sri Lanka 1985/6 (not first-class), 1986/7, to England 1986, 1990, to Sharjah (not first-class) 1985/6, 1987/8, 1989/90, to Australia 1987/8, 1990/1 (not first-class), to India 1987/8 (World Cup), 1988/9, to Pakistan 1990/1. *Tests* New Zealand (1984/5 to 1991/2, 30 matches).
Career batting
130–222–21–8108–317–40.33–20–*ct* 104
Bowling 1000–22–45.45–1–0–5/72
Test batting
30–49–4–831–107*–18.46–1–*ct* 21
Bowling 161–1–161.00–0–0–1/38
In 1986 he played in one Test v England, but hit 317 for the tourists v D. B. Close's XI at Scarborough; in 1990 injury early on affected his confidence and he achieved little in the Tests.

Rutnagar, Richard Sohrab
Cricketer. *b:* 9.8.1964, Bombay, India. Lower order right-hand batsman, right-arm medium pace bowler. *Sch* Westminster. *Team* Oxford U (1985–86, blue both years).
Career batting
17–24–2–334–66–15.18–0–*ct* 5
Bowling 1256–29–43.31–1–0–5/112
His father is a well-known cricket correspondent.

Rutter, Rev Allan Edward Henry
Amateur. *b:* 24.12.1928, Bickley, Kent. Opening or middle order right-hand batsman. *Sch* Dauntsey's and Monkton Combe. *Team* Cambridge U (1953).
Career batting
3–4–0–49–45–12.25–0–*ct* 0
His County cricket was for Wiltshire (1948–56) and Norfolk (1962–65). His final first-class match was for Free Foresters in 1955.

Rutter, Edward
Amateur. *b:* 3.8.1842, Hillingdon, Middlesex. *d:* 4.2.1926, Halliford, Middlesex. Brother of F. J. (Lancashire), uncle of E. F. (Europeans). Lower order right-hand batsman, slow left-arm bowler. *Sch* Rugby. *Team* Middlesex (1862–76, 32 matches).
Career batting
45–77–12–733–64–11.27–0–*ct* 29
Bowling 3173–181 + 2–17.53–15–5–7/47

He was a prominent member of the Free Foresters, being Hon Secretary of that Club for some years. A noted rugby footballer, he played for Richmond and was a member of the original Committee set up by the Rugby Union.

Rutter, Frederick John
Amateur. *b:* 12.9.1840, Hillingdon, Middlesex. *d:* 19.1.1907, Abbey Wood, Kent. Brother of Edward (Middlesex), father of E. F. (Europeans). Opening batsman. *Sch* Rugby. *Team* Lancashire (1868, 2 matches).
Career batting
2–4–1–15–8*–5.00–0–*ct* 0
Bowling 11–0

Rutter, Ronald Howard
Amateur. *b:* 13.7.1910, Amersham, Buckinghamshire. *d:* 8.8.1974, Beaconsfield, Buckinghamshire. He died after a long illness. Lower order right-hand batsman, right-arm fast medium bowler. *Sch* Tonbridge. *Teams* Minor Counties (1929–36); MCC (1932–33).
Career batting
6–9–3–66–37*–11.00–0–*ct* 3
Bowling 408–13–31.38–0–0–3/27

His County cricket was for Buckinghamshire (1928–47). For Buckinghamshire v Oxfordshire at High Wycombe in 1932 he hit 106 in 45 minutes.

Rutty, Arthur William Forder
Amateur. *b:* 22.8.1872, Reading, Berkshire. *d:* 10.1.1932, West Jesmond, Newcastle upon Tyne, Northumberland. Lower order right-hand batsman, off break bowler. *Sch* St John's Leatherhead, Sherborne. *Team* Surrey (1910, 1 match).
Career batting
1–2–2–18–12*–no av–0–*ct* 1

He played in trials at Oxford U, but not in first-class matches.

Ryan, Francis Peter
Professional. *b:* 14.11.1888, New Jersey, USA. *d:* 5.1.1954, Highfields, Leicester. Tail end left-hand batsman, slow left-arm bowler. *Sch* Bedford GS. *Teams* Hampshire (1919–20, 23 matches); Glamorgan (1922–31, 215 matches); Wales (1923–30).
Career batting
247–357–118–1908–52*–7.98–0–*ct* 103
Bowling 21311–1013–21.03–86–18–8/41

He took 100 wickets in a season five times (best 120, av 14.58, in 1924).

Ryan, James Henry Aloysius
Amateur. *b:* 15.9.1892, Roade, Northamptonshire. *d:* 25.9.1915, Loos, France. He was killed in action. Middle order right-hand batsman, right-arm medium pace bowler. *Sch* Downside. *Teams* Northamptonshire (1911–14, 8 matches); Ireland (1912).
Career batting
9–15–1–119–41–8.50–0–*ct* 2
Bowling 152–4–38.00–0–0–2/51

Ryan, Melville
Professional. *b:* 23.6.1933, Huddersfield, Yorkshire. Lower order right-hand batsman, right-arm fast medium bowler. *Team* Yorkshire (1954–65, 150 matches). *Tour* Yorkshire to North America and Bermuda 1964 (not first-class).
Career batting
150–149–58–682–26*–7.49–0–*ct* 59
Bowling 9466–413–22.92–12–2–7/45

Ryder, John
Amateur. *b:* 8.8.1889, Collingwood, Melbourne, Victoria, Australia. *d:* 3.4.1977, Fitzroy, Melbourne, Victoria, Australia Aggressive middle order right-hand batsman, right-arm fast medium bowler. *Team* Victoria (1912/13 to 1931/2, 80 matches). *Tours* Australia to England 1921, 1926, to South Africa 1914/15 (tour cancelled), 1921/2; Australians to India and Ceylon 1935/6. *Tests* Australia (1920/1 to 1928/9, 20 matches).
Career batting
177–274–37–10501–295–44.30–24–*ct* 133
Bowling 7064–238–29.68–9–1–7/53
Test batting
20–32–5–1394–201*–51.67–3–*ct* 17
Bowling 743–17–43.70–0–0–2/20

His batting in England was a shadow of what he achieved at home – he did not reach 1,000 runs either in 1921 or 1926. In the former year he was not picked for any of the Tests, but in 1926 appeared in four, though making only 73 runs in them. His highest score was 295 for Victoria v New South Wales at Melbourne in 1926/7. He hit 1,045 runs, av 69.66, in the 1928/9 Australian season. He captained Australia in five Tests.

Ryder, Louis
Professional. *b:* 28.8.1900, Thirsk, Yorkshire. *d:* 24.1.1955, Rygill Farm, Summer Bridge, Yorkshire. Lower order right-hand batsman, right-arm fast bowler. *Team* Yorkshire (1924, 2 matches).
Career batting
2–2–1–1–1–1.00–0–*ct* 2
Bowling 151–4–37.75–0–0–2/75

Ryder, Reginald Talbot
Amateur. *b:* 18.6.1875, Crewe, Cheshire. *d:* 6.11.1923, Stockport, Cheshire. Middle order batsman. *Sch* Denstone. *Team* Derbyshire (1903, 1 match).
Career batting
1–1–0–10–10–10.00–0–*ct* 1
He played no first-class matches at Cambridge U.

Rydon, Robert Anthony
Cricketer. *b:* 27.11.1964, Greatham, Sussex. Lower order left-hand batsman, right-arm medium pace bowler. *Sch* Sherborne. *Team* Oxford U (1986–87, blue 1986).
Career batting
6–10–1–72–20–8.00–0–*ct* 2
Bowling 518–6–86.33–0–0–3/106
He was awarded his blue for rugby football.

Rylott, Arnold
Professional. *b:* 18.2.1839, Grantham, Lincolnshire. *d:* 17.4.1914, Sandy, Bedfordshire. Lower order right-hand batsman, left-arm fast bowler. *Team* MCC (1872–88).
Career batting
85–137–26–703–45–6.33–0–*ct* 64
Bowling 5333–456–11.69–39–14–9/30
His first-class debut was for Left Handed v Right Handed in 1870. His County cricket was for Leicestershire (pre first-class, 1875–90) and Staffordshire (1877). He was on the ground staff at Lord's from 1872. His best bowling was 9/30 for MCC v Cambridge U at Cambridge in 1873. He was author of a book of verse 'Our Bobby Rykitt when a Boy.'

Rymill, Kenneth James
Amateur. *b:* 30.8.1906, Northampton. *d:* 31.5.1977, Northampton. Middle order right-hand batsman. *Team* Northamptonshire (1926–32, 4 matches).
Career batting
4–6–0–35–28–5.83–0–*ct* 1

S

Sabine, David John
Cricketer. *b:* 2.6.1966, Papakura, Auckland, New Zealand. Middle order right-hand batsman, right-arm medium pace bowler. *Team* Kent (1988, 1 match).
Career batting
1–2–0–8–7–4.00–0–*ct* 1
Bowling 29–0

Sabine, Peter Noel Barrington
Cricketer. *b:* 21.9.1941, Cookham Dean, Berkshire. Middle order right-hand batsman, leg break bowler. *Sch* Marlborough. *Team* Oxford U (1962–63, blue 1963).
Career batting
12–23–3–420–56–21.00–0–*ct* 10
Bowling 553–15–36.86–0–0–4/51

Sadiq Mohammad
Cricketer. *b:* 5.5.1945, Junagadh, India. Brother of Hanif (Pakistan), Mushtaq (Pakistan), Wazir (Pakistan) and Raees (Karachi), uncle of Shoaib (Pakistan), Shahid (PIA) and Asif (PIA). Opening left-hand batsman, leg break and googly bowler. *Teams* Karachi (1960/1 to 1972/3); PIA (1961/2 to 1966/7); Essex (1970, 1 match); Gloucestershire (1972–82, 193 matches); Tasmania (1974/5, 2 matches); United Bank (1976/7 to 1984/5). *Tours* Pakistan to England 1971, 1974, 1975 (World Cup), 1978, 1979 (World Cup), to Ceylon, Australia and New Zealand 1972/3, to Australia 1976/7, to West Indies 1976/7, to India 1979/80; Pakistan Eaglets to England 1963; PIA to East Africa 1964/5; Rest of World to England 1970, 1985. *Tests* Pakistan (1969/70 to 1980/1, 41 matches).
Career batting
387–684–40–24160–203–37.51–50–*ct* 326
Bowling 7476–235–31.81–8–0–7/34
Test batting
41–74–2–2579–166–35.81–5–*ct* 28
Bowling 98–0
Of his three Test tours to England, his best was 1978 when he headed both Test and first-class batting averages, his figures for the latter being 675 runs, av 37.50. On the 1974 tour he completed 1,000 runs: 1,007, av 45.77. In all he hit 1,000 runs in an English season seven times (best 1,759, av 47.54, in 1976). He also hit 1,000 runs in a Pakistan season. His only double century in England is 203 for Gloucestershire v Sri Lanka in 1981. According to his published date of birth he was 14 years 9 months old when making his first-class debut, for Fazal Mahmood's XI in 1959/60. His last first-class match was for D. B. Close's XI in 1986. He also played for Cornwall (1984).

Sadiq, Zahid Asa
Cricketer. *b:* 6.5.1965, Nairobi, Kenya. Cousin of A. Habib (Middlesex). Middle order right-hand batsman. *Sch* Rutlish. *Teams* Surrey (1988–89, 7 matches); Derbyshire (1990, 1 match).
Career batting
8–12–0–213–64–17.75–0–*ct* 5

Sadler, Thomas William
Professional. *b:* 15.1.1892, Chesterton, Cambridgeshire. *d:* 20.1.1973, Brandon, Suffolk. Lower order right-hand batsman, left-arm bowler. *Team* Wales (1930).
Career batting
1–2–1–18–17–18.00–0–*ct* 1
Bowling 55–3–18.33–0–0–3/55

His County cricket was for Cambridgeshire (1913–27) and Monmouthshire (1930). In the Minor Counties match between Monmouthshire and Dorset in 1930 he took all ten wickets (for 31) in an innings.

Sadler, William Cecil Holborn
Professional. *b:* 24.9.1896, Kings Cross, London. *d:* 12.2.1981, Wandsworth, London. Lower order right-hand batsman, right-arm fast bowler. *Team* Surrey (1923–25, 51 matches).
Career batting
51–65–22–646–68–15.02–0–*ct* 20
Bowling 3907–167–23.39–7–2–6/50
He also played for Durham (pre first-class, 1928–29).

Saeed Ahmed
Amateur. *b:* 1.10.1937, Jullundur, India. Half-brother of Younis (Pakistan). Attacking middle order right-hand batsman, off break bowler. *Teams* Punjab (1954/5 to 1957/8); Railways (1955/6); Universities (1958/9); Lahore (1959/60); PIA (1961/2 to 1962/3); Karachi (1961/2 to 1971/2); PWD (1971/2). *Tours* Pakistan to England 1962, 1967, 1971, to Australia and New Zealand 1964/5, 1972/3, to West Indies 1957/8, to India 1960/1; International XI to Rhodesia 1961/2; Rest of World to England 1968. *Tests* Pakistan (1957/8 to 1972/3, 41 matches).
Career batting
213–346–25–12847–203*–40.02–34–*ct* 122
Bowling 8217–332–24.75–15–2–8/41
Test batting
41–78–4–2991–172–40.41–5–*ct* 13
Bowling 802–22–36.45–0–0–4/64
On his 1962 tour to England he hit 1,294 runs, av 34.97, and appeared in all five Tests. In 1967, on the shortened tour, he made 845 runs, av 33.80, again playing in all the Tests. He was unable to find his form until late on in the 1971 visit and played only in the last Test. His only double century was 203* for Karachi v PWD at Karachi in 1970/1. He hit 1,012 runs, av 56.22, in 1970/1 in Pakistan. Apart from his cricket for Pakistan, he played in England in 1966 for MCC. His final first-class match was for NWFP XI v England in 1977/8. He captained Pakistan in three Tests.

Saggers, Ronald Arthur
Amateur. *b:* 15.5.1917, Sydenham, Sydney, New South Wales, Australia. *d:* 17.3.1987, Harbord, Sydney, New South Wales, Australia. Lower order right-hand batsman, wicket-keeper. *Team* New South Wales (1939/40 to 1950/1, 40 matches). *Tours* Australia to England 1948, to South Africa 1949/50. *Tests* Australia (1948 to 1949/50, 6 matches).
Career batting
77–93–14–1888–104*–23.89–1–*ct* 146–*st* 75
Test batting
6–5–2–30–14–10.00–0–*ct* 16–*st* 8
The reserve wicket-keeper to D. Tallon on the 1948 tour, he played in one Test.

Sainsbury, Edward
Amateur. *b:* 5.7.1851, Bath, Somerset. *d:* 28.10.1930, Weston-super-Mare, Somerset. Uncle of E. A. P. (Hawke's Bay). Opening or middle order right-hand batsman, slow under-arm bowler. *Sch* Sherborne. *Teams* Somerset (1882–85, 25 matches); Gloucestershire (1891–92, 18 matches).
Career batting
46–85–4–1213–116–14.97–1–*ct* 20
Bowling 644–25–25.76–0–0–4/74
He captained Somerset 1885–88 and played for the County 1878–87.

Sainsbury, Gary Edward
Cricketer. *b:* 17.1.1958, Wanstead, Essex. Tail end right-hand batsman, left-arm medium pace bowler. *Teams* Essex (1979–80, 3 matches); Gloucestershire (1983–87, 71 matches). *Tour* Gloucestershire to Sri Lanka 1986/7.
Career batting
74–70–38–179–14*–5.59–0–*ct* 15
Bowling 5717–172–33.23–7–0–7/38

Sainsbury, John Popham
Amateur. *b:* 8.1.1927, Weston-super-Mare, Somerset. Attacking middle order right-hand batsman, good outfield. *Sch* Clifton. *Team* Somerset (1951, 2 matches).
Career batting
2–4–0–16–16–4.00–0–*ct* 0
He was a good rugby footballer, playing at left-wing for Somerset.

Sainsbury, Peter James
Professional. *b:* 13.6.1934, Chandlers Ford, Hampshire. Middle order right-hand batsman, slow left-arm bowler, excellent field. *Team* Hampshire (1954–76, 593 matches). *Tours* MCC to Pakistan, 1955/6; Robins to West Indies 1974/5 (not first-class); International Wanderers to South Africa 1974/5.
Career batting
618–948–197–20176–163–26.86–7–*ct* 617
Bowling 31777–1316–24.14–36–5–8/76
He hit 1,000 runs in a season six times (best 1,533, av 30.05, in 1961) and took 100 wickets in a season twice (best 107, av 17.51, in 1971). He was Hampshire coach 1977–91.

Saint, Norman Hunt
Amateur. *b:* 22.4.1901, Tollington Park, Islington, London. *d:* 15.8.1930, Whitechapel, London. Middle order right-hand batsman, left-arm medium bowler. *Sch* Merchant Taylors. *Team* Essex (1920–23, 44 matches).
Career batting
44–72–7–757–36–11.64–0–*ct* 10
Bowling 800–17–47.05–0–0–3/32

St Hill, Wilton H.
Amateur. *b:* 6.7.1893, Port of Spain, Trinidad. *d:* 1957, Trinidad. Brother of E. L. (West Indies) and Cyl (Trinidad). Entertaining middle order right-hand batsman, right-arm medium pace bowler. *Team* Trinidad (1911/12 to 1929/30). *Tour* West Indies to England 1928. *Tests* West Indies (1928 to 1929/30, 3 matches).
Career batting
43–74–3–1928–144–27.15–5–*ct* 14
Bowling 209–5–41.80–0–0–2/14
Test batting
3–6–0–117–38–19.50–0–*ct* 1
Bowling 9–0
He had a very moderate tour to England, being too anxious to attack the bowling from the start of each innings.

Salah-ud-din Mulla
Amateur. *b:* 14.2.1947, Aligarh, India. Middle order right-hand batsman, off break bowler. *Teams* Karachi (1964/5 to 1971/2); PIA (1972/3 to 1979/80). *Tours* Pakistan Eaglets to England 1963; Pakistan to England 1967. *Tests* Pakistan (1964/5 to 1969/70, 5 matches).
Career batting
111–168–31–5729–256–41.81–14–*ct* 63
Bowling 4436–155–28.61–4–0–6/76
Test batting
5–8–2–117–34*–19.50–0–*ct* 3
Bowling 187–7–26.71–0–0–2/36
He achieved very little on the 1967 tour to England and did not appear in the Tests. His highest score was 256 for Karachi v East Pakistan at Karachi in 1968/9.

Salam-ud-din, Khan
Amateur. *b:* 16.10.1888, Basty Sheikh Darwesh, Jullundur, India. Middle order right-hand batsman, right-arm fast bowler. *Team* Muslims (1912/13). *Tour* India to England 1911.
Career batting
15–29–5–362–50–15.08–0–*ct* 17
Bowling 1143–36–31.75–3–0–6/64
He proved to be a useful all-rounder on the 1911 tour.

Sale, Henry George
Amateur. *b:* 26.3.1889, Shipston-on-Stour, Warwickshire. *d:* 30.8.1975, Shipston-on-Stour, Warwickshire. Middle order right-hand batsman. *Sch* Wellingborough. *Team* Worcestershire (1921–25, 4 matches).
Career batting
4–8–3–74–28*–14.80–0–*ct* 1

Sale, Richard (sen)
Amateur. *b:* 21.6.1889, Broughty Ferry, Angus, Scotland. *d:* 7.9.1970, East Hanney, Berkshire. Father of Richard jun (Derbyshire and Warwickshire). Middle order left-hand batsman, right-arm fast medium bowler. *Sch* Repton. *Teams* Derbyshire (1908–12, 23 matches); Oxford U (1909–11, blue 1910).
Career batting
39–70–2–961–69–14.13–0–*ct* 12
Bowling 471–10–47.10–0–0–2/25
He also won a blue for soccer, and also played amateur internationals for England.

Sale, Richard (jun)
Amateur. *b:* 4.10.1919, Atcham, Shrewsbury, Shropshire. *d:* 3.2.1987, Beccles, Suffolk. Son of Richard sen (Derbyshire). Stylish opening left-hand batsman, good field. *Sch* Repton. *Teams* Oxford U (1939 and 1946, blue both years); Warwickshire (1939–47, 19 matches); Derbyshire (1949–54, 24 matches).
Career batting
66–115–8–2923–157–27.31–3–*ct* 28
Bowling 4–1–4.00–0–0–1/4
He hit 1,047 runs, av 34.90, in 1946.

Saleem Altaf Bokhari
Cricketer. *b:* 23.3.1944, Lahore, India. Brother of Naeem Altaf (Punjab U). Lower order right-hand batsman, right-arm fast medium bowler. *Teams* Lahore (1963/4); Punjab University (1964/5 to 1967/8); PIA (1967/8 to 1978/9). *Tours* Pakistan to England 1967, 1971, to Australia and New Zealand 1972/3, to Australia 1976/7, to West Indies 1976/7; PIA to Ireland 1969 (not first-class). *Tests* Pakistan (1967 to 1976/7, 21 matches).
Career batting
143–184–50–3067–111–22.88–1–*ct* 61
Bowling 9479–335–28.29–8–1–7/69
Test batting
21–31–12–276–53*–14.52–0–*ct* 3
Bowling 1710–46–37.17–0–0–4/11
He played in two Tests on both 1967 and 1971 tours, and proved a useful bowler, but in both years missed matches through injury or illness.

Saleem Jaffar
Cricketer. *b:* 19.11.1962, Karachi, Pakistan. Lower order right-hand batsman, left-arm fast medium bowler. *Teams* Karachi (1983/4 to 1991/2); United Bank (1985/6 to 1990/1). *Tours* Pakistan to India 1986/7, to Sharjah (not first-class) 1986/7, 1988/9, to Australia 1986/7 (not first-class), 1991/2, to England 1987, 1992, to West Indies 1987/8, to New Zealand 1988/9. *Tests* Pakistan (1986/7 to 1991/2, 14 matches).
Career batting
69–61–27–332–33*–9.76–0–*ct* 18
Bowling 5956–240–24.81–12–2–7/29
Test batting
14–14–6–42–10*–5.25–0–*ct* 2
Bowling 1139–36–31.63–1–0–5/40
On his 1987 tour to England he suffered a groin injury early in the tour and played in only one first-

class match; on his second England visit in 1992 he appeared in four first-class matches and again returned home injured.

Saleem Malik
Cricketer. *b:* 16.4.1963, Lahore, Pakistan. Attractive middle order right-hand batsman, right-arm medium pace or leg break bowler, good field. *Teams* Lahore (1978/9 to 1985/6); Habib Bank (1982/3 to 1990/1); Essex (1991, 24 matches); Sargodha (1991/2). *Tours* Pakistan to Australia 1981/2, 1983/4, 1984/5 (not first-class), 1988/9, 1989/90, 1991/2, to England 1982, 1987, 1992, to India 1983/4, 1986/7, 1989/90 (not first-class), to Sharjah (not first-class) 1983/4, 1984/5, 1985/6, 1986/7, 1988/9, 1989/90, 1990/1, 1991/2, to New Zealand 1984/5, 1988/9, to Sri Lanka 1985/6, to West Indies 1987/8, to Bangladesh (not first-class) 1988/9, to Australia and New Zealand (World Cup) 1991/2; Pakistan Under 23 to Sri Lanka 1984/5. *Tests* Pakistan (1981/2 to 1992, 71 matches).
Career batting
190–289–46–11875–215–48.86–31–*ct* 124
Bowling 1714–57–30.07–2–0–5/19
Test batting
71–101–18–3743–165–45.09–10–*ct* 48
Bowling 118–5–23.60–0–0–1/3
Having toured England in 1982 without being required for any Tests, he returned in 1987 and proved the linchpin of the side batting at number 5, where he played very sensibly. In 1992 he was even more successful, topping the Test averages with 488 runs, av 81.33, and in first-class matches hitting 1,184, av 78.93. This glut of runs echoed his batting for Essex in 1991, when he hit 1,972 runs, av 73.03, including 215 v Leicestershire at Ilford.

Saleem Yousuf
Cricketer. *b:* 7.12.1959, Karachi, Pakistan. Middle order right-hand batsman, wicket-keeper. *Teams* Karachi (1978/9 to 1991/2); Sind (1978/9); Industrial Development Bank of Pakistan (1979/80 to 1981/2); Allied Bank (1982/3 to 1984/5). *Tours* Pakistan to England 1982, 1987, to Sharjah (not first-class) 1985/6, 1986/7, 1988/9, 1989/90, to Australia 1986/7 (not first-class), 1988/9 (not first-class), 1989/90, to India 1986/7, 1989/90 (not first-class), to West Indies 1987/8, to New Zealand 1988/9, to Bangladesh (not first-class) 1988/9. *Tests* Pakistan (1981/2 to 1990/1, 32 matches).
Career batting
118–181–22–4553–145*–28.63–6–*ct* 298–*st* 41
Bowling 16–1–16.00–0–0–1/16
Test batting
32–44–5–1055–91*–27.05–0–*ct* 91–*st* 13
The reserve wicket-keeper on the 1982 tour to England, he appeared in only four first-class matches. Returning to England in 1987 he was the only wicket-keeper chosen in the original squad, though Zulqarnain was co-opted later as a reserve. Saleem played in all five Tests and had a batting record of 187 runs, av 62.33.

Salim-ud-din
Amateur. *b:* 28.8.1938, Ajmer, India. Brother of Alimuddin (Pakistan) and Azimuddin (Rajputana). Middle order right-hand batsman, useful bowler. *Team* Karachi (1957/8 to 1962/3). *Tour* Pakistan Eaglets to England 1963.
Career batting
9–13–0–467–137–35.92–1–*ct* 2
Bowling 40–1–40.00–0–0–1/16
His first-class debut was for Combined Schools in 1954/5.

Salisbury, Ian David Kenneth
Cricketer. *b:* 21.1.1970, Northampton. Lower order right-hand batsman, leg break and googly bowler. *Teams* Sussex (1989–92, 70 matches). *Tours* England A to Pakistan and Sri Lanka 1990/1, to West Indies 1991/2. *Tests* England (1992, 2 matches).
Career batting
80–87–29–939–68–16.18–0–*ct* 52
Bowling 8168–210–38.89–9–2–7/54
Test batting
2–3–0–66–50–22.00–0–*ct* 0
Bowling 306–5–61.20–0–0–3/49
He took 87 wickets, av 28.96, in 1992.

Salmon, Edward Henry Pearse
Amateur. *b:* 23.12.1853, Fort George, Madras, India. *d:* 1.2.1907, Cliftonville, Kent. Middle order right-hand batsman, wicket-keeper. *Sch* Victoria College, Jersey. *Team* Middlesex (1878–79, 9 matches).
Career batting
11–18–3–171–49–11.40–0–*ct* 13–*st* 15

Salmon, Gordon Hedley
Amateur. *b:* 1.8.1894, Leicester. *d:* 13.6.1978, Exmouth, Devon. Middle order right-hand batsman. *Sch* Wyggeston. *Team* Leicestershire (1913–24, 47 matches).
Career batting
47–86–5–1273–72–15.71–0–*ct* 12
Bowling 31–0
It was thought that an injury to his arm during the First World War would finish his cricket, but despite this disability he continued to bat successfully in both County and Club cricket.

Salmond, George
Cricketer. *b:* 1.12.1969, Dundee, Angus, Scotland. Middle order right-hand batsman. *Team* Scotland (1991–92).
Career batting
2–3–0–279–118–93.00–1–*ct* 2

Salter, George
Professional. *b:* 18.4.1834. *d:* 15.8.1911, Chichester, Sussex. Opening batsman. *Team* Sussex (1864, 1 match).

Salter, Malcolm Gurney

Career batting
1–2–1–19–15–19.00–0–*ct* 1
He was scorer to Sussex CCC for many years.

Salter, Malcolm Gurney
Amateur. *b:* 10.5.1887, Cheltenham, Gloucestershire. *d:* 15.6.1973, Chesham Bois, Buckinghamshire. Middle order right-hand batsman. *Sch* Cheltenham. *Teams* Gloucestershire (1907–25, 34 matches); Oxford U (1908–10, blue 1909–10); Europeans (1913/4 to 1925/6); Rajputana (1926/7).
Career batting
65–119–4–2486–152–21.61–2–*ct* 44–*st* 1

Salvi, Neil Vijay
Cricketer. *b:* 21.5.1965, Gwalior, India. Middle order right-hand batsman, leg break bowler. *Sch* Rossall. *Team* Oxford U (1986–87, blue 1986).
Career batting
5–8–1–131–36–18.71–0–*ct* 2

Samaranayake, Aluthge Don Anusha
Cricketer. *b:* 25.2.1962, Colombo, Ceylon. Lower order right-hand batsman, right-arm fast medium bowler. *Team* Sri Lanka (1983/4 to 1984). *Tour* Sri Lanka to England 1984.
Career batting
6–2–1–14–9*–14.00–0–*ct* 3
Bowling 499–9–55.44–0–0–4/142

Samarasekera, Maitipage Athula Rohitha
Cricketer. *b:* 5.8.1961, Colombo, Ceylon. Middle order right-hand batsman, right-arm medium pace bowler. *Team* Colombo CC (1988/9 to 1991/2). *Tours* Sri Lanka to England 1983 (World Cup), 1988, to Australia 1987/8, 1989/90, to Bangladesh (not first-class) 1988/9, to Sharjah (not first-class) 1988/9, 1989/90, to India 1989/90 (not first-class), 1990/1, to Pakistan 1991/2, to Australia and New Zealand (World Cup) 1991/2; Sri Lanka B to Zimbabwe 1987/8. *Tests* Sri Lanka (1988 to 1991/2, 4 matches).
Career batting
40–60–3–1765–133–30.96–4–*ct* 22
Bowling 1021–29–35.20–0–0–3/31
Test batting
4–7–0–118–57–16.85–0–*ct* 3
Bowling 104–3–34.66–0–0–2/38
He proved a useful all-rounder on the 1988 tour to England and played in the Test match. His first-class debut was for Sri Lanka in 1982/3.

Sampson, Henry
Professional. *b:* 13.3.1813, Hallam, Sheffield, Yorkshire. *d:* 29.3.1885, Sheffield, Yorkshire. Father of G. H. (Otago). Excellent middle order right-hand batsman, who relied entirely on back play. *Team* Yorkshire (1845–55, 13 matches).
Career batting
38–69–9–965–55–16.08–0–*ct* 15
Bowling 44–4 + 7–11.00–0–0–4/25
His first-class debut was for the North in 1840, and his last match for the North in 1857.

Sampson, Richard King
Amateur. *b:* 15.5.1860, Lewes, Sussex. *d:* 12.7.1927, Ringmer, Sussex. Middle order right-hand batsman, wicket-keeper. *Team* Sussex (1886, 1 match).
Career batting
1–2–0–7–5–3.50–0–*ct* 1

Samson, Oswald Massey
Amateur. *b:* 8.8.1881, Taunton, Somerset. *d:* 7.9.1918, near Peronne, France. He died of wounds. Middle order left-hand batsman, slow left-arm bowler. *Sch* Cheltenham. *Teams* Somerset (1900–13, 45 matches); Oxford U (1902–03, blue 1903).
Career batting
49–85–5–1464–105–18.30–1–*ct* 32
Bowling 88–5–17.60–0–0–2/4

Samuel, Glyndwr Ninian Thomas Watkin
Amateur. *b:* 26.10.1917, Swansea, Glamorgan. *d:* 14.4.1985, Hastings, Sussex. Middle order right-hand batsman. *Sch* Uppingham. *Team* Glamorgan (1936, 3 matches).
Career batting
3–4–0–41–22–10.25–0–*ct* 0

Sandeman, George Amelius Crawshay
Amateur. *b:* 18.4.1883, Westminster, London. *d:* 26.4.1915, Zonnebeke, Belgium. He was killed in action. Lower order left-hand batsman, slow left-arm bowler. *Sch* Eton. *Team* Hampshire (1913, 3 matches).
Career batting
6–11–7–18–5*–4.50–0–0–*ct* 3
Bowling 242–5–48.40–0–0–2/73
He played in the Oxford Freshmen's match of 1903, but no first-class matches for the University. His final first-class match was for MCC in 1914.

Sanders, Arthur Thomas
Amateur. *b:* 21.12.1900, Pimlico, Westminster, London. *d:* 22.11.1920, Westminster, London. He died by his own hand. Middle order batsman. *Sch* Harrow. *Team* Somerset (1919, 1 match).
Career batting
1–1–0–0–0–0.00–0–*ct* 0

Sanders, Ian Edward Wakefield
Cricketer. *b:* 26.2.1961, Edinburgh, Scotland. Lower order right-hand batsman, right-arm fast medium bowler. *Sch* Cheltenham. *Team* Cambridge U (1984).
Career batting
1–2–0–9–9–4.50–0–*ct* 0
Bowling 93–3–31.00–0–0–2/78
His County cricket was for Dorset (1985–86). He was dismissed 'timed out' in a Minor County match v Oxfordshire in 1985, the first such dismissal under the new laws.

Sanders, Wilfred
Professional. *b:* 4.4.1910, Chilvers Coton, Warwickshire. *d:* 22.5.1965, Nuneaton, Warwickshire. Lower order right-hand batsman, right-arm medium pace bowler. *Team* Warwickshire (1928–34, 84 matches).
Career batting
84–100–18–706–64–8.60–0–*ct* 46
Bowling 4663–119–39.18–0–0–4/44

Sanderson, Gerald Barry
Amateur. *b:* 12.5.1881, Princes Park, Toxteth Park, Liverpool, Lancashire. *d:* 3.10.1964, Westminster, London. Son of R. W. B. (Lancashire). Middle order right-hand batsman. *Sch* Malvern. *Teams* Warwickshire (1901, 1 match); Worcestershire (1923, 1 match).
Career batting
2–2–0–16–16–8.00–0–*ct* 0

Sanderson, John Frederick Waley
Cricketer. *b:* 10.9.1954, Highgate, Middlesex. Lower order right-hand batsman, right-arm medium pace bowler. *Sch* Westminster. *Team* Oxford U (1979–80, blue 1980).
Career batting
6–6–2–18–9–4.50–0–*ct* 2
Bowling 282–10–28.20–1–0–6/67

Sanderson, Sir Lancelot
Amateur. *b:* 24.10.1863, Ellel, Lancaster, Lancashire. *d:* 9.3.1944, Ward House, Ellel, Lancaster, Lancashire. Defensive lower order right-hand batsman, right-arm slow bowler, useful field. *Sch* Harrow. *Team* Lancashire (1884, 1 match).
Career batting
2–3–0–71–61–23.66–0–*ct* 1

He played in the Freshmen's match at Cambridge, but no first-class matches for the University. His final first-class match was for MCC in 1888. He also won a blue for rackets. From 1910 to 1915 he was MP for Appleby; he later went to India where he was the Chief Justice of Bengal.

Sanderson, Richard Withington Bromiley
Amateur. *b:* 15.1.1847, Cheetham Hill, Manchester, Lancashire. Father of G. B. (Warwickshire and Worcestershire). Middle order batsman. *Team* Lancashire (1870, 1 match)
Career batting
1–2–0–7–6–3.50–0–*ct* 0

Sandford, John Douglas
Amateur. *b:* 3.8.1832, Chillingham, Northumberland. *d:* 26.5.1892, Windsor, Berkshire. Brother of E. G. (Oxford U 1859), uncle of T. C. G. (Oxford U). Middle order batsman. *Sch* Rugby. *Team* Oxford U (1855–56).
Career batting
3–5–0–45–20–9.00–0–*ct* 1

His final first-class match was for MCC in 1869. His County cricket was for Warwickshire (pre first-class, 1851).

Sandford, Temple Charles Gabriel
Amateur. *b:* 16.5.1877, Landkey, Devon. *d:* 27.12.1942, Marlborough, Wiltshire. Son of E. G. (Oxford U 1859), nephew of J. D. (Oxford U). Middle order right-hand batsman. *Team* Oxford U (1900).
Career batting
2–3–0–19–11–6.33–0–*ct* 1

His County cricket was for Devon (1901–04) and Wiltshire (1908–31). He won a blue for hockey.

Sandham, Andrew
Professional. *b:* 6.7.1890, Streatham, London. *d:* 20.4.1982, Westminster, London. Sound opening right-hand batsman. *Team* Surrey (1911–37, 526 matches). *Tours* MCC to South Africa 1922/3, 1930/1, to Australia 1924/5, to India, Burma and Ceylon 1926/7, to West Indies 1929/30; Cahn to Jamaica 1928/9; Brinckman to South America 1937/8. *Tests* England (1921 to 1929/30, 14 matches).
Career batting
643–1000–79–41284–325–44.82–107–*ct* 158
Bowling 560–18–31.11–0–0–3/27
Test batting
14–23–0–879–325–38.21–2–*ct* 4

He hit 1,000 runs in a season eighteen times in England and twice overseas, going on to 2,000 eight times (best 2,565, av 51.30, in 1929). His highest innings was 325 for England v West Indies at Kingston in 1929/30 and his highest in England 282* for Surrey v Lancashire at Old Trafford in 1928. He hit nine other double centuries, all for Surrey. On 63 occasions he assisted J. B. Hobbs to record a century partnership for the first wicket. From 1946 to 1958 he was coach to Surrey CCC and for the following 12 years was County scorer.

Sandiford, David Charles
Cricketer. *b:* 24.12.1970, Bolton, Lancashire. Middle order right-hand batsman, wicket-keeper. *Team* Oxford U (1991–92, blue 1991).
Career batting
10–11–1–210–83–21.00–0–*ct* 11–*st* 1

Sands, Jeremy Nigel
Cricketer. *b:* 9.1.1944, Carshalton, Surrey. Middle order right-hand batsman, wicket-keeper. *Sch* Edinburgh Academy. *Team* Scotland (1965).
Career batting
4–5–0–37–17–7.40–0–*ct* 1

His final first-class match was for MCC in 1967.

Sanger, Percival Bertram
Amateur. *b:* 19.10.1899, Reading, Berkshire. *d:* 17.9.1968, Avebury, Wiltshire. Lower order right-hand batsman, wicket-keeper. *Sch* Cheltenham. *Team* Army (1925).

Santall, Frederick Reginald

Career batting
1–1–0–2–2–2.00–0–*ct* 2–*st* 1

Santall, Frederick Reginald
Amateur, turned professional in 1923. *b:* 12.7.1903, Acocks Green, Birmingham, Warwickshire. *d:* 3.11.1950, Cheltenham, Gloucestershire. Son of Sydney (Warwickshire), brother of J. F. E. (Worcestershire). Hard hitting middle order right-hand batsman, right-arm medium pace bowler, excellent field. *Team* Warwickshire (1919–39, 496 matches). *Tour* Brinckman to South America 1937/8.
Career batting
500–797–86–17730–201*–24.93–21–*ct* 268
Bowling 12257–283–43.31–2–0–5/47

He hit 1,000 runs in a season seven times (best 1,727, av 46.67, in 1933). His only double century was 201* for Warwickshire v Northamptonshire at Northampton in 1933.

Santall, John Frank Eden
Professional. *b:* 3.12.1907, King's Heath, Birmingham. *d:* 24.5.1986, Bournemouth, Hampshire. Son of Sydney (Warwickshire), brother of F. R. (Warwickshire). Middle order right-hand batsman, right-arm medium bowler. *Team* Worcestershire (1930, 8 matches).
Career batting
8–13–1–117–36*–9.75–0–*ct* 2
Bowling 124–2–62.00–0–0–2/29

He became a professional ice skater.

Santall, Sydney
Professional. *b:* 10.6.1873, Peterborough, Northamptonshire. *d:* 19.3.1957, Northborne, Ensbury Park, Bournemouth, Hampshire. Father of F. R. (Warwickshire) and J. F. E. (Worcestershire). Lower order right-hand batsman, right-arm medium pace bowler. *Sch* Kings, Peterborough. *Teams* Warwickshire (1894–1914, 371 matches); London County (1900).
Career batting
374–539–119–6516–73–15.51–0–*ct* 175
Bowling 29250–1220–23.97–63–5–8/23

He exceeded 100 wickets in a season once – 101, av 16.62, in 1907. Before appearing for Warwickshire he played as an amateur for Northamptonshire (pre first-class, 1891).

Saravanamuttu, Sabdharatnajyoti
Amateur. *b:* 1898, Colombo, Ceylon. *d:* 17.7.1957, Colombo, Ceylon. Middle order right-hand batsman, right-arm medium fast bowler. *Teams* Cambridge U (1923); Ceylon (1926/7); Engineer's XI in India (1947/8).
Career batting
6–9–0–148–63–16.44–0–*ct* 2
Bowling 76–2–38.00–0–0–2/26

His County cricket was for Cambridgeshire (1923). He was President of the Ceylon CA.

Sardesai, Dilip Narayan
Amateur. *b:* 8.8.1940, Margao, Goa, India. Father of R. D. (Oxford U). Stylish middle order right-hand batsman, good cover field. *Team* Bombay (1960/1 to 1972/3). *Tours* India to England 1967, 1971, to Australia and New Zealand 1967/8, to West Indies 1961/2, 1970/1; ACC to Pakistan 1961/2. *Tests* India (1961/2 to 1972/3, 30 matches).
Career batting
179–271–26–10230–222–41.75–25–*ct* 85
Bowling 552–8–69.00–0–0–2/15
Test batting
30–55–4–2001–212–39.23–5–*ct* 4
Bowling 45–0

A broken finger resulted in him being sent home half way through the 1967 tour to England, but he played in one Test and had the best first-class batting average – 288 runs, av 41.14. He played some good innings on the 1971 visit, but his overall figures were not impressive. His highest score was 222 for ACC v Indian Starlets at Hyderabad in 1964/5. He scored 1,000 runs in an Indian season three times (best 1,429, av 62.13, in 1964/5).

Sardesai, Rajdeep Dilip
Cricketer. *b:* 24.5.1965, Ahmedabad, India. Son of D. N. (India). Middle order right-hand batsman, off break bowler. *Team* Oxford U (1987, blue).
Career batting
7–9–1–222–63*–27.75–0–*ct* 2

Sarel, William Godfrey Molyneux
Amateur. *b:* 15.12.1875, Dover, Kent. *d:* 5.4.1950, Whitechapel, London. Stylish middle order right-hand batsman, off break bowler. *Teams* Surrey (1904–09, 4 matches); Kent (1912–14, 9 matches); Sussex (1919–21, 12 matches); Trinidad (1904/5 to 1905/6).
Career batting
35–63–5–1313–103–22.63–1–*ct* 19
Bowling 197–3–65.66–0–0–1/1

He also played for Northumberland (1907), but not in the Minor Counties Championship. From 1919 to 1922 he was Secretary to Sussex CCC.

Sarfraz Nawaz, Malik
Cricketer. *b:* 1.12.1948, Lahore, Pakistan. Attacking lower order right-hand batsman, right-arm fast medium bowler. *Teams* Lahore (1967/8 to 1984/5); Punjab Univ (1968/9 to 1971/2); Northamptonshire (1969–82, 151 matches); Punjab (1974/5); Railways (1975/6); United Bank (1976/7 to 1977/8). *Tours* Pakistan to England 1971, 1974, 1975 (World Cup), 1978, 1979 (World Cup), 1982, 1983 (World Cup), to Australia and New Zealand 1972/3, 1978/9, to Australia 1976/7, 1981/2, 1983/4, to West Indies 1976/7, to Ceylon 1972/3, 1975/6, to Sharjah (not first-class) 1983/4. *Tests* Pakistan (1968/9 to 1983/4, 55 matches).

Career batting
299–367–72–5709–90–19.35–0–*ct* 163
Bowling 24750–1005–24.62–46–4–9/86
Test batting
55–72–13–1045–90–17.71–0–*ct* 26
Bowling 5798–177–32.75–4–1–9/86

Owing to injury he appeared in only three matches on the 1971 Pakistan tour to England. In 1974 he played in all three Tests and headed the Test bowling averages. He was again injured in 1978, but when available was the most effective bowler in the side. His Test career was affected by a number of disagreements with the Pakistan Board of Control. In 1975 he took 101 wickets, av 20.30. His best bowling was 9/86 for Pakistan v Australia at Melbourne in 1978/9; in a spell of 33 balls during that innings he took 7 wickets for one run.

Sargeant, Neil Fredrick
Cricketer. *b:* 8.11.1965, Hammersmith, London. Lower order right-hand batsman, wicket-keeper. *Team* Surrey (1989–92, 41 matches).
Career batting
41–52–9–612–49–14.23–0–*ct* 91–*st* 16
Bowling 88–1–88.00–0–0–1/88

Sargent, Arthur Harry Thomas
Professional. *b:* 24.3.1908, Northampton. *d:* 10.2.1990, Northampton. Lower order right-hand batsman, right-arm medium pace off break bowler. *Team* Northamptonshire (1932, 4 matches).
Career batting
4–7–1–41–18–6.83–0–*ct* 3
Bowling 286–7–40.85–1–0–5/88

Sargent, Murray Alfred James
Professional. *b:* 23.8.1928, North Adelaide, South Australia. Middle order right-hand batsman, right-arm medium pace or leg break bowler. *Teams* Leicestershire (1951–52, 13 matches); South Australia (1960/1, 9 matches).
Career batting
22–38–4–804–164–23.64–1–*ct* 5
Bowling 204–3–68.00–0–0–2/18

Sarwate, Chandrasekhar Trimbak
Amateur. *b:* 22.7.1920, Saugor, Vidarbha, India. Defensive middle order right-hand batsman, right-arm leg break, or occasional off break, bowler. *Teams* Central Provinces and Berar (1936/7); Maharashtra (1938/9 to 1946/7); Hindus (1941/2 to 1944/5); Bombay (1943/4); Holkar (1944/5 to 1954/5); Madhya Bharat (1955/6 to 1956/7); Madhya Pradesh (1958/9 to 1967/8); Vidarbha (1968/9). *Tours* Holkar to Ceylon 1947/8; India to England 1946, 1952, to Australia 1947/8. *Tests* India (1946 to 1951/2, 9 matches).
Career batting
171–257–30–7430–246–32.73–14–*ct* 91
Bowling 11633–494–23.54–26–3–9/61
Test batting
9–17–1–208–37–13.00–0–*ct* 0
Bowling 374–3–124.66–0–0–1/16

On the 1946 tour to England he assisted S. N. Banerjee in a record 10th wicket partnership of 249 v Surrey at the Oval; this innings was in fact the only one of note he achieved during the visit. His bowling seemed to lack confidence. In 1952 he was completely out of form. His highest score was 246 for Holkar v Bengal at Calcutta in 1950/1 and his best bowling 9/61 for Holkar v Mysore at Indore in 1945/6.

Saunders, Sir Alan Arthur
Amateur. *b:* 15.12.1892, Brighton, Sussex. *d:* 26.2.1957, Hove, Sussex. Middle order right-hand batsman, useful bowler. *Team* Sussex (1922–23, 12 matches).
Career batting
12–20–4–186–36–11.62–0–*ct* 7
Bowling 129–2–64.50–0–0–1/6

Saunders, Christopher John
Cricketer. *b:* 7.5.1940, West Worthing, Sussex. Lower order right-hand batsman, wicket-keeper. *Sch* Lancing. *Teams* Cambridge U (1962–63); Oxford U (1964, blue).
Career batting
12–14–8–69–21–11.50–0–*ct* 10–*st* 3

His County cricket was for Berkshire (1971). He also won a blue for soccer at Oxford.

Saunders, Henry Banyard
Professional. *b:* 29.12.1841, Impington, Cambridgeshire. *d:* 18.3.1904, Stanley, Kirkdale, Liverpool. Brother of William (Cambridgeshire). Attacking middle order right-hand batsman wicket-keeper. *Teams* Cambridgeshire (1865–66, 9 matches).
Career batting
9–15–0–151–39–10.06–0–*ct* 4–*st* 2
Bowling 47–1–47.00–0–0–1/47

Saunders, Henry William
Amateur. *b:* 1883. *d:* 24.4.1942, Uphill, Weston-super-Mare, Somerset. Middle order left-hand batsman. *Team* Somerset (1911–22, 4 matches).
Career batting
4–8–1–50–17–7.14–0–*ct* 4

Saunders, J.
Professional. Lower order left-hand batsman. *Team* Middlesex (1891, 2 matches).
Career batting
2–3–1–16–7*–8.00–0–*ct* 0

He also played for Buckinghamshire (1896–1900).

Saunders, James
Professional. *b:* 27.5.1802, Haslemere, Surrey. *d:* 27.3.1832, Haslemere, Surrey. He died of consumption. Cousin of W. Searle (Kent and Surrey) and R. Searle (Sussex). Middle order left-hand batsman,

wicket-keeper. *Teams* Sussex (1823–25); Kent (1827); Surrey (1828–30).
Career batting
54–97–7–2180–100*–24.22–1–*ct* 43–*st* 31
Bowling 2 wickets (no analyses)–0–0–2/?

Haygarth in *Scores & Biographies* states: 'His career was short but most brilliant; and, considering the early age at which he died, his performances with the bat will be found exceeded by few, if, indeed, by any.' His first-class debut was for Godalming in 1822 and his final match for England in 1831.

Saunders, John Graham
Cricketer. *b:* 30.11.1936, Johannesburg, South Africa. Lower order right-hand batsman, off break bowler. *Team* Oxford U (1966).
Career batting
2–4–1–48–47*–16.00–0–*ct* 1
Bowling 163–10–16.30–2–1–5/50

Saunders, John Victor
Amateur. *b:* 21.3.1876, Melbourne, Victoria, Australia. *d:* 21.12.1927, Toorak, Melbourne, Victoria, Australia. He died during an operation. Tail end left-hand batsman, left-arm medium pace spin bowler. *Teams* Victoria (1899/1900 to 1909/10, 51 matches); Wellington (1910/11 to 1913/14). *Tours* Australia to England 1902, to South Africa 1902/3. *Tests* Australia (1901/2 to 1907/8, 14 matches).
Career batting
107–170–47–586–29*–4.76–0–*ct* 71
Bowling 12064–553–21.81–48–9–8/106
Test batting
14–23–6–39–11*–2.29–0–*ct* 5
Bowling 1796–79–22.73–6–0–7/34

He was most successful on the 1902 tour to England, taking 123 wickets, av 16.95, a figure only bettered by Trumble. His bowling action however came in for some criticism.

Saunders, Martyn
Cricketer. *b:* 16.5.1958, Worcester. Lower order right-hand batsman, right-arm fast medium bowler. *Team* Worcestershire (1980, 3 matches).
Career batting
3–2–0–12–12–6.00–0–*ct* 0
Bowling 212–6–35.33–0–0–3/57

Saunders, Philip Frederick
Professional. *b:* 28.4.1929, Adelaide, South Australia. Lower order right-hand batsman, right-arm fast or leg break bowler. *Team* Leicestershire (1951–52, 9 matches).
Career batting
9–11–4–93–30–13.28–0–*ct* 2
Bowling 190–6–31.66–0–0–3/57

Saunders, William
Professional. *b:* 29.3.1840, Histon, Cambridgeshire. *d:* 10.12.1923, Histon, Cambridgeshire. Brother of H. B. (Cambridgeshire). Lower order right-hand batsman, right-hand slow round-arm bowler, slip field. *Team* Cambridgeshire (1865, 3 matches).
Career batting
3–5–2–21–11*–7.00–0–*ct* 4
Bowling 183–10–18.30–0–0–4/50

Savage, John Scholes
Cricketer. *b:* 3.3.1929, Ramsbottom, Lancashire. Lower order right-hand batsman, off break bowler. *Teams* Leicestershire (1953–66, 281 matches); Lancashire (1967–69, 58 matches).
Career batting
347–460–161–2154–33–7.20–0–*ct* 98
Bowling 23777–965–24.63–46–7–8/50

He took 100 wickets in a season three times (best 122, av 18.93, in 1961). He has been joint Lancashire coach since 1973.

Savage, Richard Le Quesne
Cricketer. *b:* 10.12.1955, Waterloo, London. Lower order right-hand batsman, right-arm medium pace off break bowler. *Sch* Marlborough. *Teams* Oxford U (1976–78, blue all three years); Warwickshire (1976–79, 23 matches).
Career batting
44–52–25–196–22*–7.25–0–*ct* 14
Bowling 3787–127–29.81–6–1–7/50

Savile, George
Amateur. *b:* 26.4.1847, Methley, Yorkshire. *d:* 4.9.1904, Tetbury, Gloucestershire. Nephew of Arthur (Cambridge U 1839). Excellent middle order right-hand batsman, good deep field. *Sch* Rossall and Eton. *Teams* Cambridge U (1867–68, blue 1868); Yorkshire (1867–74, 5 matches); Canterbury (1871/2).
Career batting
16–24–1–529–105–23.00–1–*ct* 10–*st* 1

Savill, Leslie Austin
Professional. *b:* 30.6.1935, Brentwood, Essex. Opening right-hand batsman. *Team* Essex (1953–61, 125 matches).
Career batting
125–200–16–3919–115–21.29–4–*ct* 50
Bowling 26–1–26.00–0–0–1/26

He hit 1,197 runs, av 32.35, in 1959. He also played for Devon (1964).

Saville, Clifford Allen
Amateur. *b:* 5.2.1892, Bruce Grove, Tottenham, Middlesex. *d:* 8.11.1917, Fresnoy Le Grand, Aisne, France. He was killed in action. Brother of S. H. (Middlesex). Middle order right-hand batsman. *Sch* Marlborough. *Team* Middlesex (1914, 3 matches).
Career batting
3–5–0–57–32–11.40–0–*ct* 0

Saville, Graham John
Cricketer. *b:* 5.2.1944, Leytonstone, Essex. Cousin of G. A. Gooch (Essex). Middle order right-hand batsman, leg break and googly bowler, good slip field. *Team* Essex (1963–74, 124 matches).
Career batting
126–218–29–4474–126*–23.67–3–*ct* 103
Bowling 76–3–25.33–0–0–2/30
He left Essex in 1966 and appeared for Norfolk 1967 to 1969, returning to Essex in 1970. In 1970 he hit 1,133 runs, av 29.81. He was appointed Assistant Secretary to Essex CCC at the close of the 1973 season.

Saville, Stanley Herbert
Amateur. *b:* 21.11.1889, Bruce Grove, Tottenham, Middlesex. *d:* 22.2.1966, Upperton, Eastbourne, Sussex. Brother of C. A. (Middlesex). Middle order right-hand batsman, slow right-arm bowler. *Sch* Marlborough. *Teams* Middlesex (1910–28, 50 matches); Cambridge U (1911–14, blue all four years).
Career batting
90–140–12–2784–141*–21.75–2–*ct* 60
Bowling 197–4–49.25–0–0–2/29
A fine hockey player, he won his blue, captained England and appeared in 37 internationals.

Savory, Henry Jarvis
Amateur. *b:* 4.3.1914, Chipping Sodbury, Gloucestershire. Middle order right-hand batsman, right-arm medium pace bowler. *Team* Gloucestershire (1937, 1 match).
Career batting
1–1–0–16–16–16.00–0–*ct* 0

Savory, Rev James Henry
Amateur. *b:* 20.3.1855, Binfield, Bracknell, Berkshire. *d:* 5.8.1903, Bayham Abbey, Sussex. Brother-in-law of A. H. Heath (Gloucestershire and Middlesex). Attacking middle order right-hand batsman, good cover point. *Sch* Winchester. *Team* Oxford U (1877–78, blue both years).
Career batting
13–24–1–231–36–10.04–0–*ct* 7
His last first-class match was for MCC in 1883. For many years he was a prominent member of the Free Foresters. He also won a blue for soccer.

Sawyer, Charles Montague
Amateur. *b:* 20.3.1856, Rusholme, Manchester, Lancashire. *d:* 30.3.1921, Ormskirk, Lancashire. Lower order batsman, bowler. *Team* Lancashire (1884, 2 matches).
Career batting
2–2–1–21–11*–21.00–0–*ct* 0
Bowling 65–0
A brilliant rugby three-quarter he represented Lancashire and England.

Saxelby, Kevin
Cricketer. *b:* 23.2.1959, Worksop, Nottinghamshire. Brother of Mark (Nottinghamshire). Lower order right-hand batsman, right-arm fast bowler. *Team* Nottinghamshire (1978–90, 136 matches).
Career batting
136–137–42–1112–59*–11.70–0–*ct* 31
Bowling 9705–300–32.35–6–1–6/49

Saxelby, Mark
Cricketer. *b:* 4.1.1969, Worksop, Nottinghamshire. Brother of Kevin (Nottinghamshire). Opening or middle order left-hand batsman, right-arm medium pace bowler. *Sch* Nottingham HS. *Team* Nottinghamshire (1989–92, 24 matches).
Career batting
24–40–7–982–73–29.75–0–*ct* 4
Bowling 765–9–85.00–0–0–3/41

Saxena, Ramesh Chand
Amateur. *b:* 20.9.1944, Delhi, India. Middle order right-hand batsman, leg break bowler. *Teams* Delhi (1960/1 to 1965/6); Bihar (1966/7 to 1981/2). *Tours* India to England 1967, to East Africa 1967, to Australia and New Zealand 1967/8; State Bank of India to Ceylon 1966/7. *Test* India (1967, 1 match).
Career batting
149–231–29–8155–202*–40.37–17–*ct* 65
Bowling 933–33–28.27–0–0–4/24
Test batting
1–2–0–25–16–12.50–0–*ct* 0
Bowling 11–0
A brilliant schoolboy batsman, he achieved little on the 1967 tour to England, though playing in one Test. His highest score was 202* for Bihar v Assam at Dhanbad in 1969/70.

Sayen, William Henry
Amateur. *b:* January 1883, St Davids, Pennsylvania, USA. *d:* January 1965, Princeton, New Jersey, USA. Tail end right-hand batsman, right-arm fast bowler. *Team* Gentlemen of England (1908). *Tour* Philadelphia to England 1908.
Career batting
7–13–2–136–29–12.36–0–*ct* 5
Bowling 406–12–33.83–0–0–4/44
He played for the USA v Canada in 1907. His reminiscences 'A Yankee Looks at Cricket' were published in 1956.

Sayer, David Michael
Amateur. *b:* 19.9.1936, Romford, Essex. Lower order right-hand batsman, right-arm fast bowler. *Sch* Maidstone. *Teams* Kent (1955–76, 154 matches); Oxford U (1958–60, blue all three years). *Tours* MCC to South America 1958/9 (not first-class), to New Zealand 1960/1.
Career batting
204–237–86–1252–62–8.29–0–*ct* 76
Bowling 14397–613–23.48–19–2–7/37

Sayer, John Druce
Amateur. *b:* 29.10.1920, Hong Kong. Lower order batsman, slow left-arm bowler, good slip field. *Sch* Shrewsbury. *Team* Combined Services (1950–52).
Career batting
4–7–0–81–49–11.57–0–*ct* 3
Bowling 274–7–39.14–0–0–4/38

Sayers, Denis
Cricketer. *b:* 17.3.1934, St Pancras, London. Lower order right-hand batsman, right-arm medium pace bowler. *Team* Essex (1967, 1 match).
Career batting
1–1–1–0–0*–no av–0–*ct* 0
Bowling 64–1–64.00–0–0–1/22

Sayres, Rev Edward
Amateur. *b:* 19.12.1815, North Stoke, Sussex. *d:* 11.1.1888, Cold Ashton, Gloucestershire. Brother of John (MCC 1841). Lower order right-hand batsman, right-hand slow round-arm bowler. *Teams* Cambridge U (1838–41, blue all four years); Cambridge Town Club (1838); Sussex (1840, 1 match).
Career batting
24–43–9–103–19–3.02–0–*ct* 7
Bowling 100 wickets (no analyses)–5–1–5/?
His final first-class match was for MCC in 1842.

Scattergood, Joseph Henry
Amateur. *b:* 26.1.1877, Philadelphia, USA. *d:* 15.6.1953, Wynnewood, Philadelphia, USA. Brother of Alfred (USA v Canada). Tail end right-hand batsman, wicket-keeper. *Team* Philadelphia (1897–1903). *Tours* Philadelphia to England 1897, 1903.
Career batting
15–26–8–104–13–5.77–0–*ct* 25–*st* 9
He was the principal wicket-keeper on the 1897 tour, but in 1903 played in only four matches due to injury.

Schepens, Martin
Cricketer. *b:* 12.8.1955, Barrow-upon-Soar, Leicestershire. Middle order right-hand batsman, leg break bowler. *Team* Leicestershire (1973–80, 19 matches).
Career batting
19–28–5–407–57–17.69–0–*ct* 12
Bowling 13–0

Schofield, Dennis
Cricketer. *b:* 9.10.1947, Holmfirth, Yorkshire. Lower order right-hand batsman, right-arm medium pace bowler. *Team* Yorkshire (1970–74, 3 matches).
Career batting
3–4–4–13–6*–no av–0–*ct* 0
Bowling 112–5–22.40–1–0–5/42

Schofield, J.
Amateur. Lower order batsman, wicket-keeper. *Team* Lancashire (1876, 4 matches).
Career batting
4–6–2–27–11–6.75–0–*ct* 7–*st* 1

Scholey, John Colin
Professional. *b:* 28.9.1930, Beeston, Leeds, Yorkshire. Defensive lower order right-hand batsman, wicket-keeper. *Sch* Leeds GS. *Team* Worcestershire (1952–53, 10 matches).
Career batting
10–7–2–32–16–6.40–0–*ct* 20–*st* 5

Scholfield, Frank Beaumont
Amateur. *b:* 16.11.1886, Whitefield, Bury, Lancashire. *d:* 1.3.1950, Chelsea, London. Middle order batsman. *Sch* Sedbergh. *Team* Lancashire (1911, 1 match).
Career batting
1–2–1–17–17–17.00–0–*ct* 0
Bowling 2–0
He also played for Cheshire (1912).

Schultz, Sandford Spence
(changed name to Storey)
Amateur. *b:* 29.8.1857, Birkenhead, Cheshire. *d:* 18.12.1937, South Kensington, London. Lower order right-hand batsman, right-hand fast round-arm bowler, good slip field. *Sch* Uppingham. *Teams* Cambridge U (1876–77, blue 1877); Lancashire (1877–82, 9 matches). *Tour* Harris to Australia 1878/9. *Test* England (1878/9, 1 match).
Career batting
42–70–9–1046–90–17.14–0–*ct* 29
Bowling 1143–28–40.82–0–0–4/37
Test batting
1–2–1–20–20–20.00–0–*ct* 0
Bowling 26–1–26.00–0–0–1/16
His final match was for C. I. Thornton's XI in 1885. He also played for Huntingdonshire (1873–75) and Lincolnshire (1875).

Schwann, Henry Sigismund
(changed name to Henry Bagehot Swann)
Amateur. *b:* 19.11.1868, North Houghton, Stockbridge, Hampshire. *d:* 27.5.1931, Meads, Eastbourne, Sussex. Sound middle order right-hand batsman. *Sch* Clifton. *Team* Oxford U (1890, blue).
Career batting
6–11–0–204–70–18.54–0–*ct* 1

Schwarz, Reginald Oscar
Amateur. *b:* 4.5.1875, Lee, London. *d:* 18.11.1918, Etaples, France. He died of influenza. Attacking lower order right-hand batsman, originally right-arm medium pace, but later off break bowler with a leg break action. *Sch* St Paul's. *Teams* Middlesex (1901–05, 14 matches); Transvaal (1902/3 to 1909/10). *Tours* Bosanquet to North America 1901; MCC to North America 1907; South Africa to England 1904, 1907 and 1912, to Australia 1910/11; Leveson-Gower to Rhodesia 1909/10. *Tests* South Africa (1905/06 to 1912, 20 matches).
Career batting
125–192–24–3798–102–22.60–1–*ct* 108

Bowling 7000–398–17.58–25–3–8/55
Test batting
20–35–8–374–61–13.85–0–*ct* 18
Bowling 1417–55–25.76–2–0–6/47

He played in the Freshmen's match at Cambridge in 1894 and the Seniors' match of 1895, but no first-class matches. On the 1904 South African tour to England he surprised everyone by taking 65 wickets, av 18.26, and topping the bowling table. In 1907 he was the leading bowler in England with 137 wickets, av 11.79; he achieved little on the 1912 tour. His last first-class match was for L. Robinson's XI in 1914. He also played for Oxfordshire (1899–1900). A noted rugby football full back, he represented both Cambridge and England.

Sclater, Arthur William Bassett
Amateur. *b:* 27.7.1859, Auburn, Co Cavan, Ireland. *d:* 16.6.1882, River Titirau, Tortois Station, Otago, New Zealand. He died in a shooting accident. Middle order right-hand batsman, right-arm medium pace bowler, good point field. *Sch* Cheltenham. *Team* Sussex (1879–80, 9 matches).
Career batting
9–14–5–107–18*–11.88–0–*ct* 12
Bowling 687–35–19.62–1–1–7/45

He was 6 ft 6½in tall, being, perhaps, the tallest cricketer of his day.

Scobell, Rev John Frederick
Amateur. *b:* 22.2.1844, Plymouth, Devon. *d:* 8.7.1898, St Leonards-on-Sea, Sussex. Hard hitting middle order right-hand batsman. *Sch* Marlborough. *Team* Oxford U (1865–67).
Career batting
4–7–1–73–44–12.16–0–*ct* 2
Bowling 10–0

His County cricket was for Devon (1866–69), and in 1866 he hit 269 for that County v Dorset, but curiously was dismissed for 'a pair' in the next match. He lived in Cawnpore, India, for some years commencing about 1870.

Scobie, Charles Smith
Amateur. *b:* 21.2.1895, Edinburgh, Scotland. *d:* 2.9.1965, Trinity, Edinburgh, Scotland. Lower order right-hand batsman, leg break and googly bowler. *Team* Scotland (1923–28).
Career batting
8–15–3–95–26–7.91–0–*ct* 4
Bowling 583–20–29.15–1–0–5/112

Scoggins, Air Vice Marshal Roy
Amateur. *b:* 13.3.1908, West Ham, Essex. *d:* 19.1.1970, Middleton-on-Sea, Sussex. Lower order batsman, useful bowler. *Team* RAF (1932).
Career batting
1–2–0–1–1–0.50–0–*ct* 0
Bowling 112–5–22.40–1–0–5/112

His County cricket was for Buckinghamshire (1933).

Scorer, Reginald Ivor
Amateur. *b:* 6.1.1892, Middlesbrough, Yorkshire. *d:* 19.3.1976, Birmingham. Middle order right-hand batsman, right-arm fast medium pace bowler. *Sch* KES, Birmingham. *Team* Warwickshire (1921–26, 29 matches).
Career batting
29–52–8–718–113–16.31–1–*ct* 9
Bowling 659–18–36.61–0–0–3/1

He also played for Staffordshire (1932). He was a noted rugby footballer and was on the Committee of the Rugby Union for 16 years.

Scothern, Michael Graeme
Cricketer. *b:* 9.3.1961, Skipton, Yorkshire. Lower order right-hand batsman, right-arm fast medium bowler. *Team* Worcestershire (1985, 1 match).
Career batting
1 match, did not bat–*ct* 0
Bowling 42–1–42.00–0–0–1/42

He also played for Cumberland (1983–92).

Scotland, Kenneth James Forbes
Amateur. *b:* 29.8.1936, Warriston, Edinburgh, Scotland. Middle order right-hand batsman, wicket-keeper. *Team* Scotland (1958).
Career batting
1–1–0–0–0–0.00–0–*ct* 0

A noted rugby footballer, he was capped for Scotland and toured Australia and New Zealand with the British Lions in 1959.

Scott, Alastair Martin Gordon
Cricketer. *b:* 31.3.1966, Guildford, Surrey. Tail end right-hand batsman, left-arm medium pace bowler. *Teams* Cambridge U (1985–88, blue 1985–87); Sussex (1986, 1 match).
Career batting
28–31–15–67–11*–4.18–0–*ct* 10
Bowling 2822–72–39.19–2–0–5/68

Scott, Andrew Archibald Steele
Amateur. *b:* 26.1.1918, Liberton, Midlothian, Scotland. Middle order right-hand batsman. *Sch* Sedbergh. *Team* Scotland (1947).
Career batting
1–2–0–12–12–6.00–0–*ct* 0

Scott, Arthur Avison
Amateur. *b:* 3.12.1883, Bootle, Lancashire. *d:* 6.1.1968, Westcar, Attleborough, Norfolk. Son of A. T. (Cambridge U), brother of G. A. (Cambridge U). Lower order right-hand batsman, right-arm fast bowler. *Team* Royal Navy (1912).
Career batting
1–2–0–9–9–4.50–0–*ct* 1
Bowling 96–2–48.00–0–0–1/46

Scott, Arthur Pickett
Amateur. *b:* 1.9.1885, Poplar, London. *d:* 3.6.1933, Boxgrove, Sussex. Middle order batsman, useful bowler. *Sch* Marlborough. *Team* MCC (1929).
Career batting
1–2–1–40–25–40.00–0–*ct* 0

Scott, Ven Avison Terry
Amateur. *b:* 18.7.1848, Cambridge. *d:* 18.6.1925, Marylebone, London. Father of A. A. (Royal Navy) and G. A. (Cambridge U), uncle of E. D. Tillard (Somerset), brother-in-law of C. Tillard (Surrey). Middle order right-hand batsman. *Sch* Brighton. *Teams* Cambridgeshire (1867–71, 4 matches); Cambridge U (1870–71, blue both years).
Career batting
11–21–3–393–76–21.83–0–*ct* 8
He also played for Norfolk (1870–72). Whilst at Cambridge he won the pole-jump and later became a noted golfer.

Scott, Christopher John
Cricketer. *b:* 16.9.1959, Swinton, Manchester, Lancashire. Lower order left-hand batsman, wicket-keeper. *Team* Lancashire (1977–82, 46 matches).
Career batting
46–51–13–262–27*–6.89–0–*ct* 94–*st* 10

Scott, Christopher Wilmot
Cricketer. *b:* 27.1.1964, Thorpe-on-the-Hill, Lincolnshire. Middle order right-hand batsman, wicket-keeper. *Teams* Nottinghamshire (1981–91, 63 matches); Durham (1992, 18 matches).
Career batting
81–96–23–1696–78–23.23–0–*ct* 162–*st* 11
Bowling 10–0

Scott, Colin James
Professional. *b:* 1.5.1919, Syston Common, Gloucestershire. Hard hitting lower order right-hand batsman, right-arm medium fast bowler. *Team* Gloucestershire (1938–54, 235 matches).
Career batting
235–326–43–3375–90–11.92–0–*ct* 193
Bowling 16766–531–31.57–22–2–8/90
He took 100 wickets in a season twice (best 121, av 22.89, in 1939).

Scott, Donald Edward
Amateur. *b:* 5.6.1898, West Ham, Essex. *d:* 9.1.1981, Sturminster-Newton, Dorset. Middle order batsman. *Team* Somerset (1936, 1 match).
Career batting
1–2–1–12–11*–12.00–0–*ct* 0

Scott, Dr Edward Keith
Amateur. *b:* 14.6.1918, Truro, Cornwall. Middle order right-hand batsman, leg break bowler. *Sch* Clifton. *Teams* Gloucestershire (1937, 2 matches); Oxford U (1938). *Tour* MCC to Canada 1951.
Career batting
9–15–1–136–31–9.71–0–*ct* 4
Bowling 444–12–37.00–0–0–2/21
He also played for Cornwall (1938–54) and his last first-class match in England was for Minor Counties in 1949. A noted rugby footballer, he played for Oxford and England.

Scott, Emanuel
Professional. *b:* 6.7.1834, Birkenshaw, Yorkshire. *d:* 3.12.1898, Birkenshaw, Yorkshire. Lower order right-hand batsman, right-hand medium pace round-arm bowler. *Team* Yorkshire (1864, 1 match).
Career batting
1–1–0–8–8–8.00–0–*ct* 1
Bowling 27–2–13.50–0–0–1/6

Scott, Gary Michael
Cricketer. *b:* 8.3.1960, Bulawayo, Rhodesia. Middle order right-hand batsman, right-arm medium pace bowler. *Team* Rhodesia/Zimbabwe (1979/80 to 1982). *Tour* Zimbabwe to England 1982.
Career batting
2–2–0–31–21–15.50–0–*ct* 2

Scott, Rev George Arbuthnot
Amateur. *b:* 12.4.1879, Wimbledon, Surrey. *d:* 8.6.1927, Ore, Hastings, Sussex. Son of A. T. (Cambridge U), brother of A. A. (Royal Navy). Tail end right-hand batsman, right-arm fast bowler. *Sch* Tonbridge. *Team* Cambridge U (1900–01).
Career batting
5–7–1–40–10–6.66–0–*ct* 1
Bowling 265–8–33.12–1–0–5/72
His County cricket was for Norfolk (1901).

Scott, Lord George William Montagu-Douglas
Amateur. *b:* 31.8.1866. Bowhill, Selkirk, Scotland. *d:* 23.2.1947, Gladswood, Melrose, Roxburghshire, Scotland. Brother of H. F. M. (Philipson's XI) and Earl of Dalkeith (MCC), grandson of Viscount Drumlanrig (MCC 1841), uncle of D. F. Brand (Cambridge U). Middle order right-hand batsman, good deep field. *Sch* Eton. *Teams* Oxford U (1887–89, blue all three years); Middlesex (1888, 2 matches).
Career batting
27–44–4–882–100–22.05–1–*ct* 14
Bowling 12–0
His debut was for MCC in 1886 and his final first-class match was for MCC in 1905. Whilst serving in the Army in the Boer War, he ran up the Union Jack over Bloemfontein when it was captured.

Scott, Harold Eldon
Amateur. *b:* 4.9.1907, Crowborough, Sussex. Son of Osmund (Gloucestershire), brother of K. B. (Sussex), son-in-law of F. H. Liebenrood (MCC). Middle order right-hand batsman, right-arm fast medium bowler. *Sch* Winchester. *Team* Sussex (1937, 2 matches).

Career batting
4–8–0–48–16–6.00–0–*ct* 2
Bowling 158–2–79.00–0–0–1/21

Scott, Henry
Professional. *b:* 28.10.1851, Sutton-in-Ashfield, Nottinghamshire. *d:* 11.11.1941, Sutton-in-Ashfield, Nottinghamshire. Tail end right-hand batsman, off break bowler. *Team* Somerset (1882, 2 matches).
Career batting
2–4–1–12–6–4.00–0–*ct* 1
Bowling 99–2–49.50–0–0–2/49

Scott, Lord Henry Francis Montagu-Douglas
Amateur. *b:* 15.1.1868, Bowhill, Selkirk, Scotland. *d:* 19.4.1945, Gladswood, Melrose, Roxburghshire, Scotland. Brother of G. W. M. (Middlesex) and Earl of Dalkeith (MCC), grandson of Viscount Drumlanrig (MCC 1841), uncle of D. F. Brand (Cambridge U). Middle order batsman. *Sch* Eton. *Team* H. Philipson's XI (1891).
Career batting
1–2–1–25–23*–25.00–0–*ct* 0

Scott, Dr Henry James Herbert
Amateur. *b:* 26.12.1858, Toorak, Melbourne, Victoria, Australia. *d:* 23.9.1910, Scone, New South Wales, Australia. He died of typhoid fever. Cautious middle order right-hand batsman, right-arm medium fast bowler, good field. *Team* Victoria (1877/8 to 1885/6, 12 matches). *Tours* Australia to England 1884, 1886. *Tests* Australia (1884–86, 8 matches).
Career batting
85–141–15–2863–123–22.72–4–*ct* 56
Bowling 494–18–27.44–1–0–6/33
Test batting
8–14–1–359–102–27.61–1–*ct* 8
Bowling 26–0

He batted well on his 1884 tour to England, the highlight being his 102 in the Test at the Oval. In 1886 he captained the tourists and his responsibilities in that direction affected his batting. He led Australia in three Tests.

Scott, Hugh Wilson
Amateur. *b:* 18.12.1927, Belfast, Ireland. Lower order right-hand batsman, right-arm medium pace bowler. *Team* Ireland (1958).
Career batting
1 match, did not bat–*ct* 0
Bowling 9–0

Scott, John Gordon Cameron
Amateur. *b:* 14.3.1888, Upperton, Eastbourne, Sussex. *d:* 21.3.1946, Warsash, Southampton, Hampshire. Middle order right-hand batsman. *Sch* Marlborough. *Teams* Sussex (1907–10, 4 matches); Europeans (1914/15 to 1917/18).
Career batting
13–21–3–347–137–19.27–1–*ct* 6

In 1908 he played in the Freshmen's match at Cambridge and in the Seniors' matches of the two following years. On his first-class debut, for Sussex v Oxford U at Eastbourne in 1907, he hit 137. His final first-class match in England was for H. D. G. Leveson-Gower's XI in 1912.

Scott, Kenneth
Cricketer. *b:* 16.6.1964, Dechmont, West Lothian, Scotland. Opening right-hand batsman. *Team* Scotland (1987).
Career batting
1–2–1–47–33–47.00–0–*ct* 0

Scott, Kenneth Bertram
Amateur. *b:* 17.8.1915, High Brooms, Uckfield, Sussex. *d:* 9.8.1943, Bronte, near Syracuse, Sicily. Son of Osmund (Gloucestershire), brother of H. E. (Sussex). Middle order right-hand batsman, right-arm medium pace bowler. *Sch* Winchester. *Teams* Oxford U (1935–37, blue 1937); Sussex (1937, 6 matches).
Career batting
14–22–4–274–56–15.22–0–*ct* 3
Bowling 715–12–59.58–0–0–2/13

Scott, Lothian Kerr
Amateur. *b:* 24.5.1841, Paris, France. *d:* 7.7.1919, Farnborough, Hampshire. Middle order right-hand batsman, right-hand medium pace round-arm bowler, deep field. *Sch* Winchester. *Team* Gentlemen of Kent (1864).
Career batting
1–2–0–16–16–8.00–0–*ct* 3
Bowling 22–0

He was most successful in military matches in the 1860s.

Scott, Malcolm Ernest
Professional. *b:* 8.5.1936, Westoe, Co Durham. Lower order right-hand batsman, slow left-arm bowler. *Team* Northamptonshire (1959–69, 183 matches).
Career batting
185–253–63–2445–62–12.86–0–*ct* 92
Bowling 11397–461–24.72–20–4–7/32

He took 113 wickets, av 19.27, in 1964. His first-class debut was for Combined Services in 1958. His bowling action was reported by the umpires in 1967 and he was temporarily banned from County cricket. He also played for Durham (pre first-class, 1953–56). A good soccer player, he was half back for Newcastle United, York City and Darlington.

Scott, Mark Stephen
Cricketer. *b:* 10.3.1959, Muswell Hill, Middlesex. Middle order right-hand batsman. *Team* Worcestershire (1981–83, 32 matches).
Career batting
32–60–3–1383–109–24.26–1–*ct* 9
Bowling 37–0

Scott, Michael David
Amateur. *b:* 14.11.1933, Marylebone, London. Middle order right-hand batsman, wicket-keeper. *Sch* Winchester. *Team* Oxford U (1956–57, blue 1957).
Career batting
21–38–5–499–52–15.12–0–*ct* 24–*st* 11
His final first-class match was for MCC in 1963. His County cricket was for Wiltshire (1959).

Scott, Oscar Charles
Amateur. *b:* 14.8.1893, Franklyn Town, Kingston, Jamaica. *d:* 15.6.1961, Matildas Corner, Kingston, Jamaica. Father of A. H. P. (West Indies). Middle order right-hand batsman, leg break and googly bowler. *Team* Jamaica (1910/11 to 1934/5). *Tours* West Indies to England 1928, to Australia 1930/1. *Tests* West Indies (1928 to 1930/1, 8 matches).
Career batting
45–66–12–1317–94–24.38–0–*ct* 14
Bowling 5556–182–30.52–14–5–8/67
Test batting
8–13–3–171–35–17.10–0–*ct* 0
Bowling 925–22–42.04–1–0–5/266
He played in two Tests on the 1928 tour, but he was only moderately successful. He was known as Tommy because when he first played for Jamaica he appeared in short trousers, so spectators dubbed him Tom Thumb.

Scott, Hon Osmund
Amateur. *b:* 24.3.1876, Encombe House, Wareham, Dorset. *d:* 9.9.1948, Marylebone, London. Father of H. E. (Sussex) and K. B. (Sussex). Lower order right-hand batsman, slow left-arm bowler. *Sch* Winchester. *Team* Gloucestershire (1905, 2 matches).
Career batting
2–4–1–29–23*–9.66–0–*ct* 0
Bowling 11–0
A noted golfer, he represented England and was the losing finalist in the British Amateur championship of 1905.

Scott, Peter Marriott Raleigh
Amateur. *b:* 1.2.1912, Paddington, London. *d:* 13.6.1944, Villers-Bocage, France. Brother of R. S. G. (Sussex), grandson of C. Marriott (Oxford U). Hard hitting lower order left-hand batsman, left-arm fast bowler. *Sch* Winchester. *Team* Oxford U (1932–33).
Career batting
5–8–1–114–37–16.28–0–*ct* 1
Bowling 321–5–64.20–0–0–2/22

Scott, Richard John
Cricketer. *b:* 2.11.1963, Bournemouth, Hampshire. Middle order left-hand batsman, right-arm medium pace bowler. *Teams* Hampshire (1988–90, 27 matches); Gloucestershire (1991–92, 39 matches).
Career batting
66–111–8–2516–127–24.42–3–*ct* 33
Bowling 1830–40–45.75–0–0–3/43
He also played for Dorset (1981–85).

Scott, Robert Strickland Gilbert
Amateur. *b:* 26.4.1909, Paddington, London. *d:* 26.8.1957, Paddington, London. Brother of P. M. R. (Oxford U), grandson of C. Marriott (Oxford U). Dashing middle order right-hand batsman, right-arm fast medium bowler. *Sch* Winchester. *Teams* Oxford U (1930–31, blue 1931); Sussex (1931–34, 66 matches).
Career batting
86–113–10–2042–116–19.82–2–*ct* 54
Bowling 3595–134–26.82–5–0–6/64
His final first-class match was for Free Foresters in 1939. He captained Sussex in 1933.

Scott, Stanley Winckworth
Amateur. *b:* 24.3.1854, Bombay, India. *d:* 8.12.1933, Kent House, Beckenham, Kent. Middle order right-hand batsman, right-arm fast bowler. *Sch* Brentwood and Epsom. *Team* Middlesex (1878–93, 97 matches).
Career batting
104–192–19–4432–224–25.61–4–*ct* 61
Bowling 207–3–69.00–0–0–1/15
He hit 224 for Middlesex v Gloucestershire at Lord's in 1892, and in the same year scored 1,015 runs, av 39.03. After 1893 he gave up regular County cricket owing to business. He also played for Herefordshire (1874–77).

Scott, Verdun John
Amateur. *b:* 31.7.1916, Devonport, Auckland, New Zealand. *d:* 2.8.1980, Devonport, Auckland, New Zealand. Brother of A. H. (Auckland). Solid opening right-hand batsman, good field. *Team* Auckland (1937/8 to 1952/3). *Tour* New Zealand to England 1949. *Tests* New Zealand (1945/6 to 1951/2, 10 matches).
Career batting
80–130–17–5620–204–49.73–16–*ct* 42
Bowling 271–10–27.10–0–0–3/22
Test batting
10–17–1–458–84–28.62–0–*ct* 7
Bowling 14–0
He played in all four Tests on the 1949 tour and in first-class matches hit 1,572 runs, av 40.30. His highest score in England was 203 v Combined Services at Gillingham, his highest in New Zealand being 204 for Auckland v Otago at Dunedin in 1947/8. He scored 122 on debut for Auckland v Canterbury at Auckland in 1937/8.

Scott, William Ainslie
Amateur. *b:* 1845. *d:* 17.6.1899, Queen's Park, Bolton, Lancashire. Middle order batsman. *Team* Lancashire (1874, 1 match).
Career batting
1–2–1–14–9–14.00–0–*ct* 0

Scott, William Ernest Newnham
Amateur. *b:* 31.5.1903, Binstead, Isle of Wight. *d:* 6.8.1989, Albany, Newport, Isle of Wight. Lower order right-hand batsman, slow right-arm bowler. *Team* Hampshire (1927, 5 matches).
Career batting
5–7–2–102–35–20.40–0–*ct* 0
Bowling 131–4–32.75–0–0–2/66

Scott, Dr William Jerman
Amateur. *b:* 4.4.1864, Hartley Wintney, Hampshire. *d:* 18.7.1920, Windsor, Berkshire. Middle order right-hand batsman. *Sch* Merchant Taylor's. *Team* Middlesex (1894–95, 3 matches).
Career batting
4–6–0–119–107–19.83–1–*ct* 2

Scott, William Martin
Amateur. *b:* 27.3.1870, Gateshead, Co Durham. *d:* 26.2.1944, Horsham, Sussex. Hard hitting opening or middle order right-hand batsman, right-arm medium pace bowler. *Team* Cambridge U (1891–92).
Career batting
6–11–0–158–56–14.36–0–*ct* 5
Bowling 140–3–46.66–0–0–2/47
His County cricket was for Northumberland (1890–91). A noted rugby footballer, he played for Cambridge and England. He was uncle of Brough Scott, the jockey and TV racing presenter.

Scott-Chad, George Norman
(changed name from G. N. Chad)
Amateur. *b:* 1.11.1899, Kensington, London. *d:* 4.7.1950, Paddington, London. Lower order right-hand batsman, useful bowler. *Sch* Eton. *Team* Army (1923–24). *Tour* Tennyson to Jamaica 1931/2 (he did not play in first-class matches).
Career batting
3–5–0–49–24–9.80–0–*ct* 4
Bowling 213–6–35.50–0–0–2/43
His County cricket was for Norfolk (1920–32) and Lincolnshire (1936).

Scott-Malden, Christopher Edward
Amateur. *b:* 2.9.1890, Windlesham House, Washington, Sussex. *d:* 27.7.1956, Highden, Washington, Sussex. Lower order batsman, useful bowler. *Sch* Brighton. *Team* Sussex (1920, 2 matches).
Career batting
2–3–0–6–6–2.00–0–*ct* 0
Bowling 20–0

Scotton, William Henry
Professional. *b:* 15.1.1856, Nottingham. *d:* 9.7.1893, St John's Wood, London. He died by his own hand. Defensive opening left-hand batsman, left-arm fast medium bowler. *Team* Nottinghamshire (1875–90, 153 matches). *Tours* Lilleywhite, Shaw and Shrewsbury to Australia 1881/2, 1884/5, 1886/7. *Tests* England (1881/2 to 1886/7, 15 matches).
Career batting
237–377–33–6527–134–18.97–4–*ct* 122
Bowling 410–8–51.25–0–0–1/7
Test batting
15–25–2–510–90–22.17–0–*ct* 4
Bowling 20–0
His best season was 1886 with 979 runs, av 26.45, and his final first-class match was for MCC in 1891. He was noted for his defensive batting and on two occasions in first-class matches batted for an hour without scoring a single run.

Scoulding, Frederick John
Professional. *b:* 26.8.1887, Bow, London. *d:* 25.8.1928, Whitechapel, London. Lower order batsman, slow left-arm bowler. *Team* Essex (1912–20, 22 matches).
Career batting
22–28–11–92–21–5.41–0–*ct* 6
Bowling 1252–32–39.12–0–0–4/50
He also played for Monmouthshire (1923–24).

Scriven, Timothy John Adam
Cricketer. *b:* 15.12.1965, High Wycombe, Buckinghamshire. Lower order right-hand batsman, slow left-arm bowler. *Team* Somerset (1988–89, 3 matches).
Career batting
3–2–0–11–7–5.50–0–*ct* 0
Bowling 392–7–56.00–0–0–2/67
He also played for Buckinghamshire (1986–92).

Seabrook, Frederick James
Amateur. *b:* 9.1.1899, Brockworth, Gloucester. *d:* 7.8.1979, Cirencester, Gloucestershire. Brother of W. G. (Gloucestershire). Opening or middle order left-hand batsman, slow left-arm bowler. *Sch* Haileybury. *Teams* Gloucestershire (1919–35, 104 matches); Cambridge U (1926–28, blue all three years). *Tour* Tennyson to Jamaica 1927/8.
Career batting
143–225–15–5335–136–25.40–8–*ct* 82
Bowling 274–8–34.25–0–0–4/77
His best season was 1928 with 1,406 runs, av 40.17. He also completed 1,000 runs in one other season. He captained Cambridge in 1928. A schoolmaster at Haileybury his County cricket was mainly confined to the school holidays.

Seabrook, Walter George
Amateur. *b:* 12.2.1904, Brockworth, Gloucester. *d:* 13.6.1988, Bourne End, Buckinghamshire. Brother of F. J. (Gloucestershire), brother-in-law of A. L. Spens (Europeans). Lower order left-hand batsman, left-arm fast medium bowler. *Sch* Haileybury. *Team* Gloucestershire (1928, 1 match).
Career batting
1–2–0–0–0–0.00–0–*ct* 0
Bowling 10–0

Seager, Christopher Paul
Cricketer. *b:* 5.4.1951, Salisbury, Rhodesia. Brother of M. A. J. (Rhodesia). Middle order right-hand batsman. *Team* Cambridge U (1971, blue).
Career batting
8–11–1–104–23–10.40–0–*ct* 2
His County cricket was for Berkshire (1970).

Seal, Alfred
Professional. *b:* 10.8.1875, Millbrook, Hampshire. *d:* 13.2.1961, South Chailey, Sussex. Lower order batsman, useful bowler. *Team* Sussex (1904, 2 matches).
Career batting
2–2–0–0–0–0.00–0–*ct* 1
Bowling 17–0

Sealey, Benjamin James
Amateur. *b:* 12.8.1899, St Joseph, Trinidad. *d:* 12.9.1963, Port of Spain, Trinidad. Middle order right-hand batsman, right-arm medium pace bowler. *Team* Trinidad (1923/4 to 1940/1). *Tour* West Indies to England 1933. *Test* West Indies (1933, 1 match).
Career batting
51–84–12–2115–116–29.37–4–*ct* 22
Bowling 2026–78–25.97–2–0–5/22
Test batting
1–2–0–41–29–20.50–0–*ct* 0
Bowling 10–1–10.00–0–0–1/10
He hit 1,072 runs, av 39.70, on the 1933 tour and played in one Test. He played for Barbados Born (although born in Trinidad) in 1927/8.

Sealy, Arthur John Edmund
Amateur. *b:* 30.11.1903, Woolwich, London. *d:* 11.11.1944, Portsmouth, Hampshire. Stepson of A. C. Pawson (Oxford U). Lower order right-hand batsman, right-arm medium pace bowler. *Sch* Winchester. *Team* Oxford U (1924).
Career batting
8–11–7–62–17*–15.50–0–*ct* 6
Bowling 547–20–27.35–0–0–3/25

Sealy, James Edward Derrick
(birth registered as J. E. D. Sealey)
Amateur. *b:* 11.9.1912, Collymore Rock, St Michael, Barbados. *d:* 3.1.1982, Palo Seco, Trinidad. Attractive hard-hitting middle order right-hand batsman, right-arm medium pace bowler, wicket-keeper. *Teams* Barbados (1928/9 to 1943/4); Trinidad (1935/6 to 1948/9). *Tours* West Indies to Australia 1930/1, to England 1939. *Tests* West Indies (1929/30 to 1939, 11 matches).
Career batting
80–134–8–3831–181–30.40–8–*ct* 67–*st* 13
Bowling 1802–63–28.60–2–1–8/8
Test batting
11–19–2–478–92–28.11–0–*ct* 6–*st* 1
Bowling 94–3–31.33–0–0–2/7
On his Test debut at Bridgetown in 1929/30 v England, he was the youngest cricketer to play in a Test – 17 years 122 days. His batting was rather uneven on the 1939 tour to England, but he played all three Tests and took over as wicket-keeper in the Second and Third. He returned the remarkable analysis of 6.7–2–8–8 for Barbados v Trinidad at Bridgetown in 1941/2.

Seamer, John Wemyss
Amateur. *b:* 23.6.1913, Shapwick, Somerset. Steady middle order right-hand batsman, googly bowler. *Sch* Marlborough. *Teams* Somerset (1932–48, 59 matches); Oxford U (1934–36, blue all three years).
Career batting
81–134–12–2483–194–20.35–4–*ct* 44
Bowling 171–4–42.75–0–0–2/6
His final first-class match was for Free Foresters in 1949. He also played for Wiltshire (1956). He was joint Somerset captain in 1948. He gained a blue for hockey.

Searby, John Epton
Amateur. *b:* 1.11.1900, Croft, Lincolnshire. *d:* 12.10.1956, Crown Farm, Croft, Lincolnshire. Opening right-hand batsman. *Sch* Magdalen College School. *Team* East of England (1927).
Career batting
1–2–0–17–10–8.50–0–*ct* 0
His County cricket was for Lincolnshire (1923–35).

Searle, Andrew Munro
Cricketer. *b:* 11.11.1968, Stamford, Lincolnshire. Lower order left-hand batsman, off break bowler. *Sch* Malvern. *Team* Oxford U (1988).
Career batting
1–1–0–2–2–2.00–0–*ct* 0
Bowling 76–0

Searle, Cyril John
Amateur. *b:* 12.5.1921, Battersea, London. Lower order batsman, wicket-keeper. *Team* Essex (1947, 1 match).
Career batting
1–1–1–5–5*–no av–0–*ct* 1–*st* 1

Searle, William
Professional. *c:* 14.2.1796, Thursley, Surrey. *d:* February 1837, East Clandon, Surrey. Brother of Richard (Sussex), cousin of J. Saunders (Sussex, Kent and Surrey). Steady middle order left-hand batsman, right-arm bowler. *Teams* Kent (1828–29); Surrey (1828–30).
Career batting
48–91–7–1537–87–18.29–0–*ct* 15
Bowling 8 wickets (no analyses)–0–0–2/?
His first-class debut was for Godalming in 1821, and his last match for Left-Handed in 1833.

Sears, Leslie Daniel
Amateur. *b:* 12.1.1901, Wokingham, Berkshire. *d:* 27.6.1992, Amesbury Abbey, Wiltshire. Middle order left-hand batsman. *Team* Essex (1925, 2 matches).

Career batting
2–4–0–18–16–4.50–0–*ct* 0
He also played for Berkshire (1933–35).

Seaton, Geoffrey Stuart
Amateur. *b:* 6.3.1926, Kemp Town, Brighton, Sussex. Middle order right-hand batsman, slow left-arm bowler. *Sch* Denstone. *Teams* Cambridge U (1946–47); Oxford U (1957).
Career batting
8–15–2–196–51–15.07–0–*ct* 6

Seaton, John
Professional. *b:* 15.1.1844, Nottingham. *d:* 14.10.1918, Oldham, Lancashire. Lower order right-hand batsman, right-arm medium pace bowler. *Team* Nottinghamshire (1872, 4 matches).
Career batting
4–7–0–80–27–11.42–0–*ct* 1
Bowling 12–1–12.00–0–0–1/12

Seddon, Rev Richard
Amateur. *b:* 11.2.1825, Leicester. *d:* 13.7.1884, Bournemouth, Hampshire. Middle order batsman. *Teams* Nottinghamshire (1845, 1 match); Cambridge U (1846–47, blue both years).
Career batting
14–24–0–165–26–6.87–0–*ct* 4
He played for Leicestershire (pre first-class, 1847), but it is believed did not appear in any matches of note after leaving Cambridge.

Sedgley, John Brian
Professional. *b:* 17.2.1939, West Bromwich, Staffordshire. Middle order right-hand batsman. *Team* Worcestershire (1959–61, 15 matches).
Career batting
15–27–2–389–95–15.56–0–*ct* 7

Sedgwick, Herbert Amos
Professional. *b:* 8.4.1883, Richmond, Yorkshire. *d:* 28.12.1957, Stoke-on-Trent, Staffordshire. Lower order right-hand batsman, right-arm fast bowler. *Team* Yorkshire (1906, 3 matches).
Career batting
3–5–2–53–34–17.66–0–*ct* 2
Bowling 327–16–20.43–1–0–5/8
He also played for Staffordshire (1910–31).

Seeley, Gerald Henry
Amateur. *b:* 9.5.1903, Port Blair, Andaman Islands. *d:* 23.7.1941, at sea off Belgium. Middle order right-hand batsman. *Sch* Marlborough. *Team* Worcestershire (1921, 1 match).
Career batting
1–1–0–7–7–7.00–0–*ct* 0

Seitz, John Arnold
Amateur. *b:* 19.9.1883, Carlton, Melbourne, Victoria, Australia. *d:* 1.5.1963, South Melbourne, Victoria, Australia. Middle order right-hand batsman. *Teams* Oxford U (1909, blue); Victoria (1910/11 to 1912/13, 15 matches).
Career batting
20–35–1–981–120–28.85–3–*ct* 18
Bowling 12–1–12.00–0–0–1/7

Selby, John
(birth registered as John Burrows)
Professional. *b:* 1.7.1849, Nottingham. *d:* 11.3.1894, Standard Hill, Nottingham. Son of W. W. (Nottinghamshire 1848), son-in-law of J. Hogg (Nottinghamshire). Opening or middle order right-hand batsman, right-arm medium pace bowler. *Team* Nottinghamshire (1870–87, 164 matches). *Tours* Lillywhite to Australia 1876/7; Daft to North America 1879 (not first-class); Lillywhite, Shaw and Shrewsbury to Australia 1881/2. *Tests* England (1876/7 to 1881/2, 6 matches).
Career batting
222–355–25–6215–128*–18.83–4–*ct* 128–*st* 4
Bowling 188–5–37.60–0–0–2/27
Test batting
6–12–1–256–70–23.27–0–*ct* 1
His best season was 1878 with 938 runs, av 31.26 – he was the leading batsman in England.

Selby, Thomas Gothard
Professional. *b:* 19.2.1851, North Wingfield, Derbyshire. *d:* 6.11.1924, Shirebrook, Derbyshire. Middle order right-hand batsman, right-arm fast bowler. *Team* Derbyshire (1885, 1 match).
Career batting
1–2–0–3–2–1.50–0–*ct* 0
Bowling 7–0

Sellar, Kenneth Anderson
Amateur. *b:* 11.8.1906, Lewisham, London. *d:* 15.5.1989, Cape Town, South Africa. Middle order right-hand batsman, useful change bowler. *Team* Sussex (1928, 8 matches).
Career batting
19–32–1–616–119–19.87–1–*ct* 12
Bowling 37–0
His first-class debut was for the Royal Navy in 1924 and his final first-class match for H. D. G. Leveson-Gower's XI in 1935. A noted rugby footballer, he represented the Royal Navy and England.

Sellers, Arthur
Amateur. *b:* 30.5.1870, Keighley, Yorkshire. *d:* 25.9.1941, Keighley, Yorkshire. Father of A. B. (Yorkshire). Aggressive opening right-hand batsman, good close field. *Team* Yorkshire (1890–99, 51 matches).
Career batting
53–95–2–1852–105–19.91–2–*ct* 47
Bowling 149–2–74.50–0–0–2/28
The demands of business restricted his first-class cricket. He was a member of the Yorkshire Committee 1903–31.

Sellers, Arthur Brian, MBE
Amateur. *b:* 5.3.1907, Keighley, Yorkshire. *d:* 20.2.1981, Eldwick, Bingley, Yorkshire. Son of Arthur (Yorkshire). Middle order right-hand batsman, off break bowler, brilliant close field. *Sch* St Peters, York. *Team* Yorkshire (1932–48, 334 matches).
Career batting
344–455–53–9270–204–23.05–4–*ct* 273
Bowling 676–9–75.11–0–0–2/10
He captained Yorkshire from 1933 to 1947. He hit 1,143 runs, av 27.21, in 1938 and his only double century was 204 for Yorkshire v Cambridge U at Cambridge in 1936. He was on the Yorkshire Committee until 1972 and often in the forefront of the storms to which Yorkshire was subjected in post-war years. He was a Test Selector 1938–46, 1949–50 and 1955.

Sellers, Arthur Ernest
Amateur. *b:* 23.2.1876, Mansfield, Nottinghamshire. *d:* 9.2.1949, Edinburgh, Scotland. Lower order right-hand batsman, right-arm medium pace bowler. *Team* Scotland (1920–22).
Career batting
2–3–0–29–17–9.66–0–*ct* 0
Bowling 153–8–19.12–1–0–5/22

Sellers, Reginald Hugh Durning
Amateur. *b:* 20.8.1940, Bulsar, India. Lower order right-hand batsman, leg break and googly bowler. *Team* South Australia (1959/60 to 1966/7, 39 matches). *Tours* Australia to England 1964, to India 1964/5. *Test* Australia (1964/5, 1 match).
Career batting
53–80–20–1089–87–18.15–0–*ct* 41
Bowling 4653–121–38.45–4–1–5/36
Test batting
1–1–0–0–0–0.00–0–*ct* 1
Bowling 17–0
An injury before the team landed in England prevented him from making the most of the 1964 tour.

Sellick, Arthur Samuel
Professional. *b:* 20.9.1878, South Hamlet, Gloucester. *d:* 16.1.1958, St Helier, Carshalton, Surrey. Middle order batsman. *Teams* Gloucestershire (1903–04, 11 matches); Somerset (1905, 6 matches).
Career batting
17–30–6–298–49–12.41–0–*ct* 8
Bowling 57–0
He also played for Wiltshire (1910–26). He was a first-class umpire (1929).

Sells, Hugh Michael
Amateur. *b:* 23.3.1922, Southend-on-Sea, Essex. *d:* 17.1.1978, Chelsea, London. Middle order left-hand batsman, wicket-keeper. *Sch* Malvern. *Team* RAF (1946).
Career batting
1–2–0–46–26–23.00–0–*ct* 1

Selvey, Michael Walter William
Cricketer. *b:* 25.4.1948, Chiswick, Middlesex. Lower order right-hand batsman, right-arm fast medium bowler. *Teams* Surrey (1968–71, 6 matches); Cambridge U (1971, blue); Middlesex (1972–82, 213 matches); Orange Free State (1973/4); Glamorgan (1983–84, 39 matches). *Tours* MCC to India and Australia 1976/7; Middlesex to Zimbabwe 1980/1; International XI to Pakistan 1981/2. *Tests* England (1976 to 1976/7, 3 matches).
Career batting
278–278–88–2405–67–12.65–0–*ct* 79
Bowling 20582–772–26.66–38–4–7/20
Test batting
3–5–3–15–5*–7.50–0–*ct* 1
Bowling 343–6–57.16–0–0–4/41
In 1978 he took 101 wickets, av 19.09. He was appointed captain of Glamorgan in 1983 and 1984 but was forced to retire from first-class cricket in 1984 due to injury. He is now a well-known sporting journalist.

Selwood, Timothy
Cricketer. *b:* 1.9.1944, Prestatyn, Flint. Opening right-hand batsman, right-arm medium pace bowler. *Teams* Middlesex (1966–73, 18 matches); Central Districts (1972/3).
Career batting
20–35–4–603–89–19.45–0–*ct* 9
Bowling 1–0
He also played for Durham (pre first-class, 1974).

Semmence, Derek John
Professional. *b:* 20.4.1938, Worthing, Sussex. Middle order right-hand batsman, right-arm medium bowler. *Teams* Sussex (1956–68, 35 matches); Essex (1962, 1 match).
Career batting
39–63–2–890–108–14.59–1–*ct* 24
Bowling 123–1–123.00–0–0–1/43
He played for Sussex until 1960, made a single appearance for Essex in a non-Championship match in 1962, then reappeared for Sussex in 1967. He also played for Devon (1963–66), Northumberland (1973–75) and Cambridgeshire (1976).

Sen, Probir Kumar
Amateur. *b:* 31.5.1926, Comilla, India. *d:* 27.1.1970, South Calcutta, India. He died from a heart attack. Brother of Ranbir (Bengal). Defensive lower order right-hand batsman, wicket-keeper. *Team* Bengal (1943/4 to 1957/8). *Tours* India to Australia 1947/8, to England 1952. *Tests* India (1947/8 to 1952/3, 14 matches).
Career batting
82–118–7–2580–168–23.24–3–*ct* 107–*st* 36
Bowling 106–7–15.14–0–0–3/4
Test batting
14–18–4–165–25–11.78–0–*ct* 20–*st* 11

He played in the last two Tests of the 1952 series in England. A specialist wicket-keeper, he was put on to bowl in the second innings of the match between Bengal and Orissa at Cuttack in 1954/5 and performed the hat-trick.

Senescall, John
Professional. *b:* 31.5.1853, Greetham, Rutland. *d:* 4.11.1937, Melton, Yorkshire. Lower order right-hand batsman, right-arm fast bowler, good field. *Team* Sussex (1882–83, 6 matches).
Career batting
6–10–1–26–8–2.88–0–*ct* 1
Bowling 274–18–15.22–1–0–6/23

Senghera, Ravinder
Cricketer. *b:* 25.1.1947, Kamla Nagar, Delhi, India. Lower order right-hand batsman, off break bowler. *Team* Worcestershire (1974–76, 23 matches).
Career batting
24–25–7–281–36*–15.61–0–*ct* 7
Bowling 2303–58–39–70–1–0–5/81

Senior, Eric Malcolm
Amateur. *b:* 6.10.1920, Shaftesbury, Dorset. *d:* 24.4.1970, Oxford. Middle order batsman. *Team* Combined Services (1961).
Career batting
1–2–0–1–1–0.50–0–*ct* 0
His County cricket was for Oxfordshire (1939–46) and Lincolnshire (1957–58).

Serjeant, Arthur Thomas
Amateur. *b:* 16.9.1856, Clifton, Bristol. *d:* 8.10.1916, Horfield, Bristol. Middle order batsman. *Team* Gloucestershire (1883, 3 matches).
Career batting
3–6–0–41–25–6.83–0–*ct* 1

Serjeant, Craig Stanton
Cricketer. *b:* 1.11.1951, Nedlands, Perth, Western Australia. Middle order right-hand batsman. *Team* Western Australia (1976/7 to 1982/3, 51 matches). *Tours* Australia to England 1977, to West Indies 1977/8. *Tests* Australia (1977 to 1977/8, 12 matches).
Career batting
80–134–19–4030–159–35.04–9–*ct* 90
Bowling 4–0
Test batting
12–23–1–522–124–23.72–1–*ct* 13
Although he appeared in three Tests on the 1977 tour, he was only moderately successful, and in all first-class matches hit 663 runs, av 33.15.

Serrurier, Louis Roy
Amateur. *b:* 7.2.1905, Sea Point, Cape Town, South Africa. *d:* 16.1.1990, Hermanus, Cape Province, South Africa. Middle order right-hand batsman, right-arm medium pace bowler. *Teams* Oxford U (1925–27); Worcestershire (1927, 7 matches); Western Province (1927/8 to 1929/30); Transvaal (1931/2).
Career batting
30–46–8–1281–171–33.71–3–*ct* 17
Bowling 1127–42–26.83–1–0–5/103
He won a blue for lawn tennis.

Seshachari, Kilvidi
Amateur. *b:* 2.1.1876, Madras, India. *d:* 25.1.1917, Calcutta, India. He died of pneumonia. Lower order right-hand batsman, wicket-keeper. *Team* Hindus (1905/6 to 1912/13). *Tour* India to England 1911.
Career batting
19–34–10–138–29–5.75–0–*ct* 20–*st* 16

Sethi, Ramesh Kumar
Cricketer. *b:* 4.9.1941, Kenya. Middle order right-hand batsman, off break bowler. *Team* East Africa (1975). *Tour* East Africa to England 1975.
Career batting
1–2–0–12–12–6.00–0–*ct* 1
Bowling 27–0
His County cricket was for Shropshire (1976–81).

Seth-Smith, Derek John
Amateur. *b:* 11.8.1920, Church Crookham, Hampshire. *d:* 24.6.1964, Chelsea, London. Lower order right-hand batsman, right-arm fast medium bowler. *Sch* Charterhouse. *Team* Free Foresters (1950).
Career batting
1–2–0–3–3–1.50–0–*ct* 0
Bowling 23–0

Seton, Walter John
Amateur. *b:* 29.12.1864, Calcutta, India. *d:* 30.10.1912, Fleet, Hampshire. Nephew of J. Seton Kerr (Oxford U 1837). Middle order batsman. *Sch* Eton. *Team* Oxford U (1894).
Career batting
1–2–1–1–1–1.00–0–*ct* 0

Severn, Arthur
Professional. *b:* 23.6.1893, Alfreton, Derbyshire. *d:* 10.1.1949, Stainforth, Yorkshire. Middle order batsman. *Team* Derbyshire (1919–20, 13 matches).
Career batting
13–24–2–342–73–15.54–0–*ct* 5

Sewell, Cyril Otto Hudson
Amateur. *b:* 19.12.1874, Pietermaritzburg, South Africa. *d:* 19.8.1951, Bexhill-on-Sea, Sussex. Son of J. J. (Middlesex). Hard hitting middle order right-hand batsman, slow right-arm bowler, brilliant off side field. *Team* Gloucestershire (1895–1919, 158 matches). *Tours* Warner to North America 1898; South Africa to England 1894 (not first-class).
Career batting
173–303–13–7562–165–26.07–9–*ct* 118
Bowling 308–5–61.60–0–0–2/35
He hit 1,000 runs in a season twice (best 1,142, av 26.55, in 1914). He captained Gloucestershire in 1913 and 1914, and was County Secretary from 1912 to 1914.

Sewell, Edward Humphrey Dalrymple
Amateur generally, but professional with Essex. *b:* 30.9.1872, Lingsugur, India. *d:* 20.9.1947, Westbourne Park, Paddington, London. Punishing middle order right-hand batsman, right-arm medium pace bowler. *Sch* Bedford GS. *Teams* India (1892/3); London County (1900–04); Essex (1902–04, 55 matches).
Career batting
87–147–7–3430–181–24.50–5–*ct* 70
Bowling 807–17–47.47–0–0–3/73
He hit 1,080 runs, av 28.42 in 1904. His final first-class match was for MCC in 1922. He was coach to Surrey CCC 1908–10 and also played for Bedfordshire (1891) and Buckinghamshire (1912–14), also acting as the latter County's Secretary. He was a good rugby footballer, playing for Blackheath and Harlequins. The author of twelve books on cricket, he also wrote for various newspapers on both cricket and rugby.

Sewell, Frederic John
Amateur. *b:* 29.9.1913, Great Barrington, Gloucestershire. Middle order left-hand batsman. *Sch* Cheltenham. *Team* Gloucestershire (1937, 4 matches).
Career batting
4–7–0–113–56–16.14–0–*ct* 3

Sewell, Frederick Alexander Seymour
Amateur. *b:* 6.10.1881, Leamington Spa, Warwickshire. *d:* 5.6.1964, Parkstone, Dorset. Middle order right-hand batsman, slow right-arm bowler. *Sch* Weymouth. *Team* Cambridge U (1901–02).
Career batting
5–8–2–69–19*–11.50–0–*ct* 4
Bowling 213–6–35.50–0–0–3/71
His County cricket was for Dorset (1912–13) and Bedfordshire (1921–22).

Sewell, John Joseph
Amateur. *b:* 10.2.1844, Cirencester, Gloucestershire. *d:* 8.6.1897, Pietermaritzburg, Natal, South Africa. Father of C. O. H. (Gloucestershire). Attractive opening right-hand batsman, right-arm fast medium bowler. *Sch* Marlborough. *Team* Middlesex (1863–67, 9 matches).
Career batting
12–18–2–419–166–26.18–1–*ct* 4
Bowling 24–1–24.00–0–0–1/22
He emigrated to South Africa after the 1867 season and thus was lost to County cricket, though it was not clear what qualifications he had for representing Middlesex. He also played for Wiltshire (1863) and Norfolk (1869).

Sewell, Robert Page
Amateur. *b:* 3.9.1866, Maldon, Essex. *d:* 7.2.1901, Surbiton, Surrey. Attacking middle order right-hand batsman, good field. *Sch* Blackheath. *Team* Kent (1884, 2 matches). *Tour* Lucas to West Indies 1894/5.
Career batting
10–15–1–281–77–20.07–0–*ct* 11
Bowling 189–11–17.18–0–0–4/29
He also played for Essex (pre first-class, 1885–91).

Sewell, Thomas (sen)
Professional. *b:* 5.5.1806, Mitcham, Surrey. *d:* 1.11.1888, Riverhead, Kent. Father of Thomas jun (Surrey and Kent). Middle order right-hand batsman, under-arm bowler, good field. *Teams* Middlesex (1830, 2 matches); Surrey (1839–49, 9 matches); Kent (1852, 2 matches).
Career batting
117–210–14–1956–66*–9.97–0–*ct* 56–*st* 4
Bowling 2–0 + 3–no av–0–0–2/?
His final first-class match was for a Combined Kent and Sussex XI in 1853.

Sewell, Thomas (jun)
Professional. *b:* 15.3.1830, Mitcham, Surrey. *d:* 13.6.1871, St John's, Sevenoaks, Kent. Son of Thomas sen (Surrey, Kent and Middlesex). Lower order right-hand batsman, right-arm fast bowler. *Teams* Kent (1856–66, 20 matches); Surrey (1859–68, 109 matches). *Tour* Stephenson to Australia 1861/2.
Career batting
158–266–51–2542–62–11.82–0–*ct* 73
Bowling 6301–330 + 8–19.09–14–1–8/45
His first-class debut was for Under 30 in 1851.

Seymour, Adam Charles Hilton
Cricketer. *b:* 7.12.1967, Royston, Hertfordshire. Opening left-hand batsman, right-arm medium pace bowler. *Sch* Millfield. *Teams* Essex (1988–89, 14 matches); Worcestershire (1992, 11 matches).
Career batting
25–45–4–1253–157–30.56–2–*ct* 17
Bowling 27–0

Seymour, Alfred
Amateur. *b:* 16.2.1843. *d:* 31.1.1897, Folkestone, Kent. Middle order batsman. *Sch* Rugby. *Teams* Lancashire (1869, 1 match); Hampshire (1870, 1 match).
Career batting
2–4–0–47–25–11.75–0–*ct* 1

Seymour, Charles Read
Amateur. *b:* 6.2.1855, Winchfield, Hampshire. *d:* 6.11.1934, Weeke, Winchester, Hampshire. Brother-in-law of B. W. Bentinck (Hampshire). Middle order right-hand batsman. *Sch* Harrow. *Team* Hampshire (1880–85, 15 matches).
Career batting
16–31–3–485–77*–17.32–0–2–*ct* 12
His first-class debut was for MCC in 1879. He last played for Hampshire (not first-class) in 1888. He played no first-class cricket at Oxford U, but did win a blue for royal tennis.

Seymour, Edward Neville
Amateur. *b:* 14.1.1906, Dublin, Ireland. *d:* 12.2.1980, Dublin, Ireland. Lower order right-hand batsman, right-arm fast medium bowler. *Team* Ireland (1927–28).
Career batting
3–5–0–9–3–1.80–0–*ct* 1
Bowling 147–4–36.75–0–0–2/26

Seymour, James
Professional. *b:* 25.10.1879, West Hoathly, Sussex. *d:* 30.9.1930, Marden, Kent. Brother of John (Sussex). Sound middle order right-hand batsman, off break bowler, excellent slip. *Teams* London County (1900–01); Kent (1902–26, 536 matches). *Tour* Kent to United States 1903.
Career batting
553–911–62–27237–218*–32.08–53–*ct* 675
Bowling 805–17–47.35–0–0–4/62
He reached 1,000 runs in a season sixteen times, going on to 2,000 once – 2,088, av 38.66, in 1913. His three double centuries were all for Kent, the highest being 218 * v Essex at Leyton in 1911. His benefit match, Kent v Hampshire at Canterbury in 1920, was used as a test court case, which went to the House of Lords. The final ruling was that cricketers' benefit proceeds should not be subject to tax.

Seymour, John
Professional. *b:* 24.8.1881, Brightling, Sussex. *d:* 1.12.1967, Daventry, Northamptonshire. Brother of James (Kent). Attacking middle order right-hand batsman, slow left-arm bowler. *Teams* Sussex (1904–07, 42 matches); Northamptonshire (1908–19, 94 matches).
Career batting
136–221–20–3430–136*–17.06–1–*ct* 104
Bowling 3231–113–28.59–3–0–6/58
He also played for Berkshire (1931).

Shackle, Thomas
Amateur. *b:* 28.7.1834, Hillingdon, Middlesex. *d:* 12.3.1887, The Lake, Hayes, Middlesex. Lower order right-hand batsman, right-arm fast bowler. *Team* Middlesex (1868, 3 matches).
Career batting
3–5–1–67–41*–16.75–0–*ct* 1
He also played for Buckinghamshire (1857).

Shackleton, Derek
Professional. *b:* 12.8.1924, Todmorden, Yorkshire. Father of J. H. (Gloucestershire). Lower order right-hand batsman, right-arm medium pace bowler. *Team* Hampshire (1948–69, 583 matches). *Tours* MCC to India, Pakistan and Ceylon 1951/2; Commonwealth to India and Ceylon 1950/1. *Tests* England (1950–63, 7 matches).
Career batting
647–852–197–9574–87*–14.61–0–*ct* 221
Bowling 53303–2857–18.65–194–38–9/30
Test batting
7–13–7–113–42–18.83–0–*ct* 1
Bowling 768–18–42.66–0–0–4/72
He took 100 wickets in a season twenty times (best 172, av 20.15, in 1962). His sequence of 20 consecutive seasons (1949 to 1968) with at least 100 wickets in each is a record. His best bowling was 9/30 for Hampshire v Warwickshire at Portsmouth in 1960; he also returned the remarkable figures of 8 wickets for 4 runs for Hampshire v Somerset at Weston-super-Mare in 1955. He also played for Dorset (1971–74). He became a first-class umpire (1979–81). After he retired it was revealed he had sight in only one eye.

Shackleton, Julian Howard
Cricketer. *b:* 29.1.1952, Todmorden, Yorkshire. Son of Derek (Hampshire). Lower order right-hand batsman, right-arm medium pace bowler. *Sch* Millfield. *Team* Gloucestershire (1971–78, 48 matches).
Career batting
48–64–20–596–41*–13.54–0–*ct* 36
Bowling 2242–49–45.75–0–0–4/38
He also played for Dorset (1989–92).

Shackleton, William Allan
Professional. *b:* 9.3.1908, Keighley, Yorkshire. *d:* 16.11.1971, Bridlington, Yorkshire. Lower order right-hand batsman, right-arm medium pace or leg break bowler. *Team* Yorkshire (1928–34, 5 matches).
Career batting
5–6–0–49–25–8.16–0–*ct* 3
Bowling 130–6–21.66–0–0–4/18

Shacklock, Francis Joseph
Professional. *b:* 22.9.1861, Crich, Derbyshire. *d:* 1.5.1937, Christchurch, New Zealand. Lower order right-hand batsman, right-arm fast bowler. *Teams* Nottinghamshire (1883–93, 117 matches); Derbyshire (1884–85, 18 matches); Otago (1903/4 to 1904/5).
Career batting
156–231–26–2438–71–11.89–0–*ct* 92
Bowling 9458–497–19.03–39–8–8/32
His best season was 1889 with 80 wickets, av 14.60. He took four wickets in four balls for Nottinghamshire v Somerset at Trent Bridge in 1893. He emigrated to New Zealand about 1902.

Shaddick, Dr Rowland Allen
Amateur. *b:* 26.3.1920, Clapton, London. Lower order right-hand batsman, off break bowler. *Sch* City of London. *Team* Middlesex (1946–47, 7 matches).
Career batting
20–25–13–62–12*–5.16–0–*ct* 6
Bowling 1418–49–28.93–1–0–5/34
His final first-class match was for Free Foresters in 1955.

Shadwell, Francis Bradby
Amateur. *b:* 4.5.1851, Barnes, Surrey. *d:* 9.2.1915, Old Windsor, Berkshire. Middle order batsman, good bowler. *Sch* Uppingham. *Team* Surrey (1880, 1 match).
Career batting
3–5–1–58–18*–14.50–0–*ct* 1
Bowling 86–7–12.28–1–0–5/35
His final first-class match was for MCC in 1881.

Shafiq Ahmed
Cricketer. *b:* 28.3.1949, Lahore, Pakistan. Opening right-hand batsman, right-arm medium pace bowler. *Teams* Punjab University (1967/8 to 1971/2); Lahore (1968/9 to 1986/7); Punjab (1972/3 to 1977/8); National Bank (1974/5 to 1982/3); United Bank (1983/4 to 1990/1). *Tours* Pakistan Under 25 to Sri Lanka 1973/4; Pakistan to England 1974, to Sri Lanka 1975/6. *Tests* Pakistan (1974 to 1980/1, 6 matches).
Career batting
266–449–58–19555–217*–50.01–53–*ct* 211
Bowling 3270–98–33.36–0–0–4/27
Test batting
6–10–1–99–27*–11.00–0–*ct* 0
Bowling 1–0
He hit 451 runs, av 50.11, in first-class matches on the 1974 tour, but after playing in the first Test, lost his place and was given few opportunities in later matches. A prolific batman in Pakistan first-class cricket, he scored 1,000 runs in a season nine times (best 1,498, av 51.65, in 1986/7). His highest score was 217* for National Bank v MCB at Karachi in 1978/9.

Shafqat Hussain
Amateur. *b:* 17.7.1885, Meerut, India. Lower order right-hand batsman, useful bowler. *Tour* India to England 1911.
Career batting
8–16–3–80–21–6.15–0–*ct* 1
Bowling 282–4–70.50–0–0–2/73
He achieved very little on the 1911 tour to England. Curiously he did not appear in first-class matches in India.

Shafqat Rana
Amateur. *b:* 10.8.1943, Simla, India. Brother of Azmat (Pakistan), Shakoor (Lahore) and Sultan (Habib Bank), uncle of Mansoor (Lahore) and Maqsood (Lahore). Middle order right-hand batsman, off break bowler. *Teams* Lahore (1959/60 to 1968/69); PIA (1966/7 to 1978/9). *Tours* Pakistan Eaglets to Ceylon 1960/1, to England 1963; PIA to East Africa 1964/5, to Ireland 1969 (not first-class); Pakistan to Australia and New Zealand 1964/5, to Ceylon 1964/5, to England 1971. *Tests* Pakistan (1964/5 to 1969/70, 5 matches).
Career batting
107–158–18–4947–174–35.33–9–*ct* 83
Bowling 560–16–35.00–0–0–2/8
Test batting
5–7–0–221–95–31.57–0–*ct* 5
Bowling 9–1–9.00–0–0–1/2
He achieved little on the 1971 tour to England and was not required for the Tests.

Shah, A. H.
(*see under* Omarshah, A. H.)

Shahid Mahmood
Amateur. *b:* 17.3.1939, Lucknow, India. Middle order left-hand batsman, left-arm medium pace bowler. *Teams* Karachi (1956/7 to 1969/70); Universities (1958/9); PWD (1964/5). *Tour* Pakistan to England 1962. *Test* Pakistan (1962, 1 match).
Career batting
66–107–9–3117–220–31.80–5–*ct* 25
Bowling 1927–89–21.65–3–1–10/58
Test batting
1–2–0–25–16–12.50–0–*ct* 0
Bowling 23–0
He was given only limited opportunities on the 1962 tour to England. His best bowling in an innings was 10 for 58 for Karachi Whites v Khairpur at Karachi in 1969/70. His highest score was 220 for Karachi U v Peshawar U at Karachi in 1958/9.

Shahid, Nadeem
Cricketer. *b:* 23.4.1969, Karachi, Pakistan. Middle order right-hand batsman, leg break bowler. *Team* Essex (1989–92, 48 matches).
Career batting
49–68–11–1966–132–34.49–2–*ct* 42
Bowling 947–24–39.45–0–0–3/91
He also played for Suffolk (1986–88). He scored 1,003 runs, av 45.59, in 1990.

Shakespeare, William Harold Nelson
Amateur. *b:* 24.8.1893, Worcester. *d:* 10.7.1976, Whittington, Worcestershire. Middle order right-hand batsman. *Sch* Worcester RGS. *Team* Worcestershire (1919–31, 26 matches).
Career batting
26–44–4–789–67*–19.72–0–*ct* 11
Bowling 8–0
He was President of Worcestershire CCC from 1974 until he died.

Shakoor Ahmed
Amateur. *b:* 15.9.1928, Kampala, Uganda. Opening right-hand batsman, wicket-keeper. *Teams* Punjab University (1947/8 to 1948/9); Punjab (1951/2 to 1957/8); Multan (1958/9); Lahore (1959/60 to 1967/8). *Tours* Pakistan to England 1954; Pakistan Eaglets to Ceylon 1960/1.
Career batting
53–84–4–2958–280–36.97–8–*ct* 54–*st* 17
Bowling 20–0

He had few opportunities of the 1954 tour, playing in only nine first-class matches. His highest score was 280 for Lahore Greens v Railways at Lahore in 1964/5.

Shalders, William Alfred
Amateur. *b:* 12.2.1880, Kimberley, South Africa. *d:* 18.3.1917, Cradock, Cape Province, South Africa. Opening right-hand batsman. *Teams* Griqualand West (1897/8); Cape Colony (1898/9); Transvaal (1902/3 to 1906/7); London County (1904). *Tours* South Africa to England 1901, 1904, 1907. *Tests* South Africa (1898/9 to 1907, 12 matches).
Career batting
88–152–8–3351–105–23.27–2–*ct* 38
Bowling 139–6–23.16–0–0–3/30
Test batting
12–23–1–355–42–16.13–0–*ct* 3
Bowling 6–1–6.00–0–0–1/6
Although having no outstanding innings to his name on any visit to England, he proved a most consistent batsman. His final first-class match was for Wanderers CC in 1908/9.

Shand, Francis Livingstone
Amateur. *b:* 23.6.1855, Old Charlton, Kent. *d:* 5.6.1921, Denham, Buckinghamshire. Lower order left-hand batsman, left-arm fast bowler, slip field. *Sch* Harrow. *Team* Gentlemen of England (1874–89). *Tours* Vernon to Ceylon and India 1889/90 (not first-class); Hawke to Ceylon and India 1892/3 (he played in emergency, but not in first-class matches).
Career batting
5–6–2–49–17–12.25–0–*ct* 2
Bowling 168–17–9.88–1–0–6/32
He resided for many years in Ceylon, being a noted figure in local cricket there. An excellent footballer, he represented Surrey.

Shantry, Brian Keith
Cricketer. *b:* 26.5.1955, Southmead, Bristol. Tail end left-hand batsman, left-arm fast bowler. *Team* Gloucestershire (1978–79, 3 matches).
Career batting
3 matches, did not bat–*ct* 0
Bowling 167–3–55.66–0–0–2/63
He also played for Dorset (1983–86) and Shropshire (1990–91).

Shapcott, Morton Swan
Amateur. *b:* 27.9.1901, Camberwell, London. *d:* 15.4.1977, St Pancras, London. Middle order right-hand batsman. *Sch* Alleyn's School, Dulwich. *Team* RAF (1927–32).
Career batting
4–8–1–246–68–35.14–0–*ct* 2

Shardlow, Bertie
Professional. *b:* 15.12.1909, Stone, Staffordshire. *d:* 30.4.1976, Stoke-on-Trent, Staffordshire. Lower order left-hand batsman, slow left-arm bowler. *Team* Minor Counties (1949–50).
Career batting
2–4–1–45–24*–15.00–0–*ct* 3
Bowling 89–6–14.83–1–0–5/25
His County cricket was for Staffordshire (1936–60).

Shardlow, Wilfred
Professional. *b:* 30.9.1902, Clowne, Derbyshire. *d:* 21.6.1956, Burton-on-Trent, Staffordshire. Lower order left-hand batsman, right-arm fast medium bowler. *Team* Derbyshire (1925–28, 38 matches).
Career batting
38–42–14–201–39*–7.17–0–*ct* 16
Bowling 1939–56–34.62–1–0–5/41

Sharland, Alfred Percival
Amateur. *b:* 24.10.1890, Croydon, Surrey. *d:* 18.7.1944, Locks Bottom, Farnborough, Kent. Lower order right-hand batsman, leg break bowler. *Team* Civil Service (1927).
Career batting
1–2–0–2–2–1.00–0–*ct* 0
Bowling 67–1–67.00–0–0–1/67

Sharma, Chetan
Cricketer. *b:* 3.1.1966, Ludhiana, India. Nephew of Yashpal Sharma (India). Middle order right-hand batsman, right-arm fast medium bowler. *Team* Haryana (1982/3 to 1991/2). *Tours* India to Pakistan 1984/5, to Sharjah (not first-class) 1983/4, 1985/6, 1986/7, 1987/8, 1989/90, to England 1986, to Sri Lanka 1985/6, to Australia 1984/5 (not first-class), 1985/6, to West Indies 1988/9; Rest of World to England 1988, 1990. *Tests* India (1984/5 to 1988/9, 23 matches).
Career batting
93–105–28–2317–98–30.09–0–*ct* 50
Bowling 8611–325–26.49–20–1–7/72
Test batting
23–27–9–396–54–22.00–0–*ct* 7
Bowling 2163–61–35.45–4–1–6/58
On the 1986 tour to England he was the most successful bowler, taking 16 wickets, av 18.75, in Tests and 31, av 23.74, in all first-class matches.

Sharma, Rajeshwar
Cricketer. *b:* 27.6.1962, Nairobi, Kenya. Brother-in-law of R. P. Davis (Kent). Middle order right-hand batsman, right-arm medium pace or off break bowler. *Team* Derbyshire (1985–89, 70 matches).
Career batting
70–107–20–2196–111–25.24–1–*ct* 61
Bowling 2187–53–41.26–2–0–6/80

Sharma, Sanjeev Kumar
Cricketer. *b:* 25.8.1965, Delhi, India. Middle order right-hand batsman, right-arm medium pace bowler. *Teams* Delhi (1983/4 to 1990/1); Railways (1991/2).

Sharman, Graham John

Tours India to Sharjah (not first-class) 1987/8, 1988/9, 1989/90, to West Indies 1988/9, to Bangladesh (not first-class) 1988/9, to England 1990. *Tests* India (1988/9 to 1990, 2 matches).
Career batting
59–61–21–1622–111*–40.55–1–*ct* 19
Bowling 5164–139–37.15–4–0–8/76
Test batting
2–3–1–56–38–28.00–0–*ct* 1
Bowling 247–6–41.16–0–0–3/37
He played in one Test on the 1990 tour to England, but achieved only modest success.

Sharman, Graham John
Amateur. *b:* 30.5.1938, St Pancras, London. Middle order right-hand batsman, leg break and googly bowler. *Sch* Lancing. *Team* Oxford U (1958).
Career batting
2–4–0–9–6–2.25–0–*ct* 0
He was awarded his blue for squash.

Sharood, Arthur John
Amateur. *b:* 9.8.1856, Hurstpierpoint, Sussex. *d:* 31.3.1895, Axim, Gold Coast. He died of fever. Lower order right-hand batsman, right-arm fast medium bowler. *Sch* Hurstpierpoint. *Team* Sussex (1879, 1 match).
Career batting
1 match, did not bat–*ct* 0
Bowling 51–2–25.50–0–0–2/51
He did not appear in first-class matches whilst at Oxford University. He was for some years the Solicitor-General for the Gold Coast.

Sharp, Aubrey Temple
Amateur. *b:* 23.3.1889, Whitwick, Leicestershire. *d:* 15.2.1973, Leicester. He died following a road accident. Father of J. A. T. (Leicestershire). Middle order right-hand batsman. *Sch* Repton. *Team* Leicestershire (1908–35, 130 matches).
Career batting
131–230–25–5263–216–25.67–8–*ct* 66
Bowling 78–0
His only double century was 216 for Leicestershire v Derbyshire at Chesterfield in 1911. He captained Leicestershire in 1921. He was Hon Secretary of Leicestershire 1930–35.

Sharp, Charles
Amateur. *b:* 6.9.1848, Horsham, Sussex. *d:* 23.9.1903. Lower order left-hand batsman, slow left-arm bowler. *Team* Sussex (1873–79, 17 matches).
Career batting
17–31–0–345–54–11.12–0–*ct* 10
Bowling 214–14–15.28–1–0–6/34
He captained Sussex in 1879.

Sharp, George
Cricketer. *b:* 12.3.1950, West Hartlepool, Co Durham. Lower order right-hand batsman, left-arm medium pace bowler, wicket-keeper. *Team* Northamptonshire (1968–85, 305 matches).
Career batting
306–396–81–6254–98–19.85–0–*ct* 565–*st* 90
Bowling 70–1–70.00–0–0–1/47
He became a first-class umpire in 1992.

Sharp, Harry Philip Hugh
Professional. *b:* 6.10.1917, Kentish Town, London. Sound opening right-hand batsman, off break bowler. *Team* Middlesex (1946–55, 162 matches).
Career batting
167–276–30–6422–165–26.10–10–*ct* 61
Bowling 1670–52–32.11–1–0–5/52
He hit 1,000 runs in a season three times (best 1,564, av 32.58, in 1953). His final first-class match was for MCC in 1957. He has been scorer for Middlesex since 1974.

Sharp, John
Professional to 1914, then amateur from 1919. *b:* 15.2.1878, Hereford. *d:* 28.1.1938, Wavertree, Liverpool, Lancashire. Attractive middle order right-hand batsman, left-arm fast medium bowler, brilliant cover point. *Team* Lancashire (1899–1925, 518 matches). *Tests* England (1909, 3 matches).
Career batting
534–805–75–22715–211–31.11–38–*ct* 236
Bowling 12088–441–27.41–18–3–9/77
Test batting
3–6–2–188–105–47.00–1–*ct* 1
Bowling 111–3–37.00–0–0–3/67
His only double century was 211 for Lancashire v Leicestershire at Old Trafford in 1912. He hit 1,000 runs in a season ten times, going on to 2,000 once – 2,099, av 40.36, in 1911. His best season as a bowler was 1901 with 112 wickets, av 22.43, and his best bowling 9/77 for Lancashire v Worcestershire at Worcester in the same season. He captained Lancashire from 1923 to 1925. He appeared occasionally for Herefordshire. He was a Test selector in 1924. A noted soccer player, he was outside right for Aston Villa, Everton and England.

Sharp, General Sir John Aubrey Taylor
Amateur. *b:* 6.9.1917, Blaby, Leicestershire. *d:* 15.1.1977, Oslo, Norway. Son of A. T. (Leicestershire). Middle order right-hand batsman, useful bowler. *Sch* Repton. *Teams* Leicestershire (1937–46, 4 matches); Cambridge U (1939).
Career batting
5–10–0–64–36–6.40–0–*ct* 0
Bowling 172–7–24.57–0–0–4/63
He was also a good hockey player.

Sharp, Kevin
Cricketer. *b:* 6.4.1959, Leeds, Yorkshire. Middle order left-hand batsman, off break bowler. *Teams* Yorkshire (1976–90, 195 matches); Griqualand West (1981/2 to 1983/4). *Tours* Robins to New Zealand

1979/80; Yorkshire to Windward Islands 1986/7.
Career batting
218–361–38–9962–181–30.84–14–*ct* 107
Bowling 887–12–73.91–0–0–2/13
He hit 1,445 runs, av 39.05, in 1984.

Sharp, Marcus Anthony
Cricketer. *b:* 1.6.1970, Oxford. Lower order left-hand batsman, right-arm medium pace bowler. *Team* Lancashire (1991, 1 match).
Career batting
1 match, did not bat–*ct* 0
Bowling 21–1–21.00–0–0–1/21

Sharp, Norman
Amateur. *b:* 15.4.1901, Derby. *d:* 14.7.1977, Sutton Coldfield, Warwickshire. Middle order right-hand batsman. *Team* Warwickshire (1923, 1 match).
Career batting
1–1–0–3–3–3.00–0–*ct* 1

Sharp, Robert Henry
Amateur. *b:* 11.6.1893, Doncaster, Yorkshire. *d:* 15.3.1961, Bradford-on-Avon, Wiltshire. Lower order right-hand batsman, right-arm fast medium bowler. *Team* Essex (1925–28, 16 matches).
Career batting
16–25–7–169–36*–9.38–0–*ct* 16
Bowling 696–16–43.50–1–0–5/66

Sharp, Thomas Murray
Amateur. *b:* 23.1.1916, Gisborne, East Coast, New Zealand. Lower order right-hand batsman, leg break bowler. *Team* Canterbury (1936/7 to 1945/6). *Tour* New Zealand Services in England 1945.
Career batting
4–7–2–74–28–14.40–0–*ct* 0
Bowling 222–6–37.00–0–0–3/65
His first first-class match was for North Island (New Zealand) in 1934/5.

Sharpe, Rev Charles Molesworth
Amateur. *b:* 6.9.1851, Codicote, Hertfordshire. *d:* 25.6.1935, Ilkley, Yorkshire. Lower order right-hand batsman, slow right-hand round-arm bowler, good deep field. *Teams* Cambridge U (1875, blue); Yorkshire (1875, 1 match).
Career batting
9–12–3–129–29–14.33–0–*ct* 10
Bowling 945–67 + 3–14.10–9–4–7/43
He also played for Hertfordshire (1869–90) and Cambridgeshire (1874). His first-class career is remarkable for the fact that in his nine appearances he took 70 wickets, 69 of them in 7 matches for Cambridge U. A good soccer player, he was won a blue.

Sharpe, Cloudesley Brereton
Amateur. *b:* 5.2.1904, Hampstead, London. Lower order right-hand batsman, slow left-arm medium bowler. *Sch* Sherborne. *Team* Middlesex (1923, 3 matches).
Career batting
3–5–1–5–3–1.25–0–*ct* 1
Bowling 109–1–109.00–0–0–1/18
He also played for Dorset (1921).

Sharpe, Harry Wetherherd
Amateur. *b:* 14.8.1901, Wolstanton, Staffordshire. *d:* 8.7.1950, Stubbington, Portsmouth, Hampshire. Lower order right-hand batsman, wicket-keeper. *Team* Royal Navy (1929).
Career batting
3–5–0–35–17–7.00–0–*ct* 6–*st* 3

Sharpe, John William
Professional. *b:* 9.12.1866, Ruddington, Nottinghamshire. *d:* 19.6.1936, Ruddington, Nottinghamshire. Son of Samuel (Nottinghamshire). Lower order right-hand batsman, right-arm fast medium bowler. *Teams* Surrey (1889–93, 59 matches); Nottinghamshire (1894, 5 matches). *Tour* Sheffield to Australia 1891/2. *Tests* England (1890 to 1891/2, 3 matches).
Career batting
82–116–39–657–36–8.53–0–*ct* 48
Bowling 5430–338–16.06–22–7–9/47
Test batting
3–6–4–44–26–22.00–0–*ct* 2
Bowling 305–11–27.72–1–0–6/84
His best season was 1890 when he took 139 wickets, av 12.61; he also took over 100 wickets in 1891. He played soccer for Notts County. His best bowling was 9/47 for Surrey v Middlesex at the Oval in 1891. His lost the sight of one eye as a child.

Sharpe, Philip John
Cricketer. *b:* 27.12.1936, Shipley, Yorkshire. Aggressive opening right-hand batsman, off break bowler, brilliant slip field. *Sch* Bradford GS and Worksop. *Teams* Yorkshire (1958–74, 411 matches); Derbyshire (1975–76, 40 matches). *Tours* Cavaliers to South Africa 1962/3, to West Indies 1969/70; MCC to India 1963/4; Yorkshire to North America and Bermuda 1964 (not first-class); Duke of Norfolk XI to West Indies 1969/70. *Tests* England (1963–69, 12 matches).
Career batting
493–811–78–22530–228–30.73–29–*ct* 617
Bowling 197–3–65.66–0–0–1/1
Test batting
12–21–4–786–111–46.23–1–*ct* 17
His first-class debut was for Combined Services in 1956. He hit 1,000 runs in a season twelve times, going on to 2,000 once – 2,252, av 40.94, in 1962. He scored three double centuries, the highest being 228 for Derbyshire v Oxford U at Oxford in 1976. He also played for Norfolk (1977–82). He was a Test selector 1983–88.

Sharpe, Samuel
Professional. *b:* 13.1.1839, Ruddington, Nottinghamshire. *d:* 5.11.1924, Ruddington, Nottinghamshire.

Father of J. W. (Nottinghamshire and Surrey). Opening or middle order right-hand batsman, right-arm medium pace bowler. *Team* Nottinghamshire (1868, 2 matches).
Career batting
2–3–0–29–13–9.66–0–*ct* 3

Sharples, J. E.
Amateur. Middle order batsman. *Team* Glamorgan (1922, 1 match).
Career batting
1–1–0–0–0–0.00–0–*ct* 0
Bowling 1–0

Sharpless, Dr Frederic Cope
Amateur. *b:* 1.10.1880, Haverford, Philadelphia, USA. *d:* 16.11.1971, West Chester, Pennsylvania, USA. Defensive middle order right-hand batsman. *Team* Philadelphia (1903–13). *Tour* Philadelphia to England 1903.
Career batting
13–23–1–383–54–17.40–0–*ct* 6
Bowling 232–5–46.40–0–0–2/7

Sharratt, J.
Professional. Middle order batsman, wicket-keeper. *Team* North (1880).
Career batting
1–2–0–6–5–3.00–0–*ct* 0–*st* 2

Shastri, Ravishankar Jayadritha
Cricketer. *b:* 27.5.1962, Bombay, India. Opening or middle order right-hand batsman, slow left-arm bowler. *Teams* Bombay (1979/80 to 1990/1); Glamorgan (1987–91, 62 matches). *Tours* India to New Zealand 1980/1, 1989/90, to England 1982, 1983 (World Cup), 1986, 1990, to Pakistan 1982/3, 1984/5, 1989/90, to West Indies 1982/3, 1988/9, to Sharjah (not first-class) 1983/4, 1984/5, 1985/6, 1986/7, 1987/8, 1988/9, 1989/90, 1991/2, to Australia 1984/5 (not first-class), 1985/6, 1991/2, to Sri Lanka 1985/6; Young India to Zimbabwe 1983/4; Rest of World to England 1989. *Tests* India (1980/1 to 1991/2, 76 matches).
Career batting
225–325–54–11986–217–44.22–30–*ct* 127
Bowling 15859–471–33.67–16–3–9/101
Test batting
76–115–14–3760–206–37.22–11–*ct* 36
Bowling 6027–148–40.72–2–0–5/75

On his three tours to England he played in all the nine Tests possible, but only once showed the form with which his reputation was made elsewhere. This one success was an innings of 187 against England in the Third Test at the Oval in 1990. He had acted as vice-captain on the 1986 tour. His most famous innings was 200* in 113 minutes, including six sixes in one over, for Bombay v Baroda at Bombay in 1984/5. His highest innings was 217 for Rest of India v Bengal at Bangalore in 1990/1. He hit 1,000 runs in an English season twice (best 1,108, av 48.17, in 1991). His best bowling was 9/91 for Bombay v Rest at Indore in 1981/2. He captained India in one Test.

Shaw, Alexander Armstrong
Amateur. *b:* 7.9.1907, Shardlow, Derbyshire. *d:* 19.7.1945, New Delhi, India. Tail end right-hand batsman, wicket-keeper. *Sch* Eastbourne. *Team* Sussex (1927, 1 match).
Career batting
1–1–0–6–6–6.00–0–*ct* 4–*st* 3

Shaw, Alfred
Professional. *b:* 29.8.1842, Burton Joyce, Nottinghamshire. *d:* 16.1.1907, Gedling, Nottinghamshire. Lower order right-hand batsman, right-arm medium, later slow medium, bowler. *Teams* Nottinghamshire (1864–97, 193 matches); Sussex (1894–95, 10 matches). *Tours* Willsher to North America 1868 (not first-class); Lillywhite to Australia 1876/7; Daft to North America 1879 (not first-class); Lillywhite, Shaw and Shrewsbury to Australia 1881/2, 1884/5, 1886/7 (no first-class matches in last two); Sheffield to Australia 1891/2 (manager). *Tests* England (1876/7 to 1881/2, 7 matches).
Career batting
404–630–101–6585–88–12.44–0–*ct* 368
Bowling 24577–2026 + 1–12.13–176–44–10/73
Test batting
7–12–1–111–40–10.09–0–*ct* 4
Bowling 285–12–23.75–1–0–5/38

A master of line and length, he was the most economical bowler of his generation, bowling more overs than he conceded runs. He took 100 wickets in a season eight times going on to 200 once – 201, av 10.96, in 1878. His best bowling was 10/73 for MCC v North at Lord's in 1874, but perhaps his most outstanding figures were 41.2–36–7–7 for Nottinghamshire v MCC in 1875, also at Lord's. He captained Nottinghamshire to four successive Championship titles – 1883 to 1886 – after which his connection with his native county virtually ended. For some years he was employed by Lord Sheffield to coach young Sussex cricketers and in 1894, having been absent from county cricket for six years, he turned out for Sussex at the age of 51 and ended the season at the top of the county averages. He also played for Northamptonshire (pre first-class, 1871).

A joint promoter of four tours to Australia, he captained the 1881/2 team to Australia and led England in four Tests. From 1898 to 1905 he umpired in first-class matches and he was for many years a partner in the sports goods firm of Shaw and Shrewsbury.

Shaw, Christopher
Cricketer. *b:* 17.2.1964, Hemsworth, Yorkshire. Lower order right-hand batsman, right-arm fast medium bowler. *Team* Yorkshire (1984–88, 61 matches).

Career batting
61–58–27–340–31–10.96–0–*ct* 9
Bowling 4101–123–33.34–3–0–6/64
He was forced to retire due to injury.

Shaw, Dennis George
Professional. *b:* 16.2.1931, Salford, Lancashire. Lower order right-hand batsman, leg break and googly bowler. *Team* Warwickshire (1949, 1 match).
Career batting
1–1–0–17–17–17.00–0–*ct* 0
Bowling 106–2–53.00–0–0–2/60

Shaw, Edward Alfred
Amateur. *b:* 16.5.1892, Bishops Stortford, Hertfordshire. *d:* 7.10.1916, Le Sars, France. He was killed in action. Son of E. D. (Middlesex), brother of R. J. (Royal Navy). Middle order right-hand batsman, wicket-keeper. *Sch* Marlborough. *Team* Oxford U (1912–14, blue 1912 and 1914).
Career batting
13–22–2–424–57*–21.20–0–*ct* 12–*st* 8
His County cricket was for Buckinghamshire (1908–14) and he scored a century in his last match.

Shaw, Rt Rev Edward Domett
Amateur. *b:* 5.10.1860, Passage West, Co Cork, Ireland. *d:* 5.11.1937, Bisham, Berkshire. Father of E. A. (Oxford U) and R. J. (Royal Navy). Lower order right-hand batsman, right-arm fast or medium pace bowler. *Sch* Forest. *Teams* Oxford U (1882–83, blue 1882); Middlesex (1882, 1 match).
Career batting
11–21–1–315–78*–15.75–0–*ct* 3
Bowling 358–19–18.84–1–0–5/29
He also played for Essex (pre first-class, 1881), Hertfordshire (1895) and Buckinghamshire (1897–1909). He was Bishop of Buckingham.

Shaw, Dr Frederick Roland Studdert
Amateur. *b:* 29.2.1892, Dublin, Ireland. *d:* 2.12.1935, K3 Pipe Line Station, near Haditha, Iraq. Lower order right-hand batsman, right-arm fast medium bowler. *Teams* Ireland (1913–14); Europeans (1922/3); Army (1923–24).
Career batting
7–12–1–193–65–17.54–0–*ct* 8
Bowling 290–21–13.80–2–1–7/30

Shaw, George
Professional. *b:* 20.5.1839, Sutton-in-Ashfield, Nottinghamshire. *d:* 17.8.1905, Loose, Kent. Lower order batsman, left-hand fast round-arm bowler. *Team* Kent (1872, 2 matches).
Career batting
2–4–2–17–13*–8.50–0–*ct* 3
Bowling 178–11–16.18–1–0–5/89

Shaw, George Bernard
Professional. *b:* 24.10.1931, Treharris, Glamorgan. *d:* 2.8.1984, near Port Pirie, South Australia. He died in a motor accident. Lower order right-hand batsman, off break bowler. *Team* Glamorgan (1951–55, 16 matches).
Career batting
16–20–13–30–11–4.28–0–*ct* 4
Bowling 706–26–27.15–2–1–5/38

Shaw, Henry
Professional. *b:* 21.5.1854, Mansfield, Nottinghamshire. *d:* 8.11.1932, Derby. Lower order right-hand batsman, right-hand medium round-arm bowler. *Team* Derbyshire (1875–84, 14 matches).
Career batting
14–25–7–121–22–6.72–0–*ct* 5
Bowling 158–10–15.80–1–0–5/34
He also played for Staffordshire (1888–92) and Lincolnshire (1890). He was a first-class umpire (1902).

Shaw, James
Professional. *b:* 12.3.1865, Linthwaite, Yorkshire. *d:* 22.1.1921, Armley, Leeds, Yorkshire. Lower order right-hand batsman, slow left-arm bowler. *Team* Yorkshire (1896–97, 3 matches).
Career batting
3–3–0–8–7–2.66–0–*ct* 2
Bowling 181–7–25.85–0–0–4/119
He also played for Durham (pre first-class, 1900–02).

Shaw, James Coupe
Professional. *b:* 11.4.1836, Sutton-in-Ashfield, Nottinghamshire. *d:* 7.3.1888, Sutton-in-Ashfield, Nottinghamshire. Tail end right-hand batsman, left-hand fast round-arm bowler. *Team* Nottinghamshire (1865–75, 69 matches).
Career batting
115–176–66–467–18*–4.24–0–*ct* 62
Bowling 9184–637 + 5–14.41–59–18–9/86
In his debut season of 1865 he headed the first-class averages with 44 wickets, av 10.75; he took his most wickets in 1870 with 96, av 10.31. His best bowling was 9/86 for Nottinghamshire v Gloucestershire at Trent Bridge in 1871, though for XIV of Nottinghamshire v England in 1870 he took 10 for 20 (not first-class). He was generally regarded as the worst batsman in first-class county cricket about 1870.

Shaw, John Monson
Amateur. *b:* 1.10.1832, Cuxton, Rochester, Kent. *d:* 4.9.1912, Kirkley, Suffolk. Middle order right-hand batsman. *Sch* Eton. *Team* Kent (1865–66, 3 matches).
Career batting
3–6–0–31–13–5.16–0–*ct* 2

Shaw, Robert John
Amateur. *b:* 10.2.1900, High Wycombe, Buckinghamshire. Son of E. D. (Middlesex), brother of E. A. (Oxford U). Opening right-hand batsman, wicket-keeper. *Teams* Royal Navy (1926–28); Combined Services (1931–37).
Career batting
7–13–0–531–119–40.84–1–*ct* 4
Bowling 12–0
His County cricket was for Buckinghamshire (1928) and Oxfordshire (1933).

Shaw, Vero Kemball
(changed name to Shaw-MacKenzie)
Amateur. *b:* 14.1.1854, Belgaum, Bombay, India. *d:* 18.12.1905, Hastings, Sussex. Lower order right-hand batsman, left-hand fast round-arm bowler, good field. *Sch* Haileybury. *Teams* Kent (1875–78, 25 matches); Cambridge U (1875–76, blue 1876).
Career batting
34–56–8–559–74–11.64–0–*ct* 36
Bowling 959–38 + 1–25.23–0–0–4/11

Shaw, William
Professional. *b:* 5.8.1827, Burton Joyce, Nottinghamshire. *d:* 13.2.1890, Burton Joyce, Nottinghamshire. Lower order right-hand batsman, right-arm medium pace bowler. *Team* Nottinghamshire (1866, 1 match).
Career batting
1–1–0–1–1–1.00–0–*ct* 0

Shawe, Charles
Amateur. *b:* 15.11.1878, Weddington Hall, Warwickshire. *d:* 9.2.1951, The Hermitage, Witham Friary, Frome, Somerset. Middle order batsman. *Sch* Eton. *Team* Leveson-Gower's XI (1919).
Career batting
1–1–0–0–0–0.00–0–*ct* 0
Bowling 32–0

Shea, Alfred James
Professional. *b:* 7.11.1898, Briton Ferry, Glamorgan. *d:* 21.5.1969, Neath, Glamorgan. Uncle of W. D. (Glamorgan). Lower order right-hand batsman, right-arm medium pace bowler. *Team* Glamorgan (1928, 2 matches).
Career batting
2–3–0–22–10–7.33–0–*ct* 0
Bowling 171–1–171.00–0–0–1/130

Shea, William Dennis
Professional. *b:* 7.2.1924, Briton Ferry, Glamorgan. *d:* 22.9.1982, Ormskirk, Lancashire. Nephew of A. J. (Glamorgan). Lower order right-hand batsman, leg break and googly bowler. *Team* Glamorgan (1947–48, 3 matches).
Career batting
3–3–1–27–18*–13.50–0–*ct* 0
Bowling 180–5–36.00–0–0–4/68

Sheahan, Andrew Paul
Cricketer. *b:* 30.9.1946, Werribee, Victoria, Australia. Great-grandson of W. H. Cooper (Australia). Middle order right-hand batsman. *Team* Victoria (1965/6 to 1973/4, 47 matches). *Tours* Australia to England 1968, 1972, to India 1969/70, to South Africa 1969/70, to New Zealand 1973/4. *Tests* Australia (1967/8 to 1973/4, 31 matches).
Career batting
133–206–33–7987–202–46.16–19–*ct* 89
Bowling 66–1–66.00–0–0–1/19
Test batting
31–53–6–1594–127–33.91–2–*ct* 17
Although he played in all five Tests on the 1968 tour to England, he scored only 817 runs, av 28.17, in first-class matches. In 1972 he hit 788, av 41.47, but appeared in just two of the Tests. His highest score was 202 for Victoria v South Australia at Melbourne in 1966/7, and he hit 1,002 runs, av 83.50, in 1972/3.

Shearer, Edgar Donald Reid
Amateur. *b:* 6.6.1909, Harrow-on-the-Hill, Middlesex. Middle order right-hand batsman. *Sch* Aldenham. *Team* Ireland (1933–52).
Career batting
14–27–1–628–72–24.15–0–*ct* 12
He played amateur soccer for England and in the 1936 Olympic Games.

Shearwood, Kenneth Arthur
Amateur. *b:* 5.9.1921, Derby. Lower order right-hand batsman, wicket-keeper. *Sch* Shrewsbury. *Teams* Oxford U (1949–51); Derbyshire (1949, 1 match).
Career batting
5–6–1–45–28–9.00–0–*ct* 5–*st* 4
He also played for Cornwall (1947). A noted soccer player, he played centre half for Oxford and Pegasus, playing in the FA Amateur Cup Final in 1950/1.

Sheepshanks, Ernest Richard
Amateur. *b:* 22.3.1910, Arthington, Yorkshire. *d:* 31.12.1937, Caude, Tervel, Spain. He was killed whilst a journalist reporting on the civil war. Middle order right-hand batsman. *Sch* Eton. *Team* Yorkshire (1929, 1 match).
Career batting
1–1–0–26–26–26.00–0–*ct* 0
He played in trials at Cambridge U, but not in first-class matches. He was the Reuter correspondent in Spain at the time of his death, which occurred when his car was hit by a shell. A fellow journalist, who accompanied him and escaped with minor injuries, was Kim Philby.

Sheffield, Edward James
Professional. *b:* 20.6.1908, New Eltham, Kent. *d:* 28.4.1971, Chobham, Surrey. Lower order right-hand batsman, right-arm fast medium bowler. *Teams* Surrey (1930–32, 23 matches); Kent (1933, 5 matches).

Career batting
28–26–3–319–64*–13.86–0–*ct* 17
Bowling 1871–78–23.98–2–0–7/123

Sheffield, James Roy
Professional. *b:* 19.11.1906, Barking, Essex. Lower order right-hand batsman, wicket-keeper. *Teams* Essex (1929–36, 177 matches); Wellington (1938/9).
Career batting
180–277–40–3914–108–16.51–1–*ct* 196–*st* 54
Bowling 28–0

Sheldrake, Edgar Francis Talman
Amateur. *b:* 18.1.1864, Aldershot, Hampshire. *d:* 14.12.1950, Surbiton, Surrey. Middle order right-hand batsman, right-arm fast bowler. *Team* Hampshire (1884–85, 3 matches).
Career batting
3–5–0–52–20–10.40–0–*ct* 0
Bowling 78–1–78.00–0–0–1/41

Shelmerdine, George Owen
Amateur. *b:* 7.9.1899, Pendleton, Manchester, Lancashire. *d:* 31.7.1967, Roedean, Brighton, Sussex. Middle order right-hand batsman, right-arm medium fast bowler. *Sch* Cheltenham. *Teams* Lancashire (1919–25, 31 matches); Cambridge U (1920–22, blue 1922).
Career batting
53–77–8–1614–105–23.39–1–*ct* 19
Bowling 205–3–68.33–0–0–2/24

He was for many years on the Committee of Lancashire and was President at the time of his death. He was also Chairman of the Forty Club.

Shelmerdine, Neville
Amateur. *b:* 23.12.1909, Manchester, Lancashire. Lower order right-hand batsman, right-arm medium pace or off break bowler. *Team* RAF (1945).
Career batting
1 match, did not bat–*ct* 0

Shenton, John Charles
Amateur. *b:* 20.1.1862, Bethnal Green, London. *d:* 26.1.1900, Harlow, Essex. Middle order right-hand batsman. *Team* Middlesex (1888, 1 match).
Career batting
1–2–0–8–5–4.00–0–*ct* 0

Shenton, Peter Anthony
Professional. *b:* 5.5.1936, Redcar, Yorkshire. Lower order right-hand batsman, off break bowler. *Teams* Northamptonshire (1958, 1 match); Kent (1960, 7 matches).
Career batting
8–8–3–68–33–13.60–0–*ct* 1
Bowling 442–17–26.00–1–0–5/68

Shepherd, David Robert
Cricketer. *b:* 27.12.1940, Bideford, Devon. Middle order right-hand batsman, right-arm medium pace bowler. *Team* Gloucestershire (1965–79, 282 matches).
Career batting
282–476–40–10672–153–24.47–12–*ct* 95
Bowling 106–2–53.00–0–0–1/1

He hit 1,000 runs in a season twice (best 1,079, av 26.97, in 1970). He also played for Devon (1959–64). He scored 108 on debut for Gloucestershire v Oxford U at Oxford in 1965. In 1981 he joined the first-class umpires' list and has umpired in 15 Test matches (1985–92).

Shepherd, Donald Arthur
Amateur. *b:* 10.3.1916, Whitkirk, Yorkshire. Middle order right-hand batsman, off break bowler. *Sch* Leeds GS. *Team* Yorkshire (1938, 1 match).
Career batting
1–1–0–0–0–0.00–0–*ct* 0

Shepherd, Donald John
Professional. *b:* 12.8.1927, Port Eynon, Glamorgan. Lower order right-hand batsman, right-arm medium pace or off break bowler. *Team* Glamorgan (1950–72, 647 matches). *Tours* Brown to East Africa 1961/2 (not first-class); Glamorgan to West Indies 1969/70; MCC to Ceylon 1969/70; Commonwealth to Pakistan 1967/8, 1970/1; Gloucestershire to Zambia 1971/2 (not first-class).
Career batting
668–837–248–5696–73–9.67–0–*ct* 251
Bowling 47302–2218–21.32–123–28–9/47

He took 100 wickets in a season twelve times (best 177, av 15.36, in 1956) and was the first Glamorgan bowler to reach 2,000 wickets in a career. No other bowler has taken as many first-class wickets and yet failed to be selected for Test cricket. His best innings analysis was 9/47 for Glamorgan v Northamptonshire at Cardiff in 1954.

Shepherd, John Neil
Cricketer. *b:* 9.11.1943, Belleplaine, St Andrew, Barbados. Middle order right-hand batsman, right-arm medium pace bowler. *Teams* Barbados (1964/5 to 1970/1); Kent (1966–81, 303 matches); Rhodesia (1975/6); Gloucestershire (1982–87, 71 matches). *Tours* West Indies to England 1969; Kent to West Indies 1972/3 (not first-class); Robins to South Africa 1973/4, 1974/5, to West Indies 1974/5 (not first-class); International Wanderers to South Africa 1974/5, 1975/6, to Rhodesia 1975/6. *Tests* West Indies (1969 to 1970/1, 5 matches).
Career batting
423–613–106–13359–170–26.34–10–*ct* 292
Bowling 32068–1157–27.71–54–2–8/40
Test batting
5–8–0–77–32–9.62–0–*ct* 4
Bowling 479–19–25.21–1–0–5/104

His best English season was 1968, when he hit 1,157 runs, av 29.66, and took 96 wickets, av 18.72. He hit 1,000 runs in one other season. He was

Gloucestershire coach 1985–89 during which time he appeared only twice in first-class matches.

Shepherd, Sydney George
Professional. *b:* 23.8.1908, York. *d:* 20.12.1987, Graigadwywynt, Ruthin, Denbighshire. Middle order right-hand batsman, right-arm medium fast bowler. *Team* Worcestershire (1936, 1 match).
Career batting
1–2–0–9–9–4.50–0–*ct* 0
Bowling 4–0
He also played for Cheshire (1946–59).

Shepherd, Thomas Frederick
Professional. *b:* 5.12.1889, Headington Quarry, Oxfordshire. *d:* 13.2.1957, Norbiton, Kingston-upon-Thames, Surrey. Sound middle order right-hand batsman, right-arm medium pace bowler, excellent slip field. *Team* Surrey (1919–32, 354 matches).
Career batting
363–531–61–18715–277*–39.81–42–*ct* 274
Bowling 13678–445–30.73–12–0–6/78
He hit 1,000 runs in a season twelve times, going on to 2,000 once – 2,145, av 55.00, in 1927. His five double centuries were all for Surrey, the highest being 277* v Gloucestershire at the Oval in 1927.

Shepherd, William
Professional. *b:* 9.8.1840, Kennington, London. *d:* 27.5.1919, Tooting, London. Lower order left-hand batsman, left-arm medium pace bowler. *Team* Surrey (1864–65, 13 matches).
Career batting
13–17–6–56–18–5.09–0–*ct* 8
Bowling 709–38–18.65–2–0–8/49

Sheppard, Rt Rev David Stuart
Amateur. *b:* 6.3.1929, Reigate, Surrey. Great-nephew of T. W. (Hampshire and Worcestershire). Stylish opening right-hand batsman, slow left-arm bowler, brilliant close field. *Sch* Sherborne. *Teams* Sussex (1947–62, 141 matches); Cambridge U (1950–52, blue all three years). *Tours* MCC to Australia and New Zealand 1950/1, 1962/3. *Tests* England (1950 to 1962/3, 22 matches).
Career batting
230–395–31–15838–239*–43.51–45–*ct* 195
Bowling 88–2–44.00–0–0–1/5
Test batting
22–33–2–1172–119–37.80–3–*ct* 12
Whilst at Cambridge he created a new record by hitting 1,281, with seven centuries, in 1952 and he scored a record 3,545 in his University career. He hit 1,000 runs in a season six times, going on to 2,000 three times (best 2,270, av 45.40, in 1953). He hit one double century for Sussex and two for Cambridge, his highest being 239* for Cambridge U v Worcestershire at Worcester in 1952. He captained Cambridge in 1952 and Sussex in 1953, but after that season ceased to play regular first-class cricket, though captaining England twice in 1954. From 1969 to 1975 he was Bishop Suffragan of Woolwich and from 1975 Bishop of Liverpool.

Sheppard, Edward Cecil John
Amateur. *b:* 2.3.1891, Clifton, Bristol, Gloucestershire. *d:* 23.12.1962, Bristol, Gloucestershire. Middle order batsman. *Team* Gloucestershire (1921–22, 5 matches).
Career batting
5–9–0–117–29–13.00–0–*ct* 3

Sheppard, Geoffrey Allan
Amateur. *b:* 18.12.1890, Glasgow, Scotland. *d:* 22.5.1940, Henwick, Newbury, Berkshire. Middle order batsman. *Sch* Charterhouse. *Team* Worcestershire (1919, 2 matches).
Career batting
2–4–0–18–11–4.50–0–*ct* 2

Sheppard, Harold Frederick
Amateur. *b:* 11.9.1917, Glasgow, Scotland. Son of H. H. (Scotland). Opening or middle order right-hand batsman. *Team* Scotland (1938–52).
Career batting
13–24–1–509–72–22.13–0–*ct* 11
Bowling 7–0

Sheppard, Harold Holmes
Amateur. *b:* 20.5.1889, Pewsey, Wiltshire. *d:* 28.7.1978, Sherborne, Dorset. Father of H. F. (Scotland). Lower order right-hand batsman, left-arm medium pace bowler. *Team* Scotland (1924).
Career batting
1–2–0–15–9–7.50–0–*ct* 1
Bowling 63–0

Sheppard, Robert Alexander
Amateur. *b:* 24.8.1879, Croydon, Surrey. *d:* 28.1.1953, Carshalton Beeches, Surrey. Lower order right-hand batsman, off break bowler. *Sch* Whitgift. *Team* Surrey (1904–05, 12 matches).
Career batting
14–18–1–403–82–23.70–0–*ct* 10
Bowling 602–22–27.36–0–0–4/33

Sheppard, Thomas Winter
(changed name to Sheppard-Graham in 1919)
Amateur. *b:* 4.3.1873, Havant, Hampshire. *d:* 7.6.1954, Callander, Perthshire, Scotland. great-uncle of D. S. (Sussex). Middle order right-hand batsman. *Sch* Haileybury. *Teams* Hampshire (1905, 1 match); Worcestershire (1909, 1 match).
Career batting
2–3–0–53–22–17.66–0–*ct* 0

Shepperd, John
Professional. *b:* 8.5.1937, Willesden, Middlesex. Lower order right-hand batsman, right-arm fast medium bowler. *Team* Middlesex (1959–60, 3 matches).

Career batting
4–6–2–32–13–8.00–0–*ct* 0
Bowling 253–4–63.25–0–0–3/35
He also played for Norfolk (1963–68).

Shepstone, George Harold
Amateur. *b:* 9.4.1876, Pietermaritzburg, South Africa. *d:* 3.7.1940, Springkell, Germiston, Transvaal, South Africa. He died by his own hand. Middle order right-hand batsman, right-arm fast bowler. *Sch* Repton. *Teams* Transvaal (1897/8 to 1904/5); MCC (1904). *Tour* South Africa to England 1904. *Tests* South Africa (1895/6 to 1898/9, 2 matches).
Career batting
22–34–1–693–104–21.00–1–*ct* 11
Bowling 682–42–16.23–3–1–5/17
Test batting
2–4–0–38–21–9.50–0–*ct* 2
Bowling 47–0
He appeared in only six first-class matches on the 1904 tour. His first-class debut was for South Africa v England in 1895/6.

Sheridan, Keith Lamont Paton
Cricketer. *b:* 26.3.1971, Glasgow, Scotland. Lower order right-hand batsman, slow left-arm bowler. *Team* Scotland (1992).
Career batting
1 match, did not bat–*ct* 0
Bowling 104–1–104.00–0–0–1/62

Sherman, Howard Richard
Cricketer. *b:* 15.6.1943, Seven Kings, Essex. Middle order right-hand batsman, off break bowler. *Sch* Chigwell. *Team* Essex (1967–69, 13 matches).
Career batting
13–21–3–448–66–24.88–0–*ct* 4
Bowling 23–0

Sherman, John
Professional. *b:* 17.10.1788, Crayford, Kent. *d:* 31.8.1861, Manchester, Lancashire. Brother of James (Surrey 1810), father of Thomas (Surrey). Middle order right-hand batsman, slow right-hand under-arm bowler. *Team* Surrey (1810–17).
Career batting
27–46–7–470–88–12.05–0–*ct* 13
Bowling 149–16 + 21–9.33–3–1–6/13
His career in first-class matches was a very long one extending some 44 seasons, his first match being for Lord F. Beauclerk's XI in 1809, and his last for Manchester in 1852.

Sherman, Thomas
Professional. *b:* 1.12.1825, Mitcham, Surrey. *d:* 10.10.1911, Croydon, Surrey. Son of John (Surrey), nephew of James (Surrey 1810). Lower order right-hand batsman, right-arm fast bowler. *Teams* Surrey (1847–70, 51 matches); Lancashire (1851, 1 match as given man).
Career batting
82–137–35–713–41–6.99–0–*ct* 61
Bowling 2438–168 + 176–14.51–29–8–8/?
His first-class debut was for Manchester in 1846. He also played for Cheshire (1855) and Herefordshire (1959).

Sherrard, Patrick
Amateur. *b:* 7.1.1919, Mickleover, Derbyshire. Middle order right-hand batsman. *Sch* Stowe. *Teams* Cambridge U (1938); Leicestershire (1938, 1 match).
Career batting
2–3–0–60–53–20.00–0–*ct* 0
He also played for Berkshire (1946). He won a blue for rugby.

Sherwell, Noel Benjamin
Amateur. *b:* 16.3.1904, Hendon, Middlesex. *d:* 29.12.1960, Flims, near Chur, Switzerland. He was killed while skiing. Lower order right-hand batsman, wicket-keeper. *Sch* Tonbridge. *Teams* Cambridge U (1923–25, blue all three years); Middlesex (1925–26, 3 matches).
Career batting
36–56–10–670–53*–14.56–0–*ct* 36–*st* 25
His final first-class match was for Free Foresters in 1939.

Sherwell, Percy William
Amateur. *b:* 17.8.1880, Isipingo, Natal, South Africa. *d:* 17.4.1948, Bulawayo, Southern Rhodesia. Opening or middle order right-hand batsman, wicket-keeper. *Sch* Bedford County. *Team* Transvaal (1902/3 to 1906/7). *Tours* South Africa to England 1907, to Australia 1910/11; Leveson-Gower to Rhodesia 1909/10. *Tests* South Africa (1905/6 to 1910/11, 13 matches).
Career batting
58–91–16–1808–144–24.10–3–*ct* 67–*st* 53
Test batting
13–22–4–427–115–23.72–1–*ct* 20–*st* 16
He captained the 1907 South African touring team to England and hit 806 runs, av 23.02, his only innings of note being 115 in the first Test at Lord's. In all he captained South Africa in 13 Tests. He lived in England for some years and played for Cornwall. His final first-class match was for P. W. Sherwell's XI in 1913/14. He played tennis for South Africa.

Sherwin, Arthur West
Amateur. *b:* 22.7.1879, Derby. *d:* 10.10.1947, Duffield, Derbyshire. Brother of C. B. (Derbyshire). Middle order right-hand batsman, right-arm medium bowler. *Team* Derbyshire (1908, 11 matches).
Career batting
11–21–2–152–24–8.00–0–*ct* 4

Sherwin, Charles Bakewell
Amateur. *b:* 9.8.1877, Derby. *d:* 8.6.1950, Derby. Brother of A. W. (Derbyshire). Middle order right-hand batsman. *Team* Derbyshire (1907, 1 match).

Sherwin, Howard

Career batting
1–2–0–7–7–3.50–0–*ct* 0

Sherwin, Howard
Professional. *b:* 22.7.1911, Chesterfield, Derbyshire. Lower order left-hand batsman. *Team* Derbyshire (1937, 1 match).
Career batting
1–2–2–12–9*–no av–0–*ct* 0
Bowling 32–0

Sherwin, Mordecai
Professional. *b:* 26.2.1851, Greasley, Nottinghamshire. *d:* 3.7.1910, Nottingham. Tail end right-hand batsman, occasional right-arm fast bowler, wicket-keeper. *Team* Nottinghamshire (1876–96, 206 matches). *Tour* Lillywhite, Shaw and Shrewsbury to Australia 1886/7. *Tests* England (1886/7 to 1888, 3 matches).
Career batting
328–454–147–2332–37–7.59–0–*ct* 611–*st* 225
Bowling 108–8–13.50–0–0–2/7
Test batting
3–6–4–30–21*–15.00–0–*ct* 5–*st* 2

He captained Nottinghamshire in 1887 and 1888. He was later a first-class umpire (1896–1901), standing in one Test match (1899). A good soccer player, he kept goal for Notts County.

Shield, Ian Noel Ridley
Amateur. *b:* 24.12.1914, Ayot St Lawrence, Hertfordshire. Lower order left-hand batsman, right-arm fast medium bowler. *Sch* Rugby. *Team* Hampshire (1939, 4 matches).
Career batting
4–5–1–16–6–4.00–0–*ct* 0
Bowling 274–4–68.50–0–0–2/91

He played in trials at Oxford U, but not in first-class matches.

Shields, John
Amateur. *b:* 1.2.1882, Loudoun, Ayrshire, Scotland. *d:* 11.5.1960, Isley Walton, Leicestershire. Lower order right-hand batsman, wicket-keeper. *Sch* Derby. *Team* Leicestershire (1906–23, 129 matches).
Career batting
133–215–44–1401–63–8.19–0–*ct* 176–*st* 60
Bowling 4–0

He captained Leicestershire 1911–13.

Shillingford, Grayson Cleophas
Cricketer. *b:* 25.9.1944, Macoucherie, Dublanc, Dominica. Cousin of I. T. (West Indies). Tail end left-hand batsman, right-arm fast medium bowler. *Team* Windward Islands (1967/8 to 1978/9). *Tours* West Indies to England 1969, 1973. *Tests* West Indies (1969 to 1971/2, 7 matches).
Career batting
81–106–28–791–42–10.14–0–*ct* 22
Bowling 5760–217–26.54–6–0–6/49
Test batting
7–8–1–57–25–8.14–0–*ct* 2
Bowling 537–15–35.80–0–0–3/63

He took 36 wickets, av 18.58, on the 1969 tour, playing in two Tests, but injury meant that he missed several matches. In 1973 he was ineffective and not selected for the Tests.

Shilton, John Edward
(birth registered as J. E. Shelton)
Professional. *b:* 2.10.1861, Horbury Junction, Yorkshire. *d:* 27.9.1899, Sedbergh, Yorkshire. Lower order right-hand batsman, slow left-arm bowler. *Team* Warwickshire (1894–95, 19 matches).
Career batting
24–32–10–203–30–9.22–0–*ct* 17
Bowling 1631–71–22.97–4–0–7/75

His first-class debut was for the North of England in 1884. He played for Yorkshire in 1883 in non-first-class cricket and also for Worcestershire (pre first-class, 1881), Durham (pre first-class, 1882) and Northumberland (1884). He played for Warwickshire under the identity of John Shilton (who was born at Coventry in 1857) a first cousin, and first played (pre first-class) in 1885.

Shinde, Sadashiv Ganpatrao
Amateur. *b:* 18.8.1923, Bombay, India. *d:* 22.6.1955, Bombay, India. He died of typhoid. Attacking lower order right-hand batsman, leg break and googly bowler. *Teams* Maharashtra (1940/1 to 1949/50); Hindus (1945/6); Baroda (1947/8 to 1948/9); Bombay (1950/1 to 1954/5). *Tours* India to England 1946, 1952. *Tests* India (1946–52, 7 matches).
Career batting
79–95–33–871–50*–14.04–0–*ct* 16
Bowling 7496–230–32.59–12–0–8/162
Test batting
7–11–5–85–14–14.16–0–*ct* 0
Bowling 717–12–59.75–1–0–6/91

He was disappointing on both his tours to England, but appeared in both Test series.

Shine, Eustace Beverley
Amateur. *b:* 9.7.1873, Port of Spain, Trinidad. *d:* 11.11.1952, Ashley, New Milton, Hampshire. Lower order right-hand batsman, right-arm fast bowler. *Teams* Cambridge U (1895–97, blue 1896–97); Kent (1896–99, 23 matches).
Career batting
46–68–13–576–49–10.47–0–*ct* 45
Bowling 3909–165–23.69–8–2–7/45

He played a major part in changing the follow-on law from being compulsory to being optional. In the University match of 1896 he deliberately bowled three deliveries to the boundary in order to concede 12 runs and avoid letting Oxford follow-on.

Shine, Kevin James
Cricketer. *b:* 22.2.1969, Bracknell, Berkshire. Lower order right-hand batsman, right-arm fast medium bowler. *Team* Hampshire (1989–92, 41 matches).
Career batting
41–33–16–204–26*–12.00–0–*ct* 3
Bowling 3384–95–35.62–5–1–8/47
He also played for Berkshire (1986).

Shingler, George
Professional. *b:* 15.5.1882, Leicester. *d:* 5.5.1946, New Queniborough, Leicestershire. Middle order right-hand batsman. *Team* Leicestershire (1920–21, 4 matches).
Career batting
4–8–0–76–26–9.50–0–*ct* 5
Bowling 85–0

Shipman, Alan Wilfred
Professional. *b:* 7.3.1901, Ratby, Leicestershire. *d:* 12.12.1979, Leicester. Brother of William (Leicestershire). Middle order right-hand batsman, right-arm fast bowler. *Team* Leicestershire (1920–36, 383 matches).
Career batting
386–661–72–13682–226–23.22–15–*ct* 97
Bowling 15394–607–25.36–16–0–7/62
He hit 1,000 runs in a season eight times (best 1,621, av 33.77, in 1928). His only double century was 226 for Leicestershire v Kent at Tonbridge in 1928.

Shipman, William
Professional. *b:* 1.3.1886, Ratby, Leicestershire. *d:* 26.8.1943, Ratby, Leicestershire. Brother of A. W. (Leicestershire). Lower order right-hand batsman, right-arm fast bowler. *Team* Leicestershire (1908–21, 111 matches).
Career batting
113–190–14–2497–69–14.18–0–*ct* 83
Bowling 10006–367–27.26–16–3–9/83
His best bowling was 9/83 for Leicestershire v Surrey at the Oval in 1911. He took 110 wickets, av 26.95, in 1911.

Shippey, Peter Anthony
Amateur. *b:* 31.8.1939. Newton, Wisbech, Cambridgeshire. Middle order left-hand batsman. *Teams* MCC (1967); Minor Counties (1969–71).
Career batting
4–7–1–187–94*–31.16–0–*ct* 0
His County cricket was for Cambridgeshire (1957–83).

Shipston, Frank William
Professional. *b:* 29.7.1906, Bulwell, Nottinghamshire. Middle order right-hand batsman, off break bowler. *Team* Nottinghamshire (1925–33, 49 matches).
Career batting
49–72–8–1183–118*–18.48–2–*ct* 13
He was a first-class umpire (1956). He was coach to Nottinghamshire from 1958 to 1965.

Shipton, William Louis
Amateur. *b:* 19.3.1861, Buxton, Derbyshire. *d:* 21.10.1941, Buxton, Derbyshire. Lower order right-hand batsman, right-arm fast bowler. *Sch* Repton. *Team* Derbyshire (1884, 1 match).
Career batting
1–2–0–4–3–2.00–0–*ct* 0
He did not play in first-class matches whilst at Cambridge University. He last played for Derbyshire (not first-class) in 1893.

Shirley, William Robert de la Cour
Amateur. *b:* 13.10.1900, Marylebone, London. *d:* 23.4.1970, Bognor Regis, Sussex. Opening right-hand batsman, right-arm fast medium bowler. *Sch* Eton. *Teams* Hampshire (1922–25, 49 matches); Cambridge U (1924, blue).
Career batting
62–93–11–1458–90–17.78–0–*ct* 31
Bowling 1912–81–23.60–0–0–4/10

Shirreff, Alexander Campbell
Amateur. *b:* 12.2.1919, Ealing, Middlesex. Sound middle order right-hand batsman, right-arm medium pace bowler. *Sch* Dulwich. *Teams* Cambridge U (1939, blue); Hampshire (1946–47, 12 matches); Kent (1950–56, 46 matches); Somerset (1958, 2 matches).
Career batting
119–203–24–3887–115*–21.71–1–*ct* 89
Bowling 9575–304–31.49–11–0–8/111
Being in the RAF his County cricket was very intermittant, but he played frequently for Combined Services and for the RAF XI. He was Somerset coach in 1958.

Shivram, Babaji Palwankar
Amateur. *b:* 6.3.1878, Bhuj, India. *d:* 28.12.1941, Bombay, India. Brother of P. Baloo (Hindus), P. Ganpat (Hindus) and P. Vithal (Hindus), uncle of Y. B. Palwankar (Bombay). Middle order right-hand batsman, off break bowler. *Team* Hindus (1905/6 to 1924/5). *Tour* India to England 1911.
Career batting
39–67–7–1130–113*–18.83–1–*ct* 18
Bowling 1090–53–20.56–0–0–4/31
He hit 631 runs, av 28.68, on the 1911 tour, being second in the first-class averages.

Shoaib Mohammad
Cricketer. *b:* 8.1.1961, Karachi, Pakistan. Son of Hanif (Pakistan), nephew of Wazir (Pakistan), Sadiq (Pakistan), Mushtaq (Pakistan) and Raees (Karachi), cousin of Shahid (PIA) and Asif (PIA). Opening right-hand batsman, off break bowler. *Teams* PIA

(1976/7 to 1991/2); Karachi (1983/4 to 1991/2). *Tours* Pakistan to India 1983/4, 1986/7, 1989/90 (not first-class), to New Zealand 1984/5, 1988/9, to Sri Lanka 1985/6, to Australia 1986/7 (not first-class), 1988/9 (not first-class), 1989/90, to England 1987, 1992, to West Indies 1987/8, to Sharjah (not first-class) 1984/5, 1986/7, 1988/9, 1989/90, to Bangladesh (not first-class) 1988/9. *Tests* Pakistan (1983/4 to 1992, 39 matches).
Career batting
144–242–33–8801–208*–42.11–27–*ct* 65
Bowling 616–12–51.33–0–0–2/8
Test batting
39–58–6–2443–203*–46.98–7–*ct* 20
Bowling 113–5–22.60–0–0–2/8

On the 1987 tour to England he played in four Tests, but was too impetuous. In first-class matches he hit 727 runs, av 40.28. In 1992 he appeared in only one Test, but scored 761 runs, av 44.71, in all first-class games. His highest score was 208* for Pakistanis v Board XI at Georgetown in 1987/8. He scored 113 on his first-class debut for PIA v Baluchistan at Karachi in 1976/7.

Shoesmith, George
Professional. *b:* 19.10.1842, Storrington, Sussex. *d:* 27.7.1877, Sutton, Pulborough, Sussex. He died of bronchitis. Lower order left-hand batsman, right-hand fast round-arm bowler, slip field. *Team* Sussex (1869–71, 11 matches).
Career batting
11–20–7–91–17*–7.00–0–*ct* 5
Bowling 467–20–23.35–1–0–5/48

Shoosmith, Joseph
Professional. *b:* 17.6.1859, Kemp Town, Brighton, Sussex. *d:* 9.4.1901, Brighton, Sussex. Lower order batsman, useful bowler. *Team* Sussex (1881, 1 match).
Career batting
1–2–1–2–2–2.00–0–*ct* 0
Bowling 23–1–23.00–0–0–1/23

Shooter, Thomas
Professional. *b:* 11.3.1845, Hucknall Torkard, Nottinghamshire. *d:* 14.7.1919, Hucknall Torkard, Nottinghamshire. Middle order right-hand batsman, right-arm fast bowler. *Team* Nottinghamshire (1881, 2 matches).
Career batting
2–4–1–23–15*–7.66–0–*ct* 1
Bowling 57–0

Shore, Charles
Professional. *b:* 21.11.1858, Sutton-in-Ashfield, Nottinghamshire. *d:* 5.6.1912, Sutton-in-Ashfield, Nottinghamshire. Lower order left-hand batsman, slow left-arm bowler. *Teams* Nottinghamshire (1881–85, 10 matches); Lancashire (1886, 1 match).
Career batting
13–21–9–159–42*–13.25–0–*ct* 9
Bowling 938–41–22.87–2–0–5/36

His final first-class match was for Liverpool and District in 1887. He also played for Herefordshire (1886) and Norfolk (1889–1901). He took all 10 wickets (for 50) for Norfolk v Durham at Norwich in 1897 (not first-class).

Shore, Richard Graham
Amateur. *b:* 9.3.1941, Winton, Bournemouth, Hampshire. Lower order right-hand batsman, right-arm medium pace bowler. *Sch* Blundells. *Team* Oxford U (1962).
Career batting
4–8–2–46–24–7.66–0–*ct* 1
Bowling 395–10–39.50–0–0–3/57

Shorrocks, Ernest
Professional. *b:* 12.3.1875, Rhodes, Lancashire. *d:* 20.7.1916, Thiepval, France. He was killed in action. Lower order batsman, useful bowler. *Team* Somerset (1905, 1 match).
Career batting
1–2–1–16–16*–16.00–0–*ct* 0
Bowling 60–2–30.00–0–0–2/60

Short, Arthur Martin
Cricketer. *b:* 27.9.1947, Graaff-Reinet, Cape Province, South Africa. Opening right-hand batsman. *Teams* Eastern Province (1966/7 to 1974/5); Natal (1969/70 to 1972/3). *Tours* South African Universities to England 1967; South Africa to England 1970 (tour cancelled), to Australia 1971/2 (tour cancelled).
Career batting
66–123–4–3318–118–27.88–2–*ct* 51
Bowling 62–3–20.66–0–0–2/2

Short, John David
Amateur in 1957, then professional. *b:* 13.6.1934, Chesterfield, Derbyshire. Brother of R. L. (Cambridge U). Middle order right-hand batsman, off break bowler. *Sch* Denstone. *Team* Derbyshire (1957–60, 11 matches).
Career batting
11–19–0–271–86–14.26–0–*ct* 6
Bowling 11–0

Short, John Francis
Cricketer. *b:* 12.4.1951, Cork, Ireland. Opening right-hand batsman. *Team* Ireland (1974–84).
Career batting
11–18–2–533–114–33.31–1–*ct* 10

Short, Robert Leslie
Cricketer. *b:* 24.9.1948, Chesterfield, Derbyshire. Brother of J. D. (Derbyshire). Middle order right-hand batsman. *Sch* Denstone. *Team* Cambridge U (1969–70, blue 1969).
Career batting
11–20–1–355–58–18.68–0–*ct* 4

Shorter, Richard Nicholas
Amateur. *b:* 26.7.1906, Loughton, Essex. *d:* 20.1.1984, Drogheda, Co Meath, Ireland. Tail end left-hand batsman, right-arm medium bowler. *Sch* Repton. *Team* Essex (1927–29, 23 matches).
Career batting
23–29–11–104–21–5.77–0–*ct* 12
Bowling 695–15–46.33–0–0–3/14

Shorting, Wilfred Lionel
Amateur. *b:* 12.3.1904, Tenbury, Worcestershire. *d:* 10.10.1982, Hastings, Sussex. Middle order right-hand batsman. *Sch* King's, Worcester. *Team* Worcestershire (1922–26, 9 matches).
Career batting
9–17–1–165–27–10.31–0–*ct* 2
He played hockey for England.

Shortland, Norman Arthur
Professional until 1939, then amateur. *b:* 6.7.1916, Coventry, Warwickshire. *d:* 14.3.1973, Finham, Warwickshire. Middle order right-hand batsman, right-arm medium pace bowler. *Team* Warwickshire (1938–50, 23 matches).
Career batting
23–40–5–487–70–13.91–0–*ct* 4
Bowling 50–0

Shortt, Roland Henry
Amateur. *b:* 7.8.1898, Dublin, Ireland. *d:* 8.8.1963, Dublin, Ireland. Tail end right-hand batsman, right-arm medium pace bowler. *Team* Ireland (1934).
Career batting
1–2–0–0–0–0.00–0–*ct* 0
Bowling 66–3–22.00–0–0–3/22

Shotton, William
Professional. *b:* 1.12.1840, Lascelles Hall, Yorkshire. *d:* 26.5.1909, Kirkheaton, Yorkshire. Opening right-hand batsman, right-hand medium pace round-arm bowler, good point field. *Team* Yorkshire (1865–74, 2 matches).
Career batting
2–4–0–13–7–3.25–0–*ct* 0

Shoubridge, Thomas Edward
Professional. *b:* 8.9.1868, Horsham, Sussex. *d:* 22.10.1937, Prescot, Lancashire. Lower order batsman, right-hand fast round-arm bowler. *Team* Sussex (1890, 2 matches).
Career batting
3–6–2–14–10–3.50–0–*ct* 0
Bowling 77–1–77.00–0–0–1/35

Showers, Charles James
Amateur. *b:* 12.1.1848, Fort William, Calcutta, India. Opening right-hand batsman, right-hand medium pace round-arm bowler. *Sch* Cheltenham and Wellington. *Team* MCC (1881).
Career batting
3–5–0–82–39–16.40–0–*ct* 0
Bowling 48–1–48.00–0–0–1/48
He played for the United South of England Eleven during 1877, but later went to Assam as a tea planter. His first-class debut was for the South in 1877.

Shrewsbury, Arthur
Professional. *b:* 11.4.1856, New Lenton, Nottinghamshire. *d:* 19.5.1903, Gedling, Nottinghamshire. He died by his own hand. Brother of William (Nottinghamshire), uncle of Arthur (Nottinghamshire). Very sound opening right-hand batsman, good point field. *Team* Nottinghamshire (1875–1902, 357 matches). *Tours* Daft to North America 1879 (not first-class); Lillywhite, Shaw and Shrewsbury to Australia 1881/2, 1884/5, 1886/7, 1887/8. *Tests* England (1881/2 to 1893, 23 matches).
Career batting
498–813–90–26505–267–36.65–59–*ct* 377
Bowling 2–0
Test batting
23–40–4–1277–164–35.47–3–*ct* 29
Bowling 2–0
The principal professional batsman in England in the 1880s and early 1890s, he topped the first-class batting averages in 1886, 1887, 1890, 1891, 1892 and 1902. His outstanding summer was 1887 when he hit 1,653 runs, av 78.71, which was then the highest average ever recorded by a batsman playing regular first-class cricket. In all he completed 1,000 runs in a season thirteen times. He hit ten double centuries, seven of which were for Nottinghamshire and three in Australia. Twice he made 267, both times for the County – v Middlesex at Trent Bridge in 1887 and v Sussex at Trent Bridge in 1890. In the latter match, with W. Gunn, he created a new first-class second wicket partnership record of 398 which stood for years.
With Lillywhite and Shaw he sponsored several tours to Australia and captained the tourists in 1884/5 and 1886/7, also leading England in seven Test matches.
He committed suicide in 1903. This tragic act was due, at least in part, to the belief that ill-health would prevent him from continuing to play in first-class cricket – he had headed the batting averages in the previous season.

Shrewsbury, Arthur
Professional. *b:* 4.7.1874, Nottingham. *d:* 6.10.1917, Nottingham. Son of William (Nottinghamshire), nephew of Arthur (Nottinghamshire). Lower order right-hand batsman, right-arm medium pace bowler. *Team* Nottinghamshire (1892, 3 matches).
Career batting
3–5–3–63–31*–31.50–0–*ct* 1
Bowling 31–0

Shrewsbury, William
Professional. *b:* 30.4.1854, New Lenton, Nottinghamshire. *d:* 14.11.1931, Fiskerton, Nottinghamshire. Brother of Arthur (Nottinghamshire), father of Arthur (Nottinghamshire). Lower order right-hand batsman, right-arm fast bowler. *Team* Nottinghamshire (1875–79, 9 matches).
Career batting
9–13–2–77–34–7.00–0–*ct* 5
He was a first-class umpire (1896–1904).

Shrimpton, Herbert John Donald
Amateur. *b:* 12.4.1903, Worcester. *d:* 12.3.1979, Southwark, London. Lower order right-hand batsman, leg break bowler. *Team* Gloucestershire (1923, 3 matches).
Career batting
3–6–1–26–14–5.20–0–*ct* 1

Shuckburgh, Sir Charles Gerald Stewkley
Amateur. *b:* 28.2.1911, Shuckburgh, Warwickshire. *d:* 4.5.1988, White Colne, Colchester, Essex. Brother-in-law of C. W. S. Lubbock (Northamptonshire). Middle order right-hand batsman. *Sch* Harrow. *Team* Warwickshire (1930, 1 match).
Career batting
1–1–0–0–0–0.00–*ct* 1
He played in trials at Oxford U, but not in first-class matches.

Shufflebotham, David Howell
Cricketer. *b:* 11.3.1968, Neath, Glamorgan. Lower order right-hand batsman, right-arm medium pace bowler. *Team* Cambridge U (1989–90, blue both years).
Career batting
9–10–3–149–29–21.28–0–*ct* 1
Bowling 572–7–81.71–0–0–3/60
He made his first-class debut in the 1989 University match.

Shuja-ud-din Butt
Amateur. *b:* 10.4.1930, Lahore, India. Middle order right-hand batsman, slow left-arm bowler, good field. *Teams* Northern India (1946/7); Punjab U (1947/8); Services (1953/4 to 1963/4); Bahawalpur (1957/8 to 1969/70); Rawalpindi (1965/6). *Tours* Pakistan to England 1954, to India 1960/1. *Tests* Pakistan (1954 to 1961/2, 19 matches).
Career batting
98–156–21–3342–147–24.75–6–*ct* 69
Bowling 6715–298–22.53–15–3–8/53
Test batting
19–32–6–395–47–15.19–0–*ct* 8
Bowling 801–20–40.05–0–0–3/18
On the 1954 tour he took 67 wickets, av 28.85, and played in three Tests.

Shuja-ud-din Butt
Amateur. Middle order right-hand batsman, useful bowler. *Teams* Punjab (1953/4); Railways (1954/5 to 1959/60); Lahore (1959/60). *Tour* Pakistan to England 1962.
Career batting
18–32–6–625–77–24.03–0–*ct* 9
Bowling 436–9–48.44–0–0–2/49
He was co-opted into the 1962 touring team for one first-class match. His final first-class match in Pakistan was for Railways and Quetta in 1960/1.

Shuker, Abraham
Amateur. *b:* 6.7.1848, Stockton, Shropshire. *d:* 11.2.1909, Chell, Tunstall, Staffordshire. Steady middle order right-hand batsman. *Sch* Brewood. *Team* Derbyshire (1874–82, 22 matches).
Career batting
22–40–2–601–86–15.81–0–*ct* 12
He did not play in any first-class matches whilst at Cambridge U. He also played for Staffordshire (1873).

Shuldham, Walter Frank Quantock
Amateur. *b:* 17.6.1892, Norton Manor, Stoke-sub-Hamdon, Somerset. *d:* 7.2.1971, East Stoke House, Stoke-sub-Hamdon, Somerset. Nephew of H. M. Colegrave (London County). Middle order right-hand batsman. *Sch* Marlborough. *Teams* Somerset (1914–24, 6 matches); Rajputana (1926/7).
Career batting
8–13–1–126–25–10.50–0–*ct* 0

Shuter, John
Amateur. *b:* 9.2.1855, Thornton Heath, Surrey. *d:* 5.7.1920, Blackheath, London. Brother of L. A. (Surrey), uncle of L. R. W. A. (MCC). Stylish opening right-hand batsman, good field. *Sch* Winchester. *Teams* Kent (1874, 1 match); Surrey (1877–1909, 274 matches). *Test* England (1888, 1 match).
Career batting
306–503–23–10206–135–21.26–8–*ct* 157
Bowling 49–0
Test batting
1–1–0–28–28–28.00–0–*ct* 0
His best season was 1884 when he hit 968 runs, av 26.88. He captained Surrey from 1880 to 1893 and was appointed Secretary to the County Club in 1920, unfortunately dying before he had completed a year in office; he had been however a very active member of the Club from his retirement as captain in 1893. He was a Test selector in 1912.

Shuter, Leonard Allen
Amateur. *b:* 25.5.1852, Thornton Heath, Surrey. *d:* 13.7.1928, Eastbourne, Sussex. Brother of John (Surrey), father of L. R. W. A. (MCC). Middle order right-hand batsman, right-arm fast or slow left-arm bowler, good field. *Sch* Rugby. *Team* Surrey (1876–83, 37 matches).

Career batting
38–66–2–1073–88–16.76–0–*ct* 16
Bowling 75–1–75.00–0–0–1/10

Shuter, Leonard Robert Warner Allen
Amateur. *b:* 21.3.1887, Horton-Kirby Grange, Dartford, Kent. *d:* 21.11.1960, Aldeburgh, Suffolk. Son of L. A. (Surrey), nephew of John (Surrey). Opening batsman. *Sch* Tonbridge. *Team* MCC (1908).
Career batting
1–2–0–15–11–7.50–0–*ct* 0

Shutt, Albert
Cricketer. *b:* 21.9.1952, Stockton-on-Tees, Co Durham. Lower order right-hand batsman, right-arm medium fast bowler. *Team* Worcestershire (1972, 2 matches).
Career batting
2 matches, did not bat–*ct* 1
Bowling 181–2–90.50–0–0–1/36
He also played for Durham (pre first-class, 1977).

Shutt, Herbert
Professional. *b:* 3.9.1879, Ardwick, Lancashire. *d:* 19.11.1922, Whitehaven, Cumberland. Lower order batsman, good bowler. *Team* Hampshire (1906, 4 matches).
Career batting
4–5–3–7–6–3.50–0–*ct* 0
Bowling 231–8–28.87–0–0–4/29
He also played for Cumberland (1910–21).

Shuttleworth, Guy Mitchell
Amateur. *b:* 6.11.1926, Revidge, Blackburn, Lancashire. Middle order right-hand batsman. *Team* Cambridge U (1946–48, blue all three years).
Career batting
25–39–5–786–96–23.11–0–*ct* 7
He played amateur soccer for England.

Shuttleworth, Kenneth
Cricketer. *b:* 13.11.1944, St Helens, Lancashire. Lower order right-hand batsman, right-arm fast bowler. *Teams* Lancashire (1964–75, 177 matches); Leicestershire (1977–80, 41 matches). *Tours* Commonwealth to Pakistan 1967/8; MCC to Australia and New Zealand 1970/1. *Tests* England (1970/1 to 1971, 5 matches).
Career batting
239–241–85–2589–71–16.59–0–*ct* 128
Bowling 15270–623–24.51–21–1–7/41
Test batting
5–6–0–46–21–7.66–0–*ct* 1
Bowling 427–12–35.58–1–0–5/47

Sibbles, Frank Marshall
Professional. *b:* 15.3.1904, Oldham, Lancashire. *d:* 20.7.1973, Wilmslow, Cheshire. Lower order right-hand batsman, right-arm medium pace off break bowler. *Team* Lancashire (1925–37, 308 matches).
Career batting
315–316–79–3478–71*–14.67–0–*ct* 181
Bowling 21087–940–22.43–41–4–8/24
He took 100 wickets in a season twice (best 131, av 18.25, in 1932). He was elected to the Committee of Lancashire CCC in 1950 and was Chairman for two years.

Siddiqi, Dr Shah Naweed
Cricketer. *b:* 13.9.1959, Islington, London. Middle order right-hand batsman, off break bowler. *Sch* City of London. *Team* Cambridge U (1984–85).
Career batting
7–13–0–219–52–16.84–0–*ct* 1
Bowling 102–5–20.40–1–0–5/90

Siddons, Anthony
Professional. *b:* 29.12.1941, Lenton, Nottingham. Tail end right-hand batsman, off break bowler. *Team* Nottinghamshire (1959–60, 5 matches).
Career batting
5–8–3–36–8–7.20–0–*ct* 1
Bowling 266–8–33.25–0–0–4/37

Sidebottom, Arnold
Cricketer. *b:* 1.4.1954, Shawlands, Barnsley, Yorkshire. Lower order right-hand batsman, right-arm fast medium bowler. *Teams* Yorkshire (1973–91, 216 matches); Orange Free State (1981/2 to 1983/4). *Tours* SAB England XI to South Africa 1981/2 (he did not play in first-class matches); Yorkshire to Windward Islands 1986/7. *Test* England (1985, 1 match).
Career batting
228–263–62–4508–124–22.42–1–*ct* 63
Bowling 14558–596–24.42–23–3–8/72
Test batting
1–1–0–2–2–2.00–0–*ct* 0
Bowling 65–1–65.00–0–0–1/65
He took 68 wickets, av 23.38, in 1989. A good soccer player, he has appeared for Manchester United, Huddersfield Town and Halifax.

Sidgwick, Robert
Amateur. *b:* 7.8.1851, Embsay Kirk, Yorkshire. *d:* 1934, Kingston, Jamaica. Middle order right-hand batsman, brilliant field. *Sch* Leeds GS and Wellington. *Teams* Yorkshire (1882, 9 matches); Jamaica (1894/5).
Career batting
10–15–0–72–17–4.80–0–*ct* 7
He emigrated to Jamaica in 1892, where he became a coffee planter.

Sidhu, Navjot Singh
Cricketer. *b:* 20.10.1963, Patiala, India. Opening right-hand batsman. *Team* Punjab (1981/2 to 1991/2). *Tours* India to Sharjah (not first-class) 1987/8, 1988/9, 1989/90, 1991/2, to West Indies 1988/9, to Bangladesh (not first-class) 1988/9, to Pakistan

1989/90, to New Zealand 1989/90, to England 1990, to Australia 1991/2. *Tests* India (1983/4 to 1991/2, 20 matches).
Career batting
71–108–6–3948–286–38.70–11–*ct* 24
Bowling 36–0
Test batting
20–33–2–894–116–28.83–2–*ct* 3
Bowling 9–0

He played in three Tests on the 1990 tour to England, but made few runs. His highest score was 286 for Indians v Jamaica at Kingston in 1988/9.

Sidwell, Thomas Edgar
Professional. *b:* 30.1.1888, Belgrave, Leicestershire. *d:* 8.12.1958, Braunstone Frith, Leicestershire. Sound right-hand batsman, wicket-keeper. *Team* Leicestershire (1913–33, 388 matches).
Career batting
392–605–87–7929–105–15.30–3–*ct* 583–*st* 137

He hit 1,153 runs, av 29.56, in 1928.

Siedle, Ivan Julian
Amateur. *b:* 11.1.1903, Berea, Durban, South Africa. *d:* 26.8.1982, Durban, South Africa. Brother of K. O. (Natal), father of J. R. (Western Province). Solid opening right-hand batsman. *Team* Natal (1922/3 to 1936/7). *Tours* South Africa to England 1929, 1935. *Tests* South Africa (1927/8 to 1935/6, 18 matches).
Career batting
123–204–11–7730–265*–40.05–17–*ct* 57–*st* 1
Bowling 35–1–35.00–0–0–1/7
Test batting
18–34–0–977–141–28.73–1–*ct* 7
Bowling 7–1–7.00–0–0–1/7

In first-class matches on the 1929 tour he hit 1,579 runs, av 35.88, but failed in the Tests. In 1935 he hit 1,346 runs, av 39.58, but again had only a modest return in the Tests. His highest score was 265* for Natal v Orange Free State at Durban in 1929/30. He played rugby for Natal.

Sievwright, Robert Willis
Amateur. *b:* 16.6.1882, Arbroath, Angus, Scotland. *d:* 12.7.1947, Arbroath, Angus, Scotland. He died batting for Arbroath v Perthshire. Lower order left-hand batsman, slow left-arm bowler. *Team* Scotland (1912–30).
Career batting
13–19–6–98–13*–7.53–0–*ct* 2
Bowling 1298–65–19.96–5–1–7/71

Sikander Bakht
Cricketer. *b:* 25.8.1957, Karachi, Pakistan. Tail end right-hand batsman, right-arm medium fast bowler. *Teams* PWD (1974/5); Sind (1975/6); PIA (1975/6); United Bank (1975/6 to 1989/90); Karachi (1983/4). *Tours* Pakistan to Australia 1976/7, 1978/9, 1981/2, to West Indies 1976/7, to England 1978, 1979 (World Cup), 1982, to New Zealand 1978/9, 1988/9, to India 1979/80. *Tests* Pakistan (1976/7 to 1982/3, 26 matches).
Career batting
186–202–65–1944–67–14.18–0–*ct* 82
Bowling 14167–553–25.61–29–3–8/69
Test batting
26–35–12–146–22*–6.34–0–*ct* 7
Bowling 2411–67–35.98–3–1–8/69

He played in all three Tests on the 1978 tour, but had only a modest record. In 1982 he played in two Tests, and in all first-class matches took 27 wickets, av 35.51.

Silcock, Frank
Professional. *b:* 2.10.1838, Sawbridgeworth, Hertfordshire. *d:* 26.5.1897, Marden Ash, Chipping Ongar, Essex. Stylish middle order right-hand batsman, right-hand fast medium round-arm bowler, slip field. *Team* Players (1868–69).
Career batting
41–76–8–776–66–11.41–0–*ct* 31
Bowling 1630–79–20.63–5–0–7/132

He made his first-class debut for UEE in 1864 and his final match for the South in 1879. His County cricket was for Hertfordshire (1870–73) and Essex (pre first-class, 1876–87). He was a first-class umpire (1889–92).

Silcock, William
Professional. *b:* 22.2.1868, Croston, Chorley, Lancashire. *d:* 30.7.1933, Leyland, Lancashire. Lower order batsman, good bowler. *Team* Lancashire (1899–1902, 6 matches).
Career batting
6–7–1–82–43–13.66–0–*ct* 5
Bowling 367–5–73.40–0–0–2/62

Silk, Dennis Raoul Whitehall
Amateur. *b:* 8.10.1931, Eureka, California, USA. Brother-in-law of J. P. K. Asquith (Cambridge U). Opening right-hand batsman, right-arm leg break bowler. *Sch* Christ's Hospital. *Teams* Cambridge U (1952–55, blue 1953–55); Somerset (1956–60, 33 matches). *Tours* MCC to East Africa 1957/8, to South America 1958/9, to North America 1959 (none first-class), to New Zealand 1960/1.
Career batting
83–140–11–3845–126–29.80–7–*ct* 45
Bowling 240–1–240.00–0–0–1/22

He captained Cambridge in 1955 and the MCC teams in North America and in New Zealand. He was President of MCC 1992/3. A good rugby footballer, he played for Cambridge and Sussex; he also represented the University at rugby fives.

Silkin, Rt Hon Lord Samuel Charles
Amateur. *b:* 6.3.1918, Neath, Glamorgan. *d:* 17.8.1988, Oxford. Lower order right-hand batsman, leg break and googly bowler. *Sch* Dulwich. *Teams* Cambridge U (1938); Glamorgan (1938, 1 match).

Career batting
2–3–0–4–2–1.33–0–*ct* 2
Bowling 119–2–59.50–0–0–1/27

He was Labour MP for Camberwell (1964–83); from 1974 to 1979 he served as Attorney-General, having previously been Chairman of the Council of Europe Legal Committee.

Silva, Sampathwaduge Amal Rohitha
Cricketer. *b:* 12.12.1960, Moratuwa, Ceylon. Opening left-hand batsman, wicket-keeper. *Team* Nondescripts CC (1988/9 to 1991/2). *Tours* Sri Lanka to Australia 1982/3, 1984/5, to New Zealand 1982/3, to England 1984, 1988, to Pakistan 1985/6. *Tests* Sri Lanka (1982/3 to 1988, 9 matches).
Career batting
43–69–5–1745–161*–27.26–4–*ct* 92–*st* 4
Bowling 7–0
Test batting
9–16–2–353–111–25.21–2–*ct* 33–*st* 1

On the 1984 tour to England he headed the first-class batting averages with 558 runs, av 62.00, and hit 102* in the Test match. On the 1988 tour he played in the Test match, but generally was not so successful as on the previous visit. He claimed 18 dismissals in two consecutive Tests v India 1985/6.

Silvester, Stephen
Cricketer. *b:* 12.3.1951, Hull, Yorkshire. Lower order right-hand batsman, right-arm fast medium bowler. *Team* Yorkshire (1976–77, 6 matches).
Career batting
6–7–4–30–14–10.00–0–*ct* 2
Bowling 313–12–26.08–0–0–4/86

He also played for Northumberland (1979).

Sim, Archibald Millar Robertson
Cricketer. *b:* 8.1.1942, Johannesburg, South Africa. Middle order right-hand batsman. *Teams* North Eastern Transvaal (1962/3); Northamptonshire (1964–66, 4 matches).
Career batting
7–12–1–196–66*–17.81–0–*ct* 2
Bowling 12–1–12.00–0–0–1/12

Sime, Judge William Arnold
Amateur. *b:* 8.2.1909, Wepener, Orange Free State, South Africa. *d:* 5.5.1983, Wymeswold, Leicestershire. Attacking middle order right-hand batsman, slow left-arm bowler. *Sch* Bedford. *Teams* Oxford U (1931); Nottinghamshire (1935–50, 91 matches).
Career batting
96–138–17–2473–176*–20.43–1–*ct* 55
Bowling 2300–49–46.93–0–0–4/51

He also played for Bedfordshire (1927–34) and made his first-class debut for the Minor Counties in 1929. Whilst in South Africa during the war he played in a single first-class match for the Air Force in 1942/3. He captained Nottinghamshire 1947–50. He was on the Committee of Nottinghamshire and in 1976–77 President of the County Club. A noted rugby footballer he played for Bedford, Notts and East Midlands and had a trial for England. In the legal profession he was appointed a Judge in 1972.

Simmonds, Rev Arthur
Amateur. *b:* 1.2.1848, Godalming, Surrey. *d:* 2.8.1933, Ascot, Berkshire. Middle order right-hand batsman, point field. *Sch* Brighton. *Teams* Cambridge U (1871); Surrey (1872–73, 6 matches).
Career batting
7–14–0–183–50–13.07–0–*ct* 1

Simmonds, William Henry
Amateur. *b:* 5.5.1892, Ashley Down, Bristol. *d:* 11.3.1957, Bishopston, Bristol. Middle order batsman. *Team* Gloucestershire (1924–25, 2 matches).
Career batting
2–3–0–57–44–19.00–0–*ct* 0

Simmons, C. H.
Professional. Lower order batsman, opening bowler. *Team* Sussex (1920, 1 match).
Career batting
1–2–0–0–0–0.00–0–*ct* 0
Bowling 42–1–42.00–0–0–1/18

Simmons, Jack, MBE
Cricketer. *b:* 28.3.1941, Clayton-le-Moors, Lancashire. Attacking lower order right-hand batsman, off break bowler. *Teams* Lancashire (1968–89, 429 matches); Tasmania (1972/3 to 1978/9, 20 matches). *Tours* Overseas XI to India 1980/1; Lancashire to Jamaica 1987/8, to Zimbabwe 1988/9.
Career batting
450–564–146–9417–112–22.52–6–*ct* 341
Bowling 28084–1033–27.18–41–6–7/59

The most popular Lancashire player of his generation, his benefit in 1980 realised £128,000. The fact that he had a fish and chip supper named after him places him on a pedestal as perhaps the last of the old breed of Northern professional. He did not start County cricket until he was 27 and his best seasons were after his 40th birthday. He took 68 wickets in 1972 and 1983, av 23.01 and 26.57 respectively.

Simmons, Philip Verant
Cricketer. *b:* 18.4.1963, Arima, Trinidad. Opening right-hand batsman, right-arm medium pace bowler. *Team* Trinidad (1982/3 to 1991/2). *Tours* Young West Indies to Zimbabwe 1986/7; West Indies to India 1987/8, 1989/90 (not first-class), to India and Pakistan (World Cup) 1987/8, to England 1988, 1991, to Sharjah (not first-class) 1989/90, 1991/2, to Australia and New Zealand (World Cup) 1991/2; Rest of World to England 1992. *Tests* West Indies (1987/8 to 1991/2, 8 matches).
Career batting
85–151–6–4943–202–34.08–9–*ct* 83
Bowling 1538–38–40.47–1–0–5/24

Simms, Harry Lester

Test batting
8–16–0–268–38–16.75–0–*ct* 5
Bowling 20–0

On his 1988 tour to England he was hit on the head by a ball whilst batting helmetless in his first first-class match v Gloucestershire. A blood clot on the brain resulted and only prompt action saved his life. He did not reappear on that tour. In 1991 he played in all five Tests against England, but had a very modest Test record; in first-class matches he hit 1,031 runs, av 38.18. He played for Durham in the NatWest Trophy (pre first-class, 1989–90). His highest score was 202 for Trinidad v Guyana at Pointe-a-Pierre in 1991/2.

Simms, Harry Lester
Amateur. *b:* 31.1.1888, Adelaide, South Australia. *d:* 9.6.1942, Oatlands Park, Weybridge, Surrey. Brother of R. K. (Sussex). Middle order right-hand batsman, right-arm fast bowler. *Sch* Malvern. *Teams* Sussex (1905–13, 79 matches); Europeans (1909/10 to 1916/17); Cooch-Behar's XI (1917/18); Bengal Governor's XI (1918/19); Warwickshire (1921–22, 5 matches).
Career batting
110–186–10–3154–126–17.92–1–*ct* 70
Bowling 4284–220–19.47–12–0–7/84

He performed the 'double' in 1912 with 1,099 runs, av 20.73, and 110 wickets, av 22.68.

Simms, Royston Knox
Amateur. *b:* 1.1.1894, Hyde Park, Adelaide, South Australia. *d:* 12.3.1978, South Petherton, Somerset. Brother of H. L. (Sussex and Warwickshire). Lower order batsman, useful bowler. *Sch* Lancing. *Team* Sussex (1912, 2 matches).
Career batting
2–2–0–5–4–2.50–0–*ct* 0
Bowling 64–2–32.00–0–0–1/23

Simons, Robert George
Amateur. *b:* 23.3.1922, Watford, Hertfordshire. Middle order right-hand batsman, wicket-keeper. *Sch* Berkhamsted. *Team* Minor Counties (1959).
Career batting
1–1–0–0–0–0.00–0–*ct* 1–*st* 1

His County cricket was for Hertfordshire (1939–69).

Simpkins, David Paul
Cricketer. *b:* 28.3.1962, Chippenham, Wiltshire. Lower order right-hand batsman, off break bowler. *Team* Gloucestershire (1982, 1 match).
Career batting
1–2–1–1–1*–1.00–0–*ct* 0
Bowling 15–0

He also played for Wiltshire (1981–92).

Simpkins, Peter Anthony
Amateur. *b:* 27.11.1928, Dover, Kent. Lower order right-hand batsman, slow left-arm bowler. *Team* Free Foresters (1962).
Career batting
1 match, did not bat–*ct* 2
Bowling 114–3–38.00–0–0–3/69

His County cricket was for Berkshire (1958–76).

Simpson, Alexander Russell
Amateur. *b:* 28.2.1905, Dunfermline, Fife, Scotland. *d:* 10.11.1975, Weston-super-Mare, Somerset. Lower order right-hand batsman, wicket-keeper. *Team* Scotland (1925–34).
Career batting
12–22–6–101–19*–6.31–0–*ct* 14–*st* 10

Simpson, B. B. (*see under* Gregory, B. B.)

Simpson, Cyril Charles
Amateur. *b:* 19.4.1874, Erpingham, Norfolk. *d:* 5.6.1953, Hove, Sussex. Lower order batsman, useful bowler. *Sch* Wellingborough. *Team* Northamptonshire (1908, 1 match).
Career batting
1–2–0–3–3–1.50–0–*ct* 0
Bowling 36–1–36.00–0–0–1/36

Simpson, David John
Cricketer. *b:* 23.2.1961, Irvine, Ayr, Scotland. Middle order right-hand batsman. *Team* Scotland (1984–85).
Career batting
2–4–1–19–9–6.33–0–*ct* 1

Simpson, Edward Thornhill Beckett
Amateur. *b:* 5.3.1867, Crofton, Wakefield, Yorkshire. *d:* 20.3.1944, Walton, Wakefield, Yorkshire. Middle order right-hand batsman. *Sch* Harrow. *Teams* Oxford U (1888, blue); Yorkshire (1889, 2 matches).
Career batting
11–19–3–205–82–12.81–0–*ct* 13

Simpson, Ernest Herbert
Amateur. *b:* 17.12.1875, Clapton, London. *d:* 2.10.1917, St Omer, France. Brother-in-law of C. O. Cooper (Kent). Middle order right-hand batsman, good field. *Sch* Malvern. *Team* Kent (1896, 7 matches).
Career batting
7–14–0–219–94–15.64–0–*ct* 1

Simpson, Frank William
Amateur. *b:* 27.3.1909, Theberton, Suffolk. *d:* 13.8.1992. Opening right-hand batsman, right-arm medium pace bowler. *Sch* Merchant Taylors. *Teams* Army (1931); Combined Services (1948).
Career batting
2–4–0–92–40–23.00–0–*ct* 1

He played no first-class matches at Cambridge U, but did win a blue for rugby.

Simpson, George Hayward Thomas
(changed name to Simpson-Hayward in 1898)
Amateur. *b:* 7.6.1875, Stoneleigh, Kenilworth, Warwickshire. *d:* 2.10.1936, Icomb Place, Gloucestershire. Forcing middle order right-hand batsman, right-hand slow under-arm bowler. *Sch* Malvern. *Teams* Cambridge U (1895–97); Worcestershire (1899–1914, 156 matches). *Tours* Oxford Authentics to India 1902/3; Brackley to West Indies 1904/5; MCC to New Zealand 1906/7, to North America 1907, to Egypt 1909 (not first-class), to South Africa 1909/10; Leveson-Gower to Rhodesia 1909/10. *Tests* England (1909/10, 5 matches).
Career batting
200–325–26–5556–130–18.58–3–*ct* 133
Bowling 10762–503–21.39–31–1–7/54
Test batting
5–8–1–105–29*–15.00–0–*ct* 1
Bowling 420–23–18.26–2–0–6/43

He was one of the last of the major under-arm bowlers to appear regularly in first-class cricket. His best season was 1908 when he took 68 wickets, av 18.61. He first played for Worcestershire (pre first-class) in 1895. He captained Worcestershire 1911–12. A good soccer player, he appeared for Cambridge.

Simpson, Gerard Amyatt
Amateur. *b:* 30.3.1886, Trinity, Edinburgh, Scotland. *d:* 22.2.1957, Chartham Down, Kent. Middle order batsman. *Sch* Wellington. *Teams* Kent (1929–31, 3 matches); Argentina (1911/12).
Career batting
4–6–1–50–26–10.00–0–*ct* 0

Simpson, Harold Benjamin
Amateur. *b:* 27.1.1879, Higham Ferrers, Northamptonshire. *d:* 16.3.1924, Chelveston-cum-Caldecott, Northamptonshire. Middle order right-hand batsman, useful bowler. *Sch* Wellingborough. *Team* Northamptonshire (1905–11, 8 matches).
Career batting
8–15–1–128–44–9.14–0–*ct* 3
Bowling 413–9–45.88–0–0–4/29

He first played for Northamptonshire (pre first-class) in 1904.

Simpson, Jack
Amateur. *b:* 1.12.1920, Lisburn, Co Antrim, Ireland. Lower order right-hand batsman, right-arm fast medium bowler. *Team* Ireland (1954).
Career batting
1–1–0–26–26–26.00–0–*ct* 0
Bowling 50–0

Simpson, Reginald Thomas
Amateur. *b:* 27.2.1920, Sherwood Rise, Nottingham. Attractive opening right-hand batsman, off break bowler. *Sch* Nottingham HS. *Teams* Nottinghamshire (1946–63, 366 matches); Sind (1944/5 to 1945/6); Europeans (1944/5 to 1945/6). *Tours* MCC to South Africa 1948/9, to Australia and New Zealand 1950/1, 1954/5; Commonwealth to India 1953/4; Howard to India 1956/7. *Tests* England (1948/9 to 1954/5, 27 matches).
Career batting
495–852–55–30546–259–38.32–64–*ct* 193
Bowling 2227–59–37.74–0–0–3/22
Test batting
27–45–3–1401–156*–33.35–4–*ct* 5
Bowling 22–2–11.00–0–0–2/4

He hit 1,000 runs in England thirteen times, going on to 2,000 five times (best 2,576, av 62.82, in 1950). Of his ten double centuries, nine were for Nottinghamshire, but the highest was 259 for MCC v New South Wales at Sydney in 1950/1, and perhaps his most noteworthy innings was on the same tour, when he hit 156* for England v Australia at Melbourne in the fifth Test. He captained Nottinghamshire from 1951 to 1960 and since his retirement has been a member of the Nottinghamshire Committee, being President in 1991 and 1992.

Simpson, Robert Baddeley
Amateur. *b:* 3.2.1936, Marrickville, Sydney, New South Wales, Australia. Father-in-law of A. M. J. Hilditch (Australia). Attractive right-hand opening batsman, leg break and googly bowler, brilliant slip field. *Teams* New South Wales (1952/3 to 1977/8, 67 matches); Western Australia (1956/57 to 1960/1, 24 matches). *Tours* Australia to England 1961, 1964, to South Africa 1957/8, 1966/7, to West Indies 1964/5, 1977/8, to India and Pakistan 1964/5, to New Zealand 1956/7, 1959/60; Commonwealth to South Africa 1959/60, to India, Pakistan and New Zealand 1961/2; Cavaliers to South Africa 1960/1; Rest of World to England 1966. *Tests* Australia (1957/8 to 1977/8, 62 matches).
Career batting
257–436–62–21029–359–56.22–60–*ct* 383
Bowling 13287–349–38.07–6–0–5/33
Test batting
62–111–7–4869–311–46.81–10–*ct* 110
Bowling 3001–71–42.26–2–0–5/57

On the 1961 tour to England he hit 1,947 runs, av 51.23, and played in all five Tests, but without any noteworthy innings. He captained the 1964 tourists to England and headed both Test and first-class averages with 458 runs, av 76.33, and 1,714 runs, av 57.13, respectively. His great innings was 311 in the fourth Test at Old Trafford, when he and W. M. Lawry added 201 for the first wicket. This innings was his only score over 200 in England, though he made ten other double centuries and one triple century, namely 359 for New South Wales v Queensland at Brisbane in 1963/4. He hit 1,000 runs in Australia four times (best 1,541, av 64.20, in 1960/1) and once in South Africa. He captained Australia in 39 Tests in all. He came out of retirement in 1977/8 to lead Australia when most of the side had joined the rival WSC organisation set up by Kerry Packer. He was Cricket Manager of Leicestershire CCC in 1991 and coach of the 1989 Australian tourists.

Simpson, Thomas
Professional. *b:* 13.8.1879, Keyworth, Nottinghamshire. *d:* 19.12.1961, West Hulme, Oldham, Lancashire. Middle order left-hand batsman, left-arm medium pace bowler. *Team* Nottinghamshire (1903–05, 5 matches).
Career batting
5–8–1–38–14–5.42–0–*ct* 0
Bowling 85–2–42.50–0–0–1/28
He also played for Cheshire (1914). A good soccer player, he appeared for Notts County and Everton.

Simpson, Valentine
Amateur. *b:* 15.8.1849, Newington, London. *d:* 2.11.1915, Fareham, Hampshire. Middle order batsman. *Teams* Hampshire (1885, 1 match).
Career batting
1–2–0–10–7–5.00–0–0–*ct* 2

Simpson-Hayward, G. H. T.
(*see under* Simpson, G. H. T.)

Sims, Rev Herbert Marsh
Amateur. *b:* 15.3.1853, Mount Tavy, Tavistock, Devon. *d:* 5.10.1885, Thorpe, Whitby, Yorkshire. Middle order right-hand batsman, right-arm fast bowler. *Sch* St Peter's, York. *Teams* Cambridge U (1873–75, blue all three years); Yorkshire (1875–77, 5 matches).
Career batting
23–40–8–484–71–15.12–0–*ct* 18
Bowling 1224–63 + 2–19.42–3–0–6/76

Sims, James Morton
Professional. *b:* 13.5.1903, Leyton, Essex. *d:* 27.4.1973, Canterbury, Kent. Attacking lower order right-hand batsman, leg break bowler. *Team* Middlesex (1929–52, 381 matches). *Tours* MCC to Australia and New Zealand 1935/6, 1936/7; Brinckman to South America 1937/8. *Tests* England (1935 to 1936/7, 4 matches).
Career batting
462–635–116–8983–123–17.30–4–*ct* 253
Bowling 39401–1581–24.92–98–21–10/90
Test batting
4–4–0–16–12–4.00–0–*ct* 6
Bowling 480–11–43.63–1–0–5/73
He took 100 wickets in a season eight times (best 159, av 20.30, in 1939). His best bowling was 10/90 for East v West at Kingston-upon-Thames in 1948. His final first-class match was for MCC in 1953. He was Middlesex coach 1958–60 and scorer 1960–72.

Sims, Robin Jason
Cricketer. *b:* 22.11.1970, Hillingdon, Middlesex. Middle order left-hand batsman, wicket-keeper. *Team* Middlesex (1992, 1 match).
Career batting
1–1–0–3–3–3.00–0–*ct* 0

Sinclair, Barry Whitley
Amateur. *b:* 23.10.1936, Wellington, New Zealand. Determined middle order right-hand batsman, excellent cover field. *Team* Wellington (1955/6 to 1970/1). *Tours* New Zealand to England 1965, to India and Pakistan 1964/5, to Australia 1967/8. *Tests* New Zealand (1962/3 to 1967/8, 21 matches).
Career batting
118–204–18–6114–148–32.87–6–*ct* 45
Bowling 86–2–43.00–0–0–2/32
Test batting
21–40–1–1148–138–29.43–3–*ct* 8
Bowling 32–2–16.00–0–0–2/32
He was second in the first-class averages of the 1965 tour with 807 runs, av 36.68, and appeared in all three Tests. He captained New Zealand in three Tests.

Sinclair, Edward Wortley
Amateur. *b:* 4.1.1889, Paddington, London. *d:* 22.12.1966, Orpington, Kent. Lower order right-hand batsman, right-arm medium pace bowler. *Sch* Clifton. *Team* Royal Navy (1913–19).
Career batting
3–6–1–23–19–4.60–0–*ct* 1
Bowling 310–9–34.44–0–0–4/162

Sinclair, Erroll Hamish Lindsay Graeme
Amateur. *b:* 10.9.1904, Goring-on-Thames, Oxfordshire. *d:* 24.2.1954, at sea aboard SS *Orion.* Attractive middle order left-hand batsman, leg break bowler. *Sch* Winchester. *Teams* Oxford U (1924, blue); Ceylon (1926/7).
Career batting
7–11–1–126–37–12.60–0–*ct* 2
Bowling 639–19–33.63–0–0–4/56

Sinclair, James Hugh
Amateur. *b:* 16.10.1876, Swellendam, Cape Province, South Africa. *d:* 23.2.1913, Yeoville, Johannesburg, South Africa. Brother of D. M. (Transvaal). Hard hitting middle order right-hand batsman, right-arm medium pace or leg break bowler. *Teams* Transvaal (1892/3 to 1911/12); London County (1901–04). *Tours* South Africa to England 1901, 1904, 1907, to Australia 1910/11. *Tests* South Africa (1895/6 to 1910/11, 25 matches).
Career batting
129–214–6–4483–136–21.55–6–*ct* 65
Bowling 10527–491–21.43–33–10–8/32
Test batting
25–47–1–1069–106–23.23–3–*ct* 9
Bowling 1996–63–31.68–1–0–6/26
He was the most successful bowler of the 1901 tour to England taking 61 wickets, av 19.85; in 1904 he took 92, av 23.19 (98, av 23.76, in total), but on his final visit he was not so prominent. He played rugby for South Africa.

Sinfield, Reginald Albert
Professional. *b:* 24.12.1900, Benington, Stevenage, Hertfordshire. *d:* 17.3.1988, Ham Green, Bristol. Middle order right-hand batsman, right-arm fast medium, later off break bowler. *Team* Gloucestershire (1924–39, 423 matches). *Test* England (1938, 1 match).
Career batting
430–696–86–15674–209*–25.69–16–*ct* 178
Bowling 28734–1173–24.49–66–9–9/111
Test batting
1–1–0–6–6–6.00–0–*ct* 0
Bowling 123–2–61.50–0–0–1/51
He hit 1,000 runs in a season ten times (best 1,740, av 35.51, in 1935). He took 100 wickets in a season four times (best 161, av 19.14, in 1936) and completed the 'double' in 1934 and 1937. His only double century was 209* for Gloucestershire v Glamorgan at Cardiff in 1935, and his best bowling in an innings was 9 for 111 for Gloucestershire v Middlesex at Lord's in 1936. His first-class debut was for MCC in 1921 and he also played for Hertfordshire (1920–23).

Singh, Maharaj Kumar Bhalindra
Amateur. *b:* 9.10.1919, Patiala, India. *d:* 16.4.1992, New Delhi, India. Son of Maharaja of Patiala (India), brother of Yuvraj of Patiala (India). Middle order right-hand batsman, slow right-arm bowler. *Teams* Cambridge U (1939); Southern Punjab (1939/40 to 1946/7); Patiala (1953/4).
Career batting
13–21–3–392–109–21.77–1–*ct* 4
Bowling 675–25–27.00–0–0–4/34

Singh, Dr Kanwar Shumshere
Amateur. *b:* 21.6.1879, Bahraich, Oud, India. *d:* 12.5.1975, New Delhi, India. Sound middle order right-hand batsman, good field. *Sch* Rugby. *Teams* Kent (1901–02, 4 matches); Cambridge U (1901).
Career batting
5–9–0–174–45–19.33–0–*ct* 4

Singh, Swaranjit
Amateur. *b:* 18.7.1932, Amritsar, India. Middle order left-hand batsman, right-arm medium pace bowler. *Teams* Cambridge U (1954–56, blue 1955–56); Warwickshire (1956–62, 27 matches); East Punjab (1950/1 to 1958/9); Madras (1958/9); Bengal (1959/60 to 1961/2). *Tours* Madras to Ceylon 1958/9; Swanton to West Indies 1955/6.
Career batting
88–154–17–3709–146–27.07–4–*ct* 33
Bowling 5470–183–29.89–7–1–6/20

Singleton, Alexander Parkinson
Amateur. *b:* 5.8.1914, Repton, Derbyshire. Brother of G. M. (Worcestershire). Middle order right-hand batsman, off break bowler. *Sch* Shrewsbury. *Teams* Oxford U (1934–37, blue all four years); Worcestershire (1934–46, 58 matches); Rhodesia (1946/7 to 1949/50). *Tours* MCC to Canada 1937 (not first-class); Martineau to Egypt 1939 (not first-class).
Career batting
114–191–21–4700–164–27.64–4–*ct* 90
Bowling 7317–240–30.48–8–1–6/44
He hit 1,773 runs, av 34.09, in 1946. He captained Oxford in 1937 and Worcestershire in 1946.

Singleton, George Michael
Amateur. *b:* 12.5.1913, Repton, Derbyshire. Brother of A. P. (Worcestershire). Lower order right-hand batsman, slow left-arm bowler. *Sch* Uppingham. *Team* Worcestershire (1946, 2 matches).
Career batting
3–5–1–34–23–8.50–0–*ct* 1
Bowling 146–5–29.20–0–0–1/1

Sinker, Nigel Dalcour
Cricketer. *b:* 19.4.1946, Writtle, Chelmsford, Essex. Lower order left-hand batsman, slow left-arm bowler. *Sch* Winchester. *Team* Cambridge U (1966–67, blue 1966).
Career batting
13–23–4–188–31*–9.89–0–*ct* 2
Bowling 711–22–32.31–0–0–4/10

Sismey, Stanley George
Amateur. *b:* 15.7.1916, Junee, New South Wales, Australia. Lower order right-hand batsman, wicket-keeper. *Teams* New South Wales (1938/9 to 1950/1, 20 matches); Scotland (1952). *Tours* Australian Services to England 1945, to Ceylon and India 1945/6.
Career batting
35–52–11–725–78–17.68–0–*ct* 88–*st* 18

Siviter, Kenneth
Cricketer. *b:* 10.12.1953, Southport, Lancashire. Lower order right-hand batsman, right-arm fast medium bowler. *Sch* Liverpool College. *Team* Oxford U (1974–77, blue 1976).
Career batting
16–28–9–138–26–7.26–0–*ct* 3
Bowling 964–25–38.56–0–0–4/67

Skala, Steven Michael
Cricketer. *b:* 6.10.1955, Brisbane, Queensland, Australia. Lower order right-hand batsman, wicket-keeper. *Team* Oxford U (1979).
Career batting
2–3–0–18–11–6.00–0–*ct* 6–*st* 1

Skeet, Challen Hasler Lufkin
Amateur. *b:* 17.8.1895, Oamaru, Otago, New Zealand. *d:* 20.4.1978, West Tytherley, Hampshire. Middle order right-hand batsman, right-arm fast bowler. *Sch* St Paul's. *Teams* Oxford U (1919–20, blue 1920); Middlesex (1920–22, 19 matches).
Career batting
33–55–10–945–106–21.00–1–*ct* 19
Bowling 27–0

Skelding, Alexander
Professional. *b:* 5.9.1886, Leicester. *d:* 18.4.1960, Westcoates, Leicester. Lower order right-hand batsman, right-arm fast bowler. *Team* Leicestershire (1912–29, 177 matches).
Career batting
177–257–92–1117–33–6.76–0–*ct* 48
Bowling 14630–593–24.67–35–4–8/44
His best season was 1927, when he took 102 wickets, av 20.80. He was appointed to the first-class umpires' list in 1931 and did not retire until 1958 at the age of 72. Noted for his eccentricities, he used his own system of umpiring signals and had a particular aversion to dogs on the cricket field.

Skene, Robert Worboys
Amateur. *b:* 20.5.1908, Belmont, Surrey. *d:* 15.4.1988, Blickling, Norfolk. Sound middle order left-hand batsman, slow left-arm bowler. *Sch* Sedbergh. *Team* Oxford U (1928–30, blue 1928).
Career batting
21–32–7–644–105–25.76–1–*ct* 14
Bowling 1230–26–47.30–0–0–3/53

Skey, Dr Arthur Richard Harrie
Amateur. *b:* 13.2.1873, Lucknow, India. *d:* 13.7.1942, Haslar, Hampshire. Lower order right-hand batsman, slow left-arm bowler. *Sch* Dulwich. *Team* Royal Navy (1912).
Career batting
1–2–1–4–4–4.00–0–*ct* 0
Bowling 117–6–19.50–1–0–5/27

Skinner, Alan Frank
Amateur. *b:* 22.4.1913, Brighton, Sussex. *d:* 28.2.1982, Bury St Edmunds, Suffolk. Brother of D. A. (Derbyshire). Opening or middle order right-hand batsman. *Sch* Leys School. *Teams* Derbyshire (1931–38, 83 matches); Cambridge U (1934); Northamptonshire (1949, 1 match).
Career batting
86–142–7–3537–102–26.20–1–*ct* 60
Bowling 250–6–41.66–0–0–2/12
He hit 1,019 runs, av 27.54, in 1934. He also played for Suffolk (1954–55).

Skinner, Alfred Graham
Amateur. *b:* 11.8.1910, Calcutta, India. Middle order right-hand batsman, off break bowler. *Sch* Oundle. *Teams* Minor Counties (1933); Bengal (1935/6 to 1938/9); Europeans (1935/6 to 1936/7); Services (1943/4).
Career batting
13–22–3–490–125–25.78–1–*ct* 10
Bowling 475–9–52.77–0–0–3/44
His County cricket was for Buckinghamshire (1928–52).

Skinner, David Anthony
Amateur. *b:* 22.3.1920, Duffield, Derbyshire. Brother of A. F. (Derbyshire). Middle order right-hand batsman, off break bowler. *Sch* Leys. *Team* Derbyshire (1947–49, 23 matches).
Career batting
23–36–1–475–63–13.57–0–*ct* 11
Bowling 182–2–91.00–0–0–1/41
He captained Derbyshire in 1949.

Skinner, Edward Alfred
Professional. *b:* 18.1.1847, Mitcham, Surrey. *d:* 10.2.1919, Brighton, Sussex. Lower order right-hand batsman, right-hand fast round-arm bowler, slip field. *Team* Surrey (1871–81, 3 matches).
Career batting
3–6–1–37–10–7.40–0–*ct* 1
Bowling 112–3–37.33–0–0–2/33

Skinner, Ivor John
Professional. *b:* 1.4.1928, Walthamstow, Essex. Lower order right-hand batsman, right-arm fast medium bowler. *Team* Essex (1950, 13 matches).
Career batting
13–21–7–28–7*–2.00–0–*ct* 5
Bowling 808–21–38.47–0–0–4/56
He also played for Cornwall (1956–59).

Skinner, John
Professional. *b:* 16.7.1850, Steyning, Sussex. *d:* 17.2.1926, Steyning, Sussex. Lower order right-hand batsman, left-hand fast round-arm bowler. *Team* Sussex (1873–82, 10 matches).
Career batting
10–20–4–41–10–2.56–0–*ct* 6
Bowling 479–16–29.93–0–0–4/95

Skinner, Lonsdale Ernest
Cricketer. *b:* 7.9.1950, Plaisance, British Guiana. Middle order right-hand batsman, wicket-keeper. *Teams* Surrey (1971–77, 71 matches); Guyana (1973/4 to 1976/7).
Career batting
79–127–17–2503–93–22.75–0–*ct* 119–*st* 16

Slack, Hiram
Professional. *b:* 23.7.1843, Bradford, Yorkshire. *d:* 29.10.1918, Crumpsall, Lancashire. Nephew of Hiram (Nottingham 1831). Lower order right-hand batsman, right-hand medium pace round-arm bowler. *Team* North of England (1866).
Career batting
1–2–1–7–4–7.00–0–*ct* 0
His County cricket was for Warwickshire (pre first-class, 1878).

Slack, John Kenneth Edward
Amateur. *b:* 23.12.1930, Marylebone, London. Middle order right-hand batsman. *Sch* University College School, London. *Team* Cambridge U (1954, blue). *Tour* Surridge to Bermuda 1961 (not first-class).

Career batting
7–14–0–434–135–31.00–1–*ct* 4

He hit 135 for Cambridge U v Middlesex at Fenner's on his first-class debut in 1954. His County cricket was for Buckinghamshire (1964–69). A useful rugby footballer, he represented Middlesex.

Slack, Wilfred Norris
Cricketer. *b:* 12.12.1954, Troumaca, St Vincent. *d:* 15.1.1989, Banjul, The Gambia. Opening left-hand batsman, right-arm medium pace bowler. *Teams* Middlesex (1977–88, 210 matches); Windward Islands (1981/2 to 1982/3). *Tours* Middlesex to Zimbabwe 1980/1; International XI to Pakistan 1981/2; England B to Sri Lanka 1985/6; England to West Indies 1985/6, to Australia 1986/7. *Tests* England (1985/6 to 1986, 3 matches).
Career batting
237–398–40–13950–248*–38.96–25–*ct* 174
Bowling 688–21–32.76–0–0–3/17
Test batting
3–6–0–81–52–13.50–0–*ct* 3

He hit 1,000 runs in a season eight times (best 1,900, av 54.28, in 1985). He was co-opted onto the England tour to West Indies in 1985/6 when Gatting was forced home through injury and Slack then made his Test debut. He did not play in any Tests on the 1986/7 tour to Australia. On that tour he had passed out whilst batting in the nets. He collapsed on three subsequent occasions whilst playing for Middlesex, but no cause could be found for these blackouts. He had been batting about an hour in an exhibition match in The Gambia when he suddenly collapsed and died, the reason given being a heart attack. His highest score was 248* for Middlesex v Worcestershire at Lord's in 1981. He also played for Buckinghamshire (1976).

Sladdin, Richard William
Cricketer. *b:* 8.1.1969, Halifax, Yorkshire. Lower order right-hand batsman, slow left-arm bowler. *Team* Derbyshire (1991–92, 21 matches).
Career batting
21–25–6–199–39*–10.47–0–*ct* 12
Bowling 2361–66–35.77–2–0–6/58

Slade, Douglas Norman Frank
(birth registered as N. F. D. Slade)
Professional. *b:* 24.8.1940, Feckenham, Worcestershire. Lower order right-hand batsman, slow left-arm bowler. *Team* Worcestershire (1958–71, 266 matches). *Tours* Commonwealth to Pakistan 1963/4, 1970/1; Worcestershire World Tour (Rhodesia first-class) 1964/5, to Jamaica 1965/6.
Career batting
280–395–103–5275–125–18.06–1–*ct* 193
Bowling 11785–502–23.47–14–1–7/47

His best season was 1960, when he took 97 wickets, av 19.83. He also played for Shropshire (1973–78).

Slade, William Douglas
Professional. *b:* 27.9.1941, Briton Ferry, Glamorgan. Lower order right-hand batsman, right-arm medium bowler, fine close field. *Team* Glamorgan (1961–67, 67 matches).
Career batting
67–116–11–1482–73*–14.11–0–*ct* 100
Bowling 1493–32–46.65–0–0–4/144

He played for Wales in the ICC Trophy in 1979.

Sladen, Arthur Redman
Professional. *b:* 22.7.1877, Manningham, Bradford, Yorkshire. *d:* 25.7.1934, Lake Side, Lancashire. Lower order batsman, slow left-arm bowler. *Teams* London County (1901–02); Lancashire (1903–04, 2 matches).
Career batting
5–7–3–10–5–2.50–0–*ct* 2
Bowling 450–19–23.68–2–0–5/50

Slater, Archibald Gilbert
Professional. *b:* 22.11.1890, Pilsley, Derbyshire. *d:* 22.7.1949, Manchester, Lancashire. Son of Henry (Derbyshire), brother of Herbert (Derbyshire). Lower order right-hand batsman, right-arm medium pace bowler. *Team* Derbyshire (1911–31, 210 matches).
Career batting
211–327–28–5943–105–19.87–1–*ct* 124
Bowling 10548–500–21.09–28–2–8/24

He took 108 wickets, av 16.25, in 1931. His final first-class match was for Sir L. Parkinson's XI in 1933.

Slater, Henry
Professional. *b:* 23.2.1855, Heanor, Derbyshire. *d:* 20.11.1916, Worksop, Nottinghamshire. Father of A. G. (Derbyshire) and Herbert (Derbyshire). Lower order right-hand batsman, right-arm medium pace bowler. *Team* Derbyshire (1882–87, 5 matches).
Career batting
5–9–3–22–11–3.66–0–*ct* 2
Bowling 185–3–61.66–0–0–1/35

Slater, Herbert
Professional. *b:* 11.11.1881, Langley Mill, Derbyshire. *d:* 2.12.1958, Creswell, Derbyshire. Brother of A. G. (Derbyshire), son of Henry (Derbyshire). Lower order right-hand batsman, right-arm fast medium or off break bowler. *Team* Derbyshire (1907, 5 matches).
Career batting
5–9–2–39–21–5.57–0–*ct* 0
Bowling 38–2–19.00–0–0–2/15

Slater, Leonard
Amateur. *b:* 11.10.1875, Barnstaple, Devon. *d:* 14.9.1914, Aisne, France. Middle order batsman. *Sch*

Marlborough. *Team* Gentlemen of the South (1909).
Career batting
1–2–0–15–15–7.50–0–*ct* 0

His County cricket was for Devon (1904).

Slater, Philip Hugh
Amateur. *b:* 1.4.1876, Canterbury, Kent. *d:* 20.8.1958, Fleet, Hampshire. Middle order batsman. *Sch* King's, Canterbury. *Team* Surrey (1911, 1 match).
Career batting
1–1–0–1–1–1.00–0–*ct* 0

Slater, R.
Amateur. Lower order right-hand batsman, right-hand fast round-arm bowler. *Team* Lancashire (1865, 1 match).
Career batting
1–2–0–0–0–0.00–0–*ct* 0
Bowling 3–0

Slater, William
Professional. *b:* 17.11.1790, Storrington, Sussex. *d:* 9.3.1852, Brighton, Sussex. Brother of John (Sussex). Middle order left-hand batsman, wicket-keeper. *Team* Sussex (1815–29, 20 matches).
Career batting
31–54–7–494–44–10.51–0–*ct* 23–*st* 30

His last first-class match was for Lord F. Beauclerk's XI in 1814.

Slatter, Air Marshal Sir Leonard Horatio
Amateur. *b:* 8.12.1894, Durban, South Africa. *d:* 14.4.1961, Uxbridge, Middlesex. Lower order right-hand batsman, right-arm bowler. *Team* RAF (1928).
Career batting
1–1–1–1–1*–no av–0–*ct* 2
Bowling 33–0

In his obituary published in Wisden 1962, his surname is incorrectly given as 'Slater'.

Slaven, Francis Ferguson
Amateur. *b:* 3.3.1931, Bulawayo, Southern Rhodesia. Brother of M. D. (Rhodesia). Middle order right-hand batsman, good cover field. *Team* Oxford U (1955).
Career batting
2–2–0–13–13–6.50–0–*ct* 2

Sleep, Peter Raymond
Cricketer. *b:* 4.5.1957, Penola, South Australia. Middle order right-hand batsman, leg break and googly bowler. *Team* South Australia (1976/7 to 1991/2, 135 matches). *Tours* Australia to India 1979/80, to Pakistan 1982/3, 1988/9; Rest of World to England 1990, 1991, 1992. *Tests* Australia (1978/9 to 1989/90, 14 matches).
Career batting
162–264–46–7600–182–34.86–14–*ct* 95–*st* 1
Bowling 13380–341–39.23–8–0–8/33
Test batting
14–21–1–483–90–24.15–0–*ct* 4
Bowling 1397–31–45.06–1–0–5/72

Although he has not toured England with the Australians, he has been very successful in English league cricket and has therefore been selected for the Rest of the World in England.

Slight, James
Amateur. *b:* 20.10.1855, Ashby, Geelong, Victoria, Australia. *d:* 9.12.1930, Elsternwick, Melbourne, Victoria, Australia. Brother of William (Victoria) and A. F. (South Australia). Sound middle order right-hand batsman, good field. *Team* Victoria (1874/5 to 1887/8, 14 matches). *Tour* Australia to England 1880. *Test* Australia (1880, 1 match).
Career batting
19–34–1–415–53–12.57–0–*ct* 4
Bowling 37–3–12.33–0–0–2/4
Test batting
1–2–0–11–11–5.50–0–*ct* 0

Owing to illness, his opportunities on the 1880 tour were restricted, but he did appear in the Test.

Slinger, Edward
Cricketer. *b:* 2.2.1938, Accrington, Lancashire. Opening batsman. *Team* MCC (1967).
Career batting
1–1–1–12–12*–no av–0–*ct* 1

Slinn, William
Professional. *b:* 13.12.1826, Sheffield, Yorkshire. *d:* 19.6.1888, Wortley, Sheffield, Yorkshire. Tail end right-hand batsman, right-hand fast round-arm bowler. *Team* Yorkshire (1861–64, 15 matches).
Career batting
19–31–8–46–11–2.00–0–*ct* 11
Bowling 1466–111–13.20–9–4–8/33

A brilliant bowler, his poor showing both as a batsman and fielder very much reduced his appearances in first-class cricket. His greatest bowling feat was to take all ten wickets in an innings when bowling for XXII of Scarborough against the All England Eleven in 1862. His first-class debut was for United England XI in 1860. He also played for Buckinghamshire (1859), Rutland (1859), Monmouthshire (1860), Northamptonshire (pre first-class, 1860) and Shropshire (1865).

Slocock, Ernest Frederic
(death registered as Ernest Frederick Slocock)
Amateur. *b:* 7.3.1865, Winterbourne, Berkshire. *d:* 11.1.1940, Waldershaigh, Bolsterstone, Yorkshire. Lower order right-hand batsman, wicket-keeper. *Sch* Lancing. *Team* Cambridge U (1886).
Career batting
1–2–0–4–4–2.00–0–*ct* 2

Slocombe, Philip Anthony
Cricketer. *b:* 6.9.1954, Weston-super-Mare, Somerset. Middle order right-hand batsman, right-arm medium pace bowler. *Sch* Millfield. *Team* Somerset

(1975–83, 135 matches). *Tour* Robins to South Africa 1975/6.
Career batting
139–233–29–5640–132–27.64–7–*ct* 65
Bowling 54–3–18.00–0–0–1/2

He hit 1,000 runs in a season twice (best 1,221, av 38.15, in 1978).

Sloman, William Henry
Professional. *b:* 2.12.1871, Launceston, Cornwall. *d:* 10.8.1926, South Molton, Devon. Middle order batsman, useful bowler. *Team* Somerset (1895–96, 4 matches).
Career batting
4–8–0–97–48–12.12–0–*ct* 2
Bowling 7–1–7.00–0–0–1/7

Sly, Gerald Brian
Professional. *b:* 21.10.1932, Ealing, Middlesex. Lower order batsman, useful fast medium bowler. *Team* Sussex (1953, 1 match).
Career batting
1 match, did not bat–*ct* 1
Bowling 29–1–29.00–0–0–1/24

Smail, Alastair Harold Kurt
Cricketer. *b:* 3.7.1964, Kingston-upon-Thames, Surrey. Lower order right-hand batsman, left-arm medium pace bowler. *Team* Oxford U (1983).
Career batting
6–6–1–24–13*–4.80–0–*ct* 1
Bowling 222–5–44.40–0–0–3/49

Smailes, Thomas Francis
Professional. *b:* 27.3.1910, Ripley, Yorkshire. *d:* 1.12.1970, Starbeck, Harrogate, Yorkshire. Lower order left-hand batsman, right-arm medium pace bowler. *Sch* Pocklington. *Team* Yorkshire (1932–48, 262 matches). *Tour* Yorkshire to Jamaica 1935/6. *Test* England (1946, 1 match).
Career batting
269–349–43–5892–117–19.25–3–*ct* 154
Bowling 17114–822–20.81–41–6–10/47
Test batting
1–1–0–25–25–25.00–0–*ct* 0
Bowling 62–3–20.66–0–0–3/44

He took 100 wickets in a season four times (best 130, av 17.54, in 1936). His best bowling was 10/47 for Yorkshire v Derbyshire at Bramall Lane in 1939. He hit 1,002 runs, av 25.05, in 1938.

Smales, Kenneth
Professional. *b:* 15.9.1927, Horsforth, Yorkshire. Lower order right-hand batsman, off break bowler. *Teams* Yorkshire (1948–50, 13 matches; Nottinghamshire (1951–58, 148 matches).
Career batting
161–229–55–2512–64–14.43–0–*ct* 60
Bowling 11946–389–30.70–20–5–10/66

His best bowling was 10/66 for Nottinghamshire v Gloucestershire at Stroud in 1956 and his best season was 1955 with 117 wickets, av 24.12. After retiring from first-class cricket he became Secretary to Nottingham Forest FC. He is also a well-known soccer historian.

Small, Gladstone Cleophas
Cricketer. *b:* 18.10.1961, Brighton, St George, Barbados. Lower order right-hand batsman, right-arm fast medium bowler. *Teams* Warwickshire (1980–92, 229 matches); South Australia (1985/6, 10 matches). *Tours* Robins to New Zealand 1979/80; International XI to Pakistan 1981/2; England to Australia 1986/7, 1990/1, to Sharjah (not first-class) 1986/7, to India and Pakistan (World Cup) 1987/8, to India 1989/90 (not first-class), to West Indies 1989/90, to New Zealand 1990/1 (not first-class), to Australia and New Zealand (World Cup) 1991/2. *Tests* England (1986 to 1990/1, 17 matches).
Career batting
272–351–82–4033–70–14.99–0–*ct* 83
Bowling 21497–750–28.66–27–2–7/15
Test batting
17–24–7–263–59–15.47–0–*ct* 9
Bowling 1871–55–34.01–2–0–5/48

He took 80 wickets, av 20.06, in 1988. His opportunities of a Test career were hampered by injury and his best series for England was in West Indies in 1989/90. However he bowled well for England in one-day internationals.

Small, John (sen)
Professional. *b:* 19.4.1737, Empshott, Hampshire. *d:* 31.12.1826, Petersfield, Hampshire. Father of John jun (Hampshire) and Eli (Hampshire). Middle order right hand batsman, good field. *Team* Hampshire (1773–98).

He is said to have commenced playing in great matches in 1755, though no details of these early games have yet been discovered, and since his final important match was in 1798, his career was very long. An original member of the Hambledon Club, he was one of the leading batsmen of his day.

Small, John (jun)
Professional. *b:* 1766, Petersfield, Hampshire. *d:* 21.1.1836, Petersfield, Hampshire. Son of John sen (Hampshire), brother of Eli (Hampshire). Middle order right-hand batsman. *Team* Hampshire (1787–1807).
Career batting
40–74–4–744–42–10.62–0–*ct* 21

His last first-class match was for England in 1810.

Small, Joseph A.
Amateur. *b:* 3.11.1892, Princes Town, Trinidad. *d:* 26.4.1958, Forest Reserve, Trinidad. Attractive middle order right-hand batsman, right-arm medium fast bowler, brilliant slip field. *Team* Trinidad (1909/10 to

1931/2). *Tours* West Indies to England 1923, 1928. *Tests* West Indies (1928 to 1929/30, 3 matches).
Career batting
77–128–11–3063–133–26.17–4–*ct* 72
Bowling 4589–165–27.81–7–0–7/49
Test batting
3–6–0–79–52–13.16–0–*ct* 3
Bowling 184–3–61.33–0–0–2/67

On the 1923 tour he hit 776 runs, av 31.04, but in 1928 his batting was not so successful, though his bowling greatly improved with 50 wickets, av 28.88.

Small, Milton Aster
Cricketer. *b:* 12.2.1964, Blades Point, St Philip, Barbados. Tail end right-hand batsman, right-arm fast medium bowler. *Team* Barbados (1983/4 to 1991/2). *Tour* West Indies to England 1984. *Tests* West Indies (1983/4 to 1984, 2 matches).
Career batting
18–17–5–51–15–4.25–0–*ct* 5
Bowling 1581–56–28.23–2–0–6/55
Test batting
2–1–1–3–3*–no av–0–*ct* 0
Bowling 153–4–38.25–0–0–3/40

His opportunities were limited on the 1984 tour to England, but he appeared in one Test.

Smalley, J.
Professional. Middle order batsman. *Team* Lancashire (1869, 2 matches).
Career batting
2–4–0–24–17–6.00–0–*ct* 0

Smart, Cyril Cecil
Professional. *b:* 23.7.1898, Lacock, Wiltshire. *d:* 21.5.1975, Abertillery, Glamorgan. Brother of J. A. (Warwickshire). Attacking middle order right-hand batsman, leg break bowler, good field. *Teams* Warwickshire (1920–22, 45 matches); Glamorgan (1927–46, 190 matches).
Career batting
236–383–46–8992–151*–26.68–9–*ct* 163
Bowling 7505–180–41.69–1–0–5/39

He hit 1,000 runs in a season five times (best 1,560, av 36.27, in 1935). He hit 32 runs off one over from G. Hill of Hampshire at Cardiff in 1935.

Smart, John Abbotts
(death registered as Jack Abbott Smart)
Professional. *b:* 12.4.1891, Forest Hill, Marlborough, Wiltshire. *d:* 3.10.1979, Bulkington, Nuneaton, Warwickshire. Brother of C. C. (Warwickshire and Glamorgan). Lower order right-hand batsman, wicket-keeper, right-arm off break bowler. *Team* Warwickshire (1919–36, 238 matches).
Career batting
238–340–43–3425–68*–11.53–0–*ct* 317–*st* 107
Bowling 1262–22–57.36–0–0–2/13

He also played for Wiltshire (1908–10). He was a first-class umpire (1937–48), standing in four Tests (1946–47).

Smedley, Michael John
Cricketer. *b:* 28.10.1941, Maltby, Yorkshire. Stylish middle order right-hand batsman. *Team* Nottinghamshire (1964–79, 357 matches).
Career batting
360–604–76–16482–149–31.21–28–*ct* 261
Bowling 4–0

He hit 1,000 runs in a season nine times (best 1,718, av 38.17, in 1971). From 1975 to June 1979 he captained Nottinghamshire.

Smethers, Michael Charles
Cricketer. *b:* 18.8.1947, Southgate, Middlesex. Lower order right-hand batsman, wicket-keeper. *Sch* Highgate. *Team* Cambridge U (1967).
Career batting
2–3–0–19–14–6.33–0–*ct* 1–*st* 1

Smith, A.
Professional. *b:* 1892, Beckenham, Kent. Lower order batsman, left-arm medium pace bowler. *Team* G. J. V. Weigall's XI (1914).
Career batting
1–2–0–9–8–4.50–0–*ct* 0
Bowling 102–3–34.00–0–0–3/102

Smith, Alan Christopher
Amateur. *b:* 25.10.1936, Hall Green, Birmingham. Middle order right-hand batsman, occasional right-arm fast medium bowler, wicket-keeper. *Sch* KES, Birmingham. *Teams* Warwickshire (1958–74, 358 matches); Oxford U (1958–60, blue all three years). *Tours* MCC to North America 1959 (not first-class), to Australia and New Zealand 1962/3, to New Zealand 1974/5 (assistant manager, but played in emergency); Swanton to West Indies 1960/1. *Tests* England (1962/3, 6 matches).
Career batting
428–612–85–11027–145–20.92–5–*ct* 715–*st* 61
Bowling 3074–131–23.46–2–0–5/32
Test batting
6–7–3–118–69–29.50–0–*ct* 20

He hit 1,201 runs, av 31.60, in 1962, as well as dismissing 82 batsmen as wicket-keeper. For Warwickshire v Essex at Clacton in 1965, he was in the team as wicket-keeper, but was put on to bowl and performed the hat-trick. He captained Oxford 1959–60 and Warwickshire 1968–74 and was Secretary of Warwickshire 1976–86, when he was appointed Chief Executive of the TCCB. He was a Test selector 1969–73, 1981–86 and since 1989. He also won a blue for soccer.

Smith, Alexander
Professional. *b:* 15.8.1865, Blackburn Lancashire. Lower order batsman, opening bowler. *Team* Liver-

pool and District (1894).
Career batting
2–4–0–38–21–9.50–0–*ct* 1
Bowling 170–7–24.28–0–0–4/57
His County cricket was for Cheshire (1894–95) and Worcestershire (pre first-class, 1895).

Smith, Alexander Victor
Cricketer. *b:* 11.5.1945, Shanganagh, Co Dublin, Ireland. Middle order left-hand batsman. *Team* Ireland (1978–79).
Career batting
2–1–1–11–11*–no av–0–*ct* 1
He played soccer for Shamrock Rovers and Sligo Rovers.

Smith, Alfort
Professional. *b:* 7.7.1846, Bank Lane, Bury, Lancashire. *d:* 21.12.1908, Glossop, Derbyshire. Lower order right-hand batsman, wicket-keeper. *Teams* Lancashire (1867–71, 4 matches); Derbyshire (1873–80, 49 matches).
Career batting
55–98–34–305–30–4.76–0–*ct* 70–*st* 12
Bowling 7–0
He was a first-class umpire (1887–94).

Smith, Alfred
Amateur. *b:* 6.11.1909, Kilmarnock, Ayrshire, Scotland. *d:* 28.2.1977, Fleet, Hampshire. Middle order right-hand batsman, off break bowler. *Team* Scotland (1934–37).
Career batting
3–6–1–96–36*–19.20–0–*ct* 2
Bowling 114–3–38.00–0–0–1/3

Smith, Alfred Farrer
Amateur in 1868, then professional. *b:* 7.3.1847, Birstall, Yorkshire. *d:* 6.1.1915, Ossett, Yorkshire. Very steady opening right-hand batsman, right-hand fast medium round-arm bowler. *Team* Yorkshire (1868–74, 28 matches).
Career batting
29–51–4–796–99–16.93–0–*ct* 10
He was a first-class umpire (1892–1901).

Smith, Andrew Michael
Cricketer. *b:* 1.10.1967, Dewsbury, Yorkshire. Lower order right-hand batsman, left-arm fast medium bowler. *Sch* Queen Elizabeth GS, Wakefield. *Team* Gloucestershire (1991–92, 26 matches).
Career batting
26–27–7–229–51*–11.45–0–*ct* 3
Bowling 1818–53–34.30–0–0–4/41

Smith, Anthony John Shaw
Cricketer. *b:* 8.2.1951, Johannesburg, South Africa. Brother-in-law of R. G. Lumb (Yorkshire), cousin of P. R. J. Dewes (Natal). Middle order right-hand batsman, wicket-keeper. *Team* Natal (1972/3 to 1983/4).
Career batting
103–168–25–3909–150*–27.33–2–*ct* 309–*st* 11
Bowling 35–1–35.00–0–0–1/4
His first-class debut was for South African Universities in 1971/2. His only first-class match in England was for D. H. Robins' XI in 1974.

Smith, Anthony Mervyn
Cricketer. *b:* 26.2.1930, Castle Combe, Wiltshire. Middle order left-hand batsman, slow left-arm bowler. *Team* Minor Counties (1965).
Career batting
1–2–0–20–12–10.00–0–*ct* 0
His County cricket was for Wiltshire (1955–69).

Smith, Sir Archibald Levin
Amateur. *b:* 27.8.1836, Salt Hill, Chichester, Sussex. *d:* 20.10.1901, Wester Elchies House, Aberlour, Morayshire, Scotland. Steady opening right-hand batsman, right-hand fast under-arm bowler. *Sch* Eton. *Team* MCC (1861–64).
Career batting
2–4–0–16–7–4.00–0–*ct* 0
Bowling 1 wicket (no analyses)–0–0–1/?
He was not in the Eleven whilst at Cambridge, but rowed against Oxford, and in 1859 was a member of the Cambridge boat which sank. Unable to swim he was fortunate to be rescued with the aid of a lifebuoy. He was President of MCC in 1899. He was appointed a Lord Justice of Appeal in 1892 and Master of the Rolls in 1900.

Smith, Arthur
Amateur. *b:* 28.5.1851, Hurstpierpoint, Sussex. *d:* 8.3.1923, Amberley, Sussex. Brother of C. H. (Sussex), uncle of C. L. A. (Sussex), nephew of Alfred (Sussex 1841–52). Lower order right-hand batsman, left-hand medium slow round-arm bowler. *Sch* Brighton. *Team* Sussex (1874–80, 19 matches).
Career batting
19–30–8–94–13–4.27–0–*ct* 7
Bowling 1086–61–17.80–3–1–7/47

Smith, Arthur
Professional. *b:* 1872, Barlestone, Leicestershire. *d:* 3.10.1952, Melton Mowbray, Leicestershire. Tail end right-hand batsman, right-arm fast bowler. *Team* Leicestershire (1897–1901, 4 matches).
Career batting
4–7–1–16–9–2.66–0–*ct* 0
Bowling 135–5–27.00–0–0–3/40

Smith, Arthur Frederick
Amateur. *b:* 13.5.1853, Regent's Park, London. *d:* 18.1.1936, Kimberley, South Africa. Brother of C. J. (Middlesex). Middle order right-hand batsman, right-hand fast round-arm bowler. *Sch* Wellington and Harrow. *Teams* Middlesex (1874–77, 6 matches); Cambridge U (1875, blue).

Smith, Arthur Price

Career batting
14–23–3–193–48*–9.65–0–*ct* 15
Bowling 30–0
His first-class debut was for An England XI in 1873 and his final first-class appearance for Gentlemen in 1878. He also won a blue for rugby.

Smith, Arthur Price
Professional. *b:* 3.12.1857, Ruddington, Nottinghamshire. *d:* 3.6.1937, Tottenham, Middlesex. Steady middle order right-hand batsman, right-arm medium pace bowler. *Teams* Nottinghamshire (1883, 2 matches); Lancashire (1886–94, 48 matches).
Career batting
50–79–5–1475–124–19.93–2–*ct* 31
Bowling 517–29–17.82–1–0–5/49
He was a first-class umpire (1885).

Smith, Benjamin Charles
Professional. *b:* 10.7.1859, Daventry, Northamptonshire. *d:* 29.11.1942, Northampton. Lower order right-hand batsman, wicket-keeper. *Team* Northamptonshire (1905–06, 31 matches).
Career batting
31–55–25–393–38*–13.10–0–*ct* 43–*st* 4
Bowling 2–0
He first played for Northamptonshire (pre first-class) in 1887. He was a first-class umpire (1908).

Smith, Benjamin Francis
Cricketer. *b:* 3.4.1972, Corby, Northamptonshire. Middle order right-hand batsman, right-arm medium pace bowler. *Team* Leicestershire (1990–92, 32 matches).
Career batting
32–45–9–1134–100*–31.50–1–*ct* 13
Bowling 91–1–91.00–0–0–1/5

Smith, Bertrand Nigel Bosworth
(birth registered as Nigel Bosworth Smith; known as Bosworth-Smith)
Amateur. *b:* 20.6.1873, Harrow, Middlesex. *d:* 19.2.1947, Hove, Sussex. Nephew of A. P. Wickham (Somerset). Middle order right-hand batsman, slow left-arm bowler. *Sch* Harrow. *Teams* Oxford U (1895–96); Middlesex (1895, 1 match); Europeans (1900/1); Gentlemen of India (1902/3).
Career batting
11–19–0–323–45–17.00–0–*ct* 6
Bowling 24–0
His final first-class match in England was for MCC in 1901. He also played for Dorset (1909). He won a blue for soccer.

Smith, Cameron Wilberforce
Amateur. *b:* 29.7.1933, Upper Dayrells Road, St Michael, Barbados. Opening right-hand batsman, wicket-keeper. *Team* Barbados (1951/2 to 1964/5). *Tours* West Indies to Australia 1960/1; West Indian XI to England 1964; Commonwealth to India 1964/5. *Tests* West Indies (1960/1 to 1961/2, 5 matches).
Career batting
37–64–3–2277–140–37.32–5–*ct* 32–*st* 3
Bowling 97–3–32.33–0–0–2/24
Test batting
5–10–1–222–55–24.66–0–*ct* 4–*st* 1

Smith, Cedric Ivan James
Professional. *b:* 25.8.1906, Corsham, Wiltshire. *d:* 9.2.1979, Mellor, Lancashire. Brother of W. A. (Minor Counties). Lower order right-hand batsman, right-arm fast bowler. *Team* Middlesex (1934–39, 152 matches). *Tour* MCC to West Indies 1934/35. *Tests* England (1934/5 to 1937, 5 matches).
Career batting
208–304–31–4007–101*–14.67–1–*ct* 99
Bowling 16271–845–19.25–47–8–8/102
Test batting
5–10–0–102–27–10.20–0–*ct* 1
Bowling 393–15–26.20–1–0–5/16
He also played for Wiltshire (1926–33) and his first-class debut was for the Minor Counties in 1930. He took 100 wickets in a season four times (best 172, av 18.88, in 1934). He was a noted big hitter and scored many sixes in first-class matches.

Smith, Charles
Professional. *b:* 24.8.1861, Calverley, Yorkshire. *d:* 2.5.1925, Calverley, Yorkshire. Lower order right-hand batsman, wicket-keeper. *Team* Lancashire (1893–1902, 167 matches).
Career batting
168–236–50–2251–81–12.10–0–*ct* 316–*st* 120
Bowling 18–1–18.00–0–0–1/18
He appeared for Yorkshire in a non-first-class match in 1885.

Smith, Sir Charles Aubrey
Amateur. *b:* 21.7.1863, City of London. *d:* 20.12.1948, Beverly Hills, California, USA. Lower order right-hand batsman, right-arm fast bowler. *Sch* Charterhouse. *Team* Cambridge U (1882–85, blue all four years); Sussex (1882–96, 99 matches); Transvaal (1889/90). *Tours* Lillywhite, Shaw and Shrewsbury to Australia 1887/8; Warton to South Africa 1888/9. *Test* England (1888/9, 1 match).
Career batting
143–247–28–2986–85–13.63–0–*ct* 97
Bowling 7730–346–22.34–19–1–7/16
Test batting
1–1–0–3–3–3.00–0–*ct* 0
Bowling 61–7–8.71–1–0–5/19
He captained Sussex in 1887–88 and 1890 and also led the 1887/8 team to Australia. He captained England in one Test. After the 1888/9 tour to South Africa he remained in that country setting up a business there, but much later he gained fame as an actor and, based in Hollywood, appeared in numerous films

in the 1930s and 1940s. He was knighted for services to acting in 1944.

Smith, Charles Hamlin
Amateur. *b:* 31.8.1838, Albourne, Sussex. *d:* 12.3.1909, Henfield, Sussex. Brother of Arthur (Sussex), father of C. L. A. (Sussex), nephew of Alfred (Sussex 1841–52). Middle order right-hand batsman, good close field. *Team* Sussex (1861–74, 62 matches).
Career batting
63–111–7–1705–95–16.39–0–*ct* 45
Bowling 206–4–51.50–0–0–2/61
He captained Sussex from 1864 to 1874, jointly in the first and last of those seasons. He was Sussex Secretary 1869–78.

Smith, Charles John
Amateur. *b:* 19.1.1849, Marylebone, London. *d:* 8.5.1930, Hendon, Middlesex. Brother of A. F. (Middlesex). Stylish middle order right-hand batsman, right-hand fast round-arm bowler. *Sch* Harrow. *Team* Middlesex (1868–76, 3 matches).
Career batting
10–19–2–172–43–10.11–0–*ct* 3
Bowling 147–8–18.37–0–0–4/34
His first-class debut was for MCC in 1867 and his final first-class match for MCC in 1878. He was a talented athlete, specialising in the half mile and mile.

Smith, Charles Lawrence Arthur
Amateur. *b:* 1.1.1879, Henfield, Sussex. *d:* 22.11.1949, Wineham, Henfield, Sussex. Son of C. H. (Sussex), nephew of Arthur (Sussex). Middle order right-hand batsman, right-arm medium fast bowler. *Sch* Brighton. *Team* Sussex (1898–1911, 218 matches).
Career batting
220–336–37–5844–103*–19.54–2–*ct* 149
Bowling 585–9–65.00–0–0–1/0
He hit 1,032 runs, av 24.57, in 1906. He captained Sussex in 1909, and during part of 1906 when C. B. Fry was injured.

Smith, Charles Neville Strode
Amateur. *b:* 26.12.1898, Wedmore, Somerset. *d:* 9.9.1955, Instow, Devon. He died whilst playing cricket. Middle order batsman. *Team* Royal Navy (1929).
Career batting
1–2–0–54–47–27.00–0–*ct* 0
His County cricket was for Devon (1931).

Smith, Christopher Lyall
Cricketer. *b:* 15.10.1958, Durban, South Africa. Brother of R. A. (Hampshire), grandson of V. L. Shearer (Natal). Opening right-hand batsman, off break bowler. *Teams* Natal (1977/8 to 1982/3); Glamorgan (1979, 1 match); Hampshire (1980–91, 222 matches). *Tours* England to New Zealand and Pakistan 1983/4; England B to Sri Lanka 1985/6. *Tests* England (1983–86, 8 matches).
Career batting
269–466–60–18028–217–44.40–47–*ct* 176
Bowling 2685–50–53.70–1–0–5/69
Test batting
8–14–1–392–91–30.15–0–*ct* 5
Bowling 39–3–13.00–0–0–2/31
Qualifying as an English player in May 1983, he quickly gained a place in the Test side. The following winter he went to New Zealand and Pakistan, playing in five of the six Tests, but was not chosen for England at home in either 1984 or 1985. He was given one chance in 1986, then injury ruled him out of further selection and despite continuing to score runs at County level, he was not capped for England again. In 1991 he decided to emigrate to Australia, taking a post with the Western Australia CA. He hit 1,000 runs in a season ten times, going on to 2,000 once: 2,000, av 57.14, in 1985. His highest score was 217 for Hampshire v Warwickshire at Edgbaston in 1987.

Smith, Clifford John
Professional. *b:* 6.10.1902, Shadwell, London. *d:* 4.6.1959, Cambridge. Lower order left-hand batsman, right-arm medium pace bowler. *Team* Minor Counties (1937).
Career batting
1–2–0–29–21–14.50–0–*ct* 2
Bowling 39–2–19.50–0–0–1/18
His County cricket was for Cambridgeshire (1923–50).

Smith, Colin Milner
Amateur. *b:* 2.11.1936, Mottingham, Kent. Brother of M. G. M. (Cambridge U). Lower order right-hand batsman, wicket-keeper. *Sch* Tonbridge. *Team* Oxford U (1958).
Career batting
1–2–0–16–12–8.00–0–*ct* 1–*st* 1

Smith, Colin Stansfield
Amateur. *b:* 1.10.1932, Didsbury, Manchester, Lancasahire. Brother of D. J (Lancashire). Lower order right-hand batsman, right-arm fast medium bowler. *Sch* William Hulme's GS. *Teams* Lancashire (1951–57, 45 matches); Cambridge U (1954–57, blue all four years).
Career batting
106–153–28–2339–103*–18.71–1–*ct* 48
Bowling 7179–293–24.50–9–1–6/35
His final first-class match was for D. R. Jardine's XI in 1958. He also played for Cheshire (1949–50).

Smith, D.
Amateur. Lower order batsman, useful bowler. *Team* Combined Services (1947).
Career batting
1–2–0–23–22–11.50–0–*ct* 0
Bowling 50–0

Smith, David Bertram Miller
Amateur. *b:* 14.9.1884, Richmond, Melbourne, Victoria, Australia. *d:* 29.7.1963, Hawthorn, Melbourne, Victoria, Australia. Uncle of S. A. J. (Victoria). Middle order right-hand batsman. *Team* Victoria (1908/9 to 1911/12, 19 matches). *Tours* Australia to New Zealand 1909/10, to England and North America 1912. *Tests* Australia (1912, 2 matches).
Career batting
46–77–3–1764–146–23.83–3–*ct* 16
Bowling 22–1–22.00–0–0–1/22
Test batting
2–3–1–30–24*–15.00–0–*ct* 0
Although he played in two Tests, he achieved little on the 1912 tour to England.

Smith, David Henry Kilner
Cricketer. 29.6.1940, Shipley, Yorkshire. Father of L. K. (Worcestershire). Opening left-hand batsman, occasional wicket-keeper. *Team* Derbyshire (1965–70, 112 matches); Orange Free State (1976/7 to 1977/8).
Career batting
114–202–14–4995–136–26.56–4–*ct* 84
Bowling 23–1–23.00–0–0–1/1
He hit 1,000 runs in a season three times (best 1,397, av 28.51, in 1968).

Smith, David James
Cricketer. *b:* 28.4.1962, Brighton, Sussex. Lower order left-hand batsman, wicket-keeper. *Team* Sussex (1981–84, 14 matches).
Career batting
14–14–2–29–13–2.41–0–*ct* 24

Smith, David Lind Addison
Amateur. *b:* 9.1.1873, Edinburgh, Scotland. *d:* 2.11.1937, Leith, Midlothian, Scotland. Opening batsman, slow left-arm bowler. *Team* Scotland (1905).
Career batting
1–2–0–59–45–29.50–0–*ct* 2
Bowling 108–1–108.00–0–0–1/91

Smith, David Mark
Cricketer. *b:* 9.1.1956, Balham, London. Middle order left-hand batsman, right-arm medium pace bowler. *Teams* Surrey (1973–88, 169 matches); Worcestershire (1984–86, 56 matches); Sussex (1989–92, 67 matches). *Tours* England to West Indies 1985/6, 1989/90 (not first-class). *Tests* England (1985/6, 2 matches).
Career batting
297–476–87–14137–213–36.34–27–*ct* 183
Bowling 1574–30–52.46–0–0–3/40
Test batting
2–4–0–80–47–20.00–0–*ct* 0
He hit 1,000 runs in a season seven times (best 1,305, av 45.00, in 1989). He was called to the West Indies in 1989/90 as replacement when Gooch was injured but he himself injured his thumb in the only match he played in. His highest score was 213 for Sussex v Essex at Southend in 1992.

Smith, David Martin
Cricketer. *b:* 21.1.1962, Keresley, Coventry, Warwickshire. Lower order left-hand batsman, slow left-arm bowler. *Team* Warwickshire (1981–83, 4 matches).
Career batting
4–5–2–148–100*–49.33–1–*ct* 2
Bowling 201–2–100.50–0–0–1/44
He also played for Hertfordshire (1989–92).

Smith, David Robert
Professional. *b:* 5.10.1934, Fishponds, Bristol, Gloucestershire. Lower order right-hand batsman, right-arm medium pace bowler. *Team* Gloucestershire (1956–70, 357 matches). *Tours* MCC to New Zealand 1960/1, to India and Pakistan 1961/2; Gloucestershire to Bermuda 1962 (not first-class). *Tests* England (1961/2, 5 matches).
Career batting
386–520–116–4970–74–12.30–0–*ct* 292
Bowling 29654–1250–23.72–51–6–7/20
Test batting
5–5–1–38–34–9.50–0–*ct* 2
Bowling 359–6–59.83–0–0–2/60
He took 100 wickets in a season five times (best 143, av 20.30, in 1960). A good soccer player, he was outside right for Bristol City and Millwall.

Smith, Denis
Professional. *b:* 24.1.1907, Somercotes, Derbyshire. *d:* 12.9.1979, Derby. Sound opening left-hand batsman, right-arm medium pace bowler, occasional wicket-keeper. *Team* Derbyshire (1927–52, 420 matches). *Tour* MCC to Australia and New Zealand 1935/6. *Tests* England (1935, 2 matches).
Career batting
443–753–63–21843–225–31.65–32–*ct* 381–*st* 5
Bowling 734–20–36.70–1–0–5/37
Test batting
2–4–0–128–57–32.00–0–*ct* 1
He hit 1,000 runs in a season twelve times, going on to 2,000 once: 2,175, av 39.54, in 1935. Both his double centuries were for Derbyshire, the highest being 225 v Hampshire at Chesterfield in 1935. From 1952 to 1971 he was coach to Derbyshire CCC.

Smith, Donald James
Professional. *b:* 1.5.1929, Accrington, Lancashire. Brother of C. S. (Lancashire). Lower order right-hand batsman, left-arm fast medium bowler. *Team* Lancashire (1951–52, 3 matches).
Career batting
3–4–0–26–14–6.50–0–*ct* 2
Bowling 205–4–51.25–0–0–1/19

Smith, Donald Joseph
Amateur. *b:* 19.10.1933, Stockport, Cheshire. Tail end left-hand batsman, right-arm fast medium bowler. *Sch* Stockport GS. *Team* Cambridge U (1955–57, blue 1955–56).
Career batting
28–37–21–128–18*–8.00–0–*ct* 6
Bowling 2297–73–31.46–2–0–7/55
His County cricket was for Cheshire (1949–71).

Smith, Donald Victor
Professional. *b:* 14.6.1923, Broadwater, Sussex. Sound opening left-hand batsman, left-arm medium pace bowler. *Team* Sussex (1946–62, 360 matches). *Tour* Norfolk to Jamaica 1956/7. *Tests* England (1957, 3 matches).
Career batting
377–625–66–16960–206*–30.33–19–*ct* 234
Bowling 9670–340–28.44–6–1–7/40
Test batting
3–4–1–25–16*–8.33–0–*ct* 0
Bowling 97–1–97.00–0–0–1/12
He hit 1,000 runs in a season eight times, going on to 2,000 once: 2,088, av 42.61, in 1957. His only double century was 206* for Sussex v Nottinghamshire at Trent Bridge in 1950.

Smith, Douglas James
Professional. *b:* 29.5.1873, Batley, Yorkshire. *d:* 16.8.1949, Grahamstown, Cape Province, South Africa. Brother of William (Somerset), son of John (Yorkshire and Lancashire). Middle order right-hand batsman, right-arm slow bowler. *Teams* Somerset (1896–98, 21 matches); Worcestershire (1901–04, 9 matches).
Career batting
30–52–4–558–62–11.62–0–*ct* 24–*st* 1
Bowling 24–0
He also played for Glamorgan (pre first-class, 1905–07). He was cricket coach at St Andrew's College, Grahamstown, where from his small salary he endowed a scholarship to Cambridge U.

Smith, Douglas Maxwell
Professional. *b:* 14.9.1915, Cuckfield, Sussex. Lower order right-hand batsman, right-arm fast bowler. *Team* Sussex (1938–46, 6 matches).
Career batting
6–10–2–55–34–6.87–0–*ct* 5
Bowling 401–19–21.10–1–0–5/25

Smith, Rev Edward Paske
Amateur. *b:* 9.9.1854, Mussoorie, India. *d:* 2.1.1909, Seaford, Sussex. Lower order right-hand batsman, right-arm medium pace bowler. *Sch* Sherborne. *Team* Oxford U (1876).
Career batting
1–2–0–6–6–3.00–0–*ct* 0
Bowling 42–3–14.00–0–0–2/24
He was a missionary in Calgary and Saskatchewan.

Smith, Edwin
Professional. *b:* 11.6.1860, Peatling Magna, Leicestershire. *d:* 30.5.1939, Ashby Magna, Leicestershire. Lower order right-hand batsman, right-arm fast medium bowler. *Team* Liverpool and District (1886–94).
Career batting
9–17–3–118–32–8.42–0–*ct* 5
Bowling 487–25–19.48–1–1–7/59
He played for Leicestershire (pre first-class, 1884–86) and Cheshire (1888–95).

Smith, Edwin
Professional. *b:* 2.1.1934, Grassmoor, Chesterfield, Derbyshire. Lower order right-hand batsman, off break bowler. *Team* Derbyshire (1951–71, 497 matches).
Career batting
503–674–144–6998–90–13.20–0–*ct* 207
Bowling 31448–1217–25.84–51–4–9/46
His best season was 1955 when he took 105 wickets, av 17.65, and his best bowling was 9/46 for Derbyshire v Scotland in the same year. He was Derbyshire coach 1972–75.

Smith, Edwin George
Amateur. *b:* 29.8.1848, Cheltenham, Gloucestershire. *d:* 5.4.1880, Cheltenham, Gloucestershire. Middle order right-hand batsman, right-arm medium pace bowler. *Team* Gloucestershire (1875–76, 2 matches).
Career batting
2–3–0–26–14–8.66–0–*ct* 0

Smith, Ernest
Amateur. *b:* 19.10.1869, Morley, Leeds, Yorkshire. *d:* 9.4.1945, Eastbourne, Sussex. Attacking middle order right-hand batsman, right-arm fast bowler. *Sch* Clifton. *Teams* Yorkshire (1888–1907, 154 matches); Oxford U (1889–91, blue 1890 and 1891).
Career batting
242–391–33–7686–164*–21.46–6–*ct* 174
Bowling 11666–454–25.69–22–3–7/40
A schoolmaster, his County cricket was confined mainly to August and he usually captained Yorkshire when Lord Hawke was absent. His final first-class match was for H. D. G. Leveson-Gower's XI in 1928. He was a useful golfer and rugby footballer.

Smith, Ernest
Professional. *b:* 11.7.1888, Barnsley, Yorkshire. *d:* 2.1.1972, Blackburn, Lancashire. Lower order right-hand batsman, left-arm medium slow bowler. *Team* Yorkshire (1914–26, 16 matches).
Career batting
16–21–5–169–49–10.56–0–*ct* 5
Bowling 1090–46–23.69–2–0–6/40
He is generally referred to as E. Smith of Ossett, being associated with that Yorkshire team for many years.

Smith, Ernest James
Professional. *b:* 6.2.1886, Highgate, Birmingham, Warwickshire. *d:* 31.8.1979, Northfield, Birmingham, Warwickshire. Sound opening right-hand batsman, wicket-keeper. *Team* Warwickshire (1904–30, 444 matches). *Tours* MCC to Australia 1911/12, to South Africa 1913/14, to West Indies 1925/6. *Tests* England (1911/12 to 1913/14, 11 matches).
Career batting
496–814–55–16997–177–22.39–20–*ct* 722–*st* 156
Bowling 102–2–51.00–0–0–1/0
Test batting
11–14–1–113–22–8.69–0–*ct* 17–*st* 3
He hit 1,000 runs in a season six times (best 1,477, av 31.42, in 1925). He was a first-class umpire (1931–39) and stood in 8 Test matches (1933–39). From 1946 to 1955 he was appointed coach to Warwickshire, and remained at Edgbaston until 1970.

Smith, Frank Brunton
Amateur. *b:* 13.3.1922, Rangiora, Canterbury, New Zealand. Father of G. B. (Canterbury), son of F. A. (Canterbury). Middle order right-hand batsman, off break bowler, good field. *Team* Canterbury (1946/7 to 1952/3). *Tour* New Zealand to England 1949. *Tests* New Zealand (1946/7 to 1951/2, 4 matches).
Career batting
49–85–5–2643–153–33.03–4–*ct* 21
Bowling 76–1–76.00–0–0–1/6
Test batting
4–6–1–237–96–47.40–0–*ct* 1
He hit 1,008 runs, av 28.00, on the 1949 tour, playing in two Tests. His great success was in the first Test when he scored 96 and 54*. His first-class debut was for South Island Army XI in New Zealand in 1942/3.

Smith, Frank Ernest
Professional. *b:* 13.5.1872, Bury St Edmunds, Suffolk. *d:* 3.12.1943, Sedbergh, Yorkshire. Lower order left-hand batsman, slow left-arm bowler. *Teams* Surrey (1893–1908, 56 matches); London County (1901–02); Transvaal (1906/7).
Career batting
68–87–28–578–45–9.79–0–*ct* 31
Bowling 3951–194–20.36–9–3–6/12
He took 95 wickets, av 13.94, in 1894. He also played for Suffolk (1909). He umpired 5 Test matches in South Africa (1902/3 to 1909/10).

Smith, Fred
Professional. *b:* 18.12.1879, Yeadon, Yorkshire. *d:* 20.10.1905, Nelson, Lancashire. He died of pneumonia caught whilst playing rugby football. Middle order left-hand batsman. *Team* Yorkshire (1903, 13 matches).
Career batting
13–19–1–292–55–16.22–0–*ct* 3

Smith, Fred
Professional. *b:* 26.12.1885, Idle, Yorkshire. Middle order batsman. *Team* Yorkshire (1911, 1 match).
Career batting
1–1–0–11–11–11.00–0–*ct* 0
Bowling 45–2–22.50–0–0–1/12

Smith, Frederick Aitken Leeston
(also known as Leeston-Smith)
Amateur. *b:* 10.5.1854, Kensington, London. *d:* 27.1.1894, Parkstone, Dorset. Middle order right-hand batsman, right-arm fast bowler. *Sch* Malvern and Christ College, Brecon. *Team* Somerset (1884–85, 3 matches).
Career batting
3–6–0–130–37–21.66–0–*ct* 0
He first played for Somerset (pre first-class) in 1879.

Smith, Gareth
Cricketer. *b:* 20.7.1966, Jarrow, Co Durham. Lower order right-hand batsman, left-arm fast medium bowler. *Teams* Northamptonshire (1986–89, 9 matches); Warwickshire (1990, 1 match).
Career batting
10–11–2–90–30–10.00–0–*ct* 3
Bowling 633–21–30.14–1–0–6/72

Smith, Geoffrey
Amateur. *b:* 30.11.1925, Huddersfield, Yorkshire. Lower order right-hand batsman, strong right-arm medium fast bowler. *Sch* Christ's Hospital. *Team* Kent (1951–58, 42 matches).
Career batting
42–71–12–728–60–12.33–0–*ct* 29
Bowling 3766–165–22.82–10–0–8/110

Smith, Geoffrey John
Professional. *b:* 2.4.1935, Braintree, Essex. Opening right-hand batsman, off break bowler. *Team* Essex (1955–66, 239 matches).
Career batting
243–419–30–8796–148–22.61–5–*ct* 133
Bowling 951–33–28.81–1–0–5/39
He hit 1,000 runs in a season four times (best 1,908, av 32.89, in 1961). He also played for Hertfordshire (1967–69).

Smith, George
Professional. *b:* 17.12.1844, Cambridge. *d:* 22.9.1876, Cambridge. He died of a complication of disorders. Brother of John (Cambridgeshire). Lower order right-hand batsman, right-hand fast round-arm bowler. *Team* Cambridgeshire (1868–71, 4 matches).
Career batting
4–8–1–23–7–3.28–0–*ct* 2
Bowling 384–23–16.69–1–0–6/32

Smith, George
Professional. *b:* 19.1.1875, Thorp Arch, Boston Spa, Yorkshire. *d:* 16.1.1929, Thorp Arch, Boston Spa,

Yorkshire. Tail end batsman. *Team* Yorkshire (1901–06, 2 matches).
Career batting
2–1–0–7–7–7.00–0–*ct* 3
Bowling 62–0

Smith, George William Oswald
Amateur. *b:* 7.3.1906, Halstead, Essex. *d:* 25.11.1989, Worthing, Sussex. Lower order right-hand batsman, wicket-keeper. *Sch* Bishop's Stortford. *Team* Essex (1929–30, 10 matches).
Career batting
10–18–3–206–39*–13.73–0–*ct* 2
He played in the Seniors' match whilst at Cambridge. He also played for Suffolk (1937–38).

Smith, Gilbert Oswald
Amateur. *b:* 25.11.1872, Croydon, Surrey. *d:* 6.12.1943, Yaldhurst, Lymington, Hampshire. Middle order right-hand batsman, right-arm fast medium pace bowler. *Sch* Charterhouse. *Teams* Oxford U (1893–96, blue 1895–96); Surrey (1896, 3 matches).
Career batting
17–29–3–778–132–29.92–2–*ct* 11
He also played for Hertfordshire (1898), but played little important cricket after leaving Oxford. Regarded as the greatest centre forward of his day, he represented Oxford v Cambridge four times and England in 20 internationals. He appeared in the FA Amateur Cup Final with Old Carthusians in 1895 and 1897 and later played for Corinthians.

Smith, Graham Stuart
Amateur. *b:* 4.7.1923, Leicester. Middle order right-hand batsman. *Sch* Bedford and Stoneygate. *Team* Leicestershire (1949, 1 match).
Career batting
1–2–0–29–22–14.50–0–*ct* 0

Smith, Hamilton Augustus Haigh
(also known as Haigh-Smith)
Amateur. *b:* 21.10.1884, Sandown, Isle of Wight. *d:* 28.10.1955, Paddington, London. Middle order right-hand batsman, leg break and googly bowler. *Sch* Marlborough. *Team* Hampshire (1909–14, 27 matches).
Career batting
27–41–10–327–43*–10.54–0–*ct* 9
Bowling 574–14–41.00–0–0–3/95
A noted rugby footballer, he played for Barbarians and also represented Hampshire; he appeared for the County's hockey team as well.

Smith, Harold Edward
Amateur. *b:* 21.4.1884, Cradock, Cape Colony, South Africa. *d: circa* 1925, Johannesburg, South Africa. Half-brother of C. J. E. (South Africa). Middle order right-hand batsman. *Team* Transvaal (1905/6 to 1906/7). *Tour* South Africa to England 1907.
Career batting
15–23–2–395–53–18.80–0–*ct* 2
His final first-class match was for Wanderers CC in 1908/9.

Smith, Harry
Professional. *b:* 21.5.1891, Fishponds, Bristol. *d:* 12.11.1937, Downend, Bristol. Sound middle order right-hand batsman. *Team* Gloucestershire (1912–35, 393 matches). *Test* England (1928, 1 match).
Career batting
402–656–56–13413–149–22.35–10–*ct* 457–*st* 265
Bowling 7–0
Test batting
1–1–0–7–7–7.00–0–*ct* 1
He hit 1,000 runs in a season five times (best 1,573, av 28.08, in 1926). He also played soccer for Bolton Wanderers.

Smith, Harry Thomas Oliver
Amateur. *b:* 5.3.1906, Warley, Essex. Lower order right-hand batsman, right-arm fast medium bowler. *Team* Essex (1929–35, 23 matches).
Career batting
25–40–5–400–38–11.42–0–*ct* 20
Bowling 1740–63–27.61–3–0–6/56
His final first-class match was for H. D. G. Leveson-Gower's XI in 1936.

Smith, Harry Watson
(also known as Watson-Smith)
Amateur. *b:* 30.9.1886, Chesterfield, Derbyshire. *d:* 24.6.1955, Ruthin, Denbighshire. Lower order right-hand batsman, wicket-keeper. *Sch* Worksop. *Teams* Warwickshire (1912, 1 match); Derbyshire (1920, 1 match).
Career batting
2–3–1–49–24*–24.50–0–*ct* 0

Smith, Harry William
Professional. *b:* 6.9.1890, Mile End, London. Lower order right-hand batsman, right-arm fast medium bowler. *Team* Essex (1912–22, 20 matches).
Career batting
20–31–12–195–22–10.26–0–*ct* 12
Bowling 1055–35–30.14–1–0–5/59

Smith, Haydon Arthur
Professional. *b:* 29.3.1901, Groby, Leicestershire. *d:* 7.8.1948, Groby, Leicestershire. He died from heart failure. Uncle of C. T. Spencer (Leicestershire). Lower order right-hand batsman, right-arm fast bowler. *Team* Leicestershire (1925–39, 341 matches).
Career batting
341–500–82–4603–100*–11.01–1–*ct* 257
Bowling 27968–1076–25.99–66–11–8/40
He took 100 wickets in a season five times (best 150, av 19.66, in 1935).

Smith, Hugh Purefoy
Amateur. *b:* 16.10.1856, Lasham, Hampshire. *d:* 9.9.1939, Brighton, Sussex. Lower order right-hand batsman, right-arm medium pace bowler. *Sch* Bradfield. *Team* Sussex (1878, 1 match).
Career batting
1–2–0–10–10–5.00–0–*ct* 1
Bowling 82–1–82.00–0–0–1/82

Smith, Ian
Cricketer. *b:* 11.3.1967, Chopwell, Co Durham. Middle order right-hand batsman, right-arm medium pace bowler. *Teams* Glamorgan (1985–91, 63 matches); Durham (1992, 12 matches). *Tours* Glamorgan to Zimbabwe 1990/1.
Career batting
75–99–14–2158–116–25.38–4–*ct* 29
Bowling 2692–60–44.86–0–0–3/48

Smith, Ian David Stockley
Cricketer. *b:* 28.2.1957, Nelson, New Zealand. Lower order right-hand batsman, wicket-keeper *Teams* Central Districts (1977/8 to 1986/7); Auckland (1987/8 to 1991/2). *Tours* New Zealand to Australia 1981/2, 1984/5 (not first-class), 1985/6, 1987/8, 1989/90, to England 1983, 1986, 1990, to Sri Lanka 1983/4, 1984/5 (not first-class), 1986/7, to Pakistan 1984/5, to West Indies 1984/5, to India 1987/8 (World Cup), 1988/9, to Sharjah (not first-class) 1987/8, 1989/90. *Tests* New Zealand (1980/1 to 1990/1, 63 matches).
Career batting
178–250–42–5570–173–26.77–6–*ct* 417–*st* 36
Bowling 38–0
Test batting
63–88–17–1815–173–25.56–2–*ct* 168–*st* 8
Bowling 5–0

He was most unfortunate on his three tours to England. In 1983 he gained his Test place at the expense of Lees, then broke a finger and missed the final Test. In 1986, having played in two Tests, he went home early due to an injury and in 1990 he missed one Test through injury.

Smith, Irving Wilmot
Amateur. *b:* 5.2.1884, Harborne, Birmingham, Warwickshire. *d:* 21.10.1971, Sutton Coldfield, Warwickshire. Middle order right-hand batsman, right-arm medium pace and leg break bowler. *Sch* KES, Birmingham. *Team* Warwickshire (1905, 1 match).
Career batting
1–1–0–1–1–1.00–0–*ct* 0
Bowling 13–0

Smith, Jack
Cricketer. *b:* 7.3.1936, Stotfold, Bedfordshire. Middle order right-hand batsman, off break bowler. *Sch* Bedford School. *Team* Minor Counties (1965).
Career batting
1–2–0–17–17–8.50–0–*ct* 0
Bowling 99–4–24.75–0–0–2/47

His County cricket was for Bedfordshire (1959–75).

Smith, James Crosbie
Professional. *b:* 26.9.1894, Ledbury, Herefordshire. *d:* 19.2.1980, Ledbury, Herefordshire. Middle order left-hand batsman. *Team* Worcestershire (1923–25, 16 matches).
Career batting
16–27–1–313–70–12.03–0–*ct* 15
Bowling 10–0

Smith, John
Professional. *b:* 23.3.1833, Yeadon, Yorkshire. *d:* 12.2.1909, Worcester. Father of D. J. (Somerset and Worcestershire) and William (Somerset). Lower order left-hand batsman, left-hand fast round-arm bowler. *Teams* Yorkshire (1865, 2 matches); Lancashire (1865–69, 6 matches).
Career batting
8–15–1–181–40*–12.92–0–*ct* 7
Bowling 362–18–20.11–0–0–4/46

From 1883 to 1897 he was a professional for Worcestershire, initially as player and later as groundsman.

Smith, John
Professional. *b:* 8.11.1835, Ruddington, Nottinghamshire. *d:* 29.5.1889, Bury, Lancashire. Middle order right-hand batsman, right-arm medium bowler. *Team* Nottinghamshire (1864, 2 matches).
Career batting
2–4–0–30–27–7.50–0–*ct* 1
Bowling 21–1–21.00–0–0–1/21

He umpired in first-class matches in the 1870s and 1880s.

Smith, John
Amateur. *b:* 27.10.1841, Clifton, Derbyshire. *d:* 26.11.1898, Derby. Opening right-hand batsman, right-hand slow medium round-arm bowler. *Team* Derbyshire (1871–78, 22 matches).
Career batting
22–38–2–403–35–11.19–0–*ct* 14
Bowling 162–6–27.00–0–0–3/38

Smith, John
Professional. *b:* 20.11.1843, Cambridge. *d:* 15.4.1873, Stratford-by-Bow, Essex. Brother of George (Cambridgeshire). Attractive middle order right-hand batsman, brilliant cover point. *Team* Cambridgeshire (1863–71, 25 matches).
Career batting
75–135–2–2274–97–17.09–0–*ct* 36
Bowling 9–0

His final first-class match was for MCC in 1872.

Smith, John Westwood Rowley
Amateur. *b:* 28.7.1924, Clarendon Park, Leicester. *d:* 12.12.1991, Bruntingthorpe, Leicestershire. Lower order right-hand batsman, wicket-keeper. *Sch* Stoney-

gate and Repton. *Team* Leicestershire (1950–55, 3 matches).
Career batting
3–3–0–5–4–1.66–0–*ct* 1–*st* 1

Smith, John Willoughby Dixie
(also known as Dixie-Smith)
Amateur. *b:* 11.3.1882, Blaby, Leicestershire. *d:* 2.10.1959, Harrow-on-the-Hill, Middlesex. Middle order right-hand batsman. *Team* Leicestershire (1921, 2 matches).
Career batting
2–4–0–30–25–7.50–0–*ct* 0
Bowling 17–0

Smith, Kenneth David
Cricketer. *b:* 9.7.1956, Newcastle upon Tyne, Northumberland. Son of K. D. (Leicestershire), brother of P. A. (Warwickshire), son-in-law of A. S. M. Oakman (Sussex). Opening or middle order right-hand batsman. *Team* Warwickshire (1973–85, 197 matches).
Career batting
197–346–29–8734–140–27.55–9–*ct* 70
Bowling 3–0
He hit 1,000 runs in a season four times (best 1,582, av 36.79, in 1980).

Smith, Kenneth Desmond
Professional. *b:* 30.4.1922, Bishop Auckland, Co Durham. Father of K. D. (Warwickshire) and P. A. (Warwickshire). Middle order right-hand batsman. *Team* Leicestershire (1950–51, 26 matches).
Career batting
26–43–7–621–70*–17.25–0–*ct* 12
Bowling 103–3–34.33–0–0–2/37
He also played for Northumberland (1949 and 1953–61).

Smith, Kevin Brian
Cricketer. *b:* 28.8.1957, Brighton, Sussex. Nephew of G. L. Cogger (Sussex). Middle order left-hand batsman, slow left-arm bowler. *Team* Sussex (1978, 4 matches).
Career batting
4–8–1–90–43–12.85–0–*ct* 1

Smith, Lawrence Kilner
Cricketer. *b:* 6.1.1964, Mirfield, Yorkshire. Son of D. H. K. (Derbyshire). Middle order right-hand batsman. *Team* Worcestershire (1985–87, 4 matches).
Career batting
4–7–1–62–28–10.33–0–*ct* 2
Bowling 20–1–20.00–0–0–1/20
He also played for Wiltshire (1991–92).

Smith, Lemuel Strutt Tugby
Professional. *b:* 5.6.1880, Tibshelf, Derbyshire. *d:* 30.12.1927, South Kirkby, Yorkshire. Lower order right-hand batsman, wicket-keeper. *Team* Derbyshire (1909, 2 matches).
Career batting
2–3–0–9–5–3.00–0–*ct* 1

Smith, Lewis Alfred
Amateur. *b:* 12.7.1913, Brentford, Middlesex. *d:* 10.9.1978, Ealing, Middlesex. Lower order right-hand batsman, right-arm fast medium bowler. *Teams* Middlesex (1934–37, 3 matches); Northamptonshire (1947, 2 matches).
Career batting
5–8–2–92–55–15.33–0–*ct* 2
Bowling 397–11–11–36.09–0–0–4/55

Smith, Dr Martin Graham Milner
Amateur. *b:* 28.9.1941, Otford, Kent. Brother of C. M. (Oxford U). Lower order right-hand batsman, wicket-keeper. *Sch* Tonbridge. *Team* Cambridge U (1961).
Career batting
1–2–1–24–18*–24.00–0–*ct* 1–*st* 1
He was the British Open Rackets Champion in 1973.

Smith, Michael John
Professional. *b:* 4.1.1942, Enfield, Middlesex. Sound opening right-hand batsman, slow left-arm bowler. *Team* Middlesex (1959–80, 399 matches). *Tours* Robins to South Africa 1972/3, 1973/4, to West Indies 1974/5 (not first-class), to Sri Lanka 1977/8.
Career batting
422–704–78–19814–181–31.65–40–*ct* 218
Bowling 1866–57–32.73–0–0–4/13
He hit 1,000 runs in a season eleven times (best 1,705, av 39.65, in 1970). He played for England in one-day international matches.

Smith, Michael John Knight, OBE
Amateur. *b:* 30.6.1933, Westcotes, Leicester. Father of N. M K. (Warwickshire). Stylish middle order right-hand batsman, right-arm slow medium bowler, brilliant short leg field. *Sch* Stamford. *Teams* Leicestershire (1951–55, 28 matches); Oxford U (1954–56, blue all three years); Warwickshire (1956–75, 430 matches). *Tours* MCC to East Africa 1957/8 (not first-class), to South America 1958/9 (not first-class), to West Indies 1959/60, to India and Pakistan 1961/2, to East Africa 1963/4, to India 1963/4, to South Africa 1964/5, to Australia and New Zealand 1965/6; Cavaliers to South Africa 1960/1. *Tests* England (1958–72, 50 matches).
Career batting
637–1091–139–39832–204–41.84–69–*ct* 593
Bowling 305–5–61.00–0–0–1/0
Test batting
50–78–6–2278–121–31.63–3–*ct* 53
Bowling 128–1–128.00–0–0–1/10
One of the most prolific scorers in post-war English cricket, he was most successful whilst at Oxford, hitting three centuries, including one double century against Cambridge, and went on to a long and bril-

liant career with Warwickshire. He reached 1,000 runs in a season 19 times, going to 2,000 six times and to 3,000 once: 3,245, av 57.94, in 1959. Apart from his double century for Oxford he hit 200* for Warwickshire v Worcestershire at Edgbaston in 1959 and 204 for Cavaliers v Natal at Durban in 1960/1.

He captained Oxford in 1956, Warwickshire from 1957 to 1967 and led England in 25 Tests, also captaining the MCC on three Test tours – to India, to South Africa and to Australia and New Zealand. He was Chairman of Warwickshire CCC Cricket Committee from 1988.

He was also an excellent rugby footballer, gaining a blue as fly-half and being capped for England.

Smith, Michael Jonathon
Cricketer. *b:* 30.3.1966, Edinburgh, Scotland. Middle order right-hand batsman, right-arm medium pace bowler. *Team* Scotland (1987–89).
Career batting
3–5–1–145–79–36.25–0–*ct* 3
Bowling 51–2–25.50–0–0–2/30

Smith, Neil
Cricketer. *b:* 1.4.1949, Ossett, Yorkshire. Lower order right-hand batsman, wicket-keeper. *Teams* Yorkshire (1970–71, 8 matches); Essex (1973–81, 178 matches).
Career batting
187–239–53–3336–126–17.93–2–*ct* 395–*st* 51
He also played for Cheshire (1987–89).

Smith, Neil Michael Knight
Cricketer. *b:* 27.7.1967, Solihull, Warwickshire. Son of M. J. K. (Leicestershire and Warwickshire), great grandson of R. C. Leach (Lancashire). Middle order right-hand batsman, off break bowler. *Sch* Warwick. *Team* Warwickshire (1987–92, 40 matches). *Tour* Warwickshire to South Africa 1991/2.
Career batting
40–61–10–1399–161–27.43–1–*ct* 14
Bowling 2763–57–48.47–1–0–5/61

Smith, Oliver Charles Kennedy
Cricketer. *b:* 29.10.1967, Meriden, Warwickshire. Middle order left-hand batsman, off break bowler. *Sch* Cotham. *Team* Gloucestershire (1987, 1 match).
Career batting
1–2–0–15–14–7.50–0–*ct* 0

Smith, O'Neil Gordon
Amateur. *b:* 5.5.1933, Denham Town, Kingston, Jamaica. *d:* 9.9.1959, Stoke-on-Trent, Staffordshire. He died following a motor-car accident. Half-brother of L. N. G. Wright (Jamaica). Middle order right-hand batsman, off break bowler, brilliant field. *Team* Jamaica (1954/5 to 1957/8). *Tours* West Indies to New Zealand 1955/6, to England 1957, to India and Pakistan 1958/9. *Tests* West Indies (1954/5 to 1958/9, 26 matches).
Career batting
70–112–12–4031–169–40.31–10–*ct* 39
Bowling 3754–121–31.02–2–0–5/63
Test batting
26–42–0–1331–168–31.69–4–*ct* 9
Bowling 1625–48–33.85–1–0–5/90
He headed the West Indies Test batting averages on the 1957 tour to England with 396 runs, av 39.60, and in all first-class matches hit 1,483 runs, av 41.19. Regarded as the most promising of young West Indian cricketers he tragically died after being injured in a car crash. About 60,000 people attended his funeral in Jamaica. His final first-class match in England was for a Commonwealth XI in 1958 – in 1958 and 1959 he was professional for Burnley.

Smith, Paul Andrew
Cricketer. *b:* 15.4.1964, Gosforth, Newcastle upon Tyne, Northumberland. Son of K. D. (Leicestershire), brother of K. D. (Warwickshire). Middle order right-hand batsman, right-arm fast medium bowler. *Team* Warwickshire (1982–92, 193 matches). *Tour* Warwickshire to South Africa 1991/2.
Career batting
193–311–38–7377–140–27.02–4–*ct* 53
Bowling 8768–243–36.08–7–0–6/91
He hit 1,000 runs in a season twice (best 1,508, av 37.70, in 1986).

Smith, Peter Bruce
Cricketer. *b:* 18.3.1944, Headington, Oxford. Lower order right-hand batsman, right-arm medium pace bowler. *Sch* Magdalen Coll School, Oxford. *Team* Oxford U (1967).
Career batting
5–6–1–36–18–7.20–0–*ct* 0
Bowling 291–7–41.57–0–0–4/92
His County cricket was for Oxfordshire (1963–77).

Smith, Peter Thomas
Professional. *b:* 5.10.1934, Leicester. Middle order right-hand batsman. *Team* Leicestershire (1956–57, 15 matches).
Career batting
15–24–2–152–40–6.90–0–*ct* 4

Smith, Raymond
Professional. *b:* 10.8.1914, Boreham, Essex. Cousin of T. P. B. Smith (Essex). Aggressive middle order right-hand batsman, right-arm medium pace or off break bowler. *Team* Essex (1934–56, 419 matches). *Tour* Commonwealth to India, Ceylon and Pakistan 1949/50.
Career batting
445–682–88–12041–147–20.27–8–*ct* 191
Bowling 41265–1350–30.56–73–10–8/63
He hit 1,000 runs in a season four times (best 1,386, av 28.87, in 1947) and took 100 wickets in a season seven times (best 136, av 28.87, in 1952). He completed the 'double' in 1947, 1950 and 1952.

Smith, Raymond Charles
Professional. *b:* 3.8.1935, Duddington, Northamptonshire. Lower order right-hand batsman, slow left-arm bowler. *Sch* Stamford. *Team* Leicestershire (1956–64, 104 matches).
Career batting
104–156–37–1115–36–9.36–0–*ct* 28
Bowling 5514–203–27.16–11–1–7/54

Smith, Dr Reginald
(also known as Starkey-Smith)
Amateur. *b:* 1.5.1868, Warrington, Lancashire. *d:* 5.10.1943, Scarborough, Yorkshire. Middle order batsman, useful bowler. *Team* Lancashire (1893, 1 match).
Career batting
1–1–0–6–6–6.00–0–*ct* 0
Bowling 11–0
He also played for Norfolk (1897).

Smith, Robert Posnett
(changed name to Stevens in September 1885)
Amateur. *b:* 1.11.1848, Sawley, Derbyshire. *d:* 1.5.1899, Staunton Grange, Nottinghamshire. Sound middle order right-hand batsman, right-hand fast round-arm, or slow under-arm bowler. *Team* Derbyshire (1871–84, 90 matches).
Career batting
103–190–3–2719–87–14.54–0–*ct* 74
Bowling 23–0
He captained Derbyshire from 1876 to 1883. He also played for Nottinghamshire (not first-class) in 1874.

Smith, Robin Arnold
Cricketer. *b:* 13.9.1963, Durban, South Africa. Brother of C. L. (Glamorgan and Hampshire), grandson of V. L. Shearer (Natal). Middle order right-hand batsman, off break bowler. *Teams* Natal (1980/1 to 1984/5); Hampshire (1982–92, 149 matches). *Tours* England to India 1988/9 (tour cancelled), 1989/90 (not first-class), to West Indies 1989/90, to Australia 1990/1, to New Zealand 1990/1 (not first-class), 1991/2, to Australia and New Zealand (World Cup) 1991/2. *Tests* England (1988–92, 36 matches).
Career batting
230–390–68–14227–209*–44.18–33–*ct* 153
Bowling 691–12–57.58–0–0–2/11
Test batting
36–66–14–2645–148*–50.86–7–*ct* 26
Bowling 6–0
One of the hardest hitting batsmen in English cricket, his first full season with Hampshire was 1985, but not until 1988 did he establish himself in the English Test team. He topped the Test averages in the 1989 series against Australia, 553 runs, av 61.44, again in 1990 v India, 361 runs, av 180.50 and a third time in 1991 v West Indies, 416, av 83.20. He hit 1,000 runs in a season six times (best 1,577, av 58.40, in 1989). His highest score was 209* for Hampshire v Essex at Southend in 1987.

Smith, Rodney
Cricketer. *b:* 6.4.1944, Batley, Yorkshire. Middle order right-hand batsman, slow left-arm bowler. *Team* Yorkshire (1969–70, 5 matches).
Career batting
5–8–3–99–37*–19.80–0–*ct* 0

Smith, Ronald
Amateur. *b:* 16.2.1926, Dudley, Worcestershire. Lower order right-hand batsman, right-arm fast medium bowler. *Team* Northamptonshire (1954, 1 match).
Career batting
1–2–1–19–19*–19.00–0–*ct* 0
Bowling 38–1–38.00–0–0–1/38

Smith, Roy
Amateur. *b:* 20.1.1910, Stoke-on-Trent, Staffordshire. *d:* 19.10.1971, Great Chell, Staffordshire. Middle order right-hand batsman. *Team* Minor Counties (1949).
Career batting
1–2–0–29–29–14.50–0–*ct* 1
His County cricket was for Staffordshire (1931–54).

Smith, Roy
Professional. *b:* 14.4.1930, Taunton, Somerset. Middle order right-hand batsman, slow left-arm bowler. *Team* Somerset (1949–55, 96 matches).
Career batting
96–173–21–2600–100–17.10–1–*ct* 31
Bowling 1083–19–57.00–0–0–4/91
He hit 1,176 runs, av 26.13, in 1953. He also played for Devon (1957–61).

Smith, S. C.
Amateur. Middle order left-hand batsman. *Team* Ireland (1907–08).
Career batting
3–6–0–19–11–3.16–0–*ct* 2

Smith, Sidney
Professional. *b:* 14.1.1929, Heywood, Lancashire. *d:* 25.4.1985, Middleton, Lancashire. Middle order right-hand batsman. *Team* Lancashire (1952–56, 38 matches).
Career batting
44–66–5–1117–101*–18.31–1–*ct* 10
His first-class debut was for Combined Services in 1950.

Smith, Sydney Francis
Amateur. *b:* 30.9.1892, Northampton. Middle order batsman. *Team* Northamptonshire (1914, 2 matches).
Career batting
2–4–0–16–6–4.00–0–*ct* 0

Smith, Sydney Gordon
Amateur. *b:* 15.1.1881, San Fernando, Trinidad. *d:* 25.10.1963, Auckland, New Zealand. Nephew of A. E. (Barbados) and F. B. (Barbados). Fast scoring middle order left-hand batsman, slow left-arm bowler. *Teams* Trinidad (1899/1900 to 1905/6); Northamptonshire (1907–14, 119 matches); Auckland (1917/18 to 1925/6). *Tours* West Indies to England 1906; MCC to West Indies 1910/11, 1912/13.
Career batting
211–379–30–10920–256–31.28–14–*ct* 158
Bowling 17271–955–18.08–71–19–9/34

He hit 1,000 runs in a season four times (best 1,522, av 37.12, in 1913) and took 100 wickets in a season four times, performing the 'double' three times. His best season was 1909 with 115 wickets, av 19.51. He proved the best all-rounder on the 1906 West Indies tour to England and after the visit remained in England to qualify for Northamptonshire. He captained that County in 1913 and 1914. In 1915 he emigrated to New Zealand and played with much success there, appearing in the representative New Zealand team against English and Australian touring sides. His highest score was 256 for Auckland v Canterbury at Auckland in 1919/20, and his best bowling 9/34 for a West Indies XI v Bennett's XI at Port of Spain in 1901/2.

Smith, Thomas
Professional. *b:* 26.8.1848, Glossop, Derbyshire. Opening right-hand batsman, right-hand medium pace round-arm bowler, slip field. *Team* Lancashire (1867, 2 matches).
Career batting
2–3–0–18–12–6.00–0–*ct* 2
Bowling 36–1–36.00–0–0–1/8

Smith, Thomas
Amateur. *b:* 6.4.1854, Guildford, Surrey. Middle order right-hand batsman, left-arm bowler. *Team* Surrey (1876, 1 match).
Career batting
1–2–0–16–13–8.00–0–*ct* 1
Bowling 20–0

Smith, Thomas Assheton
Amateur. *b:* 2.8.1776, Westminster, London. *d:* 9.9.1858, Vaenol, Caernarvonshire. Hard hitting middle order right-hand batsman. *Sch* Eton. *Teams* Surrey (1802); Hampshire (1803–20).
Career batting
36–68–8–965–86–16.08–0–*ct* 23–*st* 1
Bowling 5 wickets (no analyses)–0–0–2/?

He was sent to Eton at the age of seven (being the youngest boy in the school) and remained eleven years. He was known as the 'British Nimrod', being a crack shot and notable hunter. He was MP for Andover 1821–31 and Caernarfonshire 1832–41.

Smith, Thomas George Harrison
Professional. *b:* 6.3.1905, Northampton. Middle order right-hand batsman. *Team* Northamptonshire (1931, 1 match).
Career batting
1–1–0–11–11–11.00–0–*ct* 0
Bowling 28–0

Smith, Thomas Michael
Amateur. *b:* 16.5.1899, Lambeth, London, *d:* 17.11.1965, Taunton, Somerset. Middle order batsman. *Team* Hampshire (1923–24, 9 matches).
Career batting
9–11–1–89–18–8.90–0–*ct* 3

Smith, Thomas Peter Bromley
Professional. *b:* 30.10.1908, Ipswich, Suffolk. *d:* 4.8.1967, Hyères, France. He died following a fall whilst on holiday. Cousin of Raymond (Essex). Lower order right-hand batsman, leg break and googly bowler. *Team* Essex (1929–51, 434 matches). *Tours* Tennyson to India 1937/8; Cahn to New Zealand 1938/9; MCC to India 1939/40 (tour cancelled), to Australia and New Zealand 1946/7. *Tests* England (1946 to 1946/7, 4 matches).
Career batting
465–690–123–10142–163–17.88–8–*ct* 346
Bowling 45059–1697–26.55–120–28–9/77
Test batting
4–5–0–33–24–6.60–0–*ct* 1
Bowling 319–3–106.33–0–0–2/172

He hit 1,000 runs in a season once – 1,065, av 23.66, completing the 'double' in the same year. He took 100 wickets in a season six times (best 172, av 27.13, in 1947). In the same year he hit 163 for Essex v Derbyshire at Chesterfield, adding 218 for the last wicket with F. H. Vigar – Smith came in as last man. His best bowling was 9/77 for Essex v Middlesex at Colchester in 1947. His last first-class match was for T. N. Pearce's XI in 1952.

Smith, Timothy Stewart
Cricketer. *b:* 29.12.1953, Henham, Essex. Middle order right-hand batsman, slow left-arm bowler. *Team* Minor Counties (1985).
Career batting
1–1–0–9–9–9.00–0–*ct* 1
Bowling 137–7–19.57–1–0–5/79

His County cricket was for Hertfordshire (1979–90).

Smith, Vivian Ian
Amateur. *b:* 23.2.1925, Durban, South Africa. Tail end right-hand batsman, leg break bowler. *Team* Natal (1945/6 to 1957/8). *Tours* South Africa to England 1947, 1955. *Tests* South Africa (1947 to 1957/8, 9 matches).
Career batting
97–114–61–547–37–10.32–0–*ct* 37
Bowling 8233–365–22.55–26–8–9/88

Test batting
9–16–6–39–11*–3.90–0–*ct* 3
Bowling 769–12–64.08–0–0–4/143

He headed the first-class bowling figures for the 1947 tour with 58 wickets, av 23.17, and against Derbyshire returned an analysis of 4.5–3–1–6; in 1955 he was overshadowed by Tayfield and given few opportunities. His best bowling was 9/88 for Natal v Border at Pietermaritzburg in 1946/7.

Smith, Walker
Professional. *b:* 14.8.1847, Ossett, Yorkshire. *d:* 11.7.1900, Drightlington, Yorkshire. Aggressive middle order right-hand batsman, mid-wicket field. *Team* Yorkshire (1874, 5 matches).
Career batting
5–9–0–152–59–16.88–0–*ct* 2

Smith, Walter Alfred
Amateur. *b:* 23.2.1913, Evington, Leicester. Middle order right-hand batsman, slow right-arm bowler. *Sch* Wyggeston GS. *Team* Leicestershire (1930–46, 27 matches).
Career batting
27–44–4–754–125*–18.85–1–*ct* 13
Bowling 122–3–40.66–0–0–1/4

Smith, Walter Frederick Sundius
Amateur. *b:* 8.2.1889, Portslade, Brighton, Sussex. *d:* 30.12.1969, Hove, Sussex. Lower order batsman, useful bowler. *Sch* Oundle. Team Oxford U (1920).
Career batting
1–2–0–12–12–6.00–0–*ct* 0
Bowling 47–2–23.50–0–0–2/38

He won a blue for hockey.

Smith, William
Professional. *b:* 1.11.1839, Darlington, Co Durham. *d:* 19.4.1897, South Bank, Middlesbrough, Yorkshire. Attacking middle order right-hand batsman. *Team* Yorkshire (1865–74, 11 matches).
Career batting
11–19–3–260–90–16.25–0–*ct* 8

He also played for Durham (pre first-class, 1874).

Smith, William
Professional. *b:* 23.4.1871, Batley, Yorkshire. Brother of D. J. (Somerset), son of John (Yorkshire and Lancashire). Middle order right-hand batsman, right-arm medium pace bowler. *Team* Somerset (1895–98, 6 matches).
Career batting
8–13–2–97–21–8.81–0–*ct* 1
Bowling 88–0

His final first-class match was for MCC in 1902. He also played for Wiltshire (1894–1913).

Smith, William
Amateur. *b:* 1875. *d:* 20.3.1942, Chittlehambolt, Devon. Middle order right-hand batsman, useful bowler. *Team* London County (1901–04).
Career batting
30–45–6–1191–143–30.53–2–*ct* 17
Bowling 67–2–33.50–0–0–1/6

His County cricket was for Oxfordshire (1895–1905).

Smith, William Albert
Professional. *b:* 15.9.1937, Salisbury, Wiltshire. Middle order left-hand batsman, right-arm batsman, right-arm medium pace bowler. *Team* Surrey (1961–70, 144 matches).
Career batting
144–242–18–5024–103–22.42–2–*ct* 52
Bowling 1–0

He hit 1,002 runs, av 24.43, in 1968. He also played for Wiltshire (1971–76).

Smith, William Alexander Bremner
Amateur. *b:* 22.7.1902, Greenock, Renfrewshire, Scotland. *d:* 21.12.1937, Kuala Lumpur, Malaya. Lower order right-hand batsman, right-arm fast medium bowler. *Team* Scotland (1927).
Career batting
1–2–0–1–1–0.50–0–*ct* 1
Bowling 71–1–71.00–0–0–1/29

Smith, William Alfred
Professional. *b:* 29.9.1900, Corsham, Wiltshire. *d:* 6.1.1990, Trowbridge, Wiltshire. Brother of C. I. J. (Middlesex). Lower order right-hand batsman, right-arm fast medium bowler. *Team* Minor Counties (1935–36).
Career batting
2–4–1–47–35–15.66–0–*ct* 1
Bowling 208–9–23.11–1–0–5/95

His County cricket was for Wiltshire (1929–39). He played soccer for West Ham.

Smith, William Charles
Professional. *b:* 4.10.1877, Oxford. *d:* 15.7.1946, Bermondsey, London. Lower order right-hand batsman, off break bowler. *Teams* Surrey (1900–14, 229 matches); London County (1900). *Tour* MCC to West Indies 1912/13.
Career batting
245–343–71–3453–126–12.69–1–*ct* 157
Bowling 18910–1077–17.55–95–27–9/31

He took 100 wickets in a season three times, going on to 200 once: 247 av 13.05, in 1910. His best bowling was 9/31 for Surrey v Hampshire in 1904 at the Oval. Ill-health marred his career and his very sparse figure earned him the nickname 'Razor'. He also played for Oxfordshire (1897). He was Surrey coach 1926–28.

Smith, William John
Professional. *b:* 13.5.1882, Freasley, Warwickshire. Lower order right-hand batsman, right-arm fast medium bowler. *Team* Warwickshire (1906, 1 match).

Smith, Willie

Career batting
1–1–0–0–0–0.00–*ct* 0
Bowling 93–2–46.50–0–0–2/83

Smith, Willie
Professional. *b:* 12.5.1885, Gringley-on-the-Hill, Nottinghamshire. *d:* 8.5.1964, Scawsby, Yorkshire. Middle order right-hand batsman. *Team* Derbyshire (1913, 2 matches).
Career batting
2–4–0–13–8–3.25–0–*ct* 0

Smith-Barry, Arthur Hugh
(created 1st Lord Barrymore in 1902)
Amateur. *b:* 17.1.1843, Leamington, Warwickshire. *d:* 22.2.1925, Westminster, London. Middle order right-hand batsman, wicket-keeper. *Sch* Eton. *Team* MCC (1873–75).
Career batting
2–4–0–14–9–3.50–0–*ct* 1

He was not in the Eleven whilst at Oxford. His County cricket was for Cheshire (1862–74) and Warwickshire (pre first-class, 1873). He also played for Ireland (not first-class) in 1868. He was MP for Co Cork from 1867 to 1874, and for South Huntingdonshire from 1886 to 1900.

Smith-Masters, William Allan
(name changed from Cowburn in April 1862)
Amateur. *b:* 13.3.1850, Humber, Herefordshire. *d:* 27.8.1937, Camer, Meopham, Kent. Son of A. Cowburn (Oxford U 1841), brother-in-law of S. W. Gore (Surrey) and F. I. Edwards (I Zingari). Middle order batsman. *Sch* Marlborough. *Team* Kent (1875, 1 match).
Career batting
1–1–0–7–7–7.00–0–*ct* 0

Smithson, Gerald Arthur
Professional. *b:* 1.11.1926, Spofforth, Yorkshire. *d:* 6.9.1970, Abingdon, Berkshire. Middle order left-hand batsman, right-arm medium pace bowler. *Teams* Yorkshire (1946–50, 39 matches); Leicestershire (1951–56, 154 matches). *Tour* MCC to West Indies 1947/8. *Tests* England (1947/8, 2 matches).
Career batting
200–333–27–6940–169–22.67–8–*ct* 131
Bowling 117–1–117.00–0–0–1/26
Test batting
2–3–0–70–35–23.33–0–*ct* 0

He hit 1,351 runs, av 27.57, in 1952. He also played for Hertfordshire (1957–62). He was a conscript in the mines in 1947 when he was selected to tour West Indies with MCC and after his case had been debated in the House of Commons he was granted permission by the Government to take part in the tour.

Smith-Turberville, Harry Turberville
(changed name from Smith in 1884)
Amateur. *b:* 18.1.1848, Westminster, London. *d:* 28.7.1934, Hove, Sussex. Lower order batsman, useful bowler. *Team* MCC (1886). *Tour* Lucas to West Indies 1894/5.
Career batting
2–4–1–31–14–10.33–0–*ct* 0
Bowling 28–1–28.00–0–0–1/28

Smithurst, Isaiah
Professional. *b:* 6.11.1920, Hill Top, Eastwood, Nottinghamshire. Lower order left-hand batsman, slow left-arm bowler. *Team* Nottinghamshire (1946, 1 match).
Career batting
1–2–0–1–1–0.50–0–*ct* 0
Bowling 48–0

Smithyman, Michael James
Cricketer. *b:* 17.11.1945, Pietermaritzburg, South Africa. Steady middle order right-hand batsman, right-arm medium fast bowler. *Team* Natal (1965/6 to 1974/5). *Tours* South African Universities to England 1967; Isaacs to England 1969 (not first-class).
Career batting
40–59–10–1162–73–23.71–0–*ct* 15
Bowling 2027–79–25.65–0–0–4/25

He was most successful on his visit to England in 1967, heading the batting and bowling averages in all matches with 562 runs, av 93.66, and 51 wickets, av 13.98.

Smoker, George
Professional. *b:* 30.12.1856, Winchester, Hampshire. *d:* 23.5.1925, Brookwood, Alresford, Hampshire. Middle order batsman. *Team* Hampshire (1885, 2 matches).
Career batting
2–4–1–17–13–5.66–0–*ct* 2

Smoker, Henry George
Professional. *b:* 1.3.1881, Alresford, Hampshire. *d:* 7.9.1966, Wallasey, Cheshire. Brother-in-law of D. V. Norbury (Hampshire and Lancashire). Lower order left-hand batsman, right-arm medium fast bowler. *Team* Hampshire (1901–07, 31 matches).
Career batting
31–50–15–334–39*–9.54–0–*ct* 18
Bowling 733–33–22.21–2–0–7/35

He also played for Cheshire (1909–25).

Smurthwaite, James
Professional. *b:* 17.10.1916, North Ormesby, Yorkshire. *d:* 20.10.1989, Middlesbrough, Yorkshire. Tail end right-hand batsman, right-arm fast medium or off break bowler. *Team* Yorkshire (1938–39, 7 matches).
Career batting
7–9–5–29–20*–7.25–0–*ct* 4
Bowling 237–12–19.75–1–0–5/7

Smyth, Richard Ian
Cricketer. *b:* 19.11.1951, Sunderland, Co Durham. Middle order right-hand batsman, leg break bowler.

Sch Sedbergh. *Team* Cambridge U (1973–75, blue all three years).
Career batting
21–41–2–711–61–18.23–0–*ct* 4
His County cricket was for Durham (pre first-class, 1974).

Smyth, Richard Nicholas Paul
Cricketer. *b:* 27.6.1950, Chichester, Sussex. Middle order right-hand batsman. *Sch* Brighton. *Team* Sussex (1970, 3 matches).
Career batting
3–5–0–42–25–8.40–0–*ct* 0

Smyth, Stephen Gordon
Cricketer. *b:* 22.12.1968, Londonderry, Ireland. Middle order left-hand batsman. *Team* Ireland (1991).
Career batting
1–2–1–21–14–21.00–0–*ct* 0
Bowling 7–0

Smythe, David
Amateur. *b:* 4.12.1889, Rockingham, Northamptonshire. *d:* 6.3.1962, Edinburgh, Scotland. Lower order batsman, right-arm fast bowler. *Sch* Repton. *Team* Cambridge U (1912).
Career batting
3–3–0–15–12–5.00–0–*ct* 0
Bowling 149–6–24.83–0–0–2/43

Smythe, J. W.
Amateur. Middle order batsman. *Team* MCC (1878–85).
Career batting
5–10–1–122–35–13.55–0–*ct* 3
Bowling 24–2–12.00–0–0–2/24

Snaith, John Collis
Amateur. *b:* 24.2.1876, Nottingham. *d:* 8.12.1936, Hampstead Garden Suburb, London. Middle order left-hand batsman, left-arm medium pace bowler. *Team* Nottinghamshire (1900, 1 match).
Career batting
1–1–0–21–21–21.00–0–*ct* 1
A well-known popular novelist of his day, he wrote one noteworthy book on cricket: 'Willow the King'.

Snape, Jeremy Nicholas
Cricketer. *b:* 27.4.1973, Stoke-on-Trent, Staffordshire. Lower order right-hand batsman, off break bowler. *Sch* Denstone. *Team* Northamptonshire (1992, 1 match).
Career batting
1 match, did not bat–*ct* 1
Bowling 62–1–62.00–0–0–1/20

Snape, Maurice Desmond
Professional *b:* 7.7.1923, Creswell, Derbyshire. *d:* 17.4.1992, Kilton Hill, Worksop, Nottinghamshire. Middle order right-hand batsman. *Team* Derbyshire (1949, 2 matches).
Career batting
2–3–1–0–0*–0.00–0–*ct* 0

Snary, Horace Charles
Professional. *b:* 22.9.1897, Whissendine, Rutland. *d:* 26.12.1966, Whissendine, Rutland. Stubborn middle order right-hand batsman, right-arm medium-slow bowler. *Team* Leicestershire (1921–33, 183 matches).
Career batting
183–249–114–2156–124*–15.97–1–*ct* 115
Bowling 10170–419–24.27–12–1–7/31
He took 101 wickets, av 18.11, in 1931.

Snedden, Martin Colin
Cricketer. *b:* 23.11.1958, Mount Eden, Auckland, New Zealand. Son of W. N. (Auckland), grandson of A. N. C. (Auckland), nephew of C. A. (Auckland). Lower order left-hand batsman, right-arm medium fast bowler. *Team* Auckland (1977/8 to 1989/90). *Tours* New Zealand to Australia 1980/1, 1982/3, 1984/5 (not first-class), 1985/6, 1987/8, 1989/90, to England 1983, 1990, to Pakistan 1984/5, to Sri Lanka 1984/5 (not first-class), 1985/6 (not first-class), 1986/7, to Sharjah (not first-class) 1985/6, 1989/90, to India 1987/8 (World Cup), 1988/9; Young New Zealand to Zimbabwe 1983/4. *Tests* New Zealand (1980/1 to 1990, 25 matches).
Career batting
118–124–29–1792–69–18.86–0–*ct* 55
Bowling 9918–387–25.62–15–2–8/73
Test batting
25–30–8–327–33*–14.86–0–*ct* 7
Bowling 2199–58–37.91–1–0–5/68
He had only modest success on the 1983 tour to England, but in 1990 his accurate medium pace bowling made him an essential member of the side and he played in all three Tests.

Snell, Edward
Amateur. *b:* 22.4.1906, Brighton, Sussex. *d:* 6.9.1973, Hove, Sussex. Middle order right-hand batsman, slow right-arm bowler. *Sch* Winchester. *Team* Sussex (1927–28, 3 matches).
Career batting
3–3–0–13–13–4.33–0–*ct* 1
He played no first-class cricket at Oxford U, but did win a blue for rugby fives.

Snell, Harold Saxon
Amateur. *b:* 6.12.1876, Highworth, Wiltshire. *d:* 9.7.1942, Daventry, Northamptonshire. Middle order batsman. *Sch* Dean Close, Cheltenham. *Team* Northamptonshire (1909–13, 3 matches).
Career batting
3–5–0–119–52–23.80–0–*ct* 2
He also played for Wiltshire (1897–1908). He played no first-class cricket at Cambridge U, but did win a blue for soccer.

Snell, Richard Peter
Cricketer. *b:* 12.9.1968, Durban, South Africa. Middle order right-hand batsman, right-arm fast medium bowler. *Teams* Transvaal (1987/8 to 1991/2); Somerset (1992, 16 matches). *Tours* South Africa to India (not first-class) 1991/2, to Australia and New Zealand (World Cup) 1991/2, to West Indies 1991/2. *Test* South Africa (1991/2, 1 match).
Career batting
41–53–10–724–81–16.83–0–*ct* 12
Bowling 3401–124–27.42–5–0–6/58
Test batting
1–2–0–6–6–3.00–0–*ct* 0
Bowling 157–8–19.62–0–0–4/74

Snellgrove, Kenneth Leslie
Cricketer. *b:* 12.11.1941, Shepton Mallet, Somerset. Middle order right-hand batsman, off break bowler. *Team* Lancashire (1965–74, 105 matches).
Career batting
106–172–16–3948–138–25.30–2–*ct* 36
Bowling 27–3–9.00–0–0–2/23
His best season was 1971 with 991 runs, av 31.96.

Snodgrass, David Lang
Cricketer. *b:* 21.11.1958, Partick Hill, Glasgow, Scotland. Lower order right-hand batsman, right-arm medium pace bowler. *Team* Scotland (1982–89).
Career batting
5–6–0–91–49–15.16–0–*ct* 6
Bowling 139–5–27.80–0–0–2/26

Snooke, Sibley John
Amateur. *b:* 1.2.1881, St Mark's, Tembuland, South Africa. *d:* 14.8.1966, Humewood, Port Elizabeth, South Africa. Brother of S. D. (South Africa), grandfather of W. J. McAdam (Western Province and Eastern Province) and S. J. McAdam (Eastern Province, Western Province and Transvaal). Middle order right-hand batsman, right-arm fast medium bowler. *Teams* Border (1897/8 to 1908/9); Western Province (1903/4 to 1907/8); MCC (1907–12); Transvaal (1909/10 to 1923/4). *Tours* South Africa to England 1904, 1907, 1912, to Australia 1910/11; MCC to North America 1907. *Tests* South Africa (1905/6 to 1922/3, 26 matches).
Career batting
124–202–16–4821–187–25.91–7–*ct* 82
Bowling 3017–120–25.14–3–1–8/70
Test batting
26–46–1–1008–103–22.40–1–*ct* 24
Bowling 702–35–20.05–1–1–8/70
His most successful visit to England was in 1907 when he hit 943 runs, av 29.46, in first-class matches. He captained South Africa in five Tests.

Snooke, Stanley De La Courtte
(death registered as Stanley Delacourtte Snooke)
Amateur. *b:* 11.11.1878, St Mark's, Tembuland, South Africa. *d:* 6.4.1959, Wynberg, Cape Town, South Africa. Brother of S. J. (South Africa). Middle order right-hand batsman, bowler. *Teams* Western Province (1904/5 to 1910/11); Transvaal (1920/1). *Tour* South Africa to England 1907. *Test* South Africa (1907, 1 match).
Career batting
32–53–5–798–74–16.62–0–*ct* 31
Bowling 224–19–11.78–1–1–7/29
Test batting
1–1–0–0–0–0.00–0–*ct* 2
He achieved little on the 1907 visit to England.

Snow, Albert Henry Percival
Amateur. *b:* 9.8.1852, Bedford. *d:* 5.4.1909, Gunnersbury, Middlesex. Lower order batsman, left-arm fast bowler. *Team* Middlesex (1875–76, 4 matches).
Career batting
4–8–3–9–3–1.80–0–*ct* 1
Bowling 308–22–14.00–2–0–5/35
He also played for Bedfordshire (1879–80).

Snow, John Augustine
Professional. *b:* 13.10.1941, Peopleton, Worcestershire. Lower order right-hand batsman, right-arm fast medium bowler. *Sch* Christ's Hospital. *Team* Sussex (1961–77, 267 matches). *Tours* MCC to West Indies 1967/8, to Ceylon and Pakistan 1968/9, to Australia 1970/1; Robins to South Africa 1972/3; Cavaliers to West Indies 1969/70; International Wanderers to Rhodesia 1975/6. *Tests* England (1965–76, 49 matches).
Career batting
346–451–110–4832–73*–14.17–0–*ct* 125
Bowling 26675–1174–22.72–56–9–8/87
Test batting
49–71–14–772–73–13.54–0–*ct* 16
Bowling 5387–202–26.66–8–1–7/40
He took 100 wickets in a season twice (best 126, av 19.09, in 1966). A controversial cricketer, his greatest Test series were those in the West Indies in 1967/8 and in Australia in 1970/1; his best series in England being in 1975 against Australia. At his peak he was the leading fast bowler in England, but was too often at loggerheads with authority. When he signed for Kerry Packer's WSC his first-class cricket virtually ended. His autobiography was entitled 'Cricket Rebel'. He was joint Sussex coach in 1987. He also published two volumes of poetry.

Snow, Philip Sidney
Amateur. *b:* 2.7.1907, Kendal, Westmorland. *d:* 13.2.1985, Reading, Berkshire. Middle order right-hand batsman, right-arm medium pace off break bowler. *Sch* Shrewsbury. *Team* Oxford U (1928–29).
Career batting
2–4–0–41–22–10.25–0–*ct* 1
Bowling 119–5–23.80–0–0–2/31
He won a blue for soccer.

Snowden, Alexander William
Amateur. *b:* 15.8.1913, Peterborough, Northamptonshire *d:* 7.5.1981, Peterborough, Northamptonshire. Opening right-hand batsman, left-arm medium pace bowler, good short leg. *Sch* King's, Peterborough. *Team* Northamptonshire (1931–39, 136 matches).
Career batting
136–250–10–4343–128–18.09–2–*ct* 46
Bowling 22–2–11.00–0–0–1/5

He was originally a left-hand batsman, but was persuaded at school to change to right. He hit 1,000 runs, av 20.40, in 1934.

Snowden, Arthur Owen
Amateur. *b:* 7.5.1885, Ramsgate, Kent. *d:* 22.5.1964, Canterbury, Kent. Middle order right-hand batsman, left-arm medium pace bowler. *Sch* Rugby. *Teams* Oxford U (1905); Kent (1911, 1 match).
Career batting
6–11–1–142–54–14.20–0–*ct* 2
Bowling 38–0

His final first-class match was for MCC in 1912.

Snowden, William
Cricketer. *b:* 27.9.1952, Whiston, Prescot, Lancashire. Opening right-hand batsman, right-arm medium pace bowler. *Sch* Merchant Taylor's, Crosby. *Team* Cambridge U (1972–75, blue all four years).
Career batting
37–69–3–1413–108*–21.40–3–*ct* 10
Bowling 13–0

He captained Cambridge in 1974.

Soames, Henry
Amateur. *b:* 18.1.1843, Brighton, Sussex. *d:* 30.8.1913, Laverstock, Salisbury, Wiltshire. Brother of W. A. (Sussex). Middle order batsman. *Sch* Brighton. *Team* Hampshire (1867, 1 match).
Career batting
1–2–0–54–52–27.00–0–*ct* 0

Soames, William Aldwin
Amateur. *b:* 10.7.1850, Brighton, Sussex. *d:* 27.12.1916, Bank Station, City of London. Brother of Henry (Hampshire). Middle order right-hand batsman, good deep field. *Sch* Brighton. *Team* Sussex (1875, 3 matches).
Career batting
3–5–0–17–17–3.40–0–*ct* 2

He played in trials at Cambridge U, but not in first-class matches.

Soar, Thomas
Professional. *b:* 3.9.1865, Whitemoor, Nottinghamshire. *d:* 17.5.1939, Llandovery, Carmarthenshire. Lower order right-hand batsman, right-arm fast bowler. *Team* Hampshire (1895–1904, 101 matches).
Career batting
101–173–29–1927–95–13.38–0–*ct* 49
Bowling 7697–323–23.82–23–7–8/38

He made his debut for Hampshire in 1888, so that for several seasons he played only second-class County cricket. He also played for Carmarthenshire (1908).

Sobers, Sir Garfield St Aubrun
Professional. *b:* 28.7.1936, Chelsea Road, Bay Land, Bridgetown, Barbados. Cousin of D. A. J. Holford (West Indies). Brilliant middle order left-hand batsman, left-arm fast medium or slow bowler, good field. *Teams* Barbados (1952/3 to 1973/4); South Australia (1961/2 to 1963/4, 26 matches); Nottinghamshire (1968–74, 107 matches). *Tours* West Indies to England 1957, 1963, 1966, 1969, 1973, to Australia 1960/1, 1968/9, to New Zealand 1955/6, 1968/9, to Ceylon and India 1966/7, to India and Pakistan 1958/9; West Indian XI to England 1964; Rest of World to England 1965, 1967, 1968, 1970, to Pakistan 1970/1, to Australia 1971/2; Swanton to India 1963/4; Cavaliers to India 1962/3. *Tests* West Indies (1953/4 to 1973/4, 93 matches).
Career batting
383–609–93–28315–365*–54.87–86–*ct* 407
Bowling 28941–1043–27.74–36–1–9/49
Test batting
93–160–21–8032–365*–57.78–26–*ct* 109
Bowling 7999–235–34.03–6–0–6/73

The outstanding all-rounder of post war cricket, his records in Test cricket alone speak for themselves. He was the first Test cricketer to hit over 8,000 runs in his career, a total which included 365* for West Indies v Pakistan at Kingston in 1957/8, creating a new record for the highest individual innings in Test cricket. He is one of the few bowlers to capture over 200 Test wickets, and this fact, allied to his 109 catches, demonstrates his standing amongst the greatest players of all time. He captained the West Indies in 39 Tests, which was, at the time, yet another record.

Of his five West Indian tours to England the outstanding visit came in 1966, when his Test record was quite incredible – 722 runs, av 103.14, and 20 wickets, av 27.25.

He joined Nottinghamshire in 1968 and remained with the County until he retired in 1974. He was captain 1968–71 and 1973. He hit 1,000 runs in a season in England nine times, his best season being 1970 with 1,742 runs, av 75.73, when he also captained the Rest of the World in five matches against England. His most famous feat in County cricket was to hit 6 sixes off a single six-ball over delivered by M. A. Nash of Glamorgan at Swansea in 1968. His best bowling was 9/49 for West Indies v Kent at Canterbury in 1966. He hit 1,000 runs in an overseas season five times.

On retiring from first-class cricket he was knighted for his services to the game.

Soden, Frederick Brewer
Amateur. *b:* 30.3.1846, Clapham Common, London. *d:* 13.4.1877, Clapham Common, London. Middle order right-hand batsman, right-hand medium pace round-arm bowler. *Sch* Brighton. *Team* Surrey (1870–71, 3 matches).
Career batting
3–6–1–35–18*–7.00–0–*ct* 1
Bowling 17–2–8.50–0–0–1/2

Soga, Dennis William
(changed name to Grandison)
Amateur. *b:* 13.5.1917, Elliotdale, Cape Province, South Africa. Middle order right-hand batsman, off break bowler. *Team* Scotland (1936).
Career batting
1–2–0–25–24–12.50–0–*ct* 0

Sohoni, Sriranga Wasudev
Amateur. *b:* 5.3.1918, Nimbora, India. Lower order right-hand batsman, right-arm medium fast or off break bowler. *Teams* Maharashtra (1935/6 to 1959/60); Hindus (1941/2 to 1945/6); Baroda (1948/9); Bombay (1951/2 to 1954/5). *Tours* India to England 1946, to Australia 1947/8. *Tests* India (1946 to 1951/2, 4 matches).
Career batting
108–164–14–4307–218*–28.71–8–*ct* 69
Bowling 7647–232–32.96–11–2–7/20
Test batting
4–7–2–83–29*–16.60–0–*ct* 2
Bowling 202–2–101.00–0–0–1/16

Although he appeared in two of the three Tests in England in 1946, his bowling was not very penetrative and in all first-class matches he took only 14 wickets, av 44.07. His final first-class match was for Bombay Governor's XI in 1963/4. His highest score was 218* for Maharashtra v Western India at Rajkot in 1940/1.

Solanky, John William
Cricketer. *b:* 30.6.1942, Dar-es-Salaam, Tanganyika. Middle order right-hand batsman, right-arm medium pace off break bowler. *Teams* Glamorgan (1972–76, 82 matches); East Africa (1963/4 to 1964/5).
Career batting
84–138–22–2374–73–20.46–0–*ct* 17
Bowling 4639–183–25.34–8–0–6/63

He also played for Devon (1967–69).

Solbé, Edward Philip
Amateur. *b:* 10.5.1902, Bromley, Kent. *d:* 29.12.1961, Standard Hill, Nottingham. Son of F. de L. (Kent). Middle order right-hand batsman, left-arm medium pace bowler. *Sch* Tonbridge. *Team* Kent (1921–24, 15 matches). *Tour* Cahn to North America 1933 (not first-class).
Career batting
15–24–2–371–66–16.86–0–*ct* 8
Bowling 6–0

Solbé, Frank de Lisle
Amateur. *b:* 1.6.1871, Che-foo, China. *d:* 12.1.1933, Bromley, Kent. Father of E. P. (Kent). Middle order right-hand batsman, slow under-arm bowler. *Sch* Dulwich and Blair Lodge. *Team* Kent (1891–92, 4 matches).
Career batting
5–7–0–14–9–2.00–0–*ct* 0

His final first-class match was for MCC in 1898. He played hockey for England.

Solkar, Eknath Dhondu
Cricketer. *b:* 18.3.1948, Bombay, India. Brother of A. D. (Maharashtra and Railways). Attractive middle order left-hand batsman, left-arm medium pace or slow left-arm bowler, excellent field. *Teams* Bombay (1966/7 to 1980/1); Sussex (1969, 1 match). *Tours* India to England 1971, 1974, 1975 (World Cup), to West Indies 1970/1, 1975/6, to Sri Lanka 1973/4, to New Zealand 1975/6. *Tests* India (1969/70 to 1976/7, 27 matches).
Career batting
189–270–36–6851–145*–29.27–8–*ct* 190
Bowling 8282–276–30.00–10–1–6/38
Test batting
27–48–6–1068–102–25.42–1–*ct* 53
Bowling 1070–18–59.44–0–0–3/28

He was most successful on the 1971 tour to England, being second in the batting averages for both the Test series and first-class matches, in the latter hitting 802 runs, av 44.55. He was not so useful in 1974. His first-class debut was for Vazir Sultan Colts XI in 1965/6.

Solly, Edward Walter
Professional. *b:* 7.5.1882, Eastry, Kent. *d:* 12.2.1966, Cefn Mably, Glamorgan. Lower order left-hand batsman, left-arm fast medium bowler. *Team* Worcestershire (1903–07, 8 matches).
Career batting
8–10–1–78–43–8.66–0–*ct* 1
Bowling 665–14–47.50–0–0–3/25

Solly, George Edward
Amateur. *b:* 27.3.1855, West Heath, Congleton, Cheshire. *d:* 10.3.1930, Mentone, France. Lower order batsman, useful bowler. *Sch* Winchester. *Team* Oxford U (1877).
Career batting
1–2–0–8–6–4.00–0–*ct* 0
Bowling 59–3–19.66–0–0–3/44

His County cricket was for Cheshire. He won a blue for athletics.

Solomon, Joseph Stanislaus
Amateur. *b:* 26.8.1930, Corentyne, British Guiana. Sound middle order right-hand batsman, leg break bowler. *Team* British Guiana (1956/7 to 1968/9). *Tours* West Indies to England 1963, 1966, to India and Pakistan 1958/9, to Australia 1960/1. *Tests* West

Indies (1958/9 to 1964/5, 27 matches).
Career batting
104–156–28–5318–201*–41.54–12–*ct* 46
Bowling 1950–51–38.23–0–0–4/28
Test batting
27–46–7–1326–100*–34.00–1–*ct* 13
Bowling 268–4–67.00–0–0–1/20

His first-class career commenced in a spectacular fashion with three successive centuries for British Guiana – the first time a batsman had achieved such a feat. His figures on the 1963 tour to England were modest, but he was employed mainly in a defensive role as a foil to his more aggressive colleagues; he appeared in all five Tests. In 1966 he did not take part in any of the Tests. His only double century was 201* for Berbice v MCC at Blairmont in 1959/60. His throw, which ran out the last Australian batsman, led to the first tied Test at Brisbane in 1960.

Somaia, Kamal Anilkumar
Cricketer. *b:* 22.7.1968, Brent, London. Lower order right-hand batsman, slow left-arm bowler. *Team* Glamorgan (1989, 3 matches).
Career batting
3–6–0–50–15–8.33–0–*ct* 1
Bowling 245–8–30.62–1–0–5/87

He also played for Staffordshire (1989).

Somani, Addil
Cricketer. *b:* 22.10.1967, Kampala, Uganda. Lower order right-hand batsman, leg break bowler. *Teams* Nottinghamshire (1987, 1 match); Northern Districts (1988/9).
Career batting
4–4–1–59–26*–19.66–0–*ct* 0
Bowling 210–6–35.00–0–0–2/7

He was brought up and educated in New Zealand.

Somers, Lord Arthur Herbert Tennyson
(born A. H. T. Somers-Cocks, he succeeded as 6th Baron Somers in 1896)
Amateur. *b:* 20.3.1887, Freshwater, Isle of Wight. *d:* 14.7.1944, Eastnor Castle, Hereford. Middle order right-hand batsman. *Sch* Charterhouse. *Team* Worcestershire (1923–25, 16 matches).
Career batting
17–30–1–390–52–13.44–0–*ct* 10
Bowling 4–0

His first-class debut was for MCC in 1906. He was Governor of Victoria 1926–31 and Acting Governor-General of Australia in 1930. He was President of MCC in 1936.

Somerset, Arthur Plantagenet Francis Cecil
Amateur. *b:* 28.9.1889, Castle Goring, Worthing, Sussex. *d:* 13.10.1957, Worthing, Sussex. Son of A. W. F. (Sussex). Middle order right-hand batsman, right-arm medium pace bowler. *Sch* Rugby. *Team* Sussex (1911–19, 9 matches). *Tours* MCC to West Indies 1910/11, 1912/13.
Career batting
29–52–10–439–39*–10.45–0–*ct* 10
Bowling 954–33–28.90–1–0–5/62

Somerset, Arthur William Fitzroy
Amateur. *b:* 20.9.1855, Brompton, Chatham, Kent. *d:* 8.1.1937, Castle Goring, Worthing, Sussex. Father of A. P. F. C. (Sussex). Middle order right-hand batsman, right-arm fast bowler, occasional wicket-keeper. *Sch* Wellington. *Teams* Sussex (1892–1905, 5 matches); London County (1900). *Tours* Brackley to West Indies 1904/5; MCC to West Indies 1910/11, 1912/13.
Career batting
48–80–19–1221–68*–20.01–0–*ct* 41–*st* 7
Bowling 53–2–26.50–0–0–2/37

His first-class debut was for Sheffield's XI in 1891, and his final first-class match in England for MCC in 1906. He captained the two MCC tours to West Indies. He was President of Sussex in 1936. He was also a heavyweight boxer of some note. He lived in Australia from 1873 to 1881.

Somers-Smith, Ernest
(registered as E. S. Smith at birth and death)
Amateur. *b:* 8.11.1895, Ecclesall, Sheffield, Yorkshire. *d:* 2.4.1950, Odsal, Yorkshire. Middle order right-hand batsman. *Team* Worcestershire (1921, 2 matches).
Career batting
2–4–0–33–22–8.25–0–*ct* 0

Somerville, Reginald James
Amateur. *b:* 9.10.1918, Camberwell, London. *d:* 13.8.1979, Lambeth, London. Middle order right-hand batsman, wicket-keeper. *Team* D. R. Jardine's XI (1955).
Career batting
1–1–0–3–3–3.00–0–*ct* 1

Soppitt, William John Blair
Amateur. *b:* 1857. *d:* 29.10.1910, Shepherd's Bush, Fulham, London. Lower order right-hand batsman, right-arm fast medium bowler. *Team* Middlesex (1887, 1 match).
Career batting
2–4–0–15–10–3.75–0–*ct* 3
Bowling 159–5–31.80–1–0–5/159

Sorrie, James Webster
Amateur. *b:* 31.12.1885, Brechin, Angus, Scotland. *d:* 31.7.1955, Blackpool, Lancashire. Opening right-hand batsman, useful change bowler. *Team* Scotland (1912–24).
Career batting
9–18–0–346–61–19.22–0–*ct* 4
Bowling 23–2–11.50–0–0–1/2

Souness, James McGill
Amateur. *b:* 9.11.1928, Leith, Midlothian, Scotland. *d:* 2.9.1990, Jungfrau, Switzerland. He died in a

climbing accident. Lower order right-hand batsman, right-arm fast medium bowler. *Team* Scotland (1954–55).
Career batting
3–5–0–11–7–2.20–0–*ct* 0
Bowling 301–4–75.25–0–0–2/63

Soutar, Kenneth Hannam
Amateur. *b:* 11.10.1888, Barnwood, Gloucester. *d:* 2.9.1914, Marylebone, London. Middle order batsman. *Sch* Marlborough. *Team* Gloucestershire (1908, 3 matches).
Career batting
3–5–0–59–16–11.80–0–*ct* 1

Souter, James Stewart
Amateur. *b:* 9.2.1924, Kanpur, India. Middle order right-hand batsman. *Sch* Haileybury. *Team* Oxford U (1948).
Career batting
3–2–0–47–30–23.50–0–*ct* 2

Southall, Harry
Amateur. Middle order right-hand batsman. *Team* Worcestershire (1907, 1 match).
Career batting
1–1–0–11–11–11.00–0–*ct* 0

Southby, Sir Archibald Richard Charles
Amateur. *b:* 18.6.1910, Devonport, Devon. *d:* 4.4.1988, Ashford, Kent. Opening right-hand batsman. *Sch* Eton. *Teams* Madras (1935/6 to 1936/7); Army (1939).
Career batting
7–12–0–158–33–13.16–0–*ct* 3

Southcombe, Richard
Amateur. *b:* 22.11.1909, Taunton, Somerset. Middle order right-hand batsman, off break bowler. *Team* Somerset (1936–37, 2 matches).
Career batting
2–4–0–20–10–5.00–0–*ct* 0

Southern, John Dunlop
Amateur. *b:* 5.11.1899, Derby. *d:* 7.2.1972, Seend Head House, Melksham, Wiltshire. Son-in-law of T. M. Usborne (Europeans). Middle order right-hand batsman. *Sch* Malvern. *Team* Derbyshire (1919–34, 5 matches).
Career batting
5–10–0–95–43–9.50–0–*ct* 0

Southern, John William
Cricketer. *b:* 2.9.1952, King's Cross, London. Lower order right-hand batsman, slow left-arm bowler. *Team* Hampshire (1975–83, 164 matches).
Career batting
164–179–71–1653–61*–15.30–0–*ct* 59
Bowling 12283–412–29.81–17–0–6/46

Southerton, James
Professional. *b:* 16.11.1827, Petworth, Sussex. *d:* 16.6.1880, Mitcham, Surrey. Tail end right-hand batsman, slow right-hand round-arm bowler. *Teams* Surrey (1854–79, 152 matches); Sussex (1858–72, 50 matches); Hampshire (1861–67, 13 matches). *Tours* Grace to Australia 1873/4 (not first-class); Lillywhite to Australia 1876/7. *Tests* England (1876/7, 2 matches).
Career batting
286–480–130–3159–82–9.02–0–*ct* 215–*st* 3
Bowling 24280–1681–14.44–192–59–9/30
Test batting
2–3–1–7–6–3.50–0–*ct* 2
Bowling 107–7–15.28–0–0–4/46

He took 100 wickets in a season ten times, going on to 200 once: 210, av 14.63, in 1870. His best bowling was 9/30 for South v North at Lord's in 1875. He had the curious experience of playing for three counties – Hampshire, Sussex and Surrey in the same season, but this was before the qualification rules were introduced. He also played for Buckinghamshire (1867). He was aged 49 years 119 days on his Test debut – the oldest player on debut.

Southwood, Albert Henry Howard
Amateur. *b:* 19.7.1882, Taunton, Somerset. *d:* 13.7.1965, Taunton, Somerset. Middle order right-hand batsman, slow right-arm bowler. *Team* Somerset (1911–13, 3 matches).
Career batting
3–6–0–96–33–16.00–0–*ct* 0

He was Somerset Chairman 1954–59.

Sowden, Abraham
(birth registered as Abram Sowden)
Professional. *b:* 1.12.1853, Great Horton, Bradford, Yorkshire. *d:* 5.7.1921, Heaton, Bradford, Yorkshire. Middle order right-hand batsman, right-hand fast round-arm bowler. *Team* Yorkshire (1878–87, 8 matches).
Career batting
10–14–0–163–37–11.64–0–*ct* 1
Bowling 70–0

His final first-class match was for an England XI in 1902.

Sowter, Unwin
Amateur. *b:* 22.4.1839, Derby. *d:* 14.4.1910, Derby. Middle order right-hand batsman, good point field. *Sch* Derby School. *Team* Derbyshire (1871–76, 7 matches).
Career batting
7–11–1–128–47*–12.80–0–*ct* 7

He assisted in the founding of Derbyshire CCC and was for some years on the Committee.

Spanswick, John George
Professional. *b:* 30.9.1933, Folkestone, Kent. He married a niece of L. E. G. Ames (Kent). Lower order

right-hand batsman, right-arm medium fast bowler. *Team* Kent (1955–56, 16 matches).
Career batting
16–22–1–135–24–6.42–0–*ct* 7
Bowling 1175–36–32.63–0–0–4/64

Sparkes, George
Professional. *b:* 8.8.1845, Westbourne, Sussex. *d:* 9.3.1908, Old Fishbourne, Bosham, Sussex. Middle order batsman. *Team* Sussex (1875, 1 match).
Career batting
1–2–0–0–0–0.00–*ct* 0

Sparks, John
Professional. *c:* 9.4.1778, Bramley, Surrey. *d:* 5.3.1854, Edinburgh, Scotland. Hard hitting batsman, slow under-arm bowler, but with the arm extended somewhat from his side. *Teams* Surrey (1803–29); Middlesex (1807–16); Kent (1822).
Career batting
50–93–14–1016–89–12.86–0–*ct* 34
Bowling 41 wickets (no analyses)–3–1–5/?

Sparks, John Barnes
Amateur. *b:* 31.5.1873, Morar, India. *d:* 29.3.1920, Marylebone, London. Middle order right-hand batsman, wicket-keeper. *Team* Royal Navy (1913).
Career batting
1–2–0–17–13–8.50–0–*ct* 0

Sparling, John Trevor
Amateur. *b:* 24.7.1938, Mount Eden, Auckland, New Zealand. Middle order right-hand batsman, off break bowler. *Team* Auckland (1956/7 to 1970/1). *Tours* New Zealand to England 1958, to South Africa and Australia 1961/2. *Tests* New Zealand (1958 to 1963/4, 11 matches).
Career batting
127–215–26–4606–105–24.37–2–*ct* 86
Bowling 7223–318–22.71–17–3–7/49
Test batting
11–20–2–229–50–12.72–0–*ct* 3
Bowling 327–5–65.40–0–0–1/9
He took 38 wickets, av 20.28, on the 1958 tour to England and played in three Tests.

Sparrow, Adolphus James
Amateur. *b:* 10.5.1869, Alverstoke, Hampshire. *d:* 6.9.1936, Minster, Kent. Middle order batsman. *Team* Hampshire (1902, 1 match).
Career batting
1–1–0–1–1–1.00–0–*ct* 0

Sparrow, Guy Ratcliff
Amateur. *b:* 2.7.1877, Aston, Birmingham. *d:* 4.1.1958, Burton-on-Trent, Staffordshire. Middle order right-hand batsman. *Team* Derbyshire (1905, 2 matches).
Career batting
2–4–0–75–64–18.75–0–*ct* 0

Speak, Gary John
Cricketer. *b:* 26.4.1962, Chorley, Lancashire. Tail end right-hand batsman, right-arm fast medium bowler. *Team* Lancashire (1981–82, 5 matches).
Career batting
5–6–4–27–15*–13.50–0–*ct* 3
Bowling 230–1–230.00–0–0–1/78

Speak, Nicholas Jason
Cricketer. *b:* 21.11.1966, Manchester, Lancashire. Middle order right-hand batsman, right-arm medium pace or off break bowler. *Team* Lancashire (1986/7 to 1992, 53 matches). *Tour* Lancashire to Jamaica 1986/7.
Career batting
53–92–7–3380–232–39.76–6–*ct* 35
Bowling 92–2–46.00–0–0–1/0
He hit 1,892 runs, av 57.33, in 1992, including 232 for Lancashire v Leicestershire at Leicester.

Speak, Walter John
Amateur. *b:* 20.2.1873, Ripon, Yorkshire. *d:* 21.6.1943, Victoria, British Columbia, Canada. Lower order left-hand batsman, leg break bowler. *Team* Nottinghamshire (1905, 3 matches).
Career batting
3–6–0–39–19–6.50–0–*ct* 0
Bowling 54–0

Speed, Andrew Watson
Amateur. *b:* 19.1.1899, Glasgow, Scotland. *d:* 17.7.1990, Bromsgrove, Worcestershire. Lower order right-hand batsman, right-arm fast medium bowler. *Team* Warwickshire (1927–28, 8 matches).
Career batting
8–7–3–29–11*–7.25–0–*ct* 1
Bowling 538–29–18.55–2–0–6/81

Speed, Francis Elmer
Amateur. *b:* 28.2.1859, Paddington, London. *d:* 23.8.1928, Knowlton Court, Sandwich, Kent. Middle order right-hand batsman, wicket-keeper. *Sch* Rugby. *Team* MCC (1882–84).
Career batting
3–5–0–30–16–6.00–0–*ct* 0
His County cricket was for Herefordshire (1881).

Speight, Martin Peter
Cricketer. *b:* 24.10.1967, Walsall, Staffordshire. Middle order right-hand batsman, wicket-keeper. *Sch* Hurstpierpoint. *Teams* Sussex (1986–92, 78 matches); Wellington (1989/90).
Career batting
80–130–12–4164–179–35.28–8–*ct* 58
Bowling 32–2–16.00–0–0–1/2
He hit 1,000 runs in a season twice (best 1,375, av 40.44, in 1990).

Spelman, Guy Dennis
Cricketer. *b:* 18.10.1958, Westminster, London. Lower order left-hand batsman, right-arm medium

pace bowler. *Sch* Sevenoaks. *Team* Kent (1980–82, 7 matches).
Career batting
7–7–1–9–4–1.50–0–*ct* 2
Bowling 357–10–35.70–0–0–2/27

Spence, Lawrence Arthur
Professional. *b:* 14.1.1932, Blaby, Leicestershire. Middle order right-hand batsman, leg break bowler, good outfield. *Team* Leicestershire (1952–54, 20 matches).
Career batting
20–34–6–326–44–11.64–0–*ct* 4
Bowling 9–0

Spencer, Alan Horace
Professional. *b:* 4.7.1936, Lee Green, London. Middle order right-hand batsman, off break bowler, slip field. *Team* Worcestershire (1957–61, 27 matches).
Career batting
27–52–1–934–85–18.31–0–*ct* 22
Bowling 23–0

Spencer, Charles Richard
Amateur. *b:* 21.6.1903, Llandough, Cardiff. *d:* 29.9.1941, South Havant, Hampshire. Lower order right-hand batsman, wicket-keeper. *Sch* Clifton. *Teams* Oxford U (1923); Glamorgan (1925, 1 match).
Career batting
4–6–2–46–17–11.50–0–*ct* 1–*st* 1

Spencer, Charles Terence
Professional. *b:* 18.8.1931, Braunstone, Leicester. Nephew of H. A. Smith (Leicestershire). Lower order right-hand batsman, right-arm medium pace bowler. *Team* Leicestershire (1952–74, 496 matches).
Career batting
506–687–142–5871–90–10.77–0–*ct* 379
Bowling 36486–1367–26.69–47–6–9/63

He took 123 wickets, av 19.56, in 1961. His best bowling was 9/63 for Leicestershire v Yorkshire at Huddersfield in 1954. He was a first-class umpire (1979–83).

Spencer, Harry Norman Ernest
Amateur. *b:* 1.10.1901, Shipston-on-Stour, Warwickshire. *d:* 13.8.1954, Hammersmith, London. Lower order right-hand batsman, right-arm medium bowler. *Teams* Worcestershire (1927, 1 match); Warwickshire (1930, 3 matches).
Career batting
4–4–1–32–26–10.66–*ct* 3
Bowling 214–3–71.33–0–0–1/34

Spencer, Helm
Professional. *b:* 31.12.1891, Padiham, Lancashire. *d:* 7.12.1974, Burnley Lane Head, Burnley, Lancashire. Lower order right-hand batsman, right-arm fast bowler. *Teams* Lancashire (1914, 2 matches); Glamorgan (1923–25, 39 matches); Wales (1923–24).
Career batting
43–73–4–799–56–11.57–0–*ct* 40
Bowling 2517–111–22.67–4–0–7/33

Spencer, Henry
Professional. *b:* 1872. *d:* 4.12.1936, Willesden Green, Middlesex. Middle order right-hand batsman. *Team* Derbyshire (1895, 1 match).
Career batting
1–1–0–0–0–0.00–0–*ct* 0

Spencer, John
Cricketer. *b:* 6.10.1949, Brighton, Sussex. Lower order right-hand batsman, right-arm medium pace bowler. *Teams* Sussex (1969–80, 186 matches), Cambridge U (1970–72, blue all three years).
Career batting
215–286–80–2787–79–13.52–0–*ct* 75
Bowling 14622–554–26.39–21–1–6/19

Spencer, Ralph
Amateur. *b:* 14.4.1861, Newburn-on-Tyne, Northumberland. *d:* 23.8.1926, Netherwitton Hall, Morpeth, Northumberland. Great-nephew of W. B Trevelyan (Cambridge U 1842). Middle order right-hand batsman, right-arm fast bowler, slip field. *Sch* Harrow. *Team* Cambridge U (1881–82, blue 1881).
Career batting
12–20–0–181–57–9.05–0–*ct* 23
Bowling 461–19–24.26–0–0–3/19

His County cricket was for Northumberland (1882–99).

Spencer, Thomas
Amateur. *b:* 10.6.1850. *d:* 28.11.1933, Bishopsteignton, Devon. Middle order batsman. *Team* Somerset (1891–93, 3 matches).
Career batting
3–5–1–30–14–7.50–0–*ct* 5

He first played for Somerset (not first-class) in 1887. He was Somerset joint Hon Secretary 1890–94.

Spencer, Thomas William, OBE
Professional. *b:* 22.3.1914, Deptford, London. Middle order right-hand batsman, right-arm medium pace bowler. *Team* Kent (1935–46, 76 matches).
Career batting
76–120–13–2152–96–20.11–0–*ct* 36
Bowling 19–1–19.00–0–0–1/19

He was a first-class umpire 1950–80, standing in 17 Test matches (1954–78).

Spencer, Walter Gordon
Amateur. *b:* 2.8.1912, Chingford, Essex. *d:* 20.7.1971, Chelmsford, Essex. Middle order right-hand batsman, slow left-arm bowler. *Sch* Bancroft's. *Team* Essex (1938–48, 3 matches).
Career batting
3–5–1–52–25–13.00–0–*ct* 0
Bowling 8–1–8.00–0–0–1/8

He also played for Suffolk (1936).

Spencer-Smith, Gilbert Joshua
Amateur. *b:* 17.12.1843, Brooklands, Hampshire. *d:* 4.2.1928, Maidenstone Heath, Bursledon, Hampshire. Twin brother of Orlando (Hampshire), uncle of R. C. Gosling (Essex), nephew of H. W. Wilder (Old Etonians 1817). Middle order right-hand batsman, slow right-arm bowler. *Sch* Eton. *Team* Hampshire (1864, 1 match).
Career batting
1–2–0–20–11–10.00–0–*ct* 0

Spencer-Smith, Rev Orlando
Amateur. *b:* 17.12.1843, Brooklands, Hampshire. *d:* 23.11.1920, Swanwick, Southampton, Hampshire. Twin brother of G. J. (Hampshire), uncle of R. C. Gosling (Essex), nephew of H. W. Wilder (Old Etonians). Middle order right-hand batsman, slow right-arm bowler. *Sch* Eton. *Teams* Hampshire (1866, 1 match); Oxford U (1866, blue).
Career batting
7–11–1–354–98–35.40–0–*ct* 0
Bowling 130–3–43.33–0–0–2/53
He also played for Dorset (1873).

Spens, Major General James
Amateur. *b:* 30.3.1853, Subathoo, India. *d:* 19.6.1934, Folkestone, Kent. Middle order right-hand batsman, right-hand medium pace round-arm bowler, good cover point. *Sch* Rugby and Haileybury. *Team* Hampshire (1884–99, 10 matches).
Career batting
13–25–1–581–118*–24.20–1–*ct* 6
Bowling 16–0

Sperry, James
Professional. *b:* 19.3.1910, Thornton, Leicestershire. Lower order left-hand batsman, left-arm fast medium bowler. *Team* Leicestershire (1937–52, 187 matches).
Career batting
188–265–99–1193–35–7.18–0–*ct* 52
Bowling 13958–492–28.36–19–4–7/19
His best season was 1948 with 81 wickets, av 23.55.

Spicer, Norman
Amateur. *b:* 10.4.1879, Eltham, Kent. *d:* 1.9.1936, Paddington, London. Lower order batsman, useful bowler. *Sch* The Leys. *Team* Cambridge U (1901).
Career batting
1–2–0–7–6–3.50–0–*ct* 2
Bowling 52–2–26.00–0–0–1/1
An all-round athlete, he represented Cambridge at rugby football, athletics and lacrosse. He also played rugby for Kent.

Spicer, Peter Alfred
Professional. *b:* 11.5.1939, Ilford, Essex. *d:* 18.8.1969, Hainault, Essex. He was killed in a road accident. Middle order left-hand batsman, slow left-arm bowler. *Team* Essex (1962–63, 17 matches).
Career batting
17–29–2–526–86–19.48–0–*ct* 4
Bowling 55–2–27.50–0–0–2/1

Spicer, William Baldwin
Professional. *b:* 18.5.1846, Kensington, London. *d:* 22.9.1892, Kennington, London. Lower order batsman, left-hand medium pace round-arm bowler, slip field. *Team* Surrey (1870, 1 match).
Career batting
1–2–0–16–14–8.00–0–*ct* 0
Bowling 17–1–17.00–0–0–1/17

Spiller, Cecil Willmington
Amateur. *b:* 19.8.1900, Cardiff, Glamorgan. *d:* 5.4.1974, Canton, Cardiff, Glamorgan. Lower order batsman, useful bowler. *Team* Glamorgan (1922, 2 matches).
Career batting
2–4–0–20–14–5.00–0–*ct* 0
Bowling 144–4–36.00–0–0–3/50

Spiller, William John
Amateur. *b:* 8.7.1886, St Fagans, Cardiff, Glamorgan. *d:* 9.6.1970, St Fagans, Cardiff, Glamorgan. Middle order right-hand batsman. *Team* Glamorgan (1921–23, 13 matches).
Career batting
13–22–0–411–104–18.68–1–*ct* 7
Bowling 31–0
He first played for Glamorgan (pre first-class) in 1905. A noted rugby footballer, he was a centre threequarter for Cardiff and Wales.

Spillman, George
Professional. *b:* 24.10.1856, Strand, London. *d:* 18.4.1911, Brighton, Sussex. Middle order right-hand batsman, wicket-keeper. *Sch* King's College, London. *Team* Middlesex (1886, 10 matches).
Career batting
12–20–0–477–87–23.85–0–*ct* 14–*st* 3
Bowling 12–1–12.00–0–0–1/12
About 1902 he fell down the cabin stairs of a passenger steamer and so damaged his right leg that it had to be amputated, thus ending his cricket career – he was a coach in Jersey at the time.

Spilsbury, John William Edward
Amateur. *b:* 27.10.1933, Worcester. Grandson of G. F. Wheldon (Worcestershire). Lower order right-hand batsman, right-arm fast medium bowler. *Team* Worcestershire (1952, 1 match).
Career batting
1–1–0–16–16–16.00–0–*ct* 1
Bowling 86–0

Spinks, Edwin Frederick
Professional. *b:* 3.8.1902, Bermuda. *d:* 19.10.1982, Orsett, Essex. Lower order batsman, useful bowler. *Team* Essex (1926, 2 matches).

Career batting
2–3–1–2–2–1.00–0–*ct* 1
Bowling 81–0

Spiro, Douglas Gray
Amateur. *b:* 21.12.1863, Melbourne, Victoria, Australia. *d:* 16.1.1935, Westminster, London. Hard-hitting middle order right-hand batsman, right-arm medium pace bowler, good deep field. *Sch* Harrow. *Team* Cambridge U (1883–85, blue 1884).
Career batting
12–21–1–207–47–10.35–0–*ct* 3
Due to an accident he played little cricket in 1883. His final first-class match was for MCC in 1890.

Spofforth, Frederick Robert
Amateur. *b:* 9.9.1853, Balmain, Sydney, New South Wales, Australia. *d:* 4.6.1926, Ditton Hill Lodge, Long Ditton, Surrey. Brother-in-law of G. W. S. Lyttelton (Cambridge U). Hard-hitting lower order right-hand batsman, right-arm fast medium bowler. *Teams* New South Wales (1874/5 to 1884/5, 12 matches); Victoria (1885/6 to 1887/8, 5 matches). *Tours* Australia to England 1878, 1880, 1882, 1884, 1886, to North America 1878. *Tests* Australia (1876/7 to 1886/7, 18 matches).
Career batting
155–236–41–1928–56–9.88–0–*ct* 83
Bowling 12759–853–14.95–84–32–9/18
Test batting
18–29–6–217–50–9.43–0–*ct* 11
Bowling 1731–94–18.41–7–4–7/44
His record on his tours to England was quite outstanding. In 1884 he took 207 wickets, av 12.82; in 1882, 157, av 13.24; and in 1878, 97, av 11.00. He was known as the 'Demon' bowler. In 1888 he emigrated to England and played for Derbyshire from 1889 to 1891 (not first-class), captaining the County in 1890. His best bowling was 9/18 for Australians v Oxford U at Oxford in 1886. He appeared regularly in the Scarborough Festival matches from 1888, and his final first-class match was for MCC v Yorkshire at Scarborough in 1897.

Spooner, Archibald Franklin
Amateur. *b:* 21.5.1886, Litherland, Lancashire. *d:* 11.1.1965, Dartmouth, Devon. Brother of R. H. (Lancashire). Stylish middle order right-hand batsman. *Sch* Haileybury. *Team* Lancashire (1906–09, 18 matches).
Career batting
18–33–1–500–83–15.62–0–*ct* 8

Spooner, Reginald Herbert
Amateur. *b:* 21.10.1880, Litherland, Lancashire. *d:* 2.10.1961, Lincoln. Brother of A. F. (Lancashire). Stylish opening right-hand batsman, slow right-arm bowler. *Sch* Marlborough. *Team* Lancashire (1899–1921, 170 matches). *Tests* England (1905–12, 10 matches).
Career batting
237–393–16–13681–247–36.28–31–*ct* 142
Bowling 582–6–97.00–0–0–1/5
Test batting
10–15–0–481–119–32.06–1–*ct* 4
He hit 1,000 runs in a season six times, going on to 2,000 once: 2,312, av 51.37, in 1911. Each of his five double centuries was for Lancashire, the highest being 247 v Nottinghamshire at Trent Bridge in 1903. His final first-class match was for MCC in 1923. Because of his elegant driving and stroke-play, he has come to be regarded as the supreme example of the amateur batsman of the 'Golden Age'. He was a Test selector in 1921 and President of Lancashire 1945–46. A noted rugby footballer, he was a centre three-quarter for Liverpool and England.

Spooner, Richard Thompson
Professional. *b:* 30.12.1919, Stockton-on-Tees, Co Durham. Forceful opening left-hand batsman, wicket-keeper. *Team* Warwickshire (1948–59, 312 matches). *Tours* MCC to India, Pakistan and Ceylon 1951/2, to West Indies 1953/4; Commonwealth to India 1950/1. *Tests* England 1951/2 to 1955, 7 matches).
Career batting
359–580–72–13851–168*–27.26–12–*ct* 589–*st* 178
Bowling 46–0
Test batting
7–14–1–354–92–27.23–0–3–*ct* 10–*st* 2
He hit 1,000 runs in a season six times (best 1,767, av 43.09, in 1951). He also played for Durham (pre first-class, 1946–47).

Spottiswoode, William Hugh
Amateur. *b:* 12.7.1864, Belgravia, London. *d:* 20.8.1915, Llandrindod Wells, Radnorshire. Nephew of R. J. H. Arbuthnot (Kent), father-in-law of G. E. V. Crutchley (Middlesex). Hard-hitting middle order right-hand batsman, slow under-arm bowler. *Sch* Eton. *Team* Kent (1890, 2 matches).
Career batting
2–3–0–51–37–17.00–0–*ct* 1
He was a partner in the publishing company of Eyre and Spottiswoode.

Spowart, Thomas
Amateur. *b:* 24.3.1903, Dunfermline, Fife, Scotland. *d:* 12.5.1971, Edinburgh, Scotland. Middle order right-hand batsman. *Team* Scotland (1932–38).
Career batting
4–7–0–98–66–14.00–0–*ct* 0

Spray, Philip Henry
Cricketer. *b:* 28.9.1945, Bedford. Middle order right-hand batsman. *Sch* Bedford. *Team* Oxford U (1967–68).
Career batting
9–13–2–135–54–12.27–0–*ct* 4
His County cricket was for Bedfordshire (1964–73).

Spring, Trevor Coleridge
Amateur. *b:* 6.2.1882, Kidderpore, Bengal, India. *d:* 13.3.1926, Westminster, London. He died suddenly after an operation. Middle order right-hand batsman, useful bowler. *Sch* Blundells. *Team* Somerset (1909–10, 8 matches).
Career batting
11–19–1–324–117–18.00–1–*ct* 3
Bowling 71–3–23.66–0–0–3/59
He final first-class match was for the Army in 1919. He also played for Devon (1904) and Northumberland (1912).

Spring, William Amos
Professional. *b:* 17.5.1880, Dulwich, Surrey. *d:* 14.3.1958, Chase Side, Enfield, Middlesex. Middle order right-hand batsman, right-arm fast medium bowler. *Team* Surrey (1906–13, 68 matches).
Career batting
68–106–13–1968–135–21.16–2–*ct* 54
Bowling 2093–71–29.47–3–1–6/38

Springall, John Denis
Professional. *b:* 19.9.1932, Southwark, London. Opening or middle order right-hand batsman, right-arm medium pace bowler, occasional wicket-keeper. *Team* Nottinghamshire (1955–63, 119 matches).
Career batting
121–224–24–5176–107–25.88–2–*ct* 51
Bowling 3312–80–41.40–2–0–6/43
He hit 1,000 runs in a season twice (best 1,488, av 35.42, in 1959).

Sprinks, Henry Robert James
Amateur. *b:* 19.8.1905, Alexandria, Egypt. *d:* 23.5.1986, Bramshaw, Hampshire. Lower order right-hand batsman, right-arm fast bowler. *Team* Hampshire (1925–29, 21 matches).
Career batting
21–27–9–167–40–9.27–0–*ct* 14
Bowling 1338–29–46.13–0–0–4/56

Sprot, Edward Mark
Amateur. *b:* 4.2.1872, Edinburgh, Scotland. *d:* 8.10.1945, Lower Bourne, Farnham, Surrey. Forcing middle order right-hand batsman, right-arm medium pace bowler, good close field. *Sch* Harrow. *Team* Hampshire (1898–1914, 267 matches).
Career batting
270–458–28–12328–147–28.66–13–*ct* 228
Bowling 1865–55–33.90–1–0–5/28
He hit 1,000 runs in a season four times (best 1,272, av 33.47, in 1907). He captained Hampshire 1903–14. A talented all-round sportsman, he won the Army Rackets Challenge Cup, was a good golfer, a keen shot and fisherman and a noted billiards player.

Sproule, Wallace
Amateur. *b:* 17.4.1891, Killyleagh, Co Down, Ireland. *d:* 10.5.1957, Belfast, Ireland. Lower order right-hand batsman, right-arm medium pace bowler. *Team* Ireland (1923).
Career batting
1–2–0–1–1–0.50–0–*ct* 2
Bowling 83–6–13.83–0–0–4/64

Spry, Edward James
Professional. *b:* 31.7.1881, Bristol, Gloucestershire. *d:* 18.11.1958, Knowle, Somerset. Lower order right-hand batsman, leg break bowler. *Team* Gloucestershire (1899–1921, 89 matches).
Career batting
89–154–24–1447–76–11.13–0–*ct* 44
Bowling 4307–149–28.90–13–3–8/52

Spurr, Harold
Amateur. *b:* 17.6.1889, Leytonstone, Essex. *d:* 21.12.1962, Dunmow, Essex. Middle order right-hand batsman. *Sch* Merchant Taylors'. *Team* Essex (1923, 1 match).
Career batting
1–2–0–13–9–6.50–0–*ct* 0

Spurway, Rev Edward Popham
Amateur. *b:* 4.4.1863, Heathfield, Somerset. *d:* 8.2.1914, Heathfield, Somerset. Brother of R. P. (Somerset), father of F. E. (Somerset) and M. V. (Somerset). Middle order right-hand batsman. *Sch* Charterhouse. *Team* Somerset (1885–98, 2 matches).
Career batting
2–4–0–26–15–6.50–0–*ct* 1
He played in trials at Cambridge U, but not in first-class matches.

Spurway, Rev Francis Edward
Amateur. *b:* 8.8.1894, Winchester, Hampshire. *d:* 30.12.1980, Mount House, Halse, Taunton, Somerset. Son of E. P. (Somerset), brother of M. V. (Somerset), nephew of R. P. (Somerset). Lower order right-hand batsman, wicket-keeper. *Sch* King's Bruton. *Team* Somerset (1920–29, 23 matches).
Career batting
23–39–4–328–35–9.37–*ct* 29–*st* 14

Spurway, Michael Vyvyan
Amateur. *b:* 24.1.1909, Heathfield, Somerset. Son of E. P. (Somerset), brother of F. E. (Somerset), nephew of R. P. (Somerset). Lower order right-hand batsman, wicket-keeper. *Sch* St Edward's, Oxford. *Team* Somerset (1929, 3 matches).
Career batting
3–5–2–22–10–7.33–0–*ct* 4–*st* 1

Spurway, Robert Popham
Amateur. *b:* 16.7.1866, Heathfield, Somerset. *d:* 4.12.1898, Woolwich, London. Brother of E. P. (Somerset), uncle of F. E. (Somerset) and M. V. (Somerset). Middle order right-hand batsman, off break bowler. *Sch* Haileybury and Sherborne. *Teams* Natal (1889/90); Somerset (1893–98, 16 matches).

Spyers, Thomas Roper

Career batting
19–34–3–578–108*–18.64–1–*ct* 3

Spyers, Thomas Roper
Amateur. *b:* 7.12.1868, Faversham, Kent. *d:* 19.2.1961, Chelsea, London. Middle order right-hand batsman, wicket-keeper. *Sch* Radley. *Team* MCC (1890).
Career batting
1–2–0–9–9–4.50–0–*ct* 0

He played no first-class cricket at Oxford U, but did win a blue for rackets. In a very varied life he was an actor, a theatrical producer, schoolmaster and hotel proprietor.

Squire, Dick
(birth registered as Dick Squires)
Professional. *b:* 31.12.1864, Cleckheaton, Yorkshire. *d:* 28.4.1922, Scholes, Yorkshire. Lower order right-hand batsman, slow left-arm bowler. *Team* Yorkshire (1893, 1 match).
Career batting
1–2–0–0–0–0.00–0–*ct* 0
Bowling 25–0

Squire, Samuel Gimson
Amateur. *b:* 14.1.1879, Leicester. *d:* 18.9.1962, Duston, Northamptonshire. Tail end batsman, useful bowler. *Sch* Wyggeston GS. *Team* Cambridge U (1900).
Career batting
1–2–0–12–12–6.00–0–*ct* 0
Bowling 61–2–30.50–0–0–2/61

Squires, Harry Stanley
Amateur, turned professional in 1930. *b:* 22.2.1909, Kingston-upon-Thames, Surrey. *d:* 24.1.1950, Old Deer Park, Richmond, Surrey. He died following a short illness from a virus. Stylish middle order right-hand batsman, right-arm medium pace off break or leg break bowler. *Team* Surrey (1928–49, 402 matches).
Career batting
410–658–44–19186–236–31.24–37–*ct* 140
Bowling 10817–306–35.34–7–0–8/52

He hit 1,000 runs in a season eleven times (best 1,847, av 36.94, in 1947). His three double centuries were all for Surrey, the highest being 236 v Lancashire at the Oval in 1933.

Squires, Peter John
Cricketer. *b:* 4.8.1951, Ripon, Yorkshire. Middle order right-hand batsman. *Team* Yorkshire (1972–76, 49 matches).
Career batting
49–84–8–1271–70–16.72–0–*ct* 14
Bowling 32–0

A noted rugby footballer, he played for Harrogate, Yorkshire and England, touring South Africa in 1973.

Srikkanth, Krishnamachari
Cricketer. *b:* 12.12.1959, Madras, India. Opening right-hand batsman, right-arm medium pace bowler. *Team* Tamil Nadu (1978/9 to 1991/2). *Tours* India to Pakistan 1982/3, 1989/90, to Sri Lanka 1985/6, to Australia 1984/5 (not first-class), 1985/6, 1991/2, to England 1983 (World Cup), 1986, to Sharjah (not first-class) 1984/5, 1985/6, 1986/7, 1987/8, 1988/9, 1989/90, to West Indies 1988/9, to Bangladesh (not first-class) 1988/9, to Australia and New Zealand (World Cup) 1991/2; Young Indians to Zimbabwe 1983/4. *Tests* India (1981/2 to 1991/2, 43 matches).
Career batting
125–199–3–6860–172–35.00–10–*ct* 80
Bowling 1401–28–50.03–0–0–3/14
Test batting
43–72–3–2062–123–29.88–2–*ct* 40
Bowling 114–0

An attacking batsman, he played in all three Tests on the 1986 tour to England, but impetuosity led too often to his downfall. He captained India in four Tests.

Stacey, Charles Frederick
Professional. *b:* 27.4.1878, Chalfont St Giles, Buckinghamshire. *d:* 1950, Scotland. Lower order batsman, useful bowler. *Team* Surrey (1901, 1 match).
Career batting
1–1–1–0–0*–no av–0–*ct* 0
Bowling 148–1–148.00–0–0–1/78

Stackpole, Keith Raymond, MBE
Amateur. *b:* 10.7.1940, Collingwood, Melbourne, Victoria, Australia. Son of K. W. (Victoria). Excellent opening right-hand batsman, leg break bowler, good slip field. *Team* Victoria (1959/60 to 1973/4, 75 matches). *Tours* Australia to South Africa 1966/7, 1969/70, to India and Ceylon 1969/70, to England 1972, to West Indies 1972/3, to New Zealand 1973/4. *Tests* Australia (1965/6 to 1973/4, 43 matches).
Career batting
167–279–22–10100–207–39.29–22–*ct* 166
Bowling 5814–148–39.28–2–0–5/38
Test batting
43–80–5–2807–207–37.42–7–*ct* 47
Bowling 1001–15–66.73–0–0–2/33

On his only tour to England he topped the Test batting averages with 485 runs, av 53.88, and in first-class matches hit 1,309 runs, av 43.63, altogether being the success of the tour. His highest score was 207 for Australia v England at Brisbane in 1970/1. He hit 1,000 runs in an Australian season once.

Staddon, Ernest Henry
Amateur. *b:* 2.12.1882, Westbury-on-Trym, Bristol, Gloucestershire. *d:* 23.7.1965, Bristol, Gloucestershire. Middle order batsman. *Team* Gloucestershire (1912, 1 match).

Career batting
1–2–0–16–12–8.00–0–*ct* 0

Stafford, James Pratt
Professional. *b:* 1.1.1844, Godalming, Surrey. *d:* 24.8.1919, Fratton, Portsmouth, Hampshire. Lower order batsman, useful bowler. *Team* Surrey (1864, 1 match).
Career batting
1–2–0–0–0–0.00–0–*ct* 0
Bowling 31–0

Staines, Alfred
Professional. *b:* 22.5.1838, Charlton, London. *d:* 13.6.1910, Sydenham, London. Tail end right-hand batsman, wicket-keeper. *Team* Kent (1863–64, 5 matches).
Career batting
5–10–4–6–2–1.00–0–*ct* 4–*st* 5

Stainton, Robert George
Amateur. *b:* 23.5.1910, Whitstable, Kent. Middle order right-hand batsman, slow right-arm bowler. *Sch* Malvern. *Teams* Oxford U (1932–34, blue 1933); Sussex (1936–47, 45 matches).
Career batting
61–104–8–2330–89–24.27–0–*ct* 27
Bowling 25–1–25.00–0–0–1/12

Stallard, George
Amateur. *b:* 14.1.1856, Northwick, Worcester. *d:* 21.8.1912, North Tawton, Devon. Middle order right-hand batsman. *Sch* Rossall. *Team* An England XI (1875).
Career batting
1 match, did not bat –*ct* 0
He played in trials at Cambridge U, but his only first-class match was against the University. He was Chief Justice of Sierra Leone, 1897 to 1901.

Stallibrass, Michael James Dahl
Cricketer. *b:* 28.6.1951, Poltimore, Exeter, Devon. Lower order left-hand batsman, off break bowler. *Sch* Lancing. *Team* Oxford U (1972–74, blue 1974).
Career batting
21–31–7–194–24–8.08–0–*ct* 7
Bowling 993–22–45.13–1–0–5/80

Stanbury, Richard Vivian Macaulay
Amateur. *b:* 5.2.1916, Madras, India. Lower order right-hand batsman, wicket-keeper. *Sch* Shrewsbury. *Team* Somerset (1935–36, 2 matches).
Career batting
2–4–1–31–21–10.33–0–*ct* 2

Standen, James Alfred
Professional. *b:* 30.5.1935, Edmonton, Middlesex. Lower order right-hand batsman, right-arm medium pace bowler. *Team* Worcestershire (1959–70, 133 matches).
Career batting
133–174–28–2092–92*–14.32–*ct* 83
Bowling 7934–313–25.34–13–0–7/30
His best season was 1964, with 64 wickets, av 13.00. He also played for Hertfordshire (1956–57 and 1971–73). A noted goalkeeper, he played soccer for Arsenal, Luton, West Ham United, Millwall and Portsmouth and Detroit Cougars. In 1964 he was in West Ham's FA Cup-winning side and Worcestershire's Championship-winning side.

Standing, David Kevin
Cricketer. *b:* 21.10.1963, Brighton, Sussex. Middle order right-hand batsman, off break bowler. *Team* Sussex (1983–88, 43 matches).
Career batting
43–70–10–1130–65–18.83–0–*ct* 17
Bowling 725–6–120.83–0–0–2/28

Standring, Kenneth Brooks
Amateur. *b:* 17.2.1935, Clitheroe, Lancashire. Lower order left-hand batsman, right-arm fast bowler. *Team* Lancashire (1955–59, 8 matches).
Career batting
13–22–5–255–41–15.00–0–*ct* 2
Bowling 867–25–34.68–0–0–4/61

Stanford, Ross Milton
Amateur. *b:* 25.9.1917, Fulham Gardens, Adelaide, South Australia. Middle order right-hand batsman, right-arm medium pace bowler. *Team* South Australia (1935/6 to 1947/8, 10 matches). *Tours* Australian Services to England 1945, to India and Ceylon 1945/6.
Career batting
23–35–3–832–153–26.00–1–*ct* 4
Bowling 25–0

Stanhope, Rt Hon Edward
Amateur. *b:* 24.9.1840, Belgravia, Westminster, London. *d:* 21.12.1893, Chevening, Sevenoaks, Kent. Middle order right-hand batsman. *Sch* Harrow. *Team* Kent (1861, 1 match).
Career batting
3–6–1–44–17–8.80–0–*ct* 1
His final first-class match was for MCC in 1879. He was MP for Mid Lincolnshire from 1874 and Horncastle from 1885 and held at one time the offices of Secretary of State for the Colonies and Secretary of State for War.

Stanley, Edward
Amateur. *b:* 29.6.1852, Wincanton, Somerset. *d:* 7.4.1896, Accra, Gold Coast. Middle order batsman. *Sch* Tonbridge and Victoria College, Guernsey. *Team* Somerset (1884, 1 match).
Career batting
1–1–0–0–0–0.00–0–*ct* 0

Stanley, Ernest Arthur William
Professional. *b:* 27.9.1926, Leyton, Essex. Middle order right-hand batsman, off break bowler. *Team* Essex (1950–52, 13 matches).
Career batting
13–21–3–226–35–12.55–0–*ct*2
Bowling 8–0

Stanley, Harry Cecil
Amateur. *b:* 16.2.1888, Rotherham, Yorkshire. *d:* 18.5.1934, Scarborough, Yorkshire, Middle order right-hand batsman. *Team* Yorkshire (1911–13, 8 matches).
Career batting
8–13–0–155–42–11.92–0–*ct* 6

Stanley, Henry Thomas
Amateur. *b:* 20.8.1873, Westminster, London. *d:* 16.9.1900, Hekpoort, Transvaal, South Africa. He died whilst on active service in the Boer War. Uncle of L. Heathcoat-Amory (Oxford U), cousin of J. Heathcoat-Amory (Oxford U). Middle order right-hand batsman. *Sch* Eton. *Team* Somerset (1894–99, 50 matches). *Tour* Priestley to West Indies 1896/7.
Career batting
63–117–4–1691–127–14.96–1–*ct* 27
Bowling 250–9–27.77–0–0–2/11

Stanley, Neil Alan
Cricketer. *b:* 16.5.1968, Bedford. Middle order right-hand batsman, right-arm medium pace bowler. *Sch* Bedford Modern. *Team* Northamptonshire (1988–92, 21 matches). *Tour* Northamptonshire to South Africa 1991/2.
Career batting
21–35–4–1019–132–32.87–1–*ct* 9
Bowling 19–0
He also played for Bedfordshire (1987–89).

Stanley-Clarke, Arthur Christopher Lancelot
(changed name from A. C. L. Clarke)
Amateur. *b:* 30.6.1886, Brighton, Sussex. *d:* 8.1.1983, Shiel, Baily, Co Dublin, Ireland. Middle order right-hand batsman. *Sch* Winchester. *Team* Army (1923–24).
Career batting
5–8–1–262–66–37.42–0–*ct* 1
His County cricket was for Dorset (1909). He played in trials at Oxford U, but not in first-class matches.

Stannard, George Arthur
Professional. *b:* 9.7.1892, Steyning, Sussex. *d:* 28.6.1971, Brighton, Sussex. Middle order right-hand batsman, right-arm slow medium bowler. *Team* Sussex (1914–25, 73 matches).
Career batting
73–121–14–1437–114–13.42–1–*ct* 15
Bowling 724–14–51.71–0–0–4/70

Stanning, Henry Duncan
Amateur. *b:* 14.11.1881, Broadfield, Leyland, Lancashire. *d:* 5.3.1946, Kampi-Ya-Moto, Kenya. Brother of John sen (Lancashire), uncle of John jun (Worcestershire). Middle order right-hand batsman. *Sch* Rugby. *Team* Lancashire (33 matches).
Career batting
33–54–1–898–86–16.94–0–*ct* 10
Bowling 3–0

Stanning, John (sen)
Amateur. *b:* 10.10.1877, Broadfield, Leyland, Lancashire. *d:* 19.5.1929, Nakwin, Kenya. He died in a motor accident. Brother of H. D. (Lancashire), father of John jun (Worcestershire). Sound opening or middle order right-hand batsman, good field. *Sch* Rugby. *Teams* Cambridge U (1900, blue); Lancashire (1900–03, 4 matches). *Tour* Hawke to Australia and New Zealand 1902/3.
Career batting
26–45–5–964–120–24.10–1–*ct* 19
Bowling 15–0
His first-class debut was for MCC in 1899. He also played for Cheshire (1902).

Stanning, John (jun)
Amateur. *b:* 24.6.1919, Nairobi, Kenya. Son of John sen (Lancashire), nephew of H. D. (Lancashire). Middle order right-hand batsman. *Sch* Winchester. *Teams* Oxford U (1939, blue); Worcestershire (1939–46, 9 matches).
Career batting
16–22–3–403–56*–21.21–0–*ct* 7

Stanton, John Latham
Amateur. *b:* 8.3.1901, Bristol. *d:* 27.6.1973, Hoyle, Heyshott, Midhurst, Sussex. Middle order right-hand batsman. *Sch* Marlborough. *Team* Gloucestershire (1921–22, 4 matches).
Career batting
4–7–0–80–47–11.42–0–*ct* 0

Stanworth, John
Cricketer. *b:* 30.9.1960, Oldham, Lancashire. Lower order right-hand batsman, wicket-keeper. *Team* Lancashire (1983–92, 44 matches).
Career batting
44–40–11–266–50*–9.17–0–*ct* 63–*st* 10

Stanyard, Anthony Roy
Professional. *b:* 5.4.1938, Plaistow, West Ham, Essex. Middle order right-hand batsman, right-arm medium pace bowler. *Team* Essex (1960, 2 matches).
Career batting
2–3–0–47–26–15.66–0–*ct* 0

Stanyforth, Ronald Thomas
Amateur. *b:* 30.5.1892, Chelsea, London. *d:* 20.2.1964, Kirk Hammerton Hall, Yorkshire. Lower order right-hand batsman, wicket-keeper. *Sch* Eton. *Teams* Oxford U (1914); Yorkshire (1928, 3

matches). *Tours* MCC to South America 1926/7, to South Africa 1927/8, to West Indies 1929/30. *Tests* England (1927/8, 4 matches).
Career batting
61–79–16–1092–91–17.33–0–*ct* 72–*st* 21
Test batting
4–6–1–13–6*–2.60–0–*ct* 7–*st* 2
He captained MCC on the 1927/8 tour to South Africa and led England in four Tests – an unusual appointment since, at that time, he had never appeared in first-class County cricket, most of his matches being military ones. His final first-class match was in 1933 for MCC.

Staple, Richard Wayne
Cricketer. *b:* 25.11.1969, Jamaica. Middle order right-hand batsman, right-arm medium pace bowler. *Team* Jamaica (1989/90 to 1991/2). *Tour* West Indies to England 1991.
Career batting
8–15–0–366–79–24.40–0–*ct* 7
Bowling 90–0
He appeared in a match at the Scarborough Festival after the West Indies tour had officially ended.

Staples, Arthur
Professional. *b:* 4.2.1899, Newstead Colliery, Nottinghamshire. *d:* 9.9.1965, Redhill, Nottinghamshire. Brother of S. J. (Nottinghamshire). Sound middle order right-hand batsman, right-arm medium pace bowler. *Team* Nottinghamshire (1924–38, 353 matches).
Career batting
358–512–59–12763–153*–28.17–12–*ct* 215
Bowling 18942–635–29.82–14–1–7/20
He hit 1,000 runs in a season seven times (best 1,531, av 38.27, in 1932). A useful soccer player, he kept goal for Mansfield Town.

Staples, Cyril Vernon
Amateur. *b:* 1877, Melbourne, Victoria, Australia. *d:* 21.5.1936, Beaumont Hill, Jersey. Lower order batsman, wicket-keeper. *Teams* W. G. Grace's XI (1906); Gentlemen of England (1908).
Career batting
4–6–2–35–14–8.75–0–*ct* 4–*st* 3

Staples, Samuel James
Professional. *b:* 18.9.1892, Newstead Colliery, Nottinghamshire. *d:* 4.6.1950, Standard Hill, Nottingham. Brother of Arthur (Nottinghamshire). Lower order right-hand batsman, off break bowler, good slip field. *Team* Nottinghamshire (1920–34, 368 matches). *Tours* MCC to South Africa 1927/8; to Australia 1928/9 (he returned without playing a first-class match, owing to illness). *Tests* England (1927/8, 3 matches).
Career batting
385–475–95–6470–110–17.02–1–*ct* 339
Bowling 30421–1331–22.85–72–11–9/141
Test batting
3–5–0–65–39–13.00–0–*ct* 0
Bowling 435–15–29.00–0–0–3/50
He took 100 wickets in a season five times (best 132, av 23.03, in 1927). His best bowling was 9/141 for Nottinghamshire v Kent at Canterbury in 1927. He was coach to Hampshire CCC in 1939–48 and a first-class umpire in 1949.

Stapleton, Ernest
Professional. *b:* 15.1.1869, New Basford, Nottinghamshire. *d:* 14.12.1938, Nottingham. Brother-in-law of J. R. Gunn (Nottinghamshire) and G. Gunn (Nottinghamshire), uncle of G. V. Gunn (Nottinghamshire). Opening right-hand batsman. *Team* Derbyshire (1902, 1 match).
Career batting
1–2–0–3–2–1.50–0–*ct* 0
He also played for Glamorgan (pre first-class, 1908–09).

Stapleton, James
Professional. *b:* 8.8.1879, Eastwood, Nottinghamshire. *d:* 10.7.1944, Brinsley, Nottinghamshire. Lower order right-hand batsman, wicket-keeper. *Team* Nottinghamshire (1899–1911, 10 matches).
Career batting
10–15–2–152–21–11.69–0–*ct* 22–*st* 3

Starkie, Sydney
Professional. *b:* 4.4.1926, Burnley, Lancashire. Lower order right-hand batsman, off break bowler, slip field. *Team* Northamptonshire (1951–56, 95 matches).
Career batting
95–110–30–857–60–10.71–0–*ct* 64
Bowling 5685–166–34.24–6–1–6/33

Starmer, Clement Edwin
Professional. *b:* 2.12.1895, Cosby, Leicestershire. *d:* 25.7.1978, Preston Village, North Shields, Northumberland. Middle order right-hand batsman. *Team* Leicestershire (1925, 3 matches).
Career batting
3–4–0–19–8–4.75–0–*ct* 0

Statham, John Brian, CBE
Professional. *b:* 17.6.1930, Gorton, Manchester, Lancashire. Lower order left-hand batsman, right-arm fast medium bowler. *Team* Lancashire (1950–68, 430 matches). *Tours* MCC to Australia and New Zealand 1950/1, 1954/5, 1958/9, 1962/3, to India, Pakistan and Ceylon 1951/2, to West Indies 1953/4, 1959/60, to South Africa 1956/7; Cavaliers to South Africa 1960/1; President's XI to India 1967/8. *Tests* England (1950/1 to 1965, 70 matches).
Career batting
559–647–145–5424–62–10.80–0–*ct* 230
Bowling 36999–2260–16.37–123–11–8/34

Test batting
70–87–28–675–38–11.44–0–*ct* 28
Bowling 6261–252–24.84–9–1–7/39

For a period of about ten years between 1953 and 1963, he was one of England's opening bowlers; he headed the Test averages on the 1953/4 tour to West Indies, being partnered by Trueman, then on the 1954/5 tour to Australia he partnered Tyson, with equal success. This partnership continued in 1955 in England against South Africa. On the 1958/9 tour to Australia he completely outshone both Trueman and Tyson in the Test series. On his fourth visit to Australia in 1962/3, he had lost his nip off the wicket, but he ended the tour standing second in the list of those taking most wickets in a Test career.

He took 100 wickets in an English season 13 times, his best year being 1959 with 139 wickets, av 15.01. The best analysis of his career was 8/34 for Lancashire v Warwickshire at Coventry in 1957, when he took 15/89 in the match. From 1965 to 1967 he captained Lancashire, and in 1966 was awarded the CBE for his services to cricket.

Staunton, Rev Harvey
Amateur. *b:* 21.11.1870, Staunton Hall, Nottinghamshire. *d:* 14.1.1918, Arzizieh, Mesopotamia. Middle order right-hand batsman. *Sch* Bromsgrove. *Team* Nottinghamshire (1903–05, 16 matches).
Career batting
16–24–0–456–78–19.00–0–*ct* 8
Bowling 48–0

He also played for Bedfordshire. He played no first-class cricket at Cambridge U, but did win a blue for rugby.

Staveley, Miles
Professional. *b:* 12.8.1846, St Pancras, London. Lower order right-hand batsman, right-hand fast round-arm bowler. *Team* Surrey (1870, 1 match).
Career batting
1–2–0–3–3–1.50–0–*ct* 0
Bowling 51–1–51.00–0–0–1/24

Staziker, Michael William
Cricketer. *b:* 7.11.1947, Croston, Lancashire. Tail end right-hand batsman, right-arm medium fast bowler. *Team* Lancashire (1970, 2 matches).
Career batting
2–2–2–1–1*–no av–0–*ct* 0
Bowling 269–1–269.00–0–0–1/114

He also played for Cumberland (1976).

Stead, Barry
Professional. *b:* 21.6.1939, Leeds, Yorkshire. *d:* 15.4.1980, Drighlington, Yorkshire. Lower order left-arm batsman, left-arm fast medium bowler. *Teams* Yorkshire (1959, 2 matches); Essex (1962, 1 match); Nottinghamshire (1962–76, 215 matches); Northern Transvaal (1975/6).
Career batting
232–253–77–2166–58–12.30–0–*ct* 59
Bowling 18318–653–28.05–24–2–8/44

His best season was 1972 when he took 98 wickets, av 20.38. He is credited with a match for Essex in 1962, being shown in the scorecard as 'did not bat', but in fact he was not at the ground, as he was playing for Nottinghamshire 2nd XI on the same day.

Stead, Peter
Amateur. *b:* 1930, Yorkshire. Tail end right-hand batsman, right-arm fast medium bowler. *Team* Canada (1954). *Tour* Canada to England 1954
Career batting
3–4–3–6–4*–6.00–0–*ct* 0
Bowling 177–9–19.66–0–0–4/52

Stedman, Fred
Professional. *b:* 4.3.1870. Cobham, Surrey. *d:* 5.2.1918, Bray, Co Wicklow, Ireland. He was accidently killed on the railway. Lower order right-hand batsman, wicket-keeper. *Teams* Surrey (1899–1908, 134 matches); London County (1900–03); Ireland (1912).
Career batting
140–192–68–1535–62–12.37–0–*ct* 266–*st* 50
Bowling 53–0

He was a professional at Woodbrook in Ireland after leaving Surrey.

Stedman, Rev Harry Charles Plumer
Amateur. *b:* 11.10.1848, Great Budworth, Cheshire. *d:* 30.7.1904, Leire, Leicestershire. Lower order right-hand batsman, right-hand fast round-arm bowler, cover point. *Team* Cambridge U (1871, blue).
Career batting
4–8–1–98–22–14.00–0–*ct* 2

His County cricket was for Cheshire (1866–68), Bedfordshire (1876–82) and Leicestershire (pre first-class, 1883).

Steel, Allan Gibson
(birth registered as Alan Gibson Steel)
Amateur. *b:* 24.9.1858, West Derby, Liverpool, Lancashire. *d:* 15.6.1914, Hyde Park, London. Brother of H. B. (Lancashire), D. Q. (Lancashire) and E. E. (Lancashire), father of A. I. (Middlesex). Attacking middle order right-hand batsman, right-arm slow medium, or occasionally fast medium bowler. *Sch* Marlborough. *Teams* Lancashire (1877–93, 47 matches); Cambridge U (1878–81, blue all four years). *Tour* Bligh to Australia 1882/3. *Tests* England (1880–88, 13 matches).
Career batting
162–261–23–7000–171–29.41–8–*ct* 137
Bowling 11665–789–14.78–64–20–9/63
Test batting
13–20–3–600–148–35.29–2–*ct* 5
Bowling 605–29–20.86–0–0–3/27

He was outstandingly successful in 1878, his first full season in first-class cricket, taking 164 wickets, av 9.43, as well as hitting 537 runs, av 22.37. It was to prove the best season of his career, though he took 130 wickets, av 13.41, in 1881. His best bowling was 9/63 for Lancashire v Yorkshire at Old Trafford in 1878. He captained Cambridge in 1880 and England in four Tests, including the three of 1886, when England won each match. His final first-class match was for I Zingari in 1895. He was President of MCC in 1902. He also won a blue for rackets.

Steel, Allan Ivo
Amateur. *b:* 27.9.1892, Toxteth Park, Liverpool, Lancashire. *d:* 8.10.1917, Langemark, Belgium. He was killed in action. Son of A. G. (Lancashire); nephew of H. B. (Lancashire), D. Q. (Lancashire) and E. E. (Lancashire). Lower order right-hand batsman, slow right-arm bowler. *Sch* Eton. *Team* Middlesex (1912, 2 matches).
Career batting
5–8–0–116–26–14.50–0 –*ct* 2
Bowling 39–0

He took up a business appointment in India on leaving Eton and played for Calcutta CC.

Steel, Douglas Quintin
Amateur. *b:* 19.6.1856, West Derby, Liverpool, Lancashire. *d:* 2.12.1933, Upton, Cheshire. Brother of A. G. (Lancashire), H. B. (Lancashire) and E. E. (Lancashire), uncle of A. I. (Middlesex). Stylish middle order right-hand batsman, right-hand slow round-arm bowler, wicket-keeper. *Sch* Uppingham. *Teams* Cambridge U (1876–79, blue all four years); Lancashire (1876–87, 22 matches).
Career batting
57–89–3–1674–158–19.46–1–*ct* 28–*st* 4
Bowling 173–7–24.71–1–0–5/65

A noted footballer, he represented Cambridge at both rugby and association.

Steel, Ernest Eden
Amateur. *b:* 25.6.1864, West Derby, Liverpool, Lancashire. *d:* 14.7.1941, Southport, Lancashire. Brother of A. G. (Lancashire), D. Q. (Lancashire) and H. B. (Lancashire), uncle of A. I. (Middlesex). Middle order right-hand batsman, slow right-arm bowler, good field. *Sch* Marlborough. *Teams* Lancashire (1884–1903, 40 matches); Europeans (1892/3).
Career batting
47–69–4–1133–111–17.43–1–*ct* 42
Bowling 2877–129 + 2–22.30–11–2–6/69

In 1890 he went to live in Bombay and his County cricket was therefore very limited. His final first-class match was for I Zingari in 1904.

Steel, Harold Banner
Amateur. *b:* 9.4.1862, South Hill, Liverpool, Lancashire. *d:* 29.6.1911, Burnham, Somerset. Brother of A. G. (Lancashire), D. Q. (Lancashire) and E. E. (Lancashire), uncle of A. I. (Middlesex). Powerful middle order right-hand batsman, right-arm medium pace bowler. *Sch* Repton and Uppingham. *Team* Lancashire (1883–96, 22 matches).
Career batting
36–63–3–1042–100–17.36–1–*ct* 20
Bowling 83–1–83.00–0–0–1/15

He might have played more often for Lancashire, but preferred local club matches. Owing to a football injury he played no cricket whilst at Cambridge University.

Steele, Alexander
Cricketer. *b:* 25.2.1941, Salisbury, Rhodesia. Opening right-hand batsman, wicket-keeper. *Team* Scotland (1967–80).
Career batting
14–25–0–621–97–24.84–0–*ct* 11–*st* 2

Steele, Air Marshal Sir Charles Ronald
Amateur. *b:* 9.11.1897, Netheredge, Sheffield, Yorkshire. *d:* 14.2.1973, Trumpington, Cambridge. Middle order right-hand batsman. *Sch* Oundle. *Team* RAF (1929).
Career batting
2–3–0–147–63–49.00–0–*ct* 0

Steele, David Aubrey
Amateur. *b:* 3.6.1869, Southampton, Hampshire. *d:* 25.3.1935, Caterham, Surrey. Stubborn middle order right-hand batsman, slow right-arm bowler, wicket-keeper. *Team* Hampshire (1895–1906, 163 matches).
Career batting
164–279–33–3448–80–14.01–0–*ct* 133–*st* 4
Bowling 4628–135–34.28–4–0–5/32

He first played for Hampshire (not first-class) in 1887.

Steele, David Stanley
Cricketer. *b:* 29.9.1941, Bradeley, Staffordshire. Brother of J. F. (Leicestershire), cousin of B. S. Crump (Northamptonshire). Sound middle order right-hand batsman, slow left-arm bowler, good close field. *Teams* Northamptonshire (1963–84, 416 matches); Derbyshire (1979–81, 64 matches); Leicestershire (1980/1, 3 matches). *Tours* Robins to South Africa 1975/6; Leicestershire to Zimbabwe 1980/1. *Tests* England (1975–76, 8 matches).
Career batting
500–812–124–22346–140*–32.47–30–*ct* 546
Bowling 15511–623–24.89–26–3–8/29
Test batting
8–16–0–673–106–42.06–1–*ct* 7
Bowling 39–2–19.50–0–0–1/1

He hit 1,000 runs in a season ten times (best 1,756, av 48.77, in 1975). He was appointed captain of Derbyshire when he joined the County at the beginning of the 1979 season, but resigned at the end of June. He played for Leicestershire as a guest player on their tour of Zimbabwe. In 1982 he rejoined Northamptonshire. He also played for Staffordshire (1958–62) and Bedfordshire (1985).

Steele, Frederick
Professional. *b:* 14.5.1847, London. *d:* 22.1.1915, Hackney, London. Left-hand batsman, left-arm fast bowler. *Team* Middlesex (1877–79, 10 matches).
Career batting
13–23–3–33–6–1.65–0–*ct* 3
Bowling 751–43–17.46–1–0–5/22
He also played for Northumberland (1876). His final first-class match was for MCC in 1880.

Steele, Howard Keith Chillingworth
Cricketer. *b:* 6.4.1951, Epsom, Auckland, New Zealand. Middle order right-hand batsman, right-arm medium pace bowler. *Teams* Cambridge U (1970–72, blue 1971–72); Auckland (1974/5).
Career batting
26–40–4–711–103*–19.75–1–*ct* 13
Bowling 1276–30–42.53–0–0–4/71
His County cricket was for Cambridgeshire (1971). He also won a blue for rugby.

Steele, John Frederick
Cricketer. *b:* 23.7.1946, Brown Edge, Staffordshire. Brother of D. S. (Northamptonshire and Derbyshire), cousin of B. S. Crump (Northamptonshire). Opening right-hand batsman, slow left-arm bowler. *Teams* Leicestershire (1970–83, 312 matches); Natal (1973/4 to 1977/8); Glamorgan (1984–86, 48 matches). *Tour* Robins to South Africa 1974/5.
Career batting
379–605–85–15054–195–28.95–21–*ct* 413
Bowling 15793–584–27.04–16–0–7/29
He hit 1,000 runs in a season six times (best 1,347, av 31.32, in 1972). He also played for Staffordshire (1965–69). He was forced through injury to retire from first-class cricket in the middle of 1986 and became a member of the Glamorgan coaching staff.

Steele, Rev John William Jackson
Amateur. *b:* 30.7.1905, Wistaston, Cheshire. *d:* 29.3.1990, Powderham, Devon. Lower order right-hand batsman, right-arm medium pace bowler. *Team* Hampshire (1938–39, 17 matches).
Career batting
19–28–2–434–44–16.69–0–*ct* 9
Bowling 1710–66–25.90–3–0–6/62
He also played in military cricket.

Steeples, Albert
Professional. *b:* 28.7.1870, Somercotes, Derbyshire. *d:* 14.8.1945, Derby. Brother of Richard (Derbyshire). Lower order batsman, right-arm fast medium bowler. *Team* Derbyshire (1899, 1 match).
Career batting
1–2–0–18–16–9.00–0–*ct* 0
Bowling 21–0

Steeples, Richard
(birth registered as Richard Steeple)
Professional. *b:* 30.4.1873, Somercotes, Derbyshire. *d:* 2.8.1946, Somercotes, Derbyshire. Brother of Albert (Derbyshire). Lower order batsman, right-arm fast medium bowler. *Team* Derbyshire (1897, 3 matches).
Career batting
3–5–0–20–16–4.00–0–*ct* 1
Bowling 214–9–23.77–0–0–4/73
He also played for Monmouthshire (1901–08).

Stemp, Richard David
Cricketer. *b:* 11.12.1967, Erdington, Birmingham. Lower order right-hand batsman, slow left-arm bowler. *Team* Worcestershire (1990–92, 22 matches).
Career batting
22–16–11–103–16*–20.60–0–*ct* 5
Bowling 1602–46–34.82–3–1–6/67

Stenner, Jonathan Maurice Crathorne
Cricketer. *b:* 18.1.1966, RAF Newton, Bingham, Nottinghamshire. Middle order right-hand batsman. *Sch* Perse. *Team* Cambridge U (1988).
Career batting
1–2–0–23–13–11.50–0–*ct* 0
His County cricket was for Cambridgeshire (1987).

Stenton, John Derek
Amateur. *b:* 26.10.1924, Sheffield, Yorkshire. Lower order right-hand batsman, slow left-arm bowler. *Team* Somerset (1953, 1 match).
Career batting
1–2–0–19–18–9.50–0–*ct* 0
Bowling 44–1–44.00–0–0–1/18

Stephen, Norman Kenneth
Amateur. *b:* 24.6.1865, Kinloss, Morayshire, Scotland. *d:* 4.7.1948, Swiss Cottage, Hampstead, London. Brother-in-law of J. T. Welldon (Kent). Middle order right-hand batsman, slow right-arm bowler. *Sch* Fettes. *Team* Cambridge U (1887).
Career batting
4–5–2–6–3*–2.00–0–*ct* 1
Bowling 261–15–17.40–1–0–5/52

Stephens, Eric James
Professional. *b:* 23.3.1909, Gloucester. *d:* 3.4.1983, Gloucester. Dashing middle order left-hand batsman, right-arm bowler, good field. *Team* Gloucestershire (1927–37, 216 matches).
Career batting
216–313–54–4593–92–17.73–0–*ct* 167
Bowling 1171–29–40.38–1–1–6/59
He hit 1,134 runs, av 28.35, in 1935. He played rugby football for Gloucester and soccer for Hereford Town and Bristol Rovers.

Stephens, Frank Garfield
Amateur. *b:* 26.4.1889, Edgbaston, Birmingham. *d:* 9.8.1970, Moseley, Birmingham. Twin brother of

G. W. (Warwickshire). Middle order right-hand batsman, leg break bowler. *Sch* Rossall. *Team* Warwickshire (1907–12, 32 matches).
Career batting
32–50–7–1102–144–25.62–1–*ct* 17
Bowling 205–3–68.33–0–0–2/24
He was for some time on the Committee of Warwickshire CCC.

Stephens, Frederick
Amateur. *b:* 4.2.1836, Caversham, Berkshire. *d:* 1.4.1909, Chawton, Hampshire. Father of F. G. R. B. (Weigall's XI) and B. J. B. (Europeans), uncle of A. M. Byng (Hampshire) and J. A. Byng (Transvaal). Middle order batsman. *Sch* Winchester. *Team* MCC (1865).
Career batting
1–2–1–9–9*–9.00–0–*ct* 1
His County cricket was for Berkshire (1858–59) and Huntingdonshire (1871).

Stephens, Frederick Geoffrey Roger Byng
Amateur. *b:* 27.5.1886, Chawton, Alton, Hampshire. *d:* 9.5.1967, Northallerton, Yorkshire. Son of Frederick (MCC), brother of B. J. B. (Europeans), cousin of A. M. Byng (Hampshire) and J. A. Byng (Transvaal). Lower order right-hand batsman, useful bowler. *Sch* Winchester. *Team* G. J. V. Weigall's XI (1908).
Career batting
1–2–1–8–4*–8.00–0–*ct* 0
Bowling 47–2–23.50–0–0–2/47
He did not play in any first-class matches whilst at Oxford.

Stephens, George William
Amateur. *b:* 26.4.1889, Edgbaston, Birmingham. *d:* 17.3.1950, Knowle, Solihull, Warwickshire. Twin brother of F. G. (Warwickshire). Middle order right-hand batsman, leg break bowler. *Sch* Rossall. *Team* Warwickshire (1907–25, 123 matches).
Career batting
127–209–15–4171–143–21.50–4–*ct* 51
Bowling 80–4–20.00–0–0–2/25
His final first-class match was for F. S. G. Calthorpe's XI in 1926. He captained Warwickshire in 1919.

Stephens, Rev John Patrick Rhodes Felix
Cricketer. *b:* 6.8.1942, Montpellier, Cheltenham, Gloucestershire. Opening right-hand batsman. *Sch* Ampleforth. *Team* Oxford U (1966–67).
Career batting
3–6–0–73–27–12.16–0–*ct* 2

Stephenson, Edwin
Professional. *b:* 5.6.1832, Sheffield, Yorkshire. *d:* 5.7.1898, Tue Brook, Liverpool, Lancashire. Very sound middle order right-hand batsman, right-hand fast round-arm bowler, wicket-keeper. *Team* Yorkshire (1861–73, 42 matches). *Tour* Stephenson to Australia 1861/2.
Career batting
82–142–11–1940–69–14.80–0–*ct* 56–*st* 48
Bowling 24–0
His first-class debut was for Sheffield in 1854.

Stephenson, Franklyn Dacosta
Cricketer. *b:* 8.4.1959, Halls, Holders, St James, Barbados. Middle order right-hand batsman, right-arm fast bowler. *Teams* Tasmania (1981/2, 7 matches); Barbados (1981/2 to 1989/90); Gloucestershire (1982–83, 9 matches); Nottinghanshire (1988–91, 82 matches); Orange Free State (1991/2); Sussex (1992, 18 matches). *Tours* West Indian XI to South Africa 1982/3, 1983/4; Rest of World to England 1985.
Career batting
142–215–28–5108–165–27.31–6–*ct* 60
Bowling 12884–536–24.03–32–8–8/47
A remarkable all-rounder, he chose to tour South Africa in 1982/3 and thus lost the opportunity of Test cricket, though he returned to domestic first-class cricket in Barbados in 1989/90 when the ban imposed by the West Indies Board was lifted. His outstanding season in English cricket was 1988. He performed the 'double' with 1,018 runs, av 29.08, amd 125 wickets, av 18.31; the season finished with the Nottinghamshire match against Yorkshire at Trent Bridge in which he performed the brilliant feat of scoring 111 and 117 as well as taking 11 for 222. He also played for Staffordshire (1980).

Stephenson, Frederick
Professional. *b:* 24.4.1853, Todmorden, Yorkshire. *d:* July 1927. Lower order left-hand batsman, left-hand fast round-arm bowler. *Team* Lancashire (1875–77, 2 matches).
Career batting
2–4–1–0–0*–0.00–0–*ct* 2
Bowling 17–1–17.00–0–0–1/17
At 5ft 2in tall, he was one of the shortest of all first-class cricketers.

Stephenson, George Robert
Cricketer. *b:* 19.11.1942, Derby. Lower order right-hand batsman, wicket-keeper. *Sch* Derby. *Teams* Derbyshire (1967–68, 9 matches); Hampshire (1969–80, 263 matches).
Career batting
272–357–66–4781–100*–16.42–1–*ct* 584–*st* 77
Bowling 39–0
His best season as wicket-keeper was 1970 when he had 80 dismissals (73ct 7st). He captained Hampshire in 1979. A good soccer player, he appeared for Derby County, Shrewsbury and Rochdale.

Stephenson, Harold William
(birth registered as W. H. Stephenson)
Professional. *b:* 18.7.1920, Haverton Hill, Co Durham. Middle order right-hand batsman, wicket-

keeper. *Team* Somerset (1948–64, 427 matches). *Tours* Commonwealth to India and Ceylon 1950/1; International XI to India, Pakistan and Rhodesia 1961/2.
Career batting
463–747–90–13195–147*–20.08–7–*ct* 746–*st* 334
Bowling 135–1–135.00–0–0–1/0

He hit 1,000 runs in a season five times (best 1,143, av 21.56, in 1953). From 1960 to 1964 he captained Somerset. He also played for Durham (pre first-class, 1947) and Dorset (1965–68).

Stephenson, Heathfield Harman
Professional. *b:* 3.5.1833, Esher, Surrey. *d:* 17.12.1896, Uppingham, Rutland. Uncle of F. H. Read (Surrey) and J. M. Read (Surrey). Middle order right-hand batsman, right-hand fast round-arm bowler, wicket-keeper. *Team* Surrey (1853–71, 179 matches). *Tours* Parr to North America 1859 (not first-class); Stephenson to Australia 1861/2.
Career batting
256–452–41–7360–119–17.90–3–*ct* 152–*st* 25
Bowling 4920–300 + 2–16.40–17–4–8/28

His best season was 1864, when he came second in the first-class averages with 824 runs, av 39.23. He captained the first English Team to Australia in 1861/2. He umpired the first Test match ever played in England in 1880. Unusually for an early professional, he was the son of a doctor.

Stephenson, John Patrick
Cricketer. *b:* 14.3.1965, Stebbing, Essex. Opening right-hand batsman, right-arm medium pace bowler. *Sch* Felsted. *Teams* Essex (1985–92, 138 matches); Boland (1988/9). *Tours* England A to Zimbabwe 1989/90, to West Indies 1991/2. *Test* England (1989, 1 match).
Career batting
155–265–29–8684–202*–36.79–15–*ct* 84
Bowling 2903–89–32.61–2–0–6/54
Test batting
1–2–0–36–25–18.00–0–*ct* 0

He scored 1,000 runs in a season four times (best 1,887, av 57.18, in 1990). His highest score was 202* for Essex v Somerset at Bath in 1990.

Stephenson, John Stewart
Amateur. *b:* 10.11.1903, Brough, Yorkshire. *d:* 7.10.1975, Horsham, Sussex. Brother of R. H. (Royal Navy). Middle order right-hand batsman, right-arm medium pace bowler. *Sch* Shrewsbury. *Teams* Oxford U (1923–26, blue 1925 and 1926); Yorkshire (1923–26, 16 matches).
Career batting
35–53–5–949–72–19.77–0–*ct* 21
Bowling 521–11–47.36–0–0–3/44

He was also awarded his blue for soccer and golf. He was the father of Lt-Col J. R. (MCC Secretary since 1987).

Stephenson, John William Arthur
Amateur. *b:* 1.8.1907, Hong Kong. *d:* 20.5.1982, Mare Hill, Pulborough, Sussex. Attacking middle lower order right-hand batsman, right-arm fast medium bowler. *Teams* Europeans (1928/9 to 1929/30); Madras (1930/1); Essex (1934–39, 61 matches); Worcestershire (1947, 1 match).
Career batting
103–158–37–2582–135–21.33–2–*ct* 60
Bowling 7521–312–24.10–16–2–9/46

His first-class debut in England was for the Army in 1931 and his final first-class match for South of England in 1948. His best bowling was 9/46 for Gentlemen v Players at Lord's in 1936. He was joint captain of Essex in 1939. His career in the Army prevented him from appearing regularly in County cricket. He also played for Buckinghamshire (1927–32).

Stephenson, Robert Hearfield
Amateur. *b:* 3.6.1906, Brough, Yorkshire. *d:* 9.11.1942. He was drowned when HMS *Cromer* sank off Marsa Matruh, Egypt. Brother of J. S. (Yorkshire). Middle order right-hand batsman. *Team* Royal Navy (1927–28).
Career batting
3–6–0–122–75–20.33–0–*ct* 3

Stephenson-Jellie, James Parker
Amateur. *b:* 1875. *d:* 1960, Australia. Middle order batsman. *Team* Gloucestershire (1896–1908, 6 matches).
Career batting
6–10–0–88–27–8.80–0–*ct* 1

Stevens, Bertie Grosvenor
Amateur. *b:* 9.4.1886, Thingoe, Suffolk. *d:* 9.3.1943, Tipton, Staffordshire. Middle order right-hand batsman, leg break bowler, wicket-keeper. *Sch* Cheltenham and Worcester RGS. *Team* Worcestershire (1905–14, 18 matches).
Career batting
19–33–2–379–41–12.22–0–*ct* 15
Bowling 18–0

His final first-class match was for H. K. Foster's XI in 1919.

Stevens, Edward
Professional, *b:* 1735, Send, Surrey. *d:* 7.9.1819, Walton-on-Thames, Surrey. Tail end right-hand batsman, right-hand medium pace under-arm bowler. *Team* Surrey (1773–89).

He was generally known under the appellation 'Lumpy' and was famous as a bowler in matches organized by the Hambledon Club 'being able to deliver more balls of a length than other men, and he never used to tire.'

Stevens, Geoffrey Alden
Amateur. *b:* 17.10.1890, Norwich, Norfolk. *d:* 24.3.1963, Norwich, Norfolk. Middle order right-hand batsman. *Sch* Norwich. *Team* Minor Counties (1912–24).
Career batting
3–5–0–56–20–11.20–0–*ct* 6
His County cricket was for Norfolk (1906–30). He hit 201 for Norfolk v Berkshire in the Minor Counties Championship Match of 1910, which resulted in Norfolk taking the title. From 1952 to 1961 he was Secretary of Norfolk CCC.

Stevens, Greville Thomas Scott
Amateur. *b:* 7.1.1901, Hampstead, London. *d:* 19.9.1970, Islington, London. Middle order right-hand batsman, leg break bowler, good close field. *Sch* University College School. *Teams* Middlesex (1919–32, 127 matches); Oxford U (1920–23, blue all four years). *Tours* MCC to South Africa 1922/3, 1927/8, to West Indies 1929/30; Tennyson to Jamaica 1931/2. *Tests* England (1922/3 to 1929/30, 10 matches).
Career batting
243–387–36–10376–182–29.56–12–*ct* 213
Bowling 18364–684–26.84–29–5–8/38
Test batting
10–17–0–263–69–15.47–0–*ct*9
Bowling 48–20–32.40–2–1–5/90
He created a sensation in 1919 when he hit 466 in a House match at school and was then selected to play for the Gentlemen v Players at Lord's. He hit 1,000 runs in a season twice (best 1,434, av 33.34, in 1923), but after leaving University he could not spare the time for regular County cricket. He captained Oxford in 1923 and England in one Test. His last first-class matches were for MCC and H. D. G. Leveson-Gower's XI in 1933.

Stevens, James Norman
Amateur. *b:* 4.6.1910, Bexhill-on-Sea, Sussex. Lower order right-hand batsman, right-arm fast medium bowler. *Sch* Northampton. *Team* Northamptonshire (1937, 5 matches).
Career batting
7–12–1–76–19–6.90–0–*ct* 1
Bowling 571–9–63.44–0–0–3/85
His final first-class match was for Free Foresters in 1953. He also played for Wiltshire (1936) and Suffolk (1949–55).

Stevens, John
Amateur. *b:* 5.10.1854, Guildford, Surrey. Middle order right-hand batsman, good deep field. *Team* Surrey (1874–75, 3 matches).
Career batting
3–4–0–36–16–9.00–0–*ct* 1

Stevens, John Elgar
Amateur. *b:* 21.3.1875, Broad Chalke, Salisbury, Wiltshire. *d:* 10.4.1923, Woking, Surrey. He died by his own hand. Capable middle order right-hand batsman, right-arm medium fast bowler. *Sch* Sherborne. *Team* MCC (1902).
Career batting
1–1–0–4–4–4.00–0–*ct* 0
He played in the Freshmen's match in 1895, but no first-class matches for Oxford U. His County cricket was for Wiltshire (1894–1912). He was also a useful boxer, rugby footballer and steeplechase jockey.

Stevens, Keith Brian Havelock
Amateur. *b:*22.8.1942, Bombay, India. Middle order right-hand batsman. *Sch* Bradfield. *Team* Oxford U (1962).
Career batting
5–10–0–102–52–10.20–0–*ct* 4
His County cricket was for Berkshire (1960–62).

Stevens, Roy Gilbert
Cricketer. *b:* 6.2.1933, Walmer, Kent. *d:* 6.10.1992, Ipswich, Suffolk. Middle order batsman. *Team* Combined Services (1962).
Career batting
1–2–0–38–29–19.00–0–*ct* 2
Bowling 47–2–23.50–0–0–1/23
He was Secretary of Somerset CCC 1975 to 1979 and of Sussex CCC 1980 to 1983.

Stevenson, Alan William John
Cricketer. *b:* 2.10.1962, Coatbridge, Lanarkshire, Scotland. Lower order right-hand batsman, off break bowler. *Team* Scotland (1985–87).
Career batting
3–1–0–9–9–9.00–0–*ct* 3
Bowling 225–11–20.45–0–0–4/28

Stevenson, Alexander James
Amateur. *b:* 15.7.1901, Blackhall, Edinburgh, Scotland. *d:* 2.9.1970, Edinburgh, Scotland. Middle order batsman, lob bowler. *Sch* Edinburgh Academy. *Team* Scotland (1925–28).
Career batting
4–7–0–190–54–27.14–0–*ct* 2
Bowling 15–0
He played in trials at Cambridge U, but not in first-class matches.

Stevenson, David Craig
Amateur. *b:* 3.5.1890, Kilmarnock, Ayrshire, Scotland. *d:* 21.3.1977, Dundee, Angus, Scotland, Lower order left-hand batsman, slow left-arm bowler. *Team* Scotland (1922–25).
Career batting
6–11–0–96–35–8.72–0–*ct* 1
Bowling 171–4–40.25–0–0–2/29
His County cricket was for Cumberland (1924) and Northumberland (1932).

Stevenson, George Stanley
Professional. *b:* 20.7.1876, Derby. *d:* 25.7.1938, Fritchley, Derbyshire. Lower order batsman, left-arm

fast medium bowler. *Team* Derbyshire (1904, 2 matches).
Career batting
2–4–0–10–9–2.50–0–*ct* 1
Bowling 92–1–92.00–0–0–1/79

Stevenson, Graham Barry
Cricketer. *b:* 16.12.1955, Ackworth, Yorkshire. Lower order right-hand batsman, right-arm medium pace bowler. *Teams* Yorkshire (1973–86, 177 matches); Northamptonshire (1987, 1 match). *Tours* England to Australia and India 1979/80, to West Indies 1980/1. *Tests* England (1979/80 to 1980/1, 2 matches).
Career batting
188–229–34–3965–115*–20.33–2–*ct* 73
Bowling 14075–488–28.84–18–2–8/57
Test batting
2–2–1–28–27*–28.00–0–*ct* 0
Bowling 183–5–36.60–0–0–3/111
He scored 115* for Yorkshire v Warwickshire at Edgbaston in 1982 batting at number 11. His best season with the ball was 1980, 72 wickets, av 23.18.

Stevenson, Henry James
Amateur. *b:* 12.7.1867, Edinburgh, Scotland. *d:* 8.8.1945, Corstorphine, Edinburgh, Scotland. Lower order right-hand batsman, slow under-arm bowler. *Sch* Edinburgh Academy *Team* Scotland (1905).
Career batting
5–9–0–1–4–35–11.55–0–*ct* 5
Bowling 269–4–67.25–0–0–3/77
His first-class debut was for MCC in 1901. He also played for Ireland (not first-class). A noted rugby footballer, he represented Scotland 1888–93.

Stevenson, James Alexander
Amateur. *b:* 24.6.1915, Coates, Edinburgh, Scotland. Middle order right-hand batsman, right-arm medium pace bowler. *Sch* Edinburgh Academy. *Team* Scotland (1937–51).
Career batting
4–8–2–127–45*–21.16–0–*ct* 2

Stevenson, John Francis
Amateur. *b:* 18.3.1888, Handsworth, Warwickshire, *d:* 5.12.1951, Edgbaston, Birmingham. Middle order right-hand batsman. *Team* Warwickshire (1919, 1 match).
Career batting
1–2–0–18–18–9.00–0–*ct* 0

Stevenson, Keith
Cricketer. *b:* 6.10.1950, Derby. Lower order right-hand batsman, right-arm fast medium bowler. *Teams* Derbyshire (1974–77, 47 matches); Hampshire (1978–83, 99 matches).
Career batting
146–167–58–1046–33–9.59–0–*ct* 48
Bowling 10536–355–29.67–16–0–7/22

Stevenson, Michael Hamilton
Amateur. *b:* 13.6.1927, Chinley, Derbyshire. Sound middle order right-hand batsman, slow left-arm bowler. *Sch* Rydal. *Teams* Cambridge U (1949–52, blue all four years); Derbyshire (1950–52, 3 matches); Ireland (1952–64).
Career batting
66–106–7–2467–122–24.91–4–*ct* 26
Bowling 1882–50–37.64–1–0–5/36
He also played for Staffordshire (1947) and Denbighshire (1949). His final first-class match was for MCC in 1967. He was a well-known sports journalist and commentator mainly associated with *The Daily Telegraph.*

Stevenson, Ronald Leckie
Amateur. *b:* 26.11.1938, Ayr, Scotland. Lower order right-hand batsman, off break bowler. *Sch* Bedford Modern. *Team* Combined Services (1962).
Career batting
2–4–1–33–17*–11.00–0–*ct* 1
Bowling 230–3–76.66–0–0–3/86
His County cricket was for Bedfordshire (1962).

Steward, Exley Anthony Whitefoord
Cricketer. *b:* 27.6.1941, Durban, South Africa. Middle order right-hand batsman, leg break bowler, wicket-keeper. *Teams* Essex (1964–65, 15 matches); Natal (1967/8).
Career batting
18–27–3–310–47–12.91–0–*ct* 20

Stewart, Alec James
Cricketer. *b:* 8.4.1963, Merton, Surrey. Son of M. J. (Surrey). Middle order right-hand batsman, wicket-keeper. *Sch* Tiffin. *Team* Surrey (1981–92, 187 matches). *Tours* England to India 1989/90 (not first-class), to West Indies 1989/90, to Australia 1990/1, to New Zealand 1990/1 (not first-class), 1991/2, to Australia and New Zealand (World Cup) 1991/2. *Tests* England (1989/90 to 1992, 22 matches).
Career batting
222–366–43–12608–206*–39.27–23–*ct* 273–*st* 6
Bowling 352–3–117.33–0–0–1/7
Test batting
22–40–4–1493–190–41.47–4–*ct* 27
To date his best Test series was in 1992 against Pakistan, when he topped the England batting averages with 397 runs, av 56.71. He hit 1,000 runs in a season seven times (best 1,665, av 46.25, in 1986). His highest score was 206* for Surrey v Essex at the Oval in 1989. He captained Surrey in 1992. He held 11 catches in the match keeping wicket for Surrey v Leicestershire at Leicester in 1989.

Stewart, Rev Alexander Lamont
Amateur. *b:* 2.6.1858, Port of Spain, Trinidad. *d:* 17.2.1904, Marylebone, London. Brother of J. M. (Middlesex). Middle order right-hand batsman, right-arm fast bowler. *Sch* Clifton. *Teams* Middlesex

(1880, 1 match); Oxford U (1883).
Career batting
4–8–2–27–12*–4.50–0–*ct* 5
Bowling 154–6–25.66–0–0–2/33
He also played for Norfolk (1884).

Stewart, David
Amateur. *b:* 21.5.1924, Perth, Scotland. Tail end right-hand batsman, right-arm medium pace bowler. *Team* Scotland (1950).
Career batting
1–2–1–7–5*–7.00–0–*ct* 0
Bowling 21–2–10.50–0–0–2/12

Stewart, David Ernest Robertson
Cricketer. *b:* 22.5.1948, Bombay, India. Opening right-hand batsman, off break bowler. *Teams* Scotland (1969–79); Worcestershire (1970–73, 23 matches).
Career batting
32–51–3–854–69–17.79–0–*ct* 17
Bowling 72–0

Stewart, Haldane Campbell
Amateur. *b:* 28.2.1868, Notting Hill, London. *d:* 16.6.1942, Headington, Oxford. Stylish middle order right-hand batsman, useful bowler. *Sch* Magdalen College School, Oxford. *Team* Kent (1892–1903, 73 matches). *Tour* Kent to North America 1903.
Career batting
75–128–3–2829–142–22.63–2–*ct* 42
Bowling 97–3–32.33–0–0–1/2
He did not play in any first-class matches whilst at Oxford.

Stewart, Maj-Gen Sir Herbert
Amateur. *b:* 30.6.1843, Sparsholt, Hampshire. *d:* 16.2.1885, Gakdul, Sudan. He was wounded in the battle of Abu Klea and died from his injuries. Brother of W. A. (Hampshire), brother-in-law of C. H. Everett (Hampshire 1861). Lower order right-hand batsman, wicket-keeper. *Sch* Winchester and Brighton. *Team* Hampshire (1869, 1 match).
Career batting
4–7–0–19–8–2.71–0–0–*ct* 2–*st* 1

Stewart, Hugh Lambert
Amateur. *b:* 2.5.1907, Struthers Barns, Ceres, Fife, Scotland. Middle order right-hand batsman, right-arm fast medium bowler. *Team* Scotland (1932).
Career batting
2–4–0–42–25–10.50–0–*ct* 2
Bowling 71–1–71.00–0–0–1/31

Stewart, Maj-Gen Sir James Marshall
Amateur. *b:* 9.8.1861, Blythswood, Glasgow, Scotland. *d:* 20.7.1943, Home Down House, Whitchurch, Devon. Brother of A. L. (Middlesex). Lower order right-hand batsman, right-arm medium pace bowler. *Sch* Clifton and Malvern. *Team* Middlesex (1880, 1 match).
Career batting
1–2–0–8–8–4.00–0–*ct* 0
Bowling 11–1–11.00–0–0–1/11

Stewart, Michael James, OBE
Professional. *b:* 16.9.1932, Herne Hill, London. Father of A. J. (Surrey). Neat opening right-hand batsman, right-arm medium pace bowler, brilliant close field. *Sch* Alleyn's. *Team* Surrey (1954–72, 498 matches). *Tours* Swanton to West Indies 1955/6; Surrey to Rhodesia 1959/60; MCC to East Africa 1963/4, to India 1963/4; International XI to India, Pakistan and Ceylon 1967/8; Cavaliers to South Africa and India 1962/3. *Tests* England (1962 to 1963/4, 8 matches).
Career batting
530–898–93–26492–227*–32.90–49–*ct* 634
Bowling 99–1–99.00–0–0–1/4
Test batting
8–12–1–385–87–35.00–0–*ct* 6
He hit 1,000 runs in a season 15 times, going on to 2,000 once: 2,045, av 44.45, in 1962. Both his double centuries were for Surrey, the higher being 227* v Middlesex at the Oval in 1964. In 1957 he held 77 catches, and in the same year held 7 catches in an innings for Surrey v Northamptonshire at Northampton. From 1963 to 1972 he captained Surrey and from 1979 to 1986 he was manager of the County Club. He was England team manager from 1987 until 1992. A good soccer player he was inside right for Wimbledon, Hendon and Corinthian Casuals as an amateur, and was then professional with Charlton Athletic.

Stewart, Richard William
Cricketer. *b:* 28.2.1945, Portland, Jamaica. Lower order right-hand batsman, right-arm fast medium bowler. *Teams* Gloucestershire (1966, 1 match); Middlesex (1966–68, 51 matches).
Career batting
52–36–11–107–19–4.28–0–*ct* 17
Bowling 3133–131–23.91–5–0–6/65
He appeared for both Gloucestershire and Middlesex in 1966.

Stewart, Theophile Lecompte
Amateur. *b:* 9.5.1891, Brisbane, Queensland, Australia. *d:* 14.12.1952, Morriston, Glamorgan. Middle order batsman. *Team* Glamorgan (1923, 1 match).
Career batting
1–2–0–4–4–2.00–0–*ct* 0

Stewart, Rev William Anthony
Amateur. *b:* 19.5.1847, Sparsholt, Hampshire. *d:* 31.7.1883, Twyford, Hampshire. Brother of Herbert (Hampshire), brother-in-law of C. H. Everett (Hampshire 1861). Tail end right-hand batsman, wicket-keeper. *Sch* Winchester. *Teams* Oxford U (1869–70, blue both years); Hampshire (1869–78, 2 matches).
Career batting
9–17–5–46–12–3.83–0–*ct* 15–*st* 9

Stewart, William James Perver
Professional. *b:* 31.8.1934, Llanelly, Carmarthenshire. Middle order right-hand batsman, off break bowler. *Teams* Warwickshire (1955–69, 279 matches); Northamptonshire (1971, 1 match). *Tour* MCC to New Zealand 1960/1.
Career batting
290–491–56–14826–182*–34.08–25–*ct* 132
Bowling 15–2–7.50–0–0–2/4
He hit 1,000 runs in a season six times, going on to 2,000 once: 2,318, av 43,73, in 1962. A noted hitter of sixes, he hit ten in one innings of 155 for Warwickshire v Lancashire at Blackpool in 1959. A useful rugby footballer, he was centre three quarter for Coventry.

Stewart-Brown, Philip Harman
Amateur. *b:* 30.4.1904, Bromborough, Cheshire. *d:* 21.12.1960, Marylebone London. Opening or middle order right-hand batsman. *Sch* Harrow. *Team* Oxford U (1924–26, blue 1925 and 1926).
Career batting
17–31–1–845–99–28.16–0–*ct* 9
His final first-class match was for H. D. G. Leveson-Gower's XI in 1927.

Stileman-Gibbard, Leonard Gibbard
(changed name from Stileman in September 1877)
Amateur. *b:* 22.6.1856, Bombay, India. *d:* 19.9.1939, Sharnbrook, Bedfordshire. Middle order right-hand batsman, right-hand slow round-arm bowler. *Sch* Brighton. *Team* South of England (1886).
Career batting
1–2–0–55–46–27.50–0–*ct* 1
His County cricket was for Bedfordshire (1880–1905). Though at Cambridge, he did not appear for the University in any first-class matches.

Still, Stuart John
Cricketer. *b:* 14.12.1957, Hove, Sussex. Lower order right-hand batsman, right-arm medium pace bowler. *Team* Sussex (1975, 1 match).
Career batting
1–2–0–6–6–3.00–0–*ct* 0
Bowling 42–1–42.00–0–0–1/42

Stimpson, Peter John
Cricketer. *b:* 25.5.1947, Aberfan, Glamorgan. Opening right-hand batsman, right-arm medium pace bowler. *Team* Worcestershire (1971–72, 30 matches).
Career batting
30–54–3–1327–103–26.01–1–*ct* 8
Bowling 19–0

Stinchcombe, Frederick William
Professional. *b:* 12.3.1930, Barnby Moor, Nottinghamshire. *d:* 19.9.1984, Worksop, Nottinghamshire. Lower order right-hand batsman, leg break and googly bowler. *Team* Nottinghamshire (1950–51, 6 matches).
Career batting
6–8–2–87–48–14.50–0–*ct* 1
Bowling 539–4–134.75–0–0–1/42

Stirling, Derek Alexander
Cricketer. *b:* 5.10.1961, Upper Hutt, Wellington, New Zealand. Lower order right-hand batsman, right-arm fast medium bowler. *Teams* Central Districts (1981/2 to 1987/8); Wellington (1988/9 to 1991/2). *Tours* New Zealand to Sri Lanka 1983/4, 1984/5 (not first-class), to Pakistan 1984/5, to West Indies 1984/5, to England 1986; Young New Zealand to Zimbabwe 1984/5; Rest of World to England 1985. *Tests* New Zealand (1984/5 to 1986, 6 matches).
Career batting
84–106–30–1651–75–21.72–0–*ct* 27
Bowling 6948–206–33.72–5–0–6/75
Test batting
6–9–2–108–26–15.42–0–*ct* 1
Bowling 601–13–46.23–0–0–4/88
He played in two Tests in the 1986 tour, but his bowling achieved little; he did however bat usefully on occasion.

Stirling, Haycroft
Amateur. *b:* 8.2.1908, Barnet, Hertfordshire. *d:* 7.5.1952, West Byfleet, Surrey. Lower order right-hand batsman, right-arm fast medium bowler. *Sch* Bishop's Stortford. *Team* Middlesex (1932–33, 2 matches).
Career batting
2–3–1–4–3–2.00–0–*ct* 1
Bowling 195–0

Stirling, William Stuart
Amateur. *b:* 19.3.1891, Jamestown, South Australia. *d:* 18.7.1971, Adelaide, South Australia. Middle or lower order right-hand batsman, left-arm medium pace bowler. *Team* South Australia (1908/9 to 1920/1, 14 matches). *Tours* AIF to England 1919, to South Africa 1919/20.
Career batting
47–72–7–931–62–14.32–0–*ct* 32
Bowling 1891–61–31.00–3–0–5/26
He was a useful all-rounder for AIF in 1919.

Stockley, Anthony John
Cricketer. *b:* 4.4.1940, Kingston-upon-Thames, Surrey. *d:* 29.5.1991, Adelaide, South Australia. Tail end right-hand batsman, off break bowler. *Team* Surrey (1968, 3 matches).
Career batting
3–2–0–5–5–2.50–0–*ct* 3
Bowling 194–10–19.40–0–0–4/74

Stocks, Edward William
Amateur. *b:* 27.5.1856, Norwich, Norfolk. *d:* 26.10.1876, Norwich, Norfolk. He died of typhoid fever. Attacking opening right-hand batsman, right-hand medium pace round-arm bowler, slip field. *Sch*

Clergy Orphan School, Canterbury. *Team* Cambridge U (1875–76).
Career batting
4–5–0–18–11–3.60–0–*ct* 1
Bowling 22–0

He represented Cambridge in the athletic sports of 1875. His County cricket was for Norfolk (1876).

Stocks, Francis Wilfrid
Amateur. *b:* 10.12.1873, Market Harborough, Leicestershire. *d:* 21.5.1929, Framlingham, Suffolk. Lower order left-hand batsman, left-arm medium bowler, good field. *Sch* Lancing and Denstone. *Teams* Leicestershire (1894–1903, 44 matches); Oxford U (1896–99, blue 1898 and 1899). *Tour* Warner to North America 1897.
Career batting
63–102–19–834–58–10.04–0–*ct* 70
Bowling 5205–208–25.02–14–3–8/22

He first played for Leicestershire (pre first-class) in 1892. He also won a blue for hockey.

Stocks, Frederick
Professional. *b:* 23.5.1883, Shireoaks, Nottinghamshire. *d:* 2.1.1954, Hucknall, Nottinghamshire. Father of F. W. (Nottinghamshire). Middle order batsman, useful bowler. *Team* Northamptonshire (1906, 2 matches)
Career batting
2–4–0–24–13–6.00–0–*ct* 1
Bowling 37–0

Stocks, Frederick Wilfred
Professional. *b:* 6.11.1918, Carcroft, Yorkshire. Son of Frederick (Northamptonshire). Attacking middle order left-hand batsman, right-arm medium pace bowler. *Team* Nottinghamshire (1946–57, 283 matches).
Career batting
284–430–45–11397–171–29.60–13–*ct* 158
Bowling 9794–223–43.91–6–0–6/37

He hit 1,000 runs in a season five times (best 1,396, av 34.04, in 1951). He hit a century on his first-class debut in 1946 and took a wicket with his first ball in first-class cricket, although not in the same match.

Stoddart, Andrew Ernest
Amateur. *b:* 11.3.1863, Westoe, South Shields, Co Durham. *d:* 4.4.1915, St John's Wood, London. He shot himself through the head. Stylish opening right-hand batsman, right-arm medium pace bowler, excellent field. *Team* Middlesex (1885–1900, 170 matches). *Tours* Vernon to Australia 1887/8; Sheffield to Australia 1891/2; Stoddart to Australia 1894/5, 1897/8; Priestley to West Indies 1896/7; Ranjitsinhji to North America 1899. *Tests* England (1887/8 to 1897/8, 16 matches).
Career batting
309–537–16–16738–221–32.12–26–*ct* 257
Bowling 6571–278–23.63–10–2–7/67
Test batting
16–30–2–996–173–35.57–2–*ct* 6
Bowling 94–2–47.00–0–0–1/10

He hit 1,000 runs in a season six times, going on to 2,000 once: 2,072, av 42.28, in 1893. Both his double centuries were for Middlesex, the higher being 221 v Somerset at Lord's in 1900. He took two teams to Australia, acting as captain on both tours and led England in eight Tests. He was joint Middlesex captain in 1898. An excellent rugby footballer he played for Middlesex and England in the three-quarter line and toured Australia and New Zealand with the British team in 1888.

Stoddart, Peter Laurence Bowring
Amateur. *b:* 24.6.1934, Regent's Park, London. Opening right-hand batsman. *Sch* Eton. *Team* MCC (1958).
Career batting
1–2–0–22–11–11.00–0–*ct* 0

His County cricket was for Buckinghamshire (1955–67).

Stoddart, Wilfred Bowring
Amateur. *b:* 27.4.1871, West Derby, Liverpool, Lancashire. *d:* 8.1.1935, Wood End Park, Grassendale, Liverpool, Lancashire. Lower order right-hand batsman, leg break bowler. *Team* Lancashire (1898–99, 15 matches).
Career batting
19–32–5–410–43*–15.18–0–*ct* 7
Bowling 1122–48–23.37–3–0–6/121

He was a member of the Committee of Lancashire CCC. A good forward, he played rugby football for Lancashire and England.

Stogdon, Rev Edgar
Amateur. *b:* 30.7.1870, Harrow, Middlesex. *d:* 30.6.1951, Northwood, Middlesex. Brother of J. H. (Middlesex). Middle order right-hand batsman. *Sch* Harrow. *Team* Cambridge U (1893).
Career batting
2–4–0–19–12–4.75–0–*ct* 1

He won a blue for athletics.

Stogdon, John Hubert
Amateur. *b:* 25.4.1876, Harrow, Middlesex. *d:* 17.12.1944, Pinner, Middlesex. Brother of Edgar (Cambridge U). Middle order right-hand batsman. *Sch* Harrow. *Teams* Cambridge U (1896–99, blue 1897–99); Middlesex (1899–1907, 14 matches).
Career batting
44–78–1–1347–101–17.49–1–*ct* 49
Bowling 10–0

His final first-class match was for H. D. G. Leveson-Gower's XI in 1909. He also won a blue for rackets.

Stokes, Dennis Wilfrid
Amateur. *b:* 26.1.1911, Reading. Berkshire. Opening right-hand batsman, wicket-keeper. *Sch* Wellingborough. *Team* Minor Counties (1937–38).
Career batting
2–4–0–47–39–11.75–0–*ct* 1
His County cricket was for Berkshire (1928–53).

Stokes, Frederic
Amateur. *b:* 12.7.1850, Greenwich, London. *d:* 7.2.1929, Inhurst House, Berkshire. Brother of Graham (Kent) and Lennard (Kent), uncle of F. Penn jun (Kent), brother-in-law of F. Penn sen (Kent). Middle order right-hand batsman, right-hand fast round-arm bowler, long-stop. *Sch* Rugby. *Team* Kent (1871–75, 4 matches).
Career batting
8–12–1–167–65–15.18–0–*ct* 3
Bowling 335–13–25.76–0–0–3/36
A noted rugby footballer, he captained England v Scotland in 1872.

Stokes, Graham
Amateur. *b:* 22.3.1858, Greenwich, London. *d:* 19.12.1921, Blackheath, London. Brother of Frederic (Kent) and Lennard (Kent). Middle order batsman. *Team* Kent (1880–81, 4 matches).
Career batting
4–8–0–39–27–4.87–0–*ct* 3

Stokes, Dr Lennard
Amateur. *b:* 12.2.1856, Greenwich, London. *d:* 3.5.1933, Upton, Hampshire. Brother of Frederic (Kent) and Graham (Kent). Hard hitting lower order right-hand batsman, right-hand slow under-arm bowler. *Sch* Bath. *Team* Kent (1877–80, 4 matches).
Career batting
4–6–1–43–17–8.60–0–*ct* 2
Bowling 135–6–22.50–0–0–3/56
A noted rugby footballer, he played for Blackheath and England and in 1886 was President of the Rugby Football Union.

Stollmeyer, Jeffrey Baxter
Amateur. *b:* 11.3.1921, Santa Cruz, Trinidad. *d:* 10.9.1989, Melbourne, Florida, USA. He was shot by intruders who broke into his home in Port of Spain and, although taken to Florida for treatment, died of his wounds. Brother of V. H. (West Indies). Elegant opening right-hand batsman, leg break and googly bowler. *Team* Trinidad (1938/9 to 1956/7). *Tours* West Indies to England 1939, 1950, to India, Pakistan and Ceylon 1948/9, to Australia and New Zealand 1951/2. *Tests* West Indies (1939 to 1954/5, 32 matches).
Career batting
117–194–16–7942–324–44.61–14–*ct* 93
Bowling 2482–55–45.12–0–0–3/32
Test batting
32–56–5–2159–160–42.33–4–*ct* 20
Bowling 507–13–39.00–0–0–3/32
In 1939 in England he hit 916 runs, av 30.53, and in 1950, 1,334 runs, av 37.05. He played in all Tests on both tours. He captained West Indies in 13 Tests and afterwards became a noted member of the West Indies Board of Control and Test Selector. His highest innings was 324 for Trinidad v British Guiana at Port of Spain in 1946/7 and of his four double centuries three were made in the West Indies and one in India. He also hit 1,000 runs on the 1948/9 tour. He scored 118 on debut for R. S. Grant's XI v British Guiana at Georgetown in 1938/9.

Stollmeyer, Victor Humphrey
Amateur. *b:* 24.1.1916, Santa Cruz, Trinidad. Brother of J. B. (West Indies). Opening right-hand batsman, leg break and googly bowler. *Team* Trinidad (1935/6 to 1945/6). *Tour* West Indies to England 1939. *Test* West Indies (1939, 1 match).
Career batting
33–58–9–2096–139–42.77–4–*ct* 16
Bowling 612–15–40.80–0–0–3/38
Test batting
1–1–0–96–96–96.00–0–*ct* 0
Troubled by illness, he missed a number of matches in the 1939 tour and played in only one Test. In first-class games he hit 542 runs, av 30.11.

Stone, Charles Cecil
Amateur. *b:* 13.6.1865, Knighton, Leicester. *d:* 11.11.1951, Eastbourne, Sussex. Middle order right-hand batsman, right-arm medium pace bowler. *Sch* Uppingham. *Team* Leicestershire (1895–96, 7 matches). *Tour* Priestley to West Indies 1896/7.
Career batting
14–28–3–203–55–8.12–0–*ct* 4
Bowling 8–0
He first played for Leicestershire (pre first-class) in 1884. His first-class debut was for MCC in 1894. He also played for Oxfordshire (1899).

Stone, Donald Harry
Professional. *b:* 9.1.1927, Clayton, Manchester, Lancashire. Lower order left-hand batsman, right-arm fast medium bowler. *Team* Lancashire (1949–50, 6 matches).
Career batting
6–8–2–86–46–14.33–0–*ct* 1
Bowling 472–9–52.44–0–0–4/30

Stone, James
Professional. *b:* 29.11.1876, Southampton, Hampshire. *d:* 15.11.1942, Maidenhead, Berkshire. Middle order right-hand batsman, right-arm medium pace bowler, wicket-keeper. *Teams* Hampshire (1900–14, 274 matches); Glamorgan (1922–23, 27 matches).
Career batting
306–524–63–10341–174–22.43–6–*ct* 394–*st* 130
Bowling 104–1–104.00–0–0–1/77

He hit 1,000 runs in a season three times (best 1,249, av 25.48, in 1913). He was a first-class umpire (1925–34).

Stoner, Arthur
Professional. *b:* 11.5.1871, Streatham, Surrey. Lower order batsman, useful bowler. *Team* Surrey (1899–1900, 6 matches).
Career batting
6–9–0–98–61–10.88–0–*ct* 2
Bowling 344–14–24.57–0–0–4/16
He also played for Durham (pre first-class, 1904–08). He was a first-class umpire (1919).

Storer, Enoch
Professional. *b:* 18.5.1838, Clay Cross, Derbyshire. *d:* 1.7.1880, Hulme, Lancashire. Lower order left-hand batsman, right-hand fast round-arm bowler, slip field. *Team* Lancashire (1865–78, 6 matches).
Career batting
6–11–5–46–23–7.66–0–*ct* 2
Bowling 245–15–16.33–1–0–5/12

Storer, Harry (sen)
Professional. *b:* 24.7.1870, Butterley, Derbyshire. *d:* 25.4.1908, Holloway, Derbyshire. He died of consumption. Brother of William (Derbyshire), father of Harry jun (Derbyshire). Middle order right-hand batsman. *Team* Derbyshire (1895, 6 matches).
Career batting
6–10–1–92–35–10.22–0–*ct* 3
Bowling 13–0
A noted soccer player, he played for Liverpool and Arsenal.

Storer, Harry (jun)
Professional. *b:* 2.2.1898, West Derby, Liverpool, Lancashire. *d:* 1.9.1967, California, Derby. Son of Harry sen (Derbyshire), nephew of William (Derbyshire). Sound opening right-hand batsman, leg break bowler, occasional wicket-keeper. *Team* Derbyshire (1920–36, 302 matches).
Career batting
302–517–28–13513–232–27.63–18–*ct* 214–*st* 1
Bowling 7525–232–32.43–9–0–7/26
He hit 1,000 runs in a season six times (best 1,652, av 36.71, in 1929). Both his double centuries were for Derbyshire, the higher being 232 v Essex at Derby in 1933. An excellent wing-half, he played soccer for Derby County, Grimsby, Burnley and England. He later managed several League clubs.

Storer, Richard Elliott Daniel
Cricketer. *b:* 9.5.1948, Nottingham. Lower order right-hand batsman, wicket-keeper. *Sch* Nottingham HS. *Team* Oxford U (1972).
Career batting
4–6–3–13–9–4.33–0–*ct* 2

Storer, William
Professional. *b:* 25.1.1867, Butterley, Derbyshire. *d:* 28.2.1912, Derby. Brother of Harry sen (Derbyshire), uncle of Harry jun (Derbyshire). Sound middle order right-hand batsman, leg break bowler, wicket-keeper. *Teams* Derbyshire (1887–1905, 209 matches); London County (1900). *Tour* Stoddart to Australia, 1897/8. *Tests* England (1897/8 to 1899, 6 matches).
Career batting
289–490–41–12966–216*–28.87–17–*ct* 376–*st* 55
Bowling 7863–232–33.89–4–0–5/20
Test batting
6–11–0–215–51–19.54–0–*ct* 11
Bowling 108–2–54.00–0–0–1/24
He hit 1,000 runs in a season seven times (best 1,548, av 41.43, in 1898). His only double century was 216* for Derbyshire v Leicestershire at Chesterfield in 1899. A useful soccer player he appeared for Derby County, Loughborough Town and Glossop.

Storey, Stewart James
Professional. *b:* 6.1.1941, Worthing, Sussex. Middle order right-hand batsman, right-arm medium pace bowler, good close field. *Teams* Surrey (1960–74, 315 matches); Sussex (1978, 16 matches).
Career batting
332–492–62–10776–164–25.06–12–*ct* 325
Bowling 13175–496–26.56–11–2–8/22
He hit 1,000 runs in a season five times (best 1,184, av 35.87, in 1971). He took 104 wickets, av 18.39, in 1966, achieving the 'double' that season. He was the Sussex coach (1979–86).

Storie, Alastair Caleb
Cricketer. *b:* 25.7.1965, Bishopbriggs, Glasgow, Scotland. Middle order right-hand batsman, right-arm medium pace bowler. *Teams* Northamptonshire (1985–86, 15 matches); Warwickshire (1987–88, 25 matches); Orange Free State (1987/8); Scotland (1990); Oxford U (1992, blue).
Career batting
53–86–13–1495–106–20.47–1–*ct* 34
Bowling 199–2–99.50–0–0–1/17
He scored 106 for Northamptonshire v Hampshire at Northampton in 1985 on his first-class debut.

Storrie, James
Amateur. *b:* 7.2.1885, Hawick, Roxburghshire, Scotland. *d:* 23.7.1951, Hawick, Roxburghshire, Scotland. Brother of Walter (Scotland). Lower order right-hand batsman, off break bowler. *Team* Scotland (1911).
Career batting
2–3–0–53–26–17.66–0–*ct* 0
Bowling 86–1–86.00–0–0–1/10

Storrie, Walter
Amateur. *b:* 2.1.1875, Hawick, Roxburghshire, Scotland. *d:* 3.12.1945, Hawick, Roxburghshire, Scotland. Brother of James (Scotland). Middle order right-hand

batsman. *Team* Scotland (1911).
Career batting
1–2–0–8–8–4.00–0–*ct* 0

Story, William Frederick
Amateur. *b:* 3.4.1852, Stockport, Cheshire. *d:* 1.12.1939, Marylebone, London. Lower order right-hand batsman, right-arm fast bowler, wicket-keeper. *Sch* Repton. *Team* Nottinghamshire (1878–79, 6 matches).
Career batting
8–13–1–41–16–3.41–0–*ct* 6–*st* 4
His final first-class match was for MCC in 1883. He was on the Committee of Nottinghamshire CCC in 1920 and President of the Club in 1929. He was a well-known racehorse owner.

Stott, William Bryan
Professional. *b:* 18.7.1934, Yeadon, Yorkshire. Aggressive opening left-hand batsman, right-arm medium pace bowler. *Team* Yorkshire (1952–63, 187 matches).
Career batting
190–314–20–9248–186–31.45–17–*ct* 91
Bowling 112–7–16.00–0–0–4/34
He hit 1,000 runs in a season five times (best 2,034, av 37.66, in 1959).

Stovold, Andrew Willis
Cricketer. *b:* 19.3.1953, Southmead, Bristol. Brother of M. W. (Gloucestershire). Opening or middle order right-hand batsman, wicket-keeper. *Teams* Gloucestershire (1973–90, 346 matches); Orange Free State (1974/5 to 1975/6). *Tours* Gloucestershire to Sri Lanka 1986/7.
Career batting
354–630–35–17705–212*–29.75–20–*ct* 289–*st* 45
Bowling 218–4–54.50–0–0–1/0
He hit 1,000 runs in a season eight times (best 1,671, av 42.84, in 1983). His highest score was 212* for Gloucestershire v Northamptonshire at Northampton in 1982.

Stovold, Martin Willis
Cricketer. *b:* 28.12.1955, Almondsbury, Bristol. Brother of A. W. (Gloucestershire). Middle order left-hand batsman. *Team* Gloucestershire (1979–82, 25 matches).
Career batting
25–37–6–518–75*–16.70–0–*ct* 5
Bowling 19–0

Stow, Montague Haslam
Amateur. *b:* 21.7.1847, Red Hall, Whinmoor, Roundhay, Leeds, Yorkshire. *d:* 7.9.1911, Monifieth, Angus, Scotland. Brother-in-law of W. W. C. Lane (Surrey). Stylish middle order right-hand batsman, wicket-keeper. *Sch* Harrow. *Team* Cambridge U (1867–69, blue all three years).
Career batting
16–26–3–303–41–13.17–0–*ct* 18–*st* 1
His final first-class match was for Gentlemen of the North in 1871. He captained Cambridge in 1869. He represented Cambridge at rackets in 1868 and 1870.

Stow, Vincent Aubrey Stewart
Amateur. *b:* 27.7.1883, Kensington, London. *d:* 21.4.1968, St Pancras, London. Lower order batsman, wicket-keeper. *Sch* Winchester. *Team* Oxford U (1904). *Tour* MCC to North America 1905.
Career batting
3–5–1–47–23–11.75–0–*ct* 2
His final first-class match in England was for Gentlemen of England in 1905.

Strachan, George
Amateur. *b:* 21.11.1850, Prestbury, Gloucestershire. *d:* 29.12.1901, Middelburg, Transvaal, South Africa. He died of fever. Lower order right-hand batsman, slow right-arm bowler. *Sch* Cheltenham. *Teams* Gloucestershire (1870–82, 13 matches); Middlesex (1870–71, 3 matches); Surrey (1872–80, 54 matches).
Career batting
99–159–17–2014–84–14.18–0–*ct* 94
Bowling 3344–179 + 3–18.68–7–0–6/31
He was Surrey captain 1872–75 and 1877–79.

Strachan, George Robson
Cricketer. *b:* 29.8.1932, Blackridge, West Lothian, Scotland. Lower order right-hand batsman, right-arm medium pace bowler. *Team* Scotland (1965).
Career batting
2–1–1–17–17*–no av–0–*ct* 0
Bowling 34–2–17.00–0–0–1/14

Strachan, John Harold
Amateur. *b:* 8.3.1896, Walton-on-Thames, Surrey. *d:* 1.12.1988, Collingwood, Ontario, Canada. Middle order right-hand batsman. *Sch* Charterhouse. *Team* Free Foresters (1926).
Career batting
1–2–0–53–26.50–0–*ct* 0

Straker, Arthur Coppin
Amateur. *b:* 12.8.1893, High Warden, Hexham, Northumberland. *d:* 14.10.1961, Pawston, Northumberland. Middle order batsman. *Sch* Harrow. *Team* Cambridge U (1913).
Career batting
1–2–0–21–21–10.50–0–*ct* 0
His County cricket was for Denbighshire (1934–35). He won a blue for athletics.

Strang, Dr Robert
Amateur. *b:* 30.9.1901, Rainham Lodge, Hacton, Hornchurch, Essex. *d:* 15.3.1976, Tylers Green, Buckinghamshire. Middle order right-hand batsman, right-arm medium pace bowler. *Sch* Whitgift. *Team* Scotland (1925).

Career batting
1–2–0–34–23–17.00–0–*ct* 0
Bowling 66–2–33.00–0–0–2/47
His County cricket was for Berkshire (1924–25).

Stratford, Alfred Hugh
Amateur. *b:* 5.9.1853, Kensington, London. *d:* 2.5.1914, Newark, New Jersey, USA. Brother of F. W. (USA). Lower order right-hand batsman, slow right-arm bowler. *Sch* Malvern. *Teams* Middlesex (1877–80, 18 matches); USA (1884).
Career batting
34–55–8–577–55*–12.27–0–*ct* 10
Bowling 1367–83–16.46–5–2–6/44
He also played for Herefordshire. He emigrated to the USA about 1890 and played much cricket for New York and other clubs there. A good soccer player, he appeared for Wanderers when they won the FA Cup in 1876, 1877 and 1878, and for England.

Strathavon, Lord
(*see under* Aboyne, Earl of)

Stratton, Henry Duncan
Amateur. *b:* 10.5.1870, Wolverhampton, Staffordshire. *d:* 26.2.1958, Bexhill-on-Sea, Sussex. Middle order right-hand batsman. *Team* MCC (1904–14).
Career batting
4–8–3–75–20–15.00–0–*ct* 1
His County cricket was for Staffordshire (1898–1911).

Stratton, John William
Amateur. *b:* 31.8.1875, Turweston House, Buckinghamshire. *d:* 29.10.1919, Repton, Derbyshire. Lower order right-hand batsman, right-arm fast bowler. *Sch* Cheltenham. *Team* Oxford U (1896).
Career batting
1–2–0–8–7–4.00–0–*ct* 1
Bowling 93–3–31.00–0–0–3/93
His County cricket was for Buckinghamshire (1895–1901).

Stratton, Robert Arthur
Amateur. *b:* 10.10.1924, Edgbaston, Birmingham. Tail end right-hand batsman, wicket-keeper. *Sch* St Peter's, York. *Team* Cambridge U (1946).
Career batting
3–4–3–23–12*–23.00–0–*ct* 0–*st* 1
He played against Oxford U in 1944 and 1945 wartime matches. He won a blue for hockey.

Straw, David Sorby
Cricketer. *b:* 28.5.1935, South Croydon, Surrey. Middle order right-hand batsman, wicket-keeper. *Sch* Whitgift. *Team* MCC (1964).
Career batting
1–1–0–10–10–10.00–0–*ct* 0

Straw, Thomas
Professional. *b:* 1.9.1870, Hucknall Torkard, Nottinghamshire. *d:* 8.9.1959, Hucknall Torkard, Nottinghamshire. Lower order right-hand batsman, wicket-keeper. *Team* Worcestershire (1899–1907, 61 matches).
Career batting
61–94–38–600–32–10.71–0–*ct* 122–*st* 12
He was dismissed twice in first-class County matches 'obstructing field' – for Worcestershire against Warwickshire in 1899 and in 1901. He first played for Worcestershire (pre first-class) in 1895.

Streak, Denis Hilton
Cricketer. *b:* 21.6.1949, Bulawayo, Rhodesia. Lower order right-hand batsman, right-arm fast medium bowler. *Team* Rhodesia/Zimbabwe (1976/7 to 1985). *Tour* Zimbabwe to England 1985.
Career batting
13–17–5–225–29–18.75–0–*ct* 5
Bowling 647–16–40.43–0–0–4/81
He played in only three first-class games on the 1985 tour.

Streatfeild, Alexander McNeill
(changed name to Streatfeild-Moore in 1885)
Amateur. *b:* 17.10.1863, Charts Edge, Westerham, Kent. *d:* 30.12.1940, Oakhanger Park, Shefford Woodlands, Newbury, Berkshire. Brother of E. C. (Surrey), brother-in-law of G. D. Barne (Somerset). Middle order right-hand batsman, slow right-arm bowler. *Sch* Charterhouse. *Team* Kent (1885–88, 7 matches).
Career batting
7–14–0–127–36–9.07–0–*ct* 5
He also played for Buckinghamshire (1897).

Streatfeild, Edward Champion
Amateur. *b:* 16.6.1870, Nutfield, Surrey. *d:* 22.8.1932, Eastbourne, Sussex. Brother of A. M. (Kent), brother-in-law of G. D. Barne (Somerset). Sound middle order right-hand batsman, right-arm medium bowler, good slip field. *Sch* Charterhouse. *Teams* Cambridge U (1890–93, blue all four years); Surrey (1890–92, 9 matches).
Career batting
38–66–9–1414–145–24.80–2–*ct* 39
Bowling 2232–123–18.14–6–2–6/34
He was also awarded his soccer blue.

Streatfeild, Granville Gerald Champion
Amateur. *b:* 5.11.1904, Westerham, Kent. *d:* 28.9.1954, Kadang Valley, Kenya. Attractive middle order right-hand batsman, left-arm fast medium bowler. *Sch* Marlborough. *Teams* Cambridge U (1925); Burma (1926/7); Rangoon Gymkhana (1926/7).
Career batting
5–7–1–72–18–12.00–0–*ct* 0

Street, Alfred Edward
Professional. *b:* 7.7.1869, Godalming, Surrey. *d:* 18.2.1951, Exmouth, Devon. Son of James (Surrey). Middle order right-hand batsman, right-arm medium pace bowler. *Team* Surrey (1892–98, 50 matches).
Career batting
50–66–6–1356–161*–22.60–1–*ct* 16
Bowling 393–15–26.20–0–0–3/44
He was a first-class umpire (1909–24) and stood in seven Test matches (1912–22). Whilst umpiring at Taunton in 1919 he gave a Sussex batsman, Heygate, out for failing to reach the wicket within two minutes – a decision which caused much controversy at the time.

Street, Francis Edward
Amateur. *b:*16.2.1851, Hampstead, London. *d:* 4.6.1928, Armidale, New South Wales, Australia. Opening right-hand batsman, good deep field. *Sch* Uppingham. *Team* Kent (1875–77, 4 matches).
Career batting
4–7–0–21–12–3.00–0–*ct* 2

Street, Frank
Amateur. *b:* 31.5.1870, Kensington, London. *d:* 7.7.1916, Ovilliers la Boiselle, France. Middle order right-hand batsman, right-arm medium pace bowler. *Sch* Westminster. *Team* Essex (1898–99, 9 matches).
Career batting
9–11–0–246–76–22.36–0–*ct* 4
Bowling 14–0
He did not play in first-class cricket whilst at Oxford, but was awarded his blue for soccer.

Street, George Benjamin
Professional. *b:* 6.12.1889, Charlwood, Surrey. *d:* 24.4.1924, Portslade, Sussex. He was killed in a motor-cycle accident. Middle order right-hand batsman, wicket-keeper. *Team* Sussex (1909–23, 192 matches). *Tour* MCC to South Africa 1922/3. *Test* England (1922/3, 1 match).
Career batting
197–304–73–3984–109–17.24–1–*ct* 308–*st* 121
Bowling 66–3–22.00–0–0–3/26
Test batting
1–2–1–11–7*–11.00–0–*ct* 0–*st* 1
On the 1922/3 tour to South Africa, Livsey, the wicket-keeper, was injured and Street was sent out as a replacement, but played in only four first-class matches, including the third Test.

Street, Henry
Professional. *b:* 18.4.1863, Riddings, Derbyshire. *d:* 12.3.1953, Riddings, Derbyshire. Middle order right-hand batsman. *Team* Derbyshire (1887, 2 matches).
Career batting
2–4–1–24–15*–8.00–0–*ct* 1

Street, James
Professional. *b:* 10.3.1839, Cranleigh, Surrey. *d:* 17.9.1906, Godalming, Surrey. Father of A. E. (Surrey). Lower order right-hand batsman, right-hand fast round-arm bowler. *Team* Surrey (1863–78, 139 matches).
Career batting
143–247–73–1308–50–7.51–0–*ct* 74
Bowling 11578–540–21.44–36–6–7/141
His best season was 1872, when he took 60 wickets, av 15.11. He later umpired in first-class matches (1883–99), standing in one Test match in 1890.

Street, Lawrence Charles
Professional. *b:* 4.2.1920, Erdington, Birmingham. Lower order right-hand batsman, right-arm fast medium bowler. *Team* Warwickshire (1946, 4 matches).
Career batting
4–7–2–17–8*–3.40–0–*ct* 2
Bowling 146–3–48.66–0–0–2/15

Street, Norman Kingsley
Amateur. *b:* 13.8.1881, Edgbaston, Birmingham. *d:* 10.8.1915, Sari Bair, Suvla Bay, Gallipoli Peninsula, Turkey. Middle order right-hand batsman. *Sch* Bromsgrove. *Team* Warwickshire (1908, 5 matches).
Career batting
5–9–0–43–14–4.77–0–*ct* 3

Stretton, Sidney
(death registered as Sydney Stretton)
Professional. *b:* 20.11.1902, Stamford, Lincolnshire. *d:* 14.1.1984, Kings Mill, Sutton-in-Ashfield, Nottinghamshire. Tail end left-hand batsman, left-arm fast bowler. *Team* Northamptonshire (1928, 1 match).
Career batting
1–2–0–1–1–0.50–0–*ct* 1
Bowling 120–2–60.00–0–0–2/120

Stretton, Terry Kevin
Cricketer. *b:* 23.5.1953, Cosby, Leicestershire. Lower order right-hand batsman, right-arm medium pace bowler. *Team* Leicestershire (1972–75, 6 matches).
Career batting
6–7–3–20–6*–5.00–0–*ct* 2
Bowling 338–4–84.50–0–0–2/71

Stricker, Louis Anthony
Amateur. *b:* 26.5.1884, Beaconsfield, Kimberley, South Africa. *d:* 5.2.1960, Rondebosch, Cape Town, South Africa. Brother of H. B. (Transvaal). Opening right-hand batsman. *Team* Transvaal (1906/7 to 1911/12). *Tours* South Africa to Australia 1910/11, to England 1912. *Tests* South Africa (1909/10 to 1912, 13 matches).
Career batting
60–96–4–2105–146–22.88–2–*ct* 29–*st* 2
Bowling 303–8–37.87–0–0–3/13
Test batting
13–24–0–342–48–14.25–0–*ct* 3

Bowling 105–1–105.00–0–0–1/36

He hit 875 runs, av 19.88, in all matches on the 1912 visit to England.

Stringer, Peter Michael
Cricketer. *b:* 23.2.1943, Gipton, Leeds, Yorkshire. Lower order left-hand batsman, right-arm fast medium bowler. *Teams* Yorkshire (1967–69, 19 matches); Leicestershire (1970–72, 37 matches).
Career batting
56–63–21–333–22–7.92–0–*ct* 28
Bowling 2772–88–31.50–1–0–5/43

Stringer, Thomas
Professional. *b:* 1874, Lascelles Hall, Yorkshire. Tail end batsman, leg break bowler. *Team* Worcestershire (1909, 1 match).
Career batting
1–2–1–0–0*–0.00–*ct* 0
Bowling 103–1–103.00–0–0–1/103

Stripp, David Arthur
Professional. *b:* 4.4.1935, Crawley Down, Sussex. Middle order right-hand batsman, right-arm fast medium bowler. *Team* Sussex (1956–57, 12 matches).
Career batting
12–20–3–183–32*–10.76–0–*ct* 10
Bowling 297–6–49.50–0–0–2/12

Stroud, Eric Gundry
Amateur. *b:* 11.7.1904, Caterham, Surrey. *d:* 14.8.1944, Farnham, Surrey. Lower order right-hand batsman, right-arm medium bowler. *Team* Surrey (1930, 7 matches).
Career batting
10–13–3–157–24–15.70–0–*ct* 6
Bowling 832–38–21.89–2–0–7/92

His final first-class match was for H. D. G. Leveson-Gower's XI in 1932.

Strudwick, Herbert
Professional. *b:* 28.1.1880, Mitcham, Surrey. *d:* 14.2.1970, Shoreham, Sussex. Lower order right-hand batsman, excellent wicket-keeper. *Team* Surrey (1902–27, 554 matches). *Tours* MCC to Australia 1903/4, 1911/12, 1920/1, 1924/5, to South Africa 1909/10, 1913/14. *Tests* England (1909/10 to 1926, 28 matches).
Career batting
674–835–243–6445–93–10.88–0–*ct* 1242–*st* 254
Bowling 102–1–102.00–0–0–1/9
Test batting
28–42–13–230–24–7.93–0–*ct* 60–*st* 12

One of the best wicket-keepers of his day, he set up a career record for the most dismissals by a wicket-keeper, which stood for nearly 50 years, before being beaten by J. T. Murray. He was Surrey scorer 1946–57.

Strutt, Hon Henry
(succeeded to the title 2nd Lord Belper in 1880)
Amateur. *b:* 20.5.1840, Westminster, London. *d:* 26.7.1914, Kingston-upon-Soar Hall, Nottinghamshire. Brother-in-law of K. E. Digby (Oxford U). Hard hitting lower order right-hand batsman, wicket-keeper. *Sch* Harrow. *Team* Cambridge U (1862).
Career batting
5–7–1–97–31*–16.16–0–*ct* 1

He was President of MCC in 1882 and of Nottinghamshire CCC in 1885 and 1886. His final first-class match was for MCC in 1865. When travelling in Greece in 1865 he was taken prisoner by brigands and forced to pay £1,000 ransom for his release. He was MP for East Derbyshire 1868 to 1874 and Berwick-on-Tweed in 1880.

Strutton, Benjamin Thomas
Professional. *b:* 1892. *d:* 9.2.1968, Southwark, London. Lower order batsman, slow left-arm bowler. *Team* Essex (1914–19, 4 matches).
Career batting
4–6–1–64–19–12.80–0–*ct* 1
Bowling 197–0

Stuart, Pascoe William Grenfell
(changed name to Stuart-French in 1917)
Amateur. *b:* 25.10.1868, Woolwich, London. *d:* 5.2.1954, Marino, Cobh, Co Cork, Ireland. Middle order right-hand batsman. *Sch* Sherborne. *Team* London County (1904).
Career batting
3–5–0–67–50–13.40–0–*ct* 2

His final first-class match was for MCC in 1906. He played for Ireland (not first-class) 1872–1904.

Stuart, Robert Livingstone
Amateur. *b:* 30.12.1908, Buenos Aires, Argentina. *d:* 6.6.1986, Buenos Aires, Argentina. Middle order right-hand batsman, right-arm medium pace bowler. *Sch* Highgate. *Team* Argentina (1929/30 to 1937/8). *Tour* South America to England 1932.
Career batting
9–17–1–405–133–25.31–1–*ct* 4
Bowling 58–1–58.00–0–0–1/35

Stuart, William Grant Spruell
Amateur. *b:* 8.6.1889, Gartly, Aberdeen, Scotland. *d:* 23.4.1917, Arras, France. He was killed in action. Middle order batsman. *Sch* George Watson's College. *Team* Scotland (1914).
Career batting
1–2–0–27–17–13.50–0–*ct* 2

Stuart-King, R. J. (*see under* King, R. J. S.)

Stubberfield, Henry
Professional. *b:* 16.3.1835, Brighton, Sussex. *d:* 14.2.1918, Brighton, Sussex. Lower order right-hand batsman, right-hand fast medium round-arm bowler, good slip field. *Team* Sussex (1857–74, 57 matches).

Stubbings, James

Career batting
61–99–27–518–40–7.19–0–*ct* 55
Bowling 2522–141–17.88–8–2–7/10

He also played for Lincolnshire (1860). After retiring from County cricket, he became a well-known umpire.

Stubbings, James
Professional. *b:* 27.4.1856, Whitwell, Derbyshire. *d:* 17.7.1912, Huddersfield, Yorkshire. Brother of Walter (Derbyshire). Lower order right-hand batsman, right-arm fast bowler. *Team* Derbyshire (1880–85, 4 matches).
Career batting
5–10–3–26–10*–3.71–0–*ct* 1
Bowling 142–7–20.28–1–0–5/51

His first-class debut was for Players of North in 1877. He last played for Derbyshire (not first-class) in 1893.

Stubbings, Walter
Professional. *b:* 4.9.1870, Whitwell, Derbyshire. *d:* 28.11.1949, Wakefield, Yorkshire. Brother of James (Derbyshire). Lower order batsman, useful bowler. *Team* Derbyshire (1900, 1 match).
Career batting
1–2–1–9–9*–9.00–0–*ct* 0
Bowling 80–0

Stubbs, Thomas Alfred
Amateur. *b:* 13.3.1872, West Derby, Liverpool. Middle order batsman. *Team* Liverpool and District (1893–94).
Career batting
4–8–1–168–43–24.00–0–*ct* 2

Stubbs, Thomas Walker
Amateur. *b:* 11.9.1856, Ashton-upon-Mersey, Cheshire. *d:* 5.6.1899, Stow-on-the-Wold, Gloucestershire. Hard hitting lower order right-hand batsman, right-hand fast round-arm bowler. *Sch* Clifton. *Team* Oxford U (1877).
Career batting
1–1–0–1–1–1.00–0–*ct* 0
Bowling 41–3–13.66–0–0–2/26

He played for Gloucestershire in non-first-class matches in 1889.

Stuchbury, Stephen
Cricketer. *b:* 22.6.1954, Sheffield, Yorkshire. Lower order left-hand batsman, left-arm fast medium bowler. *Team* Yorkshire (1978–81, 3 matches).
Career batting
3–3–2–7–4*–7.00–0–*ct* 0
Bowling 236–8–29.50–0–0–3/82

Studd, Arthur Haythorne
Amateur. *b:* 19.11.1863, Hallaton Hall, Billesdon, Leicestershire. *d:* 26.1.1919, Marylebone, London. Half-brother of E. J. C. (MCC), brother of J. E. K. (Middlesex), G. B. (Middlesex), C. T. (Middlesex), H. W. (Middlesex and Hampshire) and R. A. (Hampshire). Opening or middle order right-hand batsman, right-arm slow bowler, good cover point. *Sch* Eton. *Team* MCC (1887–88).
Career batting
5–8–0–104–47–13.00–0–*ct* 4
Bowling 23–0

He played in the 1885 Cambridge Freshmen's match, but no first-class games at the University. His County cricket was for Hampshire (not first-class, 1888–89). His first-class debut was for A. J. Webbe's XI in 1885. He was 'an artist in London and Samoa'.

Studd, Charles Thomas
Amateur. *b:* 2.12.1860, Spratton, Northamptonshire. *d:* 16.7.1931, Ibambi, Belgian Congo. Half-brother of E. J. C. (MCC), brother of A. H. (MCC), J. E. K. (Middlesex), G. B. (Middlesex), H. W. (Middlesex and Hampshire) and R. A. (Hampshire). Stylish middle order right-hand batsman, right-arm medium fast bowler. *Sch* Eton. *Teams* Middlesex (1879–84, 34 matches); Cambridge U (1880–83, blue all four years); Gentlemen of India (1902/3). *Tour* Bligh to Australia 1882/3. *Tests* England (1882 to 1882/3, 5 matches).
Career batting
99–167–23–4391–175*–30.49–8–*ct* 73
Bowling 7659–441 + 3–17.36–32–9–8/40
Test batting
5–9–1–160–48–20.00–0–*ct* 5
Bowling 8–3–32.66–0–0–2/35

The most talented of the Studd family, he topped the first-class batting averages in 1882 with 1,249 runs, av 32.86, and came second in 1883 with 1,193, av 41.13. He took 100 wickets in a season twice (best 128 + 3, av 16.38, in 1883) and performed the 'double' in both years. He captained Cambridge in 1883. After 1884 however he left England to become a missionary in China, remaining there until ill-health forced him home in 1895. In 1900 he went out to India to do similar work and later went to the Belgian Congo where he founded the Heart of Africa Mission and stayed for the remainder of his life, despite numerous illnesses and hardship. He also won a blue for rackets.

Studd, Edward Basil Turnour
Amateur. *b:* 20.10.1878, Dhoolie, Tirhoot, India. *d:* 2.3.1951, Stanton, Cheltenham, Gloucestershire. Son of E. J. C. (MCC). Middle order right-hand batsman. *Sch* Harrow. *Teams* Europeans (1917/8); Gloucestershire (1919, 2 matches).
Career batting
3–6–0–69–25–11.50–0–*ct* 2

Studd, Edward John Charles
Amateur. *b:* 13.2.1849, Tirhoot, India. *d:* 1.3.1909, Folkestone, Kent. Half-brother of J. E. K. (Middlesex), G. B. (Middlesex), C. T. (Middlesex), A. H.

(MCC), H. W. (Middlesex and Hampshire) and R. A. (Hampshire), father of E. B. T. (Gloucestershire). Middle order right-hand batsman, good field. *Sch* Cheltenham. *Team* MCC (1879–85).

Career batting
21–34–1–621–110–18.81–1–*ct* 17

His final first-class match was for C. I. Thornton's XI in 1888. For 16 years he lived in India, being an indigo planter and therefore had little opportunity for good class cricket.

Studd, George Brown
Amateur. *b:* 20.10.1859, Netheravon, Wiltshire. *d:* 13.2.1945, Pasadena, California, USA. Half-brother of E. J. C. (MCC), brother of J. E. K. (Middlesex), C. T. (Middlesex), A. H. (MCC), H. W. (Middlesex and Hampshire) and R. A. (Hampshire). Middle order right-hand batsman, brilliant field. *Sch* Eton. *Teams* Cambridge U (1879–82, blue all four years); Middlesex (1879–86, 29 matches). *Tour* Bligh to Australia 1882/3. *Tests* England (1882/3, 4 matches).

Career batting
87–142–10–2892–120–21.90–3–*ct* 74–*st* 1
Bowling 29–2–14.50–0–0–1/5
Test batting
4–7–0–31–9–4.42–0–*ct* 8

His best season was 1881 with 647 runs, av 30.90. He captained Cambridge in 1882. A good royal tennis player he represented Cambridge. After leaving University he became, like his brother C. T., a missionary in China and later in India and America at the Los Angeles Gospel Mission.

Studd, Brig-Gen Herbert William
Amateur. *b:* 26.12.1870, Tidworth House, Wiltshire. *d:* 8.8.1947, Bayswater, London. Half-brother of E. J. C. (MCC), brother of J. E. K. (Middlesex), C. T. (Middlesex), A. H. (MCC), G. B. (Middlesex) and R. A. (Hampshire). Middle order right-hand batsman. *Sch* Eton. *Teams* Middlesex (1890, 1 match); Hampshire (1898, 4 matches).

Career batting
8–13–0–352–71–27.07–0–*ct* 5
Bowling 71–1–71.00–0–0–1/23

He played in the Freshmen's match of 1890, but no first-class matches for Cambridge. He first played for Hampshire (not first-class) in 1891.

Studd, Sir John Edward Kynaston
Amateur. *b:* 26.7.1858, Netheravon, Wiltshire. *d:* 14.1.1944, Marylebone, London. Half-brother of E. J. C. (MCC), brother of C. T. (Middlesex), A. H. (MCC), G. B. (Middlesex), H. W. (Middlesex and Hampshire) and R. A. (Hampshire). Middle order right-hand batsman, right-arm fast bowler. *Sch* Eton. *Teams* Middlesex (1878–84, 11 matches); Cambridge U (1881–84, blue all four years).

Career batting
54–96–3–1681–154–18.07–1–*ct* 22
Bowling 322–12–26.83–0–0–3/32

His final first-class match was for MCC in 1885. He captained Cambridge in 1884. He was President of MCC in 1930. He took a prominent part in the founding and running of the London Polytechnic and was President from 1903 to his death. In 1928/9 he was Lord Mayor of London.

Studd, Sir Peter Malden
Amateur. *b:* 15.9.1916, Dublin, Ireland. He married the widow of C. P. Hamilton (Kent). Attacking middle order right-hand batsman, good field. *Sch* Harrow. *Team* Cambridge U (1936–39, blue 1937–39).

Career batting
28–46–4–1075–80*–25.59–0–*ct* 12

He was Lord Mayor of London in 1970/1.

Studd, Reginald Augustus
Amateur. *b:* 18.12.1873, Tidworth House, Wiltshire. *d:* 3.2.1948, Northampton. Half-brother of E. J. C. (MCC), brother of C. T. (Middlesex), A. H. (MCC), G. B. (Middlesex), H. W. (Middlesex and Hampshire) and J. E. K. (Middlesex). Middle order right-hand batsman. *Sch* Eton. *Teams* Cambridge U (1895, blue); Hampshire (1895, 3 matches). *Tour* Mitchell to North America 1895.

Career batting
15–26–2–603–96*–25.12–0–*ct* 3

His first-class debut was for MCC in 1894.

Sturgeon, S. M.
Amateur. Lower order batsman, wicket-keeper. *Team* Scotland (1922–23).

Career batting
2–3–0–1–1–0.33–0–*ct* 5–*st* 1

Sturman, Walter
Professional. *b:* 29.8.1882, Leicester. *d:* 24.7.1958, Aylestone, Leicester. Lower order right-hand batsman, wicket-keeper. *Team* Leicestershire (1909–12, 24 matches).

Career batting
24–36–9–273–46–10.11–0–*ct* 27–*st* 5

Sturt, Michael Ormonde Cleasby
Amateur. *b:* 12.9.1941, Wembley, Middlesex. Lower order right-hand batsman, wicket-keeper. *Team* Middlesex (1961–78, 33 matches).

Career batting
33–35–9–202–26–7.76–0–*ct* 61–*st* 10

Sturt, Montague Alfred Sliney
Amateur. *b:* 11.11.1876, Sunderland, Co Durham. *d:* 16.1.1961, Buckland, Dover, Kent. Middle order right-hand batsman. *Sch* Taunton. *Team* Somerset (1896–1910, 10 matches).

Career batting
10–17–1–199–35–12.43–0–*ct* 3
Bowling 15–1–15.00–0–0–1/15

He also played for Devon (1900).

Style, Sir William Henry Marsham
Amateur. *b:* 3.9.1826, Bicester House, Oxfordshire. *d:* 31.1.1904, Folkestone, Kent. Brother-in-law of H. Tubb (MCC). Lower order batsman, wicket-keeper. *Sch* Eton. *Team* Hampshire (1865, 1 match).
Career batting
1–2–0–1–1–0.50–0–*ct* 0–*st* 1

He also played for Wiltshire (1863) and Brecon (1872).

Styler, Sidney William
Professional. *b:* 26.8.1908, Cotteridge, Warwickshire. *d:* 27.1.1980, Worcester. Lower order right-hand batsman, wicket-keeper. *Team* Worcestershire (1929–31, 18 matches).
Career batting
18–31–6–134–24–5.36–0–*ct* 23–*st* 3

Subba Row, Raman, CBE
Amateur. *b:* 29.1.1932, Streatham, London. Sound opening or middle order left-hand batsman, slow leg break and googly bowler, excellent slip field. *Sch* Whitgift. *Teams* Cambridge U (1951–53, blue all three years); Surrey (1953–54, 41 matches); Northamptonshire (1955–61, 113 matches). *Tours* MCC to Australia and New Zealand 1958/9, to West Indies 1959/60; Commonwealth to India 1953/4; International XI to India and Pakistan 1961/2; President's XI in India 1967/8. *Tests* England (1958–61, 13 matches).
Career batting
260–407–65–14182–300–41.46–30–*ct* 176
Bowling 3363–87–38.65–2–0–5/21
Test batting
13–22–1–984–137–46.85–3–*ct* 5
Bowling 2–0

He hit 1,000 runs in a season six times (best 1,917, av 46.75, in 1959). His highest innings was 300 for Northamptonshire v Surrey at the Oval in 1958, and he also hit one double century for Northamptonshire. From 1958 to 1961 he captained Northamptonshire. In 1981/2 he was manager of the England team to India. From 1974 to 1978 he was Chairman of Surrey CCC. He was Chairman of the TCCB and the Cricket Council from 1985 to 1990.

Subramanya, Venkataraman
Amateur. *b:* 16.7.1936, Bangalore, India. Brother of V. Ramadas (Mysore) and V. Krishnaprasad (Mysore). Middle order right-hand batsman, right-arm medium, or leg break and googly bowler, good close field. *Team* Mysore (1959/60 to 1969/70). *Tours* India to England 1967, to Australia and New Zealand 1967/8, to East Africa 1967/8; State Bank of India to Ceylon 1968/9. *Tests* India (1964/5 to 1967/8, 9 matches).
Career batting
101–150–16–4219–213*–31.48–8–*ct* 121
Bowling 3093–70–44.18–1–0–7/78
Test batting
9–15–1–263–75–18.78–0–*ct* 9
Bowling 201–3–67.00–0–0–2/32

He played in two Tests on the 1967 tour, but his overall figures were very modest. His highest score was 213* for Mysore v Madras at Madras in 1966/7.

Such, Peter Mark
Cricketer. *b:* 12.6.1964, Helensburgh, Dunbartonshire, Scotland. Tail end right-hand batsman, off break bowler. *Teams* Nottinghamshire (1982–86, 52 matches); Leicestershire (1987–89, 39 matches); Essex (1990–92, 40 matches).
Career batting
132–105–40–315–35*–4.84–0–*ct* 50
Bowling 9034–301–30.01–9–0–6/17

Suckling, Ernest
Professional. *b:* 27.3.1890, Balsall Heath, Birmingham. *d:* 24.2.1962, Stanley Park, Blackpool, Lancashire. Middle order left-hand batsman, slow left-arm bowler. *Teams* Warwickshire (1919, 2 matches); Worcestershire (1923–24, 3 matches).
Career batting
5–8–1–130–58–18.57–*ct* 1
Bowling 129–4–32.25–0–0–4/71

Sueter, Thomas
Professional. *c:* 17.4.1750, Hambledon, Hampshire. *d:* 17.2.1827, Hambledon, Hampshire. Middle order left-hand batsman, wicket-keeper. *Teams* Hampshire (1772–86); Surrey (1788–89).

He was one of the leading batsmen of the Hambledon Club.

Sugden, Henry Emanuel
Amateur. *b:* 16.7.1859, Edmonton, Middlesex. *d:* 4.9.1935, Chilworth, Hampshire. Brother of A. S. (Derbyshire, not first-class). Middle order right-hand batsman. *Team* Derbyshire (1882, 2 matches).
Career batting
2–4–0–13–9–3.25–0–*ct* 0

Sugden, Mark
Amateur. *b:* 11.2.1902, Leek, Staffordshire. *d:* 21.1.1990, near Dartmouth, Devon. Middle order right-hand batsman, right-arm fast medium bowler. *Sch* Denstone. *Teams* Dublin University (1922–26); Ireland (1924–30).
Career batting
8–16–1–263–51–17.53–0–*ct* 3
Bowling 255–6–42.50–0–0–3/98

A noted rugby footballer, he was capped for Dublin University and Ireland.

Sugden, Ronald Scott
Amateur. *b:* 25.5.1896, Aintree, Liverpool, Lancashire. *d:* 26.3.1971, Dinas Powys, Glamorgan. Lower order batsman, useful bowler. *Team* RAF (1929).

Career batting
2–3–0–17–12–5.66–0–*ct* 0
Bowling 33–0

Sugg, Frank Howe
Professional. *b:* 11.1.1862, Ilkeston, Derbyshire. *d:* 29.5.1933, Waterloo, Liverpool, Lancashire. Brother of Walter (Yorkshire and Derbyshire). Attacking middle order right-hand batsman, brilliant outfield. *Teams* Yorkshire (1883, 8 matches); Derbyshire (1884–86, 33 matches); Lancashire (1887–99, 235 matches). *Tests* England (1888, 2 matches).
Career batting
305–515–30–11859–220–24.45–16–*ct* 167–*st* 1
Bowling 273–10–27.30–0–0–2/12
Test batting
2–2–0–55–31–27.50–0–*ct* 0
He hit 1,000 runs in a season five times (best 1,439, av 31.26, in 1896). His only double century was 220 for Lancashire v Gloucestershire at Bristol in 1896. He was a first-class umpire (1926–27). A noted soccer player, he captained Sheffield Wednesday, Derby County and Burnley, also playing for Everton and Bolton Wanderers. Other sports at which he excelled were long distance swimming, billiards, rifle shooting, putting the shot and weight lifting.

Sugg, Walter
Professional. *b:* 21.5.1860, Ilkeston, Derbyshire. *d:* 21.5.1933, Dore, Yorkshire. Brother of F. H. (Yorkshire, Derbyshire and Lancashire). Middle order right-hand batsman, right-arm medium bowler, good cover point. *Teams* Yorkshire (1881, 1 match); Derbyshire (1884–1902, 128 matches).
Career batting
129–218–16–3469–107–17.17–2–*ct* 64
Bowling 1560–50–31.20–0–0–4/61

Sulley, Joseph
Professional. *b:* 28.5.1850, Arnold, Nottinghamshire. *d:* 14.2.1932, Daybrook, Nottinghamshire. Lower order batsman, left-hand fast round-arm bowler. *Team* Nottinghamshire (1887–88, 2 matches).
Career batting
3–6–1–57–31–11.40–0–*ct* 2
Bowling 251–15–16.73–1–0–5/46
His first-class debut was as a given man for Gentlemen of the North in 1880.

Sullivan, Rev Arnold Moon
Amateur. *b:* 30.8.1878, Kirby Moorside, Yorkshire. *d:* 27.6.1943, Meads, Eastbourne, Sussex. Brother of J. H. B. (Yorkshire). Middle order right-hand batsman. *Sch* St Peter's, York. *Teams* Cambridge U (1899–1900); Sussex (1901, 4 matches).
Career batting
13–23–3–341–63–17.05–0–*ct* 10

Sullivan, Dennis
Professional. *b:* 28.1.1883, Mitcham, Surrey. *d:* 28.12.1968, Harold Wood, Essex. Lower order right-hand batsman, wicket-keeper. *Teams* Surrey (1914–21, 8 matches); Glamorgan (1922–28, 115 matches); Wales (1923–28). *Tours* Tennyson to Jamaica 1926/7, 1927/8.
Career batting
136–192–63–971–47*–7.52–0–*ct* 152–*st* 93

Sullivan, John
Cricketer. *b:* 5.2.1945, Stalybridge, Cheshire. Lower order right-hand batsman, right-arm medium pace bowler. *Team* Lancashire (1963–76, 154 matches).
Career batting
154–241–32–4286–81*–20.50–0–*ct* 85
Bowling 2216–76–29.15–0–0–4/19

Sullivan, John Patrick
Cricketer. *b:* 11.3.1948, Bristol. Middle order right-hand batsman, occasional wicket-keeper. *Team* Gloucestershire (1968–77, 23 matches).
Career batting
23–40–1–480–53–12.30–0–*ct* 14
Bowling 50–2–25.00–0–0–2/50

Sullivan, Joseph Hubert Baron
Amateur. *b:* 21.9.1890, York. *d:* 8.2.1932, Parkgate, Chester, Cheshire. Brother of A. M. (Sussex). Sound opening right-hand batsman, right-arm medium fast bowler. *Sch* Rossall and St Peter's, York. *Teams* Yorkshire (1912, 1 match); Cambridge U (1912); Europeans (1921/2 to 1924/5).
Career batting
8–15–0–209–44–13.93–0–*ct* 3
Bowling 194–7–27.71–0–0–3/24

Sully, Haydn
Professional. *b:* 1.11.1939, Sampford Brett, Somerset. Lower order left-hand batsman, off break bowler. *Teams* Somerset (1959–63, 12 matches); Northamptonshire (1964–69, 110 matches).
Career batting
122–134–50–722–48–8.59–0–*ct* 63
Bowling 8686–314–27.66–16–2–7/29
He took 101 wickets, av 21.23, in 1966. He also played for Devon (1970–71).

Sumar, Shiraz
Cricketer. *b:* 1950, Tanganyika. Middle order right-hand batsman. *Team* East Africa (1975). *Tour* East Africa to England 1975.
Career batting
1–2–0–25–15–12.50–0–*ct* 1

Summers, Douglas Walter Levi
Professional. *b:* 12.10.1911, Smethwick, Staffordshire. Son of F. T. (Worcestershire). Lower order right-hand batsman, slow left-arm bowler. *Team* Worcestershire (1930, 1 match).

Summers, Francis Theodore

Career batting
1–1–0–4–4–4.00–0–*ct* 0
Bowling 11–0

Summers, Francis Theodore
Professional. *b:* 25.1.1887, Alcester, Warwickshire. *d:* 27.10.1967, Inkberrow, Worcestershire. Father of D. W. L. (Worcestershire). Lower order right-hand batsman, wicket-keeper. *Team* Worcestershire (1921–28, 57 matches).
Career batting
57–91–27–409–36–6.39–0–*ct* 76–*st* 8
In a local club match he removed the first five batsmen as a wicket-keeper and then took off his pads and dismissed the remaining five as a bowler.

Summers, George
Professional. *b:* 21.6.1844, Nottingham. *d:* 19.6.1870, Nottingham. Opening right-hand batsman. *Team* Nottinghamshire (1867–70, 18 matches).
Career batting
32–59–1–922–57–15.89–0–*ct* 15
Batting for Nottinghamshire v MCC at Lord's in 1870 he was hit on the head by a ball from Platts and died a few days later from the injury.

Summers, Gerald Frank
Amateur. *b:* 9.1.1905, Richmond, Surrey. *d:* 12.8.1983, Harrogate, Yorkshire. Attacking middle order right-hand batsman. *Team* Cahn's XI (1932–38). *Tours* Cahn to North America 1933 (not first-class), to Ceylon 1936/7.
Career batting
5–9–1–119–54*–14.87–0–*ct* 1
Bowling 213–6–35.50–0–0–3/18
He also played for Surrey 2nd XI.

Summers, Leonard Shelton Heath
Amateur. *b:* 25.6.1904, Fulham, London. *d:* 26.2.1977, Barnes, Surrey. Opening batsman, leg break bowler. *Sch* Emanuel. *Teams* Leveson-Gower's XI (1932); Minor Counties (1933).
Career batting
2–4–0–103–57–25.75–0–*ct* 1
Bowling 154–4–38.50–0–0–3/99
He was a noted club cricketer in the London area, being particularly associated with Dulwich and Surrey 2nd XI.

Summers, Rev Walter
Amateur. *c:* 4.6.1833, Bishop's Stortford, Hertfordshire. *d:* 14.10.1917, Uckfield, Sussex. Middle order batsman. *Team* Lord Sheffield's XI (1881).
Career batting
1–2–1–2–2*–2.00–0–*ct* 0

Sunnucks, Peter Regan
Professional. *b:* 22.6.1916, Boughton-Monchelsea, Kent. Middle order right-hand batsman. *Team* Kent (1934–46, 68 matches).

Career batting
68–121–8–2016–162–17.84–1–*ct* 11

Surendranath
Amateur. *b:* 4.1.1937, Meerut, India. Lower order right-hand batsman, right-arm medium pace bowler. *Team* Services (1955/6 to 1968/9). *Tour* India to England 1959. *Tests* India (1958/9 to 1960/1, 11 matches).
Career batting
88–115–29–1351–119–15.70–1–*ct* 32
Bowling 7055–278–25.37–15–1–7/14
Test batting
11–20–7–136–27–10.46–0–*ct* 4
Bowling 1053–26–40.50–2–0–5/75
On the 1959 tour he took 79 wickets, av 28.60, in first-class matches and headed the Test bowling with 16 wickets, av 26.62, but was heavily criticised for bowling very negatively down the leg side.

Surfleet, Dr Desmond Ford
Amateur. *b:* 5.2.1912, Dublin, Ireland. Middle order right-hand batsman, right-arm medium pace bowler. *Sch* University College School. *Teams* Middlesex (1931–33, 10 matches); Cambridge U (1931–32).
Career batting
14–21–1–337–86–16.85–0–*ct* 7
Bowling 34–0

Surman, Godfrey Pearce
Amateur. *b:* 18.7.1914, Uckington, Gloucestershire. *d:* 29.5.1987, Southampton, Hampshire. Lower order right-hand batsman, right-arm fast medium bowler. *Sch* Cheltenham. *Team* Gloucestershire (1936–37, 2 matches).
Career batting
2–4–3–11–5*–11.00–0–*ct* 0
Bowling 99–2–49.50–0–0–2/60

Surridge, David
Cricketer. *b:* 6.1.1956, Bishop's Stortford, Hertfordshire. Lower order right-hand batsman, right-arm fast medium bowler. *Team* Cambridge U (1979, blue); Gloucestershire (1980–82, 25 matches).
Career batting
35–30–18–104–14*–8.66–0–*ct* 7
Bowling 2660–89–29.88–1–0–5/78
He also played for Hertfordshire (1977–79 and 1983–92), and his last first-class match was for Minor Counties in 1986.

Surridge, Dr John Giles
Amateur. *b:* 10.8.1935, Sutton, Surrey. Middle order right-hand batsman, right-arm medium pace bowler. *Sch* Marlborough. *Team* Oxford U (1956).
Career batting
1–2–0–1–1–0.50–0–*ct* 1
Bowling 3–0
His County cricket was for Berkshire (1955–58). He won a blue for hockey and also played for Wales.

Surridge, Stuart Spicer
Cricketer. *b:* 28.10.1951, Westminster, London. Son of W. S. (Surrey). Lower order right-hand batsman, wicket-keeper. *Sch* Westminster. *Team* Surrey (1978, 1 match).
Career batting
1–1–1–2–2*–no av–0–*ct* 1

Surridge, Walter Stuart
Amateur. *b:* 3.9.1917, Herne Hill, London. *d:* 13.4.1992, Glossop. Derbyshire. Father of S. S. (Surrey). Lower order right-hand batsman, right-arm fast medium bowler, brilliant close field. *Sch* Emanuel. *Team* Surrey (1947–59, 254 matches). *Tours* Surrey to Rhodesia 1959/60; Surridge to Bermuda 1961 (not first-class).
Career batting
267–333–33–3882–87–12.94–0–*ct* 375
Bowling 14623–506–28.89–22–1–7/49
He captained Surrey from 1952 to 1956 and led the County to the Championship title in all five seasons. His best bowling season was 1952 with 78 wickets, av 25.21. He was President of Surrey in 1981.

Surti, Rusi Framroze
Amateur. *b:* 25.5.1936, Surat, India. Dashing middle order left-hand batsman, left-arm medium pace bowler, good outfield. *Teams* Gujarat (1956/7 to 1968/9); Rajasthan (1959/60 to 1960/1); Queensland (1968/9 to 1972/3, 35 matches). *Tours* India to England 1967, to Australia and New Zealand 1967/8, to West Indies 1961/2. *Tests* India (1960/1 to 1969/70, 26 matches).
Career batting
160–278–17–8066–246*–30.90–6–*ct* 121
Bowling 10529–284–37.07–10–0–5/42
Test batting
26–48–4–1263–99–28.70–0–*ct* 26
Bowling 1962–42–46.71–1–0–5/74
He appeared in two Tests on the 1967 tour to England, but made little impact – the very wet weather telling against him. His highest score was 246* for Rajasthan v Uttar Pradesh at Udaipur in 1959/60. His final first-class match in India was the first Test at Bombay in 1969/70.

Susskind, Manfred John
Amateur. *b:* 8.6.1891, Johannesburg, South Africa. *d:* 9.7.1957, Johannesburg, South Africa. He collapsed and died in the Stock Exchange. Brother of B. V. (Orange Free State). Steady middle order right-hand batsman. *Sch* University College School, London. *Teams* Middlesex (1909–10, 6 matches); Cambridge U (1910–12); Transvaal (1912/13 to 1936/7). *Tour* South Africa to England 1924. *Test* South Africa (1924, 5 matches).
Career batting
97–149–11–4775–171–34.60–11–*ct* 85–*st* 3
Bowling 81–1–81.00–0–0–1/13
Test batting
5–8–0–268–65–33.50–0–*ct* 1
He hit 1,413 runs, av 33.64, on the 1924 tour and came second in the Test batting averages. He won a blue for athletics.

Sutcliffe, Bert, MBE
Amateur. *b:* 17.11.1923, Ponsonby, Auckland, New Zealand. Excellent opening later middle order left-hand batsman, slow left-arm bowler, good field. *Teams* Auckland (1941/2 to 1948/9); Otago (1946/7 to 1961/2); Northern Districts (1962/3 to 1965/6). *Tours* New Zealand to England 1949, 1958, 1965, to South Africa and Australia 1953/4, to India and Pakistan 1955/6, 1964/5; Commonwealth to South Africa 1959/60. *Tests* New Zealand (1946/7 to 1965, 42 matches).
Career batting
233–407–39–17447–385–47.41–44–*ct* 160–*st* 1
Bowling 3273–86–38.05–2–0–5/19
Test batting
42–76–8–2727–230*–40.10–5–*ct* 20
Bowling 344–4–86.00–0–0–2/38
The outstanding New Zealand cricketer of his generation, he hit 2,627 runs, av 59.70, on the 1949 tour to England in first-class matches and 423, av 60.42, in Tests; in 1958 he hit 1,085 runs, av 31.00, in first-class matches; coming out of retirement for the 1965 tour he achieved little. His highest score was 385 for Otago v Canterbury at Christchurch in 1952/3. He also hit 355 for Otago, but not one of his six double centuries was made in England. He hit 1,000 runs in an overseas season twice. He captained New Zealand in four Tests.

Sutcliffe, Herbert
Professional. *b:* 24.11.1894, Summerbridge, Harrogate, Yorkshire. *d:* 22.1.1978, Cross Hills, Yorkshire. Father of W. H. H. (Yorkshire). Excellent opening right-hand batsman, right-arm medium pace bowler. *Team* Yorkshire (1919–45, 602 matches). *Tours* MCC to Australia 1924/5, 1928/9, to Australia and New Zealand 1932/3, to South Africa 1927/8; Yorkshire to Jamaica 1935/6; Vizianagram to India and Ceylon 1930/1. *Tests* England (1924–35, 54 matches).
Career batting
754–1098–124–50670–313–52.02–151–*ct* 473
Bowling 563–14–40.21–0–0–3/15
Test batting
54–84–9–4555–194–60.73–16–*ct* 23
One of the greatest of all opening batsman, he had the technique and the determination to score runs even on the worst of wickets, and in fact became more determined as the bowler or the wicket grew more difficult. Unlike many obdurate players, however, he was equally at home when fast scoring and sixes were needed. His career began in 1919 and he completed 1,000 runs in every season from then until

1939, when he retired – though he made a brief appearance in 1945. He went on to reach 2,000 runs in fifteen seasons and then on to 3,000 three times, his best year being 1932 with 3,336 runs, av 74.13; his highest average, however, came the previous summer with 3,006 runs, av 96.96 – in both years he was the leading English player. He also hit 1,000 runs twice in Australia and once in South Africa.

His highest innings was 313 for Yorkshire v Essex at Leyton in 1932, in the course of which he and P. Holmes added a record-breaking 555 for the first wicket. He hit 16 double centuries, all but one for Yorkshire. With Holmes, he put on a century partnership for the first wicket 69 times, and with Hobbs he compiled eleven century first wicket partnerships, including three in consecutive innings in Australia in 1924/5. Perhaps his most famous partnership with Hobbs was the one during the fifth Test at the Oval in 1926, which realised 172 runs and virtually won the Ashes for England. In that series Sutcliffe scored 472 runs, av 78.66. In the next home series against Australia in 1930 he hit 436 runs, av 87.20, and in his final series in 1934, 304 runs, av 50.66. He was equally at ease in Australia, his figures in first-class matches for his three tours being most impressive: 1924/5, 1,250, av 69.44; 1928/9, 852, av 53.25; 1932/3, 1,345, av 64.05. He was a Test selector 1959–61.

Sutcliffe, James Frederick
Amateur. *b:* 12.12.1876, Medway, Kent. *d:* 14.7.1915, Helles, Gallipoli Peninsula, Turkey. Middle order batsman. *Team* Hampshire (1911, 1 match).
Career batting
1–2–0–24–16–12.00–0–*ct* 0

Sutcliffe, Richard John
Cricketer. *b:* 18.9.1954, Rochdale, Lancashire. Lower order right-hand batsman, right-arm medium pace bowler. *Team* Lancashire (1978, 1 match).
Career batting
1–2–2–10–10*–no av–0–*ct* 0
Bowling 37–1–37.00–0–0–1/37
He also played for Cheshire (1979).

Sutcliffe, Simon Paul
Cricketer. *b:* 22.5.1960, Watford, Hertfordshire. Lower order right-hand batsman, off break bowler. *Sch* Bedford Modern. *Teams* Oxford U (1980–81, blue both years); Warwickshire (1981–83, 20 matches).
Career batting
38–47–11–141–20–3.91–0–*ct* 6
Bowling 4020–96–41.87–2–0–6/19

Sutcliffe, William Herbert Hobbs
Amateur. *b:* 10.10.1926, Pudsey, Yorkshire. Son of Herbert (Yorkshire). Forcing middle order right-hand batsman, right-arm medium, or leg break bowler. *Sch* Rydal. *Team* Yorkshire (1948–57, 177 matches). *Tours* Commonwealth to India and Ceylon 1950/1, MCC to Pakistan 1955/6.
Career batting
210–326–41–7530–181–26.42–6–*ct* 90
Bowling 334–15–22.26–0–0–2/12
He hit 1,261 runs, av 33.18, in 1955. He was captain of Yorkshire in 1956 and 1957. His final first-class match was for MCC in 1959. He was a Test selector 1969–70.

Sutherland, Henry Boyd
Amateur. *b:* 4.12.1844, Croydon, Surrey. *d:* 27.8.1915, Silverhill, St Leonard's-on-Sea, Sussex. Tail end batsman, right-hand medium pace round-arm bowler, good point field. *Sch* Eton. *Team* Kent (1871, 1 match).
Career batting
2–3–0–29–22–9.66–0–*ct* 2
Bowling 55–2–27.50–0–0–2/32
His final first-class match was for MCC in 1873. He also played for Cheshire (1869–70).

Sutherland, Ian
Amateur. *b:* 7.7.1926, Leicester. Middle order right-hand batsman, leg break and googly bowler. *Sch* Wyggeston GS. *Team* Cambridge U (1949).
Career batting
1–1–0–9–9–9.00–0–*ct* 0
Bowling 23–0

Sutherland, Thomas
Professional. *b:* 17.2.1880. Lower order right-hand batsman, right-arm fast bowler. *Team* Hampshire (1898–99, 9 matches).
Career batting
9–14–9–74–21–14.80–0–*ct* 6
Bowling 446–11–40.54–1–0–6/111

Sutor, John Allan
Amateur. *b:* 1.7.1909, Knighton-upon-Teme, Tenbury, Worcestershire. *d:* 2.12.1966, Sydney, New South Wales, Australia. Middle order right-hand batsman, right-arm medium pace bowler. *Sch* Uppingham. *Team* Worcestershire (1928, 1 match).
Career batting
1–2–0–3–2–1.5–0–*ct* 0

Sutthery, Arthur Melbourne
Amateur. *b:* 25.3.1864, Clifton-Reynes, Buckinghamshire. *d:* 15.5.1937, Chelsea, London. Aggressive opening or middle order right-hand batsman, right-arm fast medium bowler, good field. *Sch* Oundle and Uppingham. *Team* Cambridge U (1886–87, blue 1887).
Career batting
20–34–2–658–73–20.56–0–*ct* 11
Bowling 622–23–27.04–1–0–5/51
His County cricket was for Northamptonshire (pre first-class), Devon and Shropshire (1898). His final first-class match was for an England XI in 1888.

Suttle, Kenneth George
Professional. *b:* 25.8.1928, Brook Green, Kensington, London. Attractive middle order left-hand batsman, slow left-arm bowler, brilliant outfield. *Team* Sussex (1949–71, 601 matches). *Tours* MCC to West Indies 1953/4; International XI to India, Pakistan and Ceylon 1967/8.
Career batting
612–1064–92–30225–204*–31.09–49–*ct* 384–*st* 3
Bowling 8727–266–32.80–1–0–6/64
He hit 1,000 runs in a season 17 times, going on to 2,000 once: 2,326, av 39.42, in 1962. He appeared in 423 consecutive County Championship matches between August 1954 and July 1969. He hit 204* for Sussex v Kent at Tunbridge Wells in 1962. He also played for Suffolk (1973–74). He was a useful soccer player with Brighton and Hove Albion, later being player-manager to several non-League clubs.

Sutton, Cecil Alfred Leonard
Amateur. *b:* 6.1.1886, Brixton, London. *d:* 10.2.1965, Whatton, Nottinghamshire. Hard hitting lower order right-hand batsman, right-arm medium pace bowler. *Sch* Nottingham HS. *Team* Nottinghamshire (1907, 1 match).
Career batting
1–1–0–1–1–1.00–0–*ct* 0
Bowling 26–0
A well-known local architect he designed the pavilion of Sir Julien Cahn's ground in West Bridgford, Nottingham.

Sutton, Charles Henry
Amateur. *b:* 1907, Vina del Mar, Chile. *d:* 29.7.1945, Gosport, Hampshire. Lower order batsman, useful bowler. *Sch* Leys. *Team* South America (1932). *Tour* South Americans to England 1932.
Career batting
1–1–0–10–10–10.00–0–*ct* 0
Bowling 23–0
He only played in one first-class match on the 1932 tour.

Sutton, Charles Lexington Manners
Amateur. *b:* 26.4.1891, Chichester, Sussex. *d:* 8.10.1962, Mount Ephraim, Tunbridge Wells, Kent. Lower order batsman, useful bowler. *Team* Army (1920–23).
Career batting
5–8–5–90–30*–30.00–0–*ct* 4
Bowling 396–10–39.60–0–0–3/15

Sutton, Edmund George Gresham
Amateur. *b:* 12.10.1844, Marylebone, London. *d:* 7.10.1903, Tring, Hertfordshire. Middle order right-hand batsman. *Team* Middlesex (1868, 1 match).
Career batting
25–39–4–483–40–13.80–0–*ct* 26
Bowling 21–0
His debut in first-class cricket was for MCC in 1864, and his final match for MCC in 1873. He also played for Buckinghamshire (1864–68) and Hertfordshire (1868–78).

Sutton, George Thomas
Professional. *b:* 1.10.1887, West Ham, Essex. *d:* 16.1.1949, Penge, Kent. Middle order batsman. *Team* Essex (1912, 1 match).
Career batting
1–1–0–0–0–0.00–0–*ct* 0

Sutton, John Arthur
Cricketer. *b:* 26.6.1938, Longsight, Manchester, Lancashire. Middle order left-hand batsman, off break bowler. *Team* Minor Counties (1969–72).
Career batting
4–8–0–164–57–20.50–0–*ct* 2
Bowling 197–4–49.25–0–0–2/44
His County cricket was for Cheshire (1959–86).

Sutton, Leonard Cecil Leicester
Amateur. *b:* 14.4.1890, Half Way Tree, Jamaica. *d:* 3.6.1916, Zillebeke, France. Middle order left-hand batsman, left-arm slow medium bowler. *Sch* King's Bruton. *Team* Somerset (1909–12, 17 matches).
Career batting
17–29–5–171–30–7.12–0–*ct* 10
Bowling 6–0

Sutton, Michael Antony
Amateur. *b:* 29.3.1921, Weymouth, Dorset. Lower order right-hand batsman, off break bowler. *Sch* Ampleforth. *Teams* Oxford U (1946–47, blue 1946); Somerset (1948, 1 match).
Career batting
19–26–8–144–30–8.00–0–*ct* 23
Bowling 1218–47–25.91–1–0–5/63
He also played for Devon (1954).

Sutton-Mattocks, Christopher John
Cricketer. *b:* 10.7.1951, Hammersmith, London. Middle order left-hand batsman. *Sch* Winchester. *Team* Oxford U (1972–73).
Career batting
6–12–0–107–37–8.91–0–*ct* 2

Swaffer, John
Professional. *b:* 10.11.1851, Ruckinge, Kent. *d:* 26.7.1936, Orsett, Essex. Sound middle order right-hand batsman. *Team* Kent (1873, 1 match).
Career batting
1–2–0–18–18–9.00–0–*ct* 0

Swain, William
Professional. *b:* 8.9.1830, Burley, Otley, Yorkshire. *d:* 5.10.1910, East Brisbane, Queensland, Australia. Stylish middle order right-hand batsman, right-hand fast, or slow, round-arm bowler. *Team* MCC (1864).
Career batting
2–4–2–22–13*–11.00–0–*ct* 0

Swallow, Ian Geoffrey
Cricketer. *b:* 18.12.1962, Barnsley, Yorkshire. Middle order right-hand batsman, off break bowler. *Teams* Yorkshire (1983–89, 61 matches); Somerset (1990–91, 27 matches).
Career batting
88–104–28–1550–114–20.39–1–*ct* 43
Bowling 5798–106–54.69–1–0–7/95

Swallow, Raymond
Professional. *b:* 15.6.1935, Southwark, London. Middle order right-hand batsman, good cover field. *Team* Derbyshire (1959–63, 37 matches).
Career batting
38–68–2–1323–115–20.04–1–*ct* 13
Bowling 8–0
His first-class debut was for MCC in 1957. A good soccer player, he appeared at outside-right for Arsenal and Derby County.

Swalwell, Reginald Sawdon
Amateur. *b:* 25.6.1873, York. *d:* 20.9.1930, Broomhall, Sunningdale, Berkshire. Middle order left-hand batsman, useful bowler. *Team* Worcestershire (1907–20, 18 matches).
Career batting
26–45–2–665–72–15.46–0–*ct* 8
Bowling 156–3–52.00–0–0–3/49
His final first-class match was for MCC in 1925. He also played for Dorset (1903–05) and Berkshire (1925).

Swan, John James
Professional. *b:* 24.9.1848, Oadby, Leicestershire. *d:* 22.2.1924, Maidstone, Kent. Middle order right-hand batsman, right-hand medium pace round-arm bowler. *Team* Surrey (1870–76, 32 matches).
Career batting
35–65–5–662–62–11.03–0–*ct* 22
Bowling 83–2–41.50–0–0–1/15

Swan, Richard Gilroy
Cricketer. *b:* 6.12.1951, Duns, Berwickshire, Scotland. Middle order right-hand batsman, right-arm medium pace bowler. *Sch* Merchiston. *Team* Scotland (1980–91).
Career batting
12–18–1–374–77–22.00–0–*ct* 8
Bowling 0–0

Swann, Charles Frederick
Professional. *b:* 6.8.1883, Leyton, Essex. *d:* 7.3.1960, Harrow Green, Leytonstone, Essex. Middle order right-hand batsman. *Team* Essex (1912, 1 match).
Career batting
1–1–0–0–0–0.00–0–*ct* 0

Swann, John Lassam
Amateur. *b:* 3.10.1926, Ealing, Middlesex. Lower order left-hand batsman, leg break bowler. *Team* Middlesex (1949–51, 4 matches).
Career batting
4–6–3–69–23*–23.00–0–*ct* 0
Bowling 220–6–36.66–0–0–3/39

Swann-Mason, Rev Richard Swann
Amateur. *b:* 4.3.1871, Haslingfield, Cambridgeshire. *d:* 21.2.1942, St Pancras, London. Middle order batsman. *Sch* Perse. *Team* MCC (1909–14).
Career batting
3–5–1–67–25–16.75–0–*ct*4
Bowling 36–0
His County cricket was for Cambridgeshire (1895–1908).

Swanton, Ernest William, OBE
Amateur. *b:* 11.2.1907, Forest Hill, London. Son-in-law of R. H. De Montmorency (Oxford U). Middle order right-hand batsman. *Sch* Cranleigh. *Team* Middlesex (1937–38, 3 matches). *Tour* Cahn to North America 1933 (not first-class).
Career batting
3–5–0–67–26–13.40–*ct* 1
He organised several tours abroad in the 1950s and 1960s. One of the best-known cricket journalists and commentators, he wrote mainly for the London *Evening Standard* and *Daily Telegraph*. He is also the author of numerous books on cricket. He was President of Kent in 1981.

Swarbrook, Frederick William
Cricketer. *b:* 17.12.1950, Derby. Middle order left-hand batsman, slow left-arm bowler. *Teams* Derbyshire (1967–79, 199 matches); Griqualand West (1972/3 to 1987/8); Orange Free State (1979/80).
Career batting
254–376–94–6191–104*–21.95–1–*ct* 149
Bowling 13998–467–29.97–15–2–9/20
His best bowling was 9/20 for Derbyshire v Sussex at Hove in 1975. He gave up bowling late in his career in South Africa.

Swart, Peter Douglas
Cricketer. *b:* 27.4.1946, Bulawayo, Rhodesia. Middle order right-hand batsman, right-arm medium pace bowler. *Teams* Rhodesia (1965/6); Western Province (1967/8 to 1984/5); Boland (1981/2 to 1982/3); Glamorgan (1978–79, 44 matches).
Career batting
167–267–29–6093–122–25.60–6–*ct* 114
Bowling 9365–370–25.31–5–1–6/85
His debut in England was for International Cavaliers in 1969; he also played for D. H. Robins' XI in England in 1974. In 1978 he hit 1,078 runs, av 31.70. He also played for Cambridgeshire (1974–76).

Swayne, Harry Walter
Amateur. *b:* 3.3.1869, Glastonbury, Somerset. *d:* 25.11.1911, Pertapur, Mairwa, Bengal, India. Middle order batsman. *Sch* Winchester. *Team* Somerset (1894, 1 match).

Career batting
1–2–1–27–19*–27.00–0–*ct* 0

Sweet, Rev Charles Francis Long
Amateur. *b:* 29.11.1860, Bath, Somerset. *d:* 24.1.1932, Teignmouth, Devon. Middle order batsman. *Sch* Winchester. *Team* Somerset (1882–83, 5 matches).
Career batting
5–9–5–67–19*–16.75–0–*ct* 3
He also played for Dorset (1891) and Wiltshire (1894). He played no first-class cricket at Oxford U, but did win a blue for soccer. He first played for Somerset (pre first-class) in 1880.

Sweet-Escott, Edward Rhys
(birth registered as E. R. Escott)
Amateur. *b:* 27.7.1879, Brompton-Ralph, Somerset. *d:* 1.7.1956, Penarth, Glamorgan. Brother-in-law of W. I. Hancock (Somerset). Middle order right-hand batsman. *Team* Glamorgan (1921, 1 match).
Career batting
1–2–0–13–13–6.50–0–*ct* 0
He first played for Glamorgan (pre first-class) in 1902.

Sweetland, Edward Henry
Professional. *b:* 25.4.1903, Westminster, London. *d:* 18.7.1978, Middleton-on-Sea, Sussex. Lower order batsman, wicket-keeper. *Team* Middlesex (1927, 2 matches).
Career batting
5–5–3–19–8*–9.50–0–*ct* 5
His final first-class match was for MCC in 1933.

Swetman, Roy
Professional. *b:* 25.10.1933, Westminster, London. Lower order right-hand batsman, wicket-keeper, occasional off break bowler. *Teams* Surrey (1954–61, 129 matches); Nottinghamshire (1966–67, 56 matches); Gloucestershire (1972–74, 45 matches). *Tours* MCC to Pakistan 1955/6, to Australia and New Zealand 1958/9, to West Indies 1959/60; Surrey to Rhodesia 1959/60; Cavaliers to India and South Africa 1962/3; Commonwealth to Rhodesia 1962/3. *Tests* England (1958/9 to 1959/60, 11 matches).
Career batting
286–411–73–6495–115–19.21–2–*ct* 530–*st* 66
Bowling 69–1–69.00–0–0–1/10
Test batting
11–17–2–254–65–16.93–0–*ct* 24–*st* 2
His first-class debut was for Combined Services in 1953.

Swift, Brian Tennant
Amateur. *b:* 9.9.1937, Adelaide, South Australia. *d:* 8.3.1958, Higham, Suffolk. He died in a motor-car accident. Lower order right-hand batsman, wicket-keeper. *Team* Cambridge U (1957, blue).

Career batting
17–23–7–160–25–10.00–0–*ct* 37–*st* 10

Swinburne, John Warwick
Cricketer. *b:* 4.12.1939, Wath-on-Dearne, Yorkshire. Lower order right-hand batsman, off break bowler. *Team* Northamptonshire (1970–74, 29 matches).
Career batting
29–36–8–160–25–5.71–0–*ct* 13
Bowling 2281–83–27.48–4–1–6/57
He also played for Devon (1964–69) and Shropshire (1975–77).

Swindell, Robert Stephen
Cricketer. *b:* 22.1.1950, Derby. Lower order right-hand batsman, off break bowler. *Team* Derbyshire (1972–77, 23 matches).
Career batting
23–32–11–242–38–11.52–0–*ct* 11
Bowling 1665–50–33.30–4–0–6/79

Swinford, Thomas Francis
Amateur. *b:* 9.5.1839, Minster, Margate, Kent. *d:* 23.1.1915, Polegate, Eastbourne, Sussex. Opening right-hand batsman, good long-stop. *Sch* Blackheath. *Team* Kent (1874, 4 matches).
Career batting
4–8–0–89–50–11.12–0–*ct* 0
He also played for Northumberland (1870).

Swinstead, Frank Hillyard
Amateur. *b:* 6.8.1862, Chelsea, London. *d:* 6.12.1937, Hornsey, Middlesex. Stylish middle order batsman. *Team* MCC (1900).
Career batting
2–4–0–37–15–9.25–0–*ct* 1
Bowling 22–0
His first-class debut was for Gentlemen of England in 1888. His County cricket was for Herefordshire (1888).

Swire, Samuel Henry
Amateur. *b:* 3.1.1839, Ashton-under-Lyne, Lancashire. *d:* 29.12.1905, Southport, Lancashire. Middle order right-hand batsman, useful bowler, cover-point field. *Team* Lancashire (1865–68, 5 matches).
Career batting
5–9–1–93–18*–11.62–0–*ct* 1
Bowling 37–0
He was Honorary Secretary of Lancashire CCC from 1873 until his death in 1905.

Swyer, Basil James
Amateur. *b:* 6.6.1898, West Ham, Essex. *d:* 7.7.1964, Sherwood, Nottingham. Lower order batsman, right-arm medium pace bowler. *Sch* Bancroft's. *Team* Essex (1923, 1 match).
Career batting
1–2–0–12–7–6.00–0–*ct* 0
Bowling 56–0

Sydenham, David Alfred Donald
Professional. *b:* 6.4.1934, Surbiton, Surrey. Lower order right-hand batsman, left-arm fast medium bowler. *Team* Surrey (1957–72, 142 matches).
Career batting
145–133–65–487–24*–7.16–0–*ct* 52
Bowling 9732–487–19.98–26–3–9/70
He took 100 wickets in a season twice (best 115, av 17.65, in 1962). His best innings analysis was 9 for 70 for Surrey v Gloucestershire at the Oval in 1964. After 1965 he made only one further first-class appearance – in 1972.

Syed Hussain
Amateur. *b:* 1888, Moradabad, United Provinces, India. Middle order right-hand batsman, wicket-keeper. *Tour* India to England 1911.
Career batting
8–16–4–52–14–4.33–0–*ct* 2–*st* 2
He did not appear in first-class matches in India.

Syfret, Admiral Sir Edward Neville
Amateur. *b:* 20.6.1889, Newlands, Cape Town, South Africa. *d:* 10.12.1972, Highgate Village, Middlesex. Middle order right-hand batsman. *Team* Royal Navy (1912).
Career batting
1–2–0–30–30–15.00–0–*ct* 0

Sygrove, Malcolm Robert
Cricketer. *b:* 17.2.1966, Lutterworth, Leicestershire. Lower order right-hand batsman, right-arm medium pace bowler. *Team* Oxford U (1986–88, blue 1988).
Career batting
8–10–3–37–8*–5.28–0–*ct* 0
Bowling 933–20–46.65–0–0–3/91

Sykes, Charles Percy
Amateur. *b:* 9.8.1862, Westminster, London. *d:* 17.6.1899, Chelsea, London. Middle order batsman. *Sch* Harrow. *Team* MCC (1890).
Career batting
1–2–0–14–10–7.00–0–*ct* 0

Sykes, Eric
Amateur in 1925, professional in 1932. *b:* 23.6.1906, Bolsover, Derbyshire. *d:* 7.12.1989, Athersley North, Barnsley, Yorkshire. Son of E. C. (Hampshire). Middle order right-hand batsman. *Team* Derbyshire (1925–32, 5 matches).
Career batting
5–10–1–105–50–11.66–0–*ct* 0
Bowling 2–0

Sykes, Ernest Castle
Professional. *b:* 31.5.1869, Sheffield, Yorkshire. *d:* 30.11.1925, Bolsover, Derbyshire. Father of Eric (Derbyshire). Lower order right-hand batsman, wicket-keeper. *Team* Hampshire (1896, 1 match).
Career batting
1–2–2–5–5*–no av–0–*ct* 0

Sykes, James Frederick
Cricketer. *b:* 30.12.1965, Shoreditch, London. Middle order right-hand batsman, off break bowler. *Team* Middlesex (1983–89, 30 matches).
Career batting
30–38–7–696–126–22.45–1–*ct* 16
Bowling 1157–30–38.56–0–0–4/49
He also played for Durham (pre first-class, 1990).

Sylvester, Steven Antony
Cricketer. *b:* 26.9.1968, Chalfont St Giles, Buckinghamshire. Lower order right-hand batsman, left-arm fast medium bowler. *Team* Middlesex (1991–92, 5 matches).
Career batting
5–2–1–0–0*–0.00–0–*ct* 2
Bowling 320–4–80.00–0–0–2/34
He also played for Buckinghamshire (1991–92).

Syme, Ian Alexander Hastie
Amateur. *b:* 29.12.1929, King's Park, Stirling, Scotland. Lower order right-hand batsman, right-arm fast medium bowler. *Sch* Edinburgh Academy. *Team* Scotland (1950).
Career batting
1–2–0–12–12–6.00–0–*ct* 0
Bowling 7–0

Symes-Thompson, Rev Francis
Amateur. *b:* 2.2.1875, Marylebone, London. *d:* 3.3.1948, Teignmouth, Devon. Brother of H. E. (Cambridge U), brother-in-law of A. Page (Oxford U). Lower order right-hand batsman, wicket-keeper. *Sch* Harrow. *Team* Oxford U (1898).
Career batting
1–1–1–7–7*–no av–0–*ct* 0
His County cricket was for Buckinghamshire (1905–07).

Symes-Thompson, Dr Henry Edmund
Amateur. *b:* 22.6.1873, Marylebone, London. *d:* 18.1.1952, Oxford. Brother of Francis (Oxford U), brother-in-law of A. Page (Oxford U). Middle order right-hand batsman. *Sch* Winchester. *Team* Cambridge U (1894–95).
Career batting
8–16–1–174–31–11.60–0–*ct* 6
His final first-class match was for MCC in 1906.

Symington, Stuart Johnston
Amateur. *b:* 16.9.1926, Bexhill-on-Sea, Sussex. Middle order right-hand batsman, right-arm fast medium pace bowler. *Sch* Canford. *Team* Leicestershire (1948–49, 23 matches).
Career batting
23–40–6–744–65–21.88–0–*ct* 13
Bowling 1448–36–40.22–1–0–5/45
He was captain of Leicestershire in 1949.

Symonds, Henry George
Amateur. *b:* 24.6.1889, Cardiff, Glamorgan. *d:* 1.1.1945, Canton, Cardiff, Glamorgan. Middle order left-hand batsman, slow left-arm bowler. *Teams* Glamorgan (1921–25, 22 matches); Wales (1925–29).
Career batting
27–48–2–766–76–16.65–0–*ct* 5
Bowling 307–8–38.37–0–0–4/32
He first played for Glamorgan (pre first-class) in 1908. His first-class debut was for South Wales in 1912.

Syrée, Dr Anton Hugh
Amateur. *b:* 21.10.1859, Port Corrie, South Africa. *d:* 9.1.1924, Cheslyn Hay, Staffordshire. He died by his own hand. Middle order right-hand batsman, slow right-arm bowler. *Sch* St John's, Leatherhead. *Team* Kent (1879, 1 match).
Career batting
1–2–0–7–7–3.50–0–*ct* 0
Bowling 10–0

T

Taber, Hedley Brian
Cricketer. *b:* 29.4.1940, Wagga Wagga, New South Wales, Australia. Lower order right-hand batsman, occasional leg break bowler, wicket-keeper. *Team* New South Wales (1964/5 to 1973/4, 73 matches). *Tours* Australia to England 1968, 1972, to South Africa 1966/7, 1969/70, to India and Sri Lanka 1969/70. *Tests* Australia (1966/7 to 1969/70, 16 matches).
Career batting
129–182–35–2648–109–18.01–1–*ct* 345–*st* 50
Bowling 6–0
Test batting
16–27–5–353–48–16.04–0–*ct* 56–*st* 4
He was the reserve wicket-keeper on both visits to England, but appeared in one Test in 1968.

Taberer, Henry Melville
Amateur. *b:* 7.10.1870, Keiskama Hoek, Cape Province, South Africa. *d:* 5.6.1932, Stormfontein, Colesberg, Cape Province, South Africa. Brother of W. S. (Rhodesia). Middle order right-hand batsman, right-arm fast bowler, good field. *Teams* Oxford U (1891–92); Natal (1893/4 to 1894/5). *Test* South Africa (1902/3, 1 match).
Career batting
11–20–3–222–47*–13.05–0–*ct* 5
Bowling 446–22–20.27 –0–0–4/14
Test batting
1–1–0–2–2–2.00–0–*ct* 0
Bowling 48–1–48.00–0–0–1/25
He played for Essex 1891 to 1893 (pre-first-class) and also Rhodesia and Transvaal in non-first-class matches. He captained South Africa in his only Test, which was also his final first-class match. A noted rugby footballer, he was awarded his blue at Oxford and also represented the University in the long-jump. At the time of his death he was a member of the South Africa Board of Control and vice-chairman of the South African Cricket Association.

Tabor, Alfred
Amateur. *b:* 24.2.1850, Trent, Middlesex. *d:* 16.12.1925, Eastbourne, Sussex. Brother of A. S. (Middlesex and Surrey). Sound defensive opening right-hand batsman, good field. *Sch* Harrow. *Team* Middlesex (1872, 1 match). *Tour* Ceylon to India 1884/5 (not first-class).
Career batting
1–2–0–49–42–24.50–0–*ct* 0
His opportunity for County cricket was very limited, since he went to Ceylon as a coffee planter in 1873, not returning until 1890. He did however play in Ceylon, being for some time captain of the Ceylon team. He did not appear in any first-class matches whilst at Cambridge, though he played in the Freshmen's match of 1870.

Tabor, Arthur Sydney
Amateur. *b:* 9.11.1852, Trent, Middlesex. *d:* 14.10.1927, Earl's Court, London. Brother of Alfred (Middlesex). Attractive opening right-hand batsman, good deep field. *Sch* Eton. *Teams* Cambridge U (1872–74, blue all three years); Middlesex (1872–74, 6 matches); Surrey (1878, 1 match).
Career batting
28–49–1–682–59–14.20–0–*ct* 9

Tagart, Noel Ongley
(birth registered as Ernest Ongley Tagart)
Amateur. *b:* 24.12.1878, Paddington, London. *d:* 8.10.1913, Molyneux Park, Tunbridge Wells, Kent. Opening right-hand batsman, point field. *Sch* Clifton. *Teams* Cambridge U (1900); Gloucestershire (1900–01, 6 matches).
Career batting
8–11–0–140–30–12.72–0–*ct* 4

Tahir Naqqash
Cricketer. *b:* 6.6.1959, Lahore, Pakistan. Brother of Arif Naqqash (Lahore). Lower order right-hand batsman, originally slow, later right-arm fast medium bowler. *Teams* Lahore (1975/6 to 1985/6); Servis Industries (1976/7); Punjab (1975/6); Muslim Commercial Bank (1976/7 to 1988/9). *Tours* Pakistan to Australia 1981/2, 1983/4, 1984/5 (not first-class), to England 1982, 1983 (World Cup), to New Zealand 1984/5, to Sharjah (not first-class) 1984/5. *Tests* Pakistan (1981/2 to 1984/5, 15 matches).
Career batting
68–84–11–1346–60–18.43–0–*ct* 37
Bowling 5285–163–32.42–6–1–9/45

Tait, Alan

Test batting
15–19–5–300–57–21.42–0–*ct* 3
Bowling 1398–34–41.11–2–0–5/40

He played in two Tests on the 1982 tour, but his record in all first-class matches was only 15 wickets, av 35.80. His best bowling was 9/45 for Muslim Commercial Bank v Karachi at Karachi in 1980/1.

Tait, Alan

Cricketer. *b:* 27.12.1953, Washington, Co Durham. Opening left-hand batsman. *Teams* Northamptonshire (1971–75, 52 matches); Gloucestershire (1978, 11 matches).
Career batting
63–104–1–1897–99–18.41–0–*ct* 15
Bowling 0–0

He also played for Cambridgeshire (1976–77).

Tait, John Robert

Amateur. *b:* 20.11.1886, Lerwick, Shetland Islands, Scotland. *d:* 13.4.1945, Clifton, Bristol. Aggressive middle order right-hand batsman. *Teams* Glamorgan (1921–26, 43 matches); Wales (1923).
Career batting
44–82–1–1477–96–18.23–0–*ct* 21
Bowling 87–1–87.00–0–0–1/5

He first played for Glamorgan (pre first-class) in 1911. He played rugby for Swansea and soccer for Newport County, playing for Wales in amateur internationals.

Tait, Robert Garland Work

Amateur. *b:* 28.6.1885, Aberdeen, Scotland. *d:* 18.8.1973, Dundee, Angus, Scotland. Opening right-hand batsman. *Team* Scotland (1907–13).
Career batting
13–25–1–590–59–24.58–0–*ct* 9
Bowling 125–2–62.50–0–0–1/8

Tait, Thomas

Professional. *b:* 7.10.1872, Langley Moor, Co Durham. *d:* 6.9.1954, Brierley, Hemsworth, Yorkshire. Opening or middle order right-hand batsman. *Team* Yorkshire (1898–99, 2 matches).
Career batting
2–3–1–7–3–3.50–0–*ct* 1

Talat Ali Malik

Cricketer. *b:* 29.5.1950, Lahore, Pakistan. Opening right-hand batsman, right-arm medium pace off break bowler. *Teams* Lahore (1967/8 to 1970/1); Punjab University (1969/70 to 1971/2); PIA (1973/4 to 1978/9); United Bank (1977/8). *Tours* Pakistan to England 1971, 1978, to Australia and New Zealand 1972/3, 1978/9; Pakistan Under-25 to Sri Lanka 1973/4. *Tests* Pakistan (1972/3 to 1978/9, 10 matches).
Career batting
115–205–15–7296–258–38.40–15–*ct* 42
Bowling 247–2–123.50–0–0–1/32

Test batting
10–18–2–370–61–23.12–0–*ct* 4
Bowling 7–0

He had only a modest tour of England in 1971, not appearing in the Tests; in 1978 he played in two Tests, but in first-class matches only hit 278 runs, av 25.27. His highest score was 258 for PIA v Rawalpindi at Rawalpindi in 1975/6. He hit 1,124 runs, av 34.06, in Pakistan in 1973/4.

Talbot, Basil Lynch

Amateur. *b:* 23.2.1903, Southsea, Hampshire. *d:* 18.2.1962, Shitterton, Wareham, Dorset. Lower order batsman, wicket-keeper. *Team* Sussex (1947, 1 match).
Career batting
1–2–0–35–25–17.50–0–*ct* 2

Talbot, Henry Lynch

Amateur. *b:* 2.10.1863, Greenwich, London. *d:* 1911, Perak, Federated Malay States. Middle order right-hand batsman. *Sch* Wellington. *Team* MCC (1895).
Career batting
1–2–0–9–7–4.50–0–*ct* 1

His County cricket was for Bedfordshire (1882).

Talbot, Hon Milo George

Amateur. *b:* 14.9.1854, Malahide Castle, Co Dublin, Ireland. *d:* 3.9.1931, Bifrons, Canterbury, Kent. Nephew of C. W. A. Napier (Oxford U 1838). Opening right-hand batsman, right-hand medium pace round-arm bowler. *Sch* Wellington. *Team* Gentlemen of the South (1875).
Career batting
1–2–0–1–1–0.50–*ct* 2

Talbot, Rev Bishop Neville Stuart

Amateur. *b:* 21.8.1879, Headington, Oxfordshire. *d:* 3.4.1943, Henfield, Sussex. Nephew of A. Lyttelton (Middlesex), E. Lyttelton (Middlesex), C. G. Lyttelton (Cambridge U), R. H. Lyttelton (MCC), A. T. Lyttelton (MCC) and G. W. S. Lyttelton (Cambridge U). Lower order batsman, useful bowler. *Sch* Haileybury. *Team* Oxford U (1907).
Career batting
1–2–0–30–26–15.00–0–*ct* 0
Bowling 44–3–14.66–0–0–2/18

Talbot, Ronald Osmond

Amateur. *b:* 26.11.1903, Christchurch, New Zealand. *d:* 5.1.1983, Auckland, New Zealand. Cousin of G. L. (Canterbury). Middle order right-hand batsman, right-arm medium pace bowler. *Team* Canterbury (1922/3 to 1935/6). *Tour* New Zealand to England 1931.
Career batting
51–86–7–1946–117–24.63–3–*ct* 31
Bowling 2005–54–37.12–1–0–5/106

On his tour to England he hit 759 runs, av 23.71, but proved ineffective as a bowler. He scored 105 on debut for Canterbury v Otago at Dunedin in 1922/3.

Tallon, Donald
Amateur. *b:* 17.2.1916, Bundaberg, Queensland, Australia. *d:* 7.9.1984, Bundaberg, Queensland, Australia. Brother of L. W. T. (Queensland). Lower order right-hand batsman, wicket-keeper. *Team* Queensland (1933/4 to 1953/4, 86 matches). *Tours* Australia to England 1948, 1953, to New Zealand 1945/6, 1949/50. *Tests* Australia (1945/6 to 1953, 21 matches).
Career batting
150–228–21–6034–193–29.14–9–*ct* 302–*st* 131
Bowling 202–0
Test batting
21–26–3–394–92–17.13–0–*ct* 50–*st* 8

He was the principal wicket-keeper of the 1948 Australian touring team, but lost his Test place to Langley on the 1953 visit.

Tamhane, Narendra Shankar
Amateur. *b:* 4.8.1931, Bombay, India. Lower order right-hand batsman, wicket-keeper. *Team* Bombay (1953/4 to 1963/4). *Tours* India to Pakistan 1954//5, to Ceylon 1956/7, to England 1959. *Tests* India (1954/5 to 1960/1, 21 matches).
Career batting
93–96–16–1459–109*–18.23–1–*ct* 175–*st* 78
Bowling 43–2–21.5–0–0–2/43
Test batting
21–27–5–225–54*–10.22–0–*ct* 35–*st* 16

He played in two of the four Tests on the 1959 tour. His first-class debut was for Indian Universities in 1951/2 and his final match for Bandokar's XI in 1968/9.

Tamplin, Cyril
Amateur. *b:* 27.5.1921, Cardiff, Glamorgan. Lower order right-hand batsman, wicket-keeper. *Teams* Bengal (1942/3); Glamorgan (1947, 3 matches).
Career batting
4–5–2–56–40*–18.66–0–*ct* 8–*st* 2

Tancred, Augustus Bernard
Amateur. *b:* 20.8.1865, Port Elizabeth, South Africa. *d:* 23.11.1911, Maitland, Cape Town, South Africa. He died after an operation. Brother of L. J. (South Africa) and V. M. (South Africa). Sound opening right-hand batsman. *Teams* Kimberley (1889/90 to 1890/1); Griqualand West (1890/1); Transvaal (1896/7 to 1898/9); MCC (1897). *Tests* South Africa (1888/9, 2 matches).
Career batting
11–21–1–708–106–35.40–1–*ct* 6
Bowling 220–8–27.50–0–0–3/22
Test batting
2–4–1–87–29–29.00–0–*ct* 2

Owing to business commitments he was unable to come to England with the 1894 South African touring team – his single appearance in England was for MCC in 1897. His first-class debut was in the first Test match v England in 1888/9.

Tancred, Louis Joseph
Amateur. *b:* 7.10.1876, Port Elizabeth, South Africa. *d:* 28.7.1934, Parktown, Johannesburg, South Africa. Brother of A. B. (South Africa) and V. M. (South Africa). Steady opening right-hand batsman. *Teams* Transvaal (1896/7 to 1919/20); London County (1901). *Tours* South Africa to England 1901, 1904, 1907, 1912. *Tests* South Africa (1902/3 to 1913/14, 14 matches).
Career batting
130–219–12–5695–160–27.51–11–*ct* 73
Bowling 190–8–23.75–0–0–4/43
Test batting
14–26–1–530–97–21.20–0–*ct* 3

During his four tours to England he achieved greatest success in 1904 when, in all first-class matches, he scored 1,269 runs, av 40.93. He reached 1,000 runs in one other English season. He captained South Africa in the three Tests of 1912.

Tandy, Brig-General Ernest Napper
Amateur. *b:* 13.5.1879, Axbridge, Somerset. *d:* 6.5.1953, St Pancras, London. Brother of M. O. (Europeans). Middle order right-hand batsman, good field. *Sch* Wellington. *Team* Somerset (1904–05, 2 matches).
Career batting
3–5–0–81–30–16.20–0–*ct* 1

His final first-class match was for MCC in 1908.

Tankerville, 4th Earl of, Charles Bennett
Amateur. *b:* 15.11.1743, Westminster, London. *d:* 10.12.1822, Walton-on-Thames, Surrey. Middle order right-hand batsman. *Sch* Eton. *Team* Surrey (1773–79).

He was a great patron of cricket and many matches were played under his auspices at Laleham-Burway. Among professional cricketers whom he employed on his estate were Lumpy Stevens and W. Bedster.

Tanner, Arthur Ralph
Amateur. *b:* 25.12.1889, Bromley, Kent. *d:* 16.8.1966, Stone Grove, Edgware, Middlesex. Lower order right-hand batsman, left-arm medium or slow bowler. *Team* Middlesex (1920–27, 45 matches).
Career batting
47–68–10–764–81*–13.17–0–*ct* 56
Bowling 1969–71–27.73–1–0–5/13

His final first-class appearance was for Free Foresters in 1929.

Tanner, John
Amateur. *b:* 1772. *d:* 23.3.1858, Sutton, Surrey. 'A bowler of some repute'. *Teams* Surrey (1802–10);

Middlesex (1815–19).
Career batting
40–72–11–380–34–6.22–0–*ct* 27–*st 1*
Bowling 41 wickets (no analyses)–1–0–5/?
His last match was for MCC in 1826.

Tanner, John Denys Parkin
Amateur. *b:* 2.7.1921, Harrogate, Yorkshire. *d:* 25.10.1987, Ben Rydding, Yorkshire. Lower order left-hand batsman, wicket-keeper. *Sch* Charterhouse. *Team* Oxford U (1947–49).
Career batting
7–13–4–112–25*–12.44–0–*ct* 8–*st* 3
His final first-class match was for MCC in 1955. His County cricket was for Oxfordshire (1951). He played soccer for Huddersfield Town, and played amateur internationals for England.

Tanner, William
Professional. *b:* 11.4.1841, Weybridge, Surrey. Tail end right-hand batsman, right-hand fast round-arm bowler, mid-wicket field. *Team* Surrey (1866–68, 2 matches).
Career batting
3–6–2–2–1*–0.50–0–*ct* 1
Bowling 26–0
His first-class debut was for Players of Surrey in 1863. He also played for Devon (1865).

Tanvir Mehdi
Cricketer. *b:* 7.11.1972, Lahore, Pakistan. Lower order right-hand batsman, right-arm fast medium bowler. *Teams* United Bank (1990/1 to 1991/2); Lahore (1991/2). *Tours* Pakistan A to Sri Lanka 1990/1; Pakistan to England 1992.
Career batting
28–25–10–166–21*–11.06–0–*ct* 9
Bowling 2268–101–22.45–6–1–7/74
He played in only five first-class matches in the 1992 tour to England and a one-day international, but did not appear in any Tests.

Tapling, Thomas Keay
Amateur. *b:* 30.10.1855, Norwood, Surrey. *d:* 11.4.1891, Gumley Hall, Leicestershire. Hard-hitting middle order right-hand batsman. *Sch* Harrow and Brighton. *Team* MCC (1886). *Tour* Vernon to India and Ceylon 1889/90 (not first-class).
Career batting
1–2–0–5–5–2.50–0–*ct* 0
His County cricket was for Leicestershire (pre first-class, 1886). He did not appear in first-class cricket whilst at Cambridge. He was Conservative MP for the Harborough Division of Leicestershire from 1886 to his death. He was a famous stamp collector.

Tapp, Theodore Arthur
Amateur. *b:* 5.4.1883, Shortlands, Bromley, Kent. *d:* 21.10.1917, near Dozingham, Belgium. Middle order right-hand batsman, right-arm fast bowler. *Sch* Rugby. *Team* London County (1904).
Career batting
1–2–0–9–5–4.50–0–*ct* 0
Bowling 99–5–19.80–1–0–5/99

Tapsfield, Rev Hugh Alexander
Amateur. *b:* 31.1.1870, Windsor, Berkshire. *d:* 3.3.1945, Weybridge, Surrey. Middle order right-hand batsman. *Sch* Bradfield. *Team* Somerset (1892, 1 match).
Career batting
1–2–0–1–1–0.50–0–*ct* 0
He appeared in the Seniors match at Oxford, but no first-class matches.

Tarbox, Charles Victor
Professional. *b:* 2.7.1891, Hemel Hempstead, Hertfordshire. *d:* 15.6.1978, Peacehaven, Sussex. Middle order right-hand batsman, right-arm medium pace bowler. *Team* Worcestershire (1921–29, 226 matches).
Career batting
226–398–31–5824–109–15.86–2–*ct* 122
Bowling 13256–375–35.34–11–1–7/55
He also played for Hertfordshire (1931–34). He was a first-class umpire (1937–47).

Tarilton, Percy Hamilton
Amateur. *b:* 8.2.1885, St Margaret's, St John, Barbados. *d:* 18.2.1953, Bayville, St Michael, Barbados. Brother of A. F. (Jamaica). Opening right-hand batsman, right-arm slow bowler, wicket-keeper. *Team* Barbados (1905/6 to 1929/30). *Tour* West Indies to England 1923.
Career batting
51–79–7–2777–304*–38.56–8–*ct* 33–*st* 5
Bowling 0–1–0.00–0–0–1/0
He hit 554 runs, av 21.30, on the 1923 tour. His innings of 304* for Barbados v Trinidad at Bridgetown in 1919/20 was a new first-class record for the West Indies.

Tarrant, Edward
Professional. *b:* 11.2.1846, Barnwell, Cambridge. *d:* 19.7.1885, Cambridge. Brother of G. F. (Cambridgeshire). Lower order batsman, useful bowler. *Team* Cambridgeshire (1866, 1 match).
Career batting
1–2–0–4–4–2.00–0–*ct* 1
Bowling 25–0

Tarrant, Francis Alfred
Professional. *b:* 11.12.1880, Fitzroy, Melbourne, Victoria, Australia. *d:* 29.1.1951, Upper Hawthorn, Melbourne, Victoria, Australia. Father of L. B. (Australians in India), nephew of W. A. (Victoria). Cautious middle order right-hand batsman, left-arm slow medium bowler, good slip field. *Teams* Victoria (1898/9 to 1925/6, 13 matches); Middlesex (1904 to 1914, 206 matches); Europeans (1915/16 to 1936/7);

Patiala (1926/7 to 1933/4). *Tour* Australians to India 1935/6.
Career batting
329–541–48–17952–250*–36.41–33–*ct* 303
Bowling 26450–1512–17.49–133–38–10/90

He hit 1,000 runs in a season nine times, going on to 2,000 once: 2,030, av 46.13, in 1911. Eight times he exceeded 100 wickets in a season (best 183, av 15.70, in 1907) – in all eight of these summers he achieved the 'double'. He was regarded by some as the greatest all-rounder of his generation, but as an Australian living in England was never selected for Test matches. Three of his four double centuries were for Middlesex, the other being for Victoria, and his highest innings was 250* for Middlesex v Essex at Leyton in 1914. He took nine wickets in an innings seven times, going on to take all ten once (for 90) – for Maharaja of Cooch Behar's XI v Lord Willingdon's XI at Poona in 1918/19; he also hit 182* in this match. His first-class debut in England was for MCC in 1903. He umpired one Test match in 1933/4.

Tarrant, George Frederick
(registered at death as G. F. Wood)
Professional. *b:* 7.12.1838, Cambridge. *d:* 2.7.1870, Cambridge. He died of pleurisy. Brother of Edward (Cambridgeshire). Hard-hitting lower order right-hand batsman, right-hand fast round-arm bowler, good field. *Teams* Cambridgeshire (1861–68, 31 matches); Cambridge Town Club (1861). *Tours* Parr to Australia 1863/4; Willsher to North America 1868 (not first-class).
Career batting
71–119–9–1633–108–14.84–1–*ct* 58
Bowling 4887–416 + 5–11.74–41–16–10/40

His first-class debut was for AEE in 1860, and his final first-class match for AEE in 1869. He was for a few seasons perhaps the best fast bowler in England – in 1862 he took 96 wickets, av 10.07, in 1864 67, av 8.80, in 1865 45, av 14.15, in 1866 61, av 13.26, and in 1867 44, av 8.70. His best bowling was 10/40 for England v XIII of Kent at Lord's in 1863.

Tasker, Alfred George Ernest
Professional. *b:* 16.6.1934, Southwark, London. Lower order right-hand batsman, wicket-keeper. *Team* Worcestershire (1956, 1 match).
Career batting
1 match, did not bat – *ct* 1

Tasker, John
Amateur. *b:* 4.2.1887, South Kirkby, Yorkshire. *d:* 24.8.1975, Greenham Common, Berkshire. Middle order right-hand batsman. *Team* Yorkshire (1912–13, 31 matches).
Career batting
33–47–4–644–67–14.97–0–*ct* 15
Bowling 16–0

His final first-class match was for the Army in 1919.

Tate, Cecil Frederick
Professional. *b:* 1.5.1908, Gillingham, Kent. Son of F. W. (Sussex), brother of M. W. (Sussex). Middle order right-hand batsman, slow left-arm bowler. *Teams* Derbyshire (1928, 4 matches); Warwickshire (1931–33, 7 matches).
Career batting
11–12–3–82–21–9.11–0–*ct* 5
Bowling 409–8–51.12–0–0–3/65

Tate, Edward
Professional. *b:* 30.8.1877, Lyndhurst, Hampshire. *d:* 4.1.1953, Malvern, Worcestershire. Lower order right-hand batsman, right-arm medium pace bowler. *Team* Hampshire (1898–1902, 29 matches).
Career batting
35–62–17–326–34*–7.24–0–*ct* 13
Bowling 2054–66–31.12–2–1–8/51

He also played for Devon (1911–20). For fifty years he was cricket professional and manager of the college store at Malvern.

Tate, Frederick
Professional. *b:* 6.6.1844, Lyndhurst, Hampshire. *d:* 24.4.1935, Lyndhurst, Hampshire. Brother of H. W. (Hampshire). Lower order right-hand batsman, right-hand fast round-arm bowler, slip field. *Team* Hampshire (1870–76, 4 matches).
Career batting
4–8–3–50–18*–10.00–0–*ct* 5
Bowling 147–13–11.30–2–0–6/63

Tate, Frederick William
Professional. *b:* 24.7.1867, Brighton, Sussex. *d:* 24.2.1943, Burgess Hill, Sussex. Father of M. W. (Sussex) and C. F. (Derbyshire and Warwickshire). Tail end right-hand batsman, right-arm medium pace bowler, slip field. *Team* Sussex (1887–1905, 312 matches). *Test* England (1902, 1 match).
Career batting
320–458–150–2952–84–9.58–0–*ct* 236
Bowling 28691–1331–21.55–104–29–9/73
Test batting
1–2–1–9–5*–9.00–0–*ct* 2
Bowling 51–2–25.50–0–0–2/7

He took 100 wickets in a season five times (best 180, av 15.71, in 1902). His best bowling was 9/73 for Sussex v Leicestershire at Leicester in 1902. On his only appearance in Test cricket (having been chosen instead of G. H. Hirst on the morning of the match), he went in to bat as England's last man with eight runs needed for victory – he was dismissed for 4 and England lost by three runs.

Tate, Harry George
Amateur. *b:* 18.7.1862, East Knoyle, Wiltshire. *d:* 9.3.1949, Bishop's Hull, Somerset. Middle order

batsman. *Team* Somerset (1882, 1 match).
Career batting
1–2–0–0–0–0.00–0–*ct* 1

Tate, Henry William
Professional. *b:* 4.10.1849, Lyndhurst, Hampshire. *d:* 9.5.1936, Richmond, Surrey. Brother of Frederick (Hampshire). Lower order right-hand batsman, right-hand fast round-arm bowler, good slip field. *Team* Hampshire (1869–85, 29 matches).
Career batting
29–54–9–499–61*–11.08–0–*ct* 26
Bowling 1744–96–18.16–6–1–6/51

He also played for Huntingdonshire (1872). He last played for Hampshire (not first-class) in 1886.

Tate, Maurice William
Professional. *b:* 30.5.1895, Brighton, Sussex. *d:* 18.5.1956, Wadhurst, Sussex. Son of F. W. (Sussex), brother of C. F. (Derbyshire and Warwickshire). Hard-hitting middle order right-hand batsman, slow off break, changed in 1922 to right-arm fast medium, or medium pace, bowler. *Team* Sussex (1912–37, 525 matches). *Tours* MCC to Australia 1924/5, 1928/9, to Australia and New Zealand 1932/3, to India, Burma and Ceylon 1926/7, to South Africa 1930/1; Brinckman to South America 1937/8 (injured on outward voyage and did not play in a match). *Tests* England (1924–35, 39 matches).
Career batting
679–970–103–21717–203–25.04–23–*ct* 284
Bowling 50571–2784–18.16–195–44–9/71
Test batting
39–52–5–1198–100*–25.48–1–*ct* 11
Bowling 4055–155–26.16–7–1–6/42

Until 1922 an off break bowler, Tate then developed into the most effective medium fast bowler of his generation. He was the first bowler to thoroughly exploit the use of the seam and his deceptive swerve combined with his nip off the pitch troubled even the best batsmen. He took over 100 wickets in a season 13 times in England, plus once overseas, going on to 200 three times with his best being 228, av 14.97, in 1925. His best bowling was 9/71 for Sussex v Middlesex at Lord's in 1926. In Test cricket he was England's most effective bowler on two tours of Australia – in 1924/5 and 1928/9 – on the former visit he took 77 wickets, av 19.01. He hit 1,000 runs in a season 11 times and once overseas (when he performed the 'double').

Tate's batting was also most effective – in three seasons he achieved the exceptional 'double' of 1,000 runs and 200 wickets and the more ordinary 1,000 runs and 100 wickets in five other seasons. His best summer with the bat was 1927 with 1,713 runs, av 36.44, and his highest innings 203 for Sussex v Northamptonshire at Hove in 1921.

Tate, Walter William Giffard
Amateur. *b:* 27.8.1863, Axminster, Devon. Middle order batsman. *Team* Somerset (1882, 1 match).
Career batting
1–2–0–19–9.50–0–*ct* 0
Bowling 27–0

Tattersall, Geoffry
Amateur. *b:* 21.4.1882, Ripon, Yorkshire. *d:* 29.6.1972, Harrogate, Yorkshire. Middle order right-hand batsman. *Team* Yorkshire (1905, 1 match).
Career batting
1–2–0–26–26–13.00–0–*ct* 0

He played rugby for Harrogate and Yorkshire.

Tattersall, J. M. (*see under* Musgrave, J. M.)

Tattersall, Keith
Cricketer. *b:* 6.3.1946, Tunbridge Wells, Kent. Opening left-hand batsman, slow left-arm bowler. *Teams* Western Province (1965/6 to 1969/70); Rhodesia (1973/4 to 1976/7). *Tour* South African Universities to England 1967.
Career batting
33–58–2–1275–112–22.76–1–*ct* 39
Bowling 101–1–101.00–0–0–1/0

Tattersall, Roger Hartley
Cricketer. *b:* 12.3.1952, Nelson, Lancashire. Lower order left-hand batsman, left-arm medium pace bowler. *Sch* The Leys. *Team* Lancashire (1971, 2 matches).
Career batting
2 matches, did not bat – *ct* 0
Bowling 219–1–219.00–0–0–1/44

Tattersall, Roy
Professional. *b:* 17.8.1922, Tonge Moor, Bolton, Lancashire. Lower order left-hand batsman, off break bowler. *Team* Lancashire (1948–60, 277 matches). *Tours* MCC to Australia and New Zealand 1950/1, to India, Pakistan and Ceylon 1951/2. *Tests* England (1950/1 to 1954, 16 matches).
Career batting
328–369–151–2040–58–9.35–0–*ct* 146
Bowling 24692–1369–18.03–99–18–9/40
Test batting
16–17–7–50–10*–5.00–0–*ct* 8
Bowling 1513–58–26.08–4–1–7/52

He took 100 wickets in a season eight times (best 193, av 13.59, in 1950). His best bowling was 9/40 for Lancashire v Nottinghamshire at Old Trafford in 1953. His final first-class match was for MCC in 1964.

Tauseef Ahmed
Cricketer. *b:* 10.5.1960, Karachi, Pakistan. Lower order right-hand batsman, off break bowler. *Teams* PWD (1978/9); United Bank (1980/1 to 1991/2); Karachi (1983/4 to 1989/90). *Tours* Pakistan to Sri Lanka 1985/6, to Sharjah (not first-class) 1984/5,

1985/6, 1986/7, 1988/9, to India 1986/7, to England 1987, to West Indies 1987/8, to Australia 1988/9, 1989/90, to New Zealand 1988/9, to Bangladesh (not first-class) 1988/9. *Tests* Pakistan (1979/80 to 1990/1, 33 matches).
Career batting
134–144–50–1478–77–15.72–0–*ct* 61
Bowling 12523–548–22.85–36–5–8/52
Test batting
33–37–19–297–35*–16.50–0–*ct* 9
Bowling 2888–93–31.05–3–0–6/45

He did not play in any Tests on the 1987 tour to England; he rarely came to terms with English wickets and a broken finger reduced his opportunities. He made his Test debut after playing just one first-class match when spotted bowling in the nets.

Tavaré, Christopher James
Cricketer. *b:* 27.10.1954, Orpington, Kent. Sound opening or middle order right-hand batsman, off break bowler. *Sch* Sevenoaks. *Teams* Kent (1974–88, 259 matches); Oxford U (1975–77, blue all three years); Somerset (1989–92, 89 matches). *Tours* England to India and Sri Lanka 1981/2, to Australia 1982/3, to New Zealand 1982/3 (not first-class), 1983/4, to Pakistan 1983/4 (not first-class). *Tests* England (1980–89, 31 matches).
Career batting
418–692–74–24278–219–39.28–47–*ct* 396
Bowling 720–5–144.00–0–0–1/3
Test batting
31–56–2–1755–149–32.50–2–*ct* 20
Bowling 11–0

He hit 1,000 runs in a season 16 times (best 1,770, av 53.63, in 1981). His highest score was 219 for Somerset v Sussex at Hove in 1990. For England v Australia at Manchester in 1981 he scored 147 in 710 minutes in his two innings (69 in 287 minutes and 78 in 423) – this created a new record for slow scoring. Between 1980 and 1984 he played fairly regularly for England, usually opening though his normal position in county cricket was first wicket down. After a break of five years he reappeared in one Test in 1989, standing in for Gatting who was absent due to a family bereavement. He captained Kent in 1983 and 1984, then Somerset from 1990 to 1992.

Tayfield, Hugh Joseph
Amateur. *b:* 30.1.1929, Durban, South Africa. Brother of Arthur (Transvaal) and Cyril (Griqualand West and Transvaal), cousin of I. R. (Transvaal and Griqualand West) and H. Martin (Transvaal and New South Wales), nephew of S. H. Martin (Worcestershire). Lower order right-hand batsman, brilliant off break bowler. *Teams* Natal (1945/6 to 1946/7); Rhodesia (1947/8 to 1948/9); Transvaal (1956/7 to 1962/3). *Tours* South Africa to England 1951, 1955, 1960, to Australia and New Zealand 1952/3. *Tests* South Africa (1949/50 to 1960, 37 matches).
Career batting
187–259–47–3668–77–17.30–0–*ct* 149
Bowling 18890–864–21.86–67–16–9/113
Test batting
37–60–9–862–75–16.90–0–*ct* 26
Bowling 4405–170–25.91–14–2–9/113

He was flown in as a reinforcement for the 1951 touring team and did not play in the Tests. In 1955, however, he carried all before him, heading the first-class bowling table with 143 wickets, av 15.75, and in Tests 26 wickets, av 21.84. In 1960 he took over 100 first-class wickets, but was very expensive in the Tests. His best bowling was 9/113 for South Africa v England at Johannesburg in 1956/7.

Tayler, Frederick Ernest
Amateur. *b:* 18.7.1889, Aston-Blank, Gloucestershire. *d:* 30.4.1954, Cold Aston, Gloucestershire. Brother of H. W. (Gloucestershire and Glamorgan). Middle order batsman. *Sch* Wellingborough. *Team* Warwickshire (1910, 4 matches); Gloucestershire (1911, 4 matches).
Career batting
8–16–0–165–44–10.31–0–*ct* 0
Bowling 12–0

Tayler, Herbert William
Amateur. *b:* 6.12.1887, Aldsworth, Gloucestershire. *d:* 17.4.1984, Dawlish, Devon. Brother of F. E. (Warwickshire and Gloucestershire). Middle order right-hand batsman, right-arm medium pace bowler. *Sch* Wellingborough. *Teams* Gloucestershire (1914, 2 matches); Glamorgan (1921–27, 10 matches).
Career batting
12–23–4–344–44–18.10–0–*ct* 3

Tayler, Robert Frederick
Amateur. *b:* 17.3.1836, Wendover, Hastings, Sussex. *d:* 1.1.1888, Woking Village, Surrey. Solid opening right-hand batsman, good short leg. *Teams* Kent (1865, 2 matches); Hampshire (1866, 2 matches).
Career batting
5–10–0–107–42–10.70–0–*ct* 1

Taylor, Albert Edward
Professional. *b:* 14.6.1894, Chilvers Coton, Nuneaton, Warwickshire. *d:* 19.8.1960, Moorgate, Rotherham, Yorkshire. Lower order right-hand batsman, right-arm medium fast bowler. *Team* Warwickshire (1927, 1 match).
Career batting
1–1–0–0–0–0.00–0–*ct* 0
Bowling 7–0

Taylor, Alfred George
Amateur. *b:* 29.12.1891, West Ham, Essex. Lower order batsman, useful bowler. *Team* Essex (1923, 2 matches).

Taylor, Andrew

Career batting
2–3–0–7–7–2.33–0–*ct* 0
Bowling 77–1–77.00–0–0–1/40

Taylor, Andrew
Professional. *b:* 20.4.1838, Camberwell, London. *d:* 5.4.1901, Aston, Birmingham. Attacking middle order right-hand batsman, right-hand medium pace round-arm bowler, long stop. *Team* Surrey (1865, 1 match).
Career batting
1–1–0–1–1–1.00–0–*ct* 0
Bowling 13–1–13.00–0–0–1/13
He also played for Brecon (1868).

Taylor, Arthur
Professional. *b:* 1880, Maltby, Yorkshire. *d:* 13.11.1956, Winson Green, Birmingham. Tail end right-hand batsman, right-arm medium fast bowler. *Team* Warwickshire (1913, 6 matches).
Career batting
6–11–2–83–17–9.22–0–*ct* 3
Bowling 137–4–34.25–0–0–2/10

Taylor, Benjamin Williamson
Professional. *b:* 16.6.1873, Kimberley, Nottinghamshire. *d:* 24.8.1938, Eastwood, Nottinghamshire. Lower order right-hand batsman, right-arm fast medium bowler. *Team* Nottinghamshire (1902–09, 31 matches).
Career batting
31–41–11–379–54*–12.63–0–*ct* 19
Bowling 2790–85–32.82–3–0–6/109

Taylor, Brian
Professional. *b:* 19.6.1932, West Ham, Essex. Middle order left-hand batsman, wicket-keeper. *Team* Essex (1949–73, 539 matches). *Tours* MCC to South Africa 1956/7, to Bangladesh 1976/7 (not first-class).
Career batting
572–949–73–19094–135–21.79–9–*ct* 1083–*st* 211
Bowling 30–1–30.00–0–0–1/16
He hit 1,000 runs in a season eight times (best 1,837, av 30.61, in 1959). In 1962 he dismissed 91 batsmen (ct 81, st 10). Between 1961 and 1972 he appeared in 301 consecutive Championship matches for Essex. He captained Essex 1967–73. In 1973 and 1974 he was appointed to the Test Selection Committee. A good soccer player, he appeared for Brentford.

Taylor, Bruce Richard
Amateur. *b:* 12.7.1943, Timaru, Canterbury, New Zealand. Forcing middle order left-hand batsman, right-arm fast medium bowler, good slip. *Team* Canterbury (1964/5 to 1969/70); Wellington (1970/1 to 1979/80). *Tours* New Zealand to England 1965, 1969, 1973, to West Indies 1971/2, to India and Pakistan 1964/5, 1969/70, to Australia 1967/8, 1969/70, 1970/1. *Tests* New Zealand (1964/5 to 1973, 30 matches).
Career batting
141–210–25–4579–173–24.75–4–*ct* 66
Bowling 10605–422–25.13–15–0–7/74
Test batting
30–50–6–898–124–20.40–2–*ct* 10
Bowling 2953–111–26.60–4–0–7/74
After a moderate tour in 1965, he headed the Test bowling in 1969 with 10 wickets, av 15.50. In 1973 however he was not so successful. His first-class debut was for New Zealand Under 23 in 1964/5.

Taylor, Charles George
Amateur. *b:* 21.11.1816, Turnham Green, Middlesex. *d:* 10.9.1869, Frensham Hill, Surrey. He died of apoplexy. Stylish opening right-hand batsman, right-hand slow round-arm bowler, good deep field. *Sch* Eton. *Teams* Cambridge U (1836–39, blue 1836, 1838 and 1839); Sussex (1837–54, 41 matches); Cambridge Town Club (1838).
Career batting
125–227–11–3088–114–14.29–2–*ct* 70
Bowling 816–61 + 226–13.37–22–6–8/?
He was one of the first batsmen to move to the pitch of the ball and in addition the most polished amateur of his time. His final first-class match was for Gentlemen of England in 1859. He captained Cambridge 1838–39 and Sussex 1839–46. He excelled at both billiards and tennis.

Taylor, Charles James
Professional. *b:* 8.6.1881, Bedminster, Somerset. *d:* 25.8.1960, Leek, Staffordshire. Father of Frederick (Warwickshire). Lower order right-hand batsman, right-arm fast medium bowler. *Team* Warwickshire (1908–09, 3 matches).
Career batting
3–4–0–6–5–1.50–0–*ct* 1
Bowling 257–9–28.55–0–0–4/99
He also played for Staffordshire (1920–32).

Taylor, Charles William
Cricketer. *b:* 12.8.1966, Banbury, Oxfordshire. Lower order left-hand batsman, left-arm medium fast bowler. *Team* Middlesex (1990–92, 27 matches).
Career batting
27–21–8–147–21–11.30–0–*ct* 5
Bowling 2044–59–34.64–1–0–5/33
He also played for Oxfordshire (1986).

Taylor, Chilton Richard Vernon
Cricketer. *b:* 3.10.1951, Birkenhead, Cheshire. Lower order right-hand batsman, wicket-keeper. *Sch* Birkenhead. *Teams* Warwickshire (1970, 1 match); Cambridge U (1971–73, blue all three years); Middlesex (1981, 2 matches).
Career batting
33–45–5–276–25–6.90–0–*ct* 56–*st* 9
He appeared for Middlesex without being registered and the County were penalised. He also played for Cheshire (1969–72).

Taylor, Claude Hilary
Amateur. *b:* 6.2.1904, Leicester. *d:* 28.1.1966, North Foreland, Sherfield-on-Loddon, Hampshire. Solid, stylish middle order right-hand batsman, leg break and googly bowler. *Sch* Westminster. *Teams* Leicestershire (1922–27, 45 matches); Oxford U (1923–26, blue all four years).
Career batting
88–147–11–3378–123–24.83–9–*ct* 66
Bowling 920–21–43.80–0–0–2/6
He was the first Oxford Freshman to hit a century in the University match, in 1923. He also played for Buckinghamshire (1946–48). With D. H. Macindoe, he was joint author of *Cricket Dialogue*.

Taylor, Dr Clifford John
(birth registered as J. C. Taylor)
Amateur. *b:* 1.8.1875, Clifton, Bristol. *d:* 10.11.1952, Camberwell, London. Lower order batsman, useful bowler. *Team* Gloucestershire (1899–1900, 4 matches).
Career batting
4–5–0–72–25–14.40–0–*ct* 0
Bowling 44–2–22.00–0–0–2/33

Taylor, Darren Philip
Cricketer. *b:* 15.2.1965, Burnley, Lancashire. Lower order right-hand batsman, wicket-keeper. *Team* Oxford U (1985–86).
Career batting
8–12–2–44–17–4.40–0–*ct* 7–st 2

Taylor, Derek John Somerset
Cricketer. *b:* 12.11.1942, Amersham, Buckinghamshire. Twin brother of M. N. S. (Nottinghamshire and Hampshire). Middle or lower order, occasional opening, right-hand batsman, wicket-keeper. *Teams* Surrey (1966–69, 10 matches); Somerset (1970–82, 280 matches); Griqualand West (1970/1 to 1971/2).
Career batting
302–420–95–7404–179–22.78–4–*ct* 621–*st* 84
Bowling 16–0
He scored 1,121 runs, av 28.02, in 1975. He also played for Buckinghamshire (1961–63). He played soccer for Corinthian Casuals.

Taylor, Derief David Samuel
Professional. *b:* 10.9.1910, Kingston, Jamaica. *d:* 17.3.1987, Cross Roads, Kingston, Jamaica. Middle order left-hand batsman, slow left-arm bowler. *Team* Warwickshire (1948–50, 16 matches).
Career batting
16–23–7–519–121–32.43–1–*ct* 4
Bowling 607–15–40.46–0–0–3/41
He was juniors coach to Warwickshire 1951–81.

Taylor, Donald Dougald
Professional. *b:* 2.3.1923, Auckland, New Zealand. *d:* 5.12.1980, Epsom, Auckland, New Zealand. Attractive opening or middle order right-hand batsman, off break bowler. *Teams* Auckland (1946/7 to 1960/1); Warwickshire (1949–53, 45 matches). *Tests* New Zealand (1946/7 to 1955/6, 3 matches).
Career batting
95–168–6–3772–143–23.28–1–*ct* 62
Bowling 1063–32–33.21–0–0–4/24
Test batting
3–5–0–159–77–31.80–0–*ct* 2

Taylor, Edmund Judkin
Amateur. *b:* 30.12.1853, Stoke Bishop, Bristol. *d:* 25.12.1936, Redland, Bristol. Middle order right-hand batsman, good cover field. *Sch* Clifton and Rugby. *Team* Gloucestershire (1876–86, 24 matches).
Career batting
24–35–3–319–33–9.96–0–*ct* 7–*st* 1

Taylor, Edward Fairfax
Amateur. *b:* 10.7.1845, Holborn, London. *d:* 27.1.1902, Ewell, Surrey. Lower order right-hand batsman, right-hand fast medium round-arm bowler, slip field. *Sch* Marlborough. *Team* Surrey (1865–67, 2 matches).
Career batting
2–4–0–48–27–12.00–0–*ct* 2
Bowling 135–7–19.28–0–0–4/59
Owing to his position at the House of Lords, where latterly he was Taxing Master, he was unable to appear often in County cricket.

Taylor, Francis Henry
Amateur. *b:* 14.6.1890, Wirksworth, Derbyshire. *d:* 6.12.1963, California, Derby. Brother of W. T. (Derbyshire). Middle order right-hand batsman. *Team* Derbyshire (1908–11, 8 matches).
Career batting
8–16–1–95–18–6.33–0–*ct* 3

Taylor, Frank
Amateur. *b:* 4.5.1855, Rochdale, Lancashire. *d:* 14.8.1936, Heald Green, Cheadle, Cheshire. Stylish middle order right-hand batsman, round-arm bowler, good deep field. *Sch* Clifton. *Teams* Gloucestershire (1873, 3 matches); Lancashire (1874–88, 52 matches).
Career batting
55–89–4–1492–96–17.55–0–*ct* 25
Bowling 73–3–24.33–0–0–1/4

Taylor, Fred
Professional. *b:* 1891, Oldham, Lancashire. *d:* 4.7.1968, Clitheroe, Lancashire. Lower order batsman, left-arm medium pace bowler. *Team* Lancashire (1920–22, 15 matches).
Career batting
15–18–6–188–29*–15.66–0–*ct* 7
Bowling 1026–40–25.65–3–0–6/65

Taylor, Frederick
Professional. *b:* 29.4.1916, Leek, Staffordshire. Son of C. J. (Warwickshire). Lower order right-hand bats-

man, right-arm fast medium bowler. *Team* Warwickshire (1939, 1 match).
Career batting
2–3–0–8–2.66–0–*ct* 3
Bowling 142–8–17.75–1–0–5/71
He also played for Staffordshire (1937–50). His final first-class match was for Minor Counties v Australians at Stoke in 1953.

Taylor, George Rammell
Amateur. *b:* 25.11.1909, Havant, Hampshire. *d:* 21.10.1986, Romsey, Hampshire. Middle order right-hand batsman, slow right-arm bowler. *Sch* Lancing. *Team* Hampshire (1935–39, 24 matches).
Career batting
24–37–4–306–41–9.27–0–*ct* 15
Bowling 21–1–21.00–0–0–1/8
He captained Hampshire in 1939.

Taylor, Harold William Frank
Amateur. *b:* 27.12.1909, Chesterton, Cambridgeshire. *d:* 26.8.1990, Cambridge. Middle order right-hand batsman. *Sch* Perse. *Team* Minor Counties (1939).
Career batting
2–3–1–58–38–29.00–0–*ct* 2
His County cricket was for Cambridgeshire (1925–56).

Taylor, Harry
Professional. *b:* 18.12.1900, Idle, Yorkshire. *d:* 28.10.1988, Bradford, Yorkshire. Middle order right-hand batsman, right-arm medium pace bowler. *Team* Yorkshire (1924–25, 9 matches).
Career batting
9–13–0–153–36–11.76–0–*ct* 1

Taylor, Henry Blair Johnson
Amateur. *b:* 1.6.1875, Dalhousie, India. *d:* 29.5.1903, Bengeo, Hertfordshire. Middle order right-hand batsman. *Sch* Newton College. *Team* Cambridge U (1897).
Career batting
2–2–0–3–3–1.50–0–*ct* 1
He won a blue for rugby.

Taylor, Henry John Corbett
Cricketer. *b:* 16.4.1949, Solihull, Warwickshire. Middle order right-hand batsman, off break bowler. *Sch* Solihull. *Team* Cambridge U (1968–69).
Career batting
13–25–1–246–50–10.25–0–*ct* 4
Bowling 5–0

Taylor, Henry Storm
Professional. *b:* 11.12.1856, Scarborough, Yorkshire. *d:* 16.11.1896, Great Lever, Lancashire. Middle order right-hand batsman, right-arm medium pace bowler, close field. *Team* Yorkshire (1879, 3 matches).
Career batting
3–5–0–36–22–7.20–0–*ct* 0

Taylor, Henry Thomas
Amateur. *b:* 7.7.1911, Cardiff, Glamorgan. *d:* 20.7.1970, Pontypridd, Glamorgan. Middle order batsman. *Team* Glamorgan (1932–34, 3 matches).
Career batting
3–4–1–17–16*–5.66–0–*ct* 1
Bowling 11–0

Taylor, Herbert
Amateur. *b:* 22.2.1910, Accrington, Lancashire. Tail end right-hand batsman, right-arm fast bowler. *Team* Middlesex (1933, 3 matches).
Career batting
3–4–0–11–6–2.75–0–*ct* 2
Bowling 181–3–60.33–0–0–1/17

Taylor, Herbert Wilfred
Amateur. *b:* 5.5.1889, Durban, South Africa. *d:* 8.2.1973, Newlands, Cape Town, South Africa. Son of Daniel sen (Natal), brother of Daniel jun (Natal). Stylish opening right-hand batsman, bowler, splendid field. *Teams* Natal (1909/10 to 1934/5); Transvaal (1925/6 to 1930/1); Western Province (1935/6). *Tours* South Africa to England 1912, 1924, 1929, to Australia and New Zealand 1931/2. *Tests* South Africa (1912 to 1931/2, 42 matches).
Career batting
206–339–26–13105–250*–41.86–30–*ct* 75
Bowling 560–22–25.45–0–0–4/36
Test batting
42–76–4–2936–176–40.77–7–*ct* 19
Bowling 156–5–31.20–0–0–3/15
He exceeded 1,000 runs on each of his three tours to England and in both 1924 and 1929 he headed the batting averages – his best figures were in 1924 (as captain) with 1,898 runs, av 42.17. He also played in England in 1919, having served in the First World War, and appeared for L. Robinson's XI v AIF. His final first-class match in England was for Rest of England in 1932. His highest score was 250* for Natal v Transvaal at Johannesburg in 1912/13. He captained South Africa in 18 Tests. A noted rugby half-back, he represented Natal.

Taylor, Horace James
Amateur. *b:* 26.12.1895, Sevenoaks, Kent. *d:* 13.10.1961, Tunbridge Wells, Kent. Middle order right-hand batsman, right-arm medium pace bowler. *Sch* Sevenoaks. *Team* Kent (1922–25, 12 matches).
Career batting
12–13–3–181–33–18.10–0–*ct*2

Taylor, Howard
Amateur. *b:* 5.4.1908, Old Charlton, London. *d:* 30.12.1985, Tunbridge Wells, Kent. Lower order right-hand batsman, right-arm medium pace bowler. *Sch* Mill Hill. *Team* Kent (1937, 3 matches).
Career batting
3–6–0–53–29–8.83–0–*ct* 0
Bowling 121–2–60.50–0–0–1/34

Taylor, James
Professional. *b:* 25.5.1846, Littleborough, Lancashire. *d:* 16.8.1915, Smallbridge, Rochdale, Lancashire. Middle order right-hand batsman, right-hand fast round-arm bowler, point field. *Team* Lancashire (1871–73, 3 matches).
Career batting
3–6–0–52–33–8.66–0–*ct* 0
Bowling 13–0

Taylor, James Alexander Simson
Amateur. *b:* 19.6.1917, Weston-super-Mare, Somerset. Middle order right-hand batsman, right-arm medium pace bowler. *Sch* Oakham and Wyggeston GS. *Teams* Leicestershire (1937, 3 matches); Scotland (1952–54).
Career batting
9–10–0–198–78–19.80–0–*ct* 12
Bowling 58–1–58.00–0–0–1/11
Whilst at Cambridge he did not appear in any first-class matches for the University.

Taylor, James Robert Niven
Amateur. *b:* 11.8.1929, Calcutta, India. Middle order right-hand batsman. *Teams* Scotland (1949); Bengal (1952/3).
Career batting
4–8–1–129–41–18.42–0–*ct* 0

Taylor, John
Professional, *b:* 2.7.1849, Beeston, Nottinghamshire. *d:* 2.3.1921, Beeston, Nottinghamshire. Middle order right-hand batsman, right-hand medium pace round-arm bowler. *Team* Nottinghamshire (1876, 1 match).
Career batting
1–2–0–2–2–1.00–0–*ct* 1

Taylor, John
Professional, *b:* 2.4.1850, Pudsey, Yorkshire. *d:* 27.5.1924, Boston Spa, Yorkshire. Steady middle order right-hand batsman, right-hand medium pace round-arm bowler. *Team* Yorkshire (1880–81, 9 matches).
Career batting
10–15–1–110–44–7.85–0–*ct* 4
His first-class debut was for North v South in 1875.

Taylor, John Denis
Professional. *b:* 18.12.1923, Ipswich, Suffolk. Middle order right-hand batsman, right-arm medium pace bowler. *Team* Hampshire (1947–49, 4 matches).
Career batting
4–8–3–76–27*–15.20–0–*ct* 0
Bowling 24–0

Taylor, John Frederick
Professional. *b:* 9.6.1937, West Ham, Essex. Middle order right-hand batsman, wicket-keeper. *Team* Essex (1960–61, 14 matches).
Career batting
15–24–7–461–86–27.11–0–*ct* 22–*st* 5

His final first-class match was for MCC in 1967. A useful soccer player, he appeared for Grays Athletic.

Taylor, John Morris
Amateur. *b:* 10.10.1895, Stanmore, Sydney, New South Wales, Australia. *d:* 12.5.1971, Turramurra, Sydney, New South Wales, Australia. Polished middle order right-hand batsman, brilliant cover point. *Team* New South Wales (1913/14 to 1926/7, 27 matches). *Tours* AIF to England 1919, to South Africa 1919/20; Australia to England 1921, 1926, to South Africa 1921/2. *Tests* Australia (1920/1 to 1926, 20 matches).
Career batting
135–195–7–6274–180–33.37–11–*ct* 68
Bowling 53–1–53.00–0–0–1/25
Test batting
20–28–0–997–108–35.60–1–*ct* 11
Bowling 45–1–45.00–0–0–1/25
He was probably at his best, so far as his three visits to England were concerned, in 1919, when he hit 1,187 runs, av 31.23. In 1921 he just reached 1,000 runs in first-class matches, but in 1926 showed little form in the important fixtures.

Taylor, Jonathan Paul
Cricketer. *b:* 8.8.1864, Ashby-de-la-Zouch, Leicestershire. Lower order left-hand batsman, left-arm fast medium bowler. *Teams* Derbyshire (1984–86, 7 matches); Northamptonshire (1991–92, 36 matches).
Career batting
43–37–14–239–74*–10.39–0–*ct* 16
Bowling 3479–105–33.13–4–1–7/23
He also played for Staffordshire (1989–90).

Taylor, Kenneth
Professional. *b:* 21.8.1935, Primrose Hill, Huddersfield, Yorkshire. Father of N. S. (Yorkshire, Surrey and Somerset). Opening or middle order right-hand batsman, right-arm medium pace or leg break bowler. *Teams* Yorkshire (1953–68, 303 matches); Auckland (1963/4). *Tours* MCC to Bangladesh 1978/9 (not first-class); Swanton to India 1963/4. *Tests* England (1959–64, 3 matches).
Career batting
313–524–36–13053–203*–26.74–16–*ct* 150
Bowling 3763–131–28.72–1–0–6/75
Test batting
3–5–0–57–24–11.40–0–*ct* 1
Bowling 6–0
He hit 1,000 runs in a season six times (best 1,494, av 34.74, in 1961). His only double century was 203* for Yorkshire v Warwickshire at Edgbaston in 1961. He also played for Norfolk (1972–74). An excellent soccer player, he was centre half for Huddersfield Town and Bradford.

Taylor, Kenneth Alexander
Professional. *b:* 29.9.1916, Muswell Hill, Middlesex. Steady opening right-hand batsman, right-arm med-

ium pace bowler. *Team* Warwickshire (1946–49, 87 matches).
Career batting
87–155–10–3145–102–21.68–1–*ct* 42
Bowling 33–1–33.00–0–0–1/18
He hit 1,259 runs, av 26.22, in 1947. He was on the Committee of Nottinghamshire CCC from 1963 to 1978, and Cricket Manager from 1978 to 1990.

Taylor, Leslie Brian
Cricketer. *b:* 25.10.1953, Earl Shilton, Leicestershire. Lower order right-hand batsman, right-arm fast medium bowler. *Teams* Leicestershire (1977–90, 192 matches); Natal (1981/2 to 1983/4). *Tours* Leicestershire to Zimbabwe 1980/1; SAB England XI to South Africa 1981/2; England to West Indies 1985/6. *Tests* England (1985, 2 matches).
Career batting
218–199–86–1061–60–9.38–0–*ct* 53
Bowling 14648–581–25.21–18–1–7/28
Test batting
2–1–1–1–1*–no av–0–*ct* 1
Bowling 178–4–44.50–0–0–2/34
He took 75 wickets, av 21.70, in 1981. He was banned from Test cricket following his decision to tour South Africa, but gained an England cap soon after the ban was lifted. On the 1985/6 tour to West Indies he bowled well in the one-day international prior to the First Test, but was given few opportunities on the rest of the tour.

Taylor, Malcolm Lees
Professional. *b:* 16.7.1904, Heywood, Lancashire. *d:* 14.3.1978, Wimborne, Dorset. Stylish middle order left-hand batsman. *Team* Lancashire (1924–31, 95 matches).
Career batting
96–112–15–2216–107*–22.84–1–*ct* 42
Bowling 26–0
He also played for Dorset (1934–48).

Taylor, Mark Anthony
Cricketer. *b:* 27.10.1964, Leeton, New South Wales, Australia. Sound opening left-hand batsman, right-arm medium pace bowler. *Team* New South Wales (1985/6 to 1991/2, 67 matches). *Tours* New South Wales to Zimbabwe 1985/6, 1987/8; Australia to England 1989, to New Zealand 1989/90, to Sharjah (not first-class) 1989/90, to West Indies 1990/1; Australia B to Zimbabwe 1991/2. *Tests* Australia (1988/9 to 1991/2, 30 matches).
Career batting
115–199–8–8883–219–46.50–23–*ct* 156
Bowling 2–0
Test batting
30–56–4–2694–219–51.80–8–*ct* 38
He came to England in 1989 almost as an unknown, but by the close of the tour had established himself as one of the leading batsmen of the day. In the Test series he hit 839 runs, av 83.90, and on two occasions batted through the whole of the first day. The first was on a difficult wicket at Headingley, when he made 136, the second at Trent Bridge when he hit 219 and added 329 with G. R. Marsh, a first wicket record for England v Australia matches. In all first-class matches on the tour he scored 1,669 runs, av 57.55. He scored 1,000 runs in Australia twice (best 1,403, av 70.15, in 1989/90).

Taylor, Michael Norman Somerset
Cricketer. *b:* 12.11.1942, Amersham, Buckinghamshire. Twin brother of D. J. S. (Surrey and Somerset). Middle or lower order right-hand batsman, right-arm medium pace bowler. *Teams* Nottinghamshire (1964–72, 230 matches); Hampshire (1973–80, 145 matches).
Career batting
375–518–116–8031–105–19.97–3–*ct* 213
Bowling 22016–830–26.52–24–0–7/23
His best bowling season was 1968 with 99 wickets, av 21.00. He also played for Buckinghamshire (1961–62). He has been Marketing Manager of Hampshire CCC since 1984.

Taylor, Neil Raymond
Cricketer. *b:* 9.2.1964, Boscombe, Hampshire. Lower order right-hand batsman, right-arm medium fast bowler. *Team* Middlesex (1990, 1 match).
Career batting
2–2–0–0–0–0.00–0–*ct* 1
Bowling 131–4–32.75–0–0–3/44
He also played for Dorset (1987–92) and made his first-class debut for Minor Counties in 1990.

Taylor, Neil Royston
Cricketer. *b:* 21.7.1959, Farnborough, Kent. Opening right-hand batsman, off break bowler. *Team* Kent (1979–92, 263 matches).
Career batting
264–450–61–15622–204–40.15–38–*ct* 143
Bowling 891–16–55.68–0–0–2/20
He hit 1,000 runs in a season nine times (best 1,979, av 61.84, in 1990). He scored 110 for Kent v Sri Lankans at Canterbury on his first-class debut in 1979. His highest score was 204 for Kent v Surrey at Canterbury in 1990, and he twice scored a 200 and 100 in the same match.

Taylor, Nicholas Simon
Cricketer. *b:* 2.6.1963, Holmfirth, Yorkshire. Son of Kenneth (Yorkshire). Lower order right-hand batsman, right-arm fast medium bowler. *Sch* Gresham's, Holt. *Teams* Yorkshire (1982–83, 8 matches); Surrey (1984–85, 10 matches); Somerset (1986, 16 matches).
Career batting
34–33–11–180–24*–8.18–0–*ct* 7
Bowling 2775–79–35.12–2–0–7/44
He also played for Norfolk (1989–90).

Taylor, Paul Adrian
Professional. *b:* 9.3.1939, East Kirkby, Nottinghamshire. Tail end left-hand batsman, left-arm fast medium bowler. *Team* Nottinghamshire (1958, 6 matches).
Career batting
6–10–5–34–13–6.80–0–*ct* 5
Bowling 335–7–47.85–0–0–2/82

Taylor, Philip Henry
Professional. *b:* 18.9.1917, Greenbank, Bristol. Middle order right-hand batsman. *Team* Gloucestershire (1938, 1 match).
Career batting
1–2–0–14–12–7.00–0–*ct* 0
He played soccer for Liverpool, Bristol Rovers and England, captaining Liverpool in the 1950 FA Cup Final.

Taylor, Reginald Minshall
Professional, amateur in 1946. *b:* 30.11.1909, Southend, Essex. *d:* 7.1.1984, Hillbrow, Johannesburg, South Africa. Stylish middle order right-hand batsman, slow left-arm bowler. *Team* Essex (1931–46, 206 matches).
Career batting
206–349–21–6755–193–20.59–5–*ct* 185
Bowling 2933–92–31.88–3–0–7/99
He hit 1,000 runs in a season twice (best 1,181, av 24.10, in 1933).

Taylor, Robert Joseph
Professional. *b:* 1.11.1873, Liverpool, Lancashire. Lower order right-hand batsman, right-arm medium pace bowler. *Teams* Lancashire (1898, 2 matches); Worcestershire (1900, 1 match).
Career batting
3–5–0–7–6–1.40–0–*ct* 0
Bowling 137–2–68.50–0–0–1/25
He also played for Suffolk (1906–07).

Taylor, Robert William, MBE
Professional. *b:* 17.7.1941, Stoke-on-Trent, Staffordshire. Lower order right-hand batsman, right-arm medium pace bowler, brilliant wicket-keeper. *Team* Derbyshire (1961–84, 514 matches). *Tours* MCC to Ceylon 1969/70, to Australia and New Zealand 1970/1, 1974/5, to West Indies 1973/4; England to Pakistan 1977/8, 1983/4, to New Zealand 1977/8, 1982/3 (not first-class), 1983/4, to Australia 1978/9, 1979/90, 1982/3, to India 1979/80, 1981/2, to Sri Lanka 1981/2; Rest of World to Australia 1971/2; International Wanderers to South Africa 1975/6. *Tests* England (1970/1 to 1983/4, 57 matches).
Career batting
639–880–167–12065–100–16.92–1–*ct* 1473–*st* 176
Bowling 75–1–75.00–0–0–1/23
Test batting
57–83–12–1156–97–16.28–0–*ct* 167–*st* 7
Bowling 6–0
He also played for Staffordshire (1958–60), making his first-class debut for Minor Counties in 1960. In 1975–76 he captained Derbyshire. During the 1970s he vied with A. P. E. Knott as the leading wicket-keeper in England, but gained a regular England Test place only when Knott was banned. For England v India at Bombay in 1979/80, he made 7 dismissals in an innings and 10 in the match. He made more dismissals in his first-class career than any other wicket-keeper. His final appearance during a Test match occurred in rather bizarre circumstances in the Lord's Test of 1986 v New Zealand when he was working for the match sponsors, but came on as substitute wicket-keeper for B. N. French until R. J. Parks could be located and brought to the ground. His last first-class match was for Rest of the World at Scarborough in 1988.

Taylor, Ronald Alfred
Professional. *b:* 25.3.1909, The Meadows, Nottingham. *d:* 29.8.1986, Nottingham. Cousin of G. Duckworth (Lancashire). Opening or middle order right-hand batsman, right-arm medium or leg break bowler. *Team* Nottinghamshire (1932–35, 23 matches).
Career batting
23–35–2–599–107–18.15–1–*ct* 7–*st* 1
Bowling 1–0

Taylor, Stanley Shelbourne
Amateur. *b:* 2.3.1875, Islington, London. *d:* 22.7.1965, Oakley House, Basingstoke, Hampshire. Middle order batsman. *Sch* Aldenham. *Team* Middlesex (1901, 2 matches).
Career batting
2–3–0–24–16–8.00–0–*ct* 3
He played no first-class cricket at Cambridge U, but did win a blue for soccer.

Taylor, Thomas
Professional. *c:* 18.10.1753, Ropley, Hampshire. *d:* 29.4.1806, Alresford, Hampshire. Attacking right-hand batsman, useful bowler, fine field. *Team* Hampshire (1775–98).
He was 'shabby enough to put his leg in front of his wicket', which caused the leg before wicket law to be instituted.

Taylor, Timothy John
Cricketer. *b:* 28.3.1961, Romiley, Cheshire. Lower order right-hand batsman, slow left-arm bowler. *Sch* Stockport GS. *Teams* Oxford U (1981–82, blue both years); Lancashire (1981–82, 4 matches).
Career batting
14–17–7–115–28*–11.50–0–*ct* 2
Bowling 1272–37–34.37–2–0–5/81
He also played for Cheshire (1980–82).

Taylor, Tom Launcelot
Amateur. *b:* 25.5.1878, Headingley, Leeds, Yorkshire. *d:* 16.3.1960, Chapel Allerton, Leeds, Yorkshire. Brother-in-law of H. R. Parkes (Warwickshire). Sound middle order right-hand batsman, wicket-keeper. *Sch* Uppingham. *Teams* Cambridge (1897–1900, blue 1898–1900); Yorkshire (1899–1906, 82 matches). *Tour* Hawke to New Zealand and Australia 1902/3.
Career batting
130–202–16–5968–156–32.08–13–*ct* 86–*st* 6
He hit 1,000 runs in a season three times (best 1,517, av 37.92, in 1902). He captained Cambridge in 1900. He was President of Yorkshire CCC from 1948 until his death. He played hockey for Cambridge and was also a good tennis player.

Taylor, W. H.
Professional. Lower order batsman, right-arm fast bowler. *Team* Somerset (1910–11, 18 matches).
Career batting
18–34–5–220–33–7.58–0–*ct* 8
Bowling 1704–52–32.76–2–0–6/82

Taylor, William
Cricketer. *b:* 24.1.1947, Manchester, Lancashire. Lower order right-hand batsman, right-arm fast medium bowler. *Team* Nottinghamshire (1971–77, 95 matches).
Career batting
95–97–39–374–26*–6.44–0–*ct* 14
Bowling 6291–211–29.81–6–1–6/42

Taylor, William Herbert
Amateur. *b:* 23.6.1885, Sale, Cheshire. *d:* 27.5.1959, Birlingham, Worcestershire. Brother-in-law of M. F. S. Jewell (Sussex and Worcestershire). Lower order right-hand batsman, right-arm fast medium bowler. *Team* Worcestershire (1909–25, 107 matches).
Career batting
110–194–40–1792–59*–11.63–0–*ct* 35
Bowling 5877–164–35.83–5–0–7/64
He captained Worcestershire in 1914 and 1922 and was on the County Committee at the time of his death.

Taylor, William Thomas
Amateur. *b:* 14.4.1885, Wirksworth, Derbyshire. *d:* 17.8.1976, Breadsall, Derbyshire. Brother of F. H. (Derbyshire). Lower right-hand batsman, right-arm medium pace bowler. *Team* Derbyshire (1905–10, 4 matches).
Career batting
4–8–1–53–11–7.57–0–*ct* 2
Bowling 56–2–28.00–0–0–1/19
He was Secretary to Derbyshire CCC from 1908 to 1959, his tenure of 51 years being the longest served in that post in first-class County cricket, and then Hon Secretary from 1962 to 1973.

Taylor-Jones, Rev Edward William Tetley
(changed name from Jones in September 1891)
Amateur. *b:* 28.5.1866, Sydenham, London. *d:* 15.9.1956, Sittingbourne, Kent. Attacking middle order left-hand batsman, right-arm fast bowler, slip field. *Team* Kent (1894, 2 matches).
Career batting
3–6–0–22–11–3.66–0–*ct* 2
Bowling 12–0
His final first-class match was for MCC in 1901. He did not appear in any first-class matches whilst at Cambridge.

Tazelaar, Dirk
Cricketer. *b:* 13.1.1963, Ipswich, Queensland, Australia. Lower order right-hand batsman, left-arm fast medium bowler. *Teams* Queensland (1985/6 to 1990/1, 52 matches); Surrey (1989, 4 matches).
Career batting
56–68–22–730–56–15.86–0–*ct* 25
Bowling 5530–183–30.21–6–1–6/48
Injury restricted his opportunities for Surrey during 1989.

Teape, Arthur Stanley
Amateur. *b:* 28.1.1843, Blackheath, Kent. *d:* 1.3.1885, Haverstock Hill, London. Brother of C. A. (Middlesex). Tail end right-hand batsman, right-hand fast round-arm bowler, short leg. *Sch* Eton. *Team* Oxford U (1863–66, blue 1863–65).
Career batting
16–20–9–111–19–10.09–0–*ct* 8
Bowling 462–46 + 8–10.04–5–1–6/19

Teape, Charles Ashley
Amateur. *b:* 16.2.1844, Blackheath, Kent. *d:* 1.8.1925, Chelsea, London. Brother of A. S. (Oxford U). Lower order batsman, useful bowler. *Sch* Eton. *Team* Middlesex (1872, 1 match).
Career batting
1–2–1–2–2*–2.00–0–*ct* 1
Bowling 42–4–10.50–0–0–4/38
He played in some trials but no first-class matches whilst at Oxford.

Tebay, Henry
Professional. *b:* 5.10.1866, East Grinstead, Sussex. *d:* 4.6.1946, Bromley, Kent. Middle order right-hand batsman. *Team* Sussex (1886–90, 18 matches).
Career batting
18–36–0–265–43–7.36–0–*ct* 18

Tebay, Kevan
Professional. *b:* 2.2.1936, Bolton, Lancashire. Middle order right-hand batsman. *Team* Lancashire (1961–63, 15 matches).
Career batting
15–27–2–509–106–20.36–1–*ct* 3

Tebbitt, Gilbert George
Amateur. *b:* 13.9.1908, Welton, Northamptonshire. Middle order right-hand batsman, off break bowler. *Sch* Wellingborough. *Team* Northamptonshire (1934–38, 11 matches).
Career batting
11–21–3–248–41–13.77–0–*ct* 4
Bowling 29–0

Tebbs, Reginald Kearsley
Amateur. *b:* 8.5.1908, Headingley, Leeds, Yorkshire. Lower order batsman, left-arm medium fast bowler. *Sch* Leeds GS. *Team* Cambridge U (1929).
Career batting
1–1–0–0–0–0.00–0–*ct* 1
Bowling 87–1–87.00–0–0–1/70
His County Cricket was for Berkshire (1946).

Tebbut, Charles Mansfield
Amateur. *b:* 24.12.1839, Wanstead, Essex. *d:* 27.9.1898, South Hampstead, London. Middle order batsman. *Team* Middlesex (1866–70, 6 matches).
Career batting
6–9–1–38–10–4.75–0–*ct* 0
He also played for Essex (pre first-class, 1868). A great patron of cricket, he was for many years on the Committees of both Middlesex and Essex and advanced a considerable sum of money to the latter County Club which saved it from extinction. A noted soccer player, he was one of the first to establish the game on a firm basis.

Tedder, Ernest Cranfield
Amateur. *b:* 5.9.1915, Woodford Green, Essex. *d:* 9.9.1972, Ipswich, Suffolk. Middle order right-hand batsman. *Sch* Chigwell. *Team* Essex (1946, 8 matches).
Career batting
8–14–0–208–55–14.85–0–*ct* 3

Tedstone, Geoffrey Alan
Cricketer. *b:* 19.1.1961, Southport, Lancashire. Brother of Janet Aspinall (England Women). Lower order right-hand batsman, occasional off break bowler, wicket-keeper. *Teams* Warwickshire (1982–88, 32 matches); Gloucestershire (1989–90, 18 matches).
Career batting
50–67–9–935–67*–16.12–0–*ct* 82–*st* 14
Bowling 1–0

Teesdale, Hugh
Amateur. *b:* 12.2.1886, Addlestone, Surrey. *d:* 31.3.1971, Hove, Sussex. Sound opening right-hand batsman. *Sch* Winchester. *Teams* Surrey (1906–08, 2 matches); Oxford U (1908, blue).
Career batting
12–21–0–637–149–30.33–2–*ct* 4
His final first-class match was for MCC in 1910.

Teggin, Alfred
Amateur. *b:* 22.10.1860, Broughton, Lancashire. *d:* 23.7.1941, Cleveleys, Blackpool, Lancashire. Lower order right-hand batsman, leg break bowler. *Team* Lancashire (1886, 6 matches).
Career batting
6–8–0–31–9–3.87–0–*ct* 4
Bowling 176–16–11.00–2–1–6/53
A noted rugby footballer, he represented England.

Tendulkar, Sachin Ramesh
Cricketer. *b:* 24.4.1973, Bombay, India. Stylish middle order right-hand batsman, right-arm medium pace bowler. *Teams* Bombay (1988/9 to 1990/1); Yorkshire (1992, 16 matches). *Tours* India to Pakistan 1989/90, to New Zealand 1989/90, to Sharjah (not first-class) 1989/90, 1991/2, to England 1990, to Australia 1991/2, to Australia and New Zealand (World Cup) 1991/2; Rest of World to England 1991. *Tests* India (1989/90 to 1991/2, 16 matches).
Career batting
60–97–11–4708–159–54.74–10–*ct* 28
Bowling 1172–16–73.25–0–0–3/60
Test batting
16–25–2–956–148*–41.56–3–*ct* 10
Bowling 119–3–39.66–0–0–2/10
On the 1990 tour to England he hit a hundred in the Test at Old Trafford and, aged 17 years and 112 days, became the youngest batsman to make a Test century in England. He appeared in all three Tests on that tour and in all first-class matches scored 945 runs, av 63.00.
Yorkshire picked him as the first overseas registered player to represent the County (when C. J. McDermott withdrew due to injury) in 1992, during which season he scored 1,070 runs, av 46.52. He scored 100* for Bombay v Gujarat at Bombay in 1988/9 on his first-class debut when aged 15. He shared a partnership of 664* with V. G. Kambli in a schools match in India in 1987/8, the record for any wicket in a minor match.

Tennant, Lloyd
Cricketer. *b:* 9.4.1968, Walsall, Staffordshire. Lower order right-hand batsman, right-arm medium fast bowler. *Team* Leicestershire (1986–91, 10 matches).
Career batting
10–13–5–110–23*–13.75–0–*ct* 1
Bowling 503–15–33.53–0–0–4/54
He joined the Essex staff for 1992, but did not make any first-class appearances for his new County during the season.

Tennant, Peter Norie
Cricketer. *b:* 17.4.1942, Sutton Coldfield, Warwickshire. Lower order right-hand batsman, wicket-keeper. *Sch* Solihull. *Team* Warwickshire (1964, 1 match).

Tennekoon, Anura Punchi Banda

Career batting
1 match, did not bat–*ct* 3–*st* 1

He was also a useful hockey player.

Tennekoon, Anura Punchi Banda
Cricketer. *b:* 29.10.1946, Anuradhapura, Ceylon. Middle order right-hand batsman, slow left-arm bowler. *Team* Ceylon/Sri Lanka (1965/6 to 1979). *Tours* Sri Lanka to England 1975, 1979, to India 1966/7, 1968/9, 1970/1, 1975/6, to Pakistan 1966/7, 1973/4.
Career batting
61–107–11–3481–169*–36.26–5–*ct* 60
Bowling 60–2–30.00–0–0–2/23

He captained Sri Lanka in England 1975 and 1979 and played for Sri Lanka in one-day international matches.

Tennent, Hector Norman
Amateur. *b:* 6.4.1842, Hobart, Tasmania, Australia. *d:* 19.4.1904, Westminster, London. Brother of J. P. (Victoria) and W. M. (Lancashire). Middle order right-hand batsman, cover point. *Sch* Merchiston Castle and Loretto. *Team* Lancashire (1865–70, 2 matches). *Tour* Australia to England 1878 (in emergency).
Career batting
19–31–3–344–45*–12.28–0–*ct* 8
Bowling 20–0

He was also noted as a sprinter, excelling in the 100 yards. At the time of his death he was Secretary of the Empire Theatre, Leicester Square, being a member of the well-known theatrical family.

Tennent, James M'William
Amateur. *b:* 7.9.1888, Glasgow, Scotland. *d:* 20.3.1955, Westminster, London. Middle order right-hand batsman. *Sch* Merchiston. *Team* Scotland (1922–28).
Career batting
3–5–0–44–26–8.80–*ct* 3

A noted rugby footballer, he represented Scotland.

Tennent, William Middleton
Amateur. *b:* 6.10.1845, Hobart, Tasmania, Australia. *d:* 5.7.1883, Hastings, Sussex. Brother of H. N. (Lancashire) and J. P. (Victoria). Middle order batsman. *Sch* Merchiston. *Team* Lancashire (1867, 1 match).
Career batting
1–2–0–3–3–1.50–0–*ct* 0

Tennyson, Hon Lionel Hallam
(succeeded as 3rd Baron Tennyson in 1928)
Amateur. *b:* 7.11.1889, Westminster, London. *d:* 6.6.1951, Bexhill-on-Sea, Sussex. Grandson of the poet, nephew of C. W. Boyle (Oxford U). Attacking middle order right-hand batsman, right-arm fast bowler. *Sch* Eton. *Team* Hampshire (1913–35, 347 matches). *Tours* MCC to South Africa 1913/14, to West Indies 1925/6; Joel to South Africa 1924/5; Tennyson to Jamaica 1926/7, 1927/8, 1931/2; Cahn to Jamaica 1928/9; Tennyson to India 1937/8. *Tests* England (1913/14 to 1921, 9 matches).
Career batting
477–759–38–16828–217–23.33–19–*ct* 172
Bowling 2976–55–54.10–0–0–3/50
Test batting
9–12–1–345–74*–31.36–0–*ct* 6
Bowling 1–0

He hit 1,000 runs in a season seven times (best 1,335, av 30.34, in 1925). His only double century was 217 for Hampshire v West Indies at Southampton in 1928. He captained Hampshire from 1919 to 1933 and England in three Tests in 1921. As well as captaining his own touring sides, he led Joel's Team to South Africa in 1924/5. His final first-class match in England was for MCC in 1937. He scored 110 on debut for MCC v Oxford U at Lord's in 1913. He played in trials at Cambridge U, but not in first-class matches.

Terry, Rev Francis William
Amateur. *b:* 26.10.1860, Wells, Somerset. *d:* 5.10.1936, Mimico, Ontario, Canada. Middle order right-hand batsman, right-arm medium pace bowler, wicket-keeper. *Sch* St Edward's, Oxford. *Team* Somerset (1882–85, 10 matches).
Career batting
10–18–1–552–121–32.47–1–*ct* 13–*st* 2

He played in the Oxford Freshmen's match of 1881, but no first-class matches for the University. After leaving Oxford he emigrated to Canada and was for many years one of the leading cricketers there, playing against the United States between 1891 and 1907.

Terry, Vivian Paul
Cricketer. *b:* 14.1.1959, Osnabrück, West Germany. Middle order right-hand batsman, right-arm medium pace bowler. *Sch* Millfield. *Team* Hampshire (1978–92, 223 matches). *Tour* English Counties to Zimbabwe 1984/5. *Tests* England (1984, 2 matches).
Career batting
227–379–38–12281–190–36.01–27–*ct* 250
Bowling 58–0
Test batting
2–3–0–16–8–5.33–0–*ct* 2

He hit 1,000 runs in a season eight times (best 1,382, av 43.18, in 1987). He was batting in brilliant form in the early part of 1984 and gained selection for two Tests, but broke his arm so badly in his second Test that he not only missed the rest of the season but was unavailable for selection for the England winter tour which followed.

Tester, William Abraham
Professional. *b:* 8.6.1857, Brighton, Sussex. *d:* 9.6.1890, Brighton, Sussex. Middle order right-hand batsman, right-hand slow round-arm bowler. *Team*

Sussex (1878–88, 100 matches).
Career batting
103–191–7–2675–130–14.53–2–*ct* 52
Bowling 3712–154–24.10–2–0–7/40

Tew, Anthony Martin
Amateur. *b:* 24.8.1908, Wiggington Hall, Haxby, Yorkshire. *d:* 23.6.1987, Okus, Swindon, Wiltshire. Brother of J. E. (Oxford U), nephew of M. B. Hawke (Yorkshire). Lower order right-hand batsman, right-arm fast medium bowler. *Sch* Winchester. *Team* Oxford U (1928).
Career batting
2–3–0–15–15–5.00–0–*ct* 1
Bowling 221–3–73.66–0–0–2/80

Tew, John Edward
Amateur. *b:* 3.9.1905, Wiggington Hall, Haxby, Yorkshire. *d:* 28.12.1992. Brother of A. M. (Oxford U), nephew of M. B. Hawke (Yorkshire). Middle order right-hand batsman. *Sch* Eton. *Teams* Oxford U (1927–28); Europeans (1928/9 to 1947/8).
Career batting
11–22–1–348–76–16.57–0–*ct* 9
He won a blue for squash.

Thackara, Anthony Leonard Samuel Salter
Amateur. *b:* 14.3.1917, Portsmouth, Hampshire. Opening right-hand batsman. *Team* Combined Services (1949–55).
Career batting
4–6–0–112–42–18.66–0–*ct* 3
His County cricket was for Cornwall (1950–52).

Thackeray, Rev Frederick
Amateur. *b:* 23.2.1817, Cambridge. *d:* 28.7.1892, Chappel, Essex. Half-brother of Charles (Cambridge Town Club). Lower order batsman, fast right-hand round-arm bowler. *Sch* Eton. *Teams* Cambridge U (1837–43, blue 1838–40); Cambridge Town Club (1841–54).
Career batting
38–67–11–567–73–10.12–0–*ct* 12
Bowling 27 wickets (no analyses)–1–0–5/?
His County cricket was for Hertfordshire (1841–42).

Thackeray, Peter Robert
Cricketer. *b:* 26.9.1950, Kilalishwa, Nairobi, Kenya. Middle order right-hand batsman, right-arm medium pace bowler. *Sch* St Edward's, Oxford. *Team* Oxford U (1974, blue).
Career batting
8–15–4–315–65*–28.63–0–*ct* 3
Bowling 1–0
His County cricket was for Devon (1972).

Thain, Caryl
Amateur. *b:* 11.4.1895, Catherington, Hampshire. *d:* 24.9.1969, Lambeth, London. Lower order right-hand batsman, right-arm fast medium bowler. *Team* Surrey (1923, 2 matches).
Career batting
2–2–1–4–4*–4.00–0–*ct* 0
Bowling 88–3–29.33–00–0–3/38
He was a member of the Surrey Committee for 40 years, being Hon Treasurer and, in 1969, President. A useful soccer player, he appeared for Chelsea.

Tharp, Arthur Keane
Amateur. *b:* 15.9.1848, Chippenham Park, Cambridgeshire. *d:* 17.11.1928, Midanbury, Bitterne Park, Hampshire. Middle order right-hand batsman, right-hand medium pace round-arm bowler. *Sch* Haileybury. *Team* Cambridgeshire (1868–71, 3 matches).
Career batting
3–6–0–37–16–6.16–0–*ct* 3
He appeared in the Freshmen's match at Cambridge in 1868, but no first-class matches for the University. He also played for Suffolk (1866–69) and Norfolk (1876).

Thayer, Harry Chapman
Amateur. *b:* 31.12.1872, Stafford, Philadelphia, USA. *d:* 3.8.1936, Haverford, Philadelphia, USA. Brother of J. B. (Philadelphians to England 1884). Middle order right-hand batsman, wicket-keeper. *Team* Philadelphia (1890–99). *Tour* Philadelphia to England 1897.
Career batting
18–32–2–435–59–14.50–0–*ct* 6
He achieved only modest results on the 1897 tour. A noted American footballer, he appeared in the All American Team of 1892.

Theobald, F. A.
Amateur. Middle order batsman. *Team* H. K. Foster's XI (1919).
Career batting
1–1–0–4–4–4.00–0–*ct* 0
Bowling 28–0

Theobald, Harold Ernest
Amateur. *b:* 18.3.1896, Norwich, Norfolk. *d:* 20.7.1982, Norwich, Norfolk. Middle order right-hand batsman. *Sch* Taunton. *Team* Minor Counties (1938).
Career batting
1–2–0–42–42–21.00–0–*ct* 1
His County cricket was for Norfolk (1930–47).

Thesiger, Hon Frederic John Napier
(succeeded to the title 3rd Lord Chelmsford in 1905, created Viscount in 1921)
Amateur. *b:* 12.8.1868, Westminster, London. *d:* 1.4.1933, Ardington, Berkshire. Nephew of A. H. (MCC 1861). Attacking middle order right-hand batsman, slow round-arm bowler. *Sch* Winchester. *Teams* Oxford U (1888–91, blue 1888, 1890 and 1891); Middlesex (1888–92, 6 matches).

Thewlis, Herbert

Career batting
33–58–3–870–88–15.81–0–*ct* 22
Bowling 154–8–19.25–0–0–3/6

He fielded before lunch on the first day of the 1891 University match, but injured his hand and retired, his place in the eleven being taken by T. B. Case. He also played for Worcestershire (pre first-class, 1884). He was President of MCC in 1922. He was Governor of Queensland 1905 to 1909, Governor of New South Wales 1909 to 1913, Viceroy of India 1916 to 1921 and First Lord of the Admiralty in the Labour Government of 1924. He was the uncle of Wilfred Thesiger, the well-known explorer.

Thewlis, Herbert
Professional. *b:* 31.8.1865, Lascelles Hall, Yorkshire. *d:* 30.11.1920, Lascelles Hall, Yorkshire. Middle order right-hand batsman. *Team* Yorkshire (1888, 2 matches).
Career batting
2–4–1–4–2*–1.33–0–*ct* 2

Thewlis, John
Professional. *b:* 30.6.1828, Kirkheaton, Yorkshire. *d:* 29.12.1899, Lascelles Hall, Yorkshire. Uncle of John (Yorkshire) and E. Lockwood (Yorkshire). Sound opening right-hand batsman, right-hand medium pace round-arm bowler, good long stop. *Team* Yorkshire (1862–75, 47 matches).
Career batting
56–104–4–1548–108–15.48–1–*ct* 30–*st* 1

Thewlis, John
Professional. *b:* 21.9.1850, Lascelles Hall, Yorkshire. *d:* 9.8.1901, Lascelles Hall, Yorkshire. Nephew of John (Yorkshire), cousin of E. Lockwood (Yorkshire). Middle order right-hand batsman, right-hand round-arm bowler, good cover point. *Team* Yorkshire (1879, 3 matches).
Career batting
3–4–0–21–10–5.25–0–*ct* 0

Thewlis, Joseph
Amateur. *b:* 14.4.1939, Percy Main, Northumberland. Middle order right-hand batsman. *Team* Combined Services (1962).
Career batting
1–2–0–18–17–9.00–0–*ct* 0

His County cricket was for Northumberland (1963–81).

Thomas, A. F.
Amateur. Middle order batsman. *Team* Gentlemen of England (1878).
Career batting
1–2–0–3–3–1.50–0–*ct* 0

Thomas, Alan
Cricketer. *b:* 7.1.1947, Bolton, Lancashire. Lower order right-hand batsman, off break bowler. *Team* Lancashire (1966, 1 match).
Career batting
1–2–0–4–4–2.00–0–*ct* 0
Bowling 7–0

Thomas, Albert Edward
Professional. *b:* 7.6.1893, Ruthin, Denbighshire. *d:* 21.3.1965, Kidderminster, Worcestershire. Hard hitting lower order right-hand batsman, right-arm fast medium bowler, good slip field. *Team* Northamptonshire (1919–33, 284 matches); Wales (1927).
Career batting
288–467–106–4872–84–13.49–0–*ct* 121
Bowling 21237–832–25.52–30–5–9/30

His best season was 1928 with 101 wickets, av 25.36 and his best bowling 9/30 for Northamptonshire v Yorkshire at Bradford in 1920. A useful soccer player, he appeared for Denbigh, Norwich City and Northampton Nomads as a forward.

Thomas, Arthur Emlyn
Amateur. *b:* 7.5.1895, Briton Ferry, Glamorgan. *d:* 11.2.1953, Briton Ferry, Glamorgan. Middle order right-hand batsman. *Team* Glamorgan (1925, 1 match).
Career batting
1–2–0–15–11–7.50–0–*ct* 0

He first played for Glamorgan (pre first-class) in 1913.

Thomas, David James
Cricketer. *b:* 30.6.1959, Solihull, Warwickshire. Middle order left-hand batsman, left-arm medium pace bowler. *Teams* Surrey (1977–87, 135 matches); Northern Transvaal (1980/1); Natal (1983/4); Gloucestershire (1988, 3 matches).
Career batting
150–193–41–3044–119–20.02–2–*ct* 50
Bowling 11415–336–33.97–7–1–6/36

He was once selected in an England twelve, but never played a Test match. He was forced to retire due to injury.

Thomas, David John
Amateur. *b:* 25.11.1911, Swansea, Glamorgan. Tail end right-hand batsman, right-arm medium pace bowler. *Team* Glamorgan (1932, 1 match).
Career batting
1–1–1–10–10*–no av–0–*ct* 0
Bowling 63–0

Thomas, David Robert
Cricketer. *b:* 26.1.1963, Swardeston, Norfolk. Lower order left-hand batsman, right-arm fast medium bowler. *Team* Minor Counties (1990).
Career batting
1–1–0–27–27–27.00–0–*ct* 0
Bowling 65–0

His County cricket was for Norfolk (1983–92).

Thomas, Dillwyn
Professional. *b:* 13.2.1905, Neath Abbey, Glamorgan. Lower order left-hand batsman, right-arm medium fast bowler. *Team* Glamorgan (1939, 2 matches).
Career batting
2–2–1–14–14*–14.00–0–*ct* 1
Bowling 99–5–19.80–1–0–5/64

Thomas, Edgar Lang
Amateur. *b:* 2.11.1875, Clifton, Bristol. *d:* 20.3.1936, Hammersmith, London. Brother of F. E. (Gloucestershire). Middle order right-hand batsman. *Sch* Clifton. *Team* Gloucestershire (1895–1907, 27 matches).
Career batting
27–45–0–571–109–12.68–1–*ct* 14

Thomas, Frank Edgecumbe
Amateur. *b:* 5.4.1877, Clifton, Bristol. *d:* 20.5.1924, Clifton, Bristol. Brother of E. L. (Gloucestershire). Stylish middle order right-hand batsman, right-arm medium pace bowler, good field. *Sch* Clifton. *Team* Gloucestershire (1901–06, 51 matches).
Career batting
51–87–3–1874–138–22.30–3–*ct* 31
Bowling 330–10–33.00–0–0–3/22

Thomas, Frederick Oswald
Amateur. *b:* 19.11.1917, Corstorphine, Midlothian, Scotland. Middle order right-hand batsman, right-arm fast medium bowler. *Team* Scotland (1951).
Career batting
1–2–0–21–21–10.50–0–*ct* 0

Thomas, Freeman
(changed to Freeman-Thomas in 1892; created 1st Lord Willingdon 1910)
Amateur. *b:* 12.9.1866, Ratton Park, Eastbourne, Sussex. *d:* 12.8.1941, Westminster, London. Son of F. F. (Sussex). Steady middle order right-hand batsman, slow under-arm bowler. *Sch* Eton. *Teams* Cambridge U (1886–89, blue all 4 years); Sussex (1886–90, 18 matches); England XII in India (1915/16); Willingdon's XI in India (1918/19).
Career batting
40–72–3–1587–114–23.00–1–*ct* 19
Bowling 13–0

He was President of Sussex in 1911. He was Liberal MP for Hastings 1900–1906 and for Bodmin 1906–1910. From 1909 to 1912 he was Junior Lord of the Treasury; from 1913 to 1919 Governor of Bombay; from 1919 to 1924 Governor of Madras and from 1924 Governor-General of Canada. From 1931 to 1936 was Viceroy of India.

Thomas, Freeman Frederick
Amateur. *b:* 11.4.1838, Lymington, Hampshire. *d:* 1.12.1868, San Remo, Italy. He died of consumption. Father of Freeman (Sussex), brother-in-law of H. R. Brand (Sussex). Lower order right-hand batsman, brilliant cover point. *Team* Sussex (1860–67, 9 matches).
Career batting
9–18–0–89–18–4.94–0–*ct* 6

Thomas, Gary Philip
Cricketer. *b:* 8.11.1958, Birmingham. Middle order right-hand batsman, right-arm medium pace bowler. *Teams* Warwickshire (1978–81, 8 matches); Boland (1987/8).
Career batting
11–20–1–377–52–19.84–0–*ct* 8

Thomas, Grahame
Cricketer. *b:* 21.3.1938, Croydon Park, Sydney, New South Wales, Australia. Opening right-hand batsman. *Team* New South Wales (1957/8 to 1965/6, 68 matches). *Tours* Australia to New Zealand 1959/60, to West Indies 1964/5, to South Africa 1966/7; Rest of World to England 1966. *Tests* Australia (1964/5 to 1965/6, 8 matches).
Career batting
100–154–12–5726–229–40.32–17–*ct* 92–*st* 2
Bowling 30–0
Test batting
8–12–1–325–61–29.54–0–*ct* 3

His appearances in England were limited to one at Scarborough in 1966. His highest score was 229 for New South Wales v Victoria at Melbourne in 1965/6. He hit 1,171 runs, av 58.55, in 1965/6.

Thomas, John
Amateur. *b:* 1879. *d:* 1.6.1949, Taunton, Somerset. Lower order batsman, useful bowler. *Team* Somerset (1901–05, 3 matches).
Career batting
3–4–1–27–23–9.00–0–*ct* 1
Bowling 130–1–130.00–0–0–1/63

Thomas, John Gregory
Cricketer. *b:* 12.8.1960, Trebanos, Glamorgan. Lower order right-hand batsman, right-arm fast bowler. *Teams* Glamorgan (1979–88, 106 matches); Border (1983/4 to 1986/7); Eastern Province (1987/8 to 1988/9); Northamptonshire (1989–91, 44 matches). *Tours* England to West Indies 1985/6; England XI to South Africa 1989/90. *Tests* England (1985/6 to 1986, 5 matches).
Career batting
192–253–45–3419–110–16.43–2–*ct* 74
Bowling 16303–525–31.05–18–1–7/75
Test batting
5–10–4–83–31*–13.83–0–*ct* 0
Bowling 504–10–50.40–0–0–4/70

His best season was 1989 with 67 wickets, av 29.04. He was a surprise selection for the 1985/6 tour to West Indies; his only Test in England came in 1986 at Trent Bridge when Dilley and Botham were both absent through injury. He was forced to retire due to injury.

Thomas, John Leslie Gwyn
Amateur. *b:* 14.3.1891, Neath, Glamorgan. *d:* 10.4.1932, Neath, Glamorgan. Middle order right-hand batsman. *Team* Glamorgan (1922, 1 match).
Career batting
1–2–0–27–21–13.50–0–*ct* 0
He first played for Glamorgan (pre first-class) in 1910.

Thomas, Kevin Oliver
Cricketer. *b:* 20.6.1963, Mile End, London. Lower order right-hand batsman, right-arm fast medium bowler. *Team* Essex (1990, 1 match).
Career batting
1–1–0–2–2–2.00–0–*ct* 0
Bowling 81–0
He also played for Cambridgeshire (1991–92).

Thomas, Leopold Ernest
Amateur. *b:* 16.2.1865. *d:* 28.5.1937, Marylebone, London. Lower order batsman, wicket-keeper. *Sch* Clifton. *Team* Middlesex (1893, 1 match).
Career batting
1–2–1–0–0*–0.00–0–*ct* 5

Thomas, Neill Peter
Cricketer. *b:* 26.5.1964, Tenterden, Kent. Middle order left-hand batsman, slow left-arm bowler. *Sch* Sevenoaks. *Team* Cambridge U (1984).
Career batting
1–2–0–0–0–0.00–0–*ct* 1

Thomas, Rhodri James Alban
Cricketer. *b:* 13.3.1942, St Dogmaels, Pembroke. Opening or middle order right-hand batsman. *Sch* Radley. *Team* Oxford U (1963–65, blue 1965).
Career batting
15–28–2–622–135*–23.92–1–*ct* 9
Bowling 5–1–5.00–0–0–1/4

Thomas, Richard
Professional. *b:* 15.7.1867, Wales. *d:* 18.12.1918, Werneth, Oldham, Lancashire. Lower order batsman, wicket-keeper. *Team* Lancashire (1894–1902, 20 matches).
Career batting
20–22–5–60–17–3.52–0–*ct* 22–*st* 8

Thomas, Richard James
Cricketer. *b:* 18.6.1944, Griffithstown, Monmouthshire. Lower order right-hand batsman, right-arm medium pace bowler. *Team* Glamorgan (1974, 1 match).
Career batting
1–1–1–8–8*–no av–0–*ct* 0
Bowling 40–1–40.00–0–0–1/40

Thomas, Stuart Darren
Cricketer. *b:* 25.1.1975, Morriston, Swansea, Glamorgan. Lower order left-hand batsman, right-arm medium pace bowler. *Team* Glamorgan (1992, 6 matches).
Career batting
6–7–2–25–10–5.00–0–*ct* 1
Bowling 404–18–22.44–2–0–5/79

Thomas, William Owen
Amateur. *b:* 27.4.1921, Linthorpe, Middlesbrough, Yorkshire. Lower order left-hand batsman, slow left-arm bowler. *Sch* Dulwich. *Team* Cambridge U (1948).
Career batting
4–5–4–44–19*–44.00–0–*ct* 2
Bowling 145–3–48.33–0–0–1/10
His final first-class match was for MCC in 1954. His County cricket was for Norfolk (1952–59).

Thomas, William Richard Keay
Cricketer. *b:* 22.7.1960, Redditch, Worcestershire. Middle order right-hand batsman, right-arm medium pace bowler. *Sch* Dean Close. *Team* Worcestershire (1981, 1 match).
Career batting
1–2–1–57–44–57.00–0–*ct* 0
Bowling 54–0

Thomas, Wyndham Rowland
Professional. *b:* 1.6.1911, Bedford. Lower order batsman, slow left-arm bowler. *Team* Somerset (1928, 1 match).
Career batting
1 match, did not bat–*ct* 0

Thompson, Alexander Richard
Amateur. *b:* 1.12.1876, Stamford, Lincolnshire. *d:* 16.12.1951, Durban, South Africa. Reliable opening right-hand batsman. *Sch* Malvern. *Team* Northamptonshire (1905–08, 17 matches).
Career batting
17–29–2–358–48*–13.25–0–*ct* 8

Thompson, Alexander William
Professional. *b:* 17.4.1916, Toxteth Park, Liverpool, Lancashire. Attacking middle order right-hand batsman, off break bowler, good outfield. *Team* Middlesex (1939–55, 195 matches).
Career batting
202–329–30–7915–158–26.47–5–*ct* 68
Bowling 831–12–69.25–0–0–2/35
He hit 1,000 runs in a season three times (best 1,245, av 31.92, in 1953).

Thompson, Arthur Paul
Amateur. *b:* 1.3.1914, Leicester. Neat middle order left-hand batsman, right-arm medium pace bowler. *Sch* Shrewsbury. *Team* Leicestershire (1937, 2 matches).
Career batting
2–4–1–11–5–3.66–0–*ct* 0

Thompson, Eddie Clarke
Professional. *b:* 27.2.1907, Leyton, Essex. *d:* 18.3.1982, Torquay, Devon. Stylish middle order left-hand batsman, slow left-arm bowler. *Team* Essex (1926–29, 44 matches).
Career batting
44–61–17–696–45*–15.81–0–*ct* 10
Bowling 938–17–55.17–0–0–2/12

Thompson, Eric Richard
Cricketer. *b:* 6.10.1938, Kirkwall, Orkney, Scotland. *d:* 4.9.1992, Edinburgh, Scotland. Lower order right-hand batsman, right-arm fast medium bowler. *Team* Scotland (1965–74).
Career batting
16–20–7–135–29*–10.38–0–*ct* 11
Bowling 1118–35–31.94–2–0–5/11

Thompson, George Joseph
Amateur in 1895, professional commencing 1897. *b:* 27.10.1877, Cogenhoe, Northampton. *d:* 3.3.1943, Clifton, Bristol. Steady middle order right-hand batsman, right-arm fast medium bowler, close field. *Sch* Wellingborough. *Teams* Northamptonshire (1905–22, 222 matches); Auckland (1911/12). *Tours* Hawke to New Zealand and Australia 1902/3; Brackley to West Indies 1904/5; MCC to South Africa 1909/10. *Tests* England (1909 to 1909/10, 6 matches).
Career batting
352–606–60–12018–131*–22.01–9–*ct* 251
Bowling 30058–1591–18.89–147–40–9/64
Test batting
6–10–1–273–63–30.33–0–*ct* 5
Bowling 638–23–27.73–0–0–4/50
He hit 1,000 runs in a season three times (best 1,080, av 31.76, in 1914), completing the 'double' in 1906 and 1910. In all he took 100 wickets eight times (best 163, av 14.67, in 1909). For a short time after the First World War, he was player-coach to Northamptonshire, but injury received in the war effectively ended his first-class career. He first played for Northamptonshire (pre first-class) in 1895. His first-class debut was for MCC in 1897. His best bowling was 9/64 for Northamptonshire v Derbyshire at Northampton in 1906. He umpired two Tests in South Africa in 1922/3.

Thompson, Herbert
Professional. *b:* 6.12.1869, West Norwood, London. *d:* 22.10.1947, Caterham, Surrey. Lower order right-hand batsman, leg break and googly bowler. *Team* Surrey (1894–1919, 12 matches).
Career batting
12–20–4–138–44*–8.62–0–*ct* 4
Bowling 663–31–21.38–2–1–5/59
He was Surrey coach 1914–23 and later became a first-class umpire (1928–29).

Thompson, Herbert
Amateur. *b:* 14.5.1886, Knighton, Leicester. *d:* 8.8.1941, Sevenoaks, Kent. Aggressive middle order right-hand batsman, good field. *Sch* Rugby. *Team* Leicestershire (1908–10, 10 matches).
Career batting
10–18–0–233–72–12.94–0–*ct* 4
He did not appear in first-class matches whilst at Oxford U. For many years he was Honorary Secretary to the Incogniti CC.

Thompson, Hugh Reginald Patrick
Amateur. *b:* 11.4.1934, Scunthorpe, Lincolnshire. Lower order right-hand batsman, off break bowler. *Sch* Cheltenham. *Team* Hampshire (1953–54, 2 matches).
Career batting
2–1–0–16–16–16.00–0–*ct* 1
Bowling 259–2–129.50–0–0–2/106
He was also a useful hockey player.

Thompson, John Charles Peace
Amateur. *b:* 14.4.1870, Chester, Cheshire. *d:* 31.12.1945, Tarset, Northumberland. Brother-in-law of L. Garnett (Southgate). Middle order batsman. *Sch* Harrow. *Team* Liverpool and District (1892).
Career batting
1–1–0–14–14–14.00–0–*ct* 1
His County cricket was for Cheshire (1892).

Thompson, John Ross
Amateur. *b:* 10.5.1918, Berkhamsted, Hertfordshire. Attractive opening right-hand batsman, off break bowler. *Sch* Tonbridge. *Teams* Cambridge U (1938–39, blue both years); Warwickshire (1938–54, 44 matches). *Tours* MCC to North America 1951, 1959 (not first-class).
Career batting
68–116–5–3455–191–31.12–6–*ct* 32
Bowling 13–0
He also played for Wiltshire (1955–63). He was five times the Amateur Rackets Champion.

Thompson, Leslie Baines
Amateur. *b:* 12.11.1908, Brentford, Middlesex. *d:* 23.4.1990, Canada. Lower order right-hand batsman, off break bowler. *Team* Middlesex (1946–49, 6 matches).
Career batting
6–4–2–16–13–8.00–0–*ct* 3
Bowling 248–5–49.60–0–0–3/50

Thompson, M.
Amateur. Middle order batsman. *Team* Middlesex (1866, 2 matches).
Career batting
2–3–1–9–5–4.50–0–*ct* 1

Thompson, Neil Powney
Amateur. *b:* 10.10.1938, Colombo, Ceylon. Tail end left-hand batsman, left-arm fast medium bowler. *Sch*

Thompson, Nigel Ernest

Christ's Hospital. *Team* Oxford U (1961).
Career batting
7–7–3–16–4*–4.00–0–*ct* 3
Bowling 637–17–37.47–0–0–4/72

Thompson, Nigel Ernest
Cricketer. *b:* 25.6.1964, Londonderry, Ireland. Lower order right-hand batsman, right-arm medium pace bowler. *Team* Ireland (1988–91).
Career batting
3–6–1–79–38–15.80–0–*ct* 1
Bowling 193–3–64.33–0–0–2/67

Thompson, Roland George
Professional. *b:* 26.9.1932, Binley, Coventry, Warwickshire. Lower order right-hand batsman, right-arm fast medium bowler. *Team* Warwickshire (1949–62, 157 matches).
Career batting
158–187–71–657–25*–5.66–0–*ct* 51
Bowling 10901–479–22.75–21–5–9/65
His best analysis in an innings was 9 for 65 for Warwickshire v Nottinghamshire at Edgbaston in 1952.

Thompson, Thomas
Cricketer. *b:* 24.2.1934, Workington, Cumberland. Lower order right-hand batsman, off break bowler. *Team* Leicestershire (1963–64, 9 matches).
Career batting
9–14–5–43–12–4.77–0–*ct* 2
Bowling 497–17–29.23–0–0–3/53
He also played for Cumberland (1955–74).

Thompson, W. H.
Amateur. Middle order batsman. *Team* Liverpool and District (1892).
Career batting
1–1–0–10–10–10.00–0–*ct* 0
Bowling 24–1–24.00–0–0–1/24

Thompson, William Holloway
Professional. *b:* 24.6.1882, Spondon, Derbyshire. *d:* 19.10.1954, Spondon, Derbyshire. Middle order right-hand batsman. *Team* Derbyshire (1908, 1 match).
Career batting
1–2–0–17–17–8.50–0–*ct* 0

Thomson, Alpin Erroll
Amateur. *b:* 14.5.1893, Perth, Western Australia. *d:* 6.3.1960, Hawridge Place, Chesham, Buckinghamshire. Lower order right-hand batsman, useful bowler. *Team* Somerset (1922–23, 2 matches).
Career batting
3–5–3–7–7*–3.50–0–*ct* 1
Bowling 189–4–47.25–0–0–3/90
A noted rugby footballer, he represented Scotland.

Thomson, Edmund Peel
Amateur. *b:* 22.4.1874, Moss Side, Manchester, Lancashire. *d:* 21.12.1914, near La Bassee, France. Middle order right-hand batsman. *Sch* Fettes. *Team* MCC (1913–14).
Career batting
6–12–1–201–53–18.27–0–*ct* 1
His County cricket was for Wiltshire (1912).

Thomson, Graeme Bruce
Cricketer. *b:* 31.7.1951, Invercargill, New Zealand. Lower order left-hand batsman, left-arm medium pace bowler. *Team* Otago (1974/5 to 1980/1). *Tour* New Zealand to England 1978.
Career batting
47–59–22–340–34*–9.18–0–*ct* 23
Bowling 3180–110–28.90–3–1–6/41
He achieved very little on the 1978 visit and did not appear in the Tests.

Thomson, Henry Shepherd
Amateur. *b:* 4.6.1854, Ramsgate, Kent. Lower order left-hand batsman, left-hand fast round-arm bowler. *Sch* Hurstpierpoint. *Team* Kent (1876, 2 matches).
Career batting
2–3–0–44–27–14.66–0–*ct* 2
Bowling 86–3–28.66–0–0–1/14

Thomson, James
Amateur. *b:* 13.2.1940, Kilmarnock, Ayrshire, Scotland. Lower order right-hand batsman, slow left-arm bowler. *Team* Scotland (1962–85).
Career batting
3–3–2–1–1*–1.00–0–*ct* 2
Bowling 297–7–42.42–0–0–4/116
His second match was 22 years after his debut.

Thomson, Jeffrey Robert
Cricketer. *b:* 16.8.1950, Greenacre, Sydney, New South Wales, Australia. Lower order right-hand batsman, right-arm fast bowler. *Teams* New South Wales (1972/3 to 1973/4, 7 matches); Queensland (1974/5 to 1985/6, 86 matches); Middlesex (1981, 8 matches). *Tours* Australia to England 1975, 1977, 1980, 1983 (World Cup), 1985, to West Indies 1977/8, to New Zealand 1981/2, to Pakistan 1982/3. *Tests* Australia (1972/3 to 1985, 51 matches).
Career batting
187–216–64–2065–61–13.58–0–*ct* 61
Bowling 17864–675–26.46–28–3–7/27
Test batting
51–73–20–679–49–12.81–0–*ct* 20
Bowling 5601–200–28.00–8–0–6/46
On the 1975 tour, which followed his success against England in Australia, he played in all four Tests, but was very erratic. In 1977, with 23 wickets, av 25.34, in the five Tests, he took most wickets, but was troubled by injury. In 1980 he proved totally ineffective and did not play in the Test. In 1985 after a break of three years he made a comeback to Test

cricket during that season's tour to England, but his bite had gone and he achieved little in two Tests. During the 1981 season he was engaged by Middlesex, but due to injury played little. All in all he did not bowl up to his Australian form whilst in England.

Thomson, Kevin
Cricketer. *b:* 24.12.1971, Dundee, Angus, Scotland. Lower order right-hand batsman, right-arm medium pace bowler. *Team* Scotland (1992).
Career batting
1 match, did not bat–*ct* 0
Bowling 82–2–41.00–0–0–1/27

Thomson, Norman Ian
Amateur 1952, turned professional 1953. *b:* 23.1.1929, Walsall, Staffordshire. Lower order right-hand batsman, right-arm medium pace bowler. *Sch* Forest. *Team* Sussex (1952–72, 403 matches). *Tours* MCC to Pakistan 1955/6, to South Africa 1964/5. *Tests* England (1964/5, 5 matches).
Career batting
425–583–100–7120–77–14.74–0–*ct* 135
Bowling 32867–1597–20.58–73–8–10/49
Test batting
5–4–1–69–39–23.00–0–*ct* 3
Bowling 568–9–63.11–0–0–2/55
He took 100 wickets in a season twelve times (best 134, av 20.98, in 1961). His best bowling was 10/49 for Sussex v Warwickshire at Worthing in 1964. He retired after the 1965 season, but reappeared in 1972. He was joint Sussex coach in 1987.

Thomson, Richard Harry
Amateur. *b:* 19.10.1938, Bexhill-on-Sea, Sussex. Middle order left-hand batsman. *Teams* Cambridge U (1961–62, blue both years); Sussex (1961, 2 matches).
Career batting
25–48–5–883–84–20.53–0–*ct* 15
Bowling 13–0

Thomson, Samuel Johnstone
Amateur. *b:* 27.5.1911, Johnstone, Renfrewshire, Scotland. Lower order right-hand batsman, leg break and googly bowler. *Team* Scotland (1938–51).
Career batting
4–7–2–75–21*–15.00–0–*ct* 3
Bowling 246–17–14.47–1–0–5/54

Thomson, Shane Alexander
Cricketer. *b:* 27.1.1969, Hamilton, Auckland, New Zealand. Middle order right-hand batsman, right-arm fast medium bowler. *Team* Northern Districts (1987/8 to 1991/2). *Tours* Young New Zealand to Zimbabwe 1988/9; New Zealand to Sharjah (not first-class) 1989/90, to England 1990. *Tests* New Zealand (1989/90 to 1991/2, 4 matches).
Career batting
50–82–25–2410–166–42.28–3–*ct* 24
Bowling 2669–70–38.12–1–0–5/49
Test batting
4–8–2–242–80*–40.33–0–*ct* 3
Bowling 282–6–47.00–0–0–3/63
He played in only five first-class matches on the 1990 tour to England, and achieved little with either bat or ball.

Thorburn, Robert Murray
Amateur. *b:* 22.3.1883, Peebles, Scotland. *d:* 8.5.1943, Edinburgh, Scotland. Middle order batsman, useful bowler. *Team* Scotland (1924).
Career batting
1–2–0–11–11–5.50–0–*ct* 0
Bowling 32–0

Thorburn, Walter Hunter
Amateur. *b:* 7.10.1884, Glenormiston House, Innerleithen, Peebleshire, Scotland. *d:* 27.3.1957, Peebles, Scotland. Middle order batsman. *Sch* Marlborough. *Team* Scotland (1909–12).
Career batting
5–8–2–183–90*–30.50–0–*ct* 1
Bowling 21–0

Thorley, Joseph James
Amateur. *b:* 7.8.1894, Ringdale Manor, Fernham, Berkshire. *d:* 26.12.1962, Marylebone, London. Middle order right-hand batsman, right-arm medium pace bowler. *Sch* Tonbridge. *Teams* Gentlemen (1925); Tennyson's XI (1926).
Career batting
2–3–1–47–27–23.50–0–*ct* 0
Bowling 22–0
His County cricket was for Hertfordshire (1923–24).

Thorn, Hubert Wethered
Amateur. *b:* 21.4.1909, Tiptree, Essex. *d:* 20.5.1982, Colchester, Essex. Middle order batsman, useful bowler. *Team* Essex (1928, 1 match).
Career batting
1–2–0–12–7–6.00–0–*ct* 0
Bowling 42–1–42.00–0–0–1/42

Thorn, Philip Leslie
Cricketer. *b:* 17.11.1951, St George, Bristol. Lower order right-hand batsman, slow left-arm bowler. *Team* Gloucestershire (1974, 4 matches).
Career batting
4–6–2–45–25–11.25–0–*ct* 4
Bowling 227–4–56.75–0–0–2/53
He also played for Wiltshire (1980–84).

Thornber, Harry
Amateur. *b:* 9.11.1851, Manchester, Lancashire. *d:* 28.7.1913, St Pancras, London. Sound middle order right-hand batsman. *Team* Lancashire (1874, 1 match).
Career batting
1–2–0–0–0–0.00–0–*ct* 0

He also played for Cheshire (1883–91), being captain of the County for several seasons.

Thorne, David Anthony
Cricketer. *b:* 12.12.1964, Coventry, Warwickshire. Lower order right-hand batsman, left-arm medium pace bowler. *Sch* Bablake. *Teams* Warwickshire (1983–89, 43 matches); Oxford U (1984–86, blue all three years).
Career batting
69–113–15–2523–124–25.74–2–*ct* 54
Bowling 2078–41–50.68–1–0–5/39
He captained Oxford in 1986.

Thorne, Major General Sir David Calthrop
Cricketer. *b:* 13.12.1933, Hertford. Nephew of G. C. (Army). Lower order right-hand batsman, slow left-arm bowler. *Sch* St Edwards, Oxford. *Team* Combined Services (1964).
Career batting
2–4–1–98–59–32.66–0–*ct* 0
Bowling 133–2–66.50–0–0–2/74
His County cricket was for Norfolk (1954–62).

Thorne, Gordon Calthrop
Amateur. *b:* 3.3.1897, Chelsea, London. *d:* on or after 2.3.1942, lost at sea in the Indian Ocean. He was captured by the Japanese and was on board a ship which was never heard of again. Uncle of D. C. (Combined Services). Middle order right-hand batsman. *Sch* Haileybury. *Team* Army (1927).
Career batting
1–2–0–24–17–12.00–0–*ct* 0
His County cricket was for Norfolk (1914–25).

Thorne, Robert
Amateur. *b:* 1.3.1860, Southampton, Hampshire. *d:* 11.2.1930, Bitterne Park, Southampton, Hampshire. Opening batsman. *Team* Hampshire (1883, 2 matches).
Career batting
2–4–0–9–6–2.25–0–*ct* 0

Thorneycroft, Charles Bedford
Professional. *b:* 27.7.1879, Litchborough, Northamptonshire. Lower order batsman, right-arm fast bowler. *Team* Northamptonshire (1907, 2 matches).
Career batting
2–4–0–5–3–1.25–0–*ct* 1
Bowling 50–2–25.00–0–0–1/14
He first played for Northamptonshire (pre first-class) in 1899.

Thornhill, Frederick
Professional. *b:* 25.9.1846, Beeston, Nottinghamshire. *d:* 23.7.1876, Toton Sidings, Nottinghamshire. He was killed crossing a railway line. Middle order batsman. *Team* Derbyshire (1876, 1 match).
Career batting
1–2–0–0–0–0.00–0–*ct* 0

Thornhill, Robert Victor
Amateur. *b:* 1901. *d:* 28.7.1963, Merton, Surrey. Middle order right-hand batsman. *Team* Leveson-Gower's XI (1934).
Career batting
1–2–0–64–52–32.00–0–*ct* 0

Thornton, Albert James
Amateur. *b:* 17.1.1856, Folkestone, Kent. *d:* 14.6.1931, Kensington, London. Brother of R. T. (Kent) and W. A. (Oxford U). Free hitting middle order right-hand batsman, right-hand slow under-arm bowler. *Sch* Winchester. *Teams* Sussex (1880–81, 5 matches); Kent (1884–91, 21 matches). *Tour* Sanders to North America 1885.
Career batting
30–52–7–947–137–21.04–1–*ct* 13
Bowling 667–27–24.70–0–0–4/20
He did not appear in first-class matches whilst at Oxford, his first-class debut being for MCC in 1879. He also played for Devon (1874–77) and for the Gentlemen of Hampshire.

Thornton, Arthur
Professional. *b:* 20.7.1854, Wilsden, Yorkshire. *d:* 19.4.1915, Saltaire, Yorkshire. Middle order right-hand batsman. *Team* Yorkshire (1881, 3 matches).
Career batting
3–4–0–21–7–5.25–0–*ct* 2

Thornton, Charles Inglis
Amateur. *b:* 20.3.1850, Llanwarne, Herefordshire. *d:* 10.12.1929, Marylebone, London. Cousin of P. M. Thornton (Middlesex). Very powerful middle order right-hand batsman, right-hand fast under-arm bowler, good long leg. *Sch* Eton. *Teams* Kent (1867–72, 18 matches); Middlesex (1875–85, 29 matches); Cambridge U (1869–72, blue all four years).
Career batting
216–374–16–6928–124–19.35–5–*ct* 119
Bowling 945–47–20.10–0–0–4/19
His first-class debut was for Gentlemen of Kent in 1866 and his final first-class appearance for his own Eleven v Cambridge U in 1897. He also played for Lincolnshire (1871–72). He captained Cambridge in 1872. He was regarded as the greatest hitter of his day, his most effective stroke being the drive, during which he moved out to meet the ball, in contrast to the usual firm footed methods employed by his contemporaries. In practice he hit a ball 168 yards and 162 yards, and in a match at Canterbury 152 yards. He was for many years a leading figure in the Scarborough Festival.

Thornton, Edward
Amateur. *b:* 27.10.1893, Woodhurst, Pease Pottage, Crawley, Sussex. *d:* 18.10.1970, Stockport, Cheshire. Middle order batsman. *Team* combined Services (1922).

Career batting
1–2–0–59–38–29.50–0–*ct* 0
He held the old Portugese title of the Count de Cassilas.

Thornton, Frank Kenneis
Amateur. *b:* 25.10.1898, Stoneygate, Leicester. *d:* 8.9.1987, Fareham, Hampshire. Brother of J. A. C. (Leicestershire). Middle order right-hand batsman. *Sch* Oakham. *Team* Northamptonshire (1937, 2 matches).
Career batting
2–4–1–27–13–9.00–0–*ct* 0

Thornton, Dr George
Amateur. *b:* 24.12.1867, Skipton, Yorkshire. *d:* 31.1.1939, Kensington, London. Father of P. A. (Ireland and Border). Robust middle order left-hand batsman, slow left-arm bowler. *Teams* Yorkshire (1891, 3 matches); Middlesex (1893–99, 32 matches). *Tour* Ceylon to India 1909/10 (not first-class). *Test* South Africa (1902/3, 1 match).
Career batting
41–67–11–1263–161–22.55–1–*ct* 13
Bowling 1007–32–31.46–1–0–5/20
Test batting
1–1–1–1–1*–no av–0–*ct* 1
Bowling 20–1–20.00–0–0–1/20
He lived for several years in South Africa and played for Transvaal, though not in a first-class match. Later he moved to Ceylon and was President of the Colombo Cricket Club.

Thornton, James Richard
Amateur. *b:* 11.1.1861, Horsham, Sussex. *d:* 1.3.1916, Burgess Hill, Sussex. Lower order right-hand batsman, right-arm fast bowler, good field. *Team* Sussex (1880–83, 3 matches).
Career batting
3–5–0–73–29–14.60–0–*ct* 2
Bowling 42–1–42.00–0–0–1/30

Thornton, John Arthur Curzon
Amateur. *b:* 24.2.1902, Stoneygate, Leicester. Brother of F. K. (Northamptonshire). Middle order right-hand batsman, right-arm fast medium bowler. *Sch* Uppingham. *Team* Leicestershire (1921, 3 matches).
Career batting
3–5–3–53–19*–26.50–0–*ct* 1
Bowling 72–1–72.00–0–0–1/21

Thornton, Dr Patrick Alban
Amateur. *b:* 4.5.1904, Cape Town, South Africa. *d:* 1.2.1961, East London, South Africa. Son of George (Yorkshire and Middlesex). Middle order right-hand batsman, right-arm medium pace bowler. *Teams* Ireland (1928–29); Border (1933/4).
Career batting
6–11–1–119–37–11.90–0–*ct* 3
Bowling 212–10–21.20–0–0–4/64

Thornton, Percy Melville
Amateur. *b:* 29.12.1841, Mayfair, Westminster, London. *d:* 8.1.1918, South Kensington, London. Cousin of C. I. (Middlesex). Lower order right-hand batsman, right-hand fast round-arm bowler, good long stop. *Sch* Harrow. *Teams* Cambridge U (1864); Middlesex (1872, 1 match).
Career batting
4–5–1–34–27*–8.50–0–*ct* 0
Bowling 3–0
Commencing 1870 he was Hon Secretary of Middlesex CCC, not retiring until 1898, though he continued on the County Committee. He was a noted athlete and as Hon Secretary of the Cambridge University Athletic Club was one of the founders of the inter-University Sports in 1864. He was also MP for Clapham from 1892 to 1910.

Thornton, Rev Richard Thornton
Amateur. *b:* 28.3.1853, Folkestone, Kent. *d:* 30.5.1928, Eastbourne, Sussex. Brother of A. J. (Sussex and Kent) and W. A. (Oxford U). Middle order right-hand batsman, right-hand slow round-arm, or under-arm, bowler. *Team* Kent (1881–88, 45 matches). *Tour* Sanders to North America 1885.
Career batting
66–112–11–2021–107–20.00–1–*ct* 42
Bowling 104–3–34.66–0–0–2/16
He did not appear in first-class cricket whilst at Oxford, but was awarded his soccer blue. His final first-class match was for MCC in 1893. He also played for Dorset (1872), Devon (1873–77) and Wiltshire (1875).

Thornton, Thomas
Amateur. *b:* 29.5.1922, Elland, Yorkshire. Opening right-hand batsman. *Team* RAF (1946).
Career batting
1–2–0–29–23–14.50–0–*ct* 0

Thornton, Walter Alfred
Amateur. *b:* 23.2.1858, London. *d:* 2.2.1915, Blakedown, Kidderminster, Worcestershire. Brother of A. J. (Kent and Sussex) and R. T. (Kent), his widow married T. R. Hine-Haycock (Kent). Middle order right-hand batsman, right-arm fast bowler. *Sch* Winchester. *Team* Oxford U (1879–82, blue all four years).
Career batting
24–47–2–843–70–18.73–0–*ct* 9
Bowling 561–27–20.77–0–0–4/29
His final first-class match was for MCC in 1883. His County cricket was for Devon (1874–85). He also won a blue for billiards.

Thornycroft, Guy Mytton
Amateur. *b:* 1.4.1917, Blawith, Grange-over-Sands, Lancashire. Middle order right-hand batsman. *Sch* Shrewsbury. *Team* Worcestershire (1947, 1 match).
Career batting
1–2–0–3–3–1.50–0–*ct* 0

Thorp, Charles
Amateur. *b:* 11.8.1882, Fotheringhay, Northamptonshire. *d:* 5.5.1953, Fotheringhay, Northamptonshire. Middle order right-hand batsman. *Sch* Oundle. *Team* Northamptonshire (1908–09, 9 matches).
Career batting
9–17–0–195–50–11.47–0–*ct* 1
Bowling 16–0

Thorp, Philip
Amateur. *b:* 6.5.1911, Kidderminster, Worcestershire. Middle order right-hand batsman. *Team* Worcestershire (1935, 2 matches).
Career batting
2–4–0–19–11–4.75–0–*ct* 0

Thorpe, George
Professional. *b:* 20.2.1834, Sheffield, Yorkshire. *d:* 2.3.1899, Lowfield, Sheffield, Yorkshire. Middle order right-hand batsman. *Team* Yorkshire (1862–64, 2 matches).
Career batting
2–4–1–19–9*–6.33–0–*ct* 3
Bowling 4–0

Thorpe, Graham Paul
Cricketer. *b:* 1.8.1969, Farnham, Surrey. Middle order left-hand batsman, right-arm medium pace bowler. *Team* Surrey (1988–92, 83 matches). *Tours* England A to Zimbabwe 1989/90, to Pakistan and Sri Lanka 1990/1, to West Indies 1991/2.
Career batting
96–157–26–5650–216–43.12–10–*ct* 60
Bowling 738–13–56.76–0–0–2/31
He reached 1,000 runs three times (best 1,895, av 51.21, in 1992). His highest score was 216 for Surrey v Somerset at the Oval in 1992.

Thorpe, Thomas
Professional. *b:* 19.5.1881, Attercliffe, Sheffield, Yorkshire. *d:* 28.9.1953, Worksop, Nottinghamshire. Middle order batsman. *Team* Northamptonshire (1913, 3 matches).
Career batting
3–4–1–11–6–3.66–0–*ct* 2
A useful soccer player, he kept goal for Northampton Town and Barnsley.

Thoy, Reginald Ernest
Amateur. *b:* 12.5.1921, Singapore. Opening right-hand batsman. *Team* D. R. Jardine's XI (1955–57).
Career batting
2–3–0–24–13–8.00–0–*ct* 3

Threapleton, Joseph William
Professional. *b:* 20.7.1857, Pudsey, Yorkshire. *d:* 30.7.1918, Low Town, Pudsey, Yorkshire. Sound lower order right-hand batsman, wicket-keeper. *Team* Yorkshire (1881, 1 match).
Career batting
1–1–1–8–8*–no av–0–*ct* 2–*st* 1

Threlfall, Philip Walter
Cricketer. *b:* 11.2.1967, Barrow-in-Furness, Lancashire. Lower order right-hand batsman, right-arm medium fast bowler. *Team* Sussex (1988–91, 3 matches).
Career batting
3 matches, did not bat–*ct* 0
Bowling 130–7–18.57–0–0–3/45
He also played for Cumberland (1987).

Thresher, Philip
Amateur. *b:* 1.3.1844, South Stoneham, Hampshire. *d:* 11.4.1883, Shepherd's Bush, London. Opening batsman. *Sch* Winchester. *Team* Hampshire (1865–69, 5 matches).
Career batting
5–9–1–93–47*–11.62–0–*ct* 0
Bowling 19–1–19.00–0–0–1/19
Whilst at Oxford University he played in some Trial matches, but no first-class contests.

Thresher, Ronald Stanley
Amateur. *b:* 31.12.1930, Tonbridge, Kent. Lower order right-hand batsman, right-arm fast bowler. *Team* Kent (1957, 2 matches).
Career batting
5–9–4–51–19–10.20–0–*ct* 0
Bowling 407–14–29.07–0–0–4/29
His final first-class match was for D. R. Jardine's XI in 1958.

Thring, Charles Henry Meredith
Amateur. *b:* 21.1.1861, Uppingham, Rutland. *d:* 11.4.1939, Chilcompton, Somerset. Nephew of Theodore (MCC 1840). Middle order batsman. *Sch* Marlborough. *Team* MCC (1889).
Career batting
1–1–0–12–12–12.00–0–*ct* 0
His County cricket was for Wiltshire (1883–85) and Bedfordshire (1894).

Throwley, Viscount George Edward Milles
(succeeded to the title 2nd Earl Sondes in 1894)
Amateur. *b:* 11.5.1861, Lees Court, Faversham, Kent. *d:* 1.10.1907, Marylebone, London. He died after an operation. Son of G. W. Milles (Gentlemen of Kent 1849), brother of H. A. Milles (Kent), brother-in-law of F. W. G. Gore (I Zingari). Middle order right-hand batsman, right-arm medium pace bowler. *Sch* Eton. *Team* Kent (1882–84, 6 matches). *Tour* Hawke to North America 1891.

Career batting
8–12–2–168–82–16.80–0–*ct* 7
Bowling 125–5–25.00–0–0–3/29

He did not appear in any first-class matches whilst at Cambridge. He was President of Kent in 1891.

Thursfield, John Hunt
Amateur. *b:* 16.6.1892, Alvechurch, Worcestershire. *d:* 26.4.1951, Shenstone, Lichfield, Staffordshire. Middle order right-hand batsman. *Sch* Shrewsbury. *Team* Worcestershire (1922–25, 3 matches).
Career batting
3–6–0–70–35–11.66–0–*ct* 1

Thursfield, Martin John
Cricketer. *b:* 14.12.1971, South Shields, Co Durham. Lower order right-hand batsman, right-arm medium pace bowler. *Teams* Middlesex (1990, 2 matches); Hampshire (1992, 1 match).
Career batting
3 matches, did not bat–*ct* 0
Bowling 165–4–41.25–0–0–1/11

Thursting, Laurence Denis
Professional. *b:* 9.9.1915, Lambeth, London. Opening or middle order right-hand batsman, slow left-arm bowler. *Team* Leicestershire (1938–47, 29 matches).
Career batting
29–45–10–882–94–25.20–0–*ct* 10
Bowling 660–13–50.76–0–0–3/34

Thwaites, Guy Edward
Cricketer. *b:* 19.1.1971, Brighton, Sussex. Son of I. G. (Cambridge U). Middle order right-hand batsman. *Sch* Eastbourne. *Team* Cambridge U (1991–92).
Career batting
4–6–0–68–32–11.33–0–*ct* 2

Thwaites, Dr Ian Guy
Cricketer. *b:* 4.3.1943, Brighton, Sussex. Father of G. E. (Cambridge U). Middle order right-hand batsman. *Sch* Eastbourne. *Team* Cambridge U (1963–64, blue 1964).
Career batting
22–38–4–769–61–22.61–0–*ct* 3
Bowling 127–4–31.75–0–0–1/1

Tidy, Thomas
Professional. *b:* 6.10.1847, Hurstpierpoint, Sussex. *d:* 11.9.1918, Hildenborough, Kent. Middle order right-hand batsman. *Team* Kent (1868, 1 match).
Career batting
1–2–0–21–16–10.50–0–*ct* 0

Tidy, Warwick Nigel
Cricketer. *b:* 10.2.1953, Birmingham. Tail end right-hand batsman, leg break and googly bowler. *Team* Warwickshire (1970–74, 36 matches).
Career batting
36–34–14–70–12*–3.50–0–*ct* 17
Bowling 2775–81–34.25–3–0–5/24

Tillakaratne, Hashan Prasantha
Cricketer. *b:* 14.7.1967, Colombo, Ceylon. Middle order left-hand batsman, occasional off break bowler, wicket-keeper. *Team* Nondescripts (1988/9 to 1991/2). *Tours* Sri Lanka to Sharjah (not first-class) 1986/7, 1988/9, 1989/90, 1990/1, to Australia 1987/8 (not first-class), 1989/90, to England 1988, 1990, 1991, to Bangladesh (not first-class) 1988/9, to India 1989/90 (not first-class), 1990/1, to New Zealand 1990/1, to Pakistan 1991/2, to Australia and New Zealand (World Cup) 1991/2; Sri Lanka B to Zimbabwe 1987/8. *Tests* Sri Lanka (1989/90 to 1991/2, 9 matches).
Career batting
65–88–18–2759–151–39.41–8–*ct* 88–*st* 4
Bowling 146–3–48.66–0–0–1/9
Test batting
9–15–1–306–55–21.85–0–*ct* 25

He batted well on the 1990 and 1991 tours to England, when he was also the first choice wicket-keeper. His first-class debut was for Sri Lanka Under 23 in 1984/5.

Tillard, Alfred Edmund
Amateur. *b:* 20.4.1847, Conington, Cambridgeshire. *d:* 9.8.1926, Tooting Bec, London. Middle order batsman. *Sch* Norwich. *Team* Cambridgeshire (1868, 1 match).
Career batting
1–2–1–27–14–27.00–0–*ct* 2

Tillard, Charles
Amateur. *b:* 18.4.1851, Wimbledon, Surrey. *d:* 7.3.1944, Bathford, Somerset. Father of E. D. (Somerset), son-in-law of E. W. Dowell (Cambridge U 1844), brother-in-law of A. T. Scott (Cambridge U), his niece married P. V. Williams (Sussex). Lower order right-hand batsman, right-hand fast round-arm bowler, good cover point. *Sch* Repton. *Teams* Cambridge U (1871–74, blue 1873–74); Surrey (1874–75, 3 matches).
Career batting
16–26–2–328–62*–13.66–0–*ct* 6
Bowling 958–54–17.74–4–1–7/35

He also played for Norfolk (1868–95) and Huntingdonshire (1872). He was a good athlete, especially in the long and high jumps.

Tillard, Elliot Dowell
Amateur. *b:* 22.7.1880, Cheltenham, Gloucestershire. *d:* 19.2.1967, Flexbury, Bude, Cornwall. Son of Charles (Surrey), nephew of A. T. Scott (Cambridge U). Middle order batsman, useful bowler. *Sch* Malvern. *Teams* Europeans (1907/8 to 1922/3); Somerset (1912, 9 matches).
Career batting
16–30–1–357–39–12.31–0–*ct* 3
Bowling 221–14–15.78–2–0–6/40

Tillard, John Robert
Amateur. *b:* 26.5.1924, Kensington, London. Middle order right-hand batsman. *Sch* Winchester. *Team* Sussex (1949, 1 match).
Career batting
1–2–0–3–3–1.50–0–*ct* 0
He played no first-class matches at Oxford U, but did win a soccer blue.

Tilley, Eric Warrington
Amateur. *b:* 22.9.1913, Whatstandwell, Derbyshire. *d:* 1.12.1977, New Humberstone, Leicester. Lower order right-hand batsman, right-arm fast medium bowler. *Team* Leicestershire (1946, 4 matches).
Career batting
4–3–0–3–2–1.00–0–*ct* 2
Bowling 256–10–25.60–0–0–3/33

Tilly, Henry William
Professional. *b:* 25.5.1932, Edmonton, Middlesex. Lower order right-hand batsman, right-arm fast medium bowler. *Team* Middlesex (1954–61, 59 matches).
Career batting
64–88–13–814–49*–10.85–0–*ct* 18
Bowling 3502–134–26.13–4–0–6/33
After leaving Middlesex he played for Hertfordshire (1963–73) and his final first-class appearance was for the Minor Counties in 1967.

Tilson, John
Professional. *b:* 27.3.1845, Ilkeston, Derbyshire. *d:* 4.11.1895, Ilkeston, Derbyshire. Middle order right-hand batsman, right-hand medium pace round-arm bowler. *Team* Derbyshire (1871–76, 3 matches).
Career batting
3–5–0–26–14–5.20–0–*ct* 0

Timm, Christopher William
Cricketer. *b:* 17.11.1968, Didsbury, Cheshire. Lower order left-hand batsman, wicket-keeper. *Sch* William Hulme's GS. *Team* Oxford U (1989).
Career batting
2–2–0–10–5–5.00–0–*ct* 0–*st* 1

Timmis, Peter John
Cricketer. *b:* 30.7.1942, Stoke-on-Trent, Staffordshire. Lower order right-hand batsman, right-arm fast medium bowler. *Team* Minor Counties (1971).
Career batting
1 match, did not bat–*ct* 0
Bowling 36–0
His County cricket was for Staffordshire (1962–79).

Timms, Brian Stanley Valentine
Professional. *b:* 17.12.1940, Ropley, Hampshire. Lower order right-hand batsman, wicket-keeper. *Teams* Hampshire (1959–68, 208 matches); Warwickshire (1969–71, 24 matches).
Career batting
232–306–74–3657–120–15.76–1–*ct* 456–*st* 70

Timms, Herbert Harry
(death registered as Herbert Henry Timms)
Professional. *b:* 6.7.1890, Moreton-in-Marsh, Gloucestershire. *d:* 1.3.1973, Eynsham, Oxfordshire. Middle order left-hand batsman, right-arm fast medium bowler. *Team* Gloucestershire (1911–12, 3 matches).
Career batting
3–6–0–33–12–5.50–0–*ct* 0

Timms, John Edward
Amateur, turned professional in 1927. *b:* 3.11.1906, Silverstone, Northamptonshire. *d:* 18.5.1980, Buckingham. Attractive middle order right-hand batsman, right-arm medium pace bowler, excellent cover point. *Sch* Wellingborough. *Team* Northamptonshire (1925–49, 468 matches).
Career batting
472–848–30–20509–213–25.07–31–*ct* 153
Bowling 6626–149–44.46–2–0–6/18
He hit 1,000 runs in a season 11 times (best 1,632, av 34.72, in 1934). His only double century was 213 for Northamptonshire v Worcestershire at Stourbridge in 1934.

Timms, Wilfrid Walter
Amateur. *b:* 28.9.1902, Northampton. *d:* 30.9.1986, Godalming, Surrey. Sound opening right-hand batsman, leg break bowler. *Sch* Northampton CG. *Teams* Northamptonshire (1921–32, 99 matches); Cambridge U (1922–25).
Career batting
106–196–15–4083–154*–22.55–4–*ct* 25
Bowling 175–0
He hit 1,008 runs, av 27.24, in 1925. He was the master in charge of cricket at Charterhouse 1932–46 and transformed the school's cricket in that period.

Tindall, Christian
Amateur. *b:* 18.5.1878, Leighton Buzzard, Bedfordshire. *d:* 13.4.1951, Littleham, Devon. Middle order batsman. *Sch* Malvern and Clifton. *Team* London County (1904).
Career batting
1–2–1–10–9*–10.00–0–*ct* 0

Tindall, Rev Henry Charles Lenox
Amateur. *b:* 4.2.1863, Margate, Kent. *d:* 10.6.1940, Peasmarsh, Sussex. Brother of S. M. (Lancashire), brother-in-law of G. K. Papillon (Gentlemen). Stylish middle order right-hand batsman, right-arm fast bowler, good field. *Team* Kent (1893–95, 3 matches).
Career batting
5–6–1–71–32–14.20–0–*ct* 3
Bowling 166–4–41.50–0–0–2/56
He did not appear in first-class cricket whilst at Cambridge, but was a noted athlete, obtaining his blue and winning the 880, 440 and 100 yards. In 1889 he won the 440 yards Amateur Championship. Also a good rugby footballer, he appeared for Rosslyn Park.

Tindall, Mark
Amateur. *b:* 31.3.1914, Marylebone, London. Father of R. M. (Northamptonshire). Middle order right-hand batsman, left-arm fast-medium bowler. *Sch* Harrow. *Teams* Middlesex (1933–38, 16 matches); Cambridge U (1935–37, blue all three years).
Career batting
51–92–3–2202–117–24.74–3–*ct* 15
Bowling 65–3–21.66–0–0–2/21
He hit 1,018 runs, av 29.08, in 1936. He captained Cambridge in 1937.

Tindall, Richard Geoffrey
Amateur. *b:* 20.2.1912, Sherborne, Dorset. *d:* 22.1.1942, Jadabia, Libya. Lower order right-hand batsman, right-arm fast bowler. *Sch* Winchester. *Team* Oxford U (1933–34, blue both years).
Career batting
18–30–3–610–113–22.59–1–*ct* 11
Bowling 1581–50–31.62–2–0–5/73
His County cricket was for Dorset (1931–39).

Tindall, Robert Michael
Cricketer. *b:* 16.6.1959, Harrow-on-the-Hill, Middlesex. Son of Mark (Middlesex). Middle order left-hand batsman, slow left-arm bowler. *Sch* Harrow. *Team* Northamptonshire (1980–81, 14 matches).
Career batting
14–22–4–330–60*–18.33–0–*ct* 6
Bowling 331–4–82.75–0–0–2/1

Tindall, Ronald Albert Ernest
Professional. *b:* 23.9.1935, Streatham, London. Middle order right-hand batsman, off break bowler. *Team* Surrey (1956–66, 172 matches).
Career batting
173–257–38–5446–109*–24.86–2–*ct* 129
Bowling 4857–150–32.38–2–0–5/41
He hit 1,126 runs, av 28.15, in 1963. A useful soccer player, he was centre forward for Chelsea, West Ham United, Reading and Portsmouth.

Tindall, Sidney Maguire
Amateur. *b:* 18.2.1867, Margate, Kent. *d:* 19.9.1922, Sydney, New South Wales. Australia. He died after fracturing his skull whilst falling from a moving tram. Brother of H. C. L. (Kent). Attacking middle order right-hand batsman, good outfield. *Teams* Lancashire (1894–98, 42 matches); London County (1900–01).
Career batting
56–86–1–1304–86–15.34–0–*ct* 24
Bowling 69–2–34.50–0–0–1/11
He emigrated to Australia in 1911 and was for a short time Secretary of Melbourne CC. A noted hockey player, he was regarded as one of the best in England about 1890.

Tindill, Eric William Thomas
Amateur. *b:* 18.12.1910, Nelson, New Zealand. Father of Paul (Wellington). Opening or lower order left-hand batsman, wicket-keeper. *Team* Wellington (1932/3 to 1949/50). *Tours* New Zealand to England 1937, to Australia 1937/8. *Tests* New Zealand (1937 to 1946/7, 5 matches).
Career batting
69–116–13–3127–149–30.35–6–*ct* 95–*st* 33
Test batting
5–9–1–73–37*–9.12–0–*ct* 6–*st* 1
He kept wicket in all three Tests on the 1937 tour. He scored 106 on debut for Wellington v Auckland at Auckland in 1932/3. He umpired one Test in New Zealand in 1958/9. A good rugby footballer, he represented New Zealand.

Tinkler, Edgar
Amateur. *b:* 11.3.1921, Burnley, Lancashire. Stylish middle order right-hand batsman, right-arm medium pace bowler. *Sch* Worcester RGS. *Team* Worcestershire (1953, 1 match).
Career batting
3–5–0–15–7–3.00–0–*ct* 1
Bowling 14–0
His final first-class match was for MCC in 1961.

Tinley, Francis Eastward
Professional. *b:* 3.3.1819, Southwell, Nottinghamshire. *d:* 2.6.1889, Birmingham. Brother of R. C. (Nottinghamshire) and Vincent (Nottinghamshire). Hard hitting lower order right-hand batsman, right-hand medium pace round-arm bowler. *Team* Nottinghamshire (1845–56, 13 matches).
Career batting
19–32–7–188–23*–7.52–0–*ct* 7
Bowling 589–63+2–9.34–5–1–6/29
His debut was for Players of Nottinghamshire in 1844. He also played for Leicestershire (pre first-class, 1851), Lincolnshire (1853–61), Norfolk (1853), Derbyshire (pre first-class, 1857–58) and Rutland (1859).

Tinley, Robert Crispin
Professional. *b:* 25.10.1830, Southwell, Nottinghamshire. *d:* 11.12.1900, Burton-on-Trent, Staffordshire. Brother of F. E. (Nottinghamshire) and Vincent (Nottinghamshire). Attacking lower order right-hand batsman, right-hand fast round-arm, but after 1858 slow under-arm bowler, good point field. *Teams* Nottinghamshire (1847–69, 54 matches); Lancashire (1851, 1 match as given man). *Tour* Parr to Australia 1863/4.
Career batting
117–199–23–2004–56–11.38–0–*ct* 143–*st* 2
Bowling 4249–294 + 15–14.45–22–5–8/12
His last first-class match was AEE v Yorkshire in 1874. He was for some years the leading exponent of 'lob' bowling in England. He umpired in important matches after retiring from first-class cricket. He also

played for Derbyshire (pre first-class, 1848–49), Devon (1851–53) and Staffordshire (1852–53).

Tinley, Vincent
Professional. *b:* 26.1.1828, Southwell, Nottinghamshire. *d:* 19.11.1899, Sneinton, Nottingham. Brother of F. E. (Nottinghamshire) and R. C. (Nottinghamshire). Middle order right-hand batsman, right-hand slow under-arm bowler, wicket-keeper. *Teams* Lancashire (1851, 2 matches); Nottinghamshire (1864, 1 match).
Career batting
3–5–1–41–13–10.25–0–*ct* 1
He also played for Devon (1852) and Lincolnshire (1861–62).

Tinsley, Alfred
Professional. *b:* 12.3.1867, Welham, Malton, Yorkshire. *d:* 25.9.1933, Musselburgh, Midlothian, Scotland. Brother of H. J. (Lancashire and Yorkshire). Middle order right-hand batsman, good deep field. *Team* Lancashire (1890–95, 58 matches).
Career batting
58–91–10–1348–65–16.64–0–*ct* 27
Bowling 7–0
He also played in one non-first-class match for Yorkshire in 1887 and later for Staffordshire (1905–06).

Tinsley, Henry James
Professional. *b:* 20.2.1865, Welham Grange, Malton, Yorkshire. *d:* 10.12.1938, Heworth, Yorkshire. Brother of Alfred (Lancashire). Middle order right-hand batsman, right-arm fast bowler. *Teams* Yorkshire (1890–91, 9 matches); Lancashire (1894–96, 4 matches).
Career batting
14–21–0–122–18–5.80–0–*ct* 4
Bowling 57–4–14.25–0–0–3/15

Tipper, Benjamin Claude Cecil
Amateur. *b:* 7.7.1896, King's Norton, Birmingham. *d:* 11.7.1970, Norton Lindsey, Warwickshire. Middle order right-hand batsman, bowler. *Sch* KES, Birmingham. *Team* Worcestershire (1919, 5 matches).
Career batting
5–10–1–137–43–15.22–0–*ct* 7
Bowling 80–4–20.00–0–0–2/0

Tissera, Michael Hugh
Cricketer. *b:* 23.3.1939, Colombo, Ceylon. Middle order right-hand batsman, leg break bowler. *Team* Ceylon/Sri Lanka (1958/9 to 1975). *Tours* Ceylon to India 1959/60, 1961/2, 1964/5, to Pakistan 1966/7, to England 1975.
Career batting
30–54–5–1394–122–28.44–2–*ct* 15
Bowling 856–27–31.70–1–0–5/95
He captained Ceylon in the 1960s. He played for Sri Lanka in one-day internationals.

Titchard, Stephen Paul
Cricketer. *b:* 17.12.1967, Warrington, Lancashire. Middle order right-hand batsman, right-arm medium pace bowler. *Team* Lancashire (1990–92, 25 matches).
Career batting
25–44–4–1343–135–33.57–1–*ct* 16

Titchmarsh, Charles Harold
Amateur. *b:* 18.2.1881, Royston, Hertfordshire. *d:* 23.5.1930, Royston, Hertfordshire. He died following a stroke. Middle order right-hand batsman, wicket-keeper. *Sch* Bishop's Stortford. *Team* MCC (1920–28). *Tours* MCC to Australia and New Zealand 1922/3.
Career batting
42–72–6–2589–171–39.22–4–*ct* 16
Bowling 4–0
His County cricket was for Hertfordshire (1900–29) and he proved the mainstay of that County. In 1921 and 1925 he was chosen to represent the Gentlemen v Players and would no doubt have made a name for himself in first-class cricket if he had forsaken Hertfordshire for one of the major counties.

Titchmarsh, Valentine Adolphus
Amateur, turned professional 1880. *b:* 14.2.1853, Royston, Hertfordshire. *d:* 11.10.1907, St Albans, Hertfordshire. He died of locomotor ataxy. Lower order left-hand batsman, right-arm fast bowler. *Team* MCC (1885–91).
Career batting
8–12–0–82–23–6.83–0–*ct* 5
Bowling 187–9–20.77–1–0–5/69
He made his first-class debut for South of England in 1880. His County cricket was for Hertfordshire (1877–97). He was one of the best known County umpires (1896–1907), standing in three Test matches (1899–1905).

Titley, Edward George
Amateur. *b:* 7.8.1911, Carlton, Nottinghamshire. *d:* 17.7.1943, while flying on active service. Lower order right-hand batsman, wicket-keeper. *Sch* Uppingham. *Team* Cambridge U (1932).
Career batting
2–4–0–4–3–1.00–0–*ct* 2

Titmus, Frederick John, MBE
Professional. *b:* 24.11.1932, Kentish Town, London. Middle order right-hand batsman, off break bowler. *Teams* Middlesex (1949–82, 642 matches); Surrey (1978, 1 match); Orange Free State (1975/6). *Tours* MCC to Pakistan 1955/6, to Australia and New Zealand 1962/3, 1965/6, 1974/5, to India 1963/4, to South Africa 1964/5, to West Indies 1967/8; Robins to South Africa 1975/6; MCC to Far East 1981/2 (not first-class); Cavaliers to West Indies 1969/70. *Tests* England (1955 to 1974/5, 53 matches).

Career batting
792–1142–208–21588–137*–23.11–6–*ct* 473
Bowling 63313–2830–22.37–168–26–9/52
Test batting
53–76–11–1449–84*–22.29–0–*ct* 35
Bowling 4931–153–32.22–7–0–7/79

Although he made his debut in 1949, aged 16, it was not until 1953 that he really hit the headlines. In that year he took 100 wickets for the first of sixteen times. His best season came in 1955 with 191 wickets, av 16.31, and in that year he first appeared in Test cricket and achieved the 'double' for the first of eight times. His best season with the bat was 1961 with 1,703 runs, av 37.02, and he topped 1,000 runs in seven other seasons.

After his initial games for England in 1955, he did not reappear until 1962, then played regularly until his visit to West Indies in 1967/8, when in a swimming accident he lost four toes. He recovered sufficiently to resume County cricket, but never played again in Test cricket in England, his only other Tests being in Australia in 1974/5.

His best bowling performances were both for Middlesex, namely 9/52 v Cambridge U in 1962 at Fenner's and 9/57 v Lancashire in 1964 at Lord's. In 1965 he was chosen as captain of Middlesex, but his leadership did not prove a success and he resigned midway through the 1968 season. In 1977 he moved to the Oval as Surrey's coach, but again found the position uncomfortable and left in 1979 – he played once for Surrey. He reappeared for Middlesex in 1979, 1980 and 1982. He was a Test selector 1986–88.

Tobin, Rev Frederic
Amateur. *b:* 5.7.1849, Liscard, Birkenhead, Cheshire. *d:* 28.9.1914, Folkestone, Kent. Middle order right-hand batsman, good field. *Sch* Rugby. *Team* Cambridge U (1870–72, blue all three years).
Career batting
13–24–2–369–77–16.77–0–*ct* 8

His County cricket was for Lincolnshire (1868), Huntingdonshire (1868–71) and Warwickshire (pre first-class, 1885).

Tod, Ben Ross
Amateur. *b:* 6.8.1908, Edinburgh, Scotland. *d:* 3.6.1967, Belmont, Surrey. Middle order right-hand batsman, off break bowler. *Sch* Edinburgh Academy. *Team* Scotland (1930–39).
Career batting
11–20–3–387–143*–22.76–1–*ct* 5
Bowling 23–1–23.00–0–0–1/17

Todd, James Henry
Amateur. *b:* 16.12.1867, Forest Hill, London. *d:* 11.8.1956, Marylebone, London. Middle order right-hand batsman. *Sch* Mill Hill. *Team* London County (1901).
Career batting
3–6–0–66–24–11.00–0–*ct* 6

His final first-class match was for W. G. Grace's XI in 1906.

Todd, Leslie John
Professional. *b:* 19.6.1907, Catford, Kent. *d:* 20.8.1967, Buckland, Dover, Kent. Sound opening left-hand batsman, slow left-arm bowler, changing to medium pace in 1933. *Team* Kent (1927–50, 426 matches).
Career batting
437–727–93–20087–174–31.68–38–*ct* 236
Bowling 15883–572–27.76–20–1–6/26

He hit 1,000 runs in a season ten times, going on to 2,000 once: 2,312, av 46.24, in 1947. He achieved the 'double' in 1936, when he took 100 wickets for the only time in his career (103 wickets, av 21.93). He was a first-class umpire (1963–64). He played soccer as an amateur for Dulwich Hamlet and represented England at table tennis.

Todd, Norman Douglas
Amateur. *b:* 11.6.1884, Hetton-le-Hole, Co Durham. *d:* 12.5.1959, Brook Hill, Ruddington, Nottinghamshire. Middle order right-hand batsman. *Sch* King William's, Isle of Man. *Team* Derbyshire (1906–08, 2 matches).
Career batting
2–4–0–6–6–1.50–0–*ct* 0

Todd, Paul Adrian
Cricketer. *b:* 12.3.1953, Morton, Southwell, Nottinghamshire. Opening right-hand batsman, right-arm medium pace bowler. *Teams* Nottinghamshire (1972–82, 156 matches); Glamorgan (1987, 14 matches).
Career batting
171–302–16–7663–178–26.79–9–*ct* 119
Bowling 7–0

He scored 1,000 runs in a season three times (best 1,181, av 29.52, in 1978). He also played for Lincolnshire (1985–87) and Minor Counties in a first-class match in 1986.

Toft, David Penn
Cricketer. *b:* 1.3.1945, Tunbridge Wells, Kent. Opening right-hand batsman. *Sch* Tonbridge. *Team* Oxford U (1965–67, blue 1966 and 1967).
Career batting
27–48–4–1222–145–27.77–1–*ct* 10

Tolchard, Jeffrey Graham
Cricketer. *b:* 17.3.1944, Torquay, Devon. Brother of R. W. (Leicestershire). Uncle of R. G. Twose (Warwickshire). Middle order right-hand batsman, right-arm medium pace bowler, occasional wicket-keeper. *Sch* Malvern. *Team* Leicestershire (1970–77, 77 matches).
Career batting
78–109–17–1865–78–20.27–0–*ct* 24

Bowling 5–0

He also played for Devon (1963–69) and 1979–83) and his final first-class match was for Minor Counties in 1981. A good soccer player, he appeared for Torquay United and Exeter City.

Tolchard, Roger William
Cricketer. *b:* 15.6.1946, Torquay, Devon. Brother of J. G. (Leicestershire), uncle of R. G. Twose (Warwickshire). Middle order right-hand batsman, occasional off break bowler, wicket-keeper. *Sch* Malvern. *Team* Leicestershire (1965–83, 431 matches). *Tours* International XI to Pakistan, India and Ceylon 1967/8; MCC to India, Pakistan and Sri Lanka 1972/3, to India, Sri Lanka and Australia 1976/7; Robins to South Africa 1973/4, 1974/5, 1975/6, to Sri Lanka 1977/8; International Wanderers to South Africa 1974/5, to Rhodesia 1975/6; England to Australia 1978/9; Leicestershire to Zimbabwe 1980/1; Overseas XI to India 1980/1. *Tests* England (1976/7, 4 matches).
Career batting
483–680–189–15288–126*–31.13–12-*ct* 912-*st* 125
Bowling 34–1–34.00–0–0–1/4
Test batting
4–7–2–129–67–25.80–0–*ct* 5

His best season as a batsman was 1970 with 998 runs, av 30.24. He was taken to India in 1976/7 as reserve wicket-keeper but his batting ability against the slow bowlers resulted in his playing purely as a batsman. From 1981 to 1983 he captained Leicestershire. He also played for Devon (1963–64). A useful soccer player, he had a trial with Leicester City.

Tolfree, Edward
Professional. *b:* 12.7.1881, Southampton, Hampshire. *d:* 20.3.1966, Moor Green, West End, Southampton, Hampshire. Lower order batsman, useful bowler. *Team* Hampshire (1906–19, 5 matches).
Career batting
5–8–2–53–22*–8.83–0–*ct* 0
Bowling 185–2–92.50–0–0–2/13

Tollemache, Hon Mortimer Granville
Amateur. *b:* 12.4.1872, Westminster, London. *d:* 27.3.1950, Sudbury, Suffolk. Nephew of Lord Garlies (MCC), brother-in-law of J. R. Head (Middlesex). Middle order right-hand batsman. *Sch* Eton. *Team* Cambridge U (1891–93).
Career batting
9–16–1–151–28–10.06–0–*ct* 10

His County cricket was for Cheshire and Suffolk (1902).

Toller, Montagu Henry
Amateur. *b:* 1.1.1871, Barnstaple, Devon. *d:* 5.8.1948, Meon Beach, Titchfield, Hampshire. Middle order right-hand batsman, right-arm fast bowler. *Sch* Blundells. *Team* Somerset (1897, 6 matches).
Career batting
6–11–1–77–17–7.70–0–*ct* 1
Bowling 15–1–15.00–0–0–1/15

He also played for Devon (1899). He played in the 1900 Olympic cricket match, winning a gold medal.

Tolley, Christopher Mark
Cricketer. *b:* 30.12.1967, Kidderminster, Worcestershire. Lower order right-hand batsman, left-arm medium fast bowler. *Team* Worcestershire (1989–92, 33 matches). *Tour* Worcestershire to Zimbabwe 1990/1.
Career batting
33–32–11–432–37–20.57–0–*ct* 14
Bowling 1641–42–39.07–0–0–4/69

Tolley, Robert
Amateur. *b:* 14.3.1849, Radford, Nottingham. *d:* 2.1.1901, Mapperley Park, Nottingham. Steady middle order right-hand batsman, right-hand fast, or slow, round-arm bowler. *Team* Nottinghamshire (1871–78, 29 matches).
Career batting
30–47–3–556–54–12.63–0–*ct* 20
Bowling 98–0

Tomblin, Charles Bryan
Professional. *b:* 29.6.1891, Walgrave, Brixworth, Northamptonshire. *d:* 1.6.1916, near Sissonne, France. He was declared officially dead two years later. Middle order batsman. *Team* Northamptonshire (1914, 2 matches).
Career batting
2–4–0–8–3–2.00–0–*ct* 2

Tomkins, Eric Feltham
Amateur. *b:* 18.12.1892, Rushden, Northamptonshire. *d:* 20.7.1980, Rushden, Northamptonshire. Middle order right-hand batsman. *Team* Northamptonshire (1920–21, 13 matches).
Career batting
13–22–2–204–50*–10.20–0–*ct* 3

Tomkinson, Francis Martin
Amateur. *b:* 21.10.1883, Franche Hall, Kidderminster, Worcestershire. *d:* 24.11.1963, Chilton, Cleobury Mortimer, Shropshire. Brother of G. S. (Worcestershire). Middle order right-hand batsman. *Sch* Eton. *Team* Worcestershire (1902, 1 match).
Career batting
1–1–0–0–0–0.00–0–*ct* 1

Tomkinson, Sir Geoffrey Stewart
Amateur. *b:* 7.11.1881, Franche Hall, Kidderminster, Worcestershire. *d:* 8.2.1963, Kidderminster, Worcestershire. Brother of F. M. (Worcestershire). Middle order batsman. *Sch* Winchester. *Team* Worcestershire (1903–26, 2 matches).
Career batting
2–3–0–12–10–4.00–0–*ct* 0

He did not appear in any first-class matches whilst at Cambridge. From 1956 to 1958 he was President of

Worcestershire CCC. A noted rugby footballer, he captained Kidderminster RFC.

Tomkinson, Robert Edward
Amateur. *b:* 14.8.1847, Willington Hall, Chester, Cheshire. *d:* 27.7.1928, Burnham-on-Sea, Somerset. Uncle of J. E. (Oxford U Authentics in India). Robust opening right-hand batsman. *Sch* Marlborough. *Team* MCC (1873).
Career batting
3–6–1–81–52–16.20–0–*ct* 3
His County cricket was for Cheshire (1867–73).

Tomlin, William
Professional. *b:* 15.9.1866, Broughton Astley, Leicestershire. *d:* 11.5.1910, Leicester. He died of cancer. Graceful middle order right-hand batsman, right-arm medium pace bowler, good field. *Team* Leicestershire (1894–99, 68 matches).
Career batting
68–127–11–2353–140–20.28–4–*ct* 30
Bowling 346–8–43.25–0–0–3/49
His best season was 1895 when he scored 787 runs, av 23.14. He first played for Leicestershire (pre first-class) in 1887.

Tomlins, Keith Patrick
Cricketer. *b:* 23.10.1957, Kingston-upon-Thames, Surrey. Middle order right-hand batsman, right-arm medium pace bowler. *Teams* Middlesex (1977–85, 84 matches); Gloucestershire (1986–87, 24 matches). *Tours* Middlesex to Zimbabwe 1980/1; Gloucestershire to Sri Lanka 1986/7.
Career batting
108–163–20–3880–146–27.13–5–*ct* 66
Bowling 360–4–90.00–0–0–2/28

Tomlinson, Denis Stanley
Amateur. *b:* 4.9.1910, Umtali, Rhodesia. Brother of R. N. (Rhodesia). Lower order right-hand batsman, leg break and googly bowler. *Teams* Rhodesia (1927/8 to 1947/8); Border (1928/9). *Tour* South Africa to England 1935. *Test* South Africa (1935, 1 match).
Career batting
48–73–19–912–109–16.88–1–*ct* 17
Bowling 4418–156–28.32–9–1–6/56
Test batting
1–1–0–9–9–9.00–0–*ct* 0
Bowling 38–0

Tomlinson, Harry
Professional. *b:* 18.2.1886, Earl Shilton, Leicestershire. *d:* 29.11.1944, Briton Ferry, Glamorgan. Middle order left-hand batsman, off break bowler. *Team* Glamorgan (1921–23, 8 matches).
Career batting
8–16–0–244–36–15.25–0–*ct* 2
Bowling 163–1–163.00–0–0–1/30
He first played for Glamorgan (pre first-class) in 1920.

Tomlinson, Dr John Derek Williams
Amateur. *b:* 26.3.1926, South Normanton, Derbyshire. Middle order right-hand batsman. *Team* Derbyshire (1946, 1 match).
Career batting
1–1–0–2–2–2.00–0–*ct* 1
He played no first-class matches whilst at Cambridge U.

Tomlinson, William James Vincent
Amateur. *b:* 10.8.1901, Winshill, Burton-on-Trent, Staffordshire. *d:* 16.5.1984, Elsing, Norfolk. Middle order right-hand batsman, right-arm medium pace bowler. *Sch* Felsted. *Teams* Derbyshire (1920–24, 26 matches); Cambridge U (1922–23, blue 1923).
Career batting
38–65–8–852–66–14.94–0–*ct* 10
Bowling 1870–58–32.24–1–0–5/53

Tompkin, Maurice
Professional. *b:* 17.2.1919, Countesthorpe, Leicestershire. *d:* 27.9.1956, Leicester. He died following an operation. Polished middle order right-hand batsman. *Team* Leicestershire (1938–56, 349 matches). *Tour* MCC to Pakistan 1955/6.
Career batting
378–655–29–19927–186–31.83–31–*ct* 113
Bowling 106–1–106.00–0–0–1/1
He hit 1,000 runs in a season ten times, going to 2,000 once: 2,190, av 37.11, in 1955. A useful soccer player, he appeared for Leicester City, Bury and Huddersfield at either outside or inside right.

Tonge, John Norton
Amateur. *b:* 9.7.1865, Otford, Kent. *d:* 8.7.1903, Morants Court, Chevening, Kent. Brother of W. C. (Gloucestershire), father-in-law of W. T. Brooks (Leveson-Gower's XI). Sound middle order right-hand batsman, bowler. *Sch* Cheltenham. *Team* Kent (1884–97, 36 matches). *Tour* Warner to USA 1897.
Career batting
38–68–3–895–60–13.76–0–*ct* 7
Bowling 356–9–39.55–0–0–3/14

Tonge, William Corrie
Amateur. *b:* 14.4.1862, Starborough, Dormans Land, Surrey. *d:* 2.5.1943, Fulmer, Buckinghamshire. Brother of J. N. (Kent). Middle order right-hand batsman, right-arm medium pace bowler, good field. *Sch* Tonbridge and Cheltenham. *Team* Gloucestershire (1880, 2 matches).
Career batting
2–2–0–8–5–4.00–0–*ct* 0
He also played for Norfolk (1895–96).

Tongue, Christopher Hugh
Cricketer. *b:* 2.4.1943, Uppingham, Rutland. Middle order right-hand batsman, off break bowler. *Sch*

Toogood, Dr Giles John

Kingswood, Bath. *Team* Cambridge U (1963).
Career batting
1–2–0–20–13–10.00–0–*ct* 0
Bowling 23–0
His first ball in first-class cricket was hit for six by C. C. Inman (Leicestershire).

Toogood, Dr Giles John
Cricketer. *b:* 19.11.1961, West Bromwich, Staffordshire. Middle order right-hand batsman, off break, later medium pace bowler. *Team* Oxford U (1982–89, blue 1982–85).
Career batting
34–57–6–1403–149–27.50–2–*ct* 11
Bowling 1182–26–45.46–1–1–8/52
He captained Oxford in 1985. In the 1985 University match he scored 149 and took 10 for 93. He reappeared for the university in emergency in 1989, having left in 1985. His County cricket was for Shropshire (1991–92).

Toogood, Thomas Hector
Professional. *b:* 29.12.1872, Clifton, Bristol. *d:* 23.9.1953, Stapleton, Bristol. Lower order right-hand batsman, right-arm slow medium bowler. *Team* Gloucestershire (1900–14, 8 matches).
Career batting
8–11–3–30–12–3.75–0–*ct* 5
Bowling 488–16–30.50–1–0–6/115

Tooker, E. W.
(*see under* Whalley-Tooker, E.)

Toole, Charles Laurence
Cricketer. *b:* 9.1.1939, Paddington, London. Middle order right-hand batsman, right-arm medium fast bowler. *Team* MCC (1967). *Tour* MCC to Bangladesh 1978/9 (not first-class).
Career batting
1–2–0–78–54–39.00–0–*ct* 0
Bowling 56–1–56.00–0–0–1/31

Tooley, Christopher Donald Michael
Cricketer. *b:* 19.4.1964, Bromley, Kent. Middle order right-hand batsman, right-arm medium pace bowler. *Sch* St Dunstan's. *Team* Oxford U (1985–87, blue all three years).
Career batting
25–36–2–667–66–19.61–0–*ct* 10
Bowling 37–2–18.50–0–0–1/16
He captained Oxford in 1987.

Toon, James Harry Cecil
Amateur. *b:* 17.1.1916, Oundle, Northamptonshire. *d:* 26.12.1987, Wellingborough, Northamptonshire. Lower order batsman, useful bowler. *Sch* Oundle. *Team* Northamptonshire (1946, 1 match).
Career batting
1–2–0–1–1–0.50–0–*ct* 0
Bowling 126–4–31.50–0–0–3/79

Toon, Joseph
Professional. *b:* 5.6.1879, Ratby, Leicestershire. *d:* 7.3.1950, Braunstone, Leicestershire. Lower order right-hand batsman, right-arm medium pace bowler. *Team* Leicestershire (1902–09, 10 matches).
Career batting
10–19–4–159–39–10.60–0–*ct* 6
Bowling 477–10–47.70–0–0–4/114

Toone, Percy
Professional. *b:* 27.7.1883, Colchester, Essex. *d:* 4.2.1955, Isleworth, Middlesex. Lower order right-hand batsman, right-arm fast bowler. *Team* Essex (1912–22, 29 matches).
Career batting
29–42–13–215–24–7.41–0–*ct* 23
Bowling 1954–62–31.51–2–1–6/51
He was a first-class umpire (1930).

Tootell, Dr Edward
Amateur. *b:* 22.11.1849, Thurnham, Maidstone, Kent. *d:* 20.3.1878, Mitri, Sind, India. Middle order right-hand batsman, right-arm medium pace bowler. *Sch* Chatham House. *Team* Kent (1872, 3 matches).
Career batting
3–6–0–42–24–7.00–0–*ct* 2
Bowling 55–2–27.50–0–0–1/27

Topham, Rev Harry Gillespie
Amateur. *b:* 17.2.1862, Ladbroke, Warwickshire. *d:* 28.2.1925, Middleham, Yorkshire. Lower order left-hand batsman, slow left-arm bowler, good slip field. *Sch* Repton. *Teams* Derbyshire (1881, 1 match); Cambridge U (1883–84, blue both years).
Career batting
16–28–12–95–12–5.93–0–*ct* 15
Bowling 1120–60–18.66–4–1–7/62

Topham, Robert Denham Nigel
Cricketer. *b:* 17.7.1952, Trowbridge, Wiltshire. Middle order right-hand batsman. *Sch* Shrewsbury. *Team* Oxford U (1976, blue).
Career batting
4–7–1–91–31–15.16–0–*ct* 2

Topley, Peter Aland
Cricketer. *b:* 29.8.1950, Canterbury, Kent. Brother of T. D. (Surrey and Essex). Lower order right-hand batsman, slow left-arm bowler. *Team* Kent (1972–75, 18 matches).
Career batting
19–19–4–184–38*–12.26–0–*ct* 19
Bowling 741–15–49.40–0–0–2/28

Topley, Thomas Donald
Cricketer. *b:* 25.2.1964, Canterbury, Kent. Brother of P. A. (Kent). Lower order right-hand batsman, right-arm medium fast bowler. *Teams* Surrey (1985, 1 match); Essex (1985–92, 104 matches); Griqualand West (1987/8).

Career batting
111–125–28–1536–66–15.83–0–*ct* 67
Bowling 9473–351–26.98–15–2–7/75

He took 77 wickets, av 24.03, in 1989. He had the curious experience of playing first-class cricket for both Surrey and Essex in 1985. He also played for Norfolk (1984–85). He was coach to the Zimbabwe team in the 1991/2 World Cup.

Toppin, Charles
Amateur. *b:* 9.8.1864, Musgrave Hall, Skelton, Cumberland. *d:* 8.6.1928, Great Malvern, Worcestershire. Father of C. G. (Worcestershire) and J. F. T. (Worcestershire), brother-in-law of A. P. Day (Kent), S. E. Day (Kent) and S. H. Day (Kent), father-in-law of B. C. B. Brooke (Royal Navy). Lower order right-hand batsman, right-arm fast bowler, good field. *Sch* Sedbergh. *Team* Cambridge U (1885–87, blue all three years).
Career batting
25–40–4–319–39–8.86–0–*ct* 14
Bowling 2059–81–25.41–2–0–7/51

His County cricket was for Cumberland (1884–87) and Worcestershire (pre first-class, 1888–91). His final first-class match was for MCC in 1891. A master at Malvern College for 42 years, he was in charge of cricket there for 37 years and to him belongs the credit for developing a great many cricketers who subsequently became famous.

Toppin, Charles Graham
Amateur. *b:* 17.4.1906, Great Malvern, Worcestershire. *d:* 20.5.1972, Leamington Spa, Warwickshire. Son of Charles (Cambridge U), brother of J. F. T. (Worcestershire), nephew of A. P. Day (Kent), S. E. Day (Kent) and S. H. Day (Kent), brother-in-law of B. C. B. Brooke (Royal Navy). Attacking middle order right-hand batsman, off break bowler. *Sch* Malvern. *Team* Worcestershire (1927–28, 4 matches).
Career batting
4–5–0–17–10–3.40–0–*ct* 0

He lost the sight of one eye at the age of 14, when hit by a ball.

Toppin, John Fallowfield Townsend
Amateur. *b:* 25.2.1900, Great Malvern, Worcestershire. *d:* 22.11.1965, Ascot, Berkshire. Son of Charles (Cambridge U), brother of C. G. (Worcestershire), nephew of A. P. Day (Kent), S. E. Day (Kent) and S. H. Day (Kent), brother-in-law of B. C. B. Brooke (Royal Navy). Lower order right-hand batsman, right-arm medium fast bowler. *Sch* Winchester. *Team* Worcestershire (1920, 1 match).
Career batting
1–2–0–8–6–4.00–0–*ct* 0
Bowling 5–0

Tordoff, George Gerald
Amateur. *b:* 6.12.1929, Whitwood, Yorkshire. Sound middle order left-hand batsman, right-arm medium pace bowler, good field. *Teams* Somerset (1950–55, 54 matches); Cambridge U (1952, blue).
Career batting
85–155–13–3975–156*–27.99–5–*ct* 47
Bowling 1959–40–48.97–0–0–4/43

He captained Somerset in 1955. His final first-class match was for Combined Services in 1962 and he was one of the leading Royal Navy cricketers for some years. He also played for Berkshire (1962). He hit 1,000 runs in a season twice (best 1,196, av 22.56, in 1955). A useful soccer player, he gained his blue at Cambridge.

Torkington, Harold Fleming
Cricketer. *b:* 4.12.1959, Poynton, Cheshire. Middle order right-hand batsman. *Sch* Stockport GS. *Team* Cambridge U (1981).
Career batting
1–2–0–9–9–4.50–0–*ct* 1

Torrens, Attwood Alfred
Amateur. *b:* 13.2.1874, Baston Manor, Hayes, Kent. *d:* 8.12.1916, Pozieres, France. He was killed in action. Brother of W. M. (Kent), son of Alfred (MCC 1855). Middle order right-hand batsman, right-arm medium pace bowler, good deep field. *Sch* Harrow. *Team* MCC (1907). *Tour* MCC to New Zealand 1906/7.
Career batting
9–13–0–183–87–14.07–0–*ct* 2
Bowling 335–11–30.45–0–0–3/41

His final first-class match was for Free Foresters in 1913.

Torrens, Robert
Cricketer. *b:* 17.5.1948, Londonderry, Ireland. Lower order right-hand batsman, right-arm fast medium bowler. *Team* Ireland (1966–82).
Career batting
6–8–1–42–17–6.00–0–*ct* 1
Bowling 402–26–15.46–2–0–7/40

Torrens, William Matt
Amateur. *b:* 19.10.1869, Sundridge Park, Bromley, Kent. *d:* 18.2.1931, Westminster, London. Brother of A. A. (MCC), son of Alfred (MCC 1855). Middle order right-hand batsman, wicket-keeper. *Sch* Harrow. *Team* Kent (1890, 4 matches).
Career batting
4–7–1–86–43–14.33–0–*ct* 2

Tosetti, Gilbert
Amateur. *b:* 1.8.1879, Bromley, Kent. *d:* 16.4.1923, Plateau, Eldoret, Kenya. Middle order right-hand batsman, right-arm medium pace bowler. *Sch* Bancroft's. *Team* Essex (1898–1905, 41 matches).
Career batting
41–63–6–1054–132*–18.49–1–*ct* 15
Bowling 891–16–55.68–0–0–3/67

Toshack, Ernest Raymond Herbert
Amateur. *b:* 8.12.1914, Cobar, New South Wales, Australia. Lower order right-hand batsman, left-arm medium pace bowler. *Team* New South Wales (1945/6 to 1949/50, 21 matches). *Tours* Australia to New Zealand 1945/6, to England 1948. *Tests* Australia (1945/6 to 1948, 12 matches).
Career batting
48–45–13–185–20*–5.78–0–*ct* 10
Bowling 3973–195–20.37–12–1–7/81
Test batting
12–11–6–73–20*–14.60–0–*ct* 4
Bowling 989–47–21.04–4–1–6/29

He broke down with cartilage trouble during the fourth Test of the 1948 tour, but until that point proved a most useful member of the attack, especially used as a bowler keeping down the run rate.

Toulmin, Evelyn Murrough O'Brien
Amateur. *b:* 13.8.1877, Hatfield-Peverel, Essex. *d:* 7.1.1945, Boissiere, Paris, France. Middle order left-hand batsman, slow right-arm bowler. *Sch* King's School, Canterbury. *Teams* Essex (1899–1912, 2 matches); Argentina (1911/12).
Career batting
5–8–0–134–59–16.75–0–*ct* 4
Bowling 250–17–14.70–1–1–6/60

He played in trials at Oxford U, but not in first-class games.

Tovey, Gordon Charles
Amateur. *b:* 4.7.1912, Salisbury, Wiltshire. Middle order right-hand batsman. *Sch* Clifton. *Team* Cambridge U (1933).
Career batting
1–2–0–3–2–1.50–0–*ct* 0

His County cricket was for Dorset (1929–53).

Tovey, Wilson Gardner
Amateur. *b:* 16.10.1874, Cirencester, Gloucestershire. *d:* 4.3.1950, Cirencester, Gloucestershire. Middle order batsman, useful bowler. *Sch* Wellingborough. *Team* Gloucestershire (1901, 1 match).
Career batting
1–2–0–8–8–4.00–0–*ct* 0
Bowling 42–2–21.00–0–0–2/42

Towell, Edgar Fremantle
Amateur. *b:* 5.7.1901, Kettering, Northamptonshire. *d:* 2.6.1972, Kettering, Northamptonshire. Lower order left-hand batsman, right-arm medium fast bowler. *Team* Northamptonshire (1923–34, 70 matches).
Career batting
70–111–17–1199–66–12.75–0–*ct* 11
Bowling 3379–102–33.12–0–0–4/42

Townsend, Alan
Professional. *b:* 26.8.1921, Stockton-on-Tees, Co Durham. Middle order right-hand batsman, right-arm medium pace bowler, good close field. *Team* Warwickshire (1948–60, 340 matches).
Career batting
342–553–70–12054–154–24.95–6–*ct* 413
Bowling 9374–325–28.84–7–1–7/84

He hit 1,000 runs in a season five times (best 1,227, av 29.92, in 1953). He also played for Durham (pre first-class, 1947).

Townsend, Arnold Frederick
Professional. *b:* 29.3.1912, Long Eaton, Derbyshire. Brother of L. F. (Derbyshire). Sound opening right-hand batsman. *Teams* Derbyshire (1934–50, 116 matches); South African Air Force (1942/3).
Career batting
117–200–13–4327–142*–23.13–5–*ct* 30
Bowling 39–0

He hit 1,000 runs in a season twice (best 1,348, av 30.63, in 1947).

Townsend, Arthur Fenton Miles
Amateur. *b:* 1.8.1885, Clifton, Bristol. *d:* 24.8.1948, Brompton, Kensington, London. Son of Frank (Gloucestershire), brother of C. L. (Gloucestershire) and F. N. (Gloucestershire), uncle of D. C. H. (Oxford U) and P. N. (Oxford U), great-uncle of J. R. A. (Oxford U). Middle order right-hand batsman, slow under-arm bowler. *Sch* Blair Lodge. *Teams* Gloucestershire (1903–06, 9 matches); Essex (1910, 1 match).
Career batting
10–14–0–200–28–14.28–0–*ct* 6
Bowling 171–3–57.00–0–0–1/23

Townsend, Charles Lucas
Amateur. *b:* 7.11.1876, Clifton, Bristol. *d:* 17.10.1958, Elton Manor, Stockton-on-Tees, Co Durham. Son of Frank (Gloucestershire), brother of A. F. M. (Gloucestershire and Essex) and F. N. (Gloucestershire), father of D. C. H. (Oxford U) and P. N. (Oxford U), grandfather of J. R. A. (Oxford U). Sound middle order left-hand batsman, leg break bowler, good close field. *Sch* Clifton. *Teams* Gloucestershire (1893–1922, 161 matches); London County (1900). *Tour* Ranjitsinhji to North America 1899. *Tests* England (1899, 2 matches).
Career batting
199–342–28–9512–224*–30.29–21–*ct* 193
Bowling 16761–725–23.11–68–18–9/48
Test batting
2–3–0–51–38–17.00–0–*ct* 0
Bowling 75–3–25.00–0–0–3/50

He created a sensation in 1895, when, on leaving Clifton College, he joined the Gloucestershire Eleven and ended the summer with 131 wickets, av 13.94, making him the bowler of the season. His best year with the ball was 1898 with 145 wickets, av 20.64. Altogether he took 100 wickets in a season four times. He hit 2,440 runs, av 51.91, in 1899, but only exceeded 1,000 runs in two other years. He performed the 'double' in 1898 and 1899. After 1900 he moved to Stockton-on-Tees and his first-class cricket was very limited. His highest score was 224* for Gloucestershire v Essex at Clifton in 1899 and his best bowling 9/48 for Gloucestershire v Middlesex at Lord's in 1898.

Townsend, Christopher James
Cricketer. *b:* 1.12.1972, Wokingham, Berkshire. Lower order right-hand batsman, wicket-keeper. *Sch* Dean Close. *Team* Oxford U (1992, blue).
Career batting
5–4–1–8–8–2.66–0–*ct* 8

Townsend, David Charles Humphery
Amateur. *b:* 20.4.1912, Norton-on-Tees, Co Durham. Son of C. L. (Gloucestershire), grandson of Frank (Gloucestershire), nephew of A. F. M. (Gloucestershire and Essex) and F. N. (Gloucestershire), brother of P. N. (Oxford U), father of J. R. A. (Oxford U). Attractive opening right-hand batsman, right-arm medium pace bowler. *Sch* Winchester. *Team* Oxford U (1933–34, blue both years). *Tours* MCC to West Indies 1934/5; Martineau to Egypt 1936 (not first-class). *Tests* England (1934/5, 3 matches).
Career batting
37–64–2–1801–195–29.04–4–*ct* 16
Bowling 501–6–83.50–0–0–2/31
Test batting
3–6–0–77–36–12.83–0–*ct* 1
Bowling 9–0

His County cricket was for Durham (pre first-class, 1935–50) and his final first-class match for Free Foresters in 1948. He was the last cricketer to play for England without having appeared in the County Championship.

Townsend, Frank
Amateur. *b:* 17.10.1847, Clifton, Bristol. *d:* 25.10.1920, Lambeth, London. Father of A. F. M. (Gloucestershire and Essex), C. L. (Gloucestershire) and F. N. (Gloucestershire); grandfather of D. C. H. (Oxford U) and P. N. (Oxford U), great-grandfather of J. R. A. (Oxford U). Free scoring middle order right-hand batsman, right-hand slow under-arm bowler, good field. *Team* Gloucestershire (1870–91, 169 matches).
Career batting
179–288–19–5110–136–18.99–2–*ct* 131
Bowling 2551–101–25.25–2–0–6/31

Being in the scholastic profession his first-class cricket was restricted mainly to August.

Townsend, Frank Norton
Amateur. *b:* 16.9.1875, Clifton, Bristol. *d:* 25.5.1901, Kimberley, South Africa. Son of Frank (Gloucestershire), brother of A. F. M. (Gloucestershire and Essex) and C. L. (Gloucestershire), uncle of D. C. H. (Oxford U) and P. N. (Oxford U), great-uncle of J. R. A. (Oxford U). Middle order right-hand batsman, wicket-keeper. *Sch* Blair Lodge and Marlborough. *Teams* Gloucestershire (1896–1900, 11 matches); Transvaal (1898/9).
Career batting
12–20–4–230–56–14.37–0–*ct* 13–*st* 3

Townsend, Gareth Terence John
Cricketer. *b:* 28.6.1968, Tiverton, Devon. Opening right-hand batsman. *Sch* Tiverton. *Team* Somerset (1990–92, 12 matches).
Career batting
12–22–2–414–53–20.70–0–*ct* 10

Townsend, Jonathan Richard Arthur
Cricketer. *b:* 30.11.1942, Filkins, Gloucestershire. Great-grandson of Frank (Gloucestershire), grandson of C. L. (Gloucestershire), son of D. C. H. (Oxford U), nephew of P. N. (Oxford U), great-nephew of A. F. M. (Gloucestershire and Essex) and F. N. (Gloucestershire). Middle order right-hand batsman. *Sch* Winchester. *Team* Oxford U (1964–65).
Career batting
10–18–0–245–64–13.61–0–*ct* 1

His County cricket was for Durham (pre first-class, 1964), Wiltshire (1967–68) and Suffolk (1973–75).

Townsend, Leslie Fletcher
Professional. *b:* 8.6.1903, Long Eaton, Derbyshire. Brother of A. F. (Derbyshire). Middle order right-hand batsman, right-arm medium pace off break bowler. *Teams* Derbyshire (1922–39, 446 matches); Auckland (1934/5 to 1935/6). *Tours* MCC to West Indies 1929/30, to India and Ceylon 1933/4. *Tests* England (1929/30 to 1933/4, 4 matches).
Career batting
493–786–75–19555–233–27.50–22–*ct* 237
Bowling 22985–1088–21.12–51–16–8/26
Test batting
4–6–0–97–40–16.16–0–*ct* 2
Bowling 205–6–34.16–0–0–2/22

He hit 1,000 runs in a season nine times, going on to 2,000 once: 2,268, av 44.47, in 1933. He took 100 wickets in a season four times (best 117, av 18.45, in 1932). In the seasons 1928, 1932 and 1933 he performed the 'double'. His only double century was 233 for Derbyshire v Leicestershire at Loughborough in 1933. He also played for Northumberland (1946–48).

Townsend, Peter Norton
Amateur. *b:* 15.2.1910, Norton-on-Tees, Co Durham. Son of C. L. (Gloucestershire), grandson of Frank (Gloucestershire), brother of D. C. H. (Oxford U), nephew of A. F. M. (Gloucestershire and Essex) and F. N. (Gloucestershire), uncle of J. R. A. (Oxford U). Lower order right-hand batsman, leg break bowler.

Townshend, Rev William

Sch Winchester. *Team* Oxford U (1929).
Career batting
2–3–0–16–12–5.33–0–*ct* 1
Bowling 152–3–50.66–0–0–2/18

Townshend, Rev William
Amateur. *b:* 16.11.1849, Sehore, Bhopal, India. *d:* 19.7.1923, Kirkby Mallory, Leicestershire. Attacking middle order right-hand batsman, good long stop. *Sch* Rossall. *Team* Oxford U (1870–72, blue all three years).
Career batting
16–31–2–460–55–15.86–0–*ct* 6

His final first-class match was for MCC in 1874. His County cricket was for Cheshire (1866–78), Denbighshire (1867), Shropshire (1869), Herefordshire (1879) and Leicestershire (pre first-class, 1881–85).

Townsley, Richard Andrew John
Cricketer. *b:* 24.6.1952, Castleford, Yorkshire. Middle order left-hand batsman, right-arm medium pace bowler. *Team* Yorkshire (1974–75, 2 matches).
Career batting
2–4–0–22–12–5.50–0–*ct* 1
Bowling 0–0

He also played for Oxfordshire (1980).

Towse, Anthony David
Cricketer. *b:* 22.4.1968, Bridlington, Yorkshire. Lower order left-hand batsman, right-arm medium fast bowler. *Team* Yorkshire (1988, 1 match).
Career batting
1–1–0–1–1–1.00–0–*ct* 1
Bowling 50–3–16.66–0–0–2/26

Toynbee, Geoffrey Percy Robert
Amateur. *b:* 18.5.1885, Paddington, London. *d:* 15.11.1914, Ploegstraete, Armentieres, France. He was killed in action. Nephew of W. T. (MCC). Opening right-hand batsman. *Sch* Winchester. *Team* Hampshire (1912, 2 matches).
Career batting
3–3–0–18–14–6.00–0–*ct* 1

He made many runs in military matches, first at Sandhurst and later for the Green Jackets.

Toynbee, Walter Turner
Amateur. *b:* 23.12.1852, Lincoln. *d:* 26.12.1930, Hyde Park, London. Uncle of G. P. R. (Hampshire), brother-in-law of A. H. Heath (Gloucestershire and Middlesex) and J. Heath (MCC). Middle order batsman. *Team* MCC (1879).
Career batting
1 match, did not bat–*ct* 0

His County cricket was for Huntingdonshire (1871) and Lincolnshire (1873–83).

Toyne, Stanley Mease
Amateur. *b:* 13.6.1881, Bournemouth, Hampshire. *d:* 22.2.1962, Broxbourne, Hertfordshire. Uncle of H. D. Hake (Hampshire). Middle order right-hand batsman, slow under-arm bowler. *Sch* Haileybury. *Team* Hampshire (1905, 1 match).
Career batting
2–4–1–17–9–5.66–0–*ct* 2

His final first-class appearance was for MCC in 1928, 23 seasons after his previous first-class match. He played in trials at Oxford U, but not in first-class matches.

Tracy, Sean Robert
Cricketer. *b:* 7.6.1963, Auckland, New Zealand. Lower order right-hand batsman, right-arm fast medium bowler. *Teams* Auckland (1982/3 to 1984/5); Gloucestershire (1983, 1 match); Canterbury (1985/6); Otago (1990/1). *Tours* New Zealand to England 1983; Young New Zealand to Zimbabwe 1984/5.
Career batting
30–34–8–124–33–4.76–0–*ct* 7
Bowling 2316–81–28.59–3–0–5/19

He was co-opted into the 1983 New Zealand touring team for two matches.

Traicos, Athanasios John
Cricketer. *b:* 17.5.1947, Zagazig, Egypt. Lower order right-hand batsman, off break bowler, good field. *Team* Rhodesia/Zimbabwe (1967/8 to 1991/2). *Tours* South African Universities to England 1967; South Africa to England 1970 (tour cancelled); Zimbabwe to England 1982, 1983 (World Cup), 1985, 1990, to Sri Lanka 1983/4, to India (World Cup) 1987/8, to Australia and New Zealand (World Cup) 1991/2. *Tests* South Africa (1969/70, 3 matches).
Career batting
116–159–61–1178–43–12.02–0–*ct* 104
Bowling 9189–272–33.78–7–0–6/66
Test batting
3–4–2–8–5*–4.00–0–*ct* 4
Bowling 207–4–51.75–0–0–2/70

He has been the leading off spinner in Zimbabwean cricket since UDI and independence.

Traill, Major General George Balfour
Amateur. *b:* 20.6.1833, Lewisham, London. *d:* 20.11.1913, Battersea Park, London. Brother of W. F. (Kent) and J. C. (Oxford U 1848), brother-in-law of W. W. Hartopp (Gentlemen of England 1857). Middle order batsman. *Team* MCC (1864).
Career batting
1–2–1–5–4–5.00–0–*ct* 0

Traill, William Frederick
Amateur. *b:* 7.1.1838, Lewisham, London. *d:* 3.10.1905, South Hampstead, London. Brother of G. B. (MCC) and J. C. (Oxford U 1848), brother-in-law of W. W. Hartopp (Gentlemen of England 1857). Lower order right-hand batsman, right-hand medium fast round-arm bowler, slip field. *Sch* Merchant Taylors. *Teams* Oxford U (1858–60, blue all three years); Kent (1860–66, 11 matches).

Career batting
35–59–5–541–49–10.01–0–*ct* 17
Bowling 1248–66 + 6–18.90–6–1–6/35

His final first-class match was for the Gentlemen in 1867.

Tranter, Enoch
Professional. *b:* 27.4.1842, Old Park, Shropshire. *d:* 23.9.1910, Donnington Wood, Lilleshall, Shropshire. Lower order left-hand batsman, left-hand fast round-arm bowler. *Team* Lancashire (1875–76, 3 matches).
Career batting
3–5–0–9–5–1.80–0–*ct* 2
Bowling 94–3–31.33–0–0–2/11

He also played for Staffordshire (1873).

Trapnell, Barry Maurice Waller
Amateur. *b:* 18.5.1924, Hampstead, London. Middle order right-hand batsman, right-arm medium pace bowler. *Sch* University College School. *Teams* Cambridge U (1946, blue); Middlesex (1946, 1 match).
Career batting
11–20–3–283–41–16.64–0–*ct* 4
Bowling 621–16–38.81–1–0–5/73

Trask, Dr John Ernest
Amateur. *b:* 27.10.1861, Brympton, Yeovil, Somerset. *d:* 25.7.1896, Kosheh, Sudan. He died of cholera. Cousin of William (Somerset). Attacking middle order right-hand batsman, right-arm medium pace bowler, deep field. *Sch* Somerset College. *Teams* Somerset (1884–95, 9 matches); Europeans (1892/3 to 1894/5).
Career batting
16–29–2–515–78–19.07–0–*ct* 9
Bowling 9–0

He was stationed for 4½ years in India and played a great deal of cricket there, being largely responsible for instituting the inter-Presidency matches. At the time of his death he was a Surgeon-Captain in the Egyptian Army.

Trask, William
Amateur. *b:* 15.7.1859, Norton-sub-Hamdon, Ilminster, Somerset. *d:* 24.6.1949, Frome, Somerset. Cousin of J. E. (Somerset). Stylish middle order right-hand batsman, right-arm slow bowler. *Sch* Sherborne. *Team* Somerset (1882–1900, 47 matches).
Career batting
48–90–5–1225–76–14.41–0–*ct* 20
Bowling 454–12–37.83–0–0–3/33

Travers, Basil Holmes
Amateur. *b:* 7.7.1919, Mosman, Sydney, New South Wales, Australia. Lower order right-hand batsman, right-arm medium pace bowler. *Team* Oxford U (1946–48, blue 1946 and 1948).
Career batting
24–37–9–718–65*–25.64–0–*ct* 27
Bowling 1450–48–30.20–0–0–4/65

His County cricket was for Oxfordshire (1946–47). A noted rugby footballer, he played for Oxford and England.

Travers, Timothy James
Cricketer. *b:* 28.12.1962, Wimbledon, Surrey. Opening right-hand batsman, off break bowler. *Sch* Wimbledon. *Team* Cambridge U (1984).
Career batting
1–2–0–20–15–10.00–0–*ct* 0

Tredcroft, Edward
Amateur. *b:* 15.12.1828, Warnham Court, Horsham, Sussex. *d:* 8.4.1888, Westminster, London. Lower order right-hand batsman, right-hand under-arm fast, or slow, bowler, good long leg. *Sch* Eton. *Team* Sussex (1852–60, 19 matches).
Career batting
53–96–10–759–44*–8.82–0–*ct* 32–*st*1
Bowling 161–5 + 6–32.00–0–0–3/?

His first-class debut was for Gentlemen of England in 1851 and his last first-class match was for MCC in 1865.

Treglown, Claude Jesse Helby
Amateur. *b:* 13.2.1893, Herne Bay, Kent. *d:* 7.5.1980, Worthing, Sussex. Opening or middle order right-hand batsman. *Sch* Norwich. *Team* Essex (1922–28, 34 matches).
Career batting
34–55–3–792–77–15.23–0–*ct* 11

He also played for Norfolk (1910–13).

Trelor, (Arthur) Thomas Edward
Professional. *b:* 29.10.1846, St Austell, Cornwall. Lower order right-hand batsman, right-hand fast round-arm bowler. *Team* Middlesex (1872, 1 match).
Career batting
1–2–0–10–6–5.00–0–*ct* 0
Bowling 27–1–27.00–0–0–1/27

He was best known as the manager and captain of the 'Imperial Clown Cricketers', a travelling team of players who mixed serious cricket with circus tricks. In 1876 he took his team on tour to North America.

Trembath, Christopher Richard
Cricketer. *b:* 27.9.1961, Willesden, Middlesex. Lower order right-hand batsman, right-arm medium pace bowler. *Sch* Dulwich and Clifton. *Team* Gloucestershire (1982–84, 4 matches).
Career batting
4–4–3–33–17*–33.00–0–*ct* 1
Bowling 444–11–40.36–1–0–5/91

He also played for Wiltshire (1985–91).

Tremellen, Jonathon Michael
Cricketer. *b:* 30.10.1965, Pendine, Carmarthenshire. Middle order right-hand batsman, right-arm medium pace bowler. *Sch* Bradfield. *Team* Cambridge U (1986–88, blue 1987–88).

Tremenheere, James Henry Apperley

Career batting
12–20–3–269–39–15.82–0–*ct* 4
Bowling 224–2–112.00–0–0–1/13

He played for Wales in the Minor Counties Championship (1988).

Tremenheere, James Henry Apperley
Amateur. *b:* 30.10.1853, Poona, India. *d:* 28.10.1912, Inglismaldie, Edzell, Kincardine, Scotland. Middle order right-hand batsman, right-hand medium pace round-arm bowler. *Sch* Lancing and Cheltenham. *Team* Gloucestershire (1872, 1 match).
Career batting
1–1–0–7–7–7.00–0–*ct* 0

Tremlett, Major General Erroll Arthur Edwin
Amateur. *b:* 22.12.1893, Brentford, Middlesex. *d:* 24.12.1982, Bickham, Kenn, Devon. Nephew of T. D. (Cambridge U 1853). Middle order right-hand batsman, right-arm medium pace bowler. *Team* MCC (1929–34).
Career batting
2–4–0–35–23–8.75–0–*ct* 1
Bowling 31–1–31.00–0–0–1/1

Tremlett, Maurice Fletcher
Professional. *b:* 5.7.1923, Stockport, Cheshire. *d:* 30.7.1984, Southampton, Hampshire. Father of T. M. (Hampshire). Attacking middle order right-hand batsman, right-arm fast medium bowler. *Teams* Somerset (1947–60, 353 matches); Central Districts (1951/2). *Tours* MCC to West Indies 1947/8, to South Africa 1948/9. *Tests* England (1947/8, 3 matches).
Career batting
389–681–49–16038–185–25.37–16–*ct* 257
Bowling 10778–351–30.70–11–0–8/31
Test batting
3–5–2–20–18*–6.66–*ct* 0
Bowling 226–4–56.50–0–0–2/98

He hit 1,000 runs in a season ten times, going on to 2,000 once: 2,101, av 35.61, in 1951. He captained Somerset 1956 to 1959.

Tremlett, Timothy Maurice
Cricketer. *b:* 26.7.1956, Wellington, Somerset. Son of M. F. (Somerset). Lower order right-hand batsman, right-arm medium pace bowler. *Team* Hampshire (1976–91, 201 matches). *Tours* English Counties to Zimbabwe 1984/5; England B to Sri Lanka 1985/6.
Career batting
207–250–66–3864–102*–21.00–1–*ct* 73
Bowling 10798–450–23.99–11–0–6/53

His best season was 1985 with 75 wickets, av 21.60. He was appointed Hampshire coach in 1992.

Tremlin, Bert
Professional. *b:* 18.9.1877, Bristol, Gloucestershire. *d:* 12.4.1936, Essex. Lower order right-hand batsman, right-arm medium pace bowler. *Team* Essex (1900–19, 132 matches).
Career batting
136–200–64–1843–61–13.55–0–*ct* 64
Bowling 12058–467–25.82–23–4–9/126

His best season was 1914 when he took 101 wickets, av 26.00. His best bowling was 9/126 for Essex v Derbyshire at Leyton in 1905. In 1923 and 1924 he was on the first-class umpires' list.

Trenerry, William Leo
Amateur. *b:* 29.11.1892, Queanbeyan, New South Wales, Australia. *d:* 4.9.1975, Mosman, Sydney, New South Wales, Australia. Brother of Edwin (New South Wales). Opening or middle order right-hand batsman, leg break bowler. *Team* New South Wales (1920/1 to 1924/5, 3 matches). *Tours* AIF to England 1919, to South Africa 1919/20.
Career batting
38–61–3–1547–82–26.67–0–*ct* 22
Bowling 337–10–33.70–0–0–3/28

He proved a sound batsman in 1919 with 961 runs, av 28.26.

Tresawna, Dr William Samson
Amateur. *b:* 14.4.1880, Lamellyn, Probus, Cornwall. *d:* 21.8.1945, Abergavenny, Monmouth. Middle order right-hand batsman. *Team* H. K. Foster's XI (1919).
Career batting
1–2–0–76–55–38.00–0–*ct* 0

His County cricket was for Cornwall (1904–21) and Monmouthshire. He played in trials at Cambridge U, but not in first-class matches.

Trestrail, Alfred Ernest Yates
Amateur. *b:* 24.1.1876, Hallatrow, Somerset. *d:* 5.2.1935, New Milton, Hampshire. Middle order batsman. *Sch* Amersham Hall School. *Team* Somerset (1905, 1 match).
Career batting
1–2–0–7–4–3.50–0–*ct* 0

He did not appear in any first-class matches whilst at Cambridge.

Trestrail, Kenneth Basil
Amateur. *b:* 26.11.1927, Curepipe, Trinidad. *d:* 24.12.1992, Toronto, Ontario, Canada. Brother of A. L. (Trinidad). Attacking middle order right-hand batsman, leg break bowler. *Team* Trinidad (1943/4 to 1949/50). *Tours* West Indies to England 1950; Canada to England 1954.
Career batting
41–65–8–2183–161*–38.29–5–*ct* 22
Bowling 114–4–28.50–0–0–3/20

His opportunities were limited on the 1950 tour and he did not appear in the Tests. In 1954 with the Canadians he scored freely and was the best batsman.

Trevelyan, Robert William Dixey
Cricketer. *b:* 28.11.1970, Folkestone, Kent. Lower order right-hand batsman, wicket-keeper. *Sch* Marlborough. *Team* Oxford U (1990, blue).

Career batting
3–1–0–0–0–0.00–0–*ct* 2

Trevett, John Charles Pullman
Amateur. *b:* 30.7.1942, Woking, Surrey. Lower order right-hand batsman, slow left-arm bowler. *Team* Oxford U (1962).
Career batting
2–3–1–1–1–0.50–0–*ct* 0
Bowling 139–0

Trevor, Arthur Hill
Amateur. *b:* 14.11.1858, Fort William, Calcutta, India. *d:* 27.9.1924, Newton House, Elvanfoot, Lanarkshire, Scotland. Free hitting opening or middle order right-hand batsman, slow under-arm bowler, good deep field. *Sch* Winchester. *Teams* Oxford U (1879–81, blue 1880–81); Sussex (1880–82, 12 matches).
Career batting
31–61–2–1064–103–18.03–1–*ct* 18
Bowling 52–1–52.00–0–0–1/5

His final first-class match was for MCC in 1885. At Twickenham in 1882, he scored 338 for Orleans Club v Rickling Green and with G. F. Vernon added 603 runs for the second wicket.

Trevor, Frederick George Brunton
Amateur. *b:* 28.10.1838, India. *d:* 20.2.1925, Richmond Hill, Surrey. Middle order batsman, useful bowler. *Sch* Marlborough and St Peter's, York. *Team* MCC (1864).
Career batting
1–2–0–12–8–6.00–0–*ct* 0
Bowling 5–0

Trevor, Brigadier General Herbert Edward
Amateur. *b:* 16.12.1871, Paddington, London. *d:* 23.3.1939, Kemp Town, Brighton, Sussex. Middle order batsman. *Sch* Winchester. *Teams* Bombay (1892/3); Sussex (1908, 2 matches).
Career batting
3–6–2–51–22*–12.75–0–*ct* 1

Tribe, George Edward
Professional. *b:* 4.10.1920, Yarraville, Melbourne, Victoria, Australia. Aggressive middle order left-hand batsman, slow left-arm off break and chinaman bowler. *Teams* Victoria (1945/6 to 1946/7, 13 matches); Northamptonshire (1951–59, 233 matches). *Tours* Commonwealth to India, Pakistan and Ceylon 1949/50, to India and Ceylon 1950/1; Howard to India 1956/7; Norfolk to Jamaica 1956/7. *Tests* Australia (1946/7, 3 matches).
Career batting
308–454–82–10177–136*–27.35–7–*ct* 242
Bowling 28321–1378–20.55–93–23–9/43
Test batting
3–3–1–35–25*–17.50–0–*ct* 0
Bowling 330–2–165.00–0–0–2/48

He hit 1,000 runs in a season seven times (best 1,260, av 36.00, in 1953) and took 100 wickets eight times (best 176, av 19.12, in 1955). He completed the 'double' seven times. His best bowling analyses were 9/43 for Northamptonshire v Worcestershire at Northampton in 1958, 9/45 for Victoria v Queensland at Brisbane in 1945/6 and 9/45 for Northamptonshire v Yorkshire at Bradford in 1955.

Trick, Stanley Arthur
Amateur. *b:* 3.6.1884, Stoke Newington, London. *d:* 11.2.1958, Worcester Park, Surrey. Uncle of W. M. S. (Glamorgan). Middle order right-hand batsman. *Sch* Merchant Taylors. *Team* Essex (1905–19, 5 matches).
Career batting
5–9–0–69–26–7.66–0–*ct* 1

Trick, William Mervyn Stanley
Amateur. *b:* 31.10.1916, Briton Ferry, Glamorgan. Nephew of S. A. (Essex). Lower order right-hand batsman, left-arm medium pace spin bowler. *Team* Glamorgan (1946–50, 19 matches).
Career batting
19–22–11–52–15–4.72–0–*ct* 9
Bowling 1087–56–19.41–4–2–6/29

Trim, Geoffrey Edward
Cricketer. *b:* 6.4.1956, Openshaw, Manchester, Lancashire. Middle order right-hand batsman, leg break bowler. *Team* Lancashire (1976–80, 15 matches).
Career batting
15–25–0–399–91–15.96–0–*ct* 10
Bowling 13–0

Trimborn, Patrick Henry Joseph
Cricketer. *b:* 18.5.1940, Glenwood, Durban, South Africa. Father of P. P. H. (Natal). Lower order right-hand batsman, right-arm fast bowler, good close field. *Team* Natal (1961/2 to 1975/6). *Tours* South Africa to England 1970 (tour cancelled), to Australia 1971/2 (tour cancelled). *Tests* South Africa (1966/7 to 1969/70, 4 matches).
Career batting
94–111–37–880–52–11.89–0–*ct* 79
Bowling 7102–314–22.61–12–1–6/36
Test batting
4–4–2–13–11*–6.50–0–*ct* 7
Bowling 257–11–23.36–0–0–3/12

His only appearance in England was for International Cavaliers in 1969.

Tripp, Graham Malcolm
Professional. *b:* 29.6.1932, Clevedon, Somerset. Middle order right-hand batsman, good outfield. *Team* Somerset (1955–59, 34 matches).
Career batting
34–62–7–700–62–12.72–0–*ct* 29
Bowling 10–0

He also played for Devon (1960–64).

Tristram, Henry Barrington
Amateur. *b:* 5.9.1861, Greatham, Co Durham. *d:* 1.10.1946, St Helier, Jersey. Middle order right-hand batsman, right-arm fast bowler, good cover point. *Sch* Loretto and Winchester. *Team* Oxford U (1883).
Career batting
1–2–0–7–6–3.50–0–*ct* 0
His County cricket was for Durham (pre first-class, 1883–93). A noted rugby footballer, he played for Oxford and England.

Tritton, Edward William
Amateur. *b:* 3.8.1844, Marylebone, London. *d:* 1.12.1901, Paignton, Devon. Brother-in-law of J. H. Bridges (Surrey). Sound middle order right-hand batsman. *Sch* Eton. *Teams* Middlesex (1864–67, 6 matches); Oxford U (1864–67, blue all four years).
Career batting
39–65–5–1000–114–16.66–2–*ct* 20
Bowling 50–1–50.00–0–0–1/34
His final first-class match was for MCC in 1875. He appeared for Surrey in 1864 in a non-first-class match. He captained Oxford in 1866. A talented athlete he took part in the 1865 inter-University athletic meeting.

Trodd, Thomas
Professional. *b:* 1852. *d:* 26.7.1908, Macclesfield, Cheshire. Lower order batsman, useful bowler. *Team* Surrey (1879–80, 4 matches).
Career batting
5–10–6–13–5–3.25–0–*ct* 1
Bowling 152–12–12.66–1–0–6/35

Trodd, William
Professional. *c:* 7.8.1836, Stoke-next-Guildford, Surrey. *d:* 9.4.1880, Bow, London. Brother of John (Surrey Club 1855). Middle order batsman, useful bowler. *Team* Surrey (1869, 6 matches).
Career batting
6–11–0–65–16–5.90–0–*ct* 1
Bowling 146–3–48.66–0–0–2/38

Trollope, William Stapleton
Amateur. *b:* 31.7.1854, South Lambeth, London. *d:* 20.9.1895, Bellevue, Southampton, Hampshire. Attacking middle order right-hand batsman, right-hand medium pace round-arm bowler. *Sch* Westminster. *Team* Surrey (1877–82, 7 matches).
Career batting
7–14–0–154–35–11.00–0–*ct* 3
Bowling 99–4–24.75–0–0–2/2

Trott, Albert Edwin
Professional. *b:* 6.2.1873, Abbotsford, Melbourne, Victoria, Australia. *d:* 30.7.1914, Harlesden, Willesden, Middlesex. He shot himself, having been ill for some time with little hope of recovery. Brother of G. H. S. (Victoria). Very hard hitting middle order right-hand batsman, right-arm fast medium or medium pace off break bowler, good field. *Teams* Victoria (1892/3 to 1895/6, 13 matches); Middlesex (1898–1910, 223 matches); London County (1900–04); Hawke's Bay (1901/2). *Tours* Hawke to South Africa 1898/9, to Australia 1902/3 (co-opted). *Tests* Australia (1894/5, 3 matches); England (1898/9, 2 matches).
Career batting
375–602–53–10696–164–19.48–8–*ct* 452
Bowling 35317–1674–21.09–131–41–10/42
Test batting
5–9–3–228–85*–38.00–0–*ct* 4
Bowling 390–26–15.00–2–0–8/43
He hit 1,000 runs in a season twice (best 1,337, av 23.87, in 1900) – in 1899 and 1900 he achieved the feat of 1,000 runs and 200 wickets. In all he took 100 wickets in a season seven times, going on to 200 twice (best 239, av 17.09, in 1899). His best bowling was 10/42 for Middlesex v Somerset in 1900 at Taunton. Disappointed at not being selected to tour England with the 1896 Australians, he paid his own fare and then obtained a position on the ground staff at Lord's. For MCC v Australians in 1899 he hit a ball from M. A. Noble over the pavilion at Lord's. His final first-class match was for MCC in 1911. He was a first-class umpire (1912–14).

Trott, George Henry Stevens
Amateur. *b:* 5.8.1866, Collingwood, Melbourne, Victoria, Australia. *d:* 10.11.1917, Albert Park, Melbourne, Victoria, Australia. Brother of A. E. (Victoria and Middlesex). Excellent opening or middle order right-hand batsman, leg break bowler, good point field. *Team* Victoria (1885/6 to 1907/8, 59 matches). *Tours* Australia to England 1888, 1890, 1893, 1896, to North America 1893, 1896. *Tests* Australia (1888 to 1897/8, 24 matches).
Career batting
222–393–19–8804–186–23.54–9–*ct* 183
Bowling 9699–386–25.12–17–2–8/63
Test batting
24–42–0–921–143–21.92–1–*ct* 21
Bowling 1019–29–35.13–0–0–4/71
He proved a useful all-rounder on each of his tours to England, but his greatest distinction came in 1896 when he proved one of the best of all Australian captains – he was able to inspire even the most despondent of his team. Although Australia lost the 1896 Test series 2 to 1, Trott then led Australia to a 4–1 victory in the 1897/8 series, after which a serious illness compelled him to retire from regular first-class matches. In all he captained Australia in 8 Tests. He hit 1,000 runs in a season four times (best 1,297, av 26.51, in 1896).

Trotter, David North
Amateur. *b:* 24.5.1858, Forkhill, Co Down, Ireland. *d:* 17.3.1912, Dublin, Ireland. Middle order right-hand batsman, good point. *Team* North of England

(1877). *Tours* Gentlemen of Ireland to North America 1879 (not first-class).
Career batting
1–2–0–42–33–21.00–0–*ct* 1
He played for Ireland 1875 to 1890 (not first-class).

Troughton, Lionel Holmes Wood
Amateur. *b:* 17.5.1879, Seaford, Sussex. *d:* 31.8.1933, Southwark, London. Cousin of M. A. (Kent). Resolute middle order right-hand batsman, right-arm medium pace bowler, good field. *Sch* Dulwich. *Team* Kent (1907–23, 164 matches). *Tour* MCC to Argentine 1911/12.
Career batting
180–265–31–4013–104–17.14–1–*ct* 80
Bowling 20–0
He captained Kent 1914 to 1923 and from 1924 to his death was General Manager of the County Club.

Troughton, Medhurst Albert
Amateur. *b:* 25.12.1839, Milton-next-Gravesend, Kent. *d:* 1.1.1912, Campden Hill, London. Cousin of L. H. W. (Kent). Middle order right-hand batsman, right-hand slow round-arm or under-arm bowler, occasional wicket-keeper. *Team* Kent (1864–73, 39 matches).
Career batting
46–84–11–1197–87–16.39–0–*ct* 33
Bowling 218–10–21.80–1–0–5/70
His first-class debut was for Gentlemen of Kent in 1862.

Trouncer, Charles Albert
Amateur. *b:* 14.8.1866, Uckfield, Sussex. *d:* 13.3.1938, Benllech Bay, Anglesey. Opening left-hand batsman, left-arm medium pace bowler, wicket-keeper. *Sch* Cranbrook. *Teams* Cambridge U (1887–88); Surrey (1888, 3 matches).
Career batting
9–16–2–205–30*–14.64–0–*ct* 8
Bowling 54–0
His final first-class match was for Oxford and Cambridge, Past and Present v Australians in 1890.

Troup, Frank Colin
Amateur. *b:* 27.9.1896, Mussoorie, India. *d:* 19.1.1924, Murray Bridge, South Australia. He died in a motor accident. Son of Walter (Gloucestershire). Middle order right-hand batsman. *Sch* Cheltenham and Brighton. *Team* Gloucestershire (1914–21, 3 matches).
Career batting
3–5–0–10–7–2.00–0–*ct* 0

Troup, Gary Bertram
Cricketer. *b:* 3.10.1952, Taumarunui, Auckland, New Zealand. Lower order right-hand batsman, left-arm fast medium bowler. *Team* Auckland (1974/5 to 1986/7). *Tours* Robins to South Africa 1975/6; New Zealand to India and Pakistan 1976/7, to England 1978, 1979 (World Cup), to Australia 1980/1, 1982/3, to West Indies 1984/5. *Tests* New Zealand (1976/7 to 1985/6, 15 matches).
Career batting
100–115–39–925–60*–12.17–0–*ct* 39
Bowling 7541–272–27.72–5–1–6/48
Test batting
15–18–6–55–13*–4.58–0–*ct* 2
Bowling 1454–39–37.28–1–1–6/95
He was co-opted into the 1978 team to England for one match.

Troup, Walter
Amateur, *b:* 16.10.1869, Meerut, India. *d:* 14.12.1940, Isleworth, Middlesex. Father of F. C. (Gloucestershire). Defensive middle order right-hand batsman, good cover point. *Teams* Gloucestershire (1887–1911, 80 matches); All India (1892/3); Gentlemen of India (1902/3).
Career batting
85–144–15–3366–180–26.09–7–*ct* 26
Bowling 4–0
He hit 1,073 runs, av 29.00, in 1899. He took over as Gloucestershire captain in 1899 when W. G. Grace resigned.

Trubshaw, Ernest Brian
Amateur. *b:* 29.1.1924, Liverpool, Lancashire. Middle order right-hand batsman. *Sch* Winchester. *Team* RAF (1946).
Career batting
1–2–0–2–1–1.00–0–*ct* 0
He was a noted test pilot, and among the aircraft with which he was concerned was the Concorde.

Trueman, Frederick Sewards, OBE
Professional. *b:* 6.2.1931, Stainton, Yorkshire. Hard hitting lower order right-hand batsman, aggressive right-arm fast bowler. *Team* Yorkshire (1949–68, 459 matches). *Tours* MCC to West Indies 1953/4, 1959/60, to Australia and New Zealand 1958/9, 1962/3; Howard to India 1956/7; Cavaliers to South Africa 1960/1, to Jamaica 1963/4, 1964/5; Yorkshire to North America 1964 (not first-class); Prime Minister's XI in India 1967/8. *Tests* England (1952–65, 67 matches).
Career batting
603–713–120–9231–104–15.56–3–*ct* 439
Bowling 42154–2304–18.29–126–25–8/28
Test batting
67–85–14–981–39*–13.81–0–*ct* 64
Bowling 6625–307–21.57–17–3–8/31
A fast bowler whose belligerence made him the most feared by batsmen in England in the 1950s and early 1960s, Trueman took 29 wickets in his first Test series v India in 1952 and finally ended his international career with a record (since broken) of 307 Test wickets. His reputation for being difficult to handle and outspoken caused him to miss a number of Tests,

however. He took 100 wickets in a season 12 times with 175, av 13.98, in 1960 best. Of his four hat-tricks in first-class cricket, curiously three were for Yorkshire against Nottinghamshire. His best bowling was 8/28 for Yorkshire v Kent at Dover in 1954, all the wickets being taken before lunch on the first day. His last first-class appearance was for Cavaliers in 1969.

After leaving Yorkshire, he played for Derbyshire in Sunday League matches in 1972 and has since become a regular commentator on cricket and a notable after-dinner speaker.

Truman, Thomas Archibald
Amateur. *b:* 29.12.1880, Newton Abbot, Devon. *d:* 14.9.1918, No. 1 Canadian Casualty Clearing Station, near Etrun, France. He died of pneumonia. Middle order batsman, useful bowler. *Team* Gloucestershire (1910–13, 4 matches).
Career batting
4–8–2–39–12*–6.50–0–*ct* 5
Bowling 11–1–11.00–0–0–1/10

Trumble, Frederick Hugh Geoffrey
Amateur. *b:* 9.10.1893, Brading, Isle of Wight. *d:* 10.5.1918, at sea on board HMS *Warwick*. Middle order right-hand batsman. *Team* Royal Navy (1914).
Career batting
1–2–0–8–8–4.00–0–*ct* 0

Trumble, Hugh
Amateur. *b:* 12.5.1867, Abbotsford, Melbourne, Victoria, Australia. *d:* 14.8.1938, Hawthorn, Melbourne, Victoria, Australia. Brother of J. W. (Victoria). Middle order right-hand batsman, right-arm medium pace off break bowler, good slip field. *Team* Victoria (1887/8 to 1903/4, 47 matches). *Tours* Australia to England 1890, 1893, 1896, 1899, 1902, to North America 1893, 1896, to South Africa 1902/3. *Tests* Australia (1890 to 1903/4, 32 matches).
Career batting
213–344–67–5395–107–19.47–3–*ct* 328
Bowling 17134–929–18.44–69–25–9/39
Test batting
32–57–14–851–70–19.79–0–*ct* 45
Bowling 3072–141–21.78–9–3–8/65

Except on his first visit in 1890, he was most successful in England, and his record reads: 1893, 108 wickets, av 16.61; 1896, 148, 15.81; 1899, 142, 18.43; and 1902, 137, 14.02. In 1899 he hit 1,183 runs, av 27.51, thus completing the 'double' that season. His best bowling was 9/39 for Australians v South of England at Bournemouth in 1902. In 1912 he was appointed Secretary of Melbourne CC, a position he held for some 20 years. He captained Australia in two Tests.

Trumble, John William
Amateur. *b:* 16.9.1863, Kew, Melbourne, Victoria, Australia. *d:* 17.8.1944, Brighton, Melbourne, Victoria, Australia. Brother of Hugh (Victoria). Stylish middle order right-hand batsman, off break bowler. *Teams* Victoria (1883/4 to 1889/90, 18 matches); Gentlemen of England (1893). *Tour* Australia to England 1886. *Tests* Australia (1884/5 to 1886, 7 matches).
Career batting
63–104–11–1761–87–18.93–0–*ct* 33
Bowling 2627–109–24.10–5–1–6/33
Test batting
7–13–1–243–59–20.25–0–*ct* 3
Bowling 222–10–22.20–0–0–3/29

He had only modest all-round success on the 1886 tour. In 1893 on a visit to England he played in some first-class matches.

Trump, Harvey Russell John
Cricketer. *b:* 11.10.1968, Taunton, Somerset. Lower order right-hand batsman, off break bowler. *Sch* Millfield. *Team* Somerset (1988–92, 65 matches).
Career batting
66–66–18–429–48–8.93–0–*ct* 42
Bowling 6033–158–38.21–6–1–7/52

Trumper, Victor Thomas
Amateur. *b:* 2.11.1877, Darlinghurst, Sydney, New South Wales, Australia. *d:* 28.6.1915, Darlinghurst, Sydney, New South Wales, Australia. He died of Bright's disease. Father of Victor (New South Wales), he married sister-in-law of J. J. Kelly (Australia). Brilliant opening right-hand batsman, right-arm medium pace bowler. *Team* New South Wales (1894/5 to 1913/14, 73 matches). *Tours* Australia to England 1899, 1902, 1905, 1909, to South Africa 1902/3, to New Zealand 1904/5, 1913/14. *Tests* Australia (1899 to 1911/12, 48 matches).
Career batting
255–401–21–16939–300*–44.57–42–*ct* 171
Bowling 2008–64–31.37–2–0–5/19
Test batting
48–89–8–3163–214*–39.04–8–*ct* 31
Bowling 317–8–39.62–0–0–3/60

Regarded by his contemporaries as the greatest of all Australian batsmen, his form in England, with the exception of the 1902 season, cannot be compared with that of Bradman. He reached 2,000 runs only in 1902 – 2,570, av 48.49 – and scored over 1,000 on each of the three other visits. In 1905 he was most disappointing, failing completely in the Tests. His highest score in England was 300* v Sussex at Hove in 1899, but none of his other seven double centuries was hit in England. He also hit 1,246, av 69.22, in Australia in 1910/11.

Truswell, John Richard
Amateur. *b:* 14.1.1841, Farnsfield, Nottinghamshire. *d:* 6.8.1892, Farnsfield, Nottinghamshire. Lower order right-hand batsman, right-hand slow round-arm bowler. *Team* Nottinghamshire (1868, 2 matches).

Career batting
2–4–0–18–9–4.50–0–*ct* 2
Bowling 51–6–8.50–1–0–5/45

Tryon, Richard
Amateur. *b:* 31.8.1837, Bulwick Park, Oundle, Northamptonshire. *d:* 12.12.1905, Marylebone, London. Middle order batsman. *Sch* Harrow. *Team* MCC (1871).
Career batting
1–1–0–7–7–7.00–0–*ct* 1
His County cricket was for Northamptonshire (pre first-class, 1864) and Rutland (1881–83).

Tubb, Henry
Amateur. *b:* 16.6.1851, Bicester, Oxfordshire. *d:* 8.2.1924, Chesterton, Bicester, Oxfordshire. Father-in-law of E. C. Mordaunt (Middlesex and Kent), brother-in-law of W. H. M. Style (Hampshire). Middle order right-hand batsman, right-hand medium pace round-arm bowler. *Sch* Rugby. *Team* MCC (1873–77).
Career batting
5–9–0–93–24–10.33–0–*ct* 2
Bowling 22–0
His County cricket was for Oxfordshire and he captained the team for some years commencing 1894.

Tubb, Sampson
(registered at death as Samson Tubb)
Professional. *b:* 11.10.1840, Broughton, Hampshire. *d:* 27.1.1891, Southsea, Hampshire. Lower order right-hand batsman, left-hand fast round-arm bowler. *Team* Hampshire (1864–67, 10 matches).
Career batting
10–19–5–170–24*–12.14–0–*ct* 5
Bowling 746–37–20.16–2–0–7/32
He also played for Devon (1862) and Wiltshire (1863).

Tuck, George Hustler
Amateur. *b:* 28.4.1843, Norwich, Norfolk. *d:* 13.12.1920, Bracondale, Norwich, Norfolk. Opening or middle order right-hand batsman, wicket-keeper. *Sch* Eton. *Team* Cambridge U (1863–66, blue all four years).
Career batting
18–32–0–375–51–11.71–0–*ct* 9–*st* 1
His County cricket was for Norfolk (1862–72). His final first-class match was for MCC in 1876.

Tuck, Gerald Seymour
Amateur. *b:* 5.5.1902, Hartley Wintney, Hampshire. *d:* 27.7.1984, Chichester, Sussex. Middle order right-hand batsman. *Team* Royal Navy (1927–29).
Career batting
6–10–0–314–125–31.40–1–*ct* 2
His County cricket was for Northumberland (1928). He scored 125 on debut for Royal Navy v New Zealanders at Portsmouth in 1927.

Tuck, James Jeffry
Professional. *b:* 3.6.1853, Ringwood, Hampshire. *d:* 20.1.1918, Devizes, Wiltshire. Solid lower order right-hand batsman, right-hand medium pace round-arm bowler, good cover point. *Team* Hampshire (1877–82, 9 matches).
Career batting
9–17–2–176–32*–11.73–0–*ct* 4
Bowling 36–2–18.00–0–0–1/11
Playing football in the winter of 1882/3, he broke his knee cap and this ended his cricket, but he later became well-known as an umpire (1886–99).

Tuckett, Lindsay
Amateur. *b:* 6.2.1919, Durban North, South Africa. Son of L. R. (South Africa), nephew of J. L. Cox (South Africa). Lower order right-hand batsman, right-arm medium fast bowler. *Team* Orange Free State (1934/5 to 1954/5). *Tour* South Africa to England 1947. *Tests* South Africa (1947 to 1948/9, 9 matches).
Career batting
61–101–16–1496–101–17.60–1–*ct* 38
Bowling 5191–225–23.07–18–2–8/32
Test batting
9–14–3–131–40*–11.90–0–*ct* 9
Bowling 980–19–51.57–2–0–5/68
He began the 1947 tour in good form, and despite a strain proved the best bowler of his type during the season. He played in all five Tests and came second in the Test bowling table with 15 wickets, av 44.26.

Tudor, Claud Lechmere St John
Amateur. *b:* 27.12.1888, Willingdon, Sussex. *d:* 3.8.1977, Halton, Oxford. Brother of R. G. (Sussex). Middle order right-hand batsman. *Sch* Eastbourne. *Team* Sussex (1910–11, 7 matches).
Career batting
19–34–4–640–116–21.33–1–*ct* 12
Bowling 16–0
His final first-class match was for the Army in 1927.

Tudor, Richard Thornhill
Cricketer. *b:* 27.9.1948, Shrewsbury, Shropshire. Lower order right-hand batsman, right-arm medium pace bowler. *Sch* Shrewsbury. *Team* Warwickshire (1976, 1 match).
Career batting
1–1–0–6–6–6.00–0–*ct* 0
Bowling 42–0
He also played for Shropshire (1975–77).

Tudor, Roland Grimston
Amateur. *b:* 4.12.1890, Willingdon, Sussex. *d:* 11.10.1973, Lewes, Sussex. Brother of C. L. St J. (Sussex). Middle order batsman. *Sch* Eastbourne. *Teams* Sussex (1912–19, 3 matches); Cambridge U (1913).

Career batting
5–10–1–94–25*–10.44–0–*ct* 2

Tudway, Hervey Robert Charles
Amateur. *b:* 23.9.1888, Westminster, London. *d:* 18.11.1914, Boulogne, France. Grandson of F. T. A. Hervey-Bathurst (Hampshire), great-grandson of F. H. Hervey-Bathurst (Hampshire). Middle order batsman. *Sch* Eton. *Team* Somerset (1910, 1 match).
Career batting
1–2–0–12–6–6.00–0–*ct* 0

Tuff, Frank Noel
Amateur. *b:* 26.11.1889, Rochester, Kent. *d:* 5.11.1915, Imtarfa, Malta. He died of wounds. Lower order right-hand batsman, right-arm medium fast bowler. *Sch* Malvern. *Team* Oxford U (1910–11, blue 1910).
Career batting
11–20–7–190–35–14.61–0–*ct* 6
Bowling 670–25–26.80–2–0–7/47
His final first-class match was for Free Foresters in 1914. He also won a blue for soccer and played for Corinthians.

Tufnell, Carleton Fowell
Amateur. *b:* 20.2.1856, Northfleet, Kent. *d:* 26.5.1940, Chelsea, London. Father of N. C. (Surrey). Middle order right-hand batsman, right-hand slow or medium pace round-arm bowler, good slip. *Sch* Eton. *Team* Kent (1878–79, 7 matches).
Career batting
8–13–3–108–26–10.80–0–*ct* 2
Bowling 285–15–19.00–0–0–3/31

Tufnell, Neville Charsley
Amateur. *b:* 13.6.1887, Simla, India. *d:* 3.8.1951, Whitechapel, London. Son of C. F. (Kent), son-in-law of C. F. C. Clarke (Surrey). Lower order right-hand batsman, right-arm slow bowler, wicket-keeper. *Sch* Eton. *Teams* Cambridge U (1908–10, blue 1909–10); Surrey (1922, 1 match). *Tours* MCC to New Zealand 1906/7, to South Africa 1909/10, to Argentina 1911/12. *Test* England (1909/10, 1 match).
Career batting
70–120–14–1514–102–14.28–1–*ct* 59–*st* 40
Bowling 118–1–118.00–0–0–1/54
Test batting
1–1–0–14–14–14.00–0–*ct* 0–*st* 1
His first-class debut in England was for MCC in 1907. His final first-class match was for Free Foresters in 1924. He also played for Norfolk (1924–25).

Tufnell, Philip Clive Roderick
Cricketer. *b:* 29.4.1966, Barnet, Hertfordshire. Lower order right-hand batsman, slow left-arm bowler. *Sch* Highgate. *Team* Middlesex (1986–92, 97 matches). *Tours* England to Australia 1990/1, 1991/2 (World Cup), to New Zealand 1990/1 (not first-class), 1991/2. *Tests* England (1990/1 to 1992, 10 matches).
Career batting
114–113–45–722–37–10.61–0–*ct* 49
Bowling 11975–377–31.76–19–2–7/47
Test batting
10–13–8–23–8–4.60–0–*ct* 4
Bowling 1091–38–28.71–4–1–7/47
He took 88 wickets, av 25.21, in 1991. The most promising slow left-arm bowler of his generation, his early career in Test and County cricket has sometimes been overshadowed by his temperament.

Tufton, Hon John Sackville Richard
(succeeded to the title 2nd Lord Hothfield in 1926)
Amateur. *b:* 8.11.1873, Hothfield Place, Ashford, Kent. *d:* 21.12.1952, Bayswater, London. Middle order right-hand batsman. *Sch* Eton. *Team* Kent (1897–98, 8 matches).
Career batting
13–19–2–243–33*–14.29–0–*ct* 5
His final first-class match was for MCC in 1899.

Tuke, Dr Charles Molesworth
Amateur. *b:* 23.5.1857, Chiswick, Middlesex. *d:* 24.1.1925, Chiswick, Middlesex. Lower order right-hand batsman, right-arm fast bowler. *Sch* Merchant Taylor's. *Team* Middlesex (1882, 7 matches).
Career batting
8–12–4–29–8–3.62–0–*ct* 4
Bowling 505–15–33.66–0–0–3/38
His final first-class match was for the Gentlemen in 1890.

Tulk, Derek Thomas
Professional. *b:* 21.4.1934, Southampton, Hampshire. Lower order right-hand batsman, right-arm medium pace bowler. *Team* Hampshire (1956–57, 2 matches).
Career batting
2–2–2–8–8*–no av–0–*ct* 1
Bowling 70–0

Tunnicliffe, Colin John
Cricketer. *b:* 11.8.1951, Derby. Lower order right-hand batsman, left-arm fast medium bowler. *Team* Derbyshire (1973–83, 150 matches).
Career batting
150–176–30–2092–91–14.32–0–*ct* 65
Bowling 10265–319–32.17–6–0–7/36

Tunnicliffe, Howard Trevor
Cricketer. *b:* 4.3.1950, Derby. Middle or lower order right-hand batsman, right-arm medium pace bowler. *Sch* Malvern. *Team* Nottinghamshire (1973–80, 65 matches).
Career batting
65–110–27–2116–100*–25.49–1–*ct* 37
Bowling 1601–42–38.11–0–0–4/30

Tunnicliffe, John
Professional. *b:* 26.8.1866, Low Town, Pudsey, Yorkshire. *d:* 11.7.1948, Westbury Park, Bristol. Attacking opening right-hand batsman, slow right-

arm bowler, brilliant slip field, occasional wicket-keeper. *Team* Yorkshire (1891–1907, 475 matches).
Career batting
498–811–59–20310–243–27.00–23–*ct* 695
Bowling 405–7–57.85–0–0–1/6

He hit 1,000 runs in a season 12 times (best 1,804, av 41.00, in 1898). His only double century was 243 for Yorkshire v Derbyshire at Chesterfield in 1898, when together with J. T. Brown he added a record 554 for the first wicket. Altogether he and J. T. Brown realised 26 century first-wicket partnerships. After retiring he was coach at Clifton College and later a member of Gloucestershire CCC Committee, his son being the Secretary of the County Club.

Tuppin, Alfred George
Professional. *b:* 17.12.1911, Brighton, Sussex. Lower order right-hand batsman, right-arm medium pace bowler. *Team* Sussex (1935–39, 23 matches).
Career batting
23–31–6–294–31*–11.76–0–*ct* 11
Bowling 1626–56–29.03–4–0–5/30

Turland, Herbert
Professional. *b:* 29.8.1894, Stapleford, Nottinghamshire. *d:* 23.5.1973, Illogan North, Redruth, Cornwall. Middle order right-hand batsman, left-arm medium pace bowler. *Teams* Derbyshire (1921, 1 match); Nottinghamshire (1924, 1 match).
Career batting
2–4–0–30–29–7.50–0–*ct* 0
Bowling 14–0

Turnbull, Bertrand
Amateur. *b:* 19.4.1887, Cardiff, Glamorgan. *d:* 17.11.1943, Canton, Cardiff, Glamorgan. Middle order batsman, wicket-keeper. *Team* Gloucestershire (1911, 1 match).
Career batting
1–2–1–35–28*–35.00–0–*ct* 0–*st* 1

He also played for Glamorgan (pre first-class, 1911–14). He was Glamorgan Chairman 1928–39.

Turnbull, Charles Lane
Amateur. *b:* 25.2.1851, Kingsholm, Gloucester. *d:* 24.3.1920, Swindon, Wiltshire. Middle order batsman. *Team* Gloucestershire (1873, 1 match).
Career batting
1–1–0–0–0–0.00–0–*ct* 0

Turnbull, Jonathan Richard
Cricketer. *b:* 13.11.1962, Northwood, Middlesex. Lower order right-hand batsman, right-arm medium pace bowler. *Sch* Merchant Taylors. *Team* Oxford U (1983–84).
Career batting
12–16–7–17–6–1.88–0–*ct* 8
Bowling 778–15–51.86–0–0–4/51

Turnbull, Maurice Joseph Lawson
Amateur. *b:* 16.3.1906, Cardiff, Glamorgan. *d:* 5.8.1944, near Montchamp, France. He was killed in action. Brother-in-law of E. R. K. Glover (Glamorgan). Attractive middle order right-hand batsman. *Sch* Downside. *Teams* Glamorgan (1924–39, 314 matches); Cambridge U (1926–29, blue 1926, 1928 and 1929); Wales (1928). *Tours* MCC to Australia and New Zealand 1929/30, to South Africa 1930/1. *Tests* England (1929/30 to 1936, 9 matches).
Career batting
388–626–37–17544–233–29.78–29–*ct* 280
Bowling 355–4–88.75–0–0–1/4
Test batting
9–13–2–224–61–20.36–0–*ct* 1

He hit 1,000 runs in a season ten times (best 1,650, av 33.00, in 1935). Each of his three double centuries was made for Glamorgan, the highest being 233 v Worcestershire at Swansea in 1937. In conjunction with M. J. C. Allom he wrote accounts of both his MCC tours. He captained Cambridge in 1929 and Glamorgan 1930–39. He was Secretary of Glamorgan 1933–39 and a Test selector 1938–39. A noted rugby half back, he played for Cardiff and Wales.

Turnbull, Rivers Montagu
Amateur. *b:* 6.1.1855, Bullundshuhr, North West Provinces, India. *d:* 24.2.1927, Westminster, London. Lower order right-hand batsman, right-hand slow round-arm bowler. *Team* Sussex (1877–79, 2 matches).
Career batting
2–4–0–2–2–0.50–0–*ct* 1
Bowling 54–2–27.00–0–0–2/23

Turnbull, William Fleming
Amateur. *b:* 26.1.1879, Falkirk, Stirlingshire, Scotland. *d:* 26.12.1959, Edinburgh, Scotland. Middle order right-hand batsman. *Team* Scotland (1911–12).
Career batting
4–7–1–78–41*–13.00–0–*ct* 1
Bowling 12–0

Turner, Alan
Cricketer. *b:* 23.7.1950, Camperdown, Sydney, New South Wales, Australia. Opening left-hand batsman. *Team* New South Wales (1968/9 to 1977/8, 76 matches). *Tours* Australia to England 1975, to New Zealand 1969/70, 1976/7. *Tests* Australia (1975 to 1976/7, 14 matches).
Career batting
105–196–10–5744–156–30.88–7–*ct* 80
Bowling 10–1–10.00–0–0–1/6
Test batting
14–27–1–768–136–29.53–1–*ct* 15

On the 1975 tour to England he hit 654 runs, av 34.42, and played in three of the four Tests, but with little success.

Turner, Alban
Professional. *b:* 2.9.1885, Darton, Barnsley, Yorkshire. *d:* 29.8.1951, Goldthorpe, Yorkshire. Middle order right-hand batsman. *Team* Yorkshire (1910–11, 9 matches).
Career batting
9–16–1–163–37–10.86–0–*ct* 7

Turner, Allen
Professional. *b:* 24.10.1891, Heath, Derbyshire. *d:* 7.1.1961, Holmewood, Derbyshire. Tail end right-hand batsman, right-arm fast medium bowler. *Team* Derbyshire (1920, 2 matches).
Career batting
2–4–0–4–2–1.00–0–*ct* 1
Bowling 138–6–23.00–0–0–3/66

Turner, Arthur Jervois
Amateur. *b:* 10.6.1878, Mussorie, India. *d:* 8.9.1952, Graffham, Sussex. Brother of W. M. F. (Essex) and J. T. (Europeans). Middle order right-hand batsman, right-arm medium pace lob bowler, wicket-keeper. *Sch* Bedford Modern. *Team* Essex (1897–1910, 68 matches).
Career batting
77–134–15–4053–124–34.05–11–*ct* 31–*st* 2
Bowling 484–15–32.26–0–0–3/47

In his first season in first-class cricket he hit 590 runs, av 42.14, and in 1899, 804, av 40.20, but owing to military duties was not able to play regularly. His final first-class match was for Free Foresters in 1914. He also played for Bedfordshire (1895). His father was a member of the Hong Kong team which was drowned in a ship wreck returning from the annual match with Shanghai. A noted rugby footballer he played for Blackheath and Kent.

Turner, Brian
Professional. *b:* 25.7.1938, Sheffield, Yorkshire. Son of Cyril (Yorkshire), nephew of F. I. (Yorkshire). Lower order left-hand batsman, right-arm medium pace bowler. *Team* Yorkshire (1960–61, 2 matches).
Career batting
2–4–2–7–3*–3.50–0–*ct* 2
Bowling 47–4–11.75–0–0–2/9

Turner, Charles
Amateur. *b:* 11.3.1862, Gringley, Retford, Nottinghamshire. *d:* 20.5.1926, Thatcham House, Berkshire. Lower order batsman, useful bowler. *Sch* Uppingham. *Team* Gloucestershire (1886–89, 3 matches).
Career batting
3–5–0–33–17–6.60–0–*ct* 2
Bowling 119–3–39.66–0–0–1/16

From 1904 until his death he was Hon Secretary of Berkshire CCC.

Turner, Charles Thomas Biass
Amateur. *b:* 16.11.1862, Bathurst, New South Wales, Australia. *d:* 1.1.1944, Manly, Sydney, New South Wales, Australia. Brother-in-law of A. E. A. Goldman (Queensland). Forcing middle order right-hand batsman, right-arm medium fast bowler. *Team* New South Wales (1882/3 to 1909/10, 43 matches). *Tours* Australia to England 1888, 1890, 1893. *Tests* Australia (1886/7 to 1894/5, 17 matches).
Career batting
155–261–13–3856–103–15.54–2–*ct* 85
Bowling 14157–993–14.25–102–35–9/15
Test batting
17–32–4–323–29–11.53–0–*ct* 8
Bowling 1670–101–16.53–11–2–7/43

On his first visit to England in 1888 he was immensely successful, taking 283 wickets, av 11.68. In 1890 he had 179, av 14.21, and in 1893, 148, av 13.63. On each tour he headed the Australians' bowling averages and in 1893 proved to be the leading bowler in first-class cricket. In Australia in 1887/8, he took 106 first-class wickets, av 13.59, a number which remains a seasonal record. His best bowling was 9/15 for Australians v An England XI at Stoke-on-Trent in 1888.

Turner, Cyril
Professional. *b:* 11.1.1902, Wombwell, Yorkshire. *d:* 19.11.1968, Wath-on-Dearne, Yorkshire. Father of Brian (Yorkshire), brother of F. I. (Yorkshire). Middle order left-hand batsman, right-arm medium pace bowler. *Team* Yorkshire (1925–46, 200 matches). *Tour* Yorkshire to Jamaica 1935/6.
Career batting
201–266–32–6132–130–26.20–2–*ct* 181
Bowling 5354–173–30.94–4–0–7/54

He hit 1,153 runs, av 28.82, in 1934. He was Yorkshire scorer 1953–61.

Turner, David Roy
Cricketer. *b:* 5.2.1949, Corsham, Wiltshire. Middle order left-hand batsman, right-arm medium pace bowler. *Teams* Hampshire (1966–89, 416 matches); Western Province (1977/8). *Tour* Robins to South Africa 1972/3.
Career batting
426–696–74–19005–184*–30.55–28–*ct* 191
Bowling 357–9–39.66–0–0–2/7

He hit 1,000 runs in a season nine times (best 1,365, av 41.36, in 1984). He also played for Wiltshire (1965 and 1990–92).

Turner, Francis Gordon
Amateur. *b:* 1.3.1890, Kensington, London. *d:* 21.11.1979, Deal, Kent. Middle order right-hand batsman, leg break bowler. *Sch* Westminster. *Team* Hampshire (1912, 1 match).
Career batting
1–1–0–14–14–14.00–0–*ct* 1

Turner, Francis Irving
Professional. *b:* 3.9.1894, Barnsley, Yorkshire. *d:* 18.10.1954, Killearn, Stirlingshire, Scotland. Brother

of Cyril (Yorkshire), uncle of Brian (Yorkshire). Lower order right-hand batsman, right-arm medium pace bowler. *Team* Yorkshire (1924, 5 matches).
Career batting
5–7–0–33–12–4.71–0–*ct* 2
He also played for Scotland in a non-first-class match in 1935.

Turner, Francis Michael
Professional. *b:* 8.8.1934, Leicester. Middle order right-hand batsman, leg break and googly bowler. *Team* Leicestershire (1954–59, 10 matches).
Career batting
10–16–5–196–28*–17.81–0–*ct* 2
Bowling 223–3–74.33–0–0–3/56
He was appointed Secretary of Leicestershire CCC in 1960, Secretary-Manager in 1970 and Chief Executive in 1988.

Turner, Frederick Harding
Amateur. *b:* 29.5.1888, Sefton Park, Liverpool, Lancashire. *d:* 10.1.1915, near Kemmel, Belgium. He was killed in action. Lower order batsman, useful bowler. *Sch* Sedbergh. *Team* Oxford U (1909).
Career batting
5–9–2–67–44–9.57–0–*ct* 2
Bowling 272–17–16.00–0–0–4/46
A noted rugby footballer, he won a blue and was capped for Scotland.

Turner, Glenn Maitland
Cricketer. *b:* 26.5.1947, Dunedin, New Zealand. Very sound opening right-hand batsman, off break bowler. *Teams* Otago (1964/5 to 1982/3); Worcestershire (1967–82, 284 matches); Northern Districts (1976/7). *Tours* New Zealand to England 1969, 1973, 1975 (World Cup), 1979 (World Cup), to India and Pakistan 1969/70, 1976/7, to Australia 1969/70, 1973/4, 1974/5 (not first-class), 1982/3 (not first-class), to West Indies 1971/2; International Wanderers to Rhodesia 1972/3, 1975/6, to South Africa 1974/5, 1975/6. *Tests* New Zealand (1968/9 to 1982/3, 41 matches).
Career batting
455–792–101–34346–311*–49.70–103–*ct* 410
Bowling 189–5–37.80–0–0–3/18
Test batting
41–73–6–2991–259–44.64–7–*ct* 42
Bowling 5–0
He hit 1,000 runs in a season 15 times, going on to 2,000 three times (best 2,416, av 67.11, in 1973). In 1973 he hit 1,018 runs by May 31. He also completed 1,000 runs in three overseas seasons, including a New Zealand record of 1,244, av 77.75, in 1975/6. His highest innings of 311* for Worcestershire v Warwickshire at Worcester in 1982 was also his 100th century – he hit nine other scores over 200. He captained Worcestershire in 1981 and New Zealand in 10 Tests.

Turner, Graeme John
Cricketer. *b:* 5.8.1964, Bulawayo, Rhodesia. Middle order left-hand batsman, off break bowler. *Teams* Western Province (1984/5 to 1986/7); Northern Transvaal (1986/7 to 1987/8); Oxford U (1990–91, blue both years).
Career batting
42–67–5–1741–101*–28.08–1–*ct* 26
Bowling 1539–27–57.00–0–0–4/94
He captained Oxford in 1991, when he also topped the University batting averages. His last first-class match in South Africa was for SA Defence Force in 1988/9.

Turner, Harry
Professional. *b:* 6.4.1879, Birkenshaw, Yorkshire. *d:* 23.10.1939, Porthill, Shrewsbury, Shropshire. Lower order right-hand batsman, right-arm fast medium bowler. *Team* Scotland (1913).
Career batting
2–4–0–32–22–8.00–0–*ct* 5
Bowling 89–1–89.00–0–0–1/14

Turner, Ian John
Cricketer. *b:* 18.7.1968, Denmead, Hampshire. Lower order right-hand batsman, slow left-arm bowler. *Team* Hampshire (1989–92, 20 matches).
Career batting
20–22–7–142–39*–9.46–0–*ct* 9
Bowling 1628–46–35.39–1–0–5/81

Turner, James
Professional. *b:* 23.7.1865, Teversal, Nottinghamshire. *d:* 30.1.1945, Sutton-in-Ashfield, Nottinghamshire. Lower order batsman, right-arm medium pace bowler. *Team* Nottinghamshire (1894, 2 matches).
Career batting
2–3–0–30–26–10.00–0–*ct* 3
Bowling 72–1–72.00–0–0–1/11

Turner, James William Cecil
Amateur. *b:* 2.10.1886, Bromley, Kent. *d:* 29.11.1968, Girton, Cambridge. Middle order right-hand batsman, useful bowler. *Team* Worcestershire (1911–21, 46 matches).
Career batting
48–91–6–1266–106–14.89–1–*ct* 13
Bowling 32–2–16.00–0–0–1/14
He played in trial matches at Cambridge U, but not in first-class matches.

Turner, John
Amateur. *b:* 1854. *d:* 22.10.1912, Bexhill-on-Sea, Sussex. Opening right-hand batsman. *Team* MCC (1876–83).
Career batting
20–36–2–417–65–12.26–0–*ct* 9
His County cricket was for Northamptonshire (pre first-class, 1873–88) and Bedfordshire (1881–94).

Turner, John Alfred
Amateur. *b:* 10.4.1863, Leicester. *d:* 23.7.1924, Roehampton, London. Steady middle order right-hand batsman, right-arm fast bowler, good field. *Sch* Uppingham. *Team* Cambridge U (1883–86, blue all four years). *Tours* Sanders to North America 1885, 1886.
Career batting
36–63–8–1060–174–19.27–2–*ct* 24
Bowling 1136–33–34.42–0–0–4/46
His County cricket was for Leicestershire (pre first-class, 1883–92). His final first-class match was for Cambridge Past and Present in 1890. His County cricket ended when he lost an eye whilst playing rackets. He also won a blue for athletics.

Turner, John Bernard
Cricketer. *b:* 2.1.1949, Princes Risborough, Buckinghamshire. Opening right-hand batsman, slow left-arm bowler. *Team* Minor Counties (1974).
Career batting
1–2–0–127–106–63.50–1–*ct* 1
On his first-class debut and only first-class match for Minor Counties v Pakistan at Jesmond in 1974 he hit 106 in the second innings. His County cricket was for Buckinghamshire (1968–83).

Turner, Lennox James
Amateur. *b:* 24.10.1863, Croydon, Surrey. *d:* 2.12.1914, Croydon, Surrey. Lower order batsman, useful bowler. *Sch* Whitgift. *Team* MCC (1896).
Career batting
1–2–0–17–11–8.50–0–*ct* 0
Bowling 15–0

Turner, Montague
Amateur. *b:* 21.9.1843, Acton, Middlesex. *d:* 25.1.1908, Cuckfield, Sussex. Lower order right-hand batsman, wicket-keeper. *Sch* Cheltenham. *Team* Middlesex (1863–78, 29 matches).
Career batting
53–93–14–952–82–12.05–0–*ct* 79–*st* 64
He served on the Committee of both MCC and Middlesex CCC. He also played for Lincolnshire (1873).

Turner, Murray Stewart
Cricketer. *b:* 27.1.1964, Shaftesbury, Dorset. Lower order right-hand batsman, right-arm fast medium bowler. *Team* Somerset (1984–86, 12 matches).
Career batting
12–14–6–144–24*–18.00–0–*ct* 2
Bowling 788–15–52.53–0–0–4/74

Turner, Nigel Frederick
Amateur. *b:* 8.8.1914, Paddington, London. *d:* 31.1.1962, Okus, Swindon, Wiltshire. Lower order right-hand batsman, right-arm fast medium bowler. *Sch* Eton. *Team* Middlesex (1937, 1 match).
Career batting
1–1–0–0–0–0.00–0–*ct* 0
Bowling 43–2–21.50–0–0–2/38
He did not appear in any trials whilst at Cambridge University.

Turner, Noel Vernon Cyril
Amateur. *b:* 12.5.1887, Langley Mill, Eastwood, Nottinghamshire. *d:* 13.6.1941, Hungerford Park, Berkshire. Brother of R. H. T. (Nottinghamshire). Middle order right-hand batsman. *Sch* Repton. *Team* Nottinghamshire (1906–09, 23 matches).
Career batting
24–38–2–553–73*–15.36–0–*ct* 11
His final first-class match was for Free Foresters in 1912. A good goalkeeper, he played for Corinthian Casuals and for England in an amateur international.

Turner, Richard Ernest
Professional. *b:* 4.5.1886, Mitcham, Surrey. *d:* 16.3.1967, Hastings, Sussex. Middle order right-hand batsman, right-arm medium pace bowler. *Team* Worcestershire (1909–22, 52 matches).
Career batting
52–96–8–1010–66–11.47–0–*ct* 29
Bowling 225–4–56.25–0–0–3/7

Turner, Rev Richard Vinson
Amateur. *b:* 6.4.1932, Torquay, Devon. Middle order right-hand batsman. *Sch* Clifton. *Team* Cambridge U (1953–54).
Career batting
10–16–4–213–113*–17.75–1–*ct* 3
His County cricket was for Devon (1953–55). he won a blue for soccer.

Turner, Robert Frewen
Professional. *b:* 15.7.1885, Leicester. *d:* 15.2.1959, Darlington, Co Durham. Middle order right-hand batsman, bowler. *Team* Leicestershire (1909–11, 20 matches).
Career batting
20–34–1–525–41–15.90–0–*ct* 7
Bowling 367–9–40.77–0–0–2/2
A good soccer player, he appeared for Leicester Fosse, Everton, Preston North End and Darlington.

Turner, Robert Harrison Tom
Amateur. *b:* 26.10.1888, Langley Mill, Eastwood, Nottinghamshire. *d:* 13.9.1947, Shipley, Derbyshire. Brother of N. V. C. (Nottinghamshire). Stylish middle order right-hand batsman. *Sch* Repton. *Team* Nottinghamshire (1906–27, 26 matches).
Career batting
26–48–6–755–84–17.97–0–*ct* 6

Turner, Robert Julian
Cricketer. *b:* 25.11.1967, Malvern, Worcestershire. Brother of S. J. (Somerset). Middle order right-hand batsman, wicket-keeper. *Sch* Millfield. *Teams* Cambridge U (1988–91, blue all four years); Somerset

(1991–92, 8 matches).
Career batting
41–64–14–1245–101*–24.90–1–*ct* 42–*st* 12
Bowling 26–0
He captained Cambridge in 1991. He also played for Cambridgeshire (1990).

Turner, Ronald
Amateur. *b:* 19.6.1885, Gillingham, Kent. *d:* 15.8.1915, Suvla Bay, Gallipoli Peninsula, Turkey. Middle order batsman. *Sch* Hurstpierpoint. *Team* Gloucestershire (1906, 3 matches).
Career batting
3–6–0–30–19–5.00–0–*ct* 0
He played no first-class cricket at Cambridge U, but did win a blue for soccer.

Turner, Simon Jonathan
Cricketer. *b:* 28.4.1960, Cuckfield, Sussex. Brother of R. J. (Somerset). Lower order left-hand batsman, wicket-keeper. *Team* Somerset (1984–85, 6 matches).
Career batting
6–7–4–84–27*–28.00–*ct* 14–*st* 5

Turner, Stuart
Cricketer. *b:* 18.7.1943, Chester, Cheshire. Middle or lower order right-hand batsman, right-arm fast medium bowler. *Teams* Essex (1965–86, 354 matches); Natal (1976/7 to 1977/8). *Tour* Robins to South Africa 1974/5.
Career batting
361–513–101–9411–121–22.84–4–*ct* 217
Bowling 21351–821–26.00–27–1–6/26
He also played for Cambridgeshire (1987–92) and against Cumberland in 1987 he took all ten wickets for 11, the best ever analysis in the Minor Counties Championship.

Turner, Walter Martin FitzHerbert
Amateur. *b:* 4.4.1881, Meerut, India. *d:* 1.2.1948, Roxeth, Harrow, Middlesex. Brother of A. J. (Essex) and J. T. (Europeans). Middle order right-hand batsman, right-arm medium pace bowler. *Sch* Wellington. *Teams* Essex (1899–1926, 48 matches); Europeans (1910/11).
Career batting
51–86–7–2090–172–26.45–2–*ct* 62
Bowling 205–5–41.00–0–0–2/12

Turnour, Viscount Edward
(succeeded as 5th Earl of Winterton in 1879)
Amateur. *b:* 15.8.1837, Shillinglee Park, Petworth, Sussex. *d:* 5.9.1907, Shillinglee Park, Petworth, Sussex. Son of 4th Earl of Winterton (Sussex 1834), brother-in-law of G. F. Hamilton (MCC) and G. H. Field (Kent 1856). Hard hitting middle order right-hand batsman, right-hand fast round-arm bowler, cover point. *Sch* Eton. *Team* Sussex (1862–67, 5 matches).
Career batting
7–13–1–49–27*–4.08–0–*ct* 6–*st* 1
He also played for Norfolk (1868). He was on the Committee of MCC and of Sussex and President of MCC in 1884.

Turrall, Percy Wakeford
Amateur. *b:* 16.6.1883, Brentwood, Essex. *d:* 17.5.1941, Chelmsford, Essex. Opening batsman. *Team* Essex (1927, 1 match).
Career batting
1–1–0–45–45–45.00–0–*ct* 0

Tutt, Andrew
Cricketer. *b:* 21.2.1968, Bermondsey, London. Lower order right-hand batsman, right-arm medium pace bowler. *Team* Kent (1992, 1 match).
Career batting
1 match, did not bat–*ct* 0
Bowling 53–0

Tweats, Timothy Andrew
Cricketer. *b:* 18.4.1974, Stoke-on-Trent, Staffordshire. Middle order right-hand batsman, right-arm medium pace bowler. *Team* Derbyshire (1992, 1 match).
Career batting
1–1–0–24–24–24.00–0–*ct* 1
He also played for Staffordshire (1992).

Tweed, Thomas Edward
Amateur. *b:* 11.12.1904, Colombo, Ceylon. *d:* 23.3.1973, Colombo, Sri Lanka. Lower order right-hand batsman, right-arm medium pace bowler. *Team* Cambridge U (1925–26).
Career batting
4–6–1–97–24–19.40–0–*ct* 3
Bowling 177–5–35.40–0–0–2/30
He won a blue for athletics.

Twining, Richard Haynes
Amateur. *b:* 3.11.1889, St Pancras, London. *d:* 3.1.1979, Kensington, London. Opening right-hand batsman, wicket-keeper. *Sch* Eton. *Teams* Oxford U (1910–13, blue all four years); Middlesex (1910–28, 32 matches).
Career batting
78–137–8–2963–135–22.96–3–*ct* 40–*st* 10
Bowling 23–0
He captained Oxford in 1912. He served on the MCC Committee commencing 1933, was a Trustee of the Club from 1952 to 1969 and President in 1964, afterwards being elected a Life Vice-President. From 1950 to 1957 he was President of Middlesex CCC, having been Treasurer from 1936.

Twizell, Peter Henry
Cricketer. *b:* 18.6.1959, Rothbury, Northumberland. Lower order right-hand batsman, right-arm fast medium bowler. *Team* Gloucestershire (1985–86, 2 matches).

Twose, Roger Graham

Career batting
2–1–0–0–0–0.00–0–*ct* 0
Bowling 136–2–68.00–0–0–2/65

He also played for Northumberland (1978–84).

Twose, Roger Graham
Cricketer. *b:* 17.4.1968, Torquay, Devon. Nephew of R. W. Tolchard (Leicestershire) and J. G. Tolchard (Leicestershire). Opening left-hand batsman, right-arm medium pace bowler. *Sch* King's, Taunton. *Teams* Warwickshire (1989–92, 37 matches); Northern Districts (1989/90); Central Districts (1991/2). *Tours* Warwickshire to South Africa 1991/2.
Career batting
56–96–12–2900–233–34.52–3–*ct* 36
Bowling 1802–55–32.76–1–0–6/63

He hit 1,412 runs, av 40.34, in 1992 and scored 233 for Warwickshire v Leicestershire at Edgbaston. He also played for Devon (1988–91).

Tye, John
Professional. *b:* 10.7.1848, Bulwell, Nottinghamshire. *d:* 19.11.1905, Rastrick, Yorkshire. Tail end right-hand batsman, right-hand fast round-arm bowler, slip field. *Teams* Derbyshire (1874, 3 matches); Nottinghamshire (1876–81, 17 matches).
Career batting
24–38–8–226–48–7.53–0–*ct* 20
Bowling 1102–45–24.48–2–0–5/41

Tylden, James Richard
Amateur. *b:* 26.4.1889, Milstead Manor, Kent. *d:* 24.2.1949, Whitechapel, London. Brother-in-law of W. Findlay (Lancashire), he married niece of D. H. Forbes (Oxford U). Middle order left-hand batsman. *Sch* Rugby. *Team* Kent (1923, 1 match).
Career batting
1–2–0–19–19–9.50–0–*ct* 0

He appeared in the Oxford Freshmen's match of 1908 and the Seniors' match of 1909.

Tyldesley, George Ernest
Professional. *b:* 5.2.1889, Roe Green, Worsley, Lancashire. *d:* 5.5.1962, Rhos-on-Sea, Denbighshire. Brother of J. T. (Lancashire). Excellent middle order right-hand batsman, slow medium right-arm bowler. *Team* Lancashire (1909–36, 573 matches). *Tours* Joel to South Africa 1924/5; Tennyson to Jamaica 1926/7; MCC to South Africa 1927/8, to Australia 1928/9. *Tests* England (1921 to 1928/9, 14 matches).
Career batting
648–961–106–38874–256*–45.46–102–*ct* 293
Bowling 346–6–57.66–0–0–3/33
Test batting
14–20–2–990–122–55.00–3–*ct* 2
Bowling 2–0

He hit 1,000 runs in a season 18 times in England and once in South Africa going on to 2,000 six times and thence to 3,000 once: 3,024, av 79.57, in 1928. All his seven double centuries were for Lancashire, the highest being 256* v Warwickshire at Old Trafford in 1930.

Tyldesley, Harry
Professional. *b:* 4.7.1892, Kearsley, Bolton, Lancashire. *d:* 30.8.1935, Sandylands, Morecambe, Lancashire. Brother of J. D. (Lancashire), R. K. (Lancashire) and W. K. (Lancashire). Lower order right-hand batsman, right-arm slow bowler. *Team* Lancashire (1914–22, 4 matches). *Tour* MCC to Australia and New Zealand 1922/3.
Career batting
9–15–3–102–33*–8.50–0–*ct* 7
Bowling 500–18–27.77–1–0–5/100

Tyldesley, James Derbyshire
Professional. *b:* 10.8.1889, Ashton-in-Makerfield, Lancashire. *d:* 31.3.1923, Queens Park, Bolton, Lancashire. He died during an operation. Brother of Harry (Lancashire), R. K. (Lancashire) and W. K. (Lancashire). Middle order right-hand batsman, right-arm fast bowler. *Team* Lancashire (1910–22, 116 matches).
Career batting
116–169–16–2885–112*–18.85–3–*ct* 97
Bowling 8092–309–26.18–15–0–7/34

He also played for Cumberland.

Tyldesley, John Thomas
Professional. *b:* 22.11.1873, Roe Green, Worsley, Lancashire. *d:* 27.11.1930, Monton, Salford, Lancashire. He collapsed and died whilst putting on his boots to go to work. Brother of G. E. (Lancashire). Attractive middle order right-hand batsman, excellent outfield. *Team* Lancashire (1895–1923, 507 matches). *Tours* Hawke to South Africa 1898/9; MacLaren to Australia 1901/2; MCC to Australia 1903/4. *Tests* England (1898/9 to 1909, 31 matches).
Career batting
608–994–62–37897–295*–40.66–86–*ct* 355
Bowling 211–3–70.33–0–0–1/4
Test batting
31–55–1–1661–138–30.75–4–*ct* 16

Appearing for Lancashire in the middle of the 1895 season, he hit 152* in his second game (v Warwickshire) and almost at once established himself in the County side. In 1901 he scored 3,041 runs, av 55.29, which was to remain his best aggregate, but in all he exceeded 1,000 runs in a season 19 times and went on to 2,000 five times. All of his 13 double centuries were for Lancashire, his highest being 295* for Lancashire v Kent at Old Trafford in 1906.

Very quick on his feet, he could score all round the wicket, as well as having an excellent defence. For ten years he played regularly for England, his best series being in 1905 against the Australians, when he hit 424 runs, average 53.00. After retiring he became coach at Old Trafford until 1929.

Tyldesley, Richard Knowles
Professional. *b:* 11.3.1897, Westhoughton, Lancashire. *d:* 17.9.1943, Over Hulton, Bolton, Lancashire. Brother of Harry (Lancashire), J. D. (Lancashire) and W. K. (Lancashire). Lower order right-hand batsman, right-arm slow bowler. *Team* Lancashire (1919–31, 374 matches). *Tour* MCC to Australia 1924/5. *Tests* England (1924–30, 7 matches).
Career batting
397–464–54–6419–105–15.65–1–*ct* 337
Bowling 25980–1509–17.21–101–22–8/15
Test batting
7–7–1–47–29–7.83–0–*ct* 1
Bowling 619–19–32.57–0–0–3/50
He took 100 wickets in a season 10 times (best 184, av 13.98, in 1924). He was easily the leading Lancashire bowler during the 1931 season, but a disagreement over terms with the Lancashire Committee brought a sudden end to his County career. His final first-class match was for Sir L. Parkinson's XI in 1935.

Tyldesley, William Knowles
Professional. *b:* 12.8.1887, Aspull, Wigan, Lancashire. *d:* 26.4.1918, Kemmel, Belgium. He was killed in action. Brother of Harry (Lancashire), J. D. (Lancashire) and R. K. (Lancashire). Middle order left-hand batsman, left-arm medium fast bowler. *Team* Lancashire (1908–14, 87 matches).
Career batting
87–137–7–2979–152–22.91–3–*ct* 52
Bowling 383–8–47.87–0–0–2/0

Tylecote, Edward Ferdinando Sutton
Amateur. *b:* 23.6.1849, Marston Moretaine, Bedfordshire. *d:* 15.3.1938, New Hunstanton, Norfolk. Brother of H. G. (Oxford U). Middle order right-hand batsman, wicket-keeper. *Sch* Clifton. *Teams* Oxford U (1869–72, blue all four years); Kent (1875–83, 22 matches). *Tour* Bligh to Australia 1882/3. *Tests* England (1882/3 to 1886, 6 matches).
Career batting
93–158–10–3065–107–20.70–3–*ct* 127–*st* 58
Bowling 14–0
Test batting
6–9–1–152–66–19.00–0–*ct* 5–*st* 5
In 1868 he hit 404* for Classical v Modern at Clifton College, a record in any match at that date. He also played for Bedfordshire (1870–77). His final first-class match was for MCC in 1886. He captained Oxford in 1871 and 1872.

Tylecote, Henry Grey
Amateur. *b:* 24.7.1853, Marston Moretaine, Bedfordshire. *d:* 8.3.1935, Summertown, Oxford. Brother of E. F. S. (Kent). Sound, patient middle order right-hand batsman, right-hand medium pace round-arm bowler, wicket-keeper. *Sch* Clifton. *Team* Oxford U (1874–77, blue all four years).
Career batting
29–46–9–442–54–11.94–0–*ct* 25–*st* 5
Bowling 776–45–17.24–3–0–8/51
His final first-class match was for MCC in 1886. His County cricket was for Bedfordshire (1876–83) and Hertfordshire (1884–1900). He took a prominent part in athletics at Oxford, being a noted middle distance runner.

Tyler, Arthur Wellesley
Amateur. *b:* 18.6.1907, Charlton, London. *d:* 23.1.1985, Farnham, Surrey. Middle order right-hand batsman, wicket-keeper. *Sch* Cheltenham. *Team* Army (1931–32).
Career batting
3–5–1–77–26–19.25–0–*ct* 4–*st* 2
His County cricket was for Norfolk (1932).

Tyler, Bernard
Professional. *b:* 29.4.1902, Ridlington, Rutland. *d:* 10.11.1987, Bath, Somerset. Lower order right-hand batsman, right-arm fast bowler. *Teams* Northamptonshire (1923–24, 9 matches); Leicestershire (1926–28, 5 matches).
Career batting
14–25–6–135–26–7.10–0–*ct* 9
Bowling 553–11–50.27–0–0–2/13

Tyler, Charles Herbert
Amateur. *b:* 13.9.1887, Northampton. *d:* 17.5.1942, Stanley Park, Blackpool, Lancashire. Son of Frederick (Northamptonshire captain 1892). Middle order right-hand batsman, good field. *Team* Northamptonshire (1910–23, 27 matches).
Career batting
27–48–7–582–63–14.19–0–*ct* 21
He captained Northamptonshire in 1922.

Tyler, Cyril
Amateur. *b:* 26.1.1911, Ossett, Yorkshire. Lower order right-hand batsman, right-arm medium pace off break, occasionally leg break bowler. *Team* Gloucestershire (1936–38, 16 matches).
Career batting
16–22–4–113–22–6.27–0–*ct* 7
Bowling 1122–33–34.00–1–0–5/116

Tyler, Edwin James
Professional. *b:* 13.10.1864, Kidderminster, Worcestershire. *d:* 25.1.1917, North Town, Taunton, Somerset. Lower order left-hand batsman, slow left-arm bowler, good field. *Team* Somerset (1891–1907, 177 matches). *Tour* Hawke to South Africa 1895/6. *Test* England (1895/6, 1 match).
Career batting
185–310–52–2952–66–11.44–0–*ct* 118
Bowling 19779–895–22.09–77–22–10/49
Test batting
1–1–0–0–0–0.00–0–*ct* 0
Bowling 65–4–16.25–0–0–3/49

He took 100 wickets in a season three times (best 124, av 22.58, in 1895). In 1900 he was no-balled for throwing. He also played for Worcestershire (pre first-class, 1885–86) before making his debut for Somerset (not first-class) in 1888. His best bowling was 10/49 for Somerset v Surrey at Taunton in 1895.

Tyrwhitt-Drake, Thomas William
Amateur. *b:* 5.11.1926, Paddington, London. Opening right-hand batsman, wicket-keeper. *Sch* Haileybury. *Team* Cambridge U (1946–48).
Career batting
4–8–0–122–38–15.25–0–*ct* 1
His county cricket was for Hertfordshire (1946–58). His final first-class match was for Free Foresters in 1957.

Tyson, Cecil Thomas
Professional. *b:* 24.1.1889, Brompton-by-Sawdon, Scarborough, Yorkshire. *d:* 3.4.1940, Leeds, Yorkshire. Middle order left-hand batsman, right-arm fast medium bowler. *Teams* Yorkshire (1921, 3 matches); Glamorgan (1926, 2 matches).
Career batting
5–9–2–320–100*–45.71–1–*ct* 1
Bowling 32–0
He hit 100 not out for Yorkshire v Hampshire at Southampton on his first-class debut in 1921, but owing to a disagreement over terms, his County cricket was very limited.

Tyson, Frank Holmes
Professional. *b:* 6.6.1930, Farnworth, Lancashire. Lower order right-hand batsman, hostile right-arm fast bowler. *Team* Northamptonshire (1952–60, 170 matches). *Tours* MCC to Australia and New Zealand 1954/5, 1958/9, to West Indies 1955/6, to South Africa 1956/7; Commonwealth to South Africa 1959/60. *Tests* England (1954 to 1958/9, 17 matches).
Career batting
244–316–76–4103–82–17.09–0–*ct* 85
Bowling 16030–767–20.89–34–5–8/60
Test batting
17–24–3–230–37*–10.95–0–*ct* 4
Bowling 1441–76–18.56–4–1–7/27
He took 101 wickets, av 21.47, in 1957. His best bowling was 8/60 for Northamptonshire v Surrey at the Oval in 1957. For a few years the most aggressive fast bowler in England, his greatest triumphs were during the 1954/5 tour to Australia, when he took 28 wickets, av 20.82, in the Tests and 64 wickets, av 17.81, in all first-class matches. After retiring from County cricket he emigrated to Australia where he was appointed coach to the Victorian Cricket Association and also became a well-known sports commentator.

Tyssen, Rev Charles Amherst Daniel
Amateur. *b:* 11.12.1856, Sandgate, Kent. *d:* 26.12.1940, Sandgate, Kent. Opening batsman. *Sch* Harrow and Tonbridge. *Team* Gentlemen of England (1877).
Career batting
1–2–0–2–2–1.00–0–*ct* 2
He played in the Freshmen's match and Seniors' match at Oxford.

U

Ubsdell, George
Professional. *b:* 4.4.1844, Southampton, Hampshire. *d:* 15.10.1905, Garston, Liverpool, Lancashire. Lower order right-hand batsman, right-arm medium bowler, wicket-keeper. *Team* Hampshire (1864–70, 15 matches).
Career batting
15–29–4–170–29–6.80–0–*ct* 4–*st* 13

Udal, Geoffrey Francis Uvedale
Amateur. *b:* 23.2.1908, Holborn, London. *d:* 5.12.1980, Frimley, Surrey. Grandson of J. S. (MCC), grandfather of S. D. (Hampshire), nephew of N. R. (Oxford U). Tail end right-hand batsman, right-arm fast bowler. *Teams* Middlesex (1932, 1 match); Leicestershire (1946, 2 matches).
Career batting
4–8–3–4–2*–0.80–0–*ct* 2
Bowling 216–3–72.00–0–0–2/105

Udal, John Symonds
Amateur. *b:* 10.11.1848, West Bromwich, Staffordshire. *d:* 13.3.1925, St John's Wood, London. Father of N. R. (Oxford U), grandfather of G. F. U. (Middlesex and Leicestershire), great-great-grandfather of S. D. (Hampshire). Middle order right-hand batsman, right-arm bowler. *Sch* Bromsgrove. *Team* MCC (1871–75). *Tour* Fiji to New Zealand 1894/5.
Career batting
9–17–1–215–50–13.43–0–*ct* 3
Bowling 5–0
He did not play in any first-class matches whilst at Oxford U. His County cricket was for Dorset and Somerset. As Attorney-General of Fiji he did much to promote cricket there, as later he did in the Leeward Islands when Chief Justice.

Udal, Nicholas Robin
Amateur. *b:* 16.10.1883, Richmond, Surrey. *d:* 27.2.1964, Pembury, Kent. Son of J. S. (MCC), uncle of G. F. U. (Middlesex and Leicestershire). Lower order right-hand batsman, right-arm fast bowler. *Sch* Winchester. *Team* Oxford U (1904–06, blue 1905–06).
Career batting
14–24–5–387–49*–20.36–0–*ct* 17
Bowling 1439–65–22.13–5–2–7/133
His final first-class match was for MCC in 1914. His County cricket was for Dorset (1905–12) and

Devon. A member of the Sudan Civil Service from 1906 to 1930, his opportunities for first-class cricket were very limited.

Udal, Shaun David
Cricketer. *b:* 18.3.1969, Cove, Farnborough, Hampshire. Grandson of G. F. U. Udal (Middlesex and Leicestershire), great-great-grandson of J. S. (MCC). Lower order right-hand batsman, off break bowler. *Team* Hampshire (1989–92, 32 matches).
Career batting
32–36–12–479–44–19.95–0–*ct* 6
Bowling 3050–82–37.19–2–0–8/50

Ufton, Derek Gilbert
Professional. *b:* 31.5.1928, Crayford, Kent. Sound lower order left-hand batsman, wicket-keeper. *Team* Kent (1949–62, 148 matches).
Career batting
149–244–48–3919–119*–19.99–1–*ct* 270–*st* 44
A good soccer player, he appeared for Charlton Athletic and England at centre-half.

Ullathorne, Charles Edward
Professional. *b:* 11.4.1845, Hull, Yorkshire. *d:* 4.5.1904, Cheetham Hill, Manchester, Lancashire. Middle order right-hand batsman, right-hand fast round-arm bowler, splendid cover point. *Team* Yorkshire (1868–75, 27 matches).
Career batting
31–53–9–326–28–7.40–0–*ct* 23
He was also a noted athlete.

Ulyett, George
Professional. *b:* 21.10.1851, Crabtree, Pitsmoor, Sheffield, Yorkshire. *d:* 18.6.1898, Pitsmoor, Sheffield, Yorkshire. He died of pneumonia contracted whilst watching Yorkshire play Kent at Bramall Lane. Forceful opening right-hand batsman, right-hand fast round-arm bowler, good field. *Team* Yorkshire (1873–93, 359 matches). *Tours* Lillywhite to Australia 1876/7; Harris to Australia 1878/9; Daft to North America 1879 (not first-class); Lillywhite, Shaw and Shrewsbury to Australia 1881/2, 1884/5, 1887/8; Warton to South Africa 1888/9. *Tests* England (1876/7 to 1890, 25 matches).
Career batting
537–928–40–20823–199*–23.44–18–*ct* 368
Bowling 13157–653–20.14–23–3–7/30
Test batting
25–39–0–949–149–24.33–1–*ct* 19
Bowling 1020–50–20.40–1–0–7/36
He hit 1,000 runs in a season ten times (best 1,562, av 31.87, in 1883). At the time of his death he was regarded as the greatest batsman that Yorkshire had produced and was particularly noted for his opening partnerships with L. Hall. He was a first-class umpire (1894–95). He kept goal for Sheffield Wednesday.

Umrigar, Pahlan Ratanji
Amateur. *b:* 28.3.1926, Sholapur, Maharashtra, India. Attacking middle order right-hand batsman, right-arm medium pace off break bowler. *Teams* Parsis (1944/5 to 1945/6); Bombay (1946/7 to 1962/3); Gujarat (1950/1 to 1951/2). *Tours* India to England 1952, 1959, to West Indies 1952/3, 1961/2, to Pakistan 1954/5, to Ceylon 1956/7; ACC to Pakistan 1961/2. *Tests* India (1948/9 to 1961/2, 59 matches).
Career batting
243–350–41–16155–252*–52.28–49–*ct* 216
Bowling 8348–325–25.68–14–2–7/32
Test batting
59–94–8–3631–223–42.22–12–*ct* 33
Bowling 1473–35–42.08–2–0–6/74
Although he completely failed in the Tests on the 1952 tour, he was the leading batsman in first-class matches with 1,688 runs, av 48.22, including no fewer than three double centuries; on the 1959 tour he hit 1,826 runs, av 55.33, with another three double centuries and hit 118 in the Old Trafford Test; owing to injury he missed the last part of the tour as well as the last Test. He captained India in eight Tests, though not in England. His highest score was 252* for Indians v Cambridge U at Cambridge in 1959. He also hit 1,000 runs in a season twice in India (best 1,065, av 62.64, in 1962/3). His final first-class match was for Dungarpur XI in 1967/8. His first match in England was for a Commonwealth XI in 1950.

Underdown, George
Amateur. *b:* 12.5.1859, Petersfield, Hampshire. *d:* 29.5.1895, Petersfield, Hampshire. Middle order batsman, useful bowler. *Team* Hampshire (1882–85, 9 matches).
Career batting
10–18–0–231–63–12.83–0–*ct* 3
Bowling 80–1–80.00–0–0–1/15

Underwood, Arthur Joseph
Professional. *b:* 21.9.1927, Wiseton, Nottinghamshire. Lower order right-hand batsman, left-arm medium pace bowler. *Team* Nottinghamshire (1949–54, 14 matches).
Career batting
16–15–4–109–39–9.90–0–*ct* 12
Bowling 907–10–90.70–0–0–2/72

Underwood, Derek Leslie, MBE
Cricketer. *b:* 8.6.1945, Bromley, Kent. Lower order right-hand batsman, left-arm spin, either slow medium or medium, bowler. *Team* Kent (1963–87, 520 matches). *Tours* MCC Under 25 to Pakistan 1966/7; MCC to Ceylon and Pakistan 1968/9, to Australia and New Zealand 1970/1, 1974/5, to West Indies 1973/4, to India, Sri Lanka and Australia 1976/7; England to Australia and India 1979/80, to India and Sri Lanka 1981/2; International XI to India, Pakistan and Ceylon 1967/8; Norfolk to West Indies 1969/70; Interna-

tional Wanderers to South Africa 1975/6; SAB England XI to South Africa 1981/2. *Tests* England (1966 to 1981/2, 86 matches).
Career batting
676–710–200–5165–111–10.12–1–*ct* 261
Bowling 49993–2465–20.28–153–47–9/28
Test batting
86–116–35–937–45*–11.56–0–*ct* 44
Bowling 7674–297–25.83–17–6–8/51

The leading spin bowler in England for some 20 years, his accuracy combined with his ability to vary the pace of his deliveries give him the edge over other left-arm spin bowlers of the present generation. But for the fact that he left Test cricket to join World Series Cricket in 1977 and then after the reconciliation between Packer and the Establishment toured South Africa with the 1981/2 SAB side, resulting in a three-year ban, Underwood possibly would have been the leading wicket-taker in Test cricket.

His career began in 1963 in sensational fashion when he became the youngest player to take 100 wickets in a debut season. He took 100 wickets in a season ten times (best 157 wickets, av 13.80, in 1966). He reached the milestone of 1,000 wickets in a career at the age of 25 – only two cricketers have improved on this record. The best bowling analyses of his career were 9/28 for Kent v Sussex at Hastings in 1964 and 9/32 for Kent v Surrey at the Oval in 1978.

Underwood, William
Professional. *b:* 26.2.1852, Ruddington, Nottinghamshire. *d:* 9.5.1914, Blackcliffe Farm, Bradmore, Nottinghamshire. He died by his own hand. Middle order right-hand batsman, slow right-arm bowler. *Team* Nottinghamshire (1881, 1 match).
Career batting
1–1–0–10–10–10.00–0–*ct* 0

He also played for Devon (1880–83).

Unsworth, James
Professional. *b:* 4.3.1844, Everton, Liverpool, Lancashire. *d:* 1.1.1893, Warrington, Lancashire. Lower order right-hand batsman, right-hand fast round-arm bowler. *Team* Lancashire (1871, 2 matches).
Career batting
2–3–0–25–23–8.33–0–*ct* 2
Bowling 75–3–25.00–0–0–3/52

Unwin, Ernest James
Amateur. *b:* 18.9.1912, Birdbrook, Essex. Brother of F. St G. (Essex). Middle order right-hand batsman, right-arm fast medium bowler. *Sch* Haileybury. *Team* Essex (1932–39, 7 matches).
Career batting
7–14–0–152–48–10.85–0–*ct* 2
Bowling 103–0

He also played for Suffolk (1951–56). A noted rugby footballer, he played for Rosslyn Park and England and toured South Africa with the British Lions in 1938.

Unwin, Frederick St George
Amateur. *b:* 23.4.1911, Baythorne Hall, Halstead, Essex. *d:* 4.10.1990, Braintree, Essex. Brother of E. J. (Essex). Forcing right-hand batsman, right-arm medium pace bowler. *Sch* Haileybury. *Team* Essex (1932–50, 52 matches). *Tour* Martineau to Egypt 1938 (not first-class).
Career batting
53–87–9–1138–60–14.58–0–*ct* 33
Bowling 41–0

He was joint captain of Essex in 1939. His final first-class match was for Free Foresters in 1951. He also played for Suffolk (1933).

Unwin, Paul David
Cricketer. *b:* 9.6.1967, Waipawa, Hawke's Bay, New Zealand. Lower order right-hand batsman, off break bowler. *Teams* Central Districts (1986/7 to 1990/1); Somerset (1989, 1 match).
Career batting
23–22–9–215–34–16.53–0–*ct* 20
Bowling 2127–47–45.25–1–1–6/42

Upton, Mark
Cricketer. *b:* 30.6.1950, Poole, Dorset. Tail end right-hand batsman, slow left-arm bowler. *Team* Sussex (1971, 1 match).
Career batting
1–1–1–2–2*–no av–0–*ct* 0
Bowling 120–1–120.00–0–0–1/72

Urquhart, John Rankin
Amateur. *b:* 29.5.1921, Chelmsford, Essex. Lower order right-hand batsman, right-arm medium fast bowler. *Team* Cambridge U (1948, blue).
Career batting
4–6–2–13–6*–3.25–0–*ct* 0
Bowling 231–15–15.40–0–0–4/21

Usher, John
Professional. *b:* 26.2.1859, Staincliffe, Yorkshire. *d:* 8.8.1905, Haslingden, Lancashire. He died by his own hand. Lower order left-hand batsman, slow left-arm bowler, slip field. *Team* Yorkshire (1888, 1 match).
Career batting
1–2–0–7–5–3.50–0–*ct* 1
Bowling 31–2–15.50–0–0–2/11

Utley, Father Richard Peter Hugh
Amateur. *b:* 11.2.1906, Havant, Hampshire. *d:* 28.8.1968, Ampleforth, Yorkshire. Lower order right-hand batsman, right-arm fast bowler. *Sch* Ampleforth. *Team* Hampshire (1927–28, 27 matches).
Career batting
31–38–9–210–30–7.24–0–*ct* 12
Bowling 2370–90–26.33–4–1–6/43

V

Valentine, Alfred Louis

Amateur. *b:* 28.4.1930, Kingston, Jamaica. Tail end right-hand batsman, slow left-arm bowler. *Team* Jamaica (1949/50 to 1964/5). *Tours* West Indies to England 1950, 1957, 1963, to Australia and New Zealand 1951/2, to New Zealand 1955/6, to Australia 1960/1. *Tests* West Indies (1950 to 1961/2, 36 matches).
Career batting
125–142–48–470–24*–5.00–0–*ct* 45
Bowling 12451–475–26.21–32–6–8/26
Test batting
36–51–21–141–14–4.70–0–*ct* 13
Bowling 4215–139–30.32–8–2–8/104

He created a sensation on his first tour to England – completely unknown before the visit, he took 123 wickets, av 17.94, in first-class matches and was the leading bowler in the Tests with 33 wickets, av 20.42. On his second tour to England he took 60 wickets, av 19.66, but was unable to retain his Test place – playing two games against England without taking a wicket. On his third English tour he was not a success and did not play in the Tests.

Valentine, Bryan Herbert

Amateur. *b:* 17.1.1908, Blackheath, Kent. *d:* 2.2.1983, Otford, Kent. Forceful middle order right-hand batsman, right-arm medium pace bowler, good field. *Sch* Repton. *Teams* Kent (1927–48, 308 matches); Cambridge U (1928–29, blue 1929). *Tours* Tennyson to Jamaica 1931/2; Martineau to Egypt 1933, 1935, 1938 (not first-class); MCC to India and Ceylon 1933/4, to South Africa 1938/9. *Tests* England (1933/4 to 1938/9, 7 matches).
Career batting
399–645–38–18306–242–30.15–35–*ct* 289
Bowling 1125–27–41.66–0–0–3/58
Test batting
7–9–2–454–136–64.85–2–*ct* 2

He hit 1,000 runs in a season nine times (best 1,738, av 33.42, in 1933). Both his double centuries were for Kent, the highest being 242 v Leicestershire at Oakham in 1938. He was joint captain of Kent in 1937 and sole captain from 1946 to 1948. His final first-class match was for Free Foresters in 1950. He was President of Kent in 1967. He was also an excellent lawn tennis player, and won a blue for soccer.

Valentine, Vincent Adolphus

Amateur. *b:* 4.4.1908, Buff Bay, Jamaica. *d:* 6.7.1972, Hope, Kingston, Jamaica. Attacking lower order right-hand batsman, right-arm fast medium bowler. *Team* Jamaica (1931/2 to 1938/9). *Tour* West Indies to England 1933. *Tests* West Indies (1933, 2 matches).
Career batting
24–33–5–500–59*–17.85–0–*ct* 11
Bowling 1980–49–40.40–0–0–4/83
Test batting
2–4–1–35–19*–11.66–0–*ct* 0
Bowling 104–1–104.00–0–0–1/55

He played in two Tests on the 1933 tour but made little impression, and his wickets in the first-class games were terribly expensive – 36, av 42.80.

Valiant, James

Professional. *b:* 17.7.1884, Wavertree, Liverpool, Lancashire. *d:* 28.10.1917, Gaza, Palestine. Lower order batsman, useful bowler. *Team* Essex (1912, 1 match).
Career batting
1–2–1–3–3–3.00–0–*ct* 0
Bowling 20–0

Van der Bijl, Pieter Gerhard Vintcent

Amateur. *b:* 21.10.1907, Kenilworth, Cape Town, South Africa. *d:* 16.2.1973, Kalk Bay, Cape Province, South Africa. Son of V. A. (Western Province), father of V. A. P. (Middlesex), nephew of V. A. W. (Western Province). Steady opening right-hand batsman. *Teams* Oxford U (1931–32, blue 1932); Western Province (1925/6 to 1939/40). *Tests* South Africa (1938/9, 5 matches).
Career batting
44–76–9–2692–195–40.17–5–*ct* 36–*st* 2
Bowling 158–5–31.60–0–0–2/20
Test batting
5–9–0–460–125–51.11–1–*ct* 1

His final first-class match was for the 1st South African Division XI in 1942/3. He also won a blue for boxing.

Van der Bijl, Vintcent Adriaan Pieter

Cricketer. *b:* 19.3.1948, Rondebosch, Cape Town, South Africa. Grandson of V. A. (Western Province), son of P. G. V. (South Africa), great-nephew of V. A. W. (Western Province). Lower order right-hand batsman, right-arm fast medium bowler. *Teams* Natal (1968/9 to 1981/2); Middlesex (1980–81, 21 matches); Transvaal (1982/3). *Tours* Isaacs to England 1969 (not first-class); South Africa to Australia 1971/2 (tour cancelled).
Career batting
156–188–48–2269–87–16.20–0–*ct* 51
Bowling 12692–767–16.54–46–12–8/35

His first-class debut was for South African Universities in 1967/8. He headed the averages in 1980, his single full year in County cricket.

Van der Bijl, Voltelin Albert William

Amateur. *b:* 31.1.1872, Salt River, Cape Town, South Africa. *d:* 2.10.1941, Cape Town, South Africa. Brother of V. A. (Western Province), uncle of P. G. V. (South Africa), great-uncle of V. A. P. (Middlesex). Lower order batsman, useful bowler. *Sch*

Wellington. *Teams* Western Province (1890/1 to 1895/6); G. J. V. Weigall's XI (1904).
Career batting
7–11–1–176–61–17.60–0–*ct* 5
Bowling 421–19–22.15–1–0–6/56

Vanderbyl, Philip Breda
Amateur. *b:* 11.11.1867, Kensington, London. *d:* 20.3.1930, Cairo, Egypt. Middle order batsman. *Sch* Christ's College, Finchley. *Team* MCC (1900).
Career batting
1–1–0–38–38.00–0–*ct* 0

Van der Gucht, Paul Ian
Amateur. *b:* 2.11.1911, Worksop, Nottinghamshire. Lower order right-hand batsman, wicket-keeper. *Sch* Radley. *Teams* Gloucestershire (1932–33, 33 matches); Bengal (1935/6 to 1947/8); Europeans (1935/6 to 1936/7).
Career batting
51–80–11–1587–115–23.00–1–*ct* 74–*st* 25
Bowling 5–0
His final match in England was for MCC in 1939.

Van der Knaap, David Saunders
Cricketer. *b:* 7.9.1948, Sandton, Johannesburg, South Africa. Lower order right-hand batsman, off break bowler. *Teams* Lancashire (1967, 1 match); Transvaal (1967/8 to 1978/9).
Career batting
43–43–16–289–44–10.70–0–*ct* 39
Bowling 3389–121–28.00–7–0–6/61

Van der Merwe, Edward Alexander
Amateur. *b:* 9.11.1904, Rustenburg, Transvaal, South Africa. *d:* 26.2.1971, Emmarentia, Johannesburg, South Africa. He died from a gunshot wound. Lower order right-hand batsman, wicket-keeper. *Team* Transvaal (1928/9 to 1937/8). *Tours* South Africa to England 1929, to Australia 1931/2. *Tests* South Africa (1929 to 1935/6, 2 matches).
Career batting
27–36–9–287–35*–10.62–0–*ct* 35–*st* 29
Test batting
2–4–1–27–29–9.00–0–*ct* 3
The reserve wicket-keeper on the 1929 tour to England, he appeared in one Test. A good rugby footballer, he represented Transvaal.

Van der Merwe, Peter Laurence
Amateur. *b:* 14.3.1937, Paarl, Cape Province, South Africa. Brother-in-law of J. H. B. Waite (South Africa). Steady middle order right-hand batsman, slow left-arm bowler, good field. *Teams* Western Province (1958/9 to 1965/6); Eastern Province (1966/7 to 1968/9). *Tours* SA Fezela to England 1961; South Africa to Australia and New Zealand 1963/4, to England 1965. *Tests* South Africa (1963/4 to 1966/7, 15 matches).
Career batting
94–152–12–4086–128–29.18–4–*ct* 73
Bowling 2108–82–25.70–3–0–6/40
Test batting
15–23–2–533–76–25.38–0–*ct* 11
Bowling 22–1–22.00–0–0–1/6
He captained the South Africans on the 1965 tour and played in all three Tests, but his batting only proved moderately successful with 363 runs, av 16.50, in first-class matches. In all he captained South Africa in eight Tests. His first-class debut was for South African Universities in 1956/7.

Van der Merwe, Willem Maré
Cricketer. *b:* 20.7.1960, Rustenburg, Transvaal, South Africa. Middle order left-hand batsman, right-arm medium fast bowler. *Teams* Orange Free State (1978/9 to 1984/5); Western Province (1985/6 to 1986/7); Oxford U (1990, blue).
Career batting
44–67–15–1274–96–24.50–0–*ct* 14
Bowling 3388–130–26.06–4–0–5/35
His last first-class match in South Africa was for SA Defence Force 1987/8. He also won a blue for rugby and played for Western Province.

Vanderspar, George Augustus Hunter
Amateur. *b:* 1858. *d:* 23.5.1940, Dean Park, Bournemouth, Hampshire. Middle order right-hand batsman. *Sch* Southampton College. *Team* MCC (1893). *Tours* Ceylon to Calcutta 1884/5, to Madras 1885/6, 1891/2 (none first-class).
Career batting
1–1–0–7–7–7.00–0–*ct* 0
He played County cricket for Somerset 1880 (pre first-class). From 1884 to 1908 he was the organiser and promoter of cricket in Ceylon.

Van Geloven, Jack
(birth registered as Jack Geloven)
Professional. *b:* 4.1.1934, Guiseley, Yorkshire. Middle order right-hand batsman, right-arm medium pace bowler. *Teams* Yorkshire (1955, 3 matches); Leicestershire (1956–65, 244 matches).
Career batting
247–431–44–7522–157*–19.43–5–*ct* 137
Bowling 13912–486–28.62–14–1–7/56
He hit 1,000 runs in a season three times (best 1,324, av 23.22, in 1959). In 1962 he took 100 wickets, av 28.11, performing the 'double'. He also played for Northumberland (1966–73). He was a first-class umpire (1977–83).

Van Geyzel, Carl Theodore
Amateur. *b:* 19.12.1902, Colombo, Ceylon. *d:* 18.1.1971, Lunnwila, Ceylon. Brother of F. C. W. (Ceylon). Stylish middle order right-hand batsman. *Sch* Royal College, Colombo. *Teams* Cambridge U (1924); Ceylon (1926/7).

Career batting
2–4–0–74–66–18.50–0–*ct* 3
He gained an athletics blue and established a new high jump record of 6 ft 1½ in.

Vann, Denis William Arthur
Amateur. *b:* 21.11.1916, Northampton. *d:* 20.1.1961, Kettering, Northamptonshire. Middle order right-hand batsman. *Team* Northamptonshire (1936–37, 4 matches).
Career batting
4–6–0–47–16–7.83–0–*ct* 1
Bowling 104–2–52.00–0–0–2/26

Van Ryneveld, Anthony John
Amateur. *b:* 17.11.1925, Plumstead, Cape Town, South Africa. Brother of C. B. (South Africa), nephew of J. M. Blanckenberg (South Africa) and S. E. L. West (Europeans). Middle order right-hand batsman, right-arm fast medium bowler. *Team* Oxford U (1947).
Career batting
1–2–0–69–50–34.50–0–*ct* 0
Bowling 2–0

Van Ryneveld, Clive Berrange
Amateur. *b:* 19.3.1928, St James, Cape Town, South Africa. Brother of A. J. (South Africa), nephew of J. M. Blanckenberg (South Africa) and S. E. L. West (Europeans). Enterprising middle order right-hand batsman, leg break bowler, good field. *Teams* Oxford U (1948–50, blue all three years); Western Province (1946/7 to 1962/3). *Tour* South Africa to England 1951. *Tests* South Africa (1951 to 1957/8, 19 matches).
Career batting
101–171–12–4803–150–30.20–4–*ct* 71
Bowling 6230–206–30.24–9–0–8/48
Test batting
19–33–6–724–83–26.81–0–*ct* 14
Bowling 671–17–39.47–0–0–4/67
On the 1951 tour to England he hit 983 runs, av 29.78, and played in all five Tests. He later captained South Africa in eight Tests in South Africa. He captained Oxford in 1949. An outstanding rugby footballer he played at stand off half for Oxford and England. After retiring from active sport he was elected to the South African Parliament.

Van Straubenzee, Maj-Gen Sir Casimir Cartwright
Amateur. *b:* 11.11.1867, Kingston, Ontario, Canada. *d:* 28.3.1956, Lansdown, Bath, Somerset. Middle order batsman. *Team* MCC (1899).
Career batting
1–1–0–20–20–20.00–0–*ct* 0

Van Straubenzee, Henry Hamilton
Amateur. *b:* 7.3.1914, Parktown, Johannesburg, South Africa. Lower order right-hand batsman, slow left-arm bowler. *Sch* Winchester. *Team* Essex (1938, 1 match).
Career batting
4–4–2–56–38–28.00–0–*ct* 0
Bowling 185–10–18.50–0–0–4/96
His final first-class match was for the Army in 1939.

Van Troost, Adrianus Pelrus
Cricketer. *b:* 2.10.1972, Schiedam, Holland. Tail end right-hand batsman, right-arm fast medium bowler. *Team* Somerset (1991–92, 15 matches).
Career batting
15–10–6–42–12–10.50–0–*ct* 4
Bowling 1033–27–38.25–2–0–6/48
He represented Holland in the 1990 ICC Trophy competition.

Van Zyl, Cornelius Johannes Petrus Gerthardus
Cricketer. *b:* 1.10.1961, Bloemfontein, South Africa. Lower order right-hand batsman, right-arm fast medium bowler. *Teams* Orange Free State (1981/2 to 1991/2); Glamorgan (1987–88, 12 matches). *Tour* South Africa to West Indies 1991/2 (not first-class).
Career batting
88–130–23–1825–119–17.05–1–*ct* 29
Bowling 7127–308–23.13–12–2–8/84
An injury to his foot meant that he missed half of the 1987 season and in 1988 he quickly lost his place in the Glamorgan side and returned to South Africa. He played in one unofficial Test v Australia in 1985/6.

Varey, David William
Cricketer. *b:* 15.10.1961, Darlington, Co Durham. Twin brother of J. G. (Oxford U). Opening right-hand batsman. *Sch* Birkenhead. *Teams* Cambridge U (1981–83, blue 1982–83); Lancashire (1984–87, 44 matches). *Tour* Lancashire to Jamaica 1986/7.
Career batting
66–112–12–2723–156*–27.23–2–*ct* 25–*st* 1
Bowling 10–0
He also played for Cheshire (1982–92).

Varey, Jonathan Guy
Cricketer. *b:* 15.10.1961, Darlington, Co Durham. Twin brother of D. W. (Lancashire). Middle order right-hand batsman, right-arm medium pace bowler. *Sch* Birkenhead. *Team* Oxford U (1982–83, blue both years).
Career batting
13–22–8–426–69*–30.42–0–*ct* 3
Bowling 866–6–144.33–0–0–3/69
His County cricket was for Cheshire (1982).

Varley, P.
Professional. Middle order batsman. *Team* North of England (1866).
Career batting
1–2–1–15–8*–15.00–0–*ct* 0

Vasey, Percy Walter
Amateur. *b:* 29.7.1883, Highbury, London. *d:* 11.9.1952, Upton Hellions, Crediton, Devon. Brother of G. H. (Europeans). Middle order right-hand batsman, slow right-arm bowler. *Sch* Merchant Taylors'. *Team* Somerset (1913, 1 match).
Career batting
1–2–0–13–10–6.50–0–*ct* 0
He also played for Hertfordshire (1906).

Vassall, Gilbert Claude
Amateur. *b:* 5.4.1876, Hardington Mandeville, Somerset. *d:* 19.9.1941, Park Town, Oxford. Middle order batsman, useful bowler. *Sch* Charterhouse. *Team* Somerset (1902–05, 6 matches).
Career batting
6–10–1–46–27*–5.11–0–*ct* 4
Bowling 72–1–72.00–0–0–1/56
He played no first-class cricket at Oxford U, but did win blues for athletics and soccer.

Vassila, George Charles
(death registered as G. C. Vassilas)
Professional. *b:* 21.8.1857, Richmond, Surrey. *d:* 27.11.1915, Epsom, Surrey. Lower order right-hand batsman, right-arm fast bowler. *Team* Middlesex (1880, 1 match).
Career batting
1–2–1–0–0*–0.00–0–*ct* 0
Bowling 37–0

Vaughan, Justin Thomas Caldwell
(birth registered as T. J. C. Vaughan)
Cricketer. *b:* 30.8.1967, Hereford. Middle order left-hand batsman, right-arm medium pace bowler. *Teams* Auckland (1989/90 to 1991/2); Gloucestershire (1992, 11 matches).
Career batting
33–53–12–1462–106*–35.65–1–*ct* 32
Bowling 1462–43–34.00–1–0–5/72
He scored 106* on his first-class debut for Auckland v Wellington at Wellington in 1989/90. He was brought up in New Zealand and was 12th man for the national side in 1991/2, but did not lose his English qualification.

Vaughan, Richard Thomas
Amateur. *b:* 28.5.1908, Mazatlán, Mexico. *d:* 1.4.1966, Woodborough, Wiltshire. Lower order right-hand batsman, wicket-keeper. *Sch* Repton. *Team* Cambridge U (1928).
Career batting
2–3–0–16–13–5.33–0–*ct* 2
His County cricket was for Berkshire (1928–30) and Wiltshire (1937–51). He won a blue for soccer.

Vaughan-Thomas, Hugh Wyndham
Amateur. *b:* 13.5.1910, Swansea, Glamorgan. *d:* 20.10.1986, Framfield, Sussex. Middle order right-hand batsman. *Team* Glamorgan (1933, 1 match).
Career batting
1–1–0–3–3–3.00–0–*ct* 1
He was the brother of the author and broadcaster Wynford Vaughan-Thomas.

Vaulkhard, Patrick
Amateur. *b:* 15.9.1911, Nottingham. Attacking middle order right-hand batsman, leg break bowler, wicket-keeper. *Sch* Oakham. *Teams* Nottinghamshire (1934, 9 matches); Derbyshire (1946–52, 65 matches).
Career batting
77–122–7–2460–264–21.39–1–*ct* 64–*st*4
Bowling 124–1–124.00–0–0–1/30
He hit 264 for Derbyshire v Nottinghamshire at Trent Bridge in 1946. In 1950 he captained Derbyshire. He also played for Northumberland (1939) and was also a prominent member of Sir Julien Cahn's XI. A useful amateur soccer player, he represented Nottinghamshire.

Vavasour, Sir Geoffrey William
Amateur. *b:* 5.9.1914, Queenstown, Co Cork, Ireland. Middle order right-hand batsman. *Team* Combined Services (1947).
Career batting
1–2–0–14–8–7.00–0–*ct* 0

Veal, Charles Lewis
Amateur. *b:* 29.8.1876, Bridgend, Glamorgan. *d:* 1.6.1929, Kensington, London. Middle order batsman. *Sch* Charterhouse and Repton. *Team* MCC (1906–10).
Career batting
6–11–0–145–41–13.18–0–*ct* 4
His County cricket was for Glamorgan (pre first-class, 1910).

Veivers, Thomas Robert
Amateur. *b:* 6.4.1937, Beenleigh, Queensland, Australia. Middle order left-hand batsman, off break bowler. *Team* Queensland (1958/9 to 1967/8, 55 matches). *Tours* Australia to England 1964, to India and Pakistan 1964/5, to South Africa 1966/7. *Tests* Australia (1963/4 to 1966/7, 21 matches).
Career batting
106–162–24–5100–137–36.95–4–*ct* 52
Bowling 7393–191–38.70–3–0–5/63
Test batting
21–30–4–813–88–31.26–0–*ct* 7
Bowling 1375–33–41.66–0–0–4/68
He proved to be a useful all-rounder on the 1964 visit to England, playing in all five Tests, and in first-class games hitting 725 runs, av 34.52, and taking 52 wickets, av 36.17.

Veletta, Michael Robert John
Cricketer. *b:* 30.10.1963, Subiaco, Perth, Western Australia. Opening or middle order right-hand batsman, occasional wicket-keeper. *Team* Western Aus-

tralia (1983/4 to 1991/2, 95 matches). *Tours* Young Australia to Zimbabwe 1985/6; Australia to India 1986/7, to Sharjah (not first-class) 1986/7, to India and Pakistan (World Cup) 1987/8, to Pakistan 1988/9, to England 1989, to West Indies 1990/1; Western Australia to India 1989/90. *Tests* Australia (1987/8 to 1989/90, 8 matches).
Career batting
119–193–21–7152–262–41.58–18–*ct* 147–*st* 1
Bowling 12–0
Test batting
8–11–0–207–39–18.81–0–*ct* 12

His career has been marred by misfortune and the 1989 tour to England was no exception, a broken finger meaning that he missed the second half of the season. He did not appear in any of the Tests. His highest score was 262 for Western Australia v Victoria at Perth in 1986/7. He scored 1,004 runs, av 47.80, in Australia in 1988/9.

Venables, Rowland George
Amateur. *b:* 18.1.1846, Truro, Cornwall. *d:* 9.3.1920, Oakhurst, Oswestry, Shropshire. Lower order right-hand batsman, left-hand medium pace round-arm bowler, mid off field. *Sch* Rugby. *Team* Oxford U (1866–69).
Career batting
2–3–1–26–24*–13.00–0–*ct* 0
Bowling 92–4–23.00–0–0–3/25

He was a prominent member of the Free Foresters. His County cricket was for Shropshire (1869–71) and Cornwall (1870).

Venes, Richard Stephen
Amateur. *b:* 12.3.1885, Battersea, London. *d:* 10.6.1959, Northampton. Lower order right-hand batsman, leg break and googly bowler. *Team* Northamptonshire (1922, 4 matches).
Career batting
4–8–2–8–4*–1.33–0–*ct* 1
Bowling 105–5–21.00–0–0–4/60

Vengsarkar, Dilip Balwant
Cricketer. *b:* 6.4.1956, Rajapur, Bombay, India. Stylish opening or middle order right-hand batsman, right-arm medium pace bowler. *Team* Bombay (1975/6 to 1991/2). *Tours* India to New Zealand 1975/6, 1980/1, 1989/90, to West Indies 1975/6, 1982/3, 1988/9, to Australia 1977/8, 1980/1, 1984/5 (not first-class), 1985/6, 1991/2, to Pakistan 1978/9, 1982/3, 1984/5, to England 1979, 1982, 1983 (World Cup), 1986, 1990, to Sharjah (not first-class) 1983/4, 1984/5, 1985/6, 1986/7, 1988/9, 1989/90, to Sri Lanka 1985/6, to Bangladesh (not first-class) 1988/9; Rest of World to England 1987. *Tests* India (1975/6 to 1991/2, 116 matches).
Career batting
260–390–52–17868–284–52.86–55–*ct* 179
Bowling 126–1–126.00–0–0–1/31
Test batting
116–185–22–6868–166–42.13–17–*ct* 78
Bowling 36–0

A fluent stroke making batsman, he made an immediate impression on his first visit to England in 1979, hitting 751 runs, av 41.72, and playing in all four Tests. In 1982 he was again among the leading run scorers with 610, av 55.45, which included 157 in the Lord's Test. On the 1986 visit he was India's best batsman with 536 runs, av 67.00, in first-class matches and 360, av 90.00, in the three Tests, for the third time scoring a hundred at Lord's. Although he did not compile any large innings on the 1990 tour, he again played a useful role and appeared in all the Tests. His highest first-class score was 284 for Bombay v Madhya Pradesh at Bombay in 1991/2. He hit 1,000 runs in a season in India five times (best 1,495, av 57.50, in 1979/80). He scored 966 runs, av 107.33, in Tests in India in 1986/7. He captained India in 10 Test matches. He also played for Staffordshire (1985).

Venkatapathy Raju, Sagi Lakshmi
Cricketer. *b:* 9.7.1969, Hyderabad, India. Lower order right-hand batsman, slow left-arm bowler. *Team* Hyderabad (1985/6 to 1991/2). *Tours* India to New Zealand 1989/90, to England 1990, to Australia 1991/2, to Sharjah (not first-class) 1991/2, to Australia and New Zealand (World Cup) 1991/2. *Tests* India (1989/90 to 1991/2, 7 matches).
Career batting
50–56–18–679–54–14.14–0–*ct* 21
Bowling 4765–176–27.07–6–0–6/12
Test batting
7–12–3–151–31–16.77–0–*ct* 3
Bowling 588–20–29.40–1–0–6/12

He returned modest figures on the 1990 tour to England, his season being cut short when he injured his hand.

Venkataraghavan, Srinivasaraghavan
Cricketer. *b:* 21.4.1945, Madras, India. Tail end right-hand batsman, off break bowler. *Teams* Madras/Tamil Nadu (1963/4 to 1984/5); Derbyshire (1973–75, 46 matches). *Tours* India to England 1967, 1971, 1974, 1975 (World Cup), 1979, to West Indies 1970/1, 1975/6, 1982/3, to Ceylon 1973/4, to New Zealand 1975/6, to Australia 1977/8, to Pakistan 1978/9; Madras to Ceylon 1965/6, 1967/8, 1969/70, 1971/2. *Tests* India (1964/5 to 1983/4, 57 matches).
Career batting
341–457–84–6617–137–17.73–1–*ct* 317
Bowling 33568–1390–24.14–85–21–9/93
Test batting
57–76–12–748–64–11.68–0–*ct* 44
Bowling 5634–156–36.11–3–1–8/72

Although coming to England on four Test playing tours, he impressed only on the 1971 visit when he took 63 wickets, av 24.90, in first-class matches and

13, av 26.92, in the Tests, being second in both sets of bowling averages. He captained India on the 1979 tour and in 5 Tests in all. His best season with Derbyshire was 1975 with 68 wickets, av 21.42, and his best bowling was 9/93 for Indians v Hampshire at Bournemouth in 1971. He later became a first-class umpire in India.

Venn, Horace
Amateur. *b:* 4.7.1892, Coventry, Warwickshire. *d:* 23.11.1953, Keresley, Coventry, Warwickshire. Middle order right-hand batsman. *Team* Warwickshire (1919–25, 34 matches).
Career batting
34–60–0–1047–151–17.45–2–*ct* 14
Bowling 28–0
He scored 151 on debut for Warwickshire v Worcestershire at Edgbaston in 1919.

Vere Hodge, Dr Nicholas
Amateur. *b:* 31.10.1912, Woodford Green, Essex. Middle order right-hand batsman, wicket-keeper. *Sch* Uppingham. *Team* Essex (1936–39, 23 matches).
Career batting
23–38–6–713–108–22.28–2–*ct* 11
He did not appear in any first-class matches whilst at Cambridge U.

Verelst, Harry William
Amateur. *b:* 2.7.1846, Claughton, Cheshire. *d:* 5.4.1918, Aston Hall, Aston-cum-Aughton, Yorkshire. Middle order right-hand batsman, long stop. *Sch* Rugby. *Team* Yorkshire (1868–69, 3 matches).
Career batting
11–18–4–215–78–15.35–0–*ct* 3–*st* 2
His first-class debut was for Gentlemen of the North in 1867 and his last first-class match for I Zingari in 1878.

Verghese, Thomas Mathew
Cricketer. *b:* 9.7.1963, Mulanthurthy, India. Lower order right-hand batsman, right-arm medium pace bowler. *Sch* Oakham. *Team* Cambridge U (1987).
Career batting
1–1–0–2–2–2.00–0–*ct* 0
Bowling 110–1–110.00–0–0–1/36

Verity, Hedley
Professional. *b:* 18.5.1905, Headingley, Leeds, Yorkshire. *d:* 31.7.1943, Caserta, Italy. He died of wounds. Lower order right-hand batsman, slow left-arm bowler, good short leg. *Team* Yorkshire (1930–39, 278 matches). *Tours* MCC to Australia and New Zealand 1932/3, 1936/7, to Ceylon and India 1933/4, to South Africa 1938/9; Yorkshire to Jamaica 1935/6. *Tests* England (1931–39, 40 matches).
Career batting
378–416–106–5605–101–18.08–1–*ct* 269
Bowling 29146–1956–14.90–164–54–10/10
Test batting
40–44–12–669–66*–20.90–0–*ct* 30
Bowling 3510–144–24.37–5–2–8/43
The best left-arm spin bowler in England in the 1930s, he took 100 wickets in a season nine times, going on to 200 three times (best 216, av 13.18, in 1936). His best bowling was a record 10/10 for Yorkshire v Nottinghamshire at Headingley in 1931; he also took 10/36 for Yorkshire v Warwickshire at Headingley in 1931 and in addition had nine wickets in an innings seven times, all for Yorkshire.

Verity, Stuart Anthony
Cricketer. *b:* 11.11.1948, Bradford, Yorkshire. Lower order right-hand batsman, right-arm medium pace bowler. *Sch* Bradford GS. *Team* Oxford U (1970).
Career batting
4–7–2–55–15–11.00–0–*ct* 0
Bowling 260–4–65.00–0–0–3/42

Vernon, George Frederick
Amateur. *b:* 20.6.1856, Marylebone, London. *d:* 10.8.1902, Elmina, Gold Coast. He died of malarial fever. Attractive middle order right-hand batsman, occasional slow under-arm bowler, excellent deep field. *Sch* Rugby. *Team* Middlesex (1878–95, 103 matches). *Tours* Bligh to Australia 1882/3; Vernon to Australia 1887/8, to Ceylon and India 1889/90 (not first-class); Hawke to India 1892/3. *Test* England (1882/3, 1 match).
Career batting
239–391–21–7070–160–19.10–4–*ct* 171
Bowling 69–2–34.50–0–0–1/11
Test batting
1–2–1–14–11*–14.00–0–*ct* 0
He captained the 1887/8 team to Australia and the 1889/90 team to India. A noted rugby footballer, he played for Blackheath and England. His first-class debut was for MCC in 1876, and his last first-class match for MCC in 1898.

Vernon, Henry
Amateur. *b:* 16.12.1828. *d:* 19.2.1855, Tixover Hall, Rutland. He died very suddenly whilst staying with C. O. Eaton (MCC 1847). Stylish opening batsman, brilliant cover field. *Sch* Harrow. *Team* Cambridge U (1850–52, blue all three years).
Career batting
34–59–3–763–59–13.62–0–*ct* 22
Bowling 4 wickets (no analyses)–0–0–3/?
At Harrow he was regarded as the best player of cricket, football and rackets. His first-class debut was for Gentlemen of England in 1848, and his last match was for MCC in 1854. His County cricket was for Dorset (1849).

Vernon, John Michael
Amateur. *b:* 27.7.1922, Port Said, Egypt. Middle order right-hand batsman, right-arm medium pace bowler. *Sch* Tonbridge. *Team* Combined Services

(1949–52).
Career batting
8–13–0–290–83–22.30–0–*ct* 5
Bowling 100–2–50.00–0–0–1/8

Vernon, Martin Jeffrey
Cricketer. *b:* 9.7.1951, Marylebone, London. Lower order right-hand batsman, right-arm fast medium bowler. *Teams* Middlesex (1974–76, 16 matches); Gloucestershire (1977, 5 matches).
Career batting
22–27–5–146–27–6.63–0–*ct* 5
Bowling 1198–31–38.64–2–1–6/58

Verrinder, Alan Otto Charles
Cricketer. *b:* 28.7.1955, Henley-on-Thames, Oxfordshire. Lower order right-hand batsman, right-arm fast medium bowler. *Teams* Surrey (1974–76, 3 matches); Kent (1977, 1 match).
Career batting
4–4–1–24–23–8.00–0–*ct* 3
Bowling 144–4–36.00–0–0–2/42

Vials, George Alfred Turner
Amateur. *b:* 18.3.1887, Northampton. *d:* 26.4.1974, Northampton. Middle order right-hand batsman. *Sch* Wellingborough. *Team* Northamptonshire (1905–22, 122 matches).
Career batting
122–220–10–3808–129–18.13–2–*ct* 105
Bowling 19–0
He first played for Northamptonshire (pre first-class) in 1904. He captained Northamptonshire from 1911 to 1913 and was President of the County Club from 1956 to 1968. He also played soccer for Northampton Town and hockey for the County.

Vickery, Anthony
Amateur. *b:* 26.8.1925, Taunton, Somerset. Middle order right-hand batsman. *Team* Somerset (1947–48, 6 matches).
Career batting
6–12–1–89–21–8.09–0–*ct* 2
He also played for Cheshire (1949–59).

Vidler, John Lionel Symonds
Amateur. *b:* 30.3.1890, Rye, Sussex. *d:* 15.10.1967, Playden, Rye, Sussex. Middle order right-hand batsman, right-arm medium pace bowler. *Sch* Repton. *Teams* Oxford U (1910–12, blue all three years); Sussex (1910–19, 7 matches).
Career batting
29–52–6–682–55–14.82–0–*ct* 21
Bowling 1861–81–22.97–3–1–7/23
He also played for Oxfordshire (1923–24). He also won a blue for golf.

Vigar, Frank Henry
Professional. *b:* 14.7.1917, Bruton, Somerset. Sound middle order right-hand batsman, leg break bowler, good close field. *Team* Essex (1938–54, 256 matches).
Career batting
257–399–62–8858–145–26.28–12–*ct* 197
Bowling 9135–241–37.90–8–0–8/128
He hit 1,000 runs in a season three times (best 1,735, av 35.40, in 1947).

Vigar, Herbert Evelyn
Professional. *b:* 29.11.1883, Redhill, Surrey. *d:* 27.10.1946, Earlswood, Redhill, Surrey. Lower order right-hand batsman, wicket-keeper. *Team* Surrey (1906–11, 15 matches).
Career batting
15–21–2–226–33*–11.89–0–*ct* 21–*st* 2

Vigne, Thomas
Amateur. *b:* 1771. *d:* 30.3.1841, Woodford Wells, Essex. Father of G. T. (Hampshire). Middle order batsman, wicket-keeper. *Sch* Winchester. *Teams* Surrey (1809–31); Hampshire (1818–21); Norfolk (1820).
Career batting
60–103–9–564–41*–6.00–0–*ct* 37–*st* 36
Bowling 12 wickets (no analyses)–0–0–2/?
His first-class debut was for MCC & Homerton in 1804. He was about 58 years old when he played in the Gentlemen v Players match of 1829, and his last match was for MCC in 1832.

Viljoen, Jan Neil
Cricketer. *b:* 4.7.1962, Wepener, Orange Free State, South Africa. Lower order right-hand batsman, right-arm slow medium bowler. *Team* Cambridge U (1991).
Career batting
1–1–1–1–1*–no av–0–*ct* 0
Bowling 99–1–99.00–0–0–1/34
He represented Western Province at rugby.

Viljoen, Kenneth George
Amateur. *b:* 14.5.1910, Windsorton, Griqualand West, South Africa. *d:* 21.1.1974, Krugersdorp, Transvaal, South Africa. Brother of S. F. (Transvaal and Griqualand West). Sound right-hand middle order batsman, excellent outfield. *Teams* Griqualand West (1926/7 to 1930/1); Orange Free State (1933/4 to 1935/6); Transvaal (1936/7 to 1948/9). *Tours* South Africa to Australia and New Zealand 1931/2, to England 1935, 1947. *Tests* South Africa (1930/1 to 1948/9, 27 matches).
Career batting
133–209–25–7964–215–43.28–23–*ct* 50
Bowling 722–29–24.89–0–0–4/23
Test batting
27–50–2–1365–124–28.43–2–*ct* 5
Bowling 23–0
He headed the first-class batting averages on the 1935 tour with 1,454 runs, av 46.90, and in the Tests hit 280 runs, av 40.00. On his return in 1947 he had a very similar record with 1,441 runs, av 49.68, though

he was not quite so successful in the Tests. His highest innings in England was 201 v Sussex at Hove in 1947. His two other double centuries were made in South Africa, the highest being 215 for Griqualand West v Western Province at Kimberley in 1929/30. After retiring he was President of the South African Cricket Association. He was manager of the South African touring sides to Australia and New Zealand in 1952/3 and 1963/4 and to England in 1955.

Vince, John
Professional. *b:* 31.12.1849, Hackbridge, Surrey. *d:* 5.5.1886, Beddington Corner, Croydon, Surrey. Lower order right-hand batsman, right-arm fast bowler. *Team* Surrey (1870, 11 matches).
Career batting
11–22–1–60–10*–2.85–0–*ct* 11
Bowling 454–15–30.26–0–0–4/58

Vincent, Cyril Leverton
Amateur. *b:* 16.2.1902, Johannesburg, South Africa. *d:* 24.8.1968, Mayville, Durban, South Africa. Lower order right-hand batsman, slow left-arm bowler. *Team* Transvaal (1920/1 to 1930/1). *Tours* South Africa to England 1929, 1935, to Australia and New Zealand 1931/2. *Tests* South Africa (1927/8 to 1935, 25 matches).
Career batting
85–117–29–1582–83–17.97–0–*ct* 68
Bowling 7006–293–23.91–16–2–7/36
Test batting
25–38–12–526–60–20.23–0–*ct* 27
Bowling 2631–84–31.32–3–0–6/51

In England in 1929 he took 69 wickets, av 28.39, and appeared in four Tests. On his second tour he took 92 wickets, av 20.90, and again played in four Tests. His final first-class match was for the South African Air Force XI in 1942/3. He was Chairman of the South African Selection Committee, as well as being on the Transvaal Committee. A noted baseball player, he represented South Africa.

Vincent, Deryck Andrew
Cricketer. *b:* 16.9.1964, Dublin, Ireland. Middle order left-hand batsman, wicket-keeper. *Team* Ireland (1988).
Career batting
1–2–0–24–16–12.00–0–*ct* 0

Vincent, Sir Harold Graham
Amateur. *b:* 13.11.1891, Harlesden, Middlesex. *d:* 5.11.1981, Tonbridge, Kent. Middle order right-hand batsman. *Sch* Haileybury. *Team* Cambridge U (1914, blue).
Career batting
4–8–0–106–41–13.25–0–*ct* 11
Bowling 2–0

Vincett, John Herbert
Professional, but amateur in 1921. *b:* 24.5.1883, Hastings, Sussex. *d:* 28.12.1953, Lambeth, London. Lower order right-hand batsman, right-arm medium pace bowler. *Teams* Sussex (1907–19, 169 matches); Surrey (1921, 2 matches).
Career batting
172–260–49–3464–90*–16.41–0–*ct* 116
Bowling 8984–342–26.26–19–0–7/41

He played soccer for Grimsby, Leicester Fosse and Barnsley.

Vine, Joseph
Professional. *b:* 15.5.1875, Willingdon, Sussex. *d:* 25.4.1946, Aldrington, Hove, Sussex. Forcing opening right-hand batsman, leg break bowler. *Teams* Sussex (1896–1922, 506 matches); London County (1901–04). *Tours* MCC to Australia 1911/12. *Tests* England (1911/12, 2 matches).
Career batting
547–920–79–25171–202–29.92–34–*ct* 240
Bowling 19533–685–28.51–27–3–8/68
Test batting
2–3–2–46–36–46.00–0–*ct* 0

He hit 1,000 runs in a season fourteen times (best 1,871, av 34.01, in 1905). His only double century was 202 for Sussex v Northamptonshire at Hastings in 1920. He appeared in 421 consecutive matches for Sussex. In 1901 he took 113 wickets, av 29.72, and completed the 'double'.

Virgin, Roy Thomas
Professional. *b:* 26.8.1939, Taunton, Somerset. Opening right-hand batsman, leg break bowler, occasional wicket-keeper. *Teams* Somerset (1957–72, 321 matches); Western Province (1972/3); Northamptonshire (1973–77, 103 matches). *Tour* Commonwealth to Pakistan 1970/1.
Career batting
437–773–39–21930–179*–29.87–37–*ct* 415
Bowling 340–4–85.00–0–0–1/6

He hit 1,000 runs in a season twelve times, going on to 2,000 once: 2,223, av 47.29, in 1970. He was appointed County captain of Northamptonshire in 1975, but resigned midway through the season.

Viswanath, Gundappa Rangnath
Cricketer. *b:* 12.2.1949, Bhadravati, Mysore, India. Brother-in-law of S. M. Gavaskar (India). Attractive middle order right-hand batsman, leg break bowler. *Team* Mysore/Karnataka (1967/8 to 1987/8). *Tours* India to England 1971, 1974, 1975 (World Cup), 1979, 1982, to Sri Lanka 1973/4, to Australia 1977/8, to Australia and New Zealand 1980/1, to West Indies 1970/1, 1975/6, to New Zealand 1975/6, to Pakistan 1978/9, 1982/3; Wadekar to Sri Lanka 1975/6; Rest of World to England 1985. *Tests* India (1969/70 to 1982/3, 91 matches).

Career batting
308–486–47–17970–247–40.93–44–*ct* 226
Bowling 729–15–48.60–0–0–2/21
Test batting
91–155–10–6080–222–41.93–14–*ct* 63
Bowling 46–1–46.00–0–0–1/11

He played in all the Tests on each of his four tours to England, his most successful visit being in 1982 when he hit 561 runs, av 62.33, in first-class matches and 189 runs, av 47.25, in the three Tests. In 1979 his figures were 757, av 50.46, and 341, av 48.71. In 1971 and 1974 his record was not so impressive. None of his double centuries was scored in England. His greatest feat was perhaps to score 230 on his first-class debut for Mysore v Andhra at Vijayawada in 1967/8, though he also hit a century on his Test debut, in the second innings v Australia at Kanpur in 1969/70.

His highest score was 247 for Karnataka v Uttar Pradesh at Mohan Nagar in 1977/8. He hit 1,000 runs in a season in India three times (best 1,538, av 53.33, in 1974/5). He played in a record 87 consecutive Test matches and captained India in two.

Vivian, Graham Ellery
Cricketer. *b:* 28.2.1946, Auckland, New Zealand. Son of H. G. (New Zealand). Dashing middle order left-hand batsman, leg break bowler. *Team* Auckland (1966/7 to 1978/9). *Tours* New Zealand to India 1964/5, to England 1965, to Australia 1969/70, 1972/3, to West Indies 1971/2. *Tests* New Zealand (1964/5 to 1971/2, 5 matches).
Career batting
88–140–25–3259–137*–28.33–3–*ct* 41
Bowling 2128–56–38.00–1–0–5/59
Test batting
5–6–0–110–43–18.33–0–*ct* 3
Bowling 107–1–107.00–0–0–1/14

On the 1965 tour to England he played in only eight matches and no Tests. He made his first-class debut at Calcutta in the Second Test v India in 1964/5.

Vivian, Henry Gifford
Amateur. *b:* 4.11.1912, Auckland, New Zealand. *d:* 12.8.1983, Auckland, New Zealand. Father of G. E. (New Zealand). Attractive middle order left-hand batsman, slow left-arm bowler, good field. *Team* Auckland (1930/1 to 1938/9). *Tours* New Zealand to England 1931, 1937, to Australia 1937/8. *Tests* New Zealand (1931–37, 7 matches).
Career batting
85–143–15–4443–165–34.71–6–*ct* 71
Bowling 6160–223–27.62–12–2–6/49
Test batting
7–10–0–421–100–42.10–1–*ct*4
Bowling 633–17–37.23–0–0–4/58

In 1931 he hit 1,002 runs, av 30.36, and played in two Tests, whilst in 1937 he made 1,118 runs, av 29.42, and appeared in all three Tests, his bowling also being useful.

Vizard, Walter Oswald
Amateur. *b:* 16.11.1861, Bellary, India. *d:* 10.1.1929, Bayswater, London. Lower order right-hand batsman, wicket-keeper. *Sch* Clifton. *Team* Gloucestershire (1882–90, 18 matches).
Career batting
18–32–2–256–49*–8.53–0–*ct* 11–*st* 1

He also played for Hertfordshire (1897).

Vizianagram, The Rajkumar of, Sir Vijaya Anand
Amateur. *b:* 28.12.1905, Benares, India. *d:* 2.12.1965, Benares, India. Father of A. N. Venkatesh Singh (Andhra). Stylish middle order right-hand batsman. *Teams* Vizianagram's XI (1930/1 to 1935/6); Indians (Madras) (1930/1 to 1933/4); United Provinces (1934/5 to 1935/6). *Tours* India to England 1936; Vizianagram's XI to India and Ceylon 1930/1. *Tests* India (1936, 3 matches).
Career batting
47–73–7–1228–77–18.60–0–*ct* 18
Bowling 139–4–34.75–0–0–1/1
Test batting
3–6–2–33–19*–8.25–0–*ct* 1

He was a great patron of Indian cricket and organised his own Team, which played first-class matches. He captained the 1936 Indian side to England and led India in the three Tests. In first-class matches on the tour he scored 600 runs, av 16.21. During the tour he received a knighthood. From 1954 to 1956 he was President of the Indian Cricket Board of Control. He was also a member of the Indian Parliament. For several seasons he broadcast Test match commentaries.

Voce, William
Professional. *b:* 8.8.1909, Annesley Woodhouse, Nottinghamshire. *d:* 6.6.1984, Nottingham. Attacking lower order right-hand batsman, left-arm fast medium, or slow medium, bowler. *Team* Nottinghamshire (1927–52, 345 matches). *Tours* MCC to West Indies 1929/30, to South Africa 1930/1, to Australia and New Zealand 1932/3, 1936/7, 1946/7. *Tests* England (1929/30 to 1946/7, 27 matches).
Career batting
426–525–130–7590–129–19.21–4–*ct* 286
Bowling 35961–1558–23.08–84–20–8/30
Test batting
27–38–15–308–66–13.39–0–*ct* 15
Bowling 2733–98–27.88–3–2–7/70

He took 100 wickets in a season six times (best 139, av 21.58, in 1935). He hit 1,020 runs, av 35.17, in 1933. His best remembered Test series was in 1932/3 in Australia when he partnered Larwood, but his best record came in the 1936/7 series when he was England's best bowler with 26 wickets, av 21.53. Because of the controversial 'bodyline' tour, he did not play for England for nearly four years between

1932/3 and the final Test of 1936. He retired from regular County cricket in 1947 and from then until 1952 was coach to Nottinghamshire CCC.

Vogler, Albert Edward Ernest
Professional in 1906, but reverted to amateur in 1907. *b:* 28.11.1876, Swartwater, Queenstown, Cape Province, South Africa. *d:* 9.8.1946, Fort Napier, Pietermaritzburg, South Africa. Middle order right-hand batsman, leg break and googly bowler. *Teams* Natal (1903/4); Transvaal (1904/5 to 1909/10); Eastern Province (1905/6 to 1906/7); Middlesex (1906, 1 match). *Tours* South Africa to England 1907, to Australia 1910/11. *Tests* South Africa (1905/6 to 1910/11, 15 matches).
Career batting
83–136–19–2375–103–20.29–1–*ct* 81
Bowling 7182–393–18.27–31–7–10/26
Test batting
15–26–6–340–65–17.00–0–2–*ct* 20
Bowling 1455–64–22.73–5–1–7/94

On his tour to England in 1907 he took 119 wickets, av 15.62, in first-class matches and 15, av 19.66, in the Tests. The previous year he had been on the groundstaff at Lord's with the intention of qualifying for Middlesex, but returned to South Africa at the end of that season. His final first-class match was for Woodbrook Club and Ground in 1912. His best bowling was 10/26 for Eastern Province v Griqualand West at Johannesburg in 1906/7. His final first-class match in South Africa was for L. J. Tancred's XI in 1911/12.

Von Ernsthausen, Adolph Christian Ernest
(changed name to Howeson in 1914)
Amateur. *b:* 17.10.1880, Belsize Park, London. *d:* 29.5.1928, Ditton Hill, Surrey. Hard hitting lower order right-hand batsman, right-arm fast bowler. *Sch* Uppingham. *Teams* Surrey (1900–01, 2 matches); Oxford U (1902–04, blue all three years).
Career batting
30–49–7–506–45–12.04–0–*ct* 25
Bowling 2605–94–27.71–4–0–7/80

A skilled chess player, he represented Oxford v Cambridge from 1901 to 1904.

Vonhagt, Dudley Marlon
Cricketer. *b:* 31.3.1965, Kalutara, Ceylon. Opening right-hand batsman, right-arm medium pace bowler. *Team* Moors SC (1988/9). *Tours* Sri Lanka to England 1984, to Australia 1984/5 (not first-class).
Career batting
15–24–2–595–88–27.95–0–*ct* 9
Bowling 23–0

He played with moderate success on the 1984 tour to England. His first-class debut was for Sri Lanka in 1983/4. He played in one-day internationals for Sri Lanka.

Vorster, Louis Phillippus
Cricketer. *b:* 2.11.1966, Potchefstroom, Transvaal, South Africa. Middle order left-hand batsman, off break bowler. *Teams* Transvaal (1985/6 to 1989/90); Worcestershire (1988, 1 match); Northern Transvaal (1990/1 to 1991/2).
Career batting
56–97–13–2655–174–31.60–3–*ct* 40
Bowling 41–1–41.00–0–0–1/10

Voss, Ralph
Professional. *b:* 30.3.1860, Croydon, Surrey. *d:* 16.11.1900, Croydon, Surrey. Lower order right-hand batsman, useful bowler. *Team* Surrey (1883–86, 3 matches).
Career batting
3–5–2–10–7–3.33–0–*ct* 0
Bowling 53–2–26.50–0–0–2/31

Voss, Richard Zahn Hartwig
Amateur. *b:* 10.11.1880, Altrincham, Cheshire. *d:* 3.9.1948, Flixton, Lancashire. Middle order right-hand batsman. *Teams* Oxford U (1901–03); London County (1903).
Career batting
8–16–1–276–50–18.40–0–*ct* 2
Bowling 32–0

His County cricket was for Cheshire (1909–14).

Voules, Rev Stirling Cooksley
Amateur. *b:* 4.1.1843, Middle Chinnock, Somerset. *d:* 6.5.1923, Maida Hill, London. Forcing middle order right-hand batsman, right-hand fast round-arm bowler. *Sch* Marlborough. *Team* Oxford U (1863–66, blue all four years).
Career batting
24–37–3–664–78–19.52–0–*ct* 24
Bowling 503–35 + 5–14.37–3–0–7/26

He retired from first-class cricket on entering the Church. His County cricket was for Dorset (1870–72), Devon (1871), Somerset (pre first-class, 1875–77) and Staffordshire (1885). His first-class debut was for Gentlemen of the South in 1862 and his final first-class match for Southgate in 1867. A good athlete he was best known as a sprinter in the 100 and 440 yards.

Vowles, Roger Charles
Professional. *b:* 5.4.1932, Grimsby, Lincolnshire. Middle order right-hand batsman, right-arm medium pace bowler. *Sch* Brentwood. *Team* Nottinghamshire (1957–61, 16 matches).
Career batting
16–28–3–292–54–11.68–0–*ct* 7
Bowling 920–23–40.00–0–0–4/106

Vyse, Edmund Waller
Amateur. *b:* 20.2.1831, Luton, Bedfordshire. *d:* 11.4.1890, Westgate-on-Sea, Kent. Middle order right-hand batsman. *Team* Surrey (1857, 2 matches).

Career batting
13–22–4–116–24–6.44–0–*ct* 5

His first-class debut was for the Surrey Club in 1854 and his final match for Southgate in 1866. He also played for Bedfordshire (1855–68) and Buckinghamshire (1859).

W

Waddington, Abraham
(known as Abram Waddington)
Professional. *b:* 4.2.1893, Clayton, Thornton, Yorkshire. *d:* 28.10.1959, Throxenby, Scarborough, Yorkshire. Tail end right-hand batsman, left-arm fast medium bowler. *Team* Yorkshire (1919–27, 255 matches). *Tour* MCC to Australia 1920/1. *Tests* England (1920/1, 2 matches).
Career batting
266–265–69–2527–114–12.89–1–*ct* 232
Bowling 16833–852–19.75–51–10–8/34
Test batting
2–4–0–16–7–4.00–0–*ct* 1
Bowling 119–1–119.00–0–0–1/35

He took 100 wickets in a season five times (best 141, av 16.79, in 1920). He kept goal for Bradford City and Halifax and was also a skilful golfer.

Waddington, John Ernest Walter
Amateur. *b:* 22.5.1910, Woodford Green, Essex. Middle order right-hand batsman. *Sch* Chigwell. *Team* Essex (1931, 1 match).
Career batting
1–1–0–8–8–8.00–0–*ct* 0

Waddy, Bernard Broughton
Amateur. *b:* 3.7.1911, Parramatta, Sydney, New South Wales, Australia. *d:* 7.8.1981, Winchester, Hampshire. Son of P. S. (Oxford U), nephew of E. F. (Warwickshire and New South Wales) and E. L. (New South Wales). Lower order right-hand batsman, right-arm medium pace bowler. *Team* Oxford U (1932).
Career batting
4–6–0–49–26–8.16–0–*ct* 0
Bowling 206–7–29.42–0–0–2/11

His final first-class match was for MCC in 1936.

Waddy, Rev Ernest Frederick
Amateur. *b:* 5.10.1880, Morpeth, New South Wales, Australia. *d:* 23.9.1958, South Littleton, Evesham, Worcestershire. Brother of E. L. (New South Wales) and P. S. (Oxford U), uncle of B. B. (Oxford U). Middle order right-hand batsman, right-arm medium pace bowler. *Teams* New South Wales (1902/3 to 1910/11, 28 matches); Warwickshire (1919–22, 26 matches). *Tour* Waddy to Ceylon 1913/4 (not first-class).
Career batting
55–87–5–2326–129–28.36–4–*ct* 44
Bowling 23–0

Waddy, Canon Percival Stacy
Amateur. *b:* 8.1.1875, Carcoa, New South Wales, Australia. *d:* 8.2.1937, St Pancras, London. Brother of E. F. (New South Wales and Warwickshire) and E. L. (New South Wales), father of B. B. (Oxford U). Middle order right-hand batsman, right-arm medium pace bowler. *Team* Oxford U (1896–97, blue both years).
Career batting
13–20–3–400–107*–23.52–1–*ct* 13
Bowling 914–39–23.43–1–0–5/96

He was Secretary of the Society for the Propagation of the Gospel.

Wade, Herbert Frederick
Amateur. *b:* 14.9.1905, Durban, South Africa. *d:* 23.11.1980, Inanda, Sandton, Johannesburg, South Africa. Brother of W. W. (South Africa). Forceful opening or middle order right-hand batsman. *Team* Natal (1924/5 to 1936/7). *Tour* South Africa to England 1935. *Tests* South Africa (1935 to 1935/6, 10 matches).
Career batting
74–118–9–3858–190–35.39–9–*ct* 50
Test batting
10–18–2–327–40*–20.43–0–*ct* 4

He captained the 1935 touring team and led South Africa in the five Tests. He hit 1,042 runs, av 28.94, in 1935. In all he captained South Africa in 10 Tests.

Wade, Saul
Professional. *b:* 8.2.1858, Farsley, Leeds, Yorkshire. *d:* 5.11.1931, Oldham, Lancashire. Middle order right-hand batsman, slow right-arm off break bowler. *Team* Yorkshire (1886–90, 66 matches).
Career batting
70–120–24–1616–74*–16.83–0–*ct* 31
Bowling 2607–139–18.75–7–2–7/28

His first-class debut was for L. Hall's XI in 1885. He was a first-class umpire (1905).

Wade, Thomas Henry
Professional. *b:* 24.11.1910, Maldon, Essex. *d:* 25.7.1987, Colchester, Essex. Lower order left-hand batsman, off break bowler, neat wicket-keeper. *Team* Essex (1929–50, 318 matches). *Tour* MCC to Australia 1936/7 (co-opted for 2 matches).
Career batting
321–476–135–5024–96–14.73–0–*ct* 414–*st* 178
Bowling 1418–48–29.54–1–0–5/64

A useful soccer player, he appeared for Southend United.

Wadekar, Ajit Laxman
Amateur. *b:* 1.4.1941, Bombay, India. Stylish middle order left-hand batsman, left-arm medium pace or

slow left-arm bowler. *Team* Bombay (1958/9 to 1974/5). *Tours* India to England 1967, 1971, 1974, to Australia and New Zealand 1967/8, to West Indies 1970/1, to Sri Lanka 1973/4, to East Africa 1967/8; State Bank of India to Ceylon 1966/7, 1968/9. *Tests* India (1966/7 to 1974, 37 matches).
Career batting
237–360–33–15380–323–47.03–36–*st* 271
Bowling 908–21–43.23–0–0–2/0
Test batting
37–71–3–2113–143–31.07–1–*ct* 46
Bowling 55–0

He batted well on all three visits to England, being captain in both 1971 and 1974. His best batting came in 1971 with 1,057 runs, av 40.65. In all he led India in 16 Tests. His highest innings was 323 for Bombay v Mysore at Bombay in 1966/7 and both his double centuries were scored in India. He hit 1,000 runs in India three times (best 1,321, av 60.40, in 1966/7).

Wadey, Alan Nigel Charles
Cricketer. *b:* 12.9.1950, Billingshurst, Sussex. Lower order right-hand batsman, right-arm medium pace bowler. *Sch* Seaford College. *Team* Sussex (1975, 1 match).
Career batting
1–2–2–0–0*–no av–0–*ct* 0
Bowling 44–1–44.00–0–0–1/44

Wadsworth, Ernest
Professional. *b:* 30.9.1850, Manchester, Lancashire. *d:* 7.1.1918, Hale, Bowdon, Cheshire. Middle order right-hand batsman, right-hand fast round-arm bowler, long-leg. *Team* Lancashire (1871–79, 7 matches).
Career batting
7–13–0–69–30–5.30–0–*ct* 1
Bowling 13–0

Wadsworth, Kenneth John
Cricketer. *b:* 30.11.1946, Nelson, New Zealand. *d:* 19.8.1976, Nelson, New Zealand. He died of cancer. Middle order right-hand batsman, wicket-keeper, occasional slow medium right-arm bowler. *Teams* Central Districts (1968/9 to 1971/2); Canterbury (1972/3 to 1975/6). *Tours* New Zealand to England 1969, 1973, 1975 (World Cup), to Australia 1969/70, 1970/1, 1973/4, 1974/5 (not first-class), to India and Pakistan 1969/70, to West Indies 1971/2. *Tests* New Zealand (1969 to 1975/6, 33 matches).
Career batting
118–166–23–3664–117–25.62–2–*ct* 265–*st* 26
Bowling 10–0
Test batting
33–51–4–1010–80–21.48–0–*ct* 92–*st* 4

He was the principal wicket-keeper on both his tours to England and played in all Tests on both visits but had only a modest batting record.

Wagener, Jack Gordon
Amateur. *b:* 20.1.1905, Upperton, Eastbourne, Sussex. *d:* 18.6.1986, Eastbourne, Sussex. Lower order left-hand batsman, slow left-arm bowler. *Sch* Bradfield. *Teams* Cambridge U (1927); Sussex (1927–30, 9 matches).
Career batting
12–15–3–310–80*–25.83–0–*ct* 3
Bowling 476–8–59.50–0–0–3/74

His final first-class match was for the Gentlemen of England in 1931.

Waghorn, Leslie Arthur
Professional. *b:* 29.7.1906, Robertsbridge, Sussex. *d:* 22.8.1979, Robertsbridge, Sussex. Lower order left-hand batsman, slow left-arm bowler. *Team* Sussex (1926–27, 4 matches).
Career batting
5–8–1–14–7–2.00–0–*ct* 4
Bowling 265–4–66.25–0–0–2/34

His final first-class match was for MCC in 1928.

Wagstaff, Hugh
Professional. *b:* 15.10.1895, Romford, Essex. *d:* 2.3.1970, Hornchurch, Essex. Tail end batsman, right-arm medium pace bowler. *Team* Essex (1920–21, 5 matches).
Career batting
5–6–4–19–17*–9.50–0–*ct* 0
Bowling 135–2–67.50–0–0–1/19

Wagstaffe, Michael Christopher
Cricketer. *b:* 26.9.1945, Kohat, India. Lower order left-hand batsman, slow left-arm bowler. *Sch* Rossall. *Team* Oxford U (1972, blue).
Career batting
13–23–7–233–42–14.56–0–*ct* 5
Bowling 870–28–31.07–0–0–4/96

His County cricket was for Devon (1972–80) and Dorset (1981–88).

Wainwright, Edward
Professional. *b:* 8.4.1865, Tinsley, Sheffield, Yorkshire. *d:* 28.10.1919, Sheffield, Yorkshire. He died after a long illness. Brother of Walker (Yorkshire). Middle order right-hand batsman, right-arm medium off break bowler. *Team* Yorkshire (1888–1902, 355 matches). *Tour* Stoddart to Australia 1897/8. *Tests* England (1893 to 1897/8, 5 matches).
Career batting
391–607–32–12513–228–21.76–19–*ct* 353
Bowling 19536–1071–18.24–63–15–9/66
Test batting
5–9–0–132–49–14.66–0–*ct* 2
Bowling 73–0

He hit 1,000 runs in a season three times (best 1,612, av 35.82, in 1897) and he took 100 wickets in a season five times (best 166, av 12.73, in 1894). In 1897 he performed the 'double'. His only double century was 228 for Yorkshire v Surrey at the Oval in

1899 and his best bowling 9/66 for Yorkshire v Middlesex at Bramall Lane in 1894.

Wainwright, Thomas Dodsworth
Amateur. *b:* 12.11.1940, Bombay, India. Middle order right-hand batsman. *Sch* Eastbourne. *Team* L. C. Stevens' XI (1961).
Career batting
1–2–0–37–28–18.50–0–*ct* 0

Wainwright, Walker
Professional. *b:* 21.1.1882, Rotherham, Yorkshire. *d:* 31.12.1961, Winchester, Hampshire. Brother of Edward (Yorkshire). Middle order left-hand batsman, slow left-arm bowler. *Team* Yorkshire (1903–05, 24 matches).
Career batting
25–38–3–652–62–18.62–0–*ct* 21
Bowling 582–19–30.63–1–0–6/49
He umpired one Test in South Africa in 1922/3, but was only a Minor County umpire in England.

Wait, Owen John
Amateur. *b:* 2.8.1926, Dulwich, London. *d:* 26.4.1981, Bromley, Kent. Lower order right-hand batsman, right-arm fast medium bowler. *Sch* Dulwich. *Teams* Cambridge U (1949–51, blue 1949 and 1951); Surrey (1950–51, 7 matches).
Career batting
45–40–17–132–19–5.73–0–*ct* 17
Bowling 3280–125–26.24–6–1–6/18
His final first-class match was for MCC in 1961. He was elected to the MCC Committee in 1977.

Waite, Anthony Charles
Professional. *b:* 29.5.1943, Pinner, Middlesex. Lower order right-hand batsman, right-arm fast medium bowler. *Team* Middlesex (1962–64, 11 matches).
Career batting
12–14–8–58–29–9.66–0–*ct* 1
Bowling 691–18–38.38–0–0–4/25
He also played for Buckinghamshire (1965–74).

Waite, John Henry Bickford
Amateur. *b:* 19.1.1930, Johannesburg, South Africa. Brother-in-law of P. L. Van der Merwe (South Africa). Sound defensive opening or middle order right-hand batsman, wicket-keeper. *Teams* Eastern Province (1948/9 to 1951/2); Transvaal (1953/4 to 1965/6). *Tours* South Africa to England 1951, 1955, 1960, to Australia and New Zealand 1952/3, 1963/4; Isaacs to England 1969 (not first-class). *Tests* South Africa (1951 to 1964/5, 50 matches).
Career batting
199–314–34–9812–219–35.04–23–*ct* 427–*st* 84
Bowling 8–0
Test batting
50–86–7–2405–134–30.44–4–*ct* 124–*st* 17
Although he completed 1,000 runs only on his 1951 tour to England (1,011, av 33.70) he proved very effective in the Tests and actually topped the Test averages in 1960 with 267 runs, av 38.14. He missed only one of the 15 Tests which were played on the three tours and was the leading wicket-keeper-batsman of his day. His highest score was 219 for Eastern Province v Griqualand West at Kimberley in 1950/1.

Waite, Mervyn George
Amateur. *b:* 7.1.1911, Kent Town, Adelaide, South Australia. *d:* 16.12.1985, Georgetown, South Australia. Middle or lower order right-hand batsman, right-arm medium pace bowler. *Team* South Australia (1930/1 to 1945/6, 72 matches). *Tour* Australia to England 1938. *Tests* Australia (1938, 2 matches).
Career batting
103–155–15–3888–137–27.77–1–*ct* 66
Bowling 6071–192–31.61–5–0–7/101
Test batting
2–3–0–11–8–3.66–0–*ct* 1
Bowling 190–1–190.00–0–0–1/150
He proved a useful all-rounder on the 1938 tour and appeared in two Tests.

Wake, William Robert
Amateur. *b:* 21.5.1852, Sheffield, Yorkshire. *d:* 14.3.1896, Norwood, Sheffield, Yorkshire. Nephew of Bernard (Yorkshire 1849–51). Middle order right-hand batsman, right-arm slow bowler. *Team* Yorkshire (1881, 3 matches).
Career batting
3–3–0–13–11–4.33–0–*ct* 2

Wakefield, Mark
Cricketer. *b:* 17.11.1968, Rochdale, Lancashire. Lower order right-hand batsman, slow left-arm bowler. *Team* Derbyshire (1987, 1 match).
Career batting
1–1–0–4–4–4.00–0–*ct* 1
Bowling 30–1–30.00–0–0–1/30

Wakefield, Percy Harold
Amateur. *b:* 3.9.1888, Pill, Somerset. *d:* 20.12.1973, Worcester. Middle order right-hand batsman, right-arm medium pace bowler. *Sch* Taunton. *Team* Worcestershire (1922, 1 match).
Career batting
1–2–0–8–8–4.00–0–*ct* 1
Bowling 13–0

Wakelin, Edwin
Professional. *b:* 18.10.1880, Cowley St John, Oxford. *d:* 13.8.1925, St Giles, Oxford. Middle order right-hand batsman. *Team* Worcestershire (1910, 1 match).
Career batting
1–1–0–6–6–6.00–0–*ct* 0
He also played for Oxfordshire (1902–03 and 1922–24).

Walcott, Clyde Leopold, OBE
Amateur. *b:* 17.1.1926, New Orleans, St Michael, Barbados. Brother of K. E. (Barbados), father of

Walden, Frederick Ingram

M. A. C. (Barbados). Attacking middle order right-hand batsman, right-arm fast medium bowler, wicket-keeper or slip field. *Teams* Barbados (1941/2 to 1955/6); British Guiana (1954/5 to 1963/4). *Tours* West Indies to India, Pakistan and Ceylon 1948/9, to England 1950, 1957, to Australia and New Zealand 1951/2. *Tests* West Indies (1947/8 to 1959/60, 44 matches).
Career batting
146–238–29–11820–314*–56.55–40–*ct* 174–*st* 33
Bowling 1269–35–36.25–1–0–5/41
Test batting
44–74–7–3798–220–56.68–15–*ct* 53–*st* 11
Bowling 408–11–37.09–0–0–3/50

On the 1950 tour he hit 1,674 runs, av 55.80, his highest innings being 168* in the Lord's Test. On his second visit he made 1,414 runs, av 45.61. His highest innings was 314* for Barbados v Trinidad in Port of Spain in 1945/6 and each of his three double centuries were also scored in the West Indies. He also hit 1,000 runs on the 1948/9 tour. He was manager of the 1969, 1976 and 1980 West Indian tours to England.

Walden, Frederick Ingram

Professional. *b:* 1.3.1888, Wellingborough, Northamptonshire. *d:* 3.5.1949, Northampton. Attacking middle order right-hand batsman, right-arm slow bowler, brilliant cover point. *Team* Northamptonshire (1910–29, 258 matches).
Career batting
259–436–36–7538–128–18.84–5–*ct* 132
Bowling 4276–119–35.93–0–0–4/35

Only 5 ft 2 in tall, he was one of the smallest players to appear in County cricket. After retiring he joined the first-class umpires' list (1930–39) and officiated in 11 Tests (1934–39). A noted right-winger, he played soccer for Tottenham Hotspur, Northampton Town and England.

Waldock, Frederic Alexander

Amateur. *b:* 16.3.1898, Colombo, Ceylon. *d:* 4.7.1959, Galmington, Taunton, Somerset. Brother of H. F. (H. K. Foster's XI). Middle order left-hand batsman, left-arm slow bowler. *Sch* Uppingham. *Teams* Oxford U (1919–20, blue both years); Somerset (1920–24, 17 matches); Ceylon (1926/7 to 1933/4).
Career batting
40–72–1–1634–85–23.01–0–*ct* 22
Bowling 924–24–38.50–1–0–7/46

He lived in Ceylon for many years and captained the Ceylon team. He was also a good rugby footballer at stand-off half, winning his blue.

Waldock, Harold Francis

Amateur. *b:* 17.5.1899, Colombo, Ceylon. *d:* 4.9.1923, Colombo, Ceylon. Brother of F. A. (Somerset). Middle order batsman. *Sch* Uppingham. *Team* H. K. Foster's XI (1919).
Career batting
2–4–1–65–43*–21.66–0–*ct* 1
Bowling 45–0

He played no first-class cricket at Oxford U, but did win a blue for rugby.

Waldron, Alan Noel Edwin

Amateur. *b:* 23.12.1920, Southsea, Hampshire. Hard hitting lower order right-hand batsman, right-arm fast medium bowler. *Sch* St Edwards, Oxford. *Team* Hampshire (1948, 2 matches).
Career batting
4–7–0–91–52–13.00–0–*ct* 3
Bowling 204–3–68.00–0–0–2/66

Waldron, Patrick Henry Pearse

Amateur. *b:* 5.2.1917, Limerick, Ireland. Opening right-hand batsman. *Team* Ireland (1946–47).
Career batting
4–8–0–99–52–12.37–0–*ct* 0

Wales, Peter John

Amateur. *b:* 30.10.1928, Hove, Sussex. Opening right-hand batsman, right-arm medium pace bowler. *Team* Sussex (1951, 1 match).
Career batting
1–2–1–38–29–38.00–0–*ct* 1
Bowling 13–5–2.60–0–0–3/12

Walford, John Erskine Scott

Amateur. *b:* 14.8.1899, Hanbury Mount, Worcestershire. *d:* 22.8.1961, Ravenscourt Park, London. Lower order right-hand batsman, right-arm fast medium bowler. *Sch* Malvern. *Team* Worcestershire (1923–30, 6 matches).
Career batting
11–18–0–198–31–11.00–0–*ct* 6
Bowling 468–29–16.13–2–0–6/27

His final first-class match was for the Army in 1932.

Walford, Michael Moore

Amateur. *b:* 27.11.1915, Norton-on-Tees, Co Durham. Attractive opening right-hand batsman, slow left-arm bowler, excellent cover point. *Sch* Rugby. *Teams* Oxford U (1935–38, blue 1936 and 1938); Somerset (1946–53, 52 matches). *Tours* Oxford and Cambridge to Jamaica 1938/9; MCC to Canada 1951.
Career batting
97–169–11–5327–264–33.71–9–*ct* 50
Bowling 249–8–31.12–1–0–6/49

His highest innings was 264 for Somerset v Hampshire at Weston-super-Mare at 1947; his only other double century was for Oxford U. A master at Sherborne School, his County cricket was mainly confined to August. He also played for Durham (pre first-class, 1935–37) and Dorset (1954–62). He was a triple blue at Oxford – rugby and hockey as well as cricket – and captained the England hockey team, representing Great Britain in the 1948 Olympics.

Walkden, George Godfrey
Amateur. *b:* 10.3.1883, Derby. *d:* 16.5.1923, Derby. He died following a motor cycle accident. Middle order batsman. *Sch* Uppingham. *Team* Derbyshire (1905–06, 7 matches).
Career batting
7–13–0–114–33–8.76–0–*ct* 2

Walker, Alan
Cricketer. *b:* 7.7.1962, Emley, Yorkshire. Lower order left-hand batsman, right-arm fast medium bowler. *Team* Northamptonshire (1983–92, 96 matches). *Tour* Northamptonshire to South Africa 1991/2.
Career batting
96–91–45–664–41*–14.43–0–*ct* 37
Bowling 6871–221–31.09–2–0–6/50

Walker, Alan Keith
Professional. *b:* 4.10.1925, Manly, Sydney, New South Wales, Australia. Attacking lower order right-hand batsman, left-arm fast bowler. *Teams* New South Wales (1948/9 to 1952/3, 26 matches); Nottinghamshire (1954–58, 49 matches). *Tour* Australia to South Africa 1949/50.
Career batting
94–118–26–1603–73–17.42–0–*ct* 37
Bowling 6072–221–27.47–9–0–7/56

He took four wickets in four balls for Nottinghamshire v Leicestershire at Leicester in 1956, namely the last wicket of the first innings and a hat-trick with the first three deliveries of the second innings. A good rugby union footballer, he toured England with the 1947/8 Australian team, and later played rugby league for Leigh.

Walker, Alfred
Amateur. *b:* 8.9.1827, Southgate, Middlesex. *d:* 4.9.1870, Arnos Grove, Middlesex. Brother of A. H. (Middlesex), Frederic (Middlesex), I. D. (Middlesex), John (Middlesex), R. D. (Middlesex) and V. E. (Middlesex), nephew of Henry (MCC 1832). Hard hitting lower order right-hand batsman, right-hand fast under-arm 'daisy-cutter' bowler, good field. *Teams* Cambridge U (1846–48); Middlesex (1851–59, 4 matches).
Career batting
14–23–3–95–20–4.75–0–*ct* 9
Bowling 83–6+30–13.83–3–0–7/?

His final first-class match was for Gentlemen of the South in 1860. He also played for Buckinghamshire (1859).

Walker, Arthur Henry
Amateur. *b:* 30.6.1833, Southgate, Middlesex. *d:* 4.10.1878, Arnos Grove, Middlesex. Brother of Alfred (Middlesex), Frederic (Middlesex), I. D. (Middlesex), John (Middlesex), R. D. (Middlesex) and V. E. (Middlesex), nephew of Henry (MCC 1832). Middle order right-hand batsman, right-hand round-arm bowler, good point field. *Sch* Harrow. *Team* Middlesex (1859–62, 4 matches).
Career batting
23–39–3–601–90–16.69–0–*ct* 22
Bowling 351–14–25.07–0–0–4/79

His first-class debut was for MCC in 1855. He suffered a badly broken leg whilst playing football in December 1862 and this ended his career in important cricket. He also played for Buckinghamshire (1859).

Walker, Arthur Walton
Amateur. *b:* 10.9.1891, Belfast, Ireland. *d:* 13.1.1968, Bangor, Co Down. Brother of Laurence (Ireland). Lower order right-hand batsman. *Team* Ireland (1913).
Career batting
1–1–0–3–3–3.00–0–*ct* 0

Walker, Ashley
Amateur. *b:* 22.6.1844, Bowling, Bradford, Yorkshire. *d:* 26.5.1927, Harrold, Bedfordshire. Cousin of C. W. (Gentlemen of North). Stylish opening right-hand batsman, right-hand slow round-arm bowler, good deep field. *Sch* Westminster. *Teams* Yorkshire (1863–70, 9 matches); Cambridge U (1864–66, blue all three years).
Career batting
20–36–2–531–65–15.61–0–*ct* 6
Bowling 289–18–16.05–2–0–6/89

He lived for many years in Ceylon and captained Ceylon against Madras in 1885 and Bombay in 1886 (not first-class). He also played for Staffordshire (1872).

Walker, Charles William
Amateur. *b:* 11.1.1851, Bowling, Bradford, Yorkshire. *d:* 2.3.1915, Palmerston North, New Zealand. Cousin of Ashley (Yorkshire). Middle order right-hand batsman, slow right-arm bowler. *Sch* Harrow. *Team* Gentlemen of the North (1870).
Career batting
1–2–0–59–40–29.50–0–*ct* 0
Bowling 85–0

He went to Madras in 1871 and later moved to New Zealand.

Walker, Charles William
Amateur. *b:* 19.2.1909, Brompton, Adelaide, South Australia. *d:* 18.12.1942, Soltau, Germany, on active service. Lower order right-hand batsman, wicket-keeper. *Team* South Australia (1928/9 to 1940/1, 78 matches). *Tour* Australia to England 1930, 1938.
Career batting
109–152–35–1754–71–14.99–0–*ct* 171–*st* 149

He was the reserve wicket-keeper on the tours of 1930 and 1938 – on the latter tour he played in only nine first-class matches owing to injury. He did not appear in Test cricket.

Walker, Clifford
Professional. *b:* 27.6.1919, Golcar, Huddersfield, Yorkshire. *d:* 3.12.1992, Huddersfield, Yorkshire. Sound middle order right-hand batsman, right-arm medium pace bowler, good slip field. *Teams* Yorkshire (1947–48, 5 matches); Hampshire (1949–54, 126 matches).
Career batting
131–224–34–5258–150*–27.67–8–*ct* 89
Bowling 2615–53–49.33–2–0–5/40
He hit 1,000 runs in a season four times (best 1,302, av 36.16, in 1953).

Walker, David Frank
Amateur. *b:* 31.5.1913, Loddon, Norfolk. *d:* 7.2.1942. He was killed on a flight over Norway, and buried at Trondheim. Stylish opening right-hand batsman, slow left-arm bowler. *Sch* Uppingham. *Team* Oxford U (1933–35, blue all three years).
Career batting
37–66–2–1880–118–29.37–2–*ct* 18
Bowling 299–6–49.83–0–0–2/36
His County cricket was for Norfolk (1931–39). His final first-class match was for P. F. Warner's XI in 1938. He captained Oxford in 1935.

Walker, Donald Frederick
Amateur with Surrey 2nd XI, turned professional 1937. *b:* 15.8.1912, Wandsworth Common, London. *d:* 18.6.1941. He was killed flying over Holland. Patient middle order left-hand batsman. *Sch* KCS, Wimbledon. *Team* Hampshire (1937–39, 73 matches).
Career batting
73–126–11–3004–147–26.12–4–*ct* 75–*st* 1
Bowling 22–0
He hit 1,149 runs, av 28.72, in 1939.

Walker, Edwin William
Amateur. *b:* 27.12.1909, Coalville, Leicestershire. Lower order right-hand batsman, right-arm fast medium bowler. *Team* Leicestershire (1930, 1 match).
Career batting
1–2–1–2–1*–2.00–0–*ct* 0
Bowling 21–1–21.00–0–0–1/21

Walker, Frederic
Amateur. *b:* 4.12.1829, Southgate, Middlesex. *d:* 20.12.1889, Arnos Grove, Middlesex. Brother of Alfred (Middlesex), A. H. (Middlesex), I. D. (Middlesex), John (Middlesex), R. D. (Middlesex) and V. E. (Middlesex), nephew of Henry (MCC 1832). Aggressive middle order right-hand batsman, good point field. *Teams* Cambridge U (1849–52, blue all four years); Middlesex (1859, 2 matches).
Career batting
34–62–4–726–71–12.51–0–*ct* 20–*st* 2
Bowling 10–0 + 13–no av–2–0–6/?
Owing to illness he did not appear in important matches as frequently as his talents warranted. His final first-class match was for Gentlemen of the South in 1860.

Walker, George Arthur
Professional. *b:* 25.1.1919, West Bridgford, Nottingham. Lower order right-hand batsman, right-arm fast medium bowler. *Team* Nottinghamshire (1937, 2 matches).
Career batting
2–4–3–24–10*–24.00–0–*ct* 1
Bowling 176–1–176.00–0–0–1/98
He played soccer for West Ham and Lincoln City.

Walker, George Glossop
Amateur. *b:* 14.6.1860, Harthill, Yorkshire. *d:* 11.1.1908, Whitwell, Derbyshire. Lower order left-hand batsman, left-arm slow, later fast, bowler. *Team* Derbyshire (1881–98, 70 matches).
Career batting
75–128–24–1141–66–10.97–0–*ct* 26
Bowling 5063–202–25.06–10–3–9/68
His best bowling was 9/68 for Derbyshire v Leicestershire at Leicester in 1895.

Walker, Gilbert
Amateur. *b:* 15.2.1888, Olton, Solihull, Warwickshire. *d: circa* 1938, Maryborough, Victoria, Australia. Middle order right-hand batsman. *Team* Warwickshire (1912, 1 match).
Career batting
1–2–0–13–13–6.50–0–*ct* 0

Walker, Harold
Amateur. *b:* 12.6.1918, Desborough, Northamptonshire. Middle order right-hand batsman, right-arm medium pace bowler. *Team* Northamptonshire (1947, 1 match).
Career batting
1–2–0–8–7–4.00–0–*ct* 0

Walker, Harry
Professional. *b:* 1760, Churt, Surrey. *d:* July 1805, Brook, Witley, Surrey. Brother of Thomas (Surrey and Hampshire). Middle order left-hand batsman. *Teams* Hampshire (1784–93); Surrey (1788–1802).
Career batting
3–6–0–20–9–3.33–0–*ct* 5
A noted hard hitting batsman of his day, but he was not as famous as his brother.

Walker, Isaac Donnithorne
Amateur. *b:* 8.1.1844, Southgate, Middlesex. *d:* 6.7.1898, Regent's Park, London. Brother of Alfred (Middlesex), A. H. (Middlesex), Frederic (Middlesex), John (Middlesex), R. D. (Middlesex) and V. E. (Middlesex), nephew of Henry (MCC 1832). Excellent stylish middle order right-hand batsman, right-hand fast, later slow, under-arm bowler, good deep field. *Sch* Harrow. *Team* Middlesex (1862–84, 144 matches).

Career batting
294–508–43–11400–179–24.51–7–*ct* 250–*st* 3
Bowling 4755–215+3–22.11–9–1–6/42

His best season was 1868 with 661 runs, av 34.78, which placed him second in the first-class batting averages, but he remained one of the leading batsmen throughout his first-class career – even in his last season of 1884 he hit 674 runs, av 28.08. He captained Middlesex from 1873 to 1884 and was a member of the County Committee at the time of his death, having been associated with the running of the Club since its foundation. He scored 102 on debut for Middlesex v Surrey Club at the Oval in 1862.

Walker, Jack
Amateur. *b:* 2.3.1914, Cobham, Kent. *d:* 29.5.1968, Cobham, Kent. Lower order right-hand batsman, wicket-keeper. *Team* Kent (1949, 1 match).
Career batting
2–4–1–60–26–20.00–0–*ct* 2–*st* 2

His final first-class match was for D. R. Jardine's XI in 1957.

Walker, James George
Amateur. *b:* 9.10.1859, Tradeston, Glasgow, Scotland. *d:* 24.3.1923, Nether Auchendrane, Ayrshire, Scotland. Steady middle order right-hand batsman, point field. *Sch* Loretto. *Teams* Oxford U (1880–83, blue 1882–83); Middlesex (1886–90, 44 matches). *Tour* Vernon to Ceylon and India 1889/90 (not first-class).
Career batting
96–167–5–3321–111–20.50–1–*ct* 69
Bowling 52–0

His final first-class match was for MCC in 1892. A noted rugby footballer, he represented Oxford and Scotland.

Walker, John
Amateur. *b:* 15.9.1826, Palmers Green, Middlesex. *d:* 14.8.1885, Arnos Grove, Middlesex. Brother of Alfred (Middlesex), A. H. (Middlesex), Frederic (Middlesex), I. D. (Middlesex), R. D. (Middlesex) and V. E. (Middlesex), nephew of Henry (MCC 1832). Middle order right-hand batsman, right-hand slow, round-arm or under-arm bowler, wicket-keeper. *Teams* Cambridge U (1846–49, blue 1847–49); Middlesex (1850–66, 9 matches).
Career batting
87–145–20–1355–98–10.84–0–*ct* 50–*st* 20
Bowling 381–16+2–23.81–0–0–4/55

He captained Cambridge in 1848 and was joint captain of Middlesex in 1864 and 1865 and assisted in the founding of the County Club. His final first-class match was for Southgate in 1868. He also played for Cambridgeshire (1852) and Bedfordshire (1865).

Walker, John
Professional. *b:* 1854, Harrow, Middlesex. Lower order batsman, right-hand fast medium round-arm bowler. *Team* Middlesex (1879, 1 match).
Career batting
1–2–1–6–6–6.00–0–*ct* 0
Bowling 26–0

Walker, John Barnhill
Amateur. *b:* 30.10.1883, Greenock, Renfrewshire, Scotland. *d:* 21.11.1953, Bearsden, Dunbartonshire, Scotland. Brother of W. N. (Scotland). Opening right-hand batsman. *Team* Scotland (1912).
Career batting
2–4–0–45–34–11.25–0–*ct* 3

Walker, Keith Gordon Eldridge
Amateur. *b:* 30.11.1922, Wimbledon, Surrey. *d:* 7.11.1989, Goring-on-Thames, Oxfordshire. Middle order left-hand batsman, leg break bowler. *Team* D. R. Jardine's XI (1955).
Career batting
1–1–0–13–13–13.00–0–*ct* 0
Bowling 82–0

Walker, Laurence
Amateur. *b:* 17.7.1901, Belfast, Ireland. Brother of A. W. (Ireland). Lower order right-hand batsman, right-arm fast medium bowler. *Team* Ireland (1922–26).
Career batting
3–4–2–27–13*–13.50–0–*ct* 0
Bowling 284–9–31.55–1–0–5/125

Walker, Livingstone
Amateur. *b:* 14.6.1879, Urmston, Lancashire. *d:* 10.10.1940, Tonbridge, Kent. Middle order right-hand batsman, off break bowler. *Sch* The Leys. *Teams* Surrey (1900–03, 57 matches); London County (1900–04).
Career batting
94–147–14–3061–222–23.01–2–*ct* 56–*st* 1
Bowling 911–19–47.94–0–0–4/41

His double century (222) was for London County v MCC at Crystal Palace in 1901. In the same year he hit 1,180 runs, av 31.89. He captained Surrey in 1903.

Walker, Malcolm
Professional. *b:* 14.10.1933, Mexborough, Yorkshire. *d:* 2.9.1986, Retford, Nottinghamshire, in a motorcycle accident. Middle order right-hand batsman, off break bowler. *Team* Somerset (1952–58, 29 matches).
Career batting
29–52–3–574–100–11.71–1–*ct* 8
Bowling 976–28–34.85–2–0–5/45

Walker, Maxwell Henry Norman
Cricketer. *b:* 12.9.1948, West Hobart, Tasmania, Australia. Lower order right-hand batsman, right-arm fast medium bowler. *Team* Victoria (1968/9 to 1981/2, 70 matches). *Tours* Australia to England 1975, 1977, to West Indies 1972/3, to New Zealand 1973/4, 1976/7; Robins to South Africa 1974/5; International Wanderers to South Africa 1975/6. *Tests*

Australia (1972/3 to 1977, 34 matches).
Career batting
135–170–40–2014–78*–15.49–0–*ct* 49
Bowling 13209–499–26.47–21–0–8/143
Test batting
34–43–13–586–78*–19.53–0–*ct* 12
Bowling 3792–138–27.47–6–0–8/143

In 1975 in England he took 36 wickets in first-class matches, av 29.88, and played in all four Tests. In 1977 he had 53, av 22.33, but was very expensive in the Test matches with 14 wickets, av 39.35.

Walker, Niel Alexander McDonald
Amateur. *b:* 22.8.1895, Poona, India. *d:* 10.8.1960. Sheffield, Yorkshire. Middle order right-hand batsman, right-arm medium pace bowler. *Teams* Europeans (1923/4 to 1926/7); Derbyshire (1931–36, 2 matches).
Career batting
4–6–0–48–18–8.00–0–*ct* 1
Bowling 77–2–38.50–0–0–1/12

Walker, Peter Michael
Professional. *b:* 17.2.1936, Clifton, Bristol. Middle order right-hand batsman, left-arm medium or slow bowler, brilliant short leg field. *Teams* Glamorgan (1956–72, 437 matches); Transvaal (1956/7 to 1957/8); Western Province (1962/3). *Tours* Brown to East Africa 1961/2 (not first-class); Glamorgan to West Indies 1969/70; Swanton to West Indies 1960/1; Commonwealth to Pakistan 1967/8. *Tests* England (1960, 3 matches).
Career batting
469–788–110–17650–152*–26.03–13–*ct* 697
Bowling 23881–834–28.63–25–2–7/58
Test batting
3–4–0–128–52–32.00–0–*ct* 5
Bowling 34–0

He hit 1,000 runs in a season 11 times (best 1,564, av 34.00, in 1959) and took 100 wickets in a season once: 101, av 24.04, in 1961, achieving the 'double' that season. In the same year he held 73 catches. He became a cricket commentator after retiring from the first-class game.

Walker, Roger
Amateur. *b:* 18.9.1846, Bury, Lancashire. *d:* 11.11.1919, Reading, Berkshire. Lower order right-hand batsman, wicket-keeper. *Team* Lancashire (1874–75, 2 matches).
Career batting
2–4–1–27–19–9.00–0–*ct* 1–*st* 1

A noted rugby footballer, he appeared five times for England.

Walker, Russell Donnithorne
Amateur. *b:* 13.2.1842, Southgate, Middlesex. *d:* 29.3.1922, Regent's Park, London. Brother of Alfred (Middlesex), A. H. (Middlesex), Frederic (Middlesex), John (Middlesex), I. D. (Middlesex) and V. E. (Middlesex), nephew of Henry (MCC 1832). Attacking opening or middle order right-hand batsman, right-hand slow round-arm bowler, good field. *Sch* Harrow. *Teams* Oxford U (1861–65, blue all five years); Middlesex (1862–77, 45 matches).
Career batting
122–202–8–3840–104–19.79–2–*ct* 90
Bowling 5514–313+21–17.61–17–4–8/43

His best season was 1865 with 770 runs, av 24.83. His final first-class match was for MCC in 1878. He was on the Committee of both Middlesex and MCC until he died, being President of the Middlesex Club (1906–22) and a Trustee of MCC. A noted rackets player, he represented Oxford.

Walker, Stanley George
Professional. *b:* 18.5.1908, Pinxton, Derbyshire. Lower order right-hand batsman, left-arm fast medium bowler. *Team* Derbyshire (1932, 1 match).
Career batting
1–2–0–8–7–4.00–0–*ct* 0
Bowling 6–1–6.00–0–0–1/6

He also played for Scotland (not first-class).

Walker, Thomas
Professional. *b:* 16.11.1762, Churt, Surrey. *d:* 1.3.1831, Chiddingfold, Surrey. Brother of Harry (Surrey and Hampshire). Steady opening right-hand batsman, right-hand fast round-arm, later slow under-arm bowler. *Teams* Hampshire (1787–93); Surrey (1788–1810).
Career batting
46–89–4–1111–61–13.07–0–*ct* 25–*st* 2
Bowling 41 wickets (no analyses)–0–0–4/?

The most famous defensive batsman of his day, he was reported to have received 170 balls from David Harris and scored just one run. He was perhaps the first player to bowl round-arm – it was then banned by the Hambledon Club because of the tremendous pace of Walker's deliveries.

Walker, Thomas
Amateur until 18.8.1879, then professional. *b:* 3.4.1854, Mill Green, Holbeck, Leeds, Yorkshire. *d:* 28.8.1925, Roundhay, Leeds, Yorkshire. Hard hitting middle order right-hand batsman, slow right-arm bowler. *Team* Yorkshire (1879–80, 14 matches).
Career batting
15–24–2–189–30–8.59–0–*ct* 3
Bowling 7–0

His final first-class match was for T. Emmett's XI in 1883.

Walker, Vyell Edward
Amateur. *b:* 20.4.1837, Southgate, Middlesex. *d:* 3.1.1906, Arnos Grove, Middlesex. Brother of Alfred (Middlesex), A. H. (Middlesex), Frederic (Middlesex), I. D. (Middlesex), John (Middlesex) and R. D. (Middlesex), nephew of Henry (MCC 1832). Fine middle order right-hand batsman, right-hand slow

under-arm bowler, good field. *Sch* Harrow. *Team* Middlesex (1859–77, 52 matches).
Career batting
145–228–32–3384–108–17.26–1–*ct* 188
Bowling 4797–304+30–15.77–27–8–10/74

His first-class debut was for Gentlemen v Players at Lord's in 1856. He was, around 1860, the best all-round amateur cricketer in England and in 1859 for England v Surrey at the Oval scored 20* and 108 as well as taking 10/74 and 4/17. He also took 10/104 Middlesex v Lancashire at Old Trafford in 1865. He captained Middlesex from 1864 to 1872. He was President of MCC in 1891 and at the time of his death had been Middlesex treasurer since 1897 and President since 1898, having previously been President in 1869. He also played for Bedfordshire (1863).

Walker, William Norman
Amateur. *b:* 23.1.1894, Greenock, Renfrewshire, Scotland. *d:* 14.9.1960, Greenock, Renfrewshire, Scotland. Brother of J. B. (Scotland). Opening right-hand batsman, right-arm medium pace bowler. *Sch* Glasgow Academy. *Team* Scotland (1922–25).
Career batting
6–11–0–200–58–18.18–0–*ct* 5
Bowling 502–18–27.88–0–0–4/55

Walker, William Percy
Amateur. *b:* 11.4.1889, Northampton. *d:* 6.2.1938, Kingsley, Northampton. Middle order right-hand batsman. *Team* Northamptonshire (1908–20, 6 matches).
Career batting
7–13–0–113–48–8.69–0–*ct* 1

His final first-class match was for V. W. C. Jupp's XI in 1926.

Walker, Willis
Professional. *b:* 24.11.1892, Gosforth, Northumberland. *d:* 3.12.1991, Keighley, Yorkshire. Sound middle order right-hand batsman, right-arm medium pace bowler, good deep field. *Team* Nottinghamshire (1913–37, 405 matches).
Career batting
406–624–60–18259–165*–32.37–31–*ct* 110
Bowling 97–2–48.50–0–0–2/20

He hit 1,000 runs in a season 10 times (best 1,730, av 39.31, in 1933). A good soccer player, he kept goal for South Shields, Sheffield United, Doncaster, Bradford and Leeds. He was the oldest living County cricketer at the time of his death.

Walkinshaw, Frank
Amateur. *b:* 28.2.1861, Hong Kong. *d:* 14.7.1934, Bramley, Hampshire. Lower order batsman, wicket-keeper. *Sch* Eton. *Team* Hampshire (1885, 3 matches).
Career batting
3–5–0–15–11–3.00–0–*ct* 4–*st* 1

He last played for Hampshire (not first-class) in 1892.

Wall, Henry
Amateur. *b:* 20.4.1852, Wallgate, Wigan, Lancashire. *d:* 13.10.1914, Southport, Lancashire. Brother of Thomas (Lancashire) and William (Lancashire). Middle order right-hand batsman, right-hand fast round-arm bowler. *Team* Lancashire (1877, 3 matches).
Career batting
3–4–0–24–15–6.00–0–*ct* 2

Wall, Stephen
Cricketer. *b:* 10.12.1959, Ulverston, Lancashire. Lower order right-hand batsman, right-arm medium fast bowler. *Team* Warwickshire (1984–85, 19 matches).
Career batting
19–25–9–175–28–10.93–0–*ct* 6
Bowling 1518–37–41.02–0–0–4/59

He also played for Cumberland (1983–92).

Wall, Thomas
Amateur. *b:* 27.11.1841, Wigan, Lancashire. *d:* 19.4.1875, Wallgate, Wigan, Lancashire. Brother of Henry (Lancashire) and William (Lancashire). Middle order right-hand batsman, right-hand slow round-arm bowler, wicket-keeper. *Team* Lancashire (1868, 2 matches).
Career batting
2–4–0–48–37–12.00–0–*ct* 1
Bowling 17–0

Wall, Thomas Welbourn
Amateur. *b:* 13.5.1904, Semaphore, Adelaide, South Australia. *d:* 26.3.1981, Adelaide, South Australia. Tail end right-hand batsman, right-arm fast bowler, short leg field. *Team* South Australia (1924/5 to 1935/6, 53 matches). *Tours* Australia to England 1930, 1934. *Tests* Australia (1928/9 to 1934, 18 matches).
Career batting
108–135–33–1071–53*–10.50–0–*ct* 54
Bowling 9877–330–29.93–10–2–10/36
Test batting
18–24–5–121–20–6.36–0–*ct* 11
Bowling 2010–56–35.89–3–0–5/14

The fastest bowler in Australian Test cricket, he took 56 wickets, av 29.25, on the 1930 tour to England and 42, av 30.71, in 1934. He played in all five Tests in 1930 and in four in 1934, but his wickets were very expensive. His best bowling was 10/36 for South Australia v New South Wales at Sydney in 1932/3.

Wall, William
Amateur. *b:* 8.1.1854, Wigan, Lancashire. *d:* 18.4.1922, Southport, Lancashire. Brother of Henry (Lancashire) and Thomas (Lancashire). Lower order right-hand batsman, wicket-keeper. *Team* Lancashire

Wallace, Charles William

(1877, 1 match).
Career batting
1–2–1–17–17*–17.00–0–*ct* 2–*st* 2

Wallace, Charles William
Amateur. *b:* 24.11.1884, Calcutta, India. *d:* 5.9.1946, Awbridge, Hampshire. Middle order batsman. *Sch* Winchester. *Team* Worcestershire (1921–22, 4 matches).
Career batting
4–7–1–66–39*–11.00–0–*ct* 1

Wallace, Gary Charles
Cricketer. *b:* 8.2.1958, Salisbury, Rhodesia. Middle order left-hand batsman, left-arm medium pace bowler. *Team* Rhodesia/Zimbabwe (1978/9 to 1986/7). *Tour* Zimbabwe to England 1982.
Career batting
20–38–3–943–111–26.94–1–*ct* 8
Bowling 238–5–47.60–0–0–3/61

Wallace, George Henry
Amateur. *b:* 18.9.1854, Great Budworth, Cheshire. *d:* 24.11.1927, Notting Hill, London. Middle order right-hand batsman. *Sch* Clergy Orphan School, Canterbury. *Team* Cambridge U (1876).
Career batting
1–2–0–13–8–6.50–0–*ct* 1

Wallace, Kenneth William
Cricketer. *b:* 27.8.1936, Romford, Essex. Middle order right-hand batsman, right-arm medium pace bowler. *Team* Essex (1967–72, 10 matches).
Career batting
10–16–0–219–55–13.68–0–*ct* 2

Wallace, Nesbit Willoughby
Amateur. *b:* 20.4.1839, Halifax, Nova Scotia, Canada. *d:* 31.7.1931, Guildford, Surrey. Middle order right-hand batsman, right-hand slow under-arm bowler, deep field. *Sch* Rugby. *Teams* Gloucestershire (1871, 2 matches); Hampshire (1884, 2 matches).
Career batting
6–9–1–66–25–8.25–0–*ct* 4
Bowling 6–0

His first-class debut was for Gentlemen of the South in 1863 and his final first-class match for MCC in 1885. He was mainly instrumental in the organising of the English tour of North America in 1872. He also helped to found the Green Jackets CC and was Hon Secretary of that Club until 1894. He played for Ireland (not first-class) in 1865.

Wallace, Paul
Cricketer. *b:* 4.5.1962, Londonderry, Ireland. Lower order right-hand batsman, left-arm fast medium bowler. *Team* Ireland (1988).
Career batting
1–2–0–0–0–0.00–0–*ct* 0
Bowling 91–2–45.50–0–0–2/91

Wallace, Walter Mervyn
Amateur. *b:* 19.12.1916, Grey Lynn, Auckland, New Zealand. Father of G. M. (Auckland), brother of G. F. (Auckland). Forceful middle order right-hand batsman, off break bowler, good field at mid-off or mid-on. *Team* Auckland (1933/4 to 1956/7). *Tours* New Zealand to England 1937, 1949, to Australia 1937/8. *Tests* New Zealand (1937 to 1952/3, 13 matches).
Career batting
121–192–17–7757–211–44.32–17–*ct* 68
Bowling 18–0
Test batting
13–21–0–439–66–20.90–0–*ct* 5
Bowling 5–0

He hit 1,000 runs on both tours to England (best 1,722, av 49.02, in 1949), but, although he appeared in all Tests on both visits, he made little impact against England. His final first-class match was for the Governor-General's XI in 1960/1. His highest score was 211 for Auckland v Canterbury at Auckland in 1939/40. He captained New Zealand in two Tests.

Wallach, Benjamin
Amateur. *b:* 18.9.1873, Queenstown, South Africa. *d:* 25.5.1935, Troyeville, Johannesburg, South Africa. Tail end right-hand batsman, wicket-keeper. *Teams* Transvaal (1897/8 to 1904/5); London County (1902–04). *Tour* South Africa to England 1904.
Career batting
15–18–7–100–30–9.09–0–*ct* 16–*st* 11

The reserve wicket-keeper on the 1904 tour, he appeared in only three first-class matches.

Waller, Andrew Christopher
Cricketer. *b:* 25.9.1959, Salisbury, Rhodesia. Middle order right-hand batsman. *Team* Zimbabwe (1984/5 to 1991/2). *Tours* Zimbabwe to England 1985, to India (World Cup) 1987/8, to Australia and New Zealand (World Cup) 1991/2.
Career batting
22–36–4–784–99–24.50–0–*ct* 14
Bowling 2–1–2.00–0–0–1/1

He played in only two first-class matches on the 1985 tour of England.

Waller, Christopher Edward
Cricketer. *b:* 3.10.1948, Guildford, Surrey. Lower order right-hand batsman, slow left-arm bowler. *Teams* Surrey (1967–73, 40 matches); Sussex (1974–85, 227 matches).
Career batting
267–266–111–1481–51*–9.55–0–*ct* 133
Bowling 18312–630–29.06–22–1–7/61

His best season was 1976 when he took 71 wickets, av 25.95. He was subsequently on the coaching staff at both Sussex and Surrey.

Waller, Edmund
Amateur. *b:* 7.12.1838, Bishops Tachbrook, Leamington Spa, Warwickshire. *d:* 6.2.1871, Pimlico, Westminster, London. Opening batsman. *Sch* Marlborough. *Team* Gentlemen of Kent (1865).
Career batting
1–2–0–22–16–11.00–0–*ct* 1

Waller, George
Professional. *b:* 3.12.1864, Pitsmoor, Sheffield, Yorkshire. *d:* 11.12.1937, Ecclesfield, Sheffield, Yorkshire. Lower order right-hand batsman, right-arm medium pace bowler. *Team* Yorkshire (1893–94, 3 matches).
Career batting
3–4–0–17–13–4.25–0–*ct* 1
Bowling 70–4–17.50–0–0–2/10
A noted soccer player, he played for Sheffield Wednesday in the FA Cup Final of 1890. Later he played and then acted as trainer for Sheffield United.

Waller, Guy de Warrenne
Cricketer. *b:* 10.2.1950, Savernake, Wiltshire. Middle order right-hand batsman, off break bowler. *Sch* Hurstpierpoint. *Team* Oxford U (1973–74, blue 1974).
Career batting
13–25–1–203–29–8.45–0–*ct* 10
Bowling 4–0
He also won a blue for hockey.

Waller, Richard Beaumont
Cricketer. *b:* 5.12.1969, Islington, London. Lower order right-hand batsman, right-arm medium fast bowler. *Sch* Radley. *Team* Cambridge U (1991, blue).
Career batting
5–4–3–12–6*–12.00–0–*ct* 1
Bowling 363–7–51.85–0–0–3/31

Waller, Richmond Campbell Shakespear
Amateur. *b:* 26.7.1879, Barton Regis, Bristol. *d:* 28.6.1950, Colchester, Essex. Lower order batsman, bowler. *Sch* Haileybury. *Team* Navy and Army (1910).
Career batting
1–1–0–1–1–1.00–0–*ct* 0
Bowling 22–0
His County cricket was for Devon (1909–10).

Wallgate, Lamplough
Amateur. *b:* 12.11.1849, Norton, Yorkshire. *d:* 9.5.1887, Harrogate, Yorkshire. Opening right-hand batsman, right-hand round-arm bowler. *Team* Yorkshire (1875–77, 2 matches).
Career batting
2–2–0–3–3–1.50–0–*ct* 2
Bowling 17–1–17.00–0–0–1/17

Wallington, Sir Edward William
Amateur. *b:* 7.12.1854, Oakley Hall, near Basingstoke, Hampshire. *d:* 12.12.1933, Widcombe, Bath, Somerset. Great-nephew of J. C. (Sussex and Hampshire). Steady middle order right-hand batsman, right-hand slow under-arm bowler. *Sch* Sherborne. *Team* Oxford U (1875–77, blue 1877).
Career batting
6–9–1–100–38–12.50–0–*ct* 3
His final first-class match was for MCC in 1885. He lived for many years in Australia, being at one time Private Secretary to the Governor of New South Wales. His County cricket was for Wiltshire (1875–95) and Dorset (1877).

Wallis, Arthur Knight
Amateur. *b: circa* 1868, Donnycarney, Dublin, Ireland. *d:* 27.11.1905, Dublin, Ireland. Lower order batsman, useful bowler. *Team* Dublin University (1895).
Career batting
3–5–2–7–5*–2.33–0–*ct* 1
Bowling 319–6–53.16–0–0–3/110
He was a noted rugby footballer, playing for Dublin University and Ireland.

Wallis Mathias
Amateur. *b:* 4.2.1935, Karachi, India. Middle order right-hand batsman, right-arm medium pace bowler, good slip field. *Teams* Sind (1953/4 to 1955/6); Karachi (1956/7 to 1969/70); National Bank (1969/70 to 1976/7). *Tours* Pakistan to West Indies 1957/8, to India 1960/1, to England 1962. *Tests* Pakistan (1955/6 to 1962, 21 matches).
Career batting
146–206–37–7520–278*–44.49–16–*ct* 130
Bowling 532–13–40.92–0–0–2/4
Test batting
21–36–3–783–77–23.72–0–*ct* 22
Bowling 20–0
He achieved little on his tour to England in 1962.

Wallis, William Alfred
Amateur. *b:* 14.12.1878, Long Eaton, Derbyshire. *d:* 12.11.1939, Wilsthorpe, Long Eaton, Derbyshire. Middle order right-hand batsman. *Sch* Trent College. *Team* Derbyshire (1906, 1 match).
Career batting
1–2–0–17–11–8.50–0–*ct* 1

Wallroth, Conrad Adolphus
Amateur. *b:* 17.5.1851, Lee, London. *d:* 22.2.1926, Compton Grange, Godalming, Surrey. Brother-in-law of A. Lubbock (Kent). Steady middle order right-hand batsman, good long stop. *Sch* Harrow. *Teams* Kent (1872, 1 match); Oxford U (1872–74, blue all three years); Derbyshire (1879, 3 matches).
Career batting
21–36–1–596–109–17.02–1–*ct* 8
His first-class debut was for MCC in 1871.

Wallwork, Mark Andrew
Cricketer. *b:* 14.12.1960, Urmston, Lancashire. Lower order right-hand batsman, wicket-keeper. *Team* Lancashire (1982, 1 match).
Career batting
1 match, did not bat –*ct* 3

Walmsley, Walter Thomas
Amateur. *b:* 16.3.1916, Homebush, New South Wales, Australia. *d:* 25.2.1978, Hamilton, Auckland, New Zealand. Lower order right-hand batsman, leg break and googly bowler. *Teams* New South Wales (1945/6, 1 match); Tasmania (1947/8, 3 matches); Queensland (1954/5 to 1958/9, 28 matches); Northern Districts (1959/60).
Career batting
37–50–11–1064–180*–27.28–2–*ct* 8
Bowling 3861–122–31.64–3–0–6/56
His only match in England was for a Commonwealth XI at Kingston-upon-Thames in 1953. His first-class debut in New Zealand was for Combined Northern and Central Districts XI in 1958/9.

Walrond, Sir William Hood
(created 1st Baron Waleran of Uffculme in 1905)
Amateur. *b:* 26.2.1849, Bradfield, Cullompton, Devon. *d:* 17.5.1925, Victoria, London. Uncle of W. H. Holbech (Warwickshire). Middle order right-hand batsman, deep field. *Sch* Eton. *Team* MCC (1868).
Career batting
1–2–1–26–13*–26.00–0–*ct* 0
He did not appear in any first-class matches whilst at Cambridge. His County cricket was for Devon (1866–68). He played for Ireland (not first-class) in 1869. From 1880 to 1885 he was Conservative MP for East Devonshire and then until 1905 for Tiverton. He held various Government offices including Chancellor of the Duchy of Lancaster.

Walsh, Courtney Andrew
Cricketer. *b:* 30.10.1962, Kingston, Jamaica. Lower order right-hand batsman, right-arm fast bowler. *Teams* Jamaica (1981/2 to 1991/2); Gloucestershire (1984–92, 123 matches). *Tours* Young West Indies to Zimbabwe 1983/4; West Indies to England 1984, 1988, 1991, to Australia 1984/5, 1986/7, 1988/9, to Sharjah (not first-class) 1985/6, 1986/7, 1988/9, 1989/90, 1991/2, to Pakistan 1985/6 (not first-class), 1986/7, 1990/1, to New Zealand 1986/7, to India 1987/8, 1989/90 (not first-class), to India and Pakistan (World Cup) 1987/8; Rest of World to England 1987. *Tests* West Indies (1984/5 to 1991/2, 51 matches).
Career batting
252–306–72–2969–63*–12.68–0–*ct* 68
Bowling 22244–989–22.49–55–11–9/72
Test batting
51–69–22–456–30*–9.70–0–*ct* 7
Bowling 4444–178–24.96–5–1–6/62
On his first tour to England in 1984 he did not play in any Test matches; in both 1988 and 1991 he appeared in all five Tests, proving a very useful back up to Marshall and Ambrose. He has been a most successful bowler for Gloucestershire and had an outstanding season in 1986 when he took 118 wickets, av 18.17, including 9/72 v Somerset at Bristol. In 1992 he topped the first-class bowling averages with 92 wickets, av 15.96.

Walsh, David Robert
Cricketer. *b:* 17.12.1946, Bombay, India. Middle order right-hand batsman, right-arm medium pace bowler. *Sch* Marlborough. *Team* Oxford U (1966–69, blue 1967–69).
Career batting
39–69–10–1508–207–25.55–2–*ct* 13
Bowling 129–6–21.50–0–0–3/34
He hit 207 for Oxford U v Warwickshire at Oxford in 1969.

Walsh, George
Amateur. *b:* 16.2.1852, Over Darwen, Blackburn, Lancashire. *d:* 22.5.1904, Darwen, Lancashire. Middle order batsman. *Sch* Rugby. *Team* Lancashire (1874–77, 2 matches).
Career batting
2–3–0–16–15–5.33–0–*ct* 0
He also played for Cheshire (1876).

Walsh, John Edward
Professional. *b:* 4.12.1912, Sydney, New South Wales, Australia. *d:* 20.5.1980, Wallsend, New South Wales, Australia. Attacking lower order left-hand batsman, slow left-arm bowler with chinaman, good close field. *Teams* Leicestershire (1937–56, 279 matches); New South Wales (1939/40, 2 matches). *Tours* Cahn to Ceylon 1936/7, to New Zealand 1938/9.
Career batting
296–460–52–7247–106–17.76–2–*ct* 209
Bowling 29226–1190–24.55–98–26–9/101
His first-class debut was for Sir J. Cahn's XI in 1936. He took 100 wickets in a season seven times (best 174, av 19.56, in 1948). In 1952 he hit 1,106 runs, av 24.04, completing the 'double' in the same season. His best bowling was 9/101 for Sir J. Cahn's XI v Glamorgan at Newport in 1938.

Walshe, Aubrey Peter
Amateur. *b:* 1.1.1934, Salisbury, Rhodesia. Lower order right-hand batsman, wicket-keeper. *Team* Oxford U (1953–56, blue 1953, 1955 and 1956).
Career batting
46–69–8–900–77–14.75–0–*ct* 49–*st* 12

Walter, Arthur Fraser
Amateur. *b:* 12.9.1846, Wokingham, Berkshire. *d:* 22.2.1910, Bearwood, Berkshire. Son-in-law of T. A.

Anson (Cambridge U). Middle order right-hand batsman, right-hand medium pace round-arm bowler, good deep field. *Sch* Eton. *Team* Oxford U (1867–69, blue 1869).
Career batting
5–9–0–12–3–1.33–0–*ct* 0
Bowling 200–11–18.18–1–0–5/35

He was Chairman of Times Publishing Company.

Walters, Charley
Professional. *b:* 1.4.1897, Headington, Oxfordshire. *d:* 13.5.1971, Kidlington, Oxfordshire. Middle order batsman, useful bowler. *Team* Minor Counties (1930–34).
Career batting
4–4–0–47–25–11.75–0–*ct* 2
Bowling 148–3–49.33–0–0–2/72

His County cricket was for Oxfordshire (1922–52).

Walters, Cyril Frederick
Amateur. *b:* 28.8.1905, Bedlinog, Glamorgan. *d:* 23.12.1992, Neath, Glamorgan. Stylish opening right-hand batsman. *Teams* Glamorgan (1923–28, 75 matches); Wales (1927–29); Worcestershire (1928–35, 137 matches). *Tours* Tennyson to Jamaica 1931/2; MCC to India 1933/4. *Tests* England (1933–34, 11 matches).
Career batting
245–427–32–12145–226–30.74–21–*ct* 101
Bowling 380–5–76.00–0–0–2/22
Test batting
11–18–3–784–102–52.26–1–*ct* 6

He hit 1,000 runs in a season five times, going on to 2,000 twice (best 2,404, av 50.08, in 1933). His only double century was 226 for Worcestershire v Kent at Gravesend in 1933. He captained Worcestershire 1931 to 1935 and England in one Test. He moved to Worcestershire in 1928 when appointed Secretary, retaining the position until 1935, and played for both his counties in 1928. He played rugby for Swansea.

Walters, Francis Henry
Amateur. *b:* 9.2.1860, East Melbourne, Victoria, Australia. *d:* 1.6.1922, at sea off Bombay, India. Sound middle order right-hand batsman, right-arm medium pace bowler. *Teams* Victoria (1880/1 to 1893/4, 22 matches); New South Wales (1895/6, 5 matches). *Tour* Australia to England 1890. *Test* Australia (1884/5, 1 match).
Career batting
56–96–9–1755–150–20.17–4–*ct* 31
Bowling 81–1–81.00–0–0–1/17
Test batting
1–2–0–12–7–6.00–0–*ct* 2

He was very disappointing on his tour to England.

Walters, John
Cricketer. *b:* 7.8.1949, Brampton, Yorkshire. Middle order left-hand batsman, right-arm fast medium bowler. *Team* Derbyshire (1977–80, 58 matches).
Career batting
58–80–15–1296–90–19.93–0–*ct* 26
Bowling 1935–47–41.17–0–0–4/100

Walters, Joseph Arthur
Professional. *b:* 12.2.1940, Bolsover, Derbyshire. Tail end right-hand batsman, leg break bowler. *Team* Nottinghamshire (1958–59, 5 matches).
Career batting
5–9–8–64–21*–64.00–0–*ct* 4
Bowling 464–10–46.40–1–0–6/139

Walters, Kevin Douglas, MBE
Cricketer. *b:* 21.12.1945, Marshdale, Dungog, New South Wales, Australia. Attacking middle order right-hand batsman, right-arm medium pace bowler. *Team* New South Wales (1962/3 to 1980/1, 103 matches). *Tours* Australia to England 1968, 1972, 1975, 1977, to Ceylon, India and South Africa 1969/70, to West Indies 1972/3, to New Zealand 1973/4, 1976/7. *Tests* Australia (1965/6 to 1980/1, 74 matches).
Career batting
258–426–57–16180–253–43.84–45–*ct* 149
Bowling 6782–190–35.69–6–0–7/63
Test batting
74–125–14–5357–250–48.26–15–*ct* 43
Bowling 1425–49–29.08–1–0–5/66

A brilliant batsman in Australia, he rarely succeeded in England – on the tours of 1972 and 1977 his record was very poor in the Tests and altogether his best visit came in 1975 with 784 first-class runs, av 60.30. He played in 18 Tests in England. Of his four double centuries, three were made in Australia and the fourth in New Zealand. His highest score was 253 for New South Wales v South Australia at Adelaide in 1964/5. He hit 1,000 runs in a season twice (best 1,332, av 70.10, in 1965/6).

Walters, Percy Melmoth
Amateur. *b:* 30.9.1863, Ewell, Surrey. *d:* 3.10.1936, Ashtead, Surrey. Lower order right-hand batsman, wicket-keeper. *Sch* Charterhouse. *Team* Oxford U (1885).
Career batting
1–1–0–9–9–9.00–0–*ct* 0

A good soccer player, he appeared as left-back for Old Carthusians in the FA Amateur Cup final of 1895, won his blue, and was capped for England.

Walton, Arthur Christopher
Amateur. *b:* 26.9.1933, Georgetown, British Guiana. Middle order right-hand batsman. *Sch* Radley. *Teams* Oxford U (1955–57, blue all three years); Middlesex (1957–59, 35 matches).
Career batting
85–155–2–3797–152–24.81–3–*ct* 47
Bowling 8–0

He hit 1,200 runs, av 38.70, in 1956. His first-class debut was for Combined Services in 1953. He also played for Berkshire (1951–56). He captained Oxford in 1957.

Walton, Francis
Amateur. *b:* 1832. *d:* 14.7.1871, Surbiton, Surrey. Attacking middle order right-hand batsman, right-hand fast round-arm bowler. *Team* Hampshire (1864–66, 3 matches).
Career batting
3–6–1–55–16–11.00–0–*ct* 1
Bowling 165–6–27.50–0–0–3/48

Walton, George
Professional. *b:* 3.12.1863, Belgrave, Leicester. *d:* 30.6.1921, Belgrave, Leicester. Lower order right-hand batsman, right-arm fast medium bowler. *Team* Leicestershire (1894–95, 9 matches).
Career batting
9–14–1–88–24–6.76–0–*ct* 9
Bowling 424–17–24.94–0–0–4/64
He first played for Leicestershire (pre first-class) in 1889.

Walton, Herbert
Amateur. *b:* 21.5.1868, Scarborough, Yorkshire. *d:* 28.2.1930, Scarborough, Yorkshire. Lower order right-hand batsman, right-arm medium fast bowler. *Team* Yorkshire (1893, 1 match).
Career batting
1–1–0–5–5–5.00–0–*ct* 1
Bowling 135–5–27.00–0–0–3/93

Walton, J. C.
Amateur. Opening right-hand batsman, right-arm medium pace bowler. *Team* Ireland (1925).
Career batting
1–2–0–52–48–26.00–0–*ct* 0
Bowling 26–0
His County cricket was for Suffolk (1938).

Walton, James Richard
Professional. *b:* 25.3.1857, Woolwich Dockyard, London. Lower order batsman, useful bowler. *Team* Kent (1875, 1 match).
Career batting
1–2–0–13–13–6.50–0–*ct* 1
Bowling 15–1–15.00–0–0–1/15

Walton, Kevin Gordon
Cricketer. *b:* 20.10.1956, Umtali, Rhodesia. Middle order right-hand batsman. *Team* Zimbabwe (1983/4 to 1986/7). *Tour* Zimbabwe to England 1985.
Career batting
10–18–1–223–37–13.11–0–*ct* 10
He had little success on the 1985 tour to England.

Walton, Matthew
Professional. *b:* 10.12.1837, Cross Cliffe, Glossop, Derbyshire. *d:* 7.1.1888, Glossop, Derbyshire. Father of William (Derbyshire). Opening batsman. *Team* Lancashire (1867, 1 match).
Career batting
1–2–0–6–6–3.00–0–*ct* 0

Walton, William
Professional. *b:* 7.8.1862, Glossop, Derbyshire. *d:* 16.2.1925, Glossop, Derbyshire. Son of Matthew (Lancashire). Opening right-hand batsman. *Team* Derbyshire (1887, 1 match).
Career batting
1–2–0–4–3–2.00–0–*ct* 0
His last match for Derbyshire (not first-class) was in 1893.

Walusimbi, Samuel
Cricketer. *b:* 1948, Uganda. Middle order right-hand batsman, left-arm medium pace bowler. *Team* East Africa (1973/4 to 1975). *Tour* East Africa to England 1975.
Career batting
2–4–0–78–54–19.50–0–*ct* 1

Wanklyn, James Leslie
Amateur. *b:* 14.4.1860, Holdenhurst, Hampshire. *d:* 6.7.1919, Northampton. Middle order batsman. *Team* MCC (1885).
Career batting
1–1–0–0–0–0.00–0–*ct* 1
He was MP for Bradford Central 1895–1906.

Wanostrocht, N. (*see under* Felix, N.)

Waqar Ahmed
Cricketer. *b:* 19.12.1946, Lahore, India. Son of Dilawar Hussain (India), brother of Nadeem Ahmed (Lahore). Middle order right-hand batsman. *Teams* Punjab University (1964/5 to 1968/9); Lahore (1966/7 to 1972/3); Punjab (1972/3). *Tour* Pakistan to England 1967.
Career batting
33–51–6–1705–199–37.88–3–*ct* 18
Bowling 67–1–67.00–0–0–1/19
In seven matches he hit 306 runs, av 38.25, on the 1967 tour to England, but was then forced to return home due to the death of his father.

Waqar Hassan Mir
Amateur. *b:* 12.9.1932, Amritsar, India. Brother of Pervez Sajjad (Pakistan). Stylish middle order right-hand batsman, good outfield. *Teams* Punjab University (1948/9); Karachi (1951/2 to 1965/6). *Tours* Pakistan to India 1952/3, to England 1954, to West Indies 1957/8; Pakistan Services to Ceylon 1953/4. *Tests* Pakistan (1952/3 to 1959/60, 21 matches).
Career batting
97–141–11–4620–201*–35.53–8–*ct* 45
Bowling 172–2–86.00–0–0–1/9
Test batting
21–35–1–1071–189–31.50–1–*ct* 10
Bowling 10–0

He hit 1,263 runs, av 32.38, on the 1954 tour to England and played in all four Tests. His highest score was 201* for Air Vice Marshal Cannon's XI v Hasan Mahmood's XI at Karachi in 1953/4.

Waqar Younis
Cricketer. *b:* 16.11.1971, Vehari, Pakistan. Lower order right-hand batsman, right-arm fast bowler. *Teams* Multan (1987/8 to 1990/1); United Bank (1988/9 to 1990/1); Surrey (1990–91, 32 matches). *Tours* Pakistan to Australia 1989/90, to India 1989/90 (not first-class), to Sharjah (not first-class) 1989/90, 1990/1, 1991/2, to England 1992. *Tests* Pakistan (1989/90 to 1992, 19 matches).
Career batting
80–78–31–634–51–13.48–0–*ct* 18
Bowling 7261–355–20.45–32–8–7/64
Test batting
19–21–5–127–20*–7.93–0–*ct* 1
Bowling 1908–93–20.51–10–2–7/76

Waqar combined an ability to swing the ball with great pace. These qualities made him perhaps the most deadly bowler of the early 1990s. In 1991 he was the leading bowler in England with 113 wickets, av 14.65, taking his wickets at five runs fewer than any other player. In 1992 he joined with Wasim Akram to form the spearhead of the Pakistan touring side to England and proved just as successful in the Test series. He has met with equal success in cricket overseas.

Warburton, David
Amateur. *b:* 30.5.1919, Huddersfield, Yorkshire. Lower order right-hand batsman, right-arm fast bowler. *Sch* Leeds GS. *Team* Oxford U (1939).
Career batting
1–2–0–4–4–2.00–0–*ct* 0
Bowling 39–0

Warburton, Leslie
Professional. *b:* 30.4.1910, Haslingden, Lancashire. *d:* 11.2.1984, Gloucester. Middle order right-hand batsman, right-arm fast medium bowler, good slip field. *Team* Lancashire (1929–38, 6 matches).
Career batting
8–8–2–171–74*–28.50–0–*ct* 1
Bowling 289–7–41.28–0–0–3/47

He was unexpectedly selected for the Test Trial of 1936 on the strength of his performances in League cricket. He achieved little in the Trial.

Ward, Alan
Cricketer. *b:* 10.8.1947, Dronfield, Derbyshire. Lower order right-hand batsman, right-arm fast bowler. *Teams* Derbyshire (1966–76, 115 matches); Border (1971/2); Leicestershire (1977–78, 22 matches). *Tours* Norfolk to West Indies 1969/70; MCC to Australia 1970/1. *Tests* England (1969–76, 5 matches).
Career batting
163–157–47–928–44–8.43–0–*ct* 51
Bowling 10495–460–22.81–15–4–7/42
Test batting
5–6–1–40–21–8.00–0–*ct* 3
Bowling 453–14–32.35–0–0–4/61

Regarded as the best fast bowling prospect in England in 1969, his career was marred by injury.

Ward, Albert
Professional. *b:* 21.11.1865, Waterloo, Leeds, Yorkshire. *d:* 6.1.1939, Heaton, Bolton, Lancashire. Steady opening right-hand batsman, slow right-arm bowler, good field. *Teams* Yorkshire (1886, 4 matches); Lancashire (1889–1904, 330 matches). *Tour* Stoddart to Australia 1894/5. *Tests* England (1893 to 1894/5, 7 matches).
Career batting
385–642–51–17783–219–30.08–29–*ct* 169
Bowling 2473–71–34.83–4–0–6/29
Test batting
7–13–0–487–117–37.46–1–*ct* 1

He hit 1,000 runs in a season nine times (best 1,790, av 42.61, in 1895). His only double century was 219 for A. E. Stoddart's XI v South Australia at Adelaide in 1894/5.

Ward, Albert Paine
Professional. *b:* 9.11.1896, Highgate, Middlesex. *d:* 5.3.1979, Jersey. Lower order right-hand batsman, right-arm fast bowler. *Team* Hampshire (1921, 1 match).
Career batting
1–2–1–11–6–11.00–0–*ct* 1
Bowling 57–1–57.00–0–0–1/28

Ward, Arnold Sandwith
Amateur. *b:* 8.11.1876, Headington, Oxfordshire. *d:* 1.1.1950, Kensington, London. Lower order right-hand batsman, right-arm medium pace bowler. *Sch* Eton and Uppingham. *Team* Oxford U (1899).
Career batting
1–2–0–8–6–4.00–0–*ct* 1
Bowling 52–0

His County cricket was for Hertfordshire (1896–99) and Buckinghamshire (1900–05). He was MP for West Hertfordshire from 1910 to 1918.

Ward, Basil Jordain
Amateur. *b:* 6.8.1889, Dublin, Ireland. *d:* 29.3.1972, Clapham, London. Lower order left-hand batsman, left-arm fast bowler. *Team* Ireland (1912–20).
Career batting
4–7–2–56–17–11.20–0–*ct* 3
Bowling 273–13–21.00–0–0–4/66

Ward, Brian
Cricketer. *b:* 28.2.1944, Chelmsford, Essex. Middle order right-hand batsman, right-arm medium pace bowler. *Team* Essex (1967–72, 128 matches).

Career batting
128–222–19–4799–164*–23.64–4–*ct* 60
Bowling 68–5–13.60–0–0–2/5

His best season was 1971 with 968 runs, av 27.65. He played for Argentine in ICC Trophy (1979).

Ward, Rev Charles Gordon
Amateur. *b:* 23.9.1875, Braughing, Hertfordshire. *d:* 27.6.1954, South Ormsby Hall, Lincolnshire. Brother of H. F. (Hampshire), nephew of C. B. (Oxford U 1860), cousin of L. F. (Derbyshire). Lower order right-hand batsman, useful bowler. *Sch* Aldenham and Denstone. *Team* Hampshire (1897–1901, 14 matches).
Career batting
14–23–0–186–30–8.08–0–*ct* 3
Bowling 135–2–67.50–0–0–1/17

He also played for Lincolnshire (1903–11) and Hertfordshire (1912–22).

Ward, David Mark
Cricketer. *b:* 10.2.1961, Croydon, Surrey. Middle order right-hand batsman, off break bowler, wicket-keeper. *Team* Surrey (1985–92, 121 matches).
Career batting
121–192–31–6430–263–39.93–14–*ct* 100–*st* 3
Bowling 113–2–56.50–0–0–2/66

He reached 1,000 runs twice, going on to 2,072, av 76.74, in 1990. His highest score was 263 for Surrey v Kent at Canterbury in 1990.

Ward, Donald John
Professional. *b:* 30.8.1934, Trealaw, Tonypandy, Glamorgan. Lower order right-hand batsman, off break bowler, fine cover-point. *Team* Glamorgan (1954–62, 135 matches).
Career batting
135–206–33–2496–86–14.42–0–*ct* 65
Bowling 4987–187–26.66–5–0–7/60

Ward, Rev Edward Ewer
(changed name from E. E. Harrison in 1868)
Amateur. *b:* 16.7.1847, Timworth Hall, Suffolk. *d:* 25.3.1940, Gorleston, Norfolk. Tail end right-hand batsman, left-hand fast round-arm bowler. *Sch* Bury St Edmund's. *Team* Cambridge U (1868–71, blue 1870 and 1871).
Career batting
11–18–5–30–5–2.30–0–*ct* 5
Bowling 548–37–14.81–1–0–6/29

His County cricket was for Suffolk (1868–77).

Ward, Francis Anthony
Amateur. *b:* 23.2.1909, Sydney, New South Wales, Australia. *d:* 25.3.1974, Brooklyn, Sydney, New South Wales, Australia. Stubborn lower order right-hand batsman, leg break and googly bowler. *Team* South Australia (1935/6 to 1940/1, 38 matches). *Tour* Australia to England 1938. *Tests* Australia (1936/7 to 1938, 4 matches).
Career batting
66–80–17–871–62–13.82–0–*ct* 42
Bowling 7900–320–24.68–24–5–7/51
Test batting
4–8–2–36–18–6.00–0–*ct* 1
Bowling 574–11–52.18–1–0–6/102

In first-class matches on the 1938 tour he came second in the bowling table with 92 wickets, av 19.27, but was chosen for only one Test.

Ward, Frank
Professional. *b:* 9.1.1865, Carlisle, Cumberland. Stylish middle order right-hand batsman, right-arm medium pace bowler. *Team* Lancashire (1884–96, 47 matches).
Career batting
47–74–6–986–145–14.50–1–*ct* 11
Bowling 538–27–19.92–0–0–4/14

Ward, Frank
Amateur. *b:* 3.6.1888, Kensington, London. *d:* 1.3.1952, Worthing, Sussex. Middle order batsman, useful bowler. *Team* Army (1926–27).
Career batting
4–6–0–28–10–4.66–0–*ct* 0
Bowling 84–2–42.00–0–0–1/9

Ward, Frederick
Professional. *b:* 31.8.1881, Heckmondwike, Yorkshire. *d:* 28.2.1948, Dewsbury, Yorkshire. Lower order left-hand batsman, slow left-arm bowler. *Team* Yorkshire (1903, 1 match).
Career batting
1–1–0–0–0–0.00–0–*ct* 1
Bowling 16–0

Ward, Geoffrey Hubert
Professional. *b:* 22.11.1926, Rainham, Kent. Lower order right-hand batsman, wicket-keeper. *Sch* Sutton Valence. *Teams* Kent (1949, 2 matches); Essex (1950, 1 match).
Career batting
3–6–2–23–6*–5.75–0–*ct* 3–*st* 1

Ward, Hon Gerald Ernest Francis
Amateur. *b:* 9.11.1877, Himley Hall, Staffordshire. *d:* 30.10.1914, Zandvoorde, Belgium. He was killed in action. Son of Lord Ward (Oxford U 1838), grandson of T. Moncrieffe (MCC 1841), brother-in-law of D. H. B. H. Blundell (MCC). Tail end right-hand batsman, right-arm fast bowler, moderate field. *Sch* Eton. *Team* MCC (1903).
Career batting
1–1–0–8–8–8.00–0–*ct* 0

Ward, Herbert Foster
Amateur. *b:* 24.3.1873, Hammersmith, London. *d:* 6.6.1897, Northwood, Winchester, Hampshire. He died of typhoid fever. Brother of C. G. (Hampshire), nephew of C. B. (Oxford U 1860), cousin of L. F. (Derbyshire). Stylish middle order right-hand bats-

man. *Team* Hampshire (1895–97, 33 matches).
Career batting
34–63–1–1367–113–22.04–2–*ct* 20
Bowling 553–19–29.10–0–0–4/17

He also played for Hertfordshire (1891–93).

Ward, Humphrey Plowden
Amateur. *b:* 20.1.1899, Amotherby, Malton, Yorkshire. *d:* 16.12.1946, Thornton-le-Dale, Yorkshire. Fine forcing middle order right-hand batsman, wicket-keeper. *Sch* Shrewsbury. *Teams* Oxford U (1919–21, blue 1919 and 1921); Yorkshire (1920, 1 match); Europeans (1921/2 to 1945/6); Madras (1926/7 to 1938/9).
Career batting
66–120–10–3571–173–32.46–4–*ct* 67–*st* 18
Bowling 35–1–35.00–0–0–1/13

He went to India in 1922 and played much cricket in Madras. His final first-class match in England was for H. D. G. Leveson-Gower's XI in 1931. A good soccer player, he won his blue, was an Amateur International and played for Huddersfield Town.

Ward, Ian James
Cricketer. *b:* 30.9.1972, Plymouth, Devon. Lower order left-hand batsman, right-arm medium pace bowler. *Sch* Millfield. *Team* Surrey (1992, 1 match).
Career batting
1–1–0–0–0–0.00–0–*ct* 1
Bowling 35–0

Ward, John
Amateur. Lower order batsman, fast round-arm bowler. *Team* Hampshire (1877, 1 match).
Career batting
1–2–0–14–11–7.00–0–*ct* 0
Bowling 77–0

Ward, John Daniel
Amateur. *b:* 21.5.1931, Sea Point, Cape Town, South Africa. Lower order batsman, right-arm medium fast bowler. *Team* Cambridge U (1954).
Career batting
1–1–1–5–5*–no av–0–*ct* 0
Bowling 79–1–79.00–0–0–1/39

Ward, John Michael
Cricketer. *b:* 14.9.1948, Sandon, Staffordshire. Middle order right-hand batsman. *Sch* Newcastle-under-Lyme HS. *Teams* Oxford U (1970–73, blue 1971–73); Derbyshire (1973–75, 20 matches).
Career batting
49–87–4–1743–104–21.00–1–*ct* 24

He also played for Staffordshire (1969–73). A useful rugby footballer, he represented Staffordshire.

Ward, John Thomas
Amateur. *b:* 11.3.1937, Timaru, Canterbury, New Zealand. Father of B. J. (Canterbury). Steady lower order right-hand batsman, wicket-keeper. *Team* Canterbury (1959/60 to 1970/1). *Tours* New Zealand to England 1958, 1965, to South Africa 1961/2, to India and Pakistan 1964/5. *Tests* New Zealand (1963/4 to 1967/8, 8 matches).
Career batting
95–129–39–1117–54*–12.41–0–*ct* 227–*st* 27
Bowling 7–0
Test batting
8–12–6–75–35*–12.50–0–*ct* 16–*st* 1

The reserve wicket-keeper, he played in only 13 matches on the 1958 tour and in none of the Tests. In 1965 he appeared in just six matches, but in one Test. His first-class debut was for South Island in 1957/8.

Ward, Lancelot Edward Seth
Amateur. *b:* 7.8.1875, Hemel Hempstead, Hertfordshire. *d:* 27.8.1929, Lambeth, London. Father-in-law of P. J. Keen (Europeans). Middle order batsman. *Sch* Felsted. *Team* Somerset (1913–20, 3 matches).
Career batting
3–5–0–18–11–3.60–0–*ct* 0

Ward, Rev Leonard Foster
Amateur. *b:* 24.3.1866, Oldham, Lancashire. *d:* 1.9.1945, St Helier, Jersey. Son of C. B. (Oxford U 1860), cousin of C. G. (Hampshire) and H. F. (Hampshire). Middle order batsman. *Sch* Denstone. *Team* Derbyshire (1899, 1 match).
Career batting
1–2–0–0–0–0.00–0–*ct* 1

Ward, Leslie Maynard
Amateur. *b:* 2.5.1908, Coventry, Warwickshire. *d:* 13.1.1981, Bideford, Devon. Lower order right-hand batsman, right-arm medium pace off break bowler. *Sch* Bablake. *Team* Warwickshire (1930, 1 match).
Career batting
1–1–0–5–5–5.00–0–*ct* 1
Bowling 29–1–29.00–0–0–1/29

Ward, Merrik de Sampajo Cecil
Amateur. *b:* 15.7.1908, Westminster, London. *d:* 13.2.1981, Bath, Somerset. Hard hitting middle order left-hand batsman, left-arm medium or slow bowler. *Sch* Eton. *Team* Hampshire (1927–29, 5 matches).
Career batting
5–10–1–141–48–15.66–0–*ct* 3
Bowling 135–0

Ward, Michael John Paul
Cricketer. *b:* 12.9.1971, Oldham, Lancashire. Lower order right-hand batsman, off break bowler. *Sch* Manchester GS. *Team* Lancashire (1991, 1 match).
Career batting
1 match, did not bat–*ct* 0
Bowling 6–0

Ward, R. W. (*see under* Wright, R.)

Ward, Reginald Valentine
Professional. *b:* 14.2.1902, Biggleswade, Bedfordshire. *d:* 1.5.1968, Yeovil, Somerset. Lower order

right-hand batsman, useful bowler. *Team* Minor Counties (1931).
Career batting
1–1–0–4–4–4.00–0–*ct* 0
Bowling 77–2–38.50–0–0–2/77
His County cricket was for Bedfordshire (1929–39).

Ward, Thomas Alfred
Amateur. *b:* 2.8.1887, Rawalpindi, India. *d:* 16.2.1936, East Springs Gold Mine, Transvaal, South Africa. He was accidentally electrocuted whilst working. Steady opening or middle order right-hand batsman, wicket-keeper. *Team* Transvaal (1909/10 to 1925/6). *Tours* South Africa to England 1912, 1924. *Tests* South Africa (1912–24, 23 matches).
Career batting
92–137–31–1635–75–15.42–0–*ct* 107–*st* 68
Bowling 11–0
Test batting
23–42–9–459–64–13.90–0–*ct* 19–*st* 13
He played in five out of six Tests on the 1912, but achieved little as a batsman. In 1924 he played in all the Tests and, promoted to open the innings, proved a very stubborn defender. His return of 484 runs, av 14.66, does not convey his worth to the team.

Ward, Thomas Fitzgerald
Amateur. *b:* 14.2.1905, Armagh, Ireland. *d:* 2.7.1989, Dublin, Ireland. Tail end right-hand batsman, right-arm fast bowler. *Team* Ireland (1936–39).
Career batting
2–4–3–7–3*–7.00–0–*ct* 1
Bowling 139–5–27.80–0–0–2/31

Ward, Trevor Robert
Cricketer. *b:* 18.1.1968, Farningham, Kent. Opening right-hand batsman, off break bowler. *Team* Kent (1986–92, 93 matches).
Career batting
93–160–12–5683–235*–38.39–13–*ct* 71
Bowling 535–6–89.16–0–0–2/48
He reached 1,000 runs in a season three times (best 1,648, av 48.47, in 1992). His highest score was 235* for Kent v Middlesex at Canterbury in 1991.

Ward, William
Amateur. *b:* 24.7.1787, Islington, Middlesex. *d:* 30.6.1849, Westminster, London. Father of Henry (Strathavon's XI 1832), Matthew (MCC 1835) and A. R. (Cambridge U 1852). Attacking middle order right-hand batsman, slow under-arm bowler, point field. *Sch* Winchester. *Teams* Surrey (1815–17); Hampshire (1816–45).
Career batting
130–235–23–4022–278–18.97–3–*ct* 49–*st* 4
Bowling 49 wickets (no analyses)–0–0–4/?
At Lord's in 1820 he hit 278 for MCC v Norfolk, which was the highest innings recorded at that time and the first double century. He was for many years regarded as one of the leading batsmen in England. His first first-class match was for England in 1810. He was for MP for the City of London from 1826 to 1831.

Ward, William
Professional. *b:* 24.5.1874, Birmingham. *d:* 13.12.1961, Birmingham. Lower order batsman, slow left-arm bowler. *Team* Warwickshire (1895–1904, 11 matches).
Career batting
11–16–5–79–26–7.18–0–*ct* 3
Bowling 965–30–32.16–2–0–5/61

Ward, Sir William Erskine
Amateur. *b:* 4.2.1838, Bath, Somerset. *d:* 24.12.1916, Ealing, Middlesex. Brother of E. W. (New South Wales), father of L. B. (Europeans). Middle order batsman. *Team* MCC (1871).
Career batting
1–2–0–6–6–3.00–0–*ct* 0

Wardall, Thomas Arthur
Professional. *b:* 19.4.1862, Eston Junction, Middlesbrough, Yorkshire. *d:* 20.12.1932, Burnley, Lancashire. Steady middle order right-hand batsman, right-arm slow bowler, usually 'donkey-drops'. *Team* Yorkshire (1884–94, 45 matches).
Career batting
47–80–3–1163–112–15.10–3–*ct* 30
Bowling 695–30–23.16–1–0–5/13

Warde, Frederick
Amateur. *b:* 18.3.1852, West Farleigh, Kent. *d:* 14.5.1899, Aldington, Kent. Lower order right-hand batsman, right-hand fast medium round-arm bowler. *Sch* Tonbridge and Maidstone. *Team* Kent (1871–77, 6 matches).
Career batting
6–10–1–65–18–7.22–0–*ct* 1
Bowling 56–3–18.66–0–0–2/5

Warden, Jehangir Sorabji
Amateur. *b:* 13.1.1885, Bombay, India. *d:* 16.1.1928, Bombay, India. Middle order left-hand batsman, slow left-arm bowler. *Team* Parsis (1905/6 to 1924/5). *Tour* India to England 1911.
Career batting
41–71–7–1208–115*–18.87–1–*ct* 38
Bowling 2813–183–15.37–17–4–8/91
He was the leading all-rounder on the 1911 tour with 429 runs, av 15.32, and 44 wickets, av 25.59, in first-class matches. In a minor match in Calcutta in 1920 he took five wickets with the first five balls of the match. He was author of 'Knotty Cricket Problems Solved.'

Wardill, Benjamin Johnson
Amateur. *b:* 15.10.1842, Everton, Lancashire. *d:* 15.10.1917, Sandringham, Victoria, Australia. Brother of R. W. (Victoria). Lower order right-hand

batsman, wicket-keeper. *Sch* Liverpool College *Team* Victoria (1866/7, 1 match). *Tours* Manager of Australia to England 1886, 1899, 1902.
Career batting
2–3–1–21–17–10.50–0–*ct* 2

He played in one first-class match on the 1886 tour to England. He was Secretary to Melbourne Cricket Club from 1878 to 1910.

Wardle, Charles
Professional. *b:* 20.2.1837, Arnold, Nottinghamshire. *d:* 10.8.1907, Arnold, Nottinghamshire. Lower order right-hand batsman, right-hand fast round-arm bowler, slip field. *Team* Lancashire (1867–72, 3 matches).
Career batting
3–5–2–25–7*–8.33–0–*ct* 4
Bowling 17–0

Wardle, John Henry
Professional. *b:* 8.1.1923, Ardsley, Yorkshire. *d:* 23.7.1985, Hatfield, Doncaster, Yorkshire. Hard hitting lower order left-hand batsman, slow left-arm orthodox and chinaman bowler. *Team* Yorkshire (1946–58, 330 matches). *Tours* MCC to West Indies 1947/8, 1953/4, to Australia and New Zealand 1954/5, to South Africa 1956/7; selected for MCC to Australia 1958/9, but invitation withdrawn following his outspoken newspaper articles. *Tests* England (1947/8 to 1957, 28 matches).
Career batting
412–527–71–7333–79–16.08–0–*ct* 256
Bowling 35027–1846–18.97–134–29–9/25
Test batting
28–41–8–653–66–19.78–0–*ct* 12
Bowling 2080–102–20.39–5–1–7/36

He took 100 wickets in a season 10 times (best 195, av 16.14, in 1955). His best bowling was 9/25 for Yorkshire v Lancashire at Old Trafford in 1954. The newspaper articles referred to above caused his dismissal from Yorkshire at the height of his career and the virtual end of his first-class cricket. He later played for Cambridgeshire (1963–69). His final first-class appearance was in a National Defence Fund Match in India in 1967/8.

Ware, Rev John Hubert
Amateur. *b:* 9.1.1863, Ullingswick, Herefordshire. *d:* 28.11.1907, Minehead, Somerset. Tail end right-hand batsman, slow leg break bowler. *Team* Oxford U (1886).
Career batting
1–2–1–14–10–14.00–0–*ct* 0
Bowling 43–0

His County cricket was for Herefordshire (1881). He won a blue for athletics.

Waring, Ian Charles
Cricketer. *b:* 6.12.1963, Chesterfield, Derbyshire. Lower order left-hand batsman, right-arm fast medium bowler. *Team* Sussex (1985–87, 4 matches).
Career batting
4–3–2–0–0*–0.00–0–*ct* 2
Bowling 217–3–72.33–0–0–2/76

Waring, John Shaw
Cricketer. *b:* 1.10.1942, Ripon, Yorkshire. Lower order right-hand batsman, right-arm fast medium bowler. *Teams* Yorkshire (1963–66, 28 matches); Warwickshire (1967, 1 match).
Career batting
29–29–15–152–26–10.85–0–*ct* 17
Bowling 1251–55–22.74–2–1–7/40

He also played for Cumberland (1970–73).

Waring, Seth
Amateur. *b:* 4.11.1838, Darfield, Yorkshire. *d:* 17.4.1919, Keighley, Yorkshire. Middle order right-hand batsman, right-arm medium fast bowler. *Team* Yorkshire (1870, 1 match).
Career batting
1–1–0–9–9–9.00–0–*ct* 0

Warke, Dr Laurence
Amateur. *b:* 6.5.1927, North Belfast, Ireland. *d:* 22.1.1989, Belfast, Ireland. Father of S. J. S. (Ireland). Middle order right-hand batsman, right-arm medium pace bowler. *Sch* Royal Belfast Academical Institution. *Team* Ireland (1950–61).
Career batting
17–29–0–405–120–13.96–1–*ct* 20
Bowling 326–7–46.57–0–0–1/0

Warke, Stephen John Simon
Cricketer. *b:* 11.7.1959, North Belfast, Ireland. Son of Laurence (Ireland). Opening right-hand batsman. *Sch* Royal Belfast Academical Institution. *Team* Ireland (1981–92).
Career batting
11–20–2–832–144*–46.22–2–*ct* 7

Warley, Simon Nicholas
Cricketer. *b:* 6.1.1972, Sittingbourne, Kent. Middle order right-hand batsman, right-arm medium fast bowler. *Sch* Kent College. *Team* Oxford U (1991–92).
Career batting
9–13–2–132–35–12.00–0–*ct* 3

Warnapura, Bandula
Cricketer. *b:* 1.3.1953, Rambukkana, Ceylon. Opening right-hand batsman, right-arm medium pace bowler. *Team* Sri Lanka (1970/1 to 1982/3). *Tours* Sri Lanka to India 1972/3, 1975/6, 1976/7, 1982/3, to Pakistan 1973/4, 1981/2, to England 1975, 1979, 1981; Arosa Sri Lankan XI to South Africa 1982/3. *Tests* Sri Lanka (1981/2 to 1982/3, 4 matches).
Career batting
57–99–8–2280–154–25.05–2–*ct* 23
Bowling 628–13–48.30–0–0–2/33

Test batting
4–8–0–96–38–12.00–0–*ct* 2
Bowling 46–0

Captain of Sri Lanka, he led his country in its first Test, but his decision to tour South Africa ended his brief Test career.

Warne, Frank Belmont
Professional. *b:* 3.10.1906, North Carlton, Melbourne, Victoria, Australia. Son of T. S. (Victoria). Middle order left-hand batsman, leg break bowler. *Teams* Victoria (1926/7 to 1928/9, 2 matches); Worcestershire (1934–38, 78 matches); Europeans (1934/5 to 1937/8); Transvaal (1941/2). *Tour* Australia to India 1935/6.
Career batting
95–168–15–3275–115–21.40–3–*ct* 31
Bowling 4801–138–34.78–4–1–6/51

His final first-class match was for Rest of South Africa in 1942/3. He hit 1,000 runs, av 20.40, in 1935.

Warner, Alan Esmond
Cricketer. *b:* 12.5.1957, Winson Green, Birmingham. Lower order right-hand batsman, right-arm fast medium bowler. *Teams* Worcestershire (1982–84, 28 matches); Derbyshire (1985–92, 135 matches).
Career batting
163–221–40–3164–91–17.48–0–*ct* 39
Bowling 10591–326–32.48–2–0–5/27

Warner, Charles Simon
Amateur. *b:* 19.11.1938, Liverpool, Lancashire. Opening left-hand batsman. *Sch* Repton. *Team* Oxford U (1962).
Career batting
7–14–0–365–77–26.07–0–*ct* 2

Warner, Christopher John
Cricketer. *b:* 15.1.1945, Waverley, Bloemfontein, South Africa. Son of E. W. (Orange Free State). Middle order left-hand batsman. *Team* Scotland (1978–84).
Career batting
8–14–1–391–70–30.07–0–*ct* 7

He played hockey for South Africa.

Warner, Claude Charles
Amateur. *b:* 31.3.1882, Cardiff, Glamorgan. *d:* 29.12.1965, Llanelly, Carmarthenshire. Lower order batsman, useful bowler. *Team* Glamorgan (1923, 1 match).
Career batting
1–2–1–14–7*–14.00–0–*ct* 0
Bowling 47–0

Warner, Graham Sydney
Cricketer. *b:* 27.11.1945, Darlaston, Staffordshire. Middle order right-hand batsman, right-hand off break bowler. *Team* Warwickshire (1966–71, 30 matches).
Career batting
30–48–7–965–118*–23.53–2–*ct* 13
Bowling 14–0

He also played for Staffordshire (1976–87).

Warner, Sir Pelham Francis
Amateur. *b:* 2.10.1873, The Hall, Port of Spain, Trinidad. *d:* 30.1.1963, West Lavington, Sussex. Brother of C. W. P. (Trinidad) and R. S. A. (Trinidad). Stylish opening right-hand batsman, right-arm slow bowler, good field. *Sch* Rugby. *Teams* Oxford U (1894–96, blue 1895 and 1896); Middlesex (1894–1920, 345 matches). *Tours* Hawke to West Indies 1896/7, to South Africa 1898/9, to Australia and New Zealand 1902/3; Warner to North America 1897; 1898; MCC to Australia 1903/4, 1911/12, to South Africa 1905/6, to South America 1926/7; joint manager of MCC to Australia and New Zealand 1932/3. *Tests* England (1898/9 to 1912, 15 matches).
Career batting
519–875–75–29028–244–36.28–60–*ct* 183
Bowling 636–15–42.40–0–0–2/26
Test batting
15–28–2–622–132*–23.92–1–*ct* 3

He hit 1,000 runs in a season 14 times, going on to 2,000 once: 2,123, av 46.15, in 1911. His highest innings was 244 for Rest of England v Warwickshire at the Oval in 1911, and he hit two other double centuries, one in New Zealand and one for MCC v Sussex. He captained England in 10 Test matches and the MCC on three major tours, two to Australia and one to South Africa. He led Middlesex from 1908 to 1920. His final first-class match was for MCC v Royal Navy in 1929. He was Middlesex Hon Secretary 1920–22 and President 1937–46. From 1905 to 1938 he was intermittantly a Test selector and in 1937 he was knighted for his services to cricket. In 1950 he was President of MCC and from 1946 to 1961 a Trustee of the Club. He wrote many books on the game, besides being Editor of *The Cricketer* and cricket correspondent for the *Morning Post* from 1921 to 1932.

Warner, Rev William Sidney Oke
Amateur. *b:* 29.8.1844, Swansea, Glamorgan. *d:* 22.10.1871, Laverstock House, Salisbury, Wiltshire. He died from tetanus. Brother of G. T. (Cambridge U 1861). Attacking middle order right-hand batsman, long stop or long leg. *Team* Cambridge U (1865–68, blue 1867 and 1868).
Career batting
13–22–2–323–50–16.15–0–*ct* 7

His County cricket was for Devon (1862–70). He represented Cambridge at rackets 1866 to 1868.

Warr, Antony Lawley
Amateur. *b:* 15.5.1913, Selly Oak, Birmingham. Lower order right-hand batsman, wicket-keeper. *Sch* Bromsgrove. *Team* Oxford U (1933–34).

Career batting
5–7–1–54–24–9.00–0–*ct* 6–*st* 1

His final first-class match was for MCC in 1950. A noted rugby footballer, he played for Oxford and England.

Warr, John James
Amateur. *b:* 16.7.1927, Ealing, Middlesex. Tail end right-hand batsman, right-arm fast medium bowler. *Teams* Cambridge U (1949–52, blue all four years); Middlesex (1949–60, 260 matches). *Tours* MCC to Australia and New Zealand 1950/1, to Canada 1951, to East Africa 1957/8 (not first-class); Swanton to West Indies 1955/6; Norfolk to Jamaica 1956/7. *Tests* England (1950/1, 2 matches).
Career batting
344–454–119–3838–54*–11.45–0–*ct* 117
Bowling 21796–956–22.79–35–5–9/65
Test batting
2–4–0–4–4–1.00–0–*ct* 0
Bowling 281–1–281.00–0–0–1/76

He took 116 wickets, av 18.17, in 1956 and also exceeded 100 wickets in one other season. His best bowling was 9/65 for Middlesex v Kent at Lord's in 1956. He captained Cambridge in 1951 and Middlesex 1958–60. In 1991 he was elected a Trustee of the MCC, having previously served on the MCC Committee and been President 1987/8. He is a well-known after-dinner speaker.

Warren, Arnold (R.)
(his second initial was used only to distinguish him from another of the same name in his locality)
Professional. *b:* 2.4.1875, Codnor Park, Derbyshire. *d:* 3.9.1951, Codnor, Derbyshire. Lower order right-hand batsman, right-arm fast bowler. *Team* Derbyshire (1897–1920, 250 matches). *Test* England (1905, 1 match).
Career batting
255–445–44–5507–123–13.73–1–*ct* 195
Bowling 23061–939–24.55–72–15–8/69
Test batting
1–1–0–7–7–7.00–0–*ct* 1
Bowling 113–6–18.83–1–0–5/57

He took 100 wickets in a season three times (best 124, av 20.94, in 1904). He was a first-class umpire (1923–26). He played soccer for Derby County, Brentford and Glossop.

Warren, Rev Charles
Amateur. *b:* 20.12.1843, Cambridge. *d:* 29.4.1919, Sidmouth, Devon. Forceful opening right-hand batsman, good deep field. *Sch* Oakham. *Teams* Cambridgeshire (1865–67, 11 matches); Cambridge U (1866, blue).
Career batting
20–35–4–577–73–18.61–0–*ct* 5

He was on the Committee of Cambridgeshire CCC in 1866. His final first-class match was for an England Eleven in 1874, but he rarely appeared in important cricket after being ordained. He also played for Lincolnshire (1871).

Warren, Russell John
Cricketer. *b:* 10.9.1971, Northampton. Middle order right-hand batsman, off break bowler. *Team* Northamptonshire (1992, 2 matches).
Career batting
2–3–1–27–19–13.50–0–*ct* 0

Warren, Thomas Henry
Professional. *b:* 8.10.1859, Hathern, Leicestershire. *d:* 22.4.1936, Evington, Leicester. Attractive middle order right-hand batsman, right-hand fast medium round-arm bowler, good cover point. *Team* Leicestershire (1894–95, 13 matches).
Career batting
15–27–3–313–33–13.04–0–*ct* 7
Bowling 34–2–17.00–0–0–2/34

He first played for Leicestershire (pre first-class) in 1882. His first-class debut was in 1886 for North v South at Lord's.

Warrington, Anthony George
Cricketer. *b:* 28.3.1947, Ipswich, Suffolk. Opening right-hand batsman. *Team* Minor Counties (1973–74).
Career batting
2–4–0–152–92–38.00–0–*ct* 0

His County cricket was for Suffolk (1965–89).

Warrington, John Michael
Amateur. *b:* 7.3.1924, Northampton. Lower order right-hand batsman, right-arm medium pace bowler. *Team* Northamptonshire (1951, 2 matches).
Career batting
2–1–0–18–18–18.00–0–*ct* 1
Bowling 164–3–54.66–0–0–1/30

Warsop, Brian
Professional. *b:* 12.1.1904, Willesden, Middlesex. Middle order right-hand batsman, slow left-arm bowler. *Team* Essex (1931–32, 5 matches).
Career batting
5–10–2–128–51–16.00–0–*ct* 1
Bowling 18–0

Warsop, Thomas
Professional. *c:* 29.9.1778, Nottingham. *d:* 28.2.1845, Nottingham. He died of gout in the brain. Useful middle order batsman, right-hand slow under-arm bowler. *Team* Nottingham (1791–1823).
Career batting
1–2–0–24–18–12.00–0–*ct* 2
Bowling 2 wickets (no analyses)–0–0–2/?

The most famous of four brothers, all of whom played for Nottingham in the late 18th century, he was a good all-rounder and his under-arm bowling was afterwards imitated with great success by William Clarke. He played for 22 of Nottinghamshire v

MCC in 1791 when aged only 12. His only 19th century first-class match was Nottinghamshire and Leicestershire v Hampshire in 1803.

Washbrook, Cyril, CBE
Professional. *b:* 6.12.1914, Barrow, Clitheroe, Lancashire. Sound opening right-hand batsman, right-arm medium pace bowler, brilliant cover field. *Team* Lancashire (1933–59, 500 matches). *Tours* MCC to Australia and New Zealand 1946/7, 1950/1, to South Africa 1948/9. *Tests* England (1937–56, 37 matches).
Career batting
592–906–107–34101–251*–42.67–76–*ct* 212
Bowling 309–7–44.14–0–0–2/8
Test batting
37–66–6–2569–195–42.81–6–*ct* 12
Bowling 33–1–33.00–0–0–1/25

With L. Hutton he formed England's opening pair in the Tests immediately following the Second World War, and together they proved most successful. In 1946/7 in Australia they added over 100 for the first wicket in three consecutive innings and in 1948/9 against South Africa at Johannesburg added 359 for the first England wicket.

Washbrook hit 1,000 runs 17 times in England and three times in overseas seasons. He went on to 2,000 twice, with his highest aggregate being 2,662, av 68.25, in 1947. All his seven double centuries were for Lancashire, the highest being 251* v Surrey at Old Trafford in 1947. He was a Test selector in 1956 and 1957 and in the former year was brought back into the England side, having been absent for six years; he hit 98. His benefit in 1948 produced a record, at the time, of £14,000. From 1954 to 1959 he captained Lancashire, being the first professional officially to hold that post. His last first-class match was for MCC in 1964. In 1971 and 1972 he was again chosen for the Test match panel. He was President of Lancashire CCC in 1989–90, having previously served on the County Committee.

Washington, William Arthur Irving
Professional. *b:* 11.12.1879, Mitchell Main, Wombwell, Yorkshire. *d:* 20.10.1927, Wombwell, Yorkshire. Uncle of N. Kilner (Yorkshire and Warwickshire) and R. Kilner (Yorkshire). Stylish middle order left-hand batsman. *Teams* Yorkshire (1900–02, 44 matches); Griqualand West (1904/5); Transvaal (1906/7).
Career batting
48–69–6–1384–100*–21.96–1–*ct* 18
Bowling 32–0

He hit 1,029 runs, av 26.38, in 1902, but owing to ill-health could not continue in first-class cricket in England after that season.

Wasim Akram
Cricketer. *b:* 3.6.1966, Lahore, Pakistan. Middle order left-hand batsman, left-arm fast bowler. *Teams* PACO (1984/5); Lahore (1985/6); Lancashire (1988–91, 44 matches). *Tours* Pakistan Under 23 to Sri Lanka 1984/5; Pakistan to New Zealand 1984/5, to Australia 1984/5 (not first-class), 1986/7 (not first-class), 1988/9, 1989/90, 1991/2, to Sri Lanka 1985/6, to Sharjah (not first-class) 1984/5, 1985/6, 1986/7, 1988/9, 1989/90, 1990/1, 1991/2, to India 1986/7, 1989/90 (not first-class), to England 1987, 1992, to West Indies 1987/8, to Bangladesh (not first-class) 1988/9, to Australia and New Zealand (World Cup) 1991/2. *Tests* Pakistan (1984/5 to 1992, 44 matches).
Career batting
122–158–24–2981–123–22.24–3–*ct* 39
Bowling 10167–455–22.34–36–7–7/42
Test batting
44–56–9–971–123–20.66–1–*ct* 12
Bowling 4100–169–24.26–11–2–6/62

An outstanding seam bowler, capable of bowling very fast on occasions, Wasim was the leading wicket-taker on the 1987 Pakistan tour of England, and, though there were some early doubts about his fitness, proved the outstanding bowler of the 1992 tour. He has also proved very effective for Lancashire, being third in the first-class bowling table in 1989 and fourth in 1991. In 1992, he took 82 wickets, av 16.22, and came second in the table.

Wasim Bari
Cricketer. *b:* 23.3.1948, Karachi, Pakistan. Lower order right-hand batsman, wicket-keeper. *Teams* Karachi (1964/5 to 1980/1); PIA (1967/8 to 1980/1); Sind (1973/4). *Tours* Pakistan to England 1967, 1971, 1974, 1975 (World Cup), 1978, 1979 (World Cup), 1982, 1983 (World Cup), to Ceylon 1972/3, 1975/6, to Australia and New Zealand 1972/3, 1978/9, to Australia 1976/7, 1981/2, 1983/4, to West Indies 1976/7, to India 1979/80, 1983/4; PIA to Ireland 1969 (not first-class). *Tests* Pakistan (1967 to 1983/4, 81 matches).
Career batting
286–357–92–5749–177–21.69–2–*ct* 674–*st* 145
Bowling 30–1–30.00–0–0–1/11
Test batting
81–112–26–1366–85–15.88–0–*ct* 201–*st* 27
Bowling 2–0

He has been the wicket-keeper on five Test tours to England, playing in all three Tests on each tour and was captain of the 1978 team. In all he captained Pakistan in 6 Tests. His last first-class match in Pakistan was in 1982/3 in a Test match.

Wasim Hasan Raja
Cricketer. *b:* 3.7.1952, Multan, Pakistan. Son of Raja Saleem Akhtar (Sargodha), brother of Rameez Raja (Pakistan) and Zaeem Raja (National Bank), cousin of Atif Rauf (ADBP). Middle order left-hand batsman, leg break bowler. *Teams* Lahore (1967/8 to 1985/6); Sargodha (1969/70); Punjab University (1969/70); Combined Universities (1972/3); PIA

(1973/4); Punjab (1973/4); National Bank (1974/5 to 1987/8). *Tours* Pakistan to New Zealand 1972/3, 1978/9, 1984/5, to Sri Lanka 1973/4, 1975/6, to England 1974, 1975 (World Cup), 1978, 1979 (World Cup), 1982, to West Indies 1976/7, to Australia 1978/9, 1981/2, 1983/4, 1984/5 (not first-class), to India 1979/80, 1983/4. *Tests* Pakistan (1972/3 to 1984/5, 57 matches).
Career batting
250–378–54–11408–165–35.20–17–*ct* 155
Bowling 16195–558–29.02–31–7–8/65
Test batting
57–92–14–2821–125–36.16–4–*ct* 20
Bowling 1826–51–35.80–0–0–4/50

On his first tour to England in 1974 he topped the batting averages with 486 runs, av 54.00, but he was nothing like as successful in 1978 or 1982, though playing in the Test matches. He has played County cricket for Durham (pre first-class, 1978–87) and Northumberland (1983). In the 1973/4 season he hit 1,010 runs, av 32.58, and took 99 wickets, av 22.41. His last first-class match in England was for D. B. Close's XI in 1984.

Wass, George
Professional. *b:* 6.2.1882, Worksop, Nottinghamshire. *d:* 15.6.1966, Liverpool, Lancashire. Lower order right-hand batsman, right-arm medium pace leg break bowler, slip field. *Team* Nottinghamshire (1910, 1 match).
Career batting
1–1–0–0–0–0.00–0–*ct* 0
Bowling 34–3–11.33–0–0–3/34

Wass, Horace
Professional. *b:* 26.8.1903, Chesterfield, Derbyshire. Middle order right-hand batsman, change bowler. *Team* Derbyshire (1929, 1 match).
Career batting
1–1–0–9–9–9.00–0–*ct* 0

He played for Scotland in eight non-first-class matches between 1935 and 1938. A good soccer player, he appeared for Chesterfield and Southport.

Wass, Thomas George
Professional. *b:* 26.12.1873, Sutton-in-Ashfield, Nottinghamshire. *d:* 27.10.1953, Sutton-in-Ashfield, Nottinghamshire. Tail end right-hand batsman, right-arm fast medium leg break bowler. *Team* Nottinghamshire (1896–1920, 308 matches).
Career batting
312–395–101–2138–56–7.27–0–*ct* 115
Bowling 34092–1666–20.46–159–45–9/67

He took 100 wickets in a season ten times (best 163, av 14.28, in 1907). His best bowling was 9/67 for Nottinghamshire v Derbyshire at Blackwell in 1911.

Wassan, Atul Satish
Cricketer. *b:* 23.3.1968, Delhi, India. Lower order right-hand batsman, right-arm fast medium bowler. *Team* Delhi (1986/7 to 1991/2). *Tours* India to New Zealand 1989/90, to England 1990; Rest of World to England 1991. *Tests* India (1989/90 to 1990, 4 matches).
Career batting
41–33–8–533–110–21.32–1–*ct* 17
Bowling 4529–150–30.19–9–3–7/36
Test batting
4–5–1–94–53–23.50–0–*ct* 1
Bowling 504–10–50.40–0–0–4/108

He had a modest tour of England in 1990, but played in the third Test.

Wassell, Alan Robert
Professional. *b:* 15.4.1940, Fareham, Hampshire. Lower order left-hand batsman, slow left-arm bowler. *Team* Hampshire (1957–66, 121 matches).
Career batting
122–160–25–1209–61–8.95–0–*ct* 96
Bowling 8667–320–27.08–11–1–7/87

Wassell, Albert
(birth registered as A. Wassall)
Professional. *b:* 14.6.1892, Aston, Warwickshire. *d:* 27.4.1975, Erdington, Birmingham. Lower order batsman, slow left-arm bowler. *Team* Warwickshire (1923, 7 matches).
Career batting
7–11–3–24–10–3.00–0–*ct* 4
Bowling 344–10–34.40–0–0–3/67

Waterman, Alfred George
Amateur. *b:* 13.5.1911, Walthamstow, Essex. Lower order right-hand batsman, right-arm fast medium bowler. *Sch* Bancroft's. *Team* Essex (1937–38, 10 matches).
Career batting
10–15–1–380–103–27.14–1–*ct* 7
Bowling 348–11–31.63–0–0–4/79

He was Essex Chairman 1978–84.

Waterman, Peter Andrew
Cricketer. *b:* 26.3.1961, Pinner, Middlesex. Lower order right-hand batsman, right-arm medium fast bowler. *Team* Surrey (1983–85, 11 matches).
Career batting
11–6–3–7–6*–2.33–0–*ct* 4
Bowling 727–18–40.38–0–0–3/22

He also played for Bedfordshire (1987–88) and Hertfordshire (1990–92).

Waters, Albert Edward
Amateur. *b:* 8.5.1902, Stoke Bishop, Bristol. *d:* 28.6.1985, Bristol. Middle order right-hand batsman, bowler. *Sch* Bristol GS. *Team* Gloucestershire (1923–25, 16 matches).

Waters, Robin Hugh Clough

Career batting
16–24–3–270–42–12.85–0–*ct* 9
Bowling 377–5–75.40–0–0–2/13
He also played for Wiltshire (1928–31).

Waters, Robin Hugh Clough
Amateur. *b:* 6.12.1937, Calcutta, India. Lower order right-hand batsman, wicket-keeper. *Sch* Shrewsbury. *Teams* Oxford U (1961–62); Sussex (1961–65, 8 matches); Bengal (1962/3); Ireland (1968–69).
Career batting
38–62–11–929–70–18.21–0–*ct* 52–*st* 3
His first-class debut was for L. C. Stevens' XI in 1960. He was injured in a road accident just prior to the 1961 University Match and thus missed his blue.

Waterton, Stuart Nicholas Varney
Cricketer. *b:* 6.12.1960, Dartford, Kent. Lower order right-hand batsman, wicket-keeper. *Teams* Kent (1980–85, 25 matches); Northamptonshire (1986–87, 15 matches); Lancashire (1990, 1 match).
Career batting
41–48–10–757–58*–19.92–0–*ct* 79–*st* 15
He also played for Oxfordshire (1989–92).

Wathen, Arthur Cave
Amateur. *b:* 27.3.1841, Streatham, London. *d:* 14.3.1937, Bradfield, Berkshire. Brother of W. H. (Kent). Lower order right-hand batsman, wicket-keeper. *Sch* Blackheath Proprietary. *Team* Kent (1863–64, 9 matches).
Career batting
13–24–1–206–42*–8.95–0–*ct* 3–*st* 3
His first-class debut was for Gentlemen of the South in 1861.

Wathen, William Hulbert
Amateur. *b:* 5.5.1836, Streatham, Surrey. *d:* 29.3.1913, Westerham, Kent. Brother of A. C. (Kent), grandfather of P. H. Bonham-Carter (Royal Navy). Middle order right-hand batsman, right-hand slow round-arm bowler, slip field. *Sch* Blackheath Proprietary and Rugby. *Team* Kent (1863, 1 match).
Career batting
6–11–0–139–38–12.63–0–*ct* 0
Bowling 100–7–14.28–0–0–2/16
His first-class debut was for Gentlemen of Kent in 1862, and his last for the same team in 1866.

Watkin, Dennis
Professional. *b:* 28.6.1912, Stapleford, Nottinghamshire. *d:* 23.3.1983, Bramcote, Nottingham. Tail end right-hand batsman, leg break bowler. *Team* Nottinghamshire (1937–39, 9 matches).
Career batting
9–12–4–47–14–5.87–0–*ct* 4
Bowling 748–15–49.86–1–0–6/48
A good soccer player, he appeared for Aston Villa and Reading as outside-right.

Watkin, Steven Llewellyn
Cricketer. *b:* 15.9.1964, Duffryn Rhondda, Maesteg, Glamorgan. Lower order right-hand batsman, right-arm medium fast bowler. *Team* Glamorgan (1986–92, 105 matches). *Tours* England A to Zimbabwe 1989/90, to Pakistan and Sri Lanka 1990/1, to West Indies 1991/2; Glamorgan to Zimbabwe 1990/1. *Tests* England (1991, 2 matches).
Career batting
117–122–33–738–41–8.29–0–*ct* 24
Bowling 11532–374–30.83–16–3–8/59
Test batting
2–3–0–8–6–2.66–0–*ct* 0
Bowling 153–5–30.60–0–0–3/38
He took 94 wickets, av 25.09, in 1989.

Watkins, Albert John
(known as Allan John Watkins)
Professional. *b:* 21.4.1922, Usk, Monmouthshire. Sound middle order left-hand batsman, left-arm medium fast bowler, good short-leg field. *Team* Glamorgan (1939–62, 408 matches). *Tours* MCC to South Africa 1948/9, to India, Pakistan and Ceylon 1951/2, to Pakistan 1955/6. *Tests* England (1948–52, 15 matches).
Career batting
484–753–87–20361–170*–30.57–32–*ct* 462
Bowling 20393–833–24.48–25–0–7/28
Test batting
15–24–4–810–137*–40.50–2–*ct* 17
Bowling 554–11–50.36–0–0–3/20
He hit 1,000 runs in a season 13 times (best 1,640, av 34.89, in 1954) and took 100 wickets in a season twice (best 114, av 20.49, in 1955). He achieved the 'double' twice. His final first-class match was for MCC in 1963. He also played for Suffolk (1965–66). He played soccer for Plymouth Argyle.

Watkins, Bertram Thomas Lewis
Professional. *b:* 25.6.1902, Gloucester. *d:* 22.12.1982, Badminton, Gloucestershire. Lower order right-hand batsman, wicket-keeper. *Team* Gloucestershire (1932–38, 30 matches).
Career batting
30–44–9–211–25–6.02–0–*ct* 35–*st* 18

Watkins, David
Amateur. *b:* 18.8.1928, St Albans, Hertfordshire. Lower order right-hand batsman, right-arm medium pace bowler. *Sch* Westcliff HS. *Team* Essex (1949–54, 12 matches).
Career batting
12–17–4–210–32–16.15–0–*ct* 5
Bowling 421–8–52.62–0–0–2/45
He played for Essex in 1949, but not again until 1953.

Watkins, Stephen George
Cricketer. *b:* 23.3.1959, Hereford. Opening right-hand batsman, right-arm medium pace bowler. *Team*

Worcestershire (1983, 1 match).
Career batting
1–2–0–105–77–52.50–0–*ct* 0
He also played for Wales (1988–91) in the Minor Counties Championship, and for Herefordshire (1992).

Watkins, William Martin
Amateur. *b:* 18.1.1923, Swansea, Glamorgan. Middle order right-hand batsman. *Team* Glamorgan (1950, 1 match).
Career batting
1–1–0–3–3–3.00–0–*ct* 0

Watkins, William Richard
Professional. *b:* 22.6.1904, Ealing, Middlesex. *d:* 15.10.1986, Norwood Green, Middlesex. Middle order right-hand batsman, slow right-arm bowler. *Team* Middlesex (1930–37, 27 matches). *Tour* MCC to East Africa 1957/8, as baggage master.
Career batting
32–53–7–867–115–18.84–1–*ct* 7
Bowling 376–18–20.88–1–0–5/31
His final first-class match was for MCC in 1947.

Watkinson, Michael
Cricketer. *b:* 1.8.1961, Westhoughton, Lancashire. Lower order right-hand batsman, right-arm medium pace or off break bowler. *Team* Lancashire (1982–92, 199 matches).
Career batting
200–292–36–6192–138–24.18–3–*ct* 99
Bowling 15486–460–33.66–21–1–7/25
He also played for Cheshire (1982).

Watson, Alexander
Professional. *b:* 4.11.1844, Coatbridge, Lanarkshire, Scotland. *d:* 26.10.1920, Old Trafford, Manchester, Lancashire. Lower order right-hand batsman, originally right-hand fast, but after about 1877, slow round-arm bowler. *Team* Lancashire (1871–93, 283 matches).
Career batting
303–453–96–4492–74–12.58–0–*ct* 277
Bowling 18423–1384–13.31–106–27–9/118
He took 100 wickets, av 14.82, in 1887, but his two best seasons, in both of which he headed the averages, were 1883 with 96 wickets, av 11.82, and 1886 with 99, av 11.20. By some his bowling action was regarded as unfair and for this reason he was rarely chosen for the representative matches of his day. His best bowling was 9/118 for Lancashire v Derbyshire at Old Trafford in 1874.

Watson, Alexander Garth MacLaren
Cricketer. *b:* 27.2.1945, Lucknow, India. Lower order left-hand batsman, right-arm fast medium bowler. *Sch* St Lawrence College. *Team* Oxford U (1965–68, blue 1965, 1966 and 1968).
Career batting
42–67–16–666–65*–13.05–0–*ct* 13
Bowling 2708–68–39.82–1–0–5/44
His County cricket was for Dorset (1973–79). He also won a blue for hockey.

Watson, Arthur Campbell
Amateur. *b:* 17.3.1884, Henfold, Newdigate, Surrey. *d:* 16.1.1952, Shermanbury, Partridge Green, Sussex. Hard hitting middle order right-hand batsman, right-arm fast bowler. *Sch* Uppingham. *Teams* Essex (1913–14, 2 matches); Sussex (1922–28, 104 matches).
Career batting
106–178–15–2724–111–16.71–1–*ct* 38
Bowling 209–5–41.80–0–0–3/42
He also played for Norfolk (1906).

Watson, Arthur Kenelm
Amateur. *b:* 23.3.1867, Harrow, Middlesex. *d:* 2.1.1947, Harrow-on-the-Hill, Middlesex. Brother of H. D. (Oxford U), nephew of K. E. Digby (Oxford U) and R. Digby (Oxford U). Attacking middle order right-hand batsman, slow right-arm bowler. *Sch* Harrow. *Teams* Oxford U (1886–89, blue 1889); Middlesex (1890–94, 15 matches).
Career batting
34–57–0–847–91–14.85–0–*ct* 13
Bowling 38–1–38.00–0–0–1/38
He also played for Norfolk (1904–09) and Suffolk (1910–12).

Watson, Arthur Lacon
Amateur. *b:* 27.8.1866, West Cowes, Isle of Wight. *d:* 28.6.1955, Westwood, Wootton, Isle of Wight. Son of Arthur (Cambridge U 1858). Opening right-hand batsman, right-arm fast medium bowler, mid off field. *Sch* Winchester. *Teams* Hampshire (1885, 1 match); Cambridge U (1888).
Career batting
2–4–0–26–22–6.50–0–*ct* 0

Watson, Darsie
Amateur. *b:* 15.7.1889, Teddington, Middlesex. *d:* 19.11.1964, Charing Cross, Westminster, London. Attacking middle order right-hand batsman. *Sch* Rugby. *Team* Sussex (1920, 1 match).
Career batting
1–2–0–3–3–1.50–0–*ct* 0

Watson, David James Falshaw
Amateur. *b:* 18.11.1919, St Pancras, London. *d:* 3.10.1943, USA. He was killed in a Fleet Air Arm accident. Middle order right-hand batsman, good field. *Sch* Sedbergh. *Team* Oxford U (1939).
Career batting
2–4–1–83–35–27.66–0–*ct* 0

Watson, Frank (Bramley)
Professional. *b:* 17.9.1898, Nottingham. *d:* 1.2.1976, Warrington, Lancashire. Steady opening right-hand

batsman, right-arm medium pace bowler, good slip field. *Team* Lancashire (1920–37, 456 matches). *Tour* MCC to West Indies 1925/6.
Career batting
470–688–50–23596–300*–36.98–50–*ct* 292
Bowling 13083–407–32.14–5–0–5/31
He hit 1,000 runs in a season twelve times, going on to 2,000 three times (best 2,583, av 61.50, in 1928). His highest innings was 300 not out for Lancashire v Surrey at Old Trafford in 1928 and his three double centuries were also for Lancashire.

Watson, Frederic
Amateur. *b:* 3.1.1840, Bitteswell, Leicestershire. *d:* 9.9.1885, Cork, Ireland. Middle order right-hand batsman, wicket-keeper. *Sch* Harrow. *Team* MCC (1869–74).
Career batting
12–20–1–222–47–11.68–0–*ct* 7–*st* 1
His first-class debut was for Gentlemen of the North in 1862. His County cricket was for Devon (1880).

Watson, George Sutton
Amateur, turned professional in 1934. *b:* 10.4.1907, Milton Regis, Kent. *d:* 1.4.1974, Guildford, Surrey. Sound middle order right-hand batsman, left-arm medium pace bowler, good outfield. *Sch* Shrewsbury. *Teams* Kent (1928–29, 8 matches); Leicestershire (1934–50, 225 matches).
Career batting
236–393–20–8566–145–22.96–5–*ct* 87
Bowling 51–1–51.00–0–0–1/21
He hit 1,000 runs in a season three times (best 1,314, av 25.76, in 1947). A good soccer player, he appeared for Corinthians and won an Amateur International cap for England, before becoming a professional with Charlton Athletic, Crystal Palace and West Ham.

Watson, Graeme Donald
Cricketer. *b:* 8.3.1945, Kew, Melbourne, Victoria, Australia. Opening or middle order right-hand batsman, right-arm medium pace bowler. *Teams* Victoria (1964/5 to 1970/1, 40 matches); Western Australia (1971/2 to 1974/5, 25 matches); New South Wales (1976/7, 5 matches). *Tours* Australia to South Africa 1966/7, to New Zealand 1969/70, to England 1972. *Tests* Australia (1966/7 to 1972, 5 matches).
Career batting
107–162–19–4674–176–32.68–7–*ct* 73
Bowling 4709–186–25.31–8–0–6/61
Test batting
5–9–0–97–50–10.77–0–*ct* 1
Bowling 254–6–42.33–0–0–2/67
He hit 915 runs, av 36.60, on the 1972 tour to England, but failed in both the Tests in which he played.

Watson, Gregory George
Cricketer. *b:* 29.1.1955, Mudgee, New South Wales, Australia. Lower order right-hand batsman, right-arm fast medium bowler. *Teams* New South Wales (1977/8 to 1978/9, 14 matches); Worcestershire (1978–79, 30 matches); Western Australia (1979/80, 1 match).
Career batting
45–58–15–552–38–12.83–0–*ct* 12
Bowling 3832–102–37.56–1–0–6/45

Watson, Harold
Professional. *b:* 1887. *d:* 14.3.1969, Cambridge. Dashing lower order right-hand batsman, right-arm fast medium bowler. *Teams* MCC (1913–21); Minor Counties (1924).
Career batting
13–21–1–189–42–9.45–0–*ct* 5
Bowling 926–37–25.02–1–0–5/70
His County cricket was for Norfolk (1910–27). He was a first-class umpire (1931).

Watson, Dr Harold Boyes
Amateur. *b:* 23.10.1893, St Margarets, Twickenham, Middlesex. *d:* 19.3.1972, Thorpe Bay, Essex. Middle order batsman, useful bowler. *Team* Oxford U (1919).
Career batting
1–1–0–2–2–2.00–0–*ct* 0
Bowling 35–2–17.50–0–0–2/35

Watson, Haworth
Professional. *b:* 26.9.1880, Barnoldswick, Yorkshire. *d:* 24.11.1951, Doncaster, Yorkshire. Lower order right-hand batsman, wicket-keeper. *Team* Yorkshire (1908–14, 29 matches).
Career batting
30–37–12–189–41–7.56–0–*ct* 46–*st* 10

Watson, Hubert Digby
Amateur. *b:* 31.12.1869, Harrow, Middlesex. *d:* 9.10.1947, Inkpen, Berkshire. Brother of A. K. (Middlesex), nephew of K. E. Digby (Oxford U) and R. Digby (Oxford U). Attacking middle order right-hand batsman, right-hand slow under-arm bowler. *Sch* Harrow. *Team* Oxford U (1891–92, blue 1891).
Career batting
10–19–0–248–40–13.05–0–*ct* 6
He joined the Indian Civil Service in 1893 and therefore was lost to English first-class cricket.

Watson, Admiral Sir Hugh Dudley Richards
Amateur. *b:* 20.4.1872, Saltfleetby St Peter, Lincolnshire. *d:* 29.5.1954, New Windsor, Berkshire. Middle order right-hand batsman. *Team* MCC (1908).
Career batting
1–2–0–12–12–6.00–0–*ct* 0
His County cricket was for Wiltshire (1905).

Watson, Ian Ronald
Cricketer. *b:* 9.6.1947, Teddington, Middlesex. Middle order right-hand batsman. *Teams* Middlesex (1969, 1 match); Northamptonshire (1971, 1 match); Hampshire (1973, 1 match).
Career batting
3–5–1–37–16–9.25–0–*ct* 3
He had a unique career, playing one match only for three different Counties.

Watson, James Mackman
Amateur. *b:* 17.6.1936, Rotherham, Yorkshire. Middle order right-hand batsman. *Sch* Uppingham. *Team* Cambridge U (1957–59).
Career batting
5–9–0–74–31–8.22–0–*ct* 1
Bowling 1–1–1.00–0–0–1/1

Watson, John Russell
Amateur. *b:* 22.8.1910, Caundle-Purse, Sherborne, Dorset. *d:* 7.3.1980, Yeovil, Somerset. Middle order right-hand batsman. *Sch* Stowe. *Team* Somerset (1933–36, 19 matches).
Career batting
19–33–2–375–56–12.09–0–*ct* 4
He also played for Dorset (1946).

Watson, John Thomas
Amateur. *b:* 1877. *d:* 2.9.1916, Chesterfield, Derbyshire. Middle order batsman. *Team* MCC (1902–03).
Career batting
2–4–1–66–24–22.00–0–*ct* 0

Watson, Dr Joseph Riley
Amateur. *b:* 28.3.1859, Steeton-in-Craven, Yorkshire. *d:* 18.10.1915, Harrogate, Yorkshire. Lower order batsman, useful bowler. *Team* Cambridge U (1882).
Career batting
2–3–0–2–1–0.66–0–*ct* 1
Bowling 25–0
His final first-class match was for An England Eleven at Harrogate in 1888.

Watson, Richard Martin
Amateur. *b:* 31.12.1921, Bakewell, Derbyshire. *d:* 1.10.1987, Penrhosgarnedd, Caernarvon. Middle order left-hand batsman, leg break bowler. *Sch* Trent. *Team* Derbyshire (1947, 6 matches).
Career batting
6–11–3–68–25*–8.50–0–*ct* 3

Watson, Roger Graeme
Cricketer. *b:* 14.1.1964, Rawtenstall, Lancashire. Middle order left-hand batsman, off break bowler. *Team* Lancashire (1982–85, 2 matches).
Career batting
2–3–0–33–18–11.00–0–*ct* 0

Watson, Hon Ronald Bannatyne
Amateur. *b:* 28.9.1883, Edinburgh, Scotland. *d:* 22.1.1966, Edinburgh, Scotland. Middle order batsman. *Sch* Marlborough. *Team* Scotland (1913).
Career batting
1–2–0–11–6–5.50–0–*ct* 0
He played hockey for Scotland.

Watson, Thomas
Amateur. *b:* 13.10.1896, Larkhall, Lanarkshire, Scotland. *d:* 17.5.1974, Stonehouse, Lanarkshire, Scotland. Lower order right-hand batsman, right-arm fast medium bowler. *Team* Scotland (1928–31).
Career batting
5–6–2–60–25*–15.00–0–*ct* 3
Bowling 300–13–23.07–0–0–3/54

Watson, Rev Thomas Herman
Amateur. *b:* 14.11.1880, Water Orton, Warwickshire. *d:* 15.2.1944, Singleton, Blackpool, Lancashire. Tail end right-hand batsman, right-arm fast medium bowler. *Sch* St Bees. *Teams* Cambridge U (1903); Warwickshire (1904, 2 matches).
Career batting
3–5–0–18–12–3.60–0–*ct* 0
Bowling 169–0

Watson, Thomas Mead
Amateur. *b:* 22.5.1913, Lewisham, London. Forceful middle order left-hand batsman. *Sch* Monkton Combe. *Team* Oxford U (1933–34).
Career batting
3–6–1–92–27–18.40–0–*ct* 1

Watson, William
Cricketer. *b:* 31.8.1965, Auckland, New Zealand. Tail end right-hand batsman, right-arm fast medium bowler. *Team* Auckland (1984/5 to 1991/2). *Tours* New Zealand to Sri Lanka 1985/6 (not first-class), to Sharjah (not first-class) 1985/6, 1987/8, to England 1986, 1990, to Australia 1987/8, 1989/90, 1990/1 (not first-class), to India 1987/8 (World Cup), 1988/9, to Pakistan 1990/1 (not first-class); Young New Zealand to Zimbabwe 1988/9. *Tests* New Zealand (1986 to 1991/2, 10 matches).
Career batting
68–56–23–249–27*–7.54–0–*ct* 17
Bowling 5671–185–20.65–7–0–7/60
Test batting
10–14–5–54–11–6.00–0–*ct* 3
Bowling 1100–30–36.66–1–0–6/78
He played in two Tests on the 1986 tour to England, when he came as a promising youngster; in 1990 he was co-opted into the side, when injury depleted the tourists, and appeared in two first-class games.

Watson, William Kenneth
Cricketer. *b:* 21.5.1955, Port Elizabeth, South Africa. Attacking lower order right-hand batsman, right-arm fast medium bowler. *Teams* Border (1974/5 to 1991/2); Northern Transvaal (1975/6); Nottinghamshire (1976–80, 22 matches); Eastern Province

(1976/7 to 1986/7).
Career batting
143–189–59–1827–99*–14.05–0–*ct* 39
Bowling 11034–446–24.73–16–0–7/50

He played for South Africa in unoffical Tests against West Indies 1983/4.

Watson, Willie
Professional. *b:* 7.3.1920, Bolton-on-Dearne, Yorkshire. Sound and stylish middle order left-hand batsman, fine outfield. *Teams* Yorkshire (1939–57, 283 matches); Leicestershire (1958–64, 117 matches). *Tours* MCC to West Indies 1953/4, to Australia and New Zealand 1958/9, to New Zealand 1960/1, to East Africa 1963/4 (he did not play in first-class match); Howard to India 1956/7; Norfolk to Jamaica 1956/7; Commonwealth to Rhodesia 1962/3. *Tests* England (1951 to 1958/9, 23 matches).
Career batting
468–753–109–25670–257–39.86–55–*ct* 295
Bowling 127–0
Test batting
23–37–3–879–116–25.85–2–*ct* 8

He hit 1,000 runs in a season 14 times, going on to 2,000 once: 2,212, av 55.30, in 1959. His highest innings was 257 for MCC v British Guiana at Georgetown in 1953/4 and he hit one other double century for Yorkshire and one for Leicestershire. From 1958 to 1961 he captained Leicestershire and in 1962 was appointed a Test Selector, retiring in 1964. A noted soccer player, he appeared at left half for Huddersfield Town, Sunderland and Halifax Town and gained four caps for England.

Watson-Smith, H. (*see under* Smith, H. W.)

Watt, Alan Edward
Professional. *b:* 19.6.1907, Limpsfield Chart, Westerham, Kent. *d:* 3.2.1974, Pembury, Kent. Swashbuckling lower order right-hand batsman, right-arm fast medium bowler. *Team* Kent (1929–39, 226 matches).
Career batting
230–330–37–4098–96–13.98–0–*ct* 134
Bowling 17586–610–28.82–34–6–8/100

He took 108 wickets, av 27.09, in 1938. He hit 42 all in boundaries – five sixes and three fours – for Kent v Nottinghamshire at Trent Bridge in 1933. His final first-class match was for M. Leyland's XI in 1947. A useful soccer player, he kept goal for Folkestone.

Watt, Jonathan
Amateur. *b:* 11.9.1937, Eastbourne, Sussex. Opening right-hand batsman, off break bowler. *Sch* Eastbourne. *Team* L. C. Stevens' XI (1960–61).
Career batting
2–3–0–69–34–23.00–0–*ct* 1

Watt, Thomas Douglas
Amateur. *b:* 21.12.1891, Edinburgh, Scotland. *d:* 13.6.1949, Edinburgh, Scotland. Lower order right-hand batsman, right-arm medium pace bowler. *Team* Scotland (1912–24).
Career batting
11–20–6–149–23–10.64–0–*ct* 5
Bowling 821–21–39.09–0–0–3/47

Watts, Alfred William
Amateur. *b:* 5.4.1859, Millbrook, Hampshire. Lower order batsman, useful bowler. *Team* Hampshire (1882, 2 matches).
Career batting
2–3–0–26–11–8.66–0–*ct* 0
Bowling 42–2–21.00–0–0–1/9

Watts, Andrew
Cricketer. *b:* 4.10.1960, Chapeltown, Yorkshire. Lower order left-hand batsman, right-arm medium pace bowler. *Teams* Derbyshire (1982–83, 3 matches); Boland (1985/6 to 1986/7).
Career batting
12–16–5–301–57–27.36–0–*ct* 7
Bowling 581–19–30.57–0–0–4/54

Watts, Charles George
Amateur. *b:* 4.9.1894, Hinckley, Leicestershire. *d:* 30.1.1979, Hinckley, Leicestershire. Uncle of G. J. Lord (Warwickshire and Worcestershire). Middle order right-hand batsman. *Team* Leicestershire (1924, 1 match).
Career batting
1–1–0–16–16–16.00–0–*ct* 0

Watts, Charles John Manning
Amateur. *b:* 30.9.1905, Kislingbury, Northampton. *d:* 8.2.1985, Northampton. Middle order right-hand batsman, wicket-keeper. *Sch* Repton. *Team* Essex (1928, 8 matches).
Career batting
8–11–0–119–41–10.81–0–*ct* 2–*st* 2
Bowling 4–0

He also played for Suffolk (1937).

Watts, Edward Alfred
Professional. *b:* 1.8.1911, Peckham, London. *d:* 2.5.1982, Cheam, Surrey. Brother-in-law of A. R. Gover (Surrey). Middle order right-hand batsman, right-arm fast medium pace bowler. *Sch* Tiffin. *Team* Surrey (1933–49, 240 matches). *Tours* Brinckman to South America 1937/8; Cahn to New Zealand 1938/9.
Career batting
244–357–69–6158–123–21.38–2–*ct* 155
Bowling 19004–729–26.06–24–2–10/67

He took 100 wickets in a season twice (best 129, av 18.47, in 1938). His best bowling was 10/67 for Surrey v Warwickshire at Edgbaston in 1939.

Watts, Fred Henry George
Amateur. *b:* 29.7.1904, Northampton. Middle order right-hand batsman. *Team* Northamptonshire (1932–37, 4 matches).
Career batting
4–5–0–12–6–2.40–0–*ct* 0

Watts, Frederic Arthur
Amateur. *b:* 9.9.1884, Cinderford, Gloucestershire. *d:* 20.2.1968, Northampton. Lower order batsman, useful bowler. *Team* Gloucestershire (1905, 1 match).
Career batting
1–2–0–0–0–0.00–0–*ct* 0
Bowling 125–3–41.66–0–0–3/125

Watts, George Herbert
Professional. *b:* 18.2.1867, Fenner's, Cambridge. *d:* 22.4.1949, Cambridge. Son of Walter (Cambridgeshire). Lower order right-hand batsman, right-arm fast bowler, wicket-keeper. *Team* Surrey (1890–92, 8 matches).
Career batting
8–16–2–79–20–5.64–0–*ct* 13–*st* 4
Bowling 21–0
He also played for Cambridgeshire (1896–1914).

Watts, Hugh Edmund
Amateur. *b:* 4.3.1922, Stratton-on-the-Fosse, Somerset. Middle order left-hand batsman, leg break bowler. *Sch* Downside. *Teams* Somerset (1939–52, 61 matches); Cambridge U (1947, blue).
Career batting
72–124–8–2958–110–25.50–1–*ct* 24
Bowling 117–1–117.00–0–0–1/15

Watts, Lawrence Dursley
Amateur. *b:* 2.5.1935, Bristol. Middle order right-hand batsman. *Sch* Bristol GS. *Teams* Oxford U (1957–58); Gloucestershire (1958, 1 match).
Career batting
11–20–0–361–69–18.05–0–*ct* 3
A noted rugby footballer, he appeared for Oxford, Bristol and Gloucestershire.

Watts, Patrick James
Professional. *b:* 16.6.1940, Henlow, Bedfordshire. Brother of P. D. (Northamptonshire and Nottinghamshire). Middle order left-hand batsman, right-arm medium pace bowler. *Team* Northamptonshire (1959–80, 372 matches).
Career batting
375–607–90–14449–145–27.94–10–*ct* 279
Bowling 8710–333–26.15–7–0–6/18
He hit 1,000 runs in a season seven times (best 1,798, av 43.85, in 1962). From 1971 to 1974 he captained Northamptonshire, but then retired, playing a few matches in 1975, none in 1976 or 1977; in 1978 he was reappointed captain, retiring a second time in 1980. He also played for Bedfordshire (1976–77).

Watts, Peter David
Professional. *b:* 31.3.1938, Henlow, Bedfordshire. Brother of P. J. (Northamptonshire). Lower order left-hand batsman, leg break and googly bowler. *Sch* Bedford Modern. *Teams* Northamptonshire (1958–66, 158 matches); Nottinghamshire (1967, 23 matches).
Career batting
183–277–60–4567–91–21.04–0–*ct* 174
Bowling 10067–307–32.79–12–1–7/77
He also played for Bedfordshire (1955 and 1971).

Watts, Thomas
Professional. *b:* 21.8.1899, Kennington, London. *d:* 19.1.1976, St Helens, Lancashire. Lower order right-hand batsman, useful bowler. *Team* Surrey (1922–26, 6 matches).
Career batting
6–8–5–42–21*–14.00–0–*ct* 3
Bowling 327–8–40.87–0–0–2/32

Watts, Walter
Professional. *b:* 7.3.1827, Wimpole, Cambridgeshire. *d:* 29.7.1910, Cambridge. Father of G. H. (Surrey). Tail end right-hand batsman, right-hand slow round-arm bowler, short leg field. *Team* Cambridgeshire (1866–69, 11 matches).
Career batting
11–18–5–23–9*–1.76–0–*ct* 4
Bowling 752–43–17.48–4–1–7/46
He was groundsman at Fenner's (later called the University Ground) at Cambridge for fifty years.

Waud, Brian Wilkes
Amateur. *b:* 4.6.1837, Chester Court, Selby, Yorkshire. *d:* 30.5.1889, Toronto, Canada. Stylish middle order right-hand batsman, wicket-keeper. *Sch* Eton. *Teams* Oxford U (1857–60, blue all four years); Yorkshire (1862–64, 7 matches).
Career batting
19–34–7–432–42–16.00–0–*ct* 15–*st* 7
He played for Canada v United States in 1881.

Waugh, Hubert Percy
Amateur. *b:* 24.12.1898, West Ham, Essex. *d:* 13.12.1954, Dollis Hill, Middlesex. Opening right-hand batsman, right-arm medium pace bowler. *Sch* Forest. *Team* Essex (1919–29, 8 matches).
Career batting
9–16–0–251–128–15.68–1–*ct* 9
Bowling 168–4–42.00–0–0–1/6
He also played for Suffolk (1934–39), being captain of that County for five years. His final first-class match was for the Minor Counties in 1937.

Waugh, Mark Edward
Cricketer. *b:* 2.6.1965, Canterbury, Sydney, New South Wales, Australia. Twin brother of S. R. (New South Wales). Attractive middle order right-hand batsman, right-arm medium pace bowler. *Teams* New South Wales (1985/6 to 1991/2, 58 matches); Essex

(1988–92, 65 matches). *Tours* New South Wales to Zimbabwe 1987/8; Australia to West Indies 1990/1, to New Zealand (World Cup) 1991/2. *Tests* Australia (1990/1 to 1991/2, 11 matches).
Career batting
139–217–33–10448–229*–56.78–35–*ct* 175
Bowling 3882–105–36.77–1–0–5/37
Test batting
11–17–2–637–139*–42.46–2–*ct* 21
Bowling 298–9–33.11–0–0–4/80

He was very successful in County cricket for Essex and in 1990 hit 2,072 runs, av 76.74. He did not play for the County in 1991, but reappeared in 1992 and was second in the first-class batting table. His highest score was 229* for New South Wales v Western Australia at Perth in 1990/1, when he shared a 5th wicket partnership of 464* with his brother, the highest for any wicket in Australia.

Waugh, Stephen Rodger
Cricketer. *b:* 2.6.1965, Canterbury, Sydney, New South Wales, Australia. Twin brother of M. E. (New South Wales). Middle order right-hand batsman, right-arm medium pace bowler. *Teams* New South Wales (1984/5 to 1991/2, 52 matches); Somerset (1987–88, 19 matches). *Tours* Young Australia to Zimbabwe 1985/6; Australia to New Zealand 1985/6, 1989/90, 1991/2 (World Cup), to Sharjah (not first-class) 1985/6, 1986/7, 1989/90, to India 1986/7, 1989/90 (not first-class), to India and Pakistan (World Cup) 1987/8, to Pakistan 1988/9, to England 1989, to West Indies 1990/1. *Tests* Australia (1985/6 to 1990/1, 44 matches).
Career batting
139–210–32–7978–216*–44.82–22–*ct* 123
Bowling 5610–173–32.42–4–0–6/51
Test batting
44–67–11–2097–177*–37.44–3–*ct* 32
Bowling 1980–44–45.00–2–0–5/69

Signed by Somerset as an understudy for M. D. Crowe in 1987, Waugh played in only four matches, but hit two hundreds. In 1988 he hit 1,314 runs, av 73.00, and was second to G. A. Hick in the batting averages. Touring England in 1989 he topped the Test averages with 506 runs, av 126.50, and in first-class matches hit 1,030 runs, av 64.37. His highest score was 216* for New South Wales v Western Australia at Perth in 1990/1, when he shared a 5th wicket partnership of 464* with his brother, the highest for any wicket in Australia.

Wazir Ali, Syed
Amateur. *b:* 15.9.1903, Jullundur, India. *d:* 17.6.1950, Karachi, Pakistan. He died following an operation for appendicitis. Brother of S. Nazir Ali (India), father of Khalid Wazir (Pakistan). Sound opening right-hand batsman, right-arm medium pace bowler, good field. *Teams* Muslims (1922/3 to 1940/1); Southern Punjab (1926/7 to 1939/40); Patiala (1932/3); Central India (1934/5 to 1937/8). *Tours* India to England 1932, 1936; Indian University Occasionals to Ceylon 1935/6. *Tests* India (1932–36, 7 matches).
Career batting
120–207–23–7193–268*–39.09–22–*ct* 59
Bowling 1043–34–30.67–1–0–5/22
Test batting
7–14–0–237–42–16.92–0–*ct* 1
Bowling 25–0

In 1932 he hit 1,229 runs, av 32.34, in first-class matches, also playing in the Test. In 1936, although he appeared in all three Tests, his record was a poor one. His highest score was 268* for Indian University Occasionals v Viceroy's XI at Calcutta in 1935/6. He hit 1,072 runs, av 71.60, in India in 1935/6.

Wazir Mohammad
Amateur. *b:* 22.12.1929, Junagadh, India. Brother of Hanif (Pakistan), Sadiq (Pakistan), Mushtaq (Pakistan) and Raees (Karachi), uncle of Shahid (PIA), Asif (PIA) and Shoaib (Pakistan). Determined middle order right-hand batsman, good field. *Teams* Karachi (1949/50 to 1963/4); Bahawalpur (1953/4). *Tours* Pakistan to India 1952/3, to England 1954, to West Indies 1957/8; Pakistan Eaglets to England 1963. *Tests* Pakistan (1952/3 to 1959/60, 20 matches).
Career batting
105–149–26–4952–189–40.26–11–*ct* 35
Bowling 41–0
Test batting
20–33–4–801–189–27.62–2–*ct* 5
Bowling 15–0

He topped the first-class averages on the 1954 tour with 628 runs, av 39.25, but owing to injury played in only two Tests.

Weale, Simon David
Cricketer. *b:* 16.9.1967, Knightsbridge, London. Lower order right-hand batsman, slow left-arm bowler. *Team* Oxford U (1986–90, blue 1987–88).
Career batting
20–24–2–392–76–17.81–0–*ct* 3
Bowling 1459–15–97.26–0–0–3/130

Weatherby, Charles Thomas
Amateur. *b:* 7.5.1860, Kensington, London. *d:* 24.6.1913, Lindfield, Sussex. Brother of Francis (Oxford U) and J. T. (Europeans), uncle of J. C. Atkinson-Clark (Middlesex). Middle order right-hand batsman. *Sch* Winchester. *Team* MCC (1882).
Career batting
1–2–0–16–15–8.00–0–*ct* 0

He did not appear in first-class cricket whilst at Oxford U.

Weatherby, Sir Francis
Amateur. *b:* 15.9.1885, Oatlands Park, Weybridge, Surrey. *d:* 17.11.1969, Ettington, Warwickshire. Brother of C. T. (MCC) and J. T. (Europeans), uncle

of J. C. Atkinson-Clark (Middlesex). Opening right-hand batsman. *Sch* Winchester. *Team* Oxford U (1904).
Career batting
4–6–0–69–24–11.50–0–*ct* 2
His final first-class match was for Gentlemen of England in 1905.

Weaver, Frederick Charles
Amateur. *b:* 10.3.1878, Gloucester. *d:* 29.12.1949, Limpley Stoke, Wiltshire. Middle order batsman, useful bowler. *Team* Gloucestershire (1897–1909, 5 matches).
Career batting
5–10–3–31–18*–4.42–0–*ct* 2
Bowling 177–8–22.12–1–0–5/63
He was a notable figure in West Country Club cricket scoring over 35,000 runs and taking more than 5,000 wickets.

Weaver, Philip Humphrey Peter
Amateur. *b:* 12.3.1912, Kalimpong, India. *d:* 28.6.1991, Poole, Dorset. Middle order right-hand batsman, right-arm medium pace bowler. *Sch* King's, Bruton. *Team* Hampshire (1938, 2 matches).
Career batting
2–3–0–55–37–18.33–0–*ct* 1
He played hockey for England.

Weaver, Samuel
Professional. *b:* 8.2.1909, Pilsley, Derbyshire. *d:* 15.4.1985, Basford, Nottinghamshire. Lower order left-hand batsman, left-arm bowler. *Team* Somerset (1939, 2 matches).
Career batting
2–4–2–25–19–12.50–0–*ct* 2
Bowling 63–0
A good soccer player, he appeared for Hull, Newcastle United, Chelsea and England.

Webb, Arthur Geoffrey Gascoyne
Amateur. *b:* 17.8.1896, Newington, Sittingbourne, Kent. *d:* 6.4.1981, Oakham, Rutland. Middle order left-hand batsman, occasional wicket-keeper. *Sch* Wellington. *Team* Leicestershire (1933–38, 3 matches).
Career batting
5–9–0–123–57–13.66–0–*ct* 5
Bowling 22–0
From 1933 to 1938 he was Secretary of Leicestershire CCC. His first-class debut was for the Royal Navy in 1919. He married the niece of H. Rider Haggard, the author.

Webb, Arthur Stuart
Professional but amateur in 1912. *b:* 6.8.1868, Bridge, Kent. *d:* 3.12.1952, Briton Ferry, Glamorgan. Middle order right-hand batsman, right-arm medium pace bowler. *Team* Hampshire (1895–1904, 149 matches).
Career batting
151–272–16–5515–162*–21.54–2–*ct* 83
Bowling 1023–22–46.50–0–0–2/18
He also played for Glamorgan (pre first-class, 1912) and his final first-class match was for South Wales v South Africans in 1912. He hit 1,020 runs, av 34.00, in 1901.

Webb, Rev Charles Johnston Bourne
Amateur. *b:* 24.11.1874, Bloemfontein, Orange Free State, South Africa. *d:* 18.11.1963, St John's Wood, London. Brother-in-law of R. A. Bennett (Hampshire). Lower order right-hand batsman, slow right-arm bowler. *Sch* Radley. *Team* Middlesex (1902, 2 matches).
Career batting
2–3–1–18–14–9.00–0–*ct* 1
Bowling 58–0
He also played for Dorset (1907–14). He was the father of Allan Webb, the actor and opera singer.

Webb, George
Professional. *b:* 7.3.1859, Tonbridge, Kent. Lower order batsman, bowler. *Team* Kent (1892, 1 match).
Career batting
1–2–1–0–0*–0.00–0–*ct* 1
Bowling 45–1–45.00–0–0–1/30
He was a first-class umpire (1910–13), standing in three Test matches (1912).

Webb, George William
Professional. *b:* 23.10.1857, Barham, Kent. *d:* 26.12.1931, Stoke-by-Nayland, Suffolk. Lower order right-hand batsman, right-arm fast medium bowler. *Team* Kent (1880, 1 match).
Career batting
1–1–1–5–5*–no av–0–*ct* 3
Bowling 30–0

Webb, Herbert George
Amateur. *b:* 1.7.1913, Headington, Oxfordshire. *d:* 7.8.1947, Hill End, St Albans, Herts. Middle order right-hand batsman, wicket-keeper. *Team* Oxford U (1935).
Career batting
3–6–1–88–38–17.60–0–*ct* 1
His County cricket was for Oxfordshire (1934–37) and his final first-class match for Minor Counties in 1936.

Webb, Dr Hubert Eustace
Amateur. *b:* 30.5.1927, Tonk, India. Uncle of M. C. L. MacPherson (Oxford U), nephew of A. H. Du Boulay (Kent and Gloucestershire). Middle order right-hand batsman, leg break bowler. *Sch* Winchester. *Teams* Oxford U (1946–48, blue 1948); Hampshire (1954, 1 match).
Career batting
15–23–1–461–145*–20.95–1–*ct* 7
Bowling 15–1–15.00–0–0–1/10

Webb, Dr John Kingdon Guy
Amateur. *b:* 29.10.1918, Chingford, Essex. Sound opening right-hand batsman. *Sch* Highgate. *Team* Oxford U (1938).
Career batting
1–2–0–5–5–2.50–0–*ct* 0
He won a blue for soccer.

Webb, Peter Mitchell
Amateur. *b:* 5.2.1932, St Stephen's Green, Dublin, Ireland. Lower order right-hand batsman, right-arm medium pace bowler. *Team* Ireland (1953).
Career batting
2–2–1–3–3*–3.00–0–*ct* 3
Bowling 59–4–14.75–0–0–2/11

Webb, Robert
Professional. Lower order right-hand batsman, wicket-keeper. *Team* Kent (1864, 1 match).
Career batting
1–2–0–2–1–1.00–0–*ct* 0

Webb, Rupert Thomas
Professional. *b:* 11.7.1922, Harrow, Middlesex. Lower order right-hand batsman, wicket-keeper. *Team* Sussex (1948–60, 255 matches).
Career batting
256–333–104–2685–49*–11.72–0–*ct* 325–*st* 129
Bowling 43–1–43.00–0–0–1/34
He is married to the actress Barbara Whatley.

Webb, Sidney
Professional. *b:* 1.2.1875, Brompton, Kensington, London. *d:* 4.4.1923, Ilford, Essex. Lower order right-hand batsman, right-arm medium pace bowler. *Teams* Middlesex (1897–98, 9 matches); Lancashire (1899–1903, 73 matches); Griqualand West (1904/5).
Career batting
83–110–31–554–38*–7.01–0–*ct* 58
Bowling 6093–302–20.17–17–4–8/36
He took 112 wickets, av 23.18, in 1901.

Webb, William Louis Taggart
Amateur. *b:* 6.2.1898, Camberwell, London. *d:* 3.4.1969, Southport, Lancashire. Middle order right-hand batsman. *Team* Civil Service (1927).
Career batting
1–2–0–76–59–38.00–0–*ct* 0

Webbe, Alexander Josiah
Amateur. *b:* 16.1.1855, Bethnal Green, London. *d:* 19.2.1941, Fulvens, Hoe, Abinger Hammer, Surrey. Brother of H. R. (Middlesex) and G. A. (MCC). Stylish opening right-hand batsman, right-arm fast bowler, good mid wicket. *Sch* Harrow. *Teams* Oxford U (1875–78, blue all four years); Middlesex (1875–1900, 247 matches). *Tour* Harris to Australia 1878/9. *Test* England (1878/9, 1 match).
Career batting
370–641–58–14465–243*–24.81–14–*ct* 228–*st* 10
Bowling 2748–109–25.21–2–0–5/23
Test batting
1–2–0–4–4–2.00–0–*ct* 2
His best season was 1887 with 1,244 runs, av 47.84; in the same year he hit his only double century, 243* for Middlesex v Yorkshire at Huddersfield. He captained Oxford in 1877 and 1878, and Middlesex from 1885 to 1898, being joint leader in the last season. He was Middlesex Hon Secretary 1900–22 and President 1923–36. He represented Oxford at rackets and was a useful footballer.

Webbe, George Allan
Amateur. *b:* 15.1.1854, Westminster, London. *d:* 19.2.1925, Ascot, Berkshire. Brother of A. J. (Middlesex) and H. R. (Middlesex). Middle order right-hand batsman, good cover point, occasional wicket-keeper. *Sch* Harrow. *Team* MCC (1874–78).
Career batting
2–3–1–37–19*–18.50–0–*ct* 0
He was not in the Eleven whilst at Oxford. His County cricket was for Dorset (1874), but for several years he was abroad with his regiment.

Webbe, Herbert Ross
Amateur. *b:* 18.5.1856, Westminster, London. *d:* 9.5.1886, Paddington, London. He collapsed and died from heart disease whilst conducting prayers. Brother of A. J. (Middlesex) and G. A. (MCC). Stylish middle order right-hand batsman, good cover point. *Sch* Winchester. *Teams* Middlesex (1875–79, 21 matches); Oxford U (1877–79, blue all three years).
Career batting
43–81–6–1387–63–18.49–0–*ct* 16
He also played for Dorset (1874). He captained Oxford in 1879.

Webster, Andrew John
Cricketer. *b:* 5.3.1959, Rolleston-on-Dove, Staffordshire. Lower order left-hand batsman, right-arm medium pace bowler. *Team* Worcestershire (1981–82, 9 matches).
Career batting
9–11–5–81–25–13.50–0–*ct* 3
Bowling 734–15–48.93–1–0–5/87
He also played for Staffordshire (1980–81 and 1985–89).

Webster, Charles
Professional. *b:* 9.6.1838, Ecclesall, Sheffield, Yorkshire. *d:* 6.1.1881, Sheffield, Yorkshire. Middle order right-hand batsman. *Team* Yorkshire (1861–68, 4 matches).
Career batting
4–7–1–36–10–6.00–0–*ct* 2

Webster, David
Cricketer. *b:* 22.5.1946, Sheffield, Yorkshire. Middle order left-hand batsman, right-arm medium pace bowler. *Team* Derbyshire (1975, 1 match).

Career batting
1–1–0–26–26–26.00–0–*ct* 0
Bowling 28–1–28.00–0–0–1/28

Webster, Fred
Professional. *b:* 7.5.1897, Accrington, Lancashire. *d:* 28.7.1931, Burnley, Lancashire. Tail end left-hand batsman, left-arm fast medium bowler. *Team* Lancashire (1925–27, 2 matches).
Career batting
2–3–1–12–10–6.00–0–*ct* 1
Bowling 122–7–17.42–0–0–3/34

Webster, Frederick
Professional. *b:* 19.1.1885, Ecclesall, Sheffield, Yorkshire. *d:* 23.3.1938. Lower order batsman, useful bowler. *Team* Derbyshire (1906, 1 match).
Career batting
1–2–0–11–10–5.50–0–*ct* 0
Bowling 65–1–65.00–0–0–1/65

Webster, Harold Wynne
Amateur. *b:* 17.2.1889, Sydney, New South Wales, Australia. *d:* 7.10.1949, Randwick, Sydney, New South Wales, Australia. Lower order right-hand batsman, wicket-keeper. *Team* South Australia (1910/11 to 1911/12, 6 matches). *Tours* Australia to England 1912, to North America 1912.
Career batting
19–29–5–346–54–14.41–0–*ct* 21–*st* 4
He was the reserve wicket-keeper on the 1912 tour and did not play in the Tests.

Webster, Henry Haywood
Professional. *b:* 8.5.1844, Handsworth, Sheffield, Yorkshire. *d:* 1914, Port Elizabeth, South Africa. Middle order right-hand batsman, right-arm medium pace bowler. *Team* Yorkshire (1868, 2 matches).
Career batting
2–3–0–10–10–3.33–0–*ct* 0
He also played for Staffordshire (1877).

Webster, Jack
Amateur. *b:* 28.10.1917, Tyersall, Bradford, Yorkshire. Lower order right-hand batsman, right-arm medium fast bowler, good field. *Sch* Bradford GS. *Teams* Cambridge U (1938–39, blue 1939); Northamptonshire (1946–55, 60 matches).
Career batting
71–95–15–617–65–7.71–0–*ct* 52
Bowling 4649–145–32.06–6–0–7/78
A master at Harrow School, he played County cricket mainly in August. He also won a blue for soccer.

Webster, Patrick Greenway
(also known as P. G. Fairfield)
Amateur. *b:* 26.11.1907, South Africa. *d:* 21.6.1937, Le Mans, France. He was killed in a motor racing accident. Lower order left-hand batsman, left-arm fast bowler. *Team* Cambridge U (1929).
Career batting
2–3–1–21–12–10.50–0–*ct* 2
Bowling 233–6–38.83–0–0–4/86

Webster, Dr Rudi Valentine
Amateur. *b:* 10.6.1939, Marchfield, St Philip, Barbados. Lower order right-hand batsman, right-arm fast medium bowler. *Teams* Scotland (1961–64); Warwickshire (1962–66, 60 matches); Otago (1966/7 to 1967/8).
Career batting
70–82–19–867–47–13.76–0–*ct* 21
Bowling 5290–272–19.44–13–4–8/19

Webster, William
Amateur. *b:* 28.6.1876, Aberdeen, Scotland. *d:* 11.4.1948, New Aberdour, Aberdeenshire, Scotland. Middle order right-hand batsman, right-arm fast medium bowler. *Team* Scotland (1907–12).
Career batting
5–9–1–102–65–12.75–0–*ct* 0
Bowling 209–8–26.12–0–0–3/30

Webster, William
Professional. *b:* 1880. *d:* 10.3.1931, Dinnington, Yorkshire. Middle order batsman. *Team* Derbyshire (1911, 1 match).
Career batting
1–2–0–3–3–1.50–0–*ct* 0

Webster, William Hugh
Amateur. *b:* 22.2.1910, Hackney, London. *d:* 19.6.1986, Marylebone, London. Opening or middle order right-hand batsman, left-arm medium pace bowler. *Sch* Highgate. *Teams* Cambridge U (1930–33, blue 1932); Middlesex (1930–47, 45 matches).
Career batting
65–103–9–1870–111–19.89–1–*ct* 17
Bowling 478–21–22.76–0–0–3/12
He was President of MCC 1976/7 and Middlesex 1980–82. He also won a blue for soccer and won amateur international caps for England.

Wedel, George
Amateur. *b:* 18.5.1900, Leigh, Lancashire. *d:* 16.4.1981, Amberley, Gloucestershire. Lower order left-hand batsman, leg break bowler. *Team* Gloucestershire (1925–29, 45 matches).
Career batting
45–71–10–545–53–8.93–0–*ct* 37
Bowling 1629–51–31.94–0–0–4/4

Weeding, T. W.
(*See under* Baggallay, T. W.)

Weedon, Mark John Hayley
Amateur. *b:* 28.10.1940, Singapore. Lower order right-hand batsman, right-arm medium pace bowler. *Sch* Harrow. *Team* Cambridge U (1961–62, blue 1962).

Weekes, Donald James

Career batting
17–24–11–164–35–12.61–0–*ct* 8
Bowling 1604–45–35.64–2–0–5/67

Weekes, Donald James
Professional. *b:* 8.5.1930, Horsham, Sussex. Son-in-law of L. T. A. Bates (Warwickshire). Tail end right-hand batsman, right-arm fast bowler. *Team* Sussex (1952, 1 match).
Career batting
1–1–0–0–0–0.00–0–*ct* 0
Bowling 34–0

Weekes, Everton de Courcy, MBE
Amateur. *b:* 26.2.1925, Pickwick Gap, Westbury, St Michael, Barbados. Cousin of K. H. (West Indies). Attacking middle order right-hand batsman, leg break bowler, excellent field. *Team* Barbados (1944/5 to 1963/4). *Tours* West Indies to England 1950, 1957, to India, Pakistan and Ceylon 1948/9, to Australia and New Zealand 1951/2, to New Zealand 1955/6; Swanton to West Indies 1960/1; International XI to India, Pakistan, New Zealand and Rhodesia 1961/2. *Tests* West Indies (1947/8 to 1957/8, 48 matches).
Career batting
152–241–24–12010–304*–55.34–36–*ct* 125–*st* 1
Bowling 731–17–43.00–0–0–4/38
Test batting
48–81–5–4455–207–58.61–15–*ct* 49
Bowling 77–1–77.00–0–0–1/8

In 1950 he headed the tourists batting averages with 2,310 runs, av 79.65, including 304* v Cambridge U at Fenner's. On his visit in 1957, however, he was not so successful and just topped 1,000 runs in first-class matches – sinus trouble and a broken finger considerably hampered him on the tour. He hit 1,000 runs on the 1948/9 tour. He played bridge for Barbados.

Weekes, Kenneth Hunnell
Amateur. *b:* 24.1.1912, USA. Cousin of E. de C. (West Indies). Aggressive middle order left-hand batsman, wicket-keeper. *Team* Jamaica (1938/9 to 1947/8). *Tour* West Indies to England 1939. *Tests* West Indies (1939, 2 matches).
Career batting
30–47–4–1731–146–40.25–4–*ct* 21–*st* 1
Bowling 464–12–38.66–0–0–3/84
Test batting
2–3–0–173–137–57.66–1–*ct* 0

He hit 803 runs, av 29.74, on the 1939 tour. He scored 106 on debut for Jamaica v Combined Oxford and Cambridge U at Kingston in 1938/9.

Weekes, Paul Nicholas
Cricketer. *b:* 8.7.1969, Hackney, London. Middle order left-hand batsman, off break bowler. *Team* Middlesex (1990–92, 26 matches).
Career batting
26–35–8–863–95–31.96–0–*ct* 23
Bowling 1047–23–45.52–0–0–3/57

Weeks, Donald
Professional. *b:* 5.2.1903, Lewisham, London. *d:* 11.4.1967, Rye Foreign, Sussex. Lower order right-hand batsman, useful bowler. *Team* Surrey (1933, 2 matches).
Career batting
2–2–0–2–1–1.00–0–*ct* 0
Bowling 165–2–82.50–0–0–1/25

Weeks, Frederick James
Amateur. *b:* 7.6.1903, Stapleton, Bristol. *d:* 20.2.1990, Ladywell, Wrington, Somerset. Middle order left-hand batsman, right-arm fast bowler. *Sch* Clifton. *Team* Gloucestershire (1925–28, 7 matches).
Career batting
7–12–1–122–35*–11.09–0–*ct* 3
Bowling 22–0

Weeks, Raymond Thomas
Professional. *b:* 30.4.1930, Camborne, Cornwall. Lower order right-hand batsman, slow left-arm bowler. *Team* Warwickshire (1950–57, 105 matches).
Career batting
107–141–36–1051–51–10.00–0–*ct* 42
Bowling 6198–236–26.26–8–0–7/70

His best season was 1951 with 94 wickets, av 21.75. He also played for Cornwall (1947–48 and 1960–65).

Weigall, Evelyn Henry Villiers
Amateur. *b:* 29.6.1876, Marylebone, London. *d:* 3.9.1946, Tonbridge, Kent. Brother of G. J. V. (Kent) and L. A. F. (Europeans). Middle order right-hand batsman, right-arm medium pace bowler. *Sch* Wellington. *Team* G. J. V. Weigall's XI (1908).
Career batting
1–2–0–14–14–7.00–0–*ct* 0
Bowling 48–0

He played in trials at Oxford U, but not in first-class matches. He was President of Kent in 1946.

Weigall, Gerald John Villiers
Amateur. *b:* 19.10.1870, Wimbledon, Surrey. *d:* 17.5.1944, Dublin, Ireland. He died following an operation. Brother of E. H. V. (Weigall's XI) and L. A. F. (Europeans). Stylish middle order right-hand batsman, good point field. *Sch* Wellington. *Teams* Cambridge U (1891–92, blue both years); Kent (1891–1903, 127 matches); Europeans (1917/18 to 1919/20). *Tours* Kent to United States 1903; MCC to South America 1926/7; Tennyson to Jamaica 1927/8.
Career batting
232–398–44–6866–138*–19.39–3–*ct* 92
Bowling 45–1–45.00–0–0–1/4

His final first-class match in England was for MCC in 1920. Commencing 1923, he was coach to Kent CCC. A noted rackets player, he represented Cambridge.

Weighell, Rev William Bartholomew
Amateur. *b:* 21.6.1846, Cheddington, Buckinghamshire. *d:* 29.10.1905, Shilton, Oxfordshire. Effective lower order right-hand batsman, right-hand fast round-arm bowler, good deep field. *Sch* Bedford GS. *Teams* Cambridge U (1866–69, blue 1866, 1868 and 1869); Sussex (1868–78, 13 matches).
Career batting
26–49–7–388–38–9.23–0–*ct* 15
Bowling 588–25–23.52–0–0–4/23
He also played for Bedfordshire (1863) and Norfolk (1882–83). His name is pronounced 'Weel'.

Weightman, Neil Ivan
Cricketer. *b:* 5.10.1960, Normanton-on-Trent, Nottinghamshire. Opening left-hand batsman, off break bowler. *Team* Nottinghamshire (1981–82, 4 matches).
Career batting
4–6–0–175–105–29.16–1–*ct* 3
Bowling 4–0

Weir, Donald St Clair
Amateur. *b:* 23.1.1900, Trinity, Edinburgh, Scotland. *d:* 1.4.1950, Edinburgh, Scotland. Middle order right-hand batsman, right-arm medium pace bowler. *Sch* Edinburgh Academy. *Team* Scotland (1923–26).
Career batting
4–7–0–64–28–9.14–0–*ct* 3
Bowling 306–5–61.20–0–0–2/63

Weir, Gordon Lindsay
Amateur. *b:* 2.6.1908, Auckland, New Zealand. Brother of A. F. (Auckland). Sound opening or middle order right-hand batsman, right-arm medium pace bowler, good field. *Team* Auckland (1927/8 to 1946/7). *Tours* New Zealand to England 1931, 1937; to Australia 1937/8. *Tests* New Zealand (1929/30 to 1937, 11 matches).
Career batting
107–172–16–5022–191–32.19–10–*ct* 70
Bowling 3997–107–37.35–2–0–6/56
Test batting
11–16–2–416–74*–29.71–0–*ct* 3
Bowling 209–7–29.85–0–0–3/38
He hit 1,035 runs, av 25.87, in 1931 and played in all three Tests. He was not so successful in 1937 and appeared in only one Test.

Weir, Robert Scott
Cricketer. *b:* 1.5.1953, Glasgow, Scotland. Middle order right-hand batsman, right-arm medium pace bowler. *Team* Scotland (1975–82).
Career batting
4–8–2–187–65–31.16–0–*ct* 1

Welch, Thomas Bacon Gascoigne
Amateur. *b:* 31.7.1906, Reigate, Surrey. *d:* 16.3.1972, City of London. Son of T. H. G. (Northamptonshire captain 1889). Middle order right-hand batsman, right-arm fast medium bowler. *Sch* Malvern. *Teams* Northamptonshire (1922–31, 23 matches); Oxford U (1926).
Career batting
33–58–6–767–69–14.75–0–*ct* 9
Bowling 227–5–45.40–0–0–1/4

Welch, William Mark
Amateur. *b:* 12.8.1911. *d:* 25.5.1940, Calais, France. Middle order right-hand batsman, right-arm medium pace off break bowler, good slip field. *Sch* Harrow. *Team* Free Foresters (1935–39).
Career batting
4–5–0–170–104–34.00–1–*ct* 1
Bowling 221–8–27.62–1–0–5/43

Weldrick, George
Professional. *b:* 1.1.1882, Brighouse, Yorkshire. *d:* 14.4.1953, Brighouse, Yorkshire. Middle order right-hand batsman. *Team* Warwickshire (1906–07, 8 matches).
Career batting
8–11–1–53–12–5.30–0–*ct* 3

Welford, James William
Professional. *b:* 27.3.1869, Barnard Castle, Co Durham. *d:* 17.1.1945, Glasgow, Scotland. Middle order right-hand batsman, right-arm fast bowler. *Team* Warwickshire (1896, 13 matches).
Career batting
13–23–2–459–118–21.85–1–*ct* 2
Bowling 180–2–90.00–0–0–1/13
He also played for Durham (pre first-class, 1891–95). A good soccer player, he appeared for Aston Villa and Celtic.

Wellard, Arthur William
Professional. *b:* 8.4.1902, Southfleet, Kent. *d:* 31.12.1980, Eastbourne, Sussex. Hard hitting lower order right-hand batsman, right-arm fast medium or off break bowler, good slip field. *Team* Somerset (1927–50, 391 matches). *Tours* Tennyson to India 1937/8; selected for MCC to India 1939/40 (tour cancelled because of war). *Tests* England (1937–38, 2 matches).
Career batting
417–679–46–12485–112–19.72–2–*ct* 376
Bowling 39302–1614–24.35–108–24–8/52
Test batting
2–4–0–47–38–11.75–0–*ct* 2
Bowling 237–7–33.85–0–0–4/81
He hit 1,000 runs in a season four times (best 1,347, av 31.32, in 1935) and took 100 wickets eight times (best 172, av 20.29, in 1938). He completed the 'double' in 1933, 1935 and 1937. Regarded as the biggest hitter in first-class cricket in the late 1930s, he twice hit five sixes off consecutive balls – v Derbyshire at Wells in 1936 and v Kent at Wells in 1938. In the seasons of 1933, 1935, 1936 and 1938 he hit over 50 sixes.

Welldon, James Turner
Amateur. *b:* 3.8.1847, Felsted, Essex. *d:* 6.2.1927, Ashford, Kent. Brother-in-law of N. K. Stephen (Cambridge U). Middle order right-hand batsman, good deep field. *Sch* Tonbridge. *Teams* Kent (1867–69, 4 matches); Cambridge U (1869).
Career batting
7–11–2–88–37–9.77–0–*ct* 3
He also played for Lincolnshire (1868) and Essex (pre first-class, 1878).

Wellham, Dirk MacDonald
Cricketer. *b:* 13.3.1959, Summer Hill, Sydney, New South Wales, Australia. Nephew of W. A. (New South Wales). Middle order right-hand batsman. *Team* New South Wales (1980/1 to 1987/8, 68 matches); Tasmania (1988/9 to 1990/1, 32 matches); Queensland (1991/2, 10 matches). *Tours* Australia to England 1981, 1985; Young Australia to Zimbabwe 1982/3. *Tests* Australia (1981 to 1986/7, 6 matches).
Career batting
135–216–32–8101–167–44.02–15–*ct* 57
Bowling 17–1–17.00–0–0–1/11
Test batting
6–11–0–257–103–23.36–1–*ct* 5
On the 1981 tour to England he topped the first-class averages with 497 runs, av 55.22, but played in only one Test, scoring 103 on his debut. He visited England a second time in 1985 and batted well in first-class matches with 669 runs, av 55.75, but was selected only for the Sixth Test. He was one of the players who had agreed to go to South Africa with the Australian 'rebel' tourists, but was persuaded to change his mind.

Wellings, Evelyn Maitland
Amateur. *b:* 6.4.1909, Sidi Gaba, Alexandria, Egypt. *d:* 10.9.1992, Basingstoke, Hampshire. Lower order right-hand batsman, off break bowler. *Sch* Cheltenham. *Teams* Oxford U (1928–31, blue 1929 and 1931); Surrey (1931, 4 matches).
Career batting
36–47–6–836–125–20.39–1–*ct* 10
Bowling 3256–108–30.14–5–0–6/75
His final first-class match was for MCC in 1946. He was for many years cricket correspondent of the London *Evening News* and wrote eight books on cricket.

Wellington, Livern
Cricketer. *b:* 5.1.1950, Kingston, Jamaica. Lower order right-hand batsman, right-arm fast medium bowler. *Team* Jamaica (1969/70 to 1970/1). *Tour* Jamaica to England 1970.
Career batting
11–14–6–208–49–26.00–0–*ct* 7
Bowling 483–12–40.25–0–0–3/29

Wells, Alan Peter
Cricketer. *b:* 2.10.1961, Newhaven, Sussex. Brother of C. M. (Sussex). Middle order right-hand batsman, right-arm medium pace bowler. *Teams* Sussex (1981–92, 229 matches); Border (1981/2). *Tour* England XI to South Africa 1989/90.
Career batting
234–386–64–12481–253*–38.76–26–*ct* 131
Bowling 690–9–76.66–0–0–3/67
He hit 1,000 runs in a season seven times (best 1,784, av 59.46, in 1991). His highest score was 253* for Sussex v Yorkshire at Middlesbrough in 1991. He captained Sussex in 1992.

Wells, Arthur Luty
Amateur. *b:* 23.11.1909, Headingley, Leeds, Yorkshire. *d:* 13.5.1988, Northampton. Lower order right-hand batsman, right-arm medium pace bowler. *Team* Northamptonshire (1954–55, 5 matches).
Career batting
5–6–1–28–18–5.60–0–*ct* 0
Bowling 333–8–41.62–0–0–4/67

Wells, Bryan Douglas
Professional. *b:* 27.7.1930, Gloucester. Hard hitting tail end right-hand batsman, off break bowler. *Teams* Gloucestershire (1951–59, 141 matches); Nottinghamshire (1960–65, 151 matches). *Tour* Swanton to West Indies 1960/1.
Career batting
302–423–100–2413–55–7.47–0–*ct* 112
Bowling 24219–998–24.26–46–7–8/31
He took 100 wickets in a season three times (best 123, av 18.60, in 1956).

Wells, Clifford
Amateur. *b:* 17.10.1872, St Pancras, London. *d:* 27.2.1952, Dukes Ride, Crowthorne, Berkshire. Brother of C. M. (Surrey and Middlesex) and L. S. (Middlesex). Middle order batsman, useful bowler. *Sch* Dulwich. *Team* Cambridge U (1894).
Career batting
1–2–0–24–24–12.00–0–*ct* 1
Bowling 46–0

Wells, Colin Mark
Cricketer. *b:* 3.3.1960, Newhaven, Sussex. Brother of A. P. (Sussex). Middle order right-hand batsman, right-arm medium pace bowler. *Teams* Sussex (1979–92, 269 matches); Border (1980/1); Western Province (1984/5). *Tour* England to Sharjah (not first-class) 1984/5.
Career batting
276–436–69–12203–203–33.25–20–*ct* 86
Bowling 13410–392–34.20–7–0–7/42
He hit 1,000 runs in a season six times (best 1,456, av 45.50, in 1987). He played for England in one-day internationals, but no Tests. His highest score was 203 for Sussex v Hampshire at Hove in 1984.

Wells, Cyril Mowbray
Amateur. *b:* 21.3.1871, St Pancras, London. *d:* 22.8.1963, St John's Wood, London. Brother of L. S. (Middlesex) and Clifford (Cambridge U). Attractive middle order right-hand batsman, off break bowler with occasional leg breaks, good slip field. *Sch* Dulwich. *Teams* Cambridge U (1891–93, blue all three years); Surrey (1892–93, 4 matches); Middlesex (1895–1909, 113 matches).
Career batting
143–219–27–4229–244–22.02–4–*ct* 122
Bowling 9235–465–19.86–27–3–8/35
His only double century was 244 for Middlesex v Nottinghamshire at Trent Bridge in 1899. A noted rugby footballer, he played for Cambridge, Harlequins, Middlesex and England.

Wells, Frederick
Professional. *c:* 1.7.1796, Dorking, Surrey. *d:* 27.1.1849, Brighton, Sussex. Middle order batsman. *Teams* Surrey (1828, 1 match); Sussex (1832–39, 24 matches).
Career batting
29–56–1–407–67–7.40–0–*ct* 8
Bowling 1 wicket (no analyses)–0–0–1/?

Wells, Frederick
Professional. *b:* 1.6.1868, St John's, Burgess Hill, Sussex. Son of George (Sussex). Lower order right-hand batsman, right-arm medium pace bowler. *Team* Sussex (1891, 2 matches).
Career batting
2–2–0–7–7–3.50–0–*ct* 0
He also played for Hertfordshire (1894–98).

Wells, George
Professional. *b:* 2.11.1830, Whitechapel, London. *d:* 23.1.1891, Shoreham-by-Sea, Sussex. Father of Frederick (Sussex). Lower order right-hand batsman, right-hand medium round-arm, or slow under-arm bowler, good point field. *Teams* Sussex (1854–69, 79 matches); Middlesex (1859–64, 7 matches). *Tour* Stephenson to Australia 1861/2.
Career batting
103–181–15–2772–90–16.69–0–*ct* 102–*st* 13
Bowling 1580–85–18.55–3–0–9/105
His best bowling was 9/105 for Sussex v Surrey at Hove in 1860.

Wells, John
Professional. *c:* 5.1.1760, Wrecclesham, Surrey. *d:* 15.2.1835, Wrecclesham, Surrey. Brother of James (Surrey), brother-in-law of W. Beldham (Surrey). Middle order right-hand batsman, fast under-arm bowler, good field. *Team* Surrey (1788–1815).
Career batting
46–87–9–618–42–7.92–0–*ct* 34–*st* 2
Bowling 159 wickets (no analyses)–3–0–7/?
For several seasons he was one of the 'crack' players of England.

Wells, Joseph
Professional. *b:* 14.7.1828, Penshurst, Kent. *d:* 14.10.1910, Liss, Hampshire. Nephew of T. Duke (Kent 1823). Lower order right-hand batsman, right-hand fast round-arm bowler, slip field. *Team* Kent (1862–63, 7 matches).
Career batting
8–14–3–48–10–4.36–0–*ct* 6
Bowling 128–14 + 1–9.14–1–0–6/35
He took four wickets with successive balls for Kent v Sussex in 1862. His son was the well-known novelist H. G. Wells.

Wells, Lionel Seymour
Amateur. *b:* 3.2.1870, St Pancras, London. *d:* 26.4.1928, Kennington, London. Brother of C. M. (Surrey and Middlesex) and Clifford (Cambridge U). Forcing middle order right-hand batsman, slow right-arm bowler. *Sch* Dulwich. *Teams* Middlesex (1898–1905, 6 matches); London County (1900–04).
Career batting
13–21–1–196–42–9.80–0–*ct* 17
Bowling 203–11–18.45–0–0–4/46
His final first-class match was for W. G. Grace's XI in 1906.

Wells, Richard Raymond Collingwood
Cricketer. *b:* 19.1.1956, Salisbury, Rhodesia. Middle order right-hand batsman. *Sch* Cranleigh. *Team* Oxford U (1977–78).
Career batting
11–17–1–212–85–13.25–0–*ct* 4

Wells, Thomas Umfrey
Amateur. *b:* 6.2.1927, Panmure, Auckland, New Zealand. Middle order left-hand batsman, right-arm bowler, good outfield. *Teams* Cambridge U (1950–52, blue 1950); Worcestershire (1950, 1 match).
Career batting
21–28–1–446–77*–16.51–0–*ct* 8
Bowling 119–5–23.80–0–0–2/25
He also won a blue for rugby.

Wells, Vincent John
Cricketer. *b:* 6.8.1965, Dartford, Kent. Middle order right-hand batsman, right-arm medium pace bowler, occasional wicket-keeper. *Teams* Kent (1988–91, 14 matches); Leicestershire (1992, 17 matches).
Career batting
31–48–7–1008–58–24.58–0–*ct* 13
Bowling 1165–51–22.84–1–0–5/43

Wells, William
Professional. *b:* 14.3.1881, Daventry, Northamptonshire. *d:* 18.3.1939, Daventry, Northamptonshire. Hard hitting lower order right-hand batsman, right-arm fast medium bowler. *Team* Northamptonshire (1905–26, 269 matches).
Career batting
269–441–75–6324–119–17.27–2–*ct* 114

Bowling 16202–751–21.57–51–10–8/35

He first played for Northamptonshire (pre first-class) in 1904.

Welman, Frederic Tristram
Amateur. *b:* 19.2.1849, Norton Manor, Taunton, Somerset. *d:* 30.12.1931, South Ascot, Berkshire. Lower order right-hand batsman, wicket-keeper. *Teams* Middlesex (1880–88, 17 matches); Somerset (1882–1901, 19 matches). *Tour* Sanders to North America 1886.
Career batting
65–109–27–737–43–8.98–0–*ct* 83–*st* 24

His first-class debut was for MCC in 1874. He also played for Devon (1873). He first played for Somerset (pre first-class) in 1875.

Wenlock, David Alan
Cricketer. *b:* 16.4.1959, Leicester. Lower order right-hand batsman, right-arm medium pace bowler. *Team* Leicestershire (1980–82, 10 matches). *Tour* Leicestershire to Zimbabwe 1980/1.
Career batting
10–13–4–148–62–16.44–0–*ct* 3
Bowling 268–7–38.28–0–0–3/50

He also played for Staffordshire (1985–86).

Wenman, Edward Gower
Professional. *b:* 18.8.1803, Benenden, Kent. *d:* 28.12.1879, Benenden, Kent. Father of William (Kent), brother of Charles (Kent), cousin of George (Kent) and J. G. (Kent). Opening or middle order right-hand batsman, wicket-keeper, slow under-arm bowler. *Teams* Kent (1825–54, 61 matches); Cambridge Town Club (1840); Hampshire (1842, 1 match as given man).
Career batting
146–255–15–3204–73*–13.35–0–*ct* 118–*st* 87
Bowling 45 wickets (no analyses)–2–0–6/?

He was regarded as the best wicket-keeper of his day. Although his career with Kent spanned 30 years, he did not play regularly after 1844.

Wenman, William
Professional. *b:* 22.5.1832, Benenden, Kent. *d:* 23.11.1921, Souris, Manitoba, Canada. Son of E. G. (Kent), nephew of Charles (Kent). Middle order right-hand batsman. *Team* Kent (1862–64, 11 matches).
Career batting
11–22–3–179–29–9.42–0–*ct* 6

Wensley, Albert Frederick
Professional. *b:* 24.5.1898, Brighton, Sussex. *d:* 17.6.1970, Ware, Hertfordshire. Hard hitting lower order right-hand batsman, accurate right-arm medium fast bowler, good close field. *Teams* Sussex (1922–36, 373 matches); Auckland (1929/30 to 1930/1); Nawanagar (1936/7 to 1939/40); Europeans (1938/9 to 1947/8).
Career batting
400–595–64–10875–154–20.48–9–*ct* 264–*st* 1
Bowling 30251–1142–26.48–56–10–9/36

He hit 1,000 runs in a season four times (best 1,672, av 30.96, in 1928) and took 100 wickets in a season five times (best 126, av 25.04, in 1933). He achieved the 'double' in 1929. He played for Scotland in non-first class matches. His best bowling was 9/36 for Auckland v Otago at Auckland in 1929/30.

Went, Gwilym John Hubert
Amateur. *b:* 25.3.1914, Barry, Glamorgan. Lower order right-hand batsman, leg break bowler. *Team* Glamorgan (1934, 1 match).
Career batting
1–2–1–14–14*–14.00–0–*ct* 1
Bowling 14–0

Wentworth, Bruce Canning Vernon
Amateur. *b:* 14.12.1862, Portobello, Edinburgh, Scotland. *d:* 12.11.1951, Dall House, Rannoch Station, Perthshire, Scotland. Middle order batsman. *Sch* Harrow. *Team* MCC (1897–1900).
Career batting
3–5–0–133–36–26.60–0–*ct* 0

He was MP for Brighton from 1893 to 1906.

Wenyon, Herbert John
Amateur. *b:* 18.4.1888, Canton, China. *d:* 19.8.1944, Northwood, Middlesex. Middle order right-hand batsman, slow right-arm bowler. *Sch* Kingswood, Bath. *Team* Middlesex (1921–24, 11 matches).
Career batting
11–14–1–158–51*–12.15–0–*ct* 5
Bowling 71–2–35.50–0–0–2/31

Wesley, Colin
Amateur. *b:* 5.9.1937, Durban, South Africa. Aggressive middle order left-hand batsman, slow left-arm bowler, good field. *Team* Natal (1957/8 to 1965/6). *Tour* South Africa to England 1960. *Tests* South Africa (1960, 3 matches).
Career batting
51–79–9–1892–131–27.02–3–*ct* 20
Bowling 354–15–23.60–0–0–4/51
Test batting
3–5–0–49–35–9.80–0–*ct* 1

He appeared in three Tests on the 1960 tour but made little impact, and in all first-class games hit 595 runs, av 22.03. His first-class debut was for South African Universities in 1956/7. A noted baseball player, he represented Natal.

Wessels, Kepler Christoffel
Cricketer. *b:* 14.9.1957, Bloemfontein, South Africa. Opening left-hand batsman, right-arm medium pace or off break bowler. *Teams* Orange Free State (1973/4 to 1975/6); Sussex (1976–80, 53 matches); Western Province (1976/7); Northern Transvaal (1977/8); Queensland (1979/80 to 1985/6, 62

matches); Eastern Province (1986/7 to 1991/2). *Tours* Australia to Sri Lanka 1982/3, to England 1983 (World Cup), 1985, to West Indies 1983/4, to India 1984/5 (not first-class), to Sharjah (not first-classs) 1984/5; Australian XI to South Africa 1986/7; South Africa to India 1991/2 (not first-class), to Australia and New Zealand (World Cup) 1991/2, to West Indies 1991/2. *Tests* Australia (1982/3 to 1985/6, 24 matches); South Africa (1991/2, 1 match).
Career batting
237–410–35–19042–254–50.77–52–*ct* 194
Bowling 545–12–45.41–0–0–2/25
Test batting
25–44–1–1894–179–44.04–4–*ct* 19
Bowling 42–0

On the 1985 tour with Australia to England he played in all six Tests and in first-class matches hit 905 runs, av 36.20. He hit 1,000 runs in a season in England twice (best 1,800, av 52.94, in 1979), in Australia four times (best 1,325, av 57.60, in 1982/3) and in South Africa once (1,160, av 64.44, in 1986/7). He scored 162 for Australia v England at Brisbane 1982/3 on his Test debut. His highest score was 254 for Sussex v Middlesex at Hove in 1980. Having agreed to tour South Africa with the 'rebel' Australians, he then moved back to his native country and was captain when South Africa reappeared in Test cricket in 1991/2.

West, Albert Richard
Professional. *b:* 7.11.1920, Earl Shilton, Leicestershire. *d:* 8.6.1985, Earl Shilton, Leicestershire. Lower order left-hand batsman, slow left-arm bowler. *Team* Leicestershire (1939, 3 matches).
Career batting
3–5–0–50–22–10.00–0–*ct* 1
Bowling 205–2–102.50–0–0–2/46

West, Gordon Harry Sinclair
Professional. *b:* 7.8.1923, Upton Park, Essex. Sound middle order right-hand batsman, good field. *Team* Essex (1949–53, 2 matches).
Career batting
2–4–0–79–55–19.75–0–*ct* 0

West, John
Professional. *b:* 16.10.1844, Little Sheffield, Yorkshire. *d:* 27.1.1890, Little Sheffield, Yorkshire. Lower order left-hand batsman, left-hand fast round-arm bowler. *Team* Yorkshire (1868–76, 38 matches).
Career batting
52–88–17–605–41–8.52–0–*ct* 16
Bowling 1097–75–14.62–5–0–7/42

His final first-class match was for MCC in 1883. At the time of his death he had been on the staff at Lord's for over 20 years and for many years had been standing as umpire in County matches. He umpired one Test match in 1886.

West, John Edward
Professional. *b:* 11.11.1861, Stepney, London. *d:* 14.3.1920, Bow, London. Lower order right-hand batsman, right-arm medium pace bowler, wicket-keeper. *Team* Middlesex (1885–96, 76 matches).
Career batting
86–143–15–1523–83–11.89–0–*ct* 78–*st* 25
Bowling 2213–89–24.86–4–0–6/31

He was on the Lord's ground staff from 1886 to 1908 and in his later years a well-known first-class umpire (1902–11), standing in one Test match in 1905. He also played for Durham (pre first-class, 1884).

West, Leslie Harold
Professional. *b:* 24.1.1905, Leytonstone, Essex. *d:* 12.11.1982, Leytonstone, Essex. Middle order right-hand batsman. *Team* Essex (1928, 3 matches).
Career batting
3–5–0–33–30–6.60–0–*ct* 0

West, Richard
Amateur. *b:* 8.4.1916, Berkhamsted, Hertfordshire. *d:* 18.6.1983, Dry Sandford, Berkshire. Lower order right-hand batsman, right-arm fast medium bowler. *Sch* Rugby. *Team* Oxford U (1936–37).
Career batting
8–11–2–43–18–4.77–0–*ct* 5
Bowling 689–28–24.60–1–0–5/74

West, William Arthur John
Amateur, turned professional 1886. *d:* 17.11.1863, Birmingham. *d:* 22.2.1938, Northampton. Middle order right-hand batsman, right-arm fast bowler, slip. *Team* MCC (1888–91).
Career batting
5–8–1–182–74–26.00–0–*ct* 1
Bowling 100–5–20.00–0–0–3/42

His County cricket was for Northamptonshire (pre first-class, 1883–90) and Warwickshire (pre first-class, 1891). He was a first-class umpire (1896–1925), standing in nine Test matches (1896–1912). A noted boxer, he won the Queensberry Heavyweight Cup in 1884.

Westcott, Albert Harold
Professional. *b:* 6.11.1870, Bridgwater, Somerset. *d:* 6.2.1929, Salisbury, Wiltshire. Lower order batsman, useful bowler. *Team* Somerset (1894–1902, 6 matches).
Career batting
6–11–6–46–14*–9.20–0–*ct* 3
Bowling 28–0

Westerman, Peter
Amateur. *b:* 12.8.1920, East Sheen, Surrey. *d:* 3.2.1992, Hampton, Middlesex. Lower order right-hand batsman, right-arm fast bowler. *Team* Surrey (1949–51, 9 matches).

Western, Edward

Career batting
9–12–5–25–10–3.57–0–*ct* 1
Bowling 596–21–28.38–2–0–5/49

Western, Edward
Amateur. *b:* 12.5.1845, Taunton, Somerset. *d:* 16.10.1919, Minehead, Somerset. Middle order right-hand batsman. *Team* Somerset (1882–84, 2 matches).
Career batting
3–4–1–19–13–6.33–0–*ct* 0
He was Hon Secretary of Somerset CCC 1875–85 and Hon Treasurer 1880–81. He first played for Somerset (pre first-class) in 1875.

Westhorp, John White
Amateur. *b:* 9.1.1868, St Pancras, London. *d:* 24.3.1935, Purley, Surrey. Lower order right-hand batsman, right-arm medium pace bowler. *Sch* Ipswich. *Team* Middlesex (1893–94, 7 matches).
Career batting
7–11–0–97–39–8.81–0–*ct* 1
Bowling 123–3–41.00–0–0–1/7

Westley, Roger Bancroft
Cricketer. *b:* 21.3.1947, Preston, Lancashire. *d:* 12.5.1982, Haileybury, Hertfordshire. Twin brother of S. A. (Gloucestershire). Lower order right-hand batsman, off break bowler. *Sch* Lancaster GS. *Team* Oxford U (1969).
Career batting
5–7–0–32–14–4.57–0–*ct* 1
Bowling 270–4–67.50–0–0–2/65

Westley, Stuart Alker
Cricketer. *b:* 21.3.1947, Preston, Lancashire. Twin brother of R. B. (Oxford U). Lower order right-hand batsman, wicket-keeper. *Sch* Lancaster GS. *Teams* Oxford U (1968–69, blue both years); Gloucestershire (1969–71, 10 matches).
Career batting
34–55–18–577–93*–15.59–0–*ct* 71–*st* 9
He also played for Suffolk (1973–84) and his final first-class match was for Minor Counties in 1976. A noted rugby footballer, he played for Oxford and Fylde.

Weston, Alan Gibbons
Amateur. *b:* 30.9.1907, Leicester. Middle order right-hand batsman. *Sch* Ratcliffe College. *Team* Leicestershire (1933–34, 5 matches).
Career batting
5–9–1–72–31*9.00–0–*ct* 0

Weston, Henry
Amateur. *b:* 2.1.1888, Hurlingham, Putney, London. Middle order left-hand batsman, left-arm slow medium pace bowler. *Team* Middlesex (1910–14, 19 matches).
Career batting
19–27–7–402–79*–20.10–0–*ct* 7
Bowling 736–30–24.53–0–0–4/49

Weston, Martin John
Cricketer. *b:* 8.4.1959, Worcester. Opening or middle order right-hand batsman, right-arm medium pace bowler. *Team* Worcestershire (1979–92, 154 matches).
Career batting
154–245–23–5320–145*–23.96–3–*ct* 73
Bowling 3108–80–38.85–0–0–4/24
He hit 1,061 runs, av 27.92, in 1984.

Weston, William Philip Christopher
Cricketer. *b:* 16.6.1973, Durham. Opening left-hand batsman, left-arm medium pace bowler. *Sch* Durham. *Team* Worcestershire (1991–92, 16 matches).
Career batting
16–26–5–703–66*–33.47–0–*ct* 2
Bowling 237–2–118.50–0–0–2/39
He refused a place at Oxford U because his college would not allow him to captain England Under 19 on tour. His father, M. P., played for Durham (pre first-class) and was an England rugby international.

Wettimuny, Sidath
Cricketer. *b:* 12.8.1956, Colombo, Ceylon. Brother of S. R. de S. (Sri Lanka) and M. de S. (Sri Lanka). Opening right-hand batsman, right-arm medium pace bowler. *Team* Sri Lanka (1975/6 to 1986/7). *Tours* Sri Lanka to India 1976/7, 1980/1, 1982/3 (not first-class), 1986/7, to England 1981, 1983 (World Cup), 1984, to Pakistan 1981/2, 1985/6, to Zimbabwe 1982/3, to Australia 1982/3, to New Zealand 1982/3, to Sharjah (not first-class) 1983/4. *Tests* Sri Lanka (1981/2 to 1985/6, 23 matches).
Career batting
55–90–5–2859–227*–33.63–6–*ct* 21
Bowling 75–2–37.50–0–0–1/7
Test batting
23–43–1–1221–190–29.07–2–*ct* 10
Bowling 37–0
On his second tour to England in 1984 he hit 190 in the Test match. He batted 10 hours and 42 minutes, at the time the longest innings in a Test at Lord's and the highest by any batsman on his Test debut in England. His highest score was 227* for Sri Lankans v President's XI at Gwalior in 1986/7.

Wettimuny, Sunil Ramsay de Silva
Cricketer. *b:* 2.2.1949, Colombo, Ceylon. Brother of Sidath (Sri Lanka) and M. de S. (Sri Lanka). Sound right-hand opening batsman, right-arm medium pace bowler, wicket-keeper or good slip field. *Team* Ceylon/Sri Lanka (1969/70 to 1981/2). *Tours* Sri Lanka to India 1970/1, 1974/5, 1975/6, to Pakistan 1973/4, to England 1975, 1979.
Career batting
39–70–1–1693–121–24.53–2–*ct* 17–*st* 1
Bowling 49–1–49.00–0–0–1/10
He played for Sri Lanka in one-day international matches.

Whale, George
Professional. *b:* 27.3.1833, Littleton, Guildford, Surrey. *d:* 22.11.1896, Lambeth, London. Lower order left-hand batsman, right-arm fast medium pace bowler. *Team* Surrey (1861–67, 4 matches).
Career batting
5–7–1–46–26–7.66–0–*ct* 2
Bowling 288–5+10–57.60–1–1–6/?

Whalley-Tooker, Edward
Amateur. *b:* 15.1.1863, Wem, Shropshire. *d:* 23.11.1940, Hambledon, Hampshire. Middle order right-hand batsman, slow under-arm bowler. *Sch* Eton. *Team* Hampshire (1883–85, 2 matches).
Career batting
3–5–0–20–7–4.00–0–*ct* 0
His final first-class match was for Hambledon v An England XII in 1908.

Wharmby, George Edward
Professional, changed to amateur in 1914. *b:* 7.12.1870, Sutton-in-Ashfield, Nottinghamshire. *d:* 15.11.1951, Rustington, Sussex. Lower order right-hand batsman, right-arm medium pace bowler. *Teams* Nottinghamshire (1891–93, 4 matches); Lancashire (1894, 6 matches).
Career batting
10–15–2–36–11–2.76–0–*ct* 4
Bowling 298–9–33.11–0–0–3/35
From 1902 to 1923 he played with success for Bedfordshire.

Wharton, Alan
Professional. *b:* 30.4.1923, Heywood, Lancashire. Dashing opening or middle order left-hand batsman, right-arm medium pace bowler. *Teams* Lancashire (1946–60, 392 matches); Leicestershire (1961–63, 79 matches). *Tour* Howard to India 1956/7. *Test* England (1949, 1 match).
Career batting
482–745–69–21796–199–32.24–31–*ct* 288
Bowling 7488–237–31.59–2–0–7/33
Test batting
1–2–0–20–13–10.00–0–*ct* 0
He hit 1,000 runs in a season eleven times, going on to 2,000 once: 2,157, av 40.69, in 1959. He also played for Cumberland (1964–65). A good rugby league footballer, he played for Salford.

Wharton, Louis Edgar
Amateur. *b:* 18.1.1896, Port of Spain, Trinidad. *d:* 31.12.1957, Port of Spain, Trinidad. Middle order right-hand batsman. *Sch* Douai. *Teams* Oxford U (1920); Somerset (1921–22, 11 matches).
Career batting
12–24–1–513–86–22.30–0–*ct* 3
Bowling 235–3–78.33–0–0–1/28
He won a blue for soccer.

Whately, Ellis George
Amateur. *b:* 27.7.1882, Kensington, London. *d:* 4.9.1969, Chelsea, London. Middle order right-hand batsman, off break bowler. *Sch* Eton. *Teams* Oxford U (1902–03); Somerset (1904, 1 match).
Career batting
13–21–1–115–20*–5.75–0–*ct* 5
Bowling 1078–43–25.06–1–0–5/66
He also played for Hertfordshire (1901–02).

Whatford, George Lumley
Amateur. *b:* 20.7.1878, Eastbourne, Sussex. *d:* 22.11.1915, Ctesiphon, Mesopotamia. Middle order batsman. *Sch* Harrow. *Team* Sussex (1904, 2 matches).
Career batting
2–2–0–21–13–10.50–0–*ct* 0

Whatmough, Francis John
(birth registered as F. J. Whatmuff)
Professional. *b:* 4.12.1856, Wilsden, Bingley, Yorkshire. *d:* 3.6.1904, Rastrick, Yorkshire. Tail end right-hand batsman, right-hand fast round-arm bowler. *Team* Yorkshire (1878–82, 7 matches).
Career batting
7–11–1–51–20–5.10–0–*ct* 4
Bowling 111–5–22.20–0–0–3/58

Whatmough, Thomas
Professional. *b:* 26.3.1844, Manchester, Lancashire. *d:* 19.3.1911, Newton Heath, Manchester, Lancashire. Lower order right-hand batsman, right-hand fast round-arm bowler, wicket-keeper. *Team* Lancashire (1871, 2 matches).
Career batting
2–4–2–42–28*–21.00–0–*ct* 1
Bowling 79–3–26.33–0–0–2/52
He also played for Cheshire (1878–86). He was a first-class umpire (1892–93).

Wheat, Arthur Bradley
Professional. *b:* 13.5.1898, Halam, Nottinghamshire. *d:* 20.5.1973, Kirkby-in-Ashfield, Nottinghamshire. Tail end left-hand batsman, wicket-keeper. *Team* Nottinghamshire (1927–39, 91 matches).
Career batting
91–115–31–1127–52*–13.41–0–*ct* 152–*st* 21
He was Nottinghamshire CCC scorer from 1947 until his death.

Wheater, Charles Henry
Amateur. *b:* 4.3.1860, Hunmanby, Yorkshire. *d:* 11.5.1885, Scarborough, Yorkshire. Middle order right-hand batsman, right-arm medium pace bowler, point field. *Team* Yorkshire (1880, 2 matches).
Career batting
2–4–1–45–27–15.00–0–*ct* 3
At Cambridge he played in the Freshmen's match of 1881.

Wheatley, Garth Angus
Amateur. *b:* 28.5.1923, Twickenham, Middlesex. Middle order right-hand batsman, wicket-keeper. *Sch* Uppingham. *Teams* Oxford U (1946, blue); Surrey (1947, 5 matches).
Career batting
18–30–2–478–66–17.07–0–*ct* 20–*st* 8
His final first-class match was for Free Foresters in 1950.

Wheatley, Jack Brian
Amateur. *b:* 12.10.1903, Wandsworth, London. *d:* 29.4.1982, Sedlescombe, Sussex. Correct middle order right-hand batsman, left-arm slow medium bowler. *Sch* St Paul's. *Team* Middlesex (1925–28, 8 matches).
Career batting
10–15–1–216–62–15.42–0–*ct* 4
Bowling 169–6–28.16–0–0–3/49
His final first-class match was for Free Foresters in 1930. He appeared in some trial matches for Oxford U, but no first-class games.

Wheatley, Keith James
Cricketer. *b:* 20.1.1946, Guildford, Surrey. Middle order right-hand batsman, off break bowler, good field. *Team* Hampshire (1965–70, 79 matches).
Career batting
79–110–14–1781–79*–18.55–0–*ct* 32
Bowling 1954–69–28.31–0–0–4/1

Wheatley, Oswald Stephen
Amateur. *b:* 28.5.1935, Low Fell, Gateshead, Co Durham. Lower order right-hand batsman, right-arm fast medium bowler. *Sch* KES, Birmingham. *Teams* Cambridge U (1957–58, blue both years); Warwickshire (1957–60, 63 matches); Glamorgan (1961 to 1969/70, 206 matches). *Tours* MCC to South America 1958/9 (not first-class); Swanton to West Indies 1960/1; Glamorgan to West Indies 1969/70.
Career batting
316–362–145–1251–34*–5.76–0–*ct* 110
Bowling 22910–1099–20.84–56–5–9/60
His first-class debut was for Free Foresters in 1956. He took 100 wickets in a season five times (best 136, av 19.32, in 1962). His best bowling was 9/60 for Glamorgan v Sussex at Ebbw Vale in 1968. From 1961 to 1966 he captained Glamorgan. He was Chairman of Glamorgan CCC 1977–83 and since 1986 Chairman of the TCCB Cricket Committee. He was a Test selector in 1973 and 1974, and since 1988.

Wheeler, Alfred
Professional. *b:* 2.10.1845, Croydon, Surrey. Lower order right-hand batsman, wicket-keeper. *Team* Surrey (1872–73, 2 matches).
Career batting
2–3–0–15–9–5.00–0–*ct* 0

Wheeler, Heneage Gibbes
Amateur. *b:* 24.2.1870, Axbridge, Somerset. *d:* 4.8.1965, Preston, Brighton, Sussex. Middle order batsman. *Sch* St Lawrence College. *Team* Somerset (1904, 1 match).
Career batting
1–2–0–8–5–4.00–0–*ct* 0

Wheeler, Henry James William
Amateur. *b:* 27.3.1840, Gibraltar. *d:* 29.10.1908, Westminster, London. Opening batsman. *Sch* Harrow. *Team* Middlesex (1864, 1 match).
Career batting
1–2–0–44–27–22.00–0–*ct* 1

Wheeler, James Anthony
Amateur. *b:* 10.4.1913, Lacock, Wiltshire. *d:* 30.8.1977, Horwood, Devon. Stylish middle order right-hand batsman. *Team* Minor Counties (1949).
Career batting
1–2–0–75–54–37.50–0–*ct* 0
His County cricket was for Wiltshire (1932–55).

Wheeler, John
Professional. *b:* 9.12.1844, Sutton Bonington, Nottinghamshire. *d:* 22.9.1908, Sutton Bonington, Nottinghamshire. Middle order right-hand batsman, right-hand fast round-arm bowler, wicket-keeper. *Team* Nottinghamshire (1873–77, 2 matches).
Career batting
22–38–3–367–66–10.48–0–*ct* 18–*st* 1
Bowling 68–0
His County cricket was mainly for Leicestershire (pre first-class), his career with that County lasting from 1876 to 1892. From 1877 to 1908 he was also on the groundstaff at Lord's and his final first-class match was for MCC in 1887. Between 1895 and 1901 he umpired regularly in first-class matches.

Wheeler, Matthew Benjamin Harold
Cricketer. *b:* 14.8.1962, Windlesham, Surrey. Lower order right-hand batsman, right-arm medium fast bowler. *Sch* Winchester. *Team* Northamptonshire (1985, 2 matches).
Career batting
2 matches, did not bat–*ct* 0
Bowling 117–1–117.00–0–0–1/87

Wheeler, Walter Charles
Professional. *b:* 30.12.1841, Newport, Isle of Wight. *d:* 10.10.1907, Kennington, London. Lower order right-hand batsman, right-hand medium pace round-arm bowler, good field. *Teams* Middlesex (1873, 1 match); Surrey (1875, 5 matches); Hampshire (1878–80, 3 matches).
Career batting
10–20–2–80–15–4.44–0–*ct* 2
Bowling 331–14–23.64–1–0–6/133

Wheelhouse, Alan
Amateur. *b:* 4.3.1934, Nottingham. Lower order left-hand batsman, right-arm medium fast bowler. *Sch* Nottingham HS. *Teams* Cambridge U (1958–59, blue 1959); Nottinghamshire (1961, 1 match).
Career batting
17–26–7–133–17–7.00–0–*ct* 10
Bowling 1705–48–35.52–0–0–4/69

Wheldon, George Frederick
Professional. *b:* 1.11.1869, Langley Green, Worcestershire. *d:* 13.1.1924, Worcester. Grandfather of J. W. E. Spilsbury (Worcestershire). Sound middle order right-hand batsman, occasional wicket-keeper. *Team* Worcestershire (1899–1906, 138 matches).
Career batting
138–244–25–4938–112–22.54–3–*ct* 95–*st* 1
Bowling 77–0
He first played for Worcestershire (pre first-class) in 1895. He also played for Carmarthenshire (1910). A brilliant inside-left he played soccer for Aston Villa, Queen's Park Rangers, West Bromwich Albion, Portsmouth and Coventry City and was capped for England.

Whetherly, Robin Evelyn
Amateur. *b:* 23.7.1916, Westminster, London. *d:* 27.11.1943, near Glamoc, Yugoslavia. He was killed in action. Lower order right-hand batsman, wicket-keeper. *Sch* Harrow. *Team* Oxford U (1937–38). *Tour* Combined Oxford and Cambridge Univ to Jamaica 1938/9.
Career batting
11–16–4–146–63–12.16–0–*ct* 20–*st* 6

Whewell, John William
Professional. *b:* 8.5.1887, Rishton, Lancashire. *d:* 2.7.1948, Blackpool, Lancashire. Lower order right-hand batsman, wicket-keeper. *Team* Lancashire (1921–27, 12 matches).
Career batting
14–17–6–54–25–4.90–0–*ct* 14–*st* 7

Whiley, Richard Kingscote
Amateur. *b:* 10.10.1935, Gloucester. Sound middle order right-hand batsman. *Sch* Malvern. *Teams* Gloucestershire (1954, 1 match); Oxford U (1958).
Career batting
2–4–2–17–7*–8.50–0–*ct* 0
He also played for Dorset (1964–67).

Whitaker, John James
Cricketer. *b:* 5.5.1962, Skipton, Yorkshire. Middle order right-hand batsman, off break bowler. *Sch* Uppingham. *Team* Leicestershire (1983–92, 216 matches). *Tours* England to Australia 1986/7, to Sharjah (not first-class) 1986/7; England A to Zimbabwe 1989/90. *Test* England (1986/7, 1 match).
Career batting
225–357–43–12003–200*–38.22–24–*ct* 142
Bowling 268–2–134.00–0–0–1/29
Test batting
1–1–0–11–11–11.00–0–*ct* 1
He hit 1,000 runs in a season eight times (best 1,767, av 45.30, in 1990). His highest score was 200* for Leicestershire v Nottinghamshire at Leicester in 1986. A series of exciting fast scoring innings in 1986 gained him a place on the Australian tour the following winter, but since then he has not made the jump from county to Test level and has remained a valuable batsman for Leicestershire, rather than an England star.

Whitaker, Mark Robin
Cricketer. *b:* 20.9.1946, Walton-on-Thames, Surrey. Tail end right-hand batsman, right-arm fast medium bowler. *Sch* Bryanston. *Team* Cambridge U (1965–67).
Career batting
12–20–7–16–4*–1.23–0–*ct* 2
Bowling 699–20–34.95–1–0–5/62

Whitby, Hugh Owen
Amateur. *b:* 12.4.1864, Ottery St Mary, Devon. *d:* 14.10.1934, Tonbridge, Kent. Lower order right-hand batsman, right-arm fast bowler. *Sch* Leamington College. *Team* Oxford U (1884–87, blue all four years). *Tour* Sanders to North America 1885.
Career batting
29–46–12–224–24–6.58–0–*ct* 17
Bowling 2341–119–19.67–10–2–8/82
His County cricket was for Warwickshire (pre first-class, 1884–89).

Whitby, Robert Lionel
Amateur. *b:* 29.10.1928, Eden Gardens, Calcutta, India. Lower order right-hand batsman, right-arm medium fast bowler. *Sch* Charterhouse. *Team* Cambridge U (1950).
Career batting
2–2–0–23–12–11.50–0–*ct* 0
Bowling 140–0
His final first-class match was for MCC in 1957.

Whitcher, William
Professional. *b:* 1832, Emsworth, Hampshire. *d:* 9.3.1910, Shirley, Southampton, Hampshire. Middle order batsman, useful bowler. *Team* Hampshire (1864–67, 2 matches).
Career batting
2–4–2–27–17*–13.50–0–*ct* 0
Bowling 30–0

Whitcombe, Henry Maurice
Amateur. *b:* 15.8.1900, Hardwick, Buckinghamshire. *d:* 2.4.1984, Ware, Hertfordshire. Brother of P. S. (Essex), uncle of P. A. (Middlesex). Tail end right-hand batsman, left-arm fast medium bowler. *Sch* Haileybury. *Team* Essex (1922, 3 matches).

Career batting
3–4–2–13–7*–6.50–0–*ct* 1
Bowling 199–1–199.00–0–0–1/34

Whitcombe, Philip Arthur
Amateur. *b:* 23.4.1923, Kensington, London. Son of P. S. (Essex), nephew of H. M. (Essex). Hard hitting lower order right-hand batsman, right-arm fast medium bowler. *Sch* Winchester. *Teams* Oxford U (1947–49, blue all three years); Middlesex (1948, 3 matches).
Career batting
37–56–5–956–68–18.74–0–*ct* 23
Bowling 2489–112–22.22–5–0–7/51

His final first-class match was for the Free Foresters in 1960. He also played for Wiltshire (1947 and 1962).

Whitcombe, Philip John
Amateur. *b:* 11.11.1928, Worcester. Sound opening right-hand batsman, wicket-keeper. *Sch* Worcester RGS. *Teams* Worcestershire (1949–52, 8 matches); Oxford U (1950–52, blue 1951–52).
Career batting
34–53–6–1156–104–24.59–1–*ct* 30–*st* 8
Bowling 10–1–10.00–0–0–1/8

Whitcombe, Major-General Philip Sidney
Amateur. *b:* 3.10.1893, Windsor, Berkshire. *d:* 9.8.1989, Hindhead, Surrey. Father of P. A. (Middlesex), brother of H. M. (Essex). Middle order right-hand batsman, right-arm fast medium bowler. *Sch* Winchester. *Teams* Essex (1922, 1 match); Europeans (1928/9 to 1930/1).
Career batting
4–7–2–81–32*–16.20–0–*ct* 1
Bowling 37–0

He also played for Berkshire (1925–33).

White, A. B. (*see under* Blair-White, A.)

White, A. C.
Amateur. Middle order right-hand batsman. *Team* Surrey (1881, 1 match).
Career batting
1–2–1–15–9*–15.00–0–*ct* 0

White, Albert Winterton
Amateur. *b:* 10.1.1889, Earls Barton, Wellingborough, Northamptonshire. *d:* 9.3.1965, Rushden, Northamptonshire. Middle order right-hand batsman. *Sch* Wellingborough. *Team* Northamptonshire (1914–23, 8 matches).
Career batting
8–15–0–139–29–9.26–0–*ct* 5
Bowling 24–0

White, Alfred Henry Ebsworth
Amateur. *b:* 18.10.1901, Scone, New South Wales, Australia. *d:* 6.3.1964, Darling Point, Sydney, New South Wales, Australia. Lower order right-hand batsman, right-arm fast medium bowler. *Teams* Cambridge U (1922–24, blue 1924); New South Wales (1925/6, 1 match).
Career batting
20–25–6–279–53*–14.68–0–*ct* 9
Bowling 1299–45–28.86–1–0–5/66

White, Alison Kingsley Gordon
(later Gordon-White)
Amateur. *b:* 2.1.1881. *d:* 20.3.1962, Crowborough, Sussex. Middle order right-hand batsman, right-arm fast medium bowler. *Sch* Cheltenham. *Team* Gloucestershire (1913–19, 11 matches).
Career batting
13–24–1–442–54–19.21–0–*ct* 7
Bowling 3–0

He also played for Northumberland (1913).

White, Allan Frederick Tinsdale
Amateur. *b:* 5.9.1915, Earlsdon, Coventry, Warwickshire. Opening right-hand batsman. *Sch* Uppingham. *Teams* Cambridge U (1936–37, blue 1936); Warwickshire (1936–37, 9 matches); Worcestershire (1939–49, 110 matches).
Career batting
142–247–17–5035–95–21.89–0–*ct* 46
Bowling 26–0

He hit 1,179 runs, av 26.79, in 1946 and also reached 1,000 runs in one other season. He captained Worcestershire 1947–48 and jointly in 1949.

White, Anthony Wilbur
Amateur. *b:* 20.11.1938, Brighton, St Michael, Barbados. Attacking lower order right-hand batsman, right-arm medium pace off break bowler. *Team* Barbados (1958/9 to 1965/6). *Tour* West Indies to England 1963. *Tests* West Indies (1964/5, 2 matches).
Career batting
31–46–7–996–75–25.53–0–*ct* 32
Bowling 2665–95–28.05–1–0–6/80
Test batting
2–4–1–71–57*–23.66–0–*ct* 1
Bowling 152–3–50.66–0–0–2/34

He was co-opted into the 1963 touring team to England due to injury, and appeared in nine matches.

White, Sir Archibald Woollaston
Amateur. *b:* 14.10.1877, Tickhill, Yorkshire. *d:* 16.12.1945, Torhousemuir, Wigtown, Scotland. Nephew of W. J. Humble (Derbyshire). Middle order right-hand batsman, right-arm medium pace bowler. *Sch* Wellington. *Team* Yorkshire (1908–20, 97 matches).
Career batting
98–130–28–1471–55–14.42–0–*ct* 52
Bowling 7–0

He captained Yorkshire 1912 to 1914.

White, Colin Derek
Amateur. *b:* 4.4.1937, Chiswick, Middlesex. Middle order left-hand batsman. *Sch* Cranleigh. *Team* Cambridge U (1958–60).
Career batting
23–41–2–606–64–15.53–0–*ct* 7
Bowling 24–0
His final first-class match was for Free Foresters in 1961.

White, Craig
Cricketer. *b:* 16.12.1969, Morley, Yorkshire. Middle order right-hand batsman, off break bowler, occasional wicket-keeper. *Teams* Yorkshire (1990–92, 30 matches); Victoria (1990/1, 2 matches). *Tour* Yorkshire to South Africa 1991/2.
Career batting
32–41–10–1045–79*–33.70–0–*ct* 20
Bowling 700–15–46.66–1–0–5/74
Although born in Yorkshire, he was brought up and educated in Australia.

White, David William
Professional. *b:* 14.12.1935, Sutton Coldfield, Warwickshire. Lower order left-hand batsman, right-arm fast bowler. *Teams* Hampshire (1957–71, 315 matches); Glamorgan (1972, 1 match). *Tours* MCC to India and Pakistan 1961/2; Cavaliers to West Indies 1964/5. *Tests* England (1961/2, 2 matches).
Career batting
337–395–104–3080–58*–10.58–0–*ct* 106
Bowling 26913–1143–23.54–57–5–9/44
Test batting
2–2–0–0–0–0.00–0–*ct* 0
Bowling 119–4–29.75–0–0–3/65
He took 100 wickets in a season four times (best 124, av 19.10, in 1960). His best innings analysis was 9/44 for Hampshire v Leicestershire at Portsmouth in 1966.

White, Edmund
Amateur. *b:* 29.1.1928, Lee, London. Middle order right-hand batsman, wicket-keeper. *Sch* Wellingborough. *Team* Northamptonshire (1946–48, 3 matches).
Career batting
3–4–0–44–16–11.00–0–*ct* 1

White, Edward Albert
Amateur. *b:* 16.3.1844, Yalding, Kent. *d:* 3.5.1922, Stamford Bridge, Chiswick, Middlesex. Cousin of L. A. (Kent). Stylish opening right-hand baseman. *Sch* Marlborough. *Team* Kent (1867–75, 29 matches).
Career batting
31–60–7–827–81–15.60–0–*ct* 12

White, Edward Clive Stewart
Amateur. *b:* 17.4.1913, Mosman, Sydney, New South Wales, Australia. Son of A. B. S. (New South Wales). Lower order right-hand batsman, left-arm slow medium bowler. *Team* New South Wales (1934/5 to 1938/9, 32 matches). *Tour* Australia to England 1938.
Career batting
56–81–22–1316–108*–22.30–1–*ct* 37
Bowling 3072–115–26.71–2–0–8/31
He had few opportunities on the 1938 tour.

White, Francis Sims
Amateur. *b:* 26.8.1883, Philadelphia, USA. *d:* 5.4.1962, Germantown, Philadelphia, USA. Middle order right-hand batsman. *Team* Philadelphia (1903–09). *Tour* Philadelphia to England 1908.
Career batting
17–29–1–588–118–21.00–1–*ct* 8
He played for USA v Canada in 1904. On the 1908 tour he hit 346 runs, av 19.22, coming second in the batting table.

White, Air Vice Marshal George Holford
Amateur. *b:* 16.10.1904, Dorchester, Dorset. *d:* 18.1.1965, Uxbridge, Middlesex. Opening right-hand batsman. *Sch* Felsted. *Team* RAF (1932).
Career batting
1–2–0–50–25–25.00–0–*ct* 0
His County cricket was for Dorset (1932–35).

White, Gilbert William
Amateur. *b:* 6.7.1912, Farnham, Surrey. *d:* 14.10.1977, La Plaine, Dominica. Son of W. N. (Hampshire), son-in-law of H. B. G. Austin (Barbados). Attractive middle order batsman. *Sch* Winchester. *Team* Army (1938).
Career batting
1–1–0–10–10–10.00–0–*ct* 0
Bowling 12–0

White, Giles William
Cricketer. *b:* 23.3.1972, Barnstaple, Devon. Middle order right-hand batsman, leg break bowler. *Sch* Millfield. *Team* Somerset (1991, 1 match).
Career batting
1–1–0–42–42–42.00–0–*ct* 0
Bowling 30–1–30.00–0–0–1/30
He also played for Devon (1988–92).

White, Gordon Charles
Amateur. *b:* 5.2.1882, Port St Johns, Pondoland, Cape Province, South Africa. *d:* 17.10.1918, Gaza, Palestine. He died of wounds. Attractive middle order right-hand batsman, leg break bowler. *Team* Transvaal (1902/3 to 1911/12). *Tours* South Africa to England 1904, 1907 and 1912. *Tests* South Africa (1905/6 to 1912, 17 matches).
Career batting
97–152–17–3740–162*–27.70–4–*ct* 46
Bowling 3109–155–20.05–8–2–7/33
Test batting
17–31–2–872–147–30.06–2–*ct* 10
Bowling 301–9–33.44–0–0–4/47
On the 1904 visit he hit 773 runs, av 29.73, and in 1907 862 runs, av 22.10. On the latter tour he took 56

wickets, av 14.73. In 1912, though he played in five out of six Tests, he was not successful. He played soccer for South Africa.

White, Rev Harold
Amateur. *b:* 16.6.1876, Kirkstall, Yorkshire. *d:* 11.1.1965, North Town, Taunton, Somerset. Lower order right-hand batsman, right-arm fast bowler. *Sch* Denstone. *Team* Oxford U (1900–01, blue 1900).
Career batting
11–14–5–77–26–8.55–0–*ct* 3
Bowling 725–31–23.38–1–0–6/10
His County cricket was for Northumberland (1909–13).

White, Henry Albert
Professional. *b:* 8.8.1895, Watford, Hertfordshire. *d:* 27.11.1972, Barrow Gurney, Somerset. Lower order right-hand batsman, off break bowler. *Team* Warwickshire (1923, 8 matches).
Career batting
8–15–3–107–32–8.91–0–*ct* 2
Bowling 33–0
He also played for Hertfordshire (1921). A good soccer player, he appeared for Arsenal, Blackpool and Walsall.

White, Horace Arthur
Amateur. *b:* 26.3.1894, Earls Barton, Wellingborough, Northamptonshire. *d:* 3.1.1969, Earls Barton, Wellingborough, Northamptonshire. Middle order right-hand batsman, useful bowler. *Team* Northamptonshire (1923, 5 matches).
Career batting
5–10–2–51–15*–6.37–0–*ct* 1
Bowling 126–1–126.00–0–0–1/35

White, Jack
Amateur. *b:* 9.7.1893, Putney, London. *d:* 6.11.1968, Blackwell, East Grinstead, Sussex. Lower order right-hand batsman, right-arm fast bowler. *Sch* Wellingborough. *Teams* Cambridge U (1913–14); Surrey (1926, 1 match).
Career batting
3–3–1–26–15*–13.00–0–*ct* 3
Bowling 289–6–48.16–1–0–5/75

White, John
Professional. *b:* Bulwell, Nottinghamshire. Lower order batsman, wicket-keeper. *Teams* North of England (1886); Liverpool and District (1886–90).
Career batting
3–4–0–73–62–18.25–0–*ct* 4–*st* 2
He appeared for Nottinghamshire in a non-first-class match in 1887.

White, John Cornish
Amateur. *b:* 19.2.1891, Holford, Somerset. *d:* 2.5.1961, Yarde Farm, Combe-Florey, Somerset. Lower order right-hand batsman, slow left-arm bowler. *Sch* Taunton. *Team* Somerset (1909–37, 409 matches). *Tours* MCC to South America 1926/7, to Australia 1928/9, to South Africa 1930/1. *Tests* England (1921 to 1930/1, 15 matches).
Career batting
472–765–102–12202–192–18.40–6–*ct* 426
Bowling 43759–2356–18.57–193–58–10/76
Test batting
15–22–9–239–29–18.38–0–*ct* 6
Bowling 1581–49–32.26–3–1–8/126
He took 100 wickets in a season 14 times (best 168, av 15.76, in 1929) and hit 1,000 runs twice (best 1,179, av 27.41, in 1929). In 1929 and 1930 he completed the 'double'. His best bowling was 10/76 for Somerset v Worcestershire at Worcester in 1921; he took nine wickets in an innings on four other occasions. From 1927 to 1931 he captained Somerset and he led England in four Tests, as well as being a Test Selector in 1929 and 1930. He was President of Somerset in 1961.

White, John William
Professional. *b:* 1.8.1877, Annesley, Nottinghamshire. *d:* 2.12.1958, Mansfield, Nottinghamshire. Lower order right-hand batsman, wicket-keeper. *Teams* Nottinghamshire (1902–04, 3 matches); Scotland (1906).
Career batting
4–8–1–74–31–10.57–0–*ct* 8–*st* 2
A useful soccer player, he appeared for Nottingham Forest at full-back.

White, Lionel Algernon
Amateur. *b:* 9.11.1850, Wateringbury, Kent. *d:* 25.6.1917, Tunbridge Wells, Kent. Cousin of E. A. (Kent). Careful middle order right-hand batsman, good deep field. *Sch* St Paul's. *Team* Kent (1869, 4 matches).
Career batting
4–8–0–84–34–10.50–0–*ct* 1

White, Hon Luke Robert
(succeeded as 5th Baron Annaly in 1970)
Amateur. *b:* 15.3.1927, Marylebone, London. *d:* 30.9.1990, Alton, Hampshire. Nephew of D. O'Brien (Ireland). Opening or middle order right-hand batsman. *Sch* Eton. *Team* Middlesex (1946–47, 3 matches).
Career batting
6–10–1–134–46–14.88–0–*ct* 2
His first-class debut was for England in 1945 and his final first-class match for MCC in 1950.

White, Malcolm Frank
Amateur. *b:* 15.5.1924, Walsall, Staffordshire. Lower order right-hand batsman, wicket-keeper. *Team* Warwickshire (1946, 1 match).
Career batting
1–2–0–0–0–0.00–0–*ct* 3–*st* 1
He also played for Staffordshire (1954).

White, Montague Eric
Professional. *b:* 21.1.1908, London. *d:* 21.6.1970, Irby, Cheshire. Lower order right-hand batsman, right-arm fast medium bowler. *Sch* Worcester RGS. *Team* Worcestershire (1931–34, 34 matches).
Career batting
34–46–12–238–37–7.00–0–*ct* 11
Bowling 2076–66–31.45–1–0–5/34

White, Oliver Claude
Amateur. *b:* 11.3.1880, Eton, Buckinghamshire. *d:* 12.1.1956, Earlswood, Redhill, Surrey. Lower order right-hand batsman, slow right-arm bowler. *Sch* Merchant Taylors. *Team* Northamptonshire (1920, 5 matches).
Career batting
5–9–3–57–15*–9.50–0–*ct* 1
Bowling 279–10–27.90–0–0–3/49
He also played for Buckinghamshire (1906).

White, Raymond Christopher
Amateur. *b:* 29.1.1941, Johannesburg, South Africa. Attacking middle order right-hand batsman, right-arm medium pace bowler. *Teams* Cambridge U (1962–65, blue all four years); Gloucestershire (1962–64, 40 matches); Transvaal (1965/6 to 1972/3).
Career batting
141–248–4–6824–205–27.96–10–*ct* 67
Bowling 589–17–34.64–0–0–3/17
His first-class debut was for South African Universities in 1960/1. His highest score was 205 for Transvaal B v Griqualand West at Johannesburg in 1965/6. He hit 1,000 runs in a season twice (best 1,696, av 29.24, in 1962). He captained Cambridge in 1965.

White, Reginald Strelley Moresby
Amateur. *b:* 22.2.1893, Grantham, Lincolnshire. *d:* 3.3.1947, Nairobi, Kenya. Lower order batsman, wicket-keeper. *Sch* Malvern. *Teams* Oxford U (1913–14); Europeans (1924/5).
Career batting
7–10–4–90–36–15.00–0–*ct* 4–*st* 2
His final first-class match was for the Army in 1930. His County cricket was for Lincolnshire (1913). He won a blue for soccer.

White, Robert Arthur
Professional. *b:* 6.10.1936, Fulham, London. Sound opening, later middle order left-hand batsman, off break bowler. *Teams* Middlesex (1958–65, 114 matches); Nottinghamshire (1966–80, 298 matches).
Career batting
413–642–105–12452–116*–23.18–5–*ct* 190
Bowling 21138–693–30.50–28–4–7/41
He hit 1,355 runs, av 33.87, in 1963; his best bowling season was 1971 with 81 wickets, av 26.21. His career was remarkable in that he did not take a single wicket during his eight seasons with Middlesex. In 1983 he joined the first-class umpires' list.

White, Roger Frank
Cricketer. *b:* 22.11.1943, Perivale, Middlesex. Lower order right-hand batsman, slow left-arm bowler. *Team* Middlesex (1964–66, 13 matches).
Career batting
13–11–6–18–7*–3.60–0–*ct* 4
Bowling 518–17–30.47–0–0–4/79

White, Sidney Grayling
Amateur. *b:* 11.8.1892, Sunbury-on-Thames, Middlesex. *d:* 1.5.1949, Chipstead, Surrey. Lower order lefthand batsman, left-arm bowler. *Team* Middlesex (1921–23, 2 matches).
Career batting
2–3–1–23–20–11.50–0–*ct* 2
Bowling 33–0

White, Thomas
Professional. *b:* 1740, Reigate, Surrey. *d:* 28.7.1831, Reigate, Surrey. Middle order right-hand batsman. *Team* Surrey (1773–78).
He represented England against Hampshire and in 1771 he used a bat the width of the wicket, and this innnovation caused the Laws of the game to be altered to include a clause stating that the bat should not be more than four and a quarter inches in width.

White, Thomas Reginald
Amateur. *b:* 3.7.1892, Basingstoke, Hampshire. *d:* 7.5.1979, Camden, London. Middle order right-hand batsman, right-arm fast medium bowler. *Sch* Cranleigh. *Team* Sussex (1928, 1 match).
Career batting
1–2–0–13–9–6.50–0–*ct* 0
Bowling 25–0

White, William Michael Eastwood
Amateur. *b:* 22.5.1913, Barnes, Surrey. Grandson of J. Brockbank (MCC). Lower order right-hand batsman, right-arm medium fast bowler. *Sch* Dover. *Teams* Cambridge U (1937); Northamptonshire (1947–49, 5 matches).
Career batting
21–35–6–398–48–13.72–0–*ct* 15
Bowling 1524–42–36.28–0–0–4/67

White, William Neil
Amateur. *b:* 2.5.1920, Troon, Ayrshire, Scotland. *d:* 19.2.1990, Cambridge. Middle order right-hand batsman, slow left-arm bowler. *Sch* The Leys. *Team* Cambridge U (1948).
Career batting
2–3–0–19–19–6.33–0–*ct* 1
Bowling 106–4–26.50–0–0–4/16
His County cricket was for Cambridgeshire (1947–49).

White, William Nicholas
Amateur. *b:* 10.9.1879, St Pancras, London. *d:* 27.12.1951, Poltimore, Devon. Father of G. W. (Army). Middle order right-hand batsman. *Sch* Mal-

vern. *Teams* Hampshire (1903–14, 61 matches); Barbados (1903/4 to 1905/6).
Career batting
72–128–5–3225–160*–26.21–2–*ct* 42
Bowling 39–0
His final first-class match was for the Combined Services in 1922. A good soccer player, he captained the Army team.

Whitehead, Alan Geoffrey Thomas
Professional. *b:* 28.10.1940, Butleigh, Somerset. Tail end left-hand batsman, slow left-arm bowler. *Team* Somerset (1957–61, 38 matches).
Career batting
38–49–25–137–15–5.70–0–*ct* 21
Bowling 2306–67–34.41–3–0–6/74
He was appointed to the first-class umpires' list in 1970 and stood in five Test matches (1982–87).

Whitehead, George William Edendale
Amateur. *b:* 27.8.1895, Bromley, Kent. *d:* 17.10.1918, Lanwe, near Menin, France. He was killed in action. Brother of J. H. E. (MCC). Stylish middle order right-hand batsman, leg break and googly bowler. *Sch* Clifton. *Team* Kent (1914, 2 matches).
Career batting
2–4–0–12–5–3.00–0–*ct* 3

Whitehead, Harry
Professional. *b:* 19.9.1874, Barlestone, Leicestershire. *d:* 14.9.1944, Newfoundpool, Leicester. Attractive opening right-hand batsman, right-arm medium pace bowler, good field. *Team* Leicestershire (1898–1922, 380 matches).
Career batting
382–680–25–15112–174–23.07–14–*ct* 407
Bowling 3401–106–32.08–1–0–5/80
He hit 1,000 runs in a season four times (best 1,391, av 30.91, in 1911). A good soccer player, he appeared for Leicester Fosse.

Whitehead, James George
Professional. *b:* 1877, Cape Town, South Africa. *d:* 23.1.1940, Mowbray, Cape Town, South Africa. Lower order left-hand batsman, left-arm medium fast bowler. *Teams* Warwickshire (1902, 1 match); Western Province (1904/5 to 1920/1); Griqualand West (1912/13 to 1913/14).
Career batting
30–47–16–351–42–11.32–0–*ct* 10
Bowling 2228–118–18.88–7–2–7/58

Whitehead, James Hugh Edendale
Amateur. *b:* 8.7.1890, Bromley, Kent. *d:* 13.3.1919, Westminster, London. Brother of G. W. E. (Kent). Middle order batsman, leg break bowler. *Sch* Clifton. *Team* MCC (1912).
Career batting
1–2–0–3–2–1.50–0–*ct* 1

Whitehead, John Parkin
Professional. *b:* 3.9.1925, Upper Mill, Yorkshire. Lower order right-hand batsman, right-arm fast medium bowler. *Teams* Yorkshire (1946–51, 37 matches); Worcestershire (1953–55, 33 matches).
Career batting
74–91–26–1246–71–19.16–0–*ct* 25
Bowling 4297–147–29.23–4–0–5/10

Whitehead, Lees
Professional. *b:* 14.3.1864, Birchen Bank, Friarmere, Yorkshire. *d:* 22.11.1913, West Hartlepool, Co Durham. He died of pneumonia. Lower order right-hand batsman, right-arm fast bowler. *Team* Yorkshire (1889–1904, 119 matches).
Career batting
136–202–43–2433–67*–15.30–0–*ct* 79
Bowling 2799–109–25.67–3–0–6/45

Whitehead, Luther
Professional. *b:* 25.6.1869, Hull, Yorkshire. *d:* 17.1.1931, Buenos Aires, Argentine. Middle order right-hand batsman, deep field. *Team* Yorkshire (1893, 2 matches).
Career batting
2–4–0–21–13–5.25–0–*ct* 0

Whitehead, Philip James
Amateur. *b:* 2.3.1881, Deddington, Oxfordshire. *d:* 26.6.1957, Greenwich, London. Middle order batsman. *Team* Northamptonshire (1908–09, 2 matches).
Career batting
2–4–2–24–10*–12.00–0–*ct* 0
Bowling 11–1–11.00–0–0–1/11

Whitehead, Ralph
Professional. *b:* 16.10.1883, Ashton-under-Lyne, Lancashire. *d:* 23.8.1956, Winwick, Lancashire. Patient middle order right-hand batsman, right-arm medium fast bowler. *Team* Lancashire (1908–14, 107 matches).
Career batting
108–160–36–2578–131*–20.79–4–*ct* 37
Bowling 7260–300–24.20–17–5–8/77
He had a sensational debut – Lancashire v Nottinghamshire at Old Trafford in 1908 – when he hit 131* and later was no-balled four times in one over for throwing.

Whitehead, Stephen James
Professional. *b:* 2.9.1860, Enfield Highway, Middlesex. *d:* 9.6.1904, Small Heath, Birmingham. Lower order right-hand batsman, right-arm medium pace off break bowler. *Team* Warwickshire (1894–1900, 55 matches).
Career batting
58–78–29–519–46–10.59–0–*ct* 34
Bowling 4380–183–23.93–11–4–8/47
He first played for Warwickshire (pre first-class) in 1889. His first-class debut was for Liverpool and Dis-

trict in 1891. He died the day following the match between Warwickshire and Essex at Edgbaston, the proceeds of which had been set aside for the benefit of himself and Richards. Whitehead had attended the match and seemed in good health.

Whitehead, Thomas
Amateur. *b:* 1852. *d:* 2.11.1937, Brindle Lodge, Preston, Lancashire. Lower order batsman, useful bowler. *Team* Lancashire (1884, 1 match).
Career batting
1–1–0–8–8–8.00–0–*ct* 0
Bowling 20–0

Whitehill, William Kenneth
Professional. *b:* 13.6.1934, Newport, Monmouthshire. Lower order right-hand batsman, wicket-keeper. *Team* Glamorgan (1960, 7 matches).
Career batting
7–11–3–60–16–7.50–0–*ct* 8

Whitehouse, John
Cricketer. *b:* 8.4.1949, Nuneaton, Warwickshire. Stylish middle order right-hand batsman, off break bowler. *Team* Warwickshire (1971–80, 179 matches).
Career batting
180–309–38–8693–197–32.07–15–*ct* 120
Bowling 471–6–78.50–0–0–2/55

He hit 1,000 runs in a season three times (best 1,543, av 42.86, in 1977). In 1978 and 1979 he captained Warwickshire. He scored 173 on debut for Warwickshire v Oxford U at Oxford in 1971.

Whitehouse, Percy Gilbert
Amateur. *b:* 1.8.1893, Edgbaston, Warwickshire. *d:* 24.9.1959, Knowle, Solihull, Warwickshire. Lower order right-hand batsman, off break bowler. *Team* Warwickshire (1926, 3 matches).
Career batting
3–6–3–41–13–13.66–66–0–*ct* 6
Bowling 122–8–15.25–0–0–4/23

Whitehouse, Peter Michael William
Amateur. *b:* 27.4.1917, Birchington, Kent. *d:* 19.11.1943, Archi, Italy. He was killed in action. Middle order right-hand batsman, right-arm medium pace bowler. *Sch* Marlborough. *Teams* Oxford U (1936–38, blue 1938); Kent (1937–38, 8 matches).
Career batting
24–39–7–927–91*–28.96–0–*ct* 4
Bowling 1267–43–29.46–1–0–5/33

He also played for Berkshire (1935).

Whitelaw, William Frederick Martin
Amateur. *b:* 16.6.1906, Edinburgh, Scotland. *d:* 3.5.1982, Polton, Midlothian, Scotland. Lower order right-hand batsman, right-arm medium pace bowler. *Sch* Merchiston. *Team* Scotland (1932)
Career batting
1–2–0–1–1–0.50–0–*ct* 0
Bowling 54–2–27.00–0–0–2/48

Whiteley, John Peter
Cricketer. *b:* 28.2.1955, Otley, Yorkshire. Lower order right-hand batsman, off break bowler. *Team* Yorkshire (1978–82, 45 matches).
Career batting
45–38–17–231–20–11.00–0–*ct* 21
Bowling 2410–70–34.42–0–0–4/14

Whiteley, Peter
Professional. *b:* 12.8.1935, Rochdale, Lancashire. *d:* 28.10.1989, Crompton, Lancashire. He died whilst playing golf. Middle order right-hand batsman, slow left-arm bowler. *Team* Lancashire (1957–58, 5 matches).
Career batting
5–8–2–86–32–14.33–0–*ct* 2
Bowling 266–9–29.55–0–0–3/70

Whiteside, John Parkinson
Professional. *b:* 11.6.1861, Fleetwood, Lancashire. *d:* 8.3.1946, Leicester. Tail end right-hand batsman, wicket-keeper. *Teams* Lancashire (1888–90, 6 matches); Leicestershire (1894–1906, 215 matches).
Career batting
231–362–141–1362–50–6.16–0–*ct* 340–*st* 98

He was on the Lord's ground staff from 1889 to 1920. He was a first-class umpire (1921–22). He first played for Leicestershire (pre first-class) in 1893.

Whiteside, Rev Peter George
Amateur. *b:* 21.2.1930, New Malden, Surrey. Lower order right-hand batsman, wicket-keeper. *Sch* Denstone. *Team* Cambridge U (1955).
Career batting
2–2–0–1–1–0.50–0–*ct* 3

Whitfeld, Francis Barry
Amateur. *b:* 23.5.1852, Hamsey, Lewes, Sussex. *d:* 8.1.1924, Lewes, Sussex. Father of G. S. (Sussex), brother of Herbert (Sussex). Middle order batsman, excellent field. *Sch* Uppingham. *Team* Sussex (1878, 1 match).
Career batting
2–4–0–7–5–1.75–0–*ct* 3

His final first-class match was for G. N. Wyatt's XI in 1886.

Whitfeld, George Sulivan
Amateur. *b:* 20.3.1878, Lewes, Sussex. *d:* 29.7.1945, Kensington, London. Son of F. B. (Sussex), nephew of Herbert (Sussex). Hard hitting middle order batsman. *Sch* Eton. *Team* Sussex (1908, 3 matches).
Career batting
3–5–2–191–71*–63.66–0–*ct* 0

Whitfeld, Herbert
Amateur. *b:* 15.11.1858, Hamsey, Lewes, Sussex. *d:* 6.5.1909, Chailey, Sussex. Brother of F. B. (Sussex), uncle of G. S. (Sussex). Opening or middle order right-hand batsman, left-hand medium pace round-arm bowler, good slip field. *Sch* Eton. *Teams* Cam-

bridge U (1878–81, blue all four years); Sussex (1878–85, 39 matches).
Career batting
75–133–14–2400–116–20.16–1–*ct* 65
Bowling 282–6–47.00–0–0–2/35

He captained Sussex in 1883 and 1884. His final first-class match was for I Zingari in 1889. An all-round athlete, he represented Cambridge in the mile and at soccer, also being in the royal tennis doubles with Hon Ivo Bligh. He played soccer for England.

Whitfield, Edward Walter
Professional. *b:* 31.5.1911, Stockwell, London. Middle order right-hand batsman, right-arm medium pace bowler. *Teams* Surrey (1930–39, 106 matches); Northamptonshire (1946, 19 matches).
Career batting
125–189–21–3995–198–23.77–6–*ct* 36
Bowling 1562–35–44.62–0–0–4/63

He hit 1,005 runs, av 38.89, in 1938.

Whiting, Algernon Oswald
Amateur. *b:* 23.4.1861, Kensington, London. *d:* 23.1.1931, Worcester Park, Surrey. Stylish middle order right-hand batsman, wicket-keeper. *Sch* Sherborne and Charterhouse. *Team* Oxford U (1881–82, blue both years).
Career batting
9–17–0–317–80–18.64–0–*ct* 6

He was for many years a tea planter in Ceylon and played much cricket there.

Whiting, Charles Percival
Professional. *b:* 18.4.1888, Dringhoe, Skipsea, Yorkshire. *d:* 14.1.1959, Great Driffield, Yorkshire. Lower order right-hand batsman, right-arm fast bowler. *Team* Yorkshire (1914–20, 6 matches).
Career batting
6–10–2–92–26–11.50–0–*ct* 2
Bowling 416–15–27.73–1–0–5/46

Whiting, John George Benjamin
Amateur. *b:* 19.2.1894, Newport Pagnell, Buckinghamshire. *d:* 15.7.1975, Newport Pagnell, Buckinghamshire. Lower order batsman, useful bowler. *Sch* Wellingborough. *Team* Leveson-Gower's XI (1921).
Career batting
2–4–0–34–27–8.50–0–*ct* 0
Bowling 272–6–45.33–0–0–4/76

His County cricket was for Buckinghamshire (1920–22).

Whiting, Norman Harry
Professional. *b:* 2.10.1920, Wollaston, Worcestershire. Middle order right-hand batsman, off break bowler. *Team* Worcestershire (1947–52, 59 matches).
Career batting
59–96–11–1583–118–18.62–2–*ct* 32
Bowling 657–13–50.53–0–0–2/27

Whiting, Walter Sydney
Amateur. *b:* 23.10.1888, Bath, Somerset. *d:* 15.1.1952, Combe Park, Bath, Somerset. Lower order right-hand batsman, leg break bowler. *Team* Somerset (1921–23, 8 matches).
Career batting
8–12–3–133–28–14.77–0–*ct* 9
Bowling 646–27–23.92–0–0–4/28

Whitington, Richard Smallpeice
Amateur. *b:* 30.6.1912, Unley Park, Adelaide, South Australia. *d:* 13.3.1984, Sydney, New South Wales, Australia. Opening right-hand batsman. *Team* South Australia (1932/3 to 1939/40, 36 matches). *Tours* Australian Services to England 1945, to India 1945/6.
Career batting
54–90–4–2782–155–32.34–4–*ct* 32
Bowling 91–1–91.00–0–0–1/4

His final first-class match was for Australian Services in Australia in 1945/6. He was a noted author and journalist, having written a number of books on cricket, several of them jointly with K. R. Miller.

Whitley, Robert Thomas
Professional. *b:* 1837, Pimlico, London. *d:* 26.10.1887, Fulham, London. Middle order batsman. *Team* Surrey (1873, 1 match).
Career batting
1–2–0–8–5–4.00–0–*ct* 2

Whitman, Eric Ioan Emlyn
Amateur. *b:* 31.7.1909, Barry, Glamorgan. *d:* 5.12.1990, Norwich, Norfolk. Lower order batsman, fast bowler. *Team* Glamorgan (1932, 2 matches).
Career batting
2–3–0–27–16–9.00–0–*ct* 0
Bowling 172–3–57.33–0–0–2/113

He also played for Cambridgeshire (1937).

Whitney, Michael Roy
Cricketer. *b:* 24.2.1959, Surry Hills, Sydney, New South Wales, Australia. Lower order right-hand batsman, left-arm fast medium bowler. *Teams* New South Wales (1980/1 to 1991/2, 86 matches); Gloucestershire (1981, 3 matches). *Tours* Australia to England 1981, to West Indies 1990/1; Young Australia to Zimbabwe 1982/3; New South Wales to Zimbabwe 1985/6, 1987/8; Rest of World to England 1990. *Tests* Australia (1981 to 1991/2, 9 matches).
Career batting
105–105–38–349–28*–5.20–0–*ct* 45
Bowling 9955–379–26.26–18–1–7/27
Test batting
9–14–7–31–12–4.42–0–*ct* 1
Bowling 1107–35–31.62–2–1–7/27

He was just about to play for Gloucestershire v Hampshire at Cheltenham on 11 August 1981 when he was summoned to Old Trafford to play for Australia in the fifth Test, a move which created a talking point at the time. He also played for D.B.Close's XI at Scarborough in 1983.

Whittaker, Charles Gustavus
Amateur. *b:* 8.9.1819, Barming, Kent. *d:* 15.11.1886, Barming Place, Kent. Lower order right-hand batsman, right-hand fast round-arm bowler. *Sch* Westminster. *Team* Kent (1839–47, 36 matches).
Career batting
70–125–20–844–55–8.03–0–*ct* 26
Bowling 12–0 + 45–no av–1–0–6/?
His final important match was for Gentlemen of Kent in 1848 when he sustained a compound fracture of his right thumb and was unable to continue to appear in great matches.

Whittaker, David
Professional. *b:* 25.10.1857, Church, Lancashire. *d:* 17.12.1901, Rishton, Lancashire. He was found drowned in the canal. Middle order left-hand batsman, left-arm medium pace bowler, good point field. *Team* Lancashire (1884–88, 9 matches).
Career batting
9–14–1–128–26–9.84–0–*ct* 4
Bowling 46–1–46.00–0–0–1/26

Whittaker, Edwin
Amateur. *b:* 4.12.1834, Ashton-under-Lyne, Lancashire. *d:* 25.6.1880, Rock Vale House, Matlock, Derbyshire. Stylish middle order right-hand batsman, occasional wicket-keeper. *Sch* Wesley College, Sheffield. *Team* Lancashire (1865–68, 11 matches).
Career batting
14–25–2–291–39–12.65–0–*ct* 4
Bowling 125–1–125.00–0–0–1/26
He was a notable player for Gentlemen of Lancashire. His first-class debut was for North of England in 1863.

Whittaker, Geoffrey James
Professional. *b:* 29.5.1916, Peckham, London. Aggressive middle order right-hand batsman. *Team* Surrey (1937–53, 124 matches).
Career batting
129–191–20–4988–185*–29.16–8–*ct* 48
Bowling 47–1–47.00–0–0–1/31
He hit 1,439 runs, av 39.97, in 1951, and also completed 1,000 runs in 1949.

Whittaker, Robert Christopher Cornwallis
Amateur. *b:* 26.8.1908, Melton, Suffolk. *d:* 11.2.1990, Fulham, London. Lower order right-hand batsman, slow left-arm bowler. *Sch* Eton. *Team* Sussex (1927, 2 matches).
Career batting
3–3–1–31–31–15.50–0–*ct* 2
Bowling 84–6–14.00–1–0–5/36
His final first-class match was for the Army in 1929.

Whitticase, Philip
Cricketer. *b:* 15.3.1965, Marston Green, Solihull, Warwickshire. Middle order right-hand batsman, wicket-keeper. *Team* Leicestershire (1984–92, 129 matches).
Career batting
129–169–39–2963–114*–22.79–1–*ct* 302–*st* 13
Bowling 7–0

Whitting, Edward Jewel
Amateur. *b:* 1.9.1872, Falmouth, Cornwall. *d:* 8.3.1938, Abergavenny, Monmouthshire. Forceful lower order right-hand batsman, right-arm fast bowler. *Sch* Rugby. *Team* H. T. Hewett's XI (1892).
Career batting
1–2–1–6–5–6.00–0–*ct* 0
He played in the Cambridge Freshmen's match of 1892. His County cricket was for Somerset (not first-class, 1890).

Whittingham, Norman Barrie
Professional. *b:* 22.10.1940, Silsden, Yorkshire. Middle order left-hand batsman, off break bowler. *Team* Nottinghamshire (1962–66, 77 matches).
Career batting
77–141–7–2964–133–22.11–2–*ct* 41
Bowling 122–1–122.00–0–0–1/9
He also played for Cumberland (1967–71).

Whittington, Jonathan Mark Smith
Cricketer. *b:* 17.8.1973, Marylebone, London. Lower order left-hand batsman, slow left-arm bowler. *Sch* Eton. *Team* Middlesex (1992, 1 match).
Career batting
1 match, did not bat–*ct* 0
Bowling 44–0

Whittington, Thomas Aubrey Leyson
Amateur. *b:* 29.7.1881, Neath, Glamorgan. *d:* 19.7.1944, St Pancras, London. Opening right-hand batsman. *Sch* Weymouth and Merchiston. *Teams* Glamorgan (1921–23, 47 matches); Wales (1923). *Tours* MCC to West Indies 1910/11 and 1912/13.
Career batting
70–124–8–2302–154–19.84–2–*ct* 23
Bowling 12–0
His first-class debut was for West of England in 1910 and he appeared regularly for Glamorgan prior to the First World War, making his debut for the County (pre first-class) in 1901. He captained the County in 1922 and 1923. He was Glamorgan Secretary 1909–32.

Whittle, Albert Edward Mark
Professional. *b:* 16.9.1877, Bristol. *d:* 18.3.1917, Charminster, Dorset. Middle order right-hand batsman, right-arm medium pace bowler. *Teams* Warwickshire (1900–06, 60 matches); Somerset (1907–11, 29 matches).

Whittle, Charles James Richardson

Career batting
89–134–18–2552–104–22.00–1–*ct* 38
Bowling 2421–64–37.82–2–0–5/28

Whittle, Charles James Richardson
Amateur. *b:* 26.9.1921, Oxton, Cheshire. Middle order right-hand batsman, leg break bowler. *Sch* Sedbergh. *Team* Oxford U (1947).
Career batting
2–4–0–23–10–5.75–0–*ct* 1
His County cricket was for Oxfordshire (1947).

Whitty, John Henry Hamlyn
Amateur. *b:* 4.2.1910, Sydney, New South Wales, Australia. *d:* 23.10.1944, Vicchio, Florence, Italy. He died on active service. Attacking lower order right-hand batsman, right-arm bowler. *Sch* Clifton. *Team* Army (1936).
Career batting
1–2–0–23–22–11.50–0–*ct* 0
Bowling 46–4–11.50–0–0–2/19

Whitty, William James
Amateur. *b:* 15.8.1886, Elizabeth Street, Sydney, New South Wales, Australia. *d:* 30.1.1974, Tantanoola, South Australia. Lower order right-hand batsman, left-arm fast medium bowler. *Teams* New South Wales (1907–08, 1 match); South Australia (1908/9 to 1925/6, 43 matches). *Tours* Australia to England 1909, 1912, to New Zealand 1909/10, to North America 1912, to South Africa 1914/15 (tour cancelled). *Tests* Australia (1909–12, 14 matches).
Career batting
119–171–44–1465–81–11.53–0–*ct* 35
Bowling 11491–491–23.40–26–4–8/27
Test batting
14–19–7–161–39*–13.41–0–*ct* 4
Bowling 1373–65–21.12–3–0–6/17
On his 1909 tour to England he had moderate success, but in 1912 was the leading Australian bowler with 109 wickets, av 18.08, in first-class games and 25 wickets, av 19.80, in the Tests.

Whitwell, Joseph Fry
Amateur. *b:* 22.2.1869, Saltburn-by-the-Sea, Yorkshire. *d:* 6.11.1932, Langbaurgh Hall, Great Ayton, Yorkshire. Brother of W. F. (Yorkshire). Middle order right-hand batsman, right-arm medium pace bowler. *Sch* Uppingham. *Team* Yorkshire (1890, 1 match).
Career batting
1–2–0–8–4–4.00–0–*ct* 0
Bowling 11–1–11.00–0–0–1/11
He also played for Durham (pre first-class, 1889–1902), being captain from 1899 to 1902.

Whitwell, William Fry
Amateur. *b:* 12.12.1867, Stockton-on-Tees, Durham. *d:* 12.4.1942, Leazes Park, Newcastle upon Tyne, Northumberland. Brother of J. F. (Yorkshire). Lower order right-hand batsman, right-arm fast bowler. *Sch* Uppingham. *Team* Yorkshire (1890, 10 matches). *Tour* Hawke to North America 1894.
Career batting
13–19–3–93–26–5.81–0–*ct* 8
Bowling 682–38–17.94–2–0–5/25
He also played for Durham (pre first-class, 1887–1902), being captain from 1893 to 1896. His final first-class match was for Gentlemen in 1900.

Whyatt, Christopher
Cricketer. *b:* 12.6.1954, Old Whittington, Chesterfield, Derbyshire. Lower order right-hand batsman, wicket-keeper. *Team* Derbyshire (1976, 1 match).
Career batting
1–1–0–6–6–6.00–0–*ct* 2

Whysall, William Wilfrid
Professional. *b:* 31.10.1887, Woodborough, Nottinghamshire. *d:* 11.11.1930, Nottingham. He died of blood poisoning after a fall on a dance floor. Sound opening right-hand batsman, right-arm medium pace bowler, wicket-keeper. *Team* Nottinghamshire (1910–30, 346 matches). *Tours* MCC to Australia 1924/5; Cahn to Jamaica 1928/9. *Tests* England (1924/5 to 1930, 4 matches).
Career batting
371–601–44–21592–248–38.76–51–*ct* 316–*st* 16
Bowling 200–6–33.33–0–0–3/49
Test batting
4–7–0–209–76–29.85–0–*ct* 7
Bowling 9–0
He hit 1,000 runs in a season ten times, going on to 2,000 five times (best 2,716, av 51.24, in 1929). He hit three double centuries, all for Nottinghamshire, the highest being 248 v Northamptonshire at Trent Bridge in 1930.

Wickham, Preb Archdale Palmer
Amateur. *b:* 9.11.1855, South Holmwood, Surrey. *d:* 13.10.1935, East Brent, Highbridge, Somerset. Uncle of B. N. B. Smith (Middlesex). Lower order right-hand batsman, wicket-keeper. *Sch* Marlborough. *Teams* Oxford U (1876–78, blue 1878); Somerset (1891–1907, 82 matches).
Career batting
93–152–66–760–28–8.83–0–*ct* 91–*st* 59
Bowling 3–0
He also played for Norfolk (1882–90). He was Somerset President in 1927.

Wickramasinghe, Gallage Pramodya
Cricketer. *b:* 14.8.1971, Matara, Ceylon. Lower order right-hand batsman, right-arm fast medium bowler. *Teams* Burgher RC (1988/9); Sinhalese SC (1991/2). *Tours* Sri Lanka to England 1990, to India 1990/1 (not first-class), to Pakistan 1991/2, to Australia and New Zealand (World Cup) 1991/2. *Tests* Sri Lanka (1991/2, 3 matches).

Career batting
26–23–5–180–36–10.00–0–*ct* 7
Bowling 2047–83–24.66–4–1–10/41
Test batting
3–3–1–1–1*–0.50–0–*ct* 1
Bowling 273–8–34.12–1–0–5/73

His best bowling was 10/41 for Sinhalese SC v Kalutara at Colombo in 1991/2.

Wicks, Frank Cowlin
Amateur. *b:* 30.1.1892, Bristol. *d:* 26.4.1965, Ham Green, Somerset. Lower order batsman, wicket-keeper. *Team* Gloucestershire (1912, 1 match).
Career batting
1–2–0–2–2–1.00–0–*ct* 2

Wickstead, Archibald
Professional. *b:* 6.11.1884, Meltham Mills, Yorkshire. *d:* 1.2.1966, Strawberry Hill, Mansfield, Nottinghamshire. Steady middle order left-hand batsman. *Team* Derbyshire (1911–12, 14 matches).
Career batting
14–26–3–385–68–16.73–0–*ct* 3
Bowling 2–0

Widdowson, Albert
Professional. *b:* 31.3.1864, Bingham, Nottinghamshire. *d:* 28.4.1938, Duffield, Derbyshire. Lower order batsman. *Team* Derbyshire (1894, 1 match).
Career batting
1–1–0–1–1–1.00–0–*ct* 0

He was the groundsman on the County Ground at Derby and was pressed into service in emergency in one match. He also played for Staffordshire (1897).

Widdowson, Sam Weller
Amateur. *b:* 16.4.1851, Hucknall Torkard, Nottinghamshire. *d:* 9.5.1927, Beeston, Nottinghamshire. Middle order right-hand batsman, right-hand fast round-arm bowler. *Team* Nottinghamshire (1878, 1 match).
Career batting
1–2–0–15–11–7.50–0–*ct* 0

An excellent soccer player, he appeared as centre-forward for Nottingham Forest and England; he was also well-known on the athletic field as a hurdler and sprinter.

Wigan, Denis Grey
Amateur. *b:* 21.6.1893, Walton-on-Thames, Surrey. *d:* 31.12.1958, Loudham Hall, Pettistree, Suffolk. Brother-in-law of G. R. R. Colman (Oxford U) and C. F. Lyttelton (Worcestershire). Stylish middle order right-hand batsman, slow right-arm bowler. *Sch* Eton. *Team* Oxford U (1913–14).
Career batting
6–10–2–119–73*–14.87–0–*ct* 4
Bowling 45–4–11.25–0–0–3/14

Wigginton, Searson Harry
Professional. *b:* 26.3.1909, Leicester. *d:* 15.9.1977, Bulawayo, Rhodesia. Opening or middle order right-hand batsman, right-arm medium pace bowler. *Sch* Wyggeston. *Team* Leicestershire (1930–34, 49 matches).
Career batting
49–85–4–1426–120*–17.60–1–*ct* 20
Bowling 90–3–30.00–0–0–2/14

He emigrated to Rhodesia in 1947, having become coach to the Rhodesian Cricket Association.

Wigglesworth, Cecil George
Amateur. *b:* 17.10.1893, Tadcaster, Yorkshire. *d:* 8.8.1961, Lymington, Hampshire. Middle order right-hand batsman. *Team* RAF (1927).
Career batting
1–1–0–19–19–19.00–0–*ct* 0
Bowling 9–0

Wiggs, Rev Robert James
Cricketer. *b:* 6.9.1950, Woodford Green, Essex. Lower order right-hand batsman, slow left-arm bowler. *Sch* Chigwell. *Team* Cambridge U (1970).
Career batting
1–2–1–6–6–6.00–0–*ct* 0
Bowling 44–1–44.00–0–0–1/44

Wight, Claude Vibart
Amateur. *b:* 28.7.1902, Georgetown, British Guiana. *d:* 4.10.1969, Kingston, Georgetown, Guyana. Brother of O. S. (British Guiana). Middle order right-hand batsman. *Team* British Guiana (1925/6 to 1938/9). *Tour* West Indies to England 1928. *Tests* West Indies (1928 to 1929/30, 2 matches).
Career batting
40–61–11–1547–130–30.94–3–*ct* 20
Bowling 209–3–69.66–0–0–1/18
Test batting
2–4–1–67–23–22.33–0–*ct* 0
Bowling 6–0

He had only a moderately successful visit to England in 1928 and played in one Test.

Wight, Peter Bernard
Professional. *b:* 25.6.1930, Georgetown, British Guiana. Brother of G. L. (West Indies), H. A. (British Guiana) and Norman (British Guiana), uncle of R. M. (Cambridge U). Middle order right-hand batsman, off break bowler. *Teams* British Guiana (1950/1); Somerset (1953–65, 321 matches); Canterbury (1963/4). *Tour* Brown to East Africa 1961/2 (not first-class).
Career batting
333–590–53–17773–222*–33.09–28–*ct* 203
Bowling 2262–68–33.26–1–0–6/29

He hit 1,000 runs in a season ten times going on to 2,000 twice (best 2,375 runs, av 41.66, in 1960). Both his double centuries were for Somerset, the highest being 222* v Kent at Taunton in 1959. He was appointed to the first-class umpires' list in 1966.

Wight, Robert Marcus
Cricketer. *b:* 12.9.1969, Kensington, London. Nephew of P. B. (Somerset). Middle order right-hand batsman, off break bowler. *Sch* KCS Wimbledon. *Team* Cambridge U (1992, blue).
Career batting
10–17–3–388–62*–27.71–0–*ct* 3
Bowling 748–19–39.36–0–0–3/65

Wignall, Eric William Edward
Professional. *b:* 25.12.1932, Harrow, Middlesex. *d:* 2.1.1991, Oxhey, Hertfordshire. Son of W. H. (Middlesex). Lower order right-hand batsman, leg break bowler. *Team* Gloucestershire (1952–53, 3 matches).
Career batting
3–4–1–24–14–8.00–0–*ct* 2
Bowling 63–2–31.50–0–0–2/50

Wignall, William Harold
Professional. *b:* 24.12.1908, Harrow, Middlesex. *d:* 1.6.1982, Northwick Park, Middlesex. Father of E. W. E. (Gloucestershire). Lower order right-hand batsman, right-arm bowler. *Team* Middlesex (1934–36, 4 matches).
Career batting
6–11–4–152–72–21.71–0–*ct* 5
Bowling 153–3–51.00–0–0–1/9
His first-class debut was for MCC in 1932 and his final first-class match for MCC in 1938. He also played for Dorset (1930) and Berkshire (1946).

Wigram, Sir Clive
(later 1st Baron Wigram)
Amateur. *b:* 5.7.1873, Madras, India. *d:* 3.9.1960, Westminster, London. Brother of Kenneth (Europeans), brother-in-law of H. W. Kaye (Middlesex). Lower order right-hand batsman, right-hand medium pace bowler. *Sch* Winchester. *Teams* MCC (1897); Europeans (1906/7).
Career batting
3–5–1–47–22*–11.75–0–*ct* 3
Bowling 165–4–41.25–0–0–1/3
He was stationed in India for some years, being ADC to the Viceroy. In 1910 he was appointed Assistant Private Secretary to the King.

Wigram, Rev Ernest Money
Amateur. *b:* 20.11.1862, Kensington, London. *d:* 10.6.1906, Eastry, Kent. Lower order batsman, useful bowler. *Sch* Winchester. *Team* Orleans Club (1883).
Career batting
1–2–1–9–6–9.00–0–*ct* 1
Bowling 40–0
He played no first-class cricket at Oxford U, but did win a blue for athletics.

Wijegunawardene, Kapila Indaka Weerakkody
Cricketer. *b:* 23.11.1964, Colombo, Ceylon. Lower order right-hand batsman, right-arm fast medium bowler. *Team* Colombo CC (1988/9 to 1991/2). *Tours* Sri Lanka B to Zimbabwe 1987/8; Sri Lanka to Bangladesh (not first-class) 1988/9, to Sharjah (not first-class) 1988/9, to Australia 1989/90, to England 1990, 1991, to India 1990/1 (not first-class), to New Zealand 1990/1, to Pakistan 1991/2, to Australia and New Zealand (World Cup) 1991/2. *Tests* Sri Lanka (1991 to 1991/2, 2 matches).
Career batting
44–40–15–231–26–9.24–0–*ct* 15
Bowling 3154–126–25.03–5–0–7/28
Test batting
2–4–1–14–6*–4.66–0–*ct* 0
Bowling 147–7–21.00–0–0–4/51
Although he played in the 1991 Test, both his tours to England received modest results, his very long run being criticised. His first-class debut was for Sri Lanka President's XI in 1986/7.

Wijesuriya, Roger Gerard Christopher Ediriweera
Cricketer. *b:* 18.2.1960, Moratuwa, Ceylon. Lower order right-hand batsman, slow left-arm bowler. *Team* Moratuwa (1988/9 to 1989/90). *Tours* Sri Lanka to England 1979, 1981, to Pakistan 1981/2, 1985/6, to Australia 1982/3; Sri Lanka B to Zimbabwe 1987/8. *Tests* Sri Lanka (1981/2 to 1985/6, 4 matches).
Career batting
37–42–15–421–77*–15.59–0–*ct* 25
Bowling 2608–97–26.88–3–1–6/51
Test batting
4–7–2–22–8–4.40–0–*ct* 1
Bowling 294–1–294.00–0–0–1/68
His first-class debut was for Sri Lanka in 1978/9.

Wijetunge, Piyal Kashyapa
Cricketer. *b:* 6.8.1971, Badulla, Ceylon. Lower order right-hand batsman, slow left-arm bowler. *Team* Sinhalese CC (1990/1 to 1991/2). *Tour* Sri Lanka to England 1990.
Career batting
29–25–14–85–17*–7.72–0–*ct* 10
Bowling 2084–71–29.35–1–0–7/51
He looked a promising prospect on the 1990 tour to England. His first-class debut was for Sri Lanka Youth XI in 1988/9.

Wilcock, Howard Gordon
Cricketer. *b:* 26.2.1950, New Malden, Surrey. Lower order right-hand batsman, wicket-keeper. *Team* Worcestershire (1971–78, 99 matches).
Career batting
99–137–31–1697–74–16.00–0–*ct* 177–*st* 17
Bowling 3–0

Wilcox, Alfred George Sidney
Amateur in 1939, then professional. *b:* 10.7.1920, Swindon Village, Cheltenham, Gloucestershire. *d:* 30.7.1986, Cheltenham, Gloucestershire. Enterprising middle order left-hand batsman. *Team* Gloucestershire (1939–49, 39 matches).

Career batting
39–58–5–835–73–15.75–0–*ct* 21

Wilcox, Denys Robert
Amateur. *b:* 4.6.1910, Westcliff-on-Sea, Essex. *d:* 6.2.1953, Westcliff-on-Sea, Essex. Father of J. W. T. (Essex). Stylish middle order right-hand batsman, off break bowler. *Sch* Dulwich. *Teams* Essex (1928–47, 118 matches); Cambridge U (1931–33, blue all three years). *Tours* Martineau to Egypt 1934, 1935, 1936, 1937, 1938 (not first-class).
Career batting
179–296–11–8399–157–29.47–15–*ct* 130
Bowling 136–3–45.33–0–0–1/0

He hit 1,000 runs in a season four times (best 1,390, av 44.83, in 1937). Owing to his scholastic duties he was unable to play regularly in County cricket, but was joint captain of Essex from 1933 to 1939. His final first-class match was for Free Foresters in 1951. He captained Cambridge in 1933.

Wilcox, John Warren Theodore
Amateur. *b:* 16.8.1940, Newton Abbot, Devon. Son of D. R. (Essex). Middle order right-hand batsman, off break bowler, good outfield. *Sch* Malvern. *Teams* Cambridge U (1961–62); Essex (1964–67, 19 matches).
Career batting
31–54–7–903–87–19.21–0–*ct* 15

Wilcox, Sidney Charles
Professional. *b:* 28.2.1893, Maesteg, Glamorgan. *d:* 21.10.1973, Maesteg, Glamorgan. Lower order right-hand batsman, wicket-keeper. *Team* Wales (1930).
Career batting
1–2–1–7–6–7.00–0–*ct* 3–*st* 1

His County cricket was for Monmouthshire (1921–34).

Wild, Duncan James
Cricketer. *b:* 28.11.1962, Queen's Park, Northampton. Son of John (Northamptonshire). Lower order left-hand batsman, right-arm medium pace bowler. *Team* Northamptonshire (1980–90, 119 matches).
Career batting
119–167–21–3688–144–25.26–5–*ct* 40
Bowling 2910–66–44.09–0–0–4/4

Wild, F. (*see under* Wyld, F.)

Wild, Harold
Professional. *b:* 3.2.1891, Hadfield, Derbyshire. *d:* 8.8.1977, Glossop, Derbyshire. Middle order right-hand batsman, right-arm medium pace bowler. *Team* Derbyshire (1913–20, 32 matches).
Career batting
32–59–7–628–68–12.07–0–*ct* 29
Bowling 129–2–64.50–0–0–1/3

Wild, John
Professional. *b:* 24.2.1935, Parklands, Northampton. Father of D. J. (Northamptonshire). Middle order right-hand batsman, off break bowler. *Team* Northamptonshire (1953–61, 39 matches).
Career batting
41–51–4–664–95–14.12–0–*ct* 26
Bowling 2588–57–45.40–0–0–4/44

Wild, John Vernon
Amateur. *b:* 26.4.1915, Wallasey, Cheshire. Middle order right-hand batsman, right-arm slow bowler. *Sch* Taunton. *Team* Cambridge U (1938, blue).
Career batting
11–17–0–193–34–11.35–0–*ct* 5
Bowling 1047–29–36.10–2–0–6/125

Wild, T.
Professional. Opening batsman. *Team* Hampshire (1880, 2 matches).
Career batting
2–3–0–40–25–13.33–0–*ct* 0

Wild, William
Professional. *b:* 21.2.1846, Thorncombe, Dorset. Lower order right-hand batsman, right-hand fast round-arm bowler. *Team* Hampshire (1877, 1 match).
Career batting
1–2–1–10–8–10.00–0–*ct* 0
Bowling 11–0

Wilde, David
Cricketer. *b:* 3.7.1950, Glossop, Derbyshire. Tail end left-hand batsman, left-arm fast medium bowler. *Team* Derbyshire (1971–72, 13 matches).
Career batting
13–15–5–31–12–3.10–0–*ct* 1
Bowling 860–23–37.39–0–0–3/27

Wilde, Thomas Montague Morrison
(succeeded as 3rd Baron Truro in 1891)
Amateur. *b:* 11.3.1856, Brunswick, Manchester, Lancashire. *d:* 8.3.1899, Mentone, France. Middle order right-hand batsman, right-arm medium pace bowler. *Sch* Harrow. *Team* MCC (1881–83).
Career batting
4–7–2–117–37–23.40–0–*ct* 2
Bowling 23–0

Wilde, Walter Stanley
Professional. *b:* 27.2.1908, Long Ashton, Somerset. *d:* 21.8.1968, Clevedon, Somerset. Tail end batsman, wicket-keeper. *Team* Somerset (1929, 7 matches).
Career batting
7–13–5–45–21–5.62–0–*ct* 9–*st* 1

Wilder, George
Amateur. *b:* 9.6.1876, Stansted Park, Emsworth, Hampshire. *d:* 10.6.1948, Las Vegas, USA. Middle order batsman, useful bowler. *Sch* Eton. *Teams* Sus-

sex (1905–06, 6 matches); Hampshire (1909, 1 match).
Career batting
8–16–1–203–43–13.53–0–*ct* 2
Bowling 51–4–12.75–0–0–3/14

Wileman, Jonathan Ritchie
Cricketer. *b:* 19.8.1970, Sheffield, Yorkshire. Opening right-hand batsman, right-arm medium pace bowler. *Sch* Malvern. *Team* Nottinghamshire (1992, 1 match).
Career batting
1–1–0–109–109–109.00–1–0–*ct* 2
He scored 109 on his first-class debut, for Nottinghamshire v Cambridge U at Trent Bridge in 1992.

Wilenkin, Boris Charles Gregory
Amateur. *b:* 20.6.1933, Belgravia, Westminster, London. Middle order right-hand batsman, right-arm bowler. *Sch* Harrow and Loretto. *Teams* Free Foresters (1955–59); Cambridge U (1956, blue).
Career batting
16–28–1–661–105–24.48–1–*ct* 4
Bowling 4–0
His County cricket was for Oxfordshire (1951–56).

Wiles, Charles Archibald
Amateur. *b:* 11.8.1892, Bridgetown, Barbados. *d:* 4.11.1957, Diego Martin, Trinidad. Stylish middle order right-hand batsman. *Team* Trinidad (1919/20 to 1935/6). *Test* West Indies (1933, 1 match).
Career batting
38–69–5–1766–192–27.59–2–*ct* 7
Test batting
1–2–0–2–2–1.00–0–*ct* 0
Although playing in one Test, he achieved little on the 1933 tour. He played for Barbados Born in 1927/8.

Wiley, John Walter Edington
Amateur. *b:* 7.2.1927, St James, Cape Town, South Africa. *d:* 29.3.1987, Noordhoek, Cape Town, South Africa. He died by his own hand. Brother of W. G. A. (Oxford U). Middle order right-hand batsman. *Teams* Western Province (1947/8); Oxford U (1949–51).
Career batting
12–23–1–410–70–18.63–0–*ct* 8
His final first-class match in South Africa was for South African Universities in 1948/9. He was an MP in South Africa from 1966, and later a Cabinet Minister.

Wiley, William Gordon Antony
Amateur. *b:* 14.11.1931, St James, Cape Town, South Africa. Brother of J. W. E. (Oxford U). Opening right-hand batsman, leg break and googly bowler. *Teams* Oxford U (1952, blue); Western Province (1952/3 to 1953/4).
Career batting
16–29–0–666–100–22.96–1–*ct* 14
Bowling 5–0
His County cricket was for Oxfordshire (1952).

Wilkes, Alexander John
Amateur. *b:* 4.11.1900, Kidderminster, Worcestershire. *d:* 12.7.1937, Kidderminster, Worcestershire. Middle order right-hand batsman. *Team* Worcestershire (1925–27, 11 matches).
Career batting
11–22–2–113–25–5.65–0–*ct* 12

Wilkes, William Harry Walters
Amateur. *b:* 1866, Aston, Birmingham. *d:* 18.2.1940, Birmingham. Middle order right-hand batsman. *Team* Worcestershire (1899–1902, 14 matches).
Career batting
14–25–1–419–109–17.45–1–*ct* 5
He first played for Worcestershire (pre first-class) in 1892.

Wilkin, Charles Lucien Arthur
Cricketer. *b:* 9.1.1949, Basseterre, St Kitts. Son of C. (Leeward Islands, pre first-class). Lower order right-hand batsman, slow left-arm bowler. *Teams* Cambridge U (1969–70, blue 1970); Leeward Islands (1973/4 to 1976/7).
Career batting
19–30–10–302–26–15.10–0–*ct* 4
Bowling 1440–30–48.00–0–0–3/74

Wilkins, Alan Haydn
Cricketer. *b:* 22.8.1953, Rhiwbina, Cardiff, Glamorgan. Lower order right-hand batsman, left-arm medium pace bowler. *Teams* Glamorgan (1976–83, 65 matches); Gloucestershire (1980–81, 40 matches); Northern Transvaal (1981/2). *Tour* Overseas XI to India 1980/1.
Career batting
107–124–29–902–70–9.49–0–*ct* 34
Bowling 7511–243–30.90–9–0–8/57
He played rugby for Cardiff and Bristol.

Wilkins, Christopher Peter
Cricketer. *b:* 31.7.1944, King William's Town, South Africa. Brother of A. D. (Border), nephew of A. L. (Border). Middle order right-hand batsman, right-arm medium pace bowler, occasional wicket-keeper. *Teams* Border (1962/3 to 1970/1); Derbyshire (1970–72, 71 matches); Eastern Province (1972/3 to 1977/8); Natal (1978/9 to 1982/3).
Career batting
198–357–21–10966–156–32.63–18–*ct* 211–*st* 6
Bowling 5013–142–35.30–0–0–4/19
He hit over 1,000 runs in each of his three seasons with Derbyshire (best 1,638, av 39.95, in 1970).

Wilkins, Donald Albert
Amateur. *b:* 13.10.1903, Bristol. *d:* 22.1.1972, Saltford, Somerset. Middle order right-hand batsman. *Team* Somerset (1927, 2 matches).

Career batting
2–3–0–6–3–2.00–0–*ct* 1

Wilkinson, Anthony John Anstruther
Amateur. *b:* 28.5.1835, Mount Oswald, Co Durham. *d:* 11.12.1905, Anerley, Kent. Father of C. T. A. (Surrey). Steady opening or middle order right-hand batsman, right-hand slow round-arm bowler, good third man. *Sch* Shrewsbury. *Teams* Middlesex (1864–74, 19 matches); Yorkshire (1865–68, 5 matches).
Career batting
61–103–4–1351–84*–13.64–0–*ct* 43
Bowling 1199–53–22.62–2–0–6/52

His first-class debut was for Gentlemen of the South in 1862. He did not play in any important matches whilst at Cambridge U. In 1874 he took the chair at the meeting during which the Durham County Cricket Club was formed. He also played for Lincolnshire (1873) and Durham (pre first-class, 1874).

Wilkinson, Arthur
Professional. *b:* 28.12.1872, Nottingham. Dashing lower order right-hand batsman, right-arm medium pace bowler. *Team* Nottinghamshire (1894–95, 19 matches).
Career batting
19–35–5–293–62–9.76–0–*ct* 9
Bowling 926–33–28.06–1–0–5/56

Wilkinson, Burton
Amateur. *b:* 25.4.1900, Burton, Nebraska, USA. *d:* 16.10.1985, Peterborough, Northamptonshire. Tail end left-hand batsman, slow left-arm bowler. *Team* Northamptonshire (1932, 1 match).
Career batting
1–1–0–0–0–0.00–0–*ct* 1
Bowling 22–1–22.00–0–0–1/22

Wilkinson, Craig William
Cricketer. *b:* 19.3.1963, Wardle, Lancashire. Lower order right-hand batsman, right-arm medium pace bowler. *Team* Leicestershire (1991, 14 matches).
Career batting
14–13–2–138–41–12.54–0–*ct* 7
Bowling 1009–23–43.86–0–0–4/59

He was brought up and educated in Australia.

Wilkinson, Cyril Theodore Anstruther
Amateur. *b:* 4.10.1884, Elvet Hill, Durham. *d:* 16.12.1970, Honiton, Devon. Son of A. J. A. (Middlesex and Yorkshire). Middle order right-hand batsman, slow left-arm bowler. *Sch* Blundell's. *Team* Surrey (1909–20, 53 matches).
Career batting
54–78–8–1773–135–25.32–3–*ct* 25
Bowling 724–23–31.47–1–0–6/43

He captained Surrey in 1914 and in 1919–20. A great club cricketer, he took all ten wickets for Sidmouth in 1953, when he was 69. A brilliant hockey player, he captained England and appeared for Great Britain in the 1920 Olympics, where won a gold medal. He was Registrar of the Probate and Divorce Registry from 1936 to 1959.

Wilkinson, Donald John
Cricketer. *b:* 14.2.1955, Irvine, Ayrshire, Scotland. Lower order left-hand batsman, leg break bowler. *Sch* Lancaster RGS. *Team* Oxford U (1975–76).
Career batting
4–8–2–11–4–1.83–0–*ct* 3
Bowling 350–7–50.00–0–0–4/89

Wilkinson, Edward Obert Hindley
Amateur. *b:* 16.10.1853, Chesfield, Stevenage, Hertfordshire. *d:* 8.2.1881, Scheins Hoogte, Natal, South Africa. He drowned crossing a flooded stream after the Battle of Ingogo. Nephew of C. A. (Cambridge U 1833). Middle order right-hand batsman, wicket-keeper. *Sch* Eton. *Team* Cambridge U (1873).
Career batting
5–8–1–39–22*–5.57–0–*ct* 2–*st* 2

His final match was for MCC in 1875. His County cricket was for Hertfordshire (1871). He was very successful in military matches for his Regiment.

Wilkinson, Francis William
Amateur. *b:* 4.10.1895, Norton-on-Tees, Co Durham. *d:* 26.10.1987, Ely, Cambridgeshire. Lower order right-hand batsman, leg break bowler. *Team* Minor Counties (1939).
Career batting
1 match, did not bat–*ct* 0
Bowling 24–1–24.00–0–0–1/24

In his only first-class match – v Oxford U – he was forced to retire injured after bowling 8 overs and took no further part in the match, a substitute batting for him. His County cricket was for Cambridgeshire (1923–46). He played no first-class cricket at Cambridge U, but he did win a blue for billiards. He played soccer for Corinthians.

Wilkinson, Frank
Professional. *b:* 23.5.1914, Hull, Yorkshire. *d:* 26.3.1984, Hull, Yorkshire. Lower order right-hand batsman, right-arm medium fast bowler. *Team* Yorkshire (1937–39, 14 matches).
Career batting
14–14–1–73–18*–5.61–0–*ct* 12
Bowling 590–26–22.69–1–1–7/68

Wilkinson, Henry
Amateur. *b:* 11.12.1877, Hillhouse, Huddersfield, Yorkshire. *d:* 15.4.1967, Simonstown, Cape Province, South Africa. Stylish middle order right-hand batsman. *Team* Yorkshire (1903–05, 48 matches).
Career batting
51–80–3–1467–113–19.05–1–*ct* 21
Bowling 121–3–40.33–0–0–2/28

His final first-class match was for C. B. Fry's XI in 1912.

Wilkinson, John
Amateur. *b:* 16.7.1876, Wyke Regis, Dorset. *d:* 15.5.1948, Kensington, London. Tail end right-hand batsman, right-arm fast bowler. *Team* Gloucestershire (1899–1920, 10 matches).
Career batting
10–16–7–64–17*–7.11–0–*ct* 9
Bowling 587–17–34.52–0–0–4/39

Wilkinson, John William
Amateur. *b:* 20.4.1892, Dudley, Worcestershire. *d:* 3.8.1967, Edgbaston, Birmingham. Lower order right-hand batsman, useful bowler. *Team* Worcestershire (1927, 1 match).
Career batting
1–2–2–4–4*–no av–0–*ct* 0
Bowling 45–1–45.00–0–0–1/45
He also played for Devon (1925–36).

Wilkinson, Keith William
Cricketer. *b:* 15.1.1950, Fenton, Stoke-on-Trent, Staffordshire. Middle order left-hand batsman, left-arm medium pace bowler. *Team* Worcestershire (1969–75, 49 matches).
Career batting
49–77–11–1657–141–25.10–2–*ct* 29
Bowling 1651–48–34.39–1–0–5/60

Wilkinson, Kenneth
Amateur. *b:* 11.1.1908, Newbold, Derbyshire. *d:* 15.12.1943, Caldari, near Naples, Italy. Lower order batsman, right-hand fast medium bowler. *Sch* Uppingham. *Team* Cambridge U (1927).
Career batting
1 match, did not bat –*ct* 0
Bowling 99–0

Wilkinson, Leonard Litton
Professional. *b:* 5.11.1916, Northwich, Cheshire. Lower order right-hand batsman, slow leg break bowler, good close field. *Team* Lancashire (1937–47, 63 matches). *Tour* MCC to South Africa 1938/9. *Tests* England (1938/9, 3 matches).
Career batting
77–69–27–321–48–7.64–0–*ct* 53
Bowling 7121–282–25.25–17–3–8/53
Test batting
3–2–1–3–2–3.00–0–*ct* 0
Bowling 271–7–38.71–0–0–2/12
He created a great impression during his first full season of County cricket, taking 151 wickets, av 23.38; selected for the winter tour to South Africa in 1938/9, he topped the averages with 44 wickets, av 18.86. In 1939 however he fell away, and after the Second World War very little of him was seen in first-class cricket.

Wilkinson, Philip Alan
Cricketer. *b:* 23.8.1951, Hucknall, Nottinghamshire. Lower order right-hand batsman, right-arm medium pace bowler. *Team* Nottinghamshire (1971–77, 92 matches).
Career batting
92–117–38–949–77–12.01–0–*ct* 28
Bowling 6335–175–36.20–2–0–6/81

Wilkinson, Robert William
Professional. *b:* 23.12.1939, Rotherhithe, London. Great-nephew of R. Abel (Surrey). Middle order right-hand batsman, right-arm medium pace bowler. *Team* Kent (1959–63, 23 matches).
Career batting
23–39–7–635–63–19.84–0–*ct* 11
Bowling 626–10–62.60–0–0–2/31

Wilkinson, Stephen George
Cricketer. *b:* 12.1.1949, Hounslow, Middlesex. Opening right-hand batsman, slow left-arm bowler. *Team* Somerset (1972–74, 18 matches).
Career batting
18–27–5–452–69–20.54–0–*ct* 11
Bowling 9–0

Wilkinson, William
Professional. *b:* 5.7.1859, Kimberley, Nottinghamshire. *d:* 6.10.1940, Standard Hill, Nottingham. Lower order batsman, right-arm fast medium bowler. *Team* Nottinghamshire (1892–93, 5 matches).
Career batting
5–7–2–34–16*–6.80–0–*ct* 4
Bowling 133–5–26.60–0–0–3/41
He also played for Glamorgan (pre first-class, 1889).

Wilkinson, William Alexander Camac
Amateur. *b:* 6.12.1892, Sydney, New South Wales, Australia. *d:* 19.9.1983, Storrington, Sussex. Son of W. O'B. C. (Middlesex). Opening or middle order right-hand batsman, slow right-arm bowler. *Sch* Eton. *Team* Oxford U (1913–14, blue 1913). *Tour* MCC to Australia and New Zealand 1922/3.
Career batting
89–162–10–4785–129–31.48–8–*ct* 49
Bowling 385–12–32.08–0–0–4/32
His first-class debut was for H. K. Foster's XI in 1912 and his final match for MCC in 1939. He was a noted batsman in military matches between the wars. He also won a blue for athletics.

Wilkinson, William Herbert
Professional. *b:* 12.3.1881, Thorpe Hesley, Yorkshire. *d:* 4.6.1961, Winson Green, Birmingham. Sound middle order left-hand batsman, slow left-arm bowler, moderate field. *Team* Yorkshire (1903–10, 126 matches).
Career batting
127–194–14–3912–103–21.73–1–*ct* 93

Bowling 971–31–31.32–0–0–4/23

He hit 1,382 runs, av 29.40, in 1908. He was also a noted soccer player for Sheffield United.

Wilkinson, Dr William O'Brien Camac
Amateur. *b:* 15.9.1857, Glebe Point, Sydney, New South Wales, Australia. *d:* 2.2.1946, Virginia Water, Surrey. Father of W. A. C. (Oxford U). Middle order right-hand batsman, right-arm medium pace bowler. *Team* Middlesex (1881–82, 5 matches).
Career batting
8–14–2–189–52–15.75–0–*ct* 2
Bowling 156–8–19.50–0–0–4/49

His final first-class match was for A. J. Webbe's XI in 1899.

Willard, Michael James Lewis
Amateur. *b:* 24.3.1938, Hawkhurst, Kent. Middle order left-hand batsman, right-arm medium pace bowler. *Team* Cambridge U (1959–61, blue all three years).
Career batting
41–75–1–1866–101*–25.21–1–*ct* 33
Bowling 2326–72–32.30–3–1–7/62

Willatt, Guy Longfield
Amateur. *b:* 7.5.1918, The Park, Nottingham. Father of J. M. G. (Cambridge U). Sound opening left-hand batsman, right-arm slow bowler. *Sch* Repton. *Teams* Cambridge U (1938–47, blue 1946, 1947); Nottinghamshire (1939–48, 22 matches); Scotland (1948–50); Derbyshire (1950–56, 125 matches).
Career batting
185–303–17–8325–146–29.10–13–*ct* 51
Bowling 135–3–45.00–0–0–2/18

He hit 1,000 runs in a season four times (best 1,624, av 35.30, in 1952). From 1951 to 1954 he captained Derbyshire, but after 1954 he was unable to play regular first-class cricket owing to his profession. His final first-class match was for MCC in 1961. He also played for Cumberland. He captained Cambridge in 1947. He was Chairman of Derbyshire Cricket Committee 1986–90. A good soccer player, he obtained his blue at Cambridge.

Willatt, Jonathan Myles Gardiner
Cricketer. *b:* 8.7.1961, Kendal, Westmorland. Son of G. L. (Nottinghamshire and Derbyshire). Middle order left-hand batsman. *Sch* Repton. *Team* Cambridge U (1989, blue).
Career batting
9–14–1–172–45–13.23–0–*ct* 1

Willes, Canon Edmund Henry Lacon
Amateur. *b:* 7.7.1832, Dibden, Hythe, Southampton, Hampshire. *d:* 9.9.1896, Monk Sherborne, Dorset. Cousin of G. E. (Cambridge U). Middle order right-hand batsman, right-hand fast round-arm bowler, deep field. *Sch* Winchester. *Teams* Hampshire (1850–65, 2 matches); Oxford U (1852–54, blue all three years); Kent (1852–53, 2 matches).
Career batting
22–34–4–416–69–13.86–0–*ct* 12
Bowling 22–3 + 17–7.33–0–0–4/?

He also played for Oxfordshire (1852–56), Northamptonshire (pre first-class, 1866–67) and Warwickshire (pre first-class, 1866). He captained Oxford U in 1852 and 1853.

Willes, Rev George Edward
Amateur. *b:* 16.8.1844, Hamstall Ridware, Rugeley, Staffordshire. *d:* 8.9.1901, Burnham, Buckinghamshire. Cousin of E. H. L. (Hampshire and Kent). Middle order right-hand batsman, long stop. *Sch* Rugby. *Team* Cambridge U (1865–66).
Career batting
5–9–1–114–51–14.25–0–*ct* 0

His County cricket was for Warwickshire (pre first-class, 1864–76) and Buckinghamshire (1868–69).

Willes, John
Amateur. *b:* 1778, Headcorn, Kent. *d:* 5.8.1852. Staunton, near Gloucester. Brother of William (Kent 1807). Middle order batsman, fast round-arm bowler. *Team* Kent (1806–22).
Career batting
5–7–0–9–5–1.28–0–*ct* 2
Bowling 6 wickets (no analyses)–0–0–3/?

He tried to introduce round-arm bowling during the early years of the 19th century, but in 1822 when playing for Kent v MCC he was no-balled for throwing and was so annoyed by the umpire's ruling that he left the match, vowing that he would never play again.

Willett, Elquemedo Tonito
Cricketer. *b:* 1.5.1953, Charlestown, Nevis. Lower order left-hand batsman, slow left-arm bowler. *Team* Leeward Islands (1970/1 to 1988/9). *Tours* West Indies to England 1973, to India, Sri Lanka and Pakistan 1974/5. *Tests* West Indies (1972/3 to 1974/5, 5 matches).
Career batting
98–131–46–1100–56–12.94–0–*ct* 66
Bowling 8132–286–28.43–10–3–8/73
Test batting
5–8–3–74–26–14.80–0–*ct* 0
Bowling 482–11–43.81–0–0–3/33

He took 30 wickets, av 23.13, on his tour to England, but did not play in any Tests.

Willett, Dr Frederic Stovin Dealtry
Amateur. *b:* 10.11.1853, Marylebone, London. *d:* 23.4.1884, Ventnor, Isle of Wight. Middle order right-hand batsman, right-hand fast round-arm bowler, cover point field. *Sch* Rugby. *Team* MCC (1882).
Career batting
1–2–0–9–5–4.50–0–*ct* 0

He did not play in any first-class matches whilst at Cambridge.

Willett, Michael David
Professional. *b:* 21.4.1933, West Norwood, London. Middle order right-hand batsman, right-arm medium pace bowler. *Team* Surrey (1955–67, 172 matches).
Career batting
172–273–45–6535–126–28.66–8–*ct* 95
Bowling 1105–23–48.04–0–0–3/36

He hit 1,000 runs in a season three times (best 1,789, av 45.87, in 1964). A good soccer player, he was inside-right for Corinthian Casuals.

Willetts, Frank Terence
Cricketer. *b:* 20.11.1939, Birmingham. Middle order left-hand batsman. *Team* Somerset (1964–67, 16 matches).
Career batting
16–30–0–333–38–11.10–0–*ct* 4

He also played for Shropshire (1968) and Cornwall (1977–90).

Willey, Peter
Cricketer. *b:* 6.12.1949, Sedgefield, Co Durham. Middle order right-hand batsman, off break bowler. *Teams* Northamptonshire (1966–83, 319 matches); Eastern Province (1982/3 to 1984/5); Leicestershire (1984–91, 161 matches). *Tours* Robins to South Africa 1972/3, to Sri Lanka 1977/8; England to Australia 1979/80, to West Indies 1980/1, 1985/6; SAB England XI to South Africa 1981/2. *Tests* England (1976–86, 26 matches).
Career batting
559–918–121–24361–227–30.56–44–*ct* 235
Bowling 23400–756–30.95–26–3–7/37
Test batting
26–50–6–1184–102*–26.90–2–*ct* 3
Bowling 456–7–65.14–0–0–2/73

He hit 1,000 runs in a season ten times (best 1,783, av 50.94, in 1982). He captained Leicestershire in 1987. He was banned from Test cricket for three years following his 1981/2 tour to South Africa. His highest score was 227 for Northamptonshire v Somerset at Northampton in 1976. He also played for Northumberland (1992).

Williams, Alfred Edward Augustus
Professional. *b:* 20.11.1844, Ashford, Kent. *d:* 7.1.1914, Lyminge, Kent. Lower order left-hand batsman, right-hand fast round-arm bowler. *Team* Kent (1865, 3 matches).
Career batting
3–5–2–28–13*–9.33–0–*ct* 1
Bowling 16–3–5.33–0–0–3/9

Williams, Ambrose Causer
Professional. *b:* 1.3.1887, Middlewood, Darfield, Yorkshire. *d:* 1.6.1966, Morecambe, Lancashire. Tail end right-hand batsman, right-arm fast bowler. *Team* Yorkshire (1911–19, 12 matches).
Career batting
12–14–10–95–48*–23.75–0–*ct* 6
Bowling 678–30–22.60–2–1–9/29

He took 9 wickets for 29 in the first innings for Yorkshire v Hampshire at Dewsbury in 1919, but after two further matches was dropped from the County side!

Williams, Cecil Beaumont
Amateur. *b:* 8.3.1926, Cats Castle, St Michael, Barbados. Lower order right-hand batsman, leg break and googly bowler. *Team* Barbados (1947/8 to 1956/7). *Tour* West Indies to England 1950.
Career batting
37–39–5–987–133–29.02–2–*ct* 27
Bowling 2183–75–29.10–4–0–7/55

He took 31 wickets, av 27.61, on the 1950 tour. After the visit he remained in England to go to Durham University. He was appointed Barbados High Commissioner to Britain in 1976.

Williams, Lord Charles Cuthbert Powell
Amateur. *b:* 9.2.1933, Oxford. Middle order right-hand batsman. *Sch* Westminster. *Teams* Oxford U (1952–55, blue 1953–55); Essex (1954–59, 40 matches).
Career batting
87–153–8–4090–139*–28.20–6–*ct* 60
Bowling 61–1–61.00–0–0–1/33

He hit 1,000 runs in a season twice (best 1,219, av 31.25, in 1955). He also played for Oxfordshire (1950–52). He captained Oxford U in 1955. He was created a life peer in 1985.

Williams, Charles Derek
Amateur. *b:* 24.11.1924, Cardiff, Glamorgan. Middle order right-hand batsman, right-arm medium pace bowler. *Team* Oxford U (1946).
Career batting
1–2–0–3–3–1.50–0–*ct* 0
Bowling 9–0

His County cricket was for Berkshire (1949). He played rugby for Wales.

Williams, Christopher Mark Bebb
Cricketer. *b:* 11.1.1955, Stamford Hill, Middlesex. Middle order right-hand batsman, leg break and googly bowler. *Sch* Highgate. *Team* Cambridge U (1976).
Career batting
1–2–0–31–29–15.50–0–*ct* 0

His County cricket was for Shropshire (1981–86). His mother is Gwen Watford, the actress.

Williams, David
Cricketer. *b:* 25.5.1948, Barnsley, Yorkshire. Lower order right-hand batsman, slow left-arm bowler. *Team* Oxford U (1968–73).

Career batting
29–50–10–497–52–12.42–0–*ct* 15
Bowling 847–24–35.29–1–0–5/19
His County cricket was for Oxfordshire (1972–73).

Williams, David
Cricketer. *b:* 4.11.1963, San Fernando, Trinidad. Lower order right-hand batsman, wicket-keeper. *Team* Trinidad (1982/3 to 1991/2). *Tours* Young West Indies to Zimbabwe 1986/7, 1989/90; West Indies to India 1987/8, to England 1988, 1991, to Australia 1988/9, 1991/2, to Pakistan 1990/1, 1991/2 (not first-class), to Australia and New Zealand (World Cup) 1991/2. *Tests* West Indies (1991/2, 1 match).
Career batting
73–99–11–1438–57–16.34–0–*ct* 149–*st* 24
Test batting
1–2–0–6–5–3.00–0–*ct* 4–*st* 1
He came to England in 1988 and 1991 as the reserve wicket-keeper and did not play in any Tests.

Williams, David Lawrence
Cricketer. *b:* 20.11.1946, Tonna, Neath, Glamorgan. Tail end left-hand batsman, right-arm fast medium bowler. *Team* Glamorgan (1969–76, 150 matches). *Tour* Glamorgan to West Indies 1969/70.
Career batting
151–146–73–403–37*–5.52–0–*ct* 38
Bowling 9883–364–27.15–13–1–7/60
He was also a good rugby footballer.

Williams, David Philip
Amateur. Tail end batsman, useful bowler. *Team* London County (1901).
Career batting
1 match, did not bat–*ct* 0
Bowling 46–0

Williams, Dennis Stanley
Amateur. *b:* 15.11.1936, Sutton, Surrey. Middle order right-hand batsman, left-arm medium pace bowler. *Team* Combined Services (1959–64).
Career batting
8–15–1–225–82–16.07–0–*ct* 6
His County cricket was for Berkshire (1958).

Williams, Dyson Bransby
(changed name to Dyson Brock Williams)
Amateur. *b:* 13.10.1877, Killay, Sketty, Swansea, Glamorgan. *d:* 18.4.1922, City of London. He died by his own hand. Middle order right-hand batsman. *Sch* Malvern. *Team* Glamorgan (1921, 1 match).
Career batting
1–2–0–14–9–7.00–0–*ct* 0
He first played for Glamorgan (pre first-class) in 1901. He was Glamorgan Treasurer 1913–21.

Williams, Edward Lovell
Amateur. *b:* 15.9.1925, Shaftesbury, Dorset. Lower order left-hand batsman, right-arm fast medium bowler. *Sch* Charterhouse. *Team* Leicestershire (1949, 1 match).
Career batting
1–2–0–17–14–8.50–0–*ct* 0
Bowling 33–2–16.50–0–0–2/33

Williams, Edward Stephen Bruce
Amateur. *b:* 2.11.1892, Pinhoe, Devon. *d:* 20.1.1977, Winchester, Hampshire. Forceful opening right-hand batsman, slow right-arm bowler. *Sch* Winchester. *Teams* Services (1922–31); Army (1922–33). *Tour* Martineau to Egypt 1931 (not first-class).
Career batting
29–51–2–2029–228–41.40–4–*ct* 13–*st* 1
Bowling 23–0
Both his double centuries were for the Army, his highest being 228 v Royal Navy at Lord's in 1928. He was for some years captain of the Army team and the leading batsman of that side. His final first-class match was for Free Foresters in 1935. His County cricket was for Devon (1930).

Williams, Ernest Albert Vivian
Amateur. *b:* 10.4.1914, Bank Hall, St Michael, Barbados. Attacking middle order right-hand batsman, right-arm fast medium bowler. *Team* Barbados (1934/5 to 1948/9). *Tour* West Indies to England 1939. *Tests* West Indies (1939 to 1947/8, 4 matches).
Career batting
42–63–8–1479–131*–26.89–2–*ct* 19
Bowling 3387–116–29.19–1–0–5/73
Test batting
4–6–0–113–72–18.83–0–*ct* 2
Bowling 241–9–26.77–0–0–3/51
He hit 370 runs, av 30.83, and took 14 wickets, av 32.92, in first-class matches on the 1939 tour, playing in one Test.

Williams, G. E.
Amateur. Middle order batsman. *Team* Hampshire (1904, 1 match).
Career batting
1–2–0–16–15–8.00–0–*ct* 0
He also played for Berkshire (1908–09).

Williams, Gwynfor Lloyd
Amateur. *b:* 30.5.1925, Kidwelly, Carmarthenshire. Middle order right-hand batsman, good close field. *Sch* Christ College, Brecon. *Team* Somerset (1955, 3 matches).
Career batting
3–6–0–30–24–5.00–0–*ct* 4

Williams, H.
Professional. Lower order batsman, slow left-arm bowler. *Team* Worcestershire (1927, 4 matches).
Career batting
4–6–3–7–4–2.33–0–*ct* 0
Bowling 185–2–92.50–0–0–1/13

Williams, Harry
Amateur. *b:* 30.10.1903, Islington, London. *d:* 2.6.1989, Koping, Sweden. Lower order batsman, useful bowler. *Sch* Berkhamsted. *Teams* Northamptonshire (1923–24, 6 matches); Europeans in Ceylon (1930/1).
Career batting
7–13–1–104–27–8.66–0–*ct* 2
Bowling 125–5–25.00–0–0–2/29

Williams, Herbert Reginald Hewett
Amateur. *b:* 7.6.1900, Hendon, Middlesex. *d:* 17.7.1974, Denmark Hill, London. Lower order right-hand batsman, wicket-keeper. *Sch* Charterhouse. *Team* Essex (1919–20, 10 matches).
Career batting
10–12–2–67–23*–6.70–0–*ct* 18–*st* 7

Williams, Herbert Scott
(later known as Scott-Williams)
Amateur. *b:* 4.9.1860, Woolland House, Dorset. *d:* 30.11.1942, Dorchester, Dorset. Grandson of C. M. (MCC 1823), brother-in-law of F. J. Poynton (Somerset). Lower order batsman, wicket-keeper. *Sch* Harrow. *Team* Middlesex (1890, 1 match).
Career batting
1–2–0–1–1–0.50–*ct* 1–*st* 1

Williams, Ievan
Amateur. *b:* 17.3.1909, Brynamman, Carmarthenshire. *d:* 3.3.1964, Eastbourne, Sussex. Middle order batsman. *Team* Glamorgan (1931, 2 matches).
Career batting
2–4–0–10–7–2.50–0–*ct* 0

Williams, John Nathaniel
Amateur. *b:* 24.1.1878, Kensington, London. *d:* 25.4.1915, Gaba Tepe, Gallipoli Peninsula, Turkey. He was killed in action. Brother of P. F. C. (Gloucestershire). Hard hitting middle order right-hand batsman. *Sch* Eton. *Teams* Hawke's Bay (1903/4); Gloucestershire (1908, 3 matches). *Tour* Hawke to New Zealand 1902/3 (he appeared in emergency in non-first-class matches only).
Career batting
4–7–0–52–20–7.42–0–*ct* 2

He did not appear in any first-class matches whilst at Oxford and after leaving the University emigrated to New Zealand. He also played for Dorset (1904–10). He won a blue for royal tennis.

Williams, John Stewart
Amateur. *b:* 4.1.1911, South Croydon, Surrey. *d:* 12.12.1964, Haywards Heath, Sussex. Lower order left-hand batsman, right-arm slow bowler. *Sch* Repton. *Team* Oxford U (1931).
Career batting
4–2–2–16–16*–no av–0–*ct* 0
Bowling 229–6–38.16–0–0–2/49

Williams, Joseph
Professional. *b:* 1892, Bromborough Pool, Cheshire. *d:* 10.7.1916, Thiepval, France. Lower order batsman, useful bowler. *Team* MCC (1914).
Career batting
1–2–1–19–11*–19.00–0–*ct* 0
Bowling 26–0

His County cricket was for Cheshire (1909–14).

Williams, Leoline
Amateur. *b:* 15.5.1900, Wootton-under-Edge, Gloucestershire. *d:* 29.2.1984, Lower Sticker, Cornwall. Brother of P. V. (Sussex). Middle order right-hand batsman, wicket-keeper. *Sch* Winchester. *Teams* Sussex (1919–30, 24 matches); Gloucestershire (1922, 11 matches); Army (in India) (1926/7).
Career batting
43–70–7–1440–107–22.85–3–*ct* 20–*st* 5
Bowling 5–0

His final first-class match was for the Army in 1931.

Williams, Lewis Erskine Wyndham
Amateur. *b:* 28.11.1900, Bonvilston, Cardiff, Glamorgan. *d:* 24.4.1974, St Hilary, Glamorgan. Son-in-law of R. L. Knight (Oxford U). Middle order batsman, useful bowler. *Sch* Oratory. *Team* Glamorgan (1928–30, 4 matches).
Career batting
4–8–2–145–53*–24.16–0–*ct* 1
Bowling 42–0

Williams, Neil FetzGerald
Cricketer. *b:* 2.7.1962, Hopewell, St Vincent. Lower order right-hand batsman, right-arm fast medium bowler. *Teams* Middlesex (1982–92, 169 matches); Windward Islands (1982/3 to 1991/2); Tasmania (1983/4, 7 matches). *Tour* English Counties to Zimbabwe 1984/5. *Test* England (1990, 1 match).
Career batting
198–232–46–3629–77–19.51–0–*ct* 54
Bowling 15141–515–29.40–16–2–8/75
Test batting
1–1–0–38–38–38.00–0–*ct* 0
Bowling 148–2–74.00–0–0–2/148

His best season was 1983 with 63 wickets, av 26.33. He played for England in one Test when C. C. Lewis was forced to withdraw due to a migraine attack.

Williams, Norman Roy
Amateur. *b:* 4.1.1931, March, Cambridgeshire. Lower order right-hand batsman, right-arm fast medium bowler, slip field. *Team* Combined Services (1961).
Career batting
1–1–0–5–5–5.00–0–*ct* 1
Bowling 101–5–20.20–0–0–4/67

Not a member of the armed forces, he played in emergency. He played for Nottinghamshire 2nd XI.

Williams, Owen Leslie
Cricketer. *b:* 8.4.1932, Claremont, Cape Town, South Africa. Lower order right-hand batsman, slow left-arm bowler. *Team* Warwickshire (1967, 1 match).
Career batting
1–2–1–6–6*–6.00–0–*ct* 0
Bowling 60–1–60.00–0–0–1/32

Williams, Peter Victor
Amateur. *b:* 10.7.1897, Dublin, Ireland. *d:* 1.4.1971, Epsom, Auckland, New Zealand. Brother of Leoline (Sussex and Gloucestershire), he married the niece of C. Tillard (Surrey). Sound middle order right-hand batsman, wicket-keeper. *Sch* Winchester. *Team* Sussex (1919, 10 matches).
Career batting
23–40–0–810–146–20.25–2–*ct* 13–*st* 2
His final first-class match was for the Army in 1927.

Williams, Rev Philip
Amateur. *b:* 7.9.1824, Eton, Buckinghamshire. *d:* 18.11.1899, Sion Hill, Bath, Somerset. Middle order batsman. *Sch* Winchester. *Teams* Oxford U (1844–47, blue all four years); Nottinghamshire (1845, 2 matches).
Career batting
20–35–2–174–20–5.27–0–*ct* 16
His final first-class match was for MCC in 1849.

Williams, Sir Philip Francis Cunningham
Amateur. *b:* 6.7.1884, Kensington, London. *d:* 6.5.1958, Westminster, London. Brother of J. N. (Gloucestershire), his daughter married a grandson of J. P. F. Gundry (Oxford U 1857). Attractive middle order right-hand batsman, slow under-arm bowler. *Sch* Eton. *Team* Gloucestershire (1919–25, 112 matches). *Tour* MCC to New Zealand 1906/07 (played in emergency).
Career batting
113–199–10–3084–87–16.31–0–*ct* 45
Bowling 173–2–86.50–0–0–1/10
His first-class debut was for MCC in New Zealand in 1906/07. He appeared in the Oxford Freshmen's match of 1904, but no first-class matches for the University. He also played for Dorset (1903–12). He captained Gloucestershire 1922–23.

Williams, Ralph Augustin
Amateur. *b:* 2.2.1879, Reading, Berkshire. *d:* 1.12.1958, Earley, Reading, Berkshire. Sound lower order right-hand batsman, right-arm medium pace bowler. *Sch* Winchester. *Team* Oxford U (1899–1902, blue 1901–02). *Tour* Oxford University Authentics to India 1902/3.
Career batting
15–25–1–584–105–24.33–1–*ct* 14
Bowling 1099–40–27.47–3–0–5/30
His County cricket was for Buckinghamshire (1895), Oxfordshire (1896) and Berkshire (1897–1904). He also won a blue for rackets.

Williams, Ricardo Cecil
Cricketer. *b:* 3.2.1968, Camberwell, London. Middle order right-hand batsman, right-arm medium pace bowler. *Team* Gloucestershire (1991–92, 8 matches).
Career batting
8–13–1–130–44–10.83–0–*ct* 0
Bowling 381–6–63.50–0–0–3/44

Williams, Richard Charles James
Cricketer. *b:* 8.8.1969, Southmead, Bristol. Lower order left-hand batsman, wicket-keeper. *Sch* Millfield. *Team* Gloucestershire (1990–92, 23 matches).
Career batting
23–25–8–278–55*–16.35–0–*ct* 54–*st* 11

Williams, Richard Grenville
Cricketer. *b:* 10.8.1957, Bangor, Caernarvonshire. Middle order right-hand batsman, off break bowler. *Team* Northamptonshire (1974–92, 278 matches). *Tours* Robins to New Zealand 1979/80; English Counties to Zimbabwe 1984/5.
Career batting
284–447–65–11817–175*–30.93–18–*ct* 99
Bowling 12722–376–33.83–9–0–7/73
He hit 1,000 runs in a season six times (best 1,305, av 43.50, in 1983).

Williams, Richard Harry
Amateur. *b:* 23.4.1901, Brockmoor, Staffordshire. *d:* 19.12.1982, Stourbridge, Worcestershire. Middle order left-hand batsman. *Team* Worcestershire (1923–32, 37 matches).
Career batting
37–68–4–713–81–11.14–0–*ct* 17

Williams, Robert Graham
Amateur. *b:* 4.4.1911, St Peters, Adelaide, South Australia. *d:* 31.8.1978, Adelaide, South Australia. Lower order right-hand batsman, right-arm fast medium bowler. *Team* South Australia (1932/3 to 1947/8, 18 matches). *Tour* Australian Services to England 1945.
Career batting
26–41–8–531–75*–16.09–0–*ct* 12
Bowling 1957–67–29.20–3–0–6/21

Williams, Robert James
Amateur. *b:* 12.4.1912, Viljoen's Drift, Orange Free State, South Africa. *d:* 16.5.1984, Durban, South Africa. Lower order right-hand batsman, wicket-keeper. *Team* Natal (1930/1 to 1950/1). *Tour* South Africa to England 1935.
Career batting
53–68–16–1156–117*–22.23–1–*ct* 77–*st* 55
The reserve wicket-keeper on the 1935 tour, he played in only seven first-class matches. At the end

of the visit he accepted a business appointment in England.

Williams, Rowland
(changed name to Powell-Williams in April 1900)
Amateur. *b:* 8.1.1872, Stratford-on-Avon, Warwickshire. *d:* 16.12.1951, Yelverton, Devon. Middle order right-hand batsman. *Sch* KES, Birmingham. *Teams* Warwickshire (1897–98, 5 matches); London County (1902).
Career batting
7–12–1–105–38–9.54–0–*ct* 9
Bowling 20–0
His final first-class match was for Gentlemen of England in 1905.

Williams, Stephen
Cricketer. *b:* 11.3.1954, Rodbourne Cheney, Wiltshire. Middle order right-hand batsman, leg break bowler. *Team* Gloucestershire (1978, 1 match).
Career batting
1–0–0–0–0–0.00–0–*ct* 0
He also played for Wiltshire (1975–90).

Williams, Thomas Brinsmead
Amateur. *b:* 18.6.1884, Newport, Monmouthshire. *d:* 12.1.1954, Llandaff, Glamorgan. Middle order batsman. *Team* Wales (1926).
Career batting
1–1–0–43–43.00–0–*ct* 1
His County cricket was for Monmouthshire (1903–34).

Williams, Thomas Christopher
Amateur. *b:* 13.12.1908, Dublin, Ireland. *d:* 14.8.1982, Clonmel, Co Tipperary, Ireland. Middle order left-hand batsman, right-arm medium pace, or leg break, bowler. *Team* Ireland (1939).
Career batting
1–2–0–25–23–12.50–0–*ct* 2
Bowling 50–1–50.00–0–0–1/36

Williams, William
Amateur. *b:* 25.11.1844, Arnold Grove, Nottingham. *d:* 12.3.1885, Wandsworth, London. Middle order right-hand batsman, right-hand fast round-arm bowler. *Sch* Oundle. *Team* Nottinghamshire (1864–75, 9 matches).
Career batting
15–28–2–239–31–9.19–0–*ct* 4
Bowling 92–3–30.66–0–0–2/27
His debut in first-class cricket was for Gentlemen of the North in 1862 and his final first-class match for an England XI in 1878.

Williams, William
Amateur. *b:* 12.4.1861. *d:* 14.4.1951, Hampton Wick, Middlesex. Lower order right-hand batsman, leg break bowler, wicket-keeper. *Team* Middlesex (1885–1902, 27 matches). *Tour* Priestley to West Indies 1896/7.
Career batting
38–64–10–465–40–8.61–0–*ct* 32–*st* 4
Bowling 1127–63–17.88–3–1–7/38
A noted figure in club cricket, he is reputed to have taken 100 wickets each season for 55 years and appeared for MCC at the age of 74. He was a noted rugby footballer for Harlequins and later a well-known referee. It was mainly due to him that the Twickenham ground was laid out and it was for some time known as 'Billy Williams' cabbage patch'.

Williamson, Archibald Carmichael
Amateur. *b:* 11.11.1892, Hurlingham, Argentine. *d:* 17.9.1972, South Rubery, Birmingham. Opening batsman. *Sch* Fettes. *Team* Oxford U (1913).
Career batting
1–2–0–18–10–9.00–0–*ct* 0
His County cricket was for Cheshire (1913). He won a blue for rugby.

Williamson, John Gordon
(changed name to Barkass-Williamson in 1965)
Professional. *b:* 4.4.1936, Norton-on-Tees, Co Durham. Lower order right-hand batsman, right-arm fast medium bowler. *Team* Northamptonshire (1959–62, 55 matches).
Career batting
56–67–19–820–106*–17.08–1–*ct* 28
Bowling 3921–120–32.67–3–0–6/47
His first-class debut was for Combined Services in 1958. He also played for Durham (pre first-class, 1954–56 and 1963–69) and Cheshire (1974).

Willis, Carl Bleackley
Amateur. *b:* 23.3.1893, Daylesford, Victoria, Australia. *d:* 12.5.1930, Berrigan, New South Wales, Australia. Middle order right-hand batsman, excellent field. *Team* Victoria (1913/4 to 1928/9, 36 matches). *Tours* AIF to England 1919, to South Africa 1919/20; Victoria to New Zealand 1924/5.
Career batting
72–116–12–3707–156*–35.64–8–*ct* 38
Bowling 352–7–50.28–0–0–2/10
He was very successful in England in 1919 coming second in the AIF batting averages with 1,652 runs, av 41.30.

Willis, Rev Charles Francis
Amateur. *b:* 15.4.1827, Hawkhurst, Kent. *d:* 19.11.1895, Bassingham, Lincolnshire. Brother of Henry (Surrey). Lower order batsman, useful bowler. *Sch* Tonbridge. *Teams* Oxford U (1847–49, blue all three years); Kent (1850, 1 match).
Career batting
10–19–2–83–16*–4.88–0–*ct* 4
Bowling 53 wickets (no analyses)–3–2–8/?
He also played for Oxfordshire (1850).

Willis, Henry
Amateur. *b:* 17.3.1841, Sydenham, London. *d:* 29.9.1926, Horton, Epsom, Surrey. Brother of C. F. (Kent). Middle order batsman. *Sch* Tonbridge. *Team* Surrey (1868, 1 match).
Career batting
1–2–0–7–7–3.50–0–*ct* 0

Willis, John William
Amateur. *b:* 31.8.1886, Rothwell, Kettering, Northamptonshire. *d:* 21.9.1963, Rothwell, Kettering, Northamptonshire. Lower order right-hand batsman, useful bowler. *Team* Northamptonshire (1919, 1 match).
Career batting
1–2–0–4–4–2.00–0–*ct* 0
Bowling 35–0

Willis, Robert George (Dylan), MBE
Cricketer. *b:* 30.5.1949, Sunderland, Co Durham. Tail end right-hand batsman, right-arm fast bowler. *Teams* Surrey (1969–71, 34 matches); Warwickshire (1972–84, 136 matches); Northern Transvaal 1972/3. *Tours* MCC to Australia and New Zealand 1970/1, to West Indies 1973/4, to Australia 1974/5, to India, Sri Lanka and Australia 1976/7; England to Pakistan and New Zealand 1977/8, 1983/4, to Australia 1978/9, 1979/80, to West Indies 1980/1, to India and Sri Lanka 1981/2, to Australia and New Zealand 1982/3 (New Zealand not first-class); Robins to South Africa 1972/3. *Tests* England (1970/1 to 1984, 90 matches).
Career batting
308–333–145–2690–72–14.30–0–*ct* 134
Bowling 22468–899–24.99–34–2–8/32
Test batting
90–128–55–840–28*–11.50–0–*ct* 39
Bowling 8190–325–25.20–16–0–8/43

Despite an erratic first few years in County and Test cricket, Willis developed into one of the best fast bowlers to play for England. His three outstanding Test series have all been against Australia – in 1977 with 27 wickets, av 19.77, in 1978/9 with 20, av 23.05, and in 1981 with 29, av 22.96. He was vice-captain on three England tours overseas, but succeeded to the post of captain in his own right only when Botham proved unsuitable and Brearley retired. Willis led England in the home series of 1982 and then to Australia and New Zealand in 1982/3 and the following home series of 1983, proving to be better equipped for the task than some had suggested. He captained England on the 1983/4 tour to New Zealand and Pakistan, but missed the last two Tests v Pakistan due to illness and returned home early. In 1984 he played in three Tests v West Indies under the captaincy of D. I. Gower, but withdrew from the Fourth due to illness. At the time of his final Test he was England's leading wicket taker. In all he captained England in 18 Tests. Injury and Test calls restricted his appearances in County cricket, and his best season in England was 1978 with 65 wickets, av 18.41. He was appointed captain of Warwickshire 1980–84 and in 1982 received the MBE for his services to cricket. He added his third Christian name after the singer, Bob Dylan.

Willmer, Arthur Franklin
Amateur. *b:* 10.1.1890, Claughton, Birkenhead, Cheshire. *d:* 20.9.1916, Rouen, France. Lower order batsman, fast bowler. *Sch* Birkenhead. *Team* Oxford U (1912).
Career batting
1–2–2–12–7*–no av–0–*ct* 0
Bowling 36–0

His County cricket was for Cheshire (1914).

Willock, Charles Johnstone
Amateur. *b:* 8.4.1862, Shahjehanpore, India. *d:* 19.3.1919, Ryde, Isle of Wight. Lower order right-hand batsman, right-arm medium pace bowler. *Sch* Wellington. *Teams* Sussex (1883, 1 match); Cambridge U (1883).
Career batting
2–4–1–14–8*–4.66–0–*ct* 2
Bowling 34–3–11.33–0–0–2/18

Willoughby, Frederick George
Professional. *b:* 25.4.1862, Edinburgh, Scotland. *d:* 16.4.1952, Eastleigh, Hampshire. Tail end right-hand batsman, left-arm medium pace bowler. *Team* Hampshire (1885, 8 matches).
Career batting
8–15–3–60–19–5.00–0–*ct* 5
Bowling 564–25–22.56–0–0–4/39

He last played for Hampshire (not first-class) in 1886. He also played for Worcestershire (pre first-class, 1890–92). Later he was on the first-class umpires' list (1906).

Willows, Alan
Cricketer. *b:* 24.4.1961, Portslade, Sussex. Lower order right-hand batsman, slow left-arm bowler. *Team* Sussex (1980–83, 5 matches).
Career batting
5–3–1–5–4–2.50–0–*ct* 0
Bowling 253–8–31.62–0–0–4/33

He also played for Dorset (1990–92).

Wills, Alec Percy Stanley
Amateur. *b:* 11.3.1911, Guykit, Trincomalee, Ceylon. *d:* 7.11.1941, Singapore. He was killed in action. Tall end right-hand batsman, useful bowler. *Sch* Haileybury. *Team* Combined Services (1937).
Career batting
1–2–2–3–3*–no av–0–*ct* 0
Bowling 36–0

Wills, Arnold Cass Lycett
Amateur. *b:* 17.7.1906, Pimlico, Westminster, London. *d:* 28.2.1978, Northampton. Steady opening right-hand batsman, right-arm medium pace bowler. *Sch* Harrow. *Teams* Northamptonshire (1926–29, 15 matches); Cambridge U (1929).
Career batting
16–27–2–338–68–13.52–0–*ct* 5
Bowling 428–6–71.33–0–0–3/68

Wills, James Robertson
Amateur. *b:* 2.5.1899, Killala, Co Mayo, Ireland. *d:* 16.4.1949, St Saviour, Jersey. Lower order right-hand batsman, right-arm fast medium bowler. *Teams* Dublin University (1922–26); Ireland (1922).
Career batting
4–8–1–66–28–9.42–0–*ct* 1
Bowling 236–7–33.71–0–0–3/5

Wills, Robert Thomas
Cricketer. *b:* 19.7.1950, Belfast, Ireland. Middle order right-hand batsman. *Team* Ireland (1981–85).
Career batting
5–7–0–121–48–17.28–0–*ct* 0

Wills, Roy
Cricketer. *b:* 5.12.1944, Abington, Northampton. Middle order left-hand batsman, slip field. *Team* Northamptonshire (1963–69, 33 matches).
Career batting
33–54–6–824–151*–17.16–1–*ct* 26

Wills, Thomas Wentworth (Spencer)
Amateur. *b:* 19.12.1835, Molonglo Plains, New South Wales, Australia. *d:* 2.5.1880, Heidelberg, Melbourne, Victoria, Australia. He stabbed himself to death. Cousin of T. W. Antill (Victoria). Lower order right-hand batsman, right-hand fast round-arm, or slow under-arm bowler. *Sch* Rugby. *Teams* Kent (1855–56, 3 matches); Cambridge U (1856, blue); Victoria (1856/7 to 1875/6, 16 matches).
Career batting
32–57–8–602–58–12.28–0–*ct* 20
Bowling 1221–121 + 9–10.09–15–3–7/44

He played for Cambridge against Oxford in 1856 when Cambridge arrived a man short. He had been entered for Cambridge but was never in residence. His first-class debut was for Gentlemen of Kent in 1854. He was the first to train the aborigines to play cricket, on his father's sheep stations.

Willsher, Edgar
Professional. *b:* 22.11.1828, Little Halden Farm, Rolvenden, Kent. *d:* 7.10.1885, Lewisham, London. Brother of William (Kent). Steady middle order left-hand batsman, left-hand fast round-arm bowler. *Team* Kent (1850–75, 145 matches). *Tour* Willsher to North America 1868 (not first-class).
Career batting
267–473–63–5089–89–12.41–0–*ct* 233
Bowling 16488–1290 + 39–12.78–107–30–8/16

He took 113 wickets, av 9.98, in 1868 and for a period of about ten years was regarded as one of the best bowlers in England. He was a first-class umpire (1883–85).

Willson, Bernard John
Cricketer. *b:* 20.6.1935, Strood, Kent. Lower order right-hand batsman, left-arm medium paced bowler. *Team* Combined Services (1964).
Career batting
2–4–0–87–53–21.75–0–*ct* 2
Bowling 197–7–28.14–0–0–4/87

Willson, Erasmus Albert
Amateur. *b:* 13.10.1878, Sittingbourne, Kent. *d:* 17.4.1948, Sittingbourne, Kent. Lower order right-hand batsman, right-arm fast bowler. *Team* Kent (1898, 1 match).
Career batting
1–2–0–9–8–4.50–0–*ct* 1
Bowling 46–1–46.00–0–0–1/21

Willson, Ronald Henry
Professional. *b:* 14.7.1933, Seaford, Sussex. Middle order left-hand batsman, slow left-arm bowler. *Teams* Sussex (1955–57, 19 matches); Rhodesia (1961/2).
Career batting
22–34–5–411–113*–14.17–1–*ct* 10
Bowling 390–4–97.50–0–0–1/27

He also played for Devon (1959).

Wilmot, Rev Arthur Alfred
Amateur. *b:* 14.2.1845, Chaddesden, Derbyshire. *d:* 12.5.1876, Morley, Derbyshire. Opening batsman. *Sch* Repton. *Team* Derbyshire (1871, 1 match).
Career batting
1–2–0–0–0–0.00–0–*ct* 1

He played no first-class cricket at Cambridge U. He also played for Staffordshire (1872) and Northamptonshire (pre first-class, 1891).

Wilmot, Kilburn
Professional. *b:* 3.4.1911, Chilvers Coton, Nuneaton, Warwickshire. Lower order right-hand batsman, right-arm fast pace bowler. *Team* Warwickshire (1931–39, 75 matches).
Career batting
75–101–25–871–54–11.46–0–*ct* 23
Bowling 5018–154–32.58–2–1–7/34

A good soccer player, he appeared for Coventry and Walsall.

Wilmot, William
Professional. *b:* 25.12.1869, Denby, Derbyshire. *d:* 19.5.1957, Wade Hill, Leyland, Lancashire. Lower order right-hand batsman, wicket-keeper. *Team* Derbyshire (1897–1901, 10 matches).
Career batting
10–16–3–155–25*–11.92–0–*ct* 11–*st* 1

Wilson, Alan
Professional. *b:* 24.4.1920, Newton-le-Willows, Lancashire. Tail end right-hand batsman, wicket-keeper. *Team* Lancashire (1948–62, 171 matches).
Career batting
171–186–59–760–37*–5.98–0–*ct* 287–*st* 59
He lost his place in Lancashire side in 1959, but made a fleeting reappearance in 1962.

Wilson, Arthur Edward
Professional. *b:* 18.5.1910, Paddington, London. Dependable opening or middle order left-hand batsman, occasional slow left-arm bowler, wicket-keeper. *Teams* Middlesex (1932–33, 7 matches); Gloucestershire (1936–55, 318 matches).
Career batting
328–502–77–10744–188–25.28–7–*ct* 425–*st* 176
Bowling 1–0
He hit 1,000 runs in a season six times (best 1,327, av 31.59, in 1947). For Gloucestershire v Hampshire at Portsmouth in 1953 he held 10 catches in the match. From 1950 to 1954 he was appointed Gloucestershire County coach.

Wilson, Arthur Keith
Amateur. *b:* 26.8.1894, Brighton, Sussex. *d:* 8.11.1977, Brighton, Sussex. Middle order right-hand batsman, leg break bowler. *Sch* Brighton. *Team* Sussex (1914–34, 16 matches).
Career batting
17–30–2–546–134–19.50–1–*ct* 4
Bowling 221–3–73.66–0–0–2/39
His final appearance for Sussex in 1934 came after an absence of nine years. He was Chairman of Sussex CCC.

Wilson, Ben Ambler
Professional. *b:* 22.9.1921, Knaresborough, Yorkshire. Son of B. B. (Yorkshire). Lower order left-hand batsman, slow left-arm bowler. *Team* Warwickshire (1951, 1 match).
Career batting
1–1–0–0–0–0.00–0–*ct* 0
Bowling 75–1–75.00–0–0–1/75
He also played for Suffolk (1955–59).

Wilson, Benjamin Birdsall
Professional. *b:* 11.12.1879, Scarborough, Yorkshire. *d:* 14.9.1957, Harrogate, Yorkshire. Father of B. A. (Warwickshire). Sound opening right-hand batsman, right-arm fast medium bowler. *Team* Yorkshire (1906–14, 185 matches).
Career batting
185–308–12–8053–208–27.20–15–*ct* 53
Bowling 278–2–139.00–0–0–1/16
He hit 1,000 runs in a season five times (best 1,608, av 32.74, in 1914). His only double century was 208 for Yorkshire v Sussex at Bradford in 1914.

Wilson, Rt Rev Cecil
Amateur. *b:* 9.9.1860, Canonbury, London. *d:* 20.1.1941, Perth, Western Australia. Brother of Leslie (Kent). Attractive middle order right-hand batsman. *Sch* Tonbridge. *Team* Kent (1882–90, 28 matches).
Career batting
33–56–6–1193–127–23.86–1–*ct* 28
Bowling 222–5–44.40–0–0–1/2
He did not appear in any first-class matches whilst at Cambridge. From 1894 to 1917 he was appointed Bishop of Melanesia, and 1917–37 Bishop of Bunbury (Western Australia).

Wilson, Charles Plumpton
Amateur. *b:* 12.5.1859, Roydon, Norfolk. *d:* 9.3.1938, Eckling Grange, East Dereham, Norfolk. Great-uncle of R. G. Newman (Cambridge U). Middle order right-hand batsman, right-arm medium pace bowler. *Sch* Uppingham and Marlborough. *Team* Cambridge U (1880–81, blue both years).
Career batting
10–18–7–157–24*–14.27–0–*ct* 6
Bowling 439–22–19.95–1–0–5/34
His County cricket was for Lincolnshire (1880) and Norfolk (1881–84). A remarkable all-round sportsman, he played rugby for Cambridge and England in 1881 and soccer for England in 1884. Also a noted cyclist, he raced for Cambridge in the 25 miles in 1878.

Wilson, Claude William
Amateur. *b:* 9.9.1858, Banbury, Oxfordshire. *d:* 7.7.1881, Reigate, Surrey. Middle order right-hand batsman, wicket-keeper. *Sch* Brighton. *Teams* Oxford U (1881); Surrey (1881, 1 match).
Career batting
2–4–0–66–51–16.50–0–*ct* 2
He won a blue for soccer and played for England.

Wilson, Rev Clement Eustace Macro
Amateur. *b:* 15.5.1875, Bolsterstone, Yorkshire. *d:* 8.2.1944, Calverhall, Shropshire. Brother of E. R. (Yorkshire) and R. A. (Cambridge U), father of D. C. (Cambridge U). Steady middle order right-hand batsman, right-arm fast medium bowler, also slow left-arm (changing from one to the other in the course of a match). *Sch* Uppingham. *Teams* Cambridge U (1895–98, blue all four years); Yorkshire (1896–99, 9 matches). *Tours* Mitchell to North America 1895; Hawke to South Africa 1898/9. *Tests* England (1898/9, 2 matches).
Career batting
52–80–10–1665–115–23.78–1–*ct* 34
Bowling 2337–125–18.69–6–2–7/24
Test batting
2–4–1–42–18–14.00–0–*ct* 0
On being ordained he retired from first-class cricket, his final first-class match being for MCC in

1900. He captained Cambridge in 1898. He also won a blue for athletics.

Wilson, David Clement
Amateur. *b:* 1.3.1917, Eccleston, Chester, Cheshire. Son of C. E. M. (Yorkshire), nephew of E. R. (Yorkshire) and R. A. (Cambridge U). Lower order right-hand batsman, right-arm medium pace bowler. *Sch* Winchester. *Team* Cambridge U (1938–39). *Tour* Combined Oxford and Cambridge Univ to Jamaica 1938/9.
Career batting
10–17–8–98–23*–10.88–0–*ct* 8
Bowling 729–15–48.60–1–0–5/81

Wilson, Donald
Professional. *b:* 7.8.1937, Settle, Yorkshire. Lower order left-hand batsman, slow left-arm bowler. *Team* Yorkshire (1957–74, 392 matches). *Tours* MCC to New Zealand 1960/1, to India 1963/4, to Ceylon 1969/70, to Australia and New Zealand 1970/1; Yorkshire to North America 1964 (not first-class). *Tests* England (1963/4 to 1970/1, 6 matches).
Career batting
422–533–91–6230–112–14.09–1–*ct* 250
Bowling 24977–1189–21.00–50–8–8/36
Test batting
6–7–1–75–42–12.50–0–*ct* 1
Bowling 466–11–42.36–0–0–2/17
He took 100 wickets in a season five times (best 109, av 13.95, in 1968). From 1975 to 1977 he played for Lincolnshire. He was chief coach at Lord's until 1991.

Wilson, Edward Wardlaw
Amateur. *b:* 19.8.1907, Burntisland, Fife, Scotland. *d:* 16.4.1982, Edinburgh, Scotland. Middle order left-hand batsman. *Team* Scotland (1936).
Career batting
1–2–0–1–1–0.50–0–*ct* 0

Wilson, Ernest Frederick
Professional. *b:* 24.6.1907, Godstone, Surrey. *d:* 3.3.1981, Swansea, Glamorgan. Sound middle order right-hand batsman. *Team* Surrey (1928–36, 81 matches).
Career batting
81–120–12–2516–110–23.29–1–*ct* 16
Bowling 43–0

Wilson, Evelyn Rockley
Amateur. *b:* 25.3.1879, Bolsterstone, Yorkshire. *d:* 21.7.1957, Winchester, Hampshire. Brother of C. E. M. (Yorkshire) and R. A. (Cambridge U), uncle of D. C. (Cambridge U). Sound middle or lower order right-hand batsman, right-arm slow bowler turning the ball either way. *Sch* Rugby. *Teams* Cambridge U (1899–1902, blue all four years); Yorkshire (1899–1923, 66 matches). *Tours* Bosanquet to North America 1901; Bennett to West Indies 1901/2; MCC to Argentine 1911/12, to Australia 1920/1. *Test* England (1920/1, 1 match).
Career batting
136–190–28–3565–142–22.00–4–*ct* 106
Bowling 8234–467–17.63–26–5–7/16
Test batting
1–2–0–10–5–5.00–0–*ct* 0
Bowling 36–3–12.00–0–0–2/28
A master at Winchester College, his County cricket was mainly confined to matches in August, though for eleven years between 1903 and 1913 he did not play for Yorkshire. He scored 117* on debut for A. J. Webbe's XI v Cambridge U at Cambridge in 1899. He captained Cambridge in 1902.

Wilson, Francis Tyrwhitt Drake
Amateur. *b:* 9.4.1876, Cottesbrooke, Guilsborough, Northamptonshire. *d:* 19.3.1964, Great Horkesley, Essex. Brother of H. L. (Sussex). Lower order right-hand batsman, leg break bowler. *Teams* MCC (1914); Army (1913–20).
Career batting
5–7–0–103–39–14.71–0–*ct* 2
Bowling 297–18–16.50–2–0–5/57
His County cricket was for Suffolk (1908–11). His first-class debut was for the Navy and Army in 1910.

Wilson, Frederic Bonhote
Amateur. *b:* 21.9.1881, Bayswater, London. *d:* 19.1.1932, Kensington, London. Middle order right-hand batsman, right-arm slow bowler. *Sch* Harrow. *Team* Cambridge U (1902–04, blue all three years).
Career batting
27–49–7–1130–76–26.90–0–*ct* 15
Bowling 181–4–45.25–0–0–2/64
His final first-class match was for Leveson-Gower's XI in 1906. He captained Cambridge in 1904. He also won blues for rackets and royal tennis. A well known sporting journalist, he began with the *Daily Mirror*, but was associated with *The Times* after the First World War. He was father of Peter Wilson, the journalist, and grandfather of Julian Wilson, the racing commentator.

Wilson, Geoffrey
Amateur. *b:* 21.8.1895, Potternewtown, Leeds, Yorkshire. *d:* 29.11.1960, Southsea, Hampshire. Hard hitting opening or middle order right-hand batsman, right-arm medium pace bowler. *Sch* Harrow. *Teams* Cambridge U (1919–20, blue 1919); Yorkshire (1919–24, 92 matches). *Tour* MCC to Australia and New Zealand 1922/3.
Career batting
115–129–18–1801–142*–16.22–1–*ct* 44
Bowling 55–1–55.00–0–0–1/44
He captained Yorkshire from 1922 to 1924.

Wilson, George
Amateur. *b:* 30.6.1916, Ligoniel, Belfast, Ireland. Middle order right-hand batsman, off break bowler.

Team Ireland (1948–51).
Career batting
3–6–0–116–39–19.33–0–*ct* 0
Bowling 12–2–6.00–0–0–2/12

Wilson, George Alfred
Professional. *b:* 5.4.1877, Amersham, Buckinghamshire. *d:* 3.3.1962, Abbots Langley, Hertfordshire. Father of G. C. (Worcestershire). Lower order right-hand batsman, right-arm fast bowler. *Team* Worcestershire (1899–1906, 154 matches).
Career batting
160–239–42–2238–78–11.36–0–*ct* 57
Bowling 17615–732–24.06–58–18–9/75
He took 100 wickets in a season three times (best 120, av 22.79, in 1901). His best bowling was 9/75 for Worcestershire v Oxford U at Oxford in 1904. He also played for Buckinghamshire (1907–08) and Staffordshire (1912–14). He first played for Worcestershire (pre first-class) in 1898.

Wilson, George Arthur
Amateur. *b:* 2.2.1916, Whitkirk, Leeds, Yorkshire. Middle order right-hand batsman, slow left-arm bowler. *Team* Yorkshire (1936–39, 15 matches).
Career batting
15–25–5–352–55*–17.60–0–*ct* 7
Bowling 138–1–138.00–0–0–1/5

Wilson, George Clifford
Professional. *b:* 27.7.1902, Kidderminster, Worcestershire. *d:* 18.5.1957, Elswick, Newcastle upon Tyne, Northumberland. Son of G. A. (Worcestershire). Lower order right-hand batsman, right-arm fast bowler. *Team* Worcestershire (1924–26, 70 matches).
Career batting
70–119–34–609–40–7.16–0–*ct* 30
Bowling 4049–150–26.99–8–1–8/81
He also played for Northumberland (1935–47).

Wilson, George Lindsay
Amateur. *b:* 27.4.1868, Fitzroy, Melbourne, Victoria, Australia. *d:* 9.3.1920, St Kilda, Melbourne, Victoria, Australia. Sound middle order right-hand batsman, right-arm fast medium bowler, slip field. *Sch* Brighton and Repton. *Teams* Sussex (1887–95, 49 matches); Oxford U (1888–91, blue 1890 and 1891); Victoria (1898/9, 2 matches).
Career batting
75–136–7–2605–174–20.19–3–*ct* 41
Bowling 2042–34–60.05–0–0–4/47
His first-class debut was for G. N. Wyatt's XI in 1886. He also won a blue for soccer.

Wilson, Gerald Charles
Professional. *b:* 25.12.1936, Hayes, Middlesex. Tail end right-hand batsman, right-arm medium pace bowler. *Team* MCC (1957).
Career batting
2–2–2–10–7*–no av–0–*ct* 2
Bowling 211–3–70.33–0–0–2/85

Wilson, Grenville Thomas Owen
(birth registered as T. G. O. Wilson)
Professional. *b:* 9.4.1932, Elmley Lovett, Worcestershire. Tail end left-hand batsman, left-arm fast bowler. *Team* Worcestershire (1951–53, 13 matches).
Career batting
13–16–7–10–4*–1.11–0–*ct* 2
Bowling 1000–18–55.55–0–0–3/42

Wilson, Guy Denis
Amateur. *b:* 30.11.1882, Melbourne, Derbyshire. *d:* 30.11.1917, Cambrai, France. He was killed in action. Middle order batsman. *Sch* Derby School. *Team* Derbyshire (1902–05, 2 matches).
Career batting
2–4–0–19–9–4.75–0–*ct* 0
Bowling 15–0

Wilson, Harry
Professional. *b:* 1873, Yorkshire. *d:* 13.8.1906, Kidderminster, Worcestershire. He died from a brain tumor. Lower order batsman, slow left-arm bowler. *Team* Worcestershire (1901–06, 6 matches).
Career batting
6–11–3–64–21–8.00–0–*ct* 2
Bowling 373–13–28.69–1–0–6/86
He played for Yorkshire in a non-first-class match in 1900.

Wilson, Harry
Amateur. *b:* 1897. *d:* 25.4.1960, Peterborough, Northamptonshire. Tail end right-hand batsman, right-arm medium pace bowler. *Team* Northamptonshire (1931, 1 match).
Career batting
1–2–0–0–0–0.00–0–*ct* 0
Bowling 45–1–45.00–0–0–1/19

Wilson, Herbert
Professional. *b:* 22.5.1892, Eastwood, Nottinghamshire. *d:* 3.6.1972, Macclesfield, Cheshire. Lower order right-hand batsman, right-arm fast medium bowler, slip field. *Team* Nottinghamshire (1911–19, 6 matches).
Career batting
6–7–3–49–19–12.25–0–*ct* 3
Bowling 318–4–79.50–0–0–1/21
He also played for Cheshire (1924–34).

Wilson, Herbert Langford
Amateur. *b:* 27.6.1881, Cottesbrooke, Guilsborough, Northamptonshire. *d:* 15.3.1937, Halland, Uckfield, Sussex. Brother of F. T. D. (MCC). Stylish middle order right-hand batsman, slow right-arm bowler. *Sch* Framlingham. *Team* Sussex (1913–24, 140 matches).
Career batting
145–264–12–6226–187–24.70–6–*ct* 57

Bowling 1250–26–48.07–0–0–4/19

He hit 1,000 runs in a season four times (best 1,352, av 29.39, in 1913). He captained Sussex 1919 to 1921. He also played for Suffolk (1905–12). His final first-class match was for H. D. G. Leveson-Gower's XI in 1930.

Wilson, Ian Barclay Justly
Amateur. *b:* 13.10.1932, Clonmel, Co Tipperary, Ireland. Lower order left-hand batsman, slow left-arm bowler. *Sch* Wrekin. *Team* Ireland (1956–61).
Career batting
3–5–0–49–18–9.80–0–*ct* 1
Bowling 117–7–16.71–0–0–3/7

Wilson, John
Amateur. *b:* 30.6.1857, Hoyland, Yorkshire. *d:* 11.11.1931, Millhouses, Sheffield, Yorkshire. Attacking middle order right-hand batsman, right-hand slow under-arm bowler. *Sch* Trent College. *Team* Yorkshire (1887–88, 4 matches).
Career batting
4–5–1–17–13*–4.25–0–*ct* 3
Bowling 165–12–13.75–0–0–3/28

Wilson, John Devakumar
Cricketer. *b:* 4.9.1944, Jaffna, Ceylon. Middle order left-hand batsman, leg break bowler. *Team* Oxford U (1977).
Career batting
1–2–0–19–18–9.50–0–*ct* 0
Bowling 6–0

Wilson, John Philip
Amateur. *b:* 3.4.1889, Gilling Castle, East Gilling, Yorkshire. *d:* 3.10.1959, Tickton, Beverley, Yorkshire. Brother-in-law of F. S. Jackson (Yorkshire). Middle order right-hand batsman, slow right-arm bowler. *Sch* Harrow. *Team* Yorkshire (1911–12, 9 matches).
Career batting
11–18–1–172–36–10.11–0–*ct* 2
Bowling 24–1–24.00–0–0–1/20

He did not play in first-class cricket whilst at Cambridge. His final first-class match was for Leveson-Gower's XI in 1913. A noted steeplechase jockey, he won the Grand National on Double Chance in 1925.

Wilson, John Stuart
Amateur. *b:* 22.1.1932, Middleton, Manchester, Lancashire. Tail end right-hand batsman, right-arm fast medium bowler. *Team* Scotland (1957–64).
Career batting
16–19–6–66–22–5.07–0–*ct* 8
Bowling 1109–44–25.20–1–0–5/51

Wilson, John Victor
Professional. *b:* 17.1.1921, Scampston, Malton, Yorkshire. Middle order left-hand batsman, right-arm medium pace bowler, fine field. *Team* Yorkshire (1946–62, 477 matches). *Tour* MCC to Australia and New Zealand 1954/5.
Career batting
502–770–79–21650–230–31.33–30–*ct* 548
Bowling 435–9–48.33–0–0–2/1

He hit 1,000 runs in a season 14 times, going on to 2,000 once: 2,027, av 48.26, in 1951. Both his double centuries were for Yorkshire, the higher being 230 v Derbyshire at Sheffield in 1952. He captained Yorkshire 1960 to 1962. His final first-class match was for MCC in 1963. He also played for Lincolnshire (1964–66).

Wilson, John William
Amateur. *b:* 20.8.1921, Albert Park, Melbourne, Victoria, Australia. *d:* 13.10.1985, Melbourne, Victoria, Australia. Tail end right-hand batsman, slow left-arm bowler. *Teams* Victoria (1949/50, 1 match); South Australia (1950/1 to 1957/8, 55 matches). *Tours* Australia to England 1956, to India 1956/7. *Test* Australia (1956/7, 1 match).
Career batting
78–97–47–287–19*–5.74–0–*ct* 17
Bowling 7019–230–30.51–9–1–7/11
Test batting
1 match, did not bat –*ct* 0
Bowling 64–1–64.00–0–0–1/25

He took 43 wickets, av 23.06, on the 1956 tour to England and did not appear in the Tests.

Wilson, Leslie
Amateur. *b:* 16.3.1859, Canonbury, London. *d:* 15.4.1944, Bohemia, Hastings, Sussex. Brother of Cecil (Kent). Stylish middle order right-hand batsman, right-arm medium pace bowler, good deep field. *Sch* Tonbridge. *Team* Kent (1883–97, 105 matches).
Career batting
110–193–10–3554–132–19.42–1–*ct* 78
Bowling 265–6–44.16–0–0–2/17

Wilson, Mark
Amateur. *b:* 25.11.1890, Whitburn, West Lothian, Scotland. *d:* 3.8.1984, Scotland. Lower order left-hand batsman, left-arm fast medium bowler. *Team* Scotland (1925).
Career batting
1–2–0–4–4–2.00–0–*ct* 0
Bowling 23–0

Wilson, Peter Hugh L'Estrange
Cricketer. *b:* 17.8.1958, Guildford, Surrey. Lower order right-hand batsman, right-arm fast medium bowler. *Sch* Wellington. *Teams* Surrey (1978–82, 37 matches); Northern Transvaal (1979/80); Somerset (1983–84, 15 matches). *Tours* MCC to Bangladesh 1980/1, to East Africa 1981/2 (neither first-class).
Career batting
61–50–25–261–29–10.44–0–*ct* 11
Bowling 3394–110–30.85–1–0–5/36

Wilson, Peter James
Cricketer. *b:* 9.8.1942, Weston-super-Mare, Somerset. Lower order left-hand batsman, useful bowler. *Team* Oxford U (1964).
Career batting
2–3–0–56–30–18.66–0–*ct* 1

Wilson, Peter Robert Bain
Cricketer. *b:* 31.10.1944, Bulawayo, Rhodesia. Middle order right-hand batsman, leg break bowler. *Team* Oxford U (1968–70, blue 1968 and 1970).
Career batting
23–39–1–664–94–17.47–0–*ct* 9
Bowling 233–7–33.28–0–0–4/60

Wilson, Robert
Amateur. *b:* 8.4.1916, Edinburgh, Scotland. Tail end right-hand batsman, right-arm fast medium bowler. *Team* Scotland (1952).
Career batting
3–3–2–5–4–5.00–0–*ct* 1
Bowling 167–8–20.87–0–0–2/16

Wilson, Robert
Amateur. *b:* 12.2.1935, Paisley, Renfrewshire, Scotland. Opening left-hand batsman, slow left-arm bowler. *Team* Scotland (1955–56).
Career batting
3–5–0–64–29–12.80–0–*ct* 3

Wilson, Robert Colin
Professional. *b:* 18.2.1928, Bapchild, Kent. Father-in-law of S. A. Marsh (Kent). Sound middle order left-hand batsman, right-arm medium pace bowler. *Team* Kent (1952–67, 365 matches).
Career batting
367–647–39–19515–159*–32.09–30–*ct* 201
Bowling 90–4–22.50–0–0–3/38
He hit 1,000 runs in a season 13 times, going on to 2,000 once: 2,038, av 46.31, in 1964.

Wilson, Robert Greenwood
Amateur. *b:* 20.12.1922, Arnside, Westmorland. *d:* 6.3.1980, Swindon, Wiltshire. Aggressive lower order right-hand batsman, right-arm fast medium bowler. *Team* Combined Services (1948–52).
Career batting
14–25–2–662–100–28.78–1–*ct* 6
Bowling 655–24–27.29–1–0–5/41
He was Secretary of Nottinghamshire CCC 1972 to 1977.

Wilson, Robert Warley
Amateur. *b:* 15.7.1934, Warley, Worcestershire. Lower order right-hand batsman, off break bowler. *Sch* Warwick. *Team* Oxford U (1956–57, blue 1957).
Career batting
13–24–6–169–36*–9.38–0–*ct* 10
Bowling 1265–34–37.20–0–0–4/42
He also obtained his rugby blue.

Wilson, Roger Graham
Cricketer. *b:* 13.1.1943, Maidstone, Kent. Lower order right-hand batsman, slow left-arm and chinaman bowler. *Team* Cambridge U (1964).
Career batting
1–1–1–3–3*–no av–0–*ct* 1
Bowling 65–2–32.50–0–0–2/35

Wilson, Rev Rowland Alwyn
Amateur. *b:* 18.7.1868, Bolsterstone, Yorkshire. *d:* 1.10.1959, Hartlebury, Worcestershire. Brother of C. E. M. (Yorkshire) and E. R. (Yorkshire), uncle of D. C. (Cambridge U). Hard hitting lower order right-hand batsman, right-arm fast medium bowler. *Sch* Rugby. *Team* Cambridge U (1888–89).
Career batting
3–4–1–18–15–6.00–0–*ct* 3
Bowling 48–1–48.00–0–0–1/13
His County cricket was for Worcestershire (pre first-class, 1896–97).

Wilson, Sidney John
Amateur. *b:* 22.9.1858, Paddington, London. *d:* 1.2.1917, Flushing, Cornwall. Son of Alfred (Oxford U 1848). Middle order right-hand batsman, right-arm medium pace bowler. *Sch* Winchester. *Team* MCC (1882).
Career batting
1–2–0–8–6–4.00–0–*ct* 0
Bowling 2–0

Wilson, T.
Professional. Tail end batsman, useful bowler. *Team* Middlesex (1880, 1 match).
Career batting
1–1–0–5–5–5.00–0–*ct* 0
Bowling 31–0

Wilson, Theophilus Stuart Beatty
Amateur. *b:* 15.8.1870, Orion Downs, Springsure, Queensland, Australia. *d:* 19.5.1941, Orion Downs, Springsure, Queensland, Australia. Lower order right-hand batsman, right-arm fast bowler. *Sch* Bath College. *Team* Oxford U (1892–93, blue both years).
Career batting
17–31–2–186–36–6.41–0–*ct* 12
Bowling 1013–46–22.02–0–0–4/23
His County cricket was for Monmouthshire (1895).

Wilson, Thomas Crichton
Amateur. *b:* 18.11.1936, Eastbourne, Sussex. Lower order right-hand batsman, right-arm medium fast bowler. *Sch* Eastbourne. *Team* L. C. Stevens' XI (1960).
Career batting
1–1–1–0–0*–no av–0–*ct* 0
Bowling 42–1–42.00–0–0–1/25

Wilson, Thomas Henry
Amateur. *b:* 10.6.1841, Cheltenham, Gloucestershire. *d:* 31.1.1929, Tucuman, Argentine. Lower order bats-

man, wicket-keeper. *Sch* Harrow. *Team* Hampshire (1870, 2 matches).
Career batting
3–6–0–23–9–3.83–0–*ct* 0–*st* 1
His first-class debut was for MCC in 1869. He also played for Huntingdonshire (1866–67), Lincolnshire (1872) and Northamptonshire (pre first-class).

Wilson, Thomas Ward
Amateur. *b:* 1.4.1849, Nocton, Lincolnshire. *d:* 4.1.1924, Broadstone, Dorset. Tail end right-hand batsman, right-hand fast or medium pace round-arm bowler. *Sch* Repton. *Team* Cambridge U (1869–71, blue 1869).
Career batting
8–13–2–171–50–15.54–0–*ct* 1
Bowling 304–17–17.88–1–0–5/25
His County cricket was for Lincolnshire (1869–74), Norfolk (1870) and Dorset (1873–77). For 36 years he was a master at Sherborne School.

Wiltshire, Edgar
Amateur. *b:* 25.9.1877, Addiscombe, Surrey. *d:* 25.8.1912, Forest Hill, London. Middle order left-hand batsman, left-arm bowler. *Sch* Dulwich. *Team* Surrey (1902–03, 13 matches).
Career batting
13–22–2–219–33–10.95–0–*ct* 3

Wiltshire, Graham George Morley
Professional. *b:* 16.4.1931, Chipping Sodbury, Gloucestershire. Lower order right-hand batsman, right-arm medium fast bowler. *Team* Gloucestershire (1953–60, 19 matches). *Tour* Gloucestershire to Zambia 1971/2 (not first-class).
Career batting
19–30–4–218–39–8.38–0–*ct* 3
Bowling 835–25–33.40–1–0–7/52
He was coach to the Gloucestershire County Club 1962–84 and since then has been youth coach.

Wincer, Robert Colin
Cricketer. *b:* 2.4.1952, Portsmouth, Hampshire. Lower order left-hand batsman, right-arm fast medium bowler. *Team* Derbyshire (1978–80, 23 matches).
Career batting
23–21–8–131–26–10.07–0–*ct* 8
Bowling 1653–46–35.93–0–0–4/42

Winchester, Angus Lewis Charles
Cricketer. *b:* 28.11.1969, Newcastle upon Tyne, Northumberland. Lower order right-hand batsman, right-arm medium pace bowler. *Sch* Rugby. *Team* Oxford U (1990).
Career batting
1–1–1–1–0–0*–no av–0–*ct* 0
Bowling 81–0

Winchilsea, 9th Earl of, George Finch
Amateur. *b:* 4.11.1752, London. *d:* 2.8.1826, Mayfair, London. Middle order right-hand batsman. *Sch* Eton. *Teams* Hampshire (1787); Surrey (1801); MCC (1804).
Career batting
2–3–1–7–4–3.50–0–*ct* 0
He was President of Hambledon Club in 1787 and 1789 and was a member of the White Conduit Club. He, with others, persuaded Thomas Lord to found his cricket ground and thus was amongst the founding members of the MCC. He also staged matches at his country seat at Burley in Rutland. He is incorrectly given as the 8th Earl in volume XV of *Scores and Biographies.*

Windaybank, Stephen James
Cricketer. *b:* 20.10.1956, Pinner, Middlesex. Opening right-hand batsman. *Team* Gloucestershire (1979–82, 15 matches).
Career batting
15–19–4–385–53–25.66–0–*ct* 3

Winder, George Alexander
Amateur. *b:* 16.7.1850, Bolton, Lancashire. *d:* 1.2.1913, Fairmile, Ottery St Mary, Devon. Middle order right-hand batsman, good deep field. *Sch* Rossall. *Teams* Lancashire (1869, 2 matches); Cambridge U (1871).
Career batting
4–8–1–64–22–9.14–0–*ct* 1
In January 1872, when he was out shooting, his gun exploded and he lost his left hand as a result. This ended his serious cricket, but he continued to take part in minor matches. His final first-class match was for Gentlemen of the North in 1871.

Windows, Anthony Robin
Amateur. *b:* 25.9.1942, Clifton, Bristol. Father of M. G. N. (Gloucestershire). Middle order right-hand batsman, right-arm medium bowler. *Sch* Clifton. *Teams* Gloucestershire (1960–68, 98 matches); Cambridge U (1962–64, blue all three years). *Tour* MCC Under 25 to Pakistan 1966/7.
Career batting
149–241–33–3537–82–17.00–0–*ct* 42
Bowling 8308–286–29.04–9–0–8/78
He hit 1,003 runs, av 20.89, in 1962.

Windows, Matthew Guy Newman
Cricketer. *b:* 5.4.1973, Bristol. Son of A. R. (Gloucestershire). Middle order right-hand batsman. *Sch* Clifton. *Team* Gloucestershire (1992, 1 match).
Career batting
1–1–0–71–71–71.00–0–*ct* 1

Windridge, James Edwin
Professional. *b:* 21.10.1882, Sparkbrook, Birmingham. *d:* 23.9.1939, Hall Green, Birmingham. Lower order right-hand batsman, right-arm medium pace

bowler. *Team* Warwickshire (1909–13, 7 matches).
Career batting
7–12–1–161–34*–14.63–0–*ct* 2
Bowling 13–1–13.00–0–0–1/13

He played soccer for Chelsea, Middlesbrough, Birmingham and England.

Windsor, Raymond Thomas Albert
Cricketer. *b:* 9.2.1943, Wellington, Somerset. Middle order right-hand batsman. *Team* Somerset (1969, 1 match).
Career batting
1–1–0–0–0–0.00–0–*ct* 0

Windsor-Clive, Hon Archer
Amateur. *b:* 6.11.1890, Hewell Grange, Redditch, Worcestershire. *d:* 25.8.1914, Landrecies, France. Brother-in-law of H. F. Charteris (Gloucestershire). Lower order batsman, left-arm medium pace bowler. *Sch* Eton. *Team* Cambridge U (1910–12).
Career batting
7–14–1–108–22–8.30–0–*ct* 1
Bowling 217–3–72.33–0–0–3/56

His County cricket was for Glamorgan (pre first-class, 1908–12).

Winfield, Hugh Mervyn
Professional. *b:* 13.6.1933, Gainsborough, Lincolnshire. Sound middle order right-hand batsman. *Team* Nottinghamshire (1954–66, 172 matches).
Career batting
172–311–16–6799–134–23.04–7–*ct* 131
Bowling 5–0

He hit 1,000 runs in a season four times (best 1,552, av 30.43, in 1959). He also played for Shropshire (1967–69) and Lincolnshire (1970–71). He was a noted table tennis player.

Wing, Derek Charles
Cricketer. *b:* 11.2.1943, Wisbech, Cambridgeshire. Lower order right-hand batsman, right-arm fast medium bowler. *Sch* Kimbolton. *Teams* MCC (1967–68); Minor Counties (1969–76). *Tours* MCC to West Africa 1975/6, to Bangladesh 1976/7, to Far East 1981/2 (none first-class).
Career batting
5–5–1–59–42–14.75–0–*ct* 1
Bowling 375–7–53.57–0–0–3/20

His County cricket was for Cambridgeshire (1964–88).

Wingfield, W.
Professional. Middle order batsman. *Team* Surrey (1881, 3 matches).
Career batting
3–6–0–13–5–2.16–0–*ct* 2

Wingfield, Rev William
Amateur. *b:* 30.9.1834, Newtown, Montgomeryshire. *d:* 18.4.1913, Coton Hill, Shrewsbury, Shropshire. Attacking middle order right-hand batsman, wicket-keeper. *Sch* Rossall. *Teams* Cambridge U (1855–57, blue all three years); Cambridgeshire (1857, 2 matches).
Career batting
14–25–1–314–69–13.08–0–*ct* 9–*st* 4

He also played for Shropshire (1853–81). His final first-class match was for Gentlemen of the South in 1862. He was coxswain of the Cambridge boat in 1855 and 1856.

Wingfield Digby, Rev Andrew Richard
Cricketer. *b:* 25.7.1950, Sherborne, Dorset. Lower order left-hand batsman, right-arm medium pace bowler. *Sch* Sherborne. *Team* Oxford U (1971–77, blue 1971 and 1975–77).
Career batting
39–62–4–720–69–12.41–0–*ct* 20
Bowling 3252–96–33.87–4–0–5/79

His County cricket was for Dorset (1972–92). After being at Oxford in 1971 and 1972, he returned in 1974 to study theology. He is a leading figure in the Christians in Sport movement.

Winlaw, Ashley William Edgell
Amateur. *b:* 8.2.1914, Sydenham, London. *d:* 13.2.1988, Portsmouth, Hampshire. Brother of R. de W. K. (Surrey). Middle order right-hand batsman, wicket-keeper. *Sch* Winchester. *Team* Minor Counties (1936).
Career batting
1–2–0–13–13–6.50–0–*ct* 1

He appeared in the Cambridge Freshmen's match of 1934 and his County cricket was for Bedfordshire (1935–39).

Winlaw, Roger de Winton Kelsall
Amateur. *b:* 28.3.1912, Morden, Surrey. *d:* 31.10.1942, Caernarvon. Brother of A. W. E. (Minor Counties). Middle order right-hand batsman. *Sch* Winchester. *Teams* Cambridge U (1932–34, blue all three years); Surrey (1932–34, 17 matches).
Career batting
52–89–13–2708–161*–35.63–7–*ct* 17
Bowling 31–0

He hit 1,330 runs, av 42.90, in 1934. His final first-class match was for an England XI in 1937. He also played for Bedfordshire (1932–39). He was killed in the same flying incident as C. T. Ashton (Essex).

Winn, Christopher Elliott
Amateur. *b:* 13.11.1926, Beckenham, Kent. Forceful middle order left-hand batsman. *Sch* KCS Wimbledon. *Teams* Oxford U (1948–51, blue all four years); Sussex (1948–52, 15 matches).
Career batting
59–100–2–2449–146*–24.98–2–*ct* 40–*st* 1
Bowling 34–1–34.00–0–0–1/21

His final first-class match was for MCC in 1961. A rugby footballer, he played for Oxford and for England. He married the well-known athlete Valerie Ball.

Winning, Charles Samuel
Amateur. *b:* 17.7.1889, Paddington, Sydney, New South Wales, Australia. *d:* 20.4.1967, Newport, Sydney, New South Wales, Australia. Lower order right-hand batsman, right-arm medium pace bowler. *Team* AIF (1919 to 1919/20). *Tours* AIF to England 1919, to South Africa 1919/20.
Career batting
28–35–17–253–30–14.05–0–*ct* 22
Bowling 1605–67–23.95–3–0–6/30
He took 51 wickets, av 22.82, for the AIF in 1919. His final first-class match was for AIF in Australia in 1919/20.

Winnington, John Francis Sartorius
Amateur. *b:* 17.9.1876, Charlton Kings, Gloucestershire. *d:* 22.9.1918, near Kefar Kassin, Ramle, Palestine. Middle order right-hand batsman. *Team* Worcestershire (1908, 1 match).
Career batting
1–2–0–20–20–10.00–0–*ct* 0

Winrow, Frederick Henry
Professional. *b:* 17.1.1916, Manton, Nottinghamshire. *d:* 19.8.1973, Amalinda, East London, South Africa. Brother of Robert (Nottinghamshire). Sound middle order left-hand batsman, slow left-arm bowler. *Team* Nottinghamshire (1938–51, 113 matches).
Career batting
113–180–20–4769–204*–29.80–6–*ct* 34
Bowling 4009–95–42.20–3–0–6/65
He hit 1,000 runs in a season twice (best 1,459, av 37.41, in 1950). His only double century was 204* for Nottinghamshire v Derbyshire at Trent Bridge in 1947. He emigrated to South Africa in 1952/3.

Winrow, Robert
Professional. *b:* 30.12.1910, Manton, Nottinghamshire. Brother of F. H. (Nottinghamshire). Middle order left-hand batsman, slow left-arm bowler. *Teams* Nottinghamshire (1932–35, 5 matches); Scotland (1949).
Career batting
7–10–1–237–137–26.33–1–*ct* 2
Bowling 76–1–76.00–0–0–1/27

Winslow, Lyndhurst
Amateur. *b:* 10.1.1855, Leamington, Warwickshire. *d:* 1910, Queenstown, Cape Province, South Africa. Cousin of O. E. (Sussex), grandfather of P. L. (South Africa). Attacking middle order right-hand batsman. *Sch* Somerset College. *Team* Sussex (1875, 5 matches).
Career batting
8–11–0–337–124–30.63–1–*ct* 4
Bowling 13–0
He emigrated to South Africa about 1876 and was a noted cricketer there, appearing in the Champion Bat Tournament and against the English touring team of 1888/9, but not in first-class matches. He scored 124 on debut for Sussex v Gloucestershire at Hove in 1875.

Winslow, Dr Lyttelton Stewart Forbes
(changed name to L. S. Forbes-Winslow in 1874)
Amateur. *b:* 31.1.1844, Marylebone, London. *d:* 8.6.1913, Marylebone, London. Middle order batsman. *Sch* Rugby. *Team* MCC (1864).
Career batting
1–2–0–3–3–1.50–0–*ct* 0
Bowling 13–0

Winslow, Octavius Evans
Amateur. *b:* 10.9.1850, Leamington, Warwickshire. *d:* 13.10.1896, Bermondsey, London. Cousin of Lyndhurst (Sussex). Opening right-hand batsman, right-hand medium pace round-arm bowler, point field. *Sch* Somerset College. *Team* Sussex (1869, 5 matches).
Career batting
5–10–0–207–56–20.70–0–*ct* 1
Owing to a knee injury he rarely played after 1869. He also played for Somerset (pre first-class, 1866).

Winslow, Paul Lyndhurst
Amateur. *b:* 21.5.1929, Johannesburg, South Africa. Grandson of Lyndhurst (Sussex). Forcing middle order right-hand batsman, leg break bowler, good field. *Teams* Sussex (1949, 1 match); Transvaal (1949/50 to 1955/6); Rhodesia (1956/7 to 1959/60). *Tour* South Africa to England 1955. *Tests* South Africa (1949/50 to 1955, 5 matches).
Career batting
75–124–6–2755–139–23.34–2–*ct* 85
Bowling 61–1–61.00–0–0–1/12
Test batting
5–9–0–186–108–20.66–1–*ct* 1
He was moderately successful on the 1955 tour to England and appeared in three Tests. His final first-class match was for a Rhodesian Invitation XI in 1961/2.

Winstone, Alec Ethelbert
Professional. *b:* 14.3.1879, Staple Hill, Bristol. *d:* 29.3.1963, Staple Hill, Bristol. Middle order right-hand batsman, slow right-arm bowler. *Team* Gloucestershire (1906–09, 44 matches).
Career batting
44–80–3–975–58–12.66–0–*ct* 19
Bowling 130–4–32.50–0–0–1/12

Winter, Rev Arthur Henry
Amateur. *b:* 4.12.1844, Clapham Green, London. *d:* 31.12.1937, Hemingford Abbots, Huntingdonshire. Brother of William (Middlesex), uncle of G. E. (Middlesex) and C. E. (Cambridge U). Stylish opening right-hand batsman, wicket-keeper. *Sch* Westminster. *Teams* Cambridge U (1865–67, blue all three years); Middlesex (1866–67, 3 matches).

Career batting
29–55–0–1155–121–21.00–1–*ct* 24–*st* 3

His final first-class match was for MCC in 1870. He also played for Huntingdonshire (1884).

Winter, Cecil Esdaile
Amateur. *b:* 1.9.1879, Deal, Kent. *d:* 20.7.1964, Hove, Sussex. Son of William (Middlesex), brother of G. E. (Middlesex), nephew of A. H. (Middlesex). Lower order right-hand batsman, wicket-keeper. *Sch* Uppingham. *Team* Cambridge U (1901–02, blue 1902).
Career batting
10–13–5–53–18–6.62–0–*ct* 7–*st* 11

Winter, Charles Arthur
Amateur. *b:* 24.12.1903, Edmonton, Middlesex. *d:* 4.3.1982, Farnham Common, Buckinghamshire. Son of C. E. (Somerset). Lower order right-hand batsman, right-arm fast medium bowler. *Sch* Repton. *Team* Somerset (1921–25, 26 matches).
Career batting
26–47–7–437–44*–10.92–0–*ct* 5
Bowling 572–15–38.13–0–0–4/61

Winter, Charles Edgar
Amateur. *b:* 9.10.1866, Bermondsey, London. *d:* 3.4.1954, Northwood, Middlesex. Father of C. A. (Somerset). Lower order batsman, right-arm fast bowler. *Team* Somerset (1882–95, 25 matches).
Career batting
25–45–8–319–62–8.62–0–*ct* 11
Bowling 1107–50–22.14–0–0–4/20

He first played for Somerset (pre first-class) in 1881.

Winter, Charles Henry
Amateur. *b:* 17.2.1890, Philadelphia, USA. *d:* 25.1.1969, Wilmington, Delaware, USA. Tail end right-hand batsman, wicket-keeper. *Team* Philadelphia (1908–13). *Tours* Philadelphia to England 1908, to Jamaica 1908/9.
Career batting
13–22–10–70–18*–5.83–0–*ct* 13–*st* 16

He appeared in four matches for USA v Canada and was regarded as the leading wicket-keeper in America for some years.

Winter, Gerald Esdaile
(birth registered as E. G. Winter)
Amateur. *b:* 29.11.1876, Kensington, London. *d:* 17.1.1923, Marylebone, London. Son of William (Middlesex), brother of C. E. (Oxford U), nephew of A. H. (Middlesex). Free scoring middle order right-hand batsman, right-hand slow under-arm bowler. *Sch* Winchester. *Teams* Cambridge U (1898–99, blue both years); Middlesex (1900, 2 matches). *Tour* Warner to North America 1898.
Career batting
22–37–2–738–86–21.08–0–*ct* 19
Bowling 527–22–23.95–1–1–6/59

His final first-class match was for H. D. G. Leveson-Gower's XI in 1902. He also played for Cambridgeshire (1896).

Winter, H. E.
Amateur. Lower order batsman. *Team* Somerset (1884, 1 match).
Career batting
1–2–1–24–24*–24.00–0–*ct* 0
Bowling 9–0

Winter, John Arundell
Amateur. *b:* 28.7.1851, Ash Priors, Taunton, Somerset. *d:* 15.5.1914, Hampton Wick, Middlesex. Middle order batsman. *Team* Somerset (1884, 1 match).
Career batting
1–2–0–4–4–2.00–0–*ct* 1

He first played for Somerset (not first-class) in 1878. He was Somerset Treasurer 1881–85.

Winter, William
Amateur. *b:* 24.4.1843, Clapham Green, London. *d:* 22.8.1905, Rosenlaui, near Meiringen, Berne, Switzerland. He was killed while mountaineering. Father of G. E. (Middlesex) and C. E. (Oxford U), brother of A. H. (Middlesex). Opening right-hand batsman, right-hand slow under-arm bowler, wicket-keeper. *Sch* Westminster. *Team* Middlesex (1873, 1 match).
Career batting
1–2–1–14–14*–14.00–0–*ct* 1–*st* 2

He also played for Huntingdonshire (1884).

Winterborne, Gary
Cricketer. *b:* 26.6.1967, Hammersmith, London. Lower order right-hand batsman, right-arm medium pace bowler. *Team* Surrey (1986, 1 match).
Career batting
1 match, did not bat–*ct* 0
Bowling 47–0

Winterbotham, Arthur Strachan
Amateur. *b:* 28.6.1864, Dursley, Gloucestershire. *d:* 15.6.1936, Stonehouse, Gloucestershire. Middle order right-hand batsman, right-arm slow bowler. *Sch* Rugby. *Team* Gloucestershire (1885, 3 matches).
Career batting
3–5–1–53–35–13.25–0–*ct* 0
Bowling 28–0

Winterbotham, James Percival
Amateur. *b:* 21.6.1883, Pittville, Cheltenham, Gloucestershire. *d:* 2.12.1925, Marle Hill, Cheltenham, Gloucestershire. Lower order left-hand batsman, slow left-arm bowler. *Sch* Cheltenham. *Teams* Gloucestershire (1902, 1 match); Oxford U (1903–04).
Career batting
3–6–3–25–12*–8.33–0–*ct* 3
Bowling 206–4–51.50–0–0–2/68

He represented Gloucestershire at both hockey and golf. He won a blue for hockey.

Winterburn, Frederick
Professional. *b:* 10.12.1857, London. *d:* 21.4.1926, Kingsland, Hackney, London. Tail end right-hand batsman, wicket-keeper. *Team* Middlesex (1883, 4 matches).
Career batting
4–5–1–19–8–4.75–0–*ct* 6–*st* 5

Winterflood, Thomas
Amateur. *c:* 20.7.1832, Lambeth, London. *d:* 20.2.1900, Brixton Hill, London. Middle order batsman. *Team* Surrey Club (1866).
Career batting
1 match, did not bat–*ct* 0
Bowling 6–0
He was on the Committee of Surrey CCC for many years.

Winwood, Thomas Lawson
Amateur. *b:* 7.2.1910, Dudley, Worcestershire. Middle order right-hand batsman, right-arm medium pace bowler. *Team* Worcestershire (1930–34, 18 matches).
Career batting
18–30–4–404–104–15.53–1–*ct* 6
Bowling 10–0

Wisden, John
Professional. *b:* 5.9.1826, Brighton, Sussex. *d:* 5.4.1884, Westminster, London. Lower order right-hand batsman, originally right-hand fast round-arm, but after about 1857, medium pace round-arm, or slow under-arm, bowler, good slip field. *Team* Sussex (1845–63, 82 matches); Kent (1854, 1 match as given man); Middlesex (1859–63, 3 matches). *Tour* Parr to North America 1859 (not first-class).
Career batting
186–326–33–4140–148–14.12–2–*ct* 169–*st* 1
Bowling 7073–681 + 428–10.38–111–39–10/58
He took 100 wickets in a season three times (best 129 in 1849). He twice took 10 wickets in an innings, once against odds, and once for North v South at Lord's in 1850 (all bowled). In 1864 he published for the first time *John Wisden's Cricketers' Almanack*. He also played for Norfolk (1848), Essex (pre first-class, 1848), Warwickshire (pre first-class, 1849–52) and Northamptonshire (pre first-class, 1852).

Wisdom, Nicholas
Cricketer. *b:* 18.3.1953, Potters Bar, Hertfordshire. Lower order right-hand batsman, right-arm medium pace bowler. *Sch* Charterhouse. *Team* Sussex (1974, 2 matches).
Career batting
2–2–1–35–31*–35.00–0–*ct* 0
Bowling 33–2–16.50–0–0–1/0
He is the son of the comedian, Norman Wisdom.

Wisson, Philip Wesley
Amateur. *b:* 26.4.1935, Everton, Bedfordshire. Middle order right-hand batsman, wicket-keeper. *Sch* Enfield GS. *Team* Cambridge U (1958).
Career batting
2–4–0–24–14–6.00–0–*ct* 0
He was a goalkeeper with Cambridge Falcons.

Witchell, Henry Gough
Amateur. *b:* 8.4.1906, Dursley, Gloucestershire. *d:* 24.8.1965, Cotham Hill, Bristol. Middle order batsman. *Team* Gloucestershire (1923, 1 match).
Career batting
3–3–0–9–5–3.00–0–*ct* 0
He also played for Wiltshire (1934–38) and his final first-class match was for Minor Counties in 1935.

Witherden, Edwin George
Professional. *b:* 1.5.1922, Goudhurst, Kent. Middle order right-hand batsman, off break bowler, slip field. *Team* Kent (1951–55, 40 matches).
Career batting
40–71–9–1380–125*–22.25–2–*ct* 13
Bowling 371–9–41.22–1–0–5/32
He also played for Norfolk (1956–62).

Witherington, Denys March
Amateur. *b:* 25.7.1921, Hendon, Sunderland, Co Durham. *d:* 16.2.1944, near Anzio, Italy. Middle order right-hand batsman, wicket-keeper. *Sch* The Leys. *Team* Cambridge U (1939).
Career batting
4–7–2–147–52*–29.40–0–*ct* 5–*st* 1

Wolfe-Murray, James Archibald
Amateur. *b:* 25.4.1936, West End, Edinburgh, Scotland. Son-in-law of Lord Dunglass (Middlesex). Lower order right-hand batsman, right-arm fast medium bowler. *Sch* Eton. *Team* Oxford U (1957).
Career batting
3–5–2–43–25–14.33–0–*ct* 3
Bowling 155–3–51.66–0–0–1/20

Wolfson, Andrew Cecil
Amateur. *b:* 1.5.1890, Santa Cruz, Canary Islands. *d:* 26.7.1978, Forest Row, Sussex. Lower order batsman, right-arm medium pace bowler. *Sch* Marlborough. *Team* Leveson-Gower's XI (1920).
Career batting
2–3–2–14–8–14.00–0–*ct* 0
Bowling 53–2–26.50–0–0–1/4

Wollocombe, Richard Henry
Amateur. *b:* 12.1.1926, Pachmarhi, India. Middle order right-hand batsman, leg break bowler. *Sch* Wellington. *Team* Oxford U (1951–52).
Career batting
9–16–2–314–119–22.42–1–*ct* 1
Bowling 623–10–62.30–0–0–2/33
His County cricket was for Berkshire (1950).

Wolton, Albert Victor George
Professional. *b:* 12.6.1919, Maidenhead, Berkshire. *d:* 9.9.1990, Solihull, Warwickshire. Middle order right-hand batsman, off break bowler, good cover field. *Team* Warwickshire (1947–60, 296 matches).
Career batting
297–478–61–12930–165–31.00–12–*ct* 117
Bowling 1226–37–33.13–0–0–4/15
He hit 1,000 runs in a season seven times (best 1,809, av 34.13, in 1955). He also played for Berkshire (1937–39).

Womersley, Leonard Dale
Amateur. *b:* 10.9.1891, Frynerning Green, Ingatestone, Essex. *d:* 10.2.1971, Chelmsford, Essex. Middle order batsman. *Sch* Marlborough. *Team* Essex (1910, 1 match).
Career batting
1–2–0–9–9–4.50–0–*ct* 0
He played no first-class matches at Oxford U, but did win a blue for billiards.

Wood, Alfred Herbert
Amateur. *b:* 23.4.1866, Portsmouth, Hampshire. *d:* 19.4.1941, Southsea, Hampshire. Middle order batsman. *Sch* Wellington. *Team* Hampshire (1901, 1 match).
Career batting
1–2–0–22–11–11.00–0–*ct* 1

Wood, Arthur
Professional. *b:* 25.8.1898, Fagley, Bradford, Yorkshire. *d:* 1.4.1973, Middleton, Ilkley, Yorkshire. Lower order right-hand batsman, wicket-keeper. *Team* Yorkshire (1927–46, 408 matches). *Tours* Yorkshire to Jamaica 1935/6; Brinckman to South America 1937/8. *Tests* England (1938–39, 4 matches).
Career batting
420–500–83–8842–123*–21.20–1–*ct* 631–*st* 257
Bowling 33–1–33.00–0–0–1/33
Test batting
4–5–1–80–53–20.00–0–*ct* 10–*st* 1
He hit 1,249 runs, av 30.46, in 1935. His final first-class match was for an England XI in 1948.

Wood, Rear-Admiral Arthur Edmund
Amateur. *b:* 23.2.1875, Hartley Wintney, Hampshire. *d:* 30.1.1961, Ryton, Co Durham. Middle order batsman. *Team* Royal Navy (1912).
Career batting
1–2–1–16–11*–16.00–0–*ct* 1
Bowling 12–0

Wood, Arthur Hardy
Amateur. *b:* 25.5.1844, Thedden Grange, Alton, Hampshire. *d:* 10.7.1933, Hove, Sussex. Middle order right-hand batsman, wicket-keeper. *Sch* Eton. *Team* Hampshire (1870–85, 28 matches).
Career batting
30–52–3–876–82–17.87–0–*ct* 25–*st* 5
Bowling 17–0
He captained Hampshire in 1870 and from 1883 to 1885 and was President of the County Club in 1886. Well-known on the hunting field, he was Secretary of the Hampshire Hunt.

Wood, Arthur John
Amateur. *b:* 7.2.1892, Derby. *d:* 1.3.1951, Norwood, Surrey. Opening right-hand batsman, right-arm fast medium bowler. *Sch* Denstone. *Team* Derbyshire (1911–12, 13 matches).
Career batting
13–19–1–264–52–14.66–0–*ct* 5
Bowling 64–0
He appeared in the Cambridge Freshmen's match of 1912.

Wood, Arthur Machin
Amateur for Derbyshire, but professional 1880 to 1885, then reverted to amateur. *b:* 21.2.1861, Pye Bridge, Derbyshire. *d:* 25.8.1947, Philadelphia, USA. Sound opening right-hand batsman, right-arm slow bowler, occasional wicket-keeper, excellent field. *Sch* Nottingham HS. *Teams* Derbyshire (1879, 2 matches); Philadelphia (1892–1909). *Tours* Philadelphia to England 1897, 1903, 1908.
Career batting
70–122–4–2648–182–22.44–3–*ct* 96
Bowling 348–13–26.76–1–0–6/31
He played for Nottinghamshire v Leicestershire (not first-class) in 1878. He was for many years one of the principal batsmen in Philadelphia and represented USA v Canada seven times commencing 1892. His most successful tour to England was in 1897 when he hit 702 runs, av 28.08. His first first-class match in America was for English Residents in 1881.

Wood, Barry
Cricketer. *b:* 26.12.1942, Ossett, Yorkshire. Brother of Ronald (Yorkshire). Sound opening right-hand batsman, right-arm medium pace bowler. *Teams* Yorkshire (1964, 5 matches); Lancashire (1966–79, 260 matches); Derbyshire (1980–83, 63 matches); Eastern Province (1971/2 to 1973/4). *Tours* MCC to India, Pakistan and Sri Lanka 1972/3, to New Zealand 1974/5; English Counties to West Indies 1974/5 (not first-class); International Wanderers to Rhodesia 1975/6. *Tests* England (1972–78, 12 matches).
Career batting
357–591–75–17453–198–33.82–30–*ct* 283
Bowling 9160–298–30.73–8–0–7/52
Test batting
12–21–0–454–90–21.61–0–*ct* 6
Bowling 50–0
He hit 1,000 runs in a season eight times (best 1,492, av 38.25, in 1971). His Testimonial in 1979 raised £62,429. He was appointed Derbyshire captain

during the 1981 season, and resigned during 1983. He also played for Cheshire (1986–88).

Wood, Benjamin Shaw
Cricketer. *b:* 25.1.1971, Dewsbury, Yorkshire. Tail end right-hand batsman, right-arm medium fast bowler. *Team* Oxford U (1991–92, blue both years).
Career batting
13–10–2–37–13–4.62–0–*ct* 0
Bowling 1017–16–63.56–0–0–2/24

Wood, Cecil John Burditt
Amateur to 1895, professional 1896, reverted to amateur 1897. *b:* 21.11.1875, Northampton. *d:* 5.6.1960, Leicester. Stubborn opening right-hand batsman, right-arm slow bowler. *Sch* Wellingborough. *Teams* Leicestershire (1896–1923, 423 matches); London County (1900–04).
Career batting
456–823–54–23879–225–31.05–37–*ct* 180
Bowling 6782–172–39.43–3–0–6/79

He hit 1,000 runs in a season 13 times, going on to 2,000 once: 2,033, av 41.48, in 1901. Both his double centuries were for Leicestershire the higher being 225 v Worcestershire at Worcester in 1906. He captained the County in 1914, 1919 and 1920. He carried his bat through the completed Leicestershire innings no fewer than 17 times and in the match v Yorkshire at Bradford in 1911 in both innings. He also played for Northamptonshire (pre first-class, 1895). He was Leicestershire Secretary in 1940 and 1941. A good soccer player, he appeared for Leicester Fosse.

Wood, Christopher Harland
Professional. *b:* 23.7.1934, Manningham, Bradford, Yorkshire. Lower order right-hand batsman, right-arm fast medium bowler. *Team* Yorkshire (1959, 4 matches).
Career batting
4–4–1–22–10–7.33–0–*ct* 1
Bowling 319–11–29.00–0–0–4/39

Wood, David John
Cricketer. *b:* 10.1.1965, Cuckfield, Sussex. Opening left-hand batsman, slow left-arm bowler. *Team* Sussex (1984, 2 matches).
Career batting
2–3–0–32–15–10.66–0–*ct* 0

Wood, Douglas James
Professional. *b:* 19.5.1914, Horsted Keynes, Sussex. *d:* 12.3.1989, Horsted Keynes, Sussex. Tail end right-hand batsman, left-arm fast medium bowler. *Team* Sussex (1936–55, 213 matches).
Career batting
214–251–72–1305–42–7.29–0–*ct* 89
Bowling 18140–589–30.79–21–1–7/24

He took 103 wickets, av 24.56, in 1952. He was a first-class umpire (1957–62).

Wood, Major General Edward Alexander
Amateur. *b:* 8.5.1841, Kensington, London. *d:* 22.5.1898, Shorncliffe, Kent. Middle order batsman. *Sch* Radley and Eton. *Team* MCC (1875).
Career batting
1–2–1–8–8–8.00–0–*ct* 1

Wood, Edwin James
Professional. *b:* 25.11.1868, Wymeswold, Leicestershire. Lower order batsman, wicket-keeper. *Team* Leicestershire (1907, 1 match).
Career batting
1–2–0–1–1–0.50–0–*ct* 2–*st* 1

Wood, Geoffrey Dayrell
Amateur. *b:* 17.8.1891, Hampstead, London. *d:* 13.10.1915, Hohenzollern, near Loos, France. He was killed in action. Lower order batsman, slow left-arm bowler. *Sch* Cheltenham. *Team* Oxford U (1912).
Career batting
1–1–0–0–0–0.00–0–*ct* 0
Bowling 36–2–18.00–0–0–1/16

His County cricket was for Suffolk (1910–11).

Wood, George Edward Charles
Amateur. *b:* 22.8.1893, Blackheath, Kent. *d:* 18.3.1971, Christchurch, Hampshire. Opening or middle order right-hand batsman, occasional right-arm medium pace bowler, excellent wicket-keeper. *Sch* Cheltenham. *Teams* Cambridge U (1913–20, blue 1914, 1919 and 1920); Kent (1919–27, 41 matches). *Tour* Martineau to Egypt 1929 (not first-class). *Tests* England (1924, 3 matches).
Career batting
101–157–18–2773–128–19.94–1–*ct* 116–*st* 53
Bowling 9–0
Test batting
3–2–0–7–6–3.50–0–*ct* 5–*st* 1

His final first-class match was for H. D. G. Leveson-Gower's XI in 1936. He captained Cambridge in 1920. Whilst at Cambridge he also gained blues for rugby football and hockey.

Wood, George Henry
Amateur. *b:* 21.5.1846, Liverpool, Lancashire. Lower order batsman, useful bowler. *Team* MCC (1880–82).
Career batting
2–3–1–2–2–1.00–0–*ct* 0
Bowling 22–0

Wood, Rev George Robert
Amateur. *b:* 7.12.1865, Reading, Berkshire. *d:* 3.9.1948, Lyme Regis, Dorset. Nephew of W. E. Goschen (Oxford U). Middle order right-hand batsman. *Sch* Haileybury. *Team* Somerset (1893–94, 3 matches).
Career batting
3–5–0–84–52–16.80–0–*ct* 1

He also played for Oxfordshire (1893–1902).

Wood, George William
Professional. *b:* 18.11.1862, Huddersfield, Yorkshire. *d:* 4.12.1948, Mold Green, Huddersfield, Yorkshire. Lower order batsman, wicket-keeper. *Team* Yorkshire (1895, 2 matches).
Career batting
2–2–0–2–2–1.00–0–*ct* 0–*st* 1

Wood, Graeme Malcolm
Cricketer. *b:* 6.11.1956, East Fremantle, Perth, Western Australia. Brother-in-law of M. R. J. Veletta (Western Australia). Opening left-hand batsman, right-arm medium pace bowler. *Team* Western Australia (1976/7 to 1991/2, 125 matches). *Tours* Australia to West Indies 1977/8, 1983/4, to India 1979/80, 1984/5 (not first-class), to England 1980, 1981, 1983 (World Cup), 1985, to New Zealand 1981/2, to Pakistan 1982/3, 1988/9, to Sri Lanka 1980/1, 1982/3, to Sharjah (not first-class) 1984/5; Western Australia to India 1989/90. *Tests* Australia (1977/8 to 1988/89, 59 matches).
Career batting
227–375–41–13353–186*–39.97–35–*ct* 155
Bowling 156–6–26.00–0–0–3/18
Test batting
59–112–6–3374–172–31.83–9–*ct* 41

On the 1981 tour to England he hit 690 runs, av 31.36, and played in all six Tests, but with only moderate success. On the 1985 tour to England he was too often dismissed attempting to hook and in five Tests his only innings of note was 172 at Trent Bridge. He scored 1,050 runs, av 70.00, in Australia in 1987/8.

Wood, Henry
Professional. *b:* 14.12.1853, Dartford, Kent. *d:* 30.4.1919, Waddon, Surrey. Middle order right-hand batsman, right-hand fast round-arm bowler, excellent wicket-keeper. *Teams* Kent (1876–82, 9 matches); Surrey (1884–1900, 286 matches). *Tours* Warton to South Africa 1888/9; Read to South Africa 1891/2. *Tests* England (1888 to 1891/2, 4 matches).
Career batting
316–422–96–5523–134*–16.94–1–*ct* 556–*st* 118
Bowling 42–0
Test batting
4–4–1–204–134*–68.00–1–*ct* 2–*st* 1

His only first-class century was scored in the 1891/2 Test match at Cape Town. He was a first-class umpire (1910–12).

Wood, Henry
Amateur. *b:* 7.4.1872, Bath, Somerset. *b:* 1.12.1950, Bath, Somerset. Middle order batsman. *Team* Somerset (1904, 1 match).
Career batting
1–2–2–16–12*–no av–0–*ct* 0

Wood, Rev Henry Thellusson
Amateur. *b:* 1850, Aldbury, Hertfordshire. *d:* 21.7.1928, Aldbury, Hertfordshire. Middle order right-hand batsman. *Team* An All England Eleven (1872).
Career batting
1–2–0–43–43–21.50–0–*ct* 2

His County cricket was for Hertfordshire (1876–78).

Wood, Rev Hugh
Amateur. *b:* 22.3.1855, Ecclesall, Sheffield, Yorkshire. *d:* 31.7.1941, Whitchurch, Buckinghamshire. Lower order right-hand batsman, slow left-arm bowler, close field. *Teams* Cambridge U (1878–79, blue 1879); Yorkshire (1879–80, 10 matches).
Career batting
21–26–3–217–36–9.43–0–*ct* 16
Bowling 759–67–11.32–5–1–7/41

Wood, J. H.
Amateur. Middle order batsman, long stop. *Team* Yorkshire (1881, 2 matches).
Career batting
2–1–0–14–14–14.00–0–*ct* 0

Wood, James
Professional. *b:* 26.6.1933, Royton, Lancashire. *d:* 30.6.1977, Blackpool, Lancashire. Lower order right-hand batsman, bowler. *Team* Lancashire (1956, 1 match).
Career batting
1 match, did not bat–*ct* 1
Bowling 103–4–25.75–0–0–3/56

Wood, John
Cricketer. *b:* 22.7.1970, Wakefield, Yorkshire. Lower order right-hand batsman, right-arm fast medium bowler. *Team* Durham (1992, 8 matches).
Career batting
8–6–1–80–28–16.00–0–*ct* 1
Bowling 534–17–31.41–1–0–5/68

He first played for Durham (pre first-class) in 1991. In 1990/1 he appeared for Griqualand West in limited overs cricket.

Wood, Sir John Barry
Amateur. *b:* 27.4.1870, Cheltenham, Gloucestershire. *d:* 10.2.1933, Virginia Water, Surrey. Middle order right-hand batsman, right-hand slow under-arm bowler, good field. *Sch* Marlborough. *Team* Oxford U (1891–93, blue 1892 and 1893).
Career batting
16–30–3–384–50–14.22–0–*ct* 10
Bowling 1399–53–26.39–3–0–6/68

His County cricket was for Warwickshire (pre first-class, 1890–91).

Wood, Julian Ross
Cricketer. *b:* 21.11.1968, Winchester, Hampshire. Middle order left-hand batsman, right-arm medium pace bowler. *Team* Hampshire (1989–92, 26 matches).

Wood, Lindsay Jonathan

Career batting
26–35–3–935–96–29.21–0–*ct* 13
Bowling 38–1–38.00–0–0–1/5

Wood, Lindsay Jonathan
Cricketer. *b:* 12.5.1961, Ruislip, Middlesex. Lower order left-hand batsman, slow left-arm bowler. *Teams* Kent (1981–82, 2 matches); Derbyshire (1986, 2 matches).
Career batting
4–4–0–12–5–3.00–0–*ct* 0
Bowling 277–6–46.16–0–0–4/124

Wood, Sir Matthew
Amateur. *b:* 21.9.1857, Isle of Wight. *d:* 13.7.1908, Brompton, Kensington, London. Middle order right-hand batsman, slow under-arm bowler. *Sch* Winchester. *Team* Hampshire (1876, 1 match).
Career batting
1–2–0–0–0–0.00–0–*ct* 0
He also played for Essex (pre first-class, 1879).

Wood, Maurice
Professional. *b:* 6.7.1933, Nottingham. *d:* 18.3.1978, Nottingham. Lower order right-hand batsman, right-arm fast medium bowler. *Team* Nottinghamshire (1955, 4 matches).
Career batting
4–5–2–5–4–1.66–0–*ct* 2
Bowling 231–4–57.75–0–0–2/68

Wood, Maxmillian David Francis
Amateur. *b:* 22.2.1873, Kamptee, India. *d:* 22.8.1915, near Ismail Oglu Tepe, Gallipoli Peninsula, Turkey. He married the widow of D. H. B. H. Blundell (MCC). Middle order right-hand batsman, right-arm fast medium bowler, good outfield. *Sch* Wellington. *Teams* Europeans (1897/8 to 1902/3); Hampshire (1907, 1 match).
Career batting
10–19–0–196–30–10.31–0–*ct* 8
Bowling 483–34–14.20–1–0–6/51
His final first-class match was for H. D. G. Leveson-Gower's XI in 1909.

Wood, Reginald
Amateur. *b:* 7.3.1860, Woodchurch, Cheshire. *d:* 6.1.1915, Manly, Sydney, New South Wales, Australia. Middle order left-hand batsman, left-arm medium pace bowler. *Sch* Charterhouse. *Teams* Lancashire (1880–84, 6 matches); Victoria (1886/7, 2 matches). *Tour* Lillywhite, Shaw and Shrewsbury to Australia 1886/7 (co-opted into the team for three matches). *Test* England (1886/7, 1 match).
Career batting
12–20–5–235–52–15.66–0–*ct* 5
Bowling 134–8–16.75–0–0–3/19
Test batting
1–2–0–6–6–3.00–0–*ct* 0

Wood, Ronald
Professional. *b:* 3.6.1929, Ossett, Yorkshire. *d:* 22.5.1990, Stanley, Wakefield, Yorkshire. Brother of Barry (Yorkshire, Lancashire and Derbyshire). Lower order right-hand batsman, slow left-arm bowler. *Team* Yorkshire (1952–56, 22 matches).
Career batting
22–18–4–60–17–4.28–0–*ct* 5
Bowling 1346–51–26.39–3–0–8/45

Wood, Russell Brown
Amateur. *b:* 15.12.1929, Ashley Hill, Bristol. Solid lower order right-hand batsman, wicket-keeper. *Team* Gloucestershire (1950–51, 8 matches).
Career batting
8–12–3–110–48–12.22–0–*ct* 1–*st* 2

Wood, Sir Samuel Hill
(changed name to Hill-Wood in 1910)
Amateur. *b:* 21.3.1872, Glossop, Derbyshire. *d:* 4.1.1949, Westminster, London. Father of B. S. H. (Derbyshire), C. K. H. (Derbyshire), D. J. C. H. (Derbyshire) and W. W. H. (Derbyshire), grandfather of P. D. (Free Foresters). Middle order right-hand batsman. *Sch* Eton. *Team* Derbyshire (1894–1902, 34 matches).
Career batting
34–54–11–758–81*–17.62–0–*ct* 12
Bowling 50–0
He captained Derbyshire 1899 to 1901. He also played for Suffolk (1908–11). A noted figure in football, he built up his own club at Glossop, which played in the Football League prior to the 1914–18 war. In 1927 he became Chairman of Arsenal and remained in office until his death. From 1910 to 1929 he was Conservative MP for the High Peak Division of Derbyshire.

Wood, T.
Amateur. Middle order batsman. *Team* Somerset (1894, 1 match).
Career batting
1–1–0–11–11–11.00–0–*ct* 0
He first played for Somerset (not first-class) in 1887.

Wood, W.
Professional. Lower order batsman, useful bowler. *Team* Surrey (1883, 2 matches).
Career batting
2–4–0–9–8–2.25–0–*ct* 1
Bowling 44–1–44.00–0–0–1/22

Woodcock, Arthur
Professional. *b:* 23.9.1865, Northampton. *d:* 14.5.1910, Billesdon, Leicestershire. He died from self-administered poison. Tail end right-hand batsman, right-arm fast bowler. *Teams* Leicestershire (1894–1908, 121 matches); London County (1900).

Career batting
137–227–41–1547–62*–8.31–0–*ct* 35
Bowling 12211–548–22.28–38–9–9/28

He took 102 wickets, av 19.29, in 1895. His best innings analysis was 9/28 for Leicestershire v MCC in 1899 at Lord's. For a few years he was regarded as the fastest bowler in England (bar Kortright). His debut for Leicestershire was in 1889. He was a first-class umpire (1906).

Woodcock, Rev George
Amateur. *b:* 21.4.1894, Warrington, Lancashire. *d:* 22.2.1968, Bruton, Somerset. Lower order right-hand batsman, right-arm medium pace bowler. *Team* Somerset (1921, 1 match).
Career batting
1–2–0–68–63–34.00–0–*ct* 0
Bowling 119–4–29.75–0–0–4/119

Woodcock, Roy Gordon
Amateur. *b:* 26.11.1934, Stoneyholme, Burnley, Lancashire. Lower order right-hand batsman, slow left-arm bowler. *Sch* Worcester RGS. *Team* Oxford U (1956–58, blue 1957 and 1958).
Career batting
29–52–9–779–57–18.11–0–*ct* 17
Bowling 1793–53–33.83–0–0–4/54

Woodford, John Douglas
Cricketer. *b:* 9.9.1943, Little Horton, Bradford, Yorkshire. Opening right-hand batsman, right-arm medium pace bowler. *Team* Yorkshire (1968–72, 38 matches).
Career batting
38–61–2–1204–101–20.40–1–*ct* 12
Bowling 185–4–46.25–0–0–2/20

He also played for Northumberland (1975–84).

Woodfull, William Maldon
Amateur. *b:* 22.8.1897, Maldon, Victoria, Australia. *d:* 11.8.1965, Tweed Heads South, New South Wales, Australia. He collapsed and died while playing golf. Defensive opening right-hand batsman. *Team* Victoria (1921/2 to 1933/4, 59 matches). *Tours* Australia to England 1926, 1930, 1934, to New Zealand 1927/8; Victoria to New Zealand 1924/5. *Tests* Australia (1926–34, 35 matches).
Career batting
174–245–39–13388–284–64.99–49–*ct* 78
Bowling 24–1–24.00–0–0–1/12
Test batting
35–54–4–2300–161–46.00–7–*ct* 7

He captained Australia on both the 1930 and 1934 tours, as well as during the controversial 1932/3 Bodyline series in Australia. As a batsman he proved successful on all three visits to England, averaging over 50 and scoring over 1,000 runs on each visit (best 1,672, av 57.65, in 1926). His highest score was 284 for Australians v New Zealand XI at Auckland in 1927/8. He played in all Tests on each tour. Of his seven double centuries three were hit in England, the highest being 228* v Glamorgan at Swansea in 1934. In all he led Australia in 25 Tests. His last first-class match was for W. M. Woodfull's XI in 1934/5.

Woodgate, Thomas William
Amateur. *b:* 12.5.1857, Holborn, London. *d:* 30.1.1929, Shepherd's Bush, London. Middle order right-hand batsman. *Sch* Uppingham. *Team* Surrey (1877, 1 match).
Career batting
1–2–0–11–11–5.50–0–*ct* 0

Woodhams, Edwin Fehrsen
Amateur. *b:* 22.2.1880, Seaford, Sussex. *d:* 8.2.1933, Withdean, Brighton, Sussex. Middle order batsman. *Team* Sussex (1905, 1 match).
Career batting
1–2–1–14–14*–14.00–0–*ct* 1

Woodhead, David Leonard
Cricketer. *b:* 17.3.1940, Moseley, Birmingham. Middle order right-hand batsman, leg break bowler. *Team* Cambridge U (1968).
Career batting
8–15–1–190–68–13.57–0–*ct* 2
Bowling 190–0

Woodhead, Francis Gerald
Professional. *b:* 30.10.1912, Edwinstowe, Nottinghamshire. *d:* 24.5.1991, Nottingham. Lower order right-hand batsman, right-arm fast medium bowler. *Team* Nottinghamshire (1934–50, 141 matches).
Career batting
141–174–44–1100–52*–8.46–0–*ct* 80
Bowling 10550–320–32.96–11–1–7/24

His best season was 1938 when he took 69 wickets, av 25.04. From 1971 to 1980 he was coach to Nottinghamshire CCC.

Woodhead, Frank Ellis
Amateur. *b:* 29.5.1868, Woodthorpe, Huddersfield, Yorkshire. *d:* 25.8.1943, Marsh, Huddersfield, Yorkshire. Sound middle order right-hand batsman, right-arm medium fast bowler. *Sch* Loretto. *Teams* Cambridge U (1889); Yorkshire (1893–94, 4 matches).
Career batting
5–10–0–57–18–5.70–0–*ct* 4
Bowling 4–1–4.00–0–0–1/4

Woodhouse, Arthur James Powys
Amateur. *b:* 20.10.1933, Sidcup, Kent. Middle order right-hand batsman, right-arm medium pace bowler. *Sch* Oundle. *Team* Free Foresters (1957).
Career batting
1–2–0–29–17–14.05–0–*ct* 0
Bowling 20–1–20.00–0–0–1/20

He was Chief Executive of Kent CCC in 1989.

Woodhouse, George Edward Sealy
Amateur. *b:* 15.2.1924, Blandford, Dorset. *d:* 19.1.1988, Letton Park, Blandford, Dorset. Stylish middle order right-hand batsman, right-arm medium pace bowler. *Sch* Marlborough. *Team* Somerset (1946–53, 58 matches).
Career batting
65–118–14–2048–109–19.69–1–*ct* 18–*st* 1
Bowling 8–1–8.00–0–0–1/8
He played for Cambridge U in 1943 (not first-class). In 1948 he was joint-captain of Somerset and sole captain in 1949. He also played for Dorset (1954–64). A good rugby footballer, he gained a war-time blue at Cambridge and also appeared for Dorset and Wiltshire.

Woodhouse, William Henry
Amateur. *b:* 16.4.1856, Bradford, Yorkshire. *d:* 4.3.1938, Bradford, Yorkshire. Middle order right-hand batsman. *Team* Yorkshire (1884–85, 9 matches).
Career batting
9–13–0–218–63–16.76–0–*ct* 6

Woodland, Albert William
Professional. *b:* 10.6.1895, Conisbrough, Yorkshire. *d:* 31.1.1955, Mansfield, Nottinghamshire. Lower order right-hand batsman, right-arm fast medium bowler. *Team* Derbyshire (1920, 2 matches).
Career batting
2–4–1–27–19*–9.00–0–*ct* 1
Bowling 69–0

Woodman, Reginald George
Amateur. *b:* 11.8.1905, Bristol. *d:* 20.5.1980, Bristol. Middle order right-hand batsman. *Team* Gloucestershire (1925, 2 matches).
Career batting
2–3–0–4–2–1.33–0–*ct* 0

Woodroffe, Alfred
Professional. *b:* 1.9.1918, West Bromwich, Staffordshire. *d:* 23.7.1964, Whitehouse, Sutton Coldfield, Warwickshire. Middle order left-hand batsman. *Team* Warwickshire (1947–48, 4 matches).
Career batting
4–7–0–77–41–11.00–0–*ct* 3

Woodroffe, Kenneth Herbert Clayton
Amateur. *b:* 9.12.1892, Wallands Park, Lewes, Sussex. *d:* 13.5.1915, near Neuve Chapelle, France. He was killed in action. Lower order right-hand batsman, right-arm fast bowler. *Sch* Marlborough. *Teams* Hampshire (1912–13, 2 matches); Cambridge U (1913–14, blue both years); Sussex (1914, 2 matches).
Career batting
18–29–8–172–22*–8.19–0–*ct* 5
Bowling 1500–55–27.27–2–0–6/43

Woods, Basil Joseph Pontifex
Amateur. *b:* 28.8.1922, Umtata, Cape Province, South Africa. Cousin of A. P. (Natal). Lower order right-hand batsman, leg break and googly bowler. *Team* Cambridge U (1951).
Career batting
2–2–0–1–1–0.50–0–*ct* 0
Bowling 108–3–36.00–0–0–2/61

Woods, Charles Pound
Amateur. *b:* 12.9.1878, Swinton, Lancashire. d. 1.7.1940, Llandudno, Caernarvonshire. Middle order right-hand batsman. *Team* Wales (1930).
Career batting
1–2–0–9–5–4.50
His County cricket was for Cheshire (1910–14). He later captained Caernarvonshire, being also Secretary of the North Wales Cricket Association.

Woods, Samuel Moses James
Amateur. *b:* 13.4.1867, Ashfield, Sydney, New South Wales, Australia. *d:* 30.4.1931, Taunton, Somerset. Attacking middle order right-hand batsman, right-arm fast medium bowler. *Sch* Brighton. *Teams* Cambridge U (1888–91, blue all four years); Somerset (1891–1910, 299 matches). *Tours* Australia to England 1888; Hawke to North America 1891, to South Africa 1895/6; Priestley to West Indies 1896/7; Ranjitsinhji to North America 1899; MacLaren to Australia 1901/2 (he did not play in first-class matches). *Tests* Australia (1888, 3 matches); England (1895/6, 3 matches).
Career batting
401–690–35–15345–215–23.42–19–*ct* 279
Bowling 21653–1040–20.82–77–21–10/69
Test batting
6–10–0–154–53–15.40–0–0–*ct* 5
Bowling 250–10–25.00–0–0–3/28
He hit 1,000 runs in a season four times (best 1,405, av 34.26, in 1895). He took 100 wickets in a season twice (best 153, av 16.83, in 1892). His only double century was 215 for Somerset v Sussex at Hove in 1895, and his best bowling was 10/69 for Cambridge U v C. I. Thornton's XI at Fenner's in 1890. He captained Cambridge in 1890 and Somerset from 1894 to 1906. He was Secretary of Somerset 1895–1907 and 1920–22. His first-class debut was for G. N. Wyatt's XI in 1886. He first played for Somerset (not first-class) in 1887. An excellent rugby footballer, he played for Cambridge, Somerset and England as wing forward. He also played soccer for Sussex.

Wood-Sims, William Wood
(changed name from W. W. Sims)
Amateur, changed to professional in 1884. *b:* 10.2.1858, Ironville, Derbyshire. *d:* 30.11.1926, Lambeth, London. Sound opening right-hand batsman. *Team* Derbyshire (1879–86, 23 matches).

Career batting
25–45–2–518–46–12.04–0–*ct* 13
Bowling 70–5–14.00–0–0–3/22

He last played for Derbyshire (not first-class) in 1891.

Woodward, Edwin
Professional. *b:* 17.9.1864, Sutton-in-Ashfield, Nottinghamshire. *d:* 15.12.1953, Mansfield, Nottinghamshire. Lower order right-hand batsman, right-arm medium pace bowler. *Team* Liverpool and District (1888–90).
Career batting
2–4–0–19–13–4.75–0–*ct* 1
Bowling 50–2–25.00–0–0–2/38

His County cricket was for Cheshire (1886–93).

Woodward, Kenneth Alexander
Amateur. *b:* 23.12.1874, Sefton Park, Liverpool, Lancashire. d. 24.12.1950, Charlton Kings, Gloucestershire. Middle order right-hand batsman, right-arm medium pace bowler, excellent deep field. *Sch* Harrow. *Teams* Oxford U (1896); Derbyshire (1909, 2 matches).
Career batting
3–6–1–23–7–4.60–0–*ct* 0

He also played for Herefordshire (1893).

Woof, William Albert
Professional. *b:* 9.7.1858, Gloucester. *d:* 4.4.1937, Montpellier, Cheltenham, Gloucestershire. Tail end right-hand batsman, originally fast, then slow left-arm bowler, slip field. *Sch* Bedford GS. *Team* Gloucestershire (1878–1902, 140 matches).
Career batting
160–258–63–1274–43–6.53–0–*ct* 119
Bowling 13369–754–17.73–69–11–8/70

He took 100 wickets in a season twice (best 116, av 18.21, in 1884). He played very little County cricket after 1894 and for some years was a first-class umpire (1895–99).

Wookey, Rev Stephen Mark
Cricketer. *b:* 2.9.1954, Upavon, Wiltshire. Lower order right-hand batsman, right-arm medium pace bowler. *Sch* Malvern. *Teams* Cambridge U (1975–76, blue both years); Oxford U (1978–80, blue 1978).
Career batting
19–27–6–260–48–12.35–0–*ct* 5
Bowling 1158–28–41.33–0–0–3/61

He attained the unusual distinction of being awarded his cricket blue at both Universities. His County cricket was for Wiltshire (1974–78).

Wooler, Charles Robert Dudley
Professional. *b:* 30.6.1930, Bulawayo, Rhodesia. Brother of R. C. (Transvaal), uncle of D. G. W. Alers (Eastern Province and Border). Lower order right-hand batsman, right-arm fast medium bowler. *Teams* Leicestershire (1949–51, 51 matches); Rhodesia (1951/2 to 1956/7).
Career batting
60–93–16–835–49*–10.84–0–*ct* 16
Bowling 4030–130–31.00–3–0–5/47

Wooley, Gilbert George
Amateur. *b:* 1896. *d:* 8.2.1953, Gloucester. Middle order right-hand batsman. *Team* Gloucestershire (1920, 1 match).
Career batting
1–2–0–0–0–0.00–0–*ct* 0

Woolfries, Simon Andrew
Cricketer. *b:* 10.1.1953, Moreton-in-Marsh, Gloucestershire. Middle order right-hand batsman, off break bowler. *Sch* Ipswich. *Team* Cambridge U (1972).
Career batting
1–1–0–3–3–3.00–0–*ct* 0

Woolhouse, William Henry
Professional. *b:* 21.1.1791, Sheffield, Yorkshire. *d:* 14.7.1837, London. Opening left-hand batsman, left-hand round-arm bowler. *Team* Yorkshire (1833–34, 3 matches).
Career batting
17–33–2–440–51–14.19–0–*ct* 18

His debut was for Sheffield and Leicester in 1826. He was the most influential Yorkshire cricketer of his day and was responsible of the laying out of two early Sheffield cricket grounds at Darnall and at Hyde Park. He went to London in 1837 to seek medical advice for an ailment, but died before he could return home.

Woollatt, Randal James
Amateur. *b:* 19.7.1909, Surbiton, Surrey. *d:* 9.4.1984, Cheltenham, Gloucestershire. Middle order right-hand batsman. *Sch* Cheltenham. *Team* Minor Counties (1930).
Career batting
1–1–0–13–13–13.00–0–*ct* 0

He played for Surrey 2nd XI (1929–32).

Wooller, Wilfred
Amateur. *b:* 20.11.1912, Rhos-on-Sea, Denbighshire. Militant middle order right-hand batsman, right-arm medium fast bowler, brilliant close field. *Sch* Rydal. *Teams* Cambridge U (1935–36, blue both years); Glamorgan (1938–62, 400 matches).
Career batting
430–679–77–13593–128–22.57–5–*ct* 413
Bowling 25830–958–26.96–43–5–8/45

He hit 1,000 runs in a season five times (best 1,270, av 27.02, in 1947) and took 100 wickets twice (best 120, av 24.55, in 1949). In 1954 he completed the 'double'. He captained Glamorgan from 1947 to 1960, was Secretary of the County Club from 1947 until 1977 and President since 1991. From 1955 to 1961 he was a Test Selector. He also played for Denbighshire (1930–34). A noted rugby footballer, he played for Cambridge and Wales.

Woollett, Anthony Frank
Professional. *b:* 20.9.1927, Lambeth, London. Opening left-hand batsman. *Team* Kent (1950–54, 44 matches).
Career batting
44–81–4–1445–96–18.76–0–*ct* 16
He also played for Berkshire (1958).

Woolley, Albert
Professional. *b:* 26.9.1902, Salford, Lancashire. *d:* 5.1.1978, Doncaster, Yorkshire. Lower order right-hand batsman, right-arm fast medium bowler. *Team* Lancashire (1926, 7 matches).
Career batting
7–9–0–61–24–6.77–0–*ct* 9
Bowling 351–11–31.90–0–0–4/56

Woolley, Claud Neville
Professional. *b:* 5.5.1886, Tonbridge, Kent. *d:* 3.11.1962, Abington, Northampton. Brother of F. E. (Kent). Sound opening right-hand batsman, right-arm slow medium bowler. *Teams* Gloucestershire (1909, 1 match); Northamptonshire (1911–31, 362 matches).
Career batting
365–658–33–15395–204*–24.63–13–*ct* 137
Bowling 11654–352–33.10–12–1–6/30
He hit 1,000 runs in a season seven times (best 1,602, av 29.66, in 1928). His highest score was 214 for Northamptonshire v Worcestershire at Northampton in 1921. He was on the first-class umpires' list (1932–49) and stood in one Test (1938). In 1949 he became groundsman at the County Ground, Northampton, retiring in 1961.

Woolley, Frank Edward
Professional. *b:* 27.5.1887, Tonbridge, Kent. *d:* 18.10.1978, Halifax, Nova Scotia, Canada. Brother of C. N. (Gloucestershire and Northamptonshire). Attractive middle order left-hand batsman, left-arm medium pace, later slow left-arm bowler, brilliant slip field. *Team* Kent (1906–38, 764 matches). *Tours* MCC to South Africa 1909/10, 1913/14, 1922/3, to Australia 1911/12, 1920/1, 1924/5, to Australia and New Zealand 1929/30. *Tests* England (1909–34, 64 matches).
Career batting
978–1530–84–58959–305*–40.77–145–*ct* 1018
Bowling 41058–2066–19.87–132–28–8/22
Test batting
64–98–7–3283–154–36.07–5–*ct* 64
Bowling 2815–83–33.91–4–1–7/76
One of the greatest of the game's all-rounders, he holds the record for the most catches taken by a fielder in a first-class career. As a batsman he was both elegant and fast scoring and his bowling was a feature of the early part of his career – for his final ten seasons he was rarely used due to a back injury.

No fewer than 28 times he scored over 1,000 runs in a season, going on to 2,000 13 times and thence to 3,000 once: 3,352, av 60.94, in 1928. He hit six double centuries for Kent, one for the MCC in Australia and one for the Rest of England v Yorkshire, but his highest innings was 305 not out for MCC v Tasmania at Hobart in 1911/12.

Eight times he reached 100 wickets in a season, his best year being 1920 with 185 wickets, av 14.23. In each of those eight seasons he also completed the 'double' and in four of them the feat of 2,000 runs and 100 wickets – no other cricketer achieved this feat on four occasions.

Although he first appeared for England in the fifth Test of the 1909 series, his first real opportunity for England in England came in 1912 when he headed the Test bowling averages with 17 wickets, av 8.94, and scored 246 runs, av 30.75. His next home series was not until 1921 when he hit 343 runs, av 42.87. In the 1926 series he scored 237 runs, av 39.50, and that was his last Test series against Australia as a regular member of the England side, though he appeared twice in 1930 and made a final appearance, aged 47, in the Oval Test of 1934.

His most successful tour overseas was in 1911/12 in Australia, when he hit 781 runs, av 55.78.

Woolley, Kenneth McDowell
Amateur. *b:* 9.12.1924, Cape Town, South Africa. Lower order right-hand batsman, right-arm medium pace bowler. *Team* Cambridge U (1947).
Career batting
1–2–0–4–4–2.00–0–*ct* 0
Bowling 56–0

Woolmer, Robert Andrew
Cricketer. *b:* 14.5.1948, Kanpur, India. Son of C. S. (Uttar Pradesh). Stylish middle order, later opening right-hand batsman, right-arm medium pace bowler. *Teams* Kent (1968–84, 279 matches); Natal (1973/4 to 1975/6); Western Province (1980/1). *Tours* Robins to South Africa 1973/4; England to India, Sri Lanka and Australia 1976/7; SAB England XI to South Africa 1981/2. *Tests* England (1975–81, 19 matches).
Career batting
350–545–75–15772–203–33.55–34–*ct* 239–*st* 1
Bowling 10868–420–25.87–12–1–7/47
Test batting
19–34–2–1059–149–33.09–3–*ct* 10
Bowling 299–4–74.75–0–0–1/8
He hit 1,000 runs in a season five times (best 1,749, av 47.27, in 1976). Following his 1981/2 tour to South Africa he was banned from Test cricket for three years, but in fact he lost his place in the England team during the 1981 series v Australia. His highest innings was 203 for Kent v Sussex at Tunbridge Wells in 1982. A back injury ended his county career midway through the 1984 season. After retiring he spent some years coaching multi-racial cricket

in South Africa, was Kent coach in 1987 and has been Warwickshire coach since 1991.

Woolston, Robert George
Cricketer. *b:* 23.5.1968, Enfield, Middlesex. Lower order right-hand batsman, slow left-arm bowler. *Team* Somerset (1987, 1 match).
Career batting
1–1–0–0–0–0.00–0–*ct* 0
Bowling 107–2–53.50–0–0–2/70

Woosnam, Maxwell
Amateur. *b:* 6.9.1892, Liverpool, Lancashire. *d:* 14.7.1965, Marylebone, London. Nephew of H. Philipson (Middlesex). Opening batsman. *Sch* Winchester. *Team* Cambridge U (1912).
Career batting
2–2–0–14–13–7.00–0–*ct* 4

His County cricket was for Cheshire (1928). A brilliant all-round sportsman, he played soccer for Manchester City and England at centre-half. In 1921 he won the tennis doubles at Wimbledon, and later captained the English Davis Cup Team and he also won an Olympic Gold Medal in Antwerp in 1920 in the men's doubles. He won blues for golf, soccer, lawn tennis and royal tennis.

Wooster, Reginald
Amateur. *b:* 19.1.1903, Kettering, Northamptonshire. *d:* 12.9.1968, Kettering, Northamptonshire. Lower order right-hand batsman, right-arm medium pace bowler. *Team* Northamptonshire (1925, 1 match).
Career batting
1–1–0–6–6–6.00–0–*ct* 0
Bowling 77–6–12.83–1–0–5/54

He performed the hat-trick in his only first-class match for Northamptonshire v Dublin University at Northampton in 1925.

Wootton, George
Professional. *b:* 16.10.1834, Clifton, Nottinghamshire. *d:* 15.6.1924, Ruddington, Nottinghamshire. Lower order left-hand batsman, left-hand fast round-arm bowler. *Team* Nottinghamshire (1861–71, 52 matches).
Career batting
186–301–68–2431–64*–10.43–0–*ct* 143
Bowling 12500–962 + 22–12.99–87–34–10/54

He took 100 wickets in a season four times (best 142, av 11.58, in 1867). His best bowling was 10/54 for AEE v Yorkshire at Sheffield in 1865. He also played for Northamptonshire (pre first-class, 1869). He was a first-class umpire (1883).

Wootton, James
Professional. *b:* 9.3.1860, Sutton-at-Hone, Kent. *d:* 21.2.1941, Leytonstone, Essex. Tail end left-hand batsman, left-arm medium pace bowler, good slip field. *Teams* Kent (1880–90, 115 matches); Hampshire (1895–1900, 24 matches).
Career batting
168–277–73–1628–53–7.98–0–*ct* 92
Bowling 13826–761–18.16–60–17–8/27

He took 100 wickets in a season three times (best 143, av 15.95, in 1886).

Wootton, Simon Howard
Cricketer. *b:* 24.2.1959, Perivale, Middlesex. Middle order left-hand batsman, slow left-arm bowler. *Teams* Warwickshire (1981–83, 11 matches); Gloucestershire (1984, 4 matches).
Career batting
15–24–3–558–104–26.57–1–*ct* 8
Bowling 7–0

Worger, Frederick Joseph
Professional. *b:* 1869. *d:* 18.11.1954, Elm Grove, Brighton, Sussex. Middle order batsman. *Team* Sussex (1892, 1 match).
Career batting
1–2–0–1–1–0.50–0–*ct* 2

Workman, James Allen
Amateur. *b:* 17.3.1917, Peterhead, South Australia. *d:* 23.12.1970, Westminster, London. He died on a London bus on his way home from work. Opening right-hand batsman. *Team* Australia Services (1945 to 1945/6). *Tours* Australian Services to England 1945, to India and Ceylon 1945/6.
Career batting
16–29–2–549–76–20.33–0–*ct* 5
Bowling 6–1–6.00–0–0–1/6

His final first-class match was for Australian Services in Australia in 1945/6.

Wormald, Alfred
Professional. *b:* 10.5.1855, Morley, Yorkshire. *d:* 6.2.1940, Gomersal, Yorkshire. Middle order right-hand batsman, wicket-keeper. *Team* Yorkshire (1885–91, 7 matches).
Career batting
7–11–3–161–80–20.12–0–*ct* 10–*st* 2

Wormald, Edward
Amateur. *b:* 4.12.1848, Islington, London. *d:* 16.10.1928, Brighton, Sussex. Lower order right-hand batsman, right-arm fast bowler. *Sch* Eton. *Team* Kent (1870, 1 match).
Career batting
1–2–0–16–15–8.00–0–*ct* 1
Bowling 11–0

He played in the Cambridge Freshmen's match of 1868.

Wormald, John
Amateur. *b:* 23.2.1882, Westminster, London. *d:* 13.11.1957, East Dereham, Norfolk. His wife was earlier married to a son of E. S. Garnier (Oxford U). Sound middle order right-hand batsman. *Sch* Eton. *Team* Middlesex (1910–12, 22 matches).

Worrall, John

Career batting
23–35–1–548–61–16.11–0–*ct* 8
He also played for Norfolk (1921–22).

Worrall, John
Amateur. *b:* 21.6.1861, Chinamans Flat, Maryborough, Victoria, Australia. *d:* 17.11.1937, Fairfield Park, Melbourne, Victoria, Australia. Aggressive middle order, later opening, right-hand batsman, right-hand slow round-arm bowler, good close field. *Team* Victoria (1883/4 to 1901/2, 65 matches). *Tours* Australia to England 1888, 1899. *Tests* Australia (1884/5 to 1899, 11 matches).
Career batting
142–245–23–4660–128–20.99–7–*ct* 101
Bowling 2426–105–23.10–4–0–5/20
Test batting
11–22–3–478–76–25.15–0–*ct* 13
Bowling 127–1–127.00–0–0–1/97
He achieved little on the 1888 tour, but in 1899 hit 1,202 runs, av 35.35, and played in four Tests. For many years he was a noted journalist in Melbourne.

Worrell, Sir Frank Mortimer Maglinne
Amateur. *b:* 1.8.1924, Bank Hall, Bridgetown, Barbados. *d:* 13.3.1967, Mona, Kingston, Jamaica. He died of leukaemia. Cousin of L. R. (Hampshire). Stylish opening or middle order right-hand batsman, left-arm medium, or slow, bowler. *Teams* Barbados (1941/2 to 1946/7); Jamaica (1947/8 to 1963/4). *Tours* West Indies to England 1950, 1957, 1963, to Australia and New Zealand 1951/2, to Australia 1960/1; Commonwealth to India, Pakistan and Ceylon 1949/50, to India and Ceylon 1950/1, 1953/4; West Indian XI to England 1964. *Tests* West Indies (1947/8 to 1963, 51 matches).
Career batting
208–326–49–15025–308*–54.24–39–*ct* 139
Bowling 10115–349–28.98–13–0–7/70
Test batting
51–87–9–3860–261–49.48–9–*ct* 43
Bowling 2672–69–38.72–2–0–7/70
He achieved great success on his first tour to England in 1950, heading the Test batting averages with 539 runs, av 89.83, and in all first-class matches hitting 1,775 runs, av 68.26. He was no less successful in 1957 with 350 Test runs, av 39.60, and 1,470 first-class runs, av 58.80. He led the 1963 touring side which won the rubber 3 to 1, his main contribution being his captaincy. He had already led West Indies on the 1960/1 tour to Australia, and in all captained West Indies in 15 Tests. His highest Test innings was 261 for West Indies v England at Trent Bridge in 1950. He hit 1,000 runs in India, Pakistan and Ceylon twice (best 1,900, av 63.33, in 1950/1). His highest first-class innings was 308* for Barbados v Trinidad at Bridgetown in 1943/4. He was knighted for his services to cricket in 1964 and was a Senator in the Jamaican Parliament.

Worrell, Lawrence Roosevelt
Cricketer. *b:* 28.8.1943, St Thomas, Barbados. Cousin of F. M. M. (West Indies). Lower order right-hand batsman, off break bowler. *Team* Hampshire (1969–72, 32 matches).
Career batting
32–42–17–289–50–11.56–0–*ct* 21
Bowling 2116–65–32.55–1–0–5/67
He also played for Dorset (1969).

Worsley, Arthington
Amateur. *b:* 9.12.1861, Marylebone, London. *d:* 13.1.1943, Parkhurst, Newport, Isle of Wight. Nephew of G. A. Cayley (Cambridge U 1854). Middle order right-hand batsman. *Team* MCC (1888–90).
Career batting
2–4–0–29–17–7.25–0–*ct* 1

Worsley, Arthur Edward
Amateur. *b:* 10.10.1882, Evenley, Brackley, Northamptonshire. *d:* 10.8.1969, Watchet, Somerset. Brother of C. E. A. (Northamptonshire). Middle order right-hand batsman. *Sch* Malvern. *Teams* Oxford U (1903–06); Northamptonshire (1905, 3 matches).
Career batting
16–31–0–478–86–15.41–0–*ct* 6
Bowling 156–4–39.00–0–0–3/20
He first played for Northamptonshire (pre first-class) in 1903.

Worsley, Charles Edward Austen
Amateur. *b:* 30.5.1902, Evenley, Northamptonshire. *d:* 2.12.1990, Cove, Devon. Brother of A. E. (Northamptonshire). Middle order right-hand batsman. *Sch* Radley. *Team* Northamptonshire (1921, 2 matches).
Career batting
2–4–0–34–23–8.50–0–*ct* 1

Worsley, Duncan Robert
Amateur. *b:* 18.7.1941, Farnworth, Bolton, Lancashire. Steady left-hand opening batsman, off break bowler. *Sch* Bolton. *Teams* Lancashire (1960–67, 62 matches); Oxford U (1961–64, blue all four years).
Career batting
113–205–11–5062–139–26.09–4–*ct* 68
Bowling 1520–37–41.08–0–0–4/21
He hit 1,498 runs, av 31.87, in 1964. He captained Oxford in 1964.

Worsley, Francis Frederick
Amateur. *b:* 2.6.1902, Kensington, London. *d:* 15.9.1949, Mile End, Stepney, London. Brother of T. C. (Cambridge U). Middle order batsman. *Sch* Brighton. *Team* Glamorgan (1922–23, 2 matches).
Career batting
2–3–0–34–21–11.33–0–*ct* 1
He did not appear in any first-class matches whilst at Oxford. He became well-known as the producer of the radio programme 'Itma'.

Worsley, Thomas Cuthbert
Amateur. *b:* 10.12.1907, Durham. *d:* 23.2.1977, Kemp Town, Brighton, Sussex. Brother of F. F. (Glamorgan). Lower order right-hand batsman, wicket-keeper. *Sch* Marlborough. *Team* Cambridge U (1928).
Career batting
1–1–0–1–1–1.00–0–*ct* 0
He was a well-known author and journalist.

Worsley, William
Professional. *b:* 11.9.1869, Wandsworth, London. *d:* 13.11.1918, Accrington, Lancashire. Lower order right-hand batsman, wicket-keeper. *Team* Lancashire (1903–13, 136 matches).
Career batting
136–167–63–628–37*–6.03–0–*ct* 239–*st* 45

Worsley, Sir William Arthington
Amateur. *b:* 5.4.1890, Hovingham Hall, Yorkshire. *d:* 4.12.1973, Hovingham Hall, Yorkshire. Great-nephew of G. A. Cayley (Cambridge U 1854). Middle order right-hand batsman. *Sch* Eton. *Team* Yorkshire (1928–29, 60 matches).
Career batting
60–50–4–722–60–15.69–0–*ct* 32
He did not play in any first-class matches whilst at Oxford. In 1928 and 1929 he captained Yorkshire. He was President of MCC in 1961/2 and of Yorkshire from 1961 until his death. His daughter is the present Duchess of Kent.

Worthington, Dr Charles Robert
Amateur. *b:* 28.2.1877, Surbiton, Surrey. *d:* 7.12.1950, Victoria, British Columbia, Canada. Stylish middle order right-hand batsman, right-arm medium pace bowler. *Sch* Tonbridge. *Teams* Cambridge U (1898); Kent (1898, 1 match).
Career batting
8–13–0–156–42–12.00–0–*ct* 4
Bowling 66–3–22.00–0–0–2/11

Worthington, Thomas Stanley
Professional. *b:* 21.8.1905, Bolsover, Derbyshire. *d:* 31.8.1973, Kings Lynn, Norfolk. He died whilst on holiday. Uncle of F. E. Marsh (Derbyshire). Vigorous middle order right-hand batsman, right-arm fast medium bowler. *Team* Derbyshire (1924–47, 406 matches). *Tours* MCC to Australia and New Zealand 1929/30, 1936/7; Tennyson to India 1937/8. *Tests* England (1929/30 to 1936/7, 9 matches).
Career batting
453–720–59–19221–238*–29.07–31–*ct* 340
Bowling 19939–682–29.23–16–2–8/29
Test batting
9–11–0–321–128–29.18–1–*ct* 8
Bowling 316–8–39.50–0–0–2/19
He hit 1,000 runs in a season ten times (best 1,774, av 41.25, in 1937). Both his double centuries were for Derbyshire the higher being 238* v Sussex at Derby in 1937. His best bowling season was 1929 with 89 wickets, av 23.51. After leaving Derbyshire he played for Northumberland (1949) and was chief coach to Lancashire CCC 1952–62.

Wrathall, Harry
Professional. *b:* 1.2.1869, Cheltenham, Gloucestershire. *d:* 1.6.1944, Salisbury, Wiltshire. Powerful opening right-hand batsman, right-arm medium pace bowler. *Teams* Gloucestershire (1894–1907, 263 matches); London County (1900).
Career batting
288–509–20–11023–176–22.54–9–*ct* 195–*st* 3
Bowling 1358–30–45.26–0–0–4/37
He hit 1,000 runs in a season four times (best 1,508, av 31.44, in 1901). He also played for Northumberland (1914). He was a first-class umpire (1923).

Wrathmell, Lewis Franklin
Professional. *b:* 22.1.1855, House Hill, Kirkheaton, Yorkshire. *d:* 16.9.1928, Upper Hopton, Dewsbury, Yorkshire. Middle order right-hand batsman. *Team* Yorkshire (1886, 1 match).
Career batting
1–2–0–18–17–9.00–0–*ct* 0

Wreford-Brown, Anthony John
Amateur. *b:* 26.10.1912, Thames Ditton, Surrey. Son of Charles (Gloucestershire), nephew of O. E. (Gloucestershire). Opening right-hand batsman. *Sch* Charterhouse. *Teams* Oxford U (1934); Sussex (1934, 1 match).
Career batting
5–10–1–146–39–16.22–0–*ct* 2
His first-class debut was for Leveson-Gower's XI in 1933.

Wreford-Brown, Charles
Amateur. *b:* 9.10.1866, Clifton, Bristol. *d:* 26.11.1951, Paddington, London. Father of A. J. (Sussex), brother of O. E. (Gloucestershire), brother-in-law of W. J. H. Curwen (Surrey). Lower order right-hand batsman, right-arm slow bowler, good field. *Sch* Charterhouse. *Teams* Gloucestershire (1886–98, 5 matches); Oxford U (1887–88). *Tour* Hawke to North America 1891.
Career batting
19–32–6–252–51–9.69–0–*ct* 10
Bowling 969–39–24.84–1–0–5/62
He was a noted soccer player, appearing at centre-half for Oxford, Old Carthusians, Corinthians and England. Later he became Vice-President of the Football Association and Chairman of the FA Selection Committee. He is said to be the first to use the word 'soccer' for Association football.

Wreford-Brown, Oswald Eric
Amateur. *b:* 21.7.1877, Clifton, Bristol. *d:* 7.7.1916, near Corbie, France. He died of wounds. Brother of Charles (Gloucestershire), uncle of A. J. (Sussex).

Wreghitt, Peter Hadfield

Steady middle order right-hand batsman, good cover-point. *Sch* Charterhouse. *Team* Gloucestershire (1900, 1 match).
Career batting
1–1–0–5–5–5.00–0–*ct* 0

Wreghitt, Peter Hadfield
Amateur. *b:* 15.5.1929, Netheredge, Sheffield, Yorkshire. Middle order right-hand batsman, right-arm medium pace bowler. *Sch* KES, Sheffield. *Team* Oxford U (1951).
Career batting
1–1–0–1–1–1.00–0–*ct* 3
Bowling 105–3–35.00–0–0–3/64

Wren, Timothy Neil
Cricketer. *b:* 26.3.1970, Folkestone, Kent. Lower order right-hand batsman, left-arm medium pace bowler. *Team* Kent (1990–92, 7 matches).
Career batting
7–5–2–23–16–7.66–0–*ct* 4
Bowling 629–15–41.93–0–0–3/14

Wright, Alan Jack Barton
Amateur. *b:* 3.3.1905, Semilong, Northampton. *d:* 29.7.1989, Catford, London. Brother of R. C. B. (Northamptonshire). Middle order right-hand batsman. *Sch* Wellingborough. *Team* Northamptonshire (1922–23, 2 matches).
Career batting
2–4–0–4–3–1.00–0–*ct* 0

Wright, Albert
Amateur. *b:* 8.8.1899, Kettering, Northamptonshire. *d:* 1.10.1987, Bognor Regis, Sussex. Brother of E. V. (Northamptonshire), Stephen (Northamptonshire) and R. L. (Northamptonshire). Middle order right-hand batsman, right-arm medium pace bowler. *Sch* Wellingborough. *Team* Northamptonshire (1919–20, 3 matches).
Career batting
3–6–0–81–27–13.50–0–*ct* 4
Bowling 106–6–17.66–0–0–3/6

Wright, Albert
Professional. *b:* 25.8.1941, Arley, Warwickshire. Lower order right-hand batsman, right-arm medium pace bowler. *Team* Warwickshire (1960–64, 76 matches).
Career batting
76–76–27–315–27–6.42–0–*ct* 29
Bowling 5953–236–25.22–11–2–6/58

Wright, Albert Charles
Professional. *b:* 4.4.1895, Borstal, Kent. *d:* 26.5.1959, Westminster, London. Hard hitting lower order right-hand batsman, right-arm fast medium bowler. *Team* Kent (1921–31, 225 matches).
Career batting
225–298–49–3260–81–13.09–0–*ct* 127
Bowling 14463–596–24.26–24–1–7/31

He took 100 wickets in a season twice (best 107, av 20.38, in 1927).

Wright, Albert Edward
Amateur. *b:* 11.8.1902, Great Leighs, Essex. *d:* 8.11.1984, Great Leighs, Essex. Lower order right-hand batsman, right-arm fast bowler. *Team* Essex (1931–34, 3 matches).
Career batting
3–5–1–45–14–11.25–0–*ct* 1
Bowling 86–0

Wright, Anthony John
Cricketer. *b:* 27.6.1962, Stevenage, Hertfordshire, Middle order right-hand batsman, right-arm medium pace bowler. *Team* Gloucestershire (1982–92, 205 matches). *Tour* Gloucestershire to Sri Lanka 1986/7.
Career batting
205–352–26–9337–161–28.64–12–*ct* 140
Bowling 68–1–68.00–0–0–1/16

He hit 1,000 runs in a season four times (best 1,596, av 45.60, in 1991). He captained Gloucestershire 1990–92.

Wright, Arthur Edward Hext
Amateur. *b:* 7.2.1886, Georgetown, British Guiana. *d:* 13.11.1970, Coburg, Chudleigh, Devon. Son of E. F. (Gloucestershire). Middle order right-hand batsman. *Team* Royal Navy (1914).
Career batting
1–2–0–87–57–43.50–0–*ct* 0

His County cricket was for Devon (1921–23).

Wright, Bertie
Amateur. *b:* 7.2.1897, Kettering, Northamptonshire. *d:* 2.4.1955, Kettering, Northamptonshire. Brother of N. E. (Northamptonshire) and P. A. (Northamptonshire). Middle order right-hand batsman. *Sch* Wellingborough. *Team* Northamptonshire (1919–22, 5 matches).
Career batting
5–8–0–28–12–3.50–0–*ct* 3
Bowling 254–6–42.33–0–0–2/11

Wright, Charles William
Amateur. *b:* 27.5.1863, Harewood, Yorkshire. *d:* 10.1.1936, Saxelby Park, Melton Mowbray, Leicestershire. Steady opening right-hand batsman, wicket-keeper. *Sch* Charterhouse. *Teams* Cambridge U (1882–85, blue all four years); Nottinghamshire (1882–99, 117 matches). *Tours* Hawke to North America 1891, 1894, to India 1892/3, to South Africa 1895/6. *Tests* England (1895/6, 3 matches).
Career batting
265–461–21–6989–114–15.88–2–*ct* 195–*st* 41
Bowling 55–0
Test batting
3–4–0–125–71–31.25–0–*ct* 0

His final first-class match was for MCC in 1901. He was for some years on the Committee of Nottinghamshire CCC, being Treasurer 1911–35 and a Trustee in 1900. He lost the sight of one eye whilst partridge shooting and this ended his serious cricket.

Wright, Cyril Carne Glenton
Amateur. *b:* 7.3.1887, Oporto, Portugal. *d:* 15.9.1960, Hampstead, London. Opening right-hand batsman. *Sch* Tonbridge. *Team* Cambridge U (1907–09, blue 1907 and 1908).
Career batting
23–44–2–677–87–16.11–0–*ct* 22
His final first-class match was for G. J. V. Weigall's XI in 1914. A noted rugby footballer, he played for Cambridge and England.

Wright, Douglas Alexander
Amateur. *b:* 1894. *d:* 1.10.1953, Marylebone, London. Brother of O. A. (Europeans). Middle order right-hand batsman, wicket-keeper. *Sch* Christ's Hospital. *Teams* Ceylon (1926/7 to 1936/7); MCC (1928).
Career batting
5–6–1–149–82–29.80–0–*ct* 7–*st* 5

Wright, Douglas Vivian Parson
Professional. *b:* 21.8.1914, Sidcup, Kent. Lower order right-hand batsman, right-arm medium leg break and googly bowler. *Team* Kent (1932–57, 397 matches). *Tours* MCC to South Africa 1938/9, 1948/9, to Australia and New Zealand 1946/7, 1950/1; Norfolk to Jamaica 1956/7. *Tests* England (1938 to 1950/1, 34 matches).
Career batting
497–703–225–5903–84*–12.34–0–*ct* 182
Bowling 49307–2056–23.98–150–42–9/47
Test batting
34–39–13–289–45–11.11–0–*ct* 10
Bowling 4224–108–39.11–6–1–7/105
Bowling leg breaks at a much greater speed than the normal practitioner of that art, Wright was the only bowler of his type in first-class cricket. On his day he was virtually unplayable, but often he was very erratic in length and direction. His figures in Test cricket are not at all impressive, but the selectors were always mindful that he could produce the unexpected and therefore he played fairly regularly for England between 1938 and 1950.
In first-class cricket he took 100 wickets in a season 10 times, his best year being 1947 with 177 wickets, av 21.12. Some idea of his occasional effectiveness can be gauged by the fact that he achieved the hat-trick seven times. His best bowling was 9/47 for Kent v Gloucestershire at Bristol in 1939. He was captain of Kent 1954–56.

Wright, Edward Campbell
Amateur. *b:* 23.4.1874, South Shields, Co Durham. *d:* 28.7.1947, Granary, Budleigh Salterton, Devon. Middle order right-hand batsman, right-arm slow bowler. *Sch* Clergy Orphan School, Canterbury. *Teams* Gloucestershire (1894–98, 7 matches); Oxford U (1897–99, blue 1897); Kent (1902, 2 matches).
Career batting
23–35–8–420–83–15.55–0–*ct* 17
Bowling 1149–52–22.09–1–0–5/44

Wright, Edward Fortescue
Amateur. *b:* 11.3.1858, Coburg, Chudleigh, Devon. *d:* 23.11.1904, Kingston, Jamaica. He was murdered after a riot whilst serving with the Jamaica police. Father of A. E. H. (Royal Navy). Vigorous lower order right-hand batsman, right-hand fast round-arm bowler. *Sch* Sydney College, Bath. *Teams* Gloucestershire (1878, 4 matches); British Guiana (1882/3 to 1896/7); Jamaica (1901/2).
Career batting
18–32–0–759–123–23.71–1–*ct* 11
Bowling 602–47–12.80–3–2–7/15
He also played for Somerset (pre first-class, 1875) and Devon (1876–84).

Wright, Egerton Lowndes
Amateur. *b:* 15.11.1885, Adington, Chorley, Lancashire. *d:* 11.5.1918, Barly, France. He was killed in action. Father of J. E. L. (Free Foresters). Attractive middle order right-hand batsman, wicket-keeper. *Sch* Winchester. *Teams* Oxford U (1905–08, blue all four years); Lancashire (1905–10, 4 matches).
Career batting
37–68–2–1638–95–24.81–0–*ct* 26–*st* 3
Bowling 40–1–40.00–0–0–1/6
He captained Oxford in 1907 and 1908. A good soccer player, he was awarded his blue.

Wright, Ernest Vincent
Amateur. *b:* 24.10.1894, Kettering, Northamptonshire. *d:* 16.12.1977, Kettering, Northamptonshire. Brother of Albert (Northamptonshire), Stephen (Northamptonshire) and R. L. (Northamptonshire). Middle order right-hand batsman. *Sch* Wellingborough. *Team* Northamptonshire (1919, 2 matches).
Career batting
2–2–0–2–2–1.00–0–*ct* 0

Wright, Frank
(known as Francis Moult Wright)
Professional. *b:* 4.5.1870, Ilkeston, Derbyshire. *d:* 9.12.1943, Cotmanhay, Derbyshire. Middle order right-hand batsman. *Team* Derbyshire (1899, 1 match).
Career batting
1–2–0–4–4–2.00–0–*ct* 0
Bowling 37–0

Wright, Rev Frank Wynyard
Amateur. *b:* 6.4.1844, Woodstock, Oxfordshire. *d:* 15.2.1924, Eastbourne, Sussex. Son of F. B. (Oxford U 1829), cousin of E. G. Wynyard (Hampshire). Stylish middle order right-hand batsman. *Sch* Rossall. *Teams* Oxford U (1863–65, blue all three years); Lan-

cashire (1869–75, 14 matches).
Career batting
37–57–4–917–120*–17.30–1–*ct* 41–*st* 9
Bowling 156–3–52.00–0–0–2/44

His first-class debut was for Gentlemen of the North in 1861. He gave up first-class cricket entirely in 1875 when he took up a scholastic post in Eastbourne. He also played for Oxfordshie (1863) and Cheshire (1867–73).

Wright, Frederick
Amateur. *b:* 20.6.1855, Sysonby, Melton Mowbray, Leicestershire. *d:* 20.11.1929, Ankle Hill, Melton Mowbray, Leicestershire. Attacking middle order right-hand batsman, right-arm fast bowler. *Team* Leicestershire (1895–97, 5 matches).
Career batting
5–10–0–110–31–11.00–0–*ct* 4
Bowling 365–17–21.47–1–0–5/78

Most of his County cricket was played before Leicestershire was raised to first-class status, his County debut being in 1887.

Wright, George Henry
Professional. *b:* 15.11.1822, Highfield, Sheffield, Yorkshire. *d:* 28.11.1893, Ecclesall, Sheffield, Yorkshire. Steady middle order right-hand batsman, good bowler, good point field. *Team* Yorkshire (1849–55, 12 matches).
Career batting
43–76–3–741–68–10.15–0–*ct* 48
Bowling 546–53 + 35–10.30–4–0–7/?

In 1866 he was appointed groundsman at Bramall Lane, Sheffield, and remained there until his death. His first-class debut was for England in 1847 and his final match for Manchester in 1858. He also played for Northumberland (1851–52).

Wright, H. W.
Professional. Lower order batsman, useful bowler. *Team* Hampshire (1885, 1 match).
Career batting
1–2–0–12–6.00–0–*ct* 1
Bowling 70–1–70.00–0–0–1/70

Wright, Harold
Amateur. *b:* 19.2.1884, Barrow-on-Soar, Leicestershire. *d:* 14.9.1915, Marylebone, London. He died of wounds received in the Dardanelles. Middle order left-hand batsman, slow left-arm bowler, good slip field. *Sch* Mill Hill. *Team* Leicestershire (1912–14, 10 matches).
Career batting
11–21–4–243–44–14.29–0–*ct* 10
Bowling 20–0

Wright, Henry
Professional. *b:* 19.4.1852, Bopeep, St Leonards-on-Sea, Sussex. Lower order batsman, useful bowler. *Team* An England Eleven (1888).
Career batting
1–2–1–4–4–4.00–0–*ct* 2
Bowling 10–1–10.00–0–0–1/10

Wright, Henry FitzHerbert
Amateur. *b:* 9.10.1870, The Hayes, Swanwick, Derbyshire. *d:* 23.2.1947, Yeldersley Hall, Ashbourne, Derbyshire. Father-in-law of J. G. Leaf (Army), brother-in-law of G. A. T. Foljambe (MCC). Middle order right-hand batsman, right-arm medium pace bowler. *Sch* Eton. *Team* Derbyshire (1904–05, 9 matches). *Tour* Hawke to India 1892/3.
Career batting
13–22–4–349–55–19.38–0–*ct* 6

He played in the Cambridge Freshmen's match of 1890 and the Seniors' match of the following year. He first played for Derbyshire (not first-class) in 1891. From 1912 to 1918, he was Unionist MP for North Herefordshire. His great-granddaughter is Sarah Ferguson, who became Duchess of York.

Wright, J.
Amateur. Middle order batsman. *Team* MCC (1882).
Career batting
1–2–1–2–2–2.00–0–*ct* 0

Wright, James
Professional. *b:* 25.3.1874, Newbold, Leicestershire. *d:* 20.8.1961, Sheffield, Yorkshire. Middle order right-hand batsman. *Team* Derbyshire (1898–1905, 6 matches).
Career batting
6–10–1–93–53*–10.33–0–*ct* 0
Bowling 16–0

Wright, James Egerton Lowndes
Amateur. *b:* 10.5.1912, London. *d:* 14.1.1987, Ashford Hill, Newbury, Berkshire. Son of E. L. (Lancashire). Middle order right-hand batsman. *Sch* Winchester. *Team* Free Foresters (1937).
Career batting
1–2–0–48–24.00–0–*ct* 1

Wright, John
Professional. *b:* 23.9.1861, Nantwich, Cheshire. *d:* 23.12.1912, Willaston, Nantwich, Cheshire. Middle order right-hand batsman, right-arm fast medium bowler. *Team* North of England (1885).
Career batting
1–2–0–3–3–1.50–0–*ct* 2
Bowling 16–0

His County cricket was for Cheshire (1884–95).

Wright, John Geoffrey, MBE
Cricketer. *b:* 5.7.1954, Darfield, Christchurch, New Zealand. Brother of M. J. E. (Northern Districts), son of G. T. (Canterbury). Sound opening left-hand batsman, right-arm medium pace bowler. *Teams* Northern Districts (1975/6 to 1983/4); Derbyshire (1977–88, 156 matches); Canterbury (1984/5 to 1988/9); Auckland (1989/90 to 1991/2). *Tours* New Zealand to Eng-

land 1978, 1979 (World Cup), 1983, 1986, 1990, to Australia 1980/1, 1982/3 (not first-class), 1984/5 (not first-classs), 1985/6, 1987/8, 1989/90, 1990/1 (not first-class), to Sri Lankla 1983/4, 1984/5 (not first-class), 1985/6 (not first-class), to West Indies 1984/5, to Pakistan 1984/5, to Sharjah (not first-class) 1985/6, 1987/8, to India 1987/8 (World Cup), 1988/9; Robins to Sri Lanka 1977/8; International XI to Jamaica 1982/3. *Tests* New Zealand (1977/8 to 1991/2, 77 matches).
Career batting
357–619–43–24360–192–42.29–58–*ct* 188
Bowling 339–2–169.50–0–0–1/4
Test batting
77–138–6–4964–185–37.60–12–*ct* 36
Bowling 5–0

New Zealand's most accomplished opening batsman, he was the first of his country to reach 4,000 Test runs and toured England four times, the last time as captain. On the first visit in 1978 he had moderate success and illness forced him to miss one Test. In 1983 he again missed one Test, this time due to a broken toe. In 1986 and in 1990 he appeared in all three Tests. In all he captained New Zealand in 14 Test matches. He completed 1,000 runs in England six times (best 1,830, av 55.45, in 1982). He scored 1,019 runs, av 53.65, in New Zealand in 1986/7.

Wright, John Vaughan
Cricketer. *b:* 31.12.1935, Colchester, Essex. Middle order right-hand batsman. *Team* Essex (1962–67, 4 matches).
Career batting
4–6–0–60–40–10.00–0–*ct* 2

Wright, Leslie
Professional. *b:* 20.1.1903, Durham. *d:* 6.1.1956, Mitcham, Surrey. Middle order right-hand batsman, right-arm medium pace bowler. *Team* Worcestershire (1925–33, 193 matches).
Career batting
193–348–18–6593–134–19.97–5–*ct* 60
Bowling 3649–76–48.01–0–0–3/6

He hit 1,000 runs in a season twice (best 1,402, av 24.17, in 1928).

Wright, Levi George
Amateur. *b:* 15.1.1862, Oxford. *d:* 11.1.1953, Normanton, Derby. Attacking opening right-hand batsman, brilliant point field, occasional wicket-keeper. *Team* Derbyshire (1883–1909, 317 matches).
Career batting
325–593–12–15166–195–26.10–20–*ct* 237–*st* 6
Bowling 204–1–204.00–0–0–1/4

He hit 1,000 runs in a season six times (best 1,855, av 42.15, in 1906). In 1906 he was joint-captain of Derbyshire and in 1907 sole captain. He was also a useful soccer player, representing Derby County and Notts County.

Wright, Lyndel Norman Gordon
Cricketer. *b:* 18.4.1950, Kingston, Jamaica. Half-brother of O. G. Smith (West Indies). Lower order right-hand batsman, leg break bowler. *Team* Jamaica (1968/9 to 1978/9). *Tour* Jamaica to England 1970.
Career batting
24–30–11–316–33–16.63–0–*ct* 23
Bowling 1073–40–26.82–2–0–5/36

Wright, Malcolm Graeme
Amateur. *b:* 2.6.1926, Kandy, Ceylon. Son of S. W. (Ceylon, pre first-class). Forcing middle order left-hand batsman. *Team* Oxford U (1950).
Career batting
2–4–0–35–17–8.75–0–*ct* 1

Wright, Matthew William
Professional. *b:* 24.7.1858, Keyworth, Nottinghamshire. *d:* 13.5.1949, Spital, Windsor, Berkshire. Middle order batsman, useful bowler. *Team* Nottinghamshire (1889, 1 match).
Career batting
1–2–0–6–6–3.00–0–*ct* 0
Bowling 7–0

He played for Buckinghamshire as an all-rounder from 1891 to 1913, and was coach at Eton College.

Wright, Nicholas Edward
Amateur. *b:* 28.8.1901, Kettering, Northamptonshire. *d:* 20.5.1974, Corby, Northamptonshire. Brother of Bertie (Northamptonshire) and P. A. (Northamptonshire). Lower order right-hand batsman, useful bowler. *Sch* Wellingborough. *Team* Northamptonshire (1921–22, 8 matches).
Career batting
8–14–3–30–8–2.72–0–*ct* 0
Bowling 147–2–73.50–0–0–2/59

Wright, Oswald Walter
Amateur. *b:* 20.3.1877, Maxton, Dover, Kent. *d:* 19.12.1933, Montpellier, Cheltenham, Gloucestershire. Attacking tail end batsman, originally left-arm fast, later slow left-arm bowler, good field. *Sch* Malvern. *Teams* Cambridge U (1899); Somerset (1902, 1 match).
Career batting
3–5–0–21–14–4.20–0–*ct* 2
Bowling 89–2–44.50–0–0–1/16

Wright, Philip Alan
Amateur. *b:* 16.5.1903, Kettering, Northamptonshire. *d:* 21.12.1968, Kettering, Northamptonshire. Brother of Bertie (Northamptonshire) and N. E. (Northamptonshire). Forceful lower order right-hand batsman, right-arm medium pace bowler. *Sch* Wellingborough. *Teams* Northamptonshire (1921–29, 59 matches); Cambridge U (1922–24, blue all three years).
Career batting
93–151–27–1459–83–11.76–0–*ct* 45
Bowling 8078–343–23.55–19–2–6/37

Wright, Richard Leslie

In 1925, his only full year of first-class County cricket, he took 108 wickets, av 23.27. He also won a blue for soccer.

Wright, Richard Leslie
Amateur. *b:* 28.10.1903, Kettering, Northamptonshire. *d:* 31.7.1991, Bournemouth, Hampshire. Brother of Albert (Northamptonshire), E. V. (Northamptonshire) and Stephen (Northamptonshire). Steady middle order right-hand batsman, right-arm medium pace bowler. *Sch* Wellingborough. *Team* Northamptonshire (1923–26, 54 matches).
Career batting
54–101–6–1507–112–15.86–2–*ct* 32
Bowling 194–5–38.80–0–0–1/11

Wright, Robert
(real name Robert Wright Ward)
Professional. *b:* 19.7.1852, Adwalton, Yorkshire. *d:* 2.1.1891, Oldham, Lancashire. Lower order right-hand batsman, right-hand slow round-arm bowler. *Team* Yorkshire (1877, 2 matches).
Career batting
3–6–1–37–22–7.40–0–*ct* 0
His first-class debut was for North of England in 1875.

Wright, Ronald Charles Barton
Amateur. *b:* 13.3.1903, Semilong, Northampton. *d:* 3.7.1992, Northampton. Brother of A. J. B. (Northamptonshire). Middle order left-hand batsman, slow left-arm bowler. *Sch* Wellingborough. *Team* Northamptonshire (1923–31, 10 matches).
Career batting
10–17–1–160–56*–10.00–0–*ct* 4
Bowling 1–0

Wright, Dr Samuel Reginald
Amateur. *b:* 4.1.1869, Markfield, Leicestershire. *d:* 25.1.1947, Romford, Essex. Lower order left-hand batsman, left-arm fast medium bowler. *Sch* Epsom. *Team* Leicestershire (1896–97, 3 matches).
Career batting
3–4–0–75–65–18.75–0–*ct* 0
Bowling 185–2–92.50–0–0–1/14
His debut for Leicestershire (pre first-class) was in 1886.

Wright, Stephen
Amateur. *b:* 6.8.1897, Kettering, Northamptonshire. *d:* 24.6.1975, Weston-super-Mare, Somerset. Brother of Albert (Northamptonshire), E. V. (Northamptonshire) and R. L. (Northamptonshire). Middle order right-hand batsman. *Sch* Wellingborough. *Team* Northamptonshire (1922–23, 9 matches).
Career batting
9–18–0–188–44–10.44–0–*ct* 5

Wright, Stephen
Cricketer. *b:* 4.2.1952, Muswell Hill, Middlesex. Middle order right-hand batsman. *Sch* Mill Hill. *Team* Cambridge U (1973, blue).
Career batting
10–19–0–277–41–14.57–0–*ct* 2

Wright, Thomas
Amateur. *b:* 29.4.1842, Willington, Derbyshire. Steady middle order right-hand batsman, right-hand slow medium round-arm bowler, good field. *Team* Nottinghamshire (1868–74, 9 matches).
Career batting
9–15–0–138–25–9.20–0–*ct* 4

Wright, Thomas John
Amateur. *b:* 5.3.1900, North Ormesby, Middlesbrough, Yorkshire. Middle order batsman. *Sch* St Peter's, York. *Team* Yorkshire (1919, 1 match).
Career batting
1–1–0–12–12–12.00–0–*ct* 0

Wright, Walter
Professional. *b:* 29.2.1856, Hucknall Torkard, Nottinghamshire. *d:* 22.3.1940, Leigh, Lancashire. Lower order right-hand batsman, left-arm fast medium bowler, deep field. *Teams* Nottinghamshire (1879–86, 72 matches); Kent (1888–99, 191 matches).
Career batting
289–441–110–4075–127*–12.31–1–*ct* 136
Bowling 19057–976–19.52–60–13–9/72
He took 114 wickets, av 12.86, in 1889. His best bowling was 9/72 for Kent v MCC at Lord's in 1889. He also played for Berkshire (1904) and was on the first-class umpires' list for five seasons (1900–04). A noted athlete in his younger days, he won the Sheffield Handicap twice.

Wright, William Henry
Amateur. *b:* 10.8.1841, Drayton-Parslow, Buckinghamshire. *d:* 28.12.1916, Pimlico, Westminster, London. Middle order batsman. *Sch* Marlborough. *Team* MCC (1866).
Career batting
2–3–0–5–3–1.66–0–*ct* 0
His County cricket was for Warwickshire (pre first-class, 1871).

Wright, William John
Professional. *b:* 24.2.1909, Danesmoor, Clay Cross, Derbyshire. *d:* 12.8.1988, Poole, Dorset. Middle order right-hand batsman. *Team* Derbyshire (1932, 2 matches).
Career batting
2–3–0–58–28–19.33–0–*ct* 0

Wrightson, Roger Wilfrid
Cricketer. *b:* 29.10.1939, Elsecar, Yorkshire. *d:* 13.9.1986, Carlisle, Cumberland. Middle order left-hand batsman, wicket-keeper. *Team* Essex (1965–67, 12 matches).
Career batting
12–20–4–332–84–20.75–0–*ct* 8
He also played for Cumberland (1970–71).

Wrigley, Michael Harold
Amateur. *b:* 30.7.1924, Rostherne, Cheshire. Lower order right-hand batsman, right-arm fast medium bowler. *Sch* Harrow. *Team* Oxford U (1948–50, blue 1949).
Career batting
16–17–5–71–17–5.91–0–*ct* 6
Bowling 1076–48–22.41–3–0–6/57
His first-class debut was for Combined Services in 1946.

Wyatt, Francis Joseph Caldwell
Amateur. *b:* 10.7.1882, Trichinopoly, India. *d:* 5.5.1971, Chichester, Sussex. Brother-in-law of A. P. Douglas (Surrey and Middlesex). Lower order right-hand batsman, right-arm medium pace bowler. *Sch* Dulwich and Glenalmond. *Teams* Hampshire (1905–19, 11 matches); Orange Free State (1906/7).
Career batting
21–35–6–168–26–5.79–0–*ct* 16
Bowling 1843–90–20.47–6–0–6/31
His first-class debut was for Gentlemen of England in 1904 and his final first-class match in 1920 for the Army.

Wyatt, George Nevile
Amateur. *b:* 25.8.1850, Champaran, India. *d:* 16.2.1926, Clifton, Bristol. Dashing middle order right-hand batsman, right-hand medium pace round-arm bowler, good deep field. *Sch* Cheltenham. *Teams* Gloucestershire (1871–76, 10 matches); Surrey (1877–79, 10 matches); Sussex (1883–86, 40 matches).
Career batting
72–129–6–2015–112–16.38–1–*ct* 38
Bowling 127–3–42.33–0–0–1/4
He captained Sussex in 1885.

Wyatt, Gerald
Professional. *b:* 4.6.1933, New Mills, Derbyshire. Lower order right-hand batsman, wicket-keeper. *Team* Derbyshire (1954–60, 11 matches).
Career batting
11–20–4–184–59–11.50–0–*ct* 7
Bowling 2–0

Wyatt, Dr Harold Douglas
Amateur. *b:* 12.1.1880, Enfield, Middlesex. *d:* 24.11.1949, Southwark, London. Middle order batsman. *Sch* The Leys. *Team* Middlesex (1905–09, 4 matches).
Career batting
4–6–1–67–23*–13.40–0–*ct* 2

Wyatt, Julian George
Cricketer. *b:* 19.6.1963, Paulton, Somerset. Opening right-hand batsman, right-arm medium pace bowler. *Team* Somerset (1983–89, 69 matches).
Career batting
69–115–5–2789–145–25.35–3–*ct* 27
Bowling 97–3–32.33–0–0–1/0

Wyatt, Robert Elliott Storey
Amateur. *b:* 2.5.1901, Milford, Surrey. Sound middle order right-hand batsman, right-arm medium-fast bowler. *Sch* King Henry VIII, Coventry. *Teams* Warwickshire (1923–39, 404 matches); Worcestershire (1946–51, 86 matches). *Tours* MCC to India, Burma and Ceylon 1926/7, to South Africa 1927/8, 1930/1, to West Indies 1929/30, 1934/5, to Australia and New Zealand 1932/3, 1936/7; Brinckman to South America 1937/8; Martineau to Egypt 1936, 1939 (not first-class); selected for MCC to India 1939/40 (cancelled because of the war). *Tests* England (1927/8 to 1936/7, 40 matches).
Career batting
739–1141–157–39405–232–40.04–85–*ct* 415–*st* 1
Bowling 29597–901–32.84–31–2–7/43
Test batting
40–64–6–1839–149–31.70–2–*ct* 16
Bowling 642–18–35.66–0–0–3/4
A very consistent, as well as determined, batsman whose career spanned 35 seasons, he hit over 1,000 runs in a season 17 times, plus once overseas, going on to 2,000 five times, with his best year being 1929 with 2,630 runs, av 53.66. His two double centuries were both for Warwickshire, the higher being 232 v Derbyshire at Edgbaston in 1937.
He captained England in the final Test of 1930 v Australia, in four of the five Tests of the 1934 series, during the 1934/5 tour to West Indies and against South Africa in 1935. In all he captained England in 16 Tests. From 1930 to 1937 he led Warwickshire and then was joint captain of Worcestershire in 1949 and sole captain in 1950 and 1951. He was a Test Selector from 1949 to 1954, being Chairman in 1950.
His final appearance in first-class cricket was for Free Foresters in 1957.

Wyatt, Rev William
Amateur. *b:* 12.11.1842, Islington, London. *d:* 1.3.1908, Scarborough, Yorkshire. Tail end batsman, useful bowler. *Sch* Repton. *Team* Oxford U (1864).
Career batting
3–4–3–3–2*–3.00–0–*ct* 0
Bowling 72–2 + 3–36.00–0–0–2/?

Wyers, Alick
Amateur. *b:* 15.12.1907, Droitwich, Worcestershire. *d:* 28.11.1980, Kidderminster, Worcestershire. Middle order right-hand batsman. *Team* Worcestershire (1927, 1 match).
Career batting
1–1–0–3–3–3.00–0–*ct* 0

Wykes, Geoffrey Noel
Amateur. *b:* 22.11.1890, Clarendon Park, Leicester. *d:* 1.5.1926, Hull, Yorkshire. Middle order batsman.

Wykes, James Cochrane

Sch Charterhouse. *Team* Leicestershire (1923, 2 matches).
Career batting
2–4–0–2–2–0.50–0–*ct* 0

Wykes, James Cochrane
Amateur. *b:* 19.10.1913, Leigh-on-Sea, Essex. *d:* 19.10.1992, Harrogate, Yorkshire. Brother of N. G. (Essex). Middle order right-hand batsman, wicket-keeper. *Sch* Oundle. *Team* Scotland (1946).
Career batting
1–2–0–38–23–19.00–0–*ct* 1
He played in trials at Cambridge U, but not in first-class matches.

Wykes, Norman Gordon
Amateur. *b:* 19.3.1906, Woodford, Essex. *d:* 4.12.1991, Bridport, Dorset. Brother of J. C. (Scotland). Opening or middle order left-hand batsman, left-arm medium pace bowler, good field. *Sch* Oundle. *Teams* Essex (1925–36, 30 matches); Cambridge U (1926–28, blue 1928). *Tour* MCC to Canada 1937 (not first-class).
Career batting
42–60–6–1277–162–23.64–2–*ct* 13
Bowling 150–1–150.00–0–0–1/5

Wyld, Frederick
(also known as F. Wild)
Professional. *b:* 28.8.1847, Eastwood, Nottinghamshire. *d:* 11.2.1893, Nottingham. Forceful opening or middle order right-hand batsman, right-hand fast round-arm bowler, wicket-keeper. *Team* Nottinghamshire (1868–81, 109 matches).
Career batting
180–297–20–3967–104*–14.32–2–*ct* 185–*st* 53
Bowling 109–8–13.62–0–0–4/33
His final first-class match was for MCC in 1885.

Wyld, Hugh James
Amateur. *b:* 16.4.1880, Kensington, London. *d:* 9.12.1961, Beverstone, Gloucestershire. Father-in-law of W. W. H. Hill-Wood (Derbyshire). Middle order right-hand batsman, slow left-arm bowler. *Sch* Harrow. *Teams* Oxford U (1900–03, blue 1901–03); Middlesex (1900–01, 5 matches). *Tour* MCC to North America 1905.
Career batting
36–65–5–1124–85–18.73–0–*ct* 21
Bowling 42–2–21.00–0–0–1/10
His final first-class match in England was for Gentlemen of England in 1904. He also was awarded his soccer blue whilst at Oxford.

Wyld, William George
Amateur. *b:* 3.12.1859, Stirling, Scotland. *d:* 16.7.1900, South Kensington, London. Middle order right-hand batsman, right-arm medium pace, or slow under-arm, bowler. *Sch* Dulwich. *Team* Surrey (1879–87, 10 matches).
Career batting
10–16–1–169–34*–11.26–0–*ct* 4
Bowling 113–3–37.66–0–0–1/12

Wynch, Charles George
Amateur. *b:* 24.7.1833, Calcutta, India. *d:* 21.5.1876, Westminster, London. Attractive middle order right-hand batsman, good deep field. *Sch* Rugby. *Team* Sussex (1852–59, 24 matches).
Career batting
24–42–6–758–87–21.05–0–*ct* 9
Bowling 4–0 + 2–no av–0–0–1/?
He resided in India from 1855 to 1858; his first-class cricket was therefore very restricted. His final first-class match was for MCC in 1865. He also played for Essex (pre first-class, 1859–60) and Suffolk (1863–68).

Wynne-Finch, Edward Heneage
(changed name from E. H. Wynne in 1863)
Amateur. *b:* 9.12.1842, Voelas, Denbighshire. *d:* 7.1.1914, Stokesley Manor, Yorkshire. Son of C. G. (Oxford U 1836), nephew of J. H. G. (Oxford U 1838). Middle order right-hand batsman, off break bowler. *Sch* Eton. *Team* MCC (1864–66).
Career batting
3–6–1–24–20–4.80–0–*ct* 0
Bowling 76–2–38.00–0–0–2/68
He played for Cambridge U in 1864 but not in first-class matches, but he did win a blue for athletics. His County cricket was for Norfolk (1864).

Wynyard, Edward George
Amateur. *b:* 1.4.1861, Saharanpur, India. *d:* 30.10.1936, Knotty Green, Beaconsfield, Buckinghamshire. Cousin of F. W. Wright (Lancashire). Forcing opening or middle order right-hand batsman, slow under-arm bowler, fine cover-point or slip. *Sch* Charterhouse and St Edward's, Oxford. *Team* Hampshire (1878–1908, 71 matches). *Tours* Brackley to West Indies 1904/5; MCC to South Africa 1905/6, 1909/10, to New Zealand 1906/7, to North America 1907, to Egypt 1909 (not first-class). *Tests* England (1896 to 1905/6, 3 matches).
Career batting
154–272–20–8318–268–33.00–13–*ct* 163–*st* 5
Bowling 2130–66–32.27–1–0–6/63
Test batting
3–6–0–72–30–12.00–0–*ct* 0
Bowling 17–0
He hit 1,000 runs in a season twice (best 1,281, av 41.32, in 1899). In 1896 he came second in the first-class batting averages with 1,038, av 49.42. He captained Hampshire 1896 to 1899. His two double centuries were both for Hampshire, the higher being 268 v Yorkshire at Southampton in 1896.
His final first-class match was for MCC in 1912. In the 1880s he played many fine innings whilst

stationed in India. A good soccer player, he appeared in the forward line for the winners, Old Carthusians, in the FA Cup Final of 1881. He was also a noted figure skater.

Y

Yadav, Nandlal Shivlal
Cricketer. *b:* 26.1.1957, Hyderabad, India. Brother of N. R. (Hyderabad). Lower order right-hand batsman, off break bowler. *Team* Hyderabad (1977/8 to 1989/90). *Tours* India to Australia 1980/1, 1985/6, to New Zealand 1980/1, to England 1982, 1986, to Pakistan 1984/5. *Tests* India (1979/80 to 1986/7, 35 matches).
Career batting
112–114–32–1502–97*–18.31–0–*ct* 53
Bowling 10609–330–32.14–15–0–6/30
Test batting
35–40–12–403–43–14.39–0–*ct* 10
Bowling 3580–102–35.09–3–0–5/76
He achieved very little on the 1982 tour to England and did not appear in the Tests. Although he bowled well on his second tour in 1986, his off spin was again not required for the Tests.

Yajurvindra Singh
Cricketer. *b:* 1.8.1952, Rajkot, India. Middle order right-hand batsman, right-arm medium pace bowler, good close field. *Teams* Maharashtra (1971/2 to 1978/9); Saurashtra (1979/80 to 1981/2). *Tour* India to England 1979. *Tests* India (1976/7 to 1979/80, 4 matches).
Career batting
78–115–26–3765–214–42.30–9–*ct* 83
Bowling 1552–50–31.04–2–1–7/20
Test batting
4–7–1–109–43*–18.16–0–*ct* 11
Bowling 50–0
He appeared in one Test on the 1979 tour of England and in only nine first-class matches. His highest score was 214 for Saurashtra v Maharashtra at Satara in 1979/80.

Yaldren, Charles Henry
Professional. *b:* 8.12.1891, Southampton, Hampshire. *d:* 23.10.1916, Thiepval, France. Tail end batsman, useful bowler. *Team* Hampshire (1912, 1 match).
Career batting
1–1–0–8–8–8.00–0–*ct* 0
Bowling 60–1–60.00–0–0–1/52

Yalland, William Stanley
Amateur. *b:* 27.6.1889, Fishponds, Bristol. *d:* 23.10.1914, Ypres, Belgium. He was killed in action. Middle order right-hand batsman. *Sch* Clifton. *Team* Gloucestershire (1910, 1 match).
Career batting
1–1–0–1–1–1.00–0–*ct* 0

Yallop, Graham Neil
Cricketer. *b:* 7.10.1952, Balwyn, Melbourne, Victoria, Australia. Hard hitting middle order left-hand batsman. *Team* Victoria (1972/3 to 1984/5, 87 matches). *Tours* Australia to England 1979 (World Cup), 1980, 1981, 1983 (World Cup), to West Indies 1977/8, to India 1979/80, 1984/5 (not first-class), to Sri Lanka 1980/1, 1982/3, to Pakistan 1979/80; Australian XI to South Africa 1985/6, 1986/7. *Tests* Australia (1975/6 to 1984/5, 39 matches).
Career batting
164–283–30–11615–268–45.90–30–*ct* 120–*st* 1
Bowling 876–14–62.57–0–0–4/63
Test batting
39–70–3–2756–268–41.13–8–*ct* 23
Bowling 116–1–116.00–0–0–1/21
He played in the Centenary Test on the brief 1980 tour to England and in all six Tests on the 1981 tour, but apart from an innings of 114 in the Old Trafford Test in 1981, his form was not impressive. He captained Australia in 7 Test matches. He hit 1,418 runs, av 67.52, in Australia in 1982/3, and 1,132, av 113.20, in 1983/4. His highest score was 268 for Australia v Pakistan at Melbourne in 1983/4.

Yardley, Norman Walter Dransfield
Amateur. *b:* 19.3.1915, Gawber, Barnsley, Yorkshire. *d:* 3.10.1989, Lodge Moor, Sheffield, Yorkshire. Sound middle order right-hand batsman, right-arm medium pace swing bowler. *Sch* St Peter's, York. *Teams* Cambridge U (1935–38, blue all four years); Yorkshire (1936–55, 302 matches). *Tours* Tennyson to India 1937/8, MCC to South Africa 1938/9, to Australia and New Zealand 1946/7. *Tests* England (1938–50, 20 matches).
Career batting
446–658–75–18173–183*–31.17–27–*ct* 328–*st* 1
Bowling 8506–279–30.48–5–0–6/29
Test batting
20–34–2–812–99–25.37–0–*ct* 14
Bowling 707–21–33.66–0–0–3/67
He hit 1,000 runs in a season eight times (best 1,906, av 44.32, in 1947). He captained Cambridge in 1938, Yorkshire 1948–55 and England in 14 Tests. A Test Selector from 1951 to 1953, he was Chairman of the Committee in 1951–52. He was also a member of the Yorkshire Committee and President 1981–84. An all-round athlete he gained a hockey blue and was six times North of England squash champion.

Yardley, Thomas James
Cricketer. *b:* 27.10.1946, Chaddesley Corbett, Worcestershire. Middle order left-hand batsman, right-arm medium pace bowler, occasional wicket-keeper. *Teams* Worcestershire (1967–75, 153 matches); Northamptonshire (1976–82, 107 matches).

Yardley, William

Career batting
260–390–69–8287–135–25.81–5–*ct* 232–*st* 2
Bowling 38–0

He hit 1,066 runs, av 30.45, in 1971.

Yardley, William
Amateur. *b:* 10.6.1849, Altomont, Bombay, India. *d:* 28.10.1900, Kingston-upon-Thames, Surrey. He died very suddenly at the Sun Hotel. Middle order right-hand batsman, right-hand fast round-arm, or left-hand slow under-arm, bowler, cover point or wicket-keeper. *Sch* Rugby. *Teams* Kent (1868–78, 34 matches); Cambridge U (1869–72, blue all four years).
Career batting
83–151–11–3609–130–25.77–3–*ct* 43–*st* 6
Bowling 227–7–32.42–0–0–2/10

He was the first batsman to hit a century in the University match – in 1870 and in 1872 he scored another century in the same fixture. He captained Cambridge in 1871. He was rackets champion whilst at Cambridge. Well-known in theatrical circles, he was the author of several plays and also a dramatic critic. The first Champion County v The Rest match in 1901 was played for the benefit of his widow.

Yarnold, Henry
Professional. *b:* 6.7.1917, Worcester. *d:* 13.8.1974, Leamington Spa, Warwickshire. He was killed in a car accident travelling after umpiring. Lower order right-hand batsman, wicket-keeper. *Team* Worcestershire (1938–55, 283 matches).
Career batting
287–417–69–3741–68–10.75–0–*ct* 466–*st* 230

In 1949 he claimed 110 victims behind the wicket – ct 63, st 47. For Worcestershire v Scotland in 1951 he stumped six batsmen in one innings. He was on the first-class umpires' list (1957–74) after retiring from County cricket and stood in three Test matches (1967–68).

Yarnold, Walter Keith
Amateur. *d:* 8.10.1978, Monaco. Lower order right-hand batsman, wicket-keeper. *Team* Northamptonshire (1928, 1 match).
Career batting
1–2–0–3–2–1.50–0–*ct* 1

Yashpal Sharma
Cricketer. *b:* 11.8.1954, Ludhiana, India. Uncle of Chetan Sharma (India). Attractive middle order right-hand batsman, right-arm medium pace bowler, occasional wicket-keeper. *Teams* Punjab (1973/4 to 1986/7); Haryana (1987/8 to 1989/90); Railways (1991/2). *Tours* India to Pakistan 1978/9, 1982/3, to England 1979, 1982, 1983 (World Cup), to Australia and New Zealand 1980/1, to West Indies 1982/3. *Tests* India (1979 to 1983/4, 37 matches).
Career batting
158–242–46–8848–201*–45.14–21–*ct* 89–*st* 2
Bowling 1507–46–32.76–1–0–5/106
Test batting
37–59–11–1606–140–33.45–2–*ct* 16
Bowling 17–1–17.00–0–0–1/6

Although not very prolific in the Tests, he headed the first-class batting averages on the 1979 tour to England with 884 runs, av 58.93. In 1982 he played in all three Tests, but was not so successful in either the Tests or first-class matches. His highest score was 201* for Indians v Victoria at Geelong in 1980/1.

Yates, Calvert
Professional. *b:* 28.11.1851, Oswaldtwistle, Lancashire. *d:* 10.6.1904, Church, Lancashire. Middle order batsman. *Team* Lancashire (1882, 1 match).
Career batting
1–2–0–28–24–14.00–0–*ct* 0

Yates, Gary
Cricketer. *b:* 20.9.1967, Ashton-under-Lyne, Lancashire. Lower order right-hand batsman, off break bowler. *Team* Lancashire (1990–91, 25 matches).
Career batting
25–30–15–480–106–32.00–2–*ct* 10
Bowling 2334–39–59.84–0–0–4/94

He scored 106 on his first-class debut for Lancashire v Nottinghamshire at Trent Bridge in 1990.

Yates, George
Professional. *b:* 6.6.1856, Haslingden, Lancashire. *d:* 21.8.1925, Marple, Cheshire. Middle order right-hand batsman, right-hand fast round-arm bowler. *Team* Lancashire (1885–94, 92 matches).
Career batting
92–135–15–1632–74–13.60–0–*ct* 41
Bowling 934–30–31.13–0–0–4/112

Yates, George
Professional. *b:* 21.8.1858, Bolsover, Derbyshire. *d:* 21.7.1933, Bolsover, Derbyshire. Lower order batsman, useful bowler. *Team* Derbyshire (1883, 1 match).
Career batting
1–1–0–0–0–0.00–0–*ct* 0
Bowling 9–0

Yates, Humphrey William Maghull
Amateur. *b:* 25.3.1883, Ellesmere Park, Eccles, Lancashire. *d:* 21.8.1956, Abbotsford, Johannesburg, South Africa. Son of J. M. (Cambridge U). Dashing middle order right-hand batsman, right-arm medium pace bowler, good field. *Sch* Winchester. *Team* Hampshire (1910–13, 13 matches).
Career batting
20–32–7–646–97–0–25.84–*ct* 10
Bowling 87–1–87.00–0–0–1/25

His final first-class match was for the Army in 1920. From 1945 to 1956 he was scorer to the Transvaal Cricket Union.

Yates, Joseph Maghull
Amateur. *b:* 19.6.1844, Chorlton-cum-Hardy, Lancashire. *d:* 17.4.1916, Dunham Woodhouses, Cheshire. Father of H. W. M. (Hampshire). Neat middle order right-hand batsman, round-arm bowler, good long stop. *Sch* Westminster. *Team* Cambridge U (1866).
Career batting
1–1–0–10–10–10.00–0–*ct* 1
His County cricket was for Cheshire (1866).

Yates, Kenneth Clement
Amateur. *b:* 4.8.1938, Keetmanshoop, South-West Africa. Lower order right-hand batsman, wicket-keeper. *Team* Cambridge U (1961).
Career batting
1–1–1–0–0*–no av–0–*ct* 3
His County cricket was for Cambridgeshire (1963).

Yates, Walter Gerald
Professional. *b:* 18.6.1919, Warsop, Nottinghamshire. Middle order right-hand batsman, right-arm medium pace bowler. *Team* Nottinghamshire (1937–38, 6 matches).
Career batting
6–8–1–69–19–9.85–0–*ct* 1
Bowling 54–1–54.00–0–0–1/43

Yawar Saeed
Professional. *b:* 22.1.1935, Lahore, India. Son of Mohammad Saeed (Northern India), brother-in-law of Fazal Mahmood (Pakistan). Lower order right-hand batsman, right-arm medium pace bowler. *Teams* Somerset (1953–55, 50 matches); Punjab (1953/4 to 1956/7).
Career batting
59–106–6–1547–64–15.47–0–*ct* 30
Bowling 3610–106–34.05–5–0–5/32
His final first-class match was for Central Zone in 1958/9. He was a member of the Pakistan Test Selection Committee.

Yeabsley, Douglas Ian
Amateur. *b:* 3.1.1942, Exeter, Devon. Lower order left-hand batsman, left-arm medium fast bowler. *Sch* Exeter. *Team* Minor Counties (1974–81). *Tour* Minor Counties to Kenya 1977/8 (not first-class).
Career batting
4–6–3–27–14*–9.00–0–*ct* 1
Bowling 389–13–29.92–0–0–3/45
His County cricket was for Devon (1959–89).

Yeadon, James
Professional. *b:* 10.12.1861, Yeadon, Yorkshire. *d:* 30.5.1914, Yeadon, Yorkshire. Lower order right-hand batsman, wicket-keeper. *Team* Yorkshire (1888, 3 matches).
Career batting
3–6–2–41–22–10.25–0–*ct* 5–*st* 3
He was a first-class umpire (1898).

Yeatman, Rex Herbert
Amateur. *b:* 4.10.1919, Kew, Surrey. Middle order right-hand batsman, right-arm medium pace bowler. *Sch* St Pauls. *Team* Surrey (1946–47, 5 matches).
Career batting
6–9–1–53–21–6.62–0–*ct* 1
Bowling 18–0

Yonge, Gerald Edward
Amateur. *b:* 4.7.1824, Eton, Berkshire. *d:* 27.12.1904, Stoke Lodge, Bishopstoke, Hampshire. Lower order batsman, fast round-arm bowler. *Sch* Eton. *Team* Oxford U (1844–50, blue 1844–48).
Career batting
26–45–12–228–36–6.90–0–*ct* 10
Bowling 165–13 + 133–12.69–13–3–8/?
His last first-class match was for England in 1853. He captained Oxford in 1848. His County cricket was for Berkshire (1853) and Buckinghamshire (1865).

Yorke, Gerald Joseph
Amateur. *b:* 10.12.1901, Forthampton Court, Tewkesbury, Gloucestershire. *d:* 29.4.1983, Forthampton Court, Tewkesbury, Gloucestershire. Son of V. W. (Gloucestershire). Middle order batsman. *Sch* Eton. *Team* Gloucestershire (1925, 1 match).
Career batting
1–2–0–6–6–3.00–0–*ct* 0

Yorke, Vincent Wodehouse
Amateur. *b:* 21.5.1869, Pimlico, Westminster, London. *d:* 27.11.1957, Paddington, London. Father of G. J. (Gloucestershire). Middle order batsman. *Sch* Eton. *Team* Gloucestershire (1898, 1 match).
Career batting
1–1–0–10–10–10.00–0–*ct* 0
He played no first-class cricket at Cambridge U, but did win a blue for royal tennis.

Youll, Michael
Professional. *b:* 26.4.1939, Jesmond, Newcastle upon Tyne, Northumberland. Lower order left-hand batsman, slow left-arm bowler, good close field. *Team* Warwickshire (1956–57, 4 matches).
Career batting
4–2–0–15–9–7.50–0–*ct* 2
Bowling 302–14–21.57–1–0–5/99
He also played for Northumberland (1962–81). He was also a good soccer player.

Young, Sir Alfred Joseph Karney
Amateur. *b:* 1.8.1865, Victoria, British Columbia, Canada. *d:* 5.1.1942, Tamboerskloof, Cape Town, South Africa. Middle order right-hand batsman. *Team* Kent (1890, 1 match).
Career batting
1–2–0–10–6–5.00–0–*ct* 0

Young, Archibald
Professional. *b:* 6.11.1890, Bathwick, Bath, Somerset. *d:* 2.4.1936, Odd Down, Bath. Middle order right-hand batsman, slow right-arm bowler, good field. *Team* Somerset (1911–33, 310 matches).
Career batting
312–539–22–13159–198–25.45–11–*ct* 217
Bowling 9928–388–25.58–9–2–8/30
He hit 1,000 runs in a season five times (best 1,219 runs, av 25.93, in 1930).

Young, Brian Andrew
Cricketer. *b:* 3.11.1964, Whangarei, Auckland, New Zealand. Middle order right-hand batsman, wicket-keeper. *Team* Northern Districts (1983/4 to 1991/2). *Tours* Rest of World to England 1985; New Zealand to Australia 1990/1 (not first-class).
Career batting
77–125–34–3089–129–33.94–2–*ct* 169–*st* 11
He has played for New Zealand in one-day international matches.

Young, Charles Robertson
Amateur and professional at various times. *b:* 2.2.1852, Dharwar, India. Lower order left-hand batsman, left-arm medium pace bowler, slip field. *Team* Hampshire (1867–85, 38 matches).
Career batting
38–67–7–717–48–11.95–0–*ct* 35
Bowling 3258–149–21.86–8–3–7/19
He is believed to be the youngest cricketer to appear for a first-class county, being 15 years and 131 days on his debut for Hampshire. He last played for Hampshire (not first-class) in 1890.

Young, Douglas Edmund
Amateur. *b:* 7.5.1917, Wandsworth, London. Lower order right-hand batsman, leg break bowler. *Sch* KCS Wimbledon. *Team* Oxford U (1938–39, blue 1938).
Career batting
20–31–6–442–36–17.68–0–*ct* 16
Bowling 1374–50–27.48–2–0–6/58
His County cricket was for Berkshire (1953–59).

Young, Douglas Martin
Professional. *b:* 15.4.1924, Coalville, Leicestershire. Sound opening right-hand batsman, right-arm slow bowler. *Sch* Wellingborough. *Teams* Worcestershire (1946–48, 31 matches); Gloucestershire (1949–64, 435 matches). *Tour* Commonwealth to Rhodesia 1962/3.
Career batting
475–842–42–24555–198–30.69–40–*ct* 177
Bowling 172–4–43.00–0–0–2/35
He hit 1,000 runs in a season 13 times, going on to 2,000 twice (best 2,179, av 41.11, in 1959). His highest score was 198 for Gloucestershire v Oxford U at Oxford in 1962, when he assisted R. B. Nicholls in an opening partnership of 395.

Young, Goodwin
Amateur. *b:* 1850, Leemount, Carrigrohane, Co Cork, Ireland. *d:* 9.1.1915, Cork, Ireland. Tail end batsman, slow left-arm bowler. *Sch* Shrewsbury. *Team* Cambridge U (1873).
Career batting
3–6–3–17–12*–5.66–0–*ct* 2
Bowling 254–16–15.87–2–1–5/24

Young, Harding Isaac
Professional. *b:* 5.2.1876, Leyton, Essex. *d:* 12.12.1964, Rochford, Essex. Lower order right-hand batsman, left-arm medium pace bowler. *Team* Essex (1898–1912, 128 matches). *Tour* MCC to West Indies 1910/11. *Tests* England (1899, 2 matches).
Career batting
171–257–65–2303–81–11.99–0–*ct* 80
Bowling 12014–514–23.37–27–4–8/54
Test batting
2–2–0–43–43–21.50–0–*ct* 1
Bowling 262–12–21.83–0–0–4/30
He took 139 wickets, av 21.79, in 1899. Owing to muscular rheumatism he was unable to play regularly in first-class cricket. After retiring he was on the first-class umpires' list (1921–31), standing in three Test matches (1924–26).

Young, John Albert
Professional. *b:* 14.10.1912, Paddington, London. Lower order right-hand batsman, slow left-arm bowler, fine gully field. *Team* Middlesex (1933–56, 292 matches). *Tour* MCC to South Africa 1948/9. *Tests* England (1947–49, 8 matches).
Career batting
341–392–114–2485–62–8.93–0–*ct* 148
Bowling 26795–1361–19.68–82–17–9/55
Test batting
8–10–5–28–10*–5.60–0–0–*ct* 5
Bowling 757–17–44.52–0–0–3/65
He took 100 wickets in a season eight times (best 163, av 19.88, in 1952). His best bowling was 9/55 for an England XI v Commonwealth at Hastings in 1951.

Young, John Henry
Professional. *b:* 2.7.1876, Melbourne, Derbyshire. *d:* 2.8.1913, Melbourne, Derbyshire. Lower order right-hand batsman, right-arm fast medium bowler. *Team* Derbyshire (1899–1901, 28 matches).
Career batting
28–48–9–379–42*–9.71–0–*ct* 3
Bowling 996–28–35.57–1–0–5/65

Young, John Villiers
Amateur. *b:* 16.8.1884, Dharwar, India. *d:* 8.9.1960, Eastbourne, Sussex. Brother of R. A. (Sussex). Middle order batsman. *Sch* Eastbourne. *Team* Sussex (1908, 3 matches).
Career batting
3–5–0–105–84–21.00–0–*ct* 0

Bowling 28–0

He played no first-class cricket at Cambridge U, but did win a blue for rugby.

Young, John William
Professional. *b:* 24.5.1863, Clay Cross, Derbyshire. *d:* 9.5.1933, Bolsover, Derbyshire. Middle order right-hand batsman. *Team* Derbyshire (1894, 2 matches).
Career batting
2–2–0–0–0–0.00–0–*ct* 0

Young, Richard Alfred
Amateur. *b:* 16.9.1885, Dharwar, India. *d:* 1.7.1968, Hastings, Sussex. Brother of J. V. (Sussex). Consistent middle order right-hand batsman, wicket-keeper. *Sch* Repton. *Teams* Cambridge U (1905–08, blue all four years); Sussex (1905–25, 86 matches). *Tour* MCC to Australia 1907/8. *Tests* England (1907/8, 2 matches).
Career batting
139–242–11–6653–220–28.80–11–*ct* 115–*st* 29
Bowling 114–3–38.00–0–0–2/32
Test batting
2–4–0–27–13–6.75–0–0–*ct* 6

He hit 1,000 runs in a season twice (best 1,430, av 35.07, in 1908). His highest innings was 220 for Sussex v Essex at Leyton in 1905. He captained Cambridge in 1908. A noted soccer outside right, he played for Cambridge and Corinthians and won an amateur international cap.

Young, Richard James Caldwell
Amateur. *b:* 2.2.1845, Ireland. *d:* 25.1.1885, Coolkeiragh House, Londonderry, Ireland. Middle order batsman. *Team* MCC (1873).
Career batting
1–2–0–11–11–5.50–0–*ct* 0

Young, Robert William
Amateur. *b:* 2.1.1933, Perth, Scotland. Middle order right-hand batsman. *Team* Scotland (1962–64).
Career batting
6–9–0–358–96–39.77–0–*ct* 6

Young, Stuart Harrison
Professional. *b:* 6.7.1938, Blackhall, Co Durham. Lower order left-hand batsman, right-arm fast bowler. *Team* Minor Counties (1959–69).
Career batting
3–4–2–16–14–8.00–0–*ct* 1
Bowling 289–12–24.08–0–0–4/44

His County cricket was for Durham (pre first-class, 1956–72).

Young, Rev Wilfrid Alec Radford
Amateur. *b:* 5.10.1867, Brighton, Sussex. *d:* 19.3.1947, Kimcote, Leicestershire. Middle order right-hand batsman, right-arm slow bowler. *Sch* Harrow. *Team* Somerset (1891–93, 2 matches).
Career batting
2–3–0–13–13–4.33–0–*ct* 1

He did not play in any first-class matches whilst at Cambridge U. He first played for Somerset (not first-class) in 1889.

Young, William
Professional. *b:* 8.3.1861, Speedwell, Staveley, Derbyshsire. *d:* 6.10.1933, Staveley, Derbyshire. Lower order batsman, wicket-keeper. *Team* Liverpool and District (1891).
Career batting
1–2–1–21–21*–21.00–0–*ct* 1

His County cricket was for Derbyshire (not first-class, 1891).

Young, William Sturrock
Amateur. *b:* 15.11.1896, Dundee, Angus, Scotland. *d:* 2.1.1966, Dundee, Angus, Scotland. Middle order right-hand batsman. *Team* Scotland (1924).
Career batting
1–1–0–5–5–5.00–0–*ct* 0

Younger, Charles Frearson
Amateur. *b:* 9.9.1885, Tillicoultry, Clackmannanshire, Scotland. *d:* 21.3.1917, St Leger, near Aveluy, France. He died of wounds. Lower order batsman, left-arm medium pace bowler. *Sch* Winchester. *Teams* Oxford U (1907); Scotland (1912).
Career batting
2–3–1–42–27–21.00–0–*ct* 3
Bowling 80–4–20.00–0–0–2/18

Youngson, George William
Amateur. *b:* 12.12.1919, Aberdeen, Scotland. *d:* 8.12.1982, Aberdeen, Scotland. Tail end right-hand batsman, right-arm fast medium bowler. *Team* Scotland (1947–55).
Career batting
19–31–14–64–18–3.76–0–*ct* 7
Bowling 1861–75–24.81–3–1–7/42

Younis Ahmed, Mohammad
Cricketer. *b:* 20.10.1947, Jullundur, India. Brother of Saeed Ahmed (Pakistan). Middle order left-hand batsman, left-arm medium, or slow left-arm bowler. *Teams* Lahore (1963/4 to 1986/7); Surrey (1965–78, 262 matches); Karachi (1967/8); PIA (1969/70); South Australia (1972/3, 6 matches); Worcestershire (1979–83, 85 matches); Glamorgan (1984–86, 58 matches). *Tours* Cavaliers to Jamaica 1969/70; Commonwealth to Pakistan 1970/1; Robins to South Africa 1973/4, 1974/5; International Wanderers to South Africa 1974/5, to Rhodesia 1975/6; Pakistan to India 1986/7. *Tests* Pakistan (1969/70 to 1986/7, 4 matches).
Career batting
460–762–118–26073–221*–40.48–46–*ct* 244
Bowling 2101–49–42.87–0–0–4/10

Test batting
4–7–1–177–62–29.50–0–*ct* 0
Bowling 6–0

He hit 1,000 runs in a season 13 times (best 1,760, av 47.56, in 1969). His highest score was 221* for Worcestershire v Nottinghamshire at Trent Bridge in 1979. He was capped for all three counties. His first-class debut was for Pakistan Inter-Board XI in 1961/2. In February 1987 he returned to the Pakistan Test side after a break of 17 years 111 days.

Yuile, Bryan William
Amateur. *b:* 29.10.1941, Palmerston North, Wellington, New Zealand. Lower order right-hand batsman, slow left-arm bowler. *Team* Central Districts (1959/60 to 1971/2). *Tours* New Zealand to South Africa and Australia 1961/2, to England 1965, 1969, to Australia 1967/8, to Pakistan and India 1964/5, 1969/70. *Tests* New Zealand (1962/3 to 1969/70, 17 matches).
Career batting
123–187–31–3850–146–24.67–1–*ct* 73
Bowling 8209–375–21.89–17–2–9/100
Test batting
17–33–6–481–64–17.81–0–*ct* 12
Bowling 1213–34–35.67–0–0–4/43

Although completely ineffectual in the Tests, he headed the bowling averages on the 1965 tour to England with 24 wickets, av 22.91. In 1969 he did not play in any of the Tests. His best bowling was 9/100 for Central Districts v Canterbury at New Plymouth in 1965/6.

Yusuf, Mumtaz Mohamed
Cricketer. *b:* 1.6.1949, Colombo, Ceylon. Lower order right-hand batsman, off break bowler. *Team* Sri Lanka (1983/4 to 1984). *Tour* Sri Lanka to England 1984.
Career batting
5–1–1–2–2*–no av–0–*ct* 0
Bowling 282–1–282.00–0–0–1/25

Z

Zaheer Abbas, Syed
Cricketer. *b:* 24.7.1947, Sialkot, India. Brother of Tatheer Abbas (PWD) and Sagheer Abbas (Karachi). Attractive middle order right-hand batsman, off break bowler. *Teams* Karachi (1965/6 to 1975/6); PWD (1968/9); PIA (1969/70 to 1986/7); Gloucestershire (1972–85, 206 matches); Sind (1975/6 to 1976/7); Dawood Club (1975/6). *Tours* PIA to Ireland 1969 (not first-class); Pakistan to England 1971, 1974, 1975 (World Cup), 1979 (World Cup), 1982, 1983 (World Cup), to Sri Lanka 1972/3, 1975/6, to Australia 1972/3, 1976/7, 1978/9, 1981/2, 1983/4, 1984/5 (not first-class), to New Zealand 1972/3, 1978/9, 1984/5, to West Indies 1976/7, to India 1979/80, 1983/4, to Sharjah (not first-class) 1983/4; Rest of World to Australia 1971/2. *Tests* Pakistan (1969/70 to 1985/6, 78 matches).
Career batting
459–768–92–34843–274–51.54–108–*ct* 278
Bowling 1146–30–38.20–1–0–5/15
Test batting
78–124–11–5062–274–44.79–12–*ct* 34
Bowling 132–3–44.00–0–0–2/21

He scored 1,000 runs in a season in England eleven times (best 2,554, av 75.11, in 1976). On his first tour to England in 1971 he was outstandingly successful with 1,508 runs, av 55.85, in first-class matches and 386, av 96.50, in Tests, including 274 in the first Test at Edgbaston; in 1974 he again topped the Test batting averages and hit 240 in the Oval Test. On the 1982 tour he hit 664 runs, av 73.77, in first-class matches but was not so prolific in the Tests. In 1982/3 he became the first Pakistan player to hit 100 centuries in his first-class career. He scored 1,000 runs in a season in Pakistan four times (best 1,597, av 84.16, in 1973/4). He captained Pakistan in 14 Tests.

Zahid Fazal
Cricketer. *b:* 10.11.1973, Sialkot, Pakistan. Middle order right-hand batsman, off break bowler. *Team* PACO (1989/90). *Tours* Pakistan B to Zimbabwe 1990/1; Pakistan A to Sri Lanka 1990/1; Pakistan to Sharjah (not first-class) 1990/1, 1991/2, to Australia 1991/2, to England 1992. *Tests* Pakistan (1990/1 to 1991/2, 6 matches).
Career batting
29–42–7–1197–115–34.20–3–*ct* 19
Bowling 89–0
Test batting
6–10–0–223–78–22.30–0–*ct* 4

He was given few opportunities in the 1992 tour to England and did not appear in any of the Tests.

Zakir Khan
Cricketer. *b:* 3.4.1963, Bannu, Pakistan. Lower order right-hand batsman, right-arm fast medium bowler. *Teams* Peshawar (1983/4 to 1991/2); ADBP (1985/6 to 1991/2). *Tours* Pakistan to Sri Lanka 1985/6, to India 1986/7, to England 1987, to West Indies 1987/8, to Sharjah (not first-class) 1989/90; Pakistan B to Zimbabwe 1986/7, to Kenya 1986/7. *Tests* Pakistan (1985/6 to 1989/90, 2 matches).
Career batting
83–88–35–631–100*–11.90–1–*ct* 26
Bowling 6287–253–24.84–14–1–8/85
Test batting
2–2–2–9–9*–no av–0–*ct* 1
Bowling 259–5–51.80–0–0–3/80

He had few opportunities on the 1987 tour to England and did not appear in the Test series. His first-class debut was for NWFP XI 1982/3.

Zoehrer, Timothy Joseph
Cricketer. *b:* 25.9.1961, Armadale, Perth, Western Australia. Middle order right-hand batsman, leg break and googly bowler, wicket-keeper. *Team* Western Australia (1980/1 to 1991/2, 95 matches). *Tours* Australia to New Zealand 1985/6, to Sharjah (not first-class) 1985/6, 1986/7, to India 1986/7, to England 1989. *Tests* Australia (1985/6 to 1986/7, 10 matches).
Career batting
116–162–20–4287–168–30.19–6–*ct* 338–*st* 32
Bowling 740–17–43.52–1–0–5/58
Test batting
10–14–2–246–52*–20.50–0–*ct* 18–*st* 1
As reserve wicket-keeper he appeared in only seven first-class matches on the 1989 tour to England and was not required for the Tests.

Zuill, Andrew Morison
Amateur. *b:* 22.4.1937, Falkirk, Stirlingshire, Scotland. Middle order right-hand batsman. *Sch* Merchiston. *Team* Scotland (1962–79).
Career batting
9–17–2–231–62–15.40–0–*ct* 1

Zulfiqar Ahmed
Amateur. *b:* 22.11.1926, Lahore, India. Brother-in-law of A. H. Kardar (Pakistan). Steady lower order right-hand batsman, off break, occasional leg break bowler. *Teams* Bahawalpur (1953/4 to 1959/60); PIA (1964/5). *Tours* Pakistan to India 1952/3, to England 1954, to West Indies 1957/8. *Tests* Pakistan (1952/3 to 1956/7, 9 matches).
Career batting
60–70–19–969–73–19.00–0–*ct* 21
Bowling 3527–163–21.63–12–3–7/69
Test batting
9–10–4–200–63*–33.33–0–*ct* 5
Bowling 366–20–18.30–2–1–6/42
In England in 1954 he took 64 wickets, av 18.50, in first-class matches and appeared in two Tests, but achieved little. His first-class debut was for Punjab Governor's XI in 1948/9.

Zulfiqar Ali
Cricketer. *b:* 1947, Mombasa, Kenya. Lower order right-hand batsman, right-arm medium pace bowler. *Team* East Africa (1973/4 to 1975). *Tour* East Africa to England 1975.
Career batting
2–4–0–30–20–7.50–0–*ct* 1
Bowling 290–8–36.25–0–0–3/43

Zulqarnain
Cricketer. *b:* 25.5.1962, Lahore, Pakistan. Lower order right-hand batsman, wicket-keeper. *Teams* Lahore (1980/1 to 1986/7); Railways (1981/2 to 1987/8); HBFC (1989/90 to 1990/1). *Tours* Pakistan Under 23 to Sri Lanka 1984/5; Pakistan to Sri Lanka 1985/6, to Sharjah (not first-class) 1985/6, to India 1986/7, to England 1987; Pakistan B to Zimbabwe 1986/7, to Kenya 1986/7. *Tests* Pakistan (1985/6, 3 matches).
Career batting
94–122–30–922–44–10.02–0–*ct* 207–*st* 55
Bowling 13–0
Test batting
3–4–0–24–13–6.00–0–*ct* 8–*st* 2
He was co-opted into the 1987 touring team to England and played in one first-class match.